Collins
internet-linked
dictionary of

Anagrams

William Collins' dream of knowledge for all began with the publication of his first book in 1819. A self-educated mill worker, he not only enriched millions of lives, but also founded a flourishing publishing house. Today, staying true to this spirit, Collins books are packed with inspiration, innovation, and practical expertise. They place you at the centre of a world of possibility and give you exactly what you need to explore it.

Language is the key to this exploration, and at the heart of Collins Dictionaries is language as it is really used. New words, phrases, and meanings spring up every day, and all of them are captured and analysed by the Collins Word Web. Constantly updated, and with over 2.5 billion entries, this living language resource is unique to our dictionaries.

Words are tools for life. And a Collins Dictionary makes them work for you.

Collins. Do more

Collins
internet-linked dictionary of
Anagrams

Collins

HarperCollins Publishers
Westerhill Road
Bishopbriggs
Glasgow
G64 2QT

First Edition 2005

UK Edition ISBN 0-00-719467-6

www.collins.co.uk

A catalogue record for this book is
available from the British Library.

Prepared in conjunction with,
and typeset by
Market House Books Ltd,
Aylesbury, England

Printed in Great Britain by Clays Ltd, St Ives plc

Acknowledgements
We would like to thank those authors and publishers who kindly gave permission for copyright material to be used in the Collins Word Web. We would also like to thank Times Newspapers Ltd for providing valuable data.

EDITORIAL STAFF

EDITORS
Justin Crozier
Cormac McKeown

FOR THE PUBLISHERS
Morven Dooner
Elaine Higgleton
Lorna Knight

CONTENTS

vi
Foreword

vii
Using the internet safely

viii
Tips for safe use of the internet and chatrooms

1–872
Collins internet-linked dictionary of Anagrams

1–32
Supplement: Word Play

FOREWORD

Whether you're stuck for words on Scrabble, crosswords or, indeed, any word game, Collins *internet-linked Dictionary of Anagrams* is your ideal reference. Packed with words and phrases, and based on Collins' extensive word games list, this book comprises over 100,000 anagrams.

The letter sets in the book are split into sections according to length, from 4-letter words to 15-letter words, and then according to alphabetical order of their component letters (eg all sets containing A come before those with B, but no A). All conceivable anagram solutions for the letter sets are listed next to the letter sets.

In addition to all this, Collins *internet-linked dictionary of Anagrams* contains a useful supplement with handy tips on internet crossword-solving resources, an introduction to solving cryptic crosswords, how to create anagrams and other –grams, and helpful words for word games.

USING THE INTERNET SAFELY

This section offers advice chiefly to parents concerned with the online safety of their children. Hints and tips for safe surfing are provided as is a list of websites dealing with this subject in more detail.

The internet contains an inconceivably large amount of information, much of it free, on a vast range of topics. It does not belong to and is not controlled by any single organization, government, or nation. Although the absence of centralized control is occasionally lamented as anarchic, the lack of a top-down structure provides many benefits.

The internet offers the chance for anyone with a computer and a modem to communicate with and learn from any person, group, or organization similarly equipped. Libraries, museums, art galleries, governments, universities, research institutes, and many other bodies provide open access to their data and links to the online resources of other organizations.

This availability of information and the unparalleled potential for communication and the spread of ideas provides internet users with incalculable benefits, but there are downsides. As the internet is unregulated and decentralized there is no quality-control mechanism; the only barrier preventing someone from setting up a website is technical ability. There is much of little merit on the internet.

More worrying is the potential for criminal misuse. The internet's accessibility and inclusiveness is exploited by those who wish to disseminate hate or obscenity or to take advantage of the vulnerable or gullible. As 70 per cent of UK households with school-age children are online it is important that parents and carers are aware of the potential dangers as well as the benefits.

TIPS FOR SAFE USE OF THE INTERNET AND CHATROOMS

- Find out as much as possible about the internet, chatrooms, instant messaging, and email. A number of websites dealing with the concerns of parents are listed at the bottom of this section.
- Make internet surfing a family event as often as possible.
- Limit the amount of time your children spend online. Encourage them to maintain their other interests and hobbies.
- Keep the computer in a family room so that you can check how long your children have been using the internet.
- Make sure your child doesn't give out personal details, phone numbers, addresses, or any other information that could be used to identify him or her, such as information about your family or the school he or she goes to.
- Make sure that any chatroom used by your child is monitored to prevent publication of offensive material or personal contact details.
- Online contacts should not be taken at face value. They may not be what they seem.
- Warn children never to arrange to meet someone only ever previously met on the internet without first telling you. Accompany your child to any meetings and make sure they are held in a public place.
- Children should not accept files from people they don't know and trust offline, since the files could contain viruses or self-extracting software which could reveal personal information to the sender.
- Video-conferencing and webcams allow the transmission of voice and live images. Children should be discouraged from using this technology unsupervised and with people they don't know and trust offline.
- Warn your children never to respond directly to anything they find disturbing. Encourage them to log off and report what they found to an adult.
- Consider using internet filtering software and child-friendly search engines. Use your browser's controls, as some offer varying degrees of security for each family member.
- Investigate your internet service provider's (ISP) child-protection services. Do they filter out spam (unwanted email), for instance?
- Investigate internet safety in greater detail at the following websites:

www.chatdanger.com
http://safety.ngfl.gov.uk
www.childnet-int.org/links/index.html
www.internetcrimeforum.org.uk/chatwise_streetwise.html
www.nspcc.org.uk/html/home/needadvice/
helpyourchildsurfinsafety.htm

Four Letters

AABB abba
baba
AABC abac
AABH Ahab
AABI Abia
AABL alba
baal
Bala
AABS abas
baas
Saba
AACM cama
AACN Cana
AACP capa
paca
AACS caas
AACV cava
AACW waac
AADD dada
AADM Adam
AADN Dana
nada
AADR Adar
Arad
AADT data
AAEG Gaea
AAEL alae
AAER area
AAFH haaf
AAFJ jafa
AAFL alfa
AAFR afar
AAFS faas
AAGG gaga
AAGH agha
AAGI Gaia
AAGJ jaga
AAGL alga
gala
AAGM agma
gama
AAGN naga
AAGR agar
Agra
raga
AAGS agas
saga
AAGY Gaya
AAGZ Gaza
AAHH haha
AAHK haka
AAHM amah
Hama
AAHN Naha
AAHR haar
AAHY ayah
AAIL Alai
AAIM Maia
AAIP Apia
AAIR aria
raia
AAIS Asia
AAJP jaap
AAJR ajar
raja
AAJV java
AAJX Ajax
AAJY Jaya
AAKK kaka
AAKL kaal
AAKM kama
AAKN kana
AAKR arak
kara
AAKT kata
taka
AAKV kava
AAKW kawa
waka
AALM lama
mala
AALN anal
AALP alap
paal
AALR alar
Lara
AALS alas
AALT taal
tala
AALV Alva
lava
Vaal
AALW Waal
AAMM mama
AAMN Anam
mana
AAMR Aram
maar
mara
Rama
AAMS maas
AAMY maya
AAMZ Zama
AANN anna
naan
nana
AANO anoa
AANR Aran
Nara
AANS anas
San'a
AANT anta
tana
AANZ azan
AAPP papa
AAPR arpa
para
Pará
AAPT tapa
AAPU paua
AAQU aqua
AARS Aras
Saar
AART rata
Tara
AARU aura
AARV vara
AASV Sava
vasa
AATU atua
AATW tawa
AATX taxa
AAWW wawa
AAWY away
ABBE abbe
abbé
Abbe
babe
ABBI Abib
Babi
ABBL blab
ABBO boab
ABBR barb
ABBU babu
ABBY baby
ABCH bach
ABCK back
ABCN banc
ABCR carb
crab
ABCS cabs
scab
ABCU Cuba
ABDE abed
bade
bead
ABDI Bida
ABDL bald
ABDN band
ABDO doab
ABDR bard
brad
drab
ABDS dabs
ABDU baud
daub
ABDW bawd
ABEK bake
beak
ABEL Abel
able
bael
bale
Bâle
blae
Elba
Labe
ABEM beam
bema
ABEN bane
bean
ABER bare
bear
brae
ABES base
ABET abet
bate
beat
beta
ABEU Aube
beau
ABEY abye
ABEZ Baez
Beza
ABFL flab
ABFR barf
ABGH bagh
ABGL blag
ABGN bang
ABGO Gabo
ABGR brag
garb
grab
ABGS bags
gabs
ABGY gaby
ABHI Bhai
ABHL blah
ABHS bash
ABHT baht
bath
ABHU habu
ABIK Biak
ABIL Albi
bail
Bali
ABIM bima
iamb
ABIN bani
ABIR abri
Bari
rabi
riba
ABIS bias
ABIT bait
ABJM jamb
ABJO Joab
ABJS jabs
ABJU juba
ABKL balk
ABKN bank
ABKO boak
ABKR bark
brak
krab

ABKS bask
kabs
ABKU Baku
ABLL ball
ABLM balm
lamb
ABLO bola
ABLS albs
labs
slab
ABLT blat
ABLW bawl
ABLY ably
ABMO ambo
boma
Moab
ABMR barm
ABMU Baum
ABNO bona
Oban
ABNR barn
bran
ABNS bans
nabs
ABNT bant
ABNU buna
ABOR baro
boar
bora
ABOS abos
boas
obas
soba
ABOT boat
ABOZ Boaz
ABPS baps
ABRS bars
bras
ABRT Bart
brat
ABRU bura
ABRW braw
warb
ABRY bray
ABSS bass
ABST bast
bats
stab
tabs
ABSW swab
ABSY abys
bays
ABTT batt
ABTU abut
tabu
tuba
ACCE ceca
ACCO coca
ACCS SACC
ACDE aced
cade
dace
ecad
ACDH chad
ACDI acid
cadi
ACDK dack
ACDL clad
ACDO coda
ACDR card
drac
ACDS cads
scad
ACEF cafe
face
ACEG cage
ACEH Aceh
ache
each
ACEK cake
ACEL alec
Cela
lace
ACEM acme
came
mace
ACEN acne
ance
Caen
cane
ACEP cape
pace
ACER acer
acre
care
race
ACES aces
case
ACET tace
ACEV cave
ACEW Wace
ACFF caff
ACFL calf
ACFT fact
ACGL clag
ACGN cang
ACGR crag
ACGS cags
scag
ACGY cagy
ACHI chai
ACHK hack
ACHM cham
mach
ACHP chap
ACHR arch
char
ACHS Asch
cash
ACHT chat
ACHW chaw
ACHY achy
ACIL Cali
laic
ACIM mica
ACIN cain
ACIO ciao
ACIP pica
ACIS Acis
asci
Sica
ACJK jack
ACKL calk
lack
ACKM mack
ACKP pack
ACKR cark
rack
ACKS cask
sack
ACKT tack
ACKW wack
ACKY caky
yack
ACLL call
ACLM calm
clam
ACLN clan
ACLO alco
coal
cola
ACLP clap
ACLR carl
ACLS lacs
ACLT clat
talc
ACLU caul
ACLW claw
ACLX calx
ACLY acyl
clay
lacy
ACMN Manc
ACMO camo
coma
ACMP camp
ACMR cram
marc
ACMS cams
macs
scam
ACMY cyma
YMCA
ACNR cran
narc
ACNS cans
scan
ACNT cant
ACNY cyan
ACOP capo
ACOR Caro
Roca
ACOS ocas
soca
ACOT Cato
coat
octa
taco
ACOX coax
coxa
ACPP Capp
ACPR carp
crap
ACPS caps
ACPT pact
ACPY pacy
ACRR carr
ACRS arcs
cars
scar
ACRT cart
ACRW craw
ACRY Cary
cray
racy
ACRZ czar
ACSS sacs
ACST acts
cast
cats
scat
ACSV vacs
ACSW caws
ACSY cays
ACTT tact
ACVY cavy
ACWY YWCA
ADDD Dadd
ADDE dead
Edda
ADDO dado
ADDS adds
dads
ADDU daud
duad
ADDY addy
dyad
ADEF deaf
fade
ADEG aged
egad
gaed
ADEH hade
haed
head
ADEI Adie
aide
idea
ADEJ jade
ADEK Deak
ADEL dale
deal
lade
lead
Leda
ADEM dame
Edam
made
mead
ADEN Aden
dean
ADEO odea
ADEP aped
ADER dare
dear
read
ADES daes
sade
ADET date
ADEU Aude
ADEV deva
Veda
ADEW awed
wade
ADEX axed
ADEZ adze
daze
ADFF daff
ADFO fado
ADFR fard
ADFS fads
ADFT daft
ADGL glad
ADGM AMDG
ADGN dang
Gand
ADGO dago
goad
ADGR darg
drag
Gard
grad
ADGS dags
gads
ADGU gaud
ADHJ hadj
ADHK dhak
ADHL dahl
dhal
ADHN hand
ADHO Doha
ADHR hard
ADHS dahs
dash
shad
ADHU haud
ADIK kadi
ADIL dali
dial
laid
ADIM amid
maid
ADIP paid
ADIQ qadi
ADIR arid
raid
ADIS aids
dais
Dias
sadi

said
ADIT adit
dita
ADIV avid
diva
ADIW wadi
ADIZ Diaz
ADKN dank
ADKR dark
ADKS daks
ADKU duka
ADKW dawk
ADLN land
ADLO load
ADLR lard
ADLS dals
lads
ADLU auld
dual
laud
Lüda
udal
ADLY lady
ADMN damn
ADMP damp
ADMR dram
ADMS dams
mads
ADMU duma
maud
ADMW dwam
ADNO dona
ADNR darn
nard
rand
ADNS dans
nads
sand
ADNU Duna
ADNW dawn
wand
ADOP dopa
ADOR Odra
road
ADOS sado
soda
ADOT dato
doat
toad
ADOW woad
ADPR drap
pard
ADPS daps
pads
ADQU quad
ADRS Ards
rads
sard
ADRT dart
drat
trad
ADRU daur
dura
ADRW draw
ward
ADRY dray
yard
ADST tads
ADSU Saud
ADSW daws
wads
ADSY days
yads
ADUV Vaud
ADVY davy
ADWY wady
ADYZ Yazd
AEEG agee
AEEJ ajee
AEEK akee
AEEL alee
Elea
AEES ease
AEFK fake
AEFL feal
flea
leaf
AEFM fame
AEFN fane
AEFR fare
fear
frae
AEFS safe
AEFT fate
feat
feta
AEFV fave
AEFZ faze
AEGG gage
AEGL gale
AEGM game
mage
mega
AEGN agen
gane
gean
AEGP gape
page
peag
AEGR areg
gear
Gera
rage
AEGS ages
gaes
sage
AEGT gate
AEGU ague
AEGV gave
vega
AEGW wage
AEGY Gaye
AEGZ gaze
AEHK hake
AEHL hale
heal
Leah
AEHM ahem
haem
hame
Mahé
AEHP epha
heap
AEHR hare
hear
Hera
rhea
AEHS Ashe
haes
shea
AEHT haet
hate
heat
AEHV have
AEHW whae
AEHY yeah
AEHZ haze
AEIL Elia
ilea
AEIM amie
AEIN eina
AEIR Aire
AEJK jake
AEJL Jael
AEJN Jaén
jane
jean
Jena
AEJP jape
AEKL kale
lake
leak
AEKM kame
make
AEKN Kean
AEKP peak
AEKR rake
AEKS keas
sake
AEKT take
teak
AEKW wake
weak
weka
AELL leal
AELM Elam
lame
male
Malé
meal
mela
AELN elan
lane
lean
Lena
AELO aloe
olea
AELP leap
pale
peal
plea
AELR earl
lear
rale
real
AELS ales
lase
leas
sale
Salé
seal
AELT Elat
late
leat
tael
tale
teal
tela
AELU Laue
AELV avel
lave
leva
vale
veal
vela
AELW wale
weal
AELX axel
axle
AELY yale
AELZ laze
zeal
AEMN amen
mane
mean
name
AEMR mare
ream
AEMS mesa
same
seam
AEMT mate
meat
meta
tame
team
Tema
AEMW wame
AEMX exam
AEMY Aymé
Eyam
AEMZ maze
AENN Anne
nane
AENO aeon
AENP nape
neap
pane
pean
AENR Arne
earn
near
rean
AENS sane
sena
AENT ante
Aten
etna
neat
AENV nave
Neva
vane
vena
AENW anew
wane
wean
AENY yean
AENZ naze
AEOR aero
AEOT toea
AEOZ zoea
AEPR pare
Paré
pear
Pera
rape
reap
AEPS apes
apse
pase
peas
spae
AEPT pate
peat
tape
AEPV pave
AEPX apex
AEPZ Páez
AERR rare
rear
AERS ares
arse
ears
eras
rase
sear
sera
AERT rate
tare
tear
AERU Auer
urea
AERV aver
rave
AERW ware
wear
AERY aery
Ayer
eyra
yare

year
AERZ Ezra
raze
AESS seas
AEST east
eats
etas
sate
seat
seta
taes
teas
AESU Esau
AESV aves
save
vase
AESW awes
waes
AESX axes
Saxe
AESY ayes
easy
eyas
AETT tate
teat
AETW twae
weta
AETY yate
AETZ zeta
AEUV uvea
AEVW wave
AFFF faff
AFFG gaff
AFFN naff
AFFO Offa
AFFR raff
AFFW waff
AFGL flag
AFGN fang
AFGR frag
Graf
AFGS fags
AFHL half
AFHS fash
AFHT haft
AFHU hauf
AFIK kaif
AFIL fail
fila
AFIN fain
naif
AFIP Piaf
AFIR fair
AFIS Safi
AFIT fiat
AFIW waif
AFKL flak
AFLL fall
AFLM flam
AFLN flan
AFLO foal
loaf
AFLP flap
AFLR farl
AFLS alfs
AFLT flat
AFLW flaw
AFLX flax
AFLY flay
AFMO foam
AFMR farm
AFNS fans
AFNU faun
AFNW fawn
AFOR afro
faro
fora
AFOS oafs
sofa
AFOY ofay
Yafo
AFPR frap
AFRS fras
AFRT fart
frat
raft
AFRU faur
frau
Urfa
AFRY fray
AFRZ zarf
AFST fast
fats
saft
AFSX Sfax
AFSY fays
AFTT Taft
AFTU faut
tufa
AFTW waft
AGGI giga
AGGJ jagg
AGGN gang
AGGO agog
AGGR ragg
AGGS gags
AGHI Haig
AGHN hang
AGHS gash
hags
shag
AGHT gath
ghat
AGIL gila
glia
AGIM magi
AGIN agin
Agni
gain
AGIO agio
AGIR gari
ragi
Riga
AGIT gait
taig
AGIV vagi
AGIY yagi
AGIZ Gîza
AGJS jags
AGKN knag
AGKS skag
AGKU kagu
AGKW gawk
AGLL gall
AGLM glam
AGLN lang
AGLO gaol
goal
AGLS gals
lags
slag
AGLT Galt
AGLU aglu
Gaul
AGMO ogam
AGMP gamp
AGMR gram
marg
AGMS gams
mags
AGMU Guam
AGMY gamy
AGNO agon
AGNP pang
AGNR gnar
gran
rang
AGNS gans
nags
sang
snag
AGNT gnat
tang
AGNU gaun
guan
AGNV vang
AGNW gnaw
AGNY Nagy
yang
AGOR Argo
AGOS goas
sago
AGOT goat
Göta
toga
AGOY Goya
yoga
AGPS gaps
gasp
spag
AGPU gaup
AGPW gawp
AGPY gapy
AGQU quag
AGRS gars
rags
AGRT grat
AGRU gaur
guar
ruga
Urga
AGRV grav
AGRY Gary
gray
AGRZ Graz
AGSS sags
AGST gats
stag
tags
AGSV vags
AGSW swag
wags
AGSY gays
AGUY yuga
AHHN Hahn
AHHS hash
shah
AHHT hath
AHIJ haji
AHIK haik
AHIL hail
hila
AHIR hair
AHIU huia
AHIY hiya
AHJJ hajj
AHKL lakh
AHKN ankh
hank
Kahn
khan
AHKO koha
AHKP kaph
AHKR hark
AHKS hask
AHKT khat
AHKW hawk
AHLL hall
AHLM halm
AHLO halo
AHLR harl
AHLS Hals
lahs
lash
AHLT halt
lath
AHLU haul
hula
AHLY hyla
AHMM Hamm
AHMO homa
AHMR harm
AHMS hams
mash
sham
AHMT math
AHMW wham
AHMY Mahy
YMHA
AHNO noah
AHNS Nash
shan
AHNT tanh
than
AHNW hwan
AHOP opah
AHOR hoar
hora
AHOT oath
AHOU Oahu
AHOW whoa
AHOX hoax
AHOY ahoy
hoya
AHPR harp
AHPS haps
hasp
pash
AHPT path
phat
Ptah
AHPU hapu
puha
AHPW whap
AHRS rash
AHRT hart
rath
tahr
thar
AHRZ Harz
AHSS sash
AHST hast
hats
shat
AHSW haws
shaw
shwa
wash
AHSY ashy
hays
shay
AHTT that
AHTU Utah
AHTW thaw
what
AHWY YWHA
AHYZ hazy
AIIL ilia
Ilía
AIIS Iaşi
AIIX ixia
AIJL jail
AIJN Jain
AIKK kaik
kaki
AIKL ilka
kail
kali
laik
AIKM kami

	maik
AIKN	akin
	ikan
	kain
	kina
AIKP	pika
AIKR	raki
AIKS	saki
	sika
AIKT	ikat
	tika
AIKU	kuia
AIKV	kiva
AILM	lima
	mail
	mali
AILN	anil
	lain
	nail
AILO	Liao
AILP	lipa
	pail
AILR	aril
	lair
	lari
	liar
	lira
	rail
	rial
AILS	ails
	sail
	sial
AILT	alit
	Atli
	lati
	tail
	tali
AILV	vail
	vial
AILW	wail
	wali
AILX	axil
AILZ	zila
AIMM	imam
	maim
AIMN	amin
	main
	mani
	mina
AIMO	moai
AIMR	amir
	rami
AIMS	aims
	amis
	Siam
	sima
AIMU	Maui
AIMX	maxi
AINO	Iona
	naoi
AINP	nipa
	pain
	pina
AINR	Iran
	rain
	rani
AINS	ains
	anis
	isna
	sain
	Sian
AINT	anti
	tain
AINV	vain
	vina
AINW	wain
AINX	Xi'an
AINY	ayin
AINZ	nazi
AIOT	iota
	Oita
AIOW	Iowa
AIPP	pipa
AIPR	pair
AIPS	Apis
	Pisa
AIPT	pita
AIQR	Iraq
AIRS	airs
	Asir
	Isar
	rais
	rias
	sair
	sari
AIRT	airt
	arti
AIRV	vair
AIRY	airy
	Iyar
AISS	sais
	Saïs
AIST	aits
	Asti
	Sita
	tais
	Tisa
AISV	Siva
	visa
AISX	axis
AITT	Tati
AITV	vita
AITW	wait
AITX	taxi
AIVV	viva
AJKS	jaks
AJLR	jarl
AJMS	jams
AJNO	Joan
AJOT	jato
	jota
	Tajo
AJPR	jarp
AJPS	japs
AJPU	jaup
	puja
AJRS	jars
AJRU	jura
AJSW	jaws
AJSY	jays
AJXY	jaxy
AJZZ	jazz
AKLN	lank
AKLO	alko
	kola
AKLR	lark
AKLS	Salk
AKLT	talk
AKLU	kula
AKLW	walk
AKLY	alky
	laky
AKMO	amok
	mako
AKMR	mark
AKMS	maks
	mask
AKNO	Kano
	kaon
	koan
AKNP	knap
AKNR	knar
	nark
	rank
AKNS	sank
AKNT	kant
	tank
AKNU	kuna
AKNW	wank
AKNY	yank
AKOR	kora
	okra
AKOS	koas
	oaks
	okas
	soak
AKOT	Kota
	okta
AKOY	kayo
	oaky
	okay
AKPR	park
AKRS	arks
	Rask
	sark
AKRT	kart
AKRU	Kura
AKRW	wark
AKRY	yark
AKSS	asks
AKST	kats
	skat
	task
AKSU	auks
	skua
AKSV	kvas
AKSW	skaw
AKSY	yaks
AKTY	kyat
AKTZ	Katz
AKUW	wauk
ALLM	mall
ALLO	Lalo
	olla
ALLP	pall
ALLT	tall
ALLW	wall
ALLY	ally
ALMM	malm
ALMO	loam
	mola
ALMP	lamp
	palm
ALMR	marl
ALMS	alms
	lams
	slam
ALMT	malt
ALMU	alum
	luma
	maul
ALMY	amyl
ALNO	loan
ALNP	plan
ALNR	larn
ALNU	luna
	ulan
	ulna
ALNW	lawn
ALOP	opal
	Pola
ALOR	oral
ALOS	also
	Laos
	sola
ALOT	alto
	lota
	tola
ALOV	oval
ALOW	alow
	awol
ALOZ	Özal
	Zola
ALPP	palp
ALPS	alps
	laps
	pals
	slap
ALPT	plat
ALPU	paul
	pula
ALPW	pawl
ALPY	paly
	play
ALRU	Ural
ALRY	aryl
	lyra
ALSS	lass
	sals
ALST	alts
	last
	lats
	salt
	slat
ALSU	saul
ALSV	lavs
ALSW	awls
	laws
	slaw
ALSY	lays
	slay
	Syal
ALTU	Lü-ta
	Tula
ALUU	luau
ALUW	waul
ALUY	Yalu
ALWW	wawl
ALWY	yawl
ALYZ	lazy
AMMO	ammo
AMMS	mams
AMNN	Mann
AMNO	Amon
	moan
	mona
	noma
	Oman
AMNS	mans
AMNU	Amūn
	maun
AMNX	Manx
AMNY	many
	myna
AMOR	mora
	Omar
	roam
	roma
AMOS	Amos
	moas
	soma
AMOT	atom
	moat
AMOU	ouma
AMOX	moxa
AMOY	Amoy
	mayo
	moya
AMPR	pram
	ramp
AMPS	amps
	maps
	samp
	spam
AMPT	tamp
AMPU	puma
AMPV	vamp
AMRS	arms
	mars
	rams

AMRT mart
tram
AMRU Amur
arum
Umar
AMRW warm
AMRX Marx
AMRY army
mary
AMSS mass
sams
AMST mast
mats
tams
AMSW maws
swam
AMSX Xmas
AMSY mays
yams
AMTT matt
AMTY maty
AMUX Axum
AMUZ Mazu
AMYZ mazy
ANNO anon
nona
ANNS nans
ANOR Arno
Oran
roan
ANOS naos
ANOT Aton
nota
ANOV Avon
nova
ANOX axon
ANOZ Zoan
ANPS naps
pans
snap
span
ANPT pant
ANPU puna
ANPW pawn
ANRT rant
tarn
ANRW warn
ANRY nary
yarn
ANSS sans
ANST ants
nats
tans
ANSU anus
ANSV vans
ANSW awns
sawn
swan
wans
ANSY nays
Nysa
ANTU aunt
tuan
tuna
ANTW want
ANUU unau
ANUY yuan
Yüan
ANVY navy
ANWY wany
yawn
ANYZ zany
AOPR proa
AOPS soap
AOPT atop
AOPU oupa
AORR orra
roar
AORS oars
osar
Rosa
soar
sora
AORT rato
rota
taro
AORV arvo
AOSS ossa
AOST oast
oats
stoa
tosa
AOSY soya
AOTU auto
AOVW avow
AOVZ Azov
APPS paps
APPU pupa
APRR parr
APRS raps
rasp
spar
APRT part
prat
rapt
tarp
trap
APRU prau
APRW warp
wrap
APRY pray
APSS asps
pass
saps
spas
APST past
pats
spat
taps
APSU upas
APSV pavs
APSW paws
swap
wasp
APSY pays
pyas
spay
yaps
APSZ zaps
APTU patu
tapu
upta
APTY pyat
APUY yaup
APWY yawp
AQUY quay
ARSS ASSR
ARST arts
rats
star
tars
tsar
ARSU Asur
sura
ursa
ARSV vars
ARSW wars
ARSY rays
ARTT tart
ARTW wart
ARTY arty
tray
ARTZ tzar
ARUW waur
ARVY vary
ARWY awry
wary
ARZZ razz
ASSS sass
ASST tass
ASSU Susa
ASSV savs
ASSW saws
ASSY says
ASTT stat
tats
ASTU saut
taus
ASTV tavs
vast
vats
ASTW swat
taws
twas
wast
wats
ASTY stay
tays
ASUV Suva
ASVV vavs
ASWW waws
ASWY sway
ways
yaws
ATTU Attu
taut
ATTW twat
watt
ATUV vatu
AVWY wavy
AWXY waxy
BBBI bibb
BBCO cobb
BBDI DBib
BBEL bleb
BBES ebbs
BBEW Webb
BBIJ jibb
BBIS bibs
BBLO blob
BBLU blub
bulb
BBMO bomb
BBOO boob
BBOS bobs
BBOU bubo
BBSU bubs
BBUU bubu
BCEH Cheb
BCEI bice
BCEK beck
BCEU Cebu
cube
BCHO Cóbh
BCHU chub
BCIR crib
BCKO bock
BCKU buck
BCLO bloc
BCLU club
BCMO comb
BCOS cobs
BCRU curb
BCSU cubs
BDEE bede
debe
BDEI bide
BDEL bled
BDEN bend
BDEO bode
BDER bred
BDES beds
debs
BDET debt
BDEY byde
BDIN bind
BDIR bird
BDIS bids
dibs
BDLO bold
BDMU dumb
BDNO bond
BDNU bund
BDOO doob
BDOR dorb
BDOS bods
dobs
BDOY body
Boyd
doby
BDRU drub
BDRY Byrd
BDSU buds
dubs
BEEF beef
BEEH hebe
BEEL Elbe
BEEN been
BEEP beep
BEER beer
bree
BEES bees
BEET beet
BEGI gibe
BEGR berg
BEGS begs
BEGY gybe
BEHN Behn
BEHR herb
BEHT beth
BEIJ jibe
BEIK bike
kibe
BEIL Biel
bile
BEIN beni
bine
BEIR bier
brei
brie
BEIS bise
BEIT bite
BEIV vibe
BEIX ibex
BEJU jube
BEKO boke
Kobe
BEKR berk
kerb
BEKY byke
BELL bell
BELO bole
lobe
Loeb
BELP pleb
BELR Brel
BELS bels
BELT belt
blet
BELU blue
BELW blew
BEMO mobe
BEMR berm
BENN Benn
BENO bone
Bône
ebon
Nebo
BENR Bern
bren

BENS	bens
	nebs
BENT	bent
BENZ	Benz
BEOO	oboe
BEOR	bore
	Ebro
	robe
BEOS	Bose
BEOT	boet
BEOY	obey
	yebo
BEPU	pube
BERR	brer
BERS	rebs
	Serb
BERU	rube
BERV	verb
BERW	brew
BERY	brey
	byre
BEST	best
	bets
BESW	webs
BESY	beys
	byes
BETU	bute
	tube
BETY	byte
BEUZ	zebu
BEVY	bevy
BFFI	biff
BFFO	boff
BFFU	buff
BFIR	frib
BFIS	fibs
BFMU	bumf
BFOR	forb
BFOS	fobs
BFOY	boyf
BGIL	glib
BGIN	bing
BGIO	Gobi
BGIR	brig
BGIS	bigs
	gibs
BGLO	blog
	glob
BGNO	bong
BGNU	bung
BGNY	Byng
BGOO	gobo
BGOR	Borg
	brog
BGOS	bogs
	gobs
BGOY	bogy
	goby
BGRU	burg
	grub
BGSU	bugs
BHIS	bish
BHLU	buhl
BHMO	Böhm
BHOO	boho
	hobo
BHOR	Bohr
BHOS	bosh
	hobs
BHOT	both
BHRU	buhr
BHSU	bush
	hubs
BIIS	ibis
BIJS	jibs
BIKL	bilk
BIKO	Biko
BIKR	birk
	brik
BIKS	bisk
BILL	bill
BILM	limb
BILN	blin
BILO	boil
BILP	blip
BILR	birl
BIMR	brim
BINS	bins
	nibs
	snib
BINT	bint
BINY	inby
BIOR	brio
BIOS	bios
	obis
BIOT	obit
BIOZ	Zibo
BIRR	birr
BIRS	bris
	ribs
BIRT	brit
BISS	sibs
BIST	bist
	bits
BITT	bitt
BJOS	jobs
BKLO	Blok
BKLU	bulk
BKNO	bonk
	knob
BKNU	bunk
BKOO	book
BKOS	bosk
	kobs
BKOY	kybo
BKRU	burk
BKSU	busk
BLLO	boll
	Böll
BLLU	bull
BLMU	Blum
BLOO	bolo
	bool
	lobo
	obol
BLOS	lobs
	slob
BLOT	blot
	bolt
BLOW	blow
	bowl
BLRU	blur
	burl
BLSU	slub
BMNU	numb
BMOO	boom
BMOR	borm
BMOS	mobs
BMOT	tomb
BMOU	Bomu
	umbo
BMOW	womb
BMOY	moby
BMPU	bump
BMSU	bums
BNNO	Bonn
BNOO	boon
BNOR	born
	Brno
BNOS	nobs
	snob
BNOY	bony
BNRU	burn
BNSU	buns
	nubs
	snub
BNTU	bunt
BOOR	boor
BOOS	boos
BOOT	boot
BOOY	boyo
BOOZ	bozo
BOPS	bops
BORS	bors
	bros
	orbs
	robs
	sorb
BORT	bort
BORW	brow
BORZ	Broz
BOSS	boss
	sobs
BOST	bots
	stob
BOSW	bows
	swob
BOSY	boys
	sybo
	yobs
BOTT	bott
BOTU	bout
BOTY	toby
BOUY	buoy
BOXY	boxy
BPRU	burp
BPSU	pubs
BRRU	burr
BRSU	burs
	rubs
BRTU	brut
BRUY	bury
	ruby
BSSU	buss
	subs
BSTU	bust
	buts
	stub
	tubs
BSUY	busy
	buys
BTTU	butt
BUZZ	buzz
CCHI	chic
CCKO	cock
CCOO	coco
CCOR	croc
CDEE	cede
CDEI	cedi
	cide
	dice
	iced
CDEK	deck
CDEO	code
	coed
CDER	cred
CDEU	cued
	duce
CDHI	chid
	dich
CDIK	dick
CDIO	odic
CDIS	disc
CDKO	dock
CDKU	duck
CDLO	clod
	cold
CDOO	doco
CDOR	cord
CDOS	cods
	docs
CDOU	douc
CDOY	Cody
CDRU	crud
	curd
CDSU	scud
CDTU	duct
CEER	cere
	cree
CEET	cete
CEFH	chef
CEFK	feck
CEFL	clef
CEFO	C of E
CEGL	cleg
CEHK	heck
CEHL	lech
CEHO	echo
	oche
CEHP	pech
CEHR	cher
CEHS	sech
CEHT	echt
	etch
	tech
CEHW	chew
CEHZ	chez
CEIL	ceil
	Içel
	lice
CEIM	mice
CEIN	cine
	nice
CEIP	epic
	pice
CEIR	cire
	eric
	rice
CEIS	ices
	sice
CEIT	cite
CEIV	vice
CEKK	keck
CEKM	meck
CEKN	neck
CEKO	coke
CEKP	peck
CEKR	reck
CEKY	Eyck
CELL	cell
CELM	clem
CELO	cole
CELS	cels
CELT	celt
CELU	clue
	luce
CELW	clew
CEMO	come
CEMY	cyme
CENO	Coen
	cone
	once
CENT	cent
CEOP	cope
CEOR	cero
	core
CEOT	cote
CEOU	Coué
CEOV	cove
CEPS	ceps
	pecs
	Pécs
	spec
CEPU	puce
CERS	recs
CERT	cert
CERU	cure
	curé
	ecru
CERW	crew

CESS cess
secs
CEST sect
tecs
CESU cues
ecus
CESY syce
CETU cute
CETY cyte
CEXY Ceyx
CFFO coff
CFFU cuff
CFHO Foch
CFIO C of I
coif
fico
foci
CFIS fisc
CFIU fuci
CFKU fuck
CFLO floc
CFOR corf
CFOS C of S
CFOT coft
CGHO chog
CGHU chug
CGIS cigs
CGKU guck
CGLO clog
CGOR crog
CGOS cogs
CHIK hick
CHIL lich
CHIM mich
CHIN chin
inch
CHIP chip
CHIR rich
CHIT chit
itch
CHIV chiv
CHKO hock
Koch
CHKU huck
CHLO loch
CHLY lych
CHMU chum
much
CHNO chon
CHOO coho
CHOP chop
CHOS cosh
CHOT coth
Toc H
CHOU chou
ouch
CHOW chow
CHRU Chur
CHSU cush
such
CHWY wych
CIKK kick
CIKL lick
CIKM mick
CIKN nick
CIKP pick
CIKR rick
CIKS sick
CIKT tick
CIKW wick
CIKY icky
CILL cill
CILO Clio
coil
loci
CILP clip
CIMR crim
CINO coin
coni
icon
CINU unci
CINZ zinc
CIOR coir
Cori
CIOT coit
otic
CIOV Vico
CIOZ zoic
CIPS pics
spic
CIRU uric
CISS sics
CIST cist
tics
CITY city
CJKO jock
CJLU Cluj
CKLO lock
CKLU luck
CKMO mock
CKMU muck
CKNO conk
nock
CKOO cook
CKOP pock
CKOR cork
rock
CKOS sock
CKOW cowk
CKPS SPCK
CKPU puck
CKRU ruck
CKSU cusk
suck
CKTU tuck
CKUY yuck
CLLU cull
CLMU culm
CLOO cool
loco
CLOP clop
CLOS cols
CLOT clot
colt
CLOW cowl
CLOY cloy
coly
CLRU curl
CLTU cult
CLUY Lucy
CMOO Como
coom
CMOP comp
CMOR corm
CMOS coms
CMSU scum
CMSW cwms
CNNO conn
CNOO coon
CNOR corn
CNOS cons
CNOU unco
CNOY cony
CNSY sync
CNTU Cnut
cunt
COOP coop
poco
COOS coos
COOT coot
COPR crop
COPS cops
scop
COPT Copt
COPU coup
COPW cowp
COPY copy
CORS orcs
rocs
CORT torc
CORW crow
COSS coss
COST cost
cots
scot
COSW cows
scow
COSY cosy
COYZ cozy
CPSU cups
cusp
scup
CPUY Cuyp
CRSU crus
curs
scur
CRSY scry
CRTU curt
CRUX crux
CSSU cuss
CSTU cuts
scut
CSTY cyst
DDDO Dodd
DDEE deed
DDEI deid
died
DDEO eddo
DDER redd
DDEU dude
DDEY dyed
eddy
DDIK Kidd
DDIO dido
DDOO dodo
DDOS odds
DDOT Todd
DDRU rudd
DDSU duds
sudd
DEEF feed
DEEG edge
geed
DEEH heed
DEEK deek
deke
eked
DEEL dele
DEEM deem
deme
meed
DEEN dene
Eden
need
DEEP deep
peed
DEER deer
de re
dere
dree
rede
reed
DEES dees
seed
DEET teed
DEEW weed
DEEY eyed
DEFI deif
DEFL fled
DEFN fend
DEFO feod
DEFS feds
DEFT deft
DEFU feud
DEFY defy
DEGI Gide
gied
DEGL geld
gled
DEGO doge
DEGR dreg
DEGS degs
DEGY edgy
DEHI heid
hide
hied
DEHL held
DEHO hoed
DEHR herd
DEHS edhs
shed
DEHU hued
DEHY Hyde
DEIJ jedi
DEIK dike
DEIL deil
deli
idle
lied
DEIM dime
idem
DEIN deni
dine
Enid
nide
DEIP pied
DEIR dire
Reid
ride
DEIS dies
ides
side
DEIT diet
edit
tide
tied
DEIV Devi
dive
vide
vied
DEIW wide
DEJN Nejd
DEJU Jude
DEKO doek
DEKS desk
keds
DEKU duke
DEKY dyke
DELL dell
DELM meld
DELN lend
DELO delo
dole
lode
DELP pled
DELS sled
DELU duel
DELV veld
DELW lewd
weld
DELY yeld
DEMN mend
DEMO demo
dome
Edom
mode
DEMR derm
DEMY demy
DENO done
node

DENP pend
DENR nerd
rend
DENS dens
ends
send
sned
DENT dent
tend
DENU dune
nude
DENV vend
DENW wend
DENY deny
dyne
DENZ Zend
DEOP dope
oped
DEOR dero
doer
dore
Doré
Oder
redo
rode
DEOS does
dose
odes
DEOT dote
toed
DEOV dove
DEOW owed
DEOZ doze
DEPS sped
DEPU dupe
DERS reds
DERU rude
rued
urde
DERV derv
Revd
DERW drew
DERY drey
dyer
DEST teds
DESU deus
dues
Duse
sued
used
DESW dews
weds
DESY deys
dyes
DESZ zeds
DETU duet
DEWY dewy
DEYZ Yezd
DFFO doff
DFFU duff
DFIN find
DFIS fids
DFLO fold
DFNO fond
DFNU fund
DFOO food
DFOR ford
DFRY fyrd
DFUU Du Fu
DFUY Dufy
DGIL gild
DGIN ding
DGIR gird
grid
DGIS digs
DGIU guid
DGLO gold
DGNO dong
DGNU dung
DGOO good
DGOS dogs
gods
DGOY dogy
DGRU drug
DGSU dugs
DHII Idhi
DHIN hind
DHIS dish
DHLO hold
DHOO hood
DHOS dohs
dosh
hods
shod
DHOT doth
DHOU Oudh
DHOW dhow
DHOY yodh
DHRU Hurd
DHTU thud
DIIL Dili
DIIM midi
DIIN nidi
DIIR irid
DIIV divi
DIKN dink
kind
DIKR dirk
DIKS disk
kids
skid
DILL dill
DILM mild
DILN lind
DILO diol
idol
lido
Lodi
olid
DILS lids
sild
slid
DILW wild
DILY idly
idyl
DIMN mind
DIMS dims
mids
DINO Indo-
nodi
Odin
DINR Drin
rind
DINS dins
sind
DINT dint
DINU Idun
DINW wind
DIOR Dior
DIOT doit
DIOV Ovid
void
DIPR drip
DIPS dips
DIQU quid
DIRS rids
DIRT dirt
DISS diss
DIST dits
DISV divs
vids
DISY yids
DITY tidy
DITZ ditz
DIUW Wu Di
DJLO Jodl
DJOO dojo
Jodo
DJOU judo
DJUY judy
DKNU dunk
DKOO dook
DKOR dork
DKOU douk
DKSU dusk
DKUU kudu
DLLO doll
DLLU dull
DLMO mold
DLNU Lund
DLOP plod
DLOR lord
DLOS dols
sold
DLOT dolt
told
DLOU loud
ludo
DLOW wold
DLOY odyl
DLOZ Łódź
DLSU luds
DLUY duly
DMOO doom
mood
DMOR dorm
DMOS doms
mods
DMOU doum
DMPU dump
DMRU drum
DMSU muds
DNOO doon
Ondo
DNOP pond
DNOR Nord
DNOS dons
nods
DNOU doun
udon
undo
DNOW down
DNOY yond
DNRU durn
nurd
DNSU duns
DNSY synd
DNTU dunt
DNWY wynd
DOOP pood
DOOR door
odor
rood
DOOS doos
DOOW wood
DOPR dorp
drop
prod
DOPS dops
pods
DOPU doup
DOPY dopy
DOQU quod
DORS dors
rods
DORT dort
trod
DORU dour
duro
DORW word
DORY dory
DOSS doss
sods
DOST dost
dots
tods
DOSU duos
ouds
udos
DOSW dows
DOSY doys
yods
DOSZ dzos
DOTY tody
DOXY doxy
DOYZ dozy
DPSU dups
puds
spud
DPUU pudu
DRSU surd
urds
DRSY drys
DRTU turd
DSSU suds
DSTU dust
stud
DTUY duty
DUUW wudu
EEEP epee
EEFJ jefe
EEFK keef
EEFL feel
flee
EEFM feme
EEFR fere
free
reef
EEFS fees
EEFT feet
fete
EEGH ghee
EEGK geek
EEGL glee
EEGN gene
EEGO ogee
EEGR eger
gree
EEGS gees
EEHL heel
hele
EEHM heme
EEHR here
Rhee
EEHT thee
EEHW whee
EEIR Eire
Erie
EEJP jeep
EEJR jeer
EEJT jete
EEKK keek
EEKL keel
Klee
leek
EEKM meek
EEKN keen
knee
EEKP keep
peek
peke
EEKR reek
EEKS ekes
seek
EEKW week
EELN Néel
EELP peel
pele
Pelé
EELR leer

reel
EELS eels
else
lees
seel
EELT leet
tele
EELU Uele
EELW weel
EELY eely
EEMM meme
EEMN neem
EEMR mere
EEMS seem
seme
EEMT meet
mete
teem
EEMZ meze
mzee
EENN nene
EENP neep
peen
pene
EENR erne
reen
EENS seen
EENT teen
EENV even
neve
EENW ween
EEPP peep
EEPR peer
pere
EEPS pees
seep
EEPV veep
EEPW weep
EERS seer
sere
EERT Erté
rete
tree
EERU Eure
EERV erev
ever
veer
EERW ewer
weer
were
EERY eyre
EESS esse
sees
EEST Este
tees
EESV eves
EESW ewes
wees
EESX exes
EESY eyes
EESZ zees
EETW twee
EFFI fief
fife
EFFJ jeff
EFFS effs
EFFT teff
EFGN Genf
EFHT heft
EFIK kief
EFIL file
lief
life
EFIN fine
nife
EFIR fier
fire
rife
EFIS seif
EFIV five
EFIW wife
EFKR kerf
EFKY fyke
EFLL fell
EFLO floe
EFLP pelf
EFLS self
EFLT felt
left
EFLU flue
fuel
EFLW flew
EFLX flex
EFLY fley
EFMU fume
EFNR fern
EFNS fens
EFOR fore
froe
orfe
EFOS foes
EFOX Foxe
EFRS refs
serf
EFRT fret
reft
tref
EFRU Urfé
EFRY Frey
EFSS fess
EFST efts
fest
EFSU feus
fuse
EFTW weft
EFUZ fuze
EGGS eggs
EGGY yegg
EGHU huge
EGIL glei
EGIN gien
Inge
EGIS egis
gies
EGIT gite
EGIV give
EGKN Genk
EGKS kegs
skeg
EGLN glen
EGLO loge
ogle
EGLS gels
legs
EGLT gelt
EGLU glue
luge
EGLY gley
EGMR germ
EGMS gems
EGMU geum
EGNO gone
EGNS engs
gens
EGNT gent
EGNU genu
EGOR ergo
goer
gore
ogre
rego
Roeg
EGOS egos
geos
goes
EGOV vego
EGPS pegs
EGPU Pegu
EGRS ergs
Gers
EGRU grue
urge
EGRW grew
EGRX grex
EGRY grey
gyre
EGST gest
gets
tegs
EGTZ Getz
EGVY gyve
EHHT heth
EHIK hike
EHIR heir
hire
EHIS hies
EHIV hive
EHJU jehu
EHKO hoke
EHKS kesh
EHKU kueh
EHLL hell
EHLM helm
EHLO hole
EHLP help
EHLR herl
lehr
EHMO home
EHMP hemp
EHMR herm
EHMS hems
mesh
Shem
EHMT meth
them
EHMU Hume
EHNO hone
EHNR hern
EHNS hens
nesh
EHNT hent
then
EHNW hewn
when
EHOP hope
EHOR hero
hoer
EHOS hoes
hose
shoe
EHOT theo-
EHOV hove
EHOW howe
EHPT hept
EHPW phew
EHPY hype
EHRS hers
resh
EHSS Hess
sesh
shes
EHST eths
hest
hets
Seth
EHSU hues
EHSW hews
shew
EHSY heys
EHTT teth
EHTW thew
whet
EHTY they
EHWW whew
EHWY whey
EIIV Veii
EIJV jive
EIKK kike
EIKL Kiel
like
EIKM mike
EIKN kine
Nike
EIKP kepi
pike
EIKR kier
EIKS Eisk
seik
sike
EIKT kite
tike
EIKV Kiev
EIKY yike
EILM lime
mile
EILN lien
line
Nile
EILO Leo I
EILP pile
plie
EILR lire
riel
rile
EILS Elis
isle
leis
lies
sile
EILT lite
tile
EILU lieu
EILV evil
Levi
live
veil
vile
vlei
EILW weil
wile
EILX ilex
Leix
EIMM mime
EIMN Emin
mien
mine
EIMR emir
Meir
mire
rime
EIMS mise
semi
EIMT emit
item
mite
time
EINN nine
EINO onie
EINP pine
EINR Erin
Neri
rein
Reni
EINS sine
EINT tine
EINU Niue
EINV nevi
vein
vine
EINW Wien

wine
EINZ zein
zine
EIOS Oise
EIPP pipe
EIPR peri
pier
ripe
EIPS pies
pise
EIPW wipe
EIPZ pize
EIRS Eris
reis
rise
sire
EIRT Réti
rite
tier
tire
EIRV rive
vier
EIRW weir
wire
EISS sies
EIST site
ties
EISV Ives
vies
vise
EISW wise
EISZ size
EITU etui
EITW wite
EITX exit
EITY yeti
yite
EIVV vive
EIVW view
wive
EJKO joke
EJKR jerk
EJLL jell
EJLO Joel
EJOS joes
EJOT Tejo
EJOV Jove
EJOY joey
EJSS jess
EJST jest
jets
EJSU Jesu
EJSW jews
EJTU jute
EKKS keks
EKLM Melk
EKLO koel
EKLP kelp
EKLS elks
leks
EKLT kelt
EKLU luke
EKLW kewl
EKLY kyle
yelk
EKMO moke
EKMP kemp
EKNO keno
EKNR kern
renk
EKNS kens
neks
sken
EKNT kent
EKNU neuk
nuke
EKNW knew
EKOP poke
EKOR kero
EKOS Keos
okes
soke
EKOT keto
toke
EKOW woke
EKOY yoke
EKPR perk
EKPS keps
skep
spek
EKPT kept
EKPU puke
EKPY kype
EKRR Kerr
EKRS erks
EKRT trek
EKRU Kure
EKST sekt
sket
EKSW skew
EKSY esky
keys
Skye
EKTY kyte
tyke
ELLS ells
sell
ELLT tell
ELLU Elul
ELLW well
ELLY Lely
Lyle
yell
ELMO lome
Lomé
mole
ELMR merl
ELMS elms
ELMT melt
ELMU mule
ELMW mewl
ELMY lyme
ylem
ELNO enol
leno
León
lone
noel
ELNS lens
ELNT lent
ELNU lune
ELOO oleo
ELOP lope
pole
ELOR lore
Orel
orle
role
ELOS lose
oles
sloe
sole
ELOT Leto
tole
ELOV levo
love
ovel
vole
ELOW lowe
Löwe
ELOX Leo X
ELPT lept
pelt
ELPU plue
pule
ELPW plew
ELPY yelp
ELRU lure
rule
ELRY lyre
rely
Ryle
ELSS less
sels
ELST lest
lets
ELSU lues
slue
ELSW slew
Wels
ELSY lyes
lyse
ELTU lute
ELTW welt
ELTY lyte
ELUX luxe
ELUY yule
ELVY levy
ELWY Weyl
EMMO memo
EMMS mems
EMNO meno
nome
omen
EMNT ment
EMNU menu
neum
EMOP mope
poem
pome
EMOR moer
more
omer
Rome
EMOS some
EMOT mote
tome
EMOU moue
EMOV move
EMOW meow
EMPR perm
EMPT empt
temp
EMRT term
EMRU mure
EMSS mess
EMST stem
EMSU emus
meus
muse
EMSW mews
smew
EMTU mute
EMTZ Metz
EMZZ mezz
ENNO neon
none
ENNP Penn
ENOP nope
open
peon
pone
ENOR Nero
oner
Orne
Reno
rone
ENOS Enos
eons
noes
nose
ones
sone
ENOT Eton
note
Teno
tone
ENOV oven
ENOW enow
Owen
ENOX exon
Nexø
oxen
ENOZ zone
ENPS pens
ENPT pent
ENPU Pune
ENRS erns
ENRT rent
tern
ENRU rune
ENRW wren
ENSS ness
ENST nest
nets
sent
sten
tens
ENSW news
sewn
wens
ENSY nyes
snye
syne
yens
ENTT nett
tent
ENTU tune
ENTV vent
ENTW newt
went
ENTX next
ENTY tyne
ENVY envy
EOOS oose
EOOZ ooze
EOPP pepo
poep
pope
EOPR pore
repo
rope
EOPS epos
opes
peso
pose
EOPT poet
tope
EOPX expo
EORS eros
ores
roes
rose
sore
EORT rote
tore
EORU euro
roue
EORV over
rove
EORW ower
owre
Rowe
wero
wore
EORY oyer
yore
EORZ zero
EOST toes
EOSU Ouse

EOSV	voes
EOSW	owes
	woes
EOSY	oyes
EOTT	tote
EOTV	veto
	vote
EOTY	eyot
	toey
EOVW	wove
EOWY	yowe
EOYZ	oyez
EPPR	prep
	repp
EPPS	peps
EPRS	reps
EPRT	pert
EPRU	Peru
	pure
EPRV	perv
EPRY	prey
	pyre
EPST	pest
	pets
	sept
	step
EPSU	spue
EPSW	pews
	spew
EPSY	espy
	pyes
	Spey
EPTW	wept
EPTY	pyet
	type
ERRS	errs
ERRU	ruer
ERSS	sers
ERST	erst
	rest
	rets
ERSU	Reus
	rues
	ruse
	suer
	sure
	user
ERSV	revs
	vers
ERSY	ryes
	Yser
ERTT	tret
ERTU	true
ERTV	Tver
	vert
ERTW	wert
ERTY	trey
	tyre
ERTZ	Retz
ERUV	eruv
ERUY	Urey
ERVY	very
ESST	sets
ESSU	sues
	uses
ESSW	sews
ESTT	sett
	stet
	test
ESTU	suet
	utes
ESTV	vest
	vets
ESTW	stew
	west
	wets
ESTX	sext
ESTY	stye
ESTZ	zest
ESUZ	Suez
	Zeus
ESWY	yews
ESXY	sexy
ETTX	text
ETTY	yett
FFGU	guff
FFHU	huff
FFII	fifi
FFIJ	jiff
FFIM	miff
FFIN	niff
FFIR	riff
FFIT	tiff
FFIY	iffy
FFIZ	ziff
FFLU	luff
FFMU	muff
FFOR	Orff
FFOT	toff
FFPU	puff
FFRU	ruff
FFTU	tuff
FGIR	frig
FGIS	figs
FGIT	gift
FGIU	Gifu
FGLO	flog
	golf
FGLU	gulf
FGNU	fung
FGOO	goof
FGOR	frog
FGOS	fogs
FGOY	fogy
FGSU	fugs
FHIS	fish
FHNO	fohn
FHOO	hoof
FHOW	howf
FIIJ	Fiji
FIIN	Ifni
FIJU	fuji
FIKN	fink
FILL	fill
FILM	film
	flim
FILO	filo
	foil
FILP	flip
FILS	fils
FILT	flit
	lift
FIMR	firm
FINN	Finn
FINO	fino
	foin
	info
FINR	firn
FINS	fins
FIPS	spif
FIRS	firs
	rifs
FIRT	frit
	rift
FIST	fist
	fits
	sift
FISU	Sufi
FIZZ	fizz
FKLO	folk
FKNU	funk
FKOR	fork
FKOU	Kofu
FLLU	full
FLOO	fool
FLOP	flop
FLOR	rolf
FLOT	loft
FLOU	foul
FLOW	flow
	fowl
	wolf
FLRU	furl
FLUX	flux
FMOO	mofo
FMOR	form
	from
FMUY	fumy
FNOT	font
FNSU	funs
FOOP	poof
FOOR	roof
FOOT	foot
FOOW	woof
FOOY	oofy
	yoof
FOPR	prof
FOPS	fops
FOPU	pouf
FORT	fort
FORU	four
FORW	frow
FOSS	foss
FOST	soft
FOTT	toft
FOTU	tofu
FOXY	foxy
FRSU	furs
	surf
FRTU	turf
FRUY	fury
FSSU	fuss
FSUU	Sufu
FTTU	tuft
FTUU	Tu Fu
FUZZ	fuzz
GGHO	Gogh
	hogg
GGIN	ging
GGIR	grig
GGIS	gigs
GGLU	glug
GGNO	gong
	nogg
GGOO	gogo
	goog
GGOR	grog
GGUV	vugg
GHHI	high
GHIN	nigh
GHIS	Gish
	sigh
GHIW	whig
GHNO	hong
GHNU	hung
GHOS	gosh
	hogs
GHOU	Hugo
GHOY	yogh
GHSU	gush
	hugs
GHTU	thug
GHUV	vugh
GIIR	Rigi
GIJS	jigs
GIKN	gink
	king
GIKO	Kogi
GILL	gill
GILM	glim
GILN	ling
GILR	girl
GILS	ligs
GILT	gilt
GILU	iglu
GIMN	ming
GIMP	gimp
GIMR	grim
GIMS	migs
GINO	ingo
GINP	ping
GINR	girn
	grin
	ring
GINS	gins
	sign
	sing
	snig
GINT	ting
GINW	wing
GINZ	zing
GIOR	giro
GIOS	gios
GIOV	Vigo
GIOY	yogi
GIOZ	Zog I
GIPR	grip
	prig
GIPS	gips
	pigs
GIRR	girr
GIRS	gris
	rigs
GIRT	girt
	grit
	trig
GIRY	gyri
GIST	gist
	gits
	tigs
GISW	swig
	wigs
GITW	twig
GJNO	jong
GJNU	Jung
GJOS	jogs
GJSU	jugs
GKNO	gonk
GKNU	gunk
	Küng
GKOO	gook
GKOW	gowk
GLLU	gull
GLMO	glom
GLMU	glum
GLNO	long
GLNU	lung
GLOO	logo
GLOS	Glos
	logs
	slog
GLOU	Lugo
GLOW	glow
	gowl
GLOY	logy
GLPU	gulp
	plug
GLSU	lugs
	slug
GLTU	glut
GLUY	ugly
GMNO	mong
GMNU	mung
GMOR	gorm
GMOS	mogs
	smog
GMSU	gums
	mugs
	smug
GMSY	gyms

GNNO nong
GNNU Gunn
GNOO goon
GNOP pong
GNOS gons
nogs
snog
song
GNOT tong
GNOU Ogun
GNOW gnow
gown
GNPU pung
GNRU gurn
rung
GNSU gnus
guns
snug
sung
GNTU tung
GNWY Gwyn
GNYY gyny
GOOP goop
pogo
GOOS goos
GOOT Togo
GOPR prog
GOPY pogy
GORS Gros
GORT grot
trog
GORW grow
GORY gory
Györ
gyro
orgy
GORZ Görz
GOSS goss
GOST togs
GOSW wogs
GOSY goys
GOTU gout
GOUZ Zoug
GPSU pugs
spug
GPSY gyps
GRSU rugs
GRTU trug
GRUU guru
GSTU gust
guts
tugs
GSUV guvs
vugs
GSUY guys
HHJV JHVH
HHSU hush
HHUU huhu
HHVY YHVH
HIIM mihi
HIKS kish
Sikh
HIKT kith
HILL hill
HILO Holi
HILT hilt
lith
HIMS Hims
shim
HIMW whim
HINS hins
nish
shin
sinh
HINT hint
thin
HINW whin
HIOO Ohio
HIOP Ipoh
HIOR hori
HIOT thio
HIPS hips
phis
pish
ship
HIPT pith
HIPW whip
HIPZ phiz
HIRW whir
HISS hiss
HIST hist
hits
shit
sith
this
HISV shiv
HISW wish
HITW whit
with
HIWZ whiz
HJNO john
HJOS josh
HKLO kohl
HKLU hulk
HKNO honk
HKNU hunk
HKOO hook
HKOP koph
HKOW howk
HKSU husk
Kush
HLLU hull
HLMO holm
HLOP holp
HLOS hols
HLOT holt
loth
HLOW howl
HLOY holy
HLRU hurl
HLSU lush
shul
HLWY hwyl
HMNY hymn
HMOO homo
HMOR Röhm
HMOS Homs
mhos
mosh
ohms
shmo
HMOT moth
HMOW whom
HMOY homy
HMPU hump
HMSU hums
mush
HMTY myth
HNOO hoon
HNOP phon
HNOR horn
HNOS nosh
HNOT thon
HNSU huns
shun
HNTU hunt
Thun
HOOP hoop
pooh
HOOS shoo
soho
HOOT hoot
HOPQ qoph
HOPS hops
posh
shop
HOPT phot
HOPW whop
HOPY hypo
HORS rhos
HORT Roth
Thor
thro
HORU hour
HOSS sohs
HOST host
hots
shot
tosh
HOSW hows
show
HOSY hoys
HOSZ zhos
HOTU thou
HPSU push
HPSY hyps
HPTU phut
HPUW whup
HRRU Ruhr
HRSU rhus
rush
HRSY Rhys
HRTU hurt
ruth
thru
HSSU huss
HSTU huts
shut
thus
tush
HSWY whys
HUUW Wuhu
IIKT tiki
IIKW kiwi
IILP pili
IIMN mini
IIMP impi
IIMR miri
IINP I-pin
IINR INRI
IINS nisi
IINT inti
IIPP pipi
IIPT tipi
IIRS iris
IISS Isis
IISW iwis
IITT titi
IIXZ Zi Xi
IJKN jink
IJLL jill
IJLT jilt
IJMS jism
IJNN jinn
IJNO join
IJNR Rijn
IJNX jinx
IJZZ jizz
IKKN kink
IKKR kirk
IKLL kill
IKLM milk
IKLN kiln
link
IKLO kilo
Loki
IKLS ilks
silk
IKLT kilt
IKLU Luik
IKMN mink
IKMO moki
IKMR mirk
IKMS skim
IKNO ikon
kino
oink
IKNP pink
IKNR rink
IKNS inks
kins
sink
skin
IKNT knit
IKNW wink
IKNY inky
IKOR Okri
IKOS oiks
IKPP kipp
IKPS kips
skip
spik
IKRS irks
kris
risk
IKRU kuri
IKSS kiss
skis
IKST kist
kits
skit
IKUV Kivu
ILLM mill
ILLO lilo
ILLP pill
ILLR rill
ILLS ills
sill
ILLT lilt
till
ILLW will
ILLY lily
ILMN limn
ILMO limo
milo
moil
ILMP limp
ILMS mils
slim
ILMT milt
ILMY limy
ILNN linn
ILNO lino
lion
loin
noil
ILNT lint
ILNY inly
liny
ILNZ Linz
ILOO olio
ILOP Li Po
ILOR roil
ILOS oils
silo
soil
soli
ILOT loti
toil
ILOV viol
ILOY oily
ILPS lips
lisp
slip
ILPU puli
ILST list
lits
silt
slit
ILTT tilt

ILTU	litu
ILTW	wilt
ILVV	Lviv
ILVY	Livy
ILWY	wily
IMMO	momi
IMNO	mino
	Miño
IMNT	mint
IMNX	minx
IMOO	mooi
IMOR	Miró
IMOS	miso
IMOT	omit
IMOZ	Mo-Zi
IMPP	pimp
IMPR	prim
IMPS	imps
	simp
IMPW	wimp
IMQU	quim
IMRS	rims
	smir
IMRT	trim
IMRU	muir
	rimu
IMRV	mirv
IMRY	miry
	rimy
	Ymir
IMSS	isms
	miss
IMST	mist
	smit
	stim
IMSW	swim
IMTT	mitt
IMTU	muti
INNS	inns
INOP	pion
INOR	iron
	noir
	nori
INOS	ions
	Sion
INOT	into
INOV	vino
INOW	wino
INOY	yoni
INOZ	Zion
INPR	pirn
INPS	nips
	pins
	snip
	spin
INPT	pint
INPY	piny
INQU	quin
INRU	ruin
INSS	sins
INST	nits
	snit
	tins
INSU	unis
INSW	wins
INTT	tint
INTU	unit
INTW	twin
INTY	tiny
INVY	viny
INWY	winy
IOPR	Pori
IOPS	pois
IOPT	topi
IORS	sori
IORT	riot
	roti
	tiro
	tori
	trio
IOSS	Ossi
IOTT	Tito
IOVV	vivo
IPPS	pips
IPPY	pipy
IPQU	quip
IPRS	rips
IPRT	trip
IPRU	puir
	puri
IPSS	piss
	psis
	sips
IPST	pits
	spit
	tips
IPSV	spiv
IPSW	wisp
IPSY	yips
IPSZ	zips
IPTT	Pitt
IPTY	pity
IPUY	Pu-yi
IPXY	pixy
IQTU	quit
IQUZ	quiz
IRRY	yirr
IRSS	sirs
IRST	stir
IRTW	writ
IRTZ	ritz
IRWY	wiry
ISST	sits
ISTT	tits
ISTU	suit
	tuis
ISTW	wist
	wits
ISTZ	sitz
	zits
ISWY	ywis
ISWZ	swiz
ISYZ	sizy
ITTW	twit
	Witt
ITUW	Wu Ti
ITZZ	tizz
IUWX	Wuxi
IZZZ	zizz
JJUU	juju
JKNU	junk
JKOO	jook
JKOU	jouk
JKOY	joky
JLOO	Jolo
JLOS	jols
JLOT	jolt
JLOW	jowl
JMOO	mojo
JMPU	jump
JNOU	Juno
JOOT	Tojo
JOSS	joss
JOST	jots
JOSY	joys
JRUY	jury
JSTU	just
	juts
KKOO	kook
KLNO	Köln
KLNU	lunk
KLOO	kolo
	look
KLOP	polk
KLOS	skol
KLOV	volk
KLOY	yolk
KLRU	lurk
KLSU	sulk
KMNO	monk
KMOO	moko
	mook
KMOS	Omsk
KMRU	murk
KMRY	Krym
KMSU	musk
KNOO	nook
KNOP	knop
KNOR	nork
KNOT	knot
	tonk
KNOW	know
	wonk
KNOX	Knox
KNPU	punk
KNRU	knur
KNSU	sunk
KNTU	knut
KNUU	Nuuk
KOOP	pook
KOOR	rook
KOOS	sook
KOOT	koto
	took
KOPR	pork
KOPS	kops
KOPY	poky
KORS	Orsk
KORU	koru
KORW	work
KORY	york
KOSU	souk
KOSW	woks
KOUZ	zouk
KRSU	rusk
KRTU	turk
KRUU	kuru
KSTU	tusk
KSUY	kyus
KTUU	kutu
LLLO	loll
LLLU	lull
LLMO	moll
LLMU	mull
LLNU	null
LLOP	poll
LLOR	roll
LLOT	toll
LLPU	pull
LLTU	Tull
LLUU	lulu
LLYY	Lyly
LMOO	loom
LMOS	olms
LMOT	molt
LMOU	Lomu
LMOY	moly
LMPU	lump
	plum
LMSU	lums
	slum
LNNY	Lynn
LNOO	loon
LNOR	lorn
LNOY	Lyon
	only
LNRU	nurl
LNUY	luny
LNXY	lynx
LOOP	loop
	polo
	pool
LOOS	loos
	Oslo
	solo
	sool
LOOT	loot
	tool
LOOW	wool
LOPP	plop
LOPS	lops
	slop
LOPT	plot
LOPU	loup
LOPW	lowp
	plow
LOPY	ploy
	poly
LORT	rotl
LORU	lour
LORY	lory
	Orly
LOSS	loss
	sols
LOST	lost
	lots
	slot
LOSU	lous
	soul
LOSW	lows
	owls
	slow
LOSY	loys
LOTU	lout
	tolu
	Toul
LOTV	volt
LOUU	Oulu
LOVV	Lvov
LOWW	Lwów
LOWY	yowl
LPPU	pulp
LPRU	purl
LPSU	plus
	puls
LRSU	slur
LRUY	ruly
LSTU	lust
	slut
LSUU	sulu
LTUZ	lutz
LUUZ	zulu
MMMU	mumm
MMOS	moms
MMPU	mump
MMSU	mums
MNOO	mono
	moon
MNOR	morn
	norm
MNOS	mons
MNOU	muon
MNOW	mown
MNOY	mony
MNTU	munt
MOOR	moor
	Moro
	room
MOOS	moos
MOOT	moot
MOOZ	zoom
MOPP	pomp
MOPR	prom
	romp
MOPS	mops
	poms
MOPY	mopy
	yomp
MORS	mors
MORT	mort

MORW	worm
MOSS	moss
MOST	most
	mots
	toms
MOSU	muso
	sumo
MOSW	mows
MOSY	somy
MOTU	motu
MOUV	ovum
MOXY	myxo
MOZZ	mozz
MPPU	pump
MPRU	rump
MPSU	sump
MPTU	tump
MPUY	umpy
MRSU	smur
MSSU	muss
	sums
MSTU	must
	muts
	smut
	stum
	tums
MSUW	swum
MSUY	Sumy
MTTU	mutt
MUZZ	muzz
NNNU	Nunn
NNOO	Nono
	noon
NNOR	Norn
NNOU	noun
NNSU	nuns
	sunn
NOOP	poon
NOOS	soon
NOOT	onto
	oont
	toon
NOOX	Oxon
NOOZ	zoon
NOPR	porn
NOPS	pons
NOPT	pont
NOPU	upon
NOPY	pony
NORS	sorn
NORT	torn
	tron
NORW	worn
NORZ	Zorn
NOSS	sons
NOST	snot
	tons
NOSU	nous
	onus
	Osun
NOSW	owns
	snow
	sown
	wons
NOSY	nosy
NOTU	toun
	unto
NOTW	nowt
	town
	wont
NOTY	tony
NOXY	onyx
NPSU	puns
	spun
NPTU	punt
NPUY	puny
NRSU	runs
	urns
NRTU	runt
	turn
NSSU	suns
NSTU	nuts
	stun
	tuns
NTXY	Xnty
OOPP	poop
OOPR	poor
OOPS	oops
OOPT	topo
OORS	roos
OORT	Oort
	root
	roto
OOST	soot
	Soto
OOSW	woos
OOSY	oosy
OOSZ	zoos
OOTT	otto
	toot
OOTZ	zoot
OOUZ	ouzo
OOYZ	oozy
OPPR	prop
OPPS	pops
OPRS	pros
OPRT	port
OPRU	pour
	roup
OPRW	prow
OPRY	pyro
	ropy
	yorp
OPSS	poss
	sops
OPST	opts
	post
	pots
	spot
	stop
	tops
OPSU	opus
	soup
OPSW	pows
	swop
	wops
OPSY	posy
OPTT	pott
OPTU	pout
OPTY	pyot
	typo
OPXY	poxy
ORRT	rort
	torr
ORSS	Ross
ORST	orts
	rots
	sort
	tors
ORSU	ours
	sour
ORSW	rows
ORSY	rosy
	Syro-
ORTT	tort
	trot
ORTU	rout
	tour
ORTW	trow
	wort
ORTY	ryot
	tory
	troy
	tyro
ORUV	vrou
ORUX	roux
ORUY	your
ORXY	oryx
OSSS	soss
OSST	sots
	toss
OSSU	sous
OSSW	sows
OSTT	stot
	tots
OSTU	oust
	outs
OSTW	stow
	swot
	tows
	twos
OSTY	toys
OSUX	Oxus
OSUY	yous
OSVW	vows
OSWW	wows
OTTU	tout
OTWY	towy
PPSU	pups
PRRU	purr
PRSU	spur
PRSY	spry
PRTU	Prut
PSST	psst
PSSU	puss
	sups
PSTU	puts
	tups
PTTU	putt
PTUZ	putz
QSSU	suqs
RRTY	Tyrr
RRUU	ruru
RSSU	USSR
RSTT	Trst
RSTU	rust
	ruts
RSUU	urus
RTUY	yurt
SSSU	suss
SSUU	susu
SSUW	wuss
STTU	tuts
STXY	Styx
	xyst
TTUU	tutu

Five Letters

AAABC abaca
Caaba
AAABK Kaaba
AAABQ Aqaba
AAADN Adana
AAAGM agama
AAAGN Agaña
AAAIS A'asia
AAAMP Amapá
AAANS asana
AAANT anata
AAANZ Azaña
AAARU Aarau
AAASV Vaasa
AAATT taata
AABBR Babar
AABBS abbas
babas
AABBY yabba
AABCK aback
AABCL cabal
AABCR barca
AABCS abacs
AABCU Bacău
AABDE baaed
Baeda
AABDN banda
AABEK Bekaa
AABEM abeam
ameba
AABES abase
AABET abate
AABFT abaft
AABGL Galba
AABGM gamba
AABGR Braga
Gabar
AABHI Baha'í
Bahia
AABHM hamba
AABHS abash
Sabah
Shaba
AABIL labia
AABIR braai
Rabia
AABJN bajan
AABJR Rajab
AABJU Abuja
AABKN banak
Banka
AABKR Akbar
bakra
Barak
AABLN Alban
banal
Laban
nabla
AABLR labra
AABLS balas
balsa
basal
AABLT tabla
AABMM mamba
AABMP abamp
AABMS samba
AABNT Banat
AABNW bwana
nawab
AABRR barra
AABRS Basra
sabra
AABRT rabat
AABRU Aruba
AABRY Araby
AABRZ bazar
AACCD Accad
AACCE caeca
AACCO cacao
AACCR Accra
AACCU Cauca
AACCY yacca
AACDE caaed
AACDH dacha
AACDI Dacia
AACDU cauda
AACEI aecia
AACEN Canea
AACEP apace
AACER areca
Ceará
AACFI facia
AACGN Gäncä
AACHK Chaka
kacha
AACHP pacha
AACIR acari
Arica
Caria
AACIS Isaac
AACJL Cajal
AACKL alack
AACKY yacka
AACLL calla
AACLN canal
Lacan
AACLS scala
AACLT Talca
AACMN caman
AACMO Macao
AACMS camas
AACMU Macáu
AACMW macaw
AACNN canna
AACNT tacan
AACNV Cavan
AACPR Capra
AACPS pacas
scapa
AACPU Capua
AACRS sacra
AACRT carat
AACSW waacs
AACUV vacua
AADDH dadah
AADDX addax
AADEF faaed
AADEG adage
AADEH ahead
AADEN Danaë
AADFR daraf
farad
AADGG dagga
AADGN Dagan
AADGR garda
AADHK Dhaka
AADHL hadal
AADHN adhan
Dahna
AADHW dawah
AADIM Amida
AADIN Aidan
Diana
naiad
AADIS Saadi
Saida
AADIW Wadai
AADJJ Djaja
AADJW Wajda
AADKK Akkad
AADKR Dakar
Kádár
AADLN Aldan
AADLS salad
AADLT datal
AADLU Lauda
AADLW dwaal
AADMM madam
AADMN adman
daman
AADMO Damão
AADMR damar
drama
AADMS Adams
AADNP panda
AADNR Nadar
AADNV vanda
V and A
AADNY dayan
AADOV Davao
AADOW Adowa
AADPR Arpád
AADPT adapt
AADPU Padua
AADRR radar
AADRV Drava
AADRW award
AADSS Assad
AADST Sadat
AADTW Waadt
AADTY adyta
AADUW Aduwa
AAEFN faena
AAEGL algae
galea
AAEGP agape
AAEGT agate
AAEGV agave
AAEHK hakea
AAEKL akela
AAEKP apeak
AAEKW awake
AAELP palea
AAELR areal
AAELT alate
AAEMR maare
marae
AAEMZ amaze
AAENP apnea
paean
AAENR anear
arena
AAENT Aetna
antae
AAEOZ zoaea
AAEQU aquae
AAERS areas
AAERU aurae
AAERW aware
AAFFJ Jaffa
AAFHI Haifa
AAFHS haafs
AAFIL Faial
AAFIM mafia
AAFIT tafia
AAFJN Najaf
AAFJS jafas
AAFKK Kafka
AAFKN nakfa
AAFLL Falla
AAFLS alfas
AAFLT fatal
AAFLY Fayal
AAFNU fauna
AAFRS Safar
AAFTW fatwa
AAGGR ragga
AAGGW wagga
AAGHL galah
AAGHN Ghana
AAGHR Hagar
AAGHS aghas
AAGHT Gatha
AAGIN again
AAGIS saiga

AAGIT taiga
AAGJN ganja
AAGJS jagas
AAGKN kanga
AAGLL algal
AAGLN lagan
AAGLO Laoag
AAGLR argal
AAGLS galas
AAGLV vagal
AAGLY gayal
AAGMM gamma
magma
AAGMN manga
AAGMR Agram
grama
AAGMS agmas
AAGMT tagma
AAGNP pagan
panga
AAGNS nagas
Sagan
AAGNT tanga
AAGOR agora
AAGPR apgar
AAGRS ragas
AAGSS sagas
AAGUV guava
AAHHS hahas
AAHHT hatha
AAHIN Hania
AAHIS Aisha
AAHJR rajah
AAHKM Khama
AAHKS hakas
kasha
Shaka
AAHLL Allah
halal
AAHLM halma
hamal
AAHLN nahal
AAHLO aloha
AAHLP alpha
AAHLR lahar
AAHLS Lhasa
AAHLT latah
AAHLV halva
AAHMO Omaha
AAHMR haram
AAHMS amahs
AAHMZ hamza
AAHNN Hanna
AAHNS hansa
AAHNU Hanau
AAHNZ hazan
AAHOR aroha
AAHPR Praha
AAHPS pasha
AAHRR Harar
AAHRS haars
Sarah
AAHRT arhat
ratha
AAHRV Varah
AAHRY rayah
AAHSW awash
AAHSY ayahs
AAHWZ Ahwaz
AAIIL aalii
AAIKK kaiak
AAIKS Kasai
sakai
AAIKT akita
kiaat
AAIKU Kauai
AAILM lamia
AAILN lanai
liana
AAILR laari
AAILS alias
AAILV avail
Ávila
AAILX axial
AAIMN amain
amnia
anima
mania
AAIMR maria
AAIMT Amati
matai
AAIMZ zamia
AAINP apian
AAINR Arian
naira
AAINS Asian
AAINV avian
AAIPR Praia
AAIPS paisa
AAIPV Pavia
AAIRS arias
raias
AAIRT aarti
atria
raita
tiara
AAIRV varia
AAIRZ Zaria
AAISS assai
AAIST satai
AAISV Saiva
AAITW await
tawai
AAJKS Askja
AAJLP jalap
AAJNP japan
AAJNV Javan
AAJNW jawan
AAJPS jaaps
AAJRS rajas
AAKKS kakas
AAKKY kayak
yakka
AAKLO koala
AAKLP kalpa
AAKLR kraal
AAKLS laksa
AAKLT Kalat
AAKMR karma
makar
marka
AAKNN Nanak
AAKNR Karan
AAKNT tanka
AAKNZ Kazan
AAKOS Asoka
Osaka
AAKOT Takao
AAKPP kappa
AAKPR parka
AAKPS Spaak
AAKRS araks
karas
Sarka
AAKRT karat
Katar
AAKRW Kwara
AAKSS Kassa
AAKST katas
takas
AAKSV kavas
AAKSW wakas
AAKTZ zakat
AALLM llama
AALLO Alloa
AALLU alula
AALLV Laval
Valla
AALLW walla
AALLY allay
AALMM malam
AALMO alamo
AALMP Palma
AALMR alarm
malar
Mälar
AALMS lamas
malas
AALMT Malta
AALMU ulama
AALMW malwa
AALNN annal
AALNS nasal
AALNT natal
AALNV naval
AALNY nyala
AALOT Aalto
AALPP appal
papal
AALPS paals
plaas
salpa
AALPT Plata
AALPU Palau
AALPY playa
AALPZ La Paz
plaza
AALQT talaq
AALRT altar
artal
ratal
AALRU aural
AALRV larva
AALRY alary
AALRZ lazar
AALSS Lassa
salsa
AALST Aalst
atlas
Salta
talas
AALTY Yalta
AALWY alway
AAMMM mamma
AAMMN amman
AAMMS mamas
AAMNN Annam
manna
AAMNS Masan
AAMNT atman
manat
manta
AAMNX axman
AAMNY mayan
AAMOR aroma
AAMOS omasa
Samoa
AAMPR Parma
AAMPT Tampa
AAMRS maars
maras
Maraş
Samar
AAMRT Marat
AAMSS amass
assam
massa
AAMSY mayas
AAMTU amaut
AAMTZ matza
AANNN Annan
nanna
AANNS annas
naans
nanas
AANNW wanna
AANNY Yanan
AANOR Aaron
AANOS anoas
AANOX xoana
AANPP nappa
AANPR prana
AANPT Patna
AANPV pavan
AANPY Panay
AANRR Arran
AANRS saran
AANRT antra
ratan
AANRV Narva
navar
varna
AANRY Arany
AANST Santa
Satan
tanas
Tsana
AANSU sauna
AANSW Aswan
AANSY Nyasa
AANSZ azans
AANTT Tanta
AANTV avant
AAORT aorta
AAOST Aosta
AAPPS papas
AAPPU Papua
AAPPW papaw
AAPPZ Zappa
AAPRR parra
AAPRS paras
AAPRT apart
AAPST pasta
tapas
AAPSU pauas
AAPSY Pasay
AAPTW watap
AAQRT Qatar
AAQRZ Zarqa
AAQSU aquas
AARRS arras
AARRU Arrau
aurar
AARRY array
AARST rasta
ratas
AARSU auras
AARSV varas
AARTT attar
tatar
AARTW Warta
AARTY tayra
AARTZ Taraz
Tzara
AASSY assay
AASTV avast
AASTW tawas
AASTY satay
AASWW wawas
AASWY aways
AATXY ataxy
AATZZ tazza
ABBCO cabob
ABBCY cabby
ABBDE abbed
ABBEK kebab
ABBEL babel
ABBER Baber
ABBES abbes
babes

ABBEY abbey
ABBGY gabby
ABBIM bambi
ABBIR rabbi
ABBKO kabob
ABBLO Balbo
ABBLS blabs
ABBLU babul
bubal
ABBNO nabob
ABBOS boabs
ABBOT abbot
ABBRS barbs
ABBRU Babur
ABBRY barby
ABBSU babus
ABBTY tabby
ABBYY yabby
ABCCY baccy
ABCEH beach
ABCEI ceiba
ABCEK Baeck
ABCEL cable
ABCER Barce
brace
caber
ABCHI Chiba
ABCHR brach
ABCHT batch
ABCIN cabin
ABCIO cobia
ABCIR baric
rabic
ABCIS basic
ABCJO Jacob
ABCKL black
ABCKR brack
ABCKS backs
ABCLN Blanc
ABCMS Cambs
ABCNO bacon
banco
ABCNU Cuban
ABCOR Broca
carbo
carob
cobra
ABCOT Cabot
ABCOV vocab
ABCRS crabs
ABCRT bract
ABCRY carby
ABCSS scabs
ABCSU scuba
ABDDY baddy
ABDEG badge
begad
debag
ABDEI abide
ABDEK baked
ABDEL abled
baled
blade
ABDEN Baden
Benda
ABDEO abode
adobe
ABDER ardeb
Bader
barde
bared
beard
bread
Breda
debar
ABDES based
beads
ABDET bated
ABDEU daube
ABDEY bayed
beady
ABDHN bandh
ABDIL Blida
ABDIR Baird
braid
rabid
ABDIU Dubai
ABDLN bland
ABDLO dobla
ABDLY badly
baldy
ABDNR brand
ABDNS bands
ABDNU Dubna
ABDNY bandy
Danby
ABDOR bardo
board
broad
dobra
dorba
ABDOS doabs
ABDRS bards
brads
drabs
ABDRY Darby
ABDSU bauds
daubs
ABDSW bawds
ABDUY dauby
ABDWY bawdy
ABEEL abele
albee
Beale
ABEFL fable
ABEFR Fabre
ABEGI bagie
ABEGL bagel
belga
gable
ABEGN began
ABEGR barge
ABEGS Gabès
ABEGT begat
ABEHJ hejab
ABEHL belah
ABEHN Behan
ABEHO bohea
obeah
ABEHR Brahe
rehab
ABEHS saheb
Sheba
ABEHT bathe
ABEIR Beira
Beria
ABEIS Basie
ABEIZ baize
ABEJM jambe
ABEJR Jerba
ABEKL Blake
bleak
ABEKR baker
brake
break
ABEKS bakes
beaks
ABEKY beaky
ABELL label
ABELM amble
blame
Melba
ABELR abler
baler
belar
blare
blear
ABELS baels
bales
Basel
Basle
blaes
blase
sable
ABELT bleat
table
Taleb
ABELU Belau
ABELY bayle
belay
ABELZ blaze
ABEMP Pemba
ABEMR amber
bream
ABEMS beams
ABEMY beamy
embay
maybe
ABENO beano
ABENS Asben
banes
beans
ABENV Bevan
ABENY beany
ABEOV above
ABERR Arber
barer
barre
Berar
ABERS bares
baser
bears
braes
saber
sabre
ABERU Auber
ABERV brave
ABERY barye
yerba
ABERZ braze
zebra
ABESS bases
ABEST abets
baste
bates
beast
beats
betas
tabes
ABESU abuse
beaus
ABESY abyes
bayes
ABETT betta
ABETU beaut
tubae
ABETY beaty
ABEUX beaux
ABFFN Banff
ABFRU fubar
ABFRY Fabry
ABGGR Bragg
ABGGY baggy
ABGHN bhang
ABGHS baghs
ABGIR Bragi
ABGLS blags
ABGNO bogan
Gabon
ABGNS bangs
ABGOR Gabor
garbo
ABGRS brags
garbs
grabs
ABHIJ bhaji
hijab
ABHIM bimah
ABHIO Bohai
ABHIR Bihar
ABHIS sahib
ABHIT habit
ABHKL Balkh
ABHLS blahs
ABHMO abohm
ABHOR abhor
ABHOS basho
ABHOT Botha
ABHRS brash
ABHRT Barth
ABHST bahts
baths
ABHSU habus
subah
subha
ABIIL alibi
Libia
ABIIM iambi
ABIIT tibia
ABIIZ Ibiza
ABIJM Jambi
ABIKL kibla
ABIKR Kabir
ABIKT batik
ABILN binal
blain
ABILQ Iqbal
qibla
ABILR Arbil
Blair
brail
libra
ABILS bails
basil
ABILT balti
ABILU Libau
ABILY Libya
ABIMR mbira
ABIMS bimas
iambs
simba
ABIMT ambit
ABINQ niqab
ABINR bairn
brain
Brian
Rabin
ABINS basin
nabis
sabin
ABINU nubia
ABIOT biota
ABIQS Qabis
ABIRR briar
ABIRS abris
rabis
ABISS basis
bassi
ABIST baits
basti
ABJLU Jubal
ABJMO jambo
ABJMS jambs
ABJNO banjo
ABJOT jabot
ABJSU jubas
ABKLN blank
ABKLS balks
ABKLU baulk
Kabul

ABKLY	balky
ABKNS	banks
ABKNU	Kuban
ABKOR	borak
ABKOS	boaks
ABKRS	barks
ABKRU	burka
ABKSS	basks
ABKST	Bakst
ABLLS	balls
ABLLU	bulla
ABLLY	bally
ABLMS	balms
	lambs
ABLMU	album
ABLMY	balmy
ABLNU	balun
ABLOR	labor
	lobar
ABLOS	bolas
ABLOT	bloat
ABLOY	boyla
ABLRT	blart
ABLRU	lubra
ABLRW	brawl
ABLSS	slabs
ABLST	blast
	blats
ABLSW	bawls
ABLTU	tubal
ABLWY	bylaw
ABMMO	mambo
ABMOS	ambos
	bomas
	sambo
ABMOT	Tambo
ABMOZ	Zomba
ABMRS	barms
ABMRU	Burma
	rumba
	umbra
ABMRY	ambry
	barmy
ABMSU	Sumba
ABMSY	abysm
ABMTU	Batum
ABMUY	mauby
ABNNS	banns
ABNNU	unban
ABNOR	baron
ABNOT	baton
ABNRS	barns
ABNRT	brant
ABNRU	Braun
	buran
	unbar
	urban
ABNRW	brawn
ABNTU	bantu
	tabun
ABNUY	bunya
ABOOT	taboo
ABOOZ	bazoo
ABORR	arbor
	barro
ABORS	boars
	boras
	Borås
ABORT	abort
	boart
	tabor
ABORV	bravo
ABORX	borax
ABORY	boyar
ABOSS	basso
ABOST	boast
	boats
	sabot
ABOSV	Basov
ABOTU	about
ABOUY	bayou
ABPST	Pabst
ABQRU	burqa
ABQSU	squab
ABRRU	Burra
ABRRY	barry
ABRSS	brass
ABRST	brats
	trabs
ABRSU	Arbus
	Brusa
	buras
	bursa
	Busra
ABRSW	warbs
ABRSY	brays
ABRWY	warby
ABRXY	braxy
ABSST	stabs
ABSSW	swabs
ABSSY	abyss
ABSTT	batts
ABSTU	abuts
	tabus
	tubas
ABTTY	batty
	Byatt
ABUZZ	abuzz
ABWYY	byway
ACCDY	cycad
ACCEH	cache
ACCEL	cecal
ACCEM	mecca
ACCHO	chaco
	coach
ACCHT	catch
ACCIR	circa
	craic
ACCIT	cacti
ACCIW	wicca
ACCKL	clack
ACCKR	crack
ACCKY	cacky
ACCLU	Lucca
ACCMO	occam
ACCNZ	CCANZ
ACCOO	cocoa
ACCOS	cocas
	Sacco
ACCUY	yucca
ACDDY	caddy
ACDEF	decaf
	faced
ACDEG	cadge
	caged
ACDEH	ached
ACDEK	caked
ACDEL	clade
	decal
	laced
ACDEM	maced
ACDEN	caned
	dance
ACDEP	paced
ACDER	acred
	arced
	cadre
	cared
	cedar
	raced
ACDES	cades
	cased
	daces
	ecads
ACDET	acted
	cadet
ACDEV	caved
ACDEW	cawed
ACDEY	decay
ACDHO	chado
ACDHR	chard
ACDHT	Tchad
ACDHY	daych
ACDIN	canid
	nicad
ACDIR	acrid
	caird
	cardi
	daric
	Dirac
ACDIS	acids
	asdic
	cadis
ACDIT	dicta
ACDIY	acidy
ACDIZ	Cádiz
ACDKR	drack
ACDKS	dacks
ACDLS	clads
	scald
ACDLU	cauld
	ducal
ACDNY	candy
ACDOR	draco
ACDOS	codas
ACDOT	octad
ACDRS	cards
ACDRY	cardy
	darcy
ACDSS	scads
ACDSU	scaud
ACDTU	ducat
ACEEK	ackee
ACEEP	peace
ACEES	cease
ACEFH	chafe
ACEFL	fecal
ACEFR	facer
	farce
ACEFS	cafes
	faces
ACEFT	facet
ACEGL	glace
ACEGN	Gance
ACEGR	grace
ACEGS	cages
ACEGY	cagey
ACEHK	cheka
ACEHL	chela
	leach
ACEHN	hance
ACEHP	chape
	cheap
	peach
ACEHR	reach
ACEHS	aches
	chase
ACEHT	cheat
	tache
	teach
	theca
ACEIL	Alice
	ileac
ACEIM	amice
ACEIN	Caine
ACEIR	ceria
	erica
ACEIS	saice
ACEIV	cavie
ACEKL	aleck
ACEKP	Čapek
ACEKR	acker
	crake
	creak
ACEKS	cakes
ACEKW	wacke
ACEKY	cakey
ACELL	cella
ACELM	camel
	macle
ACELN	Celan
	clean
	lance
ACELP	Calpe
	place
ACELR	carle
	Clare
	clear
	lacer
ACELS	alecs
	claes
	laces
	scale
ACELT	cleat
	eclat
ACELV	calve
	cavel
	clave
ACEMO	cameo
	comae
ACEMR	Carme
	Ceram
	cream
	macer
	Merca
ACEMS	acmes
	cames
	maces
ACEMY	cymae
ACENO	canoe
	ocean
ACENP	pecan
ACENR	caner
	Carné
	crane
	nacre
	rance
ACENS	canes
	scena
ACENT	enact
ACEOR	ocrea
ACEOX	coxae
ACEPR	caper
	crape
	pacer
	recap
ACEPS	capes
	paces
	scape
	space
ACEPT	Capet
	epact
ACEPY	pacey
ACERR	carer
	racer
ACERS	acers
	acres
	cares
	carse
	races
	scare
	serac
ACERT	caret
	carte
	cater
	crate
	react
	recta
	trace
ACERV	carve

caver
crave
varec
ACERW Carew
ACERY Carey
ACERZ craze
ACESS cases
ACEST caste
cates
taces
ACESU cause
sauce
ACESV caves
ACESY Cayes
ACETT tacet
ACETU acute
Ceuta
ACETX exact
ACFFH chaff
ACFFS caffs
ACFHU chufa
ACFIL calif
ACFIR farci
ACFKL flack
ACFLO focal
ACFNR franc
ACFNY fancy
ACFRS scarf
ACFRT craft
ACFRU furca
ACFRY farcy
ACFST facts
ACGHN chang
ACGIM gamic
magic
ACGIN acing
ACGIR cigar
craig
ACGLN clang
ACGLS clags
ACGNO conga
ACGNS cangs
ACGOR cargo
ACGOU guaco
ACGRS crags
scrag
ACGSS scags
ACHHT hatch
ACHIK haick
ACHIL Haliç
ACHIM Micah
ACHIN chain
Chian
china
ACHIR chair
Chari
ACHIT aitch
Chita
ACHKL chalk
ACHKS hacks
shack
ACHKW chawk
whack
ACHLO loach
ACHLR larch
ACHLS clash
ACHLT latch
ACHLU luach
ACHMO choma
macho
mocha
ACHMP champ
ACHMR charm
march
ACHMS chams
chasm
ACHMT match
ACHNO nacho
ACHNR ranch
ACHNT chant
natch
ACHNU nauch
nucha
ACHOP poach
ACHOR orach
roach
ACHOS chaos
ACHOT Catho
tacho
ACHOV havoc
ACHPR parch
ACHPS chaps
Pasch
ACHPT patch
ACHRR charr
ACHRS chars
crash
ACHRT chart
ACHRY chary
ACHSS Sachs
ACHST chats
ACHSU sauch
ACHSW chaws
schwa
ACHTW watch
ACHTY yacht
ACHUV vauch
ACIIL cilia
iliac
ACIIN acini
ACILL lilac
ACILM claim
malic
ACILN linac
ACILP plica
ACILR Clair
ACILS laics
salic
ACILT ictal
tical
ACILU aulic
ACILV cavil
ACILX calix
ACILY Lycia
ACIMN manic
ACIMR micra
ACIMS micas
ACINN Cinna
ACINO Ciano
ACINP panic
ACINR cairn
ACINT actin
antic
ACINV vinca
ACIOR Cairo
coria
ACIOT coati
ACIOZ azoic
ACIPR Capri
carpi
ACIPS aspic
Pašić
picas
spica
ACIPZ capiz
ACIRT artic
ACIRU auric
curia
ACIRV vicar
ACIRX Craxi
ACISU Caius
ACITT attic
tacit
ACITU Utica
ACITV vatic
ACJKS jacks
ACJKY jacky
ACJNU cajun
ACKKN knack
ACKLN clank
ACKLO cloak
ACKLR Clark
ACKLS calks
lacks
slack
ACKLU caulk
ACKMS macks
smack
ACKMU amuck
ACKNR crank
ACKNS snack
ACKOR croak
ACKOW wacko
ACKPS packs
ACKPU pucka
ACKQU quack
ACKRS carks
racks
ACKRT track
ACKRW wrack
ACKSS casks
sacks
ACKST stack
tacks
ACKSW wacks
ACKSY yacks
ACKTY tacky
ACKWY wacky
ACLLO local
ACLLS calls
scall
ACLMO cloam
comal
ACLMP clamp
ACLMS calms
clams
ACLNS clans
Lancs
ACLNU Lucan
ACLOP copal
ACLOR carol
claro
coral
Lorca
ACLOS alcos
coals
colas
ACLOT octal
ACLOV vocal
ACLOW cowal
ACLOX coxal
ACLOY coaly
ACLOZ colza
ACLPS claps
clasp
scalp
ACLPU culpa
ACLRS carls
ACLRW crawl
ACLRY clary
ACLSS class
ACLST talcs
ACLSU cauls
Lucas
ACLSW claws
ACLSY clays
scaly
ACLXY calyx
ACMMO comma
ACMNO macon
Mâcon
Nam Co
ACMOP campo
ACMOR carom
macro
Maroc
ACMOS comas
ACMPR cramp
ACMPS camps
scamp
ACMPY campy
ACMRS crams
marcs
scram
ACMRY cymar
ACMSS scams
ACMSU camus
musca
sumac
ACMSY cymas
ACNNO ancon
canon
ACNNY canny
nancy
ACNOP capon
Copán
ACNOR acorn
narco
racon
ACNOS canso
ACNOT acton
canto
cotan
ACNOY cyano
ACNPU pucan
uncap
ACNRS crans
narcs
scran
ACNRY carny
ACNSS scans
ACNST canst
cants
scant
ACNTY canty
ACOPR copra
ACOPS capos
scopa
ACOPT capot
ACORS oscar
ACORT actor
Croat
ACORY oracy
ACOST ascot
coast
coats
costa
octas
tacos
ACOTT cotta
ACPPU cuppa
ACPRS carps
craps
scarp
scrap
ACPRY crapy
ACPST pacts
ACPSU scaup
ACPTU caput
ACRRS carrs
ACRRU crura
ACRRY carry
ACRSS crass
scars
ACRST carts
scart
ACRSU scaur
ACRSW craws
scraw
ACRSY crays

scary
ACRSZ czars
ACRTT tract
ACRTY Tracy
ACRYZ crazy
ACSST casts
scats
ACSSU ascus
ACSTU scuta
ACSUY saucy
ACTTY catty
ADDDE added
ADDDY daddy
ADDEF faded
ADDEH haded
ADDEI aided
ADDEJ jaded
Jedda
ADDEL addle
daled
dedal
laded
ADDER adder
dared
dread
readd
ADDET dated
ADDEW waded
ADDEZ dazed
ADDFY faddy
ADDGI gadid
ADDIJ Jidda
ADDIV David
ADDLY Lydda
ADDNY dandy
ADDOS dados
saddo
ADDPY paddy
ADDRY dryad
ADDSU dauds
duads
ADDSY dyads
ADDWY waddy
ADEEM edema
Meade
Medea
ADEEN Deane
ADEER eared
Reade
ADEES aedes
eased
ADEEV deave
evade
ADEFG fadge
ADEFK faked
ADEFM famed
ADEFR fader
fared
ADEFS fades
ADEFT fated
ADEFX faxed
ADEFY fayed
ADEFZ fazed
ADEGG gaged
ADEGI Adige
ADEGL glade
ADEGM gamed
ADEGP gaped
paged
ADEGR Edgar
grade
radge
raged
ADEGS degas
ADEGT gated
ADEGW waged
ADEGZ gazed
ADEHJ jehad
ADEHK Kedah
kheda
ADEHL haled
ADEHN Haden
ADEHR hared
heard
ADEHS hades
heads
sadhe
shade
ADEHT death
hated
ADEHW hawed
ADEHX hexad
ADEHY hayed
heady
ADEHZ hazed
ADEIL ailed
ideal
ADEIM aimed
amide
media
ADEIR aider
aired
irade
redia
ADEIS aides
aside
Desai
ideas
ADEIU adieu
ADEIZ azide
ADEJP japed
ADEJS jades
ADEJU Judea
ADEJW jawed
ADEKN knead
naked
ADEKR drake
Radek
raked
ADEKS asked
ADELL ladle
ADELM lamed
medal
ADELN Dalén
eland
laden
ADELP paled
pedal
plead
ADELR Adler
alder
lader
ADELS dales
deals
lades
lased
leads
ADELT dealt
delta
lated
ADELV laved
ADELW dwale
waled
weald
ADELY delay
leady
ADELZ lazed
ADEMN admen
amend
deman
maned
Medan
menad
named
ADEMR armed
derma
dream
ADEMS dames
meads
ADEMT mated
tamed
ADEMZ mazed
ADENO anode
ADENP paned
Penda
ADENR André
Arden
denar
Nader
redan
ADENS Andes
deans
sedan
Sedna
Snead
ADENT anted
Dante
ADENU Auden
ADENV daven
vaned
Venda
ADENW awned
dewan
waned
ADEOR adore
oared
oread
ADEPR drape
padre
pared
raped
ADEPS spade
spaed
ADEPT adept
taped
ADEPV paved
ADEPW pawed
ADEPY payed
ADERR darer
drear
ADERS arsed
dares
dears
rased
reads
ADERT rated
tared
trade
tread
ADERV drave
raved
ADERW dewar
wader
wared
ADERX raxed
ADERY deary
rayed
ready
ADERZ razed
ADESS sades
ADEST dates
sated
stead
tsade
ADESV devas
saved
ADESW Dawes
sawed
wades
ADESZ adzes
dazes
ADETW tawed
ADETX taxed
ADEVW waved
ADEWX waxed
ADEWY yawed
ADFFR draff
ADFFS daffs
ADFFY daffy
ADFIU Fuad I
ADFLO Faldo
ADFNO fonda
ADFOS fados
ADFRT draft
ADFRU fraud
ADFRW dwarf
ADGGY daggy
ADGIL algid
ADGIU Gaudí
ADGLN gland
ADGLS glads
ADGMO dogma
ADGNO Dagon
donga
gonad
ADGNR grand
ADGNW dwang
ADGNY gandy
ADGOS dagos
goads
ADGOU Gouda
ADGRS dargs
drags
grads
ADGRU Durga
guard
ADGSU gauds
ADGUY gaudy
ADHIJ hadji
jihad
ADHIK khadi
ADHIL halid
ADHIM Mahdi
ADHIN Dinah
ADHIO Idaho
ADHIP aphid
ADHIS dashi
ADHJU Judah
ADHKS dhaks
ADHLS dhals
ADHNO donah
ADHNS hands
ADHNU hudna
ADHNY handy
Haydn
ADHOR hoard
ADHRS hards
shard
ADHRY hardy
hydra
ADHSS shads
ADHST hadst
ADHSU hauds
sadhu
ADHSY shady
ADIIL iliad
ADIIN Aidin
India
ADIIO oidia
ADIIR radii
ADIKS kadis
ADIKU aduki
ADILN nidal
ADILP plaid
ADILR drail
laird
liard
ADILS dials
ADILT Dalit
tidal

ADILU dulia
ADILV valid
Vidal
ADILY daily
Lydia
ADIMN admin
mandi
ADIMO amido
ADIMS maids
Midas
ADIMT admit
ADIMX admix
ADINN Dinan
dinna
ADINO danio
ADINR dinar
drain
Indra
nadir
ADINV divan
Dvina
viand
ADINW diwan
ADINY Aydin
ADIOP podia
ADIOR aroid
Dario
radio
ADIOS adios
ADIOU audio
Douai
Ouida
ADIOV avoid
ADIOZ diazo
ADIPR rapid
ADIPS sapid
ADIPV pavid
vapid
ADIQS qadis
ADIRS raids
Sidra
ADIRT triad
ADIRX radix
ADIRY dairy
diary
ADIRZ izard
ADISS saids
ADIST adits
ditas
staid
ADISU Saudi
ADISV Davis
divas
ADISY daisy
sayid
ADITU audit
ADITV davit
ADJNU Dunaj
ADJOU Oujda
ADJSU judas
ADKKU dukka
ADKLS skald
ADKLY alkyd
ADKNR drank
ADKNY kandy
ADKOR Korda
ADKOV vodka
ADKRS darks
ADKRY darky
ADKSU dukas
ADKSW dawks
ADLLO aldol
allod
ADLLU Udall
ADLLY dally
ADLMO dolma
modal
ADLMY madly
ADLNO Ndola
nodal
Öland
ADLNS lands
ADLNY Dylan
ADLOS loads
ADLOT dotal
ADLOU aloud
doula
ADLOW waldo
woald
ADLRS lards
ADLRU dural
ADLRW drawl
ADLRY lardy
Rydal
ADLSU duals
lauds
ADLSY sadly
ADLTU adult
ADLUY yauld
ADMNO monad
nomad
ADMNS damns
ADMNU maund
ADMOR Radom
ADMOU douma
ADMPS damps
ADMRS drams
ADMRU mudra
ADMRY mardy
ADMSU adsum
dumas
mauds
ADMSW dwams
ADMTU datum
ADMUW dwaum
ADNNO donna
ADNNY danny
ADNOO doona
ADNOR adorn
Donar
radon
ADNOS donas
ADNOU Donau
ADNPY pandy
Pydna
ADNRS darns
nards
rands
ADNRU Durán
ADNRW drawn
ADNRY randy
ADNSS sands
ADNST stand
ADNSU Sudan
ADNSW dawns
wands
ADNSY sandy
ADNTU daunt
ADOPR Prado
ADOPT adopt
ADORR ardor
ADORS dorsa
roads
sarod
ADORT troad
ADORU doura
ADOSS sodas
ADOST datos
doats
toads
ADOSV Davos
ADOTY toady
today
ADPRS draps
pards
ADPRU purda
ADPSU Padus
ADQSU quads
squad
ADRRU durra
ADRST darts
strad
ADRSU daurs
duras
Sudra
ADRSW draws
sward
wards
ADRSY drays
yards
ADRTY tardy
ADSTU adust
ADUVZ Vaduz
AEEFZ feaze
AEEGL aglee
eagle
AEEGP peage
AEEGR agree
eager
eagre
AEEHV heave
hevea
AEEIL Eleia
AEEIR aerie
AEEKN akene
AEEKP Peake
AEEKR rakee
AEEKS akees
AEELN anele
AEELS easel
lease
AEELT elate
telae
AEELV leave
AEEMN enema
Nemea
AEEMR ameer
ramee
AEENR arene
ranee
AEENT eaten
enate
AEENV venae
AEEOZ zoeae
AEEPR perea
AEEPS pease
AEEPY payee
AEERR raree
AEERS easer
erase
saree
AEERT arete
eater
AEERV reave
AEERZ razee
AEESS eases
AEEST setae
tease
AEESV eaves
AEETX exeat
AEEVW weave
AEFFG gaffe
AEFGN ganef
AEFHS sheaf
AEFIR afire
feria
AEFKL flake
AEFKN kenaf
AEFKR faker
freak
AEFKS fakes
AEFLL fella
AEFLM flame
fleam
AEFLR farle
feral
flare
AEFLS false
fleas
leafs
AEFLT fetal
AEFLY leafy
AEFMR frame
AEFMS fames
AEFNR frena
AEFNS fanes
AEFOR afore
AEFOV fovea
AEFPR frape
AEFRR farer
AEFRS fares
fears
safer
AEFRT after
AEFRU Fauré
feuar
AEFRW wafer
AEFRY faery
fayre
Freya
AEFSS safes
AEFST fates
feast
feats
AEFSX faxes
AEFSZ fazes
AEFUV fauve
AEGGR agger
eggar
gager
AEGGS gages
AEGGU gauge
AEGHM Egham
AEGHN Hagen
Neagh
AEGHP phage
AEGHR gerah
AEGHU Hague
AEGIL agile
AEGIM image
AEGIR Aegir
AEGIS aegis
AEGJR jager
AEGLL Galle
legal
AEGLM gleam
AEGLN angel
angle
Galen
glean
Lange
AEGLP plage
AEGLR Alger
Elgar
glare
lager
large
regal
AEGLS gales
AEGLT aglet
AEGLV gavel
Gävle
AEGLY agley
AEGLZ glaze
AEGMM gemma
AEGMN mange
AEGMO omega
AEGMR gamer
marge
AEGMS games

	mages
AEGMY	gamey
AEGNO	agone
	genoa
	Onega
AEGNR	anger
	range
AEGNS	Agnes
	geans
AEGNT	agent
	Tange
AEGNU	genua
AEGNV	ganev
	vegan
AEGNW	Agnew
AEGNY	gynae
AEGPR	gaper
	grape
	pager
AEGPS	gapes
	pages
AEGRS	gears
	rages
	sarge
AEGRT	grate
	great
	targe
	terga
AEGRU	argue
	auger
	rugae
AEGRV	grave
AEGRW	wager
AEGRY	gayer
AEGRZ	gazer
	graze
AEGSS	gases
	sages
AEGST	gates
	stage
AEGSU	usage
AEGSW	swage
	wages
AEGSZ	gazes
AEGTT	Atget
AEGTU	Taegu
AEGUV	vague
AEGUZ	gauze
AEHHP	ephah
AEHHT	heath
AEHJZ	Hejaz
AEHKL	Hekla
AEHKS	hakes
	Hašek
	shake
AEHKW	Hawke
AEHKY	Hayek
AEHLL	Halle
	Hallé
AEHLM	hemal
AEHLP	aleph
AEHLR	haler
	Lehár
AEHLS	hales
	heals
	leash
	selah
	shale
AEHLT	lathe
AEHLV	halve
	Havel
AEHLW	whale
	wheal
AEHLY	Haley
	Healy
AEHLZ	hazel
AEHMR	harem
	herma
AEHMS	hames
	shame
	Shema
AEHMT	meath
	Mehta
AEHNN	Henan
	henna
AEHNR	Ahern
AEHNS	ashen
	hanse
	Nashe
AEHNT	neath
	thane
AEHNV	haven
AEHNY	hyena
AEHOR	Horae
AEHOS	Hosea
AEHOT	Tahoe
AEHOV	hovea
AEHPR	raphe
AEHPS	ephas
	heaps
	phase
	shape
AEHRS	Asher
	hares
	hears
	rheas
	share
	shear
AEHRT	earth
	Harte
	heart
	Herat
	rathe
	Thera
AEHRV	haver
	Havre
AEHRW	whare
AEHRZ	hazer
AEHSS	ashes
	sheas
AEHST	ashet
	haste
	hates
	heats
AEHSV	haves
	shave
AEHSW	hawse
AEHSY	Hayes
AEHSZ	hazes
AEHTT	theta
AEHTW	wheat
AEHVY	heavy
AEIJK	Ikeja
AEIJX	jaxie
AEIKL	alike
	alkie
AEIKN	Aiken
AEILL	ileal
AEILM	email
AEILN	alien
	aline
	anile
	Laine
	liane
AEILP	pilea
AEILR	ariel
AEILS	aisle
	Elias
AEILT	Eilat
	telia
AEILV	alive
AEILX	axile
AEIMN	amine
	anime
	Maine
	minae
AEIMR	Marie
	ramie
AEIMS	amies
	Seami
AEIMZ	maize
	Zeami
AEINN	inane
AEINP	Paine
AEINS	Aisne
	anise
	isnae
	Siena
AEINT	entia
	Taine
	tenia
	tinea
AEINV	naevi
	naive
AEINX	xenia
AEINZ	azine
AEIPS	paise
	sepia
AEIPT	pieta
	pietà
AEIPV	Piave
AEIRS	aesir
	Aries
	arise
	raise
	serai
AEIRT	irate
	retia
	terai
AEIRU	aurei
AEIRZ	zaire
	Zaïre
AEIST	Saite
	Satie
AEITV	vitae
AEITW	waite
AEIVW	waive
AEJKS	jakes
AEJLV	javel
AEJMR	Ajmer
AEJMS	james
AEJNS	janes
	jeans
AEJNT	Janet
AEJPR	japer
AEJPS	japes
	jaspe
AEJST	tajes
AEKKM	Mekka
AEKLN	ankle
AEKLR	laker
AEKLS	kales
	lakes
	leaks
	slake
AEKLW	kwela
AEKLY	leaky
AEKMN	Ekman
AEKMR	kerma
	maker
AEKMS	kames
	makes
AEKMT	Kamet
AEKNO	oaken
AEKNP	pekan
AEKNR	naker
AEKNS	skean
	snake
	sneak
AEKNT	taken
AEKNV	knave
AEKNW	waken
AEKNY	Kenya
AEKOR	Korea
AEKOW	awoke
AEKPR	Perak
AEKPS	peaks
	spake
	speak
AEKPY	peaky
AEKQU	quake
AEKRR	raker
AEKRS	asker
	eskar
	rakes
	saker
AEKRT	taker
AEKRU	Akure
AEKRW	waker
	wreak
AEKSS	sakes
AEKST	Keats
	skate
	stake
	steak
	takes
AEKSU	ukase
AEKSW	askew
	wakes
	wekas
	Wesak
AEKSY	Askey
AEKTW	tweak
AELLM	Malle
AELLN	Allen
AELLP	lapel
	Pella
AELLS	Ellás
	Sella
AELLU	Luleå
AELLY	alley
AELMM	lemma
AELMN	leman
	Léman
AELMP	ample
	maple
	Palme
AELMR	lamer
	realm
AELMS	lames
	males
	meals
	melas
	Salem
AELMT	metal
AELMU	ulema
AELMY	mealy
AELNO	alone
	anole
AELNP	Nepal
	panel
	penal
	plane
	plena
AELNR	Larne
	learn
	neral
	renal
AELNS	lanes
	leans
AELNT	leant
AELNU	ulnae
AELNV	navel
	venal
AELNY	Lenya
AELOS	aloes
AELOV	laevo
AELOZ	azole
AELPP	appel
	apple

pepla
AELPR lepra
paler
pearl
AELPS lapse
leaps
pales
peals
pleas
salep
sepal
AELPT leapt
lepta
petal
plate
pleat
tepal
AELPY Paley
AELQU equal
quale
AELRS arles
earls
lares
laser
rales
reals
AELRT alert
alter
artel
later
ratel
taler
AELRU ureal
AELRV laver
ravel
Reval
velar
AELRW waler
AELRX relax
AELRY early
layer
leary
relay
AELSS lases
sales
seals
AELST least
leats
salet
setal
slate
Staël
stale
steal
stela
taels
tales
teals
tesla
AELSV avels
laves
salve
selva
slave
vales
valse
AELSW Lawes
swale
wales
weals
AELSX axels
axles
AELSY lyase
AELSZ lazes
AELTT latte
AELTV valet
AELTX exalt
latex
AELUV uveal
value
AELVV valve
AELWY Waley
AELZZ lezza
AEMMN Menam
AEMMT Mamet
AEMMY mamey
AEMNN Namen
Neman
AEMNR Marne
ramen
reman
AEMNS amens
manes
manse
means
mensa
names
AEMNT ament
manet
meant
AEMNV maven
AEMNX axmen
AEMNY meany
yamen
AEMOR morae
Morea
AEMOV voema
AEMOW Maewo
AEMRR rearm
AEMRS mares
maser
reams
Seram
smear
AEMRT armet
mater
tamer
AEMRW Mewar
AEMRY Mayer
AEMRZ mazer
AEMSS mases
masse
mesas
seams
AEMST mates
meats
satem
steam
tames
teams
AEMSU amuse
AEMSW wames
AEMSX exams
AEMSY samey
seamy
AEMSZ mazes
smaze
AEMTT matte
AEMTY etyma
matey
meaty
AEMUV mauve
AEMYZ mazey
AENNP panne
penna
AENNR Renan
AENNS senna
AENNT anent
AENNX annex
AENNY Yenan
AENOP paeon
AENOS aeons
Saône
Soane
AENOT Aneto
atone
oaten
AENOV novae
AENOX axone
AENPP nappe
Papen
AENPS aspen
napes
neaps
panes
peans
AENPT paten
AENPZ Penza
AENQU quean
AENRR reran
AENRS earns
nares
nears
reans
saner
snare
AENRT antre
AENRV Nerva
raven
AENRW Warne
AENRY yearn
AENSS Assen
sensa
AENST antes
nates
stane
AENSV avens
Evans
naves
Sevan
vanes
AENSW sewan
wanes
weans
AENSY yeans
AENSZ senza
AENTX Texan
AENTZ zante
AENVW navew
AENWX waxen
AENWY waney
Wayne
AENZZ zazen
AEOPR opera
AEOPS Aesop
AEOPT potae
AEORS arose
AEORT Erato
orate
AEORV Évora
AEOSS oases
AEOST Oates
stoae
toeas
AEOSV soave
AEOSZ zoeas
AEOTV ovate
AEOTZ azote
AEPPR paper
rappe
AEPPU pupae
AEPRR parer
AEPRS asper
pares
parse
pears
prase
presa
rapes
reaps
spare
spear
AEPRT apter
pater
peart
Petra
prate
taper
AEPRU Apure
pareu
AEPRV parev
parve
paver
AEPRY apery
payer
Peary
repay
AEPSS apses
pases
passe
spaes
AEPST paste
pates
peats
septa
spate
tapes
AEPSU pause
AEPSV paves
AEPSX paxes
AEPTU taupe
AEPTX expat
AEPTY peaty
AEPVY peavy
AEQRU quare
AERRR rarer
AERRS raser
rears
Sarre
serra
AERRT terra
AERRV raver
verra
AERRY yarer
AERRZ razer
AERSS arses
rases
rasse
saser
sears
AERST aster
rates
reast
resat
stare
tares
tears
AERSV avers
raves
saver
AERSW sawer
swear
wares
wears
AERSX raxes
AERSY arsey
eyras
sayer
years
AERSZ razes
AERTT tater
tetra
treat
AERTU urate
AERTV avert
trave
AERTW Ewart
tawer
water
AERTX extra

taxer
AERTY teary
AERUZ azure
AERVV varve
AERVW waver
AERWX waxer
AERWY weary
AESSS asses
AESST asset
sates
seats
tasse
AESSV saves
vases
AESSX saxes
AESSY essay
AESSZ assez
AESTT state
taste
teats
testa
AESTU saute
AESTV stave
vesta
AESTW sweat
tawse
twaes
waste
wetas
AESTX taxes
texas
AESTY yates
yeast
Yeats
AESTZ zetas
AESUV suave
uveas
AESVW waves
AESWX waxes
AESXZ zaxes
AETTV Evatt
AEVWY wavey
AFFFS faffs
AFFGS gaffs
AFFIX affix
AFFLO offal
AFFLU luffa
AFFNY nyaff
AFFQU quaff
AFFST staff
AFFSW waffs
AFFTY taffy
AFGHU faugh
AFGLO oflag
AFGLS flags
AFGLU fugal
AFGNO fango
ganof
AFGNS fangs
AFGOR Fargo
AFGOT fagot
AFGRS frags
AFGRT graft
AFHIR Farhi
AFHIT faith
AFHIZ hafiz
AFHLS flash
AFHRW wharf
AFHST hafts
shaft
AFHSU haufs
AFIKL kalif
AFIKR fakir
kafir
AFILL flail
AFILN final
AFILO folia
Olaf I
AFILP pilaf
AFILR filar
flair
frail
Lifar
AFILS fails
AFINR infra
AFINS fains
naifs
AFINT faint
AFIOS Sofia
AFIQR faqir
AFIRR friar
AFIRS fairs
AFIRT afrit
iftar
AFIRY fairy
AFIST fiats
AFISW waifs
AFKLN flank
AFKLS flaks
flask
AFKLY flaky
AFKNR frank
AFKOT kofta
AFKRT kraft
AFLLS falls
AFLMS flams
AFLMY flamy
AFLNS flans
AFLNU Falun
AFLOO aloof
loofa
AFLOR flora
AFLOS foals
loafs
AFLOT aloft
float
AFLOU afoul
AFLOV Olaf V
AFLPS flaps
AFLRS farls
AFLST flats
AFLSW flaws
AFLSY flays
AFLTU fault
AFLTY fatly
AFLUW awful
AFLWY flawy
AFLXY flaxy
AFMOR foram
AFMOS foams
AFMOY foamy
AFMRS farms
AFMSU Musaf
AFMUY Fayum
AFNNO fanon
AFNNY fanny
AFNRS snarf
AFNRU furan
AFNRY Frayn
AFNSU fauns
snafu
AFNSW fawns
AFOOT afoot
AFORS afros
sofar
AFORV favor
AFORY foray
AFORZ forza
AFOSS fossa
sofas
AFOST fatso
softa
AFOSY ofays
AFPRS fraps
AFRSS frass
AFRST farts
frats
rafts
AFRSU fraus
AFRSW swarf
AFRSY frays
AFRSZ zarfs
AFSST fasts
AFSTU Faust
fauts
AFSTW wafts
AFSUV favus
AFTTY fatty
AGGGO gogga
AGGIN aging
AGGIW wigga
AGGJS jaggs
AGGJY jaggy
AGGLU gulag
AGGMO Magog
AGGMU mugga
AGGNS gangs
AGGOR aggro
Gogra
AGGRS raggs
AGGRY raggy
AGHHU haugh
AGHIN hangi
AGHIZ ghazi
AGHLU laugh
AGHMO ogham
Omagh
AGHNO hogan
AGHNS gnash
hangs
sangh
Shang
AGHNW whang
AGHOT Gotha
AGHPR graph
AGHRT garth
AGHSS shags
AGHST ghats
AGHSU saugh
AGHTU aught
ghaut
AGHUW waugh
AGIIT atigi
AGIIV vigia
AGIKN kiang
AGILL glial
AGILN algin
align
Laing
ligan
linga
AGILO logia
AGILR argil
glair
grail
AGILS glias
sigla
AGILU ugali
AGILW wilga
AGILY gaily
AGIMN gamin
AGIMO amigo
imago
AGIMS agism
sigma
AGINO gonia
ngaio
AGINP aping
AGINR grain
AGINS gains
Siang
AGINT giant
ngati
tangi
AGINW awing
wigan
AGINX axing
Xiang
AGIOS agios
Goiás
AGIRT tragi
AGIRV virga
AGIST agist
gaits
taigs
AGISU Gaius
AGJLU jugal
AGKNS knags
AGKOP gopak
AGKSU kagus
AGKSW gawks
AGKWY gawky
AGLLS galls
AGLMU mulga
AGLNO along
logan
AGLNR gnarl
AGLNS glans
slang
AGLOO agloo
AGLOP galop
AGLOR algor
argol
goral
largo
AGLOS gaols
goals
Lagos
AGLOT gloat
AGLOV galvo
Volga
AGLOW aglow
AGLRU glaur
gular
AGLRY glary
gyral
AGLSS glass
slags
AGLSU aglus
AGLTU gault
AGLYZ glazy
AGMMU gumma
AGMMY gammy
AGMNO among
mango
ngoma
AGMNU munga
AGMNY mangy
AGMOT magot
AGMPS gamps
AGMRS grams
AGMSU magus
AGMTU gamut
AGNNO Agnon
gonna
AGNNW gnawn
AGNOP ponga
AGNOR argon
groan
nagor
orang
organ
AGNOT tango
tonga
AGNOU guano
AGNOW gowan
wagon
wonga
AGNOY agony
AGNPR prang

AGNPS	pangs
	spang
AGNPU	Pan Gu
	punga
AGNRS	gnars
	grans
AGNRT	grant
AGNRW	wrang
AGNRY	angry
	rangy
AGNSS	sangs
	snags
AGNST	angst
	gnats
	stang
	tangs
AGNSU	Angus
	Gansu
	guans
	sugan
AGNSV	vangs
AGNSW	gnaws
AGNTU	gaunt
AGNTW	twang
AGNTY	tangy
AGOOT	Otago
AGORS	Argos
AGORT	argot
	groat
AGOSS	sagos
AGOST	goats
	togas
AGOSY	yogas
AGOTT	gotta
AGOTV	gavot
AGOYZ	gyoza
AGPPY	gappy
AGPRS	grasp
	sprag
AGPRY	grapy
AGPSS	gasps
	spags
AGPSU	gaups
AGPSW	gawps
AGQSU	quags
AGRSS	grass
AGRSU	argus
	gaurs
	sugar
AGRSV	gravs
AGRSY	grays
AGRUU	augur
AGRVY	gravy
AGSST	stags
AGSSU	gauss
AGSSW	swags
AGSSY	gassy
AGSTU	Tagus
AGSTY	stagy
AGSUV	vagus
AGTTU	gutta
AGUYZ	gauzy
AHHIS	Shiah
AHHNS	Shahn
AHHOS	hohas
AHHOX	Hoxha
AHHPY	hypha
AHHRS	harsh
AHHSS	shahs
AHIIS	shiai
AHIIT	Haiti
AHIJJ	hajji
AHIJS	hajis
AHIJZ	Hijaz
AHIKK	khaki
AHIKM	hakim
AHIKS	haiks
	Kashi
AHIKU	haiku
AHIKV	Khiva
AHIKZ	khazi
AHILL	Hilla
AHILP	phial
AHILR	hilar
AHILS	hails
AHILT	Lahti
	lathi
	thali
AHIMR	Hiram
	ihram
AHIMS	Amish
AHINO	Hanoi
AHINS	Hsian
	nashi
AHINU	Anhui
AHIOP	Pohai
AHIPS	aphis
	apish
	spahi
AHIRS	hairs
	Shari
AHIRT	airth
AHIRU	rahui
	Uriah
AHIRY	hairy
AHIST	saith
	Thaïs
AHISU	huias
AHISV	shiva
AHITW	Tihwa
AHJNO	Jonah
AHJTU	thuja
AHKLS	lakhs
AHKMO	Mokha
AHKNS	ankhs
	hanks
	khans
	shank
AHKNT	thank
AHKNY	hanky
AHKOO	hooka
AHKOS	kohas
	shako
AHKPS	kaphs
AHKRS	harks
	shark
AHKSS	hasks
AHKST	khats
AHKSW	hawks
AHKSY	shaky
AHLLO	hallo
	holla
AHLLS	halls
	shall
AHLMS	halms
AHLMU	haulm
AHLNO	halon
	lohan
AHLNU	uhlan
AHLOR	horal
AHLOS	halos
	shoal
AHLOT	loath
	lotah
AHLPS	plash
AHLPT	Plath
AHLPY	haply
	phyla
AHLRS	harls
AHLSS	slash
AHLST	halts
	laths
	shalt
AHLSU	hauls
AHLSW	shawl
	Walsh
AHLSY	hylas
	shaly
AHLTY	lathy
AHMMU	Ummah
AHMMY	hammy
AHMNU	human
	Nahum
AHMNY	mynah
AHMOS	Shamo
AHMPS	pashm
AHMRS	harms
	marsh
AHMSS	shams
	smash
AHMST	maths
AHMSW	shawm
	whams
AHMSY	mashy
AHNNO	honan
AHNNU	Hunan
AHNOS	noahs
AHNOT	Hotan
AHNPT	Panth
AHNSS	shans
AHNST	Hants
	snath
AHNTT	Thant
AHNTU	haunt
AHNUW	Wuhan
AHOOW	wahoo
AHOOY	yahoo
AHOPS	opahs
AHORS	Horsa
AHORT	Horta
	torah
AHORY	hoary
AHORZ	Zohar
AHOST	Athos
	hoast
	hosta
	oaths
	shoat
AHOSY	hoyas
AHOTZ	azoth
AHPPY	happy
AHPRS	harps
	sharp
AHPRT	Tharp
AHPRY	harpy
AHPSS	hasps
AHPST	paths
	staph
AHPSU	hapus
	puhas
AHPSW	pshaw
	whaps
AHPUW	whaup
AHQSU	quash
AHRRY	harry
AHRST	harts
	Rasht
	raths
	tahrs
	thars
	trash
AHRSU	Århus
	Ashur
	shura
	surah
AHRSY	syrah
AHRTW	wrath
AHRTY	rhyta
AHRUW	whaur
AHRXY	hyrax
AHSST	stash
AHSSU	Susah
	Ushas
AHSSW	shaws
	shwas
	swash
AHSSY	shays
AHSTW	swath
	thaws
AHSTY	hasty
AHSWY	washy
AHTUY	thuya
AIIKR	ariki
AIILM	milia
AIILO	aioli
AIILT	litai
AIIMM	Miami
AIINO	Ionia
AIINS	Sinai
AIIPU	Piauí
AIIQR	Iraqi
AIISX	ixias
AIIVZ	Iviza
AIJJN	Jinja
AIJKN	kanji
AIJKT	Kitaj
AIJLS	jails
AIJNN	Jinan
	ninja
AIJOR	rioja
AIJOU	ouija
AIKKM	kamik
AIKKS	kaiks
	kakis
AIKKT	tikka
AIKLS	kails
	laiks
	Laski
AIKLT	tilak
AIKMO	maiko
AIKMS	maiks
AIKMU	umiak
AIKNS	kinas
	Nasik
AIKNT	takin
AIKNU	nikau
AIKOP	okapi
AIKPP	kippa
AIKPS	pikas
AIKPU	pikau
AIKRR	karri
AIKRT	krait
AIKRU	kauri
AIKSS	sakis
	sikas
AIKST	Sakti
	sitka
AIKSV	kivas
AIKSZ	Ziska
AILLV	villa
AILLZ	zilla
AILMN	Milan
AILMS	Islam
	mails
	salmi
	Simla
AILMU	miaul
AILMY	My Lai
AILNO	aloin
AILNP	plain
AILNS	anils
	nails
	slain
	snail
AILNT	Latin
AILNV	anvil
	nival
AILNW	lawin
AILNY	inlay
AILOP	pilao

AILOS	Laois
AILOT	Italo-
AILOV	viola
AILOZ	Lao Zi
	Lazio
AILPP	palpi
	pipal
AILPS	lapis
	pails
AILPT	plait
AILPU	Pauli
	Paul I
	pilau
AILPW	pilaw
AILQU	quail
AILRS	arils
	lairs
	laris
	liars
	liras
	rails
	rials
AILRT	trail
	trial
AILRU	Luria
AILRV	rival
	viral
AILRY	lairy
	riyal
AILRZ	Rizal
AILSS	lassi
	sails
	sisal
AILST	litas
	tails
AILSU	Aulis
	Laius
AILSV	silva
	vails
	vials
AILSW	wails
	Wisła
AILSX	axils
AILSY	Islay
AILSZ	zilas
AILTT	atilt
AILTV	vital
AILTY	Italy
	laity
AIMMS	imams
	maims
AIMMU	imaum
AIMMX	maxim
AIMNN	Minna
AIMNO	amino
	Naomi
	Omani
AIMNR	Arnim
	Marin
AIMNS	mains
	minas
AIMNT	matin
AIMNV	mavin
AIMNY	Minya
AIMNZ	Mainz
	nizam
AIMOR	moira
AIMOU	miaou
AIMOW	miaow
AIMOX	axiom
AIMPR	Priam
	prima
AIMRR	marri
AIMRS	amirs
	simar
AIMRT	amrit
	Tarim
AIMRU	mauri
	Urmia
AIMRY	Mary I
AIMRZ	mirza
AIMSS	amiss
AIMST	maist
	tamis
AIMSV	mavis
AIMSW	swami
AIMSX	maxis
AIMSY	Mysia
AIMTY	amity
AINNO	anion
AINNP	pinna
AINNS	Nisan
AINOP	piano
AINOR	noria
AINOW	Iowan
AINOX	axion
AINOZ	Anzio
AINPS	nipas
	pains
	spain
AINPT	inapt
	paint
	patin
	pinta
AINRS	naris
	rains
	ranis
	sarin
AINRT	intra
	riant
	Tiran
	train
AINRV	invar
	ravin
	Vanir
AINRY	rainy
AINSS	sains
	sasin
AINST	antis
	saint
	satin
	stain
	Tanis
AINSV	savin
	Sivan
	vinas
AINSW	swain
	wains
AINSY	ayins
AINSZ	nazis
AINTT	taint
	titan
AINTU	Uniat
AINTW	twain
	witan
AINUX	auxin
AINYZ	zayin
AIOPT	patio
AIORT	ratio
AIORX	orixa
AIOSS	oasis
AIOST	iotas
	ostia
AIPPP	pappi
AIPPS	pipas
AIPRS	pairs
	paris
	Sapir
	Sarpi
AIPRT	atrip
	tapir
AIPRU	Piura
AIPSS	apsis
AIPST	tapis
AIPSV	pavis
AIPTT	Patti
	pitta
AIPZZ	pizza
AIQRU	quair
AIQSU	quasi
AIQUY	Yaqui
AIRRS	arris
AIRRW	wirra
AIRSS	arsis
	saris
AIRST	airts
	astir
	sitar
	stair
	stria
	tarsi
AIRSU	Arius
AIRSV	vairs
AIRSY	Syria
AIRSZ	sizar
AIRTT	trait
AIRVX	varix
AISSV	Sivas
	visas
AISTT	Attis
AISTV	vista
AISTW	waist
	waits
AISTX	taxis
AISTZ	Tisza
AISVV	vivas
AITTV	vitta
AITWZ	Waitz
AITZZ	izzat
	Ta'izz
AJKNR	Kranj
AJKOR	rojak
AJLOP	jalop
AJLOU	joual
AJLRS	jarls
AJLRU	jural
AJMMU	Jammu
AJMMY	jammy
AJMNU	Jumna
AJMOR	major
AJMRU	jumar
AJNNY	janny
AJNOS	Jason
AJNOU	Anjou
AJNSU	Janus
AJNTU	jaunt
	junta
AJOPP	Joppa
AJOST	jatos
	jotas
AJPRS	jarps
AJPSU	jaups
	pujas
AJRRY	Jarry
AJRTU	jurat
AJRUU	Juruá
AJSSY	Jassy
AJYZZ	jazzy
AKKLU	kulak
AKKNS	skank
AKKOP	kapok
AKKOW	wokka
AKKPU	pukka
AKLLY	alkyl
AKLNP	plank
AKLNU	kulan
AKLNY	lanky
AKLOP	polka
AKLOS	alkos
	kolas
	skoal
AKLRS	larks
AKLRT	Trakl
AKLRY	larky
AKLSS	Śląsk
AKLST	stalk
	talks
AKLSU	kulas
AKLSW	lawks
	walks
AKLTU	taluk
AKLTY	talky
AKLUW	waulk
AKMNY	manky
AKMOR	korma
AKMOS	makos
AKMOU	oakum
AKMRS	marks
AKMSS	masks
AKMSU	Aksum
AKNOR	Akron
	Koran
	krona
AKNOS	kaons
	koans
AKNOT	tonka
AKNOY	Konya
AKNPR	prank
AKNPS	knaps
	spank
AKNPU	punka
AKNRS	knars
	krans
	narks
	ranks
AKNRY	narky
AKNST	stank
	tanks
AKNSU	ankus
	Kansu
AKNSW	swank
	wanks
AKNSY	snaky
	yanks
AKNUZ	kanzu
AKNWY	wanky
AKOOR	karoo
AKOOZ	kazoo
AKOPP	koppa
AKOPY	yapok
AKORS	koras
	okras
AKORT	korat
AKOSS	soaks
AKOST	oktas
AKOSY	kayos
	okays
AKOTY	tokay
AKPRS	parks
	spark
AKPRY	parky
AKPTU	kaput
AKPWY	pawky
AKQRU	quark
AKQUY	quaky
AKRSS	sarks
AKRST	karst
	karts
	stark
AKRSW	warks
AKRSY	sarky
AKRTU	kraut
	kurta
AKSST	tasks
AKSSU	skuas
AKSSV	kvass
AKSTY	kyats
AKSUW	wauks
ALLLY	allyl
ALLMO	molal

ALLMS malls
small
ALLMU mulla
ALLMY myall
ALLNO llano
ALLOS ollas
salol
ALLOT allot
atoll
ALLOW allow
ALLOY alloy
loyal
ALLPS palls
spall
ALLPY pally
ALLRY rally
ALLST stall
ALLSU Sulla
ALLSW walls
ALLSY sally
ALLTY tally
ALLWY wally
ALLXY laxly
ALMMO Malmö
ALMNO monal
ALMNY manly
ALMOR molar
moral
ALMOS loams
molas
ALMOT matlo
ALMOX Lomax
ALMOY loamy
ALMPS lamps
palms
plasm
psalm
ALMPY amply
palmy
ALMQU qualm
ALMRS marls
ALMRU larum
mural
ALMRY marly
ALMSS slams
ALMST malts
smalt
ALMSU alums
mauls
ALMTY malty
ALMUX Uxmal
ALNNO Nolan
ALNNU annul
ALNOP nopal
ALNOR Arlon
loran
ALNOS loans
salon
sloan
solan
ALNOT notal
talon
tolan
tonal
ALNOW lowan
ALNOZ zonal
ALNPS plans
ALNPT plant
ALNRS larns
snarl
ALNRU lunar
ulnar
ALNST slant
ALNSU Lanús
ulans
ulnas
ALNSW lawns
ALNUY unlay
yulan
ALNWY Alwyn
lawny
wanly
ALNXY xylan
ALOPR parol
polar
ALOPS opals
Palos
salop
ALOPT Plato
ploat
ALORS orals
solar
ALORT tolar
ALORV valor
volar
ALORY royal
ALOSS lasso
ALOST Alost
altos
lotas
salto
Talos
tolas
ALOSV ovals
salvo
ALOTT total
ALOTV lovat
volta
ALOVV volva
ALPPS palps
ALPPU pupal
ALPPY apply
ALPSS slaps
ALPST plast
plats
splat
ALPSU pulas
ALPSW pawls
ALPSY palsy
plays
splay
ALPTU tulpa
ALPTY aptly
platy
typal
ALPUY layup
ALRRU rural
ALRST slart
ALRSU sural
ALRSY lyras
ALRTU ultra
ALRTW trawl
ALRWY rawly
ALSST lasts
salts
slats
ALSSY lyssa
slays
ALSTU talus
Tulsa
ALSTY salty
slaty
ALSUU luaus
usual
ALSUW wauls
ALSVY sylva
ALSWW wawls
ALSWY yawls
ALTTY lytta
ALTUV vault
ALTWZ waltz
ALUUV uvula
ALUVV vulva
AMMMO momma
AMMMY mammy
AMMNO ammon
AMMOY myoma
AMMRS smarm
AMMRY rammy
AMMSU summa
AMMSY sammy
AMMTY tammy
AMNNU unman
AMNNY Nyman
AMNOR manor
norma
roman
AMNOS mason
moans
monas
nomas
soman
AMNOT toman
AMNOW woman
AMNOY anomy
Mayon
AMNOZ Monza
AMNRU Namur
unarm
AMNSU manus
AMNSY mynas
AMOQR qorma
AMORR armor
Morar
AMORS Maros
moras
roams
AMORU amour
AMORY mayor
moray
AMOSS Samos
somas
AMOST atoms
moats
stoma
AMOSU oumas
AMOTU Omuta
AMOTW amowt
AMOTY atomy
AMOTZ matzo
motza
AMPRS prams
ramps
AMPRT tramp
AMPSS spams
spasm
AMPST stamp
tamps
AMPSU pumas
AMPSV vamps
AMPSW swamp
AMPYY yampy
AMRRU murra
AMRRY marry
AMRST marts
smart
trams
AMRSU musar
ramus
Sarum
AMRSW swarm
warms
AMRTU Murat
AMRTY tryma
AMRUU aurum
AMRUY Maury
AMSST masts
AMSSY massy
AMSTT matts
AMSTU Matsu
AMSTY mayst
AMTTU Tatum
ANNNY nanny
ANNOY annoy
ANNSU sunna
ANOOP Poona
ANOPR apron
ANOPT panto
Paton
ANOPW powan
ANOPY yapon
ANORS arson
roans
sonar
ANORT rotan
trona
ANORW rowan
ANORY rayon
ANOST Aston
ANOSV novas
ANOSX axons
Naxos
Saxon
ANOTT tanto
ANOTU tauon
ANOTW Wotan
ANOTX taxon
ANOTY atony
ayont
ANOUY noyau
ANOWY noway
ANPPY nappy
ANPRW prawn
ANPRY pyran
ANPSS snaps
spans
ANPST pants
ANPSU punas
Pusan
ANPSW pawns
spawn
ANPSY pansy
ANPTU unapt
ANPTY panty
ANQRU Qur'an
ANQTU quant
ANRST rants
tarns
trans
ANRSW warns
ANRSY yarns
ANRUU Nauru
ANRUY unary
ANSST Stans
ANSSW swans
ANSTU aunts
staun
tuans
tunas
ANSTW wants
ANSTY antsy
nasty
tansy
ANSUU unaus
ANSUY unsay
ANSWY yawns
ANTTU taunt
ANTTY natty
ANTUV vaunt
ANTUY aunty
ANTWY tawny
ANVVY navvy
AOORZ razoo
AOPRS aspro
Páros
proas
sapor
AOPRT aport
porta
Prato

AOPRV	vapor
AOPSS	psoas
	soaps
AOPST	Pasto
AOPSU	oupas
AOPSY	soapy
AOPTU	Taupo
AOPTY	atopy
AOPTZ	topaz
AOQTU	quota
AORRS	roars
AORRV	Varro
AORRW	arrow
AORRZ	razor
AORSS	saros
	soars
	soras
AORST	Astor
	roast
	rotas
	Sarto
	taros
	Troas
AORSV	savor
AORTT	ottar
	tarot
	troat
AORVY	ovary
AOSST	oasts
	stoas
	Tasso
	tosas
AOSSU	Sousa
AOSTT	stoat
	toast
AOSTU	autos
AOSVW	avows
AOSVY	savoy
AOTWY	Otway
APPPY	pappy
APPSU	pupas
APPSY	sappy
APPYY	yappy
APPYZ	zappy
APRRS	parrs
APRRY	parry
APRSS	rasps
	spars
APRST	parts
	prats
	sprat
	strap
	tarps
	traps
APRSU	praus
	supra
APRSW	warps
	wraps
APRSY	prays
	raspy
	spray
APRTY	party
APSST	pasts
	spats
APSSW	swaps
	wasps
APSSY	Passy
	spays
APSTU	patus
	sputa
	stupa
APSTY	pasty
	patsy
	pyats
APSUY	yaups
APSWY	waspy
	yawps
APTTY	patty
APZZZ	pzazz
AQRTU	quart
AQSSU	quass
AQSTU	squat
AQSUW	squaw
AQSUY	quays
ARRST	starr
ARRSU	surra
ARRTY	tarry
ARSST	stars
	trass
	tsars
ARSSU	Assur
	suras
ARSTT	start
	tarts
ARSTU	surat
	sutra
ARSTW	straw
	swart
	warts
ARSTY	satyr
	stray
	trays
ARSTZ	tzars
ARSUV	varus
ARSUY	saury
ARTTU	Tartu
	tuart
ARTTY	ratty
	tarty
ARTWY	warty
ASSSY	sassy
ASSTU	sauts
ASSTW	swats
ASSTY	stays
ASSWY	sways
ASTTW	twats
	watts
ASTTY	tasty
ASTUY	Asyut
ASTVY	vasty
ASVVY	savvy
ATTTY	tatty
ATTWY	Wyatt
BBBIS	bibbs
BBBOY	bobby
BBCEU	cubeb
BBCOS	cobbs
BBCUY	cubby
BBDEE	ebbed
BBDOU	dubbo
BBDOY	dobby
BBEEL	Bebel
BBEER	rebbe
BBEIL	bible
BBEIR	bribe
BBELS	blebs
BBEMO	Bembo
	bombe
BBEOP	bebop
BBERU	Buber
BBEWY	webby
BBGIO	gobbi
BBGIS	Gibbs
BBGOY	gobby
BBHOS	Hobbs
BBHOY	hobby
BBHUY	hubby
BBIJS	jibbs
BBILO	bilbo
BBILY	bilby
	Libby
BBIMO	bimbo
BBLOO	bobol
BBLOS	blobs
BBLOY	lobby
BBLRU	blurb
BBLSU	blubs
	bulbs
BBMOS	bombs
BBNOY	nobby
BBNUY	nubby
BBOOS	boobs
BBOOY	booby
	yobbo
BBRSU	burbs
BBRUY	rubby
BBSUU	bubus
BBSUY	busby
BBTUY	tubby
BCCEO	bocce
BCCIO	bocci
BCCIU	cubic
BCDEU	cubed
BCEEH	beech
BCEEL	celeb
BCEER	rebec
BCEEX	xebec
BCEEZ	zebec
BCEHL	belch
BCEHN	bench
BCEHO	boche
BCEIR	Brice
BCEIS	bices
BCEKS	becks
BCELO	coble
BCEMO	combe
BCENO	bonce
BCEOY	Boyce
BCERU	Bruce
	cuber
BCESU	cubes
BCHIM	chimb
BCHIR	birch
BCHIT	bitch
BCHLO	Bloch
BCHNU	bunch
BCHOR	broch
BCHOS	Bosch
BCHOT	botch
BCHRU	Bruch
BCHSU	chubs
BCHTU	butch
BCHUU	buchu
BCIKR	brick
BCILM	climb
BCIOR	boric
BCIPU	pubic
BCIRS	cribs
BCITU	cubit
BCKLO	block
BCKOR	brock
BCKOS	bocks
BCKOU	bucko
BCKSU	bucks
BCLMO	clomb
BCLOS	blocs
BCLSU	clubs
BCMOO	combo
	coomb
BCMOS	combs
BCMRU	crumb
BCNOU	bunco
BCORY	corby
BCRSU	curbs
	scrub
BDDEI	bided
BDDEO	boded
BDDEU	debud
BDDEY	byded
BDDIY	biddy
BDDUY	buddy
BDEEL	bedel
	bleed
BDEEM	embed
BDEER	brede
	breed
BDEES	debes
BDEEW	bedew
	dweeb
BDEEY	debye
BDEGI	gibed
BDEGO	bodge
BDEGU	budge
	debug
BDEGY	gybed
BDEIJ	jibed
BDEIK	biked
BDEIL	bield
	biled
BDEIM	bedim
	imbed
BDEIP	biped
BDEIR	breid
	bride
	rebid
BDEIS	bides
BDEIT	bidet
	debit
BDEKO	boked
BDEKY	byked
BDELN	blend
BDELU	blued
BDEMO	demob
BDENO	boned
BDENS	bends
BDENY	bendy
BDEOO	booed
BDEOR	bored
	orbed
	robed
BDEOS	bodes
BDEOW	bowed
BDEOX	boxed
BDERY	derby
BDEST	debts
BDESU	bused
	debus
BDESY	bydes
BDETU	debut
	tubed
BDFII	bifid
BDHIO	dhobi
BDHNU	bundh
BDIIN	bindi
BDIIR	Irbid
BDILN	blind
BDILU	build
BDINO	Bondi
BDINS	binds
BDIOP	bipod
BDIOV	bovid
BDIRS	birds
	dribs
BDLNO	blond
BDLOO	blood
BDMOU	dumbo
BDNOS	bonds
BDNOU	bound
BDNSU	bunds
BDNUU	bundu
BDNUY	bundy
BDOOR	brood
	droob
BDORS	dorbs
BDOSU	Doubs
BDOTU	doubt
BDRSU	drubs
BDRSY	Byrds
BEEFS	beefs
BEEFY	beefy

BEEGI beige
BEEGL glebe
BEEGR Geber
grebe
BEEGT beget
BEEHI Hebei
BEEHP Phebe
BEEHT Bethe
thebe
BEEIL belie
BEEJL jebel
BEEJM jembe
BEEKL Keble
BEELL belle
BEELM Belém
BEELN leben
BEELP bleep
plebe
BEELR rebel
BEELT betel
BEELV bevel
BEELZ bezel
BEEMR berme
ember
BEENN benne
BEENS Beneš
BEENT benet
Benét
BEENU Benue
BEEOR boree
BEEOS obese
BEEPS beeps
BEERS beers
brees
BEERT beret
Ebert
BEERV breve
BEERW weber
BEERY beery
BEEST beets
beset
BEETT Tebet
BEFGO befog
BEFIR brief
fiber
fibre
BEFIT befit
BEFOU boeuf
BEGIL bilge
BEGIN begin
being
binge
BEGIO bogie
BEGIR giber
BEGIS gibes
BEGLO bogle
globe
BEGLU bugle
bulge
BEGMU begum
BEGNU begun
BEGOT begot
BEGOY bogey
BEGRS bergs
BEGSY gybes
BEHIU Hubei
BEHMO Böhme
BEHOR Horeb
BEHOT Bothe
BEHRS herbs
BEHRT berth
BEHRY herby
BEHST beths
BEIIK bikie
BEIJR jiber
BEIJS jibes
BEIKM Mbeki
BEIKR biker
BEIKS bikes
kibes
BEILL libel
BEILO obeli
BEILR Erbil
liber
BEILS biles
Eblis
BEILY Belyi
BEIMO biome
mobie
BEIMT Témbi
BEIMU imbue
BEINN Benin
BEINO Niobe
BEINR brine
BEINS benis
bines
Ibsen
BEINV Bevin
BEINX Benxi
BEIOR Berio
Ibero-
BEIOS Boise
BEIOW bowie
BEIRR brier
BEIRS biers
breis
bries
BEIRT biter
Ibert
Tiber
tribe
BEISS bises
BEIST bites
BEISV vibes
BEITT Betti
Tibet
BEITZ Bizet
zibet
BEIVY vibey
BEJSU jubes
BEKLO bloke
BEKOR berko
broke
BEKOS bokes
BEKRS berks
kerbs
Krebs
BEKRU burke
BEKSY bykes
BELLS bells
BELLY belly
BELMU umbel
umble
BELNO Nobel
noble
BELNT blent
BELOO Boole
BELOR roble
BELOS boles
lobes
BELOT botel
BELOU boule
BELOW below
bowel
elbow
BELOY Boyle
BELPS plebs
BELRT blert
BELRU bluer
brule
ruble
BELRY beryl
BELSS bless
BELST belts
blest
blets
BELSU blues
BELSY Selby
BELTU bluet
BELUY bluey
BEMOP pombe
BEMOR brome
omber
ombre
BEMOS besom
mobes
BEMOW embow
BEMRS berms
BEMRU brume
umber
BEMSU embus
sebum
BENNO bonne
BENNY benny
BENOO Boone
BENOR boner
borne
BENOS bones
BENOT bento
BENOW Bowen
BENOY Boyne
ebony
BENOZ bonze
Bozen
BENRT brent
BENST bents
BEOOS oboes
BEOOT Obote
BEOOZ booze
BEOPR probe
BEORR borer
BEORS bores
brose
robes
sober
BEORW bower
BEORX boxer
BEORY Boyer
Robey
BEOST boets
BEOSU bouse
BEOSW bowse
BEOSX boxes
BEOSY obeys
syboe
BEOTT botte
BEOTV Bovet
BEOTY Tobey
BEPSU pubes
BERRS brers
BERRY berry
BERST Brest
BERSU burse
rebus
rubes
BERSV verbs
BERSW brews
BERSY breys
byres
BERTU brute
buret
rebut
tuber
BERUY buyer
BESST bests
BESSU buses
BESTU tubes
BESTY bytes
BESUY Beuys
BESUZ zebus
BETTU butte
BEVVY bevvy
BFFIO biffo
BFFIS biffs
BFFIU buffi
BFFLU bluff
BFFOO boffo
BFFOU buffo
BFFSU buffs
BFIOR fibro
BFIRS fribs
BFLYY flyby
BFOOY boofy
BFORS forbs
BFORY forby
BFOSY boyfs
BFSUY fubsy
BGGOY boggy
BGGUY buggy
BGHIL Bligh
BGHIT bight
BGHOU bough
BGHRU burgh
BGIIL gibli
BGILN bling
BGILY bilgy
BGINO bingo
BGINR bring
BGINS bings
BGINY bingy
BGIOT bigot
BGIRS brigs
BGISU gibus
BGLOS blogs
globs
BGLUY bulgy
BGMOO gombo
BGMOU gumbo
BGNOO bongo
boong
BGNOS bongs
BGNSU bungs
BGNUY bungy
BGOOR Bogor
BGOOS gobos
BGOOY gooby
BGORS brogs
BGORU bourg
BGOSU bogus
BGRSU burgs
grubs
BGRUY rugby
BHILU Hubli
BHIMO himbo
BHIOS Bisho
BHIRT birth
brith
BHLOO Bohol
BHLSU blush
buhls
BHLTY Blyth
BHMOR rhomb
BHMPU bumph
BHMRU rhumb
BHMTU thumb
BHOOS bohos
hobos
BHOOT booth
BHORT broth
throb
BHOTY bothy
BHRSU brush
buhrs
shrub
BHSUY bushy
BIIKS Biisk
BIILM limbi
BIILN blini
BIILR Irbil
BIIMN nimbi

BIINY Yibin
BIIOR oribi
BIISU Sibiu
BIJOU bijou
BIKLN blink
BIKLS bilks
BIKNR brink
BIKOO Bioko
BIKRS birks
briks
brisk
BIKSS bisks
BIKSY Biysk
BILLR brill
BILLS bills
BILLY billy
BILMO limbo
BILMP blimp
BILMS limbs
BILNY bliny
BILOO oboli
BILOR broil
BILOS Blois
boils
BILPS blips
BILRS birls
BILSS bliss
BILST stilb
BILSY sibyl
BILTU built
BILTZ blitz
BIMOZ zombi
BIMRS brims
BINNU Bunin
BINOR robin
BINOS bison
BINRU bruin
burin
rubin
BINRY briny
BINSS snibs
BINST bints
BIOOT Boito
BIORT orbit
BIOST obits
BIOTT Tobit
BIOZZ bizzo
BIPSU pubis
BIQSU squib
BIRRS birrs
BIRST brits
BIRTU bruit
Tibur
BISSY byssi
BISTT bitts
BISTU busti
BISVY Visby
BITTY bitty
BIVVY bivvy
BIYZZ bizzy
BJMOU jumbo
BKLSU bulks
BKLUY bulky
BKMOU kombu
BKNOS bonks
knobs
BKNOU bunko
konbu
BKNSU bunks
BKOOR brook
BKOOS books
BKOSS bosks
BKOSY bosky
BKRSU burks
BKSSU busks
BKSUU Üsküb
BLLOS bolls
BLLSU bulls
BLLUY bully
BLMOO bloom
BLMPU plumb
BLNOW blown
BLNOY nobly
BLNTU blunt
BLOOS bolos
bools
lobos
obols
BLOOT Tobol
BLOOY looby
BLOSS slobs
BLOST blots
bolts
BLOSU bolus
BLOSW blows
bowls
BLOTU boult
BLOUW Bülow
BLOWY blowy
BLRSU blurs
burls
BLRTU blurt
BLRUY burly
BLSSU slubs
BLTUY butyl
BMMOU mumbo
BMNSU numbs
BMOOR bromo
broom
BMOOS booms
bosom
BMORS borms
BMOST tombs
BMOSU umbos
BMOSW wombs
BMOTY Bytom
BMOUX buxom
BMPSU bumps
BMPUY bumpy
BNNOY bonny
BNNRU Brünn
BNNUY bunny
BNOOR Borno
boron
BNOOS boons
boson
BNORU bourn
Bruno
BNORW brown
BNORX Bronx
BNORY Byron
BNOSS snobs
BNOSU bonus
bosun
BNRSU burns
BNRTU brunt
burnt
BNSSU snubs
BNSTU bunts
BOORS boors
sorbo
BOORT robot
BOORU buroo
BOOST boost
boots
BOOSY boyos
BOOSZ bozos
BOOTY booty
BOOWX oxbow
BOOYZ boozy
BOPUW upbow
BORRU burro
BORSS sorbs
BORSW brows
BORTU turbo
BORTY borty
BORTZ bortz
BOSST stobs
BOSSW swobs
BOSSY bossy
BOSTT botts
BOSTU bouts
BOSUY buoys
BOSWY sybow
BOSYY boysy
BPRSU burps
BRRSU burrs
BRRUY burry
BRSTU burst
BSSTU busts
stubs
BSTTU butts
BSTUY busty
BTTUU butut
BTTUY butty
CCCIO cocci
CCDEO codec
CCEEL Lecce
CCEER recce
CCEHK check
CCEHY Čechy
CCEHZ Czech
CCEIL Cecil
CCEIR cerci
ceric
Circe
CCEKL cleck
CCELY cycle
leccy
CCEMU cecum
CCEOR Croce
CCEOS cosec
secco
CCERY Crécy
CCESU cusec
CCHIK chick
CCHIN cinch
CCHIO chico
CCHKO chock
CCHKU chuck
CCHLU culch
CCHNO conch
CCHOO choco
CCHOU couch
CCHRU curch
CCHTU cutch
CCHTW cwtch
CCIIR Ricci
CCIIV civic
CCIKL click
CCIKR crick
CCILO colic
CCIMO comic
CCIMU mucic
CCINO conic
CCINY cynic
CCIOS cisco
CCIRS circs
CCKLO clock
CCKLU cluck
CCKOR crock
CCKOS cocks
CCKOY cocky
CCKRU cruck
CCLOY cyclo
CCMOY McCoy
CCOOS cocos
CCORS crocs
CCORU occur
CCOSU Cusco
CCOUZ Cuzco
CDDEE ceded
CDDEI diced
CDDEO coded
CDDUY cuddy
CDEEI deice
CDEER ceder
cered
creed
CDEES cedes
CDEEU deuce
educe
CDEHI chide
CDEHN Dench
CDEIM medic
CDEIR cider
cried
dicer
riced
CDEIS dices
CDEIT cited
edict
CDEIV Vedic
viced
CDEIY dicey
CDEKO coked
CDEKR dreck
CDEKS decks
CDELO dolce
CDELU clued
CDELY Clyde
CDEMO Médoc
CDENO Condé
coned
CDENS scend
CDENU dunce
CDEOO cooed
CDEOP coped
CDEOR coder
cored
credo
decor
CDEOS codes
coeds
CDEOT coted
CDEOU coude
douce
CDEOV coved
CDEOW cowed
CDEOX codex
coxed
CDEOY decoy
CDERU crude
cured
CDERY cyder
decry
CDESU duces
CDETU educt
CDHIL child
CDHIT ditch
CDHOR chord
CDHTU dutch
CDHUY duchy
CDIIO iodic
CDIIS disci
CDIKS dicks
CDIKY dicky
CDILU lucid
ludic
CDIMU mucid
CDIOS disco
CDIOT dicot
CDIPU cupid
pudic
CDISS discs
CDISU scudi
CDKOS docks
CDKSU ducks
CDKUY ducky
CDLOS clods

scold
CDLOU cloud
could
CDLWY Clwyd
CDNOO codon
condo
CDOOS docos
CDORS cords
scrod
CDORU duroc
CDORW crowd
CDOSU doucs
scudo
CDOSY scody
CDRSU cruds
curds
CDRUY curdy
CDSSU scuds
CDSTU ducts
CEEEM emcee
CEEFN fence
CEEFS feces
CEEHK cheek
CEEHL Elche
leech
CEEHN hence
CEEHP cheep
CEEHR cheer
CEEIN niece
CEEIP piece
CEEJT eject
CEEKL cleek
CEEKN Encke
CEEKR creek
CEELL Celle
CEELP clepe
CEELR creel
CEELT elect
CEELX excel
CEELY lycee
CEEMR creme
CEENP pence
CEENS cense
scene
CEEOO cooee
CEEPR creep
crepe
CEERS ceres
crees
scree
CEERT Crete
erect
terce
CEERW crewe
CEEST cetes
CEESY sycee
CEEUV cuvee
CEFHI chief
fiche
CEFHS chefs
CEFHT fecht
fetch
CEFIT fecit
CEFKL fleck
CEFLS clefs
CEFLT cleft
CEFOR force
CEGIN genic
CEGIR grice
CEGKN Genck
CEGKO gecko
CEGLS clegs
CEGNO conge
CEGOR Greco
CEHHT cheth
CEHIL chiel
chile
CEHIM chime
hemic
CEHIN chine
niche
CEHIR Reich
CEHIT ethic
CEHIV chive
CEHJU Cheju
CEHKO choke
CEHKR Kerch
CEHKS hecks
CEHKT ketch
CEHLO Chloe
CEHLP chelp
CEHLT letch
CEHLW welch
CEHLY chyle
CEHMO chemo
CEHMY chyme
CEHNO Cohen
Enoch
CEHNT tench
CEHNW wench
CEHOP epoch
CEHOR chore
ocher
ochre
CEHOS chose
oches
Soche
CEHPR perch
CEHPS pechs
CEHRT chert
retch
CEHRU ruche
CEHSS chess
CEHST chest
techs
CEHSW chews
CEHTU chute
CEHTV vetch
CEHTY techy
Tyche
CEHVY chevy
CEHWY chewy
CEIIR icier
CEIJU juice
CEIKL cleik
ickle
CEIKT Tieck
CEILM clime
melic
CEILN cline
CEILO oleic
CEILR relic
CEILS ceils
Leics
slice
CEILT telic
CEILV Clive
CEIMN mince
CEIMR crime
Meriç
CEIMS mesic
CEIMT metic
CEIMX cimex
CEINR nicer
CEINS Cenis
since
CEINW wince
CEIOR Coire
CEIOV voice
CEIPR price
CEIPS epics
spice
CEIPT Tepic
CEIRR crier
ricer
CEIRS cires
cries
erics
rices
CEIRT citer
recti
trice
CEIRU curie
ureic
CEIRX xeric
CEISS sices
CEIST cites
CEISV vices
CEITU cutie
CEITV civet
evict
CEITW twice
CEJOY Joyce
CEKKS kecks
CEKLO Locke
CEKLR clerk
CEKLY Lecky
CEKMS mecks
CEKNS necks
sneck
CEKOO Cooke
CEKOR Korçë
ocker
CEKOS cokes
CEKPS pecks
speck
CEKRS recks
CEKRW wreck
CELLO cello
CELLS cells
CELMO celom
CELMS clems
CELNO Cleon
clone
CELNU uncle
CELOR ceorl
CELOS close
coles
socle
CELOT Colet
telco
CELOU leuco
CELOV clove
CELOY coley
CELOZ cloze
CELPT clept
CELPU cupel
CELPY clype
CELRU cruel
lucre
ulcer
CELST celts
CELSU clues
luces
CELSW clews
CELTU culet
CELUX culex
CEMOR comer
crome
CEMOS comes
CEMOT comet
comte
CEMRY mercy
CEMSY cymes
CENNO nonce
CENOP ponce
CENOR Creon
crone
oncer
CENOS cones
scone
CENOT cento
conte
CENOU Cuneo
ounce
CENOV coven
CENOY coney
CENOZ cozen
CENPU punce
CENST cents
scent
CEOOR cooer
CEOOY cooey
CEOPR coper
CEOPS copes
copse
Pecos
scope
CEOPU coupe
CEORR crore
CEORS ceros
cores
corse
score
CEORT recto
CEORU Coeur
CEORV cover
CEORW cower
Crowe
CEORY Royce
CEORZ croze
CEOST coset
cotes
CEOSV coves
voces
CEOSW Cowes
CEOSX coxes
CEOTT octet
CEOTV covet
CEOVY covey
CEPRT crept
CEPRY crepy
Percy
CEPSS specs
CEQRS Sercq
CERRU curer
recur
CERSS cress
CERST certs
crest
CERSU cruse
cures
curse
sucre
CERSW crews
screw
CERTU cruet
curet
cuter
eruct
truce
CERUV curve
CESST sects
CESSY syces
CESTU cutes
scute
CETUY cutey
CFFHU chuff
CFFIL cliff
CFFOS coffs
scoff
CFFSU cuffs
scuff
CFHIL filch
CFHIN finch
CFHIT fitch
CFHIU fichu
CFHOO choof
CFHSU Fuchs
CFIKL flick

CFILO folic
CFIOS coifs
CFISS fiscs
CFISU ficus
CFKLO flock
CFKOR frock
CFKSU fucks
CFLOS flocs
CFMOY comfy
CFORT croft
CFORU Corfu
CFOSU focus
CFRSU scurf
CFRTU Cruft
CFSUU fucus
CGGIY ciggy
CGHLU gulch
CGHOO Gooch
CGHOU cough
CGHSU chugs
CGIIN icing
CGILN cling
CGILO logic
CGINO coign
CGIOR corgi
CGIOY yogic
CGKLU Gluck
CGLNU clung
CGLOO colog
CGLOS clogs
CGNOO cogon
congo
CGOOR Coorg
CGORS crogs
CHHIT hitch
CHHIW which
CHHNU hunch
CHHOO hooch
CHHTU hutch
CHIIL chili
lichi
CHIKN chink
CHIKO hoick
Kochi
CHIKS hicks
CHIKT thick
CHILL chill
CHILM milch
CHILO choli
CHILP pilch
CHILT licht
CHILZ zilch
CHIMN Minch
CHIMO ohmic
CHIMP chimp
CHIMR chirm
CHIMS misch
CHIMT micht
mitch
CHIMU humic
CHINO chino
Chino-
CHINP pinch
CHINS chins
CHINT nicht
CHINW winch
CHIOR chiro
choir
ichor
CHIOS Chios
Sochi
CHIPR chirp
CHIPS chips
CHIPT pitch
CHIRR chirr
CHIRT richt
CHIRU chiru
CHIST chits
sicht
stich
CHISU cuish
CHISV chivs
CHITW witch
CHITY itchy
tichy
CHIUX Chu Xi
CHIVY chivy
vichy
CHKNU chunk
CHKOO choko
chook
CHKOS hocks
shock
CHKOW chowk
CHKOY choky
CHKSU shuck
CHKTU kutch
CHLMU mulch
CHLNU lunch
CHLNY lynch
CHLOS lochs
CHLOT cloth
CHLRU churl
lurch
CHLSU schul
CHMNU munch
CHMOO choom
mooch
CHMOP chomp
CHMOS schmo
CHMPU chump
CHMSU chums
CHMTU mutch
CHNOT notch
CHNPU punch
CHNRU churn
runch
CHNSY synch
CHOOP pooch
CHOOS cohos
CHOPR porch
CHOPS chops
CHOPT potch
CHOPU pouch
CHORT torch
CHORY ochry
CHOST coths
CHOSU hocus
CHOSW chows
CHOTT chott
CHOTU couth
touch
CHOUV vouch
CHOUX choux
CHPSY psych
CHRRU churr
CHRSU crush
CHRTW crwth
CHSUY cushy
CIILT licit
CIILV civil
CIILY icily
CIIMM mimic
CIINO ionic
CIINR ricin
CIINV Vinci
vinic
CIIRR cirri
CIJUY juicy
CIKKS kicks
CIKLN clink
CIKLS licks
slick
CIKMS micks
CIKMY micky
CIKNS nicks
snick
CIKOS sicko
CIKPR prick
CIKPS picks
spick
CIKPY picky
CIKQU quick
CIKRS ricks
CIKRT trick
CIKRW wrick
CIKSS sicks
CIKST stick
ticks
CIKSW wicks
CIKVY Vicky
CILLS cills
CILNO nicol
CILNS Lincs
CILNT clint
CILOS coils
CILOT lotic
CILOW wilco
CILPS clips
CILPU picul
Pulci
CILRU curli
CILRY Cyril
lyric
CILSU sulci
CILTU culti
CILTY lytic
CILXY cylix
CIMNO Cimon
nomic
CIMNU cumin
mucin
CIMOR micro
CIMOS osmic
CIMPR crimp
CIMRS crims
scrim
CIMSU music
CINNO conin
CINOR orcin
CINOS coins
icons
scion
sonic
CINOT tonic
CINOV covin
CINOZ zinco
CINRU incur
runic
CINSU incus
CINTT tinct
CINTU cutin
tunic
CINYZ zincy
CIOPT optic
picot
topic
CIORS crios
CIORT toric
CIORU curio
CIOST coits
stoic
CIOTX toxic
CIPRS crisp
scrip
CIPRY pricy
CIPSS spics
CIPSY spicy
CIPTY typic
CISST cists
CISSY cissy
CISTU cutis
ictus
CIVVY civvy
CJKOO jocko
CJKOS jocks
CJNOU junco
CKKNO knock
CKLNO clonk
CKLNU clunk
CKLOP Płock
CKLOS locks
CKLPU pluck
CKLSU lucks
CKLUY lucky
CKMNO Monck
CKMOS mocks
smock
CKMSU mucks
CKMUY mucky
CKNOR cronk
CKNOS conks
nocks
CKNSU snuck
CKOOR crook
CKOOS cooks
CKOOY cooky
CKOPS pocks
Spock
CKOPY pocky
CKORS corks
rocks
CKORY corky
rocky
CKOSS socks
CKOST stock
CKOSW cowks
CKOTY tocky
CKOUY yucko
CKPSU pucks
CKRSU rucks
CKRTU truck
CKSSU cusks
sucks
CKSTU stuck
tucks
CKUYY yucky
CLLOY colly
CLLSU culls
scull
CLLUY cully
CLMOP clomp
CLMOU Colum
locum
CLMPU clump
CLMSU culms
CLMTU mulct
CLNOO colon
Colón
CLNOW clown
CLNUY Cluny
CLOOR color
crool
CLOOS cools
locos
CLOOY cooly
CLOPS clops
CLOST clots
colts
CLOSU locus
CLOSW cowls
scowl
CLOSY cloys
CLOTU clout
CLOVY coyly
CLPSU sculp
CLRSU curls
CLRUY curly
CLSTU cults
CLTUY culty

CMMOO	commo
CMMOS	comms
CMMOY	commy
CMOOP	compo
CMOPS	comps
CMORS	corms
CMORU	mucor
	mucro
CMOSU	comus
CMPRU	crump
CMRSU	scrum
CMRUY	Cymru
CMSSU	scums
CMSUU	mucus
CNNOS	conns
CNOOR	corno
	croon
CNOOS	coons
CNOOT	conto
CNOPY	poncy
CNORS	corns
	scorn
CNORT	tronc
CNORU	cornu
CNORW	crown
CNORY	corny
	crony
CNOSU	conus
	uncos
CNOTU	count
CNOWY	Conwy
CNSSY	syncs
CNSTU	cunts
CNSUU	uncus
CNTUU	uncut
COOPS	coops
	scoop
COOPT	coopt
COORS	corso
COORT	Corot
COORV	Corvo
COOST	coots
	scoot
COPRS	corps
	crops
COPRU	croup
COPSS	scops
COPSU	coups
COPSW	cowps
COPUY	coypu
CORRU	cruor
CORSS	cross
CORST	torcs
CORSU	Orcus
	scour
CORSW	crows
	Worcs
CORTU	court
CORWY	cowry
CORYZ	Orczy
COSST	costs
	scots
COSSW	scows
COSTT	Scott
COSTU	scout
CPRTY	crypt
CPSSU	cusps
	scups
CPTUU	cutup
CRRUY	curry
CRSTU	crust
	curst
CRSUY	Cyrus
CRUVY	curvy
CSSTU	scuts
CSSTY	cysts
CTTUY	cutty
DDDIY	diddy
DDEEG	edged
DDEEL	deled
DDEEN	ended
DDEER	dreed
	reded
DDEES	deeds
DDEEW	dewed
DDEFY	Dyfed
DDEGO	dodge
DDEHI	hided
DDEIK	diked
DDEIL	idled
DDEIN	dined
DDEIO	diode
DDEIR	dried
	redid
DDEIS	sided
DDEIT	tided
DDEIV	dived
DDEKY	dyked
DDELO	doled
DDEMO	domed
DDENY	neddy
DDEOP	doped
DDEOR	odder
	roded
DDEOS	dosed
DDEOT	doted
DDEOW	dowed
DDEOZ	dozed
DDEPU	duped
DDERS	redds
DDERU	udder
DDESU	dudes
DDETY	teddy
DDGIY	giddy
DDGOY	dodgy
DDHUU	hudud
DDIKY	kiddy
DDILO	dildo
DDIMX	Middx
DDIMY	middy
DDINU	undid
DDINY	d'Indy
	Indy, d'
DDIOS	didos
DDIRU	druid
DDIST	didst
DDLOY	oddly
DDMUY	muddy
DDNOY	noddy
DDNUY	nuddy
DDOOS	dodos
DDOPY	poddy
DDOSY	soddy
DDOTY	toddy
DDOWY	dowdy
DDRSU	rudds
DDRUY	ruddy
DEEFF	effed
DEEFO	Defoe
DEEFR	defer
	freed
DEEFS	feeds
DEEFT	feted
DEEGG	egged
DEEGH	hedge
DEEGK	kedge
DEEGL	glede
	gleed
	ledge
DEEGO	geode
DEEGR	edger
	greed
DEEGS	edges
	sedge
DEEGW	wedge
DEEHL	heled
DEEHR	heder
DEEHS	heeds
DEEHW	hewed
DEEHX	hexed
DEEIL	edile
	elide
DEEIN	diene
DEEIR	eider
DEEIT	Teide
DEEJW	jewed
DEEKN	kneed
DEEKR	Derek
DEEKY	keyed
DEELR	elder
DEELS	deles
	Leeds
DEELU	elude
DEELV	delve
	Velde
DEEMN	Emden
	emend
DEEMS	deems
	demes
	meeds
DEEMT	meted
DEEMW	mewed
DEENO	donee
DEENR	ender
DEENS	denes
	dense
	needs
DEENU	endue
DEENY	needy
DEENZ	Enzed
DEEOP	epode
DEEOR	erode
DEEPS	deeps
	pedes
	speed
DEERR	erred
DEERS	deers
	drees
	redes
	reeds
	seder
	sered
DEERT	deter
	treed
DEERU	urdee
DEERV	Verde
DEERY	redye
	reedy
DEESS	seeds
DEEST	steed
DEESU	suede
DEESW	sewed
	swede
	weeds
DEESX	desex
	sexed
DEESY	seedy
DEETU	etude
DEETW	de Wet
	tweed
DEETY	Teyde
DEEUX	exude
DEEVX	vexed
DEEWY	Dewey
	weedy
DEFFI	fifed
DEFFO	deffo
DEFGI	fidge
DEFGU	fudge
DEFIL	felid
	field
	filed
DEFIN	fiend
	fined
DEFIR	fired
	fried
DEFIT	fetid
DEFIX	fixed
DEFIY	deify
	edify
DEFJL	fjeld
DEFLT	delft
DEFLU	flued
DEFLY	Fylde
DEFMR	fremd
DEFMU	fumed
DEFNS	fends
DEFNU	unfed
DEFOS	feods
DEFOX	foxed
DEFRU	Freud
DEFSU	feuds
	fused
DEFUZ	fuzed
DEGHY	hedgy
DEGIL	gelid
	glide
DEGIM	midge
DEGIN	deign
	dinge
DEGIO	dogie
	geoid
DEGIR	dirge
	gride
	ridge
DEGIU	guide
DEGJU	judge
DEGLO	Gödel
	lodge
	ogled
DEGLS	gelds
	gleds
DEGLU	glued
	luged
DEGLY	ledgy
DEGMO	modge
DEGNO	Ogden
DEGNU	nudge
DEGOP	podge
DEGOR	gored
DEGOS	doges
DEGOT	godet
DEGOW	wodge
DEGOY	dogey
DEGPU	pudge
DEGRS	dregs
DEGRU	grued
	urged
DEGRY	gyred
DEGSY	sedgy
DEGUY	guyed
DEGVY	gyved
DEGWY	wedgy
DEHIK	hiked
DEHIL	Delhi
DEHIR	hider
	hired
DEHIS	heids
	hides
	shied
	sidhe
DEHIV	hived
DEHKO	hoked
DEHLO	dhole
	holed
DEHMO	homed
DEHNO	honed
DEHNS	shend
DEHOP	ephod
	hoped

DEHOR Herod
horde
DEHOS hosed
DEHPT depth
DEHPY hyped
DEHRS herds
sherd
shred
DEHSS sheds
DEHUZ Zhu De
DEIIM imide
DEIIN indie
DEIIV ivied
DEIIX dixie
DEIJR jerid
DEIJV jived
DEIKL liked
DEIKM miked
DEIKN inked
DEIKP piked
DEIKR irked
DEIKS dikes
skied
DEIKT kited
DEIKY yiked
DEILM limed
DEILN lined
DEILO oiled
oldie
DEILP lepid
piled
plied
DEILR idler
riled
DEILS deils
delis
idles
sidle
siled
slide
DEILT tilde
tiled
DEILV devil
lived
DEILW wield
Wilde
wiled
DEILY yield
DEIMM mimed
DEIMN denim
mined
DEIMP imped
DEIMR dimer
mired
rimed
DEIMS deism
dimes
DEIMT demit
timed
DEIMX mixed
DEINO Dione
DEINP pined
DEINR diner
Indre
DEINS Denis
dines
nides
snide
DEINT ident
teind
tined
DEINU indue
Udine
DEINV vined
DEINW Edwin
widen
wined
DEINX index
nixed
DEINZ dizen
DEIOV video
DEIOW dowie
DEIOX doxie
oxide
DEIPP piped
DEIPR pride
pried
DEIPS spied
DEIPT tepid
DEIPW wiped
DEIPZ pized
DEIRR drier
rider
DEIRS dries
rides
sider
sired
DEIRT tired
tried
DEIRV diver
drive
rived
Verdi
DEIRW weird
wider
wired
wried
DEISS sides
DEIST deist
diets
edits
sited
stied
tides
DEISV dives
vised
DEISW wides
wised
DEISZ sized
DEITY deity
DEIVW wived
DEJKO joked
DEJOY joyed
DEKKO dekko
DEKNO kendo
DEKNU nuked
DEKOP poked
DEKOS doeks
DEKOT toked
DEKOY yoked
DEKPU puked
DEKSS desks
DEKSU dukes
DEKSY dykes
DELLN Lendl
DELLS dells
DELLW dwell
DELMO model
DELMS melds
DELNO Eldon
loden
Nolde
olden
DELNS lends
DELOO looed
DELOP loped
poled
DELOR older
DELOS delos
doles
lodes
DELOU loued
DELOV loved
DELOW dowel
lowed
DELOY Doyle
odyle
yodel
yodle
DELPU duple
puled
DELRU lured
ruled
DELRY redly
DELSS sleds
DELSU duels
dulse
slued
DELSV velds
DELSW welds
DELSY lysed
DELTU luted
DELTV veldt
DELTW dwelt
DEMMO modem
DEMNO demon
DEMNS mends
DEMOO mooed
DEMOP moped
DEMOR drome
Drôme
DEMOS demos
domes
modes
DEMOU odeum
DEMOV moved
DEMOW mowed
DEMRS derms
DEMRU demur
mured
DEMSU mused
sedum
DEMTU muted
DENNO donne
DENOO odeon
DENOR drone
redon
DENOS nodes
nosed
sonde
DENOT noted
toned
DENOV devon
DENOW endow
owned
Woden
DENOY doyen
DENOZ dozen
zoned
DENPS pends
spend
DENPU upend
DENRS nerds
rends
DENRT trend
DENRU Düren
under
DENRY nerdy
DENSS sends
sneds
DENST dents
tends
DENSU dunes
nudes
DENSV vends
DENSW wends
DENSY Denys
dynes
syned
DENTU tuned
DENUU undue
DENUW unwed
DEOOR rodeo
DEOOW wooed
DEOOZ oozed
DEOPR pedro
pored
roped
DEOPS dopes
posed
spode
DEOPT depot
opted
toped
DEOPY dopey
DEORR derro
order
DEORS deros
doers
doser
rodes
rosed
DEORT doter
trode
DEORU Duero
uredo
DEORV dover
drove
roved
DEORW dower
rowed
DEORX redox
DEORZ dozer
DEOSS doses
DEOST dotes
Odets
DEOSU douse
DEOSV doves
DEOSW dowse
sowed
DEOSZ dozes
DEOTT toted
DEOTU outed
DEOTV voted
DEOTW towed
DEOTX detox
DEOTY toyed
DEOVW vowed
DEOWW wowed
DEOXY deoxy
DEPPU upped
DEPRU drupe
duper
du Pré
Dupré
perdu
prude
DEPSU dupes
pseud
spued
DEPTY typed
DERRU Dürer
ruder
DERRY derry
dryer
redry
Ryder
DERSS dress
DERSU druse
DERSY dreys
dyers
DERTU trued
DERTY tyred
DESTU duets
DESUX duxes
DETUV duvet
DFFOS doffs
DFFSU duffs
DFFUY Duffy
DFILU fluid

DFINS finds
DFINU fundi
DFIOR fiord
DFIRT drift
DFJOR fjord
DFLOO flood
DFLOS folds
DFNOR frond
DFNOS fonds
DFNOU found
DFNSU funds
DFNUY fundy
DFOOR fordo
DFOOS foods
DFOOY foody
DFORS fords
DFRSY fyrds
DGGOO doggo
DGGOY doggy
DGHIT dight
DGHOU dough
DGIIR rigid
DGIIT digit
DGILS gilds
DGILU guild
DGIMY midgy
DGINO dingo
doing
DGINR grind
DGINS dings
DGINY dingy
dying
DGIRS girds
grids
DGIRY ridgy
DGLOS golds
DGLOU Gould
DGLOY godly
DGNOO Ogdon
DGNOS dongs
DGNSU dungs
DGNUY dungy
DGOOS goods
DGOOY Godoy
goody
DGOPY podgy
DGORU gourd
DGPUY pudgy
DGRSU drugs
DHIMU humid
DHINS hinds
DHINU Hindu
DHIOT dhoti
DHIOY hyoid
DHIRT third
DHISY dishy
DHITU dhuti
DHITW width
DHLLO dholl
DHLOS holds
DHNOO Hondo
DHNOU hound
DHOOS hoods
DHORY hydro
DHOSW dhows
showd
DHOSY yodhs
DHOWY howdy
DHRSU hurds
DHSTU thuds
DIILL dilli
DIILP lipid
DIILV livid
DIIMO idiom
DIIMS midis
DIIMT timid
DIINR indri
DIINT nitid
DIIOT idiot
DIIVV vivid
DIJNN djinn
DIJNO Dijon
DIKNR drink
DIKNS dinks
kinds
DIKNY dinky
kindy
DIKOS Disko
DIKRS dirks
DIKSS disks
skids
DILLR drill
DILLS dills
DILLY dilly
idyll
DILMS milds
DILMY dimly
DILNO Dolin
indol
DILOS diols
idols
lidos
soldi
solid
DILOY doily
DILRU lurid
DILRY drily
DILSS silds
DILSW wilds
DILSY idyls
DIMNS minds
DIMOU odium
DIMRU mudir
DIMST midst
DIMTU tumid
DINOP poind
DINOR Rodin
DINOS Sidon
DINOT tondi
DINOX Dixon
DINRS rinds
DINST dints
DINSU Indus
nidus
DINSW winds
DINWY windy
DIOOT ootid
DIOOV ovoid
DIOOZ zooid
DIOPR Prodi
DIOPS dipso
DIOPY pyoid
DIORS doris
DIORT droit
DIOST doits
DIOSV voids
DIOSY Doisy
DIOTT ditto
DIOTV divot
DIOWW widow
DIPPY dippy
DIPRS drips
DIQSU quids
squid
DIRTY dirty
DIRUZ durzi
DISTY ditsy
DITTY ditty
DITYZ ditzy
DIVVY divvy
DIYZZ dizzy
DJNOR Njord
DJOOS dojos
DKKOO Kodok
DKNOO donko
kondo
DKNRU drunk
DKNSU dunks
DKOOR drook
DKOOS dooks
DKORS dorks
DKORU drouk
DKORY dorky
DKOSU douks
kudos
DKSSU dusks
DKSUU kudus
DKSUY dusky
DKUUZ kudzu
DLLOR droll
DLLOS dolls
DLLOY dolly
Lloyd
DLLSU dulls
DLLUY dully
DLMOS molds
DLMOU mould
DLMOY moldy
DLNUY Lundy
DLOOR dolor
drool
DLOOS dolos
soldo
DLOPS plods
DLORS lords
DLORW world
DLORY lordy
DLOST dolts
DLOSW wolds
DLOUW would
DLOWY dowly
DLOYY doyly
DLRYY dryly
DMMUY dummy
DMNOU mound
DMOOS dooms
moods
sodom
DMOOY doomy
moody
DMORS dorms
DMORY dormy
DMPSU dumps
DMPUY dumpy
DMRSU drums
DMRUU durum
DNNOU dunno
DNNOY donny
DNNUY dunny
DNOOR donor
doorn
rondo
DNOOS snood
DNOOT tondo
DNOPS ponds
DNOPU pound
DNORU N'Dour
round
DNORW drown
DNOSU nodus
sound
DNOSW downs
DNOSY Dyson
synod
DNOTU donut
DNOUW wound
DNOWY downy
DNRSU nurds
DNRUY nurdy
DNSSY synds
DNSTU dunts
DNSWY wynds
DNTUW Wundt
DOOPR droop
DOOPS poods
DOORS doors
odors
roods
DOORU Douro
odour
DOOST stood
DOOSW woods
DOOTU outdo
DOOWY woody
DOOYZ doozy
DOPRS dorps
drops
prods
DOPRU proud
DOQSU quods
DORSS dross
DORSU duros
sudor
DORSW sword
words
DORTU Tudor
DORTY dorty
DORUY Oudry
DORWY dowry
rowdy
wordy
DOTTY dotty
DPPUY duppy
DPSSU spuds
DPSUU pudus
DRRUY durry
DRSSU surds
DRSTU durst
turds
DSSTU dusts
studs
DSSUY sudsy
DSTUY dusty
study
EEEFZ feeze
EEEGL gelee
Gelée
EEEGS geese
EEEIR eerie
EEELM melee
EEELP Peele
Pelée
EEELV levee
EEEMS semee
EEEPS epees
EEEPT tepee
EEEPV peeve
EEEPW pewee
EEERV reeve
EEFGR Frege
EEFHI Hefei
EEFIL Eifel
EEFIR fiere
EEFJS jefes
EEFLR fleer
EEFLS feels
flees
EEFLT fleet
EEFMM femme
EEFMS femes
EEFRR freer
refer
EEFRS feres
frees
reefs
sefer
EEFRV fever
EEFRW fewer
EEFSS fesse
EEFST fetes

EEFSU	fusee
EEFUZ	fuzee
EEGGR	egger
EEGHL	Hegel
EEGHN	henge
EEGIL	liege
	Liège
EEGIN	Eigen
	genie
EEGIR	Eiger
EEGIS	siege
EEGIV	vegie
EEGKR	greek
EEGKS	geeks
EEGKY	geeky
EEGLR	leger
	Léger
EEGLS	glees
	leges
EEGLT	gleet
EEGLY	elegy
EEGMR	merge
EEGNR	genre
	green
EEGNS	genes
EEGNT	genet
	tenge
EEGNV	Negev
	venge
EEGNW	ngwee
EEGOS	ogees
EEGRR	Greer
	Reger
EEGRS	grees
	Segrè
	serge
EEGRT	egret
	greet
EEGRV	verge
EEGST	egest
	geest
	geste
EEGSU	segue
EEHIN	Heine
	Henie
EEHLL	Helle
EEHLN	Helen
EEHLS	heels
	heles
EEHLT	lethe
EEHLV	helve
EEHLW	wheel
EEHMR	rehem
	rheme
EEHMT	theme
EEHNR	Herne
EEHNS	sheen
EEHNW	wheen
EEHNZ	Henze
EEHPS	sheep
EEHRS	Esher
	heres
	sheer
EEHRT	ether
	there
	three
EEHRW	hewer
	where
EEHRX	hexer
EEHRY	Heyer
EEHSS	Hesse
EEHST	sheet
	these
EEHSX	hexes
EEHTT	teeth
EEIJT	eejit
EEIJW	jewie
EEILM	elemi
EEILT	elite
EEILX	exile
EEINR	Irene
EEINS	seine
EEINV	nieve
EEINX	exine
EEIPR	Ieper
EEIRS	Isère
EEIRT	retie
	Tiree
EEIRV	reive
EEIRY	eyrie
EEISS	seise
EEISV	sieve
EEISZ	seize
EEITV	evite
EEJLW	jewel
EEJLY	jeely
EEJPS	jeeps
EEJRS	jeers
EEJRZ	Jerez
EEJSS	jesse
EEJST	jetes
EEKKS	keeks
EEKLN	kneel
EEKLR	kerel
EEKLS	keels
	leeks
	sleek
EEKLV	kevel
EEKMP	Kempe
EEKNR	kerne
EEKNS	keens
	knees
EEKNT	kente
EEKOP	pekoe
EEKOV	evoke
EEKPS	keeps
	peeks
	pekes
EEKRS	esker
	reeks
EEKRY	reeky
	rekey
EEKSS	seeks
EEKST	skeet
EEKSW	weeks
EEKSX	kexes
EEKSY	Kesey
EELLV	level
EELMM	Memel
EELMR	merle
EELNO	leone
EELNP	Le Pen
EELNS	lenes
EELNV	Leven
EELNW	newel
EELOP	elope
EELOW	Loewe
EELPR	leper
	repel
EELPS	peels
	sleep
	speel
EELPX	expel
EELRS	leers
	reels
EELRT	relet
EELRU	Euler
EELRV	elver
	lever
	revel
EELRY	leery
EELSS	seels
	seles
EELST	leets
	sleet
	steel
	stele
EELSV	elves
EELSW	Lewes
EELTU	elute
EELTX	telex
EELTY	Leyte
EELTZ	Etzel
	Tezel
EEMMN	Emmen
EEMMR	emmer
EEMMT	emmet
EEMNS	menes
	mesne
	neems
	semen
EEMNU	neume
EEMNY	enemy
	Yemen
EEMOR	Meroë
EEMOT	emote
EEMPT	Tempe
EEMRS	meres
	merse
EEMRT	meter
	metre
EEMRX	remex
EEMRY	emery
EEMSS	seems
EEMST	meets
	metes
	teems
EEMSU	meuse
EEMSZ	mezes
	mzees
EENNP	penne
EENNS	nenes
EENPR	neper
	preen
EENPS	neeps
	peens
	penes
EENQU	queen
EENRS	ernes
	reens
	sneer
EENRT	enter
	rente
	terne
	treen
EENRU	enure
EENRV	erven
	nerve
	never
	Verne
EENRW	newer
	renew
EENSS	Essen
	sense
EENST	steen
	teens
	tense
EENSU	ensue
EENSV	evens
	neves
	seven
EENSW	sewen
	weens
EENSY	Syene
EENTT	tenet
EENTV	event
EENTW	tween
EENTY	teeny
EENUV	venue
EENWY	weeny
EEOPT	topee
EEORS	erose
EEOXY	oxeye
EEPPS	peeps
EEPRS	peers
	peres
	perse
	prese
	speer
	spree
EEPRT	peter
EEPRU	puree
	rupee
EEPRV	perve
EEPSS	seeps
EEPST	steep
EEPSW	sweep
	weeps
EEPWY	weepy
EEQRU	queer
EEQUU	queue
EERSS	seers
	seres
EERST	ester
	reest
	reset
	steer
	stere
	terse
	trees
EERSU	reuse
EERSV	erevs
	serve
	sever
	veers
	verse
EERSW	ewers
	sewer
	sweer
	Weser
EERSX	Xeres
EERSY	eyres
EERTV	evert
	revet
EERTX	exert
EERUV	revue
EERVV	verve
EERVX	vexer
EERVY	every
	veery
EESSX	Essex
	sexes
EESSY	yeses
EESTW	sweet
	weest
EESVX	vexes
EETTU	tutee
EETTV	Tevet
EETTW	tweet
EFFFO	feoff
EFFIR	fifer
EFFIS	fiefs
	fifes
EFFOR	offer
	reffo
EFFRU	ruffe
EFGIN	feign
EFGIR	grief
EFGOR	forge
	gofer
EFGOY	fogey
EFGUU	fugue
EFHIO	Hofei
EFHIT	thief
EFHLS	flesh
	shelf
EFHNO	foehn
EFHPY	Phyfe
EFHRS	fresh
EFHST	hefts

EFHTT theft
EFHTY hefty
EFIKN knife
EFILN elfin
EFILR filer
flier
lifer
rifle
EFILS files
flies
EFILT filet
flite
EFIMR fermi
EFIMU Fiume
EFINR finer
infer
EFINS fines
EFINT feint
EFIOX foxie
EFIRR Er Rif
firer
frier
EFIRS fiers
fires
fries
frise
serif
EFIRT refit
treif
EFIRV fiver
EFIRX fixer
EFIRY fiery
reify
EFISV fives
EFISX fixes
EFKLS skelf
EFKLU fluke
EFKRS kerfs
EFKSY fykes
EFLLS fells
EFLLY felly
EFLMU flume
EFLNO felon
EFLOR Rolfe
EFLOS floes
EFLOT flote
EFLOW Wolfe
EFLOX flexo
EFLOY foley
EFLRY ferly
flyer
EFLST felts
lefts
EFLSU flues
fuels
fusel
EFLSW flews
EFLSY fleys
EFLTU flute
EFLTY flyte
lefty
EFLUY fluey
EFMMY femmy
EFMOR forme
Frome
EFMOS fomes
EFMRU femur
fumer
EFMSU fumes
EFMTU fumet
EFNNU Funen
EFNNY fenny
EFNOR freon
EFNOT often
EFNRS ferns
EFNRY ferny
EFORR frore
EFORS froes
orfes
EFORT fetor
forte
EFORX forex
EFORY foyer
EFORZ froze
EFOSS fosse
EFOSX foxes
EFOWY Fowey
EFRRY ferry
fryer
refry
EFRSS serfs
EFRST frets
EFRUZ furze
EFSST fests
EFSSU fuses
EFSTU fetus
EFSTW wefts
EFSTY festy
EFSUZ fuzes
EGGIN ginge
EGGIR Grieg
EGGIU gigue
EGGLY leggy
EGGNU gunge
EGGOP pogge
EGGOR gorge
EGGOU gouge
EGGSY yeggs
EGHIL Leigh
EGHIN hinge
neigh
EGHIT eight
EGHIW weigh
EGHNT Ghent
thegn
EGHOU Hogue
EGHRU huger
EGHRY Gehry
EGIIN genii
EGIJR rejig
EGIKL klieg
EGIKN eking
EGIKR grike
EGILM gimel
EGILN Elgin
ingle
EGILO Egoli
EGILR liger
EGILS Giles
gleis
EGILT gilet
legit
EGILU guile
EGIMM gimme
EGIMN minge
EGIMR grime
EGINP genip
EGINR niger
Regin
reign
EGINS segni
singe
EGINT tinge
EGINV given
EGINY eying
EGIOV ogive
EGIPR gripe
EGIRT tiger
Tigré
EGIRV giver
EGIST gites
EGISU guise
EGISV gives
EGIWZ Zweig
EGKRY gryke
EGKSS skegs
EGLLY gelly
EGLMO golem
Gomel
EGLMU glume
EGLNN Glenn
EGLNO Elgon
longe
EGLNS glens
EGLNU lunge
EGLOO Goole
EGLOR ogler
EGLOS loges
ogles
EGLOV glove
Vogel
EGLOZ gloze
EGLRU gluer
gruel
luger
EGLSU glues
gules
luges
EGLSY gleys
EGLUY gluey
EGMMY gemmy
EGMNO genom
gnome
EGMNU Meung
EGMOT gemot
EGMRS germs
EGMSU geums
EGNNO ennog
EGNOP pengo
EGNOR genro
goner
negro
Norge
EGNOS segno
EGNOY Goyen
Yonge
EGNPU unpeg
EGNRZ grenz
EGNST gents
EGNSU genus
negus
EGNSY Synge
EGNTW Gwent
EGNUU Enugu
EGOOS goose
EGOOY gooey
EGOPR grope
EGOPY pogey
EGORR roger
EGORS goers
gores
gorse
ogres
regos
EGORT ergot
Grote
Roget
EGORU rogue
rouge
EGORV grove
EGORW Gower
EGORY Gorey
EGOSS gesso
gosse
EGOSV vegos
EGOUV vogue
vouge
EGPRU purge
EGPSU speug
EGPTU getup
Puget
EGPTY Egypt
EGPUY Péguy
EGRRU urger
EGRSU grues
Suger
surge
urges
EGRSY greys
gyres
EGRUW Gweru
EGSST gests
EGSSU guess
EGSTU guest
EGSVY gyves
EGTTY Getty
EHHOP Hopeh
EHHPU Hupeh
EHHST heths
EHIKR hiker
EHIKS hikes
sheik
EHILO helio
EHILS shiel
EHILT Leith
lithe
EHILW while
EHILX helix
EHIMN hemin
EHIMO homie
EHINR Rhein
rhine
EHINS Hines
shine
EHINT thine
EHINW whine
EHIRR hirer
EHIRS heirs
hires
shier
shire
EHIRT ither
Reith
their
EHISS shies
EHIST heist
shite
EHISV hives
shive
EHITT tithe
EHITW white
withe
EHJLO Jehol
EHKLW whelk
EHKNO Kohen
EHKOO Hooke
EHKOS hokes
EHKOY hokey
EHLLO hello
EHLLS hells
shell
EHLMO mohel
EHLMS helms
EHLMU Hulme
EHLMW whelm
EHLOS holes
sheol
EHLOT helot
hotel
thole
EHLOV hovel
EHLOW whole
EHLOY holey
hoyle
EHLPS helps
EHLPW whelp
EHLPY phyle
EHLRS herls
lehrs
EHLRZ Herzl

EHLSW	welsh
EHLTU	Thule
EHLTY	ethyl
EHLXY	hexyl
EHMNY	hymen
EHMOR	homer
	horme
EHMOS	homes
EHMOT	metho
EHMOY	homey
EHMPS	hemps
EHMQS	Qeshm
EHMRS	herms
EHMRT	therm
EHMRU	rheum
EHMRY	rhyme
EHMST	meths
EHMSY	meshy
EHMTY	thyme
EHNOP	phone
EHNOR	heron
	rhone
	Rhône
EHNOS	hones
	hosen
	shone
EHNOY	honey
EHNRS	herns
EHNRU	Nehru
EHNRY	henry
EHNST	hents
	shent
EHNSW	shewn
	whens
EHNTT	tenth
EHOOY	hooey
EHOPR	ephor
	hoper
EHOPS	hopes
EHORS	hoers
	horse
	hoser
	shoer
	shore
EHORT	other
	throe
EHORV	hover
EHORW	whore
EHOSS	hoses
	shoes
EHOST	ethos
	shote
	those
EHOSU	house
EHOSV	shove
EHOSW	howes
	whose
EHPRT	Perth
EHPRY	hyper
EHPSY	hypes
EHRST	Herts
	Resht
EHRSU	usher
EHRSW	shrew
	wersh
EHRSY	shyer
EHRTU	Uther
EHRTW	threw
EHRTZ	hertz
EHSST	hests
EHSSW	shews
EHSTT	teths
EHSTU	shute
EHSTW	thews
	whets
EHTWY	thewy
EIIJM	Meiji
EIIKR	reiki
EIILP	pilei
EIIMN	imine
EIINS	nisei
EIINX	nixie
EIIPX	pixie
EIISV	ivies
EIITY	yitie
EIJKO	Keijo
EIJRV	jiver
EIJSV	jives
EIKKS	kikes
EIKLN	inkle
	Klein
	Kline
	liken
EIKLR	Rilke
EIKLS	likes
EIKLY	kiley
	kylie
EIKMN	minke
EIKMS	mikes
EIKNO	eikon
	koine
EIKNP	pekin
	Penki
EIKNR	inker
EIKNS	skein
	Skien
EIKOP	pokie
EIKPR	piker
EIKPS	kepis
	pikes
	spike
EIKRS	kiers
	skier
EIKRT	kiter
	trike
EIKSS	sikes
	skies
EIKST	kites
	skite
	tikes
EIKSV	skive
EIKSY	Yeisk
	yikes
EIKTW	Kitwe
EILLL	Lille
EILLN	Neill
EILLO	ollie
EILLR	rille
EILLS	Ellis
	lisle
EILLW	Weill
EILMN	Ilmen
	limen
	Milne
EILMP	impel
EILMR	miler
EILMS	limes
	miles
	slime
	smile
EILMU	ileum
EILMY	limey
EILNN	Lenin
	linen
EILNO	eloin
	olein
EILNR	liner
EILNS	lenis
	lines
EILNT	inlet
EILNV	levin
	liven
EILNY	liney
EILOR	Loire
	oiler
	oriel
	reoil
EILOT	Eliot
	toile
EILOV	olive
	voile
EILOW	Loewi
EILOX	Leo IX
EILPP	Lippe
EILPR	peril
	plier
EILPS	piles
	plies
	Siple
	slipe
	spiel
	spile
EILPX	pixel
EILRS	riels
	riles
	slier
EILRT	liter
	litre
	relit
	tiler
EILRU	Lurie
	Uriel
EILRV	liver
	livre
	viler
EILRY	riley
EILSS	isles
	siles
EILST	islet
	istle
	lites
	stile
	tiles
EILSU	ileus
EILSV	elvis
	evils
	lives
	veils
	vleis
EILSW	lewis
	wiles
EILSX	lexis
	silex
EILTT	title
EILTU	utile
EILTX	ixtle
EIMMR	mimer
EIMMS	mimes
EIMNR	miner
EIMNS	miens
	mines
	Nîmes
EIMNV	vimen
EIMNY	meiny
EIMNZ	mizen
EIMOR	moire
EIMOV	movie
EIMOX	moxie
	oxime
EIMPR	prime
EIMPT	tempi
EIMPU	umpie
EIMRR	rimer
EIMRS	emirs
	mires
	miser
	Reims
	rimes
EIMRT	merit
	miter
	mitre
	remit
	timer
EIMRX	mixer
	remix
EIMSS	mises
	seism
	semis
EIMST	emits
	items
	metis
	mites
	smite
	times
EIMSX	mixes
EIMTX	mixte
EINNP	penni
EINNR	inner
	renin
EINNS	Ennis
	nines
EINNU	ennui
EINNV	Niven
	venin
EINNW	Ne Win
EINOP	opine
EINOS	eosin
	noise
EINOV	envoi
	ovine
EINPR	repin
	ripen
EINPS	penis
	pines
	snipe
	spine
EINPT	inept
	nepit
EINQU	quine
EINRS	reins
	resin
	rinse
	risen
	serin
	siren
EINRT	inert
	inter
	niter
	nitre
	Terni
	trine
EINRU	inure
	urine
EINRV	Nervi
	riven
	Viren
EINRX	nixer
EINSS	sines
EINST	inset
	stein
	Stine
	tines
EINSV	Nevis
	veins
	vines
EINSW	sewin
	sinew
	swine
	wines
EINSX	nixes
EINSZ	zeins
	zines
EINTU	unite
	untie
EINTW	twine
EINVX	vixen
EINVY	veiny
EINWY	winey
EINWZ	winze
	wizen

EIOPS poise
EIOPZ piezo
EIORS osier
EIORV vireo
EIOSS Ossie
EIOTW towie
EIOWY yowie
EIOZZ ozzie
EIPPR piper
EIPPS pipes
EIPQU equip
pique
EIPRR prier
riper
EIPRS peris
piers
pries
prise
speir
spier
spire
EIPRT piert
tripe
EIPRV viper
EIPRW wiper
EIPRZ prize
EIPSS spies
EIPST piste
spite
stipe
EIPSW swipe
wipes
EIPSY yipes
EIPSZ pizes
EIPTT petit
EIPTW pewit
EIPTY piety
EIPXY pyxie
EIQRU quire
EIQTU quiet
quite
EIRRS riser
EIRRT trier
EIRRV river
EIRRW wirer
wrier
EIRRY eyrir
EIRSS rises
sires
EIRST resit
rites
Siret
tiers
tires
tries
EIRSV rives
siver
viers
vires
Vries
EIRSW sweir
weirs
wires
wiser
wries
EIRSX sixer
EIRSZ sizer
EIRTT titer
titre
trite
EIRTU uteri
EIRTV rivet
EIRTW write
EISSS sises
EISST sites
sties
EISSU issue
EISSV vises
EISSW wises
EISSX sixes
EISSZ sizes
EISTU etuis
suite
EISTX exist
exits
sixte
EISTY yetis
yites
EISTZ Zeist
EISUV Viseu
EISVW swive
views
wives
EITTW twite
Witte
EIVWY viewy
EJKOP kopje
EJKOR joker
EJKOS jokes
EJKOY jokey
EJKRS jerks
EJKRY jerky
EJLLO jello
EJLLS jells
EJLLY jelly
EJLOP polje
EJLOU joule
EJLPU julep
EJLRU jurel
EJMMY jemmy
EJNNY jenny
EJNOS jones
EJNOY enjoy
EJOSY joeys
EJRRY jerry
EJRWY Jewry
EJSST jests
EJSSU jesus
EJSTU jutes
EJTTY jetty
EKKOP kopek
EKKRY kerky
EKLLN knell
EKLLS kells
EKLLY kelly
EKLMS skelm
EKLNO Knole
EKLNT knelt
EKLOS koels
EKLOY kyloe
yokel
EKLPS skelp
spelk
EKLPY kelpy
EKLST kelts
EKLSY kyles
yelks
EKMOS mokes
smoke
EKMPS kemps
EKMPT kempt
EKMPY kempy
EKMRS Krems
EKNNY Kenny
EKNOR krone
EKNOS snoek
EKNOT token
EKNOW woken
EKNRS kerns
EKNSS skens
EKNSU neuks
nukes
EKOOT Tooke
EKOPR poker
EKOPS pokes
spoke
EKOPY pokey
EKORT toker
EKORY yoker
EKOSS sokes
EKOST stoke
tokes
EKOSY yokes
EKPRS perks
EKPRY perky
EKPSS skeps
EKPSU pukes
EKPSY kypes
pesky
EKPTU tupek
EKRRY kerry
EKRST treks
EKSST skets
EKSSW skews
EKSTY kytes
tykes
EKSYY Yeysk
ELLLY Lyell
ELLMS smell
ELLNS snell
ELLNY nelly
ELLOR oller
ELLOS losel
ELLPS spell
ELLQU quell
ELLSS sells
ELLST stell
tells
ELLSW swell
wells
ELLSY yells
ELLSZ Szell
ELLTU tulle
ELLTY telly
ELLWY welly
ELMMU lumme
ELMNO lemon
melon
ELMNU lumen
ELMOR morel
ELMOS Melos
moles
ELMOT metol
motel
ELMOU oleum
ELMOY moyle
ELMPU plume
ELMRS merls
ELMRU lemur
ELMST melts
smelt
ELMSU mules
ELMSW mewls
ELMUV velum
ELMUY muley
ELMXY xylem
ELNOR enrol
loner
Loren
ELNOS enols
lenos
noels
Olsen
ELNOT Elton
lento
ELNOV novel
Venlo
ELNPZ Plzeň
ELNSU lunes
ELNWY newly
ELOOP Poole
ELOOS loose
ELOPR loper
poler
prole
ELOPS lopes
poles
slope
ELOPU loupe
ELOPY poley
ELOPZ Lopez
ELORS lores
loser
orles
roles
sorel
ELORV lover
Vlorë
ELORW lower
rowel
ELOSS loess
loses
sloes
soles
ELOST stole
ELOSU louse
ousel
Seoul
ELOSV loves
ovels
solve
voles
ELOSW lowse
ELOSY Losey
ELOTV volte
ELOTW owlet
towel
ELOTX extol
ELOTY Elyot
ELOUV ovule
ELOUZ ouzel
ELOVW vowel
ELOVY lovey
ELPRU puler
ELPRY reply
ELPST pelts
slept
spelt
ELPSU plues
pules
pulse
ELPSW plews
ELPSY slype
yelps
ELPTU letup
ELRRU lurer
ruler
ELRSU lures
luser
rules
ELRSY lyres
slyer
ELRTY tyler
ELSSU slues
ELSSW slews
ELSSY lyses
Yssel
ELSTU lutes
ELSTW welts
ELSTY style
ELSUY yules
ELTUX exult
ELTWY Welty
wetly
EMMOS memos
Somme
EMNNO Menon
nomen
EMNNU numen
EMNOS meson

nomes
omens
EMNOT Monet
monte
EMNOV venom
EMNOW women
EMNOY money
EMNRU rumen
EMNSU menus
neums
EMOOR Moore
romeo
EMOOS moose
EMOPR moper
proem
EMOPS Epsom
mopes
poems
pomes
EMOPT tempo
EMOPY myope
EMORR ormer
EMORS Moers
mores
morse
omers
EMORT metro
EMORV mover
vomer
EMORW mower
EMOSS moses
EMOST moste
motes
smote
tomes
EMOSU moues
mouse
EMOSV moves
EMOSW meows
EMOSY mosey
EMOSZ mozes
EMOTT motet
motte
totem
EMOZZ mezzo
EMPRS perms
sperm
EMPST empts
temps
EMPSU spume
EMPTT tempt
EMPTY empty
EMRRU murre
EMRRY merry
EMRST terms
EMRSU mures
Mureş
muser
Remus
serum
Sumer
EMRSY Myers
EMRUW Mweru
EMRUX murex
EMSST stems
EMSSU muses
EMSSW smews
EMSSY messy
EMSTU mutes
ENNOS nones
ENNOT nonet
tenno
tenon
tonne
ENNOX xenon
ENNOY Yonne
ENNPY penny
ENOOR roneo
ENOOS noose
ENOOZ ozone
ENOPR Perón
prone
ENOPS Nepos
opens
peons
pones
Posen
snoep
ENOPY peony
ENORS Ensor
Norse
oners
rones
senor
snore
ENORT tenor
toner
ENORU rouen
ENORW owner
rowen
ENOSS noses
sones
ENOST notes
onset
seton
steno
stone
tones
ENOSV ovens
ENOSW Owens
ENOSX exons
ENOSY nosey
ENOSZ zones
ENOVW woven
ENOVY envoy
ENPRU prune
ENPST spent
ENQRU quern
ENRRU rerun
ENRST Ernst
rents
stern
terns
ENRSU nurse
runes
ENRSW wrens
ENRTT Trent
ENRTU tuner
ENRTY entry
ENRVY nervy
Verny
ENRWY Newry
ENSST nests
ENSSU Neuss
ENSSY snyes
synes
ENSTT stent
tents
ENSTU suent
tunes
unset
ENSTV vents
ENSTW newts
ENSUV nevus
venus
ENSUX nexus
unsex
ENSWY newsy
Sweyn
ENTTY netty
EOOPS Espoo
EOOPV poove
EOORS roose
EOORW wooer
EOOSZ oozes
EOPPS pepos
poeps
popes
EOPRR repro
EOPRS pores
poser
prose
ropes
Soper
spore
EOPRT repot
toper
trope
EOPRV prove
EOPRW power
EOPRY ropey
EOPSS pesos
poses
posse
speos
EOPST estop
pesto
poets
stoep
stope
topes
EOPSX expos
poxes
EOPSY poesy
posey
sepoy
EOPXY epoxy
EOQRU roque
EOQTU quote
toque
EORRR error
EORRT retro
EORRV rover
EORRW rower
EORSS roses
sores
EORST resto
rotes
store
tores
EORSU euros
roues
rouse
EORSV Évros
overs
roves
servo
verso
EORSW serow
sower
swore
worse
EORSZ zeros
EORTT otter
torte
toter
EORTU outer
outre
route
Touré
EORTV overt
trove
voter
EORTW tower
wrote
EORTX oxter
EORTY toyer
EORVW vower
EORXX xerox
EOSSU souse
EOSTT totes
EOSTV stove
votes
EOSTW Stowe
EOSTX sexto
EOSTY eyots
EOSUY youse
EOSVV Svevo
EOSWY yowes
EOTTV Ovett
EPPPY peppy
EPPRS preps
EPPRU upper
EPPSY Pepys
EPRRU purer
EPRRY perry
pryer
EPRSS press
EPRST prest
strep
EPRSU purse
sprue
spuer
super
EPRSV pervs
EPRSY preys
Ypres
EPRTU erupt
upter
EPRTW twerp
EPSST pests
septs
steps
EPSSU spues
EPSSW spews
EPSTU setup
stupe
upset
EPSTW swept
EPSTY pyets
types
EPSUY Pusey
EPSXY pyxes
EPTTY petty
EQRUY query
EQSTU quest
EQTUU tuque
ERRSU ruers
surer
ERRTU truer
ERRTY retry
terry
ERRWY wryer
ERSST rests
tress
ERSSU ruses
suers
users
ERSTT trets
ERSTU trues
ERSTV verst
verts
ERSTW strew
trews
wrest
ERSTY Steyr
treys
tyres
ERSUU Eurus
ERSUV eruvs
ERSVY syver
ERTTU utter
ERTUV vertu
ERTWY twyer
ERUVY Yurev
ESSTT setts
stets
tests
ESSTV vests
ESSTW stews

ESSTY	styes
ESSTZ	zests
ESTTX	texts
ESTTY	testy
	yetts
ESTUY	suety
ESTYZ	zesty
FFFLU	fluff
FFGIR	griff
FFGRU	gruff
FFGSU	guffs
FFHIT	fifth
FFHIW	whiff
FFHOU	Hofuf
FFHOW	howff
FFHSU	huffs
FFHUU	Hufuf
FFHUY	huffy
FFIJS	jiffs
FFIJY	jiffy
FFIKS	skiff
FFIMS	miffs
FFIMY	miffy
FFINS	niffs
	sniff
FFINY	niffy
FFIQU	quiff
FFIRS	riffs
FFIST	stiff
	tiffs
FFISZ	ziffs
FFITY	fifty
FFLSU	luffs
	sluff
FFMSU	muffs
FFNSU	snuff
FFOST	toffs
FFOTY	toffy
FFPSU	puffs
FFPUY	puffy
FFRSU	ruffs
FFSTU	stuff
FGGIR	Frigg
FGGOY	foggy
FGGUY	fuggy
FGHIT	fight
FGILN	fling
FGINO	gonif
FGINU	fungi
FGIOU	fugio
FGIRS	frigs
FGIST	gifts
FGLNO	flong
FGLNU	flung
FGLOS	flogs
	golfs
FGLSU	gulfs
FGLUY	gulfy
FGNOO	gonof
FGOOR	forgo
FGOOS	goofs
FGOOY	goofy
FGORS	frogs
FHILT	filth
FHIRT	firth
	frith
FHIST	shift
FHISY	fishy
FHKUU	Khufu
FHLSU	flush
FHOOS	hoofs
FHOOT	Hooft
FHORT	forth
	froth
FHORW	Whorf
FHOSW	howfs
FHRTU	furth
	Fürth
FHSUU	Shufu
FIILO	Ofili
FIINS	finis
FIINX	infix
FIINZ	Finzi
FIKLU	kulfi
FIKNR	Frink
FIKNS	finks
FIKRS	frisk
FILLR	frill
FILLS	fills
FILLY	filly
FILMS	films
FILMU	filum
FILMY	filmy
FILNT	flint
FILOO	folio
FILOR	Forlì
FILOS	filos
	foils
FILPS	flips
FILRT	flirt
FILST	flits
	lifts
FILSU	fusil
FILTY	fitly
FIMOS	Foism
FIMOT	motif
FIMRS	firms
FIMTU	mufti
FINNY	finny
FINOS	finos
	foins
FINRS	firns
FINTU	unfit
FINTY	nifty
FINUX	unfix
FINUY	unify
FIOST	foist
FIPSS	spifs
FIRRY	firry
FIRST	first
	frits
	rifts
FIRTT	fritt
FIRTU	fruit
FIRZZ	frizz
FISST	fists
	sifts
FISTW	swift
FIYZZ	fizzy
FKLNU	flunk
FKLOO	kloof
FKLOS	folks
FKLOY	folky
FKLUY	fluky
FKNSU	funks
FKNUY	funky
FKORS	forks
FLLOY	folly
FLLSU	fulls
FLLUY	fully
FLNNY	Flynn
FLNOW	flown
FLOOR	floor
FLOOS	fools
FLOOW	Woolf
FLOPS	flops
FLORU	flour
	fluor
FLORY	flory
FLOSS	floss
FLOST	lofts
FLOSU	fouls
FLOSW	flows
	fowls
	wolfs
FLOTU	flout
FLOTY	lofty
FLRSU	furls
FLTUY	fluty
FMMOR	Fromm
FMOOS	mofos
FMORS	forms
FMORU	forum
FMORY	FYROM
FMPRU	frump
FNNUY	funny
FNORS	frons
FNORT	front
FNORW	frown
FNOST	fonts
FNOTU	fount
	futon
FOOPR	proof
FOOPS	poofs
	spoof
FOOPY	poofy
FOORS	roofs
FOOST	foots
FOOSW	woofs
FOOTY	footy
FOPRS	profs
FOPSU	poufs
FORRU	furor
FORST	forts
	frost
FORSU	fours
FORTY	forty
FOSST	softs
FOSTT	tofts
FOSTY	softy
FRRSS	RSFSR
FRRUY	furry
FRSSU	surfs
FRSTU	turfs
FRSUY	surfy
FRTUY	turfy
FRUYZ	furzy
FSSUY	fussy
FSTTU	tufts
FSTUY	fusty
FTTUY	tufty
FUYZZ	fuzzy
GGGLO	glogg
GGHOS	hoggs
GGHUY	huggy
GGIIL	Gigli
GGIJY	jiggy
GGILO	Golgi
GGINO	going
GGINS	gings
GGIOT	gigot
GGIPY	piggy
GGIRS	grigs
GGLOO	Gogol
GGLSU	glugs
GGMOY	moggy
GGMUY	muggy
GGNOS	gongs
	noggs
GGNUY	gungy
GGOOS	googs
GGOSY	soggy
GGPUY	puggy
GGSUV	vuggs
GGUVY	vuggy
GHHIS	highs
GHHIT	hight
	thigh
GHHOO	Hoogh
GHHOU	hough
GHILT	light
GHIMT	might
GHINO	hongi
GHINS	Singh
GHINT	night
	thing
GHINY	hying
GHIRT	girth
	grith
	right
GHISS	sighs
GHIST	sight
GHISW	whigs
GHITT	tight
GHITW	wight
GHLLY	ghyll
GHLOU	ghoul
	lough
GHLPY	glyph
GHNOS	hongs
GHNOT	thong
GHORU	rough
GHOST	ghost
GHOSU	sough
GHOSY	yoghs
GHOTU	ought
	tough
GHRSU	shrug
GHSTU	thugs
GHSUV	vughs
GHSUY	gushy
GHUVY	vughy
GIILS	sigil
GIILV	vigil
GIINP	piing
GIJNO	Gijón
	jingo
GIKNS	ginks
	kings
GIKOR	Gorki
GILLR	grill
GILLS	gills
GILLY	gilly
GILMS	glims
GILNO	lingo
	login
GILNS	lings
	sling
GILNT	glint
GILNU	lungi
GILNY	lingy
	lying
GILOO	igloo
GILOS	Sligo
GILRS	girls
GILRY	girly
GILST	gilts
GILSU	iglus
GILTU	guilt
GILTZ	glitz
GIMMR	Grimm
GIMNY	mingy
GIMOS	gismo
GIMOY	goyim
GIMOZ	gizmo
GIMPS	gimps
GIMPY	gimpy
	pigmy
GIMRY	grimy
GINOP	gipon
	oping
	pingo
GINOR	giron
	groin
GINOT	ingot
	tigon
	toing
GINOW	owing
GINOY	yogin
GINPS	pings

GINPU Pugin
GINRS girns
grins
rings
GINRU ruing
unrig
GINRW wring
GINSS signs
sings
snigs
GINST sting
tings
GINSU suing
using
GINSW swing
wings
GINSZ zings
GINTY tying
GINUX Xingú
GINVY Vigny
vying
GINVZ zingy
GIOPP gippo
GIOPR pirog
GIORR rigor
GIORS giros
GIORT griot
GIORV vigor
Virgo
GIOSY yogis
GIPPY gippy
GIPRS grips
prigs
sprig
GIPSY gipsy
GIRRS girrs
GIRST girts
grist
grits
trigs
GISST gists
GISSW swigs
GISTW twigs
GJMUU jugum
GJOSU jougs
GKLNO klong
GKOOS gooks
GKORY Gorky
GKOSW gowks
GLLOY golly
GLLSU gulls
GLLUY gully
GLMOO gloom
GLMOU mogul
GLNOO logon
GLNOS longs
GLNOU gluon
GLNSU lungs
slung
GLOOS logos
GLOOY gooly
ology
GLORW growl
GLORY glory
GLOSS gloss
slogs
GLOSW glows
GLPSU gulps
plugs
GLPUY gulpy
GLRUY lurgy
GLSSU slugs
GLSTU gluts
GMMUY gummy
GMNOO mongo
GMNOS mongs
GMNOU mungo
GMOOR groom
GMOSS smogs
GMPRU grump
GMPYY pygmy
GNNOS nongs
GNNUY gunny
GNOOP pongo
GNOOS goons
Soong
GNOOZ gonzo
GNOPR prong
GNOPS pongs
GNOPY pongy
GNORW grown
wrong
GNORY gyron
GNOSS snogs
songs
GNOST tongs
GNOSW gnows
gowns
GNOUY young
GNPSU pungs
GNRSU gurns
rungs
GNRTU grunt
GNRUW wrung
GNSSU snugs
GNSTU stung
GNSUW swung
GOOPS goops
pogos
GOOPY goopy
GOORS sorgo
GOORY goory
GOOSY goosy
GOOTU outgo
GOPPY gyppo
GOPRS progs
sprog
GOPRU group
GOPRY porgy
GORSS gross
GORST grots
trogs
GORSW grows
GORSY gorsy
gyros
GORSZ grosz
GORTU grout
trugo
GOSTU gouts
gusto
GOSTV Vogts
GOSTY stogy
GOTUY gouty
guyot
GPPUY guppy
GPSSU spugs
GPSYY gypsy
GRSTU trugs
GRSUU gurus
GRSUY gyrus
GSSTU gusts
GSTUY gusty
gutsy
GTTUY gutty
HHISS shish
HHISW whish
HHMPU humph
HHOTT Thoth
HHSSU shush
HHSUU huhus
HIIKO hikoi
HIILN nihil
HIIRS Irish
HIJNO John I
HIJOS shoji
HIKLW whilk
HIKNS knish
HIKNT think
HIKOS Khíos
HIKRS shirk
HIKSW whisk
HILLS hills
shill
HILLT thill
HILLY hilly
HILMU hilum
HILOT litho
thiol
HILRT thirl
HILRW whirl
HILST hilts
liths
HILSU hilus
HILSY shily
HILTT tilth
HIMNO Minho
HIMQS Qishm
HIMRT mirth
HIMSS shims
HIMST smith
HIMSW whims
HIMTY thymi
HINNO Nihon
HINNT ninth
HINNY hinny
HINOR rhino
HINOT Othin
HINPU unhip
HINSS shins
HINST hints
thins
HINSY shiny
HINWY whiny
HIOOT Otho I
HIOPP hippo
HIOPR Ophir
HIOPT tophi
HIORS horis
HIORU houri
HIOST hoist
HIPPY hippy
HIPSS ships
HIPST piths
HIPSW whips
HIPTY pithy
HIRRS shirr
HIRRW whirr
HIRST Hirst
shirt
HIRSU shiur
HIRSW whirs
HISST shits
HISSU sushi
HISSV shivs
HISSW swish
HISTW whist
wisht
HISTX sixth
HITWY whity
withy
HIWZZ whizz
HJNOS johns
HKKOU hokku
HKLSU hulks
HKLUY hulky
HKMOU hokum
HKNOS honks
HKNOY honky
HKNSU hunks
HKNTU thunk
HKOOS hooks
shook
HKOOY hooky
HKOPS kophs
HKOSW howks
HKSSU husks
HKSUY husky
HLLOO hollo
HLLOU hullo
HLLOY holly
HLLSU hulls
HLMOS holms
HLMPY lymph
HLNOO holon
HLNSU shuln
HLOOS shool
HLOPX phlox
HLORW whorl
HLOSS slosh
HLOST Holst
holts
sloth
HLOSW howls
HLOTU Louth
HLOTY hotly
HLPSU plush
HLPSY sylph
HLRSU hurls
HLSSU slush
HLSYY shyly
HMNOT month
HMNPY nymph
HMNSY hymns
HMOOP oomph
HMOOS homos
HMOPR morph
HMORU humor
mohur
HMOST moths
HMOTU mouth
HMOTY mothy
mytho-
HMPSU humps
sumph
HMPTU thump
HMPUW whump
HMPUY humpy
HMRRY myrrh
HMRTU thrum
HMSTU musth
HMSTY myths
Smyth
HMSUU humus
HMSUY mushy
HMTYY thymy
HNOOP phono
HNOOR honor
HNOOS hoons
shoon
HNOOW nohow
HNOPS phons
HNOPY phony
HNORS horns
shorn
HNORT north
thorn
HNORU Huron
HNORY horny
HNOSU Oshun
HNOSW shown
HNOSY hyson
HNSSU shuns
HNSTU hunts
shunt
HNSTY synth
HOOPS hoops
poohs
posho
HOOPT photo
HOOPW whoop

HOORT ortho
HOOSS shoos
HOOST hoots
shoot
sooth
HOOSW whoso
woosh
HOOTT tooth
HOPQS qophs
HOPRT thorp
HOPSS shops
HOPST phots
HOPSW whops
HOPSY hypos
sophy
HOQTU quoth
HORST horst
short
HORSU Horus
hours
HORSY horsy
HORTT troth
HORTU routh
HORTW rowth
throw
whort
worth
wroth
HOSST hosts
shots
HOSSW shows
HOSTT shott
HOSTU shout
south
thous
HOSUY shoyu
HOSWY showy
HOTTY hotty
HOTUY youth
HOUUW Wu Hou
HPSTU phuts
HPSUW whups
HPSUY pushy
HRRUY hurry
HRSTU hurst
hurts
HRSUY rushy
HRTTU truth
HRUUU uhuru
HSSTU shuts
HSSUY hussy
IIJJU Ujiji
IIJLN Jilin
IIJNN jinni
IIKKO kikoi
IIKLM kilim
IIKNN kinin
IIKNR Kirin
IIKNZ Iznik
IIKRT Kríti
IIKST tikis
IIKSW kiwis
IILLV villi
IILMT limit
IILMU ilium
IILNN linin
IILNO Ilion
IILPP Lippi
IILPS pilis
IIMMN minim
IIMMR Mimir
IIMMX immix
IIMNS minis
IIMPR primi
IIMPS impis
IIMRZ Izmir
IIMST Misti
mitis
IIMTZ Izmit
IINNO inion
IINOX Ixion
IINST intis
IIORT torii
IIPPS pipis
IIPPT pipit
IIPST tipis
IISTT titis
IISTV visit
IJKMU mujik
IJKNS jinks
IJLLS jills
IJLST jilts
IJMMY jimmy
IJNOS joins
IJNOT joint
IJOST joist
IKKNO Nikko
IKKNS kinks
skink
IKKNY kinky
IKKOS kiosk
IKKRS kirks
IKKRU kukri
IKLLR krill
IKLLS kills
skill
IKLMO milko
IKLMS milks
IKLMT Klimt
IKLMY milky
IKLNP plink
IKLNS kilns
links
slink
IKLNT Klint
IKLNY kylin
IKLOS kilos
IKLRS skirl
IKLSS silks
IKLST kilts
IKLSY silky
IKLXY kylix
IKMNS minks
Minsk
IKMOS mokis
IKMPS skimp
IKMRS smirk
IKMRY mirky
IKMSS skims
IKNOP pinko
IKNOS ikons
nkosi
IKNPR prink
IKNPS pinks
Pinsk
IKNPY pinky
IKNRS rinks
IKNSS sinks
skins
IKNST knits
skint
stink
IKNSW swink
winks
IKNTW twink
IKNYZ zinky
IKOOR iroko
koori
IKOOT Kioto
IKORV Kirov
IKPSS skips
spiks
IKPSY spiky
IKPTU tupik
IKQRU quirk
IKRRS skirr
IKRRU Rurik
IKRSS risks
IKRST skirt
stirk
IKRSU kuris
IKRSY risky
IKSST kists
skits
IKSSY kissy
IKTTY kitty
ILLMS mills
ILLOS lilos
ILLPR prill
ILLPS pills
spill
ILLPU pulli
ILLQU quill
ILLRS rills
ILLRT trill
ILLSS sills
ILLST lilts
still
tills
ILLSW swill
wills
ILLSY silly
slily
ILLTW twill
ILLTY tilly
ILLWY willy
ILMNS limns
ILMNU linum
ILMOO mooli
ILMOS limos
milos
Mílos
moils
ILMPS limps
ILMPY imply
ILMSS slims
ILMST milts
ILMSU Musil
simul
ILMSY slimy
ILNNS linns
ILNOS linos
lions
loins
ILNOW Wilno
ILNPU lupin
ILNPY Pliny
ILNSY lysin
ILNTU unlit
until
ILNTY linty
ILNVY vinyl
ILOOP polio
ILOOS olios
ILOOV ovoli
ILOPS Pílos
polis
spoil
ILOPT pilot
ILOPU poilu
ILOPX oxlip
ILORS loris
roils
ILORT Tirol
triol
ILORY roily
ILORZ zoril
ILOSS silos
soils
ILOST Solti
toils
ILOSU louis
ILOSV viols
ILPPU pupil
ILPPY lippy
ILPSS lisps
slips
ILPST spilt
split
ILPSU pilus
pulis
ILPTU tulip
ILQTU quilt
ILRSW swirl
ILRTW twirl
ILSST lists
silts
slits
ILSSY lysis
ILSTT stilt
tilts
ILSTW wilts
ILSTY silty
styli
ILSTZ Liszt
ILSUU Iulus
IMMOS Moism
IMMSY mimsy
IMNOR minor
IMNOS minos
Simon
IMNOU onium
IMNPS nimps
IMNRU Nurmi
IMNST mints
IMNSU minus
IMNTY minty
IMOPR primo
IMOPU opium
IMORT Timor
IMORZ Imroz
IMOST moist
omits
IMOSU Suomi
IMOSX sixmo
IMOTV vomit
IMPPR primp
IMPPS pimps
IMPRS prims
prism
IMPRU purim
IMPSS simps
IMPST timps
IMPSW wimps
IMPUX mixup
IMPWY wimpy
IMQSU quims
IMRRS smirr
IMRRU murri
IMRSS smirs
IMRST trims
IMRSU muirs
rimus
IMRSV mirvs
IMRTU murti
Timur
IMSST mists
stims
IMSSW swims
IMSSY missy
IMSTT mitts
IMSTY misty
INNNO ninon
INNNY ninny
INNOO onion
INNOR ronin
INNOT niton
INNOU Inönü
union
INNOX Nixon

INNPU unpin
INNPY pinny
INNQU Quinn
INNRU inurn
INNSU Ninus
Sunni
INNTY tinny
INOOR Orion
INOPP ippon
INOPR orpin
prion
Ripon
INOPS opsin
pions
INOPT pinto
piton
point
INOQU quoin
INORS irons
ornis
rosin
INORT intro
Niort
nitro
INORY irony
INOSV vinos
INOSW winos
INOSY noisy
INOTX toxin
INOXX Xixón
INPPU pinup
INPPY nippy
INPRS pirns
INPRT print
INPRU purin
unrip
INPSS snips
spins
INPST pints
INPSY spiny
INPTU input
Putin
INPUZ unzip
INQSU quins
INQTU quint
INRSU ruins
INRTU Turin
INSST snits
INSSU nisus
sinus
INSTT stint
tints
INSTU suint
Tunis
units
INSTW twins
INTTY nitty
INTUY unity
INUXZ Xun Zi
IOOPT topoi
IOOTT Otto I
IOPRR prior
IOPST posit
topis
IOPSU pious
IOPTV pivot
IOQTU Quito
quoit
IORRS orris
IORST riots
tiros
torsi
trios
IORSV visor
IORVY ivory
IORVZ vizor
IPPYZ zippy
IPQSU quips
IPQUU quipu
IPRST spirt
sprit
strip
trips
IPRSU sirup
IPRSY spiry
IPRTW twirp
IPRVY privy
IPSST spits
IPSSU Ipsus
IPSSV spivs
IPSSW wisps
IPSTU situp
IPSTY tipsy
IPSTZ spitz
IPSUV Pius V
IPSUX Pius X
IPSWY wispy
IPSXY pyxis
IPTTU putti
IQRTU quirt
IQSTU quist
quits
squit
IQSUZ squiz
IRRSY yirrs
IRSST stirs
IRSTW wrist
writs
IRSUV virus
IRTUV virtu
IRTYZ ritzy
ISSSU Issus
ISSSW swiss
ISSSY sissy
ISSTU situs
suits
ISTTU Titus
ISTTW twist
twits
ISTXY sixty
ISWZZ swizz
ITTTU tutti
ITTWX twixt
ITTWY witty
ITYZZ tizzy
JJSUU jujus
JKNSU junks
JKNUY junky
JKOOS jooks
JKOSU jouks
JLLOY jolly
JLOST jolts
JLOSW jowls
JLOTY jolty
JMOOS mojos
JMORU jorum
JMPSU jumps
JMPUY jumpy
JNOPU jupon
JNOTU jotun
junto
JORRU juror
JOSTU joust
KKLSU skulk
KKNSU skunk
KKOOS kooks
KKOOY kooky
KKRSU Kursk
KKUYY yukky
KLLNO knoll
KLLSU skull
KLNOP plonk
KLNPU plunk
KLNRU knurl
KLNSU slunk
KLNUU Kulun
KLOOP plook
KLOOS kolos
looks
skool
KLOPU plouk
KLOSY yolks
KLOYY yolky
KLRSU lurks
KLSSU sulks
KLSUY sulky
KLTUZ klutz
KMNOO Nkomo
KMNOS monks
KMOOP Mokpo
KMOOS mokos
smoko
KMOST Tomsk
KMOSY smoky
KMRUY murky
KMSSU musks
KMSUY musky
KNNOW known
KNOOR kroon
KNOOS nooks
snook
KNOOV Kovno
KNOOY nooky
KNOPS knops
KNORS norks
KNORT tronk
KNOST knots
stonk
tonks
KNOSW knows
wonks
KNOSY yonks
KNOTU knout
KNOUY Yukon
KNOWY wonky
KNPSU punks
spunk
KNRRU knurr
KNRSU knurs
KNRTU trunk
KNSSU sunks
KNSTU stunk
KNSUU Nukus
KOOPS spook
KOORS rooks
KOORY rooky
KOOSS sooks
KOOST kotos
stook
KOOTY Kyoto
Tokyo
KOPRY porky
KOPSV Pskov
KORST stork
torsk
KORSW works
KORSY yorks
KOSSU souks
KPPRU Krupp
KRSSU rusks
KRSTU turks
KRSUU kurus
KRTUU Turku
KSSTU tusks
KSTUU kutus
KTTUU tuktu
LLLOS lolls
LLLOY lolly
LLLSU lulls
LLLUY Lully
LLMOS molls
LLMOY molly
LLMSU mulls
LLOOP L'pool
LLOOR Rollo
LLOPS polls
LLOPY polly
LLOQU quoll
LLORS rolls
LLORT troll
LLOST tolls
LLOSY lysol
LLOTY tolly
tolyl
LLOWY lowly
wolly
LLOXY xylol
LLPSU pulls
LLRTU trull
LLSTU stull
LLSUU lulus
LLSUY sully
LLSYY slyly
LLTUY Tully
LLXYY xylyl
LMMUY lummy
LMOOS looms
LMOOT molto
LMORS slorm
LMOST molts
smolt
LMOSU Mosul
solum
LMOTU moult
LMPPU plump
LMPSU lumps
plums
slump
LMPUY lumpy
plumy
LMRUY rumly
LMSSU slums
LNNOY nylon
LNOOS loons
solon
LNOOY loony
LNOPY pylon
LNOSY Lyons
LNOTU Luton
LNOUZ Luzon
LNRSU nurls
LOOOV ovolo
LOOPR orlop
LOOPS loops
polos
pools
sloop
spool
LOOPY loopy
LOORV Orlov
LOORY Oryol
LOOSS solos
sools
LOOST loots
lotos
sloot
stool
tools
LOOSV Vólos
LOOSW wools
LOOTT lotto
LOOWY wooly
LOPPS plops
LOPPY loppy
polyp
LOPRW prowl
LOPSS slops
LOPST plots
LOPSU loups
LOPSW lowps

plows
LOPSY ploys
polys
Pylos
LOPTU Pluto
poult
LOPUU Upolu
LORRY lorry
LORST rotls
LORSU lours
LORTY Tylor
Tyrol
LORUX Luxor
LORWY lowry
LOSST slots
LOSSU solus
souls
LOSSW slows
LOSSY lossy
LOSTU lotus
louts
Soult
LOSTV volts
LOSTY stylo
LOSUY lousy
LOSWY yowls
LOTYZ zloty
LPPSU pulps
LPPUY pulpy
LPRSU purls
slurp
LPSUU lupus
LRSSU slurs
LRSUY surly
LRTUY truly
LRUUU Uluru
LRWYY wryly
LSSTU lusts
sluts
LSTUY lusty
LSUUZ zulus
LUVVY luvvy
MMMUY mummy
MMOPY pommy
MMOSU momus
MMOTY tommy
MMOUY yummo
MMPSU mumps
MMRUY rummy
MMSUY mumsy
MMTUY tummy
MMUYY yummy
MNOOR moron
MNOOS monos
moons
MNOOY moony
MNORS morns
norms
MNORU mourn
Munro
MNORY Myron
MNOSU muons
MNOTT Nottm
MNOTU mount
notum
MNSTU munts
MOOPR promo
MOORR morro
MOORS moors
rooms
MOORT motor
MOORV vroom
MOORY moory
roomy
MOOSS mosso
MOOST moots
MOOSZ zooms
MOOTT motto
MOPPS pomps
MOPRS proms
romps
MOPRT tromp
MOPST stomp
MOPSY yomps
MORRU rumor
MORST morts
storm
MORSW worms
MORTU tumor
MORUZ Ormuz
MORWY wormy
MOSSU musos
MOSSY mossy
MOSTU motus
smout
MOSTW smowt
MOSUY mousy
MOTTY motty
MOTUZ Mo-tzu
MPPSU pumps
MPRSU rumps
MPRTU trump
MPSSU sumps
MPSTU stump
tumps
MPSUY spumy
MRSSU smurs
MRSTU strum
MSSTU musts
smuts
stums
MSSUY mussy
MSTTU mutts
MSTUY musty
MSTYY stymy
MUYZZ muzzy
NNNUY nunny
NNOOS noons
NNOOY Noyon
NNOSU nouns
NNOSY sonny
NNRUY runny
NNSUY sunny
NNTUY tunny
NOOPR porno
NOOPS poons
snoop
spoon
NOORT Orton
roton
NOOST oonts
snoot
toons
NOOSW swoon
NOOSZ zoons
NOPST ponts
NOPTU puton
NORSS sorns
NORST snort
trons
NORSW sworn
NORTU Toruń
NOSST snots
NOSSW snows
NOSSY sonsy
NOSTT Notts
NOSTU Notus
nutso
snout
tonus
touns
NOSTW nowts
towns
wonts
NOSTY stony
Tyson
NOSWY snowy
NOTUZ Utzon
NOTWY nowty
towny
NPRSU spurn
NPSTU punts
NPSUU sunup
NPTUY punty
NRSTU runts
turns
NRTUY runty
NSSTU stuns
NSTTU stunt
NTTUY nutty
OOOPP Poopó
OOPPS poops
OOPPV Popov
OOPRS sopor
spoor
OOPRT poort
Porto
troop
OOPST stoop
topos
OOPSW swoop
OOPTT potto
OORRT rotor
OORRU Oruro
OORST roost
roots
stoor
torso
OORTU outro
OORTY rooty
OOSST soots
OOSTT toots
OOSTY sooty
OOWYZ woozy
OPPPY poppy
OPPRS props
OPPSY popsy
soppy
OPRST ports
prost
sport
strop
OPRSU pours
roups
OPRSW prows
OPRSY prosy
OPRTU Prout
OPRUY roupy
OPRXY proxy
OPSST posts
spots
stops
OPSSU soups
OPSSW swops
OPSSY sysop
OPSTU pouts
spout
stoup
OPSTW stowp
OPSTY pyots
typos
OPSUY soupy
OPSWY Powys
OPTTU putto
OPTTY potty
OPTUY pouty
OPTUZ Tzu-po
OPYZZ pozzy
ORRST rorts
ORRSY sorry
ORRTU Truro
ORRTY rorty
ORRWY worry
ORSST sorts
ORSSU sorus
sours
ORSTT torts
trots
ORSTU roust
routs
stour
torus
tours
ORSTW strow
trows
worst
worts
ORSTY ryots
story
stroy
tyros
ORSUV vrous
ORSUY yours
ORTTU trout
tutor
OSSST stoss
OSSTT stots
OSSTU ousts
OSSTW stows
swots
OSTTU stout
touts
OSUYZ soyuz
OTTTY totty
PPPUY puppy
PPUYY yuppy
PRRSU purrs
PRSSU spurs
PRSTU spurt
turps
PRSUU Purús
usurp
PRSUY pursy
syrup
PSSUY pussy
PSTTU putts
PTTUY putty
RRSUU rurus
RSSTU rusts
truss
RSTTU strut
sturt
trust
RSTTY tryst
RSTUW wurst
RSTUY rusty
yurts
RSUUY usury
RTTUY rutty
SSSUU susus
SSTXY xysts
SSUWY wussy
STTUU tutus
TTTUY tutty
TTUVY vutty

Six Letters

AAABBN Banaba
AAABCL cabala
AAABCN cabana
AAABCS abacas
casaba
AAABDN Abadan
AAABHN Habana
AAABIR Arabia
AAABKK kabaka
AAABKL kabala
AAABKN Abakan
AAABLM Ambala
Balaam
AAABLR labara
AAABLT albata
balata
AAABNN Annaba
banana
AAABNS anabas
AAABNT Bataan
AAABRT Atbara
braata
AAABRZ baraza
bazaar
AAABTT batata
AAACCI acacia
AAACDG cadaga
AAACDI Acadia
AAACDN canada
AAACEH Achaea
AAACJN jacana
AAACLP alpaca
AAACMP Macapá
AAACMR maraca
AAACNN Canaan
AAACNR arcana
Canara
AAACOX Oaxaca
AAADGL Ala Dağ
AAADGM Da Gama
AAADLM Almada
AAADMR armada
AAADMS Masada
AAADNN Ananda
AAADNP panada
AAAELZ azalea
AAAFRT Arafat
AAAGIL Aglaia
AAAGLM Málaga
AAAGLN Alagna
AAAGLT Galata
AAAGMS agamas
AAAGNN nagana
AAAGNR Angara
AAAGRU Aargau
AAAHIK Akhaïa
AAAHIT taiaha
AAAHKR akhara
AAAHMR Amhara
AAAHNV Havana
vahana
AAAHRS Sahara
AAAHTY Yahata
AAAILL alalia
AAAILN Alania
AAAILR aralia
AAAINZ Azania
AAAITX ataxia
AAAJLP Jalapa
AAAJMP pajama
AAAJMU ujamaa
AAAJRW Jawara
AAAKKN kanaka
AAAKLM kamala
AAAKLS alaska
AAAKNR Ankara
Kanara
AAAKRT Rakata
AAALMS masala
salaam
AAALMY Malaya
AAALQS al-Aqsa
AAAMMN Manama
AAAMNN manana
AAAMNP panama
AAAMNT ataman
AAAMRS Asmara
samara
AAANNS ananas
AAANNT Tanana
AAANPR Paraná
AAANRT Ratana
AAANSS asanas
AAANST Astana
AAAPPY papaya
AAAPTZ zapata
AAARRT Ararat
AAARTV avatar
AAARTW Tarawa
AAASTT taatas
AAATWY Yawata
AABBBO baobab
AABBCO babaco
AABBCY abbacy
AABBDO Abbado
AABBIS Abbas I
AABBLL lablab
AABBLO balboa
AABBST sabbat
AABCEO cobaea
AABCHM ambach
AABCHS casbah
AABCIM cambia
AABCIR arabic
AABCIU Cuiabá
AABCLR Cabral
AABCLS cabals
AABCLU bacula
AABCLZ Balzac
AABCMN cabman
AABCMT tambac
AABCMY Cambay
AABCRS scarab
AABCSU abacus
AABCUY Cuyabá
AABDDG Bagdad
AABDER abrade
AABDES abased
AABDET abated
AABDEU aubade
AABDGO dagoba
AABDIN Ibadan
indaba
AABDIS Abdias
AABDLL ballad
AABDLM lambda
AABDMN badman
AABDOR aboard
abroad
Baroda
AABDRT tabard
AABDRY bayard
AABDSS badass
AABEEM amebae
AABEGM ambage
AABEGS seabag
AABEKM Makeba
AABELM mabela
AABELR arable
Arbela
AABELT ablate
AABELZ ablaze
AABEMO amoeba
AABEMS amebas
AABERU bauera
AABERZ zareba
AABESS abases
AABEST abates
AABETU bateau
AABFIR Biafra
AABGGR ragbag
AABGGS gasbag
AABGIM gambia
AABGIN baaing
AABGKN Bangka
AABGMN bagman
AABGMR Bagram
AABGMS gambas
AABGRT ratbag
AABHJN bhajan
AABHKS kasbah
sabkha
AABHLR bharal
AABHMR brahma
AABHMS shamba
AABHNS Bashan
Shaban
AABHNV bhavan
AABHNW bhawan
AABHRT Bharat
AABHSW bashaw
Wabash
AABIKL Baikal
Kabila
AABIKR Kariba
AABILL labial
AABILR Brăila
AABILU abulia

AABILV	Libava
AABIMR	ambari
	Bairam
	marabi
AABIMZ	Zambia
AABINN	banian
AABINT	Aintab
AABINZ	banzai
AABIRS	arabis
	braais
AABIRT	Tabari
AABIST	abatis
	Bastia
AABISW	Swabia
	wasabi
AABJNS	bajans
AABJOR	Baroja
AABKLN	Balkan
AABKLR	Barkla
AABKMO	Bamako
AABKNN	kanban
AABKNR	barkan
AABKNS	banaks
AABKRS	bakras
AABLMO	Malabo
AABLMS	balsam
AABLNS	nablas
AABLNU	Labuan
AABLNY	Albany
AABLOR	aboral
AABLOV	lavabo
AABLRU	Rabaul
AABLSS	balsas
AABLST	basalt
	tablas
AABLTU	ablaut
AABMMS	mambas
AABMNR	barman
AABMNT	bantam
	batman
AABMRS	sambar
AABMRY	ambary
AABMSS	sambas
AABNNY	banyan
AABNRY	Bárány
AABNSW	nawabs
AABNUV	Vauban
AABNYY	bayyan
AABORR	arroba
AABORT	abator
	rabato
AABOSU	oubaas
AABRRS	Barras
AABRSS	sabras
AABRSZ	bazars
AABRTY	baryta
AABTTW	abwatt
AACCDI	cicada
AACCEL	caecal
AACCHM	chacma
AACCIL	alcaic
	cicala
AACCIN	anicca
AACCLO	cloaca
AACCLP	calpac
AACCLR	calcar
AACCMO	macaco
AACCNN	cancan
AACCNR	Carnac
AACCOS	cacaos
AACDDU	caudad
AACDEF	facade
AACDEI	acedia
AACDEL	alcade
AACDER	arcade
AACDFR	cafard
AACDGI	cadagi
AACDHS	dachas
AACDHT	datcha
AACDHU	Dachau
AACDIN	Candia
AACDIR	acarid
AACDLU	caudal
AACDMP	madcap
AACDNR	canard
	cardan
AACDOP	da capo
AACEFI	faciae
AACEFL	faecal
AACEFR	carafe
AACEHP	apache
AACEHT	chaeta
AACEIN	Nicaea
AACEJR	jacare
AACELN	anlace
AACELP	palace
AACELS	Alsace
AACELT	acetal
AACELY	Celaya
AACEMO	caeoma
AACEMR	camera
AACENN	cannae
AACENP	canape
AACENR	arcane
AACENT	catena
AACEPR	Parcae
AACERS	arecas
	caesar
AACETV	caveat
	vacate
AACFIL	facial
AACFIR	Africa
AACFIS	fascia
AACFLU	facula
	faucal
AACFNT	caftan
AACFRS	fracas
AACFRX	carfax
AACFVY	Cavafy
AACGGM	cagmag
AACGIM	agamic
AACGIN	caaing
AACGIR	agaric
AACGIU	guaiac
AACGLY	galyac
AACHIN	Chania
AACHIT	Ithaca
AACHKR	chakra
	charka
AACHKW	kwacha
AACHLS	calash
AACHMN	machan
AACHMS	Ascham
	Schama
AACHNO	Chaoan
AACHNR	anarch
AACHNS	ashcan
AACHNT	acanth
	Tanach
AACHNZ	chazan
AACHPS	pachas
AACHRS	charas
AACHRT	Cathar
AACHTT	attach
AACHTY	Cathay
AACIIR	Icaria
AACIJM	jicama
AACILL	laical
AACILM	calami
	camail
AACILP	apical
AACILR	Alaric
	racial
AACILS	Calais
AACIMN	caiman
	maniac
AACINR	arnica
	carina
	crania
AACIPS	capias
AACIPT	capita
AACIRV	caviar
AACISS	cassia
AACITT	Attica
AACITV	atavic
AACITX	ataxic
AACJKL	jackal
AACJOU	acajou
AACKMY	Mackay
AACKRR	arrack
AACKSY	yackas
AACKTT	attack
AACLLN	callan
AACLLO	Callao
AACLLS	callas
AACLLU	calalu
AACLMN	Alcman
AACLMT	lactam
AACLMU	macula
AACLNO	canola
AACLNR	carnal
AACLNS	canals
AACLNT	Cantal
AACLNU	canula
	lacuna
AACLOT	catalo
AACLOX	coaxal
AACLPR	carpal
AACLPS	pascal
AACLPU	paucal
AACLRS	lascar
	rascal
	sacral
	scalar
AACLSS	Casals
AACLSU	casual
	causal
AACLTU	actual
AACMNR	carman
AACMNS	camans
AACMNU	Cumaná
AACMNY	cayman
AACMOT	Tacoma
AACMRT	tarmac
AACMSS	camass
AACMSW	macaws
AACNNO	Ancona
AACNNS	cannas
AACNOV	Canova
AACNPR	Carnap
AACNPT	catnap
AACNRT	arctan
AACNRY	canary
AACNST	sancta
	tacans
AACNSV	canvas
AACNTT	actant
AACNTV	vacant
AACNUX	Cunaxa
AACPPY	papacy
AACPRS	Caspar
AACRST	carats
AACRSU	acarus
AACRTV	cravat
AADDEL	daedal
AADDIL	alidad
AADDLN	adland
AADDMS	Addams
AADDOU	aoudad
AADEFR	afeard
AADEGJ	jagaed
AADEGL	gelada
AADEGM	damage
AADEGN	agenda
AADEGS	adages
AADEIT	ideata
AADEJU	Judaea
AADEKW	awaked
AADELS	salade
AADEMM	madame
AADEMN	anadem
	maenad
AADEMZ	amazed
AADENN	Andean
AADENT	adnate
AADENV	Nevada
AADENX	adnexa
AADEOR	Oradea

AADEPR	parade
AADERV	Veadar
AADEWW	wawaed
AADFIR	afraid
AADFMU	madafu
AADFRS	darafs
	farads
AADGHR	dargah
AADGIM	agamid
AADGIO	adagio
AADGIR	Agadir
	gardai
AADGLO	Ladoga
AADGNN	Da Nang
AADGNP	padang
AADGNR	argand
AADGNU	Uganda
AADGOP	pagoda
AADGRS	Asgard
AADGRY	gaydar
AADHIL	dahlia
AADHIM	Amidah
AADHKN	khanda
AADHMM	dhamma
AADHMR	dharma
AADHNR	dharna
AADHRZ	hazard
AADILN	Dalian
AADILO	alodia
AADILR	radial
AADILS	dalasi
AADIMN	maidan
AADIMT	Matadi
AADINO	Adonai
AADINR	Adrian
	radian
AADINS	naiads
AADIST	stadia
AADJLN	jandal
AADJMU	Jumada
AADKMS	damask
AADKNU	Kaduna
	Kaunda
AADKOT	Dakota
AADKPU	padauk
AADLLS	Dallas
AADLMW	wadmal
AADLMY	malady
AADLNO	anodal
	Loanda
AADLNR	Darlan
AADLNS	sandal
AADLNU	landau
	Luanda
AADLNV	vandal
AADLOP	apodal
AADLOS	Salado
AADLOU	Douala
AADLRU	radula
AADLRY	Layard
AADLSS	salads
AADMMN	madman
AADMMR	dammar
AADMMS	madams
AADMNO	Manado
AADMNS	damans
AADMOU	amadou
AADMOV	Adamov
AADMRS	dramas
	madras
AADMRU	Madura
	maraud
AADMRZ	mazard
AADMSS	admass
AADMYY	mayday
AADNNR	randan
AADNPS	pandas
AADNRU	Arnaud
AADNRW	Rwanda
AADNRY	Anadyr
AADNSU	Danaüs
AADNSV	vandas
AADNSY	dayans
AADOPS	posada
AADOPV	Padova
AADOSW	Sadowa
AADPRS	Prasad
AADPST	adapts
AADPSW	padsaw
AADPYY	payday
AADRRS	radars
	sardar
AADRRV	Vardar
AADRSW	awards
AADRTU	Artaud
	datura
AADRTY	datary
AAEEGL	galeae
AAEEGN	Aegean
AAEEGR	Graeae
AAEEGT	eatage
AAEELP	paleae
AAEENS	Aeneas
AAEEOZ	zoaeae
AAEEPR	peraea
AAEERT	aerate
AAEFGR	agrafe
AAEFLM	aflame
AAEFLV	favela
AAEFNR	fraena
AAEFNS	faenas
AAEFNU	faunae
AAEFNZ	Faenza
AAEGGR	garage
AAEGGV	gavage
AAEGIN	Aegina
AAEGIR	Graiae
AAEGKR	Kagera
AAEGLM	agleam
AAEGLN	anlage
	galena
	lagena
AAEGLR	alegar
	laager
AAEGLV	lavage
AAEGLZ	Alagez
AAEGMN	manage
AAEGMR	Gemara
	megara
AAEGNR	Reagan
AAEGNT	agnate
AAEGOR	agorae
AAEGPV	pavage
AAEGRV	ravage
AAEGST	agates
AAEGSV	agaves
	savage
AAEGTU	gateau
AAEHKP	pakeha
AAEHKS	hakeas
AAEHKT	takahe
AAEHLM	haemal
AAEHLT	althea
AAEHMT	athame
	hamate
AAEHNT	Athena
AAEHNY	hyaena
AAEHPR	raphae
AAEHRR	Harare
AAEHSY	Ayesha
AAEILM	amelia
	lamiae
AAEILR	aerial
	realia
AAEILX	alexia
AAEIMN	anemia
AAEINT	taenia
AAEITV	aviate
AAEKLN	alkane
AAEKLR	Kerala
AAEKLS	akelas
AAEKNN	ananke
AAEKNW	awaken
AAEKRT	karate
AAEKSW	awakes
AAELLP	paella
AAELLU	alulae
AAELMN	Alemán
AAELMT	malate
	tamale
AAELNN	anneal
AAELNT	lanate
AAELOR	areola
AAELPP	appeal
AAELPR	earlap
AAELPS	salpae
AAELPT	palate
AAELPY	Lepaya
AAELRT	relata
AAELRV	larvae
	Valera
AAELRZ	Azrael
AAELSW	Wałęsa
AAELTV	valeta
AAELZZ	Azazel
AAEMMM	mammae
AAEMNP	apeman
AAEMNR	Amen-Ra
AAEMNS	seaman
AAEMNX	axeman
AAEMRS	maraes
AAEMRU	Rameau
AAEMSZ	amazes
AAENNZ	zenana
AAENOP	apnoea
AAENPS	España
	paeans
AAENPV	pavane
AAENRS	arenas
AAENST	ansate
AAENSU	nausea
AAENSW	seawan
AAEORT	aortae
AAEOSZ	zoaeas
AAEPPR	appear
AAEPTT	tapeta
AAERRT	errata
AAERSX	Araxes
AAERWX	earwax
AAESTV	Avesta
	savate
AAESWY	seaway
AAFFIM	maffia
AAFFIR	affair
	raffia
AAFFIT	taffia
AAFFJN	Jaffna
AAFFRY	affray
AAFFST	Staffa
AAFGHN	afghan
AAFGIN	faaing
AAFHTW	fatwah
AAFIKS	sifaka
AAFILM	Amalfi
AAFIMT	Fatima
	Fátima
AAFINN	Fianna
AAFINR	farina
AAFINX	Fa Xian
AAFIRS	safari
AAFIST	fatsia
AAFKNS	nakfas
AAFKNT	kaftan
AAFLLL	fallal
AAFLNU	faunal
AAFLOT	afloat
AAFNSU	faunas
AAFSTW	fatwas
AAGGHI	Haggai
AAGGLO	galago
AAGGQU	quagga
AAGGRS	saggar
AAGGRT	ragtag
AAGGSW	waggas
AAGHKN	kangha
	khanga
AAGHLS	galahs
AAGHMR	Armagh

graham
AAGHNP Pahang
AAGHNR hangar
AAGHNS Sangha
AAGHST aghast
AAGIJW Jigawa
AAGIKN kainga
AAGILL Gallia
AAGILN agnail
Anglia
AAGILP Paglia
palagi
AAGILR argali
garial
AAGILT Galați
AAGILV gavial
AAGIMN magian
AAGINN angina
inanga
AAGINR nagari
AAGINU Guiana
iguana
AAGINV vagina
AAGIOS asiago
AAGIRW waragi
AAGISS Agassi
AAGJRU jaguar
AAGKLN Kalgan
AAGKLU Kaluga
AAGKLY galyak
AAGKNS kangas
AAGLLN lalang
AAGLLP plagal
AAGLMN Malang
AAGLNO analog
angola
AAGLNR langar
raglan
AAGLNT galant
AAGLRS argals
AAGLRT tragal
AAGLST stalag
AAGLSY gayals
AAGLWY Galway
AAGLXY galaxy
AAGMMS gammas
magmas
AAGMMT gammat
AAGMNR ragman
AAGMNS gasman
AAGMOT Gotama
AAGMRW Wagram
AAGMRY magyar
margay
AAGNNO goanna
Nagano
AAGNNY Anyang
AAGNOR angora
Aragon
organa
AAGNOT taonga
AAGNOY Nagoya
AAGNPR parang
AAGNPS pagans
pangas
AAGNRS sangar
AAGNRT Granta
AAGNRY angary
AAGNST satang
tangas
AAGNTU taguan
AAGNUV Ungava
AAGNUY Guyana
AAGORS agoras
AAGPPR grappa
AAGPRS Gaspar
AAGRRY garrya
AAGRSU Ragusa
AAGRSV Vargas
AAGRUV avruga
AAGRVY vagary
AAGSUV guavas
AAHHJJ hajjah
AAHHLL hallah
AAHHLV halvah
AAHHMZ hamzah
AAHHNN Hannah
AAHHPT aphtha
AAHHWW Haw-Haw
AAHIIS Isaiah
AAHIIW Hawaii
AAHIKN Khaniá
AAHIKP pakahi
AAHILT hiatal
Thalia
AAHILY aliyah
AAHIMS ahimsa
AAHINN Hainan
Nanhai
AAHINT tahina
AAHIOT taihoa
AAHIPR pariah
raphia
AAHIRR harira
AAHIRS sharia
AAHITW tawhai
AAHJKT jhatka
AAHJRR jarrah
AAHJRS rajahs
AAHKKM Makkah
AAHKKT kathak
AAHKLS Khalsa
AAHKLY khayal
AAHKMO Oakham
AAHKPS pashka
AAHKPU hapuka
AAHKST Shakta
AAHLLL hallal
AAHLLO halloa
AAHLLS halals
AAHLLW wallah
AAHLMM hammal
AAHLMS hamals
AAHLMT maltha
AAHLMU hamaul
AAHLNS nahals
AAHLNT Anhalt
AAHLPS alphas
AAHLRS ashlar
lahars
AAHLRT hartal
AAHLSV halvas
AAHMMM hammam
AAHMNS shaman
AAHMPY mayhap
AAHMRS ashram
harams
AAHMRT Martha
AAHMST asthma
AAHMTZ matzah
AAHNNS Anshan
AAHNNT Nathan
AAHNSS hansas
AAHNSZ hazans
AAHNTU Utahan
AAHNTV Havant
AAHNUW whanau
AAHNZZ hazzan
AAHOSW Oshawa
AAHPPR paraph
AAHPRS Parsha
Saphar
AAHPSS pashas
AAHPTY apathy
AAHRSS harass
AAHRST arhats
rathas
AAHRSU Aarhus
Ashura
AAHRSY rayahs
AAHSSY sashay
AAIIKR Ikaría
AAIILS aaliis
AAIILT Italia
AAIINY Aíyina
AAIISV Savaii
AAIJNN Janina
AAIJNP Panaji
AAIJRV Javari
AAIKKS kaiaks
AAIKLL alkali
AAIKLM kalmia
AAIKLN kalian
AAIKMT Katmai
AAIKNO aikona
AAIKRS askari
AAIKRT Katari
AAIKRZ Karzai
AAIKSS sakais
AAIKST akitas
kiaats
AAILLP pallia
AAILLX axilla
AAILMN animal
lamina
manila
AAILMP impala
AAILMS lamias
salami
AAILMW Malawi
AAILNR narial
AAILNS lanais
lianas
nasial
salina
AAILNT antlia
Latina
AAILNY inyala
AAILPU Apulia
AAILQU Aquila
qualia
AAILRS laaris
Larisa
AAILRT atrial
lariat
latria
AAILSS assail
AAILSV avails
saliva
salvia
Valais
AAILTT Attila
AAILTV Latvia
AAIMMS miasma
AAIMMX maxima
AAIMNR airman
Armani
Marian
marina
AAIMNS manias
Manisa
Samian
AAIMNY Yamani
AAIMRR marari
AAIMRT amrita
tamari
AAIMRV Ma'ariv
AAIMST matais
AAIMSZ zamias
AAIMTT tatami
AAINNT Tainan
AAINNY Yanina
AAINOX anoxia
AAINPP papain
AAINPR parian
pirana
AAINPS Saipan
AAINPT patina
pinata
taipan
AAINRS nairas
Sarnia
AAINRT antiar
Tirana
AAINRU anuria
urania
AAINST istana
AAINTT attain

AAINTW Taiwan
AAINTY Yantai
AAIOPR aporia
AAIOTU Aouita
AAIPRY apiary
AAIPZZ piazza
AAIQRT Qatari
AAIRST arista
tarsia
tiaras
AAIRSV Vasari
AAIRUW wairua
AAIRVY aviary
Yavarí
AAIRWY airway
AAIRZZ razzia
AAISSS assais
AAISST satais
AAISTW awaits
tawais
AAISVY Vaisya
AAITUY yautia
AAJKNS sanjak
AAJLMR Al Marj
AAJLNO janola
AAJLPS jalaps
AAJMNP jampan
AAJMNR Jarman
AAJMOR Marajó
AAJMPY pyjama
AAJNPR prajna
AAJNPS japans
AAJNRT Trajan
AAJNRU Arjuna
AAJNSW jawans
AAJPRU Japurá
AAJRSW swaraj
AAKKLP kalpak
AAKKMR markka
AAKKNR Karnak
AAKKOP kakapo
AAKKRU Krakau
AAKKSY kayaks
AAKLMO Akmola
AAKLMR Kalmar
AAKLMU Makalu
AAKLOS koalas
AAKLRS kraals
AAKLSS laksas
AAKLSU Lusaka
AAKLTU taluka
AAKMNU manuka
AAKMRS makars
markas
AAKMRU kumara
AAKMTU makuta
AAKNNS Kansan
AAKNOR anorak
AAKNRT kantar
AAKNSS Kansas
AAKNST askant
tankas

AAKNSU Kaunas
AAKNWZ kwanza
AAKOPR pakora
AAKPPS kappas
AAKPRS parkas
AAKRST karats
AAKSST Saktas
AAKTVY Vyatka
AAKUWY Yukawa
AAKUYZ yakuza
AALLLN lallan
AALLMM mallam
AALLMS llamas
AALLNY anally
AALLPP appall
palpal
AALLRU alular
AALLRV larval
AALLSW wallas
AALLSY allays
AALMMM mammal
AALMMS Lammas
malams
AALMNP napalm
AALMNT Altman
AALMNU alumna
manual
AALMNW lawman
AALMNY layman
AALMOQ Aqmola
AALMOR amoral
AALMOT amatol
AALMPR palmar
AALMPS lampas
Palmas
plasma
AALMRS alarms
malars
AALMRU alarum
AALMTY Almaty
amytal
AALNNS annals
AALNNU annual
AALNOS Solana
AALNOT atonal
Latona
AALNOV Avalon
Avlona
Valona
AALNOX axonal
AALNOZ azonal
AALNPR planar
AALNPT platan
AALNRT antral
tarnal
AALNRU ranula
AALNRW narwal
AALNRX larnax
AALNSS nasals
AALNST aslant
AALNSY nyalas
AALOPY payola

AALORT aortal
AALOVW avowal
AALPPS appals
AALPPU papula
AALPRR parral
AALPRY parlay
AALPSS salpas
AALPSU pausal
Upsala
AALPSY playas
AALPSZ plazas
AALRST altars
astral
ratals
tarsal
AALRSY salary
AALRSZ lazars
AALSSS salsas
AALSSV vassal
AALSWY always
AALTUV valuta
AALTVV Vltava
AALWYY waylay
AAMMMS mammas
AAMMRR marram
AAMMRT tammar
AAMMUZ mazuma
AAMNNR Mannar
AAMNOS Manáos
Samoan
AAMNOZ amazon
AAMNPS sampan
AAMNPX Paxman
AAMNRT mantra
AAMNST mantas
Tasman
AAMNSU Manaus
AAMNTU mantua
AAMNTX taxman
AAMOPR paramo
AAMORS aromas
Masora
AAMORV Morava
AAMORZ Zamora
AAMOSS samosa
AAMOST somata
AAMOTY Toyama
AAMPPS pampas
AAMQST Masqat
AAMQSU squama
AAMRSU asarum
AAMRSW aswarm
AAMRSY Ramsay
AAMRTU trauma
AAMSSS assams
AAMSTU amauts
AAMSTZ matzas
AAMTTU Umtata
AANNNS nannas
AANNRU anuran
AANNTT natant
AANNYZ nyanza

AANORV Novara
AANOST sonata
AANOSV Savona
AANOTT anatto
AANPPS nappas
AANPPU Papuan
AANPRT partan
tarpan
trapan
AANPRU purana
AANPSV pavans
AANQTU quanta
AANRRT arrant
AANRRY yarran
AANRSS sarans
AANRST ratans
AANRSV varnas
AANRTT rattan
tantra
tartan
AANRTZ tarzan
AANRUV Varuna
AANRYZ Ryazan
AANSSU Assuan
Nassau
saunas
AANSTV savant
AANSTZ stanza
AANTUV avaunt
AANWYY anyway
AAOPST sapota
AAORRU aurora
AAORST aortas
Sorata
AAORTT totara
AAOTTV ottava
AAOTTW Ottawa
AAPPSW papaws
AAPPWW pawpaw
AAPRRS parras
AAPRST Patras
satrap
Sparta
AAPRUY Yapurá
AAPSST pastas
AAPSTW wataps
AAPWXX paxwax
AAPZZZ pazazz
AAQQWW Qwaqwa
AAQRSU quasar
AARRSY arrays
AARRTT tartar
AARSST sastra
AARSTT strata
tatars
AARSTY astray
tayras
AARSWW warsaw
AARTTY Tatary
AASSSY assays
AASTZZ tazzas
ABBBEL babble

ABBCEI cabbie
ABBCER Crabbe
ABBCIR bicarb
ABBCOS cabobs
ABBCOT bobcat
ABBCRY crabby
ABBCSY scabby
ABBDDE dabbed
ABBDEG gabbed
ABBDEI babied
ABBDEJ jabbed
ABBDEL dabble
ABBDEN nabbed
ABBDER barbed
dabber
ABBDET tabbed
ABBDEU bedaub
ABBEEW bawbee
ABBEFU Babeuf
ABBEGL gabble
ABBEGR gabber
ABBEIR barbie
ABBEIS babies
ABBEIY yabbie
ABBEJR jabber
ABBEKS kebabs
ABBELR barbel
rabble
ABBELS babels
ABBELU bauble
ABBELW wabble
ABBERR barber
ABBERT barbet
rabbet
ABBERY yabber
ABBESS abbess
ABBESY abbeys
ABBFLY flabby
ABBGMU bumbag
ABBGOR gabbro
ABBGRY grabby
ABBHJU jubbah
ABBHSY shabby
ABBIJL jilbab
ABBILO Bilbao
ABBIMS Babism
bambis
ABBIOR Robbia
ABBIRS rabbis
ABBIRT rabbit
ABBITW wabbit
ABBKOS kabobs
ABBLRU bulbar
ABBLSU babuls
bubals
ABBLWY wabbly
ABBMOO bamboo
ABBMOY Bombay
ABBNOO baboon
ABBNOS nabobs
ABBORS absorb
ABBOST abbots
ABBRRU Rubbra
ABBRSU busbar
ABCCIO boccia
ABCCLU buccal
ABCDEH bached
ABCDEK backed
ABCDEL cabled
ABCDER braced
ABCDIR bardic
ABCDTU abduct
ABCEEH Achebe
ABCEEM became
ABCEGO bocage
ABCEGU cubage
ABCEHL bleach
ABCEHN Chenab
ABCEHR Béchar
breach
ABCEHS baches
ABCEHU Hecuba
ABCEIK backie
ABCEIM amebic
ABCEIS ceibas
ABCEJT abject
ABCEKR backer
ABCELS cables
ABCELT cablet
ABCEMN cabmen
ABCEMR camber
ABCEMW webcam
ABCENO beacon
ABCENU cubane
ABCERR bracer
ABCERS braces
cabers
ABCFIR fabric
ABCFNO confab
ABCHIU Bauchi
ABCHLN blanch
ABCHMO Cobham
ABCHNR branch
ABCHNU Buchan
ABCHOR broach
ABCHPR Archbp
ABCHPU hubcap
ABCHRU Baruch
ABCIIM iambic
ABCIJO Jacobi
ABCILT Baltic
ABCILU abulic
ABCINS cabins
ABCIOS cobias
ABCISS basics
ABCISU Baucis
ABCISY Biscay
ABCKLS blacks
ABCKPU backup
ABCKRS bracks
ABCKRU buckra
ABCLMY cymbal
ABCLNO Balcon
blanco
ABCLOT cobalt
ABCMOP mobcap
ABCMOR crambo
ABCMOT combat
tombac
ABCMRS scramb
ABCNOR carbon
corban
ABCNOS bacons
ABCORS brasco
carobs
cobras
ABCORX boxcar
ABCORY carboy
ABCOSV vocabs
ABCRST bracts
ABDDEE beaded
ABDDEI abided
baddie
ABDDEL bladed
ABDDEN banded
ABDDER badder
barded
ABDDEU daubed
ABDDEY daybed
ABDDHU buddha
ABDEEH behead
ABDEEK beaked
debeak
ABDEEL beadle
ABDEEM beamed
ABDEEN beaned
ABDEER beared
ABDEES debase
ABDEET debate
ABDEFL fabled
ABDEGG bagged
ABDEGL gabled
ABDEGN banged
ABDEGO bodega
ABDEGR badger
barged
garbed
ABDEGS badges
debags
ABDEHL blahed
ABDEHS bashed
ABDEHT bathed
ABDEIL bailed
ABDEIR abider
bardie
ABDEIS abides
biased
ABDEIT baited
ABDEIZ baized
ABDEJR Djerba
ABDEKL balked
ABDEKN banked
ABDEKO boaked
ABDEKR barked
braked
debark
ABDEKS basked
ABDELL balled
ABDELM ambled
bedlam
beldam
blamed
lambed
ABDELO albedo
doable
ABDELR balder
blared
ABDELS blades
ABDELT tabled
ABDELW bawled
ABDELY dyable
ABDELZ blazed
ABDEMN badmen
ABDENN banned
ABDENP bedpan
ABDENU Danube
ABDEOS abodes
adobes
ABDEOT boated
ABDERR barred
ABDERS ardebs
bardes
beards
breads
debars
sabred
serdab
ABDERU dauber
ABDERV adverb
braved
ABDERY brayed
ABDERZ brazed
ABDEST basted
ABDESU abused
daubes
ABDETT batted
ABDETU tabued
ABDFOR forbad
ABDHNS bandhs
ABDHOY hobday
ABDIJM Djambi
ABDILR bridal
labrid
ribald
ABDINR Briand
riband
ABDINT bandit
ABDIRR briard
ABDIRS braids
disbar
ABDLLY baldly
ABDLNO Boland
ABDLOS doblas
ABDLRY drably
ABDNOR Brando
roband
ABDNOU abound
ABDNRS brands

ABDNRT	Brandt
ABDNRU	Dunbar
	Durban
ABDNRY	brandy
ABDORS	adsorb
	boards
	broads
	dobras
	dorbas
ABDORT	Bardot
ABDORY	byroad
ABDOSY	Abydos
ABDOYY	dayboy
ABDRRU	durbar
ABDRSU	absurd
ABDRWY	bawdry
ABEEGL	beagle
ABEEGR	barege
	bargee
ABEEHV	behave
ABEEIL	bailee
ABEEIN	beanie
ABEEKR	beaker
ABEEKT	betake
ABEELN	baleen
	enable
ABEELS	abeles
ABEEMN	bemean
	bename
ABEEMR	beamer
ABEENT	beaten
ABEENU	Beaune
ABEEOR	aerobe
ABEEOU	Euboea
ABEERR	bearer
ABEERT	beater
	berate
	rebate
ABEERV	beaver
ABEERW	beware
ABEERY	Baeyer
ABEFFL	baffle
ABEFHL	behalf
ABEFLL	befall
ABEFLM	flambe
ABEFLR	fabler
ABEFLS	fables
ABEFMR	ferbam
ABEFPR	prefab
ABEGGR	beggar
ABEGIS	bagies
	gabies
ABEGIU	Ibagué
ABEGLL	Elbląg
ABEGLM	gamble
ABEGLN	bangle
	Bengal
ABEGLR	garble
ABEGLS	bagels
	belgas
	gables
ABEGLT	gablet
ABEGLU	beluga
	blague
ABEGMN	bagmen
ABEGMR	bregma
ABEGMU	Mugabe
ABEGNR	banger
	graben
ABEGOR	borage
ABEGOZ	gazebo
ABEGRS	barges
ABEGRZ	Zagreb
ABEGTU	baguet
ABEHIL	habile
ABEHLR	herbal
ABEHLS	belahs
ABEHLU	Beulah
ABEHNT	Theban
ABEHOS	obeahs
ABEHRS	basher
	rehabs
ABEHRT	bather
	bertha
	breath
ABEHSS	bashes
	sahebs
ABEHST	bathes
	Shebat
ABEIIL	bailie
ABEIIR	Iberia
ABEIIT	tibiae
ABEIKK	bakkie
ABEILL	alible
	Belial
	labile
	liable
ABEILM	lambie
ABEILR	bailer
	librae
ABEILS	abseil
	isabel
ABEILT	albeit
	albite
ABEILV	viable
ABEILW	bewail
ABEILY	bailey
ABEIMN	Namibe
ABEINR	Braine
ABEINS	sabine
ABEINT	binate
ABEINZ	Azbine
	Ibáñez
ABEIOT	boatie
ABEIRR	barrie
	Ribera
ABEIRS	braise
	rabies
	Serbia
ABEIRT	barite
	terbia
ABEISS	biases
ABEISZ	baizes
ABEJMR	jamber
ABEJMS	jambes
ABEJOR	jerboa
ABEJRT	Béjart
ABEJRU	abjure
ABEKKZ	Kazbek
ABEKLM	kembla
ABEKLR	balker
ABEKLY	Blakey
ABEKMN	embank
ABEKMR	embark
ABEKNR	banker
ABEKNT	banket
ABEKOT	Aktobe
ABEKOU	Bouaké
ABEKRR	barker
ABEKRS	bakers
	brakes
	breaks
ABEKRY	bakery
ABEKST	basket
ABELLS	labels
ABELLT	ballet
ABELLU	bullae
ABELLY	Bellay
ABELMM	embalm
ABELMR	ambler
	Balmer
	marble
	ramble
ABELMS	ambles
	blames
ABELMW	wamble
ABELNR	branle
ABELNU	nebula
	unable
ABELNY	bylane
ABELOR	boreal
ABELOT	boatel
	lobate
	oblate
ABELOW	Lebowa
ABELPU	Puebla
ABELRR	barrel
ABELRS	Albers
	balers
	belars
	blares
	blears
ABELRT	albert
	labret
ABELRV	verbal
ABELRW	bawler
	warble
ABELRY	barely
	barley
	bleary
ABELRZ	blazer
ABELSS	sables
ABELST	ablest
	bleats
	stable
	tables
ABELSU	suable
	usable
ABELSY	basely
	belays
ABELSZ	blazes
ABELTT	battle
	tablet
ABELTY	Batley
ABELWY	byelaw
ABEMNO	bemoan
ABEMNR	barmen
ABEMNT	batmen
ABEMOS	Soemba
ABEMRS	ambers
	breams
	Sambre
ABEMRU	umbrae
ABEMSU	Mabuse
ABEMSY	embays
	maybes
ABENNR	banner
ABENOR	borane
ABENOS	beanos
ABENOT	Beaton
	onbeat
ABENRR	barren
ABENRS	Barnes
ABENRT	banter
	barnet
ABENRU	urbane
ABENRY	barney
	Bayern
	nearby
ABENRZ	brazen
ABENST	absent
	Besant
ABENSY	Naseby
ABENTT	batten
ABENTU	butane
ABENTZ	bezant
ABEORS	Boreas
ABEORT	boater
	borate
	rebato
ABEORZ	bezoar
ABEOSS	Sasebo
ABEPTU	upbeat
ABEQRU	barque
	Braque
ABEQSU	basque
ABERRS	barres
	Barrès
ABERRT	barret
	barter
ABERRV	braver
ABERRW	brawer
ABERRY	brayer
ABERRZ	brazer
ABERSS	sabers
	sabres
ABERST	barest
	breast

	Tarbes
ABERSU	abuser
	bursae
	busera
ABERSV	braves
ABERSY	baryes
	yerbas
ABERSZ	brazes
	zebras
ABERTT	batter
ABERTX	baxter
ABERTY	betray
ABERUU	bureau
ABERUY	Aubrey
ABERWY	bewray
ABERZZ	Zabrze
ABESSS	basses
ABESST	basest
	basset
	bastes
	beasts
ABESSU	abuses
ABESTT	bettas
ABESTU	beauts
ABETTU	battue
	tubate
ABETTY	Beatty
ABETUY	beauty
ABEUXY	Bayeux
ABEZZZ	bezazz
ABFGLU	bagful
ABFILU	fibula
ABFISY	basify
ABFLRY	barfly
ABFOOR	foobar
ABGGIW	bagwig
ABGHTU	hagbut
ABGIKN	baking
ABGIKT	kitbag
ABGILM	gimbal
ABGILN	baling
ABGIMR	gambir
ABGIMT	gambit
ABGIMY	bigamy
ABGINO	bagnio
	gabion
	Gobian
ABGINR	baring
	Gibran
ABGINS	basing
ABGINT	bating
ABGINU	Bangui
ABGINY	abying
	baying
ABGIOR	Borgia
ABGIOS	biogas
ABGIOU	baguio
ABGKOO	bogoak
ABGLLO	global
ABGLMO	gambol
ABGLOR	Ålborg
	brolga
ABGMNO	bogman
ABGNOO	boonga
	gaboon
ABGNOR	Bangor
	barong
	brogan
ABGNOS	bogans
ABGOOT	Bogotá
	Tobago
ABGORS	garbos
ABGORT	bogart
ABGRSU	Burgas
ABHIIR	Bihari
ABHIJS	bhajis
ABHIKL	kiblah
ABHIKT	bhakti
ABHIMR	mihrab
ABHIMS	bimahs
ABHINR	Harbin
ABHINS	banish
ABHIOO	boohai
ABHIOP	phobia
ABHISS	sahibs
ABHIST	habits
ABHLOP	Bhopal
ABHMNO	bonham
ABHMOS	abohms
ABHMOT	Botham
ABHMOU	Huambo
ABHMRS	Brahms
ABHMRU	rhumba
ABHMSU	ambush
ABHNOT	Naboth
ABHNRU	Hurban
ABHNTU	Bhutan
ABHORR	harbor
ABHORS	abhors
ABHORT	Hobart
ABHOST	bathos
ABHOTX	hatbox
ABHOXY	haybox
ABHPTY	bypath
ABHRSY	brashy
ABHSSU	subahs
ABIIKL	Bialik
	Bikila
ABIILS	alibis
	Basil I
ABIILT	tibial
ABIINN	bainin
ABIIST	tibias
ABIJRS	Srbija
ABIJRU	jabiru
ABIKKU	kabuki
ABIKLS	Balkis
ABIKMO	akimbo
ABIKRS	Biskra
ABIKTT	battik
ABILLO	Baliol
ABILMT	timbal
ABILMU	labium
ABILNO	albino
	Albion
	Alboin
ABILNS	blains
ABILNY	Libyan
ABILOR	bailor
ABILRS	brails
	brasil
ABILRT	tribal
ABILRU	burial
ABILRZ	brazil
ABILSS	basils
ABILST	baltis
ABILSY	Baylis
ABIMMU	Mumbai
ABIMNN	binman
ABIMPT	bitmap
ABIMRS	mbiras
ABIMRU	barium
	Umbria
ABIMSS	simbas
ABIMST	ambits
ABIMSU	iambus
ABINNU	Nubian
ABINOS	basion
	bonsai
	Bosnia
ABINOT	obtain
ABINRS	bairns
	brains
ABINRY	binary
	brainy
ABINSS	basins
	sabins
ABINSU	Anubis
ABIORR	barrio
ABIORS	isobar
ABIOST	biotas
ABIRRS	briars
ABIRRY	briary
ABIRSU	airbus
ABIRTZ	Tabriz
ABISST	bastis
ABISSU	Bissau
ABJJOO	jojoba
ABJLMU	jumbal
ABJLNU	Banjul
ABJNOS	banjos
ABJNPU	Punjab
ABJOST	jabots
ABKLNS	blanks
ABKLSU	baulks
ABKLSY	skylab
ABKLUY	baulky
ABKNRS	branks
ABKORS	boraks
ABKORT	Bartók
ABKRSU	burkas
ABKUUV	Bukavu
ABLLOO	lobola
ABLLOT	ballot
ABLLPU	ballup
ABLLSY	ballsy
ABLMOO	abloom
ABLMOP	aplomb
	Pombal
ABLMOR	bromal
ABLMRU	brumal
	labrum
	lumbar
	umbral
ABLMRY	marbly
ABLMSU	albums
ABLMTY	tymbal
ABLMWY	wambly
ABLNOZ	blazon
ABLNSU	baluns
	Nablus
ABLNTU	buntal
ABLOOR	robalo
ABLORS	labors
ABLORU	labour
ABLOST	bloats
	oblast
ABLOSY	boylas
ABLOTT	talbot
ABLOTV	abvolt
ABLPRU	burlap
ABLPYY	byplay
ABLRST	blarts
ABLRSU	bursal
	lubras
ABLRSW	brawls
ABLRTU	brutal
ABLRWY	brawly
ABLSST	blasts
ABLSTY	stably
ABLSUY	usably
ABLSWY	bylaws
ABMMOO	Moomba
ABMMOS	mambos
ABMNOW	bowman
ABMNRU	Barnum
ABMNSU	busman
ABMNTU	numbat
	Tubman
ABMOSS	sambos
ABMOTV	Tambov
ABMOTW	wombat
ABMRSU	sambur
	umbras
ABMRUY	aumbry
ABMSSY	abysms
ABNNUY	Bunyan
ABNORS	barons
ABNORT	barton
ABNORY	barony
	baryon
ABNOST	batons
ABNOTY	botany
ABNRST	brants
ABNRSU	burans
	unbars
ABNRTU	turban
ABNRTY	Bryant

ABNRUU	auburn
ABNRUY	anbury
ABNRWY	brawny
ABNSTU	bantus
ABNSUY	bunyas
ABNTYZ	byzant
ABOOST	taboos
ABOOSZ	bazoos
ABOOTU	Baotou
ABORRS	arbors
	Barros
ABORRU	arbour
ABORRW	barrow
ABORSS	Brassó
ABORST	aborts
	Strabo
	tabors
ABORSV	Braşov
	bravos
ABORSY	boyars
ABORTU	rubato
	tabour
ABORTW	towbar
ABORTY	tarboy
	Torbay
ABOSSS	bassos
ABOSST	boasts
	sabots
ABOSUY	bayous
ABOSWW	bowsaw
ABPRTU	abrupt
ABPSSY	bypass
ABPSTY	bypast
ABQSSU	squabs
ABRRSU	bursar
ABRSSU	bursas
ABRSSY	brassy
ABSUWY	subway
ABSWYY	byways
ACCCIL	calcic
ACCCLO	coccal
ACCDEE	accede
ACCDEH	cached
ACCDEN	Deccan
ACCDII	acidic
ACCDOR	accord
ACCDSY	cycads
ACCEHN	chance
ACCEHS	caches
ACCEHT	cachet
ACCEIL	celiac
	cicale
ACCEIP	icecap
	ipecac
ACCEIT	acetic
ACCEKL	cackle
ACCELN	cancel
ACCELR	cercal
ACCELS	calces
ACCEMU	caecum
ACCENR	cancer
ACCENT	accent
ACCENU	Cuenca
ACCEPT	accept
ACCERS	scarce
ACCERU	accrue
ACCESS	access
ACCESU	accuse
ACCGNO	cognac
ACCHIK	chiack
ACCHIR	Chirac
ACCHKY	chyack
ACCHNO	concha
ACCHNY	chancy
ACCHOU	cachou
ACCHRT	cratch
ACCHSU	succah
ACCHTY	catchy
ACCHUY	Cauchy
ACCIIN	acinic
ACCILO	calico
ACCILT	lactic
ACCINO	cocain
ACCINT	cantic
ACCINY	cyanic
ACCIOT	ocicat
ACCIPR	capric
ACCIRR	ricrac
ACCIRS	siccar
ACCIRT	arctic
ACCITT	tactic
ACCKLO	Alcock
ACCKLS	clacks
ACCKRS	cracks
ACCKSU	Cusack
ACCLNY	Clancy
ACCLOU	coucal
ACCNNU	Cancún
ACCORS	arccos
	corsac
ACCORW	Cracow
ACCOST	accost
ACCRUY	curacy
ACCSTU	cactus
ACCSUU	caucus
ACCSUY	yuccas
ACCTUU	Cúcuta
ACDDEE	decade
ACDDEG	cadged
ACDDEI	caddie
ACDDEN	danced
ACDDER	carded
ACDDEU	adduce
ACDDII	diacid
ACDDIN	candid
ACDDIS	caddis
ACDDIT	addict
ACDDIY	dyadic
ACDDTU	adduct
ACDEEF	deface
ACDEEN	decane
ACDEEP	peaced
ACDEER	decare
ACDEES	ceased
ACDEFH	chafed
ACDEFR	farced
ACDEGR	cadger
	graced
ACDEGS	cadges
ACDEGT	gedact
ACDEHK	hacked
ACDEHR	arched
	echard
ACDEHS	chased
ACDEHT	detach
ACDEHW	chawed
ACDEIN	decani
ACDEIR	cardie
ACDEIS	de Sica
ACDEIV	advice
ACDEJK	jacked
ACDEKL	calked
	lacked
ACDEKP	packed
ACDEKR	arcked
	carked
	racked
ACDEKS	sacked
ACDEKT	tacked
ACDEKY	yacked
ACDELL	called
ACDELM	calmed
ACDELN	candle
	lanced
ACDELO	coaled
ACDELP	placed
ACDELR	Calder
	cradle
	credal
ACDELS	clades
	decals
	scaled
ACDELT	talced
ACDELU	caudle
	Claude
ACDELV	calved
ACDELW	clawed
ACDELY	clayed
ACDEMN	Camden
ACDEMP	camped
	decamp
ACDENN	canned
ACDENO	acnode
	canoed
	deacon
ACDENR	craned
	dancer
	nacred
ACDENS	ascend
	dances
ACDENT	cadent
	canted
	decant
ACDENY	dancey
ACDEOT	coated
ACDEOX	coaxed
ACDEPP	capped
ACDEPR	carped
	craped
	redcap
ACDEPS	scaped
	spaced
ACDERR	carder
ACDERS	cadres
	cedars
	sacred
	scared
ACDERT	carted
	crated
	redact
	traced
ACDERV	carved
	craved
ACDERZ	crazed
ACDEST	cadets
ACDESU	caused
	sauced
ACDESY	decays
ACDETT	catted
ACDEUX	caudex
ACDHIR	chadri
	diarch
ACDHMR	drachm
ACDHOR	chador
ACDHRS	chards
ACDIIM	amidic
ACDIIP	adipic
ACDIJU	Judaic
ACDILM	Mladic
ACDILP	placid
ACDILS	discal
ACDILY	acidly
ACDINO	anodic
ACDINR	Andrić
	Cardin
	rancid
ACDINY	cyanid
ACDIOT	dacoit
ACDIOZ	zodiac
ACDIPR	Picard
ACDIPS	capsid
ACDIRS	cairds
	darics
ACDIST	dicast
ACDLNU	unclad
ACDLSS	scalds
ACDLTY	dactyl
ACDMSU	Cadmus
ACDMTU	mudcat
ACDNNU	Duncan
ACDNOR	candor
	Conrad
ACDNRY	Drancy
ACDORR	Rocard
ACDORS	Dorcas
	dracos
ACDORW	coward
ACDORY	Corday

ACDOST	octads
ACDPRU	Duparc
ACDRSU	Cardus
ACDSSU	scauds
ACDSTU	ducats
ACEEFF	efface
ACEEFN	enface
ACEEFR	reface
ACEEFS	faeces
ACEEGN	encage
ACEEHL	chelae
ACEEHN	achene
ACEEHT	Hecate
	thecae
ACEEIP	apiece
ACEEJT	ejecta
ACEEKS	ackees
ACEELL	cellae
ACEELN	enlace
ACEELR	alerce
	cereal
ACEELV	cleave
ACEEMN	menace
ACEEMR	amerce
	careme
	Carême
	raceme
ACEEMZ	eczema
ACEENR	careen
ACEENS	Cesena
	encase
	seance
	seneca
ACEENT	cetane
	tenace
ACEEOR	ocreae
ACEEOT	coatee
ACEEPS	escape
	peaces
ACEERR	career
ACEERS	crease
ACEERT	cerate
	create
	ecarte
ACEESS	ceases
ACEFFT	affect
ACEFHR	chafer
ACEFHS	chafes
ACEFIL	facile
ACEFIN	fiance
ACEFIR	fiacre
ACEFIS	facies
ACEFLU	fecula
ACEFNR	France
ACEFRS	facers
	farces
	Scarfe
ACEFRU	furcae
ACEFSS	fasces
ACEFST	facets
ACEFSU	fauces
ACEFSY	casefy
ACEFTU	faucet
ACEGHN	change
ACEGHR	charge
ACEGHU	gauche
ACEGIL	Gaelic
ACEGIR	cagier
ACEGLN	glance
ACEGLS	glaces
ACEGLU	Glauce
ACEGLY	legacy
ACEGNU	cangue
ACEGNY	agency
	Cagney
ACEGOS	socage
ACEGOW	cowage
ACEGRS	graces
ACEHHS	Shache
ACEHHT	chetah
ACEHIK	hackie
ACEHIM	haemic
ACEHIP	phaeic
ACEHIR	achier
	cahier
	eriach
ACEHIS	chaise
ACEHKL	hackle
ACEHKR	hacker
ACEHLM	Machel
ACEHLN	Chanel
ACEHLP	chapel
	pleach
ACEHLR	Rachel
ACEHLS	chelas
	laches
ACEHLT	chalet
	thecal
ACEHLV	cheval
ACEHMN	manche
ACEHMR	macher
	Marche
ACEHMS	sachem
	schema
ACEHNS	encash
	hances
ACEHNU	nuchae
ACEHOP	cheapo
ACEHOR	chorea
	Horace
	ochrea
	orache
ACEHPR	eparch
	preach
ACEHPS	chapes
	Pesach
ACEHPT	hepcat
ACEHPY	peachy
ACEHRR	archer
ACEHRS	arches
	chaser
	eschar
	search
ACEHRT	Cather
	Thrace
ACEHRW	chawer
ACEHRX	exarch
ACEHSS	chases
	chasse
ACEHST	chaste
	cheats
	sachet
	scathe
	taches
ACEHSU	Huesca
ACEHSW	cashew
ACEILM	maleic
	malice
ACEILN	inlace
ACEILP	plaice
	plicae
ACEILR	eclair
	lacier
ACEIMN	anemic
	cinema
	iceman
ACEIMO	Maceió
ACEIMR	Crimea
	Mercia
ACEIMS	amices
	camise
ACEIMU	aecium
ACEINN	canine
	neanic
ACEINR	carnie
	Racine
ACEINS	casein
	incase
ACEINT	centai
	enatic
ACEINX	axenic
ACEIPR	pacier
ACEIPS	apices
	spicae
ACEIQU	caique
ACEIRR	racier
ACEIRS	caries
ACEIRU	curiae
ACEISS	saices
ACEISV	cavies
	vesica
ACEITT	cattie
ACEITV	active
	Cavite
ACEIVV	vivace
ACEJKT	jacket
ACEJLO	cajole
ACEKLM	mackle
ACEKLR	calker
	Clarke
	lacker
ACEKLS	alecks
ACEKLT	tackle
ACEKLY	lackey
ACEKMN	McKean
ACEKNR	canker
	Neckar
ACEKPR	packer
	repack
ACEKPT	packet
ACEKRR	racker
ACEKRS	crakes
	creaks
	sacker
	screak
ACEKRT	racket
	tacker
ACEKRW	wacker
ACEKRY	creaky
	yacker
ACEKST	casket
ACEKSW	wackes
ACEKTT	tacket
ACEKTY	tackey
ACELLO	locale
ACELLR	caller
	cellar
	recall
ACELLV	Cavell
ACELMR	calmer
	Carmel
	marcel
ACELMS	camels
	mascle
	mescal
ACELMT	camlet
ACELMU	almuce
	macule
ACELMZ	mezcal
ACELNN	cannel
ACELNR	lancer
ACELNS	cleans
	lances
	Senlac
ACELNT	cantle
	cental
	lancet
ACELNU	cuneal
	launce
	unlace
ACELOR	coaler
	oracle
ACELOS	solace
ACELOT	Alecto
	locate
ACELOV	alcove
	coeval
ACELPR	carpel
	parcel
	placer
ACELPS	places
ACELPT	caplet
	placet
ACELPU	culpae
ACELQU	calque
	claque
ACELRR	carrel
ACELRS	carles

	clears
	lacers
	scaler
	sclera
ACELRT	cartel
	claret
	rectal
ACELRV	carvel
	claver
ACELRW	clawer
ACELSS	Cassel
	scales
ACELST	castle
	cleats
ACELSU	caules
	clause
	Leucas
ACELSV	calves
	cavels
	claves
ACELSX	calxes
ACELTT	cattle
ACELTY	acetyl
ACELWY	Cawley
ACELYY	Cayley
	clayey
ACEMNP	encamp
ACEMNR	carmen
ACEMNU	acumen
ACEMNW	McEwan
ACEMOP	pomace
ACEMOS	cameos
ACEMOT	comate
ACEMPR	camper
ACEMRS	creams
	macers
	scream
ACEMRT	mercat
ACEMRY	creamy
ACEMSU	muscae
ACEMTU	acetum
ACEMUX	exacum
ACENNO	ancone
ACENNR	canner
ACENNS	Cannes
ACENNU	nuance
ACENNY	Annecy
ACENOP	Capone
ACENOR	cornea
ACENOS	canoes
	oceans
ACENOT	octane
ACENPR	prance
ACENPS	pecans
ACENRS	caners
	casern
	cranes
ACENRT	canter
	carnet
	centra
	Cretan
	nectar
	recant
	trance
ACENRV	carven
	cavern
	craven
ACENRY	carney
ACENST	ascent
	centas
	enacts
	secant
	stance
ACENSU	usance
ACENTU	Canute
ACEOPS	scopae
ACEOPT	capote
	toecap
ACEOPW	cowpea
ACEORR	correa
ACEORS	Açôres
	coarse
	rosace
ACEORW	crowea
ACEORX	coaxer
ACEOST	coates
	costae
ACEOSW	ECOWAS
ACEOSX	coaxes
ACEOSY	O'Casey
ACEOTV	avocet
	octave
ACEPPR	capper
ACEPRR	carper
ACEPRS	capers
	crapes
	escarp
	pacers
	parsec
	recaps
	scrape
	spacer
ACEPRT	carpet
ACEPRU	apercu
ACEPSS	scapes
	spaces
ACEPST	aspect
	epacts
ACEPSY	spacey
ACEPTU	teacup
ACEQSU	casque
	sacque
ACERRS	carers
	racers
	scarer
ACERRT	carter
	crater
	tracer
ACERRU	curare
ACERRV	carver
	craver
ACERRY	Carrey
ACERSS	caress
	carses
	crases
	scares
	seracs
ACERST	carets
	caster
	caters
	crates
	reacts
	recast
	traces
ACERSU	causer
	cesura
	saucer
ACERSV	carves
	cavers
	craves
ACERSY	carsey
	creasy
ACERSZ	crazes
ACERTU	curate
ACESST	castes
ACESSU	causes
	sauces
ACESTT	stacte
	tacets
ACESTU	acutes
	cuesta
	Escaut
ACESTX	exacts
ACESUY	causey
	cayuse
ACFFHS	chaffs
ACFFHY	chaffy
ACFFLS	sclaff
ACFGIN	facing
ACFHLN	flanch
ACFHRT	fratch
ACFHSU	chufas
ACFILS	califs
	fiscal
ACFIOS	fiasco
ACFIPY	pacify
ACFISS	fascis
ACFKLS	flacks
ACFKNR	Franck
ACFLNO	falcon
	flacon
ACFLNU	canful
ACFLRU	fulcra
	furcal
ACFNOR	franco
ACFNRS	francs
ACFORT	factor
ACFRSS	scarfs
ACFRST	crafts
ACFRTY	crafty
ACGGIN	caging
ACGGIO	agogic
ACGGLY	claggy
ACGGRY	craggy
ACGHIN	aching
	Ichang
ACGHOU	gaucho
ACGHRU	curagh
ACGHTU	caught
ACGIKN	caking
ACGILL	gallic
ACGILN	lacing
ACGILR	garlic
ACGILS	glacis
ACGILY	cagily
ACGIMN	macing
ACGIMS	magics
ACGINN	caning
ACGINO	agonic
ACGINP	pacing
ACGINR	arcing
	caring
	racing
ACGINS	casing
	Signac
ACGINT	acting
ACGINV	caving
ACGINW	cawing
ACGIOR	Gorica
ACGIRS	cigars
	craigs
ACGIRT	tragic
ACGIUU	Iguaçú
ACGLNS	clangs
ACGLNU	glucan
ACGNOR	garcon
ACGNOS	congas
	gascon
ACGNOU	cougan
ACGORS	cargos
ACGORU	cougar
ACGOSU	guacos
ACGOWY	cogway
ACGRSS	scrags
ACGTTU	catgut
ACHHNU	haunch
ACHHTT	thatch
ACHIIS	ischia
ACHIJK	hijack
ACHIKO	kochia
ACHIKS	haicks
ACHIKW	Hawick
ACHILM	l'chaim
ACHILO	lochia
ACHILP	caliph
ACHILR	archil
	chiral
ACHILT	chital
ACHIMN	Mincha
ACHIMR	chimar
ACHIMS	chiasm
ACHINN	Chinan
ACHINR	inarch
	Ranchi
ACHINS	chains
	chinas
ACHINT	canthi
ACHIPS	phasic

ACHIPT haptic
pathic
phatic
ACHIQU quaich
ACHIRS chairs
rachis
ACHKKU chukka
ACHKLS chalks
ACHKLY chalky
ACHKMO Ockham
ACHKOS shacko
ACHKOW whacko
ACHKRU chukar
ACHKSS shacks
ACHKSW chawks
whacks
ACHKTW thwack
ACHKWY whacky
ACHLLO cholla
ACHLMU Culham
ACHLNO lochan
ACHLNU launch
nuchal
ACHLOR choral
ACHLRY archly
ACHLTU Clutha
ACHMMY chammy
ACHMOR chroma
morcha
ACHMOS machos
ACHMPS champs
ACHMRS charms
ACHMSS chasms
ACHMST smatch
ACHMSU sumach
ACHNOR anchor
archon
Charon
rancho
ACHNOS nachos
ACHNOT Can Tho
ACHNPU paunch
ACHNRU raunch
ACHNST chants
snatch
stanch
ACHNSU Usnach
ACHNTU chaunt
nautch
ACHNTY chanty
ACHOPR carhop
ACHOSV havocs
ACHOUV avouch
ACHPTY patchy
ACHRRS charrs
ACHRST charts
starch
ACHSSU sauchs
ACHSSW schwas
ACHSTU cushat
ACHSTW swatch
ACHSTY yachts
ACHTTY chatty
ACIILS sialic
silica
ACIILT italic
ACIINN niacin
ACIINS Nicias
ACIIRT iatric
ACIIST Saitic
ACIKLN calkin
ACIKMR karmic
ACIKNT catkin
ACIKPX pickax
ACILLN clinal
ACILLP plical
ACILLS lilacs
scilla
ACILLY lacily
ACILMO Colima
ACILMS claims
ACILMX climax
ACILNO alnico
oilcan
ACILNP caplin
ACILNR carlin
ACILNS linacs
ACILNT tincal
ACILNU Alcuin
Lucian
Lucina
uncial
ACILNV Calvin
ACILNY Lycian
ACILOR caroli
lorica
ACILOS social
ACILOT coital
ACILOX oxalic
ACILRT citral
rictal
ACILRU curial
lauric
uracil
ACILRY racily
ACILST ticals
ACILSU caulis
ACILSV cavils
ACIMNO anomic
camion
manioc
ACIMNP Campin
ACIMNS manics
ACIMNT mantic
ACIMOO oomiac
ACIMOS mosaic
ACIMOT atomic
ACIMPS scampi
ACIMPT impact
ACIMRS racism
ACIMRT matric
ACIMRU Murcia
ACIMRY myrica
ACIMST mastic
ACIMTU Actium
ACINNT tannic
ACINNY cyanin
ACINOP Pacino
ACINOS casino
ACINOT action
atonic
cation
ACINOX anoxic
ACINPS panics
ACINPT catnip
ACINRS arcsin
cairns
ACINRT Cintra
ACINRU uranic
ACINST antics
nastic
ACINSU acinus
ACINSV vincas
ACINTT intact
ACINTU tunica
ACINUV vicuna
ACIOPT atopic
copita
ACIORS scoria
ACIORT aortic
ACIOST coatis
scotia
ACIOSV ovisac
ACIOTZ azotic
ACIPRS capris
ACIPRY piracy
ACIPSS aspics
spicas
ACIPTT tipcat
ACIQTU acquit
ACIRRU curari
ACIRSS crasis
crissa
ACIRST artics
crista
racist
ACIRSU Icarus
ACIRSV vicars
ACIRTU uratic
ACISSS cassis
ACISTT attics
static
ACITUY acuity
ACITVY cavity
ACJKSY jacksy
ACKKNS knacks
ACKLNP Planck
ACKLNS clanks
ACKLOS cloaks
ACKLSS slacks
ACKLSU caulks
Lukács
ACKMSS smacks
ACKNOR Cranko
ACKNPU unpack
ACKNRS cranks
ACKNRY cranky
ACKNSS snacks
ACKNTU untack
ACKORS croaks
ACKORY croaky
ACKOSW wackos
ACKQSU quacks
ACKRST tracks
ACKRSW wracks
ACKSST stacks
ACLLMY calmly
ACLLNO clonal
ACLLOO alcool
ACLLOP callop
ACLLOR collar
ACLLOS Laclos
locals
ACLLOW callow
ACLLSS scalls
ACLLSU callus
ACLLSY scally
Scylla
ACLMMY clammy
ACLMOP copalm
ACLMOR clamor
Colmar
ACLMPS clamps
ACLMTU talcum
ACLNOT coltan
ACLNOX claxon
ACLNOY Lycaon
ACLNUV vulcan
ACLNUY lunacy
ACLOPU copula
cupola
ACLORR corral
ACLORS Carlos
carols
claros
corals
ACLORT crotal
ACLORU ocular
ACLORW Carlow
ACLORY calory
ACLOST costal
ACLOSU oscula
ACLOSV vocals
ACLOSW cowals
ACLOTT Alcott
ACLOTU Toluca
ACLPSS clasps
scalps
ACLPUU cupula
ACLRRU crural
ACLRST clarts
ACLRSW crawls
scrawl
ACLRTU curtal
ACLRTY clarty
ACLRWY crawly
ACLSSY classy
ACMMOS commas

ACMNOO Monaco
ACMNOR macron
ACMNOS mascon
socman
ACMNOT Cotman
ACMNOW cowman
ACMOPS campos
ACMORS caroms
macros
Marcos
ACMOST mascot
scamto
ACMOSU mucosa
ACMPRS cramps
ACMPSS scamps
ACMPSU campus
ACMRSS scrams
ACMRSU sacrum
ACMRSY cymars
ACMSSU sumacs
ACMSTU muscat
ACMUUV vacuum
ACNNNO cannon
ACNNOS canons
ACNNOT cannot
canton
ACNNOY canyon
ACNNRY cranny
ACNOOR corona
racoon
ACNOPS capons
ACNOPY canopy
ACNORR carron
rancor
ACNORS acorns
Carson
racons
ACNORT cantor
Carnot
carton
contra
craton
ACNORU cornua
ACNORY crayon
ACNOSS Casson
ACNOST actons
cantos
octans
ACNOTT octant
ACNOTU toucan
ACNOTX Caxton
ACNPSU pucans
uncaps
ACNSST scants
ACNSTU cantus
ACNSTY scanty
ACOOTV octavo
ACOPRS copras
ACOPRT captor
ACOPSS scopas
ACOPST capots
ACOPTW cowpat
ACORRT carrot
trocar
ACORSS across
oscars
ACORST actors
castor
Castro
costar
scrota
ACORSU Caruso
ACORTT cottar
ACORTU turaco
ACORTV cavort
ACORUV Cavour
ACORYZ coryza
ACOSST ascots
coasts
ACOSTT cottas
ACOSZZ scozza
ACOTTU outact
ACPPSU cuppas
ACPRSS scarps
scraps
ACPRSU carpus
ACPRSW scrawp
ACPSSU scaups
ACPSTU catsup
upcast
ACRRTU cratur
ACRSST scarts
ACRSSU scaurs
ACRSSW scraws
ACRSTT tracts
ACSTTY scatty
ADDDEG gadded
ADDDEL addled
ADDDEM madded
ADDDEN addend
ADDDEO dadoed
ADDDEP padded
ADDDEW wadded
ADDDOO doodad
ADDEEH headed
ADDEEL leaded
ADDEEN deaden
ADDEER Eadred
ADDEEV deaved
evaded
ADDEFF daffed
ADDEFG fadged
ADDEFN Fadden
ADDEGG dagged
ADDEGO goaded
ADDEGR gadder
graded
ADDEHI haddie
ADDEHK keddah
ADDEHN handed
ADDEHS dashed
shaded
ADDEHU hauded
ADDEIL dialed
laddie
ADDEIM diadem
mediad
ADDEIR raided
ADDEIS addies
ADDEKR darked
ADDELL ladled
ADDELN dandle
landed
ADDELO loaded
ADDELP paddle
ADDELR ladder
larded
raddle
ADDELS addles
daleds
saddle
ADDELU lauded
ADDELW dawdle
waddle
ADDELY deadly
ADDEMM dammed
ADDEMN damned
demand
madden
ADDEMP damped
ADDEMR madder
ADDENR dander
darned
ADDENS dedans
sadden
sanded
ADDENU undead
ADDENW dawned
ADDEOR adored
deodar
ADDEOS dadoes
ADDEOT doated
ADDEOW woaded
ADDEPP dapped
ADDEPR draped
ADDEPS spaded
ADDERR radder
ADDERS adders
dreads
readds
sadder
ADDERT darted
traded
ADDERU daured
ADDERW Edward
wadder
warded
ADDERY yarded
ADDETU Daudet
ADDGIN adding
ADDGIO gadoid
ADDGIP giddap
ADDGIS gadids
ADDGIY gidday
ADDGMO goddam
ADDGOO ogdoad
ADDGOR Godard
ADDGRU du Gard
ADDHOO doodah
ADDHOS Ashdod
ADDHSU saddhu
ADDIIV David I
ADDIMR Madrid
ADDIMS misadd
ADDIMY midday
ADDLNO Donald
ADDLWY waddly
ADDMOO Dodoma
ADDNOO Dodona
ADDOOR dorado
ADDORS dorsad
ADDORT dotard
ADDRSY dryads
ADDSWY swaddy
ADEEFL leafed
ADEEFM defame
ADEEFN deafen
ADEEFR deafer
feared
ADEEFT defeat
ADEEFZ feazed
ADEEGG degage
ADEEGR agreed
dragee
geared
ADEEHL Hadlee
healed
ADEEHP heaped
ADEEHR adhere
header
hedera
ADEEHT heated
ADEEHV heaved
ADEEIL aedile
Eliade
ADEEIM mediae
ADEEIR dearie
rediae
ADEEIS easied
ADEEIT ideate
ADEEJY deejay
ADEEKL leaked
ADEEKP peaked
ADEELN aneled
leaden
leaned
ADEELP leaped
pealed
ADEELR dealer
leader
ADEELS leased
sealed
ADEELT delate
elated
ADEELV leaved
ADEEMN amende
demean
ADEEMO oedema

ADEEMR	reamed
	remade
ADEEMS	seamed
ADEEMT	teamed
ADEENN	ennead
ADEENR	earned
	endear
	neared
ADEENT	anteed
ADEENW	weaned
ADEENY	yeaned
ADEEPR	reaped
ADEEPS	pesade
ADEEPT	pedate
ADEERR	dearer
	reader
	reared
	reread
ADEERS	erased
	Red Sea
	reseda
	seared
ADEERT	derate
ADEERV	evader
	reaved
ADEERW	drawee
ADEERX	exedra
ADEERZ	razeed
ADEESS	Edessa
ADEEST	seated
	sedate
	teased
ADEESV	deaves
	evades
ADEESX	axseed
ADEEVW	weaved
ADEFFF	faffed
ADEFFG	gaffed
ADEFFW	waffed
ADEFGG	fagged
ADEFGN	fanged
ADEFGS	fadges
ADEFHS	fashed
ADEFHT	hafted
ADEFIL	afield
	failed
ADEFIR	faired
ADEFKL	flaked
ADEFLM	flamed
ADEFLO	foaled
	loafed
ADEFLR	fardel
	flared
ADEFLU	feudal
ADEFLW	flawed
ADEFLY	deafly
	flayed
ADEFMO	foamed
ADEFMR	farmed
	framed
ADEFMT	mafted
ADEFNN	fanned
ADEFNW	fawned
ADEFOR	fedora
ADEFRS	faders
ADEFRT	dafter
	farted
	rafted
ADEFRY	defray
	frayed
ADEFST	fasted
ADEFTT	fatted
ADEFTU	fauted
ADEFTW	wafted
ADEGGG	gagged
ADEGGI	gadgie
ADEGGJ	jagged
ADEGGL	lagged
ADEGGM	magged
ADEGGN	ganged
	nagged
ADEGGR	dagger
	ragged
ADEGGS	sagged
ADEGGT	gadget
	tagged
ADEGGU	gauged
ADEGGV	vagged
ADEGGW	wagged
ADEGHN	hanged
ADEGHS	gashed
ADEGIL	Gilead
ADEGIM	imaged
ADEGIN	daeing
	gained
ADEGIT	gaited
ADEGIW	Eadwig
ADEGKN	Kang-de
ADEGKW	gawked
ADEGLL	galled
ADEGLN	angled
	dangle
ADEGLO	gaoled
ADEGLR	glared
ADEGLS	glades
ADEGLZ	glazed
ADEGMM	gammed
ADEGNN	ganned
ADEGNO	Ogaden
ADEGNR	danger
	gander
	garden
	ranged
ADEGNU	augend
ADEGNW	gnawed
ADEGOR	dogear
ADEGOS	dagoes
	dosage
	seadog
ADEGOT	dotage
	togaed
ADEGPP	gapped
ADEGPS	gasped
ADEGPU	gauped
ADEGPW	gawped
ADEGRR	garred
	Gérard
	grader
	regard
ADEGRS	grades
ADEGRT	grated
ADEGRU	argued
ADEGRV	graved
ADEGRY	grayed
ADEGRZ	grazed
ADEGSS	gassed
ADEGST	staged
ADEGSW	swaged
ADEHHK	khedah
ADEHHS	hashed
ADEHIL	hailed
	halide
ADEHIR	haired
	Hardie
ADEHJS	hadjes
	jehads
ADEHJZ	Hedjaz
ADEHKN	hanked
ADEHKR	harked
ADEHKS	khedas
ADEHKW	hawked
ADEHLM	lamedh
ADEHLN	Handel
	handle
ADEHLO	haloed
ADEHLR	harled
	herald
ADEHLS	lashed
ADEHLT	daleth
	halted
	lathed
ADEHLU	hauled
ADEHLV	halved
ADEHLW	whaled
ADEHMM	hammed
ADEHMR	harmed
ADEHMS	mashed
	shamed
ADEHNP	daphne
ADEHNR	harden
ADEHNU	hauden
ADEHOX	hoaxed
ADEHPP	happed
ADEHPR	harped
ADEHPS	hasped
	pashed
	phased
	shaped
ADEHPT	heptad
ADEHRR	Erhard
	harder
ADEHRS	dasher
	Ershad
	shared
ADEHRT	dearth
	hatred
	red hat
	thread
ADEHRY	hydrae
ADEHSS	dashes
	sadhes
	sashed
	shades
ADEHST	deaths
	hasted
ADEHSV	shaved
ADEHSW	hawsed
	shawed
	washed
ADEHSX	hexads
ADEHSY	Hyades
ADEHTT	hatted
ADEHTW	thawed
ADEHYY	heyday
ADEIJL	jailed
ADEIKL	laiked
ADEIKN	Deakin
ADEIKR	darkie
ADEILL	allied
	Lleida
ADEILM	mailed
	medial
ADEILN	Aldine
	alined
	Daniel
	Delian
	denial
	nailed
ADEILO	eidola
ADEILP	aliped
	elapid
	pleiad
ADEILR	derail
	laired
	Lérida
	railed
	redial
	relaid
ADEILS	aisled
	deasil
	ideals
	ladies
	sailed
ADEILT	detail
	dilate
	tailed
ADEILU	audile
ADEILV	vailed
ADEILW	wailed
ADEIMM	maimed
ADEIMN	Damien
	maiden
	median
	medina
ADEIMR	admire
	Mérida
ADEIMS	amides
	mesiad

ADEINO	Oneida
ADEINP	pained
ADEINR	Dairen
	Darien
	Derain
	rained
	read in
ADEINS	sained
	Sendai
ADEINT	detain
ADEINV	invade
ADEINZ	Zidane
ADEIOR	roadie
ADEIOT	iodate
ADEIPR	diaper
	paired
	repaid
ADEIRR	raider
ADEIRS	aiders
	irades
	raised
ADEIRT	tirade
ADEIRU	uredia
ADEIRV	varied
ADEISS	asides
	daises
	dassie
ADEISU	adieus
ADEISV	advise
	davies
	visaed
ADEISW	wadies
ADEISZ	azides
ADEITV	dative
ADEITW	waited
ADEITX	taxied
ADEIUX	adieux
ADEIVV	vivaed
ADEIVW	waived
ADEJMM	jammed
ADEJOU	Judaeo-
ADEJPR	jarped
ADEJPU	jauped
ADEJRR	jarred
ADEJRU	adjure
ADEJZZ	jazzed
ADEKKY	yakked
ADEKLN	Kendal
ADEKLR	darkle
	larked
ADEKLS	slaked
ADEKLT	talked
ADEKLW	walked
ADEKMR	marked
ADEKMS	masked
ADEKNR	danker
	darken
	narked
	ranked
ADEKNS	kneads
	sandek
	Sendak
ADEKNT	tanked
ADEKNW	wanked
ADEKNY	yanked
ADEKOS	soaked
ADEKOY	kayoed
	okayed
ADEKPR	parked
ADEKPY	keypad
ADEKQU	quaked
ADEKRR	darker
ADEKRS	drakes
ADEKRY	darkey
ADEKST	skated
	staked
	tasked
ADEKUW	wauked
ADELLP	palled
ADELLR	ladler
ADELLS	dalles
	ladles
ADELLU	allude
	aludel
ADELLW	walled
ADELMM	lammed
ADELMO	loamed
ADELMP	palmed
ADELMR	Del Mar
	dermal
	marled
	medlar
ADELMS	damsel
	lameds
	medals
ADELMT	malted
ADELMU	dumela
	mauled
ADELNO	loaned
ADELNP	planed
ADELNR	darnel
	lander
	larned
ADELNS	elands
	landes
	sendal
ADELNT	dental
ADELNU	unlade
	unlead
ADELOP	pedalo
ADELOR	Laredo
	loader
	ordeal
	reload
ADELOS	aldose
ADELPP	dapple
	lapped
ADELPR	pedlar
ADELPS	lapsed
	pedals
	pleads
ADELPT	plated
ADELPW	dewlap
ADELPY	played
ADELRR	larder
ADELRS	alders
	laders
ADELRU	aulder
	Éluard
	lauder
ADELRY	dearly
ADELST	deltas
	desalt
	lasted
	salted
	slated
	staled
ADELSV	salved
	slaved
ADELSW	wealds
ADELSY	delays
ADELUV	valued
ADELUW	wauled
ADELWW	wawled
ADELWY	yawled
ADELZZ	dazzle
ADEMMN	madmen
ADEMMR	dammer
	rammed
ADEMMS	sammed
ADEMNN	manned
ADEMNO	daemon
	Menado
	moaned
	modena
ADEMNP	dampen
ADEMNR	randem
	remand
ADEMNS	amends
	demans
	desman
	menads
ADEMNT	tandem
ADEMNU	unmade
ADEMOP	pomade
ADEMOR	radome
	roamed
ADEMOT	moated
ADEMOW	meadow
ADEMPP	mapped
ADEMPR	damper
	ramped
ADEMPT	tamped
ADEMPV	vamped
ADEMRR	marred
ADEMRS	dermas
	dreams
ADEMRT	dreamt
ADEMRW	warmed
ADEMRY	dreamy
ADEMSS	massed
ADEMST	masted
ADEMSU	amused
	medusa
ADEMTT	matted
ADEMWY	Medway
ADENNP	panned
ADENNT	tanned
ADENNU	duenna
ADENNW	wanned
ADENOS	anodes
ADENOT	atoned
	donate
ADENOY	noyade
ADENPP	append
	napped
ADENPR	pander
	repand
ADENPT	panted
	pedant
	pentad
ADENPW	pawned
ADENPX	expand
ADENRR	darner
	errand
ADENRS	denars
	redans
	sander
	snared
ADENRT	ardent
	Arendt
	ranted
ADENRU	Neruda
	unread
ADENRW	Andrew
	wander
	warden
	warned
ADENRY	denary
	yarned
ADENRZ	zander
ADENSS	sedans
ADENSU	sundae
ADENSV	davens
ADENSW	dewans
ADENTT	attend
ADENTV	advent
ADENTW	wanted
ADENUY	Yaunde
ADENWY	dawney
	yawned
ADEOPS	soaped
ADEORR	adorer
	roared
ADEORS	adores
	oreads
	soared
ADEORT	doater
	orated
ADEORW	redowa
ADEOSS	Odessa
ADEOSV	vadose
ADEOVW	avowed
ADEPPR	dapper
	rapped
ADEPPS	sapped
ADEPPT	tapped
ADEPPY	yapped

ADEPPZ	zapped
ADEPRR	draper
ADEPRS	drapes
	padres
	parsed
	rasped
	spader
	spared
	spread
ADEPRT	depart
	parted
	petard
	prated
ADEPRW	warped
ADEPRY	prayed
ADEPSS	passed
	spades
ADEPST	adepts
	pasted
ADEPSU	paused
ADEPSY	spayed
ADEPTT	patted
ADEPTU	update
ADEPUY	yauped
ADEPWY	yawped
ADERRS	darers
ADERRT	darter
	retard
	tarred
	trader
ADERRW	drawer
	redraw
	reward
	warder
	warred
ADERRY	dreary
ADERSS	Esdras
ADERST	stared
	trades
	treads
ADERSW	sawder
	Seward
	waders
ADERTT	ratted
	tetrad
ADERTV	advert
ADERTW	warted
ADERZZ	razzed
ADESSS	sassed
ADESST	steads
	tsades
ADESSU	Dessau
ADESTT	stated
	tasted
ADESTU	sauted
ADESTV	staved
ADESTW	tawsed
	wadset
	wasted
ADESTY	stayed
	steady
ADESWY	swayed
ADETTT	tatted
ADETTV	vatted
ADFFOR	afford
ADFFRS	draffs
ADFFRY	draffy
ADFGIN	fading
ADFGLY	gadfly
ADFGRU	Fugard
ADFHSU	shaduf
ADFILY	ladify
ADFIRT	adrift
ADFLTY	daftly
ADFLYY	dayfly
	ladyfy
ADFNOT	fantod
ADFRRU	Darfur
ADFRST	drafts
ADFRSU	frauds
ADFRSW	dwarfs
ADFRTY	drafty
ADGGRY	draggy
ADGHIN	Gandhi
	hading
ADGHRU	durgah
ADGIIN	aiding
ADGIJN	jading
ADGIJO	adjigo
ADGILN	lading
	ligand
ADGILO	algoid
	dialog
ADGIMY	digamy
ADGINO	ganoid
ADGINR	daring
	gradin
ADGINT	dating
ADGINW	wading
ADGINY	Gdynia
ADGINZ	Danzig
	dazing
ADGIOV	Godiva
ADGIRU	Giraud
	Guardi
ADGIRV	gravid
ADGKMO	Domagk
ADGKNS	Gdańsk
ADGLLY	gladly
ADGLNS	glands
ADGLOP	lapdog
ADGMNO	dogman
	God man
ADGMOS	dogmas
ADGNNO	Andong
ADGNOP	dognap
ADGNOR	dragon
	Gondar
ADGNOS	dongas
	gonads
ADGNRS	grands
ADGNSW	dwangs
ADGRSU	gradus
	guards
ADGRTU	Utgard
ADHHIT	hadith
ADHHIW	whidah
ADHHKU	duhkha
ADHHOU	houdah
ADHHOW	howdah
ADHHWY	whydah
ADHIIJ	jihadi
ADHIJS	hadjis
	jadish
	jihads
ADHIKU	haiduk
ADHILO	haloid
ADHILS	halids
ADHIMR	dirham
ADHINS	danish
	sandhi
ADHIOO	hoodia
ADHIOR	hairdo
ADHIPS	aphids
ADHIRS	radish
	Rashid
ADHIRY	hydria
	Riyadh
ADHISS	Hassid
ADHKKU	dukkah
	dukkha
ADHLMO	Oldham
ADHLNU	Uhland
ADHLRY	hardly
ADHMNO	hodman
ADHMNU	numdah
ADHMRU	Durham
ADHNNU	unhand
ADHNOO	Doohan
ADHNOR	hadron
ADHNOS	donahs
ADHNOU	houdan
ADHNOY	Haydon
ADHNRU	dhurna
ADHNSY	shandy
ADHORS	hoards
ADHORU	dourah
ADHORW	Howard
ADHOSW	shadow
ADHPRU	purdah
ADHRSS	shards
ADHRSY	hydras
ADHSSU	sadhus
ADIIKO	aikido
ADIILM	miladi
ADIILN	inlaid
ADIILW	Diwali
ADIIMN	Midian
ADIIMO	daimio
ADIIMR	midair
ADIINN	Indian
ADIINV	avidin
ADIINZ	diazin
ADIIPR	diapir
ADIJLS	Djilas
ADIJMS	masjid
ADIJNO	adjoin
ADIKKO	Kodiak
ADIKKS	Skikda
ADIKMN	Kidman
ADIKMO	mikado
ADIKNO	daikon
ADIKNP	kidnap
ADIKSU	adsuki
ADIKTT	diktat
ADIKUZ	adzuki
ADILLP	pallid
ADILMO	amidol
ADILMS	dismal
ADILMY	milady
ADILNN	inland
ADILNO	dolina
	ladino
ADILNR	aldrin
ADILNS	island
ADILNT	tindal
ADILNU	unlaid
ADILNY	Lydian
ADILPS	plaids
ADILRS	drails
	lairds
	liards
ADILRV	aridly
ADILRZ	lizard
ADILSS	Aldiss
ADILST	distal
ADILVY	avidly
ADIMMT	dammit
ADIMNO	daimon
	domain
ADIMNR	mandir
ADIMNS	admins
	mandis
ADIMNT	mantid
ADIMOT	diatom
ADIMOY	daimyo
ADIMRS	disarm
ADIMRU	radium
ADIMRY	myriad
ADIMSS	sadism
ADIMST	admits
	amidst
ADIMSY	dismay
ADIMWY	midway
ADINNP	pindan
ADINNT	Dinant
ADINNU	induna
ADINOR	inroad
	ordain
ADINOS	adonis
	danios
ADINOX	dioxan
ADINPR	Pindar
ADINPT	pandit
ADINPU	unpaid
ADINQR	qindar
ADINRS	dinars
	drains

nadirs
ADINRU durian
ADINRW Darwin
inward
ADINSU unsaid
ADINSV divans
viands
ADINSW diwans
ADINTY dainty
ADIORS radios
ADIORT adroit
Doráti
ADIOSV avoids
ADIOSZ diazos
ADIPRS rapids
sparid
ADIPSX spadix
ADIRRS sirdar
ADIRSS Sardis
ADIRST triads
ADIRSU radius
ADIRSZ izards
ADIRTZ Tizard
ADIRVZ vizard
ADIRWZ wizard
ADIRZZ izzard
ADISST sadist
ADISSY sayids
ADISTU audits
ADISTV davits
ADISYY sayyid
ADJKOU judoka
ADJNOR jordan
ADJSTU adjust
ADKKNO Kokand
ADKLNY dankly
ADKLOY Kodály
ADKLRY darkly
ADKLSS skalds
ADKMRU Marduk
ADKNRU Durkan
ADKOPS padkos
ADKOPU padouk
ADKORV Dvořák
ADKOSV vodkas
ADLLOR dollar
ADLLOS aldols
allods
ADLLUY dually
ADLMNO almond
dolman
Maldon
old man
ADLMOS dolmas
ADLMOU Moldau
ADLMPY damply
ADLMTU talmud
ADLNOO doolan
ADLNOP Poland
ADLNOR Arnold
Landor
lardon
Roland
ADLNOS soldan
ADLNOT dalton
ADLNOU unload
ADLNPU upland
ADLNRU lurdan
ADLNSU Lasdun
ADLOPU upload
ADLORS dorsal
ADLOSS dossal
ADLOSU doulas
ADLOSW Oswald
waldos
ADLRSW drawls
ADLRWY drawly
ADLSTU adults
ADMNOR random
ADMNOS damson
monads
nomads
ADMNOY dynamo
ADMNSU maunds
ADMNUY maundy
ADMORR ramrod
ADMORT Tadmor
ADMORU maduro
ADMORZ Ormazd
ADMOSU doumas
ADMRSU mudras
ADMSUW dwaums
ADMTUY adytum
Dumyat
ADNNOS donnas
ADNNOT danton
ADNNOU adnoun
ADNNTU Dunant
ADNOOR Adorno
nardoo
ADNOOS doonas
ADNOOW wandoo
ADNOPR pardon
ADNOPT dopant
ADNORS adorns
Andros
nadors
ADNORU around
Nordau
ADNORV Vardon
ADNORW onward
ADNOSU soudan
ADNOSW Dawson
ADNOTY Dayton
ADNRST strand
ADNRTU tundra
ADNRUW undraw
ADNSST stands
ADNSTU daunts
ADNSTY dynast
ADNSUY Sunday
ADOOTW Atwood
ADOPRT Dorpat
ADOPRY parody
ADOPST adopts
ADORRU ardour
ADORSS sarods
ADORSU Sardou
ADORTW toward
ADPRSU purdas
ADPRUW upward
ADQSSU squads
ADRSST strads
ADRSSW swards
ADRTWY tawdry
AEEEHL healee
AEEEST Aeëtes
AEEFIR faerie
feriae
AEEFKR fakeer
AEEFLM female
AEEFOV foveae
AEEFRR fearer
AEEFRT afreet
feater
AEEFSZ feazes
AEEGGN engage
AEEGGR raggee
reggae
AEEGHZ geezah
AEEGIR Ariège
AEEGJR jaeger
AEEGKN Keegan
AEEGLL allege
AEEGLP pelage
AEEGLR galere
regale
AEEGLS eagles
Le Sage
AEEGLT eaglet
legate
telega
AEEGLU league
AEEGMM gemmae
AEEGMN manege
menage
AEEGMR meager
meagre
AEEGMT gamete
metage
AEEGNN ennage
AEEGNR enrage
genera
AEEGNS senega
AEEGNT negate
AEEGNV avenge
geneva
AEEGNW New Age
AEEGOP apogee
AEEGOT goatee
AEEGRS agrees
eagers
eagres
grease
AEEGRV greave
AEEGST egesta
AEEGSU Aegeus
AEEGSW sewage
AEEHHW heehaw
AEEHKM hakeem
AEEHKT Hekate
AEEHLN Helena
AEEHLR healer
AEEHLW awheel
AEEHLX exhale
AEEHLY Healey
AEEHMR hareem
hermae
AEEHMU heaume
AEEHNP peahen
AEEHNT ethane
AEEHNV heaven
AEEHNX hexane
AEEHNY Heaney
AEEHPR heaper
AEEHPS spahee
AEEHRR hearer
rehear
AEEHRS haeres
hearse
AEEHRT aether
heater
hereat
reheat
AEEHRV heaver
AEEHSV heaves
heveas
sheave
AEEILM mealie
AEEIMN meanie
AEEINT teniae
AEEIRR aerier
AEEIRS aeries
easier
AEEISS easies
AEEKLN alkene
AEEKLR leaker
AEEKLY Leakey
AEEKMR remake
AEEKMZ kameez
AEEKNS akenes
AEEKNW weaken
AEEKRT retake
AEEKRU eureka
AEEKRW rewake
weaker
AEELLL allele
AEELLM mallee
AEELLR lealer
AEELLS sallee
AEELMN enamel
AEELMP empale
AEELNR leaner
AEELNS aneles
AEELNT lateen
AEELNV leaven
AEELOR areole
AEELOT oleate

AEELPR	leaper
	repeal
AEELPS	asleep
	elapse
	please
	sapele
AEELRS	leaser
	reales
	resale
	reseal
	sealer
	Searle
AEELRT	elater
	relate
	Tralee
AEELRV	leaver
	reveal
	vealer
AEELSS	easels
	leases
AEELST	elates
	stelae
	teasel
AEELSV	leaves
	sleave
AEELSW	weasel
AEELSZ	sleaze
AEELTT	Attlee
AEELTU	eluate
AEELTV	velate
	veleta
AEELTZ	teazel
	teazle
AEELWY	leeway
AEEMMM	mammee
AEEMNN	Nemean
AEEMNP	apemen
AEEMNR	meaner
	rename
AEEMNS	enemas
	mensae
	seamen
AEEMNX	axemen
	examen
AEEMPR	ampere
	Ampère
AEEMRR	reamer
AEEMRS	ameers
	seamer
AEEMSS	sesame
AEEMTX	taxeme
AEENNP	pennae
AEENNT	neaten
AEENNX	annexe
AEENPR	paneer
AEENPT	nepeta
AEENPU	eupnea
AEENPW	pawnee
AEENRR	earner
	nearer
AEENRS	arenes
	ranees
AEENRT	entera
	neater
	rateen
AEENRV	Erevan
AEENRW	weaner
AEENST	enates
	Santee
	sateen
	senate
AEENSU	unease
AEENSW	Swanee
AEENTW	atween
AEENUV	avenue
AEEPPR	rappee
AEEPRR	reaper
AEEPRS	Parsee
	Pearse
	serape
AEEPRT	repeat
AEEPRV	pareve
	repave
AEEPST	peseta
AEEPSV	Pavese
AEEPSW	pesewa
AEEPSX	apexes
AEEPSY	payees
AEEPTT	pattee
AEEPVY	peavey
AEEQRU	quaere
AEEQTU	equate
AEERRR	rearer
AEERRS	eraser
	serrae
AEERRT	tearer
AEERRW	wearer
AEERSS	easers
	erases
	sarees
AEERST	aretes
	easter
	eaters
	reseat
	seater
	teaser
	Teresa
AEERSU	reseau
	urease
AEERSV	averse
	reaves
	Varese
	Varèse
AEERSZ	razees
AEERTY	eatery
AEERVW	weaver
AEESST	teases
AEESSW	seesaw
AEESSY	eyases
AEESTT	estate
	testae
AEESTX	exeats
AEESVW	weaves
AEEWXY	waxeye
AEFFGR	gaffer
AEFFGS	gaffes
AEFFIN	affine
AEFFIP	piaffe
AEFFLR	raffle
AEFFLW	waffle
AEFFLY	yaffle
AEFFNR	naffer
AEFFRZ	zaffer
	zaffre
AEFGLN	flange
AEFGNS	ganefs
AEFGOR	forage
AEFHKR	Khafre
AEFHLL	fellah
AEFHRS	afresh
AEFHRT	father
	hafter
AEFHSS	fashes
AEFIJO	feijoa
AEFILL	faille
AEFILN	finale
AEFILR	ferial
AEFILS	Feisal
AEFILT	fetial
AEFIMN	famine
AEFINN	fainne
	Fenian
AEFINR	infare
AEFIRR	fairer
AEFIRS	ferias
	fraise
AEFIRT	treifa
AEFIRY	aerify
AEFIST	fastie
	fiesta
AEFITX	fixate
AEFJNT	fanjet
AEFKLN	fankle
AEFKLR	flaker
AEFKLS	flakes
AEFKLY	flakey
AEFKNS	kenafs
AEFKRS	fakers
	freaks
AEFKRY	fakery
	freaky
AEFKSW	Fawkes
AEFLLN	fallen
AEFLLR	faller
AEFLLS	fellas
AEFLMN	flamen
AEFLMR	flamer
AEFLMS	flames
	fleams
AEFLNU	Le Fanu
AEFLNV	Alfvén
AEFLNX	flaxen
AEFLOR	florae
	loafer
AEFLOT	foetal
AEFLOV	foveal
AEFLRS	falser
	farles
	flares
AEFLRT	falter
AEFLRU	earful
	ferula
AEFLRY	flayer
AEFLST	festal
AEFLSY	safely
AEFLTY	fealty
	featly
AEFMNO	foeman
AEFMOR	femora
AEFMRR	farmer
	framer
AEFMRS	frames
AEFMRT	Fermat
AEFNNR	fanner
AEFNRW	fawner
AEFNST	fasten
AEFNSU	unsafe
AEFNTT	fatten
AEFNZZ	Fezzan
AEFORS	Faroes
AEFOSS	fossae
AEFOSV	favose
AEFPPR	frappe
AEFRRR	Ferrar
AEFRRS	farers
	Fraser
AEFRRT	frater
	rafter
AEFRRU	faurer
AEFRRY	rarefy
AEFRRZ	Frazer
AEFRST	afters
	faster
	safter
	strafe
AEFRSU	feuars
AEFRSW	wafers
AEFRTT	fatter
AEFRTW	wafter
AEFRWY	wafery
AEFSST	feasts
	safest
AEFSTY	safety
AEFSUV	fauves
AEGGGL	gaggle
AEGGGR	gagger
AEGGHL	haggle
AEGGIM	maggie
AEGGIN	ageing
AEGGJR	jagger
AEGGLR	gargle
	raggle
AEGGLW	waggle
AEGGNR	ganger
	grange
	nagger
AEGGNS	Ganges
AEGGNU	gangue

AEGGRS aggers
eggars
gagers
sagger
AEGGRT garget
AEGGRU gauger
AEGGSU gauges
AEGGWW gewgaw
AEGHIN haeing
AEGHIR hegira
AEGHIS geisha
AEGHIW aweigh
AEGHIY Hygeia
AEGHMO homage
ohmage
AEGHNR hanger
rehang
AEGHNS Ganesh
AEGHNW Hwange
AEGHOR gherao
AEGHPS phages
AEGHRS gerahs
AEGHRT gather
AEGHSS gashes
AEGILM milage
AEGILN genial
linage
AEGILO goalie
AEGILP paigle
AEGILS ligase
silage
AEGILT aiglet
ligate
AEGILV glaive
AEGILZ El Gîza
AEGIMN enigma
gamine
AEGIMP magpie
AEGIMR gamier
maigre
mirage
AEGIMS ageism
images
AEGINR earing
gainer
reagin
regain
regina
AEGINS Agnesi
easing
AEGINT eating
tagine
AEGINU guinea
AEGIPP pipage
AEGIPT Piaget
AEGIRT aigret
gaiter
triage
AEGIRV Argive
rivage
AEGIRW earwig
AEGIRZ Gezira
AEGIST ageist
AEGISV visage
AEGITU augite
AEGITY gaiety
AEGJLN jangle
AEGJRS jagers
AEGJTU jugate
AEGKNS Skagen
AEGKST gasket
AEGLLN Angell
AEGLLU Gaulle
ullage
AEGLLY galley
AEGLMN legman
mangel
mangle
AEGLMS gleams
AEGLMV maglev
AEGLMY gamely
gleamy
AEGLNR Algren
angler
erlang
langer
largen
regnal
AEGLNS angels
angles
gleans
AEGLNT tangle
AEGLNU lagune
langue
AEGLNW wangle
AEGLOR galore
gaoler
AEGLOT legato
AEGLOV lovage
AEGLPS plages
AEGLPU plague
AEGLRR larger
AEGLRS glares
Glaser
lagers
regals
AEGLRT tergal
AEGLRV gravel
AEGLRY argyle
AEGLRZ glazer
AEGLST aglets
AEGLSV gavels
AEGLSY sagely
AEGLSZ glazes
AEGLTU Tugela
AEGLTW talweg
AEGMMR gammer
gramme
AEGMMS smegma
AEGMNO gamone
AEGMNR engram
german
manger
ragmen
AEGMNS gasmen
AEGMNT magnet
AEGMNY mangey
AEGMOS omegas
AEGMPS sepmag
AEGMRS marges
AEGMRU mauger
maugre
murage
AEGMRW mawger
AEGMSS megass
AEGMST gamest
AEGMUY maguey
AEGMUZ zeugma
AEGNNO nonage
AEGNNP penang
AEGNNT gannet
AEGNOR Gerona
onager
orange
AEGNOS agones
genoas
AEGNOV Genova
AEGNRR garner
ranger
AEGNRS angers
ranges
sanger
serang
AEGNRT argent
garnet
AEGNRV graven
AEGNRW gnawer
Wagner
AEGNRY anergy
AEGNST agents
AEGNSV ganevs
vegans
AEGNSY gansey
AEGOPT potage
AEGORT orgeat
Ortega
Tagore
toerag
AEGORU aerugo
AEGOTU outage
AEGOTW towage
AEGOVY voyage
AEGPRS gapers
gasper
grapes
pagers
sparge
AEGPRT parget
AEGPRU Prague
AEGPRW gawper
AEGPRY grapey
AEGRRT garret
garter
grater
AEGRRU arguer
AEGRRV graver
AEGRRY grayer
AEGRRZ grazer
AEGRSS gasser
AEGRST grates
greats
stager
targes
AEGRSU argues
augers
sauger
AEGRSV graves
AEGRSW swager
wagers
AEGRSY greasy
AEGRSZ gazers
grazes
AEGRTT target
AEGRTU rugate
AEGRTY gyrate
AEGRUV vaguer
AEGRVY garvey
AEGSSS gasses
AEGSST stages
AEGSSU usages
AEGSSW swages
AEGSTY gayest
stagey
AEGSUZ gauzes
AEGTTU guttae
AEGTYY gayety
AEHHJV Jahveh
AEHHLT health
AEHHMS HaShem
AEHHPS ephahs
AEHHPY hyphae
AEHHRS rehash
AEHHRT hearth
AEHHSS hashes
AEHHST heaths
sheath
AEHHTY heathy
AEHHWY Yahweh
AEHIIW Weihai
AEHIJL Elijah
AEHIJR hejira
AEHIKN hankie
AEHILM hiemal
lehaim
AEHILN inhale
AEHILP Philae
AEHILR hailer
AEHILS Elisha
Ilesha
sheila
AEHILT halite
AEHILW awhile
AEHIMM maihem
AEHIMN haemin
AEHIMR hermai
AEHIMS mashie
AEHINR hernia
AEHINW wahine

AEHIRS ashier
sheria
AEHIRZ hazier
AEHIST Hestia
saithe
AEHJJS hajjes
AEHKLT Khelat
AEHKMS samekh
AEHKNR hanker
harken
AEHKNS shaken
AEHKRS kasher
shaker
AEHKRW hawker
AEHKSS shakes
AEHKSY ashkey
AEHKWY hawkey
AEHLLL hallel
AEHLLR Haller
AEHLLS Hellas
AEHLLT lethal
AEHLLY Halley
AEHLMN Hameln
AEHLMP pelham
AEHLMR Harlem
Mahler
AEHLMT hamlet
AEHLNS hansel
AEHLOR Lahore
AEHLOS haloes
AEHLOT loathe
AEHLPS alephs
AEHLPY phylae
AEHLRS ashler
halers
lasher
AEHLRT halter
lather
thaler
Thrale
AEHLRU haleru
hauler
AEHLRW whaler
AEHLRY Harley
AEHLSS hassle
lashes
shales
AEHLST haslet
lathes
shelta
Thales
AEHLSV halves
AEHLSW whales
wheals
AEHLSY Ashley
AEHLSZ hazels
AEHLTW wealth
AEHLTY hyetal
AEHLUV Huelva
AEHLVY Halévy
AEHMMR hammer
AEHMMY mayhem

AEHMNR Arnhem
Mähren
AEHMNT anthem
hetman
AEHMNU humane
AEHMNW Newham
AEHMPR hamper
AEHMRR harmer
AEHMRS harems
masher
AEHMSS mashes
shames
AEHMST Thames
AEHMUW mahewu
AEHMWY Mayhew
AEHNNS hennas
AEHNPP happen
AEHNPT hapten
AEHNRT anther
Tehran
thenar
AEHNSS hanses
AEHNST Athens
hasten
snathe
thanes
AEHNSV havens
shaven
AEHNSW whenas
AEHNSY hyenas
Seyhan
AEHNTT Thanet
AEHNUW whenua
AEHORS ashore
hoarse
AEHORX hoaxer
AEHOSV hoveas
AEHOSX hoaxes
AEHPRR harper
AEHPRS phrase
seraph
shaper
sherpa
AEHPRT tephra
teraph
threap
AEHPSS pashes
phases
shapes
AEHPST spathe
AEHRRR Harrer
AEHRRS rasher
sharer
AEHRRT rather
AEHRSS rashes
shares
shears
AEHRST earths
Hearst
hearts
Sarthe
AEHRSV havers

shaver
AEHRSW hawser
rewash
washer
whares
AEHRSZ hazers
AEHRTT hatter
threat
AEHRTV thrave
AEHRTW thawer
wreath
AEHRTY earthy
hearty
AEHRVW wharve
AEHRVY Harvey
AEHSSS sashes
AEHSST ashets
hastes
AEHSSV shaves
AEHSSW hawses
washes
AEHSTT thetas
AEHSTV Shevat
AEHSTW swathe
wheats
AEIILR Leiria
AEIILS liaise
AEIIPR Pieria
AEIIPT Taipei
AEIIRR airier
AEIJKR Rijeka
AEIJLR jailer
AEIJMS James I
AEIJNR injera
AEIJNT Netaji
tajine
AEIJRV jarvie
AEIJSX jaxies
AEIKLR lakier
AEIKLS alkies
alsike
AEIKLT talkie
AEIKNS Eakins
kinase
AEIKNT Aitken
intake
kentia
AEIKNW Wankie
AEIKNZ kaizen
AEIKOR oakier
AEIKOS oakies
AEIKPR parkie
AEIKRS kaiser
AEIKRV Kaveri
AEILLM mallei
AEILLN lienal
lineal
AEILLR Allier
AEILLS allies
AEILLT taille
telial
AEILMN menial

AEILMP impale
AEILMR mailer
remail
AEILMS emails
mesial
samiel
AEILNO eolian
AEILNP alpine
Nepali
pineal
AEILNR aliner
larine
linear
nailer
AEILNS aliens
alines
lianes
saline
AEILNT entail
tineal
AEILNV alevin
alvine
valine
veinal
venial
AEILNX alexin
xenial
AEILOS Aeolis
AEILPS espial
laipse
lipase
Pelias
pileas
AEILPT aplite
Pilate
AEILQU equali
AEILRR railer
AEILRS ariels
Israel
sailer
serail
serial
AEILRT retail
retial
AEILRW wailer
AEILRZ lazier
AEILSS aisles
lassie
AEILST saltie
AEILSV Leavis
silvae
valise
AEILSY easily
AEILUV eluvia
AEIMMM mammie
AEIMMN ammine
AEIMMR maimer
AEIMNO anomie
AEIMNP pieman
AEIMNR airmen
marine
Namier

remain
AEIMNS Amiens
amines
animes
AEIMNT etamin
inmate
AEIMNX Xiamen
AEIMNY Niamey
AEIMPY pyemia
AEIMRS armies
maries
sarmie
AEIMRT imaret
matier
AEIMRU uremia
AEIMRW Weimar
AEIMRY rimaye
AEIMRZ mazier
AEIMST maties
samite
AEIMXX maxixe
AEINNO eonian
AEINNP pennia
pinnae
AEINNR narine
AEINNS inanes
insane
sienna
AEINNT innate
tannie
AEINNU Niuean
AEINNV Vienna
AEINOS Naoise
AEINPR Napier
rapine
AEINPT patine
Pétain
pineta
AEINRS arisen
arsine
sarnie
AEINRT ratine
retain
retina
AEINRV Erivan
ravine
vainer
AEINRZ zanier
AEINSS sanies
sasine
AEINST tisane
AEINSV naives
navies
savine
AEINSZ azines
zanies
AEINTU auntie
AEINTV native
AEINTY Yentai
AEIOPR Peoria
AEIOPS soapie
AEIOPT opiate
AEIOPZ epizoa
AEIORS ariose
AEIORV Aveiro
AEIOSV Savoie
AEIOVV Évvoia
AEIPPT Petipa
AEIPRR pairer
rapier
repair
AEIPRS aspire
paries
Persia
praise
spirea
AEIPRT pirate
AEIPSS sepias
AEIPST petsai
pietas
AEIPSV pavise
AEIRRS arsier
raiser
sairer
sierra
AEIRRT artier
AEIRRV arrive
Rivera
AEIRRW warier
AEIRSS arises
raises
serais
Sisera
AEIRST satire
striae
terais
AEIRSV Servia
varies
AEIRTT attire
ratite
AEIRTW waiter
AEIRVW waiver
wavier
AEIRVX Xavier
AEIRWX waxier
AEISST siesta
tassie
AEISSU Aussie
AEISSX axises
AEISSZ assize
AEISTX taxies
AEISTY aseity
AEISUY Ieyasu
AEISVW waives
AEITTT tattie
AEITTV vittae
AEJMMR jammer
AEJMRT ramjet
AEJMST jetsam
AEJMSV James V
AEJNNS Jansen
AEJNOT Taejon
AEJNST sejant
AEJNUU Juneau
AEJPRS japers
jasper
AEJPRY japery
AEJRSU Jaurès
AEJRUZ Juárez
AEJRVY jarvey
AEJRZZ jazzer
AEJSZZ jazzes
AEKKNR kraken
AEKKRY yakker
AEKLNR lanker
rankle
AEKLNS ankles
AEKLNT anklet
AEKLNW knawel
AEKLNY alkyne
AEKLOY Oakley
AEKLPS splake
AEKLRR larker
AEKLRS lakers
Lasker
slaker
AEKLRT talker
AEKLRW walker
AEKLSS Kassel
slakes
AEKLST lasket
AEKLSU Leukas
AEKLSV Levkás
AEKLTU auklet
AEKLWY weakly
AEKMNR Kerman
AEKMNU unmake
AEKMOT matoke
AEKMPU makeup
AEKMRR marker
remark
AEKMRS kermas
makers
masker
AEKMRT market
AEKMRU kumera
AEKNNY Kenyan
AEKNOR Korean
AEKNOT Keaton
AEKNOW awoken
AEKNPS pekans
AEKNRR ranker
AEKNRS nakers
AEKNRT tanker
AEKNRW Newark
wanker
AEKNSS skeans
snakes
sneaks
AEKNSV knaves
AEKNSW wakens
AEKNSY Sankey
sneaky
AEKOPT Topeka
AEKORS arkose
soaker
AEKOSY kayoes
AEKPRR parker
AEKPRS Parkes
AEKPSS speaks
AEKPTU takeup
uptake
AEKQRU quaker
AEKQSU quakes
squeak
AEKRRS rakers
AEKRSS askers
eskars
sakers
AEKRST skater
strake
streak
takers
tasker
AEKRSW wakers
wreaks
AEKSST skates
stakes
steaks
AEKSSU ukases
AEKSTW tweaks
AEKTWY tweaky
AEKWYY keyway
AELLLY leally
AELLMO Almelo
AELLMT mallet
AELLMU Lemalu
AELLMY lamely
AELLNY leanly
AELLPS lapels
AELLPT pallet
AELLPY palely
AELLRT taller
AELLRU allure
laurel
AELLRW waller
AELLRY really
AELLST sallet
AELLSY alleys
AELLTT tallet
AELLTU luteal
AELLTW wallet
AELLTY lately
lealty
AELLVW Wavell
AELLVY valley
AELMMR rammel
rammle
AELMMS lemmas
AELMNO melano
AELMNS Anselm
lemans
Le Mans
mensal
AELMNT lament
mantel
mantle
mental

AELMNW lawmen
AELMNY laymen
Manley
meanly
namely
AELMOR morale
AELMOS Salome
AELMPR lamper
palmer
AELMPS maples
sample
AELMPU ampule
AELMRS realms
AELMRT armlet
martel
AELMRU mauler
AELMRV marvel
AELMRY Marley
AELMST lamest
metals
AELMSU Samuel
ulemas
AELMSY measly
AELMTU amulet
muleta
AELMTY tamely
AELNNR lanner
AELNOR loaner
reloan
AELNOS anoles
lanose
AELNOT etalon
tolane
AELNPR planer
replan
AELNPS Naples
panels
planes
AELNPT planet
platen
AELNPU Plauen
AELNRS learns
nerals
AELNRT antler
learnt
rental
AELNRU Lauren
neural
unreal
AELNRV nerval
verlan
vernal
AELNRY larney
nearly
AELNSU unseal
AELNSV navels
Valens
AELNSY sanely
AELNTT latent
latten
talent
AELNTU eluant
lunate
AELNTV levant
AELNTY neatly
AELOPP Aleppo
AELOPR parole
AELOPS aslope
El Paso
AELOPT pelota
AELOPX poleax
AELORS solera
AELOST osteal
AELOSU Aeolus
AELOSV loaves
AELOSZ azoles
AELOTZ zealot
AELOVV volvae
AELPPR lapper
rappel
AELPPS appels
apples
AELPPT applet
lappet
AELPPU papule
AELPPY appley
AELPQU plaque
AELPRR parrel
AELPRS lapser
pearls
AELPRT palter
plater
AELPRU pleura
AELPRY parley
pearly
player
replay
AELPSS lapses
passel
sepals
AELPST palest
pastel
petals
plates
pleats
septal
staple
tepals
AELPTT Platte
AELQSU equals
squeal
AELQUY Quayle
AELQUZ quezal
AELRRT retral
AELRRY rarely
AELRSS lasers
AELRST alerts
alters
artels
estral
laster
ratels
salter
slater
staler
stelar
talers
AELRSU saurel
AELRSV lavers
ravels
salver
serval
slaver
AELRSW walers
warsle
AELRSY layers
relays
slayer
AELRTT latter
rattle
AELRTV travel
varlet
AELRTW Walter
AELRTY elytra
lyrate
raylet
realty
AELRUV valuer
AELRVY Valéry
AELRWY lawyer
Warley
AELRYY yarely
yearly
AELRZZ razzle
AELSSS Elsass
lasses
AELSST salets
slates
stales
steals
tassel
teslas
AELSSV salves
selvas
slaves
valses
AELSSW awless
swales
AELSTT latest
lattes
AELSTU salute
AELSTV valets
vestal
AELSTX exalts
AELSTY slatey
AELSUV values
AELSUX sexual
AELSVV valves
AELSVY slavey
sylvae
AELSYZ sleazy
AELTTT tattle
AELTTW wattle
AELTTY lyttae
AELTUX luxate
AELUUV uvulae
AELUVV vulvae
AEMMMT mammet
AEMMNR merman
AEMMOR Mamoré
AEMMRR rammer
AEMMRY yammer
AEMMRZ mamzer
AEMMST stemma
AEMMSU summae
AEMMSY mameys
AEMMTU maumet
AEMNNP penman
AEMNNR manner
AEMNNW Newman
AEMNNY Nyeman
AEMNOP mopane
AEMNOR enamor
Merano
moaner
AEMNOT omenta
AEMNOU Nouméa
AEMNOY yeoman
AEMNPU pneuma
AEMNQU manque
AEMNRS Mearns
remans
AEMNRT marten
AEMNRU manure
AEMNSS manses
AEMNST aments
mantes
stamen
AEMNSU unseam
AEMNSV mavens
AEMNSY yamens
AEMNTX taxmen
AEMORR remora
roamer
AEMORS ramose
AEMORT omerta
AEMORU Moreau
AEMORW womera
AEMORX xeroma
AEMPPR mapper
pamper
preamp
AEMPRR prearm
AEMPRT tamper
AEMPRV revamp
vamper
AEMQRU marque
AEMQSU masque
AEMRRR marrer
AEMRRS rearms
AEMRRU armure
AEMRRW rewarm
warmer
AEMRSS masers
Ramses
smears
AEMRST armets
master

maters
stream
tamers
AEMRSU Maseru
AEMRSY Ramsey
smeary
AEMRSZ mazers
AEMRTT matter
AEMRTU mature
Mutare
AEMSSS masses
AEMSST steams
AEMSSU amuses
assume
AEMSSY Massey
AEMSSZ smazes
AEMSTT mattes
tamest
AEMSTU meatus
AEMSTY mayest
steamy
AEMSUV mauves
AEMSYZ zymase
AEMTTU mutate
AENNNS Nansen
AENNOV novena
AENNOY anyone
AENNRS Sarnen
Sennar
AENNRT tanner
AENNRV Vänern
AENNRW wanner
AENNSS sennas
AENNST Nantes
AENNTT tenant
AENOPS paeons
AENOPW weapon
AENOPY paeony
AENORS reason
senora
AENORT atoner
ornate
AENORV Averno
Verona
AENOSS season
AENOST atones
AENOSX axones
AENOTT notate
AENOTZ zonate
AENPPR napper
parpen
AENPPS nappes
AENPRT arpent
entrap
parent
trepan
AENPRW enwrap
AENPRY napery
AENPRZ panzer
AENPSS aspens
AENPST patens
AENPTT patent
patten
AENPTU peanut
AENQSU queans
AENRRS snarer
AENRRT errant
ranter
AENRRW warner
warren
AENRSS Nasser
sarsen
snares
AENRST antres
astern
Santer
sterna
AENRSV Anvers
ravens
AENRSW answer
AENRSY senary
yearns
AENRTT natter
AENRTU nature
AENRTV tavern
Traven
AENRTW wanter
AENRWY yawner
AENSST assent
sanest
stanes
AENSSU anuses
AENSTU Austen
unseat
AENSTX sextan
AENSUV naevus
AENSUY uneasy
AENSVW navews
AENSWY sawney
AENTTU attune
tauten
Tetuán
AENTTX extant
AENTTY tetany
AENTWY tawney
AEOPPS appose
AEOPQU opaque
AEOPRS operas
Pesaro
AEOPRT Pareto
protea
AEOPRU Europa
AEOPSS Pessoa
AEOPST potaes
AEOPTT teapot
AEOPTY teapoy
AEORRR roarer
AEORRS soarer
AEORSS serosa
soares
AEORST orates
AEORSU arouse
Roseau
AEORSZ Azores
AEORTT rotate
AEORVW avower
AEORZZ Arezzo
AEOSTZ azotes
AEOTTU outate
outeat
AEOUVZ zouave
AEPPRR rapper
AEPPRS papers
sapper
AEPPRT tapper
AEPPRU pauper
AEPPRY papery
prepay
yapper
AEPPTT tappet
AEPPTU pupate
AEPRRS parers
parser
rasper
sparer
AEPRRT prater
AEPRRU parure
uprear
AEPRRW prewar
rewrap
warper
AEPRRY prayer
AEPRSS aspers
parses
repass
spares
sparse
spears
AEPRST paters
prates
repast
tapers
trapes
AEPRSU pareus
pauser
AEPRSV pavers
AEPRSX praxes
AEPRSY payers
repays
AEPRTT patter
AEPRTU uprate
AEPRUY yauper
AEPRWY yawper
AEPSSS passes
AEPSST pastes
spates
stapes
AEPSSU pauses
upases
AEPSTT aptest
AEPSTX expats
AEPSUX auspex
AEQRRU quarer
AEQRSU square
AEQRTU quarte
quatre
AEQRUV quaver
AEQSUY queasy
AEQTTU Quetta
AERRSS rasers
AERRST arrest
rarest
raster
Sartre
starer
AERRSV ravers
AERRSZ razers
AERRTT ratter
AERRTY artery
AERSSS rasses
sasers
AERSST assert
asters
reasts
stares
AERSSU assure
AERSSV savers
AERSSW sawers
swears
wrasse
AERSSY sayers
AERSTT stater
taster
taters
tetras
treats
AERSTU Atreus
Seurat
urates
AERSTV averts
starve
traves
vaster
AERSTW tawers
waster
waters
AERSTX extras
taxers
AERSTY estray
stayer
yarest
AERSTZ ersatz
AERSUU aureus
uraeus
AERSUV suaver
AERSUZ azures
Suárez
AERSVV varves
AERSVW wavers
AERSVY Savery
AERSWX waxers
AERSWY sawyer
swayer
AERSZZ razzes
AERTTT tatter
AERTTY treaty
yatter
AERTUU auteur

AERTWY watery
AERTYZ azerty
AESSSS assess
sasses
AESSST assets
tasses
AESSSY essays
AESSTT states
tasset
tastes
AESSTU sautes
AESSTV staves
vestas
AESSTW sweats
tawses
wastes
AESSTY yeasts
AESTTT attest
AESTTU astute
statue
AESTWY sweaty
AESTYY yeasty
AESVWY waveys
AFFGUW guffaw
AFFHIO Offiah
AFFIKR kaffir
AFFILP pilaff
AFFIMR affirm
AFFINR Fafnir
AFFIRT tariff
AFFLOY layoff
Offaly
AFFLSU luffas
AFFLUX afflux
AFFLWY waffly
AFFNSY nyaffs
AFFOPY payoff
AFFORR Forfar
AFFQSU quaffs
AFFSST staffs
AFGGIO Foggia
AFGGLY flaggy
AFGGOT faggot
AFGIJM figjam
AFGIKN faking
AFGIMN faming
AFGINO Fangio
AFGINR faring
AFGINT fating
AFGINX faxing
AFGINY faying
AFGINZ fazing
AFGISY gasify
AFGLNO flagon
AFGLNU fungal
AFGLOS oflags
AFGLRU frugal
AFGMNU Fa Ngum
AFGNOS ganofs
AFGORT forgat
AFGOST fagots
AFGOTU fugato
AFGRST grafts
AFGRUY argufy
AFHIIR hairif
AFHIKL khalif
AFHIKR kharif
AFHIMS famish
AFHIOS oafish
AFHIRS sharif
AFHIST faiths
AFHLMU fulham
AFHLOO loofah
AFHLSY flashy
AFHMOT fathom
AFHNOS Foshan
AFHORS shofar
AFHRSW wharfs
AFHSST shafts
AFIIJN Fijian
AFIILL filial
AFIILN finial
AFIILO Olaf II
AFIIMN infima
AFIJNU Fujian
AFIKLS kalifs
AFIKRS fakirs
kafirs
AFIKRU Faruk I
AFILLS flails
AFILMU famuli
AFILMY family
AFILNS finals
AFILNU infula
AFILNV flavin
AFILNY Finlay
naifly
AFILOR foliar
AFILRS flairs
frails
AFILRY fairly
AFILRZ frazil
AFILSY salify
AFIMNR firman
AFIMNY infamy
AFIMRT maftir
AFIMRY ramify
AFIMSS massif
AFIMUY Faiyûm
AFIMUZ umfazi
AFINNN finnan
AFINNO fanion
AFINNT infant
AFINRU unfair
AFINST faints
AFINSU fusain
AFINYZ nazify
AFIQRS faqirs
AFIRRS friars
AFIRRY friary
AFIRST afrits
AFIRTY ratify
AFJLRU jarful
AFKLNS flanks
AFKLSS flasks
AFKNRS franks
AFKOST koftas
AFLLOR floral
AFLLOW fallow
AFLLPU lapful
AFLLTY flatly
AFLLUW lawful
AFLMNU manful
AFLMNY flyman
AFLMOR formal
AFLMOU Malouf
AFLMRU armful
fulmar
AFLMYY mayfly
AFLNOT fontal
AFLNPU panful
AFLNTU flaunt
AFLOOS loofas
AFLORS floras
AFLORV flavor
AFLOST floats
AFLOTY floaty
AFLRTU artful
AFLSTU faults
flatus
AFLSWY sawfly
AFLTUY faulty
AFLWYY flyway
AFMNOR Forman
AFMNOT fantom
AFMOOS samfoo
AFMORT format
AFMOSU famous
AFNNOS fanons
AFNPRY frypan
AFNRSS snarfs
AFNSUU Faunus
AFORRW farrow
AFORRY orfray
AFORSV favors
AFORSY forays
AFORSZ Sforza
AFORUV favour
AFOSSS fossas
AFOSST fatsos
softas
AFRSTU frusta
AGGGIN gaging
AGGGOS goggas
AGGHIS haggis
AGGHSY shaggy
AGGIIL gilgai
AGGILO loggia
AGGIMN gaming
AGGINP gaping
paging
AGGINR raging
AGGINT gating
AGGINW waging
AGGINZ gazing
AGGIWW wigwag
AGGIZZ zigzag
AGGLNY gangly
AGGLSY slaggy
AGGLWY waggly
AGGMOT maggot
AGGMRU muggar
AGGNOW waggon
AGGNRU nuggar
AGGNSY snaggy
AGGQUY quaggy
AGHHSU haughs
AGHILN haling
AGHILT alight
AGHINR haring
AGHINS hangis
Hsiang
AGHINT hating
AGHINV having
AGHINW hawing
AGHINY haying
AGHINZ hazing
AGHIPS Pisgah
AGHIQU quaigh
AGHIRR gharri
AGHIRS garish
AGHIRT aright
AGHISU aguish
AGHISZ ghazis
AGHKNU Hanguk
AGHLNY Lynagh
AGHLSU laughs
AGHNNU hungan
AGHNOS hogans
Shango
AGHNPU hangup
AGHNRT thrang
AGHNSW whangs
AGHNTU naught
AGHNUY gunyah
AGHOQU quahog
AGHPRS graphs
AGHRRY gharry
AGHRST garths
AGHSSU saughs
AGHSTU aughts
ghauts
AGHTTU taught
AGIIJN gaijin
AGIIKL Kigali
AGIILN ailing
Iligan
nilgai
AGIIMN aiming
AGIINR airing
AGIIST atigis
AGIISV vigias
AGIIUX Xia Gui
AGIJNP japing
AGIJNW jawing
AGIJSW jigsaw
AGIKLN Glinka
AGIKMN making

AGIKNN Anking
AGIKNR raking
AGIKNS asking
gaskin
kiangs
Sikang
AGIKNT taking
AGIKNW waking
AGILLU ligula
AGILMN laming
lingam
malign
AGILMO glioma
AGILMP magilp
AGILMY gamily
AGILNP paling
AGILNS algins
aligns
lasing
lingas
signal
AGILNU lingua
AGILNV laving
AGILNW lawing
waling
AGILNY gainly
laying
AGILNZ lazing
AGILOR gloria
AGILOS oilgas
AGILOT galiot
AGILOV ogival
AGILPU Puglia
AGILRS glairs
AGILRY glairy
AGILSS siglas
AGILSW wilgas
AGIMNN naming
AGIMNR arming
margin
AGIMNS gamins
AGIMNT mating
taming
AGIMNY maying
AGIMNZ mazing
AGIMOS amigos
AGIMSS sigmas
AGIMST stigma
AGIMWW wigwam
AGINNP paning
AGINNQ Anqing
AGINNT anting
AGINNW awning
waning
AGINOR Girona
oaring
onagri
origan
AGINOS ngaios
Saigon
AGINPR paring
raping
AGINPT taping
AGINPV paving
AGINPW pawing
AGINPY paying
AGINRR raring
AGINRS arsing
grains
rasing
AGINRT gratin
rating
taring
AGINRV raving
AGINRW waring
AGINRX raxing
AGINRY grainy
raying
AGINRZ razing
AGINSS assign
AGINST gainst
giants
sating
tangis
AGINSV saving
AGINSW sawing
AGINSY saying
AGINTW tawing
AGINTX taxing
AGINVW waving
AGINWX waxing
AGINWY yawing
AGIORU giaour
AGIORV virago
AGIOTU agouti
AGIRST gratis
AGIRSV virgas
AGIRTU guitar
AGISST agists
AGJLMO logjam
AGJLSU jugals
AGJNOR jargon
AGKLNO kalong
AGKLOT kgotla
AGKLOU kagoul
AGKNOR Angkor
AGKNRU kurgan
AGKOPS gopaks
AGLLNO gallon
AGLLOP gallop
AGLLPU Gallup
AGLLSU gallus
AGLMMO Glomma
AGLMOR glamor
AGLMSU mulgas
AGLNNO longan
AGLNNU lungan
AGLNOO lagoon
AGLNOP Pagnol
AGLNOS logans
slogan
AGLNOT Galton
AGLNOU lanugo
Lugano
AGLNOY Loyang
AGLNRS gnarls
AGLNRU langur
AGLNRY gnarly
AGLNSS slangs
AGLNSY slangy
AGLNTY tangly
AGLNUU ungual
ungula
AGLOOS agloos
AGLOOT galoot
AGLOPS galops
AGLORS argols
gorals
Goslar
largos
AGLOSS glossa
AGLOST gloats
AGLOSV galvos
AGLOWY logway
AGLPUY plaguy
AGLRSU Glarus
AGLRUV vulgar
AGLRUY glaury
AGLRYY grayly
AGLSSY glassy
AGLSUV valgus
AGMMNO gammon
AGMMNU magnum
AGMMSU gummas
AGMNNU gunman
AGMNOR morgan
AGMNOS mangos
ngomas
AGMNOX magnox
AGMNSU magnus
mungas
AGMNUY maungy
AGMOOY oogamy
AGMORS orgasm
AGMORV vagrom
AGMOST magots
AGMOYZ zygoma
AGMPUZ gazump
AGMRTU Targum
AGMSTU gamuts
AGNNOY Yangon
AGNNRU Gunnar
AGNNRY granny
AGNNTU Antung
AGNOPS pongas
AGNOQU quango
AGNORR garron
AGNORS groans
nagors
orangs
organs
sarong
AGNOST sontag
tangos
tongas
AGNOSW gowans
wagons
AGNOTU nougat
AGNOWY gowany
AGNPRS prangs
sprang
AGNPRU Nagpur
AGNPSU pungas
AGNRST grants
AGNRSW wrangs
AGNRTY gantry
AGNSST stangs
AGNSSU sugans
AGNSTW twangs
AGNSTY angsty
AGNTUY Tanguy
AGNTWY twangy
AGOORT agorot
AGORST argots
groats
AGORSY argosy
AGORTU ragout
AGOSTU outgas
AGOSTV gavots
AGOSYZ gyozas
AGOTTU tautog
AGPRSS grasps
sprags
AGRSSU sugars
AGRSSY grassy
AGRSTU tragus
AGRSUU augurs
AGRSUY sugary
AGRUUY augury
AGSTUU august
AHHIJR hijrah
AHHISV shivah
AHHKOO hookah
AHHLPY hyphal
AHHOOR hoorah
AHHORT Hathor
AHHORW Howrah
AHHPPU huppah
AHHRRU hurrah
AHHRST thrash
AHHUZZ huzzah
AHIILT lithia
AHIINT tahini
AHIISS shiais
AHIITT Tahiti
AHIJJS hajjis
AHIJNN Jinnah
AHIJNS Jhansi
AHIJOS Josiah
AHIKKS khakis
AHIKMO Kohima
AHIKMS hakims
AHIKMV mikvah
AHIKOW kowhai
AHIKRS rakish
shikar
AHIKSS shiksa
AHIKST Shakti

AHIKSZ khazis
AHILLP phalli
AHILLT thalli
AHILLZ zillah
AHILMP Imphal
AHILMU hamuli
AHILNR rhinal
AHILNU inhaul
AHILNY hyalin
linhay
AHILOS Lashio
AHILPS palish
phials
AHILPT Lapith
AHILPZ Zilpah
AHILST lathis
latish
tahsil
AHILSV lavish
AHILTW withal
AHILYZ hazily
AHIMNO Namhoi
AHIMNS Mishna
AHIMOR mohair
AHIMPS mishap
AHIMRS ihrams
marish
Shamir
AHINPT hatpin
AHINRS Shinar
AHINRU unhair
AHINSS nashis
Shansi
AHINSU Husain
AHINSV vanish
AHINSW washin
AHINSX Shanxi
AHIOPS Sophia
AHIORS orisha
AHIORT thoria
AHIOST Taisho
AHIPRS parish
raphis
AHIPRU rupiah
AHIPSS spahis
AHIPTY Pythia
AHIRRS arrish
Harris
sirrah
AHIRRW wirrah
AHIRST airths
Ishtar
AHIRSV ravish
AHIRSW rawish
wairsh
AHIRSZ Shiraz
AHIRTW wraith
AHISSW siwash
AHISTU hiatus
AHISTV Vashti
AHJOSU Joshua
AHJSTU thujas
AHKKSU sukkah
AHKLNU Khulna
AHKMOS moksha
AHKMOW mohawk
AHKNOT Khotan
AHKNOW Hankow
AHKNPU punkah
AHKNRS shrank
AHKNSS shanks
AHKNST thanks
AHKOOS hookas
AHKOSS shakos
AHKPUU hapuku
AHKRSS sharks
AHKRTU khurta
AHLLMO mollah
AHLLMU mullah
AHLLNU nullah
AHLLOO halloo
holloa
AHLLOS hallos
hollas
AHLLOT hallot
AHLLOW hallow
AHLLRT thrall
AHLLUX hallux
AHLMNY Hamlyn
hymnal
AHLMOO moolah
AHLMOS shalom
AHLMSU haulms
AHLNOS halons
lohans
AHLNOT Halton
AHLNSU uhlans
unlash
AHLOOP hoopla
AHLORT harlot
AHLORW Harlow
Warhol
AHLOSS shoals
AHLOST lotahs
AHLOSY shoaly
AHLPSS splash
AHLPSU sulpha
AHLPSY plashy
AHLRSY rashly
AHLSSW shawls
AHLTUZ halutz
AHMMSY shammy
AHMMWY whammy
AHMNNU numnah
AHMNOS hansom
AHMNPY nympha
AHMNSU Hamsun
humans
AHMNSY mynahs
AHMNTU Uthman
AHMOOP oompah
AHMORY moryah
AHMORZ mahzor
AHMOST Thomas
AHMOSV moshav
AHMOTU mahout
AHMOTZ matzoh
AHMOWY haymow
AHMPSU mashup
AHMRSY marshy
AHMRTW warmth
AHMSSU samshu
shamus
AHMSSW shawms
AHNNSY shanny
AHNOPR orphan
AHNOPY aphony
AHNORS sharon
shoran
AHNOST Ashton
AHNOWY anyhow
AHNRTW thrawn
AHNRVY hryvna
AHNSST snaths
AHNSTU haunts
sunhat
Ushant
AHNSTY shanty
AHNTTU U Thant
AHOORS shoora
AHOORY hooray
AHOOSW wahoos
AHOOSY yahoos
AHOPPS Paphos
Sappho
AHOPRS pharos
phasor
AHOPST pathos
potash
AHOQTU quotha
AHORRW harrow
AHORRY horary
AHORTT throat
AHORTU author
AHORTX thorax
AHOSST hoasts
hostas
shoats
Thásos
AHOTWZ howzat
AHPRRY Pyrrha
AHPRSS sharps
AHPSUW washup
whaups
AHQSSU squash
AHRRTU Arthur
AHRRUY hurray
AHRSSU Asshur
hussar
AHRSTT strath
AHRSTW swarth
wraths
AHRSTY trashy
AHRTTW thwart
AHRTWY wrathy
AHSSTU tussah
AHSSTW swaths
AHSTUY thuyas
AIIJSV Sivaji
AIIKLS Likasi
AIILMN limina
AIILRY airily
AIIMMN minima
AIIMMR Miriam
AIIMNS simian
AIIMNT intima
AIIMNV vimina
AIIMOR moirai
AIIMPR impair
AIIMRY Mary II
AIIMST samiti
AIINNN Ninian
AIINNO Ionian
AIINNZ zinnia
AIINRS raisin
AIINRZ Rinzai
AIINST isatin
AIINSX sixain
AIINTT titian
AIINVV Ivan IV
Vivian
AIIORS ariosi
AIIPTW wapiti
AIIRST Istria
AIIRTV trivia
AIISSS Assisi
AIITUW tauiwi
AIJJNU Ujjain
AIJKNS kanjis
AIJLMS majlis
AIJLNU Julian
AIJLOR jailor
AIJLOV jovial
AIJMNP Panjim
AIJMOR romaji
AIJNNS ninjas
AIJNOV Jovian
AIJPRU Jaipur
AIKLMN malkin
AIKLNO kaolin
AIKLNR Larkin
AIKLST tilaks
AIKLSU saluki
AIKLSZ Kalisz
AIKLTU likuta
AIKMNS kamsin
AIKMNW mawkin
AIKMOO oomiak
AIKMOP Maikop
AIKMOT Komati
AIKMSU Kumasi
umiaks
AIKNNN nankin
AIKNNP napkin
AIKNPR kirpan
parkin
AIKNRT kirtan
AIKNRU Kiruna

AIKNRV Narvik
AIKNST Atkins
Kistna
takins
AIKNSU nikaus
Suakin
AIKOPS okapis
AIKOPT katipo
AIKORT troika
AIKOTW kwaito
AIKPPS kippas
AIKPSU pikaus
AIKRRS karris
AIKRST kraits
AIKRSU kauris
AIKSST sitkas
AIKTUW Kuwait
AILLMU allium
AILLMY Millay
AILLPR pillar
AILLST tallis
AILLSV villas
AILLSW Wallis
AILLSZ zillas
AILLTT tallit
AILLUZ lazuli
AILLYZ lazily
AILMNO Molina
oilman
AILMNR marlin
AILMNU alumni
lumina
AILMNY mainly
AILMOP lipoma
AILMOS Siloam
Somali
AILMOT maloti
Tolima
AILMPR primal
AILMRT mitral
ramtil
AILMSS missal
salmis
AILMST mistal
smalti
AILMSU miauls
AILMSX smilax
AILMSY mislay
AILMTU Latium
ultima
Umtali
AILMYZ mazily
AILNNU annuli
AILNOP Napoli
AILNOS alison
AILNOT latino
talion
AILNPS plains
spinal
AILNPT plaint
pliant
AILNPU Ulpian

AILNRT ratlin
trinal
AILNRU urinal
AILNSS snails
AILNST instal
Stalin
AILNSU insula
AILNSV anvils
silvan
AILNSY inlays
AILNTY litany
AILNVY vainly
AILNYZ zanily
AILOPS pilaos
AILORS sailor
AILORT rialto
tailor
AILORU Auriol
AILOSS assoil
AILOSV Valois
violas
AILOSX oxalis
AILOTX oxtail
AILPPS pipals
AILPRS spiral
AILPST pastil
plaits
spital
AILPUV Paul VI
AILQSU quails
AILRRW Wirral
AILRST trails
trials
AILRSV rivals
AILRSY riyals
AILRTU ritual
AILRWY warily
AILSSS sisals
AILSSV silvas
AILSSY Lysias
AILSTU situla
AILSTV vitals
AILSUV visual
AILSVZ vizsla
AILTXY laxity
AILVWY wavily
AILWXY waxily
AIMMOS mimosa
AIMMSU imaums
AIMMSX maxims
AIMNNO amnion
nomina
AIMNNU numina
AIMNNY minyan
AIMNOP mopani
AIMNOS Osman I
AIMNOT manito
AIMNPT pitman
AIMNPY paynim
AIMNRT Antrim
martin
AIMNRU rumina

AIMNST mantis
matins
AIMNSU animus
AIMNSV mavins
AIMNSY Mysian
AIMNSZ nizams
AIMNTT mattin
titman
AIMNTU manitu
AIMNUZ mizuna
AIMOPT optima
AIMOPY myopia
AIMOST Taoism
AIMOSU miaous
AIMOSV Asimov
AIMOSW miaows
AIMOSX axioms
AIMPRS Pamirs
AIMPRT armpit
impart
AIMPSS passim
AIMQSU maquis
AIMRRS marris
AIMRSS simars
AIMRST amrits
Marist
AIMRSU Marius
mauris
AIMRSW Wismar
AIMRSZ mirzas
AIMRTU atrium
Timaru
AIMRTX matrix
AIMSSW swamis
AIMSTU autism
AINNNT tannin
AINNOS anions
nasion
AINNOT anoint
nation
AINNPS inspan
pinnas
AINNST Tsinan
AINOPR porina
AINOPS pianos
Pisano
AINOQU Aquino
AINORS norias
AINORT aroint
ration
AINORZ Azorín
AINOSS Ossian
AINOSX axions
AINPRS sprain
AINPRW inwrap
AINPST paints
patins
ptisan
AINPSV spavin
AINPTU tipuna
AINPTY painty
AINQRT qintar

AINQTU quaint
quinta
AINRST instar
Sintra
strain
trains
AINRSV ravins
AINRSY Syrian
AINRTU nutria
AINSSS sasins
AINSST saints
satins
stains
AINSSW swains
AINSTT statin
taints
tanist
titans
AINSTU Austin
AINSTW witans
AINSTY sanity
satiny
AINSYZ zayins
AINTVY vanity
AIOORS arioso
AIOPRV pavior
AIOPST patios
patois
AIOPTU utopia
AIORSS Orissa
AIORST aorist
aristo
Artois
ratios
satori
AIORSV savior
AIORSX orixas
AIORTV viator
AIOSYZ zoysia
AIPPRR riprap
AIPPRY papyri
AIPPST papist
AIPRST rapist
tapirs
AIPRSV parvis
AIPRSW ripsaw
AIPRSX praxis
AIPRTY parity
AIPRUY pyuria
AIPSST pastis
AIPSTW pitsaw
sawpit
AIPSZZ pizzas
AIPZZZ pizazz
AIQRSU quairs
AIRRTY rarity
AIRSST sistra
sitars
stairs
AIRSSU russia
AIRSSZ sizars
AIRSTT artist

strait
strati
traits
AIRSTU aurist
AIRSTY Styria
AIRTTT attrit
AIRTTY yttria
AISSST assist
stasis
AISSTU Assiut
AISSTV vistas
AISSTW waists
AJKNSY jansky
AJKORS rojaks
AJKORT Rajkot
AJLOPS jalops
AJLOPY jalopy
AJMORS majors
AJMRSU jumars
AJNSTU jaunts
juntas
AJNTUY jaunty
AJORRW Jarrow
AJPRTU Rajput
AJRSTU jurats
AKKKOO kokako
AKKLSU kulaks
AKKNSS skanks
AKKNSY skanky
AKKOOP pakoko
AKKOQU quokka
AKKORU Kokura
AKKORW Kraków
AKLLNY lankly
AKLLSY alkyls
AKLMOR Kolmar
AKLMOY Kolyma
AKLMUU Maluku
AKLNOX klaxon
AKLNPS planks
AKLNRY rankly
AKLNSU kulans
AKLOPS polkas
Polska
AKLOSV Slovak
AKLOVY Kvaløy
AKLPTU uptalk
AKLPUW walkup
AKLRVY valkyr
AKLSST stalks
AKLSTU taluks
AKLSTY stalky
AKLSUW waulks
AKMNSU unmask
AKMORS kormas
AKMOSV Moskva
AKMPRU markup
AKNNNO Kannon
AKNNOO nanook
AKNORU koruna
AKNORY ryokan
AKNPRS pranks
AKNPRU Kanpur
AKNPSS spanks
AKNPSU punkas
AKNRRY knarry
AKNRSY snarky
AKNRUU Nakuru
AKNSST stanks
AKNSSW swanks
AKNSUZ kanzus
AKNSWY swanky
AKOORR karroo
AKOORS karoos
AKOOSZ kazoos
AKOPPS koppas
AKOPRV Karpov
AKOPSY yapoks
AKORSS kaross
AKORSU kouras
AKOSTY tokays
AKOTWY towkay
AKPRSS sparks
AKPRSY sparky
AKPSSU Puskas
AKQRSU quarks
AKQSUW squawk
AKRSTU krauts
kurtas
ALLMOS slalom
ALLMOW mallow
ALLMSS smalls
ALLMSU mullas
ALLMSY myalls
ALLMUV vallum
ALLNOP pollan
ALLNOS llanos
ALLNUU lunula
ALLOOP apollo
palolo
ALLOOY Loyola
ALLOPR pallor
ALLOPW wallop
ALLORY orally
ALLOSS salols
ALLOST allots
atolls
ALLOSW allows
sallow
ALLOSY alloys
ALLOTW tallow
ALLOUY allyou
ALLOVY ovally
ALLOWW wallow
ALLPRU plural
ALLPSS spalls
ALLPSY psylla
ALLQSU squall
ALLRUY lauryl
ALLSST stalls
ALLSTY lastly
ALLUVV vulval
ALMMOW Mowlam
ALMMUW wammul
ALMMUY amylum
ALMNOR Molnár
normal
ALMNOS monals
salmon
ALMNOU monaul
ALMNTU Multan
ALMORS molars
morals
ALMORT mortal
ALMORU morula
ALMORY Malory
ALMOST almost
matlos
smalto
ALMOTW matlow
ALMPSS plasms
psalms
ALMQSU qualms
ALMRSU larums
murals
ALMRWY warmly
ALMSUY asylum
ALMTUU mutual
umlaut
ALNNOU nounal
ALNNSU annuls
ALNOOS saloon
ALNOOZ zoonal
ALNOPS nopals
ALNORS lorans
ALNOSS salons
solans
ALNOST talons
ALNOSW Lawson
lowans
ALNOTV volant
ALNOTW Walton
ALNPST plants
ALNRSS snarls
ALNRSY snarly
ALNRUY uranyl
ALNRXY larynx
ALNSST slants
ALNSTU sultan
ALNSUY unlays
yulans
ALNSVY sylvan
ALNTUW walnut
ALOOPS saloop
ALOPPR poplar
ALOPPT laptop
ALOPRR parlor
ALOPRS parols
ALOPRT patrol
portal
ALOPST ploats
postal
ALOPVV Pavlov
ALOQTU loquat
ALORST sortal
ALORSV salvor
ALORSY royals
ALORTU Latour
La Tour
ALORTY Taylor
ALORUV louvar
ovular
valour
ALOSSS lassos
ALOSSV salvos
ALOSTT totals
ALOSVV volvas
ALOTUW outlaw
ALOTUY layout
outlay
ALPPSU palpus
ALPRRU larrup
ALPRSU pulsar
ALPRSW sprawl
ALPRTY paltry
partly
raptly
ALPSST splats
ALPSSU lapsus
ALPSSY splays
ALPSTY platys
ALRSST slarts
ALRSTU lustra
ultras
ALRSTW trawls
ALRSTY stylar
ALRSUU Ursula
ALRSUW walrus
ALRTTY rattly
tartly
ALRUUV uvular
ALRUVV vulvar
ALSSSU lassus
ALSSTU saltus
tussal
ALSSUU usuals
ALSSVY sylvas
ALSTTY lyttas
ALSTUV vaults
ALSTVY vastly
ALSUUV uvulas
ALSUVV vulvas
ALTTUY tautly
ALTUUV Tuvalu
AMMMNO mammon
AMMMOS mommas
AMMORT marmot
AMMOSU omasum
AMMOSY myomas
AMMOXY myxoma
AMMPUW wampum
AMMRSS smarms
AMMRSY smarmy
AMMSTU summat
AMMTUZ Tammuz
AMNNOR norman
AMNNOS Manson
AMNNOY anonym

AMNNSU unmans
AMNOOP Pomona
AMNOOR maroon
romano
AMNOPT potman
tampon
AMNORR marron
AMNORS manors
ransom
romans
AMNORT matron
AMNORY mornay
AMNOSS masons
Samson
AMNOST Nam Tso
tomans
AMNOSW Mawson
womans
AMNOTU amount
outman
AMNPTU Putnam
AMNPTY tympan
AMNQRU Qumran
AMNRSU Mansur
unarms
AMNRSY Smyrna
AMNRTU antrum
Truman
AMNSSU Samsun
AMNTTU mutant
AMNTUU autumn
AMOOTT tomato
AMOPST Patmos
AMOPTU Maputo
AMOQRS qormas
AMORRS armors
AMORRT mortar
AMORRU armour
AMORRW marrow
AMORRY armory
AMORSS morass
AMORST stroma
AMORSU amours
ramous
AMORSY mayors
morays
AMORTU Outram
AMORTZ Mozart
AMOSTW amowts
AMOSTZ matzos
motzas
AMPRRU Rampur
AMPRST tramps
AMPRUW warmup
AMPSSS spasms
AMPSST stamps
AMPSSW swamps
AMPSWY swampy
AMRRTY martyr
AMRRUY murray
AMRSST smarts
AMRSSU musars
AMRSSW swarms
AMRSTU struma
AMRSTY smarty
AMRTTU Muttra
AMSSSY Massys
AMSSTY Matsys
ANNNUY Yünnan
ANNOOX xoanon
ANNOPZ Poznań
ANNORT natron
ANNOST sonant
ANNOSW Wõnsan
ANNOSY annoys
ANNOTW wanton
ANNOTY Antony
tannoy
ANNPSU pannus
unsnap
ANNRTY tranny
ANNSTU suntan
ANNTTU nutant
ANOORS Sonora
ANOORT ratoon
ANOPRS aprons
parson
sanpro
ANOPRT parton
patron
tarpon
ANOPST pantos
ANOPSW powans
ANOPSY yapons
ANOPTT Patton
ANOPTX Paxton
ANOPTY Payton
ANOPUY yaupon
ANORRW narrow
ANORSS sonars
ANORST rotans
ANORSV sovran
ANORSW rowans
ANORSY rayons
ANORTT attorn
ANORTU outran
ANORTW Tarnów
Warton
ANORTY notary
ANORWY Norway
ANORYZ zonary
ANOSST santos
ANOSTU tauons
ANOSTW Watson
ANOSUY noyaus
ANOSWY noways
ANOSXY saxony
ANPPSY snappy
ANPRSW prawns
ANPRTY pantry
trypan
ANPRUW unwrap
ANPSSW spawns
ANPTUU tupuna
ANQSTU quants
ANRSTU Saturn
ANRSUU Uranus
ANRSUY sunray
ANRSYZ Syzran
ANRTTU truant
ANRTTY tyrant
ANRUWY runway
unwary
ANSSTU stauns
ANSSUY unsays
ANSTTU taunts
tutsan
ANSTUV vaunts
ANSTXY syntax
ANSYZZ snazzy
AOOPTT potato
AOOPTW Paotow
AOORRT orator
AOORRY arroyo
AOORSZ razoos
AOOTTT tattoo
AOPPRT apport
AOPRRT parrot
raptor
AOPRRU uproar
AOPRRW prowar
AOPRSS aspros
sapors
AOPRST pastor
portas
AOPRSU parous
AOPRSV vapors
AOPRUV vapour
AOPRVY vapory
AOPTUY payout
AOQRTU quarto
AOQSTU quotas
AORRST rostra
sartor
AORRSW arrows
AORRSY rosary
AORRSZ razors
AORRTY rotary
AORRWY yarrow
AORSST assort
roasts
AORSSV savors
AORSTT stator
tarots
troats
AORSTU soutar
AORSTX storax
AORSUU aurous
AORSUV savour
AORSVY savory
AORTVY votary
AOSSTT stoats
toasts
AOSSVY savoys
AOSTTU outsat
AOSTTY toasty
AOSTWW Swatow
APPPSU pappus
APRRSY sparry
APRSST sprats
straps
APRSSY sprays
APRSTY pastry
APSSSU passus
APSSTU stupas
APSSUW wassup
AQRRUY quarry
AQRSTU quarts
AQRTUZ quartz
AQSSTU squats
AQSSUW squaws
AQUYZZ quazzy
ARRSTY starry
ARSSST strass
ARSSTT starts
ARSSTU Straus
sutras
tarsus
ARSSTW straws
ARSSTY satyrs
strays
ARSTTU Stuart
tuarts
ARSTUU Taurus
ARSTUX surtax
ARSTWY strawy
ARSTXY styrax
ASSTTU status
BBBDEI bibbed
BBBDEO bobbed
BBBEIL bibble
BBBEIR bibber
BBBELO bobble
BBBELU bubble
BBBELY blebby
BBBHUU hubbub
BBBINO bobbin
BBBLOY blobby
BBBLUY bubbly
BBCDEO cobbed
BBCDEU cubbed
BBCEIR Cibber
BBCELO cobble
BBCEOR cobber
BBCEOW cobweb
BBCESU cubebs
BBCHUY chubby
BBCLUY clubby
BBDDEI dibbed
BBDDEO dobbed
BBDDEU dubbed
BBDEEW webbed
BBDEFI fibbed
BBDEFO fobbed
BBDEGI gibbed
BBDEGO gobbed
BBDEGU bedbug
BBDEHO hobbed

BBDEIJ jibbed
BBDEIL dibble
BBDEIN nibbed
BBDEIR bribed
dibber
ribbed
BBDEJO jobbed
BBDELO lobbed
BBDEMO bombed
mobbed
BBDEOO boobed
BBDEOR dobber
robbed
BBDEOS sobbed
BBDEPU pubbed
BBDERU rubbed
BBDESU subbed
BBDETU tubbed
BBDIKU dibbuk
BBDINO dobbin
BBDINU dubbin
BBDKUY dybbuk
BBDOSU dubbos
BBEEHL Hebbel
BBEEIW webbie
BBEELP pebble
BBEERS rebbes
BBEFIR fibber
BBEGIN Big Ben
ebbing
BBEGIR gibber
BBEGIT gibbet
BBEGLO gobble
BBEGNU Bengbu
BBEGOT gobbet
BBEHLO hobble
BBEHLU Hubble
BBEHOS Hobbes
BBEIIM imbibe
BBEIJR jibber
BBEIKL kibble
BBEILN nibble
BBEILR Ribble
BBEILS bibles
BBEILW wibble
BBEIRR briber
BBEIRS bribes
BBEJOR jobber
BBELLU bulbel
BBELMU bumble
BBELNO nobble
BBELNU nubble
BBELOT boblet
BBELOW wobble
BBELPY pebbly
plebby
BBELRU burble
lubber
rubble
BBEMNU benumb
BBEMOR bomber
mobber
BBEMOS bombes
BBENOW Benbow
BBEORR robber
BBEORS sobber
BBEOSU buboes
BBERRU rubber
BBERTU tubber
BBGINO gibbon
BBGRUY grubby
BBHIOT hobbit
BBHNOO hobnob
BBIIOO Bío-Bío
BBIIUU buibui
BBIKOS skibob
BBILLU bulbil
BBILOS bilbos
BBIMOS bimbos
BBINNU nubbin
BBINOR ribbon
robbin
BBKNOY knobby
BBLLUU bulbul
BBLNUY nubbly
BBLOOS bobols
BBLOWY blowby
wobbly
BBLRSU blurbs
BBLRUY rubbly
BBMRUY brumby
Bumbry
BBNNOO bonbon
BBNOOO bonobo
BBNOSY snobby
BBNOTU nobbut
BBNSUY snubby
BBOOOO booboo
BBOOSY yobbos
BBOOUU boubou
BBORTU burbot
BBOSUY busboy
BBRSUU suburb
BBSSTU Stubbs
BBSTUY stubby
BCCEIO boccie
BCDEEK bedeck
BCDEIO bodice
BCDEKO bocked
BCDEKU bucked
Dubček
BCDEMO combed
BCDENO Cobden
BCDERU curbed
BCDIOU cuboid
BCEEHR breech
BCEEHT Bechet
BCEEHY beechy
BCEEIR Bierce
BCEEKR Becker
rebeck
BCEEKT becket
BCEEKZ zebeck
BCEELS celebs
BCEELY Cybele
BCEEMO become
BCEEQU Quebec
BCEERS rebecs
BCEESX xebecs
BCEESZ zebecs
BCEHLN blench
BCEHNU Bunche
BCEHNY benchy
BCEHOR broche
BCEHOS boches
BCEHRT Brecht
BCEHRU cherub
BCEIIK bickie
BCEIIS ibices
BCEIKR bicker
BCEIKU buckie
BCEIKW Bewick
BCEIOR corbie
BCEIOX icebox
BCEIPS biceps
BCEIRS scribe
BCEIRT terbic
BCEIST bisect
BCEJOT object
BCEKLU buckle
Lübeck
BCEKNO beckon
BCEKRU bucker
BCEKTU bucket
BCELLO Belloc
BCELOR corbel
BCELOS cobles
BCELOU boucle
BCEMOO coombe
BCEMOR comber
BCEMOS combes
BCEMRU cumber
BCENOR Brecon
BCENOS bonces
BCENOU bounce
BCEOTT obtect
BCERSU cubers
BCGINU cubing
BCGORU coburg
BCGORY cyborg
BCHILO chibol
BCHIMS chimbs
BCHINY Binchy
BCHIOP phobic
BCHIRT bricht
BCHITY bitchy
BCHLOT blotch
BCHLSU schlub
BCHMOU Bochum
BCHNRU brunch
BCHNUY bunchy
BCHOOR brocho
brooch
BCHORS borsch
brochs
BCHOTY botchy
BCHSUU buchus
BCIILM limbic
BCIINO bionic
niobic
BCIINU incubi
BCIIOP biopic
BCIIOT biotic
BCIKNO kincob
BCIKRS bricks
BCIKRY bricky
BCILMO Imbolc
BCILMS climbs
BCILPU public
BCIMOR bromic
BCIMSU cubism
BCINOR bicorn
BCIORS borsic
sorbic
BCIRRU rubric
BCISTU cubist
cubits
BCKLOS blocks
BCKLOY blocky
BCKORS brocks
BCMOOS combos
coombs
BCMORY corymb
BCMRSU crumbs
BCMRUY crumby
BCNOOR bronco
BCNOSU buncos
BCNOTU cobnut
BCNOUY bouncy
BCOOSY scooby
BCOOWY cowboy
BCORSY Crosby
BCRSSU scrubs
BDDDEE bedded
BDDDEU budded
BDDEER bedder
breded
BDDEGO bodged
BDDEGU budged
BDDEIL Biddle
BDDEIN bidden
BDDEIO bodied
BDDEIR bidder
BDDELU buddle
BDDENO bonded
BDDERU redbud
BDDESU debuds
BDDISU disbud
BDEEEF beefed
BDEEEN bendee
BDEEEP beeped
BDEEGG begged
BDEEGR Edberg
BDEEHL beheld
BDEEIL belied
edible
BDEEIR bredie
BDEEIS beside

BDEEIT betide
BDEEJL djebel
BDEEJM djembe
BDEEKR kerbed
BDEELL bedell
belled
BDEELN blende
BDEELS bedels
bleeds
BDEELT belted
BDEEMS embeds
BDEENR bender
BDEEOY obeyed
BDEERS bredes
breeds
BDEERW brewed
BDEERY breyed
BDEEST bested
BDEESW bedews
dweebs
BDEETT betted
BDEEWY dweeby
BDEFFI biffed
BDEFFU buffed
BDEFIR fibred
BDEGGI bigged
BDEGGO bogged
BDEGGU bugged
BDEGIL bilged
BDEGIN binged
BDEGIO bodgie
bogied
BDEGIR begird
bridge
BDEGIU budgie
BDEGLO globed
BDEGLU bludge
bugled
bulged
BDEGNO bonged
BDEGNU bunged
BDEGOR bodger
BDEGOS bodges
BDEGRU redbug
BDEGSU budges
debugs
BDEGTU budget
BDEHIN behind
BDEHLO behold
BDEHOT hotbed
BDEHSU bushed
BDEIIR birdie
bridie
BDEIKL bilked
BDEILL billed
BDEILM limbed
BDEILO boiled
bolide
BDEILR birled
bridle
BDEILS bields
BDEIMS bedims
imbeds
BDEIMU imbued
BDEINN binned
BDEINR binder
brined
inbred
rebind
BDEINU beduin
BDEIOR boride
BDEIOS bodies
BDEIPS bipeds
BDEIRR birder
birred
BDEIRS breids
brides
debris
rebids
BDEIRU buried
BDEIRV verbid
BDEIST bedsit
bidets
debits
BDEISU busied
BDEITT bitted
BDEKLU bulked
BDEKNO bonked
BDEKNU bunked
debunk
BDEKOO booked
BDEKRU burked
BDEKSU busked
BDELLO Dobell
BDELLU bulled
BDELNO blonde
bolden
BDELNS blends
BDELNU bundle
BDELOO boodle
booled
BDELOR bolder
bordel
BDELOT bolted
BDELOU double
BDELOW blowed
bowled
BDELRU burled
BDEMMU bummed
BDEMNU numbed
BDEMOO boomed
BDEMOR bormed
BDEMOS demobs
BDEMOT tombed
BDEMOW wombed
BDEMOY embody
BDEMPU bumped
BDEMRU dumber
BDENNU unbend
BDENOR bonder
BDENOY beyond
BDENRU burden
burned
unbred
BDENTU bunted
BDEOOT booted
BDEOOZ boozed
BDEOPP bopped
BDEOPR probed
BDEORR border
BDEORS desorb
BDEORT Bordet
debtor
BDEORW browed
BDEOSS bossed
BDEOSU boused
BDEOSW bowsed
BDEOTT botted
BDEOUY buoyed
BDEPRU burped
BDERRU burred
deburr
BDESSU bussed
BDESTU busted
debuts
BDESUU subdue
BDETTU butted
BDEUZZ buzzed
BDFIOR forbid
BDGIIN biding
BDGIIR Brigid
BDGINO boding
BDGINY byding
BDHIIN bhindi
bindhi
BDHIOS dhobis
BDHIRY hybrid
BDHNSU bundhs
BDIILO libido
BDIIMR midrib
BDIITT tidbit
BDIKNO bodkin
BDILNS blinds
BDILNU Dublin
BDILOY bodily
BDILSU builds
BDIMNO Bodmin
BDIMOR morbid
BDINNU unbind
BDINOU boudin
BDIOOT biodot
BDIOPS bipods
BDIOSU Dubois
BDIOSV bovids
BDIOTU outbid
BDIRTU turbid
BDKLOO kobold
BDLLOY boldly
BDLMUY dumbly
BDLNOO doblon
BDLNOS blonds
BDLOOS bloods
BDLOOY bloody
BDLOUY doubly
BDNOOY nobody
BDNORY Drobny
BDNOSU bounds
BDNOTU obtund
BDOORS broods
droobs
BDOORY broody
BDORWY byword
BDOSTU doubts
BEEEFL feeble
BEEEHP ephebe
BEEELT beetle
BEEEMS beseem
BEEEPR beeper
BEEERZ beezer
breeze
BEEESV beeves
BEEFIL belief
BEEFLL befell
BEEFLY feebly
BEEFOR before
BEEFRT bereft
BEEGHR Gheber
BEEGIL beigel
BEEGIS beiges
BEEGIY bigeye
BEEGLS glebes
BEEGNO begone
BEEGNR bergen
BEEGOR greebo
BEEGRS grebes
BEEGRT Egbert
BEEGRU burgee
BEEGST begets
BEEHLT bethel
BEEHMS Shembe
BEEHOP phoebe
BEEHOV behove
BEEHRT Hébert
BEEHRY hereby
BEEHST behest
Thebes
BEEIKL belike
BEEILR belier
BEEILS belies
BEEILZ Belize
BEEIMR bemire
bireme
BEEINN Bienne
BEEINW newbie
BEEIST betise
BEEISV bevies
BEEISX ibexes
BEEJLS jebels
BEEJMS jembes
BEEKLM Kemble
BEEKLR Kléber
BEEKOR reebok
BEEKRS breeks
BEEKRU rebuke
BEEKSY Békésy
BEELLS belles
BEELMM emblem
BEELNO Leoben

BEELNS Belsen
BEELNV Veblen
BEELPS bleeps
plebes
BEELRS rebels
BEELRT belter
Elbert
treble
BEELRY berley
BEELSS Bessel
BEELSV bevels
BEELSZ bezels
BEELXY Bexley
BEEMMR member
BEEMNR Bremen
BEEMRS bermes
embers
BEEMRU embrue
BEEMSU bemuse
BEENNT bennet
BEENOR boreen
enrobe
BEENOT beento
Beeton
BEENRU Reuben
BEENRW Webern
BEENTU butene
BEEOOT bootee
BEEOPP bopeep
BEEORR rebore
BEEORS borees
BEEORY obeyer
BEERRU Breuer
BEERRV reverb
BEERRW brewer
BEERST berets
breest
BEERSU Erebus
BEERSV breves
BEERSW webers
BEERTT better
BEERTV brevet
BEERYZ breezy
BEESST besets
BEESTU bustee
BEFFIR biffer
BEFFOU bouffe
BEFFRU buffer
rebuff
BEFFTU buffet
BEFGOS befogs
BEFHOO behoof
BEFILM fimble
BEFILO foible
BEFIRS briefs
fibers
fibres
BEFIRT bifter
BEFIST befits
BEFLMU fumble
BEFLOO befool
BEFLOU befoul
BEFLRY belfry
BEFORS Forbes
BEFORY forbye
BEFRUY rubefy
BEGGIR bigger
BEGGLO boggle
BEGGOR bogger
BEGGRU bugger
BEGIIL Liebig
BEGILN bingle
BEGILO oblige
BEGILR gerbil
BEGILS bilges
BEGINN benign
Bingen
BEGINO biogen
Gibeon
BEGINR Bering
BEGINS begins
beings
binges
BEGINU beguin
BEGIOO boogie
BEGIOS bogies
gobies
BEGIOU bougie
BEGIRS gibers
BEGIRT begirt
BEGLNO belong
BEGLNU blunge
bungle
BEGLOR Bolger
BEGLOS bogles
globes
BEGLOT goblet
BEGLOW weblog
BEGLRU bugler
burgle
BEGLSU bugles
bulges
BEGMNO bogmen
BEGMSU begums
BEGNOY bygone
BEGNRU bunger
BEGOOR goober
BEGOOS goboes
BEGORS Borges
BEGORU brogue
BEGOSY bogeys
BEGRRU burger
Bürger
BEGRSU Bruges
BEHILT blithe
BEHINT henbit
BEHISS bishes
BEHIST Thisbe
BEHISU bushie
BEHKOR rhebok
BEHLMU humble
BEHLRU burhel
BEHLSU bushel
BEHMOR hombre
BEHMRU Humber
BEHNOR Hebron
BEHOOS hoboes
BEHORT bother
BEHOSS boshes
BEHRST berths
BEHSSU bushes
BEIIKR birkie
BEIIKS bikies
BEIIRS iberis
BEIIRV vibier
BEIISS ibises
BEIJLR jerbil
BEIJRS jibers
BEIKLR bilker
BEIKOO bookie
BEIKRS bikers
BEILLR biller
BEILLS libels
BEILLT billet
BEILMN nimble
BEILMO emboli
mobile
BEILMR limber
BEILMW wimble
BEILMY blimey
BEILNO boline
Nobile
BEILNR berlin
BEILNU nubile
BEILNX Blixen
BEILNY byline
BEILOR boiler
libero
reboil
BEILOT boleti
BEILOW blowie
BEILSY Bisley
BEIMNN binmen
BEIMOS biomes
mobies
BEIMOZ zombie
BEIMRT timber
timbre
BEIMRU erbium
imbrue
BEIMSU imbues
BEINNO Benoni
BEINNZ benzin
BEINOR bonier
O'Brien
BEINOV bovine
BEINOX bonxie
BEINRS brines
BEINRU Brunei
BEINRY byrnie
BEINST Nesbit
BEINTT bitten
BEINVZ Ben-Zvi
BEIOOT bootie
BEIORS ribose
BEIORX boxier
BEIOST sobeit
tobies
BEIOSW bowies
bowsie
BEIPPU buppie
BEIQSU bisque
BEIRRS briers
BEIRRU burier
BEIRRY briery
BEIRSS brises
BEIRST bestir
bister
bistre
biters
bitser
breist
tribes
BEIRSU bruise
buries
busier
rubies
BEIRSV brevis
BEIRSW brewis
BEIRTT bitter
BEIRTU Beirut
BEISSU busies
BEISTZ zibets
BEITUY ubiety
BEJJUU jujube
BEJLMU jumble
BEJORU objure
BEKKRY brekky
BEKLOS blokes
BEKLOY blokey
BEKLRU bulker
BEKNOR broken
BEKNRU bunker
BEKOOR booker
Brooke
BEKOOT betook
BEKORR broker
BEKOST bosket
BEKRSU burkes
busker
BELLOU boulle
lobule
BELLOW bellow
BELLTU bullet
BELLUY bluely
BELMMU mumble
BELMOY emboly
BELMRU lumber
rumble
BELMSU umbels
umbles
BELMTU tumble
BELNNY blenny
BELNOR nobler
BELNOS nobles
BELNOY Boleyn
BELNOZ benzol
BELNRU Brunel

Lebrun
BELNTU unbelt
BELNUU Buñuel
BELNYZ benzyl
BELOOR bolero
BELOOS sobole
BELOOT Bootle
BELOOV Belovo
BELOPU pueblo
BELORS robles
BELORT bolter
BELORU rouble
BELORW blower
bowler
BELOSS lesbos
BELOST botels
BELOSU blouse
boules
obelus
BELOSW bowels
Bowles
elbows
BELOTT bottle
BELOUZ Boulez
BELRRU burler
BELRST blerts
BELRSU Elbrus
rubles
BELRSY beryls
BELRTU butler
BELRTY trebly
BELRUY burley
BELSTU bluest
bluets
bustle
sublet
subtle
BELSUY bluesy
blueys
BELTUU tubule
BEMMRU bummer
BEMNOT entomb
BEMNOW bowmen
enwomb
BEMNRU number
BEMOOR boomer
BEMOPS pombes
BEMORS bromes
somber
sombre
BEMORY embryo
BEMOSS besoms
emboss
BEMOSW embows
BEMPRU bumper
BEMRSU brumes
umbers
BENNOS Benson
bonnes
BENNOT Benton
bonnet
BENNSU bunsen
BENNTU bunnet
unbent
BENOOR Borneo
Oberon
BENORR reborn
BENORS boners
BENORT breton
Brontë
BENORU bourne
BENORW Browne
BENORZ bonzer
bronze
BENOST bentos
BENOSZ bonzes
BENOTY betony
BENRRU burner
Burren
BENRST brents
BENRSU Rubens
BENRTU brunet
burnet
BENRUY Burney
BEOORR Örebro
BEOORT reboot
BEOORZ boozer
rebozo
BEOOSZ boozes
BEOPPR bopper
BEOPRR prober
BEOPRS probes
BEORRS borers
resorb
BEORSS sobers
BEORST sorbet
strobe
BEORSU bourse
BEORSW bowers
bowser
browse
BEORSX boxers
BEORTT bettor
BEORTV obvert
BEORVV bovver
BEORWY bowery
bowyer
BEOSSS bosses
obsess
BEOSST bosset
BEOSSU bouses
BEOSSW bowses
BEOSSY syboes
BEOSTT bottes
obtest
BEOSTU obtuse
BEOSTW bestow
BEPRSU superb
BERRUY rebury
BERSSU burses
BERSTU brutes
burets
buster
rebuts
tubers
BERSUX exurbs
BERSUY buyers
BERTTU butter
BERUZZ buzzer
BESSSU busses
BESSTU subset
BESTTU buttes
BESUZZ buzzes
BFFIIN biffin
BFFINO boffin
BFFLSU bluffs
BFFNOU Buffon
BFFORU ruboff
BFFOSU buffos
BFGOOW fogbow
BFIILR fibril
BFIINR fibrin
BFIMOR biform
BFINOW bowfin
BFIORS rosbif
BFLOTY botfly
BFLOUX boxful
BFLSYY flybys
BFLTUU tubful
BFMORY Formby
BGGIIN biggin
gibing
BGGIIW bigwig
BGGINO biggon
BGGINY gybing
BGGIRS Briggs
BGGNOO bogong
BGGNOU bugong
BGHIIL ghibli
BGHIIN binghi
BGHILT blight
BGHIRT bright
BGHIST bights
BGHMUU humbug
BGHOSU boughs
BGHOTU bought
BGHRSU burghs
BGIIJN jibing
BGIIKN biking
BGIILN biling
BGIILS giblis
BGIINN Binnig
BGIINT biting
BGIKNO boking
BGIKNY byking
BGILLY glibly
BGILNO globin
goblin
BGILNU bluing
BGINNO boning
Ningbo
BGINOO booing
BGINOR boring
orbing
robing
BGINOS bingos
gibson
BGINOW bowing
BGINOX boxing
BGINRS brings
BGINSU busing
BGINTU tubing
BGINUY buying
BGIORV Viborg
BGIOST bigots
BGLMOO moblog
BGLNOO oblong
BGLOSU globus
BGLRUU bulgur
BGMOOS gombos
BGMOSU gumbos
BGNOOS bongos
boongs
BGNTUU Butung
BGOORU burgoo
BGORSU bourgs
Burgos
BGORVY Vyborg
BHHIKU bhikhu
BHIKOS kibosh
BHILPY Philby
BHILSU bluish
BHIMOR rhombi
BHIMTU Thimbu
BHIOPS bishop
BHIOSY boyish
BHIRST births
briths
BHIRSU hubris
BHIRSY hybris
BHITWY Whitby
BHKNOU bohunk
BHKOSY kybosh
BHLMUY humbly
BHLOSY bolshy
BHMORS rhombs
BHMRSU rhumbs
BHMSTU thumbs
BHNORY Hornby
BHOOOO boohoo
BHOOST booths
BHORST broths
throbs
BHOTTU Bhutto
BHRSSU shrubs
BHRSUY brushy
BIIIKN bikini
BIIKTZ kibitz
BIILNS blinis
BIILTW twibil
BIIMOS obiism
BIIMOZ imbizo
BIINOT biotin
BIINOU biniou
BIIORS Boris I
oribis
BIIORV vibrio
BIISTV vibist

BIITTT titbit
BIJLOT Bitolj
BIJOUX bijoux
BIKKRY Kirkby
BIKLNS blinks
BIKMNU bumkin
BIKNRS brinks
BIKNSU buskin
BIKRSS brisks
BILLNO billon
BILLNU Lublin
BILLOW billow
BILLOX bollix
BILLOY billyo
BILLRS brills
BILMNY nimbly
BILMOS limbos
BILMPS blimps
BILMSU limbus
BILNOS Lisbon
BILNTZ blintz
BILOOT Lobito
BILORS broils
BILRTY trilby
BILSST stilbs
BILSSY sibyls
BILSUY busily
BIMMOO miombo
BIMNOS bonism
BIMNSU nimbus
BIMORS Imbros
BIMOSZ zombis
BIMSTU submit
BINNOR inborn
BINNOU bunion
BINNOY Binyon
BINNRY brinny
BINOOT bonito
BINORS robins
BINORY briony
BINOST bonist
BINPUY bunyip
BINRSU bruins
burins
BIOORZ borzoi
BIOOST oboist
BIOPSY biopsy
BIORST bistro
orbits
BIOSTU subito
BIOSZZ bizzos
BIQSSU squibs
BIRSTU bruits
BIRTTU turbit
BISSTU bustis
BJLMUY jumbly
BJMOSU jumbos
BKLMOO Lombok
BKMNUU bunkum
BKNOSU bunkos
konbus
BKOORS brooks
BKOOSY booksy
BKORTU Korbut
Tobruk
BKOSXY skybox
BLLOOO lobolo
BLLORY brolly
BLMNUY numbly
BLMOOS blooms
BLMOOY bloomy
BLMOSY symbol
BLMPSU plumbs
BLNOOS bolson
BLNOOT Bolton
BLNOTU unbolt
BLNOTY Blyton
BLNSTU blunts
BLOOSU obolus
BLOOTT blotto
BLOOWY lowboy
BLOPUW blowup
BLOSTU boults
BLOSWY blowsy
BLOWYZ blowzy
BLRRUY blurry
BLRSTU blurts
BLSTUY subtly
BMOORS brooms
BMOOSS bosoms
BMOOSY bosomy
BMOOTT bottom
BMOOTY tomboy
BMOTUU Mobutu
BNNORU unborn
BNOORS Robson
BNOOSS bosons
BNOOST boston
BNORSU bourns
suborn
BNORSW browns
BNORTU Bruton
burton
BNORWY browny
BNORYY bryony
BNORYZ bronzy
BNOSSU bosuns
BNOSUW sunbow
BNOTTU button
BNOTUX Buxton
BNOTUY bounty
BNRSTU brunts
BNRTUY Tyburn
BOOPTY potboy
BOORRW borrow
BOORRY Rob Roy
BOORST robots
BOORSU buroos
BOOSST boosts
BOOSWX oxbows
BOOTUX outbox
BOOWWW bowwow
BORRSU burros
BORRUW burrow
BORSTU robust
BORTTU turbot
BORTUU rubout
BOSSWY sybows
BOTUUY buyout
BRSSTU bursts
BRSTUU Brutus
BSSSUY byssus
BSTTUU bututs
CCCCIO coccic
CCCDIO coccid
CCCHOY choccy
CCCILY cyclic
CCCOSU coccus
CCCOXY coccyx
CCDEER recced
CCDEKO cocked
CCDELY cycled
CCDEOS codecs
CCDEOT decoct
CCEEHR creche
crèche
CCEELS Eccles
CCEEOR coerce
CCEERS recces
CCEHIL chicle
cliche
CCEHIO choice
echoic
CCEHIT hectic
CCEHKS checks
CCEHKY checky
CCEHLN clench
CCEHLO cloche
CCEHOS cosech
CCEIIL cilice
icicle
CCEILR circle
cleric
CCEILY cicely
CCEINS scenic
CCEIOR cicero
CCEIPT pectic
CCEIRS cercis
CCEIRT cretic
CCEITY cecity
CCEKLO cockle
CCEKLS clecks
CCEKLY clecky
CCEKOP copeck
CCEKOR cocker
CCELRY cycler
CCELSY cycles
CCENOS sconce
CCEORS soccer
CCEOSS seccos
CCERSU cercus
cruces
CCESSU cusecs
CCFILO flocci
CCHHII chichi
CCHHIN chinch
CCHHRU church
CCHIKS chicks
CCHILN clinch
CCHILO cholic
CCHILY chicly
Clichy
CCHINO cochin
CCHIOR choric
CCHIOS chicos
CCHIPU hiccup
CCHKOO chocko
CCHKOS chocks
CCHKSU chucks
CCHLTU clutch
cultch
CCHNOS conchs
CCHNOY conchy
CCHNRU crunch
CCHOOS chocos
CCHOOT cootch
CCHORS scorch
CCHORT crotch
CCHORU crouch
CCHOST scotch
CCHRTU crutch
CCHSTU scutch
CCIILN clinic
CCIILT clitic
CCIINO iconic
CCIINP picnic
CCIINZ zincic
CCIIOR Riccio
CCIIPR picric
CCIIRT citric
critic
CCIISV civics
CCIKLS clicks
CCIKRS cricks
CCILNO clonic
CCILTU cultic
CCIMOS comics
cosmic
CCIMRY Cymric
CCINOS conics
CCINSY cynics
CCIOPT Coptic
CCIOSS ciscos
CCIPRU cupric
CCIRSU circus
CCISTY cystic
CCKLOS clocks
CCKLSU clucks
CCKLUY clucky
CCKOOU cuckoo
CCKOPU cockup
CCKORS crocks
CCKRSU crucks
CCLOTU occult
CCNOOO cocoon
CCNORU concur
CCOOOR rococo
CCOPUY occupy

CCORSU crocus
occurs
succor
CCOSTU stucco
CCSSUU cuscus
CDDDEO codded
CDDEEI decide
deiced
CDDEEK decked
CDDEEO decode
CDDEEU deduce
deuced
educed
CDDEHI chided
CDDEIS disced
CDDEIU cuddie
CDDEKO docked
CDDEKU ducked
CDDELO coddle
CDDELU cuddle
CDDEOR codder
corded
CDDERU curded
CDDETU deduct
CDDHUY chuddy
CDDLOY cloddy
CDDLUY cuddly
CDDRUY cruddy
CDEEEM emceed
CDEEER decree
recede
CDEEES secede
CDEEEX exceed
CDEEFN fenced
CDEEFT defect
CDEEHL leched
CDEEHO echoed
CDEEHP peched
CDEEHR cheder
CDEEHT etched
CDEEHW chewed
CDEEIL ceiled
decile
CDEEIN edenic
CDEEIP pieced
CDEEIR deicer
CDEEIS deices
CDEEIT deceit
CDEEIV device
CDEEIX excide
CDEEJT deject
CDEEKK kecked
CDEEKL deckel
deckle
CDEEKN necked
CDEEKO decoke
CDEEKP pecked
CDEEKR decker
recked
CDEELP cleped
CDEELW clewed
CDEENO encode

CDEENR decern
CDEENS censed
CDEENT decent
CDEEOO cooeed
CDEEPR creped
CDEERS ceders
creeds
screed
CDEERU reduce
CDEERW crewed
CDEESS cessed
CDEESU deuces
educes
seduce
CDEETT detect
CDEFFO coffed
CDEFFU cuffed
CDEFII deific
CDEFKU fucked
CDEFNU fecund
CDEFOR forced
CDEGGO cogged
CDEGIN ceding
CDEGIO geodic
CDEGLU cudgel
CDEGOR codger
CDEHIL childe
CDEHIM chimed
miched
CDEHIN chined
inched
niched
CDEHIR chider
dreich
herdic
CDEHIS chides
CDEHIT itched
CDEHKO choked
hocked
CDEHNR drench
CDEHOR ochred
CDEHOS coshed
CDEHOU douche
CDEIIL Lidice
CDEIIM Medici
CDEIIR dicier
CDEIJU juiced
CDEIKK kicked
CDEIKL licked
CDEIKM medick
CDEIKN nicked
CDEIKP picked
CDEIKR dicker
ricked
CDEIKS sicked
CDEIKT ticked
CDEIKU duckie
CDEIKW wicked
CDEIKY dickey
CDEILO coiled
coldie
docile

CDEILS sliced
CDEILT delict
deltic
CDEILU Euclid
CDEIMN minced
CDEIMO medico
CDEIMR dermic
CDEIMS medics
CDEINO coined
CDEINR cinder
CDEINU induce
CDEINW winced
CDEIOP copied
CDEIOT coedit
CDEIOV voiced
CDEIPR priced
CDEIPS spiced
CDEIPT depict
CDEIRS ciders
dicers
scried
CDEIRT credit
direct
triced
CDEIRV cervid
CDEIST edicts
CDEKLO locked
CDEKLU lucked
CDEKMO mocked
CDEKMU mucked
CDEKNO conked
docken
nocked
CDEKOO cooked
CDEKOR corked
docker
redock
rocked
CDEKOS socked
CDEKOT docket
CDEKOW cowked
CDEKPU pucked
CDEKRS drecks
CDEKRU ducker
rucked
CDEKRY drecky
CDEKSU sucked
CDEKTU tucked
CDELLU culled
CDELNO cloned
CDELOO cooled
locoed
CDELOR colder
CDELOS closed
CDELOW cowled
CDELOY cloyed
CDELPY clyped
CDELRU curdle
curled
CDELTU dulcet
CDEMOO comedo
CDEMOP comped

CDEMOY comedy
CDENNO conned
CDENOP ponced
CDENOR corned
CDENOS second
CDENOT docent
CDENPU punced
CDENRU Cruden
CDENSS scends
CDENSU dunces
secund
CDENSY synced
CDEOOP cooped
CDEOPP copped
CDEOPU couped
CDEOPW cowped
CDEORR corder
record
CDEORS coders
credos
decors
scored
CDEORW crowed
CDEOST costed
CDEOSU escudo
CDEOSY decoys
CDEOTT cotted
CDEOYZ zydeco
CDEPPU cupped
CDEPSU cusped
CDERRU cruder
CDERSU cursed
CDERSY cyders
descry
CDERUV curved
CDERUY decury
CDESSU cussed
CDESTU educts
CDFINU fundic
CDFIOU fucoid
CDFIOY codify
CDGIIN dicing
CDGINO coding
CDHIOR orchid
rhodic
CDHIRY hydric
CDHORS chords
CDIIIM imidic
CDIIIR iridic
CDIINT indict
CDIIOY idiocy
CDIISV viscid
CDILNO codlin
CDIMOU mucoid
CDIMOY cymoid
CDIMSU muscid
CDIMTU dictum
CDINOO conoid
CDINOR nordic
CDINSU Cnidus
CDINSY syndic
CDINTU induct

CDIOSS	discos
CDIOTT	cottid
CDIPSU	cuspid
CDISSU	discus
CDJNOU	jocund
CDLLOY	coldly
CDLOSS	scolds
CDLOSU	clouds
CDLOUY	cloudy
CDMNOO	condom
CDMOOO	comodo
CDMOOT	dotcom
CDNOOR	condor
	cordon
CDNOOS	codons
	condos
CDNSUY	Cydnus
CDOORT	doctor
CDOORY	corody
CDORSS	scrods
CDORSU	durocs
CDORSW	crowds
CEEEFL	fleece
CEEEGR	greece
CEEEHS	cheese
CEEELS	Cleese
CEEEMS	emcees
CEEERS	creese
CEEFFO	coffee
CEEFFT	effect
CEEFHL	fleche
CEEFIR	fierce
	Recife
CEEFLY	fleecy
CEEFNN	fennec
CEEFNR	fencer
CEEFNS	fences
CEEFSU	fescue
CEEHIL	eliche
	lichee
CEEHIS	seiche
CEEHIT	techie
CEEHIW	chewie
CEEHKL	heckle
CEEHKS	cheeks
CEEHKY	cheeky
CEEHLR	lecher
CEEHLS	leches
CEEHLY	lychee
CEEHMS	scheme
	smeech
CEEHNT	thence
CEEHNW	whence
CEEHNY	Cheney
CEEHOR	cohere
	reecho
CEEHOS	echoes
CEEHPS	cheeps
	speech
CEEHQU	cheque
CEEHRS	cheers
CEEHRT	etcher
CEEHRU	euchre
CEEHRV	chevre
CEEHRW	chewer
CEEHRY	cheery
CEEHST	etches
CEEHSW	eschew
CEEHSY	cheesy
CEEHTV	chevet
CEEIKL	Kielce
CEEILN	Céline
CEEILS	siecle
CEEIMT	emetic
CEEINN	Nicene
CEEINP	Niepce
CEEINS	nieces
CEEINT	entice
CEEINV	evince
	Venice
CEEIPR	Peirce
	piecer
	pierce
	recipe
CEEIPS	pieces
	specie
CEEIRS	cerise
CEEIRT	recite
	tierce
CEEIRU	ecurie
CEEISS	ecesis
CEEISX	excise
CEEITV	Ecevit
CEEITX	excite
CEEJRT	reject
CEEJST	ejects
CEEKLS	cleeks
CEEKNR	necker
CEEKNU	Eucken
CEEKPR	pecker
CEEKRS	creeks
CEEKRT	Eckert
CEELMO	cleome
CEELNP	pencel
CEELNR	crenel
CEELOR	creole
CEELOU	coulee
CEELOV	veloce
CEELPS	clepes
CEELRS	creels
	sclere
CEELRT	tercel
CEELRV	clever
CEELRW	crewel
CEELRY	celery
CEELST	elects
	select
CEELSX	excels
CEELSY	lycees
CEEMNT	cement
CEEMNY	cymene
CEEMRR	mercer
CEEMRS	cremes
CEEMRT	cermet
CEENOR	encore
CEENOS	Enesco
CEENOT	cenote
CEENPS	spence
CEENPT	pecten
CEENRS	censer
	screen
	secern
CEENRT	center
	centre
	recent
	tenrec
CEENRY	Cyrene
CEENSS	censes
	scenes
CEEOOS	cooees
CEEORV	corvee
CEEPRS	creeps
	crepes
CEEPRT	recept
CEEPRY	creepy
	crepey
CEEPTX	except
	expect
CEEPTY	ectype
CEEPUY	eyecup
CEERSS	cesser
	recess
	screes
CEERST	certes
	erects
	resect
	screet
	secret
CEERSU	cereus
	ceruse
	Creuse
	rescue
	secure
CEERTT	tercet
CEERTU	Teucer
CEESSS	cesses
CEESSX	excess
CEESSY	cyeses
CEESTX	exsect
CEESUV	cuvees
CEESUX	excuse
CEFFIO	office
CEFFLO	coffle
CEFFOR	coffer
CEFHIS	chiefs
	fiches
CEFHIT	fetich
	Fichte
CEFHLN	flench
CEFHLT	fletch
CEFHNR	french
CEFHOO	Chefoo
CEFHST	fechts
CEFIKL	fickle
CEFINT	infect
CEFIOS	ficoes
CEFIRR	ferric
CEFKLS	flecks
CEFKRU	fucker
CEFLST	clefts
CEFNOR	confer
CEFORR	forcer
CEFORS	forces
	fresco
CEFRUW	curfew
CEGGLO	coggle
CEGGPU	eggcup
CEGHIO	chigoe
CEGINO	coigne
CEGINR	cering
	cringe
CEGINU	cueing
CEGIRR	gricer
CEGIRS	grices
CEGKOS	geckos
CEGLRY	clergy
CEGNOR	conger
CEGNOS	conges
CEGNOT	cogent
CEGNSU	scunge
CEGNTY	cygnet
CEGORR	grocer
CEHHSU	sheuch
CEHHTU	Chu Teh
CEHIIN	echini
CEHIKY	hickey
CEHILN	lichen
CEHILS	chiels
	chiles
	chisel
CEHIMR	chimer
CEHIMS	chimes
	miches
CEHIMU	echium
CEHINP	Penchi
CEHINR	enrich
CEHINS	chines
	inches
	niches
CEHINT	ethnic
CEHINY	hyenic
CEHIOR	coheir
	heroic
CEHIPR	cipher
CEHIQU	quiche
CEHIRR	chirre
	richer
CEHIRS	riches
CEHIRT	cither
	thrice
CEHIST	ethics
	itches
CEHISU	cushie
CEHISV	chives
CEHITT	thetic
CEHKLO	hockle
CEHKLU	huckle
CEHKNU	kuchen

CEHKOR	choker
	hocker
CEHKOS	chokes
CEHKOY	chokey
	hockey
CEHKST	sketch
CEHKTV	kvetch
CEHLMO	Molech
CEHLOR	choler
CEHLOT	clothe
CEHLOU	louche
CEHLPS	chelps
	schlep
CEHLPU	pleuch
CEHLSY	lyches
CEHMMY	chemmy
CEHMOR	chrome
CEHNOO	ochone
CEHNOS	chosen
CEHNOT	techno
CEHNOU	cohune
CEHNQU	quench
CEHNRT	trench
CEHNRW	wrench
CEHNST	stench
CEHNUU	eunuch
CEHOOS	choose
CEHOPS	Cheops
	epochs
CEHORS	chores
	cosher
	ochers
	ochres
CEHORT	hector
	rochet
	tocher
	troche
CEHORU	rouche
CEHORY	ochery
CEHOSS	choses
	coshes
CEHOSU	ouches
CEHOTU	touche
CEHPRY	chypre
	cypher
CEHPSY	psyche
CEHRRY	cherry
CEHRSU	ruches
CEHRTW	wretch
CEHRTY	cherty
CEHSST	chests
CEHSTU	chutes
	tusche
CEHSTY	chesty
	scythe
CEHTTY	tetchy
CEIIKR	ickier
CEIIKS	Ciskei
	sickie
CEIILT	elicit
CEIILX	exilic
CEIINR	irenic
CEIINS	incise
CEIINT	incite
CEIIST	cities
	iciest
CEIISV	civies
CEIJMO	Méjico
CEIJNT	inject
CEIJRU	juicer
CEIJSU	juices
CEIKKR	kicker
CEIKLM	melick
	mickle
CEIKLN	nickel
CEIKLP	pickle
CEIKLR	licker
	rickle
CEIKLS	cleiks
	sickle
CEIKLT	tickle
CEIKMY	mickey
CEIKNR	nicker
CEIKNS	sicken
CEIKOO	cookie
CEIKOS	Košice
CEIKPR	picker
CEIKPT	picket
CEIKRR	ricker
CEIKRS	sicker
CEIKRT	ticker
CEIKRW	wicker
CEIKRY	crikey
	rickey
CEIKTT	ticket
CEIKTW	wicket
CEIKTY	tickey
CEILLM	micell
CEILLO	collie
	ocelli
CEILLR	Çiller
CEILMS	climes
CEILNO	cineol
	enolic
CEILNP	pencil
CEILNS	clines
CEILNT	client
	lectin
	lentic
CEILNU	leucin
	nuclei
CEILNY	nicely
CEILOO	coolie
CEILOP	police
CEILOR	coiler
	recoil
CEILOS	colies
CEILOT	citole
CEILPS	splice
CEILPV	pelvic
CEILPY	clypei
CEILQU	clique
CEILRS	relics
	slicer
CEILRT	relict
CEILSS	slices
CEILSU	sluice
CEILSV	clevis
CEILTU	luetic
CEIMMO	commie
CEIMNO	income
CEIMNR	mincer
CEIMNS	cnemis
	minces
CEIMNU	neumic
CEIMOX	Mexico
CEIMPU	pumice
CEIMPY	pyemic
CEIMRS	crimes
CEIMRT	metric
CEIMRU	cerium
	uremic
CEIMST	metics
CEIMSU	cesium
	miscue
CEINNO	conine
CEINOR	coiner
	orcein
	recoin
CEINOS	conies
	cosine
	oscine
CEINOT	noetic
	notice
CEINOV	novice
CEINOX	exonic
CEINPR	pincer
	prince
CEINPT	incept
	pectin
CEINQU	cinque
	quince
CEINRT	cretin
CEINRU	Runcie
CEINRV	Cervin
CEINRW	wincer
CEINST	incest
	insect
	nicest
CEINSU	incuse
CEINSW	winces
CEINTY	nicety
CEINWY	wincey
CEIOOR	coorie
CEIOOT	cootie
CEIOPR	copier
CEIOPS	copies
CEIOPT	poetic
CEIORR	corrie
	orrice
CEIORS	cosier
CEIORT	erotic
CEIORU	courie
CEIORV	voicer
CEIORW	cowrie
CEIORZ	cozier
CEIOSS	cosies
	cossie
CEIOSV	voices
CEIOSZ	cozies
CEIOTX	exotic
CEIPPT	peptic
CEIPRR	pricer
CEIPRS	cripes
	precis
	prices
	spicer
CEIPRY	pricey
CEIPSS	Pisces
	spices
CEIPST	septic
CEIQRU	cirque
CEIRRS	criers
	ricers
CEIRSS	crises
	scries
CEIRST	citers
	steric
	trices
CEIRSU	cruise
	crusie
	curies
CEIRTU	uretic
CEIRUV	Cuvier
CEIRUZ	cruzie
CEIRVX	cervix
CEISSU	cuisse
CEISSY	cyesis
CEISTU	cuties
CEISTV	civets
	evicts
CEJKOY	jockey
CEJNOU	jounce
CEJOOS	jocose
CEKKOP	kopeck
CEKLMU	muckle
CEKLOR	locker
CEKLOT	locket
CEKLRS	clerks
CEKLRU	ruckle
CEKLSU	suckle
CEKMOR	mocker
CEKMRU	mucker
CEKMRX	Merckx
CEKNOR	conker
	reckon
CEKNSS	snecks
CEKOOR	cooker
CEKOPT	pocket
CEKORR	corker
	rocker
CEKORS	ockers
CEKORT	rocket
CEKOST	socket
CEKPRU	pucker
CEKPSS	specks
CEKRSU	sucker
CEKRSW	wrecks

CEKRTU tucker
CEKTTU tucket
CELLNU Cullen
CELLOS cellos
CELLOT collet
CELLOU locule
CELLOW Cowell
CELLRU culler
CELLTU cullet
CELMOO coelom
CELMOP compel
CELMOR cormel
CELMOS celoms
CELMOY comely
CELMSU muscle
CELMUY lyceum
CELNNU nuncle
CELNOR cornel
CELNOS clones
CELNOV cloven
CELNOY Ceylon
CELNSU uncles
CELNTU lucent
CELOOR cooler
CELOOT ocelot
CELOPU couple
CELOPY Copley
Coypel
CELOQU cloque
CELORS ceorls
closer
cresol
CELORT colter
lector
CELORU colure
CELORV clover
CELOSS closes
socles
CELOST closet
telcos
CELOSU coleus
CELOSV cloves
CELOSX scolex
CELOSY coleys
CELOTU Clouet
CELOWY Cowley
CELPSU cupels
CELPSY clypes
CELPTY yclept
CELPUU cupule
CELRRU curler
CELRSU cruels
ulcers
CELRTU cutler
reluct
CELRUU curule
CELRUV culver
CELRUW curlew
CELSTU culets
CELTTU cutlet
cuttle
CELTUY cutely
CEMNOS socmen
CEMNOW cowmen
CEMNTU centum
CEMOOS comose
CEMOPR comper
CEMORR Cromer
CEMORS comers
scrome
CEMOST comets
CEMOSU mucose
CEMOSY cymose
CEMOTU Temuco
CEMRTU rectum
CENNOS nonces
CENOOP poonce
CENOPR Procne
CENOPS ponces
CENOPU pounce
CENOPY poncey
CENORR corner
CENORS censor
crones
oncers
CENORT cornet
CENORU conure
uncoer
CENOSS scones
CENOST centos
contes
CENOSU ounces
CENOSV covens
CENOSY coneys
CENOSZ cozens
CENOVX convex
CENOVY convey
CENPSU punces
CENRYZ Czerny
CENSST scents
CENSSU census
CENSTY encyst
CENSUU cuneus
CEOOPR cooper
CEOORS cooers
CEOOSY cooeys
CEOOTY coyote
oocyte
CEOPPR copper
CEOPRS copers
corpse
CEOPRT copter
CEOPRU croupe
recoup
CEOPRW Cowper
CEOPRY recopy
CEOPSS copses
scopes
CEOPSU coupes
CEOPTY cotype
CEOQTU coquet
CEORRS crores
scorer
CEORRT rector
CEORRW crower
CEORSS corses
crosse
scores
CEORST corset
Cortés
coster
escort
rectos
scoter
sector
CEORSU cerous
course
crouse
source
CEORSV corves
covers
CEORSW cowers
escrow
CEORSY corsey
CEORSZ crozes
CEORTT cotter
CEORTU croute
CEORTV covert
vector
CEORTX cortex
CEOSSS cosses
CEOSST cestos
cosets
cosset
CEOSSU scouse
CEOSTT octets
CEOSTV covets
CEOSVY coveys
CEPPRU cupper
CEPRSU spruce
CEPRSY cypres
CERRSU curers
curser
recurs
CERSST crests
CERSSU cruses
curses
sucres
CERSSW screws
CERSSY Cressy
CERSTU cruets
curets
Custer
eructs
rectus
truces
CERSUV curves
CERSUX cruxes
CERSWY screwy
CERTTU cutter
CERTUV curvet
CESSSU cusses
CESSTU cestus
scutes
CESTTU cutest
CESTUY cutesy
cuteys
CFFHIS Schiff
CFFHSU chuffs
CFFHUY chuffy
CFFILS cliffs
CFFILY cliffy
CFFINO coffin
CFFOSS scoffs
CFFOTU cutoff
offcut
CFFRSU scruff
CFFRUY Cruyff
CFFSSU scuffs
CFGINU fungic
CFHILN flinch
CFHILT flitch
CFHIRS Frisch
CFHISU fichus
CFHLSY flysch
CFHOOS choofs
CFHOUU Fu-chou
CFIILM filmic
CFIINO Ficino
CFIINU unific
CFIIST fistic
CFIITY citify
CFIKLS flicks
CFILOR frolic
CFIMOR formic
CFIMOT comfit
CFINOT confit
CFISTU fustic
CFITYY cityfy
CFKLOS flocks
CFKLOY flocky
CFKORS frocks
CFKPUU fuckup
CFLPUU cupful
CFORST crofts
CFOSUU fucous
CFRSUY scurfy
CGGLOY cloggy
coggly
CGGORY croggy
CGHHOU chough
CGHIIN I Ching
CGHILT glitch
CGHINR grinch
CGHIOT gothic
CGHLOU clough
CGHORU grouch
CGHOSU coughs
CGIILT tiglic
CGIINO congii
CGIINR ricing
CGIINS icings
CGIINT citing
CGIINV vicing
CGIKNO coking
CGILNS clings
CGILNU cluing
CGILNY clingy

CGIMNO	coming
	gnomic
CGINNO	coning
CGINOO	cooing
CGINOP	coping
	picong
CGINOR	coring
CGINOS	coigns
CGINOT	coting
CGINOV	coving
CGINOW	cowing
CGINOX	coxing
CGINRU	curing
CGINRY	crying
CGIOOT	cogito
CGIORS	corgis
CGLLOY	glycol
CGLNOU	unclog
CGLOOU	colugo
CGNOOS	cogons
	congos
CGNOOU	congou
CGNSUY	scungy
CHHIIL	Chihli
CHHNOO	honcho
CHHOOS	cohosh
CHHOOT	hootch
CHIILL	chilli
	Illich
CHIILS	lichis
CHIILT	litchi
	lithic
CHIINS	nicish
CHIINT	chitin
CHIKKO	Hickok
CHIKNS	chinks
CHIKNY	chinky
CHIKOS	hoicks
CHIKOT	thicko
CHIKOX	Hickox
CHIKRS	kirsch
CHIKST	kitsch
	shtick
	skitch
CHIKTY	thicky
CHILLS	chills
CHILLY	chilly
CHILMO	holmic
CHILOR	orchil
CHILOS	cholis
CHILPY	phylic
CHILRY	richly
CHILST	lichts
CHIMNU	Munich
CHIMNY	hymnic
CHIMOR	hormic
CHIMPS	chimps
CHIMRS	chirms
	chrism
	smirch
CHIMSS	schism
CHIMTY	mythic
	thymic
CHINNO	Inchon
CHINOP	chopin
	phonic
CHINOR	Chiron
CHINOS	chinos
CHINOT	chiton
CHINRU	urchin
CHINST	nichts
	snitch
CHINTZ	chintz
CHIOPR	orphic
CHIOPS	Phocis
CHIOPT	photic
CHIORS	chiros
	choirs
	ichors
	orchis
CHIORT	rhotic
	thoric
CHIOSY	coyish
CHIOSZ	schizo
CHIPPY	chippy
CHIPRS	chirps
CHIPRY	chirpy
CHIPSY	physic
	scyphi
CHIPTY	pitchy
CHIQTU	quitch
CHIRRS	chirrs
CHIRST	Christ
	richts
CHIRSU	chirus
CHIRUZ	Zürich
CHISST	schist
	sichts
	stichs
CHISTT	stitch
CHISTW	switch
CHITTW	twitch
CHITTY	chitty
	titchy
CHIVVY	chivvy
CHJMOU	Jochum
CHJNOU	Chŏnju
CHKLOO	klooch
CHKNSU	chunks
CHKNUY	chunky
CHKOOS	chokos
	chooks
CHKOSS	shocks
CHKOSW	chowks
CHKSSU	shucks
CHLMOO	moloch
CHLNOO	Cholon
CHLOOS	school
CHLOOT	Clotho
	coolth
CHLORS	schorl
CHLOST	cloths
CHLOSU	slouch
CHLRSU	churls
CHLSSU	schuls
CHLSTU	slutch
CHMMUY	chummy
CHMOOR	chromo
CHMOOS	chooms
	smooch
CHMOPS	chomps
CHMPSU	chumps
CHMSTU	smutch
CHNOOP	poncho
CHNOOS	Chosŏn
CHNOTY	notchy
CHNPUY	punchy
CHNRSU	churns
CHNSSY	synchs
CHNTUU	tuchun
CHOORT	cohort
CHOOSS	scoosh
CHOOSY	choosy
CHOPPY	choppy
CHOPSY	psycho
CHOPUY	pouchy
CHORSU	chorus
CHORTU	trouch
CHOSTT	chotts
CHOSUU	Su-chou
CHOSUW	Süchow
CHOTUY	couthy
	touchy
CHPSSY	psychs
CHPSTU	putsch
CHRRSU	churrs
CHRSTW	crwths
CHSSSU	schuss
CHSTUY	cushty
CHSTUZ	Schütz
CHSWYZ	Schwyz
CIIIRT	iritic
CIIKNP	pickin
CIILMU	cilium
CIILOP	lipoic
CIILSY	Sicily
CIIMMS	mimics
CIIMOT	miotic
CIIMSV	civism
CIIMTV	victim
CIINNU	uncini
CIINOR	ironic
CIINOS	ionics
CIINOT	Ticino
CIINQU	quinic
CIINRT	citrin
	nitric
CIIOPS	Scipio
CIIPRS	Crispi
CIIRSS	crisis
CIIRTV	vitric
CIKKPU	kickup
CIKLNS	clinks
CIKLSS	slicks
CIKLSY	sickly
CIKLTY	tickly
CIKNPU	unpick
CIKNPY	pyknic
CIKNSS	snicks
CIKNYZ	zincky
CIKOSS	sickos
CIKOSY	yoicks
CIKPPU	pickup
CIKPRS	pricks
CIKPSS	spicks
CIKPTU	uptick
CIKQSU	quicks
CIKRST	strick
	tricks
CIKRSW	wricks
CIKRTY	tricky
CIKSST	sticks
CIKSTY	sticky
CIKWYZ	Zwicky
CILLOU	loculi
CILLSU	cullis
CILMUU	cumuli
CILNOU	uncoil
CILNST	clints
CILNTU	incult
CILOPU	oilcup
CILOPY	policy
CILORS	Locris
CILORT	lictor
CILOSU	coulis
CILOSV	clovis
CILOSY	cosily
CILOTU	toluic
CILOYZ	cozily
CILPSU	piculs
CILQUY	cliquy
CILRSY	lyrics
CIMMNU	cummin
CIMMOS	commis
CIMMOT	commit
CIMMOX	commix
CIMNOR	micron
CIMNOS	cosmin
CIMNOU	conium
	muonic
CIMNRU	crinum
CIMNSU	mucins
CIMOPY	myopic
CIMORS	micros
CIMORU	corium
CIMOST	sitcom
CIMOTY	comity
	myotic
CIMPRS	crimps
	scrimp
CIMPRY	crimpy
CIMRSS	scrims
CIMRUU	curium
CIMSTY	mystic
CINNOR	Cronin
CINNOU	nuncio
CINOOZ	ozonic
CINOPT	pontic

CINORT citron
CINORZ zircon
CINOSS scions
sonics
CINOST tocsin
tonics
CINOSU cousin
CINOSV covins
CINOSY Sicyon
CINOSZ zincos
CINPSU Pincus
CINRSU incurs
CINRTU Curtin
CINSTT tincts
CINSTU cutins
tunics
CIOORT octroi
CIOPRT tropic
CIOPST optics
picots
topics
CIOPTT ptotic
CIOPWY wicopy
CIORSU curios
CIORTT tricot
CIORTV victor
CIOSST stoics
CIOSTU coitus
CIPPRS Cripps
CIPRSS crisps
scrips
CIPRST script
CIPRSY crispy
CIRRSU cirrus
CIRSTT strict
CIRSTU citrus
rictus
rustic
CIRTTY yttric
CISSSU cissus
CISSTU cistus
CISSUV viscus
CJKOOS jockos
CJNOSU juncos
CKKNOS knocks
CKLNOS clonks
CKLNOU unlock
CKLNSU clunks
CKLNUY clunky
CKLOPU lockup
CKLPSU plucks
CKLPUY plucky
CKMOPU mockup
CKMOSS smocks
CKNORU uncork
CKNTUU untuck
CKOORS crooks
CKOSST stocks
CKOSTY stocky
CKRSTU struck
trucks
CKRSUU ruckus

CLLOOP collop
CLLOOY coolly
CLLORS scroll
CLLSSU sculls
CLMNOU column
CLMOPS clomps
CLMOPY comply
CLMOSU locums
CLMPSU clumps
CLMPUY clumpy
CLMSTU mulcts
CLMSUY clumsy
muscly
CLNOOS colons
CLNOOU uncool
CLNOOY colony
CLNOSU clonus
consul
CLNOSW clowns
CLNRUU uncurl
CLOORS colors
crools
CLOORU colour
CLOORY colory
CLOSSW scowls
CLOSTU clouts
locust
CLOSTY costly
CLPSSU sculps
CLPSTU sculpt
CLRTUY curtly
CLSSUU sulcus
CLSTUU cultus
CMMNOO common
CMMOOR romcom
CMMOOS commos
CMMRUY crummy
CMMSUY scummy
CMNNOO noncom
CMNOSY syncom
CMOOPS compos
CMOOSS cosmos
CMOOSW Moscow
CMOSTU custom
CMOSUU mucous
CMPRSU crumps
scrump
CMPRUU cuprum
CMRSSU scrums
CMSTUU scutum
CNOOPU coupon
CNOORS croons
CNOORT croton
CNOOST contos
nostoc
oncost
CNOOTT cotton
CNOOTY tycoon
CNOOVY convoy
CNORSS scorns
CNORST troncs
CNORSU Cronus

CNORSW crowns
CNORSY synroc
CNORUW Curnow
CNORUZ Curzon
CNOSTU counts
Tucson
CNOTUY county
COOORZ corozo
Orozco
COOPRS scroop
COOPSS scoops
COOPST coopts
COOPWX cowpox
COORTT Cortot
COORUU roucou
COOSST scoots
COOSTY oocyst
COPRRS scrorp
COPRSU corpus
croups
COPRTY crypto
COPRUY croupy
COPSSU Scopus
COPSUY coypus
CORRSU cursor
CORSSU scours
CORSSY Scyros
CORSTU courts
CORSUV corvus
CORTUY outcry
COSSTU custos
Scotus
scouts
COSTTU cottus
COTTUU cutout
CPRSTY crypts
CPRSUY cyprus
CPSTUU cutups
CRRSUY scurry
CRSSTU crusts
CRSTUY crusty
curtsy
CRSUVY scurvy
CSUYZZ scuzzy
DDDEEE deeded
DDDEEI eddied
DDDEER redded
DDDEET tedded
DDDEEW wedded
DDDEGO dodged
DDDEIK kidded
DDDEIL diddle
lidded
DDDEIR ridded
DDDELO doddle
DDDEMU mudded
DDDENO nodded
DDDEOP podded
DDDEOR dodder
DDDEOS sodded
DDEEEH heeded
DDEEEM deemed

DDEEEN needed
DDEEER reeded
DDEEES seeded
DDEEEW weeded
DDEEFI de fide
defied
DDEEFN defend
fended
DDEEFU feuded
DDEEGG degged
DDEEGH hedged
DDEEGK kedged
DDEEGL gelded
ledged
DDEEGR dredge
DDEEGW wedged
DDEEHL heddle
DDEEHR herded
DDEEIL elided
DDEEIN denied
indeed
DDEEIR deride
diedre
DDEEIS eddies
DDEEIT dieted
edited
DDEELM meddle
melded
DDEELP peddle
DDEELR reddle
DDEELS sleded
DDEELU delude
dueled
eluded
DDEELV delved
DDEELW welded
DDEEMN mended
DDEEMO demode
DDEENN denned
DDEENP depend
pended
DDEENR redden
DDEENT dented
tended
DDEENU denude
dudeen
Dundee
endued
DDEENV vended
DDEENW wended
DDEEOR eroded
DDEEOS eddoes
DDEERR redder
DDEERT tedder
DDEERY Eddery
redyed
DDEEUV de Duve
DDEEUX exuded
DDEFFO doffed
DDEFFU duffed
DDEFGI fidged
DDEFGU fudged

DDEFIL fiddle
DDEFLO folded
DDEFLU fuddle
DDEFNU funded
DDEFOR fodder
forded
DDEGGI digged
DDEGGO dogged
DDEGIL gilded
glided
DDEGIN dinged
DDEGIR girded
grided
ridged
DDEGIT geddit
DDEGIU guided
DDEGJU judged
DDEGLO lodged
DDEGLU guddle
DDEGMO dodgem
modged
DDEGNO donged
DDEGNU dunged
nudged
DDEGOR dodger
DDEGOS dodges
DDEGRU drudge
DDEHIN hidden
DDEHIS dished
DDEHLU huddle
DDEHNO hodden
DDEHOO hooded
DDEHOR horded
DDEIIK kiddie
DDEIIO iodide
DDEIIT tidied
DDEIIV divide
DDEIKL kiddle
DDEIKN dinked
DDEIKR dirked
kidder
DDEIKS disked
DDEILM middle
DDEILO dildoe
DDEILP piddle
DDEILR riddle
DDEILS sidled
DDEILW widdle
DDEIMM dimmed
DDEIMN midden
minded
DDEIMS desmid
DDEINN dinned
DDEINR ridden
DDEINT dinted
DDEINU indued
DDEINW winded
DDEIOS didoes
diodes
DDEIOT doited
DDEIOV devoid
voided

DDEIPP dipped
DDEIPR prided
DDEIRR ridder
DDEISS dissed
DDEJRU judder
DDEKNU dunked
DDEKOO dooked
DDEKOU douked
DDEKSU dusked
DDELLO dolled
DDELLU dulled
DDELMO molded
DDELMU muddle
DDELNO noddle
DDELOO doodle
DDELOP poddle
DDELOT toddle
DDELPU puddle
DDELRU ruddle
DDELUY Dudley
DDEMNU Edmund
DDEMOO doomed
DDEMOR Modred
DDEMPU dumped
DDENNO donned
DDENNU dunned
DDENOR donder
droned
DDENOS Seddon
sodden
DDENOW downed
DDENOY dynode
DDENRY Dryden
DDENSU sudden
DDENSY synded
DDENTU dunted
DDENUY undyed
DDEOOS dodoes
DDEOOW wooded
DDEORV droved
DDEORW worded
DDEOSS dossed
DDEOST oddest
DDEOSU doused
DDEOSW dowsed
DDEOTT dotted
DDEPPU dupped
DDERRU rudder
DDERSU udders
DDESTU dusted
DDFILY fiddly
DDFIOR fordid
DDHINO hoddin
DDHISU dudish
DDHOSY shoddy
DDIIKK dikdik
DDIKSY skiddy
DDILNR dirndl
DDILOS dildos
DDILTY tiddly
DDIOPY dipody
DDIORS sordid

DDIOTU outdid
DDIOTY oddity
DDIRSU druids
siddur
DDLMUY muddly
DDLPUY puddly
DDMMUU dumdum
DEEEFR feeder
reefed
DEEEFZ feezed
DEEEGR degree
DEEEHL heeled
DEEEHR heeder
DEEEJR jeered
jereed
DEEEKK keeked
DEEEKL keeled
DEEEKN keened
DEEEKP peeked
DEEEKR reeked
DEEELN needle
DEEELP peeled
DEEELR leered
reeled
DEEELS seeled
DEEELT delete
DEEEMR redeem
DEEEMS seemed
DEEEMT teemed
DEEENP deepen
peened
DEEENV evened
vendee
Vendée
DEEENW weened
DEEEPP peeped
DEEEPR deeper
peered
DEEEPS seeped
DEEEPV peeved
DEEERS seeder
DEEERV reeved
veered
DEEERW weeder
DEEERY redeye
DEEFGL fledge
DEEFHT hefted
DEEFIL defile
DEEFIN define
DEEFIR defier
deifer
DEEFIS defies
DEEFLL felled
DEEFLT felted
DEEFLU fueled
DEEFLX flexed
DEEFLY fleyed
DEEFNR fender
DEEFRS defers
DEEFRT defter
DEEFRY redefy
DEEFSU defuse

DEEFUZ defuze
DEEFZZ fezzed
DEEGGI gidgee
DEEGGL legged
DEEGGP pegged
DEEGGV vegged
DEEGHR hedger
DEEGHS hedges
DEEGIJ gidjee
DEEGIN deeing
DEEGIR edgier
DEEGIS sieged
DEEGKS kedges
DEEGLL gelled
DEEGLN legend
DEEGLP pledge
DEEGLR gelder
ledger
redleg
DEEGLS gledes
ledges
sledge
DEEGLU deluge
DEEGMM gemmed
DEEGMR merged
DEEGNR gender
DEEGNU dengue
DEEGNV venged
DEEGOS geodes
DEEGRS edgers
greeds
DEEGRV verged
DEEGRY greedy
greyed
DEEGSS sedges
DEEGSU segued
DEEGSW wedges
DEEGSZ Szeged
DEEHLM helmed
DEEHLP helped
DEEHLV helved
DEEHMM hemmed
DEEHMS meshed
DEEHMT themed
DEEHNT hented
DEEHRR herder
DEEHSW shewed
DEEILN Leiden
DEEILR lieder
relied
DEEILS diesel
ediles
elides
DEEILV levied
veiled
DEEILX exiled
DEEILY eyelid
DEEIMP impede
DEEIMS demies
demise
DEEIMT itemed
DEEINN indene

DEEINR denier
Edirne
nereid
reined
DEEINS denies
dienes
seined
DEEINV Devine
endive
envied
veined
DEEIPP Dieppe
DEEIPS espied
DEEIRS desire
eiders
reside
DEEIRT dieter
reedit
retied
tiered
DEEIRU ureide
DEEIRV derive
reived
DEEIRW dewier
DEEISS dieses
seised
DEEISV devise
sieved
DEEISZ seized
DEEITV evited
DEEITX exited
DEEIVW viewed
DEEJKR jerked
DEEJLL jelled
DEEJSS jessed
DEEJST jested
DEEJTT jetted
DEEKKR Dekker
DEEKNN kenned
DEEKNR kerned
DEEKOV evoked
DEEKPR perked
DEEKSW skewed
DEELLR Deller
DEELLW welled
DEELLY yelled
DEELMN Mendel
DEELMT melted
DEELMW mewled
DEELMY medley
DEELNR lender
DEELNS Selden
DEELNW wedeln
DEELNY Leyden
DEELOP eloped
DEELPR pedler
DEELPT pelted
DEELPY deeply
yelped
DEELRS elders
DEELRU eluder
DEELRV delver
DEELRW lewder
reweld
welder
DEELST eldest
DEELSU eludes
DEELSV delves
DEELSW slewed
DEELTT letted
DEELTU eluted
teledu
DEELTW welted
DEELUX deluxe
DEEMNO omened
DEEMNR mender
remend
DEEMNS emends
Mendes
DEEMNT dement
DEEMOT demote
emoted
DEEMOW meowed
DEEMPR permed
premed
DEEMPT empted
temped
DEEMRT termed
DEEMRU demure
DEEMRY remedy
DEEMSS messed
DEEMTU Te Deum
DEENNO donnee
DEENNP penned
DEENNY yenned
DEENOP depone
opened
DEENOR redone
DEENOS donees
Odense
DEENOT denote
DEENOV ovened
DEENPX expend
DEENRR render
DEENRS denser
enders
sender
DEENRT rented
tender
DEENRU Deurne
endure
enured
DEENRV Denver
nerved
vender
DEENSS sensed
DEENST nested
tensed
DEENSU endues
ensued
DEENSW Sweden
DEENTT detent
netted
tented
DEENTV vented
DEENTX dentex
extend
DEENUV vendue
DEEOPS depose
epodes
speedo
DEEORS erodes
redoes
DEEORT teredo
DEEORV devore
DEEORZ zeroed
DEEOTV devote
vetoed
DEEPPP pepped
DEEPPR repped
DEEPRU perdue
pureed
DEEPRV perved
DEEPRY preyed
DEEPSS speeds
DEEPSW spewed
DEEPSY speedy
DEEPTT petted
DEEPTU depute
DEEQUU queued
DEERRW redrew
DEERSS seders
DEERST desert
deters
rested
DEERSU reused
DEERSV served
versed
DEERSY redyes
DEERTT retted
DEERTX dexter
DEERVV revved
DEESST steeds
DEESSW swedes
DEESTT detest
tested
DEESTU etudes
DEESTV devest
vested
DEESTW stewed
tweeds
DEESTZ zested
DEESUX exudes
DEETTV vetted
DEETTW wetted
DEETWY tweedy
DEFFHU huffed
DEFFIM miffed
DEFFIN niffed
DEFFIR differ
riffed
DEFFIT tiffed
DEFFLU duffel
duffle
luffed
DEFFMU muffed
DEFFNO offend
DEFFOR doffer
DEFFPU puffed
DEFFRU duffer
ruffed
DEFGGI figged
DEFGGO fogged
DEFGIR fridge
DEFGIS fidges
DEFGIT fidget
gifted
DEFGLO Geldof
golfed
DEFGLU gulfed
DEFGLY fledgy
DEFGOO goofed
DEFGOR forged
DEFGSU fudges
DEFHIS fished
DEFHOO hoofed
DEFIKN finked
knifed
DEFILL filled
DEFILM filmed
DEFILO foiled
DEFILR rifled
DEFILS fields
DEFILT flited
lifted
DEFIMR firmed
DEFINN finned
DEFINO foined
DEFINR finder
friend
redfin
DEFINS fiends
DEFINU fundie
DEFIOO foodie
DEFIOT foetid
DEFIRT rifted
DEFIRV fervid
DEFIST fisted
sifted
DEFITT fitted
DEFIZZ fizzed
DEFJLS fjelds
DEFKLU fluked
DEFKNU funked
DEFKOR forked
DEFLLU fulled
DEFLMU flumed
DEFLMY medfly
DEFLNO enfold
fondle
DEFLOO fooled
DEFLOR folder
refold
DEFLOT lofted
DEFLOU fouled
DEFLOW flowed
fowled
wolfed

DEFLRU furled
DEFLTU fluted
DEFLTY deftly
flyted
DEFLUX fluxed
DEFMOR deform
formed
DEFNNU funned
DEFNOR fonder
DEFNOU fondue
DEFNRU funder
refund
DEFOOR foredo
roofed
DEFOOT footed
DEFOOW woofed
DEFORU Froude
DEFRRU furred
DEFRSU surfed
DEFRTU turfed
DEFSSU fussed
DEFTTU tufted
DEFUZZ fuzzed
DEGGGI gigged
DEGGHO hogged
DEGGHU hugged
DEGGIJ jigged
DEGGIL ligged
DEGGIN edging
DEGGIO doggie
DEGGIP pigged
DEGGIR digger
rigged
DEGGIT tigged
DEGGIW wigged
DEGGJO jogged
DEGGJU jugged
DEGGLO dogleg
logged
DEGGLU lugged
DEGGMU mugged
DEGGNO gonged
DEGGNU gunged
DEGGOR dogger
gorged
DEGGOT togged
DEGGOU gouged
DEGGPU pugged
DEGGRU grudge
rugged
DEGGRY dreggy
DEGGTU tugged
DEGHIN hinged
DEGHIR dreigh
DEGHIS sighed
DEGHSU gushed
DEGIIW widgie
DEGIKN kinged
DEGILL gilled
DEGILN dingle
DEGILR gilder
girdle
glider
regild
ridgel
DEGILS glides
DEGILY edgily
DEGIMR grimed
DEGIMS midges
smidge
DEGIMT midget
DEGINN ending
ginned
DEGINO Gideon
DEGINP pinged
DEGINR dinger
girned
reding
ringed
DEGINS deigns
design
dinges
signed
singed
DEGINT tinged
DEGINW dewing
winged
DEGINY dingey
dyeing
DEGINZ zinged
DEGIOS dogies
geoids
DEGIPP gipped
DEGIPR griped
DEGIRR girder
DEGIRS dirges
grides
ridges
DEGIRT girted
DEGIRU guider
DEGIST digest
DEGISU guides
guised
DEGITU dugite
DEGITW widget
DEGJRU judger
DEGJSU judges
DEGLLU gulled
DEGLNO dongle
golden
longed
DEGLNU gulden
lunged
DEGLOP plodge
DEGLOR dogrel
lodger
DEGLOS lodges
DEGLOV gloved
DEGLOW glowed
DEGLOZ glozed
DEGLPU gulped
DEGLSU sludge
DEGMMU gummed
DEGMNO dogmen
monged
DEGMOS modges
DEGMSU smudge
DEGNNU gunned
DEGNOP ponged
DEGNOT tonged
DEGNOW gowned
DEGNRU dunger
gerund
gurned
nudger
DEGNSU nudges
DEGOOP pogoed
DEGOOS goosed
DEGOPR groped
DEGOPS podges
DEGORS sodger
DEGORU drogue
gourde
rogued
rouged
DEGOSS gossed
DEGOST godets
stodge
DEGOSW wodges
DEGOSY dogeys
DEGPPY gypped
DEGPRU purged
DEGPSU pudges
DEGRSU surged
DEGRTU trudge
DEGSTU degust
gusted
DEGTTU gutted
DEHHSU hushed
DEHILL hilled
DEHILP Delphi
DEHILS shield
DEHILT hilted
DEHILW whiled
DEHIMN mehndi
DEHIMO hemoid
DEHINO hoiden
honied
DEHINR hinder
DEHINS shined
DEHINT hinted
DEHINW whined
DEHIOO hoodie
DEHIOS Hesiod
DEHIOX oxhide
DEHIPP hipped
DEHIPS pished
DEHIPT pithed
DEHIRS hiders
shired
DEHIRT dither
DEHISS dishes
hissed
DEHIST shited
DEHISW wished
DEHITT tithed
DEHITW whited
withed
DEHJOS joshed
DEHKLU hulked
DEHKNO honked
DEHKOO hooked
DEHKOW howked
DEHKSU husked
DEHLLU hulled
DEHLNO holden
DEHLOR holder
DEHLOS dholes
DEHLOT tholed
DEHLOW howled
DEHLPU upheld
DEHLRU hurdle
hurled
DEHLSU lushed
DEHMMU hummed
DEHMNO hodmen
DEHMNY hymned
DEHMOS moshed
DEHMOT method
DEHMPU humped
DEHMRY rhymed
DEHMSU mushed
DEHNOP phoned
DEHNOR dehorn
horned
DEHNOS noshed
DEHNOY hoyden
DEHNRY Hendry
DEHNSS shends
DEHNSU unshed
DEHNTU hunted
DEHOOP hooped
DEHOOS shooed
DEHOOT hooted
DEHOPP hopped
DEHOPS ephods
DEHORS hordes
horsed
reshod
Rhodes
shored
DEHORW whored
DEHOST hosted
DEHOSU housed
DEHOSV shoved
DEHOSW showed
DEHOTT hotted
DEHPST depths
DEHPSU pushed
DEHRSS sherds
shreds
DEHRSU rushed
DEHRSW shrewd
DEHTTU hutted
DEIIKN dinkie
kindie
DEIIKR Kediri
DEIILP lipide

DEIIMS	imides
DEIINO	iodine
DEIINS	indies
	inside
DEIINT	indite
	tineid
DEIINV	divine
DEIIOS	iodise
DEIIOZ	iodize
DEIIPT	pitied
DEIIRS	irides
DEIIRT	tidier
DEIISS	diesis
DEIIST	tidies
DEIISX	deixis
	dixies
DEIJKN	jinked
DEIJLT	jilted
DEIJNO	joined
DEIJNX	jinxed
DEIJRS	jerids
DEIJSU	judies
DEIKLL	killed
DEIKLM	milked
DEIKLN	kilned
	kindle
	linked
DEIKLO	keloid
DEIKLS	silked
DEIKLT	kilted
DEIKNP	pinked
DEIKNR	kinder
DEIKNW	winked
DEIKNY	kidney
DEIKPP	kipped
DEIKPS	spiked
DEIKPU	Updike
DEIKRS	risked
DEIKRU	duiker
DEIKSS	kissed
DEIKST	skited
DEIKSV	skived
DEIKTT	kitted
DEILLM	milled
DEILLP	pilled
DEILLT	lilted
	tilled
DEILLU	illude
DEILLW	willed
DEILMN	limned
	milden
DEILMO	meloid
	moiled
DEILMP	dimple
	limped
DEILMR	milder
DEILMS	misled
	slimed
	smiled
DEILMT	milted
DEILMW	mildew
DEILNN	linden
DEILNO	doline
	indole
DEILNT	dentil
	Tilden
DEILOP	diploe
	dipole
DEILOR	roiled
DEILOS	Isolde
	oldies
	soiled
DEILOT	toiled
DEILOV	livedo
DEILPP	lipped
DEILPS	dispel
	lisped
	spiled
DEILPX	diplex
DEILRS	idlers
	sidler
	slider
DEILRV	drivel
DEILRW	wilder
DEILRY	direly
	ridley
DEILSS	sidles
	slides
DEILST	delist
	idlest
	listed
	silted
	tildes
DEILSU	Delius
DEILSV	devils
DEILSW	wields
DEILSY	yields
DEILTT	tilted
	titled
DEILTU	dilute
DEILTW	wilted
DEILWY	dewily
	widely
	wieldy
DEIMMR	dimmer
	rimmed
DEIMMU	medium
DEIMNO	monied
DEIMNP	impend
DEIMNR	minder
	remind
DEIMNS	denims
DEIMNT	minted
DEIMOR	dormie
	moider
DEIMOW	mowdie
DEIMPP	pimped
DEIMPR	primed
DEIMPW	wimped
DEIMRS	dermis
	dimers
DEIMRT	mitred
DEIMSS	missed
DEIMST	demist
	demits
	misted
DEIMTU	tedium
DEINNP	pinned
DEINNR	dinner
DEINNS	Dennis
	sinned
DEINNT	dentin
	indent
	intend
	tinned
DEINNU	undine
DEINNW	enwind
DEINOP	opined
DEINOR	De Niro
	Indore
	ironed
DEINOS	Edison
	noised
	onside
DEINOV	nevoid
DEINOZ	D'Inzeo
DEINPP	nipped
DEINPS	sniped
	spined
DEINRS	diners
	rinsed
	snider
DEINRT	rident
	tinder
DEINRU	inured
	ruined
DEINRV	driven
	verdin
DEINRW	rewind
	winder
DEINST	teinds
DEINSU	indues
	undies
DEINSW	widens
	Widnes
	Wisden
DEINSY	Disney
	Sidney
	snidey
DEINSZ	dizens
DEINTT	tinted
DEINTU	dunite
	united
	untied
DEINTW	de Wint
	twined
DEIOOR	oroide
DEIOOV	Oviedo
DEIOPR	dopier
	Pedro I
	period
DEIOPS	poised
DEIORS	dories
DEIORT	editor
	rioted
	tierod
	triode
DEIORV	voider
DEIORW	dowier
	weirdo
DEIORZ	dozier
DEIOST	todies
DEIOSV	videos
DEIOSX	doxies
	oxides
DEIPPP	pipped
DEIPPR	dipper
	ripped
DEIPPS	sipped
DEIPPT	tipped
DEIPPZ	zipped
DEIPQU	piqued
DEIPRS	prides
	prised
	spider
	spired
DEIPRZ	prized
DEIPSS	pissed
DEIPST	spited
DEIPSU	upside
DEIPSV	vespid
DEIPSW	swiped
	wisped
DEIPTT	pitted
DEIRRS	derris
	driers
	riders
DEIRRU	durrie
DEIRRV	driver
DEIRRY	yirred
DEIRST	driest
	stride
DEIRSU	diseur
DEIRSV	divers
	drives
DEIRSW	weirds
DEIRTV	divert
DEISSS	disses
DEISST	deists
	desist
DEISSU	disuse
	issued
DEISTU	duties
	suited
DEISTV	divest
DEISTW	widest
DEISVW	swived
DEITTW	de Witt
	witted
DEIZZZ	zizzed
DEJKNU	junked
DEJKOO	jooked
DEJKOU	jouked
DEJLLO	jolled
DEJLOT	jolted
DEJLOW	jowled
DEJMPU	jumped
DEJOTT	jotted

DEJTTU jutted
DEKKOS dekkos
DEKLOO looked
DEKLRU lurked
DEKLSU sulked
DEKMNU Mukden
DEKMOS smoked
DEKNOR Kedron
DEKNOY donkey
DEKNOZ zonked
DEKNRU dunker
DEKOOR rooked
DEKOOS sooked
DEKOOT dooket
DEKOPS spoked
DEKORW worked
DEKORY yorked
DEKOST stoked
DEKOSU souked
DEKRUY duyker
DEKSTU tusked
DELLLO lolled
DELLLU lulled
DELLMU mulled
DELLOP polled
DELLOR rolled
DELLOT tolled
DELLOU duello
DELLOW Dowell
DELLPU pulled
DELLRU duller
DELLSU Dulles
DELLSW dwells
DELLWY lewdly
DELMNO dolmen
DELMOO loomed
DELMOR molder
DELMOS models
seldom
DELMOT molted
DELMOU module
DELMOY melody
DELMPU lumped
plumed
DELNOO noodle
DELNOR rondel
DELNOU louden
nodule
DELNOV Vondel
DELNOW Weldon
DELNRU nurled
rundle
DELNUY nudely
DELOOP looped
poodle
pooled
DELOOS loosed
oodles
soloed
sooled
DELOOT looted
toledo
tooled
DELOPP lopped
DELOPR polder
DELOPS sloped
DELOPU louped
DELOPW lowped
plowed
DELOPY deploy
DELORS Delors
resold
solder
DELORT retold
DELORU louder
loured
DELORW weldor
DELORY yodler
DELOSS dossel
DELOST oldest
DELOSU loused
DELOSV solved
DELOSW dowels
lowsed
slowed
DELOSY yodels
yodles
DELOTT dottel
dottle
lotted
DELOTU louted
DELOWY yowled
DELOYY doyley
DELPPU pulped
DELPRU drupel
purled
DELPSU pulsed
DELPTU duplet
DELPUX duplex
DELRUY rudely
DELSSU dulses
DELSTU lusted
DELSTV veldts
DELSTY styled
DEMMMU mummed
DEMMOS modems
DEMMPU mumped
DEMMSU summed
DEMNOO mooned
DEMNOR modern
DEMNOS demons
DEMOOR moored
roomed
DEMOOT mooted
DEMOOZ zoomed
DEMOPP mopped
DEMOPR romped
DEMOPS mopeds
DEMOPY yomped
DEMORR dormer
DEMORW wormed
DEMOST modest
DEMOTT domett
DEMPPU pumped
DEMPRU dumper
DEMPSU spumed
DEMRRU murder
DEMRSU demurs
DEMSSU mussed
sedums
DEMUZZ muzzed
DENNOS donnes
DENNOT Denton
tendon
DENNOU undone
DENNOW wonned
DENNPU punned
DENNRU dunner
DENNSU sunned
DENNTU tunned
DENOOS nodose
noosed
odeons
DENOOW wooden
DENOPR ponder
DENOPT Top End
DENORS drones
snored
sorned
DENORT rodent
DENORU undoer
DENORV vendor
DENORW downer
wonder
DENORY Rodney
yonder
DENOSS sondes
DENOST Donets
Ostend
stoned
DENOSU undoes
DENOSV devons
DENOSW endows
snowed
DENOSY doyens
DENOSZ dozens
DENOTW wonted
DENPRU pruned
DENPSS spends
DENPSU sendup
upends
DENPTU punted
DENRST trends
DENRSU nursed
sunder
DENRTU turned
DENRTY trendy
DENRUV Verdun
DENRUW undrew
DENSTU Undset
DENSUU unused
DENSUW sundew
DENSYY Sydney
DENTTU nutted
DEOOPP pooped
DEOORS rodeos
roosed
DEOORT rooted
DEOORV overdo
DEOOST De Soto
sooted
DEOOTT tooted
DEOPPP popped
DEOPPR dopper
DEOPPS sopped
DEOPPT topped
DEOPPW wopped
DEOPRS prosed
spored
DEOPRT deport
ported
redtop
DEOPRU poured
rouped
DEOPRV proved
DEOPRW powder
DEOPSS possed
DEOPST depots
despot
posted
stoped
DEOPSU pseudo
DEOPTT potted
DEOPTU pouted
DEOQTU quoted
DEORRS derros
orders
DEORRT retrod
DEORRU ordure
DEORRV drover
DEORRW reword
DEORSS dosers
dosser
sordes
DEORST Dorset
doters
sorted
stored
strode
DEORSU douser
roused
soured
DEORSV droves
DEORSW dowers
dowser
drowse
DEORSZ dozers
DEORTT dotter
rotted
DEORTU detour
routed
toured
DEORTW trowed
DEORTX dextro
DEORUV devour
DEOSSS dosses
DEOSST tossed
DEOSSU douses

soused
DEOSSW dowses
DEOSTU ousted
DEOSTV stoved
DEOSTW stowed
DEOSUX exodus
DEOSXY desoxy
DEOTTT totted
DEOTTU touted
DEOTUV devout
DEOTUX tuxedo
DEPPPU pupped
DEPPSU supped
DEPPTU tupped
DEPRRU purred
DEPRSU drupes
dupers
perdus
prudes
pursed
DEPRUY dupery
DEPSSU pseuds
DEPSUY pudsey
DEPTTU putted
DEPTUY deputy
DERRSU Durrës
DERRSY dryers
DERRTV Rt Revd
DERRUY rudery
DERSSU druses
duress
DERSSY dressy
DERSTU duster
rudest
rusted
DERSTY dryest
DERTTU rutted
DESSSU sussed
DESTUV duvets
DETTTU tutted
DFGGOO fogdog
DFGIIR frigid
DFGILU fulgid
DFIINY nidify
DFIIRT trifid
DFILNO infold
DFILOR florid
DFILSU fluids
DFIMOY modify
DFINSU fundis
DFIORS fiords
DFIRST drifts
DFIRTY drifty
DFJORS fjords
DFLNOU unfold
DFLNOY fondly
DFLOOS floods
DFLORU Rudolf
DFNORS fronds
DFNOSU founds
DFNSUU fundus
DFOORX oxford
DFOOSU doofus
DGGNOU dugong
gundog
DGGRUY druggy
DGHIIN hiding
DGHINY dinghy
DGHIST dights
DGHOOT hotdog
DGHOSU doughs
DGHOTU dought
DGHOUY doughy
DGIIKN diking
DGIILN idling
DGIINN dining
indign
DGIINO indigo
DGIINP pidgin
DGIINR riding
DGIINS siding
DGIINT tiding
DGIINV diving
DGIIST digits
DGIJOU judogi
DGIKNY dyking
DGILNO doling
DGILOT diglot
DGILSU guilds
DGIMNO doming
DGIMOO omigod
DGIMTU midgut
DGINOP doping
pongid
DGINOR roding
DGINOS doings
dosing
DGINOT doting
DGINOU guidon
DGINOW dowing
Godwin
DGINOZ dozing
DGINPU duping
DGINRS grinds
DGINRU during
DGINRY drying
DGIOTW godwit
DGIRSU Sigurd
DGIRTU turgid
DGLOOU duolog
DGLOOY goodly
DGLSUY sludgy
DGMSUY smudgy
DGNOOR Dorgon
drongo
Gordon
Grodno
DGNOOS godson
DGNOOU Gounod
DGNOOW godown
DGNORU ground
DGNOSU sundog
sun-god
DGNRUU Gudrun
DGORSU gourds
DGOSTY stodgy
DGOTUU dugout
DHIIPS hispid
DHIISW widish
DHIJTU Judith
DHILOS Dhílos
oldish
DHIMOS modish
DHINOO Hindoo
DHINSY shindy
DHIOOT dhooti
DHIOPY hypoid
DHIORR horrid
DHIOST dhotis
DHIOSV dovish
DHIOSY hyoids
DHIRST thirds
DHIRSU rudish
DHISTU dhutis
DHISTW widths
DHLLOS dholls
DHLOPU holdup
uphold
DHLOSU should
DHLTUU Duluth
DHNOOU Houdon
DHNORT Northd
DHNOSU hounds
Hudson
unshod
DHOOOO hoodoo
DHOORS Rhodos
Ródhos
DHOORT hotrod
DHORSU shroud
DHORSY hydros
DHORTU drouth
DHOSSW showds
DIIJNN djinni
DIILMP limpid
DIILOP lipoid
DIILOS solidi
DIILPS lipids
DIILQU liquid
DIILST distil
DIILTY tidily
DIIMNU indium
DIIMOS idioms
iodism
DIIMOU oidium
DIIMTW dimwit
DIIMTY dimity
DIINOX dioxin
DIINRS indris
DIIOOP opioid
DIIORV viroid
DIIOST idiots
DIIOTT doitit
DIJMSU musjid
DIJNNY djinny
DIKKLU kudlik
DIKKOP dikkop
DIKLNY kindly
DIKLTU kidult
DIKMNU dinkum
DIKNNU unkind
DIKNOR Kidron
DIKNRS drinks
DIKNSV Dvinsk
DIKOOS skidoo
DILLMY mildly
DILLRS drills
DILLSY idylls
DILLWY wildly
DILMOR milord
DILMOU idolum
moduli
DILMPY dimply
DILNNU dunlin
DILNTU indult
DILNUU Ulundi
DILOPY dopily
ploidy
DILOSS solids
DILOST stolid
DILOXY xyloid
DILOYZ dozily
DIMNOO domino
DIMNOR nimrod
DIMNRU Nimrud
DIMNSU nudism
DIMOPU podium
DIMOSU sodium
DIMOSW wisdom
DIMOSY disomy
DIMPSY dimpsy
DIMRSU mudirs
DINNUW unwind
DINOOR indoor
DINOPS poinds
DINOPU dupion
unipod
DINORU durion
DINOSU Dunois
DINOSW disown
DINOTZ Dönitz
DINOWW window
DINPSU Pindus
DINPTU pundit
DINPUW upwind
windup
DINRUU Urundi
DINSTU nudist
DINTUY nudity
untidy
DIOOPP doppio
DIOOPS isopod
DIOORT toroid
DIOOST ootids
DIOOSU iodous
odious
DIOOSV ovoids
DIOOSZ zooids

DIOOTX	toxoid
DIOPRT	torpid
	tripod
DIORRT	torrid
DIORST	droits
DIOSTT	dittos
DIOSTU	studio
DIOSTV	divots
DIOSWW	widows
DIPPRY	drippy
DIPRTU	putrid
DIPSTU	stupid
DIQSSU	squids
DIRSUZ	durzis
DJNNOO	donjon
DKNOOP	pondok
DKNOOS	donkos
	kondos
DKNRSU	drunks
DKOOOO	koodoo
DKOORS	drooks
DKORSU	drouks
DKORSY	drosky
DLLOOP	dollop
DLLORY	drolly
	lordly
DLLOUW	Ludlow
DLLOUY	loudly
DLMNOO	Lomond
DLMOSU	moulds
DLMOUY	mouldy
DLNNOO	London
DLNOPU	Dunlop
DLNOSU	unsold
DLNOTU	untold
DLNOUV	Völund
DLNUUY	unduly
DLOOPS	podsol
DLOOPZ	podzol
DLOORS	drools
DLOORU	dolour
DLORSW	worlds
DLORUY	dourly
DMMRUY	drummy
DMNOOR	dromon
DMNOOY	monody
DMNOSU	mounds
	osmund
DMNOTU	Du Mont
DMOOSS	sodoms
DMOOSY	sodomy
DMORSU	dorsum
DNNOOU	Dunoon
DNOORS	donors
	rondos
DNOOSS	snoods
DNOOSU	nodous
DNOOSW	Dowson
DNOPSU	pounds
DNORSU	rounds
DNORSW	drowns
DNORTU	rotund
	untrod
DNOSSU	sounds
DNOSSY	synods
DNOSTU	donuts
	stound
DNOSUW	swound
	wounds
DNOSUZ	zounds
DNOTTU	Dutton
DNRSUY	sundry
DOOOOV	voodoo
DOOPRS	droops
DOOPRU	uropod
DOOPRY	droopy
DOORSU	odours
DOOSWY	woodsy
DOPRSY	dropsy
DORSSW	swords
DORSSY	drossy
DORSTU	stroud
DORSWY	drowsy
DPSTUU	dustup
DRSTUY	sturdy
EEEEPT	teepee
EEEEPW	peewee
EEEEWW	weewee
EEEFFT	effete
EEEFLR	feeler
EEEFRR	reefer
EEEFRZ	freeze
EEEFSZ	feezes
EEEGMR	emerge
EEEGNR	Greene
	renege
EEEGNU	Eugène
EEEGNV	Genève
EEEGRS	Seeger
EEEGRZ	geezer
EEEHLR	heeler
	reheel
EEEHNS	Sheene
EEEHNT	ethene
EEEHST	seethe
EEEHTT	teethe
EEEHWZ	wheeze
EEEIJL	jeelie
EEEIKL	keelie
EEEILS	seelie
EEEINW	weenie
EEEIPR	peerie
EEEIRR	eerier
EEEJRR	jeerer
EEEKLU	ekuele
EEEKMR	meeker
EEEKNR	keener
EEEKNT	ketene
EEEKPR	keeper
EEEKRS	seeker
EEELMS	melees
	Semele
EEELMX	lexeme
EEELNS	Selene
EEELNV	eleven
EEELPR	peeler
EEELRR	reeler
EEELSS	lessee
EEELST	Steele
EEELSV	levees
	sleeve
EEELSY	Elysée
EEELTY	eyelet
EEEMMS	sememe
EEEMNR	meneer
EEEMRS	seemer
EEEMRT	meeter
	teemer
EEEMST	esteem
	mestee
EEENRS	serene
EEENRT	entree
	eterne
	retene
EEENRV	evener
	veneer
EEENSS	Essene
EEENSZ	sneeze
EEEOPP	epopee
EEEPPR	peeper
EEEPRV	peever
EEEPRW	weeper
EEEPST	tepees
EEEPSV	peeves
EEEPSW	pewees
EEERRV	revere
EEERSV	reeves
	severe
EEERTT	teeter
	terete
EEERTV	Tevere
EEERTX	Exeter
EEERVW	weever
EEESTT	settee
EEESTV	steeve
EEETWZ	tweeze
EEFFIL	Eiffel
EEFFOT	toffee
EEFFSU	effuse
EEFGIN	feeing
EEFGRU	refuge
EEFHIR	heifer
EEFHOR	hereof
EEFHRT	hefter
EEFILN	feline
	fleein
EEFILR	ferlie
	refile
	relief
EEFINR	ferine
	refine
EEFINW	Newfie
EEFIRR	refire
EEFIRS	fieres
EEFIRZ	frieze
EEFLLO	felloe
EEFLLR	feller
EEFLNN	fennel
EEFLNS	flense
EEFLRS	fleers
EEFLRT	reflet
	telfer
	Terfel
EEFLRU	ferule
	fueler
	refuel
EEFLRW	Werfel
EEFLRX	reflex
EEFLRY	freely
EEFLST	fleets
EEFLSX	flexes
EEFLTT	fettle
EEFLUY	eyeful
EEFMMS	femmes
EEFMNO	foemen
EEFPRR	prefer
EEFPTY	tepefy
EEFRRS	refers
EEFRRT	ferret
EEFRST	fester
	freest
EEFRSU	refuse
EEFRSV	fevers
EEFRTT	fetter
EEFRTU	refute
EEFSSS	fesses
EEFSSU	fusees
EEFSTW	fewest
EEFSUZ	fuzees
EEFSZZ	fezzes
EEGGGI	geggie
EEGGIN	geeing
EEGGIR	Geiger
	greige
EEGGIV	veggie
EEGGLR	eggler
EEGGOR	George
EEGGRS	eggers
EEGGSV	vegges
EEGHNS	henges
EEGHOT	Goethe
EEGIIK	Geikie
EEGILS	lieges
EEGIMR	emigre
	regime
EEGINN	engine
EEGINP	peeing
EEGINS	genies
	seeing
	Siegen
EEGINT	teeing
EEGINW	weeing
EEGINY	eyeing
EEGIRV	grieve
EEGISS	sieges
EEGKLR	kegler
EEGLMN	legmen
EEGLMU	legume

EEGLNS Engels
EEGLNT gentle
EEGLNU lungee
EEGLRT reglet
EEGLRU reglue
EEGLST gleets
EEGLTY gleety
EEGMNO genome
EEGMNR germen
EEGMNT tegmen
EEGMOT gemote
EEGMRR merger
EEGMRS merges
EEGNNT gennet
EEGNOP pongee
EEGNRS genres
greens
EEGNRT gerent
regent
EEGNRY energy
greeny
Ygerne
EEGNST genets
gentes
EEGNSV venges
EEGPRU pugree
EEGRRT regret
EEGRRV verger
EEGRRW regrew
EEGRRY greyer
EEGRSS egress
EEGRST egrets
greets
EEGRSV verges
EEGRSX grexes
EEGRSY geyser
EEGRTT getter
EEGRUZ Greuze
EEGSST egests
geests
gestes
EEGSSU segues
EEHHSS sheesh
EEHHSW wheesh
EEHINR herein
inhere
EEHINT theine
EEHIRR rehire
EEHIRT either
EEHIST sithee
EEHITV thieve
EEHKLS shekel
EEHLLN Hellen
EEHLLR heller
EEHLLS Helles
EEHLMR helmer
EEHLMT helmet
EEHLPR helper
EEHLQS sheqel
EEHLSV helves
shelve
EEHLSW wheels

EEHLWY wheely
EEHMMR hemmer
EEHMNP hempen
EEHMNS enmesh
EEHMPT tempeh
EEHMRS Hermes
rehems
rhemes
EEHMSS meshes
EEHMST themes
EEHMUX exhume
EEHNOR hereon
EEHNOX hexone
EEHNPS sphene
EEHNPW nephew
EEHNRT nether
EEHNRZ Herzen
EEHNSS sheens
EEHNSY sheeny
EEHNTY ethyne
EEHNWW whenwe
EEHOPS sheepo
EEHORS heroes
reshoe
EEHORT hereto
hetero
Hotere
EEHOSX hexose
EEHOTW towhee
EEHPPR hepper
EEHPRS herpes
sphere
EEHPRT threep
EEHRSS reshes
sheers
EEHRST Esther
threes
EEHRSW hewers
shewer
wheres
EEHRSX hexers
EEHRSY heresy
EEHRTT tether
EEHRTW wether
EEHSST sheets
theses
EEHSVY Hevesy
EEHWYY wheyey
EEHWYZ wheezy
EEIIKK kiekie
EEIILM mielie
EEIIMN meinie
EEIINW wienie
EEIJNN jinnee
EEIJSS jessie
EEIJST eejits
EEIJSW jewies
EEIKLP kelpie
EEIKLS selkie
EEIKLT Keitel
EEIKPW kewpie
EEIKRS seiker

EEIKSS eskies
EEILLL Lillee
EEILMS elemis
Méliès
EEILNP penile
EEILNR lierne
reline
EEILNS enisle
ensile
senile
silene
EEILOR loerie
EEILPT pelite
EEILRS relies
resile
EEILRV levier
relive
revile
veiler
EEILRY eerily
EEILST elites
EEILSV levies
EEILSW Wiesel
EEILSX exiles
ilexes
EEILTV levite
EEILVW weevil
EEILZZ lezzie
EEIMMN Eminem
EEIMNN Niemen
EEIMNP piemen
EEIMNR ermine
EEIMNT emetin
EEIMNY Yemeni
EEIMPR empire
epimer
permie
premie
EEIMRS Mieres
misere
remise
EEIMRT metier
tremie
EEIMSS emesis
EEINNP pinene
EEINNR nerine
Rennie
EEINNS Esenin
EEINNV Vienne
EEINOS eosine
EEINPR repine
EEINQU equine
EEINRS nereis
serein
serine
EEINRT entire
triene
EEINRV envier
Nièvre
EEINRW wiener
EEINSS Neisse
seines

EEINSV envies
nieves
EEINSX exines
EEINTT nettie
EEINTV venite
EEINTX extine
EEINTZ Iténez
EEIORS soiree
EEIPPT tippee
EEIPPY yippee
EEIPQU equipe
EEIPRR Pierre
EEIPRS espier
EEIPRT Peter I
Petrie
EEIPRX expire
EEIPSS espies
EEIPTT petite
EEIPTW peewit
EEIRRS sirree
EEIRRT etrier
retire
EEIRRV reiver
EEIRRW rewire
EEIRSS seiser
series
EEIRST resite
reties
Steier
EEIRSV reives
revise
EEIRSX sexier
EEIRSY eyries
EEIRTV verite
EEIRVV revive
EEIRVW review
viewer
EEISSS seises
EEISSV sieves
EEISSY Sieyès
EEISSZ seizes
EEISTV evites
EEITTW wettie
EEITTY yettie
EEJJNU jejune
EEJKRR jerker
EEJLSW jewels
EEJMOR Jerome
EEJNNR Jenner
EEJNNS Jensen
EEJNNT jennet
EEJRST jester
EEJRSY jersey
EEJSSS jesses
EEJSSW Jewess
EEKKLR lekker
EEKKNO koneke
EEKLLR Keller
EEKLMY meekly
EEKLNN kennel
EEKLNR kernel
EEKLNS kneels

EEKLNY	keenly
EEKLPR	Kepler
EEKLRS	kerels
EEKLRT	kelter
EEKLRW	kewler
EEKLSS	sleeks
EEKLSV	kevels
EEKLSY	sleeky
EEKLTT	kettle
EEKLWY	weekly
EEKMNS	Meknès
EEKMRR	Kremer
EEKMRS	kermes
EEKNOT	ketone
EEKNRR	renker
EEKNRS	kernes
EEKNST	kentes
EEKNSY	Keynes
EEKORV	evoker
	revoke
EEKORW	rewoke
EEKOST	ketose
EEKOSV	evokes
EEKPPU	upkeep
EEKPRU	peruke
EEKRSS	eskers
EEKRSW	skewer
	Wesker
EEKRSY	kersey
	rekeys
EELLPS	Pelles
EELLPT	pellet
EELLRS	resell
	seller
EELLRT	retell
	teller
EELLRV	yeller
EELLSV	levels
EELLSW	Sewell
	Welles
EELMOT	omelet
EELMPR	Lemper
EELMPT	pelmet
	temple
EELMRS	merles
EELMRT	melter
	remelt
EELMRU	relume
EELMRW	mewler
EELMRY	merely
EELMSY	seemly
EELMTT	mettle
EELMTY	meetly
EELNNT	lenten
EELNNV	vennel
EELNOS	leones
EELNOV	elevon
EELNPS	pensel
	spleen
EELNPV	Pleven
EELNRR	Lerner
EELNRT	relent
EELNRU	unreel
EELNSS	lenses
	lessen
EELNST	nestle
EELNSV	Velsen
EELNSW	newels
EELNTT	nettle
EELNTU	eluent
EELNUV	Leuven
	venule
EELNVY	Evelyn
	evenly
EELNXY	xylene
EELOPP	people
EELOPR	eloper
EELOPS	elopes
EELORS	resole
EELORZ	Lozère
EELOVV	evolve
EELPPU	peepul
EELPRS	lepers
	repels
EELPRT	pelter
	petrel
EELPRY	yelper
EELPSS	sleeps
	speels
EELPST	pestle
EELPSU	Peleus
EELPSV	pelves
EELPSX	expels
EELPSY	sleepy
EELQSU	sequel
EELRSS	lesser
EELRST	relets
	streel
EELRSV	elvers
	levers
	revels
EELRTT	letter
EELRTU	Teruel
EELRTW	welter
EELRUV	velure
EELSST	sleets
	steels
	steles
EELSSV	selves
	vessel
EELSTT	settle
EELSTU	elutes
EELSTV	svelte
EELSTY	sleety
	steely
EELSWY	Wesley
EELTTZ	Tetzel
EELTVV	velvet
EELTVW	twelve
EELTWY	tweely
EEMMNO	moneme
EEMMNR	mermen
EEMMRY	yemmer
EEMMST	emmets
EEMNNP	penmen
EEMNOR	moreen
EEMNOT	toneme
EEMNOY	yeomen
EEMNSS	menses
EEMNSU	neumes
EEMNTU	unmeet
EEMNYZ	enzyme
EEMOPT	metope
EEMORS	Oresme
EEMORT	emoter
	meteor
	remote
EEMORV	remove
EEMOST	emotes
EEMPRS	sempre
EEMPRT	temper
EEMPRY	empery
EEMPTX	exempt
EEMRRT	termer
EEMRRU	murree
EEMRSS	merses
EEMRST	merest
	mester
	meters
	metres
EEMRSU	resume
	Semeru
EEMRSV	vermes
EEMRSY	Mersey
EEMRTU	Meerut
EEMSSS	messes
EEMSTU	mustee
EENNOO	Oenone
EENNPY	Penney
EENNRS	rennes
EENNRT	rennet
	tenner
EENNST	sennet
EENNSU	unseen
EENNUV	uneven
EENNUY	ennuye
EENOPR	opener
	reopen
	repone
EENOPT	poteen
EENORS	Orense
EENORZ	rezone
EENOSV	venose
EENOTV	Veneto
EENOTW	townee
EENOVZ	evzone
EENPRS	nepers
	preens
EENPRT	repent
EENPRY	pyrene
EENPSU	Peneus
EENQSU	queens
EENRRT	renter
EENRRW	Werner
EENRSS	sneers
EENRST	enters
	nester
	resent
	Sterne
	tenser
EENRSU	ensure
	enures
	Nereus
EENRSV	nerves
	Nevers
	Severn
EENRSW	renews
EENRSY	sneery
EENRTT	tenter
EENRTU	neuter
	retune
	tenure
	tureen
EENRTV	venter
EENRTX	extern
EENRVY	venery
EENSSS	nesses
	senses
EENSST	tenses
EENSSU	ensues
EENSSV	sevens
EENSSW	sewens
EENSTT	tenets
EENSTU	tenues
EENSTV	events
EENSTW	newest
EENSUV	venues
EENSVW	sweven
EENSWY	sweeny
	weensy
EENSYZ	sneezy
EENTTX	extent
EENTUX	exeunt
EENTWY	tweeny
EEOOTT	toetoe
EEOPRS	repose
EEOPRU	Europe
EEOPST	topees
EEOPSX	expose
EEOPTU	toupee
EEOPTY	peyote
EEORST	stereo
EEORSV	soever
EEORSZ	zeroes
EEORTV	vetoer
EEORUV	oeuvre
EEOSST	setose
EEOSSV	Seveso
EEOSTV	vetoes
EEOSXY	oxeyes
EEPPPR	pepper
EEPPST	steppe
EEPRRY	preyer
EEPRSS	speers
	sprees
EEPRST	pester
	peters
	preset

	Streep
EEPRSU	peruse
	purees
	rupees
EEPRSV	perves
	vesper
EEPRSW	spewer
EEPRSY	Speyer
EEPRTT	petter
EEPRTU	repute
EEPRTW	pewter
EEPRTX	expert
EEPRTY	retype
EEPRUV	prevue
EEPSST	steeps
EEPSSW	sweeps
EEPSTT	septet
EEPSWY	sweepy
EEPTTU	puttee
EEQRSU	queers
EEQSUU	queues
EERRST	rester
	terser
EERRSV	revers
	server
EERRTT	terret
EERRTU	Reuter
	ureter
EERRTV	revert
EERRVY	revery
EERSST	esters
	reests
	resets
	steers
	steres
EERSSU	reuses
EERSSV	serves
	severs
	verses
EERSSW	sewers
	sweers
EERSTT	retest
	setter
	street
	tester
EERSTU	retuse
	Tereus
EERSTV	everts
	revest
	revets
	Trèves
EERSTW	wester
EERSTX	exerts
	exsert
EERSTY	yester
EERSTZ	zester
EERSUV	revues
EERSVW	swerve
EERSVX	vexers
EERTTT	tetter
EERTTW	wetter
EERTTX	texter
EERTUY	tuyere
EERTVV	vervet
EERTVX	vertex
EERUVX	Évreux
EESSTT	sestet
	testes
EESSTW	sweets
EESSWX	Wessex
EESTTU	suttee
	tutees
EESTTW	tweets
EESTTX	sextet
EFFFOS	feoffs
EFFGIN	effing
EFFGIR	griffe
EFFGIY	effigy
EFFGOR	goffer
EFFIIR	iffier
EFFILP	piffle
EFFILR	riffle
EFFILY	Liffey
EFFIMO	moffie
EFFIRS	fifers
EFFJOR	Joffre
EFFKOY	offkey
EFFLMU	muffle
EFFLRU	ruffle
EFFLUX	efflux
EFFOPU	pouffe
EFFORS	offers
	reffos
EFFORT	effort
EFFORX	forfex
EFFOST	offset
	setoff
EFFPRU	puffer
EFFRSU	ruffes
	suffer
EFFTTU	tuffet
EFGGRU	Fugger
EFGINR	finger
	fringe
EFGINS	feigns
EFGINT	feting
EFGIOS	fogies
EFGIRS	griefs
EFGIRU	figure
EFGLNU	engulf
EFGLOR	golfer
EFGOOR	forego
EFGORR	forger
EFGORS	forges
	gofers
EFGORT	forget
EFGOSY	fogeys
EFGRSU	Fergus
EFGSUU	fugues
EFHILS	elfish
EFHIRS	fisher
	sherif
EFHISS	fishes
EFHIST	fetish
EFHLSS	shelfs
EFHLSY	fleshy
EFHOOR	hoofer
EFHRRU	fuhrer
EFHSTT	thefts
EFIINT	finite
EFIKLO	folkie
EFIKNO	Fokine
EFIKNR	knifer
EFIKNS	knifes
EFIKSV	five Ks
EFILLR	filler
	refill
EFILLT	fillet
EFILMR	refilm
EFILNO	olefin
EFILNY	finely
EFILOS	filose
EFILOU	foulie
EFILPP	fipple
EFILPR	pilfer
EFILRR	rifler
EFILRS	filers
	fliers
	lifers
	rifles
EFILRT	filter
	lifter
	trifle
EFILRU	ireful
EFILRY	rifely
EFILST	filets
	flites
	itself
	stifle
EFILSU	Fuseli
	fusile
EFILTU	futile
EFILWY	wifely
EFILZZ	fizzle
EFIMRR	firmer
EFIMRS	fermis
EFINNR	finner
EFINNS	Finsen
EFINNY	Finney
EFINPR	perfin
EFINRR	Fenrir
EFINRS	infers
EFINRY	finery
EFINST	feints
	finest
	infest
EFINSU	infuse
EFIOOT	footie
EFIOPT	Petöfi
EFIORX	foxier
EFIOST	softie
EFIOSX	foxies
EFIPRX	prefix
EFIRRS	firers
	friers
EFIRSS	serifs
EFIRST	refits
	sifter
	strife
EFIRSU	furies
	surfie
EFIRSV	fivers
EFIRSX	fixers
EFIRTT	fitter
	titfer
EFIRTY	ferity
EFIRVY	verify
EFIRZZ	fizzer
EFISTY	feisty
EFISZZ	fizzes
EFKKOR	Fokker
EFKLSS	skelfs
EFKLSU	flukes
EFKLUY	flukey
EFKNRU	funker
EFLLOT	flotel
EFLLOW	fellow
EFLLRU	fuller
EFLMNY	flymen
EFLMSU	flumes
EFLMSY	myself
EFLNNU	funnel
EFLNOS	felons
EFLNOY	felony
EFLNTU	fluent
	unfelt
EFLOOT	footle
EFLOOZ	foozle
EFLORR	Ferrol
EFLORS	Flores
EFLORT	floret
	lofter
EFLORU	fouler
EFLORW	flower
	fowler
	wolfer
EFLORX	flexor
EFLORY	Florey
EFLOSW	Fowles
EFLOSY	foleys
EFLOUW	woeful
EFLPRU	purfle
EFLRRU	furler
EFLRSY	flyers
EFLRTU	fluter
EFLRUU	rueful
EFLRUX	reflux
EFLRUY	fleury
EFLSTU	flutes
EFLSTY	flyest
	flytes
EFLSUU	useful
EFLSUX	fluxes
EFMNOT	foment
EFMNRU	frenum
EFMORR	Fermor
	former
	reform

EFMORS	formes
EFMRSU	femurs
	fumers
EFMSTU	fumets
EFMTUY	tumefy
EFNNOT	Fenton
EFNORS	Fresno
EFNORZ	frozen
EFNOST	Sefton
	soften
EFNRUZ	Frunze
EFNRYZ	frenzy
EFOORR	reroof
	roofer
EFOORT	foetor
	footer
EFOORW	woofer
EFOQUU	Fouqué
EFORRU	furore
EFORRV	fervor
EFORST	fetors
	forest
	fortes
	foster
	softer
EFORSY	foyers
EFORTU	fouter
EFOSSS	fosses
EFOSTU	foetus
EFRRSU	surfer
EFRRSY	fryers
EFRRTU	Erfurt
	returf
EFRSSU	fusser
EFRTTU	tufter
EFRTUU	future
EFSSSU	fusses
EFSUZZ	fuzzes
EGGGIL	giggle
EGGGIN	egging
EGGGLO	goggle
EGGGNO	eggnog
EGGHIL	higgle
EGGHOR	hogger
EGGHOT	hogget
EGGHRU	hugger
EGGIIN	gieing
EGGIJL	jiggle
EGGIJR	jigger
EGGILN	niggle
EGGILO	loggie
EGGILR	ligger
EGGILW	wiggle
EGGINR	ginger
	nigger
EGGIRR	rigger
EGGIRW	wigger
EGGISU	gigues
EGGJLO	joggle
EGGJLU	juggle
EGGJOR	jogger
EGGLOO	google
EGGLOR	logger
EGGLOT	goglet
	toggle
EGGLOW	woggle
EGGLRU	gurgle
	lugger
EGGLTU	guglet
EGGMRU	mugger
EGGNRU	grunge
EGGNSU	gunges
EGGNTU	nugget
EGGOPS	pogges
EGGORR	gorger
EGGORS	gorges
EGGORT	gorget
	togger
EGGORU	gouger
EGGOSU	gouges
EGGPRY	preggy
EGGRRU	rugger
EGGRTU	tugger
EGHHIR	higher
EGHHIT	eighth
	height
EGHHSU	Hughes
	sheugh
EGHIIN	hieing
EGHILN	heling
EGHILS	sleigh
EGHINO	hoeing
EGHINR	Hering
EGHINS	hinges
	neighs
EGHINW	hewing
	whinge
EGHINX	hexing
EGHIOT	hogtie
EGHIRS	sigher
EGHIST	eights
EGHISW	weighs
EGHITW	weight
EGHITY	eighty
EGHLMP	phlegm
EGHLNT	length
EGHLPU	Guelph
	pleugh
EGHLUY	hugely
EGHMMO	megohm
EGHNOS	Goshen
EGHNOU	enough
EGHNPU	Penghu
EGHNRU	hunger
	rehung
EGHNST	thegns
EGHOPR	gopher
EGHORZ	Herzog
EGHOTT	ghetto
EGHRSU	gusher
EGHSSU	gushes
EGHSTU	hugest
EGIILL	gillie
EGIILR	girlie
EGIILT	Ligeti
EGIIMN	gemini
EGIINP	pieing
EGIINT	ignite
EGIJLN	jingle
EGIJNW	jewing
EGIJRS	rejigs
EGIKLS	kliegs
EGIKNP	Peking
EGIKNY	keying
EGIKRS	grikes
EGILLR	grille
EGILLU	ligule
EGILMN	mingle
EGILMP	megilp
EGILMS	gimels
EGILMT	gimlet
EGILNN	ginnel
EGILNO	eloign
	legion
EGILNP	Li Peng
EGILNR	linger
EGILNS	ingles
	single
EGILNT	tingle
EGILOO	goolie
EGILOR	logier
EGILPT	piglet
EGILRS	grilse
	ligers
EGILRU	gluier
	ligure
	reguli
	uglier
EGILRV	Vergil
EGILST	gilets
	legist
EGILSU	guiles
	uglies
EGILTU	glutei
EGIMMR	megrim
EGIMNR	mering
	minger
EGIMNS	minges
EGIMNT	meting
EGIMNW	mewing
EGIMNZ	Mengzi
EGIMOS	egoism
EGIMPU	guimpe
EGIMPY	gympie
EGIMRS	grimes
EGINNR	ginner
EGINNS	ensign
EGINOP	epigon
	pigeon
EGINOR	eringo
	ignore
	Origen
	region
EGINOS	soigne
EGINOT	toeing
EGINOW	wigeon
EGINPP	Epping
	pigpen
EGINPR	pinger
EGINPS	genips
EGINRR	erring
	ringer
EGINRS	Ingres
	reigns
	resign
	sering
	signer
	singer
EGINRW	Wigner
	winger
EGINSS	gneiss
	singes
EGINST	ingest
	signet
	tinges
EGINSU	genius
EGINSV	givens
EGINSW	sewing
	swinge
EGINSX	sexing
EGINTU	gunite
EGINTW	twinge
EGINVX	vexing
EGIOOR	gooier
	goorie
EGIOPS	pogies
EGIORR	gorier
EGIORS	orgies
EGIORT	goiter
	goitre
EGIOST	egoist
EGIOSV	ogives
EGIPPR	grippe
EGIPRR	griper
EGIPRS	gripes
EGIRST	tigers
EGIRSU	guiser
	regius
EGIRSV	givers
EGIRTV	grivet
EGISSU	guises
EGJLNU	jungle
EGKMNO	Mekong
EGKMSU	muskeg
EGKRRU	Kruger
EGKRSY	grykes
EGLLTU	gullet
EGLLUY	gulley
EGLMOS	golems
EGLMSU	glumes
EGLNNU	gunnel
EGLNOR	longer
EGLNOS	longes
EGLNOU	lounge
EGLNPU	plunge
EGLNRU	lunger
EGLNSU	gunsel
	lunges

EGLNTU englut
gluten
EGLNTY gently
EGLOPR proleg
EGLOPS gospel
EGLORS oglers
EGLORU regulo
EGLORV glover
grovel
EGLORW glower
EGLOSV gloves
EGLOSZ glozes
EGLOUY eulogy
EGLPRU gulper
EGLRSU gluers
gruels
lugers
EGLRYY greyly
EGLUZZ guzzle
EGMNNU gunmen
EGMNOO mongoe
EGMNOR monger
morgen
EGMNOS genoms
gnomes
EGMNOT Egmont
EGMNOU eumong
EGMNTU nutmeg
EGMNUU eumung
EGMOOS smooge
EGMORU morgue
EGMOST gemots
EGMRTU tergum
EGNNOO nonego
EGNNOS ennogs
EGNNOU guenon
EGNNRU gunner
EGNOOR Oregon
orgone
EGNOOT gentoo
EGNOOY gooney
EGNOPS pengos
sponge
EGNORS goners
Negros
EGNORV govern
EGNORY eryngo
Geryon
groyne
EGNOSS gnoses
EGNOTT gotten
EGNOTU tongue
EGNOXY oxygen
EGNPPU Pengpu
EGNPRU repugn
EGNPSU unpegs
EGNRTU gunter
gurnet
urgent
EGNRTY gentry
EGNRUY gurney
EGNSUU ungues

EGOOOU Ogooué
EGOOPR pogoer
EGOORV groove
EGOOSS gooses
EGOOST stooge
EGOOSY goosey
EGOPRR groper
EGOPRS gropes
EGOPSY pogeys
EGORRS rogers
EGORRW grower
regrow
EGORSS gorses
ogress
EGORST goster
EGORSU grouse
rogues
rouges
rugose
EGORSV groves
EGORSY gyrose
EGORTV grovet
EGOSSV Vosges
EGOSTY stogey
EGOSUV vouges
EGOSYZ zygose
EGOTYZ zygote
EGPRRU purger
EGPRSU purges
spurge
EGPSSU speugs
EGPSTU getups
EGRRSU surger
urgers
EGRSSU surges
EGRSTU gutser
EGRTTU gutter
EGSSTU guests
gusset
EHHIKS sheikh
EHHIRT hither
EHHISW Hewish
EHHNPY hyphen
EHHRST thresh
EHHSSU hushes
EHIIJM Himeji
EHIIPP hippie
EHIIST Shiite
EHIKKS kishke
EHIKMV mikveh
EHIKRS hikers
shriek
shrike
EHIKSS sheiks
EHILLL Hillel
EHILLR hiller
EHILMO Elohim
EHILMU helium
EHILNN Linnhe
EHILOO hoolie
EHILOR holier
EHILOS helios

holies
isohel
EHILOT eolith
EHILPR hirple
EHILRS hirsel
relish
EHILRT Hitler
EHILSS shiels
EHILSV elvish
EHILSW whiles
EHIMMS immesh
EHIMNR menhir
EHIMNS inmesh
EHIMNU inhume
EHIMOR homier
EHIMOS homies
EHIMRS Rheims
EHIMRT hermit
mither
EHIMRU humeri
EHIMST theism
Themis
EHINOR heroin
EHINOT Hotien
EHINPX phenix
EHINRS shiner
shrine
EHINRT hinter
nither
EHINRW whiner
EHINRY Henry I
EHINSS Shensi
shines
EHINSW newish
whines
EHINTW whiten
EHINTZ zenith
EHIOPR ephori
EHIOPT ophite
EHIORS hosier
EHIORT heriot
EHIOST hostie
EHIOTT hottie
EHIPPR hipper
EHIPRS perish
reship
seriph
EHIPSS pishes
EHIPSZ phizes
EHIRRS hirers
EHIRSS hisser
shiers
shires
EHIRST theirs
Thiers
EHIRSV shiver
shrive
EHIRSW wisher
EHIRSX rhexis
EHIRTT hitter
tither
EHIRTV thrive

EHIRTW whiter
wither
writhe
EHIRTZ zither
EHISSS hisses
EHISST heists
shiest
shites
thesis
EHISSV shives
EHISSW wishes
EHISTT theist
Thetis
tithes
EHISTW whites
withes
EHITTW Hewitt
EHITWY whitey
EHJLMU Jhelum
EHJOOR Johore
EHJOPS joseph
EHJORS josher
EHJORT Jethro
EHJOSS joshes
EHKLOR Köhler
EHKLPT klepht
EHKLSW whelks
EHKLWY whelky
EHKNOR honker
EHKNRU hunker
EHKOOR hooker
EHKOOY hookey
EHKORS kosher
EHKORY horkey
EHKPTU Phuket
EHKRSU husker
EHLLOR holler
EHLLOS hellos
EHLLRU huller
EHLLSS shells
EHLLSY shelly
EHLMMU hummel
EHLMNU unhelm
EHLMOP phloem
EHLMOS Holmes
mohels
EHLMOY homely
EHLMSW whelms
EHLMTY methyl
EHLNOP holpen
phenol
EHLNPY phenyl
EHLOOY hooley
EHLOPP hopple
EHLORW howler
Wöhler
EHLOSS Sholes
EHLOST helots
hostel
hotels
tholes
EHLOSU housel

EHLOSV hovels
shovel
EHLOSW wholes
EHLOTW howlet
EHLPSW whelps
EHLRRU hurler
EHLRTU hurtle
Luther
EHLRUY hurley
EHLSSU lushes
EHLSTT shtetl
EHLSTU hustle
sleuth
EHLSTY shelty
EHLUXY Huxley
EHMMRU hummer
EHMNOP phenom
EHMNOR Hermon
EHMNSY hymens
EHMORS homers
EHMORT mother
EHMOSS moshes
shmoes
EHMOST methos
EHMRRY rhymer
EHMRST therms
EHMRSU musher
rheums
EHMRSY rhymes
EHMRUY rheumy
EHMSSU mushes
EHNNUW unhewn
EHNOPR phoner
EHNOPS phones
EHNOPY phoney
EHNORS herons
nosher
EHNORT hornet
Theron
throne
EHNOSS noshes
EHNOST honest
Stheno
EHNOSY honeys
EHNPRY Phryne
EHNRSY henrys
EHNRTU hunter
EHNRVY Henry V
EHNSTT tenths
EHOOOP hoopoe
EHOOPR hooper
EHOOPY phooey
EHOORT hooter
EHOORV hoover
EHOOST soothe
EHOOSV hooves
EHOPPR hopper
EHOPRS ephors
hopers
posher
EHOPRT pother
thorpe

EHOPRU uphroe
EHOPTT Tophet
EHOPUV uphove
EHORRT rhetor
EHORSS horses
hosers
shoers
shores
EHORST others
throes
EHORSV hovers
shover
shrove
EHORSW shower
whores
EHORSY horsey
EHORTT hotter
tother
EHORTV throve
EHORTX exhort
EHORTY theory
EHORTZ zeroth
EHOSST shotes
EHOSSU houses
shouse
EHOSSV shoves
EHPRSU pusher
EHPRSY hypers
sphery
sypher
EHPRYZ zephyr
EHPSSU pushes
EHRRSU rusher
EHRRSY sherry
EHRRTU hurter
EHRRWY wherry
EHRSSU rhesus
rushes
ushers
Ussher
EHRSSW shrews
EHRSSY shyers
EHRSTY thyrse
EHSSSU Sesshu
EHSSTU tushes
EHSSTY shyest
EHSTTY Tethys
EIIILO Leo III
EIIKLS silkie
EIIKNP pinkie
EIIKNR inkier
EIILLN nielli
EIILLP pillie
EIILLS lilies
EIILLT illite
EIILLW willie
EIILMR limier
EIILMS simile
EIILMU milieu
EIILNR inlier
EIILNT lintie
EIILOR oilier

EIILOT iolite
EIILPP lippie
EIILRV virile
EIILRW wilier
EIILRX elixir
EIIMNS imines
EIIMPS impies
EIIMRR rimier
EIINNT intine
tinnie
EIINOS ionise
EIINOZ ionize
EIINPR pinier
EIINPT pinite
tiepin
EIINRT tinier
EIINRV Irvine
EIINRW winier
EIINRZ Rienzi
EIINSS niseis
seisin
EIINSX nixies
EIINSZ seizin
EIINTV invite
EIIPRS pieris
EIIPRU euripi
EIIPST pities
EIIPSX pixies
EIIRRW wirier
EIIRSS irises
EIIRVZ vizier
EIISTY yities
EIJKNR jerkin
jinker
EIJKNT inkjet
EIJKNU junkie
EIJKOR jokier
EIJKOS Osijek
EIJLRT jilter
EIJLSS IJssel
EIJNNO enjoin
EIJNOR joiner
rejoin
EIJNRU injure
EIJNSX jinxes
EIJNTY jitney
EIJRSU juries
EIJRSV jivers
EIJRTT jitter
EIJSTU jesuit
EIJSZZ jizzes
EIKKOO kookie
EIKKRS skrike
EIKLLR killer
EIKLLY Ilkley
likely
EIKLMR milker
EIKLNO Elikón
EIKLNR linker
EIKLNS likens
silken
EIKLNT tinkle

EIKLNU unlike
EIKLNV kelvin
EIKLNW welkin
winkle
EIKLRT kilter
kirtle
EIKLSS kissel
EIKLST Kleist
EIKLSV Kislev
EIKLSW Wilkes
EIKLSY kileys
kylies
EIKLTT kittel
kittle
EIKMNR merkin
EIKMOR Mörike
EIKMPS Kempis
EIKMRS kermis
EIKMST kismet
EIKMSU muskie
EIKMTU kumite
EIKNOO nookie
EIKNOS eikons
EIKNOV invoke
EIKNPR perkin
Pernik
EIKNRS inkers
sinker
EIKNRT tinker
EIKNRW winker
Wrekin
EIKNSS skeins
EIKNSV knives
Nevski
EIKNSY Kinsey
EIKNTT kitten
EIKOOR rookie
EIKOPP koppie
EIKOPR pokier
EIKOPS pokies
EIKORY yorkie
EIKOTW Koweit
EIKPPR kipper
EIKPPT keppit
EIKPRS pikers
EIKPSS spikes
EIKRRS risker
EIKRSS kisser
krises
skiers
EIKRST kiters
strike
trikes
EIKRSV skiver
EIKSSS kisses
EIKSST skites
EIKSSV skives
EIKSTW weskit
EILLMR miller
EILLMT millet
EILLMU illume
EILLNO niello

O'Neill
EILLNP penill
EILLNT lentil
lintel
tellin
EILLOT tollie
EILLPU pilule
EILLRS rilles
siller
EILLRT rillet
tiller
EILLRW willer
EILLST listel
EILLTT little
EILLTW willet
EILLTY Tilley
EILLVY evilly
lively
vilely
EILMNO moline
oilmen
EILMNR limner
merlin
EILMNS limens
simnel
EILMNY myelin
EILMOR moiler
EILMOS molies
Molise
EILMOT motile
EILMPP pimple
EILMPR limper
EILMPS impels
simple
EILMPT limpet
EILMPU pileum
EILMPW wimple
EILMRS milers
smiler
EILMRT milter
EILMSS missel
slimes
smiles
EILMST mistle
EILMSU muesli
EILMSY limeys
smiley
EILMTU telium
EILMTY timely
EILMZZ mizzle
EILNNO online
EILNNS linens
EILNNT linnet
EILNNY linney
EILNOO loonie
EILNOP Pelion
pinole
EILNOR neroli
EILNOS eloins
insole
lesion
Silone
EILNOT entoil
EILNPP nipple
EILNPS pensil
Pilsen
spinel
spline
EILNPT leptin
pintle
EILNPU lineup
lupine
EILNRS liners
EILNRT linter
EILNRU lunier
EILNST enlist
inlets
listen
silent
tinsel
EILNSU lunies
EILNSV livens
snivel
EILNSY lysine
EILNTU lutein
EILNTY lenity
EILNUV unlive
unveil
EILOOR oriole
EILOOT oolite
EILOPS pilose
poleis
EILOPT piolet
polite
EILORS lories
oilers
oriels
reoils
Serlio
EILORT Loiret
loiter
toiler
EILORU lourie
EILORV oliver
EILORW lowrie
EILOST toiles
EILOSV lovies
olives
voiles
EILOSX isolex
EILOTT toilet
EILOTV violet
EILPPR ripple
EILPPT tipple
EILPPU pileup
EILPRS lisper
perils
Perlis
pliers
EILPRT triple
EILPRY ripely
Ripley
EILPSS plisse
slipes
spiels
spiles
EILPST stipel
EILPSU epulis
pileus
EILPSV pelvis
EILPSW swiple
EILPSX pixels
EILPZZ pizzle
EILRST lister
liters
litres
relist
tilers
EILRSV livers
livres
silver
sliver
EILRSW swiler
EILRTT litter
tilter
EILRTU rutile
EILRUW wurlie
EILRVY livery
verily
EILSST islets
sliest
stiles
EILSSY Sisley
EILSTT titles
EILSTU Iseult
EILSTV vilest
EILSTX ixtles
EILSTY Elytis
stylie
EILSVW swivel
EILSWY wisely
EILSXY sexily
EILSZZ sizzle
EILTTT tittle
EILTTU lutite
EILTTV vittle
EILTVY levity
EILUVV luvvie
EIMMNU immune
EIMMOR memoir
EIMMRS mimers
simmer
EIMMRU immure
EIMMRZ zimmer
EIMMST semmit
EIMNNX meninx
EIMNOO Moonie
EIMNOR merino
EIMNOS eonism
Miseno
monies
Simeon
EIMNPT pitmen
EIMNRS Mersin
miners
EIMNRT minter
remint
EIMNRU murine
EIMNRV vermin
EIMNSX minxes
EIMNSZ mizens
EIMNTT mitten
titmen
EIMNTU minuet
minute
EIMNTY enmity
EIMNZZ mizzen
EIMOPS impose
EIMORS isomer
moires
rimose
EIMOSS mioses
mossie
EIMOST somite
EIMOSV movies
EIMOSX oximes
EIMOTV motive
EIMOTY moiety
EIMOZZ mozzie
EIMPRR primer
EIMPRS primes
simper
EIMPRT permit
EIMPRU impure
umpire
EIMPRX premix
EIMPSU umpies
EIMPTU impute
uptime
EIMRRS rimers
EIMRRT retrim
trimer
EIMRSS misers
remiss
EIMRST merits
mister
miters
mitres
remits
smiter
timers
EIMRSV verism
vermis
EIMRSX mixers
EIMRSY misery
EIMSSS misses
seisms
EIMSST smites
tmesis
EIMSSU misuse
EIMSSX sexism
EIMSTY stymie
EINNNR rennin
EINNOO ionone
EINNOT intone
EINNOY yonnie
EINNPR pinner
EINNPS pennis

EINNPT tenpin
EINNRS inners
sinner
EINNRT intern
tinner
EINNRW winner
EINNST sennit
tennis
EINNSU Ennius
EINNSV venins
EINNTT intent
EINNTV invent
EINNTY ninety
EINOOT toonie
EINOPR orpine
Pinero
EINOPS opines
ponies
EINOPT pointe
EINORR ironer
Renoir
EINORS nosier
senior
EINORT Ireton
norite
orient
tonier
EINORV enviro
renvoi
EINOSS enosis
noesis
noises
ossein
sonsie
EINOST tonies
EINOSV envois
EINOSW nowise
EINOTW townie
twonie
EINOVW inwove
EINPPR nipper
EINPPS pepsin
EINPRR Perrin
EINPRS repins
ripens
sniper
EINPRT Pinter
EINPRU punier
purine
unripe
EINPRV Previn
EINPRY pinery
EINPSS snipes
spines
EINPST instep
nepits
spinet
EINPSU puisne
supine
EINQSU quines
sequin
EINQTU quinte
EINQUU unique
EINQUZ quinze
EINRRS rinser
EINRRU ruiner
EINRSS resins
rinses
serins
sirens
EINRST estrin
insert
inters
sinter
trines
EINRSU erinus
insure
inures
ursine
EINRSX nixers
EINRTT tinter
Trient
EINRTU triune
uniter
EINRTV invert
EINRTW twiner
winter
EINRVW wivern
EINRVY vinery
EINRWY winery
EINSST insets
steins
Tessin
EINSSW sewins
sinews
swines
EINSTU tenuis
unites
unties
EINSTV invest
EINSTW twines
wisent
EINSUW unwise
EINSUX unisex
EINSVX vixens
EINSWY sinewy
EINSWZ winzes
wizens
EINTTY entity
yitten
EIOORT toorie
EIOORZ oozier
EIOOST otiose
EIOPPT potpie
EIOPRR ropier
EIOPRX poxier
EIOPSS poises
posies
possie
EIOPST postie
EIOPTT tiptoe
EIORRS rosier
EIORRT rioter
EIORRW Owerri
EIORSS osiers
EIORST sortie
tories
triose
EIORSV vireos
EIORTU tourie
EIOSTV soviet
EIOTTT tottie
EIOTVV votive
EIPPRR ripper
EIPPRS pipers
sipper
EIPPRT Pripet
tipper
EIPPRZ zipper
EIPPST sippet
EIPPSU Peipus
EIPPTT tippet
EIPPUY yuppie
EIPQSU equips
piques
EIPQTU piquet
EIPRRS priers
sprier
EIPRRU puirer
EIPRSS pisser
prises
speirs
spiers
spires
EIPRST esprit
priest
ripest
sprite
stripe
EIPRSU Epirus
uprise
EIPRSV vipers
EIPRSW wipers
EIPRSZ prizes
EIPRTV privet
EIPRTY pyrite
EIPRXY expiry
EIPSSS pisses
sepsis
speiss
EIPSST pistes
spites
stipes
EIPSSW swipes
EIPSTW pewits
EIPSXY pyxies
EIQRSU quires
risque
squire
EIQRUV quiver
EIQSTU quiets
EIQTUY equity
EIRRSS risers
EIRRST triers
EIRRSV rivers
EIRRSW werris
wirers
EIRRTT triter
EIRRTW writer
EIRSST resist
resits
sister
EIRSSU issuer
EIRSSW sweirs
EIRSSX sixers
EIRSSZ sizers
EIRSTT sitter
titers
titres
triste
EIRSTU suiter
EIRSTV rivets
stiver
strive
verist
EIRSTW wriest
writes
EIRTTT titter
EIRTTV trivet
EIRTTW witter
EIRTUV virtue
EIRTVY verity
EISSSU issues
Suisse
EISSSW wisses
EISSTT testis
EISSTU suites
tissue
EISSTW wisest
EISSTX exists
sexist
EISSVW swives
EISTTW twites
EISTZZ tizzes
EISUXZ Zeuxis
EISWZZ wizzes
EISZZZ zizzes
EJKLLY Jekyll
EJKNRU junker
EJKNTU junket
EJKOPS kopjes
Skopje
EJKORS jokers
EJLLOS jellos
EJLOPS poljes
EJLORT jolter
EJLOST jostle
EJLOSU joules
EJLPSU juleps
EJLRSU jurels
EJLSTU justle
Sutlej
EJMOOS mojoes
EJMOST jetsom
EJMPRU jumper
EJNOSV Jevons
EJNOSY enjoys
EJNOTT jetton

EJOPRT projet
EJORSS josser
EJORTT jotter
EJOSSS josses
EJOTTW Jowett
EKKOPS kopeks
EKKOPU pukeko
EKLLNS knells
EKLLSY skelly
EKLMMU kummel
EKLMOT Moltke
EKLMOW Welkom
EKLMSS skelms
EKLNOS kelson
EKLOOR looker
EKLOSY kyloes
yokels
EKLPSS skelps
spelks
EKLRRU lurker
EKLRSU sulker
EKMNOY monkey
EKMOOP mopoke
EKMORS smoker
EKMOSS smokes
EKMSTU musket
EKNNOR kronen
EKNNOT nekton
EKNNSU sunken
EKNNTU unkent
EKNOPS spoken
EKNORR kroner
EKNORW knower
EKNORY Orkney
EKNOSS snoeks
EKNOST tokens
EKNOUY unyoke
EKNPTU unkept
EKOORR korero
EKOORT retook
EKOPRR porker
EKOPRS pokers
EKOPSS spokes
EKOPSY pokeys
EKORRW rework
worker
EKORRY yorker
EKORST stoker
stroke
EKORSY yokers
EKOSST stokes
EKPSTU tupeks
EKRRSY skerry
EKRSTU tusker
EKRTUY turkey
ELLLOR loller
ELLLOV Lovell
ELLLOW Lowell
ELLMNU mullen
ELLMOW mellow
ELLMPU pellum
ELLMRU muller
Müller
ELLMSS smells
ELLMSY smelly
ELLMTU mullet
ELLMUV vellum
ELLMUY mulley
ELLNOP pollen
ELLNOR enroll
ELLNOY lonely
ELLNSU sullen
ELLNUU lunule
ELLNUW unwell
ELLOPW Powell
ELLOPX pollex
ELLORR roller
ELLORT toller
ELLORW Orwell
ELLOSS losels
ELLOSY solely
ELLOTX extoll
ELLOVY lovely
volley
ELLOWY yellow
ELLPRU puller
ELLPSS spells
ELLPTU pullet
ELLPUY pulley
ELLQSU quells
ELLSSW swells
ELLSTU tellus
ELMMOP pommel
ELMMOR Rommel
ELMMOS Moslem
ELMMPU pummel
ELMNOR merlon
ELMNOS Lemnos
lemons
melons
solemn
ELMNOT loment
melton
molten
ELMNOY lemony
ELMNPU lumpen
plenum
ELMNSU lumens
ELMOOP pomelo
ELMOPR Plomer
ELMOPY employ
ELMORS morels
morsel
ELMORT merlot
molter
ELMORY Morley
ELMOST molest
motels
ELMOSU oleums
ELMOSY Mosley
ELMOTT mottle
ELMOTY motley
ELMOUV volume
ELMOZZ mozzle
ELMPPU peplum
ELMPRU lumper
rumple
ELMPSU plumes
ELMRSU lemurs
ELMRTY myrtle
termly
ELMSST smelts
ELMSSU mussel
ELMSUY muleys
ELMTUU mutuel
mutule
ELMTUW umwelt
ELMTUY mutely
ELMUZZ muzzle
ELNNNO Lennon
ELNNOS nelson
ELNNRU runnel
ELNNTU tunnel
ELNOOS loosen
ELNOOV Leonov
ELNOOW woolen
ELNOOY looney
ELNOPT lepton
ELNOPY openly
poleyn
ELNORS enrols
loners
ELNORZ Lorenz
ELNOSS lesson
ELNOST lentos
Solent
stolen
telson
ELNOSU ensoul
ELNOSV novels
sloven
ELNOUZ zonule
ELNOZZ nozzle
ELNPTU n-tuple
penult
ELNPTY pentyl
plenty
ELNRTU runlet
ELNRUZ luzern
ELNSSU unless
ELNSSY selsyn
ELNSXY lynxes
ELNTTU nutlet
ELNTTY nettly
ELNTUZ Lützen
ELNUZZ nuzzle
ELOOOT O'Toole
ELOOPR looper
ELOOPT pootle
ELOORS looser
ELOORT looter
retool
rootle
tooler
ELOOSS looses
ELOOTT tootle
ELOPPP popple
ELOPPR lopper
propel
ELOPPS Pelops
peplos
ELOPPT topple
ELOPRS lopers
polers
proles
sloper
splore
ELOPRT petrol
ELOPRV plover
ELOPRW plower
ELOPRX plexor
ELOPSS slopes
ELOPSU loupes
ELOPTT pottle
ELOPTU tupelo
ELORRS sorrel
ELORSS lessor
losers
ELORST Ortles
ostler
sterol
ELORSU louser
ELORSV lovers
solver
ELORSW lowers
lowser
rowels
slower
ELORSY sorely
ELORTV revolt
ELORTW trowel
ELORUV louver
louvre
velour
ELORVW wolver
ELORVY overly
ELORWY Rowley
yowler
ELOSSS losses
ELOSST stoles
ELOSSU louses
ousels
ELOSSV Lésvos
solves
ELOSSW lowses
ELOSTU solute
tousle
ELOSTV voltes
ELOSTW lowest
owlets
towels
ELOSTX extols
ELOSUV ovules
ELOSUZ ouzels
ELOSVW vowels
wolves
ELOSWY Wolsey
ELOSXY xylose

ELOTTU outlet
ELOTUV volute
ELOTUZ touzle
ELOTWY owelty
ELPPRU pulper
purple
ELPPSU peplus
supple
ELPQUU pulque
ELPRRU purler
ELPRSU pulers
ELPRTY peltry
pertly
ELPRUY purely
ELPSSU pluses
pulses
ELPSSY slypes
ELPSTU letups
ELPSUX plexus
suplex
ELPUZZ puzzle
ELRRSU lurers
rulers
ELRSSU lusers
ELRSTU luster
lustre
result
rustle
Sluter
sutler
ulster
ELRSTY styler
ELRSUY surely
ELRTTU turtle
ELRTTY tetryl
ELRUWY wurley
ELSSTU tussle
ELSSTY slyest
styles
ELSTTY stylet
ELSTUX exults
ELSTUY Yseult
EMMMRU mummer
EMMNNO Memnon
EMMNOT moment
EMMORY memory
EMMOST mestom
EMMRRU rummer
EMMRSU summer
EMMSUU museum
EMNNOT Menton
Monnet
EMNOOR Monroe
EMNOPS Empson
EMNOPT potmen
EMNOPY eponym
EMNORS sermon
EMNORT mentor
Merton
EMNORY Romney
EMNOSS mesons
EMNOST montes
EMNOSV venoms
EMNOSY moneys
EMNOTY etymon
EMNOTZ Montez
EMNOXY exonym
EMNRSU rumens
EMNRTU munter
EMNSSU sensum
EMNTUY Tyumen
EMOORR roomer
EMOORS morose
romeos
EMOORT mooter
EMOORX Exmoor
EMOOSS osmose
EMOPPT moppet
EMOPPY pompey
EMOPRR romper
EMOPRS mopers
proems
EMOPRT trompe
EMOPST tempos
EMOPSY myopes
EMOQSU mosque
EMOQUY Quemoy
EMORRS ormers
EMORRT termor
tremor
EMORRW wormer
EMORSS morses
EMORST metros
motser
EMORSU mouser
EMORSV movers
vomers
EMORSW mowers
EMORSY Mysore
EMORUV mevrou
EMOSSS mosses
EMOSSU mousse
EMOSSY moseys
myoses
EMOSTT motets
mottes
totems
EMOSUY mousey
EMOSZZ mezzos
mozzes
EMPPTU muppet
EMPRSS sperms
EMPSSU spumes
EMPSTT tempts
EMPSTU septum
EMRRSU murres
EMRRUY murrey
EMRSSU musers
serums
EMRSTU estrum
muster
stumer
Sumter
EMRTTU mutter
EMSSSU musses
EMSSTU Musset
EMSSTY Metsys
system
EMSUZZ muzzes
ENNNOP pennon
ENNOPU unopen
ENNORU neuron
ENNORW renown
ENNOST nonets
sonnet
tennos
tenons
tonnes
ENNOSU nonuse
ENNOTW newton
ENNPRU punner
ENNPRY Prynne
ENNPTU punnet
ENNRRU runner
ENNRST Nernst
ENNTUY Tunney
ENOOPR operon
ENOORS roneos
sooner
ENOORT enroot
ENOORY Rooney
ENOOSS nooses
ENOOSZ snooze
ENOPRR perron
ENOPRS person
ENOPRT Repton
ENOPRV proven
ENOPRY pyrone
ENOPST pontes
ENOPTT potent
ENORRS snorer
ENORRY ornery
ENORSS senors
sensor
snores
ENORST nestor
stoner
tenors
tensor
toners
ENORSW owners
rowens
worsen
ENORTT rotten
Trento
ENORTY Tyrone
ENORUV unrove
ENOSST onsets
stenos
stones
ENOSSU onuses
ENOSSW sowens
ENOSTT teston
ENOSTW Townes
ENOSTX sexton
ENOSTY stoney
ENOSUV venous
ENOSVY envoys
ENOTTU tenuto
ENPPRU prenup
ENPRRU pruner
ENPRSU prunes
ENPRTU punter
ENPRUY penury
ENPSTU unstep
ENPTUU tuneup
ENPTUW unwept
ENQRSU querns
ENRRSU reruns
ENRRTU return
turner
ENRSST sterns
ENRSSU nurses
ENRSTU tuners
unrest
ENRSTW strewn
ENRSTY sentry
ENRSUU unsure
ENRTTU nutter
ENRTUU untrue
ENRVWY wyvern
ENSSSU Nessus
ENSSTU sunset
ENTTWY twenty
EOOPPS oppose
EOOPRR poorer
EOOPSV pooves
EOORRS rooser
EOORRT rooter
torero
EOORSS rooses
EOORST torose
EOORSW wooers
EOORTT tooter
EOOSTV Eötvös
EOOSTW Soweto
EOPPPR popper
EOPPPT poppet
EOPPRR proper
EOPPRT topper
EOPPRY popery
pyrope
yopper
EOPRRS repros
EOPRRT porter
pretor
report
EOPRRU pourer
EOPRSS posers
posser
proses
spores
EOPRST poster
presto
repots
topers
tropes
EOPRSU poseur

	uprose
EOPRSV	proves
EOPRSW	powers
EOPRSY	osprey
EOPRTT	potter
EOPRTU	pouter
	troupe
EOPRTX	export
EOPRTY	poetry
EOPRXY	peroxy
EOPSSS	posses
EOPSST	estops
	posset
	ptoses
	stoeps
	stopes
EOPSSU	opuses
	spouse
EOPSSY	sepoys
EOPSTX	sexpot
EOQRTU	roquet
	torque
EOQSTU	quotes
	toques
EORRRS	errors
EORRRT	rorter
	terror
EORRRY	orrery
EORRST	resort
	retros
	roster
	sorter
EORRSU	rouser
EORRSV	rovers
EORRSW	rowers
	worser
EORRSY	rosery
EORRTT	retort
	rotter
EORRTU	router
	tourer
EORRTV	Trevor
	trover
EORRZZ	rozzer
EORSST	restos
	stores
	tosser
EORSSU	rouses
	serous
EORSSV	servos
	versos
EORSSW	serows
	sowers
EORSTT	otters
	tortes
	toters
EORSTU	ouster
	outers
	routes
	souter
	trouse
EORSTV	stover
	strove
	troves
	voters
EORSTW	towers
EORSTX	oxters
EORSTY	oyster
	storey
	toyers
	Troyes
EORSTZ	zoster
EORSVW	vowers
EORSWW	wowser
EORSXY	oryxes
EORTTT	totter
EORTTU	touter
EORTTX	extort
EORTVX	vortex
EORUVY	voyeur
EOSSST	Sestos
	tosses
EOSSSU	souses
	Sousse
EOSSTV	stoves
EOSSTX	sextos
EOSTTU	outset
	setout
EOSUUV	uveous
EOSVYY	Voysey
EPPPRY	preppy
EPPPTU	puppet
EPPRSU	supper
	uppers
EPRRSU	purser
EPRRSY	pryers
	spryer
EPRRTU	Rupert
EPRSST	prests
	streps
EPRSSU	purses
	sprues
	spuers
	supers
EPRSTU	erupts
	purest
EPRSTW	twerps
EPRSUU	pursue
EPRTTU	putter
EPRTTY	pretty
EPRTUZ	Perutz
EPRUVY	purvey
EPSSSU	pusses
EPSSTU	setups
	stupes
	upsets
EQRTWY	qwerty
EQSSTU	quests
EQSTUU	tuques
ERRSUU	usurer
ERRSUY	surrey
ERRTTU	turret
ERRTUY	Ruyter
ERSSST	stress
ERSSTU	estrus
	russet
	surest
	tusser
ERSSTV	versts
ERSSTW	strews
	wrests
ERSSTY	tressy
ERSSUU	uruses
ERSSUV	versus
ERSSVY	syvers
ERSTTU	truest
	utters
ERSTUU	suture
	uterus
ERSTUV	Struve
	turves
	vertus
ERSTUY	surety
ERSTVY	vestry
ERSTWY	twyers
	wryest
ERSTXY	xyster
ERSUVY	survey
ERTTUX	urtext
ESSSSU	susses
ESSSUW	wusses
ESSSUX	Sussex
FFFLSU	fluffs
FFFLUY	fluffy
FFGIIN	fifing
FFGINO	offing
FFGLOO	logoff
FFHIOS	offish
FFHIST	fifths
FFHISW	whiffs
FFHIWY	whiffy
FFHORS	shroff
FFHOSW	howffs
FFIINT	tiffin
FFIIUZ	Uffizi
FFIKSS	skiffs
FFILLU	fulfil
FFILPS	spliff
FFILTU	fitful
FFIMNU	muffin
FFINPU	puffin
FFINSS	sniffs
FFINSY	sniffy
FFIOPR	ripoff
FFIOPT	tipoff
FFIOST	soffit
FFIPSY	spiffy
FFIQSU	quiffs
FFISST	stiffs
FFISTY	stiffy
FFISUX	suffix
FFLOTY	fylfot
FFLSSU	sluffs
FFNORU	runoff
FFNSSU	snuffs
FFNSUY	snuffy
FFOPTU	putoff
FFRRUU	furfur
FFSSTU	stuffs
FFSTUY	stuffy
FGGIIZ	fizgig
FGGORY	froggy
FGHILT	flight
FGHIRT	fright
FGHIST	fights
FGHOTU	fought
FGIILN	filing
FGIINN	fining
FGIINR	firing
FGIINX	fixing
FGILNS	flings
FGILNU	ingulf
FGILNY	flying
FGILUY	uglify
FGIMNU	fuming
FGINOS	gonifs
FGINOX	foxing
FGINRY	fringy
	frying
FGINSU	fusing
FGINUZ	fuzing
FGIOSU	fugios
FGJLUU	jugful
FGLMUU	mugful
FGLNOS	flongs
FGNOOS	gonofs
FGNSUU	fungus
FGOORT	forgot
FHHISU	Fushih
FHIINS	finish
FHILTY	filthy
FHIMUY	humify
FHIRST	firths
	friths
	shrift
FHIRTT	thrift
FHISST	shifts
FHISTU	shufti
FHISTY	shifty
FHNSUU	Fushun
FHORST	froths
FHORTU	fourth
FHORTY	frothy
FHORWY	forwhy
FHOUUZ	Fuzhou
FHPRUY	furphy
FHSTUY	shufty
FIIKNR	firkin
FIILLN	infill
FIILLP	fillip
FIILRU	Friuli
FIILST	Tiflis
FIILVY	vilify
FIIMNR	infirm
FIIMNV	minify
FIIMST	misfit
FIINOR	fiorin
FIITXY	fixity

FIIVVY	vivify
FIJLOR	frijol
FIKLSU	kulfis
FIKRSS	frisks
FIKRSY	frisky
FILLRS	frills
FILLRY	frilly
FILLUW	wilful
FILMOU	folium
FILMRY	firmly
FILMSY	flimsy
FILNOR	florin
FILNOW	inflow
FILNST	flints
FILNSU	sinful
FILNTU	tinful
FILNTY	flinty
FILNUX	influx
FILOOR	Florio
FILOOS	folios
FILORV	frivol
FILOSS	fossil
FILOTW	Wolfit
FILOXY	foxily
FILPPY	flippy
FILPTU	uplift
FILRST	flirts
FILRTY	flirty
FILSSU	fusils
FIMNOR	inform
FIMOST	motifs
FIMSSU	Sufism
FIMSTU	muftis
FINOOS	foison
FINORT	forint
FINORX	fornix
FINOSU	fusion
FINOTY	notify
FINSTU	unfits
FIOPRT	profit
FIORST	fortis
FIOSST	foists
FIOSSY	ossify
FIOTTU	outfit
FIPRUY	purify
FIPTYY	typify
FIRSST	firsts
FIRSTT	fritts
FIRSTU	fruits
FIRTUY	fruity
FIRYZZ	frizzy
FISSTW	swifts
FISTWY	swifty
FJLOUY	joyful
FKLNSU	flunks
FKLNUY	flunky
FKLOOS	kloofs
FKLOSY	folksy
FLLOOW	follow
FLLOUY	foully
FLMOOR	formol
FLMORY	formyl
FLNOTU	Fulton
FLNRUU	unfurl
FLOORS	floors
FLOOTW	Flotow
FLOOYZ	floozy
FLOPPY	floppy
FLOPTU	potful
FLORSU	flours
FLORUY	floury
FLOSSY	flossy
FLOSTU	flouts
FLOSTY	softly
FLOTUY	outfly
FLRRUY	flurry
FLRSUU	sulfur
FMORSU	forums
FMPRSU	frumps
FMPRUY	frumpy
FNORST	fronts
FNORSW	frowns
FNOSTU	founts
	futons
FOOPRS	proofs
FOOPSS	spoofs
FOOTUX	outfox
FORRSU	furors
FORRUW	furrow
FORSST	frosts
FORSTW	frowst
FORSTY	frosty
FORSUU	rufous
FORSWY	frowsy
FORUYZ	frouzy
FORWYZ	frowzy
GGGILY	giggly
GGGLOS	gloggs
GGGLOY	goggly
GGGORY	groggy
GGHINO	hoggin
GGHORU	grough
GGHSUY	shuggy
GGIINP	piggin
GGIINV	giving
GGIIRR	grigri
GGIJLY	jiggly
GGIKNO	gingko
	ginkgo
GGILNO	ogling
GGILNU	gluing
	luging
GGILNY	niggly
GGILOO	gigolo
GGILWY	wiggly
GGINNO	noggin
GGINOQ	qigong
GGINOR	goring
	Göring
	gringo
GGINOS	goings
GGINOZ	Zigong
GGINRU	urging
GGINRY	gyring
GGINUY	guying
GGINVY	gyving
GGIOOR	gorgio
GGIOST	gigots
GGITWY	twiggy
GGLLOO	loglog
GGLOOO	googol
GGLOOY	googly
GGMOSY	smoggy
GGMRUU	muggur
GGNOOR	gorgon
GGNOOY	gongyo
GGNRUY	grungy
GGPSUY	spuggy
GGRRUU	grugru
GHHILY	highly
GHHIST	thighs
GHHOSU	houghs
GHHOTU	though
GHIIKN	hiking
GHIINR	hiring
GHIINV	hiving
GHIKNO	hoking
GHIKNT	knight
GHILNO	holing
GHILPT	plight
GHILST	lights
	slight
GHIMNO	homing
GHIMTY	mighty
GHINNO	honing
GHINOP	hoping
GHINOS	hosing
GHINPY	hyping
GHINST	nights
	things
GHINSY	shying
GHINTY	nighty
GHIOPZ	phizog
GHIORT	righto
GHIOSY	goyish
GHIRST	girths
	griths
	rights
GHIRTW	wright
GHISST	sights
GHISTT	tights
GHISTW	wights
GHLLSY	ghylls
GHLOPU	plough
GHLOSU	ghouls
	loughs
	slough
GHLPSY	glyphs
GHNORT	throng
GHNOST	thongs
GHNOSU	shogun
GHNOTU	hognut
	nought
GHNOUW	Hong-wu
GHNRUY	hungry
GHNUUW	Hung-wu
GHOORS	sorgho
GHORSU	roughs
GHORTU	trough
GHORTW	growth
GHOSST	ghosts
GHOSSU	soughs
GHOSTU	oughts
	sought
	toughs
GHRSSU	shrugs
GIIJNV	jiving
GIIKLN	liking
GIIKMN	miking
GIIKNN	inking
GIIKNP	piking
GIIKNR	irking
GIIKNS	Siking
	skiing
GIIKNT	kiting
GIIKNV	viking
GIIKNY	yiking
GIILMN	liming
GIILNN	lignin
	lining
GIILNO	oiling
GIILNP	piling
GIILNR	riling
GIILNS	siling
GIILNT	tiling
GIILNU	Guilin
GIILNV	living
GIILNW	wiling
GIILOS	sigloi
GIILRV	Virgil
GIILSS	sigils
GIILSV	vigils
GIIMMN	miming
GIIMNN	mining
GIIMNP	imping
GIIMNR	miring
	riming
GIIMNT	timing
GIIMNX	mixing
GIINNN	inning
GIINNP	pining
GIINNS	sining
GIINNW	wining
GIINNX	nixing
	Xining
GIINOR	origin
GIINOY	yogini
GIINPP	piping
GIINPW	wiping
GIINPZ	pizing
GIINRS	rising
	siring
GIINRT	tiring
GIINRV	Irving
	riving
	virgin
GIINRW	wiring
GIINST	siting

GIINSV	vising
GIINSW	wising
GIINSZ	sizing
GIINVW	wiving
GIIOPR	pirogi
GIIRST	Tigris
GIJKNO	joking
GIJLNO	Jilong
GIJLNY	jingly
GIJNOY	joying
GIKLNU	Kilung
	Lungki
GIKLNY	kingly
GIKNNU	nuking
GIKNOP	poking
GIKNOT	toking
GIKNOW	Woking
GIKNOY	yoking
GIKNOZ	Kong Zi
GIKNPU	puking
GIKNSY	skying
GIKRTU	tugrik
GILLOO	Gilolo
GILLRS	grills
GILLUY	uglily
GILMNU	lignum
GILMRY	grimly
GILNOO	logion
	looing
GILNOP	loping
	poling
GILNOS	losing
GILNOT	tiglon
GILNOU	louing
GILNOV	loving
GILNOW	lowing
GILNPU	puling
GILNPY	plying
GILNRU	luring
	ruling
GILNSS	slings
GILNST	glints
GILNSU	lungis
	nisgul
GILNSY	lysing
	singly
GILNTU	luting
GILNTY	tingly
GILOOS	igloos
GILOOY	gooily
GILORY	gorily
GILOSS	siglos
GILRSY	grisly
GILRTY	trigly
GILSTU	guilts
GILTUY	guilty
GILTYZ	glitzy
GIMNNO	mignon
GIMNOO	mooing
GIMNOP	moping
GIMNOU	gonium
GIMNOV	moving
GIMNOW	mowing
GIMNPU	impugn
GIMNRU	muring
GIMNSU	Mingus
	musing
GIMNTU	muting
GIMOSS	gismos
GIMOSZ	gizmos
GIMOTU	gomuti
GINNOO	gonion
GINNOS	nosing
GINNOT	noting
	toning
GINNOW	owning
GINNOZ	zoning
GINNRU	urning
GINNSY	syning
GINNTU	tuning
GINOOS	isogon
GINOOW	wooing
GINOOZ	oozing
GINOPR	poring
	roping
GINOPS	gipons
	pingos
	posing
GINOPT	opting
	toping
GINORS	girons
	grison
	groins
	rosing
	signor
GINORT	trigon
GINORV	roving
GINORW	rowing
GINOSS	gnosis
GINOST	ingots
	stingo
	tigons
	toings
GINOSW	sowing
GINOTT	toting
GINOTU	outing
GINOTV	voting
GINOTW	towing
GINOTY	toying
GINOVW	vowing
GINOWW	wowing
GINPPU	upping
GINPRS	spring
GINPRY	prying
GINPSU	spuing
GINPSY	spying
GINPTU	pignut
GINPTY	typing
GINRRU	runrig
GINRST	string
GINRSU	unrigs
GINRSW	wrings
GINRTU	truing
	Turing
GINRTY	trying
	tyring
GINRWY	wrying
GINSST	stings
GINSSW	swings
GINSTY	stingy
	stying
GINSUU	unguis
GINSWY	swingy
GIOORV	vigoro
GIOOTT	Giotto
GIOPSS	gossip
GIOPST	spigot
GIOPTU	pigout
GIORRS	rigors
GIORRU	rigour
GIORST	griots
GIORTU	rigout
GIORUV	vigour
GIOSTT	Tostig
GIOSTU	giusto
GIOTUZ	Guizot
GIPRSS	sprigs
GIPSTY	pigsty
GIRTTY	gritty
GIRTUY	Guitry
GJLNUY	jungly
GJMSUU	jugums
GJNOOU	goujon
GJNRUU	gurjun
GKLNOS	klongs
GKNRUU	Kungur
GLLMUY	glumly
GLLOOP	gollop
GLMNOO	mongol
GLMOOS	glooms
GLMOOY	gloomy
GLMOSU	moguls
GLMSUY	smugly
GLNOOO	oolong
GLNOOY	Yong Lo
GLNOSU	gluons
	Longus
GLNOUY	Yung-lo
GLNPUU	unplug
GLNSUY	snugly
GLOOOY	oology
GLOOPR	prolog
GLOOTU	logout
GLOPTU	putlog
GLORSW	growls
GLOSSY	glossy
GMNNOO	gnomon
GMNOOS	mongos
GMNOST	mongst
GMNOSU	mungos
GMNTUU	gumnut
GMNUUZ	mzungu
GMOOPR	pogrom
GMOORS	grooms
GMPRSU	grumps
GMPRUY	grumpy
GMPSUY	gypsum
GNNOOR	rognon
GNNSUU	unsung
GNOOPS	pongos
GNOORT	Gorton
	trogon
GNOPPU	oppugn
	popgun
GNOPRS	prongs
GNOPSY	spongy
GNORST	strong
GNORSW	wrongs
GNORSY	gyrons
GNORYZ	Grozny
GNOTUU	outgun
GNPRSU	sprung
GNQRUU	Qungur
GNRSTU	grunts
	strung
GNRTUU	Guntur
GOORSS	sorgos
GOORTT	grotto
GOORVY	groovy
GOPRSS	sprogs
GOPRSU	groups
GORRTU	turgor
GORSTU	grouts
GORSUU	rugous
GORSYZ	groszy
GORTTU	rotgut
	Turgot
GORTTY	grotty
GORTUY	grouty
	yogurt
GOSTUY	guyots
GSYYYZ	syzygy
HHHOOT	Hohhot
HHILOS	Shiloh
HHISTW	whisht
HHMRTY	rhythm
HHNOSU	Honshu
HHOOSW	whoosh
HHORTY	Horthy
HHRSTU	thrush
HIIJNO	John II
HIILLT	Lilith
HIILPP	Philip
HIIMMS	mishmi
HIIMPS	impish
HIIMSS	Shiism
HIIMST	isthmi
	mishit
HIINTW	within
HIIOPT	pithoi
HIIRST	Tishri
HIITZZ	zizith
HIJNOV	John IV
	John VI
HIJNSU	shinju
HIJOSS	shojis
HIKMUZ	muzhik
HIKNRS	shrink

HIKNST	thinks
HIKRSS	shirks
HIKSSW	whisks
HIKSUU	Kiushu
HIKSWY	whisky
HILLOY	holily
HILLPU	uphill
HILLRS	shrill
HILLRT	thrill
HILLSS	shills
HILLST	thills
HILMOS	holism
HILMOW	whilom
HILMOY	homily
HILMSU	mulish
HILNOT	Hilton
HILNPT	plinth
HILNTY	thinly
HILOOT	oolith
	tholoi
HILOPS	polish
HILOST	lithos
	thiols
HILOSW	owlish
HILRST	thirls
HILRSW	whirls
HILSTW	whilst
HIMMSY	shimmy
HIMNOY	hominy
HIMORS	morish
	Romish
HIMOTY	mythoi
HIMPRS	shrimp
HIMSST	smiths
HIMSTY	smithy
HIMSWY	whimsy
HINNST	ninths
HINNSY	shinny
HINNTU	Ithunn
HINNWY	whinny
HINOPS	siphon
HINORS	rhinos
HINOST	Shinto
HINPSU	punish
	unship
HINPSX	sphinx
HINRSU	inrush
HINSTY	shinty
HINSUV	Vishnu
HINSUW	unwish
HIOPPS	hippos
	popish
HIOPST	pithos
HIOPSY	physio
HIORSU	houris
HIOSST	hoists
HIOTTU	outhit
HIOTWZ	howzit
HIPPSU	uppish
HIPRST	thrips
HIQSSU	squish
HIRRSS	shirrs
HIRRSW	whirrs
HIRSST	shirts
HIRSTT	thirst
HIRSTY	Irtysh
	shirty
	thyrsi
HIRTTY	thirty
HISSTW	whists
HISSTX	sixths
HISSWY	swishy
HISTTY	shitty
	stithy
HIWYZZ	whizzy
HJNNOY	johnny
HKNOOU	unhook
HKNOSY	shonky
HKNRSU	shrunk
HKOOPU	hookup
HKOORT	Rothko
HKOOSS	shooks
HKOUVZ	Zhukov
HKSUUY	Kyushu
HLLOOS	hollos
HLLOOW	hollow
HLLOPY	phyllo
HLLOSU	hullos
HLLOWY	wholly
HLLSUY	lushly
HLMOTY	thymol
HLMPUY	phylum
HLNOOS	holons
HLNOUY	unholy
HLNSUU	Lüshun
HLOOSS	shools
HLOOST	tholos
HLOPSS	splosh
HLOPSU	Ophüls
HLORSW	whorls
HLORUY	hourly
HLOSST	sloths
HLOSSY	sloshy
HLPSSY	sylphs
HLPSUY	plushy
HLPSYY	sylphy
HLSSUY	slushy
HMMSUU	hummus
HMNOPY	nympho
HMNOST	months
HMNPSY	nymphs
HMOOPR	morpho
HMOOST	shtoom
	smooth
HMOPRS	morphs
HMOPRY	Morphy
HMORSU	humors
	mohurs
HMORUU	humour
HMORUZ	Hormuz
HMOSTU	mouths
HMOSTY	mythos
HMOSUU	houmus
HMOTUY	mouthy
HMPRUY	murphy
HMPSSU	sumphs
HMPSTU	thumps
HMPTUY	humpty
HMRSTU	thrums
HMSTUY	thymus
HNNOOP	phonon
HNOOPT	photon
HNOORS	honors
HNOORT	thoron
HNOORU	honour
HNOPSY	Hypnos
	syphon
HNOPTY	phyton
	python
	typhon
HNORST	norths
	thorns
HNORSU	onrush
HNORTW	thrown
HNORTY	rhyton
	thorny
HNOSTU	Huston
HNOTTU	Hutton
HNRTUU	unhurt
HNSSTU	shunts
HNSSTY	synths
HOOOOR	hooroo
HOOPSS	poshos
HOOPST	photos
HOOPSW	whoops
HOOPSY	shypoo
HOOPTT	hotpot
HOORRR	horror
HOOSST	shoots
	sooths
HOOSSW	swoosh
HOOSTT	tooths
HOOTTY	toothy
HOPRRY	Pyrrho
HOPRST	thorps
HOPRTY	trophy
HOPSSY	hyssop
	phossy
HOPSTU	tophus
	upshot
HORSST	horsts
	shorts
HORSTT	troths
HORSTU	rouths
HORSTW	rowths
	throws
	worths
HORSTY	shorty
HORTWY	worthy
HOSSTT	shotts
HOSSTU	shouts
	stoush
HOSTUY	shouty
	youths
HOSUUZ	Suzhou
HOUUXZ	Xuzhou
HPPSUU	pushup
HPRSUU	uprush
HPSTUY	typhus
HRSSTU	hursts
HRSTTU	thrust
	truths
HSTUUX	Xuthus
IIIMNR	Rimini
IIIPSU	Pius II
IIIRST	iritis
IIKKMS	Sikkim
IIKKOS	kikois
IIKLMS	kilims
IIKNNS	kinins
IIKNPP	pipkin
IIKNSS	siskin
IIKPUW	wikiup
IIKRTT	Tikrit
IILLMU	limuli
IILLOO	Iloilo
IILLOY	oilily
IILLSW	Willis
IILMMU	milium
IILMST	limits
IILNNS	linins
IILNNU	inulin
IILNOP	Pílion
IILNOR	Ilorin
IILNOV	violin
IILNST	instil
IILNTY	tinily
IILOSU	Louis I
IILOTV	Tivoli
IILPST	pistil
IILRWY	wirily
IILSTT	Tilsit
IILTTW	twilit
IIMMNS	minims
IIMMNU	minium
IIMNNO	minion
IIMNOU	ionium
IIMNTZ	Nimitz
IIMOSS	miosis
IIMRST	smriti
IIMRSU	surimi
IIMSSS	missis
IINNOP	pinion
IINNOS	inions
IINNPY	pinyin
IINOPS	Piniós
IINOPT	poitin
IINORS	Orsini
IINORV	virino
	virion
IINOSV	vision
IINPPP	pippin
IINPTX	pinxit
IINSST	insist
IINTTU	intuit
IINTTW	nitwit
IIOOTT	toitoi
IIOPZZ	Piozzi

IIORSS Osiris
IIORZZ Rizzio
IIOSTT otitis
IIPPST pipits
IIPPUU piupiu
IIPRRU puriri
IIPRST spirit
IIPRTU pituri
IIPSUV Pius IV
Pius VI
IIPSUX Pius IX
Pius XI
IISSTV visits
IJKMOU moujik
IJKMSU mujiks
IJLLOO Jilolo
IJLNOP Joplin
IJMNOS jimson
IJMOSS jissom
IJNOPS Jospin
IJNORU junior
IJNOST joints
IJNRUY injury
IJNSUU Junius
IJOSST joists
IJRSTU jurist
IKKKRU Kirkuk
IKKNSS skinks
IKKOSS kiosks
IKKRSU kukris
IKKUUY kikuyu
IKLLSS skills
IKLLSY skilly
IKLMOS milkos
IKLNNU unlink
IKLNPS plinks
IKLNPU linkup
uplink
IKLNSS slinks
IKLNSY kylins
slinky
IKLNTY tinkly
IKLOPY pokily
IKLRSS skirls
IKLSSU suslik
IKMNOO kimono
IKMOSU koumis
IKMPSS skimps
IKMPSY skimpy
IKMRSS smirks
IKMSSU kumiss
IKMSUU Kisumu
IKNNOT Tonkin
IKNNSY skinny
IKNNTU unknit
IKNOOR krooni
IKNOPS pinkos
IKNOST stinko
IKNPRS prinks
IKNRSU Ruskin
IKNSST stinks
IKNSSW swinks
IKNSTW twinks
IKNSTY stinky
IKOOPU Kuopio
IKOORS irokos
IKORSS Skíros
IKORYZ Yizkor
IKPRSU prusik
spruik
IKPSTU tupiks
IKQRSU quirks
IKQRUY quirky
IKRRSS skirrs
IKRRUY Ryurik
IKRSST skirts
stirks
IKSUUY Suu Kyi
IKSVVY skivvy
ILLMPY limply
ILLMSY slimly
ILLNOV Villon
ILLOPW pillow
ILLOWW willow
ILLPRS prills
ILLPSS spills
ILLQSU quills
squill
ILLRST trills
ILLSST stills
ILLSSW swills
ILLSTW twills
ILLSTY stilly
ILLSUV villus
ILMMSU Muslim
ILMNOS Límnos
ILMNOT Milton
ILMNOU moulin
ILMNSU muslin
ILMOOS moolis
ILMOOV moolvi
ILMOSS lissom
ILMOSZ Miłosz
ILMOTU ultimo
ILMPPY pimply
ILMPRY primly
ILMPSY simply
ILMRSY lyrism
ILMRTY trimly
ILMSSU simuls
ILMSSY slimsy
ILMSTU litmus
ILMTUU tumuli
ILMYZZ mizzly
ILNOOT lotion
ILNOPP poplin
ILNOPT pontil
ILNOQU quinol
ILNOST Liston
tonsil
ILNOSU insoul
ILNOSW Wilson
ILNOSY nosily
ILNPRU purlin
ILNPST splint
ILNPSU lupins
ILNPUY punily
ILNSSY lysins
ILNSTU insult
sunlit
ILNSVY vinyls
ILOOYZ oozily
ILOPPY polypi
ILOPRX prolix
ILOPRY pylori
ropily
ILOPSS spoils
ILOPST pilots
pistol
postil
spoilt
ILOPSU pilous
poilus
ILOPSX oxlips
ILOPTY polity
ILOQRU liquor
ILORRS Lorris
ILORST triols
ILORSY rosily
ILORSZ zorils
ILOSUV Louis V
ILOTTW wittol
ILPPRY ripply
ILPPSU pupils
slipup
ILPPSY slippy
ILPPTU pulpit
ILPRTY triply
ILPSST splits
ILPSTU tulips
ILPTTU uptilt
ILQSTU quilts
ILRSSW swirls
ILRSTW twirls
ILRSTY lyrist
ILRSWY swirly
ILSSTT stilts
ILSTTU lutist
IMMMOS momism
IMMNOS monism
nomism
IMMOOS simoom
IMMOSU osmium
IMMOTW wommit
IMMSTU mutism
summit
IMNNOW minnow
IMNNTU muntin
IMNOOR morion
Moroni
IMNOOS simoon
IMNOOT motion
IMNORS minors
IMNOST inmost
monist
IMNOSY myosin
simony
IMNTUY mutiny
IMOPRS porism
primos
IMOPRT import
IMOPRV improv
IMOPST impost
IMORRR mirror
IMORRS morris
IMOSSX sixmos
IMOSSY myosis
IMOSTU ostium
IMOSTV vomits
IMOTTT tomtit
IMPPRS primps
IMPRSS prisms
IMPRSU primus
purims
purism
IMPSUX mixups
IMQRSU squirm
IMRRSS smirrs
IMRRSU murris
IMRSTU murtis
truism
IMSSSU missus
INNNOS ninons
INNOOS onions
INNOOT notion
INNOOY oniony
INNOPP Nippon
INNOPZ Pinzón
INNORS ronins
INNORT intron
INNOSU unions
unison
INNOWW winnow
INNPSU unpins
INNRSU inurns
INOOPS poison
INOOPT option
potion
INOORS orison
INOORT Torino
INOPPS ippons
INOPRS orpins
prions
prison
INOPST pintos
piston
pitons
points
INOPTT tinpot
INOPTY pointy
INOQSU quoins
INORSS rosins
INORST intros
INORSY rosiny
INORTT triton
INORTU turion
INOSTT stotin
INOSTX toxins

INOSUV	vinous
INPPRU	Nippur
INPPSU	pinups
INPPSY	snippy
INPRST	prints
	sprint
INPRSU	unrips
INPRTU	turnip
	Turpin
INPSTU	inputs
INPSUZ	unzips
INQSTU	quints
	squint
INQSUY	quinsy
INRSXY	syrinx
INRTWY	wintry
INSSTT	stints
INSTUW	Wutsin
IOOPST	Potosí
IOOPTU	Poitou
IOOTTV	Otto IV
IOPPTT	tiptop
IOPRRS	priors
IOPRRY	priory
IOPRST	prosit
	ripost
	tripos
IOPSST	posits
	ptosis
IOPSSY	pyosis
IOPSTV	pivots
IOQSTU	quoits
IORRTW	worrit
IORSSV	visors
IORSTU	suitor
IORSVZ	vizors
IOSSTT	Tissot
	tsotsi
IOSTTU	outsit
IOTTUW	outwit
IPPQUU	quippu
IPPRTY	trippy
IPPTUY	uppity
IPQSUU	quipus
IPRRTU	irrupt
IPRSST	spirts
	sprits
	stirps
	strips
IPRSSU	sirups
IPRSSY	prissy
IPRSTU	purist
	spruit
IPRSTW	twirps
IPRSTY	stripy
IPRTUY	purity
IPSSTU	situps
IPSTTY	typist
IPSVVY	spivvy
IPTTTU	tittup
IQRSTU	quirts
	squirt
IQSSTU	quists
	squits
IRSSTW	wrists
IRSSTY	syrtis
IRSSUU	Ussuri
IRSTWY	wristy
ISSSTU	tussis
ISSTTW	twists
ISTTWY	twisty
JLLOOP	jollop
JLNOOS	Jolson
JLSTUY	justly
JMORSU	jorums
JNNOOS	Jonson
JNNOTU	jotunn
JNOORU	journo
JNOPSU	jupons
JNOSTU	jotuns
	juntos
JNSTUU	unjust
JOOPPY	joypop
JOOSUY	joyous
JORRSU	jurors
JOSSTU	jousts
KKLMUU	mukluk
KKLOOZ	kolkoz
KKLSSU	skulks
KKMTUU	muktuk
KKNSSU	skunks
KKOTUU	kotuku
KLLNOS	knolls
KLLNOY	knolly
KLLOSY	skolly
KLLSSU	skulls
KLNNUU	Kunlun
KLNOOP	plonko
KLNOPS	plonks
KLNPSU	plunks
KLNRSU	knurls
KLNRUY	knurly
KLOOPS	plooks
KLOOPU	lookup
KLOOPY	plooky
KLOOSS	skools
KLOPSU	plouks
KLOPUY	plouky
KLRTUU	kultur
KLTUYZ	klutzy
KMOOOR	mokoro
KMOOSS	smokos
KNNOTU	unknot
KNOORR	kronor
KNOORS	Kronos
	kroons
KNOOSS	snooks
KNORRU	kronur
KNORST	tronks
KNORUY	koruny
KNOSST	stonks
KNOSTU	knouts
KNOTTY	knotty
KNPSSU	spunks
KNPSUY	spunky
KNRRSU	knurrs
KNRSTU	trunks
KOOOST	Sokoto
KOOOSV	Kosovo
KOOPSS	spooks
KOOPSY	spooky
KOORUU	Kourou
KOORVV	Kovrov
KOOSST	stooks
KOOTTU	tuktoo
KOOTWW	kowtow
KOPRUW	workup
KORSST	storks
	torsks
KORSSY	Skyros
KSTTUU	tuktus
LLLOOP	lollop
LLNORU	unroll
LLOOTU	toluol
LLOOWY	woolly
LLOPUX	Pollux
LLORST	stroll
	trolls
LLOSWY	slowly
LLOSXY	xylols
LLOTUY	toluyl
LLPPUU	pullup
LLPSUU	pullus
LLRSTU	trulls
LLSSTU	stulls
LLSXYY	xylyls
LMMOUX	lummox
LMMPUY	plummy
LMMSUY	slummy
LMOOOO	mooloo
LMOOOP	Molopo
LMOORU	ormolu
LMORSS	slorms
LMOSST	smolts
LMOSSU	solums
LMOSTU	moults
LMOSTY	mostly
LMOTUZ	Olmütz
LMPPSU	plumps
LMPRUY	rumply
LMPSSU	slumps
LMTTUU	tumult
LNNOSY	nylons
LNOOPY	polony
LNOOST	stolon
LNOOTU	Toulon
LNOPSY	pylons
LNOPTU	pluton
LNOTTY	Lytton
LNRUUY	unruly
LOOPPT	Pol Pot
LOOPRS	orlops
LOOPRY	poorly
LOOPSS	sloops
	spools
LOOSST	sloots
	stools
LOOSTV	volost
LOOVVX	volvox
LOPPRY	propyl
LOPPSY	polyps
	sloppy
LOPRSW	prowls
LOPRTY	portly
	protyl
LOPSTU	poults
LORSUY	sourly
LORTTY	trotyl
LOSTYZ	zlotys
LPPRUY	purply
LPPSUY	supply
LPRRUY	plurry
LPRSSU	slurps
LPRSYY	spryly
LPSTUU	Plutus
LRRSUY	slurry
LRSTUY	sultry
LRUUXY	luxury
LSSTUY	stylus
MMNOOR	Mormon
MMNOSU	summon
MMOOPP	pompom
MMOOTT	motmot
MMRRUU	murmur
MMUUUU	muumuu
MNNOUW	unmown
MNOOPP	pompon
MNOORS	morons
MNOORT	Morton
MNOORU	unmoor
MNOOTU	mouton
MNORSU	mourns
MNOSSU	Somnus
MNOSSY	Symons
MNOSTU	mounts
MNOTTU	mutton
MNPTUY	numpty
MOOPRS	promos
MOORRS	morros
MOORRW	morrow
MOORST	motors
	Tromsø
MOOSSU	osmous
MOOSTT	mottos
MOOTVY	yom tov
MOPPRT	prompt
MOPSST	stomps
MOPSSU	possum
MOPSTU	upmost
MOQRUU	quorum
MORRSU	rumors
MORRUU	rumour
MORSST	storms
MORSTU	tumors
MORSTY	stormy
MORTUU	tumour
MOSSTU	smouts
MOSSTW	smowts

MOSTTU	utmost
MPRSTU	trumps
MPRSUU	rumpus
MPSSTU	stumps
MPSTUU	sputum
MPSTUY	stumpy
MRSSTU	strums
MSTTUY	smutty
NNOORT	Norton
NNOOTW	wonton
NNORUW	unworn
NNORUY	Runyon
NNOSUW	unsown
NOOPRS	Porson
NOOPRT	pronto
	proton
NOOPSS	snoops
	spoons
NOOPSY	snoopy
	spoony
NOORST	nostro
	rotons
NOORTU	notour
	unroot
NOOSST	snoots
NOOSSW	swoons
NOOSTY	snooty
NOOSYZ	snoozy
NOOTTW	Wotton
NOPSTU	Pontus
	putons
	unstop
NOPTUW	uptown
NORSST	snorts
NORSTW	strown
NORTUU	outrun
	runout
NOSSTU	snouts
NOSTTU	Sutton
NOSTTY	snotty
NPRSSU	spurns
NPRTUU	turnup
	upturn
NPSSUU	sunups
NSSTTU	stunts
OOOPRT	Oporto
OOPPRT	troppo
OOPRRT	torpor
OOPRSS	sopors
	spoors
OOPRST	poorts
	troops
OOPRSU	porous
OOPRTU	uproot
OOPSST	stoops
OOPSSW	swoops
OOPSTT	pottos
OOPWWW	powwow
OORRST	rotors
OORRSW	sorrow
OORSST	roosts
	stoors
	torsos
OORSTU	outros
	torous
OORSTV	Rostov
OORSTY	rootsy
OOSTTY	tootsy
OPPSSY	psyops
OPRSST	sports
	strops
OPRSTU	Proust
	sprout
	stupor
OPRSTY	sporty
OPSSTU	spouts
	stoups
	tossup
OPSSTW	stowps
OPSTTY	spotty
OPTTUU	output
	putout
ORSSTU	rousts
	stours
ORSSTW	strows
	worsts
ORSSTY	stroys
ORSTTU	trouts
	tutors
ORTTUY	tryout
OSSTTU	stouts
OSSTXY	xystos
OSTTWY	swotty
PRRSUY	spurry
PRSSTU	spurts
PRSSUU	usurps
PRSSUY	syrups
PRSUYY	syrupy
RSSTTU	struts
	trusts
RSSTTY	trysts
RSSTUW	wursts
RSTTUY	trusty
SSTUXY	xystus

Seven Letters

AAAABLM	Alabama
AAAALMT	Alma-Ata
AAABBCL	cabbala
AAABBKL	kabbala
AAABBLS	babalas
AAABBNN	Banaban
AAABCIR	arabica
AAABCLR	Calabar
AAABCLS	cabalas
AAABCLV	baclava
AAABCNS	cabanas
AAABCOR	carabao
AAABCSS	casabas
	cassaba
AAABCTW	catawba
AAABDFR	abfarad
AAABDLM	lambada
AAABDLR	Aldabra
AAABDNN	bandana
AAABDNR	Narbada
AAABENS	Sabaean
AAABFLL	falbala
AAABHJL	Halabja
AAABHLQ	qabalah
AAABHMR	Abraham
AAABHMS	Bahamas
AAABILN	Albania
AAABILX	abaxial
AAABINR	Arabian
AAABIPR	Paraíba
AAABIRV	Bavaria
AAABITV	batavia
AAABKKS	kabakas
AAABKLR	Karbala
AAABKLS	kabalas
AAABKLV	baklava
AAABKPS	baaskap
AAABLLU	Lualaba
AAABLST	balatas
AAABMNR	Anambra
AAABMOS	abomasa
AAABMST	mastaba
AAABNNS	bananas
AAABNRS	Banaras
AAABORR	araroba
AAABRST	braatas
AAABRSX	abrasax
	abraxas
AAABRSZ	barazas
	bazaars
AAABSTT	batatas
AAACCIS	acacias
AAACCLM	malacca
AAACCLP	alpacca
AAACCLR	caracal
AAACCRS	Caracas
	cascara
AAACDGS	cadagas
AAACDIN	Acadian
AAACDIR	arcadia
AAACDLU	acaudal
AAACDMM	macadam
AAACENP	panacea
AAACHHL	halacha
AAACHLZ	chalaza
AAACHRY	acharya
AAACIJM	Jamaica
AAACILM	malacia
AAACINT	Catania
AAACJMR	jacamar
AAACJNS	jacanas
AAACJRU	Aracajú
AAACLLS	La Scala
AAACLLV	cavalla
AAACLMN	almanac
AAACLNT	Alacant
	cantala
	Catalan
AAACLPS	alpacas
AAACLPT	catalpa
AAACLRZ	alcazar
AAACMRS	maracas
	marasca
	mascara
AAACMRY	Maracay
AAACNPU	Capuana
AAACNRS	arcanas
AAACNRV	caravan
AAACNST	canasta
AAACNTT	cantata
AAACRRR	Carrara
AAACRWY	caraway
AAACSST	cassata
AAACSSV	cassava
AAADDMO	amadoda
AAADELM	alameda
AAADFRY	faraday
AAADGGH	Aggadah
AAADGHL	Galahad
AAADGNR	Granada
AAADGUV	Daugava
AAADHHS	shahada
AAADHMN	Hamadān
AAADHNS	sadhana
AAADHWY	hadaway
AAADILX	adaxial
AAADIRT	radiata
AAADLLN	Laaland
AAADLMN	amandla
	mandala
AAADMNR	Narmada
	Ramadan
AAADMNT	adamant
AAADMNZ	Zaandam
AAADMRS	armadas
	madrasa
AAADWYY	awayday
AAAEGLT	galatea
AAAEGNP	apanage
AAAEHLT	althaea
AAAEIMN	anaemia
AAAEKRS	Kara Sea
AAAELPT	Plataea
AAAELRS	Aral Sea
AAAELSZ	azaleas
AAAENST	anatase
AAAERWY	areaway
AAAFFLL	alfalfa
AAAFHLS	Falasha
AAAFIRT	ratafia
AAAFRWY	faraway
AAAGHIP	aphagia
AAAGHKN	Aga Khan
AAAGHNT	ataghan
AAAGHPR	agrapha
AAAGILN	analgia
AAAGILT	Galatia
AAAGINR	Niagara
AAAGINZ	gazania
AAAGIPT	patagia
AAAGISS	assagai
AAAGKNN	Kananga
AAAGKNR	karanga
AAAGKNT	Katanga
AAAGLMM	amalgam
AAAGLNS	lasagna
AAAGLOS	Alagoas
AAAGMMT	magmata
AAAGMNR	anagram
AAAGMNU	Managua
AAAGMTT	tagmata
AAAGMTU	Gautama
AAAGNRR	ngarara
AAAGNRT	tanagra
AAAGRST	Aragats
AAAHHKL	halakha
AAAHHLV	halavah
AAAHIKP	aphakia
AAAHIKW	kahawai
AAAHIPS	aphasia
AAAHIST	taiahas
AAAHKRS	akharas
AAAHLNN	alannah
AAAHMMT	mahatma
AAAHMST	Athamas
	tamasha
AAAHNRS	Saharan
AAAHNRY	Haryana
AAAHNSV	vahanas
AAAHPPR	Harappa
AAAHPRT	paratha
AAAHRTW	waratah
AAAIKKR	karakia
AAAIKLT	latakia
AAAIKRS	akrasia
AAAILMR	malaria
AAAILNX	anaxial
AAAILPS	aplasia
AAAILPT	Patiala
AAAILRT	talaria
AAAILST	Alsatia
AAAIMNT	amanita
AAAIMRS	Samaria
AAAINNS	Ananias
AAAINNZ	Azanian
AAAIPRX	apraxia
AAAIPSS	Aspasia
AAAIQRU	aquaria

AAAJKNR	Karajan
AAAJKRT	Jakarta
AAAJMPS	pajamas
AAAKKMR	markkaa
AAAKKNS	kanakas
AAAKLLV	Kaválla
AAAKLMP	Kampala
AAAKLMR	Alkmaar
AAAKLMS	kamalas
AAAKLNS	Alaskan
AAAKLSS	Kassala
AAAKMOY	Okayama
AAAKMPR	Karmapa
AAAKMRS	Makasar
AAAKNRS	Sankara
AAAKNTY	Antakya
AAAKPPU	kaupapa
AAAKRSW	Sarawak
AAALLMP	La Palma
AAALLPT	La Plata
	palatal
AAALMNY	Malayan
AAALMRS	marsala
AAALMSS	salaams
AAALMTY	Malatya
AAALNNT	lantana
AAALNPW	Palawan
AAALNTT	Atlanta
AAALNTY	Antalya
AAALRRY	arrayal
AAALRSZ	Salazar
AAALWYY	layaway
AAAMMPR	mampara
AAAMMRR	Marmara
AAAMNNT	anatman
AAAMNPS	panamas
AAAMNPT	Matapan
AAAMNRT	maranta
AAAMNST	atamans
AAAMORT	tamarao
AAAMRSS	samaras
	samsara
AAAMRTU	tamarau
AAAMSSW	Massawa
AAANNRY	Narayan
AAANNSV	savanna
AAANPPY	papayan
AAANRTT	tantara
AAAOPRZ	parazoa
AAAPPRT	apparat
AAAPPSY	papayas
AAAPSST	passata
AAARRST	Tarrasa
AAARSTV	avatars
AAARTTT	ratatat
AAARTTU	tuatara
AAARTXY	ataraxy
AABBBEG	Babbage
AABBBOS	baobabs
AABBCEG	cabbage
AABBCOS	babacos
AABBDIS	Abbasid
AABBDRU	Barbuda
AABBEGN	beanbag
AABBEKL	Baalbek
AABBEMN	Mbabane
AABBERR	Barbera
AABBERT	barbate
AABBHMR	Brabham
AABBHST	sabbath
	Shabbat
AABBLLS	lablabs
AABBLOS	balboas
AABBNRT	Brabant
AABBRRY	Barbary
AABBSST	sabbats
AABBSSU	babassu
AABCCEH	Bacchae
AABCCET	baccate
AABCDIN	Cabinda
AABCDIR	carabid
AABCEFR	facebar
AABCELL	Caballé
AABCELN	balance
AABCELP	capable
AABCELT	actable
AABCEMR	macabre
AABCEMS	ambsace
AABCEOS	cobaeas
AABCERT	abreact
	bearcat
	cabaret
AABCFKT	fatback
AABCHHR	brachah
AABCHIL	Laibach
AABCHIR	brachia
AABCHMT	ambatch
AABCHNR	barchan
AABCHOR	abroach
AABCHSS	casbahs
AABCIIP	Picabia
AABCILM	cambial
AABCIMR	Cambrai
	Cambria
AABCIMS	Cabimas
AABCINR	carabin
AABCIOP	copaiba
AABCIRT	Bactria
AABCITX	taxicab
AABCKLY	layback
AABCKPY	backpay
	payback
AABCKRR	barrack
AABCKSW	backsaw
AABCLPY	capably
AABCLRY	Barclay
AABCMMU	macumba
AABCORT	acrobat
AABCOST	Tabasco
AABCOTT	catboat
AABCRSS	scarabs
AABDDER	abraded
AABDDGH	Baghdad
AABDDIK	kabaddi
AABDDNO	Abaddon
AABDDNS	sanddab
AABDEFL	fadable
AABDEGM	gambade
AABDEGN	bandage
AABDEHS	abashed
AABDEIR	braaied
AABDEIS	diabase
AABDEKW	dawbake
AABDELL	ballade
AABDELR	Abelard
AABDELT	ablated
	datable
AABDELW	wadable
AABDEMS	sambaed
AABDENU	bandeau
AABDERR	abrader
AABDERS	abrades
AABDESU	aubades
AABDEWZ	Bezwada
AABDGHN	handbag
AABDGMO	gambado
AABDGNS	sandbag
AABDGNU	Buganda
AABDGOS	dagobas
AABDHIO	Obadiah
AABDHNT	hatband
AABDHRU	bahadur
AABDIIS	basidia
AABDIJN	Abidjan
AABDIKR	bidarka
AABDIMR	barmaid
AABDINS	indabas
AABDINT	tabanid
AABDIOT	biodata
AABDJOZ	Badajoz
AABDLLR	Ballard
AABDLLS	ballads
AABDLMS	lambdas
AABDLRW	bradawl
AABDLRY	Arblay, d'
	d'Arblay
AABDLSU	Salduba
AABDMNR	armband
	Bradman
AABDNNO	abandon
AABDNRR	Barnard
AABDNRS	sandbar
AABDORV	bravado
AABDRRW	drawbar
AABDRST	bastard
	tabards
AABDRSU	subadar
AABDRSY	bayards
AABEELT	eatable
AABEEMO	amoebae
AABEERZ	zareeba
AABEFFL	affable
AABEFGL	fleabag
AABEFNR	Aberfan
AABEFNS	fanbase
AABEGGG	baggage
AABEGGR	garbage
AABEGLR	algebra
AABEGMS	ambages
AABEGRR	barrage
AABEGSS	bagasse
AABEHLT	hatable
AABEHRS	earbash
AABEHSS	abashes
AABEIKN	ikebana
AABEILM	amiable
AABEILN	abelian
AABEILT	labiate
AABEIOR	aerobia
AABEIRS	airbase
AABEJLL	jellaba
AABEJMU	jambeau
AABEKLM	makable
AABEKLT	takable
AABEKRY	kerbaya
AABELLL	labella
AABELLN	balneal
AABELLR	earball
AABELLS	salable
AABELMN	namable
AABELMT	tamable
AABELNO	abalone
AABELNS	bansela
AABELPR	parable
AABELPY	payable
AABELRS	arables
AABELRT	Alberta
	ratable
AABELSS	balases
AABELST	ablates
	astable
AABELSV	savable
AABELTT	abettal
AABELTU	tableau
AABELTX	taxable
AABEMNS	baseman
AABEMOS	amoebas
AABEMRR	Braemar
AABEMST	Masbate
AABENNW	wannabe
AABENRT	antbear
AABENRV	Barnave
AABENTY	abeyant
AABERST	abreast
AABERSU	subarea
AABERSZ	zarebas
AABERTT	tabaret
AABETUX	bateaux
AABFFLY	affably
AABFILU	fabliau
AABFINR	Biafran
AABGGRS	ragbags
AABGGSS	gasbags
AABGHNR	bhangra
	Branagh
AABGHSW	bagwash
AABGIIL	abigail

AABGILM	mailbag
AABGIMN	Gambian
AABGINR	bargain
AABGINS	abasing
AABGINT	abating
AABGLOR	Aalborg
AABGRST	ratbags
AABHHIW	Wahhabi
AABHIMS	Baha'ísm
AABHINR	Bahrain
AABHITT	habitat
AABHKNR	barkhan
AABHKOR	Bokhara
AABHKRS	Bhaskar
AABHKRU	Bukhara
AABHKSS	kasbahs
	sabkhas
AABHLRS	bharals
AABHLTY	bathyal
AABHMNR	Brahman
AABHMRS	brahmas
AABHMSS	shambas
AABHNSV	bhavans
AABHNSW	bhawans
AABHOST	Sabaoth
AABHSSW	bashaws
AABIILX	biaxial
AABIIMN	Namibia
AABIKNS	banksia
AABILLR	barilla
AABILLS	labials
AABILMN	Balmain
AABILMY	amiably
AABILNS	Basilan
AABILNT	Taliban
AABILOU	aboulia
AABILRS	basilar
AABIMMR	marimba
AABIMNO	amboina
AABIMNZ	Zambian
AABIMRS	ambaris
AABIMST	basmati
AABINNS	banians
AABINOU	ouabain
AABINST	abstain
AABINSW	Swabian
AABIORT	airboat
AABIORZ	Orizaba
AABIRSS	Brassaï
AABIRST	barista
	bartsia
AABISSY	Bisayas
AABISTT	abattis
	Batista
AABJMRT	jambart
AABKMRU	Mubarak
AABKNPR	Brakpan
AABKNRS	barkans
AABKNRT	tanbark
AABKOOZ	bazooka
AABLLNY	banally
AABLLST	ballast
AABLLSY	basally
	salably
AABLLWY	wallaby
AABLMOS	Absalom
AABLMRU	labarum
AABLMSS	balsams
AABLMST	lambast
AABLMSY	abysmal
	balsamy
AABLNOT	Balaton
AABLNRU	Barnaul
AABLNSS	San Blas
AABLNTT	blatant
AABLORT	ablator
AABLOSV	lavabos
AABLRTU	tabular
AABLRTY	ratably
AABLSST	basalts
AABLSSY	abyssal
AABLTTU	abuttal
AABLTXY	taxably
AABMMOS	Mombasa
AABMNOT	boatman
AABMNOY	amboyna
	Bayamón
AABMNST	bantams
	batsman
AABMORT	Tambora
AABMORU	marabou
AABMRSS	sambars
AABMSUW	Sumbawa
AABNNOZ	bonanza
AABNNSY	banyans
AABNOSY	sabayon
AABORRS	arrobas
	rasbora
AABORST	abators
	rabatos
AABOTTY	attaboy
AABQSUU	subaqua
AABRRUV	bravura
AABSSSY	sassaby
AABSTTW	abwatts
AACCDEI	cicadae
AACCDES	cascade
	saccade
AACCDIR	cardiac
AACCDIS	cicadas
AACCDOR	Accardo
AACCELO	cloacae
AACCERS	carcase
AACCEST	saccate
AACCHIR	archaic
AACCHLN	clachan
AACCHLS	Calchas
AACCHMP	champac
AACCHMS	chacmas
AACCHNR	Cranach
AACCHPU	Pachuca
AACCIJO	Ajaccio
AACCILM	acclaim
AACCILS	alcaics
	cicalas
AACCILU	acicula
AACCIOR	carioca
AACCITT	atactic
AACCJKR	carjack
AACCKLP	calpack
AACCKRR	carrack
AACCLLO	cloacal
AACCLLT	catcall
AACCLOP	polacca
AACCLOR	caracol
AACCLPS	calpacs
AACCLRU	accrual
	caracul
AACCLSU	accusal
AACCMOS	macacos
AACCNNS	cancans
AACCNVY	vacancy
AACCORU	curacao
	Curaçao
AACCOTT	toccata
AACCRSS	carcass
AACDDEL	decadal
AACDDIN	candida
AACDEEM	academe
AACDEFS	facades
AACDEHL	Chaldea
AACDEHM	chamade
AACDEHR	charade
AACDEHT	cathead
AACDEII	aecidia
AACDEIL	alcaide
AACDELL	alcalde
AACDELN	canaled
	candela
	decanal
AACDELR	caldera
AACDELS	alcades
	scalade
AACDEMY	academy
AACDENV	advance
AACDENZ	cadenza
AACDERS	arcades
AACDERV	cadaver
AACDERY	daycare
AACDETU	caudate
AACDETV	vacated
AACDFIR	faradic
AACDGIS	cadagis
AACDHMO	Machado
AACDHMR	drachma
AACDHST	datchas
AACDIIS	ascidia
AACDIJU	Judaica
AACDILR	radical
AACDINT	antacid
AACDINV	vanadic
AACDIOR	acaroid
AACDIRS	acarids
	ascarid
AACDJKW	jackdaw
AACDLNO	acnodal
	calando
AACDLNS	scandal
AACDLOS	scalado
AACDLPR	placard
AACDMPS	madcaps
AACDNRS	canards
	cardans
AACDOOV	avocado
AACDPRU	crapaud
AACDRSZ	czardas
AACEEGR	acreage
AACEEHR	earache
AACEEHT	chaetae
AACEEKT	teacake
AACEELN	anelace
AACEEMN	Camenae
AACEEMR	camerae
AACEEMS	amesace
AACEENT	catenae
AACEERT	acerate
AACEESS	casease
AACEEST	caseate
AACEETT	acetate
AACEFIS	fasciae
AACEFLT	falcate
AACEFLU	faculae
AACEFRR	carfare
AACEFRS	carafes
AACEGKP	package
AACEGLS	scalage
AACEGNR	caganer
	carnage
	cranage
AACEGRT	cartage
AACEHLP	acaleph
AACEHLR	alchera
AACEHNP	panache
AACEHNR	Arachne
AACEHOP	Phocaea
AACEHPS	apaches
AACEHPU	chapeau
AACEHRT	trachea
AACEHST	achates
AACEHTT	attache
AACEHTU	chateau
AACEILN	Caelian
AACEIMN	anaemic
AACEIMR	America
AACEINN	Nicaean
AACEINO	Oceania
AACEINR	carinae
AACEIRV	avarice
	caviare
AACEIST	ectasia
AACEJKN	Janáček
AACEJRS	jacares
AACEKNP	pancake
AACEKNS	askance
AACEKOT	oatcake
AACELLN	canella
AACELLP	Laplace
AACELLT	lacteal

AACELLW Wallace
AACELMN Maclean
manacle
AACELMR cameral
caramel
ceramal
maceral
AACELMU maculae
AACELNS anlaces
AACELNU canulae
lacunae
AACELNV valance
AACELPR carpale
AACELPS palaces
AACELPT placate
AACELRS scalare
AACELRV caravel
AACELST acetals
lactase
AACELSU Alcaeus
AACELTT lactate
AACELTV clavate
AACEMMR macrame
AACEMNV caveman
AACEMQU macaque
AACEMRS cameras
AACEMRU Marceau
AACENOT Actaeon
Caetano
AACENPS canapes
AACENRT cateran
AACENTY cyanate
AACEOPT peacoat
AACEORS rosacea
AACEPRS Pescara
AACEPWY paceway
AACEQTU Caquetà
AACERSS caesars
AACERST Caserta
AACERSU caesura
AACERSZ sazerac
AACERTT teacart
AACERTU arcuate
AACERWY raceway
AACESTV caveats
vacates
AACETTU actuate
AACFILS facials
fascial
AACFILU faucial
AACFINR African
AACFINT fanatic
AACFLLT catfall
AACFLLU falcula
AACFLLY fallacy
AACFLPT flatcap
AACFLRT fractal
AACFLRU facular
AACFLTU factual
AACFNST caftans
AACGGMS cagmags
AACGHLL Chagall
AACGHNN Changan
AACGIIL Galicia
AACGILL glacial
AACGILM magical
AACGINT agnatic
AACGIRS agarics
AACGLOT catalog
AACGLOU coagula
AACGLRY Calgary
AACGLSY galyacs
AACGNOR Orcagna
AACGNOU guanaco
AACHHKR charkha
AACHHLL challah
AACHHMT Chatham
AACHIKN kachina
AACHIKR Karachi
AACHILM Malachi
AACHILR rachial
AACHILT calathi
AACHIMR machair
AACHIMS chiasma
AACHINT acanthi
Ithacan
tachina
AACHIPR charpai
AACHIPS aphasic
Chiapas
AACHIPT chapati
AACHIRT cithara
AACHKMN Hackman
AACHKMP champak
AACHKMR Rackham
AACHKNR Harnack
AACHKRS chakras
charkas
AACHKRY hayrack
AACHKSW hacksaw
kwachas
AACHLLN Lachlan
AACHLMS chasmal
AACHLMY Malachy
AACHLNT canthal
AACHLPP chappal
AACHLPS paschal
AACHMNP chapman
AACHMNR Cam Ranh
AACHMNS machans
AACHMSY yashmac
AACHMTU Machaut
AACHNOP panocha
AACHNPX panchax
AACHNRS anarchs
AACHNRY anarchy
AACHNSU anchusa
AACHNSZ chazans
AACHRRT catarrh
AACHRSU Huáscar
AACHRSW Crashaw
AACHRWY archway
AACIINR Icarian
AACIINT actinia
AACIIST Asiatic
AACIITV viatica
AACIJLP jalapic
AACIKLL alkalic
AACIKLR clarkia
AACIKNN canakin
AACIKPR Rapacki
AACIKRT akratic
AACILLS callais
AACILMR mailcar
AACILMS camails
AACILNO Laconia
AACILNR cranial
AACILNT actinal
antical
AACILNU Lucania
AACILOS asocial
AACILOX coaxial
AACILPS spacial
AACILPT capital
AACILRR railcar
AACILUY Ucayali
AACIMNO manioca
AACIMNS caimans
maniacs
AACIMOR acromia
AACIMRU Mauriac
AACIMTY cymatia
AACINNT cantina
AACINOR Aaronic
ocarina
AACINPT captain
AACINRS arnicas
carinas
AACINRZ czarina
AACINST satanic
AACINTV Vatican
AACIOPT tapioca
AACIOPV copaiva
AACIORT Croatia
AACIORV Craiova
AACIOTV Octavia
AACIPRX apraxic
AACIQTU aquatic
AACIRSV caviars
AACISSS cassias
AACISTT astatic
AACJKLS jackals
AACJKMN manjack
AACJKSS jackass
AACJMOR Majorca
AACJOST Jocasta
AACJOSU acajous
AACKKLO Kaolack
AACKLMR Lamarck
AACKLTW catwalk
AACKNRS ransack
AACKPRR carpark
AACKPRT ratpack
AACKSTT attacks
AACLLNS callans
AACLLNT callant
AACLLNU lacunal
AACLLOO calaloo
AACLLSU clausal
AACLLVY cavally
AACLMNT clamant
AACLMRU macular
AACLMST lactams
AACLMSU calamus
AACLNNO anconal
AACLNNU cannula
AACLNOR Alarcón
Alcoran
AACLNPY claypan
AACLNRU canular
lacunar
AACLNSU canulas
lacunas
AACLOPR caporal
crapola
AACLORT Carlota
coaltar
AACLOST catalos
coastal
AACLOTT cattalo
AACLPRS carpals
AACLPRT caltrap
AACLPSS pascals
AACLPSU paucals
scapula
AACLPTY playact
AACLRSS lascars
rascals
scalars
AACLRTY lactary
AACLRVY calvary
cavalry
AACLSSU casuals
AACLSTU actuals
AACLSUV vascula
AACLSUX Lascaux
AACLTTU tactual
AACMNNO Monacan
AACMNRU arcanum
AACMNSY caymans
AACMORR camorra
AACMORS sarcoma
AACMORT marcato
AACMRRT tramcar
AACMRSS sarcasm
AACMRST tarmacs
AACNNOZ canzona
AACNORU A Coruña
AACNOSS Canossa
AACNOST sacaton
Toscana
AACNPST capstan
catnaps
AACNRTU curtana
AACNSSV canvass
AACNSTT actants
AACNTUY Yucatán
AACOPPR apocarp

AACPSTW	catspaw
AACRSTV	cravats
AACRTTT	attract
AACRTUY	actuary
AACSSTT	Cassatt
AACTUWY	cutaway
AADDDEN	addenda
AADDEES	Dead Sea
AADDEGM	damaged
AADDEHH	hadedah
AADDEIL	alidade
AADDEMN	deadman
AADDENP	deadpan
AADDEPR	paraded
AADDEPT	adapted
AADDERW	awarded
AADDESX	addaxes
AADDFGI	Gaddafi
AADDFIQ	Qaddafi
AADDGNR	grandad
AADDHKR	khaddar
AADDIIK	didakai
AADDILS	alidads
AADDIMN	Miandad
AADDIMS	dadaism
AADDIST	dadaist
AADDLYY	Lady Day
AADDMOR	Damodar
AADDNVV	dvandva
AADDOSU	aoudads
AADDRST	dastard
AADEEFR	afeared
AADEELT	dealate
AADEEMT	edemata
AADEERT	aerated
AADEERW	awardee
AADEFHT	fathead
AADEFLY	al Fayed
AADEGGR	aggrade
	garaged
AADEGHN	Den Haag
AADEGLS	geladas
AADEGMN	managed
AADEGMR	damager
AADEGMS	damages
AADEGNR	Grenada
AADEGNS	agendas
	Sandage
AADEGRT	gradate
AADEGRV	ravaged
AADEGRY	drayage
	yardage
AADEGSV	savaged
AADEHIR	airhead
AADEHLN	Haldane
AADEHMN	headman
AADEHMS	ashamed
AADEHPR	Phaedra
AADEHPS	saphead
AADEHRW	warhead
AADEHWY	headway
AADEILV	availed
	vedalia
AADEIMR	madeira
AADEINR	araneid
	Ariadne
AADEINS	naiades
AADEIRT	radiate
	tiaraed
AADEITV	aviated
AADEITW	awaited
AADEJMR	jemadar
AADEJNU	Judaean
AADEKLR	kraaled
AADEKMR	kamerad
AADEKPR	parkade
AADELLY	allayed
AADELMN	Almadén
	Mandela
AADELMO	alamode
AADELMR	alarmed
AADELNR	adrenal
AADELNW	danelaw
AADELNX	adnexal
AADELNZ	Zealand
AADELRU	radulae
AADELRY	already
AADELSS	salades
AADELTU	adulate
AADEMMN	manmade
AADEMNO	adenoma
AADEMNS	anadems
	maenads
AADEMNT	mandate
AADEMNY	name day
AADEMRW	Medawar
AADEMSS	amassed
AADENNP	Pandean
AADENNT	andante
AADENRU	Dunărea
AADENRV	veranda
AADENSW	weasand
AADENTV	Vedanta
AADEPRR	parader
AADEPRS	parades
AADEPRT	adapter
	readapt
AADEPSS	passade
AADERRW	awarder
AADERRY	arrayed
AADERSW	seaward
AADESSY	assayed
AADFHOS	Fashoda
AADGGHR	haggard
AADGGLR	laggard
AADGHNZ	Gandzha
AADGHOR	darogha
AADGHRS	dargahs
AADGIKZ	Kaz Daği
AADGIMM	digamma
AADGIMR	diagram
AADGIMS	agamids
AADGINN	Dingaan
AADGIOS	adagios
AADGLLW	gadwall
AADGLNO	gonadal
AADGLNR	garland
AADGLRU	gradual
AADGMNR	grandam
	grandma
AADGMOT	dogmata
AADGMRS	smaragd
AADGNNU	Ugandan
AADGNPR	grandpa
AADGNPS	Dapsang
	padangs
AADGNRT	gardant
AADGOPR	podagra
AADGOPS	pagodas
AADGRSY	gaydars
AADHHMS	Mashhad
AADHHNR	Dhahran
AADHHRT	hardhat
AADHILR	Harald I
AADHILS	dahlias
AADHIMR	hadarim
AADHIMS	samadhi
AADHINO	Idahoan
AADHINP	daphnia
AADHINR	Hadrian
AADHKNS	dhansak
	khandas
AADHLRY	halyard
AADHMNR	hardman
AADHNPR	hardpan
AADHNSW	handsaw
AADHOYY	Ayodhya
AADHRSZ	hazards
AADHRWY	hayward
AADHSWY	washday
AADIINN	Indiana
AADIINO	dianoia
AADIIPS	adipsia
AADILLO	alodial
AADILMR	admiral
AADILMT	matilda
AADILNP	paladin
AADILNR	laniard
AADILNS	Saladin
AADILNU	Laudian
AADILPS	apsidal
AADILRS	radials
AADILSS	dalasis
AADILTV	datival
AADILWY	waylaid
AADIMNR	Miranda
AADIMNS	maidans
AADIMOR	diorama
AADIMOT	domatia
AADIMRU	Madurai
AADINRS	radians
AADINRT	radiant
AADINRV	Andvari
AADINRW	wardian
AADIRSU	sudaria
AADISST	stadias
AADJLNS	jandals
AADKLNO	Oakland
AADKMNR	Danmark
AADKMSS	damasks
AADKNOT	Dakotan
AADKNRT	tankard
AADKNRY	Yarkand
AADKPSU	padauks
AADKRWW	awkward
AADLLMR	mallard
AADLLNP	Lapland
AADLLPU	paludal
AADLMMU	Malamud
AADLMNO	mandola
AADLMNU	ladanum
AADLNRY	lanyard
AADLNSS	sandals
AADLNSU	landaus
AADLNSV	vandals
AADLNWY	Wayland
AADLOPY	payload
AADLPPU	applaud
AADLRRU	radular
AADLRWY	Aylward
AADMNNO	madonna
AADMNNS	sandman
AADMNOR	madrona
	monarda
AADMNRS	mansard
AADMNTU	tamandu
AADMORT	matador
AADMOYY	Omayyad
AADMRRY	yardarm
AADMRSU	marauds
AADMRSZ	mazards
AADMRZZ	mazzard
AADMUYY	Umayyad
AADNNRS	randans
AADNNRW	Rwandan
AADNOPR	pandora
AADNORR	Andorra
AADNORY	anyroad
AADNRVW	vanward
AADOPRR	parador
AADOPRS	parados
AADOPRT	adaptor
AADOPRX	paradox
AADOPSS	posadas
AADORWY	roadway
AADOSTT	tostada
AADPSSW	padsaws
AADPSYY	paydays
AADPTTU	dupatta
AADQRTU	quadrat
AADRRSS	sardars
AADRSTU	daturas
AADRSTY	daystar
AADRWWY	wayward
AAEEFGL	leafage
AAEEFRT	ratafee
AAEEGKL	leakage
AAEEGLT	galeate

AAEEGMR Megaera
AAEEGMT agamete
AAEEGNO Neogaea
AAEEGRV average
AAEEHRT hetaera
AAEEINT taeniae
AAEEKLS seakale
AAEELMT maleate
AAEELOR areolae
AAEEMNT emanate
enemata
manatee
AAEEMRT amreeta
AAEEMTX meataxe
AAEEPPS appease
AAEERST aerates
AAEERSW seaware
AAEERTU aureate
AAEERTX exarate
AAEFFGR agraffe
AAEFFIR affaire
AAEFFLL falafel
AAEFFNR fanfare
AAEFFTT taffeta
AAEFGNR Fergana
AAEFGRS agrafes
AAEFGTW waftage
AAEFHMR Fareham
AAEFHNS Eşfahān
AAEFKLO oakleaf
AAEFLPR earflap
AAEFLSV favelas
AAEFMRT fermata
AAEFNST Santa Fe
AAEFRRR Ferrara
AAEFRRW warfare
AAEFRST Far East
AAEGGNO anagoge
AAEGGRS garages
AAEGHLU haulage
AAEGHMR Grahame
AAEGHNT thanage
AAEGILR Algeria
lairage
regalia
AAEGILS algesia
AAEGINV vaginae
AAEGISS assegai
AAEGISU ageusia
AAEGITT agitate
AAEGKNT tankage
AAEGKOS soakage
AAEGLLT tallage
AAEGLMN gamelan
AAEGLMT gametal
AAEGLNN anlagen
AAEGLNS anlages
lagenas
lasagne
AAEGLNU leguaan
AAEGLRR realgar
AAEGLRS laagers
AAEGLRV Algarve
AAEGLSV lavages
salvage
AAEGMNR manager
AAEGMNS manages
AAEGMNT magenta
magnate
AAEGMPR rampage
AAEGMRT Margate
AAEGMSS massage
AAEGNNP pannage
AAEGNNT tannage
AAEGNOP apogean
AAEGNPT pageant
AAEGNPW pawnage
AAEGNRR arrange
AAEGNRT tanager
AAEGNST agnates
AAEGNSU guanase
AAEGNTV vantage
AAEGPRR parerga
AAEGPRW warpage
AAEGPSS passage
AAEGQUY quayage
AAEGRRV ravager
AAEGRST teargas
AAEGRSV ravages
AAEGRTT regatta
AAEGRUV Guevara
AAEGSSU assuage
sausage
AAEGSSV savages
AAEGSTW wastage
AAEGTTW wattage
AAEGTUX gateaux
AAEGTWY gateway
getaway
AAEHHIL Hialeah
AAEHHPT aphthae
AAEHILP aphelia
AAEHIMN Anaheim
AAEHIRT hetaira
Rhaetia
AAEHKNT khanate
AAEHKPS pakehas
AAEHKST takahes
AAEHLLL allheal
AAEHLMR Haarlem
AAEHLNT ethanal
AAEHLPR Raphael
AAEHLPS phaseal
AAEHLPX hexapla
AAEHLRT trehala
AAEHLST altheas
AAEHMST athames
AAEHNPR hanaper
AAEHNPS saphena
AAEHNSY hyaenas
AAEHRRT Earhart
AAEHRSY hearsay
AAEHSTT hastate
AAEIJLP Liepāja
AAEIKLN akenial
AAEIKLR Karelia
AAEIKLU Kilauea
AAEIKRT Karaite
AAEILLN La Línea
AAEILLX axillae
AAEILMN Alamein
laminae
AAEILMR Almería
AAEILMS malaise
AAEILNN alanine
AAEILNO aeolian
AAEILNT antliae
AAEILNU El Aaiún
AAEILOR olearia
AAEILOT Aetolia
AAEILRS aerials
AAEILRV velaria
AAEILSS aliases
AAEIMMT imamate
AAEIMNR Armenia
AAEIMNS amnesia
AAEIMNT amentia
animate
AAEIMPY pyaemia
AAEIMRR armeria
AAEIMRT amirate
AAEIMRU uraemia
AAEIMTV amative
AAEINNO aeonian
AAEINPR Pienaar
AAEINPT patinae
AAEINST entasia
AAEIPRR pareira
AAEIPRS spiraea
AAEIPRT Tarpeia
AAEIPTT apatite
AAEIRST aristae
Astaire
atresia
AAEIRSU Eurasia
AAEIRTT arietta
AAEIRTV variate
AAEISTT satiate
AAEISTV aviates
AAEITUX eutaxia
AAEJOPR aparejo
AAEKKOR karaoke
AAEKLNS alkanes
AAEKLNT alkanet
AAEKMRR earmark
AAEKMRS seamark
AAEKNSW awakens
AAEKPRT partake
AAELLLM lamella
AAELLLS La Salle
AAELLPS paellas
AAELLPT patella
AAELLRT lateral
AAELLSW seawall
AAELMMR almemar
AAELMMT lemmata
AAELMNU alumnae
AAELMOT oatmeal
AAELMPT palmate
AAELMST malates
maltase
tamales
AAELMSY amylase
AAELNNS anneals
AAELNRS arsenal
AAELNRT Lateran
AAELNST sealant
AAELNSY analyse
AAELNTT tetanal
AAELNYZ analyze
AAELORR areolar
AAELORS areolas
AAELORU aureola
AAELOTX oxalate
AAELPPR apparel
AAELPPS appeals
AAELPPT palpate
AAELPPU papulae
AAELPRS earlaps
AAELPRT apteral
AAELPRV palaver
AAELPSS plaases
AAELPST palates
AAELPTT tapetal
AAELPTU plateau
AAELPTY apetaly
AAELRST tarseal
AAELRTZ lazaret
AAELRVZ Alvarez
AAELSST atlases
AAELSTV valetas
AAELSUX asexual
AAELTTV Valetta
AAELTUV valuate
AAELTVV valvate
AAEMMMR maremma
AAEMNPP pampean
AAEMNRS Manresa
AAEMNRT ramenta
AAEMNSS Masséna
AAEMNST Eastman
Smetana
AAEMNTU manteau
AAEMQSU squamae
AAEMRSS amasser
AAEMRTU amateur
AAEMSSS amasses
AAENNNT antenna
AAENNRV Ravenna
AAENNST annates
AAENNSZ zenanas
AAENNTT tannate
AAENPST anapest
peasant
AAENPSV pavanes
AAENPTT epatant
AAENRRT narrate
AAENRRV Navarre

AAENRSZ	Sarazen
AAENRTU	taurean
AAENRTV	taverna
AAENRUW	unaware
AAENSST	Nastase
AAENSSW	Swansea
AAENSTU	Antaeus
AAENSTV	Avestan
	savante
AAEORRT	aerator
AAEORRU	aurorae
AAEPPRS	appears
AAEPPRT	parapet
AAERRRS	arrears
AAERRSS	arrases
AAERRTT	tartare
AAERSSY	assayer
AAERSTT	Astarte
AAESSTV	savates
AAESSWY	seaways
AAETTUW	Watteau
AAFFINS	saffian
AAFFINT	affiant
AAFFIRS	affairs
	raffias
AAFFIRX	Fairfax
AAFFRSY	affrays
AAFGHIN	afghani
AAFGHNS	afghans
AAFGLMN	flagman
AAFGORR	farrago
AAFHILX	Halifax
AAFHINS	Isfahan
AAFHLWY	halfway
AAFHMNR	Farnham
AAFHNST	Fatshan
AAFHSTW	fatwahs
AAFIILR	filaria
AAFIILS	Faisal I
AAFIJST	fajitas
AAFIKSS	sifakas
AAFILNT	fantail
	tailfan
AAFIMRY	Mayfair
AAFINNT	infanta
AAFIPRT	parfait
AAFIRSS	safaris
AAFIRUY	rufiyaa
AAFIRWY	fairway
AAFISST	fatsias
AAFJLOR	alforja
AAFKMNU	Kaufman
AAFKNST	kaftans
AAFLLLS	fallals
AAFLLTY	fatally
AAFLMNX	Flaxman
AAFLNUU	faunula
AAFLWYY	flyaway
AAFMNST	fantasm
AAFNSTT	fantast
AAFNSTY	fantasy
AAGGIJN	jagaing
AAGGILN	ganglia
AAGGINR	Gagarin
AAGGIZZ	Zagazig
AAGGJRY	jaggary
AAGGLMO	magalog
AAGGLOS	galagos
AAGGLRY	graylag
AAGGNOY	anagogy
AAGGNST	gangsta
AAGGNWY	gangway
AAGGQSU	quaggas
AAGGRSS	saggars
AAGHHZZ	Ghazzah
AAGHILR	Aligarh
	gharial
AAGHILZ	Ghazali
AAGHINN	anhinga
AAGHITU	Gauhati
AAGHKNS	kanghas
	khangas
AAGHKNT	thangka
AAGHLNT	gnathal
AAGHLSU	Agulhas
AAGHMMU	Maugham
AAGHMNN	hangman
AAGHMRS	grahams
AAGHNNY	Hanyang
AAGHNRS	hangars
AAGHNST	sanghat
AAGHNUV	Vaughan
AAGHRSW	washrag
AAGIINO	Goiânia
AAGIINT	Niigata
AAGIKNS	kaingas
AAGIKNT	tikanga
AAGIKNW	awaking
AAGILMY	myalgia
AAGILNN	anginal
AAGILNP	paginal
AAGILNS	agnails
AAGILNV	Galvani
	vaginal
AAGILOT	otalgia
AAGILPS	palagis
AAGILRS	argalis
	garials
AAGILSV	gavials
AAGILTW	wagtail
AAGIMNO	angioma
AAGIMNS	siamang
AAGIMNZ	amazing
AAGINNS	inangas
AAGINOS	agnosia
AAGINRR	arraign
AAGINRS	sangria
	sarangi
AAGINRT	Gratian
AAGINRU	guarani
AAGINRZ	zingara
AAGINST	against
AAGINSU	iguanas
AAGINSV	vaginas
AAGINSY	gainsay
AAGINTU	Antigua
AAGINWW	wawaing
AAGIOTT	agitato
AAGIPPR	Agrippa
AAGIPRU	piragua
AAGIRST	Artigas
	Stagira
AAGISSZ	Agassiz
AAGISTT	sagitta
AAGJMNU	Majunga
AAGJRSU	jaguars
AAGJRTU	Gujarat
AAGKLSY	galyaks
AAGKNRS	Angarsk
AAGLLNT	gallant
AAGLNNO	Angolan
AAGLNOS	analogs
AAGLNOY	analogy
AAGLNPS	lapsang
AAGLNRS	langars
	raglans
AAGLNRU	angular
AAGLNTY	galanty
AAGLRUU	arugula
	augural
AAGLRVX	gravlax
AAGLSST	stalags
AAGMMNS	magsman
AAGMMRR	grammar
AAGMMST	gammats
AAGMMTU	gummata
AAGMMUY	mamaguy
AAGMNOR	Romagna
AAGMNOS	sangoma
AAGMNOT	agamont
AAGMNPR	pangram
AAGMNRT	tangram
AAGMNSW	swagman
AAGMOPY	apogamy
AAGMRRY	gramary
AAGMRSY	margays
AAGNNOS	goannas
AAGNOPR	paragon
AAGNORS	angoras
AAGNORZ	organza
AAGNOST	taongas
AAGNPRS	parangs
AAGNRRY	granary
AAGNRSS	sangars
AAGNRTT	Grattan
AAGNRTV	vagrant
AAGNSTU	taguans
AAGOPSS	sapsago
AAGORSU	saguaro
AAGPPRS	grappas
AAGRRSY	garryas
AAGSTUU	Augusta
AAHHJJS	hajjahs
AAHHLLS	hallahs
AAHHLSV	halvahs
AAHHMSS	Shamash
AAHHNPT	naphtha
AAHHOPR	pharaoh
AAHIIKW	Hawaiki
AAHIIMT	himatia
AAHIINT	Haitian
AAHIJNR	harijan
AAHIKMT	Khatami
AAHIKPS	pakahis
AAHIKRT	kithara
AAHILMT	thalami
AAHILPV	pahlavi
AAHIMNO	mahonia
AAHIMNR	Ahriman
AAHIMNS	Samhain
	shamina
AAHIMNZ	hazanim
AAHIMRT	Marathi
AAHINNU	Huainan
AAHINOP	aphonia
AAHINOR	Honiara
AAHINPP	paphian
AAHINPR	piranha
AAHINST	Ashanti
	shaitan
AAHINSX	Shaanxi
AAHINTU	Hainaut
AAHINTW	taniwha
AAHIPRS	pariahs
	raphias
AAHIPRT	Parthia
AAHIPTY	Hypatia
AAHIRRS	hariras
AAHISTW	tawhais
AAHJRRS	jarrahs
AAHKLRS	lashkar
AAHKMMR	Markham
AAHKMSY	yashmak
AAHKMYY	Khayyám
AAHKNPU	Punakha
AAHKNRS	Shankar
AAHKNSY	Sankhya
AAHKPSS	pashkas
AAHKPSU	hapukas
AAHLLLS	hallals
AAHLLOS	halloas
AAHLLSW	wallahs
AAHLLWY	hallway
	Whyalla
AAHLMMS	hammals
AAHLMPR	Ramphal
AAHLMRS	marshal
AAHLMRU	hamular
AAHLMST	malthas
AAHLMSU	hamauls
AAHLNPX	phalanx
AAHLNRW	narwhal
AAHLPRS	phrasal
AAHLPST	asphalt
AAHLRSS	ashlars
AAHLRSW	shalwar
AAHLSWW	Shawwal
AAHMNNU	hanuman

AAHMNSS	shamans
AAHMOPR	amphora
AAHMQSU	quamash
AAHMRSS	ashrams
AAHMRTU	Mathura
AAHMSTZ	matzahs
AAHNNNS	Nan Shan
AAHNNOS	hosanna
AAHNRTX	anthrax
AAHNRTY	rhatany
AAHNSUW	whanaus
AAHNSZZ	hazzans
AAHORSU	sahuaro
AAHPPRS	paraphs
AAHPRTW	warpath
AAHPTWY	pathway
AAHRSST	shastra
AAHRSTY	ashtray
AAHRTTW	athwart
AAHSSSY	sashays
AAIIKNR	Nikaria
AAIILMN	Iliamna
AAIILMR	airmail
AAIILNT	Italian
AAIILPT	tilapia
AAIINNR	Iranian
AAIINRZ	Zaïrian
AAIINTT	titania
AAIIRSU	Isauria
AAIIRVV	vivaria
AAIJLNU	Juliana
AAIJNTU	Tijuana
AAIKLLS	alkalis
AAIKLMS	kalmias
AAIKLNP	palinka
AAIKLNS	kalians
AAIKLPR	palikar
AAIKMNN	manakin
AAIKNNT	Kantian
AAIKNOW	Okinawa
AAIKNST	Katsina
AAIKOTW	Waikato
AAIKPPR	paprika
AAIKPTZ	Kapitza
AAIKRSS	askaris
AAIKTVV	akvavit
AAILLMM	mamilla
AAILLMN	manilla
AAILLMX	maxilla
AAILLNV	vanilla
AAILLPP	papilla
AAILLRX	axillar
AAILLXY	axially
AAILMMN	mailman
AAILMMS	Lamaism
	miasmal
AAILMMX	maximal
AAILMNR	laminar
AAILMNS	animals
	laminas
AAILMNT	matinal
AAILMNU	alumina
AAILMOS	Somalia
AAILMPR	Palmira
AAILMPS	impalas
AAILMRR	Ar Rimal
AAILMRT	marital
	martial
AAILMSS	salamis
AAILNOS	Sinaloa
AAILNOT	Laotian
AAILNOV	valonia
AAILNPT	platina
AAILNPU	Naipaul
AAILNRY	laniary
AAILNSS	salinas
AAILNSY	inyalas
AAILNTV	Latvian
	valiant
AAILORS	solaria
AAILORV	variola
AAILOST	solatia
AAILPRT	partial
	patrial
AAILPRY	airplay
AAILPST	spatial
AAILQWW	qawwali
AAILRRV	arrival
AAILRST	Al Sirat
	lariats
AAILRTT	rattail
AAILRTV	travail
AAILRWY	railway
AAILSSS	assails
AAILSSV	salvias
AAILSSW	wassail
AAILSTU	Lusatia
AAIMMNO	ammonia
AAIMMSS	miasmas
AAIMNOR	Romania
AAIMNOS	anosmia
AAIMNOT	animato
AAIMNRS	marinas
AAIMNRT	martian
	tamarin
AAIMNRU	Rumania
AAIMNRZ	Mazarin
AAIMNST	stamina
AAIMORR	Roraima
AAIMORV	Moravia
AAIMRRS	mararis
AAIMRST	amritas
	Maritsa
AAIMRSU	Masuria
	samurai
AAIMSTT	tatamis
AAIMSTV	atavism
AAINNRU	uranian
AAINNRV	navarin
	nirvana
AAINNWX	Wanxian
AAINOPS	paisano
AAINORV	ovarian
AAINORZ	Arizona
AAINPRS	parians
	piranas
AAINPRT	Trapani
AAINPRU	Rapa Nui
AAINPST	patinas
	taipans
AAINQRW	Qairwan
AAINQSU	Aquinas
AAINRST	antiars
	artisan
	Sinatra
	tsarina
AAINRSU	saurian
AAINRTV	variant
AAINRTW	antiwar
AAINRTY	Nayarit
AAINSST	istanas
AAINSSY	sanyasi
AAINSTT	attains
AAINTTT	attaint
AAINTUY	Taiyuan
AAIOPRS	aporias
AAIORRS	rosaria
AAIORST	Astoria
AAIORTV	aviator
AAIPPRU	puparia
AAIPPTT	pitapat
AAIPRTT	partita
AAIPRTV	Parvati
AAIPSZZ	piazzas
AAIQQZZ	Zaqaziq
AAIQSSU	quassia
AAIQTUV	aquavit
AAIRSSS	Sassari
AAIRSST	tarsias
AAIRSSY	Assyria
AAIRSTU	Austria
AAIRSWY	airways
AAIRSZZ	razzias
AAISTTV	atavist
AAISTUY	yautias
AAITWXY	taxiway
AAJKLWY	jaywalk
AAJKNSS	sanjaks
AAJMNPS	jampans
AAJMPSY	pyjamas
AAJNNSU	San Juan
AAJOPST	Tapajós
AAJOPSU	sapajou
AAKKLOT	Kolkata
AAKKLPS	kalpaks
AAKKLRU	karakul
AAKKMOT	tokamak
AAKKMRU	Kara Kum
AAKKOPS	kakapos
AAKKSUZ	zakuska
AAKLMRY	malarky
AAKLNOR	Alkoran
AAKLOOP	palooka
AAKLOOT	talooka
AAKLRSU	kursaal
AAKLSTU	talukas
AAKLWWY	walkway
AAKMNSU	manukas
AAKMNSW	Waksman
AAKMNUU	Manukau
AAKMORV	Markova
AAKMOSU	mousaka
AAKMRSU	kumaras
AAKMRSY	Masaryk
AAKMRUZ	mazurka
AAKMRWY	waymark
AAKNNTU	nunatak
AAKNORS	anoraks
AAKNRSS	Saransk
AAKNRST	kantars
AAKNRTU	Turkana
AAKNSWZ	kwanzas
AAKOOPP	pakapoo
AAKOPRS	pakoras
AAKPRWY	parkway
AAKRTTU	Atatürk
AAKRTUY	autarky
AALLLNS	lallans
AALLLSW	Walsall
AALLMMS	mallams
AALLMPU	ampulla
AALLNPU	planula
AALLNSY	nasally
AALLOPR	Rapallo
AALLORW	Oral Law
AALLOTV	lavolta
AALLOWY	Alloway
AALLPPS	appalls
AALLPPY	papally
AALLRUY	aurally
AALMMMS	mammals
AALMMNO	ammonal
AALMMNS	almsman
AALMNOY	anomaly
	Layamon
AALMNPS	napalms
AALMNSU	manuals
AALMOPR	Palomar
AALMORY	mayoral
AALMPRY	palmary
	palmyra
AALMRSU	alarums
AALMRTU	Umar Tal
AALMRUX	Malraux
AALNNRU	annular
AALNNSU	annuals
AALNOUV	Ulanova
AALNPRT	plantar
AALNPST	platans
	saltpan
AALNQTU	quantal
AALNRSW	narwals
AALNRTU	natural
AALNSTT	saltant
AALNSTU	sultana
AALNSTY	analyst
AALOPRS	parasol
AALOPST	Spalato

AALOPSY payolas
AALOPTV Poltava
AALOPVV pavlova
AALORRU auroral
AALORSU arousal
AALOSTT Astolat
AALOSVW avowals
AALPPRU papular
AALPPSU Uppsala
AALPRRS parrals
AALPRSY parlays
AALPRTY laptray
AALPSTU spatula
AALRSST tarsals
AALRSTT stratal
AALRSTU austral
AALRSTY astylar
AALRSUZ Lazarus
AALSSSV vassals
AALSSTU assault
AALSTUV valutas
AALSWYY waylays
AAMMMRY mammary
AAMMNNX Manxman
AAMMNRY Myanmar
AAMMOTY myomata
AAMMRST ramstam
tammars
AAMNNOR Marañón
AAMNNOT Montana
AAMNORR marrano
orraman
AAMNORS oarsman
AAMNORZ romanza
AAMNOSZ amazons
AAMNOTV Mantova
AAMNOTY anatomy
AAMNPRT mantrap
rampant
AAMNPSS sampans
AAMNPTY tympana
AAMNRST Mansart
mantras
AAMNRSU Mansûra
AAMNSTU mantuas
AAMOPRS paramos
AAMORSV samovar
AAMORTU Utamaro
AAMORTY amatory
AAMOSSS samosas
AAMOSTT stomata
AAMOTTU automat
AAMPRRT rampart
AAMPRSS Sampras
AAMRRSU Maurras
AAMRRTY Marryat
AAMRSST matrass
AAMRSTU sumatra
traumas
AAMRTTY trymata
AAMRTWY tramway
AAMSSTU satsuma

AANNOTT annatto
AANNRSU anurans
AANNRUU Nauruan
AANNSSU Susanna
AANNSYZ nyanzas
AANNTUY Yuan Tan
AANORTT Taranto
AANOSST sonatas
AANOSTT anattos
AANPRST partans
spartan
tarpans
trapans
AANPRUU Uruapan
AANPSST passant
AANQRTU quartan
AANRRSY yarrans
AANRRTW warrant
AANRSTT rattans
tartans
AANRSTZ tarzans
AANRUWY runaway
AANSSTT tsantsa
AANSSTV savants
AANSSTZ stanzas
AANSTTT statant
AANSWYY anyways
AANTUUV Vanuatu
AAOPSST sapotas
AAORRSU auroras
AAORSTT totaras
AAORSTV Ostrava
Saratov
AAORSVV vavasor
AAOSTTV ottavas
AAOTTUY tatouay
AAPPSWW pawpaws
AAPRRTT rattrap
AAPRSST satraps
AAPRSTY satrapy
AAPRTUU raupatu
AAPRTWY partway
AAPZZZZ pazzazz
AAQRSSU quasars
AARRSTT tartars
AARRTTY Tartary
AARSSST sastras
ABBBDEL babbled
blabbed
ABBBELR babbler
blabber
brabble
ABBBELS babbles
ABBBITT babbitt
ABBCDER crabbed
ABBCDES scabbed
ABBCEHI babiche
ABBCEIS cabbies
ABBCELS scabble
ABBCERR crabber
ABBCIKT backbit
ABBCKUY buyback

ABBCOST bobcats
ABBCOTY abbotcy
ABBCRYY crybaby
ABBDDEL dabbled
ABBDDER drabbed
ABBDEGL gabbled
ABBDEGR grabbed
ABBDEIY yabbied
ABBDELR dabbler
drabble
rabbled
ABBDELS dabbles
slabbed
ABBDELW wabbled
ABBDERR drabber
ABBDERS dabbers
ABBDERT drabbet
ABBDEST stabbed
ABBDESU bedaubs
ABBDESW swabbed
ABBDGIN dabbing
ABBDILO Boabdil
ABBDINR ribband
ABBDMOR bombard
ABBDNOX bandbox
ABBEERR Berbera
ABBEESW bawbees
ABBEGIR gabbier
ABBEGLR gabbler
grabble
ABBEGLS gabbles
ABBEGMR Bamberg
ABBEGNO bogbean
ABBEGNU bugbane
ABBEGRR grabber
ABBEGRS gabbers
ABBEGRU bugbear
Burbage
ABBEHMO Hobbema
ABBEINT Babinet
ABBEIRS barbies
ABBEIST tabbies
ABBEISY yabbies
ABBEJRS jabbers
ABBEKRU Abu-Bekr
ABBELLR barbell
ABBELMR bramble
ABBELOR belabor
ABBELRR rabbler
ABBELRS barbels
rabbles
slabber
ABBELRU barbule
ABBELRW wabbler
ABBELSU baubles
ABBELSW wabbles
ABBEOTX beatbox
ABBERRS barbers
ABBERST barbets
rabbets
stabber
ABBERSW swabber

ABBERSY yabbers
ABBESSU subbase
ABBGGIN gabbing
ABBGIJN jabbing
ABBGINN nabbing
ABBGINR barbing
ABBGINT tabbing
ABBGINY babying
ABBGOOU bugaboo
ABBGORS gabbros
ABBHISY babyish
ABBHJSU jubbahs
ABBHRRU rhubarb
ABBHTTU bathtub
ABBIIMN bambini
ABBIJLS jilbabs
ABBILOT bobtail
ABBILSU bubalis
ABBIMNO bambino
ABBIORT rabbito
ABBIRST rabbits
ABBKLOU blaubok
ABBLLTU bullbat
ABBLMRY brambly
ABBLNOY Babylon
ABBMOOR bombora
ABBMOOS bamboos
ABBMOST bombast
ABBMOTU bumboat
ABBNOOS baboons
ABBNRUY Banbury
ABBOORU rubaboo
ABBORRU Barbour
ABBORSS absorbs
ABBOSTY bobstay
ABBQSUY squabby
ABBRSSU busbars
ABBSSSU subbass
ABCCCHI bacchic
ABCCEER Rebecca
ABCCEIR acerbic
breccia
ABCCEIS baccies
sebacic
ABCCHII bacchii
ABCCHSU Bacchus
ABCCHTY bycatch
ABCCILU cubical
ABCCIMR cambric
ABCCIOR boracic
ABCCKOW bawcock
ABCCKTU cutback
ABCCOOT tobacco
ABCCSUU succuba
ABCDEEH beached
ABCDEEL debacle
ABCDEHT batched
ABCDEHU debauch
ABCDEIK dieback
ABCDEIN cabined
ABCDEIP pedicab
ABCDEIR carbide

ABCDEKL	blacked
ABCDEKR	redback
ABCDEOR	brocade
ABCDERU	cudbear
ABCDIIS	dibasic
ABCDILR	baldric
ABCDIRS	scabrid
ABCDIRT	catbird
ABCDISU	subacid
ABCDLOO	Bacolod
ABCDNOS	abscond
ABCDOOR	cordoba
	Córdoba
ABCDRUY	Cadbury
ABCDSTU	abducts
ABCEEHM	Beecham
ABCEEHS	beaches
ABCEEMR	embrace
ABCEENR	carbeen
	carbene
ABCEENS	absence
ABCEERR	cerebra
ABCEESU	because
ABCEGIR	ribcage
ABCEGOS	boscage
ABCEHIL	Labiche
ABCEHIT	Thebaic
ABCEHKM	Beckham
ABCEHLO	chaebol
ABCEHLU	bauchle
ABCEHMR	chamber
	chambre
ABCEHMT	Macbeth
ABCEHRS	braches
ABCEHRT	brachet
ABCEHST	batches
ABCEIIT	abietic
ABCEIKS	backies
ABCEIKT	tieback
ABCEILM	alembic
	cembali
ABCEILR	caliber
	calibre
ABCEILT	citable
ABCEIMO	amoebic
ABCEIMU	Cimabue
ABCEINR	carbine
ABCEINT	cabinet
ABCEIOR	aerobic
ABCEIOT	iceboat
ABCEIRS	ascribe
	Brescia
	carbies
ABCEIRZ	zebraic
ABCEISS	abscise
	scabies
ABCEITT	tabetic
ABCEKLN	blacken
ABCEKLR	blacker
ABCEKNR	bracken
ABCEKRS	backers
ABCEKRT	bracket
ABCEKRW	Warbeck
ABCEKST	setback
ABCEKTW	wetback
ABCELLN	Leblanc
ABCELLU	bullace
ABCELMO	cembalo
ABCELMR	cambrel
	clamber
ABCELOP	placebo
ABCELOV	vocable
ABCELPU	bluecap
ABCELRU	curable
ABCELST	cablets
ABCELSU	bascule
ABCEMRS	cambers
ABCEMSW	webcams
ABCENOR	baconer
ABCENOS	beacons
ABCENOW	cowbane
ABCENOZ	cabezon
ABCENRU	unbrace
ABCEOOS	caboose
ABCEORS	boraces
ABCEORV	cabover
ABCERRS	bracers
ABCERSU	subrace
ABCESSS	abscess
ABCESTW	webcast
ABCESTY	Catesby
ABCFIKN	finback
ABCFILO	bifocal
ABCFIOT	biofact
ABCFIRS	fabrics
ABCFKLY	flyback
ABCFLOO	cobloaf
ABCFNOS	confabs
ABCGHIN	baching
ABCGHKO	hogback
ABCGIKN	backing
ABCGILN	cabling
ABCGINR	bracing
ABCGKLO	backlog
ABCGMSU	scumbag
ABCHHII	hibachi
ABCHILS	chablis
ABCHILU	Baluchi
ABCHIOT	cohabit
ABCHKTU	hackbut
ABCHLOR	Chabrol
ABCHNRU	Churban
ABCHNRY	branchy
ABCHOTT	chatbot
ABCHPSU	hubcaps
ABCIILL	bacilli
ABCIILN	albinic
ABCIILS	basilic
ABCIILT	albitic
ABCIIMN	minicab
ABCIIMS	iambics
ABCIIOR	ciboria
ABCIIOT	abiotic
ABCIJNO	jacobin
ABCIKLT	backlit
ABCIKSY	sickbay
ABCILRS	scribal
ABCILST	Baltics
ABCILTU	cubital
ABCIMMU	cambium
ABCIMOR	Coimbra
ABCIMRU	Cumbria
ABCIMST	cambist
ABCINOT	botanic
ABCIOOR	Cariboo
ABCIORU	caribou
ABCIOUV	bivouac
ABCIRTY	barytic
ABCJOSU	jacobus
ABCKLLY	blackly
ABCKLOT	backlot
ABCKMRU	buckram
ABCKMUZ	zambuck
ABCKNNO	bannock
ABCKNOT	Bantock
ABCKOSW	sowback
ABCKOTU	backout
	outback
ABCKSTU	sackbut
ABCKSUW	bucksaw
	sawbuck
ABCLLOY	callboy
ABCLMNU	clubman
ABCLMOU	Columba
ABCLMOY	cymbalo
ABCLMSY	cymbals
ABCLMUU	baculum
ABCLNOY	balcony
ABCLNSU	subclan
ABCLOVY	vocably
ABCLRUY	curably
ABCMNRW	Cwmbran
ABCMOPS	mobcaps
ABCMOST	combats
ABCMRSS	scrambs
ABCNORS	carbons
	corbans
ABCORRW	crowbar
ABCORSS	brascos
ABCORSX	boxcars
ABCORSY	carboys
ABDDEER	bearded
	breaded
ABDDEES	debased
ABDDEET	debated
ABDDEIN	bandied
ABDDEIR	braided
ABDDEIS	baddies
ABDDELR	bladder
ABDDENR	branded
ABDDEOR	boarded
	roadbed
ABDDEOY	deadboy
ABDDEST	baddest
ABDDHIS	baddish
ABDDHSU	buddhas
ABDDINS	disband
ABDDLLO	oddball
ABDEEFG	feedbag
ABDEEGL	beagled
ABDEEGR	rebadge
ABDEEHS	beheads
ABDEEHV	behaved
ABDEEIR	beadier
ABDEELL	labeled
ABDEELM	beldame
ABDEELN	enabled
ABDEELR	bleared
ABDEELS	beadles
ABDEELT	belated
	bleated
ABDEELY	belayed
	dyeable
ABDEEMN	benamed
ABDEEMR	breamed
ABDEEMY	embayed
ABDEENR	Bardeen
ABDEERR	barreed
ABDEERS	debaser
	sabered
ABDEERT	berated
	debater
	rebated
ABDEERW	bewared
ABDEESS	debases
ABDEEST	bestead
	debates
ABDEETT	abetted
ABDEFFL	baffled
ABDEFLT	flatbed
ABDEFOR	forbade
ABDEFST	bedfast
ABDEGGL	blagged
ABDEGGR	bragged
ABDEGHI	bighead
ABDEGHR	beghard
ABDEGIN	beading
ABDEGIR	abridge
	brigade
ABDEGLM	gambled
ABDEGLR	garbled
ABDEGNO	bondage
	dogbane
ABDEGOR	Beograd
	Bogarde
ABDEGOS	bodegas
ABDEGRS	badgers
ABDEHIL	hidable
ABDEHIT	habited
	Thebaid
ABDEHLR	halberd
ABDEHOR	Deborah
ABDEHOW	bowhead
ABDEHRT	breadth
ABDEHSU	subhead
ABDEIIL	alibied
ABDEILP	bipedal
	piebald

ABDEILR bedrail
brailed
ridable
ABDEILS baldies
disable
ABDEILU audible
ABDEILY beadily
ABDEIMO ameboid
ABDEINR bandier
brained
ABDEINS bandies
ABDEIRR braider
ABDEIRS abiders
bardies
braised
darbies
seabird
ABDEIRT tribade
ABDEIRW bawdier
ABDEIRX axebird
ABDEISS biassed
ABDEJRU abjured
ABDEKLN blanked
ABDEKLU baulked
ABDEKRS debarks
ABDELMR marbled
rambled
ABDELMS bedlams
beldams
ABDELMW wambled
ABDELNR blander
ABDELOR labored
ABDELOS albedos
ABDELOT bloated
lobated
ABDELOW dowable
ABDELPU dupable
ABDELRT blarted
ABDELRU durable
ABDELRW brawled
warbled
ABDELRY Bradley
dryable
ABDELST baldest
blasted
stabled
ABDELTT battled
blatted
ABDEMMO mamboed
ABDEMNO abdomen
ABDEMRU Bermuda
ABDENOR bandore
broaden
ABDENPS bedpans
ABDENRR Bernard
brander
rebrand
ABDENSS badness
ABDENTU unbated
ABDEOOT tabooed
ABDEOPY Peabody
ABDEORR boarder
broader
ABDEORT aborted
borated
ABDEOST boasted
ABDEOTU boutade
ABDERSS serdabs
ABDERST dabster
ABDERSU daubers
ABDERSV adverbs
ABDERUY daubery
ABDETTU abutted
ABDGIIN abiding
ABDGILN balding
blading
ABDGINN banding
ABDGINO Baoding
ABDGINR barding
brigand
ABDGINT dingbat
ABDGINU daubing
ABDGINW windbag
ABDGLNO Bagnold
ABDGLUY ladybug
ABDGNNU Bandung
ABDHIIT adhibit
ABDHILS baldish
ABDHMTU mudbath
ABDHNOR bodhran
ABDHNSU husband
ABDHOSY hobdays
ABDIINO anobiid
ABDIKOR Kobarid
ABDILMO bimodal
ABDILNW Baldwin
ABDILOO diabolo
ABDILOR labroid
ABDILOT tabloid
ABDILRS bridals
labrids
ribalds
ABDILRY rabidly
ABDILTU Bidault
ABDILUY audibly
ABDILWY bawdily
ABDIMNR birdman
ABDIMOR ambroid
ABDIMRU Rimbaud
ABDINOR inboard
ABDINRS ribands
ABDINRT antbird
ABDINST bandits
ABDINSU ibn-Saud
ABDIOOR Boiardo
ABDIPRU upbraid
ABDIRRS briards
ABDIRSS disbars
ABDIRSU subarid
ABDJORU Dobruja
ABDKOOY daybook
ABDLLNY blandly
ABDLLOR bollard
ABDLMOR Lombard
ABDLNOY Blaydon
ABDLORY broadly
ABDLOYY ladyboy
ABDLRUY durably
ABDLSUU subdual
ABDNNOR Bonnard
ABDNOPR proband
ABDNORS robands
ABDNOSS Donbass
ABDNOSU abounds
ABDNOSX sandbox
ABDNOSY sandboy
ABDNOUU Audubon
ABDNOYY anybody
ABDNSTY standby
ABDOOWY baywood
ABDORSS adsorbs
ABDORSY byroads
ABDOSYY dayboys
ABDRRSU durbars
ABDRRUY du Barry
ABDRSTU bustard
ABDRUZZ buzzard
ABEEELS seeable
ABEEERV bereave
ABEEFFL effable
ABEEFGR Fabergé
ABEEFLM flambee
ABEEGHR herbage
ABEEGLL gabelle
ABEEGLS beagles
ABEEGLT getable
ABEEGRR gerbera
ABEEGRS bargees
ABEEGRU auberge
ABEEGRW brewage
ABEEHNN henbane
ABEEHNS banshee
shebean
ABEEHNT beneath
ABEEHRT breathe
ABEEHSV behaves
ABEEHTY eyebath
ABEEILN Abilene
ABEEILS bailees
ABEEINS beanies
ABEEINT betaine
ABEEIRT beatier
ABEEIST beastie
ABEEKLR bleaker
Kerbela
ABEEKNT betaken
ABEEKNY eyebank
ABEEKPS bespeak
ABEEKRR breaker
ABEEKRS beakers
ABEEKST betakes
ABEELLR relabel
ABEELLY eyeball
ABEELMZ emblaze
ABEELNR enabler
ABEELNS enables
ABEELNT Beltane
tenable
ABEELNU nebulae
ABEELOR earlobe
ABEELQU equable
ABEELRR blearer
ABEELRT bleater
retable
ABEELSU useable
ABEEMNS basemen
bemeans
benames
ABEEMRS beamers
besmear
ABEENNW bawneen
ABEENOU Euboean
ABEENRS Benares
ABEENRV verbena
ABEENRY beanery
ABEEORS aerobes
ABEERRS bearers
ABEERRT rebater
ABEERST beaters
berates
rebates
ABEERSV beavers
ABEERSW bewares
ABEERTT abetter
ABEESWX beeswax
ABEFFIS baffies
ABEFFLR baffler
ABEFFLS baffles
ABEFFOT offbeat
ABEFGST gabfest
ABEFILN finable
ABEFILR friable
ABEFILU fibulae
ABEFILX fixable
ABEFITY beatify
ABEFLLS befalls
ABEFLLU baleful
ABEFLLY flyable
ABEFLMS flambes
ABEFLNU baneful
ABEFLRS fablers
ABEFLST Belfast
ABEFORR forbear
ABEFPRS prefabs
ABEGGIR baggier
ABEGGIS baggies
ABEGGLR blagger
ABEGGMO gamboge
ABEGGRR bragger
ABEGGRS beggars
ABEGGRU burgage
ABEGGRY beggary
ABEGHMR Maghreb
ABEGHNS shebang
ABEGHOT Bagehot
ABEGHRU bearhug
ABEGILN Belgian
Bengali

ABEGILR Gabriel
ABEGILV givable
ABEGIMN beaming
ABEGIMR gambier
ABEGIMT megabit
ABEGINN beaning
ABEGINO begonia
ABEGINR bearing
ABEGINT beating
ABEGIPP bagpipe
ABEGKOS boskage
ABEGLMR gambler
gambrel
ABEGLMS gambles
ABEGLMU Belgaum
ABEGLNS bangles
ABEGLOT globate
ABEGLRR Arlberg
garbler
ABEGLRS garbles
ABEGLRU blaguer
ABEGLSS bagless
ABEGLST gablets
ABEGLSU belugas
ABEGMNR Bergman
ABEGMOR Bergamo
embargo
ABEGMRU umbrage
ABEGNOS nosebag
ABEGNRS bangers
grabens
ABEGOPY pageboy
ABEGORR begorra
ABEGORS borages
Seaborg
ABEGORX gearbox
ABEGOSZ gazebos
ABEGOUY buoyage
ABEGSTU baguets
ABEHILR hirable
ABEHIMO bohemia
ABEHINO Bien Hoa
ABEHIRS bearish
ABEHITU habitue
ABEHKRU hauberk
ABEHKTU ketubah
ABEHLMS shamble
ABEHLMT Lambeth
ABEHLNT benthal
ABEHLRS herbals
ABEHLRT blather
halbert
ABEHMNT Bentham
ABEHNRY abhenry
ABEHNTY Bethany
ABEHRRS brasher
ABEHRSS bashers
ABEHRST Barthes
bathers
berthas
breaths
ABEHRTY breathy

ABEIILL baillie
ABEIILR Liberia
ABEIILS bailies
ABEIINR Iberian
ABEIINT bainite
ABEIIRS Siberia
ABEIJNS basenji
ABEIKKS bakkies
ABEIKLL likable
ABEIKLR balkier
ABEIKLS skiable
ABEIKLT batlike
ABEIKNR Bikaner
ABEIKNT beatnik
ABEILLN linable
ABEILLO lobelia
ABEILLP pliable
ABEILLR braille
liberal
ABEILLV livable
ABEILMN minable
ABEILMR balmier
remblai
ABEILMS ableism
lambies
ABEILMT limbate
timbale
ABEILMX mixable
ABEILNP biplane
ABEILNS lesbian
ABEILNZ Albéniz
ABEILOU Boileau
ABEILRS bailers
ABEILRT Alberti
Albert I
librate
triable
ABEILSS abseils
ABEILST astilbe
bestial
stabile
ABEILSW bewails
ABEILSY baileys
ABEILSZ sizable
ABEILVV bivalve
ABEIMNT ambient
ABEIMOS Amboise
ABEIMOT Moabite
ABEIMRR barmier
ABEIMRS ambries
ABEIMSU maubies
ABEIMZZ Zambezi
ABEINNR Bernina
ABEINOR Bonaire
ABEINOZ Zenobia
ABEINRS Serbian
ABEINRT atebrin
ABEINRZ ibn-Ezra
ABEINSS Bassein
sabines
ABEINST Antibes
basinet

ABEIOOT Boeotia
ABEIOST boaties
ABEIOTV obviate
ABEIPST baptise
ABEIPTZ baptize
ABEIRRR barrier
ABEIRRS barries
brasier
ABEIRRT arbiter
rarebit
ABEIRRW warbier
ABEIRRZ bizarre
brazier
ABEIRSS braises
brassie
ABEIRST terbias
ABEIRTT battier
biretta
ratbite
ABEIRTV vibrate
ABEIRTX Beatrix
ABEIRUX exurbia
ABEISSS biasses
ABEISTT batiste
ABEISUV abusive
ABEITUX bauxite
ABEJLUY bluejay
ABEJMRS jambers
ABEJNOS banjoes
ABEJNOW jawbone
ABEJORS jerboas
ABEJRRU abjurer
ABEJRSU abjures
ABEKLLY bleakly
ABEKLNR blanker
ABEKLNT blanket
ABEKLRS balkers
ABEKLRU baulker
ABEKMNS embanks
ABEKMRS embarks
ABEKNRS bankers
ABEKNSU sunbake
ABEKPRU breakup
ABEKRRS barkers
ABEKRST Stębark
ABEKSST baskets
ABELLMN bellman
ABELLMY Bellamy
ABELLNO Bellona
ABELLNT netball
ABELLNY Allenby
ABELLOS losable
ABELLOV lovable
ABELLRU rubella
rulable
ABELLST ballets
ABELLTU bullate
ABELMMS embalms
ABELMNT beltman
lambent
ABELMNU albumen
ABELMOV movable

ABELMRR marbler
rambler
ABELMRS amblers
marbles
rambles
ABELMRT lambert
ABELMSW wambles
ABELMTU mutable
ABELNNO Lebanon
ABELNOS Abelson
bonsela
ABELNOT notable
ABELNOY baloney
ABELNRS branles
ABELNRU nebular
ABELNRY blarney
ABELNSU nebulas
ABELNSY bylanes
ABELNTU tunable
ABELNTY tenably
ABELOPR ropable
ABELOPT potable
ABELORR laborer
ABELORT bloater
ABELORU rubeola
ABELOSS bolases
ABELOST boatels
oblates
ABELOSV absolve
ABELOSW sowable
ABELOTV votable
ABELOTW towable
ABELPPY Appleby
ABELQUY equably
ABELRRS barrels
ABELRRW brawler
warbler
ABELRST alberts
blaster
labrets
ABELRSU Belarus
Breslau
ABELRSV verbals
ABELRSW bawlers
warbles
ABELRSY barleys
ABELRSZ blazers
ABELRTT battler
ABELRVY bravely
ABELSST stables
ABELSSU subsale
ABELSTT battels
battles
tablets
ABELSTU Setúbal
ABELSTY beastly
ABELSUY useably
ABELSWY byelaws
ABELTWY beltway
ABEMNOS ambones
bemoans
ABEMNOT boatmen

ABEMNST	batsmen
ABEMNSU	sunbeam
ABEMORS	Ambrose
ABEMORT	bromate
ABEMRRT	Rambert
ABEMSSY	embassy
ABENNNR	Brennan
ABENNOR	Bornean
ABENNOY	Bayonne
ABENNRS	banners
ABENORS	boranes
ABENORT	baronet
ABENOST	onbeats
ABENOSY	soybean
ABENOTY	bayonet
ABENQTU	banquet
ABENRRS	barrens
ABENRRU	Raeburn
ABENRST	banters
	barnets
ABENRSY	barneys
ABENRSZ	brazens
ABENRUX	exurban
ABENSST	absents
ABENSTT	battens
ABENSTZ	bezants
ABENTUZ	Bautzen
ABENTZZ	bezzant
ABEOOTV	obovate
ABEOPRS	saprobe
ABEOPRT	probate
ABEOQRU	baroque
ABEORRT	taborer
ABEORST	boaster
	boaters
	borates
	rebatos
ABEORSV	bravoes
ABEORSX	boraxes
ABEORSY	rosebay
ABEORSZ	bezoars
ABEORTT	abettor
	taboret
ABEPRTY	typebar
ABEPSTU	upbeats
ABEQRSU	barques
ABEQSSU	basques
ABERRST	barrets
	barters
ABERRSY	brayers
ABERRSZ	brazers
ABERRVY	bravery
ABERSSS	brasses
ABERSST	breasts
ABERSSU	abusers
	buseras
	surbase
ABERSTT	batters
ABERSTV	bravest
ABERSTW	brawest
ABERSTY	barytes
	betrays

ABERSUU	bureaus
ABERSWY	bewrays
ABERTTU	abutter
ABERTTY	battery
ABERUUX	bureaux
ABERUVY	Avebury
ABESSST	bassets
ABESSSY	abysses
ABESTTU	battues
ABFFIIL	bailiff
ABFFINO	banoffi
ABFFLOU	buffalo
ABFGILN	fabling
ABFGLSU	bagfuls
ABFHIST	batfish
ABFHLSU	bashful
ABFIILR	bifilar
ABFIIMR	fimbria
ABFIKNR	Firbank
ABFILRU	fibular
ABFILSU	fibulas
ABFIMOR	fibroma
ABFLORU	Balfour
ABFLOTW	batfowl
ABFLOTY	flyboat
ABFOOTY	foyboat
ABGGGIN	bagging
ABGGILY	baggily
ABGGINN	banging
ABGGINR	barging
	garbing
ABGGISW	bagwigs
ABGGORT	boggart
ABGHILN	blahing
ABGHINS	bashing
ABGHINT	bathing
ABGHLRU	burghal
ABGHMRU	hamburg
ABGHOTU	abought
ABGHSTU	hagbuts
ABGIILN	bailing
ABGIINS	biasing
ABGIINT	baiting
ABGIINZ	baizing
ABGIKLN	balking
ABGIKNN	banking
ABGIKNO	boaking
ABGIKNR	barking
	braking
ABGIKNS	bakings
	basking
ABGIKST	kitbags
ABGILLN	balling
ABGILMN	ambling
	blaming
	lambing
ABGILMS	gimbals
ABGILNR	blaring
ABGILNT	tabling
ABGILNW	bawling
ABGILNZ	blazing
ABGILOR	garboil

ABGIMST	gambits
ABGINNN	banning
ABGINNT	banting
ABGINOS	bagnios
	gabions
ABGINOT	boating
ABGINRR	barring
ABGINRS	sabring
ABGINRV	braving
ABGINRY	braying
ABGINRZ	brazing
ABGINST	basting
ABGINSU	abusing
ABGINTT	batting
ABGINTU	tabuing
ABGINTW	batwing
ABGITTU	Bugatti
ABGKKNO	bangkok
ABGKORW	workbag
ABGLMNU	Balmung
ABGLMOS	gambols
ABGLMOU	lumbago
ABGLNOO	bologna
ABGLORS	brolgas
	Gorbals
ABGLORT	ragbolt
ABGLORU	Borlaug
ABGLRRU	burglar
ABGMORW	bagworm
ABGMRRU	Marburg
ABGNOOS	boongas
	gaboons
ABGNOPR	probang
ABGNORS	barongs
	brogans
ABGNOTU	gunboat
ABGOORT	botargo
ABGOPST	postbag
ABGORST	bogarts
ABGOTTU	tugboat
ABGRRUW	Warburg
ABHHKTU	khutbah
ABHHSUY	hushaby
ABHIINT	inhabit
ABHIKTW	hawkbit
ABHILNO	hobnail
ABHILOS	abolish
ABHILTU	halibut
ABHIMNR	Brahmin
ABHIMRS	mihrabs
ABHINOT	Bothnia
ABHINRS	Bas-Rhin
ABHINST	absinth
ABHIOOS	boohais
ABHIOPS	phobias
ABHIORS	boarish
ABHIOST	isobath
ABHIOSU	haubois
ABHIRTY	Yathrib
ABHISTU	habitus
ABHLOUX	boxhaul
ABHLRSY	brashly

ABHLSTU	Balthus
ABHMNOS	bonhams
ABHMNSU	bushman
ABHMRSU	rhumbas
ABHNSTU	sunbath
ABHORRS	harbors
ABHORRU	harbour
ABHOTUY	hautboy
ABHPSTY	bypaths
ABHRSTU	tarbush
ABHSTUW	washtub
ABIIINR	biriani
ABIIKKT	kibitka
ABIILMU	bulimia
ABIILNO	Lin Biao
ABIILNQ	inqilab
ABIILOV	bolivia
ABIILRY	biliary
ABIILST	stibial
ABIILTY	ability
ABIIMNR	minibar
ABIINNS	bainins
	ibn-Sina
ABIINOR	Nairobi
	robinia
ABIINRT	Britain
ABIINRU	Urban II
ABIINRY	biryani
ABIIOSS	abiosis
ABIJLNR	brinjal
ABIJNPU	Punjabi
ABIJPRU	Bijapur
ABIJRSU	jabirus
ABIKLLY	balkily
ABIKLMN	lambkin
ABIKNNU	Bakunin
ABIKRST	britska
ABIKRTZ	britzka
ABILLLO	Balliol
ABILLMY	balmily
ABILLNP	pinball
ABILLPY	pliably
ABILLSW	sawbill
ABILLSY	syllabi
ABILLWX	waxbill
ABILLWY	waybill
ABILMNU	albumin
ABILMOX	mailbox
ABILMST	timbals
ABILNOS	albinos
ABILNQU	Blanqui
ABILNSU	Albinus
ABILOPR	bipolar
	parboil
ABILORS	bailors
ABILORT	Bartoli
	orbital
ABILORV	bolivar
ABILOTU	bailout
ABILRRY	library
ABILRSS	brasils
ABILRSU	burials

ABILRSZ	brazils
ABILSYZ	sizably
ABIMNRU	Umbrian
ABIMORR	Maribor
ABIMOSS	biomass
ABIMPST	baptism
	bitmaps
ABIMRTT	trimtab
ABINNOS	Bosnian
ABINOOR	boronia
ABINORT	taborin
ABINORW	rainbow
ABINOSS	basions
ABINOST	bastion
	obtains
ABINRST	brisant
ABINRTV	vibrant
ABINRUV	Urban VI
ABIORRS	barrios
ABIORSS	isobars
ABIORTV	vibrato
ABIORUX	Roubaix
ABIORZZ	Barozzi
ABIPSTT	baptist
ABIRSSY	Sybaris
ABIRUZZ	Abruzzi
ABISSST	bassist
ABJJOOS	jojobas
ABJKMOS	sjambok
ABJLMSU	jumbals
ABKLLNY	blankly
ABKLOTX	talkbox
ABKLRUW	bulwark
ABKNOOV	Nabokov
ABKNRSY	Bryansk
ABKNRUU	bunraku
ABLLLOW	lowball
ABLLLUY	lullaby
ABLLNOO	balloon
ABLLOOS	lobolas
ABLLORR	rollbar
ABLLORU	lobular
ABLLOST	ballots
ABLLOTY	tallboy
ABLLOVY	lovably
ABLLPSU	ballups
ABLMMOU	bummalo
ABLMMUU	Lumumba
ABLMNOU	umbonal
ABLMOOT	tombola
ABLMOVY	movably
ABLMPUU	pabulum
ABLMSTU	Stambul
ABLMSTY	tymbals
ABLMTUY	mutably
ABLNOOZ	Bolzano
ABLNOSZ	blazons
ABLNOTU	butanol
ABLNOTY	notably
ABLOORS	robalos
ABLOPYY	playboy
ABLORST	borstal
ABLORSU	labours
	suboral
ABLORTT	Rotblat
ABLOSST	oblasts
ABLOSTT	talbots
ABLOSTV	abvolts
ABLOSTX	saltbox
ABLPRSU	burlaps
ABLPSYY	byplays
ABLRTUU	tubular
ABMNNOR	Bormann
ABMNSTU	numbats
ABMOORR	barroom
ABMORTU	tambour
ABMOSTW	wombats
ABMRSSU	samburs
ABNNORS	Branson
ABNOORZ	borazon
ABNOOSS	bassoon
ABNORST	bartons
ABNORSY	baryons
ABNORTY	baryton
ABNORTZ	Trabzon
ABNOTUY	buoyant
ABNRSTU	turbans
ABNSTYZ	byzants
ABOOPSX	soapbox
ABOORRT	Borotra
ABOORTW	rowboat
ABOOTTW	towboat
ABORRSU	arbours
ABORRSW	barrows
ABORSTU	robusta
	rubatos
	tabours
ABORSTW	towbars
ABOSSWW	bowsaws
ABPRSTU	subpart
ABRRSSU	bursars
ABRRSUY	bursary
ABRRTUY	turbary
ABRSTUU	arbutus
ABRSTUY	Astbury
ABSSUWY	subways
ACCCILY	acyclic
ACCDDEE	acceded
ACCDDEI	caddice
ACCDEEN	cadence
ACCDEER	acceder
ACCDEES	accedes
ACCDEHN	chanced
ACCDEHO	coached
ACCDEII	accidie
ACCDEIU	caducei
ACCDEKL	cackled
	clacked
ACCDEKO	cockade
ACCDEKR	cracked
ACCDENY	cadency
ACCDEOP	Cape Cod
ACCDERU	accrued
ACCDESU	accused
ACCDFIL	flaccid
ACCDHIL	chalcid
ACCDILS	scaldic
ACCDINS	scandic
ACCDIOT	octadic
ACCDIPR	Piccard
ACCDLOY	cacodyl
ACCDORS	accords
ACCEEHL	caleche
ACCEEHO	coachee
ACCEELN	cenacle
ACCEERS	Cáceres
ACCEERT	accrete
ACCEFIT	factice
ACCEFLU	felucca
ACCEHIL	caliche
	chalice
ACCEHIN	chicane
ACCEHLN	chancel
ACCEHLO	cochlea
ACCEHNO	conchae
ACCEHNR	chancer
	chancre
ACCEHNS	chances
ACCEHNY	chancey
ACCEHOR	caroche
	coacher
ACCEHOS	coaches
ACCEHPU	capuche
ACCEHRT	catcher
ACCEHRU	Chaucer
ACCEHST	cachets
	catches
ACCEHTU	catechu
ACCEHXY	cachexy
ACCEIIL	Cecilia
ACCEIKP	icepack
ACCEIKR	cackier
ACCEILL	calicle
ACCEILN	calcine
ACCEILO	coeliac
ACCEILS	calices
ACCEILT	calcite
ACCEIMR	ceramic
	racemic
ACCEINO	cocaine
	oceanic
ACCEINV	vaccine
ACCEIPR	caprice
ACCEIPS	icecaps
	ipecacs
ACCEIPV	peccavi
ACCEIQU	cacique
ACCEIST	ascetic
ACCEITT	ectatic
ACCEKLO	Leacock
ACCEKLR	cackler
	clacker
	crackle
ACCEKLS	cackles
ACCEKOP	peacock
ACCEKOS	seacock
ACCEKPU	cupcake
ACCEKRR	cracker
ACCEKRT	cracket
ACCELLY	calycle
ACCELNO	conceal
ACCELNS	cancels
ACCELOR	coracle
ACCELSU	saccule
ACCELSY	calyces
ACCENOR	conacre
ACCENOV	concave
ACCENPT	peccant
ACCENRS	cancers
ACCENST	accents
ACCEOPY	cacoepy
ACCEOTU	Cocteau
ACCEPRY	peccary
ACCEPST	accepts
ACCERRS	scarcer
ACCERSU	accrues
	accuser
ACCESSU	accuses
ACCFIIP	pacific
ACCFILY	calcify
ACCGHIN	caching
ACCGHIO	Chicago
ACCGNOS	cognacs
ACCHIKS	chiacks
ACCHILS	Chalcis
ACCHIMS	chasmic
ACCHINO	chicano
ACCHIOT	chaotic
ACCHIOU	acouchi
ACCHKNO	Hancock
ACCHKOY	haycock
ACCHKSY	chyacks
ACCHLNO	conchal
ACCHNRU	craunch
ACCHOPU	capouch
	pachuco
ACCHORT	Charcot
ACCHOSU	cachous
ACCHOTW	choctaw
ACCHOUY	acouchy
ACCHPTU	catchup
ACCHRRU	currach
ACCHRST	scratch
ACCHSSU	succahs
ACCIIIL	Cilicia
ACCIILN	aclinic
ACCIINT	actinic
ACCIIST	ascitic
	sciatic
ACCIKRR	carrick
ACCIKRS	carsick
ACCILLU	calculi
ACCILMO	comical
ACCILMU	calcium
ACCILNO	conical
	laconic
ACCILNU	Cluniac
ACCILNY	cynical

ACCILOR	caloric
ACCILOS	calicos
ACCILOV	vocalic
ACCILRU	crucial
ACCILRY	acrylic
ACCILSS	classic
ACCILST	clastic
ACCILSU	sacculi
ACCILTU	Calicut
ACCINNO	canonic
ACCINRU	crucian
ACCIOPR	caproic
ACCIORS	Corsica
ACCIOST	ocicats
ACCIRRS	ricracs
ACCIRST	arctics
ACCISTT	tactics
ACCISTU	caustic
ACCKNNO	Cannock
ACCKOPR	caprock
ACCKOSS	cassock
	cossack
ACCKPRU	crackup
ACCKTTU	Cuttack
ACCLNOT	Clacton
ACCLOSU	coucals
ACCMOOY	cocoyam
ACCMOPT	compact
ACCMRUU	curcuma
ACCNNOO	cooncan
ACCNOOP	cocopan
ACCNOOR	raccoon
ACCNOTT	contact
ACCNOTU	account
ACCOPTY	copycat
ACCOQSU	squacco
ACCORRY	Corcyra
ACCORSS	corsacs
ACCOSST	accosts
ACCRSTU	accurst
ACDDDEI	caddied
ACDDDEU	adduced
ACDDEEF	defaced
ACDDEEL	decaled
ACDDEES	decades
ACDDEEY	decayed
ACDDEHI	Didache
ACDDEHR	cheddar
ACDDEHY	dayched
ACDDEIN	candied
ACDDEIS	caddies
ACDDEIU	decidua
ACDDELN	candled
ACDDELO	cladode
ACDDELR	cradled
ACDDELS	scalded
ACDDEOP	decapod
ACDDESU	adduces
	scauded
ACDDHHU	chuddah
ACDDHIS	caddish
ACDDHKO	haddock
ACDDHRU	chuddar
ACDDIIS	diacids
ACDDIRS	discard
ACDDIRY	dryadic
ACDDIST	addicts
ACDDISY	dyadics
ACDDKOP	paddock
ACDDSTU	adducts
ACDEEES	decease
ACDEEFF	effaced
ACDEEFN	enfaced
ACDEEFR	defacer
	refaced
ACDEEFS	defaces
ACDEEFT	faceted
ACDEEGL	glaceed
ACDEEGN	encaged
ACDEEHL	leached
ACDEEHP	peached
ACDEEHR	Ardèche
	reached
ACDEEHT	cheated
ACDEEIR	deciare
ACDEEJT	dejecta
ACDEEKR	creaked
ACDEELL	cadelle
ACDEELN	cleaned
	enlaced
ACDEELR	cleared
	creedal
	declare
ACDEELS	descale
ACDEELT	cleated
ACDEELV	cleaved
ACDEEMN	menaced
ACDEEMR	amerced
	creamed
ACDEEMV	medevac
ACDEENS	encased
ACDEENT	enacted
ACDEENV	vendace
ACDEEPR	capered
ACDEEPS	escaped
ACDEERS	creased
	decares
ACDEERT	catered
	cerated
	created
	reacted
ACDEETT	taceted
ACDEETU	educate
ACDEETX	exacted
ACDEFFH	chaffed
ACDEFIN	fancied
ACDEFRS	scarfed
ACDEFRT	crafted
ACDEGGL	clagged
ACDEGGR	cragged
ACDEGGS	scagged
ACDEGHN	Changde
	changed
ACDEGHR	charged
ACDEGKO	dockage
ACDEGLN	clanged
	glanced
ACDEGNO	congaed
	decagon
ACDEGNU	uncaged
ACDEGOR	cordage
ACDEGRS	cadgers
ACDEGST	gedacts
ACDEHHT	hatched
ACDEHIN	chained
	echidna
ACDEHIP	edaphic
ACDEHIR	chaired
ACDEHIX	hexadic
ACDEHKL	hackled
ACDEHKS	shacked
ACDEHKW	whacked
ACDEHLS	clashed
ACDEHMP	champed
ACDEHMR	charmed
	marched
ACDEHMT	matched
ACDEHNR	endarch
	ranched
ACDEHNT	chanted
ACDEHOP	poached
ACDEHOR	roached
ACDEHOT	cathode
ACDEHPP	chapped
ACDEHPR	parched
ACDEHPT	patched
ACDEHRR	charred
ACDEHRS	crashed
ACDEHRT	charted
ACDEHSS	chassed
ACDEHST	scathed
ACDEHSY	dayches
ACDEHTT	chatted
ACDEHTW	watched
ACDEHTY	yachted
ACDEILL	cedilla
ACDEILM	camelid
	claimed
	decimal
	declaim
	medical
ACDEILN	Iceland
	inlaced
ACDEILR	decrial
	radicel
	radicle
ACDEILS	Alcides
ACDEILT	citadel
	deltaic
	dialect
	edictal
ACDEILV	caviled
ACDEIMV	medivac
ACDEIMY	mediacy
ACDEINO	oceanid
ACDEINR	carnied
	dancier
ACDEINS	candies
	incased
ACDEINY	cyanide
ACDEIPR	peracid
ACDEIRR	carried
ACDEIRS	cardies
	darcies
	radices
	sidecar
ACDEISV	advices
ACDEITT	dictate
ACDEITY	edacity
ACDEJLO	cajoled
ACDEKKN	knacked
ACDEKLM	mackled
ACDEKLN	clanked
ACDEKLO	cloaked
ACDEKLS	slacked
ACDEKLT	tackled
	talcked
ACDEKLU	caulked
ACDEKMS	smacked
ACDEKNR	cranked
ACDEKNS	snacked
ACDEKOR	croaked
ACDEKQU	quacked
ACDEKRT	tracked
ACDEKRW	wracked
ACDEKST	stacked
ACDEKSW	swacked
ACDELLN	Cleland
ACDELLS	scalled
ACDELLU	Claudel
ACDELMM	clammed
ACDELMO	Macleod
ACDELMP	clamped
ACDELNO	celadon
ACDELNR	candler
ACDELNS	calends
	candles
ACDELNU	unlaced
ACDELOP	pedocal
ACDELOR	caroled
ACDELOS	solaced
ACDELOT	located
ACDELPP	clapped
ACDELPS	clasped
	scalped
ACDELQU	calqued
ACDELRR	cradler
ACDELRS	cradles
	scalder
ACDELRU	caulder
ACDELRW	crawled
ACDELSS	classed
	declass
ACDELST	castled
ACDELWW	dewclaw
ACDEMMR	crammed
ACDEMMS	scammed
ACDEMNO	Cædmon

	Macedon
ACDEMOR	comrade
ACDEMPR	cramped
ACDEMPS	decamps
	scamped
ACDENNS	scanned
ACDENNT	candent
ACDENOR	dracone
ACDENOS	acnodes
	deacons
ACDENOT	tacnode
ACDENPR	pranced
ACDENPT	pandect
ACDENRS	dancers
ACDENRT	Tancred
	tranced
ACDENRU	Cernuda
	durance
ACDENRY	ardency
ACDENSS	ascends
ACDENST	decants
	descant
	scanted
ACDENTU	unacted
ACDEOOR	Odoacer
ACDEOPS	peascod
ACDEORR	corrade
ACDEORT	cordate
	redcoat
ACDEORU	Ecuador
ACDEOST	coasted
ACDEOUV	couvade
ACDEPPR	crapped
ACDEPRS	redcaps
	scarped
	scraped
ACDEQSU	casqued
ACDERRS	carders
	scarred
ACDERST	redacts
	scarted
ACDERSU	crusade
ACDERTT	detract
ACDERTU	Decatur
	traduce
ACDERWY	Cawdrey
ACDESTT	scatted
ACDFFIR	Cardiff
ACDFIIT	fatidic
ACDFIIY	acidify
ACDFIOT	factoid
ACDGGIN	cadging
ACDGINN	dancing
ACDGINO	gonadic
ACDGINR	carding
ACDGKLO	daglock
ACDGORT	dogcart
ACDHIIL	chiliad
ACDHINR	Chardin
ACDHIRR	Richard
ACDHIRY	diarchy
ACDHISS	Chassid
ACDHLOR	chordal
ACDHMPU	Duchamp
ACDHMRS	drachms
ACDHNOW	cowhand
ACDHOPR	pochard
ACDHORR	orchard
ACDHORS	chadors
ACDHRYY	dyarchy
ACDIIIN	indicia
ACDIINN	indican
ACDIINO	conidia
ACDIINV	da Vinci
ACDIIRT	arctiid
	triacid
	triadic
ACDIITY	acidity
ACDIKLS	skaldic
ACDILMO	domical
ACDILMS	cladism
ACDILNO	nodical
ACDILNU	incudal
ACDILOP	placoid
ACDILOR	cordial
ACDILOT	cotidal
ACDILRY	acridly
ACDILST	cladist
ACDILTW	wildcat
ACDIMMU	cadmium
ACDIMNO	monacid
	monadic
	nomadic
ACDIMNY	dynamic
ACDIMOO	camoodi
ACDINNU	Duncan I
ACDINOT	Candiot
ACDINRU	iracund
ACDINST	discant
ACDINSU	Sudanic
ACDINSY	cyanids
ACDIOPR	parodic
	picador
ACDIORR	corrida
	Ricardo
ACDIORS	sarcoid
ACDIORT	carotid
ACDIOST	dacoits
ACDIOSZ	zodiacs
ACDIOTY	dacoity
ACDIOXY	oxyacid
ACDIPRY	Picardy
ACDIPSS	capsids
ACDIQRU	quadric
ACDIRST	drastic
ACDISST	dicasts
ACDITUV	viaduct
ACDJNTU	adjunct
ACDKLOP	padlock
ACDKMPU	mudpack
ACDKNVY	Van Dyck
ACDLLOR	collard
ACDLLUY	ducally
ACDLNOP	Copland
ACDLNOR	caldron
ACDLSTY	dactyls
ACDMMNO	command
ACDMOOW	camwood
ACDMORZ	czardom
ACDMSTU	mudcats
ACDNOOR	cardoon
ACDNORU	candour
ACDOORS	Cardoso
ACDOORV	Cordova
ACDORST	costard
ACDORSU	crusado
ACDORSW	cowards
ACDORUZ	cruzado
ACDRSTU	custard
ACEEEPS	escapee
ACEEEUV	evacuee
ACEEFFR	effacer
ACEEFFS	effaces
ACEEFIN	faience
	fiancee
ACEEFLU	feculae
ACEEFNS	enfaces
ACEEFPR	preface
ACEEFRS	refaces
ACEEGIL	elegiac
ACEEGNS	encages
ACEEGSU	escuage
ACEEHHT	cheetah
ACEEHIV	achieve
ACEEHKL	Haeckel
ACEEHLR	leacher
ACEEHLS	Chelsea
	leaches
ACEEHLT	chelate
ACEEHMR	machree
ACEEHMT	machete
ACEEHNN	enhance
ACEEHNP	cheapen
ACEEHNS	achenes
	enchase
ACEEHOR	ochreae
ACEEHPR	cheaper
	peacher
ACEEHPS	peaches
ACEEHRR	reacher
ACEEHRS	reaches
ACEEHRT	cheater
	hectare
	reteach
	teacher
ACEEHST	escheat
	teaches
ACEEHTT	thecate
ACEEILP	calipee
ACEEILT	Eleatic
ACEEINR	Cairene
ACEEINU	eucaine
ACEEISV	vesicae
ACEEJKN	jackeen
ACEEKNP	kneecap
ACEELLN	nacelle
ACEELMN	Alcmene
ACEELMP	emplace
ACEELMR	reclame
ACEELNN	Laënnec
ACEELNO	Celaeno
ACEELNR	cleaner
ACEELNS	cleanse
	enlaces
	scalene
ACEELNV	enclave
	valence
ACEELPR	percale
	replace
ACEELRR	clearer
	Le Carré
ACEELRS	alerces
	cereals
ACEELRT	Electra
	treacle
ACEELRV	cleaver
ACEELST	celesta
	selecta
ACEELSV	cleaves
ACEELVX	exclave
ACEEMNR	menacer
ACEEMNS	menaces
ACEEMNV	cavemen
ACEEMNY	Mayence
	Mycenae
ACEEMPS	Campese
ACEEMRR	amercer
	creamer
ACEEMRS	amerces
	racemes
ACEEMRT	cremate
ACEENNP	penance
ACEENNR	narceen
ACEENNT	canteen
ACEENNY	cayenne
ACEENNZ	Cézanne
ACEENOR	corneae
ACEENOT	acetone
ACEENRS	careens
	caserne
ACEENRT	centare
	crenate
	reenact
ACEENRV	cervena
ACEENSS	encases
	seances
	senecas
ACEENST	tenaces
ACEENTU	cuneate
ACEEORS	acerose
ACEEORT	ocreate
ACEEOSS	caseose
ACEEOST	acetose
	coatees
ACEEPRR	caperer
ACEEPRS	escaper
ACEEPSS	escapes
ACEEPST	pectase

ACEEPTT	pectate
ACEERRS	careers
	creaser
ACEERRT	caterer
	retrace
	terrace
ACEERSS	creases
ACEERST	creates
ACEERSU	cesurae
ACEERSV	Versace
ACEERTX	exacter
	excreta
ACEESSS	asceses
ACEFFHI	affiche
ACEFFHR	chaffer
ACEFFIN	caffein
ACEFFST	affects
ACEFGIP	pigface
ACEFHMR	chamfer
ACEFHRS	chafers
ACEFHRU	chaufer
ACEFILL	icefall
ACEFILM	malefic
ACEFINN	finance
ACEFINR	fancier
ACEFINS	fancies
	fascine
	fiances
ACEFIRS	farcies
	fiacres
ACEFITV	factive
ACEFITY	acetify
ACEFLRU	careful
ACEFNNO	faconne
ACEFNOS	Fonseca
ACEFNRU	furnace
ACEFOTU	outface
ACEFRRT	refract
ACEFRRU	farceur
ACEFRSU	surface
ACEFRTU	facture
	furcate
ACEFSTU	faucets
ACEFTTW	Fawcett
ACEGHNR	changer
ACEGHNS	changes
ACEGHOU	gouache
ACEGHOW	cowhage
ACEGHRR	charger
ACEGHRS	Chagres
	charges
ACEGIIR	Craigie
ACEGILN	angelic
	anglice
	galenic
	Legnica
ACEGILP	pelagic
ACEGILR	glacier
	gracile
ACEGILS	algesic
ACEGILT	algetic
ACEGIMO	camogie
ACEGIMR	grimace
ACEGIMT	gametic
ACEGINO	coinage
ACEGINP	peacing
ACEGINR	anergic
	grecian
ACEGINS	ceasing
ACEGINY	gynecia
ACEGIRT	cigaret
ACEGIST	cagiest
ACEGKLO	lockage
ACEGKLR	grackle
ACEGKOR	corkage
ACEGLLO	collage
ACEGLNO	congeal
ACEGLNR	clanger
ACEGLNS	glances
ACEGLOU	cagoule
ACEGNOR	acrogen
ACEGNOT	cognate
ACEGNSU	cangues
ACEGORS	cargoes
	corsage
	socager
ACEGORU	courage
ACEGOTT	cottage
ACEGSTU	scutage
ACEHHLR	Harlech
ACEHHLT	hatchel
ACEHHMS	Meshach
ACEHHRT	hatcher
ACEHHRU	hachure
ACEHHST	chetahs
	hatches
ACEHHTT	hatchet
ACEHIKS	hackies
ACEHILL	challie
	helical
ACEHILM	lechaim
	Meilhac
	Michael
ACEHILN	Chilean
ACEHILR	charlie
ACEHILT	alethic
	ethical
ACEHIMN	machine
ACEHIMP	impeach
ACEHIMR	chimera
ACEHIMT	hematic
ACEHINN	Chennai
	enchain
ACEHINR	archine
ACEHINY	hyaenic
ACEHIPP	chappie
ACEHIPT	aphetic
	hepatic
ACEHIRR	charier
ACEHIRS	cahiers
	cashier
	eriachs
ACEHIRT	theriac
ACEHIRV	archive
ACEHISS	chaises
ACEHIST	achiest
	aitches
ACEHITY	yachtie
ACEHKLR	hackler
ACEHKLS	hackles
	shackle
ACEHKNY	hackney
ACEHKRS	hackers
ACEHKRT	Eckhart
ACEHKRW	whacker
ACEHKRY	hackery
ACEHLLS	shellac
ACEHLLT	hellcat
ACEHLMY	alchemy
ACEHLNN	channel
ACEHLNO	chalone
ACEHLNR	charnel
ACEHLOP	epochal
ACEHLOR	cholera
	chorale
	choreal
ACEHLOS	loaches
ACEHLOT	cathole
ACEHLPS	chapels
ACEHLPT	chaplet
ACEHLPY	cheaply
ACEHLRS	Charles
	clasher
	larches
ACEHLRY	charley
ACEHLSS	clashes
ACEHLST	chalets
	latches
	satchel
ACEHLSV	chevals
ACEHLTT	chattel
	latchet
ACEHMNP	chapmen
ACEHMPR	champer
ACEHMPS	Sempach
ACEHMRR	charmer
	marcher
ACEHMRS	machers
	marches
	mesarch
	schmear
ACEHMRT	matcher
	rematch
ACEHMSS	sachems
ACEHMST	matches
ACEHMTT	matchet
ACEHMTY	ecthyma
ACEHMTZ	chametz
ACEHNNT	enchant
ACEHNOR	Acheron
ACEHNOS	Acheson
ACEHNRR	rancher
ACEHNRS	ranches
ACEHNRT	chanter
	tranche
ACEHNSS	Sachsen
ACEHNST	chasten
ACEHNSU	nauches
ACEHNTT	etchant
ACEHNTU	unteach
ACEHNTY	chantey
ACEHOOT	ootheca
ACEHOPR	Pechora
	poacher
ACEHOPS	cheapos
	poaches
ACEHORS	choreas
	oraches
	roaches
ACEHOTY	chayote
ACEHPPS	schappe
ACEHPRS	eparchs
	parches
ACEHPRT	chapter
	patcher
ACEHPRY	eparchy
	preachy
ACEHPSS	chapess
ACEHPST	hepcats
	patches
ACEHRRS	archers
	crasher
ACEHRRT	charter
	rechart
ACEHRRV	charver
ACEHRRX	xerarch
ACEHRRY	archery
ACEHRSS	chasers
	crashes
	eschars
ACEHRSW	chawers
ACEHRSX	exarchs
ACEHRSY	hyraces
ACEHRTT	chatter
	ratchet
ACEHRTW	watcher
ACEHRTY	Cythera
ACEHRXY	exarchy
ACEHSSS	chasses
ACEHSST	sachets
	scathes
ACEHSSW	cashews
ACEHSTW	watches
ACEIILS	laicise
ACEIILT	ciliate
ACEIILZ	laicize
ACEIJKS	jackies
	jacksie
ACEIKLS	saclike
ACEIKLT	catlike
ACEIKMR	keramic
ACEIKPX	pickaxe
ACEIKRT	tackier
ACEIKRW	wackier
ACEIKSS	seasick
ACEIKST	tackies
ACEILLL	allelic
ACEILLM	micella

ACEILLX lexical
ACEILMN cnemial
melanic
ACEILMR claimer
miracle
reclaim
ACEILMT climate
ACEILMX exclaim
ACEILMY mycelia
ACEILNP capelin
panicle
pelican
ACEILNR carline
Linacre
ACEILNS inlaces
sanicle
scaleni
ACEILNU cauline
ACEILOR calorie
cariole
loricae
ACEILOS celosia
ACEILOT aloetic
ACEILPR caliper
replica
ACEILPS plaices
special
ACEILPT plicate
ACEILRS claries
eclairs
scalier
ACEILRT article
recital
ACEILRU auricle
ACEILRV clavier
valeric
ACEILST Castile
elastic
laciest
latices
salicet
ACEILSV vesical
ACEILTT lattice
tactile
ACEIMNO encomia
ACEIMNP pemican
ACEIMNR carmine
Crimean
ACEIMNS amnesic
cinemas
ACEIMNT nematic
ACEIMNX Mexican
ACEIMPR campier
ACEIMPY pyaemic
ACEIMRU Maurice
uraemic
ACEIMST sematic
ACEIMSU caesium
ACEIMTX taxemic
ACEINNP pinnace
ACEINNR cannier
ACEINNS canines
nancies
ACEINNT ancient
ACEINNY cyanine
ACEINOP paeonic
ACEINOS acinose
ACEINOT aconite
ACEINPR caprine
ACEINPS inscape
ACEINRS arsenic
carnies
ACEINRT cantier
ceratin
certain
creatin
ACEINSS incases
ACEINTT Canetti
nictate
tetanic
ACEINTV venatic
ACEINTX inexact
ACEINTY cyanite
ACEINTZ zincate
ACEINVZ Vicenza
ACEIOPT ectopia
ACEIORS cariose
scoriae
ACEIORT erotica
ACEIOTX exotica
ACEIPPR crappie
epicarp
ACEIPRS scrapie
spacier
ACEIPRT paretic
picrate
ACEIPST aseptic
paciest
spicate
ACEIPSU auspice
ACEIPSZ capizes
capsize
ACEIPTV captive
ACEIQRU acquire
Quercia
ACEIQSU caiques
ACEIQUZ cazique
ACEIRRR carrier
ACEIRRS carries
scarier
ACEIRRT Cartier
cirrate
erratic
ACEIRRW aircrew
ACEIRRZ crazier
ACEIRST cristae
raciest
stearic
ACEIRSU saucier
ACEIRSV varices
viscera
ACEIRTT cattier
citrate
ACEISSS ascesis
ACEISST ascites
ectasis
ACEISTT catties
statice
ACEISTV actives
ACEITTV cavetti
ACEJKST jackets
ACEJLOR cajoler
ACEJLOS cajoles
ACEJNOT jaconet
ACEJNOY joyance
ACEJPTU cajeput
ACEJRTT traject
ACEKKNR knacker
ACEKLMS mackles
ACEKLNS slacken
ACEKLPT placket
ACEKLRS calkers
lackers
slacker
ACEKLRT tackler
ACEKLRU caulker
ACEKLST tackles
ACEKLSY lackeys
ACEKMNN McKenna
ACEKMRS smacker
ACEKNRR cranker
ACEKNRS cankers
ACEKNVY van Eyck
ACEKORR croaker
ACEKORU Kerouac
ACEKPPR prepack
ACEKPRS packers
repacks
ACEKPST packets
ACEKRRS rackers
ACEKRRT tracker
ACEKRSS sackers
screaks
ACEKRST rackets
restack
stacker
tackers
ACEKRSW wackers
ACEKRSY screaky
ACEKRTY rackety
ACEKSST caskets
ACEKSTT tackets
ACEKTTY tackety
ACELLMO calomel
ACELLMY mycella
ACELLNY cleanly
ACELLOR corella
ocellar
ACELLOS callose
locales
ACELLOT collate
ACELLPS scalpel
ACELLPY clypeal
ACELLRR carrell
ACELLRS callers
cellars
recalls
ACELLRY Carlyle
clearly
ACELMNO Coleman
ACELMOT camelot
ACELMOU leucoma
ACELMPR clamper
ACELMRS marcels
ACELMSS mascles
mescals
ACELMST calmest
camlets
ACELMSU almuces
macules
ACELMSZ mezcals
ACELMTU calumet
ACELNNO alencon
Alençon
ACELNNU unclean
ACELNNY lyncean
ACELNOR corneal
ACELNOT lactone
ACELNOY Alcyone
ACELNOZ calzone
ACELNPS enclasp
spancel
ACELNPT clapnet
ACELNPU cleanup
ACELNRS lancers
ACELNRT central
ACELNRU lucarne
nuclear
unclear
ACELNRY larceny
ACELNST cantles
centals
lancets
ACELNSU censual
launces
unlaces
ACELNTY latency
ACELNVY valency
ACELOPR polacre
ACELOPT polecat
ACELOPU copulae
ACELOQU coequal
ACELORR caroler
ACELORS claroes
coalers
escolar
oracles
solacer
ACELORT locater
ACELORY caloyer
ACELOSS solaces
ACELOST alecost
lactose
locates
talcose
ACELOSV alcoves
coevals
ACELOTT calotte

ACELOTU oculate
ACELOTY acolyte
ACELOUV vacuole
ACELPPR clapper
ACELPRS carpels
clasper
parcels
scalper
ACELPRT plectra
ACELPRY prelacy
ACELPST placets
ACELPSU capsule
specula
upscale
ACELPSY cypsela
ACELPTY ectypal
ACELQRU lacquer
ACELQSU calques
claques
ACELQUY lacquey
ACELRRS carrels
ACELRRW crawler
ACELRSS classer
scalers
ACELRST cartels
clarets
scarlet
ACELRSU cesural
secular
ACELRSV carvels
clavers
ACELRSW clawers
ACELRTT clatter
ACELRTU Lautrec
Leuctra
ACELRTV Calvert
ACELRTY treacly
ACELRWY Crawley
ACELSSS classes
ACELSST castles
ACELSSU clauses
ACELSTU sulcate
ACELSUU aculeus
ACELSXY calyxes
ACELTUY acutely
ACELTXY exactly
ACEMMRR crammer
ACEMMRS scammer
ACEMNOR Cameron
cremona
Menorca
romance
ACEMNOS Camoëns
ACEMNPS encamps
ACEMNRR Cranmer
ACEMOPR compare
ACEMORU morceau
ACEMOSU mucosae
ACEMPRR cramper
ACEMPRS campers
scamper
ACEMRSS screams

ACEMRST mercats
ACEMRSU Marcuse
ACEMSUX exacums
ACENNOS ancones
sonance
ACENNOT connate
ACENNOZ canzone
ACENNRS canners
scanner
ACENNRY cannery
ACENNST nascent
ACENNSU nuances
ACENNTY tenancy
ACENOOR coronae
ACENORS coarsen
corneas
ACENORT enactor
ACENOSU Oceanus
ACENOSZ Cosenza
ACENOTV centavo
ACENPRR prancer
ACENPRS prances
ACENPTY patency
ACENRRY errancy
ACENRSS caserns
ACENRST canters
carnets
Castner
nectars
recants
trances
ACENRSV caverns
cravens
ACENRSY carneys
ACENRTU centaur
ACENRTY nectary
ACENSST ascents
stances
ACENSSU usances
ACENSTU nutcase
ACEOOPP apocope
ACEOPRX exocarp
ACEOPSS scapose
ACEOPST capotes
toecaps
ACEOPSW cowpeas
ACEOPTU outpace
ACEORRS coarser
correas
ACEORRT acroter
creator
reactor
ACEORSS rosaces
ACEORST coaster
ACEORSU acerous
carouse
ACEORSX coaxers
ACEORTU outrace
ACEORTV overact
ACEORTX exactor
ACEOSSU caseous
ACEOSTT costate

ACEOSTU acetous
ACEOSTV avocets
octaves
ACEOTTV cavetto
ACEOTUU autocue
couteau
ACEPPRS cappers
ACEPRRS carpers
scarper
scraper
ACEPRSS escarps
parsecs
scrapes
spacers
ACEPRST carpets
precast
spectra
ACEPRSU apercus
scauper
ACEPRTU capture
ACEPSST aspects
ACEPSTU cuspate
teacups
ACEQRTU racquet
ACEQSSU casques
sacques
ACERRSS scarers
ACERRST carters
craters
tracers
ACERRSU curares
ACERRSV carvers
cravers
ACERRTT retract
ACERRTY tracery
ACERRUV verruca
ACERRVY carvery
ACERSST actress
casters
recasts
ACERSSU causers
cesuras
saucers
sucrase
ACERSSV scarves
ACERSSY carseys
ACERSTT scatter
ACERSTU curates
ACERSTY sectary
ACERTTU curtate
ACERTTX extract
ACERTTY cattery
ACERTUY cautery
ACERUVY Cauvery
ACESSTU caestus
cuestas
ACESSTY ecstasy
ACESSUY causeys
cayuses
ACESTTU scutate
ACESTTY testacy
ACFFIIT caitiff

ACFFIKM maffick
ACFFILT afflict
ACFFIRT traffic
ACFFLSS sclaffs
ACFFLTU factful
ACFFOST castoff
ACFGHIN chafing
ACFGINR farcing
ACFGINS facings
ACFHIST catfish
ACFHISU fuchsia
ACFHLNU flaunch
Funchal
ACFHRTU futharc
ACFHRTY fratchy
ACFIILN finical
ACFILNO folacin
ACFILNY fancily
ACFILRY clarify
ACFILSS fiscals
ACFIMRU fumaric
ACFIMSS fascism
ACFINNY infancy
ACFINOT faction
ACFINRS Francis
ACFINRT frantic
infarct
infract
ACFINRY carnify
ACFIOSS fiascos
ACFIRSY scarify
ACFISST fascist
ACFKLSU sackful
ACFLLOY focally
ACFLNOS falcons
flacons
ACFLNSU canfuls
ACFLRTU cartful
ACFLRUU furcula
ACFLTTU tactful
ACFLTUY faculty
ACFNRTU fructan
ACFORST factors
ACFORTY factory
ACGGINR gracing
ACGGRSY scraggy
ACGHIKN hacking
ACGHINR arching
chagrin
charing
ACGHINS chasing
ACGHINT gnathic
ACGHINW chawing
chinwag
ACGHINY Yichang
ACGHIOR choragi
ACGHIPR graphic
ACGHLOY Chogyal
ACGHMRT McGrath
ACGHNRU graunch
ACGHNUW Wuchang
ACGHOSU gauchos

ACGHRRU curragh
ACGHRSU curaghs
ACGIILN alginic
ACGIITU augitic
ACGIJKN jacking
ACGIKLN calking
lacking
ACGIKNP packing
ACGIKNR arcking
carking
racking
ACGIKNS sacking
ACGIKNT tacking
ACGIKNY yacking
ACGIKRR Garrick
ACGILLN calling
ACGILLO logical
ACGILMN calming
ACGILMY myalgic
ACGILNN lancing
ACGILNO coaling
ACGILNP placing
ACGILNR carling
ACGILNS lacings
scaling
ACGILNT catling
talcing
ACGILNU cingula
ACGILNV calving
ACGILNW clawing
ACGILNY claying
ACGIMNO coaming
ACGIMNP camping
ACGIMRS Gramsci
ACGINNN canning
ACGINNR craning
ACGINNS canings
ACGINNT canting
ACGINOP Cipango
ACGINOR organic
ACGINOS agnosic
ACGINOT coating
cotinga
ACGINOX coaxing
ACGINPP capping
ACGINPR carping
craping
ACGINPS scaping
spacing
ACGINRS sacring
scaring
ACGINRT carting
crating
tracing
ACGINRV carving
craving
ACGINRZ crazing
ACGINSS casings
ACGINST casting
ACGINSU causing
saucing
ACGINTT catting

ACGIORT argotic
ACGIRST gastric
ACGKLLO gallock
ACGLNOR clangor
ACGLNSU glucans
ACGNNOR crannog
ACGNOOT octagon
ACGNORS garcons
ACGNOSS gascons
ACGNOSU cougans
ACGNOSY Gascony
ACGORSU cougars
ACGOSWY cogways
ACHHIIT Hitachi
ACHHIRS rhachis
ACHHIRW Harwich
ACHHMSU chumash
ACHHPPU chuppah
ACHHTTY thatchy
ACHIILS ischial
ACHIIMS chiasmi
ACHIINT chianti
ACHIIPS pachisi
ACHIITW Wichita
ACHIJKS hijacks
ACHIJMO Joachim
ACHIJNT jacinth
ACHIKLN Nalchik
ACHIKOS kochias
ACHIKRS ricksha
ACHIKRY hayrick
ACHILLN Chillán
ACHILLO lochial
ACHILLP phallic
ACHILLS challis
ACHILLT thallic
ACHILLV Villach
ACHILNP Chaplin
ACHILOR chorial
ACHILOS scholia
ACHILOV Covilhã
ACHILPS caliphs
ACHILRS archils
ACHILRY charily
ACHILST chitals
ACHILSY clayish
ACHIMNO mohican
ACHIMOS chamois
ACHIMRS charism
chimars
ACHIMSS chiasms
ACHINNU unchain
ACHINOP aphonic
ACHINOT Antioch
ACHINOY onychia
ACHINPS spinach
ACHINSU Sichuan
ACHINTX xanthic
ACHINTY Cynthia
ACHIOPS isopach
ACHIOPT aphotic
ACHIORT chariot
haricot

ACHIOST isotach
ACHIPPS sapphic
ACHIPST pathics
spathic
ACHIQRU charqui
ACHIQSU quaichs
ACHIRTU haircut
ACHIRTY charity
ACHISSS chassis
ACHISTT cattish
ACHISTY Scythia
ACHKKSU chukkas
ACHKLOV Chkalov
ACHKMMO hammock
ACHKOPS hopsack
ACHKOSS hassock
shackos
ACHKRSU chukars
ACHKSTW thwacks
ACHLLOO alcohol
ACHLLOR chloral
ACHLLOS chollas
ACHLLOU Cholula
ACHLMNU McLuhan
ACHLMSZ schmalz
ACHLNOS lochans
ACHLNOW Lanchow
ACHLNOY halcyon
ACHLNTU unlatch
ACHLORS chorals
scholar
ACHLORT trochal
ACHLOSW salchow
ACHLTUZ chalutz
ACHMMNO McMahon
ACHMNOR monarch
nomarch
ACHMNSU Schuman
ACHMOPR camphor
ACHMORS chromas
morchas
ACHMORZ machzor
ACHMOST stomach
ACHMPTU matchup
ACHMSSU sumachs
ACHMSUW cumshaw
ACHNNSW Schwann
ACHNOOY chanoyo
ACHNORS anchors
archons
ranchos
ACHNOTY tachyon
ACHNOUY chanoyu
ACHNOVY anchovy
ACHNPSS schnaps
ACHNPUY paunchy
ACHNRTY chantry
ACHNRUY raunchy
ACHNSTU canthus
chaunts
staunch

ACHNSTY snatchy
ACHOOST cahoots
ACHOPRS carhops
ACHOPRT toparch
ACHOPRY charpoy
ACHORSU aurochs
ACHRSTY starchy
ACHSSTU cushats
ACHSSTY stachys
ACIIILS Sicilia
ACIIKNN canikin
ACIIKRS airsick
ACIILMS laicism
ACIILNO Nicolai
ACIILNR clarini
ACIILNS salicin
ACIILNV vicinal
ACIILOR Carol II
ACIILPT aplitic
ACIILRY ciliary
ACIILST italics
ACIIMMS miasmic
ACIIMOT comitia
ACIIMST simatic
ACIINNO anionic
ACIINOS Nicosia
ACIINOV avionic
ACIINPS piscina
ACIINSS Cassini
ACIINTT titanic
ACIIORS Oscar II
ACIIPPR priapic
ACIIPRT piratic
ACIIRST satiric
ACIJKLN Jacklin
ACIJLOS Jalisco
ACIJUZZ jacuzzi
ACIKLNS calkins
ACIKLOR airlock
ACIKLTY tackily
ACIKLWY wackily
ACIKNPY panicky
ACIKNST catkins
ACIKPRT patrick
ACIKRST karstic
ACIKRWW Warwick
ACIKUWZ Zwickau
ACILLMS miscall
ACILLRY lyrical
ACILLSS scillas
ACILMNO limacon
malonic
ACILMPS plasmic
psalmic
ACILMSU musical
ACILNNY cannily
ACILNOR clarino
clarion
Locrian
ACILNOS oilcans
ACILNOU inocula
ACILNOV Calvino

ACILNPS	caplins
ACILNPY	pliancy
ACILNRS	carlins
ACILNST	tincals
ACILNSU	uncials
ACILNTU	lunatic
ACILNTY	cantily
ACILNUV	vincula
ACILOPT	capitol
	optical
	topical
ACILOSS	socials
ACILOST	stoical
ACILOTV	voltaic
ACILPRT	clipart
ACILPST	plastic
ACILPSU	spicula
ACILPTY	typical
ACILRSS	crissal
ACILRTU	curtail
	trucial
ACILRTY	clarity
ACILRVY	vicarly
ACILRYZ	crazily
ACILSSS	classis
ACILSUY	saucily
ACILTTY	cattily
	tacitly
ACILTUV	victual
ACIMMNO	ammonic
ACIMNOP	campion
ACIMNOR	marconi
	minorca
ACIMNOS	anosmic
	camions
	masonic
ACIMNRS	narcism
ACIMNRU	cranium
	cumarin
ACIMNTT	catmint
ACIMOOS	oomiacs
ACIMOPT	apomict
	potamic
	Tampico
ACIMOSS	mosaics
ACIMOST	somatic
ACIMPRY	primacy
ACIMPST	impacts
ACIMRSS	racisms
ACIMRST	matrics
ACIMRSZ	czarism
ACIMSST	mastics
	miscast
ACINNOT	actinon
	contain
ACINNOZ	canzoni
ACINNST	stannic
ACINNSY	cyanins
ACINOPT	caption
	Pontiac
ACINOQU	coquina
ACINORR	carrion
ACINORS	saronic
ACINORT	carotin
ACINOSS	caisson
	casinos
	cassino
ACINOST	actions
	atonics
	cations
ACINOSU	acinous
ACINOSY	syconia
ACINOTT	taction
ACINOTU	auction
	caution
ACINPRT	cantrip
ACINPRU	puranic
ACINPRY	cyprian
ACINQTU	quantic
ACINRTT	tantric
ACINRTU	curtain
ACINSUV	vicunas
ACIOPRS	prosaic
ACIOPRT	apricot
	aprotic
	parotic
ACIOPSS	Picasso
ACIOPST	copitas
ACIOPTY	opacity
ACIORRS	corsair
ACIORSU	carious
	curiosa
ACIORTT	ricotta
ACIOSST	scotias
ACIOSSV	ovisacs
ACIPRSS	casspir
ACIPRSY	piscary
ACIPRVY	privacy
ACIPSST	spastic
ACIPTUY	paucity
ACIQRTU	quartic
ACIQSTU	acquits
ACIRRSU	curaris
ACIRSST	racists
	sacrist
ACIRSSU	cuirass
ACIRSTT	astrict
ACIRSTU	Scutari
ACIRSTY	satyric
ACIRSTZ	czarist
ACIRTUY	raucity
ACISSTT	statics
ACISSTU	casuist
ACISTTU	catsuit
	Tacitus
ACITUVY	vacuity
ACJKKSY	skyjack
ACJKLOW	lockjaw
ACJKNNO	jannock
ACJKNOS	Jackson
ACJKOPT	jackpot
ACJLORU	jocular
ACJMNTU	muntjac
ACJPTUU	cajuput
ACKLLOP	pollack
ACKLLOR	Rockall
ACKLLSY	slackly
ACKLMOT	Matlock
ACKLOOR	oarlock
ACKLORW	warlock
ACKMMMO	mammock
ACKMNRU	ruckman
ACKMOST	stomack
ACKMOTT	mattock
ACKNORY	Conakry
ACKNPSU	unpacks
ACKNSTU	untacks
ACKOWZZ	wazzock
ACLLLOY	locally
ACLLMMO	Malcolm
ACLLOOR	corolla
ACLLOOS	alcools
ACLLOPS	callops
	scallop
ACLLORR	Carroll
ACLLORS	collars
ACLLORU	locular
ACLLOSU	callous
ACLLOVY	vocally
ACLLRYY	acrylyl
ACLMNOO	locoman
ACLMNUY	calumny
ACLMOPS	copalms
ACLMORS	clamors
ACLMORU	clamour
ACLMOSU	mucosal
ACLNOOO	Laocoon
ACLNOOR	coronal
	Locarno
ACLNOOT	coolant
ACLNOOV	volcano
ACLNOPT	Clapton
ACLNORT	Carlton
ACLNORU	cornual
	courlan
ACLNOSX	claxons
ACLNPSU	unclasp
ACLNSTY	scantly
ACLOOPP	alcopop
	Coppola
ACLOPRT	caltrop
ACLOPRU	copular
ACLOPSU	copulas
	cupolas
	scopula
ACLOPSY	calypso
ACLORRS	corrals
ACLORST	crotals
	scrotal
ACLORSU	carolus
	oculars
	oscular
ACLORWW	Wrocław
ACLOSTU	talcous
ACLOTTW	Walcott
ACLPRTY	cryptal
ACLPRUU	cupular
ACLRSSW	scrawls
ACLRSSY	crassly
ACLRSTU	crustal
	curtals
ACLRSTY	crystal
ACLRSWY	scrawly
ACLSSTU	cutlass
ACMNOPR	crampon
ACMNOPY	company
ACMNORS	macrons
ACMNORY	acronym
ACMNOSS	mascons
ACMNSTU	sanctum
ACMNTUU	Tucumán
ACMOOPT	Potomac
ACMOOST	scotoma
ACMOPSS	compass
ACMORTW	catworm
ACMOSST	mascots
ACMQTUU	cumquat
ACMSSTU	muscats
ACMSUUV	vacuums
ACNNNOS	cannons
ACNNNUY	uncanny
ACNNORU	Corunna
ACNNORY	canonry
ACNNOST	cantons
ACNNOSY	canyons
ACNOORS	coronas
	racoons
ACNOORT	cartoon
	coranto
	Cortona
ACNOPSU	Canopus
ACNOPSW	snowcap
ACNORRS	Scarron
ACNORRU	rancour
ACNORRY	carryon
ACNORST	cantors
	cartons
	cratons
ACNORSY	crayons
ACNOSTT	octants
ACNOSTU	conatus
	toucans
ACNPRSY	syncarp
ACNRRTU	currant
ACNRSWY	scrawny
ACNRTUY	truancy
ACNSSTU	Sanctus
ACNSSUU	Cusanus
ACNSTUY	Tuscany
ACOOPRR	corpora
ACOOPTT	topcoat
ACOORST	Socotra
ACOORTU	touraco
ACOOSTV	octavos
ACOPPRR	procarp
ACOPRRT	carport
ACOPRST	captors
ACOPSTW	cowpats

ACORRST	carrots
	trocars
ACORRTT	tractor
ACORRTU	curator
ACORRTY	carroty
ACORSST	castors
	costars
ACORSSU	sarcous
ACORSTT	cottars
ACORSTU	surcoat
	turacos
ACORSTV	cavorts
ACORSUU	raucous
ACOSSZZ	scozzas
ACOSTTU	outacts
	outcast
ACOSUUV	vacuous
ACPPRSY	scrappy
ACPSSTU	catsups
	upcasts
ACRRSTU	craturs
ACRSSSU	Crassus
ADDDEEL	Deledda
ADDDEER	dreaded
	readded
ADDDEGL	gladded
ADDDEIS	daddies
ADDDEIW	waddied
ADDDELN	dandled
ADDDELP	paddled
ADDDELR	raddled
ADDDELS	saddled
ADDDELW	dawdled
	waddled
ADDDENO	deodand
ADDDENS	addends
ADDDGOR	Goddard
ADDDOOS	doodads
ADDEEEY	deadeye
ADDEEFM	defamed
ADDEEGR	degrade
ADDEEHR	adhered
	redhead
ADDEEKN	kneaded
ADDEELM	medaled
ADDEELP	pedaled
	pleaded
ADDEELT	delated
ADDEELY	delayed
ADDEEMN	amended
	deadmen
ADDEEMR	dreamed
ADDEENS	deadens
ADDEERT	derated
ADDEEST	sedated
	steaded
ADDEFHN	handfed
ADDEFIR	faddier
ADDEFRT	drafted
ADDEFRU	defraud
ADDEFRW	dwarfed
ADDEGGR	dragged
ADDEGHO	godhead
ADDEGIL	gladdie
ADDEGJU	adjudge
ADDEGLN	dangled
	gladden
ADDEGLO	Delgado
ADDEGLR	gladder
ADDEGRS	gadders
ADDEGRU	guarded
ADDEHIO	Hodeida
ADDEHIR	diehard
ADDEHKS	keddahs
ADDEHLN	handled
ADDEHOR	hoarded
ADDEIIS	daisied
ADDEILL	dallied
	dialled
ADDEILR	drailed
ADDEILS	laddies
ADDEILT	dilated
ADDEIMR	admired
ADDEIMS	diadems
ADDEIMX	admixed
ADDEINO	adenoid
ADDEINP	pandied
ADDEINR	dandier
	drained
ADDEINS	dandies
ADDEINU	unaided
ADDEINV	invaded
ADDEIOR	radioed
ADDEIOT	iodated
	toadied
ADDEIOV	avoided
ADDEIPS	paddies
ADDEIRR	Derrida
ADDEIRW	Edward I
ADDEISV	advised
ADDEISW	swaddie
	waddies
ADDEITU	audited
ADDEJLY	jadedly
ADDEJRU	adjured
ADDEKLR	darkled
ADDELLU	alluded
	dualled
ADDELNR	dandler
ADDELNS	dandles
ADDELNU	unladed
ADDELPP	dappled
ADDELPR	paddler
ADDELPS	paddles
ADDELRS	ladders
	raddles
	saddler
ADDELRW	dawdler
	drawled
	waddler
ADDELSS	saddles
ADDELST	staddle
ADDELSW	dawdles
	swaddle
	waddles
ADDELTW	twaddle
ADDELYZ	dazedly
ADDELZZ	dazzled
ADDEMMW	dwammed
ADDEMNS	demands
	maddens
ADDEMOP	pomaded
ADDEMRY	dramedy
ADDEMST	maddest
ADDEMUW	dwaumed
ADDENOR	adorned
ADDENOT	donated
ADDENOU	duodena
ADDENPU	pudenda
ADDENRS	danders
ADDENSS	saddens
ADDENTU	daunted
	undated
ADDEOPT	adopted
ADDEORS	deodars
ADDEPTU	updated
ADDERSS	address
ADDERST	addrest
	raddest
ADDERSW	Edwards
	swarded
	wadders
ADDERSY	dryades
ADDERTT	dratted
ADDERVW	Edward V
ADDESST	saddest
ADDFHIS	faddish
ADDFIMS	faddism
ADDFINY	dandify
ADDFIST	faddist
ADDGGIN	gadding
ADDGILN	addling
ADDGIMN	madding
ADDGIMR	Midgard
ADDGINO	dadoing
ADDGINP	padding
ADDGINW	wadding
ADDGIOS	gadoids
ADDGLNO	gladdon
ADDGMNO	goddamn
ADDGNNO	Dandong
ADDGOOS	ogdoads
ADDGOSY	dogdays
ADDHIKS	kaddish
ADDHILS	laddish
ADDHIMS	maddish
ADDHIQS	Qaddish
ADDHITY	hydatid
ADDHNOR	Rhondda
ADDHOOS	doodahs
ADDHOTY	athodyd
ADDHSSU	saddhus
ADDIIIV	David II
ADDIINS	disdain
ADDIKTY	katydid
ADDILMN	midland
ADDILNY	dandily
ADDIMNO	diamond
ADDIMSS	misadds
ADDINOR	android
ADDINOS	Addison
ADDKLNU	Dundalk
ADDLLRU	dullard
ADDLNOO	Dandolo
ADDLNOW	Dowland
ADDNNOR	donnard
ADDOORS	dorados
ADDORST	dotards
ADDQSUY	squaddy
ADEEEFY	fedayee
ADEEESW	seaweed
ADEEFKR	freaked
ADEEFLR	federal
ADEEFLT	deflate
ADEEFMR	defamer
ADEEFMS	defames
ADEEFNS	deafens
ADEEFRT	draftee
ADEEFRW	wafered
ADEEFST	deafest
	defeats
	feasted
ADEEFUY	Feydeau
ADEEGGH	egghead
ADEEGGN	engaged
ADEEGLL	alleged
ADEEGLM	gleamed
ADEEGLN	gleaned
ADEEGLR	lagered
	regaled
ADEEGLU	leagued
ADEEGLZ	deglaze
ADEEGMN	endgame
ADEEGNR	angered
	derange
	enraged
	grandee
	grenade
ADEEGNT	negated
ADEEGNV	avenged
ADEEGOT	goateed
ADEEGRR	regrade
ADEEGRS	dragees
	greased
ADEEGRU	guardee
ADEEGRV	greaved
ADEEGRW	ragweed
	wagered
ADEEGSS	degases
ADEEHIR	headier
ADEEHLS	leashed
ADEEHLX	exhaled
ADEEHMN	headmen
ADEEHNN	hennaed
ADEEHNS	dasheen
ADEEHNT	nethead
ADEEHNV	havened
ADEEHPR	ephedra

ADEEHRR	reheard
ADEEHRS	adheres
	headers
	sheared
ADEEHRT	earthed
	hearted
ADEEHRV	havered
ADEEHSS	Édhessa
ADEEHST	headset
ADEEHSV	sheaved
ADEEHSY	hayseed
ADEEIJT	jadeite
ADEEILM	emailed
	limeade
ADEEILN	aliened
	delaine
ADEEILS	aediles
ADEEIMT	mediate
ADEEINN	adenine
ADEEINS	aniseed
ADEEIRR	readier
ADEEIRS	dearies
	readies
ADEEIRW	wearied
ADEEISS	disease
	seaside
ADEEITV	deviate
ADEEJSY	deejays
ADEEKNP	kneepad
ADEEKNR	kneader
ADEEKNS	sneaked
ADEEKNW	wakened
ADEEKRW	rewaked
	wreaked
ADEEKTW	tweaked
ADEEKWY	weekday
ADEELLN	Allende
ADEELLS	allseed
ADEELMN	Edelman
ADEELMP	empaled
ADEELMR	emerald
ADEELMS	measled
ADEELMT	metaled
ADEELNP	deplane
	paneled
ADEELNR	Leander
	learned
ADEELNS	Seeland
ADEELNZ	Zeeland
ADEELPR	pearled
	pleader
ADEELPS	elapsed
	pleased
ADEELPT	pleated
ADEELQU	equaled
ADEELRS	dealers
	leaders
ADEELRT	alerted
	altered
	related
	treadle
ADEELRV	raveled
ADEELRW	leeward
ADEELRX	relaxed
ADEELRY	delayer
	layered
	relayed
ADEELST	delates
ADEELSV	sleaved
ADEELTT	ladette
ADEELTV	valeted
ADEELTX	exalted
ADEELTZ	teazled
ADEELUV	devalue
	Uvedale
ADEELYZ	laydeez
ADEEMNR	amender
	meander
	reedman
	renamed
ADEEMNS	demeans
ADEEMRR	dreamer
	rearmed
ADEEMRS	smeared
ADEEMST	steamed
ADEEMSU	medusae
ADEEMWY	mayweed
ADEENNS	enneads
ADEENNX	annexed
ADEENRS	endears
ADEENRV	ravened
ADEENRY	deanery
	yearned
ADEENST	East End
	standee
ADEENTT	dentate
ADEEOPT	adoptee
ADEEORW	oarweed
ADEEPPR	papered
ADEEPRS	speared
ADEEPRT	predate
	tapered
ADEEPRV	deprave
	pervade
	repaved
ADEEPSS	pesades
ADEEQTU	equated
ADEERRS	readers
	rereads
ADEERRT	retread
	treader
ADEERRV	averred
ADEERRW	redware
ADEERSS	resedas
ADEERST	dearest
	derates
	estrade
	reasted
ADEERSV	adverse
	evaders
ADEERSW	drawees
ADEERTT	treated
ADEERTV	averted
ADEERTW	watered
ADEERVW	wavered
ADEESST	sedates
ADEESSY	essayed
ADEESTU	sauteed
ADEESTW	sweated
ADEESTY	yeasted
ADEETUX	exudate
ADEFFIN	affined
ADEFFIR	daffier
ADEFFIX	affixed
ADEFFLO	leadoff
ADEFFLR	raffled
ADEFFLW	waffled
ADEFFQU	quaffed
ADEFFST	staffed
ADEFGGL	flagged
ADEFGGR	fragged
ADEFGLN	flanged
ADEFGOR	foraged
ADEFGOT	fagoted
ADEFGRT	grafted
ADEFHLS	flashed
ADEFHRW	wharfed
ADEFHST	shafted
ADEFILL	flailed
ADEFINR	Friedan
ADEFINT	defiant
	fainted
ADEFITX	fixated
ADEFKLN	fankled
	flanked
ADEFKNR	franked
ADEFLLN	elfland
ADEFLMM	flammed
ADEFLOT	floated
ADEFLPP	flapped
ADEFLRS	fardels
ADEFLTT	flatted
ADEFLTU	default
	faulted
ADEFNRS	snarfed
ADEFNSU	snafued
ADEFNUZ	unfazed
ADEFOOS	seafood
ADEFORS	fedoras
ADEFORV	favored
ADEFORY	forayed
ADEFPPR	frapped
ADEFRRT	drafter
	redraft
ADEFRST	strafed
ADEFRSY	defrays
ADEFSTT	daftest
ADEGGGL	gaggled
ADEGGHL	haggled
ADEGGHS	shagged
ADEGGIR	daggier
ADEGGLR	draggle
	gargled
ADEGGLS	slagged
ADEGGLW	waggled
ADEGGMO	demagog
ADEGGNS	snagged
ADEGGOP	pedagog
ADEGGPS	spagged
ADEGGRS	daggers
ADEGGRY	raggedy
ADEGGST	gadgets
	stagged
ADEGGSW	swagged
ADEGGTY	gadgety
ADEGHIN	heading
ADEGHLU	laughed
ADEGHMO	homaged
ADEGHNS	gnashed
ADEGHNW	whanged
ADEGHPR	graphed
ADEGILN	aligned
	dealing
	leading
ADEGILR	glaired
ADEGILT	ligated
ADEGILV	glaived
ADEGINR	deraign
	gradine
	grained
	reading
ADEGINV	deaving
	evading
ADEGINW	windage
ADEGIOT	godetia
ADEGIRU	gaudier
ADEGIRV	Rig-Veda
ADEGIST	agisted
ADEGISU	gaudies
ADEGISV	visaged
ADEGJLN	jangled
ADEGLLU	ullaged
ADEGLMN	mangled
ADEGLNN	England
ADEGLNO	Donegal
ADEGLNR	dangler
	gnarled
ADEGLNS	dangles
	glandes
	slanged
ADEGLNT	tangled
ADEGLNW	wangled
ADEGLOT	gloated
ADEGLPU	plagued
ADEGLRY	gradely
ADEGLSS	glassed
ADEGLTY	dalgyte
	Lydgate
ADEGMNU	agendum
ADEGNNU	dunnage
ADEGNOR	groaned
ADEGNOS	sondage
ADEGNOT	tangoed
ADEGNOV	dogvane
ADEGNOW	gowaned
ADEGNPR	pranged
ADEGNPU	unpaged
ADEGNRR	Gardner

	gnarred
	grander
ADEGNRS	dangers
	ganders
	gardens
ADEGNRT	dragnet
	granted
ADEGNRW	wranged
ADEGNST	stanged
ADEGNSU	augends
ADEGNTW	twanged
ADEGNUW	unwaged
ADEGNWY	Weygand
ADEGORS	dogears
ADEGORW	dowager
	wordage
ADEGOSS	dosages
	seadogs
ADEGOST	dotages
ADEGOVY	voyaged
ADEGPRS	grasped
	spadger
	sparged
ADEGPRU	upgrade
ADEGRRS	graders
	regards
ADEGRRU	guarder
ADEGRSS	grassed
ADEGRSU	sugared
ADEGRTY	gyrated
	tragedy
ADEGRUU	augured
ADEGRUY	gaudery
ADEGSSU	degauss
ADEHHKS	khedahs
ADEHHOP	hophead
ADEHHOT	hothead
ADEHILL	Delilah
ADEHILN	hieland
	inhaled
ADEHILP	helipad
ADEHILS	halides
ADEHILY	headily
ADEHIMO	haemoid
ADEHINP	headpin
	pinhead
ADEHINR	handier
ADEHIPR	raphide
ADEHIPS	aphides
	diphase
ADEHIPT	pithead
ADEHIRR	hardier
	harried
ADEHIRS	hardies
	shadier
ADEHIRW	rawhide
ADEHKNS	shanked
ADEHKNT	thanked
ADEHKRS	sharked
ADEHLLO	halloed
	hollaed
ADEHLLP	lapheld
ADEHLMN	Helmand
ADEHLMS	lamedhs
ADEHLMU	Duhamel
ADEHLNR	handler
ADEHLNS	handles
	handsel
ADEHLOS	shoaled
ADEHLOT	loathed
ADEHLPS	plashed
ADEHLRS	heralds
ADEHLSS	hassled
	slashed
ADEHLST	daleths
ADEHLTY	deathly
ADEHMMS	shammed
ADEHMMW	whammed
ADEHMNP	Hampden
ADEHMOY	Dahomey
ADEHMSS	smashed
ADEHNPS	daphnes
ADEHNRS	hardens
ADEHNRU	unheard
ADEHNST	handset
ADEHNTU	haunted
ADEHNUY	Da Yunhe
ADEHOPT	pothead
ADEHOPX	hexapod
ADEHORR	hoarder
ADEHOST	hoasted
ADEHOTW	towhead
ADEHPPW	whapped
ADEHPRS	phrased
	sharped
	Shepard
ADEHPST	heptads
	spathed
ADEHQSU	quashed
ADEHRSS	dashers
ADEHRST	dearths
	hardest
	hatreds
	threads
	trashed
ADEHRTY	hydrate
	thready
ADEHSST	stashed
ADEHSSW	swashed
ADEHSTW	swathed
ADEHSYY	heydays
ADEIILR	deliria
ADEIILS	dailies
	liaised
	sedilia
ADEIIMN	diamine
ADEIINR	denarii
ADEIINZ	diazine
ADEIIPR	peridia
ADEIIRR	Airdrie
ADEIIRS	airside
	dairies
	diaries
ADEIISS	daisies
ADEIJUZ	Judaize
ADEIKLR	Kildare
ADEIKRS	darkies
ADEILLR	dallier
	dialler
	rallied
ADEILLS	dallies
	sallied
ADEILLT	tallied
ADEILLY	ideally
ADEILMM	dilemma
ADEILMP	impaled
	implead
ADEILMR	Daimler
ADEILMS	medials
	misdeal
	mislead
ADEILMU	miauled
ADEILNN	annelid
	lindane
ADEILNP	plained
ADEILNR	Ireland
ADEILNS	denials
ADEILNU	aliunde
	unideal
ADEILNW	Wieland
ADEILOP	oedipal
ADEILOR	dariole
ADEILOZ	diazole
ADEILPP	applied
ADEILPR	predial
ADEILPS	alipeds
	elapids
	laipsed
	palsied
	pleiads
ADEILPT	plaited
	taliped
ADEILQU	quailed
ADEILRS	derails
	redials
ADEILRT	dilater
	trailed
ADEILRU	uredial
ADEILRV	rivaled
ADEILRY	readily
ADEILSS	deasils
ADEILST	details
	dilates
ADEILSU	audiles
ADEILSV	devisal
ADEILSY	dialyse
ADEILYZ	dialyze
ADEIMMR	mermaid
ADEIMMT	tammied
ADEIMNS	maidens
	medians
	medinas
	sideman
ADEIMNT	mediant
ADEIMNU	unaimed
ADEIMOU	miaoued
ADEIMOW	miaowed
ADEIMPR	dampier
ADEIMRR	admirer
	married
ADEIMRS	admires
	misread
ADEIMRT	readmit
ADEIMRU	Daumier
ADEIMRY	midyear
ADEIMST	Mideast
	misdate
ADEIMSX	admixes
ADEIMTU	ideatum
ADEIMTY	daytime
ADEINNN	nannied
ADEINNS	dannies
ADEINOR	aneroid
ADEINOS	anodise
ADEINOV	naevoid
ADEINOX	dioxane
ADEINOZ	anodize
ADEINPS	pandies
ADEINPT	painted
ADEINRR	drainer
	randier
ADEINRS	randies
	sandier
	sardine
ADEINRT	detrain
	trained
ADEINRU	unaired
	uranide
ADEINRV	invader
	ravined
ADEINST	detains
	instead
	sainted
	stained
ADEINSV	invades
ADEINTT	tainted
ADEINTV	deviant
ADEIOPS	adipose
ADEIOPT	opiated
ADEIORS	roadies
	soredia
ADEIORV	avoider
ADEIORX	exordia
ADEIOST	iodates
	toadies
ADEIOSX	oxidase
ADEIOSZ	diazoes
ADEIOTX	oxidate
ADEIPPR	drappie
	prepaid
ADEIPRR	parried
ADEIPRS	aspired
	despair
	diapers
	praised
ADEIPRT	partied
	pirated
ADEIPSS	apsides

ADEIRRS	raiders
ADEIRRT	tardier
	tarried
ADEIRRV	arrived
ADEIRST	astride
	diaster
	disrate
	tirades
ADEIRSU	residua
ADEIRSV	adviser
ADEIRSX	radixes
ADEIRTT	attired
ADEIRTY	dietary
ADEISSS	dassies
ADEISSV	advises
ADEISTV	datives
	vistaed
ADEISTW	waisted
ADEISVV	savvied
ADEISWY	wayside
ADEITUZ	deutzia
ADEITWY	tideway
ADEJMOR	majored
ADEJMRU	jumared
	mudejar
ADEJNTU	jaunted
ADEJRRU	adjurer
ADEJRSU	adjures
ADEJSSU	judases
ADEKKNS	skanked
ADEKLLN	Kendall
ADEKLNP	planked
ADEKLNR	rankled
ADEKLNS	kalends
ADEKLNY	nakedly
ADEKLOP	polkaed
ADEKLRS	darkles
ADEKLST	stalked
ADEKLUW	waulked
ADEKMNR	Denmark
ADEKNPP	knapped
ADEKNPR	pranked
ADEKNPS	spanked
ADEKNRR	knarred
ADEKNRS	darkens
ADEKNRU	Kundera
ADEKNSS	sandeks
ADEKNST	dankest
	stanked
ADEKNSU	unasked
ADEKNSW	swanked
ADEKNVY	vandyke
ADEKPRS	sparked
ADEKPSY	keypads
ADEKRST	darkest
ADEKRSY	darkeys
ADELLMU	medulla
ADELLNR	landler
ADELLOW	allowed
ADELLOY	alloyed
ADELLPS	spalled
ADELLRS	ladlers
ADELLRU	allured
ADELLST	stalled
ADELLSU	alludes
	aludels
ADELMMS	slammed
ADELMMY	Malmédy
ADELMNO	Mondale
ADELMNR	mandrel
ADELMNT	mantled
ADELMOR	earldom
ADELMOS	damosel
ADELMOZ	damozel
ADELMPS	sampled
ADELMRS	medlars
ADELMSS	damsels
ADELNNP	planned
ADELNNU	unladen
ADELNOR	ladrone
	Leonard
ADELNOT	taloned
ADELNPT	planted
ADELNPY	endplay
ADELNRR	Lardner
ADELNRS	darnels
	slander
	snarled
ADELNRU	Arundel
	launder
	rundale
ADELNRY	Darnley
ADELNSS	sendals
ADELNST	dentals
	slanted
ADELNSU	Ålesund
	unlades
	unleads
ADELNTU	lunated
ADELNTW	wetland
ADELNTY	Tyndale
ADELNTZ	Zetland
ADELNUU	Ulan-Ude
ADELOPR	leopard
	paroled
ADELOPS	deposal
	pedalos
ADELOPT	ploated
	tadpole
ADELORS	loaders
	ordeals
	reloads
ADELORT	delator
	leotard
ADELORU	roulade
ADELORX	Axelrod
ADELOSS	aldoses
	lassoed
ADELOSW	waldoes
ADELOTT	totaled
ADELPPR	Leppard
ADELPPS	dapples
	slapped
ADELPRS	pedlars
ADELPST	stapled
ADELPSW	dewlaps
ADELPSY	splayed
ADELPTT	platted
ADELPTY	adeptly
ADELRRS	larders
ADELRRU	ruderal
ADELRRW	drawler
ADELRST	slarted
ADELRSU	lauders
ADELRSW	warsled
ADELRTT	rattled
ADELRTW	trawled
ADELRTX	dextral
ADELRTY	lyrated
ADELSST	desalts
ADELSTT	slatted
ADELSTU	auldest
	saluted
ADELSZZ	dazzles
ADELTTT	tattled
ADELTTW	wattled
ADELTUV	vaulted
ADELTUX	luxated
ADELTWZ	waltzed
ADELUVX	Delvaux
ADEMMNR	Drammen
ADEMMPS	spammed
ADEMMRS	smarmed
ADEMMRT	trammed
ADEMNNS	sandmen
ADEMNNU	mundane
	unnamed
ADEMNOR	madrone
ADEMNOS	daemons
	masoned
	monades
ADEMNOW	womaned
ADEMNOZ	Mendoza
ADEMNPS	dampens
ADEMNRS	randems
	remands
ADEMNRU	duramen
	manured
	maunder
	unarmed
ADEMNSS	desmans
	madness
ADEMNST	tandems
ADEMNSU	medusan
ADEMNTU	untamed
ADEMOPS	pomades
ADEMORR	armored
ADEMORS	radomes
ADEMOSW	meadows
ADEMOSY	someday
ADEMOWY	meadowy
ADEMPRS	dampers
ADEMPRT	tramped
ADEMPST	dampest
	stamped
ADEMPSW	swamped
ADEMRRU	eardrum
ADEMRST	smarted
ADEMRSW	swarmed
ADEMRTU	matured
ADEMSSU	assumed
	medusas
ADEMSTU	Admetus
ADEMTTU	mutated
ADENNOY	annoyed
	anodyne
ADENNPS	spanned
ADENNPT	pendant
ADENNSU	duennas
ADENNSW	swanned
ADENOPR	aproned
	operand
	padrone
	pandore
ADENOPS	dapsone
ADENOPT	Da Ponte
	notepad
ADENORR	Reardon
ADENORU	rondeau
ADENOST	donates
ADENOSY	noyades
ADENOTT	notated
ADENOTZ	zonated
ADENOUY	Yaoundé
ADENPPR	parpend
ADENPPS	appends
	snapped
ADENPRR	pardner
ADENPRS	panders
ADENPST	pedants
	pentads
ADENPSW	spawned
ADENPSX	expands
	spandex
ADENPSY	dyspnea
ADENPUV	unpaved
ADENQTU	quanted
ADENRRS	darners
	errands
	Randers
ADENRRW	redrawn
ADENRRY	reynard
ADENRSS	sanders
ADENRST	stander
ADENRSU	asunder
	danseur
ADENRSW	Andrews
	wanders
	wardens
ADENRSZ	zanders
ADENRTU	daunter
	Durante
	untread
ADENRTV	verdant
ADENRTX	dextran
ADENRUY	Reynaud
	unready
ADENSSS	sadness

ADENSSU	sundaes
ADENSTT	attends
ADENSTU	stauned
	unsated
ADENSTV	advents
ADENSUV	unsaved
ADENSWY	endways
ADENTTU	attuned
	taunted
ADENTUV	vaunted
ADENTUX	untaxed
ADENUWX	unwaxed
ADEOPPS	apposed
ADEOPQU	opaqued
ADEOPRR	eardrop
ADEOPRT	readopt
ADEOPRV	vapored
ADEOPST	podesta
ADEORRS	adorers
ADEORST	doaters
	roasted
	torsade
ADEORSU	aroused
ADEORSV	savored
ADEORTT	rotated
	troated
ADEORTU	outdare
	readout
ADEORYZ	zedoary
ADEOSTT	toasted
ADEOTTU	outdate
ADEPPRT	trapped
ADEPPRW	wrapped
ADEPPSW	swapped
ADEPPTU	pupated
ADEPRRS	drapers
	sparred
ADEPRRY	drapery
ADEPRSS	spaders
	spreads
ADEPRST	departs
	petards
ADEPRSY	sprayed
ADEPRTU	updater
	uprated
ADEPSTT	spatted
ADEPSTU	updates
ADEQRSU	squared
ADERRST	darters
	retards
	starred
	traders
ADERRSW	drawers
	redraws
	rewards
	warders
ADERSSU	assured
ADERSSW	sawders
ADERSTT	started
	tetrads
ADERSTV	adverts
	starved
ADERSTW	steward
	strawed
ADERSTY	strayed
ADERSUY	dasyure
ADERSVW	dwarves
ADERTUU	Trudeau
ADESSTW	wadsets
ADESTTU	statued
ADESTTW	swatted
ADFFGIN	daffing
ADFFHNO	handoff
	offhand
ADFFIST	distaff
ADFFLOO	offload
ADFFORS	affords
ADFGGIN	fadging
ADFGINS	fadings
ADFHLNU	handful
ADFHLNY	flyhand
ADFHOOS	shadoof
ADFHORS	Ashford
ADFHSSU	shadufs
ADFILLU	fluidal
ADFILNN	Finland
ADFILOR	Florida
ADFIMNY	damnify
ADFINRT	indraft
ADFLMTU	mudflat
ADFLNOP	plafond
ADFLNSY	sandfly
ADFLORS	Salford
ADFLORT	Altdorf
ADFLORU	foulard
ADFNNOT	fondant
ADFNOST	fantods
ADFOOPT	footpad
ADFORRW	forward
	froward
ADFORTW	Watford
ADGGGIN	dagging
ADGGHNO	hangdog
ADGGINO	goading
ADGGINR	grading
	niggard
ADGHILO	hidalgo
ADGHINN	handing
ADGHINR	Harding
ADGHINS	dashing
	shading
ADGHINU	hauding
ADGHIPR	digraph
ADGHNNU	handgun
ADGHNOS	sandhog
ADGHRSU	durgahs
ADGHRTU	draught
ADGIILN	dialing
	gliadin
ADGIILT	digital
ADGIINO	gonidia
ADGIINR	raiding
ADGIINU	iguanid
ADGIIPY	pygidia
ADGIJOS	adjigos
ADGIKNR	darking
ADGILLN	ladling
ADGILNN	landing
ADGILNO	digonal
	loading
ADGILNR	darling
	larding
ADGILNS	ligands
ADGILNU	languid
	lauding
ADGILOR	goliard
ADGILOS	dialogs
ADGILUY	gaudily
ADGIMMN	damming
ADGIMNN	damning
ADGIMNP	damping
ADGIMNR	mridang
ADGINNR	darning
ADGINNS	sanding
ADGINNW	dawning
ADGINOQ	Qingdao
ADGINOR	adoring
ADGINOS	ganoids
	Sogdian
ADGINOT	doating
ADGINPP	dapping
ADGINPR	draping
ADGINPS	spading
ADGINRS	gradins
ADGINRT	darting
	trading
ADGINRU	dauring
ADGINRW	drawing
	warding
ADGINRY	yarding
ADGINST	datings
ADGINWY	gwyniad
ADGIPRU	pagurid
ADGIRZZ	gizzard
ADGLMNO	mangold
ADGLNOO	dongola
	gondola
ADGLNOR	goldarn
ADGLNOT	Gotland
ADGLNOY	daylong
ADGLNRY	grandly
ADGLOOV	Vologda
ADGLOPS	lapdogs
ADGLOSU	Douglas
ADGMNOO	goodman
ADGMNOR	gormand
ADGMOOR	Mogador
ADGNOOR	dragoon
	gadroon
ADGNORS	dragons
ADGNORU	aground
	Durango
ADGNORY	organdy
ADGNRRU	gurnard
ADGOOPS	gospoda
ADHHISW	whidahs
ADHHMOS	shahdom
ADHHOSU	houdahs
ADHHOSW	howdahs
ADHHSWY	whydahs
ADHIIKS	dashiki
ADHIIMS	maidish
ADHIIPS	Phidias
ADHIJMS	Jamshid
ADHIKRS	darkish
ADHIKSU	haiduks
ADHILMO	halidom
ADHILMU	Milhaud
ADHILNY	handily
ADHILOP	haploid
ADHILOR	Harold I
ADHILOS	haloids
ADHILOY	holiday
	hyaloid
	hyoidal
ADHILRY	hardily
ADHILSY	shadily
ADHIMPS	dampish
	phasmid
ADHIMQS	Dimashq
ADHIMRS	dirhams
	midrash
ADHINOR	Rhodian
ADHINPS	Daphnis
	dishpan
ADHINPU	dauphin
ADHINSS	sandhis
ADHINUY	Hunyadi
ADHIOOS	hoodias
ADHIORS	hairdos
ADHIOST	toadish
ADHJKNU	Khujand
ADHLLLO	holdall
ADHLLNO	holland
ADHLOYY	holy day
	holyday
ADHMMNO	Hammond
ADHMNOO	manhood
ADHMNOU	Mahound
ADHMNSU	numdahs
ADHMNWY	Wyndham
ADHMORY	hydroma
ADHNNSU	unhands
ADHNNUY	unhandy
ADHNORS	hadrons
ADHNOSU	houdans
ADHNOSW	Ashdown
ADHNOTU	handout
ADHNOVZ	Zhdanov
ADHNRTY	hydrant
ADHOPRT	hardtop
ADHOPST	dashpot
ADHOSSW	shadows
ADHOSWY	shadowy
ADHPRSU	purdahs
ADIIJNU	Jundiaí
ADIILMS	mislaid
ADIILNO	lianoid

ADIILNV	invalid
ADIILOS	sialoid
ADIILRW	wirilda
ADIILUV	diluvia
ADIILVV	Vivaldi
ADIIMNU	Numidia
ADIIMOS	daimios
ADIINSU	indusia
ADIINSZ	diazins
ADIIPRS	diapirs
ADIIPXY	pyxidia
ADIIRST	diarist
ADIIRSU	Darius I
ADIIRTY	aridity
ADIITVY	avidity
ADIJMSS	masjids
ADIJMSU	Judaism
ADIJNOS	adjoins
ADIJNOT	adjoint
ADIKLOS	odalisk
ADIKMNN	mankind
ADIKMOS	mikados
ADIKMOU	daimoku
ADIKMRU	Makurdi
ADIKNPS	kidnaps
	skidpan
ADIKNSW	Dawkins
ADIKSTT	diktats
ADIKSWY	skidway
ADILLMM	milldam
ADILLTY	tidally
ADILLVY	validly
ADILLYY	daylily
ADILMNO	mondial
ADILMNR	mandril
ADILMNU	maudlin
ADILMOP	diploma
ADILMOU	alodium
ADILMOY	amyloid
ADILMPS	plasmid
ADILMSU	dualism
ADILNNV	Vinland
ADILNOR	ordinal
ADILNOS	dolinas
	ladinos
ADILNRU	diurnal
ADILNRY	randily
ADILNSS	islands
ADILNSU	sundial
ADILNSY	Lindsay
ADILOOZ	zooidal
ADILOPR	dipolar
ADILORT	dilator
ADILOTU	outlaid
ADILPRY	pyralid
	rapidly
ADILPST	plastid
ADILPSY	display
ADILPTU	plaudit
ADILPVY	vapidly
ADILQSU	squalid
ADILRSZ	lizards
	Szilard
ADILRTY	tardily
ADILSTU	dualist
ADILSTY	staidly
ADILTUY	duality
ADIMNNO	mondain
ADIMNOS	daimons
	domains
	madison
ADIMNRS	mandirs
ADIMORR	mirador
ADIMOST	diatoms
	mastoid
ADIMOSY	daimyos
ADIMOTT	mattoid
ADIMPRY	pyramid
ADIMRSS	disarms
ADIMRSY	myriads
ADIMSST	dismast
ADIMSSY	dismays
ADIMSTU	stadium
ADIMSWY	midways
ADINNOP	dipnoan
ADINNOR	andiron
ADINNPS	pindans
ADINNRS	innards
ADINNRW	indrawn
	winnard
ADINNSU	indunas
ADINOPP	oppidan
ADINOPR	padroni
	poniard
ADINOPT	pintado
ADINORS	inroads
	Nidaros
	ordains
	sadiron
ADINOSV	Novi Sad
ADINOTX	oxidant
ADINPST	pandits
	sandpit
ADINQRS	qindars
ADINRSU	durians
ADINRSW	inwards
ADINSTT	distant
ADINTTY	dittany
ADIOOSW	woodsia
ADIOPRR	airdrop
ADIOPRS	sparoid
ADIOPRT	parotid
ADIORST	astroid
ADIORSV	advisor
ADIORTU	auditor
ADIOSUV	Vaudois
ADIOSVW	disavow
ADIPRSS	sparids
ADIPRUU	Udaipur
ADIRRSS	sirdars
ADIRSSU	sardius
ADIRSTY	satyrid
ADIRSUY	dysuria
ADIRSVZ	vizards
ADIRSWZ	wizards
ADIRSZZ	izzards
ADISSST	sadists
ADISSYY	sayyids
ADJKOSU	judokas
ADJLLNY	Jylland
ADJLMOR	jarldom
ADJLNTU	Jutland
ADJNNOU	Don Juan
ADJNORU	adjourn
ADJORRU	adjuror
ADJSSTU	adjusts
ADKLMRU	mudlark
ADKLNRU	Kurland
ADKOPSU	padouks
ADKORWY	workday
ADKORYY	Aykroyd
ADKRSUU	Üsküdar
ADKRSWY	skyward
ADLLLNO	Lolland
ADLLMOY	modally
ADLLNOR	Rolland
ADLLNOW	lowland
ADLLNOY	nodally
ADLLNTY	Tyndall
ADLLOPR	pollard
ADLLORS	dollars
ADLMNOS	almonds
	dolmans
ADLMOOV	Moldova
ADLMORU	modular
ADLNNOR	norland
ADLNOOR	lardoon
	Orlando
ADLNOOS	doolans
ADLNOPU	poundal
ADLNORS	lardons
ADLNORU	nodular
ADLNOSS	soldans
ADLNOST	daltons
	sandlot
ADLNOSU	unloads
ADLNOSY	synodal
ADLNOTU	outland
ADLNPRT	Prandtl
ADLNPSU	uplands
ADLNRSU	lurdans
ADLNRTU	Rutland
ADLNRUY	laundry
ADLNSYY	Lyndsay
ADLOORW	Larwood
ADLOPRU	poulard
ADLORRW	warlord
ADLORSU	sudoral
ADLORUY	Our Lady
ADLOSSS	dossals
ADLOSTW	Ostwald
ADMMNSU	summand
ADMNOOR	doorman
	madrono
ADMNOOW	woodman
ADMNOOZ	madzoon
ADMNOQU	quondam
ADMNORT	dormant
	mordant
ADMNORY	Ormandy
ADMNOSS	damsons
ADMNOSU	osmunda
ADMNOSY	dynamos
ADMNSTU	dustman
ADMOORT	doormat
ADMOORY	dayroom
ADMOPST	Potsdam
ADMORRS	ramrods
ADMORST	stardom
	tsardom
ADMORSU	maduros
ADMORTW	madwort
ADMRSTU	durmast
	mustard
ADNNOOY	noonday
ADNNOSU	adnouns
ADNNRTU	dunnart
ADNNRUW	undrawn
ADNNSTU	Dunstan
ADNNSUY	Dunsany
ADNOORS	nardoos
ADNOORT	donator
	tandoor
	tornado
ADNOOSW	wandoos
ADNOPRS	pardons
ADNOPRU	pandour
ADNOPST	dopants
ADNORRS	Ronsard
ADNORST	Rostand
ADNORSW	onwards
ADNORTU	rotunda
ADNORTY	Drayton
ADNOSTU	astound
	Donatus
ADNPSTU	dustpan
	standup
ADNRSST	strands
ADNRSUW	sunward
	undraws
ADNSSTY	dynasts
ADNSTYY	dynasty
ADOOPSU	apodous
ADOOPSW	sapwood
ADOORWY	doorway
ADOOSTT	tostado
ADORSTW	towards
ADORSUU	arduous
ADORTUW	outward
ADORUZZ	Durazzo
ADPRSUW	upwards
ADSSTUU	Tussaud
ADSSTUW	sawdust
AEEEGGN	engagee
AEEEGKL	keelage
AEEEGLT	legatee
AEEEGNT	teenage
AEEEGPR	peerage

AEEEGPS seepage
AEEEGRT etagere
AEEEHLS healees
AEEEILN alienee
AEEEIRT eaterie
AEEELRS release
AEEELTV elevate
AEEEPPT Papeete
AEEFFLL felafel
AEEFHRT feather
AEEFILR leafier
AEEFILW alewife
AEEFIRS faeries
freesia
AEEFKRS fakeers
AEEFLLT fellate
leaflet
AEEFLMS females
AEEFLRT reflate
AEEFLRU ferulae
AEEFLRW welfare
AEEFLSU easeful
AEEFMNR freeman
AEEFMRR reframe
AEEFMRT fermate
AEEFNRS Farnese
AEEFNRU Freneau
AEEFORS Faeroes
Faroese
AEEFOTV foveate
AEEFRRS fearers
AEEFRRT ferrate
AEEFRST afreets
feaster
AEEFRTU feature
AEEFRWY freeway
AEEFSTT featest
AEEGGLT gateleg
AEEGGNR engager
AEEGGNS engages
AEEGGRU regauge
AEEGHNN Gehenna
AEEGHNW whangee
AEEGHSZ geezahs
AEEGILL galilee
AEEGILM mileage
AEEGILN lineage
AEEGILP epigeal
AEEGILW weigela
AEEGINP epigean
AEEGINR Erigena
AEEGIRT Reigate
AEEGIRU eugarie
AEEGJRS jaegers
AEEGLLS alleges
AEEGLLZ gazelle
AEEGLMN gleeman
melange
AEEGLMT meltage
AEEGLNR enlarge
general
gleaner
AEEGLNS Senegal
AEEGLNT elegant
AEEGLNU euglena
AEEGLNV evangel
AEEGLOR aerogel
AEEGLPS pelages
AEEGLRS galeres
regales
AEEGLRU leaguer
AEEGLRY eagerly
AEEGLRZ reglaze
AEEGLSS ageless
AEEGLST eaglets
legates
telegas
AEEGLSU leagues
AEEGLSV selvage
AEEGLTV vegetal
AEEGMMT gemmate
tagmeme
AEEGMNR germane
AEEGMNS maneges
menages
AEEGMSS megasse
message
AEEGMST gametes
metages
AEEGNNS ennages
AEEGNNV Genevan
AEEGNOP peonage
AEEGNPP genappe
AEEGNRS enrages
AEEGNRT grantee
greaten
negater
reagent
AEEGNRV avenger
engrave
AEEGNST negates
AEEGNSV avenges
AEEGNTT tentage
AEEGNTV ventage
AEEGNTW Newgate
AEEGOPS apogees
AEEGORV overage
AEEGOST goatees
AEEGPRS presage
AEEGPRU pugaree
AEEGRRS greaser
AEEGRRT greater
regrate
AEEGRRU reargue
AEEGRRW wagerer
AEEGRSS greases
AEEGRST restage
AEEGRSV greaves
AEEGRUZ guereza
AEEGSTT gestate
tagetes
AEEGTTZ gazette
AEEHHNT heathen
AEEHHRT heather
AEEHHST sheathe
AEEHINR herniae
AEEHIRV heavier
AEEHISV heavies
AEEHKMS hakeems
AEEHKNR hearken
AEEHLNT lethean
AEEHLPT heeltap
AEEHLRS healers
AEEHLRT haltere
leather
AEEHLRV Le Havre
AEEHLSS leashes
AEEHLSX exhales
AEEHLSY eyelash
AEEHLTT athlete
AEEHMNT methane
AEEHMRS hareems
mahseer
AEEHMRT thermae
AEEHMSU heaumes
AEEHMSV Evesham
AEEHNPS peahens
AEEHNPT haptene
heptane
AEEHNRT earthen
hearten
AEEHNSV heavens
AEEHNTW wheaten
AEEHPRS heapers
reshape
AEEHPRT preheat
AEEHPSS spahees
AEEHPUV upheave
AEEHRRS hearers
rehears
shearer
AEEHRSS hearses
AEEHRST aethers
heaters
reheats
Theresa
AEEHRSV heavers
AEEHRSW whereas
AEEHRTT theater
theatre
thereat
AEEHRTW weather
whereat
wreathe
AEEHSSV sheaves
AEEHSWY eyewash
AEEIKLP apelike
pealike
AEEIKLR earlike
leakier
AEEILMR Lamerie
mealier
AEEILMS mealies
AEEILNT lineate
AEEILPT epilate
pileate
AEEILRR earlier
learier
AEEILRS realise
AEEILRT atelier
AEEILRZ realize
AEEILTV elative
AEEIMNS meanies
nemesia
AEEIMNT etamine
matinee
AEEIMNX examine
AEEIMRS seamier
seriema
AEEIMRT emirate
meatier
AEEIMSS siamese
AEEIMST steamie
AEEINPR perinea
AEEINRT Aintree
arenite
retinae
trainee
AEEINST etesian
AEEINTV naivete
Venetia
AEEINVW inweave
AEEINVZ Venezia
AEEIORT etaerio
AEEIPRR pereira
AEEIPRS aperies
AEEIPSV peavies
AEEIPTX expiate
AEEIRRT Eretria
Eritrea
tearier
AEEIRRW wearier
AEEIRST aeriest
seriate
AEEIRSW wearies
AEEIRTT ariette
iterate
AEEISST easiest
AEEISVV evasive
AEEIUVX exuviae
AEEJKSS jakeses
AEEJNST sejeant
AEEKKNO kokanee
AEEKLNS alkenes
AEEKLRS leakers
AEEKMNS kamseen
AEEKMRS remakes
AEEKMRT meerkat
AEEKNNN nankeen
AEEKNNP kneepan
AEEKNRT retaken
AEEKNRW rewaken
wakener
AEEKNSW weakens
AEEKPRS speaker
AEEKRRT retaker
AEEKRRW wreaker
AEEKRST retakes

AEEKRSW	rewakes
AEEKRTW	tweaker
AEEKSTW	weakest
AEELLLS	alleles
AEELLMS	mallees
AEELLPS	Apelles
AEELLSS	sallees
AEELLST	lealest
AEELLWY	walleye
AEELMNP	empanel
	emplane
AEELMNR	reelman
AEELMNS	enamels
AEELMNV	velamen
AEELMNY	amylene
AEELMPR	empaler
AEELMPS	empales
AEELMPX	example
	exempla
AEELMSS	measles
AEELMST	Maltese
AEELMTU	emulate
AEELNNP	enplane
AEELNPS	spelean
AEELNRR	learner
	relearn
AEELNRT	enteral
	eternal
	teleran
AEELNRW	renewal
AEELNST	leanest
AEELNSV	enslave
	leavens
AEELNSW	Salween
AEELOPR	parolee
AEELOPX	poleaxe
AEELORS	areoles
AEELORU	aureole
AEELOST	oleates
AEELPRR	pearler
AEELPRS	leapers
	pleaser
	presale
	relapse
	repeals
AEELPRT	pleater
	prelate
AEELPRU	pleurae
AEELPSS	elapses
	pleases
AEELPTT	palette
	peltate
AEELPTU	epaulet
AEELQRU	lequear
AEELQSU	sequela
AEELRRT	realter
	relater
AEELRRX	relaxer
AEELRSS	earless
	leasers
	resales
	reseals
	sealers
AEELRST	elaters
	Laertes
	relates
	stealer
AEELRSV	leavers
	reveals
	several
	vealers
AEELRSX	relaxes
AEELRSY	sealery
AEELRTX	exalter
AEELRUV	revalue
AEELRUY	Euryale
AEELSST	teasels
AEELSSV	sleaves
AEELSSW	aweless
	weasels
AEELSTT	Seattle
AEELSTU	eluates
AEELSTV	veletas
AEELSTX	latexes
AEELSTZ	teazels
	teazles
AEELTTY	layette
AEELTVW	wavelet
AEEMMMR	maremme
AEEMMMS	mammees
AEEMMPY	empyema
AEEMMRT	ammeter
	metamer
AEEMNNO	anemone
AEEMNNP	penname
AEEMNNY	Mayenne
AEEMNRS	renames
AEEMNST	meanest
AEEMNSX	examens
AEEMORT	erotema
AEEMOSW	awesome
AEEMPRS	amperes
AEEMPRT	Tampere
	tempera
AEEMPTU	amputee
AEEMQRU	marquee
AEEMRRS	reamers
	smearer
AEEMRSS	Rameses
	seamers
AEEMRST	steamer
AEEMRSU	measure
AEEMSTX	taxemes
AEENNOT	neonate
AEENNOV	novenae
AEENNPT	pennate
	pentane
AEENNRS	ensnare
AEENNST	neatens
AEENNSX	annexes
AEENNTU	uneaten
AEENOPU	eupnoea
AEENOSU	aeneous
AEENPST	nepetas
	penates
AEENPSW	pawnees
AEENPSX	expanse
AEENQUU	Queneau
AEENRRS	earners
AEENRRT	terrane
AEENRRV	ravener
AEENRRY	yearner
AEENRST	earnest
	eastern
	nearest
AEENRSW	weaners
AEENRTT	entreat
	ratteen
	ternate
AEENRTV	nervate
	Tavener
	veteran
AEENRVY	Yerevan
AEENSST	entases
	sateens
	senates
	sensate
AEENSTT	neatest
AEENSUV	avenues
AEEOPRT	operate
AEEORST	roseate
AEEORSV	oversea
AEEORTV	overate
	overeat
AEEORVW	overawe
AEEPPRR	paperer
	prepare
	repaper
AEEPRRS	reapers
	spearer
AEEPRRT	taperer
AEEPRSS	asperse
	pareses
	serapes
AEEPRST	repeats
AEEPRSV	repaves
AEEPRTZ	trapeze
AEEPSST	pesetas
AEEPSSW	pesewas
AEEPSTT	septate
AEEPSVY	peaveys
AEEQRSU	quaeres
AEEQSTU	equates
AEERRRS	rearers
AEERRSS	erasers
AEERRST	serrate
	tearers
AEERRSU	erasure
AEERRSW	swearer
	wearers
AEERRTT	retreat
	treater
AEERRTW	waterer
AEERRUX	Auxerre
AEERRVW	waverer
AEERSST	easters
	reseats
	teasers
	tessera
AEERSSU	reseaus
AEERSTT	estreat
	restate
AEERSTU	austere
AEERSTW	sweater
AEERSUX	reseaux
AEERSVW	weavers
AEESSSW	seesaws
AEESSTT	estates
AEESTTT	testate
AEESWXY	waxeyes
AEFFGIL	fig leaf
AEFFGIR	giraffe
AEFFGRS	gaffers
AEFFGRU	gauffer
AEFFHRS	Shaffer
AEFFIPS	piaffes
AEFFIST	taffies
AEFFISX	affixes
AEFFKOP	offpeak
AEFFKOR	rakeoff
AEFFKOT	takeoff
AEFFLLY	flyleaf
AEFFLNS	snaffle
AEFFLRR	raffler
AEFFLRS	raffles
AEFFLRU	fearful
AEFFLRW	waffler
AEFFLSW	waffles
AEFFLSY	yaffles
AEFFLTU	fateful
AEFFMRU	earmuff
AEFFNST	naffest
AEFFOVW	waveoff
AEFFQRU	quaffer
AEFFRST	restaff
	staffer
AEFGGGO	foggage
AEFGGLR	flagger
AEFGIKN	Kaifeng
AEFGILN	finagle
	leafing
AEFGILO	foliage
AEFGILR	fragile
AEFGINR	fearing
AEFGINU	Fuegian
AEFGINZ	feazing
AEFGIRT	frigate
AEFGIRU	refugia
AEFGITU	fatigue
AEFGLMN	flagmen
AEFGLNR	flanger
AEFGLNS	flanges
AEFGLOT	flotage
AEFGLOW	flowage
AEFGNRR	franger
AEFGNRT	engraft
AEFGOOT	footage
AEFGORR	forager

AEFGORS forages
AEFGORV forgave
AEFGRRT grafter
AEFGRTY Freytag
AEFHINS Fa-hsien
AEFHIRT faither
AEFHIRW wharfie
AEFHLLS fellahs
AEFHLRS flasher
AEFHLSS flashes
AEFHLTU hateful
AEFHRRT farther
AEFHRST fathers
hafters
AEFIILR Alfieri
Falerii
AEFIILT filiate
AEFIIRS fairies
AEFIJOS feijoas
AEFIKLN fanlike
AEFIKLR flakier
AEFIKLT fatlike
AEFILLM famille
AEFILMN inflame
AEFILNS finales
AEFILNT inflate
AEFILNU infulae
AEFILNV flavine
AEFILOT foliate
AEFILPT fleapit
AEFILRR frailer
AEFILRU failure
AEFILRV favrile
AEFILSS falsies
AEFILTT flattie
AEFIMNR fireman
AEFIMNS famines
AEFIMOR foamier
AEFIMRR firearm
AEFINNS fainnes
fannies
AEFINNT infante
AEFINNZ fanzine
AEFINPR firepan
AEFINRR refrain
AEFINRS infares
AEFINRT fainter
AEFINTX antefix
AEFIQRU aquifer
AEFIRRR farrier
Ferrari
AEFIRRZ Frazier
AEFIRSS fraises
AEFIRST fairest
AEFIRTT fattier
AEFISST fasties
fiestas
AEFISTT fatties
AEFISTX fixates
AEFJNST fanjets
AEFKLNR Falkner
flanker
AEFKLNS fankles
AEFKLOS Lefkoşa
AEFKLRS flakers
AEFKLRT fartlek
AEFKLST flasket
AEFKLUW wakeful
AEFKNRR franker
AEFKORS forsake
AEFLLNN flannel
AEFLLOT floatel
AEFLLRR Farrell
AEFLLRS fallers
AEFLLSY falsely
AEFLLTT flatlet
AEFLMNS flamens
AEFLMOR femoral
AEFLMRS flamers
AEFLNOV flavone
AEFLNRU flaneur
frenula
funeral
AEFLNTT flatten
AEFLNUU faunule
AEFLOOV foveola
AEFLOPW peafowl
AEFLORS loafers
safrole
AEFLORT floater
floreat
refloat
AEFLPPR flapper
AEFLPRS felspar
AEFLPRY palfrey
AEFLRST Falster
falters
AEFLRSU ferulas
refusal
AEFLRSY flayers
AEFLRTT flatter
AEFLRTU tearful
AEFLRZZ frazzle
AEFLSST falsest
fatless
AEFMNNY Feynman
AEFMNOR foramen
foreman
AEFMNRU fraenum
AEFMORR forearm
AEFMORT formate
AEFMRRS farmers
framers
AEFNNOT Fontane
AEFNNRS fanners
AEFNOPR profane
AEFNORR foreran
AEFNORT Torfaen
AEFNRSS farness
AEFNRSW fawners
AEFNSST fastens
fatness
AEFNSSU snafues
AEFNSTT fattens
AEFOPRW forepaw
AEFORRV favorer
overfar
AEFORRY forayer
AEFORSW foresaw
AEFOSST fatsoes
AEFPPRS frappes
AEFRRST fraters
rafters
strafer
AEFRSST fasters
strafes
AEFRSTU faurest
AEFRSTW fretsaw
wafters
AEFRTTU tartufe
AEFRTUW wafture
AEFRWYZ frawzey
AEFSSTT fastest
saftest
AEFSTTT fattest
AEGGGLS gaggles
AEGGGLU luggage
AEGGGRS gaggers
AEGGGRY gaggery
AEGGHLR haggler
AEGGHLS haggles
AEGGHMO hemagog
AEGGIJR jaggier
AEGGIMS maggies
AEGGINR gearing
AEGGINS signage
AEGGIOR Georgia
AEGGIOS isagoge
AEGGIRU garigue
AEGGISW swaggie
AEGGJRY jaggery
AEGGLNO agelong
AEGGLNR gangrel
AEGGLRR gargler
AEGGLRS gargles
raggles
AEGGLRW waggler
AEGGLRY greylag
AEGGLSW waggles
AEGGNRS gangers
granges
naggers
AEGGNTU Gauteng
AEGGRSS aggress
saggers
AEGGRST stagger
taggers
AEGGRSU gaugers
AEGGRSW swagger
AEGGRTY gargety
AEGGRWY waggery
AEGGSWW gewgaws
AEGHHNU Huang He
AEGHHUY Haughey
AEGHIKL haglike
AEGHILN healing
AEGHILR Raleigh
AEGHINP heaping
AEGHINR hearing
AEGHINT gahnite
heating
AEGHINV heaving
AEGHINZ genizah
AEGHIRS hegiras
AEGHISS geishas
AEGHLNO halogen
AEGHLOU La Hogue
AEGHLRU laugher
AEGHLTW thalweg
AEGHMNN hangmen
AEGHMOS homages
ohmages
AEGHMRS Gresham
AEGHMSU meshuga
AEGHNOX hexagon
AEGHNRS hangers
rehangs
sherang
AEGHNSS gnashes
AEGHNST stengah
AEGHOPY hypogea
AEGHORS gheraos
AEGHOST hostage
AEGHRST gathers
AEGIIMN imagine
AEGIINR Igraine
Nigeria
AEGIKLN leaking
linkage
AEGIKLT glaiket
AEGIKNP peaking
AEGIKNS sinkage
AEGIKNT Keating
AEGIKPR garpike
AEGIKRW gawkier
AEGILLL illegal
AEGILLN nigella
AEGILLO Galileo
AEGILLP pillage
AEGILLR Allegri
AEGILLT tillage
AEGILLU ligulae
AEGILLV village
AEGILLY agilely
AEGILMR gremial
AEGILMS milages
AEGILNN aneling
leaning
AEGILNP leaping
pealing
AEGILNR engrail
nargile
realign
AEGILNS leasing
sealing
AEGILNT elating
gelatin
genital

AEGILNU	linguae
AEGILNV	leaving
AEGILOS	goalies
	soilage
AEGILOU	eulogia
AEGILPS	Legaspi
	paigles
AEGILRR	glarier
AEGILRS	Algiers
AEGILRZ	glazier
AEGILSS	ligases
AEGILST	aiglets
	ligates
AEGILSV	glaives
AEGILTU	glutaei
AEGIMMR	gammier
AEGIMNN	meaning
	Meninga
AEGIMNR	germina
	mangier
	reaming
AEGIMNS	enigmas
	gamines
	seaming
AEGIMNT	mintage
	teaming
	tegmina
AEGIMOS	imagoes
AEGIMPR	epigram
	primage
AEGIMPS	magpies
AEGIMPT	pigmeat
AEGIMRR	armiger
AEGIMRS	gisarme
	mirages
AEGIMRT	migrate
	ragtime
AEGIMRY	imagery
AEGIMST	gamiest
	sigmate
AEGIMSV	misgave
AEGINNR	earning
	engrain
	grannie
	nearing
AEGINNT	anteing
	antigen
	gentian
AEGINNU	anguine
	guanine
AEGINNV	Angevin
AEGINNW	weaning
AEGINNY	yeaning
AEGINOR	iron age
AEGINOS	agonies
	agonise
AEGINOZ	agonize
AEGINPP	genipap
AEGINPR	reaping
AEGINPS	spaeing
AEGINRR	angrier
	earring

	grainer
	rangier
	rearing
AEGINRS	earings
	erasing
	gainers
	regains
	searing
	seringa
AEGINRT	granite
	ingrate
	tangier
	tearing
AEGINRV	reaving
	vinegar
AEGINRW	wearing
AEGINRZ	zingare
AEGINST	easting
	ingesta
	seating
	teasing
AEGINSU	guineas
AEGINSY	easying
AEGINTV	vintage
AEGINTW	Wingate
AEGINTZ	tzigane
AEGINVW	weaving
AEGIORV	Argovie
AEGIOSV	Segovia
AEGIPPR	gappier
AEGIPRR	grapier
AEGIPRS	prisage
AEGIPRU	Perugia
AEGIRRZ	grazier
AEGIRSS	gassier
AEGIRST	aigrets
	gaiters
	seagirt
	stagier
AEGIRSV	Gervais
	gravies
	rivages
AEGIRSW	earwigs
AEGIRTU	Gautier
AEGIRTV	virgate
AEGIRUY	yugarie
AEGIRUZ	gauzier
AEGISST	ageists
AEGISSV	visages
AEGJLNR	jangler
AEGJLNS	jangles
AEGKLLS	Gaskell
AEGKLOU	kagoule
AEGKMRY	kerygma
AEGKNOS	Kaesŏng
AEGKSST	gaskets
AEGLLLY	legally
AEGLLNO	galleon
AEGLLNR	langrel
AEGLLNY	langley
AEGLLOR	allegro
AEGLLOT	tollage

AEGLLRY	allergy
	gallery
	largely
	regally
AEGLLSU	seagull
	sullage
	ullages
AEGLLSY	galleys
AEGLLTU	gluteal
AEGLMNR	mangler
AEGLMNS	mangels
	mangles
AEGLMPU	plumage
AEGLMSV	maglevs
AEGLNOT	tangelo
AEGLNOU	Angelou
AEGLNPR	grapnel
AEGLNPS	spangle
AEGLNRS	anglers
	erlangs
	largens
AEGLNRT	tangler
AEGLNRU	granule
AEGLNRW	wangler
	wrangle
AEGLNST	langest
	tangles
AEGLNSU	angelus
	lagunes
AEGLNSW	wangles
AEGLNTT	gantlet
AEGLNTU	languet
AEGLNUU	ungulae
AEGLNUW	gunwale
AEGLOPR	pergola
AEGLORS	gaolers
AEGLORT	gloater
	legator
	Ortegal
AEGLORV	vorlage
AEGLOSS	glossae
AEGLOST	legatos
AEGLOTV	voltage
AEGLPPR	grapple
AEGLPRU	earplug
	graupel
	plaguer
AEGLPSS	gapless
AEGLPSU	plagues
AEGLPUY	plaguey
AEGLRRU	regular
AEGLRSS	largess
AEGLRST	largest
AEGLRSV	gravels
	verglas
AEGLRSY	argyles
AEGLRSZ	glazers
AEGLRTU	tegular
AEGLRTY	greatly
AEGLRVY	gravely
AEGLSSS	gasless
	glasses

AEGLSTT	gestalt
AEGLSTW	talwegs
AEGLTUV	vulgate
AEGLUUY	guayule
AEGLUVY	vaguely
AEGMMRS	gammers
	grammes
AEGMMRU	rummage
AEGMNNO	agnomen
AEGMNOR	marengo
	megaron
AEGMNOS	gamones
	mangoes
AEGMNOT	magneto
	megaton
	montage
AEGMNPY	pygmean
AEGMNRS	engrams
	germans
	mangers
AEGMNRT	garment
	margent
AEGMNRY	Germany
AEGMNST	magnets
AEGMNSW	swagmen
AEGMNTU	augment
	mutagen
AEGMOOR	moorage
AEGMOXY	exogamy
AEGMRSU	murages
AEGMSUY	magueys
AEGMSUZ	zeugmas
AEGNNOR	Argonne
	Garonne
AEGNNOT	tonnage
AEGNNRT	regnant
AEGNNRU	gunnera
AEGNNST	gannets
AEGNNTT	tangent
AEGNNTU	tunnage
AEGNOOR	oregano
AEGNORR	groaner
AEGNORS	onagers
	oranges
AEGNORT	negator
AEGNORW	wagoner
AEGNOST	tangoes
AEGNOSY	nosegay
AEGNPRT	trepang
AEGNRRS	garners
	rangers
AEGNRRT	granter
AEGNRST	garnets
	Sargent
	strange
AEGNRSW	gnawers
AEGNRTT	Garnett
AEGNSSY	ganseys
	gayness
AEGNTYZ	Yangtze
AEGOPRT	portage
	potager

AEGOPRU	Guaporé
AEGOPST	gestapo
	postage
AEGOPTT	pottage
AEGORRT	garrote
AEGORST	storage
	toerags
AEGORTT	garotte
AEGORTU	outrage
AEGORVY	voyager
AEGOSSU	gaseous
AEGOSTU	outages
AEGOSTW	stowage
	towages
AEGOSVY	voyages
AEGOTTV	gavotte
AEGPRRS	grasper
	sparger
AEGPRSS	gaspers
	sparges
AEGPRST	pargets
AEGPRSW	gawpers
AEGPSSU	pegasus
AEGPSTU	upstage
AEGRRST	garrets
	garters
	graters
AEGRRSU	arguers
AEGRRSV	gravers
AEGRRSZ	grazers
AEGRRTT	Garrett
AEGRRUV	gravure
AEGRSSS	gassers
	grasses
AEGRSST	stagers
AEGRSSU	arguses
	saugers
AEGRSSW	swagers
AEGRSTT	targets
AEGRSTV	gravest
AEGRSTY	grayest
	gyrates
AEGRSUZ	Zagreus
AEGSTUU	auguste
AEGSTUV	vaguest
AEGTTTU	guttate
AEHHJOV	Jehovah
AEHHJPT	Japheth
AEHHLTY	healthy
AEHHMSY	Heysham
AEHHNSV	Heshvan
AEHHRRS	harsher
AEHHRST	hearths
AEHHSST	sheaths
AEHIIRR	hairier
AEHIJRS	hejiras
AEHIKLT	hatlike
AEHIKNS	hankies
AEHIKPS	peakish
AEHIKRS	shakier
AEHIKST	shitake
AEHIKSW	weakish
AEHILMO	hemiola
AEHILMS	Ishmael
AEHILNR	hernial
	inhaler
AEHILNS	inhales
AEHILNT	Antheil
AEHILNY	hyaline
AEHILOR	airhole
AEHILPR	harelip
AEHILPT	haplite
AEHILRS	hailers
AEHILRT	lathier
AEHILRU	haulier
AEHILSS	sheilas
AEHILSW	shawlie
AEHILTY	hyalite
AEHILUV	vihuela
AEHILVY	heavily
AEHIMMR	hammier
AEHIMNR	Manhire
AEHIMNS	Hsia-men
AEHIMNT	hematin
AEHIMNY	hymenia
AEHIMPR	Ephraim
AEHIMPS	phaeism
AEHIMRS	mishear
AEHIMSS	mashies
	messiah
AEHIMST	atheism
AEHINPR	heparin
AEHINPS	Pahsien
AEHINRS	hernias
AEHINRT	hairnet
	inearth
AEHINSS	hessian
AEHINSV	evanish
AEHINSW	wahines
AEHIORR	hoarier
AEHIPPR	happier
AEHIPPT	epitaph
AEHIPRS	harpies
	sharpie
AEHIPSS	aphesis
AEHIQSU	quashie
AEHIRRR	harrier
AEHIRRS	harries
AEHIRST	hastier
AEHIRSU	Herisau
AEHIRSW	washier
AEHIRWY	haywire
AEHISST	ashiest
	saithes
	stashie
AEHISTT	atheist
AEHISTZ	haziest
AEHISVY	yeshiva
AEHITTW	thwaite
AEHKLOY	Hoylake
AEHKMSS	samekhs
AEHKMWY	Wykeham
AEHKNRS	hankers
	harkens
AEHKOSS	shakoes
AEHKPSU	shakeup
AEHKRSS	kashers
	shakers
AEHKRSW	hawkers
AEHKRTY	Kythera
AEHKSSY	ashkeys
AEHLLMN	Hellman
AEHLLRW	Harwell
AEHLLUV	helluva
AEHLMNN	Lehmann
AEHLMNO	manhole
AEHLMNY	hymenal
AEHLMOP	Omphale
AEHLMOR	armhole
AEHLMPS	pelhams
AEHLMRT	thermal
AEHLMRU	humeral
AEHLMST	hamlets
AEHLNOT	ethanol
AEHLNRT	enthral
AEHLNSS	hansels
AEHLNSU	unleash
AEHLOPR	ephoral
AEHLOPT	taphole
AEHLORT	loather
AEHLOSS	asshole
AEHLOST	loathes
AEHLPRS	spheral
AEHLPSS	hapless
	plashes
AEHLPSU	Alpheus
AEHLPSY	shapely
	Shapley
AEHLRSS	ashlers
	lashers
	slasher
AEHLRST	halters
	harslet
	lathers
	slather
	thalers
AEHLRSU	haulers
AEHLRSW	whalers
AEHLRTU	Hérault
AEHLRTY	earthly
	Hartley
	lathery
AEHLSSS	hassles
	slashes
AEHLSST	haslets
	Hasselt
	hatless
AEHLSTT	stealth
AEHLTWY	wealthy
AEHMMOT	Mahomet
AEHMMRS	hammers
	shammer
AEHMMSS	shammes
AEHMMTT	Hammett
AEHMNNR	Hermann
AEHMNOR	menorah
AEHMNPY	nymphae
AEHMNRS	Sherman
AEHMNST	anthems
	hetmans
AEHMOPT	apothem
AEHMPRS	hampers
AEHMPTY	empathy
AEHMRRS	harmers
AEHMRSS	marshes
	mashers
	smasher
AEHMRST	Amherst
	hamster
AEHMRWX	Wrexham
AEHMSSS	smashes
AEHMSTT	shmatte
AEHMTTW	Matthew
AEHMUZZ	mezuzah
AEHNOPT	phaeton
	phonate
AEHNORS	hoarsen
AEHNORT	another
AEHNORV	Hanover
AEHNOSX	hexosan
AEHNPPS	happens
AEHNPRS	sharpen
AEHNPRT	panther
AEHNRSS	harness
AEHNRST	anthers
	thenars
AEHNRTU	haunter
	unearth
	urethan
AEHNRTX	narthex
AEHNSST	hastens
	snathes
AEHNSTW	Tshwane
AEHNSTY	astheny
	shantey
AEHOORT	toheroa
AEHOPST	teashop
AEHORRS	hoarser
AEHORST	earshot
AEHORSX	hoaxers
AEHORTU	Thoreau
AEHPPRS	perhaps
AEHPPSU	shapeup
AEHPRRS	harpers
	sharper
AEHPRSS	phrases
	seraphs
	shapers
	sherpas
AEHPRST	threaps
AEHPRSW	prewash
AEHPRTY	therapy
AEHPSST	spathes
AEHPSTY	Pytheas
AEHQSSU	quashes
AEHRRSS	rashers
	sharers
AEHRRTU	urethra

AEHRSST	shaster	**AEIKLMR**	armlike	**AEILMMS**	melisma	**AEILNSV**	alevins
	trashes	**AEIKLNO**	kaoline	**AEILMNN**	Lemnian		valines
AEHRSSV	shavers	**AEIKLNR**	lankier		lineman	**AEILNSY**	elysian
AEHRSSW	hawsers	**AEIKLNT**	antlike		melanin	**AEILNTU**	alunite
	washers	**AEIKLNU**	unalike	**AEILMNP**	impanel	**AEILNTV**	ventail
AEHRSTT	hatters	**AEIKLOR**	oarlike		maniple	**AEILNVY**	naively
	shatter	**AEIKLOT**	keitloa	**AEILMNR**	manlier	**AEILOPR**	peloria
	threats	**AEIKLRR**	larkier		marline	**AEILORV**	variole
AEHRSTV	harvest	**AEIKLRT**	ratlike		mineral	**AEILOST**	isolate
	thraves		talkier	**AEILMNS**	malines	**AEILOTV**	violate
AEHRSTW	thawers	**AEIKLRW**	warlike		menials	**AEILPPR**	applier
	wreaths	**AEIKLST**	lakiest		seminal	**AEILPPS**	applies
AEHRSVW	wharves		talkies	**AEILMNT**	ailment	**AEILPRT**	platier
AEHRSWY	washery	**AEIKLSW**	sawlike		aliment	**AEILPRV**	prevail
AEHRSXY	hyraxes	**AEIKLWX**	waxlike	**AEILMNU**	Manuel I	**AEILPSS**	espials
AEHRTUU	hauteur	**AEIKMNP**	pikeman	**AEILMNY**	El Minya		lipases
AEHSSST	stashes	**AEIKMNR**	mankier	**AEILMOR**	Morelia		palsies
AEHSSSW	swashes		ramekin	**AEILMPR**	impaler	**AEILPST**	platies
AEHSSTW	swathes	**AEIKMST**	mistake		impearl		talipes
AEHSTUX	exhaust	**AEIKNRR**	narkier		lempira	**AEILPSY**	paisley
AEIIJMS	James II	**AEIKNRS**	snakier		palmier	**AEILQTU**	liquate
AEIIKNT	kainite	**AEIKNRT**	Katrine	**AEILMPS**	impales		tequila
AEIIKWZ	Azikiwe		Kénitra	**AEILMRS**	mailers	**AEILRRS**	railers
AEIILMP	lipemia		keratin		realism	**AEILRRT**	retiral
AEIILNN	aniline	**AEIKNRU**	Ukraine		remails		retrial
AEIILNR	airline	**AEIKNSS**	kinases	**AEILMRT**	Latimer		trailer
AEIILNX	exilian	**AEIKNST**	intakes		maltier	**AEILRRU**	Laurier
AEIILRR	lairier		kentias		marlite	**AEILRSS**	airless
AEIILRS	Israeli	**AEIKNSX**	Xenakis	**AEILMSS**	aimless		sailers
	Salieri	**AEIKNSY**	kyanise		samiels		serails
AEIILSS	liaises	**AEIKNTY**	kyanite	**AEILMTY**	meatily		serials
	silesia	**AEIKNYZ**	kyanize	**AEILNNY**	inanely	**AEILRST**	realist
AEIIMNT	intimae	**AEIKOST**	oakiest	**AEILNOP**	opaline		retails
AEIIMPR	imperia	**AEIKPRR**	parkier	**AEILNOR**	aileron		saltier
AEIIMRT	airtime	**AEIKPRW**	pawkier		alienor		saltire
AEIIMRV	viremia	**AEIKQRU**	quakier	**AEILNOS**	anisole		slatier
AEIIMST	amities	**AEIKRRS**	sarkier	**AEILNOT**	elation	**AEILRSV**	revisal
AEIIMTT	imitate	**AEIKRSS**	kaisers		toenail	**AEILRSW**	wailers
AEIINNR	Aneirin	**AEIKRSY**	Kayseri	**AEILNPR**	plainer	**AEILRTT**	tertial
AEIINNS	asinine	**AEILLLM**	Melilla		praline	**AEILRTU**	uralite
AEIINPR	Pierian	**AEILLMN**	manille	**AEILNPS**	alpines	**AEILRTY**	irately
AEIINRR	rainier	**AEILLNR**	ralline		spaniel		reality
AEIINRT	inertia	**AEILLNU**	uillean	**AEILNPT**	pantile		tearily
AEIINST	isatine	**AEILLOV**	alveoli	**AEILNPU**	Pauline	**AEILRVV**	revival
AEIINTX	axinite	**AEILLPR**	pallier	**AEILNPX**	explain	**AEILRVY**	virelay
AEIIPRR	prairie	**AEILLPY**	epyllia	**AEILNRS**	aliners	**AEILRWY**	wearily
AEIIRRV	riviera	**AEILLQU**	Lalique		Linares	**AEILSSS**	lassies
AEIIRST	airiest	**AEILLRR**	rallier		nailers	**AEILSSV**	valises
AEIISSV	Eivissa	**AEILLRS**	rallies	**AEILNRT**	latrine	**AEILSTU**	situlae
AEIITTV	vitiate		sallier		ratline	**AEILSTV**	estival
AEIJKLW	jawlike	**AEILLRT**	literal		reliant	**AEILSTZ**	laziest
AEIJKMN	Eijkman		tallier		retinal	**AEILTTU**	Lutetia
AEIJLNV	javelin		triella		trenail	**AEILTUV**	Lietuva
AEIJLRS	jailers	**AEILLSS**	sallies	**AEILNRV**	ravelin	**AEILTVV**	Tel Aviv
AEIJMMR	jammier	**AEILLST**	Liestal	**AEILNRX**	relaxin	**AEILTVY**	vilayet
AEIJMNS	jasmine		sitella	**AEILNRY**	inlayer	**AEILUVX**	exuvial
AEIJMSV	James IV		tailles	**AEILNST**	elastin	**AEIMMMS**	mammies
	James VI		tallies		entails	**AEIMMNS**	misname
AEIJRSV	jarvies	**AEILLSW**	wallies		nailset	**AEIMMPS**	spammie
AEIJRZZ	jazzier	**AEILLUV**	eluvial		salient	**AEIMMRS**	maimers
AEIKKST	takkies	**AEILLVX**	vexilla		slainte		rammies
AEIKLMN	manlike	**AEILMMN**	mailmen	**AEILNSU**	insulae	**AEIMMRT**	marmite

	trammie
AEIMMSS	sammies
AEIMMST	tammies
AEIMNNR	Riemann
AEIMNNT	mannite
AEIMNOR	moraine
	romaine
AEIMNOT	amniote
AEIMNRR	mariner
AEIMNRS	marines
	remains
	seminar
AEIMNRT	meranti
	minaret
	raiment
AEIMNRV	Minerva
AEIMNRW	wireman
AEIMNSS	Massine
	Messina
	samisen
AEIMNST	inmates
AEIMNSW	Wiseman
AEIMNTV	Vietnam
AEIMNTY	amenity
AEIMOOP	ipomoea
AEIMOPR	emporia
AEIMORR	armoire
AEIMOST	atomies
	atomise
AEIMOTX	toxemia
AEIMOTZ	atomize
AEIMPRS	impresa
AEIMPRT	primate
AEIMPRV	vampire
AEIMPSS	impasse
AEIMPST	impaste
	pastime
AEIMRRR	marrier
AEIMRRS	marries
AEIMRSS	massier
	sarmies
AEIMRST	Artemis
	imarets
	maestri
	Maistre
	smartie
AEIMRSY	rimayes
AEIMRTU	muriate
AEIMRTW	wartime
AEIMSST	Matisse
	tamises
AEIMSSV	massive
	mavises
AEIMSSW	swamies
AEIMSSY	myiases
AEIMSTT	matiest
AEIMSTZ	maziest
	mestiza
AEIMSXX	maxixes
AEINNNS	nannies
AEINNPR	pannier
AEINNPT	pinnate
AEINNRS	insnare
AEINNRT	entrain
	trannie
AEINNRU	aneurin
AEINNSW	swannie
AEINOPZ	epizoan
AEINORS	erasion
AEINORT	Aretino
AEINOST	Estonia
AEINOSV	evasion
AEINOXZ	oxazine
AEINPPR	nappier
AEINPPS	nappies
AEINPRT	painter
	pertain
	repaint
AEINPSS	pansies
AEINPST	panties
	patines
	sapient
AEINPSZ	Penzias
AEINPTT	patient
AEINPTU	petunia
AEINQTU	antique
	quinate
AEINRRS	sierran
AEINRRT	retrain
	terrain
	trainer
AEINRSS	Resnais
	sarnies
AEINRST	antsier
	nastier
	retains
	retinas
	retsina
	stainer
	stearin
AEINRSV	ravines
	Servian
AEINRTT	intreat
	iterant
	nattier
	nitrate
	tertian
AEINRTU	taurine
	uranite
	urinate
AEINRTW	tinware
AEINRVV	vervain
AEINSST	entasis
	nasties
	sestina
	Staines
	tansies
	tisanes
AEINSSV	vinasse
AEINSTT	instate
	satinet
AEINSTU	aunties
	sinuate
AEINSTV	natives
	vainest
AEINSTX	sextain
AEINSTZ	zaniest
AEINSVV	navvies
AEINSWY	anywise
AEINTVY	naivety
AEINTXY	anxiety
AEIOPRS	soapier
AEIOPST	opiates
AEIOQSU	sequoia
AEIORSV	ovaries
AEIOSST	Ossetia
	sosatie
AEIOSTT	toastie
AEIOSTZ	azotise
AEIOTZZ	azotize
AEIPPPR	pappier
AEIPPPS	pappies
AEIPPRS	apprise
	sappier
AEIPPRT	periapt
AEIPPRZ	apprize
	zappier
AEIPRRS	aspirer
	parries
	praiser
	rapiers
	repairs
AEIPRSS	aspires
	paresis
	praises
	Serapis
AEIPRST	pairest
	parties
	pastier
	piaster
	piastre
	pirates
	traipse
AEIPRSU	Piraeus
	upraise
AEIPRSV	parvise
AEIPRTT	partite
AEIPRTV	private
AEIPRTW	wiretap
AEIPRXY	pyrexia
AEIPSSS	asepsis
AEIPSST	pasties
	patsies
AEIPSSV	passive
	pavises
AEIPSTT	patties
AEIPTXY	epitaxy
AEIRRRT	tarrier
AEIRRRV	arriver
AEIRRSS	arrises
	raisers
	sierras
AEIRRST	tarries
	tarsier
AEIRRSV	arrives
AEIRRTT	rattier
	tartier
AEIRRTU	Etruria
AEIRRTY	retiary
AEIRSSS	sassier
AEIRSST	arsiest
	sairest
	satires
AEIRSSU	sauries
AEIRSTT	artiest
	artiste
	attires
	ratites
	striate
	tastier
AEIRSTV	vastier
AEIRSTW	waiters
	wariest
AEIRSVV	savvier
AEIRSVW	waivers
AEIRTTT	tattier
	titrate
AEIRTUZ	azurite
AEIRTVY	variety
AEISSST	siestas
	tassies
AEISSSW	wiseass
AEISSSZ	assizes
AEISSUV	suasive
AEISSUX	auxesis
AEISSVV	savvies
AEISTTT	tatties
AEISTTU	situate
AEISTTV	stative
AEISTTY	satiety
AEISTVW	waviest
AEISTWX	waxiest
AEISUVY	Iyeyasu
AEITTTV	vittate
AEJJLNU	jejunal
AEJLLOV	Vallejo
AEJLNUV	juvenal
AEJLOSU	jalouse
	jealous
AEJMMRS	jammers
AEJMNOS	Jameson
AEJMRST	ramjets
AEJMSTY	majesty
AEJNNOS	joannes
AEJNORT	Tanjore
AEJNOSS	San Jose
	San José
AEJPRSS	jaspers
AEJRRTT	Jarrett
AEJRSVY	jarveys
AEJRSZZ	jazzers
AEKKNRS	krakens
AEKKRRY	Kérkyra
AEKLNRS	rankles
AEKLNST	anklets
	lankest
AEKLNSY	alkynes
AEKLOST	skatole

AEKLOTU Tokelau
AEKLPRS sparkle
AEKLPSS splakes
AEKLRRS larkers
AEKLRSS slakers
AEKLRST stalker
talkers
AEKLRSW walkers
AEKLSST laskets
AEKLSTU auklets
AEKMNOS sokeman
AEKMNRU Kamerun
unmaker
AEKMNSU unmakes
AEKMPSU makeups
AEKMRRS markers
remarks
AEKMRSS maskers
AEKMRST markets
AEKMRSU kumeras
AEKNNRT Kärnten
AEKNOPS Spokane
AEKNPPR knapper
AEKNPRS spanker
AEKNPSU unspeak
AEKNRRS rankers
AEKNRSS kranses
AEKNRST rankest
tankers
AEKNRSW wankers
AEKNRVY knavery
AEKNSSU ankuses
AEKOPRS presoak
AEKOPTZ Zátopek
AEKORSS soakers
AEKOSTV voetsak
AEKOTTU outtake
takeout
AEKPSSY passkey
AEKPSTU uptakes
AEKQRSU quakers
AEKQSSU squeaks
AEKQSUY squeaky
AEKRRST starker
AEKRSST skaters
strakes
streaks
taskers
AEKRSTY Starkey
streaky
AEKSWYY keyways
AELLMNS Mansell
AELLMNU lumenal
AELLMRS smaller
AELLMRV Marvell
AELLMST mallets
AELLMSU malleus
AELLMWX maxwell
AELLNOV novella
AELLNPR Parnell
AELLNPY penally
AELLNUU lunulae
AELLNVY venally
AELLOPW Walpole
AELLORS rosella
AELLORT reallot
AELLORV allover
overall
AELLOSS loessal
AELLPRU pleural
AELLPST pallets
AELLPTY playlet
AELLQUY equally
AELLRRU allurer
AELLRST stellar
AELLRSU allures
laurels
AELLRTY alertly
AELLRVY ravelly
AELLSST sallets
AELLSSW lawless
AELLSTT tallest
AELLSTW wallets
AELLSTY stalely
AELLSVY valleys
AELLTUU ululate
AELLUVV valvule
AELMMNO mamelon
AELMMNS almsmen
AELMMOY myeloma
AELMMRS slammer
AELMMRT trammel
AELMMST stammel
AELMMSY malmsey
AELMNOR almoner
AELMNOT lomenta
Montale
telamon
AELMNPR lampern
Perlman
AELMNRU numeral
AELMNRV Malvern
AELMNSS manless
AELMNST laments
mantels
mantles
AELMNTT mantlet
AELMOPR Palermo
AELMOPU ampoule
AELMOPY maypole
AELMORT molerat
AELMORU morulae
AELMORV removal
AELMORW Marlowe
AELMOSS molasse
AELMOST maltose
AELMOSY amylose
AELMOTT matelot
AELMPRS lampers
palmers
sampler
AELMPRT templar
trample
AELMPRY lamprey
AELMPSS mapless
samples
AELMPSU ampules
AELMPTU plumate
AELMRSS armless
AELMRST armlets
AELMRSU maulers
serumal
AELMRSV marvels
AELMRTT martlet
AELMRTU relatum
AELMSST matless
AELMSTU amulets
muletas
AELNNPR planner
AELNNRS lanners
AELNNRT lantern
AELNNRU unlearn
AELNNTU annulet
AELNOPT Lepanto
polenta
AELNOPU apolune
AELNORS loaners
orleans
Orléans
reloans
Salerno
AELNORU aleuron
AELNORV veronal
AELNOST etalons
AELNOUV von Laue
AELNPPR preplan
AELNPPY playpen
AELNPRS planers
replans
AELNPRT planter
replant
AELNPRY plenary
AELNPST planets
platens
AELNPTX explant
AELNPTY aplenty
penalty
AELNQUU unequal
AELNRRS snarler
AELNRST antlers
rentals
saltern
slanter
sternal
AELNRSY larneys
AELNRTU neutral
AELNRTV ventral
AELNRUV unravel
venular
AELNSSU sensual
unseals
AELNSSW awnless
AELNSSX laxness
AELNSTT talents
AELNSTU eluants
lunates
AELNSTV levants
AELNSTY Stanley
AELOORS aerosol
roseola
AELOPRS paroles
reposal
AELOPRT prolate
AELOPRV overlap
AELOPST apostle
pelotas
AELOPSX exposal
AELOPTT paletot
AELOPTU outleap
AELORRT realtor
relator
AELORSS lassoer
oarless
AELORST Oastler
oestral
AELORTV levator
AELORUU rouleau
AELORVY layover
overlay
AELOSSS lassoes
AELOSSV salvoes
AELOSTV solvate
AELOSTZ zealots
AELOSUZ zealous
AELOSVY saveloy
AELOTTU toluate
AELOTUV ovulate
AELOTVV volvate
AELOTVY ovately
AELPPRS lappers
rappels
slapper
AELPPRY reapply
AELPPST lappets
AELPPSU appulse
papules
AELPQSU plaques
AELPRRS parrels
AELPRSS lapsers
AELPRST palters
persalt
plaster
platers
psalter
stapler
AELPRSU perusal
AELPRSY parleys
parsley
players
replays
sparely
AELPRTT partlet
platter
prattle
AELPRTY peartly
pteryla
AELPSSS passels
sapless

AELPSST	pastels
	staples
AELPSSY	Plassey
AELPSTT	peltast
AELPSTU	pulsate
AELQRRU	quarrel
AELQRSU	Quarles
AELQSSU	squeals
AELQSUZ	quezals
AELQTUZ	quetzal
AELRRSU	surreal
AELRRSW	warsler
AELRRTT	rattler
AELRRTW	trawler
AELRSST	artless
	lasters
	salters
	slaters
AELRSSU	saurels
AELRSSV	salvers
	servals
	slavers
AELRSSW	warsles
AELRSSY	rayless
	slayers
AELRSTT	rattles
	starlet
	startle
AELRSTU	saluter
AELRSTV	travels
	varlets
	vestral
AELRSTW	warstle
	wastrel
AELRSTY	raylets
AELRSUV	valuers
AELRSVY	slavery
AELRSWY	lawyers
AELRTTT	tartlet
	tattler
AELRTTU	tutelar
AELRTUV	vaulter
AELRTWZ	waltzer
AELSSST	tassels
AELSSTT	stalest
AELSSTU	salutes
	taluses
AELSSTV	vestals
AELSSTX	taxless
AELSSUU	Sulu Sea
AELSSVY	slaveys
AELSTTT	tattles
AELSTTW	wattles
AELSTTY	stately
AELSTUX	luxates
AELSTWZ	waltzes
AELSUVY	suavely
AELSWZZ	swazzle
AELTTTW	twattle
AELTTUX	textual
AELTUVV	vulvate
AELTUYY	Lyautey
AEMMMST	mammets
AEMMNOT	momenta
AEMMNTU	amentum
AEMMOPR	mampoer
AEMMPRS	spammer
AEMMRRS	rammers
AEMMRST	stammer
AEMMRSY	yammers
AEMMRSZ	mamzers
AEMMSST	stemmas
AEMMSTU	maumets
AEMNNNU	Neumann
AEMNNOS	mannose
AEMNNOT	montane
AEMNNOU	noumena
AEMNNOY	many-one
	one-many
AEMNNRS	manners
AEMNNRT	remnant
AEMNNSW	newsman
AEMNNTU	unmeant
AEMNOPP	pampoen
AEMNOPR	manrope
AEMNOPS	mopanes
AEMNORR	orramen
AEMNORS	enamors
	moaners
	oarsmen
	Ransome
	San Remo
AEMNORT	tonearm
AEMNORU	enamour
	neuroma
AEMNORV	overman
AEMNORY	anymore
AEMNOTT	tomenta
AEMNPSU	pneumas
AEMNPTU	putamen
AEMNPTY	payment
AEMNRRU	manurer
AEMNRST	martens
	smarten
AEMNRSU	manures
	surname
AEMNRTU	trueman
AEMNSST	stamens
AEMNSSU	unseams
AEMNSTY	amnesty
AEMOORT	tearoom
AEMOORW	woomera
AEMOOST	osteoma
AEMOOSV	vamoose
AEMOPPR	pampero
AEMOPRS	Pasmore
AEMOPRT	Patmore
AEMOPST	Petsamo
AEMORRR	armorer
AEMORRS	remoras
	roamers
AEMORRV	overarm
AEMORRW	earworm
AEMORST	maestro
AEMORSW	womeras
AEMOSWY	someway
AEMOTTY	Mayotte
AEMOTTZ	mozetta
AEMPPRS	mappers
	pampers
AEMPRRS	prearms
AEMPRRT	tramper
AEMPRRW	prewarm
AEMPRST	stamper
	tampers
AEMPRSV	revamps
	vampers
AEMPRSW	swamper
AEMPRTU	tempura
AEMPSTU	Paestum
AEMPTTT	attempt
AEMPTTU	tapetum
AEMQRSU	marques
	masquer
AEMQRUZ	Márquez
AEMQSSU	masques
AEMRRRS	marrers
AEMRRRY	remarry
AEMRRST	armrest
	smarter
AEMRRSW	rewarms
	warmers
AEMRRTU	erratum
AEMRSST	masters
	streams
AEMRSSU	assumer
	Erasmus
	masseur
AEMRSTT	matters
	smatter
AEMRSTU	matures
	strumae
AEMRSTW	warmest
AEMRSTY	mastery
	streamy
AEMRTTY	mattery
AEMRTTZ	Zermatt
AEMRTUU	trumeau
AEMSSSU	assumes
AEMSTTU	mutates
AENNNPT	pennant
AENNORY	annoyer
AENNOTU	tonneau
AENNPRS	spanner
AENNRST	tanners
AENNRTT	entrant
AENNRTY	tannery
AENNSSW	wanness
AENNSTT	tannest
	tenants
AENNSTW	wannest
AENOOTZ	entozoa
AENOPPR	propane
AENOPRS	Pearson
	persona
	Porsena
AENOPRT	operant
	pronate
	protean
AENOPSW	weapons
AENORRV	overran
AENORSS	reasons
	senoras
AENORST	atoners
	senator
	treason
AENORSY	Reynosa
AENORTU	Tourane
AENORVY	Aveyron
AENORWZ	warzone
AENOSSS	seasons
AENOSTT	notates
AENOSTU	soutane
AENOUUV	nouveau
AENPPRS	nappers
	parpens
	snapper
AENPRRT	partner
AENPRRW	prawner
AENPRST	arpents
	entraps
	parents
	pastern
	trepans
AENPRSW	enwraps
	spawner
AENPRSZ	panzers
AENPRTT	pattern
	reptant
AENPRTW	Antwerp
AENPRUV	parvenu
AENPSST	aptness
AENPSSY	synapse
AENPSTT	patents
	pattens
AENPSTU	peanuts
AENQSUY	Quesnay
AENRRSS	snarers
AENRRST	ranters
AENRRSW	warners
	warrens
AENRRTY	ternary
AENRSSS	sarsens
AENRSSW	answers
	rawness
AENRSTT	natters
AENRSTU	natures
	saunter
AENRSTV	servant
	taverns
	versant
AENRSTW	wanters
AENRSUW	unswear
AENRSWY	yawners
AENRTTU	taunter
AENRTTV	Vättern
AENRTUV	vaunter
AENRUWY	unweary

AENSSST assents
AENSSTU unseats
AENSSTX sextans
AENSSWY sawneys
AENSTTU attunes
tautens
tetanus
AENSTTX sextant
AENSTUZ Neusatz
AEOOPPS papoose
AEOPPPS pappose
AEOPPRV approve
AEOPPSS apposes
AEOPQSU opaques
AEOPRRT praetor
prorate
AEOPRRV vaporer
AEOPRST esparto
proteas
seaport
AEOPRVY overpay
AEOPSST petasos
AEOPSTT teapots
AEOPSTY teapoys
AEOPSTZ topazes
AEOQRTU equator
quorate
AEOQSUU aqueous
AEORRRS roarers
AEORRSS soarers
AEORRST roaster
AEORRSU arouser
AEORSSS Ross Sea
saroses
serosas
AEORSSU arouses
AEORSTT Rosetta
rotates
toaster
AEORSVW avowers
oversaw
AEORTUW outwear
AEORTVX overtax
AEOSTTU outeats
AEOSUVZ zouaves
AEPPRRS rappers
AEPPRRT trapper
AEPPRRW wrapper
AEPPRSS sappers
AEPPRST tappers
AEPPRSU paupers
AEPPRSW swapper
AEPPRSY prepays
yappers
AEPPSTT tappets
AEPPSTU pasteup
pupates
AEPQRTU parquet
AEPRRSS parsers
raspers
sparers
sparser

AEPRRST praters
AEPRRSU parures
uprears
AEPRRSW rewraps
warpers
AEPRRSY prayers
respray
sprayer
AEPRRTU rapture
AEPRSST repasts
AEPRSSU pausers
AEPRSSY pessary
AEPRSTT patters
spatter
tapster
AEPRSTU Pasteur
pasture
uprates
AEPRSUX aruspex
AEPRSUY yaupers
AEPRSWY yawpers
AEPRTXY apteryx
AEPSSTU petasus
AEPSTTU upstate
AEQRRSU squarer
AEQRRTU quarter
AEQRSSU squares
AEQRSTU quarest
quatres
AEQRSUV quavers
AEQRTTU quartet
AEQRUVY quavery
AERRSST arrests
rasters
starers
AERRSSU assurer
AERRSTT ratters
restart
starter
AERRSTV starver
Travers
AERRSTY strayer
AERSSST asserts
AERSSSU assures
AERSSSW wrasses
AERSSTT staters
tasters
AERSSTV starves
AERSSTW wasters
AERSSTY estrays
stayers
AERSSWY sawyers
swayers
AERSTTT stretta
tatters
AERSTTU stature
AERSTTW Stewart
swatter
AERSTTY yatters
AERSTUU auteurs
AERSTUY estuary
AERSTVY strayve

AESSSTT tassets
AESSTTT attests
AESSTTU statues
AESSTTV vastest
AESSTUV suavest
AESSTUY eustasy
AESTTTU statute
AFFFGIN faffing
AFFFLLO falloff
AFFGGIN gaffing
AFFGINW waffing
AFFGSUW guffaws
AFFHIRS raffish
AFFHLUU Al Hufuf
AFFHMNO Hoffman
AFFIKRS kaffirs
AFFILOR riffola
AFFILSY falsify
AFFIMRS affirms
AFFIMST mastiff
AFFINRU funfair
ruffian
AFFINTY tiffany
AFFIRST tariffs
AFFKLOR Karloff
AFFLOPY playoff
AFFLOSY layoffs
AFFNORS saffron
AFFNORT affront
AFFNOYZ Zoffany
AFFOPSY payoffs
AFGGGIN fagging
AFGGOST faggots
AFGGOTY faggoty
AFGHHIS hagfish
AFGHINS fashing
AFGHINT hafting
AFGHIRS garfish
AFGHRTU fraught
AFGIILN failing
AFGIINR fairing
AFGIJMS figjams
AFGIKLN flaking
AFGILLN falling
AFGILMN flaming
AFGILNO foaling
loafing
AFGILNR flaring
AFGILNT fatling
AFGILNU gainful
AFGILNW flawing
AFGILNY anglify
flaying
AFGILRU figural
AFGIMNO foaming
AFGIMNR farming
framing
AFGIMNY magnify
AFGINNN fanning
AFGINNW fawning
AFGINRT farting
ingraft

rafting
AFGINRY fraying
AFGINST fasting
AFGINTT fatting
AFGINTU fauting
AFGINTW wafting
AFGIRTY gratify
AFGKORT koftgar
AFGLLLY gallfly
AFGLLUY fugally
AFGLNOS flagons
AFGMNOR frogman
AFGNOPU Pang-fou
AFGORTY Fogarty
AFGOSTU fugatos
AFHIIRS fairish
AFHIKLS khalifs
AFHIKRS kharifs
AFHIKUY kufiyah
AFHILTW halfwit
AFHIMNU hafnium
AFHINOS fashion
AFHIORS oarfish
AFHIRST ratfish
AFHISSW sawfish
AFHISTT fattish
AFHISWY fishway
AFHKORY hayfork
AFHKRTU futhark
AFHLMRU harmful
AFHLOOS loofahs
AFHMNNO Hofmann
AFHMOST fathoms
AFHMOUZ Mahfouz
AFHORSS shofars
AFIILNS finials
AFIILOR airfoil
AFIILRS Israfil
AFIILRT airlift
AFIIMOS mafiosi
AFIINRS Frisian
AFIKKLR Falkirk
AFIKLLY flakily
AFIKLOT flokati
AFIKNRT ratfink
AFIKORU Farouk I
AFILLNP pinfall
AFILLNY finally
AFILLPT pitfall
AFILLPU pailful
AFILLRY frailly
AFILLSU Ulfilas
AFILLUV fluvial
AFILLUW wailful
Wulfila
AFILMNT liftman
AFILMOR aliform
AFILMOY foamily
AFILMPY amplify
AFILNPU painful
AFILNTY faintly
AFILORW airflow

AFILOTX	foxtail
AFILQUY	qualify
AFILRRY	friarly
AFILRTY	frailty
AFILSSY	salsify
AFILSTU	fistula
AFILSTY	falsity
AFILTTY	fattily
AFIMNRS	firmans
AFIMOOS	mafioso
AFIMRST	maftirs
AFIMSSS	massifs
AFIMSTT	fattism
AFIMSUV	fauvism
AFIMSUZ	umfazis
AFIMTTY	mattify
AFINNOS	fanions
AFINNOT	fontina
AFINNST	infants
AFINSSU	fusains
AFINSTU	fustian
AFIORTU	faitour
AFISSTT	sitfast
AFISSTY	satisfy
AFISTTT	fattist
AFISTUV	fauvist
AFITTUY	fatuity
AFKKOUU	Fukuoka
AFKLNRY	frankly
AFKLNTU	tankful
AFKRRTU	fraktur
AFLLOOY	aloofly
AFLLORU	florula
AFLLOSW	fallows
AFLLOTU	fallout
	outfall
AFLLPSU	lapfuls
AFLLPUY	playful
AFLLUWY	awfully
AFLMNOU	moanful
AFLMORU	formula
AFLMORW	wolfram
AFLMOST	flotsam
AFLMRSU	armfuls
	fulmars
AFLMSUU	famulus
AFLNORT	frontal
AFLNPSU	panfuls
AFLNSTU	flaunts
AFLNTUY	flaunty
AFLOOTW	woolfat
AFLOPTT	flattop
AFLORSV	flavors
AFLORUV	flavour
AFLPRTY	flytrap
AFLPSTY	flypast
AFLSUWY	swayful
AFMNOOT	footman
AFMNORT	formant
AFMNOST	fantoms
AFMNRTU	turfman
AFMOORS	Formosa
AFMORST	formats
AFMORTU	foumart
AFMOSTU	sfumato
AFNORTU	Fortuna
AFNPRSY	frypans
AFNSSTU	sunfast
AFOOTWY	footway
AFORRSW	farrows
AFORRSY	orfrays
AFORSUV	favours
AFOSTUU	fatuous
AGGGGIN	gagging
AGGGIJN	jagging
AGGGILN	lagging
AGGGIMN	magging
AGGGINN	ganging
	nagging
AGGGINR	ragging
AGGGINS	sagging
AGGGINT	tagging
AGGGINU	gauging
AGGGINV	vagging
AGGGINW	wagging
AGGHHIS	haggish
AGGHIMN	gingham
AGGHINN	hanging
AGGHINS	gashing
AGGHISW	waggish
AGGHNOV	Van Gogh
AGGIILS	gilgais
AGGIIMN	imaging
AGGIINN	gaining
AGGIINT	gaiting
AGGIINV	gingiva
AGGIKNW	gawking
AGGILLN	galling
AGGILNN	angling
AGGILNO	gaoling
AGGILNR	glaring
AGGILNZ	glazing
AGGILOS	loggias
AGGIMMN	gamming
AGGINNN	ganning
AGGINNR	ranging
AGGINNW	gnawing
AGGINPP	gapping
AGGINPS	gasping
AGGINPU	gauping
AGGINPW	gawping
AGGINRR	garring
AGGINRT	grating
AGGINRU	arguing
AGGINRV	graving
AGGINRY	graying
AGGINRZ	grazing
AGGINSS	gassing
AGGINST	staging
AGGINSW	swaging
AGGINUU	Gauguin
AGGINUY	Guiyang
AGGIORS	gorgias
AGGISWW	wigwags
AGGISZZ	zigzags
AGGKNOT	Gangtok
AGGLOSW	Glasgow
AGGMORR	grogram
AGGMOST	maggots
AGGMOTY	maggoty
AGGMRSU	muggars
AGGNOSU	Angus Og
AGGNOSW	waggons
AGGNRSU	nuggars
AGHHINS	hashing
AGHHIWY	highway
AGHHMNU	Hamhung
AGHHNOW	Hwang Ho
AGHHORT	Hogarth
AGHHOSW	hogwash
AGHHTUY	haughty
AGHIILN	hailing
AGHIINQ	Qinghai
AGHIKNN	hanking
AGHIKNR	harking
AGHIKNS	shaking
AGHIKNW	hawking
AGHIKSW	gawkish
AGHILNO	haloing
AGHILNR	harling
AGHILNS	lashing
AGHILNT	halting
	lathing
AGHILNU	hauling
	nilghau
AGHILNV	halving
AGHILNW	whaling
AGHILOT	Goliath
AGHILRS	largish
AGHILRT	alright
AGHILST	alights
AGHIMMN	hamming
AGHIMNR	harming
AGHIMNS	mashing
	shaming
AGHIMRS	Grisham
AGHINOX	hoaxing
AGHINPP	happing
AGHINPR	harping
AGHINPS	hasping
	pashing
	phasing
	shaping
AGHINRS	garnish
	sharing
AGHINRT	Granthi
AGHINSS	sashing
AGHINST	hasting
AGHINSU	anguish
AGHINSV	shaving
AGHINSW	hawsing
	shawing
	washing
AGHINTT	hatting
AGHINTW	thawing
AGHIOST	goatish
AGHIPRY	Phrygia
AGHIQSU	quaighs
AGHIRSY	grayish
AGHJMNO	mahjong
AGHKOSW	goshawk
AGHLLUZ	Zaghlul
AGHLMPU	galumph
AGHLNUY	nylghau
AGHLOOS	gasohol
AGHLOSU	goulash
AGHLSTY	ghastly
AGHMNNU	Hungnam
AGHMORY	hygroma
AGHMRRU	murragh
AGHNNOU	houngan
AGHNNSU	hungans
AGHNOSU	Songhua
AGHNOTU	hangout
	tohunga
AGHNPSU	hangups
AGHNRST	thrangs
AGHNRUY	Hungary
AGHNSTU	naughts
AGHNSUY	gunyahs
AGHNTUY	naughty
AGHOQSU	quahogs
AGHORTW	warthog
AGHRTUU	Thurgau
AGIIJLN	jailing
AGIIJNX	Jiangxi
AGIIKLN	laiking
AGIIKLT	glaikit
AGIIKNS	Kiangsi
	Si Kiang
AGIILMN	mailing
AGIILNN	alining
	nailing
AGIILNR	lairing
	railing
AGIILNS	nilgais
	sailing
AGIILNT	intagli
	tailing
AGIILNV	vailing
AGIILNW	wailing
AGIILPT	pigtail
AGIILRU	Liguria
AGIILTY	agility
AGIIMMN	maiming
AGIIMMS	imagism
AGIIMOR	origami
AGIIMST	imagist
AGIINNP	paining
AGIINNR	ingrain
	raining
AGIINNS	Ningsia
	saining
AGIINPR	pairing
AGIINRS	airings
	arising
	raising
AGIINRZ	zingari

AGIINSV	visaing
AGIINTW	waiting
AGIINTX	taxiing
AGIINVV	vivaing
AGIINVW	waiving
AGIIORZ	Gorizia
AGIJMMN	jamming
AGIJNNN	Nanjing
AGIJNNU	Nu Jiang
AGIJNPR	jarping
AGIJNPU	jauping
AGIJNRR	jarring
AGIJNSU	Jiangsu
AGIJNZZ	jazzing
AGIJSSW	jigsaws
AGIKKNY	yakking
AGIKLNR	larking
AGIKLNS	slaking
AGIKLNT	talking
AGIKLNW	walking
AGIKLWY	gawkily
AGIKMNR	marking
AGIKMNS	makings
	masking
AGIKNNR	narking
	ranking
AGIKNNT	tanking
AGIKNNW	wanking
AGIKNNY	yanking
AGIKNOS	soaking
AGIKNOY	kayoing
	okaying
AGIKNPR	parking
AGIKNQU	quaking
AGIKNRS	sarking
AGIKNRT	karting
AGIKNSS	gaskins
AGIKNST	skating
	staking
	takings
	tasking
AGIKNSU	Kiangsu
AGIKNUW	wauking
AGILLMU	gallium
AGILLNP	palling
AGILLNU	lingual
AGILLNW	walling
AGILLNY	allying
AGILLOR	gorilla
AGILLOT	galliot
AGILLRU	ligular
AGILLRY	Gillray
AGILLSU	ligulas
	lugsail
AGILMMN	lamming
AGILMNO	loaming
AGILMNP	palming
AGILMNR	marling
AGILMNS	lingams
	maligns
AGILMNT	malting
AGILMNU	mauling
AGILMNY	mangily
AGILMOS	gliomas
AGILNNO	loaning
AGILNNP	planing
AGILNNR	larning
AGILNNS	Lansing
	linsang
AGILNOT	antilog
AGILNOV	Vignola
AGILNPP	lapping
AGILNPS	lapsing
	palings
	sapling
AGILNPT	plating
AGILNPU	Pauling
AGILNPW	lapwing
AGILNPY	playing
AGILNRY	angrily
	rangily
AGILNSS	signals
AGILNST	anglist
	lasting
	salting
	slating
	staling
AGILNSV	salving
	slaving
AGILNSY	slaying
AGILNUV	valuing
AGILNUW	wauling
AGILNWW	wawling
AGILNWY	yawling
AGILOPT	galipot
AGILORS	Argolis
	girasol
	glorias
AGILORW	airglow
	Gwalior
AGILOST	galiots
AGILSTY	stagily
AGILUYZ	gauzily
AGIMMNR	ramming
AGIMMNS	samming
AGIMNNN	manning
AGIMNNO	moaning
AGIMNNW	wingman
AGIMNOR	roaming
AGIMNOT	moating
AGIMNPP	mapping
AGIMNPR	ramping
AGIMNPT	tamping
AGIMNPV	vamping
AGIMNRR	marring
AGIMNRS	armings
	margins
AGIMNRT	migrant
AGIMNRW	warming
AGIMNSS	massing
AGIMNST	masting
AGIMNSU	amusing
AGIMNTT	matting
AGIMORS	isogram
AGIMORU	gourami
AGIMOSY	isogamy
AGIMSST	stigmas
AGIMSWW	wigwams
AGINNNN	Nanning
AGINNNP	panning
AGINNNT	tanning
AGINNNW	wanning
AGINNOT	atoning
AGINNOV	Avignon
AGINNPP	napping
AGINNPT	panting
AGINNPW	pawning
AGINNRS	snaring
AGINNRT	ranting
AGINNRW	warning
AGINNRY	yarning
AGINNSW	awnings
AGINNTW	wanting
AGINNWY	yawning
AGINOOO	oogonia
AGINOOP	pogonia
AGINOPR	porangi
AGINOPS	soaping
AGINOPT	Paoting
AGINORR	roaring
AGINORS	signora
	soaring
AGINORT	orating
AGINORZ	zingaro
AGINOST	agonist
AGINOVW	avowing
AGINPPR	rapping
AGINPPS	sapping
AGINPPT	tapping
AGINPPY	yapping
AGINPPZ	zapping
AGINPRS	parings
	parsing
	rasping
	sparing
AGINPRT	parting
	prating
AGINPRW	warping
AGINPRY	praying
AGINPSS	passing
AGINPST	pasting
AGINPSU	pausing
AGINPSY	spaying
AGINPTT	patting
AGINPUY	yauping
AGINPUZ	Zipangu
AGINPWY	yawping
AGINRRT	tarring
AGINRRW	warring
AGINRST	gastrin
	ratings
	staring
AGINRSU	Sungari
AGINRSV	ravings
AGINRSY	syringa
AGINRTT	ratting
AGINRTW	ringtaw
AGINRVY	varying
AGINRZZ	razzing
AGINSSS	assigns
	sassing
AGINSST	Sitsang
AGINSSV	savings
AGINSSY	sayings
AGINSTT	stating
	tasting
AGINSTU	sauting
AGINSTV	staving
AGINSTW	tawsing
	wasting
AGINSTY	staying
	stygian
AGINSVY	Savigny
AGINSWY	swaying
AGINTTT	tatting
AGINTTV	vatting
AGINTXY	taxying
AGINWWX	waxwing
AGIOPPT	agitpop
AGIORSU	giaours
AGIORSV	viragos
AGIOSTU	agoutis
AGIOUUY	ouguiya
AGIRSTU	guitars
AGIRTVY	gravity
AGJKNUW	Kwangju
AGJLRUU	jugular
AGJNOOR	jargoon
AGJNORS	jargons
AGKLMOU	Gomulka
AGKLNOS	kalongs
AGKLNSU	Lugansk
AGKLOSU	kagouls
AGKMNOP	kampong
AGLLNOO	galloon
AGLLNOS	gallons
AGLLNTU	gallnut
	nutgall
AGLLOOR	rogallo
AGLLOOT	galloot
AGLLOPS	gallops
AGLLOSS	glossal
AGLLOSU	gallous
AGLLOSW	gallows
AGLLOTT	glottal
AGLLPTY	glyptal
AGLLRYY	gyrally
AGLMORU	glamour
AGLNNOS	longans
AGLNNOT	Langton
AGLNNSU	lungans
AGLNOOO	ologoan
AGLNOOS	lagoons
AGLNORU	languor
AGLNOSS	slogans
AGLNOSU	lanugos
AGLNOUY	Luoyang
AGLNPSY	spangly

AGLNPUY	gunplay
AGLNRSU	langurs
AGLNRTY	Langtry
AGLNRUU	ungular
AGLNTUY	gauntly
AGLOOPY	apology
AGLOOST	galoots
AGLOSSS	glossas
AGLOSWY	logways
AGLSYYZ	syzygal
AGMMNOS	gammons
AGMMNSU	magnums
AGMMORY	myogram
AGMNNOR	grannom
AGMNORS	morgans
AGMNORU	organum
AGMNOST	amongst
AGMNOTU	Montagu
AGMNSTU	mustang
AGMNSTY	gymnast
	syntagm
AGMNSYY	syngamy
AGMOPRR	program
AGMORRW	ragworm
AGMORSS	orgasms
AGMORSV	vagroms
AGMPRSU	grampus
AGMPSUZ	gazumps
AGNNNOO	nonagon
AGNNNOT	Nantong
AGNNOOR	argonon
	organon
	Rangoon
AGNNTTU	Tan-tung
AGNOQSU	quangos
AGNORRS	garrons
AGNORRT	grantor
AGNORSS	sarongs
AGNOSTU	nougats
	outsang
	Sagunto
AGNRTUY	gauntry
AGOPPST	stopgap
AGORRTW	ragwort
AGORRTY	gyrator
AGORSTU	ragouts
AGORTTU	Tortuga
AGOSTTU	tautogs
AGOSUYZ	azygous
AGRUUUY	Uruguay
AGSSTUU	augusts
AHHHISS	hashish
AHHIKSW	hawkish
AHHIMNU	hahnium
AHHISSV	shivahs
AHHISTT	shittah
AHHKOOS	hookahs
AHHKSTY	Shakhty
AHHLRSY	harshly
AHHNSSU	Shushan
AHHOORS	hoorahs
AHHOPRS	shophar
AHHORTW	Haworth
AHHPPSU	huppahs
AHHPTUZ	hutzpah
AHHRRSU	hurrahs
AHHSUZZ	huzzahs
AHIIKNT	Haitink
AHIIKOT	Akihito
AHIIKRS	shikari
AHIIKRT	Kíthira
AHIIMMS	Mishima
AHIIMNT	thiamin
AHIIMSS	sashimi
AHIIMST	samithi
AHIINPR	hairpin
AHIIPRS	airship
AHIIQQR	Qiqihar
AHIJMSW	Jahwism
AHIJOUZ	Jiazhou
AHIJSTV	Jahvist
AHIKKLS	Khalkís
AHIKLMS	Lakshmi
AHIKLRS	larkish
AHIKLSY	shakily
AHIKMNS	khamsin
AHIKMRS	kashmir
AHIKMSV	mikvahs
AHIKMSW	mawkish
AHIKNRS	Krishna
AHIKNSV	knavish
AHIKNSW	Hawkins
AHIKORS	karoshi
AHIKOSU	Hokusai
AHIKOSW	kowhais
AHIKRSS	shikars
AHIKSSS	shiksas
AHILLNT	anthill
AHILLRY	Hillary
AHILLSZ	zillahs
AHILLTT	tallith
AHILMOP	omphali
AHILMOU	haloumi
AHILMTW	Whitlam
AHILNOU	Anouilh
AHILNPS	planish
AHILNSU	inhauls
AHILNSY	linhays
AHILORY	hoarily
AHILOTY	aliyoth
AHILOTZ	thiazol
AHILPPY	happily
AHILPRT	philtra
AHILPSY	apishly
AHILSST	saltish
	tahsils
AHILSSV	slavish
AHILSTY	hastily
AHILSWY	washily
AHILTTZ	Hazlitt
AHIMMRS	rammish
AHIMNNS	mannish
AHIMNNU	inhuman
AHIMNOT	Othman I
AHIMNPS	shipman
AHIMNTW	Whitman
AHIMOPR	morphia
AHIMPSS	mishaps
AHIMPSV	vampish
AHIMRST	Mithras
AHIMRSW	warmish
AHIMSSU	hassium
AHIMSWY	Yahwism
AHIMTUZ	azimuth
AHIMTVZ	mitzvah
AHINNST	tannish
AHINNTX	xanthin
AHINOST	Onitsha
AHINOTZ	hoatzin
AHINPRS	harpins
AHINPSS	Spanish
AHINPST	hatpins
AHINPTY	Pythian
AHINRST	tarnish
AHINRSU	unhairs
AHINRSV	varnish
AHINSSU	Hussain
AHINSSW	washins
AHIOOST	atishoo
AHIOPXY	hypoxia
AHIORSS	orishas
AHIORSW	airshow
AHIPRSS	raspish
AHIPRST	harpist
AHIPRSU	rupiahs
AHIPRSW	warship
AHIPSSW	waspish
AHIPSTY	Pythias
AHIPSWW	whipsaw
AHIPSWY	shipway
AHIQSTU	Asquith
AHIRRSW	wirrahs
AHIRSTT	athirst
	rattish
	tartish
AHIRSTW	trishaw
	wraiths
AHISSTU	shiatsu
AHISTTW	whatsit
AHISTWY	Yahwist
AHKKORV	Kharkov
AHKKSSU	sukkahs
AHKLNSY	Shankly
AHKLTUY	Hakluyt
AHKMNRU	Nkrumah
AHKMORR	markhor
AHKMOSW	mohawks
AHKNPSU	punkahs
AHKPSUU	hapukus
AHKRSTU	kashrut
	khurtas
AHLLMOS	mollahs
AHLLMSU	mullahs
AHLLNSU	nullahs
AHLLOOS	halloos
	holloas
AHLLOPS	shallop
AHLLOST	shallot
AHLLOSW	hallows
	shallow
AHLLOTY	loathly
	tallyho
AHLLPSU	phallus
AHLLPYY	aphylly
AHLLRST	thralls
AHLLSTU	thallus
AHLMNPY	nymphal
AHLMNSY	hymnals
AHLMNUY	humanly
AHLMORU	humoral
AHLMSTU	Malthus
AHLMSUU	hamulus
AHLNOPR	alphorn
AHLNOPT	haplont
AHLNORT	althorn
AHLNOUZ	Lanzhou
AHLOOPS	hooplas
AHLORST	harlots
AHLOTUU	outhaul
AHLPRSY	sharply
AHLPSSY	splashy
AHMMMOT	mammoth
AHMMTUZ	Thammuz
AHMNNSU	numnahs
AHMNNTU	manhunt
AHMNNUU	unhuman
AHMNOPT	Hampton
	phantom
AHMNORY	harmony
AHMNOSS	hansoms
AHMNOSU	Housman
AHMNOSW	showman
AHMNSTY	Nasmyth
AHMOOPS	shampoo
AHMOSTU	mahouts
AHMOSTZ	matzohs
AHMOSWY	haymows
AHMOTTZ	matzoth
AHMPSSU	smashup
AHNNNOS	Shannon
AHNNOTY	Anthony
AHNOOPR	harpoon
AHNOPRS	orphans
AHNORSS	shorans
AHNORSX	saxhorn
AHNORTW	Wharton
AHNOSTU	Shantou
AHNOTTW	whatnot
AHNPPUY	unhappy
AHNPRXY	pharynx
AHNRSVY	hryvnas
AHNRVYY	hryvnya
AHNSSTU	sunhats
AHNSTUX	Xanthus
AHOORSY	hoorays
AHOPRSS	phasors
AHOPRTY	atrophy
AHOPTTW	towpath

AHORRSW harrows
AHORSTT throats
AHORSTU authors
Suharto
AHORTTY throaty
AHOSTUV Shavuot
AHOSTUW outwash
washout
AHPRRTY phratry
AHPSSTU Thapsus
AHQSSUY squashy
AHRRSUY hurrays
AHRSSSU hussars
AHRSSTT straths
AHRSTTW thwarts
AHRSTWY swarthy
AHSSSTU tussahs
AIIIINV Ivan III
AIIIKKW Waikiki
AIIILMS Ismaili
AIIILMT militia
AIIILNT initial
AIIILPU Paul III
AIIILVX lixivia
AIIJMNS Jainism
AIIJMOW Iwo Jima
AIIJNNT Tianjin
AIIKLNN Kalinin
AIIKMMS skimmia
AIIKMNN manikin
AIIKNNT tankini
AIIKOTW Kowaiti
AIIKRRU rauriki
AIIKSTU Kutaisi
AIIKTUW Kuwaiti
AIILLLP lapilli
AIILLMN liminal
AIILLMS Millais
AIILLMW William
AIILLNV villain
AIILLQU quillai
AIILLRY Illyria
AIILMMN minimal
AIILMNT intimal
AIILMNV viminal
AIILMRS similar
AIILMRY miliary
AIILNOP Lin Piao
AIILNOS liaison
AIILNOV Livonia
AIILNPT pintail
Platini
AIILNPU nauplii
AIILNRY rainily
AIILNTU nautili
AIILNTY anility
AIILOPT Li T'ai-po
AIILORV ravioli
AIILPRU lipuria
AIILQSU siliqua
AIILQTU Iqaluit

AIILRST liatris
AIILRTV trivial
AIIMMNS animism
AIIMMNX maximin
minimax
AIIMNNV minivan
AIIMNOR amorini
AIIMNPS pianism
AIIMNPT timpani
AIIMNRT martini
AIIMNSS simians
AIIMNST animist
AIIMNTU minutia
AIIMNTV vitamin
AIIMNZZ Mazzini
AIIMPRS impairs
AIIMRST simitar
AIIMRUW Aruwimi
AIIMSST samitis
AIIMSSV Sivaism
AIIMSSY myiasis
AIINNSZ zinnias
AIINNTY inanity
AIINORV Ivorian
AIINOTT notitia
AIINPRS aspirin
AIINPRT Patinir
AIINPST pianist
AIINRSS raisins
AIINRST Istrian
AIINRSY raisiny
AIINRTV vitrain
AIINRTZ triazin
AIINSST isatins
AIINSSX sixains
AIINSTU Tunisia
AIIOOTV Voiotia
AIIOPRR a priori
AIIOPST Pistoia
AIIORTV Vitoria
Vitória
AIIPSTW wapitis
AIJJMMS jimjams
AIJLORS jailors
AIJLORT tolarji
AIJLYZZ jazzily
AIJNORT janitor
AIKKMNR kirkman
AIKKMOT komatik
AIKKOPY kopiyka
AIKKSUZ zakuski
AIKLLNY lankily
AIKLMMN milkman
AIKLMNN linkman
AIKLMNS malkins
AIKLMOO Molokai
AIKLNST Slatkin
AIKLNSY snakily
AIKLOST Sialkot
AIKLPWY pawkily
AIKLQUY quakily
AIKLRTT titlark

AIKLSSU salukis
AIKLSSY skysail
AIKMNNS kinsman
AIKMNSS kamsins
AIKMNSW mawkins
AIKMOOS oomiaks
AIKMRUY Kumayri
AIKMSUY Kismayu
AIKNNNS nankins
AIKNNPS napkins
AIKNNUY Kuan Yin
AIKNOSY Soyinka
AIKNPRS kirpans
parkins
AIKOORT rooikat
AIKOPST katipos
AIKORST troikas
AIKRTUZ zikurat
AILLLMO Maillol
AILLLNO linalol
AILLMNU luminal
AILLMOT maillot
AILLMPU Illampu
pallium
AILLMSU alliums
AILLMSW sawmill
AILLNNO lanolin
AILLNNT Tallinn
AILLNPY plainly
AILLNST install
AILLORZ zorilla
AILLPRS pillars
AILLPRU pilular
AILLPUV pluvial
AILLQSU squilla
AILLRSV Villars
AILLSTY saltily
AILLTVY vitally
AILMMOR immoral
AILMMSY myalism
AILMMUW mwalimu
AILMNNO nominal
AILMNOP lampion
AILMNOS malison
Soliman
AILMNOY alimony
AILMNPS plasmin
AILMNPT implant
AILMNRS marlins
AILMOOV moviola
AILMOPS lipomas
AILMOPT optimal
AILMOPY Olympia
AILMOST somital
AILMOSY isoamyl
AILMOZZ Milazzo
AILMPRU primula
AILMPST palmist
AILMPSY misplay
AILMRST mistral
ramtils
AILMRSU simular

AILMSSS missals
AILMSST mistals
AILMSSY mislays
AILMSTU ultimas
AILMSTY myalist
AILNNOT antlion
AILNNPU pinnula
AILNORR Lorrain
AILNOSS alisons
AILNOST latinos
Saint-Lô
AILNOSV Novalis
AILNOUV Louvain
AILNPST plaints
AILNPSX salpinx
AILNPTU nuptial
AILNPTY inaptly
ptyalin
AILNQTU quintal
AILNRST ratlins
AILNRSU insular
urinals
AILNRTY riantly
AILNSST instals
AILNSSV silvans
AILNSTY nastily
saintly
AILNTTY nattily
AILOORW woorali
AILOPST apostil
topsail
AILOPSY soapily
AILOPTT talipot
AILOPTV pivotal
AILOQTU aliquot
AILORSS sailors
AILORST rialtos
sliotar
tailors
AILORUX uxorial
AILORVY olivary
AILOSSS assoils
AILOSSU São Luís
AILOSTT altoist
AILOTVY ovality
AILOVVV Vavilov
AILPPSY sappily
AILPQSU pasquil
AILPRSS spirals
AILPRSU parulis
spirula
AILPSST pastils
spitals
AILPSSY Palissy
AILPSTU Pilatus
AILPSTY pastily
AILPSWY slipway
waspily
AILQTUY quality
AILRRVY rivalry
AILRSTT starlit
AILRSTU rituals

AILRSTY trysail
AILRTTU titular
AILRTTY rattily
AILRTUV virtual
AILSSSY sassily
AILSSUV visuals
AILSSVZ vizslas
AILSTTY tastily
AILSTUV Vistula
AILSTUW lawsuit
AILTTTY tattily
AILTTUU Tutuila
AIMMMUX maximum
AIMMNSU Samnium
AIMMNTU manumit
AIMMORZ Mizoram
AIMMOSS mimosas
AIMMOST atomism
AIMMSUX maximus
AIMNNOS amnions
mansion
onanism
AIMNNOZ Manzoni
AIMNNSY minyans
AIMNOOR amorino
AIMNOPR rampion
AIMNOPS mopanis
AIMNOPT maintop
ptomain
tampion
AIMNORS Romains
AIMNOST manitos
AIMNOTU manitou
tinamou
AIMNPRU Manipur
AIMNPSY paynims
AIMNPTY tympani
AIMNRRU murrain
AIMNRST martins
AIMNRSU Surinam
uranism
AIMNRTU Martinů
natrium
AIMNRTV Martin V
varmint
AIMNRUU uranium
AIMNSTT mattins
AIMNSTU manitus
tsunami
AIMNSYZ zanyism
AIMOPST impasto
AIMORST amorist
AIMORSU Maurois
AIMOSTT atomist
AIMPRRY primary
AIMPRST armpits
imparts
AIMQRSU marquis
AIMRSST tsarism
AIMRSTU Maurist
AIMRSTZ tzarism
AIMSSTT statism
AINNNST tannins
AINNOOX Oxonian
AINNOPS saponin
AINNOSS nasions
AINNOST anoints
nations
onanist
AINNPSS inspans
AINNPST snaptin
AINNQTU quinnat
quintan
AINNRTU urinant
AINNSTT instant
AINNTUY annuity
AINOORT Ontario
oration
AINOOTV ovation
AINOOVV Ivanovo
AINOPPT appoint
AINOPRS parison
porinas
soprani
AINOPRT atropin
AINOPSS passion
AINOPSZ Spinoza
AINOPTU opuntia
utopian
AINORST rations
AINORSW warison
AINORTU rainout
Tournai
AINOSSS Onassis
AINOSSU suasion
AINOSTT station
AINOSUX anxious
AINOSVY synovia
AINPPRS parsnip
AINPQTU piquant
AINPRSS sprains
AINPRST spirant
spraint
AINPRSW inwraps
AINPRTU puritan
AINQRST qintars
AINQRTU Tarquin
AINQRUY quinary
AINQSTU asquint
AINRRTY trinary
AINRRUY urinary
AINRSST instars
strains
AINRSSU Russian
AINRSTT transit
Tristan
AINRSTU nutrias
AINRTTT titrant
AINRTUY unitary
AINSSTT tanists
AINSSTU issuant
sustain
AINSUUY Suiyüan
AINTTVY tantivy
AIOORRS Rosario
AIOORSS ariosos
AIOORST Ariosto
AIOPRRT airport
AIOPRRU Porirua
AIOPRRZ Pizarro
AIOPRSV paviors
AIOPRTT patriot
AIOPRTY topiary
AIOPRUV paviour
AIOPSTU utopias
AIORRRW warrior
AIORRTT traitor
AIORSSV saviors
AIORSSY Rossiya
AIORSTV travois
AIORSTY ostiary
AIORSUV saviour
various
AIPPRSU priapus
AIPPSST papists
AIPRRTU Tripura
AIPRSST rapists
AIPRSSU Prussia
AIPRSSW ripsaws
AIPSSTW pitsaws
sawpits
AIPZZZZ pizzazz
AIRSSTT artists
straits
tsarist
AIRSSTU aurists
AIRSTTT attrits
AIRSTVY varsity
AISSSST assists
AISSTTT statist
AISSTTU Statius
AISTTVY vastity
AISTUVY suavity
AJKMNNU junkman
AJKMNTU muntjak
AJKNSSY janskys
AJLLRUY jurally
AJLMORY majorly
AJLNORU journal
AJLOPPY jaloppy
AJMNRUY juryman
AKKKOOS kokakos
AKKLRSY skylark
AKKNORY Konakry
AKKOOPS pakokos
AKKOQSU quokkas
AKKSTUY Yakutsk
AKLMNOO Kolomna
AKLNOSX klaxons
AKLOSVV Slavkov
AKLOTTU outtalk
AKLOTUW outwalk
walkout
AKLPSTU uptalks
AKLPSUW walkups
AKLRSTY starkly
AKLRSVY valkyrs
AKLUUWZ KwaZulu
AKMNORW workman
AKMNSSU unmasks
AKMORST ostmark
AKMPRSU markups
AKMQTUU kumquat
AKMRSTU muskrat
AKNNOOS nanooks
AKNORSU korunas
Sukarno
AKNORSY ryokans
AKNORTU outrank
AKOOPRT partook
AKOORRS karroos
AKOORST Sokotra
AKORRTW artwork
AKORWWX waxwork
AKOSTWY towkays
AKOUVYZ Yuzovka
AKPSSSY Spassky
AKQSSUW squawks
ALLLOYY loyally
ALLMNOY allonym
ALLMNPU pullman
ALLMORY morally
ALLMOSS slaloms
ALLMOSW mallows
ALLNOPS pollans
ALLNOST Allston
ALLNOTY tonally
ALLNOYZ zonally
ALLNRUU lunular
ALLNSTY slantly
ALLNTUU ululant
ALLOOPS apollos
ALLOOTX axolotl
ALLOPRS pallors
ALLOPRY payroll
ALLOPSW wallops
ALLORWY rollway
ALLORYY royally
ALLOSSW sallows
ALLOSTW tallows
ALLOSWW swallow
wallows
ALLOSWY sallowy
ALLOTTY totally
ALLOTWY tallowy
ALLOTYY loyalty
ALLPRSU plurals
ALLPSSY psyllas
ALLQSSU squalls
ALLQSUY squally
ALLRRUY rurally
ALLRSTU lustral
ALLSSTU Sallust
ALLSUUY usually
ALMNNUY unmanly
ALMNOOP lampoon
ALMNOPS plasmon
ALMNOPW plowman

ALMNORU unmoral
ALMNORY almonry
ALMNOSS salmons
ALMNOSU monauls
solanum
ALMNOSY Solyman
ALMNOWY womanly
ALMNPSU sunlamp
ALMNSUU alumnus
ALMOPPT palmtop
ALMORRU morular
ALMORST mortals
ALMORSU morulas
ALMORTU tumoral
ALMOSST smaltos
ALMOSSW Low Mass
ALMOSTW matlows
ALMOTTU mulatto
ALMRSTY smartly
ALMRTUU tumular
ALMSSUY alyssum
asylums
ALMSTUU umlauts
ALNNRSU unsnarl
ALNNSUU annulus
ALNOOPT platoon
ALNOORT ortolan
ALNOOSS saloons
ALNOPPY panoply
ALNOPYY polynya
ALNORUZ zonular
ALNPTUY unaptly
ALNSSTU sultans
ALNSSVY sylvans
ALNSTUW walnuts
ALNSUUU unusual
ALOOPSS saloops
ALOORTT Tortola
ALOPPRS poplars
ALOPPRU popular
ALOPPRY propyla
ALOPRRS parlors
ALOPRRU parlour
ALOPRST patrols
portals
ALOPRSU parlous
ALOPRTW Paltrow
ALOPSSU spousal
ALOPTUY outplay
ALOQRRU rorqual
ALOQRSU squalor
ALOQSTU loquats
ALORRST rostral
ALORSST sortals
ALORSSV salvors
ALORSUV louvars
ALORTUU Rouault
ALORTWW awlwort
ALORTYY royalty
ALOSTTU outlast
ALOSTUW outlaws
ALOSTUY layouts
outlays
ALOSTXY oxysalt
ALOTTUU Tutuola
ALPRRSU larrups
ALPRSSU pulsars
ALPRSSW sprawls
ALPRSWY sprawly
ALPSTUU Plautus
ALQSTUY squatly
ALRSSUU russula
ALRSTUU sutural
ALRSUUV uvulars
AMMNRUY nummary
AMMOPTU pomatum
AMMORST marmots
AMMOSXY myxomas
AMMRSUY summary
AMNNORS normans
AMNNOSW snowman
AMNNOSY anonyms
AMNNOTY antonym
AMNNOUU Unamuno
AMNNSTU stannum
AMNOOPP pompano
AMNOORS maroons
AMNOORV Romanov
AMNOOTT ottoman
AMNOOTZ matzoon
AMNOPPR propman
AMNOPRY paronym
AMNOPST postman
tampons
AMNOPTU pantoum
AMNORRS marrons
AMNORSS ramsons
ransoms
AMNORST Marston
matrons
transom
AMNORSY masonry
AMNORTU romaunt
AMNOSTU amounts
outmans
AMNPSTY tympans
AMNPTTU Puttnam
AMNPTYY tympany
AMNQTUU quantum
AMNRTTU tantrum
AMNSTTU mutants
AMNSTUU autumns
AMOOORS amoroso
AMOOPRS prosoma
AMOOPRT taproom
AMOORSU amorous
AMOORXY oxymora
AMOPSTT topmast
AMORRST mortars
AMORRSU armours
AMORRSW marrows
AMORRUY armoury
AMORRWY marrowy
AMPRSUW warmups
AMRRSTY martyrs
AMRRTYY martyry
AMRSTTU stratum
ANNOSST sonants
ANNOSTW wantons
ANNOSTY tannoys
ANNOTTU Taunton
ANNPSSU unsnaps
ANNRTYY tyranny
ANNSSTU suntans
ANNTUUV Nunavut
ANOOPRS soprano
ANOOPRT patroon
ANOORST ratoons
ANOORTT Otranto
rattoon
ANOOSSS Sassoon
ANOPRRS sporran
ANOPRSS parsons
ANOPRST partons
patrons
tarpons
ANOPSTU outspan
ANOPSUY yaupons
ANORRSW narrows
ANORSSV sovrans
ANORSTT attorns
ANORSUU anurous
uranous
ANORWWY wayworn
ANPRSTU suntrap
unstrap
ANPRSUW unwraps
ANRSSTU sunstar
ANRSSUY sunrays
ANRSTTU truants
ANRSTTY tyrants
ANRSUWY runways
AOOPPRS apropos
Sapporo
AOOPRST Atropos
AOOPRTT taproot
AOORRST orators
AOORRSY arroyos
AOORRTT rotator
AOORRTU Rotorua
AOORRTY oratory
AOOSTTT tattoos
AOPPPSU pappous
AOPPRRT rapport
AOPPRST apports
AOPRRST parrots
raptors
AOPRRSU uproars
AOPRRSW sparrow
AOPRRTY portray
AOPRSST pastors
AOPRSTW postwar
AOPRSUV vapours
AOPRUVY vapoury
AOPSSTU passout
AOPSTUY autopsy
payouts
AOPTTUU autoput
AOQRSTU quartos
AOQRTUY Torquay
AORRSST sartors
AORRSWY yarrows
AORSSST assorts
AORSSTT stators
AORSSTU soutars
AORSSUV savours
AORSSUY ossuary
AORSUVY savoury
AORUVVY vouvray
AOSTTUY outstay
APPRRUU purpura
APPRSUY papyrus
APRSSSU surpass
APRSTTU startup
upstart
AQRSTUU Suqutra
AQSTTUY squatty
ARSSSTU Strauss
ARSSTTU stratus
BBBDELO blobbed
bobbled
BBBDELU blubbed
bubbled
BBBEILS bibbles
BBBEIOS bobbies
BBBEIRS bibbers
BBBELOS bobbles
BBBELRU blubber
bubbler
BBBELSU bubbles
BBBEORY bobbery
BBBGIIN bibbing
BBBGINO bobbing
BBBHSUU hubbubs
BBBINOS bobbins
BBCCIKO bibcock
BBCDEIR cribbed
BBCDELO cobbled
BBCDELU clubbed
BBCEEIR berbice
BBCEIRR cribber
BBCEKRU Brubeck
BBCELOR clobber
cobbler
BBCELOS cobbles
BBCELRU clubber
BBCEORS cobbers
BBCEOSW cobwebs
BBCEOTT Cobbett
BBCGINO cobbing
BBCGINU cubbing
BBCHISU cubbish
BBCINOU bubonic
BBCKLOU Lubbock
BBCRSUY scrubby
BBDDEIL dibbled
BBDDERU drubbed
BBDEELP pebbled

BBDEGIR Gibberd
BBDEGLO gobbled
BBDEGRU grubbed
BBDEGSU bedbugs
BBDEHLO hobbled
BBDEIIM imbibed
BBDEIKL kibbled
BBDEILN nibbled
BBDEILO bilobed
lobbied
BBDEILR dibbler
dribble
BBDEILS dibbles
BBDEILW wibbled
BBDEINS snibbed
BBDEIOS dobbies
BBDEIRS dibbers
BBDEKNO knobbed
BBDELMU bumbled
BBDELNO nobbled
BBDELOS bobsled
BBDELOW wobbled
BBDELRU burbled
BBDELSU slubbed
BBDENSU snubbed
BBDEORS dobbers
BBDEOSW swobbed
BBDERRU drubber
BBDESTU stubbed
BBDGIIN dibbing
BBDGINO dobbing
BBDGINU dubbing
BBDIKSU dibbuks
BBDILRY dribbly
BBDINOS dobbins
BBDIRUY rubbidy
BBDKSUY dybbuks
BBEEENT Entebbe
BBEEERR berbere
BBEEERU bebeeru
BBEEIRW webbier
BBEELPS pebbles
BBEFILR fribble
BBEFIRS fibbers
BBEGILR glibber
gribble
BBEGINW webbing
BBEGIOS gibbose
BBEGIRS gibbers
BBEGIST gibbets
BBEGLOR gobbler
BBEGLOS gobbles
BBEGMOR Bomberg
BBEGOST gobbets
BBEGRRU grubber
BBEHIOS hobbies
BBEHISU hubbies
BBEHLOR hobbler
BBEHLOS hobbles
BBEIILS bilbies
BBEIIMR imbiber
BBEIIMS imbibes
BBEIJRS jibbers
BBEIKLS kibbles
BBEILNR nibbler
BBEILNS nibbles
BBEILOS bilboes
lobbies
BBEILOT bibelot
BBEILQU quibble
BBEILSW wibbles
BBEIMOS bimboes
BBEIOOS boobies
BBEIOOT bobotie
BBEIRRS bribers
BBEIRRY bribery
BBEIRSU rubbies
BBEIRTU tubbier
BBEISSU busbies
BBEISTU stubbie
BBEJORS jobbers
BBEJORY jobbery
BBEKLOS blesbok
BBELLOY bellboy
BBELLSU bulbels
BBELMRU bumbler
BBELMSU bumbles
BBELNOR nobbler
BBELNOS nobbles
BBELNSU nubbles
BBELORS slobber
BBELORU boerbul
BBELORW wobbler
BBELORY lobbyer
BBELOST boblets
BBELOSW wobbles
BBELRRU burbler
BBELRSU burbles
lubbers
BBELSTU stubble
BBEMNSU benumbs
BBEMORS bombers
mobbers
BBENRSU snubber
BBEORRS robbers
BBEORRY robbery
BBEORSS sobbers
BBEORYY yobbery
BBEPRUW brewpub
BBERRSU rubbers
BBERRUY rubbery
BBERSTU tubbers
BBFGIIN fibbing
BBFGINO fobbing
BBGGIIN gibbing
BBGGINO gobbing
BBGHINO hobbing
BBGIIJN jibbing
BBGIINN nibbing
BBGIINR bribing
ribbing
BBGIJNO jobbing
BBGILNO lobbing
BBGIMNO bombing
mobbing
BBGINOO boobing
BBGINOR robbing
BBGINOS gibbons
sobbing
BBGINPU pubbing
BBGINRU rubbing
BBGINSU gubbins
subbing
BBGINTU tubbing
BBGIOSU gibbous
BBHIMOS Hobbism
mobbish
BBHIOST hobbits
BBHIOSY yobbish
BBHIRSU rubbish
BBHNOOS hobnobs
BBHRSUY shrubby
BBIILST biblist
BBIISUU buibuis
BBIJMOO jibboom
BBIJNOS jibbons
BBIKOSS skibobs
BBIKTUZ kibbutz
BBILLSU bulbils
BBILNOY nobbily
BBINNSU nubbins
BBINORS ribbons
robbins
BBINORY ribbony
BBIRTUY rubbity
BBJLOOW blowjob
BBKLNOY knobbly
BBKOOOO boobook
BBLLSUU bulbuls
BBLOSUU bulbous
BBLSTUY stubbly
BBNNOOS bonbons
BBNOOOS bonobos
BBNOORU bourbon
BBOOOOS booboos
BBOOSSY bossboy
BBOOSUU boubous
BBORSTU burbots
BBRSSUU suburbs
BCCEILO ecbolic
BCCEILU cubicle
BCCEILY bicycle
BCCEMOR crombec
BCCILOU bucolic
BCCINOO obconic
BCCISUU succubi
BCCMOOX coxcomb
BCCMSUU succumb
BCCNOOR corncob
BCDEEHL belched
BCDEEHN benched
BCDEEIL decibel
BCDEEKS bedecks
BCDEHIR birched
BCDEHIT bitched
BCDEHNU bunched
BCDEHOT botched
BCDEHOU debouch
BCDEIIO biocide
BCDEIKR bricked
BCDEILM climbed
BCDEIMR McBride
BCDEIOS bodices
BCDEIRS scribed
BCDEKLO blocked
BCDEKLU buckled
BCDEKOR bedrock
BCDEKOY bockedy
BCDELOU becloud
BCDEMRU crumbed
BCDENOU bounced
buncoed
BCDIIRU rubidic
BCDINOW cowbind
BCDIORW cowbird
BCDIOSU cuboids
BCDKORU burdock
BCDSTUU subduct
BCEEEHN beechen
BCEEEHR Beecher
BCEEEHS beeches
beseech
BCEEELS Celebes
BCEEFIN benefic
BCEEGIR iceberg
BCEEHIP ephebic
BCEEHIT hebetic
BCEEHLS belches
BCEEHNR bencher
BCEEHNS benches
BCEEHOU bouchee
BCEEILR Liberec
BCEEIRS escribe
BCEEIRT terebic
BCEEKNU buckeen
BCEEKRS rebecks
BCEEKST beckets
BCEEKSZ zebecks
BCEEKTT Beckett
BCEEKUY buckeye
BCEELOU bouclee
BCEEMOS becomes
BCEENOS obscene
BCEHINR birchen
BCEHINT benthic
BCEHIOR brioche
BCEHIOT biotech
BCEHIRS birches
BCEHIST bitches
BCEHISW Wisbech
BCEHITW bewitch
BCEHLRU blucher
Blücher
BCEHNRU Buchner
Büchner
BCEHNSU bunches
BCEHORT botcher
BCEHORU Boucher

BCEHORW cowherb
BCEHOST botches
BCEHOSU subecho
BCEHRSU cherubs
BCEHRTU butcher
BCEHSTU butches
BCEIIKR brickie
BCEIIKS bickies
BCEIKLO blockie
BCEIKLR brickle
BCEIKRS bickers
BCEIKRW Berwick
BCEIKSU buckies
BCEILMO embolic
BCEILMR climber
BCEILOR bricole
corbeil
BCEIMNO combine
BCEIMOR microbe
BCEINOZ benzoic
BCEINRU brucine
BCEIORS corbies
BCEIRRS scriber
BCEIRSS scribes
BCEIRSU suberic
BCEISST bisects
BCEJOST objects
BCEJSTU subject
BCEKLLO bellock
BCEKLOR blocker
BCEKLRU buckler
BCEKLSU buckles
BCEKNOR Brocken
BCEKNOS beckons
BCEKORT brocket
BCEKORU roebuck
BCEKOSU buckoes
BCEKRSU buckers
BCEKSTU buckets
BCELLOW cowbell
BCELLSU subcell
BCELMNU clubmen
BCELMRU clumber
crumble
BCELMSU scumble
BCELNOZ Coblenz
BCELORS corbels
BCELORT Colbert
BCELOSU boucles
BCEMNOW Newcomb
BCEMOOS coombes
BCEMORS combers
BCEMRRU crumber
BCEMRSU cumbers
BCENORU bouncer
BCENOSU bounces
BCEORSU obscure
BCEORTU Courbet
BCESSTU subsect
BCFSSUU subfusc
BCGIKNO bocking
BCGIKNU bucking
BCGIMNO combing
BCGINRU curbing
BCGORSU coburgs
BCGORSY cyborgs
BCHHORS borshch
BCHIIOP biochip
BCHIKOU chibouk
BCHIKSU buckish
BCHIMOR rhombic
BCHINOR bronchi
BCHIOPR pibroch
BCHIOPS phobics
BCHLOTY blotchy
BCHNOOR broncho
BCHORST borscht
BCIIKLN niblick
BCIILMU bulimic
BCIILSY sibylic
BCIINOS bionics
BCIIOPS biopics
BCIIOPT bioptic
BCIISTU biscuit
BCIKKRU Kubrick
BCIKNOS kincobs
BCILMPU plumbic
BCILOOR bicolor
BCIMNOU umbonic
BCINORU rubicon
BCINSUU incubus
BCIOORT robotic
BCIORST strobic
BCIRRSU rubrics
BCIRTUY butyric
BCISSTU cubists
BCJKMUU jumbuck
BCKLLOU bullock
BCKLNOU unblock
BCKOTTU buttock
BCLMOOO Colombo
BCLMOOU coulomb
BCLMRUY crumbly
BCLOOSU colobus
BCMORSY corymbs
BCMOSTU combust
BCNOORS broncos
BCNOSTU cobnuts
BCOOSWY cowboys
BCOOTTY boycott
BCOSTTU Cottbus
BDDDEIU buddied
BDDDELU buddled
BDDEEES seedbed
BDDEEEW bedewed
BDDEEIL bielded
BDDEEIS bedside
BDDEEIT betided
debited
BDDEELN blended
BDDEEOS Beddoes
BDDEERS bedders
BDDEESU debused
BDDEETU debuted
BDDEFOR Bedford
BDDEGIN bedding
BDDEGIR bridged
BDDEGLU bludged
BDDEIIR birdied
BDDEIIS biddies
BDDEILN blinded
BDDEILR bridled
BDDEIRR redbird
BDDEIRS bidders
BDDEISU buddies
BDDELNU bundled
BDDELOO blooded
boodled
BDDELOR broddle
BDDELOU doubled
BDDELSU buddles
BDDENOU bounded
BDDEOOR brooded
BDDEOTU doubted
BDDERSU redbuds
BDDESUU subdued
BDDGIIN bidding
BDDGINU budding
BDDISSU disbuds
BDEEEEZ Zebedee
BDEEELP bleeped
BDEEELR bleeder
BDEEELT beetled
BDEEELV beveled
BDEEERR breeder
BDEEERZ breezed
BDEEFIR briefed
debrief
fibered
BDEEGOY bogeyed
BDEEHOV behoved
BDEEHRT berthed
BDEEILL bellied
libeled
BDEEILO El Obeid
BDEEILS Delibes
edibles
BDEEILV bedevil
BDEEIMR bemired
BDEEIMT bedtime
BDEEINR bendier
inbreed
BDEEINZ bedizen
BDEEIRR berried
BDEEIRS bredies
derbies
BDEEISS besides
BDEEIST betides
BDEEIVV bevvied
BDEEJLS djebels
BDEEKRU rebuked
BDEELLS bedells
BDEELNR blender
Brendel
BDEELNS blendes
BDEELOV beloved
BDEELOW elbowed
BDEELRT trebled
BDEELSS blessed
BDEEMOS besomed
BDEEMOW embowed
BDEEMRU embrued
BDEEMSU bemused
embused
BDEENOR enrobed
BDEENPR prebend
BDEENRS benders
BDEENRT Derbent
BDEEORR rebored
BDEEORS bedsore
sobered
BDEERUW burweed
BDEESSU debuses
BDEFFLU bluffed
BDEFLMU fumbled
BDEGGLO boggled
BDEGHIT bedight
bighted
BDEGILO obliged
BDEGINN bending
BDEGINO Bendigo
BDEGINR breding
BDEGIOO boogied
BDEGIOS bodgies
BDEGIOT bigoted
BDEGIRS begirds
bridges
BDEGIRT Bridget
BDEGISU budgies
BDEGLNU blunged
bungled
BDEGLRU bludger
burgled
BDEGLSU bludges
BDEGOOY goodbye
BDEGRSU redbugs
BDEGSTU budgets
BDEHINS behinds
BDEHINT Beth Din
BDEHIRT birthed
BDEHLMU humbled
BDEHLOS beholds
BDEHLSU blushed
BDEHMTU thumbed
BDEHOST hotbeds
BDEHRSU brushed
BDEIIRS birdies
bridies
BDEIKLN blinked
BDEIKRS brisked
BDEILLU bullied
BDEILMW wimbled
BDEILNR blinder
brindle
BDEILOR broiled
BDEILOS bolides
BDEILPP blipped
BDEILRR bridler

BDEILRS	bridles
BDEILRT	driblet
BDEILRU	builder
	rebuild
BDEILTZ	blitzed
BDEIMMR	brimmed
BDEIMNR	birdmen
BDEIMOR	bromide
BDEIMRU	imbrued
BDEINOU	bedouin
BDEINRS	binders
	rebinds
BDEINRY	bindery
BDEINSU	beduins
	bundies
BDEIORR	broider
BDEIORS	borides
	disrobe
BDEIORT	orbited
BDEIORV	overbid
BDEIORZ	zebroid
BDEIOSY	disobey
BDEIRRS	birders
BDEIRST	bestrid
BDEIRSU	bruised
BDEIRSV	verbids
BDEIRTU	bruited
BDEISST	bedsits
BDEISSU	subside
BDEISTU	subedit
BDEISUW	Budweis
BDEITUY	dubiety
BDEJLMU	jumbled
BDEJORU	objured
BDEKNOO	bookend
BDEKNOU	bunkoed
BDEKNSU	debunks
BDEKOOR	brooked
BDELLOR	bedroll
BDELMMU	mumbled
BDELMOO	bloomed
BDELMPU	plumbed
BDELMRU	rumbled
BDELMTU	tumbled
BDELNNU	Blunden
BDELNOR	blonder
BDELNOS	blondes
BDELNRU	blunder
	bundler
BDELNSU	bundles
BDELNTU	blunted
BDELOOS	boodles
BDELORS	bordels
BDELORU	boulder
	doubler
BDELORW	lowbred
BDELOST	boldest
BDELOSU	bloused
	doubles
BDELOTT	blotted
	bottled
BDELOTU	boulted
	doublet
BDELRRU	blurred
BDELRTU	blurted
BDELSTU	bustled
BDEMOOR	bedroom
	boredom
	broomed
BDEMOOS	bosomed
BDEMSTU	dumbest
BDENNOU	bounden
	unboned
BDENNSU	unbends
BDENORU	bounder
	rebound
BDENORW	browned
BDENORZ	bronzed
BDENOUW	unbowed
BDENRSU	burdens
BDENSTU	subtend
BDEOORR	brooder
BDEOOST	boosted
BDEOPST	bedpost
BDEORRS	borders
BDEORRU	bordure
BDEORSS	desorbs
BDEORST	debtors
	strobed
BDEORSU	rosebud
BDEORSW	browsed
BDEORTU	doubter
	obtrude
	outbred
	redoubt
BDEORUV	overdub
BDERRSU	deburrs
BDESSUU	subdues
BDESSUY	Debussy
BDFIILY	bifidly
BDFIIOR	fibroid
BDFIORS	forbids
BDGGINO	bodging
BDGGINU	budging
BDGGLOU	goldbug
BDGIINN	binding
BDGIINR	birding
BDGIIOO	gobioid
BDGILOO	globoid
BDGINNO	bonding
BDGINOS	bodings
BDGINOY	bodying
BDGLLOU	bulldog
BDGOOOW	bogwood
BDHIINS	bhindis
	bindhis
BDHIOSU	bushido
BDHIRSY	hybrids
BDHOOOY	boyhood
BDIILOR	oilbird
BDIILOS	libidos
BDIIMRS	midribs
BDIISTT	tidbits
BDIKNOS	bodkins
BDILLNY	blindly
BDILNNO	Blondin
BDILPUU	buildup
	upbuild
BDIMNPU	dumpbin
BDIMNUU	dubnium
BDINNOU	inbound
BDINNSU	unbinds
BDINOOR	Borodin
	bridoon
BDINOSU	boudins
BDINRSU	sunbird
BDINRUU	Burundi
BDINSTU	dustbin
BDIOOOV	obovoid
BDIOORU	boudoir
BDIOOST	biodots
BDIOSTU	outbids
BDIOSUU	dubious
BDIRSTU	disturb
BDISSUY	subsidy
BDKLOOS	kobolds
BDKORSY	Brodsky
BDLNOOS	doblons
BDLOOOX	oxblood
BDNNOUU	unbound
BDNOORU	bourdon
BDNOOWW	downbow
BDNORUW	rubdown
BDNOSTU	obtunds
BDOOOWX	boxwood
BDOORRY	Boyd Orr
BDORSWY	bywords
BDRSUUY	Sudbury
BEEEFIR	beefier
	freebie
BEEEFLR	feebler
BEEEFTW	webfeet
BEEEGIS	besiege
BEEEGKL	geelbek
BEEEGNR	breenge
BEEEGRR	bergere
BEEEHIV	beehive
BEEEHNS	shebeen
BEEEHPS	ephebes
BEEEILL	libelee
BEEEILN	beeline
BEEEILV	believe
BEEEIRR	beerier
BEEEJLW	bejewel
BEEEJLZ	jezebel
BEEEKLL	belleek
BEEELPR	bleeper
BEEELPS	Peebles
BEEELRV	beveler
BEEELST	beetles
BEEEMRS	berseem
BEEEMSS	beseems
BEEENNZ	benzene
BEEENTW	between
BEEEPRS	beepers
BEEERSZ	beezers
	breezes
BEEFGIN	beefing
BEEFILR	febrile
BEEFILS	beliefs
BEEFILY	beefily
BEEFINT	benefit
BEEFIRR	briefer
BEEFLOR	Froebel
BEEFLTY	beetfly
BEEGGNU	geebung
BEEGILL	legible
BEEGILO	obligee
BEEGILS	beigels
BEEGILU	beguile
BEEGIMR	begrime
BEEGINP	beeping
BEEGINR	bigener
	breinge
BEEGINT	beignet
BEEGINU	beguine
BEEGISY	bigeyes
BEEGJRS	Esbjerg
BEEGLMR	Lemberg
BEEGNRS	bergens
BEEGNRZ	Bregenz
BEEGRSU	burgees
BEEHIRR	herbier
BEEHLRT	blether
BEEHNRS	Behrens
BEEHNTU	Beuthen
BEEHOOV	behoove
BEEHOPS	phoebes
BEEHOSV	behoves
BEEHRRT	Herbert
BEEHRST	sherbet
BEEHRSW	beshrew
	Hebrews
BEEHRTY	thereby
BEEHRWY	whereby
BEEHSST	behests
BEEHSTY	bheesty
BEEIJLU	jubilee
BEEIKLW	weblike
BEEILLS	bellies
BEEILMP	epiblem
BEEILNR	berline
BEEILOS	obelise
BEEILOZ	obelize
BEEILRS	beliers
BEEILRY	beerily
BEEIMRS	bemires
	biremes
BEEIMST	betimes
BEEINNS	bennies
BEEINNZ	benzine
BEEINOS	ebonies
	ebonise
BEEINOT	ebonite
BEEINOZ	ebonize
BEEINRZ	zebrine
BEEIOSU	Eusebio
BEEIQUZ	bezique

BEEIRRS berries
BEEIRRV brevier
BEEIRSZ Béziers
BEEIRTZ Bizerte
BEEISTW website
BEEISVV bevvies
BEEJMOR Bermejo
BEEJSSU bejesus
BEEKNOT betoken
BEEKOPS bespoke
BEEKORS reeboks
BEEKRRS berserk
BEEKRRU rebuker
BEEKRSU rebukes
BEELLMN bellmen
BEELMMS emblems
BEELMOW embowel
BEELMRT tremble
BEELMWY Wembley
BEELNNO ennoble
BEELNOZ benzole
BEELNTY Bentley
BEELNUX Benelux
BEELOTY eyebolt
BEELRST belters
trebles
BEELRSY berleys
BEELSSS blesses
BEELSSW webless
BEEMMRS members
BEEMNPT benempt
BEEMORW embower
BEEMRSU Burmese
embrues
BEEMSSU bemuses
embuses
BEENNST bennets
BEENNTT Bennett
BEENORR enrober
BEENORS boreens
enrobes
BEENOST beentos
boneset
BEENOTY Toynbee
BEENSTU subteen
BEENSUV subvene
BEEOOST bootees
BEEOPPS bopeeps
BEEORRS rebores
soberer
BEEORRU bourree
BEEORSV observe
obverse
verbose
BEEORSY obeyers
BEEORWY eyebrow
BEEQSTU bequest
BEERRSV reverbs
BEERRSW brewers
BEERRWY brewery
BEERSST breests
BEERSSU rebuses
subsere
BEERSTT betters
BEERSTV brevets
BEERSTW bestrew
webster
BEERTTU burette
BEESSTU bustees
BEFFIRS biffers
BEFFLRU bluffer
BEFFRSU buffers
rebuffs
BEFFSTU buffets
BEFGIIL filibeg
BEFGIIR Fibiger
BEFGIRU firebug
BEFILMS fimbles
BEFILNU bluefin
BEFILOS foibles
BEFILOU biofuel
BEFILRT filbert
BEFILRY briefly
BEFILSU fusible
subfile
BEFINOR bonfire
BEFIOOR boofier
BEFIORX firebox
BEFIRST bifters
BEFIRSU fubsier
BEFIRVY verbify
BEFITUX tubifex
BEFLLWY flyblew
BEFLMRU fumbler
BEFLMSU fumbles
BEFLOOS befools
BEFLORT Belfort
BEFLOSU befouls
BEFOORR forbore
BEFOOTW webfoot
BEGGGIN begging
BEGGIOR boggier
BEGGIRU buggier
BEGGIST biggest
BEGGISU buggies
BEGGLOS boggles
BEGGMOR Gomberg
BEGGORS boggers
BEGGRSU buggers
BEGGRUY buggery
BEGHINR Behring
BEGHLOR Holberg
BEGHRRU burgher
BEGIIJN Beijing
BEGIILR bilgier
BEGIINN inbeing
BEGIINR breiing
BEGIINS bingies
BEGIKNR kerbing
BEGILLN belling
BEGILLY legibly
BEGILMU Belgium
BEGILNO ignoble
BEGILNS bingles
BEGILNT belting
BEGILNU blueing
BEGILNY belying
BEGILOR Broglie
obliger
BEGILOS obliges
BEGILRS gerbils
BEGILRT gilbert
BEGILST giblets
BEGINOS biogens
BEGINOY obeying
BEGINRR bringer
BEGINRW brewing
BEGINRY breying
BEGINSS bigness
BEGINST besting
BEGINSU beguins
BEGINTT betting
BEGIOOS boogies
goobies
BEGIOSU bougies
BEGIRSU Bergius
BEGISSU gibuses
BEGKMOS gemsbok
BEGLLOU globule
BEGLMRU grumble
BEGLMUU bluegum
BEGLNOS belongs
BEGLNRU blunger
bungler
BEGLNSU blunges
bungles
BEGLOOS globose
BEGLOOT bootleg
BEGLOST goblets
BEGLOSW bowlegs
weblogs
BEGLOUY Beyoğlu
BEGLRSU buglers
burgles
BEGMORR Romberg
BEGNNOY Bonynge
BEGNOOS bongoes
BEGNORS Bergson
BEGNORU burgeon
BEGNOSY bygones
BEGNOTT bettong
BEGNRSU bungers
BEGOORS goobers
BEGORSU Bourges
brogues
BEGRRSU burgers
BEGRSSU burgess
BEHIITX exhibit
BEHIKKS Bishkek
BEHIKLO hoblike
BEHIKNT bethink
BEHILLX Bexhill
BEHILMS blemish
BEHILMT thimble
BEHILNO Holbein
BEHILOS bolshie
BEHILRT Hilbert
BEHILSU blueish
BEHILSW weblish
BEHIMOR bioherm
BEHINOP hipbone
BEHINOR Hiberno-
BEHINRU Niebuhr
BEHINST henbits
BEHIOST bothies
BEHIOTW howbeit
BEHIRRT rebirth
BEHIRSU bushier
Bushire
BEHISSU bushies
BEHKKOO kokobeh
BEHKNOO Hoboken
BEHKORS rheboks
BEHLLOP bellhop
BEHLLOX hellbox
BEHLMRU humbler
BEHLMSU humbles
BEHLORT brothel
BEHLRSU blusher
burhels
BEHLSSU blushes
bushels
BEHMNSU bushmen
BEHMOOY homeboy
BEHMORS hombres
BEHMOST Tshombe
BEHNNOT benthon
BEHNORU Bonheur
BEHNOST benthos
BEHNPRU Hepburn
BEHNRTU burthen
BEHOORT theorbo
BEHOPRT potherb
BEHOPSU phoebus
BEHORRT brother
BEHORST bothers
BEHORTT betroth
BEHRRSU brusher
BEHRRTU Thurber
BEHRSSU brushes
BEIIKLN niblike
BEIIKLR riblike
BEIIKRS birkies
BEIILLN Bellini
BEIILLS billies
BEIILRS risible
BEIILSV visible
BEIINNR Bernini
BEIINOT niobite
BEIINRR brinier
BEIINST stibine
BEIIOTT biotite
BEIIRTT bittier
BEIISTT Tibesti
BEIISTV vibiest
BEIISVV bivvies
BEIISZZ bizzies
BEIJLRS jerbils

BEIKKLU	Kubelik
BEIKLNR	blinker
BEIKLOS	obelisk
BEIKLOX	boxlike
BEIKLRS	bilkers
BEIKLRU	bulkier
BEIKNRS	brisken
BEIKOOS	bookies
BEIKORS	boskier
BEIKRRS	brisker
BEIKRST	brisket
BEIKSTV	Vitebsk
BEILLST	billets
BEILLSU	bullies
BEILMNR	nimbler
BEILMOR	embroil
BEILMOS	mobiles
BEILMRS	limbers
BEILMRT	timbrel
	Trimble
BEILMSU	sublime
BEILMSW	wimbles
BEILNOS	bolines
BEILNOW	bowline
BEILNRS	berlins
BEILNSY	bylines
BEILNTZ	blintze
BEILOOS	loobies
BEILOPR	preboil
BEILOPY	epiboly
BEILOQU	oblique
BEILORR	broiler
BEILORS	boilers
	liberos
	reboils
BEILORT	Blériot
BEILORW	blowier
BEILORZ	Berlioz
BEILOSW	blowies
BEILRRU	burlier
BEILRSS	ribless
BEILRST	blister
	bristle
BEILRTT	brittle
	triblet
BEILRTU	rebuilt
BEILRTY	liberty
BEILSSS	blisses
BEILSTU	subtile
BEILSTW	blewits
BEILSTZ	blitzes
BEILTTU	bluetit
BEIMMRR	brimmer
BEIMNOR	bromine
BEIMNTU	bitumen
BEIMOSZ	zombies
BEIMPRU	bumpier
BEIMRST	timbers
	timbres
BEIMRSU	imbrues
BEIMRTU	terbium
BEIMSTU	subitem
BEINNOR	bonnier
BEINNOS	benison
BEINNOZ	benzoin
BEINNSU	bunnies
BEINOOT	eobiont
BEINORT	bornite
BEINORW	brownie
BEINOST	boniest
BEINOSV	bovines
BEINOSX	bonxies
BEINOTT	bottine
BEINRSU	suberin
BEINRSY	byrnies
BEINRTT	bittern
	Britten
BEINRTU	tribune
	turbine
BEIOOPT	biotope
BEIOORZ	boozier
BEIOOST	booties
BEIOPTY	biotype
BEIORRT	bortier
	orbiter
	Robert I
BEIORSS	bossier
BEIORSY	boysier
BEIORUV	bouvier
BEIOSSS	bossies
BEIOSSU	soubise
BEIOSSW	bowsies
BEIOSTX	boxiest
BEIOSTY	obesity
BEIQRTU	briquet
BEIQSSU	bisques
BEIRRRU	burrier
BEIRRSU	bruiser
	buriers
BEIRSST	bestirs
	bisters
	bistres
	bitsers
	breists
BEIRSSU	bruises
BEIRSTT	bitters
BEIRSTU	bustier
BEIRTTU	tribute
BEIRTVY	brevity
BEISSTU	busiest
BEISTTU	butties
BEITTWX	betwixt
BEJJSUU	jujubes
BEJKOUX	jukebox
BEJLMRU	jumbler
BEJLMSU	jumbles
BEJLOSS	jobless
BEJORSU	objures
BEKLNOZ	Koblenz
BEKLOOT	booklet
BEKLRSU	bulkers
	burlesk
BEKNORS	bonkers
BEKNRSU	bunkers
BEKORRS	brokers
BEKOSST	boskets
BEKRSSU	buskers
BELLNPU	bullpen
BELLOSU	boulles
	lobules
	soluble
BELLOSW	bellows
	Boswell
BELLOUV	voluble
BELLRRU	burrell
BELLSSU	Bussell
BELLSTU	bullets
BELMMRU	mumbler
BELMMSU	mumbles
BELMNOS	nombles
BELMNOU	nelumbo
BELMNOY	benomyl
BELMNSU	numbles
BELMOOR	bloomer
BELMOPR	problem
BELMORT	temblor
BELMORY	Bromley
BELMOSU	embolus
BELMPRU	plumber
BELMRRU	rumbler
BELMRSU	lumbers
	rumbles
	slumber
BELMRTU	tumbler
	tumbrel
BELMRTY	trembly
BELMSTU	stumble
	tumbles
BELNOOR	borneol
BELNOOY	boloney
BELNOST	noblest
BELNOYZ	benzoyl
BELNRTU	blunter
BELNRUY	Burnley
BELNSTU	sunbelt
	unbelts
BELNUUZ	Zebulun
BELOOPR	blooper
BELOORS	boleros
BELOOSS	soboles
BELOOVY	Byelovo
BELOPSU	pueblos
BELORST	bolster
	bolters
	lobster
BELORSU	roubles
BELORSW	blowers
	bowlers
BELORSY	soberly
BELORTT	blotter
	bottler
BELORTU	boulter
	trouble
BELOSSU	blouses
	boluses
BELOSTT	bottles
BELOSTU	boletus
BELRRSU	burlers
BELRSTU	bluster
	bustler
	butlers
	subtler
BELRSUU	subrule
BELRSUY	burleys
BELRTUY	butlery
BELSSTU	bustles
	sublets
BELSTUU	tubules
BEMMOOS	embosom
BEMMRSU	bummers
BEMNOST	entombs
BEMNOSU	umbones
BEMNOSW	enwombs
BEMNRSU	numbers
BEMOORS	boomers
BEMORST	mobster
BEMORSY	embryos
BEMPRSU	bumpers
BEMSSUU	subsume
BENNORT	Brenton
BENNORW	newborn
BENNOST	bonnets
BENNSTU	bunnets
BENOORS	Osborne
	Robeson
BENORRW	browner
BENORRZ	bronzer
BENORSS	Bresson
BENORST	bretons
BENORSU	bournes
BENORSZ	bronzes
BENOSSU	bonuses
BENOSWY	newsboy
BENRRSU	burners
BENRSSU	brussen
BENRSTU	burnets
BENRTTU	Burnett
BENRUWY	Newbury
BEOORSS	sorbose
BEOORST	booster
	reboots
BEOORSZ	boozers
	rebozos
BEOPPRS	boppers
BEOPRRS	probers
BEOPRRV	proverb
BEOQSTU	bosquet
BEOQSUY	obsequy
BEOQTUU	bouquet
BEORRSS	resorbs
BEORRST	Roberts
BEORRSW	browser
BEORSST	sorbets
	strobes
BEORSSU	bourses
BEORSSW	bowsers
	browses
BEORSTT	bettors

BEORSTV	obverts
BEORSUZ	subzero
BEORSWY	bowyers
BEORUVY	overbuy
BEOSSST	bossets
BEOSSTT	obtests
BEOSSTU	Bossuet
BEOSSTW	bestows
BEPRRTU	perturb
BEPRTUY	puberty
BEPSTUY	subtype
BEQRSUU	brusque
BERRSTU	burster
BERSSTU	busters
BERSTTU	butters
BERSTUV	subvert
BERSUZZ	buzzers
BERTTUY	buttery
BESSSTU	subsets
BESTTUX	subtext
BFFGIIN	biffing
BFFGINU	buffing
BFFIINS	biffins
BFFILOO	boiloff
BFFINOS	boffins
BFFLLUY	bluffly
BFFLOOW	blowoff
BFFNOOU	buffoon
BFGIORT	frogbit
BFHIOSX	boxfish
BFHIRSU	furbish
BFHLSUY	bushfly
BFIILRS	fibrils
BFIINOR	fibroin
BFILMRU	brimful
BFILOTY	liftboy
BFILSUY	fusibly
BFINOSW	bowfins
BFIORSS	rosbifs
BFIORST	Bifrost
BFIORSU	fibrous
BFIRTUY	brutify
BFKLOOY	flybook
BFLLOUW	bowlful
BFLLOWY	blowfly
	flyblow
BFLOSUX	boxfuls
BFLSTUU	tubfuls
BFOOOTY	footboy
BGGGIIN	bigging
BGGGINO	bogging
BGGGINU	bugging
BGGHIIS	biggish
BGGIILN	bilging
BGGIINN	binging
BGGIINS	biggins
BGGIISW	bigwigs
BGGILNO	globing
BGGILNU	bugling
	bulging
BGGINNO	bonging
BGGINNU	bunging
BGGINOS	biggons
BGGNOOS	bogongs
BGGNOSU	bugongs
BGHHIOY	highboy
BGHIILS	ghiblis
BGHIINS	binghis
BGHILST	blights
BGHILTY	blighty
BGHINOR	bighorn
BGHINSU	bushing
BGHIPSU	bushpig
BGHIRST	brights
BGHLRUU	burghul
BGHMORU	homburg
BGHMSUU	humbugs
BGHOOOS	Oshogbo
BGHOORU	borough
BGHORTU	brought
BGIIKLN	bilking
BGIILLN	billing
BGIILNO	boiling
BGIILNR	birling
BGIILNS	sibling
BGIIMNU	imbuing
BGIINNN	binning
BGIINNR	brining
BGIINRR	birring
BGIINTT	bitting
BGIKLNU	bulking
BGIKNNO	bonking
BGIKNNU	bunking
BGIKNOO	booking
BGIKNOR	broking
BGIKNRU	burking
BGIKNSU	busking
BGILLNU	bulling
BGILMOU	gumboil
BGILMRU	Limburg
BGILNOO	booling
BGILNOS	goblins
BGILNOT	biltong
	bolting
BGILNOW	blowing
	bowling
BGILNOY	ignobly
BGILNRU	burling
BGILNSU	bluings
BGILOOR	obligor
BGILOOY	biology
BGILRTU	Tilburg
BGIMMNU	bumming
BGIMNNU	numbing
BGIMNOO	booming
BGIMNOR	borming
BGIMNOT	tombing
BGIMNPU	bumping
BGIMRSY	Grimsby
BGINNRU	Brüning
	burning
BGINNTU	bunting
BGINOOT	booting
BGINOOZ	boozing
BGINOPP	bopping
BGINOPR	probing
BGINORS	borings
BGINORZ	zorbing
BGINOSS	bossing
	gibsons
BGINOSU	bousing
BGINOSW	bowsing
BGINOTT	botting
BGINOUY	buoying
BGINOWW	wingbow
BGINPRU	burping
BGINRRU	burring
BGINRUY	burying
BGINSSU	bussing
BGINSTU	busting
BGINSUY	busying
BGINTTU	butting
BGINUZZ	buzzing
BGIORTY	bigotry
BGKLOOO	logbook
BGKORSY	grysbok
BGLMORU	Borglum
BGLMRUY	grumbly
BGLNOOS	oblongs
BGLNOOW	longbow
BGLNOUW	blowgun
BGLOOSU	globous
BGLOSSU	bugloss
BGLOSUY	bogusly
BGNOSSU	subsong
BGOORSU	burgoos
BHHIIST	bhishti
BHHIKSU	bhikhus
BHIIINT	inhibit
BHIINRS	brinish
BHIIPSS	sibship
BHIKLOS	blokish
BHIKOOS	bookish
BHILLOY	billyoh
BHILLSU	bullish
BHILOTU	holibut
BHILPSU	publish
BHILSUY	bushily
BHIMOOS	hoboism
BHIMOPR	bimorph
BHIMORT	thrombi
BHIMORU	bohrium
BHIMSTU	bismuth
BHINRSU	burnish
BHIOORS	boorish
BHIOOST	booshit
BHIOPSS	bishops
BHIOSWZ	showbiz
BHIRSTU	brutish
BHISTTU	bushtit
BHKNOSU	bohunks
BHLRSUU	bulrush
BHMORSU	rhombus
BHOOOOS	boohoos
BHOOSTW	bowshot
BHPRSUU	brushup
BIIIKNS	bikinis
BIIILST	Tbilisi
BIIJOTU	Jibouti
BIILLNO	billion
BIILLTW	twibill
BIILNTU	inbuilt
BIILOSU	bilious
BIILRSY	risibly
BIILSTW	twibils
BIILSVY	visibly
BIIMNOU	niobium
BIIMNSU	minibus
BIIMPRS	biprism
BIIMSTU	stibium
BIINOSU	binious
BIINSTU	Bisitun
BIIORSV	vibrios
BIISSTV	vibists
BIISTTT	titbits
BIJNOSU	subjoin
BIKLLUY	bulkily
BIKLNOT	inkblot
BIKLNOY	linkboy
BIKLRSY	briskly
BIKMNOO	boomkin
BIKMNPU	bumpkin
BIKMNSU	bumkins
BIKNRSY	Rybinsk
BIKNSSU	buskins
BILLNOS	billons
BILLNOU	bullion
BILLNUY	Lyublin
BILLOPX	pillbox
BILLOSW	billows
BILLOWY	billowy
BILLRWY	wrybill
BILMNOR	nombril
BILMOOS	Ólimbos
BILMPUY	bumpily
BILMRTU	tumbril
BILNNOY	bonnily
BILNOTU	botulin
BILNRSU	Lisburn
BILNTUU	unbuilt
BILORST	bristol
BILOSSU	subsoil
BILOSSY	bossily
BILPTUU	upbuilt
BILRSTY	bristly
BILRTTY	brittly
BILRTUY	tilbury
BIMMOOS	miombos
BIMMORS	bromism
BIMNOSU	omnibus
BIMOSSS	bossism
BIMRSUX	bruxism
BIMSSSU	submiss
BIMSSTU	submits
BINNOSU	bunions
BINOORS	Orbison
BINOOST	bonitos
BINOOSU	niobous

BINOSST bonists
BINPSUY bunyips
BINRTUY butyrin
BINSTUU Bisutun
subunit
BIOOORS rooibos
BIOORSZ borzois
BIOOSST oboists
BIOOSUV obvious
BIOPRTY probity
BIORRTU burrito
BIORRTW ribwort
BIORSST bistros
Brissot
BIORSTT bistort
BIORSTW Bristow
BIORSUU rubious
BIRSTTU turbits
BISSSTU subsist
BISTUUU busuuti
BKLOOST Tobolsk
BKNOOTW bowknot
BKOORWX workbox
BLLNTUY bluntly
BLLOOOS lobolos
BLLOSUY solubly
BLLOUVY volubly
BLMMPUU plumbum
BLMOOOT tombolo
BLMOORW lobworm
BLMOOSS blossom
BLMOSSY symbols
BLMOUXY buxomly
BLNNOUW unblown
BLNOORW lowborn
BLNOOSS bolsons
BLNOOSU blouson
BLNOOTU Boulton
BLNOSTU unbolts
BLOOPWY plowboy
BLOOQUY obloquy
BLOORWW lowbrow
BLOOSWY lowboys
BLOOTUW blowout
BLOPSTU subplot
BLOPSUW blowups
BLORUVY Rublyov
BMNOOSU unbosom
BMOOORX boxroom
BMOOSTT bottoms
BMOOSTY tomboys
BMORSUU brumous
BNNRSUU sunburn
BNOORYZ Broonzy
BNOOSST bostons
BNORSSU suborns
BNORSTU burtons
BNORSUU burnous
BNORTUU burnout
BNOSSUW sunbows
BNOSTTU buttons
BNOTTUY buttony
BOOPRTT Bottrop
BOOPSTX postbox
BOOPSTY postboy
potboys
BOORRSW borrows
BOORRTY robotry
BOOSWWW bowwows
BOPSSTU postbus
BORRSUW burrows
BORSTTU turbots
BOSTUUY buyouts
CCCDIOO coccoid
CCCDIOS coccids
CCCNOOT concoct
CCCOOSU coccous
CCDEEER recceed
CCDEEHK checked
CCDEEIM ecdemic
CCDEEIO ecocide
CCDEEKL clecked
CCDEENO concede
CCDEENY decency
CCDEEOR coerced
CCDEESU succeed
CCDEHIL cliched
CCDEHIN cinched
CCDEHKO chocked
CCDEHKU chucked
CCDEHOU couched
CCDEHTW cwtched
CCDEIIL icicled
CCDEIIT deictic
CCDEIKL clicked
CCDEIKR cricked
CCDEILR circled
CCDEIMO comedic
CCDEIOS codices
CCDEKLO clocked
cockled
CCDEKLU clucked
CCDEKOR crocked
CCDELOU occlude
CCDENOS sconced
CCDENOU conduce
CCDEOST decocts
CCDHIIL cichlid
CCDIILO codicil
CCDIILU culicid
CCDIIOR cricoid
CCDILOY cycloid
CCDKLOU cuckold
CCDNOOR concord
CCDNOTU conduct
CCEEHKR checker
recheck
CCEEHOR ecorche
CCEEHRS creches
screech
CCEEILN licence
CCEEINR eccrine
CCEEINS science
CCEEIRV crevice
CCEEKOY cockeye
CCEELRY recycle
CCEENRY recency
CCEEORR coercer
CCEEORS coerces
CCEERSY secrecy
CCEFHRU curchef
CCEFNOT confect
CCEGNOY cogency
CCEHIKN chicken
CCEHIKU chuckie
CCEHILS cliches
CCEHILU culchie
CCEHINO conchie
CCEHINS cinches
CCEHINT technic
CCEHIOR choicer
choreic
CCEHIOS choices
Cochise
CCEHIRS screich
CCEHIST hectics
CCEHKLU chuckle
CCEHKOR chocker
CCEHKPU checkup
CCEHKRU chucker
CCEHLOS cloches
CCEHLRU cleruch
CCEHNOS conches
CCEHORT crochet
CCEHORU coucher
CCEHOSU couches
CCEHRSU curches
CCEHSTW cwtches
CCEIILS cilices
icicles
CCEIIMS cimices
CCEIIRT icteric
CCEIKLR clicker
CCEIKOR cockier
CCEIKOS cockies
CCEIKRT cricket
CCEILMO celomic
CCEILNU nucleic
CCEILRR circler
CCEILRS circles
clerics
CCEILRT circlet
CCEILSU culices
CCEILSY cylices
CCEILTU cuticle
CCEIMOT cometic
CCEIMST smectic
CCEINOR cornice
crocein
CCEINOS concise
CCEINOT conceit
CCEINRT centric
CCEIOPP coppice
CCEIOPT ectopic
CCEIORS ciceros
CCEIORT cerotic
orectic
CCEIOSS ciscoes
CCEIPST sceptic
CCEIRST cretics
CCEISSU succise
CCEKLOR clocker
CCEKLOS cockles
CCEKNOY cockney
CCEKOPS copecks
CCEKOPT petcock
CCEKORS cockers
CCEKORT crocket
CCELLOT collect
CCELLOU Uccello
CCELNOY cyclone
CCELRSY cyclers
CCENNOR concern
CCENNOT concent
connect
CCENOPT concept
CCENORT concert
CCENOSS sconces
CCEOOTT cocotte
CCEOPRS Cecrops
CCEORRT correct
CCEORRU reoccur
CCEORTW twoccer
CCESSSU success
CCFIRUY crucify
CCFLOSU floccus
CCGHINO gnocchi
CCGIKNO cocking
CCGIKNU cucking
CCGILNY cycling
CCGKOOR gorcock
CCHHIIS chichis
CCHHRUY churchy
CCHIIOR Chirico
CCHIIST stichic
CCHIKLS Schlick
CCHIKST schtick
CCHILOR chloric
CCHILOS Colchis
CCHIMOR chromic
CCHINOR chronic
CCHIORY chicory
CCHIOTW cowitch
CCHIPSU hiccups
CCHIPSY psychic
CCHKLOS schlock
CCHKMSU schmuck
CCHKOOS chockos
CCHKOSY cockshy
CCHNRSU scrunch
CCHNRUY crunchy
CCHOORS scrooch
CCHOSTU succoth
CCIIILS silicic
CCIILNS clinics
CCIILOT colitic
CCIILPR circlip
CCIILST clitics

CCIINPS	picnics
CCIINPU	Puccini
CCIIRST	critics
CCIIRTU	circuit
CCIKLOW	cowlick
CCIKLOY	cockily
	colicky
CCIKOPT	cockpit
CCILNOO	colonic
CCILNOU	council
CCILOOP	piccolo
CCILSTY	cyclist
CCIMOTY	mycotic
CCINOTV	convict
CCIOORS	sirocco
CCIOPTU	occiput
CCIPRTY	cryptic
CCISUYZ	Cyzicus
CCKOOSU	cuckoos
CCKOPSU	cockups
CCLOPSY	cyclops
CCLOSTU	occults
CCMOOOR	morocco
CCNOOOS	cocoons
CCNOOPU	puccoon
CCNOOTU	coconut
CCNORSU	concurs
CCNOSSU	concuss
CCORSSU	succors
CCORSUU	succour
CCORSUY	succory
CCOSSTU	stuccos
CCSSSUU	succuss
CDDDEEI	decided
CDDDEEO	decoded
CDDDEEU	deduced
CDDDELO	coddled
CDDDELU	cuddled
CDDDESU	scudded
CDDEEER	decreed
	receded
CDDEEES	seceded
CDDEEII	deicide
CDDEEIR	decider
	decried
CDDEEIS	decides
CDDEEIX	excided
CDDEEKO	decoked
CDDEENO	encoded
CDDEENS	descend
	scended
CDDEEOR	decoder
CDDEEOS	decodes
CDDEEOY	decoyed
CDDEERU	reduced
CDDEESU	deduces
	seduced
CDDEEUW	cudweed
CDDEHIN	chidden
CDDEHIT	ditched
CDDEHOR	chorded
CDDEHOU	douched
CDDEHRU	chudder
CDDEINU	induced
CDDEIOT	de dicto
CDDEISU	cuddies
CDDELOR	coddler
CDDELOS	coddles
	scolded
CDDELOU	clouded
CDDELRU	curdled
CDDELSU	cuddles
CDDEORS	codders
CDDEORW	crowded
CDDESTU	deducts
CDDGINO	codding
CDDIIKN	niddick
CDDIIOS	discoid
CDDIIOY	didicoy
CDDIIRU	druidic
CDDIKOP	piddock
CDDIKOR	Roddick
CDDIORS	discord
CDDKOPU	puddock
CDDKORU	ruddock
CDEEEFL	fleeced
CDEEEFN	defence
CDEEEHK	cheeked
CDEEEHL	leeched
CDEEEHP	cheeped
CDEEEHR	cheered
CDEEEHS	cheesed
CDEEEIV	deceive
CDEEEJT	ejected
CDEEELT	elected
CDEEEPR	precede
CDEEERR	decreer
CDEEERS	decrees
	recedes
	seceder
CDEEERT	decreet
	erected
CDEEESS	secedes
CDEEESX	exceeds
CDEEFHT	fetched
CDEEFII	edifice
CDEEFKL	flecked
CDEEFLT	clefted
	deflect
CDEEFOR	deforce
CDEEFST	defects
CDEEGHN	Chengde
CDEEGKT	gedeckt
CDEEHIP	cepheid
CDEEHIS	dehisce
CDEEHIV	chevied
CDEEHKL	heckled
CDEEHLP	chelped
CDEEHLT	letched
CDEEHLW	welched
CDEEHMS	schemed
CDEEHNW	wenched
CDEEHOR	cohered
	ochered
CDEEHPR	perched
CDEEHRS	cheders
CDEEHRT	retched
CDEEHRU	euchred
CDEEHST	chested
CDEEIIT	eidetic
CDEEILN	decline
CDEEILP	pedicel
	pedicle
CDEEILS	deciles
CDEEIMN	endemic
CDEEINO	codeine
CDEEINT	enticed
CDEEINV	evinced
CDEEIOS	diocese
CDEEIOV	devoice
CDEEIPR	pierced
CDEEIRR	decrier
CDEEIRS	decries
	deicers
CDEEIRT	recited
CDEEIST	deceits
CDEEISV	devices
CDEEISX	excides
	excised
CDEEITV	evicted
CDEEITX	excited
CDEEJST	dejects
CDEEKLS	deckels
	deckles
CDEEKNR	redneck
CDEEKNS	snecked
CDEEKOS	decokes
CDEEKPS	specked
CDEEKRS	deckers
CDEEKRW	wrecked
CDEELMM	clemmed
CDEELPU	cupeled
	decuple
CDEELPY	ycleped
CDEELSU	seclude
CDEELUX	exclude
CDEENOR	encoder
	encored
CDEENOS	encodes
	seconde
CDEENOZ	cozened
CDEENRS	decerns
CDEENRT	centred
	credent
CDEENST	descent
	scented
CDEEOOY	cooeyed
CDEEOPR	proceed
CDEEORV	covered
CDEEORW	cowered
CDEEORY	decoyer
CDEEOST	cestode
CDEEOTV	coveted
CDEERRU	reducer
CDEERSS	screeds
CDEERST	crested
CDEERSU	reduces
	rescued
	secured
	seducer
CDEERSW	screwed
CDEERTU	eructed
CDEESSU	seduces
CDEESSY	ecdyses
CDEESTT	detects
CDEESUX	excused
CDEFFHU	chuffed
CDEFFIO	coiffed
CDEFFOS	scoffed
CDEFFSU	scuffed
CDEFHIL	filched
CDEFHOO	choofed
CDEFIIT	deficit
CDEFIKL	flicked
CDEFINO	confide
CDEFKLO	flocked
CDEFKOR	defrock
	frocked
CDEFNTU	defunct
CDEFOSU	focused
CDEGGHU	chugged
CDEGGLO	clogged
	coggled
CDEGGOR	crogged
CDEGHNU	Chengdu
CDEGHOU	coughed
CDEGIIN	deicing
CDEGIKN	decking
CDEGINR	cringed
CDEGINU	educing
CDEGLSU	cudgels
CDEGNSU	scunged
CDEGORS	codgers
CDEHHIT	hitched
CDEHHNU	hunched
CDEHHTU	hutched
CDEHIIL	ceilidh
CDEHIIV	chivied
CDEHIKN	chinked
CDEHIKO	hoicked
CDEHILL	chilled
CDEHILO	cheloid
CDEHILP	delphic
CDEHILR	eldrich
CDEHIMR	chirmed
CDEHIMT	mitched
CDEHINN	chinned
CDEHINO	hedonic
CDEHINP	pinched
CDEHINW	winched
CDEHIOW	cowhide
CDEHIPP	chipped
CDEHIPR	chirped
CDEHIPT	pitched
CDEHIRR	chirred
CDEHIRS	chiders
	Driesch
	herdics

CDEHIRT ditcher
CDEHIST ditches
sichted
CDEHISU duchies
CDEHITW witched
CDEHIVV chivved
CDEHKLO hockled
CDEHKOO chooked
CDEHKOS shocked
CDEHKSU shucked
CDEHKUY heyduck
CDEHLMU mulched
CDEHLNU lunched
CDEHLNY lynched
CDEHLOT clothed
CDEHLRU lurched
CDEHLST Scheldt
CDEHMMU chummed
CDEHMNU munched
CDEHMOO mooched
CDEHMOP chomped
CDEHMOR chromed
CDEHMPU chumped
CDEHMTU mutched
CDEHNOT notched
CDEHNPU punched
CDEHNRU chunder
churned
CDEHNSY synched
CDEHOPP chopped
CDEHOPU pouched
CDEHORW chowder
cowherd
CDEHOSU douches
hocused
CDEHOTU touched
CDEHOUV vouched
CDEHPSY psyched
CDEHRRU churred
CDEHRSU crushed
CDEHSSU duchess
CDEHSTU Deutsch
dutches
CDEHSTY scythed
CDEIIKR dickier
CDEIIKS dickies
CDEIINR dineric
CDEIINS incised
indices
CDEIINT identic
incited
CDEIIOR ericoid
CDEIIST deistic
diciest
CDEIISU suicide
CDEIJST disject
CDEIKLN clinked
CDEIKLP pickled
CDEIKLS slicked
CDEIKLT tickled
CDEIKMS medicks
CDEIKNS dickens
snicked
CDEIKPR pricked
CDEIKRR derrick
CDEIKRS dickers
CDEIKRT tricked
CDEIKRU duckier
CDEIKRW wricked
CDEIKST sticked
CDEIKSU duckies
CDEIKSY dickeys
CDEILLO collide
collied
CDEILMO melodic
CDEILNU include
nuclide
CDEILOP policed
CDEILOS coldies
CDEILPP clipped
CDEILPS spliced
CDEILPU clupeid
CDEILSU sluiced
CDEILTU ductile
CDEIMNO demonic
McIndoe
CDEIMOR dormice
CDEIMOS medicos
CDEIMOT demotic
CDEIMPR crimped
CDEIMPU pumiced
CDEIMSU miscued
CDEINOS secondi
CDEINOT ctenoid
deontic
noticed
CDEINRS cinders
discern
rescind
CDEINRU inducer
CDEINRY cindery
CDEINSU incudes
incused
induces
CDEINSX exscind
CDEINTT tincted
CDEIOOR cooried
CDEIOPR percoid
CDEIORR Roderic
CDEIORS scodier
CDEIORT cordite
CDEIORU couried
CDEIORV divorce
CDEIORW crowdie
CDEIOST cestoid
coedits
CDEIPRS crisped
CDEIPRT predict
CDEIPST depicts
CDEIRRU curried
CDEIRST credits
directs
CDEIRSU cruised
CDEIRSV cervids
CDEIRTV verdict
CDEISST dissect
CDEISSY ecdysis
CDEJNOU jounced
CDEKKNO knocked
CDEKLNO clonked
CDEKLNU clunked
CDEKLOW wedlock
CDEKLPU plucked
CDEKLRU ruckled
CDEKLSU suckled
CDEKMOS smocked
CDEKNOR dorneck
CDEKNOS dockens
CDEKNSU sundeck
CDEKOOR crooked
CDEKORS dockers
redocks
CDEKOST destock
dockets
stocked
CDEKRSU duckers
CDEKRTU trucked
CDELLOU collude
CDELLSU sculled
CDELMPU clumped
CDELMSU muscled
CDELMTU mulcted
CDELNOO condole
CDELNOW clowned
CDELNOY condyle
CDELOOR colored
crooled
CDELOPP clopped
CDELOPU coupled
CDELORS scolder
CDELOST coldest
CDELOSW scowled
CDELOTT clotted
CDELOUY doucely
CDELPSU sculped
CDELRRU curdler
CDELRSU curdles
CDELRUY crudely
CDELTUU ductule
CDEMMNO commend
CDEMMOO commode
CDEMMSU scummed
CDEMNNO condemn
CDEMOOS comedos
CDEMORS scromed
CDEMORU decorum
CDEMPRU crumped
CDENNOO condone
CDENNOT contend
CDENOOP pooncned
CDENOOR crooned
CDENOOS secondo
CDENOPU pounced
CDENORS scorned
CDENORU crunode
CDENORW crowned
CDENOSS seconds
CDENOST docents
CDENOTU counted
CDENPUY pudency
CDENRUU uncured
CDEOOPP copepod
CDEOOPS scooped
CDEOOPT coopted
CDEOORR corrode
CDEOORT Côte-d'Or
CDEOORV vocoder
CDEOOST scooted
CDEOOTV dovecot
CDEOPPR cropped
CDEOPRS corpsed
CDEOPRU crouped
produce
CDEORRS corders
records
CDEORRW crowder
CDEORSS crossed
CDEORSU coursed
scoured
sourced
CDEORTU courted
CDEORUU douceur
CDEORWY Cowdrey
CDEOSSU escudos
CDEOSTU scouted
CDEPRTY decrypt
CDERSTU crudest
crusted
CDFHIOS codfish
CDFIILU fluidic
CDFILUY dulcify
CDFIOSU fucoids
CDGHIIN chiding
CDGIINO gonidic
CDGIINS discing
CDGIKNO docking
CDGIKNU ducking
CDGILNO codling
lingcod
CDGINNO condign
CDGINOR cording
CDGINRU curding
CDHIINT chindit
CDHIIST distich
CDHILLY childly
CDHILOS coldish
CDHILUW Dulwich
CDHIMST Schmidt
CDHINOR chondri
CDHIOOR choroid
ochroid
CDHIORS orchids
CDHIPTY diptych
CDHMORU Murdoch
CDIIIOT idiotic
CDIIJRU juridic
CDIILLY idyllic
CDIILMO domicil

CDIILNY	dicliny
CDIIMNO	Dominic
CDIIMOS	disomic
CDIINOR	crinoid
CDIINOT	diction
CDIINOV	vidicon
CDIINOZ	zincoid
CDIINST	indicts
CDIIORS	cirsoid
CDIIORX	corixid
CDIIOSS	cissoid
CDIIOSV	viscoid
CDIKLNO	Old Nick
CDIKNOR	dornick
CDILLOO	colloid
CDILLUY	lucidly
CDILNOS	codlins
CDILOTU	dulotic
CDILOTZ	Colditz
CDILPPU	Cudlipp
CDIMMOU	modicum
CDIMNOO	monodic
CDIMOOS	cosmoid
CDIMSSU	muscids
CDIMSTU	dictums
CDINOOS	conoids
CDINOSY	synodic
CDINOTU	conduit
	noctuid
CDINSSY	syndics
CDINSTU	inducts
CDIOPRR	ripcord
CDIOSTT	cottids
CDIOSTY	cystoid
CDIOTUV	oviduct
CDIPSSU	cuspids
CDIRSUY	dysuric
CDIRTUY	crudity
CDISSSU	discuss
CDKNNOU	dunnock
CDLOOPY	lycopod
CDLOSTU	couldst
CDMMOOO	commodo
CDMNOOS	condoms
CDMOOST	dotcoms
CDNOORS	condors
	cordons
CDNOORY	Croydon
CDNOTUW	cutdown
CDOOOPT	octopod
CDOORRY	corrody
CDOORST	doctors
CDOOTUW	woodcut
CDOPRTU	product
CDOSTUY	custody
CEEEFIL	fleecie
CEEEFLS	fleeces
CEEEHLS	leeches
	Scheele
CEEEHPR	cheeper
CEEEHRR	cheerer
CEEEHRV	Cheever
CEEEHSS	cheeses
CEEEINP	epicene
CEEEIPR	creepie
CEEEIRV	receive
CEEEITV	evictee
CEEELRT	reelect
CEEELST	celeste
CEEENRT	Terence
CEEENSS	essence
CEEEOTZ	Coetzee
CEEEPRR	creeper
CEEERRT	erecter
	reerect
CEEERSS	creeses
CEEERST	secrete
CEEERTX	excrete
CEEETUX	execute
CEEFFNO	offence
CEEFFOS	coffees
CEEFFST	effects
CEEFHLS	fleches
CEEFHNR	Fechner
CEEFHRT	fechter
	fetcher
CEEFHST	fetches
CEEFIRR	fiercer
CEEFKLR	flecker
	freckle
CEEFLRT	reflect
CEEFNNS	fennecs
CEEFNOR	enforce
CEEFNRS	fencers
CEEFPRT	perfect
	prefect
CEEFSSU	fescues
CEEGINR	generic
CEEGINT	genetic
CEEGINU	eugenic
CEEGIRZ	grecize
CEEGKOS	geckoes
CEEGLLO	college
CEEGLNO	Glencoe
CEEGLNT	neglect
CEEGLOR	El Greco
CEEGLOU	eclogue
CEEGNRY	regency
CEEGORT	cortege
CEEHHMS	Shechem
CEEHILN	elenchi
CEEHILR	Eichler
CEEHILS	helices
	lichees
	Schiele
CEEHILV	vehicle
CEEHIMR	chimere
CEEHIMS	chemise
CEEHINR	Chénier
CEEHINS	chinese
CEEHIOR	cheerio
CEEHIRT	etheric
	heretic
	techier
CEEHIRW	chewier
CEEHISS	seiches
CEEHIST	techies
CEEHISV	chevies
CEEHKLR	heckler
CEEHKLS	heckles
CEEHKNP	henpeck
CEEHKST	ketches
CEEHLNO	chelone
	echelon
CEEHLRS	lechers
CEEHLRW	welcher
CEEHLRY	cheerly
	lechery
CEEHLSS	chessel
CEEHLST	letches
CEEHLSW	welches
CEEHLSY	lychees
CEEHMRS	schemer
	schmeer
CEEHMRT	merchet
CEEHMSS	schemes
CEEHNPU	penuche
CEEHNRW	wencher
CEEHNST	tenches
CEEHNSW	wenches
CEEHORR	coherer
CEEHORS	coheres
CEEHORT	trochee
CEEHPRR	percher
CEEHPRS	perches
CEEHPSU	Cepheus
CEEHQRU	chequer
CEEHQSU	cheques
CEEHRST	Chester
	etchers
	retches
CEEHRSU	euchres
CEEHRSV	chevres
CEEHRSW	chewers
CEEHSSS	chesses
CEEHSSW	eschews
CEEHSTV	chevets
	vetches
CEEIIKL	icelike
CEEIINR	eirenic
CEEIINW	icewine
CEEIIPR	epeiric
CEEIJNT	Cetinje
CEEIJOR	rejoice
CEEIKNT	necktie
CEEILLM	micelle
CEEILNO	cineole
CEEILNR	recline
CEEILNS	license
	selenic
	silence
CEEILNT	centile
CEEILNU	leucine
CEEILPS	eclipse
CEEILRT	reticle
	tiercel
CEEILSS	iceless
	siecles
CEEILST	sectile
CEEILSV	vesicle
CEEILTU	leucite
CEEIMNT	centime
CEEIMRS	mercies
CEEIMRX	excimer
CEEIMST	emetics
CEEINNS	incense
CEEINOS	senecio
CEEINPU	eupneic
CEEINRS	ceresin
	sincere
CEEINRT	enteric
	enticer
CEEINRV	cervine
CEEINST	entices
CEEINSV	evinces
CEEINTV	Vicente
CEEIOPT	picotee
CEEIORT	coterie
CEEIORV	revoice
CEEIPRR	piercer
	reprice
CEEIPRS	piecers
	pierces
	precise
	recipes
CEEIPRT	receipt
CEEIPRU	epicure
CEEIPSS	species
CEEIPST	pectise
CEEIPTZ	pectize
CEEIRRT	reciter
CEEIRST	recites
CEEIRSU	ecuries
CEEIRSV	service
CEEIRTX	exciter
CEEISSX	excises
CEEISTX	excites
CEEITTZ	zetetic
CEEJORT	ejector
CEEJRST	rejects
CEEKLNT	necklet
CEEKLPS	speckle
CEEKMNN	Mencken
CEEKNRS	neckers
CEEKNSY	Eysenck
CEEKOSY	sockeye
CEEKPRS	peckers
CEEKRRW	wrecker
CEELLLU	cellule
CEELLNO	colleen
CEELLOS	cellose
CEELMNS	Clemens
CEELMNT	clement
	Tlemcen
CEELMOS	cleomes
CEELMOT	telecom
CEELMOW	welcome
CEELNOS	enclose

CEELNPS pencels
CEELNRS crenels
CEELNRT lectern
CEELNRU lucerne
CEELORS creoles
CEELORT elector
electro
CEELOSU coulees
CEELOTT Colette
CEELOTU elocute
CEELPRT prelect
CEELRRU crueler
CEELRSS scleres
CEELRST tercels
CEELRSU recluse
CEELRTU lecture
CEELRTY erectly
CEELSST selects
CEELTTU lettuce
CEEMMOR commere
CEEMNOR McEnroe
CEEMNQU McQueen
CEEMNRU cerumen
CEEMNST cements
CEEMOPR compeer
compere
CEEMOPT compete
CEEMRRS mercers
CEEMRRY mercery
CEEMRST cermets
CEEMSTY mycetes
CEENNOU enounce
CEENNOV convene
CEENNRT centner
CEENOOT ecotone
CEENOPT potence
CEENORS encores
necrose
CEENORZ cozener
CEENOST cenotes
CEENPRS spencer
CEENPRT percent
CEENPSS spences
CEENPST pectens
CEENRSS censers
screens
secerns
CEENRST centers
centres
tenrecs
CEENRSU censure
CEENRSY scenery
CEEOPST pectose
CEEOPTY ecotype
CEEORRT erector
CEEORRV coverer
recover
CEEORRZ Corrèze
CEEORSV corvees
CEEORTV coveter
CEEORTW cowtree
CEEOTTT octette
CEEPPRT percept
precept
CEEPPRU prepuce
CEEPRSS precess
CEEPRST recepts
respect
scepter
sceptre
specter
spectre
CEEPRTX excerpt
CEEPSTX expects
CEEPSTY ectypes
CEEPSUY eyecups
CEERRSU rescuer
securer
CEERRSW screwer
CEERRUV recurve
CEERSSS cessers
cresses
CEERSST cresset
resects
screets
secrets
CEERSSU rescues
secures
CEERSTT tercets
CEERTTU curette
CEESSTX exsects
CEESSUX excuses
CEETTUV cuvette
CEFFIOR officer
CEFFIOS offices
CEFFISU suffice
CEFFLOS coffles
CEFFLSU scuffle
CEFFORS coffers
scoffer
CEFGINN fencing
CEFHILR filcher
CEFHILS filches
CEFHILY chiefly
Chifley
CEFHINS finches
CEFHIRS Fischer
CEFHIST fitches
CEFHITT fitchet
CEFHITW fitchew
CEFIILT fictile
CEFIIOR orifice
CEFIITV fictive
CEFIKLR flicker
CEFILNT inflect
CEFILNU funicle
CEFILRU lucifer
CEFIMOR comfier
CEFINNO confine
CEFINOR conifer
CEFINST infects
CEFIPSY specify
CEFIRSS sferics
CEFIRTY certify
rectify
CEFISSU ficuses
CEFKLLO elflock
CEFKLOT fetlock
CEFKLRY freckly
CEFKRSU fuckers
CEFLNOU flounce
CEFLNUY fluency
CEFMORY comfrey
CEFNORS confers
CEFNOSS confess
CEFNOSU confuse
CEFNOTU confute
CEFOPRS forceps
CEFORRS forcers
CEFORRT crofter
CEFORSS frescos
CEFORSU focuser
refocus
CEFOSSU focuses
CEFRSUW curfews
CEFSSUU fucuses
CEGGHIR chigger
CEGGIIS ciggies
CEGGIOR georgic
CEGGLOS coggles
CEGHILN leching
CEGHINO echoing
CEGHINP peching
CEGHINT etching
CEGHINW chewing
CEGHIOS chigoes
CEGHIRS screigh
CEGHITU guichet
CEGHLSU gulches
CEGHORU cougher
CEGIILN ceiling
CEGIILW Gliwice
CEGIINP piecing
CEGIKKN kecking
CEGIKNN necking
CEGIKNP pecking
CEGIKNR recking
CEGIKOR Górecki
CEGILMP gemclip
CEGILNP cleping
CEGILNR clinger
cringle
CEGILNW clewing
CEGILNY glycine
CEGIMNO genomic
CEGIMNU mucigen
CEGIMRW McGwire
CEGINNS censing
CEGINOS cognise
coignes
CEGINOZ cognize
CEGINPR creping
CEGINRR cringer
CEGINRS cringes
CEGINRW crewing
CEGINSS cessing
CEGIRRS gricers
CEGKLOR grockle
CEGLNOO cologne
CEGLOOY ecology
CEGLOSU glucose
CEGLOSY glycose
CEGNORS congers
CEGNORY cryogen
CEGNOST congest
CEGNRUY urgency
CEGNSSU scunges
CEGNSTY cygnets
CEGOORS scrooge
CEGORRS grocers
CEGORRY grocery
CEGORSU scourge
scrouge
CEHHILR Ehrlich
CEHHIRS cherish
CEHHIRT hitcher
CEHHIST hitches
CEHHITU hutchie
CEHHKOV Chekhov
CEHHNSU hunches
CEHHOST shochet
CEHHSSU sheuchs
CEHHSTU hutches
CEHIIKT thickie
CEHIILS chilies
CEHIINR hircine
CEHIINT ichnite
CEHIIPP chippie
CEHIIRT itchier
tichier
CEHIISV chivies
CEHIJOR Jericho
CEHIKNT chetnik
kitchen
thicken
CEHIKOO chookie
CEHIKOR chokier
CEHIKOS chokies
CEHIKPS peckish
CEHIKRR Herrick
CEHIKRS shicker
CEHIKRT thicker
CEHIKRW whicker
CEHIKSY hickeys
CEHIKTT thicket
CEHILLR chiller
CEHILMN Mechlin
CEHILNO choline
helicon
CEHILNS lichens
CEHILPS pilches
CEHILRR Richler
CEHILRV chervil
CEHILSS chisels
CEHILTY ethylic
lecythi
techily
CEHIMMS chemism

CEHIMNY chimney
CEHIMOS echoism
CEHIMRS chimers
CEHIMRT thermic
CEHIMST chemist
mitches
CEHIMSU echiums
CEHINOP chopine
phocine
CEHINOR Cheiron
CEHINPR phrenic
CEHINPS pinches
sphenic
CEHINRT cithern
CEHINRW wincher
CEHINST ethnics
sthenic
CEHINSU echinus
CEHINSW winches
CEHIOPS hospice
CEHIOPT potiche
CEHIORR chorrie
CEHIORS coheirs
heroics
CEHIOTU couthie
CEHIOTV cheviot
CEHIPPR chipper
CEHIPRR chirper
CEHIPRS ciphers
spheric
CEHIPRT pitcher
CEHIPST pitches
CEHIQSU quiches
CEHIRRS chirres
CEHIRRT richter
CEHIRST cithers
richest
CEHIRSU cushier
CEHIRSZ scherzi
CEHIRTT chitter
CEHISSU cuishes
cushies
CEHISTW witches
CEHISWZ Schweiz
CEHKKRU chukker
CEHKLMO hemlock
CEHKLOS hockles
CEHKLSU huckles
CEHKNOY Hockney
CEHKORS chokers
hockers
shocker
CEHKOSY chokeys
hockeys
CEHKPTU ketchup
CEHKRSU shucker
CEHKRUY huckery
CEHKSTY sketchy
CEHKTVY kvetchy
CEHLLPU chellup
CEHLMOR chromel
CEHLMSU mulches
CEHLNNU chunnel
CEHLNOT cholent
CEHLNRU luncher
CEHLNRY lyncher
CEHLNSU lunches
CEHLNSY lynches
CEHLNTY lynchet
CEHLORT chortle
CEHLORY Chorley
CEHLOST clothes
CEHLPSS schleps
CEHLPSU pleuchs
CEHLQSU squelch
CEHLRRU lurcher
CEHLRSU lurches
CEHMNNU München
CEHMNRU muncher
CEHMNSU munches
CEHMOOR moocher
CEHMOOS mooches
CEHMORS chromes
CEHMOSS schmoes
CEHMOTZ chometz
CEHMSTU mutches
CEHNOOP hencoop
CEHNORV chevron
CEHNOST notches
CEHNOSU cohunes
CEHNPRU puncher
CEHNPSU punches
CEHNRRU churner
CEHNRTU chunter
CEHNSUU eunuchs
CEHNTUY chutney
CEHOOPS pooches
CEHOORS chooser
CEHOORT cheroot
CEHOOSS chooses
CEHOPPR chopper
CEHOPRS porches
CEHOPST potches
CEHOPSU pouches
CEHORSS coshers
CEHORST hectors
rochets
tochers
torches
troches
CEHORSU rouches
CEHORSZ scherzo
CEHORTU retouch
toucher
CEHORTW wotcher
CEHORUV voucher
CEHOSSU hocuses
CEHOSTU touches
CEHOSUV vouches
CEHPRSY cyphers
CEHPSSY psyches
CEHRRSU crusher
CEHRSSU crushes
CEHRSTT stretch
CEHRTTU Utrecht
CEHSSTY scythes
CEIIJRU juicier
CEIIKNT kinetic
CEIIKPR pickier
CEIIKQU quickie
CEIIKSS sickies
CEIIKST ekistic
ickiest
CEIILLN Cellini
CEIILLS silicle
CEIILNN incline
CEIILPP clippie
CEIILPT pelitic
CEIILST elicits
CEIILTV levitic
CEIIMMT mimetic
CEIIMNS menisci
CEIIMOT meiotic
CEIIMPR empiric
CEIIMSS seismic
CEIIMTT titmice
CEIINNO coniine
CEIINNR cinerin
CEIINOR oneiric
CEIINOS eosinic
CEIINOV invoice
CEIINPS piscine
CEIINRS irenics
sericin
CEIINRT citrine
crinite
inciter
neritic
CEIINSS iciness
incises
CEIINST incites
CEIINSU cuisine
CEIINTZ citizen
zincite
CEIIOPZ epizoic
CEIIPRR pricier
CEIIPRS spicier
CEIIPRT picrite
CEIIRST eristic
CEIIRUZ cruizie
CEIIRVX Eric XIV
CEIISSS cissies
CEIISVV civvies
CEIITUV uveitic
CEIJNST injects
CEIJRSU juicers
CEIJSTU justice
CEIKKRS kickers
CEIKKSW Keswick
CEIKLMS melicks
CEIKLNR clinker
crinkle
CEIKLNS nickels
CEIKLPR pickler
prickle
CEIKLPS pickles
CEIKLPU cuplike
CEIKLRS lickers
rickles
slicker
CEIKLRT tickler
trickle
CEIKLRU luckier
CEIKLRW Lerwick
CEIKLSS sickles
CEIKLST stickle
tickles
CEIKMRU muckier
CEIKMSY mickeys
CEIKNOT kenotic
ketonic
CEIKNQU quicken
CEIKNRS nickers
snicker
CEIKNSS sickens
CEIKNST snicket
CEIKOOS cookies
CEIKOPS pockies
CEIKORR rockier
CEIKORS Rockies
CEIKORT tockier
CEIKPRR pricker
CEIKPRS pickers
CEIKPRT pricket
CEIKPST pickets
skeptic
CEIKQRU quicker
CEIKRRS rickers
CEIKRRT tricker
CEIKRST rickets
Sickert
sticker
tickers
CEIKRSW wickers
CEIKRSY rickeys
CEIKRTU truckie
CEIKRTY rickety
CEIKRUY yuckier
CEIKSST sickest
CEIKSTT tickets
CEIKSTW wickets
CEIKSTY tickeys
CEILLMS micells
CEILLNU nucelli
CEILLOR collier
Corelli
CEILLOS collies
CEILLST cellist
CEILLSU cullies
CEILMOP compile
polemic
CEILMPR crimple
CEILNNU nuclein
CEILNOP pinocle
CEILNOS inclose
CEILNOT lection
CEILNOX lexicon
CEILNPS pencils

splenic
CEILNST clients
lectins
stencil
CEILNTU tunicle
CEILOOS coolies
CEILOPR peloric
CEILOPS polices
CEILORS coilers
recoils
CEILOSS ossicle
CEILOST citoles
CEILOTT coletit
CEILPPR clipper
cripple
CEILPRS splicer
CEILPSS splices
CEILPSU spicule
CEILQSU cliques
CEILQUV cliquey
CEILRRU curlier
CEILRSS slicers
CEILRST relicts
CEILRTU cultier
utricle
CEILSSS scissel
CEILSSU sluices
CEIMMOS commies
CEIMMRR crimmer
CEIMNOR incomer
CEIMNOS Comines
cosmine
incomes
mesonic
CEIMNOT centimo
entomic
tonemic
CEIMNRS mincers
CEIMNRU numeric
CEIMNSU Mencius
CEIMNYZ enzymic
CEIMOPT metopic
CEIMORT mortice
CEIMOSX exosmic
CEIMOTT totemic
CEIMOTV vicomte
CEIMOTX toxemic
CEIMPRR crimper
CEIMPRS spermic
CEIMPSU pumices
CEIMRST metrics
CEIMRSU murices
CEIMSSU miscues
CEINNOV connive
CEINOOS Ionesco
CEINOOT coontie
CEINOPR porcine
CEINOPT entopic
nepotic
CEINORR cornier
CEINORS coiners
cronies
Ericson
recoins
CEINORU coenuri
CEINORV corvine
CEINOSS cession
cosines
CEINOST notices
section
CEINOSV novices
CEINOTT tonetic
CEINOTX exciton
CEINOUV unvoice
CEINPPR Crippen
CEINPRS pincers
princes
CEINPST incepts
inspect
pectins
CEINQSU cinques
quinces
CEINRRU reincur
CEINRST cistern
cretins
CEINRSW wincers
CEINRTT cittern
CEINRUV incurve
CEINSST incests
insects
CEINSSU incuses
CEINSTY cystine
CEINSWY winceys
CEINTTX extinct
CEIOORS coories
CEIOOST cooties
CEIOPRS copiers
CEIOPST poetics
CEIOPSU piceous
CEIORRS cirrose
corries
crosier
CEIORRU courier
Ricoeur
CEIORRZ crozier
CEIORST erotics
CEIORSU couries
CEIORSV voicers
CEIORSW cowries
CEIORTT cottier
CEIORTV evictor
CEIORTX excitor
xerotic
CEIORVY viceroy
CEIOSSS cossies
CEIOSST cosiest
Ossetic
CEIOSSU cesious
CEIOSSV viscose
CEIOSTT scottie
CEIOSTV costive
CEIOSTX coexist
exotics
CEIOSTY society
CEIOSTZ coziest
CEIPQTU picquet
CEIPRRS crisper
pricers
CEIPRSS spicers
CEIPRST triceps
CEIPRSY spicery
CEIPRTU cuprite
picture
CEIPRTY pyretic
CEIPRXY pyrexic
CEIPSST cesspit
septics
CEIQRSU cirques
CEIRRRU currier
CEIRRSU cruiser
curries
CEIRRTT critter
CEIRRTU recruit
CEIRRTX rectrix
CEIRRUV curvier
CEIRSSU cruises
crusies
CEIRSTT trisect
CEIRSTU icterus
CEIRSUV cursive
CEIRSUZ cruzies
CEIRTTX tectrix
CEISSSU cuisses
CEISSTU cutises
ictuses
CEISTTU cutties
CEJKOSY jockeys
CEJNOOS cojones
CEJNORU conjure
CEJNOSU jounces
juncoes
CEJOPRT project
CEKKLNU knuckle
CEKKNOR knocker
CEKKOPS kopecks
CEKLLRY clerkly
CEKLNRU clunker
CEKLORS lockers
CEKLORY Lockyer
CEKLOST lockets
CEKLOTY tockley
CEKLPRU plucker
CEKLRSU ruckles
suckler
CEKLRTU truckle
CEKLSSU suckles
CEKMNOY mockney
CEKMORS mockers
CEKMORY mockery
CEKMRSU muckers
CEKNOOV convoke
CEKNORS conkers
reckons
CEKNRWY wryneck
CEKOOPR precook
CEKOOPW cowpoke
CEKOORS cookers
Crookes
CEKOORY cookery
CEKOPST pockets
CEKORRS corkers
rockers
CEKORRY rockery
CEKORST restock
rockets
stocker
CEKORTW twocker
CEKOSST sockets
CEKPRSU puckers
CEKRRTU trucker
CEKRSSU suckers
CEKRSTU tuckers
CEKSTTU tuckets
CELLMNO Clonmel
CELLNNO Connell
CELLNOO colonel
CELLOST collets
CELLOSU locules
ocellus
CELLOSY closely
CELLPRU Purcell
CELLRRU cruller
CELLRSU cullers
sculler
CELLRUY cruelly
CELMNOO locomen
monocle
CELMOOS coeloms
CELMOPS compels
CELMOPX complex
CELMORS cormels
CELMPRU crumple
CELMSSU muscles
CELMSUY lyceums
CELMTUU cumulet
CELNNOU nucleon
CELNNSU nuncles
CELNOOS Colenso
colones
console
CELNOOY Clooney
CELNOPU Poulenc
CELNORS cornels
CELNOSU counsel
unclose
CELNOTU noctule
CELNSUU nucleus
CELOORR colorer
CELOORS coolers
creosol
CELOOST coolest
ocelots
CELOPRU coupler
CELOPSU couples
CELOPTU couplet
octuple
CELORSS closers
CELORST colters

	corslet
	costrel
	lectors
CELORSU	closure
	colures
CELORSV	clovers
CELORSW	scowler
CELORTT	crottle
CELORTU	cloture
	clouter
	coulter
CELOSST	closest
	closets
CELOSSX	coxless
CELPRSU	scruple
CELPSUU	cupules
CELPSUY	clypeus
CELRRSU	curlers
CELRSTU	cluster
	cutlers
	relucts
CELRSTY	clyster
CELRSUV	culvers
CELRSUW	curlews
CELRTTU	clutter
CELRTUU	culture
CELRTUV	culvert
CELRTUY	cruelty
	cutlery
CELSTTU	cutlets
	cuttles
	scuttle
CEMMNOT	comment
CEMMNOU	commune
CEMMOOV	commove
CEMMOTU	commute
CEMMRSU	scummer
CEMNNOT	contemn
CEMNOOP	compone
CEMNOOY	economy
CEMNOSU	consume
CEMNRTU	centrum
CEMOOPS	compose
CEMOOPT	compote
CEMOOTU	outcome
CEMOPRS	compers
CEMOPTU	compute
CEMORSS	scromes
CEMOSTU	costume
CEMPRTU	crumpet
CEMRRUY	mercury
CEMRSTU	rectums
CENNOOT	connote
CENNORY	Connery
CENNOST	consent
CENNOTT	content
CENNOTV	convent
CENNRSU	scunner
CENOOPS	poonces
CENOORR	coroner
	crooner
CENOORT	coronet

	Crotone
CENOPRU	pouncer
CENOPSU	pounces
CENOPSY	syncope
CENOPTU	pouncet
CENOPTY	potency
CENOQRU	conquer
CENORRS	corners
	scorner
CENORRW	crowner
	recrown
CENORSS	censors
CENORST	cornets
	Costner
CENORSU	conures
CENORTT	cornett
CENORTU	cornute
	counter
	recount
	trounce
CENORTV	convert
CENORUV	uncover
CENOSSY	coyness
CENOSTT	Consett
	contest
CENOSTU	contuse
	uncoest
CENOSVY	conveys
CENOTTX	context
CENPRTY	encrypt
CENRRTU	current
CENRSTU	encrust
CENRSUW	unscrew
CENRTUY	century
CENSSTY	encysts
CEOOPRS	coopers
	scooper
CEOOPRY	coopery
CEOORST	scooter
CEOOSTY	coyotes
	oocytes
CEOPPRR	cropper
CEOPPRS	coppers
CEOPPRY	coppery
CEOPRRS	scorper
CEOPRRT	porrect
CEOPRRU	procure
CEOPRSS	corpses
	process
CEOPRST	copters
	Spector
CEOPRSU	croupes
	recoups
CEOPRTT	protect
CEOPRUV	coverup
CEOPSTY	cotypes
CEOQRTU	croquet
CEOQSTU	coquets
CEORRSS	crosser
	recross
	scorers
CEORRST	rectors

CEORRSU	courser
	cruores
	scourer
CEORRSW	crowers
CEORRSY	sorcery
CEORRTY	rectory
CEORSSS	crosses
CEORSST	corsets
	costers
	escorts
	scoters
	sectors
CEORSSU	courses
	Croesus
	scouser
	sources
	sucrose
CEORSSW	escrows
CEORSSY	corseys
CEORSTT	cotters
CEORSTU	croutes
	scouter
CEORSTV	coverts
	vectors
CEORTUU	couture
CEORTUV	couvert
CEOSSST	cossets
CEOSSSU	scouses
CEPPRRU	crupper
CEPPRSU	cuppers
	scupper
CEPRRSU	sprucer
CEPRSSU	percuss
	spruces
CEPRSSY	cypress
CEPRSUW	screwup
CEPSSTU	suspect
CERRSSU	cursers
CERSTTU	cutters
	scutter
CERSTUV	curvets
CERSTUY	curtsey
CFFGINO	coffing
CFFGINU	cuffing
CFFHINO	chiffon
CFFIKKO	kickoff
CFFIKOP	pickoff
CFFINOS	coffins
CFFOSTU	cutoffs
	offcuts
CFFRSSU	scruffs
CFFRSUY	scruffy
CFGIKNU	fucking
CFGINOR	forcing
CFHINSU	fuchsin
CFHIOSW	cowfish
CFHOOOW	Foochow
CFHORTU	futhorc
CFIIKNY	finicky
CFIILNT	inflict
CFIIMNO	omnific
CFIINOT	fiction

CFIKNNO	finnock
CFIKOSS	fossick
CFIKTUW	fuckwit
CFILORS	frolics
CFILORU	fluoric
CFIMNOR	confirm
CFIMOST	comfits
CFIORSY	scorify
CFISSTU	fustics
CFKNORU	unfrock
CFKOTTU	futtock
CFLMRUU	fulcrum
CFLNOUX	conflux
CFLOOOS	Foscolo
CFLOOPW	cowflop
CFMNOOR	conform
CFMOORT	comfort
CFOSSUU	fuscous
CGGGINO	cogging
CGGIINR	gricing
CGHHOSU	choughs
CGHIILM	milchig
CGHIIMN	chiming
	miching
CGHIINN	chining
	inching
	niching
CGHIINT	itching
CGHIKNO	choking
	hocking
CGHIKNU	chi kung
	Kuching
CGHILNU	Chilung
CGHILPY	glyphic
CGHINNO	chignon
CGHINOR	ochring
CGHINOS	coshing
CGHINOU	Noguchi
CGHINRU	ruching
CGHINSU	Cushing
CGHIOST	gothics
CGHLNOS	schlong
CGHLOSU	cloughs
CGHORUY	grouchy
CGIIJNU	juicing
CGIIKKN	kicking
CGIIKLN	licking
CGIIKMM	gimmick
CGIIKNN	nicking
CGIIKNP	picking
CGIIKNR	ricking
CGIIKNS	sicking
CGIIKNT	ticking
CGIIKNW	wicking
CGIILLO	illogic
CGIILNO	coiling
CGIILNS	slicing
CGIIMNN	mincing
CGIINNO	coining
CGIINNW	wincing
CGIINOV	voicing
CGIINPR	pricing

CGIINPS spicing
CGIINRT tricing
CGIINSS cissing
CGIKLNO locking
CGIKLNU lucking
CGIKMNO mocking
CGIKMNU mucking
CGIKNNO conking
nocking
CGIKNOO cooking
CGIKNOR corking
rocking
CGIKNOS socking
CGIKNOW cowking
CGIKNPU kingcup
pucking
CGIKNRU rucking
CGIKNSU sucking
CGIKNTU tucking
CGILLNU culling
CGILNNO cloning
CGILNOO cooling
locoing
CGILNOS closing
CGILNOW cowling
CGILNOY cloying
Coligny
CGILNPY clyping
CGILNRU curling
CGILORW cowgirl
CGILOTT glottic
CGILPTY glyptic
CGIMNOP comping
CGIMNOS comings
CGINNNO conning
CGINNNU cunning
CGINNOP poncing
CGINNOR corning
CGINNOS consign
CGINNPU puncing
CGINNSY syncing
CGINOOP cooping
CGINOPP copping
CGINOPS picongs
CGINOPU couping
CGINOPW cowping
CGINOPY copying
CGINORS scoring
CGINORW crowing
CGINOST costing
gnostic
CGINOSU congius
CGINOTT cotting
CGINPPU cupping
CGINRSU cursing
CGINRSY scrying
CGINRUV curving
CGINSSU cussing
CGINTTU cutting
CGIOTYZ zygotic
CGKLNOU gunlock
CGLLOSY glycols
CGLNOSU unclogs
CGLOOSU colugos
CHHINOR rhonchi
CHHINTU unhitch
CHHNOOS honchos
CHHOSUU Hsü-chou
CHHRTTU thrutch
CHIIKLM milchik
CHIIKSS sickish
CHIILLT Tillich
CHIILST litchis
CHIIMSU ischium
CHIINOT thionic
CHIIOPT ophitic
CHIIPSW Ipswich
CHIIRRS scirrhi
CHIKLLO hillock
CHIKLTY thickly
CHIKNOO chinook
CHIKORY hickory
CHIKOST thickos
CHIKPSU puckish
CHIKSST shticks
CHIKSTY kitschy
CHILLMU chillum
CHILLNO Chillon
CHILNOO holonic
CHILNOR chlorin
CHILNOS Nichols
CHILNSY lychnis
CHILOOS coolish
CHILORS orchils
CHILOST coltish
CHILPSY sylphic
CHILSTU cultish
CHIMMTU Mitchum
CHIMOPR morphic
CHIMORS chrisom
CHIMRUU Urumchi
CHIMSSS schisms
CHIMSTY tychism
CHINOOR chorion
CHINOPS chopins
phonics
CHINORS Cornish
CHINORT Corinth
CHINORW Norwich
CHINOST chitons
CHINOSU cushion
CHINQSU squinch
CHINRSU urchins
CHINSTY snitchy
CHINTYZ chintzy
CHIOORS isochor
CHIOORZ chorizo
CHIOPRT trophic
CHIOPXY hypoxic
CHIORST Christo
Christo-
ostrich
CHIORVW Virchow
CHIOSSZ schizos
CHIPRRU chirrup
CHIPRRY pyrrhic
CHIPSSY physics
CHIRRSU currish
CHIRSTY christy
CHISSST schists
CHISTTU chutist
CHITTWY twitchy
CHKLOOT klootch
CHKLOSY shylock
CHKMMOU hummock
CHKMOSY Chomsky
CHKNOOS schnook
CHLMOOS molochs
CHLMORY chromyl
CHLOOSS schools
CHLOPST splotch
CHLOSUY chylous
slouchy
CHLSTUY slutchy
CHMOORS chromos
CHMOSUY chymous
CHMSTUY smutchy
CHNNOOR chronon
CHNNOPY Pynchon
CHNNOSU nonsuch
CHNOOPS ponchos
CHNOORT torchon
CHNORSY synchro
CHNORTU cothurn
CHNOTUU uncouth
CHNSTUU tuchuns
CHOOOSW Soochow
CHOOPPS copshop
CHOOPST post hoc
CHOORST cohorts
CHOORSU ochrous
CHOORWZ Chorzów
CHOPSSY psychos
CHOPTUU touchup
CHPSSUY scyphus
CIIILLT illicit
CIIINPT incipit
CIIJLUY juicily
CIIKKLL killick
CIIKLPY pickily
CIIKNPS pickins
CIIKPUW wickiup
CIILLTY licitly
CIILLVY civilly
CIILNOP cipolin
CIILNOS silicon
CIILNOT Nilotic
CIILNUV uncivil
CIILOOT oolitic
CIILOPT politic
CIILOST colitis
solicit
CIILOSV Clovis I
CIILPSY spicily
CIIMMNO minicom
CIIMMRY mimicry
CIIMNNO nimonic
CIIMNOU Iconium
CIIMOOS Cosimo I
CIIMOST somitic
CIIMOTT mitotic
CIIMRST trismic
CIIMSTV victims
CIINOOT coition
CIINOPR porcini
CIINORS incisor
CIINPRS crispin
CIINQTU quintic
CIINSTU Ictinus
CIIORST soritic
CIIOSUV vicious
CIIPRTY pyritic
CIJNNOO conjoin
CIJNNTU injunct
CIKKLLO killock
CIKKNNO Kinnock
CIKLLOP pillock
CIKLLOR rollick
CIKLLSY slickly
CIKLLUY luckily
CIKLMOS Miskolc
CIKLMUY muckily
CIKLNRY crinkly
CIKLORY rockily
CIKLOWW Wicklow
CIKLPRY prickly
CIKLQUY quickly
CIKLRTY trickly
CIKMORR rimrock
CIKNOSW cowskin
CIKNPSU unpicks
CIKNSTU unstick
CIKOSTU sickout
CIKPPSU pickups
CIKPSTU stickup
CIKPUWY wickyup
CIKRSTY tricksy
CIKRSWY Ryswick
CILLNNO Lincoln
CILLNOS collins
CILLNSU Scullin
CILLOOR criollo
CILMNOP complin
CILMOOS locoism
CILMSTU cultism
CILNNOT Clinton
CILNOOR orcinol
CILNOSU uncoils
CILNOTU linocut
CILNPSU sculpin
CILNSTU linctus
CILOOPT copilot
CILOORU couloir
CILOOSS colossi
CILOPRY pyloric
CILOPSU oilcups
CILOPSW cowslip
CILORST lictors

CILOSTU oculist
CILPRSY crisply
CILPRTU culprit
CILSTTU cultist
CIMMOST commits
CIMNOOR Comorin
moronic
omicron
CIMNORS crimson
microns
CIMNORU Noricum
CIMNOSU coniums
CIMNRSU crinums
CIMOORS morisco
CIMOOST osmotic
CIMOPSY miscopy
CIMOSST Scotism
sitcoms
CIMOSSY mycosis
CIMOTYZ zymotic
CIMPRSS scrimps
CIMPRSY scrimpy
CIMRSSU crissum
CIMSSTY mystics
CINNNOU inconnu
CINNORU unicorn
CINNOSU nuncios
CINNOTU unction
CINNSUU uncinus
CINOOOR Orinoco
CINOOPR porcino
CINOOPS opsonic
CINORRT tricorn
CINORSS incross
CINORST cistron
citrons
CINORSZ zircons
CINORTU ruction
CINORTY tyronic
CINOSST consist
tocsins
CINOSSU cousins
Socinus
CINOSTU suction
CINOSUZ zincous
CINOTXY oxyntic
CINRSTU incrust
CIOOPRS Scorpio
CIOOPRT portico
CIOOPSU copious
CIOOQTU coquito
CIOORST octrois
CIOORSU corious
CIOPRST tropics
CIOPRTY Cypriot
CIOPSTY copyist
CIORRSU cirrous
CIORSSS scissor
CIORSSU Roscius
CIORSTT tricots
CIORSTU citrous
CIORSTV victors
CIORSUU curious
CIORTVY victory
CIOSSSY sycosis
CIOSSUV viscous
CIPRSST scripts
CIPRSSU prussic
CIPRTTY tryptic
CIPRUVY pyruvic
CIPSTTY styptic
CIRSSTU rustics
CJKNNOO jonnock
CKKLNUY knuckly
CKLLMOU mullock
CKLLOOP pollock
CKLNOSU unlocks
CKLNOTU locknut
CKLNOUW Lucknow
CKLNUUY unlucky
CKLOORW rowlock
CKLOOTU lockout
CKLOPSU lockups
CKLOPTU potluck
putlock
CKMOPSU mockups
CKNOOOR rockoon
CKNOOOS Cookson
CKNORSU uncorks
CKNSTUU unstuck
untucks
CKOOOPT cooktop
CKOOOTU cookout
CKOORST Rostock
CKORTUW cutwork
CKOSSTU tussock
CLLMOSU mollusc
CLLOOPS collops
scollop
CLLORSS scrolls
CLLOSUU loculus
CLMNOSU columns
CLMOOOU Olomouc
CLMOOPT complot
CLMOSUU osculum
CLMPRUY crumply
CLMSUUU cumulus
CLNOORT control
CLNOOSS consols
CLNOSSU consuls
CLNOSTU consult
CLNRSUU uncurls
CLOORSU colours
CLOORUY coloury
CLOOSTY cytosol
CLOPRSU Proclus
CLORSSY crossly
CLORTUY courtly
CLOSSTU locusts
CLPSSTU sculpts
CMMNOOS commons
CMMOORS romcoms
CMMRSUY scrummy
CMNNOOS noncoms
CMNNOOT Moncton
CMNOOOT monocot
CMNOOPT Compton
CMNOOPY compony
CMOOORS Comoros
CMOOPRT comport
CMOOPST compost
CMOORSU cormous
CMORSTU scrotum
CMORTUW cutworm
CMOSSTU customs
CMOSUVY Muscovy
CMPRSSU scrumps
CMPRSUY scrumpy
CNNOOOR O'Connor
CNNOORS Connors
CNNORRU Runcorn
CNNORTU nocturn
CNNORUW uncrown
CNOOOTU Cotonou
CNOOPPR popcorn
CNOOPSU coupons
soupcon
CNOORRW cornrow
CNOORST consort
crotons
CNOORTT contort
CNOORTU contour
crouton
CNOOSST oncosts
CNOOSTT cottons
CNOOSTY tycoons
CNOOSUU nocuous
CNOOSVY convoys
CNOOTTY cottony
CNORSSU uncross
CNORTUY country
CNOSSSU Cnossus
COOORSZ corozos
COOPRRT proctor
COOPRSS scroops
COOPRTU outcrop
COOPSTU octopus
COORSUU roucous
COOSTTY otocyst
COPRRSS scrorps
COPRRTU corrupt
COPRSUU cuprous
CORRSSU cursors
CORRSUY cursory
COSTTUU cutouts
DDDDEIL diddled
DDDEEGR dredged
DDDEEHS shedded
DDDEEIR derided
DDDEELM meddled
DDDEELP peddled
DDDEELR reddled
DDDEELU deluded
DDDEENS snedded
DDDEENU denuded
DDDEFIL fiddled
DDDEFLU fuddled
DDDEGII giddied
DDDEGIR gridded
DDDEGLU guddled
DDDEGRU drudged
DDDEHLU huddled
DDDEHTU thudded
DDDEIIS diddies
DDDEIIV divided
DDDEIKS skidded
DDDEILM middled
DDDEILP piddled
DDDEILR diddler
riddled
DDDEILS diddles
DDDEIMU muddied
DDDELMU muddled
DDDELNO noddled
DDDELOO doodled
DDDELOP plodded
poddled
DDDELOS doddles
DDDELOT toddled
DDDELPU puddled
DDDELRU ruddled
DDDEOPR prodded
DDDEORS dodders
DDDEORY doddery
DDDEPSU spudded
DDDESTU studded
DDEEELN needled
DDEEELT deleted
DDEEEMN emended
DDEEEPS speeded
DDEEERR Red Deer
DDEEESX desexed
DDEEFGL fledged
DDEEFII deified
edified
DDEEFIL defiled
fielded
DDEEFIN defined
DDEEFNS defends
DDEEFSU defused
DDEEFUZ defuzed
DDEEGIN deeding
deigned
DDEEGLP pledged
DDEEGLS sledged
DDEEGLU deluged
DDEEGRR dredger
DDEEGRS dredges
DDEEHLS heddles
DDEEHRS shedder
DDEEILV deviled
DDEEILW wielded
DDEEILY yielded
DDEEIMP impeded
DDEEIMS demised
misdeed
DDEEINS neddies
DDEEINT teinded

DDEEINW widened
DDEEINX deindex
indexed
DDEEINZ dizened
DDEEIOV videoed
DDEEIPS depside
DDEEIRR Deirdre
derider
redried
DDEEIRS derides
desired
diedres
resided
DDEEIRV derived
DDEEIRW weirded
DDEEIST teddies
DDEEISV devised
DDEELLU duelled
DDEELLW dwelled
DDEELMO modeled
DDEELMR meddler
DDEELMS meddles
DDEELOY yodeled
DDEELPR peddler
DDEELPS peddles
DDEELRS reddles
DDEELRU deluder
DDEELSU deludes
DDEEMOT demoted
DDEENOP deponed
DDEENOT denoted
DDEENOW endowed
DDEENPS depends
DDEENPU upended
DDEENRS Dresden
reddens
DDEENRT trended
DDEENRU denuder
endured
DDEENSU denudes
dudeens
DDEEOPS deposed
seedpod
DDEEORR ordered
DDEEORW dowered
DDEEOTV devoted
DDEEOTX detoxed
DDEEPTU deputed
DDEERRS redders
DDEERSS dressed
DDEERST reddest
tedders
DDEERTU detrude
DDEETTU duetted
DDEFILR fiddler
DDEFILS fiddles
DDEFIOR foredid
DDEFIRT drifted
DDEFLNO Flodden
fondled
DDEFLOO flooded
DDEFLSU fuddles
DDEFNOR fronded
DDEFNOU founded
DDEFORR Redford
DDEFORS fodders
DDEGGRU drugged
grudged
DDEGHIT dighted
DDEGIIR giddier
DDEGIIS giddies
DDEGILR girdled
griddle
DDEGIMO demigod
Megiddo
DDEGINO dingoed
DDEGINR redding
DDEGINT tedding
DDEGINW wedding
DDEGINY eddying
DDEGIOR dodgier
DDEGLOP plodged
DDEGLOS dogsled
DDEGLSU guddles
DDEGMOS dodgems
DDEGMSU smudged
DDEGNOS godsend
DDEGNOU dudgeon
DDEGNWY Gwynedd
DDEGORS dodgers
gorsedd
DDEGOSS goddess
DDEGOST stodged
DDEGRRU drudger
DDEGRSU drudges
DDEGRTU trudged
DDEHIRS reddish
DDEHIRY hydride
DDEHLRU huddler
hurdled
DDEHLSU huddles
DDEHNOU hounded
DDEHNRU hundred
DDEHOSW showded
DDEHRSU shudder
DDEIIKS kiddies
DDEIIMS middies
DDEIINT indited
DDEIINV divined
DDEIIOS iodides
iodised
DDEIIOX dioxide
DDEIIOZ iodized
DDEIIRT dirtied
DDEIIRV divider
DDEIISV divides
DDEIIVV divvied
DDEIIZZ dizzied
DDEIKLN kindled
DDEIKLS kiddles
DDEIKNR kindred
DDEIKRS kidders
DDEILLO dollied
DDEILLR drilled
DDEILLU illuded
DDEILMP dimpled
DDEILMS middles
DDEILNS slidden
DDEILNW dwindle
DDEILOS dildoes
DDEILOT deltoid
DDEILPR piddler
DDEILPS piddles
DDEILRR riddler
DDEILRS riddles
DDEILRT tiddler
DDEILTU diluted
DDEILTW twiddle
DDEILTY lyddite
DDEIMMU dummied
DDEIMNS middens
DDEIMNU Edmund I
DDEIMOR dermoid
DDEIMOS desmoid
DDEIMRU muddier
DDEIMSS desmids
DDEIMSU muddies
DDEINNU Dunedin
DDEINOP poinded
DDEINOS noddies
DDEINOT dentoid
DDEINPS dispend
DDEINST distend
DDEINSW swidden
DDEIOPR Perdido
DDEIOPS poddies
DDEIORT Diderot
DDEIORV overdid
DDEIORW dowdier
DDEIOST toddies
DDEIOSW dowdies
DDEIOTT dittoed
DDEIOWW widowed
DDEIPPR dripped
DDEIRRS ridders
DDEIRRU ruddier
DDEISSU disused
DDEISTU studied
DDEJRSU judders
DDEKMOU dukedom
DDEKOOR drooked
DDEKORU drouked
DDELMOT Detmold
DDELMOU moulded
DDELMRU muddler
DDELMSU muddles
DDELNOO noodled
DDELNOS noddles
DDELOOR doodler
drooled
DDELOOS doodles
DDELOPR plodder
DDELOPS poddles
DDELORT toddler
DDELOST toddles
DDELPRU puddler
DDELPSU puddles
spuddle
DDELRSU ruddles
DDEMMRU drummed
DDEMMSU smeddum
DDEMNOR Redmond
DDEMNOS Desmond
DDEMNOT oddment
DDEMNOU mounded
DDEMORR Mordred
DDENNOR dendron
DDENOOS desnood
snooded
DDENOPS despond
DDENOPU pounded
DDENORS donders
DDENORT trodden
DDENORU redound
rounded
underdo
DDENORW drowned
DDENOSS oddness
soddens
DDENOSU sounded
DDENOSY dynodes
DDENOUW wounded
DDENSSU suddens
DDEOOPR drooped
DDEOORW redwood
DDEOOWY dyewood
DDEOPPR dropped
DDEOPRR prodder
DDEOPRW dewdrop
DDEORSW drowsed
DDEPRSU spudder
DDERRSU rudders
DDGGINO dodging
DDGHOOO godhood
DDGIIKN kidding
DDGIILY giddily
DDGIINR ridding
DDGIMNU mudding
DDGINNO nodding
DDGINOP podding
DDGINOS sodding
DDGINOW Dowding
DDGINPU pudding
DDGIPUY giddyup
DDGNOOS Dodgson
DDGOOOW dogwood
DDHIKSU kiddush
DDHIORY hydroid
DDIIKKS dikdiks
DDIIKLS skidlid
DDIILOP diploid
DDILMUY muddily
DDILNRS dirndls
DDILOWY dowdily
DDILRUY ruddily
DDIMOOS dodoism
DDINOSS Siddons
DDIRSSU siddurs

DDMMSUU dumdums
DDMNOOR dromond
DEEEEWW weeweed
DEEEFLR fleered
DEEEFLT fleeted
DEEEFNS defense
DEEEFRS feeders
DEEEFRV fevered
DEEEGLP pledgee
DEEEGMR demerge
emerged
DEEEGNR greened
reneged
DEEEGRS degrees
DEEEGRT deterge
greeted
DEEEGST egested
DEEEHLW wheedle
wheeled
DEEEHNS sheened
DEEEHRS heeders
heredes
sheered
DEEEHST seethed
sheeted
DEEEHTT teethed
DEEEHWZ wheezed
DEEEINR needier
DEEEIRR reedier
DEEEIRS seedier
DEEEIRW weedier
DEEEISV devisee
DEEEJLW jeweled
DEEEJRR jerreed
DEEEJRS jereeds
DEEEKLN kneeled
DEEEKLS sleeked
DEEEKNW weekend
DEEEKRY rekeyed
DEEELLV leveled
DEEELNS needles
DEEELPT deplete
DEEELRV levered
reveled
DEEELST deletes
sleeted
steeled
DEEELSV sleeved
DEEELTX telexed
DEEEMNR reedmen
DEEEMNS demesne
DEEEMRS emersed
medrese
redeems
DEEEMRT Demeter
metered
DEEENPR preened
DEEENPS deepens
DEEENQU queened
DEEENRS sneered
DEEENRT entered
DEEENRW renewed
DEEENSV vendees
DEEENSZ sneezed
DEEENTT detente
DEEENTV evented
DEEENUV Deneuve
DEEEOTV devotee
DEEEPRS speeder
speered
DEEEPRT petered
DEEEPST deepest
steeped
DEEEQRU queered
DEEERRV revered
DEEERSS seeders
DEEERST reested
steered
DEEERSV deserve
severed
DEEERSW sewered
sweered
weeders
DEEERSY redeyes
DEEERTV everted
DEEERTX exerted
DEEESSX desexes
DEEESTV steeved
DEEETTV vedette
DEEETTW tweeted
DEEETWZ tweezed
DEEFFFO feoffed
DEEFFIN effendi
DEEFFOR offered
DEEFFSU effused
DEEFGIN feeding
feigned
DEEFGLS fledges
DEEFGRU refuged
DEEFHLS fleshed
shelfed
DEEFHLU heedful
DEEFHRS freshed
DEEFIIR deifier
edifier
reified
DEEFIIS deifies
edifies
DEEFILN Enfield
DEEFILR defiler
ferlied
fielder
refiled
DEEFILS defiles
DEEFINR definer
refined
DEEFINS defines
DEEFINT feinted
DEEFIRR ferried
refired
refried
DEEFIRS defiers
DEEFIST deifest
DEEFKLR Krefeld
DEEFLLU fuelled
DEEFLNS flensed
DEEFLNU needful
DEEFLOT feedlot
DEEFLRU feruled
DEEFLTT fettled
DEEFMOR freedom
DEEFNRS fenders
DEEFORV overfed
DEEFRSU refused
DEEFRTT fretted
DEEFRTU refuted
DEEFSSU defuses
DEEFSTT deftest
DEEFSUZ defuzes
DEEGGIS gidgees
DEEGHIN heeding
neighed
DEEGHIW weighed
DEEGHOW hogweed
DEEGHRS hedgers
DEEGIJS gidjees
DEEGILN deleing
DEEGIMN deeming
DEEGIMV demiveg
DEEGINN needing
DEEGINR dreeing
energid
reeding
reigned
DEEGINS seeding
DEEGINW weeding
DEEGIPW pigweed
DEEGIRV diverge
grieved
DEEGIRW wedgier
DEEGIST edgiest
DEEGJRU rejudge
DEEGLNR Grendel
DEEGLNS legends
DEEGLNT gentled
DEEGLOY goldeye
DEEGLPR pledger
DEEGLPS pledges
DEEGLPT pledget
DEEGLRS gelders
ledgers
redlegs
sledger
DEEGLRU reglued
DEEGLRW wergeld
DEEGLSS sledges
DEEGLSU deluges
DEEGMUW gumweed
DEEGNNO endogen
DEEGNRS genders
DEEGORR rogered
DEEGOSY geodesy
DEEGSSU guessed
DEEGSTU guested
DEEHIKV khedive
DEEHINR inhered
DEEHIRR rehired
DEEHIST heisted
DEEHITV thieved
DEEHLLS shelled
DEEHLMW whelmed
DEEHLOV hoveled
DEEHLPW whelped
DEEHLSV shelved
DEEHLSW welshed
DEEHMUX exhumed
DEEHNOY honeyed
DEEHNRT Drenthe
DEEHNVZ Dezhnev
DEEHORV hovered
DEEHPRS sphered
DEEHRRS herders
DEEHRSU ushered
DEEHTTW whetted
DEEIIRW weirdie
DEEIIST deities
DEEIJLL jellied
DEEIJMM jemmied
DEEIKLN kneidel
likened
DEEIKMW midweek
DEEIKOV dovekie
DEEILLM De Mille
DEEILMR Demirel
DEEILNO eloined
DEEILNR redline
relined
DEEILNS enisled
ensiled
linseed
DEEILNV livened
DEEILNY dyeline
DEEILOR reoiled
DEEILPR replied
DEEILPS spieled
DEEILRS resiled
DEEILRV deliver
relived
reviled
DEEILRW wielder
DEEILRY reedily
yielder
DEEILSS diesels
DEEILSY eyelids
seedily
DEEILTU dilutee
DEEILWY weedily
DEEIMNO dominee
DEEIMNS sidemen
DEEIMOT Edomite
DEEIMPR demirep
impeder
DEEIMPS impedes
DEEIMPT emptied
DEEIMRS remised
DEEIMRT demerit
dimeter
merited

	mitered
DEEIMRX	remixed
DEEIMSS	demises
DEEIMTT	emitted
DEEINNS	Dinesen
DEEINNT	dentine
DEEINNU	ennuied
DEEINNZ	denizen
DEEINPR	Dnieper
	repined
	ripened
DEEINRS	deniers
	resined
DEEINRW	rewiden
	widener
DEEINRX	indexer
DEEINST	destine
DEEINSV	endives
DEEINSW	endwise
DEEINSX	indexes
DEEINTT	dinette
DEEINTU	detinue
DEEINTV	evident
DEEINWZ	wizened
DEEIOPS	episode
DEEIOPT	epidote
DEEIOPX	epoxide
DEEIPPT	peptide
DEEIPRS	preside
	speired
DEEIPRV	deprive
DEEIPRX	expired
DEEIPSS	despise
DEEIPST	despite
DEEIQRU	queried
DEEIQTU	quieted
DEEIRRS	derries
	desirer
	Dreiser
	redries
	resider
	serried
DEEIRRT	retired
	retried
DEEIRRV	deriver
DEEIRRW	rewired
	weirder
DEEIRSS	desires
	resides
DEEIRST	dieters
	reedits
	resited
DEEIRSU	residue
	ureides
DEEIRSV	derives
	deviser
	De Vries
	diverse
	revised
DEEIRSW	sweired
DEEIRTU	erudite
DEEIRTV	riveted
DEEIRVV	revived
DEEISSU	diseuse
DEEISSV	devises
DEEISTW	dewiest
DEEISTX	existed
DEEISVZ	Devizes
DEEITTV	vidette
DEEJNOY	enjoyed
DEEKKLR	de Klerk
DEEKKRT	trekked
DEEKLLN	knelled
DEEKLPS	skelped
DEEKNNS	skenned
DEEKNNY	Kennedy
DEEKNOT	tokened
DEEKNRW	Kendrew
DEEKORV	revoked
DEEKOVY	dovekey
DEEKSTT	sketted
DEELLMS	smelled
DEELLNR	Rendell
DEELLPS	spelled
DEELLQU	quelled
DEELLRU	dueller
DEELLRW	dweller
DEELLRY	elderly
DEELLSW	swelled
DEELMOR	Delorme
	modeler
	remodel
DEELMPT	templed
DEELMPU	deplume
DEELMRU	relumed
DEELMST	smelted
DEELMSU	mulesed
DEELMSY	medleys
DEELMTT	mettled
DEELNOT	dolente
DEELNPU	pendule
DEELNRS	lenders
	slender
DEELNSS	endless
DEELNST	nestled
DEELNSW	wedelns
DEELNSY	densely
DEELNTT	nettled
DEELOPP	peopled
DEELOPR	deplore
DEELOPV	develop
DEELOPX	explode
DEELORS	resoled
DEELORU	urodele
DEELORW	lowered
	roweled
DEELOSU	delouse
DEELOTW	toweled
DEELOVV	devolve
	evolved
DEELPRS	pedlers
DEELPRU	prelude
DEELPST	pestled
DEELRSU	eluders
DEELRSV	delvers
DEELRSW	rewelds
	welders
DEELSTT	settled
DEELSTU	teledus
DEELSTW	lewdest
DEELTUX	exulted
DEELVXY	vexedly
DEEMMST	stemmed
DEEMNOR	moderne
DEEMNOU	eudemon
DEEMNOV	Vendôme
DEEMNOY	moneyed
DEEMNRS	menders
	remends
DEEMNST	dements
DEEMORV	removed
DEEMORX	exoderm
DEEMOSS	demoses
DEEMOST	demotes
DEEMOSY	moseyed
DEEMPRS	premeds
DEEMPSY	Dempsey
DEEMPTT	tempted
DEEMRSU	resumed
DEENNOS	donnees
DEENNOT	tenoned
DEENNOY	doyenne
DEENNPT	pendent
DEENNUY	ennuyed
DEENOOR	roneoed
DEENOPR	reponed
DEENOPS	depones
	spondee
DEENOPT	pentode
DEENORS	endorse
DEENORT	erodent
DEENORW	endower
	reendow
DEENORZ	rezoned
DEENOST	denotes
	Tenedos
DEENPPR	perpend
DEENPRS	spender
DEENPRT	pretend
DEENPSX	expends
DEENRRS	renders
DEENRSS	redness
	senders
DEENRST	tenders
DEENRSU	endures
	ensured
DEENRSV	venders
DEENRTU	denture
	tenured
DEENRTW	Derwent
DEENSST	densest
DEENSTT	detents
DEENSTW	West End
DEENSTX	extends
DEENSUV	vendues
DEENSUX	unsexed
DEEOPPY	popeyed
DEEOPRS	deposer
	reposed
DEEOPRW	powered
DEEOPSS	deposes
	speedos
DEEOPSX	exposed
DEEORRR	orderer
	reorder
DEEORRS	reredos
DEEORST	oersted
	teredos
DEEORSV	devores
DEEORTT	ottered
	tetrode
DEEORTW	towered
DEEORUV	overdue
DEEORVY	overdye
DEEORXX	xeroxed
DEEOSTV	devotes
DEEOSTX	detoxes
DEEPPPR	prepped
DEEPPST	stepped
DEEPPSU	speedup
DEEPRSS	depress
	des Prés
	pressed
DEEPRSU	perdues
	perused
DEEPRTU	erupted
	reputed
DEEPRTY	retyped
DEEPRUV	prevued
DEEPSTU	deputes
DEEQSTU	quested
DEERRSS	dresser
	redress
DEERRUV	verdure
DEERSSS	dresses
DEERSST	deserts
	dessert
	tressed
DEERSTW	strewed
	wrested
DEERSTX	dexters
DEERSVW	swerved
DEERTTU	uttered
DEERTUX	extrude
DEESSTT	detests
DEESSTU	Sudetes
DEESSTV	devests
DEESTTT	stetted
DEFFFLU	fluffed
DEFFHIW	whiffed
DEFFILP	piffled
DEFFILR	riffled
DEFFIMO	fiefdom
DEFFINS	sniffed
DEFFIOS	offside
DEFFIRS	differs
DEFFIST	stiffed
DEFFISU	diffuse

DEFFLMU muffled
DEFFLRU ruffled
DEFFLSU sluffed
DEFFNOR forfend
DEFFNOS offends
sendoff
DEFFNSU snuffed
DEFFORS doffers
DEFFRSU duffers
DEFFSTU duffest
stuffed
DEFGGIR frigged
DEFGGLO flogged
DEFGGOR frogged
DEFGINN fending
DEFGINR fringed
DEFGINU feuding
DEFGINY defying
DEFGIOR firedog
DEFGIRS fridges
DEFGIRU figured
DEFGIST fidgets
DEFGITY fidgety
DEFHIRS redfish
DEFHIST shifted
DEFHLSU flushed
DEFHORT frothed
DEFIILM midlife
DEFIILN infidel
infield
DEFIIMS fideism
DEFIIMW midwife
DEFIINU unified
DEFIINX infixed
DEFIIST fideist
DEFIKRS frisked
DEFILLR frilled
DEFILNT flinted
DEFILOO folioed
DEFILOW oldwife
DEFILPP flipped
DEFILRT flirted
trifled
DEFILRU direful
DEFILST stifled
DEFILTT flitted
DEFILTY fetidly
DEFILXY fixedly
DEFILZZ fizzled
DEFIMOR deiform
DEFINRS finders
friends
redfins
DEFINRU unfired
DEFINSU infused
DEFINUX unfixed
DEFIOOS foodies
DEFIOST foisted
DEFIPRY perfidy
DEFIRRT drifter
DEFIRTT fritted
DEFIRTU fruited
DEFIRZZ frizzed
DEFISTU feudist
DEFKLNU flunked
DEFLLOU doleful
DEFLNOR fondler
DEFLNOS enfolds
fondles
DEFLNOT tenfold
DEFLOOR flooder
floored
reflood
DEFLOOT footled
DEFLOOZ foozled
DEFLOPP flopped
DEFLORS folders
refolds
DEFLORT telford
DEFLORU floured
DEFLOTU flouted
DEFLPRU purfled
DEFLRUU Duruflé
DEFMORS deforms
serfdom
DEFNOOR fordone
DEFNORT fronted
DEFNORU founder
DEFNORW frowned
DEFNOST fondest
DEFNOSU fondues
DEFNRSU refunds
DEFOOPR proofed
DEFOOPS spoofed
DEFOORS fordoes
DEFOORT redfoot
DEFORST defrost
frosted
DEFORWX Wexford
DEFRSUY Dreyfus
DEGGGIL giggled
DEGGGIN degging
DEGGGLO goggled
DEGGHIL higgled
DEGGHIN hedging
DEGGIJL jiggled
DEGGIKN kedging
DEGGILN gelding
niggled
DEGGILU Gielgud
DEGGILW wiggled
DEGGINS edgings
snigged
DEGGINW wedging
DEGGIOS doggies
DEGGIPR prigged
DEGGIRS diggers
DEGGIRT trigged
DEGGIRU druggie
DEGGISW swigged
DEGGITW twigged
DEGGJLO joggled
DEGGJLU juggled
DEGGLOS doglegs
slogged
DEGGLOT toggled
DEGGLPU plugged
DEGGLRU gurgled
DEGGLSU slugged
DEGGNOO doggone
DEGGNOS snogged
DEGGNOU gudgeon
DEGGNSU snugged
DEGGOPR progged
DEGGORS doggers
DEGGORT trogged
DEGGORY doggery
DEGGRRU grudger
DEGGRSU grudges
DEGGRTU drugget
DEGHHOU houghed
DEGHILT delight
lighted
DEGHINR herding
DEGHINW whinged
DEGHIOT hogtied
DEGHIRT girthed
righted
DEGHIST sighted
DEGHORU roughed
DEGHOST ghosted
DEGHOSU soughed
DEGHOTU toughed
DEGIILN eliding
DEGIINN indigen
DEGIINR dingier
DEGIINT dieting
editing
ignited
DEGIISW widgies
DEGIJLN jingled
DEGIKLO doglike
godlike
DEGILLO gollied
DEGILLR grilled
DEGILLU gullied
DEGILLY gelidly
DEGILMN melding
mingled
DEGILNN lending
DEGILNO glenoid
DEGILNS dingles
singled
DEGILNT glinted
tingled
DEGILNU dueling
eluding
indulge
DEGILNV delving
DEGILNW welding
DEGILOR gloried
godlier
DEGILRR girdler
DEGILRS gilders
girdles
gliders
regilds
ridgels
DEGILRU guilder
DEGILRW wergild
DEGILUV divulge
DEGIMNN mending
DEGIMNS smidgen
DEGIMST midgets
DEGINNN denning
DEGINNP pending
DEGINNR grinned
rending
DEGINNS endings
sending
DEGINNT denting
tending
DEGINNU enduing
DEGINNV vending
DEGINNW wending
DEGINNY denying
DEGINOR eroding
Gironde
groined
ignored
negroid
redoing
DEGINOS dingoes
DEGINOT ingoted
DEGINOW wendigo
widgeon
DEGINRR grinder
DEGINRW redwing
DEGINSS designs
DEGINSW swinged
DEGINSY dingeys
DEGINTW twinged
DEGINUX exuding
DEGIOOS goodies
DEGIOPR podgier
DEGIORT goitred
DEGIPPR gripped
DEGIPRU pudgier
DEGIRRS girders
DEGIRSS digress
DEGIRSU guiders
DEGIRTT gritted
DEGISST digests
DEGISTU dugites
DEGISTW widgets
DEGJRSU judgers
DEGLMOO gloomed
DEGLNNO endlong
DEGLNOS dongles
DEGLNOU lounged
DEGLNPU plunged
DEGLNSU guldens
DEGLOPR pledgor
DEGLOPS plodges
splodge
DEGLORS lodgers
DEGLORW growled
DEGLOSS glossed

godless
DEGLSSU sludges
DEGLTTU glutted
DEGLUZZ guzzled
DEGMNOO goodmen
DEGMOOR groomed
DEGMOOS smoodge
smooged
DEGMPRU grumped
DEGMSSU smudges
DEGNNOU dungeon
DEGNOPR pronged
DEGNOPS sponged
DEGNORU guerdon
undergo
DEGNORW wronged
DEGNOTU tongued
DEGNRSU dungers
gerunds
nudgers
DEGNRTU grunted
trudgen
DEGOORV grooved
DEGOOST stooged
DEGOPRU grouped
DEGORRS Rodgers
DEGORSS grossed
sodgers
DEGORSU drogues
gourdes
groused
DEGORTU grouted
DEGOSST stodges
DEGRRTU trudger
DEGRSTU trudges
DEGSSTU degusts
DEHHSSU shushed
DEHIINN hinnied
DEHIIRS dishier
DEHIKRS shirked
DEHIKSW whisked
DEHILPR hirpled
DEHILRT thirled
DEHILRW whirled
DEHILSS shields
DEHILTY diethyl
DEHIMMS shimmed
DEHIMNU inhumed
DEHIMOP hemipod
DEHIMOR heirdom
DEHIMOT ethmoid
DEHIMUX humidex
DEHINNS shinned
DEHINNT thinned
DEHINOR hordein
DEHINOS hoidens
DEHINRS hinders
nerdish
shrined
DEHINRX Hendrix
DEHIOOS hoodies
DEHIOOT dhootie
DEHIORT theroid
DEHIOST hoisted
DEHIOSU hideous
DEHIOSX oxhides
DEHIOTU hideout
DEHIPPS shipped
DEHIPPW whipped
DEHIRRS shirred
DEHIRRU hurried
DEHIRRW whirred
DEHIRST dithers
DEHIRSU hurdies
Rushdie
DEHIRSV dervish
shrived
DEHIRTV thrived
DEHIRTW writhed
DEHIRTY dithery
DEHISSW Swedish
swished
DEHISTT shitted
DEHISTW whisted
DEHISVV shivved
DEHIWZZ whizzed
DEHKORS Shkodër
DEHLLOO holloed
DEHLLOU hulloed
DEHLOOT toehold
DEHLOPP hoppled
DEHLORS holders
DEHLORW whorled
DEHLOSS sloshed
DEHLRRU hurdler
DEHLRSU hurdles
DEHLRTU hurtled
DEHLSSU slushed
DEHLSTU hustled
DEHMORU humored
DEHMOST methods
DEHMOTU mouthed
DEHMPTU thumped
DEHNNSU shunned
DEHNOOR honored
DEHNOOW hoedown
woodhen
DEHNORR Hordern
DEHNORS dehorns
DEHNORT thonder
throned
DEHNORU hounder
DEHNOSY hoydens
DEHNOTZ dozenth
DEHNRTU thunder
DEHNSTU shunted
DEHOOPW whooped
DEHOOST soothed
DEHOOSW wooshed
DEHOOTT toothed
DEHOOWY Heywood
DEHOPPS shopped
DEHOPPW whopped
DEHORTW worthed
DEHOSTT shotted
DEHOSTU shouted
DEHPPUW whupped
DEIIJMM jimmied
DEIIKKL kidlike
DEIIKLS dislike
DEIIKNR dinkier
DEIIKNS dinkies
kindies
DEIILLS dillies
DEIILMP implied
DEIILMT delimit
limited
DEIILOS doilies
idolise
DEIILOZ idolize
DEIILPS lipides
DEIIMMX immixed
DEIIMNO dominie
DEIINOS ionised
DEIINOT edition
DEIINOZ ionized
DEIINRS insider
DEIINRT inditer
nitride
DEIINRU uridine
DEIINRV diviner
DEIINRW windier
DEIINSS insides
DEIINST indites
tineids
DEIINSV divines
DEIINTV invited
DEIIOPR Pedro II
DEIIORS iodiser
DEIIORT diorite
DEIIORZ iodizer
DEIIOSS iodises
DEIIOSX oxidise
DEIIOSZ iodizes
DEIIOXZ oxidize
DEIIPPR dippier
DEIIPRT riptide
tiderip
DEIIRRT dirtier
DEIIRST dirties
ditsier
DEIIRTZ ditzier
DEIIRZZ dizzier
DEIISTT ditties
tidiest
DEIISTV visited
DEIISVV divvies
DEIISYZ Yezidis
DEIISZZ dizzies
DEIJLLO jollied
DEIJNOR joinder
DEIJNOT jointed
DEIJNRU injured
DEIJORY joyride
DEIJOST joisted
DEIKLLS deskill
skilled
DEIKLNP plinked
DEIKLNR kindler
DEIKLNS kindles
DEIKLNT tinkled
DEIKLNW winkled
DEIKLOR rodlike
DEIKLOS keloids
DEIKLRS skirled
DEIKLTT kittled
DEIKMMS skimmed
DEIKMPS skimped
DEIKMRS smirked
DEIKNNS skinned
DEIKNOS doeskin
Sekondi
DEIKNOV invoked
DEIKNPR prinked
DEIKNRR drinker
DEIKNRS redskin
DEIKNST kindest
DEIKNSW swinked
DEIKNSY kidneys
DEIKNTT knitted
DEIKPPS skipped
DEIKRRS skirred
DEIKRST skirted
DEIKRSU duikers
duskier
DEIKSVY skydive
DEILLMU illumed
DEILLNW indwell
DEILLOS dollies
DEILLPR prilled
DEILLPS spilled
DEILLQU quilled
DEILLRR driller
redrill
DEILLRT trilled
DEILLSS lidless
DEILLST stilled
DEILLSU illudes
sullied
DEILLSW swilled
DEILLTW twilled
DEILMMS slimmed
DEILMNS mildens
DEILMOP implode
DEILMOR moldier
DEILMOS meloids
midsole
DEILMOY myeloid
DEILMPP pimpled
DEILMPS dimples
mispled
DEILMPW wimpled
DEILMST mildest
DEILMSW mildews
DEILMWY mildewy
DEILMXY mixedly
DEILMZZ mizzled
DEILNNS lindens

DEILNNU	unlined
DEILNOO	eidolon
DEILNOS	dolines
DEILNOT	lentoid
DEILNPS	spindle
	splined
DEILNRT	tendril
DEILNST	dentils
DEILNSW	swindle
DEILNSY	Lindsey
	snidely
DEILNTU	diluent
DEILNTW	indwelt
DEILNUV	unlived
DEILOPR	leporid
DEILOPS	despoil
	diploes
	dipoles
	spoiled
DEILOPT	piloted
DEILOPU	euploid
DEILORS	soldier
DEILORW	dowlier
DEILOSV	livedos
DEILOSY	doylies
DEILPPR	rippled
DEILPPS	slipped
DEILPPT	tippled
DEILPRT	tripled
DEILPSS	dispels
DEILPSU	Lepidus
DEILPTY	tepidly
DEILPUX	Dupleix
DEILQTU	quilted
DEILRSS	sidlers
	sliders
DEILRSV	drivels
DEILRSW	swirled
	wilders
DEILRTU	diluter
DEILRTW	twirled
DEILRTY	tiredly
DEILRVY	devilry
DEILRWY	weirdly
DEILRZZ	drizzle
DEILSTT	stilted
DEILSTU	dilutes
DEILSTW	wildest
DEILSZZ	sizzled
DEIMMPR	primmed
DEIMMRS	dimmers
DEIMMRT	midterm
	trimmed
DEIMMRU	immured
DEIMMST	dimmest
DEIMMSU	dummies
	mediums
DEIMNNU	minuend
DEIMNOR	minored
DEIMNPS	impends
	Mendips
DEIMNRS	minders
	reminds
DEIMNSS	dimness
DEIMNST	mindset
DEIMNTU	minuted
DEIMNUX	unmixed
DEIMOOR	moidore
	moodier
DEIMOPR	impedor
DEIMOPS	imposed
DEIMORS	moiders
DEIMOST	modiste
DEIMOSW	mowdies
DEIMOTT	omitted
DEIMOTV	motived
	vomited
DEIMPPR	primped
DEIMPRU	dumpier
	umpired
DEIMPTU	imputed
DEIMRRS	smirred
DEIMRSY	semidry
DEIMRUU	uredium
DEIMSST	demists
DEIMSSU	misused
DEIMSTW	Midwest
DEIMSTY	stymied
DEINNOS	donnies
DEINNOT	intoned
DEINNRS	dinners
DEINNRU	inurned
DEINNST	indents
	intends
DEINNSU	dunnies
	undines
DEINNSW	enwinds
DEINNTU	dunnite
DEINNTW	twinned
DEINOOZ	ozonide
DEINOPS	spinode
DEINOPT	pointed
DEINORS	indorse
	rosined
DEINORU	dourine
DEINORW	downier
DEINOTZ	Doenitz
DEINPPS	snipped
DEINPRT	printed
DEINPST	stipend
DEINRRU	nurdier
DEINRSU	insured
DEINRSV	verdins
DEINRSW	rewinds
	winders
DEINRTT	trident
DEINRTU	intrude
	turdine
	untried
DEINRTX	dextrin
DEINRTY	tindery
DEINSST	dissent
	snidest
DEINSSY	endysis
DEINSTT	dentist
	stinted
DEINSTY	density
	destiny
DEINSUZ	unsized
DEIOORW	woodier
DEIOOSS	isodose
DEIOOST	osteoid
DEIOPPP	poppied
DEIOPRS	periods
DEIOPRT	diopter
	dioptre
	peridot
DEIOPRV	provide
DEIOPSS	dispose
DEIOPST	deposit
	dopiest
	posited
	topside
DEIOPSU	Oedipus
	Opus Dei
DEIOPTT	tiptoed
DEIOPTV	pivoted
DEIORRT	dortier
DEIORRW	rowdier
	wordier
	worried
DEIORSS	dossier
DEIORST	editors
	sortied
	steroid
	storied
	triodes
DEIORSV	devisor
	devoirs
	visored
	voiders
DEIORSW	dowries
	rowdies
	weirdos
DEIORTT	Detroit
	dottier
DEIORTU	outride
DEIORVZ	vizored
DEIORWW	widower
DEIOSTU	outside
	tedious
DEIOSTW	dowiest
DEIOSTZ	doziest
DEIOSUV	devious
DEIPPQU	quipped
DEIPPRS	dippers
DEIPPRT	tripped
DEIPPSU	duppies
DEIPRSS	spiders
DEIPRST	striped
DEIPRSY	spidery
DEIPSSU	upsides
DEIPSSV	vespids
DEIPSTT	spitted
DEIPSTU	dispute
DEIPSXY	pyxides
DEIPTTU	puttied
DEIQRSU	squired
DEIQRTU	quirted
DEIQTTU	quitted
DEIQUZZ	quizzed
DEIRRST	stirred
	strider
DEIRRSU	durries
DEIRRSV	drivers
DEIRSST	strides
DEIRSSU	diseurs
DEIRSTU	dustier
DEIRSTV	diverts
DEISSST	desists
DEISSSU	disuses
DEISSTU	studies
	tissued
DEISSTV	divests
DEISTTW	twisted
DEITTTW	twitted
DEJLOST	jostled
DEJLSTU	justled
DEJMOUZ	Judezmo
DEJOORY	joyrode
DEJOSTU	jousted
DEKKLSU	skulked
DEKLLNO	knolled
DEKLNOP	plonked
DEKLNPU	plunked
DEKLNRU	knurled
DEKNNRU	drunken
DEKNOST	Donetsk
	stonked
DEKNOSY	donkeys
DEKNOTT	knotted
DEKNOUY	unyoked
DEKNRRU	drunker
DEKNRSU	dunkers
DEKOOPS	spooked
DEKOOST	dookets
	stooked
DEKOPST	desktop
DEKORST	stroked
DEKORWY	keyword
DEKOSVY	skydove
DEKRSUY	duykers
DELLOOW	woolled
DELLOPR	redpoll
DELLORT	trolled
DELLOSU	duellos
DELLOVW	lowveld
DELLRRU	Durrell
DELLSTU	dullest
DELMMSU	slummed
DELMNOS	dolmens
DELMORS	molders
	slormed
	smolder
DELMORU	moulder
	remould
DELMOSU	modules
DELMOTT	mottled

DELMOTU moulted
DELMOUV volumed
DELMPPU plumped
DELMPRU rumpled
DELMPSU slumped
DELMUZZ muzzled
DELNOOS noodles
DELNORS rondels
DELNORU roundel
DELNOSS oldness
DELNOSU loudens
nodules
DELNOTW letdown
DELNOTY notedly
DELNOUV unloved
DELNPRU plunder
DELNRSU rundles
DELNRTU rundlet
trundle
DELNRUU unruled
DELNSSU dulness
DELNUZZ nuzzled
DELOOPP pleopod
DELOOPS poodles
spooled
DELOOPT pootled
DELOORT rootled
DELOOSS dolosse
DELOOST stooled
DELOOTT tootled
DELOPPP plopped
poppled
DELOPPS slopped
DELOPPT toppled
DELOPRS polders
presold
DELOPRT droplet
DELOPRW prowled
DELOPSY deploys
DELOPTT plotted
DELORRY orderly
DELORSS solders
DELORST oldster
DELORSU Lourdes
DELORSW weldors
DELORSY yodlers
DELORTT dottrel
DELORUV louvred
DELOSSS dossels
DELOSTT dottels
dottles
slotted
DELOSTU loudest
tousled
DELOSYY doyleys
DELOSZZ sozzled
DELOTUV voluted
DELOTUZ touzled
DELPPSU suppled
DELPRSU drupels
slurped
DELPSTU duplets
DELPUZZ puzzled
DELRRSU slurred
DELRSTU lustred
rustled
strudel
DELRTTU turtled
DELSSTU tussled
DEMMRRU drummer
DEMMSTU stummed
DEMNOOR doormen
Ormonde
DEMNOOW woodmen
DEMNORS moderns
DEMNORT mordent
DEMNORU mourned
DEMNOST endmost
DEMNOTU demount
mounted
DEMNOUV unmoved
DEMNSTU dustmen
DEMOOPP popedom
DEMOOPR predoom
DEMOORT motored
DEMOOSS osmosed
DEMOPST stomped
DEMORRS dormers
DEMORRU rumored
DEMORST stormed
DEMOSTY modesty
DEMPRSU dumpers
DEMPRTU trumped
DEMPSTU stumped
DEMRRSU murders
smurred
DEMSTTU smutted
DENNORT donnert
DENNOST tendons
DENNOUW enwound
unowned
DENNSTU dunnest
stunned
DENOOPS snooped
spooned
DENOOSW swooned
woodens
DENOOSZ snoozed
DENOOTU duotone
outdone
DENOPPR propend
DENOPRS ponders
respond
DENOPRT portend
DENOPRU pounder
DENOPSU unposed
DENOPUX expound
DENORRU rondure
rounder
DENORRW drowner
DENORST rodents
snorted
DENORSU Øresund
resound
sounder
undoers
DENORSV vendors
DENORSW downers
wonders
DENORUW rewound
wounder
DENOSTU snouted
DENPRSU spurned
DENPRTU prudent
DENPSSU sendups
suspend
DENRSSU sunders
undress
DENRSSY dryness
DENSSUW sundews
DENSTTU student
stunted
DENTUVY duvetyn
DEOOPPS opposed
DEOOPRS spoored
DEOOPRT torpedo
trooped
DEOOPST stooped
DEOOPSW swooped
DEOORRT redroot
DEOORST roosted
DEOORTU outrode
DEOOSTU outdoes
DEOPPPR propped
DEOPPRR dropper
DEOPPRS doppers
DEOPPST stopped
DEOPPSW swopped
DEOPRRU prouder
DEOPRST deports
sported
DEOPRSW powders
DEOPRTU trouped
DEOPRWY powdery
DEOPSST despots
DEOPSSU spoused
DEOPSTT spotted
DEOPSTU spouted
DEORRSV drovers
DEORRSW rewords
DEORSSS dossers
DEORSSU dousers
DEORSSW dowsers
drowses
DEORSTT dotters
DEORSTU detours
rousted
DEORSTW strowed
worsted
DEORSTY destroy
stroyed
DEORSUV devours
DEORTTT trotted
DEORTTU tutored
DEOSSYY odyssey
DEOSTTT stotted
DEOSTTU testudo
DEOSTTW swotted
DEOSTUU duteous
DEOSTUX tuxedos
DEPRRSU spurred
DEPRRUY prudery
DEPRSTU spurted
DEPRSUU pursued
usurped
DEPRSUY syruped
DERSSTU dusters
trussed
DERSTTU trusted
DERSTTY trysted
DERSTUU sutured
DFFGINO doffing
DFFGINU duffing
DFFIIMR midriff
DFFIIRT triffid
DFFILOR Lifford
DFGGIIN fidging
DFGGINU fudging
DFGHIOS dogfish
DFGIINN finding
DFGIINY dignify
DFGILNO folding
DFGINNU funding
DFGINOR fording
Fröding
DFGINOU fungoid
DFHILSU dishful
DFHIMSU mudfish
DFIILRW Wilfrid
DFILLUY fluidly
DFILMNU mindful
DFILNOP pinfold
DFILNOS infolds
DFILORT trifold
DFILORU Rudolf I
DFILOSX sixfold
DFILTUU dutiful
DFLMOUW mudflow
DFLNOSU unfolds
DFLOOTU foldout
DFLOOTW twofold
DFMMORU Mumford
DFMORRU Rumford
DFNNOUU unfound
DFNORUY foundry
DGGGIIN digging
DGGGINO dogging
DGGHIOS doggish
DGGIILN gilding
gliding
DGGIINN dinging
DGGIINR girding
griding
ridging
DGGIINU guiding
DGGIJNU judging
DGGILNO Golding
lodging

DGGIMNO modging
DGGINNO donging
DGGINNU dunging
nudging
DGGNOSU dugongs
DGHIINS dishing
hidings
shindig
DGHIKNO Hodgkin
DGHILNO holding
DGHINOO hooding
DGHINOR hording
DGHINTU hindgut
DGHIOOS goodish
DGHOOOW Hogwood
DGHOOST hotdogs
DGHORTU drought
DGHOTUY doughty
DGIIKNN dinking
DGIIKNR dirking
DGIIKNS disking
DGIILNS sidling
sliding
DGIILNW wilding
DGIILNY dingily
DGIILRY rigidly
DGIIMMN dimming
DGIIMNN minding
DGIIMNS smidgin
DGIIMOS sigmoid
DGIINNN dinning
DGIINNT dinting
DGIINNU induing
DGIINNW winding
DGIINOS indigos
DGIINOV voiding
DGIINOW windigo
DGIINOX digoxin
DGIINPP dipping
DGIINPR priding
DGIINPS pidgins
DGIINPU pinguid
DGIINRS ridings
DGIINRV driving
DGIINSS dissing
sidings
DGIINST tidings
DGIINTY dignity
tidying
DGIJOSU judogis
DGIKLNO Kolding
DGIKMNO kingdom
DGIKNNU dunking
DGIKNOO dooking
DGIKNOU douking
DGIKNSU dusking
DGILLNO dolling
DGILLNU dulling
DGILMNO molding
DGILNOO Goldoni
DGILNOR lording
DGILOPY podgily
DGILOST diglots
DGILPUY pudgily
DGIMNOO Domingo
dooming
DGIMNPU dumping
DGIMNSU Sigmund
DGIMSTU midguts
DGINNNO donning
DGINNNU dunning
DGINNOR droning
DGINNOU undoing
DGINNOW downing
DGINNSY synding
DGINNTU dunting
DGINNUY undying
DGINOOW wooding
DGINOPS pongids
DGINORS rodings
DGINORV droving
DGINORW wording
DGINOSS dossing
DGINOSU dousing
guidons
DGINOSW dowsing
DGINOTT dotting
DGINPPU dupping
DGINSTU dusting
DGIOORR Rodrigo
DGIOPRY prodigy
DGIOSTW godwits
DGIQSUY squidgy
DGISSTU disgust
DGLNOUY ungodly
DGLOOOW logwood
DGLOOST godslot
DGLOOSU duologs
DGLOPSY splodgy
DGMOOUW gumwood
DGMOPRU gumdrop
DGNOOOP gonopod
DGNOOOR godroon
DGNOORS drongos
DGNOOSS godsons
DGNOOSW godowns
DGNOOUV Godunov
DGNORSU grounds
DGNOSSU sundogs
DGOORTT dogtrot
DGOPRRU prodrug
DGOSTUU dugouts
DHIILOT lithoid
DHIILSW wildish
DHIIMNO hominid
DHIIMPS midship
DHIINOU Houdini
DHIINRU hirudin
DHIIOPX xiphoid
DHIIORZ rhizoid
DHIIOST histoid
DHILLOS dollish
DHILLPY phyllid
DHILLSU dullish
DHILMUY humidly
DHILNOP dolphin
DHILOST doltish
DHILOSU loudish
DHILRTY thirdly
DHIMOPR dimorph
DHIMORU humidor
rhodium
DHIMPSU dumpish
DHINNOS donnish
DHINOPY hypnoid
DHINORS dronish
DHINRSU nurdish
DHIOOST dhootis
DHIOPTY typhoid
DHIORTY thyroid
DHIPRSU prudish
DHIPRSY syrphid
DHJOPRU jodhpur
DHKORSY droshky
DHLMOOU hoodlum
DHLOOTU holdout
DHLOPSU holdups
upholds
DHMMRUU humdrum
DHMNOYY hymnody
DHNNOOU nunhood
DHNOPRU Prud'hon
DHOOOOS hoodoos
DHOPRSU pushrod
DHORSSU shrouds
DHORSTU drouths
DHORSUY hydrous
DHORTUY drouthy
DHORXYY hydroxy
DIIIMRU iridium
DIIINPS insipid
DIIJNOS disjoin
DIIKKNS kidskin
DIILLST distill
DIILLVY lividly
DIILMNS dislimn
DIILMOO modioli
DIILMOS idolism
DIILMTY timidly
DIILNNU indulin
DIILNWY windily
DIILOPS lipoids
DIILOST idolist
DIILQSU liquids
DIILRSU silurid
DIILRTY dirtily
DIILSST distils
DIILSTY idylist
DIILVVY vividly
DIILYZZ dizzily
DIIMNOR midiron
DIIMSSS dismiss
DIIMSTW dimwits
DIINOQU quinoid
DIINORS sordini
DIINOSX dioxins
DIIOOPS opioids
DIIOPRS spiroid
DIIORSV divisor
viroids
DIIRSTX distrix
DIJMSSU musjids
DIJOSTU judoist
DIKKLSU kudliks
DIKKOPS dikkops
DIKLSUY duskily
DIKNOOR Doornik
DIKOORT drookit
DIKORTU droukit
DILLOSY solidly
DILLPSY psyllid
DILLRUY luridly
DILMNRU drumlin
DILMOOY doomily
moodily
DILMORS milords
DILMPUY dumpily
DILMTUY tumidly
DILNNSU dunlins
DILNOPT diplont
DILNOXY indoxyl
DILNPSY spindly
DILNSTU indults
DILOPVV Plovdiv
DILORWY rowdily
wordily
DILOSSU dulosis
solidus
DILOSTY styloid
DILOTTY dottily
DILRYZZ drizzly
DILSTUY dustily
DIMMOST midmost
DIMNOOR Mindoro
DIMNOOS dominos
DIMNOPU impound
DIMNOSU Dominus
DIMNOTW midtown
DIMNOWX mixdown
DIMOPSU podiums
DIMOSSW wisdoms
DIMRTUU triduum
DIMRUUV duumvir
DINNOPR nondrip
DINNOPW pindown
DINNOSW Swindon
DINNSUW unwinds
DINOORS indoors
sordino
DINOPSU unipods
DINORSU durions
DINORSW Windsor
DINORWW windrow
DINOSSW disowns
DINOSWW windows
DINPSTU pundits
DINPSUW windups
DINSSTU nudists

DIOOPPS doppios
DIOOPSS isopods
DIOORST toroids
DIOORTT ridotto
DIOOSTX toxoids
DIOPRST disport
tripods
DIOPRTY tripody
DIORRST stridor
DIORSTT distort
DIOSSTU studios
DIPRSTU disrupt
DIPSSTU stupids
DJNNOOS donjons
DKLOOPS Podolsk
DKNOOPS pondoks
DKOOOOS koodoos
DLLOOPS dollops
DLLORWY worldly
DLMNOOU Muldoon
DLMOSUU modulus
DLNOOWW lowdown
DLNORUY roundly
DLNOSUY soundly
DLOOOTW woodlot
DLOOPPY polypod
DLOOPTY tylopod
DLOOPUY duopoly
DLOOPWY plywood
DLOOSTU outsold
DLOPRUY proudly
DLOSTUW wouldst
DMNOORS dromons
DMNOSSU osmunds
DMNOSSY Symonds
DNNOOSW Snowdon
DNNORUW rundown
DNNOSUU unsound
DNNOSUW sundown
DNNOUUW unwound
DNOORTU orotund
DNOOTUW nutwood
DNOPRUU roundup
DNOSSTU stounds
DNOSSUW swounds
DOOOOSV voodoos
DOOORSU odorous
DOOORTU outdoor
DOOPRSU uropods
DOOPRSY prosody
DOOPRTU dropout
DPSSTUU dustups
EEEEFRR referee
EEEEFRW Wee Free
EEEEGTX exegete
EEEEPST teepees
EEEEPSW peewees
EEEESWW weewees
EEEFFFO feoffee
EEEFFKO O'Keeffe
EEEFGRU refugee
EEEFHRS shereef
EEEFLRS feelers
EEEFLRT fleeter
EEEFLSS feeless
EEEFMNR freemen
EEEFORS foresee
EEEFRRS reefers
EEEFRRZ freezer
EEEFRSZ freezes
EEEGIKR geekier
EEEGILN gleenie
EEEGILS elegies
elegise
EEEGILZ elegize
EEEGINP epigene
EEEGINR greenie
EEEGINU Eugénie
EEEGIPR perigee
EEEGKLR kegeler
EEEGLMN gleemen
EEEGLNT genteel
EEEGLRY Greeley
EEEGMRS emerges
EEEGNOS Genoese
EEEGNPR epergne
EEEGNRR greener
reneger
EEEGNRS reneges
EEEGNRU renegue
EEEGNRV revenge
EEEGNRW Wegener
EEEGNSS geneses
EEEGNTT genette
EEEGRRT greeter
EEEGRSZ geezers
EEEGRUX exergue
EEEHILW wheelie
EEEHLNR Heerlen
EEEHLOY eyehole
EEEHLRS heelers
reheels
EEEHLRW wheeler
EEEHRRS sheerer
EEEHRWZ wheezer
EEEHSST seethes
EEEHSTT esthete
teethes
EEEHSWZ wheezes
EEEIJLS jeelies
EEEIKLL eellike
EEEIKLS keelies
EEEIKLY eyelike
EEEIKLZ Ezekiel
EEEILRR leerier
EEEILRV relieve
EEEILVY evil eye
EEEIMMR Mérimée
EEEIMNS enemies
EEEIMNT emetine
EEEIMPR epimere
preemie
EEEIMRT eremite
EEEINNT Étienne
EEEINRS eserine
EEEINRT teenier
EEEINRW weenier
EEEINSW weenies
EEEINTW tweenie
EEEIPRS peeries
EEEIPRW weepier
EEEIPST epeeist
EEEIPSW weepies
EEEIRRT retiree
EEEIRRV reverie
EEEIRST eeriest
EEEIRSV veeries
EEEISTW sweetie
EEEJLRW jeweler
EEEJLRZ Jezreel
EEEJPRS jeepers
EEEJRRS jeerers
EEEKLLU ukelele
EEEKLNR kneeler
EEEKLPW ekpwele
EEEKLRS sleeker
EEEKLSW Weelkes
EEEKMST meekest
EEEKNPT keepnet
EEEKNRS keeners
EEEKNST keenest
ketenes
EEEKPRS keepers
EEEKRSS seekers
EEEKRST keester
EEELLRV leveler
EEELMNT element
EEELMSX lexemes
EEELNSV elevens
EEELPRS peelers
sleeper
EEELPRT replete
EEELPST steeple
EEELRRS reelers
EEELRTV leveret
EEELSSS lessees
EEELSSV sleeves
EEELSSY eyeless
EEELSTX telexes
EEELSTY eyelets
EEELTTX teletex
EEEMMSS meseems
sememes
EEEMNRS meneers
EEEMNSS Messene
nemeses
EEEMORT eroteme
EEEMRRV Vermeer
EEEMRSS seemers
EEEMRST meeters
teemers
EEEMRTX extreme
EEEMSST esteems
mestees
EEENNPT pentene
EEENNTT entente
EEENPRR preener
EEENPRT preteen
terpene
EEENPST steepen
EEENPSX expense
EEENRRS sneerer
EEENRRT enterer
reenter
terrene
EEENRRW renewer
EEENRRY Nyerere
EEENRST entrees
EEENRSV eveners
veneers
EEENRSZ sneezer
EEENRTV eventer
evernet
EEENRTX externe
EEENRUV revenue
unreeve
EEENSSZ sneezes
EEENSTW sweeten
EEEOPPS epopees
EEEORSV oversee
EEEORSY eyesore
EEEPPRS peepers
EEEPRSS peeress
EEEPRST steeper
EEEPRSV peevers
EEEPRSW sweeper
weepers
EEEPRTU Euterpe
EEEQRRU queerer
EEEQSUZ squeeze
EEERRRV reverer
EEERRST steerer
EEERRSV reserve
reveres
reverse
EEERRSW sweerer
EEERSSS seeress
EEERSTT teeters
EEERSTV Everest
EEERSTW sweeter
EEERSVW weevers
EEERTTW tweeter
EEERTWZ tweezer
EEESSTT settees
EEESSTV steeves
EEESTWZ tweezes
EEFFFNO enfeoff
EEFFFOR feoffer
EEFFINT fifteen
EEFFJRY Jeffrey
EEFFNOS offense
EEFFORR offerer
EEFFOST toffees
EEFFSSU effuses
EEFGILN feeling
fleeing
EEFGILT gefilte
EEFGINR feigner

freeing
reefing
EEFGINZ feezing
EEFGLLU gleeful
EEFGLOR foreleg
EEFGLOS solfege
EEFGORR reforge
EEFGRSU refuges
EEFHIRS heifers
EEFHIRT heftier
EEFHISY fisheye
EEFHITZ Heifetz
EEFHLRS flesher
herself
EEFHLSS fleshes
EEFHNRS freshen
EEFHORT thereof
EEFHORW whereof
EEFHRRS fresher
refresh
EEFHRRU fuehrer
EEFHRSS freshes
EEFHRST freshet
hefters
EEFIIRR fierier
reifier
EEFIIRS reifies
EEFIKLL elflike
EEFILLS fellies
EEFILLX flexile
EEFILNO olefine
EEFILOS Fiesole
EEFILRS ferlies
refiles
reliefs
EEFILRT fertile
EEFILST felsite
lefties
EEFIMMR femmier
EEFIMNR firemen
EEFINNS Fiennes
EEFINRR refiner
EEFINRS refines
EEFINRZ Firenze
EEFINSS finesse
EEFIRRR Ferrier
EEFIRRS ferries
refires
refries
EEFIRRT ferrite
EEFIRSS Seferis
EEFIRST festier
Seifert
EEFIRSZ friezes
EEFISTV festive
EEFLLOS felloes
EEFLLRS fellers
EEFLLRU fueller
EEFLLTY fleetly
EEFLNNO Fénelon
EEFLNOS oneself
EEFLNRS flenser
fresnel
EEFLNSS flenses
EEFLRRU ferrule
EEFLRST reflets
telfers
EEFLRSU ferules
fuelers
refuels
EEFLRTT fettler
EEFLRTU fleuret
EEFLRUX flexure
EEFLSTT fettles
EEFLSUY eyefuls
EEFMNOR foremen
EEFMNRT ferment
EEFMOTT mofette
EEFMPRU perfume
EEFNRRW Renfrew
EEFNRRY fernery
EEFNRTV fervent
EEFNSSW fewness
EEFNSSY feyness
EEFNSTU Fuentes
EEFORRV forever
EEFORRZ refroze
EEFOTTU fouette
EEFPRRS prefers
EEFPRSU perfuse
EEFRRST ferrets
EEFRRSU refuser
EEFRRTU refuter
EEFRRTY ferrety
EEFRSST festers
EEFRSSU refuses
EEFRSTT fetters
EEFRSTU refutes
EEFSSTU fetuses
EEGGGIS geggies
EEGGHTU thuggee
EEGGILN neglige
EEGGILR leggier
EEGGINR greeing
EEGGIOR George I
EEGGIRV Gergiev
EEGGISV veggies
EEGGLNO Geelong
EEGGLRS egglers
EEGGNOR engorge
EEGGORR regorge
EEGGORV George V
EEGGPRU puggree
EEGHILN heeling
EEGHINR rehinge
EEGHINY hygiene
EEGHIRW reweigh
weigher
EEGHKMO Okeghem
EEGHLNO Hengelo
EEGHMNU hegumen
EEGHNRY greyhen
EEGIJNR jeering
EEGIKKN keeking
EEGIKLL leglike
EEGIKLM gemlike
EEGIKLN keeling
EEGIKNN keening
kneeing
EEGIKNP keeping
peeking
EEGIKNR reeking
EEGIKNS seeking
EEGIKNT kitenge
EEGILNN Glennie
EEGILNP peeling
EEGILNR leering
reeling
EEGILNS seeling
EEGILNT gentile
EEGILRV veliger
EEGILST elegist
EEGIMMR immerge
EEGIMNR regimen
EEGIMNS seeming
EEGIMNT meeting
teeming
EEGIMRS emigres
regimes
remiges
EEGINNP peening
EEGINNS engines
EEGINNU genuine
Guienne
ingenue
EEGINNV evening
EEGINNW weening
EEGINOP epigone
EEGINOS soignee
EEGINPP peeping
EEGINPR peering
EEGINPS seeping
EEGINPV peeving
EEGINPW weeping
EEGINRS greisen
EEGINRT integer
treeing
EEGINRV reeving
veering
EEGINSS genesis
Giessen
EEGINSV Sévigné
EEGINTX exigent
EEGIPRS Sergipe
EEGIRRV griever
EEGIRSV grieves
Sverige
EEGISTV vestige
EEGKLNU Keelung
EEGKLRS keglers
EEGKNOR kerogen
EEGKNRU gerenuk
EEGLLNN Lenglen
EEGLLSS legless
EEGLMMU gemmule
EEGLMSU legumes
EEGLNOR erelong
EEGLNOU eugenol
EEGLNOZ lozenge
EEGLNRT gentler
EEGLNRY greenly
EEGLNST gentles
EEGLNSU lungees
EEGLRST reglets
EEGLRSU reglues
EEGMNOS genomes
EEGMNRS germens
EEGMNST segment
EEGMOST gemotes
EEGMRRS mergers
EEGMRTU gumtree
EEGNNST gennets
EEGNNUY Guyenne
EEGNORS negroes
EEGNPUX expunge
EEGNRSS negress
EEGNRST gerents
regents
EEGNRSZ grenzes
EEGNSSU genuses
neguses
EEGOPRT protege
EEGPRSU pugrees
EEGRRSS regress
EEGRRST regrets
EEGRRSU resurge
EEGRRSV vergers
EEGRRUY gruyere
EEGRSSU guesser
EEGRSSY geysers
EEGRSTT getters
EEGRSTU gesture
EEGRSTY greyest
EEGSSSU guesses
EEHHRTW whether
EEHHSTW wheesht
EEHIKLN Heinkel
EEHIKLO hoelike
EEHILMN hemline
EEHILOS Héloïse
EEHILRT Heitler
Theiler
EEHILST sheltie
EEHILSX helixes
EEHINNV Nineveh
EEHINOR heroine
EEHINOS Hesione
EEHINRR errhine
EEHINRS henries
inheres
EEHINRT neither
therein
EEHINRW wherein
EEHIPRT prithee
EEHIPSV peevish
EEHIPTT epithet
EEHIRRS rehires
EEHIRSS heiress

EEHIRST	heister
EEHIRSV	shrieve
EEHISST	hessite
EEHISTV	thieves
EEHKLOY	keyhole
EEHKLSS	shekels
EEHKOOY	eyehook
EEHKORT	Roethke
EEHLLMP	phellem
EEHLLRS	hellers
EEHLLRY	hellery
EEHLLSY	Shelley
EEHLMRS	helmers
EEHLMST	helmets
EEHLORY	holeyer
EEHLOSY	Holy See
EEHLPRS	helpers
EEHLPRT	telpher
EEHLRST	shelter
EEHLRSV	shelver
EEHLRSW	welsher
EEHLRSY	sheerly
EEHLSSV	shelves
EEHLSSW	welshes
EEHMMRS	hemmers
EEHMNOP	phoneme
EEHMNRY	mynheer
EEHMORT	theorem
EEHMRUX	exhumer
EEHMSUX	exhumes
EEHNNOS	shoneen
EEHNNRY	hennery
EEHNOPT	potheen
EEHNORT	thereon
EEHNORW	nowhere
	whereon
EEHNPST	Stephen
EEHNPSW	nephews
EEHNSTU	enthuse
EEHNSTV	seventh
EEHOOPW	whoopee
EEHOPRU	euphroe
EEHOPSS	sheepos
EEHOPST	heptose
EEHORRV	hoverer
EEHORSS	reshoes
EEHORST	heteros
EEHORSU	rehouse
EEHORTT	thereto
EEHORTW	whereto
EEHORVW	however
	whoever
EEHOSTW	towhees
EEHOSTY	eyeshot
EEHPPST	heppest
EEHPPSY	Sheppey
EEHPRSS	spheres
EEHPRST	threeps
EEHPSSU	Ephesus
EEHRRSW	wersher
EEHRRTW	wherret
EEHRSSW	shewers
EEHRSTT	tethers
EEHRSTW	wethers
EEHRTTW	whetter
EEHSSTU	Theseus
EEHSTUY	shuteye
EEIIKKS	kiekies
EEIILMS	mielies
EEIIMNS	meinies
EEIIMPR	riempie
EEIIMST	itemise
EEIIMTZ	itemize
EEIINNS	neineis
EEIINRT	niterie
EEIINSW	wienies
EEIINSY	Yenisei
EEIIPST	pieties
EEIIRRV	riviere
EEIIRVW	viewier
EEIJKRR	jerkier
EEIJLLS	jellies
EEIJMMS	jemmies
EEIJMNZ	Jiménez
EEIJNNS	jennies
EEIJRRS	jerries
EEIJSSS	jessies
EEIJSTT	jetties
EEIKKRR	kerkier
EEIKLNR	Lineker
EEIKLOT	toelike
EEIKLPS	kelpies
EEIKLPT	pikelet
EEIKLSS	selkies
EEIKLST	sleekit
EEIKMNP	pikemen
EEIKMPR	kempier
EEIKNPY	pinkeye
EEIKNRS	Erskine
EEIKNRT	kernite
EEIKPRR	perkier
EEIKPRS	peskier
EEIKPSW	kewpies
EEIKRRS	kerries
EEIKRST	keister
EEIKSST	seikest
EEIKTTT	tektite
EEILLNS	nellies
EEILLOR	Lorelei
EEILLPS	ellipse
EEILLRS	rellies
EEILLST	tellies
EEILLSV	Seville
EEILLSW	wellies
EEILMMT	meltemi
EEILMNN	linemen
EEILMNY	myeline
EEILMOR	Molière
EEILMRU	Lumière
EEILMRV	vermeil
EEILNNO	leonine
EEILNNS	Nielsen
EEILNNT	lenient
	Tenniel
EEILNNV	enliven
EEILNOR	eloiner
EEILNOV	Evil One
EEILNPS	pensile
EEILNRS	liernes
	relines
EEILNRV	livener
EEILNSS	enisles
	ensiles
	silenes
EEILNST	setline
	tensile
EEILNTT	entitle
EEILNTV	veinlet
EEILNUV	veinule
EEILOPT	petiole
EEILORS	loeries
EEILORV	overlie
	relievo
EEILOTZ	zeolite
EEILPRR	replier
EEILPRS	replies
	spieler
EEILPRT	perlite
	reptile
EEILPRU	puerile
EEILPSS	pelisse
EEILPST	epistle
	pelites
EEILPWY	weepily
EEILQRU	relique
EEILRRV	reviler
EEILRSS	ireless
	resiles
EEILRST	leister
	sterile
EEILRSU	leisure
EEILRSV	leviers
	relives
	reviles
	servile
	veilers
EEILRTT	retitle
EEILRVY	liveyer
EEILSSS	sessile
EEILSST	telesis
EEILSSU	Eleusis
EEILSSV	Elevsís
EEILSSW	lewises
EEILSTV	levites
	velites
EEILSTX	sextile
EEILSUV	elusive
EEILSVW	weevils
EEILTTX	textile
EEILVWY	weevily
EEIMMNS	immense
EEIMMRS	immerse
EEIMNNO	nominee
EEIMNNT	eminent
EEIMNOT	onetime
EEIMNRS	ermines
EEIMNRT	Meitner
EEIMNRW	wiremen
EEIMNSS	Meissen
	nemesis
	siemens
EEIMNSX	Ximenes
EEIMNSZ	Menzies
EEIMOPS	episome
EEIMOPT	epitome
EEIMOSS	meioses
EEIMOTV	emotive
EEIMPRR	premier
EEIMPRS	empires
	emprise
	epimers
	imprese
	premies
	premise
	spireme
EEIMPRT	emptier
EEIMPST	empties
	septime
EEIMQRU	requiem
EEIMRRR	merrier
EEIMRRT	trireme
EEIMRSS	messier
	miseres
	remises
EEIMRST	meister
	metiers
	tremies
EEIMRSX	remixes
EEIMRTT	emitter
	termite
EEIMSST	metisse
EEINNNP	pennine
EEINNPS	pennies
	pinenes
EEINNRS	nerines
EEINNRT	interne
EEINNRV	innerve
	nervine
EEINNST	intense
EEINNSY	Yesenin
EEINNTW	entwine
EEINNTZ	netizen
EEINOPR	pioneer
EEINOPS	peonies
EEINPPS	pepsine
EEINPRR	ripener
EEINPRS	erepsin
	repines
EEINPRT	Petrine
EEINPSS	penises
EEINPST	Epstein
EEINPSV	pensive
	vespine
EEINQRU	enquire
EEINQTU	quieten
EEINRRT	reinter
	rentier
	terrine

EEINRRV nervier
vernier
EEINRST entries
Steiner
Teniers
trienes
EEINRSV enviers
inverse
EEINRSW newsier
wieners
EEINRSY Erinyes
EEINRTU retinue
reunite
uterine
EEINSTT netties
EEINSTV tensive
EEINSTX extines
sixteen
EEINSTY syenite
EEIOPPT epitope
EEIOPSS poesies
EEIOPST poetise
EEIOPSX epoxies
EEIOPTZ poetize
EEIORSS soirees
EEIORSV erosive
EEIPPPR peppier
EEIPPST peptise
EEIPPTT pipette
EEIPPTZ peptize
EEIPQRU perique
reequip
repique
EEIPQSU equipes
EEIPRRR perrier
EEIPRRS perries
prisere
reprise
respire
EEIPRRX expirer
EEIPRSS espiers
pressie
EEIPRST respite
EEIPRSV previse
EEIPRSX expires
EEIPRTT pettier
EEIPRVW preview
EEIPRZZ prezzie
EEIPSTW peewits
EEIQRRU require
EEIQRSU esquire
queries
EEIQRTU quieter
requite
EEIQSTU equites
EEIRRRT retirer
terrier
EEIRRST etriers
retires
retries
terries
EEIRRSV reivers
reversi
reviser
EEIRRSW rewires
sweirer
EEIRRTV riveter
EEIRRTW rewrite
EEIRRVV reviver
EEIRSSS seisers
EEIRSST resites
EEIRSSU reissue
EEIRSSV revises
EEIRSTT testier
Trieste
EEIRSTV restive
sievert
veriest
EEIRSUZ seizure
EEIRSVV revives
EEIRSVW reviews
viewers
EEIRSXX Xerxes I
EEIRTVV vetiver
EEISSTX sexiest
EEISTTW wetties
EEISTTY yetties
EEJKRRS jerkers
EEJLRWY jewelry
EEJNNST jennets
EEJNORY enjoyer
EEJPRRU perjure
EEJRSST jesters
EEJRSSY jerseys
EEKKNOS konekes
EEKKRRT trekker
EEKLLNR Kneller
EEKLLSY sleekly
EEKLLUU ukulele
EEKLMRZ klezmer
EEKLNNS kennels
EEKLNOS keelson
EEKLNRS kernels
EEKLRST kestrel
EEKLSSY keyless
EEKLSTT kettles
EEKLSTW kewlest
EEKMNOS sokemen
EEKMRUZ Kurzeme
EEKNNTT kennett
EEKNOST ketones
EEKNOTY keynote
EEKNRST renkest
EEKNSST knesset
EEKNSTU netsuke
EEKORRV revoker
EEKORSV evokers
revokes
EEKOSTV voetsek
EEKPRSU perukes
EEKRRUZ kreuzer
EEKRSSW skewers
EELLLVY levelly
EELLMOS Moselle
EELLMRS smeller
EELLNOV novelle
EELLNUV unlevel
EELLORV Vellore
EELLPRS presell
speller
EELLPST pellets
EELLQRU queller
EELLRSS resells
sellers
EELLRST retells
tellers
EELLRSY yellers
EELLSWZ Wellesz
EELMNOO oenomel
EELMOPY employe
EELMORW eelworm
EELMOST omelets
EELMOSY Moseley
EELMPST pelmets
temples
EELMPTT templet
EELMRST melters
remelts
smelter
EELMRSU lemures
relumes
EELMRSW mewlers
EELMSSU muleses
EELNNSV vennels
EELNOPV envelop
EELNOPY polyene
EELNORT Le Nôtre
EELNOSV elevons
Slovene
EELNOTT notelet
EELNOTU toluene
EELNPSS pensels
spleens
EELNPSY spleeny
EELNQUY queenly
EELNRST nestler
relents
slenter
EELNRSU unreels
EELNSSS lessens
EELNSST nestles
EELNSTT nettles
EELNSTU eluents
unsteel
EELNSTY tensely
EELNSUV venules
EELNSXY xylenes
EELNTTU lunette
EELOPPS peoples
EELOPRS elopers
leprose
EELOPRX explore
EELOPTU eelpout
EELORSS resoles
EELORSU Soleure
EELORSV resolve
EELORSY erosely
EELORVV evolver
revolve
EELOSTT teleost
EELOSVV evolves
EELOTUV evolute
veloute
EELPPRX perplex
EELPPSU peepuls
EELPQRU prequel
EELPRST pelters
petrels
spelter
EELPRSU repulse
EELPRSY Presley
yelpers
EELPRTZ pretzel
EELPRVY replevy
EELPSSS Lesseps
EELPSST pestles
EELPSTY steeply
EELQRUY queerly
EELQSSU sequels
EELRRVY revelry
EELRSST streels
EELRSTT letters
settler
sterlet
trestle
EELRSTW swelter
welters
wrestle
EELRSTY restyle
tersely
EELRSTZ seltzer
EELRSUV velures
EELSSSU useless
EELSSSV vessels
EELSSSX sexless
EELSSTT settles
EELSTVV velvets
EELSTVW twelves
EELSTWY sweetly
EELTVVY velvety
EEMMNOS monemes
EEMMNOT memento
EEMMOST mestome
EEMMRST stemmer
EEMNNOV envenom
EEMNOOS someone
EEMNOOY mooneye
EEMNORS Emerson
EEMNORV overmen
EEMNORY moneyer
EEMNOST tonemes
EEMNPTU umpteen
EEMNSYZ enzymes
EEMOPRR emperor
EEMOPRW empower
EEMOPST metopes
EEMORRS remorse
EEMORRT remoter

EEMORRV remover
EEMORST emoters
meteors
EEMORSV removes
EEMPPRT preempt
EEMPRRT preterm
EEMPRSS empress
EEMPRST tempers
EEMPRSU presume
supreme
EEMPRTT tempter
EEMPRTU permute
EEMPSTT tempest
EEMPSTX exempts
EEMRRST termers
EEMRRSU murrees
resumer
EEMRSST mesters
EEMRSSU resumes
EEMSSTU mustees
EEMSTTU musette
EENNORT enteron
tenoner
EENNORU neurone
EENNOSS Essonne
oneness
EENNOTY neoteny
EENNPTU Neptune
EENNRST tenners
EENNRTU Turenne
EENNRUV unnerve
EENNSST sennets
EENNSSU unseens
EENNSSW newness
EENNSTT Sennett
EENOPPR prepone
propene
EENOPPT peptone
EENOPRS openers
Penrose
reopens
repones
EENOPST open set
pentose
EENOPTY neotype
EENORSS senores
EENORST estrone
EENORSZ rezones
EENOSTV ventose
EENOSTW townees
EENOSVZ evzones
EENPPRT perpent
EENPRSS Spenser
EENPRST present
repents
serpent
EENPRSV Pevsner
EENPRSY pyrenes
EENPRTV prevent
EENPRTY perenty
EENQSTU sequent
EENRRST renters
sterner
EENRRSU ensurer
EENRRTY reentry
EENRRUV nervure
EENRSST nesters
resents
EENRSSU ensures
EENRSTT tenters
EENRSTU neuters
tenures
tureens
EENRSTV venters
EENRSTW western
EENRSTX externs
EENRSTY styrene
yestern
EENRTUV venture
EENRUVY Nureyev
EENSSTT tensest
EENSSTV stevens
EENSSTW wetness
EENSSUX unsexes
EENSSVW swevens
EENSTTX extents
EENSTVY seventy
EENTTWY Wynette
EEOOPRS operose
EEOOSTT toetoes
EEOPPTT popette
EEOPRRS reposer
EEOPRRV reprove
EEOPRSS reposes
EEOPRSX exposer
EEOPSSS speoses
EEOPSST poetess
EEOPSSU espouse
EEOPSSX exposes
EEOPSTU toupees
EEOPSTY eyespot
EEORRST restore
EEORRSV reverso
EEORRTU reroute
EEORRTV evertor
EEORRTW rewrote
EEORSST Orestes
stereos
EEORSTT rosette
EEORSTV overset
vetoers
EEORSUV oeuvres
overuse
EEORSVW oversew
EEORSXX xeroxes
EEPPPRS peppers
EEPPPRY peppery
EEPPRST stepper
EEPPSST steppes
EEPPSUW upsweep
EEPPSUY eupepsy
EEPRRSS repress
EEPRRSU peruser
EEPRRSY preyers
EEPRRTV pervert
Prévert
EEPRSSS presses
EEPRSST pesters
presets
EEPRSSU Perseus
peruses
EEPRSSV vespers
EEPRSSW spewers
EEPRSSX express
EEPRSTT petters
pretest
EEPRSTU reputes
EEPRSTX experts
sexpert
EEPRSTY retypes
EEPRSUV prevues
EEPRTTX pretext
EEPSSTT septets
EEPSTTU puttees
EEPSTTY typeset
EEQRRUY equerry
EEQRSTU quester
request
EERRSST resters
EERRSSV servers
EERRSTT terrets
EERRSTU ureters
EERRSTV reverts
EERRSTW strewer
wrester
EERRSVW swerver
EERRTTU utterer
EERSSST tresses
EERSSTT retests
setters
streets
tersest
testers
EERSSTU Surtees
EERSSTV revests
EERSSTW westers
EERSSTX exserts
EERSSUV Severus
EERSSVW swerves
EERSTTT tetters
EERSTTU trustee
EERSTTW wetters
EERSTTX texters
EERSTUV vesture
EERSTUY tuyeres
EERSTVV vervets
EERTTUX texture
EESSSTT sestets
EESSTTU suttees
EESSTTX sextets
EESTTTW wettest
EFFFLRU fluffer
EFFFOOR feoffor
EFFGINS effings
EFFGIRS griffes
EFFGORS goffers
EFFGRRU gruffer
EFFHILW whiffle
EFFHIRS sheriff
EFFHIRU huffier
EFFHIRW whiffer
EFFHLSU shuffle
EFFIIJS jiffies
EFFIIMR miffier
EFFIINR niffier
EFFIIST fifties
iffiest
EFFIKLS skiffle
EFFILNO offline
EFFILNS sniffle
EFFILPS piffles
EFFILRR riffler
EFFILRS riffles
EFFILRY firefly
EFFIMOS moffies
EFFINRS sniffer
EFFINST stiffen
EFFIORT forfeit
EFFIORX foxfire
EFFIOST toffies
EFFIPRU puffier
EFFIRST stiffer
EFFLMRU muffler
EFFLMSU muffles
EFFLNSU snuffle
EFFLOSU souffle
EFFLRRU ruffler
EFFLRSU ruffles
EFFLRTU fretful
truffle
EFFNRSU snuffer
EFFOORR offeror
EFFOPRR proffer
EFFOPSU pouffes
EFFORST efforts
EFFOSST offsets
setoffs
EFFPRSU puffers
EFFPRUY puffery
EFFRSSU suffers
EFFRSTU stuffer
EFFSSUU suffuse
EFFSTTU tuffets
EFGGIOR foggier
EFGGIRU fuggier
EFGGLOR flogger
EFGHIMS gemfish
EFGHINT hefting
EFGHIRT fighter
freight
EFGILLN felling
EFGILMN fleming
EFGILNR flinger
EFGILNT felting
EFGILNU fueling
EFGILNX flexing
EFGILNY fleying
EFGIMNT figment

EFGINNP	pfennig
EFGINOR	foreign
EFGINPR	perfing
EFGINRS	fingers
	fringes
EFGINRU	gunfire
EFGIOOR	goofier
EFGIORV	forgive
EFGIRRU	figurer
EFGIRSU	figures
EFGLNSU	engulfs
EFGLNTU	fulgent
EFGLORS	golfers
EFGMNOR	frogmen
EFGNOOR	forgone
EFGOORR	forgoer
EFGOORS	forgoes
EFGORRS	forgers
EFGORRY	forgery
EFGORST	forgets
EFGORTU	foregut
EFHIIRS	fishier
EFHIJSW	jewfish
EFHILMS	flemish
	himself
EFHILSS	selfish
EFHILTY	heftily
EFHINST	fishnet
EFHIRSS	fishers
EFHIRST	shifter
EFHIRSY	fishery
EFHISUW	huswife
EFHLLPU	helpful
EFHLLSY	fleshly
EFHLOOX	foxhole
EFHLOPU	hopeful
EFHLRSU	flusher
EFHLRSY	freshly
EFHLSSU	flushes
EFHLSTY	thyself
EFHLTTW	twelfth
EFHRRSU	fuhrers
EFHRRTU	further
EFIILLN	Fellini
EFIILLS	fillies
EFIILMR	filmier
EFIILMS	misfile
EFIILRY	fierily
EFIILSS	fissile
EFIIMRR	rimfire
EFIIMRS	misfire
EFIINNR	finnier
EFIINPV	fivepin
EFIINRT	niftier
EFIINRU	unifier
EFIINSU	unifies
EFIINSX	infixes
EFIISTW	swiftie
EFIJLLY	jellify
EFIJLOT	jetfoil
EFIKLOS	folkies
EFIKLOX	foxlike
EFIKLRU	flukier
EFIKNRS	knifers
EFIKNRU	funkier
EFIKRRS	frisker
EFIKRST	frisket
EFILLOS	follies
EFILLOW	lowlife
EFILLRS	fillers
	refills
EFILLST	fillets
EFILMNT	liftmen
EFILMRS	refilms
EFILMST	filmset
	leftism
EFILNOS	olefins
EFILNOX	flexion
EFILNSS	finless
EFILOOS	floosie
	foliose
EFILOOZ	floozie
EFILOPR	profile
EFILORT	loftier
	trefoil
EFILOSU	foulies
EFILPPR	flipper
EFILPPS	fipples
EFILPPU	pipeful
EFILPRS	pilfers
EFILQUY	liquefy
EFILRRS	riflers
EFILRRT	flirter
	trifler
EFILRRY	riflery
EFILRST	filters
	lifters
	stifler
	trifles
EFILRTT	flitter
EFILRVV	flivver
EFILRZZ	frizzle
EFILSST	stifles
EFILSTT	leftist
EFILSZZ	fizzles
EFIMMRU	fermium
EFIMNOR	fermion
EFIMNTT	fitment
EFIMOST	fomites
EFIMRST	firmest
EFIMRTY	metrify
EFINNOR	inferno
EFINNRS	finners
EFINNRU	funnier
EFINNSU	funnies
EFINPRS	perfins
EFINRST	snifter
EFINRSU	infuser
EFINRUY	reunify
EFINSST	fitness
	infests
EFINSSU	infuses
EFINSUX	unfixes
EFIOOPR	poofier
EFIOOST	footsie
EFIORRT	rotifer
EFIORRU	Fourier
EFIORST	forties
EFIOSST	softies
EFIOSTX	foxiest
EFIPPRT	frippet
EFIPRST	presift
EFIPRTY	petrify
EFIRRRU	furrier
EFIRRSU	friseur
EFIRRTT	fritter
EFIRRTU	fruiter
	turfier
EFIRRTY	terrify
EFIRRZZ	frizzer
EFIRSST	sifters
EFIRSSU	fissure
	fussier
	surfies
EFIRSTT	fitters
	titfers
EFIRSTU	fustier
	surfeit
EFIRSTW	swifter
EFIRSVY	versify
EFIRSZZ	fizzers
	frizzes
EFIRTTU	turfite
EFIRTUV	furtive
EFIRTUX	fixture
EFIRUZZ	fuzzier
EFISTTT	fittest
EFISTTY	testify
EFJLSTU	jestful
EFKLMNO	menfolk
EFKLNUY	flunkey
EFKNRSU	funkers
EFLLORU	florule
EFLLOST	flotels
EFLLOSW	fellows
EFLLRSU	fullers
EFLLSSY	flyless
EFLLSTU	fullest
EFLMOSU	fulsome
EFLMSUU	museful
EFLNNSU	funnels
EFLNORU	fleuron
EFLNORY	felonry
EFLNSSU	fulness
EFLNTUU	tuneful
EFLOORY	foolery
EFLOORZ	foozler
EFLOOST	footles
EFLOOSZ	foozles
EFLORST	florets
	lofters
EFLORSU	ourself
EFLORSW	flowers
	fowlers
	wolfers
EFLORSX	flexors
EFLORTU	flouter
EFLORTW	felwort
EFLORVY	flyover
	overfly
EFLORWY	flowery
EFLOSTU	foulest
EFLOTUW	outflew
EFLPRSU	purfles
EFLRRSU	furlers
EFLRSSU	furless
EFLRSTU	fluster
	fluters
	restful
EFLRTTU	flutter
EFLSSUU	usefuls
EFLSTUZ	zestful
EFMNOOT	footmen
EFMNOST	foments
EFMNRTU	turfmen
EFMOPRR	perform
	preform
EFMOPRT	pomfret
EFMORRS	formers
	reforms
EFMRTUY	furmety
EFNNOTY	Fonteyn
EFNOOST	festoon
EFNORRU	forerun
EFNORRW	frowner
EFNORST	frontes
EFNORTU	fortune
EFNORTW	forwent
EFNORUZ	unfroze
EFNOSST	softens
EFNRSSU	Furness
EFOOPRR	reproof
EFOOPRS	spoofer
EFOOPRT	foretop
	poofter
EFOORRS	reroofs
	roofers
EFOORST	foetors
	footers
EFOORSW	woofers
EFOORTW	woofter
EFOPPRY	foppery
EFOPRSS	profess
EFOPRSU	profuse
EFOQTUU	Fouquet
EFORRST	Forrest
	Forster
EFORRSU	ferrous
	furores
EFORRSV	fervors
EFORRTY	torrefy
EFORRUV	fervour
EFORSST	forests
	fosters
EFORSTU	fouters
EFOSSTT	softest
EFPRTUY	putrefy
EFPSTUY	stupefy

EFRRSSU surfers
EFRRSTU returfs
EFRSSSU fussers
EFRSTTU tufters
EFRSTUU futures
EGGGILN legging
EGGGILR giggler
EGGGILS giggles
EGGGINP pegging
EGGGINV vegging
EGGGLOS goggles
EGGGNOS eggnogs
EGGHILR higgler
EGGHILS higgles
EGGHIRU huggier
EGGHORS hoggers
EGGHOST hoggets
EGGHRSU huggers
EGGIIJR jiggier
EGGIINS sieging
EGGIIPR piggier
EGGIIPS piggies
EGGIJLS jiggles
EGGIJRS jiggers
EGGILLN gelling
EGGILNR niggler
EGGILNS niggles
sniggle
EGGILNU glueing
EGGILRS liggers
EGGILRW wiggler
wriggle
EGGILSW wiggles
EGGIMMN gemming
EGGIMNR merging
EGGIMOS moggies
EGGIMRU muggier
EGGINNS ginseng
EGGINNV venging
EGGINOR Goering
EGGINRS gingers
niggers
snigger
EGGINRU grueing
gungier
EGGINRV verging
EGGINRY gingery
greying
EGGINTT getting
EGGIORS soggier
EGGIPRU puggier
EGGIPRY piggery
EGGIRRS riggers
EGGIRRT trigger
EGGIRSW swigger
EGGJLOR joggler
EGGJLOS joggles
EGGJLRU juggler
EGGJLSU juggles
EGGJORS joggers
EGGLMSU smuggle
EGGLNSU snuggle
EGGLOOY geology
EGGLORS loggers
slogger
EGGLORT toggler
EGGLOST goglets
toggles
EGGLOSW woggles
EGGLPRU plugger
EGGLRSU gurgles
luggers
slugger
EGGLRTU gurglet
EGGLSTU guglets
EGGMRSU muggers
smugger
EGGNRSU snugger
EGGNSTU nuggets
EGGNTUY nuggety
EGGORRS gorgers
EGGORRY Gregory
EGGORST gorgets
toggers
EGGORSU gougers
EGGORTY toggery
EGGRSTU tuggers
EGGSSTU suggest
EGHHIRS highers
EGHHIST eighths
heights
highest
EGHHSSU sheughs
EGHIILL ghillie
EGHIINT nightie
EGHIINV inveigh
EGHIKLO hoglike
EGHIKNR gherkin
EGHILMN helming
EGHILNP helping
EGHILNS english
shingle
EGHILNT lighten
EGHILNV helving
EGHILRT lighter
relight
EGHILSS sleighs
EGHILST sleight
EGHIMMN hemming
EGHIMNS meshing
EGHIMNT theming
EGHINNT henting
EGHINNU unhinge
EGHINOS shoeing
EGHINRR herring
EGHINRT Enright
righten
EGHINRW whinger
EGHINST Hengist
EGHINSW shewing
whinges
EGHINTT tighten
EGHIORS ogreish
EGHIORU roughie
EGHIOST hogties
EGHIOTT gothite
EGHIOTV eightvo
EGHIRRT righter
EGHIRSS sighers
EGHIRST sighter
EGHIRSU gushier
EGHIRSY greyish
EGHIRTT tighter
EGHIRTU Guthrie
EGHISTW weights
EGHISTY hygeist
EGHITWY weighty
EGHLLOU lughole
EGHLMPY phlegmy
EGHLNOR leghorn
EGHLNST lengths
EGHLNTY lengthy
EGHLOOS shoogle
EGHLPSU pleughs
EGHMMOS megohms
EGHMOSU gumshoe
EGHNOOS hognose
EGHNORS Senghor
EGHNORU roughen
EGHNOTU toughen
EGHNRSU hungers
EGHNRTU Gunther
EGHNSUY Huygens
EGHOPRS gophers
EGHORRU rougher
EGHORTU tougher
EGHORTZ Hertzog
EGHOSTT ghettos
EGHOSUU hugeous
EGHRSSU gushers
EGHRTUY theurgy
EGIIKLW wiglike
EGIILLS gillies
EGIILNT lignite
EGIILNV veiling
EGIILNX exiling
EGIILPZ Leipzig
EGIILRS girlies
EGIIMNP impinge
EGIIMNR mingier
EGIIMNT iteming
EGIIMPR gimpier
EGIIMPS pigmies
EGIIMRR grimier
EGIIMSV misgive
EGIINNR reining
EGIINNS insigne
seining
EGIINNV veining
EGIINOP epigoni
EGIINRT igniter
tiering
EGIINRV reiving
EGIINRZ zingier
EGIINSS seising
EGIINST ignites
EGIINSV sieving
EGIINSZ seizing
EGIINTV eviting
EGIINTX exiting
EGIINVW viewing
EGIIORR Roger II
EGIIPPS gippies
EGIIPRW periwig
EGIIPSS gipsies
EGIJKNR jerking
EGIJLLN jelling
EGIJLNR jingler
EGIJLNS jingles
EGIJNOS jingoes
EGIJNSS jessing
EGIJNST jesting
EGIJNTT jetting
EGIKLMU gumlike
EGIKLNR erlking
EGIKLNT kinglet
EGIKLRU ruglike
EGIKLTU gutlike
EGIKNNN kenning
EGIKNNR kerning
EGIKNOV evoking
EGIKNPP kepping
EGIKNPR perking
EGIKNSW skewing
EGILLMU Guillem
EGILLNS selling
EGILLNT gillnet
telling
EGILLNW welling
EGILLNY yelling
EGILLOR girolle
EGILLOS gollies
EGILLRR griller
EGILLRS grilles
EGILLSU gullies
ligules
EGILMMN lemming
Memling
EGILMMR glimmer
EGILMNR gremlin
mingler
EGILMNS mingles
EGILMNT melting
EGILMNU legumin
EGILMNW mewling
EGILMOR gomeril
EGILMOS Limoges
EGILMOV Mogilev
EGILMPS glimpse
EGILMST gimlets
EGILNNS ginnels
EGILNOP eloping
EGILNOS eloigns
legions
lingoes
EGILNOT lentigo
EGILNPS spignel
EGILNPT pelting

EGILNPY yelping
EGILNRS lingers
slinger
EGILNRT ringlet
tingler
EGILNRY relying
EGILNSS Lessing
singles
EGILNST glisten
singlet
tingles
EGILNSU slueing
EGILNSW slewing
swingle
EGILNTT letting
EGILNTU eluting
EGILNTW welting
winglet
EGILNVY levying
EGILOOS goolies
ologies
EGILORS glories
EGILOST logiest
EGILPST piglets
EGILRSS grilses
EGILRST glister
gristle
EGILRSU ligures
lurgies
EGILRTT glitter
EGILRUV virgule
EGILRZZ grizzle
EGILSST legists
EGILSSV Slesvig
EGILSSW wigless
EGILSTU gluiest
ugliest
EGIMMRR grimmer
EGIMMRS megrims
EGIMMRU gummier
EGIMMSU gummies
EGIMMTU gummite
EGIMNNO omening
EGIMNNW wingmen
EGIMNOT emoting
mitogen
EGIMNOU Minogue
EGIMNOW meowing
EGIMNPR perming
EGIMNPT empting
pigment
temping
EGIMNRS merings
mingers
EGIMNRT terming
EGIMNSS messing
EGIMOST egotism
EGIMPSU guimpes
EGIMPSY gympies
pygmies
EGINNNP penning
EGINNNY yenning

EGINNOP opening
EGINNOV ovening
EGINNPU penguin
EGINNRR grinner
EGINNRS ginners
EGINNRT renting
ringent
EGINNRU enuring
EGINNRV nerving
EGINNSS ensigns
sensing
EGINNST nesting
tensing
EGINNSU ensuing
gunnies
EGINNTT netting
tenting
EGINNTV venting
EGINNVY envying
EGINOOS isogone
EGINOPR perigon
pongier
EGINOPS epigons
pigeons
EGINORR ignorer
EGINORS eringos
ignores
regions
signore
EGINORT genitor
EGINORZ zeroing
EGINOSU igneous
EGINOSW wigeons
EGINOSY isogeny
EGINOTV vetoing
EGINPPP pepping
EGINPPS pigpens
EGINPRS pingers
springe
EGINPRV perving
EGINPRY preying
EGINPSW spewing
EGINPSY espying
EGINPTT petting
EGINPYY epigyny
EGINQUU queuing
EGINRRS ringers
EGINRRW wringer
EGINRSS ingress
resigns
signers
singers
EGINRST resting
stinger
EGINRSU reusing
EGINRSV serving
versing
EGINRSW swinger
wingers
EGINRSY syringe
EGINRTT gittern
retting

EGINRTY retying
EGINRVV revving
EGINSST ingests
signets
EGINSSW swinges
EGINSTT setting
testing
EGINSTV vesting
EGINSTW stewing
twinges
westing
EGINSTZ zesting
EGINTTV vetting
EGINTTW wetting
EGIOOPR goopier
EGIOORS goories
goosier
EGIOOST gooiest
EGIOPPS gippoes
EGIOPRS porgies
serpigo
EGIOPRU groupie
pirogue
EGIORST goiters
goitres
goriest
EGIORTU goutier
EGIORTV vertigo
EGIOSST egoists
stogies
EGIOSTT egotist
EGIPPRR gripper
EGIPPSU guppies
EGIPRRS gripers
EGIPRUU guipure
EGIPSSY gypsies
EGIRRRU gurrier
EGIRRTT gritter
EGIRSST tigress
EGIRSSU guisers
EGIRSTU gustier
gutsier
EGIRSTV grivets
EGIRTTU turgite
EGISTTU gutties
EGJLNSU jungles
EGKLORW legwork
EGKMSSU muskegs
EGKNTUZ Tzekung
EGKRTYZ Gretzky
EGLLNNU Gunnell
EGLLOUY yule log
EGLLSTU gullets
EGLLSUY gulleys
EGLMMRU glummer
EGLMNOR mongrel
EGLMOOR legroom
EGLMSSU gumless
EGLNNSU gunnels
EGLNOOY enology
neology
EGLNORU lounger

EGLNOST longest
EGLNOSU lounges
EGLNOYZ lozengy
EGLNPRU plunger
EGLNPSU plunges
EGLNRSU lungers
EGLNSSU gunsels
EGLNSTU engluts
EGLOORS regosol
EGLOPRS prolegs
EGLOPSS gospels
EGLORRW growler
EGLORSS glosser
EGLORSV glovers
grovels
EGLORSW glowers
EGLOSSS glosses
EGLPRSU gulpers
splurge
EGLRSUU regulus
EGLRUZZ guzzler
EGLSSTU gutless
EGLSTUU gluteus
EGLSUZZ guzzles
EGMMORT grommet
EGMMOSU gummose
EGMMRTU grummet
EGMNOOS mongoes
EGMNORS mongers
morgens
EGMNOSU eumongs
EGMNOYZ zymogen
EGMNSTU nutmegs
EGMNSUU eumungs
EGMOORR groomer
EGMOOSS smooges
EGMOPRS Gompers
EGMORSU grumose
morgues
EGMORTU gourmet
EGNNORT rontgen
Röntgen
EGNNOSU guenons
EGNNPTU pungent
EGNNRSU gunners
EGNNRUY gunnery
EGNNTUU unguent
EGNOORY orogeny
EGNOOST gentoos
EGNOOTU outgone
EGNOPRS sponger
EGNOPRY progeny
pyrogen
EGNOPSS sponges
EGNORRW regrown
wronger
EGNORSS engross
EGNORSU surgeon
EGNORSV governs
EGNORSY eryngos
groynes
EGNORUY younger

EGNOSTU tongues
EGNPRSU repugns
EGNRRTU grunter
EGNRSTU gurnets
EGNRSUY gurneys
EGNRSYY synergy
EGNRTTU grutten
turgent
EGOOPRS pogoers
EGOORSV grooves
EGOOSST stooges
EGOOSTU outgoes
EGOPRRS gropers
EGOPRRU grouper
regroup
EGORRSS grosser
EGORRSU grouser
EGORRSW growers
regrows
EGORRTU grouter
EGORRUY roguery
EGORSSS grosses
EGORSST gosters
EGORSSU grouses
EGORSTV grovets
EGORTUW outgrew
EGOSTYZ zygotes
EGPRRSU purgers
EGPRSSU spurges
EGPRSUU upsurge
EGRRSSU surgers
EGRRSUY surgery
EGRSSTU gutsers
EGRSTTU gutters
EGSSSTU gussets
EHHHOTU Huhehot
EHHIKSS sheikhs
EHHILLS hellish
EHHIMRS Rhemish
EHHINRS Rhenish
EHHIRTT thither
EHHIRTW whither
EHHISSW whishes
EHHISWY wheyish
EHHMOSS Moshesh
EHHNPSY hyphens
EHHSSSU shushes
EHIIIKT heitiki
EHIIKLP hiplike
EHIILLR hillier
EHIINNS hinnies
EHIINRS shinier
EHIINRT inherit
EHIINRW whinier
EHIINRY Henry II
EHIIPPR hippier
EHIIPPS hippies
shippie
EHIIPRT pithier
EHIISST stishie
EHIISTW whities
withies
EHIKKSS kishkes
EHIKLTU hutlike
EHIKMSV mikvehs
EHIKNOS honkies
EHIKNRT rethink
thinker
EHIKNSS knishes
EHIKPPS Pishpek
EHIKRRS shirker
EHIKRSS shrieks
shrikes
EHIKRSU huskier
EHIKRSW whisker
EHIKSSU huskies
EHIKSVZ Izhevsk
EHIKSWY whiskey
EHILLNO hellion
EHILLOS hollies
EHILLRS hillers
EHILLTY lithely
EHILMMR Himmler
EHILNOP pinhole
EHILNOT hotline
neolith
EHILNPS plenish
EHILOOS hoolies
EHILOPT hoplite
EHILOSS isohels
EHILOST Elohist
eoliths
holiest
hostile
Sithole
EHILOUZ Leizhou
EHILPRS hirples
EHILPRT philter
philtre
EHILPSS hipless
EHILRRW whirler
EHILRST slither
EHILRSV shrivel
EHILSTT thistle
EHILSTW whistle
EHILTTW whittle
EHILTWY whitely
EHIMMPS Memphis
EHIMMRS shimmer
EHIMNNU Menuhin
EHIMNPS shipmen
EHIMNRS menhirs
EHIMNRU inhumer
rhenium
EHIMNSU inhumes
EHIMNTY thymine
EHIMOPT Imhotep
EHIMORS heroism
moreish
EHIMORT moither
mothier
EHIMORZ rhizome
EHIMOST homiest
EHIMPRU humpier
EHIMPRW whimper
EHIMPSU humpies
EHIMRST hermits
mithers
EHIMRSU mushier
EHIMSWY whimsey
EHINNRT thinner
EHINOPR phonier
EHINOPS phonies
EHINOPX phoenix
EHINORR hornier
EHINORS inshore
EHINOST histone
EHINOSU heinous
EHINPRT Penrith
EHINRSS shiners
shrines
EHINRST hinters
EHINRSV shriven
EHINRSW whiners
EHINRTV thriven
EHINRTW writhen
EHINRVY Henry IV
Henry VI
EHINSSU Hussein
EHINSTW whitens
EHINSTZ zeniths
EHINSUW Wuhsien
EHINTWY Whitney
EHIOOST tooshie
EHIOPRS rosehip
EHIOPSS sophies
EHIOPST ophites
EHIORRS horsier
EHIORRT heritor
Herriot
EHIORSS hosiers
EHIORST heriots
hoister
shortie
EHIORSW showier
EHIORSY hosiery
EHIORTT thorite
EHIOSST hosties
EHIOSTT hotties
EHIOSTY isohyet
EHIPPRS shipper
EHIPPRW whipper
EHIPPST hippest
EHIPPTW whippet
EHIPRSS reships
seriphs
EHIPRST hipster
EHIPRSU pushier
EHIPRSW whisper
EHIPSST Thespis
EHIPSTT pettish
EHIRRSU hurries
rushier
EHIRRSV shriver
EHIRRTV thriver
EHIRRTW wherrit
writher
EHIRSSS hissers
EHIRSSV shivers
shrives
EHIRSSW swisher
wishers
EHIRSTT hitters
tithers
EHIRSTU hirsute
EHIRSTV thrives
EHIRSTW swither
withers
writhes
EHIRSTZ zithers
EHIRSVY shivery
EHIRTTW whitter
EHISSSU hussies
EHISSSW swishes
EHISSTT theists
EHISSTU Hussite
stushie
EHISTTW wettish
whitest
EHISTWY whiteys
EHISWZZ whizzes
EHJKNOT Khojent
EHJLOOY Holy Joe
EHJOPSS josephs
EHJORSS joshers
EHKLPST klephts
EHKMOOS smokeho
EHKNORS honkers
Kherson
EHKNRSU hunkers
EHKOORS hookers
EHKRSSU huskers
EHLLORS hollers
EHLLRSU hullers
EHLMNOT Helmont
menthol
EHLMNSU unhelms
EHLMSTY methyls
EHLNOPS phenols
EHLNRTU luthern
EHLNTTY tenthly
EHLOOPT pothole
EHLOOST Lesotho
EHLOOSY hooleys
EHLOPPR hoppler
EHLOPPS hopples
EHLOPSX phloxes
EHLOPSY spyhole
EHLORST holster
hostler
EHLORSW howlers
EHLORTY helotry
EHLOSSS sloshes
EHLOSST hostels
EHLOSSU housels
EHLOSSV shovels
EHLOSTW howlets
EHLRRSU hurlers

EHLRSSU	Husserl
EHLRSTU	hurtles
	hustler
EHLRSUY	hurleys
EHLSSSU	slushes
EHLSSTU	hustles
	sleuths
EHLSTTU	shuttle
EHMMRSU	hummers
EHMNOOR	hormone
	moorhen
EHMNOSW	showmen
EHMNPTY	nymphet
EHMNTTU	hutment
EHMOOSW	somehow
EHMOPRT	Morpeth
EHMORST	mothers
	smother
	thermos
EHMORTU	mouther
EHMORTY	mothery
EHMOTUX	Exmouth
EHMPRTU	thumper
EHMRRSY	rhymers
EHMRRTU	murther
EHMRSSU	mushers
EHMRSUU	humerus
EHNNOPR	nephron
EHNNRSU	shunner
EHNOORR	honorer
EHNOORS	onshore
EHNOPRS	phoners
EHNOPRY	hyperon
EHNOPSY	phoneys
EHNOPUY	euphony
EHNOPXY	phenoxy
EHNORRT	norther
EHNORRY	heronry
EHNORSS	Horsens
	noshers
EHNORST	hornets
	shorten
	thrones
EHNORSU	unhorse
EHNORSY	noshery
EHNOSST	hotness
EHNOSTT	shotten
EHNOSTY	honesty
EHNOUWZ	Wenzhou
EHNPRSY	phrensy
EHNRSTU	hunters
	shunter
EHNSSSY	shyness
EHOOOPS	hoopoes
EHOOPRS	hoopers
EHOOPRW	whooper
EHOOPTY	oophyte
EHOORST	hooters
	shooter
	soother
EHOORSV	hoovers
EHOOSST	soothes
EHOOSSW	wooshes
EHOPPRS	hoppers
	shopper
EHOPPRT	prophet
EHOPPRW	whopper
EHOPRRY	orphrey
EHOPRST	pothers
	strophe
	thorpes
EHOPRSU	Orpheus
	uphroes
EHOPRSY	phoresy
EHOPSST	poshest
EHORRST	rhetors
	shorter
EHORRTW	thrower
EHORSSV	shovers
EHORSSW	showers
EHORSTU	shouter
	souther
EHORSTX	exhorts
EHORSWY	showery
EHORTUX	Theroux
EHOSSST	hostess
EHOSSSU	shouses
EHOSTTT	hottest
EHOSTUY	Southey
EHPRSSU	pushers
EHPRSSY	syphers
EHPRSYZ	zephyrs
EHPRTTU	turpeth
EHRRSSU	rushers
EHRRSTU	hurters
EHRSSTY	shyster
	thyrses
EHRSTTU	shutter
EHRSTTW	strewth
EIIILOX	Leo XIII
EIIILRV	rilievi
EIIILST	ileitis
EIIINPR	ripieni
EIIJMMS	jimmies
EIIKKNR	kinkier
EIIKLLP	liplike
EIIKLMR	milkier
EIIKLMS	mislike
EIIKLNT	tinlike
EIIKLNW	Kweilin
EIIKLRS	silkier
EIIKLSS	silkies
EIIKLVY	ivylike
EIIKNPS	pinkies
EIIKNSS	kinesis
EIIKNST	inkiest
EIIKPRS	spikier
EIIKRRS	riskier
EIIKSTT	kitties
EIIKSUW	Kweisui
EIILLMM	millime
EIILLMN	milline
EIILLNV	villein
EIILLPS	pillies
EIILLRS	sillier
EIILLSS	sillies
EIILLSW	willies
EIILLTT	littlie
EIILLTV	vitelli
EIILMPR	imperil
EIILMPS	implies
EIILMPT	limepit
EIILMRS	milreis
	slimier
EIILMRT	Leitrim
	limiter
EIILMSS	missile
	similes
EIILMST	elitism
	El Misti
	limiest
	limites
EIILMSU	milieus
EIILMUX	milieux
EIILNOS	elision
	isoline
	lionise
EIILNOV	olivine
EIILNOZ	lionize
EIILNPS	splenii
EIILNRS	inliers
EIILNRT	nitrile
EIILNST	linties
EIILNTU	inutile
EIILORR	roilier
EIILORV	Olivier
	rilievo
EIILOST	oiliest
EIILPPR	lippier
EIILPPS	lippies
EIILQSU	silique
EIILRSX	elixirs
EIILSTT	elitist
EIILSTU	utilise
EIILSTW	wiliest
EIILSUX	Lisieux
EIILTUZ	utilize
EIIMMSS	mimesis
EIIMMST	mistime
EIIMMSX	immixes
EIIMNPR	primine
EIIMNRT	interim
	mintier
	termini
EIIMNRV	miniver
EIIMNTV	minivet
EIIMNTY	nimiety
EIIMOPP	Pompeii
EIIMOSS	meiosis
EIIMPRS	pismire
EIIMPRW	wimpier
EIIMPST	pietism
EIIMPTY	impiety
EIIMRST	mistier
	rimiest
EIIMSSS	missies
EIIMSSV	missive
EIIMSSZ	sizeism
EIINNNP	ninepin
EIINNNS	ninnies
EIINNPS	pinnies
EIINNQU	quinine
EIINNRT	tinnier
EIINNST	intines
	tinnies
EIINNTW	intwine
EIINOPR	ripieno
EIINORS	ioniser
	ironies
	ironise
	noisier
EIINORT	Niterói
EIINORZ	ionizer
	ironize
EIINOSS	ionises
EIINOSZ	ionizes
EIINPPR	nippier
EIINPRS	inspire
	spinier
EIINPST	piniest
	tiepins
EIINPTT	pentiti
EIINQRU	inquire
EIINQTU	inquiet
EIINRTT	nitrite
	nittier
EIINRTV	inviter
	vitrine
EIINSSS	seisins
EIINSSZ	seizins
EIINSTT	tiniest
EIINSTU	unities
	unitise
EIINSTV	invites
EIINSTW	winiest
EIINTUV	unitive
EIINTUZ	unitize
EIIOPTT	petitio
EIIORSV	ivories
EIIOSTZ	zoisite
EIIPPRZ	zippier
EIIPRRV	privier
EIIPRST	tipsier
EIIPRSV	privies
EIIPRSW	wispier
EIIPSTT	pietist
EIIQQUU	Iquique
EIIRRTZ	ritzier
EIIRSTV	revisit
EIIRSTW	wiriest
EIIRSVZ	viziers
EIIRTTW	wittier
EIISSSS	sissies
EIISSTX	sixties
EIISTUV	uveitis
EIISTZZ	tizzies
EIJKKSU	jukskei
EIJKLRY	jerkily

EIJKNNS	Jenkins
EIJKNPR	perjink
EIJKNRS	jerkins
	jinkers
EIJKNSU	junkies
EIJKOST	jokiest
EIJLLOR	jollier
EIJLLOS	jollies
EIJLLOT	Jolliet
EIJLORT	joltier
EIJLRST	jilters
EIJMPRU	jumpier
EIJNNOS	enjoins
EIJNORS	joiners
	rejoins
EIJNORT	jointer
EIJNORY	joinery
EIJNPRU	juniper
EIJNRRU	injurer
EIJNRSU	injures
EIJNSTY	jitneys
EIJPRTU	Jupiter
EIJRSTT	jitters
EIJRTTY	jittery
EIJSSTU	jesuits
EIJSSUV	jussive
EIKKLRS	Selkirk
EIKKLSY	kylikes
	skylike
EIKKMNR	kirkmen
EIKKOOR	kookier
EIKKOPS	Kopeisk
EIKKRUY	yukkier
EIKLLNW	inkwell
EIKLLOS	skollie
EIKLLOW	owllike
EIKLLRS	killers
	reskill
EIKLLST	skillet
EIKLMMN	milkmen
EIKLMNN	linkmen
EIKLMNR	kremlin
EIKLMRS	milkers
EIKLNNU	nunlike
EIKLNOS	sonlike
EIKLNOT	Tolkien
EIKLNRS	linkers
EIKLNRU	urnlike
EIKLNRW	wrinkle
EIKLNST	tinkles
EIKLNSU	sunlike
EIKLNSV	kelvins
EIKLNSW	winkles
EIKLNSY	skyline
EIKLNTU	nutlike
EIKLNTW	twinkle
EIKLOTY	toylike
EIKLPRY	perkily
EIKLPST	Lipetsk
EIKLPSY	peskily
EIKLRST	kirtles
EIKLRSU	sulkier
EIKLRTV	Kilvert
EIKLSSU	sulkies
EIKLSTT	kittels
	kittles
	skittle
EIKMMRR	krimmer
EIKMMRS	skimmer
EIKMNNS	kinsmen
EIKMNOR	moniker
EIKMNRS	merkins
EIKMORS	irksome
	smokier
EIKMOSS	smokies
EIKMRRS	smirker
EIKMRRU	murkier
EIKMRSS	kirmess
EIKMRSU	muskier
EIKMSSU	muskies
EIKNNOR	einkorn
EIKNNRS	skinner
EIKNOOR	rooinek
EIKNOOS	nookies
EIKNOPS	pinkoes
EIKNORV	invoker
EIKNORW	wonkier
EIKNOSS	kenosis
EIKNOSV	invokes
EIKNPRR	prinker
EIKNPRS	perkins
EIKNRSS	sinkers
EIKNRST	stinker
	tinkers
EIKNRSW	swinker
	winkers
EIKNRTT	knitter
	trinket
EIKNSTT	kittens
EIKNTUZ	kunzite
EIKOORR	rookier
EIKOORS	koories
	rookies
EIKOOST	stookie
EIKOPPR	porkpie
EIKOPPS	koppies
EIKOPRR	porkier
EIKOPRS	porkies
EIKOPST	pokiest
EIKORSY	yorkies
EIKOSST	ketosis
EIKPPRS	kippers
	skipper
EIKPPST	skippet
EIKRRSS	riskers
EIKRRST	skirret
	skirter
	striker
EIKRSSS	kissers
EIKRSST	strikes
EIKRSSV	skivers
EIKRSTT	skitter
EIKSSTW	weskits
EILLLOS	lollies
EILLMNU	mullein
EILLMOS	mollies
EILLMOT	melilot
EILLMOU	mouille
EILLMRS	millers
EILLMST	millets
EILLMSU	illumes
EILLMTT	Millett
EILLMTU	mullite
EILLNOS	niellos
EILLNSS	illness
EILLNST	lentils
	lintels
	tellins
EILLORW	lowlier
EILLORZ	zorille
EILLOST	tollies
EILLOSW	wollies
EILLPRS	spiller
EILLPSS	lipless
EILLPSU	pilules
EILLQTU	quillet
EILLRST	rillets
	stiller
	tillers
	trellis
EILLRSW	swiller
	willers
EILLRTT	littler
EILLSST	listels
EILLSSU	sullies
EILLSTW	Sitwell
	willets
EILMMRS	slimmer
EILMNRS	limners
	merlins
EILMOOV	moolvie
EILMOPR	implore
EILMORR	lorimer
EILMORS	moilers
EILMOSS	lissome
EILMOST	motiles
EILMPPS	pimples
EILMPRS	limpers
	prelims
	simpler
EILMPRU	lumpier
	plumier
EILMPRY	primely
EILMPSS	simples
EILMPST	limpest
	limpets
EILMPSU	impulse
EILMPSW	wimples
EILMPSX	simplex
EILMPTY	emptily
EILMQSU	Quilmes
EILMRRY	merrily
EILMRSS	smilers
EILMRST	milters
EILMRSU	misrule
EILMRSY	miserly
EILMSSU	mueslis
EILMSSY	messily
EILMSTT	smittle
EILMSTU	Miletus
EILMSUY	Elysium
EILMSZZ	mizzles
EILMUUV	eluvium
EILNNOR	onliner
EILNNPU	pinnule
EILNNRY	innerly
EILNNST	linnets
EILNOOR	loonier
EILNOOS	loonies
EILNOOV	violone
EILNOPR	plerion
	proline
EILNOPS	epsilon
EILNORR	loriner
EILNORT	Lorient
	retinol
EILNOSS	insoles
	lesions
	lioness
EILNOST	entoils
EILNOSU	elusion
EILNOTU	elution
	outline
EILNOTV	violent
EILNOTW	towline
EILNOVV	involve
EILNPPS	nipples
EILNPRS	pilsner
EILNPRU	purline
EILNPSS	pensils
	splines
EILNPST	leptins
	pintles
EILNPSU	lineups
	lupines
	spinule
EILNPTY	ineptly
EILNPUV	vulpine
EILNRST	linters
	slinter
EILNRSV	silvern
EILNRTY	inertly
EILNRVY	nervily
EILNSSS	sinless
EILNSST	enlists
	listens
	silents
	tinsels
EILNSSU	silenus
EILNSSV	snivels
EILNSTU	luniest
	utensil
EILNSTW	Winslet
EILNSTY	Yeltsin
EILNSUV	unlives
	unveils
EILNSVY	sylvine
EILNVXY	vixenly

EILOOPR loopier
EILOOPT Tiepolo
EILOORS orioles
EILOORW woolier
EILOOSS loosies
EILOOST oolites
ostiole
EILOOSW woolies
EILOPRS spoiler
EILOPST piolets
pistole
Ploeşti
EILOPSU pileous
EILOPSV plosive
EILOPTX exploit
EILORRS lorries
EILORSS rissole
EILORST Estoril
estriol
loiters
toilers
EILORSU louries
lousier
soilure
EILORSW lowries
EILORTT tortile
triolet
EILORTU outlier
EILOSTT litotes
toilets
EILOSTV violets
EILOTUV outlive
EILPPPY peppily
EILPPRR rippler
EILPPRS ripples
slipper
EILPPRT ripplet
tippler
EILPPRU pulpier
EILPPST stipple
tipples
EILPPSU pileups
EILPPSW swipple
EILPRSS lispers
EILPRST triples
EILPRTT triplet
EILPRTX triplex
EILPRUU purlieu
EILPSST stipels
tipless
EILPSSW swiples
EILPSTT spittle
EILPSTU stipule
EILPSZZ pizzles
EILPTTY pettily
EILQRTU quilter
EILQRUU liqueur
EILQTUY quietly
EILRRSU surlier
EILRRTW twirler
EILRSST listers
relists
EILRSSV silvers
slivers
EILRSSW swilers
EILRSTT litters
slitter
tilters
EILRSTU lustier
EILRSUW wurlies
EILRSVY silvery
EILRSZZ sizzler
EILRTTY tritely
EILRTUV rivulet
EILSSTW witless
EILSSTY stylise
EILSSVW swivels
EILSSZZ sizzles
EILSTTT tittles
EILSTTU lutites
EILSTTV vittles
EILSTTY stylite
testily
EILSTVY sylvite
EILSTYZ stylize
EILSUVV luvvies
EILSWZZ swizzle
EIMMMSU mummies
EIMMNSU immunes
EIMMOPS pommies
EIMMORS memoirs
EIMMOST tommies
EIMMPRR primmer
EIMMPRU premium
EIMMRRT trimmer
EIMMRRU rummier
EIMMRSS simmers
EIMMRST misterm
EIMMRSU immures
mumsier
rummies
EIMMRSW swimmer
EIMMRSZ zimmers
EIMMRUY yummier
EIMMSST semmits
EIMMSTU tummies
EIMNNOS Simenon
EIMNNOT mention
EIMNOOR moonier
EIMNOOS isonome
moonies
noisome
EIMNOOT emotion
EIMNOPS peonism
EIMNOPT pimento
EIMNORS merinos
EIMNOST moisten
EIMNOSW winsome
EIMNOTT Menotti
EIMNPTU pinetum
EIMNRRU murrine
EIMNRST minster
minters
remints
EIMNRSU murines
EIMNSSU minuses
EIMNSTT mittens
smitten
EIMNSTU minuets
minutes
EIMNSZZ mizzens
EIMNUZZ muezzin
EIMOORR roomier
EIMOPRR primero
EIMOPRS imposer
promise
semipro
EIMOPRV improve
EIMOPRW impower
EIMOPSS imposes
EIMOPST stompie
EIMORRW wormier
EIMORSS isomers
mossier
EIMORST erotism
mortise
EIMORSU mousier
EIMORSV verismo
EIMORTT omitter
EIMORTV vomiter
EIMOSSS mossies
EIMOSST somites
EIMOSTT motties
EIMOSTU timeous
EIMOSTV motives
EIMOSTZ mestizo
EIMOSYZ isozyme
EIMOSZZ mozzies
EIMOTTU timeout
EIMPQRU Quimper
EIMPRRS primers
EIMPRRU impurer
EIMPRSS impress
premiss
simpers
EIMPRST imprest
permits
EIMPRSU umpires
EIMPRTU imputer
EIMPSST misstep
EIMPSTU impetus
imputes
EIMPSTY mistype
EIMQSTU mesquit
EIMRRST retrims
trimers
EIMRSST misters
smiters
EIMRSSU misuser
mussier
surmise
EIMRSTT metrist
EIMRSTU mustier
EIMRTTU tertium
EIMRTUX mixture
EIMRUZZ muzzier
EIMSSSU misuses
EIMSSTY stymies
EINNOOS ionones
EINNOPS pension
EINNOPT pontine
EINNOQU quinone
EINNORT intoner
nointer
ternion
EINNORU reunion
Réunion
EINNORV environ
EINNOSS sonnies
EINNOST intones
tension
EINNOSV venison
EINNOSY yonnies
EINNOTT tontine
EINNOVW inwoven
EINNPRS pinners
spinner
EINNPRT enprint
EINNPST Pinsent
tenpins
EINNPSY spinney
EINNRRU runnier
EINNRSS sinners
EINNRST interns
tinners
EINNRSU sunnier
EINNRSW winners
EINNRTV vintner
EINNSST sennits
EINNSSU sunnies
EINNSTT intents
EINNSTU Sunnite
tunnies
EINNSTV invents
EINNSWY Swinney
EINNTUW untwine
EINOOPZ epizoon
EINOORS erosion
EINOOST isotone
toonies
EINOOSZ ozonise
EINOOZZ ozonize
EINOPRS orpines
EINOPRT pointer
protein
repoint
tropine
EINOPSS spinose
EINOPST pointes
EINOPTT in petto
pentito
EINOPTU poutine
EINOQUX equinox
EINORRS ironers
rosiner
EINORSS seniors
sonsier
EINORST norites

	oestrin
	orients
	stonier
EINORSU	urinose
EINORSV	enviros
	version
EINORSW	snowier
EINORTT	tritone
EINORTU	routine
EINORTV	Trevino
EINORTW	nowtier
EINOSSS	session
EINOSST	nosiest
EINOSTT	toniest
EINOSTU	Soutine
EINOSTW	townies
	twonies
EINOSUV	envious
	niveous
EINPPRS	nippers
EINPPST	snippet
EINPRRT	printer
	reprint
EINPRSS	snipers
EINPRSU	uprisen
EINPSST	insteps
	spinets
EINPSSU	supines
EINPSTU	puniest
	punties
EINPTTY	tintype
EINQRUY	enquiry
EINQSSU	sequins
EINQSTU	inquest
EINQTTU	quintet
EINQTUU	unquiet
EINRRSS	rinsers
EINRRSU	insurer
	ruiners
EINRSST	inserts
	sinters
EINRSSU	insures
	sunrise
EINRSTT	stinter
	tinters
EINRSTU	triunes
	uniters
EINRSTV	inverts
	striven
	Ventris
EINRSTW	twiners
	winters
EINRSVW	wiverns
EINRTTU	nuttier
EINRTTW	written
EINRTUV	venturi
EINRTWY	wintery
EINSSSU	Senussi
	sinuses
EINSSSY	synesis
EINSSTV	invests
EINSSTW	wisents
	witness
EINSSUW	sunwise
EINSTTT	Stettin
EINSTTW	twinset
EINSTTY	tensity
EINTTTW	twitten
EINTTUY	tenuity
EIOOPST	isotope
EIOORST	sootier
	toories
EIOORTV	Orvieto
EIOORWZ	woozier
EIOOSTT	tootsie
EIOOSTZ	ooziest
EIOPPPS	poppies
EIOPPRS	soppier
EIOPPSS	popsies
EIOPPST	potpies
EIOPRRS	prosier
EIOPRRT	pierrot
EIOPRST	reposit
	riposte
	ropiest
EIOPRSU	soupier
EIOPRSX	proxies
EIOPRTT	pottier
EIOPSSS	possies
EIOPSST	posties
EIOPSTT	potties
	spottie
	tiptoes
EIOPSTU	piteous
EIOPSTX	poxiest
EIOPSZZ	pozzies
EIOPTUW	wipeout
EIOQTUX	quixote
EIORRRS	sorrier
EIORRRT	terroir
EIORRST	rioters
	roister
EIORRSW	worries
EIORSST	rosiest
	siroset
	sorites
	sorties
	stories
EIORSSU	serious
EIORSSX	xerosis
EIORSTU	touries
EIORSTV	Treviso
EIOSSTV	soviets
	stovies
EIOSTTT	stottie
EIOSTUZ	outsize
EIPPPSU	puppies
EIPPRRS	rippers
EIPPRRT	tripper
EIPPRSS	sippers
EIPPRST	tippers
EIPPRSZ	zippers
EIPPRTT	trippet
EIPPSST	sippets
EIPPSTT	tippets
EIPPSUY	yuppies
EIPPTTT	Tippett
EIPRRST	striper
EIPRRSU	upriser
EIPRRUV	upriver
EIPRSSS	pissers
EIPRSST	persist
	priests
	spriest
	sprites
	stirpes
	stripes
EIPRSSU	pussier
	suspire
	uprises
EIPRSTT	spitter
	tipster
EIPRSTU	puirest
EIPRSTV	privets
EIPRSTY	pyrites
	stripey
EIPRSUU	euripus
EIPRUVW	purview
EIPRUZZ	Peruzzi
EIPSSSU	pussies
EIPSSTZ	spitzes
EIPSTTU	putties
EIQRSSU	squires
EIQRSTU	querist
EIQRSUV	quivers
EIQRTTU	quitter
EIQRUVY	quivery
EIQRUZZ	quizzer
EIQSTUU	quietus
EIQSUZZ	quizzes
EIRRRST	stirrer
EIRRSTU	rustier
EIRRSTV	striver
EIRRSTW	writers
EIRRTTU	ruttier
EIRSSST	resists
	sisters
EIRSSSU	issuers
EIRSSTT	sitters
EIRSSTV	stivers
	strives
	verists
EIRSSUU	usuries
EIRSSUV	viruses
EIRSTTT	stretti
	titters
	tritest
EIRSTTV	trivets
EIRSTTW	retwist
	twister
	witters
EIRSTUV	virtues
EIRSUVV	survive
EIRTTTW	twitter
EIRTTUV	vuttier
EISSSTU	tissues
EISSSTX	sexists
EISSSUW	wussies
EISSTUV	tussive
EISSWZZ	swizzes
EJJMNUU	jejunum
EJKMNNU	junkmen
EJKNRSU	junkers
EJKNSTU	junkets
EJLORST	jolters
	jostler
EJLOSST	jostles
EJLOSSY	joyless
EJLSSTU	justles
EJMNRUY	jurymen
EJMPRSU	jumpers
EJNORUY	journey
EJNOSTT	jettons
EJOORVY	overjoy
EJOPPRT	propjet
EJOPRST	projets
EJOPRTT	jetport
EJORSSS	jossers
EJORSTT	jotters
EJORSTU	jouster
EJPRRUY	perjury
EKKLRSU	skulker
EKKOPSU	pukekos
EKLLMSU	skellum
EKLLNOR	knoller
EKLLRRU	kruller
EKLNNUU	Kuenlun
EKLNOPR	plonker
EKLNORS	snorkel
EKLNOSS	kelsons
EKLNOST	Skelton
EKLNOSW	Knowles
EKLNOSY	Lysenko
EKLNPTU	Plunket
EKLOORS	lookers
EKLOSSZ	Slezsko
EKLOSTV	stokvel
EKLRRSU	lurkers
EKLRSSU	sulkers
EKLSTUZ	klutzes
EKMNORW	workmen
EKMNORY	monkery
EKMNOSY	monkeys
EKMNPTU	unkempt
EKMOOPS	mopokes
EKMORSS	smokers
EKMSSTU	muskets
EKNNSSU	Knussen
EKNOORS	snooker
EKNOPSU	unspoke
EKNORSW	knowers
EKNORSY	yonkers
EKNORTT	knotter
EKNORTW	network
EKNORUY	younker
	Yukoner
EKNORWY	New York
EKNOSUY	unyokes

EKNRTUY	turnkey
EKNSTUZ	Kuznets
EKOOPRV	provoke
EKOORRS	koreros
EKOORRY	rookery
EKOORST	stooker
EKOPRRS	porkers
EKOPRUY	kouprey
EKORRSW	reworks
	workers
EKORRSY	yorkers
EKORSST	stokers
	strokes
EKOSSTV	Sovetsk
EKPPSUU	seppuku
EKRSSTU	tuskers
EKRSTUY	turkeys
ELLLORS	lollers
ELLMNSU	mullens
ELLMOOR	morello
ELLMORR	morrell
ELLMOSW	mellows
ELLMPUU	plumule
ELLMRSU	mullers
ELLMSTU	mullets
ELLMSUY	mulleys
ELLNOOV	Novello
ELLNOOW	woollen
ELLNORS	enrolls
ELLNOST	stollen
ELLNOSW	swollen
ELLNSSU	sullens
ELLNSUU	lunules
ELLOOSY	loosely
ELLOOWY	Woolley
ELLOPTU	pollute
ELLORRS	rollers
ELLORRT	troller
ELLORTY	trolley
ELLOSTU	outsell
	sellout
ELLOSTX	extolls
ELLOSVY	volleys
ELLOSWY	yellows
ELLOWYY	yellowy
ELLPRSU	pullers
ELLPSTU	pullets
ELLPSUW	upswell
ELLPSUY	pulleys
ELLRSSU	Russell
ELMMOPS	pommels
ELMMORT	trommel
ELMMPSU	pummels
ELMMPTU	plummet
ELMMRSU	slummer
ELMMRTU	tummler
ELMNOPW	plowmen
ELMNORS	merlons
ELMNOST	loments
ELMNPSU	plenums
ELMOOPS	pomelos
ELMOORS	Morelos
ELMOORT	tremolo
ELMOPRY	polymer
ELMOPSU	plumose
ELMOPSY	employs
ELMOPTY	Ptolemy
ELMORSS	morsels
ELMORTU	moulter
ELMOSST	molests
ELMOSTT	mottles
ELMOSTY	motleys
ELMOSUU	emulous
ELMOSUV	volumes
ELMPPRU	plumper
ELMPPSU	peplums
ELMPRSU	lumpers
	rumples
ELMRSTY	myrtles
ELMRTUU	multure
ELMRTUY	elytrum
ELMRUZZ	muzzler
ELMSSSU	mussels
ELMSTUU	mutuels
	mutules
ELMSTUW	umwelts
ELMSUZZ	muzzles
ELNNOSS	nelsons
ELNNRSU	runnels
ELNNRTU	trunnel
ELNNSTU	tunnels
ELNOOPT	peloton
ELNOOSS	loosens
ELNOOSU	unloose
ELNOOSW	woolens
ELNOOSY	looneys
ELNOPRU	pleuron
ELNOPRY	pronely
ELNOPST	leptons
ELNOPSY	poleyns
ELNOPTU	opulent
ELNORTY	elytron
ELNORTZ	Lorentz
ELNOSSS	lessons
	sonless
ELNOSST	telsons
ELNOSSU	ensouls
ELNOSSV	slovens
ELNOSSW	lowness
ELNOSTV	solvent
ELNOSUZ	zonules
ELNOSZZ	nozzles
ELNOTVY	novelty
ELNPSTU	penults
ELNRSTU	runlets
ELNRSTY	sternly
ELNSSSU	sunless
ELNSSSY	selsyns
	slyness
ELNSTTU	nutlets
ELNSTUY	Lutyens
ELNSUZZ	nuzzles
ELOOPRS	loopers
ELOOPST	pootles
ELOORST	looters
	retools
	rootles
	toolers
ELOORTT	rootlet
	tootler
ELOOSST	loosest
	lotoses
ELOOSTT	tootles
ELOOSTU	outsole
ELOPPPS	popples
ELOPPRS	loppers
	propels
ELOPPST	stopple
	topples
ELOPRRW	prowler
ELOPRRY	pyrrole
ELOPRSS	plessor
	slopers
	splores
ELOPRSU	leprous
	pelorus
	sporule
ELOPRSV	plovers
ELOPRSW	plowers
ELOPRSX	plexors
ELOPRSY	leprosy
ELOPRTT	plotter
ELOPRTU	plouter
ELOPRTW	plowter
ELOPRTY	protyle
ELOPSST	topless
ELOPSTT	pottles
ELOPSTU	tupelos
ELOPTUV	Tupolev
ELORRSS	sorrels
ELORRSU	Roulers
ELORSSS	lessors
ELORSST	ostlers
	sterols
ELORSSU	lousers
ELORSSV	solvers
ELORSTT	settlor
	slotter
ELORSTV	revolts
ELORSTW	trowels
ELORSUV	louvers
	louvres
	velours
ELORSUY	elusory
ELORSVW	wolvers
ELORSWY	yowlers
ELORTTY	lottery
ELORTVY	overtly
ELOSSTU	lotuses
	solutes
	tousles
ELOSSTW	lowsest
	slowest
ELOSSTY	systole
	toyless
	tyloses
ELOSSVW	vowless
ELOSTTU	outlets
ELOSTUU	luteous
ELOSTUV	volutes
ELOSTUZ	touzles
ELOSWZZ	swozzle
ELPPRSU	pulpers
	purples
ELPPSSU	supples
ELPQSUU	pulques
ELPRRSU	purlers
ELPRUZZ	puzzler
ELPSTUU	pustule
ELPSUZZ	puzzles
ELRRSTU	rustler
ELRRTTU	turtler
ELRSSTU	lusters
	lustres
	results
	rustles
	sutlers
	ulsters
ELRSSTY	stylers
ELRSTTU	turtles
ELRSUWY	wurleys
ELRTTUY	utterly
ELRTUUV	vulture
ELSSSTU	tussles
ELSSSUY	Ulysses
ELSSTTY	stylets
EMMMNOS	Mommsen
EMMMRSU	mummers
EMMMRUY	mummery
EMMNOOR	monomer
EMMNOPR	Pommern
EMMNORY	meronym
EMMNOST	moments
EMMNOTU	omentum
EMMNOTY	metonym
EMMOOTY	myotome
EMMOSST	mestoms
EMMOSSU	momuses
EMMRRSU	rummers
EMMRSSU	summers
EMMRSTU	rummest
EMMRSUY	summery
EMMSSUU	museums
EMNNOSW	snowmen
EMNOORT	montero
EMNOOST	moonset
EMNOPPR	propmen
EMNOPST	postmen
EMNOPSU	spumone
EMNOPSY	eponyms
EMNOPYY	eponymy
EMNORRU	mourner
EMNORSS	sermons
EMNORST	mentors
	monster
EMNORTT	torment
EMNORTU	mounter
	remount

EMNORTV	Vermont
EMNOSST	stemson
EMNOSTY	etymons
EMNOSXY	exonyms
EMNOTUX	Monteux
EMNRSSU	rumness
EMNRSTU	munster
	Münster
	munters
	sternum
EMNRTUZ	Müntzer
EMOOPRS	oosperm
EMOOPRT	promote
EMOOPRZ	Pomorze
EMOORRS	roomers
EMOORST	mooters
EMOOSSS	osmoses
EMOOSTT	mottoes
EMOOSTW	twosome
EMOOSTY	myosote
EMOPPST	moppets
EMOPRRS	rompers
EMOPRST	stomper
	trompes
EMOPRSU	supremo
EMOQSSU	mosques
EMORRST	stormer
	termors
	tremors
EMORRSW	wormers
EMORRWY	wormery
EMORSST	motsers
EMORSSU	mousers
EMORSUV	mevrous
EMORSUY	Seymour
EMOSSSU	mousses
EMOSSYZ	zymoses
EMOSTVZ	zemstvo
EMPPSTU	muppets
EMPRSTU	stumper
	sumpter
EMPRTTU	trumpet
EMRRSTU	sturmer
EMRRUUZ	Erzurum
EMRSSTU	musters
	stumers
EMRSTTU	mutters
EMRSTYY	mystery
EMSSSTY	systems
ENNNOPS	pennons
ENNNRUY	nunnery
ENNORSU	neurons
	nonuser
ENNORTT	Trenton
ENNORTU	neutron
ENNOSST	sonnets
ENNOSTU	neuston
ENNOSTW	newtons
ENNOTWW	Newtown
ENNPRSU	punners
ENNPSTU	punnets
ENNRRSU	runners
ENNRSTU	stunner
ENOOPPR	propone
ENOOPRS	operons
	snooper
ENOOPSY	spooney
ENOORRT	Torreón
ENOORST	enroots
	Orontes
ENOORSU	onerous
ENOORSZ	snoozer
ENOOSST	soonest
ENOOSSZ	snoozes
ENOOSTT	testoon
ENOOTXY	oxytone
ENOPRRS	perrons
ENOPRSS	persons
ENOPRST	postern
	Preston
ENOPRSY	pyrones
ENOPRTT	portent
ENOPRTW	Newport
ENOPRTY	entropy
ENOPSST	stepson
ENOQTUU	unquote
ENORRSS	snorers
ENORRST	snorter
	Torrens
ENORRTT	torrent
ENORRUV	overrun
	runover
ENORSSS	sensors
ENORSST	stoners
	tensors
ENORSSW	worsens
ENORSSY	sensory
ENORSTT	snotter
	stentor
ENORSTU	tonsure
ENORSUV	nervous
ENORSUW	unswore
ENORTUY	tourney
ENOSSSU	Souness
ENOSSTT	stetson
	testons
ENOSSTU	outness
ENOSSTX	sextons
ENOSTUU	tenuous
ENOTTUW	outwent
ENPPRSU	prenups
ENPRRSU	pruners
	spurner
ENPRSTU	punster
	punters
ENPSSTU	unsteps
ENPSTUU	tuneups
ENRRSTU	returns
	turners
ENRRSUY	nursery
ENRRTUU	nurture
ENRRTUY	turnery
ENRSSWY	wryness
ENRSTTU	entrust
	nutters
ENRSVWY	wyverns
ENSSSTU	sunsets
EOOOPRS	oospore
EOOPPRS	opposer
	propose
EOOPPRV	popover
EOOPPSS	opposes
EOOPRRS	spoorer
EOOPRRT	trooper
EOOPRST	poorest
	stooper
EOOPRTV	overtop
EOOPRTW	towrope
EOORRSS	roosers
EOORRST	rooster
	rooters
	toreros
EOORRVW	rowover
EOORSSS	soroses
EOORSTT	tooters
EOORTUW	outwore
EOOSSSU	osseous
EOOSSTT	tootses
EOOTTUV	outvote
EOPPPRS	poppers
EOPPPST	poppets
EOPPRRS	prosper
EOPPRSS	oppress
EOPPRST	popster
	stopper
	toppers
EOPPRSU	purpose
EOPPRSW	swopper
EOPPRSY	yoppers
EOPPSSU	suppose
EOPRRSS	pressor
EOPRRST	porters
	pretors
	reports
	sporter
EOPRRSU	pourers
EOPRRTU	trouper
EOPRSST	posters
	prestos
EOPRSSU	poseurs
EOPRSSW	prowess
EOPRSSY	ospreys
EOPRSTT	potters
	protest
	spotter
EOPRSTU	petrous
	posture
	pouters
	proteus
	spouter
	troupes
EOPRSTX	exports
EOPRSUU	uprouse
EOPRTTY	pottery
EOPRTVY	poverty
EOPSSSS	possess
EOPSSSU	spouses
EOPSSTX	sexpots
EOPSTTU	outstep
EOQRSTU	questor
	roquets
	torques
EORRRST	terrors
EORRSST	resorts
	rosters
	sorters
EORRSSU	rousers
EORRSTT	retorts
	rotters
	stertor
EORRSTU	routers
	tourers
	trouser
EORRSTV	Vorster
EORRSTY	stroyer
EORRSZZ	rozzers
EORRTTT	trotter
EORRTTU	torture
EORSSST	tossers
EORSSTU	estrous
	oestrus
	ousters
	souters
	tussore
EORSSTV	votress
EORSSTY	oysters
	storeys
EORSSWW	wowsers
EORSTTT	stotter
	stretto
	totters
EORSTTU	outsert
	stouter
	touters
EORSTTW	swotter
EORSTTX	extorts
EORSUVY	voyeurs
EORTTTY	tottery
EOSSTTU	outsets
EPPPSTU	puppets
EPPRRUU	purpure
EPPRSSU	suppers
EPPSTUW	upswept
EPRRSSU	pursers
EPRRSUU	pursuer
	usurper
EPRRSUY	spurrey
EPRRTUU	rupture
EPRSSTY	spryest
EPRSSUU	pursues
EPRSTTU	putters
	sputter
EPRSUVY	purveys
ERRSSTU	trusser
ERRSSUU	usurers
ERRSSUY	surreys
ERRSTTU	truster
	turrets

ERRSTTY tryster
ERSSSTU russets
trusses
tussers
ERSSTUU sutures
ERSSTUY russety
ERSSTXY xysters
ERSSUVY surveys
ERSTTTU stutter
ERSTTUX urtexts
FFFILOT liftoff
FFGHINU huffing
FFGIIMN miffing
FFGIINN niffing
FFGIINR griffin
riffing
FFGIINT tiffing
FFGILNU luffing
FFGIMNU muffing
FFGINOR griffon
FFGINOS offings
FFGINPU puffing
FFGLRUY gruffly
FFHHISU huffish
FFHILTY fifthly
FFHILUY huffily
FFHIOST toffish
FFHOOSW showoff
FFHORSS shroffs
FFHOSTU shutoff
FFIILMY miffily
FFIINST tiffins
FFILLLU fulfill
FFILLSU fulfils
FFILNSY sniffly
FFILPSS spliffs
FFILPUY puffily
FFILRTY fritfly
FFILSTU fistful
FFILSTY stiffly
FFIMNSU muffins
FFINOOT finfoot
FFINOPS spinoff
FFINOPT pontiff
FFINPSU puffins
FFIOPRS ripoffs
FFIOPST tipoffs
FFIORTY fortify
FFIOSST soffits
FFIQSUY squiffy
FFJMOPU jumpoff
FFKLORU forkful
FFKLOSU Suffolk
FFKOOSS Kossoff
FFLNSUY snuffly
FFLOSTY fylfots
FFNORSU runoffs
FFNORTU turnoff
FFOOPST stopoff
FFOPSTU putoffs
FGGGIIN figging
FGGGINO fogging

FGGHIIS fishgig
FGGIINT gifting
FGGIISZ fizgigs
FGGILNO golfing
FGGILNU gulfing
FGGILOY foggily
FGGINOO goofing
FGGINOR forging
FGHHIOS hogfish
FGHIINS fishing
FGHIIPS pigfish
FGHILST flights
FGHILTY flighty
FGHINOO hoofing
FGHIOSY fogyish
FGHIRST frights
FGHNOOR foghorn
FGIIKNN finking
knifing
FGIILLN filling
FGIILMN filming
FGIILNO foiling
FGIILNR rifling
FGIILNS filings
FGIILNT fliting
lifting
FGIILNY lignify
FGIIMNR firming
FGIINNN finning
FGIINNO foining
FGIINRS firings
FGIINRT rifting
FGIINST fisting
sifting
FGIINSX fixings
FGIINSY signify
FGIINTT fitting
FGIINZZ fizzing
FGIKLNU fluking
FGIKNNU funking
FGIKNOR forking
FGILLNU fulling
FGILMNU fluming
FGILNOO fooling
FGILNOT lofting
FGILNOU fouling
FGILNOW flowing
fowling
wolfing
FGILNRU furling
FGILNSU ingulfs
FGILNTU fluting
FGILNTY flyting
FGILNUX fluxing
FGILOOY goofily
FGILORY glorify
FGIMNOR forming
FGIMOSY fogyism
FGINNNU funning
FGINOOR roofing
FGINOOT footing
FGINOOW woofing

FGINOSX foxings
FGINRRU furring
FGINRSU surfing
FGINRTU turfing
FGINSSU fussing
FGINTTU tufting
FGINUZZ fuzzing
FGIORTW figwort
FGISTUU fuguist
FGJLSUU jugfuls
FGLMSUU mugfuls
FGLNORU furlong
FGLNOSU songful
FGLOOUY ufology
FGNOORU fourgon
FGNOSUU fungous
FHIILSY fishily
FHIINNS Finnish
FHIINPS pinfish
FHIKLOS folkish
FHILOOS foolish
FHILOSW wolfish
FHILSUW wishful
FHINRSU furnish
FHINSSU sunfish
FHIOPPS foppish
FHIORRY horrify
FHIRSTT thrifts
FHIRTTY thrifty
FHKORTU futhork
FHLOOSY shoofly
FHLRTUU hurtful
ruthful
FHNOTUX foxhunt
FHOOOTT hotfoot
FHORSTU fourths
FHORSTY Forsyth
FIIKNRS firkins
FIILLMO milfoil
FIILLMY filmily
FIILLNS infills
FIILLPS fillips
FIILNOT tinfoil
FIILNTY niftily
FIILPTU pitiful
FIIMMNU infimum
FIIMSST misfits
FIINOSS fission
FIINRTY nitrify
FIIOPST positif
FIIRTVY vitrify
FIJLLOY jollify
FIJSTUY justify
FIKKLNO kinfolk
FIKLLSU skilful
FIKLNSU skinful
FILLLUW willful
FILLMOY mollify
FILLNUY nullify
FILLOTU toilful
FILLOTY loftily
FILMNOO monofil

FILNNUY funnily
FILNORS florins
FILNORU fluorin
FILNOSW inflows
FILNOUX fluxion
FILNSTU tinfuls
FILNTUY unfitly
FILORST florist
FILORSV frivols
FILORTU floruit
FILOSSS fossils
FILPSTU uplifts
FILRRUY furrily
FILRSTY firstly
FILRYZZ frizzly
FILSSUY fussily
FILSTTU flutist
FILSTUW wistful
FILSTUY fustily
FILSTWY swiftly
FILUYZZ fuzzily
FIMMMUY mummify
FIMNORS informs
FIMNORU uniform
FIMOORV oviform
FIMORTY mortify
FIMRTUY furmity
FIMSTYY mystify
FINOOSS foisons
FINOPSU soupfin
FINOPTY pontify
FINORSS frisson
FINORST forints
FINOSSU fusions
FIOORSU furioso
FIOPRST profits
FIOPSTX postfix
FIORSUU furious
FIOSTTU outfits
FIPPUYY yuppify
FIRSSUY russify
FKLMOOT folkmot
FKLNOOR Norfolk
FKOOORS forsook
FLLOOSW follows
FLLOPTU topfull
FLLOSUU soulful
FLLSTUU lustful
FLMMOUX flummox
FLMNOOU mouflon
FLMOOOT tomfool
FLMOORU roomful
FLMORWY wormfly
FLNOORR forlorn
FLNRSUU unfurls
FLOOTUW outflow
FLOPSTU potfuls
FLOSUUV fulvous
FMOOPRU Profumo
FMRSTUU frustum
FNNNUUY unfunny
FNNOORT fronton

FNOORRW forworn
FNOORSU sunroof
FNOPRTU upfront
FNSSUUY unfussy
FOOOPRT rooftop
FOOORTT footrot
FOOOTTU outfoot
FOORTTX foxtrot
FOPSSTU fusspot
FORRSUW furrows
FORRUWY furrowy
FORSSTW frowsts
FORSTWY frowsty
GGGGIIN gigging
GGGHINO hogging
GGGHINU hugging
GGGIIJN jigging
GGGIILN ligging
GGGIINP pigging
GGGIINR rigging
GGGIINT tigging
GGGIINW wigging
GGGIJNO jogging
GGGIJNU jugging
GGGILNO logging
GGGILNU lugging
GGGIMNU mugging
GGGINNO gonging
nogging
GGGINNU gunging
GGGINOR gorging
GGGINOT togging
GGGINOU gouging
GGGINPU pugging
GGGINSU sugging
GGGINTU tugging
GGHHIOS hoggish
GGHIINN hinging
GGHIINS Higgins
sighing
GGHIIPS piggish
GGHINSU gushing
Huggins
GGHIPSU puggish
GGHORSU groughs
GGIIILN gingili
GGIIKNN kinging
GGIILLN gilling
GGIIMNN minging
GGIIMNR griming
GGIINNN ginning
GGIINNO ingoing
GGIINNP pinging
GGIINNR girning
ringing
GGIINNS signing
singing
GGIINNT tinging
GGIINNW winging
GGIINNZ zinging
GGIINPP gipping
GGIINPR griping
GGIINPS piggins
GGIINRT girting
ringgit
GGIINSS Gissing
GGIINSU guising
GGIIRRS grigris
GGIJNSU juggins
GGILLNU gulling
GGILMUY muggily
GGILNNO longing
GGILNNU lunging
GGILNOS gosling
GGILNOV gloving
GGILNOW glowing
GGILNOZ glozing
GGILNPU gulping
GGILOOS gigolos
GGILOSY soggily
GGILRWY wriggly
GGIMMNU gumming
GGIMNSU muggins
GGINNNU gunning
GGINNOO ongoing
GGINNOP ponging
GGINNOS noggins
GGINNOT tonging
GGINNOW gowning
GGINNRU gurning
GGINOOP pogoing
GGINOOS goosing
GGINOPR groping
GGINORS gringos
GGINORU roguing
rouging
GGINORW growing
GGINORZ grozing
GGINOSS gossing
GGINPPY gypping
GGINPRU purging
GGINRSU surging
GGINSTU gusting
GGINTTU gutting
GGIOORS gorgios
GGIOPTT Piggott
GGIPRSY spriggy
GGLLOOS loglogs
GGLOOOS googols
GGMRSUU muggurs
GGNOORS gorgons
GGNOOSY gongyos
GGRRSUU grugrus
GHHINSU hushing
GHHLOOY Hooghly
GHHORTU through
GHHOTTU thought
GHIILLN hilling
GHIILNT hilting
GHIILNW whiling
GHIILRS girlish
GHIINNS Hsining
shining
GHIINNT hinting
GHIINNW whining
GHIINPS pishing
GHIINPT pithing
GHIINRS shiring
GHIINSS hissing
GHIINST insight
shiting
GHIINSW wishing
GHIINTT hitting
tithing
GHIINTW whiting
withing
GHIIRST tigrish
GHIJNOS joshing
GHIKLNU hulking
GHIKNNO honking
GHIKNOO hooking
GHIKNOW howking
GHIKNST knights
GHIKNSU husking
GHIKRTU tughrik
GHILLNU hulling
GHILLTY lightly
GHILNOS longish
GHILNOT tholing
GHILNOU Holguín
GHILNOW howling
GHILNRU hurling
GHILNSU lushing
GHILNSY shingly
GHILNTY nightly
GHILPST plights
GHILRTY rightly
GHILSST slights
GHILSTY sightly
GHILSUY gushily
GHILTTY tightly
GHIMMNU humming
GHIMNNY hymning
GHIMNOS gnomish
moshing
GHIMNPU humping
GHIMNRY rhyming
GHIMNSU mushing
GHINNOP phoning
GHINNOR horning
GHINNOS noshing
GHINNOT nothing
GHINNTU hunting
GHINOOP hooping
GHINOOS shooing
GHINOOT hooting
GHINOPP hopping
GHINORS horsing
shoring
GHINORW whoring
GHINOST hosting
GHINOSU housing
GHINOSV shoving
GHINOSW showing
GHINOTT hotting
tonight
GHINOTU houting
GHINPSU pushing
GHINRSU Grishun
rushing
GHINRTU hurting
GHINTTU hutting
GHIOPSZ phizogs
GHIORSU roguish
GHIOSUV voguish
GHIOUUZ Guizhou
GHIPRTU upright
GHIPTTU uptight
GHIRSTW wrights
GHLMOOO homolog
GHLOOSY shoogly
GHLOPSU ploughs
GHLORUY roughly
GHLOSSU sloughs
GHLOSTY ghostly
GHLOSUY sloughy
GHLOTUY toughly
GHMORSU sorghum
GHNOOTW Hogtown
GHNOPRY gryphon
GHNORST throngs
GHNOSSU shoguns
GHNOSTU gunshot
hognuts
noughts
shotgun
GHNRTUU Guthrun
GHOOOSW hoosgow
GHOORSS sorghos
GHORSTU troughs
GHORSTW growths
GHORTUW wrought
GHORTUY yoghurt
GIIILNU Giulini
GIIJKNN jinking
GIIJLNT jilting
GIIJNNO joining
GIIJNNX jinxing
GIIKLLN killing
GIIKLMN milking
GIIKLNN inkling
kilning
linking
GIIKLNP Kipling
GIIKLNS silking
GIIKLNT kilting
GIIKNNP kingpin
pinking
GIIKNNS sinking
GIIKNNW winking
GIIKNPP kipping
GIIKNPS pigskin
spiking
GIIKNRS griskin
risking
GIIKNSS kissing
GIIKNST kitings
skiting

GIIKNSV skiving
vikings
GIIKNTT kitting
GIILLMN milling
GIILLNO gillion
GIILLNP pilling
GIILLNT lilting
tilling
GIILLNW willing
GIILMNN limning
GIILMNO moiling
GIILMNP limping
GIILMNS sliming
smiling
GIILMNT milting
GIILMPR pilgrim
GIILNNS linings
GIILNNY inlying
GIILNOR ligroin
roiling
GIILNOS soiling
GIILNOT toiling
GIILNPP lipping
GIILNPS lisping
spiling
GIILNST listing
silting
GIILNSV livings
GIILNTT tilting
titling
GIILNTW wilting
witling
GIILNWZ Zwingli
GIILRST strigil
GIIMMNR rimming
GIIMNNT minting
GIIMNPP pimping
GIIMNPR priming
GIIMNPW wimping
GIIMNRT mitring
GIIMNSS missing
GIIMNST misting
smiting
timings
GIINNNP pinning
GIINNNS innings
sinning
GIINNNT tinning
GIINNNW winning
GIINNOP Nipigon
opining
GIINNOR ironing
GIINNOS noising
GIINNPP nipping
GIINNPS sniping
GIINNRS rinsing
GIINNRU inuring
ruining
GIINNSW inswing
GIINNTT tinting
GIINNTU uniting
GIINNTW twining
GIINOPS poising
GIINORS origins
signior
signori
GIINORT rioting
GIINOSY yoginis
GIINPPP pipping
GIINPPR ripping
GIINPPS sipping
GIINPPT tipping
GIINPPZ zipping
GIINPQU piquing
GIINPRS prising
spiring
GIINPRZ prizing
GIINPSS pissing
GIINPST spiting
GIINPSW swiping
wisping
GIINPTT pitting
GIINPTW wingtip
GIINPTY pitying
GIINRRY yirring
GIINRSS risings
GIINRSV virgins
GIINRTW writing
GIINSSU issuing
GIINSSW wissing
GIINSTT sitting
GIINSTU suiting
GIINSVW swiving
GIINTTW witting
GIINZZZ zizzing
GIJKNNU junking
GIJKNOO jooking
GIJKNOU jouking
GIJLLNO jolling
GIJLNOT jolting
GIJMNPU jumping
GIJNOTT jotting
GIJNTTU jutting
GIKLNOO looking
GIKLNRU lurking
GIKLNSU sulking
GIKMNNU Kunming
GIKMNOS smoking
GIKNNOO kongoni
Kooning
GIKNNOW knowing
GIKNNSU Sun King
GIKNOOR rooking
GIKNOOS Song Koi
sooking
GIKNOPS spoking
GIKNORW working
GIKNORY yorking
GIKNOST stoking
GIKNOSU souking
GIKNOSY Kosygin
GIKNOUY Yingkou
GIKNSTU tusking
GIKRSTU tugriks
GILLLNO lolling
GILLLNU lulling
GILLMNU mulling
GILLNOP polling
GILLNOR rolling
GILLNOT tolling
GILLNPU pulling
GILMMUY gummily
GILMNOO looming
GILMNOT molting
GILMNPU lumping
pluming
GILMNSU lignums
GILMPSY gymslip
GILNNRU nurling
GILNNSU unsling
GILNOOP looping
pooling
GILNOOS loosing
soloing
sooling
GILNOOT looting
tooling
GILNOPP lopping
GILNOPS sloping
GILNOPU louping
GILNOPW lowping
plowing
GILNORU louring
GILNORW Rowling
GILNOSS losings
GILNOST tiglons
GILNOSU lousing
GILNOSV solving
GILNOSW lowsing
slowing
GILNOTT lotting
GILNOTU louting
GILNOWY yowling
GILNPPU pulping
GILNPRU purling
GILNPSU pulsing
GILNRSU rulings
GILNSSU nisguls
GILNSTU lusting
GILNSTY styling
GILNVYY vyingly
GILOORS girosol
GILORTY trilogy
GILORTZ Görlitz
GILOSTT glottis
GILOTUY goutily
GILRSTY gristly
GILRTUY liturgy
GILRYZZ grizzly
GILSTUY gustily
GIMMMNU mumming
GIMMNPU mumping
GIMMNSU summing
GIMNNOO mooning
GIMNNOR morning
GIMNOOR mooring
rooming
GIMNOOT mooting
GIMNOOZ zooming
GIMNOPP mopping
GIMNOPR romping
GIMNOPY yomping
GIMNORW worming
GIMNOSU mousing
GIMNOWY Wyoming
GIMNPPU pumping
GIMNPSU impugns
spuming
GIMNSSU mussing
GIMNUZZ muzzing
GIMOSTU gomutis
GINNNOO nooning
GINNNOW wonning
GINNNPU punning
GINNNRU running
GINNNSU sunning
GINNNTU tunning
GINNOOS noosing
GINNOPS spongin
GINNORS snoring
sorning
GINNORU grunion
GINNORW ingrown
GINNORY gironny
GINNOSS nosings
GINNOST stoning
GINNOSW snowing
GINNOSZ zonings
GINNOTW wonting
GINNPRU pruning
GINNPTU punting
GINNRSU nursing
urnings
GINNRTU turning
GINNTTU nutting
GINNTUY untying
GINOOPP pooping
GINOORS roosing
GINOORT rooting
GINOOSS isogons
GINOOST sooting
GINOOSW wooings
GINOOTT tooting
GINOPPP popping
GINOPPS sopping
GINOPPT topping
GINOPPW wopping
GINOPRS prosing
sporing
GINOPRT porting
GINOPRU ingroup
pouring
rouping
GINOPRV proving
GINOPSS possing
GINOPST posting
stoping
GINOPTT potting

GINOPTU	pouting
GINOQTU	quoting
GINORSS	grisons
	signors
GINORST	sorting
	storing
	trigons
GINORSU	rousing
	souring
GINORSY	signory
GINORTT	rotting
GINORTU	routing
	touring
GINORTW	trowing
GINOSST	stingos
	tossing
GINOSSU	sousing
GINOSTU	ousting
	outings
	outsing
GINOSTV	stoving
GINOSTW	stowing
GINOTTT	totting
GINOTTU	touting
GINPPPU	pupping
GINPPSU	supping
GINPPTU	tupping
GINPRRU	purring
GINPRSS	springs
GINPRSU	pursing
GINPRSY	springy
GINPSTU	pignuts
GINPSUW	upswing
GINPTTU	putting
GINRSST	strings
GINRSTU	rusting
GINRSTY	stringy
GINRTTU	rutting
GINSSSU	sussing
GINTTTU	tutting
GIOPRRU	prurigo
GIOPRSU	Gropius
GIOPSSS	gossips
GIOPSST	spigots
GIOPSSY	gossipy
GIORRSU	rigours
GIORSTU	Grotius
	rigouts
GIOSSYZ	zygosis
GISWWYY	wysiwyg
GJNOOSU	goujons
GJNRSUU	gurjuns
GJOORTT	jogtrot
GKKNOOS	songkok
GKMOORY	Gromyko
GLLLOOR	logroll
GLLOOPS	gollops
GLMNOOS	mongols
GLMNUUU	umlungu
GLMOOYY	myology
GLMORUW	lugworm
GLNNOOR	lorgnon
GLNNSUU	unslung
GLNOOOR	Logroño
GLNOOPR	prolong
GLNOOPY	polygon
GLNORWY	wrongly
GLNOSUV	Volsung
GLNOSUW	sunglow
GLNOTTU	glutton
GLNPSUU	unplugs
GLOOORY	orology
GLOOOTY	otology
GLOOOYZ	zoology
GLOOPRS	prologs
GLOORUY	urology
GLOPSTU	putlogs
GLORSSY	grossly
GMMOSUU	gummous
GMMPUUW	mugwump
GMNNOOS	gnomons
GMNOORU	gunroom
GMNOORW	morwong
GMNSUUZ	mzungus
GMOOPRS	pogroms
GMORSUU	grumous
GMORTUW	mugwort
GMRUYYZ	zymurgy
GNNOORS	rognons
GNNORYY	gyronny
GNOOOSS	gossoon
GNOORST	trogons
GNOPPSU	oppugns
	popguns
GNOPRUW	grownup
GNOSTUU	outguns
	outsung
GNPSUUW	upswung
GOOPRST	gosport
GOORSTT	grottos
GOORTUW	outgrow
GORSTTU	rotguts
GORSTUY	yogurts
HHIISTW	whitish
HHINNSU	hunnish
HHIORSW	whorish
HHIOSTT	hottish
HHISSTW	whishts
HHMRSTY	rhythms
HHOOSTT	hotshot
HIIIJNO	John III
HIIIKRS	rikishi
HIIILPP	Philip I
HIIJKNS	hijinks
HIIKNNS	shinkin
HIIKNPS	kinship
	pinkish
HIILLPP	Phillip
HIILMTU	lithium
HIILPPV	Philip V
HIILPST	shilpit
HIILPTY	pithily
HIILRTT	trilith
HIIMMSS	mishmis
HIIMNSX	minxish
HIIMPSW	wimpish
HIIMRSU	shiurim
HIIMSST	mishits
HIIMSTT	shittim
HIINNOT	thionin
HIINSSW	swinish
HIINSTW	Swithin
HIIOPRW	powhiri
HIJNOUZ	Jinzhou
HIKKOSU	Shikoku
HIKLSUY	huskily
HIKMNOS	monkish
HIKMSUU	Sukhumi
HIKMSUZ	muzhiks
HIKNNOR	inkhorn
HIKNNTU	unthink
HIKNOOU	hokonui
HIKNOPS	Hopkins
HIKNPSU	punkish
	Pushkin
HIKNRSS	shrinks
HIKOVVZ	Zhivkov
HILLPSU	uphills
HILLRSS	shrills
HILLRST	thrills
HILLRSY	shrilly
HILLTUU	Luthuli
HILMMOU	holmium
HILMPSU	lumpish
HILMSUY	mushily
HILMTUU	thulium
HILNNTY	ninthly
HILNORY	hornily
HILNOTY	thionyl
HILNPST	plinths
HILOOST	ooliths
HILOOTT	otolith
HILORSY	horsily
HILORTU	urolith
HILOSTU	loutish
HILOSWY	showily
HILOTWW	whitlow
HILPSUY	pushily
HILSSTY	stylish
HILSTTY	thistly
HILSTXY	sixthly
HIMMMTU	Thummim
HIMMOST	Thomism
HIMMPSU	mumpish
HIMNSTY	hymnist
HIMOORS	moorish
HIMOPRS	Orphism
	rompish
HIMOPSS	sophism
HIMOPST	moshpit
HIMORSW	wormish
HIMORTU	thorium
HIMOTTY	timothy
HIMPRSS	shrimps
HIMPRTU	triumph
HIMSSTU	isthmus
HINNORT	tinhorn
HINOORZ	horizon
HINOPSS	siphons
HINORSU	nourish
HINOSTW	townish
HINPPSU	pushpin
HINPSSU	unships
HINRSTU	runtish
HINSTUW	Whitsun
HIOPRSW	worship
HIOPSST	sophist
HIOPSSY	physios
HIOPSTW	Sopwith
HIORSSU	sourish
HIORSTY	history
HIOSSTT	sottish
HIOSTTU	outhits
HIOTTUW	outwith
	without
HIPRSUX	Phrixus
HIQSSUY	squishy
HIRSSTT	thirsts
HIRSTTU	ruttish
HIRSTTY	thirsty
HJNNOOS	Johnson
HKKLOOS	kolkhos
HKKLOOZ	kolkhoz
HKKOOST	Okhotsk
HKKOSTU	sukkoth
HKNOOSU	unhooks
HKNOOWW	knowhow
HKOOOPT	pothook
HKOOPSU	hookups
HKOOSVZ	sovkhoz
HKORSWY	workshy
HKOSSTU	Kossuth
HLLOOSW	hollows
HLLPSUY	plushly
HLMNOTY	monthly
HLOOPSS	sploosh
HLOOSTY	soothly
HLORSTY	shortly
HLPRSUU	sulphur
HMMNOOY	homonym
HMMOOSU	hoummos
HMNOOST	Thomson
HMNOPSY	nymphos
HMNOPYY	hyponym
HMOOSST	smooths
HMOOSTY	smoothy
HMOOSUU	houmous
HMORSUU	humours
HNNOOPS	phonons
HNOOPST	photons
HNOOPTY	typhoon
HNOORSU	honours
HNOOSTU	Houston
HNOPSSY	syphons
HNOPSTY	phytons
	pythons
HNRTTUU	untruth
HNSTUUZ	Hsün-tzu

HOOPSSY	shypoos
HOOPSTT	hotpots
	potshot
HOORRRS	horrors
HOOSTTU	outshot
HOPRSTU	hotspur
HOPRTUW	upthrow
HOPSSSY	hyssops
HOPSSTU	upshots
HOPSTTU	shotput
HOPSTUY	typhous
HORSTUU	outrush
HOSTTUU	shutout
HPPSSUU	pushups
HPRRSUY	Pyrrhus
HRSSTTU	thrusts
HRSSTUY	thyrsus
IIIKMNN	minikin
IIILOSU	Louis II
IIIPRUV	Viipuri
IIIPSUV	Pius VII
IIIPSUX	Pius XII
IIJLLNO	jillion
IIJNSUU	Sinŭiju
IIKKLNY	kinkily
IIKKNPS	kipskin
IIKLLMY	milkily
IIKLLSY	silkily
IIKLMNP	limpkin
IIKLMRY	mirkily
IIKLNOS	oilskin
IIKLNSW	Wilkins
IIKLPSY	spikily
IIKLRSY	riskily
IIKMOUZ	Koizumi
IIKNPPS	pipkins
IIKNSSS	siskins
IIKPSUW	wikiups
IILLMNO	million
IILLMSY	slimily
IILLNOP	pillion
IILLNOZ	zillion
IILLNST	instill
IILMSTU	stimuli
IILMSTY	mistily
IILNNSU	insulin
IILNNTY	tinnily
IILNORS	sirloin
IILNOSV	violins
IILNOSY	noisily
IILNPPY	nippily
IILNPUV	pulvini
IILNSST	instils
IILNSUV	Vilnius
IILOPRT	tripoli
IILORTV	vitriol
IILOSTV	violist
IILOSUV	Louis IV
IILOSUX	Louis IX
	Louis XI
IILPRVY	privily
IILPSST	pistils
IILPSTY	tipsily
IILPSWY	wispily
IILRTYZ	ritzily
IILTTUY	utility
IILTTWY	wittily
IIMMMNU	minimum
IIMMNSU	minimus
IIMNNOS	minions
IIMNOSS	mission
IIMNOSZ	Zionism
IIMNPRT	imprint
IIMOPSU	impious
IIMOSST	mitosis
IIMOSSU	simious
IIMOSTT	Imittós
IIMRSST	smritis
IIMRTTU	tritium
IIMRTUV	trivium
IINNOOP	opinion
IINNOPS	pinions
IINOPSS	isospin
IINORSS	Rossini
IINORST	ironist
IINORSV	virinos
	virions
IINORTT	introit
IINOSSV	visions
IINOTTU	tuition
IINPPPS	pippins
IINQRUY	inquiry
IINRTTY	trinity
IINSSST	insists
IINSTTU	intuits
IINSTTW	nitwits
IIOOSTT	toitois
IIOPRSS	pissoir
IIOQSTU	Iquitos
IIORSTV	visitor
IIPPSUU	piupius
IIPRRSU	puriris
IIPRSST	spirits
IIPRSTU	pituris
IIPRTTZ	Tirpitz
IIPRTVY	privity
IITTTZZ	tzitzit
IJJMSUU	jujuism
IJJSTUU	jujitsu
	jujuist
IJKLLOY	killjoy
IJKMOSU	moujiks
IJLLOTY	jollity
IJLMPUY	jumpily
IJLNOQU	jonquil
IJLNOTY	jointly
IJNORSU	juniors
IJRSSTU	jurists
IKKMNOU	kikumon
IKKRSTU	Irkutsk
IKKSUUY	kikuyus
IKLLPSU	upskill
IKLLSUY	sulkily
IKLMOOS	lookism
IKLMOPS	milksop
IKLMOSY	smokily
IKLMRUY	murkily
IKLNNSU	unlinks
IKLNOOT	kiloton
IKLNPSU	linkups
	uplinks
IKLNRWY	wrinkly
IKLOOTT	toolkit
IKLOSSU	souslik
IKLSSSU	susliks
IKMNOOS	kimonos
	Míkonos
	monoski
IKMNPPU	pumpkin
IKMOOST	mistook
IKMOSSU	koumiss
IKNNSTU	unknits
IKNOPRW	pinwork
IKNOPST	Skipton
IKNORTW	tinwork
IKNPSTU	sputnik
IKPRSSU	prusiks
	spruiks
ILLMNOU	mullion
ILLMNRU	millrun
ILLMORU	Murillo
ILLMPUY	lumpily
ILLMSUU	limulus
ILLNOQU	quillon
ILLNORS	Rollins
ILLNPUU	lupulin
ILLNTUY	nullity
ILLOPRY	pillory
ILLOPSW	pillows
ILLORTU	Utrillo
ILLOSUV	villous
ILLOSUY	lousily
ILLOSWW	willows
ILLOWWY	willowy
ILLPPUY	pulpily
ILLQSSU	squills
ILLRSUY	surlily
ILLSTUY	lustily
ILMMSUU	mimulus
ILMNOOT	moonlit
ILMNOOY	moonily
ILMNOSU	moulins
ILMNSSU	muslins
ILMOOPP	Limpopo
ILMOORY	roomily
ILMOOSV	moolvis
ILMORTU	turmoil
ILMOSTY	moistly
ILMOSUY	mousily
ILMRSSY	lyrisms
ILMSSUY	mussily
ILMSTUY	mustily
ILMUYZZ	muzzily
ILNNOPS	nonslip
ILNNOSS	Nilsson
ILNNSUY	sunnily
ILNOOPS	plosion
ILNOORS	rosinol
ILNOORV	Livorno
ILNOOST	lotions
	soliton
ILNOPRU	purloin
ILNOPST	pontils
ILNOPSU	upsilon
ILNORST	nostril
ILNOSST	tonsils
ILNOSSU	insouls
ILNOSTY	stonily
ILNOSWY	snowily
ILNPRSU	purlins
ILNPSST	splints
ILNSSTU	insults
ILNTTUY	nuttily
ILOOPST	topsoil
ILOOSST	soloist
ILOOSTY	sootily
ILOOWYZ	woozily
ILOPPSY	soppily
ILOPRSY	prosily
ILOPSST	pistols
	postils
ILOPSTT	spotlit
ILOPSUY	piously
ILOQRSU	liquors
ILORRSY	sorrily
ILORSTU	troilus
ILOSSTY	tylosis
ILOSTTW	wittols
ILOSUVX	Louis XV
ILPPSSU	slipups
ILPPSTU	pulpits
ILPSTTU	uptilts
ILRSSTY	lyrists
ILRSTUY	rustily
ILRTTUY	ruttily
ILSSTTU	lutists
ILSSTTY	stylist
ILSTTUU	titulus
IMMOOSS	simooms
IMMOPTU	optimum
IMMOSTU	stomium
IMMSSTU	summits
IMNNNOU	munnion
IMNNOSW	minnows
IMNNSTU	muntins
IMNOOPT	tompion
IMNOORS	morions
IMNOORT	monitor
IMNOOSS	simoons
IMNOOST	motions
IMNOOSU	ominous
IMNOOSY	isonomy
IMNOOUX	oxonium
IMNOPRW	pinworm
IMNOPSS	Simpson
IMNOPSU	spumoni
IMNORST	Strimon
IMNOSST	monists

IMOOPRX	proximo
IMOORST	Morisot
IMOOSSS	osmosis
IMOOSSU	osmious
IMOPRST	imports
	tropism
IMOPRTU	protium
IMOPSST	imposts
IMORRRS	mirrors
IMORSTU	tourism
IMORSTY	trisomy
IMOSSTU	missout
IMOSSYZ	zymosis
IMOSTTT	tomtits
IMOSTUV	vomitus
IMQRSSU	squirms
IMQRSUY	squirmy
IMRSSTU	sistrum
	trismus
	truisms
IMRTTUY	yttrium
INNNOOR	noniron
INNOOPS	opsonin
INNOOST	notions
INNORST	introns
INNOSTU	nonsuit
INNOSTW	Winston
INNOSWW	winnows
INOOPRT	portion
INOOPSS	poisons
	poisson
INOOPST	options
	potions
INOORSS	orisons
INOORST	isotron
	nitroso
	torsion
INOORTT	tortoni
INOOSUX	noxious
INOPPST	topspin
INOPRSS	prisons
INOPSST	pistons
INOPSSU	poussin
	spinous
INOPSTU	spinout
INORSTT	tritons
INORSTU	nitrous
	turions
INORSUU	ruinous
	urinous
INOSSUU	sinuous
INOSTUV	Ustinov
INPRSST	sprints
INPRSTU	turnips
INPRSTY	trypsin
INQSSTU	squints
INQSTUY	squinty
INRSTTU	intrust
INSSTUU	sunsuit

INSTTUW	untwist
IOOPRSV	proviso
IOOPSTY	isotopy
IOORSSS	sorosis
IOORSTT	risotto
IOORSTU	riotous
IOOSSST	ostosis
IOPRSST	riposts
IOPRSSY	pyrosis
IOPRSTT	protist
IOQRTTU	quittor
IORRSTW	worrits
IORSSTU	suitors
IORSTTU	tourist
IOSSSTT	tsotsis
IOSSTTU	outsits
IOSTTUW	outwits
IPPQSUU	quippus
IPRRSTU	irrupts
	stirrup
IPRSSTU	purists
	spruits
IPRSTUU	pursuit
IPSSSTY	stypsis
IPSSTTY	typists
IPSTTTU	tittups
IQRSSTU	squirts
ISSTUVX	Sixtus V
JJSTUUU	jujutsu
JLLOOPS	jollops
JMOPTUU	outjump
JNNORUY	nonjury
JNNOSTU	jotunns
JNOORSU	journos
	sojourn
JOOPPSY	joypops
KKLMSUU	mukluks
KKMOOSU	skookum
KKNOOOR	Koko Nor
KKNORUU	Kuku Nor
KLLMOSU	mollusk
KLNOOOW	Kowloon
KLNOOPS	plonkos
KLOOOTU	lookout
	outlook
KMNOOSY	Mykonos
KMOOORS	mokoros
KMOSSUY	koumyss
KNNNOUW	unknown
KNNOSTU	unknots
KNOOPTT	topknot
KNOOSSS	Knossos
KNOPRTY	krypton
KNORRTY	krytron
KOOPRSW	Worksop
KOOPRTW	worktop
KOORTUW	outwork
	workout
KOOSSUU	soukous

KOOSTTU	tuktoos
KOOSTWW	kowtows
KORSTTY	Trotsky
KOTUUVZ	Kutuzov
LLLOOPS	lollops
LLMOOPR	rollmop
LLMPPUY	plumply
LLNORSU	unrolls
LLOOPRT	rolltop
	trollop
LLOORTU	rollout
LLOPTUU	pullout
LLORSST	strolls
LLPPSUU	pullups
LMNOOOS	Solomon
LMOOOOS	mooloos
LMOOOTV	Molotov
LMOPSUY	Olympus
LMORSUU	Romulus
LMRSTUU	lustrum
LMSTTUU	tumults
LMSTUUU	tumulus
LNNOPSU	nonplus
LNOOSST	stolons
LNOPSTU	plutons
LNOSTYZ	Olsztyn
LNRTUUY	untruly
LOOORRS	oloroso
LOOSSTV	volosts
LOOSTTY	Tolstoy
LOPPSUY	polypus
LOPRSUY	pylorus
LOPRTUY	poultry
LOPSSTY	stylops
LOSTTUY	stoutly
LPRSSUU	surplus
MMNNOOY	mononym
MMNOSSU	summons
MMOOPPS	pompoms
MMOOSTT	motmots
MMOPSTY	symptom
MMRRSUU	murmurs
MMSUUUU	muumuus
MNNOOOS	monsoon
MNNOSYY	synonym
MNOOPPS	pompons
MNOOPTY	toponym
MNOORSU	sunroom
	unmoors
MNOOSUY	onymous
MNORSTU	nostrum
	Urmston
MNORSTY	Strymon
MNOTTUY	muttony
MOOOTYZ	zootomy
MOOPPSU	pompous
MOOPSSU	opossum
MOOPSTT	topmost
MOORRSW	morrows

MOOSTTU	outmost
MOPPRST	prompts
MOPSSSU	possums
MOPSSUU	spumous
MOQRSUU	quorums
MORRSTU	rostrum
MORRSUU	rumours
MORSTUU	tumours
NNOOOPT	pontoon
NNOOPRS	nonpros
NNOOPRU	pronoun
NNOOPSS	sponson
NNOOPST	nonstop
NNOOSTW	wontons
NNORSUW	unsworn
NOOORTT	Toronto
NOOOSUZ	ozonous
NOOOTTW	Wootton
NOOPRSS	sponsor
NOOPRST	protons
NOOPSYZ	Pozsony
NOORSTU	unroots
NOORTUW	outworn
NOOTTWY	toytown
NOPSSTU	sunspot
	unstops
NORSTUU	outruns
	runouts
NORTTUU	outturn
	turnout
NPRSTUU	turnups
	upturns
NRSSTUU	untruss
OOOOPRT	potoroo
OOORTTU	outroot
OOPRSSU	soursop
OOPRSTU	uproots
OOPRSTV	provost
OOPRTTU	outport
OOPRTUU	outpour
OOPSSTT	tosspot
OOPSTTU	outpost
OOPSWWW	powwows
OORRSSW	sorrows
OORSUVV	Suvorov
OPPRRTU	purport
OPPRSTU	support
OPPRSTY	stroppy
OPRSSTU	sprouts
	stupors
OPSSSTU	tossups
OPSTTUU	outputs
	putouts
ORSTTUU	surtout
ORSTTUY	tryouts
RSTTUUY	Ustyurt

Eight Letters

AAAABENN anabaena
AAAABKTW Kawabata
AAAACCRR caracara
AAAACNRS anasarca
AAAADMTV amadavat
AAAADTVV avadavat
AAAAEMNR Aramaean
AAAAGIRU Araguaia
AAAAGLRT Agartala
AAAAGMTY Yamagata
AAAAHJMR maharaja
AAAAHMNY Mahayana
AAAAIMPR arapaima
AAAAINPY Ayia Napa
AAAAIRTX ataraxia
AAAAKKNT katakana
AAAAKKWW kawakawa
AAAAKMWY Wakayama
AAAAKNWZ Kanazawa
AAAALLVV lavalava
AAAALNTT Atalanta
AAAAMMTT matamata
AAAAMNRY Ramayana
AAAANNST Santa Ana
AAABBBRS Barabbas
AAABBCLS cabbalas
AAABBHKL kabbalah
AAABBILT abbatial
AAABBKLS kabbalas
AAABBNRS Barnabas
AAABCCMW maccabaw
AAABCCRT baccarat
AAABCDOZ Bozcaada
AAABCENT Ecbatana
AAABCHLS calabash
AAABCILP abapical
AAABCILR Calabria
AAABCINT anabatic
AAABCITT ciabatta
AAABCLSV baclavas
AAABCNRR barranca
AAABCNRU carnauba
AAABCORS carabaos
AAABCPRY capybara
AAABCSSS cassabas
AAABCSTW catawbas
AAABDEHH dahabeah
AAABDENS Banda Sea
AAABDEST database
AAABDFRS abfarads
AAABDHHI dahabiah
AAABDHLL Abd Allah
AAABDKNT databank
AAABDKSZ Szabadka
AAABDLMS lambadas
AAABDLNO Badalona
AAABDNNN bandanna
AAABDNNS bandanas
AAABDNRS saraband
AAABDNRT abradant
AAABEHNR habanera
AAABEHRT barathea
AAABENSS anabases
AAABFILR al-Farabi
AAABFLLS falbalas
AAABGLNY bangalay
AAABGLOR algaroba
AAABGMNQ mbaqanga
AAABGNST Batangas
AAABGRTU rutabaga
AAABHIKZ Abkhazia
AAABHIMN Bahamian
AAABHIMT Amitabha
AAABHJLV Jhabvala
AAABHLMR Alhambra
AAABHMNR Brahmana
AAABHMST mastabah
AAABHPRT Bhatpara
AAABINPR Parnaíba
AAABINRV Bavarian
AAABINSS anabasis
AAABINTV Batavian
AAABIPSS piassaba
AAABISTV batavias
AAABKLSV baklavas
AAABKPSS baasskap
AAABLLRT Ballarat
AAABLOPR parabola
AAABMNRT Martaban
AAABMSST mastabas
AAABORRS ararobas
AAABRSUY Surabaya
AAACCEPR carapace
AAACCILR calcaria
AAACCISU Caucasia
AAACCLMS malaccas
AAACCLPS alpaccas
AAACCLRS caracals
AAACCRSS cascaras
AAACCRTT cataract
AAACDEIM academia
AAACDELM aceldama
AAACDENR dracaena
AAACDEQU aquacade
AAACDETU acaudate
AAACDFIR faradaic
AAACDILR caldaria
AAACDINN Canadian
AAACDINR acaridan
arcadian
AAACDKLY lackaday
AAACDNNO anaconda
AAACDNRS sandarac
AAACDOTV advocaat
AAACEERS Caesarea
AAACEHLT calathea
AAACEHLZ chalazae
AAACELNT analecta
AAACELST catalase
AAACENNP panacean
AAACENPS panaceas
AAACGHNR charanga
AAACGLSW scalawag
AAACGMNP campagna
AAACGMNR armagnac
AAACGNRU Rancagua
AAACHILW Walachia
AAACHIPS aphasiac
Caiaphas
AAACHLLZ chalazal
AAACHLMN La Mancha
AAACHLSZ chalazas
AAACHRSY acharyas
AAACIJMN Jamaican
AAACILMN maniacal
AAACILMR calamari
AAACILRV calvaria
AAACILST Castalia
AAACILSY calisaya
AAACIMNP Campania
AAACINSU Nausicaä

AAACINTV	cavatina
AAACIRRS	sacraria
AAACIRTX	ataraxic
AAACJMRS	jacamars
AAACKLMN	almanack
AAACKMRT	tamarack
AAACLLSV	cavallas
AAACLLTX	Tlaxcala
AAACLMNS	almanacs
AAACLMUY	Macaulay
AAACLNST	cantalas
AAACLPST	catalpas
AAACLRSZ	alcazars
AAACLRTZ	Alcatraz
AAACMRSS	macassar
	marascas
AAACNOSV	Casanova
AAACNRSV	caravans
AAACNSTT	cantatas
AAACRSWY	caraways
AAACSSSV	cassavas
AAACSTWY	castaway
AAADDORV	Vadodara
AAADELMS	alamedas
	salaamed
AAADEMNN	Mandaean
AAADEMSV	Sama-Veda
AAADENPS	Pasadena
AAADENTV	vanadate
AAADEPRT	tapadera
AAADFRSY	faradays
AAADGGHH	haggadah
AAADGGHS	haggadas
AAADGIMM	gammadia
AAADGINU	Guadiana
AAADGLMY	amygdala
AAADGLNN	Nagaland
AAADHHLV	havdalah
AAADHIMN	Mahanadi
AAADHKNR	Kandahar
AAADHMRS	madrasah
AAADIKLS	Kalidasa
AAADILMT	Dalmatia
AAADILRU	adularia
AAADIMNY	adynamia
AAADIRST	radiatas
AAADJKRT	Djakarta
AAADKNNS	Sandakan
AAADKRRV	aardvark
AAADLLLN	La-La land
AAADLMNS	mandalas
AAADLMNY	Mandalay
AAADLNRS	Saarland
AAADMNOR	Maradona
AAADMNST	adamants
AAADMNTU	tamandua
AAADMRUY	Amu Darya
AAADNSTZ	Zaanstad
AAADSWYY	awaydays
AAAEGNPP	appanage
AAAEGNPS	apanages
AAAEHLMT	Amalthea
AAAEHLST	althaeas
AAAEHMNT	anathema
AAAEHNPS	anaphase
AAAEIMRV	Ave Maria
AAAEKKRT	karateka
AAAEKLLV	Kalevala
AAAEKMNU	Mauna Kea
AAAEKNTW	Te Kanawa
AAAEKTWY	takeaway
AAAELMMN	analemma
AAAELRTV	lavatera
AAAEMTTV	Tamatave
AAAENNSS	ananases
AAAENPRV	paravane
AAAENPST	anapaest
AAAEOORT	Aotearoa
AAAERSWY	areaways
AAAERTWY	tearaway
AAAFFLLS	alfalfas
AAAFHHRT	haftarah
AAAFINST	fantasia
AAAFINUV	avifauna
AAAFIRST	ratafias
AAAFLLWY	fallaway
AAAGGJLN	Ganga jal
AAAGGLLN	galangal
AAAGHINN	Ghanaian
AAAGHINR	hiragana
AAAGHIPR	agraphia
AAAGHNNT	agnathan
AAAGHNST	ataghans
AAAGHNTY	yataghan
AAAGIKNS	Nagasaki
AAAGILNT	Galatian
AAAGILRU	La Guaira
AAAGINRR	agrarian
AAAGINSZ	gazanias
AAAGISSS	assagais
AAAGJLNR	La Granja
AAAGJMNR	Jamnagar
AAAGJORY	raja yoga
AAAGKNNO	Okanagan
AAAGKRSV	Gavaskar
AAAGLMMS	amalgams
AAAGLMSY	Malagasy
AAAGLNRW	Warangal
AAAGLNSS	lasagnas
AAAGLNTV	galavant
AAAGLRST	astragal
AAAGMNNN	Namangan
AAAGMNRS	anagrams
	Samarang
AAAGMNRT	Ramat Gan
AAAGMORS	Saramago
AAAGNPRS	parasang
AAAGNRRS	ngararas
AAAGNRTU	Tauranga
AAAGORZZ	Zaragoza
AAAGPRUY	Paraguay
AAAHHITW	Hiawatha
AAAHHKLS	halakhas
AAAHHLSV	halavahs
AAAHHPRS	parashah
AAAHHSTT	tatahash
AAAHHTWY	Hathaway
AAAHIINW	Hawaiian
AAAHIKLR	Kalahari
AAAHIKSW	kahawais
AAAHILPS	Ali Pasha
AAAHIMNR	maharani
AAAHIMRT	hamartia
	Mata Hari
AAAHIMRV	Mahavira
AAAHINNY	Hinayana
AAAHJLMT	Taj Mahal
AAAHLLLV	Valhalla
AAAHLLLW	Walhalla
AAAHLLMR	Ramallah
AAAHMMST	mahatmas
AAAHMNOR	Maranhão
AAAHMNRT	amaranth
AAAHMSST	tamashas
AAAHNNSV	savannah
AAAHNOPR	anaphora
AAAHNPPR	Harappan
AAAHRSTW	waratahs
AAAHSWWY	washaway
AAAIINPR	apiarian
AAAIJNTU	Tia Juana
AAAIKKSW	Kawasaki
AAAIKMSY	Yamasaki
AAAIKNTY	Antakiya
AAAILLMR	malarial
AAAILLPT	palatial
AAAILMNR	malarian
AAAILMNW	Malawian
AAAILMRT	Altamira
AAAILMSV	malvasia
AAAILMSY	Malaysia
AAAILNOT	Anatolia
AAAILNST	Alsatian
AAAILPRX	paraxial
AAAILRSU	Laurasia
AAAIMMST	miasmata
AAAIMNOR	Marianao
AAAIMNOZ	Amazonia
AAAIMNST	amanitas
	Tasmania
AAAIMRST	Sarmatia
AAAIMRTV	Amravati
AAAINNST	Antisana
AAAINNTZ	Tanzania
AAAINOPR	paranoia
AAAINQRU	aquarian
AAAINRSV	Varanasi
AAAIPSSV	piassava
AAAJMNRU	Ramanuja
AAAJPRUY	Jayapura
AAAKKMRU	Kamakura
AAAKKORT	Krakatoa
AAAKLWWY	walkaway
AAAKMNRS	namaskar
AAAKMTUU	kaumatua
AAAKNNRS	Arkansan

AAAKNRSS Arkansas
AAAKOSWY soakaway
AAALLPRX parallax
AAALLPST palatals
AAALMNOU Mauna Loa
AAALMNTZ Mazatlán
AAALNNST lantanas
AAALNPRT rataplan
AAALNRTT tarlatan
AAALRRSY arrayals
AAAMMPRS mamparas
AAAMNOPR panorama
AAAMNOSZ Amazonas
AAAMNRRY yarraman
AAAMNRST marantas
AAAMNSSS Manassas
AAAMNSTZ Matanzas
AAAMORST tamaraos
AAAMOTTU automata
AAAMRSTU tamaraus
AAAMRTTU traumata
AAANNPRU Anapurna
AAANNSSV savannas
AAANOPRZ parazoan
AAANQTUU aquanaut
AAANRSTT tantaras
AAANSTXY Astyanax
AAAORSWY soaraway
AAAPPRST apparats
AAAPQRTU paraquat
AAAPSTTU taupatas
AAARSTTT ratatats
AAARSTTU tuataras
AABBCDEG cabbaged
AABBCDRS scabbard
AABBCEGS cabbages
AABBCEIS abbacies
AABBCEKR bareback
AABBCEKT backbeat
AABBCINR barbican
AABBCIRR barbaric
AABBCIST sabbatic
AABBDENS baseband
AABBDHIU Abu Dhabi
AABBDORS Barbados
AABBEELR bearable
AABBEELT beatable
AABBEGNS beanbags
AABBEILL bailable
AABBEKLN bankable
AABBELLM blamable
AABBELLS baseball
AABBELOS baalebos
AABBELRY bearably
AABBELTY Table Bay
AABBHKSU babushka
AABBHSST sabbaths
AABBIILL bilabial
AABBILRT barbital
AABBIRSU babirusa
AABBIRSY Baybars I
AABBLLMY blamably
AABBOORR Bora Bora
AABBSSSU babassus
AABCCEHK backache
AABCCEIR Beccaria
AABCCELS cascabel
AABCCERT braccate
AABCCHKS cashback
AABCCHKT backchat
AABCCHNT bacchant
AABCCIMR carbamic
AABCCINN cannabic
AABCCKKP backpack
AABCCKLP blackcap
AABCCKLW clawback
AABCCMOT catacomb
AABCCMOY maccaboy
AABCDEIN abidance
AABCDEIO Boadicea
AABCDEIT abdicate
AABCDEKT backdate
AABCDELL caballed
AABCDELN balanced
AABCDHKN backhand
AABCDHKR hardback
AABCDIIS diabasic
AABCDIMO Cambodia
AABCDIRS carabids
AABCDKRW backward
drawback
AABCDKRY backyard
AABCDLRS Carlsbad
AABCEEFL faceable
AABCEELT Albacete
AABCEENY abeyance
AABCEERT acerbate
AABCEFRS facebars
AABCEGOT cabotage
AABCEHLS cashable
AABCEHMS ambaches
AABCEHNR barchane
AABCEHRU Auerbach
AABCEILM amicable
AABCEIMN ambiance
AABCEINR carabine
AABCEIRT bacteria
AABCEKLM clambake
AABCEKLP packable
AABCEKLR lacebark
AABCEKLS Black Sea
sackable
AABCEKST backseat
AABCELLL callable
AABCELLN Ballance
AABCELLP placable
AABCELLS scalable
AABCELNR balancer
barnacle
AABCELNS balances
AABCELOR albacore
AABCELPS spacelab
AABCELRT bracteal
cartable
AABCELST castable
AABCELSU causable
AABCELWY cableway
AABCEMRV vambrace
AABCEMSS ambsaces
AABCENRR Canberra
AABCERST abreacts
bearcats
cabarets
AABCERTT cabretta
AABCESSU abacuses
AABCFHKL halfback
AABCFIIL bifacial
AABCFKLL fallback
AABCFKST fastback
fatbacks
AABCGIMO cambogia
AABCGKRY grayback
AABCHILR brachial
AABCHINR branchia
AABCHKLS backlash
AABCHKSW backwash
AABCHLOO coolabah
AABCHMRY chambray
AABCHNNU Buchanan
AABCHNRS barchans
AABCIILR biracial
AABCIILS basilica
AABCIINR brainiac
AABCIKLT tailback
AABCILLR bacillar
cabrilla
AABCILMS balsamic
cabalism
AABCILMY amicably
AABCILNN cannibal
AABCILNO anabolic
AABCILST basaltic
cabalist
AABCINNN cannabin
AABCINNO Baconian
AABCINNR cinnabar
AABCINNS cannabis
AABCINRS carabins
AABCINRT Bactrian
AABCINSU banausic
AABCIRSS brassica
AABCISSS abscissa
AABCISTX taxicabs
AABCKKLT talkback
AABCKLNO loanback
AABCKLNY claybank
AABCKLPY playback
AABCKLRT black art
AABCKNPS snapback
AABCKPRT bratpack
AABCKPSY paybacks
AABCKRRS barracks
AABCKSTY backstay
AABCKSWY swayback
AABCLLPY placably
AABCLLSY scalably

AABCLNTY blatancy
AABCLRRY carbaryl
AABCNORR barranco
AABCNOSU Casaubon
AABCOORS Sorocaba
AABCORST acrobats
AABCOSTT catboats
AABCRSTT abstract
AABDDEET deadbeat
AABDDEGN bandaged
AABDDEHL baldhead
AABDDEHN headband
AABDDINZ zindabad
AABDDLNS badlands
Bad Lands
AABDDMRU murdabad
AABDEELR readable
AABDEELT dateable
AABDEELV evadable
AABDEELW wadeable
AABDEEMN endameba
AABDEERR Aberdare
AABDEERT teabread
AABDEERY bayadere
AABDEGHN headbang
AABDEGIN badinage
AABDEGLR gradable
AABDEGMS gambades
AABDEGNS bandages
AABDEGRR barraged
AABDEHKN Bankhead
AABDEHKR hardbake
AABDEIOU aboideau
AABDEISS diabases
AABDEJLL djellaba
AABDEKRY daybreak
AABDEKSW dawbakes
AABDELLS ballades
Sabadell
AABDELLU laudable
AABDELMN damnable
AABDELOR adorable
AABDELPR drapable
AABDELPT baldpate
AABDELRT tradable
AABDELRW drawable
AABDELRY readably
AABDEMNS beadsman
AABDENST Banstead
AABDENTU unabated
AABDENUX bandeaux
AABDENVW waveband
AABDEORS seaboard
AABDERRS abraders
AABDFHIT bad faith
AABDFHLN fahlband
AABDGHNS handbags
AABDGHOT Godthaab
AABDGHOY Bodh Gaya
AABDGINR abrading
AABDGLNR landgrab
AABDGMOS gambados
AABDGNOV vagabond
AABDGNSS sandbags
AABDGORR garboard
AABDGOTU gadabout
AABDHLLN handball
AABDHLLR hardball
AABDHLLU Abdullah
AABDHNST hatbands
AABDHRSU bahadurs
subahdar
AABDHRUY Buraydah
AABDIILR biradial
AABDIILS basidial
AABDIKRS bidarkas
AABDIMRS barmaids
AABDINNR rainband
AABDINNU Danubian
AABDINST tabanids
AABDINVY Dvina Bay
AABDKNNS sandbank
AABDLLRY balladry
AABDLLUY laudably
AABDLMNU labdanum
AABDLMNY damnably
AABDLMRU adumbral
AABDLOOT boatload
AABDLOPR lapboard
AABDLORR labrador
larboard
AABDLORY adorably
AABDLRSV Svalbard
AABDLRSW bradawls
AABDMNNS bandsman
AABDMNRS armbands
AABDNNOS abandons
AABDNNTU abundant
AABDNORR Barnardo
AABDNPSS passband
AABDNRRY barnyard
AABDORSV bravados
AABDORWY broadway
AABDRRSS brassard
AABDRRSW drawbars
AABDRSST bastards
AABDRSSU subadars
AABDRSTY bastardy
AABEEFLN fleabane
AABEEGGL gageable
AABEEGKR breakage
AABEEGNT abnegate
AABEEHLL healable
AABEEHLR hearable
AABEEHLT hateable
AABEEHMR harambee
AABEEKLT takeable
AABEELLS leasable
saleable
sealable
AABEELMN amenable
nameable
AABEELMT tameable
AABEELPR reapable
AABEELRS erasable
AABEELRT rateable
tearable
AABEELRW wearable
AABEELST eatables
AABEELSV saveable
AABEEMNO amoebean
AABEEMNT entameba
AABEEMPR abampere
AABEENNW wannabee
AABEENOR anaerobe
AABEERSZ zareebas
AABEERTT trabeate
AABEFGLS fleabags
AABEFHKL halfbeak
AABEFLLL flabella
AABEFLMR farmable
framable
AABEFLMU flambeau
AABEFLSY False Bay
AABEFNSS fanbases
AABEGGGS baggages
AABEGGLY gageably
AABEGILN gainable
AABEGLLL glabella
AABEGLLM ballgame
AABEGLNW gnawable
AABEGLRS algebras
AABEGLRT glabrate
AABEGLRU arguable
Balaguer
AABEGMNR bargeman
AABEGMNY mangabey
AABEGMRT bregmata
AABEGMTT gambetta
AABEGNOR baronage
AABEGORT abrogate
AABEGOST sabotage
AABEGRRS barrages
AABEHIMS Maebashi
AABEHIRR herbaria
AABEHJLL jellabah
AABEHKLS shakable
AABEHLMS shamable
AABEHLPS shapable
AABEHLPT alphabet
AABEHLRS sharable
AABEHLSV shavable
AABEHLSW washable
AABEHMRS Habermas
AABEILLM mailable
AABEILLS isabella
sailable
AABEILRS Rabelais
raisable
AABEILRV variable
AABEILST labiates
satiable
AABEILTV ablative
AABEIMRS ambaries
AABEIMRU Mirabeau
AABEINST basanite

AABEIOTU	aboiteau
AABEIRST	Sabatier
AABEIRSV	abrasive
AABEIRTU	aubretia
	aubrieta
AABEISST	abatises
AABEISUV	Beauvais
AABEJLLS	jellabas
AABEJMSY	James Bay
AABEJMUX	jambeaux
AABEKLLS	slakable
AABEKLLT	talkable
AABEKLLW	walkable
AABEKMNR	brakeman
AABEKNRS	Nebraska
AABEKOTU	Abeokuta
AABEKRRS	baresark
AABEKRSY	kerbayas
AABELLMR	Marbella
AABELLMT	meatball
AABELLNO	loanable
AABELLPP	palpable
AABELLPS	lapsable
AABELLPY	playable
AABELLRS	earballs
AABELLSV	salvable
AABELLSY	saleably
AABELLUV	valuable
AABELMNY	amenably
AABELMPP	mappable
AABELMST	blastema
	lambaste
AABELMSU	amusable
AABELMTU	ambulate
AABELNNT	tannable
AABELNOS	abalones
AABELNOT	atonable
AABELNPS	anableps
AABELNRT	Albertan
AABELNRY	balneary
AABELNSS	banselas
AABELORR	arboreal
AABELOSV	lavaboes
AABELOVW	avowable
AABELPPT	tappable
AABELPRS	parables
	parsable
	sparable
AABELPSS	passable
AABELRST	arbalest
AABELRTT	Barletta
AABELRTY	betrayal
	rateably
AABELSTT	abettals
	statable
	tastable
AABELSTU	tableaus
AABELSTW	wastable
AABELSTX	taxables
AABELSWY	swayable
AABELTTU	tabulate
AABELTUX	tableaux
AABEMNRT	Bramante
AABEMOSW	Soembawa
AABENNSW	wannabes
AABENRRT	aberrant
AABENRST	ratsbane
	Strabane
AABEORRT	arboreta
AABEOSSU	oubaases
AABERSSU	subareas
AABFILUX	fabliaux
AABFLLST	fastball
AABFLOTT	faltboat
	flatboat
AABGGGNN	gangbang
AABGGRRT	braggart
AABGHINS	abashing
AABGHKRS	shagbark
AABGIILS	abigails
AABGIINR	braaiing
AABGILMS	mailbags
AABGILNT	ablating
	bangtail
AABGILRU	Bulgaria
AABGIMNS	sambaing
AABGINRS	bargains
AABGLLLO	goalball
AABGLLRY	ballyrag
AABGLMNU	galbanum
AABGLNOW	bangalow
AABGLRUY	arguably
AABGMORR	barogram
AABGNNOU	Nobunaga
AABGNORZ	garbanzo
AABHHKLS	Balkhash
AABHHORU	brouhaha
AABHIIKS	Baisakhi
AABHIINR	Bahraini
AABHIINU	bauhinia
AABHILLR	hairball
AABHILNN	Hannibal
AABHILTU	habitual
AABHILTY	Bat Hayil
AABHIMNR	Brahmani
AABHINTT	habitant
AABHISTT	habitats
AABHKKKU	Habakkuk
AABHKNRS	barkhans
AABHKNUY	Ayub Khan
AABHMMOT	Mmabatho
AABHMSWY	Byam Shaw
AABHNOTU	autobahn
AABHORRT	Arbroath
AABIIJLT	jailbait
AABIILNS	Basilian
AABIILRS	Brasília
AABIIMNN	Namibian
AABIKLMS	kabalism
AABIKLNU	Kinabalu
AABIKLST	kabalist
AABIKNSS	banksias
AABIKOSS	Bokassa I
AABILLLY	labially
AABILLRS	barillas
AABILLST	ballista
AABILMNS	bailsman
AABILMNU	bimanual
AABILNNU	biannual
AABILNOR	baronial
AABILNOT	ablation
AABILNRU	binaural
AABILNTY	banality
AABILOST	sailboat
AABILRRT	arbitral
AABILRST	arbalist
AABILRSY	basilary
AABILRVY	variably
AABILSTY	satiably
AABIMMRS	marimbas
AABIMNOT	Manitoba
AABIMNRU	manubria
AABIMORS	ambrosia
AABIMRSU	simaruba
AABINNPR	brainpan
AABINORS	abrasion
AABINRTT	Brattain
AABINRTZ	bartizan
AABINRZZ	Zanzibar
AABINSST	abstains
AABIORST	airboats
AABIORSV	bavarois
AABIORTT	abattoir
AABIOSSY	bioassay
AABIOSTV	Boa Vista
AABIRSST	baristas
	bartsias
AABIRTUY	rubaiyat
AABISTUZ	zaibatsu
AABJLPRU	Jabalpur
AABJMRST	jambarts
AABJNOOS	Obasanjo
AABKLLPR	ballpark
AABKMNNS	banksman
AABKOOSZ	bazookas
AABKOPRS	soapbark
AABKORTU	Kotabaru
AABLLMOR	balmoral
AABLLPPY	palpably
AABLLSST	ballasts
AABLLSTU	blastula
AABLLSVY	salvably
AABLLUVY	valuably
AABLMNOR	abnormal
AABLMNTU	ambulant
AABLMOST	blastoma
AABLMSST	lambasts
AABLNORW	Bonar Law
AABLORST	ablators
AABLORTY	altar boy
AABLOTUY	layabout
AABLOUWY	Bulawayo
AABLPSSY	passably
AABLRRTU	Barrault
AABLSTTU	abuttals
AABMMOSU	abomasum

AABMNOTW batwoman
AABMNRTU rambutan
AABMORSU marabous
AABMORTU marabout
tamboura
AABNNORR Ann Arbor
AABNNOST absonant
AABNNOSZ bonanzas
AABNOSSY sabayons
AABNOSTW Botswana
AABNRRUZ Zurbarán
AABORRRT barrator
AABORRSS rasboras
AABORSTT barostat
AABRRRTY barratry
AABRRSST brassart
AACCCFIO focaccia
AACCCHHU cachucha
AACCCIRR Carracci
AACCCRUY accuracy
AACCDDES cascaded
AACCDEIM academic
AACCDELO accolade
AACCDERR racecard
AACCDESS cascades
saccades
AACCDHIR characid
AACCDIRS cardiacs
AACCDOVY advocacy
AACCEENT cetacean
AACCEFLO coalface
AACCEHIX cachexia
AACCEILN calcanei
AACCEILU aciculae
AACCEIRR cercaria
AACCELOR caracole
AACCELTY calycate
AACCEMNU cumacean
AACCENRT carcanet
AACCENTU acutance
AACCERSS carcases
AACCERTU accurate
AACCFILR farcical
AACCFLTU calctufa
AACCGILT galactic
AACCHILP pachalic
AACCHINR anarchic
characin
AACCHISV viscacha
AACCHIVZ vizcacha
AACCHLLT catchall
AACCHLNS clachans
AACCHLOR charcoal
AACCHLOT cachalot
AACCHLRS clarsach
AACCHMNO coachman
AACCHMPS champacs
AACCHOUY Ayacucho
AACCIINV vaccinia
AACCIIST sciatica
AACCIITT Titicaca
AACCIKMN Mackinac
AACCILMS acclaims
AACCILNU Culiacán
AACCILNV vaccinal
AACCILRU acicular
AACCILTT tactical
AACCIMOS Masaccio
AACCINRT Carnatic
AACCIORS cariocas
AACCIPRT apractic
AACCIPTY capacity
AACCIRTY caryatic
AACCJKRS carjacks
AACCJKRW crackjaw
AACCJORU carcajou
AACCKKPS packsack
AACCKLPS calpacks
AACCKRRS carracks
AACCLLST catcalls
AACCLOPS polaccas
AACCLOPU Acapulco
AACCLORS caracols
AACCLPRS calcspar
AACCLRSU caraculs
saccular
AACCLSSU accusals
AACCLTTU Calcutta
AACCOPRS ascocarp
AACCOSTT staccato
toccatas
AACCSSUU Caucasus
AACDDEHI acidhead
AACDDEIL daedalic
AACDDENV advanced
AACDDETU caudated
AACDDINR radicand
AACDDINS candidas
AACDEEHH headache
AACDEEHR headrace
AACDEEHS headcase
AACDEELS escalade
AACDEEMS academes
AACDEEPS escapade
AACDEEST caseated
AACDEETT acetated
AACDEGKP packaged
AACDEHHY headachy
AACDEHIN hacienda
AACDEHLP cephalad
AACDEHMR drachmae
AACDEHMS chamades
AACDEHRS charades
AACDEHRT cathedra
AACDEHST catheads
AACDEHTT attached
AACDEILO Laodicea
AACDEILS alcaides
sidalcea
AACDEIMN maenadic
AACDEIMS camisade
AACDEIMT acetamid
AACDEINR radiance
AACDEJNT adjacent
AACDEKNP pancaked
AACDEKTT attacked
AACDELLN canalled
AACDELLS alcaldes
AACDELMN manacled
AACDELNR calendar
Cardenal
landrace
AACDELNS candelas
AACDELNV valanced
AACDELOS caseload
AACDELPT placated
AACDELRS calderas
AACDELSS scalades
AACDELTT lactated
AACDEMRY Macready
AACDENRS Cárdenas
AACDENRV advancer
AACDENSV advances
AACDENSZ cadenzas
AACDEOTU autocade
AACDEOTV advocate
AACDEQUY adequacy
AACDERST cadaster
cadastre
AACDERSV cadavers
AACDERTU arcuated
AACDETTU actuated
AACDGGHI haggadic
AACDGINR carangid
cardigan
AACDHHKR hardhack
AACDHHNS shadchan
AACDHHRS shadrach
AACDHIIS dichasia
AACDHILR diarchal
AACDHIMR chadarim
AACDHINP handicap
AACDHINR arachnid
AACDHKRT hardtack
AACDHLOT cathodal
AACDHLRY charlady
dyarchal
AACDHMRS drachmas
AACDHNRT handcart
AACDHPRS crashpad
AACDIINS ascidian
AACDIIRT Adriatic
AACDIKRZ Karadžić
AACDILLP palladic
AACDILMT dalmatic
AACDILMU caladium
AACDILNO diaconal
AACDILNR cardinal
AACDILNU dulciana
AACDILNV vandalic
AACDILOZ zodiacal
AACDILRR railcard
AACDILRS radicals
AACDIMNY adynamic
cyanamid
AACDIMOS camisado

AACDIMRT dramatic
AACDINRY radiancy
AACDINST antacids
AACDIOTU autacoid
AACDIRSS ascarids
AACDIRTY caryatid
AACDITUY audacity
AACDJKSW jackdaws
AACDJQRU jacquard
AACDKLNU Auckland
AACDLLUY caudally
AACDLNRT Cartland
AACDLNSS scandals
AACDLORT cartload
AACDLOSS scalados
AACDLOSV calvados
AACDLPRS placards
AACDMMOR cardamom
AACDMMRU cardamum
AACDMNOR cardamon
AACDMSSU Damascus
AACDOORV Odovacar
AACDOOSV avocados
AACDORRT cartroad
AACDPRSU crapauds
AACEEFIT facetiae
AACEEFLP paleface
AACEEGLV cleavage
AACEEGNR carageen
AACEEGNY gynaecea
AACEEGRS acreages
AACEEHLR Heraclea
AACEEHLT leachate
AACEEHRS earaches
AACEEHRT tracheae
AACEEIMT emaciate
AACEEINN encaenia
AACEEIRT acierate
AACEEKST teacakes
AACEELNS anelaces
AACEELRT lacerate
AACEELST escalate
AACEELTU aculeate
Le Cateau
AACEEMNS Maecenas
AACEEMRT macerate
AACEEMSS amesaces
AACEEMST casemate
AACEENNT catenane
AACEENRS cesarean
AACEENTT catenate
AACEEPSS seascape
AACEEPST East Cape
AACEERSU caesurae
AACEERTV acervate
AACEESST caseates
AACEESTT acetates
AACEETUV evacuate
AACEETVX excavate
AACEFFIN affiance
AACEFILM facemail
AACEFILT califate
AACEFIST fasciate
AACEFLLU falculae
AACEFRRS carfares
AACEFRSX carfaxes
AACEFRTT artefact
AACEGHRT Carthage
AACEGILN angelica
AACEGILT glaciate
AACEGINR canaigre
AACEGINY gynaecia
AACEGIRR carriage
AACEGIRV vicarage
AACEGKPR packager
AACEGKPS packages
AACEGLSS scalages
AACEGMRU Camargue
AACEGMUY Camagüey
AACEGNRS caganers
AACEGTTT Cattegat
AACEHILL achillea
heliacal
AACEHILN achenial
AACEHILP phacelia
AACEHIMR chimaera
AACEHIMT haematic
AACEHINS China Sea
AACEHIPT hepatica
AACEHIRS archaise
AACEHIRZ archaize
AACEHLMN La Manche
AACEHLNU eulachan
AACEHLPS acalephs
AACEHLRT tracheal
AACEHLRX exarchal
AACEHLSS calashes
AACEHLST alcahest
AACEHMRS marchesa
AACEHMST schemata
AACEHNPS panaches
AACEHPSU chapeaus
AACEHPUX chapeaux
AACEHRTT attacher
reattach
AACEHSTT attaches
AACEHSTU chateaus
AACEHTUX chateaux
AACEIINT actiniae
AACEIKMT kamacite
AACEILLM camellia
AACEILLN alliance
canaille
AACEILMN analcime
calamine
AACEILMT calamite
AACEILNP Palencia
AACEILNS canalise
AACEILNT Alicante
analcite
AACEILNU acauline
AACEILNV valencia
valiance
AACEILNZ canalize
AACEILOP alopecia
AACEILRT tailrace
AACEILRV cavalier
AACEIMNR American
AACEIMNS amnesiac
AACEIMTT catamite
AACEINNO Oceanian
AACEINNV Avicenna
AACEINPZ Piacenza
AACEINRS canaries
cesarian
AACEINRT carinate
craniate
AACEINRV variance
AACEINST estancia
AACEINTV cavatine
AACEIOPR capoeira
AACEIPPS papacies
AACEIPRS airspace
AACEIPSS capiases
AACEIPTT apatetic
capitate
AACEIRSV caviares
AACEITTV activate
AACEKKLW cakewalk
AACEKNPS pancakes
AACEKOST oatcakes
AACEKRTT attacker
AACELLOT allocate
AACELLST lacteals
AACELLTY alleycat
AACELMNP placeman
AACELMNS manacles
AACELMRS caramels
ceramals
macerals
AACELMTU maculate
AACELNNO anconeal
AACELNNU cannulae
AACELNPR parlance
AACELNPT placenta
AACELNPY anyplace
AACELNRT lacerant
AACELNRY arcanely
AACELNST analects
AACELNSV valances
AACELNTU canulate
tenacula
AACELORS Coral Sea
AACELOST cataloes
AACELOSU acaulose
AACELPRS carpales
AACELPST placates
AACELPSU scapulae
AACELRSS scalares
AACELRSU caesural
AACELRSV caravels
AACELRWY clearway
AACELSST lactases
AACELSTT lactates
AACELSTY catalyse
AACELTTY cattleya

AACELTYZ catalyze
AACEMNPS spaceman
AACEMQSU macaques
AACEMRSS massacre
AACENNOR Anacreon
AACENPRS pancreas
AACENPSU saucepan
AACENPTT pancetta
AACENRST canaster
caterans
AACENRTT reactant
AACENRTY catenary
AACENRVZ czarevna
AACENSSV canvases
AACENSTY cyanates
AACENTUV evacuant
AACEOPST peacoats
AACEORSU araceous
AACEORTV caveator
AACEOSST seacoast
AACEPSWY paceways
AACERRRS Carreras
AACERRTU arcature
AACERSSU caesuras
AACERSSZ sazeracs
AACERSTT castrate
teacarts
AACERSWY raceways
AACERTTT tractate
AACESTTU actuates
AACESUWY causeway
AACESUXY Aux Cayes
AACFFGHR Chargaff
AACFHMST camshaft
AACFILLY facially
AACFINST fanatics
AACFIRRT aircraft
AACFIRST frascati
AACFIRTT artifact
AACFJKLP flapjack
AACFKLPT flatpack
AACFLLST catfalls
AACFLNNR Lanfranc
AACFLRST fractals
AACGGINO anagogic
AACGHHNS Changsha
AACGHLLO agalloch
AACGHNNN Nanchang
AACGHOPZ gazpacho
AACGHORU guacharo
AACGIILN Galician
AACGIILR Cagliari
AACGIIMN magician
AACGILLN gallican
AACGILLU Caligula
AACGILNN Anglican
canaling
AACGILNO analogic
AACGILNV galvanic
AACGILOR Agricola
AACGILOU guaiacol
AACGILOX coxalgia
AACGILRT tragical
AACGIMMT magmatic
AACGIMNN manganic
AACGIMNP campaign
AACGIMNS Mascagni
AACGIMOP apogamic
AACGIMRR margaric
AACGIMUU guaiacum
AACGINOT contagia
AACGINTV vacating
AACGISTY sagacity
AACGLMOU glaucoma
AACGLOST catalogs
AACGMNRS cragsman
AACGNOSU guanacos
AACGNRVY vagrancy
AACHHILR rhachial
AACHHIMS mashiach
AACHHKNU Chanukah
AACHHKRS charkhas
AACHHLLS challahs
AACHHTWY hatchway
AACHIIMR mariachi
AACHIKNS kachinas
AACHILLR rachilla
AACHILMS chiasmal
AACHILMT thalamic
AACHILNP chaplain
AACHILOU Coahuila
AACHILPS calipash
pashalic
AACHILRV archival
AACHIMNN chainman
AACHIMNR chairman
AACHIMNS shamanic
AACHIMNZ chazanim
AACHIMRR armchair
AACHIMRS archaism
charisma
machairs
AACHIMSS chiasmas
AACHINNO Noachian
AACHINRY Hyrcania
AACHINSW chainsaw
AACHIOTU Ouachita
AACHIPRS charpais
AACHIPSS aphasics
AACHIPST chapatis
AACHIPTT chapatti
AACHIRSS Issachar
AACHIRST archaist
citharas
AACHKKOZ kazachok
AACHKMPS champaks
AACHKNSW hacksawn
AACHKRSY hayracks
AACHKSSW hacksaws
AACHKSTY haystack
AACHLMNO monachal
AACHLMOS chloasma
AACHLPPS chappals
AACHLSTU calathus
AACHMMNO Macmahon
AACHMNOU Ancohuma
AACHMNTW watchman
AACHMNUY naumachy
AACHMORT achromat
trachoma
AACHMPRY pharmacy
AACHMSSY yashmacs
AACHNNUW Wanchüan
AACHNPRS sarpanch
AACHNRST trashcan
AACHNSSU anchusas
AACHNSTU acanthus
AACHOPPR approach
AACHRSWY archways
AACHRTUY autarchy
AACIILMO maiolica
AACIILRT iatrical
AACIILRV vicarial
AACIILTV viatical
AACIINST actinias
AACIIRSV viscaria
AACIJLMO majolica
AACIJNOP japonica
AACIKLMS mailsack
AACIKLRS clarkias
AACIKMNW mackinaw
AACIKNNS canakins
AACIKRTU autarkic
AACILLLY laically
AACILLMR lacrimal
AACILLMT climatal
AACILLPY apically
AACILLRY racially
AACILMNT calamint
claimant
AACILMRS mailcars
AACILMTY calamity
AACILNNO Laconian
AACILNOR Carniola
Carolina
AACILNOY Lycaonia
AACILNRV carnival
AACILNTT Atlantic
tantalic
AACILNTU nautical
AACILNTY analytic
AACILNVY valiancy
AACILOTT coattail
tailcoat
AACILPRU piacular
AACILPST aplastic
capitals
AACILPSZ capsizal
AACILPTU capitula
AACILPTY atypical
AACILRRS railcars
AACILRTY alacrity
AACILRUU auricula
AACILSTT statical
AACILSTY salacity
AACIMMNO ammoniac

AACIMMRS	marasmic
AACIMNOR	macaroni
	Marciano
	marocain
AACIMNPS	Campinas
AACIMORR	Armorica
AACIMORS	Cimarosa
AACIMORT	aromatic
AACIMPRU	Apurimac
AACIMRST	Sarmatic
AACINNST	cantinas
AACINOPR	paranoic
AACINORS	ocarinas
AACINORT	Croatian
	raincoat
AACINOTV	Octavian
	vacation
AACINPST	captains
AACINQTU	acquaint
AACINRSZ	czarinas
AACINSSU	Ascanius
AACINSTZ	stanzaic
AACIPRST	aspartic
AACIPRTY	rapacity
AACIQSTU	aquatics
AACIRRTT	tartaric
AACIRSSU	Siracusa
AACIRSTT	castrati
AACIRTZZ	czaritza
AACJKLPS	slapjack
AACJKOOR	jackaroo
AACJKSTY	jackstay
AACKKNPS	knapsack
AACKLOWY	lockaway
AACKLSTW	catwalks
AACKMNRT	trackman
AACKMNST	tacksman
AACKNRSS	ransacks
AACKORWY	rockaway
AACKPRST	ratpacks
AACLLMOR	Mallorca
AACLLMRY	lacrymal
AACLLNRY	carnally
AACLLNST	callants
AACLLRRY	carryall
AACLLRSY	rascally
AACLLSUY	casually
	causally
AACLLTUY	actually
AACLMNNS	clansman
AACLMOTU	comatula
AACLMRRU	macrural
AACLNNOT	cantonal
AACLNNOW	canon law
AACLNNRU	cannular
AACLNNSU	cannulas
AACLNOPR	coplanar
AACLNORU	La Coruña
AACLNRSU	lacunars
AACLNRUY	lacunary
AACLNTVY	vacantly
AACLORRU	oracular
AACLORSU	carousal
AACLORUV	vacuolar
AACLPPRT	claptrap
AACLPRST	caltraps
AACLPRSU	scapular
AACLPRTY	calyptra
AACLPSSU	scapulas
AACLPSTY	playacts
AACLPTTU	catapult
AACLRSUV	vascular
AACLSTTY	catalyst
AACLSTUY	casualty
AACMNOOR	macaroon
AACMNPRY	rampancy
AACMNRRU	macruran
AACMORRS	camorras
AACMORSS	sarcomas
AACMRRST	tramcars
AACNNOSZ	canzonas
AACNPSST	capstans
AACNRSTT	transact
AACNRSTU	curtanas
AACOPPRS	apocarps
AACOPRSU	acarpous
AACOPSTV	postcava
AACORRTV	varactor
AACORSTT	castrato
AACORTTU	actuator
	autocrat
AACPSSTW	catspaws
AACRSTTT	attracts
AACSTUWY	cutaways
AADDDEEH	deadhead
AADDDGNR	granddad
AADDEEIL	Adelaide
AADDEELT	dealated
AADDEFLL	deadfall
AADDEGGR	aggraded
AADDEGRT	gradated
AADDEHHS	hadedahs
AADDEHLN	headland
AADDEHMN	handmade
AADDEHRW	headward
AADDEHRZ	hazarded
AADDEILR	Daladier
AADDEILS	alidades
AADDEINS	Danaides
AADDEIRT	radiated
AADDEKMS	damasked
AADDELSU	Daedalus
AADDELTU	adulated
AADDEMNT	mandated
AADDEMRU	marauded
AADDEMRY	daydream
AADDGNRS	grandads
AADDGNRU	graduand
AADDHILU	Id-ul-Adha
AADDHIMN	handmaid
AADDIIKS	didakais
AADDISST	dadaists
AADDLLNY	landlady
AADDLNRW	landward
AADDNRST	standard
AADDNRSU	Dardanus
AADDNSVV	dvandvas
AADDRSST	dastards
AADEEGHR	headgear
AADEEGHT	headgate
AADEEGLR	laagered
AADEEGLT	galeated
AADEEGMN	endamage
AADEEGNR	gadarene
AADEEGRV	averaged
AADEEIRT	eradiate
AADEEKNW	awakened
AADEELMR	de la Mare
AADEELNN	annealed
AADEELPP	appealed
AADEELRV	de Valera
AADEELRW	Delaware
AADEEMNR	Maeander
AADEEMNT	emanated
AADEEMOT	oedemata
AADEEMRR	demerara
AADEENPT	tapenade
AADEENRU	Adenauer
AADEENTT	antedate
AADEEPPR	appeared
AADEEPPS	appeased
AADEEQTU	adequate
AADEERSW	awardees
AADEFFRY	affrayed
AADEFHLT	flathead
AADEFHST	fatheads
	headfast
AADEFILR	fairlead
AADEFIRS	faradise
AADEFIRZ	faradize
AADEFLLR	falderal
AADEFLRY	defrayal
AADEGGRS	aggrades
AADEGHLN	danelagh
AADEGHMN	Dagenham
AADEGILL	diallage
AADEGILT	gladiate
AADEGINR	drainage
	gardenia
AADEGITT	agitated
AADEGITV	divagate
AADEGLLT	tallaged
AADEGLMN	magdalen
AADEGLMY	amygdale
AADEGLOP	galopade
AADEGLSV	salvaged
AADEGMNR	grandame
AADEGMPR	rampaged
AADEGMRS	damagers
AADEGMSS	massaged
AADEGNRR	arranged
AADEGNRS	Sardegna
AADEGPSS	passaged
AADEGRST	gradates
AADEGRTU	graduate
AADEGSSU	assuaged

AADEHILN	nailhead
AADEHILR	headrail
	railhead
AADEHILS	headsail
AADEHIRR	diarrhea
AADEHIRS	airheads
AADEHIWY	hideaway
AADEHKOT	Hakodate
AADEHLLL	halalled
AADEHLLO	halloaed
AADEHLMO	Almohade
AADEHLMP	headlamp
AADEHLNR	anhedral
AADEHLPS	slaphead
AADEHMNS	headsman
AADEHMST	masthead
AADEHNRV	verandah
AADEHPSS	sapheads
AADEHRRW	hardware
AADEHRSS	Dassehra
	harassed
AADEHRSW	warheads
AADEHSSY	sashayed
AADEIINR	Deianira
AADEIKLP	Klaipeda
AADEILMR	Armidale
AADEILMS	maladies
AADEILNT	dentalia
AADEILPR	praedial
AADEILPS	palisade
AADEILPT	lapidate
AADEILRS	salaried
AADEILSS	assailed
AADEILSV	vedalias
AADEILTV	validate
AADEIMNR	marinade
AADEIMNT	animated
	diamante
AADEIMPZ	diazepam
AADEIMRV	maravedi
AADEIMST	adamsite
	diastema
AADEIMTT	Damietta
AADEINRS	araneids
AADEINTT	attained
AADEIPRS	paradise
AADEIPSU	diapause
AADEIPTV	adaptive
AADEIRST	dataries
	radiates
AADEISST	diastase
AADEISTT	astatide
	satiated
AADEITVW	viewdata
AADEJMNN	Ndjamena
AADEJMRS	jemadars
AADEJNNP	japanned
AADEJNOT	Ondaatje
AADEKLLN	lakeland
AADEKLRY	kaleyard
AADEKMNR	mandrake
AADEKMRS	kamerads
AADEKPRS	parkades
AADELLPP	appalled
AADELMNP	napalmed
AADELMNR	alderman
AADELMNS	dalesman
	leadsman
AADELMOS	alamodes
AADELMPT	palmated
AADELNPT	peatland
AADELNRS	adrenals
AADELNSU	Aalesund
AADELNSY	analysed
AADELNUY	Delaunay
AADELNYZ	analyzed
AADELPPT	palpated
AADELPRY	parlayed
AADELRRW	De La Warr
AADELRSY	saleyard
AADELSTU	adulates
AADELTUV	valuated
AADEMNOS	adenomas
AADEMNST	mandates
AADEMRRU	marauder
AADEMRSS	madrases
AADEMWZZ	zamzawed
AADENNST	andantes
AADENNTV	Davenant
AADENRRT	narrated
AADENRSV	verandas
AADENRTT	tartaned
AADENSSW	weasands
AADENSTY	asyndeta
AADENSTZ	stanzaed
AADEPPRT	preadapt
AADEPRRS	paraders
AADEPRST	adapters
	readapts
AADEQRTU	quadrate
AADERRRW	rearward
AADERRSW	awarders
AADERSSW	seawards
AADERSTW	eastward
AADERUVY	ayurveda
AADFFLLN	Llandaff
AADFGLST	Flagstad
AADFGNNO	fandango
AADFHMNR	farmhand
AADFHNST	handfast
AADFIINT	intifada
AADFIMRS	faradism
AADFINRU	unafraid
AADFLLLN	landfall
AADFLMNR	farmland
AADFLORW	aardwolf
AADFLOTW	dataflow
AADFLOTX	toadflax
AADFLOWY	foldaway
AADFMRRY	farmyard
AADGGHRS	haggards
AADGGIMN	damaging
AADGGLNN	gangland
AADGGLRS	laggards
AADGGRST	staggard
AADGHIPR	diagraph
AADGHJNU	Junagadh
AADGHORS	daroghas
	Sargodha
AADGIINS	gainsaid
AADGILLO	gladiola
AADGILLR	gaillard
	galliard
AADGILMR	madrigal
AADGILNO	diagonal
	gonadial
AADGIMMS	digammas
AADGIMPR	paradigm
AADGIMRS	diagrams
AADGINOS	Sogdiana
AADGINPR	parading
AADGINPT	adapting
AADGINRR	darraign
AADGINRU	guardian
AADGINRW	awarding
AADGIORV	Godavari
AADGIQRU	quadriga
AADGLLNN	Langland
AADGLLSW	gadwalls
AADGLNRS	garlands
AADGLOPR	podagral
AADGLRSU	graduals
AADGMNOP	pagandom
AADGMNOR	dragoman
AADGMNRS	grandams
	grandmas
AADGMRSS	smaragds
AADGNNOO	Onondaga
AADGNNQU	quandang
AADGNORS	Granados
AADGNPRS	grandpas
AADGNRTU	guardant
AADGNRUV	vanguard
AADGNRWY	drangway
AADGOORV	Avogadro
AADGRRUW	gurdwara
AADHHIJK	Khadijah
AADHHIPS	padishah
AADHIINP	aphidian
AADHILLR	halliard
AADHILNR	handrail
AADHILNT	Thailand
AADHILNU	Ludhiana
AADHILRV	havildar
AADHINNZ	Andizhan
AADHINOT	anthodia
AADHINPS	daphnias
AADHINRR	harridan
AADHKNSS	dhansaks
AADHLMST	Halmstad
AADHLPSS	slapdash
AADHLRSY	halyards
AADHMMMU	Muhammad
AADHMNNY	handyman
AADHMNOU	omadhaun
AADHMNRU	Damanhûr

AADHNSSW	handsaws
AADHNSTT	hatstand
AADHRSWY	haywards
AADHSSWY	washdays
AADIILVV	Valdivia
AADIINRS	Sardinia
AADIINRV	Adrian IV
AADIKLLO	alkaloid
AADIKLRY	kailyard
AADIKNQR	qindarka
AADIKORT	Takoradi
AADILLLO	allodial
AADILLNR	landrail
AADILLOP	Palladio
AADILLRY	radially
AADILLSY	dyslalia
AADILMNN	mainland
AADILMNT	Maitland
AADILMOV	Moldavia
AADILMRS	admirals
AADILMVY	Limavady
AADILNPR	prandial
AADILNPS	paladins
AADILNRS	laniards
AADILNTT	dilatant
AADILORR	railroad
AADILPRY	lapidary
AADILRST	diastral
AADIMMSZ	Mazdaism
AADIMNNO	Mindanao
AADIMNNR	mandarin
AADIMNOT	manatoid
AADIMNRT	tamarind
AADIMNRY	dairyman
	mainyard
AADIMNRZ	zamindar
AADIMNUV	vanadium
AADIMORS	dioramas
AADIMPST	misadapt
AADIMSTZ	samizdat
AADINOPR	paranoid
AADINOPS	diapason
AADINOPT	adaption
AADINOTV	avoidant
AADINRST	radiants
AADIOPRS	diaspora
AADIORRT	radiator
AADIRRSY	disarray
AADISTXY	dystaxia
AADJNTTU	adjutant
AADJNTUV	adjuvant
AADKLMNR	landmark
AADKLNPR	parkland
AADKMNTU	Katmandu
AADKNRST	tankards
AADKORWY	workaday
AADLLMRS	mallards
AADLMNNS	landsman
AADLMNOR	mandorla
AADLMNOS	mandolas
AADLMNRY	Maryland
AADLMNSS	landmass
AADLMNUU	laudanum
AADLNOPR	parlando
AADLNRSY	lanyards
AADLOPRV	Pavlodar
AADLOPSY	payloads
AADLORST	loadstar
AADLORSV	Salvador
AADLORTU	adulator
AADLPPSU	applauds
AADMMNOW	madwoman
AADMMNSU	mandamus
AADMNORS	madronas
	monardas
AADMNORT	mandator
AADMNQRU	Marquand
AADMNRSS	mansards
AADMNSTU	tamandus
AADMORRT	tramroad
AADMORST	matadors
AADMRRSY	yardarms
AADMRSZZ	mazzards
AADNNORR	Andorran
AADNNORS	Sarandon
AADNNPSU	pandanus
AADNOPRS	pandoras
AADNOPSS	sandsoap
AADNOSUV	vanadous
AADNOSWY	nowadays
AADNPRSU	Pandarus
AADNPSTT	standpat
AADNPSUY	Paysandú
AADNQRTU	quadrant
AADNQRUY	quandary
AADNRSSY	Andrássy
AADOPPRR	paradrop
AADOPRRS	paradors
AADOPRST	adaptors
AADOPSUY	paduasoy
AADORSVY	savoyard
AADORSWY	roadways
AADPSTTU	dupattas
AADQRSTU	quadrats
AADRRSYY	Syr Darya
AADRSSTU	Adrastus
AAEEEHRT	hetaerae
AAEEFRRS	seafarer
AAEEFRST	ratafees
AAEEGILN	alienage
AAEEGKLS	leakages
AAEEGMPR	amperage
AAEEGMST	agametes
AAEEGNNO	Neogaean
AAEEGNRS	sangaree
AAEEGNRT	tagareen
AAEEGRSV	averages
AAEEGRTW	waterage
AAEEHIMR	haeremai
AAEEHLMR	ahemeral
AAEEHNPS	saphenae
AAEEHRTW	aweather
	wheatear
AAEEILNT	alienate
AAEEJNPS	Japanese
AAEEJNSV	Javanese
AAEEJPVY	Vajpayee
AAEEKMNS	namesake
AAEEKMRT	teamaker
AAEEKNRW	reawaken
AAEEKPRT	parakeet
AAEEKQSU	seaquake
AAEELLLM	lamellae
AAEELLMR	amarelle
AAEELLPT	patellae
AAEELMMT	metamale
AAEELMST	maleates
AAEELNNR	annealer
AAEELNPS	seaplane
	spelaean
AAEELNST	elastane
AAEELORT	areolate
AAEELPPR	appealer
AAEELRTU	laureate
AAEELSST	elastase
AAEELTUV	evaluate
AAEELVWY	wayleave
AAEEMMTT	teammate
AAEEMNNS	Annamese
AAEEMNPT	nametape
AAEEMNST	emanates
	manatees
AAEEMRST	amreetas
AAEEMSSS	Assamese
AAEEMSTX	meataxes
AAEENNNT	antennae
AAEENNRZ	Nazarene
AAEENRST	arsenate
	Near East
	serenata
AAEENRTT	anteater
AAEENSTU	nauseate
AAEEPPRR	rapparee
	reappear
AAEEPPRS	appeaser
AAEEPPSS	appeases
AAEEPRST	asperate
	separate
AAEEPSTT	aseptate
AAEERSTT	stearate
AAEFFGRS	agraffes
AAEFFIRS	affaires
AAEFFLLS	falafels
AAEFFNRS	fanfares
AAEFFSTT	taffetas
AAEFGHRW	wharfage
AAEFGLLL	flagella
AAEFGLOT	floatage
AAEFIILR	filariae
AAEFIKLT	kalifate
AAEFILTY	fayalite
AAEFIMRR	airframe
AAEFINNT	faineant
AAEFINTX	antefixa
AAEFKMST	makefast
AAEFLMTT	flatmate

AAEFLNUU faunulae
AAEFLPRS earflaps
AAEFLRTW flatware
AAEFMRST fermatas
AAEFRRWY wayfarer
AAEGGIOT agiotage
AAEGGLNR Lagrange
langrage
AAEGGLNU language
AAEGGMMR grammage
AAEGGNOS anagoges
AAEGGNRY garganey
AAEGGOPR paragoge
AAEGHIRS Hargeisa
AAEGHLNP phalange
AAEGHLSU haulages
AAEGHMRX hexagram
AAEGHNRU harangue
AAEGILLN Galilean
AAEGILLR galleria
AAEGILNP pelagian
AAEGILNR Algerian
geranial
AAEGILNT agential
alginate
AAEGILRS lairages
AAEGILSX galaxies
AAEGILTT tailgate
AAEGIMNO egomania
AAEGIMNS magnesia
AAEGIMNT agminate
AAEGIMNZ magazine
AAEGIMRR marriage
AAEGIMRT Armitage
maritage
AAEGINPS paganise
AAEGINPT paginate
AAEGINPZ paganize
AAEGINRT aerating
AAEGINTV navigate
vaginate
AAEGIRSV vagaries
AAEGISSS assegais
AAEGISTT agitates
AAEGIVWY giveaway
AAEGKNNW KaNgwane
AAEGKOSS soakages
AAEGKTTT Kattegat
AAEGLLMN Magellan
AAEGLLMS smallage
AAEGLLPR pellagra
AAEGLLSS galleass
AAEGLLST tallages
AAEGLLTU glutaeal
AAEGLMNS gamelans
AAEGLMPY gameplay
AAEGLMST almagest
AAEGLNOU analogue
AAEGLNPP lagnappe
AAEGLNSS lasagnes
AAEGLNSU leguaans
AAEGLNTU angulate
AAEGLPRV Palgrave
AAEGLRST agrestal
AAEGLRSV salvager
AAEGLSSV Las Vegas
salvages
AAEGLSVY savagely
AAEGMMNS gamesman
AAEGMNNT Mantegna
AAEGMNPY pygmaean
AAEGMNRS managers
Semarang
AAEGMNRT magnetar
AAEGMNRV gravamen
AAEGMNST magnates
AAEGMORR aerogram
AAEGMORS sagamore
AAEGMPRR rampager
AAEGMPRS rampages
AAEGMRRT Margaret
AAEGMRRV margrave
AAEGMRRY gramarye
AAEGMRSS massager
AAEGMRST megastar
Ramsgate
AAEGMRTU ageratum
AAEGMSSS massages
AAEGMTTW megawatt
AAEGMUYZ Mayagüez
AAEGNNST tannages
AAEGNOOT Notogaea
AAEGNPST pageants
AAEGNRRR arranger
AAEGNRRS arranges
AAEGNRST tanagers
AAEGNRTU runagate
AAEGNSTT stagnate
AAEGNSTV vantages
AAEGNSUY Saguenay
AAEGORRT arrogate
AAEGORTT aegrotat
AAEGPSSS passages
AAEGQSUY quayages
AAEGRRSV ravagers
AAEGRSSU assuager
AAEGRSTT regattas
AAEGRSTZ stargaze
AAEGRSVY savagery
AAEGSSSU assuages
sausages
AAEGSTTW wattages
AAEGSTWY gateways
getaways
AAEHIIMR Ihimaera
AAEHIIRT hetairai
AAEHILNP aphelian
AAEHILNT anthelia
AAEHILPR parhelia
AAEHIMNT anthemia
haematin
AAEHINNT Athenian
AAEHINPT aphanite
AAEHINRT Rhaetian
AAEHINST asthenia
AAEHIPPS Pasiphaë
AAEHKLST alkahest
AAEHKMRY haymaker
AAEHKNST khanates
AAEHLLLS allheals
AAEHLMNT methanal
AAEHLMNW whaleman
AAEHLMSY sealyham
AAEHLMTU hamulate
AAEHLNRT antheral
AAEHLNRW narwhale
AAEHLNTX exhalant
AAEHLPRS pearlash
AAEHLPRX hexaplar
AAEHLPUV upheaval
AAEHMMOT hematoma
AAEHMNRT earthman
AAEHMNSS Manasseh
AAEHMOPR amphorae
AAEHMORT atheroma
AAEHNPRS hanapers
AAEHNPST pheasant
AAEHNRTU Rathenau
AAEHNRTZ Nazareth
AAEHNTTX xanthate
AAEHPRSW Peshawar
AAEHRSSS harasses
AAEHRSTT Hatteras
AAEHRSTU arethusa
AAEHRTWX earthwax
AAEIILMP lipaemia
AAEIILQU Aquileia
AAEIIMRV viraemia
AAEIIPRS apiaries
AAEIIRSV aviaries
AAEIJNRT naartjie
AAEIKKMZ kamikaze
AAEIKLLN alkaline
AAEIKLLS alkalies
alkalise
AAEIKLLZ alkalize
AAEIKLNR Karelian
AAEIKMRR krameria
AAEILLLU alleluia
AAEILLMM mamillae
AAEILLMX maxillae
AAEILLNT allanite
AAEILLPP papillae
AAEILLPT palliate
AAEILLRT arillate
AAEILMMX axilemma
AAEILMNT laminate
AAEILMNV velamina
AAEILMRT material
AAEILNPR airplane
AAEILNPT palatine
AAEILNRU aurelian
AAEILNRV valerian
AAEILNSS nasalise
Salesian
AAEILNSZ nasalize

AAEILNTU Aleutian
AAEILOTU Alaouite
AAEILPRT parietal
AAEILPRX preaxial
AAEILPST stapelia
AAEILPSZ La Spezia
AAEILRRT arterial
AAEILRSS assailer
salaries
AAEILRTV varietal
AAEILSTV aestival
salivate
AAEILSTX saxatile
AAEILTVX laxative
AAEIMMST imamates
AAEIMNNR Armenian
AAEIMNNT Mantinea
AAEIMNOX anoxemia
AAEIMNPR pearmain
AAEIMNRT animater
marinate
AAEIMNST animates
AAEIMNTT Antietam
AAEIMOTX toxaemia
AAEIMOTZ azotemia
AAEIMPRS aspermia
AAEIMRST amirates
AAEIMRTY Maitreya
AAEINNRS Saarinen
AAEINORT aeration
AAEINORX anorexia
AAEINPPR priapean
AAEINRRW rainwear
AAEINRST antisera
artesian
Santeria
AAEINRTT reattain
AAEINRTZ atrazine
Nazarite
AAEINSST entasias
AAEINSTT astatine
AAEINSTV sanative
AAEINTTT titanate
AAEIPPRS appraise
AAEIPQRU Arequipa
AAEIPRST aspirate
parasite
septaria
AAEIPRTT patriate
AAEIPRTZ trapezia
AAEIPRXY apyrexia
AAEIRRRT terraria
AAEIRRST taraires
AAEIRSTT ariettas
aristate
AAEIRSTV variates
AAEIRSVW airwaves
AAEIRTTZ zaratite
AAEISSTT satiates
AAEJLNOP jalapeno
AAEJLNPU Jean Paul
AAEJMNNY Jan Mayen
AAEJMNRY maryjane
AAEJOPRS aparejos
AAEJORSV Sarajevo
AAEJRSTX Jaxartes
AAEKKMNR Akkerman
AAEKLMRW lawmaker
AAEKLMRY malarkey
AAEKLNNT Kelantan
AAEKLNRS larnakes
AAEKLNST alkanets
AAEKMRRS earmarks
AAEKMRSS seamarks
AAEKNPRT partaken
AAEKNTTY Kenyatta
AAEKORTY akaryote
AAEKPRRT partaker
AAEKPRST partakes
AAELLLMR lamellar
AAELLLMS lamellas
AAELLLPR parallel
AAELLLSS Lassalle
AAELLMMR Mallarmé
AAELLMPU ampullae
AAELLNNV Van Allen
AAELLNPU planulae
AAELLORV alveolar
AAELLPRT patellar
AAELLRST laterals
AAELLSWY Wallasey
AAELLTTV Valletta
AAELLWWY wellaway
AAELLWYY alleyway
AAELMMNO melanoma
AAELMMOX axolemma
AAELMMRS almemars
AAELMMTU malamute
AAELMNRT maternal
AAELMNSS salesman
AAELMNST talesman
AAELMNSY seamanly
AAELMOSU mausolea
AAELMPRT malapert
AAELMPTY playmate
AAELMRSY lamasery
AAELMRTT maltreat
AAELMSSY amylases
AAELNNNT antennal
AAELNNOT neonatal
AAELNNSU Lausanne
AAELNNTU annulate
AAELNOSS seasonal
AAELNPRT parental
paternal
prenatal
AAELNPRW warplane
AAELNPST pleasant
AAELNRSS arsenals
AAELNRST asternal
AAELNRSY analyser
AAELNRTX relaxant
AAELNRYZ analyzer
AAELNSST sealants
AAELNSSY analyses
AAELNSTT atlantes
AAELNSYZ analyzes
AAELOPRS psoralea
AAELORSU aureolas
AAELORTY aleatory
AAELOSTX oxalates
AAELPPRS apparels
AAELPPRT La Trappe
AAELPPST palpates
AAELPPSU applause
AAELPRST palestra
AAELPRSV palavers
AAELPRSY paralyse
AAELPRYZ paralyze
AAELPSTU plateaus
AAELPSTV palstave
AAELPTUX plateaux
AAELRSST tarseals
AAELRSTZ lazarets
AAELRSVY Vasarely
AAELRUZZ zarzuela
AAELRWYY waylayer
AAELSTUV valuates
AAEMMNOT ammonate
AAEMMNRT armament
AAEMMOST metasoma
AAEMNORT emanator
AAEMNOTZ metazoan
AAEMNPRS Parmesan
spearman
AAEMNPRT parament
AAEMNRRY yarramen
AAEMNRST Santarém
AAEMNRTW waterman
AAEMNSTU manteaus
AAEMNTUX manteaux
AAEMORTT amaretto
teratoma
AAEMOTTU automate
AAEMPTTU amputate
AAEMQSTU squamate
AAEMRRTU armature
AAEMRSSS amassers
AAEMRSTU amateurs
AAEMRTTU maturate
AAENNNST antennas
AAENNOTT annotate
AAENNSTT tannates
AAENORTU aeronaut
AAENPPRT apparent
trappean
AAENPRTY prytanea
AAENPSST anapests
peasants
AAENPSTY peasanty
AAENRRST narrates
AAENRSTV tavernas
tsarevna
AAENRSUW unawares
AAENSSTV savantes
AAEOPSTT apostate

AAEORRST aerators
AAEORSTT aerostat
AAEORTTV rotavate
AAEPPRST parapets
AAEPPSTT appestat
AAEPRTXY taxpayer
AAEPSWXX paxwaxes
AAERRSTU Sarraute
AAERRTTT tartrate
AAERSSSY assayers
AAERSSTV Västerås
AAERSTTU saturate
AAERTWWY waterway
AAFFGILS gaffsail
AAFFILRT taffrail
AAFFINPR paraffin
AAFFINST affiants
AAFFLSTU afflatus
AAFFMNST staffman
AAFGHINS afghanis
AAFGHNRU fraughan
AAFGLLNU langlauf
AAFGLNRT flagrant
AAFGNRRT fragrant
AAFGORRS farragos
AAFHIRST airshaft
AAFHJLLU Fallujah
AAFHLSTY layshaft
AAFHQRRU Farquhar
AAFHRSUU hausfrau
AAFIIILS Faisal II
AAFIIKLR Faliraki
AAFIILLM familial
AAFIILLR filarial
AAFIILMR familiar
AAFIILNR filarian
AAFIKLLY alkalify
AAFILLNR rainfall
AAFILMST fatalism
AAFILNST fantails
AAFILPRS Parsifal
AAFILSTT fatalist
AAFILTTY fatality
AAFIMNOR foramina
AAFINNOV favonian
AAFINNRS safranin
AAFINNST infantas
AAFINRRW warfarin
AAFINSTU faustian
AAFIPRST parfaits
AAFIRSUY rufiyaas
AAFIRSWY fairways
AAFIRTTT frittata
AAFJLORS alforjas
AAFKMUUY Fukuyama
AAFKORTU Karafuto
AAFLLNUY faunally
AAFLLPRT pratfall
AAFLNNOT nonfatal
AAFLSTWY flatways
AAFLSWYY flyaways
AAFMNSST fantasms
AAFMOPRR paraform
AAFMORST Amfortas
AAFNSSTT fantasts
AAGGGHNS gangshag
AAGGGINR garaging
AAGGILLN ganglial
AAGGILNR gangliar
AAGGIMNN managing
AAGGIMNR maraging
AAGGINRV ravaging
AAGGINSV savaging
AAGGLLLY lallygag
AAGGLRSY graylags
AAGGNORT Taganrog
AAGGNSST gangstas
AAGGNSWY gangways
AAGGOOPP Pago Pago
AAGHHINS shanghai
AAGHHINU Huang Hai
AAGHHINW Hwang Hai
AAGHHNOS oanshagh
AAGHHNUU Huang Hua
AAGHILNN hangnail
AAGHILRS gharials
AAGHINNS anhingas
AAGHINPS paganish
AAGHKMNY gymkhana
AAGHKNST thangkas
AAGHLNPY anaglyph
AAGHMNNO Monaghan
AAGHMNOY hogmanay
mahogany
AAGHMNRT Grantham
AAGHNNRT Nha Trang
AAGHNNST Tangshan
AAGHNPRY phrygana
AAGHNSST sanghats
AAGHRSSW washrags
AAGIILMN imaginal
AAGIILNS aliasing
AAGIILNV availing
AAGIIMNN magainin
AAGIIMST astigmia
AAGIINNP Paganini
AAGIINNU iguanian
AAGIINTV aviating
AAGIINTW awaiting
AAGIJRTU Gujarati
AAGIKLNO kaoliang
AAGIKLNR kraaling
AAGIKLUY Kaliyuga
AAGILLNU Anguilla
AAGILLNY allaying
AAGILLSS galliass
AAGILMNO magnolia
AAGILMNR alarming
marginal
AAGILMOT gliomata
AAGILNOT galtonia
AAGILNOY Liaoyang
AAGILNRR larrigan
AAGILNRS Sangrail
AAGILNTV galivant
AAGILOOP apologia
AAGILOPT topalgia
AAGILOSS aglossia
AAGILPRY plagiary
AAGILRRW warrigal
AAGILSTT sagittal
AAGILSTW wagtails
AAGIMMRR marigram
AAGIMNNO agnomina
AAGIMNOS angiomas
AAGIMNPS paganism
AAGIMNSS amassing
siamangs
AAGIMNSY gymnasia
AAGIMPTU patagium
AAGIMSTT stigmata
AAGINNNY nannygai
AAGINNOT agnation
AAGINNST Siangtan
AAGINNTU Antiguan
AAGINNTX Xiangtan
AAGINNUW Wanganui
AAGINORR rangiora
AAGINOST Santiago
AAGINPRU pagurian
AAGINPST paganist
AAGINRRS arraigns
Srinagar
AAGINRRY arraying
AAGINRSS sangrias
sarangis
AAGINRSU guaranis
AAGINRTT Rattigan
AAGINRUZ Zungaria
AAGINSST assignat
AAGINSSU gaussian
AAGINSSY assaying
gainsays
AAGIORTT agitator
AAGIPRSU piraguas
AAGIRSTV gravitas
stravaig
AAGKNOOR kangaroo
AAGKNOOV Okavango
AAGKNORR Ragnarök
AAGLLMOY allogamy
AAGLLNRY laryngal
AAGLLNST gallants
AAGLLOPY polygala
AAGLLOSS aglossal
AAGLLOWY Galloway
AAGLMNSS glassman
AAGLNQUU aqualung
AAGLNRRU granular
AAGLRSTU gastrula
AAGMMRRS grammars
AAGMMSUY mamaguys
AAGMNORT martagon
AAGMNOSS sangomas
AAGMNOST agamonts
AAGMNRST tangrams

AAGMNSTY	syntagma
AAGMORTY	Gayomart
AAGMOTUY	autogamy
AAGMOTYZ	zygomata
AAGMRSST	matgrass
AAGNNSTT	stagnant
AAGNNUXZ	Xuan Zang
AAGNOPRS	paragons
AAGNOPRT	tragopan
AAGNORRT	arrogant
	tarragon
AAGNORSZ	organzas
AAGNORTU	argonaut
AAGNRSTV	vagrants
AAGNRTUY	guaranty
AAGORSSS	sargasso
AAGORSSU	saguaros
AAGRSSTU	sastruga
AAGRSTUZ	zastruga
AAHHIJLR	Al Hijrah
AAHHIKNU	hanukiah
AAHHKKNU	Hanukkah
AAHHKMRS	hashmark
AAHHMMSS	shammash
AAHHNPST	naphthas
AAHHOPRS	pharaohs
AAHIIKRR	hari-kari
AAHIIKRT	tarakihi
AAHIILRT	hairtail
AAHIINPS	Hispania
AAHIINSS	Hassan II
AAHIINTT	Tahitian
AAHIJNRS	harijans
AAHIKLNS	Sakhalin
AAHIKLPS	pashalik
AAHIKNOV	Haakon IV
AAHIKNSS	Kinshasa
AAHIKRST	kitharas
AAHILLLS	shillala
AAHILMRY	Hail Mary
AAHILNNT	inhalant
AAHILNOT	halation
AAHILNPT	Naphtali
AAHILQUZ	Zia ul Haq
AAHIMNOS	mahonias
AAHIMNPS	pashmina
AAHIMNRR	Harriman
AAHIMNZZ	hazzanim
AAHIMSTT	Matthias
AAHINNST	Tian Shan
AAHINNTX	Xanthian
AAHINPRS	piranhas
AAHINPRT	Parthian
AAHINSST	shaitans
AAHIPPRS	Sapphira
AAHIPSXY	asphyxia
AAHJNNOT	Jonathan
AAHKLLMR	hallmark
AAHKLMOO	Oklahoma
AAHKLOOS	Koolhaas
AAHKMOOY	Yokohama
AAHKMOTW	tomahawk
AAHKMSSY	yashmaks
AAHKORSV	Sakharov
AAHKRSTV	Hrvatska
AAHLLMRS	marshall
AAHLLOPT	allopath
AAHLLSWY	hallways
AAHLLUVX	Vauxhall
AAHLMRSS	marshals
AAHLMSTU	thalamus
AAHLNNSU	An Lu Shan
AAHLNPST	ashplant
AAHLNRSW	narwhals
AAHLPSST	asphalts
AAHMMORR	Moharram
AAHMMRRU	Muharram
AAHMNNSU	hanumans
AAHMNORT	marathon
AAHMNOTX	xanthoma
AAHMNPST	phantasm
AAHMOPRS	amphoras
AAHMRSST	stramash
AAHNNOSS	hosannas
AAHNNSTY	Tyan-Shan
AAHNOPTW	Powhatan
AAHNOSTT	thanatos
AAHNPSTY	phantasy
AAHNRTTY	Hanratty
AAHNTUWY	huntaway
AAHOPRTU	autoharp
AAHOQSUW	aquashow
AAHORSSU	sahuaros
AAHPRSTW	warpaths
AAHPSTWY	pathways
AAHRSSTY	ashtrays
AAIIILMR	miliaria
AAIIILMS	Ismailia
AAIIJJPP	jipijapa
AAIILMNS	mainsail
AAIILMRS	airmails
AAIILNRZ	alizarin
AAIILNUX	uniaxial
AAIILPST	tilapias
AAIILRTX	triaxial
AAIILTXY	axiality
AAIIMNNR	Arminian
AAIIMNNT	maintain
AAIIMNPX	panmixia
AAIIMNQS	Si-ma Qian
AAIIMNRS	Arianism
AAIIMNRT	Maritain
AAIINNNO	Ioánnina
AAIINOTV	aviation
AAIINPRR	riparian
AAIINPRS	Parisian
AAIINRST	intarsia
AAIINRSU	Isaurian
AAIIPRST	apiarist
AAIIRSTV	aviarist
AAIIRTVX	aviatrix
AAIJNRYZ	janizary
AAIKKNOS	skokiaan
AAIKLNNN	alkannin
AAIKLNOS	Salonika
AAIKLNRS	Sri Lanka
AAIKLORU	Liákoura
AAIKLOSV	Slovakia
AAIKLPRS	palikars
AAIKMNNS	manakins
AAIKMRST	tamarisk
AAIKNNTT	antitank
AAIKNORU	Kairouan
AAIKNPST	Pakistan
AAIKSSTW	swastika
AAIKSTVV	akvavits
AAILLLUV	alluvial
AAILLMMM	mammilla
AAILLMNS	manillas
AAILLMNT	mantilla
AAILLMOR	Amarillo
AAILLMPT	taillamp
AAILLMRX	maxillar
AAILLNSV	vanillas
AAILLRXY	axillary
AAILMMNU	Maulmain
AAILMMRS	alarmism
AAILMNOR	manorial
	morainal
AAILMNOS	Somalian
AAILMNOX	monaxial
AAILMNST	staminal
	talisman
AAILMNSV	Malvinas
AAILMOPT	lipomata
AAILMORR	armorial
AAILMRSS	Marsalis
AAILMRST	alarmist
AAILMTTU	ultimata
AAILNNOT	national
AAILNNPT	plantain
AAILNNRU	lunarian
AAILNNST	annalist
AAILNOPS	salopian
AAILNOPT	talapoin
AAILNORS	orinasal
AAILNORT	notarial
	rational
AAILNOSV	Slavonia
AAILNOTV	lavation
AAILNOTX	laxation
AAILNQTU	aliquant
AAILNSSY	analysis
AAILNSTT	Atlantis
AAILNSTU	Lusatian
AAILNSTY	nasality
AAILNTTY	natality
AAILORRS	rasorial
AAILORRV	variolar
AAILPPRU	puparial
AAILPRST	partials
	patrials
AAILPRSY	airplays
AAILPRVZ	Parzival
AAILQRSU	squarial
AAILQSWW	qawwalis

AAILRRSV arrivals
AAILRSTT rattails
AAILRSTV travails
AAILRSVY salivary
AAILRSWY railways
AAILSSSW wassails
AAILSSTY staysail
AAIMMNOS ammonias
AAIMMNST mainmast
AAIMMRSU samarium
AAIMNNOR Romanian
AAIMNNRU Rumanian
AAIMNNTU Numantia
AAIMNORT animator
AAIMNORU Roumania
AAIMNORV Moravian
AAIMNORW airwoman
AAIMNOTT antiatom
AAIMNPRZ marzipan
AAIMNPTU putamina
AAIMNRRT trimaran
AAIMNRST martians
tamarins
AAIMNRSU Masurian
AAIMNSST mantissa
satanism
AAIMNSTY mainstay
AAIMNTYZ Zamyatin
AAIMOPRS mariposa
parosmia
AAIMPRST pastrami
AAIMPRSU marsupia
AAIMQRUU aquarium
AAIMRRST Amritsar
AAIMRUVX Marivaux
AAIMSSTV atavisms
AAINNNOP Pannonia
AAINNORT Ontarian
Taínaron
AAINNORV Navarino
AAINNOST sonatina
AAINNOTT natation
AAINNRSV navarins
AAINNSST naissant
AAINNSSY sannyasi
AAINOPSS paisanos
AAINORRS rosarian
AAINOTTX taxation
AAINPRST aspirant
partisan
AAINPRTZ partizan
AAINQRRU quarrian
AAINQRTU quatrain
AAINQTTU aquatint
AAINRSST artisans
tsarinas
AAINRSSU saurians
AAINRSTU Austrian
AAINRSTV variants
AAINRSTY sanitary
AAINSSSS assassin
AAINSSTT satanist
AAINSTTT attaints
AAINSTTV avantist
AAIOPRSU parousia
AAIORSTV aviators
AAIPPSTT pitapats
AAIPRSSX sparaxis
AAIPRSTT partitas
AAIQRSTU aquarist
AAIQRSUU Aquarius
AAIQSSSU quassias
AAIRSSTT tsaritsa
AAIRSSTU Asturias
AAIRSTWY stairway
AAISSTTV atavists
AAISTWXY taxiways
AAJKLSWY jaywalks
AAJMMORR marjoram
AAKKLRSU karakuls
AAKKMOST tokamaks
AAKKOSUZ zakouska
AAKLOOPS palookas
AAKLOOST talookas
AAKLRSSU kursaals
AAKLSWWY walkways
AAKMMNRS marksman
AAKMORUZ mazourka
AAKMOSSU mousakas
moussaka
AAKMRSUZ mazurkas
AAKMRSWY waymarks
AAKNNSTU nunataks
AAKOOPPS pakapoos
AAKOPRSV Kasparov
AAKORSUW Kurosawa
AAKPRSWY parkways
AALLLLMP Pall Mall
AALLMNTY tallyman
AALLMNUY manually
AALLMORY amorally
AALLMPRU ampullar
AALLNNUY annually
AALLNOTY atonally
AALLNPRU planular
AALLNRTY tarnally
AALLOOPT Palo Alto
AALLOORW wallaroo
AALLORSU allosaur
AALLORWY rollaway
AALLPRST plastral
AALLRSTY astrally
AALLRUVV valvular
AALMNOPP Pamplona
AALMNORT matronal
AALMNORU monaural
AALMNOWY laywoman
AALMNTTU tantalum
AALMNTUU autumnal
AALMOPPR malaprop
AALMOSTT stomatal
AALMPPSU paspalum
AALMPRSY palmyras
AALNNOST sonantal
AALNOORS oronasal
AALNOPRT patronal
AALNOPST postanal
AALNPSST saltpans
AALNPTWX waxplant
AALNRRTY arrantly
AALNRSTU naturals
AALNSSTU sultanas
AALNSSTY analysts
AALNSTTU tantalus
AALNTUUV Tuvaluan
AALOOPSU São Paulo
AALOPPRV approval
AALOPPST apoplast
AALOPRSS parasols
AALOPRST pastoral
AALOPSVV pavlovas
AALORSSU arousals
AALORTUV valuator
AALORTVY lavatory
AALPRSTU spatular
AALPRSTY laptrays
AALPSSTU spatulas
AALRSTTW stalwart
AALRSTUY salutary
AALSSSTU assaults
AAMMOTXY myxomata
AAMMRSSU marasmus
AAMNNNOT Montanan
AAMNORRS marranos
AAMNORSZ romanzas
AAMNPRST mantraps
AAMNQSUW squawman
AAMNRSTU Sumatran
AAMOPRRU paramour
AAMORSSU mosasaur
AAMORSSV samovars
AAMORSTT stromata
AAMOSTTU automats
AAMPRRST ramparts
AAMRSSTT mattrass
AAMRSTWY tramways
AAMSSSTU satsumas
AANNOSST assonant
AANNOSTT annattos
AANNRSTY stannary
AANORRRT narrator
AANORTTY natatory
AANPPTTY pattypan
AANPRSST spartans
AANRRSTW warrants
AANRRTTY tartanry
AANRRTWY warranty
AANRSTTU saturant
AANRSUWY runaways
AAOPSSTY apostasy
AAORSSVV vavasors
vavassor
AAORSUVV vavasour
AAOSTTUY tatouays
AAOSTWWY stowaway
AAPRRSTT rattraps

AARRSTTU	Tartarus
AARSTTUY	statuary
ABBBDELR	brabbled
ABBBEILR	bribable
ABBBELRR	brabbler
ABBBELRS	babblers
	blabbers
	brabbles
ABBBELTU	tubbable
ABBBGILN	babbling
	blabbing
ABBBHSUY	bushbaby
ABBBISTT	babbitts
ABBBOSTU	subabbot
ABBCCKMO	backcomb
ABBCDEKN	backbend
ABBCDELS	scabbled
ABBCEERU	barbecue
ABBCEGIR	cribbage
ABBCEHIS	babiches
ABBCEHTU	bathcube
ABBCEIKT	backbite
ABBCEILR	barbicel
ABBCEIRR	crabbier
ABBCEIRS	scabbier
ABBCEKNO	backbone
ABBCEKNU	buckbean
ABBCELLU	clubable
ABBCELRS	scrabble
ABBCELSS	scabbles
ABBCERRS	crabbers
ABBCGINR	crabbing
ABBCGINS	scabbing
ABBCGIOR	gabbroic
ABBCIILL	biblical
ABBCIINR	rabbinic
ABBCIKRT	brickbat
ABBCILSY	scabbily
ABBCKLOW	blowback
ABBCKLOY	blackboy
ABBCKNRU	backburn
ABBCKSUY	buybacks
ABBDDEEL	beddable
ABBDDEEU	bedaubed
ABBDDEIL	biddable
ABBDDELR	drabbled
ABBDDILY	biddably
ABBDEEER	beebread
ABBDEEJR	jabbered
ABBDEERR	barbered
ABBDEERT	rabbeted
ABBDEGLR	grabbled
ABBDEHOO	boobhead
ABBDEIRT	rabbited
ABBDELMR	brambled
ABBDELRS	dabblers
	drabbles
ABBDEMOR	bombarde
ABBDEORS	absorbed
ABBDERST	drabbest
	drabbets
ABBDGILN	dabbling
ABBDGINR	drabbing
ABBDHIRT	birdbath
ABBDHOOY	babyhood
ABBDILNO	bailbond
ABBDINRS	ribbands
ABBDMORS	bombards
ABBDNORW	browband
ABBDOORX	boxboard
ABBDRRUY	Bradbury
ABBEEJRR	jabberer
ABBEEJRS	bejabers
ABBEELLN	Ben Bella
ABBEELTU	bluebeat
ABBEELVW	Ebbw Vale
ABBEERTT	barbette
ABBEESSS	abbesses
ABBEFILR	flabbier
ABBEGIST	gabbiest
ABBEGLRR	grabbler
ABBEGLRS	gabblers
	grabbles
ABBEGNOS	bogbeans
ABBEGNSU	bugbanes
ABBEGRRS	grabbers
ABBEGRSU	bugbears
ABBEHIRS	shabbier
ABBEHORT	bathrobe
ABBEILLO	boilable
ABBEILNU	bubaline
ABBEILOT	bilobate
ABBEILRW	wabblier
ABBEILST	bistable
ABBEIMRU	berimbau
ABBEIMWZ	Zimbabwe
ABBEINRS	Brisbane
ABBEIRRT	rabbiter
ABBEIRRW	barbwire
ABBELLRS	barbells
ABBELMRS	brambles
ABBELOPR	probable
ABBELORS	belabors
ABBELORU	belabour
ABBELQSU	squabble
ABBELRRS	rabblers
ABBELRSS	slabbers
ABBELRSU	barbules
ABBELRSW	wabblers
ABBELRSY	slabbery
ABBENORS	baseborn
ABBENORY	nabobery
ABBEORRS	absorber
	reabsorb
ABBEORTW	browbeat
ABBERRRY	barberry
ABBERRYY	bayberry
ABBERSST	stabbers
ABBERSSU	Barbusse
ABBERSSW	swabbers
ABBESSSU	subbases
ABBFILLY	flabbily
ABBFLOOT	bobfloat
ABBGGILN	gabbling
ABBGGINR	grabbing
ABBGHRSU	Habsburg
ABBGILNR	rabbling
ABBGILNS	slabbing
ABBGILNW	wabbling
ABBGINST	stabbing
ABBGINSW	swabbing
ABBGINYY	yabbying
ABBGOOSU	bugaboos
ABBHILSY	shabbily
ABBHINOS	nabobish
ABBHIORT	rabbitoh
ABBHRRSU	rhubarbs
ABBHSTTU	bathtubs
ABBILLOT	boatbill
ABBILLSU	sillabub
ABBILOST	bobtails
ABBILOTU	tabbouli
ABBIMNOS	bambinos
	nabobism
ABBINORX	brainbox
ABBIORST	rabbitos
ABBIRRTY	rabbitry
ABBIRSUU	suburbia
ABBKKNOO	bankbook
ABBKLOSU	blauboks
ABBLLRSU	bullbars
ABBLLSTU	bullbats
ABBLLSUY	syllabub
ABBLOPRY	probably
ABBMOORS	bomboras
ABBMOSST	bombasts
ABBMOSTU	bumboats
ABBNRSUU	suburban
ABBOSSTY	bobstays
ABCCDHIK	dabchick
ABCCDIOU	Boudicca
ABCCEEHN	bechance
ABCCEELP	peccable
ABCCEILY	celibacy
ABCCEIRS	breccias
ABCCEKMO	comeback
ABCCESUU	succubae
ABCCHISU	bacchius
ABCCHNOO	cabochon
ABCCIKKK	kickback
ABCCILOR	carbolic
ABCCILOT	cobaltic
ABCCILUU	cubicula
ABCCINOR	carbonic
ABCCIORS	ascorbic
ABCCKLLO	ballcock
ABCCKOOT	cockboat
ABCCKOSW	bawcocks
ABCCKSTU	cutbacks
ABCCMOOY	maccoboy
ABCCOOST	tobaccos
ABCDDEOR	brocaded
ABCDDETU	abducted
ABCDEEFK	feedback
ABCDEEHL	bleached
ABCDEEHR	breached

ABCDEELM	becalmed
ABCDEELS	debacles
ABCDEELU	educable
ABCDEEMR	cambered
	embraced
ABCDEENO	beaconed
ABCDEFLO	boldface
ABCDEGIR	birdcage
ABCDEGKL	Gladbeck
ABCDEHLN	blanched
ABCDEHNR	branched
ABCDEHOR	broached
ABCDEIIT	diabetic
ABCDEIKS	backside
ABCDEILR	calibred
ABCDEIMR	MacBride
ABCDEIPS	pedicabs
ABCDEIRS	ascribed
ABCDEISS	abscised
ABCDEKLO	blockade
ABCDEKLV	backveld
ABCDEKNN	neckband
ABCDEKNU	unbacked
ABCDEKRS	redbacks
ABCDELOO	caboodle
ABCDEMNU	dumbcane
ABCDEMOT	combated
ABCDEMRS	scrambed
ABCDENRU	unbraced
ABCDENSU	abducens
ABCDENTU	abducent
ABCDEORS	brocades
ABCDFKLO	foldback
ABCDHKLO	holdback
ABCDHLNU	clubhand
ABCDHMOR	Chambord
ABCDIILO	biocidal
	diabolic
ABCDIIRT	tribadic
ABCDIKLS	backslid
ABCDILLR	birdcall
ABCDILOU	cuboidal
ABCDILRS	baldrics
ABCDIRST	catbirds
ABCDKLNU	Buckland
ABCDKNOW	backdown
ABCDKOOR	backdoor
ABCDKOPR	backdrop
ABCDKORW	backword
ABCDLLNU	clubland
ABCDNOSS	absconds
ABCDOORS	cordobas
ABCDOORW	crabwood
ABCDOPRU	cupboard
ABCDORTU	abductor
ABCDORUY	obduracy
ABCEEEFK	beefcake
ABCEEGRR	Bergerac
ABCEEHLM	bechamel
ABCEEHLR	bleacher
ABCEEHLS	bleaches
ABCEEHLW	chewable
ABCEEHRS	breaches
ABCEEILT	celibate
	citeable
ABCEEIMN	ambience
ABCEEKLY	eyeblack
ABCEELOV	evocable
ABCEELRR	cerebral
ABCEELRT	bracelet
ABCEEMRR	embracer
ABCEEMRS	embraces
ABCEENOZ	cabezone
ABCEENRS	carbeens
	carbenes
ABCEENSS	absences
ABCEFIIT	beatific
ABCEFIKL	backfile
ABCEFIKR	backfire
	fireback
ABCEFINO	boniface
ABCEGHIN	beaching
ABCEGIRS	ribcages
ABCEGKLL	blackleg
ABCEGKLO	blockage
ABCEGKMU	megabuck
ABCEGKRY	greyback
ABCEHILR	Alberich
ABCEHIRR	Chabrier
ABCEHITT	bathetic
ABCEHLNS	blanches
	Schnabel
ABCEHLOR	bachelor
ABCEHLOS	chaebols
ABCEHLSU	bauchles
	chasuble
ABCEHMOT	hecatomb
ABCEHMRS	chambers
ABCEHMRY	Chambéry
ABCEHNRS	branches
ABCEHNSW	Schwaben
ABCEHOOT	cohobate
ABCEHORR	broacher
ABCEHORS	broaches
ABCEHORU	barouche
ABCEHRST	brachets
ABCEIIRT	rabietic
ABCEIJOT	Jacobite
ABCEIKKL	kickable
ABCEIKLP	pickable
ABCEIKLS	scablike
ABCEIKST	tiebacks
ABCEIKWZ	zwieback
ABCEILLR	cribella
ABCEILLT	balletic
ABCEILMS	alembics
ABCEILNN	binnacle
ABCEILNO	coinable
ABCEILOR	cabriole
ABCEILOS	sociable
ABCEILRS	calibers
	calibres
ABCEIMRW	micawber
ABCEINRS	brisance
	carbines
ABCEINRT	bacterin
ABCEINST	bascinet
	cabinets
ABCEINTU	incubate
ABCEIORS	aerobics
ABCEIORT	boracite
ABCEIOST	iceboats
ABCEIRRT	catbrier
ABCEIRSS	ascribes
ABCEIRSW	crabwise
ABCEIRTT	brattice
ABCEIRTY	acerbity
ABCEISSS	abscises
ABCEJLTY	abjectly
ABCEJNOS	Jacobsen
ABCEKKSW	skewback
ABCEKLLO	lockable
ABCEKLMO	mockable
ABCEKLNS	blackens
ABCEKLOO	cookable
ABCEKLSS	backless
ABCEKLST	blackest
ABCEKLTT	Blackett
ABCEKMNN	Beckmann
ABCEKNRS	brackens
ABCEKOOS	bookcase
	casebook
ABCEKRST	backrest
	brackets
ABCEKSST	setbacks
ABCEKSTW	wetbacks
ABCELLMP	Campbell
ABCELLPU	culpable
ABCELLSU	bullaces
ABCELMNY	lambency
ABCELMOS	cembalos
ABCELMRS	cambrels
	clambers
	scramble
ABCELMRU	La Cumbre
ABCELMRY	cymbaler
ABCELNUU	nubecula
ABCELOOT	bootlace
ABCELOPS	placebos
ABCELORT	brocatel
ABCELOST	obstacle
ABCELOSV	vocables
ABCELPSU	bluecaps
ABCELRTT	bractlet
ABCELSSU	bascules
ABCEMOOS	camboose
ABCEMORT	combater
ABCEMORU	Eboracum
ABCEMSSY	Cambyses
ABCENNOS	Besançon
ABCENORS	baconers
ABCENOSW	cowbanes
ABCENOSZ	cabezons
ABCENRSU	unbraces
ABCEOOSS	cabooses
ABCEOSUX	saucebox

ABCERRTU	carburet
ABCERRWY	cyberwar
ABCERSSU	subraces
ABCERTUU	cubature
ABCESSTW	webcasts
ABCESTUU	subacute
ABCFIKLL	backfill
ABCFIKNS	finbacks
ABCFILOS	bifocals
ABCFIOST	biofacts
ABCFKLLU	fullback
ABCFKLLY	blackfly
ABCFKLSY	flybacks
ABCGHINT	batching
ABCGHKOS	hogbacks
ABCGHNPU	punchbag
ABCGIINN	cabining
ABCGIKLN	blacking
ABCGIKNS	backings
ABCGINRS	bracings
ABCGKLMU	blackgum
ABCGKLOS	backlogs
ABCGMSSU	scumbags
ABCHHIIS	hibachis
ABCHIIPS	biphasic
ABCHIKLS	blackish
ABCHIKRS	brackish
ABCHILOO	coolibah
ABCHIMOR	choriamb
ABCHIMRU	brachium
ABCHINOR	bronchia
ABCHIOST	cohabits
ABCHIRRT	tribrach
ABCHKLOW	howlback
ABCHKMPU	humpback
ABCHKOOP	chapbook
ABCHKOOS	cashbook
ABCHKSTU	hackbuts
ABCHLLUU	clubhaul
ABCHMOTX	matchbox
ABCHOSTT	chatbots
ABCIIKRR	airbrick
ABCIIMNS	minicabs
ABCIINRS	Scriabin
ABCIIORS	isobaric
ABCIIRST	tribasic
ABCIIRTU	Curitiba
ABCIISTY	basicity
ABCIJNOS	jacobins
ABCIKLST	backlist
ABCIKMRS	Bismarck
ABCIKNPS	backspin
ABCIKSSY	sickbays
ABCILLNY	billycan
ABCILLSU	bacillus
ABCILLSY	syllabic
ABCILMMO	cimbalom
ABCILMOO	Colombia
ABCILMOU	Columbia
ABCILNPU	publican
ABCILOSY	sociably
ABCILRRU	rubrical
ABCIMMSU	cambiums
ABCIMNRU	Cumbrian
ABCIMSST	cambists
ABCINNOS	nonbasic
ABCINORY	baryonic
ABCINOST	botanics
ABCINOUV	Bucovina
ABCINRSU	Brancusi
ABCINRVY	vibrancy
ABCIOPRS	saprobic
ABCIORSU	caribous
ABCIOSSU	scabious
ABCIOSTU	Subotica
ABCIOSUV	bivouacs
ABCJKOOT	bootjack
	jackboot
ABCKLLOS	ballocks
ABCKLLPU	pullback
ABCKLOPT	blacktop
ABCKLOST	backlots
ABCKLOTU	blackout
ABCKMOOR	backroom
ABCKMOSS	mossback
ABCKMOST	backmost
ABCKMRSU	buckrams
ABCKMSUZ	zambucks
ABCKNNOS	bannocks
ABCKOORR	roorback
ABCKOORU	buckaroo
ABCKOPST	backstop
ABCKOSSW	sowbacks
ABCKSSTU	sackbuts
ABCKSSUW	bucksaws
	sawbucks
ABCLLNOR	cornball
ABCLLOSY	callboys
ABCLLPUY	culpably
ABCLMMOY	cymbalom
ABCLMOOO	coloboma
ABCLMOSY	cymbalos
ABCLMSUU	baculums
ABCLNORY	carbonyl
ABCLNSSU	subclans
ABCLORXY	carboxyl
ABCLSSSU	subclass
ABCMOORT	mobocrat
ABCNORTY	corybant
ABCNOUYY	buoyancy
ABCORRSS	crossbar
ABCORRSW	crowbars
ABCORRTU	turbocar
ABCORSSU	scabrous
ABCRSTTU	subtract
ABDDEEEH	beheaded
ABDDEEGG	debagged
ABDDEEGR	badgered
ABDDEEHT	deathbed
ABDDEEKR	debarked
ABDDEERR	debarred
ABDDEEST	bedstead
ABDDEGIR	abridged
	brigaded
ABDDEHMO	hebdomad
ABDDEHOY	hobdayed
ABDDEILS	disabled
ABDDEILU	buddleia
ABDDEINS	sideband
ABDDELRS	bladders
ABDDELRY	bladdery
ABDDENOU	abounded
ABDDEORS	adsorbed
	roadbeds
ABDDEOSY	deadboys
ABDDFORR	Bradford
ABDDILMO	lambdoid
ABDDILRY	ladybird
ABDDIMNO	bondmaid
ABDDINSS	disbands
ABDDIRRY	yardbird
ABDDLLOS	oddballs
ABDDLNRY	Byrd Land
ABDDLUWY	bulwaddy
ABDEEEFL	feedable
ABDEEEMN	bemeaned
ABDEEENR	Aberdeen
ABDEEERV	beavered
	bereaved
ABDEEFGS	feedbags
ABDEEFLM	flambeed
ABDEEGGR	beggared
ABDEEGLL	gabelled
ABDEEGLR	Belgrade
ABDEEGNO	Abednego
ABDEEHIR	braeheid
ABDEEHLS	shedable
ABDEEHNO	bonehead
ABDEEHRR	Eberhard
ABDEEHRT	breathed
ABDEEHST	bethesda
ABDEEIKR	bidarkee
ABDEEILN	deniable
ABDEEILR	rideable
ABDEEILS	abseiled
ABDEEILW	bewailed
ABDEEIST	beadiest
	diabetes
ABDEEJMN	enjambed
ABDEEKMN	embanked
ABDEEKMR	embarked
ABDEELLL	labelled
ABDEELLW	weldable
ABDEELMM	embalmed
ABDEELMN	mendable
ABDEELMS	beldames
ABDEELMZ	emblazed
ABDEELNS	sendable
ABDEELOR	leeboard
ABDEELPT	bedplate
ABDEELRR	barreled
ABDEELZZ	bedazzle
ABDEEMNO	bemoaned
ABDEEMNS	beadsmen
	bedesman
ABDEENNR	bannered

ABDEENRT bantered
ABDEENRY barneyed
ABDEENRZ brazened
ABDEENST absented
ABDEENTT battened
ABDEEPRS bespread
ABDEERRT bartered
ABDEERRY ryebread
ABDEERSS debasers
ABDEERST breasted
debaters
ABDEERTT battered
ABDEERTW waterbed
ABDEERTY betrayed
ABDEERWY bewrayed
ABDEESST basseted
besteads
ABDEFHOO boofhead
ABDEFIIS basified
ABDEFILN findable
ABDEFLLO foldable
ABDEFLOR fordable
ABDEGHIS bigheads
ABDEGHRS beghards
ABDEGILN blindage
ABDEGILU guidable
ABDEGINR bearding
breading
ABDEGINS beadings
debasing
ABDEGINT debating
ABDEGIRR abridger
ABDEGIRS abridges
brigades
ABDEGLMO gamboled
ABDEGLOT globated
ABDEGLSU slugabed
ABDEGNOS bondages
dogbanes
ABDEGOPR pegboard
ABDEGORT bogarted
ABDEGRSU subgrade
ABDEHINS banished
ABDEHITU habitude
ABDEHKLU bulkhead
ABDEHKNO knobhead
ABDEHLLN handbell
ABDEHLLO holdable
ABDEHLLU bullhead
ABDEHLMS shambled
ABDEHLRS halberds
ABDEHMSU ambushed
ABDEHNSU Dushanbe
ABDEHORR abhorred
harbored
ABDEHOSW bowheads
ABDEHRST breadths
ABDEHSSU subheads
ABDEIIRT diatribe
ABDEIKNU baudekin
ABDEILLR brailled
ABDEILLS slidable
ABDEILMN mandible
ABDEILNN bin Laden
ABDEILNR bilander
ABDEILNW windable
ABDEILNY deniably
ABDEILOV voidable
ABDEILPS piebalds
ABDEILRS bedrails
ABDEILRT librated
ABDEILRV drivable
ABDEILSS disables
ABDEILSU audibles
ABDEILTU dutiable
ABDEIMOO amoeboid
ABDEIMOR amberoid
ABDEINNR endbrain
ABDEINOR debonair
ABDEINOT obtained
ABDEINRS brandies
ABDEINST bandiest
ABDEINSU unbiased
ABDEIOST beastoid
ABDEIOTV obviated
ABDEIPST baptised
ABDEIPTZ baptized
ABDEIRRS braiders
ABDEIRST braidest
tribades
ABDEIRSX axebirds
ABDEIRTV vibrated
ABDEISSU disabuse
ABDEISTW bawdiest
ABDEJNOW jawboned
ABDEKLSW skewbald
ABDEKNSU sunbaked
ABDEKORW beadwork
ABDEKORY keyboard
ABDELLMO moldable
ABDELLOR beadroll
ABDELLOT balloted
ABDELLUY du Bellay
ABDELNOR banderol
Oberland
ABDELNOZ blazoned
ABDELNSS baldness
ABDELNST blandest
ABDELORU laboured
ABDELOSV absolved
ABDELOSW dowsabel
ABDELRSU durables
ABDEMNNS bandsmen
ABDEMNOS abdomens
ABDEMORT bromated
ABDEMRSU bermudas
ABDEMRTU drumbeat
ABDENNOS noseband
ABDENORR Dearborn
ABDENORS bandores
broadens
ABDENORW rawboned
ABDENORY boneyard
ABDENOTW downbeat
ABDENRRS branders
ABDENRRU unbarred
ABDENRSS drabness
ABDENRTU breadnut
turbaned
ABDENTTU debutant
ABDEOORW bearwood
ABDEOPRT probated
ABDEORRS boarders
ABDEORRW wardrobe
ABDEORST broadest
ABDEORSW sowbread
ABDEORTU obdurate
ABDEORUX bordeaux
ABDEOSTU boutades
ABDEPSSY bypassed
ABDEPSTU Budapest
ABDERSST dabsters
ABDERSSU surbased
ABDERSTW bedstraw
ABDERTUW drawtube
ABDFLOOT foldboat
ABDGHINR hangbird
ABDGIINR braiding
ABDGILOO Badoglio
ABDGILOR gaolbird
ABDGIMNR Bridgman
ABDGINNO Abingdon
ABDGINNR branding
ABDGINNY bandying
ABDGINOR boarding
ABDGINRS brigands
ABDGINST dingbats
ABDGINSW windbags
ABDGINUY Daubigny
ABDGLSUY ladybugs
ABDGNRSU Sandburg
ABDGNRUU Dünaburg
ABDHHSSU shadbush
ABDHIIST adhibits
ABDHILLN handbill
ABDHILNS blandish
ABDHINRS brandish
ABDHIRTY birthday
ABDHKNOO handbook
ABDHLMUZ Dzhambul
ABDHLORW blowhard
ABDHLOST Shadbolt
ABDHMOTU badmouth
ABDHNORS bodhrans
ABDHNSSU husbands
ABDIIJLR jailbird
ABDIILLR billiard
ABDIILNW Baldwin I
ABDIIMNR midbrain
ABDIIMSU basidium
ABDIINOS anobiids
obsidian
ABDIINRR rainbird
ABDIINTT banditti
ABDIIRTY rabidity
ABDILLRY ribaldly

ABDILMOR Lombardi
ABDILNOS Basildon
ABDILOOS diabolos
ABDILORS labroids
ABDILOST tabloids
ABDILRRY ribaldry
ABDILRZZ blizzard
ABDINOTY antibody
ABDINRTY banditry
ABDIPRSU upbraids
ABDJMOOR doorjamb
ABDKOOSY daybooks
ABDLLNUW bundwall
ABDLLORS bollards
ABDLMORY Lombardy
ABDLOSYY ladyboys
ABDLRSUU subdural
ABDLRSUY absurdly
ABDMNNOS bondsman
ABDMOOPR mopboard
ABDNOPRS probands
ABDNORUY boundary
ABDNOSSY sandboys
ABDNSSTY standbys
ABDNSTUU butsudan
ABDOORTU outboard
ABDOOSSW basswood
ABDRSSTU bustards
ABDRSUZZ buzzards
ABEEEFRS freebase
ABEEEGRV beverage
ABEEEHTT hebetate
ABEEELLR reelable
ABEEELNS Lebanese
ABEEENRT tenebrae
ABEEENST absentee
ABEEERSV bereaves
ABEEFFNO banoffee
ABEEFILN fineable
ABEEFILR afebrile
balefire
fireable
ABEEFILS feasible
ABEEFILT fleabite
ABEEFLLL fellable
ABEEFLLN befallen
ABEEFLMS flambees
ABEEFORR forebear
ABEEGILV giveable
ABEEGIRV verbiage
ABEEGLLS gabelles
ABEEGLNU Benguela
ABEEGLTT gettable
ABEEGMNR bargemen
ABEEGMTY megabyte
ABEEGMUU Maubeuge
ABEEGNOS Gabonese
ABEEGNRR Béranger
ABEEGNRT Bretagne
ABEEGNTT bagnette
ABEEGOSZ gazeboes
ABEEGRRS gerberas
ABEEGRSU auberges
ABEEGRSW brewages
ABEEGTTU baguette
ABEEHILR hireable
ABEEHINT thebaine
ABEEHIRZ hebraize
ABEEHLLL heelball
ABEEHLLP helpable
ABEEHLLR harebell
ABEEHLMR Malherbe
ABEEHLPT aleph-bet
ABEEHNSS banshees
shebeans
ABEEHORS rheobase
ABEEHQTU bequeath
ABEEHRRT breather
ABEEHRST breathes
ABEEHSTY eyebaths
ABEEIKKL beaklike
ABEEIKLL likeable
ABEEIKLM beamlike
ABEEIKRS bakeries
ABEEILLN lineable
ABEEILLR reliable
ABEEILLV leviable
liveable
ABEEILMN mineable
ABEEILNP plebeian
ABEEILNS Balinese
baseline
ABEEILNU banlieue
ABEEILNV enviable
ABEEILNZ Belizean
ABEEILPX expiable
ABEEILRR blearier
ABEEILRT liberate
ABEEILRW bewailer
ABEEILSS seisable
ABEEILST seablite
ABEEILSZ seizable
sizeable
ABEEILTV evitable
ABEEILUU Beaulieu
ABEEILVW viewable
ABEEINRZ Berezina
ABEEINST betaines
ABEEISST beasties
ABEEISTT beatiest
ABEEISTU beauties
ABEEJMNT Betjeman
ABEEJMOR jamboree
ABEEKLLW Bakewell
ABEEKLOT keelboat
ABEEKLSS beakless
ABEEKLST bleakest
ABEEKMNR brakemen
ABEEKMRR reembark
ABEEKNSY eyebanks
ABEEKOOP peekaboo
ABEEKPSS bespeaks
ABEEKRRS breakers
ABEELLLR labeller
ABEELLLS sellable
ABEELLLT tellable
ABEELLMT meltable
ABEELLOV loveable
ABEELLRS relabels
ABEELLSY eyeballs
ABEELMMR embalmer
ABEELMNO bonemeal
ABEELMOV moveable
ABEELMPR preamble
ABEELMSS assemble
beamless
ABEELMSZ emblazes
ABEELMTT embattle
ABEELNOP beanpole
openable
ABEELNOV ovenable
ABEELNRS enablers
ABEELNRT rentable
ABEELNTU tuneable
ABEELOPR operable
ropeable
ABEELORX exorable
ABEELOTV voteable
ABEELRST blearest
bleaters
retables
ABEELRSU reusable
ABEELRSV servable
ABEELRTU bateleur
ABEELSSS baseless
ABEELSSU sublease
ABEELSTT testable
ABEELTTW wettable
ABEEMMNR membrane
ABEEMMRU bummaree
ABEEMNQU Queen Mab
ABEEMNRS Seremban
ABEEMNST basement
ABEEMNTT abetment
ABEEMRSS besmears
ABEENNRT banneret
ABEENNSW bawneens
ABEENNTU unbeaten
ABEENORS seaborne
ABEENOTZ benzoate
ABEENRRT banterer
ABEENRSS bareness
ABEENRST absenter
ABEENRSV verbenas
ABEENSSS baseness
ABEEORRV overbear
ABEERRRT barterer
ABEERRST rebaters
ABEERRTT barrette
batterer
berretta
ABEERRTV vertebra
ABEERRTY betrayer
teaberry
ABEERRWY bewrayer
ABEERSTT abetters

ABEFFKOR breakoff
ABEFFLRS bafflers
ABEFFOST offbeats
ABEFGSST gabfests
ABEFHILS fishable
ABEFIIMR fimbriae
ABEFIISS basifies
ABEFILLL fallible
ABEFILLO foilable
ABEFILLR fireball
ABEFILLT liftable
ABEFILOT lifeboat
ABEFILRS barflies
ABEFILSY feasibly
ABEFILTT fittable
ABEFIORT biforate
fireboat
ABEFIRRT firebrat
ABEFITUY beautify
ABEFKLNT Left Bank
ABEFLLMU blameful
ABEFLLRU furlable
ABEFLLTU tableful
ABEFLMOR formable
ABEFLRSU surfable
ABEFLRTU Flaubert
ABEFOORT barefoot
ABEFORRS forbears
ABEFORTU Beaufort
ABEGGHLU huggable
ABEGGILN beagling
ABEGGIST baggiest
ABEGGITY gigabyte
ABEGGLRS blaggers
ABEGGLRY beggarly
ABEGGMOS gamboges
ABEGGRRS braggers
ABEGHIMR Maghrebi
ABEGHINS Siegbahn
ABEGHINV behaving
ABEGHINZ Benghazi
ABEGHNSS shebangs
ABEGIILR Gabrieli
ABEGIIMS bigamies
ABEGIJTU bijugate
ABEGIKNR breaking
ABEGIKNT betaking
ABEGILLN labeling
ABEGILNN enabling
ABEGILNR blearing
ABEGILNS signable
singable
ABEGILNT bleating
tangible
ABEGILNY belaying
ABEGILOT obligate
ABEGILPP Big Apple
ABEGIMNN benaming
ABEGIMNR breaming
ABEGIMNS beamings
ABEGIMNY embaying
ABEGIMST megabits
ABEGINOS begonias
ABEGINRR barreing
berrigan
ABEGINRS bearings
sabering
ABEGINRT berating
rebating
ABEGINRU Rugbeian
ABEGINRW bewaring
ABEGINST beatings
ABEGINTT abetting
ABEGINTW wingbeat
ABEGIOSS biogases
ABEGIPPS bagpipes
ABEGKORS grosbeak
ABEGLMOR Lag b'Omer
ABEGLMRS gamblers
gambrels
ABEGLMUY mealybug
ABEGLORU Uleåborg
ABEGLORW growable
ABEGLRRS garblers
ABEGLRSS garbless
ABEGLRSU blaguers
ABEGMNOS gambeson
ABEGMNOY bogeyman
ABEGMORT bergamot
ABEGMRSU umbrages
ABEGNOOR Gaborone
ABEGNOSS nosebags
ABEGNOST Bastogne
ABEGNSTU subagent
ABEGOPSY pageboys
ABEGOSUY buoyages
ABEGRRUV burgrave
ABEGSSTU substage
ABEHIINR Hibernia
ABEHILNR hibernal
ABEHILTT tithable
ABEHIMMS memsahib
ABEHIMNO bohemian
ABEHINSS banishes
ABEHINST absinthe
ABEHIORV behavior
ABEHIRRS brashier
ABEHISTU habitues
ABEHKRSU hauberks
ABEHKSTU ketubahs
ABEHLMSS shambles
ABEHLRST blathers
halberts
ABEHMNOR hornbeam
ABEHMOOR rehoboam
ABEHMSSU ambushes
ABEHMSTU bushmeat
ABEHNSTU sunbathe
ABEHORRR abhorrer
harborer
ABEHOSTX hatboxes
ABEHOSXY hayboxes
ABEHRSST brashest
ABEHRTUY Bayreuth
ABEIILMT imitable
ABEIILNN biennial
ABEIILNR bilinear
Liberian
ABEIILNV inviable
ABEIILPT pitiable
ABEIILRT Albert II
ABEIILST sibilate
ABEIILTV vitiable
ABEIINRR brainier
ABEIINRS binaries
Siberian
ABEIIRST Tiberias
ABEIJLNO joinable
ABEIJLTU jubilate
ABEIJMNN benjamin
ABEIJNSS basenjis
ABEIKLLM balmlike
lamblike
ABEIKLLN balkline
linkable
ABEIKLNS sinkable
ABEIKLRU baulkier
ABEIKLSS kissable
ABEIKLST balkiest
ABEIKNRS bearskin
ABEIKNST beatniks
ABEILLLM millable
ABEILLLT tillable
ABEILLLW willable
ABEILLMS mislabel
ABEILLNT libelant
ABEILLNV Banville
ABEILLOS isolable
lobelias
ABEILLOV violable
ABEILLPS lapsible
ABEILLRS brailles
liberals
ABEILLRY Bareilly
blearily
reliably
ABEILLST bastille
listable
ABEILMNS bailsmen
ABEILMNT bailment
ABEILMRW wamblier
ABEILMSS missable
ABEILMST balmiest
timbales
ABEILNNW winnable
ABEILNPS biplanes
ABEILNRS rinsable
ABEILNRU ruinable
ABEILNSS lesbians
ABEILNST instable
ABEILNSU sabuline
ABEILNTV bivalent
ABEILNTY binately
ABEILNUV unviable
ABEILNVY enviably
ABEILPPR rippable

ABEILPPT	tippable
ABEILPRT	partible
ABEILPSS	passible
ABEILPST	epiblast
ABEILRRU	reburial
ABEILRST	librates
ABEILRTW	writable
ABEILRYY	biyearly
ABEILSST	astilbes
	stabiles
ABEILSSU	issuable
ABEILSTU	suitable
ABEILSUX	bisexual
ABEILSVV	bivalves
ABEILSYZ	sizeably
ABEIMORU	aerobium
ABEIMRST	barmiest
ABEIMRSU	aumbries
ABEIMRTV	ambivert
	verbatim
ABEIMSSU	iambuses
ABEINNOZ	bezonian
ABEINNRU	inurbane
ABEINOOT	Boeotian
ABEINORR	airborne
ABEINORS	baronies
	searobin
ABEINORT	baritone
	obtainer
ABEINOST	botanies
	botanise
	obeisant
ABEINOTZ	botanize
ABEINRRW	brawnier
ABEINRSU	anburies
	urbanise
ABEINRTU	braunite
	urbanite
ABEINRUZ	urbanize
ABEINSST	basinets
	bassinet
ABEINTTU	intubate
ABEIORTV	abortive
ABEIORUV	Beauvoir
ABEIOSTV	obviates
ABEIPRRS	sparerib
ABEIPSST	baptises
ABEIPSTZ	baptizes
ABEIRRRS	barriers
ABEIRRSS	brasiers
	brassier
ABEIRRST	arbiters
	rarebits
ABEIRRSU	Briareus
ABEIRRSZ	braziers
ABEIRRVY	breviary
ABEIRRYZ	braziery
ABEIRSSS	brassies
ABEIRSSU	airbuses
ABEIRSTT	birettas
	ratbites
ABEIRSTV	vibrates
ABEIRSTW	warbiest
ABEIRSTY	bestiary
	sybarite
ABEIRTTY	ytterbia
ABEISTTT	battiest
ABEJKLOU	kabeljou
ABEJLMPU	jumpable
ABEJMOOR	jeroboam
ABEJNOSW	jawbones
ABEJRRSU	abjurers
ABEKLMOS	abelmosk
	smokable
ABEKLNOW	knowable
ABEKLNST	blankest
	blankets
ABEKLNTY	blankety
ABEKLORW	workable
ABEKLRSU	baulkers
ABEKMNNS	banksmen
ABEKNNOT	banknote
ABEKNSSU	sunbakes
ABEKNSTW	West Bank
ABEKOORY	yearbook
ABEKORST	Stabroek
ABEKORTU	breakout
	outbreak
ABEKPRSU	breakups
ABEKRSTY	basketry
ABELLLMU	labellum
ABELLLSY	syllable
ABELLMRU	umbellar
	umbrella
ABELLNOT	ballonet
ABELLNST	netballs
ABELLOSV	solvable
ABELLOTU	lobulate
ABELLOTY	lobately
	oblately
ABELLOVY	loveably
ABELLRVY	verbally
ABELMNNO	nobleman
ABELMNOP	Belmopan
ABELMNOZ	emblazon
ABELMNSU	albumens
ABELMOSU	albumose
ABELMOSV	movables
ABELMOTY	metaboly
ABELMRRS	marblers
	ramblers
ABELMRST	lamberts
ABELMSSY	assembly
ABELNNOR	bannerol
ABELNORZ	blazoner
ABELNOSS	bonselas
ABELNOST	notables
	stonable
ABELNOSY	baloneys
ABELNPRU	prunable
ABELNRRY	barrenly
ABELNRSY	Barnsley
	blarneys
ABELNRTU	turnable
ABELNRUY	urbanely
ABELNRYZ	brazenly
ABELNSTU	unstable
ABELNSTY	absently
ABELNSUU	unusable
ABELOPRT	portable
ABELOPRV	provable
ABELOPRY	operably
ABELOPST	potables
ABELOQTU	quotable
ABELORRS	laborers
ABELORRU	labourer
	rubeolar
ABELORST	bloaters
	sortable
	storable
ABELORSV	absolver
ABELOSSU	sabulose
ABELOSSV	absolves
ABELOSTU	absolute
ABELOSTW	bestowal
ABELPRTU	pubertal
ABELRRSW	brawlers
	warblers
ABELRSST	blasters
ABELRSTT	battlers
ABELRSTU	baluster
ABELRTTU	rebuttal
ABELSSSU	subsales
ABELSTUU	subulate
ABELSTWY	beltways
ABELTTUU	tubulate
ABEMMNOO	moonbeam
ABEMNOTU	Beaumont
	umbonate
ABEMNOTW	batwomen
ABEMNPRU	penumbra
ABEMNRRY	Berryman
ABEMNSSU	sunbeams
ABEMNSUY	sunbeamy
ABEMNTTU	abutment
ABEMORST	bromates
ABENNNOR	Narbonne
ABENNORS	Bernanos
ABENNORT	Brentano
ABENNOTU	butanone
ABENNRUV	Van Buren
ABENOPSU	subpoena
ABENORSS	baroness
ABENORST	baronets
ABENORTT	betatron
ABENORTV	bevatron
ABENORTY	barytone
ABENOSSW	sawbones
ABENOSSY	soybeans
ABENOSTY	bayonets
ABENQSTU	banquets
ABENSTZZ	bezzants
ABEOPPRY	paperboy
ABEOPRSS	saprobes
ABEOPRST	probates
ABEOQRSU	baroques

ABEORRST taborers
ABEORRTU tabourer
ABEORSST boasters
ABEORSSY rosebays
ABEORSTT abettors
taborets
ABEORSTU saboteur
ABEORTTU obturate
tabouret
ABEORTUV outbrave
ABEOSSST asbestos
ABEOSTWX sweatbox
ABEPRSSY passerby
ABEPRSTY typebars
ABEPSSSY bypasses
ABEQRSUU arquebus
ABERRRTY barretry
ABERRTYY tayberry
ABERRWXY waxberry
ABERSSSU surbases
ABERSSTU abstruse
ABERSTTU abutters
ABERTTUY butyrate
ABFFGILN baffling
ABFFIILS bailiffs
ABFFINOS banoffis
ABFFLLPU puffball
ABFFLOST blastoff
ABFFLOSU buffalos
ABFFNOTU bouffant
ABFGLLOO goofball
ABFGORUU faubourg
ABFHIORS boarfish
ABFIILLR fibrilla
ABFIILMR fimbrial
ABFIILRR fibrilar
ABFILLLY fallibly
ABFILNSU basinful
ABFILSTU fabulist
ABFIMORS fibromas
ABFKLLOR korfball
ABFLLOOT football
ABFLLOST softball
ABFLOSTU boastful
ABFLOSTW batfowls
ABFLOSTY flyboats
ABFLOSUU fabulous
ABFNORTU turbofan
ABFOOSTY foyboats
ABFORSTU surfboat
ABGGGILN blagging
ABGGGINR bragging
ABGGILMN gambling
ABGGILNR garbling
ABGGNOOT toboggan
ABGGORST boggarts
ABGGRSUU Augsburg
ABGHHILL highball
ABGHIINT habiting
ABGHINWZ whizbang
ABGHMORU brougham
ABGHMOTU Tombaugh
ABGHMRSU hamburgs
ABGHNRUV Vanbrugh
ABGHORTU broughta
ABGHPRSU Hapsburg
ABGIIILN alibiing
ABGIILNR brailing
ABGIILOT obligati
ABGIIMST bigamist
ABGIINNO bignonia
ABGIINNR braining
ABGIINRS braising
ABGIINSS biassing
ABGIIRTT Birgitta
ABGIJNRU abjuring
ABGIKLNN blanking
ABGIKLNU baulking
ABGIKNNS bankings
ABGIKNRR ringbark
ABGILMNR marbling
rambling
ABGILMNS lambings
ABGILMNW wambling
ABGILNNT bantling
ABGILNNU Bulganin
ABGILNOR laboring
ABGILNOT bloating
ABGILNRT blarting
ABGILNRW brawling
warbling
ABGILNST blasting
stabling
ABGILNSW bawlings
ABGILNTT battling
blatting
ABGILNTY tangibly
ABGILOOT obligato
ABGILORS garboils
ABGILORW brigalow
ABGIMMNO mamboing
ABGIMOSU bigamous
subimago
ABGINNOR aborning
ABGINNRT Branting
ABGINNST bantings
ABGINOOT tabooing
ABGINORT aborting
borating
ABGINOST boasting
ABGINOUU Oubangui
ABGINTTU abutting
ABGIRRSS ribgrass
ABGKLOUV Bulgakov
ABGKOOYZ Boğazköy
ABGKORSW workbags
ABGLLLOY globally
ABGLLNUW bungwall
ABGLLORU globular
ABGLLRUY bullyrag
ABGLMOPU plumbago
ABGLNOOT longboat
ABGLNOUW bungalow
ABGLORST ragbolts
ABGLORSU glabrous
ABGLRRSU burglars
ABGLRRUY burglary
ABGLRSUZ Salzburg
ABGMORSW bagworms
ABGNOORY boongary
ABGNOPRS probangs
ABGNORSU osnaburg
ABGNOSTU gunboats
ABGNOSWY bowyangs
ABGOORST botargos
ABGOPSST postbags
ABGOSTTU tugboats
ABGRRTUW Wartburg
ABHHOSTU Shabuoth
ABHIINST inhabits
ABHIINTY Bithynia
ABHIIORZ rhizobia
ABHIKLLW hawkbill
ABHIKLOR kohlrabi
ABHIKNRU Bukharin
ABHIKSTW hawkbits
ABHIKSUZ buzkashi
ABHILNOS hobnails
ABHILNOT biathlon
ABHILOPS basophil
ABHILSST stablish
ABHILSTU halibuts
ABHIMNOR Morbihan
ABHIOSST isobaths
ABHIOSTU hautbois
ABHIRRSU airbrush
ABHKOOOT boathook
ABHLLMOT mothball
ABHLLOOY ballyhoo
ABHLLPSU pushball
ABHLOSUX boxhauls
ABHLOSWW washbowl
ABHLPSUY subphyla
ABHLSSTU saltbush
ABHMNSUU subhuman
ABHMOORT bathroom
ABHOORST tarboosh
ABHOOSTW showboat
ABHORRSU harbours
ABHOSTUY hautboys
ABHRSTTU Bathurst
ABHSSTUW washtubs
ABIIIKRT Kiribati
ABIIINRS birianis
ABIIKKST kibitkas
ABIIKLSS basilisk
ABIILLMR millibar
ABIILLTY lability
ABIILMNO binomial
ABIILMNS albinism
ABIILNNO Albinoni
ABIILNOT libation
ABIILNOV Bolivian
ABIILNRS brasilin
ABIILNRY brainily
ABIILNRZ brazilin

ABIILNST	sibilant
ABIILNVY	inviably
ABIILPTY	pitiably
ABIIMNOT	ambition
ABIIMNRS	minibars
ABIINORS	robinias
ABIINRSY	biryanis
ABIIQQUU	Qu Qiu Bai
ABIIRRRU	Ibarruri
ABIIRRTZ	Biarritz
ABIIRSSV	vibrissa
ABIJLNRS	brinjals
ABIJLNTU	jubilant
ABIJNOST	banjoist
ABIKLLUY	baulkily
ABIKLMNS	lambkins
	lambskin
ABIKLMOU	kumbaloi
ABIKNORR	ironbark
ABIKNORU	Baikonur
ABIKNOUV	Bukovina
ABIKNRSY	Skryabin
ABIKRSST	britskas
ABIKRSTZ	britzkas
ABILLLPY	playbill
ABILLOVY	violably
ABILLRTY	tribally
ABILLSSW	sawbills
ABILLSWX	waxbills
ABILLSWY	waybills
ABILMNOU	olibanum
ABILMNSU	albumins
ABILMOPS	bioplasm
ABILMORS	laborism
ABILMPSU	Ipsambul
ABILNOOT	boltonia
	oblation
ABILNOTU	ablution
	abutilon
ABILNRTU	tribunal
	turbinal
ABILNRWY	brawnily
ABILNSTU	Istanbul
ABILOPRS	parboils
ABILORST	laborist
	orbitals
	strobila
ABILORSV	bolivars
ABILRSSY	brassily
ABILRSUV	subviral
ABILSSUY	issuably
ABILSTUY	suitably
ABIMNOSU	bimanous
ABIMNRSU	urbanism
ABIMORSU	biramous
ABIMPSST	baptisms
ABINOORS	boronias
ABINOORT	abortion
ABINOPTX	paintbox
ABINORST	Ratisbon
	taborins
ABINORSW	rainbows
ABINORTU	tabourin
ABINOSST	bastions
ABINOSTT	botanist
ABINRSTV	vibrants
ABINRTTY	Brittany
ABINRTUY	urbanity
ABIOORRV	Río Bravo
ABIOPRSU	biparous
ABIOPSTU	subtopia
ABIORRST	arborist
ABIORRTV	vibrator
ABIORSTV	vibratos
ABIORTUY	obituary
ABIPSSTT	baptists
ABIRRSTU	airburst
ABISSSST	bassists
ABJKMOSS	sjamboks
ABJKNOOS	Jakobson
ABKKMOOR	bookmark
ABKLLNOR	bankroll
ABKLOOPY	playbook
ABKLRSUW	bulwarks
ABKNOPST	stopbank
ABKNPRTU	bankrupt
ABKOOPSS	passbook
ABLLMOOR	ballroom
ABLLMOPW	blowlamp
ABLLMOSY	smallboy
ABLLNOOS	balloons
ABLLNOSW	snowball
ABLLORRS	rollbars
ABLLOSTY	tallboys
ABLLRTUY	brutally
ABLLSSUY	syllabus
ABLMNNTU	Bultmann
ABLMNRUU	alburnum
	laburnum
ABLNORYZ	blazonry
ABLNRSUY	Lansbury
ABLNSTUY	unstably
ABLOORTY	oblatory
ABLOPRSU	subpolar
ABLOPRTY	portably
ABLOPRVY	provably
ABLOPSYY	playboys
ABLORSST	borstals
ABLORSSU	subsolar
ABLORSTY	sortably
ABLOSSUU	sabulous
ABLOSTTU	subtotal
ABLPRTUY	abruptly
ABMOORRS	barrooms
ABMORSTU	tambours
ABMRRSUY	burramys
ABMRSUUU	Usumbura
ABNNORUV	von Braun
ABNOORRT	roborant
ABNOORYZ	bryozoan
ABNOOSSS	bassoons
ABNORSTY	barytons
ABNORTUU	runabout
ABNOSSUU	Aubusson
ABOORSTW	rowboats
ABOOSTTU	outboast
ABOOSTTW	towboats
ABPRSSTU	subparts
ACCCDILY	Cycladic
ACCCDIRU	Carducci
ACCCENPY	peccancy
ACCCFIIL	calcific
ACCCIILT	calcitic
ACCCIIPR	capricci
ACCCILLY	cyclical
ACCDDEKO	cockaded
ACCDDEOR	accorded
ACCDDIII	diacidic
ACCDDIIT	didactic
ACCDEEER	reaccede
ACCDEELN	canceled
ACCDEENS	cadences
ACCDEENT	accented
ACCDEEPT	accepted
ACCDEERS	acceders
ACCDEERT	accreted
ACCDEESS	accessed
ACCDEGIN	acceding
ACCDEHIK	chiacked
ACCDEHIL	chaliced
ACCDEHIN	chicaned
ACCDEHKY	chyacked
ACCDEILN	calcined
ACCDEILY	delicacy
ACCDEINO	decanoic
ACCDEINT	accident
ACCDEIRT	accredit
ACCDEISU	caudices
ACCDEKLR	crackled
ACCDEKOS	cockades
ACCDELSY	Cyclades
ACCDENOV	concaved
ACCDEORR	accorder
ACCDEOST	accosted
ACCDERSU	accursed
ACCDESUU	caduceus
	caucused
ACCDGHOO	coachdog
ACCDHIIR	diarchic
ACCDHIKW	Chadwick
ACCDHILS	chalcids
ACCDHIOT	cathodic
ACCDHIRY	dyarchic
ACCDIIOT	acidotic
ACCDIIST	dicastic
ACCDILTY	dactylic
ACCDINOR	cancroid
	draconic
ACCDIOOR	coracoid
ACCDITUY	caducity
ACCDOSUU	caducous
ACCEEHLO	cochleae
ACCEEHLS	caleches
ACCEEHMP	Campeche
ACCEEILR	celeriac
ACCEEILS	ecclesia

ACCEEIMN MacNeice
ACCEEKLN necklace
ACCEELNO coenacle
ACCEELNR canceler
clarence
ACCEELNS cenacles
ACCEELOS coalesce
ACCEELRT calcrete
ACCEENNS nascence
ACCEENRT reaccent
ACCEENST acescent
ACCEEPRT accepter
reaccept
ACCEERST accretes
ACCEESSS accesses
ACCEFFIY efficacy
ACCEFILS fascicle
ACCEFLSU feluccas
ACCEGKMO gamecock
ACCEHIKP chickpea
ACCEHILM alchemic
chemical
ACCEHILP cephalic
ACCEHILS caliches
chalices
ACCEHIMN mechanic
ACCEHIMS sachemic
ACCEHINO anechoic
ACCEHINR chancier
chicaner
ACCEHINS chicanes
ACCEHINT catechin
ACCEHIRT catchier
ACCEHLNS chancels
ACCEHLOR cochlear
ACCEHLOT catechol
ACCEHMNO coachmen
ACCEHNNO chaconne
ACCEHNOR encroach
ACCEHNRS chancers
chancres
ACCEHNRY chancery
ACCEHOPT cachepot
ACCEHORS caroches
coachers
ACCEHPSU capuches
ACCEHRST catchers
cratches
ACCEIKLT ticklace
ACCEIKST cackiest
ACCEILLR clerical
ACCEILLU caulicle
ACCEILLV clavicle
ACCEILNS calcines
ACCEILNT canticle
ACCEILNY calycine
ACCEILOS calicoes
ACCEILRV cervical
ACCEILTY acetylic
ACCEIMNO Comaneci
ACCEIMRS ceramics
ACCEINOT acetonic
ACCEINRT acentric
ACCEINRY Cyrenaic
ACCEINSV vaccines
ACCEIOPR cecropia
ACCEIOTV coactive
ACCEIPRS caprices
ACCEIPRT practice
ACCEIPSV peccavis
ACCEIQSU caciques
ACCEIRRR ricercar
ACCEIRSU curacies
ACCEIRTU cruciate
ACCEISST ascetics
ACCEISTT ecstatic
ACCEKLNR cracknel
ACCEKLRS cacklers
clackers
crackles
ACCEKNOY Cockayne
ACCEKOPS peacocks
ACCEKOSS seacocks
ACCEKPSU cupcakes
ACCEKRRS crackers
ACCEKRST crackets
ACCELMNY cyclamen
ACCELNOS conceals
ACCELNOV conclave
ACCELNRU caruncle
ACCELORS coracles
ACCELRSY scarcely
ACCELSSU saccules
ACCENNSY nascency
ACCENORS conacres
ACCENORT accentor
ACCENOST cosecant
ACCENOSV concaves
ACCEOPRT acceptor
ACCEORST ectosarc
ACCEORTU accouter
accoutre
ACCERSST scarcest
ACCERSSU accusers
ACCESSTU cactuses
ACCESSUU caucuses
ACCFFLTU calctuff
ACCFHLTY catchfly
ACCFLNOO confocal
ACCFOORT cofactor
ACCGHINN chancing
ACCGHINO coaching
ACCGHINT catching
ACCGHIOR choragic
ACCGHRSU Gracchus
ACCGIKLN cackling
clacking
ACCGIKMR gimcrack
ACCGIKNR cracking
ACCGILOX coxalgic
ACCGINRU accruing
ACCGINSU accusing
ACCGLOOY cacology
ACCHHITT chitchat
ACCHHOOW Chaochow
ACCHIIMS chiasmic
ACCHIIRT rachitic
ACCHIIST chiastic
ACCHILNY chancily
ACCHILOT catholic
ACCHILOY Chiclayo
ACCHIMOR achromic
ACCHINNO cinchona
ACCHINOS chicanos
ACCHINPU capuchin
ACCHIORT thoracic
trochaic
ACCHIOSU acouchis
ACCHKLOR charlock
ACCHKOSY haycocks
ACCHMNOY Maconchy
ACCHMRTY McCarthy
ACCHNNOT Connacht
ACCHNNUY unchancy
ACCHNOOR coronach
ACCHNOTU couchant
ACCHNRUY craunchy
ACCHOPSU pachucos
ACCHORTU cartouch
ACCHORTY octarchy
ACCHOSTW choctaws
ACCHPSTU catchups
ACCHRRSU currachs
ACCHRSTY scratchy
ACCIIILN Cilician
ACCIILLN clinical
ACCIILMT climatic
ACCIILNO iconical
ACCIILRT critical
ACCIIMNN cinnamic
ACCIINNO aniconic
ACCIINNP piccanin
ACCIINOT aconitic
cationic
itaconic
ACCIINTY cyanitic
ACCIIOPT occipita
ACCIIRTX cicatrix
ACCIKKNN nicknack
ACCIKKRR rickrack
ACCIKKTT ticktack
ACCIKLOT cocktail
ACCIKRRS carricks
ACCILMUU aciculum
ACCILNOT lactonic
ACCILNOV volcanic
ACCILORT cortical
ACCILRRU circular
ACCILSSS classics
ACCILTUU cuticula
ACCIMNOS moccasin
ACCIMORU coumaric
ACCIMPSU capsicum
ACCINOOS occasion
ACCINOOT coaction
ACCINORS Corsican

ACCINORT	cratonic
	narcotic
ACCINORV	cavicorn
ACCINOTY	cyanotic
ACCINRSU	crucians
ACCIOPST	spiccato
ACCIORST	acrostic
	Socratic
ACCIORSY	isocracy
ACCIOSTU	acoustic
ACCIRRTT	trictrac
ACCIRSTY	scarcity
ACCISSTU	caustics
ACCKKRSU	rucksack
ACCKOOOT	cockatoo
ACCKOPRT	crackpot
ACCKORST	stockcar
ACCKOSSS	cassocks
	cossacks
ACCKPRSU	crackups
ACCLLNOY	cyclonal
ACCLLOSU	occlusal
ACCLLSUU	calculus
ACCLMOSU	Moluccas
ACCLSSUU	sacculus
ACCMNOOR	Moroccan
ACCMOOSY	cocoyams
ACCMOPST	compacts
ACCMOSTU	accustom
ACCMRSUU	curcumas
ACCNOOPS	cocopans
ACCNOORS	raccoons
ACCNOOTU	cocoanut
ACCNOPTU	occupant
ACCNORTT	contract
ACCNOSTT	contacts
ACCNOSTU	accounts
ACCOPSTY	copycats
ACCOQSSU	squaccos
ACCORRTY	carrycot
ACDDDEIT	addicted
ACDDDETU	adducted
ACDDEEES	deceased
ACDDEEHT	detached
ACDDEEIT	dedicate
ACDDEEIU	deciduae
ACDDEELL	decalled
ACDDEELR	declared
ACDDEELS	descaled
ACDDEEMP	decamped
ACDDEENR	credenda
ACDDEENS	ascended
ACDDEENT	decadent
	decanted
ACDDEERT	redacted
ACDDEESU	Sadducee
ACDDEETU	educated
ACDDEHIK	dickhead
ACDDEHKN	deckhand
ACDDEHRS	cheddars
ACDDEIIL	deicidal
ACDDEIIM	medicaid
ACDDEILU	decidual
ACDDEINR	riddance
ACDDEISU	deciduas
ACDDEITT	dictated
ACDDEKLO	deadlock
ACDDELOS	cladodes
ACDDENTU	adducent
ACDDEOPS	decapods
ACDDEORR	corraded
ACDDERSU	crusaded
ACDDERTU	traduced
ACDDGILN	cladding
ACDDGINU	adducing
ACDDGINY	caddying
ACDDHHSU	chuddahs
ACDDHIIO	diadochi
ACDDHIOY	diadochy
ACDDHIRY	hydracid
ACDDHKOS	haddocks
	shaddock
ACDDHRSU	chuddars
ACDDIIOR	cardioid
ACDDILNY	candidly
ACDDILTY	didactyl
ACDDIRSS	discards
ACDDKLNO	dockland
ACDDKOPS	paddocks
ACDDKORY	dockyard
ACDDLMNO	McDonald
ACDDORTU	adductor
ACDEEEFT	defecate
ACDEEEKS	seedcake
ACDEEEMR	reedmace
ACDEEENR	careened
ACDEEENT	antecede
ACDEEERR	careered
ACDEEERS	decrease
ACDEEESS	deceases
	seedcase
ACDEEFFT	affected
ACDEEFIN	defiance
ACDEEFIS	casefied
ACDEEFPR	prefaced
ACDEEFRS	defacers
ACDEEFTT	facetted
ACDEEGLY	delegacy
ACDEEHIN	echidnae
ACDEEHIR	charidee
ACDEEHIV	achieved
ACDEEHLP	pleached
ACDEEHLT	chelated
ACDEEHMR	demarche
ACDEEHNN	enhanced
ACDEEHNS	encashed
	enchased
ACDEEHPR	preached
ACDEEHRS	searched
ACDEEHRT	detacher
ACDEEHST	detaches
ACDEEIIP	epicedia
ACDEEILT	delicate
ACDEEILU	aedicule
ACDEEIMR	ceramide
	medicare
ACDEEIMT	decimate
	medicate
ACDEEINN	decennia
	enneadic
ACDEEINU	audience
ACDEEINV	deviance
ACDEEIRS	deciares
ACDEEJKT	jacketed
ACDEEKLR	lackered
ACDEEKLY	lackeyed
ACDEEKNR	cankered
ACDEEKPR	repacked
ACDEEKRS	screaked
ACDEEKRT	racketed
ACDEELLR	cellared
	recalled
ACDEELLS	cadelles
ACDEELMP	emplaced
ACDEELNR	calender
ACDEELNS	cleansed
ACDEELNT	lanceted
ACDEELPR	parceled
	replaced
ACDEELRR	declarer
ACDEELRS	declares
ACDEELRT	decretal
ACDEELRV	clavered
ACDEELSS	declasse
	descales
ACDEEMNO	codename
ACDEEMNP	encamped
ACDEEMRS	screamed
ACDEEMRT	cremated
ACDEENNP	penanced
ACDEENNT	tendance
ACDEENOT	anecdote
ACDEENRS	ascender
	reascend
ACDEENRT	cantered
	crenated
	decanter
	recanted
ACDEENRV	caverned
ACDEENRY	carneyed
	decenary
ACDEENRZ	credenza
ACDEENSV	vendaces
ACDEENTT	dancette
ACDEEOPS	peasecod
ACDEEORT	decorate
ACDEEPPR	recapped
ACDEEPRS	escarped
ACDEEPRT	carpeted
ACDEERRT	cratered
	retraced
	terraced
ACDEERSS	caressed
ACDEESTU	educates
ACDEESUX	caudexes
ACDEFFLS	sclaffed

ACDEFGIN defacing
ACDEFHKU headfuck
ACDEFIIP pacified
ACDEFILN canfield
ACDEFILR filecard
ACDEFINN financed
ACDEFNOW facedown
ACDEFORT factored
ACDEFOTU outfaced
ACDEFRSU surfaced
ACDEFRTU furcated
ACDEGGRS scragged
ACDEGIIL algicide
ACDEGIKM magicked
ACDEGILN decaling
ACDEGIMR grimaced
ACDEGINU guidance
ACDEGINY decaying
ACDEGIRS disgrace
ACDEGKOS dockages
ACDEGNOS decagons
ACDEGORS God's acre
ACDEHHNU haunched
ACDEHHRU hachured
ACDEHHTT thatched
ACDEHIJK hijacked
ACDEHILR Heraclid
heraldic
ACDEHIMM chammied
ACDEHIMN machined
ACDEHIMS schiedam
ACDEHINR inarched
Red China
ACDEHINS echidnas
ACDEHIRS rachides
ACDEHIRT tracheid
ACDEHIRV archived
ACDEHKLO headlock
ACDEHKLS shackled
ACDEHKOV havocked
ACDEHKRU archduke
ACDEHKTW thwacked
ACDEHLNR chandler
ACDEHLNU launched
ACDEHLOR Rochdale
ACDEHNOR anchored
ACDEHNPU paunched
ACDEHNST snatched
stanched
ACDEHNSU uncashed
ACDEHORR hardcore
ACDEHORT chordate
ACDEHOST cathodes
ACDEHOUV avouched
ACDEHPST despatch
ACDEHRRS chresard
ACDEHRST starched
ACDEIILN alcidine
ACDEIILS laicised
ACDEIILT ciliated
ACDEIILZ laicized
ACDEIIMU aecidium
ACDEIINR acridine
ACDEIINS sciaenid
ACDEIINT actinide
ctenidia
indicate
ACDEIITV vaticide
ACDEIJNU jaundice
ACDEIKNP panicked
ACDEIKPX pickaxed
ACDEILLM medallic
ACDEILLS cedillas
ACDEILLV cavilled
ACDEILMS decimals
declaims
medicals
ACDEILMT maledict
ACDEILMX climaxed
ACDEILNP panicled
ACDEILNU dulcinea
ACDEILNY adenylic
ACDEILPS displace
ACDEILPT plicated
ACDEILRS decrials
radicels
radicles
ACDEILRT articled
ACDEILRU auricled
ACDEILST citadels
dialects
ACDEILSY ecdysial
ACDEILTT latticed
ACDEIMNO comedian
daemonic
demoniac
ACDEIMNP pandemic
ACDEIMOR Mordecai
ACDEIMPT impacted
ACDEIMRT timecard
ACDEIMSV medivacs
ACDEINNR crannied
ACDEINOP canopied
ACDEINOS diocesan
oceanids
ACDEINOT actioned
catenoid
ACDEINOV voidance
ACDEINPT pedantic
ACDEINRT dicentra
ACDEINSS acidness
ACDEINST danciest
distance
ACDEINSY cyanides
ACDEINTT nictated
ACDEINTU incudate
ACDEINVY deviancy
ACDEIOPS diascope
ACDEIORS idocrase
ACDEIORT ceratoid
ACDEIOSS acidoses
ACDEIOSU edacious
ACDEIPRS peracids
ACDEIPSS spadices
ACDEIPSZ capsized
ACDEIQRU acquired
ACDEIRSS Cressida
sidecars
ACDEIRTT tetracid
ACDEISTT dictates
ACDEKNPU unpacked
ACDEKNTU untacked
ACDEKOST stockade
ACDELLLW Caldwell
ACDELLNO Candolle
ACDELLOR carolled
collared
ACDELLOT collated
ACDELLSU callused
ACDELMOR clamored
ACDELMOS Damocles
ACDELMSU muscadel
ACDELNOO canoodle
ACDELNOR colander
ACDELNPU unplaced
ACDELNRS candlers
ACDELOPT clodpate
ACDELRRS cradlers
ACDELRSS scalders
ACDELRSW scrawled
ACDELRSY sacredly
ACDELSTU cauldest
ACDELSWW dewclaws
ACDEMMRS scrammed
ACDEMNOR romanced
ACDEMOPR compadre
compared
ACDEMORS comrades
ACDEMORT democrat
ACDEMSTU muscadet
ACDEMUUV vacuumed
ACDENNNO cannoned
ACDENNOR ordnance
ACDENNOT cantoned
ACDENNST scandent
ACDENOPR endocarp
ACDENORS dracones
ACDENORT cartoned
ACDENORY crayoned
deaconry
ACDENOST endocast
tacnodes
ACDENOTU outdance
ACDENPPU uncapped
ACDENPST pandects
ACDENRSU durances
ACDENRTU underact
untraced
ACDENRVY verdancy
ACDENSST descants
ACDENSUU uncaused
ACDEOORS doorcase
ACDEOPRY copyread
ACDEOPSS peascods
ACDEOPTU outpaced
ACDEORRS corrades

ACDEORRT	redactor
ACDEORST	redcoats
ACDEORSU	caroused
ACDEORTU	educator
	outraced
ACDEORTV	cavorted
ACDEOTTU	outacted
ACDEPPRS	scrapped
ACDEPRSW	scrawped
ACDEPRTU	captured
ACDEPSTU	cuspated
ACDEQTUU	aqueduct
ACDERRSU	crusader
ACDERRTU	traducer
ACDERSSU	crusades
ACDERSTT	detracts
ACDERSTU	traduces
ACDFFHNU	handcuff
ACDFFIRT	diffract
ACDFFLOS	scaffold
ACDFIILU	fiducial
ACDFILOU	fucoidal
ACDFINOR	fricando
ACDFIOST	factoids
ACDFORRW	Crawford
ACDGHINY	dayching
ACDGHOTW	dogwatch
	watchdog
ACDGIILO	dialogic
ACDGILNN	candling
ACDGILNR	cradling
ACDGILNS	scalding
ACDGIMOT	dogmatic
ACDGINNY	candying
ACDGINRS	cardings
ACDGINSU	scauding
ACDGIOPR	podagric
ACDGIRSU	Guiscard
ACDGKLOS	daglocks
ACDGLNOO	golconda
ACDGORST	dogcarts
ACDHIILS	chiliads
ACDHIIPS	diphasic
ACDHIIRR	Richard I
ACDHIKNP	handpick
ACDHILPR	pilchard
ACDHINOR	hadronic
ACDHINSW	sandwich
ACDHIOPS	scaphoid
ACDHIORY	hyracoid
ACDHIPST	dispatch
ACDHIQRU	charquid
ACDHIRRS	Richards
ACDHKORR	hardrock
ACDHLNOR	chaldron
	chlordan
	chondral
ACDHMNTU	dutchman
ACDHNOSW	cowhands
ACDHOOTW	woodchat
ACDHOPRS	pochards
ACDHORRS	orchards
ACDIIILN	indicial
ACDIIJLU	judicial
ACDIILMS	disclaim
ACDIILNO	conidial
ACDIILSU	suicidal
ACDIILTY	dialytic
ACDIIMNO	daimonic
	Dominica
ACDIIMOR	dioramic
ACDIIMOT	diatomic
ACDIIMSU	ascidium
ACDIINNO	conidian
ACDIINNT	indicant
ACDIINOT	actinoid
	diatonic
ACDIINPY	pycnidia
ACDIIOPR	DiCaprio
ACDIIOSS	acidosis
ACDIIRST	arctiids
	carditis
ACDIIRTY	acridity
ACDIISST	sadistic
ACDILLOT	Clotilda
ACDILLOU	caudillo
ACDILLPY	placidly
ACDILMOU	mucoidal
ACDILMSS	cladisms
ACDILMTU	talmudic
ACDILNOO	conoidal
ACDILNOR	ironclad
ACDILNOT	daltonic
ACDILNSY	syndical
ACDILNUU	nudicaul
ACDILOPY	polyadic
ACDILORS	cordials
ACDILORT	dicrotal
ACDILOUV	oviducal
ACDILPSU	cuspidal
ACDILSST	cladists
ACDILSTW	wildcats
ACDILSUU	Claudius
ACDIMNOO	codomain
	monoacid
ACDIMNSU	scandium
ACDIMNSY	dynamics
ACDIMOOS	camoodis
ACDINOPS	spondaic
ACDINORS	sardonic
ACDINORT	tornadic
ACDINORW	cordwain
ACDINSST	discants
ACDINSTY	dynastic
ACDIOPRS	picadors
	sporadic
ACDIORRS	corridas
ACDIORSS	sarcoids
ACDIORST	carotids
ACDIORTT	dictator
ACDIOSTX	doxastic
ACDIOSTY	dystocia
ACDIOSXY	oxyacids
ACDIQRSU	quadrics
ACDIRSTT	distract
ACDISTUV	viaducts
ACDJNSTU	adjuncts
ACDKLOPS	padlocks
ACDKMPSU	mudpacks
ACDLLORS	collards
ACDLNOPU	Coupland
ACDLNORS	caldrons
	Crosland
ACDLNORU	cauldron
	Courland
ACDLNORY	condylar
ACDLNOST	Scotland
ACDLOOOR	colorado
ACDLOORT	doctoral
ACDLORWY	cowardly
ACDMMNOO	commando
ACDMMNOS	commands
ACDMNORY	dormancy
	mordancy
ACDMOOSW	camwoods
ACDMORSZ	czardoms
ACDNNORU	Cournand
ACDNOORS	cardoons
ACDNOORT	acrodont
ACDNOORV	cordovan
ACDNOSTW	downcast
ACDOORST	ostracod
ACDOPRST	postcard
ACDORSST	costards
ACDORSSU	crusados
ACDORSUZ	cruzados
ACDRSSTU	custards
ACDRSTTU	dustcart
ACEEEFRR	carefree
ACEEEGLN	elegance
ACEEEIPR	earpiece
ACEEELMR	cameleer
ACEEENRR	careener
ACEEENSV	evanesce
ACEEEPSS	escapees
ACEEERRT	recreate
ACEEERTT	etcetera
ACEEERTX	execrate
ACEEESUV	evacuees
ACEEFFIN	caffeine
ACEEFFRS	effacers
ACEEFHWY	wheyface
ACEEFINS	fiancees
ACEEFISS	casefies
ACEEFLPU	peaceful
ACEEFLSS	faceless
ACEEFPRR	prefacer
ACEEFPRS	prefaces
ACEEFPRT	praefect
ACEEFPTY	typeface
ACEEFRSU	farceuse
ACEEGHNP	Pechenga
ACEEGHNX	exchange
ACEEGHRR	recharge
ACEEGILS	elegiacs
	legacies

ACEEGINR Carnegie
ACEEGINS agencies
ACEEGINT agenetic
ACEEGIRZ graecize
ACEEGKRW wreckage
ACEEGLNY elegancy
ACEEGNOZ cozenage
ACEEGNSV scavenge
ACEEGORR racegoer
ACEEGORV coverage
ACEEGSSU escuages
ACEEHHRU heuchera
ACEEHHST cheetahs
ACEEHILM Aleichem
ACEEHINS Eisenach
ACEEHINT echinate
ACEEHIPR peachier
ACEEHIPT epitheca
petechia
ACEEHIRT hetaeric
ACEEHIRV achiever
chivaree
ACEEHISV achieves
ACEEHKTT hackette
ACEEHLOS shoelace
ACEEHLPS pleaches
ACEEHLRS Heracles
leachers
ACEEHLST chelates
ACEEHLSW eschewal
ACEEHMNP camphene
ACEEHMNR menarche
ACEEHMRS cashmere
marchese
ACEEHMST machetes
ACEEHNNR enhancer
ACEEHNNS enhances
ACEEHNPS cheapens
ACEEHNRS enchaser
ACEEHNRT Charente
ACEEHNSS encashes
enchases
ACEEHOOT oothecae
ACEEHPRR preacher
ACEEHPRS peachers
preaches
ACEEHPST cheapest
ACEEHRRS reachers
research
searcher
ACEEHRSS searches
ACEEHRST cheaters
hectares
teachers
ACEEHRTT catheter
ACEEHRTY Cytherea
ACEEHSST escheats
ACEEHSTX cathexes
ACEEIKLL lacelike
ACEEIKRR creakier
ACEEILMR Calimere
ACEEILNR careline
reliance
ACEEILNS salience
ACEEILPS especial
ACEEILSU Seleucia
ACEEIMRR creamier
rearmice
ACEEIMRS casimere
racemise
ACEEIMRZ racemize
ACEEINNR narceine
ACEEINPS sapience
ACEEINPT patience
ACEEINRS increase
ACEEINRT centiare
creatine
increate
iterance
ACEEINST cineaste
ACEEINTV enactive
ACEEINTX exitance
ACEEIPST speciate
ACEEIRRT Terceira
ACEEIRSU causerie
ACEEIRSW wiseacre
ACEEIRTV creative
reactive
ACEEISTV vesicate
ACEEJKNS jackeens
ACEEKLMR mackerel
ACEEKNPS kneecaps
ACEEKNRW neckwear
ACEELLNS nacelles
ACEELLNT lancelet
ACEELLOT ocellate
ACEELLOV Lovelace
ACEELLRR cellarer
ACEELLRT cellaret
ACEELMNP placemen
ACEELMPS emplaces
ACEELNOR Caerleon
ACEELNPR preclean
ACEELNPT pentacle
ACEELNRR larcener
ACEELNRS cleaners
cleanser
ACEELNRU cerulean
ACEELNRW Lawrence
ACEELNSS cleanses
ACEELNST cleanest
ACEELNSU nuclease
ACEELNSV enclaves
valences
ACEELNTT tentacle
ACEELNTU nucleate
ACEELOPS escalope
opalesce
ACEELORS escarole
ACEELORT relocate
ACEELPRR replacer
ACEELPRS replaces
ACEELPRV Perceval
ACEELPSY cypselae
ACEELPTU peculate
ACEELPTY clypeate
ACEELRRS clearers
ACEELRSS careless
ACEELRST clearest
treacles
ACEELRSV cleavers
ACEELRTU ulcerate
ACEELRTV cervelat
ACEELRTX excretal
ACEELSST celestas
selectas
ACEELSSY Les Cayes
ACEELSTT telecast
ACEELSVX exclaves
ACEEMNPS spacemen
ACEEMNRS menacers
ACEEMNST casement
ACEEMOPR camporee
ACEEMORS racemose
ACEEMORV overcame
ACEEMRRS amercers
creamers
screamer
ACEEMRRY creamery
ACEEMRST cremates
ACEEMRTW crewmate
ACEENNPS penances
ACEENNPZ Penzance
ACEENNRT entrance
ACEENNST canteens
ACEENORT carotene
ACEENOST notecase
ACEENPRR parcener
ACEENRRT recanter
recreant
ACEENRSS casernes
ACEENRST centares
encastre
reascent
reenacts
sarcenet
ACEENRSV cervenas
ACEEPRRS caperers
ACEEPRSS escapers
ACEEPSTT spectate
ACEEPSTY typecase
ACEERRSS caresser
creasers
ACEERRST caterers
retraces
terraces
ACEERRSU ecraseur
ACEERRTT Carteret
ACEERRTU creature
ACEERRUV verrucae
ACEERSSS caresses
ACEERSST cerastes
ACEERSSU surcease
ACEERSSV crevasse
ACEERSTX exacters
ACEERTTU eructate

ACEESSTT cassette
ACEFFGIN effacing
ACEFFHIS affiches
ACEFFHRS chaffers
ACEFFHRU chauffer
ACEFFILY Aycliffe
ACEFFLLU fullface
ACEFFLRS sclaffer
ACEFGINN enfacing
ACEFGINR refacing
ACEFGINT faceting
ACEFGIPS pigfaces
ACEFGLRU graceful
ACEFHISV cavefish
ACEFHLNS flanches
ACEFHMRS chamfers
ACEFHORU farouche
ACEFHRSU chaufers
ACEFIIPR pacifier
ACEFIIPS pacifies
ACEFIIRT artifice
ACEFILLS icefalls
ACEFILLY facilely
ACEFILOP epifocal
ACEFILOS focalise
ACEFILOZ focalize
ACEFILRY fireclay
ACEFIMPR campfire
ACEFINNS finances
ACEFINRS fanciers
ACEFINSS fascines
ACEFINST fanciest
ACEFIOSS fiascoes
ACEFIRRT craftier
ACEFIRTT trifecta
ACEFLMNO flamenco
ACEFLNOR falconer
ACEFLNOT conflate
falconet
ACEFLNRY cranefly
ACEFLORS alfresco
ACEFLRTU crateful
ACEFLRUU furculae
ACEFNNOS faconnes
ACEFNORV conferva
ACEFNRSU furnaces
ACEFOOPT footpace
ACEFORST forecast
ACEFOSTU outfaces
ACEFRRST refracts
ACEFRRSU farceurs
surfacer
ACEFRRTU fracture
ACEFRSSU surfaces
ACEFRSTU furcates
ACEGGILN cageling
glaceing
ACEGGILR claggier
ACEGGINN encaging
ACEGGINT Gangetic
ACEGGIRR craggier
ACEGHHNT Changteh

ACEGHIIT chigetai
ACEGHIKN Chekiang
ACEGHILN leaching
ACEGHILT lichgate
ACEGHINP peaching
ACEGHINR reaching
ACEGHINT cheating
teaching
ACEGHIRR Argerich
ACEGHLTY lychgate
ACEGHLUY gauchely
ACEGHNRS changers
ACEGHOSU gouaches
ACEGHRRS chargers
ACEGIIMP epigamic
ACEGIINV vicinage
ACEGIIRS Gaiseric
ACEGIKNR creaking
ACEGILLO collegia
ACEGILLR allergic
ACEGILMU mucilage
ACEGILNN cleaning
enlacing
ACEGILNO Angelico
ACEGILNR clearing
ACEGILNT cleating
ACEGILNV cleaving
ACEGILNW lacewing
ACEGILRS glaciers
Scaliger
ACEGILSS glacises
ACEGIMMT tagmemic
ACEGIMNN menacing
ACEGIMNR amercing
creaming
germanic
ACEGIMNS magnesic
ACEGIMNT magnetic
ACEGIMOX exogamic
ACEGIMRR grimacer
ACEGIMRS grimaces
ACEGIMTY megacity
ACEGINNO canoeing
ACEGINNS encasing
ACEGINNT enacting
ACEGINOS coinages
ACEGINOY gynoecia
ACEGINPR capering
ACEGINPS escaping
ACEGINRS creasing
grecians
ACEGINRT argentic
catering
creating
reacting
ACEGINRU Guernica
ACEGINSS caginess
ACEGINTT taceting
ACEGINTX exacting
ACEGIOTT cogitate
ACEGIRST agrestic
cigarets

ACEGKLOS lockages
ACEGKLRS grackles
ACEGKRTU truckage
ACEGLLNO collagen
ACEGLLOS collages
ACEGLNOS congeals
longcase
ACEGLNOT octangle
ACEGLNRS clangers
ACEGLOSU cagoules
ACEGMNOY geomancy
ACEGMNRS cragsmen
ACEGMOPS compages
ACEGMRRY gramercy
ACEGNNOR crannoge
ACEGNNOY cyanogen
ACEGNNRY regnancy
ACEGNNTY tangency
ACEGNORS acrogens
ACEGNOST cognates
ACEGOPRY geocarpy
ACEGORSS corsages
socagers
ACEGORST escargot
ACEGORSV Cosgrave
ACEGORTT cottager
ACEGORTY category
ACEGOSTT cottages
ACEGSSTU scutages
ACEHHINS Shechina
ACEHHIPS cheapish
ACEHHIRR hierarch
ACEHHIST shechita
ACEHHLST hatchels
ACEHHMNN henchman
ACEHHNRT ethnarch
ACEHHNSU haunches
ACEHHNSV Cheshvan
ACEHHPRT heptarch
ACEHHRST hatchers
ACEHHRSU hachures
ACEHHRTT thatcher
ACEHHRTY hatchery
thearchy
ACEHHSTT hatchets
thatches
ACEHIIMS ischemia
ACEHIIRT hetairic
hieratic
ACEHIJKR hijacker
ACEHIKLR chalkier
ACEHIKRW whackier
ACEHILLS Achilles
ACEHILMN inchmeal
ACEHILMS Macleish
ACEHILMV Malevich
ACEHILNP cephalin
ACEHILNT chatline
ethnical
ACEHILOR heroical
ACEHILPR parhelic
ACEHILPY peachily

ACEHILRS Charles I
charlies
ACEHILSS Lachesis
ACEHILTT athletic
ACEHIMMS chammies
ACEHIMNN chainmen
Eichmann
ACEHIMNR chairmen
ACEHIMNS machines
ACEHIMNT anthemic
ACEHIMPR camphire
ACEHIMPT empathic
emphatic
ACEHIMRS chimeras
marchesi
ACEHIMST hematics
misteach
tachisme
ACEHIMTT thematic
ACEHINNS enchains
ACEHINOT ethanoic
inchoate
ACEHINOX hexanoic
ACEHINRS archines
inarches
ACEHINRV vacherin
ACEHINSS Anchises
ACEHINST asthenic
chanties
ACEHIPPS chappies
ACEHIPRS seraphic
ACEHIPRT chapiter
patchier
phreatic
ACEHIPST hepatics
pastiche
ACEHIPTT pathetic
ACEHIPTW whitecap
ACEHIRSS cashiers
rachises
ACEHIRST chariest
ACEHIRSU eucharis
ACEHIRSV archives
ACEHIRTT chattier
ACEHISST chastise
ACEHISTX cathexis
ACEHISTY yachties
ACEHKLOV havelock
ACEHKLPR kreplach
ACEHKLRS hacklers
shackler
ACEHKLSS shackles
ACEHKLSV Alchevsk
ACEHKLTY latchkey
ACEHKNSY hackneys
ACEHKORV havocker
ACEHKOSS shackoes
ACEHKRSW whackers
ACEHKRTW thwacker
ACEHLLOO coalhole
ACEHLLPP Chappell
ACEHLLSS shellacs
ACEHLLST hellcats
ACEHLMNU Mulhacén
ACEHLNNS channels
ACEHLNOS chalones
ACEHLNOU eulachon
ACEHLNOY Halcyone
ACEHLNPT planchet
ACEHLNRS charnels
ACEHLNRU launcher
relaunch
ACEHLNRY Charnley
ACEHLNSU launches
ACEHLOOT oothecal
ACEHLORS chorales
ACEHLORT chlorate
trochlea
ACEHLOST eschalot
ACEHLOSU Achelous
ACEHLPRY chapelry
ACEHLPST chaplets
ACEHLRSS clashers
ACEHLRSV Charles V
ACEHLRSX Charles X
ACEHLRSY charleys
ACEHLRTU trauchle
ACEHLSSS cashless
ACEHLSST satchels
ACEHLSTT chattels
latchets
ACEHLSTY chastely
ACEHMNRT merchant
ACEHMNSS chessman
ACEHMNTW watchmen
ACEHMORT chromate
ACEHMPRS champers
ACEHMRRS charmers
marchers
ACEHMRST matchers
ACEHMSST smatches
ACEHMSTT matchets
ACEHMSTU mustache
ACEHNNPT penchant
ACEHNNST enchants
ACEHNOPR Cape Horn
chaperon
ACEHNOPT cenotaph
ACEHNORR ranchero
ACEHNPSU paunches
ACEHNRRS ranchers
ACEHNRSS archness
ACEHNRST chanters
snatcher
stancher
tranches
ACEHNRTU chaunter
ACEHNSST chastens
snatches
stanches
ACEHNSTT etchants
ACEHNSTU nautches
unchaste
ACEHNSTY chanteys
ACEHNSUZ Szechuan
ACEHNUVX Cuxhaven
ACEHOPRR reproach
ACEHOPRS poachers
ACEHORRV overarch
ACEHORST thoraces
ACEHORTT theocrat
ACEHORTU outreach
ACEHOSSW showcase
ACEHOSTU cathouse
soutache
ACEHOSTY chayotes
ACEHOSUV avouches
ACEHPRRT Petrarch
ACEHPRST chapters
patchers
ACEHPRSU purchase
ACEHRRSS crashers
ACEHRRST charters
Chartres
recharts
starcher
ACEHRRSV charvers
ACEHRRTT tetrarch
ACEHRSST starches
ACEHRSSU chasseur
ACEHRSTT chatters
ratchets
ACEHRSTW watchers
ACEHRSTY Strachey
ACEHRTTY chattery
trachyte
ACEHSSSU chausses
ACEHSSTW swatches
ACEIILMN limacine
ACEIILMX Mexicali
ACEIILNR irenical
ACEIILNS salicine
ACEIILNT Catiline
ACEIILNX alexinic
ACEIILSS laicises
ACEIILST ciliates
silicate
ACEIILSZ laicizes
ACEIIMSS aseismic
ACEIIMTU maieutic
ACEIINPS piscinae
ACEIINRT arenitic
ACEIINTV inactive
ACEIIPRS piracies
ACEIIRRT criteria
ACEIISTV cavities
ACEIJKSS jacksies
ACEIJMST majestic
ACEIKKLS sacklike
ACEIKLLY claylike
ACEIKLRY creakily
ACEIKMNN nickname
ACEIKMRS keramics
ACEIKMRV maverick
ACEIKNPS capeskin
ACEIKNRR crankier

ACEIKOTW Katowice
ACEIKPSX pickaxes
ACEIKSTT tackiest
ACEIKSTW wackiest
ACEILLLT clitella
ACEILLMR micellar
millrace
ACEILLMS micellas
ACEILLMT metallic
ACEILLMY mycelial
ACEILLNT cliental
ACEILLOP calliope
ACEILLOR rocaille
ACEILLOS localise
ACEILLOT teocalli
ACEILLOZ localize
ACEILLPR calliper
ACEILLPS allspice
ACEILLRS Carlisle
ACEILLRV caviller
ACEILLSS scallies
ACEILMMO camomile
ACEILMMR clammier
ACEILMNP manciple
ACEILMNS mescalin
ACEILMOS camisole
ACEILMPS misplace
ACEILMRS claimers
miracles
reclaims
ACEILMRT metrical
ACEILMRY creamily
ACEILMST clematis
climates
ACEILMSU musicale
ACEILMSX climaxes
exclaims
ACEILNNP pinnacle
ACEILNOR acrolein
lonicera
ACEILNPS capelins
panicles
pelicans
ACEILNRS carlines
ACEILNRT clarinet
ACEILNSS laciness
sanicles
ACEILNSU lunacies
ACEILNSY saliency
ACEILOPR capriole
ACEILOPT poetical
ACEILORR carriole
ACEILORS calories
carioles
Escorial
ACEILORT erotical
loricate
ACEILORZ calorize
ACEILOSS celosias
ACEILOST societal
ACEILOSV vocalise
ACEILOSX saxicole

ACEILOTV locative
ACEILOVZ vocalize
ACEILPPY pipeclay
ACEILPRS calipers
replicas
spiracle
ACEILPRT particle
prelatic
ACEILPRU peculiar
ACEILPRV Percival
ACEILPSS slipcase
specials
ACEILPST tieclasp
ACEILPXY epicalyx
ACEILRRT clartier
ACEILRRW crawlier
ACEILRSS classier
ACEILRST altrices
articles
recitals
sterical
ACEILRSU auricles
Escurial
ACEILRSV claviers
visceral
ACEILRTT tractile
ACEILRTU Lucretia
reticula
ACEILRTV vertical
ACEILRTY literacy
ACEILSST Alcestis
elastics
salicets
scaliest
ACEILSTT lattices
ACEILTVY actively
ACEIMMNP pemmican
ACEIMMOS semicoma
ACEIMMRS racemism
ACEIMMTT metamict
ACEIMNOX anoxemic
ACEIMNPS pemicans
ACEIMNRU manicure
ACEIMNSS amnesics
ACEIMNST semantic
ACEIMNSY sycamine
ACEIMOTX toxaemic
ACEIMOTZ azotemic
metazoic
ACEIMPSS escapism
ACEIMPST campiest
campsite
ACEIMRST ceramist
matrices
ACEIMRTU muricate
ACEIMSTU autecism
ACEIMTTU muticate
ACEINNOS canonise
ACEINNOT enaction
ACEINNOZ canonize
ACEINNPS pinnaces
ACEINNRS crannies

ACEINNST ancients
canniest
insectan
instance
ACEINNSU nuisance
ACEINNSY cyanines
ACEINNTU uncinate
ACEINOPR apocrine
Poincaré
procaine
ACEINOPS canopies
caponise
ACEINOPZ caponize
ACEINORS scenario
ACEINORT actioner
creation
reaction
ACEINORV veronica
ACEINORX anorexic
ACEINOST aconites
canoeist
ACEINOTT taconite
ACEINOTV conative
invocate
ACEINOTX exaction
ACEINPSS inscapes
ACEINPTT pittance
ACEINPUY picayune
ACEINRRU curarine
ACEINRRY cinerary
ACEINRSS raciness
ACEINRST canister
cisterna
scantier
ACEINRTT interact
ACEINRTU Cernăuţi
ACEINRTV navicert
ACEINRVY vicenary
ACEINSSU issuance
ACEINSTT cantiest
nictates
tetanics
ACEINSTV vesicant
ACEINSTZ zincates
ACEINTTU tunicate
ACEINTTX excitant
ACEINTTY tenacity
ACEIOPRT aporetic
operatic
ACEIORSS scariose
ACEIORSV varicose
ACEIOSSU caesious
ACEIOTVV vocative
ACEIPPRR pericarp
ACEIPPRS crappies
epicarps
ACEIPRRS perisarc
ACEIPRST crispate
picrates
practise
ACEIPRTY apyretic
ACEIPSST escapist

	spaciest
ACEIPSSU	auspices
ACEIPSSZ	capsizes
ACEIPSTV	captives
ACEIQRRU	acquirer
ACEIQRSU	acquires
ACEIQSUZ	caziques
ACEIRRRS	carriers
ACEIRRSS	Cassirer
ACEIRRST	erratics
ACEIRRSU	curarise
ACEIRRSW	aircrews
	airscrew
ACEIRRTX	creatrix
ACEIRRUZ	curarize
ACEIRSST	Castries
	scariest
ACEIRSTT	citrates
	cristate
	scattier
ACEIRSTU	suricate
ACEIRSTZ	craziest
ACEIRTTU	urticate
ACEIRTTV	tractive
ACEIRTUV	curative
ACEIRTVY	veracity
ACEISSTU	sauciest
	suitcase
ACEISTTT	cattiest
ACEISTTU	eustatic
ACEJKOOR	jackeroo
ACEJLORS	cajolers
ACEJLORY	cajolery
ACEJNOST	jaconets
ACEJNOSY	joyances
ACEJNRRY	jerrycan
ACEJPSTU	cajeputs
ACEJRSTT	trajects
ACEKKMRU	muckrake
ACEKKNRS	knackers
ACEKKNRY	knackery
ACEKLNSS	slackens
ACEKLORV	laverock
ACEKLPST	plackets
ACEKLRSS	slackers
ACEKLRST	tacklers
ACEKLRSU	caulkers
ACEKLSST	slackest
	tackless
ACEKMNRT	trackmen
ACEKMNST	tacksmen
ACEKMRSS	smackers
ACEKNPRU	unpacker
ACEKNRST	crankest
ACEKOPRY	Cape York
ACEKORRS	croakers
ACEKORSW	casework
ACEKPPRS	prepacks
ACEKPSSY	skyscape
ACEKQRUY	quackery
ACEKRRST	trackers
ACEKRSST	restacks
	stackers
ACELLLRU	cellular
ACELLNOT	Lancelot
ACELLNRU	nucellar
ACELLNRW	Cranwell
ACELLOPS	collapse
	escallop
ACELLORR	caroller
ACELLORS	corellas
ACELLORV	coverall
	overcall
ACELLOST	collates
ACELLOSW	coleslaw
ACELLOTU	loculate
ACELLOVY	coevally
ACELLPSS	scalpels
ACELLRRS	carrells
ACELLRTY	rectally
ACELLSSU	calluses
ACELLSSW	clawless
ACELLSTU	scutella
ACELMNNS	clansmen
ACELMNOR	cornmeal
ACELMNSS	calmness
ACELMOPT	compleat
ACELMORR	clamorer
ACELMORS	scleroma
ACELMORY	claymore
ACELMOSU	leucomas
ACELMPRS	clampers
ACELMSTU	calumets
	muscatel
ACELMTUU	cumulate
ACELNNRS	scrannel
ACELNOOT	ecotonal
ACELNORT	Coltrane
ACELNORV	novercal
ACELNOST	lactones
ACELNOSU	lacunose
ACELNOSZ	calzones
ACELNOTV	covalent
ACELNPSS	enclasps
	spancels
ACELNPST	clapnets
ACELNPSU	cleanups
ACELNRSU	lucarnes
ACELNRVY	cravenly
ACELNSSU	scalenus
ACELNSTY	secantly
ACELOOSS	Colossae
ACELOPPU	populace
ACELOPRS	parclose
	polacres
ACELOPRT	pectoral
ACELOPRU	opercula
ACELOPST	polecats
ACELOPSU	scopulae
ACELOPTU	copulate
ACELOPTY	calotype
ACELOQSU	coequals
ACELORRS	carolers
ACELORSS	escolars
	lacrosse
	solacers
ACELORST	locaters
	sectoral
ACELORSU	carousel
ACELORSY	caloyers
	coarsely
ACELOSST	alecosts
ACELOSTT	calottes
ACELOSTU	osculate
ACELOSTY	acolytes
ACELOSUV	vacuoles
ACELOTTY	catolyte
ACELPPRS	clappers
	scrapple
ACELPRSS	claspers
	scalpers
ACELPRST	spectral
ACELPRSU	specular
ACELPSSU	capsules
ACELPTUU	cupulate
ACELPTUY	eucalypt
ACELQRSU	lacquers
ACELQSUY	lacqueys
ACELRRSW	crawlers
	scrawler
ACELRSSS	classers
ACELRSSU	seculars
ACELRSTT	clatters
ACELRTTU	cultrate
ACELRTTY	clattery
ACELSSTT	tactless
ACELSUUV	Vaucluse
ACEMMOTY	mycetoma
ACEMMRRS	crammers
ACEMMRSS	scammers
ACEMNOOR	Cameroon
ACEMNORR	romancer
ACEMNORS	romances
ACEMNORU	Cameroun
ACEMNRUY	numeracy
ACEMOOST	comatose
ACEMOPRR	comparer
ACEMOPRS	compares
	mesocarp
ACEMOPRT	mercapto
ACEMORRT	cremator
	Mercator
ACEMORSU	racemous
ACEMORSW	caseworm
ACEMORSY	sycamore
ACEMORTY	cometary
ACEMORUX	morceaux
ACEMPRRS	crampers
ACEMPRSS	scampers
ACEMPSSU	campuses
ACEMRSST	scamster
ACENNNOU	announce
ACENNOSS	canoness
ACENNOTT	cotenant
ACENNOTV	covenant
ACENNOTZ	canzonet

ACENNRSS	scanners
ACENOPRW	Cawnpore
ACENOPST	capstone
	opencast
ACENOPTW	Cape Town
ACENOQTU	cotquean
ACENORRT	Torrance
ACENORRW	careworn
ACENORSS	coarsens
ACENORST	ancestor
	enactors
ACENORSU	nacreous
ACENORTU	courante
ACENORTY	enactory
ACENOSSV	cavesson
ACENOSTV	centavos
ACENPRRS	prancers
ACENPTTU	punctate
ACENRSTT	transect
ACENRSTU	centaurs
	recusant
ACENRSTY	ancestry
ACENRTTU	truncate
ACENRTUY	centaury
ACENSSTU	nutcases
ACENSSTW	newscast
ACEOOPSU	poaceous
ACEOORTV	evocator
	overcoat
ACEOPPRS	copperas
ACEOPRSX	exocarps
ACEOPRTT	attercop
ACEOPSTU	outpaces
ACEORRST	acroters
	creators
	reactors
ACEORRSU	carouser
ACEORRTT	retroact
ACEORRTU	eurocrat
ACEORRTV	cavorter
ACEORSST	coarsest
	coasters
	Socrates
ACEORSSU	carouses
ACEORSTU	outraces
ACEORSTV	overacts
	overcast
ACEORSTX	exactors
ACEOSTTU	outcaste
ACEOSTUU	autocues
	Cousteau
ACEOTUUX	couteaux
ACEOTUXY	auxocyte
ACEPRRSS	scarpers
	scrapers
ACEPRRSU	supercar
ACEPRRTU	capturer
ACEPRSST	precasts
ACEPRSSU	scaupers
ACEPRSTU	captures
ACEPSTTY	typecast
ACEQRSTU	racquets
ACERRSTT	retracts
ACERRSUV	verrucas
ACERRUVZ	Veracruz
ACERSSTT	scatters
ACERSSTY	actressy
ACERSSUY	Syracuse
ACERSTTX	extracts
ACERSTTY	cytaster
ACERTTUW	cutwater
ACFFGHIN	chaffing
ACFFIILO	official
ACFFIIST	caitiffs
ACFFIKMS	mafficks
ACFFILNU	fanciful
ACFFILST	afflicts
ACFFIRST	traffics
ACFFLOSW	scofflaw
ACFFOSST	castoffs
ACFGHITT	catfight
ACFGIIMN	magnific
ACFGIIPR	caprifig
ACFGINNY	fancying
ACFGINRS	scarfing
ACFGINRT	crafting
ACFGITUY	fugacity
ACFHHINW	hawfinch
ACFHIJKS	jackfish
ACFHILNO	falchion
ACFHILOS	coalfish
ACFHIRSW	crawfish
ACFHIRSY	crayfish
ACFHISSU	fuchsias
ACFHLTUW	watchful
ACFHMNOR	chamfron
ACFHNNOR	chanfron
ACFHORST	Ashcroft
ACFHRSTU	futharcs
ACFIILTY	facility
ACFIIMPS	pacifism
ACFIINRS	Francis I
ACFIIPST	pacifist
ACFIKLNS	calfskin
ACFILLSY	fiscally
ACFILNOR	fornical
ACFILNOT	califont
ACFILORT	trifocal
ACFILRTY	craftily
ACFILSSY	classify
ACFIMNRU	francium
ACFINORT	fraction
ACFINOST	factions
ACFINRST	infarcts
	infracts
ACFINSTY	sanctify
ACFIOSTU	factious
ACFISSST	fascists
ACFKLOST	lockfast
ACFKLSSU	sackfuls
ACFKOSTT	fatstock
ACFLMNOO	mooncalf
ACFLNORY	falconry
ACFLOOPS	foolscap
ACFLORSU	scrofula
ACFLOTTU	floatcut
ACFLOTUU	Foucault
ACFLRSTU	cartfuls
ACFMOTTU	factotum
ACGGGILN	clagging
ACGGGINS	scagging
ACGGHINN	changing
ACGGHINR	charging
ACGGIINT	gigantic
ACGGIIOS	isagogic
ACGGILNN	clanging
	glancing
ACGGILRY	craggily
ACGGINNO	congaing
ACGGLNOU	glucagon
ACGGLRSY	scraggly
ACGHHIIN	Chinghai
ACGHHIJK	highjack
ACGHHINT	hatching
ACGHHNOW	Hangchow
ACGHIIMN	michigan
ACGHIINN	chaining
ACGHIINR	chairing
ACGHIKLN	hackling
ACGHIKNS	shacking
ACGHIKNU	Chu Kiang
ACGHIKNW	whacking
ACGHILNS	clashing
ACGHILNY	achingly
ACGHILOR	oligarch
ACGHIMNP	champing
ACGHIMNR	charming
	marching
ACGHIMNT	matching
ACGHINNN	Nan-ching
ACGHINNR	ranching
ACGHINNT	chanting
ACGHINOP	poaching
ACGHINOT	Chingtao
ACGHINPP	chapping
ACGHINPR	parching
ACGHINPT	nightcap
	patching
ACGHINRR	charring
ACGHINRS	chagrins
	crashing
ACGHINRT	charting
ACGHINRU	churinga
ACGHINST	scathing
ACGHINSW	chinwags
ACGHINTT	chatting
ACGHINTU	Taichung
ACGHINTW	watching
ACGHINTY	yachting
ACGHIPRS	graphics
ACGHLLOR	gralloch
ACGHLOOY	chaology
ACGHNRYY	gynarchy
ACGHNTUU	uncaught
ACGHOPUV	Pugachov
ACGHORSU	choragus

ACGHRRSU curraghs
ACGIILMN claiming
ACGIILNN inlacing
ACGIILNO logician
ACGIILNV caviling
ACGIINNS incasing
ACGIINRT granitic
ACGIJLNO cajoling
ACGIKLMN mackling
ACGIKLNN clanking
ACGIKLNO cloaking
ACGIKLNS slacking
ACGIKLNT tackling
talcking
ACGIKLNU caulking
ACGIKLRY garlicky
ACGIKMNS smacking
ACGIKNNR cranking
ACGIKNNS snacking
ACGIKNOR croaking
ACGIKNPS packings
ACGIKNQU quacking
ACGIKNRT tracking
ACGIKNRW wracking
ACGIKNST stacking
ACGILLNS callings
ACGILLRS Scargill
ACGILMMN clamming
ACGILMNO gnomical
ACGILMNP clamping
ACGILMTU glutamic
ACGILNNU unlacing
ACGILNOP Polignac
ACGILNOR caroling
ACGILNOS solacing
ACGILNOT locating
ACGILNPP clapping
ACGILNPS clasping
scalping
ACGILNQU calquing
ACGILNRS carlings
ACGILNRW crawling
ACGILNSS classing
ACGILNST castling
catlings
ACGILNUY guanylic
ACGILRSU surgical
ACGIMMNR cramming
ACGIMMNS scamming
ACGIMNOS coamings
ACGIMNPR cramping
ACGIMNPS campings
scamping
ACGIMNSY syngamic
ACGIMORS orgasmic
ACGIMOUU guaiocum
ACGINNNS cannings
scanning
ACGINNPR prancing
ACGINNRT trancing
ACGINNRY carnying
ACGINNST scanting
ACGINORS organics
ACGINOST agnostic
coasting
coatings
cotingas
ACGINPPR crapping
ACGINPRS scarping
scraping
ACGINPSS spacings
ACGINRRS scarring
ACGINRRY carrying
ACGINRST scarting
tracings
ACGINRSU Granicus
ACGINRSV carvings
cravings
ACGINSST castings
ACGINSTT scatting
ACGIOORS gracioso
ACGIORST orgastic
ACGIORSU gracious
ACGIPRSY spagyric
ACGJLNOU conjugal
ACGLMOUU coagulum
ACGLNORS clangors
ACGLNORU clangour
ACGLOOPS Glooscap
ACGLOSUU glaucous
ACGLSSTU cutglass
ACGNNOOT contango
ACGNNORS crannogs
ACGNOOST octagons
ACGNORST congrats
ACHHIIMS Chishima
ACHHILMS Hamlisch
ACHHILPT phthalic
ACHHINRU Nurhachi
ACHHINTW whinchat
ACHHINTY hyacinth
ACHHIPPR hipparch
ACHHLLOT challoth
ACHHLNOR rhonchal
ACHHLORY holarchy
ACHHNTTU nuthatch
ACHHOOUZ Chaozhou
ACHHPPSU chuppahs
ACHHPTUZ chutzpah
ACHIILMS chiliasm
ACHIILPT haplitic
ACHIILST chiliast
ACHIINPS Hispanic
ACHIINRT trichina
ACHIINST chiantis
ACHIINSU Chişinău
ACHIIRST rachitis
ACHIJNST jacinths
ACHIKKSW kickshaw
ACHIKLMY hickymal
ACHIKLPT chalkpit
ACHIKNOP pachinko
ACHIKOOW Kiaochow
ACHIKQSU quackish
ACHIKRSS rickshas
ACHIKRSW rickshaw
ACHIKRSY hayricks
ACHILMRS chrismal
ACHILMTY mythical
ACHILNNS clannish
ACHILNOS Nicholas
ACHILOPU pachouli
ACHILORT acrolith
ACHILPSY physical
ACHILPTY patchily
ACHILRVY chivalry
ACHILTTY chattily
ACHIMMOS machismo
ACHIMMST mismatch
ACHIMNOP champion
ACHIMNOR harmonic
ACHIMNOS mohicans
ACHIMNOX Chamonix
ACHIMNPT pitchman
ACHIMNSU inasmuch
ACHIMOPR amphoric
ACHIMPSS scampish
ACHIMRSS charisms
ACHIMRST chartism
ACHIMSSU chiasmus
ACHINNSU anchusin
unchains
ACHINNUY Yinchuan
ACHINORS Niarchos
ACHINORT anorthic
ACHINOTZ hoactzin
ACHINSTY Scythian
ACHIOPRT atrophic
ACHIOPSS isopachs
ACHIORST chariots
haricots
ACHIORTV tovarich
ACHIOSST isotachs
ACHIPPSS sapphics
ACHIPRRT parritch
phratric
ACHIPTTU chupatti
ACHIRRTY triarchy
ACHIRSTT chartist
ACHIRSTU haircuts
ACHISTTY chastity
ACHKKORW hackwork
ACHKMMOS hammocks
ACHKMORS shamrock
ACHKNOOT canthook
ACHKOSSS hassocks
ACHLLOOS alcohols
ACHLLORY chorally
ACHLMSTZ schmaltz
ACHLNORT Charlton
ACHLNOSY halcyons
ACHLOPRT calthrop
ACHLOPTT potlatch
ACHLORSS scholars
ACHLOSSW salchows
ACHLOTWX waxcloth

ACHLPRTU Plutarch
ACHMNNSU Schumann
ACHMNORS monarchs
nomarchs
ACHMNORY monarchy
nomarchy
ACHMOORT chatroom
ACHMOSST stomachs
ACHMOSTY stomachy
ACHMOTTU outmatch
ACHMSSUW cumshaws
ACHNORXY chronaxy
ACHNOSTY tachyons
ACHNPPSS schnapps
ACHNRSYY synarchy
ACHOORTU coauthor
ACHOPRST toparchs
ACHOPRSY charpoys
ACHOPRTY toparchy
ACHOTTUW watchout
ACHPRSTU pushcart
ACHPTTUY chupatty
ACHRRTUY craythur
ACIIILMN inimical
ACIIILNS Sicilian
ACIIILNV civilian
ACIIINST isatinic
Sinaitic
ACIIKLNO kaolinic
ACIIKNNN cannikin
ACIIKNNS canikins
ACIIKNTY kyanitic
ACIIKPRT paitrick
ACIILLNV vanillic
ACIILLSU silicula
ACIILLTV villatic
ACIILMNR criminal
ACIILMOT comitial
ACIILMPT palmitic
ACIILMSS laicisms
ACIILNOR ironical
ACIILNPS piscinal
ACIILNPT platinic
ACIILNRS Sinclair
ACIILRTU uralitic
ACIILSST silastic
ACIIMNNT mannitic
ACIIMNOR morainic
ACIIMNOS simoniac
ACIIMNOT amniotic
ACIIMNST actinism
ACIIMNSU musician
ACIIMNTU actinium
ACIIMNTY intimacy
minacity
ACIIMOST iotacism
ACIIMOTT amitotic
ACIIMPRV vampiric
ACIIMRST scimitar
ACIIMRTU muriatic
ACIIMSTT atticism
ACIIMSTV activism
ACIIMTUV viaticum
ACIINNOS Socinian
ACIINNOT inaction
ACIINNQU cinquain
ACIINNRV nirvanic
ACIINOPT optician
ACIINORZ zirconia
ACIINOSV avionics
ACIINOTT citation
ACIINPRS Priscian
ACIINPSS piscinas
ACIINRSS narcissi
ACIINRTU uranitic
ACIIORST aoristic
Iscariot
ACIIORTV victoria
ACIIPPST papistic
ACIIRSTT artistic
ACIISTTT atticist
ACIISTTU autistic
ACIISTTV activist
ACIITTVY activity
ACIITVVY vivacity
ACIJKKPS skipjack
ACIJSUZZ jacuzzis
ACIKLMNV Vlaminck
ACIKLNOT antilock
ACIKLNRY crankily
ACIKLNSU Nicklaus
ACIKLORS airlocks
ACIKLORY croakily
ACIKNNPR crankpin
ACILLLNY clinally
ACILLLOP pollical
ACILLMMN McMillan
ACILLMMY clammily
ACILLMOS localism
ACILLMSS miscalls
ACILLNOO colonial
ACILLNOR carillon
ACILLNOS scallion
ACILLNUY uncially
ACILLOQU coquilla
ACILLORT clitoral
ACILLORY collyria
ACILLOST Callisto
localist
ACILLOSY socially
ACILLOTY locality
ACILLOUV colluvia
ACILLSSY classily
ACILMNOP complain
ACILMNOS laconism
limacons
ACILMOPR proclaim
ACILMOSV vocalism
ACILMSSS classism
ACILMSSU musicals
ACILMSTY mystical
ACILNOOT location
ACILNOPS salpicon
ACILNOPT platonic
ACILNORS clarinos
clarions
ACILNORT cilantro
contrail
ACILNOSU unsocial
ACILNOUV univocal
ACILNRSU cislunar
ACILNRUY culinary
uranylic
ACILNSTU lunatics
sultanic
ACILNSTY scantily
ACILOPRT tropical
ACILOPST postical
ACILORRV corrival
ACILORTV vortical
ACILOSTV vocalist
ACILOTVY vocality
ACILPSST plastics
ACILRSTU curtails
ACILRTUV cultivar
ACILSSST classist
ACILSSUU Clausius
ACILSTTY scattily
ACILSTUV victuals
ACILSTVY sylvatic
ACIMMTUY cymatium
ACIMNNNO cinnamon
ACIMNNOR Minorcan
ACIMNOOR acromion
ACIMNOPS campions
ACIMNORT romantic
ACIMNORU coumarin
ACIMNORY acrimony
ACIMNOST monastic
ACIMNOTU aconitum
ACIMNPTY tympanic
ACIMNRSU craniums
ACIMOPST apomicts
ACIMORSY cramoisy
ACIMOSST massicot
ACIMOSTT stomatic
ACIMRRSY miscarry
ACIMSSST miscasts
ACINNNOO nonanoic
ACINNOOT conation
ACINNOQU conquian
ACINNOSS scansion
ACINNOST actinons
canonist
contains
sanction
sonantic
ACINNOSU Asunción
ACINNOTU continua
ACINNRTY tyrannic
ACINNSTY instancy
ACINOOPR picaroon
ACINOOTV vocation
ACINOPPT panoptic
ACINOPRS parsonic
ACINOPST captions

ACINOPTU acupoint
ACINORSS narcosis
ACINORST cantoris
carotins
ACINORTT traction
ACINOSSS caissons
ACINOSSY cyanosis
ACINOSTT oscitant
tactions
ACINOSTU auctions
cautions
ACINOSTW wainscot
ACINOSWX coxswain
ACINOTTX toxicant
ACINPQUY piquancy
ACINPRST cantrips
ACINPRSY cyprians
ACINPSTY synaptic
ACINQSTU quantics
ACINRSTU curtains
ACINRTTU taciturn
urticant
ACINSTTY sanctity
ACINSTYY syncytia
ACIOOPST scotopia
ACIOOPTX Cotopaxi
ACIOPRST apricots
ACIOPRTT protatic
ACIOPSST potassic
ACIOPSSU spacious
ACIOPSTU captious
ACIORRSS corsairs
ACIORRTU Courtrai
ACIORSSU scarious
ACIORTTY atrocity
citatory
ACIORTVY voracity
ACIOSTUU cautious
ACIPRSSS casspirs
ACIPSSST spastics
ACIQRSTU quartics
ACIRSSST sacrists
ACIRSSTT astricts
ACIRSSTY sacristy
ACIRSSTZ czarists
ACISSSTU casuists
ACISSTTU catsuits
ACJKKSSY skyjacks
ACJKOPST jackpots
ACJMNSTU muntjacs
ACJPSTUU cajuputs
ACKKMOPR pockmark
ACKLLOPS pollacks
ACKLLPSU skullcap
ACKLNORS Clarkson
ACKLOOPW woolpack
ACKLOORS oarlocks
ACKLOOSW woolsack
ACKLORSW warlocks
ACKMMMOS mammocks
ACKMNOST stockman
ACKMOSST stomacks
ACKMOSTT mattocks
ACKOPRRT traprock
ACLLLNOY clonally
ACLLMMOX Malcolm X
ACLLNNOO nonlocal
ACLLNORW Cornwall
ACLLOORT collator
ACLLOOSS colossal
ACLLOPSS scallops
ACLLORUY ocularly
ACLLRTUU cultural
ACLLSTUU Catullus
ACLMMNOT Montcalm
ACLMMNOU communal
ACLMMORW clamworm
ACLMNOOO coolamon
ACLMNORU columnar
ACLMNORY normalcy
ACLMORSU clamours
ACLMRSUU muscular
ACLMSTUU custumal
ACLMSUUV vasculum
ACLNNOOV nonvocal
ACLNOORS coronals
ACLNOORT colorant
ACLNOOST coolants
ACLNOOSV volcanos
ACLNOOSY Colonsay
ACLNOPSY syncopal
ACLNORSU consular
courlans
ACLNORTU calutron
ACLNOSTU osculant
ACLNPSSU unclasps
ACLNPTUU punctual
ACLNSTUU Tusculan
ACLOOPPS alcopops
ACLOOPRR corporal
ACLOPPRY Polycarp
ACLOPRRU procural
ACLOPRST caltrops
ACLOPRXY xylocarp
ACLOPSSU scopulas
ACLOPSSY calypsos
ACLOSSTU outclass
ACLRSSTY crystals
ACMMNOSY scammony
ACMNOOPR monocarp
ACMNOORT monocrat
ACMNOPRS corpsman
crampons
ACMNORSS Crossman
ACMNORSY acronyms
ACMNSSTU sanctums
ACMOOPRS coprosma
ACMOORRT motorcar
ACMOOSST scotomas
ACMORSTW catworms
wormcast
ACMORSTY costmary
ACMQSTUU cumquats
ACNNNORY cannonry
ACNNORST Scranton
ACNNOSTT constant
ACNOOORT octaroon
ACNOORRY coronary
ACNOORST cartoons
corantos
ostracon
ACNOORSU canorous
ACNOORTY octonary
ACNOPSSW snowcaps
ACNORRSY carryons
ACNORRTY contrary
ACNORSTT contrast
ACNORTTU turncoat
ACNPRSSY syncarps
ACNPRSYY syncarpy
ACNRRSTU currants
ACOOPSTT topcoats
ACOORSTU touracos
ACOPPRRS procarps
ACOPRRST carports
ACOPRRTT protract
ACORRSTT tractors
ACORRSTU curators
ACORRTUY carryout
ACORSSTU surcoats
ACORSSUW curassow
ACORSSWY crossway
ACORSTTY cryostat
ACOSSTTU outcasts
ACPSSTUY pussycat
ADDDEEEN deadened
ADDDEEGR degraded
ADDDEEIM diademed
ADDDEELR laddered
ADDDEEMN demanded
maddened
ADDDEENR dandered
ADDDEENS saddened
ADDDEGJU adjudged
ADDDEIMS misadded
ADDDELSW swaddled
ADDDELTW twaddled
ADDDEMNU addendum
ADDDENOS deodands
ADDDEOOW deadwood
ADDEEEFN deafened
ADDEEEFT defeated
ADDEEEMN demeaned
ADDEEENR deadener
endeared
ADDEEESY deadeyes
ADDEEFHN handfeed
ADDEEFIL defilade
ADDEEFLT deflated
ADDEEFRY defrayed
ADDEEGGR daggered
ADDEEGHR hardedge
ADDEEGLN danegeld
ADDEEGNR deranged
gardened
ADDEEGOR dogeared

ADDEEGRR degrader
regarded
regraded
ADDEEGRS degrades
ADDEEGSS degassed
ADDEEHLR heralded
ADDEEHLY aldehyde
ADDEEHNR hardened
ADDEEHRS redheads
ADDEEHRT threaded
ADDEEILN deadline
ADDEEILR deadlier
derailed
ADDEEILT detailed
ADDEEIMT mediated
ADDEEINT detained
ADDEEIPR diapered
ADDEEISS diseased
ADDEEIST steadied
ADDEEITV deviated
ADDEEKNR darkened
ADDEELLM medalled
ADDEELLP pedalled
ADDEELNP deplaned
ADDEELNU unleaded
ADDEELOR reloaded
ADDEELRT treadled
ADDEELST desalted
ADDEELUV devalued
ADDEEMNN demanned
ADDEEMNP dampened
ADDEEMNR demander
redemand
remanded
ADDEEMNV Demavend
ADDEENPP appended
ADDEENPR pandered
ADDEENPX expanded
ADDEENRW wandered
ADDEENSS deadness
ADDEENTT attended
ADDEENTU denudate
ADDEENUV unevaded
ADDEEPRT departed
predated
ADDEEPRV depraved
pervaded
ADDEERRT retarded
ADDEERRW rewarded
ADDEERSW sawdered
ADDEERTV adverted
ADDEFFOR afforded
ADDEFIIL ladified
ADDEFILY ladyfied
ADDEFIST faddiest
ADDEFLRU dreadful
ADDEFRSU defrauds
ADDEGGLR draggled
ADDEGHOR Drogheda
ADDEGILS gladdies
ADDEGINR dreading
readding
ADDEGJSU adjudges
ADDEGLNS gladdens
ADDEGLST gladdest
ADDEGNRU ungraded
ADDEGPRU upgraded
ADDEHHLN handheld
ADDEHILR dihedral
ADDEHINW headwind
ADDEHIRS diehards
ADDEHLOS shedload
ADDEHLOW Howel Dda
ADDEHLWY Hywel Dda
ADDEHMRU drumhead
ADDEHNNU unhanded
ADDEHNRU Dehra Dun
ADDEHNSU unshaded
ADDEHOPR drophead
ADDEHORW headword
ADDEHOSW shadowed
ADDEHRTY hydrated
ADDEHSTU Thaddeus
ADDEIIRW Edward II
ADDEIITV additive
ADDEIJNO adjoined
ADDEIKNP kidnaped
ADDEILNS islanded
landside
ADDEILNT tideland
ADDEILSY dialysed
ADDEILYZ dialyzed
ADDEIMOS sodamide
ADDEIMRS disarmed
ADDEIMST misdated
ADDEIMSY dismayed
ADDEIMTT admitted
ADDEINOR ordained
ADDEINOS adenoids
anodised
ADDEINOZ anodized
ADDEINPR drepanid
ADDEINST dandiest
ADDEIOPR parodied
ADDEIORS sideroad
ADDEIOTX oxidated
ADDEIQSU squaddie
ADDEIRST disrated
ADDEIRSW sideward
ADDEIRVW Edward IV
Edward VI
ADDEIRVZ vizarded
ADDEISSU dissuade
ADDEISSW swaddies
ADDEJSTU adjusted
ADDELMOS dolmades
ADDELNNS Land's End
ADDELNOU duodenal
unloaded
ADDELNPU pudendal
ADDELNRS dandlers
ADDELNSU unsaddle
ADDELOOR eldorado
El Dorado
ADDELPRS paddlers
ADDELRSS saddlers
ADDELRST straddle
ADDELRSW dawdlers
waddlers
ADDELRSY Drysdale
saddlery
ADDELRTW twaddler
ADDELSST staddles
ADDELSSW swaddles
ADDELSTW twaddles
ADDEMNPU undamped
ADDEMOSY domesday
ADDENOPR pardoned
ADDENPRU undraped
ADDENRST stranded
ADDEORTU outdared
ADDEOTTU outdated
ADDEPRSU superadd
ADDFFILO daffodil
ADDFFINR dandriff
ADDFFNRU dandruff
ADDFIRSU Safid Rud
ADDFISST faddists
ADDFORRT Dartford
ADDGGILN gladding
ADDGILNN dandling
ADDGILNP paddling
ADDGILNR raddling
ADDGILNS saddling
ADDGILNW dawdling
waddling
ADDGINSW waddings
ADDGINWY waddying
ADDGLNOS gladdons
ADDGMRUU mudguard
ADDGOQSU godsquad
ADDHHLNO handhold
ADDHINSY dandyish
ADDHISTY hydatids
ADDHOORW hardwood
ADDHOSTY athodyds
ADDIINOT addition
ADDIINRT Trinidad
ADDIINSS disdains
ADDIKSTY katydids
ADDILMNS midlands
ADDIMNOS diamonds
ADDIMNSY dandyism
ADDINNOR ordinand
ADDINORS androids
ADDINRWW windward
ADDKLNOR Dorkland
ADDKNRRU drunkard
ADDLLNOR landlord
ADDLLRSU dullards
ADDLNNOW downland
ADDLNOOW download
woodland
ADDLNORR randlord
ADDLORSY Lord's Day
ADDLORTY dotardly

ADDMOOSY	doomsday
ADDNOPWY	pandowdy
ADDNORWW	downward
ADDOORRY	dooryard
ADDOORWW	woodward
ADDOORWY	woodyard
ADEEEFNY	fedayeen
ADEEEFRT	defeater
	federate
ADEEEGLT	delegate
ADEEEGNR	renegade
ADEEEGNT	teenaged
ADEEEGRS	degrease
ADEEEGUW	agueweed
ADEEEHRS	haeredes
ADEEEHRT	reheated
ADEEEHSY	eyeshade
ADEEEINT	detainee
ADEEEKNW	weakened
ADEEELMN	enameled
ADEEELNV	leavened
ADEEELPR	repealed
ADEEELRS	released
	resealed
ADEEELRV	revealed
ADEEELST	teaseled
ADEEELSW	weaseled
ADEEELTV	elevated
ADEEELTZ	teazeled
ADEEENNT	neatened
ADEEENRS	serenade
ADEEENTT	attendee
	edentate
ADEEEPRS	rapeseed
ADEEEPRT	repeated
ADEEERST	reseated
ADEEESSW	seesawed
ADEEFHNR	freehand
ADEEFHOR	forehead
ADEEFHRT	fathered
ADEEFIIR	aerified
ADEEFILN	enfilade
ADEEFIMS	semideaf
ADEEFIRR	rarefied
ADEEFLLT	fellated
ADEEFLOR	freeload
ADEEFLPR	pedalfer
ADEEFLRR	deferral
ADEEFLRT	faltered
	reflated
ADEEFLSS	fadeless
ADEEFLST	deflates
ADEEFLSX	flaxseed
ADEEFMNR	freedman
ADEEFMRR	reframed
ADEEFMRS	defamers
ADEEFNSS	deafness
ADEEFNST	fastened
ADEEFNTT	fattened
ADEEFOTV	foveated
ADEEFRRY	defrayer
ADEEFRST	draftees
ADEEFRTU	featured
ADEEGGHS	eggheads
ADEEGGRU	regauged
ADEEGHRT	gathered
ADEEGINN	Engadine
ADEEGINR	regained
ADEEGIRS	disagree
ADEEGLLU	de Gaulle
ADEEGLNR	enlarged
	largened
ADEEGLNT	danegelt
ADEEGLRV	graveled
ADEEGLRZ	reglazed
ADEEGLSV	selvaged
ADEEGMMT	gemmated
ADEEGMNR	gendarme
ADEEGMNS	endgames
ADEEGMNY	ganymede
ADEEGMOP	megapode
ADEEGMOS	megadose
ADEEGMSS	messaged
ADEEGNNR	endanger
ADEEGNOR	renegado
ADEEGNRR	gardener
	garnered
ADEEGNRS	deranges
	grandees
	grenades
ADEEGNRU	dungaree
	underage
ADEEGNRV	engraved
ADEEGORT	derogate
ADEEGPRS	presaged
ADEEGPRT	pargeted
ADEEGRRS	regrades
ADEEGRRT	gartered
	regrated
ADEEGRRU	Daguerre
	reargued
ADEEGRRV	Redgrave
ADEEGRSS	degasser
	dressage
ADEEGRST	restaged
ADEEGRSU	guardees
ADEEGRSW	ragweeds
ADEEGRTT	targeted
ADEEGSSS	degasses
ADEEGSTT	gestated
ADEEGSWY	edgeways
ADEEGTTZ	gazetted
ADEEHHRS	rehashed
ADEEHHST	sheathed
ADEEHIKL	headlike
ADEEHIKZ	Zedekiah
ADEEHILN	headline
ADEEHIST	headiest
ADEEHISV	adhesive
ADEEHKNR	hankered
	harkened
ADEEHKWW	hawkweed
ADEEHKWY	hawkeyed
ADEEHLLW	wellhead
ADEEHLNR	rehandle
ADEEHLNS	hanseled
ADEEHLNU	unhealed
ADEEHLRT	haltered
	lathered
ADEEHLSS	headless
ADEEHLTY	heatedly
ADEEHMMO	homemade
ADEEHMMR	hammered
ADEEHMNN	menhaden
ADEEHMNS	headsmen
ADEEHMPR	hampered
ADEEHMST	stemhead
ADEEHNPP	happened
ADEEHNRR	hardener
	reharden
ADEEHNRT	adherent
ADEEHNSS	dasheens
ADEEHNST	hastened
	netheads
ADEEHNTU	unheated
ADEEHORS	sorehead
ADEEHORV	overhead
ADEEHPRS	reshaped
ADEEHPRT	threaped
ADEEHPUV	upheaved
ADEEHRRT	rethread
	threader
ADEEHRRW	Hereward
ADEEHRST	headrest
ADEEHRSW	rewashed
ADEEHRTT	threated
ADEEHRTW	wreathed
ADEEHSST	headsets
ADEEHSSY	hayseeds
ADEEIILS	idealise
ADEEIILZ	idealize
ADEEIIRS	Dies Irae
ADEEIJKL	jadelike
ADEEIJMR	jeremiad
ADEEIJST	jadeites
ADEEILLO	oeillade
ADEEILMN	endemial
ADEEILMR	remailed
	remedial
ADEEILMS	limeades
ADEEILMV	medieval
ADEEILNS	delaines
ADEEILNT	dateline
	entailed
	lineated
ADEEILPS	pleiades
ADEEILPT	depilate
	epilated
	pileated
ADEEILRR	derailer
ADEEILRS	realised
	sidereal
ADEEILRT	elaterid
	retailed
ADEEILRZ	realized
ADEEILSS	idealess

ADEEIMNR remained
ADEEIMNT dementia
ADEEIMNX examined
ADEEIMRR dreamier
ADEEIMRT diameter
ADEEIMST mediates
Tameside
ADEEIMTT meditate
ADEEINNS adenines
andesine
ADEEINOP oedipean
ADEEINPT diapente
ADEEINRS arsenide
nearside
ADEEINRT detainer
retained
ADEEINRV reinvade
ADEEINST andesite
ADEEINVW inweaved
ADEEIPRR repaired
ADEEIPRS airspeed
ADEEIPTX expiated
ADEEIRRR drearier
ADEEIRST readiest
steadier
ADEEIRTT iterated
ADEEISSS diseases
ADEEISST steadies
ADEEISTV deviates
sedative
ADEEKKRR Kerkrade
ADEEKMRR remarked
ADEEKMRT demarket
marketed
ADEEKNPS kneepads
ADEEKNPW knapweed
ADEEKNRR darkener
ADEEKNRS kneaders
ADEEKQSU squeaked
ADEEKRST streaked
ADEEKSWY weekdays
ADEELLLP lapelled
ADEELLMT metalled
ADEELLMU medullae
ADEELLNP panelled
ADEELLNY leadenly
ADEELLPR predella
ADEELLPS sepalled
ADEELLPT petalled
ADEELLQU equalled
ADEELLRU laureled
ADEELLRV ravelled
ADEELLSS allseeds
leadless
ADEELLTY elatedly
ADEELLWY walleyed
ADEELMNO lemonade
ADEELMNP emplaned
ADEELMNR aldermen
ADEELMNS dalesmen
leadsmen
ADEELMNT lamented
ADEELMPX exampled
ADEELMRS demersal
emeralds
ADEELMRV marveled
ADEELMTU emulated
ADEELNNP enplaned
ADEELNNU unaneled
ADEELNOR oleander
reloaned
ADEELNPS deplanes
ADEELNPT endplate
ADEELNRS Landseer
ADEELNRV lavender
ADEELNRY Alderney
ADEELNSU unleased
unsealed
ADEELNSV enslaved
ADEELNTT talented
ADEELNTV levanted
ADEELOPS pedaloes
ADEELOPX poleaxed
ADEELOST desolate
ADEELPPT lappeted
ADEELPRS pleaders
relapsed
ADEELPRT paltered
ADEELPRY parleyed
replayed
ADEELPST pedestal
ADEELPTY pedately
ADEELQSU squealed
ADEELRRT treadler
ADEELRST treadles
ADEELRSV slavered
ADEELRSY delayers
ADEELRTV traveled
ADEELRUV revalued
ADEELSST dateless
tasseled
ADEELSTU adultese
ADEELSTY sedately
ADEELSUV devalues
ADEEMMRY yammered
ADEEMMSS mesdames
ADEEMMXY myxedema
ADEEMNNR mannered
Menander
remanned
ADEEMNOR demeanor
enamored
ADEEMNOT nematode
ADEEMNOU eudaemon
ADEEMNPR dampener
ADEEMNPY ependyma
ADEEMNRS amenders
meanders
ADEEMNSU unseamed
ADEEMORT moderate
ADEEMPPR pampered
ADEEMPRR prearmed
ADEEMPRT tampered
ADEEMPRV revamped
ADEEMPST stampede
stepdame
ADEEMRRS dreamers
ADEEMRRW rewarmed
ADEEMRST mastered
streamed
ADEEMRSU Madurese
measured
ADEEMRTT mattered
ADEEMSWY mayweeds
ADEENNPT pennated
ADEENNRS Andersen
Ardennes
ensnared
ADEENNRU unearned
ADEENNTT tenanted
ADEENNUW unweaned
ADEENOPW weaponed
ADEENORS reasoned
ADEENORV endeavor
ADEENORY aerodyne
ADEENOSS seasoned
ADEENOST endostea
ADEENOTT detonate
ADEENPPR endpaper
ADEENPRR panderer
ADEENPRX expander
ADEENPTT patented
ADEENRRW wanderer
ADEENRSS dearness
ADEENRSU undersea
ADEENRSW Andrewes
answered
ADEENRTT attender
nattered
ADEENRTU denature
underate
undereat
ADEENSST assented
standees
ADEENSSU danseuse
Sudanese
ADEENSTU unseated
ADEENTTU tautened
ADEENTTV vendetta
ADEEOPRT operated
ADEEOPST adoptees
ADEEORSW oarweeds
ADEEORVW overawed
ADEEPPRR prepared
ADEEPRRS spreader
ADEEPRRU upreared
ADEEPRRV depraver
pervader
ADEEPRSS aspersed
repassed
ADEEPRST pederast
predates
repasted
trapesed
ADEEPRSU persuade
ADEEPRSV depraves

	pervades
ADEEPRTT	pattered
ADEEPRTU	depurate
ADEEPSST	stapedes
ADEEPSWY	speedway
ADEEQRUV	quavered
ADEERRRT	retarder
ADEERRRW	rewarder
ADEERRST	arrested
	retreads
	serrated
	treaders
ADEERRTW	redwater
ADEERSST	asserted
	estrades
ADEERSTT	restated
ADEERTTT	tattered
ADEERTTY	yattered
ADEERVYY	everyday
ADEESSSS	assessed
ADEESTTT	attested
ADEFFGUW	guffawed
ADEFFIMR	affirmed
ADEFFIRT	tariffed
ADEFFIST	daffiest
ADEFFLNS	snaffled
ADEFFLOS	leadoffs
ADEFFORT	tradeoff
ADEFGGOT	faggoted
ADEFGIIS	gasified
ADEFGILN	finagled
ADEFGILO	foliaged
ADEFGILR	Garfield
ADEFGILS	gadflies
ADEFGIMN	defaming
ADEFGIRT	driftage
ADEFGIRU	argufied
ADEFGITU	fatigued
ADEFGLOT	gatefold
ADEFHILS	dealfish
ADEFHILT	Hatfield
ADEFHIMS	famished
ADEFHMOT	fathomed
ADEFHNOR	forehand
ADEFIILN	finialed
ADEFIILR	airfield
ADEFIILS	ladifies
	salified
ADEFIILT	filiated
ADEFIIMR	ramified
ADEFIINZ	nazified
ADEFIIRT	ratified
ADEFILMN	inflamed
ADEFILNT	inflated
ADEFILOT	foliated
ADEFILSY	dayflies
	ladyfies
ADEFIMNR	Friedman
ADEFIMPR	firedamp
ADEFINRR	infrared
ADEFINYZ	denazify
ADEFIORS	foresaid
ADEFIRRT	draftier
ADEFKSST	deskfast
ADEFLLLU	ladleful
ADEFLLOR	falderol
ADEFLLOW	fallowed
ADEFLLRY	alderfly
ADEFLMRU	dreamful
ADEFLNOR	foreland
ADEFLNRS	Flanders
ADEFLNTU	flaunted
ADEFLORT	deflator
ADEFLORV	flavored
ADEFLPRS	feldspar
ADEFLRTW	leftward
ADEFLRZZ	frazzled
ADEFLSTU	defaults
ADEFMNRU	unframed
ADEFNOPR	profaned
ADEFNSST	daftness
ADEFORRW	farrowed
ADEFORRY	foreyard
ADEFORUV	favoured
ADEFRRST	drafters
	redrafts
ADEFSSTT	stedfast
ADEGGIRR	draggier
ADEGGIST	daggiest
ADEGGJLY	jaggedly
ADEGGLNU	angledug
ADEGGLRS	draggles
ADEGGLRY	raggedly
ADEGGMOS	demagogs
ADEGGMOY	demagogy
ADEGGOPS	pedagogs
ADEGGOPY	pedagogy
ADEGGRTY	gadgetry
ADEGHHOS	hogshead
ADEGHILT	alighted
	gilthead
ADEGHINR	adhering
	Hardinge
ADEGHINS	headings
	sheading
ADEGHLNO	headlong
ADEGHNRT	thranged
ADEGHORT	goatherd
ADEGHRTU	daughter
ADEGIILN	gliadine
ADEGIILP	diplegia
ADEGIIMN	imagined
ADEGIIMS	digamies
ADEGIIRT	digerati
ADEGIITT	digitate
ADEGIKLO	goadlike
ADEGIKNN	kneading
ADEGILLP	pillaged
ADEGILMN	maligned
	medaling
ADEGILNP	pedaling
	pleading
ADEGILNR	dragline
ADEGILNS	dealings
	signaled
ADEGILNT	delating
ADEGILNY	delaying
ADEGILOU	dialogue
ADEGILSS	glissade
ADEGIMNN	amending
ADEGIMNR	dreaming
	margined
ADEGIMNT	Mitnaged
ADEGIMOR	ideogram
ADEGIMRT	migrated
ADEGINOR	organdie
ADEGINOS	agonised
	diagnose
	San Diego
ADEGINOZ	agonized
ADEGINRR	Gardiner
ADEGINRS	deraigns
	gradines
	readings
ADEGINRT	derating
	gradient
	treading
ADEGINSS	assigned
	Gassendi
ADEGINST	sedating
	steading
ADEGINSU	Agnus Dei
ADEGINSW	windages
ADEGINTV	vintaged
ADEGIOST	godetias
ADEGIRTU	Radiguet
ADEGIRWY	ridgeway
ADEGISTU	gaudiest
ADEGJNOR	jargoned
ADEGLLNU	glandule
ADEGLLOP	galloped
ADEGLMOS	gladsome
ADEGLMUY	amygdule
ADEGLNPS	spangled
ADEGLNRS	danglers
	glanders
ADEGLNRW	wrangled
ADEGLNSS	gladness
ADEGLNUZ	unglazed
ADEGLOSU	Gesualdo
ADEGLPPR	grappled
ADEGLSTY	dalgytes
ADEGMMNO	gammoned
ADEGMMRU	rummaged
ADEGMNOR	dragomen
ADEGMNOY	endogamy
ADEGMNSU	agendums
ADEGMORW	wordgame
ADEGMPUZ	gazumped
ADEGNNOR	androgen
ADEGNOPU	poundage
ADEGNORT	dragonet
ADEGNOSS	sondages
ADEGNOSV	dogvanes
ADEGNPRR	Grand Pré
ADEGNRRU	grandeur

ADEGNRST	dragnets
	grandest
ADEGNRUZ	gazunder
ADEGOORY	goodyear
ADEGOPRR	dragrope
ADEGOPRT	portaged
ADEGORRT	garroted
ADEGORSW	dowagers
ADEGORTT	garotted
ADEGORTU	outraged
	ragouted
ADEGORTW	waterdog
ADEGPRRU	upgrader
ADEGPRSU	upgrades
ADEGPSTU	upstaged
ADEGRRST	dragster
ADEGRRSU	guarders
ADEGRSSU	graduses
ADEGTTTU	guttated
ADEHHIPS	headship
ADEHHIST	shithead
ADEHHLOY	Holyhead
ADEHHOOR	hoorahed
ADEHHOPS	hopheads
ADEHHOST	hotheads
ADEHHRRU	hurrahed
ADEHHRST	thrashed
ADEHHUZZ	huzzahed
ADEHIKLN	handlike
ADEHIKLV	khedival
ADEHIKNS	skinhead
ADEHILLM	Heimdall
ADEHILMW	Waldheim
ADEHILNR	hardline
ADEHILNU	unhailed
ADEHILPS	helipads
ADEHILRY	Hyder Ali
ADEHILSV	lavished
ADEHIMOT	hematoid
ADEHIMRS	misheard
	semihard
ADEHINOP	diaphone
ADEHINOS	adhesion
ADEHINOY	hyoidean
ADEHINPS	deanship
	headpins
	pinheads
ADEHINPU	dauphine
	Dauphiné
ADEHINRS	Sheridan
ADEHINRU	unhaired
ADEHINSS	shandies
ADEHINST	handiest
ADEHINSV	vanished
ADEHIORS	Herodias
	Rhodesia
ADEHIOTT	athetoid
ADEHIPRS	raphides
	Sephardi
ADEHIPSS	pisshead
ADEHIPST	pitheads
	Spithead
ADEHIRRT	trihedra
ADEHIRSS	radishes
ADEHIRST	hardiest
ADEHIRSV	ravished
ADEHIRSW	rawhides
ADEHISST	shadiest
ADEHISSW	siwashed
ADEHKNRS	redshank
ADEHKORW	headwork
ADEHKPRY	Hyde Park
ADEHLLOO	hallooed
	holloaed
ADEHLLOW	hallowed
ADEHLLRT	thralled
ADEHLLSW	Shadwell
ADEHLLSY	dayshell
ADEHLMNO	homeland
ADEHLNRS	handlers
ADEHLNSS	handless
	handsels
ADEHLNST	shetland
	Stendhal
ADEHLNSU	unlashed
ADEHLOPS	asphodel
ADEHLPSS	splashed
ADEHLRRY	heraldry
ADEHMMMO	Mohammed
ADEHMNNY	handymen
ADEHMNOS	handsome
ADEHMNOT	methadon
ADEHMNRS	herdsman
ADEHMNRU	unharmed
ADEHMOOR	headroom
ADEHMORW	homeward
ADEHMOST	headmost
ADEHMOSU	madhouse
ADEHNOPR	orphaned
ADEHNOPT	phonated
ADEHNORV	handover
	overhand
ADEHNOSS	sandshoe
ADEHNRSS	hardness
ADEHNRSU	unshared
ADEHNRSW	swanherd
ADEHNRTU	unthread
ADEHNSST	handsets
ADEHNSSU	sunshade
ADEHNSUV	unshaved
ADEHNSUW	unwashed
ADEHOORT	Theodora
ADEHOORW	harewood
ADEHOORY	hoorayed
ADEHOPRS	rhapsode
ADEHOPST	potheads
ADEHOPSX	hexapods
ADEHOPXY	hexapody
ADEHORRS	hoarders
ADEHORRW	harrowed
ADEHORSW	shadower
ADEHORTU	authored
ADEHOSTW	towheads
ADEHPPRS	Sheppard
ADEHPRSU	Phaedrus
ADEHQSSU	squashed
ADEHRRUY	hurrayed
ADEHRSTY	hydrates
ADEHRTTW	thwarted
ADEIILMS	idealism
	miladies
ADEIILRS	Disraeli
ADEIILST	idealist
ADEIILTV	dilative
ADEIILTY	ideality
ADEIIMNN	indamine
ADEIIMNR	meridian
ADEIIMNS	diamines
ADEIIMPR	impaired
ADEIIMRS	semiarid
ADEIIMTT	imitated
ADEIINNS	sanidine
ADEIINRT	daintier
ADEIINRU	uredinia
ADEIINST	adenitis
	dainties
ADEIINSZ	diazines
ADEIIPRS	presidia
ADEIIRSS	airsides
ADEIITTV	vitiated
ADEIITUV	auditive
ADEIKLLO	keloidal
ADEIKLLR	lardlike
ADEIKLLY	ladylike
ADEIKLNS	sandlike
ADEIKLNW	dawnlike
	wandlike
ADEIKLOT	toadlike
ADEIKLPV	Kapil Dev
ADEIKLSW	sidewalk
ADEIKMRT	tidemark
ADEIKNPR	kidnaper
ADEIKNSY	kyanised
ADEIKNYZ	kyanized
ADEIKORT	keratoid
ADEILLMY	medially
ADEILLNN	landline
ADEILLNU	unallied
ADEILLNY	leylandi
ADEILLOR	arillode
ADEILLPR	pillared
ADEILLPS	spadille
ADEILLRS	dalliers
	diallers
ADEILLRT	trialled
ADEILLRV	rivalled
ADEILLSW	sidewall
ADEILMMS	dilemmas
ADEILMNO	de Molina
	melanoid
ADEILMNY	maidenly
	medianly
ADEILMOX	aldoxime
ADEILMPS	impleads
	misplead
ADEILMRY	dreamily

ADEILMSS	misdeals
	misleads
ADEILMST	medalist
	misdealt
ADEILMSV	Maldives
ADEILNNR	inlander
ADEILNNS	annelids
ADEILNNT	dentinal
ADEILNNV	Vineland
ADEILNOP	palinode
ADEILNOS	Leonidas
ADEILNOT	delation
ADEILNRS	islander
ADEILNTV	divalent
ADEILOPR	Leopardi
ADEILOPS	sepaloid
ADEILOPT	petaloid
ADEILORT	idolater
	tailored
ADEILORV	overlaid
ADEILORX	exordial
ADEILOSS	assoiled
ADEILOST	diastole
	isolated
	sodalite
ADEILOSV	de Valois
	Val-d'Oise
ADEILOSZ	diazoles
ADEILOTT	datolite
ADEILOTV	dovetail
	violated
ADEILPPP	pedipalp
ADEILPRS	spiraled
ADEILPRT	dipteral
ADEILPRU	epidural
ADEILPRV	deprival
ADEILPST	talipeds
ADEILQTU	liquated
ADEILRRY	drearily
ADEILRST	dilaters
ADEILRSU	residual
	Ruisdael
ADEILRSY	dialyser
ADEILRTT	detrital
ADEILRUV	Duvalier
ADEILRVY	variedly
ADEILRYZ	dialyzer
ADEILSSV	devisals
ADEILSSY	dialyses
ADEILSTY	diastyle
	steadily
ADEILSWY	Day-Lewis
ADEILSXY	dyslexia
ADEILSYZ	dialyzes
ADEILTTU	altitude
	latitude
ADEILTVY	datively
ADEIMMNS	misnamed
ADEIMMRS	mermaids
ADEIMNNO	mondaine
ADEIMNOP	dopamine
ADEIMNOS	nomadise

ADEIMNOT	dominate
ADEIMNOZ	nomadize
ADEIMNRY	dairymen
ADEIMNRZ	zemindar
ADEIMNSS	sidesman
ADEIMNST	mediants
ADEIMNSU	maundies
ADEIMNTY	dynamite
ADEIMORR	airdrome
ADEIMORT	mediator
ADEIMOSS	sesamoid
ADEIMOST	atomised
ADEIMOTZ	atomized
ADEIMPRT	imparted
ADEIMPST	impasted
ADEIMRRS	admirers
	disarmer
	marrieds
ADEIMRSS	misreads
	sidearms
ADEIMRST	readmits
ADEIMSST	misdates
ADEIMSTY	daytimes
ADEINNOT	anointed
	antinode
ADEINNOV	Devonian
ADEINNPT	pinnated
ADEINNRS	insnared
ADEINNRZ	rendzina
ADEINNTU	antidune
	inundate
ADEINOPT	antipode
ADEINORR	ordainer
ADEINORT	deration
	ordinate
	rationed
ADEINOSS	anodises
ADEINOST	astonied
	sedation
ADEINOSZ	anodizes
ADEINOTT	antidote
	tetanoid
ADEINOTV	donative
ADEINPPX	appendix
ADEINPRS	sprained
ADEINPRT	dipteran
ADEINPRU	unpaired
ADEINPSV	spavined
ADEINQTU	antiqued
ADEINRRS	drainers
	serranid
ADEINRSS	aridness
	sardines
ADEINRST	detrains
	randiest
	strained
ADEINRSU	denarius
	unraised
	uranides
ADEINRSV	invaders
ADEINRTT	Andretti
	nitrated

ADEINRTU	indurate
	urinated
ADEINRUV	unvaried
ADEINRVY	vineyard
ADEINSST	sandiest
ADEINSSV	vanessid
ADEINSTT	instated
ADEINSTU	sinuated
ADEINSTV	deviants
ADEIOPRS	diaspore
	parodies
ADEIOPRV	overpaid
ADEIOPST	dioptase
ADEIOPTV	adoptive
ADEIORST	asteroid
ADEIORSV	avoiders
ADEIORTT	teratoid
ADEIORTV	deviator
ADEIOSTX	oxidates
ADEIOSTZ	azotised
ADEIOTZZ	azotized
ADEIPPRS	apprised
	drappies
ADEIPPRZ	apprized
ADEIPRSS	despairs
ADEIPRST	traipsed
ADEIPRSU	upraised
ADEIPRTU	eupatrid
ADEIPTTU	aptitude
ADEIQRRU	quarried
ADEIQSUY	quayside
ADEIRRTW	tawdrier
ADEIRRWW	wiredraw
ADEIRSST	disaster
	disrates
ADEIRSSU	radiuses
ADEIRSSV	advisers
ADEIRSTT	striated
	tardiest
ADEIRTTT	titrated
ADEIRTUV	durative
ADEIRVWY	driveway
ADEISSST	assisted
ADEISSTT	distaste
ADEISSWY	sideways
	waysides
ADEISTTU	situated
ADEISTUZ	deutzias
ADEISTWY	tideways
ADEITTTU	attitude
ADEJLOSU	jaloused
ADEJNORS	Jordaens
ADEJOPRY	jeopardy
ADEJRRSU	adjurers
ADEJRSTU	adjuster
	readjust
ADEKLMRY	markedly
ADEKLNSU	unslaked
ADEKLPRS	sparkled
ADEKMNRU	unmarked
ADEKMNSU	unmasked
ADEKMORS	darksome

ADEKNNSS dankness
ADEKNOTW takedown
ADEKNRSS darkness
ADEKQSUW squawked
ADEKRTYZ Radetzky
ADELLMOS slalomed
ADELLMRU medullar
ADELLMSU medullas
ADELLNNU annulled
ADELLNRS landlers
ADELLNSS landless
ADELLNSW Sandwell
wallsend
ADELLOPW walloped
ADELLOSW sallowed
ADELLOTT allotted
totalled
ADELLOTW tallowed
ADELLOVY ladylove
ADELLOWW wallowed
ADELLQSU squalled
ADELLTUU ululated
ADELMNNS landsmen
ADELMNOO Laomedon
ADELMNRS mandrels
ADELMOPS malposed
ADELMORS earldoms
ADELMOSS damosels
ADELMOSZ damozels
ADELMOTU modulate
ADELMPRT trampled
ADELMRRU demurral
ADELMSSY massedly
ADELNNSW Newlands
ADELNORS solander
ADELNORU unloader
ADELNORV overland
rondavel
ADELNOVY Donleavy
ADELNPRS spandrel
ADELNPRY repandly
ADELNPSY dyspneal
endplays
ADELNPUY unplayed
ADELNRSS slanders
ADELNRSU launders
ADELNRSY Lysander
ADELNRTY ardently
ADELNRUY underlay
ADELNSTU unsalted
ADELNSTW wetlands
ADELNTUU undulate
ADELNUUV unvalued
ADELOOPV levodopa
ADELOORV overload
ADELOPRS leopards
ADELOPRU poularde
ADELOPSS deposals
ADELOPST tadpoles
ADELOPTY petalody
ADELORSS roadless
ADELORST delators
del Sarto
leotards
lodestar
ADELORSU roulades
ADELORTW leadwort
ADELOSTV solvated
ADELOTUV ovulated
ADELOTUW outlawed
ADELOVWY avowedly
ADELPPRY dapperly
ADELPRSW sprawled
ADELPRTT prattled
ADELPRTU preadult
ADELPSTU pulsated
ADELRRSU ruderals
ADELRRSW drawlers
ADELRRTU ultrared
ADELRSSW wardless
ADELRSTT startled
ADELRSTW warstled
ADELRSUY Ruysdael
ADELRTUY adultery
ADEMMNOW madwomen
ADEMNNNU unmanned
ADEMNNSU Amundsen
ADEMNOOR marooned
ADEMNOPR pomander
ADEMNOPT tamponed
ADEMNORS madrones
ransomed
ADEMNOTU amounted
ADEMNPSS dampness
ADEMNRRU underarm
unmarred
ADEMNRSU maunders
surnamed
ADEMNRTU undreamt
ADEMNRUW unwarmed
ADEMNSSU medusans
ADEMNSUU unamused
ADEMOORT moderato
ADEMOOST stomodea
ADEMOOSV vamoosed
ADEMOPRY pyoderma
ADEMORRT mortared
ADEMORRU armoured
ADEMORTW damewort
wardmote
ADEMOSSU Asmodeus
ADEMRRSU eardrums
ADEMRRTY martyred
ADENNORS Anderson
ADENNOSY anodynes
ADENNOTU unatoned
ADENNOTW wantoned
ADENNPST pendants
ADENNRUW unwarned
ADENNTUW unwanted
ADENOORT ratooned
ADENOORW wanderoo
ADENOPRR pardoner
ADENOPRS operands
padrones
pandores
Sarpedon
ADENOPRT pronated
ADENOPST notepads
ADENOPSY dyspnoea
ADENORRW narrowed
ADENORTT attorned
ADENORTW danewort
teardown
ADENORUX rondeaux
ADENORUY Dounreay
ADENOTUY autodyne
ADENPPRS parpends
ADENPPTU untapped
ADENPRRS pardners
ADENPRTY pedantry
ADENPRUY underpay
ADENQRSU squander
ADENRRWY wardenry
ADENRSST standers
ADENRSSU danseurs
Saunders
ADENRSTU daunters
transude
untreads
ADENRSTX dextrans
ADENRTTU truanted
ADENRTVY Daventry
ADENRUWY underway
ADENSTTU unstated
untasted
ADENSTUY unsteady
ADENSUWY unswayed
ADEOOPSS apodoses
ADEOORRT toreador
ADEOOSTW Eastwood
ADEOOTTT tattooed
ADEOPPRV approved
ADEOPRRS eardrops
ADEOPRRT parroted
predator
prorated
teardrop
ADEOPRSS Sporades
ADEOPRST readopts
ADEOPRTT tetrapod
ADEOPRUV vapoured
ADEOPSST podestas
ADEOPSTT postdate
ADEORRST roadster
ADEORRVW overdraw
ADEORSST assorted
torsades
ADEORSTU outdares
readouts
ADEORSTX extrados
ADEORSUV savoured
ADEOSTTU outdates
ADEPPRST strapped
ADEPRRTU raptured
ADEPRSTU pastured

updaters
ADEQSTTU squatted
ADERRSSW wardress
ADERRSTT redstart
ADERSSTW stewards
ADERSSUY dasyures
ADERSTUX surtaxed
ADERSTVY strayved
ADERSTWW westward
ADFFHNOS handoffs
ADFFISST distaffs
ADFFLOOS offloads
ADFFNOST standoff
ADFFORRT Trafford
ADFFORST Stafford
ADFGINNU unfading
ADFGINRT drafting
ADFGINRW dwarfing
ADFGMNOO man of God
ADFHIOST toadfish
ADFHIRSW dwarfish
ADFHLNSU handfuls
ADFHLNSY flyhands
ADFHLOST holdfast
ADFHOOSS shadoofs
ADFHORRT Hartford
ADFIILPY lapidify
ADFIIRSU Firdausi
ADFILLLN landfill
ADFILLNW windfall
ADFILMNO manifold
ADFILRTY draftily
ADFIMRSW dwarfism
ADFINRST indrafts
ADFIORSV disfavor
ADFKNOOR Kordofan
ADFLLNOW downfall
ADFLMNOR landform
ADFLNOPS plafonds
ADFLORSU foulards
ADFMORST Stamford
ADFNNOST fondants
ADFNOORZ forzando
ADFNORST Stanford
ADFOOPST footpads
ADFORRSW forwards
ADGGGINR dragging
ADGGHNOS hangdogs
ADGGIIMO DiMaggio
ADGGILNN dangling
ADGGINRS niggards
ADGGINRU guarding
ADGGLRSU sluggard
ADGHHILN highland
ADGHHIOR highroad
ADGHILLL gildhall
ADGHILLS Dalglish
ADGHILNN handling
ADGHILOS hidalgos
ADGHILTY daylight
ADGHINOR hoarding
ADGHINPR handgrip
ADGHINSS shadings
ADGHIPRS digraphs
ADGHITTW tightwad
ADGHLNNO longhand
ADGHNNOS Shandong
ADGHNNSU handguns
ADGHNOSS sandhogs
ADGHRSTU draughts
ADGHRTUY draughty
ADGIIIRT tigridia
ADGIILLN dialling
ADGIILLO gladioli
ADGIILMR Grimaldi
ADGIILNO gonidial
ADGIILNR drailing
ADGIILNS gliadins
ADGIILNT dilating
ADGIILPY pygidial
ADGIILRS Igdrasil
ADGIILST digitals
ADGIILTY algidity
ADGIIMNR admiring
ADGIIMNX admixing
ADGIIMOR idiogram
ADGIIMST digamist
ADGIINNR draining
ADGIINNU guanidin
ADGIINNV invading
ADGIINOR radioing
ADGIINOT iodating
ADGIINOV avoiding
ADGIINRY dairying
ADGIINSU iguanids
ADGIINSV advising
ADGIINTU auditing
ADGIJNRU adjuring
ADGIKLNR darkling
ADGILLNU alluding
dualling
ADGILLNW windgall
ADGILLNY dallying
ADGILLOT goldtail
ADGILMNS gildsman
ADGILMOR marigold
ADGILNNS landings
ADGILNNU unlading
ADGILNOS loadings
ADGILNPP dappling
ADGILNPS Spalding
ADGILNRS darlings
ADGILNRW drawling
ADGILNRY daringly
ADGILNZZ dazzling
ADGILOOS solidago
ADGILOPR prodigal
ADGILORS goliards
ADGILRVY gravidly
ADGIMMNW dwamming
ADGIMNOP pomading
ADGIMNRS mridangs
ADGIMNUW dwauming
ADGIMOSU digamous
ADGINNOR adorning
ADGINNOT donating
ADGINNPY pandying
ADGINNST standing
ADGINNTU daunting
ADGINOOR rigadoon
ADGINOPT adopting
ADGINORU rigaudon
ADGINOTY toadying
ADGINPTU updating
ADGINRSW drawings
swarding
ADGINRSY yardings
ADGINSWY gwyniads
ADGIORTT Titograd
ADGIPRSU pagurids
ADGIRSZZ gizzards
ADGKOOSZ gadzooks
ADGLMNOS mangolds
ADGLMNSU gumlands
ADGLNNOR Grønland
ADGLNOOS gondolas
ADGLNOOT Togoland
ADGMNORS gormands
ADGMNORU gourmand
ADGNNOQU quandong
ADGNNORS grandson
ADGNNRYY gynandry
ADGNOORS dragoons
gadroons
ADGNRRSU gurnards
ADGPRRUU Durgapur
ADHHIPRS hardship
ADHHLOOV havdoloh
ADHHMOSS shahdoms
ADHHNRTY hydranth
ADHIIJMS jihadism
ADHIIKSS dashikis
ADHIILLR Hilliard
ADHIILOR Harold II
ADHIINOP ophidian
ADHIJLSY jadishly
ADHIKKOO Hokkaido
ADHILLOT thalloid
ADHILLRY hydrilla
ADHILMOS halidoms
ADHILNOR rhodinal
ADHILOOW Hailwood
ADHILOPS haploids
shipload
ADHILOPY haploidy
ADHILOSY holidays
ADHILPSY ladyship
ADHIMNOS admonish
ADHIMNOU humanoid
ADHIMOPP amphipod
ADHIMPSS phasmids
ADHINNOY Dohnányi
ADHINOPY diaphony
ADHINPSS dishpans
ADHINPSU dauphins
ADHINSST standish

ADHINSTU	dianthus
ADHINTUV	Hindutva
ADHIOSTY	toadyish
ADHIPRSW	wardship
ADHIPRSY	shipyard
ADHIRTWW	withdraw
ADHKNORW	handwork
ADHLLLOS	holdalls
ADHLLNOS	hollands
ADHLLNOY	Holy Land
ADHLMORT	thraldom
ADHLNOPR	Randolph
ADHLNOTU	duathlon
ADHLNOUW	downhaul
ADHLNSTU	Landshut
ADHLORRY	Old Harry
ADHMORSY	hydromas
ADHNNORU	Honduran
ADHNORSU	Honduras
ADHNOSTU	handouts
	thousand
ADHNOSWW	downwash
ADHNRSTY	hydrants
ADHOOPRS	hospodar
ADHOORSW	roadshow
ADHOPRST	hardtops
	potshard
ADHOPRSY	rhapsody
ADHOPSST	dashpots
ADHORRTY	hydrator
ADIIINRV	viridian
ADIIIQRU	daiquiri
ADIIKLMM	milkmaid
ADIIKLST	tailskid
ADIIKNST	antiskid
ADIILLMR	milliard
ADIILLOP	lipoidal
ADIILLUV	diluvial
ADIILMRV	Vladimir
ADIILNOT	dilation
ADIILNSU	indusial
ADIILNSV	invalids
ADIILNSW	windsail
ADIILNTW	tailwind
ADIILNTY	daintily
ADIILNUV	diluvian
ADIILOPP	diplopia
ADIILSSY	dialysis
ADIILTVY	validity
ADIIMNNU	Numidian
ADIIMNOT	Domitian
ADIIMRST	triadism
ADIINNOS	Sidonian
ADIINNOT	nidation
ADIINOOT	iodation
ADIINOSY	Dionysia
ADIINOTU	audition
ADIINRST	distrain
ADIIPRTY	rapidity
ADIIPSTY	sapidity
ADIIPTVY	vapidity
ADIIRSST	diarists
ADIIRSTT	distrait
ADIJLLOO	Djailolo
ADIJNOST	adjoints
ADIKLLOR	roadkill
ADIKLOSS	odalisks
ADIKMOSU	daimokus
ADIKNNNU	dunnakin
ADIKNNST	inkstand
ADIKNOPY	pyinkado
ADIKNPSS	skidpans
ADIKSSWY	skidways
ADILLLNW	Lindwall
ADILLLPY	pallidly
ADILLMMS	milldams
ADILLMNR	mandrill
ADILLMOU	allodium
ADILLMSY	dismally
ADILLNPS	landslip
ADILLOSW	disallow
ADILLOSY	disloyal
ADILLRUV	Vuillard
ADILLSTY	distally
ADILMNNO	mandolin
ADILMNOS	salmonid
ADILMNRS	mandrils
ADILMOPS	diplomas
	plasmoid
ADILMOPT	diplomat
ADILMOPY	olympiad
ADILMOSY	amyloids
ADILMOTY	modality
ADILMPSS	plasmids
ADILMPSU	paludism
ADILNNOR	Londrina
ADILNNSU	disannul
ADILNOOR	doornail
ADILNOOV	vindaloo
ADILNORS	ordinals
ADILNOTY	nodality
ADILNPRS	spandril
ADILNPST	displant
ADILNRSU	diurnals
ADILNRWY	inwardly
ADILNSSU	sundials
ADILNSSW	windlass
ADILOORT	toroidal
ADILOPRT	dioptral
	tripodal
ADILOPSS	disposal
ADILORST	dilators
ADILORSY	solidary
ADILORTY	adroitly
	dilatory
	idolatry
ADILOSTY	sodality
ADILPRSY	pyralids
ADILPSST	plastids
ADILPSSY	displays
ADILPSTU	plaudits
ADILRTTY	tiltyard
ADILRTWY	tawdrily
ADILRWYZ	wizardly
ADILSSTU	dualists
ADIMMNOS	monadism
	nomadism
ADIMMNSY	dynamism
ADIMMOTU	domatium
ADIMNNOR	Mondrian
ADIMNNOS	mondains
ADIMNNOT	dominant
ADIMNOSS	madisons
ADIMNOST	donatism
	saintdom
ADIMNRSY	misandry
ADIMNSTY	dynamist
ADIMOPRY	myriapod
ADIMOPSY	sympodia
ADIMORRS	miradors
ADIMOSST	mastoids
ADIMOSTT	mattoids
ADIMOSTY	toadyism
ADIMPRSY	pyramids
ADIMRSUU	sudarium
ADIMSSST	dismasts
ADIMSSTU	stadiums
ADINNNTU	inundant
ADINNOOR	Rondônia
ADINNOOT	donation
ADINNOPS	dipnoans
ADINNORS	andirons
ADINNRSW	winnards
ADINOOPS	isopodan
ADINOOPT	adoption
ADINOORT	tandoori
ADINOOTT	dotation
ADINOPPS	oppidans
ADINOPRS	poniards
ADINOPST	satinpod
ADINORRY	ordinary
ADINORSS	sadirons
ADINORST	intrados
ADINORSU	dinosaur
ADINORTU	duration
ADINOSSV	Davisson
ADINOSTT	Donatist
ADINOSTX	oxidants
ADINOSTY	dystonia
ADINPSST	sandpits
ADIOOPRT	parotoid
ADIOOPSS	apodosis
ADIOOSSW	woodsias
ADIOPPST	postpaid
ADIOPRRS	airdrops
ADIOPRSS	sparoids
ADIOPRST	parodist
	parotids
	Port Said
ADIOPRTY	podiatry
ADIOPSTY	dystopia
ADIORRTT	traditor
ADIORSST	astroids
ADIORSSV	advisors
ADIORSTU	auditors
ADIORSVY	advisory

ADIORTUY auditory
ADIOSSVW disavows
ADIRRWYZ wizardry
ADIRSSTY satyrids
ADJKNRUY junkyard
ADJLMORS jarldoms
ADJNORSU adjourns
ADJORRSU adjurors
ADKLMRSU mudlarks
ADKLOORW woodlark
workload
ADKMNORW markdown
ADKMOORR darkroom
ADKNORTU outdrank
ADKOORRW roadwork
ADKORSWY workdays
ADKRSSWY skywards
ADLLLOOY doolally
ADLLNOSW lowlands
ADLLNUUZ Zululand
ADLLOPRS pollards
ADLLORSY dorsally
ADLMNOOR moorland
ADLMNOOV Moldovan
ADLMNORY randomly
ADLMOPSY psalmody
ADLNNORS norlands
ADLNNOTW townland
ADLNNTUU undulant
ADLNOORS lardoons
ADLNOORW loanword
ADLNOPRT portland
ADLNOPRU pauldron
ADLNOPSU poundals
ADLNOPWY downplay
playdown
ADLNOSTU outlands
ADLOOPRU uropodal
ADLOPRSU poulards
ADLOPRWY wordplay
ADLOQSUW oldsquaw
ADLORRSW warlords
ADLORTWY towardly
ADLPRUWY upwardly
ADMMNORU Omdurman
ADMMNSSU summands
ADMNNORY monandry
Normandy
ADMNOORS madronos
ADMNOOST mastodon
ADMNOOSW woodsman
ADMNORST mordants
ADMNORSW sandworm
ADMNOSSU osmundas
ADMOOPPP poppadom
ADMOORRT Dartmoor
ADMOORRW wardroom
ADMOORST doormats
ADMOPPPU poppadum
ADMORSST tsardoms
ADMRSSTU durmasts
mustards

ADNNOOSY noondays
ADNNORTY dynatron
ADNOOPRV Andropov
ADNOOQRU quadroon
ADNOORST donators
tandoors
tornados
ADNOOSVW advowson
ADNOPRSU pandours
ADNOQRSU squadron
ADNORSTU rotundas
ADNORSTW sandwort
ADNORSXY sardonyx
ADNORTUW untoward
ADNOSSTU astounds
ADNOSTTU outstand
standout
ADNPSSTU dustpans
ADNRSSUW sunwards
ADOOPPRU pauropod
ADOOPRRT trapdoor
ADOOPRSU sauropod
ADOORSWY doorways
ADOOSSSW sasswood
ADOPPRST Stoppard
ADOPRSSW password
ADOPSSSU soapsuds
ADORSTUW outwards
ADORSTUY sudatory
ADRSSTTU stardust
AEEEFORS Faeroese
AEEEFRRW freeware
AEEEGGNR reengage
AEEEGHNS Seahenge
AEEEGLLS legalese
AEEEGLMR Meleager
AEEEGLRT regelate
relegate
AEEEGLRV leverage
AEEEGLST legatees
AEEEGNRT generate
teenager
AEEEGNSS ageneses
AEEEGPRS peerages
AEEEGPSS seepages
AEEEGRST etageres
steerage
AEEEGRSW sewerage
AEEEGTTV vegetate
AEEEHLRT ethereal
AEEEHMPR ephemera
AEEEHRRS rehearse
AEEEHRRT reheater
AEEEHSTT aesthete
AEEEILNS alienees
AEEEIMNX examinee
AEEEIRST eateries
AEEEKKPS keepsake
AEEEKNRW weakener
AEEEKNTW Enewetak
AEEELLPP appellee
AEEELMNR enameler

AEEELNPS Nepalese
AEEELNRV venereal
AEEELNST selenate
AEEELPRR repealer
AEEELQSU sequelae
AEEELRRS releaser
AEEELRRV revealer
AEEELRSS releases
AEEELRTX axletree
AEEELSTV elevates
AEEEMMRT metamere
AEEEMNST easement
AEEEMPRT permeate
AEEENPTT patentee
AEEENRTV enervate
venerate
AEEEPRRT repartee
repeater
AEEEPSTW sweetpea
AEEERRTW treeware
AEEERSST esterase
tesserae
AEEFFLLS felafels
AEEFFLTT flatfeet
AEEFFNRT afferent
AEEFGILR filagree
AEEFGIRR ferriage
AEEFGLSU fuselage
AEEFHLLS selfheal
AEEFHRST feathers
AEEFHRTY feathery
AEEFIIRS aerifies
AEEFIKLL leaflike
AEEFIKRR freakier
AEEFIKRW wakerife
AEEFILMN filename
AEEFILNR flanerie
AEEFILST fealties
fetiales
leafiest
AEEFIPSW spaewife
AEEFIRRR rarefier
AEEFIRRS rarefies
AEEFIRSS freesias
AEEFISST safeties
AEEFKOPR forepeak
AEEFLLLM Flémalle
AEEFLLMT flamelet
AEEFLLNV evenfall
AEEFLLRW farewell
AEEFLLSS leafless
AEEFLLST fellates
leaflets
AEEFLMSS fameless
selfsame
AEEFLNRU funereal
AEEFLOOV foveolae
AEEFLORV overleaf
AEEFLRRR referral
AEEFLRRT falterer
AEEFLRSS fearless
AEEFLRST reflates

AEEFLTTT	flatette
AEEFMNOR	forename
AEEFMORS	fearsome
AEEFMRRS	reframes
AEEFNRST	fastener
	fenestra
	refasten
AEEFNRTT	fattener
AEEFNSSS	safeness
AEEFRRST	ferrates
AEEFRSST	feasters
AEEFRSTU	features
AEEFRSWY	freeways
AEEGGINR	agreeing
AEEGGIRV	aggrieve
AEEGGNNR	gangrene
AEEGGNRS	engagers
AEEGGPRU	puggaree
AEEGGRSU	regauges
AEEGHILN	Hegelian
AEEGHIRT	heritage
AEEGHLOT	helotage
AEEGHMPR	grapheme
AEEGHNRS	shagreen
AEEGHNSW	whangees
AEEGHRRT	gatherer
	regather
AEEGIIST	gaieties
AEEGIKLM	gamelike
AEEGIKLT	gatelike
AEEGILLS	galilees
	legalise
AEEGILLZ	legalize
AEEGILMN	liegeman
AEEGILMR	gleamier
AEEGILMS	gelsemia
	mileages
AEEGILNR	algerine
AEEGILNS	ensilage
	lineages
AEEGILNT	galenite
	gelatine
	legatine
AEEGILPR	perigeal
AEEGILRS	gaselier
AEEGILSW	weigelas
AEEGILTV	levigate
AEEGIMNT	geminate
AEEGIMRT	emigrate
AEEGINPR	perigean
AEEGINRR	regainer
AEEGINRS	gesneria
AEEGINRZ	razeeing
AEEGINSS	agenesis
	assignee
AEEGINSU	Guianese
AEEGINSV	envisage
AEEGINTV	agentive
	negative
AEEGIPQU	equipage
AEEGIRRS	greasier
AEEGIRSS	greasies
AEEGIRSU	eugaries
AEEGIRTT	aigrette
AEEGIRTV	ergative
AEEGISTY	gayeties
AEEGKMRR	regmaker
AEEGLLNR	allergen
AEEGLLSZ	gazelles
AEEGLMNS	melanges
AEEGLMOS	mesoglea
AEEGLMPX	megaplex
AEEGLMRT	telegram
AEEGLMRY	meagerly
	meagrely
AEEGLNNO	Angeleno
AEEGLNNR	Erlangen
AEEGLNNT	entangle
AEEGLNOS	gasolene
AEEGLNOT	elongate
AEEGLNRR	enlarger
	Erlanger
AEEGLNRS	enlarges
	generals
	gleaners
AEEGLNRT	regental
AEEGLNSV	evangels
AEEGLNSY	Anglesey
AEEGLRSS	eelgrass
	gearless
	largesse
AEEGLRSU	leaguers
AEEGLRSZ	reglazes
AEEGLRTU	regulate
AEEGLRUX	exergual
AEEGLSST	gateless
AEEGLSSV	selvages
AEEGLSSW	wageless
AEEGLSSY	eyeglass
AEEGLTTU	tutelage
AEEGMMNS	gamesmen
AEEGMMOS	gamesome
AEEGMMST	gemmates
	tagmemes
AEEGMNSS	gameness
AEEGMRRS	Grasmere
AEEGMRSS	Messager
AEEGMRST	gamester
AEEGMSSS	messages
AEEGMSSU	messuage
AEEGNNNO	enneagon
AEEGNPPS	genappes
AEEGNRRV	engraver
AEEGNRST	estrange
	grantees
	greatens
	negaters
	reagents
	sergeant
AEEGNRSV	avengers
	engraves
AEEGNRUV	Auvergne
AEEGNSSS	sageness
AEEGNSTT	tentages
AEEGNSTV	ventages
AEEGNSUY	Guyanese
AEEGOPRV	overpage
AEEGORRV	overgear
AEEGPRRS	presager
AEEGPRSS	asperges
	presages
AEEGPRSU	pugarees
AEEGRRRT	regrater
AEEGRRSS	greasers
AEEGRRST	regrates
AEEGRRSU	reargues
AEEGRRSW	wagerers
AEEGRSST	restages
AEEGRSTT	greatest
AEEGRSUZ	guerezas
AEEGSSTT	gestates
AEEGSTTZ	gazettes
AEEHHHSS	hasheesh
AEEHHIKZ	Hezekiah
AEEHHIMN	Nehemiah
AEEHHLNZ	hazelhen
AEEHHNST	heathens
AEEHHRSS	rehashes
AEEHHRST	heathers
AEEHHRTY	heathery
AEEHHSST	sheathes
AEEHIJMR	Jeremiah
AEEHIKLN	Alekhine
AEEHIKLR	harelike
AEEHIKMN	Khamenei
AEEHIKRS	shikaree
AEEHILRS	shiralee
AEEHILTV	Helvetia
AEEHIMNT	hematein
AEEHIMNX	hexamine
AEEHIMTT	hematite
AEEHIPRS	Hesperia
	pharisee
	sphairee
AEEHIRRT	earthier
	heartier
AEEHIRST	hearties
AEEHIRSV	shivaree
AEEHISST	esthesia
AEEHISTT	hesitate
AEEHISTV	heaviest
AEEHISTW	White Sea
AEEHKLLR	rakehell
AEEHKLLU	keelhaul
AEEHKNRR	harkener
AEEHKNRS	hearkens
AEEHLLSS	seashell
AEEHLMNW	whalemen
	wheelman
AEEHLMNY	hymeneal
AEEHLMPT	helpmate
AEEHLNOT	anethole
AEEHLNPT	elephant
AEEHLNRT	leathern
AEEHLNSS	haleness
AEEHLNVY	heavenly

AEEHLORS arsehole
halosere
AEEHLOSU alehouse
AEEHLPST heeltaps
AEEHLPTT telepath
AEEHLRST halteres
leathers
AEEHLRTY leathery
AEEHLSST heatless
AEEHLSTT athletes
AEEHLTTY ethylate
AEEHMMRR hammerer
AEEHMNRT earthmen
AEEHMNTU atheneum
AEEHMNTX exanthem
AEEHMORW homeware
AEEHMPRR hamperer
AEEHMPSS emphases
AEEHMRSS mahseers
AEEHMRTY erythema
AEEHNNTX xanthene
AEEHNNVW Newhaven
New Haven
AEEHNOPR earphone
AEEHNRRT Traherne
AEEHNRST hastener
heartens
AEEHNRTT threaten
AEEHNRTU urethane
AEEHNRTW enwreath
waterhen
AEEHNRWY anywhere
AEEHNSTW enswathe
AEEHOPRT ephorate
AEEHORRV overhear
AEEHORSS sea horse
seahorse
seashore
AEEHORTV overheat
AEEHOSTU teahouse
AEEHPPRS preshape
AEEHPRRS rephrase
AEEHPRRT threaper
AEEHPRSS reshapes
AEEHPRST preheats
AEEHPSUV upheaves
AEEHRRSS shearers
AEEHRRTU urethrae
AEEHRSSW rewashes
AEEHRSTT theaters
theatres
AEEHRSTW weathers
wreathes
AEEHRTVW whatever
AEEIKLLS seallike
AEEIKLMU leukemia
AEEIKLMZ mazelike
AEEIKLPT tapelike
AEEIKLRW weaklier
AEEIKLST leakiest
AEEIKLVW wavelike
AEEIKMNT ketamine
AEEIKNRS sneakier
AEEIKNRT ankerite
AEEIKNTW Keewatin
AEEILLNT tenaille
AEEILLRT laetrile
AEEILMMN melamine
AEEILMNT melanite
AEEILMRS measlier
AEEILMRT Lemaître
materiel
realtime
AEEILMST mealiest
AEEILMTZ metalize
AEEILNPR perineal
AEEILNPS penalise
sepaline
AEEILNPT petaline
tapeline
AEEILNPZ penalize
AEEILNRT elaterin
entailer
treenail
AEEILNRV Verlaine
AEEILORT aerolite
AEEILOTT etiolate
AEEILPRR pearlier
AEEILPRS espalier
pearlies
AEEILPRT pearlite
AEEILPST epilates
AEEILQSU equalise
AEEILQUZ equalize
AEEILRRS realiser
AEEILRRT retailer
AEEILRRZ realizer
AEEILRSS realises
AEEILRST ateliers
earliest
leariest
AEEILRSV velarise
AEEILRSY yearlies
AEEILRSZ realizes
sleazier
AEEILRTT laterite
literate
AEEILRTV levirate
relative
AEEILRVW liveware
reviewal
AEEILRVZ velarize
AEEILSTV elatives
AEEILSVW alewives
AEEILTTV levitate
AEEIMMNT meantime
AEEIMNRT antimere
AEEIMNRX examiner
AEEIMNSS Messenia
Messiaen
nemesias
AEEIMNST matinees
AEEIMNSX examines
AEEIMNUV mauveine
AEEIMORV Aviemore
AEEIMRSS seriemas
AEEIMRST emirates
steamier
AEEIMSST seamiest
steamies
AEEIMSTT estimate
meatiest
AEEINNRS anserine
AEEINNTV Aventine
venetian
AEEINOPS paeonies
AEEINPRS naperies
AEEINPRT aperient
Patenier
AEEINRRT Arretine
Eritrean
retainer
AEEINRSS Asnières
AEEINRST arenites
arsenite
resinate
stearine
Teresina
trainees
AEEINRSU uneasier
AEEINSSS easiness
AEEINSTT anisette
tetanise
AEEINSTV naivetes
AEEINSVW inweaves
AEEINTTZ tetanize
AEEIOOPP epopoeia
AEEIORST etaerios
AEEIPPSU eupepsia
AEEIPPTT appetite
AEEIPRRR rareripe
repairer
AEEIPRST parietes
AEEIPRSU Peiraeus
AEEIPSST epitases
AEEIPSTX expiates
AEEIQRSU queasier
AEEIQSTU equiseta
AEEIRRST arteries
AEEIRSTT ariettes
iterates
teariest
treaties
treatise
AEEIRSTW sweatier
weariest
AEEIRSTY yeastier
AEEIRSVV aversive
AEEISTTT steatite
AEEISTTV estivate
AEEITUVX exuviate
AEEJLNPT jetplane
AEEJMPPS Jemappes
AEEJNRST serjeant
AEEJORSV Serajevo
AEEKKLWY lykewake

AEEKKNOS	kokanees
AEEKLLNY	Keneally
AEEKLLST	skeletal
AEEKLMMU	mameluke
AEEKLMRT	telemark
AEEKLMSS	makeless
AEEKLSSW	wakeless
AEEKLSTY	eyestalk
AEEKMMRR	Kammerer
AEEKMNSS	kamseens
AEEKMORV	makeover
AEEKMRRR	remarker
AEEKMRRT	marketer
AEEKMRST	meerkats
AEEKNNNS	nankeens
AEEKNNPS	kneepans
AEEKNPSW	newspeak
AEEKNRSS	sneakers
AEEKNRSW	rewakens
	wakeners
AEEKNSSW	weakness
AEEKORST	keratose
AEEKORTV	overtake
	takeover
AEEKPRSS	speakers
AEEKPRTT	parkette
AEEKQRSU	squeaker
AEEKRRST	retakers
	streaker
AEEKRRSW	wreakers
AEEKRSTW	tweakers
AEELLLTT	telltale
AEELLMSS	mealless
AEELLOTT	allottee
AEELLPPY	Alleppey
AEELLPTT	platelet
AEELLRRV	raveller
AEELLSTT	stellate
AEELLSWY	walleyes
	weaselly
AEELLTVV	valvelet
AEELMMNU	Emmanuel
AEELMMTU	malemute
AEELMNNT	Telemann
AEELMNOT	Manolete
AEELMNPR	Perelman
AEELMNPS	empanels
	emplanes
	ensample
AEELMNRT	lamenter
AEELMNSS	lameness
	maleness
	maneless
	nameless
	salesmen
AEELMNST	talesmen
AEELMNSU	Menelaus
AEELMNTT	mantelet
AEELMOTT	matelote
AEELMPRS	empalers
AEELMPRX	exemplar
AEELMPRY	empyreal
AEELMPSX	examples
AEELMPTT	palmette
	template
AEELMRTX	extremal
AEELMSSS	seamless
AEELMSST	mateless
	meatless
	tameless
AEELMSTU	emulates
AEELNNPS	enplanes
AEELNNRT	lanneret
AEELNNSS	leanness
AEELNOPR	peroneal
AEELNOPT	antelope
AEELNORU	aleurone
AEELNPPS	spalpeen
AEELNPQU	Palenque
AEELNPSS	paleness
AEELNQSU	squalene
AEELNRRS	learners
	relearns
AEELNRSS	realness
AEELNRST	telerans
AEELNRSV	enslaver
AEELNRSW	renewals
AEELNRTV	levanter
	relevant
AEELNRTX	external
AEELNSST	lateness
AEELNSSV	enslaves
	vaneless
AEELNSWY	Wesleyan
AEELNTUV	eventual
AEELOPRS	parolees
AEELOPRV	overleap
AEELOPSX	poleaxes
AEELORST	oleaster
AEELORSU	aureoles
AEELORTT	tolerate
AEELORTV	elevator
AEELOTTT	teetotal
AEELPRRS	pearlers
	relapser
AEELPRRT	palterer
AEELPRRY	parleyer
AEELPRSS	pleasers
	relapses
AEELPRST	pleaters
	prelates
AEELPRSU	pleasure
AEELPRSV	vesperal
AEELPRTY	pterylae
AEELPSST	spatlese
AEELPSTT	palettes
AEELPSTU	epaulets
AEELQRSU	lequears
	squealer
AEELQSUZ	quezales
AEELRRST	realters
	relaters
AEELRRSV	reversal
	slaverer
AEELRRSX	relaxers
AEELRRTU	ureteral
AEELRRTV	traveler
AEELRSST	stealers
	tearless
	tesseral
AEELRSTX	exalters
AEELRSTY	easterly
AEELRSUV	revalues
AEELRSVY	aversely
AEELSSST	seatless
AEELSSVW	waveless
AEELSTTT	statelet
AEELSTTY	layettes
AEELSTVW	wavelets
AEEMMNTZ	mazement
AEEMMPSY	empyemas
AEEMMRRY	yammerer
AEEMMRST	ammeters
	metamers
AEEMMSST	messmate
AEEMNNOS	anemones
AEEMNNRT	remanent
AEEMNNSS	meanness
AEEMNPRS	spearmen
AEEMNPRT	permeant
	peterman
AEEMNPRY	empyrean
AEEMNPTV	pavement
AEEMNRST	Ansermet
AEEMNRSW	menswear
AEEMNRTU	numerate
AEEMNRTV	averment
AEEMNRTW	watermen
AEEMNRUV	maneuver
AEEMNRVY	everyman
AEEMNSSS	sameness
AEEMNSST	Massenet
	tameness
AEEMNSTW	sweetman
AEEMORST	Masorete
AEEMPPRR	pamperer
AEEMPRRT	tamperer
AEEMPRRV	revamper
AEEMPRST	temperas
AEEMPRTT	attemper
AEEMPSTU	amputees
AEEMQRRU	remarque
AEEMQRSU	marquees
AEEMQTTU	maquette
AEEMRRSS	smearers
AEEMRRST	remaster
	streamer
AEEMRRSU	measurer
AEEMRSST	masseter
	steamers
AEEMRSSU	measures
	reassume
AEEMRSTT	teamster
AEEMRSTV	Temesvár
AEEMRSTW	stemware
AEEMSSSU	masseuse

AEEMSSTU meatuses
AEENNOST neonates
AEENNPRY Pyrenean
AEENNRRS ensnarer
AEENNRRT Nanterre
AEENNRSS ensnares
nearness
AEENNRTV revenant
AEENNSSS saneness
AEENNSST neatness
AEENNSTT setenant
AEENNSUW Suwannee
AEENOPRS personae
AEENORRS reasoner
AEENORSS seasoner
AEENORST resonate
AEENORTV renovate
AEENORVW ovenware
AEENOTTU outeaten
AEENPQTU petanque
AEENPRUV parvenue
AEENPSSX expanses
AEENPTTY antetype
AEENRRRW warrener
AEENRRSS rareness
AEENRRST terranes
AEENRRSV raveners
AEENRRSY yearners
AEENRRTT natterer
AEENRRTV taverner
AEENRSST earnests
sarsenet
AEENRSTT entreats
AEENRSTV veterans
AEENRSTW Westenra
AEENRTTV antevert
AEENRTTX extranet
AEENRTTY entreaty
AEEOPRRT perorate
AEEOPRST operates
protease
AEEOPRTT operetta
AEEORRSU rearouse
AEEORRSV Averroës
AEEORRTV overrate
AEEORSSV overseas
AEEORSTV overeats
AEEORSVW overawes
AEEPPRRR preparer
AEEPPRRS paperers
prepares
repapers
AEEPRRRT parterre
AEEPRRSS asperser
spearers
AEEPRRST taperers
AEEPRRTU aperture
AEEPRSSS asperses
repasses
AEEPRSST trapeses
AEEPRSTZ trapezes
AEEQRRUV quaverer
AEERRRST arrester
rearrest
AEERRSST asserter
reassert
serrates
AEERRSSU erasures
reassure
AEERRSSW swearers
AEERRSTT retreats
treaters
AEERRSTU treasure
AEERRSTV traverse
AEERRSTW waterers
AEERRSVW waverers
AEERSSSS reassess
AEERSSTT estreats
restates
AEERSSTW sweaters
AEERSSUU uraeuses
AEERSTTT attester
AEESSSSS assesses
AEESSTTT testates
AEFFGIIL effigial
AEFFGIRS giraffes
AEFFGOST offstage
AEFFGRSU gauffers
suffrage
AEFFHIKY kaffiyeh
AEFFHILL halflife
AEFFIIPT Ipatieff
AEFFILUV effluvia
AEFFIMRR affirmer
reaffirm
AEFFKORS rakeoffs
AEFFKOST takeoffs
AEFFLNSS snaffles
AEFFLNTU affluent
AEFFLRRS rafflers
AEFFLRSW wafflers
AEFFLSTU sufflate
AEFFLSUX affluxes
AEFFMNST staffmen
AEFFMRSU earmuffs
AEFFNNSS naffness
AEFFORST afforest
AEFFOSVW waveoffs
AEFFQRSU quaffers
AEFFRSST restaffs
staffers
AEFFRTTU tartuffe
AEFGGLRS flaggers
AEFGIIRS gasifier
AEFGIISS gasifies
AEFGIKLN fanglike
AEFGIKMN Mafeking
Mafikeng
AEFGIKNR freaking
AEFGILNR finagler
AEFGILNS finagles
AEFGIMTU fumigate
AEFGINRW wafering
AEFGINST feasting
AEFGIRST frigates
AEFGIRSU argufies
AEFGIRTU figurate
fruitage
AEFGISTU fatigues
AEFGLLNO longleaf
AEFGLLOP flagpole
AEFGLLOR Lagerlöf
AEFGLLSS flagless
AEFGLMNU fugleman
AEFGLMOP megaflop
AEFGLNRS flangers
AEFGLNSS fangless
AEFGLOOR floorage
AEFGLOPR leapfrog
AEFGLORU Laforgue
AEFGLRTU grateful
AEFGMNRT fragment
AEFGNORT frontage
AEFGNRRS frangers
AEFGNRST engrafts
AEFGOORT footgear
AEFGOOST footages
AEFGORRS foragers
AEFGORTT frottage
AEFGRRST grafters
AEFHIKRS freakish
AEFHIKSW weakfish
AEFHILLN fellahin
AEFHILLR firehall
AEFHILLT tefillah
AEFHILMS fishmeal
AEFHILMT halftime
AEFHILNS shinleaf
AEFHILRS flashier
AEFHIMSS famishes
AEFHINUZ Han Fei Zu
AEFHIRST faithers
AEFHIRSW wharfies
AEFHLMSU shameful
AEFHLNOT halftone
AEFHLRRU Harfleur
AEFHLRSS flashers
AEFHLRTY fatherly
Flaherty
AEFHLSTU hasteful
AEFHMNOZ Zamenhof
AEFHMNRS freshman
AEFHMORT fathomer
AEFHRSTT farthest
AEFIIKLW waiflike
AEFIILLN nailfile
AEFIILMS families
AEFIILNS finalise
AEFIILNZ finalize
AEFIILSS salifies
AEFIILST filiates
AEFIIMNS infamies
infamise
AEFIIMNZ infamize
AEFIIMRS ramifies
AEFIINST fainites

AEFIINSZ nazifies
AEFIIPRT aperitif
AEFIIRRS friaries
AEFIIRRT ratifier
AEFIIRST ratifies
AEFIITVX fixative
AEFIKKLV Keflavík
AEFIKLMO foamlike
AEFIKLNU faunlike
AEFIKLNW fawnlike
AEFIKLRY freakily
AEFIKLST flakiest
AEFIKRUW waukrife
AEFILLLN Fall Line
AEFILLNT flatline
AEFILLOT fellatio
AEFILLRW firewall
AEFILLTT Tafilelt
AEFILMNR inflamer
rifleman
AEFILMNS flamines
inflames
AEFILMNT filament
AEFILMSY mayflies
AEFILMUY El Faiyûm
AEFILNNR infernal
AEFILNPS lifespan
AEFILNRT inflater
AEFILNRU fraulein
AEFILNST inflates
AEFILOOR aerofoil
AEFILORS foresail
AEFILORT floatier
AEFILOST foliates
AEFILPRX prefixal
AEFILPST fleapits
AEFILRST frailest
AEFILRSU failures
AEFILRTT filtrate
AEFILRTU faultier
filature
AEFILRUW weariful
AEFILSSW sawflies
AEFILSTT flatties
AEFILSTU fistulae
AEFILSTV festival
AEFILSTW flatwise
AEFILTUU fauteuil
AEFIMNST manifest
AEFIMORR aeriform
AEFIMOST foamiest
AEFIMRRS firearms
AEFIMRRW firmware
AEFINNNS Anfinsen
AEFINNSS naifness
AEFINNST infantes
AEFINNSZ fanzines
AEFINOPR pinafore
AEFINORS farinose
AEFINOTT fetation
AEFINPRS firepans
AEFINRRS refrains
AEFINRSS fairness
sanserif
AEFINRST fainters
AEFINSTT faintest
AEFIORTV favorite
AEFIPRRT firetrap
AEFIQRSU aquifers
AEFIRRRS farriers
AEFIRRRY farriery
AEFISTTT fattiest
AEFKLLOT folktale
AEFKLLST self-talk
AEFKLNRS flankers
AEFKLNRU Faulkner
AEFKLSST flaskets
AEFKNORS forsaken
AEFKNRST frankest
AEFKOPRS forspeak
AEFKORRS forsaker
AEFKORRW workfare
AEFKORSS forsakes
AEFKORTU freakout
AEFLLNNS flannels
AEFLLORT fellator
AEFLLORU florulae
AEFLLORV overfall
AEFLLOST floatels
AEFLLPTU plateful
AEFLLRUX flexural
AEFLLSSW flawless
AEFLLSTT flatlets
AEFLLSTY festally
AEFLMORU formulae
fumarole
AEFLMOSS foamless
AEFLMOSY flaysome
AEFLMOTU flameout
AEFLNNOT fontanel
AEFLNNTY fentanyl
AEFLNOPT pantofle
AEFLNORS farnesol
AEFLNORT floreant
AEFLNRSU flaneurs
funerals
AEFLNRTU flaunter
AEFLNSST flatness
AEFLNSTT flattens
AEFLNSUU faunules
AEFLOORS seafloor
AEFLOORV foveolar
AEFLOPRT teraflop
AEFLOPRY foreplay
AEFLOPSW peafowls
AEFLORRV flavorer
AEFLORST floaters
forestal
refloats
AEFLORTW fleawort
AEFLOSTT falsetto
AEFLPPRS flappers
AEFLPPRY flypaper
AEFLPRSS felspars
AEFLPRSY palfreys
AEFLRSSU refusals
AEFLRSTT flatters
AEFLRSZZ frazzles
AEFLRTTU aflutter
AEFLRTTY flattery
AEFLSSTU flatuses
AEFLSTTT flattest
AEFLSTTU tasteful
AEFLSTUW wasteful
AEFMNORS foramens
AEFMORRS forearms
AEFMORST foremast
formates
mortsafe
AEFMORVW waveform
AEFNNSTU unfasten
AEFNOPRR profaner
AEFNOPRS profanes
AEFNORRW forewarn
AEFNORST seafront
AEFNRRST transfer
AEFNRRUY funerary
AEFNRSTU aftersun
AEFNSSST fastness
saftness
AEFOORTW footwear
AEFOPRRT forepart
AEFOPRSW forepaws
AEFORRSV favorers
AEFORRSW forswear
AEFORRSY forayers
AEFORRUV favourer
AEFORSTW software
AEFORSTY forestay
AEFOSSWY Fosse Way
AEFRRSST strafers
AEFRSTTU tartufes
AEFRSTUW waftures
AEFRSWYZ frawzeys
AEGGGINN engaging
AEGGHIRS shaggier
AEGGHISS haggises
AEGGHJRY jagghery
AEGGHLRS hagglers
AEGGHMOS hemagogs
AEGGHNNY Hengyang
AEGGHOPY geophagy
AEGGHORU roughage
AEGGIINV gingivae
AEGGIJST jaggiest
AEGGILLN alleging
AEGGILLR grillage
AEGGILMN gleaming
AEGGILNN gleaning
AEGGILNR lagering
regaling
AEGGILNU leaguing
AEGGIMOR Maggiore
AEGGIMSU misgauge
AEGGINNR angering
enraging

AEGGINNT negating
AEGGINNV avenging
AEGGINOR Georgian
AEGGINOS seagoing
AEGGINRR Grainger
AEGGINRS gearings
greasing
AEGGINRW wagering
AEGGIOPR arpeggio
AEGGIOSS isagoges
AEGGIQRU quaggier
AEGGIRRU garrigue
AEGGISSW swaggies
AEGGLNPT eggplant
AEGGLNRS gangrels
AEGGLORY gargoyle
AEGGLOWY wayleggo
AEGGLRRS garglers
AEGGLRST straggle
AEGGLRSW wagglers
AEGGLRSY greylags
AEGGMORT mortgage
AEGGNORW waggoner
AEGGNRST gangster
AEGGRSST staggers
AEGGRSSW swaggers
AEGHIJNZ Zhejiang
AEGHILLM megillah
AEGHILLS shigella
AEGHILMT megalith
AEGHILNR narghile
nargileh
AEGHILNS healings
leashing
AEGHILNT atheling
AEGHILNX exhaling
AEGHILRT litharge
thirlage
AEGHILRY Rayleigh
AEGHINNN hennaing
AEGHINNV havening
AEGHINRS hearings
shearing
AEGHINRT earthing
hearting
ingather
AEGHINRV havering
AEGHINRY Haringey
AEGHINSV sheaving
AEGHINSZ genizahs
AEGHINTT gnathite
AEGHIOPS esophagi
AEGHIPPR epigraph
AEGHIPRT graphite
AEGHIRRS gharries
AEGHLNOS halogens
AEGHLOPY hypogeal
AEGHLOSS galoshes
AEGHLRSU laughers
AEGHLRTU laughter
AEGHLRTY lethargy
AEGHLSTW thalwegs
AEGHMOPT apothegm
AEGHNNSY Shenyang
AEGHNOPT heptagon
pathogen
AEGHNORV hangover
overhang
AEGHNOSX hexagons
AEGHNRSS gnashers
sherangs
AEGHNSST stengahs
AEGHOPPR prophage
AEGHOPPY apophyge
AEGHORST shortage
AEGHOSST hostages
AEGHRTTU retaught
AEGIILLU aiguille
AEGIILMN emailing
AEGIILMO oligemia
AEGIILMR remigial
AEGIILNN aliening
AEGIILNR gainlier
AEGIILTT litigate
AEGIILTV ligative
AEGIIMNR imaginer
migraine
AEGIIMNS imagines
AEGIIMTT mitigate
AEGIINNR arginine
Nigerian
AEGIINRR grainier
AEGIINTV Ignatiev
AEGIIRRT irrigate
AEGIKLNS linkages
snaglike
AEGIKLNT gnatlike
AEGIKLNW weakling
AEGIKLOT goatlike
AEGIKMNR remaking
AEGIKNNS sneaking
AEGIKNNW wakening
AEGIKNPS speaking
AEGIKNRT retaking
AEGIKNRW rewaking
wreaking
AEGIKNTW tweaking
AEGIKNWY Kweiyang
AEGIKPRS garpikes
AEGIKSTW gawkiest
AEGILLLS illegals
AEGILLMS legalism
AEGILLNY genially
AEGILLPR pillager
AEGILLPS pillages
spillage
AEGILLRU guerilla
AEGILLRV villager
AEGILLST legalist
stillage
AEGILLSV villages
AEGILLTU ligulate
AEGILLTY legality
AEGILMMR aglimmer
AEGILMNP empaling
AEGILMNR germinal
maligner
malinger
AEGILMNT ligament
metaling
tegminal
AEGILMRS gremials
AEGILMRX lexigram
AEGILNNP paneling
AEGILNNR learning
AEGILNNS leanings
AEGILNNT gantline
AEGILNNW weanling
AEGILNNY yeanling
AEGILNOR geraniol
regional
AEGILNOS gasoline
AEGILNOT gelation
legation
AEGILNPR pearling
AEGILNPS elapsing
pleasing
AEGILNPT pleating
AEGILNQU equaling
AEGILNRS engrails
nargiles
realigns
Salinger
signaler
AEGILNRT alerting
altering
integral
relating
teraglin
triangle
AEGILNRV raveling
AEGILNRX relaxing
AEGILNRY layering
relaying
yearling
AEGILNSS glassine
AEGILNST gelatins
genitals
stealing
AEGILNSV leavings
sleaving
AEGILNTV valeting
AEGILNTX exalting
AEGILNTZ teazling
AEGILOPS spoilage
AEGILOPT pilotage
AEGILORS gasolier
girasole
seraglio
AEGILOSS oilgases
AEGILPPS slippage
AEGILPPU pupilage
AEGILPSU Pelagius
AEGILRRU glaurier
AEGILRSS glassier
AEGILRST glariest

AEGILRSU	Galerius
AEGILRSY	greasily
AEGILRSZ	glaziers
AEGILRTT	aglitter
AEGILRTU	Gaultier
	ligature
AEGILRTY	regality
AEGILRVW	lawgiver
AEGILRYZ	glaziery
AEGIMMST	gammiest
AEGIMNNR	renaming
AEGIMNNS	meanings
AEGIMNRR	rearming
AEGIMNRS	smearing
AEGIMNRT	emigrant
AEGIMNRU	geranium
	maungier
AEGIMNSS	gaminess
AEGIMNST	mangiest
	mintages
	steaming
AEGIMPRS	epigrams
AEGIMPRU	umpirage
AEGIMQRU	quagmire
AEGIMRRS	armigers
AEGIMRSS	gisarmes
AEGIMRST	migrates
	sterigma
AEGIMRTT	Magritte
AEGIMSSU	misusage
AEGINNNX	annexing
AEGINNOS	anginose
AEGINNOT	Antigone
	negation
AEGINNRS	earnings
	engrains
	grannies
AEGINNRV	ravening
AEGINNRY	yearning
AEGINNST	antigens
	gentians
AEGINNSU	sanguine
AEGINOPT	pinotage
AEGINORS	organise
AEGINORT	Iron Gate
AEGINORZ	organize
AEGINOSS	agonises
AEGINOSV	Gonaïves
AEGINOSZ	agonizes
AEGINPPR	papering
AEGINPPS	genipaps
AEGINPRS	spearing
AEGINPRT	tapering
AEGINPRV	repaving
AEGINPRY	repaying
AEGINPTY	egyptian
AEGINQTU	equating
AEGINRRS	earrings
	grainers
AEGINRRU	Guarneri
AEGINRRV	averring
AEGINRSS	assigner
	reassign
	seringas
AEGINRST	angriest
	angstier
	ganister
	gantries
	granites
	ingrates
	rangiest
	reasting
AEGINRSV	vinegars
AEGINRSW	swearing
AEGINRTT	treating
AEGINRTV	averting
	vintager
AEGINRTW	watering
AEGINRVW	wavering
AEGINRVY	vinegary
AEGINRWY	wearying
AEGINSST	eastings
	giantess
AEGINSSY	essaying
AEGINSTT	tangiest
AEGINSTU	sauteing
AEGINSTV	vintages
AEGINSTW	sweating
AEGINSTY	yeasting
AEGINSTZ	tziganes
AEGIOPRR	progeria
AEGIORSS	argosies
AEGIORSV	viragoes
AEGIOSTU	agouties
AEGIOSTX	geotaxis
AEGIPPRT	griptape
AEGIPPST	gappiest
AEGIPRST	grapiest
AEGIRRSS	grassier
AEGIRRSZ	graziers
AEGIRSTV	virgates
AEGIRSUU	auguries
AEGIRSUY	yugaries
AEGISSST	gassiest
AEGISSTT	stagiest
AEGISTUZ	gauziest
AEGJLNRS	janglers
AEGJLTUU	jugulate
AEGKLLOT	lekgotla
AEGKLOSU	kagoules
AEGLLMNN	Gell-Mann
AEGLLNOS	galleons
AEGLLNRW	Wrangell
AEGLLOPR	galloper
AEGLLORS	allegros
AEGLLORY	allegory
AEGLLOSS	gaolless
	goalless
AEGLLOTT	tollgate
AEGLLRVY	gravelly
AEGLLSSU	galluses
	seagulls
AEGLMNNO	mangonel
AEGLMNRS	manglers
AEGLMNSS	glassmen
AEGLMNTU	gunmetal
AEGLMOTV	megavolt
AEGLMSSU	gaumless
AEGLNNPT	plangent
AEGLNNSY	langsyne
AEGLNNTU	untangle
AEGLNORS	Selangor
AEGLNORY	yearlong
AEGLNOST	tangelos
AEGLNOZZ	González
AEGLNPRS	grapnels
AEGLNPSS	spangles
AEGLNRRW	wrangler
AEGLNRST	strangle
	tanglers
AEGLNRSU	granules
AEGLNRSW	wanglers
	wrangles
AEGLNRSY	larynges
AEGLNSTT	gantlets
AEGLNSTU	languets
AEGLNSUW	gunwales
AEGLNTTU	gauntlet
AEGLNTUU	ungulate
AEGLOOOZ	zoogloea
AEGLOOPU	apologue
AEGLOORY	aerology
AEGLOPRS	pergolas
AEGLOPRY	playgoer
AEGLORST	gloaters
	legators
AEGLORTV	travelog
AEGLOSTV	voltages
AEGLPPRR	grappler
AEGLPPRS	grapples
AEGLPRSU	earplugs
	plaguers
AEGLRRSU	regulars
AEGLRSTU	gestural
AEGLSSTT	gestalts
AEGLSTUU	glutaeus
AEGLSTUV	vulgates
AEGLSUUY	guayules
AEGMMNOR	gammoner
AEGMMPRU	Pergamum
AEGMMRRU	rummager
AEGMMRSU	rummages
AEGMNNOT	magneton
AEGMNORV	mangrove
AEGMNOST	magnetos
	megatons
	montages
AEGMNOXY	xenogamy
AEGMNRST	garments
	margents
AEGMNRTU	argentum
	argument
AEGMNSTU	augments
	mutagens
AEGMOORS	moorages
AEGMOPRW	gapeworm

AEGMORSS gossamer
AEGMPRUZ gazumper
AEGMPSTU stumpage
AEGMRSUV Musgrave
AEGNNOPT pentagon
AEGNNORT negatron
AEGNNOST tonnages
AEGNNPRT pregnant
AEGNNRSU gunneras
AEGNNSTT tangents
AEGNNSTU tunnages
AEGNOPRR parergon
AEGNORRS groaners
AEGNORRY orangery
AEGNORSS Sargeson
AEGNORST estragon
negators
ragstone
AEGNORSW wagoners
AEGNORTT tetragon
AEGNORTU outrange
AEGNOSSY nosegays
AEGNOTUY autogeny
AEGNPPRU gunpaper
AEGNPRST trepangs
AEGNPRSU speargun
AEGNRRST granters
stranger
AEGNRSSY grayness
AEGNRSYY asynergy
AEGOPPST stoppage
AEGOPRST portages
potagers
AEGOPSTT gatepost
AEGORRRT garroter
AEGORRST garrotes
AEGORRTT garotter
garrotte
AEGORSTT garottes
AEGORSTU outrages
AEGORSVY voyagers
AEGORTTU tutorage
AEGORUVY voyageur
AEGOSSTU outgases
AEGOSSTW stowages
AEGOSTTV gavottes
AEGPRRSS graspers
spargers
AEGPSSTU upstages
AEGPSTUY Aegyptus
AEGRRSSY ryegrass
AEGRRSUV gravures
AEGRSTTY strategy
AEGSSTUU augustes
AEHHHJPT Jephthah
AEHHIKNS Shekinah
AEHHINPR Ha-erh-pin
AEHHNOPT Phaëthon
AEHHRRST thrasher
AEHHRSST harshest
thrashes
AEHIIKLR hairlike
AEHIIKRT terakihi
AEHIIKST shiitake
AEHIIKSU Hsia Kuei
AEHIILMO hemiolia
AEHIILNR hairline
AEHIIMNT thiamine
AEHIINTZ thiazine
AEHIIOPT Ethiopia
AEHIIRSS Irish Sea
AEHIIRST hairiest
AEHIKKLW hawklike
AEHIKLLL El Khalil
AEHIKLLO halolike
AEHIKLLT lathlike
AEHIKLNP kephalin
AEHIKLRS rashlike
AEHIKRTW Whitaker
AEHIKSST shakiest
AEHILMSW Lewisham
limewash
AEHILNOP aphelion
AEHILNRS inhalers
AEHILNRU inhauler
AEHILNSY hyalines
AEHILNTX anthelix
AEHILNTZ zenithal
AEHILOTZ thiazole
AEHILPRS harelips
plashier
AEHILRSS hairless
AEHILRSU hauliers
AEHILRSV lavisher
shrieval
AEHILRTY earthily
heartily
AEHILSSV lavishes
AEHILSSW shawlies
AEHILSTT lathiest
AEHILSUV vihuelas
AEHILTWW Whitelaw
AEHIMMNN Mannheim
AEHIMMSS shammies
AEHIMMST hammiest
AEHIMMSW whammies
AEHIMNNU inhumane
AEHIMNSU humanise
AEHIMNUZ humanize
AEHIMPRS samphire
seraphim
AEHIMPRT teraphim
AEHIMPSS emphasis
misshape
AEHIMPST mateship
shipmate
AEHIMRRS marshier
AEHIMRSS mishears
AEHIMSSS messiahs
AEHIMTUY euthymia
AEHINNSS shannies
AEHINNST Tien Shan
AEHINNSW Wanhsien
AEHINNTX xanthein
xanthine
AEHINORT antihero
AEHINOST Esthonia
AEHINOTT thionate
AEHINPPY epiphany
AEHINPRT perianth
AEHINPST thespian
AEHINRST hairnets
inearths
AEHINRSV vanisher
AEHINRSW sherwani
AEHINRTU Ruthenia
AEHINRTW tarwhine
AEHINSSS hessians
AEHINSST anthesis
shanties
AEHINSSV vanishes
AEHINSSZ haziness
AEHINSTT hesitant
AEHIOPRS aphorise
AEHIOPRU euphoria
AEHIOPRZ aphorize
AEHIORST hoariest
AEHIORTU thiourea
AEHIPPRS sapphire
AEHIPPST epitaphs
happiest
AEHIPRSS parishes
sharpies
AEHIPSTT Peshitta
AEHIQSSU quashies
AEHIRRRS harriers
AEHIRRST trashier
AEHIRRSV ravisher
AEHIRRSW wairsher
AEHIRRSY Ayrshire
AEHIRSSV ravishes
AEHIRSTU thesauri
AEHIRSTW waterish
AEHIRSTY hysteria
AEHIRTYZ yahrzeit
AEHISSST stashies
AEHISSSW siwashes
AEHISSTT atheists
hastiest
AEHISSTU hiatuses
AEHISSTW washiest
AEHISTTW thwaites
AEHJNNOS johannes
AEHKLOOY Holyoake
AEHKNNSU unshaken
AEHKNSTT Tashkent
AEHKNSWW newshawk
AEHKOSTU shakeout
AEHKPSSU shakeups
AEHLLLTY lethally
AEHLLMTY methylal
AEHLLNRT enthrall
Hartnell
AEHLLORW hallower
AEHLMMNS helmsman
AEHLMNNP Helpmann

AEHLMNOS	manholes
AEHLMNOT	methanol
AEHLMNSW	Welshman
AEHLMNUY	humanely
AEHLMORS	armholes
AEHLMOSU	hamulose
AEHLMPPT	pamphlet
AEHLMRSS	harmless
AEHLMRST	thermals
AEHLMSUW	Hume's law
AEHLNOTY	ethanoyl
AEHLNPRS	shrapnel
AEHLNPTY	enthalpy
AEHLNRST	enthrals
AEHLNRTU	Lutheran
AEHLNSST	nathless
AEHLNSSU	unlashes
AEHLNTUZ	hazelnut
AEHLOPRT	plethora
AEHLOPST	tapholes
AEHLOPTT	hotplate
AEHLORST	loathers
AEHLORSY	hoarsely
AEHLORUV	overhaul
AEHLORYY	Holy Year
AEHLOSSS	assholes
AEHLPPRT	thrapple
AEHLPRSS	splasher
AEHLPSSS	splashes
AEHLPSST	pathless
AEHLPSTU	sulphate
AEHLRRTU	urethral
AEHLRSSS	slashers
AEHLRSST	harslets
	slathers
AEHLSSTW	thawless
AEHLSSTY	Thessaly
AEHLSTTY	stealthy
AEHMMRSS	shammers
AEHMNNPY	nymphean
AEHMNOPR	morphean
AEHMNORS	horseman
	menorahs
AEHMNOSU	houseman
AEHMNPRU	prehuman
AEHMOPRT	metaphor
AEHMOPST	apothems
AEHMOSTT	hemostat
AEHMOSTW	somewhat
AEHMPPRY	pamphrey
AEHMRSSS	smashers
AEHMRSST	hamsters
AEHMSSSU	shamuses
AEHMSSTT	shmattes
AEHMSTTW	Matthews
AEHMSTTY	amethyst
AEHMSUZZ	mezuzahs
AEHNNOPT	pantheon
AEHNNORV	Hannover
AEHNNPSU	unshapen
AEHNNSUV	unshaven
AEHNOOPT	hanepoot
AEHNOPPY	hypopnea
	payphone
AEHNOPRT	hapteron
AEHNOPST	phaetons
	phonates
	stanhope
AEHNORSS	hoarsens
AEHNORST	North Sea
	Sheraton
AEHNORTT	Atherton
AEHNOSSX	hexosans
AEHNPRSS	sharpens
AEHNPRST	panthers
AEHNRSSS	rashness
AEHNRSTU	haunters
	unearths
AEHNRTTU	earthnut
AEHNSSTY	shanteys
AEHNSTUW	unswathe
AEHOORST	toheroas
AEHOPPRS	prophase
AEHOPRRY	pyorrhea
AEHOPSST	spathose
	teashops
AEHOPSTU	phaseout
	taphouse
AEHORRRW	harrower
AEHORRSW	warhorse
AEHORSST	hoarsest
AEHORSSW	sawhorse
AEHORSTT	rheostat
AEHORSTU	rathouse
AEHORSTX	thoraxes
AEHORSTY	Rothesay
AEHPPSSU	shapeups
AEHPRRSS	sharpers
AEHPRSST	sharpest
AEHPRSUX	haruspex
AEHPRSUY	euphrasy
AEHQRSSU	squasher
AEHQSSSU	squashes
AEHRRSTU	urethras
AEHRRSTY	trashery
AEHRRTTW	thwarter
AEHRSSTT	shatters
AEHRSSTV	harvests
AEHSSTUX	exhausts
AEIIIJMS	James III
AEIIINTT	initiate
AEIIIRRT	retiarii
AEIIJMSV	James VII
AEIIKLLT	taillike
AEIIKRTY	teriyaki
AEIILLTV	illative
AEIILMNN	mainline
AEIILMNS	alienism
AEIILMPR	imperial
AEIILMSZ	Islamize
AEIILMTT	militate
AEIILNQU	aquiline
AEIILNRR	airliner
AEIILNRS	airlines
AEIILNRT	inertial
AEIILNSS	Silesian
AEIILNST	alienist
	litanies
	Taliesin
AEIILNTZ	latinize
AEIILPPT	tailpipe
AEIILQSU	siliquae
AEIILRST	lairiest
	listeria
AEIILRTT	literati
AEIILSTV	vitalise
AEIILTVZ	vitalize
AEIIMMRT	maritime
AEIIMMSX	maximise
AEIIMMXZ	maximize
AEIIMNTT	intimate
AEIIMNTU	minutiae
AEIIMOSS	ameiosis
AEIIMPRR	impairer
AEIIMPSY	epimysia
AEIIMRSS	Ramses II
AEIIMRST	seriatim
AEIIMSTT	imitates
AEIINNRS	sirenian
AEIINNRT	triennia
AEIINPRS	Piranesi
AEIINRSS	airiness
AEIINRST	rainiest
AEIINRTZ	triazine
AEIINSST	isatines
	sanitise
	teniasis
AEIINSTV	vanities
AEIINSTZ	sanitize
AEIINSVV	invasive
AEIINTTT	titanite
AEIIPRRS	prairies
AEIIPRST	parities
AEIIPRZZ	pizzeria
AEIIPSST	epitasis
AEIIPSTX	epitaxis
AEIIRRST	rarities
AEIIRRTT	irritate
AEIIRSST	satirise
	Tiresias
AEIIRSTW	wisteria
AEIIRSTZ	satirize
AEIIRTTT	tritiate
AEIISTTV	vitiates
AEIITTTV	titivate
AEIJLLSS	jailless
AEIJLNSV	javelins
AEIJLOPS	jalopies
AEIJLOSU	jalousie
AEIJMMST	jammiest
AEIJMNSS	jasmines
AEIJNRTU	jauntier
AEIJORST	jarosite
AEIJSTZZ	jazziest
AEIKKLMS	masklike
AEIKKLNT	tanklike

AEIKKLPR parklike
AEIKLLOV Oakville
AEIKLLST saltlike
AEIKLMST mastlike
AEIKLNPS skiplane
AEIKLNSS sealskin
AEIKLNST lankiest
AEIKLNSW swanlike
AEIKLNSY sneakily
AEIKLOPS soaplike
AEIKLOST keitloas
AEIKLOSV Levkosia
AEIKLPRT traplike
AEIKLPSW wasplike
AEIKLRST larkiest
stalkier
starlike
AEIKLRTW wartlike
AEIKLRVY valkyrie
AEIKLRWY walkyrie
AEIKLSTT talkiest
AEIKMNNR Inkerman
AEIKMNRS ramekins
AEIKMNST mankiest
mistaken
AEIKMRST mistaker
sitkamer
AEIKMSST mistakes
AEIKNRST narkiest
Transkei
AEIKNRSW swankier
AEIKNRTW knitwear
AEIKNSST snakiest
AEIKNSSY kyanises
AEIKNSYZ kyanizes
AEIKPRRS sparkier
AEIKPRST parkiest
AEIKPSTW pawkiest
AEIKQSTU quakiest
AEIKRSST asterisk
sarkiest
AEIKRSTV Kristeva
AEILLLLN Llanelli
AEILLLMO malleoli
AEILLLMS allelism
AEILLLNY lineally
AEILLMNS manilles
AEILLMNY menially
AEILLMSS mailless
AEILLMSY mesially
AEILLNNO lanoline
AEILLNPS Spillane
splenial
AEILLNQU quinella
AEILLNRY linearly
AEILLNSS nailless
sensilla
AEILLNST Antilles
AEILLNUV laevulin
AEILLNVY venially
AEILLOSS loessial
AEILLOTV volatile
AEILLPST palliest
pastille
AEILLQSU squillae
AEILLRRS ralliers
AEILLRRY raillery
AEILLRSS railless
salliers
AEILLRST literals
talliers
triellas
AEILLRSY serially
AEILLRVX vexillar
AEILLSSS sailless
AEILLSST sitellas
tailless
AEILLSTT sittella
tallites
AEILLSUV allusive
AEILLSYZ sleazily
AEILLTUZ lazulite
AEILMMNS melanism
AEILMMNU Immanuel
AEILMMOR memorial
AEILMMOT immolate
AEILMMRT trilemma
AEILMMSS melismas
AEILMNNO minneola
AEILMNNS linesman
AEILMNOS laminose
semolina
AEILMNPS impanels
maniples
AEILMNRS marlines
minerals
AEILMNRT terminal
tramline
AEILMNST ailments
aliments
manliest
AEILMOPR proemial
AEILMORS moralise
AEILMORZ moralize
AEILMPRS impalers
impearls
lempiras
AEILMPRV primeval
AEILMPST palmiest
AEILMPTY playtime
AEILMRSS realisms
AEILMRSY mislayer
smearily
AEILMRTT remittal
AEILMRUV velarium
AEILMSTT maltiest
metalist
smaltite
AEILMSTU simulate
AEILMSTY steamily
AEILMSUV misvalue
AEILMTTU mutilate
ultimate
AEILNNOS solanine
AEILNNPU pinnulae
AEILNNRT internal
AEILNNSU Linnaeus
AEILNNSY insanely
AEILNNTY innately
AEILNOPS opalines
AEILNORR Lorraine
AEILNORS ailerons
alienors
AEILNORT oriental
relation
Tirolean
AEILNORV overlain
AEILNOST insolate
toenails
AEILNOSV Slovenia
AEILNOSX siloxane
AEILNPRS pralines
AEILNPRT interlap
triplane
AEILNPSS painless
spaniels
AEILNPST panelist
pantiles
plainest
AEILNPSX explains
AEILNPTT tinplate
AEILNRSS rainless
AEILNRST entrails
latrines
ratlines
reinstal
trenails
AEILNRSV ravelins
AEILNRSX relaxins
AEILNRSY inlayers
AEILNRTU tenurial
AEILNRTV interval
AEILNRTY interlay
AEILNSST salients
AEILNSSZ laziness
AEILNSTU insulate
AEILNSTV ventails
AEILNSUY uneasily
AEILNTVY natively
venality
AEILNUVV univalve
AEILOPPT oppilate
AEILOPRS polarise
AEILOPRT epilator
AEILOPRZ polarize
AEILOPST spoliate
AEILORSS solarise
AEILORSV Olivares
valorise
varioles
AEILORSZ solarize
AEILORTV violater
Voltaire
AEILORTZ triazole
AEILORVZ valorize
AEILOSST isolates

AEILOSTT	totalise
AEILOSTV	violates
AEILOTTZ	totalize
AEILPPQU	applique
AEILPPRS	appliers
AEILPRRS	reprisal
AEILPRRT	paltrier
AEILPRST	pilaster
	plaister
AEILPRSV	prevails
AEILPRSW	slipware
AEILPRTV	livetrap
AEILPRXY	pyrexial
AEILPSSY	paisleys
AEILPSTT	platiest
AEILPSUU	Apuleius
AEILPSUV	plausive
AEILQRTU	quartile
	requital
AEILQSTU	liquates
	tequilas
AEILQSUY	queasily
AEILQTUY	equality
AEILRRST	retirals
	retrials
	trailers
AEILRRSU	ruralise
AEILRRTT	rattlier
AEILRRTY	literary
AEILRRUZ	ruralize
AEILRSST	realists
	saltiers
	saltires
	slaister
AEILRSSV	revisals
AEILRSTU	uralites
AEILRSUU	Aurelius
AEILRSVV	revivals
AEILRSVY	virelays
AEILRTUZ	lazurite
AEILSSTT	saltiest
	slatiest
AEILSSUV	Vesalius
AEILSSUW	Sulawesi
AEILSTVY	vilayets
AEILSTWY	sweatily
AEILSTYY	yeastily
AEIMMNNT	immanent
AEIMMNOS	seminoma
AEIMMNOT	ammonite
AEIMMNSS	misnames
AEIMMPST	psammite
AEIMMRRS	smarmier
AEIMMRST	marmites
	trammies
AEIMMRTU	immature
AEIMNNOT	nominate
AEIMNNRS	reinsman
AEIMNNWZ	Weizmann
AEIMNOPT	ptomaine
AEIMNORS	moraines
	romaines
	romanise
AEIMNORT	Maronite
AEIMNORW	airwomen
AEIMNORZ	Marenzio
	romanize
AEIMNOST	amniotes
AEIMNOSW	womanise
AEIMNOTZ	monazite
AEIMNOWZ	womanize
AEIMNQRU	ramequin
AEIMNRRR	Marriner
AEIMNRRS	mariners
AEIMNRSS	seminars
AEIMNRST	minarets
AEIMNRSU	aneurism
	Sumerian
AEIMNRSY	seminary
AEIMNRTT	martinet
AEIMNRTU	ruminate
AEIMNRTY	tyramine
AEIMNSSS	samisens
AEIMNSST	mantises
	matiness
AEIMNSSZ	maziness
AEIMOOPS	ipomoeas
AEIMOPSX	apomixes
AEIMORRS	armoires
	armories
AEIMORST	amortise
	atomiser
	Timor Sea
AEIMORTT	amoretti
AEIMORTZ	amortize
	atomizer
AEIMOSST	atomises
AEIMOSTZ	atomizes
AEIMOTTV	motivate
AEIMPRRT	imparter
AEIMPRSS	impresas
AEIMPRST	apterism
	primates
AEIMPRSV	vampires
AEIMPRSW	swampier
AEIMPSSS	impasses
AEIMPSST	impastes
	pastimes
AEIMQRSU	marquise
AEIMRRRS	marriers
AEIMRRTU	Arretium
AEIMRSST	asterism
	smarties
AEIMRSSY	emissary
AEIMRSTT	mistreat
	teratism
AEIMRSTU	muriates
AEIMRSTX	matrixes
AEIMSSST	massiest
AEIMSSTT	misstate
AEIMSSTZ	mestizas
AEIMTTUV	mutative
AEINNOPV	pavonine
AEINNORT	anointer
AEINNOST	Estonian
AEINNOTT	intonate
AEINNOTV	innovate
	venation
AEINNPRS	panniers
AEINNRRS	insnarer
AEINNRRT	inerrant
AEINNRSS	insnares
AEINNRST	entrains
	trannies
AEINNRTT	intranet
AEINNSSV	vainness
AEINNSSZ	zaniness
AEINNSTT	stannite
AEINOPPT	antipope
AEINOPRT	atropine
AEINOPST	saponite
AEINOQTU	equation
AEINORRT	anterior
AEINORRW	ironware
AEINORSS	erasions
	sensoria
AEINORST	notaries
	notarise
	senorita
AEINORSV	aversion
AEINORTU	Touraine
AEINORTZ	notarize
AEINOSSV	evasions
AEINOSXZ	oxazines
AEINOTVX	vexation
AEINPPPS	panpipes
AEINPPRS	snappier
AEINPPST	nappiest
AEINPRRT	terrapin
AEINPRRU	unrepair
AEINPRST	painters
	pantries
	pertains
	pinaster
	repaints
AEINPRTT	triptane
AEINPRUV	Peruvian
AEINPSST	steapsin
AEINPSSU	apneusis
AEINPSTT	patients
AEINPSTU	petunias
	supinate
AEINPSTY	epinasty
AEINPTTY	antitype
AEINQRTU	quainter
AEINQSTU	antiques
	quantise
AEINQTTU	equitant
AEINQTUY	antiquey
AEINQTUZ	quantize
AEINRRST	restrain
	retrains
	strainer
	terrains
	trainers
AEINRRTV	veratrin

AEINRRTW interwar
AEINRSST artiness
stainers
AEINRSSU anuresis
AEINRSSW wariness
AEINRSTT intreats
nitrates
straiten
tertians
AEINRSTU Neustria
uranites
urinates
AEINRSUZ suzerain
AEINRSVV vervains
AEINRSZZ snazzier
AEINSSST sestinas
AEINSSSV vinasses
AEINSSTT antsiest
instates
nastiest
titaness
AEINSSTX sextains
AEINSSVW waviness
AEINSSWX waxiness
AEINSTTT nattiest
AEINSTWY Steinway
AEINSUVV vesuvian
AEINTTUU autunite
AEINTTVZ Vanzetti
AEIOPPST apposite
AEIOPRRT Pretoria
priorate
AEIOPRRW airpower
AEIOPRSV vaporise
AEIOPRTX expiator
AEIOPRVZ vaporize
AEIOPSST soapiest
AEIOPTTV optative
AEIOQSSU sequoias
AEIORRSS rosaries
AEIORRST rotaries
AEIORSSV savories
AEIORSTV viatores
votaries
AEIORTTV rotative
AEIOSSST sosaties
AEIOSSTT toasties
AEIOSSTZ azotises
AEIOSTZZ azotizes
AEIPPPST pappiest
AEIPPRSS apprises
AEIPPRST periapts
AEIPPRSZ apprizes
AEIPPSST sappiest
AEIPPSTZ zappiest
AEIPQRTU pratique
AEIPRRSS aspirers
praisers
AEIPRRSU upraiser
AEIPRSST pastries
piasters
piastres
traipses
AEIPRSSU upraises
AEIPRSSV parvises
AEIPRSSX praxises
AEIPRSTV privates
AEIPRSTW wiretaps
AEIPRSTY asperity
AEIPRSVY vespiary
AEIPRTVY varitype
AEIPSSSV passives
AEIPSSTT pastiest
AEIPTTUV putative
AEIQRRRU quarrier
AEIQRRSU quarries
AEIQRUZZ quazzier
AEIRRRST starrier
tarriers
AEIRRRSV arrivers
AEIRRSST tarsiers
AEIRRSTW strawier
AEIRRTTY tertiary
AEIRSSST assister
AEIRSSTT artistes
striates
AEIRSSTW waitress
AEIRSTTT rattiest
tartiest
titrates
tristate
AEIRSTVY vestiary
AEIRSVZZ Svizzera
AEISSSST sassiest
AEISSSTY essayist
AEISSTTT tastiest
AEISSTTU situates
AEISSTTV statives
vastiest
AEISSTVV savviest
AEISTTTT tattiest
AEJLOSSU jalouses
AEJLOSUY jealousy
AEJMOOSW Moose Jaw
AEKKMNOO kakemono
AEKLMNOV Malenkov
AEKLMRUW lukewarm
AEKLMRUY yarmulke
AEKLNNSS lankness
AEKLNOSY ankylose
AEKLNSST tankless
AEKLOPRW ropewalk
AEKLORVW walkover
AEKLPRRS sparkler
AEKLPRSS sparkles
AEKLRSST stalkers
AEKLSSST taskless
AEKMMNRS marksmen
AEKMNRSU unmakers
unmasker
AEKMNRUZ Zukerman
AEKMORTW teamwork
workmate
AEKMPRTU upmarket
AEKNNRSS rankness
AEKNOORS Soekarno
AEKNOOTY Kootenay
AEKNORSV Nekrasov
AEKNPPRS knappers
AEKNPPSS spanspek
AEKNPRSS spankers
AEKNPSSU unspeaks
AEKOPRSS presoaks
AEKOPSTU outspeak
speakout
AEKORRWW workwear
AEKORSSS karosses
AEKORSTV overtask
AEKOSTTU outtakes
stakeout
takeouts
AEKPSSSY passkeys
AEKQRSUW squawker
AEKRRSST starkers
AEKRSSTT starkest
AELLMNOO allomone
AELLMNTY mentally
tallymen
AELLMORT martello
AELLMOTY tomalley
AELLMOYZ allozyme
AELLMSST smallest
AELLMSWX maxwells
AELLNOSV novellas
AELLNPRU prunella
AELLNRUY neurally
unreally
AELLNRVY vernally
AELLNSST tallness
AELLNTTY latently
AELLNTUU lunulate
AELLOPRT preallot
AELLOPRW walloper
AELLOPTY allotype
AELLORSS rosellas
AELLORST reallots
rostella
AELLORSV overalls
AELLORSW Rosewall
sallower
AELLORWW wallower
AELLOSUV alveolus
AELLPSTY playlets
AELLQRSU squaller
AELLRRSU allurers
AELLRRTY retrally
AELLRTTY latterly
AELLRTVY trevally
AELLRTYY lyrately
AELLSSST saltless
AELLSSTY tasselly
AELLSTUU ululates
AELLSUVV valvules
AELLSUXY sexually
AELMMNOS mamelons
AELMMORW mealworm

AELMMOSY myelomas
AELMMRSS slammers
AELMMRST trammels
AELMNNOT nonmetal
AELMNNOU noumenal
AELMNNRY mannerly
AELMNOPS neoplasm
pleonasm
AELMNORS almoners
AELMNORT Montreal
AELMNOST telamons
AELMNOSU melanous
AELMNOWY laywomen
AELMNOYY yeomanly
AELMNPRS lamperns
AELMNRSU mensural
numerals
AELMNSTT mantlets
AELMNSTY mesnalty
AELMOORS saleroom
AELMOPRR premolar
AELMOPRT temporal
AELMOPSU ampoules
AELMOPSX exoplasm
AELMOPSY maypoles
AELMOPTT palmetto
AELMORSU ramulose
AELMORSV removals
AELMORSY ramosely
AELMORTU emulator
AELMOSSS molasses
AELMOSTT matelots
AELMPRRT trampler
AELMPRSS samplers
AELMPRST templars
tramples
AELMPRSY lampreys
AELMRSST tramless
AELMRSTT maltster
martlets
AELMRSTY masterly
AELMRTUY maturely
AELMSSST mastless
AELNNOOP napoleon
AELNNOOX naloxone
AELNNOQU nonequal
AELNNORU neuronal
AELNNOSU annulose
AELNNPRS planners
AELNNRST lanterns
AELNNRSU unlearns
AELNNRTU unlearnt
AELNNSTU annulets
AELNOPPT Appleton
AELNOPRS personal
AELNOPST Tonle Sap
AELNOPSU apolunes
AELNOPXY Polyxena
AELNORTT tolerant
AELNORTY ornately
AELNOSSV ovalness
AELNPPRS preplans

AELNPPSY playpens
AELNPRST planters
replants
AELNPRSU purslane
supernal
AELNPSSS snapless
AELNPSSU spansule
AELNPSTX explants
AELNPTTU petulant
AELNPTTY patently
AELNRRSS snarlers
AELNRRTY errantly
AELNRSST salterns
slanters
AELNRSTT slattern
AELNRSTU neutrals
AELNRSUV unravels
AELNRSXY larynxes
AELNRTTW trawlnet
AELNSSST saltness
AELNTTUX exultant
AELOORRS roseolar
AELOORSS aerosols
roseolas
AELOORTW waterloo
AELOORTZ zoolater
AELOPPRS prolapse
sapropel
AELOPPTU populate
AELOPPXY apoplexy
AELOPQUY opaquely
AELOPRRV reproval
AELOPRSS reposals
AELOPRST petrosal
polestar
AELOPRSV overlaps
AELOPRVY overplay
AELOPRYZ pyrazole
AELOPSSS soapless
AELOPSST apostles
AELOPSSU espousal
sepalous
AELOPSSX exposals
AELOPSTT paletots
AELOPSTU outleaps
petalous
AELOPTTU outleapt
AELORRST realtors
relators
AELORSSS lassoers
AELORSSU Larousse
AELORSTV levators
AELORSUU rouleaus
AELORSVY layovers
overlays
AELORTYZ zealotry
AELORUUX rouleaux
AELOSSTV solvates
AELOSSTY asystole
AELOSSVY saveloys
AELOSTTU toluates
AELOSTTW wastelot

AELOSTUV ovulates
AELOSTUY autolyse
AELOTUUV outvalue
AELOTUYZ autolyze
AELPPRSS slappers
AELPPSSU appulses
AELPQRTU Quelpart
AELPRRRU larruper
AELPRRSW sprawler
AELPRRTT prattler
AELPRRTU Perrault
AELPRSST persalts
plasters
psalters
staplers
AELPRSSU perusals
AELPRSSY parsleys
sparsely
AELPRSTT partlets
platters
prattles
splatter
AELPRSTY plastery
psaltery
AELPSSTT peltasts
AELPSSTU pulsates
AELQRRSU quarrels
AELQRSUV servqual
AELQRSUY squarely
AELQSTUZ quetzals
AELRRSSW warslers
AELRRSTT rattlers
startler
AELRRSTW trawlers
warstler
AELRRTVY varletry
AELRSSST starless
AELRSSTT starlets
startles
AELRSSTU saluters
AELRSSTW warstles
wastrels
AELRSSUU russulae
AELRSSUW walruses
AELRSTTT tartlets
tattlers
AELRSTTU lustrate
tutelars
AELRSTUV vaulters
vestural
AELRSTWZ waltzers
AELRTTUX textural
AELRTTUY tutelary
AELSSSTU saltuses
AELSTTUY astutely
AEMMNRTU ramentum
AEMMOORT roommate
AEMMORST marmoset
AEMMRSST stammers
AEMMRTUY maumetry
AEMNNORT ornament
AEMNNRST remnants

AEMNOORT	anteroom
AEMNOORY	aeronomy
AEMNOPPS	pampoens
AEMNOPRS	manropes
AEMNOPRW	manpower
AEMNORRS	ransomer
AEMNORST	monstera
AEMNORSU	enamours
	neuromas
AEMNORSV	overmans
AEMNORTY	monetary
AEMNORVY	overmany
AEMNORYY	yeomanry
AEMNOSTU	seamount
AEMNPRSS	pressman
AEMNPRSU	superman
AEMNPSTY	payments
AEMNRRSU	manurers
	surnamer
AEMNRRUY	numerary
AEMNRSST	smartens
AEMNRSSU	surnames
AEMNRSSW	warmness
AEMNRSTU	menstrua
AEMNRSUY	aneurysm
AEMNRTTU	Tarentum
AEMOORST	tearooms
AEMOORSW	woomeras
AEMOORTT	amoretto
AEMOOSST	maestoso
	osteomas
AEMOOSSV	vamooses
AEMOOSTT	tomatoes
AEMOOSTU	autosome
AEMOPPRS	pamperos
AEMOPRTW	tapeworm
AEMOQSSU	squamose
AEMORRRS	armorers
AEMORRRU	armourer
AEMORRST	rearmost
AEMORRSY	rosemary
AEMORSSS	morasses
AEMORSST	maestros
AEMORSSY	mayoress
AEMORTTU	tautomer
AEMORUWZ	Muzorewa
AEMOSTTZ	mozettas
AEMOTTZZ	mozzetta
AEMPRRST	trampers
AEMPRRSW	prewarms
AEMPRRSY	spermary
AEMPRSST	stampers
AEMPRSSW	swampers
AEMPRSTU	upstream
AEMPRSUX	supermax
AEMPSTTT	attempts
AEMQRSSU	marquess
	masquers
AEMRRSST	armrests
AEMRSSSU	assumers
	masseurs
AEMRSSTT	mattress
	smartest
	smatters
AEMRSSUU	Sarum use
AEMRTUUX	trumeaux
AENNNOTU	Nuneaton
AENNNPST	pennants
AENNOOTZ	entozoan
AENNOPRT	patronne
AENNOPST	pentosan
AENNORST	resonant
AENNORSU	unreason
AENNORSY	annoyers
AENNORTW	wantoner
AENNOSTU	tonneaus
AENNOSTV	Evanston
AENNOTUX	tonneaux
AENNPRSS	spanners
AENNRSTT	entrants
AENNRSWY	swannery
AENNRTTY	tenantry
AENOOPST	teaspoon
AENOPRSS	responsa
AENOPRST	operants
	Paterson
	pronates
AENOPRTT	patentor
AENOPRWY	weaponry
AENORRRW	narrower
AENORRST	antrorse
AENORSST	assentor
	senators
	treasons
AENORSSU	anserous
	arsenous
AENORSUV	ravenous
AENORSWZ	warzones
AENORTTY	attorney
AENOSSTU	Ouessant
	soutanes
AENOSSUU	nauseous
AENOUUVX	nouveaux
AENPPRSS	snappers
AENPRRST	partners
AENPRRSW	prawners
AENPRSST	pasterns
AENPRSSW	spawners
AENPRSTT	patterns
	transept
AENPRSUV	parvenus
AENPSSSY	synapses
AENQRRTU	quartern
AENRRRTY	errantry
AENRSSTT	tartness
AENRSSTU	anestrus
	saunters
AENRSSTV	servants
	versants
AENRSSUW	unswears
AENRSTTU	taunters
AENRSTUV	vaunters
AENRSTWY	sternway
AENSSSTV	vastness
AENSSTTU	tautness
AENSSTTX	sextants
AENSSTXY	syntaxes
AEOOPPPS	pappoose
AEOOPPSS	papooses
AEOOPRRT	operator
AEOOPSTT	potatoes
AEOORRST	sororate
AEOORTTT	tattooer
AEOORTTV	rotovate
AEOPPRSV	approves
AEOPRRST	praetors
	prorates
AEOPRRSV	vaporers
AEOPRRUV	vapourer
AEOPRRVW	wrapover
AEOPRSST	espartos
	protases
	seaports
AEOPRSSU	asperous
AEOPRSSV	overpass
	passover
AEOPRSTT	prostate
AEOPRSTU	apterous
AEOPRSTV	overpast
AEOPRSVY	overpays
AEOPTTUY	autotype
AEOQRSTU	equators
	quaestor
AEOQRTTU	torquate
AEORRSST	assertor
	assorter
	roasters
AEORRSSU	arousers
AEORRSTT	rostrate
AEORRTZZ	terrazzo
AEORSSSS	assessor
AEORSSTT	toasters
AEORSSTV	votaress
AEORSSUU	rousseau
AEORSTTT	attestor
	testator
AEORSTTU	outstare
AEORSTUW	outwears
AEORSTVY	overstay
AEPPRRST	strapper
	trappers
AEPPRRSW	wrappers
AEPPRSSW	swappers
AEPPSSTU	pasteups
AEPQRSTU	parquets
AEPRRSSY	resprays
	sprayers
AEPRRSTU	raptures
AEPRSSST	sparsest
	trespass
AEPRSSTT	spatters
	tapsters
AEPRSSTU	pastures
AEPRSTTU	upstater
AEPRSTTY	tapestry
AEPRSTUX	supertax

AEPSSSSU	passuses
AEPSSTTU	upstates
AEQRRSSU	squarers
AEQRRSTU	quarters
AEQRSTTU	quartets
	squatter
AEQRSTUZ	quartzes
AERRSSSU	assurers
AERRSSTT	restarts
	starters
AERRSSTV	starvers
AERRSSTY	strayers
AERRSTUY	treasury
AERSSSST	strasses
AERSSSUU	Saussure
AERSSTTT	strettas
AERSSTTU	statures
AERSSTTW	swatters
AERSSTUX	surtaxes
AERSSTVY	strayves
AERSTTVY	travesty
AERTTUXY	textuary
AESSSTTU	statuses
AESSTTTU	statutes
AFFFFIRR	riffraff
AFFGHIRT	affright
AFFGIINX	affixing
AFFGIIRT	graffiti
AFFGILNR	raffling
AFFGILNW	waffling
AFFGINQU	quaffing
AFFGINST	staffing
AFFGIORT	graffito
AFFHILLS	fallfish
AFFHILST	flatfish
AFFHILTU	faithful
AFFHNOTV	van't Hoff
AFFIINTY	affinity
AFFILLMM	flimflam
AFFILSUX	suffixal
AFFIMSST	mastiffs
AFFINOSU	affusion
AFFINRSU	funfairs
	ruffians
AFFIPSTT	tipstaff
AFFLLOOT	footfall
AFFLOOTT	flatfoot
AFFLOPSY	playoffs
AFFLRRUU	furfural
AFFNORST	affronts
AFFNRRUU	furfuran
AFFRTTUU	Truffaut
AFGGGILN	flagging
AFGGGINR	fragging
AFGGILNN	flanging
AFGGILOP	gigaflop
AFGGINOR	foraging
AFGGINOT	fagoting
AFGGINRT	grafting
AFGHILNS	flashing
AFGHILNT	fanlight
AFGHILPS	flagship
AFGHINRT	farthing
AFGHINRW	wharfing
AFGHINST	shafting
AFGHIOST	goatfish
AFGHLNSU	flashgun
AFGIILLN	flailing
AFGIILNS	failings
AFGIINNT	fainting
AFGIINRS	fairings
AFGIINTX	fixating
AFGIKLNN	fankling
	flanking
AFGIKNNR	franking
AFGIKORT	koftgari
AFGILLNT	flatling
AFGILMMN	flamming
AFGILMNO	flamingo
AFGILNOT	floating
AFGILNOW	Fowliang
AFGILNPP	flapping
AFGILNST	fatlings
AFGILNTT	flatting
AFGILNTU	faulting
AFGIMNRS	framings
AFGIMNTU	fumigant
AFGIMORS	gasiform
AFGINNRS	snarfing
AFGINNSU	snafuing
AFGINORV	favoring
AFGINORY	foraying
AFGINPPR	frapping
AFGINRST	ingrafts
	strafing
AFGINRTU	figurant
AFGIPRTW	giftwrap
AFGJNRUU	Jungfrau
AFGKORST	koftgars
AFGLLRUY	frugally
AFGLLSSU	glassful
AFGLNNOO	gonfalon
AFGNNNOO	gonfanon
AFHIILSS	sailfish
AFHIILST	fishtail
AFHIINST	faintish
AFHIKSUY	kufiyahs
AFHILLSY	flashily
AFHILOSY	oafishly
AFHILSST	saltfish
AFHILSTT	flattish
AFHILSTW	halfwits
AFHINOSS	fashions
AFHINOSY	fashiony
AFHIRSST	starfish
AFHISSWY	fishways
AFHKLNTU	thankful
AFHKORSY	hayforks
AFHKRSTU	futharks
AFHLMOTU	Falmouth
AFHLRTUW	wrathful
AFHNOOST	fantoosh
AFHNORRT	Far North
AFHOOPTT	footpath
AFIILLLY	filially
AFIILMMS	familism
AFIILMNS	finalism
AFIILMST	Familist
AFIILNRU	Friulian
	unifilar
AFIILNST	finalist
AFIILNTY	finality
AFIILORS	airfoils
AFIILRST	airlifts
AFIIMNPR	rifampin
AFIINNOS	sainfoin
	sinfonia
AFIINOTX	fixation
AFIIORRT	triforia
AFIJKRTU	jakfruit
AFIKLNNR	franklin
AFIKLOST	flokatis
AFIKMNNR	finnmark
AFIKNNPU	Panufnik
AFIKNRST	ratfinks
AFILLLOT	flotilla
AFILLNPS	pinfalls
AFILLPST	pitfalls
AFILLPSU	pailfuls
AFILLTUY	faultily
AFILMNOR	formalin
	informal
AFILMNOS	foilsman
AFILMRUU	Mufulira
AFILNORT	flatiron
	inflator
AFILNPPT	flippant
AFILNRUY	unfairly
AFILORSW	airflows
AFILOSTX	foxtails
AFILRSTU	fistular
AFILSSTU	fistulas
AFILSTTU	flautist
AFIMMNOY	ammonify
AFIMMORR	ramiform
AFIMNOPR	napiform
AFIMNOSU	infamous
AFIMOOSS	mafiosos
AFIMORRU	auriform
AFIMORRV	variform
AFINNOTU	fountain
AFINNRTY	infantry
AFINOPSY	saponify
AFINQTUY	quantify
AFINRSTX	transfix
AFIORSTU	faitours
AFIRSTTY	stratify
AFISSSTT	sitfasts
AFISSTUV	fauvists
AFKLNOTU	outflank
AFKLNSTU	tankfuls
AFKLOSWY	folkways
AFKMOORT	footmark
AFLLLORY	florally
AFLLLUWY	lawfully
AFLLMNUY	manfully

AFLLMORY	formally
AFLLNOOV	flavonol
AFLLNOSW	snowfall
AFLLNUUW	unlawful
AFLLOOTW	footwall
AFLLOSTU	outfalls
AFLLRTUY	artfully
AFLMNOPR	planform
AFLMNOST	loftsman
AFLMOPRT	platform
AFLMORSU	formulas
AFLMORTW	flatworm
AFLMORTY	Fort Lamy
AFLMOSUY	famously
AFLNORST	frontals
AFLOPSTT	flattops
AFLORSUV	flavours
AFLPRSTY	flytraps
AFLPSSTY	flypasts
AFMNNOOS	Son of Man
AFMNNORT	frontman
AFMNORST	formants
AFMOOPRR	proforma
AFMORSTU	foumarts
AFMORTUY	fumatory
AFMOSSTU	sfumatos
AFNNOTTY	nonfatty
AFOORSTZ	sforzato
AFOOSTWY	footways
AGGGGILN	gaggling
AGGGHILN	haggling
AGGGHINS	shagging
AGGGILNN	gangling
AGGGILNR	gargling
AGGGILNS	slagging
AGGGILNW	waggling
AGGGINNS	snagging
AGGGINPS	spagging
AGGGINST	stagging
AGGGINSW	swagging
AGGHILNU	laughing
AGGHILST	gaslight
AGGHILSY	shaggily
AGGHIMNO	homaging
AGGHINNS	gnashing
	hangings
AGGHINNW	whanging
AGGHINPR	graphing
AGGHISTT	gastight
AGGHJMNO	mahjongg
AGGHLOOT	golgotha
AGGIILNN	aligning
AGGIILNR	glairing
AGGIILNT	ligating
AGGIILNV	gingival
AGGIINNR	graining
AGGIINNS	gainings
AGGIINST	agisting
AGGIJLNN	jangling
AGGILLNU	ullaging
AGGILMNN	mangling
AGGILMNO	gloaming
AGGILNNO	ganglion
AGGILNNR	gnarling
AGGILNNS	slanging
AGGILNNT	tangling
AGGILNNW	wangling
AGGILNOT	gloating
AGGILNPU	plaguing
AGGILNPY	gapingly
AGGILNRY	grayling
AGGILNSS	glassing
AGGINNOR	groaning
AGGINNOT	tangoing
AGGINNPR	pranging
AGGINNRR	gnarring
AGGINNRT	granting
AGGINNRW	wranging
AGGINNST	stanging
AGGINNSW	gnawings
AGGINNTW	twanging
AGGINOOX	Gaoxiong
AGGINOVY	voyaging
AGGINPRS	grasping
	sparging
AGGINRSS	grassing
AGGINRST	gratings
AGGINRSU	sugaring
AGGINRSZ	grazings
AGGINRTY	gyrating
AGGINRUU	auguring
AGGINSSS	gassings
AGGINSST	stagings
AGGIRTUZ	ziggurat
AGGLLLOY	lollygag
AGGLLOOY	algology
AGGLMOOR	logogram
AGGLOORY	agrology
AGGLRSTY	straggly
AGGMORRS	grograms
AGGNUWZZ	zugzwang
AGHHIILT	hightail
AGHHIMSS	High Mass
AGHHINOP	Haiphong
AGHHISWY	highways
AGHHLOTU	although
AGHHNOUZ	Hangzhou
AGHIILMP	Malpighi
AGHIILNN	inhaling
AGHIILOS	Laoighis
AGHIINST	Tsinghai
AGHIIPRR	hairgrip
AGHIIRTT	airtight
AGHIJNRT	nightjar
AGHIJNUZ	Zhu Jiang
AGHIKNNS	shanking
AGHIKNNT	thanking
AGHIKNRS	sharking
AGHILLNO	halloing
	hollaing
AGHILMTY	almighty
AGHILNOO	hooligan
AGHILNOS	shoaling
AGHILNOT	loathing
AGHILNPS	plashing
AGHILNRS	harlings
	ringhals
AGHILNSS	hassling
	lashings
	slashing
AGHILNSU	languish
	nilghaus
AGHILRSY	garishly
AGHIMMNS	shamming
AGHIMMNW	whamming
AGHIMNPR	pharming
AGHIMNRS	Ram Singh
AGHIMNSS	smashing
AGHINNOT	gnathion
AGHINNTU	haunting
AGHINNTY	anything
AGHINOST	hoasting
AGHINPPW	whapping
AGHINPRS	harpings
	phrasing
	sharping
AGHINPSS	phasings
AGHINQSU	quashing
AGHINRRY	harrying
AGHINRST	trashing
AGHINSST	hastings
	stashing
AGHINSSV	shavings
AGHINSSW	swashing
	washings
AGHINSTW	swathing
AGHINUZZ	Zhuangzi
AGHIPRRT	trigraph
AGHIRSTT	straight
AGHISSTT	tightass
AGHISSTW	sightsaw
AGHJRTUU	Jugurtha
AGHKNOPT	pakthong
AGHKOSSW	goshawks
AGHLMOOR	hologram
AGHLMPSU	galumphs
AGHLNOSU	shogunal
AGHLNOTU	Laughton
AGHLNSUY	nylghaus
AGHLOOSS	gasohols
AGHLOTUU	outlaugh
AGHMMOOY	homogamy
AGHMNPSU	sphagnum
AGHMOOPY	omophagy
AGHMOORR	Gomorrah
AGHMOPRY	myograph
AGHMORSY	hygromas
AGHMRRSU	murraghs
AGHNNOSU	houngans
AGHNNSTU	shantung
AGHNOORS	shagroon
AGHNORST	staghorn
AGHNOSTU	hangouts
	tohungas
AGHNTTUU	untaught
AGHORSTW	warthogs

AGIIIKMR	kirigami
AGIIILNS	liaising
AGIIINNS	insignia
AGIIINRV	Virginia
AGIIJJNN	Jinjiang
AGIILLMN	Milligan
AGIILMNP	impaling
AGIILMNS	misalign
AGIILMNU	miauling
AGIILNNO	Liaoning
AGIILNNP	plaining
AGIILNNU	inguinal
AGIILNNY	inlaying
AGIILNOR	original
AGIILNOT	intaglio
	ligation
	taglioni
AGIILNOX	gloxinia
AGIILNPS	laipsing
AGIILNPT	plaiting
AGIILNQU	quailing
AGIILNRS	railings
AGIILNRT	ringtail
	trailing
AGIILNRU	Ligurian
AGIILNRV	rivaling
	virginal
AGIILNSS	sailings
AGIILNST	tailings
AGIILNTT	litigant
AGIILNTV	vigilant
AGIILORU	oliguria
AGIILPST	pigtails
AGIIMNOU	miaouing
AGIIMNOW	miaowing
AGIIMNST	giantism
AGIIMSST	imagists
AGIINNNO	Annigoni
AGIINNPT	painting
AGIINNRS	ingrains
AGIINNRT	training
AGIINNRV	ravining
AGIINNST	sainting
	staining
AGIINNTT	tainting
AGIINOPT	opiating
AGIINORS	Sargon II
AGIINORT	rigatoni
AGIINOST	Agostini
AGIINPRS	aspiring
	praising
AGIINPRT	pirating
AGIINRRV	arriving
AGIINRTT	attiring
AGIINSTU	Ignatius
AGIJLNPY	japingly
AGIJMNOR	majoring
AGIJMNRU	jumaring
AGIJNNTU	jaunting
AGIKKNNS	skanking
AGIKLMOR	kilogram
AGIKLNNP	planking
AGIKLNNR	rankling
AGIKLNOP	polkaing
AGIKLNST	stalking
AGIKLNTY	takingly
AGIKLNUW	waulking
AGIKMNNU	unmaking
AGIKMNRS	markings
AGIKNNPP	knapping
AGIKNNPR	pranking
AGIKNNPS	spanking
AGIKNNRS	rankings
AGIKNNST	stanking
AGIKNNSW	swanking
AGIKNOSS	soakings
AGIKNOST	goatskin
AGIKNPRS	sparking
AGIKNRSS	sarkings
AGILLMNU	mulligan
AGILLMNY	malignly
AGILLNOW	allowing
AGILLNOY	alloying
AGILLNPS	spalling
AGILLNRU	alluring
AGILLNRY	rallying
AGILLNST	stalling
AGILLNSU	linguals
AGILLNSY	sallying
	signally
	slangily
AGILLNTY	tallying
AGILLOPT	gallipot
AGILLORS	gorillas
AGILLOST	galliots
AGILLPUY	plaguily
AGILLSSU	lugsails
AGILLSSY	glassily
AGILMMNS	slamming
AGILMNNT	mantling
AGILMNOO	Mongolia
AGILMNPS	sampling
AGILMNRS	marlings
AGILMNRU	Langmuir
AGILMNST	maltings
AGILMOPR	lipogram
AGILMORS	algorism
	Margolis
AGILNNNP	planning
AGILNNOP	pangolin
AGILNNOQ	Qian Long
AGILNNOS	loanings
AGILNNPT	planting
AGILNNRS	snarling
AGILNNSS	linsangs
AGILNNST	slanting
AGILNNUY	ungainly
	unlaying
AGILNOOO	oogonial
AGILNOOS	isogonal
AGILNOPR	paroling
AGILNOPT	ploating
AGILNORT	trigonal
AGILNOSS	lassoing
AGILNOST	antilogs
AGILNOTT	totaling
AGILNOTY	antilogy
AGILNPPS	slapping
AGILNPPY	applying
AGILNPRS	sparling
AGILNPSS	saplings
AGILNPST	platings
	stapling
AGILNPSW	lapwings
AGILNPSY	palsying
	splaying
AGILNPTT	platting
AGILNRST	slarting
	starling
AGILNRSU	singular
AGILNRSW	warsling
AGILNRTT	rattling
AGILNRTW	trawling
AGILNRVY	ravingly
AGILNSST	anglists
	lastings
	saltings
	slatings
AGILNSTT	slatting
AGILNSTU	saluting
AGILNSVY	savingly
AGILNTTT	tattling
AGILNTTW	wattling
AGILNTUV	vaulting
AGILNTUX	luxating
AGILNTWZ	waltzing
AGILNTXY	taxingly
AGILOORS	gloriosa
AGILOOXY	axiology
AGILOPST	galipots
AGILORSS	girasols
AGILSYYZ	syzygial
AGIMMNPS	spamming
AGIMMNRS	smarming
AGIMMNRT	tramming
AGIMMNTY	tammying
AGIMMOSY	misogamy
AGIMNNOS	masoning
AGIMNNOW	womaning
AGIMNNRU	manuring
	unarming
AGIMNORR	armoring
	roarming
AGIMNORS	organism
AGIMNORU	origanum
AGIMNORY	agrimony
AGIMNPPS	mappings
AGIMNPRT	tramping
AGIMNPST	stamping
AGIMNPSW	swamping
AGIMNRRY	marrying
AGIMNRST	migrants
	smarting
AGIMNRSW	swarming
AGIMNRTU	maturing
AGIMNSSU	assuming

AGIMNSTT mattings
AGIMNTTU mutating
AGIMORRT migrator
AGIMORSS isograms
AGIMORSU gouramis
AGINNNNY nannying
AGINNNOY annoying
AGINNNPS spanning
AGINNNSW swanning
AGINNOPR aproning
AGINNOPT Paignton
poignant
AGINNORT ignorant
AGINNOSU anginous
AGINNOTT notating
AGINNPPS snapping
AGINNPSW spawning
wingspan
AGINNQTU quanting
AGINNRST rantings
AGINNRSW warnings
AGINNSTU stauning
AGINNSUY unsaying
AGINNTTU attuning
taunting
AGINNTUV vaunting
AGINOOPS pogonias
AGINOORT rogation
AGINOPPS apposing
AGINOPQU opaquing
AGINOPRV vaporing
AGINORRS garrison
AGINORSS assignor
signoras
AGINORST organist
roasting
AGINORSU arousing
AGINORSV savoring
AGINORTT rotating
troating
AGINORTV graviton
AGINORTY gyration
AGINOSST agonists
AGINOSTT tangoist
toasting
Tsingtao
AGINPPRS rappings
AGINPPRT trapping
AGINPPRW wrapping
AGINPPSW swapping
AGINPPTU pupating
AGINPRRS sparring
AGINPRRY parrying
AGINPRSS raspings
AGINPRST partings
AGINPRSY spraying
AGINPRTU uprating
AGINPRTY partying
AGINPSSS passings
AGINPSST pastings
AGINPSTT spatting
AGINQRSU squaring
AGINRRST starring
AGINRRTY tarrying
AGINRSST gastrins
AGINRSSU assuring
AGINRSSY syringas
AGINRSTT starting
AGINRSTV starving
AGINRSTW strawing
AGINRSTY stingray
straying
AGINRTYY gyniatry
AGINSTTT tattings
AGINSTTW swatting
AGINSVVY savvying
AGINSWWX waxwings
AGIOORTU autogiro
AGIOPPRT agitprop
AGIRSSTU sastrugi
AGIRTTUY gratuity
AGJLOSUV Jugoslav
AGJLRSUU jugulars
AGJNOORS jargoons
AGKLOORV Gorlovka
AGKMNOPS kampongs
AGKNOOOV Okovango
AGKNSTUU Tunguska
AGKORSSW gasworks
AGLLMOPW glowlamp
AGLLNOOS galloons
AGLLNSTU gallnuts
nutgalls
AGLLOORS rogallos
AGLLOOST galloots
AGLLPSTY glyptals
AGLLRUVY vulgarly
AGLMOPYY polygamy
AGLNOOOS ologoans
AGLNOSST glasnost
AGLNOSWY longways
AGLNOUVZ Glazunov
AGLNSSSU sunglass
AGLOOPST goalpost
AGLOPRTU Portugal
AGLORSSY glossary
AGLOSUVY Yugoslav
AGLPSSSY spyglass
AGLRTTUU guttural
AGLSTUUY augustly
AGMMNOOR monogram
nomogram
AGMMNOOY monogamy
AGMMORSY myograms
AGMNNORS grannoms
AGMNOORS sonogram
AGMNOORY agronomy
AGMNORST angstrom
Ångström
AGMNORSU organums
AGMNSSTU mustangs
AGMNSSTY gymnasts
syntagms
AGMOOOSU oogamous
AGMOOTVY vagotomy
AGMOPRRS programs
AGMORRSW ragworms
AGNNNOOS nonagons
AGNNOORS argonons
organons
AGNNOQTU quantong
AGNNOSSW swan song
AGNNOTUX Xuan-tong
AGNNOUXZ Xuan Zong
AGNORRST grantors
AGNORTUY nugatory
AGNPPRSU upsprang
AGOORRTY rogatory
AGOORTUY autogyro
AGOPPSST stopgaps
AGORRSTW ragworts
AGORRSTY gyrators
AGORRTYY gyratory
AGORSTTY gyrostat
AGSSTUUU Augustus
AHHIKLSS shashlik
AHHILPSW whiplash
AHHIMMSS mishmash
AHHINRTU Haut-Rhin
AHHIPRSS sharpish
AHHIRSST Tarshish
AHHISSTT shittahs
AHHKMOTW hawkmoth
AHHKRSTU kashruth
AHHLNOPT naphthol
AHHLNPTY naphthyl
AHHMPRRU harrumph
AHHNORTW hawthorn
AHHOPRSS shophars
AHHOPSTU aphthous
AHIIILMN malihini
AHIIKMRS Kashmiri
AHIIKRSS shikaris
AHIILORT Lothair I
AHIILRTY hilarity
AHIIMNOT himation
AHIIMNRU manuhiri
AHIIMNST isthmian
AHIIMOPX amphioxi
AHIIMSST samithis
AHIINPRS hairpins
AHIINSSW swainish
AHIIOPST hospitia
AHIIPRSS airships
AHIIRSTW tawhiris
AHIKLNRS rinkhals
AHIKLRSY rakishly
AHIKMNSS khamsins
AHIKNNOT Ikhnaton
AHIKNOSU Sihanouk
AHIKNPRS prankish
AHIKORSS karoshis
AHIKORST Oistrakh
AHIKOSUZ Shizuoka
AHIKPRSS sparkish
AHILLMOU halloumi

AHILLMPS phallism
AHILLMSS smallish
AHILLMTU thallium
AHILLPST phallist
AHILLSVY lavishly
AHILMNOT Hamilton
AHILMOST mailshot
AHILMOSU haloumis
AHILMQSU qualmish
AHILMTUZ halutzim
AHILNOPS siphonal
AHILNOPT oliphant
AHILNORT horntail
AHILNOST Lothians
AHILOORT lothario
AHILOPSS alphosis
haplosis
AHILOPST hospital
AHILPSSY physalis
AHILRSTY trashily
AHIMMNSU humanism
AHIMMORZ mahzorim
AHIMMOSV moshavim
AHIMNOSW womanish
AHIMNSTU humanist
AHIMNSTX xanthism
AHIMNTUY humanity
AHIMOOSY yahooism
AHIMOPRS aphorism
AHIMOPST opsimath
AHIMORRW hairworm
AHIMPPSS sapphism
AHIMPRST trampish
AHIMPSSW swampish
AHIMRSST smartish
AHIMSSTU Tsushima
AHIMSTUZ azimuths
AHIMSTVZ mitzvahs
AHINNOPT antiphon
AHINNSTX xanthins
AHINORRS Harrison
AHINOSST astonish
AHINOSTZ hoatzins
AHINPPSS snappish
AHINPRST tranship
AHINPRSU Nishapur
AHINPSWW whipsawn
AHINQSUV vanquish
AHINSTUU tauhinus
AHIOOPPT photopia
AHIOPPRT Potiphar
AHIOPRST aphorist
AHIOPRSV vaporish
AHIORSSW airshows
AHIORSTV tovarish
AHIPRSST harpists
AHIPRSSW warships
AHIPSSWW whipsaws
AHIPSSWY shipways
AHIQRSSU squarish
AHIRSSTW trishaws
AHISSTTW whatsits

AHKLOPRU Kolhapur
AHKLOPST shoptalk
AHKMOORR markhoor
AHKMORRS markhors
AHKMORTU Khartoum
AHKNOTUY thankyou
AHLLNOOS shalloon
AHLLNOTW townhall
AHLLNOUW unhallow
AHLLOPSS shallops
AHLLOSST shallots
AHLLOSSW shallows
AHLLOSTU thallous
AHLLOSTY tallyhos
AHLMMOPY lymphoma
AHLMNNRU Luhrmann
AHLMNOOR hormonal
AHLMNOST Mansholt
AHLMOOPS omphalos
AHLMOPTY polymath
AHLMOSUU hamulous
AHLNNORT lanthorn
AHLNOPRS alphorns
AHLNOPST haplonts
AHLNORST althorns
AHLOPRSU Sholapur
AHLOPSST slapshot
AHLORRTY harlotry
AHLOSTUU outhauls
AHMMMOST mammoths
AHMNNNOU nonhuman
AHMNNSTU huntsman
manhunts
AHMNOPST phantoms
AHMNORRS ramshorn
AHMNSSUY Huysmans
AHMOOPPT photomap
AHMOOPSS shampoos
AHMOORSW washroom
AHMOPTYY myopathy
AHMORTTW tamworth
AHMORTUY Yarmouth
AHMPSSSU smashups
AHMPSTYY sympathy
AHMQSSUU musquash
AHNOOPRS harpoons
AHNOORRY honorary
AHNOPPSW pawnshop
AHNOPPSY pansophy
AHNOPSST snapshot
AHNORSSX saxhorns
AHNORSTV Tórshavn
AHNOSTTW whatnots
AHNOSTUX xanthous
AHNRSVYY hryvnyas
AHOOSSTY soothsay
AHOOSTTW sawtooth
AHOPSTTW towpaths
AHOPSTUW southpaw
AHORTTUW watthour
AHOSSTUW washouts
AHQRRTUU Urquhart

AIIILLMN Illimani
AIIILLMW William I
AIIILLVX lixivial
AIIILMST militias
AIIILNST initials
AIIILRVZ vizirial
AIIKKSUY sukiyaki
AIIKLLMN Millikan
AIIKLNOR Iráklion
AIIKLNRR larrikin
AIIKMMSS skimmias
AIIKMNNN mannikin
AIIKMNNS manikins
AIIKNNNP pannikin
AIIKNNST tankinis
AIIKORTY yakitori
AIIKRRSU raurikis
AIIKTTZZ tzatziki
AIILLLUV illuvial
AIILLMNO monilial
AIILLMRY milliary
AIILLMSW Williams
AIILLNNV vanillin
AIILLNOP pollinia
AIILLNOT illation
AIILLNPT antipill
AIILLNRY Illyrian
AIILLNSV villains
AIILLNVY villainy
AIILLPRS sliprail
spirilla
AIILLQSU quillais
AIILLWWW williwaw
AIILMNPS alpinism
AIILMNPT palmitin
AIILMNTT militant
AIILMRST mistrial
AIILMRTY limitary
military
AIILMSST Islamist
AIILMSTV vitalism
AIILNNOV Livonian
AIILNOPS Pasolini
AIILNOPT Politian
AIILNOPV pavilion
AIILNOSS liaisons
AIILNOSV visional
AIILNPST alpinist
pintails
tailspin
AIILNQRU Quirinal
AIILNSTY salinity
AIILNTTY latinity
AIILORTT Littoria
AIILQSSU siliquas
AIILRSTT trialist
AIILSTTV vitalist
AIILTTVY vitality
AIIMMNNY minyanim
AIIMMNRU Ariminum
AIIMNNOS insomnia
AIIMNPSS sinapism

AIIMNPSX panmixis
AIIMNRST martinis
AIIMNRSU Arminius
AIIMNSST animists
AIIMNSTT titanism
AIIMNSTV nativism
vitamins
AIIMNTTU titanium
AIIMOPSX apomixis
AIIMORTT imitator
AIIMOSST amitosis
AIIMPPRS priapism
AIIMPRTY imparity
AIIMRSST simitars
AIIMRSTU tiramisu
AIIMRUVV vivarium
AIIMSSTT mastitis
AIINNOSV invasion
AIINNOTV nivation
AIINNQTU quintain
AIINNSTU Tunisian
AIINNSTV Vinnitsa
AIINNSTY insanity
AIINORTT antiriot
tritonia
AIINOSTT notitias
AIINPRSS aspirins
AIINPRST Priština
AIINPSST pianists
AIINRRTT irritant
AIINRSTV vitrains
AIINSTTV nativist
visitant
AIINTTVY nativity
AIIORRST sartorii
AIIORSTT aortitis
AIIORSTV ovaritis
AIIORTTV vitiator
AIIPRRST airstrip
AIIPRVVY vivipary
AIIRSSTT satirist
sitarist
AIJKKNOU kinkajou
AIJLLOOR jillaroo
AIJLLOVY jovially
AIJLNTUY jauntily
AIJMORTY majority
AIJNOPPY popinjay
AIJNORST janitors
AIKKLLRW Kirkwall
AIKKMOST komatiks
AIKKOOSW kokowais
AIKKOPSY kopiykas
AIKKOSUZ zakouski
AIKKRTUZ zikkurat
AIKLLSTY stalkily
AIKLNNPS snaplink
AIKLNOPS Polanski
AIKLNSST Stalinsk
AIKLNSWY swankily
AIKLOTTW kilowatt
AIKLRSTT titlarks
AIKLSSSY skysails
AIKMRSTZ sitzmark
AIKNNOOS nainsook
AIKNNOST Atkinson
AIKNNSSW swanskin
AIKNORTY karyotin
AIKNOSTT stotinka
AIKOORST rooikats
AIKPTTUU patutuki
AIKRSTUZ zikurats
AILLLNOO linalool
AILLLOST Saltillo
AILLLPSU lapillus
AILLMOSS Limassol
AILLMOST maillots
AILLMOSY loyalism
AILLMOTY molality
AILLMPSU palliums
AILLMSSW sawmills
AILLMUUV alluvium
AILLNOPP papillon
AILLNORT antiroll
AILLNOST stallion
AILLNOSU allusion
AILLNOUV alluvion
AILLNPSY spinally
AILLNPTY pliantly
AILLNSST installs
AILLNSUV Sullivan
AILLORSY sailorly
AILLORSZ zorillas
AILLORTT littoral
tortilla
AILLOSTY loyalist
AILLOTTT tallitot
AILLPRSY spirally
AILLPRTY paltrily
AILLPSTY playlist
AILLPSUV pluvials
AILLPSWY spillway
AILLQSSU squillas
AILLRTUY ritually
AILLSUVY visually
AILMMNOO monomial
AILMMNUU aluminum
AILMMORS moralism
AILMMORT immortal
AILMMRSY smarmily
AILMMSTU summital
AILMMSUW mwalimus
AILMNNOS nominals
AILMNNOT mannitol
AILMNNPP Lippmann
AILMNOOP palomino
AILMNOOR monorail
AILMNOOT motional
AILMNOPS lampions
AILMNOPY Olympian
palimony
AILMNOSS malisons
AILMNPST implants
AILMNPTU platinum
AILMNRUY luminary
AILMNSTU simulant
AILMOOSV moviolas
AILMOPRU Mariupol
AILMOPRX proximal
AILMORSS solarism
AILMORST moralist
AILMORSU solarium
AILMORSY royalism
AILMORTY molarity
morality
AILMOSTU solatium
AILMOSTV voltaism
AILMPPSY misapply
AILMPRSU primulas
AILMPSST palmists
psalmist
AILMPSSY misplays
AILMPSTY ptyalism
AILMRRSU ruralism
AILMRSSU simulars
AILMRSTU altruism
muralist
ultraism
AILMSSTY myalists
AILNNOOT notional
AILNNOST antlions
AILNNOSU unisonal
AILNNOSY Lyonnais
AILNNOTU lunation
AILNNPRU pinnular
AILNNSTU insulant
AILNOOPT optional
AILNOOST solation
AILNOPRU unipolar
AILNOPTY ponytail
AILNOSTY lanosity
AILNOSUV avulsion
AILNOSVY synovial
AILNOTTV volitant
AILNOTTY tonality
AILNOTUX luxation
AILNPPSY snappily
AILNPSTU nuptials
AILNPSUU nauplius
Paulinus
AILNQRTU tranquil
AILNQSTU quintals
AILNQTUY quaintly
AILNRSSU insulars
AILNRTTU rutilant
AILNRUWY unwarily
AILNSSTU stunsail
AILNSSUV Silvanus
AILNSTTU lutanist
AILNSTUU nautilus
AILNSYZZ snazzily
AILOOPZZ Paolozzi
AILOORST isolator
ostiolar
AILOORTV violator
AILOPRTU troupial

AILOPRTY	polarity
AILOPRUY	polyuria
AILOPSST	apostils
	topsails
AILOQSTU	aliquots
AILORSST	sliotars
	solarist
AILORSTY	royalist
	solitary
AILORSVY	savorily
AILORTTU	tutorial
AILORTUV	outrival
AILOSSTT	altoists
AILOSSUY	Aloysius
AILOTTTY	totality
AILPPRUY	pupilary
AILPQSSU	pasquils
AILPRSSU	spirulas
AILPRSTU	stipular
AILPSSWY	slipways
AILPSTUY	playsuit
AILRRSTU	ruralist
AILRRSTY	starrily
AILRRTUY	rurality
AILRSSTY	trysails
AILRSTTU	altruist
	titulars
	ultraist
AILRSTTY	straitly
AILRSUVV	survival
AILRTTUY	titulary
AILSSTUW	lawsuits
AIMMMNOU	ammonium
AIMMMSUX	maximums
AIMMNORS	Romanism
AIMMNORT	mortmain
AIMMNSTU	manumits
AIMMOSST	atomisms
AIMMRSUU	masurium
AIMNNOPT	pointman
AIMNNOSS	mansions
AIMNNOTU	antimuon
	mountain
AIMNNOTY	antimony
	antinomy
AIMNNRTU	ruminant
AIMNOORV	Monrovia
AIMNOOTY	myotonia
AIMNOPRS	rampions
AIMNOPST	maintops
	ptomains
	tampions
AIMNOQRU	maroquin
AIMNORST	Romanist
AIMNORTU	Minotaur
AIMNORTY	minatory
AIMNOSTU	manitous
	Mount Isa
	tinamous
AIMNOTTU	mutation
AIMNRSTT	Tantrism
	transmit
AIMNRSTU	naturism
AIMNRSTV	varmints
AIMNSSTU	tsunamis
AIMNSTUU	Manutius
AIMOPRSS	prosaism
AIMOPSSY	symposia
AIMORRST	armorist
AIMORRSU	rosarium
AIMORRUV	variorum
AIMORSST	amorists
AIMORSTY	ramosity
AIMOSSTT	atomists
AIMPPRUU	puparium
AIMRTTUY	maturity
AINNNOST	santonin
AINNOOTT	notation
AINNOOTV	novation
AINNOOTZ	zonation
AINNOPSS	saponins
AINNOSST	onanists
AINNOSTU	Antonius
AINNOTTU	nutation
AINNPSST	snaptins
AINNRSTU	Nuristan
AINNSSTT	instants
AINNSTTY	nystatin
AINOOPTT	potation
AINOORST	orations
AINOORTT	rotation
AINOOSTT	ostinato
AINOOSTV	ovations
AINOPPST	appoints
AINOPPTU	pupation
AINOPRSS	parisons
AINOPSSS	passions
AINOPSTU	opuntias
	utopians
AINOPSTW	swaption
AINOQRRU	quarrion
AINORSST	arsonist
AINORSSW	warisons
AINORSTT	strontia
AINOSSTT	stations
AINOSSUU	Ausonius
AINOSTTU	titanous
AINPPRSS	parsnips
AINPRSST	spirants
	spraints
AINPRSSU	Prussian
AINPRSTU	puritans
	Rasputin
AINPSSSY	synapsis
AINPSSTU	puissant
AINPSTTU	pantsuit
AINQTTUY	quantity
AINRSSTT	transits
AINRSTTT	titrants
AINRSTTU	antirust
	naturist
AINRSTTY	tanistry
AINSSSTU	sustains
AIOOORRT	oratorio
AIOPRRSS	Pissarro
AIOPRRST	airports
AIOPRRTT	portrait
AIOPRSST	prosaist
	protasis
AIOPRSTT	patriots
AIOPRSUV	paviours
AIORRRSW	warriors
AIORRSTT	traitors
AIORRSTV	varistor
AIORSSUV	saviours
AIORSTTV	votarist
AIOSSSTY	isostasy
AIPPRSTT	Trappist
AIPPRSTY	papistry
AIPRSSTU	upstairs
AIPRSSTY	sparsity
AIRRSTTY	artistry
AIRSSSTT	tsarists
AISSSTTT	statists
AJKMNSTU	muntjaks
AJLNORSU	journals
AJORRTUY	juratory
AKKLRSSY	skylarks
AKKOOSUY	Yokosuka
AKKORSTW	taskwork
AKLNNOPT	plankton
AKLOSTTU	outtalks
AKLOSTUW	outwalks
	walkouts
AKLPRRSU	larkspur
AKMMNOOR	monomark
AKMMNRSU	Murmansk
AKMMOOTU	Kumamoto
AKMNOOPU	mokopuna
AKMOORST	Kostroma
AKMOPRST	postmark
AKMORSST	ostmarks
AKMQSTUU	kumquats
AKMRSSTU	muskrats
AKNNOSTZ	Konstanz
AKNOOUYZ	yokozuna
AKNOPSTW	swankpot
AKNORSTU	outranks
AKOPRRTW	partwork
AKORSWWX	waxworks
ALLLOSWY	sallowly
ALLLPRUY	Lyallpur
	plurally
ALLMNORY	normally
ALLMNOSY	allonyms
ALLMNPSU	pullmans
ALLMOPSX	smallpox
ALLMORTY	mortally
ALLMOUWY	mulloway
ALLMTUUY	mutually
ALLNNOUY	nounally
ALLNOOPS	planosol
ALLNOOPY	Apollyon
ALLOOSTX	axolotls
ALLOPRSY	payrolls
ALLOPSTY	postally

ALLORSST allsorts
ALLORSWY rollways
ALLOSSWW swallows
ALLRUUVY uvularly
ALMMNRUU nummular
ALMNNOOR nonmoral
ALMNOOPS lampoons
ALMNOPSS plasmons
ALMNORTY matronly
ALMNOSSU solanums
ALMOOPRY playroom
ALMOORTU alumroot
ALMOPPST lamppost
palmtops
ALMORSUU ramulous
ALMORSUY ramously
ALMOSTTU mulattos
ALMPSSTY symplast
ALMSSSUY alyssums
ALNNORRU nonrural
ALNNOTWY wantonly
ALNNRSSU unsnarls
ALNOOPRT Tarnopol
ALNOOPST platoons
ALNOOPYZ polyzoan
ALNOORST ortolans
ALNOPRST plastron
ALNOPRTY patronly
ALNOPSYY polynyas
ALNORRWY narrowly
ALNORSVY sovranly
ALNPPSTU supplant
ALNSSUVY Sylvanus
ALOOPPRS proposal
ALOOPRST postoral
ALOORSUV valorous
ALOORTYZ zoolatry
ALOPPRSU populars
ALOPPRYY polypary
ALOPRRSU parlours
ALOPRSTU postural
pulsator
ALOPSSSU spousals
ALOPSTUU patulous
ALOPSTUY outplays
ALOQRRSU rorquals
ALORSTTW saltwort
ALORSTWW awlworts
ALORTUWY outlawry
ALOSSTTU outlasts
ALOSSTXY oxysalts
ALOSTTUZ Zlatoust
ALPPSTUY platypus
ALPRSTUU pustular
ALRSSSUU russulas
AMMNOORT motorman
AMMNPTUY tympanum
AMMOPSTU pomatums
AMMORRWY armyworm
AMNNOSTW townsman
AMNNOSTY antonyms
AMNNSTTU stuntman
AMNOOPPS pompanos
AMNOOSTT ottomans
AMNOOTUY autonomy
AMNOOTXY taxonomy
AMNOPRSY paronyms
AMNOPSTU pantoums
AMNORSST transoms
AMNORSTU romaunts
AMNOTTUY tautonym
AMNRSTTU tantrums
AMOOPRSS prosomas
AMOOPRST taprooms
AMOORRTY moratory
AMOORTWY motorway
AMOOTTUY autotomy
AMOPRSXY paroxysm
AMOPSSTT topmasts
AMOPTUUY Putumayo
AMOQSSUU squamous
AMORRTUY mortuary
AMORSTTU outsmart
AMRSSTTU stratums
ANNOORST sonorant
ANNOPRTY nonparty
ANNOSSTU stannous
ANNPRSUY spunyarn
ANOOPRRT pronator
ANOOPRSS sopranos
ANOOPRST patroons
ANOORSTT rattoons
ANOPRRSS sporrans
ANOPRTTU trapunto
ANOPSSTU outspans
ANORSSTW Strawson
ANORSTVY sovranty
ANORSUVY unsavory
ANPRSSTU suntraps
unstraps
ANPRSTUU pursuant
ANRRSTUY unstarry
ANRSSSTU sunstars
AOOOPRTZ protozoa
AOOPPRSY apospory
AOOPRSSU saporous
AOOPRSTT taproots
AOOPRSTW soapwort
AOOPRSUV vaporous
AOOPRTTY potatory
AOORRSTT rotators
AOORRTTY rotatory
AOORSSUV savorous
AOPPRRST rapports
AOPPRSST passport
AOPRRRTY parrotry
AOPRRSSW sparrows
AOPRRSTY portrays
AOPRSTTY pyrostat
AOPSTTUU autoputs
AOPTTUYY autotypy
AORRSTTW starwort
AORSUVVY vouvrays
AOSSTTUY outstays
APRSSTTU upstarts
BBBCEOWY cobwebby
BBBEILOR blobbier
BBBEILRU bubblier
BBBEINOT bobbinet
BBBELRSU blubbers
bubblers
BBBELRUY blubbery
BBBGILNO blobbing
bobbling
BBBGILNU blubbing
bubbling
BBCCIKOS bibcocks
BBCDERSU scrubbed
BBCDIMOY bombycid
BBCEEIRS berbices
BBCEHIRU chubbier
BBCEIKKR Birkbeck
BBCEILRS scribble
BBCEILRU clubbier
BBCEIRRS cribbers
BBCEKLSU blesbuck
BBCEKLUU bluebuck
BBCELORS clobbers
cobblers
BBCELRSU clubbers
BBCEMNOU buncombe
BBCERRSU scrubber
BBCGIINR cribbing
BBCGILNO cobbling
BBCGILNU clubbing
BBCHKOOS boschbok
BBCHKSUU bushbuck
BBCILLUY clubbily
BBCILRSY scribbly
BBDDEEIR dibbered
BBDDEEMO demobbed
BBDDEILR dribbled
BBDEEGIR gibbered
BBDEEGIT gibbeted
BBDEEMNU benumbed
BBDEERSU subbreed
BBDEFILR fribbled
BBDEHORT throbbed
BBDEILLR bellbird
BBDEILMY Dimbleby
BBDEILQU quibbled
BBDEILRR dribbler
BBDEILRS dibblers
dribbles
BBDEILRT dribblet
BBDEILRU bluebird
BBDEIMOV divebomb
BBDEINOR ribboned
BBDEIQSU squibbed
BBDELLMU dumbbell
BBDELLOO bobolled
BBDELOSS bobsleds
BBDELSTU stubbled
BBDERRSU drubbers
BBDERSUU suburbed
BBDGIILN dibbling

BBDGINRU drubbing
BBDOSUYY busybody
BBEEERSU bebeerus
BBEEGLOS Goebbels
BBEEHMOR Beerbohm
BBEEIIRR beriberi
BBEEILPR plebbier
BBEEIRRS berberis
BBEEISTW webbiest
BBEELLLU bluebell
BBEEOPPR bebopper
BBEFILRR fribbler
BBEFILRS fribbles
BBEFILRT flibbert
BBEFIMOR firebomb
BBEGIIST gibbsite
BBEGILNP pebbling
BBEGILRS gribbles
BBEGILST glibbest
BBEGINSW webbings
BBEGIRRU grubbier
BBEGLMRU Blumberg
BBEGLORS gobblers
BBEGMORR Bromberg
BBEGRRSU grubbers
BBEHIOTW bobwhite
BBEHLORS hobblers
BBEHLSUU bluebush
BBEIIMRS imbibers
BBEIKNOR knobbier
BBEILLLU bluebill
BBEILNRS nibblers
BBEILORW wobblier
BBEILOST bibelots
BBEILOSW wobblies
BBEILQRU quibbler
BBEILQSU quibbles
BBEILRRY bilberry
BBEIMOST bombsite
BBEIMRSU brumbies
BBEIOOST boboties
BBEIRSTU stubbier
subtribe
BBEISSTU stubbies
BBEISTTU tubbiest
BBEKLOOU bluebook
BBEKLOSS blesboks
BBEKNOOT bontebok
BBELLOSY bellboys
BBELLRUY lubberly
BBELMRSU bumblers
BBELNORS nobblers
BBELOORW bobowler
BBELORSS slobbers
BBELORSU boerbuls
BBELORSW wobblers
BBELORSY lobbyers
slobbery
BBELOTUW blowtube
BBELRRSU burblers
BBENORSY snobbery
BBENRSSU snubbers
BBEORRXY boxberry
BBGGILNO gobbling
BBGGINRU grubbing
BBGHILNO hobbling
BBGIIIMN imbibing
BBGIIKLN kibbling
BBGIILNN nibbling
BBGIILNW wibbling
BBGIINNS snibbing
BBGIINRS ribbings
BBGIKNNO knobbing
BBGILMNU bumbling
BBGILNNO nobbling
BBGILNOW wobbling
BBGILNOY lobbying
BBGILNRU burbling
BBGILNSU slubbing
BBGILRUY grubbily
BBGINNSU snubbing
BBGINOSW swobbing
BBGINRSU rubbings
BBGINSTU stubbing
BBHILOSS slobbish
BBHINOSS snobbish
BBHIORTY hobbitry
BBHIOSTY hobbyist
BBHIRSUY rubbishy
BBHRSSUU subshrub
BBIILSST biblists
BBIKLNOO bobolink
BBIKORSU Bobruisk
BBILMOSY lobbyism
BBILOSTY lobbyist
BBILOSUU bibulous
BBILSTUY stubbily
BBIMNOSS snobbism
BBKOOOOS boobooks
BBLLNNUU bulnbuln
BBLLOUYY bullyboy
BBNOORSU bourbons
BBNORSTU stubborn
BBOOSSSY bossboys
BCCCIILY bicyclic
BCCDEILY bicycled
BCCDELOU Dulbecco
BCCEEIRR cerebric
BCCEHIRU cherubic
BCCEIIIS cicisbei
BCCEIILO libeccio
BCCEIIOS cicisbeo
BCCEILOS ecbolics
BCCEILOY biocycle
BCCEILRU crucible
BCCEILRY bicycler
BCCEILSU cubicles
BCCEILSY bicycles
BCCEMORS crombecs
BCCEMRUU cucumber
BCCIIMOR microbic
BCCIINOO Boccioni
BCCIISTU cubistic
BCCILMOU columbic
BCCILOOR broccoli
BCCILOSU bucolics
BCCINORR corncrib
BCCIRTUU cucurbit
BCCMOOSX coxcombs
BCCMSSUU succumbs
BCCNOORS corncobs
BCCSSUUU succubus
BCDDEEEK bedecked
BCDDEHIL childbed
BCDEEEHR breeched
BCDEEENR Debrecen
BCDEEHLN blenched
BCDEEHOU debouche
BCDEEIKR bickered
BCDEEILR credible
BCDEEILS decibels
BCDEEILU educible
BCDEEINT benedict
BCDEEIRS describe
escribed
BCDEEIST bisected
BCDEEJOT objected
BCDEEKNO beckoned
BCDEEKRU reedbuck
BCDEEKTU bucketed
BCDEELOR corbeled
BCDEEMRU cumbered
BCDEEOTT obtected
BCDEFKOR Beckford
BCDEHLOT blotched
BCDEHNOS Den Bosch
BCDEIIOS biocides
BCDEIIRR ricebird
BCDEIKRR redbrick
BCDEILRY credibly
BCDEIMNO combined
BCDEINOU icebound
BCDEKLRU Delbrück
BCDEKORS bedrocks
BCDELMRU crumbled
BCDELMSU scumbled
BCDELOSU beclouds
BCDEMNOU uncombed
BCDEMORY corymbed
BCDENRUU uncurbed
BCDEORSU obscured
BCDIIMOR bromidic
BCDIIPSU bicuspid
BCDIKLLU duckbill
BCDILMOY molybdic
BCDILORU colubrid
BCDINOSW cowbinds
BCDINRUU rubicund
BCDIORSW cowbirds
BCDKORSU burdocks
BCDSSTUU subducts
BCEEEFIN benefice
BCEEEHRS breeches
BCEEERSU berceuse
BCEEFILN fencible
BCEEGIRS icebergs

BCEEHINR benchier
BCEEHKSU buckshee
BCEEHLNS blenches
BCEEHNRS benchers
BCEEHNTU beechnut
BCEEHOSU bouchees
BCEEIILM imbecile
BCEEIKRR bickerer
BCEEILNR bernicle
BCEEINOT cenobite
BCEEIOSX iceboxes
BCEEIRSS escribes
BCEEKNOR beckoner
BCEEKNSU buckeens
BCEEKSUY buckeyes
BCEELOOR borecole
BCEELOSU bouclees
BCEELRTU tubercle
BCEEMNOW Newcombe
BCEEMNRU encumber
BCEEMRRU cerebrum
cumberer
BCEEPRTY cyberpet
BCEERRSU Cerberus
BCEERSXY cybersex
BCEERTVY brevetcy
BCEFFIIR febrific
BCEFHISU subchief
BCEFILOR forcible
BCEGHILN belching
BCEGHINN benching
BCEGIINO biogenic
BCEGIMNO becoming
BCEGKMSU gemsbuck
BCEHIIRT bitchier
BCEHIMOT Chimbote
BCEHIMRS besmirch
BCEHIMRU cherubim
BCEHINOR Cheribon
BCEHINRU bunchier
BCEHIORS brioches
BCEHIORT botchier
BCEHIRRT brichter
BCEHIRST britches
BCEHLOST blotches
BCEHLRSU bluchers
BCEHNRSU brunches
BCEHOORS brooches
BCEHOPSU subepoch
BCEHORRT Ter Borch
BCEHORRU brochure
BCEHORST botchers
BCEHRSTU butchers
Schubert
BCEHRTTU Cuthbert
BCEHRTUY butchery
BCEHSTTU butchest
BCEIIKLN iceblink
BCEIIKRR brickier
BCEIIKRS brickies
BCEIILMS miscible
BCEIILNV vincible
BCEIILOP epibolic
BCEIINRS inscribe
BCEIKLOO booklice
BCEIKNNT Bentinck
BCEILMRS climbers
BCEILMRU Mulciber
BCEILNRU runcible
BCEILORS bricoles
corbeils
BCEILPRU republic
BCEIMNOR combiner
BCEIMNOS combines
BCEIMNRU incumber
BCEIMORS microbes
BCEIMRRU crumbier
BCEINORU bouncier
BCEINOVX biconvex
BCEIOOPS bioscope
BCEIOOSS scoobies
BCEIORRS cribrose
BCEIORST bisector
BCEIRRSS scribers
BCEJSSTU subjects
BCEKLLOS bellocks
BCEKLNUU unbuckle
BCEKLORS blockers
BCEKLRSU bucklers
subclerk
BCEKNRRU Bruckner
BCEKORST brockets
BCEKORSU roebucks
BCELLOSW cowbells
BCELLSSU subcells
BCELMOOS Colombes
BCELMRSU crumbles
BCELMSSU scumbles
BCEMRRSU crumbers
BCENORSU bouncers
BCEORRSU obscurer
BCEORRWY cowberry
BCEORSSU obscures
BCESSSTU subsects
BCFIIMOR morbific
BCFIIORT fibrotic
BCFILORY forcibly
BCFIMORU cubiform
BCFLOOTU clubfoot
BCGHIINR birching
BCGHIINT bitching
BCGHINNU bunching
BCGHINOT botching
BCGIIKNR bricking
BCGIILMN climbing
BCGIILOO biologic
BCGIINRS scribing
BCGIKLNO blocking
BCGIKLNU buckling
BCGIMNOS combings
BCGIMNRU crumbing
BCGIMNUU cumbungi
BCGINNOU bouncing
buncoing
BCGINRSU curbings
BCHIILTY bitchily
BCHIISSU hibiscus
BCHIKLOS blockish
BCHIKOSU chibouks
BCHILOTY botchily
BCHILRTU Ulbricht
BCHILSTU Lubitsch
BCHIOORY choirboy
BCHIOPRS pibrochs
BCHKNORU buckhorn
BCHKOSTU buckshot
BCHLNOUX lunchbox
BCHNOORS bronchos
BCHNORSU bronchus
BCIIILMU umbilici
BCIIIOTT biotitic
BCIIKLNS niblicks
BCIILLSY sibyllic
BCIILMSU bulimics
BCIILOTY biolytic
BCIIMNOO bionomic
BCIIMORU ciborium
BCIINORV vibronic
BCIIOPTY biotypic
BCIISSTU biscuits
BCIKKNSU buckskin
BCIKLOOT bootlick
BCIKORRW cribwork
BCIKOSTT bitstock
BCILLPUY publicly
BCILMOSY symbolic
BCILNOUY bouncily
BCILOORU bicolour
BCINORSU bursicon
BCINOSSU subsonic
BCINOSTU subtonic
BCINOSUU incubous
BCIOOPSY bioscopy
BCIOORST robotics
BCIOPSTU subtopic
BCIORRSU cribrous
BCJKMSUU jumbucks
BCKKOOOO cookbook
BCKLLOOS bollocks
BCKLLOSU bullocks
BCKLLOUY bullocky
BCKLNOSU sunblock
unblocks
BCKOOOPY copybook
BCKOSTTU buttocks
BCLMOOSU coulombs
BCLMOSUU Columbus
BCLOORTU clubroot
BCMORSUU cumbrous
BCMOSSTU combusts
BCOOORTW crowboot
BCOORSSW crossbow
BCOOSTTY boycotts
BCORSTTU obstruct
BDDDDEEU debudded
BDDDEEEM embedded

BDDDEEIM imbedded
BDDDELOR broddled
BDDEEESS seedbeds
BDDEEFLU befuddle
BDDEEGGU debugged
BDDEEGIR begirded
BDDEEGTU budgeted
BDDEEIMM bedimmed
BDDEEIMO embodied
BDDEEINT indebted
BDDEEINW bindweed
BDDEEIRR reedbird
BDDEEIRS birdseed
BDDEEISS bedsides
BDDEEKNU debunked
BDDEENRU burdened
BDDEEORR bordered
BDDEEORS desorbed
BDDEERRU deburred
BDDEESSU debussed
BDDEGINR Bridgend
BDDEGINS beddings
BDDEILNR brindled
BDDEILOO bloodied
BDDEINNU unbidden
BDDEINRU underbid
BDDEIORS disrobed
BDDEIOWY widebody
BDDEISSU subsided
BDDELOOR bloodred
BDDELORS broddles
BDDENOTU obtunded
BDDEORTU obtruded
BDDGILNU buddling
BDDGINUY buddying
BDDGOOSY dogsbody
BDDHIIRY dihybrid
BDDHIMSU Buddhism
BDEEEEMS beseemed
BDEEEGIS besieged
BDEEEGNR breenged
BDEEEHTU hebetude
BDEEEILV believed
BDEEEIRV Bedivere
BDEEEIRW dweebier
BDEEELLR rebelled
BDEEELLV bevelled
BDEEELRS bleeders
BDEEELRY berleyed
BDEEELUW blueweed
BDEEEMNS bedesmen
BDEEENOS Bodensee
BDEEERRS breeders
BDEEERTT bettered
BDEEERTV breveted
BDEEFFRU buffered
rebuffed
BDEEFFTU buffeted
BDEEFGGO befogged
BDEEFINR befriend
BDEEFIRS debriefs
BDEEFIRU rubefied
BDEEFITT befitted
BDEEFLOO befooled
BDEEFLOU befouled
BDEEFOOR forebode
BDEEFOOW beefwood
BDEEGGRU begrudge
buggered
BDEEGILN bleeding
BDEEGILU beguiled
BDEEGIMR begrimed
BDEEGINR breeding
breinged
BDEEGINW bedewing
BDEEGLNO belonged
BDEEHIRS Hebrides
BDEEHLNO beholden
BDEEHLOR beholder
BDEEHLSU busheled
BDEEHMOR homebred
BDEEHOOV behooved
BDEEHORT bothered
BDEEIILL elidible
BDEEIILN inedible
BDEEIKRS kerbside
BDEEILLL libelled
BDEEILLT billeted
BDEEILMR limbered
BDEEILNR rendible
BDEEILNU unedible
BDEEILNV vendible
BDEEILOR erodible
reboiled
BDEEILOS obelised
BDEEILOZ obelized
BDEEILRW bewilder
BDEEILSV bedevils
BDEEIMOS embodies
BDEEIMRT timbered
BDEEIMST bedtimes
BDEEINOS ebonised
BDEEINOT obedient
BDEEINOZ ebonized
BDEEINRS inbreeds
BDEEINST bendiest
BDEEINSZ bedizens
BDEEIRRU reburied
BDEEIRST bestride
BDEEIRSY birdseye
BDEEIRTT bittered
BDEEKNRU bunkered
debunker
BDEEKORR brokered
BDEELLOW bellowed
BDEELMNO embolden
BDEELMOR rebeldom
BDEELMRT trembled
BDEELMRU lumbered
BDEELNNO ennobled
BDEELNRS blenders
BDEELNTU unbelted
BDEELORU redouble
BDEELOSV beloveds
BDEELRUY burleyed
BDEELSST debtless
BDEEMNOT bodement
entombed
BDEEMNOW enwombed
BDEEMNRU numbered
BDEEMOSS embossed
BDEEMPRU bumpered
BDEEMSSU embussed
BDEENPRS prebends
BDEENSUV subvened
BDEEOORT rebooted
BDEEORRR borderer
BDEEORRS resorbed
BDEEORSS bedsores
BDEEORST bestrode
BDEEORSV observed
BDEEORTU outbreed
BDEEORTV obverted
BDEEOSSS obsessed
BDEEOSTT besotted
obtested
BDEEOSTW bestowed
BDEEPRRU purebred
BDEERRWY dewberry
BDEERSUW burweeds
BDEERTTU buttered
rebutted
BDEESSSU debusses
BDEFFTUU Dubuffet
BDEFIIRR firebird
BDEFIMOR biformed
BDEFINRR fernbird
BDEGHILT blighted
BDEGHIST bedights
BDEGIILN bielding
BDEGIINT betiding
debiting
BDEGILNN blending
BDEGINSU debusing
BDEGINTU debuting
BDEGIRUX Uxbridge
BDEGLMRU grumbled
BDEGLNOU bludgeon
BDEGLRSU bludgers
BDEGOOSY goodbyes
BDEGORRY dogberry
BDEHIKOS kiboshed
BDEHLSUV bushveld
BDEHMOOY homebody
BDEHOOOO boohooed
BDEHORTW Bedworth
BDEIIKLR birdlike
BDEIIKTZ kibitzed
BDEIILMR birdlime
BDEIILTY debility
BDEIIRTU Itúrbide
BDEILLMU bdellium
BDEILLOW billowed
BDEILLOX bollixed
BDEILMOS semibold
BDEILMSU sublimed

BDEILNOY	bodyline
BDEILNRS	blinders
	brindles
BDEILNRU	Dubliner
	unbridle
BDEILNRY	Brindley
BDEILNST	blindest
BDEILOOR	bloodier
BDEILOOS	bloodies
BDEILOQU	obliqued
BDEILORV	lovebird
BDEILOSS	bodiless
BDEILRRS	bridlers
BDEILRRY	lyrebird
BDEILRST	bristled
	driblets
BDEILRSU	builders
	rebuilds
BDEIMNOR	Benidorm
BDEIMNSU	nimbused
BDEIMNUU	unimbued
BDEIMORS	bromides
BDEIMORY	embryoid
BDEINOOS	nobodies
BDEINOOW	woodbine
BDEINORV	ovenbird
BDEINOSU	bedouins
BDEINRUU	unburied
BDEINSUX	subindex
BDEIOORR	broodier
BDEIORRS	broiders
	disrober
BDEIORSS	disrobes
BDEIORSV	overbids
BDEIOSSY	disobeys
BDEIOSUX	suboxide
BDEIRSSU	disburse
	subsider
BDEISSSU	subsides
BDEISSTU	subedits
BDELLOOR	bordello
BDELLORS	bedrolls
BDELLOUZ	bulldoze
BDELMNOO	Belmondo
BDELMOSY	symboled
BDELMSTU	stumbled
BDELNNUU	unbundle
BDELNOSS	boldness
BDELNOST	blondest
BDELNOTU	unbolted
BDELNRSU	blunders
	bundlers
BDELOORV	overbold
BDELORSU	boulders
	doublers
BDELORTU	troubled
BDELORUU	doublure
BDELORUY	bouldery
BDELOSTU	doublets
BDEMNNOS	bondsmen
BDEMNSSU	dumbness
BDEMOORS	bedrooms
BDEMOOSY	somebody
BDEMOOTT	bottomed
BDEMSSUU	subsumed
BDENNOTU	dubonnet
BDENNRUU	unburden
BDENOORU	eurobond
BDENOOTW	bentwood
BDENORSU	bounders
	rebounds
	suborned
BDENOTTU	buttoned
BDENRUUY	underbuy
BDENSSTU	subtends
BDEOORRS	brooders
BDEOORRW	borrowed
BDEOOTUX	outboxed
BDEOOWWW	bowwowed
BDEOPSST	bedposts
BDEOPSTU	subdepot
BDEORRSU	bordures
	suborder
BDEORRTU	obtruder
BDEORRUW	burrowed
BDEORSSU	rosebuds
BDEORSTU	doubters
	obtrudes
	redoubts
BDEORSUV	overdubs
BDERSUWY	Dewsbury
BDFFIPRU	puffbird
BDFGNOOU	fogbound
BDFIIITY	bifidity
BDFIIORS	fibroids
BDFILLLO	billfold
BDFILNOO	bloodfin
BDFIRRSU	surfbird
BDFLOTUU	doubtful
BDFORSUY	bodysurf
BDGGIINR	bridging
BDGGILNU	bludging
BDGGLOSU	goldbugs
BDGHOOUY	doughboy
BDGIIKNR	kingbird
BDGIILNN	blinding
BDGIILNR	bridling
BDGIILNU	building
BDGIINNS	bindings
BDGIIOOS	gobioids
BDGILNNO	blonding
BDGILNNU	bundling
BDGILNOO	blooding
	boodling
BDGILNOU	doubling
BDGILOOS	globoids
BDGINNOS	bondings
BDGINNOU	bounding
BDGINOOR	brooding
BDGINORS	birdsong
	songbird
BDGINOTU	doubting
BDGINSUU	subduing
BDGIRSUU	Duisburg
BDGKOOOO	Good Book
BDGLLOSU	bulldogs
BDGNRUUY	burgundy
BDGOOOSW	bogwoods
BDHIIPRW	whipbird
BDHILNRU	Brunhild
BDHILNRY	Brynhild
BDHIMOOR	rhomboid
BDHINRSU	ibn-Rushd
BDHIORST	birdshot
BDHKOORU	Dukhobor
BDHLMOTU	Humboldt
BDHOOOSY	boyhoods
BDIIINRS	brindisi
BDIIIORV	vibrioid
BDIIJOTU	Djibouti
BDIILLNW	windbill
BDIILORS	oilbirds
BDIIMRUU	rubidium
BDILLOOY	bloodily
BDILMORY	morbidly
BDILNNSU	sunblind
BDILNPRU	purblind
BDILPSUU	buildups
	upbuilds
BDILRTUY	turbidly
BDIMNORU	moribund
BDIMOSTU	misdoubt
BDINNORR	Dornbirn
BDINNRUW	windburn
BDINOOOR	Borodino
BDINOORS	bridoons
BDINORSW	snowbird
BDINRSSU	sunbirds
BDINSSTU	dustbins
BDIOORSU	boudoirs
BDIORUZZ	burdizzo
BDIOSTUY	bodysuit
BDIRSSTU	disturbs
BDKOOORW	wordbook
BDKOORWY	bodywork
BDKOOSTU	studbook
BDLLSTUU	bulldust
BDLNOOOU	doubloon
BDLNOOWW	blowdown
BDLOSTUW	Dust Bowl
BDNNOOTU	bunodont
BDNOORSU	bourdons
BDNOOSUX	soundbox
BDNOOSWW	downbows
BDNOOTUU	outbound
BDNORSUW	rubdowns
BDOOOSWX	boxwoods
BDORUWZZ	buzzword
BEEEEFLN	enfeeble
BEEEENRT	terebene
BEEEFIRS	freebies
BEEEFIST	beefiest
BEEEFLNT	Benfleet
BEEEFLST	feeblest
BEEEGIRS	besieger
BEEEGISS	besieges

BEEEGKLS geelbeks
BEEEGNRS breenges
BEEEGORS greeboes
BEEEGRRS bergeres
BEEEGRTT begetter
BEEEHISV beehives
BEEEHLWW webwheel
BEEEHNOY honeybee
BEEEHNSS shebeens
BEEEILLL libellee
BEEEILLS libelees
BEEEILLT billetee
BEEEILNS beelines
BEEEILRV believer
BEEEILSV believes
BEEEINNS Beninese
BEEEIRRZ breezier
BEEEIRST beeriest
BEEEJLSW bejewels
BEEEJLSZ jezebels
BEEEKLRY Berkeley
BEEELLRV beveller
BEEELMNS ensemble
BEEELMRS resemble
BEEELMZZ embezzle
BEEELPRS bleepers
BEEELRSV bevelers
BEEELRVY Beverley
BEEEMMRR remember
BEEERSTT besetter
BEEFFRTU buffeter
BEEFILLT lifebelt
BEEFILLX flexible
BEEFILNU unbelief
BEEFILRS belfries
BEEFINST benefits
BEEFIRST briefest
BEEFIRSU rubefies
BEEFLORU befouler
BEEFNORR freeborn
BEEFOORT freeboot
BEEGGNSU geebungs
BEEGHLRU Breughel
Brueghel
BEEGHORS Borghese
BEEGIILL eligible
BEEGIILX exigible
BEEGILLR gerbille
BEEGILNP bleeping
BEEGILNT beetling
BEEGILNV beveling
BEEGILOS obligees
BEEGILRU beguiler
BEEGILSU beguiles
BEEGIMRS begrimes
BEEGINNR beginner
BEEGINRS bigeners
breinges
BEEGINRW Weinberg
BEEGINRZ breezing
BEEGINSU beguines
BEEGINSW beeswing
BEEGLNOR Grenoble
BEEGMNOY bogeymen
BEEGMRSU submerge
BEEGNOTT begotten
BEEGNRRU Erenburg
Runeberg
BEEGNRSU sungrebe
BEEHHMOT behemoth
BEEHIKLR herblike
BEEHILMN Blenheim
BEEHIMOT boehmite
BEEHIRST herbiest
BEEHLLNT hellbent
BEEHLOOR borehole
BEEHLRST blethers
BEEHLRSU busheler
BEEHNOOP neophobe
BEEHNRRT brethren
BEEHNRVZ Brezhnev
BEEHOOSV behooves
BEEHRSST sherbets
BEEHRSSW beshrews
BEEIILNZ zibeline
BEEIIRSS iberises
BEEIJLSU jubilees
BEEIKKRS brekkies
BEEIKLTU tubelike
BEEIKLWY biweekly
BEEIKORS broekies
BEEILLLR libeller
BEEILLNO lobeline
BEEILLNU Blue Nile
BEEILLRT billeter
BEEILLTT belittle
BEEILLTU tullibee
BEEILMOS embolies
embolise
BEEILMOZ embolize
BEEILMPR periblem
BEEILMPS epiblems
BEEILNNS blennies
BEEILNRR Berliner
BEEILNRS berlines
BEEILNRY beryline
BEEILNSS sensible
BEEILNST stilbene
tensible
BEEILNSU nebulise
BEEILNUZ nebulize
BEEILOSS obelises
BEEILOSZ obelizes
BEEILOTV lovebite
BEEILRRT terrible
BEEILRSU bluesier
BEEILRYZ breezily
BEEIMRTT embitter
BEEINNSV Ben Nevis
BEEINOSS ebonises
BEEINOST betonies
BEEINOSZ ebonizes
BEEIORTV overbite
BEEIQSUZ beziques
BEEIRRSU reburies
BEEIRRSV breviers
BEEIRRTT bitterer
BEEIRSSU suberise
BEEIRSSV brevises
BEEIRSUZ suberize
BEEISSTW websites
BEEISSUU Eusebius
BEEKMOPR pembroke
BEEKNOPS bespoken
BEEKNOST betokens
steenbok
BEEKRRSS berserks
BEEKRRSU rebukers
BEELLORW bellower
rebellow
BEELMNNO noblemen
BEELMOSW embowels
BEELMRRT trembler
BEELMRRU lumberer
BEELMRST trembles
BEELNNOR ennobler
BEELNNOS ennobles
BEELNOSS boneless
noblesse
BEELNOSU bluenose
BEELNSSU blueness
BEELNTTU betelnut
BEELNTUY butylene
BEELOOST obsolete
BEELORVW overblew
BEELOSTY eyebolts
BEELRSSV verbless
BEELRTUU trueblue
BEELSSTU tubeless
BEEMNRRU renumber
BEEMOPRT obtemper
BEEMORSS embosser
BEEMORSW embowers
BEEMOSSS embosses
BEEMQSUU embusque
BEEMRSSU submerse
BEEMSSSU embusses
BEENNORS Berenson
BEENOPTY teenybop
BEENORRS enrobers
BEENORTV verboten
BEENOSST bonesets
BEENPRST besprent
BEENRSTW bestrewn
BEENRTTU brunette
BEENSSTU subteens
BEENSSUV subvenes
BEEOORRV overbore
BEEOORTT beetroot
BEEORRSU bourrees
BEEORRSV observer
BEEORRSY Rosebery
BEEORSST soberest
BEEORSSU suberose
BEEORSSV observes
obverses

BEEORSTU tuberose
BEEORSTW bestower
BEEORSWY eyebrows
BEEOSSSS obsesses
BEEQSSTU bequests
BEERRSTW brewster
BEERRTTU rebutter
BEERSSSU subseres
BEERSSTW bestrews
websters
BEERSSUV subserve
BEERSTTU burettes
BEERSTTY bystreet
BEFFLRSU bluffers
BEFFLSTU bluffest
BEFGIILL fillibeg
BEFGIILS filibegs
BEFGIINR briefing
BEFGILNU fungible
BEFGIRRU Freiburg
BEFGIRSU firebugs
BEFHILSU bluefish
BEFHINOS bonefish
BEFHIRSU bushfire
BEFILLXY flexibly
BEFILMOR forelimb
BEFILOST botflies
BEFILOSU biofuels
BEFILOUY lifebuoy
BEFILRST filberts
BEFILSSU subfiles
BEFINORS bonfires
BEFIOOST boofiest
BEFISSTU fubsiest
BEFLLLUY bellyful
BEFLMRSU fumblers
BEFLORUW furbelow
BEFNOORR forborne
BEGGIINN bingeing
BEGGIINO bogieing
BEGGINOY bogeying
BEGGINRS Ginsberg
BEGGIOST boggiest
BEGGISTU buggiest
BEGGOOOS goosegob
BEGGOORT Göteborg
BEGHIILP philibeg
BEGHIIRT Ghiberti
BEGHILRT blighter
BEGHILRU Burleigh
BEGHINOR neighbor
BEGHINOV behoving
BEGHINRT berthing
brighten
BEGHIOST gobshite
BEGHIRRT brighter
BEGHLNOU bunghole
BEGHLRUY Burghley
BEGHNOTU boughten
BEGHOSTU besought
BEGHOSUU bughouse
BEGHRRSU burghers
BEGIILLN libeling
BEGIILLY eligibly
BEGIILST bilgiest
BEGIIMNR bemiring
BEGIKNRS kerbings
BEGIKNRU rebuking
BEGILLLU bluegill
gullible
BEGILLNY bellying
BEGILLOU Gelibolu
BEGILNNU Nibelung
BEGILNNY benignly
BEGILNOW elbowing
BEGILNRT trebling
BEGILNSS blessing
glibness
BEGILNST beltings
BEGILNSU blueings
BEGILNTU Belitung
BEGILORS obligers
BEGILRST gilberts
BEGIMNOS besoming
BEGIMNOW embowing
BEGIMNRU embruing
BEGIMNSU bemusing
embusing
BEGIMOST misbegot
BEGINNNO nonbeing
BEGINNOR enrobing
ringbone
BEGINNTU Tübingen
BEGINORR reboring
BEGINORS Gisborne
sobering
BEGINRRS bringers
BEGINRRY berrying
BEGINRSW brewings
BEGINVVY bevvying
BEGKMOSS gemsboks
BEGLLOSU globules
BEGLMRRU grumbler
BEGLMRSU grumbles
BEGLNOOU Boulogne
BEGLNRSU blungers
bunglers
BEGLNRUU Lüneburg
BEGLOOST bootlegs
BEGNNRRU Nürnberg
BEGNOORU bourgeon
BEGNORRU Orenburg
BEGNORSU burgeons
BEGNORTU burgonet
BEGNORUY Burgoyne
BEGNOSTT bettongs
BEGNSSUU subgenus
BEGPRSUU superbug
BEHIISTX exhibits
BEHIKLOS blokeish
BEHIKNST bethinks
BEHIKOSS kiboshes
BEHILLOS shoebill
BEHILLTY blithely
BEHILMRW whimbrel
BEHILMST thimbles
BEHILNPY biphenyl
BEHILORR horrible
BEHILORS bolshier
BEHILOSS bolshies
BEHILRTU thurible
BEHIMNOO bonhomie
BEHIMORS bioherms
BEHINNOS shinbone
BEHINOPS hipbones
BEHINOSW wishbone
BEHINSTU Behistun
BEHIOSTU Boethius
BEHIRRST rebirths
BEHIRRSU brushier
BEHISSTU bushiest
BEHLLOOT bolthole
BEHLLOOW blowhole
BEHLLOPS bellhops
BEHLLOTW Bothwell
BEHLLPSU bellpush
BEHLMRSU humblers
BEHLMSTU humblest
BEHLORST brothels
BEHLRSSU blushers
BEHMOOSY homeboys
BEHNNOUY honeybun
BEHNRSTU burthens
BEHOORST theorbos
BEHOORSX horsebox
BEHOOSUY houseboy
BEHOPRST potherbs
BEHORRST brothers
BEHORSTT betroths
BEHORTUY Beyrouth
BEHRRSSU brushers
BEIIKRTZ kibitzer
BEIIKSTZ kibitzes
BEIILLST libelist
BEIILMMO immobile
BEIILMOS mobilise
BEIILMOZ mobilize
BEIILNRS rinsible
BEIILNTZ Leibnitz
BEIILRST trilbies
BEIILRTT libretti
BEIILSSU Sibelius
BEIILSSV visibles
BEIILSTT stilbite
BEIIMNNR renminbi
BEIINNRS brinnies
BEIINORS brionies
BEIINOST niobites
BEIINRST briniest
BEIINSTT stibnite
BEIIOPSS biopsies
BEIIORRT Robert II
BEIIOSTT biotites
BEIIRSTU Tiberius
BEIISSTU subitise
BEIISTTT bittiest

BEIISTUZ	subitize
BEIJMOSU	jumboise
BEIJMOUZ	jumboize
BEIJNORT	Tjirebon
BEIKKLNO	knoblike
BEIKLMOT	tomblike
BEIKLMOW	womblike
BEIKLNRS	blinkers
BEIKLOSS	obelisks
BEIKLOTY	kilobyte
BEIKLRUY	rubylike
BEIKLSTU	bulkiest
BEIKNOST	steinbok
BEIKNRRY	inkberry
BEIKNRSS	briskens
BEIKOORT	brookite
BEIKOSST	boskiest
BEIKRSST	briskest
	briskets
BEILLMRY	limberly
BEILLMSS	limbless
BEILLNRU	Lilburne
BEILLNTU	bulletin
BEILLORS	brollies
BEILLOSU	libelous
BEILLOSX	bollixes
BEILMMOS	embolism
BEILMNOR	bromelin
BEILMNOU	nobelium
BEILMNRU	unlimber
BEILMNST	nimblest
BEILMOOR	bloomier
BEILMORS	embroils
BEILMRSS	brimless
BEILMRST	timbrels
BEILMSSU	sublimes
BEILNNTU	buntline
BEILNOPS	bonspiel
BEILNOSW	bowlines
BEILNOVY	bovinely
BEILNSSY	sensibly
BEILNSTY	tensibly
BEILNSTZ	blintzes
BEILOORV	boilover
BEILOPPW	blowpipe
BEILOPRS	preboils
BEILOPSS	possible
BEILOQSU	obliques
BEILORRS	broilers
BEILORST	strobile
BEILORSW	blowsier
BEILORTT	libretto
BEILORWZ	blowzier
BEILOSTW	blowiest
BEILPRTV	blipvert
BEILRRRU	blurrier
BEILRRTT	brittler
BEILRRTY	terribly
BEILRSST	blisters
	bristles
BEILRSTT	brittles
	triblets
BEILRSTU	burliest
	subtiler
BEILRSTY	blistery
BEILRTTY	bitterly
BEILSTTU	bluetits
	subtitle
BEIMMRRS	brimmers
BEIMNSSU	nimbuses
BEIMNSTU	bitumens
BEIMOORS	ribosome
BEIMORTU	Umberto I
BEIMORTY	biometry
BEIMORYZ	ribozyme
BEIMPSTU	bumpiest
BEIMRSTU	resubmit
BEIMSSTU	subitems
BEINNOSS	benisons
	boniness
BEINNOST	bonniest
BEINNOSZ	benzoins
BEINOOST	eobionts
BEINOQRU	Quiberon
BEINORSW	brownies
BEINORSY	bryonies
BEINORTZ	bronzite
BEINOSTT	bottines
BEINOSTU	bounties
BEINRSTT	bitterns
BEINRSTU	tribunes
	turbines
BEINSSSU	business
BEIOOPST	biotopes
BEIOORST	robotise
BEIOORTZ	robotize
BEIOOSTZ	booziest
BEIOPSTY	biotypes
BEIOQTUU	boutique
BEIORRST	orbiters
BEIORSTT	bortiest
BEIORSTY	sobriety
BEIORSUV	bouviers
BEIOSSST	bossiest
BEIOSSTY	boysiest
BEIQRSTU	briquets
BEIRRSSU	bruisers
BEIRRSTU	burriest
BEIRSSTU	bustiers
BEIRSTTU	tributes
BEISSTTU	bustiest
BEJLMRSU	jumblers
BEJORTTU	turbojet
BEKLNORY	brokenly
BEKLNTTU	Blunkett
BEKLOORT	brooklet
BEKLOOST	Belostok
	booklets
BEKLRSSU	burlesks
BEKNNORU	unbroken
BEKNOOOT	notebook
BEKNOORR	Brookner
BEKOOORV	overbook
BEKOOTTX	textbook
BELLLLPU	bellpull
BELLMMRU	Brummell
BELLNORW	wellborn
BELLNOSU	bullnose
BELLNPSU	bullpens
BELLOOSU	lobulose
BELLOPTY	potbelly
BELLORTW	bellwort
BELMMRSU	mumblers
BELMNOSU	nelumbos
BELMOORS	bloomers
BELMOORY	bloomery
BELMOPRS	problems
BELMORST	temblors
BELMORSY	somberly
	sombrely
BELMPRSU	plumbers
BELMPRUY	plumbery
BELMRRSU	rumblers
BELMRRUY	mulberry
BELMRSSU	slumbers
BELMRSTU	stumbler
	tumblers
	tumbrels
BELMSSTU	stumbles
BELNOOSY	boloneys
BELNOSUU	nebulous
BELNSTTU	bluntest
BELNSTUU	unsubtle
BELOOOSX	loosebox
BELOOPRS	bloopers
BELOOPRT	boltrope
BELOORVW	overblow
BELOOSST	bootless
BELOOTUV	obvolute
BELORRTU	troubler
BELORSST	bolsters
	lobsters
BELORSTT	blotters
	bottlers
BELORSTU	boulters
	troubles
BELOSTUY	obtusely
BELPRSUY	superbly
BELRSSSU	Brussels
BELRSSTU	blusters
	bustlers
BELRSSUU	subrules
BELRSTUY	blustery
BELSSTTU	subtlest
BELSTTUY	subtlety
BEMMOOSS	embosoms
BEMNNSSU	numbness
BEMNOORT	trombone
BEMOORRS	sombrero
BEMORSST	mobsters
BEMRSSTU	bumsters
BEMSSSUU	subsumes
BENNNOTU	unbonnet
BENNOORS	Sorbonne
BENNOPYY	pennyboy
BENOORSU	burnoose

BENORRSU	suborner
BENORRTU	trueborn
BENORSTU	burstone
	rubstone
BENORSTW	brownest
BENORSUU	burnouse
BENORTTU	buttoner
	rebutton
BENOSSWY	newsboys
BENRSTUY	subentry
BENSSSUY	busyness
BEOOORTV	overboot
BEOORRRW	borrower
BEOORSST	boosters
BEOORSTY	botryose
BEOOSTUX	outboxes
BEOPRRSV	proverbs
BEOQSSTU	bosquets
BEOQSTUU	bouquets
BEORRRUW	burrower
BEORRSSW	browsers
BEORSTUU	tuberous
BEORSUVY	overbusy
	overbuys
BEPRRSTU	perturbs
BEPSSTUY	subtypes
BERRSSTU	bursters
BERSSTTU	buttress
BERSSTUV	subverts
BESSSSUY	byssuses
BFFFLMUU	bumfluff
BFFGILNU	bluffing
BFFHORSU	brushoff
BFFLOOSW	blowoffs
BFFLOTUU	outbluff
BFFNOOSU	buffoons
BFFNOSUX	snuffbox
BFGHINTU	bunfight
BFGILMNU	fumbling
BFGIORRU	Fribourg
BFGIORST	frogbits
BFGLLORU	bullfrog
BFHIILLS	billfish
BFHILOST	fishbolt
BFHILOSW	blowfish
	fishbowl
BFHIMNSU	numbfish
BFHLLSUU	blushful
BFIIORSS	fibrosis
BFILLMRU	brimfull
BFILLSSU	blissful
BFILOSTY	liftboys
BFIMORTU	tubiform
BFKLOOSY	flybooks
BFLLNOWY	flyblown
BFLLOSUW	bowlfuls
BFLLOSWY	flyblows
BFLOORSU	subfloor
BFOOOSTY	footboys
BGGGILNO	boggling
BGGHIINT	bighting
BGGIILNO	obliging
BGGIILNY	gibingly
BGGIINNR	bringing
BGGILNNU	blunging
	bungling
BGGILNRU	burgling
BGGINRUZ	Ginzburg
BGHHINOR	highborn
BGHHIORW	highbrow
BGHHIOSY	highboys
BGHIINRT	birthing
BGHILMNU	humbling
BGHILNSU	blushing
BGHILRTY	brightly
BGHIMNTU	thumbing
BGHIMOTU	bigmouth
BGHINORS	bighorns
BGHINORT	Brighton
BGHINRSU	brushing
BGHIPSSU	bushpigs
BGHMORSU	homburgs
BGHOORSU	boroughs
BGIIJLNY	jibingly
BGIIKLNN	blinking
BGIIKNRS	brisking
BGIILLNS	billings
BGIILMNW	wimbling
BGIILNOR	broiling
BGIILNOS	boilings
BGIILNPP	blipping
BGIILNRS	brisling
BGIILNSS	siblings
BGIILNTY	bitingly
BGIILNTZ	blitzing
BGIIMMNR	brimming
BGIIMNRU	imbruing
BGIINORT	orbiting
BGIINRSU	bruising
BGIINRTU	bruiting
BGIJLMNU	jumbling
BGIJNORU	objuring
BGIJOSUU	bijugous
BGIKLNOT	kingbolt
BGIKNNOS	bonkings
BGIKNNOU	bunkoing
BGIKNNOY	Nykøbing
BGIKNOOR	brooking
BGIKNOOS	bookings
BGIKNSTU	stinkbug
BGILLLUY	gullibly
BGILLNOU	globulin
BGILLNRU	bullring
BGILLNUY	bullying
BGILMMNU	mumbling
BGILMNOO	blooming
BGILMNPU	plumbing
BGILMNRU	rumbling
BGILMNTU	tumbling
BGILMORU	Limbourg
BGILMOSU	gumboils
BGILMOTU	gumbotil
BGILNNTU	blunting
BGILNORT	ringbolt
BGILNORY	boringly
BGILNOSU	blousing
BGILNOTT	blotting
	bottling
BGILNOTU	boulting
BGILNRRU	blurring
BGILNRTU	blurting
BGILNSTU	bustling
BGILOORS	obligors
BGIMNOOR	brooming
BGIMNOOS	bosoming
BGIMNORW	ringwomb
BGINNORW	browning
BGINNORZ	bronzing
BGINNRSU	burnings
BGINOOST	boosting
BGINORST	strobing
BGINORSW	browsing
BGINRSTU	bursting
BGINSUZZ	buzzings
BGKLOOOS	logbooks
BGKORSSY	grysboks
BGLNOOSW	longbows
BGLNOSUW	blowguns
BGLOORYY	bryology
BGMNOOOR	gombroon
BGMOOSTU	gumboots
BGOPRSUU	subgroup
BGRRUUWZ	Würzburg
BHIIINST	inhibits
BHIIOPRT	prohibit
BHIIPSSS	sibships
BHIKLLOO	billhook
BHILLNOR	hornbill
BHILLPUW	bullwhip
BHILLSTU	bullshit
BHILORRY	horribly
BHILOSTU	holibuts
BHILOSYY	boyishly
BHIMNORT	thrombin
BHIMOPRS	bimorphs
BHINORSW	brownish
BHINORTU	Thonburi
BHIOOPRT	biotroph
BHISSTTU	bushtits
BHKMNOOY	hymn book
	hymnbook
BHKNOOOR	hornbook
BHLLNORU	bullhorn
BHLMNOOR	Bornholm
BHLOOOTT	tolbooth
BHMMOTTU	Tom Thumb
BHMNTTUU	thumbnut
BHMORSTU	thrombus
BHNOOOST	bosthoon
BHNOORTX	boxthorn
BHOOSSTW	bowshots
BHPRSSUU	brushups
BIIKMRSS	Simbirsk
BIILLMOR	morbilli
BIILLNOS	billions
BIILLNOT	Billiton

BIILLSTW	twibills
BIILMOTY	mobility
BIILNOOV	oblivion
BIILNORU	urobilin
BIILNOTY	nobility
BIILNTUY	nubility
BIILORST	strobili
BIILOSSY	biolysis
BIILSTTW	witblits
BIIMMNSY	nimbyism
BIIMMOSZ	zombiism
BIIMNOSU	niobiums
BIIMPRSS	biprisms
BIIMSSTU	stibiums
BIIQTUUY	ubiquity
BIIRSSTU	bursitis
BIJNOSSU	subjoins
BIKLNOST	inkblots
BIKLNOSY	linkboys
BIKMNOOS	boomkins
BIKMNPSU	bumpkins
BIKMTTUU	Timbuktu
BIKOOUUZ	bouzouki
BILLNOOU	bouillon
BILLOSWY	blowsily
BILLOWYZ	blowzily
BILLRSWY	wrybills
BILLSTUU	Tibullus
BILMMPSU	plumbism
BILMNORS	nombrils
BILMOSTU	botulism
BILMRSTU	tumbrils
BILNOSTU	botulins
BILOORST	sorbitol
BILOORTT	borlotti
BILOPSSY	possibly
BILOPSUY	Polybius
BILORSST	bristols
BILOSSSU	subsoils
BILSTTUY	subtilty
BIMNOSTY	symbiont
BIMNRRUU	muirburn
BIMNRUUV	viburnum
BIMOORST	robotism
BINNOORS	Robinson
BINNOORZ	Bronzino
BINOOPRT	Bonporti
BINORSTW	Brownist
BINSSTUU	subunits
BIOPRSTW	bowsprit
BIORRSTU	burritos
BIORSSTT	bistorts
BIORSTTY	botrytis
BIORSTUY	bistoury
BISSSSTU	subsists
BISSTUUU	busuutis
BJNNOORS	Bjørnson
BKKOOORW	workbook
BKLNOORY	Brooklyn
BKMOOORW	bookworm
BKNOOSTW	bowknots
BLLLLOOY	loblolly
BLLMOORW	bollworm
BLMOOORS	Lombroso
BLMOOOST	tombolos
BLMOOOTY	lobotomy
BLMOORSW	lobworms
BLMOOSSS	blossoms
BLMOOSSY	blossomy
BLMOPSUU	plumbous
BLNOOSSU	blousons
BLOOPSWY	plowboys
BLOORSWW	lowbrows
BLOOSSTY	slyboots
BLOOSTUW	blowouts
BLOPSSTU	subplots
BLORSTUY	robustly
BLOSTUUU	tubulous
BMNOOORW	monobrow
BMNOOOTW	boomtown
BMNOORRU	moorburn
BMNOOSSU	unbosoms
BMNORTUW	mowburnt
BMOOORSX	boxrooms
BMOORSSU	sombrous
BMOORSTU	motorbus
BMOORTTY	bottomry
BNNORTUW	nutbrown
BNNOTTUU	unbutton
BNNRSTUU	sunburnt
BNOOOSUY	sonobuoy
BNOORTUW	brownout
BNORSTUU	burnouts
BNRSSTUU	sunburst
BOOPRSSU	Bosporus
BOOPSSTY	postboys
BORSTTUU	outburst
CCCDIILY	dicyclic
CCCEEILT	eclectic
CCCEGOSY	coccyges
CCCEILNY	encyclic
CCCHIORY	chiccory
CCCIINSU	succinic
CCCILNOY	cyclonic
CCCINSTU	succinct
CCCKOORW	cockcrow
CCCNOOST	concocts
CCDDEENO	conceded
CCDDEEOT	decocted
CCDDELOU	occluded
CCDDENOU	conduced
CCDEEENR	credence
CCDEEHLN	clenched
CCDEEIOP	codpiece
CCDEEIOS	ecocides
CCDEEKOR	cockered
CCDEEKOY	cockeyed
CCDEELRY	recycled
CCDEENOR	conceder
CCDEENOS	concedes
CCDEESSU	succeeds
CCDEHHRU	churched
CCDEHILN	clinched
CCDEHIPU	hiccuped
CCDEHKLU	chuckled
CCDEHLTU	clutched
	declutch
CCDEHNRU	crunched
CCDEHOOT	cootched
CCDEHORS	scorched
CCDEHORT	crotched
CCDEHORU	crouched
CCDEHOST	scotched
CCDEHRTU	crutched
CCDEHSTU	scutched
CCDEIILO	cleidoic
CCDEIINO	coincide
CCDEINOR	corniced
CCDEINOT	occident
CCDEIOPP	coppiced
CCDEIOPU	occupied
CCDEKOOU	cuckooed
CCDELNOU	conclude
CCDELOSU	occludes
CCDELOTU	occulted
CCDENOOO	cocooned
CCDENORU	conducer
CCDENOSU	conduces
CCDEORRU	occurred
CCDEORSU	succored
CCDEOSTU	stuccoed
CCDHIILO	cichloid
CCDHIILS	cichlids
CCDHIIOR	dichroic
CCDHIIOT	dichotic
CCDHINOO	conchoid
CCDIILOS	codicils
CCDIILSU	culicids
CCDIINOS	scincoid
CCDIIORS	cricoids
CCDIIORT	dicrotic
CCDILOSY	cycloids
CCDKLOSU	cuckolds
CCDKOOOW	woodcock
CCDNOORS	concords
CCDNOSTU	conducts
CCEEGINR	recceing
CCEEHKNS	schnecke
CCEEHKPR	precheck
CCEEHKRS	checkers
	rechecks
CCEEHLNS	clenches
CCEEHMOO	Ecce Homo
CCEEHORS	ecorches
CCEEHRSY	screechy
CCEEIILS	cicelies
CCEEIKLR	cleckier
CCEEILNR	encircle
CCEEILNS	licences
CCEEILNT	elenctic
CCEEILPY	epicycle
CCEEILRT	electric
CCEEIMNU	ecumenic
CCEEINOR	cicerone
CCEEINOV	conceive
CCEEINSS	sciences

CCEEIORV coercive
CCEEIRSS cercises
CCEEIRSV cervices
crevices
CCEEITTU eutectic
CCEEKLOR cockerel
CCEEKNRW crewneck
CCEEKOSY cockeyes
CCEELMNY clemency
CCEELOSS scoleces
CCEELRSY recycles
CCEEMMNO commence
CCEEMMOR commerce
CCEENNOS ensconce
CCEENORT concrete
CCEENRST crescent
CCEEORRS coercers
CCEFFHKO checkoff
CCEFHRSU curchefs
CCEFIIPS specific
CCEFIRRU crucifer
CCEFLLOU floccule
CCEFLOOS floccose
CCEFNOST confects
CCEGHIKN checking
CCEGIKLN clecking
CCEGILRY glyceric
CCEGINNO congenic
CCEGINOR coercing
CCEHHINS chinches
CCEHHRSU churches
CCEHIIMR chimeric
CCEHIIMS ischemic
CCEHIINZ zecchini
CCEHIKNS chickens
CCEHIKSU chuckies
CCEHILNR clincher
CCEHILNS clinches
CCEHILOR choleric
CCEHILOY choicely
CCEHILSU culchies
CCEHINOR corniche
enchoric
CCEHINOS conchies
CCEHINOZ zecchino
CCEHINRU crunchie
CCEHINST technics
CCEHIORT ricochet
CCEHIOST choicest
CCEHKLRU chuckler
CCEHKLSU chuckles
CCEHKORW checkrow
CCEHKOTU checkout
CCEHKPSU checkups
CCEHLMOR cromlech
CCEHLRSU cleruchs
CCEHLRUY cleruchy
CCEHLSTU clutches
CCEHNRSU crunches
CCEHOOST cootches
CCEHORRS scorcher
CCEHORSS scorches
CCEHORST crochets
crotches
CCEHORSU couchers
crouches
CCEHORTT crotchet
CCEHOSST scotches
CCEHRSTU crutches
scutcher
CCEHRTUY cutchery
CCEHSSTU scutches
CCEIIKLN nickelic
CCEIILNT enclitic
CCEIILOR licorice
CCEIILPT ecliptic
CCEIILST scilicet
CCEIILTU leucitic
CCEIINNO conicine
CCEIINOR ciceroni
CCEIINTU cicutine
CCEIKLRS clickers
CCEIKOST cockiest
CCEIKRST crickets
CCEILMOO coelomic
CCEILMOP complice
CCEILNUY unicycle
CCEILOSS scolices
CCEILRRS circlers
CCEILRRU curricle
CCEILRST circlets
CCEILRSY cresylic
CCEILRTY tricycle
CCEILRUU curlicue
CCEILSTU cuticles
CCEIMNOO economic
CCEIMOST cosmetic
CCEIMRRU mercuric
CCEIMRUV cervicum
CCEINNOV convince
CCEINOOR coercion
CCEINORS cornices
croceins
CCEINORT concerti
necrotic
CCEINOST conceits
CCEINOTT tectonic
CCEINPRT precinct
CCEINRTU cincture
CCEINSZZ Szczecin
CCEIOORT crocoite
CCEIOPPS coppices
CCEIOPRU occupier
CCEIOPSU occupies
CCEIOPTY ecotypic
CCEIORST cortices
CCEIPSST sceptics
CCEIPSUV Vespucci
CCEIRSSU circuses
CCEKLORS clockers
CCEKNOSY cockneys
CCEKOPST petcocks
CCEKORRY crockery
CCEKORST crockets
CCEKORSU cocksure
CCEKORTT Crockett
CCELLOST collects
CCELMOPT complect
CCELNOSY cyclones
CCELOPSY cyclopes
CCELOSSY cycloses
CCENNORS concerns
CCENNOST concents
connects
CCENOORT concerto
CCENOPST concepts
CCENORST concerts
CCENORTY cornetcy
CCENRRUY currency
CCEOOSTT cocottes
CCEOPRUY reoccupy
CCEORRST corrects
CCEORRSU reoccurs
succorer
CCEORSSU crocuses
CCEORSTU stuccoer
CCEOSSTU stuccoes
CCESSSUU cuscuses
CCFIIRUX crucifix
CCFIKNOY cocknify
CCFILLOU flocculi
CCFILNOT conflict
CCFKLOOT cockloft
CCGHHIOU hiccough
CCGHIINN cinching
CCGHIKNO chocking
CCGHIKNU chucking
CCGHINOU couching
CCGHINTW cwtching
CCGIIKLN clicking
CCGIIKNR cricking
CCGIILNR circling
CCGIKLNO clocking
cockling
CCGIKLNU clucking
CCGIKNOR crocking
CCGILLOY glycolic
CCGILOSU glucosic
CCGINNOS sconcing
CCGINOTW twoccing
CCGKOORS gorcocks
CCHHIITY ichthyic
CCHHINOT chthonic
CCHHINOU Chin-Chou
CCHHLRUY churchly
CCHHNRUU unchurch
CCHHOOWW chowchow
CCHIINUZ zucchini
CCHIIORT orchitic
CCHINORT Crichton
CCHIPSSY psychics
CCHKMSSU schmucks
CCHKOOST cockshot
CCIILPRS circlips
CCIIMNSY cynicism
CCIINORZ zirconic

CCIIRSTU circuits
CCIIRTUY circuity
CCIKKLOP picklock
CCIKKOTT ticktock
CCIKLOSW cowlicks
CCIKOPST cockpits
CCILNOOS colonics
CCILNOSU councils
CCILOOPS piccolos
CCILORUU curculio
CCILOSSY cyclosis
CCILSSTY cyclists
CCINOORT crotonic
CCINOPSY syncopic
CCINORSY cryonics
CCINOSTV convicts
CCIOOPST scotopic
CCIOORSS siroccos
CCIOOTXY oxytocic
CCIOPSTU occiputs
CCJNNOTU conjunct
CCKMMORU crummock
CCKMOOOR moorcock
CCKNORTU turncock
CCKOOPST stopcock
CCKOPRSU cockspur
CCLLOTUY occultly
CCNOOPSU puccoons
CCNOOSTU coconuts
CCOOSSUU couscous
CCOOTTUU tucotuco
CCORSSTU crosscut
CCORSSUU succours
CCTTUUUU tucutucu
CDDDEETU deducted
CDDDIIOY diddicoy
CDDEEEEX exceeded
CDDEEEFT defected
CDDEEEIV deceived
CDDEEEJT dejected
CDDEEENR decerned
CDDEEENT decedent
CDDEEEPR preceded
CDDEEETT detected
CDDEEFOR deforced
CDDEEGLU cudgeled
CDDEEHIS dehisced
CDDEEHIT cheddite
CDDEEHNR drenched
CDDEEIIS deicides
CDDEEIKR dickered
CDDEEILN declined
CDDEEINR cindered
CDDEEIOT coedited
CDDEEIOV devoiced
CDDEEIPT depicted
CDDEEIRS deciders
descried
CDDEEIRT credited
directed
CDDEEKNU undecked
CDDEEKOR redocked
CDDEEKOT docketed
CDDEEKUW duckweed
CDDEELPU decupled
CDDEELSU secluded
CDDEELUX excluded
CDDEELUY deucedly
CDDEENOS seconded
CDDEENSS descends
CDDEEORR recorded
CDDEEORS decoders
CDDEERUV decurved
CDDEESUW cudweeds
CDDEFIIO codified
CDDEFINO confided
CDDEGIIN deciding
CDDEGINO decoding
CDDEGINU deducing
CDDEHIRT Redditch
CDDEHISU chuddies
CDDEHRSU chudders
CDDEIINT indicted
CDDEILLO collided
CDDEILNU included
CDDEILOR cloddier
CDDEINTU inducted
CDDEIORV divorced
CDDEIRRU cruddier
CDDELLOU colluded
CDDELNOO condoled
CDDELORS coddlers
CDDENNOO condoned
CDDENOOR cordoned
CDDEOORR corroded
CDDEOORT doctored
CDDEOORW codeword
CDDEOPRU produced
CDDGHILO godchild
CDDGILNO coddling
CDDGILNU cuddling
CDDGINSU scudding
CDDHHISU shidduch
CDDHIIRY dihydric
CDDHILOS cloddish
CDDIIKNS niddicks
CDDIIOSS discoids
CDDIIOSY didicoys
CDDIISTY dytiscid
CDDIKOPS piddocks
CDDIORSS discords
CDDKOPSU puddocks
CDDKORSU ruddocks
CDDOOORW cordwood
CDEEEERX exceeder
CDEEEFFT effected
CDEEEFNS defences
CDEEEHNS Enschede
CDEEEHOR reechoed
CDEEEHSW eschewed
CDEEEINV evidence
CDEEEIRV deceiver
received
CDEEEISV deceives
CDEEEJRT rejected
CDEEELLX excelled
CDEEELST deselect
selected
CDEEEMNT cemented
CDEEENOS secondee
CDEEENRS screened
secerned
CDEEENRT centered
CDEEEPRS precedes
CDEEEPTX expected
CDEEERRS decreers
CDEEERSS recessed
seceders
CDEEERST decreets
resected
screeted
secreted
CDEEERTT detecter
CDEEERTX excreted
CDEEESTX exsected
CDEEETUX executed
CDEEFHLN flenched
CDEEFHLT fletched
CDEEFIIL icefield
CDEEFIIS edifices
CDEEFIIT feticide
CDEEFINT infected
CDEEFKLR freckled
CDEEFKOR foredeck
CDEEFLST deflects
CDEEFNOR enforced
CDEEFORS deforces
CDEEFORT defector
CDEEGIIR regicide
CDEEGINO genocide
CDEEGINR receding
CDEEGINS seceding
CDEEGIOS geodesic
CDEEGIOT geodetic
CDEEGIRU cudgerie
CDEEGIRZ grecized
CDEEGKST gedeckts
CDEEHIKL helideck
CDEEHILN lichened
CDEEHILS chiseled
CDEEHINR enriched
CDEEHIPR ciphered
decipher
CDEEHISS dehisces
CDEEHKST sketched
CDEEHLPU pleuched
CDEEHLSU schedule
CDEEHNQU quenched
CDEEHNRR drencher
CDEEHNRS drenches
CDEEHNRT trenched
CDEEHNRW wrenched
CDEEHORS coshered
CDEEHORT hectored
tochered
CDEEHPRY cyphered

CDEEHRTW	wretched
CDEEIILT	elicited
CDEEIIMN	medicine
CDEEIIMP	epidemic
CDEEIINT	indictee
CDEEIIRT	dieretic
CDEEIISV	decisive
CDEEIITT	dietetic
CDEEIJNT	injected
CDEEIJOR	rejoiced
CDEEIKLN	nickeled
CDEEIKNR	nickered
CDEEIKNS	sickened
CDEEIKPT	picketed
CDEEIKRW	wickeder
CDEEIKTT	ticketed
CDEEILNP	penciled
CDEEILNR	decliner
	reclined
CDEEILNS	declines
	licensed
	silenced
CDEEILNT	denticle
CDEEILNV	Cliveden
CDEEILOR	recoiled
CDEEILPS	eclipsed
	pedicels
	pedicles
CDEEILRT	derelict
CDEEILSU	Seleucid
CDEEIMNR	endermic
CDEEIMOR	mediocre
CDEEIMOS	comedies
CDEEIMPR	premedic
CDEEIMRV	decemvir
CDEEINNS	incensed
CDEEINNT	indecent
CDEEINOR	recoined
CDEEINPT	incepted
CDEEINRU	reinduce
CDEEINTU	inductee
CDEEIOPR	recopied
CDEEIORV	divorcee
	revoiced
CDEEIOSS	dioceses
CDEEIOSV	devoices
CDEEIPRR	repriced
CDEEIPRS	precised
CDEEIPRT	decrepit
	depicter
CDEEIPRU	pedicure
CDEEIPST	pectised
CDEEIPTZ	pectized
CDEEIRRS	decriers
	descrier
CDEEIRRT	redirect
CDEEIRSS	descries
CDEEIRST	discreet
	discrete
CDEEIRSU	decuries
CDEEIRSV	serviced
CDEEIRSY	Criseyde
CDEEIRUY	Eurydice
CDEEITUV	eductive
CDEEJKOY	jockeyed
CDEEKLPS	speckled
CDEEKNOR	reckoned
CDEEKNRS	rednecks
CDEEKOPT	pocketed
CDEEKORT	rocketed
CDEEKORW	rockweed
CDEEKOST	socketed
CDEEKPRU	puckered
CDEEKRSU	suckered
CDEEKRTU	tuckered
CDEELLOT	colleted
CDEELLPU	cupelled
CDEELMOW	welcomed
CDEELNOS	enclosed
CDEELNPU	peduncle
CDEELNTY	decently
CDEELOOW	locoweed
CDEELOPU	decouple
CDEELOST	closeted
CDEELOTU	elocuted
CDEELPRU	preclude
CDEELPSU	decuples
CDEELRTU	lectured
	relucted
CDEELRUX	excluder
CDEELSSU	secludes
CDEELSUX	excludes
CDEEMOPR	compered
CDEEMOPT	competed
CDEEMORT	ectoderm
CDEEMRTU	Decretum
CDEENNOS	condense
CDEENNOU	denounce
	enounced
CDEENNOV	convened
CDEENNPY	pendency
CDEENNTY	tendency
CDEENORR	cornered
CDEENORS	censored
	encoders
	necrosed
	seconder
CDEENOSY	ecdysone
CDEENOTX	coextend
CDEENOVX	convexed
CDEENOVY	conveyed
CDEENPRU	prudence
CDEENRSU	censured
CDEENRUV	verecund
CDEENSST	descents
CDEENSTY	encysted
CDEEOOPR	coopered
CDEEOOTV	dovecote
CDEEOPPR	coppered
CDEEOPRS	proceeds
CDEEOPRU	recouped
CDEEORRR	recorder
	rerecord
CDEEORST	corseted
	escorted
CDEEORSV	coversed
CDEEORSW	escrowed
CDEEORSY	decoyers
CDEEORTT	cottered
	detector
CDEEORTV	vectored
CDEEOSST	cestodes
	cosseted
CDEEPRST	sceptred
CDEERRRU	recurred
CDEERRSU	reducers
CDEERRUV	recurved
CDEERSSU	seducers
CDEERTTU	curetted
CDEERTUV	curveted
CDEFFISU	sufficed
CDEFFLSU	scuffled
CDEFHILN	flinched
CDEFHILT	flitched
CDEFIIIL	filicide
CDEFIIIT	citified
CDEFIIOR	codifier
CDEFIIOS	codifies
CDEFIIST	deficits
CDEFIITY	cityfied
CDEFILOS	Scofield
CDEFINNO	confined
CDEFINNU	infecund
CDEFINOR	confider
CDEFINOS	confides
CDEFIORY	recodify
CDEFKORS	defrocks
CDEFLNOU	flounced
CDEFLORY	forcedly
CDEFNORU	unforced
CDEFNOSU	confused
CDEFNOTU	confuted
CDEFOSSU	focussed
CDEGHIOR	Goderich
CDEGHORU	grouched
CDEGIILP	diplegic
CDEGIINX	exciding
CDEGIKNO	decoking
CDEGIKSW	Sedgwick
CDEGILOO	Coolidge
CDEGINNO	encoding
CDEGINNS	scending
CDEGINOS	cognised
CDEGINOY	decoying
	gynecoid
CDEGINOZ	cognized
CDEGINRU	reducing
CDEGINRY	decrying
CDEGINSU	seducing
CDEGINSY	dysgenic
CDEGORSU	scourged
	scrouged
CDEHHNOO	honchoed
CDEHIILO	helicoid
CDEHIILS	ceilidhs
CDEHIIMO	homicide

CDEHIINO echinoid
CDEHIIRT Dietrich
CDEHIIVV chivvied
CDEHIKRW herdwick
CDEHIKST skitched
CDEHILNR children
CDEHILOR chloride
CDEHILOS cheloids
CDEHILRS Childers
CDEHILRT eldritch
CDEHIMOT methodic
CDEHIMRS smirched
CDEHINOS hedonics
CDEHINST snitched
CDEHIOSW cowhides
CDEHIOTY theodicy
CDEHIRST ditchers
CDEHISTT stitched
CDEHISTW switched
CDEHITTW twitched
CDEHKLSU shelduck
CDEHKSUY heyducks
CDEHLOOS deschool
schooled
CDEHLORT chortled
CDEHLOSU slouched
CDEHMNTU dutchmen
CDEHMOOS smooched
CDEHMSTU smutched
CDEHNOOP chenopod
CDEHNRSU chunders
CDEHOOSS scooshed
CDEHORRS Schröder
CDEHORSU chorused
CDEHORSW chowders
cowherds
CDEHOSSU hocussed
CDEHSSSU schussed
CDEIIILS silicide
CDEIIIMT miticide
CDEIIIOS idiocies
CDEIIKKS sidekick
CDEIIKMM mimicked
CDEIIKST dickiest
stickied
CDEIILMM dilemmic
CDEIILMO domicile
CDEIILNN inclined
CDEIILNO indocile
CDEIILOT idiolect
CDEIILPS disciple
CDEIILRU ridicule
CDEIIMRT dimetric
CDEIINNT incident
CDEIINOS decision
CDEIINOV invoiced
CDEIINRT indicter
indirect
CDEIINTY cytidine
CDEIIOPR periodic
CDEIIOPS episodic
CDEIIOPT epidotic
CDEIIOSU diecious
CDEIIPRR cirriped
CDEIIRTU diuretic
CDEIISSU suicides
CDEIJSST disjects
CDEIKLNR crinkled
CDEIKLOR cordlike
CDEIKLPR prickled
CDEIKLRT trickled
CDEIKLRU luderick
CDEIKLST stickled
CDEIKLWY wickedly
CDEIKNPU unpicked
CDEIKOST diestock
CDEIKRRS derricks
CDEIKSTU duckiest
CDEILLOR collider
CDEILLOS collides
CDEILLOU lodicule
CDEILLOY docilely
CDEILLPU pellucid
CDEILMOP compiled
complied
CDEILMOY myceloid
CDEILMPR crimpled
CDEILMRU dulcimer
CDEILNOS inclosed
CDEILNOU uncoiled
CDEILNRY cylinder
CDEILNSU includes
nuclides
CDEILOOW woodlice
CDEILOPU clupeoid
CDEILORS scleroid
CDEILORU cloudier
CDEILOSS disclose
CDEILPPR crippled
CDEILPSU clupeids
CDEILRTY directly
CDEILSXY dyslexic
CDEIMMOT decommit
CDEIMMOX commixed
CDEIMORT morticed
CDEIMOST Docetism
domestic
CDEIMPRS scrimped
CDEINNOU uncoined
CDEINNOV connived
CDEINOOZ endozoic
CDEINORS consider
CDEINORT centroid
doctrine
CDEINORU decurion
CDEINOTU eduction
CDEINOUV unvoiced
CDEINPRS prescind
CDEINPRU unpriced
CDEINPSY dyspneic
CDEINRRU incurred
CDEINRSS discerns
rescinds
CDEINRSU inducers
CDEINRUV incurved
CDEINSSX exscinds
CDEINSTY syndetic
CDEIOORS corodies
CDEIOORT coeditor
CDEIOPRS percoids
CDEIOPRT depictor
CDEIOPST despotic
CDEIOPTY copyedit
CDEIORRT creditor
director
CDEIORRV codriver
divorcer
CDEIORST cordites
CDEIORSV discover
divorces
CDEIORTU outcried
CDEIOSST scodiest
CDEIPRST predicts
scripted
CDEIPRTU pictured
CDEIRRSU scurried
CDEIRSTU crudites
curtsied
CDEIRSTV verdicts
CDEISSST dissects
CDEISSSU discuses
CDEJNORU conjured
CDEKKLNU knuckled
CDEKLMOR clerkdom
CDEKLNOU unlocked
CDEKLRTU truckled
CDEKNOOU uncooked
CDEKNOOV convoked
CDEKNORU uncorked
CDEKNTUU untucked
CDEKOPSY copydesk
CDEKOSST destocks
CDELLNOU Culloden
CDELLOOP clodpole
CDELLORS scrolled
CDELLORU colluder
CDELLOSU colludes
CDELLOTU cloudlet
CDELLTUY dulcetly
CDELMNOO monocled
CDELMNOU columned
CDELMPRU crumpled
CDELNOOR condoler
CDELNOOS condoles
consoled
CDELNOSS coldness
CDELNOSU unclosed
CDELNOSY condyles
secondly
CDELNRUU uncurled
CDELNSUY secundly
CDELOORU coloured
decolour
CDELOPTU octupled
CDELORSS cordless
scolders

CDELORSU	closured
CDELORTU	clotured
CDELORZZ	crozzled
CDELPRSU	scrupled
CDELPSTU	sculpted
CDELRRSU	curdlers
CDELRSUY	cursedly
CDELRTUU	cultured
CDELRUVY	curvedly
CDELSSTU	ductless
CDELSSUY	cussedly
CDELSTTU	scuttled
CDELSTUU	ductules
CDEMMNOS	commends
CDEMMNOU	communed
CDEMMOOS	commodes
CDEMMOOV	commoved
CDEMMOTU	commuted
CDEMMRSU	scrummed
CDEMNNOS	condemns
CDEMNOOW	comedown
	downcome
CDEMNOSU	consumed
CDEMNOTU	document
CDEMOOPS	composed
CDEMOPTU	computed
CDEMOSTU	costumed
CDEMPRSU	scrumped
CDENNOOR	condoner
CDENNOOS	condones
CDENNOOT	connoted
CDENNOST	contends
CDENOORT	creodont
CDENOOVY	convoyed
CDENORSU	crunodes
CDENORTU	cornuted
	trounced
CDENOSTU	contused
CDENRTUU	undercut
CDEOOPPS	copepods
CDEOOPRS	scrooped
CDEOOPST	postcode
CDEOORRR	corroder
CDEOORRS	corrodes
CDEOORSU	decorous
CDEOORSV	vocoders
CDEOOSTV	dovecots
CDEOPRRU	procured
	producer
CDEOPRSU	produces
CDEORRSW	crowders
CDEORSUU	douceurs
CDEOSSTU	custodes
CDEPRSTY	decrypts
CDERSTTU	destruct
CDFIILSU	fluidics
CDFIKMNU	mindfuck
CDFIKOPR	Pickford
CDFIKORS	disfrock
CDFKOORR	Rockford
CDFKOOTU	duckfoot
CDFNNOOU	confound
CDGHIINT	ditching
CDGHILOW	Chlodwig
CDGHINOR	chording
CDGHINOU	douching
CDGIINNU	inducing
CDGIKLNU	duckling
CDGIKLOR	gridlock
CDGILNOS	codlings
	lingcods
	scolding
CDGILNOU	clouding
CDGILNRU	curdling
CDGINORW	crowding
CDGLOOOY	codology
CDGNOOTU	gonoduct
CDHHIILS	childish
CDHIINNW	Chindwin
CDHIINST	chindits
CDHIIOOR	chorioid
CDHIIORT	hidrotic
	trichoid
CDHIIOSZ	schizoid
CDHIISST	distichs
CDHILOOP	chilopod
CDHIMNOR	Richmond
CDHINNOR	chondrin
CDHIOORS	choroids
CDHIOORT	trochoid
CDHIOPRW	whipcord
CDHIPSTY	diptychs
CDHLOOPY	copyhold
CDHOOOPW	woodchop
CDHOORRU	urochord
CDHORTUW	Cudworth
CDIIIMNS	minidisc
CDIIIMNU	indicium
CDIIIORT	dioritic
CDIIKPST	dipstick
CDIILMOS	domicils
CDIILOPP	diplopic
CDIILOTY	docility
CDIILRUY	uridylic
CDIILSVY	viscidly
CDIILTUY	lucidity
CDIIMNOU	conidium
CDIIMTUY	mucidity
CDIINORS	crinoids
CDIINORT	indictor
CDIINOST	dictions
CDIINOSV	vidicons
CDIINPRY	cyprinid
CDIINSTT	distinct
CDIIOOSU	dioicous
CDIIOPRT	dioptric
CDIIORSU	Dioscuri
	sciuroid
CDIIORSX	corixids
CDIIOSSS	cissoids
CDIIPTUY	cupidity
CDIIRSTT	district
CDIJNSTU	disjunct
CDIKKNOW	kickdown
CDIKKOPR	dropkick
CDIKNORS	dornicks
CDIKNOSW	windsock
CDILLOOS	colloids
CDILLOUY	cloudily
CDILOOPS	podsolic
CDILOOPZ	podzolic
CDILOORS	discolor
CDILOORT	lordotic
CDILOOTY	cotyloid
CDIMMOSU	modicums
CDIMOORT	microdot
CDINNQUU	quidnunc
CDINORTU	inductor
CDINOSTU	conduits
	discount
	noctuids
CDIOOPRS	prosodic
CDIOORRR	corridor
CDIOPRRS	ripcords
CDIOPRSU	cuspidor
CDIOSSTY	cystoids
CDIOSTUV	oviducts
CDJLNOUY	jocundly
CDKLOOOS	ockodols
CDKNNOSU	dunnocks
CDKOOORW	corkwood
CDLLLOOP	clodpoll
CDLOOPSY	lycopods
CDMMOOSU	Commodus
CDMNOOPU	compound
CDMNORUU	corundum
CDNNOOOT	conodont
CDNNOOTY	cynodont
CDOOOPST	octopods
CDOORRUY	corduroy
CDOOSTUW	woodcuts
CDOPRSTU	products
CEEEEIPY	eyepiece
CEEEELST	selectee
CEEEFFRT	effecter
CEEEFILR	fleecier
CEEEFILS	fleecies
CEEEFNOR	conferee
CEEEGIMN	emceeing
CEEEGINX	exigence
CEEEGITX	exegetic
CEEEGMNR	mergence
CEEEGNRV	vergence
CEEEHIKR	cheekier
CEEEHIRR	cheerier
CEEEHIRS	cheesier
CEEEHLMN	Mechelen
CEEEHNNY	Cheyenne
CEEEHORS	reechoes
CEEEHPRS	cheepers
CEEEHPSS	speeches
CEEEHRRS	cheerers
CEEEHRSW	eschewer
CEEEIJTV	ejective
CEEEILNN	lenience
CEEEILNS	licensee

CEEEILNT telecine
CEEEILRT erectile
CEEEILTV cleveite
elective
CEEEIMNN eminence
CEEEIMRR reremice
CEEEINNT enceinte
CEEEINPS epicenes
CEEEIPRR creepier
creperie
CEEEIPRS creepies
CEEEIPRV perceive
CEEEIRRV receiver
CEEEIRSV receives
CEEEIRSX exercise
CEEEJRRT rejecter
CEEELLNR crenelle
CEEELOST Eteocles
CEEELPRT preelect
CEEELRRV cleverer
CEEELRST reelects
reselect
CEEELRTT electret
CEEELSST celestes
CEEEMNRT cementer
cerement
CEEEMORT ectomere
CEEEMRTY cemetery
CEEENNST sentence
CEEENNSV Cévennes
CEEENPRS presence
CEEENPRT pretence
CEEENQSU sequence
CEEENRRS screener
CEEENSSS essences
CEEEPRRS creepers
CEEERRST erecters
reerects
CEEERRTX excreter
CEEERSSS recesses
CEEERSST secretes
sesterce
CEEERSSU cereuses
CEEERSTX excretes
CEEERTUX executer
CEEESSSX excesses
CEEESTUX executes
CEEFFNOS offences
CEEFFORT effector
CEEFGILN fleecing
CEEFHIKR kerchief
CEEFHIST fetiches
CEEFHLNR flencher
CEEFHLNS flenches
CEEFHLRT fletcher
CEEFHLRU cheerful
CEEFHLST fletches
CEEFHRST fechters
fetchers
CEEFILLY fleecily
CEEFILRT telferic
CEEFILRY fiercely
CEEFINRT frenetic
infecter
reinfect
CEEFIRST fiercest
CEEFKLRS freckles
CEEFKLSS feckless
CEEFLNOR florence
CEEFLNTU feculent
CEEFLRST reflects
CEEFNORR confrere
enforcer
CEEFNORS enforces
CEEFNRVY fervency
CEEFOPRR perforce
CEEFOPRT perfecto
CEEFORSS frescoes
CEEFORTW crowfeet
CEEFPRST perfects
prefects
CEEGHIKN cheeking
CEEGHILN leeching
CEEGHINP cheeping
CEEGHINR cheering
CEEGHINS cheesing
CEEGHKMO Ockeghem
CEEGHLLS Schlegel
CEEGHLOW cogwheel
CEEGIJNT ejecting
CEEGIKRU Guericke
CEEGILNT electing
CEEGILOT eclogite
CEEGILRS clergies
CEEGINOO cooeeing
CEEGINOR erogenic
CEEGINPR creeping
CEEGINRS Genseric
CEEGINRT erecting
CEEGINST genetics
CEEGINSU eugenics
CEEGINXY exigency
CEEGIORX exoergic
CEEGIRSZ grecizes
CEEGKNOR Greenock
CEEGLLOS colleges
CEEGLNST neglects
CEEGLOSU eclogues
CEEGMNOY cymogene
CEEGNNOO oncogene
CEEGNNOR congener
CEEGNORV Congreve
converge
CEEGORST corteges
CEEHHIRS Cheshire
CEEHHLRS Herschel
CEEHHMNN henchmen
CEEHHNPR Chephren
CEEHIIST ethicise
CEEHIITZ ethicize
CEEHIKLY cheekily
CEEHILLN chenille
Hellenic
CEEHILMT Melchite
Michelet
CEEHILRW clerihew
CEEHILRY cheerily
CEEHILSV vehicles
CEEHILSW Weichsel
CEEHILTV Helvetic
CEEHIMRS chimeres
CEEHIMRT hermetic
CEEHIMSS chemises
CEEHINPR encipher
CEEHINPT phenetic
CEEHINRR enricher
CEEHINRS enriches
CEEHINRT Chrétien
CEEHINTT enthetic
CEEHIORS cheerios
CEEHIOSU icehouse
CEEHIOSV cohesive
CEEHIPRT herpetic
CEEHIRRS cherries
CEEHIRST chestier
heretics
CEEHIRTT tetchier
CEEHISTT esthetic
techiest
CEEHISTW chewiest
CEEHKLRS hecklers
CEEHKNOR Honecker
CEEHKNPS henpecks
CEEHKRST sketcher
CEEHKSST sketches
CEEHLLRW Cherwell
CEEHLMOO hemocoel
CEEHLNOS chelones
echelons
CEEHLNPU penuchle
CEEHLNSU elenchus
CEEHLORT reclothe
CEEHLOSS echoless
CEEHLRSU hercules
CEEHLRSW welchers
CEEHLSSS chessels
CEEHMNSS chessmen
CEEHMOTY hemocyte
CEEHMRSS schemers
CEEHMRST merchets
CEEHMSTU Tecumseh
CEEHNNOW nowhence
CEEHNNRT entrench
CEEHNORT coherent
CEEHNQRU quencher
CEEHNQSU quenches
CEEHNRRT retrench
trencher
CEEHNRST trenches
CEEHNRSW wenchers
wrenches
CEEHNSST stenches
CEEHOPRY coryphee
CEEHOPTT pochette
CEEHORRS coherers
CEEHORRT torchere

CEEHORST	trochees
CEEHPRRS	perchers
CEEHPRRY	perchery
CEEHQRSU	chequers
CEEHRSTW	wretches
CEEHRSTY	Chertsey
CEEHRTTU	teuchter
CEEIIKLV	vicelike
CEEIIMPR	epimeric
CEEIIMRT	eremitic
CEEIINST	niceties
CEEIINSW	icewines
CEEIINVV	evincive
CEEIJLLO	Jellicoe
CEEIJNOT	ejection
CEEIJORR	rejoicer
CEEIJORS	rejoices
CEEIJRUV	verjuice
CEEIKLNN	neckline
CEEIKLPR	pickerel
CEEIKNRS	sickener
CEEIKNST	neckties
CEEIKPRT	picketer
CEEILLLP	pellicle
CEEILLMS	micelles
CEEILLNT	lenticel
	lenticle
CEEILLRV	Vercelli
CEEILMNT	Clement I
CEEILMOR	comelier
CEEILMPS	semplice
CEEILNNY	leniency
CEEILNOT	election
CEEILNOV	violence
CEEILNPR	penciler
CEEILNRR	recliner
CEEILNRS	licenser
	reclines
	silencer
CEEILNSS	licenses
	silences
CEEILNST	centiles
CEEILORR	recoiler
CEEILPRS	eclipser
	Pericles
CEEILPRY	creepily
CEEILPSS	eclipses
CEEILQSU	liquesce
CEEILRST	reticles
	sclerite
	tiercels
CEEILRSV	versicle
CEEILRTU	reticule
CEEILRTY	celerity
CEEILSSV	clevises
	vesicles
	viceless
CEEILSTT	testicle
CEEIMMPY	empyemic
CEEIMMRS	mesmeric
CEEIMNNY	eminency
CEEIMNPS	specimen
CEEIMNST	centimes
	tenesmic
CEEIMORT	meteoric
CEEIMOTY	meiocyte
CEEIMRSX	excimers
CEEIMSTT	smectite
CEEINNOP	pinecone
CEEINNOT	neotenic
CEEINNSS	incenses
	niceness
CEEINNST	nescient
CEEINOPU	eupnoeic
CEEINORT	erection
	neoteric
CEEINORV	overnice
CEEINORX	exocrine
CEEINOSS	senecios
CEEINOST	seicento
CEEINOTV	evection
CEEINPRT	prentice
	terpenic
CEEINPST	pectines
CEEINPSX	sixpence
CEEINQRU	quercine
CEEINRST	enticers
	scienter
	secretin
CEEINRSU	insecure
	sinecure
CEEINRTT	reticent
CEEINRTU	enuretic
CEEINSTY	cysteine
CEEIOPPR	pericope
CEEIOPPS	episcope
CEEIOPRS	recopies
CEEIOPST	picotees
CEEIORST	coteries
	esoteric
CEEIORSV	revoices
CEEIORSX	exorcise
CEEIORTT	erotetic
CEEIORTX	exoteric
CEEIORXZ	exorcize
CEEIPPTU	eupeptic
CEEIPRRS	piercers
	reprices
CEEIPRSS	precises
CEEIPRST	receipts
CEEIPRSU	epicures
CEEIPSST	pectises
CEEIPSTZ	pectizes
CEEIRRST	reciters
CEEIRRSW	screwier
CEEIRRTU	ureteric
CEEIRSSV	services
CEEIRSTU	cerusite
	cutesier
CEEIRSTV	vertices
CEEIRSTX	exciters
CEEIRSVX	cervixes
CEEJORRT	rejector
CEEJORST	ejectors
CEEKLLMN	McKellen
CEEKLNPU	penuckle
CEEKLNST	necklets
CEEKLPSS	speckles
CEEKLRSS	clerkess
	reckless
CEEKNORR	reckoner
CEEKNORV	Cerenkov
CEEKOPRX	oxpecker
CEEKORRT	corktree
CEEKOSSY	sockeyes
CEEKRRSW	wreckers
CEELLLSU	cellules
CEELLMOU	molecule
CEELLNOS	colleens
CEELLNOU	nucleole
CEELLPRU	cupeller
CEELLRRU	crueller
CEELLRVY	cleverly
CEELLSSU	clueless
CEELLSTY	selectly
CEELMNTV	Clement V
CEELMOPT	complete
CEELMORW	welcomer
CEELMOST	telecoms
CEELMOSW	welcomes
CEELMRTU	electrum
CEELNOPU	opulence
CEELNORS	encloser
CEELNORT	electron
CEELNOSS	encloses
CEELNPTU	centuple
CEELNRST	lecterns
CEELNRTU	relucent
CEELNRTY	recently
CEELNSTU	esculent
CEELORSS	coreless
CEELORST	corselet
	electors
	electros
	selector
CEELORTV	coverlet
CEELOSSU	coleuses
CEELOSTU	elocutes
CEELPPRU	Culpeper
CEELPRST	prelects
CEELRRTU	lecturer
CEELRSSU	cureless
	recluses
CEELRSTU	cruelest
	lectures
CEELRSTY	secretly
CEELRSUY	securely
CEELSTTU	lettuces
CEEMMNTU	cementum
CEEMMORS	commeres
CEEMNNOW	Newcomen
CEEMNORW	newcomer
CEEMNORY	ceremony
CEEMNOYZ	coenzyme
CEEMOORV	comeover
	overcome

CEEMOOTY oomycete
CEEMOPRS compeers
comperes
CEEMOPST competes
CEENNORT cretonne
CEENNORU renounce
CEENNORV convener
CEENNOSU enounces
CEENNOSV convenes
CEENNRST centners
CEENOOST ecotones
CEENOPRV Provence
CEENOPST potences
CEENOPTW twopence
CEENORSS necroses
CEENORSV conserve
converse
CEENORSZ cozeners
CEENORTT trecento
CEENORVY conveyer
reconvey
CEENOSVX convexes
CEENPPTU tuppence
CEENPRSS spencers
CEENRRSU censurer
CEENRSST Cressent
CEENRSSU censures
CEENSSSU censuses
CEENSSTU cuteness
CEEOORST creosote
CEEOPRRT receptor
CEEOPRTY cerotype
CEEOPSTY ecotypes
CEEOQTTU coquette
CEEORRRS sorcerer
CEEORRST erectors
secretor
CEEORRSU recourse
resource
CEEORRSV coverers
recovers
CEEORRVY recovery
CEEORSSS Scorsese
CEEORSTV coveters
CEEORTTV corvette
CEEORTUX executor
CEEOSTTT octettes
CEEPPRST percepts
precepts
CEEPPRSU prepuces
CEEPRSST respects
scepters
sceptres
specters
spectres
CEEPRSTX excerpts
CEERRSSU rescuers
securers
CEERRSSW screwers
CEERRSUV recurves
CEERSSST cressets
CEERSSTW setscrew
CEERSTTU curettes
CEESSSTU cestuses
CEESTTUV cuvettes
CEFFHIRU chuffier
CEFFILWY Wycliffe
CEFFIORS officers
CEFFIORU coiffeur
coiffure
CEFFIRSU sufficer
CEFFISSU suffices
CEFFLORU forceful
CEFFLSSU scuffles
CEFFORSS scoffers
CEFGHINT fechting
fetching
CEFGIKLN flecking
CEFGILNT clefting
CEFHIIMS mischief
CEFHILNR flincher
CEFHILNS flinches
CEFHILNY Finchley
CEFHILRS filchers
CEFHILST flitches
CEFHINSU fuchsine
CEFHISTT fitchets
CEFHISTW fitchews
CEFHKOOR forehock
CEFHLSTU chestful
CEFIIIST citifies
CEFIILLM mellific
CEFIILNO olefinic
CEFIILST felsitic
CEFIILTY felicity
CEFIIORS orifices
CEFIIRRT terrific
CEFIISTY cityfies
CEFIKLOR firelock
CEFIKLRS flickers
CEFIKLRY flickery
CEFILLLO follicle
CEFILMRU merciful
CEFILNOT flection
CEFILNST inflects
CEFILNSU funicles
CEFILOUV voiceful
CEFILRSU lucifers
CEFIMOST comfiest
CEFINNOR confiner
CEFINNOS confines
CEFINORS conifers
forensic
fornices
CEFINORT infector
CEFINOTT confetti
CEFIOPRS forcipes
CEFIORTY ferocity
CEFKLLOS elflocks
CEFKLOOR forelock
CEFKLOST fetlocks
CEFKLPSY flyspeck
CEFKLRUW wreckful
CEFLNOSU flounces
CEFLNRUU furuncle
CEFLNUWY Cynewulf
CEFMORSY comfreys
CEFNORTU confuter
CEFNOSSU confuses
CEFNOSTU confutes
CEFOQTUU Foucquet
CEFORRST crofters
CEFORSSU focusers
CEFORSTU fructose
CEGGHIRS chiggers
CEGGILOO geologic
CEGGIORS croggies
georgics
CEGGLNOY glycogen
CEGGMORR McGregor
CEGHIINY hygienic
CEGHIKLN heckling
CEGHILLW Chigwell
CEGHILNP chelping
CEGHILNT letching
CEGHILNW welching
CEGHILST glitches
CEGHIMNS scheming
CEGHINNW wenching
CEGHINOR cohering
ochering
CEGHINPR perching
CEGHINRT retching
CEGHINRU euchring
CEGHINST etchings
CEGHINVY chevying
CEGHIRSS screighs
CEGHIRTU theurgic
CEGHISTU guichets
CEGHMRUY chemurgy
CEGHNORS groschen
CEGHORSU coughers
grouches
CEGIILMO oligemic
CEGIILNS ceilings
CEGIINNT enticing
CEGIINNV evincing
CEGIINOS isogenic
CEGIINPR piercing
CEGIINRT reciting
CEGIINSS gneissic
CEGIINSX excising
CEGIINTV evicting
CEGIINTX exciting
CEGIIOST egoistic
CEGIKNNS snecking
CEGIKNPS specking
CEGIKNRW wrecking
CEGILMMN clemming
CEGILMPS gemclips
CEGILNPU cupeling
CEGILNRS clingers
cringles
CEGILNRY glycerin
CEGILNSU Guesclin
CEGILNTU cultigen

CEGILRSY lysergic
CEGIMNOS genomics
CEGIMNOY myogenic
CEGIMNUY gynecium
CEGINNOR encoring
CEGINNOZ cozening
CEGINNRT centring
CEGINNST scenting
CEGINNSY ensigncy
CEGINOOP geoponic
CEGINOOR orogenic
CEGINOOY cooeying
CEGINOPY pyogenic
CEGINORT gerontic
CEGINORV covering
CEGINORW cowering
CEGINOSS cognises
CEGINOSZ cognizes
CEGINOTV coveting
CEGINOXY oxygenic
CEGINRRS cringers
CEGINRST cresting
CEGINRSU rescuing
scungier
securing
CEGINRSW screwing
CEGINRSY synergic
CEGINRTU eructing
CEGINSUX excusing
CEGKLORS grockles
CEGLLOOU collogue
CEGLLORY glycerol
CEGLLRYY glyceryl
CEGLNOOS colognes
CEGLNOTY cogently
CEGLOOOY oecology
CEGLOOTY cetology
CEGLOSSY glycoses
CEGMNNOO cognomen
CEGNNPUY pungency
CEGNOOTY gonocyte
CEGNORSS congress
CEGNORSU scrounge
CEGNOSST congests
CEGNOTYY cytogeny
CEGOORSS scrooges
CEGORRSU scourger
CEGORSSU scourges
scrouges
CEHHIRST hitchers
CEHHISTU hutchies
CEHHNSTU Cheshunt
CEHHOOSS cohoshes
CEHHOPTY hypothec
CEHHOSST shochets
CEHIIKNS chinkies
CEHIIKST thickies
CEHIILLR chillier
CEHIILLS chillies
CEHIILMN Michelin
CEHIILMO hemiolic
CEHIILNN lichenin
CEHIILNT lecithin
CEHIILOT eolithic
CEHIILTY helicity
CEHIIMOS isocheim
isochime
CEHIIMPT mephitic
CEHIIMRT hermitic
CEHIINNR Nichiren
CEHIINST ichnites
CEHIIPPR chippier
CEHIIPPS chippies
CEHIIPRR chirpier
CEHIIPRT pitchier
CEHIIRST christie
CEHIIRTT titchier
trichite
CEHIISTT chitties
ethicist
itchiest
theistic
tichiest
CEHIISVV chivvies
CEHIKLNY Hinckley
CEHIKLPT klephtic
CEHIKLRS clerkish
CEHIKLSU suchlike
CEHIKMNT Chimkent
CEHIKMOS homesick
CEHIKNRR Kirchner
CEHIKNRU chunkier
CEHIKNST chetniks
kitchens
thickens
CEHIKOOS chookies
CEHIKOST chokiest
thickoes
CEHIKOWW Kweichow
CEHIKRSW whickers
CEHIKSST skitches
CEHIKSTT thickest
thickets
thickset
CEHILLMT Mitchell
CEHILLPR prechill
CEHILLRS chillers
schiller
CEHILMOR Melchior
CEHILMOU humicole
CEHILMTY methylic
CEHILNOP phenolic
pinochle
CEHILNOR chlorine
CEHILNOS helicons
CEHILNRU Reuchlin
CEHILNSS chinless
CEHILOOS schoolie
CEHILORS ceorlish
CEHILORT chlorite
clothier
CEHILOSU Choiseul
CEHILPTY phyletic
CEHILRSV chervils
CEHILTTY tetchily
CEHIMMRU chummier
CEHIMMSS chemisms
CEHIMNOP phonemic
CEHIMNPT pitchmen
CEHIMNSU munchies
CEHIMNSY chimneys
CEHIMNTZ Chemnitz
CEHIMORT chromite
trichome
CEHIMRRS smircher
CEHIMRSS smirches
CEHIMSST chemists
CEHINNRT intrench
CEHINOOS cohesion
CEHINOPS chopines
CEHINOPT phonetic
Pinochet
CEHINOPU euphonic
CEHINORU unheroic
CEHINOSY hyoscine
CEHINPRU punchier
CEHINRSS richness
CEHINRST christen
citherns
snitcher
CEHINRSW Schwerin
winchers
CEHINRTU ruthenic
CEHINSST snitches
CEHIOORS choosier
isochore
CEHIOPPR choppier
CEHIOPRU euphoric
CEHIOPSS hospices
CEHIOPST postiche
potiches
CEHIOPTU euphotic
CEHIORRS chorries
CEHIORRT rhetoric
torchier
CEHIORRV overrich
CEHIORSS orchises
CEHIORTU touchier
CEHIOSTV cheviots
CEHIPPRS chippers
CEHIPRRS chirpers
CEHIPRSS spherics
CEHIPRST pitchers
CEHIRSTT chitters
stitcher
CEHIRSTW switcher
CEHIRSTY hysteric
CEHIRTTW twitcher
CEHIRTWY witchery
CEHISSTT stitches
CEHISSTU cushiest
CEHISSTW switches
CEHISTTW twitches
CEHKKRSU chukkers
CEHKLMOS hemlocks
CEHKLOOS klooches

CEHKLOSY Shockley
CEHKNPUY keypunch
CEHKORSS shockers
CEHKPSTU ketchups
CEHKRSSU shuckers
CEHKRSTU huckster
CEHLLORS chollers
CEHLLPSU chellups
CEHLMOPU Chemulpo
CEHLNNOU luncheon
CEHLNOST cholents
CEHLNOTU unclothe
CEHLNRSU lunchers
CEHLNRSY lynchers
CEHLNSTY lynchets
CEHLORRT chortler
CEHLORST chortles
CEHLORSU sloucher
CEHLOSSU slouches
CEHLQSUY squelchy
CEHLRRSU lurchers
CEHLSTUY lecythus
CEHMNRSU munchers
CEHMNSSU muchness
CEHMOORS moochers
CEHMOOSS smooches
CEHMOOSZ schmooze
CEHMORUV overmuch
CEHMSSTU smutches
CEHNNOPU puncheon
CEHNNOSU nonesuch
unchosen
CEHNOOPS hencoops
CEHNOORS schooner
CEHNORSV chevrons
CEHNPRSU punchers
CEHNRRSU churners
CEHNRSTU chunters
CEHNSTTU chestnut
CEHNSTUY chutneys
CEHOOORZ zoochore
CEHOORSS choosers
CEHOORST cheroots
CEHOORSU ocherous
ochreous
CEHOOSSS scooshes
CEHOPPRS choppers
CEHOPPRY prophecy
CEHOPSTW Chepstow
CEHORSSU choruses
CEHORSSZ scherzos
CEHORSTU touchers
CEHORSUV vouchers
CEHPSSTU putsches
CEHRRSSU crushers
CEHRSTTY stretchy
CEHSSSSU schusses
CEIIILSV civilise
CEIIILVZ civilize
CEIIINSV incisive
CEIIJSTU jesuitic
juiciest

CEIIKLMR limerick
CEIIKLRS sicklier
CEIIKMMR mimicker
CEIIKNSS ickiness
kinesics
CEIIKNST kinetics
CEIIKPST pickiest
CEIIKQSU quickies
CEIIKRRT trickier
CEIIKRST stickier
CEIIKSST ekistics
stickies
CEIILLNO linoleic
CEIILLPT elliptic
CEIILLSS silicles
CEIILLSU silicule
CEIILMNS lemnisci
CEIILMNT limnetic
CEIILMNY myelinic
CEIILNNR incliner
CEIILNNS inclines
CEIILNOP picoline
CEIILNOS isocline
silicone
CEIILOPS policies
CEIILORT elicitor
CEIILOTZ zeolitic
CEIILPPS clippies
CEIILPRT perlitic
CEIILPSS eclipsis
CEIILPTX explicit
CEIILPTY pyelitic
CEIILRTV verticil
CEIILSSS scissile
CEIIMOPT epitomic
CEIIMORS isomeric
CEIIMOST comities
semiotic
CEIIMOSW Oświęcim
CEIIMPRS empirics
CEIIMRRT trimeric
CEIIMRST meristic
CEIIMRTT termitic
CEIINNOP nepionic
CEIINNOR irenicon
CEIINNOT nicotine
CEIINNRS cinerins
CEIINORS recision
soricine
CEIINOSV invoices
CEIINOSX excision
CEIINOTV eviction
CEIINPPR principe
Príncipe
CEIINRST citrines
crinites
inciters
CEIINRSU incisure
sciurine
CEIINRTU neuritic
CEIINSTU cutinise
CEIINSTY syenitic

CEIINSTZ citizens
zincites
CEIINTUZ cutinize
CEIIOPRT periotic
CEIIOPSW wicopies
CEIIOSTT osteitic
CEIIPRRS crispier
CEIIPRST priciest
CEIIPSST spiciest
CEIIQRTU critique
CEIIRSST eristics
CEIIRSTV veristic
CEIIRSUZ cruizies
CEIISTVV vivisect
CEIJNORT injector
CEIJNOUV cunjevoi
CEIJSSTU justices
CEIKKLOR corklike
CEIKKNRS knickers
CEIKKRRS skerrick
CEIKLMNY McKinley
CEIKLMSU scumlike
CEIKLNRS clinkers
crinkles
CEIKLNRU clunkier
CEIKLNSZ Selznick
CEIKLOSV lovesick
CEIKLPRS picklers
prickles
CEIKLPRU pluckier
CEIKLRSS slickers
CEIKLRST stickler
strickle
ticklers
trickles
CEIKLSST slickest
stickles
CEIKLSTU luckiest
CEIKMNOR monicker
CEIKMSTU muckiest
CEIKNNOT nektonic
CEIKNNPY Pinckney
CEIKNOTY cytokine
CEIKNQSU quickens
CEIKNRSS snickers
CEIKNRST stricken
CEIKNSSS sickness
CEIKNSST snickets
CEIKORST rockiest
stockier
CEIKOSTT tockiest
CEIKPRRS prickers
CEIKPRST prickets
CEIKPSST skeptics
CEIKQSTU quickest
quickset
CEIKRRST trickers
CEIKRRTY trickery
CEIKRSST stickers
CEIKRSTU truckies
CEIKSTUY yuckiest
CEILLNOU nucleoli

CEILLOPS pollices
CEILLOQU coquille
CEILLORS colliers
CEILLORY colliery
CEILLRTU telluric
CEILLSST cellists
CEILLSSU cullises
CEILMMUY mycelium
CEILMNOP compline
CEILMOPR compiler
complier
CEILMOPS compiles
complies
polemics
CEILMOSS solecism
CEILMOSU coliseum
CEILMPRS crimples
CEILMPUU peculium
CEILMRSU clumsier
CEILMTUU lutecium
CEILNNSU nucleins
CEILNNSY syncline
CEILNOOS colonies
colonise
eclosion
CEILNOOZ colonize
CEILNOPR replicon
CEILNOPT leptonic
CEILNORS incloser
licensor
CEILNOSS incloses
CEILNOST lections
telsonic
CEILNOSX lexicons
CEILNPRY princely
CEILNRUV culverin
CEILNSST stencils
CEILNSTU tunicles
CEILOORZ colorize
CEILOPRT petrolic
CEILOPTU poultice
CEILOPTY epicotyl
CEILORST cloister
costlier
CEILORTY cryolite
CEILOSSS ossicles
CEILOSST solecist
solstice
CEILOSSU coulisse
CEILOSSV clovises
CEILOSTT coletits
CEILOTVY velocity
CEILPPRR crippler
CEILPPRS clippers
cripples
CEILPRSS splicers
CEILPRSU surplice
CEILPSSU spicules
CEILRSTU curliest
utricles
CEILSTTU cultiest
CEIMMNNO mnemonic
CEIMMNOS Commines
CEIMMNOU encomium
meconium
CEIMMORT recommit
CEIMMOSX commixes
CEIMMRRU crummier
CEIMMRSU crummies
CEIMNNOY neomycin
CEIMNOOT emoticon
CEIMNOPT pentomic
CEIMNOPY eponymic
CEIMNORS incomers
sermonic
CEIMNORT intercom
CEIMNOST centimos
CEIMNOSU Comenius
CEIMNRST centrism
CEIMNSSU meniscus
CEIMOPRS comprise
CEIMORRU Mercouri
CEIMORST mortices
CEIMORSX exorcism
CEIMOSTV vicomtes
CEIMPRRS crimpers
CEIMRRTU turmeric
CEIMSSTY systemic
CEINNNOT innocent
CEINNORU neuronic
CEINNORV conniver
CEINNOSV connives
CEINNOTU continue
CEINOOPR pecorino
CEINOOST coonties
CEINOOTZ entozoic
enzootic
CEINOPPT peptonic
CEINOPRS conspire
CEINOPRT inceptor
pretonic
CEINOPRU Couperin
CEINOPRV province
CEINOPTT entoptic
CEINOPTU unpoetic
CEINORRT tricorne
CEINORSS necrosis
CEINORST corniest
CEINORSU coinsure
CEINORTT contrite
CEINORTU neurotic
CEINORTV contrive
CEINOSSS cessions
cosiness
CEINOSST sections
CEINOSSZ coziness
CEINOSTT stenotic
CEINOSTU counties
CEINOSTX excitons
CEINOSTY cytosine
CEINOSUV unvoices
CEINPRSS princess
CEINPRST spectrin
CEINPSST inspects
CEINRRSU reincurs
CEINRSST cisterns
CEINRSTT centrist
citterns
CEINRSUV incurves
CEINRTTU intercut
tincture
CEIOOTXX exotoxic
CEIOPRRU croupier
CEIOPRSU precious
CEIOPSSU specious
CEIORRSS crosiers
CEIORRSU couriers
CEIORRSZ croziers
CEIORRTU courtier
CEIORRUZ cruzeiro
CEIORSTT cottiers
CEIORSTU citreous
outcries
CEIORSTV evictors
vortices
CEIORSTX excitors
exorcist
CEIORSVY viceroys
CEIORTTU toreutic
CEIOSSTT scotties
CEIOSSTX coexists
CEIPQSTU picquets
CEIPRRSS crispers
CEIPRRST rescript
scripter
CEIPRSST crispest
CEIPRSTU crepitus
pictures
piecrust
CEIPRSUU Epicurus
CEIPSSST cesspits
CEIRRRSU curriers
CEIRRRUY curriery
CEIRRSSU cruisers
scurries
CEIRRSTT critters
restrict
stricter
CEIRRSTU crustier
recruits
CEIRRSUV scurvier
CEIRSSSU scissure
CEIRSSTT trisects
CEIRSSTU citruses
crusties
curtsies
rictuses
CEIRSSUV cursives
CEIRSTUV curviest
CEIRSTUY security
CEIRSUZZ scuzzier
CEISSSSU cissuses
CEISSSTU cistuses
CEJLOOSY jocosely
CEJNORRU conjurer
CEJNORSU conjures

CEJNRTUU	juncture
CEJOPRST	projects
CEKKLNSU	knuckles
CEKKNORS	knockers
CEKKNTUY	Kentucky
CEKLLNOR	rollneck
CEKLLOOV	lovelock
CEKLLORW	Rockwell
CEKLLSSU	luckless
CEKLOPST	lockstep
CEKLPRSU	pluckers
CEKLRRTU	truckler
CEKLRSSU	sucklers
CEKLRSTU	truckles
CEKLSSSU	suckless
CEKMNOST	stockmen
CEKMNOSY	mockneys
CEKNOORV	convoker
CEKNOOSV	convokes
CEKNOPST	penstock
CEKNRSWY	wrynecks
CEKOOORV	overcook
CEKOOPRS	precooks
CEKOOPSW	cowpokes
CEKOORRS	rockrose
CEKOORRW	coworker
CEKOPRST	sprocket
CEKORRTY	rocketry
CEKORSST	restocks
	stockers
CEKORSTW	twockers
CEKRRSTU	truckers
CEKRSSUU	ruckuses
CELLLOVY	Clovelly
CELLMORW	Cromwell
CELLNNOO	O'Connell
CELLNOOS	colonels
CELLNORW	Cornwell
CELLNSUU	nucellus
CELLNTUU	luculent
CELLNTUY	lucently
CELLOOST	Costello
CELLRRSU	crullers
CELLRSSU	scullers
CELLRSUY	scullery
CELMNOOS	monocles
CELMOSYY	cymosely
CELMPRSU	crumples
	scrumple
CELMPRTU	plectrum
CELMPSUU	speculum
CELMSTUU	cumulets
CELNNOSU	nucleons
CELNOORS	consoler
CELNOOSS	consoles
	coolness
CELNOOVV	convolve
CELNOPRT	plectron
CELNOPUU	uncouple
CELNOPUY	opulency
CELNORWY	clownery
CELNOSSU	clonuses
	counsels
	uncloses
CELNOSTU	noctules
CELNOSUV	convulse
CELNOSVY	solvency
CELNOVXY	convexly
CELOOORV	overcool
CELOOPSS	cesspool
CELOORRS	colorers
CELOORTW	colewort
CELOOSTU	closeout
CELOPRSU	couplers
CELOPSTU	couplets
	octuples
CELOPSUU	opuscule
CELORSST	corslets
	costrels
	crosslet
CELORSSU	closures
	sclerous
CELORSSW	scowlers
CELORSTT	crottles
CELORSTU	clotures
	clouters
	coulters
CELORSUU	ulcerous
CELORTVY	covertly
CELOSSST	costless
CELOSTTU	culottes
CELPRSSU	scruples
CELPRSUY	sprucely
CELRSSTU	clusters
CELRSSTY	clysters
CELRSTTU	clutters
CELRSTUU	cultures
CELRSTUV	culverts
CELRSTUY	clustery
CELSSTTU	scuttles
CELSSTUU	cultuses
CEMMNOOR	commoner
CEMMNOOS	consomme
CEMMNOST	comments
CEMMNOSU	communes
CEMMOOSV	commoves
CEMMORTU	commuter
CEMMOSTU	commutes
CEMMRSSU	scummers
CEMNNOST	contemns
CEMNOOTY	monocyte
CEMNOPRS	corpsmen
CEMNOPTT	contempt
CEMNORSU	consumer
	mucrones
CEMNOSSU	consumes
CEMNRSTU	centrums
CEMOOPRS	composer
CEMOOPSS	composes
CEMOOPST	compotes
CEMOORSY	sycomore
CEMOOSSS	cosmoses
CEMOOSTU	outcomes
CEMOPRSS	compress
CEMOPRTU	computer
CEMOPSTU	computes
CEMORSTU	costumer
	customer
CEMOSSTU	costumes
CEMPRSTU	crumpets
	spectrum
CENNOOPR	cornpone
CENNOORV	convenor
CENNOOST	connotes
CENNORTU	nocturne
CENNOSST	consents
CENNOSTT	contents
CENNOSTV	convents
CENNRSSU	scunners
CENOORRS	coroners
	crooners
CENOORST	coronets
CENOORSU	corneous
CENOORVY	conveyor
CENOPRSU	pouncers
CENOPRSY	necropsy
CENOPSSY	syncopes
CENOQRSU	conquers
CENOQSTU	conquest
CENORRSS	scorners
CENORRSW	crowners
	recrowns
CENORSTT	cornetts
CENORSTU	construe
	counters
	recounts
	trounces
CENORSTV	converts
CENORSUU	cernuous
	coenurus
CENORSUV	uncovers
CENORSUY	cynosure
CENORTVY	Coventry
CENOSSTT	contests
CENOSSTU	contuses
	countess
CENOSTTX	contexts
CENPRSTY	encrypts
CENPRTUU	puncture
CENRRSTU	currents
CENRSSTU	curtness
	encrusts
CENRSSUW	unscrews
CEOOOPST	otoscope
CEOOPRRV	overcrop
CEOOPRSS	scoopers
CEOORSST	scooters
CEOOSTUV	covetous
CEOPPRRS	croppers
CEOPPRST	prospect
CEOPRRRU	procurer
CEOPRRSS	scorpers
CEOPRRSU	procures
CEOPRSTT	Prescott
	protects
CEOPRSTW	crowstep

	screwtop
CEOPRSUU	cupreous
CEOPRSUV	coverups
CEOQRSTU	croquets
CEOQRTUY	coquetry
CEORRSSS	crossers
CEORRSSU	coursers
	scourers
CEORRSTY	corsetry
CEORSSSU	scousers
CEORSSTU	crustose
	scouters
CEORSTUV	couverts
CEORSTUY	courtesy
CEOSSTTU	cottuses
CEPPRRSU	cruppers
CEPPRSSU	scuppers
CEPPRTUU	uppercut
CEPRSSTU	sprucest
CEPRSTUU	cutpurse
CEPSSSTU	suspects
CERSSTTU	scutters
CERSSTUY	curtseys
CERSSUUX	excursus
CFFGHINU	chuffing
CFFGIINO	coiffing
CFFGINOS	scoffing
CFFGINSU	scuffing
CFFHINOY	chiffony
CFFIKKOS	kickoffs
CFFIRTUY	fructify
CFFKKNOO	knockoff
CFGHIILN	filching
CFGHINOO	choofing
CFGIIKLN	flicking
CFGIIKNR	fricking
CFGIKLNO	flocking
CFGIKNOR	frocking
CFGINORT	crofting
CFGINOSU	focusing
CFHIINOO	finochio
CFHIIORR	horrific
CFHIKORS	rockfish
CFHIKSSU	suckfish
CFHORSTU	futhorcs
CFIIILSY	silicify
CFIILMNU	fulminic
CFIILNST	inflicts
CFIILNUU	funiculi
CFIILOPR	prolific
CFIIMNOS	somnific
CFIINORT	friction
CFIINOST	fictions
CFIKLORY	frolicky
CFIKLSTU	stickful
CFIKNNOS	finnocks
CFIKOSSS	fossicks
CFIKSTUW	fuckwits
CFILMOOR	coliform
CFILRSUU	sulfuric
CFIMNORS	confirms
CFIMNORU	unciform
CFINNOTU	function
CFKNORSU	unfrocks
CFKOSTTU	futtocks
CFLLOORU	colorful
CFLMRSUU	fulcrums
CFLMRUUU	furculum
CFLNORSU	scornful
CFLOOPSU	scoopful
CFMNOORS	conforms
CFMOORST	comforts
CFNNOORT	confront
CFOOORTW	crowfoot
CFRSTUUU	usufruct
CGGGHINU	chugging
CGGGILNO	clogging
	coggling
CGGGINOR	crogging
CGGHINOU	coughing
CGGIILNN	clinging
CGGIINNR	cringing
CGGINNSU	scunging
CGGINORS	scroggin
CGHHIINT	hitching
CGHHINNU	hunching
CGHHINTU	hutching
CGHIIKNN	chinking
CGHIIKNO	hoicking
CGHIILLN	chilling
CGHIIMNR	chirming
CGHIIMNT	mitching
CGHIINNN	chinning
CGHIINNP	pinching
CGHIINNW	winching
CGHIINPP	chipping
CGHIINPR	chirping
CGHIINPT	pitching
CGHIINRR	chirring
CGHIINST	sichting
CGHIINTW	witching
CGHIINVV	chivving
CGHIINVY	chivying
CGHIJNNO	Chŏngjin
CGHIJNNU	Chungjin
CGHIKLNO	hockling
CGHIKNNU	chunking
CGHIKNOO	chooking
CGHIKNOS	shocking
CGHIKNSU	shucking
CGHILMNU	mulching
CGHILNNU	lunching
CGHILNNY	lynching
CGHILNOT	clothing
CGHILNRU	lurching
CGHIMMNU	chumming
CGHIMNNU	munching
CGHIMNOO	mooching
CGHIMNOP	chomping
CGHIMNOR	chroming
CGHIMNPU	chumping
CGHIMNTU	mutching
CGHIMPSY	sphygmic
CGHINNOS	chignons
CGHINNOT	notching
CGHINNPU	punching
CGHINNRU	churning
CGHINNSY	synching
CGHINOOS	choosing
CGHINOPP	chopping
CGHINOPU	pouching
CGHINOSU	hocusing
CGHINOTU	touching
CGHINOUV	vouching
CGHINPSY	psyching
CGHINRRU	churring
CGHINRSU	crushing
	ruchings
CGHINSTY	scything
CGHLNOSS	schlongs
CGHNOOSU	souchong
CGIIILNT	lignitic
CGIIINNS	incising
CGIIINNT	inciting
CGIIKLNN	clinking
CGIIKLNP	pickling
CGIIKLNS	lickings
	slicking
CGIIKLNT	tickling
CGIIKMMS	gimmicks
CGIIKMMY	gimmicky
CGIIKNNS	snicking
CGIIKNPR	pricking
CGIIKNPS	pickings
CGIIKNRT	tricking
CGIIKNRW	wricking
CGIIKNST	sticking
CGIIKNSW	wickings
CGIIKPST	pigstick
CGIILMOS	logicism
CGIILNOP	policing
CGIILNPP	clipping
CGIILNPS	splicing
CGIILNSU	sluicing
CGIILOST	logistic
CGIILRTU	liturgic
CGIIMNNO	incoming
CGIIMNPR	crimping
CGIIMNPU	pumicing
CGIIMNSU	miscuing
CGIINNOT	noticing
CGIINNSU	incusing
CGIINNTT	tincting
CGIINOOS	isogonic
CGIINPRS	crisping
CGIINRSU	cruising
CGIJNNOU	jouncing
CGIKKNNO	knocking
CGIKLNNO	clonking
CGIKLNNU	clunking
CGIKLNOR	rockling
CGIKLNPU	plucking
CGIKLNRU	ruckling
CGIKLNSU	suckling
CGIKMNOS	smocking
CGIKNOOR	crooking

CGIKNORW	corkwing
CGIKNOST	stocking
CGIKNOTW	twocking
CGIKNPSU	kingcups
CGIKNRTU	trucking
CGIKPSTU	pigstuck
CGILLNOY	collying
CGILLNSU	sculling
CGILMNPU	clumping
CGILMNSU	muscling
CGILMNTU	mulcting
CGILMNUU	cingulum
	glucinum
CGILMOOY	myologic
CGILNNOW	clowning
CGILNOOR	coloring
	crooling
CGILNOOY	cooingly
CGILNOPP	clopping
CGILNOPU	coupling
CGILNOSW	cowlings
	scowling
CGILNOTT	clotting
CGILNPSU	sculping
CGILOORU	urologic
CGILORSW	cowgirls
CGILPSTY	glyptics
CGIMMNSU	Cummings
	scumming
CGIMNNOO	gnomonic
	oncoming
CGIMNOPU	upcoming
CGIMNORS	scroming
CGIMNPRU	crumping
CGIMRRUY	micrurgy
CGINNOOP	pooncing
CGINNOOR	crooning
CGINNOPU	pouncing
CGINNORS	scorning
CGINNORW	crowning
CGINNOSS	consigns
CGINNOTU	counting
CGINOOPS	scooping
CGINOOPT	coopting
CGINOOST	scooting
CGINOPPR	cropping
CGINOPRS	corpsing
CGINOPRU	crouping
CGINORSS	crossing
CGINORSU	coursing
	scouring
	sourcing
CGINORTU	courting
CGINOSTU	scouting
CGINRRUY	currying
CGINRSTU	crusting
CGINSTTU	cuttings
	tungstic
CGKLNOSU	gunlocks
CGKNOSTU	gunstock
CGLMOOYY	mycology
CGLNOOOY	oncology
CGLOOOTY	tocology
CGLOOTYY	cytology
CGLRSUUY	Lycurgus
CGNOORTU	Goncourt
CHHHHOTU	Hochhuth
CHHIIKST	thickish
CHHIIPST	phthisic
CHHILRSU	churlish
CHHIMRTY	rhythmic
CHHNORSU	rhonchus
CHHOOPTT	hotchpot
CHIIINRT	rhinitic
CHIIKLST	ticklish
CHIILNNP	linchpin
CHIILNST	chitlins
CHIILOPT	hoplitic
CHIILORT	trochili
CHIILOST	holistic
	Stilicho
CHIILPRY	chirpily
CHIILPTZ	Lipchitz
CHIILQSU	cliquish
CHIINOPS	siphonic
CHIINORT	ornithic
CHIIORST	historic
	orchitis
CHIIPPRU	hippuric
CHIIRSTT	tristich
CHIKLLOS	hillocks
CHIKLLOY	hillocky
CHIKLNUY	chunkily
CHIKLORS	horlicks
CHIKMNNU	munchkin
CHIKMNPU	chipmunk
CHIKMNTU	mutchkin
CHIKNOOR	Korchnoi
CHIKNOOS	chinooks
CHIKOPTY	kyphotic
CHIKOSST	stockish
CHIKPSYY	physicky
CHILLMSU	chillums
CHILLOOT	oilcloth
CHILMMUY	chummily
CHILMOSU	scholium
CHILMPSU	clumpish
CHILNNPY	lynchpin
CHILNOSW	clownish
CHILNPUY	punchily
CHILOOOZ	holozoic
CHILOOYZ	hylozoic
CHILOPPY	choppily
CHILOSTT	clottish
CHILOTUY	touchily
CHILOTYY	Holy City
CHIMMORU	chromium
CHIMNORW	inchworm
CHIMNOSU	insomuch
CHIMNOSY	chymosin
CHIMORSS	chrisoms
CHINOORS	chorions
	isochron
CHINOORT	orthicon
CHINOPTY	hypnotic
	pythonic
	typhonic
CHINORTU	cothurni
CHINOSSU	cushions
CHINOSTZ	schizont
CHINOSUY	cushiony
CHIOOPPT	photopic
CHIOOPTY	oophytic
CHIOORSS	isochors
CHIOORSU	ichorous
CHIOORSZ	chorizos
CHIOPRST	strophic
CHIOSSTT	Scottish
CHIPRRSU	chirrups
CHIPRRSY	pyrrhics
CHIPRRUY	chirrupy
CHIPRTTY	triptych
CHIRRSSU	scirrhus
CHISSTTU	chutists
CHKLOSSY	shylocks
CHKMMOSU	hummocks
CHKMMOUY	hummocky
CHKNOOSS	schnooks
CHKNORSU	cornhusk
CHKOOOPS	cookshop
CHKOPSTU	tuckshop
CHKORRTU	Thurrock
CHLNOOOP	colophon
CHLOORSU	chlorous
CHLOPSTY	splotchy
CHMNORRU	crumhorn
CHMOORSU	chromous
CHNNOORS	chronons
CHNOOPTT	topnotch
CHNORSSY	synchros
CHNORSTU	cothurns
CHOPSTUU	touchups
CHORSTTU	shortcut
CIIILMPT	implicit
CIIILMSU	silicium
CIIILTVY	civility
CIIINNOS	incision
CIIINTVY	vicinity
CIIJRSTU	juristic
CIIKKLLS	killicks
CIIKLPST	lipstick
CIIKLRTY	trickily
CIIKLSTY	stickily
CIIKNPPR	pinprick
CIIKNPST	stickpin
CIIKPSUW	wickiups
CIILLMTU	tillicum
CIILLNOP	pollinic
CIILLSUU	Lucilius
CIILMOPY	impolicy
CIILMOSS	sciolism
CIILMRSY	lyricism
CIILOOPT	politico
CIILOPST	colpitis
	politics
CIILORST	clitoris

CIILOSST sciolist
solicits
CIILPRSY crispily
CIILRSTY lyricist
CIILRTUU utriculi
CIILSTTY stylitic
CIIMMNOS minicoms
CIIMNOOS isonomic
CIIMNOST monistic
nomistic
CIIMORST trisomic
CIIMOSST stoicism
CIIMOSYZ isozymic
CIIMRTTU triticum
CIINNSTT instinct
CIINOOST isotonic
CIINORSS incisors
CIINORST crostini
CIINOSSS scission
CIINOSTT stiction
CIINOSTV Visconti
CIINOTTY tonicity
CIINPSTU sinciput
CIIOOPST isotopic
CIIOQTUX quixotic
CIIOTTXY toxicity
CIIPRRTU pruritic
CIIPRSTU puristic
CIIRSTTU truistic
CIISSTTY cystitis
CIJKOSTY joystick
CIJNNOOS conjoins
CIJNNOOT conjoint
CIJNNOTU junction
CIJOOSTY jocosity
CIKKLLOS killocks
CIKLLOPS pillocks
CIKLLORS rollicks
CIKLLPUY pluckily
CIKLNOST linstock
CIKLOPSU liposuck
CIKLOSTY stockily
CIKMNNNO McKinnon
CIKMOORS sickroom
CIKNNOOS coonskin
CIKNNOST nonstick
CIKNOSSW cowskins
CIKNSSTU unsticks
CIKOSSTT stockist
CIKOSSTU sickouts
CIKOSTTU stickout
CIKPSSTU stickups
CIKPSUWY wickyups
CILLMSUY clumsily
CILLNOOT cotillon
CILLNOSU scullion
CILLOOOT ocotillo
CILLOORS criollos
CILMNOPU pulmonic
CILMNOUU inoculum
CILMNUUV vinculum
CILMOPSY olympics
CILMPSUU spiculum
CILNNOOS Nicolson
CILNOORU unicolor
CILNOOST colonist
CILNOOTU locution
CILNOPTU plutonic
CILNOSTU linocuts
CILNOSUY cousinly
CILNPSSU sculpins
CILOOPST copilots
CILOOPYZ polyzoic
CILOORRT tricolor
CILOORST colorist
cortisol
CILOORSU couloirs
CILOPRRY pyrrolic
CILOPRUY polyuric
CILOPSSW cowslips
CILOSSTU oculists
CILOSSTY systolic
CILOSSUU luscious
CILPRSTU culprits
CILPSSTU sculpsit
CILRSTTY strictly
CILRSTUY crustily
CILRSUVY scurvily
CILSSTTU cultists
CIMNOORS omicrons
CIMNOOTY myotonic
CIMNORSS crimsons
CIMNORSY cronyism
CIMNOSTU miscount
CIMNOSUU mucinous
CIMNOSUY syconium
CIMOOOTZ zootomic
CIMOORSS moriscos
CIMOSTUU muticous
CIMOSTUY mucosity
CINNOOTU continuo
CINNOOTX nontoxic
CINNORSU unicorns
CINNOSTU unctions
CINNOSTY syntonic
CINNQUUX quincunx
CINOOOPT cooption
CINOOPRS scorpion
CINOOPRT protonic
CINOOTXY oxytocin
CINOPSTY synoptic
CINORRST tricorns
CINORSST cistrons
CINORSTU ructions
CINOSSST consists
CINOSTUV viscount
CINRSSTU incrusts
CINRSTTU instruct
CINRSTUY scrutiny
CIOOOPRS oosporic
CIOOOTXZ zootoxic
CIOOPRST porticos
CIOOQSTU coquitos
CIOPSSTY copyists
CIORSSSS scissors
CIPPRRUU purpuric
CIPSSTTY styptics
CIRSSTUY citrussy
CJNOORRU conjuror
CKKNOOTU knockout
CKLLMOSU mullocks
CKLLMOUY mullocky
CKLLOOPS pollocks
CKLMMOOS slommock
CKLNOSTU locknuts
CKLOORSW rowlocks
CKLOOSTU lockouts
CKLOPSTU putlocks
CKMMORUW muckworm
CKNOOORS rockoons
CKNOOSTT Stockton
CKOOOSTU cookouts
CKOOPSTT stockpot
CKOSSSTU tussocks
CKOSSTUY tussocky
CLLLSUUU Lucullus
CLLMOSSU molluscs
CLLNNOOY Connolly
CLLOOPSS scollops
CLLOOQUY colloquy
CLMMNOOY commonly
CLMOOOTY colotomy
CLMOOPST complots
CLMOSUUU cumulous
CLMSTUUU Tusculum
CLNOORST controls
CLNOSSTU consults
CLOOOPRT protocol
CLOOSSSU colossus
CLOPRSTU sculptor
CMMNNOOU uncommon
CMNOOOST monocots
CMNOOPRT Crompton
CMOOPRST comports
CMOOPSST composts
CMORSSTU scrotums
CMORSTUW cutworms
CNNORSTU nocturns
CNNORSUW uncrowns
CNOOOORT octoroon
CNOOPSSU soupcons
CNOORRTY cryotron
CNOORSST consorts
CNOORSTT contorts
CNOORSTU contours
croutons
CNOSTUUU unctuous
COOPRRST proctors
COOPRSTU outcrops
COOPRSUU croupous
COOPRSUY uroscopy
COORSSTU outcross
COOSSTTY otocysts
COPRRSTU corrupts
DDDDEEOR doddered
DDDEEEFN defended

DDDEEENP depended
DDDEEENR reddened
DDDEEFOR foddered
DDDEEHRS shredded
DDDEEIKN Dedekind
DDDEEJRU juddered
DDDEENOR dondered
DDDEENOS soddened
DDDEENUW unwedded
DDDEEORR dodderer
DDDEERTU detruded
DDDEGILR griddled
DDDEIINV dividend
DDDEILNW dwindled
DDDEILRS diddlers
DDDEILTW twiddled
DDDEINOR dendroid
DDDEINRU underdid
DDDEIQSU squidded
DDDGIILN diddling
DDEEEEMR redeemed
DDEEEENP deepened
DDEEEFIR redefied
DDEEEFLX deflexed
DDEEEFNR defender
fendered
DDEEEFRR deferred
DDEEEGLR ledgered
DDEEEGMR demerged
DDEEEGRT deterged
DDEEEHLW wheedled
DDEEEHNU unheeded
DDEEEIMR remedied
DDEEEIRT reedited
DDEEELPT depleted
DDEEELRW rewelded
DDEEEMNR remended
DDEEEMNT demented
DDEEENNU unneeded
DDEEENPX expended
DDEEENRR rendered
DDEEENRT tendered
DDEEENSU unseeded
DDEEENTX extended
DDEEENUW unweeded
DDEEERRT deterred
DDEEERST deserted
DDEEERSV deserved
DDEEESTT detested
DDEEESTV devested
DDEEFFIR differed
DDEEFFNO offended
DDEEFGIT fidgeted
DDEEFINR friended
DDEEFLNO enfolded
DDEEFLOR refolded
DDEEFMOR deformed
DDEEFNRU refunded
underfed
DDEEGILR regilded
DDEEGINS designed
DDEEGIRV diverged
DDEEGIST digested
DDEEGJRU rejudged
DDEEGOPS godspeed
DDEEGORS sodgered
DDEEGRRS dredgers
DDEEGSTU degusted
DDEEHILS shielded
DDEEHINR hindered
DDEEHIRT dithered
DDEEHNOR dehorned
DDEEHRRS shredder
DDEEHRSS shedders
DDEEIINT inedited
DDEEIIRV redivide
DDEEIKNW Wedekind
DDEEILLV devilled
DDEEILMN mildened
DDEEILMW mildewed
DDEEILNR redlined
DDEEILRV driveled
DDEEILRW wildered
DDEEIMNP impended
DDEEIMNR reminded
DDEEIMOR moidered
DDEEIMOS Diomedes
DDEEIMSS misdeeds
DDEEIMST demisted
DDEEIMTT demitted
DDEEINNT indented
intended
DDEEINNU undenied
DDEEINRT dendrite
DDEEINST destined
DDEEINTU unedited
DDEEIPRS presided
DDEEIPRV deprived
DDEEIPSS depsides
despised
DDEEIPST despited
DDEEIRRS deriders
DDEEIRTV diverted
DDEEISST desisted
DDEEISTV divested
DDEELLMO modelled
DDEELLOY yodelled
DDEELMOR moldered
DDEELMPU deplumed
DDEELMRS meddlers
DDEELNOU loudened
DDEELOPR deplored
DDEELOPX exploded
DDEELOPY deployed
DDEELORS soldered
DDEELOSU deloused
DDEELOVV devolved
DDEELPRS peddlers
DDEELPRU preluded
DDEELRSU deluders
DDEEMNNU unmended
DDEEMNOR endoderm
DDEEMRRU demurred
murdered
DDEENNOR donnered
DDEENNTU untended
DDEENOOW woodened
DDEENOPR pondered
DDEENOPW pondweed
DDEENORS endorsed
DDEENORW wondered
DDEENRSU denuders
sundered
DDEEOPRT deported
DDEEOPRW powdered
DDEEORRW reworded
DDEEORTU detoured
DDEEORUV devoured
DDEEORVY overdyed
DDEERRUV verdured
DDEERSTU detrudes
DDEERTUX extruded
DDEFFISU diffused
DDEFIIIN nidified
DDEFIILM midfield
DDEFIILR fiddlier
DDEFIIMO modified
DDEFILLO Oldfield
DDEFILNO infolded
DDEFILRS fiddlers
DDEFLNOU unfolded
DDEFNNUU unfunded
DDEFOPRT Deptford
DDEGGINR dredging
DDEGGLOY doggedly
DDEGGNOO doggoned
DDEGHINS shedding
DDEGIINR deriding
DDEGIIST giddiest
DDEGILMN meddling
DDEGILNP peddling
DDEGILNR reddling
DDEGILNU deluding
indulged
DDEGILOS dislodge
DDEGILRS griddles
DDEGILUV divulged
DDEGIMOS demigods
DDEGINNS snedding
DDEGINNU denuding
DDEGINSW weddings
DDEGINUU unguided
DDEGIOST dodgiest
DDEGLOPS splodged
DDEGLOSS dogsleds
DDEGMOOS smoodged
DDEGNOOR Dordogne
DDEGNORU grounded
underdog
DDEGNOSS godsends
DDEGNOSU dudgeons
DDEGOOTU outdodge
DDEGOOWW Wedgwood
DDEGORSS gorsedds
DDEGRRSU drudgers
DDEGRRUY drudgery

DDEHILLO Old Delhi
DDEHILNY hiddenly
DDEHINOR dihedron
DDEHIORS shoddier
DDEHIOSS shoddies
DDEHIRSY hydrides
DDEHLRSU huddlers
DDEHNRSU hundreds
DDEHOOOO hoodooed
DDEHOOSW woodshed
DDEHORSU shrouded
DDEHRSSU shudders
DDEHRSUY shuddery
DDEIIKLS disliked
DDEIILNR dieldrin
DDEIILOS idolised
DDEIILOZ idolized
DDEIILRT tiddlier
DDEIIMNU Edmund II
DDEIINTU untidied
DDEIIOPS diopside
dipodies
DDEIIOST oddities
DDEIIOSX dioxides
oxidised
DDEIIOXZ oxidized
DDEIIRSV dividers
DDEIIRUV reduviid
DDEIKSVY skydived
DDEILMOP imploded
DDEILNPS spindled
splendid
DDEILNRU unriddle
DDEILNSW dwindles
swindled
DDEILOPS displode
lopsided
DDEILOST deltoids
DDEILPRS piddlers
DDEILRRS riddlers
DDEILRST tiddlers
DDEILRTW twiddler
DDEILRZZ drizzled
DDEILSTW twiddles
DDEIMMNU undimmed
DDEIMORS dermoids
DDEIMOSS desmoids
DDEIMOSU medusoid
DDEIMSTU muddiest
DDEINNRU unridden
DDEINORS indorsed
DDEINOSW disendow
disowned
downside
DDEINOWW windowed
DDEINPSS dispends
DDEINRST stridden
DDEINRTU intruded
DDEINSST distends
DDEIOPRS dropsied
DDEIOPRV provided
DDEIOPSS disposed
DDEIORRS disorder
DDEIOSTW dowdiest
DDEIPSTU disputed
DDEIRSSU druidess
DDEIRSTU ruddiest
sturdied
DDEKMOSU dukedoms
DDELLOOP dolloped
DDELMRSU muddlers
DDELNOSY soddenly
DDELNRTU trundled
DDELNSUY suddenly
DDELOORS doodlers
DDELOPRS plodders
DDELORST toddlers
DDELPRSU puddlers
DDELPSSU spuddles
DDEMNOST oddments
DDEMNOUU duodenum
DDEMNPUU pudendum
DDEMOOTU outmoded
DDENNORS dendrons
DDENOOSS desnoods
DDENOOUW unwooded
DDENOPSS desponds
DDENORSU redounds
DDENOSUW swounded
DDEOOOOV voodooed
DDEOORSW redwoods
DDEOOSWY dyewoods
DDEOPRRS prodders
DDEOPRSW dewdrops
DDEPRSSU spudders
DDFGIILN fiddling
DDFGILNU fuddling
DDFMNOUU dumfound
DDGGIINY giddying
DDGGILNU guddling
DDGGINNO dingdong
DDGGINRU drudging
DDGHILNU huddling
DDGHINTU thudding
DDGIIINO indigoid
DDGIIINV dividing
DDGIIKNS skidding
DDGIILMN middling
DDGIILNP piddling
DDGIILNR riddling
DDGILMNU muddling
DDGILNNO noddling
DDGILNOO doodling
DDGILNOP plodding
poddling
DDGILNOT toddling
DDGILNPU puddling
DDGILNRU ruddling
DDGIMNUY muddying
DDGINOPR prodding
DDGINPSU puddings
spudding
DDGINPUY puddingy
DDGINSTU studding
DDGLORRU druglord
DDGOOOOW Goodwood
DDHILOSY shoddily
DDHILSUY dudishly
DDHIORSY hydroids
DDHIOSWY dowdyish
DDIIIIVV dividivi
DDIIKLSS skidlids
DDIILOPS diploids
DDIILOPY diploidy
DDIIMMUY didymium
DDIIMRSU druidism
siddurim
DDIINOPU dupondii
DDIIQTUY quiddity
DDILOOPP diplopod
DDILOOWW wildwood
DDILORSY sordidly
DDIMOSUY didymous
DDINNOWW downwind
DDINOOOT odontoid
DDINOOWW woodwind
DDLMORSU doldrums
DDMNOORS dromonds
DDMNORTU Dortmund
DDNOORTW downtrod
DEEEEFRR refereed
DEEEEGKR kedgeree
DEEEEHLR reheeled
DEEEEMMS meseemed
DEEEEMRR redeemer
DEEEEMST esteemed
DEEEENPR deepener
DEEEENRV veneered
DEEEERTT teetered
DEEEFHST sheetfed
DEEEFINR redefine
DEEEFIPT tepefied
DEEEFIRS redefies
DEEEFIRW fireweed
DEEEFKST keftedes
DEEEFLRU refueled
DEEEFLRX reflexed
DEEEFMNR freedmen
DEEEFNRT deferent
DEEEFNSS defenses
DEEEFORV overfeed
DEEEFRRR deferrer
referred
DEEEFRRT ferreted
DEEEFRST festered
DEEEFRTT fettered
DEEEGILS elegised
DEEEGILZ elegized
DEEEGIPR pedigree
DEEEGIRR greedier
DEEEGISW edgewise
DEEEGLNR Legendre
DEEEGLPS pledgees
DEEEGLSS edgeless
DEEEGLSV selvedge
DEEEGMRR demerger

DEEEGMRS	demerges
DEEEGNNR	engender
DEEEGNRU	renegued
DEEEGNRV	revenged
DEEEGRSS	egressed
DEEEGRST	deterges
DEEEGRTT	gettered
DEEEHHSW	wheeshed
DEEEHLMT	helmeted
DEEEHLRW	wheedler
DEEEHLSS	heedless
DEEEHLSW	wheedles
DEEEHMMR	rehemmed
DEEEHMNS	enmeshed
DEEEHPRT	threeped
DEEEHRTT	tethered
DEEEIKLS	seedlike
DEEEIKLW	weedlike
DEEEILRV	relieved
DEEEIMRS	remedies
DEEEINRR	reindeer
DEEEINRS	nereides
DEEEINST	neediest
DEEEINTV	eventide
DEEEIPRS	speedier
DEEEIPTX	expedite
DEEEIRRR	derriere
DEEEIRSS	diereses
DEEEIRST	reediest
DEEEIRTW	tweedier
DEEEIRVW	reviewed
DEEEISST	seediest
	Teesside
DEEEISSV	devisees
DEEEISTW	weediest
DEEEJLLW	jewelled
DEEEJRRS	jerreeds
DEEEKLNN	kenneled
DEEEKLNR	kerneled
DEEEKNSW	weekends
DEEEKOPW	pokeweed
DEEEKRSW	skewered
DEEELLLV	levelled
DEEELLPR	predelle
	repelled
DEEELLPT	pelleted
DEEELLPX	expelled
DEEELLRV	revelled
DEEELMRT	remelted
DEEELNRT	relented
DEEELNRU	unreeled
DEEELNSS	lessened
	needless
DEEELPST	depletes
	steepled
DEEELRTT	lettered
DEEELRTW	weltered
DEEELSSS	seedless
DEEELSSW	weedless
DEEEMNRS	Menderes
DEEEMNSS	demesnes
DEEEMPRT	tempered
DEEEMPTX	exempted
DEEEMRSS	medreses
DEEEMRST	deemster
DEEENOPR	reopened
DEEENORS	endorsee
DEEENPRT	repented
	repetend
DEEENPRX	expender
DEEENPSS	deepness
DEEENPSX	expensed
DEEENRRR	renderer
DEEENRRT	tenderer
DEEENRRV	reverend
DEEENRST	resented
DEEENRTT	tentered
DEEENRTU	neutered
DEEENRTV	Deventer
DEEENRTX	extender
DEEENRUV	revenued
	unreeved
DEEENSTT	detentes
DEEENSTX	dentexes
DEEEOPRT	deportee
DEEEOSTV	devotees
DEEEPPPR	peppered
DEEEPRSS	speeders
DEEEPRST	pestered
DEEEQSUZ	squeezed
DEEERRRV	verderer
DEEERRST	deserter
DEEERRSV	deserver
	reserved
	reversed
DEEERRTV	reverted
DEEERSSV	deserves
DEEERSTT	detester
	retested
	streeted
DEEERSTV	revested
DEEERSTW	westered
DEEERSTX	exserted
DEEERTTV	revetted
DEEERUVX	Devereux
DEEESTTV	vedettes
DEEFFGOR	goffered
DEEFFINS	effendis
DEEFFNOR	forefend
	offender
DEEFFRSU	suffered
DEEFGILR	fledgier
DEEFGILZ	Ziegfeld
DEEFGINR	fingered
DEEFGLNU	engulfed
DEEFGLOO	feelgood
DEEFGLUW	gulfweed
DEEFGORR	reforged
DEEFHLOR	freehold
DEEFHLRS	feldsher
DEEFHORR	Hereford
DEEFIINT	definite
DEEFIIRS	deifiers
	edifiers
	fireside
DEEFIIRV	verified
DEEFILLR	refilled
DEEFILLT	filleted
DEEFILMR	refilmed
DEEFILMS	medflies
DEEFILNX	inflexed
DEEFILPR	pilfered
DEEFILRS	defilers
	fielders
DEEFILRT	filtered
DEEFIMTU	tumefied
DEEFINRR	inferred
DEEFINRS	definers
DEEFINRZ	frenzied
DEEFINSS	finessed
DEEFINST	infested
DEEFIORS	foreside
DEEFIPRX	prefixed
DEEFIRTT	refitted
DEEFLLOW	fellowed
DEEFLLRU	fullered
DEEFLNNU	funneled
DEEFLNOR	enfolder
DEEFLORW	deflower
	flowered
DEEFLOST	feedlots
DEEFLRRU	ferruled
DEEFLRUX	refluxed
DEEFMNOT	fomented
DEEFMORR	deformer
	reformed
DEEFMORS	freedoms
DEEFMPRU	perfumed
DEEFNOOR	foredone
DEEFNOST	softened
DEEFNRRU	refunder
DEEFNSST	deftness
DEEFOORR	reroofed
DEEFOORS	foredoes
DEEFOORT	footered
DEEFOORW	woodfree
DEEFORST	deforest
	De Forest
	forested
	fostered
DEEFORTU	foutered
DEEFPRSU	perfused
DEEFRRTU	returfed
DEEGGHHO	hedgehog
DEEGGIJR	jiggered
	rejigged
DEEGGINR	gingered
DEEGGIRR	dreggier
DEEGGLOR	doggerel
DEEGGNOR	engorged
DEEGGNPU	unpegged
DEEGGORR	regorged
DEEGGORT	gorgeted
DEEGHHOP	hedgehop
DEEGHILL	Edgehill
DEEGHILS	sleighed

DEEGHINR rehinged
DEEGHITW weighted
DEEGHLPU pleughed
DEEGHNRU hungered
DEEGHOPS sheepdog
DEEGHORW hedgerow
DEEGHOSW hogweeds
DEEGHOTT dogteeth
DEEGIINN indigene
DEEGILMT gimleted
DEEGILNN needling
DEEGILNO eloigned
DEEGILNR lingered
reedling
DEEGILNS seedling
DEEGILNT deleting
DEEGILRW weregild
DEEGILRY greedily
DEEGIMMR immerged
DEEGIMNN emending
DEEGIMRU demiurge
DEEGINOS Diogenes
DEEGINPS speeding
DEEGINRR deringer
DEEGINRS designer
energids
redesign
reedings
resigned
DEEGINSS edginess
DEEGINST ingested
signeted
DEEGINSX desexing
DEEGIORT goitered
DEEGIPSW pigweeds
DEEGIRST digester
redigest
DEEGIRSV diverges
DEEGISTW wedgiest
DEEGJPRU prejudge
DEEGJRSU rejudges
DEEGLLUY gulleyed
DEEGLNOZ lozenged
DEEGLNRY legendry
DEEGLOPR pledgeor
DEEGLORV groveled
DEEGLORW glowered
DEEGLOSY goldeyes
DEEGLPRS pledgers
DEEGLPST pledgets
DEEGLRSS sledgers
DEEGLRSU Guelders
DEEGLRSW wergelds
DEEGMSUW gumweeds
DEEGNNOS endogens
DEEGNNOY endogeny
DEEGNOPU geepound
DEEGNORV governed
DEEGNPRU repugned
DEEGNPUX expunged
DEEGORST gostered
DEEGOTUW goutweed
DEEGRRSU resurged
DEEGRSTU gestured
DEEGRTTU guttered
DEEGSSTU gusseted
DEEHHNPY hyphened
DEEHHPRS shepherd
DEEHHRST threshed
DEEHIKLS shedlike
DEEHIKRS shrieked
DEEHILNW New Delhi
DEEHILRS relished
shielder
DEEHILSS hideless
DEEHILSV dishevel
DEEHIMMS immeshed
DEEHIMNS inmeshed
DEEHIMOP hemipode
DEEHIMRT Meredith
DEEHINPR ephedrin
DEEHINRR hinderer
DEEHINRS drisheen
DEEHINTW whitened
DEEHIOTX ethoxide
DEEHIPRS perished
DEEHIRRT ditherer
DEEHIRSV shivered
DEEHIRSW shrewdie
DEEHIRTW withered
DEEHIRTY heredity
DEEHKNOS keeshond
DEEHKNRU hunkered
DEEHLLOR hollered
DEEHLLOV hovelled
DEEHLMNU unhelmed
DEEHLNPU unhelped
DEEHLOSU houseled
DEEHLOSV shoveled
DEEHLSTU sleuthed
DEEHMNRS herdsmen
DEEHMORT mothered
DEEHNORR dehorner
DEEHNORT dethrone
threnode
DEEHNOWY honeydew
DEEHNSTU enthused
DEEHOORV hoovered
DEEHOPRT pothered
DEEHORSU rehoused
DEEHORSW showered
DEEHORTX exhorted
DEEHPRSY syphered
DEEHRRSW shrewder
DEEIIKLT tidelike
DEEIILNS sideline
DEEIILRV liveried
DEEIILRW wieldier
DEEIIMRS dimerise
DEEIIMRZ dimerize
DEEIIMST itemised
DEEIIMTZ itemized
DEEIINOZ deionize
DEEIIPRS Pierides
DEEIIPRU priedieu
DEEIIRSS dieresis
DEEIIRST siderite
DEEIIRSV derisive
DEEIIRSW weirdies
DEEIISSS disseise
DEEIISSZ disseize
DEEIJNNO enjoined
DEEIJNOR rejoined
DEEIJRTT jittered
DEEIKLLR killdeer
DEEIKLLS skellied
DEEIKLMO domelike
DEEIKLMW milkweed
DEEIKLNN enkindle
DEEIKLNR rekindle
DEEIKLOV dovelike
DEEIKLSW silkweed
DEEIKNRS deerskin
DEEIKNRT tinkered
DEEIKOSV dovekies
DEEIKPPR kippered
DEEIKSTT diskette
DEEILLMN Medellín
DEEILLMP impelled
milleped
DEEILLNO nielloed
DEEILLRT tillered
DEEILLVY veiledly
DEEILMNU demilune
DEEILMOS melodies
melodise
DEEILMOZ melodize
DEEILNOT deletion
entoiled
DEEILNRS redlines
DEEILNRU underlie
DEEILNSS idleness
DEEILNST enlisted
listened
tinseled
DEEILNSV sniveled
DEEILNTT entitled
DEEILNUV unveiled
DEEILOPT lepidote
DEEILORT dolerite
loitered
DEEILORV evildoer
DEEILPRX diplexer
DEEILPSY speedily
DEEILRST relisted
DEEILRSU leisured
DEEILRSV delivers
silvered
slivered
DEEILRSW wielders
DEEILRSY yielders
DEEILRTT littered
retitled
DEEILRVY delivery
DEEILSST tideless
DEEILSTU dilutees

DEEILSUV	delusive
DEEILSVW	swiveled
DEEIMMNS	endemism
DEEIMMOS	semidome
DEEIMMRS	immersed
	simmered
DEEIMNOR	domineer
DEEIMNOS	demonise
	dominees
DEEIMNOZ	demonize
DEEIMNPT	pediment
DEEIMNRR	reminder
DEEIMNRT	reminted
DEEIMNSS	sidesmen
DEEIMNST	sediment
DEEIMNSU	seminude
DEEIMPRR	periderm
DEEIMPRS	demireps
	impeders
	premised
	simpered
DEEIMPRX	premixed
DEEIMRST	demerits
	demister
	dimeters
	mistered
DEEIMRTT	remitted
DEEINNPR	repinned
DEEINNRT	indenter
	intender
	interned
DEEINNRV	innerved
DEEINNST	desinent
DEEINNSZ	denizens
DEEINNTV	invented
DEEINNTW	entwined
DEEINORS	indorsee
DEEINORT	oriented
DEEINOSV	nosedive
DEEINPSS	dispense
DEEINQRU	enquired
DEEINQSU	sequined
DEEINRRT	interred
	trendier
DEEINRRW	rewinder
DEEINRSS	direness
DEEINRST	Dniester
	inserted
	resident
	sintered
	trendies
DEEINRSU	uredines
DEEINRSW	rewidens
	wideners
DEEINRSX	indexers
DEEINRTU	retinued
	reunited
DEEINRTV	inverted
DEEINRTW	wintered
DEEINRTX	dextrine
DEEINSST	destines
DEEINSSW	dewiness
	wideness
DEEINSTT	dinettes
DEEINSTU	detinues
DEEINSTV	invested
DEEINSTY	Tyneside
DEEINTUV	duvetine
DEEIOPRX	peroxide
DEEIOPSS	episodes
DEEIOPST	poetised
DEEIOPSX	epoxides
DEEIOPTZ	poetized
DEEIORRV	override
DEEIORSV	overside
DEEIOTVX	videotex
DEEIPPQU	equipped
DEEIPPRZ	zippered
DEEIPPST	peptides
	peptised
DEEIPPTT	pipetted
DEEIPPTZ	peptized
DEEIPQRU	repiqued
DEEIPRRS	presider
	reprised
	respired
DEEIPRRV	depriver
DEEIPRSS	despiser
	disperse
	presides
DEEIPRST	Depretis
	priested
	respited
DEEIPRSV	deprives
	prevised
DEEIPRTT	prettied
DEEIPSSS	despises
DEEIPSST	despites
	sidestep
DEEIPSTU	deputies
	deputise
DEEIPTUZ	deputize
DEEIQRRU	required
DEEIQRSU	esquired
DEEIQRTU	requited
DEEIQRUV	quivered
DEEIQTUU	quietude
DEEIRRRV	Red River
DEEIRRSS	derrises
	desirers
	dressier
	residers
DEEIRRST	destrier
DEEIRRSV	derivers
DEEIRRTV	diverter
DEEIRRWW	wiredrew
DEEIRSST	resisted
DEEIRSSU	residues
DEEIRSSV	devisers
	disserve
	dissever
DEEIRSTW	weirdest
DEEIRTTT	tittered
DEEIRTTW	wittered
DEEISSSU	diseuses
DEEISTTV	videttes
DEEJKNTU	junketed
DEEJPRRU	perjured
DEEKKOOY	okeydoke
DEEKMNOY	monkeyed
DEEKNNNU	unkenned
DEEKNOTW	knotweed
DEEKNOTY	keynoted
DEEKORRW	reworked
DEEKOSVY	dovekeys
DEELLMOR	modeller
DEELLMOW	mellowed
DEELLMRU	mullered
DEELLNOR	enrolled
DEELLORW	rowelled
DEELLORY	yodeller
DEELLOTW	towelled
DEELLOTX	extolled
DEELLOVY	volleyed
DEELLOWY	yellowed
DEELLRSU	duellers
DEELLRSW	dwellers
DEELLSSW	weldless
DEELMMOP	pommeled
DEELMMPU	pummeled
DEELMNOO	melodeon
DEELMNTU	unmelted
DEELMOOS	dolesome
DEELMOPR	empolder
DEELMOPY	employed
DEELMORS	modelers
	remodels
DEELMOST	molested
DEELMPSU	deplumes
DEELMRUY	demurely
DEELNNTU	tunneled
DEELNOOS	loosened
DEELNORT	redolent
	rondelet
DEELNOSS	lessoned
DEELNOSU	ensouled
DEELNPSU	pendules
DEELNRTU	underlet
DEELNRTY	tenderly
DEELNSSW	lewdness
DEELNWWY	newlywed
DEELOORT	retooled
DEELOPRR	deplorer
DEELOPRS	deplores
DEELOPRV	preloved
DEELOPRX	exploder
	explored
DEELOPRY	redeploy
DEELOPSV	develops
DEELOPSX	explodes
DEELORRS	solderer
DEELORSU	urodeles
DEELORSV	resolved
DEELORTT	dotterel
DEELORTV	revolted
DEELORTW	troweled

DEELORUV louvered
DEELORVV revolved
DEELOSSU delouses
DEELOSVV devolves
DEELPRRU preluder
DEELPRSU preludes
repulsed
DEELPRTU drupelet
DEELPSUX duplexes
DEELRSTU lustered
resulted
DEELRSTW wrestled
DEELRSTY restyled
DEEMMORS mesoderm
DEEMMRSU summered
DEEMNOOS moonseed
DEEMNOQU queendom
DEEMNORT entoderm
DEEMOORT odometer
DEEMORRT tremored
DEEMORSW wormseed
DEEMORSX exoderms
DEEMORTU udometer
DEEMPRST dempster
DEEMPRSU presumed
DEEMPRTU permuted
DEEMRRRU demurrer
murderer
DEEMRSTU mustered
DEEMRTTU muttered
DEENNOPT deponent
DEENNOPU unopened
DEENNORW renowned
DEENNOST sonneted
DEENNOSY doyennes
DEENNPST pendents
DEENNRTU unrented
DEENNRUV unnerved
DEENNSSU nudeness
DEENOORT enrooted
DEENOORV overdone
DEENOOST Oostende
DEENOPSS spondees
DEENOPST pentodes
DEENORRS endorser
DEENORRW wonderer
DEENORSS endorses
DEENORST erodents
DEENORSW endowers
reendows
worsened
DEENORTU deuteron
DEENPPRS perpends
DEENPRSS spenders
DEENPRST pretends
DEENRRSU sunderer
DEENRRTU returned
DEENRSSU rudeness
DEENRSTU dentures
sederunt
underset
unrested
DEENRSUV unserved
unversed
DEENRTUV ventured
DEENSTTU untested
DEENTUVY duvetyne
DEEOORRV overrode
DEEOORSV overdoes
overdose
DEEOPPST estopped
DEEOPRRT portered
reported
DEEOPRRV reproved
DEEOPRRW powderer
DEEOPRSS deposers
DEEOPRST dopester
reedstop
DEEOPRTT pottered
repotted
DEEOPRTX exported
DEEOPSSU espoused
DEEOQRTU roqueted
DEEORRRS orderers
reorders
DEEORRST resorted
restored
rostered
DEEORRTT retorted
DEEORRTU rerouted
DEEORRUV devourer
DEEORRVW overdrew
Verwoerd
DEEORSST oersteds
DEEORSTT tetrodes
DEEORSTX dextrose
DEEORSTY oystered
storeyed
DEEORSUV overused
DEEORSVY overdyes
DEEORTTT tottered
DEEORTTX extorted
DEEOSSUX exoduses
DEEPPRSU suppered
DEEPPSSU speedups
DEEPRTTU puttered
DEEPRUVY purveyed
DEERRSSS dressers
DEERRSUV verdures
DEERRTTU turreted
DEERSSST desserts
stressed
DEERSTUV vestured
DEERSTUX extrudes
DEERSUVY surveyed
DEERTTUX textured
DEFFHILW whiffled
DEFFHLSU shuffled
DEFFHORS shroffed
DEFFILNS sniffled
DEFFILNU Nuffield
DEFFILOV fivefold
DEFFIMOS fiefdoms
DEFFIORS offsider
DEFFIOSS offsides
DEFFIQSU squiffed
DEFFIRSU diffuser
DEFFISSU diffuses
DEFFISUX suffixed
DEFFLNSU snuffled
DEFFNORS forfends
DEFFNOSS sendoffs
DEFFSSUU suffused
DEFFSTUY dyestuff
DEFGGILN fledging
DEFGHILT flighted
DEFGHIRT frighted
DEFGIILN defiling
fielding
DEFGIILU uglified
DEFGIINN defining
DEFGIINY deifying
edifying
DEFGIIST digestif
DEFGILNU ingulfed
DEFGILRU dirgeful
DEFGILTY giftedly
DEFGINSU defusing
DEFGINUZ defuzing
DEFGIOOW goodwife
DEFGIORS firedogs
DEFGJORU forjudge
DEFHIIMU humified
DEFHIINS fiendish
finished
DEFHIOOW wifehood
DEFHIRST redshift
DEFHLOOS selfhood
DEFHOORS serfhood
DEFHORRT Hertford
DEFIIILV vilified
DEFIIIMN minified
DEFIIINS nidifies
DEFIIIVV vivified
DEFIILLO oilfield
DEFIILLP filliped
DEFIILLW wildlife
DEFIILMS misfiled
DEFIILNS infidels
infields
DEFIILOR oilfired
DEFIILRW wildfire
DEFIILSU fluidise
DEFIILTY fidelity
DEFIILUZ fluidize
DEFIIMOR modifier
DEFIIMOS modifies
DEFIIMRS misfired
DEFIINOT notified
DEFIINTY identify
DEFIIOSS ossified
DEFIIOTV videofit
DEFIIPRU purified
DEFIIPSS fissiped
DEFIIPTY typified
DEFIISST fideists

DEFILLNU unfilled
DEFILNNO ninefold
DEFILNOR infolder
DEFILNRS flinders
DEFILNRU unrifled
urnfield
DEFILNRY friendly
DEFILOPR profiled
DEFILORU fluoride
DEFILORV frivoled
DEFILOTU outfield
DEFILOTY foetidly
DEFILPRU prideful
DEFILPTU uplifted
DEFILRRU flurried
DEFILRVY fervidly
DEFILRZZ frizzled
DEFIMNOR informed
DEFIMOPR pediform
DEFIMORY remodify
DEFIMRRU drumfire
DEFIMRSU Dumfries
DEFINORW forewind
DEFINRTY trendify
DEFINTTU unfitted
DEFIOPRT profited
DEFIOTXY detoxify
DEFIRRST drifters
DEFIRSSU fissured
DEFISSTU feudists
DEFKLORY forkedly
DEFLLOOR folderol
DEFLLOOW followed
DEFLMRSU Rumsfeld
DEFLNORS fondlers
DEFLNORU flounder
unfolder
DEFLNRUU unfurled
DEFLOORS flooders
refloods
DEFLOORT foretold
DEFLOORV overfold
DEFLOOSS foodless
DEFMNORU unformed
DEFMOOOR foredoom
DEFNNOSS fondness
DEFNNOUW newfound
DEFNOOPS spoonfed
DEFNOORS frondose
DEFNOORV overfond
DEFNORRU frondeur
DEFNORSU founders
DEFNORTU fortuned
DEFNRRUU underfur
DEFOORRW foreword
DEFOOTUX outfoxed
DEFORRUW furrowed
DEFORSST defrosts
DEGGHINS hedgings
DEGGHRSU shrugged
DEGGIINN deigning
DEGGILNP pledging
DEGGILNS geldings
sledging
sniggled
DEGGILNU deluging
DEGGILRW wriggled
DEGGINRU unrigged
DEGGIORS disgorge
DEGGIPRS sprigged
DEGGIRSU druggies
DEGGLMSU smuggled
DEGGLNSU snuggled
DEGGLRUY ruggedly
DEGGNOSU gudgeons
DEGGRRSU grudgers
DEGHHILV highveld
DEGHIINS dinghies
DEGHIKNT knighted
DEGHILNS shingled
DEGHILPT plighted
DEGHILST delights
slighted
DEGHINNS shending
DEGHINNU unhinged
DEGHINOT Deighton
DEGHIOPS dogeship
DEGHIORU doughier
DEGHLOOS shoogled
DEGHLOPU ploughed
DEGHLORY hydrogel
DEGHLOSU sloughed
DEGHMOSU gumshoed
DEGHNOOS hognosed
DEGHNORT thronged
DEGHNORY hydrogen
DEGHOOOP Good Hope
DEGHOOSU doghouse
DEGIIIST digitise
DEGIIITZ digitize
DEGIILNT diligent
DEGIILNV deviling
DEGIILNW wielding
DEGIILNY yielding
DEGIILTU digitule
DEGIILTY gelidity
DEGIIMNP impeding
impinged
DEGIIMNS demising
DEGIIMSU misguide
DEGIINNR nidering
DEGIINNS indigens
DEGIINNT indigent
teinding
DEGIINNW widening
DEGIINNX indexing
DEGIINNZ dizening
DEGIINOS indigoes
DEGIINOV videoing
DEGIINRS desiring
residing
ringside
DEGIINRV deriving
DEGIINRW weirding
DEGIINST dingiest
DEGIINSV devising
DEGIISSU disguise
DEGIJMSU misjudge
DEGIKLOV kidglove
DEGILLNU duelling
DEGILLNW dwelling
DEGILMNO modeling
DEGILMNS gildsmen
DEGILMPS glimpsed
DEGILNOS sidelong
DEGILNOW doweling
DEGILNOY yodeling
DEGILNRU indulger
DEGILNSU indulges
DEGILNSW swingled
DEGILOOR goodlier
DEGILOOY ideology
DEGILOST godliest
DEGILRRS girdlers
DEGILRSU guilders
DEGILRSW wergilds
DEGILRUV divulger
DEGILRZZ grizzled
DEGILSUV divulges
DEGIMNNS mendings
DEGIMNOT demoting
DEGIMNPU impugned
DEGIMNSS smidgens
DEGIMOOT goodtime
DEGIMORR Gordimer
DEGINNNU unending
DEGINNOP deponing
DEGINNOT denoting
DEGINNOW endowing
DEGINNPS spending
DEGINNPU upending
DEGINNRT trending
DEGINNRU enduring
DEGINNSU unsigned
DEGINNTU untinged
DEGINOPS deposing
DEGINORR ordering
DEGINORS negroids
DEGINORV ringdove
DEGINORW dowering
DEGINOSW widgeons
DEGINOTV devoting
DEGINOTX detoxing
DEGINPRS springed
DEGINPTU deputing
DEGINRRS grinders
DEGINRRY grindery
redrying
DEGINRSS dressing
DEGINRST stringed
DEGINRSU grundies
DEGINRSW redwings
DEGINRSY syringed
DEGINTTU duetting
DEGIOPRR porridge
DEGIOPSS gossiped

DEGIOPST podgiest
DEGIORST stodgier
DEGIPSTU pudgiest
DEGJMNTU judgment
DEGLLNOY goldenly
DEGLLOOP golloped
DEGLMNOT lodgment
DEGLNRTU gruntled
DEGLOOPR prologed
DEGLOOPY pedology
DEGLOOUU duologue
DEGLOPRS pledgors
DEGLOPSS splodges
DEGLPRSU splurged
DEGMOOSS smoodges
DEGNNOSU dungeons
DEGNOOSS goodness
DEGNOOST stegodon
DEGNOPPU oppugned
DEGNORSU guerdons
DEGNORYY gyrodyne
DEGPRSUU upsurged
DEGRRSTU trudgers
DEHHILTW withheld
DEHHISTW whishted
DEHHOOSW whooshed
DEHIIKLS dishlike
DEHIILSV devilish
DEHIIMMS shimmied
DEHIIMST ditheism
DEHIINNS shinnied
DEHIINNW whinnied
DEHIINSS shindies
DEHIINST shintied
DEHIISST dishiest
DEHIISTT ditheist
stithied
DEHIJMNO demijohn
DEHIKLOO hoodlike
DEHIKMOS sheikdom
DEHIKMRU Durkheim
DEHIKNOW Windhoek
DEHILLRS shrilled
DEHILLRT thrilled
DEHILMOS demolish
DEHILNOY honiedly
DEHILNPY diphenyl
DEHILOOR heliodor
DEHILOPS polished
DEHILOTY holytide
DEHILPSU sulphide
DEHILSTW whistled
DEHILTTW whittled
DEHIMNOS hedonism
Sondheim
DEHIMOPS hemipods
DEHIMOST ethmoids
DEHIMPRS shrimped
DEHINOPS siphoned
sphenoid
DEHINOST hedonist
DEHINPSU punished
DEHINSUW unwished
DEHIOOST dhooties
DEHIOPRS spheroid
DEHIOSSW sideshow
DEHIOSTU hideouts
DEHIQSSU squished
DEHIRSTT thirsted
DEHIRTWW withdrew
DEHKLNOU elkhound
DEHKNOOU unhooked
DEHLLOOW hollowed
DEHLLOPY phyllode
DEHLMORY hydromel
DEHLNOOW downhole
DEHLNTUY huntedly
DEHLOORV holdover
DEHLOOSS hoodless
DEHLOOST toeholds
toolshed
DEHLOOSW woolshed
DEHLOPRU upholder
DEHLOPSS sploshed
DEHLORSU shoulder
DEHLRRSU hurdlers
DEHLRSWY shrewdly
DEHLSTTU shuttled
DEHMMRTU thrummed
DEHMNRUY unrhymed
DEHMOORW whoredom
DEHMOOST smoothed
DEHMOPRY hypoderm
DEHMORUU humoured
DEHNOORU honoured
DEHNOOSW hoedowns
woodhens
DEHNOPSY syphoned
DEHNORSU enshroud
hounders
unhorsed
DEHNORTY threnody
DEHNOSSW snowshed
DEHNOSUU unhoused
DEHNRSTU thunders
DEHNRTUY thundery
DEHOOPRT theropod
DEHOORSW Sherwood
DEHOOSSW swooshed
DEHOPRST potsherd
DEHOSSTU stoushed
DEIIIMST dimities
DEIIINSV divinise
DEIIINVZ divinize
DEIIISVV divisive
DEIIKLMS misliked
DEIIKLNR kindlier
DEIIKLSS dislikes
DEIIKNST dinkiest
DEIIKSVV skivvied
DEIILMRU delirium
DEIILMST delimits
DEIILNNU induline
DEIILNOS lionised
DEIILNOT tolidine
DEIILNOZ lionized
DEIILNPV vilipend
DEIILNVY divinely
DEIILNXY xylidine
DEIILORS idoliser
DEIILORZ idolizer
DEIILOSS idolises
DEIILOSZ idolizes
DEIILPSS sideslip
DEIILSTU utilised
DEIILTUZ utilized
DEIIMMRS dimerism
DEIIMMST mistimed
DEIIMNOS dominies
DEIIMNRT diriment
DEIIMNTU mutinied
DEIIMOSS disomies
DEIIMPRU peridium
DEIIMSVW midwives
DEIINNOP pinioned
DEIINNPP pinniped
DEIINNTW intwined
DEIINORS derision
ironised
ironside
resinoid
DEIINORZ ironized
DEIINOST editions
sedition
DEIINOSV visioned
DEIINPPW windpipe
DEIINPRS inspired
DEIINPRT intrepid
DEIINPRY pyridine
DEIINPTU unpitied
DEIINQRU inquired
DEIINRSS insiders
DEIINRST disinter
inditers
nitrides
DEIINRSV diviners
DEIINRTU untidier
DEIINSST insisted
tidiness
DEIINSTU disunite
nudities
unitised
untidies
DEIINSTW windiest
DEIINTTU intuited
DEIINTTY identity
DEIINTUZ unitized
DEIIOPRS presidio
DEIIORSS iodisers
DEIIORST diorites
DEIIORSX oxidiser
DEIIORSZ iodizers
DEIIORTX trioxide
DEIIORXZ oxidizer
DEIIOSSX oxidises
DEIIOSXZ oxidizes

DEIIPPRR drippier
DEIIPPST dippiest
DEIIPRST riptides
spirited
tiderips
DEIIPRSZ disprize
DEIIPTTY tepidity
DEIIQSTU disquiet
DEIIRSSU diuresis
DEIIRSTT dirtiest
DEIISSTT ditsiest
DEIISTTZ ditziest
DEIISTZZ dizziest
DEIJNNOU unjoined
DEIJNORS joinders
DEIJORRY joyrider
DEIJORSY joyrides
DEIKKLNO klondike
DEIKLLOR lordlike
DEIKLLSS deskills
DEIKLNNU unlinked
DEIKLNOR Kol Nidre
DEIKLNRS kindlers
DEIKLNRW wrinkled
DEIKLNSS kindless
DEIKLNTW twinkled
DEIKLORS Roskilde
DEIKMNOO kimonoed
DEIKNNRU unkinder
DEIKNNSS kindness
DEIKNORU Iron Duke
DEIKNOSS doeskins
DEIKNRRS drinkers
DEIKNRSS redskins
DEIKNSSU unkissed
DEIKORSS droskies
DEIKPRSU prusiked
spruiked
DEIKRSVY skydiver
DEIKSSTU duskiest
DEIKSSVY skydives
DEILLNSW indwells
DEILLNTU untilled
DEILLNUW unwilled
DEILLOOP Leopold I
DEILLOPW pillowed
DEILLORR lordlier
DEILLRRS drillers
redrills
DEILLSTU duellist
DEILMNOO melodion
DEILMNSS mildness
mindless
DEILMOOT dolomite
DEILMOPR implored
impolder
DEILMOPS implodes
DEILMORU lemuroid
mouldier
DEILMOST melodist
moldiest
DEILMOSU emulsoid
DEILMOTV demivolt
DEILMPTU multiped
DEILMRSU misruled
DEILNNOT indolent
DEILNOOS eidolons
solenoid
DEILNOSU delusion
insouled
unsoiled
DEILNOTU outlined
DEILNOVV involved
DEILNPSS spindles
DEILNPST splinted
DEILNRST tendrils
DEILNRSW swindler
DEILNRTY trendily
DEILNSST dintless
DEILNSSW swindles
wildness
windless
DEILNSTU diluents
insulted
unlisted
DEILNTTU untitled
DEILNTUY unitedly
DEILNUWY unwieldy
DEILOOPW woodpile
DEILOPRS leporids
DEILOPSS despoils
DEILOPST pistoled
postiled
DEILOPSU euploids
DEILOPUY euploidy
DEILOQRU liquored
DEILORSS soldiers
DEILORSY soldiery
DEILORTY elytroid
DEILOSSV dissolve
DEILOSTU solitude
DEILOSTW dowliest
DEILOSVW oldwives
DEILOTUV outlived
DEILPPST stippled
DEILPPSU supplied
DEILPRSU serpulid
DEILPTTU uptilted
DEILRSSY dressily
DEILRSTU diluters
DEILRSZZ drizzles
DEILRTUZ Lüderitz
DEILRTVY deviltry
DEILSSTY stylised
DEILSTUY sedulity
DEILSTYZ stylized
DEILSWZZ swizzled
DEIMMNOS demonism
DEIMMOST immodest
DEIMMRST midterms
DEIMMRSU drummies
DEIMNNOY Endymion
DEIMNNSU minuends
DEIMNOOS dominoes
monodies
DEIMNOOT demotion
motioned
DEIMNOOX monoxide
DEIMNOPT piedmont
DEIMNOST demonist
DEIMNOTW downtime
DEIMNPSS misspend
DEIMNPTU impudent
DEIMNRTU rudiment
DEIMNSST mindsets
DEIMOORS moidores
DEIMOOSS sodomise
DEIMOOST moodiest
sodomite
DEIMOOSZ sodomize
DEIMOPRS impedors
promised
DEIMOPRT imported
DEIMOPRV improved
DEIMOPST imposted
DEIMORRR mirrored
DEIMORST mortised
DEIMORSU dimerous
soredium
DEIMORUX exordium
DEIMOSST modistes
DEIMOSTT demotist
DEIMPSTU dumpiest
DEIMPSTY mistyped
DEIMQRSU squirmed
DEIMRSSU surmised
DEIMRSUU residuum
DEINNNOU innuendo
DEINNNPU unpinned
DEINNOOT noontide
DEINNOPT endpoint
DEINNORT indentor
DEINNORU unironed
DEINNOWW winnowed
DEINNPRU underpin
DEINNRUW unwinder
DEINNTUW untwined
DEINOOPS poisoned
Poseidon
DEINOOPT optioned
DEINOOSZ ozonides
ozonised
DEINOOTV devotion
DEINOOZZ ozonized
DEINOPPW downpipe
DEINOPRT dipteron
DEINOPRY pyrenoid
DEINOPSS dopiness
spinodes
DEINOPSU unpoised
DEINOPTW dewpoint
DEINORRS indorser
DEINORSS indorses
DEINORSU sourdine
DEINORSW disowner
windrose

DEINORVW overwind
DEINOSSV voidness
DEINOSSZ doziness
DEINOSTW downiest
DEINOSWZ downsize
DEINPPRU unripped
DEINPPUZ unzipped
DEINPRST sprinted
DEINPSST stipends
DEINQSTU squinted
DEINRRTU intruder
DEINRSSU sundries
DEINRSTT strident
tridents
DEINRSTU intrudes
nurdiest
DEINRSTX dextrins
DEINSSST dissents
DEINSSSY syndesis
DEINSSTT dentists
DEINSTUU unsuited
DEIOOORR Río de Oro
DEIOORSW woodsier
DEIOOSSS isodoses
DEIOOSTW woodiest
DEIOPRRV provider
DEIOPRSS disposer
DEIOPRST diopters
dioptres
riposted
DEIOPRSV disprove
provides
DEIOPSSS disposes
DEIOPSST deposits
topsides
DEIORRSW drowsier
DEIORRSY derisory
DEIORRTU outrider
DEIORRTW worrited
DEIORSSS dossiers
DEIORSST steroids
DEIORSSU desirous
DEIORSSV devisors
DEIORSTT dortiest
DEIORSTU outrides
outsider
DEIORSTW rowdiest
wordiest
DEIORSWW widowers
DEIORTTX tetroxid
DEIOSSTU outsides
DEIOSTTT dottiest
DEIOSTUZ outsized
DEIPPRST stripped
DEIPRRTU irrupted
DEIPRSSU suspired
DEIPRSTU disputer
stupider
DEIPSSTU disputes
DEIPTTTU tittuped
DEIQRSTU squirted
DEIRRSST striders
DEIRRSTU sturdier
DEIRSSST distress
DEIRSSTU diestrus
DEIRSTTU detritus
DEIRSUVV survived
DEISSTTU dustiest
DEISTTTU duettist
DEKNORUW unworked
DEKNRSTU drunkest
DEKOOPRV provoked
DEKOOTWW kowtowed
DEKOPSST desktops
DEKORSWY keywords
DELLLOOP lolloped
DELLNNOY Donnelly
DELLNOPU unpolled
DELLNORU unrolled
DELLNSSU dullness
DELLOORS Sordello
DELLOPRS redpolls
DELLOPTU polluted
DELLORRY drollery
DELLORSS lordless
DELLORST strolled
DELLOSTY oldstyle
DELMNORY modernly
DELMNOTW meltdown
DELMNPUU pendulum
DELMORSS smolders
DELMORSU moulders
remoulds
smoulder
DELMOSTY modestly
DELNNOOR Londoner
DELNOOSU nodulose
unloosed
DELNOOWY woodenly
DELNOPRS splendor
DELNORSU roundels
DELNORSY Reynolds
DELNORTU roundlet
DELNORWW New World
DELNOSSU loudness
DELNOSTW letdowns
DELNOSUV unsolved
DELNPRSU plunders
DELNRRTU trundler
DELNRSTU rundlets
trundles
DELOOPPS pleopods
DELOORRV overlord
DELOORSS odorless
DELOORSV oversold
DELOOSSW woodless
DELOPPST stoppled
DELOPRST droplets
DELOPSTU postlude
DELORSST oldsters
DELORSSW wordless
DELORSTT dottrels
DELORSUY delusory
DELOSSUU sedulous
DELOTUVY devoutly
DELRSSTU strudels
DELSSSTU dustless
DEMMNOOO monomode
DEMMNOSU summoned
DEMMRRSU drummers
DEMMRRUU murmured
DEMMRSTU strummed
DEMNNOOT Edmonton
DEMNOOOP monopode
DEMNOORU unmoored
DEMNOOSW woodsmen
DEMNORST mordents
DEMNORSY syndrome
DEMNOSTU demounts
mudstone
DEMOOPPS popedoms
DEMOOPRR prodrome
DEMOOPRS predooms
DEMOOPRT promoted
DEMOORST doomster
DEMOORSU dormouse
DEMOORTY odometry
DEMOPPRT prompted
DEMORRUU rumoured
DENNOSTY syndeton
DENNOTUW unwonted
DENNRTUU unturned
DENOOOTW woodnote
DENOOPPR proponed
DENOORRS endorsor
DENOORTU unrooted
DENOORTX nextdoor
DENOOSTU duotones
DENOPPRS propends
DENOPRSS responds
DENOPRST portends
DENOPRSU pounders
DENOPRUV unproved
DENOPSUX expounds
DENOQTUU unquoted
DENORRSU rondures
rounders
DENORRSW drowners
DENORSSU dourness
resounds
sounders
DENORSTU roundest
tonsured
unsorted
DENORSTY drystone
DENORSUW wounders
DENORTUW undertow
DENOSSTU soundest
DENPRTUU upturned
DENPSSSU suspends
DENRRTUU nurtured
DENRSSSU sundress
DENSSTTU students
DENSTTUY studenty
DEOOORSW rosewood
DEOOPPRS proposed

DEOOPPRT pteropod
DEOOPRST doorstep
DEOOPRTU uprooted
DEOOPWWW powwowed
DEOORRST redroots
DEOORRSW sorrowed
DEOORRVW overword
DEOOSTWW Westwood
DEOOTTUV outvoted
DEOPPRRS droppers
DEOPPRST stropped
DEOPPRSU purposed
DEOPPSSU supposed
DEOPRRTU protrude
DEOPRSTU postured
proudest
sprouted
DEOPRSUU uproused
DEORRTTU tortured
DEORSSTW worsteds
DEORSSTY destroys
DEORSTUX dextrous
DEOSSSUY Odysseus
DEOSSSYY odysseys
DEPPSSYY dyspepsy
DEPRRTUU ruptured
DERSTTTU strutted
DFFIIMRS midriffs
DFFIIRST triffids
DFFIORSU diffusor
DFFLOORU fourfold
DFFOORUW woodruff
DFGGHIOT dogfight
DFGHILOS goldfish
DFGIIIRY rigidify
DFGIILRY frigidly
DFGIINNS findings
DFGIINRT drifting
DFGILNNO fondling
DFGILNOO flooding
DFGINNOU founding
DFGINOOR fordoing
DFGLNOOR Longford
DFGNOOOS son of God
DFHIIMUY humidify
DFHILSSU dishfuls
DFHIMRSU drumfish
DFHLOOOT foothold
DFHNOOUX foxhound
DFIILMTU multifid
DFIILOSY solidify
DFIILRTU Id-ul-Fitr
DFIILTUY fluidity
DFIINPRT driftpin
DFIKNOOS skinfood
DFILLOOT floodlit
DFILLORY floridly
DFILLOWW wildfowl
DFILNNOU nonfluid
DFILNOPS pinfolds
DFIMOOOR iodoform
DFINRSUW windsurf
DFIOOPRS disproof
DFLLOSSU Dollfuss
DFLMOSUW mudflows
DFLOOSTU foldouts
DFNOOPRU profound
DFNOORSU frondous
DFOOOSTW softwood
DGGGIINS diggings
DGGGINRU drugging
grudging
DGGHIINT dighting
DGGIILNR girdling
ridgling
DGGIINNO dingoing
DGGIINNR grinding
DGGIINNW wingding
DGGIINSU guidings
DGGILNOP plodging
DGGILNOS lodgings
DGGIMNSU smudging
DGGINNOT Dongting
DGGINOST stodging
DGGINRTU trudging
DGGIRSTU druggist
DGHIIMNT midnight
DGHIINSS shindigs
DGHIKNOO kinghood
DGHILLNU dunghill
DGHILNOS holdings
DGHILNRU hurdling
DGHILOOR girlhood
DGHINNOU hounding
DGHINOSW showding
DGHINSTU hindguts
DGHNOTUU doughnut
DGHOOOTT dogtooth
DGHORRUY roughdry
DGHORSTU droughts
DGHORTUY droughty
DGIIINNT inditing
DGIIINNV divining
DGIIINOS iodising
DGIIINOZ iodizing
DGIIIRTY rigidity
DGIIKLNN kindling
DGIIKNNR drinking
DGIILLNR drilling
DGIILLNU illuding
DGIILLNW wildling
DGIILLOU liguloid
DGIILMNP dimpling
DGIILNNP pindling
DGIILNSW wildings
DGIILNTU diluting
DGIIMNOU gonidium
DGIIMNSS smidgins
DGIIMOSS sigmoids
DGIIMPUY pygidium
DGIINNOP poinding
DGIINNOR nonrigid
DGIINNSW windings
DGIINORR gridiron
DGIINORT digitron
DGIINOSX digoxins
DGIINOTT dittoing
DGIINOWW widowing
DGIINPPR dripping
DGIINRST striding
DGIINRTY dirtying
DGIINVVY divvying
DGIINYZZ dizzying
DGIJKNNO Jongkind
DGIKLOOY kidology
DGIKMNOS kingdoms
DGIKNOOR drooking
DGIKNOOW kingwood
DGIKNORU drouking
DGILLNOR lordling
DGILLNOY dollying
DGILLOOW goodwill
DGILMNOS moldings
DGILMNOU moulding
DGILMNPU dumpling
DGILMSUY smudgily
DGILNNOO noodling
DGILNOOR drooling
DGILNORS lordings
DGILOSTY stodgily
DGILRTUY turgidly
DGIMMNRU drumming
DGIMMNUY dummying
DGIMNNOU mounding
DGINNOOS snooding
DGINNOPU pounding
DGINNORU rounding
DGINNORW drowning
DGINNOSU sounding
undoings
DGINNOUW wounding
DGINOOPR drooping
DGINOOPS gospodin
DGINOOTU outdoing
DGINOPPR dropping
DGINORSW drowsing
wordings
DGINSSTU dustings
DGINSTUY studying
DGISSSTU disgusts
DGLOOOSW logwoods
DGLOOOXY doxology
DGLOOSST godslots
DGMOPRSU gumdrops
DGMOPSYY gypsydom
DGNOOOPS gonopods
DGNOOORS godroons
DGNOOORV Novgorod
DHHILOTW withhold
DHIIIMNS diminish
minidish
DHIIMNOO hominoid
DHIIMNOS hominids
DHIIMNSU Hinduism
DHIIMOST isthmoid
DHIIMPSS midships

DHIIMTUY humidity
DHIIOPSX xiphoids
DHIIORSS hidrosis
DHIIORSZ rhizoids
DHIJOPRU Jodhpuri
DHIKNOOW hoodwink
DHIKORSY hydroski
DHILLNOW downhill
DHILLOPY phylloid
DHILLPSY phyllids
DHILMOPY lymphoid
DHILMOSY modishly
DHILNOPS dolphins
DHILOPRS lordship
DHILOPSS slipshod
DHILORRY horridly
DHIMNOST hindmost
DHIMOPRS dimorphs
DHIMORSU humidors
DHIMOSTU Sidmouth
DHINOORS dishonor
DHINORSU roundish
DHINOTUW whodunit
DHINTUWY whydunit
DHIOOPRZ rhizopod
DHIORSTY thyroids
thyrsoid
DHIPRSSY syrphids
DHJOPRSU jodhpurs
DHKMNOOO monkhood
DHLMOOSU hoodlums
DHLOOORY holy rood
DHLOORSY hydrosol
DHLOOSTU holdouts
DHLORXYY hydroxyl
DHLOSSTU shouldst
DHMMRSUU humdrums
DHMNOOOT homodont
DHNNOOSU nunhoods
DHNOOPRU Proudhon
DHNOOSWW showdown
DHNOSTUW shutdown
DHOOORTX orthodox
DHOOPRST dropshot
DHOORSUW woodrush
DHOPRSSU pushrods
DIIILLQU illiquid
DIIILTVY lividity
DIIIMOST idiotism
DIIIMTTY timidity
DIIINOSV division
DIIINTVY divinity
DIIIPRST dispirit
DIIIRTVY viridity
DIIJNOSS disjoins
DIIJNOST disjoint
DIIKKNSS kidskins
DIILLMNR millrind
DIILLMNW windmill
DIILLMPY limpidly
DIILLQUY liquidly
DIILLSST distills
DIILLSTY idyllist
DIILMNSS dislimns
DIILMOPP pompilid
DIILMUUV diluvium
DIILNNSU indulins
DIILNOTU dilution
DIILNTUY untidily
DIILOPRT triploid
DIILOPSS diplosis
DIILORTU utilidor
DIILOSST idolists
DIILOSTY solidity
DIILRSSU silurids
DIILSSTY idylists
DIIMMNOU dominium
DIIMNNOO dominion
DIIMNOPT midpoint
DIIMNORS midirons
DIIMNOSS Sismondi
DIIMNSUU indusium
DIIMOPRS prismoid
DIIMPUXY pyxidium
DIIMRUUV duumviri
DIIMTTUY tumidity
DIINNOSU disunion
DIINOOPS iodopsin
DIINOSSU sinusoid
DIINSTUY disunity
DIIORSST sistroid
DIIORSSV divisors
DIJOSSTU judoists
DIKLNNUY unkindly
DIKNOPUV Pudovkin
DIKNORTU outdrink
DILLMNOP millpond
DILLOORS doorsill
DILLOSTY stolidly
DILLPSSY psyllids
DILMNOSW slimdown
DILMNRSU drumlins
DILMOOSU modiolus
DILNOPST diplonts
DILOOPPY polypoid
DILOOPRY droopily
DILOORSS lordosis
DILOOSUY odiously
DILOPRTY torpidly
DILORRTY torridly
DILORSWY drowsily
DILPRTUY putridly
DILPSTUY stupidly
DILRSTUY sturdily
DIMMNORY myrmidon
DIMNOOST monodist
DIMNOPSU impounds
DIMNOSTU dismount
DIMNOSWX mixdowns
DIMOOPPU Pompidou
DIMORSWY rowdyism
DIMRSTUU triduums
DIMRSUUV duumvirs
DINOOORW ironwood
DINOORRS indorsor
DINOOSTY nodosity
DINOPRTY drypoint
DINORSWW windrows
DINOSSUY Dionysus
DINPRTUY punditry
DINRSTUY industry
DIOORSTT ridottos
DIOPRSST disports
DIORRSST stridors
DIORSSTT distorts
DIOSSTUU studious
DIPRSSTU disrupts
DIRSSTTU distrust
DKLNOOOW lookdown
DKMNOOOR komondor
DKNORTUU outdrunk
DKOOORWW woodwork
DKORSTUW studwork
DLLMORSU slumlord
DLNOOSUU nodulous
DLNOOSWW lowdowns
slowdown
DLNORTUY rotundly
DLOOORS doloroso
DLOOORSU dolorous
DLOOOSTW woodlots
DLOOPPSY polypods
DLOOPPUW pulpwood
DLOOPPYY polypody
DLOOPSTY tylopods
DMNNOOOT monodont
DMOOORWW woodworm
wormwood
DMPPPUUY mudpuppy
DNNOORTU Duntroon
DNNOOTWW downtown
DNNORSUW rundowns
DNNORTUW downturn
turndown
DNNOSSUW sundowns
DNOOPPRU propound
DNOOPRSW snowdrop
DNOOPRUW downpour
DNOORSUW wondrous
DNOOSTUW nutwoods
DNOPRSUU roundups
DNORRSUU surround
DOOOPRST doorpost
doorstop
DOOORSTU outdoors
DOOORSUW sourwood
DOOOSTTU outstood
DOOPRRTW dropwort
DOOPRSTU dropouts
EEEEFRRS referees
EEEEFRRZ refreeze
EEEEGGRR greegree
EEEEGHRT Etherege
EEEEGMRR reemerge
EEEEGQSU squeegee
EEEEGSSX exegeses

EEEGSTX exegetes
EEEHTTY eyeteeth
EEELLPX expellee
EEELLVY eyelevel
EEELNSV sleeveen
EEELPRT Peterlee
EEENRRV veneerer
EEEPTTW peetweet
EEFFFOS feoffees
EEFFLTY effetely
EEFFNRT efferent
EEFFORT forefeet
EEFFRVW feverfew
EEFGRSU refugees
EEFINRT Tenerife
EEFIPST tepefies
EEFLRSX reflexes
EEFLSST feetless
EEFNORS foreseen
EEFNRRT referent
EEFNRSS freeness
EEFNRUZ unfreeze
EEFORRS foreseer
EEFORSS foresees
EEFRRRR referrer
EEFRRRT ferreter
EEFRRSZ freezers
EEFRRTT fetterer
EEGGILN negligee
EEGHINT eighteen
EEGIKST geekiest
EEGILMN liegemen
EEGILNS gleenies
EEGILRT gleetier
EEGILSS elegises
EEGILSZ elegizes
EEGINNR engineer
EEGINRS energies
energise
greenies
EEGINRZ energize
EEGIPRS perigees
EEGIRTY tigereye
EEGISSX exegesis
EEGISTV egestive
EEGKLRS kegelers
EEGLNRT greenlet
EEGMNRT emergent
EEGMNRU merengue
EEGMORT geometer
EEGNPRS epergnes
EEGNRRS renegers
EEGNRRU reneguer
EEGNRRV revenger
EEGNRRY greenery
EEGNRST greenest
EEGNRSU renegues
EEGNRSV revenges
EEGNSTT genettes
EEGOPRT protegee
EEGRRST greeters
EEGRSSS egresses
EEGRSUX exergues
EEHHSSW wheeshes
EEHILRW erewhile
EEHILSW wheelies
EEHINSS sheenies
EEHIRSS heresies
EEHIRST etherise
EEHIRTZ etherize
EEHIRWZ wheezier
EEHKLNO kneehole
EEHLLSS heelless
EEHLMPT helpmeet
EEHLNTV eleventh
EEHLNTY ethylene
EEHLOPP peephole
EEHLOSY eyeholes
EEHLRSW wheelers
EEHMNSS enmeshes
EEHMNTV vehement
EEHNNPT nepenthe
EEHNNQU henequen
EEHNPRS ensphere
EEHNRVW whenever
EEHORST shoetree
EEHPRRT threeper
EEHRRVW wherever
EEHRSST sheerest
EEHRSWZ wheezers
EEHSSTT esthetes
EEIKLRT treelike
EEIKLSW weeklies
EEILLRV reveille
EEILMRS seemlier
EEILNPR pelerine
EEILNRY eyeliner
EEILNST selenite
EEILNSU unseelie
EEILPRS sleepier
EEILRRV reliever
EEILRST leeriest
EEILRSV relieves
EEILRVY liveyere
EEILSTV televise
EEIMNRU meuniere
EEIMNRY Niemeyer
EEIMPRR premiere
EEIMPRS emperies
epimeres
preemies
EEIMRRS miserere
EEIMRST eremites
EEIMRSZ Mézières
EEIMRTT remittee
EEINNNT nineteen
EEINNRT internee
retinene
EEINNST Estienne
EEINNSV Viennese
EEINPRT perentie
EEINRRS sneerier
EEINRSS eeriness
EEINRST eternise
EEINRSW weensier
EEINRTZ eternize
EEINSTT teeniest
EEINSTV eventise
EEINSTW tweenies
weeniest
EEINTUX euxenite
EEINTVZ eventize
EEIPRRV reprieve
EEIPSST epeeists
EEIPSTW weepiest
EEIQSUX exequies
EEIRRST retirees
EEIRRSV reveries
EEIRRTV retrieve
EEIRRVW reviewer
EEIRTVX exertive
EEISSTW sweeties
EEJKKNR kneejerk
EEJLLRW jeweller
EEJLRSW jewelers
EEKLLSS keelless
EEKLLSU ukeleles
EEKLNRS kneelers
EEKLSST sleekest
EEKMNSS meekness
EEKNNSS keenness
EEKNORS kerosene
EEKNPST keepnets
EEKNSTV Kesteven
EEKRSST keesters
EELLLRV leveller
EELLLSW sewellel
EELLNOR enrollee
EELLNQU quenelle
EELLPRR repeller
EELLPRX expeller
EELLRRV reveller
EELLRSV levelers
EELMNST elements
EELMOPY employee
EELMOTT omelette
EELMRTU muleteer
EELNOPP Penelope
EELNOPV envelope
EELNOSV novelese
EELNRSW newsreel
EELNRSY serenely
EELOPPR repeople
EELPRSS peerless
sleepers
EELPSST steeples
EELRRTT letterer
EELRSST treeless
EELRSTT resettle
EELRSTV leverets
EELRSVY severely
EELTTTX teletext
EEMMRUZ mezereum
EEMNNTT tenement
EEMNORZ mezereon
EEMNPRT petermen

EEEMNSTW	sweetmen
EEEMORRV	evermore
EEEMORST	stereome
EEEMPRRT	temperer
EEEMRSST	semester
EEEMRSTX	extremes
EEENNOPR	neoprene
EEENNOSV	venenose
EEENNSSV	evenness
EEENNSTT	ententes
EEENORSV	overseen
	Veronese
EEENORVY	everyone
EEENPPRS	prepense
EEENPRRS	preeners
EEENPRRT	repenter
EEENPRST	pretense
	terpenes
EEENPRSY	Pyrenees
EEENPSST	steepens
EEENPSSX	expenses
EEENRRSS	sneerers
EEENRRST	enterers
	reenters
	terrenes
EEENRRSW	renewers
EEENRRTU	returnee
EEENRRTV	reverent
EEENRRUV	revenuer
EEENRSSZ	sneezers
EEENRSTV	eventers
EEENRSTX	externes
EEENRSTY	yestreen
EEENRSUV	revenues
	unreeves
EEENSSTW	sweetens
	tweeness
EEEOPPSY	popeseye
EEEORRSV	overseer
EEEORRSX	xerosere
EEEORSSV	oversees
EEEORSSY	eyesores
EEEPRRST	pesterer
EEEPRRSV	perverse
	preserve
EEEPRRTW	pewterer
EEEPRSST	steepers
EEEPRSSW	sweepers
EEEPSSTT	steepest
EEEPSTTT	septette
EEEQRSTU	queerest
EEEQRSUZ	squeezer
EEEQSSUZ	squeezes
EEERRRSV	reserver
	reverers
	reverser
EEERRRTV	reverter
EEERRSST	steerers
EEERRSSV	reserves
	reverses
EEERRSTT	resetter
EEERSSTW	sweerest
EEERSTTW	tweeters
EEERSTVX	vertexes
EEERSTWZ	tweezers
EEESSTTW	sweetest
EEESTTTX	sextette
EEFFFNOS	enfeoffs
EEFFFORS	feoffers
EEFFGIIS	effigies
EEFFHIKY	keffiyeh
EEFFINST	fifteens
EEFFISUV	effusive
EEFFJRSY	Jeffreys
EEFFLNTU	effluent
EEFFMORR	freeform
EEFFNOSS	offenses
EEFFNSST	Steffens
EEFFORRS	offerers
EEFFORSX	forfexes
EEFFRRSU	sufferer
EEFGIILR	filigree
EEFGILNR	fleering
EEFGILNS	feelings
EEFGILNT	fleeting
EEFGINNP	pfennige
EEFGINRR	fingerer
EEFGINRS	feigners
EEFGINRV	fevering
EEFGINRZ	freezing
EEFGLLNR	Grenfell
EEFGLLTU	gefullte
EEFGLMNU	fuglemen
EEFGLNRY	greenfly
EEFGLNUV	vengeful
EEFGLORS	forelegs
EEFGLOSS	solfeges
EEFGNOOR	foregone
EEFGOORR	foregoer
EEFGOORS	foregoes
EEFGORRS	reforges
EEFHILLR	hellfire
EEFHILRS	fleshier
EEFHIRSV	feverish
EEFHIRTY	etherify
EEFHISST	fetishes
EEFHISTT	heftiest
EEFHLLWY	flywheel
EEFHLMST	themself
EEFHLRSS	fleshers
EEFHMNRS	freshmen
EEFHMORY	Meyerhof
EEFHNRSS	freshens
EEFHORRT	therefor
EEFHRRSS	freshers
EEFHRRSU	fuehrers
EEFHRSST	freshest
	freshets
EEFIIKLL	lifelike
EEFIIKLW	wifelike
EEFIILLN	lifeline
EEFIILMT	lifetime
EEFIIMNN	feminine
EEFIIMNS	feminise
EEFIIMNZ	feminize
EEFIINRS	fineries
EEFIIRRS	reifiers
EEFIIRRV	verifier
EEFIIRST	feistier
	ferities
	fieriest
EEFIIRSV	verifies
EEFIKLMU	fumelike
EEFIKLNR	fernlike
EEFIKLRS	serflike
EEFIKNNP	penknife
EEFILLNY	felinely
EEFILLRW	free will
	freewill
EEFILLSS	lifeless
EEFILMNR	riflemen
EEFILMST	fistmele
EEFILMTX	flextime
EEFILNOS	felonies
	olefines
EEFILPRR	pilferer
EEFILRRT	refilter
EEFILRSS	fireless
EEFILRSU	fusileer
EEFILSST	felsites
EEFILSSW	wifeless
EEFIMMST	femmiest
EEFIMORT	foretime
EEFIMSTU	tumefies
EEFINNSS	fineness
EEFINRRR	inferrer
EEFINRRS	refiners
EEFINRRY	refinery
EEFINRSS	rifeness
EEFINRST	infester
EEFINRSU	reinfuse
EEFINRSZ	frenzies
EEFINSSS	finesses
EEFIPRSX	prefixes
EEFIRRST	ferrites
EEFIRRSU	surefire
EEFIRRVY	reverify
EEFIRSTT	frisette
EEFIRSTY	esterify
EEFIRTTZ	frizette
EEFISSTT	festiest
EEFKNORW	foreknew
EEFLLLNU	fluellen
EEFLLNSS	fellness
EEFLLORR	El Ferrol
EEFLLORT	foretell
EEFLLRSU	fuellers
EEFLLSSS	selfless
EEFLMSSU	fumeless
EEFLNORU	fluorene
EEFLNOST	felstone
EEFLNRSS	flensers
	fresnels
EEFLNRSU	sneerful
EEFLNRTU	refluent
EEFLNTUV	eventful

EEFLORRW	flowerer
	reflower
EEFLORTV	leftover
EEFLORTW	floweret
EEFLORVW	overflew
EEFLORWW	werewolf
EEFLOSUX	flexuose
EEFLRRSU	ferrules
EEFLRSST	fretless
EEFLRSTT	fettlers
EEFLRSTU	fleurets
EEFLRSUX	flexures
	refluxes
EEFLSSSU	fuseless
EEFMNORT	fomenter
EEFMNRST	ferments
EEFMORRR	reformer
EEFMOSTT	mofettes
EEFMPRRU	perfumer
EEFMPRSU	perfumes
EEFNORRZ	refrozen
EEFNORST	softener
EEFNORTU	fourteen
EEFNORTW	forewent
	Freetown
EEFNQRTU	frequent
EEFNRTTU	unfetter
EEFOORRT	rooftree
EEFOPRRZ	prefroze
EEFORRST	forester
	fosterer
	reforest
EEFORRSU	ferreous
EEFORRTY	feretory
EEFORSUV	feverous
EEFOSSTT	fossette
EEFOSSTU	foetuses
EEFOSTTU	fouettes
EEFPRSSU	perfuses
EEFRRSSU	refusers
EEFRRSTU	refuters
EEGGHLLS	eggshell
EEGGHNOR	Honegger
EEGGHSTU	thuggees
EEGGIIOR	George II
EEGGIJRR	rejigger
EEGGILNS	negliges
EEGGILST	leggiest
EEGGIMNR	emerging
EEGGINNR	greening
	reneging
EEGGINRT	greeting
EEGGINST	egesting
EEGGINSU	segueing
EEGGIORV	George IV
	George VI
EEGGLOOR	geologer
EEGGNORS	engorges
EEGGORRS	regorges
EEGGPRRS	preggers
EEGGPRSU	puggrees
EEGHHINT	heighten
EEGHIIST	eighties
EEGHIKLY	Keighley
EEGHILNW	wheeling
EEGHILRS	sleigher
EEGHINNS	sheening
EEGHINRS	greenish
	rehinges
	sheering
EEGHINST	seething
	sheeting
EEGHINTT	teething
EEGHINWZ	wheezing
EEGHIOTT	goethite
EEGHIRST	Thesiger
EEGHIRSW	reweighs
	weighers
EEGHIRTW	weighter
EEGHISST	sightsee
EEGHISTY	eyesight
EEGHLNNT	lengthen
EEGHMNOY	hegemony
EEGHMNSU	hegumens
EEGHMORT	geotherm
EEGHNOPS	phosgene
EEGHNOPY	hypogene
EEGHNRSY	greyhens
EEGHNSSU	hugeness
EEGHOPTY	geophyte
EEGHORTT	together
EEGHOSTT	ghettoes
EEGIILNR	lingerie
EEGIILNV	inveigle
EEGIINNR	Nigerien
EEGIINRT	reignite
EEGIINTV	genitive
EEGIJLNW	jeweling
EEGIJMNN	Nijmegen
EEGIJNRS	jeerings
EEGIJOPR	jerepigo
EEGIKLLN	glenlike
EEGIKLLU	gluelike
EEGIKLNN	kneeling
EEGIKLNS	sleeking
EEGIKNRY	rekeying
EEGIKNST	kitenges
EEGILLNV	leveling
EEGILLRV	Greville
EEGILNOR	eloigner
EEGILNPS	peelings
	sleeping
EEGILNRR	lingerer
EEGILNRS	leerings
EEGILNRU	reguline
EEGILNRV	levering
	reveling
EEGILNST	gentiles
	sleeting
	steeling
EEGILNSV	sleeving
EEGILNTX	telexing
EEGILOPU	epilogue
EEGILOSU	eulogies
	eulogise
EEGILOUZ	eulogize
EEGILQSU	squilgee
EEGILRSV	veligers
EEGILRTV	verligte
EEGILSST	elegists
EEGIMMRS	immerges
EEGIMNNS	meninges
EEGIMNNW	Nimwegen
EEGIMNRS	regimens
EEGIMNRT	metering
	regiment
EEGIMNRU	meringue
EEGIMNST	meetings
EEGINNPR	preening
EEGINNQU	queening
EEGINNRS	sneering
EEGINNRT	entering
EEGINNRW	renewing
EEGINNRY	enginery
EEGINNSU	ingenues
	unseeing
EEGINNSV	evenings
EEGINNSZ	sneezing
EEGINNTV	eventing
EEGINOPS	epigones
EEGINORR	erigeron
EEGINORS	eringoes
EEGINOST	egestion
EEGINPRS	speering
EEGINPRT	petering
EEGINPRU	pureeing
EEGINPST	steeping
EEGINPSW	sweeping
EEGINQRU	queering
EEGINQUU	queueing
EEGINRRS	resigner
EEGINRRV	revering
EEGINRST	gentries
	integers
	reesting
	steering
EEGINRSU	seigneur
EEGINRSV	severing
EEGINRSW	sewering
	sweering
EEGINRTV	everting
EEGINRTX	exerting
EEGINSSU	geniuses
EEGINSTU	eugenist
EEGINSTV	steeving
EEGINSTW	sweeting
EEGINTTV	vignette
EEGINTTW	tweeting
EEGINTWZ	tweezing
EEGIOPSU	epigeous
EEGIPRST	prestige
EEGIRRST	register
EEGIRRSV	grievers
EEGIRSTT	grisette
EEGISSTV	vestiges
EEGKNORS	kerogens

EEGKNRSU gerenuks
EEGLMMSU gemmules
EEGLMNOR Glen More
EEGLMOSS glosseme
EEGLNOPY polygene
EEGLNOSZ lozenges
EEGLNOTY telegony
EEGLNPRS Spengler
EEGLNSTT gentlest
EEGLOOST Togolese
EEGMNOST gemstone
EEGMNSST segments
EEGMNTTU tegument
EEGMORSU gruesome
EEGMORSW grewsome
EEGMORTY geometry
EEGMRSTU gumtrees
EEGNNORT roentgen
EEGNNOSV evensong
EEGNOPTY genotype
EEGNORST estrogen
EEGNORSU generous
EEGNORSY eryngoes
EEGNOTYZ zygotene
EEGNPRUX expunger
EEGNPSUX expunges
EEGNRSSY greyness
EEGNRSUY guernsey
EEGNRTUV Turgenev
EEGOPRST proteges
EEGOPRSU superego
EEGORRRU Guerrero
EEGORRVW overgrew
EEGORSSS ogresses
EEGRRSSU resurges
EEGRRSTU gesturer
EEGRRSUY gruyeres
EEGRSSSU guessers
EEGRSSTU gestures
EEHHIPSS sheepish
EEHHIRTW herewith
EEHHKLOT Koheleth
EEHHLLLO hellhole
EEHHNOSU henhouse
EEHHRRST thresher
EEHHRSST threshes
EEHHSSTW wheeshts
EEHIIKLV hivelike
EEHIKLMO homelike
EEHIKLMP hemplike
EEHIKLWY wheylike
EEHIKNNT Kenneth I
EEHIKRRS shrieker
EEHILLMS shlemiel
EEHILLNP helpline
EEHILMNS hemlines
EEHILMNU helenium
EEHILMOR homelier
EEHILNPW pinwheel
EEHILORT hotelier
EEHILPRT herptile
EEHILRSS heirless
relishes
EEHILSST shelties
EEHILSUV Hevelius
EEHILTWY Whiteley
EEHILWYZ wheezily
EEHIMMSS immeshes
EEHIMNRT theremin
EEHIMNSS inmeshes
EEHIMRRU rheumier
EEHIMRST erethism
EEHIMRTT thermite
EEHINNQU henequin
heniquen
EEHINNRS enshrine
EEHINNRT inherent
EEHINORS heroines
nosherie
EEHINORT hereinto
EEHINPRS insphere
EEHINPRT nephrite
trephine
EEHINPSX phenixes
EEHINRRS errhines
EEHINRTT thirteen
EEHINRTW whitener
EEHIORST isothere
theories
theorise
EEHIORTZ theorize
EEHIPPST psephite
EEHIPPTY epiphyte
EEHIPRSS perishes
EEHIPRTT tephrite
EEHIPSTT epithets
EEHIQRSU queerish
EEHIRRSS sherries
EEHIRRSV shiverer
EEHIRRSW wherries
EEHIRRTW witherer
EEHIRSST heisters
EEHIRSSV shrieves
EEHIRTVY thievery
EEHISSTW sweetish
EEHKLOSY keyholes
EEHKLOWY Holy Week
EEHKOOSY eyehooks
EEHLLMSS helmless
EEHLLPSS helpless
EEHLMMNS helmsmen
EEHLMOSS homeless
EEHLNOSW Henslowe
EEHLNOTT telethon
EEHLOPSS hopeless
EEHLOPST heelpost
EEHLORST hosteler
EEHLORSV shoveler
EEHLOSTY holeyest
EEHLPRST telphers
EEHLPRSU spherule
EEHLRSST shelters
EEHLRSSV shelvers
EEHLRSSW welshers
EEHLSSTW thewless
EEHMMOPR morpheme
EEHMMORT ohmmeter
EEHMNOPS phonemes
EEHMNORS horsemen
EEHMNOSU housemen
EEHMNRSY mynheers
EEHMORST theorems
EEHMORVW whomever
EEHMRSUX exhumers
EEHNNOOT ethonone
EEHNNORT enthrone
EEHNNOSS shoneens
EEHNOPRU hereupon
EEHNOPTY neophyte
EEHNORST Hortense
EEHNORTU hereunto
EEHNPRSU unsphere
EEHNPSTU Pentheus
EEHNSSTU enthuses
EEHNSSTV sevenths
EEHOOPRS oosphere
EEHOOPSW whoopees
EEHOORSV overshoe
EEHOOTTY eyetooth
EEHOPPSW peepshow
EEHOPRSU euphroes
EEHORRSV hoverers
EEHORRTX exhorter
EEHORSSU rehouses
EEHPRSTU superhet
EEHPRSTY hypester
EEHRRSTW wherrets
EEHRSSTW wershest
EEHRSTTW whetters
EEHSSTTY Thyestes
EEIIIPRT Peter III
EEIIKLLN linelike
EEIIKLLR likelier
EEIIKLLV veillike
EEIIKLNV veinlike
vinelike
EEIIKLRW wirelike
EEIIKLSV viselike
EEIIKLSW likewise
EEIILLMM millieme
EEIILLOP eolipile
EEIILLRV livelier
EEIILMNT ilmenite
melinite
menilite
timeline
EEIILMRT timelier
EEIILNPP pipeline
EEIILNST lenities
EEIILNTV lenitive
EEIILRSV liveries
EEIILSTV levities
EEIILSTW lewisite
EEIIMMTT mimetite
EEIIMNST enmities
EEIIMOST moieties

EEIIMPRS riempies
EEIIMRSS miseries
EEIIMRTZ itemizer
EEIIMSST itemises
EEIIMSSV emissive
EEIIMSTZ itemizes
EEIINNST einstein
nineties
EEIINNTV Ninevite
EEIINPPR piperine
EEIINPRS pineries
EEIINPRV viperine
EEIINRRV riverine
EEIINRST niteries
EEIINRSV vineries
EEIINRSW wineries
EEIINRTT retinite
EEIINRTV reinvite
EEIINSSV inessive
EEIINSTT entities
EEIIOPTZ epizoite
EEIIPRSX expiries
EEIIQSTU equities
EEIIRRSV rivieres
EEIIRSTV verities
EEIISTVW viewiest
EEIJKRST jerkiest
EEIJLNNU julienne
EEIJLNRT jetliner
EEIJLNUV juvenile
EEIJNNOR enjoiner
EEIKKLRS Kirklees
EEIKKNRS Kerenski
EEIKKRST kerkiest
EEIKLLSS skellies
EEIKLMST stemlike
EEIKLNOS noselike
EEIKLNOV ovenlike
EEIKLNSS likeness
EEIKLNST nestlike
EEIKLNTT tentlike
EEIKLORS roselike
EEIKLORT lorikeet
EEIKLPST pikelets
spikelet
steplike
EEIKLRRS Kreisler
EEIKLRST triskele
EEIKLSTV vestlike
EEIKMOTX ketoxime
EEIKMPST kempiest
EEIKNORS kerosine
EEIKNORV reinvoke
EEIKNOTW Eniwetok
EEIKNPSY pinkeyes
EEIKNRRT tinkerer
EEIKOQUV equivoke
EEIKPRST perkiest
EEIKPSST peskiest
EEIKRRSS skerries
EEIKRSST keisters
EEIKSTTT tektites
EEILLLMV Melville
EEILLMPR impeller
EEILLMRS smellier
EEILLMSS smellies
EEILLNOR lonelier
EEILLNSY senilely
EEILLORV lovelier
EEILLOSV lovelies
EEILLPSS ellipses
EEILLPSY sleepily
EEILLSSV veilless
EEILLTVY velleity
EEILMNNO limonene
EEILMNNS linesmen
EEILMNRU lemurine
relumine
EEILMNSU selenium
EEILMNTY Mytilene
EEILMRSS rimeless
EEILMSST timeless
EEILMSUV emulsive
EEILNNST sentinel
EEILNNSV enlivens
EEILNOPR leporine
EEILNORS eloiners
Elsinore
EEILNOSV novelise
EEILNOVZ novelize
EEILNPPZ zeppelin
EEILNPRS pilsener
EEILNPRU perilune
EEILNPRV replevin
EEILNPST plenties
EEILNQUY equinely
EEILNRST enlister
Leinster
listener
EEILNRSV liveners
EEILNRTY entirely
lientery
EEILNSST setlines
EEILNSSV evilness
veinless
vileness
vineless
EEILNSSW wineless
EEILNSTT entitles
EEILNSTV veinlets
EEILNSUV veinules
EEILNSVY Yvelines
EEILOPST petioles
EEILORRT loiterer
EEILORST Tirolese
EEILORSV overlies
relievos
EEILORVV overlive
EEILOSSX isolexes
EEILOSTW owelties
EEILOSTZ zeolites
EEILOSVW vowelise
EEILOTTT toilette
EEILOVWZ vowelize
EEILPPSS pipeless
EEILPPSY epilepsy
EEILPRRS repliers
EEILPRSS spielers
EEILPRST epistler
peltries
reptiles
spirelet
EEILPSSS pelisses
EEILPSST epistles
EEILPSSV pelvises
EEILPSTY epistyle
EEILQRSU reliques
EEILRRSV revilers
silverer
EEILRSST leisters
tireless
EEILRSSW wireless
EEILRSTT retitles
EEILRSVY liveyers
EEILSSTX sextiles
EEILSSVW viewless
EEILSTTX textiles
EEIMMORS memories
memorise
EEIMMORZ memorize
EEIMMOST sometime
EEIMMRRS immerser
EEIMMRSS immerses
EEIMMRST meristem
EEIMNNOS nominees
EEIMNNRS reinsmen
EEIMNOPT Piemonte
EEIMNORS emersion
EEIMNORV vomerine
EEIMNOST monetise
semitone
EEIMNOTZ monetize
zonetime
EEIMNPRS spermine
EEIMNPRU perineum
EEIMNRTU mutineer
EEIMNRTV virement
EEIMNSUV Museveni
EEIMOPRS promisee
reimpose
EEIMOPSS episomes
EEIMOPST epitomes
EEIMORST tiresome
EEIMORTV overtime
EEIMOSSW somewise
EEIMPRRS premiers
simperer
EEIMPRSS emprises
impreses
premises
spiremes
EEIMPRST emptiers
EEIMPRSX premixes
EEIMPSTT emptiest
EEIMQRSU requiems
EEIMQSTU mesquite

EEIMRRST merriest
rimester
triremes
EEIMRRTT remitter
trimeter
EEIMRSTT emitters
termites
EEIMRSTU emeritus
EEIMRTTY temerity
EEIMSSST messiest
metisses
EEINNNPS pennines
EEINNPTT penitent
EEINNRST intenser
internes
EEINNRSV innerves
nervines
EEINNRTT renitent
EEINNRTV reinvent
EEINNSTT sentient
EEINNSTW entwines
EEINOPPR ronepipe
EEINOPRS isoprene
pioneers
EEINORRT reorient
EEINORST serotine
EEINORSV eversion
EEINORTT tenorite
EEINORTX exertion
EEINOSST essonite
EEINOSTT noisette
teosinte
EEINPRRS ripeners
EEINPRSS ripeness
EEINPRSU resupine
EEINPRTX inexpert
EEINQRRU enquirer
EEINQRSU enquires
squireen
EEINQSTU quietens
EEINRRST inserter
reinsert
reinters
rentiers
terrines
EEINRRSU reinsure
EEINRRSV verniers
EEINRRTU reuniter
EEINRRTV inverter
EEINRRTW winterer
EEINRRTX interrex
EEINRSST sentries
EEINRSSU enuresis
EEINRSSV inverses
EEINRSTT insetter
interest
EEINRSTU esurient
retinues
reunites
EEINRSTV nerviest
reinvest
sirvente
EEINRSTX intersex
EEINRSTY serenity
EEINRSUV universe
EEINRTTY entirety
eternity
EEINSSSW wiseness
EEINSSSX sexiness
EEINSSTW newsiest
EEINSSTX sixteens
EEINSTTW twenties
EEINSTTX existent
EEIOPRRT portiere
EEIOPRRV overripe
EEIOPSST poetises
EEIOPSTZ poetizes
EEIORRRS orreries
EEIORRSS roseries
EEIORRTV overtire
EEIORRTX exterior
EEIORSST erotesis
EEIORSVW overwise
EEIORSVZ oversize
EEIORVVW overview
EEIORVWW wirewove
EEIPPPRS preppies
EEIPPPST peppiest
EEIPPQRU equipper
EEIPPRRS perspire
EEIPPRST peptiser
EEIPPRTY peripety
EEIPPRTZ peptizer
EEIPPSST peptises
EEIPPSTT pipettes
EEIPPSTZ peptizes
EEIPQRSU reequips
repiques
EEIPRRRS perriers
EEIPRRSS priseres
reprises
respires
EEIPRRSX expirers
EEIPRRTT preterit
prettier
EEIPRSSS pressies
EEIPRSST respites
EEIPRSSV previses
EEIPRSTT pretties
EEIPRSTX preexist
EEIPRSVW previews
EEIPRSZZ prezzies
EEIPRTUV eruptive
EEIPSSTW stepwise
EEIPSTTT pettiest
EEIQRRRU requirer
EEIQRRSU requires
EEIQRRTU requiter
EEIQRRUV quiverer
EEIQRSSU esquires
EEIQRSTU requites
EEIQSTTU quietest
EEIRRRST retirers
terriers
EEIRRSST resister
EEIRRSSV revisers
EEIRRSTV riveters
EEIRRSTW rewrites
EEIRRSVV revivers
EEIRRTTT titterer
EEIRSSSU reissues
EEIRSSTU sureties
EEIRSSTV sieverts
vestries
EEIRSSTW sweirest
EEIRSSUZ seizures
EEIRSTVV vetivers
EEIRSTVY severity
EEIRTTTZ terzetti
EEISSTTT testiest
EEJJLNUY jejunely
EEJKNRTU junketer
EEJLPSTU pulsejet
EEJNORSY enjoyers
EEJPRRRU perjurer
EEJPRRSU perjures
EEKKKNNO Kekkonen
EEKKORWW workweek
EEKKRRST trekkers
EEKLLNNY Kennelly
EEKLLSUU ukuleles
EEKLNNNU unkennel
EEKLNOSS keelsons
EEKLNOST skeleton
EEKLORST Koestler
EEKLOSSY yokeless
EEKLRSST kestrels
EEKMOORV Kemerovo
EEKNNSTT kennetts
EEKNOSTY keynotes
keystone
EEKNSSSW skewness
EEKNSSTU netsukes
EEKORRSV revokers
EEKRRSUZ kreuzers
EEKRRTUZ kreutzer
EELLLLMP pellmell
EELLMORW mellower
EELLMRSS smellers
EELLNORR enroller
EELLNPRU prunelle
EELLNSSW wellness
EELLNSTU entellus
EELLORST solleret
EELLORSV oversell
EELLORTX extoller
EELLORVY volleyer
EELLORWY yellower
EELLOSSS soleless
EELLOSSV loveless
EELLOSWY Wolseley
EELLPRSS presells
spellers
EELLQRSU quellers
EELMMPUX exemplum
EELMNOOS lonesome

	oenomels
EELMNSUY	unseemly
EELMNTUY	unmeetly
EELMOPRY	employer
	reemploy
EELMOPSY	employes
EELMORST	molester
EELMORSW	eelworms
EELMORTY	remotely
EELMOTVW	twelvemo
EELMPSTT	templets
EELMRRTU	murrelet
EELMRSST	smelters
	termless
EELMRSTY	smeltery
EELNNOSS	loneness
EELNNRTU	tunneler
EELNNUVY	unevenly
EELNOORS	loosener
EELNOPPU	unpeople
EELNOPRT	petronel
EELNOPSV	envelops
EELNOPSY	polyenes
EELNOPTY	polytene
EELNOQTU	eloquent
EELNORST	entresol
EELNORUV	von Euler
EELNOSSS	noseless
	soleness
EELNOSST	noteless
	toneless
EELNOSSU	selenous
EELNOSTT	notelets
EELNRSST	nestlers
	slenters
EELNSSSW	newsless
EELNSSTT	tentless
EELNSSTU	tuneless
	unsteels
EELNSSTV	ventless
EELNSTTU	lunettes
	unsettle
EELOPPSS	peploses
EELOPPST	estoppel
EELOPRRX	explorer
EELOPRSX	explores
EELOPRTT	teleport
EELOPSTU	eelpouts
	sleepout
EELORRSV	resolver
EELORRTV	revolter
EELORRTW	troweler
EELORRUV	overrule
EELORRVV	revolver
EELORSSV	resolves
EELORSTU	resolute
EELORSTY	Tyrolese
EELORSVV	evolvers
	revolves
EELORTTU	roulette
EELORTUV	revolute
	truelove
EELOSSTT	teleosts
EELOSSTV	vetoless
	voteless
EELOSTUV	evolutes
	veloutes
EELPPSSU	pepluses
EELPPSTU	septuple
EELPQRSU	prequels
EELPRRSU	repulser
EELPRSSU	repulses
EELPRSTZ	pretzels
EELPRTXY	expertly
EELPSSUX	plexuses
	suplexes
EELPSTUX	sextuple
EELRRSTW	wrestler
EELRSSST	restless
EELRSSTT	settlers
	sterlets
	trestles
EELRSSTU	streusel
EELRSSTW	swelters
	wrestles
EELRSSTY	restyles
EELRSTWY	westerly
EELSSSTV	vestless
EELSSSTZ	zestless
EELSSTTX	textless
EEMMNORT	Mentmore
EEMMNOST	mementos
EEMMNOTV	movement
EEMMNRRY	merrymen
EEMMOSST	mestomes
EEMMRSST	stemmers
EEMNNOPR	prenomen
EEMNNOSV	envenoms
EEMNOOSY	mooneyes
EEMNORSY	moneyers
EEMNORTY	Monterey
EEMNPRSS	pressmen
EEMNPRSU	supermen
EEMNPRTU	erumpent
EEMNRSTU	muenster
EEMNSSTU	muteness
	tenesmus
EEMNSTTV	vestment
EEMOOPRT	proteome
EEMOORRT	orometer
EEMOORRV	moreover
EEMOORTT	roomette
EEMOPRRS	emperors
	premorse
EEMOPRSW	empowers
EEMOQRSU	moresque
EEMOQTTU	moquette
EEMORRSV	removers
EEMORSST	somerset
EEMORSTT	remotest
EEMOTTTU	teetotum
EEMPPRST	preempts
EEMPRRSU	presumer
EEMPRSSU	presumes
EEMPRSTT	tempters
EEMPRSTU	permutes
EEMPSSTT	tempests
EEMRRSSU	resumers
EEMRRTTU	mutterer
EEMSSTTU	musettes
EENNNOSS	nonsense
EENNNOTV	nonevent
EENNNPTY	tenpenny
EENNOORT	rotenone
EENNOPSS	openness
EENNOPTX	exponent
EENNORST	tenoners
EENNORSU	neurones
EENNRSUV	unnerves
EENOORST	oestrone
EENOORTU	euronote
EENOORTV	overtone
EENOPPST	peptones
EENOPRSS	response
EENOPRST	Peterson
EENOPRTT	entrepot
EENOPRXY	pyroxene
EENOPSST	pentoses
EENOPSTY	neotypes
EENORSSS	soreness
EENORSSU	neuroses
EENORSTX	extensor
EENORSVW	oversewn
EENOSSST	stenoses
EENOSTUV	ventouse
EENPPRST	perpents
EENPRSST	pertness
	presents
	serpents
EENPRSSU	Preussen
	pureness
EENPRSTV	prevents
EENPSSSU	suspense
EENPSTTU	petuntse
EENPTTUZ	petuntze
EENQSSTU	sequents
EENRRRTU	returner
EENRRSSU	ensurers
EENRRSUV	nervures
EENRRTUV	venturer
EENRSSSU	sureness
EENRSSTT	sternest
EENRSSTU	trueness
EENRSSTW	westerns
EENRSTUV	ventures
EEOOPRST	proteose
EEOOPRSX	exospore
EEOOPRTZ	zoetrope
EEOPPSTT	popettes
EEOPRRRT	reporter
EEOPRRRV	reprover
EEOPRRSS	reposers
EEOPRRSV	reproves
EEOPRRTT	potterer
EEOPRRTX	exporter
	reexport

EEOPRSSS espresso
EEOPRSSU espouser
repousse
EEOPRSSX exposers
expresso
EEOPRSTV overstep
EEOPRSTY serotype
EEOPRSUX exposure
EEOPSSSU espouses
EEOPSSTW sweetsop
EEOPSSTY eyespots
EEORRRST resorter
restorer
retrorse
EEORRRTT retorter
EEORRSST restores
EEORRSSV reversos
EEORRSTU reroutes
EEORRSTV evertors
EEORRSTX extrorse
EEORRTTT totterer
EEORRTTX extorter
EEORRTUV overture
trouvere
EEORSSTT rosettes
EEORSSTV estovers
oversets
EEORSSUV overuses
EEORSSVW oversews
EEORSTVX vortexes
EEORTTTZ terzetto
EEPPRSST steppers
EEPPSSUW upsweeps
EEPRRSSU perusers
pressure
EEPRRSTV perverts
EEPRRTTU putterer
EEPRSSTT pretests
EEPRSSUX supersex
EEPRSTTU upsetter
EEPRSTTX pretexts
EEPSSTTY typesets
EEQRSSTU questers
requests
EERRSSTU tressure
EERRSSTW strewers
wresters
EERRSSVW swervers
EERRSTTU utterers
EERRSUVY resurvey
EERSSSST stresses
EERSSTTU trustees
EERSSTUV Servetus
vestures
EERSTTUX textures
EFFFGINO feoffing
EFFFILRU fluffier
EFFFLRSU fluffers
EFFFOORS feoffors
EFFGINOR offering
EFFGINSU effusing
EFFGRSTU gruffest
EFFHIILS filefish
EFFHIIRW whiffier
EFFHIISW fishwife
EFFHIITT fiftieth
EFFHILRW whiffler
EFFHILSW whiffles
EFFHIRRS Sherriff
EFFHIRSS sheriffs
EFFHIRSW whiffers
EFFHISTU huffiest
EFFHLRSU shuffler
EFFHLSSU shuffles
EFFHOORS offshore
EFFIIMST miffiest
EFFIINRS sniffier
EFFIINST niffiest
EFFIIPRS spiffier
EFFIKLRU rufflike
EFFILNRS sniffler
EFFILNSS sniffles
EFFILRRS rifflers
EFFINOSU effusion
EFFINRSS sniffers
EFFINRSU snuffier
EFFINSST stiffens
EFFIORST forfeits
EFFIPSTU puffiest
EFFIRSTU stuffier
EFFISSTT stiffest
EFFISSUX suffixes
EFFLMNUU unmuffle
EFFLMRSU mufflers
EFFLNRSU snuffler
EFFLNSSU snuffles
EFFLOSSU souffles
EFFLRRSU rufflers
EFFLRSTU truffles
EFFNRSSU snuffers
EFFOOORT forefoot
EFFOORRS offerors
EFFOPRRS proffers
EFFRRSUU furfures
EFFRSSTU stuffers
EFFSSSUU suffuses
EFGGIINN feigning
EFGGILOS solfeggi
EFGGINRU refuging
EFGGIOST foggiest
EFGGISTU fuggiest
EFGGLORS floggers
EFGHHIIL highlife
EFGHIILS fleishig
EFGHILNS fleshing
shelfing
EFGHINRS freshing
EFGHINRT frighten
EFGHINSU feng shui
EFGHIOSY fogeyish
EFGHIRST fighters
freights
EFGIILNR refiling
EFGIILNU figuline
EFGIILRU uglifier
EFGIILSU uglifies
EFGIINNR infringe
refining
EFGIINNT feinting
EFGIINRR refiring
EFGIINRU figurine
EFGIINRY reifying
EFGIITUV fugitive
EFGIKLLU gulflike
EFGILLNO lifelong
EFGILLNU fuelling
EFGILLUU guileful
EFGILNNS flensing
EFGILNOR florigen
EFGILNRS flingers
EFGILNRU feruling
EFGILNRY ferlying
EFGILNTT fettling
EFGILNTW leftwing
EFGILPRU fireplug
EFGILSST giftless
EFGIMNST figments
EFGIMOSY fogeyism
EFGIMRUU refugium
EFGINNPS pfennigs
EFGINORV forgiven
EFGINORW forewing
EFGINRRY ferrying
refrying
EFGINRSU refusing
EFGINRTT fretting
EFGINRTU refuting
EFGIOOST goofiest
EFGIOPTT pettifog
EFGIORRV forgiver
EFGIORSV forgives
EFGIRRSU figurers
EFGLOOVX foxglove
EFGNORSU Ferguson
EFGNSSUU funguses
EFGOORRS forgoers
EFGORSTU foreguts
EFHIIKLS fishlike
fleishik
EFHIILMN Niflheim
EFHIILRT filthier
EFHIILST tilefish
EFHIIMSU humifies
EFHIINRS finisher
refinish
EFHIINSS finishes
EFHIIPPS pipefish
EFHIIPRS fireship
EFHIIRST shiftier
EFHIISST fishiest
EFHIKLOO hooflike
EFHILLSY elfishly
EFHILTWY whitefly
EFHINSST fishnets
EFHIORRT frothier
EFHIORSS rosefish

EFHIORSV overfish
EFHIORTT fortieth
EFHIPRSU furphies
EFHIRRTU thurifer
EFHIRSST shifters
EFHISSTU shufties
EFHKLNOU funkhole
EFHLNORS hornfels
EFHLOOSS hoofless
EFHLOOSX foxholes
EFHLOPSU hopefuls
EFHLORSY horsefly
EFHLOSUU houseful
EFHLOSUY housefly
EFHLRSSU flushers
EFHLSTTW twelfths
EFHOORSW foreshow
EFHRRSTU furthers
EFHRSTTU furthest
EFIIILRV vilifier
EFIIILSV vilifies
EFIIIMNS minifies
EFIIINNT infinite
EFIIIRVV vivifier
EFIIISTX fixities
EFIIISVV vivifies
EFIIKRRS friskier
EFIILLNT tefillin
EFIILMRS flimsier
EFIILMSS misfiles
EFIILMST filmiest
EFIILNRT flintier
EFIILNTY felinity
finitely
EFIILRST filister
EFIILRSU fusilier
EFIIMMNS feminism
EFIIMNST feminist
EFIIMRSS misfires
EFIINNOS sinfonie
EFIINNST finniest
EFIINORR inferior
EFIINORT notifier
EFIINOST notifies
EFIINPSV fivepins
EFIINPSX spinifex
EFIINRRT ferritin
EFIINRSU unifiers
EFIINSTT niftiest
EFIINSUV infusive
EFIIORSS ossifier
EFIIOSSS ossifies
EFIIPRRU purifier
EFIIPRST spitfire
EFIIPRSU purifies
EFIIPRTY typifier
EFIIPSTY typifies
EFIIRRTU fruitier
EFIIRRZZ frizzier
EFIIRVVY revivify
EFIISSTW swifties
EFIJLORS frijoles
EFIKLLOW wolflike
EFIKLMOR foremilk
EFIKLNSU flunkies
EFIKLOOR rooflike
EFIKLORS folksier
EFIKLRSU surflike
EFIKLSTU flukiest
EFIKNORS foreskin
EFIKNRSU refusnik
EFIKNSTU funkiest
EFIKORRW firework
EFIKRRSS friskers
EFIKRSST friskets
EFILLLNU fluellin
EFILLMOR Fillmore
EFILLORV overfill
EFILLOSW lowlifes
EFILLRUY irefully
EFILLSTY stellify
EFILLTUY futilely
EFILMNOS foilsmen
EFILMSST filmsets
EFILMSUY emulsify
EFILNNTU influent
EFILNORU fluorine
EFILNSUX influxes
EFILOOSS floosies
EFILOOSZ floozies
EFILOPPR floppier
EFILOPPS floppies
EFILOPRR profiler
EFILOPRS profiles
EFILORRV frivoler
EFILORSS flossier
EFILORST trefoils
EFILORTU fluorite
EFILOSTT loftiest
EFILOSTU outflies
EFILPPRS flippers
EFILPPSU pipefuls
EFILPRTU uplifter
EFILPSTU spiteful
EFILRRST flirters
triflers
EFILRRSU flurries
EFILRRVY Fly River
EFILRRZZ frizzler
EFILRSST stiflers
EFILRSTT flitters
EFILRSVV flivvers
EFILRSZZ frizzles
EFILSSTT leftists
EFILSTTW swiftlet
EFIMNORR informer
reinform
reniform
EFIMNORS ensiform
fermions
EFIMNRSS firmness
EFIMNSTT fitments
EFIMORRT retiform
EFIMORST setiform
EFIMOSST semisoft
EFIMOSTT ofttimes
EFIMRSTU fremitus
EFINNORS infernos
EFINNPSU finespun
EFINNSTU funniest
EFINOPTX pontifex
EFINORRT frontier
EFINORRU Fournier
EFINORTY renotify
EFINOSSX foxiness
EFINRSST snifters
EFINRSSU infusers
EFIOOPST poofiest
EFIOPRRT portfire
profiter
EFIORRST frostier
rotifers
EFIORRSW frowsier
EFIORRTT retrofit
EFIORRUZ frouzier
EFIORRWZ frowzier
EFIPPRRY frippery
EFIPPRST frippets
EFIPRRUY repurify
EFIPRSST presifts
EFIPRSUX superfix
EFIPRTTY prettify
EFIRRRSU furriers
EFIRRRUY furriery
EFIRRSSU friseurs
EFIRRSTT fritters
EFIRRSTU fruiters
furriest
EFIRRSZZ frizzers
EFIRSSSU fissures
EFIRSSTU surfeits
EFIRSSTW swifters
EFIRSTTU turfiest
turfites
EFIRSTUX fixtures
EFISSSTU fussiest
EFISSTTU fustiest
EFISSTTW swiftest
EFISTUZZ fuzziest
EFKLLOOR folklore
EFKLMNOS menfolks
EFKLMOOT folkmote
EFKLNSUY flunkeys
EFKLNUWY Kynewulf
EFKNOORW foreknow
EFKNRSTU funkster
EFKOOPRS forspoke
EFKORRTW fretwork
EFLLLOOW woolfell
EFLLNSSU fullness
EFLLNTUY fluently
EFLLOORW follower
EFLLORSU florules
EFLLORUV overfull
EFLLOUWY woefully
EFLLRUUY ruefully

EFLLSUUY	usefully
EFLMMRUY	flummery
EFLMNOST	loftsmen
EFLMNRUU	frenulum
EFLMORRY	formerly
EFLMORSS	formless
EFLNORSU	fleurons
EFLNORTT	frontlet
EFLNORYZ	frozenly
EFLNOSSU	foulness
EFLNOSTY	stonefly
EFLOORSS	roofless
EFLOORSZ	foozlers
EFLOORTU	footrule
EFLOORVW	overflow
EFLOOSST	footless
EFLOPRUW	powerful
EFLORSTU	flouters
EFLORSUY	yourself
EFLORSVY	flyovers
EFLOSUUX	flexuous
EFLRSSTU	flusters
EFLRSTTU	flutters
EFLRSTUU	frustule
EFLRTTUY	fluttery
EFMNORTY	fromenty
EFMNRTUY	frumenty
	furmenty
EFMOORST	foremost
EFMOORSU	foursome
EFMOPRRS	performs
	preforms
EFMOPRST	pomfrets
EFNNOOOR	forenoon
EFNNORST	fornenst
EFNNORUZ	unfrozen
EFNOOOTT	footnote
EFNOORRW	foreworn
EFNOOSST	eftsoons
	festoons
EFNOPRST	forspent
EFNORRSU	foreruns
EFNORRSW	frowners
EFNORSTU	fortunes
EFNOSSST	softness
EFOOOPRT	footrope
EFOOORST	footsore
EFOOPRRS	reproofs
EFOOPRSS	spoofers
EFOOPRST	foretops
	poofters
EFOOPSTT	footstep
EFOORRSW	forswore
EFOORSTT	footrest
EFOORSTW	woofters
EFOOSTUX	outfoxes
EFORRRUW	furrower
EFORRSST	fortress
EFORRSTY	forestry
EFORRSUV	fervours
EGGGIILR	gigglier
EGGGILNS	leggings
EGGGILRS	gigglers
EGGGIORR	groggier
EGGGNNOR	ronggeng
EGGGOOOS	goosegog
EGGHIINN	neighing
EGGHIINW	weighing
EGGHIKSW	eggwhisk
EGGHILRS	higglers
EGGHIORU	Gheorgiu
EGGHISSU	shuggies
EGGHISTU	huggiest
EGGHRTUY	thuggery
EGGIIJLR	jigglier
EGGIIJST	jiggiest
EGGIILLN	gingelli
EGGIILNR	nigglier
EGGIILRW	wigglier
EGGIINNR	reigning
EGGIINNS	singeing
EGGIINNT	tingeing
EGGIINRT	Girgenti
EGGIINRV	grieving
EGGIIPST	piggiest
EGGIIRTW	twiggier
EGGIKLNO	gonglike
EGGIKNOS	gingkoes
	ginkgoes
EGGILLNY	gingelly
EGGILNNT	gentling
EGGILNRS	nigglers
	sniggler
EGGILNRU	grueling
	regluing
EGGILNRY	gingerly
EGGILNSS	sniggles
EGGILOOS	googlies
EGGILQSU	squiggle
EGGILRRW	wriggler
EGGILRSW	wigglers
	wriggles
EGGIMSTU	muggiest
EGGINNOR	Groening
EGGINNSS	ginsengs
EGGINORR	gorgerin
	rogering
EGGINOUV	vogueing
EGGINRRU	grungier
EGGINRSS	sniggers
EGGINSSU	guessing
EGGINSTU	guesting
	gungiest
EGGIORRY	Gregory I
EGGIOSST	soggiest
EGGIPRRS	sprigger
EGGIPRRY	priggery
EGGIPSSU	spuggies
EGGIPSTU	puggiest
EGGIRRST	triggers
EGGIRSSW	swiggers
EGGJLORS	jogglers
EGGJLRSU	jugglers
EGGJLRUY	jugglery
EGGLMOOY	gemology
EGGLMRSU	smuggler
EGGLMSSU	smuggles
EGGLNSSU	snuggles
EGGLORSS	sloggers
EGGLORST	togglers
EGGLPRSU	pluggers
EGGLRSSU	sluggers
EGGLRSTU	gurglets
	struggle
EGGMRSUY	smuggery
EGGMSSTU	smuggest
EGGNOOSY	geognosy
EGGNRSUY	snuggery
EGGNSSTU	snuggest
EGGOORSU	gorgeous
EGGSSSTU	suggests
EGHHILTY	eighthly
EGHHINSS	highness
EGHHORUW	roughhew
EGHIILLS	ghillies
EGHIILNR	hireling
EGHIILNS	shieling
EGHIIMRT	mightier
EGHIINNR	inhering
EGHIINRR	rehiring
EGHIINST	heisting
	nighties
EGHIINSV	inveighs
EGHIINTV	thieving
EGHIIPRS	Respighi
EGHIIRST	tigerish
EGHIISTY	hygieist
EGHIKNRS	gherkins
EGHILLNS	shelling
EGHILLOR	Holliger
EGHILMNW	whelming
EGHILMOR	homegirl
EGHILNOT	Leighton
EGHILNOV	hoveling
EGHILNPS	helpings
EGHILNPW	whelping
EGHILNRS	shingler
EGHILNSS	shingles
EGHILNST	lightens
EGHILNSV	shelving
EGHILNSW	welshing
EGHILNUW	gluhwein
EGHILORT	regolith
EGHILPRT	plighter
EGHILRST	lighters
	relights
	slighter
EGHILSTT	lightest
EGHIMNUX	exhuming
EGHINNOY	honeying
EGHINNST	sennight
EGHINNSU	unhinges
EGHINORV	hovering
EGHINOST	histogen
EGHINPRS	Pershing
	sphering

EGHINPSS	sphinges
EGHINRRS	herrings
EGHINRRU	hungrier
EGHINRST	rightens
EGHINRSU	ushering
EGHINRSW	Gershwin
	whingers
EGHINSTT	tightens
EGHINTTW	whetting
EGHIOPSU	pishogue
EGHIORSU	roughies
EGHIOSTV	eightvos
EGHIOTUW	outweigh
EGHIRRST	righters
EGHIRSST	sighters
EGHISSTU	gushiest
EGHISSTY	hygeists
EGHISTTT	tightest
EGHLLOPU	plughole
EGHLLOSU	lugholes
EGHLNORS	leghorns
EGHLOOOR	horologe
EGHLOORY	rheology
EGHLOOSS	goloshes
	shoogles
EGHLOOTY	ethology
	theology
EGHLOPRU	plougher
EGHMNOOY	homogeny
EGHMOPUY	hypogeum
EGHMOSSU	gumshoes
EGHNOOTY	theogony
EGHNORSU	roughens
EGHNORUV	overhung
EGHNOSTU	toughens
EGHNOTUU	Huguenot
EGHNRSTT	strength
EGHOOOSW	hoosegow
EGHORRTW	regrowth
EGHORSTU	roughest
EGHOSTTU	toughest
EGIIJLNR	jinglier
EGIIKKLN	kinglike
EGIIKLNN	likening
EGIIKLNR	kinglier
EGIIKLNW	winglike
EGIIKLTW	twiglike
EGIILMMN	immingle
EGIILNNO	eloining
EGIILNNR	relining
EGIILNNS	enisling
	ensiling
EGIILNNU	linguine
EGIILNNV	livening
EGIILNOR	religion
	reoiling
EGIILNPS	spieling
EGIILNRS	resiling
	riesling
EGIILNRV	reliving
	reviling
EGIILNTZ	Liegnitz
EGIILRRS	grislier
EGIILRSS	grislies
EGIILRTU	guiltier
EGIILRTZ	glitzier
EGIILTWZ	Gleiwitz
EGIIMNPR	impinger
EGIIMNPS	impinges
EGIIMNRS	remising
EGIIMNRT	meriting
	mitering
EGIIMNRX	remixing
EGIIMNST	mingiest
EGIIMNSV	misgiven
EGIIMNTT	emitting
EGIIMOPT	impetigo
EGIIMORR	grimoire
EGIIMPST	gimpiest
EGIIMRST	grimiest
EGIIMSSV	misgives
EGIINNPR	repining
	ripening
EGIINNPW	Winnipeg
EGIINNRS	resining
EGIINNSV	veinings
EGIINNWZ	wizening
EGIINOPR	peignoir
EGIINORS	seignior
EGIINPRS	speiring
EGIINPRX	expiring
EGIINQTU	quieting
EGIINRRT	retiring
EGIINRRW	rewiring
EGIINRST	igniters
	resiting
	stingier
EGIINRSV	revising
EGIINRSW	sweiring
	swingier
EGIINRTU	intrigue
EGIINRTV	riveting
EGIINRVV	reviving
EGIINSST	stingies
EGIINSSZ	seizings
EGIINSTX	existing
EGIINSTZ	zingiest
EGIINSVW	viewings
EGIIPRSW	periwigs
EGIIPSST	pigsties
EGIIRRTT	grittier
EGIIRTTU	te igitur
EGIITUXY	exiguity
EGIJKNRS	jerkings
EGIJLLNY	jellying
EGIJLNRS	jinglers
EGIJLNRU	junglier
EGIJMMNY	jemmying
EGIJNNOY	enjoying
EGIKKNRT	trekking
EGIKLLNN	knelling
EGIKLNOS	songlike
EGIKLNPS	skelping
EGIKLNSS	kingless
EGIKLNST	kinglets
EGIKLNSY	Kingsley
EGIKNNNS	kennings
	skenning
EGIKNNOT	tokening
EGIKNORV	revoking
EGIKNSTT	sketting
EGILLMNS	smelling
EGILLNOV	livelong
EGILLNOW	Lilongwe
EGILLNPS	spelling
EGILLNQU	quelling
EGILLNSW	swelling
EGILLNTU	glutelin
EGILLOOR	gloriole
EGILLORS	girolles
EGILLRRS	grillers
EGILMMNS	lemmings
EGILMMRS	glimmers
EGILMNOT	longtime
EGILMNRS	gremlins
	minglers
EGILMNRU	reluming
EGILMNST	smelting
EGILMNSU	mulesing
EGILMOOR	gloomier
	oligomer
EGILMORS	gomerils
EGILMOUU	eulogium
EGILMPRS	glimpser
EGILMPSS	glimpses
EGILNNOS	Solingen
EGILNNST	nestling
EGILNNTT	nettling
EGILNOPP	peopling
EGILNORS	resoling
EGILNORW	lowering
	roweling
EGILNOSS	loginess
EGILNOSU	ligneous
EGILNOSW	longwise
EGILNOTW	toweling
EGILNOVV	evolving
EGILNPRY	replying
EGILNPSS	spignels
EGILNPST	pestling
EGILNRSS	slingers
EGILNRST	ringlets
	sterling
	tinglers
EGILNRSW	newsgirl
EGILNSST	glistens
	singlets
EGILNSSU	ugliness
EGILNSSW	swingles
	wingless
EGILNSTT	settling
EGILNSTW	winglets
EGILNTUX	exulting
EGILNVXY	vexingly
EGILOOSU	isologue
EGILOOTY	etiology

EGILORSS glossier
EGILOSSS glossies
EGILOSTU eulogist
EGILRRZZ grizzler
EGILRSST glisters
gristles
gritless
EGILRSTT glitters
EGILRSTY greylist
EGILRSUV virgules
EGILRSZZ grizzles
EGILRTTY glittery
EGIMMNST stemming
EGIMMRST grimmest
EGIMMSTU gummiest
EGIMNNNO mignonne
EGIMNOOR Geronimo
EGIMNORS negroism
EGIMNORV removing
EGIMNOST mitogens
EGIMNOSY moseying
EGIMNPRU impugner
EGIMNPST pigments
EGIMNPTT tempting
EGIMNPTY emptying
EGIMNRSS grimness
EGIMNRSU resuming
EGIMNRUY eryngium
EGIMORST ergotism
EGIMPRRU grumpier
EGINNNOT tenoning
EGINNOOR roneoing
EGINNOPR reponing
EGINNOPS openings
EGINNORT nitrogen
EGINNORV vigneron
EGINNORZ rezoning
EGINNPSU penguins
EGINNRRS grinners
EGINNRRU unerring
EGINNRSU ensuring
EGINNRSV nervings
EGINNSSU Guinness
EGINNSUX unsexing
EGINOORR Río Negro
EGINOOSS isogones
EGINOPRS perigons
reposing
spongier
EGINOPRU Perugino
EGINOPRW powering
EGINOPST pongiest
EGINOPSX exposing
EGINORRS Grierson
ignorers
EGINORSS goriness
EGINORST genitors
Signoret
EGINORTT ottering
EGINORTU routeing
EGINORTW towering
EGINORVW wingover
EGINORXX xeroxing
EGINPPPR prepping
EGINPPST stepping
EGINPRRS springer
EGINPRSS pressing
springes
EGINPRSU perusing
EGINPRTU erupting
reputing
EGINPRTY retyping
EGINPRUV prevuing
EGINPRYY perigyny
EGINQRUY querying
EGINQSTU questing
EGINRRST restring
ringster
stringer
EGINRRSW wringers
EGINRRTY retrying
EGINRSST stingers
tressing
trigness
EGINRSSV servings
EGINRSSW swingers
EGINRSSY syringes
EGINRSTT gitterns
EGINRSTW strewing
wresting
EGINRSVW swerving
EGINRTTU uttering
EGINSSTT settings
EGINSSTW westings
EGINSTTT stetting
EGIOOPST goopiest
EGIOORRV groovier
EGIOOSST goosiest
EGIOPRSS gossiper
EGIOPRSU groupies
pirogues
EGIORRTT grottier
EGIORRTU groutier
EGIORSST strigose
EGIORSSU griseous
EGIORSUV grievous
EGIOSSTT egotists
EGIOSTTU goutiest
EGIOSUUX exiguous
EGIPPRRS grippers
EGIPRSUU guipures
EGIRRRSU gurriers
EGIRRSTT gritters
EGIRRSTY registry
EGISSTTU gustiest
gutsiest
EGISSYYZ syzygies
EGJLNORU jongleur
EGJLNOTU jelutong
EGLLMORW gromwell
EGLLOOPR golloper
EGLMMSTU glummest
EGLMNOOY menology
EGLMNORS mongrels
EGLMNSSU glumness
EGLMOPRU promulge
EGLMORSS gormless
EGLNNOOR longeron
EGLNOOOY oenology
EGLNOOPR prolonge
EGLNOOPY penology
EGLNOORV overlong
EGLNORSU loungers
EGLNORUU longueur
EGLNOSYY lysogeny
EGLNPRSU plungers
EGLNRSSU rungless
EGLNRTUY urgently
EGLOOPRU prologue
EGLOOPTY logotype
EGLOORSY serology
EGLOOSXY sexology
EGLORRSW growlers
EGLORSSS glossers
EGLORSUY rugosely
EGLPRSSU splurges
EGLRSUZZ guzzlers
EGMMORST grommets
EGMMRSTU grummets
EGMNNOOY monogeny
EGMNOOOS gonosome
mongoose
EGMNOSYZ zymogens
EGMNSSSU smugness
EGMOORRS groomers
EGNNOOTY ontogeny
EGNNORST rontgens
EGNNOTTU ungotten
EGNNOTUV Vonnegut
EGNNSSSU snugness
EGNNSTTU tungsten
EGNNSTUU unguents
EGNOOOPR gonopore
EGNOORRV governor
EGNOOSSS Goossens
EGNOOTUX oxtongue
EGNOPPRU oppugner
EGNOPRSS spongers
EGNOPRSY pyrogens
EGNORRST stronger
EGNORRSW wrongers
EGNORSST songster
EGNORSSU surgeons
EGNORSTU sturgeon
EGNOSTUY youngest
EGNRRSTU grunters
restrung
EGNRSTUU Ten Gurus
EGOOPRRU prorogue
EGOORRVW overgrow
EGOORSTT grottoes
EGOPRRSS progress
EGOPRRSU groupers
regroups
EGOPSSUY gypseous
EGORRSSU grousers

EGORRSTU grouters
EGORSSST grossest
EGOSSTUU outguess
EGPRSSUU upsurges
EHHIIPRS heirship
EHHIISTV thievish
EHHILMNT helminth
EHHINOPT thiophen
EHHIORTT hitherto
EHHIRSSW shrewish
EHHLOOST shothole
EHHMPRUY Humphrey
EHHNOORS shoehorn
EHHOOSSW whooshes
EHHOOSTU hothouse
EHHOPRTW Hepworth
EHHRSSTU thrushes
EHIIIKST heitikis
EHIIINRY Henry III
EHIIJOPS Joseph II
EHIIKLNS Helsinki
EHIIKLPW whiplike
EHIIKMNO Khomeini
EHIIKNSV Kishinev
EHIIKSSW whiskies
EHIILLMW Wilhelm I
EHIILLST hilliest
EHIILMOS homilies
EHIILRSV liverish
EHIIMMSS shimmies
EHIIMPST mephitis
EHIIMRSW whimsier
EHIIMSST smithies
EHIIMSSW whimsies
EHIINNOS inhesion
EHIINNOT thionine
EHIINNRS inshrine
EHIINNSS shinnies
EHIINNSW whinnies
EHIINRST inherits
EHIINRVY Henry VII
EHIINSST shiniest
shinties
EHIINSTW whiniest
EHIINSVX vixenish
EHIIPPSS shippies
EHIIPPST hippiest
EHIIPRSV viperish
EHIIPSTT pithiest
EHIIRRST shirtier
EHIIRRTX heritrix
EHIIRSTT shittier
thirties
EHIIRTTW Whittier
EHIIRWZZ whizzier
EHIISSST stishies
EHIISSTT stithies
EHIISTTX sixtieth
EHIJNNOS johnnies
EHIJOSTV Jehovist
EHIKKLOO hooklike
EHIKKLSU husklike
EHIKLMNY hymnlike
EHIKLMPU humplike
EHIKLNOR hornlike
EHIKLNOS sinkhole
EHIKLOOP hooplike
EHIKLOSY yokelish
EHIKLRSU rushlike
EHIKMNST methinks
EHIKNORS shonkier
EHIKNRRS shrinker
EHIKNRST rethinks
thinkers
EHIKRRSS shirkers
EHIKRSSW whiskers
EHIKRSWY whiskery
EHIKSSTU huskiest
EHIKSSWY whiskeys
EHILLLMO molehill
EHILLMOP philomel
EHILLNOS hellions
EHILLPTY phyllite
EHILLRRS shriller
EHILLRRT thriller
EHILLSVY elvishly
EHILMNOP Philemon
EHILMNOS lemonish
EHILMOOR heirloom
EHILMOST helotism
EHILMPSY symphile
EHILNOPS pinholes
EHILNOPT tholepin
EHILNORU unholier
EHILNOSS holiness
EHILNOST holstein
hotlines
neoliths
EHILNOTX xenolith
EHILNSWY newishly
EHILOOPZ zoophile
EHILOPRS polisher
repolish
EHILOPRT heliport
EHILOPSS polishes
EHILOPST hoplites
isopleth
EHILORTY rhyolite
EHILOSST hostiles
EHILPRST philters
philtres
EHILPSTU sulphite
EHILRRSW whirlers
EHILRSST slithers
EHILRSSU slushier
EHILRSSV shrivels
EHILRSTW whistler
EHILRSTY slithery
EHILRTTW whittler
EHILSSSU slushies
EHILSSSW wishless
EHILSSTT thistles
EHILSSTW whistles
EHILSTTW whittles
EHIMMNUY hymenium
EHIMMRSS shimmers
EHIMMRSY shimmery
EHIMNOPR morphine
EHIMNORT thermion
EHIMNOSS hominess
EHIMNOTT monteith
EHIMNPST shipment
EHIMNRRU murrhine
EHIMNRSU inhumers
EHIMOOST smoothie
EHIMORST isotherm
moithers
Stroheim
EHIMORSZ rhizomes
EHIMORTU mouthier
EHIMOSTT mothiest
EHIMPRRS shrimper
EHIMPRSU murphies
EHIMPRSW whimpers
EHIMPSTU humpiest
humpties
EHIMPSUU euphuism
EHIMRSTY smithery
EHIMSSTU mushiest
EHIMSSWY whimseys
EHINNRST thinners
EHINNSST thinness
EHINNSSU sunshine
EHINNSTT thinnest
EHINOOPS isophone
EHINOPPR hornpipe
EHINOPRY Hyperion
EHINOPST phoniest
EHINORRT thornier
EHINORST horniest
EHINOSST histones
EHINOSTU outshine
EHINPPRU unhipper
EHINPRSU punisher
EHINPSSU punishes
EHINPSSX sphinxes
EHINRSSU inrushes
EHINSSUW unwishes
EHIOOPST isophote
EHIOORTT toothier
EHIOOSST stooshie
EHIOPPSU eohippus
EHIOPRSS poserish
rosehips
EHIOPRST trophies
EHIORRST heritors
EHIORRTW worthier
EHIORSST hoisters
horsiest
shorties
EHIORSTT theorist
EHIORSTU shoutier
EHIORSTW worthies
EHIORTWZ howitzer
EHIOSSTU housesit
stoushie

EHIOSSTW showiest
EHIOSSTY isohyets
EHIOTTUW whiteout
EHIPPRSS shippers
EHIPPRSW whippers
EHIPPSTW whippets
EHIPQSUY physique
EHIPRSST hipsters
EHIPRSSW whispers
EHIPRSTW whipster
EHIPSSTU pushiest
EHIPSTUU euphuist
EHIQSSSU squishes
EHIRRSSV shrivers
EHIRRSTT thirster
EHIRRSTV thrivers
EHIRRSTW wherrits
writhers
EHIRSSSW swishers
EHIRSSTU rushiest
EHIRSSTW swithers
EHIRSTTW whitters
EHIRTTTW whittret
EHISSSTU stushies
EHISSUVW huswives
EHJOPSSU Josephus
EHKLNOOT knothole
EHKLOOSS hookless
EHKMOORW homework
EHKMOOSS smokehos
EHKNNRSU shrunken
EHKNOOOS hooknose
EHLLMOPY phyllome
EHLLNSTU nutshell
EHLLOOOP loophole
EHLMOORW wormhole
EHLMORTY motherly
EHLMOSUU Mulhouse
EHLNOPSU sulphone
EHLNORSS hornless
EHLNOSST lothness
EHLNOSTY honestly
EHLNRSTU lutherns
EHLNSSSU lushness
EHLOOPRT porthole
potholer
EHLOOPST potholes
EHLOOPTY holotype
EHLOPPRS hopplers
EHLOPSSS sploshes
EHLOPSSY spyholes
EHLORSST holsters
hostlers
EHLORSTT throstle
EHLORSTY hostelry
EHLORTTT throttle
EHLRSSTU hustlers
ruthless
EHLSSTTU shuttles
EHMMRRTU thrummer
EHMNNOPP Pnom Penh
EHMNNSTU huntsmen
EHMNOORS hormones
moorhens
EHMNOOST smoothen
EHMNOOTY theonomy
EHMNOPSU homespun
EHMNPRYY hypernym
EHMNPSTY nymphets
EHMNSTTU hutments
EHMOORST smoother
EHMOPRSU Morpheus
EHMORRSU Rushmore
EHMORSST smothers
EHMORSTU mouthers
EHMORSTY smothery
EHMORTUV vermouth
EHMOTUWY Weymouth
EHMOTUZZ mezuzoth
EHMPRSTU thumpers
EHMRRSTU murthers
EHMRTUYY eurythmy
EHMSSTUY thymuses
EHMSTTUY Hymettus
EHNNOOPX Xenophon
EHNNOPRS nephrons
EHNNORRT northern
thronner
EHNNORSY Henryson
EHNNORTU unthrone
EHNNRSSU shunners
EHNOOPTY honeypot
EHNOORRS honorers
EHNOORRU honourer
EHNOORSW whoreson
EHNOORTW honewort
EHNOORVZ Voronezh
EHNOOSSW snowshoe
EHNOOSTU outshone
EHNOPRSY hyperons
EHNOPSSY hypnoses
EHNORRST northers
EHNORSST shortens
EHNORSSU onrushes
unhorses
EHNORSTU southern
EHNOSTUU nuthouse
EHNOSTUW New South
EHNRSSTU huntress
shunters
EHOOPRRT horopter
EHOOPRSW whoopers
EHOOPRTY orthoepy
EHOOPSTT photoset
EHOOPSTU housetop
pothouse
EHOOPSTY oophytes
EHOOPTYZ zoophyte
EHOORSST shooters
soothers
EHOORSTV overshot
EHOOSSSW swooshes
EHOOSTUU outhouse
EHOPPRSS shoppers
EHOPPRST prophets
EHOPPRSW whoppers
EHOPPRSY prophesy
EHOPRRSY orphreys
EHOPRSST hotpress
strophes
EHOPRSUV pushover
EHOPRTUY eutrophy
EHOPSTUY Typhoeus
EHORRSTW throwers
EHORRSTY herstory
EHORSSTT shortest
EHORSSTU shouters
southers
EHOSSSTU stoushes
EHPRSSUU uprushes
EHPRSTTU turpeths
EHPRSUYZ Zephyrus
EHRRSTTU thruster
EHRSSSTY shysters
EHRSSTTU shutters
EHRSSTUY tusherys
EHRSTTTU truth set
EIIILPPR liripipe
EIIIMMNS minimise
EIIIMMNZ minimize
EIIJNRSU injuries
EIIKKLLS silklike
EIIKKLLT kiltlike
EIIKKLNS skinlike
EIIKKNST kinkiest
EIIKLLLY lilylike
EIIKLLMN limekiln
EIIKLLSS skillies
EIIKLMRS misliker
EIIKLMSS mislikes
EIIKLMST milkiest
EIIKLNOR ironlike
EIIKLNRS slinkier
EIIKLPSW wisplike
EIIKLSST silkiest
EIIKLSTU suitlike
EIIKMPRS skimpier
EIIKMRST mirkiest
EIIKNNOS noisenik
EIIKNNRS skinnier
EIIKNNSS inkiness
EIIKNNSW wineskin
EIIKPSST spikiest
EIIKQRRU quirkier
EIIKRSST riskiest
EIIKSSVV skivvies
EIILLLVY livelily
EIILLMNN Minnelli
EIILLMNR milliner
EIILLMNS millines
slimline
EIILLMNU illumine
EIILLNST niellist
EIILLNSV villeins
EIILLNTV vitellin
EIILLOST Sillitoe

EIILLPSS ellipsis
EIILLRSV Villiers
EIILLSST silliest
EIILLSTT littlies
EIILLSUV illusive
EIILMMOT immotile
EIILMNNT liniment
EIILMNOT limonite
EIILMNSS liminess
EIILMNST Milstein
EIILMOPT impolite
EIILMPRS imperils
EIILMRSS slimsier
EIILMRST limiters
EIILMSSS missiles
EIILMSST slimiest
EIILMSTT mistitle
EIILMSTY myelitis
EIILNORS lioniser
EIILNORT triolein
EIILNORZ lionizer
EIILNOSS elisions
isolines
lionises
oiliness
EIILNOSV olivines
EIILNOSZ lionizes
EIILNQTU quintile
EIILNRST nitriles
EIILNSSW wiliness
EIILNSTY senility
EIILNTTU intitule
EIILNTUV vituline
EIILOPST pisolite
polities
EIILORST roiliest
EIILOTVV volitive
EIILPPRS slippier
EIILPPST lippiest
EIILPSST pitiless
EIILPSTY pyelitis
EIILQSSU siliques
EIILRSSS Isserlis
EIILRSTU utiliser
EIILRTUZ utilizer
EIILSSTT elitists
EIILSSTU utilises
EIILSTUZ utilizes
EIILTUVV Viti Levu
EIIMMNNO menomini
EIIMMNNT imminent
EIIMMNSU immunise
EIIMMNUZ immunize
EIIMMPRU imperium
EIIMMSST mistimes
EIIMNOPT pimiento
EIIMNORT Minorite
EIIMNOSS emission
EIIMNPRS primines
EIIMNRSS miriness
EIIMNRST interims
minister
EIIMNRTT intermit
EIIMNRTX intermix
EIIMNSTT mintiest
EIIMNSTU mutinies
EIIMNSTV minivets
EIIMOPRX mirepoix
EIIMOPST optimise
EIIMOPSZ epizoism
EIIMOPTZ optimize
EIIMOSSV omissive
EIIMOSUX eximious
EIIMOTVV vomitive
EIIMPRSS misprise
pismires
EIIMPRSZ misprize
EIIMPSTW wimpiest
EIIMQSTU quietism
EIIMRSTT metritis
EIIMSSSV missives
EIIMSSTT mistiest
semitist
EIINNNPS ninepins
EIINNOSU unionise
EIINNOSV envision
EIINNOUZ unionize
EIINNSST tininess
EIINNSTT Tientsin
tinniest
EIINNSTW intwines
EIINOPRS ripienos
EIINOPRT pointier
poitrine
EIINOPTT petition
EIINORRT interior
EIINORSS ionisers
ironises
sironise
EIINORSV revision
EIINORSZ ionizers
ironizes
sironize
EIINOSST noisiest
EIINOVVZ Zinoviev
EIINPPRS snippier
EIINPPST nippiest
EIINPRRS inspirer
EIINPRSS inspires
EIINPRST pristine
EIINPSST spiniest
EIINPSTZ pintsize
EIINPTUV punitive
EIINQRRU inquirer
EIINQRSU inquires
EIINQTUY inequity
EIINRRTW wintrier
EIINRSST insister
sinister
EIINRSSW wiriness
EIINRSTT nitrites
EIINRSTU neuritis
EIINRSTV inviters
vitrines
EIINSSTU unitises
EIINSTTT nittiest
EIINSTTZ Steinitz
EIINSTUZ unitizes
EIIOPRRS priories
EIIOPRST Poitiers
EIIOPSTV positive
EIIOSSTT osteitis
EIIOSSTZ zoisites
EIIPPSTZ zippiest
EIIPRRSS prissier
EIIPRRST stripier
EIIPRRTW tripwire
EIIPRSTV priviest
EIIPSSTT pietists
stipites
tipsiest
EIIPSSTW wispiest
EIIQSTTU quietist
EIIRRSTW wristier
EIIRSSTV revisits
EIIRSTTZ ritziest
EIISTTTW wittiest
EIJJNTUY jejunity
EIJKORRS skijorer
EIJLLOST jolliest
EIJLOSTT joltiest
EIJMPSTU jumpiest
EIJNORST jointers
EIJNORTU jointure
EIJNOSTT jettison
EIJNPRSU junipers
EIJNRRSU injurers
EIJRSTUY jesuitry
EIKKLNNY Kilkenny
EIKKLNOT knotlike
EIKKLSTU tusklike
EIKKOOST kookiest
EIKKSTUY yukkiest
EIKLLMNU Mulliken
EIKLLMPU plumlike
EIKLLNSW inkwells
EIKLLNUY unlikely
EIKLLNXY lynxlike
EIKLLOOW woollike
EIKLLORV overkill
EIKLLOSS skollies
EIKLLOSU soullike
EIKLLRSS reskills
EIKLLSSS skilless
EIKLLSST skillets
EIKLMNOS moleskin
EIKLMNRS kremlins
EIKLMORW wormlike
EIKLMOSS mosslike
EIKLNOST Ilkeston
EIKLNOSW snowlike
EIKLNPRS sprinkle
EIKLNRRU knurlier
EIKLNRSW wrinkles
EIKLNRTW twinkler
EIKLNSSS skinless

EIKLNSTW twinkles
EIKLOORT rootlike
EIKLOSYY Yeşilköy
EIKLRTUZ klutzier
EIKLSSTT skittles
EIKLSSTU sulkiest
EIKMMRSS skimmers
EIKMNOPT Potemkin
EIKMNORS monikers
EIKMNOST tokenism
EIKMORTW timework
EIKMOSST smokiest
EIKMRRSS smirkers
EIKMRSTU murkiest
EIKMSSTU muskiest
EIKNNPSS pinkness
EIKNNRSS skinners
EIKNOORS rooineks
EIKNOPSS pokiness
EIKNORSS Eriksson
EIKNORSV invokers
EIKNORTT knottier
EIKNOSTW wonkiest
EIKNPRRS prinkers
EIKNPRSU spunkier
EIKNPRTU turnpike
EIKNRSST stinkers
EIKNRSSW swinkers
EIKNRSTT knitters
trinkets
EIKNSSTT skintest
EIKOOPRS spookier
EIKOORST rookiest
EIKOOSST stookies
EIKOPRST porkiest
EIKORRWW wirework
EIKPPRSS skippers
EIKPPSST skippets
EIKPRRSU spruiker
EIKRRSST skirrets
skirters
strikers
EIKRSSTT skitters
EILLLSTW Stilwell
EILLMNOU linoleum
EILLMNSU mulleins
EILLMOPS plimsole
EILLMOST melilots
EILLMPSS misspell
EILLMPTU multiple
EILLMUVX vexillum
EILLNOPY epyllion
EILLNOTU luteolin
EILLNPSW pinswell
EILLNSTY silently
tinselly
EILLNSVY snivelly
EILLOORW woollier
EILLOOSW woollies
EILLOPTY politely
EILLORSZ zorilles
EILLOSTW lowliest

EILLPRSS spillers
EILLPSSS slipless
EILLQSTU quillets
EILLRSSW swillers
EILLSSST listless
EILLSSTT stillest
EILLSTTT littlest
EILLSTUV vitellus
EILMMNOU Moulmein
EILMMPRU plummier
EILMMRSS slimmers
EILMMSST slimmest
EILMNOQU Miquelon
EILMNOSU emulsion
EILMNOTY mylonite
EILMNPSS limpness
EILMNPTU tumpline
EILMNRST minstrel
EILMNSSS slimness
EILMNTUY minutely
untimely
EILMOOPS liposome
EILMOOSS Solimões
EILMOOST toilsome
EILMOOSV moolvies
EILMOPRR implorer
EILMOPRS implores
EILMOPST milepost
polemist
EILMOPTY Ptolemy I
EILMORRS lorimers
EILMORSY rimosely
EILMPRUY impurely
EILMPSST misspelt
simplest
EILMPSSU impulses
EILMPSTU lumpiest
plumiest
EILMRSSU misrules
EILMRSSY remissly
EILMTTUU lutetium
EILMTTUY multeity
EILNNORS onliners
EILNNOST insolent
EILNNOSW snowline
EILNNPSU pinnules
EILNNSSU luniness
EILNNTTY intently
EILNOOPS polonies
EILNOOST looniest
oilstone
EILNOOSV violones
EILNOPRS plerions
EILNOPRU neuropil
EILNOPSS epsilons
EILNORRS loriners
EILNORSS ironless
EILNORTT trotline
EILNORVV involver
EILNOSSU elusions
EILNOSSW lewisson
EILNOSTU outlines

EILNOSTV novelist
EILNOSTW towlines
EILNOSUV evulsion
EILNOSVV involves
EILNOTUV involute
EILNPRST splinter
EILNPRSU purlines
EILNPSSU spinules
splenius
EILNPSUY supinely
EILNQUUY uniquely
EILNRRUU unrulier
EILNRSST slinters
EILNRSTU insulter
EILNRSUU Ursuline
EILNRTUV virulent
EILNRTWY winterly
EILNSSTU utensils
EILNSTTU lutenist
EILNSUWY unwisely
EILOOPST loopiest
EILOORST oestriol
EILOOSST ostioles
EILOOSTW wooliest
EILOPPRS sloppier
EILOPRRT portlier
EILOPRSS spoilers
EILOPRSU perilous
EILOPRSV slipover
EILOPRTW pilewort
EILOPSST pistoles
EILOPSSV plosives
EILOPSTX exploits
EILOPSUV pluviose
EILORRTU ulterior
EILORSSS rissoles
EILORSSU soilures
EILORSTT triolets
EILORSTU outliers
EILORTTY toiletry
EILOSSTU lousiest
EILOSTTT stiletto
EILOSTUV outlives
EILOTVVY votively
EILPPRRS ripplers
EILPPRSS slippers
EILPPRST ripplets
stippler
tipplers
EILPPRSU supplier
EILPPRSY slippery
EILPPSST stipples
EILPPSSU supplies
EILPPSSW swipples
EILPPSTU pulpiest
EILPRSTT splitter
triplets
EILPRSTY priestly
EILPRSUU purlieus
EILPRSUY pleurisy
EILPRTTY prettily
EILPRTUZ Pulitzer

EILPSSTU stipules
EILQRRSU squirrel
EILQRSTU quilters
EILQRSUU liqueurs
EILRRSSU slurries
EILRRSTU sultrier
EILRRSTW twirlers
EILRRTWY writerly
EILRSSTT slitters
EILRSSTU surliest
EILRSSTV listserv
EILRSSTY sisterly
styliser
EILRSSZZ sizzlers
EILRSTTW wristlet
EILRSTUV rivulets
EILRSTYZ stylizer
EILRSUUX luxuries
EILSSSTY stylises
EILSSTTU lustiest
EILSSTTY stylites
EILSSTYZ stylizes
EILSSWZZ swizzles
EIMMNNTU muniment
EIMMNORS misnomer
EIMMOPRU emporium
EIMMORRT Mortimer
EIMMOSTT totemism
EIMMPRST primmest
EIMMPRSU premiums
EIMMRRST trimmers
EIMMRSST misterms
EIMMRSSW swimmers
EIMMRSTT trimmest
EIMMRSTU rummiest
EIMMSSTU mumsiest
EIMMSTUY yummiest
EIMNNOOT noontime
EIMNNOPT imponent
EIMNNOST mentions
EIMNNOTT ointment
EIMNOOPS empoison
EIMNOORS moonrise
EIMNOORV omnivore
EIMNOOSS isonomes
EIMNOOST emotions
mooniest
EIMNOPRT orpiment
EIMNOPST nepotism
pimentos
EIMNOPTT impotent
EIMNORSU monsieur
EIMNORTW timeworn
EIMNORTY enormity
EIMNOSST moistens
EIMNPRSS primness
EIMNPSST misspent
EIMNRSST minsters
trimness
EIMNRSTU terminus
EIMNRSTY entryism
EIMNSUZZ muezzins
EIMOORST motorise
roomiest
EIMOORTZ motorize
EIMOPPRR improper
EIMOPRRS primrose
promiser
EIMOPRRT importer
reimport
EIMOPRRV improver
EIMOPRSS imposers
promises
semipros
EIMOPRST imposter
EIMOPRSV improves
EIMOPRSW impowers
EIMOPRUU europium
EIMOPSST stompies
EIMOQSTU misquote
EIMORRST mortiser
stormier
EIMORRTT remittor
EIMORRWW wireworm
EIMORSST mortises
EIMORSTT omitters
EIMORSTU moisture
EIMORSTV vomiters
EIMORSTW wormiest
EIMORSTY isometry
EIMOSSST mossiest
EIMOSSTU mousiest
EIMOSSTZ mestizos
EIMOSSYZ isozymes
EIMOSTTT totemist
EIMOSTTU timeouts
titmouse
EIMPRSST imprests
EIMPRSSU primuses
EIMPRSTU impurest
stumpier
EIMPSSST missteps
EIMPSSTY mistypes
EIMPSSUY Puseyism
EIMQRRSU squirmer
EIMQSSTU mesquits
EIMQSTUY mystique
EIMRRSSU surmiser
EIMRSSST mistress
EIMRSSSU misusers
surmises
EIMRSSTT metrists
EIMRSTTU smuttier
EIMRSTUX mixtures
EIMSSSTU mussiest
EIMSSTTU mustiest
EIMSTUZZ muzziest
EINNOPSS pensions
EINNORST intoners
ternions
EINNORSU reunions
EINNORSV environs
EINNORTU neutrino
EINNORTV inventor
EINNORWW winnower
EINNOSSS nosiness
EINNOSST tensions
EINNOSTT tinstone
tontines
EINNPRSS spinners
EINNPRST enprints
EINNPSSU puniness
EINNPSSY spinneys
EINNPSXY sixpenny
EINNRSTU runniest
EINNRSTV vintners
EINNRTTU nutrient
EINNSSTU sunniest
EINNSTUW untwines
EINOOPRS poisoner
spoonier
EINOOPSS opsonise
spoonies
EINOOPSZ opsonize
EINOORSS erosions
EINOORST snootier
EINOORSZ ozoniser
EINOORZZ ozonizer
EINOOSST isotones
EINOOSSZ ooziness
ozonises
EINOOSZZ ozonizes
EINOOTXX exotoxin
EINOPRRS prisoner
EINOPRSS ropiness
EINOPRST pointers
proteins
repoints
EINOPRSU pruinose
EINOPRTU eruption
EINOPSTT nepotist
EINOPSTU poutines
EINOPSWX swinepox
EINOQSTU question
EINOQTTU quotient
EINORRSS rosiners
EINORRST introrse
EINORRTV invertor
EINORSSS rosiness
EINORSST oestrins
EINORSSU neurosis
resinous
EINORSSV versions
EINORSTT snottier
tritones
EINORSTU routines
EINORSTV investor
EINORSTY tyrosine
EINORSUV souvenir
EINORTTU ritenuto
EINOSSSS sessions
EINOSSST sonsiest
stenosis
EINOSSTT snotties
stoniest
EINOSSTW snowiest

EINOSTTW	nowtiest
EINOSTVY	venosity
EINPPSST	snippets
EINPPSTY	snippety
EINPRRST	printers
	reprints
	sprinter
EINPRRTU	prurient
EINPRRTY	printery
EINPRSST	spinster
EINPSTTY	tintypes
EINQRSTU	squinter
EINQRTTU	quitrent
EINQSSTU	inquests
EINQSTTU	quintets
EINRRSSU	insurers
EINRSSSU	sunrises
EINRSSTT	stinters
EINRSSXY	syrinxes
EINRSTTY	entryist
EINSSTTW	twinsets
EINSTTTU	nuttiest
EIOOPPRS	porpoise
EIOOPPST	opposite
EIOOPSST	isotopes
EIOORSTT	tortoise
EIOOSSTT	sootiest
	tootsies
EIOOSTWZ	wooziest
EIOPPRTW	pipewort
EIOPPSST	soppiest
EIOPRRSS	prioress
EIOPRRST	pierrots
	sportier
EIOPRRSU	superior
EIOPRSST	prosiest
	reposits
	ripostes
	triposes
EIOPRSTT	spottier
EIOPRSTV	sportive
EIOPRSUV	pervious
	previous
	viperous
EIOPSSTT	spotties
EIOPSSTU	soupiest
EIOPSTTT	pottiest
EIOPSTUW	wipeouts
EIORRRST	terroirs
EIORRSST	resistor
	roisters
	sorriest
EIORRSTV	servitor
EIORRSVY	revisory
EIORSSTT	Rossetti
EIORSSTY	serosity
EIORSTTW	swottier
EIORSTUV	vitreous
EIOSSTTT	stotties
EIOSSTUZ	outsizes
EIPPRRST	stripper
	trippers
EIPPRSTT	trippets
EIPQRSTU	quipster
EIPRRRSU	spurrier
EIPRRSST	stripers
EIPRRSSU	spurries
	surprise
	uprisers
EIPRRSTZ	spritzer
EIPRSSST	persists
EIPRSSSU	suspires
EIPRSSTT	spitters
	tipsters
EIPRSUVW	purviews
EIPSSSTU	pussiest
EIQRRSTU	squirter
EIQRSSTU	querists
EIQRSTTU	quitters
EIQRSUZZ	quizzers
EIQSSUZZ	squizzes
EIRRRSST	stirrers
EIRRSSTV	strivers
EIRRSTTU	trustier
EIRSSTTU	rustiest
	trusties
EIRSSTTW	retwists
	twisters
EIRSSUVV	survives
EIRSTTTU	ruttiest
EIRSTTTW	twitters
EIRTTTWY	twittery
EISSSSTU	tussises
EISSUUVV	Vesuvius
EISTTTUV	vuttiest
EJLOPSTU	pulsojet
EJLORSST	jostlers
EJNNOSWY	Wyn Jones
EJNORSUY	journeys
EJNSSSTU	justness
EJOORSVY	overjoys
EJOPPRST	propjets
EJOPRSTT	jetports
EJORSSTU	jousters
EKKLOOSZ	kolkozes
EKKLRSSU	skulkers
EKKMORSY	kromesky
EKLLMSSU	skellums
EKLLNORS	knollers
EKLLOSSY	yolkless
EKLLRRSU	krullers
EKLMNOSS	Smolensk
EKLNOOOR	onlooker
EKLNOPRS	plonkers
EKLNORSS	snorkels
EKLNOSST	knotless
EKLNOSWY	Knowsley
EKLOOORV	lookover
	overlook
EKLOOPSW	slowpoke
EKLORSSW	workless
EKLOSSTV	stokvels
EKMOOPRR	morepork
EKMRSTUY	musketry
EKNNOPSU	unspoken
EKNOOPRW	openwork
EKNOORSS	snookers
EKNORSTT	knotters
EKNORSTW	networks
EKNORSUY	younkers
EKNRSTUY	turnkeys
EKOOOPRT	pokeroot
EKOOORTV	overtook
EKOOPRSV	provokes
EKOOPSTU	outspoke
EKOORRVW	overwork
EKOORSST	stookers
EKOORTWW	kowtower
EKOPRSTU	upstroke
EKOPRSTV	Petrovsk
EKOPRSUY	koupreys
ELLLMOWY	mellowly
ELLLNSUY	sullenly
ELLLOWYY	yellowly
ELLMNOSY	solemnly
ELLMOORS	morellos
ELLMORRS	morrells
ELLMOSTT	Smollett
ELLMPSUU	plumules
ELLNOORV	lovelorn
ELLNOOSW	woollens
ELLNOPRU	prunello
ELLNOSST	stollens
ELLNOSVY	slovenly
ELLNOUVY	unlovely
ELLOOPRT	Trollope
ELLOORRV	rollover
ELLOOSST	toolless
ELLOPRST	pollster
ELLOPRTU	polluter
ELLOPRUV	pullover
ELLOPSTU	pollutes
ELLORRST	stroller
	trollers
ELLORSTY	trolleys
ELLOSSSU	soulless
ELLOSSTU	outsells
ELLPPSUY	supplely
ELLPSSUW	upswells
ELMMNOTU	lomentum
ELMMNOTY	momently
ELMMORST	trommels
ELMMOSUX	lummoxes
ELMMPSTU	plummets
ELMMRSSU	slummers
ELMMRSUY	summerly
ELMNOOOP	monopole
ELMNOOSS	moonless
ELMNORUY	Mulroney
ELMNUUZZ	unmuzzle
ELMOOPSY	polysome
ELMOORST	tremolos
ELMOORSY	morosely
ELMOOSSY	lysosome
ELMOPRSY	polymers
ELMOPSYY	polysemy

ELMORSTU moulters
ELMOSTUU tumulose
ELMOSYYZ lysozyme
ELMPPRSU plumpers
ELMPPSTU plumpest
ELMPRSSU rumpless
ELMPRSYZ Przemyśl
ELMRSTUU multures
ELMRSUZZ muzzlers
ELNNOOSU unloosen
ELNNORSS lornness
ELNNOSSU nounless
ELNNRSTU trunnels
ELNOOPRT Ternopol
ELNOOPST pelotons
ELNOOSST solonets
ELNOOSSU unlooses
ELNOOSTZ solonetz
ELNOPRVY provenly
ELNOPSTU pleuston
ELNOPTTY potently
ELNORSTU turnsole
ELNORTTY rottenly
ELNOSSSW slowness
snowless
ELNOSSTV solvents
ELNOSSTW townless
ELNOSUVY venously
ELNPRTUU purulent
ELOOPRSU superloo
ELOORSST rootless
ELOORSTT rootlets
tootlers
ELOOSSTU outsoles
ELOOSTUU Toulouse
ELOPPRRY properly
ELOPPSST stopples
ELOPRRSW prowlers
ELOPRSSS plessors
ELOPRSSU sporules
ELOPRSTT plotters
ELOPRSTU plouters
ELOPRSTW plowters
ELOPRSTY prostyle
ELOPRSUV overplus
ELOPRSYY pyrolyse
ELOPRYYZ pyrolyze
ELOPSSST spotless
ELOPSSTY stylopes
ELORSSTT settlors
slotters
ELORSTUY elytrous
urostyle
ELPPRSUY resupply
ELPRSTTU splutter
ELPRSUZZ puzzlers
ELPSSTUU pustules
ELRRSSTU rustlers
ELRRSTTU turtlers
ELRSSSTU rustless
ELRSTUUV vultures
ELSSSTUY styluses

EMMMNOTU momentum
EMMNNOTU monument
EMMNOOOS monosome
EMMNOORS monomers
EMMNOORT motormen
EMMNOOSY monosemy
EMMNORSU resummon
EMMNOSTY metonyms
EMMNOTTU tomentum
EMMNOTYY metonymy
EMMOOSTY myotomes
EMMRRRUU murmurer
EMMRRSTU strummer
EMMRSTYY symmetry
EMNNNOOU noumenon
EMNNOOOT monotone
EMNNOSTW townsmen
EMNNSTTU stuntmen
EMNOOPTY monotype
EMNOORST mesotron
monteros
Montrose
EMNOORSU enormous
EMNOORSW newsroom
EMNOOSUV venomous
EMNOOTTY tenotomy
EMNORRSU mourners
EMNORSST monsters
EMNORSTT torments
EMNORSTU mounters
remounts
EMNORSUU numerous
EMNORTUX Montreux
EMNOSSST stemsons
EMNOSUUY euonymus
EMNOSUVY evonymus
EMNRSSTU sternums
EMOOPRRT promoter
EMOOPRSS oosperms
EMOOPRST promotes
EMOOPRSZ zoosperm
EMOORRST restroom
EMOORTYZ zoometry
EMOOSSTW twosomes
EMOOSSTY myosotes
EMOPPRRT prompter
EMOPRSST stompers
EMOPRSSU spermous
supremos
EMORRSST stormers
EMORSSTU strumose
EMOSSTVZ zemstvos
EMPRRTUY trumpery
EMPRSSTU stumpers
sumpters
EMPRSSUU rumpuses
EMPRSTTU strumpet
trumpets
EMRRSSTU sturmers
ENNNOSTY Tennyson
ENNOOOTZ entozoon
ENNOOPPT opponent

ENNOORTV nonvoter
ENNOPRSU unperson
ENNOPRUV unproven
ENNOPTWY twopenny
ENNORSST sternson
ENNORSSU nonusers
ENNORSSW wornness
ENNORSTU neutrons
ENNOSSTU sunstone
ENNPPTUY tuppenny
ENNRSSTU stunners
ENOOOSSZ zoonoses
ENOOPPRS propones
ENOOPPST postpone
ENOOPRSS poorness
snoopers
ENOOPSTT potstone
ENOORRST Sorrento
ENOORSSZ snoozers
ENOOSSTT testoons
ENOPRSST posterns
ENOPRSTT portents
ENOPRTUW uptowner
ENOPSSST stepsons
ENOPSSSY synopses
ENOQSTUU unquotes
ENORRSST snorters
ENORRSTT torrents
ENORRSUV overruns
ENORRTUU Tourneur
ENORRTUV overturn
turnover
ENORSSSU sourness
ENORSSTT snotters
stentors
ENORSSTU tonsures
ENORSTUY tourneys
ENOSSSTT stetsons
ENOSSSUU sensuous
ENPRRSSU spurners
ENPRSSSY spryness
ENPRSSTU punsters
ENRRRTUU nurturer
ENRRSTUU nurtures
ENRSSTTU entrusts
EOOOPRSS oospores
EOOOPRSZ zoospore
EOOORRST roseroot
EOOPPRRS proposer
EOOPPRSS opposers
proposes
EOOPPRSV popovers
EOOPPTTY topotype
EOOPRRSS spoorers
EOOPRRST troopers
EOOPRRTU uprooter
EOOPRSST stoopers
EOOPRSTV overtops
stopover
EOOPRSTW towropes
EOOPSTTV stovetop
EOORRRSW sorrower

EOORRSST	roosters
EOORRSVW	rowovers
EOORSSTU	oestrous
EOOSTTUV	outvotes
EOPPRRSS	prospers
EOPPRRTY	property
EOPPRSST	popsters
	stoppers
EOPPRSSU	purposes
	supposer
EOPPSSSU	supposes
EOPRRSST	portress
	sporters
EOPRRSTU	posturer
	troupers
EOPRRUVY	purveyor
EOPRSSTT	protests
	spotters
EOPRSSTU	postures
	spouters
EOPRSSUU	uprouses
EOPSSTTU	outsteps
EOQRSSTU	questors
EORRRTTU	torturer
EORRSSST	stressor
EORRSSTU	trousers
EORRSSTY	stroyers
EORRSTTT	trotters
EORRSTTU	tortures
EORRSUVY	surveyor
EORRTUUV	trouveur
EORSSSTU	tussores
EORSSTTT	stotters
	strettos
EORSSTTU	outserts
EORSSTTW	swotters
EOSSTTTU	stoutest
EPPPRTUY	puppetry
EPPRSSSU	suppress
EPRRSSUU	pursuers
	usurpers
EPRRSTUU	ruptures
EPRSSTTU	sputters
ERRSSSTU	trussers
ERRSSTTU	trusters
ERRSSTTY	trysters
ERRSTTTU	strutter
ERSSTTTU	stutters
FFFGILNU	fluffing
FFFILLUY	fluffily
FFFILOST	liftoffs
FFGHIINW	whiffing
FFGHIIRT	Griffith
FFGHIORS	frogfish
FFGHIRSU	gruffish
FFGIILNP	piffling
FFGIILNR	riffling
FFGIINNS	sniffing
FFGIINPS	spiffing
FFGIINRS	griffins
FFGIINST	stiffing
FFGILMNU	muffling
FFGILNRU	ruffling
FFGILNSU	sluffing
FFGINNSU	snuffing
FFGINORS	griffons
FFGINOSW	swoffing
FFGINSTU	stuffing
FFHIISST	stiffish
FFHILOSW	wolffish
FFHILOSY	offishly
FFHOOOST	offshoot
FFHOOSSW	showoffs
FFHOSSTU	shutoffs
FFIILMOR	filiform
FFIILNSY	sniffily
FFIILPSY	spiffily
FFIKLORT	forklift
FFILLLSU	fulfills
FFILLTUY	fitfully
FFILRTUU	fruitful
FFILSSTU	fistfuls
FFILSTUY	stuffily
FFIMORSU	fusiform
FFINOOST	finfoots
FFINOPRT	offprint
FFINOPSS	spinoffs
FFINOPST	pontiffs
FFJMOPSU	jumpoffs
FFKLORSU	forkfuls
FFLMNOOU	moufflon
FFNORSTU	turnoffs
FFOOPSST	stopoffs
FFOORRUU	froufrou
FGGGIINR	frigging
FGGGILNO	flogging
FGGGINOR	frogging
FGGHIINT	fighting
FGGHIISS	fishgigs
FGGHINTU	gunfight
FGGIILNN	flinging
FGGIINNR	fringing
FGGIINRU	figuring
FGGINOOR	forgoing
FGGINORS	forgings
FGHIIKNS	kingfish
FGHIILNT	inflight
FGHIINST	shifting
FGHIITTW	Whitgift
FGHILNSU	flushing
	lungfish
FGHILRTU	rightful
FGHINORT	frothing
FGHIOTTU	outfight
FGHLORUU	furlough
FGHNOORS	foghorns
FGHNOTUU	unfought
FGIIINNX	infixing
FGIIKNRS	frisking
FGIILLNR	frilling
FGIILLNS	fillings
FGIILNNT	flinting
FGIILNOO	folioing
FGIILNPP	flipping
FGIILNRS	riflings
FGIILNRT	flirting
	trifling
FGIILNST	stifling
FGIILNTT	flitting
FGIILNZZ	fizzling
FGIINNSU	infusing
FGIINNUX	unfixing
FGIINNUY	unifying
FGIINOST	foisting
FGIINRTT	fritting
FGIINRTU	fruiting
FGIINRZZ	frizzing
FGIINSST	siftings
FGIINSTT	fittings
FGIKLNNU	flunking
FGILMNUY	fumingly
FGILNNTU	gunflint
FGILNOOR	flooring
FGILNOOT	footling
FGILNOOZ	foozling
FGILNOPP	flopping
FGILNORU	flouring
FGILNOTU	flouting
FGILNPRU	purfling
FGILNSTU	flutings
FGINNORT	fronting
FGINNORW	frowning
FGINOOPR	proofing
FGINOOPS	spoofing
FGINOOST	footings
FGINORST	frosting
FGINRRSU	furrings
FGIORSTW	figworts
FGISSTUU	fuguists
FGLLMOOU	gloomful
FGLNORSU	furlongs
FGLNORUW	wrongful
FGLOOOST	footslog
FGNOORSU	fourgons
FHHIKOOS	fishhook
	fish-hook
FHHOORST	shofroth
FHIIKLMS	milkfish
FHIIKNSS	fishskin
FHIILLTY	filthily
FHIILNOS	lionfish
FHIILSTY	shiftily
FHIKMNOS	monkfish
FHILLOOT	foothill
FHILLORT	hillfort
FHILMPSU	lumpfish
FHILMRTU	mirthful
FHILORSU	flourish
FHILORTY	frothily
FHIMNOOS	moonfish
FHIMPRSU	frumpish
FHIOOPTT	photofit
FHKORSTU	futhorks
FHLLOSTU	slothful
FHLMORUU	humorful
FHLMOTUU	mouthful

FHLORTUY fourthly
FHLOTUUY youthful
FHLRTTUU truthful
FHOOORST forsooth
FHOOSTT hotfoots
FIIILNOP Filipino
FIIIMNST finitism
FIIINNOX infixion
FIIINNTY infinity
FIIKLRSY friskily
FIILLMOS milfoils
FIILLMSY flimsily
FIILLNTY flintily
FIILMNRY infirmly
FIILMOPR piliform
FIILMPSY simplify
FIILRTUY fruitily
FIILRYZZ frizzily
FIILTTUY futility
FIIMOPRS pisiform
FIINNOSU infusion
FIINORTU fruition
FIINOSSS fissions
FIIOPSST positifs
FIKKLNOS kinsfolk
FIKLLLSU skillful
FIKLNSSU skinfuls
FILLLUWY wilfully
FILLNSUY sinfully
FILLOPPY floppily
FILMNOOS monofils
FILMPRUY frumpily
FILNOSUX fluxions
FILORSST florists
FILORSTY frostily
FILORUYZ frouzily
FILRSTTU tristful
FILSSTTU flutists
FILSTTUY stultify
FIMNORSU uniforms
FIMOPRRY pyriform
FIMORTUY fumitory
FIMRSTUU futurism
FINOOPSY opsonify
FINOPSSU soupfins
FINORSSS frissons
FIOORSSU furiosos
FIORTTUY fortuity
FIRSTTUU futurist
FIRTTUUY futurity
FJLLOUYY joyfully
FKKLOORW workfolk
FKLMOOOT folkmoot
FKLMOOST folkmots
FKLNRTUU trunkful
FKMOORRW formwork
FKNOORTX Fort Knox
FKOOORTW footwork
FLMNOOSU mouflons
FLMNORUU mournful
FLMOOORW moorfowl
FLMOOOST tomfools
FLMOORSU roomfuls
FLNOOPSU spoonful
FLNOOTUW outflown
FLOOPTTY toplofty
FLOOSTUW outflows
FLOPRSTU sportful
FLRSTTUU trustful
FMNOORTT Montfort
FMRSSTUU frustums
FNNOORST frontons
FNOOORTW footworn
FNOORRSW forsworn
FNOORSSU sunroofs
FOOOPRST rooftops
FOOOSTTU outfoots
FOORSTTX foxtrots
FOPSSSTU fusspots
GGGGIILN giggling
GGGGILNO goggling
GGGHIILN higgling
GGGIIJLN jiggling
GGGIILNN niggling
GGGIILNW wiggling
GGGIINNS snigging
GGGIINPR prigging
GGGIINRS riggings
GGGIINRT trigging
GGGIINSW swigging
wiggings
GGGIINTW twigging
GGGIJLNO joggling
GGGIJLNU juggling
GGGILNOS slogging
GGGILNOT toggling
GGGILNPU plugging
GGGILNRU gurgling
GGGILNSU slugging
GGGILORY groggily
GGGINNOS noggings
snogging
GGGINNSU snugging
GGGINOPR progging
GGGINORT trogging
GGHHINOU houghing
GGHHISTU thuggish
GGHIILNT lighting
GGHIINOS O'Higgins
GGHIINRT girthing
righting
GGHIINST sighting
GGHIIPRS priggish
GGHILSSU sluggish
GGHINORU roughing
GGHINOST ghosting
GGHINOSU soughing
GGHINOTU toughing
GGHINOTY hogtying
GGHKNNOO Hong Kong
GGHOOPRS grogshop
GGIIINNT igniting
GGIIINOR Grigioni
GGIIJLNN jingling
GGIILLNR grilling
GGIILMNN mingling
GGIILMNY ginglymi
GGIILNNS singling
slinging
GGIILNNT glinting
tingling
GGIIMPRS priggism
GGIINNNR grinning
GGIINNOR groining
ignoring
GGIINNOS ingoings
GGIINNOT ingoting
GGIINNRW wringing
GGIINNSS Sing Sing
GGIINNST stinging
GGIINNSW swinging
GGIINNTW twinging
GGIINPPR gripping
GGIINRST ringgits
GGIINRTT gritting
GGIIRRSS grisgris
gris-gris
GGILLNOY gollying
GGILLNUY gullying
GGILLOOW golliwog
GGILMNOO glooming
GGILNNOS longings
GGILNNOU lounging
GGILNNPU plunging
GGILNORW growling
GGILNORY glorying
GGILNOSS glossing
goslings
GGILNTTU glutting
GGILNUZZ guzzling
GGILQSUY squiggly
GGIMNOOR grooming
GGIMNOOS smooging
GGIMNPRU grumping
GGINNNSU gunnings
GGINNOOS ongoings
GGINNOPR pronging
GGINNOPS sponging
GGINNORW wronging
GGINNOSS singsong
GGINNOTU tonguing
GGINNRTU grunting
GGINNTTU Tungting
GGINOORV grooving
GGINOOST stooging
GGINOOTU outgoing
GGINOPRU grouping
GGINORSS grossing
GGINORSU grousing
GGINORTU grouting
GGLLPUUY plugugly
GHHIILST lightish
GHHIIRST rightish
GHHILOSU ghoulish
GHHINSSU shushing
GHHIOPST highspot

GHIORSU roughish
GHIOSTU toughish
GHHOORTU thorough
GHHOSTTU thoughts
GHIIJNOS jingoish
GHIIKNNS Hsinking
GHIIKNNT thinking
GHIIKNPS kingship
GHIIKNRS shirking
GHIIKNSW whisking
GHIILLNS shilling
GHIILMTY mightily
GHIILNPR hirpling
GHIILNRT thirling
GHIILNRW whirling
GHIILTTW twilight
GHIIMMNS shimming
GHIIMNNU inhuming
GHIIMRST rightism
GHIINNNS shinning
GHIINNNT thinning
GHIINNNY hinnying
GHIINNRS shrining
GHIINNST hintings
GHIINOST hoisting
GHIINPPS shipping
GHIINPPW whipping
GHIINRRS shirring
GHIINRRW whirring
GHIINRST shirting
GHIINRSV shriving
GHIINRTV thriving
GHIINRTW writhing
GHIINSST insights
GHIINSSW swishing
GHIINSTT shitting
tithings
GHIINSTW whisting
whitings
GHIINSVV shivving
GHIINWZZ whizzing
GHIIORSU Ishiguro
GHIIRSTT rightist
GHIKLNTY knightly
GHIKLSTY skylight
GHIKRSTU tughriks
GHILLNOO holloing
GHILLNOS Shillong
GHILLNOU hulloing
GHILLOTW lowlight
GHILLSTY slightly
GHILNOPP hoppling
GHILNOPS longship
GHILNOSS sloshing
GHILNRTU hurtling
GHILNRUY hungrily
GHILNSSU slushing
GHILNSTU hustling
sunlight
GHILORSW showgirl
GHILPRTY triglyph
GHIMNOPR morphing
GHIMNORU humoring
GHIMNOTU mouthing
GHIMNPTU thumping
GHIMNSTU gunsmith
GHIMPRSU grumpish
GHINNNSU shunning
GHINNOOR honoring
GHINNOQU Qui Nhong
GHINNORT northing
throning
GHINNOST nothings
GHINNSTU shunting
GHINOOPW whooping
GHINOOST shooting
soothing
GHINOOSW wooshing
GHINOOTT toothing
GHINOPPS hoppings
shopping
GHINOPPW whopping
GHINORTW ingrowth
throwing
worthing
GHINOSSU housings
GHINOSSW showings
GHINOSTT shotting
GHINOSTU houtings
shouting
southing
GHINOSUY youngish
GHINPPUW whupping
GHINRRUY hurrying
GHINSSTU hustings
GHINSTTU shutting
GHIORTTU outright
GHIPRSTU uprights
GHIPRSUU guruship
GHIPSSYY gypsyish
GHLMOOOS homologs
GHLMOOOY homology
GHLNNOOR longhorn
GHLNOORU hourlong
GHLOOORY horology
GHLORTUU turlough
GHMNOOOY homogony
GHMORSSU sorghums
GHNNOOOZ gohonzon
GHNOPRSY gryphons
GHNOPYYY hypogyny
GHNOSSTU gunshots
shotguns
GHNOSTUU unsought
GHOOOSSW hoosgows
GHOORTUY yoghourt
GHOPRTUW upgrowth
GHORSTUY yoghurts
GIIILMNT limiting
GIIILNNU linguini
GIIILOTV vitiligo
GIIIMMNX immixing
GIIINNOS ionising
GIIINNOT ignition
GIIINNOZ ionizing
GIIINNTV inviting
GIIINORS signiori
GIIINSTV visiting
GIIJMMNY jimmying
GIIJMNOS jingoism
GIIJNNOT jointing
GIIJNNRU injuring
GIIJNOST jingoist
joisting
GIIKKLNP kingklip
GIIKLLNS killings
skilling
GIIKLNNP plinking
GIIKLNNS inklings
slinking
GIIKLNNT tinkling
GIIKLNNW winkling
GIIKLNRS skirling
GIIKLNTT kittling
GIIKMMNS skimming
GIIKMNPS skimping
GIIKMNRS smirking
GIIKNNNS skinning
GIIKNNOV invoking
GIIKNNPR prinking
GIIKNNPS kingpins
GIIKNNST stinking
GIIKNNSW swinking
GIIKNNTT knitting
GIIKNPPS skipping
GIIKNPSS pigskins
GIIKNRRS skirring
GIIKNRSS griskins
GIIKNRST skirting
striking
GIILLMNS millings
GIILLMNU illuming
GIILLNOR grillion
GIILLNOS gillions
GIILLNPR prilling
GIILLNPS spilling
GIILLNQU quilling
GIILLNRT trilling
GIILLNST stilling
GIILLNSW swilling
GIILLNTW twilling
GIILLPSW pigswill
GIILLTUY guiltily
GIILMMNS slimming
GIILMNPW wimpling
GIILMNPY implying
GIILMNZZ mizzling
GIILMPRS pilgrims
GIILMPSU pugilism
GIILNNPS splining
GIILNNUV unliving
GIILNOPS spoiling
GIILNOPT piloting
GIILNPPR rippling
GIILNPPS slipping
GIILNPPT tippling

GIILNPRT tripling
GIILNPSS lispings
GIILNQSU quisling
GIILNQTU quilting
GIILNRST Stirling
GIILNRSW swirling
GIILNRTW twirling
GIILNSST listings
GIILNSTT slitting
stilting
GIILNSTU linguist
GIILNSTW witlings
GIILNSTY stingily
GIILNSZZ sizzling
GIILPSTU pugilist
GIILRSST strigils
GIILRTTY grittily
GIIMMNPR primming
GIIMMNRT trimming
GIIMMNRU immuring
GIIMMNSW swimming
GIIMNNOR minoring
GIIMNNOY ignominy
GIIMNNTU minuting
GIIMNOPS imposing
GIIMNOTT omitting
GIIMNOTV motiving
vomiting
GIIMNPPR primping
GIIMNPRS primings
GIIMNPRU umpiring
GIIMNPTU imputing
GIIMNRRS smirring
GIIMNSSU misusing
GIIMORRS rigorism
GIINNNOT intoning
GIINNNPS spinning
GIINNNRU inurning
GIINNNSW winnings
GIINNNTW twinning
GIINNOPT pointing
GIINNORS ironings
nigrosin
rosining
GIINNORT ignitron
GIINNPPS snipping
GIINNPRT printing
GIINNRSU insuring
GIINNRTU untiring
GIINNSTT stinting
GIINOPST positing
GIINOPTV pivoting
GIINORSS signiors
GIINORSV visoring
GIINORVZ vizoring
GIINPPQU quipping
GIINPPRT tripping
GIINPRST striping
GIINPRSU uprising
GIINPSTT spitting
GIINPTTU tituping
GIINQRSU squiring
GIINQRTU quirting
GIINQTTU quitting
GIINQUZZ quizzing
GIINRRST stirring
GIINRSTV striving
GIINRSTW writings
GIINSSTT sittings
GIINSSTU tissuing
GIINSTTW twisting
GIINTTTW twitting
GIIORRST rigorist
GIIPRSTZ spritzig
GIJKLNOY jokingly
GIJLLNOY jollying
GIJLNOST jostling
GIJLNSTU justling
GIJNOSTT jottings
GIJNOSTU jousting
GIKKLNSU skulking
GIKLLNNO knolling
GIKLNNOP plonking
GIKLNNPU plunking
GIKLNNRU knurling
GIKLNNUY unkingly
GIKNNOST Kingston
stonking
GIKNNOTT knotting
GIKNNOUY unyoking
GIKNNRTU trunking
GIKNOOPS spooking
GIKNOOST stooking
GIKNOPST kingpost
GIKNORST stroking
GIKNORSW workings
GILLMOOY gloomily
GILLNORS rollings
GILLNORT trolling
GILLNOVY lovingly
GILLNSUY sullying
GILLOOPW polliwog
GILLOSSY glossily
GILMMNSU slumming
GILMMTUY multigym
GILMNORS slorming
GILMNOTT mottling
GILMNOTU moulting
GILMNOVY movingly
GILMNPPU plumping
GILMNPRU rumpling
GILMNPSU slumping
GILMNUZZ muzzling
GILMOOSY misology
GILMPRUY grumpily
GILMPSSY gymslips
GILNNOSU Longinus
GILNNOUV unloving
GILNNRSU nursling
GILNNSSU unslings
GILNNUZZ nuzzling
GILNOOPS spooling
GILNOOPT pootling
GILNOORT rootling
GILNOOSS loosings
GILNOOST stooling
GILNOOSY sinology
GILNOOTT tootling
GILNOPPP plopping
poppling
GILNOPPS slopping
GILNOPPT toppling
GILNOPRW prowling
GILNOPSY spongily
GILNOPTT plotting
GILNOSTT slotting
GILNOSTU tousling
GILNOTUY outlying
GILNOTUZ touzling
GILNPPSU suppling
GILNPRSU slurping
GILNPUZZ puzzling
GILNRRSU slurring
GILNRSTU lustring
rustling
GILNRTTU turtling
GILNRTYY tryingly
GILNSSTU tussling
GILOOOST oologist
GILOORSS girosols
GILOORSU glorious
GILOORVY virology
GILOOSSS isogloss
GILOOSTY sitology
GILOSSST glossist
GILOSTUY gulosity
GIMMNSTU stumming
GIMMOSSU gummosis
GIMNNNSU Munnings
GIMNNORS mornings
GIMNNORU mourning
GIMNNOTU mounting
GIMNNOUV unmoving
GIMNOOOU oogonium
GIMNOORS moorings
GIMNOORT motoring
GIMNOOSS osmosing
GIMNOPST stomping
GIMNOPTU gumption
GIMNORRU rumoring
GIMNORRW ringworm
GIMNORST storming
GIMNOSSU mousings
GIMNOSYY misogyny
GIMNPRTU trumping
GIMNPSTU stumping
GIMNRRSU smurring
GIMNSTTU smutting
GIMNSTYY stymying
GINNNOOS noonings
GINNNSTU stunning
GINNOOPS snooping
spooning
GINNOOSW swooning
GINNOOSZ snoozing
GINNOPTU gunpoint

GINNOPTY poynting
GINNORST snorting
GINNORSU grunions
GINNPRSU spurning
GINNRSTU turnings
unstring
GINNSTTU nuttings
stunting
GINOOPPS opposing
GINOOPRS spooring
GINOOPRT trooping
GINOOPST stooping
GINOOPSW swooping
GINOORST roosting
GINOPPPR propping
GINOPPST stopping
toppings
GINOPPSW swopping
GINOPRST sporting
GINOPRSU ingroups
GINOPRTU trouping
GINOPSST postings
signpost
GINOPSSU spousing
GINOPSTT spotting
GINOPSTU spouting
GINORRWY worrying
GINORSTU rousting
GINORSTW strowing
worsting
GINORSTY storying
stroying
GINORTTT trotting
GINORTTU tutoring
GINOSSTU outsings
GINOSTTT stotting
GINOSTTW swotting
GINOSTUW outswing
GINPPRSU upspring
GINPRRSU spurring
GINPRSTU spurting
GINPRSUU pursuing
usurping
GINPRSUY syruping
GINPSSUW upswings
GINPTTUY puttying
GINRSSTU trussing
GINRSTTU trusting
GINRSTTY trysting
GINRSTUU suturing
GIOORRSU rigorous
GIOORSTU goitrous
GIOORSUV vigorous
GIORSTUY rugosity
GJOORSTT jogtrots
GKKNOOSS songkoks
GKLOOOTY tokology
GLLLOORS logrolls
GLLOOPTY polyglot
GLLOOPWY pollywog
GLMNOOOY monology
nomology
GLMNORUW lungworm
GLMNRTUU ngultrum
GLMNSUUU umlungus
GLMOOOPY pomology
GLMOORWW glowworm
GLMOOYYZ zymology
GLMORSUW lugworms
GLNNOORS lorgnons
GLNOOOSY nosology
GLNOOOTY ontology
GLNOOPRS prolongs
GLNOOPSY polygons
GLNOPRSU longspur
GLNOPYYY polygyny
GLNORSTY strongly
strongyl
GLNORTUW lungwort
GLNOSSUW sunglows
GLNOSTTU gluttons
GLNOTTUY gluttony
GLOOOPSY posology
GLOOOPTY topology
GLOOPSSY gossypol
GLOOPTYY logotypy
typology
GLOORSUU orgulous
GMMPSUUW mugwumps
GMNNOOYY monogyny
GMNOORSW morwongs
GMNOORTU Gourmont
GMORSTUW mugworts
GNNRSTUU unstrung
GNOOOSSS gossoons
GNOORTUW outgrown
GNOPRSUW grownups
GNPPRSUU upsprung
GOOPRTUU outgroup
GOORSTUW outgrows
HHIIOORT Hirohito
HHIIPSST phthisis
HHILMOSS shloshim
HHILPSSY sylphish
HHKKSSUU khuskhus
HHLOORUY Holy Hour
HHOOPPRS phosphor
HHOOSSTT hotshots
HIIIILPP Philip II
HIIILMNS nihilism
HIIILNST nihilist
HIIILNTY nihility
HIIILPPP Philippi
HIIILPPV Philip IV
Philip VI
HIIINRST rhinitis
HIIJNOXX John XXII
HIIKMRSS skirmish
HIIKNNSS shinkins
HIIKOPRS piroshki
HIIKOPRZ pirozhki
HIIKSSTT skittish
HIILLPPS Phillips
HIILMOST homilist
HIILMPSY impishly
HIILMTUY humility
HIILNSUY Ilyushin
HIILPSSY syphilis
HIILRSTT triliths
HIILRSTY shirtily
HIILSTTY shittily
HIIMNSTT tinsmith
HIIMOPSS phimosis
HIIMORTZ Zhitomir
HIINNNSY ninnyish
HIIPRTTU puirtith
HIISSTTT tsitsith
HIKKNSUU inukshuk
HIKNNORS inkhorns
HIKNNSTU unthinks
HIKNOOSU hokonuis
HIKNOTTU outthink
HIKOOPRZ pirozhok
HIKOOPSS spookish
HIKOORSU Kuroshio
HIKOPSSY kyphosis
HILLLOSU Solihull
HILLMSUY mulishly
HILLOOPT lopolith
HILLOOST lithosol
HILLOSWY owlishly
HILMNOOT monolith
HILMOPYY myophily
HILMPRTU philtrum
HILNORTY thornily
HILOOSTT otoliths
HILOOTTY toothily
HILOPPSY popishly
HILORSTU uroliths
HILORSUU urushiol
HILORTWY Holy Writ
worthily
HILOSTWW whitlows
HILPPRSU purplish
HILPPSUY uppishly
HILSSTTU sluttish
HIMMOPRU phormium
HIMNOSST Smithson
HIMNSSTY hymnists
HIMOOPRS isomorph
HIMOPRRT trimorph
HIMOPRSW shipworm
HIMOPRWW whipworm
HIMOPSSS sophisms
HIMOPSST moshpits
HIMORSTU humorist
HIMOTTVZ mitzvoth
HIMPRSTU triumphs
HINNORST tinhorns
HINNSSUY sunshiny
HINOORSZ horizons
HINOPRTW Winthrop
HINOPSSY hypnosis
HINOPSTW township
HINORTXY thyroxin
HINOSTTU Tithonus

HINPPSSU pushpins
HIOOPRTT poortith
HIOORSST orthosis
HIOORTWZ Horowitz
HIOPRSSW worships
HIOPRSUZ rhizopus
HIOPSSST sophists
HIOSSTTU stoutish
HIPPPSUY puppyish
HIPSSSUY Sisyphus
HKMOOORW hookworm
HKOOOPST pothooks
HKOOPRSW workshop
HKOOSVYZ sovkhozy
HLLLOOWY hollowly
HLLMNOOU monohull
HLLNOOUU Honolulu
HLMOOSTY smoothly
HLMOPTUY Plymouth
HLNOOOTU Luton Hoo
HLNOOSUW Hounslow
HLNOSTUY Olynthus
HMMNOOSY homonyms
HMMNOOTU Monmouth
HMMNOOYY homonymy
HMMOORSU mushroom
HMNOOOST moonshot
HMNOOPST Thompson
HMNOPSYY hyponyms
symphony
HMNOPYYY hyponymy
HMOOORSW showroom
HMOORSUU humorous
HNOOPRSW shopworn
HNOOPSTY typhoons
HNOORRTW hornwort
HNOORSTU southron
HNORTUWY unworthy
HNRSTTUU untruths
HOOOSTTU outshoot
shootout
HOPPRRYY porphyry
HOPRSSTU hotspurs
HOPRSTUW upthrows
HOSSTTUU shutouts
HPRSTTUU upthrust
IIIILMNT Mitilíni
IIIJLSUU Julius II
IIIKLNPS spilikin
IIIKMNNS minikins
IIILLMNP minipill
IIILLMNU illinium
IIILLNOS Illinois
IIILMRSV virilism
IIILMUVX lixivium
IIILOSUV Louis VII
IIILOSUX Louis XII
IIILRTVY virility
IIIMMPRS imprimis
IIINPRST inspirit
IIINQTUY iniquity
IIJJKRSW Rijswijk
IIJJSTUU jiujitsu
IIJKNNSY Nijinsky
IIJLLNOS jillions
IIKKNPSS kipskins
IIKKORSS Sikorski
IIKLLNOS skillion
IIKLLNSY slinkily
IIKLMNPS limpkins
IIKLMPSY skimpily
IIKLNOSS oilskins
IIKLQRUY quirkily
IIKNOSTT stotinki
IILLLPUV pulvilli
IILLMNOS millions
IILLMRTU trillium
IILLMUUV illuvium
IILLNOPS pillions
IILLNORT trillion
IILLNOSU illusion
IILLNOSZ zillions
IILLNSST instills
IILMMNOS Molinism
IILMMPSS simplism
IILMNORT mirliton
IILMNOSU Limousin
IILMORST troilism
IILMOTTY motility
IILMRSSY missilry
IILNOOST inositol
IILNOOTV volition
IILNORSS sirloins
IILNPPSY snippily
IILNRTWY wintrily
IILOOPPR liripoop
IILOPRST tripolis
IILOPSTY pilosity
IILORSTT troilist
IILORSTV vitriols
IILOSSTV violists
IILOSUVX Louis XIV
Louis XVI
IILPRSSY prissily
IILSTUUV uvulitis
IILSTUVV vulvitis
IIMMMNSU minimums
IIMMNTUY immunity
IIMMOPST optimism
IIMMOPSU opiumism
IIMMSTTU mittimus
IIMNNOOT monition
IIMNNOSU unionism
IIMNNOTU munition
IIMNOOSS omission
IIMNOPRS imprison
IIMNORTT intromit
IIMNORTY minority
IIMNOSSS missions
IIMNOSST simonist
IIMNPRST imprints
misprint
IIMNPTUY impunity
IIMNRSTY ministry
IIMOPSTT optimist
IIMORSSU Missouri
IIMORSTY rimosity
IIMOTTVY motivity
IIMPRTUY impurity
IIMRRTTU Trimurti
IIMRRTUV triumvir
IIMSSTUW swimsuit
IINNOOPS opinions
IINNOPPT pinpoint
IINNOSTU unionist
IINNPSST tinsnips
IINNSTTU tinnitus
IINOOPST position
IINOPSSS isospins
IINORSST ironists
IINORSTT introits
IINOSTVY vinosity
IINQRSUU Quirinus
IINRTTUY triunity
IIOOPSTV oviposit
IIOORRRR riroriro
IIOOSTTY otiosity
IIOPRRTY priority
IIOPRSSS pissoirs
IIORSSTV visitors
IIORSTUV virtuosi
IISSTUVX Sixtus IV
IJJMSSUU jujuisms
IJJSSTUU jujuists
IJJSTUUU jiujutsu
IJKKORRT Kortrijk
IJKLLOSY killjoys
IJLLORTU Trujillo
IJLNOQSU jonquils
IJMPSTUU jumpsuit
IKKLNORW linkwork
IKKLNOSY kolinsky
IKKLSSUY Issyk-Kul
IKKMNOSU kikumons
IKKORSSY sikorsky
IKLLMORW millwork
IKLLOOTV kilovolt
IKLLOTWZ Kollwitz
IKLLPSSU upskills
IKLMOPSS milksops
IKLMORSW silkworm
IKLMORTW milkwort
IKLNOOST kilotons
IKLNOPST slipknot
IKLNOTTY knottily
IKLNPSUY spunkily
IKLOOPST Topolski
IKLOOPSY spookily
IKLOSSSU sousliks
IKMNOOSS monoskis
IKMNPPSU pumpkins
IKNOOPRT pinkroot
IKNOORRW ironwork
IKNOPSTT stinkpot
IKNORSTW tinworks
IKNORWYZ Zworykin

IKORSSTU	kurtosis
ILLLMOPS	plimsoll
ILLLOOPP	lollipop
ILLLOOWY	woollily
ILLMNOSU	mullions
ILLMNRSU	millruns
ILLMOSSY	lissomly
ILLMPSUY	psyllium
ILLMPTUY	multiply
ILLNOQSU	quillons
ILLOPPSS	slipslop
ILLOPPSY	sloppily
ILLOPRTW	pillwort
ILLOPRXY	prolixly
ILLORSTU	trollius
ILLORSUY	illusory
ILLOSSYY	lyolysis
ILLRSTUY	sultrily
ILMNOOPU	polonium
ILMNOSUU	luminous
ILMOPPSU	populism
ILMORSTU	turmoils
ILMORSTY	stormily
ILMPPTUU	pulpitum
ILMSSTUU	stimulus
ILMSTTUY	smuttily
ILNOOPSS	plosions
ILNOOSTU	solution
ILNOOSTY	snootily
ILNOOTUV	volution
ILNOPRSU	purloins
ILNOPSSU	upsilons
ILNOPSTU	Plotinus
	unspoilt
ILNOPSTY	Stolypin
ILNORSST	nostrils
ILNORSTY	nitrosyl
ILNOSTTY	snottily
ILNPSUUV	pulvinus
ILOOPPRS	propolis
ILOOPSST	topsoils
ILOOPUZZ	Pozzuoli
ILOOSSST	soloists
ILOPPSTU	populist
ILOPRSTY	sportily
ILOPSTTY	spottily
ILOPSUUV	pluvious
ILOQRTUU	loquitur
ILPPSSUY	Lysippus
ILRSTTUY	trustily
ILSSSTTY	stylists
IMMNOORS	moronism
IMMOPSTU	optimums
IMMRSTUY	summitry
IMNNNOSU	munnions
IMNNOOTT	monotint
IMNNOSUU	numinous
IMNOOPST	tompions
IMNOORRS	Morrison
IMNOORST	monitors
IMNOORTY	monitory
	moronity
IMNOPRSW	pinworms
IMNOSTUU	mutinous
IMOOPRRS	promisor
IMOOPRST	impostor
IMOOQSTU	mosquito
IMOORSTT	motorist
IMOORSTU	timorous
IMOORTVY	vomitory
IMOOSSTY	myosotis
IMOOSTUV	vomitous
IMOPPRRU	proprium
IMRSSTTU	mistrust
INNNNOOU	nonunion
INNNORTU	trunnion
INNOOPRU	prounion
INNOOPSS	sponsion
INNOORST	notornis
INNOSSTU	nonsuits
INOOOSSZ	zoonosis
INOOOTXZ	zootoxin
INOOPRST	portions
	positron
	sorption
INOOPSTT	spittoon
INOOPTTU	outpoint
INOORSST	isotrons
INOORSTY	sonority
INOOSSSS	Soissons
INOPRTTU	printout
INOPRTUY	punitory
INOPSSSU	poussins
INOPSSSY	synopsis
INOPSSTU	spinouts
INPPRRUU	purpurin
INPRRSTU	surprint
INPRSTTU	turnspit
INRSSTTU	intrusts
INSSSTUU	sunsuits
INSSTTUW	untwists
IOOPRSSV	provisos
IOOPRSTY	isotropy
	porosity
IOORRSTY	sorority
IOORSSTT	risottos
IOORSSUV	voussoir
IOORSTTU	tortious
IOORSTTY	torosity
IOORSTUV	virtuoso
IOORSUUX	uxorious
IOOSSTTU	stotious
IOPRRSUV	provirus
IOPRSSTT	protists
IOPRSSUU	spurious
IOPRSTTU	outstrip
IOPRSTUY	pyritous
IORRSUVV	survivor
IORSSTTU	tourists
IORSSUUU	usurious
IORSTTUY	touristy
IORSTUUV	virtuous
IPRRSSTU	stirrups
IPRRSTUU	pruritus
IPRSSTUU	pursuits
JLNSTUUY	unjustly
JLOOSUYY	joyously
JMOPSTUU	outjumps
JNNOORRU	nonjuror
JNOORSSU	sojourns
KKLMUYYZ	Kyzyl Kum
KKNOORTW	knotwork
KLLMNSUU	numskull
KLLMOSSU	mollusks
KLNORSTY	klystron
KLOOOSTU	lookouts
	outlooks
KLOOPRSW	slopwork
KMOOORRW	workroom
KNNNOSUW	unknowns
KNOOPSTT	topknots
KNOORTWY	Yorktown
KOOORSTV	voorskot
KOOPRSTW	worktops
KOORSTUW	outworks
	workouts
LLMOOPRS	rollmops
LLMOPRUU	pullorum
LLOOPRST	trollops
LLOOPRTY	trollopy
LLOORSTU	rollouts
LLOPSTUU	pullouts
LLOSUUVV	volvulus
LMNOOOPY	monopoly
LMOOOOPR	poolroom
LMOOOORT	toolroom
LMOOPRTU	pulmotor
LMOORSWW	slowworm
LMOOTXYY	xylotomy
LMOPPRTY	promptly
LMOSTUUU	tumulous
LMRSSTUU	lustrums
LNOOOPRT	poltroon
LNOOPPRY	propylon
LNOORTUV	Volturno
LOOOORSS	olorosos
LOOPPSUU	populous
LOOPPSUY	polypous
LOOPRSUY	porously
LORSSTUU	lustrous
MMNNOOSY	mononyms
MMOORTTY	tommyrot
MMOPSSTY	symptoms
MNNOOOSS	monsoons
MNNOOOTY	monotony
MNNOSSYY	synonyms
MNNOSYYY	synonymy
MNOOOPRT	Pontormo
MNOOORTW	moonwort
MNOOORXY	oxymoron
MNOOPRTU	pronotum
MNOOPSTY	toponyms
MNOOPTYY	toponymy
MNOORSTT	Stormont
MNORSSTU	nostrums
MNORSTUU	surmount

MOOORRTW moorwort
tomorrow
MOOPSSSU opossums
MOORSTUU tumorous
MORRSSTU rostrums
MORSSTUU strumous
NNOOOPST pontoons
spontoon
NNOOPRSU pronouns
NNOOPSSS sponsons
NOOORSSU sonorous
NOOPRSSS sponsors
NOPSSSTU sunspots
NORSTTUU outturns
turnouts
OOOOPRST potoroos
OOORSTTU outroots
OOPRSSSU soursops
OOPRSSTV provosts
OOPRSTTU outports
OOPRSTUU outpours
OOPSSSTT tosspots
OOPSSTTU outposts
OORSTTUU tortuous
OPPRRSTU purports
OPPRSSTU supports
OPRSSSUU sourpuss
ORSSTTUU surtouts
RRSSSUUU susurrus

Nine Letters

AAAABCLLV balaclava
AAAABCLMN balmacaan
AAAABDHLL Allahabad
AAAABDJLL Jalalabad
AAAABENNS anabaenas
AAAABGNRU Guanabara
AAAABHKST Athabaska
AAAABIKLL balalaika
AAAABILMN Alabamian
AAAABJLMY jambalaya
AAAABKLLV Balaklava
AAAACCHMT tacamahac
AAAACCLLR Caracalla
AAAACCRRS caracaras
AAAACDIMM macadamia
AAAACDJNR jacaranda
AAAACDKLY alackaday
AAAACDMNR Maracanda
AAAACGILT agalactia
AAAACHILS achalasia
AAAACHKKL chakalaka
AAAACHSUY ayahuasca
AAAACINRU Araucania
AAAACIRRU araucaria
AAAACLMNS Salamanca
AAAACLNRT Alcántara
AAAACMNRT catamaran
AAAADGIMR Madariaga
AAAADGKNR Karaganda
AAAADILLM Dalai Lama
AAAADMSTV amadavats
AAAADSTVV avadavats
AAAAEHKLL Haleakala
AAAAGHJMN Mahajanga
AAAAGIKMS Amagasaki
AAAAHHJMR maharajah
AAAAHJMRS maharajas
AAAAHKPPW whakapapa
AAAAHLPTU Atahualpa
AAAAILLPR paralalia
AAAAILNPS anaplasia
AAAAIMPRS arapaimas
AAAAINSST Anastasia
AAAAJNRVY Vajrayana
AAAAKKNRT Karnataka
AAAAKKSWW kawakawas
AAAALLSVV lavalavas
AAAAMPRTT paramatta
AAAANNSTY Santayana
AAABBDINR Barbadian
AAABBINRR barbarian
AAABCCEMN Maccabean
AAABCCHHR bacharach
AAABCCHLN bacchanal
AAABCCHNR charabanc
AAABCCITT catabatic
AAABCDEHN Banda Aceh
AAABCDIIT adiabatic
AAABCDRRU barracuda
AAABCEIRS scarabaei
AAABCELTU acetabula
AAABCELTV vacatable
AAABCEMRT carbamate
AAABCESST catabases
AAABCHNNR anabranch
AAABCIKTT katabatic
AAABCILNR Calabrian
AAABCILNT abactinal
AAABCIMOR Maracaibo
AAABCISST catabasis
AAABCISTT ciabattas
AAABCLMOR carambola
AAABCLMRU ambulacra
AAABCNRRS barrancas
AAABCNRSU carnaubas
AAABCPRSY capybaras
AAABDDEHM Ahmedabad
AAABDDFIR Faridabad
AAABDDMOR Moradabad
AAABDEHHS dahabeahs
AAABDELPT adaptable
AAABDELRW awardable
AAABDENRS sarabande
AAABDESST databases
AAABDHHIS dahabiahs
AAABDHHKS Ashkhabad
AAABDILLS sabadilla
AAABDILMS Islamabad
AAABDINNT anabantid
AAABDNNNS bandannas
AAABDNRSS sarabands
AAABDNRST abradants
AAABEEMNO amoebaean
AAABEHNRS habaneras
AAABEILLV available
AAABEINOR anaerobia
AAABEJORS Soerabaja
AAABEKPRR parabrake
AAABEKRRS Skara Brae
AAABEKRWY breakaway
AAABEKSST katabases
AAABELLPT palatable
AAABELRST alabaster
AAABELSSY assayable
AAABEPRSS parabases
AAABERSST braatases
AAABGHNRV Bhavnagar
AAABGLLNO Alba Longa
AAABGLNSY bangalays
AAABGLORR algarroba
AAABGLORS algarobas
AAABGMNOZ Zamboanga
AAABGRSTU rutabagas
AAABHHLLU Baha'ullah
AAABHINNS Nana Sahib
AAABHKNRT Bakhtaran
AAABHLRTZ balthazar
AAABHMSST mastabahs
AAABIKSST katabasis
AAABILLVY availably
AAABILMNY Manila Bay
AAABILMRS Salambria
AAABIPRSS parabasis
AAABIPSSS piassabas
AAABJKLNU Banja Luka
AAABLLPTY palatably
AAABLOPRS parabolas
AAABLPRST parablast
AAABMNRTU marabunta
AAACCDEIM Accademia
AAACCDELV cavalcade
AAACCELLN calcaneal
AAACCELNN calcanean
AAACCESTZ Zacatecas
AAACCGNOU Aconcagua
AAACCHKMT tacmahack
AAACCILLU acalculia
AAACCINSU Caucasian
AAACCIRTT ataractic
AAACCLMNO calamanco
AAACCRSTT cataracts

AAACCRSTU Caratacus
AAACDEHRZ azedarach
AAACDEQSU aquacades
AAACDHIKT kadaitcha
AAACDHNRS sandarach
AAACDILNR calandria
AAACDINRS acaridans
arcadians
AAACDLRST cadastral
AAACDNNOS anacondas
AAACDNRSS Cassandra
sandaracs
AAACDOSTV advocaats
AAACEENRS caesarean
AAACEGNRT Cartagena
AAACEGORT Arctogaea
AAACEHINP Phaeacian
AAACEHLNV avalanche
AAACEHLST calatheas
AAACEIMNT catamenia
AAACEIMPR paramecia
AAACEINNT Canaanite
AAACEINOR oceanaria
AAACEINRS caesarian
AAACELNRV Canaveral
AAACEMMNR cameraman
AAACFILNT fanatical
AAACGHLLN Callaghan
AAACGHMTT Chattagam
AAACGILSU causalgia
AAACGINRU Nicaragua
AAACGLLSW scallawag
AAACGLSSW scalawags
AAACGMNPS campagnas
AAACHIKKN Aniakchak
AAACHILLW Wallachia
AAACHILNW Walachian
AAACHIMNU naumachia
AAACHIMST chiasmata
AAACHIPSS aphasiacs
AAACHIRSZ Zacharias
AAACHKKMT Kamchatka
AAACHKPRR pracharak
AAACHLNRT charlatan
AAACHLPRR chaparral
AAACHLRRT catarrhal
AAACHNPTY panchayat
AAACHNRSU Huascarán
AAACHOPRT cataphora
AAACIIRSS acariasis
AAACILLMR camarilla
AAACILLNN anaclinal
AAACILNOT Catalonia
AAACILNPT aplanatic
AAACILNRU lacunaria
AAACILNST satanical
AAACILRSV calvarias
AAACILRTU actuarial
AAACINOPR paranoiac
AAACINOTT catatonia
AAACINPRT pancratia
AAACINRSU casuarina

AAACIRSTX ataraxics
AAACKLMNS almanacks
AAACKMRST tamaracks
AAACLMNPU campanula
AAACLMPST cataplasm
AAACLRSUV avascular
AAACMORST sarcomata
AAACMRTUX taraxacum
AAACNORTZ Catanzaro
AAACSSTWY castaways
AAADDEILN daedalian
AAADDHMRY hamadryad
AAADEFIST asafetida
AAADEGLMN Magdalena
AAADEGLMY amygdalae
AAADEGNTV advantage
AAADEHRTV Theravada
AAADELMMR marmalade
AAADELNRX Alexandra
AAADEMNOT adenomata
AAADENSTV vanadates
AAADEOPTZ zapateado
AAADEPRST tapaderas
AAADFHILW Wadi Halfa
AAADGGHHS haggadahs
AAADGILRU La Guardia
AAADGLMNR Grand Lama
AAADGLRVX gravadlax
AAADGMMNR grandmama
AAADGNPPR grandpapa
AAADGNRVY Nagyvárad
AAADHHMNR Rhamadhan
AAADHHPRZ haphazard
AAADHIILR Haidar Ali
AAADHILMN Al Madinah
AAADHJLNR Jalandhar
AAADHMRSS madrasahs
AAADHMRSY hamadryas
AAADILLNP Palladian
AAADILMNT dalmatian
AAADILNSU Andalusia
AAADILPRS paradisal
AAADILRSU adularias
AAADIOPPR parapodia
AAADJJPRU Djajapura
AAADKMNRS Samarkand
AAADKRRSV aardvarks
AAADLMMOR Marmolada
AAADLMNTY adamantly
AAADLNNSY analysand
Nyasaland
AAADMNRTY mandatary
AAADMNSTU tamanduas
AAAEEEGNS Aegean Sea
AAAEEGRRR arrearage
AAAEEGRTW agateware
AAAEEHMNR maharanee
AAAEFGMNU megafauna
AAAEFNNST Santa Fean
AAAEGGRTV aggravate
AAAEGHLMY Meghalaya
AAAEGILNS analgesia

AAAEGLLPR paralegal
AAAEGLMNU malaguena
AAAEGLMTU Guatemala
AAAEGLSSV vassalage
AAAEGMNNT manganate
AAAEGNPPS appanages
AAAEHHLMR Halmahera
AAAEHIKKT kahikatea
AAAEHIMRT Arimathea
AAAEHLNNT Nathanael
AAAEHMMOT haematoma
AAAEHMNST anathemas
AAAEHNPSS anaphases
AAAEIKLPR parakelia
AAAEILPRX paralexia
AAAEILTUY Auliye-Ata
AAAEIMNOX anoxaemia
AAAEIMOTZ azotaemia
AAAEIMPRS sapraemia
AAAEKKRST karatekas
AAAEKSTWY takeaways
AAAELLNPT panatella
AAAELMMNS analemmas
AAAELMSTT Malatesta
AAAELNNTT antenatal
Atlantean
AAAELNPQU aquaplane
AAAELNTTT tantalate
AAAELPRST palaestra
AAAELRSTV lavateras
AAAEMNPRT paramenta
AAAEMNSST Tasman Sea
AAAEMPRST aspartame
AAAENPRSV paravanes
AAAENPSST anapaests
AAAENRRTT Tartarean
AAAERSTWY tearaways
AAAFFIKRR Kaffraria
AAAFGLRRT Trafalgar
AAAFGMSTU Famagusta
AAAFHHRST haftarahs
AAAFIILLR alfilaria
AAAFILNUV avifaunal
AAAFINSST fantasias
AAAFIRRST Ras Tafari
AAAFLMNST fantasmal
AAAFLORST solfatara
AAAFRSSSS sassafras
AAAGGLLNS galangals
AAAGGLOPS galapagos
AAAGHHOTY hatha yoga
AAAGHIKNV Aga Khan IV
AAAGHJNNT Jagannath
AAAGHNNST agnathans
AAAGHNSTY yataghans
AAAGHPPRR paragraph
AAAGILMNS salaaming
AAAGILNST Galatians
AAAGILRST astragali
AAAGIMNNU Guamanian
AAAGIMNOT angiomata
AAAGIMNRV gravamina

AAAGIMRRT	margarita
AAAGINOPT	Patagonia
AAAGINRRS	agrarians
AAAGINRRT	rangatira
AAAGJNNRU	Nagarjuna
AAAGLNSTV	galavants
AAAGLRSST	astragals
AAAGNORRT	Tarragona
AAAGNPRSS	parasangs
AAAGORSSS	Saragossa
AAAGPRSSU	asparagus
AAAHHHJNS	Shah Jahan
AAAHHHPRT	Haphtarah
AAAHIKKLT	kathakali
AAAHIKRTW	Kathiawar
AAAHILMNY	Himalayan
AAAHILMST	Tashi Lama
AAAHILMSY	Himalayas
AAAHIMNRS	maharanis
AAAHIMNRU	marihuana
AAAHIMRST	hamartias
AAAHIMSTY	Yamashita
AAAHINRRT	anarthria
AAAHINSVV	Vaishnava
AAAHJNRST	Rajasthan
AAAHKMOTV	Akhmatova
AAAHKNRST	astrakhan
AAAHLLOTY	ayatollah
AAAHMMSTU	Hamamatsu
AAAHMNNTT	manhattan
AAAHMNRST	amaranths
AAAHMNRTT	harmattan
AAAHNNSSV	savannahs
AAAHNOPRS	anaphoras
AAAHSSWWY	washaways
AAAHTTUYY	Ayutthaya
AAAIIJNRY	Irian Jaya
AAAIILLLP	palilalia
AAAIILMNR	laminaria
AAAIINRST	sanitaria
AAAIJMNRU	marijuana
AAAIKLLNT	antalkali
AAAILLNPS	Sillanpää
AAAILLRRW	Illawarra
AAAILMMMN	mammalian
AAAILMNSV	malvasian
AAAILMNSY	Malaysian
AAAILMORT	amatorial
AAAILNNOT	Anatolian
AAAILNNPR	planarian
AAAILNRST	artisanal
AAAILNSST	assailant
AAAILPPRS	appraisal
AAAILRSTU	Australia
AAAIMNNOZ	amazonian
AAAIMNNST	Tasmanian
AAAIMNORT	inamorata
AAAIMNOST	Toamasina
AAAIMNRST	samaritan
	Sarmatian
AAAINNNTZ	Tanzanian
AAAINOPRS	paranoias
	saponaria
AAAINORST	sanatoria
AAAINORTT	natatoria
AAAINPPWY	Appian Way
AAAINPSSU	Pausanias
AAAINPSTV	vanaspati
AAAINQRSU	aquarians
AAAINRRTV	Navaratri
AAAIPPRZZ	paparazzi
AAAIPRSTX	parataxis
AAAIPSSSV	piassavas
AAAIRSSTU	Austrasia
AAAIRSSTV	Sarasvati
AAAJNPRTU	Rajputana
AAAJPRTUY	Putrajaya
AAAKKMORR	Karakoram
AAAKLMOOZ	Kalamazoo
AAAKMSTTU	Takamatsu
AAAKOSSWY	soakaways
AAAKRRSTU	Surakarta
AAALLLPTY	palatally
AAALLMPSS	Las Palmas
AAALMNRSY	salaryman
AAALNPSTY	anaplasty
AAALNRSTV	Transvaal
AAALNRTTU	tarantula
AAAMMSTUY	Matsuyama
AAAMNOPRS	panoramas
AAAMNRRSY	yarramans
AAANNNPRU	Annapurna
AAANQSTUU	aquanauts
AAANRSSTT	tarantass
AAAOPPRZZ	paparazzo
AAAPPRSTU	apparatus
AABBBEJNO	bobbejaan
AABBCCIRR	bricabrac
AABBCDEIL	abdicable
AABBCDKOR	backboard
AABBCDRSS	scabbards
AABBCEINR	Caribbean
AABBCEKST	backbeats
AABBCGGIN	cabbaging
AABBCHKOR	Bar Kochba
AABBCILMS	cabbalism
AABBCILST	cabbalist
AABBCINRS	barbicans
AABBCKLLL	blackball
AABBCKMRR	barmbrack
AABBCKNRR	barnbrack
AABBDDNOR	broadband
AABBDEELT	debatable
AABBDELOR	boardable
AABBDELST	beadblast
AABBDENSS	basebands
AABBDEORS	baseboard
	bosberaad
AABBEEKLR	breakable
AABBEEKRT	breakbeat
AABBEELLM	blameable
AABBEELRT	rebatable
AABBEHHST	Bathsheba
AABBEHILT	habitable
AABBEIILT	bilabiate
AABBEINRT	rabbinate
AABBEIRRS	barbarise
AABBEIRRZ	barbarize
AABBELLMY	blameably
AABBELLSS	baseballs
AABBELLTU	tabulable
AABBFFINY	Baffin Bay
AABBHILTY	habitably
AABBHKSSU	babushkas
AABBIILLS	bilabials
AABBIKLMS	kabbalism
AABBIKLST	kabbalist
AABBIKRUY	Abukir Bay
AABBILLOO	boobialla
AABBILNOY	Babylonia
AABBIMRRS	barbarism
AABBINTTU	ibn-Batuta
AABBIRRTY	barbarity
AABBIRSSU	babirusas
AABBNOTYY	Botany Bay
AABBORRSU	barbarous
AABCCEEMS	Maccabees
AABCCEFKL	blackface
AABCCEHKS	backaches
AABCCEHLT	catchable
AABCCEHNT	bacchante
AABCCEKPS	backspace
AABCCELSS	cascabels
AABCCHHKT	hatchback
AABCCHKKU	huckaback
AABCCHKSS	cashbacks
AABCCHNST	bacchants
AABCCIKKP	pickaback
AABCCILOT	catabolic
AABCCIORT	acrobatic
AABCCJKKL	blackjack
AABCCKKPS	backpacks
AABCCKKRT	backtrack
AABCCKLPS	blackcaps
AABCCKLSW	clawbacks
AABCCKRRY	carryback
AABCCMOST	catacombs
AABCDDEFL	baldfaced
AABCDDEIT	abdicated
AABCDDEKT	backdated
AABCDDORR	cardboard
AABCDEEFR	barefaced
AABCDEEHH	beachhead
AABCDEELN	danceable
AABCDEELY	decayable
AABCDEERT	abreacted
	acerbated
AABCDEHKL	blackhead
AABCDEIMR	carbamide
AABCDEIRR	barricade
AABCDEIST	abdicates
AABCDEKLL	blacklead
AABCDEKLP	backpedal
AABCDEKRR	barracked
AABCDEKST	backdates
AABCDELNR	barnacled

AABCDEMRV	vambraced
AABCDEMSU	ambuscade
AABCDENNO	abondance
AABCDENNU	abundance
AABCDENOR	carbonade
AABCDENPS	spaceband
AABCDHILN	baldachin
AABCDHKNS	backhands
AABCDHKRS	hardbacks
AABCDHNTW	watchband
AABCDIMNO	Cambodian
AABCDIORS	scaraboid
AABCDIORT	abdicator
AABCDKLMP	blackdamp
AABCDKRSW	backwards
	drawbacks
AABCDLNSS	scablands
AABCDLOPR	clapboard
AABCDNOOR	carbonado
AABCDORST	broadcast
AABCEEELP	peaceable
AABCEEHLR	reachable
AABCEEHLS	chaseable
AABCEEHLT	cheatable
	teachable
AABCEEKLS	leaseback
AABCEEKNR	canebrake
AABCEELLN	cleanable
AABCEELLR	clearable
	lacerable
AABCEELLV	cleavable
AABCEELNT	enactable
AABCEELPS	escapable
AABCEELPY	peaceably
AABCEELRS	calabrese
AABCEELRT	creatable
	traceable
AABCEELTX	exactable
AABCEENRR	aberrance
AABCEERST	acerbates
AABCEERTT	bracteate
AABCEFIRT	fabricate
AABCEFOSU	fabaceous
AABCEGILR	algebraic
AABCEGKLM	blackgame
AABCEGKST	backstage
AABCEGLMR	cablegram
AABCEGPRT	carpetbag
AABCEHHLT	hatchable
AABCEHINR	branchiae
AABCEHIRT	brachiate
AABCEHITZ	chabazite
AABCEHKLW	whaleback
AABCEHLMP	Palm Beach
AABCEHLMT	matchable
AABCEHLPT	patchable
AABCEHLRT	chartable
AABCEHLTW	watchable
AABCEHMST	ambatches
AABCEHNRS	barchanes
AABCEILLM	claimable
AABCEILMN	imbalance
AABCEILMR	bicameral
AABCEILNP	incapable
AABCEILNT	cantabile
AABCEILRT	bacterial
	calibrate
AABCEILST	Baltic Sea
AABCEIMNR	mainbrace
AABCEINOR	anaerobic
AABCEINRR	carabiner
AABCEINRS	carabines
AABCEIORT	aerobatic
AABCEISSS	abscissae
AABCEJKMR	amberjack
AABCEKLMS	clambakes
AABCEKLRS	lacebarks
AABCEKLRT	trackable
AABCEKLST	stackable
AABCEKPPR	paperback
AABCEKRRR	barracker
AABCEKRTW	backwater
AABCEKSST	backseats
AABCELLOR	caballero
AABCELLOT	locatable
AABCELLSS	classable
AABCELMNU	ambulance
AABCELMRY	macabrely
AABCELNNS	scannable
AABCELNNU	unbalance
AABCELNOR	Barcelona
AABCELNRS	balancers
	barnacles
AABCELOOS	calaboose
AABCELORR	barcarole
AABCELORS	albacores
AABCELORZ	carbazole
AABCELPRS	scrapable
AABCELPSS	spacelabs
AABCELRST	Castlebar
AABCELRTT	tractable
AABCELRTU	trabecula
AABCELRTY	traceably
AABCELSWY	cableways
AABCEMRSV	vambraces
AABCENORT	carbonate
AABCENRRY	aberrancy
AABCEOSTU	sauceboat
AABCFHKLS	flashback
	halfbacks
AABCFINRT	fabricant
AABCFKSST	fastbacks
AABCGILLN	caballing
AABCGILNN	balancing
AABCGKRSY	graybacks
AABCGLOSU	calabogus
AABCGRRSS	crabgrass
AABCHIKRY	hairyback
AABCHILNR	branchial
AABCHILTY	Bat Chayil
AABCHIORS	barachois
AABCHKLSS	backslash
AABCHLOOS	coolabahs
AABCIILNS	basilican
AABCIILSS	basilicas
AABCIINOT	anabiotic
AABCIINRS	brainiacs
AABCIKLLM	blackmail
AABCIKLLT	blacktail
AABCIKLOT	katabolic
AABCIKLST	tailbacks
AABCIKRST	backstair
AABCILLRS	cabrillas
AABCILLRY	bacillary
AABCILLSY	asyllabic
	basically
AABCILNNS	cannibals
AABCILNOT	botanical
AABCILNPY	incapably
AABCILNTU	Tubal-cain
AABCILOPR	parabolic
AABCILOST	bicoastal
AABCILRUV	vibracula
AABCILSST	cabalists
AABCINNOR	carbanion
AABCINNRS	cinnabars
AABCIRSSS	brassicas
AABCISSSS	abscissas
AABCKLLMP	lampblack
AABCKLLRT	trackball
AABCKLMSS	black mass
AABCKLNOS	loanbacks
AABCKLPSY	playbacks
AABCKNPSS	snapbacks
AABCKORRZ	razorback
AABCKPRST	bratpacks
AABCKSSTY	backstays
AABCLRTTY	tractably
AABCMNOTT	combatant
AABCNOORR	barracoon
AABCNORRS	barrancos
AABCRSSTT	abstracts
AABDDEEST	deadbeats
AABDDEGLS	saddlebag
AABDDEHLS	baldheads
AABDDEHNS	headbands
AABDDEHOR	headboard
AABDDEHRY	Hyderabad
AABDDEINR	braindead
AABDDENNO	abandoned
AABDDGHUY	Buddh Gaya
AABDDHORR	hardboard
AABDDHORS	dashboard
AABDDNNST	bandstand
AABDDORRT	dartboard
AABDEEEMN	endamebae
AABDEEGNT	abnegated
AABDEEHRS	earbashed
AABDEELLP	pleadable
AABDEELLR	balladeer
AABDEELLS	Bleasdale
AABDEELMN	amendable
AABDEELPR	drapeable
AABDEELRT	tradeable
AABDEEMNO	endamoeba
AABDEEMNS	endamebas

AABDEENNO	abandonee
AABDEERST	teabreads
AABDEERSY	bayaderes
AABDEERTT	trabeated
AABDEFLOR	broadleaf
AABDEFLRT	flatbread
AABDEGGGS	gasbagged
AABDEGHNS	headbangs
AABDEGINO	gabionade
AABDEGINR	bargained
	gabardine
AABDEGLRS	gradables
AABDEGLRU	guardable
AABDEGMOS	gambadoes
AABDEGORT	abrogated
AABDEGOST	sabotaged
AABDEGRRY	graybeard
AABDEHIST	Bethsaida
AABDEHJLL	djellabah
AABDEHKNR	handbrake
AABDEHLNR	handlebar
AABDEHLSY	abashedly
AABDEHNSU	unabashed
AABDEILLT	dilatable
AABDEILMR	admirable
AABDEILNN	Leninabad
AABDEILNR	drainable
AABDEILNV	invadable
AABDEILOV	avoidable
AABDEILRV	adverbial
AABDEILSV	advisable
AABDEIMNR	Marienbad
AABDEINST	abstained
AABDEIOSU	aboideaus
AABDEIOUX	aboideaux
AABDELLNT	tableland
AABDELLST	ballasted
AABDELMST	lambasted
AABDELMTU	ambulated
AABDELORT	dolabrate
AABDELPST	baldpates
AABDELTTU	tabulated
AABDELTWY	twayblade
AABDEMORT	dreamboat
AABDEMRTU	adumbrate
AABDENSTW	sweatband
AABDENSVW	wavebands
AABDEORSS	seaboards
AABDEORST	adsorbate
AABDEORSV	bravadoes
AABDGGINN	bandaging
AABDGHLRU	Bradlaugh
AABDGIILR	garibaldi
AABDGNNOW	bandwagon
AABDGNOSV	vagabonds
AABDGORRS	garboards
AABDGOSTU	gadabouts
AABDHIORZ	biohazard
AABDHLLNS	handballs
AABDHLRSU	Hasdrubal
AABDHORSW	washboard
AABDHRSSU	subahdars
AABDIJNOR	jaborandi
AABDIKORV	Kirovabad
AABDILMNO	abdominal
AABDILMRY	admirably
AABDILNQU	baldaquin
AABDILORS	sailboard
AABDILORT	broadtail
	tailboard
AABDILOVY	avoidably
AABDILSSU	disabusal
AABDILSVY	advisably
AABDINNRT	trainband
AABDINOST	bastinado
AABDINSTW	waistband
AABDKLORW	boardwalk
AABDKNNSS	sandbanks
AABDLLORW	wallboard
AABDLNSST	sandblast
AABDLOOST	boatloads
AABDLOOSW	balsawood
AABDLOPRS	lapboards
AABDLORRS	labradors
AABDLRSTY	bastardly
AABDNRRSY	barnyards
AABDORRST	starboard
AABDRRSSS	brassards
AABDRRSTY	bastardry
AABEEEGLR	agreeable
AABEEEMNT	entamebae
AABEEFLMR	frameable
AABEEFLNS	fleabanes
AABEEFNST	beanfeast
AABEEGGLU	gaugeable
AABEEGILM	imageable
AABEEGKRS	breakages
AABEEGLLL	glabellae
AABEEGLLN	gleanable
AABEEGLLT	bagatelle
AABEEGLRY	agreeably
AABEEGLTT	getatable
AABEEGNST	abnegates
AABEEHKLS	shakeable
AABEEHLLX	exhalable
AABEEHLMS	shameable
AABEEHLPS	shapeable
AABEEHLRS	shareable
AABEEHLSV	shaveable
AABEEHMRS	harambees
AABEEHRRS	earbasher
AABEEHRSS	earbashes
AABEEHRTT	heartbeat
AABEEILLN	alienable
AABEEILRS	raiseable
AABEEINRS	bearnaise
AABEEKLLS	slakeable
AABEEKLPP	bakeapple
AABEEKLPS	speakable
AABEELLLM	malleable
AABEELLNR	learnable
AABEELLPS	pleasable
AABEELLRS	resalable
AABEELLRT	alterable
	relatable
AABEELLRX	relaxable
AABEELMNR	Lambaréné
AABEELMSU	amuseable
AABEELNNX	annexable
AABEELNOT	atoneable
AABEELNTU	uneatable
AABEELORT	elaborate
AABEELPRR	reparable
AABEELPRS	separable
AABEELPRY	repayable
AABEELQTU	equatable
AABEELRSW	wearables
AABEELRTT	treatable
AABEELRTV	avertable
AABEELRTW	tableware
AABEELSTT	stateable
AABEEMNOT	entamoeba
AABEEMNST	abasement
	entamebas
AABEEMNTT	abatement
AABEEMPRS	abamperes
AABEENNSW	wannabees
AABEENORS	anaerobes
AABEEQRSU	arabesque
AABEERSTT	Battersea
AABEFFLQU	quaffable
AABEFGILT	fatigable
AABEFHKLS	halfbeaks
AABEFIMRS	frambesia
AABEFKLNR	frankable
AABEFKRST	breakfast
AABEFLLMM	flammable
AABEFLLOT	floatable
AABEFLMSU	flambeaus
AABEFLMUX	flambeaux
AABEFLORV	favorable
AABEGGHLS	shaggable
AABEGGLUY	gaugeably
AABEGHLLU	laughable
AABEGHORR	harborage
AABEGHSSW	bagwashes
AABEGILNV	navigable
AABEGILRV	Belgravia
AABEGINRR	bargainer
AABEGIRRT	arbitrage
AABEGIRRU	bigarreau
AABEGKLOR	gaolbreak
AABEGLLLR	glabellar
AABEGLMNP	Palembang
AABEGLNOR	Bangalore
AABEGLNRT	grantable
AABEGLPRS	graspable
AABEGMNSY	mangabeys
AABEGNORS	baronages
AABEGNORT	abnegator
AABEGNRUZ	Aurangzeb
AABEGORST	abrogates
AABEGOSST	sabotages
AABEHILRR	herbarial
AABEHIMNN	Inhambane
AABEHINNS	Beni Hasan

AABEHITTU habituate
AABEHJLLS jellabahs
AABEHLMSS smashable
AABEHLOTW whaleboat
AABEHLPST alphabets
AABEHLSTW swathable
AABEHMNST abashment
AABEIILLS Isabella I
labialise
AABEIILLZ labialize
AABEIIRTU aubrietia
AABEIIRTV bivariate
AABEIJKLR jailbreak
AABEIKLNS balkanise
AABEIKLNZ balkanize
AABEIKLRV Balakirev
AABEIKNRR karabiner
AABEILLMN laminable
AABEILLNR ballerina
AABEILLRT bilateral
AABEILLST ballistae
AABEILLSW wallabies
AABEILMNR lamebrain
AABEILMNU unamiable
AABEILNOT anabolite
AABEILNRT trainable
AABEILNST stainable
AABEILPST basipetal
AABEILRSV variables
AABEILSTV ablatives
AABEILTVV bivalvate
AABEIMNOT abominate
AABEIMNZZ Zambezian
AABEIMRSU Beaumaris
AABEINORS arabinose
AABEINOSS anabioses
AABEINRST abstainer
AABEINRVW brainwave
AABEINSST Sebastian
AABEIOSTU aboiteaus
AABEIOTUX aboiteaux
AABEIRRTT arbitrate
AABEIRSSV abrasives
AABEIRSTU aubretias
aubrietas
AABEISSSS sassabies
AABEISSTT abattises
AABEKLNST beanstalk
AABEKMNRS brakesman
AABEKNNRS Nebraskan
AABEKPPRR paperbark
AABELLLMY malleably
AABELLLOW allowable
AABELLMNY Ballymena
AABELLMST meatballs
AABELLNPT plantable
AABELLNSU unsalable
AABELLOPR parolable
AABELLPPR palpebral
AABELLRTY alterably
AABELLSTU blastulae
AABELLSUV valuables
AABELMNNU unnamable
AABELMNST stableman
AABELMNTU untamable
AABELMSST blastemas
lambastes
AABELMSSU assumable
AABELMSTU ambulates
AABELNPPS snappable
AABELNSUY unsayable
AABELOPPS apposable
AABELOPRV vaporable
AABELORST astrolabe
AABELORTT rotatable
AABELPRRY reparably
AABELPRSS sparables
AABELPRSY separably
AABELRSST arbalests
AABELRSSU assurable
AABELRSTU saturable
AABELRSTY betrayals
AABELRTTU tablature
AABELSTTU tabulates
AABEMOSTT steamboat
AABEMRRSS embarrass
AABENOPRT Bonaparte
AABEOPPRT approbate
AABFGILSU basifugal
AABFIKNRS Fairbanks
AABFIMORT fibromata
AABFLORVY favorably
AABFLOSTT faltboats
flatboats
AABGGGNNS gangbangs
AABGGIMNO gambogian
AABGGINRR barraging
AABGGRRST braggarts
AABGHILRT Galbraith
AABGHKRSS shagbarks
AABGHLLUY laughably
AABGHLPRU Bhagalpur
AABGHNOUY Hu Yaobang
AABGHOPRR barograph
AABGILNRU Bulgarian
AABGILNST bangtails
AABGILNVY navigably
AABGILRRT Gibraltar
AABGIMOSU ambagious
AABGINNOR born-again
AABGLLLOS goalballs
AABGLLRSY ballyrags
AABGLNOSW bangalows
AABGMORRS barograms
AABGNORSZ garbanzos
AABGNRRUW burrawang
AABGOORRT abrogator
AABHHIKSU hibakusha
AABHHISTV Tishah b'Av
AABHHORSU brouhahas
AABHIILRZ bilharzia
AABHIIMNP amphibian
AABHIINSU bauhinias
AABHILLRS hairballs
AABHIMMRU Hammurabi
AABHINRSW brainwash
AABHINSSW washbasin
AABHINSTT habitants
AABHIPRRV vibraharp
AABHKORTU Kota Bharu
AABHNOSTU autobahns
AABIILLMS labialism
AABIILLTY labiality
AABIILNRR librarian
AABIILNRZ Brazilian
AABIILNST balanitis
AABIINNRT Britannia
AABIINOSS anabiosis
AABIINRZZ Zanzibari
AABIINSSY Abyssinia
AABIKLSST kabalists
AABILLNPT paintball
AABILLORS isallobar
AABILMNOS anabolism
AABILMNRU manubrial
AABILMOPR ambipolar
AABILMOPY amblyopia
AABILMORS ambrosial
AABILMPST baptismal
AABILNOST ablations
AABILNOTT battalion
AABILOSST sailboats
AABILRRSU bursarial
AABILRSST arbalists
AABILSVWY Walvis Bay
AABIMNNOT Manitoban
AABIMNORS ambrosian
AABIMORSS ambrosias
AABIMORSU simarouba
AABINNPRS brainpans
AABINORSS abrasions
AABINOSTW boatswain
AABINRSTZ bartizans
AABIORSTT abattoirs
AABIOSSSY bioassays
AABIRRRTY arbitrary
AABJJLLNU Ljubljana
AABKLLPRS ballparks
AABKLOTUW walkabout
AABKLSTVY Blavatsky
AABKOPRSS soapbarks
AABLLLOWY allowably
AABLLMORS balmorals
AABLLMSYY abysmally
AABLLNTTY blatantly
AABLLRSTU blastular
AABLLRSYY syllabary
AABLLRTUY tabularly
AABLLSSTU blastulas
AABLMNORY myrobalan
AABLMOSST blastomas
AABLNOPSS Bolan Pass
AABLNORTU Ulan Bator
AABLORSST albatross
AABLORTTU tabulator
AABLOSTUY layabouts

AABLRSSTU	subastral
AABMNNOTU	Montauban
AABMNRSTU	rambutans
AABMORSTU	marabouts
	tambouras
AABORRRST	barrators
AABORSSTT	barostats
AABRRSSST	brassarts
AABRSSTTU	substrata
AACCCFIOS	focaccias
AACCCHHSU	cachuchas
AACCCHIRS	saccharic
AACCCIOPR	carpaccio
AACCDDINY	candidacy
AACCDEHKR	crackhead
AACCDEIIR	acaricide
AACCDEILM	acclaimed
AACCDEIMS	academics
AACCDEIRV	cadaveric
AACCDEJNY	adjacency
AACCDELLT	catcalled
AACCDELOR	caracoled
AACCDELOS	accolades
AACCDERRS	racecards
AACCDGINS	cascading
AACCDHIRS	characids
AACCDHLRU	archducal
AACCDHORY	adhocracy
AACCDIINR	circadian
AACCDNORT	accordant
AACCEEHIN	echinacea
AACCEEIRR	cercariae
AACCEELNR	clearance
AACCEENRT	reactance
AACCEENST	cetaceans
AACCEFHKL	chalkface
AACCEFLOS	coalfaces
AACCEFNRS	Francesca
AACCEHILL	cailleach
AACCEHJKP	cheapjack
AACCEHRRT	character
AACCEHSTW	watchcase
AACCEIILN	caecilian
AACCEIINR	Cirenaica
AACCEILMR	acclaimer
AACCEILMT	acclimate
AACCEILNT	analectic
AACCEILRR	cercarial
AACCEILST	ascetical
AACCEILTU	aciculate
AACCEINRR	cercarian
AACCEINRY	Cyrenaica
AACCEINSV	vacancies
AACCEINTV	vaccinate
AACCEJKLN	lancejack
AACCEJKRR	carjacker
AACCEKNRS	crankcase
AACCEKRRT	racetrack
AACCELLRT	catcaller
AACCELLTU	calculate
AACCELMNU	calcaneum
AACCELMTY	cyclamate
AACCELNSU	calcaneus
AACCELNTU	accentual
AACCELORS	caracoles
AACCELSTU	sacculate
AACCEMNSU	cumaceans
AACCENPTT	acceptant
AACCENRST	carcanets
AACCEORTT	coarctate
AACCERSSS	carcasses
AACCERSSY	accessary
AACCGHNOR	Gran Chaco
AACCHILMO	mailcoach
AACCHILPS	pachalics
AACCHIMNO	Michoacán
AACCHIMOT	macchiato
AACCHIMSY	sciamachy
AACCHINRS	characins
	saccharin
AACCHIPRR	archicarp
AACCHIRTT	cathartic
AACCHIRTU	autarchic
AACCHISSV	viscachas
AACCHISVZ	vizcachas
AACCHLLST	catchalls
AACCHLORS	charcoals
AACCHLOST	cachalots
AACCHLRSS	clarsachs
AACCHNNWY	wanchancy
AACCIILNT	anaclitic
AACCIILNV	vaccinial
AACCIINPS	capsaicin
AACCIINTT	tactician
AACCIIRSS	Circassia
AACCILLNO	laconical
AACCILLNY	calycinal
AACCILLRU	calicular
AACCILLSS	classical
AACCILMNU	cacuminal
AACCILNNO	canonical
AACCILNOR	acronical
AACCILNRU	canicular
AACCILPRT	practical
AACCILSTU	caustical
AACCILTTY	catalytic
AACCIMNOR	carcinoma
	macaronic
	maccaroni
AACCINOTT	catatonic
AACCINPRT	pancratic
AACCINPTY	captaincy
AACCINRTT	antarctic
AACCIOPRT	capacitor
AACCIOPSU	capacious
AACCIORST	Costa Rica
AACCIRSST	sarcastic
AACCJKRSW	crackjaws
AACCJORSU	carcajous
AACCKKPSS	packsacks
AACCKMNRS	cracksman
AACCLLRUY	calycular
AACCLMORY	cyclorama
AACCLMSTY	cataclysm
AACCLNORY	acronycal
AACCMNOPY	accompany
AACCOPRRS	sarcocarp
AACCOPRSS	ascocarps
AACCORTUY	autocracy
AACDDEEGH	Dedéagach
AACDDEELS	escaladed
AACDDEHIS	acidheads
AACDDEINT	candidate
AACDDELNS	scandaled
AACDDELOP	decapodal
AACDDELPR	placarded
AACDDENOP	decapodan
AACDDEOTV	advocated
AACDDIIST	dadaistic
AACDDIMPV	Camp David
AACDDINRS	radicands
AACDDKPWY	paddywack
AACDDLMNO	Macdonald
	MacDonald
AACDDMORU	docudrama
AACDEEEFT	defaecate
AACDEEFLT	defalcate
AACDEEHHR	headreach
AACDEEHHS	headaches
AACDEEHHY	headachey
AACDEEHRS	headraces
AACDEEHSS	headcases
AACDEEIMS	academies
AACDEEIMT	acetamide
	emaciated
AACDEEIRT	acierated
	eradicate
AACDEELRS	escalader
AACDEELRT	lacerated
AACDEELSS	escalades
AACDEELST	escalated
AACDEELTU	aculeated
AACDEEMNS	damascene
AACDEEMRT	demarcate
	macerated
AACDEEMST	casemated
AACDEENTT	catenated
AACDEEPSS	escapades
AACDEETUV	evacuated
AACDEETUX	excaudate
AACDEETVX	excavated
AACDEFFIN	affianced
AACDEFFIR	fairfaced
AACDEFHRS	headscarf
AACDEFIST	fasciated
AACDEGGGM	cagmagged
AACDEGILT	glaciated
AACDEGLNO	decagonal
AACDEGLOT	cataloged
AACDEGNOS	gasconade
AACDEHILN	enchilada
AACDEHINS	haciendas
AACDEHIRS	archaised
AACDEHIRZ	archaized
AACDEHKMS	smackhead
AACDEHKSW	hacksawed

AACDEHLLN	dancehall
AACDEHLRT	cathedral
	clarthead
AACDEHORT	octahedra
AACDEHRST	cathedras
AACDEIIPR	epicardia
AACDEILLN	dalliance
AACDEILLT	dialectal
AACDEILMR	creamlaid
AACDEILNO	Caledonia
	laodicean
AACDEILNS	canalised
AACDEILNZ	canalized
AACDEILPS	asclepiad
AACDEILSS	sidalceas
AACDEILTU	acidulate
AACDEIMMS	academism
AACDEIMNO	Macedonia
AACDEIMNY	cyanamide
AACDEIMPR	paramedic
	preadamic
AACDEIMSS	camisades
AACDEIMST	steadicam
AACDEINOR	androecia
AACDEINOT	diaconate
AACDEINOV	avoidance
AACDEINPS	cispadane
AACDEINPT	captained
AACDEINRS	radiances
AACDEINRT	carinated
AACDEITTV	activated
AACDEJNST	adjacents
AACDEKMRT	tarmacked
AACDEKNRS	ransacked
AACDELLNU	calendula
AACDELLNY	decanally
AACDELLOT	allocated
AACDELMNS	Candlemas
AACDELMTU	maculated
AACDELNOT	anecdotal
AACDELNPS	landscape
AACDELNRS	calendars
AACDELNRT	declarant
AACDELNTU	canulated
AACDELOPS	loadspace
AACDELOSS	caseloads
AACDELPTY	playacted
AACDELSTY	catalysed
AACDELTYZ	catalyzed
AACDEMNRS	Scamander
AACDEMNTU	manducate
AACDEMRSS	massacred
AACDENNNO	cannonade
AACDENNST	ascendant
AACDENORR	carronade
AACDENOTU	coadunate
AACDENPPT	catnapped
AACDENRSV	advancers
AACDENSSV	canvassed
AACDEOSTU	autocades
AACDEOSTV	advocates
AACDERSST	cadasters
	cadastres
AACDERSTT	castrated
AACDERTTT	attracted
AACDFHNRT	handcraft
AACDFIILT	fatidical
AACDFIOPR	picofarad
AACDGINNV	advancing
AACDGINOR	carangoid
AACDGINRS	carangids
	cardigans
AACDGLMOR	cladogram
AACDHHKRS	hardhacks
AACDHHNSS	shadchans
AACDHIILL	chiliadal
AACDHIILR	rachidial
AACDHIILS	dichasial
AACDHILMY	chlamydia
AACDHINOR	arachnoid
AACDHINOT	acanthoid
AACDHINPS	handicaps
AACDHINRS	arachnids
AACDHINRT	cantharid
AACDHKRST	hardtacks
AACDHLMNR	marchland
AACDHLNPS	handclasp
AACDHLNPU	launchpad
AACDHLNRS	crashland
AACDHNRST	handcarts
AACDHPRRS	cardsharp
AACDIIIMR	miracidia
AACDIINNR	cnidarian
AACDIINSS	ascidians
AACDIISST	diastasic
AACDIISTT	diastatic
AACDILLRY	radically
AACDILMNO	monadical
AACDILMNY	dynamical
AACDILMRU	caldarium
AACDILMST	dalmatics
AACDILMSU	caladiums
AACDILNRS	cardinals
AACDILNSU	dulcianas
AACDILNTY	dilatancy
AACDILOPR	parodical
AACDILORT	carotidal
AACDILOTU	autocidal
AACDILRRS	railcards
AACDIMORY	myocardia
AACDIMOSS	camisados
AACDIMRST	dramatics
AACDINNOR	draconian
AACDINOTU	caudation
AACDINRTU	traducian
AACDIOSTU	autacoids
AACDIOSUU	audacious
AACDIQRTU	quadratic
AACDIRSSY	dyscrasia
AACDIRSTY	caryatids
AACDJNTUY	adjutancy
AACDJQRSU	jacquards
AACDLORST	cartloads
AACDMMORS	cardamoms
AACDMMRSU	cardamums
AACDMNORS	cardamons
AACDMOSUV	muscavado
AACEEEGNR	careenage
AACEEFINN	faineance
AACEEFIRT	cafeteria
AACEEFLPS	palefaces
AACEEFLPT	faceplate
AACEEFMRT	farcemeat
AACEEFRRT	aftercare
AACEEGKPR	repackage
AACEEGLLR	cellarage
AACEEGLSV	cleavages
AACEEGNRR	carrageen
AACEEHHRT	heartache
AACEEHLNP	encephala
AACEEHLPS	acalephes
AACEEHNOR	Chaeronea
AACEEHPRT	eparchate
AACEEHRTT	tracheate
AACEEHRTX	exarchate
AACEEILNR	Erie Canal
AACEEIMST	emaciates
AACEEINRT	ecarinate
AACEEIRST	acierates
AACEEJLTU	ejaculate
AACEEKMPR	pacemaker
AACEEKRRT	caretaker
AACEELLMU	melaleuca
AACEELNPS	pleasance
AACEELNPT	placentae
AACEELNST	elastance
AACEELPRT	paraclete
AACEELRST	lacerates
AACEELRTT	altercate
AACEELSST	escalates
AACEELTTY	acetylate
AACEEMMNR	cameramen
AACEEMPST	meatspace
AACEEMRRT	macerater
AACEEMRRW	creamware
AACEEMRST	macerates
AACEEMSST	casemates
AACEENNST	catenanes
AACEENRTU	centaurea
AACEENSTT	catenates
AACEEOPRS	aerospace
AACEEPRSS	cassareep
AACEEPSSS	seascapes
AACEESTUV	evacuates
AACEESTVX	excavates
AACEFFINS	affiances
AACEFFIRT	affricate
AACEFGLNR	flagrance
AACEFGNRR	fragrance
AACEFGORT	factorage
AACEFGOSU	fagaceous
AACEFILLS	fallacies
AACEFILST	califates
AACEFINNY	faineancy
AACEFINST	fascinate
AACEFKMPR	packframe

AACEFLLTU falculate
AACEFLPST Cape Flats
AACEFRSTT artefacts
AACEGHHMU gamahuche
AACEGHIMR archimage
AACEGHLNR archangel
AACEGHLTT Gaeltacht
AACEGHMNP champagne
AACEGHMRU gamaruche
AACEGHNOR anchorage
AACEGHRST gatecrash
AACEGILLN angelical
englacial
galenical
AACEGILNS analgesic
angelicas
AACEGILRS Algeciras
AACEGILRT cartilage
AACEGILST glaciates
AACEGIMNO egomaniac
AACEGINST caseating
AACEGIRRS carriages
AACEGIRSV vicarages
AACEGISTT castigate
AACEGKPRS packagers
AACEGKRWY graywacke
AACEGLMOU guacamole
AACEGLOST galactose
AACEGLOSU coagulase
AACEGLOTU catalogue
coagulate
AACEGNNST stagnance
AACEGNORR arrogance
AACEGNRSU sugarcane
AACEGOPST scapegoat
AACEGORTT greatcoat
AACEHHIRZ Zechariah
AACEHIIMS ischaemia
AACEHILLO echolalia
AACEHILLS achilleas
AACEHILLT alecithal
AACEHILMT malachite
AACEHILNS selachian
AACEHILNT chatelain
AACEHILPR eparchial
AACEHILPS phacelias
AACEHILPT caliphate
AACEHIMNT machinate
AACEHIMRS chimaeras
AACEHIMST haematics
AACEHIMTT athematic
AACEHINNT acanthine
AACEHINRW chinaware
AACEHIOPT apothecia
AACEHIOST taoiseach
AACEHIPST chapaties
hepaticas
AACEHIPTT apathetic
AACEHIRRS archaiser
AACEHIRRZ archaizer
AACEHIRSS archaises
AACEHIRSZ archaizes
AACEHKLNO kalanchoe
AACEHKMOR hackamore
AACEHKMPU Kampuchea
AACEHKMRR Marrakech
AACEHKRSV haversack
AACEHKRTY Thackeray
AACEHLNSU eulachans
AACEHLRTT clathrate
AACEHMNPR marchpane
AACEHNNSV Chavannes
AACEHNOTV anchoveta
AACEHNPSX panchaxes
AACEHNPTY tachypnea
AACEHNRST anthraces
AACEHPPRS scrapheap
AACEHPRTU parachute
AACEHRSST catharses
AACEHRSTT attachers
AACEIILNT laciniate
AACEIILRS racialise
AACEIILRZ racialize
AACEIINRR cineraria
AACEIIRTV vicariate
AACEIKNTW antwackie
AACEILLMS camellias
AACEILLNS alliances
AACEILLPT capitella
AACEILLRV varicella
AACEILLSV cavallies
AACEILLTV vacillate
AACEILMNP campanile
AACEILMPS eclampsia
AACEILMST calamites
AACEILMTV calmative
AACEILNNR carnelian
AACEILNNT cantilena
lancinate
AACEILNPP appliance
AACEILNPT analeptic
aplanetic
El Capitan
AACEILNRS arsenical
AACEILNRT lacertian
nectarial
AACEILNSS canalises
AACEILNSZ canalizes
AACEILNTV venatical
AACEILORT aleatoric
AACEILPRX paralexic
AACEILPSS asclepias
AACEILPTU apiculate
AACEILPTV placative
AACEILRST tailraces
AACEILRSV calvaries
cavaliers
cavalries
AACEILRUU auriculae
AACEILSTU actualise
AACEILTTU actualite
AACEILTUZ actualize
AACEIMNOX anoxaemic
AACEIMNRR Ermanaric
AACEIMNSS amnesiacs
AACEIMNTU acuminate
AACEIMOTZ azotaemic
AACEIMPRS sapraemic
AACEIMPRT metacarpi
AACEIMQRU Macquarie
AACEIMRST marcasite
AACEIMSTT catamites
masticate
AACEINNRT incarnate
AACEINOST caseation
AACEINPST anapestic
AACEINRRT tarriance
AACEINRST ascertain
Cartesian
sectarian
AACEINRSV variances
AACEINSST estancias
AACEIOSST associate
AACEIPRSS airspaces
AACEIPSTU auspicate
AACEIPTTV captivate
AACEIRSST staircase
AACEIRSTU actuaries
AACEISTTV activates
AACEISTUV causative
AACEJKLPP applejack
AACEJKSSS jackasses
AACEKKLSW cakewalks
AACEKLLMR Mackellar
AACEKLPSW spacewalk
AACEKMRRS Mackerras
AACEKNRRS ransacker
AACEKRSTT attackers
AACELLLRU acellular
AACELLLTY lacteally
AACELLLUV vallecula
AACELLNOR olecranal
AACELLNOW allowance
AACELLNPT placental
AACELLNST castellan
AACELLOST allocates
AACELLTVY clavately
AACELMNTT cattleman
AACELMOTU comatulae
AACELMSST classmate
AACELMSTU maculates
AACELNNOZ Canal Zone
AACELNNTU cannulate
AACELNOTT Canaletto
AACELNPRS parlances
AACELNPST placentas
AACELNRST ancestral
Lancaster
AACELNSTU canulates
AACELNSUZ Suez Canal
AACELOPRT acropetal
cleopatra
AACELORST escalator
AACELOSTT cattaloes
AACELOTUV autoclave
vacuolate

AACELPPRT	applecart
AACELPSTU	aspectual
	capsulate
AACELPSTY	catalepsy
AACELPTXY	cataplexy
AACELRRTU	creatural
AACELRSTY	catalyser
AACELRSWY	clearways
AACELRTUW	caterwaul
AACELRTUX	curtalaxe
AACELRTUY	arcuately
AACELRTYZ	catalyzer
AACELSSTY	catalyses
AACELSTTY	cattleyas
AACELSTYZ	catalyzes
AACEMNNOR	Connemara
AACEMNPRT	mercaptan
AACEMNPRU	Capernaum
AACEMNRST	sacrament
AACEMORRT	macerator
AACEMRRSS	massacrer
AACEMRSSS	massacres
AACENNNOY	annoyance
AACENNOSS	assonance
AACENPRRY	parcenary
AACENPSSU	saucepans
AACENPSTT	pancettas
AACENRSSU	anacruses
	assurance
AACENRSSV	canvasser
AACENRSTT	reactants
AACENRSVZ	czarevnas
AACENRTTU	cauterant
AACENSSSV	canvasses
AACENSSTT	castanets
AACENSTUV	evacuants
AACEOOPPT	apocopate
AACEORSTV	caveators
AACEORTUV	evacuator
AACEORTVX	excavator
AACEOSSST	seacoasts
AACEOSTUX	taxaceous
AACERRSTU	arcatures
AACERRTTT	attracter
AACERSSTT	castrates
AACERSTTT	tractates
AACESSUWY	causeways
AACFGLNRY	flagrancy
AACFGNRRY	fragrancy
AACFHIMNR	chamfrain
AACFHJKST	jackshaft
AACFHMSST	camshafts
AACFIILNN	financial
AACFIILRT	trifacial
AACFILNOT	factional
AACFILORT	factorial
AACFILORV	varifocal
AACFIMNST	fantasmic
AACFINNOR	Franconia
AACFINSTT	fantastic
AACFIRSTT	artifacts
AACFJKLPS	flapjacks
AACFJNOOR	Joan of Arc
AACFLLTUY	factually
AACFLOPSW	Scapa Flow
AACFLRRTU	fractural
AACFMNRST	craftsman
AACGGIKNP	packaging
AACGGIOPR	paragogic
AACGHHIRY	hagiarchy
AACGHILPR	graphical
AACGHIMNP	champaign
AACGHINTT	attaching
AACGHLLOS	agallochs
AACGHMORT	tachogram
AACGHOPRR	arcograph
AACGHOPSZ	gazpachos
AACGHORSU	guacharos
AACGIIMNS	magicians
AACGIKNNP	pancaking
AACGIKNTT	attacking
AACGILLLY	glacially
AACGILLMY	magically
AACGILLNN	canalling
AACGILLOS	scagliola
AACGILMNN	manacling
AACGILMOR	macroglia
AACGILNPT	placating
AACGILNTT	lactating
AACGIMNPS	campaigns
AACGIMOTU	autogamic
AACGIMPRT	pragmatic
AACGIMSUU	guaiacums
AACGINOOS	ascogonia
AACGINORV	Craigavon
AACGINTTU	actuating
AACGIOSSU	sagacious
AACGLLSWY	scallywag
AACGLNOOT	octagonal
AACGLNOTU	coagulant
AACGLOORY	acarology
AACGLSSUY	Gay-Lussac
AACGMORRT	cartogram
AACGNNSTY	stagnancy
AACGORSTU	sugarcoat
AACHHHIUU	chihuahua
AACHHIKNU	chanukiah
AACHHILLR	rhachilla
AACHHIRSS	Shacharis
AACHHSTWY	hatchways
AACHIILNP	Chaliapin
AACHIILPT	aliphatic
AACHIIMRS	mariachis
AACHIINRT	Carinthia
AACHIIPRS	pharisaic
AACHIIRRV	charivari
AACHIKMSY	skiamachy
AACHILLPS	callipash
AACHILMNP	Champlain
AACHILNOZ	chalazion
AACHILNPS	chaplains
AACHILOPR	parochial
AACHILOPT	chipolata
AACHILPSS	pashalics
AACHILPST	asphaltic
AACHILSST	thalassic
AACHIMNOR	harmonica
AACHIMNRR	Charminar
AACHIMNRS	anarchism
AACHIMNRU	Manchuria
AACHIMRRS	armchairs
AACHIMRRT	matriarch
AACHIMRSS	archaisms
	charismas
AACHIMSTT	asthmatic
AACHINNRY	Hyrcanian
AACHINOPR	anaphoric
	pharaonic
AACHINRST	anarchist
	cantharis
AACHIPRRT	patriarch
AACHIPSTT	chapattis
AACHIRSST	archaists
	catharsis
AACHKMMRT	matchmark
AACHKSSTY	haystacks
AACHLLMRY	lachrymal
AACHLLPTY	cataphyll
AACHLMNOR	monarchal
AACHLMRSY	marshalcy
AACHMNNOR	anchorman
AACHMNORW	charwoman
AACHMNSTY	yachtsman
AACHMORST	achromats
AACHMRRTU	Macarthur
	MacArthur
AACHNNOTY	anthocyan
AACHNOSTU	acanthous
AACHNOTTY	chatoyant
AACHOPPRY	apocrypha
AACHQSSTU	sasquatch
AACIILLNV	Cavallini
AACIILLRT	altricial
AACIILMRS	racialism
AACIILMST	lamaistic
AACIILNPT	ancipital
AACIILNSS	anaclisis
AACIILNST	Castilian
AACIILNTV	vaticinal
AACIILPRT	piratical
AACIILRST	racialist
	satirical
AACIIMMST	miasmatic
AACIIMOTX	axiomatic
AACIINNOP	poinciana
AACIINNOT	nicotiana
AACIINPRT	patrician
AACIINRRT	Trinacria
AACIINRTV	vicariant
AACIIPRST	parasitic
AACIIRRTU	urticaria
AACIIRSSV	viscarias
AACIISTTV	atavistic
AACIJNOPS	japonicas
AACIJNOTT	jactation
AACIKLMSS	mailsacks

AACIKMNNY kanamycin
AACIKMNSW mackinaws
AACIKORTY akaryotic
AACILLMMN Macmillan
MacMillan
AACILLNOT allantoic
AACILLNRY ancillary
cranially
AACILLNTU lunatical
AACILLNTV vacillant
AACILLNTY actinally
AACILLPRY capillary
AACILLPTY capitally
AACILMMNO ammonical
AACILMNST calamints
claimants
AACILMOSW Mosaic law
AACILMPST plasmatic
AACILMRSU simulacra
AACILNNOR nonracial
AACILNNUV vulcanian
AACILNOPT placation
AACILNORR carnaroli
AACILNORT cantorial
AACILNOTT lactation
AACILNOTY acylation
claytonia
AACILNPPT applicant
AACILNRST carnalist
AACILNRSV carnivals
AACILNRTY carnality
AACILNRUV navicular
AACILNSTU actual sin
AACILORTU auctorial
AACILOSSU salacious
AACILOSTT coattails
AACILPRTU capitular
AACILPRTY paralytic
AACILPSSZ capsizals
AACILQTTU acquittal
AACILRRTU articular
AACILRRUU auricular
AACILRSTT Scarlatti
AACILRSTY rascality
satyrical
AACILRSUU auriculas
AACILSSTY catalysis
AACILSTUY causality
AACILTTUY actuality
AACIMNNNU Mancunian
AACIMNOPR panoramic
AACIMNORR Armorican
AACIMNORS macaronis
marocains
AACIMNOST anosmatic
AACIMOPRS macropsia
AACIMORST aromatics
AACIMORTU amaurotic
AACIMOTTU automatic
AACIMRRSU sacrarium
AACIMRTTU traumatic
AACINNORT carnation
AACINNOST santonica
AACINOOTV avocation
AACINOPRS caparison
paranoics
AACINOPRT paratonic
AACINORST raincoats
AACINORTU arcuation
AACINOSST cassation
AACINOSTU causation
AACINOSTV vacations
AACINOTTU actuation
AACINQSTU acquaints
AACINRSST sacristan
AACINRSSU anacrusis
AACINRSTU Naucratis
rusticana
AACIOPRSU rapacious
AACIORTTV activator
AACIOSTTW waistcoat
AACIRSTZZ czaritzas
AACJKLPSS slapjacks
AACJKOORS jackaroos
AACJKSSTY jackstays
AACKKNPSS knapsacks
AACKORSWY rockaways
AACLLOPRS collapsar
AACLLOSTY coastally
AACLLRRSY carryalls
AACLLRSTU claustral
AACLLTTUY tactually
AACLNNOSU noncausal
AACLNOOSS Soo Canals
AACLNOPTU cantaloup
AACLNRUUV avuncular
AACLOPRTU portulaca
AACLOPRTY placatory
AACLOPSTV postcaval
AACLORSSU carousals
AACLPRSSU scapulars
AACLPRSTY calyptras
AACLPRSUY scapulary
AACLPSTTU catapults
AACLRRTUY cartulary
AACLSSTTY catalysts
AACMNOORS macaroons
AACMNOTTU catamount
AACMNRRSU macrurans
AACMOOSTT scotomata
AACNNORRV Carnarvon
AACNNOSTT Constanța
AACNRSSTT transacts
AACNRSTUY sanctuary
AACNRSTUZ Santa Cruz
AACOOPSTT capotasto
AACORRSTT castrator
AACORRSTV varactors
AACORRTTT attractor
AACORSSTT castratos
AACORSSWY cassowary
AACORSTTU actuators
autocrats
AACPRSSTU Spartacus
AADDDEEHS deadheads
AADDDGNRS granddads
AADDDGNRY grandaddy
AADDEEFHT fatheaded
AADDEEGMN endamaged
AADDEEHPS sapheaded
AADDEEHRT Dead Heart
AADDEEIRT eradiated
AADDEEMRY readymade
AADDEENRV verandaed
AADDEENTT antedated
AADDEEPRT readapted
AADDEFIRS faradised
AADDEFIRZ faradized
AADDEFLLS deadfalls
AADDEGIMR diagramed
AADDEGITV divagated
AADDEGLNR garlanded
AADDEGMNU undamaged
AADDEGRTU graduated
AADDEHHRS hardheads
AADDEHILU Eid-ul-Adha
AADDEHLNS headlands
AADDEHNST headstand
AADDEHRSW headwards
AADDEILNO adenoidal
AADDEILPS palisaded
AADDEILPT lapidated
AADDEILTV validated
AADDEIMNR marinaded
AADDEIMNW Wad Medani
AADDEINNV Nanda Devi
AADDEINRT andradite
AADDELLNS sandalled
AADDELMNR dreamland
AADDELPPU applauded
AADDELRST astraddle
AADDEMNNT demandant
AADDEMNOR andromeda
AADDEMRSY daydreams
AADDEMRYY daydreamy
AADDENPTU unadapted
AADDEORST roadstead
AADDEQRTU quadrated
AADDGNRSU graduands
AADDHIMNS handmaids
AADDHNNST handstand
AADDIIMRY dairymaid
AADDINPRT dandiprat
AADDIRRWY Irrawaddy
AADDLNRSW landwards
AADDLRSTY dastardly
AADDMRSTT Darmstadt
AADDNRSST standards
AADEEGHMT megadeath
AADEEGHNP phagedena
AADEEGHST Gateshead
AADEEGLMN magdalene
AADEEGMNS endamages
AADEEGNOR orangeade
AADEEGNPP appendage
AADEEHHRX hexahedra

AADEEHKNS	snakehead
AADEEHPRS	spearhead
AADEEIKWW	wideawake
AADEEILMV	mediaeval
AADEEILNT	alienated
AADEEIMNT	deaminate
AADEEIRST	eradiates
AADEEKMRR	earmarked
AADEEKMRY	makeready
AADEELLMN	allemande
AADEELNPS	esplanade
AADEELNRX	alexander
AADEELPPR	appareled
AADEELPRV	palavered
AADEELRRY	lay reader
AADEELTUV	devaluate
	evaluated
AADEEMNRT	tradename
AADEEMRRS	demeraras
AADEEMRSU	admeasure
AADEENSTT	antedates
AADEENSTU	nauseated
AADEEORTT	toadeater
AADEEPRST	paederast
	separated
AADEERRTT	retardate
AADEESTTV	devastate
AADEFGLNN	fandangle
AADEFGRSU	safeguard
AADEFHLST	flatheads
AADEFHSST	headfasts
AADEFILNT	fantailed
AADEFILRS	fairleads
AADEFINST	fantasied
AADEFIORS	aforesaid
AADEFIRRS	faradiser
AADEFIRRZ	faradizer
AADEFIRSS	faradises
AADEFIRSZ	faradizes
AADEFLLRS	falderals
AADEFLNOR	farandole
AADEFLRSY	defrayals
AADEFMPRT	afterdamp
AADEFMRST	farmstead
AADEFOSWY	Days of Awe
AADEFRRTW	afterward
AADEFSSTT	steadfast
AADEGHNRU	harangued
AADEGHNRY	hydrangea
AADEGHNST	stagehand
AADEGIIRT	Dei gratia
AADEGILRT	taligrade
AADEGILTT	tailgated
AADEGIMNT	diamagnet
AADEGINNR	Grenadian
AADEGINPS	paganised
AADEGINPT	paginated
AADEGINPZ	paganized
AADEGINRR	arraigned
AADEGINRS	drainages
	gardenias
AADEGINRT	tragedian
AADEGINTV	navigated
AADEGIPRS	disparage
AADEGIQRU	quadrigae
AADEGISTV	divagates
AADEGLLNT	gallanted
AADEGLLOP	gallopade
AADEGLMNS	magdalens
AADEGLMSY	amygdales
AADEGLNNR	rangeland
AADEGLNRV	landgrave
AADEGLNTU	angulated
AADEGLOPS	galopades
AADEGLRVW	waldgrave
AADEGMMUY	mamaguyed
AADEGMNRS	grandames
AADEGMOSV	savagedom
AADEGNOPR	paragoned
AADEGNRRT	regardant
AADEGNSTT	stagnated
AADEGORRT	arrogated
AADEGRRRU	rearguard
AADEGRRVY	graveyard
AADEGRSTU	graduates
AADEGRSTZ	stargazed
AADEHHKNS	handshake
AADEHILNS	nailheads
AADEHILRR	diarrheal
AADEHILRS	headrails
	railheads
AADEHILSS	headsails
AADEHIMOT	haematoid
AADEHIORR	diarrhoea
AADEHIPRT	apartheid
AADEHIRST	stairhead
AADEHISWY	hideaways
AADEHLLLL	hallalled
AADEHLLST	headstall
AADEHLMNN	manhandle
AADEHLMPS	headlamps
AADEHLMRS	marshaled
AADEHLMSY	ashamedly
AADEHLNNP	panhandle
AADEHLNRT	heartland
AADEHLPSS	slapheads
AADEHLPST	asphalted
AADEHMNSU	unashamed
AADEHMPST	Hampstead
AADEHMSST	mastheads
AADEHNRSV	verandahs
AADEHORRW	arrowhead
AADEHPRTT	deathtrap
AADEHRRTW	earthward
AADEHRSVW	drawshave
AADEIILMR	airmailed
AADEIIPRS	praesidia
AADEIIRRT	irradiate
AADEIIRTV	radiative
AADEIKLLS	alkalised
AADEIKLLZ	alkalized
AADEILLPT	palliated
AADEILMNN	almandine
AADEILMNT	laminated
AADEILMRT	diametral
AADEILMRV	Valdemar I
AADEILMRW	Waldemar I
AADEILNNN	annelidan
AADEILNNR	adrenalin
AADEILNNS	Inland Sea
AADEILNOT	dealation
AADEILNSS	nasalised
AADEILNSV	vandalise
AADEILNSZ	nasalized
AADEILNVZ	vandalize
AADEILPSS	palisades
AADEILPST	lapidates
	stapedial
AADEILRTV	travailed
AADEILSSW	wassailed
AADEILSTV	salivated
	validates
AADEILTUV	laudative
AADEIMMNS	maenadism
AADEIMNRS	marinades
AADEIMNRT	marinated
AADEIMRST	dramatise
AADEIMRSV	maravedis
AADEIMRTZ	dramatize
AADEIMSST	adamsites
AADEINPRT	pintadera
AADEINRST	steradian
AADEINRTT	attainder
AADEINTTT	attainted
AADEIPPRS	appraised
	disappear
AADEIPRSS	paradises
AADEIPRST	aspirated
	disparate
AADEIPSSU	diapauses
AADEISSST	diastases
AADEJKLWY	jaywalked
AADEJLLNS	Sjælland
AADEJRUVY	Yajur-Veda
AADEKLRSY	kaleyards
AADEKMNRS	mandrakes
AADEKMRRT	trademark
AADEKMRWY	waymarked
AADELLNOT	lanolated
AADELLNTU	landaulet
AADELLNUY	unallayed
AADELLQRU	quadrella
AADELLSSY	saleslady
AADELMMOR	melodrama
AADELMNOR	ealdorman
AADELMNRS	malanders
AADELMPSU	Lampedusa
AADELNNTU	annulated
AADELNPST	peatlands
AADELNRRU	rural dean
AADELNSTW	wasteland
AADELOPRT	pardalote
AADELPPRU	applauder
AADELPRSY	paralysed
AADELPRTW	drawplate
AADELPRYZ	paralyzed

AADELRSSY saleyards
AADELSSTU assaulted
AADEMMNOR memoranda
AADEMMRST Amsterdam
AADEMNPRS ampersand
AADEMNRST tradesman
AADEMOOST stomodaea
AADEMOTTU automated
AADEMPRRT ramparted
AADEMPTTU amputated
AADEMRRSU marauders
AADEMRTTU maturated
AADENNOTT annotated
AADENNPPT appendant
AADENNPRT trapanned
AADENNRST Santander
AADENNTTT attendant
AADENOWWX woadwaxen
AADENPPRS sandpaper
AADENPRTU pandurate
AADENRRTT retardant
AADENRRTW warranted
AADEOPRRS paradores
AADEOPRSS paradoses
AADEOPRSX paradoxes
AADEORTTV rotavated
AADEPPRST preadapts
AADEQRSTU quadrates
AADERRRSW rearwards
AADERRSVY adversary
AADERRTTT tartrated
AADERSSTW eastwards
AADERSTTU saturated
AADFFIITV affidavit
AADFGIRUU Guardafui
AADFGNNOS fandangos
AADFGNORR Fragonard
AADFHNSST handfasts
AADFILNRY fairyland
AADFLLLNS landfalls
AADFLOSTW dataflows
AADFMNRST draftsman
AADFMRRSY farmyards
AADGGGINR aggrading
AADGGHHOT haggadoth
AADGGHIST haggadist
AADGGHLRY haggardly
AADGGINRT gradating
AADGGLLRY laggardly
AADGGRSST staggards
AADGHIMPR diaphragm
AADGHINRT Adi Granth
AADGHINRZ hazarding
AADGHIPRS diagraphs
AADGHIPSY dysphagia
AADGIINRT radiating
AADGIKMNS damasking
AADGILLOS gladiolas
AADGILLRS galliards
AADGILMNY amygdalin
AADGILMRS madrigals
AADGILNOR girandola
AADGILNOS diagonals
AADGILNTU adulating
AADGILORT gladiator
AADGILRRU guardrail
AADGIMMNO gammadion
AADGIMNNT mandating
AADGIMNRU marauding
AADGIMORR radiogram
AADGIMORU audiogram
AADGIMPRS paradigms
AADGINORT gradation
AADGINRRS darraigns
AADGINRSU guardians
AADGINRUZ Dzungaria
AADGIQRSU quadrigas
AADGJPRUU Durga Puja
AADGLLNRU glandular
AADGLLRUY gradually
AADGLNOOW wagonload
AADGLNRSS grassland
AADGLNSSS sandglass
AADGMNORS dragomans
AADGMNRSU guardsman
AADGMRRTU dramaturg
AADGNNQSU quandangs
AADGNNRTU grandaunt
AADGNRSUV vanguards
AADGNRSWY drangways
AADGORRTU graduator
AADGRRSUW gurdwaras
AADHHJKNR Jharkhand
AADHIIILR Harald III
AADHIINPS aphidians
AADHILLNO Hollandia
AADHILLRS halliards
AADHILNRS handrails
AADHILNSV vandalish
AADHILRST tahsildar
AADHILRSV havildars
AADHINNOT danthonia
AADHINPSU Upanishad
AADHINRRS harridans
AADHIORRT arthrodia
AADHIPSSY dysphasia
AADHKLNRS landshark
AADHLLNST hallstand
AADHLMNRS marshland
AADHMNOSU omadhauns
AADHNSSTW washstand
AADHORRSU hadrosaur
AADHORSUZ hazardous
AADIIINNN Indianian
AADIILMNV Maldivian
AADIIMMOT ommatidia
AADIIMNRZ zamindari
AADIINORT radiation
AADIINRRT irradiant
AADIIORTU auditoria
AADIIQRUV quadrivia
AADIISSST diastasis
AADIJNNOR Jordanian
AADIKLLOS alkaloids
AADIKLRSY kailyards
AADILLMOR armadillo
AADILLMPU palladium
AADILLNOT allantoid
AADILLOPS sapodilla
AADILMNNO adnominal
AADILMNOR Māoriland
AADILMNOV Moldavian
AADILMNSV vandalism
AADILMNTU Tamil Nadu
AADILMOPS plasmodia
AADILMORT maladroit
AADILMPRY pyramidal
AADILMRTY admiralty
AADILNNOT antinodal
AADILNOPT antipodal
AADILNOTT antidotal
AADILNOTU adulation
laudation
AADILNRTY radiantly
AADILNSTT dilatants
AADILNSWZ Swaziland
AADILORRS railroads
AADILORTT dilatator
AADILOSVW disavowal
AADILPSSY dysplasia
AADIMNNOT damnation
AADIMNNRS mandarins
AADIMNRST tamarinds
AADIMNRSZ zamindars
AADIMNUVZ avizandum
AADIMPSST misadapts
AADIMRSTT dramatist
AADINNNOT andantino
AADINNOOT anodontia
AADINOORT adoration
AADINOPRS paranoids
AADINOPSS diapasons
AADINOPST adaptions
AADINSSTY saint's day
AADIORRST radiators
AADIORRTY radiatory
AADIORSTU sudatoria
AADIPRSXY dyspraxia
AADIPSSUY upsadaisy
AADIRRSSY disarrays
AADJNSTTU adjutants
AADJNSTUV adjuvants
AADKLMNRS landmarks
AADKLNOSW Landowska
AADKLNPRS parklands
AADKLORSV volksraad
AADKLRWWY awkwardly
AADKNORRS Krasnodar
AADLLOPSU palladous
AADLMNORS mandorlas
AADLMNPSW swampland
AADLMOORV Almodóvar
AADLORSST loadstars
AADLORSTU adulators
AADLORTUY adulatory
laudatory

AADLRWWYY	waywardly
AADMMNOOR	monodrama
AADMNORST	mandators
AADMNORTY	damnatory
	mandatory
AADMORRST	tramroads
AADNNORSU	anandrous
AADNOOPSW	sapanwood
AADNOORRS	Aaron's rod
AADNQRSTU	quadrants
AADOPPRRS	paradrops
AADOPPRST	strappado
AADOPSSUY	paduasoys
AADORSSVY	savoyards
AAEEEHLRT	aethereal
AAEEFHRTT	afterheat
AAEEFKPRT	afterpeak
AAEEFLOTV	faveolate
AAEEFLTTY	Lafayette
AAEEFRRSS	seafarers
AAEEGGGRT	aggregate
AAEEGINTV	evaginate
AAEEGIRTV	variegate
AAEEGLRVY	averagely
AAEEGMNNS	manganese
AAEEGMPRS	amperages
AAEEGNORS	Aragonese
AAEEGNPRT	parentage
AAEEGNRRR	rearrange
AAEEGNRSS	sangarees
AAEEGNRST	tagareens
AAEEGNRTU	guarantee
AAEEGNRWY	Greenaway
AAEEGPRSU	gaspereau
AAEEHIMNT	haematein
AAEEHIMTT	haematite
AAEEHISST	aesthesia
AAEEHKNNT	Akhenaten
AAEEHLMRX	hexameral
AAEEHLMTW	wheatmeal
AAEEHLRRS	rehearsal
AAEEHMNTU	athenaeum
AAEEHMNTX	exanthema
AAEEHMPST	metaphase
AAEEHRRSW	shareware
AAEEHRSTW	wheatears
AAEEIKLMT	Amalekite
AAEEIKLMU	leukaemia
AAEEILLMN	El Alamein
AAEEILLTV	alleviate
AAEEILMNS	Melanesia
AAEEILNST	alienates
AAEEILRTT	aliterate
	retaliate
AAEEIMNRT	reanimate
AAEEIMNTV	emanative
AAEEIMNTX	exanimate
AAEEINSTW	Taiwanese
AAEEIPTTX	expatiate
AAEEISTTV	aestivate
AAEEKKMVY	Makeyevka
AAEEKLNNP	palankeen
AAEEKMNSS	namesakes
AAEEKMRST	teamakers
AAEEKNPTW	wapentake
AAEEKNRSW	reawakens
AAEEKPRRT	parrakeet
AAEEKPRST	parakeets
AAEEKPSSY	speakeasy
AAEEKQSSU	seaquakes
AAEELLLMT	lamellate
AAEELLMRS	amarelles
AAEELLOTV	alveolate
AAEELLPPT	appellate
AAEELLPTT	patellate
AAEELLQRU	aquarelle
AAEELMMRT	metameral
AAEELMMST	metamales
AAEELMNPT	nameplate
AAEELMNRT	Tamerlane
AAEELMSST	matelasse
AAEELMSTT	stalemate
AAEELNNRS	annealers
AAEELNOPR	aeroplane
AAEELNPSS	seaplanes
AAEELNRTT	alternate
AAEELNSST	elastanes
AAEELPPRS	appealers
AAEELPRST	palestrae
AAEELPSTV	Laptev Sea
AAEELRSTU	laureates
AAEELRTTZ	lazarette
AAEELRTUV	revaluate
AAEELRTUY	aureately
AAEELSTUV	evaluates
AAEELSVWY	wayleaves
AAEEMMNTZ	amazement
AAEEMMPTY	empyemata
AAEEMMPTZ	temazepam
AAEEMMSTT	teammates
AAEEMNNSS	anamneses
AAEEMNPST	nametapes
AAEEMPRRT	parameter
AAEENPPRT	parapente
AAEENRRTW	warrantee
AAEENRSST	arsenates
	serenatas
AAEENRSSW	awareness
AAEENRSTT	anteaters
AAEENSSTU	nauseates
AAEENTTTU	attenuate
AAEEOPRSU	aeropause
AAEEOPRTV	evaporate
AAEEPPRRS	rapparees
	reappears
AAEEPPRSS	appeasers
AAEEPRRTY	ratepayer
AAEEPRSST	separates
AAEERRSWW	rewarewas
AAEERSSTT	stearates
AAEESTTVV	Tsvetaeva
AAEFFIILT	affiliate
AAEFFILRS	rafflesia
AAEFFINPR	paraffine
AAEFFINRT	raffinate
AAEFFLNUZ	affluenza
AAEFGHMNR	Fermanagh
AAEFGHRSW	wharfages
AAEFGINRS	seafaring
AAEFGIRSX	saxifrage
AAEFGLLLR	flagellar
AAEFGORRS	farragoes
AAEFHLRST	flatshare
AAEFHMRTT	aftermath
AAEFIILLR	alfileria
AAEFIKLST	kalifates
AAEFILNTX	antefixal
AAEFILRTY	fairytale
AAEFIMMNR	mainframe
AAEFIMNOU	meiofauna
AAEFIMRRS	airframes
AAEFINNRS	safranine
AAEFINNST	faineants
AAEFINSST	fantasies
	fantasise
AAEFINSTZ	fantasize
AAEFINTTU	infatuate
AAEFKLLST	leafstalk
AAEFKLNRR	farnarkel
AAEFKMSST	makefasts
AAEFLLLRY	fallalery
AAEFLLRTW	waterfall
AAEFLMSTT	flatmates
AAEFLNRRT	fraternal
AAEFLORTZ	Fortaleza
AAEFMNSTY	safetyman
AAEFRRSWY	wayfarers
AAEGGHIOP	geophagia
AAEGGILLN	galingale
AAEGGILNR	laagering
AAEGGILNW	Galwegian
AAEGGINOS	anagogies
AAEGGINRV	averaging
AAEGGLLNO	gallonage
AAEGGLMOU	magalogue
AAEGGLNSU	languages
AAEGGMMRS	grammages
AAEGGNRSY	garganeys
AAEGGOPRS	paragoges
AAEGGOPRU	paragogue
AAEGHIILM	hemialgia
AAEGHILNS	Saghalien
AAEGHINRW	Whangarei
AAEGHLLPY	hypallage
AAEGHLNOX	hexagonal
AAEGHLNPR	phalanger
AAEGHLNPS	phalanges
AAEGHMRSX	hexagrams
AAEGHNOPR	orphanage
AAEGHNORS	angashore
AAEGHNRRU	haranguer
AAEGHNRSU	harangues
AAEGHOPRY	aerophagy
AAEGHORRT	Harrogate
AAEGIILMO	oligaemia
AAEGIILNT	genitalia

AAEGIILQU	aquilegia
AAEGIKNNW	awakening
AAEGILLRS	gallerias
AAEGILLRV	Gällivare
AAEGILMNS	magnesial
AAEGILMRT	metralgia
AAEGILNNN	annealing
AAEGILNNT	galantine
AAEGILNOS	analogies
	analogise
AAEGILNOZ	analogize
AAEGILNPP	appealing
	lagniappe
AAEGILNPS	pelagians
AAEGILNRU	neuralgia
AAEGILNST	agentials
	alginates
AAEGILNSV	galvanise
AAEGILNVZ	galvanize
AAEGILRTT	tailgater
AAEGILSTT	tailgates
AAEGIMMNS	mismanage
AAEGIMNNS	magnesian
AAEGIMNNT	emanating
	manganite
AAEGIMNRR	margarine
AAEGIMNRT	marginate
AAEGIMNSZ	magazines
AAEGIMRRS	marriages
AAEGIMRRT	margarite
AAEGIMRST	maritages
AAEGINNRT	Argentina
AAEGINORT	aragonite
AAEGINPPR	appearing
AAEGINPPS	appeasing
AAEGINPRS	paganiser
AAEGINPRZ	paganizer
AAEGINPSS	paganises
AAEGINPST	paginates
AAEGINPSZ	paganizes
AAEGINPTZ	Gaziantep
AAEGINRRR	arraigner
AAEGINRRS	granaries
AAEGINRSY	asynergia
	gainsayer
AAEGINSTV	navigates
AAEGIRTTV	gravitate
AAEGISTTT	sagittate
AAEGISVWY	giveaways
AAEGKKRRS	Skagerrak
AAEGKLNTU	Gatún Lake
AAEGLLMPS	plasmagel
AAEGLLNRY	laryngeal
AAEGLMNOR	Mangalore
AAEGLMNTU	mangulate
AAEGLMPSY	gameplays
AAEGLMSST	almagests
AAEGLMTTU	glutamate
AAEGLNOSU	analogues
AAEGLNPPS	lagnappes
AAEGLNRTU	granulate
AAEGLNSTU	angulates
AAEGLOSST	aglossate
AAEGLPRSV	palsgrave
AAEGLRSSV	salvagers
AAEGLRSSW	glassware
AAEGLRSTU	gastrulae
AAEGLRTTU	gratulate
AAEGMMNNO	Agamemnon
AAEGMNOPT	tamponage
AAEGMNORT	matronage
AAEGMNPRT	pentagram
AAEGMNRST	magnetars
AAEGMNRTT	termagant
AAEGMORRS	aerograms
AAEGMORSS	sagamores
AAEGMPRRS	rampagers
AAEGMRRSV	margraves
AAEGMRRTT	tetragram
AAEGMRSSS	massagers
AAEGMRSST	megastars
AAEGMRSTT	stratagem
AAEGMRSTU	ageratums
AAEGMSTTW	megawatts
AAEGNNOOT	Notogaean
AAEGNOPRS	parsonage
AAEGNOPRT	patronage
AAEGNPRTY	pageantry
AAEGNRRRS	arrangers
AAEGNRSTU	runagates
AAEGNRSTV	Stavanger
AAEGNSSTT	stagnates
AAEGOPPRT	propagate
AAEGOPRSU	Areopagus
AAEGORRST	arrogates
AAEGORSTT	aegrotats
AAEGPRSTU	pasturage
AAEGRRSTZ	stargazer
AAEGRSSSU	assuagers
AAEGRSSTZ	stargazes
AAEHHINPZ	Zephaniah
AAEHHLNOT	halothane
AAEHHLPTT	phthalate
AAEHHMNNN	Hahnemann
AAEHILMMS	hamamelis
AAEHILNTV	leviathan
AAEHILRST	harestail
AAEHIMMNR	Mariehamn
AAEHIMNOT	theomania
AAEHIMRTU	hematuria
AAEHINPST	aphanites
AAEHINRST	rhatanies
AAEHKMRSY	haymakers
AAEHKNSYZ	Ashkenazy
AAEHLLNOP	allophane
AAEHLLSTU	haustella
AAEHLMRRS	marshaler
AAEHLNPSX	phalanxes
AAEHLNPSY	synalepha
AAEHLNRSW	narwhales
AAEHLNSTT	Athelstan
AAEHLNSTX	exhalants
AAEHLOPPR	phalarope
AAEHLPSUV	upheavals
AAEHMMNOT	Mahometan
AAEHMMOST	hematomas
AAEHMNRSW	washerman
AAEHMOOTZ	hematozoa
AAEHMORST	atheromas
AAEHMOSTT	haemostat
AAEHMQSSU	quamashes
AAEHMRSTU	shamateur
AAEHNNTUY	Netanyahu
AAEHNPSST	pheasants
AAEHNSSTT	Shan State
AAEHNSTTX	xanthates
AAEHRRSTT	earthstar
AAEHRSSTU	arethusas
AAEHRSSUU	Ahasuerus
AAEIILMNR	animalier
AAEIILMNS	animalise
AAEIILMNZ	animalize
AAEIILMRT	latimeria
AAEIILNNT	antialien
AAEIILNRS	laniaries
AAEIILPTX	epitaxial
AAEIILRST	aerialist
AAEIILRSV	Rea Silvia
AAEIIMNNT	inanimate
AAEIIMRST	artemisia
AAEIINNOS	Ionian Sea
AAEIINQTU	Aquitaine
AAEIINSST	taeniasis
AAEIINSTT	insatiate
AAEIJKLNW	Kwajalein
AAEIJNRST	naartjies
AAEIKKMSZ	kamikazes
AAEIKLLSS	alkalises
AAEIKLLSZ	alkalizes
AAEIKLNNN	Leninakan
AAEIKLTTV	talkative
AAEIKMNRR	rainmaker
AAEIKMRRS	kramerias
AAEIKRSTU	autarkies
AAEILLLSU	alleluias
AAEILLMMM	mammillae
AAEILLMMT	mamillate
AAEILLMNT	alimental
AAEILLNPR	enalapril
AAEILLNPS	sailplane
AAEILLNPT	tailplane
AAEILLNTV	élan vital
AAEILLPPT	papillate
AAEILLPSS	paillasse
	palliasse
AAEILLPST	palliates
AAEILMMRS	marmalise
AAEILMMRZ	marmalize
AAEILMMST	melismata
AAEILMMSX	axilemmas
AAEILMNOS	anomalies
AAEILMNRT	Lamartine
AAEILMNSS	Messalina
AAEILMNST	laminates
AAEILMNSZ	Manizales
AAEILMNTU	aluminate

AAEILMPRV	primaeval
	verapamil
AAEILMPTT	palmitate
AAEILMRST	materials
AAEILMRTU	tularemia
AAEILMTVY	amatively
AAEILNNSU	annualise
AAEILNNUZ	annualize
AAEILNORS	Orléanais
AAEILNORT	alienator
	rationale
AAEILNPRS	airplanes
AAEILNPRT	perinatal
AAEILNPST	palatines
AAEILNPTX	taxiplane
AAEILNRSV	valerians
AAEILNSSS	nasalises
AAEILNSSZ	nasalizes
AAEILNSTT	tantalise
AAEILNTTT	tantalite
AAEILNTTZ	tantalize
AAEILORTV	variolate
AAEILPPTT	palpitate
AAEILPRST	parietals
	psalteria
AAEILPRTZ	trapezial
AAEILPSST	stapelias
AAEILRSSS	assailers
AAEILRSSW	wassailer
AAEILRSTU	estuarial
AAEILRSTV	varietals
AAEILSSSV	vassalise
AAEILSSTV	salivates
AAEILSSVZ	vassalize
AAEILSTVX	laxatives
AAEIMMNOT	ammoniate
AAEIMNNOT	anamniote
	emanation
AAEIMNNSS	anamnesis
AAEIMNOPR	Pomerania
AAEIMNOST	anatomies
	anatomise
AAEIMNOTZ	amazonite
	anatomize
AAEIMNPRR	repairman
AAEIMNPRS	pearmains
AAEIMNRST	animaters
	marinates
AAEIMNRTU	Martineau
AAEIMNSTT	staminate
AAEIMOPRT	ametropia
AAEIMORST	aromatise
AAEIMORTZ	aromatize
AAEIMPRST	spermatia
AAEIMRRST	airstream
AAEIMRSTT	metatarsi
AAEINPPRT	appertain
AAEINPRST	septarian
AAEINPRTT	Antipater
AAEINPSSV	Vespasian
AAEINQTTU	antiquate
AAEINRRTV	narrative
AAEINRRTW	rainwater
AAEINRRVY	Inveraray
AAEINRSTT	reattains
AAEINSTTT	titanates
AAEIORSSU	Essaouira
AAEIPPRRS	appraiser
AAEIPPRSS	appraises
AAEIPRSST	aspirates
	parasites
	satrapies
AAEIPSSTV	passivate
AAEIRRSTT	tartarise
AAEIRRTTZ	tartarize
AAEIRSSTU	Aristaeus
AAEIRSSTV	aviatress
AAEIRSTTZ	zaratites
AAEISSSUV	assuasive
AAEJKLRWY	jaywalker
AAEJLNOPS	jalapenos
AAEKLMPRT	platemark
AAEKLMPRY	playmaker
AAEKLMRSW	lawmakers
AAEKLPRST	lapstrake
	lapstreak
AAEKMRRTW	watermark
AAEKNPRST	Pasternak
AAEKORSTY	akaryotes
AAEKPRRST	partakers
AAELLLMOR	malleolar
AAELLLPRS	parallels
AAELLLRTY	laterally
AAELLNPPT	appellant
AAELLORSV	alveolars
AAELLPPRW	wallpaper
AAELLSUXY	asexually
AAELLSWYY	alleyways
AAELMMNOS	melanomas
AAELMMORR	marmoreal
AAELMMOSX	axolemmas
AAELMMOTY	myelomata
AAELMMPST	metaplasm
AAELMMSTU	malamutes
AAELMNOSU	mausolean
AAELMNPPU	Pampeluna
AAELMNRSU	El Mansûra
AAELMNRSY	salarymen
AAELMPRST	malaperts
AAELMPSTY	playmates
AAELMRSTT	maltreats
AAELNNRTT	alternant
AAELNOPRT	rotaplane
AAELNORTZ	Lanzarote
AAELNPRST	prenatals
AAELNPRSW	warplanes
AAELNPRTY	planetary
AAELNPSTT	pantalets
AAELNRSSY	analysers
AAELNRSTT	translate
AAELNRSTX	relaxants
AAELNRSYZ	analyzers
AAELNRUWY	unawarely
AAELNSTTU	sultanate
AAELNUUVV	Vanua Levu
AAELOOPRT	tropaeola
AAELOPPRY	propylaea
AAELOPRSS	psoraleas
AAELOPRST	pastorale
AAELOPSSU	asepalous
AAELOPSTU	apetalous
AAELORRSU	rearousal
AAELORSTT	attolaser
AAELORTTZ	lazaretto
AAELORTUV	evaluator
AAELPRRSY	paralyser
AAELPRRYZ	paralyzer
AAELPRSST	palestras
AAELPRSSY	paralyses
AAELPRSYZ	paralyzes
AAELPSSTV	palstaves
AAELPSTTU	spatulate
AAELRRSTV	traversal
AAELRSSTU	assaulter
	australes
	saleratus
AAELRSTTW	saltwater
AAELRSUZZ	zarzuelas
AAELRSWYY	waylayers
AAELSSTWY	leastways
AAEMMNORR	marmorean
AAEMMNOST	ammonates
AAEMMNRST	armaments
AAEMMORTT	mattamore
AAEMMOSST	metasomas
AAEMNORST	emanators
AAEMNORTU	neuromata
AAEMNORTY	emanatory
AAEMNOSTZ	metazoans
AAEMNPRST	paraments
AAEMNPRTT	apartment
AAEMNQRSU	Marquesan
AAEMNSSTT	statesman
AAEMOOSTT	osteomata
AAEMORSSU	amauroses
AAEMORSTT	amarettos
	teratomas
AAEMOSTTU	automates
AAEMPRSTY	paymaster
AAEMPSTTU	amputates
AAEMRRSST	smartarse
AAEMRRSTU	armatures
AAEMRSSST	matrasses
AAEMRSTTU	maturates
AAENNNRTY	antennary
AAENNOSTT	annotates
AAENNPRRT	trapanner
AAENNTTTU	attenuant
AAENORRVZ	Verrazano
AAENORSTU	aeronauts
AAENPRSTY	peasantry
AAENPSTXY	anaptyxes
AAENRRRST	Stranraer
AAENRRRTW	warranter
AAENRSSTV	tsarevnas
AAENSTTTT	attestant

AAEOPRRST separator
AAEOPRSTT pastorate
AAEOPSSTT apostates
AAEORSSTT aerostats
AAEORSTTV rotavates
AAEPPSSTT appestats
AAEPRSTXY taxpayers
AAERRSTTT tartrates
AAERRSTTU saturater
AAERSSTTU saturates
AAERSTTWW Wast Water
AAERSTWWY waterways
AAFFFGLST flagstaff
AAFFGILSS gaffsails
AAFFGINRY affraying
AAFFGNRSU suffragan
AAFFILRST taffrails
AAFFIMNRT affirmant
AAFFINPRS paraffins
AAFFKMNNU Kauffmann
AAFGHNRSU fraughans
AAFGILNRS franglais
AAFGILNST falangist
AAFGINRWY wayfaring
AAFGLLORT allograft
AAFGLORSU sugarloaf
AAFGORTTU autograft
AAFHHORTT haftaroth
AAFHLSSTY layshafts
AAFHMRRSU Musharraf
AAFHRSSUU hausfraus
AAFILLNRS rainfalls
AAFILMNOR foraminal
AAFILNOTX aflatoxin
AAFILORUW rauwolfia
AAFILSSTT fatalists
AAFIMORTU fumatoria
AAFINNRSS safranins
AAFINSSTT fantasist
AAFKLNOUU Nuku'alofa
AAFLLPRST pratfalls
AAFMORRTW marrowfat
AAGGGHNSS gangshags
AAGGGINRS garagings
AAGGIINTT agitating
AAGGILLNT tallaging
AAGGILNSV salvaging
AAGGIMNOR angiogram
AAGGIMNPR rampaging
AAGGIMNSS massaging
AAGGINNRR arranging
AAGGINPSS passaging
AAGGINSSU assuaging
AAGGKLNNP gangplank
AAGGLLLSY lallygags
AAGGLMNOR Glamorgan
AAGGLNOSY synagogal
AAGGMNOOY agamogony
AAGHHILRT high altar
AAGHHINSS shanghais
AAGHHIRTT High Tatra
AAGHHNOSS oanshaghs
AAGHIKMNY haymaking
AAGHIKMOS Kagoshima
AAGHILLLN halalling
AAGHILLMN Allingham
AAGHILLNO halloaing
AAGHILNNS hangnails
AAGHILNRS ashlaring
AAGHILPSU ispaghula
AAGHIMOOP omophagia
AAGHIMPRR marigraph
AAGHINNRU Hungarian
AAGHINNSW Wang An Shi
AAGHINRSS harassing
AAGHINSSY sashaying
AAGHKMNSY gymkhanas
AAGHLLOPR allograph
AAGHLNPRY pharyngal
AAGHLNPSY anaglyphs
AAGHLNPYY anaglyphy
AAGHMNOSY hogmanays
AAGHNOOPR angophora
AAGHNOSTU agnathous
AAGHOPRTU autograph
AAGIIKNNS Kisangani
AAGIIKNRY Kirinyaga
AAGIILNSS assailing
AAGIIMNNS magainins
AAGIIMNNT animating
AAGIIMNRY imaginary
AAGIINNSU iguanians
AAGIINNTT attaining
AAGIINOTT agitation
AAGIINPPR Agrippina
AAGIINRTT antitragi
AAGIINSTT satiating
AAGIJNNNP japanning
AAGIKLNOS kaoliangs
AAGIKMRSS kissagram
AAGIKNPRT partaking
AAGILLNPP appalling
AAGILLNST Saint Gall
AAGILLNTV gallivant
AAGILLORT alligator
AAGILLPSW galliwasp
AAGILMNNO agnominal
AAGILMNNP napalming
AAGILMNNS signalman
AAGILMNNT malignant
AAGILMNOS magnolias
AAGILMNRS marginals
AAGILMNSV galvanism
AAGILMNYZ amazingly
AAGILMRST magistral
AAGILNNSY analysing
AAGILNNYZ analyzing
AAGILNOST analogist
galtonias
nostalgia
AAGILNPPT palpating
AAGILNPRY parlaying
AAGILNRRS larrigans
AAGILNRSY salarying
AAGILNRUU inaugural
AAGILNRUV vulgarian
AAGILNSTV galivants
AAGILNTUV valuating
AAGILNWYY waylaying
AAGILOOPS apologias
AAGILQUUY Guayaquil
AAGILRRSW warrigals
AAGIMMMST magmatism
AAGIMMRRS marigrams
AAGIMNOSY anisogamy
AAGIMNPRT ptarmigan
AAGIMORTU matagouri
AAGIMSSST massagist
AAGINNNSY nannygais
AAGINNRRT narrating
AAGINOOTV vagotonia
AAGINOPRS sporangia
AAGINORRS rangioras
AAGINORTV navigator
AAGINPRSU pagurians
AAGINPSST paganists
AAGINPTXY taxpaying
AAGINSTTU sitatunga
AAGIORSTT agitators
AAGIORSUV vagarious
AAGIPRSTZ Gaza Strip
AAGIRSSTV stravaigs
AAGKLNUUZ Gazankulu
AAGKMORRY karyogram
AAGKMORYY karyogamy
AAGKNNRUU Guru Nanak
AAGKNOORS kangaroos
AAGLLLNTY gallantly
AAGLLNNTU ungallant
AAGLLNRTY gallantry
AAGLLNRUY angularly
AAGLLOPSY polygalas
AAGLMMMOY mammalogy
AAGLMNORU granuloma
AAGLNNNOO nonagonal
AAGLNOOSU analogous
AAGLNQSUU aqualungs
AAGLNRTTU gratulant
AAGLNRTVY vagrantly
AAGLRRSTU gastrular
AAGLRSSTU gastrulas
AAGMMMMOR mammogram
AAGMNNOSU manganous
AAGMNORST martagons
AAGMOOPSU apogamous
AAGMRSSSU sargassum
AAGNNORTU orangutan
AAGNOORRT Rarotonga
AAGNOPRST tragopans
AAGNORRTU guarantor
AAGNORSTU angostura
argonauts
AAGNRUUUY Uruguayan
AAGOORRRT arrogator
AAGORSSSS sargassos
AAHHIIMRS maharishi

AAHHIKNSU	hanukiahs
AAHHILLNS	inshallah
AAHHIMPPT	amphipath
AAHHINPTY	hypanthia
AAHHOPRST	parashoth
AAHIIKNOV	Haakon VII
AAHIIKRST	tarakihis
AAHIILNTU	Lithuania
AAHIILRST	hairtails
AAHIIMUWY	Mu'awiyah I
AAHIINRSY	Nasiriyah
AAHIKLPSS	pashaliks
AAHIKMNNR	Imran Khan
AAHIKRSTY	Kshatriya
AAHILLLSS	shillalas
AAHILMNOT	malathion
AAHILMPPY	Pamphylia
AAHILMTUZ	azimuthal
AAHILNNST	inhalants
AAHILNORT	inhalator
AAHILNSTU	ailanthus
AAHILORTU	authorial
AAHILPSXY	asphyxial
AAHIMMNSS	shamanism
AAHIMNOPY	hypomania
AAHIMNSST	shamanist
AAHIMNSTU	amianthus
AAHINOORR	honoraria
AAHINOPRT	parathion
AAHINPTTY	antipathy
AAHINRRTU	Arthurian
AAHIOPPSS	apophasis
AAHIORSTU	haustoria
AAHIPRRSY	hairspray
AAHJNRTUV	Thanjavur
AAHKLLMRS	hallmarks
AAHKLMNOO	Oklahoman
AAHKMOSTW	tomahawks
AAHLLMOSW	Hallowmas
AAHLLOPST	allopaths
AAHLLOPTY	allopathy
AAHLLPRSY	phrasally
AAHLMNNTU	lanthanum
AAHLNNNOT	lanthanon
AAHLNPSST	ashplants
AAHLPPPSY	slaphappy
AAHLPRSSU	Pharsalus
AAHMNNPTU	Hauptmann
AAHMNNSSU	Haussmann
AAHMNORST	marathons
AAHMNOSWW	washwoman
AAHMNPPRY	paranymph
AAHMNPSST	phantasms
AAHMOPPRR	paramorph
AAHNNOOTZ	anthozoan
AAHNNOSTU	ananthous
AAHNOTTXY	anthotaxy
AAHNSTUWY	huntaways
AAHOPRSTU	autoharps
AAHOQSSUW	aquashows
AAHORTWWY	throwaway
AAIIILMRT	militaria
AAIIJJPPS	jipijapas
AAIIKNNRU	Ukrainian
AAIIKNPST	Pakistani
AAIIKPRTT	tripitaka
AAIILLMST	tallaisim
AAIILMMNS	animalism
AAIILMNNR	laminarin
AAIILMNOS	islomania
AAIILMNSS	mainsails
AAIILMNST	animalist
AAIILMNTY	animality
AAIILMPRT	impartial primatial
AAIILNOPP	palinopia
AAIILNOSU	Louisiana
AAIILNRTV	antiviral
AAIILNSTU	Lusitania
AAIILRUXY	auxiliary
AAIIMMNST	animatism
AAIIMNNOT	animation
AAIIMNNST	maintains
AAIIMNORS	Asia Minor
AAIIMNRTU	Mauritian
AAIIMNSSS	Masinissa
AAIIMORST	Timişoara
AAIIMPPRR	primipara
AAIINNRTU	unitarian
AAIINNRTV	invariant
AAIINOPRT	topiarian
AAIINORTV	variation
AAIINOSTT	satiation
AAIINPRRS	riparians
AAIINRRTU	Ruritania
AAIINRSST	intarsias
AAIIPRSST	apiarists
AAIIRSSTV	aviarists
AAIJMRSSW	swarajism
AAIJNRSSY	janissary
AAIJRSSTW	swarajist
AAIKKNOSS	skokiaans
AAIKLLOSS	alkalosis
AAIKLNNNS	alkannins
AAIKLNNRS	Sri Lankan
AAIKLNOSV	Slovakian
AAIKLOSUV	souvlakia
AAIKMNSUY	Sakyamuni
AAIKMRSST	tamarisks
AAIKNNOPT	pontianak
AAIKNOTTU	taikonaut
AAIKNQRTU	antiquark
AAIKRSTTU	autarkist
AAIKSSSTW	swastikas
AAILLLNOT	lallation
AAILLLSUV	alluvials
AAILLMMRY	mamillary
AAILLMMXY	maximally
AAILLMNST	mantillas
AAILLMOPP	papilloma
AAILLMORT	tamarillo
AAILLMPST	taillamps
AAILLMRRY	armillary
AAILLMRSY	amaryllis
AAILLMRTY	maritally martially
AAILLMRXY	maxillary
AAILLNOPT	altiplano
AAILLNOST	allantois
AAILLNOTV	vallation
AAILLNPRU	nullipara
AAILLNPSW	Aspinwall
AAILLNTVY	valiantly
AAILLOPRT	palliator
AAILLPPRY	papillary
AAILLPRTY	partially
AAILLPSTY	spatially
AAILMNNPS	plainsman
AAILMNOPT	palmation
AAILMNORT	laminator
AAILMNOST	atonalism
AAILMNPRU	manipular
AAILMNSST	talismans
AAILMNTTU	matutinal
AAILMORRS	armorials
AAILMORSU	malarious
AAILMORTY	amorality
AAILMPRSU	marsupial
AAILMPRTU	multipara
AAILMRSST	alarmists
AAILNNOPS	Annapolis
AAILNNOPT	planation
AAILNNOST	nationals santolina
AAILNNOSV	Slavonian
AAILNNPQU	palanquin
AAILNNPRU	uniplanar
AAILNNPST	plantains
AAILNNRSU	lunarians
AAILNNSST	annalists
AAILNOOTV	ovational
AAILNOPPT	palpation
AAILNOPSS	passional
AAILNOPST	talapoins
AAILNOPUW	paulownia
AAILNORSS	orinasals
AAILNORST	rationals
AAILNOSTT	saltation
AAILNOSTV	lavations salvation
AAILNOTTY	atonality
AAILNOTUV	valuation
AAILNPPTT	palpitant
AAILNPRTU	tarpaulin
AAILNPRTY	planarity
AAILNPSTU	Saint Paul
AAILNSSTW	Stanisław
AAILOPPRY	polyparia
AAILOPRRT	raptorial
AAILOPSTX	postaxial
AAILORRST	sartorial
AAILPRSSY	paralysis
AAILQRSSU	squarials
AAILSSSTY	staysails
AAIMMNNOO	monomania
AAIMMNRST	Martinmas

AAIMMNSST	mainmasts
AAIMMRSSU	samariums
AAIMNNNTU	Numantian
AAIMNNORS	San Marino
AAIMNNORU	Roumanian
AAIMNNRST	San Martín
AAIMNOORT	inamorato
AAIMNOOTY	amyotonia
AAIMNOPRY	pyromania
AAIMNORST	animators
AAIMNOSTT	anatomist
AAIMNPRSU	marsupian
AAIMNRRST	trimarans
AAIMNRSTT	tarantism
AAIMNSSST	mantissas
AAIMNSSTY	mainstays
AAIMOORRT	moratoria
AAIMOPRSS	mariposas
	parosmias
AAIMORSSU	amaurosis
	mosasauri
AAIMOSSST	Massasoit
AAIMQRSUU	aquariums
AAINNNSSY	sannyasin
AAINNNTTU	annuitant
AAINNORRT	narration
AAINNORTT	Tarantino
	tarnation
AAINNOSST	sonatinas
AAINNOSTT	natations
AAINNRSTU	Saturnian
AAINNSSSY	sannyasis
AAINOORRT	oratorian
AAINOPQRU	aquaporin
AAINOPSTT	antipasto
AAINORRSS	rosarians
AAINOSTTX	taxations
AAINPRSST	aspirants
	partisans
AAINPRSTZ	partizans
AAINPSSSY	asynapsis
AAINPSTXY	anaptyxis
AAINQRRSU	quarrians
AAINQRSTU	quatrains
AAINQRTUY	antiquary
AAINQSTTU	aquatints
AAINSSSSS	assassins
AAINSSSTT	assistant
	satanists
AAINSSTTV	avantists
AAIOPPRRT	apparitor
AAIOPRRST	aspirator
AAIOPRTTV	Pavarotti
AAIOPSTTU	autopista
AAIORRTTT	trattoria
AAIQRSSTU	aquarists
AAIRSSSTT	tsaritsas
AAIRSSTWY	stairways
AAJNORRTW	Trojan War
AAKKMORRU	Karakorum
AAKMORSUZ	mazourkas
AAKMOSSSU	moussakas
AAKNOOSST	saskatoon
AAKNOPSTV	Návpaktos
AALLMOOSS	Los Alamos
AALLMOPSS	plasmasol
AALLMPRUY	ampullary
AALLMRSYY	Sally Army
AALLNNOPY	pollyanna
AALLNNRUY	annularly
AALLNRTUY	naturally
AALLOORSW	wallaroos
AALLORRUY	aurorally
AALLORSSU	allosaurs
AALLORSVY	Yaroslavl
AALMMNOSW	almswoman
AALMNNPST	plantsman
AALMNOOSU	anomalous
AALMNOPRT	patrolman
AALMNPRTY	rampantly
AALMOOSTU	autosomal
AALMOQSSU	squamosal
AALMORTYY	mayoralty
AALMPPSSU	paspalums
AALNNOOPT	pantaloon
AALNNRTUU	unnatural
AALNOOPZZ	pozzolana
AALNOPSST	postnasal
AALNOPSTT	postnatal
AALNOPUZZ	puzzolana
AALNOSTTU	tantalous
AALNPSTWX	waxplants
AALNSSTWY	slantways
AALOPPRSV	approvals
AALOPPSST	apoplasts
AALOPRRTY	portrayal
AALOPRSST	pastorals
AALOPSSVY	Savoy Alps
AALORSTTY	saltatory
AALORSTUV	valuators
AALRSSTTW	stalwarts
AAMMOORST	Matamoros
AAMNOOTTU	automaton
AAMNOPRTU	paramount
AAMNQRRUY	quarryman
AAMOOPRST	prosomata
AAMOPRRSU	paramours
AAMOPRTTU	amputator
AAMORSSSU	mosasaurs
AANNOORTT	annotator
AANNOSSST	assonants
AANORRRST	narrators
AANORRRTW	warrantor
AANORSTTU	astronaut
AANPRSSSU	Parnassus
AANRSSTTU	saturants
AAOORRTTV	rotavator
AAOPRRSTY	raspatory
AAORRSTTU	saturator
	tartarous
AAORSSSVV	vavassors
AAORSSUVV	vavasours
AAOSSTWWY	stowaways
ABBBCELLU	clubbable
ABBBDEELR	blabbered
ABBBDEITT	babbitted
ABBBEEILR	bribeable
ABBBELRRS	brabblers
ABBBGILNR	brabbling
ABBBGILNS	babblings
	blabbings
ABBBOSSTU	subabbots
ABBCCKKLO	backblock
ABBCCKKLU	blackbuck
ABBCCKMOS	backcombs
ABBCDEERU	barbecued
ABBCDEFNO	confabbed
ABBCDEKNS	backbends
ABBCDELRS	scrabbled
ABBCDELRY	crabbedly
ABBCDIKLR	blackbird
ABBCDKLOY	blackbody
ABBCDKORU	buckboard
ABBCEEIRS	Caribbees
ABBCEERSU	barbecues
ABBCEIKRT	backbiter
ABBCEIKST	backbites
ABBCEILLM	climbable
ABBCEILRS	barbicels
ABBCEIOST	abbotcies
ABBCEIRST	crabbiest
ABBCEIRSY	crybabies
ABBCEISST	scabbiest
ABBCEKLLT	black belt
ABBCEKLNO	boneblack
ABBCEKNOS	backbones
ABBCEKNSU	buckbeans
ABBCELRRS	scrabbler
ABBCELRSS	scrabbles
ABBCGILNS	scabbling
ABBCHNRSU	subbranch
ABBCIINRS	rabbinics
ABBCIMOST	bombastic
ABBCKLLUY	buckyball
ABBCKLNRU	Blackburn
ABBCKLOOT	bootblack
ABBCKLOSW	blowbacks
ABBCKLOSY	blackboys
ABBCKLTTU	blackbutt
ABBCKNRSU	backburns
ABBCLMOOU	abcoulomb
ABBDDEMOR	bombarded
ABBDDOORY	bodyboard
ABBDEELOR	belabored
ABBDEELRS	slabbered
ABBDEELRU	bluebeard
ABBDEGINR	Banbridge
ABBDEGINU	bedaubing
ABBDEGNRU	Bundaberg
ABBDEHOOS	boobheads
ABBDEHRRU	rhubarbed
ABBDEILLU	buildable
ABBDEILOT	bobtailed
ABBDEILTU	dubitable
ABBDELLNY	bellyband
ABBDELOTU	doubtable

ABBDELQSU	squabbled
ABBDELSUU	subduable
ABBDEMORS	bombardes
ABBDENOSX	bandboxes
ABBDGILNR	drabbling
ABBDHIRST	birdbaths
ABBDHLOOT	bloodbath
ABBDILLOR	billboard
	broadbill
ABBDILTUY	dubitably
ABBDIMORR	broadbrim
ABBDLOTUY	doubtably
ABBDLSUUY	subduably
ABBDMNOOR	bombardon
ABBDNORSW	browbands
ABBDNOSTU	bandobust
ABBEEEHRS	Beersheba
ABBEEILLV	Abbeville
ABBEEJRRS	jabberers
ABBEEKLRU	rebukable
ABBEEKNOR	breakbone
ABBEELLMS	semblable
ABBEELOPR	probeable
ABBEELRRS	slabberer
ABBEELRRY	blaeberry
ABBEENRRY	baneberry
ABBEEOSTX	beatboxes
ABBEERRRY	bearberry
ABBEERSTT	barbettes
ABBEFILST	flabbiest
ABBEGIJNR	jabbering
ABBEGILLO	obligable
ABBEGINRR	barbering
ABBEGINRT	rabbeting
ABBEGLRRS	grabblers
ABBEHINOS	Hobbesian
ABBEHISST	shabbiest
ABBEHLOTU	tabbouleh
ABBEHORST	bathrobes
ABBEIKNRU	Burkinabé
ABBEILMOT	bombilate
ABBEILMRR	bramblier
ABBEILMSU	Abu Simbel
ABBEILSST	bistables
ABBEILSSU	bubalises
ABBEILSTW	wabbliest
ABBEIMNOR	Barenboim
ABBEIMNOS	bombasine
ABBEIMNOT	bombinate
ABBEIMNOZ	bombazine
ABBEIMRSU	berimbaus
ABBEINORT	barbitone
ABBEIRRST	rabbiters
ABBEKLOOR	brookable
ABBELLMPU	plumbable
ABBELLMSY	semblably
ABBELMOOZ	bamboozle
ABBELOPRS	probables
ABBELORSU	belabours
ABBELOSTY	stableboy
ABBELQRSU	squabbler
ABBELQSSU	squabbles
ABBELSTTU	battlebus
ABBENORST	absorbent
ABBEORRSS	absorbers
	reabsorbs
ABBEORSTW	browbeats
ABBERSUUU	subbureau
ABBESSSSU	subbasses
ABBFHLLSU	flashbulb
ABBFLOOST	bobfloats
ABBGGILNR	grabbling
ABBGIILOT	obbligati
ABBGIINRT	rabbiting
ABBGIJLNY	jabbingly
ABBGILLNO	billabong
ABBGILMNR	brambling
ABBGILOOT	obbligato
ABBGINNOT	Babington
ABBGINORS	absorbing
ABBGIORUU	Bourguiba
ABBHIINRT	B'nai B'rith
ABBHIOPST	abbotship
ABBHIORST	rabbitohs
ABBIIMNRS	rabbinism
ABBIINRST	rabbinist
ABBILLOST	boatbills
ABBILLSSU	sillabubs
ABBINORRU	Brian Boru
ABBJMRUUU	Bujumbura
ABBKKNOOS	bankbooks
ABBLLSSUY	syllabubs
ABBNRSSUU	suburbans
ABCCCCIOO	Boccaccio
ABCCCEFIO	beccafico
ABCCCKKLO	blackcock
ABCCDEEHN	bechanced
ABCCDHIKS	dabchicks
ABCCEEFRY	cybercafe
ABCCEEHKL	checkable
ABCCEEHNS	bechances
ABCCEENRU	buccaneer
ABCCEIIST	scabietic
ABCCEIKLL	clickable
ABCCEINOV	biconcave
ABCCEKMOS	comebacks
ABCCELNRU	carbuncle
ABCCELORY	cryocable
ABCCEMNRU	cumbrance
ABCCEMNTU	accumbent
ABCCEOOST	tobaccoes
ABCCFIINO	Fibonacci
ABCCFIMOR	bacciform
ABCCHHKNU	hunchback
ABCCHIOOR	Barocchio
ABCCHKLOT	backcloth
ABCCHKOTU	touchback
ABCCHNOOR	Conchobar
ABCCHNOOS	cabochons
ABCCIKKKS	kickbacks
ABCCIKRST	crabstick
ABCCILLOU	bucolical
ABCCILLUY	cubically
ABCCILNOO	obconical
ABCCILORU	corbicula
ABCCIRSTU	subarctic
ABCCKKOOR	crookback
ABCCKNOTU	countback
ABCCKOOST	cockboats
ABCCKORSS	backcross
ABCCKORTU	backcourt
ABCCMOORY	mobocracy
ABCDDEEHU	debauched
ABCDDEEIL	decidable
ABCDDEILU	adducible
ABCDDEKLO	blockaded
ABCDDENOS	absconded
ABCDDKORU	duckboard
ABCDEEEHL	de la Beche
ABCDEEEHU	debauchee
ABCDEEHMR	chambered
ABCDEEHRU	debaucher
ABCDEEHSU	debauches
ABCDEEILM	medicable
ABCDEEILR	calibered
ABCDEEKLN	blackened
ABCDEEKRT	bracketed
ABCDEELMR	clambered
ABCDEESSS	abscessed
ABCDEFIKL	backfield
ABCDEFIKR	backfired
ABCDEGIKR	ridgeback
ABCDEGIMR	Cambridge
ABCDEGIRS	birdcages
ABCDEHIOT	cohabited
ABCDEHKLO	blockhead
ABCDEHOOT	cohobated
ABCDEIIST	diabetics
ABCDEIJLU	judicable
ABCDEIKLS	backslide
ABCDEIKRU	rudbeckia
ABCDEIKSS	backsides
ABCDEILMY	medicably
ABCDEILNO	balconied
ABCDEILTU	decubital
ABCDEINTU	incubated
ABCDEIORT	bacteroid
ABCDEIPRU	Pardubice
ABCDEIRTT	bratticed
ABCDEKLNY	Clydebank
ABCDEKLOR	blockader
ABCDEKLOS	blockades
ABCDEKMRU	buckramed
ABCDEKNNS	neckbands
ABCDELLOS	scoldable
ABCDELMNO	Candomblé
ABCDELMRS	scrambled
ABCDEMNSU	dumbcanes
ABCDENORR	cornbread
ABCDENORS	absconder
ABCDENOSU	casebound
	subdeacon
ABCDEOORT	obcordate
ABCDGINOR	brocading
ABCDGINTU	abducting
ABCDHINRS	disbranch

ABCDHIOPR chipboard
ABCDHIRSY Charybdis
ABCDHKLOS holdbacks
ABCDIKRRY brickyard
ABCDILOPR clipboard
ABCDILSUY subacidly
ABCDINOOT bandicoot
ABCDINOTU abduction
ABCDIOOSU bodacious
ABCDKLOOR roadblock
ABCDKLOOW blackwood
ABCDKNOSW backdowns
ABCDKOORR corkboard
ABCDKOOSW backwoods
ABCDKOPRS backdrops
ABCDKORSW backsword
backwords
ABCDLNRSU scrubland
ABCDOORSW crabwoods
ABCDOPRSU cupboards
ABCDORSTU abductors
ABCEEELLR cerebella
ABCEEELLT electable
ABCEEELRT celebrate
erectable
ABCEEELRX execrable
ABCEEENRR cerberean
ABCEEERRT cerebrate
ABCEEFHRU Feuerbach
ABCEEFIRS briefcase
ABCEEFLOR forceable
ABCEEGKNR greenback
ABCEEHIOT cohabitee
ABCEEHIRT Rechabite
ABCEEHKLO chokeable
ABCEEHLLP Pachelbel
ABCEEHLLY bellyache
ABCEEHLRS bleachers
ABCEEILLS sliceable
ABCEEILNV bivalence
ABCEEILRT recitable
ABCEEILST celibates
ABCEEILSX excisable
ABCEEILTX excitable
ABCEEIMMS misbecame
ABCEEINOS obeisance
ABCEEINRR carbineer
ABCEEKKNR breakneck
ABCEEKPSW sweepback
ABCEELMNS semblance
ABCEELMRR clamberer
ABCEELMRY cymbaleer
ABCEELNRT celebrant
ABCEELNST albescent
ABCEELNUU nubeculae
ABCEELOPS placeboes
ABCEELORT bracteole
ABCEELORV coverable
revocable
ABCEELOTV covetable
ABCEELRRS cerebrals
ABCEELRST bracelets
ABCEELRSU rescuable
securable
ABCEELRXY execrably
ABCEELSUX excusable
ABCEEMMOR Morecambe
ABCEEMORR embraceor
ABCEEMORT embrocate
ABCEEMOTY amebocyte
ABCEEMRRS embracers
ABCEEMRRY embracery
ABCEENORY Conybeare
ABCEENOSZ cabezones
ABCEENRTY cybernate
ABCEENSTT tabescent
ABCEEORST obsecrate
ABCEEOSSU sebaceous
ABCEEPRRU cupbearer
ABCEESSSS abscesses
ABCEFFHNO Offenbach
ABCEFHLSU flashcube
ABCEFIKLS backfiles
ABCEFIKRS backfires
firebacks
ABCEFIRTU bifurcate
ABCEFLOSU focusable
ABCEFOSTU obfuscate
ABCEGHILN bleaching
ABCEGHINR breaching
ABCEGHLNO Long Beach
ABCEGILOR bricolage
ABCEGILOT cogitable
ABCEGIMNR cambering
embracing
ABCEGINNO beaconing
ABCEGKLLS blacklegs
ABCEGKLOS blockages
ABCEGKMSU megabucks
ABCEGKRSY greybacks
ABCEGKRTU tuckerbag
ABCEHILTY chalybite
ABCEHINOT aitchbone
ABCEHIORT cohabiter
ABCEHKLLS shellback
ABCEHKLOS shockable
shoeblack
ABCEHKMNR benchmark
ABCEHKORS horseback
ABCEHKRRY hackberry
ABCEHKTUW buckwheat
ABCEHLNTT Blanchett
ABCEHLORS bachelors
ABCEHLOTU touchable
ABCEHLRSU crushable
ABCEHLSSU chasubles
ABCEHMOST hecatombs
ABCEHOOST cohobates
ABCEHOQRU quebracho
ABCEHORRS broachers
ABCEHORSU barouches
ABCEHORTU tarbouche
ABCEHRSTU Bucharest
ABCEIILNS sibilance
ABCEIILRS irascible
ABCEIIMRT imbricate
ABCEIJLNU jubilance
ABCEIJNOT abjection
ABCEIKLLS Black Isle
ABCEIKRRV Back River
ABCEIKSWZ zwiebacks
ABCEILLOS obeliscal
ABCEILLPP clippable
ABCEILMOT metabolic
ABCEILMST blastemic
cembalist
ABCEILNNS binnacles
ABCEILNOS balconies
ABCEILNOT cobaltine
ABCEILNOV invocable
ABCEILNRU binuclear
incurable
ABCEILNVY bivalency
ABCEILORS cabrioles
carbolise
ABCEILORT cabriolet
ABCEILORZ carbolize
ABCEILOTT cobaltite
ABCEILRTU lubricate
ABCEILRUX Excalibur
ABCEILSTU bisulcate
ABCEILTXY excitably
ABCEIMOTV combative
ABCEIMRSW micawbers
ABCEIMRTU bacterium
ABCEINORS carbonise
ABCEINORT bicornate
ABCEINORZ carbonize
ABCEINRSS brisances
ABCEINRST bacterins
ABCEINSST bascinets
ABCEINSTU incubates
ABCEIOPTT betatopic
ABCEIRRSU carburise
ABCEIRRTU rubricate
ABCEIRRUZ carburize
ABCEIRSTT brattices
ABCEJNSTU subjacent
ABCEJOSSU jacobuses
ABCEKKSSW skewbacks
ABCEKLLNR Bracknell
ABCEKLMOR Blackmore
ABCEKLNSS blackness
ABCEKLPRU parbuckle
ABCEKOOSS bookcases
casebooks
ABCEKPSTW backswept
sweptback
ABCEKRTUW waterbuck
ABCELLOOR colorable
ABCELLRSU subcellar
ABCELLRSW screwball
ABCELLRUV curveball
ABCELMOOR rocambole
ABCELMRRS scrambler
ABCELMRSS scrambles

ABCELMRSY cymbalers
ABCELNOST constable
ABCELNOTU countable
ABCELOOST bootlaces
ABCELORVY revocably
ABCELOSST obstacles
ABCELOSTT ectoblast
ABCELRSST bractless
ABCELRSTT bractlets
ABCELRSTU scrutable
ABCELRTUU lucubrate
ABCELSSUU subclause
ABCELSUXY excusably
ABCEMOOSS cambooses
ABCEMORSS crossbeam
ABCEMORST combaters
ABCEMRSUV verbascum
ABCENORTY baronetcy
ABCENRRRY cranberry
ABCENRTUU bucentaur
ABCENSSTU substance
ABCEOOPRS baroscope
ABCEOPRRY reprobacy
ABCERRSTU carburets
ABCERRSWY cyberwars
ABCFGHIKT fightback
ABCFHIKLS blackfish
ABCFHRSTU bushcraft
ABCFIKLLS backfills
ABCFKLLSU fullbacks
ABCGGIKPY piggyback
ABCGHIKLT backlight
ABCGHIKST backsight
ABCGHILNN blanching
ABCGHINNR branching
ABCGHINOR broaching
ABCGHNPSU punchbags
ABCGHOORV Gorbachov
ABCGIINRS ascribing
ABCGIINSS abscising
ABCGIKLNS blackings
slingback
ABCGILNRY bracingly
ABCGIMNOT combating
ABCGIMNRS scrambing
ABCGINNRU unbracing
ABCHHIKRU Kuch Bihar
ABCHHKSUW bushwhack
ABCHIILLN chilblain
ABCHIIMOR choriambi
ABCHIIOST isobathic
ABCHIIRSU Suribachi
ABCHILMOS shambolic
ABCHILNOR bronchial
ABCHILOOS coolibahs
ABCHIMORS choriambs
ABCHIRRST tribrachs
ABCHKLOSW howlbacks
ABCHKMPSU humpbacks
ABCHKMRSU marshbuck
ABCHKMTTU thumbtack
ABCHKNORT thornback
ABCHKOOPS chapbooks
ABCHKOOSS cashbooks
ABCHKORSV boschvark
ABCHKORTW throwback
ABCHLLNPU punchball
ABCHLLSUU clubhauls
ABCHLRWYZ Wałbrzych
ABCIIIKLW bailiwick
ABCIIILPT bicipital
ABCIIKNRS brainsick
ABCIIKRRS airbricks
ABCIILLMU umbilical
ABCIILLST ballistic
ABCIILMOR microbial
ABCIILNOT albinotic
ABCIILNSY sibilancy
ABCIILORU Roubiliac
ABCIILRSY irascibly
ABCIIMNOR microbian
ABCIINRRU rubrician
ABCIIOPRY biopiracy
ABCIIOSTT biostatic
ABCIIRSTY sybaritic
ABCIJLNUY jubilancy
ABCIKLLST blacklist
ABCILLMRU lumbrical
ABCILLNSY billycans
ABCILLORU bilocular
ABCILLSSY syllabics
ABCILMMOS cimbaloms
ABCILMNOO Colombian
ABCILMNOU Columbian
ABCILMOPY amblyopic
ABCILMSTY cymbalist
ABCILMSUX subclimax
ABCILNNOU connubial
ABCILNORU binocular
ABCILNPSU publicans
ABCILNRTU lubricant
ABCILNRUY incurably
ABCILOPSY polybasic
ABCILORRU courbaril
orbicular
ABCILOSSU subsocial
ABCIMNOOS monobasic
ABCIMNORU carbonium
ABCIMOSTU subatomic
ABCIMRSTY cambistry
ABCINOORR Rio Branco
ABCINORTU incubator
ABCINOSTY obstinacy
ABCJKOOST bootjacks
jackboots
ABCKKLMNO Black Monk
ABCKLLLOP blackpoll
ABCKLLOOP Blackpool
ABCKLLPSU pullbacks
ABCKLOPST blacktops
ABCKLOSTU blackouts
ABCKMOSSS mossbacks
ABCKNORSU Osnabrück
ABCKNORUY Ayckbourn
ABCKOOPRS scrapbook
ABCKOORRS roorbacks
ABCKOORSU buckaroos
ABCKOPSST backstops
ABCLLNORS cornballs
ABCLMMOSY cymbaloms
ABCLMNNOT Mont Blanc
ABCLMNOUW clubwoman
ABCLMOOOS colobomas
ABCLNORSY carbonyls
ABCLNOWYY Colwyn Bay
ABCLOOSTU cobaltous
ABCMOORST mobocrats
ABCMOSSUU submucosa
ABCNOORSU carbonous
ABCNORSTU obscurant
ABCNORSTY corybants
ABCORRSSS crossbars
ABCORRSTU turbocars
ABCRSSTTU subtracts
ABDDDEELR bladdered
ABDDDEINS disbanded
ABDDEEEST besteaded
ABDDEEGHI bigheaded
ABDDEEHLS sheddable
ABDDEEHST deathbeds
ABDDEELLU deludable
ABDDEELMO beadledom
ABDDEELUW bulwaddee
ABDDEELZZ bedazzled
ABDDEENOR broadened
ABDDEENRR rebranded
ABDDEEPRS bedspread
ABDDEESST bedsteads
ABDDEFILN deafblind
ABDDEGLLO dodgeball
ABDDEHIIT adhibited
ABDDEHMOS hebdomads
ABDDEHNSU husbanded
ABDDEIILV dividable
ABDDEILSU buddleias
ABDDEINSS sidebands
ABDDEIORS broadside
sideboard
ABDDEIPRU upbraided
ABDDEIRRS disbarred
ABDDEISSU disabused
ABDDELOSW saddlebow
ABDDGORUY bodyguard
ABDDHINTW bandwidth
ABDDHNORU hardbound
ABDDILRSY ladybirds
ABDDIMNOS bondmaids
ABDDIRRSY yardbirds
ABDDLLUWY bullwaddy
ABDDLMOOR moldboard
ABDEEEFLR deferable
ABDEEEFRS freebased
ABDEEEGLL delegable
ABDEEEHTT hebetated
ABDEEELLR relabeled
ABDEEELMN emendable

ABDEEELRY	bleareyed
ABDEEEMRS	besmeared
ABDEEESWX	beeswaxed
ABDEEFHIR	Faidherbe
ABDEEFIIT	beatified
ABDEEFILN	definable
ABDEEFORR	freeboard
ABDEEGGLR	bedraggle
ABDEEGHIN	beheading
ABDEEGINR	gaberdine
ABDEEGJLU	judgeable
ABDEEGLLO	lodgeable
ABDEEGLLP	pledgable
ABDEEGMOR	embargoed
ABDEEGORR	garderobe
ABDEEGRRY	greybeard
ABDEEHINR	Hebridean
ABDEEHIRS	braeheids
ABDEEHIRZ	hebraized
ABDEEHLRT	blathered
ABDEEHNOS	boneheads
ABDEEHRSW	shewbread
ABDEEHSST	bethesdas
ABDEEIILR	diablerie
ABDEEIINR	badinerie
ABDEEIKRS	bidarkees
ABDEEILLW	wieldable
ABDEEILLY	yieldable
ABDEEILMS	Ambleside
	demisable
ABDEEILMT	bedlamite
ABDEEILNR	breadline
ABDEEILNS	disenable
ABDEEILRS	desirable
ABDEEILRT	liberated
ABDEEILRV	derivable
	driveable
ABDEEILSV	devisable
ABDEEINSS	beadiness
ABDEEINSW	Wiesbaden
ABDEEINTT	bidentate
ABDEEINTU	butadiene
ABDEEIRSU	dauberies
ABDEEITTU	beatitude
ABDEELLLY	Leadbelly
ABDEELLPS	speedball
ABDEELLRR	barrelled
ABDEELLRV	verballed
ABDEELLTY	belatedly
ABDEELMRT	Alembert, d'
	d'Alembert
ABDEELMSS	assembled
ABDEELMTT	embattled
ABDEELNOR	banderole
	bandoleer
ABDEELNOT	denotable
ABDEELNPR	prebendal
ABDEELNPS	spendable
ABDEELNRU	endurable
ABDEELNRY	blarneyed
ABDEELOPS	deposable
ABDEELORS	leeboards
ABDEELPST	bedplates
ABDEELRSS	beardless
ABDEELRSY	Beardsley
ABDEELSSU	subleased
ABDEELSZZ	bedazzles
ABDEEMNRT	debarment
ABDEEMNSU	sunbeamed
ABDEEMRRW	bedwarmer
ABDEEMRSY	Ember days
ABDEENOTY	bayoneted
ABDEENQTU	banqueted
ABDEENRRT	bartender
ABDEENTTU	debutante
ABDEEOPST	speedboat
ABDEEORRU	bordereau
ABDEEPRSS	bespreads
ABDEERRST	redbreast
ABDEERVYY	Berdyayev
ABDEFFLOU	buffaloed
ABDEFHOOS	boofheads
ABDEFIISX	basifixed
ABDEFILNY	definably
ABDEFINRR	firebrand
ABDEFLLOO	floodable
ABDEFLOTW	batfowled
ABDEFORRT	fretboard
ABDEFORTY	afterbody
ABDEGGGIN	debagging
ABDEGGINR	badgering
ABDEGGMOR	beggardom
ABDEGGMRU	Magdeburg
ABDEGHLRU	Aldeburgh
ABDEGIINU	biguanide
ABDEGIIRR	brigadier
ABDEGIKNR	debarking
ABDEGILOT	obligated
ABDEGINRR	debarring
ABDEGIRRS	abridgers
ABDEGLLMO	gambolled
ABDEGLSSU	slugabeds
ABDEGOPRS	pegboards
ABDEGRSSU	subgrades
ABDEGRTUY	budgetary
ABDEHIINT	inhabited
ABDEHILNO	hobnailed
ABDEHILOS	abolished
ABDEHIRTW	Whitbread
ABDEHISTU	habitudes
ABDEHKLSU	bulkheads
ABDEHKNOS	knobheads
ABDEHLLNS	handbells
ABDEHLLSU	bullheads
ABDEHLOOT	bloodheat
ABDEHLOTW	deathblow
ABDEHLOUX	boxhauled
ABDEHNRRT	Bernhardt
ABDEHNRSU	husbander
ABDEHNSTU	sunbathed
ABDEHORRU	harboured
ABDEHORSW	showbread
ABDEHRRSY	shadberry
ABDEIIIYZ	Bayezid II
ABDEIILNU	inaudible
ABDEIILNV	divinable
ABDEIILOS	diabolise
ABDEIILOZ	diabolize
ABDEIILST	sibilated
ABDEIIRST	diatribes
ABDEIJLTU	jubilated
ABDEIKLMR	Abd-el-Krim
ABDEIKLNR	drinkable
ABDEIKMRS	disembark
ABDEIKNRS	snakebird
ABDEIKNRW	windbreak
ABDEIKNSU	baudekins
ABDEILLLO	labelloid
ABDEILLLR	drillable
ABDEILLLU	lullabied
ABDEILMNS	mandibles
ABDEILMOR	bromeliad
ABDEILNNO	bandoline
ABDEILNOR	bandolier
ABDEILNRS	bilanders
ABDEILOPR	parboiled
ABDEILRSY	desirably
ABDEIMNRU	Bermudian
ABDEINNRS	endbrains
ABDEINOST	botanised
ABDEINOSY	anybodies
ABDEINOTZ	botanized
ABDEINRSS	rabidness
ABDEINRSU	urbanised
ABDEINRUZ	urbanized
ABDEINSSU	unbiassed
ABDEINSSW	bawdiness
ABDEINTTU	intubated
ABDEIOSST	beastoids
ABDEIPRRU	upbraider
ABDEIRRTW	waterbird
ABDEISSSU	disabuses
ABDEKLRUW	bulwarked
ABDEKLSSW	skewbalds
ABDEKNORW	breakdown
ABDEKORRW	wordbreak
ABDEKORSY	keyboards
ABDELLLSY	syllabled
ABDELLMOU	mouldable
ABDELLNOO	ballooned
ABDELLORS	beadrolls
ABDELLORY	laboredly
ABDELLOTU	lobulated
ABDELMNOY	baldmoney
ABDELMOTY	molybdate
ABDELNNSS	blandness
ABDELNORS	banderols
ABDELNOST	endoblast
ABDELNOSU	soundable
ABDELNOUW	woundable
ABDELNRUY	endurably
ABDELNSTU	Dunstable
ABDELORUV	boulevard
ABDELOSSW	dowsabels
ABDELTTUU	tubulated
ABDEMNRRT	Rembrandt

ABDEMORTU tamboured
ABDEMRSTU drumbeats
ABDENNNOO bandoneon
ABDENNOSS nosebands
ABDENNTTU Butenandt
ABDENOPRR Paderborn
ABDENORSS broadness
ABDENORST adsorbent
ABDENORSY boneyards
ABDENOSSX sandboxes
ABDENOSTU eastbound
ABDENOSTW downbeats
ABDENRSTU breadnuts
ABDENRSTY bystander
ABDEOORRT breadroot
ABDEOORRV overboard
ABDEOORSW bearwoods
ABDEOORWZ zebrawood
ABDEORRSW wardrobes
ABDEORTTU obturated
ABDEORTUV outbraved
ABDERSSTW bedstraws
ABDERSTUW drawtubes
ABDFGLMOO Lamb of God
ABDFIIRRR friarbird
ABDFLOOST foldboats
ABDFNORRT Brantford
ABDFOOORT footboard
ABDFORRSU surfboard
ABDGGIINR abridging
brigading
ABDGHINOY hobdaying
ABDGHINRS hangbirds
ABDGIILNS disabling
ABDGIILNY abidingly
ABDGIINRS braidings
ABDGILNNR brandling
ABDGILORS gaolbirds
ABDGINNOU abounding
ABDGINORS adsorbing
boardings
signboard
ABDGINRRY brigandry
ABDGLOPRU plugboard
ABDHIINNR hindbrain
ABDHILLNS handbills
ABDHILORT Bartholdi
ABDHIMORY hybridoma
ABDHIMRTY dithyramb
ABDHIOPRS shipboard
ABDHIRSTY birthdays
ABDHKNOOS handbooks
ABDHLORSW blowhards
ABDHMOSTU badmouths
ABDHNOSUY Hudson Bay
ABDHNRSUY husbandry
ABDHOOSWX shadowbox
ABDIIILLN libidinal
ABDIIJLRS jailbirds
ABDIILLRS billiards
ABDIILMOS diabolism
ABDIILNUY inaudibly
ABDIILOST diabolist
idioblast
ABDIIMNRS midbrains
ABDIIMPRY bipyramid
ABDIIMRST tribadism
ABDIINOUU Baudouin I
ABDIINRRS rainbirds
ABDIKMORS skimboard
ABDILLMOR millboard
ABDILRSZZ blizzards
ABDIMNNOT badminton
ABDINNOSU Nabonidus
ABDINNRUU Burundian
ABDINORUY duobinary
ABDINRSTW wristband
ABDIOORRW briarwood
ABDIRSTUY absurdity
ABDJMOORS doorjambs
ABDLLNSUW bundwalls
ABDLMOOOR broadloom
ABDLORSSU subdorsal
ABDMMNOSU ombudsman
ABDMNORTU Dumbarton
ABDMOOORR boardroom
Broadmoor
ABDNOORSW snowboard
ABDNSSTUU butsudans
ABDOORSTU outboards
ABDOOSSSW basswoods
ABEEEEFRT beefeater
ABEEEFKST beefsteak
ABEEEFLRR referable
ABEEEFLRZ freezable
ABEEEFRSS freebases
ABEEEGGRT eggbeater
ABEEEGLNR generable
ABEEEGLRU beleaguer
ABEEEGLTV vegetable
ABEEEGRSV beverages
ABEEEHLSW wheelbase
ABEEEHSTT hebetates
ABEEEINRS beaneries
ABEEEKNRV breakeven
ABEEEKPRR barkeeper
ABEEELMPR permeable
ABEEELNRT enterable
ABEEELNRV venerable
ABEEELNRW renewable
ABEEELRRV reverable
ABEEELRST steerable
ABEEELRSV serveable
severable
ABEEENSST absentees
ABEEERRTT terebrate
ABEEERRTV vertebrae
ABEEERTUX exuberate
ABEEERWYZ breezeway
ABEEESSWX beeswaxes
ABEEFFILN ineffable
ABEEFFNOS banoffees
ABEEFGLOR forgeable
ABEEFIIST beatifies
ABEEFIKRR firebreak
ABEEFILNR inferable
refinable
ABEEFILRS balefires
ABEEFILST fleabites
ABEEFLRSU refusable
ABEEFLRTU refutable
ABEEFORRR forbearer
ABEEFORRS forebears
ABEEGGLOR gorgeable
ABEEGHILW weighable
ABEEGHNOR habergeon
ABEEGHRTU hagbuteer
ABEEGILNN bengaline
ABEEGIMNN bemeaning
ABEEGINRS Bering Sea
ABEEGINRU aubergine
ABEEGINRV beavering
bereaving
ABEEGKORR brokerage
ABEEGLLRU regulable
ABEEGLMNR embrangle
ABEEGLNPR pregnable
ABEEGLNPS bespangle
ABEEGLOPR bargepole
porbeagle
ABEEGLRTT Great Belt
ABEEGLSSU guessable
ABEEGMNRW wambenger
ABEEGMORS embargoes
ABEEGMSTY megabytes
ABEEGNORS Boanerges
Gaberones
ABEEGNORZ bronze age
ABEEGNRSU subgenera
ABEEGNSTT bagnettes
ABEEGORSX gearboxes
ABEEGSTTU baguettes
ABEEHHKSS baksheesh
ABEEHILRT heritable
ABEEHILST Elisabeth
ABEEHILTZ Elizabeth
ABEEHIMSV misbehave
ABEEHIMTW whitebeam
ABEEHINRS abhenries
ABEEHINRT hibernate
inbreathe
ABEEHIRRT breathier
ABEEHIRSZ hebraizes
ABEEHKOSU bakehouse
ABEEHLLRS harebells
ABEEHLMPS blaspheme
ABEEHLNOW whalebone
ABEEHNORS horsebean
ABEEHNRTY abernethy
ABEEHNSTU Bhutanese
ABEEHORRS seborrhea
ABEEHORSS rheobases
ABEEHORTU hereabout
ABEEHQSTU bequeaths
ABEEHRRST breathers
ABEEHRSTT hartbeest

ABEEIINRT inebriate
ABEEIIRST biseriate
ABEEIKNST snakebite
ABEEILLMR mirabelle
ABEEILLRV relivable
ABEEILMPT emptiable
ABEEILMRS miserable
ABEEILMST estimable
ABEEILMTT timetable
ABEEILNPS plebeians
ABEEILNQU inequable
ABEEILNRR inerrable
ABEEILNSS baselines
ABEEILNSU banlieues
ABEEILQTU equitable
ABEEILRRW rewirable
ABEEILRST beastlier
bleariest
liberates
ABEEILRSV revisable
verbalise
ABEEILRSW bewailers
ABEEILRTT albertite
ABEEILRTV avertible
veritable
ABEEILRVV revivable
ABEEILRVZ verbalize
ABEEIMSSS embassies
ABEEINSST asbestine
ABEEIPRST rebaptise
ABEEIPRTZ rebaptize
ABEEIRRSS brasserie
brassiere
ABEEIRRST biserrate
ABEEIRSTT batteries
ABEEJLLNY jellybean
ABEEJLMSU Jebel Musa
ABEEJLNOY enjoyable
ABEEJMORS jamborees
ABEEKLMOS smokeable
ABEEKLNNO anklebone
ABEEKLNSS bleakness
ABEEKLORV revokable
ABEEKLOST keelboats
ABEEKLRSS brakeless
ABEEKMNRS brakesmen
ABEEKMRRS reembarks
ABEELLLPS spellable
ABEELLLRS labellers
ABEELLMSS blameless
ABEELLMTU umbellate
ABEELLNRT netballer
ABEELLORT tolerable
ABEELLORW lowerable
ABEELLOVV evolvable
ABEELLSST tableless
ABEELMMOR memorable
ABEELMMRS embalmers
ABEELMNRU numerable
ABEELMNST stablemen
ABEELMORV removable
ABEELMOSV moveables
ABEELMPRS preambles
ABEELMPRY permeably
ABEELMPTT temptable
ABEELMRSS assembler
ABEELMRSU resumable
ABEELMSSS assembles
ABEELMSTT embattles
ABEELNNTU untenable
ABEELNOPS beanpoles
ABEELNOST stoneable
ABEELNRVY venerably
ABEELOPSX exposable
ABEELPRRV preverbal
ABEELPRSU superable
ABEELPRTU reputable
ABEELRRTV vertebral
ABEELRRUY La Bruyère
ABEELRSVW swervable
ABEELRTTU utterable
ABEELSSSU subleases
ABEEMMNRS membranes
ABEEMMNTY embayment
ABEEMMRSU bummarees
ABEEMNPRU penumbrae
ABEEMNSST basements
ABEEMNSTT abetments
ABEEMNTTT battement
ABEEMORRT barometer
ABEEMRRSU embrasure
ABEEMRSTW webmaster
ABEENNRST bannerets
ABEENOSTZ benzoates
ABEENQRTU banqueter
ABEENQTTU banquette
ABEENRRST banterers
ABEENRRSY naseberry
ABEENRSST absenters
steenbras
ABEENRSSV braveness
ABEENRTUX exuberant
ABEEOPRRT perborate
reprobate
ABEEORRSV overbears
ABEEOSTUU beauteous
ABEEPRSTT bespatter
ABEERRRST barterers
ABEERRSTT barrettes
batterers
berrettas
ABEERRSTV vertebras
ABEERRSTY betrayers
ABEERRSWY bewrayers
ABEERSTTY Bay Street
ABEFFILNY ineffably
ABEFFKORS breakoffs
ABEFFLOSU buffaloes
ABEFGILLN befalling
ABEFGILNR frangible
ABEFHISST batfishes
ABEFIILLR fibrillae
ABEFIILNU unifiable
ABEFIILOT bifoliate
ABEFIIMRT fimbriate
ABEFILLRS fireballs
ABEFILLRT filtrable
ABEFILNRU funebrial
ABEFILNRY inferably
ABEFILOST lifeboats
ABEFILTUU beautiful
ABEFIMORS framboise
ABEFINORR forebrain
ABEFINOSX Foxe Basin
ABEFIORST fireboats
ABEFIOSTY biosafety
ABEFIRRST firebrats
ABEFKLSTU basketful
ABEFLLLMU flabellum
ABEFLLLUY balefully
ABEFLLNUY banefully
ABEFLLRRU barrelful
ABEFLLSTU tablefuls
ABEFLNOSW wolfsbane
ABEFLORTW batfowler
ABEFLRTUY refutably
ABEFORRTY ferryboat
ABEFRTTTU butterfat
ABEGGGINR beggaring
ABEGGGLLU gluggable
ABEGGINSS bagginess
ABEGGISTY gigabytes
ABEGGNOPS spongebag
ABEGHILRT rightable
ABEGHILST sightable
ABEGHINRR harbinger
ABEGHINRT breathing
ABEGHMRRU hamburger
ABEGHRSSU sagebrush
ABEGHRTTU hagbutter
ABEGIILLT litigable
ABEGIILMT mitigable
ABEGIILNS abseiling
ABEGIILNT ignitable
ABEGIILNW bewailing
ABEGIILRR irrigable
ABEGIINOR aborigine
ABEGIKMNN embanking
ABEGIKMNR embarking
ABEGILLLN labelling
ABEGILLOS globalise
ABEGILLOZ globalize
ABEGILMMN embalming
ABEGILMNZ emblazing
ABEGILNOR ignorable
ABEGILNRR barreling
ABEGILNST bleatings
tangibles
ABEGILOST obligates
ABEGIMNNO bemoaning
ABEGIMRRS ambergris
ABEGINNNT benignant
ABEGINNOW Winnebago
ABEGINNRT bantering
ABEGINNRY barneying
ABEGINNRZ brazening

ABEGINNST	absenting
ABEGINNTT	battening
ABEGINRRS	berrigans
ABEGINRRT	bartering
ABEGINRST	breasting
ABEGINRTT	battering
ABEGINRTY	betraying
ABEGINRUY	guberniya
ABEGINRWY	bewraying
ABEGINSST	basseting
	beastings
ABEGINSTW	swingbeat
ABEGJORTU	objurgate
ABEGJSTUU	subjugate
ABEGKORSS	grosbeaks
ABEGKRSTU	grubstake
ABEGLLNNY	Glen Albyn
ABEGLLNOU	Lobengula
ABEGLNORU	Boulanger
ABEGLNUUW	Bangweulu
ABEGLRSSU	bluegrass
ABEGMMMRU	brummagem
ABEGMNOOR	boomerang
ABEGMNOSS	gambesons
ABEGMNOSY	moneybags
ABEGMORST	bergamots
ABEGNSSTU	subagents
ABEGOORST	botargoes
ABEGORSTU	subrogate
ABEGRRSUV	burgraves
ABEGSSSTU	substages
ABEHHISSU	hushabies
ABEHHLLOZ	Hezbollah
ABEHHOSTU	bathhouse
ABEHIINNR	Hibernian
ABEHIITTW	whitebait
ABEHIKLNT	thinkable
ABEHILMOP	amphibole
ABEHILOPR	barophile
ABEHILOPS	basophile
ABEHILORS	abolisher
ABEHILOSS	abolishes
ABEHILOTT	batholite
ABEHILPPS	shippable
ABEHILRST	herbalist
ABEHILRSY	bearishly
ABEHILRTY	breathily
	heritably
ABEHILSST	establish
ABEHIMMSS	memsahibs
ABEHIMNOS	bohemians
ABEHIMRRU	herbarium
ABEHINOOP	neophobia
ABEHIOPRU	euphorbia
ABEHIORSV	behaviors
ABEHIORUV	behaviour
ABEHIRRTT	birthrate
ABEHIRSST	brashiest
ABEHKLLRS	shellbark
ABEHKLMMU	Kumbh Mela
ABEHKNNOV	København
ABEHLLNWY	Newby Hall
ABEHLMNSU	bushelman
ABEHLMPSY	blasphemy
ABEHLNNSU	shunnable
ABEHLNOOR	honorable
ABEHLOPRY	hyperbola
ABEHLORTT	betrothal
ABEHMNORS	hornbeams
ABEHMOORS	rehoboams
ABEHNORRT	abhorrent
	earthborn
ABEHNRRTU	heartburn
ABEHNRSSS	brashness
ABEHNRSTU	sunbather
ABEHNSSTU	sunbathes
ABEHOOSTU	boathouse
	houseboat
ABEHORRRS	abhorrers
	harborers
ABEHORRRU	harbourer
ABEHQRSUU	harquebus
ABEHRSSTU	tarbushes
ABEIIILST	abilities
ABEIILLLR	illiberal
ABEIILLMT	limitable
ABEIILNNS	biennials
ABEIILNOS	ionisable
ABEIILNOZ	ionizable
ABEIILNRS	brasilein
ABEIILNRT	nailbiter
ABEIILNRZ	brazilein
ABEIILRRS	libraries
ABEIILRRT	irritable
ABEIILRTV	vibratile
ABEIILSST	sibilates
	stabilise
ABEIILSTV	visitable
ABEIILSTZ	stabilize
ABEIIMMNO	meibomian
ABEIINNPT	bipinnate
ABEIINNRT	inebriant
ABEIINRST	brainiest
ABEIIPRTT	bipartite
ABEIIRSSV	vibrissae
ABEIIRTVV	vibrative
ABEIJLNRU	injurable
ABEIJLSTU	jubilates
ABEIJMNNS	benjamins
ABEIJRSVY	Jervis Bay
ABEIKLLNU	unlikable
ABEIKLNRT	Treblinka
ABEIKLNSS	balkiness
ABEIKLNTT	knittable
ABEIKLSTU	baulkiest
ABEIKMORR	biomarker
ABEIKNNRT	interbank
ABEIKNRSS	bearskins
ABEILLLMS	slimeball
ABEILLLNT	libellant
ABEILLLRY	liberally
ABEILLLST	labellist
ABEILLLSU	lullabies
	sulliable
ABEILLMSS	mislabels
ABEILLNST	libelants
ABEILLNUV	unlivable
ABEILLPSU	plausible
ABEILLSTY	bestially
ABEILMMOV	immovable
ABEILMMSW	swimmable
ABEILMMTU	immutable
ABEILMNSS	balminess
ABEILMNST	bailments
ABEILMOPS	imposable
ABEILMORT	Baltimore
ABEILMOSX	mailboxes
ABEILMPTU	imputable
ABEILMRSV	verbalism
ABEILMRSY	miserably
ABEILMSTU	sublimate
ABEILMSTW	wambliest
ABEILMSTY	estimably
ABEILNPRT	printable
ABEILNPSU	subalpine
ABEILNRRY	inerrably
ABEILNRSS	brainless
ABEILNRSU	insurable
ABEILNSTV	bivalents
ABEILOQSU	obsequial
ABEILORRT	liberator
ABEILORST	strobilae
ABEILORSV	bolivares
ABEILORTT	trilobate
ABEILPSST	epiblasts
ABEILQTUY	equitably
ABEILRRST	stirrable
ABEILRRSU	reburials
ABEILRRYZ	bizarrely
ABEILRSTU	brutalise
ABEILRSTV	verbalist
ABEILRTUZ	brutalize
ABEILRTVY	veritably
ABEILRVVY	revivably
ABEILSSUX	bisexuals
ABEILSTTW	twistable
ABEILSUVY	abusively
ABEIMMNRT	timberman
ABEIMNORT	brominate
ABEIMNRST	brainstem
	tribesman
ABEIMNRSU	submarine
ABEIMOSSS	biomasses
ABEIMPRST	rebaptism
ABEIMRSTV	ambiverts
ABEINNOST	sanbenito
ABEINNOSZ	bezonians
ABEINNRST	bannister
ABEINNSTT	abstinent
ABEINNTYZ	byzantine
ABEINOOPW	bioweapon
ABEINORST	baritones
	obtainers
ABEINOSST	botanises
ABEINOSTT	obstinate
ABEINOSTZ	botanizes

ABEINPRST breastpin
ABEINRSST banisters
ABEINRSSU urbanises
ABEINRSTU urbanites
ABEINRSTW brawniest
ABEINRSUZ urbanizes
ABEINRTTU tribunate
turbinate
ABEINSSST bassinets
ABEINSTTU intubates
ABEIOORSV Beriosova
ABEIOPRTV probative
ABEIPRRSS spareribs
ABEIRRRST barrister
ABEIRRSST arbitress
ABEIRRSSU bursaries
ABEIRRSTU turbaries
ABEIRSSST brassiest
ABEIRSSTY sybarites
ABEIRTTTU attribute
ABEJLNOYY enjoyably
ABEJMOORS jeroboams
ABEKKMOOR bookmaker
ABEKLMOSS abelmosks
ABEKLNNSS blankness
ABEKLOOPT bookplate
ABEKLORTW worktable
ABEKLORVY revokably
ABEKLOSTX talkboxes
ABEKNNOST banknotes
ABEKOORSY yearbooks
ABEKORSTU breakouts
outbreaks
ABELLLSSY syllables
ABELLMNTY lambently
ABELLMRSU umbrellas
ABELLNOST ballonets
ABELLNOUV unlovable
ABELLORTY tolerably
ABELMMORY memorably
ABELMNORY embryonal
ABELMNOSZ emblazons
ABELMNOTU mountable
ABELMNOUV unmovable
ABELMNPRU penumbral
ABELMNRUY numerably
ABELMNSTU submental
ABELMOORT motorable
ABELMORVY removably
ABELMOSST mesoblast
ABELMOSSU albumoses
ABELNNORS bannerols
ABELNNORV nonverbal
ABELNNTUY untenably
ABELNORSZ blazoners
ABELNOSTT entoblast
ABELNOSYZ lazybones
ABELNRSTU subaltern
ABELNRTTU turntable
ABELOOPPS opposable
ABELOPPST stoppable
ABELOPRST portables
ABELOPSTT spottable
ABELORRSU labourers
ABELORSSV absolvers
ABELORTTX rattlebox
ABELOSSTU absolutes
ABELOSSTX saltboxes
ABELOSTTY stylobate
ABELPRSUY superably
ABELPRTTU prebuttal
ABELPRTUY reputably
ABELRSSTU balusters
ABELRSTTU rebuttals
trustable
ABELRSUYY Aylesbury
ABELSTTUU tubulates
ABELSTUUX subluxate
ABEMMNOOS moonbeams
ABEMNPRSU penumbras
ABEMNSTTU abutments
ABEMOOPRR broomrape
ABEMOPRTY ambrotype
ABEMORRRY Barrymore
ABEMORRTU arboretum
ABEMORRTY barometry
ABENNORTW warbonnet
ABENNSTTU subtenant
ABENOOSTT stoneboat
ABENOPRRS barperson
ABENOPSSU subpoenas
ABENORSTT betatrons
ABENORSTV bevatrons
observant
ABENORSTY barytones
ABEOOPRTW powerboat
ABEOOPSSX soapboxes
ABEOORRSU arboreous
ABEOPPRSY paperboys
ABEOPRRSY soapberry
ABEORRSTU tabourers
ABEORSSTU saboteurs
ABEORSTTU obturates
tabourets
ABEORSTUV outbraves
ABEPRRRSY raspberry
ABEPRSSSY passersby
ABERSSTTU substrate
ABERSSTUU arbutuses
ABERSTTUY butyrates
ABFFLLPSU puffballs
ABFFLOSST blastoffs
ABFFNOSTU bouffants
ABFGIINSY basifying
ABFGIOPSY Bay of Pigs
ABFGLLOOS goofballs
ABFGORSUU faubourgs
ABFHLLSUY bashfully
ABFIILLRR fibrillar
ABFIILLRY bifilarly
ABFIIORSU bifarious
ABFILLSYY syllabify
ABFILMSUY subfamily
ABFILNOTU bufotalin
ABFILNSSU basinfuls
ABFILSSTU fabulists
ABFLLOOST footballs
ABFLLOSST softballs
ABFLOOTTX Fox Talbot
ABFLORRUW barrowful
ABFNORSTU turbofans
ABFORSSTU surfboats
ABGGGINRS braggings
ABGGILMNO gamboling
ABGGINORT bogarting
ABGGLOORY garbology
ABGGNOOST toboggans
ABGHHILLS highballs
ABGHIINNS banishing
ABGHILMNS shambling
ABGHILRTY rightably
ABGHIMNSU ambushing
ABGHINORR abhorring
harboring
ABGHINSWZ whizbangs
ABGHINWZZ whizzbang
ABGHIOPRY biography
ABGHMORSU broughams
ABGHORSTU broughtas
ABGIILLNR brailling
ABGIILLNU bilingual
ABGIILNRT librating
ABGIIMSST bigamists
ABGIIMTUY ambiguity
ABGIINNOS bignonias
ABGIINNOT obtaining
ABGIINOTV obviating
ABGIINPST baptising
ABGIINPTZ baptizing
ABGIINRTV vibrating
ABGIJNNOW jawboning
ABGIKNNSU sunbaking
ABGIKNRRS ringbarks
ABGILLNOT balloting
ABGILMNRS ramblings
ABGILNNOZ blazoning
ABGILNNST bantlings
ABGILNORU labouring
ABGILNOSV absolving
ABGILNRSW brawlings
ABGILNSST stablings
ABGILOORT obligator
ABGILOOST obligatos
ABGILORSW brigalows
ABGIMNORT bromating
ABGIMNRSU Gambrinus
ABGIMOSUU ambiguous
ABGINNRRU unbarring
ABGINOPRT probating
ABGINOSST boastings
ABGINOSTW swingboat
ABGINPSSY bypassing
ABGLLNSUW bungwalls
ABGLLRSUY bullyrags
ABGLMNOOS boomslang
ABGLMOPSU plumbagos

ABGLNOOST longboats
ABGLNOSUW bungalows
ABHHIIRUV bahuvrihi
ABHHILLOZ Hizbollah
ABHHILOTT batholith
ABHHIRRSU hairbrush
ABHIIILOP biophilia
ABHIILLMS bismillah
ABHIILMRT brit milah
ABHIIPSTU Tipu Sahib
ABHIKLLSW hawkbills
hawksbill
ABHIKMRRT birthmark
ABHILMNTU thumbnail
ABHILMOPY amphiboly
ABHILMSTU bismuthal
ABHILNOOT halobiont
ABHILNOST biathlons
ABHILNRSU nailbrush
ABHILNRTY labyrinth
ABHILOPSS basophils
ABHILORSY boarishly
ABHIOOOPZ zoophobia
ABHKMRRSU brushmark
ABHKOOOST boathooks
ABHLLMOST mothballs
ABHLLOOSY ballyhoos
ABHLNOORY honorably
ABHLOPSTY hypoblast
ABHLOSSWW washbowls
ABHLPRSUY subphylar
ABHMOORST bathrooms
ABHNORTTU Arbuthnot
ABHOOSSTW showboats
ABIIILLTY liability
ABIIILNTY inability
ABIIILTVY viability
ABIIINRUV Urban VIII
ABIIJMMUY Mbujimayi
ABIIKLSSS basilisks
ABIILLMRS millibars
ABIILLNOT ballotini
ABIILLNRT brilliant
ABIILMNNO binominal
ABIILMNOS binomials
ABIILMNSS albinisms
ABIILMRST tribalism
ABIILNOOT abolition
ABIILNOOV boliviano
ABIILNORT libration
ABIILNORY nobiliary
ABIILNOST libations
ABIILNSST sibilants
ABIILRRTY irritably
ABIILRSSV vibrissal
ABIILRSTT tribalist
ABIILSTTY stability
ABIILSTUY suability
usability
ABIIMNOST ambitions
ABIIMORSS isobarism
ABIIMOSTU ambitious

ABIINOOTV obviation
ABIINORTV vibration
ABIJNOSST banjoists
ABIKLMNSS lambskins
ABIKLOSTY Białystok
ABIKNORRS ironbarks
ABILLLPSY playbills
ABILLMSSY syllabism
ABILLNOPT ballpoint
ABILLORRZ razorbill
ABILLORTY orbitally
ABILLPSUY plausibly
ABILMMOVY immovably
ABILMMTUY immutably
ABILMOORS ribosomal
ABILMORSU labourism
ABILMORXY xylorimba
ABILMPTUY imputably
ABILMRSTU brutalism
ABILMSTTU submittal
ABILNOOST boltonias
oblations
ABILNORUV binovular
ABILNOSTU ablutions
abutilons
ABILNRSTU tribunals
turbinals
ABILNRTVY vibrantly
ABILOORSU laborious
ABILOPRRT Port Blair
ABILORRTY libratory
ABILORSST laborists
ABILORSTU labourist
ABILRSSUY Salisbury
ABILRSTTU brutalist
ABILRSTUY salubrity
ABILRTTUY brutality
ABIMMNRUU manubrium
ABIMNORTU tambourin
ABIMNTUYZ Byzantium
ABINOOPRT probation
ABINOOPST spoonbait
ABINOORST abortions
ABINOPRTU abruption
ABINOPSTU subtopian
ABINORSTU tabourins
ABINOSSTT botanists
ABINRRTUY tribunary
ABINRSSUY Sainsbury
ABIOORRRT briarroot
ABIORRSST arborists
ABIORRSTV vibrators
ABIORRSUV arbovirus
ABIORRTVY vibratory
ABIORSTTU stirabout
ABIPRSTTY baptistry
ABIRRSSTU airbursts
ABIRRTTUY tributary
ABJLLOOTY jollyboat
ABKKMOORS bookmarks
ABKLLNORS bankrolls
ABKLLOOST bookstall

ABKNOPSST stopbanks
ABKNPRSTU bankrupts
ABKOOPSSS passbooks
ABLLLOOST stoolball
ABLLMOORS ballrooms
ABLLMOPSW blowlamps
ABLLMOSSY smallboys
ABLLNOSSW snowballs
ABLLRTUUY tubularly
ABLMNNOTZ Boltzmann
ABLMNORSU subnormal
ABLMNRSUU laburnums
ABLNRSUUY sublunary
ABLOOPPSY opposably
ABLOOPRST blastopor
ABLORTTUU tubulator
ABLOSSTTU subtotals
ABMNORRST barnstorm
ABMOOOOTW Toowoomba
ABMOORTT motorboat
ABNOORRST roborants
ABNOORSYZ bryozoans
ABNOORTUZ zorbonaut
ABNORSTUU runabouts
ABNORTTUU turnabout
ABOOPRRTY probatory
ABOOPRSTT bootstrap
ABOORRTTU obturator
ABOOSSTTU outboasts
ABRRSSTTU starburst
ABRRSTTUW bratwurst
ACCCCEHIT cachectic
ACCCDEEEN accedence
ACCCDEEIN accidence
ACCCDILOY cacodylic
ACCCEEENS acescence
ACCCEENSY acescency
ACCCEGINO cacogenic
ACCCEGLOY coccygeal
ACCCEHIOT cacoethic
ACCCEHITT cathectic
ACCCEILLO calcicole
ACCCEIOPT copacetic
ACCCHKOOR cockroach
ACCCIILLY alicyclic
ACCCIILMT climactic
ACCCIIOPR capriccio
ACCCKMMOR McCormack
ACCCNOPUY occupancy
ACCDDEEEN decadence
ACCDDEEER reacceded
ACCDDEENY decadency
ACCDDEILS discalced
ACCDDIIST didactics
ACCDDIORS disaccord
ACCDEEERS reaccedes
ACCDEEHIK chickadee
ACCDEEINS cadencies
ACCDEEIST desiccate
ACCDEEKOP peacocked
ACCDEELLN cancelled
ACCDEELNO concealed

ACCDEELOS	coalesced
ACCDEFIIL	calcified
ACCDEFILS	fascicled
ACCDEFILY	decalcify
ACCDEHIKR	deckchair
ACCDEHILR	childcare
ACCDEHNRU	craunched
ACCDEHRST	scratched
ACCDEIILN	Icelandic
ACCDEIILT	dialectic
ACCDEILNR	calendric
ACCDEINOT	anecdotic
ACCDEINST	accidents
	desiccant
ACCDEIORW	cowardice
ACCDEIPRT	practiced
ACCDEIRST	accredits
ACCDEKOSS	cassocked
ACCDEMNOO	cacodemon
ACCDEMOPT	compacted
ACCDEMORR	camcorder
ACCDEMORY	democracy
ACCDENOTT	contacted
ACCDENOTU	accounted
ACCDEORRS	accorders
	scorecard
ACCDEORTU	accoutred
ACCDFILLY	flaccidly
ACCDGINOR	according
ACCDHHRUY	archduchy
ACCDHIIIL	chiliadic
ACCDHIIOR	radicchio
ACCDHINOR	chancroid
ACCDHNPRU	cardpunch
ACCDHOOOW	coachwood
ACCDHOORT	octachord
ACCDHORTW	catchword
ACCDIIINT	diactinic
ACCDIIIRT	diacritic
ACCDIIMNO	monacidic
ACCDIIOPT	apodictic
ACCDILLNO	Condillac
ACCDILLOY	cycloidal
ACCDILSTY	dactylics
ACCDINOOR	accordion
ACCDINORS	cancroids
ACCDIOORS	coracoids
ACCDKNORW	crackdown
ACCDNOORT	concordat
ACCDOOORV	Corcovado
ACCEEEILS	ecclesiae
ACCEEELRS	recalesce
ACCEEENRR	recreance
ACCEEGLMY	megacycle
ACCEEHIKR	chickaree
ACCEEHILR	chelicera
ACCEEHIST	catechise
ACCEEHITY	haecceity
ACCEEHITZ	catechize
ACCEEHKMN	namecheck
ACCEEHKMT	checkmate
ACCEEHLOT	cochleate
ACCEEHNPR	perchance
ACCEEHOST	cacoethes
ACCEEHPST	speech act
ACCEEILST	Celtic Sea
ACCEEIPRS	peccaries
ACCEEIQSU	acquiesce
ACCEEIRRR	ricercare
ACCEEIRTV	accretive
ACCEEISTX	exsiccate
ACCEEKLNS	necklaces
ACCEEKLOT	cockateel
ACCEELLNR	canceller
ACCEELLOR	clearcole
ACCEELNOR	concealer
ACCEELNOS	coenacles
ACCEELNOV	covalence
ACCEELNPR	precancel
ACCEELNRS	cancelers
	clarences
ACCEELOSS	coalesces
ACCEELPST	spectacle
ACCEENNSS	nascences
ACCEENNST	canescent
ACCEENRRY	recreancy
ACCEENRST	reaccents
ACCEENRSU	recusance
ACCEEOPSU	cepaceous
ACCEEORSU	ceraceous
ACCEEOSTU	cetaceous
ACCEEPRST	accepters
	reaccepts
ACCEESSUU	Ceaușescu
ACCEFGILU	calcifuge
ACCEFHLNU	chanceful
ACCEFHLOT	facecloth
ACCEFIILS	calcifies
ACCEFIIRS	sacrifice
ACCEFILSS	fascicles
ACCEFILSU	fascicule
ACCEGHLNO	chalcogen
ACCEGIKNO	Cockaigne
ACCEGILNN	canceling
ACCEGINNT	accenting
ACCEGINOR	acrogenic
ACCEGINPT	accepting
ACCEGINRT	accreting
ACCEGINSS	accessing
ACCEGIORT	categoric
ACCEGIOTT	geotactic
ACCEGKMOS	gamecocks
ACCEHHIRT	thearchic
ACCEHHKOT	heathcock
ACCEHIIMS	ischaemic
ACCEHIKLR	checkrail
ACCEHIKNR	raincheck
ACCEHIKPS	chickpeas
ACCEHILLO	echolalic
ACCEHILMS	chemicals
ACCEHILNO	coachline
	cochineal
ACCEHILNT	technical
ACCEHILOT	chicalote
ACCEHIMNS	mechanics
	mischance
ACCEHIMST	catechism
	schematic
ACCEHINRS	chicaners
ACCEHINRY	chicanery
ACCEHINST	catechins
	chanciest
ACCEHIOSU	acouchies
ACCEHIRST	scratchie
ACCEHIRTT	architect
ACCEHISTT	catchiest
	catechist
ACCEHLNOR	chloracne
ACCEHLOOT	chocolate
ACCEHLOPT	catchpole
ACCEHMMNU	mumchance
ACCEHMNTT	catchment
ACCEHNNOS	chaconnes
ACCEHNRSU	craunches
ACCEHOPST	cachepots
ACCEHOPSU	capouches
ACCEHORTU	cartouche
ACCEHORTY	theocracy
ACCEHRRST	scratcher
ACCEHRSST	scratches
ACCEIILMN	calcimine
ACCEIIMNT	cinematic
ACCEIINOS	cocainise
ACCEIINOZ	cocainize
ACCEIINRT	circinate
ACCEIIPRT	accipiter
ACCEIIRRR	ricercari
ACCEIIRST	cicatrise
ACCEIIRTZ	cicatrize
ACCEIISTV	siccative
ACCEIKKLP	placekick
ACCEIKLOT	cockatiel
ACCEIKLST	ticklaces
ACCEIKRSW	wisecrack
ACCEIKRTT	Catterick
ACCEILLOT	laccolite
ACCEILLRS	clericals
ACCEILLSU	caulicles
ACCEILLSV	clavicles
ACCEILMOX	cacomixle
ACCEILMPT	eclamptic
ACCEILNRT	centrical
ACCEILNST	canticles
ACCEILNTU	inculcate
ACCEILOPR	precocial
ACCEILPST	sceptical
ACCEILRTU	circulate
ACCEILTUU	cuticulae
ACCEIMNPT	impeccant
ACCEIMOSU	micaceous
ACCEINORT	accretion
	anorectic
ACCEINOSS	accession
ACCEINOST	oscitance
ACCEINSTU	encaustic
	succinate

ACCEIOPST copasetic
ACCEIORTT corticate
ACCEIPRST practices
ACCEIPSTY cityscape
ACCEIRRRS ricercars
ACCEISSTT ecstatics
ACCEJKRSW jackscrew
ACCEKLNRS cracknels
ACCEKMNRS cracksmen
ACCEKNORR corncrake
ACCELLOOT collocate
ACCELLTUU cucullate
ACCELMNSY cyclamens
ACCELNOPY cyclopean
ACCELNOSV conclaves
ACCELNOVY concavely
covalency
ACCELNPTY peccantly
ACCELNRSU caruncles
ACCELOTUY autocycle
ACCEMNRTY McCartney
ACCEMOPRT compacter
ACCEMORTY macrocyte
ACCEMPRSU creamcups
ACCENNOST Constance
ACCENNOTY cotenancy
ACCENOORS coenosarc
ACCENOPRY coparceny
ACCENORST accentors
ACCENORSU cancerous
ACCENOSST cosecants
ACCENRSUY recusancy
ACCEOPRST acceptors
ACCEORRSW scarecrow
ACCEORSSY accessory
ACCEORSTU accouters
accoutres
coruscate
ACCFFHHIN chaffinch
ACCFIILOR calorific
ACCFIILSU fasciculi
ACCFIISST fascistic
ACCFINNOU Confucian
ACCFOORST cofactors
ACCGHHINU Chu Chiang
ACCGHHNNU Changchun
ACCGHHNOW Changchow
ACCGHIIKN chiacking
ACCGHIINN chicaning
ACCGHIKNY chyacking
ACCGIILNN calcining
ACCGIKLNR crackling
ACCGIKMRS gimcracks
ACCGINNOV concaving
ACCGINOST accosting
ACCGINSUU caucusing
ACCHHISTT chitchats
ACCHHMNRU churchman
ACCHIILRV chivalric
ACCHIINNP chincapin
ACCHIKPST chapstick
ACCHILLOO alcoholic
ACCHILLOT laccolith
ACCHILNOY halcyonic
ACCHILNUU Cuchulain
ACCHILOST catholics
ACCHILPSY psychical
ACCHIMNOR monarchic
ACCHIMOPR camphoric
ACCHIMORT chromatic
ACCHIMOST stomachic
ACCHIMOSY sciomachy
ACCHINNOS cinchonas
ACCHINPSU capuchins
ACCHIORST trochaics
ACCHIRTTY trachytic
ACCHKLMOT matchlock
ACCHKLORS charlocks
ACCHKLOST sackcloth
ACCHKLSTU saltchuck
ACCHKOORW coachwork
ACCHLLOPT catchpoll
ACCHLOORT colcothar
ochlocrat
ACCHLOOSW slowcoach
ACCHLOOTY chocolaty
ACCHNOOPY cacophony
ACCHNOORS coronachs
ACCHNORSU chancrous
ACCHOSSTU succotash
ACCIIILNN clinician
ACCIILLSY salicylic
ACCIILLVY civically
ACCIILNOR conciliar
ACCIILOPT occipital
ACCIILOST cloacitis
ACCIILRTU circuital
ACCIILTVY acclivity
ACCIIMNOS cocainism
ACCIIMNPT panmictic
ACCIIMOPT apomictic
ACCIIMQSU caciquism
ACCIINNPS piccanins
ACCIINOSY isocyanic
ACCIINRTY intricacy
ACCIIOPST pasticcio
ACCIIORST isocratic
ACCIIOSTT isotactic
ACCIISSTU casuistic
ACCIKKNNS nicknacks
ACCIKKRRS rickracks
ACCIKKSTT ticktacks
ACCIKLOST cocktails
ACCIKNOSW cockswain
ACCILLMOY comically
ACCILLNOY conically
ACCILLNYY cynically
ACCILLRUY crucially
ACCILMSUU aciculums
ACCILNORV clavicorn
ACCILNOTU noctiluca
ACCILOSUV acclivous
ACCILPRTY cryptical
ACCILRRSU circulars
ACCILRRUU curricula
ACCILRTUU cuticular
ACCIMNORY acronymic
ACCIMNOSS moccasins
ACCIMNOSY sciomancy
ACCIMOORS crocosmia
ACCIMORTY timocracy
ACCIMPSSU capsicums
ACCINOOSS occasions
ACCINOOST coactions
ACCINOPRR Capricorn
ACCINORST narcotics
ACCINOSTY oscitancy
ACCINOTVY concavity
ACCINSTTY syntactic
ACCIOPRTT catoptric
ACCIORSST acrostics
ACCIOSSTU acoustics
ACCJKORSS crossjack
ACCKKMMUU muckamuck
ACCKKRSSU rucksacks
ACCKOOOST cockatoos
ACCKOPRST crackpots
ACCLLOSUU calculous
ACCLLSUUY calyculus
ACCLMOPTY compactly
ACCLNNNOO colcannon
ACCLRSSUU succursal
ACCMMOORS macrocosm
ACCMNOORY monocracy
nomocracy
ACCMNOTUY contumacy
ACCMORSTY macrocyst
ACCMOSSTU accustoms
ACCNNOSTY constancy
ACCNOORTT contactor
ACCNOOSTU cocoanuts
ACCNOPSTU occupants
ACCNORSTT contracts
ACCNORTTU cunctator
ACCOPRRUY procuracy
ACCOPRSTY cystocarp
ACCORRSTY carrycots
ACDDDEEIT dedicated
ACDDDEIRS discarded
ACDDDEKOP paddocked
ACDDEEEFT defecated
ACDDEEEIT dedicatee
ACDDEEENT anteceded
ACDDEEERS decreased
ACDDEEILM declaimed
ACDDEEIMT decimated
medicated
ACDDEEIST dedicates
ACDDEEITU deciduate
ACDDEELSS declassed
ACDDEELWW dewclawed
ACDDEENST decadents
ACDDEEORT decorated
ACDDEERTT detracted
ACDDEFIII acidified
ACDDEGIRS disgraced

ACDDEGNOO dodecagon
ACDDEHIKS dickheads
ACDDEHILY aldehydic
ACDDEIINT indicated
ACDDEIITV addictive
ACDDEIJNU jaundiced
ACDDEILPS displaced
ACDDEINST discanted
distanced
ACDDEIORT dedicator
ACDDEIRRS discarder
ACDDEKLOP padlocked
ACDDEKLOS deadlocks
ACDDEKOST deadstock
stockaded
ACDDELNOO canoodled
ACDDELNRU underclad
ACDDEMMNO commanded
ACDDENOTU outdanced
ACDDGIINT addicting
ACDDGINTU adducting
ACDDHHNSU dachshund
ACDDHIRSY hydracids
ACDDHKOSS shaddocks
ACDDIILOS discoidal
ACDDIILRU druidical
ACDDIINOT addiction
ACDDIIORS cardioids
ACDDINOTU adduction
ACDDKLNOS docklands
ACDDKORSY dockyards
ACDDLLNOU cloudland
ACDDORSTU adductors
ACDEEEFST defecates
ACDEEEHIP headpiece
ACDEEEHNP cheapened
ACDEEEHNR adherence
ACDEEEHST escheated
ACDEEEKSS seedcakes
ACDEEELSS declassee
ACDEEEMRT decameter
decametre
ACDEEENRT reenacted
ACDEEENST antecedes
ACDEEENSV evanesced
ACDEEEPRT deprecate
ACDEEEPRV Cape Verde
ACDEEERRT recreated
ACDEEERSS decreases
ACDEEERST desecrate
ACDEEERTU reeducate
ACDEEERTX execrated
ACDEEESSS seedcases
ACDEEFFHR chaffered
ACDEEFHMR chamfered
ACDEEFHWY wheyfaced
ACDEEFIIT acetified
ACDEEFINS defiances
ACDEEFKRT afterdeck
ACDEEFNTU fecundate
ACDEEFORT defecator
ACDEEFRRT refracted
ACDEEGHNX exchanged
ACDEEGHRR recharged
ACDEEGINS deceasing
ACDEEGIRZ graecized
ACDEEGLNO congealed
ACDEEGLOU decalogue
ACDEEGNSV scavenged
ACDEEGOPU decoupage
ACDEEHHLT hatcheled
ACDEEHIMP impeached
ACDEEHINN enchained
ACDEEHINT echinated
ACDEEHIRS cashiered
charidees
ACDEEHIRT tracheide
ACDEEHKNY hackneyed
ACDEEHLLN chandelle
ACDEEHLNN channeled
ACDEEHLOR Delaroche
ACDEEHLPT chapleted
ACDEEHMRS demarches
ACDEEHMRT rematched
ACDEEHNNT enchanted
ACDEEHNST chastened
ACDEEHRRT chartered
recharted
ACDEEHRST detachers
ACDEEHRTT chattered
ACDEEIINT teniacide
ACDEEIIRT diaeretic
ACDEEIJTV adjective
ACDEEILMN endemical
ACDEEILMR declaimer
reclaimed
ACDEEILMX exclaimed
ACDEEILNN celandine
decennial
ACDEEILNT declinate
ACDEEILNU euclidean
ACDEEILPR calipered
ACDEEILRT decaliter
decalitre
ACDEEILST delicates
ACDEEILSU aedicules
ACDEEILTU elucidate
ACDEEILTY acetylide
ACDEEIMNO macedoine
ACDEEIMNP impedance
ACDEEIMRS ceramides
racemised
ACDEEIMRZ racemized
ACDEEIMST decimates
medicates
ACDEEINOS oceanides
ACDEEINRS increased
ACDEEINSU audiences
ACDEEINSV deviances
ACDEEIOPR adipocere
ACDEEIPRT predicate
ACDEEIPST speciated
ACDEEIRRT traceried
ACDEEISTV vesicated
ACDEEITUV educative
ACDEEJRTT trajected
ACDEEKKNR knackered
ACDEEKLNS slackened
ACDEEKPPR prepacked
ACDEEKRST restacked
ACDEELLMR marcelled
ACDEELLNV Cleveland
ACDEELLOT decollate
ocellated
ACDEELLPR parcelled
ACDEELNNU uncleaned
ACDEELNPS enclasped
spanceled
ACDEELNRS calenders
ACDEELNSU Enceladus
ACDEELNTT tentacled
ACDEELNTU nucleated
ACDEELOPS opalesced
ACDEELORT relocated
ACDEELORV Coverdale
ACDEELPTU peculated
ACDEELQRU lacquered
ACDEELRRS declarers
ACDEELRST decretals
ACDEELRSW leadscrew
ACDEELRTT clattered
ACDEELRTU ulcerated
ACDEELSSS declasses
ACDEELSTY decastyle
ACDEEMNOS codenames
ACDEEMPRS scampered
ACDEENNRT entranced
ACDEENNRU endurance
ACDEENNRY decennary
ACDEENNST ascendent
ACDEENORS coarsened
ACDEENOSS deaconess
ACDEENOST anecdotes
ACDEENRSS ascenders
reascends
ACDEENRST decanters
descanter
ACDEENRSU ascendeur
ACDEENRSZ credenzas
ACDEENRTY daycentre
ACDEENSTT dancettes
ACDEEOPSS peasecods
ACDEEORST decorates
ACDEEORTV overacted
ACDEEPRRS scarpered
ACDEEPSTT spectated
ACDEEQRTU racqueted
ACDEERRTT retracted
ACDEERSST Descartes
ACDEERSSU surceased
ACDEERSSV crevassed
ACDEERSTT scattered
ACDEERSTU reductase
ACDEERTTU eructated
ACDEERTTX extracted
ACDEESSTU decussate

ACDEFFIKM	mafficked
ACDEFFILR	Radcliffe
ACDEFFILT	afflicted
ACDEFFIST	disaffect
ACDEFFMOR	cofferdam
ACDEFHINR	archfiend
ACDEFHLRS	feldschar
ACDEFIIIL	edificial
ACDEFIIIR	acidifier
ACDEFIIIS	acidifies
ACDEFIILR	clarified
ACDEFIILT	feticidal
ACDEFIINR	carnified
ACDEFIIRS	scarified
ACDEFILLO	coalfield
ACDEFILLU	Caulfield
ACDEFILOS	focalised
ACDEFILOZ	focalized
ACDEFILRS	filecards
ACDEFILRU	cauldrife
ACDEFINRT	infarcted
	infracted
ACDEFLNOT	conflated
ACDEFMNOO	moonfaced
ACDEFRRTU	fractured
ACDEGGIMO	demagogic
ACDEGGIOP	pedagogic
ACDEGGIRT	catrigged
ACDEGHINR	chagrined
ACDEGHINT	detaching
ACDEGHIRS	discharge
ACDEGHNNU	unchanged
ACDEGHNRU	graunched
	uncharged
ACDEGIILR	regicidal
ACDEGIILS	algicides
ACDEGILLN	decalling
ACDEGILNO	genocidal
ACDEGILNR	declaring
ACDEGILNS	descaling
ACDEGILOO	logaoedic
ACDEGIMNO	endogamic
ACDEGIMNP	decamping
ACDEGINNS	ascending
ACDEGINNT	decanting
ACDEGINOY	gynaecoid
ACDEGINRT	redacting
ACDEGINTU	educating
ACDEGIOTT	cogitated
ACDEGIRRS	disgracer
ACDEGIRRT	cartridge
ACDEGIRSS	disgraces
ACDEGLNOR	clangored
ACDEGLNOU	Languedoc
ACDEGNNOU	undecagon
ACDEHHIKT	thickhead
ACDEHHIRS	rhachides
ACDEHHNTU	unhatched
ACDEHHORX	hexachord
ACDEHIIRR	diarrheic
ACDEHIIRS	diarchies
ACDEHIITT	diathetic
ACDEHILLO	cheloidal
ACDEHINNR	hindrance
ACDEHINNU	unchained
ACDEHINOT	inchoated
ACDEHINSV	cavendish
ACDEHIOPX	hexapodic
ACDEHIPRY	hyperacid
ACDEHIPST	cadetship
ACDEHIRST	tracheids
ACDEHIRSY	dyarchies
ACDEHISST	chastised
ACDEHKLOS	headlocks
ACDEHKMOP	chokedamp
ACDEHKMPU	chempaduk
ACDEHKOST	headstock
ACDEHKRSU	archdukes
ACDEHLNOR	chlordane
ACDEHLNOT	decathlon
ACDEHLNRS	chandlers
ACDEHLNRY	chandlery
ACDEHLNTU	unlatched
ACDEHLRSU	schedular
ACDEHLRTU	trauchled
ACDEHMNTU	unmatched
ACDEHMOST	stomached
ACDEHMPRY	pachyderm
ACDEHMPSS	Deschamps
ACDEHMSTU	mustached
ACDEHNOPR	cardphone
	phonecard
ACDEHNRRT	trenchard
ACDEHNRTU	uncharted
ACDEHNSTU	staunched
	unscathed
ACDEHNTUW	unwatched
ACDEHOOPT	chaetopod
ACDEHORRV	hardcover
ACDEHORSS	crosshead
ACDEHORST	chordates
ACDEHOSSW	showcased
ACDEHPRSU	purchased
ACDEHRRSS	chresards
ACDEIIINT	dietician
ACDEIIIST	acidities
ACDEIILMN	adminicle
	medicinal
ACDEIILNO	lidocaine
ACDEIILNT	identical
ACDEIILNU	euclidian
ACDEIILNX	indexical
ACDEIILRV	larvicide
	veridical
ACDEIILST	deistical
ACDEIIMMY	immediacy
ACDEIIMRT	diametric
	matricide
ACDEIINOS	sciaenoid
ACDEIINOT	dianoetic
ACDEIINSS	sciaenids
ACDEIINST	actinides
	indicates
ACDEIINTV	vindicate
ACDEIIOPR	aperiodic
ACDEIIOST	dacoities
ACDEIIPRR	parricide
ACDEIIPRT	patricide
	pediatric
ACDEIISTV	vaticides
ACDEIJNSU	jaundices
ACDEIKLNN	calkinned
ACDEIKMNN	nicknamed
ACDEIKMNR	Mackinder
ACDEIKRST	sidetrack
ACDEILLMS	miscalled
ACDEILLMY	decimally
	medically
ACDEILLOS	localised
ACDEILLOZ	localized
ACDEILLTY	edictally
ACDEILMNU	unclaimed
ACDEILMPS	misplaced
ACDEILMST	maledicts
ACDEILNNP	candlepin
	pinnacled
ACDEILNOR	clarioned
ACDEILNOU	Deucalion
ACDEILNSU	dulcineas
ACDEILNSW	Windscale
ACDEILNTU	acidulent
ACDEILNVY	divalency
ACDEILOPR	caprioled
ACDEILOPT	petalodic
ACDEILORT	loricated
ACDEILORX	Delacroix
ACDEILORZ	calorized
ACDEILOST	dislocate
ACDEILOSV	vocalised
ACDEILOVZ	vocalized
ACDEILPRS	displacer
ACDEILPRU	pedicular
ACDEILPSS	displaces
ACDEILPTU	duplicate
ACDEILRSS	laserdisc
ACDEILRTU	curtailed
ACDEILTUV	victualed
ACDEIMNNO	dominance
ACDEIMNNT	mendicant
ACDEIMNOP	companied
	compendia
ACDEIMNOS	comedians
	demoniacs
ACDEIMNPS	pandemics
ACDEIMNRU	manicured
ACDEIMNSU	muscadine
ACDEIMNTY	mendacity
ACDEIMORT	decimator
ACDEIMRST	timecards
ACDEIMRTU	muricated
ACDEINNOR	ordinance
ACDEINNOS	canonised
ACDEINNOT	contained
ACDEINNOZ	canonized
ACDEINNST	instanced
ACDEINOPS	caponised

ACDEINOPT captioned
ACDEINOPZ caponized
ACDEINORR coriander
ACDEINORS dinoceras
ACDEINORT redaction
ACDEINOSS diocesans
ACDEINOST catenoids
ACDEINOSV voidances
ACDEINOTU auctioned
cautioned
education
ACDEINOTV advection
invocated
ACDEINPRT predicant
ACDEINRSS acridness
ACDEINRST discanter
ACDEINRTU curtained
ACDEINSST distances
ACDEINSSY anecdysis
ACDEINSTY asyndetic
syndicate
ACDEINTTU tunicated
ACDEIOPSS diascopes
ACDEIOPTY adipocyte
ACDEIPRST crispated
practised
ACDEIPRTY predacity
ACDEIPSTU cuspidate
ACDEIQTTU acquitted
ACDEIRRSU curarised
ACDEIRRUZ curarized
ACDEIRSSU cuirassed
ACDEIRSTT astricted
cristated
ACDEIRSTY dicastery
ACDEIRTTU urticated
ACDEIRUVY ayurvedic
ACDEISSTY ecdysiast
ACDEJKKSY skyjacked
ACDEKKMRU muckraked
ACDEKMMMO mammocked
ACDEKNRTU untracked
ACDEKOSST stockades
ACDELLOPS collapsed
scalloped
ACDELLORR corralled
ACDELLOST Oldcastle
ACDELLOSU calloused
ACDELMOPR placoderm
ACDELMORU clamoured
ACDELMORY comradely
ACDELMSSU muscadels
ACDELMTUU cumulated
ACDELNNOO colonnade
ACDELNNOR clarendon
ACDELNNTU candlenut
ACDELNNUU undulance
ACDELNOOR canoodler
ACDELNOOS canoodles
ACDELNOOW lancewood
ACDELNORS Androcles
colanders

ACDELNOTU unlocated
ACDELNPSU unclasped
ACDELNRUY underclay
ACDELOPST clodpates
ACDELOPTU copulated
cupolated
ACDELORTY cordately
ACDELOSTU osculated
ACDELPRSY clepsydra
ACDELRTTU cultrated
ACDEMMMNO commendam
ACDEMMNOR commander
ACDEMNOPR compander
cramponed
ACDEMOORR acrodrome
ACDEMOORT motorcade
ACDEMOPRS compadres
ACDEMOPSS compassed
ACDEMORST democrats
ACDENNNOU announced
ACDENNNSU unscanned
ACDENNRST transcend
ACDENOOOW canoewood
ACDENOOTT cottonade
ACDENOPRS endocarps
ACDENORST Doncaster
ACDENORSY secondary
ACDENORTU undercoat
ACDENOSST endocasts
ACDENOSTU outdances
ACDENPTTU punctated
ACDENRRSU unscarred
ACDENRRTU undercart
ACDENRSTU underacts
ACDENRTTU truncated
ACDEOORRT decorator
ACDEOORSS doorcases
ACDEOORTT doctorate
ACDEOPRSY copyreads
ACDEORRST costarred
redactors
ACDEORRTT detractor
ACDEORSST coatdress
ACDEORSSU crusadoes
ACDEORSTU ceratodus
educators
ACDEORSUU rudaceous
ACDEORSUZ cruzadoes
ACDEORTUY educatory
ACDEORTUZ Côte d'Azur
ACDEOSTTU outcasted
ACDEQSTUU aqueducts
ACDERRSSU crusaders
ACDERRSTU traducers
ACDFFHNSU handcuffs
ACDFFIRST diffracts
ACDFFLOSS scaffolds
ACDFHILSS scaldfish
ACDFIIILL filicidal
ACDFIIRUY fiduciary
ACDFINNOT confidant
ACDFNTTUY candytuft

ACDFOORTW woodcraft
ACDGHIILO glochidia
ACDGHIIPR digraphic
ACDGHIMOY dichogamy
ACDGHIPSY dysphagic
ACDGHOSTW watchdogs
ACDGIILNO gadolinic
ACDGIILOR goliardic
ACDGIINNY cyaniding
ACDGIINTT dictating
ACDGIIRST digastric
ACDGILNRS cradlings
ACDGIMOST dogmatics
ACDGINORR corrading
ACDGINRSU crusading
ACDGINRTU traducing
ACDGIOOPR Podgorica
ACDGLOOST Gold Coast
ACDGORRSS cordgrass
ACDHIIIRR Richard II
ACDHIILMO homicidal
ACDHIILOP acidophil
haploidic
ACDHIILST distichal
ACDHIIMRS midrashic
ACDHIIMSU dichasium
ACDHIINNO Indochina
ACDHIINOP diaphonic
ACDHIKNPS handpicks
ACDHILPRS pilchards
ACDHILRSY chrysalid
ACDHILRUY hydraulic
ACDHIMORT chromatid
ACDHIOPRS rhapsodic
ACDHIORSY hyracoids
ACDHIORYZ hydrazoic
ACDHIPSSY dysphasic
ACDHIRRSU churidars
ACDHKORRS hardrocks
ACDHLNORS chaldrons
ACDHMNOOR chondroma
ACDHMOOTW doomwatch
matchwood
ACDHOOPPS scaphopod
ACDHOOSTW woodchats
ACDHORTWW watchword
ACDIIILMT miticidal
ACDIIIMOT idiomatic
ACDIIJLRU juridical
ACDIIJRUY judiciary
ACDIILMNO dominical
ACDIILMSS disclaims
ACDIILMSX disclimax
ACDIILNOR crinoidal
ACDIILOSS dissocial
ACDIILOST diastolic
ACDIILOSV viscoidal
ACDIILPTY placidity
ACDIILSTU dualistic
ACDIIMNNO Dominican
ACDIIMPRY pyramidic
ACDIIMRTY mydriatic

ACDIINNST indicants
ACDIINORS radionics
ACDIINORT indicator
ACDIINOSY Dionysiac
ACDIINOTT dictation
ACDIINRTY rancidity
ACDIIOPRT diatropic
podiatric
ACDIIRTTX dictatrix
ACDIJORTU judicator
ACDIKKLRY Kirkcaldy
ACDIKKNST kickstand
ACDIKNQSU quicksand
ACDIKRSTY yardstick
ACDILLLOO colloidal
ACDILLOOR coralloid
ACDILLORY cordially
ACDILLOSU caudillos
ACDILMNOO monodical
ACDILMOPS psalmodic
ACDILMOPY diplomacy
ACDILMOTU comatulid
ACDILNOOR coordinal
ACDILNORS ironclads
ACDILNORT doctrinal
ACDILNOSY synodical
ACDILOORT doctorial
ACDILOPRS dropsical
ACDILORSY corydalis
ACDILOSTU custodial
ACDILOSTY dystocial
ACDILOSUU acidulous
ACDILOTUV oviductal
ACDILRTTY tridactyl
ACDIMNOOS codomains
ACDIMOPSS spasmodic
ACDIMORRU macruroid
ACDIMORTY mordacity
ACDINOOPT actinopod
ACDINOSTU custodian
ACDIORSTT dictators
ACDIRSSTT distracts
ACDJLNTUY adjunctly
ACDJOORTU coadjutor
ACDKLORTU truckload
ACDKMNNOO monadnock
ACDKORSTY stockyard
ACDLMNOOY condyloma
ACDLMNOPW clampdown
ACDLNNORW crownland
ACDLNORSU cauldrons
ACDLNSTYY syndactyl
ACDMMNOOS commandos
ACDMMNORU communard
ACDMOOPRR comprador
ACDMOOSUV muscovado
ACDNOORRT corrodant
ACDNOORSV cordovans
ACDNOSSTW downcasts
ACDOORRSS crossroad
ACDOORSST ostracods
ACDOPRSST postcards
ACDORRTUY courtyard
ACDRSSTTU dustcarts
ACEEEFIRT cafetiere
ACEEEFLNR freelance
ACEEEGHPR repechage
ACEEEGLNS elegances
ACEEEGNNV vengeance
ACEEEHIPT epithecae
petechiae
ACEEEHIRV echeveria
ACEEEHNPR cheapener
ACEEEHRST reteaches
ACEEEILMP piecemeal
ACEEEIMPT peacetime
ACEEEIPRS earpieces
ACEEEKNQU queencake
ACEEEKRRT racketeer
ACEEELMRS cameleers
ACEEELNPS Pleasence
ACEEELNRT crenelate
ACEEELNRV relevance
ACEEELNTU enucleate
ACEEELNTY acetylene
ACEEELSSS ceaseless
ACEEEMNNR remanence
ACEEEMNPR permeance
ACEEENPPT appetence
ACEEENPRS esperance
ACEEENRRS careeners
ACEEENRSV severance
ACEEENSSV evanesces
ACEEERRST recreates
ACEEERSTT etceteras
ACEEERSTX execrates
ACEEFFHRR chafferer
ACEEFFHRU rechauffe
ACEEFFITV affective
ACEEFFLNU affluence
ACEEFFLTU effectual
ACEEFHLNP halfpence
ACEEFHLPR parfleche
ACEEFHMRR chamferer
ACEEFHORR forereach
ACEEFHSTT factsheet
ACEEFHSWY wheyfaces
ACEEFIIRT acetifier
ACEEFIIST acetifies
ACEEFILPR fireplace
ACEEFINRT interface
ACEEFIRSS fricassee
ACEEFMORT forcemeat
ACEEFNNRW New France
ACEEFNORV confervae
ACEEFPRRS prefacers
ACEEFPRST praefects
ACEEFPSTY typefaces
ACEEFRRSU resurface
ACEEFRSSU farceuses
ACEEGHIOR heroic age
ACEEGHIRU gaucherie
ACEEGHLLN challenge
ACEEGHNRX exchanger
ACEEGHNSX exchanges
ACEEGHRRS recharges
ACEEGILNR generical
ACEEGILNT clientage
genetical
ACEEGILRS sacrilege
ACEEGILRV vicegeral
viceregal
ACEEGIMNT metagenic
ACEEGINNR careening
ACEEGINRR careering
ACEEGINRV grievance
ACEEGIRRV caregiver
ACEEGIRSZ graecizes
ACEEGIRTT cigarette
ACEEGKRSW wreckages
ACEEGKRWY greywacke
ACEEGLLOU colleague
ACEEGLNOR congealer
ACEEGLNRT rectangle
ACEEGLRSS graceless
ACEEGMNOR geomancer
ACEEGMNUY gynaeceum
ACEEGNORU encourage
ACEEGNRSV scavenger
ACEEGNRSY sergeancy
ACEEGNSSV scavenges
ACEEGOOPR cooperage
ACEEGORRS racegoers
ACEEGRTTU curettage
ACEEHHRSU heucheras
ACEEHHTUX Hexateuch
ACEEHIIPR hairpiece
ACEEHILMS alchemies
alchemise
ACEEHILMZ alchemize
ACEEHILPT petechial
ACEEHILRT heretical
ACEEHILRV chevalier
ACEEHIMNS achimenes
mechanise
ACEEHIMNZ mechanize
ACEEHIMPR impeacher
ACEEHIMPS impeaches
ACEEHINNV enhancive
ACEEHINPT phenacite
ACEEHINRR rancherie
ACEEHINRT Catherine
ACEEHINSS Aeschines
ACEEHINST hesitance
ACEEHIPRR preachier
ACEEHIPRS eparchies
parcheesi
ACEEHIPRT apheretic
ACEEHIPST peachiest
ACEEHIRSV achievers
chivarees
ACEEHIRSX exarchies
ACEEHISTT aesthetic
ACEEHLMNO chameleon
ACEEHLMOO haemocoel
ACEEHLMPV champleve

ACEEHLNRU herculean
ACEEHLNRW Walcheren
ACEEHLNSS seneschal
ACEEHLNST Cleanthes
ACEEHLNTU Neuchâtel
ACEEHLORT trochleae
ACEEHLOSS shoelaces
ACEEHLPSS chapeless
ACEEHLRTW cartwheel
ACEEHMMRT machmeter
ACEEHMNRY archenemy
ACEEHMOTY haemocyte
ACEEHMRST rematches
ACEEHMRSU charmeuse
ACEEHNNRS enhancers
ACEEHNNRT enchanter
ACEEHNOPR chaperone
ACEEHNPSS cheapness
ACEEHNPTY pachytene
ACEEHNRSS enchasers
ACEEHNRST chastener
ACEEHNRTT entrechat
ACEEHNSTU chanteuse
unteaches
ACEEHORRS racehorse
ACEEHORRV overreach
ACEEHOSTU theaceous
ACEEHPRRS preachers
ACEEHPRTY archetype
ACEEHPSSS chapesses
ACEEHRRRT charterer
recharter
ACEEHRRSS searchers
ACEEHRRTT chatterer
ACEEHRRTY treachery
ACEEHRSTT catheters
ACEEIILNR eirenical
ACEEIILPT tailpiece
ACEEIJQRU jacquerie
ACEEIKLLS scalelike
ACEEIKLMR creamlike
ACEEIKMNZ Mackenzie
ACEEIKRST creakiest
ACEEILLMS limescale
ACEEILLNR cleanlier
ACEEILLST celestial
ACEEILLTV vellicate
ACEEILMNS mescaline
ACEEILMNZ mezcaline
ACEEILMRR reclaimer
ACEEILMRT carmelite
ACEEILMRX exclaimer
ACEEILMST timescale
ACEEILMTT telematic
ACEEILNOR Coleraine
ACEEILNPR percaline
ACEEILNRS carelines
larcenies
reliances
ACEEILNRT interlace
reclinate
ACEEILNST latencies
ACEEILNSV valencies
ACEEILPRS periclase
prelacies
ACEEILPRT replicate
ACEEILPTX explicate
ACEEILRST cartelise
ACEEILRTZ cartelize
ACEEIMMNN immanence
ACEEIMMNT mincemeat
ACEEIMMRT metameric
ACEEIMNPR mepacrine
ACEEIMNSX exciseman
ACEEIMPRT imprecate
ACEEIMRRS careerism
ACEEIMRSS cassimere
racemises
ACEEIMRST creamiest
miscreate
ACEEIMRSZ racemizes
ACEEIMRTT metricate
ACEEIMRVW crimewave
ACEEINNRS canneries
ACEEINNRT nectarine
ACEEINNST insectean
tenancies
ACEEINNTU enunciate
ACEEINPRU epicurean
ACEEINPTT pectinate
ACEEINRRS errancies
increaser
ACEEINRSS increases
ACEEINRST centiares
cisternae
iterances
nectaries
ACEEINSST cineastes
ACEEIORTX excoriate
ACEEIOSSS ecossaise
ACEEIOTVV evocative
ACEEIPRTT crepitate
ACEEIPRTV precative
ACEEIPSST speciates
ACEEIQRRU reacquire
ACEEIRRST careerist
traceries
ACEEIRRSV carveries
ACEEIRSST sectaries
ACEEIRSSU causeries
ACEEIRSSW wiseacres
ACEEIRSTT catteries
ACEEIRSTU cauteries
cauterise
ACEEIRSTV creatives
ACEEIRTTX extricate
ACEEIRTUZ cauterize
ACEEISSST ecstasies
ACEEISSTT testacies
ACEEISSTV vesicates
ACEEKLMRS mackerels
ACEEKNSTT snackette
ACEELLLSU cellulase
ACEELLMRR marceller
ACEELLNST lancelets
ACEELLORT electoral
ACEELLPSS placeless
ACEELLRRS cellarers
ACEELLRST cellarets
ACEELMNPT placement
ACEELMNST selectman
ACEELMNTT cattlemen
ACEELMOPS someplace
ACEELMORT latecomer
ACEELNNRU cannelure
ACEELNNSS cleanness
ACEELNORT coeternal
tolerance
ACEELNPRS precleans
ACEELNPST pentacles
ACEELNPTU petulance
ACEELNRRS larceners
ACEELNRSS cleansers
clearness
ACEELNRTU calenture
crenulate
ACEELNRTY crenately
ACEELNRVY relevancy
ACEELNSSU nucleases
ACEELNSTT tentacles
ACEELNSTU nucleates
ACEELNSTW Newcastle
ACEELNTUX exultance
ACEELNTUY cuneately
ACEELOOSU oleaceous
ACEELOPRT percolate
ACEELOPSS escalopes
opalesces
ACEELORRT correlate
ACEELORSS casserole
ACEELORST relocates
ACEELORSW lowercase
ACEELORTT lectorate
ACEELORTU urceolate
ACEELPRRS replacers
ACEELPSSS spaceless
ACEELPSTU peculates
speculate
ACEELPTUX exculpate
ACEELQRRU lacquerer
ACEELRRTT clatterer
ACEELRSST traceless
ACEELRSTU ulcerates
ACEELRSTV cervelats
ACEELRTUY electuary
ACEELSSSU causeless
sauceless
ACEELSSTT telecasts
ACEEMMOOT ammocoete
ACEEMMORR macromere
ACEEMNNTT enactment
ACEEMNRRY mercenary
ACEEMNSST casements
ACEEMOPRS camporees
capsomere
ACEEMORRS sarcomere

ACEEMORTT	octameter
ACEEMORVW	creamwove
ACEEMPRRS	scamperer
ACEEMRRSS	screamers
ACEEMRRTU	mercurate
ACEEMRSTY	mercy seat
ACEENNNOR	cannoneer
ACEENNORS	resonance
ACEENNOST	Cantonese
ACEENNRST	entrances
	renascent
ACEENNRTY	centenary
ACEENORST	carotenes
ACEENOSST	notecases
ACEENPPTY	appetency
ACEENPRRS	parceners
ACEENPRRT	carpenter
ACEENPTTX	expectant
ACEENRRST	recanters
	recreants
ACEENRRTU	crenature
ACEENRSST	reascents
ACEENRSSY	necessary
ACEENRSTV	Cervantes
ACEENRTTU	utterance
ACEENSSTU	acuteness
ACEENSSTX	exactness
ACEENTTUX	executant
ACEEOOPRT	cooperate
ACEEOPRRT	procreate
ACEEORRRT	recreator
ACEEORRTT	rectorate
ACEEORRTV	overreact
ACEEORTUY	eucaryote
ACEEOSSTU	setaceous
ACEEPPRSU	uppercase
ACEEPRRTU	recapture
ACEEPSSTT	spectates
ACEEPSSTY	typecases
ACEERRSSS	caressers
ACEERRSST	creatress
ACEERRSSU	ecraseurs
ACEERRSTT	scatterer
	streetcar
ACEERRSTU	creatures
ACEERRSTY	secretary
ACEERRTUV	recurvate
ACEERSSST	actresses
ACEERSSSU	surceases
ACEERSSSV	crevasses
ACEERSSTU	secateurs
ACEERSTTU	eructates
ACEERTUXY	executary
ACEESSSTT	cassettes
ACEESSSTU	caestuses
ACEFFFLRU	carfuffle
ACEFFGINT	affecting
ACEFFHRSU	chauffers
ACEFFHRUU	chauffeur
ACEFFIIOT	officiate
ACEFFIKMR	mafficker
ACEFFINOT	affection
ACEFFIORT	forficate
ACEFFLRSS	sclaffers
ACEFFOSTU	suffocate
ACEFGHILT	lightface
ACEFGHLNU	changeful
ACEFGINPR	prefacing
ACEFGINSY	casefying
ACEFGINTT	facetting
ACEFGLNOR	gerfalcon
ACEFHIINT	chieftain
ACEFHIKLT	thickleaf
ACEFHINRS	franchise
ACEFHIPRY	preachify
ACEFHIRRT	fratchier
ACEFHISST	catfishes
ACEFHLNSU	flaunches
ACEFHOSUV	vouchsafe
ACEFIILMS	facsimile
ACEFIILRR	clarifier
ACEFIILRS	clarifies
ACEFIILRT	laticifer
ACEFIINNR	financier
ACEFIINNS	infancies
ACEFIINRS	carnifies
ACEFIIPRS	pacifiers
ACEFIIRRS	scarifier
ACEFIIRRT	artificer
ACEFIIRSS	scarifies
ACEFIIRST	artifices
ACEFIIRTV	fricative
ACEFIISST	satisfice
ACEFIITTV	factitive
ACEFIJKKN	jackknife
ACEFIKRTU	fruitcake
ACEFILNNO	falconine
ACEFILORT	fortalice
ACEFILOSS	focalises
ACEFILOSZ	focalizes
ACEFILSTU	faculties
ACEFIMORT	formicate
ACEFIMPRS	campfires
ACEFINNSS	fanciness
ACEFINORT	fornicate
ACEFINPRT	faceprint
ACEFINSTU	infuscate
ACEFINTTV	ventifact
ACEFIORST	factories
	factorise
ACEFIORTZ	factorize
ACEFIOSTU	facetious
ACEFIRSTT	craftiest
ACEFLLRUY	carefully
ACEFLMNOS	flamencos
ACEFLNORR	conferral
ACEFLNORS	falconers
ACEFLNORV	conferval
ACEFLNOST	conflates
	falconets
ACEFLPTUU	teacupful
ACEFLRSTU	cratefuls
ACEFLRSUU	saucerful
ACEFLTTUU	fluctuate
ACEFMNRST	craftsmen
ACEFNNORT	Frontenac
ACEFNORSV	confervas
ACEFNRSTT	transfect
ACEFOOPRS	roofscape
ACEFOOPST	footpaces
ACEFORRRT	refractor
ACEFORRRU	carrefour
ACEFORSST	forecasts
ACEFOSTUU	tufaceous
ACEFRRSSU	surfacers
ACEFRRSTU	fractures
ACEGGILNS	cagelings
ACEGGILST	claggiest
ACEGGINOS	Gascoigne
ACEGGIRRS	scraggier
ACEGGIRST	craggiest
ACEGGMORR	MacGregor
ACEGHHILP	high place
ACEGHHPTU	Hugh Capet
ACEGHIIMN	Chiengmai
ACEGHIINV	achieving
ACEGHIIST	chigetais
ACEGHILNP	pleaching
ACEGHILNT	chelating
ACEGHILRT	lethargic
ACEGHINNN	enhancing
ACEGHINNS	encashing
	enchasing
ACEGHINPR	preaching
ACEGHINRS	searching
ACEGHINSS	chasseing
ACEGHINST	teachings
ACEGHIRST	Reichstag
ACEGHMNOS	cheongsam
ACEGHMORT	hectogram
ACEGHNRSU	graunches
ACEGHOPRY	creophagy
ACEGHOPTY	phagocyte
ACEGHRRSU	surcharge
ACEGIILLS	gallicise
ACEGIILLZ	gallicize
ACEGIILMO	oligaemic
ACEGIILNS	anglicise
ACEGIILNT	genitalic
ACEGIILNV	vigilance
ACEGIILNZ	anglicize
ACEGIIMNT	enigmatic
ACEGIINNT	antigenic
ACEGIINSV	vicinages
ACEGIIRRT	geriatric
ACEGIJKNT	jacketing
ACEGIKLNR	lackering
ACEGIKLNY	lackeying
ACEGIKNNR	cankering
ACEGIKNPR	repacking
ACEGIKNRS	screaking
ACEGIKNRT	racketing
ACEGIKPRR	ragpicker
ACEGILLLO	collegial
ACEGILLNO	collegian
ACEGILLNR	cellaring

recalling
ACEGILLOR allegoric
ACEGILLOT colligate
ACEGILMNP emplacing
ACEGILMSU mucilages
ACEGILNNO congenial
ACEGILNNS cleansing
ACEGILNPR parceling
replacing
ACEGILNRS clearings
ACEGILNRU genicular
neuralgic
ACEGILNRV clavering
ACEGILNRW clearwing
ACEGILNSW lacewings
ACEGILNTU cingulate
ACEGILOOR aerologic
ACEGILRTU curtilage
Géricault
graticule
ACEGIMMNR engrammic
ACEGIMMRS scrimmage
ACEGIMMST tagmemics
ACEGIMNNP encamping
ACEGIMNOT geomantic
megatonic
ACEGIMNRS screaming
ACEGIMNRT centigram
cremating
ACEGIMNST magnetics
ACEGIMNTU mutagenic
ACEGIMNUY gynaecium
ACEGIMRRS grimacers
ACEGIMTUZ zeugmatic
ACEGINNNP penancing
ACEGINNOP poignance
ACEGINNOR ignorance
ACEGINNRT cantering
recanting
ACEGINNRV caverning
ACEGINNRY carneying
ACEGINNSU unceasing
ACEGINOTU autogenic
ACEGINPPR recapping
ACEGINPRS escarping
ACEGINPRT carpeting
ACEGINPRY panegyric
ACEGINRRT cratering
retracing
terracing
ACEGINRSS caressing
ACEGINRST caterings
recasting
ACEGIOPRR paregoric
ACEGIOSTT cogitates
geostatic
ACEGIRSTT strategic
ACEGJNOTU conjugate
ACEGKRSTU truckages
ACEGLMNRY clergyman
ACEGLNNPY plangency
ACEGLNOST octangles
ACEGLNOTY cognately
ACEGMMNOO commonage
ACEGMMRSU scrummage
ACEGNNORS crannoges
ACEGNNOTT cotangent
ACEGNNPRY pregnancy
ACEGORRTU corrugate
ACEGORSST escargots
ACEGORSTT cottagers
ACEHHHIST shechitah
ACEHHILPS chelaship
ACEHHIRRS hierarchs
ACEHHIRRY hierarchy
ACEHHIRSS rhachises
ACEHHISTX hexastich
ACEHHLSTT shtetlach
ACEHHMNTT hatchment
ACEHHMOTY theomachy
ACEHHNRST ethnarchs
ACEHHNRTY ethnarchy
ACEHHOOTT toothache
ACEHHOPTY hypotheca
ACEHHPRST heptarchs
ACEHHPRTY heptarchy
ACEHHRSTT thatchers
ACEHHSSTY Hesychast
ACEHIILRS Charles II
ACEHIIMNT hematinic
ACEHIIMSS ischemias
ACEHIIMTT hematitic
ACEHIINOP Phoenicia
ACEHIINPP epiphanic
ACEHIINPT epicanthi
ACEHIINRT trichinae
ACEHIINST Han Cities
ACEHIIPPT epitaphic
ACEHIIRST charities
ACEHIISTT atheistic
ACEHIJKRS hijackers
ACEHIKKLL chalklike
ACEHIKLPT Pitch Lake
ACEHIKLST chalkiest
ACEHIKNPP Peckinpah
ACEHIKORT artichoke
ACEHIKRST heartsick
ACEHIKSTW whackiest
ACEHILLLY helically
ACEHILLTY ethically
ACEHILMMO chamomile
ACEHILMST alchemist
ACEHILNNO chelonian
ACEHILNOR enchorial
ACEHILNOT chelation
ACEHILNOU Chou En-lai
ACEHILNST chatlines
ACEHILNTU unethical
ACEHILNTY thylacine
ACEHILORR Charleroi
ACEHILPRS clipshear
spherical
ACEHILRSU Heraclius
ACEHILRSV Charles IV
Charles VI
ACEHILRSX Charles IX
Charles XI
ACEHILRUV vehicular
ACEHILSTT athletics
ACEHILTTY tachylite
ACEHIMMNS mechanism
ACEHIMNOT methanoic
ACEHIMNRY machinery
ACEHIMNST mechanist
ACEHIMPST emphatics
ACEHIMRTU hematuric
rheumatic
ACEHIMSTT thematics
ACEHINORT anchorite
antechoir
ACEHINORX chronaxie
ACEHINOST inchoates
ACEHINOSV anchovies
ACEHINPST cathepsin
ACEHINRRU hurricane
raunchier
ACEHINRSS chariness
ACEHINRST chantries
snatchier
ACEHINRSV vacherins
ACEHINSST asthenics
Caithness
ACEHINSTY hesitancy
ACEHINTTU authentic
ACEHIOPRY coryphaei
ACEHIPPSS spaceship
ACEHIPRST chapiters
ACEHIPRUY eucryphia
ACEHIPSST pastiches
ACEHIPSTT patchiest
ACEHIPSTW whitecaps
ACEHIRRRT trierarch
ACEHIRRST Charteris
starchier
ACEHIRSST chastiser
ACEHIRSTT theatrics
ACEHIRSTU Eucharist
ACEHISSST chastises
ACEHISTTT chattiest
ACEHKLOSV havelocks
ACEHKLRSS shacklers
ACEHKLSTY latchkeys
ACEHKMORY chromakey
ACEHKOPRS packhorse
ACEHKORST shortcake
ACEHKORSV havockers
ACEHKRSTW thwackers
ACEHLLLMS clamshell
ACEHLLLOR chlorella
ACEHLLOPY epochally
holy place
ACEHLLRTW Chartwell
ACEHLMOPR polemarch
ACEHLMOST moschatel
ACEHLMSST matchless
ACEHLNOSU eulachons

ACEHLNOSY	anchylose
ACEHLNPST	planchets
ACEHLNPTY	phlyctena
ACEHLNRSU	launchers
ACEHLNSTU	unlatches
ACEHLOPSU	cephalous
ACEHLOPSW	showplace
ACEHLORRT	trochlear
ACEHLORST	chlorates
ACEHLORSU	housecarl
ACEHLORTT	charlotte
ACEHLOSST	eschalots
ACEHLOTTY	catholyte
ACEHLRSST	chartless
ACEHLSSUY	Aeschylus
ACEHLTTYY	tachylyte
ACEHMNNOR	anchormen
ACEHMNOPY	cymophane
ACEHMNORT	metarchon
ACEHMNORW	charwomen
ACEHMNOTY	theomancy
ACEHMNPRT	parchment
ACEHMNRST	merchants
ACEHMNSTY	yachtsmen
ACEHMNTTU	humectant
ACEHMORST	chromates
	stomacher
ACEHMORTV	overmatch
ACEHMOSTT	chemostat
ACEHMOSTU	moustache
ACEHMPRTY	champerty
ACEHMSSTU	mustaches
ACEHNNPST	penchants
ACEHNNRTT	trenchant
ACEHNOPRS	chaperons
ACEHNOPRT	North Cape
ACEHNOPST	cenotaphs
ACEHNORRS	rancheros
ACEHNORSS	anchoress
ACEHNOSTT	stonechat
ACEHNOSTU	ceanothus
ACEHNPPRS	schnapper
ACEHNPRTY	pentarchy
ACEHNRSST	snatchers
	stanchers
ACEHNRSTU	chaunters
	stauncher
ACEHNRSUZ	schnauzer
ACEHNSSTU	staunches
ACEHOOSTU	housecoat
ACEHOPPRR	hoppercar
ACEHOPRRS	sharecrop
ACEHOPRTY	pothecary
ACEHOPSST	chassepot
ACEHORRST	carthorse
	orchestra
ACEHORSTT	theocrats
ACEHORSTY	theocrasy
ACEHORTTU	rotachute
ACEHORTVW	overwatch
ACEHOSSSW	showcases
ACEHOSSTU	cathouses
	soutaches
ACEHOSTWY	Cetshwayo
ACEHPRRSU	purchaser
ACEHPRSSU	purchases
ACEHPRTTT	Pratchett
ACEHRRSST	starchers
ACEHRRSTT	tetrarchs
ACEHRRTTY	tetrarchy
ACEHRSSSU	chasseurs
ACEIIILST	italicise
ACEIIILTZ	italicize
ACEIIKLST	ekistical
ACEIIKMNT	kinematic
ACEIILLOT	ciliolate
ACEIILLTV	levitical
ACEIILMPR	empirical
ACEIILMPT	implicate
ACEIILMSS	seismical
ACEIILNNT	anticline
ACEIILNNV	vicennial
ACEIILNPS	cisalpine
ACEIILNST	inelastic
	sciential
ACEIILORT	aerolitic
ACEIILOSS	socialise
ACEIILOST	socialite
ACEIILOSZ	socialize
ACEIILPRT	pearlitic
ACEIILRST	eristical
	realistic
ACEIILRTT	lateritic
	triticale
ACEIILRTV	leviratic
ACEIILSST	silicates
ACEIILSTV	calvities
ACEIIMMNR	Cimmerian
ACEIIMMRU	americium
ACEIIMNRT	antimeric
	criminate
ACEIIMNSS	messianic
ACEIIMORS	cramoisie
ACEIIMPRS	primacies
ACEIIMPTV	impactive
ACEIIMRST	armistice
ACEIINOTV	noviciate
ACEIINPRS	precisian
ACEIINPST	epinastic
ACEIINRTT	intricate
ACEIINRTY	itineracy
ACEIINTTT	nictitate
ACEIIOPST	opacities
ACEIIPRSS	piscaries
ACEIIPSTT	epistatic
ACEIIRSTV	variscite
ACEIISTTT	steatitic
ACEIISTUV	vacuities
ACEIJKNPS	jacksnipe
ACEIKLLSV	Sackville
ACEIKLNNS	cleanskin
ACEIKLPST	skeptical
ACEIKMNNS	nicknames
ACEIKMRSV	mavericks
ACEIKNPSS	capeskins
ACEIKNRST	crankiest
ACEIKNSST	tackiness
ACEIKNSSW	wackiness
ACEIKOPSS	skiascope
ACEIKPRRT	peritrack
ACEILLLNY	cleanlily
ACEILLLXY	lexically
ACEILLMOP	polemical
ACEILLMOR	allomeric
ACEILLMOT	collimate
ACEILLMRS	millraces
	miscaller
ACEILLMSY	mesically
ACEILLNOR	collinear
	coralline
ACEILLNPS	spellican
ACEILLOPS	calliopes
ACEILLORS	localiser
ACEILLORT	corallite
ACEILLORZ	localizer
ACEILLOSS	localises
ACEILLOST	oscillate
	teocallis
ACEILLOSZ	localizes
ACEILLOTV	collative
ACEILLPRS	callipers
ACEILLPSS	allspices
ACEILLPSY	specially
ACEILLPTY	plicately
ACEILLRSV	cavillers
ACEILLRXY	xerically
ACEILMMOS	camomiles
ACEILMMST	clammiest
ACEILMNNU	luminance
ACEILMNOP	policeman
ACEILMNOT	melanotic
ACEILMNPS	manciples
ACEILMNRU	numerical
ACEILMNSU	calumnies
	masculine
ACEILMNTU	culminate
ACEILMOSS	camisoles
	coseismal
ACEILMOSV	semivocal
ACEILMPSS	misplaces
ACEILMRRU	mercurial
ACEILMRTU	tularemic
ACEILMSSU	musicales
ACEILNNNO	canneloni
ACEILNNOR	cornelian
ACEILNNOT	octennial
ACEILNNPS	pinnacles
ACEILNNTY	anciently
ACEILNOPR	porcelain
ACEILNORS	censorial
ACEILNORT	clarionet
ACEILNOST	coastline
	sectional
ACEILNOSV	volcanise
ACEILNOTU	inoculate
ACEILNOVZ	volcanize

ACEILNPTU	inculpate
ACEILNRST	cisternal
	clarinets
	larcenist
ACEILNRTU	centurial
ACEILNRTY	certainly
ACEILNSSS	scaliness
ACEILNSUV	vulcanise
ACEILNTUV	vulcanite
ACEILNTXY	inexactly
ACEILNUVZ	vulcanize
ACEILOPPS	episcopal
ACEILOPRS	caprioles
ACEILOPST	scapolite
ACEILOQUV	equivocal
ACEILORRS	carrioles
ACEILORRT	rectorial
ACEILORST	sclerotia
	sectorial
ACEILORSV	vocaliser
ACEILORSZ	calorizes
ACEILORTT	tectorial
ACEILORTV	vectorial
ACEILORVZ	vocalizer
ACEILOSSV	vocalises
ACEILOSTV	locatives
ACEILOSVZ	vocalizes
ACEILOTVY	coevality
ACEILPPPR	paperclip
ACEILPPSY	pipeclays
ACEILPRSS	spiracles
ACEILPRST	particles
ACEILPRSU	peculiars
ACEILPRTU	plicature
ACEILPSSS	slipcases
ACEILPSSU	Asclepius
	capsulise
ACEILPSTU	euplastic
	spiculate
ACEILPSTY	specialty
ACEILPSUZ	capsulize
ACEILPTUY	eucalypti
ACEILRRTU	curtailer
	reticular
ACEILRSTT	clartiest
ACEILRSTU	sterculia
ACEILRSTV	verticals
ACEILRSTW	crawliest
ACEILRSUV	vesicular
ACEILRTUV	lucrative
	revictual
ACEILSSST	classiest
ACEILSUWY	sluiceway
ACEILTTUV	cultivate
ACEIMMNNY	immanency
ACEIMMNPS	pemmicans
ACEIMMOSS	semicomas
ACEIMNOPS	companies
ACEIMNORT	cremation
	manticore
ACEIMNOST	encomiast
ACEIMNPTU	pneumatic
ACEIMNRST	miscreant
ACEIMNRSU	manicures
	muscarine
ACEIMNSST	semantics
ACEIMNSSY	sycamines
ACEIMNTYZ	enzymatic
ACEIMORST	Masoretic
ACEIMORVW	microwave
ACEIMOSTU	autoecism
ACEIMPRST	spermatic
ACEIMRSST	ceramists
ACEIMRTTU	micturate
ACEINNNRU	uncannier
ACEINNNSS	canniness
ACEINNOOV	novocaine
ACEINNOPT	pentanoic
ACEINNORS	canonries
ACEINNORT	container
	crenation
ACEINNOSS	ascension
	canonises
ACEINNOST	enactions
ACEINNOSZ	canonizes
ACEINNRRY	inerrancy
ACEINNRSU	insurance
ACEINNRTU	runcinate
	uncertain
ACEINNSST	cantiness
	incessant
	instances
ACEINNSSU	nuisances
ACEINOOST	isooctane
ACEINOOTV	evocation
ACEINOPRS	proscenia
ACEINOPRT	recaption
ACEINOPSS	caponises
ACEINOPSU	pinaceous
ACEINOPSZ	caponizes
ACEINORRT	cinerator
ACEINORRV	carnivore
ACEINORSS	scenarios
ACEINORST	actioners
	creations
	narcotise
	reactions
ACEINORSV	veronicas
ACEINORSX	anorexics
ACEINORTT	carnotite
ACEINORTU	cautioner
ACEINORTZ	narcotize
ACEINOSST	canoeists
	cessation
ACEINOSTU	tenacious
ACEINOSTV	invocates
ACEINOSTX	exactions
ACEINOSUV	vinaceous
ACEINPRTT	crepitant
ACEINPRUY	pecuniary
ACEINPSSU	puissance
ACEINPSTT	pittances
ACEINPSTU	apneustic
ACEINPSUY	picayunes
ACEINQTTU	quittance
ACEINRRSW	scrawnier
ACEINRSST	canisters
	scenarist
ACEINRSSZ	craziness
ACEINRSTT	interacts
ACEINRSTU	truancies
ACEINRSTV	navicerts
ACEINRSTY	insectary
ACEINRTTY	certainty
ACEINRTUV	incurvate
ACEINSSSU	issuances
	sauciness
ACEINSSTT	cattiness
	scantiest
	tacitness
ACEINSSTV	vesicants
ACEINSTTU	tunicates
ACEINSTTX	excitants
ACEINSTTY	intestacy
ACEIOPRRS	acrospire
ACEIOPRSU	auriscope
ACEIOPRTV	proactive
ACEIOPSTV	vitascope
ACEIOPTTT	petticoat
ACEIORRSV	corrasive
ACEIORSST	Isocrates
	ostracise
ACEIORSTZ	ostracize
ACEIORSUV	veracious
ACEIOSTUU	autecious
ACEIOSTUV	vitaceous
ACEIOSTVV	vocatives
ACEIOTTUU	autocutie
ACEIPPRRS	pericarps
	scrappier
ACEIPRRSS	perisarcs
ACEIPRSST	practises
ACEIPRSSU	aruspices
ACEIPSSST	escapists
ACEIPSSTU	spacesuit
ACEIQRRSU	acquirers
ACEIQRTTU	acquitter
ACEIQSTUY	sequacity
ACEIRRSSU	curarises
ACEIRRSSW	airscrews
ACEIRRSUZ	curarizes
ACEIRSSSU	cuirasses
ACEIRSSTU	suricates
ACEIRSTTU	rusticate
	urticates
ACEIRSTUV	curatives
ACEIRSUWY	cruiseway
ACEISSSTU	suitcases
ACEISSTTT	scattiest
ACEJKKMOS	smokejack
ACEJKKRSY	skyjacker
ACEJKLMST	jacksmelt
ACEJKNOST	jackstone
ACEJKOORS	jackeroos
ACEJLMSUU	majuscule
ACEKKMRRU	muckraker

ACEKKMRSU muckrakes
ACEKLLMMU mallemuck
ACEKLNSSS slackness
ACEKLOPRW workplace
ACEKLORSV laverocks
ACEKLRSST trackless
ACEKMNRUZ Zuckerman
ACEKMSTUW mucksweat
ACEKNNTTU Nantucket
ACEKNORSU cankerous
ACEKNPRSU unpackers
ACEKOPRRT retropack
ACEKOPRTY copytaker
ACEKORRSY Ayers Rock
ACEKPRSSU sapsucker
ACEKPSSSY skyscapes
ACEKRSTUW awestruck
ACELLLMOU columella
ACELLMORU molecular
ACELLMRSU Marcellus
ACELLNNUY uncleanly
ACELLNORU nucleolar
ACELLNOSS localness
ACELLNRTY centrally
ACELLNRUY unclearly
ACELLOPRS scalloper
ACELLOPSS collapses
escallops
ACELLOQUY coequally
ACELLORRS carollers
ACELLORSS sclerosal
ACELLORSV coveralls
overcalls
ACELLOSSU callouses
ACELLRSTU scutellar
ACELLRSUY secularly
ACELLSSSS classless
ACELMMNOS commensal
ACELMMNSU muscleman
ACELMNTUU tenaculum
ACELMOPST ectoplasm
ACELMORRS clamorers
ACELMORRU clamourer
ACELMORSS scleromas
ACELMORSY claymores
ACELMOSUU ulmaceous
ACELMSSTU muscatels
ACELMSTUU cumulates
ACELNNOOR olecranon
ACELNNOTY connately
ACELNOOSV volcanoes
ACELNOPRV Provençal
ACELNORSU larcenous
ACELNORTU nucleator
recountal
ACELNOSTU consulate
ACELNOSTY claystone
ACELNPRTU crapulent
ACELNPTUY petulancy
ACELNRTTU reluctant
ACELNTUXY exultancy
ACELOOPRR corporale
corporeal
ACELOOSTT coelostat
ACELOPRRU opercular
ACELOPRSS parcloses
ACELOPRST pectorals
ACELOPRTU peculator
ACELOPSTU copulates
scopulate
ACELOPSTY calotypes
ACELORRSU carrousel
ACELORSSU caroluses
carousels
ACELOSSTU cassoulet
osculates
ACELOSTTY catolytes
ACELPPRRU curlpaper
ACELPSTUY eucalypts
ACELRRSSW scrawlers
ACELSSSTU cutlasses
ACEMMOSTY mycetomas
ACEMMOTTU commutate
ACEMNOOPS moonscape
ACEMNOORU coumarone
ACEMNOPSS encompass
ACEMNORRS romancers
ACEMNORTU mucronate
ACEMOOPSU pomaceous
ACEMOORSU moraceous
ACEMOPRRS comparers
ACEMOPRSS mesocarps
ACEMOPSSS compasses
ACEMORRST cremators
ACEMORRTY crematory
ACEMORSSW caseworms
ACEMORSSY sycamores
ACEMOSSUU musaceous
ACEMOSTVY vasectomy
ACEMPRSUY supremacy
ACEMRSSST scamsters
ACENNNORU announcer
ACENNNOSU announces
ACENNOSTT cotenants
ACENNOSTU Antonescu
ACENNOSTV covenants
ACENNOSTZ canzonets
ACENNSSST scantness
ACENOPRRT copartner
procreant
ACENOPSST capstones
ACENOPSTW townscape
ACENOPSTY syncopate
ACENOPTYY cyanotype
ACENOQSTU cotqueans
ACENORRTU raconteur
ACENORRUY Yourcenar
ACENORSST ancestors
ACENORSTU courantes
courtesan
nectarous
ACENORSUV cavernous
ACENORTUZ courtezan
ACENORUVV Vancouver
ACENOSSSV cavessons
ACENOSSTT stonecast
ACENOSTUU cutaneous
ACENPRRTY carpentry
ACENPRSUU pursuance
ACENPTTUU punctuate
ACENRSSSS crassness
ACENRSSTT transects
ACENRSSTU recusants
ACENRSSTZ Carstensz
ACENRSTTU truncates
ACENSSSTW newscasts
ACEOOPRRT corporate
ACEOOPRSS ascospore
ACEOOPRTT Caporetto
ACEOORSSU rosaceous
ACEOORSTV evocators
overcoats
ACEOPPRST spaceport
ACEOPRRTY precatory
ACEOPRSSY caryopses
ACEOPRSTT spectator
ACEORRRTT retractor
ACEORRRVY carryover
ACEORRSSU carousers
ACEORRSTT retroacts
ACEORRSTU craterous
eurocrats
ACEORRSTV cavorters
ACEORRTTX extractor
ACEORSSTV overcasts
ACEORSTTY astrocyte
ACEORSTUU rutaceous
ACEOSSTTU outcastes
ACEOSTUXY auxocytes
ACEPRRSTU capturers
ACEPSSTTY typecasts
ACERRTUUV curvature
ACERSSTTY cytasters
ACERSTTUW cutwaters
ACFFGILNS sclaffing
ACFFIILNO officinal
ACFFIILOS officials
ACFFIINOT officiant
ACFFIIORY officiary
ACFFIKRTY trafficky
ACFFILMOR falciform
ACFFLOSSW scofflaws
ACFGHMORR frogmarch
ACFGIIMNO magnifico
ACFGIINNN financing
ACFGIINPY pacifying
ACFGIIPRS caprifigs
ACFGIKNRT kingcraft
ACFGINORT factoring
ACFGINOTU outfacing
ACFGINRSU surfacing
ACFGINRTU furcating
ACFGIOSUU fugacious
ACFGLNORY gyrfalcon
ACFHIILRT chairlift
ACFHILNOS falchions

ACFHKORST rockshaft
ACFHLORTW flowchart
ACFHMNORS chamfrons
ACFHMORSU forasmuch
ACFHNNORS chanfrons
ACFIIINRS Francis II
ACFIIISST fasciitis
ACFIILLNY finically
ACFIILNOT fictional
ACFIIMNOR aciniform
ACFIIOPRS saporific
ACFIIOPRV vaporific
ACFIIPSST pacifists
ACFIJKRTU jackfruit
ACFIKLNSS calfskins
ACFIKNRSS scarfskin
ACFIKRRTU Friar Tuck
ACFILMORU formulaic
fumarolic
ACFILMORV claviform
ACFILNNOR francolin
ACFILNOOT olfaction
ACFILNOST califonts
ACFILNPPY flippancy
ACFILNRTY franticly
ACFILNRUU funicular
ACFILORST trifocals
ACFIMORRY formicary
ACFINORRT infractor
ACFINORST fractions
ACFINORTU furcation
ACFIORSTU fractious
ACFJKORST Jack Frost
ACFKNORWY fancywork
ACFLLTTUY tactfully
ACFLMNOOR conformal
ACFLNTTUU fluctuant
untactful
ACFLOOPSS foolscaps
ACFLOORTY olfactory
ACFMOSTTU factotums
ACFOOSTUU autofocus
ACGGGINRS scragging
ACGGIIKMN magicking
ACGGIIMNR grimacing
ACGGIIOSS isagogics
ACGGILRSY scraggily
ACGGINOTT cottaging
ACGHHHIIR highchair
ACGHHIJKS highjacks
ACGHHILNT hatchling
ACGHHINOT hoatching
ACGHHINRU hachuring
ACGHHINST hatchings
ACGHHINTT thatching
ACGHIIJKN hijacking
ACGHIIKNN Chinkiang
ACGHIIMNN machining
ACGHIIMNS michigans
ACGHIINNR inarching
ACGHIINRV archiving
ACGHIIPRT graphitic
ACGHIJKLT jacklight
ACGHIKLNS shackling
ACGHIKNOV havocking
ACGHIKNTW thwacking
ACGHILNNU launching
ACGHILORS oligarchs
ACGHILORY oligarchy
ACGHILPRY graphicly
ACGHIMMNY chammying
ACGHIMOOP omophagic
ACGHINNOR anchoring
ACGHINNOT gnathonic
ACGHINNPU paunching
ACGHINNST snatching
stanching
ACGHINNUY Ch'ing-yüan
ACGHINOUV avouching
ACGHINPST nightcaps
ACGHINRST starching
ACGHINRSU churingas
ACGHKNOWW Kwangchow
ACGHLLORS grallochs
ACGHLMOOY logomachy
ACGHMOPRY cymograph
ACGHNNOTU Connaught
ACGHNOORV Goncharov
ACGHNTUUZ Chuang-tzu
ACGHOPPRY copygraph
ACGHORSTU roughcast
ACGIIILNS laicising
ACGIIILNZ laicizing
ACGIIIMST imagistic
ACGIIKNNP panicking
ACGIIKNPX pickaxing
ACGIILLLO illogical
ACGIILLMS gallicism
ACGIILLNV cavilling
ACGIILLOR cigarillo
ACGIILLPR pilgarlic
ACGIILMNS anglicism
ACGIILMNX climaxing
ACGIILMOR microglia
ACGIILNOS gasolinic
logicians
ACGIILNRT articling
ACGIILNST anglicist
ACGIILNTT latticing
ACGIILRTY gracility
ACGIIMNPT impacting
ACGIIMSTT stigmatic
ACGIINNOR inorganic
ACGIINNOT actioning
incognita
ACGIINNTT nictating
ACGIINOST agonistic
ACGIINPSZ capsizing
ACGIINQRU acquiring
ACGIIORST orgiastic
ACGIIRSTT gastritic
ACGIKNNPU unpacking
ACGIKNNTU untacking
ACGILLLOY logically
ACGILLNOR carolling
collaring
ACGILLNOT collating
ACGILLNSU callusing
ACGILLOOO oological
ACGILLOST collagist
ACGILMNOR clamoring
ACGILNNST scantling
ACGILNNTY cantingly
ACGILNORS carolings
ACGILNOST gnostical
nostalgic
ACGILNOXY coaxingly
ACGILNPRY carpingly
ACGILNRSW scrawling
ACGIMMNRS scramming
ACGIMNNOO cognomina
ACGIMNNOR romancing
ACGIMNOOR agronomic
ACGIMNOPR comparing
ACGIMNORR cairngorm
ACGIMNOTU contagium
ACGIMNSTY gymnastic
syntagmic
ACGIMNUUV vacuuming
ACGIMOPRT pictogram
ACGIMOSUU guaiocums
ACGIMOTYZ zygomatic
ACGINNNNO cannoning
ACGINNNOT cantoning
ACGINNOOT cognation
contagion
ACGINNOPY canopying
poignancy
ACGINNORT cartoning
ACGINNORY crayoning
ACGINNOST cognisant
ACGINNOTZ cognizant
ACGINNPPU uncapping
ACGINOPTU outpacing
ACGINORSU carousing
ACGINORTU outracing
ACGINORTV cavorting
ACGINOSST agnostics
ACGINOTTU outacting
ACGINPPRS scrapping
ACGINPRSS scrapings
ACGINPRSW scrawping
ACGINPRTU capturing
ACGINPSTU upcasting
ACGINPTUY pugnacity
ACGIOORSS graciosos
ACGIOORTT cogitator
ACGJNNOTU conjugant
ACGJNORRU currajong
ACGKNNSUY gunnysack
ACGLNORSU clangours
ACGLOOPRY carpology
ACGLOOSTY scatology
ACGMOPRTY cryptogam
ACGNNOOST contangos
ACGNORRUW currawong

ACGORRSUY surrogacy
ACHHIKLSS shashlick
ACHHILNOR rhonchial
ACHHILORT haircloth
ACHHINNOT chthonian
ACHHINOST chainshot
ACHHINSTW whinchats
ACHHINSTY hyacinths
ACHHIPPRS hipparchs
ACHHIPRSU pushchair
ACHHLOSTW washcloth
ACHIIIMOS Chisimaio
ACHIIKNNP chinkapin
ACHIILMOS isochimal
ACHIILMSW whimsical
ACHIILNOS Nicholas I
ACHIILRTY chirality
ACHIILSST chiliasts
ACHIIMNST machinist
ACHIINPSY physician
ACHIINRST Christian
Christina
ACHIIOPST pistachio
ACHIIORST ahistoric
ACHIIPRSV vicarship
ACHIIRRTT arthritic
ACHIIRSTV archivist
ACHIISTWY Yahwistic
ACHIKKSSW kickshaws
ACHIKLMST mahlstick
ACHIKLMSY hickymals
ACHIKLPST chalkpits
ACHIKNOST antishock
ACHIKRSSW rickshaws
ACHILLNTY Chantilly
ACHILLOST sailcloth
ACHILMOPU mailpouch
ACHILMPTY lymphatic
ACHILMTUZ chalutzim
ACHILNOPT haplontic
ACHILNORT antichlor
ACHILNOSV Nicholas V
ACHILNRUY raunchily
ACHILNSTU clianthus
ACHILNSTY snatchily
ACHILOPSU pachoulis
ACHILOPTU patchouli
ACHILORST acroliths
ACHILORTV archivolt
ACHILOSST scholiast
ACHILPSSY physicals
ACHILRSSY chrysalis
ACHILRSTY starchily
ACHILSTTY cattishly
ACHIMMNOS monachism
ACHIMMORZ machzorim
ACHIMMOSS masochism
ACHIMNOPS champions
ACHIMNOPY hypomanic
ACHIMNORS harmonics
ACHIMNORT chromatin
ACHIMNOST macintosh
monachist
ACHIMNSTW switchman
ACHIMOOTX homotaxic
ACHIMOPSU Pachomius
ACHIMORST rhotacism
ACHIMORYZ mycorhiza
ACHIMOSST masochist
ACHIMOSTU mustachio
ACHIMRSST Christmas
ACHIMRSSW scrimshaw
ACHINNOST stanchion
ACHINNOTW Chinatown
ACHINNSSU anchusins
ACHINOPPS pansophic
ACHINOPRT anthropic
ACHINOPST cashpoint
ACHINOSTZ hoactzins
ACHIOOPST sociopath
ACHIOPPRS hippocras
ACHIORSTT rhotacist
ACHIORSTV tovarisch
ACHIPRSUY haruspicy
ACHIPSTTU chupattis
ACHIRSSTT chartists
ACHISTUWZ Auschwitz
ACHKKKOOS Kokoschka
ACHKLNOOS solonchak
ACHKMNOUU Manchukuo
ACHKMORSS shamrocks
ACHKMORTU touchmark
ACHKNORRW hornwrack
ACHKOPRTW patchwork
ACHLLORSY scholarly
ACHLMNOOS schoolman
ACHLMSTYZ schmaltzy
ACHLNSTUY staunchly
ACHLOOSTU holocaust
ACHLOPRST calthrops
ACHLOPRYY polyarchy
ACHLOPTUY patchouly
ACHMOORST chatrooms
ACHMOORSU achromous
ACHNOPSTY sycophant
ACHNSTUYZ Zacynthus
ACHOORSTU coauthors
ACHOPSTTW stopwatch
ACHOPSTUY hypocaust
ACHORSSST Trossachs
ACHORTTTU cutthroat
ACHPRSSTU pushcarts
ACHRRSTUY craythurs
ACIIILNOS siciliano
ACIIILNOT ciliation
ACIIILNRT triclinia
ACIIILNSV civilians
ACIIIMNST animistic
ACIIIMNTV vitaminic
ACIIIMRSV Casimir IV
ACIIINPPR principia
ACIIINPST pianistic
sincipita
ACIIJRSTU justiciar
ACIIKNNNS cannikins
ACIIKPRST paitricks
ACIILLNOS collinsia
isoclinal
ACIILLNST scintilla
ACIILLOPT political
ACIILLSSU siliculas
ACIILMNPU municipal
ACIILMNRS criminals
ACIILMNSV Calvinism
ACIILMNTY militancy
ACIILMOSS socialism
ACIILMOSU malicious
ACIILMQTU quitclaim
ACIILNNOT clintonia
ACIILNOOT coalition
ACIILNOPT plication
ACIILNOVV convivial
ACIILNOVY inviolacy
ACIILNPPR principal
ACIILNPST cisplatin
ACIILNRSU incisural
ACIILOPRT pictorial
ACIILORST soritical
ACIILORTZ triazolic
ACIILOSST socialist
ACIILOSTY sociality
ACIILQUZZ quizzical
ACIILTTTY tactility
ACIIMMNOT ammonitic
ACIIMMPST psammitic
ACIIMNNOS insomniac
ACIIMNNOT antimonic
antinomic
ACIIMNOPT impaction
ACIIMNORT mortician
ACIIMNOSS simoniacs
ACIIMNOSU minacious
ACIIMNOTT manicotti
ACIIMNSSU musicians
ACIIMOPRS micropsia
ACIIMOPST simpatico
ACIIMORTT triatomic
ACIIMOSST mosaicist
ACIIMOSTT atomistic
ACIIMOTTY atomicity
ACIIMPRST prismatic
ACIIMRSST scimitars
ACIIMSSTT atticisms
ACIIMSTUV viaticums
ACIINNOST onanistic
Toscanini
ACIINNOTT nictation
ACIINNOTU incaution
ACIINNQSU cinquains
ACIINOPST opticians
ACIINORTV Victorian
ACIINOSTT Anticosti
citations
ACIINOTTX antitoxic
ACIINOTTY atonicity
ACIINPRTU Paricutín

puritanic
ACIINPTTY antitypic
ACIINRRTY irritancy
ACIIOPRST psoriatic
ACIIOPRTT parotitic
patriotic
ACIIOPTZZ pizzicato
ACIIORSSV varicosis
ACIIORSTV victorias
ACIIORSTY cariosity
ACIIORSUV vicarious
ACIIOSSTT isostatic
ACIIOSUVV vivacious
ACIIPRSTT patristic
ACIIPTTVY captivity
ACIISSTTT atticists
statistic
ACIISSTTU autistics
ACIISSTTV activists
ACIJKKPSS skipjacks
ACIJLMNUU Janiculum
ACIJNNORT Corantijn
ACIKKNNOT antiknock
ACIKLMPTU multipack
ACIKLMSTU maulstick
ACIKLNOTY ankylotic
ACIKLOSTT tailstock
ACIKLPSST slapstick
ACIKLPSTY plasticky
ACIKNNPRS crankpins
ACIKNOOPR pickaroon
ACIKNOSTU Kostunica
ACIKOPSSY skiascopy
ACIKRSTTU tracksuit
ACILLLOUV colluvial
ACILLLRYY lyrically
ACILLMOSS localisms
ACILLMSUY musically
ACILLNNSY synclinal
ACILLNOOS colonials
ACILLNOOT collation
ACILLNORS carillons
ACILLNOSS scallions
ACILLNOTY tonically
ACILLOOQU colloquia
ACILLOPTY optically
topically
ACILLORST cloistral
ACILLORYZ zircalloy
ACILLOSST localists
ACILLOSTY callosity
stoically
ACILLOTXY toxically
ACILLPTYY typically
ACILMMOTT committal
ACILMNNTU culminant
ACILMNOPS complains
ACILMNOPT complaint
compliant
ACILMNOSS laconisms
ACILMNOSV volcanism
ACILMNPRT McPartlin
ACILMNSUU unmusical
ACILMNSUV vulcanism
ACILMOOPY Pilcomayo
ACILMOPRS comprisal
proclaims
ACILMOSSV vocalisms
ACILMPTUU capitulum
ACILMSSTU masculist
simulcast
ACILNNNUY uncannily
ACILNNOOS nonsocial
ACILNNOTU continual
inoculant
ACILNNQTU clinquant
ACILNNRUU ranunculi
ACILNOOSS Colossian
ACILNOOST locations
ACILNOPRT prolactin
ACILNOPSS salpicons
ACILNOPSY isopycnal
ACILNORST contrails
ACILNORTT contralti
ACILNOSTT clinostat
ACILNOSTU suctional
sulcation
ACILNOSUV univocals
ACILNPTUY untypical
ACILNRSTU lincrusta
ACILNRSWY scrawnily
ACILNSTYY syncytial
ACILOOPRS acropolis
ACILOOPST apostolic
ACILOPPRT captopril
ACILOQTUY loquacity
ACILORRSU cursorial
ACILORRSV corrivals
ACILORSSU ossicular
ACILORSTU ocularist
suctorial
ACILOSSTV vocalists
ACILOSSTY asystolic
ACILOTTUY autolytic
ACILPPRSY scrappily
ACILRRTUU utricular
ACILRSTUV cultivars
ACILSSTTY systaltic
ACIMMNOOT monatomic
ACIMMORSS commissar
ACIMNNNOS cinnamons
ACIMNNOOP companion
ACIMNOOST onomastic
ACIMNOOTU autonomic
ACIMNOOTX taxonomic
ACIMNOPRY paronymic
ACIMNORST narcotism
romantics
ACIMNOSST monastics
ACIMNOSTU aconitums
ACIMNOSUU acuminous
ACIMOOTTU autotomic
ACIMOPSSY symposiac
ACIMORSST ostracism
ACIMORSTT stromatic
ACIMPRSTY sympatric
ACIMRSTTU strumatic
ACINNORST constrain
transonic
ACINNOSSS scansions
ACINNOSST canonists
sanctions
ACINNOSTT Tocantins
ACINOOPPR propanoic
ACINOOPRS picaroons
ACINOOPRT proaction
ACINOOPTZ panzootic
ACINOORRS corrasion
ACINOORST consortia
ACINOORTV invocator
ACINOOSST iconostas
ACINOOSTV vocations
ACINOOTUX auxotonic
ACINOPSTU acupoints
ACINORSST croissant
ACINORSTY crayonist
ACINOSSTW wainscots
ACINOSSWX coxswains
ACINOSTTU scutation
ACINOSTTX toxicants
ACINRSSSU narcissus
ACIOOPRSU paroicous
ACIOOPRSZ saprozoic
ACIOORSTU atrocious
ACIOORSUV voracious
ACIOOSTUU autoicous
ACIOOTTUX autotoxic
ACIOPRSSY caryopsis
ACIOPRSTT prostatic
ACIOPRSTY piscatory
ACIOPTTUY autotypic
ACIOSTTXY cytotaxis
ACIRSSTUY casuistry
ACJKOPRST jockstrap
ACJLLORUY jocularly
ACKKMOPRS pockmarks
ACKLLPSSU skullcaps
ACKLMOOOR cloakroom
ACKLNORST cornstalk
ACKLOOPSW woolpacks
ACKLOOSSW woolsacks
ACKLORSST crosstalk
ACKLORSSW crosswalk
ACLLLOSUY callously
ACLLMNOSU molluscan
ACLLOORRY corollary
ACLLOORST collators
colostral
ACLMMORSW clamworms
ACLMNOOOS coolamons
ACLMNOORU colourman
monocular
ACLMOOOPR Marco Polo
ACLMOORSS classroom
ACLMOORSU clamorous
ACLMOPSTY cytoplasm

ACLMSSUUV vasculums
ACLNNORTU nocturnal
ACLNOORST colorants
ACLNOORTT contralto
ACLNORSTU calutrons
ACLNORSUY cynosural
ACLOOORRT coralroot
ACLOOPRRS corporals
ACLOORUWY colourway
ACLOPPRYY polycarpy
ACLOPRRSU procurals
ACLOPRSTU Patroclus
ACLOPRSUU crapulous
opuscular
ACLOPRSXY xylocarps
ACLOPRTTU plutocrat
ACLORSUUY raucously
ACLOSTUUY Autolycus
ACLOSUUVY vacuously
ACMNOOPRS monocarps
ACMNOOPSY manoscopy
ACMNOORRT cormorant
ACMNOORST monocrats
ACMNOOSTU cosmonaut
ACMNOPRYY pyromancy
ACMNORSTU sanctorum
ACMOOPRSS coprosmas
ACMOORRST motorcars
ACMOORSTU macrotous
ACMORRSUU macrurous
ACMORSSTW wormcasts
ACMORSTUY customary
ACNNNOOST consonant
ACNNOSSTT constants
ACNOOORST octaroons
ACNOOPRST corposant
ACNOORRSU rancorous
ACNOORSST ostracons
ACNORSSTT contrasts
ACNORSTTU turncoats
ACNORSTTY contrasty
ACOOPPRRS sporocarp
ACOORSSTU autocross
ACOPRRSTT protracts
ACORRSTTU scrutator
ACORRSTUY carryouts
ACORSSSUW curassows
ACORSSSWY crossways
ACORSSTTY cryostats
ACOSSTTTY statocyst
ACPSSSTUY pussycats
ADDDEEEHR redheaded
ADDDEEFIL defiladed
ADDDEEFRU defrauded
ADDDEEGLN gladdened
ADDDEEHNR redhanded
ADDDEEKLS skedaddle
ADDDEENTU denudated
ADDDEERSS addressed
ADDDEFIIN dandified
ADDDEGMNO goddamned
ADDDEIINS disdained
ADDDEIMNO diamonded
ADDDEISSU dissuaded
ADDDELNSU unsaddled
ADDDELRST straddled
ADDEEEFRT federated
ADDEEEGLT delegated
ADDEEEGRS degreased
ADDEEELTW Tweeddale
ADDEEEMNR meandered
ADDEEENRS deadeners
serenaded
ADDEEENWZ Waddenzee
ADDEEEPRT depredate
ADDEEERRT retreaded
ADDEEERSS addressee
ADDEEFHNS handfeeds
ADDEEFILN enfiladed
ADDEEFILS defilades
ADDEEFLTU defaulted
ADDEEFNNT defendant
ADDEEFNSS fadedness
ADDEEFRRT redrafted
ADDEEFRRU defrauder
ADDEEGHIP pigheaded
ADDEEGINN deadening
ADDEEGINR deraigned
ADDEEGIRS disagreed
ADDEEGLNR gladdener
glandered
ADDEEGORT derogated
ADDEEGRRS degraders
ADDEEGSSU degaussed
ADDEEHHOT hotheaded
ADDEEHINP pinheaded
ADDEEHLNR rehandled
ADDEEHLNS handseled
ADDEEHLSY aldehydes
ADDEEHOTW towheaded
ADDEEHRSS headdress
ADDEEHRTY dehydrate
ADDEEIILS idealised
ADDEEIILZ idealized
ADDEEILLR redialled
ADDEEILMP impleaded
ADDEEILNS deadlines
ADDEEILPT depilated
ADDEEILRV daredevil
ADDEEILST deadliest
ADDEEIMTT meditated
ADDEEINRT detrained
ADDEEINRV reinvaded
ADDEEIPRR draperied
ADDEEIPRS despaired
ADDEEIPRU Depardieu
ADDEEJNSS jadedness
ADDEELNNR Nederland
ADDEELNPY endplayed
ADDEELNRS slandered
ADDEELNRU laundered
ADDEELOST desolated
ADDEELPPW dewlapped
ADDEEMNRS demanders
redemands
ADDEEMNRU maundered
undreamed
ADDEEMNST damnedest
ADDEEMORT moderated
ADDEEMPST stampeded
ADDEENNPT dependant
ADDEENOTT detonated
ADDEENRST darnedest
ADDEENRTU denatured
ADDEENSTU denudates
ADDEEOPRS desperado
ADDEEOPRT readopted
ADDEEPRSU persuaded
ADDEEPRTU depurated
ADDEERRSS addresser
readdress
ADDEERSSS addresses
ADDEERSTW stewarded
ADDEESTTW wadsetted
ADDEFFHNO offhanded
ADDEFFLOO offloaded
ADDEFIIMN damnified
ADDEFIINS dandifies
ADDEFIIPT pedatifid
ADDEFINNR Ferdinand
ADDEFORRW forwarded
ADDEGGINR degrading
ADDEGHILT deadlight
ADDEGHINR hagridden
ADDEGIIMN diademing
ADDEGIITT digitated
ADDEGILNR laddering
ADDEGILOU dialogued
ADDEGILSS glissaded
ADDEGIMNN demanding
maddening
ADDEGINNR dandering
ADDEGINNS saddening
ADDEGINOS diagnosed
ADDEGIRRS disregard
ADDEGLRUY guardedly
ADDEGNOOR dragooned
gadrooned
ADDEGNORW downgrade
ADDEGNRRU undergrad
ADDEGNRUU unguarded
ADDEHHOTY hydathode
ADDEHILOY holidayed
ADDEHILRS dihedrals
ADDEHINRY anhydride
ADDEHINSW headwinds
ADDEHINSY hendiadys
ADDEHIRRW hardwired
ADDEHIRYZ hydrazide
ADDEHLOSS shedloads
ADDEHMRSU drumheads
ADDEHNNRU underhand
ADDEHNORS hardnosed
ADDEHORSW headwords
ADDEIIIMT dimidiate
ADDEIIIRW Edward III

ADDEIILNV invalided
ADDEIILNX Dixieland
ADDEIIMNS desmidian
ADDEIIRVW Edward VII
ADDEIISTV additives
ADDEIKNPP kidnapped
ADDEILLNS landslide
ADDEILMMN middleman
ADDEILMNR Midlander
ADDEILNNO dandelion
ADDEILNRU underlaid
ADDEILNST tidelands
ADDEILPSY displayed
ADDEILSVY advisedly
ADDEIMNOS nomadised
ADDEIMNOT demantoid
dominated
ADDEIMNOZ nomadized
ADDEIMNTY dynamited
ADDEIMORT dermatoid
ADDEIMPRY pyramided
ADDEIMSST dismasted
ADDEINNRU undrained
ADDEINNTU inundated
ADDEINOPR poniarded
ADDEINPRS drepanids
ADDEINPRU underpaid
ADDEINRTT dittander
ADDEINRTU indurated
ADDEINSUV unadvised
ADDEIORSS sideroads
ADDEIOSVW disavowed
ADDEIQSSU squaddies
ADDEIRSSU dissuader
ADDEIRSSW sidewards
ADDEISSSU dissuades
ADDEISSTT distasted
ADDEJNORU adjourned
ADDEKNRSU underdaks
ADDELLOPR pollarded
ADDELMOTU modulated
ADDELNSSU unsaddles
ADDELNTUU undulated
ADDELRRST straddler
ADDELRSST straddles
ADDELRSTW twaddlers
ADDEMNORT mordanted
ADDEMORRY dromedary
ADDENNORU unadorned
ADDENNRTU redundant
ADDENNTUU undaunted
ADDENOORT deodorant
ADDENOPTU unadopted
ADDENORUY duodenary
ADDENOSTU astounded
ADDENRSTU transuded
ADDEOPSTT postdated
ADDEORRSS addressor
ADDEPQRUU quadruped
ADDEPRSSU superadds
ADDFFILOS daffodils
ADDFFNRUY dandruffy
ADDFIIQRU quadrifid
ADDFLNNOO land of Nod
ADDGGIJNU adjudging
ADDGHNORU draghound
ADDGIIMNS misadding
ADDGILMNY maddingly
ADDGILNSW swaddling
ADDGILNTW twaddling
ADDGINNOT Addington
ADDGMRSUU mudguards
ADDGOQSSU godsquads
ADDHHIOOR hardihood
ADDHHLNOS handholds
ADDHIIKMS kaddishim
ADDHLOOTU adulthood
ADDHNNORU roundhand
ADDHOORSW hardwoods
ADDIINOST additions
ADDINNNOU Dundonian
ADDINNORS ordinands
ADDINORSU diandrous
ADDKNRRSU drunkards
ADDLLNNOU Llandudno
ADDLLNORS landlords
ADDLNNOOP Pondoland
ADDLNOOSW downloads
woodlands
ADDLNORRS randlords
ADDLNORST landdrost
ADDNORSWW downwards
ADDOORRSY dooryards
ADDOORSWY woodyards
ADEEEFHRT feathered
ADEEEFLLT leafleted
ADEEEFNRR referenda
ADEEEFRST defeaters
federates
ADEEEFRTW feedwater
ADEEEGGNR reengaged
ADEEEGGRT gadgeteer
ADEEEGHNR greenhead
ADEEEGLRT regelated
relegated
ADEEEGLRV leveraged
ADEEEGLST delegates
ADEEEGNRS renegades
ADEEEGNRT generated
greatened
ADEEEGRSS degreases
ADEEEGSUW agueweeds
ADEEEGTTV vegetated
ADEEEHHRT heathered
ADEEEHKNR hearkened
ADEEEHLRT leathered
ADEEEHLST steelhead
ADEEEHNRT heartened
ADEEEHPRT preheated
ADEEEHRRS rehearsed
ADEEEHRTW weathered
ADEEEHSSY eyeshades
ADEEEILMN madeleine
ADEEEILNT delineate
ADEEEINRS deaneries
ADEEEINST detainees
ADEEEIRSS diaereses
ADEEEKNRW rewakened
ADEEEKNSW snakeweed
ADEEELLMN enamelled
ADEEELLST teaselled
ADEEELLSW weaselled
ADEEELLTZ teazelled
ADEEELMNP empaneled
ADEEELNRR relearned
ADEEELNRZ Zeelander
ADEEELRRT realtered
ADEEEMNRR meanderer
ADEEEMOST edematose
ADEEEMPRT permeated
ADEEEMRSV Mesa Verde
ADEEENRRS serenader
ADEEENRSS serenades
ADEEENRST East Ender
ADEEENRTT entreated
ADEEENRTV denervate
enervated
venerated
ADEEENSTT edentates
ADEEEPPRR repapered
ADEEEPRSS rapeseeds
ADEEEPRST desperate
ADEEERRTT retreated
ADEEERSTT estreated
ADEEERTTU deuterate
ADEEERTWW waterweed
ADEEFFGRU gauffered
ADEEFFILR fieldfare
ADEEFFRST restaffed
ADEEFGILR filagreed
ADEEFGINN deafening
ADEEFGINT defeating
ADEEFGLLR Lagerfeld
ADEEFGNRT engrafted
ADEEFHORS foreheads
ADEEFIKLW Wakefield
ADEEFIKRR firedrake
ADEEFILMS Masefield
ADEEFILNS enfilades
ADEEFILOT defoliate
ADEEFILSU feudalise
ADEEFILUZ feudalize
ADEEFIMST defeatism
ADEEFINRR refrained
ADEEFISTT defeatist
ADEEFLLNN flanneled
ADEEFLLRY federally
ADEEFLMST Flamsteed
ADEEFLNNR Fernandel
ADEEFLNRU underleaf
ADEEFLNTT flattened
ADEEFLORS freeloads
ADEEFLORT floreated
refloated
ADEEFLRRS deferrals
ADEEFLRTT flattered

ADEEFLRTU	defaulter
ADEEFLRTW	delftware
ADEEFLSSX	flaxseeds
ADEEFMNOR	forenamed
ADEEFMORR	forearmed
ADEEFMORT	fadometer
ADEEFRRSY	defrayers
ADEEGGINR	degearing
ADEEGGINS	disengage
ADEEGGIRV	aggrieved
ADEEGGIRW	earwigged
ADEEGGLNO	golden age
ADEEGGLNY	engagedly
ADEEGGMOU	demagogue
ADEEGGNNR	gangrened
ADEEGGNNU	unengaged
ADEEGGOPU	pedagogue
ADEEGGRSS	aggressed
ADEEGGRST	staggered
ADEEGGRSW	swaggered
ADEEGIILT	Gileadite
ADEEGIKLL	gladelike
ADEEGILLR	galleried
ADEEGILLS	legalised
ADEEGILLZ	legalized
ADEEGILNR	engrailed
	realigned
ADEEGILRR	gradelier
ADEEGILTV	levigated
ADEEGIMNN	demeaning
ADEEGIMNT	geminated
ADEEGIMRT	emigrated
ADEEGINNR	endearing
	engrained
	grenadine
ADEEGINRR	grenadier
	rereading
ADEEGINRT	denigrate
ADEEGINST	designate
ADEEGINSV	envisaged
ADEEGINTV	negatived
ADEEGIPRS	De Gasperi
ADEEGIRSS	disagrees
ADEEGIRST	tragedies
ADEEGIRSU	gauderies
ADEEGIUVW	waveguide
ADEEGLLLY	allegedly
ADEEGLLRV	gravelled
ADEEGLNNR	Greenland
ADEEGLNNT	entangled
ADEEGLNOT	elongated
ADEEGLNRW	Wergeland
ADEEGLNRY	enragedly
	legendary
ADEEGLOOW	eaglewood
ADEEGLRTU	regulated
ADEEGMNRR	germander
ADEEGMNRS	gendarmes
ADEEGMNRT	garmented
	margented
ADEEGMNTU	augmented
ADEEGMOPS	megapodes
ADEEGMOSS	megadoses
ADEEGMRRU	demurrage
ADEEGNNRS	endangers
	greensand
ADEEGNNUV	unavenged
ADEEGNORS	renegados
ADEEGNRRS	gardeners
ADEEGNRST	estranged
ADEEGNRSU	dungarees
ADEEGNRSV	Gravesend
ADEEGORST	derogates
ADEEGRRSS	deergrass
ADEEGRSSS	degassers
ADEEGSSSU	degausses
ADEEGSTTU	degustate
ADEEHHITW	whitehead
ADEEHHLRY	Heyerdahl
ADEEHIISV	Heaviside
ADEEHIKTV	khedivate
ADEEHILNR	headliner
ADEEHILNS	headlines
ADEEHIMNV	Midheaven
ADEEHINRT	herniated
	inearthed
ADEEHINSS	headiness
ADEEHINSV	evanished
ADEEHIRRT	threadier
ADEEHISST	diatheses
ADEEHISSV	adhesives
ADEEHISTT	hesitated
ADEEHKLRS	sheldrake
ADEEHKSWW	hawkweeds
ADEEHLLNS	hanselled
ADEEHLLOS	leasehold
ADEEHLLSW	wellheads
ADEEHLNRS	rehandles
ADEEHLNSU	unleashed
ADEEHLRST	slathered
ADEEHLSSS	shadeless
ADEEHLSST	deathless
ADEEHLTTY	ethylated
ADEEHMNOT	methadone
ADEEHMOST	homestead
ADEEHMSST	stemheads
ADEEHNORS	hoarsened
ADEEHNOST	headstone
ADEEHNPPR	apprehend
ADEEHNPRS	sharpened
ADEEHNRRS	hardeners
	rehardens
ADEEHNRSS	harnessed
ADEEHNRST	adherents
ADEEHNRTU	unearthed
ADEEHNSTW	enswathed
ADEEHORRV	overheard
ADEEHORSS	soreheads
ADEEHORSV	overheads
ADEEHOSWY	eyeshadow
ADEEHPPRS	preshaped
ADEEHPRRS	rephrased
ADEEHPRST	spreathed
ADEEHPRSW	prewashed
ADEEHRRST	rethreads
	threaders
ADEEHRSST	headrests
ADEEHRSTT	shattered
ADEEHRSTV	harvested
ADEEHRSTW	watershed
ADEEHSTUX	exhausted
ADEEIILRS	idealiser
ADEEIILRZ	idealizer
ADEEIILSS	idealises
ADEEIILSZ	idealizes
ADEEIIMMT	immediate
ADEEIIMNS	deaminise
ADEEIIMNZ	deaminize
ADEEIIMST	mediatise
ADEEIIMTV	mediative
ADEEIIMTZ	mediatize
ADEEIIRSS	diaeresis
ADEEIIRST	dietaries
ADEEIJMRS	jeremiads
ADEEIKLMR	dreamlike
ADEEILLOS	oeillades
ADEEILLUV	Deauville
ADEEILMNP	impaneled
ADEEILMNR	madrilene
ADEEILMNT	alimented
ADEEILMPR	epidermal
	impearled
	impleader
ADEEILMRS	misdealer
	misleader
ADEEILMTY	mediately
ADEEILMTZ	metalized
ADEEILNOT	toenailed
ADEEILNPS	penalised
ADEEILNPX	explained
ADEEILNPZ	penalized
ADEEILNSS	idealness
ADEEILNST	datelines
ADEEILOTT	etiolated
ADEEILPPR	reapplied
ADEEILPRS	pearlised
ADEEILPRV	prevailed
ADEEILPRZ	pearlized
ADEEILPSS	displease
ADEEILPST	depilates
ADEEILQSU	equalised
ADEEILQUZ	equalized
ADEEILRRS	derailers
ADEEILRST	elaterids
ADEEILRSV	velarised
ADEEILRVZ	velarized
ADEEILTTV	levitated
ADEEIMMNS	misdemean
ADEEIMMRT	dreamtime
ADEEIMNNO	menadione
ADEEIMNOU	eudemonia
ADEEIMNRR	remainder
ADEEIMNRT	minareted
ADEEIMNST	amnestied
ADEEIMRRR	remarried
ADEEIMRST	diameters

	dreamiest
ADEEIMSST	demitasse
ADEEIMSTT	estimated
	meditates
ADEEINNOS	adenosine
ADEEINNRT	entrained
ADEEINPRT	pertained
	repainted
ADEEINRRT	retrained
ADEEINRSS	nearsides
	readiness
ADEEINRST	detainers
	resinated
ADEEINRSV	reinvades
ADEEINRTT	denitrate
	intreated
ADEEINRUW	unwearied
ADEEINSTT	tetanised
ADEEINTTZ	tetanized
ADEEINTVV	adventive
ADEEIOPRT	periodate
ADEEIOPTV	videotape
ADEEIORSZ	zedoaries
ADEEIPPSS	passepied
ADEEIPPST	peptidase
ADEEIPRRS	draperies
ADEEIPRSS	airspeeds
ADEEIPRTU	repudiate
ADEEIRRST	dreariest
ADEEIRSST	steadiers
ADEEIRSTV	advertise
ADEEIRSTW	waterside
ADEEIRTTW	tidewater
ADEEIRTTX	extradite
ADEEIRTVZ	advertize
ADEEISSTT	stateside
	steadiest
ADEEISSTV	sedatives
ADEEISTTV	estivated
ADEEITUVX	exudative
	exuviated
ADEEJMRSU	mudejares
ADEEKMRST	demarkets
ADEEKNNSS	nakedness
ADEEKNPSW	knapweeds
ADEEKNRRS	darkeners
ADEEKNRTU	undertake
ADEEKOPRS	presoaked
ADEELLLRU	laurelled
ADEELLMRV	marvelled
ADEELLNRY	learnedly
ADEELLPPR	rappelled
ADEELLPSY	pleasedly
ADEELLRTV	travelled
ADEELLRXY	relaxedly
ADEELLSST	tasselled
ADEELLSTT	stellated
ADEELLTXY	exaltedly
ADEELMMRT	trammeled
ADEELMNOP	pademelon
ADEELMNOR	ealdormen
ADEELMNOS	lemonades
ADEELMNPY	ependymal
ADEELMORU	remoulade
ADEELMRSS	dreamless
ADEELNNPR	replanned
ADEELNNRU	unlearned
ADEELNORS	Esdraelon
	oleanders
ADEELNORV	overladen
ADEELNOST	endosteal
ADEELNPRT	replanted
ADEELNPST	endplates
ADEELNPTX	explanted
ADEELNQUU	unequaled
ADEELNRRS	slanderer
ADEELNRRU	launderer
ADEELNRSU	underseal
ADEELNRTU	unaltered
	unrelated
ADEELNRUV	unraveled
ADEELNSSW	Waldenses
ADEELNTTY	dentately
ADEELOPTU	outleaped
ADEELORST	desolater
ADEELORTT	tolerated
ADEELOSST	desolates
ADEELPRST	plastered
ADEELPRSU	pleasured
ADEELPSST	pedestals
ADEELQRRU	quarreled
ADEELRRST	treadlers
ADEELRRTU	adulterer
ADEELRSST	tradeless
ADEELRSTY	steelyard
ADEELRSVY	adversely
ADEEMMNNT	amendment
ADEEMMORT	dermatome
ADEEMMOXY	myxoedema
ADEEMMRST	stammered
ADEEMNOPR	promenade
ADEEMNORS	demeanors
ADEEMNORT	emendator
	Notre Dame
ADEEMNORU	demeanour
	enamoured
ADEEMNOST	nematodes
ADEEMNPRS	dampeners
ADEEMNPSY	ependymas
ADEEMNRRU	maunderer
ADEEMNRST	smartened
	tradesmen
ADEEMNRTU	numerated
ADEEMNRTY	dynameter
ADEEMNSSS	madnesses
ADEEMOORR	aerodrome
ADEEMOPRR	madrepore
ADEEMORRX	xeroderma
ADEEMORST	moderates
ADEEMORTT	trematode
ADEEMOSTU	edematous
ADEEMPRRW	prewarmed
ADEEMPRST	stampeder
ADEEMPSST	stampedes
	stepdames
ADEEMPSTU	despumate
ADEEMPTTT	attempted
ADEEMRSSU	reassumed
ADEEMRSTT	smattered
ADEENNORR	nonreader
ADEENNPRT	trepanned
ADEENNPRU	depanneur
ADEENNRSS	Anderssen
ADEENORST	resonated
ADEENORSV	endeavors
ADEENORSY	aerodynes
ADEENORTV	renovated
ADEENORUV	endeavour
ADEENOSTT	detonates
ADEENPPRS	endpapers
ADEENPPRT	entrapped
ADEENPPRW	enwrapped
ADEENPRRS	panderers
ADEENPRRT	partnered
ADEENPRSX	expanders
ADEENPRTT	patterned
ADEENPSST	adeptness
ADEENRRSW	wanderers
ADEENRRTU	underrate
ADEENRRUW	underwear
ADEENRSSU	underseas
ADEENRSTT	attenders
ADEENRSTU	denatures
	sauntered
	undereats
ADEENRSTY	sedentary
ADEENRTTU	untreated
ADEENRTTV	advertent
ADEENRTUV	adventure
ADEENSSSU	danseuses
ADEENSTTV	vendettas
ADEEOPRRT	perorated
ADEEOPRSV	eavesdrop
ADEEORRSU	rearoused
ADEEORRTV	overrated
	overtrade
ADEEORTVX	overtaxed
ADEEPPRRW	rewrapped
ADEEPPRSS	appressed
ADEEPQRTU	parqueted
ADEEPRRSS	spreaders
ADEEPRRSU	persuader
ADEEPRRSV	depravers
	pervaders
ADEEPRRSY	resprayed
ADEEPRRTU	departure
ADEEPRSST	pederasts
ADEEPRSSU	persuades
ADEEPRSTT	spattered
ADEEPRSTU	depasture
	depurates
ADEEPRSTY	pederasty
ADEEPSSUX	pseudaxes
ADEEPSSWY	speedways
ADEEQRRTU	quartered
ADEERRRST	retarders

ADEERRRSW rewarders
ADEERRSSU reassured
ADEERRSTT restarted
ADEERRSTU treasured
ADEERRSTV traversed
ADEERSTYY yesterday
ADEFFIILS falsified
ADEFFLSTU sufflated
ADEFFNORT affronted
ADEFFORST tradeoffs
ADEFGGOPW powfagged
ADEFGHORT godfather
ADEFGIILN anglified
ADEFGIIMN magnified
ADEFGIIRT gratified
ADEFGILNT deflating
ADEFGILRU lifeguard
ADEFGIMTU fumigated
ADEFGINRT ingrafted
ADEFGINRY defraying
ADEFGIRRU fireguard
ADEFGLOOT floodgate
ADEFGLOST gatefolds
ADEFGLRRU regardful
ADEFHINOS fashioned
ADEFHINRT threadfin
ADEFHIPSS spadefish
ADEFHIRST headfirst
ADEFHLOOS falsehood
ADEFHNORS forehands
ADEFIILMP amplified
ADEFIILNS finalised
ADEFIILNZ finalized
ADEFIILQU qualified
ADEFIILRS airfields
ADEFIILRT airlifted
ADEFIIMNS damnifies
infamised
ADEFIIMNZ infamized
ADEFIIMTT mattified
ADEFIISST satisfied
ADEFIKNRW drawknife
ADEFILLNT flatlined
ADEFILLSU fusillade
ADEFILMNS fieldsman
Mansfield
ADEFILMSU feudalism
ADEFILNNZ zinfandel
ADEFILNOT deflation
defoliant
ADEFILNRS Friesland
ADEFILNSS sandflies
ADEFILNTY defiantly
ADEFILORT floriated
ADEFILRTT filtrated
ADEFILSTU feudalist
ADEFILTUY feudality
ADEFINOST Di Stéfano
ADEFINRSU fundraise
ADEFIRSTT draftiest
ADEFKNNRU unfranked
ADEFKSSST deskfasts
ADEFLLLSU ladlefuls
ADEFLLMSY damselfly
ADEFLLNOV Flevoland
ADEFLLORS falderols
ADEFLMMOR malformed
ADEFLNORS forelands
ADEFLORRT Altdorfer
ADEFLORST deflators
ADEFLORUV flavoured
ADEFLORWY dayflower
ADEFLPRSS feldspars
ADEFLRSTW leftwards
ADEFMNNTU fundament
ADEFMNRST draftsmen
ADEFMOORR doorframe
ADEFMORTT formatted
ADEFNORUV unfavored
ADEFOOPRR proofread
ADEFORRRW forwarder
ADEFORRSY foreyards
ADEFORRTV overdraft
ADEFORRTW afterword
Waterford
ADEFORTUY feudatory
ADEFRRSTU fraudster
ADEGGGINR daggering
ADEGGGIWW wigwagged
ADEGGGIZZ zigzagged
ADEGGIITZ dziggetai
ADEGGILNR langridge
ADEGGIMSU misgauged
ADEGGINNR deranging
gardening
ADEGGINOR dogearing
ADEGGINRR regarding
regrading
ADEGGINSS degassing
ADEGGIRST draggiest
ADEGGLNSU angledugs
ADEGGLORY gargoyled
ADEGGLRST straggled
ADEGGMORT mortgaged
ADEGGNORU groundage
ADEGHHILT headlight
ADEGHHOSS hogsheads
ADEGHIILV Diaghilev
ADEGHILNR heralding
ADEGHILST giltheads
ADEGHINNR hardening
ADEGHINRS garnished
ADEGHINRT threading
ADEGHINSS sheadings
ADEGHINSU anguished
ADEGHIOPR ideograph
ADEGHLLNO Helgoland
ADEGHLMPU galumphed
ADEGHLORS gasholder
ADEGHNOUZ gazehound
ADEGHORST goatherds
ADEGHRRTU draughter
ADEGHRSTU daughters
ADEGIILNR derailing
grindelia
ADEGIILNS gliadines
ADEGIILNT detailing
ADEGIILOS dialogise
ADEGIILOZ dialogize
ADEGIILPT pigtailed
ADEGIILTT litigated
ADEGIIMNT mediating
ADEGIIMTT mitigated
ADEGIINNR ingrained
ADEGIINNT detaining
ADEGIINNU guanidine
ADEGIINPR diapering
ADEGIINTV deviating
ADEGIIRRT irrigated
ADEGIKLLN glandlike
ADEGIKLNV gavelkind
ADEGIKLRU guardlike
ADEGIKNNR darkening
ADEGILLMN medalling
ADEGILLNP pedalling
ADEGILLNS signalled
ADEGILLNY leadingly
ADEGILNNP deplaning
ADEGILNNR Ingerland
Leningrad
ADEGILNNU unaligned
unleading
ADEGILNOR girandole
reloading
ADEGILNOS alongside
ADEGILNPS pleadings
ADEGILNRS draglines
ADEGILNRT treadling
triangled
ADEGILNRU gerundial
ADEGILNST desalting
ADEGILNUV devaluing
ADEGILNVY evadingly
ADEGILORU dialoguer
ADEGILOSU dialogues
ADEGILRRS rigsdaler
ADEGILRSS glissader
ADEGILRTU ligatured
ADEGILSSS glissades
ADEGILTUV divulgate
ADEGIMNNN demanning
ADEGIMNNP dampening
ADEGIMNNR remanding
ADEGIMNTU magnitude
ADEGIMORS ideograms
ADEGIMOST dogmatise
ADEGIMOTZ dogmatize
ADEGINNPP appending
ADEGINNPR pandering
ADEGINNPX expanding
ADEGINNRT integrand
ADEGINNRW wandering
ADEGINNTT attending
ADEGINORR Rio Grande
ADEGINORS grandiose
organdies

	organised
ADEGINORZ	organized
ADEGINOSS	diagnoses
ADEGINPRS	spreading
ADEGINPRT	departing
	predating
ADEGINPRV	depraving
	pervading
ADEGINRRS	grandsire
ADEGINRRT	retarding
ADEGINRRW	redrawing
	rewarding
ADEGINRST	gradients
ADEGINRSW	sawdering
ADEGINRTV	adverting
ADEGINSST	steadings
ADEGINSSU	gaudiness
ADEGINSTT	digestant
ADEGINSTY	steadying
ADEGIPRRT	partridge
ADEGIRSWY	ridgeways
ADEGIRTTU	gratitude
ADEGJLTUU	jugulated
ADEGLLLOU	Dolgellau
ADEGLLNOO	gallooned
ADEGLLNSU	glandules
ADEGLNNTU	untangled
ADEGLNOOO	ologoaned
ADEGLNOST	gladstone
ADEGLNRST	strangled
ADEGLNRUW	Grünewald
ADEGLOOPY	paedology
ADEGLRSSU	guardless
ADEGMNRSU	guardsmen
ADEGMOPRR	deprogram
ADEGNNOPR	pendragon
ADEGNNORS	androgens
ADEGNNORW	downrange
ADEGNNORY	androgyne
ADEGNNRSS	grandness
ADEGNOORS	goosander
ADEGNOPPR	dognapper
ADEGNOPRT	godparent
ADEGNORSS	dragoness
ADEGNORST	dragonets
ADEGNORSU	dangerous
ADEGNORTU	outranged
ADEGNOSTW	downstage
ADEGNRRSU	grandeurs
ADEGNRSUZ	gazunders
ADEGOPRRS	dragropes
ADEGOPRRT	Petrograd
ADEGORRTT	garrotted
ADEGOSSTU	outgassed
ADEGPRRSU	upgraders
ADEGRRSST	dragsters
ADEHHISST	shitheads
ADEHHLLRS	hardshell
ADEHIIKLV	khedivial
ADEHIILNP	delphinia
ADEHIIMNS	maidenish
ADEHIINPR	nephridia
ADEHIIRRR	hairdrier
ADEHIISST	diathesis
ADEHIKKLS	Kikládhes
ADEHIKNPS	handspike
ADEHIKNSS	skinheads
ADEHIKNSW	windshake
ADEHIKRRS	shikarred
ADEHILMNS	mishandle
ADEHILMOT	ethmoidal
ADEHILNNR	Rheinland
	Rhineland
ADEHILNPR	philander
ADEHILNPS	planished
ADEHILNRR	hardliner
ADEHILOSU	Dalhousie
ADEHILRRT	trihedral
ADEHILRST	heraldist
ADEHIMNOR	rhodamine
ADEHIMNRS	mindshare
ADEHIMNSU	humanised
ADEHIMNUZ	humanized
ADEHIMOSU	housemaid
ADEHIMPSS	misshaped
ADEHIMPTW	whitedamp
ADEHIMRTY	diathermy
ADEHINNRS	Sanhedrin
ADEHINNSS	handiness
ADEHINOPS	diaphones
ADEHINOPU	audiphone
ADEHINORS	Rhodesian
ADEHINOSS	adhesions
ADEHINPRT	printhead
ADEHINPSS	deanships
ADEHINPSU	dauphines
ADEHINRRT	Reinhardt
ADEHINRSS	hardiness
ADEHINRST	tarnished
ADEHINRSV	varnished
ADEHINRTY	anhydrite
ADEHINRYZ	hydrazine
ADEHINSSS	shadiness
ADEHIOPRS	aphorised
ADEHIOPRT	Aphrodite
	atrophied
ADEHIOPRZ	aphorized
ADEHIPRST	therapsid
ADEHIPSSS	pissheads
ADEHIPSSY	diaphyses
ADEHIPSWW	whipsawed
ADEHIRRRY	hairdryer
ADEHIRSTW	dishwater
ADEHKNNTU	unthanked
ADEHKNOSW	shakedown
ADEHKNRSS	redshanks
ADEHLLOSW	shallowed
ADEHLLOTY	tallyhoed
ADEHLLSSY	dayshells
ADEHLMNOS	homelands
ADEHLOPRY	polyhedra
ADEHLOPSS	asphodels
ADEHLORST	Aldershot
ADEHLORSY	hydrolase
ADEHLPPRT	thrappled
ADEHLPSTU	sulphated
ADEHMNORS	handsomer
ADEHMOOPS	shampooed
ADEHMOORV	Hoover Dam
ADEHMORSW	homewards
ADEHMOSSU	madhouses
ADEHNOOPR	harpooned
ADEHNORSV	handovers
	overhands
ADEHNORVY	hydrovane
ADEHNOSSS	sandshoes
ADEHNRSSW	swanherds
ADEHNRSTU	unthreads
ADEHNSSSU	sunshades
ADEHNSTUW	unswathed
ADEHOORSU	roadhouse
ADEHOORTW	heartwood
ADEHOOSTT	statehood
ADEHOPPPY	poppyhead
ADEHOPRSS	rhapsodes
ADEHORRSW	shoreward
ADEHORRSY	drayhorse
ADEHORSSW	shadowers
ADEHORSTU	Stourhead
ADEIIILNT	initialed
ADEIIINTT	dietitian
	initiated
ADEIILLNY	leylandii
ADEIILMNN	mainlined
ADEIILMOZ	imidazole
ADEIILMST	Miltiades
ADEIILMTT	militated
ADEIILNRT	deliriant
	interlaid
ADEIILNST	disentail
ADEIILNTZ	latinized
ADEIILORT	editorial
ADEIILORV	D'Oliviera
ADEIILPTX	pixilated
ADEIILQTU	liquidate
ADEIILSST	idealists
ADEIILSTU	dualities
ADEIILSTV	vitalised
ADEIILTVZ	vitalized
ADEIIMMSX	maximised
ADEIIMMXZ	maximized
ADEIIMNNS	indamines
ADEIIMNOT	mediation
ADEIIMNRS	meridians
ADEIIMNRZ	zemindari
ADEIIMNTT	intimated
ADEIIMOTT	diatomite
ADEIIMSSV	admissive
ADEIINNOS	Indonesia
ADEIINOTV	deviation
ADEIINPPR	drainpipe
ADEIINSST	sanitised
ADEIINSTT	daintiest
	dittanies
ADEIINSTZ	sanitized
ADEIIOSTZ	diazotise

ADEIIOTVX oxidative
ADEIIOTZZ diazotize
ADEIIPRRS disrepair
ADEIIPRSS dispraise
ADEIIPSST dissipate
ADEIIRRTT irritated
ADEIIRSST Aristides
satirised
ADEIIRSTZ satirized
ADEIIRTTT tritiated
ADEIITTTV titivated
ADEIKKSST kidstakes
ADEIKLRSS laserdisk
ADEIKLSSW sidewalks
ADEIKMORS kaiserdom
ADEIKMRST tidemarks
ADEIKNPPR kidnapper
ADEIKNPRS spikenard
ADEIKNPRT predikant
ADEILLMNO medallion
ADEILLMOT metalloid
ADEILLMRT treadmill
ADEILLMST medallist
ADEILLNOU andouille
ADEILLNST installed
ADEILLORS arillodes
ADEILLPRS spiralled
ADEILLPRU preludial
ADEILLPSS spadilles
ADEILLQRU quadrille
ADEILLSSW sidewalls
ADEILMMOT immolated
ADEILMNNN Lindemann
ADEILMNNO mandoline
ADEILMNOP diplonema
ADEILMNPT implanted
ADEILMNST dismantle
ADEILMNTU dentalium
ADEILMOPT diplomate
ADEILMOPY polyamide
ADEILMORS moralised
ADEILMORZ moralized
ADEILMOSX aldoximes
ADEILMOTV moldavite
ADEILMPSS mispleads
ADEILMPSY misplayed
ADEILMPTU amplitude
ADEILMSST medalists
ADEILMSTU simulated
ADEILMSUV misvalued
ADEILMTTU mutilated
ADEILNNRS inlanders
ADEILNNRU underlain
ADEILNOPP panoplied
ADEILNOPS palinodes
ADEILNOPT planetoid
ADEILNOPU aneuploid
ADEILNOST delations
insolated
ADEILNPPU unapplied
ADEILNPTT tinplated
ADEILNRRT interlard
ADEILNRSS islanders
ADEILNRSU laundries
ADEILNRTT tridental
ADEILNRTU uitlander
ADEILNRUV unrivaled
ADEILNRUY unreadily
ADEILNSSV validness
ADEILNSTU insulated
ADEILNSTW Waldstein
ADEILOPPT oppilated
ADEILOPRS polarised
ADEILOPRT depilator
ADEILOPRZ polarized
ADEILOPST spoliated
ADEILOQSU odalisque
ADEILORSS solarised
ADEILORST estradiol
idolaters
steroidal
ADEILORSV valorised
ADEILORSZ solarized
ADEILORVZ valorized
ADEILOSTT datolites
totalised
ADEILOSTV dovetails
ADEILOTTZ totalized
ADEILPPPS pedipalps
ADEILPPQU appliqued
ADEILPRSS dispersal
ADEILPRSU epidurals
parulides
ADEILPRSV deprivals
ADEILPRSY displayer
ADEILPTTU platitude
ADEILRRSU ruralised
ADEILRRUZ ruralized
ADEILRSSU residuals
ADEILRSSY dialysers
ADEILRSYZ dialyzers
ADEILRTTU rutilated
ADEILSSTU lassitude
ADEILSSTY diastyles
ADEILSTTU altitudes
latitudes
ADEIMMRST midstream
ADEIMNNOS mondaines
ADEIMNNOT nominated
ADEIMNNTU indumenta
ADEIMNOPT ademption
ADEIMNORS randomise
romanised
ADEIMNORZ randomize
romanized
ADEIMNOSS nomadises
ADEIMNOST dominates
Maidstone
staminode
ADEIMNOSW womanised
ADEIMNOSZ nomadizes
ADEIMNOWZ womanized
ADEIMNPRR reprimand
ADEIMNPRS spiderman
ADEIMNRRU unmarried
ADEIMNRSU nursemaid
ADEIMNRSZ zemindars
ADEIMNRTU ruminated
ADEIMNRTY dynamiter
ADEIMNSTY dynamites
ADEIMORRS airdromes
ADEIMORST amortised
mediators
ADEIMORTT meditator
ADEIMORTY mediatory
ADEIMORTZ amortized
ADEIMOTTV motivated
ADEIMPRST spermatid
ADEIMRRSS disarmers
ADEIMRRUU Du Maurier
ADEIMRTUX admixture
ADEIMRTXY taxidermy
ADEIMSSTT misstated
ADEINNNPS inspanned
ADEINNNSU Dunsinane
ADEINNNTT intendant
ADEINNOST antinodes
ADEINNOTT dentation
intonated
ADEINNOTV innovated
ADEINNRSS randiness
ADEINNRTU untrained
ADEINNSSS sandiness
ADEINNSTU antidunes
inundates
unstained
ADEINNTTU untainted
ADEINOOTX exodontia
ADEINOPPT appointed
ADEINOPRR preordain
ADEINOPRT predation
ADEINOPST antipodes
ADEINORRS ordainers
serranoid
ADEINORST derations
notarised
ordinates
ADEINORTY arytenoid
ADEINORTZ notarized
ADEINOSST sedations
ADEINOSTT antidotes
stationed
ADEINOSTV donatives
ADEINOTUX exudation
ADEINPPRS sandpiper
ADEINPPRW inwrapped
ADEINPPST standpipe
ADEINPRSS rapidness
ADEINPRST dipterans
ADEINPSSS sapidness
ADEINPSSV vapidness
ADEINPSTU supinated
ADEINQSTU quantised
ADEINQTUZ quantized
ADEINRRSS serranids
ADEINRRWW wiredrawn

ADEINRSST	Streisand
	tardiness
ADEINRSTT	transited
ADEINRSTU	indurates
ADEINRSVY	vineyards
ADEINSSST	staidness
ADEINSSSV	vanessids
ADEINSSTU	sustained
ADEINSSTY	dynasties
ADEINSTTV	Adventist
ADEIOPRSV	vaporised
ADEIOPRTZ	trapezoid
ADEIOPRVZ	vaporized
ADEIOPSST	dioptases
ADEIORSST	asteroids
ADEIORSTT	storiated
ADEIORSTV	deviators
ADEIORSVW	disavower
ADEIORTVY	deviatory
ADEIPPSSY	dyspepsia
ADEIPRSTU	eupatrids
ADEIPRSUU	Epidaurus
ADEIPRTVY	depravity
	varityped
ADEIPSSUX	pseudaxis
ADEIPSTTU	aptitudes
ADEIQSSUY	quaysides
ADEIRRSUY	residuary
ADEIRRSWW	wiredraws
ADEIRSSST	disasters
ADEIRSSSU	sardiuses
ADEIRSTTW	tawdriest
ADEIRSTUV	duratives
ADEIRSTVY	adversity
ADEIRSVWY	driveways
ADEIRTTTT	attritted
ADEISSSTT	distastes
ADEISTTTU	attitudes
ADEISTTUV	vastitude
ADEJLNRTU	Jutlander
ADEJRSSTU	adjusters
	readjusts
ADEKKLRSY	skylarked
ADEKLNOSY	ankylosed
ADEKLNRTU	Tendulkar
ADEKLOTTU	outtalked
ADEKLOTUW	outwalked
ADEKNORRV	overdrank
ADEKNORTU	outranked
ADEKOPRSW	spadework
ADELLLOWY	allowedly
ADELLMRUY	medullary
ADELLNOOT	Donatello
ADELLNOPR	landloper
ADELLNORW	lowlander
ADELLNOUY	unalloyed
ADELLNTUU	lunulated
ADELLOPRT	patrolled
ADELLOSVY	ladyloves
ADELLOSWW	swallowed
ADELLRTXY	dextrally
ADELMNNUY	mundanely
ADELMNOOP	lampooned
ADELMNOPS	endoplasm
ADELMOOST	stomodeal
ADELMOSTU	modulates
ADELMRRSU	demurrals
ADELNNNPU	unplanned
ADELNNORW	landowner
ADELNNOSW	Lansdowne
ADELNNPTU	unplanted
ADELNNRSU	unsnarled
ADELNOOPR	Apeldoorn
ADELNOOST	loadstone
ADELNOPSY	dyspnoeal
ADELNORSS	solanders
ADELNORSU	unloaders
ADELNORSV	overlands
	rondavels
ADELNORTU	outlander
ADELNORUY	roundelay
ADELNPRSS	spandrels
ADELNPRUY	underplay
ADELNRRUY	Drury Lane
ADELNRSSU	laundress
ADELNRSUY	underlays
ADELNRTVY	verdantly
ADELNSSTU	dauntless
ADELNSTUU	undulates
ADELOORST	desolator
ADELOORSV	overloads
ADELOPPRS	prolapsed
ADELOPPTU	populated
ADELOPRSU	poulardes
	superload
ADELOPTUY	outplayed
ADELORSST	lodestars
ADELORSTW	leadworts
ADELOSTTU	outlasted
ADELOSTUY	autolysed
ADELOTUUV	outvalued
ADELOTUYZ	autolyzed
ADELPPRRU	larrupped
ADELPQRUU	quadruple
ADELRRSTY	drysalter
ADELRSSUY	assuredly
ADELRSTTU	lustrated
ADEMMORST	masterdom
ADEMNNORT	adornment
ADEMNNOTU	outmanned
ADEMNOPRS	pomanders
ADEMNORST	transomed
ADEMNORSU	meandrous
ADEMNPSTU	unstamped
ADEMNRTUU	unmatured
ADEMNSSUU	unassumed
ADEMOORRT	moderator
ADEMOORST	astrodome
ADEMOPRSY	pyodermas
ADEMORRTT	Rotterdam
ADEMORSTW	wardmotes
ADENNNSTU	suntanned
ADENNORSS	Sanderson
ADENNOSST	sandstone
ADENNOSTY	asyndeton
ADENNPPSU	unsnapped
ADENNSSTW	newsstand
ADENOORST	tornadoes
ADENOORSW	wanderoos
ADENOORTT	detonator
	rattooned
ADENOOSTT	toadstone
ADENOOWWX	woodwaxen
ADENOPRRS	pardoners
ADENOPRTV	davenport
ADENORRVW	overdrawn
ADENORSTV	standover
ADENOSTTW	downstate
ADENOTTWY	wyandotte
ADENPPRUW	unwrapped
ADENPRRTU	underpart
ADENPRSSU	underpass
ADENPRSUY	underpays
ADENQRSSU	squanders
ADENRRSTW	sternward
ADENRSSTU	transudes
ADENRSTUY	Tyndareus
ADEOOPRTT	taprooted
ADEOORRST	toreadors
ADEOORTTV	rotovated
ADEOPRRST	predators
	teardrops
ADEOPRRTU	depurator
ADEOPRRTY	portrayed
	predatory
ADEOPRSTT	tetrapods
ADEOPRSTU	outspread
ADEOPRTTY	tetrapody
ADEOPSSTT	postdates
ADEORRSST	roadsters
ADEORRSVW	overdraws
ADEORRSWW	swearword
ADEORSTTU	outstared
ADEOSTTUY	outstayed
ADEPRSSSU	surpassed
ADEPRSTTU	upstarted
ADERRSSTT	redstarts
ADERSSTWW	westwards
ADFFGINOR	affording
ADFFIIMRS	disaffirm
ADFFNOSST	standoffs
ADFFORRST	Strafford
ADFGHIRSU	Fishguard
ADFGIILNY	ladifying
ADFGILNYY	ladyfying
ADFGINORS	sangfroid
ADFGLNORY	dragonfly
ADFHINRST	firsthand
ADFHLOORY	foolhardy
ADFHLOSST	holdfasts
ADFIILNOR	Floridian
ADFILLLUY	fluidally
ADFILLNSW	windfalls
ADFILMNOS	manifolds
ADFILNOOV	flavonoid
ADFIORSSV	disfavors

ADFIORSUV	disfavour
ADFLLNOSW	downfalls
ADFLLOOST	faldstool
ADFLMNORS	landforms
ADFLORRWY	forwardly
	frowardly
ADFNOORSZ	forzandos
	sforzando
ADFNORRTW	frontward
ADGGGILNR	draggling
ADGGGNNOU	Guangdong
ADGGILNRY	niggardly
ADGGILRSY	Yggdrasil
ADGGINNOP	dognaping
ADGGINPRU	upgrading
ADGGLOORV	Volgograd
ADGGLRSSU	sluggards
ADGHHILNS	highlands
ADGHHIORS	highroads
ADGHHOOPR	hodograph
ADGHILLLS	gildhalls
ADGHILLLU	guildhall
ADGHILNNS	handlings
ADGHILNSY	dashingly
ADGHILSTY	daylights
ADGHIMOSU	Mogadishu
ADGHINNNU	unhanding
ADGHINORS	dragonish
	hoardings
ADGHINOSW	shadowing
ADGHINPRS	handgrips
ADGHINRTU	indraught
ADGHINRTY	hydrating
ADGHIRRTW	rightward
ADGHISTTW	tightwads
ADGHNOOPR	ondograph
ADGHNOSTU	staghound
ADGHPRTUU	updraught
ADGIIILNT	digitalin
ADGIIILST	digitalis
ADGIIJNNO	adjoining
ADGIIKNNP	kidnaping
ADGIILLTY	digitally
ADGIILMOS	dialogism
	sigmoidal
ADGIILNNS	islanding
ADGIILNPS	Pig Island
ADGIILNSS	glissandi
ADGIILNSY	dialysing
ADGIILNYZ	dialyzing
ADGIILOSS	diglossia
ADGIILOST	dialogist
ADGIIMNRS	disarming
ADGIIMNST	misdating
ADGIIMNSY	dismaying
ADGIIMNTT	admitting
ADGIIMORS	idiograms
ADGIIMRUU	Maiduguri
ADGIIMSST	digamists
ADGIINNNT	indignant
ADGIINNOR	ordaining
ADGIINNOS	anodising
ADGIINNOZ	anodizing
ADGIINORT	granitoid
ADGIINOSS	diagnosis
ADGIINOTX	oxidating
ADGIINRST	disrating
ADGIINRTY	dignitary
ADGIIRTVY	gravidity
ADGIJNSTU	adjusting
ADGILLNSW	windgalls
ADGILLNUY	languidly
ADGILLOST	goldtails
ADGILLOSU	gladiolus
ADGILMNSU	guildsman
ADGILMORS	marigolds
ADGILNNOT	Aldington
ADGILNNOU	unloading
ADGILNORY	adoringly
ADGILNOSS	glissando
ADGILNPPS	Gippsland
ADGILNRTY	dartingly
ADGILOORY	radiology
ADGILOOSS	solidagos
ADGILOOUY	audiology
ADGILOPRS	prodigals
ADGIMMOST	dogmatism
ADGIMOSTT	dogmatist
ADGINNOOU	iguanodon
ADGINNOPR	pardoning
ADGINNRST	stranding
ADGINNRUW	undrawing
ADGINNSST	standings
ADGINOORS	grandioso
ADGINOPRY	parodying
ADGINORTU	outdaring
ADGINOTTU	outdating
ADGINPRSY	dayspring
ADGIORUUX	Giraudoux
ADGLNOORY	andrology
ADGMNORSU	gourmands
ADGMOORRU	guardroom
ADGNNNNOU	Dungannon
ADGNNOQSU	quandongs
ADGNNORSS	grandsons
ADGNNORYY	androgyny
ADGOOPRST	gastropod
ADGOOPRSU	podagrous
ADHHIPRSS	hardships
ADHHNOORU	hoarhound
ADHHNORST	shorthand
ADHHNRSTY	hydranths
ADHHOPRTY	hydropath
ADHIILLOT	lithoidal
ADHIILORZ	rhizoidal
ADHIIMMRS	midrashim
ADHIIMPSS	amidships
ADHIINOPS	ophidians
ADHIIOPSU	aphidious
ADHIIOPTY	idiopathy
ADHIIPSSY	diaphysis
ADHIKMNNU	humankind
ADHIKNORW	handiwork
ADHILLRSY	hydrillas
ADHILMNPY	nymphalid
ADHILMSTY	Ladysmith
ADHILNOPY	hypnoidal
ADHILOPSS	shiploads
ADHILOPTY	typhoidal
ADHILPSSY	ladyships
ADHILSTTU	Dasht-i-Lut
ADHIMNOSU	humanoids
ADHIMNOTU	anthodium
ADHIMOPPS	amphipods
ADHIMSTYY	dysthymia
ADHINNOTY	hydantoin
ADHINNSTU	Hindustan
ADHINOOST	sainthood
ADHINOPSY	dysphonia
ADHINORTY	hydration
ADHINRTWW	withdrawn
ADHINSTTW	withstand
ADHIOOSST	soothsaid
ADHIOPRSY	dysphoria
ADHIPRSSW	wardships
ADHIPRSSY	shipyards
ADHIRSSTY	hydrastis
ADHIRSTWW	withdraws
ADHISTWWY	widthways
ADHKNORTW	Dankworth
ADHLLMORT	thralldom
ADHLNNORT	northland
ADHLNOSTU	duathlons
ADHLNOSUW	downhauls
ADHMNOOOW	womanhood
ADHMOORSY	hydrosoma
ADHMORTTU	Dartmouth
ADHNOORYZ	hydrozoan
ADHNORRTW	northward
ADHNORSUY	anhydrous
ADHNORTUY	hydronaut
ADHNOSSTU	thousands
ADHNRSSTU	Sandhurst
ADHOOPRRT	arthropod
ADHOOPRSS	hospodars
ADHOPRSST	potshards
ADHORRSTY	hydrators
ADHORSTTY	hydrostat
ADHORSTUW	southward
ADIIIIRSU	Darius III
ADIIINOSZ	isoniazid
ADIIINRSV	viridians
ADIIIQRSU	daiquiris
ADIIKLMMS	milkmaids
ADIIKLNNU	kundalini
ADIIKLSST	tailskids
ADIILLMRS	milliards
ADIILLNTU	lunitidal
ADIILLNVY	invalidly
ADIILLPTY	pallidity
ADIILMOPS	idioplasm
ADIILMSSS	dismissal
ADIILNOPT	platinoid
ADIILNOST	dilations
ADIILNOTU	nautiloid
ADIILNSSW	windsails

ADIILNSTW tailwinds
ADIILOORV varioloid
ADIIMNOSS admission
ADIIMNOUZ diazonium
ADIIMOPRR primordia
ADIIMRSSY mydriasis
ADIINNOST nidations
ADIINNOSY Dionysian
ADIINOOST iodations
ADIINOOTX oxidation
ADIINOQTU quotidian
ADIINORSS anidrosis
ADIINORTT tradition
ADIINOSTU auditions
ADIINRSST distrains
ADIINRSTT distraint
ADIINRSTU saturniid
ADIIPRSTY disparity
ADIISSTUY assiduity
ADIJNOOVV Vojvodina
ADIKKNNSY Kandinsky
ADIKLLORS roadkills
ADIKMNNOW womankind
ADIKNNNSU dunnakins
ADIKNNSST inkstands
ADIKNOPSY pyinkados
ADIKNRSTU Kurdistan
ADILLMNRS mandrills
ADILLMNUY maudlinly
ADILLNPSS landslips
ADILLNRUY diurnally
ADILLOSSW disallows
ADILLQSUY squalidly
ADILMMSTU talmudism
ADILMNNOS mandolins
ADILMNOOS salmonoid
ADILMNOSS salmonids
ADILMNOST daltonism
ADILMNRUU duralumin
ADILMOPSS plasmoids
ADILMOPST diplomats
ADILMOPSY olympiads
sympodial
ADILMSTTU Talmudist
ADILNNSSU disannuls
ADILNOORS doornails
ADILNOOSV vindaloos
ADILNORTW antiworld
ADILNPRSS spandrils
ADILNPSST displants
ADILNSTTY distantly
ADILOPRSV disproval
ADILOPRXY pyridoxal
ADILOPSSS disposals
ADILORSTW swordtail
ADILRSTTY tiltyards
ADIMNNOST dominants
ADIMNNTUY mundanity
ADIMNOOOP monopodia
ADIMNOORT admonitor
dominator
ADIMNOSTY staminody
ADIMNSSTY dynamists
ADIMOOQSU Quasimodo
ADIMOPRSY myriapods
ADINNNOUZ D'Annunzio
ADINNOOST donations
ADINNOOSW Snowdonia
ADINNORTU inundator
ADINNOSST dissonant
ADINOOPST adoptions
ADINOOSTW satinwood
ADINOPSTY dystopian
ADINORSSU dinosaurs
ADINORSTU durations
ADINPSTTU disputant
ADIOOPRST parotoids
ADIOPRSST parodists
ADIORRSTT traditors
ADIOSSSUU assiduous
ADJKNRSUY junkyards
ADJMMOOOR majordomo
ADKLOORSW woodlarks
workloads
ADKMNORSW markdowns
ADKMOORRS darkrooms
ADKNORRWW drawnwork
ADKNORSTT Kronstadt
ADKOORRSW roadworks
ADLLNSSUV Sundsvall
ADLMNOORS moorlands
ADLMNORTY mordantly
ADLMOOPRR prodromal
ADLMOORTU modulator
ADLMOPRUW mouldwarp
ADLNNOORW nanoworld
ADLNNOSTW townlands
ADLNOPRSU pauldrons
ADLNOPRYY polyandry
ADLNOPSWY downplays
ADLNORTUU undulator
ADLNOSUWY Low Sunday
ADLNRSSTU Stralsund
ADLOOOSTT toadstool
ADLOPRSWY swordplay
ADLORSUUY arduously
ADLORTUWY outwardly
ADLPQRUUY quadruply
ADMMORRTY martyrdom
ADMNNORSU roundsman
ADMNOORTY dynamotor
ADMNOOSST mastodons
ADMNORSST sandstorm
ADMNORSSW sandworms
swordsman
ADMOOPPPS poppadoms
ADMOOPPRU pompadour
ADMOORRSW wardrooms
ADMOPPPSU poppadums
ADNNORRUU runaround
ADNNOSSWW swansdown
ADNOOPRTW Portadown
ADNOOQRSU quadroons
ADNOOSSVW advowsons
ADNOPRRTY protandry
ADNOPRRUW wrapround
ADNOPRSTU Port Sudan
ADNOQRSSU squadrons
ADNORSSTW sandworts
ADNOSSTTU outstands
standouts
ADOOORRWW arrowwood
ADOOPPRSU pauropods
ADOOPRRST trapdoors
ADOOPRSSU sauropods
ADOOPSSSS Dos Passos
ADOPRSSSW passwords
ADOPSSSUY soapsudsy
AEEEEHMPR ephemerae
AEEEFGLRT telferage
AEEEFHLLN fellaheen
AEEEFHRRT hereafter
AEEEFLLRT leafleter
AEEEFNRST fenestrae
AEEEFRRSW freewares
AEEEFRSTT Free State
AEEEGGGNR greengage
AEEEGGNRS reengages
AEEEGGRST segregate
AEEEGHLRW gearwheel
AEEEGHMRT megathere
AEEEGIMNR menagerie
AEEEGKRTW Great Week
AEEEGLRST regelates
relegates
AEEEGMNNP empennage
AEEEGMNRT agreement
AEEEGNRSS eagerness
AEEEGNRST generates
teenagers
AEEEGNRTW tweenager
AEEEGNSTV Stevenage
AEEEGORRV overeager
AEEEGRTTZ gazetteer
AEEEGSTTV vegetates
AEEEHKNRR hearkener
AEEEHLMPR ephemeral
AEEEHLSSY eyelashes
AEEEHMPRS ephemeras
AEEEHMRTX hexameter
AEEEHNRRV Verhaeren
AEEEHRRRS rehearser
AEEEHRRSS rehearses
AEEEHRRST reheaters
AEEEHRRTW weatherer
AEEEHRSTT tearsheet
AEEEHSSTT aesthetes
AEEEILRSS sealeries
AEEEILRTT elaterite
AEEEIMNRX reexamine
AEEEIMNSX examinees
AEEEINSUX Euxine Sea
AEEEIPPRT papeterie
AEEEIRRTT reiterate
AEEEKKPSS keepsakes
AEEEKLTTT teakettle

AEEEKMRRT marketeer
AEEEKNRSW weakeners
AEEELLMNR enameller
AEEELLMNT elemental
AEEELLPPS appellees
AEEELLRST teaseller
AEEELLSST telesales
AEEELMNRS enamelers
AEEELMSTW sweetmeal
AEEELNNPP peneplane
AEEELNSST selenates
AEEELNUVZ Venezuela
AEEELORRS Roeselare
AEEELPRRS repealers
AEEELPTTU epaulette
AEEELRRSS releasers
AEEELRRSV revealers
AEEELRSTX axletrees
AEEEMMNST semanteme
AEEEMMRST metameres
AEEEMNNRT nemertean
AEEEMNRST mesentera
AEEEMNRTU enumerate
AEEEMNSST easements
AEEEMORRT aerometer
AEEEMPRST permeates
AEEEMPRTT temperate
AEEEMRRSU remeasure
AEEEMRTVW wavemeter
AEEEMSTTW sweetmeat
AEEENNPRT perennate
AEEENOPRW weaponeer
AEEENORTV overeaten
AEEENORTX exonerate
AEEENPRTT penetrate
AEEENPSTT patentees
AEEENRRST easterner
AEEENRRTW treenware
AEEENRSTV enervates
venerates
AEEENTTUV eventuate
AEEENTTUX extenuate
AEEEPRRST repartees
repeaters
AEEERSSST esterases
AEEFFILRT afterlife
AEEFGILLR fillagree
AEEFGILPR pilferage
AEEFGILRS filagrees
AEEFGINRS farseeing
AEEFGINTU teniafuge
AEEFGLLOT flageolet
AEEFGLORW flowerage
AEEFGLSSU fuselages
AEEFGORST fosterage
AEEFHLLSS selfheals
AEEFHLRTT heartfelt
AEEFIKLLM flamelike
AEEFIKRST freakiest
AEEFILMNS filenames
AEEFILNRT interleaf
AEEFILNSS leafiness

AEEFILOTX exfoliate
AEEFILRSV lifesaver
AEEFIMORT aforetime
AEEFINRRR refrainer
AEEFINSTX antefixes
AEEFIRRRS rarefiers
AEEFIRRTW firewater
AEEFKOPRS forepeaks
forespeak
AEEFLLMSS flameless
AEEFLLMST flamelets
AEEFLLRSW farewells
AEEFLLSUY easefully
AEEFLLSVY flyleaves
AEEFLMNRT Fremantle
AEEFLMRSS frameless
AEEFLNRST fenestral
AEEFLNRTT flattener
AEEFLNSSS falseness
AEEFLNSTW Westfalen
AEEFLOOTV foveolate
AEEFLORSS Flores Sea
AEEFLORST foresteal
AEEFLOSTV love feast
AEEFLPSTY splayfeet
AEEFLRRRS referrals
AEEFLRRST falterers
AEEFLRRTT flatterer
AEEFLSTTT flatettes
AEEFMNORS forenames
freemason
AEEFMNSTY safetymen
AEEFNRSST fasteners
refastens
AEEFNRSTT fatteners
AEEFOPRRT perforate
AEEFORSTT foretaste
AEEGGHMOU hemagogue
AEEGGILLR Gelligaer
AEEGGINRR gregarine
AEEGGIRSV aggrieves
AEEGGLNOY genealogy
AEEGGLNRT Great Glen
AEEGGMORT mortgagee
AEEGGNNRS gangrenes
AEEGGPRSU puggarees
AEEGGRRST staggerer
AEEGGRRSW swaggerer
AEEGGRSSS aggresses
AEEGHILST Eastleigh
AEEGHIMRT hermitage
AEEGHINRR rehearing
AEEGHINRS garnishee
AEEGHINRT reheating
AEEGHIRST heritages
AEEGHLPRT telegraph
AEEGHLRSS shearlegs
AEEGHMNOP megaphone
AEEGHMPRS graphemes
AEEGHMRTZ megahertz
AEEGHNOPT pathogene
AEEGHNRSW greenwash

AEEGHOSTU gatehouse
AEEGHRRST gatherers
regathers
AEEGIIMRS imageries
AEEGIKLPR grapelike
AEEGIKNNW weakening
AEEGILLRS allergies
galleries
AEEGILLRT treillage
AEEGILLRV grevillea
AEEGILLSS legalises
AEEGILLST legislate
AEEGILLSZ legalizes
AEEGILMNN enameling
meningeal
AEEGILMNR greenmail
AEEGILMSS imageless
AEEGILMST gleamiest
AEEGILNNT eglantine
inelegant
AEEGILNNV leavening
AEEGILNPR repealing
AEEGILNRS algerines
releasing
resealing
AEEGILNRV revealing
AEEGILNST anglesite
gelatines
teaseling
AEEGILNSW weaseling
AEEGILNTV elevating
AEEGILNTZ teazeling
AEEGILRSS gaseliers
AEEGILRSV silver age
AEEGILRTU gauleiter
AEEGILSTV levigates
AEEGIMNRT germanite
germinate
AEEGIMNRZ germanize
AEEGIMNST geminates
magnesite
magnetise
AEEGIMNTT magnetite
AEEGIMNTZ magnetize
AEEGIMOST isogamete
AEEGIMPTT pegmatite
AEEGIMRRT remigrate
AEEGIMRST emigrates
AEEGINNNT neatening
AEEGINNRT argentine
tangerine
AEEGINNUW New Guinea
AEEGINOPS espionage
AEEGINOTT negotiate
AEEGINPRT interpage
repeating
AEEGINPRV grapevine
AEEGINRRS regainers
AEEGINRSS gesnerias
AEEGINRST reseating
stingaree
AEEGINRTT argentite

	integrate
AEEGINSSS	assignees
AEEGINSSV	envisages
AEEGINSSW	seesawing
AEEGINSTU	sauteeing
AEEGINSTV	agentives
	negatives
AEEGIPQSU	equipages
AEEGIRSST	greasiest
AEEGIRSTT	aigrettes
AEEGIRSTV	ergatives
AEEGISTTV	gestative
AEEGKMRRS	regmakers
AEEGLLNOR	organelle
AEEGLLNRS	allergens
AEEGLLNRY	generally
AEEGLLNTY	elegantly
AEEGLLRSS	glareless
AEEGLMNNT	gentleman
AEEGLMNRY	germanely
AEEGLMNST	segmental
AEEGLMOOS	mesogloea
AEEGLMORT	algometer
	glomerate
AEEGLMRRW	legwarmer
AEEGLMRST	telegrams
AEEGLNNPT	pentangle
AEEGLNNRT	entangler
AEEGLNNST	entangles
AEEGLNORS	sloganeer
AEEGLNOST	elongates
AEEGLNRRS	enlargers
AEEGLNRSS	largeness
AEEGLNSSU	angeluses
AEEGLNSTT	gestalten
AEEGLORRV	overlarge
AEEGLORVZ	overglaze
AEEGLPRSS	grapeless
AEEGLRSSS	largesses
AEEGLRSSV	verglases
AEEGLRSTU	regulates
AEEGMNRRS	merganser
AEEGMNRTU	augmenter
AEEGMOPRS	megaspore
AEEGMORST	gasometer
AEEGMRSST	gamesters
AEEGMSSSU	messuages
AEEGNNNOS	enneagons
AEEGNNRST	transgene
AEEGNNSTW	newsagent
AEEGNOPRS	personage
AEEGNORRT	generator
AEEGNORTT	teratogen
AEEGNORTU	entourage
AEEGNOTTW	wagonette
AEEGNOTXY	oxygenate
AEEGNPRSS	passenger
AEEGNRRST	estranger
AEEGNRRSV	engravers
AEEGNRSST	estranges
	greatness
	sergeants
AEEGNRSSV	graveness
AEEGNSSUV	vagueness
AEEGOPPST	estoppage
AEEGOPRRT	porterage
	reportage
AEEGORRSV	overgears
AEEGORRVZ	overgraze
AEEGORSTU	Great Ouse
AEEGPRRSS	presagers
AEEGPRTUX	expurgate
AEEGRRRST	regraters
AEEGRSSTT	greatests
AEEHHIKLT	heathlike
AEEHHILRT	healthier
AEEHHLNSZ	hazelhens
AEEHHLOSW	hawsehole
AEEHHNNPT	naphthene
AEEHHNPTY	hyphenate
AEEHHNRTY	heathenry
AEEHHNSTU	unsheathe
AEEHIILPR	perihelia
AEEHIILPT	epithelia
AEEHIKNPT	phenakite
AEEHIKRSS	shikarees
AEEHILLTW	tailwheel
AEEHILMNW	meanwhile
AEEHILNTV	Helvetian
AEEHILPRS	shapelier
AEEHILRRT	earthlier
AEEHILRSS	shiralees
AEEHILRTW	wealthier
AEEHIMNST	mainsheet
AEEHIMPRY	hyperemia
AEEHIMPSS	emphasise
AEEHIMPST	empathise
AEEHIMPSZ	emphasize
AEEHIMPTZ	empathize
AEEHIMRST	hetaerism
AEEHINNPZ	phenazine
AEEHINPRS	Hesperian
AEEHINPSS	Ephesians
AEEHINRSV	haversine
AEEHINRTU	eutherian
AEEHINRTZ	Therezina
AEEHINSSV	evanishes
	heaviness
AEEHIPPSW	hawsepipe
AEEHIPRSS	apheresis
	pharisees
AEEHIPRST	therapies
AEEHIRRST	earthrise
AEEHIRSSV	shivarees
AEEHIRSSW	washeries
AEEHIRSTT	earthiest
	heartiest
	hesitater
	hetaerist
AEEHISSTT	hesitates
AEEHKLLRS	rakehells
AEEHKLLRY	rakehelly
AEEHKLLSU	keelhauls
AEEHKLPSW	sheepwalk
AEEHKMMOR	homemaker
AEEHKMORS	shoemaker
AEEHKNRRS	harkeners
AEEHLLMOW	wholemeal
AEEHLLNOW	Halloween
AEEHLLOSW	wholesale
AEEHLLSSS	seashells
AEEHLMNSW	wheelsman
AEEHLMNSY	hymeneals
AEEHLMPRY	melaphyre
AEEHLMPST	helpmates
AEEHLMRTY	erythemal
	hemelytra
AEEHLMSSS	shameless
AEEHLMTTY	methylate
AEEHLNOPS	anopheles
AEEHLNOPT	phenolate
AEEHLNOSW	Halesowen
AEEHLNPST	elephants
AEEHLNSST	natheless
AEEHLNSSU	unleashes
AEEHLNSSV	havenless
AEEHLOPST	telophase
AEEHLORSS	arseholes
	haloseres
AEEHLORST	trehalose
AEEHLOSSU	alehouses
AEEHLPRRY	hyperreal
AEEHLPSSS	phaseless
	shapeless
AEEHLPSTT	telepaths
AEEHLPTTY	telepathy
AEEHLRSST	heartless
AEEHLRTWY	weatherly
AEEHLSTTY	ethylates
AEEHLSTXY	hexastyle
AEEHMMORT	hammertoe
AEEHMMPSY	emphysema
AEEHMMRRS	hammerers
AEEHMNNOP	phenomena
AEEHMNRSW	washermen
AEEHMNSTU	atheneums
AEEHMNSTX	exanthems
AEEHMOPRS	semaphore
AEEHMORST	heartsome
AEEHMORSW	homewares
AEEHMOSST	hematoses
AEEHMOSTU	housemate
AEEHMPRRS	hamperers
AEEHMPRST	petersham
AEEHMSTTW	Westmeath
AEEHNOORT	oenothera
AEEHNOPRS	earphones
AEEHNOPTX	toxaphene
AEEHNPPRY	hyperpnea
AEEHNPRRS	sharpener
AEEHNRRSS	harnesser
AEEHNRSSS	harnesses
AEEHNRSST	hasteners
AEEHNRSTT	threatens
AEEHNRSTW	enwreaths
AEEHNRSTX	narthexes

AEEHNRSWY	anywheres
AEEHNSSTW	enswathes
AEEHOPRST	ephorates
AEEHOPRTY	aerophyte
AEEHORRSV	overhears
AEEHORSSS	seashores
AEEHORSTV	overheats
AEEHORSUW	warehouse
AEEHOSSTU	teahouses
AEEHPPRSS	preshapes
AEEHPRRSS	rephrases
AEEHPRRST	threapers
AEEHPRSSW	prewashes
AEEHPRSTU	Euphrates
	superheat
AEEHRRSTT	shatterer
AEEHRRSTV	harvester
AEEHRSTUX	exhauster
AEEHRSTYZ	Esterházy
AEEIILLOP	aeolipile
AEEIILMNT	eliminate
AEEIILQRU	reliquiae
AEEIILRSS	serialise
AEEIILRST	Israelite
	realities
AEEIILRSZ	serialize
AEEIIMNST	amenities
AEEIINNTV	Vientiane
AEEIINRTT	itinerate
AEEIINSTV	naiveties
AEEIINSTX	anxieties
AEEIIPPRT	peripetia
AEEIIRSTV	varieties
AEEIIRTTV	iterative
AEEIIRTVZ	vizierate
AEEIJMNSS	jessamine
AEEIJMSST	majesties
AEEIKKLNS	snakelike
AEEIKKPPS	Pikes Peak
AEEIKLLNS	silkalene
AEEIKLLPT	petallike
AEEIKLLVV	valvelike
AEEIKLMUW	Milwaukee
AEEIKLNNP	Lenin Peak
AEEIKLNSS	leakiness
AEEIKLPRS	sprekelia
AEEIKLSTW	weakliest
AEEIKLSTY	yeastlike
AEEIKMNOT	ketonemia
AEEIKNRSV	knaveries
AEEIKNSST	sneakiest
AEEIKQRSU	squeakier
AEEIKRRST	streakier
AEEILLMNT	metalline
AEEILLMRS	marseille
AEEILLMST	metallise
AEEILLMTZ	metallize
AEEILLNOT	lineolate
	linoleate
AEEILLNST	tenailles
AEEILLPPS	Apple Isle
AEEILLPST	palletise
AEEILLPTT	paillette
AEEILLPTZ	palletize
AEEILLRST	laetriles
AEEILLSSS	aisleless
AEEILLSTT	satellite
AEEILLTVW	wavellite
AEEILLTVX	vexillate
AEEILMMST	lemmatise
AEEILMMTZ	lemmatize
AEEILMNNT	alinement
	lineament
AEEILMNRY	minelayer
AEEILMNSS	mealiness
	messaline
AEEILMNST	enamelist
AEEILMOOS	elaiosome
AEEILMORT	meliorate
AEEILMRST	misrelate
	salimeter
AEEILMRTT	altimeter
AEEILMRTU	elaterium
AEEILMRTW	limewater
AEEILMSST	measliest
AEEILMSTZ	metalizes
AEEILMTUV	emulative
AEEILNNPP	peneplain
AEEILNNPR	perennial
AEEILNNSX	sexennial
AEEILNNTV	levantine
	valentine
AEEILNOTV	elevation
AEEILNPPP	pineapple
AEEILNPRS	plenaries
AEEILNPRX	explainer
AEEILNPSS	penalises
AEEILNPST	Palestine
	penalties
	tapelines
AEEILNPSX	expansile
AEEILNPSZ	penalizes
AEEILNRSS	earliness
	leariness
AEEILNRST	entailers
	treenails
AEEILNRSV	vernalise
AEEILNRTW	waterline
AEEILNRVZ	vernalize
AEEILNSST	essential
AEEILNSSV	aliveness
AEEILNTTV	ventilate
AEEILOPTT	petiolate
AEEILORRT	arteriole
AEEILORST	aerolites
AEEILOSTT	etiolates
AEEILPPRS	reapplies
AEEILPRRV	prevailer
AEEILPRSS	espaliers
AEEILPRST	pearliest
AEEILQRSU	equaliser
AEEILQRUZ	equalizer
AEEILQSSU	equalises
AEEILQSUZ	equalizes
AEEILRRSS	realisers
AEEILRRST	retailers
AEEILRRSZ	realizers
AEEILRRTV	retrieval
AEEILRSSV	velarises
AEEILRSSW	weariless
AEEILRSTT	laterites
	literates
	statelier
AEEILRSTV	levirates
	relatives
	versatile
AEEILRSTY	seriately
AEEILRSVW	reviewals
AEEILRSVZ	velarizes
AEEILRTTU	elutriate
AEEILSSTW	leastwise
AEEILSSTZ	sleaziest
AEEILSSUX	sexualise
AEEILSTTV	levitates
AEEILSUXZ	sexualize
AEEILSVVY	evasively
AEEIMNNPT	impennate
AEEIMNNRV	venireman
AEEIMNNZZ	mezzanine
AEEIMNPRR	repairmen
AEEIMNRST	antimeres
	Trasimene
AEEIMNRSX	examiners
AEEIMNRTT	terminate
AEEIMNSSS	seaminess
AEEIMNSST	amnesties
	meatiness
AEEIMNSTT	estaminet
AEEIMOPPR	peperomia
AEEIMORSS	isomerase
AEEIMORSW	wearisome
AEEIMPRTT	impetrate
AEEIMRRRS	remarries
AEEIMRRST	streamier
AEEIMRSST	masteries
AEEIMRSTT	tasimeter
AEEIMRTTX	taximeter
AEEIMSSTT	estimates
	steamiest
AEEINNNPS	Apennines
AEEINNPST	septennia
AEEINNRST	tanneries
AEEINNRTT	entertain
AEEINNRTV	innervate
AEEINNSST	insensate
AEEINNSSV	naiveness
AEEINNSTV	venetians
AEEINOPPT	appointee
AEEINOPRT	peritonea
AEEINOPSW	weaponise
AEEINOPWZ	weaponize
AEEINORTT	orientate
AEEINPPST	pepsinate
AEEINPRSS	passerine
AEEINPRST	aperients
	episterna

pistareen
sparteine
AEEINPSVX expansive
AEEINRRST retainers
ternaries
AEEINRRTT reiterant
AEEINRRTV veratrine
AEEINRSST arsenites
resinates
AEEINRSSW weariness
AEEINRSTT reinstate
AEEINRSTU estuarine
AEEINRSTV invertase
AEEINRSTY eyestrain
AEEINSSTT tetanises
AEEINSSTU uneasiest
AEEINSTTT enstatite
intestate
satinette
AEEINSTTU austenite
AEEINSTTZ tetanizes
AEEINTTTV attentive
tentative
AEEIOOPPS epopoeias
AEEIOPRST operatise
periostea
AEEIOPRTV evaporite
operative
AEEIOPRTZ operatize
AEEIPPRST appetiser
AEEIPPRSU pauperise
AEEIPPRTZ appetizer
AEEIPPRUZ pauperize
AEEIPPSTT appetites
AEEIPRRRS rareripes
repairers
AEEIPRRTV privateer
AEEIPRSSS pessaries
AEEIPRSSV aspersive
AEEIPRSVV pervasive
AEEIPRTTX extirpate
AEEIPSSVW spaewives
AEEIQSSTU queasiest
AEEIRSSTT sestertia
treatises
AEEIRSSTU estuaries
AEEIRSSTV assertive
AEEIRSTWW wasteweir
AEEISSTTV estivates
AEEISSTTW sweatiest
AEEISSTTY yeastiest
AEEISTUVX exuviates
AEEJKRRTW jerkwater
AEEJLMRSU Jerusalem
AEEJMORTT majorette
AEEJMRSTT jetstream
AEEJNOSTZ Zeta-Jones
AEEJNRSST serjeants
AEEKKLSWY lykewakes
AEEKLLPSW sleepwalk
AEEKLMMSU mamelukes
AEEKLMRST telemarks
AEEKLNRST Lankester
AEEKLSSTY eyestalks
AEEKMNRTW newmarket
AEEKMORSV makeovers
AEEKMRRRS remarkers
AEEKMRRST marketers
AEEKNORTV overtaken
AEEKORSTV overtakes
takeovers
AEEKORTUY eukaryote
AEEKPRSTT parkettes
AEEKQRSSU squeakers
AEEKRRSST streakers
AEELLLMOS lamellose
AEELLLSTT telltales
AEELLNPPZ Appenzell
AEELLNPRT repellant
AEELLNPTX expellant
AEELLNRTY enterally
eternally
AEELLOPST sellotape
soleplate
AEELLOSTT allottees
AEELLOSUV laevulose
AEELLOSWY Yellow Sea
AEELLPSTT platelets
AEELLPTTY peltately
AEELLRRSV ravellers
AEELLRRTV traveller
AEELLRSVY severally
AEELLRTTU tellurate
AEELLSSUV valueless
AEELLSSVV valveless
AEELLSTVV valvelets
AEELMMNRT entrammel
AEELMMRRT trammeler
AEELMMSTU malemutes
AEELMMTXY metaxylem
AEELMNOST telamones
AEELMNPRT parlement
AEELMNPSS ampleness
ensamples
AEELMNRST lamenters
AEELMNRTV ravelment
AEELMNSTT mantelets
AEELMORST elastomer
AEELMOSTT matelotes
AEELMOSWY awesomely
AEELMOTTT matelotte
AEELMPRSU supermale
AEELMPRSX exemplars
AEELMPRXY exemplary
AEELMPSTT palmettes
templates
AEELMRSST semestral
AEELMRSTT streamlet
AEELMRSTX extremals
AEELMRTTW meltwater
AEELNNNTU antennule
AEELNNPSS planeness
AEELNNRST lannerets
AEELNOPST antelopes
AEELNOPTX exoplanet
AEELNPPSS spalpeens
AEELNPRTV prevalent
AEELNRSSS snareless
AEELNRSST alertness
AEELNRSSV enslavers
AEELNRSTV levanters
AEELNRSTX externals
AEELNRSTY earnestly
AEELNRTTV tervalent
AEELNRTTY ternately
AEELNRTVY Trevelyan
AEELNSSST staleness
AEELNSSTY sensately
AEELOPRSV overleaps
AEELOPRTV overleapt
AEELORSST oleasters
AEELORSTT tolerates
AEELORSTV elevators
AEELORSTY roseately
AEELORTVY elevatory
AEELORUVV overvalue
AEELPPRRU puerperal
AEELPPRSS paperless
AEELPPRTU perpetual
AEELPRRSS relapsers
AEELPRRST palterers
plasterer
AEELPRRSY parleyers
AEELPRRTU prelature
AEELPRSSU pleasures
AEELPRSSV vesperals
AEELPRSTT saltpeter
saltpetre
AEELQRRRU quarreler
AEELQRSSU squealers
AEELQSTUZ quetzales
AEELQUVZZ Velázquez
AEELRRSSV reversals
slaverers
AEELRRSTU serrulate
AEELRRSTV travelers
AEELRSSTW waterless
AEELRSTUY austerely
AEELRSTVY severalty
AEELSSSTT stateless
tasteless
AEELSSSTW sweatless
AEELSSSTY yeastless
AEELSSTTT statelets
AEEMMNORT manometer
AEEMMNSTU amusement
AEEMMORTT atmometer
AEEMMPRUY empyreuma
AEEMMRRST stammerer
AEEMMRRSY yammerers
AEEMMSSST messmates
AEEMNNOPR praenomen
AEEMNNORT nanometre
AEEMNNOTT atonement
AEEMNNPRT permanent
AEEMNOPRT treponema

AEEMNOPSU	menopause
AEEMNOPYZ	apoenzyme
AEEMNORUV	manoeuvre
AEEMNPRTY	repayment
AEEMNPSTV	pavements
AEEMNRSST	steersman
AEEMNRSTU	numerates
AEEMNRSTV	averments
AEEMNRSUV	maneuvers
AEEMNRTTT	treatment
AEEMNSSTT	statesmen
AEEMNSSTY	mateyness
AEEMNSTTT	statement
	testament
AEEMOPSSU	mesopause
AEEMORRSU	rearmouse
AEEMORRTT	rotameter
AEEMORRTY	aerometry
AEEMORSST	Massorete
AEEMORTTU	autometer
AEEMPPRRS	pamperers
AEEMPRRST	tamperers
AEEMPRRSV	revampers
AEEMPRRTU	premature
AEEMPRSTT	attempers
AEEMPRTTT	attempter
	reattempt
AEEMPRTTU	permutate
AEEMQRRSU	remarques
AEEMQRTTU	Marquette
AEEMQSTTU	maquettes
AEEMRRSST	remasters
	streamers
AEEMRRSSU	measurers
AEEMRRSTT	smatterer
AEEMRSSST	masseters
AEEMRSSSU	reassumes
AEEMRSSTT	teamsters
AEEMRTTTW	wattmeter
AEEMSSSSU	masseuses
AEENNOPTT	panettone
AEENNPRRT	trepanner
AEENNPRTT	penetrant
	repentant
AEENNRRSS	ensnarers
AEENNRRTT	reentrant
AEENNRSTV	revenants
AEENOPPRT	notepaper
AEENOPRST	personate
AEENOPTTT	potentate
AEENORRSS	reasoners
AEENORRTV	enervator
	venerator
AEENORSSS	seasoners
AEENORSST	resonates
AEENORSTV	renovates
AEENORSTW	stoneware
AEENPPRRT	entrapper
AEENPPRSW	newspaper
AEENPRRTU	enrapture
AEENPRSSS	spareness
AEENPRSST	peartness
AEENPRSTY	septenary
AEENPRSUV	parvenues
AEENPSTTY	antetypes
AEENRRRSW	warreners
AEENRRSTT	natterers
AEENRRSTU	saunterer
AEENRRSTV	taverners
AEENRRTUV	nervature
AEENRSSTU	sauternes
AEENRSTTV	anteverts
AEENSSSUV	suaveness
AEEOOPRTZ	azeotrope
AEEOPPRSU	peasouper
AEEOPRRST	perorates
AEEOPRSST	proteases
AEEOPRSTT	operettas
	poetaster
AEEOPSSST	petasoses
AEEOQRRTU	Querétaro
AEEORRSSU	rearouses
AEEORRSTV	overrates
AEEORRSTW	rosewater
AEEORRTVW	overwater
AEEORSTTV	overstate
AEEORSTTW	twoseater
AEEORSTVX	overtaxes
AEEPPRRRS	preparers
AEEPRRRST	parterres
AEEPRRSSS	aspersers
AEEPRRSTU	apertures
AEEPRSTXY	apteryxes
AEEPSSSTU	petasuses
AEEQRRSUV	quaverers
AEEQRSSTU	sequestra
AEEQRTTTU	quartette
AEEQRTUUX	exequatur
AEERRRSST	arresters
	rearrests
AEERRRSSU	reassurer
AEERRRSTU	serrature
	treasurer
AEERRRSTV	traverser
AEERRSSST	asserters
	reasserts
AEERRSSSU	reassures
AEERRSSTU	treasures
AEERRSSTV	traverses
AEERRTTVX	extravert
AEERSSTTT	attesters
AEESTTTTU	statuette
AEFFGRSSU	suffrages
AEFFHIKSY	kaffiyehs
AEFFIILRS	falsifier
AEFFIILSS	falsifies
AEFFIKPST	pikestaff
AEFFILLUV	effluvial
AEFFIMRRS	affirmers
	reaffirms
AEFFINORS	raffinose
AEFFIRTUX	affixture
AEFFLLRUY	fearfully
AEFFLLTUY	fatefully
AEFFLNOPT	pantoffle
AEFFLNSTU	affluents
AEFFLORSW	safflower
AEFFLSSTU	sufflates
AEFFNOOSS	offseason
AEFFORSST	afforests
AEFFORSTV	overstaff
AEFFRSTTU	tartuffes
AEFGHHISS	hagfishes
AEFGHILNS	angelfish
AEFGHILST	safelight
AEFGHINRT	fathering
AEFGHIRSS	garfishes
AEFGHIRST	gearshift
AEFGHORRT	forgather
AEFGIILNS	anglifies
AEFGIIMNR	magnifier
AEFGIIMNS	magnifies
AEFGIINRY	aerifying
AEFGIIRRT	gratifier
AEFGIIRSS	gasifiers
AEFGIIRST	gratifies
AEFGILLLN	flagellin
AEFGILLLS	gallflies
AEFGILLNT	fellating
AEFGILLRY	fragilely
AEFGILMOR	galeiform
AEFGILNRS	finaglers
AEFGILNRT	faltering
	reflating
AEFGIMNRR	reframing
AEFGIMSTU	fumigates
AEFGINNST	fastening
AEFGINNTT	fattening
AEFGINRRY	rarefying
AEFGINRTU	featuring
	figurante
AEFGIORSS	ossifrage
AEFGIRRRY	Grey Friar
AEFGISTTU	fustigate
AEFGLLLMU	flagellum
AEFGLLOPS	flagpoles
AEFGLMOPS	megaflops
AEFGLNOST	flagstone
AEFGLOPRS	leapfrogs
AEFGLORTW	afterglow
AEFGLRTUU	fulgurate
AEFGMNRST	fragments
AEFGNORST	frontages
AEFGNORTX	xenograft
AEFHHISST	sheatfish
AEFHHLLTU	healthful
AEFHHLOTW	heathfowl
AEFHIKMST	makeshift
AEFHILMSS	fishmeals
AEFHILMST	halftimes
AEFHILPST	fishplate
AEFHILSST	faithless
	flashiest
AEFHIMNRS	fisherman
AEFHINORS	fashioner
	refashion

AEFHINTTT	antitheft
AEFHIORSS	oarfishes
AEFHIPRSS	spearfish
AEFHIRSST	ratfishes
AEFHISSSW	sawfishes
AEFHKNORS	foreshank
AEFHLLTUY	hatefully
AEFHLNNPY	halfpenny
AEFHLNOST	halftones
AEFHLNSSW	newsflash
AEFHLORSV	flashover
AEFHLORTY	O'Flaherty
AEFHMORST	fathomers
AEFHMORSU	farmhouse
AEFHORRTU	Our Father
AEFHORSTW	aftershow
AEFIIKLRY	fairylike
AEFIILLNS	nailfiles
AEFIILMNS	semifinal
AEFIILMPR	amplifier
AEFIILMPS	amplifies
AEFIILNNT	infantile
AEFIILNSS	finalises
AEFIILNSZ	finalizes
AEFIILQRU	qualifier
AEFIILQSU	qualifies
AEFIILRST	frailties
AEFIILSSS	salsifies
AEFIILSST	falsities
AEFIIMNSS	infamises
AEFIIMNSZ	infamizes
AEFIIMSTT	mattifies
AEFIINRTU	infuriate
AEFIIPRST	aperitifs
AEFIIRRST	ratifiers
AEFIIRSST	satisfier
AEFIISSST	satisfies
AEFIISTTU	fatuities
AEFIISTVX	fixatives
AEFIKLNSS	flakiness
AEFILLNOT	fellation
AEFILLNOX	flexional
AEFILLNST	flatlines
AEFILLOOT	foliolate
AEFILLRSW	firewalls
AEFILLRTX	fellatrix
AEFILMMOR	oriflamme
AEFILMNOS	Isle of Man
AEFILMNRS	inflamers
AEFILMNST	filaments
AEFILMNTU	fulminate
AEFILMORS	formalise
AEFILMORZ	formalize
AEFILMRSW	welfarism
AEFILNNUZ	influenza
AEFILNORT	reflation
AEFILNRSS	frailness
AEFILNRST	inflaters
AEFILNRSU	frauleins
AEFILNRTU	flauntier
AEFILOORS	aerofoils
AEFILORRT	rotiferal
AEFILORSS	foresails
AEFILOSTT	floatiest
AEFILRSTT	filtrates
AEFILRSTU	filatures
AEFILRSTW	welfarist
AEFILSSTV	festivals
AEFILSTTU	faultiest
	fistulate
AEFILSTUU	fauteuils
AEFIMMNRT	firmament
AEFIMNOSS	foaminess
AEFIMNOST	manifesto
AEFIMNOTX	tamoxifen
AEFIMNSST	manifests
AEFIMORSS	misfeasor
AEFIMORTV	formative
AEFINNSST	faintness
AEFINOOTT	foetation
AEFINOPRR	poriferan
AEFINOPRS	pinafores
AEFINORSU	nefarious
AEFINOSTY	Sainte Foy
AEFINRTZZ	frizzante
AEFINSSTT	fattiness
AEFIORSTV	favorites
AEFIORTUV	favourite
AEFIPRRST	firetraps
AEFIPRSUW	superwaif
AEFKLLUWY	wakefully
AEFKLNOSW	snowflake
AEFKLORSW	falsework
AEFKMORRW	framework
AEFKNNRSS	frankness
AEFKOPRSS	forspeaks
AEFKORRSS	forsakers
AEFLLLNNY	flannelly
AEFLLNTTU	flatulent
AEFLLORST	fellators
	forestall
AEFLLORSV	overfalls
AEFLLPSTU	platefuls
AEFLLRTUY	tearfully
AEFLLSSTU	faultless
AEFLMORSU	fumaroles
AEFLMORTU	formulate
AEFLMORWY	mayflower
AEFLMOSTU	flameouts
AEFLMRSTU	masterful
AEFLNNOST	fontanels
AEFLNNSTY	fentanyls
AEFLNOOSS	aloofness
AEFLNOPRY	profanely
AEFLNOPST	pantofles
AEFLNOPTU	pantoufle
AEFLNRSTU	flaunters
AEFLNSSUW	awfulness
AEFLOOPTT	footplate
AEFLOORSS	seafloors
AEFLORRSV	flavorers
AEFLORRUV	flavourer
AEFLORSTW	fleaworts
AEFLORTWW	waterfowl
AEFLOSSTT	falsettos
AEFLPPRSY	flypapers
AEFLPRRUY	prayerful
AEFMNOORW	forewoman
AEFMORSST	foremasts
	mortsafes
AEFMORSTT	aftermost
AEFMORSVW	waveforms
AEFNNOORT	afternoon
AEFNNSSTU	unfastens
AEFNOPRRS	profaners
AEFNORRSW	forewarns
AEFNORSST	seafronts
AEFNORTTU	fortunate
AEFNORTVW	wavefront
AEFNORTWY	Fort Wayne
AEFNRRSST	transfers
AEFNRSSTU	aftersuns
	transfuse
AEFOOPRRW	wearproof
AEFOPRRST	foreparts
AEFOPRRTY	prefatory
AEFOPSSTT	softpaste
AEFORRSSW	forswears
AEFORRSUV	favourers
AEFORSSTY	forestays
AEFRRSTTU	frustrate
AEGGGINRU	regauging
AEGGGIRWW	wigwagger
AEGGHILMS	Gilgamesh
AEGGHINNR	rehanging
AEGGHINRT	gathering
AEGGHIRTZ	gigahertz
AEGGHISST	shaggiest
AEGGHOPRR	ergograph
AEGGHOPRY	geography
AEGGIINNR	regaining
AEGGIIORV	Viareggio
AEGGILLRS	grillages
AEGGILNNR	enlarging
	largening
AEGGILNNS	gleanings
AEGGILNRV	graveling
AEGGILNRZ	reglazing
AEGGIMMNT	gemmating
AEGGIMNSS	messaging
AEGGIMSSU	misgauges
AEGGINNRR	garnering
AEGGINNRV	engraving
AEGGINOOR	gorgoneia
AEGGINORR	Gregorian
AEGGINORT	Agrigento
AEGGINOSY	easygoing
AEGGINPRS	presaging
AEGGINPRT	pargeting
AEGGINRRT	gartering
	regrating
AEGGINRRU	rearguing
AEGGINRST	restaging
AEGGINRTT	targeting
AEGGINSTT	gestating
AEGGINTTZ	gazetting

AEGGIOPRS	arpeggios
AEGGIQSTU	quaggiest
AEGGLNPST	eggplants
AEGGLNRRY	glengarry
AEGGLORSY	gargoyles
AEGGLRRST	straggler
AEGGLRSST	straggles
AEGGMORRT	mortgager
AEGGMORST	mortgages
AEGGNNRTU	Trengganu
AEGGNORSW	waggoners
AEGGNOSUY	synagogue
AEGGNRSST	gangsters
AEGGORRSS	aggressor
AEGHHINRS	rehashing
AEGHHINST	sheathing
AEGHHIRTU	haughtier
AEGHHOPTY	theophagy
AEGHIIINP	Iphigenia
AEGHIKNNR	hankering
	harkening
AEGHIKNPR	phreaking
AEGHIKNRS	shrinkage
AEGHILLMS	megillahs
AEGHILLSS	shigellas
AEGHILMST	megaliths
AEGHILNNS	hanseling
AEGHILNRS	narghiles
	nargilehs
	shearling
AEGHILNRT	earthling
	haltering
	lathering
AEGHILNST	athelings
AEGHILNSV	shaveling
AEGHILRST	ghastlier
	thirlages
AEGHILRSV	gravelish
AEGHIMMNR	hammering
AEGHIMNPR	hampering
AEGHIMNRT	nightmare
AEGHIMNWY	Hemingway
AEGHIMORR	hierogram
AEGHIMPPR	epiphragm
AEGHINNPP	happening
AEGHINNST	hastening
AEGHINOPS	siphonage
AEGHINPRS	reshaping
AEGHINPRT	threaping
AEGHINPUV	upheaving
AEGHINRRS	garnisher
AEGHINRSS	garnishes
AEGHINRST	ingathers
AEGHINRSW	rewashing
AEGHINRTT	threating
AEGHINRTU	naughtier
AEGHINRTW	nightwear
	wreathing
AEGHINSSU	anguishes
AEGHINSTT	gnathites
AEGHINSTU	naughties
AEGHIOOPS	oesophagi
AEGHIPPRS	epigraphs
AEGHIPPRY	epigraphy
AEGHIPRRS	serigraph
AEGHIPSTT	spaghetti
AEGHISSTU	Aegisthus
AEGHLLMPY	megaphyll
AEGHLMNNT	lengthman
AEGHLOOPR	oleograph
AEGHLOORR	logorrhea
AEGHLORTT	larghetto
AEGHLOSSU	goulashes
AEGHLRSTU	slaughter
AEGHMNOPR	nephogram
AEGHMOPST	apothegms
AEGHMPRYY	hypergamy
AEGHNOORR	gonorrhea
AEGHNOPST	heptagons
	pathogens
AEGHNOPTY	pathogeny
AEGHNORSV	hangovers
	overhangs
AEGHNOSTU	shogunate
AEGHNPRSY	pharynges
AEGHOPPRS	prophages
AEGHOPPSY	apophyges
AEGHOPRST	grapeshot
AEGHOPSSU	esophagus
AEGHORSST	shortages
AEGIIKLNT	giantlike
AEGIILLNN	lilangeni
AEGIILLRS	grisaille
AEGIILLRT	argillite
AEGIILLSU	aiguilles
AEGIILMNR	remailing
AEGIILMSV	vigesimal
AEGIILNNT	entailing
AEGIILNPT	epilating
AEGIILNRR	rerailing
AEGIILNRS	realising
AEGIILNRT	retailing
AEGIILNRZ	realizing
AEGIILNSS	signalise
AEGIILNST	gainliest
AEGIILNSZ	signalize
AEGIILNTV	genitival
	vigilante
AEGIILNTY	geniality
AEGIILSTT	litigates
AEGIILSTV	vestigial
AEGIIMMRT	immigrate
AEGIIMMTT	migmatite
AEGIIMNNR	remaining
AEGIIMNNX	examining
AEGIIMNRS	imaginers
	migraines
AEGIIMOSS	isogamies
AEGIIMSTT	mitigates
AEGIINNRT	retaining
AEGIINNVW	inweaving
AEGIINORT	originate
AEGIINOTT	goniatite
AEGIINPRR	repairing
AEGIINPTX	expiating
AEGIINRST	grainiest
AEGIINRTT	granitite
	iterating
AEGIINSTT	instigate
AEGIIRRST	irrigates
AEGIIRSTT	Stagirite
AEGIIRSTV	gravities
AEGIISSTV	visagiste
AEGIJNORS	jargonise
AEGIJNORZ	jargonize
AEGIJNTUU	unijugate
AEGIKKMNR	kingmaker
AEGIKLLSS	glasslike
AEGIKLLST	Gaitskell
AEGIKLNSW	weaklings
AEGIKLRSS	grasslike
AEGIKMNRR	remarking
AEGIKMNRT	marketing
AEGIKNQSU	squeaking
AEGIKNRST	streaking
AEGIKNSSW	gawkiness
AEGILLLLY	illegally
AEGILLLNU	gallinule
AEGILLMNT	metalling
AEGILLNNP	panelling
AEGILLNOS	lignaloes
AEGILLNQU	equalling
AEGILLNRS	signaller
AEGILLNRU	laureling
AEGILLNRV	Granville
	ravelling
AEGILLNTU	lingulate
AEGILLPPR	Grappelli
AEGILLPPU	pupillage
AEGILLPRS	aspergill
	pillagers
AEGILLPSS	spillages
AEGILLRRU	guerrilla
AEGILLRSS	salesgirl
AEGILLRST	allergist
	gallerist
AEGILLRSU	guerillas
AEGILLRSV	villagers
AEGILLSST	legalists
	stillages
AEGILMNNP	emplaning
AEGILMNNS	signalmen
AEGILMNNT	alignment
	lamenting
AEGILMNPX	exampling
AEGILMNRS	maligners
	malingers
AEGILMNRV	marveling
AEGILMNST	ligaments
AEGILMNTU	emulating
	glutamine
AEGILMORR	rigmarole
AEGILMORS	glamorise
AEGILMORZ	glamorize
AEGILMOSU	São Miguel
AEGILMRSX	lexigrams

AEGILNNNP	enplaning
AEGILNNOR	reloaning
AEGILNNRS	learnings
AEGILNNST	gantlines
AEGILNNSU	unsealing
AEGILNNSV	enslaving
AEGILNNSW	weanlings
AEGILNNSY	yeanlings
AEGILNNTV	levanting
AEGILNOPX	poleaxing
AEGILNORU	neuroglia
AEGILNORY	legionary
AEGILNOST	gelations
	legations
AEGILNPRS	relapsing
AEGILNPRT	paltering
AEGILNPRY	parleying
	replaying
AEGILNPSS	salpinges
AEGILNQSU	squealing
AEGILNRSS	grainless
	signalers
AEGILNRST	integrals
	teraglins
	triangles
AEGILNRSV	slavering
AEGILNRSY	layerings
	syringeal
	yearlings
AEGILNRTU	granulite
AEGILNRTV	traveling
AEGILNRTY	ingrately
AEGILNRUV	revaluing
AEGILNRWY	wearingly
AEGILNSST	tasseling
AEGILNSSW	wineglass
AEGILNSTY	teasingly
AEGILOOPS	apologies
	apologise
AEGILOOPZ	apologize
AEGILOOTY	aetiology
AEGILOPSS	spoilages
AEGILORSS	gasoliers
	girasoles
	seraglios
AEGILORSU	glaireous
AEGILORTV	levigator
AEGILPPRR	papergirl
AEGILPPSS	slippages
AEGILPRTY	pterygial
AEGILRRRU	irregular
AEGILRSTU	glauriest
	ligatures
AEGILRSUV	vulgarise
AEGILRSVW	lawgivers
AEGILRTUV	virgulate
AEGILRUVZ	vulgarize
AEGILSSST	glassiest
AEGIMMNOT	gemmation
AEGIMMNRU	germanium
AEGIMMNRY	yammering
AEGIMMNST	magnetism
AEGIMMNSU	magnesium
AEGIMNNNR	remanning
AEGIMNNNU	unmeaning
AEGIMNNOR	enamoring
	omnirange
AEGIMNNOT	Montaigne
AEGIMNNRT	germinant
AEGIMNNSS	manginess
AEGIMNNSU	unseaming
AEGIMNORT	morganite
AEGIMNOSZ	Egas Moniz
AEGIMNPPR	pampering
AEGIMNPRR	prearming
AEGIMNPRT	tampering
AEGIMNPRV	revamping
AEGIMNRRW	rewarming
AEGIMNRSS	Massinger
AEGIMNRST	emigrants
	mastering
	streaming
AEGIMNRSU	geraniums
	measuring
AEGIMNRTT	mattering
AEGIMNSTT	magnetist
AEGIMNSTU	maungiest
AEGIMOSTY	stegomyia
AEGIMQRSU	quagmires
AEGIMRSST	sterigmas
AEGIMRSTY	magistery
AEGIMSSSU	misusages
AEGINNNRS	ensnaring
AEGINNNTT	tenanting
AEGINNORS	reasoning
AEGINNORW	Norwegian
AEGINNORZ	organzine
AEGINNOSS	seasoning
AEGINNOST	negations
AEGINNOSU	guanosine
AEGINNOTT	negotiant
AEGINNPPR	Perpignan
AEGINNPRT	parenting
AEGINNPTT	patenting
AEGINNRSS	ranginess
AEGINNRST	gannister
AEGINNRSW	answering
AEGINNRSY	yearnings
AEGINNRTT	integrant
	nattering
AEGINNSST	assenting
AEGINNSSU	sanguines
AEGINNSTU	unseating
AEGINNTTU	tautening
AEGINOPRS	Singapore
AEGINOPRT	operating
AEGINOPST	pinotages
AEGINORRS	organiser
AEGINORRV	granivore
AEGINORRZ	organizer
AEGINORSS	organises
AEGINORSZ	organizes
AEGINORTT	gittarone
AEGINORVW	overawing
AEGINOSTT	gestation
AEGINOTTU	outeating
AEGINPPRR	preparing
AEGINPPRY	prepaying
AEGINPRRU	uprearing
AEGINPRSS	aspersing
	preassign
	repassing
AEGINPRST	repasting
	trapesing
AEGINPRTT	pattering
AEGINPSTY	egyptians
AEGINQRUV	quavering
AEGINRRST	arresting
	serrating
AEGINRRTU	garniture
AEGINRSSS	assigners
	reassigns
AEGINRSST	asserting
AEGINRSTT	restating
AEGINRSTU	gauntries
	signature
AEGINRSTV	vintagers
AEGINRTTT	tattering
AEGINRTTU	Ungaretti
AEGINRTTY	yattering
AEGINSSSS	assessing
	gassiness
AEGINSSST	staginess
AEGINSSTT	angstiest
AEGINSSUZ	gauziness
AEGINSTTT	attesting
AEGINSTUU	Augustine
AEGIPRTUV	purgative
AEGIRRRST	registrar
AEGIRSSST	grassiest
AEGISTTUV	gustative
AEGJLSTUU	jugulates
AEGKLNOOP	pokelogan
AEGKLNOPS	Longs Peak
AEGKORSTT	agterskot
AEGLLNOPW	alpenglow
AEGLLNOST	gallstone
AEGLLOOOZ	zoogloeal
AEGLLOPRS	gallopers
AEGLLOSSW	gallowses
AEGLLOSTT	tollgates
AEGLLRRUY	regularly
AEGLLRTUY	tegularly
AEGLLSSSS	glassless
AEGLMMORY	myelogram
AEGLMNNOS	mangonels
AEGLMNOOY	anemology
AEGLMNORW	angleworm
AEGLMORTY	algometry
AEGLMOSTV	megavolts
AEGLNNOOT	Long Eaton
AEGLNNSTU	untangles
AEGLNOPRY	gyroplane
AEGLNORSU	granulose
AEGLNOSSW	wagonless
AEGLNOSTU	langouste

AEGLNRRST strangler
AEGLNRRSW wranglers
AEGLNRSST strangles
AEGLNRSTY strangely
AEGLNSTTU gauntlets
AEGLNSTUU ungulates
AEGLOOOSZ zoogloeas
AEGLOOPSU apologues
AEGLOPPRU propagule
AEGLOPRSY playgoers
AEGLORRTU regulator
AEGLORSTV travelogs
AEGLORTTY tetralogy
AEGLPPRRS grapplers
AEGLRSSSS grassless
AEGLRSSSU sugarless
AEGMMNORS gammoners
AEGMMOPRR programme
AEGMMRRSU rummagers
AEGMNNORT magnetron
AEGMNNOST magnetons
AEGMNORRW warmonger
AEGMNORSU germanous
AEGMNORSV mangroves
AEGMNORTU augmentor
AEGMNOTTU mangetout
AEGMNRSTU arguments
AEGMOOSUX exogamous
AEGMOPRSW gapeworms
AEGMORSSS gossamers
AEGMORSSY gossamery
AEGMORSTY gasometry
AEGMPRSSU grampuses
AEGMPRSUZ gazumpers
AEGMPSSTU stumpages
AEGNNOPST pentagons
AEGNNORST negatrons
AEGNNORSY nongreasy
AEGNNPRTU repugnant
AEGNNSSTU gauntness
AEGNORRWY garryowen
AEGNORSST ragstones
AEGNORSTT tetragons
AEGNORSTU argentous
outranges
AEGNRRSST strangers
AEGNRSSTT strangest
AEGNRSSTU assurgent
AEGNSTTTU tungstate
AEGOOSWYZ wayzgoose
AEGOPPSST stoppages
AEGOPRRUW groupware
AEGOPSSTT gateposts
AEGORRRST garroters
AEGORRRTT garrotter
AEGORRSTT garotters
garrottes
AEGORRSTU surrogate
AEGORSSTU stegosaur
AEGORSTTY gestatory
AEGORSUVY voyageurs
AEGOSSSTU outgasses

AEGPRRRUY prayer rug
AEHHILLOP halophile
AEHHILLPT tephillah
AEHHILLTW Whitehall
AEHHILLTY healthily
AEHHILMST healthism
AEHHILNPT phthalein
AEHHIMPRS Hampshire
AEHHIORRS horsehair
AEHHIPPSS shipshape
AEHHISSVY yeshivahs
AEHHISTWW whitewash
AEHHLNTUY unhealthy
AEHHLOPTY halophyte
AEHHLPRTY hypethral
AEHHMOOPT homeopath
AEHHMORRT Rotherham
AEHHNOPTY theophany
AEHHNORTW Hawthorne
AEHHNRSSS harshness
AEHHOPPST phosphate
AEHHOPTTY theopathy
AEHHORSTT Ashtoreth
AEHHOSSUW washhouse
AEHHRRSST thrashers
AEHIIKRST terakihis
AEHIILMTU humiliate
AEHIILNOP neophilia
AEHIILNRS hairlines
AEHIILNTX antihelix
AEHIIMNST histamine
AEHIIMRST hetairism
AEHIIMRTY Himyarite
AEHIINOPT Ethiopian
AEHIINRSS hairiness
AEHIIPSTT hepatitis
AEHIIRSTT hetairist
AEHIJLOSU jailhouse
AEHIKKLRS sharklike
AEHIKLMNU humanlike
AEHIKLMRS marshlike
AEHIKLSWY weakishly
AEHIKNSSS shakiness
AEHILLMOP philomela
AEHILLNRT allethrin
AEHILLNSV Nashville
AEHILLPTY philately
AEHILLSTT tallithes
AEHILLTTY lethality
AEHILLTWW whitewall
AEHILLTWY wealthily
AEHILMNOP nemophila
AEHILMSTU Shulamite
AEHILNNOT anthelion
AEHILNOOZ heliozoan
AEHILNOPR parhelion
AEHILNOST hailstone
AEHILNOUZ Zhou En Lai
AEHILNPRS planisher
AEHILNPSS planishes
AEHILNQRU harlequin
AEHILNRSU inhaulers

AEHILORST horsetail
isotheral
AEHILOSTT heliostat
AEHILPPTY epiphytal
AEHILPRSS splashier
AEHILPSST plashiest
AEHILRSSV lavishers
AEHILRSTY hairstyle
AEHIMNNOT anthemion
AEHIMNORS harmonies
harmonise
AEHIMNORZ harmonize
AEHIMNPSS misshapen
AEHIMNPST pantheism
AEHIMNRSU humaniser
AEHIMNRUZ humanizer
AEHIMNSSU humanises
AEHIMNSUZ humanizes
AEHIMNTTY Hymettian
AEHIMOSST hematosis
AEHIMPSSS misshapes
AEHIMPSST shipmates
steamship
AEHIMPSTT empathist
AEHIMQSSU squeamish
AEHIMRSST marshiest
AEHINNRTU Ruthenian
AEHINNSTX xanthines
AEHINOPST pantihose
AEHINORSS hoariness
AEHINORTT anorthite
AEHINOSTT thionates
AEHINPPRU unhappier
AEHINPPSS happiness
AEHINPPTX Xanthippe
AEHINPRST perianths
AEHINPRUW wharepuni
AEHINPSSS apishness
AEHINPSST thespians
AEHINPSSY Sisyphean
AEHINPSTT pantheist
AEHINRRST tarnisher
AEHINRRSU Arrhenius
AEHINRRSV varnisher
AEHINRSST tarnishes
AEHINRSSV vanishers
varnishes
AEHINRSSW sherwanis
AEHINRSTW tarwhines
AEHINSSST hastiness
AEHINSSSW washiness
AEHIOPPRY hyperopia
AEHIOPRSS aphorises
AEHIOPRST atrophies
AEHIOPRSZ aphorizes
AEHIORRTT throatier
AEHIORSTT hesitator
AEHIORSTU authorise
AEHIORSTX rheotaxis
AEHIORTTV hortative
AEHIORTUZ authorize
AEHIOSSTT athetosis

AEHIPPRSS	sapphires
AEHIPRRST	phratries
AEHIPRSTT	therapist
AEHIQRSSU	squashier
AEHIRRSSV	ravishers
AEHIRRSTW	swarthier
AEHIRSSTT	trashiest
AEHIRSSTW	wairshest
AEHIRSSTY	hysterias
AEHJLLNOS	Hall-Jones
AEHKLNOPV	Plekhanov
AEHKLNSST	thankless
AEHKLRRSU	Karlsruhe
AEHKNSSWW	newshawks
AEHKORRTW	earthwork
AEHKOSSTU	shakeouts
AEHLLLMPS	lampshell
AEHLLMRTY	thermally
AEHLLNNOT	nonlethal
AEHLLNOOP	allophone
AEHLLNRST	enthralls
AEHLLORSW	hallowers
	shallower
AEHLLPSSU	phalluses
AEHLLPSSY	haplessly
AEHLLSSTU	thalluses
AEHLMOOST	loathsome
AEHLMOSSU	almshouse
AEHLMPPST	pamphlets
AEHLNNOPR	alpenhorn
AEHLNOSST	loathness
AEHLNPSUY	unshapely
AEHLNRTUY	unearthly
AEHLNSTUZ	hazelnuts
AEHLOPPSY	polyphase
AEHLOPRRY	pyorrheal
AEHLOPRSW	plowshare
AEHLOPRSY	horseplay
AEHLOPSTT	hotplates
AEHLOPSUY	playhouse
AEHLORSUV	overhauls
AEHLORTUU	outhauler
AEHLORTWY	holy water
AEHLPPRST	thrapples
AEHLPRRSU	spherular
AEHLPRSSS	splashers
AEHLPSSTU	sulphates
AEHLRSSTU	Althusser
AEHLRSSTW	wrathless
AEHMMOORT	harmotome
AEHMNNRTU	manhunter
AEHMNNSSU	humanness
AEHMNOSWW	washwomen
AEHMNRRWY	wherryman
AEHMOOPRS	shampooer
AEHMOPRST	metaphors
AEHMORRTW	earthworm
	heartworm
AEHMORTWW	wheatworm
AEHMOSSTT	hemostats
AEHMPPRSY	pamphreys
AEHMSSTTY	amethysts
AEHNNOPRT	Parthenon
AEHNNOPST	pantheons
AEHNNRSSU	unharness
AEHNOOPPY	hypopnoea
AEHNOOPRR	harpooner
AEHNOOPSX	saxophone
AEHNOPPSY	payphones
AEHNOPRST	hapterons
	Parthenos
AEHNOPRTU	neuropath
AEHNOPRTY	honeytrap
AEHNOPSST	stanhopes
AEHNOPSSU	saphenous
AEHNOPSTY	pantyhose
AEHNORSTT	northeast
AEHNPRSSS	sharpness
AEHNPRSXY	pharynxes
AEHNRSTTU	earthnuts
AEHNSSTUW	unswathes
AEHOOORRT	otorrhoea
AEHOOPRRY	pyorrhoea
AEHOOPSTT	osteopath
AEHOOSSTU	oasthouse
AEHOPPSSY	apophyses
AEHOPSSTT	posthaste
AEHOPSSTU	phaseouts
	taphouses
AEHOPSSTW	sweatshop
AEHOPTTUY	autophyte
AEHORRRSW	harrowers
AEHORRSSW	warhorses
AEHORSSSW	sawhorses
AEHORSSTT	rheostats
AEHORSSTU	authoress
	rathouses
AEHORSTVW	shortwave
AEHORSTVY	overhasty
AEHORSTWY	seaworthy
AEHOSSSTU	South Seas
AEHOSSTTU	southeast
AEHQRSSSU	squashers
AEHRRSTTW	thwarters
AEHRSSTUU	thesaurus
AEIIILNRT	initialer
AEIIILRVZ	vizierial
AEIIILTVX	lixiviate
AEIIIMRSS	Ramses III
AEIIIMTTV	imitative
AEIIINNST	inanities
AEIIINSTT	initiates
AEIIJLNUV	juvenilia
AEIIKKTTW	kittiwake
AEIIKLLNS	silkaline
	snaillike
AEIIKLNOT	kaolinite
AEIIKLNOZ	kaolinize
AEIIKLNST	saintlike
AEIIKLRST	triskelia
AEIIKMRSS	kaiserism
AEIIKRSTT	keratitis
AEIILLMNN	millennia
AEIILLMRS	ramillies
AEIILLRST	listerial
AEIILLSTV	illatives
AEIILLTTT	titillate
AEIILMNNR	mainliner
AEIILMNNS	mainlines
AEIILMNNT	eliminant
AEIILMNOS	alimonies
AEIILMNOZ	iminazole
AEIILMNSU	aluminise
	Suleiman I
AEIILMNUZ	aluminize
AEIILMOSV	malvoisie
AEIILMPRS	imperials
AEIILMRSS	serialism
AEIILMRTT	literatim
AEIILMSTT	militates
AEIILNNOT	lineation
AEIILNNRT	triennial
AEIILNNSV	venial sin
AEIILNNSY	asininely
AEIILNOPT	epilation
AEIILNOTV	inviolate
AEIILNPRT	reptilian
AEIILNPST	platinise
AEIILNPTV	plaintive
AEIILNPTZ	platinize
AEIILNRRS	airliners
AEIILNRRT	trilinear
AEIILNRST	saintlier
AEIILNRSU	uniserial
AEIILNRTY	linearity
AEIILNSST	alienists
AEIILNSTW	waistline
AEIILNSTZ	latinizes
AEIILNTVY	veniality
AEIILORST	solitaire
AEIILORSV	Lavoisier
AEIILORTV	variolite
AEIILOSTV	isolative
AEIILOTVV	violative
AEIILPPST	tailpipes
AEIILQSTU	qualities
AEIILRRST	triserial
AEIILRRSV	rivalries
AEIILRSTU	ritualise
AEIILRSTV	vitaliser
AEIILRTUZ	ritualize
AEIILRTVZ	vitalizer
AEIILSSTV	vitalises
AEIILSSUV	visualise
AEIILSTVZ	vitalizes
AEIILSUVZ	visualize
AEIIMMNSX	minimaxes
AEIIMMRSS	Semiramis
AEIIMMRSX	maximiser
AEIIMMRXZ	maximizer
AEIIMMSSX	maximises
AEIIMMSXZ	maximizes
AEIIMNNRT	nitramine
AEIIMNOPP	Pompeiian
AEIIMNORU	iminourea
AEIIMNPST	impatiens

AEIIMNPTT impatient
AEIIMNRTT intimater
Marinetti
AEIIMNRTU miniature
AEIIMNSTT intimates
AEIIMPRRS impairers
primaries
AEIIMPRSY perimysia
AEIIMPSSV impassive
AEIIMRRSV arrivisme
AEIINNNTV antivenin
AEIINNOST antinoise
AEIINNPTT inpatient
AEIINNRSS raininess
sirenians
AEIINNRSV Nivernais
AEIINNRTT itinerant
AEIINNRTU uraninite
AEIINNSTU annuities
insinuate
AEIINOPTX expiation
AEIINORTT iteration
AEIINOTTV novitiate
AEIINQRSU quinaries
AEIINRRSU urinaries
AEIINRRTY itinerary
AEIINRSTW West Irian
AEIINRTUV urinative
AEIINSSST sanitises
AEIINSSTZ sanitizes
AEIINSTTT titanites
AEIINSTTV tantivies
AEIIOPRST topiaries
AEIIORSST ostiaries
AEIIPRSTV privatise
AEIIPRSZZ pizzerias
AEIIPRTTV partitive
AEIIPRTVV privative
AEIIPRTVZ privatize
AEIIPSSST epistasis
AEIIPSSTX epistaxis
AEIIPSTTT stipitate
AEIIRRSST satiriser
AEIIRRSTT arteritis
irritates
AEIIRRSTU retiarius
AEIIRRSTV arriviste
AEIIRRSTZ satirizer
AEIIRSSST satirises
AEIIRSSTV varsities
AEIIRSSTW wisterias
AEIIRSSTZ satirizes
AEIIRSTTT tritiates
AEIIRTTTV attritive
AEIISSSTV assistive
AEIISTTTV titivates
AEIITTTTV tittivate
AEIJKKRVY Reykjavik
AEIJLOPPS jaloppies
AEIJLOSSU jalousies
AEIJMNNSS Jansenism
AEIJNRSST janitress
AEIJNSSZZ jazziness
AEIJNSTTU jauntiest
AEIJORSST jarosites
AEIKKLLOO lookalike
AEIKKLLST stalklike
AEIKKNNSS snakeskin
AEIKLLNPT plantlike
AEIKLLNRY Killarney
AEIKLLTUV vaultlike
AEIKLLTWZ waltzlike
AEIKLMNOS kalsomine
AEIKLMNOW womanlike
AEIKLNNSS lankiness
AEIKLNOVY Nikolayev
AEIKLNPSS skiplanes
AEIKLNSSS sealskins
AEIKLQSUY squeakily
AEIKLRSTW strawlike
AEIKLRSTY streakily
AEIKLRSVY valkyries
AEIKLRSWY walkyries
AEIKLSSTT stalkiest
AEIKMRSST mistakers
sitkamers
AEIKNNPRS spinnaker
AEIKNNSSS snakiness
AEIKNORTU ketonuria
AEIKNPRSS Speranski
AEIKNPSSW pawkiness
AEIKNQSSU quakiness
AEIKNSSTW swankiest
AEIKORSST keratosis
AEIKPPQSU pipsqueak
AEIKPRSST sparkiest
AEIKRSSST asterisks
AEILLLMSS allelisms
AEILLLRTY literally
AEILLMNRY millenary
AEILLMNSY seminally
AEILLMSSY aimlessly
AEILLMSTT metallist
AEILLNOPS Pisanello
AEILLNOPT pollinate
AEILLNPRY plenarily
AEILLNPST panellist
AEILLNPTT petillant
AEILLNRST installer
reinstall
AEILLNRTU tellurian
AEILLNRTY reliantly
AEILLNSTY saliently
AEILLOPPS papillose
AEILLOPPT papillote
popliteal
AEILLOSTV volatiles
AEILLOSTY loyalties
AEILLPRSU pluralise
AEILLPRUZ pluralize
AEILLPSST pastilles
AEILLPSTU pulsatile
AEILLRRTY artillery
AEILLRSST trailless
AEILLRSTW stairwell
AEILLRTWY waterlily
AEILLRVXY vexillary
AEILLSSTT sittellas
AEILMMNPS pelmanism
AEILMMNST mentalism
AEILMMORS memorials
AEILMMOST immolates
AEILMMRST trilemmas
AEILMNNOS minneolas
AEILMNNOT melatonin
AEILMNNPS plainsmen
AEILMNNSS manliness
AEILMNOOT emotional
AEILMNOPR prolamine
AEILMNORS almonries
normalise
AEILMNORT mentorial
AEILMNORZ normalize
AEILMNOSS loaminess
melanosis
AEILMNOTU emulation
AEILMNPRT implanter
AEILMNPSU asplenium
AEILMNPSY manyplies
AEILMNPTU penultima
AEILMNRST terminals
tramlines
AEILMNRSU semilunar
AEILMNRVY liveryman
AEILMNSST maltiness
AEILMNSTT mentalist
AEILMNTTY mentality
AEILMOPRS semipolar
AEILMORRS moraliser
AEILMORRZ moralizer
AEILMORSS moralises
AEILMORSZ moralizes
AEILMOSTU mousetail
AEILMPRST prelatism
AEILMPSTY playtimes
AEILMRRSU semirural
AEILMRSSY mislayers
AEILMRSTT remittals
AEILMRSTY salimetry
AEILMRTTY altimetry
AEILMSSTT metalists
AEILMSSTU simulates
AEILMSSUV misvalues
AEILMSSVY massively
AEILMSTTU mutilates
stimulate
ultimates
AEILMSTUU mutualise
AEILMTUUZ mutualize
AEILNNNOR nonlinear
AEILNNOOP Napoleon I
AEILNNOPR nonpareil
AEILNNOST tensional
AEILNNOSY lyonnaise
AEILNNOTV antinovel
Valentino

AEILNNPSS plainness
AEILNNPSU peninsula
AEILNNPTY pinnately
AEILNNRST internals
AEILNNTUV univalent
AEILNOOPS polonaise
AEILNOORS erosional
AEILNOPPR piperonal
AEILNOPPS panoplies
AEILNOPST sealpoint
AEILNOPSY Polynesia
AEILNOPTT peltation
potential
AEILNORSS sensorial
AEILNORST orientals
relations
serotinal
tensorial
AEILNORSV versional
AEILNORTT natrolite
AEILNOSSS sessional
AEILNOSST insolates
AEILNOSSX siloxanes
AEILNPRST interlaps
strapline
triplanes
AEILNPRTY interplay
painterly
AEILNPSST panelists
AEILNPSTT tinplates
AEILNPSTY sapiently
AEILNPTTX plaintext
AEILNPTTY patiently
AEILNPTUV pulvinate
AEILNRSST reinstals
trainless
AEILNRSTT sterilant
AEILNRSTV intervals
AEILNRSTY interlays
AEILNRSUV universal
AEILNRTTV trivalent
AEILNRTUV avirulent
AEILNRTUY unreality
AEILNSSST saintless
saltiness
slatiness
stainless
AEILNSSTT taintless
AEILNSSTU insulates
AEILNSSTW slantwise
AEILNSTUY sinuately
AEILNSTVY sylvanite
AEILNSUUX unisexual
AEILNSUVV univalves
AEILOOSTT ostiolate
AEILOPPST oppilates
AEILOPRRS polariser
AEILOPRRZ polarizer
AEILOPRSS polarises
AEILOPRST epilators
saprolite
AEILOPRSZ polarizes
AEILOPSST spoliates
AEILORRTT literator
AEILORSSS solarises
AEILORSSV valorises
AEILORSSZ solarizes
AEILORSTT aristotle
totaliser
AEILORSTV violaters
AEILORSTY royalties
AEILORSVZ valorizes
AEILORTTV levitator
AEILORTTZ totalizer
AEILOSSTT totalises
AEILOSTTZ totalizes
AEILPPQSU appliques
AEILPPRTU preputial
AEILPPSUV appulsive
AEILPRRSS reprisals
AEILPRSST pilasters
AEILPRSTT paltriest
prelatist
AEILPRSTV livetraps
AEILPRTVY privately
AEILPSSTT pastelist
AEILPSSVY passively
AEILPSTTU stipulate
AEILPSTUV pulsative
AEILQRRUY reliquary
AEILQRSTU quartiles
requitals
AEILRRSSU ruralises
AEILRRSUZ ruralizes
AEILRSSST slaisters
AEILRSSTT last rites
AEILRSSTY lay sister
AEILRSTTT rattliest
AEILRTUUX luxuriate
AEILSSSTV vistaless
AEILSSSTW waistless
AEILSTUXY sexuality
AEIMMMNOT mammonite
AEIMMNNOO monoamine
AEIMMNNRS mannerism
AEIMMNNTU minuteman
AEIMMNOPT pantomime
AEIMMNOSS seminomas
AEIMMNOST ammonites
AEIMMNSTZ mizenmast
AEIMMPSST psammites
AEIMMRSST smarmiest
AEIMMRSSU summaries
summarise
AEIMMRSTX mixmaster
AEIMMRSUZ summarize
AEIMMSTUV summative
AEIMNNNOT Maintenon
AEIMNNNQU mannequin
AEIMNNOPR prenomina
AEIMNNOPU pneumonia
AEIMNNOST Minnesota
nominates
AEIMNNOSY anonymise
AEIMNNOTT mentation
AEIMNNOYZ anonymize
AEIMNNRST mannerist
AEIMNOPRT protamine
AEIMNOPST ptomaines
AEIMNORSS masonries
romanises
AEIMNORSU uniramose
AEIMNORSW womaniser
AEIMNORSZ romanizes
AEIMNORTV normative
AEIMNORTW tirewoman
AEIMNORWZ womanizer
AEIMNOSSW womanises
AEIMNOSWZ womanizes
AEIMNPRST spearmint
AEIMNPSTY tympanies
AEIMNQRSU ramequins
AEIMNRSSU aneurisms
AEIMNRSTT martinets
AEIMNRSTU antiserum
ruminates
AEIMNRTTY maternity
AEIMNSSSS massiness
AEIMOOPPT pampootie
AEIMOPRRT imperator
AEIMOPRTX proximate
AEIMORRSU armouries
AEIMORRSV Averroism
AEIMORSST amortises
atomisers
AEIMORSTT East Timor
estimator
AEIMORSTZ amortizes
atomizers
AEIMORTTU autotimer
AEIMOSTTV motivates
AEIMPPRSU pauperism
AEIMPRRST imparters
AEIMPRSTU septarium
AEIMPRTUZ trapezium
AEIMPSSTW swampiest
AEIMQRSSU marquises
AEIMRRRTU terrarium
AEIMRRSTY martyries
martyrise
AEIMRRTYZ martyrize
AEIMRSSST asterisms
AEIMRSSTT mistreats
teratisms
AEIMRSTTY tasimetry
AEIMSSSTT misstates
AEINNNOTV nonnative
AEINNNPTU Neptunian
AEINNOPSX expansion
AEINNOPTT panettoni
AEINNORST anointers
AEINNORTV nervation
vernation
AEINNOSST sensation
AEINNOSTT intonates
AEINNOSTU Saint-Ouen

AEINNOSTV innovates
venations
AEINNOTTT attention
tentation
AEINNPPSS nappiness
AEINNPSST inaptness
AEINNRRSS insnarers
AEINNRSTT instanter
intranets
transient
AEINNRSTU Neustrian
saturnine
AEINNRSTY tyrannies
tyrannise
AEINNRTUV aventurin
AEINNRTYZ tyrannize
AEINNSSST nastiness
AEINNSSTT nattiness
AEINNSSTW tawniness
AEINOOPRT operation
AEINOOPSU ionopause
AEINOPPPR Popperian
AEINOPPRT appointer
reappoint
AEINOPPST antipopes
AEINOPRSS aspersion
AEINOPRST patronise
Petrosian
AEINOPRSV pervasion
AEINOPRSY aepyornis
AEINOPRTZ patronize
AEINOPSSS soapiness
AEINOQRTU inquorate
ortanique
AEINOQSTU equations
AEINOQTTU totaquine
AEINORRST serration
AEINORRTV overtrain
AEINORSST assertion
notarises
senoritas
AEINORSSU arsenious
AEINORSSV aversions
AEINORSTT stationer
AEINORSTZ notarizes
AEINOSTVX vexations
AEINPPSSS sappiness
AEINPPSST snappiest
AEINPRRST terrapins
transpire
AEINPRSST pinasters
AEINPRTTY paternity
AEINPSSST pastiness
AEINPSSSW waspiness
AEINPSSTU supinates
AEINPSTTY antitypes
AEINQSSTU quantises
AEINQSTTU quaintest
AEINQSTUZ quantizes
AEINRRSST restrains
strainers
tarriness

AEINRRSTT restraint
AEINRRTTV travertin
AEINRSSTT rattiness
resistant
straitens
AEINRSSTU sustainer
AEINRSSUZ suzerains
AEINSSSSS sassiness
AEINSSSTT tastiness
AEINSSTTT tattiness
AEINSSTZZ snazziest
AEINSSUVV vesuvians
AEIOORRST oratories
AEIOPRRST priorates
AEIOPRRSV vaporiser
AEIOPRRVZ vaporizer
AEIOPRSSV vaporises
AEIOPRSTX expiators
AEIOPRSVZ vaporizes
AEIOPRTTV portative
vaporetti
AEIOPRTXY expiatory
AEIOPSSTU autopsies
AEIOPSTTV optatives
AEIORSSSU ossuaries
AEIORSSTV assortive
AEIORSSUV savouries
AEIORSTTV estivator
AEIORTUVV uvarovite
AEIOSTUVX vexatious
AEIPPRRTY Tipperary
AEIPPRSTU peripatus
AEIPRRSSU upraisers
AEIPRSSTU prussiate
AEIPRSTTU petaurist
AEIPRSTUZ trapezius
AEIPRSTVY varitypes
AEIQRRRSU quarriers
AEIQRTTUZ quartzite
AEIQSTUZZ quazziest
AEIRRSSTT starriest
traitress
AEIRRTTTU triturate
AEIRSSSST assisters
AEIRSSTTU tessitura
AEIRSSTTW strawiest
AEIRSTTTX testatrix
AEIRSTTUU auteurist
AEIRSTTUY austerity
AEISSSSTY essayists
AEISSTTUW sweatsuit
AEJLLOSUY jealously
AEJMMORRT major term
AEJMNOSTW Jamestown
AEJOPSTUX juxtapose
AEKKLRRSY skylarker
AEKKMNOOS kakemonos
AEKLLSSST stalkless
AEKLMOORT toolmaker
AEKLMORSS lossmaker
AEKLMORTW metalwork
AEKLMRSUY yarmulkes

AEKLNOOPW Polokwane
AEKLNOSSY ankyloses
AEKLOPRSW ropewalks
AEKLORSVW walkovers
AEKLPRRSS sparklers
AEKMNNORY Orkneyman
AEKMNOOQU moonquake
AEKMNOORR moonraker
AEKMNOPSS spokesman
AEKMNRSSU unmaskers
AEKMOORRV voorkamer
AEKMOORSY karyosome
AEKMORSTW workmates
AEKMPRRSS pressmark
AEKNOORST snakeroot
AEKNPPSSS spanspeks
AEKNPRRST prankster
AEKNRSSST starkness
AEKNRSTTU Turkestan
AEKOPPRRW paperwork
AEKOPRTYY karyotype
AEKOPSSTU outspeaks
AEKORRWWX waxworker
AEKORSSTV overtasks
AEKOSSTTU stakeouts
AEKQRSSUW squawkers
AELLLMOSU malleolus
AELLLPTUU pullulate
AELLLRSTU stellular
AELLLSSWY lawlessly
AELLMMRUX Max Müller
AELLMNOOS allomones
AELLMNOTT allotment
AELLMNSSS smallness
AELLMOPRY permalloy
AELLMORST martellos
AELLMORTU Tullamore
AELLMORTY allometry
AELLMOSYZ allozymes
AELLNNOTW Allentown
AELLNOSSY loyalness
AELLNOSTW stonewall
AELLNQUUY unequally
AELLNRTUY neutrally
AELLNRTVY ventrally
AELLNSSUY sensually
AELLOOPRT allotrope
AELLOPRRT patroller
AELLOPRST preallots
AELLOPRSW wallopers
AELLOPRTW potwaller
AELLOPRTY prolately
AELLOPSTY allotypes
AELLORRST rostellar
AELLORSWW swallower
wallowers
AELLOSSTW sallowest
AELLOSUYZ zealously
AELLQRSSU squallers
AELLRSSTY artlessly
AELLRSSYY raylessly
AELLRSTUW Ullswater

AELLTTUXY	textually
AELMMNOSW	almswomen
AELMMORST	maelstrom
AELMMORSW	mealworms
AELMMOSUU	mausoleum
AELMNNNTU	annulment
AELMNNOOP	monoplane
AELMNNOST	nonmetals
AELMNNPST	plantsmen
AELMNOOPR	lampooner
AELMNOORT	monolater
AELMNOORY	monolayer
AELMNOPRT	patrolmen
AELMNOPSS	neoplasms
	pleonasms
AELMNOPTU	pulmonate
AELMNORST	marlstone
	mestranol
AELMNORWW	lawnmower
AELMNOSSW	womanless
AELMNRSTU	menstrual
AELMNRTTU	tremulant
AELMOORSS	salerooms
	salesroom
AELMOPRRS	premolars
AELMOPSTT	palmettos
AELMORSTU	emulators
AELMORSUV	marvelous
AELMOSSTY	atmolyses
AELMOSTTU	mulattoes
AELMPRRST	tramplers
AELMPSSSW	swampless
AELMRSSTT	maltsters
AELNNOOPS	napoleons
AELNNOOSX	naloxones
AELNNOSUX	nonsexual
AELNNSSUU	annuluses
AELNOPRSS	personals
AELNOPRSY	layperson
AELNOPSTY	neoplasty
AELNORTVW	navelwort
AELNPRSSU	purslanes
AELNPSSSU	spansules
AELNRRUVY	vulnerary
AELNRSSTT	slatterns
AELNRSTTU	resultant
AELNSSSTU	sultaness
AELNSSSUU	usualness
AELOOPRVY	parleyvoo
AELOORRTT	tolerator
AELOORSTZ	zoolaters
AELOPPRSS	prolapses
AELOPPSTU	populates
AELOPRRSV	reprovals
AELOPRRTW	pearlwort
AELOPRRTY	proletary
AELOPRSSV	vaporless
AELOPRSTU	sporulate
AELOPRSVY	overplays
AELOPSSSU	espousals
AELOPSTTU	postulate
AELORRSTX	extrorsal
AELORSSSV	savorless
AELOSSTTW	wastelots
AELOSSTUY	autolyses
AELOSTUUV	outvalues
AELOSTUYZ	autolyzes
AELPPRTUW	Wuppertal
AELPRRRSU	larrupers
AELPRRSSW	sprawlers
AELPRRSTT	prattlers
AELPRSSST	strapless
AELPRSSTT	splatters
AELPRSSTU	pertussal
AELPSTTUU	pustulate
AELQRRTUY	quarterly
AELQRSSUV	servquals
AELRRSSTT	startlers
AELRRSSTW	warstlers
AELRSSTTU	lustrates
AEMMNORTY	manometry
	momentary
AEMMOORST	roommates
AEMMORSST	marmosets
AEMMORTTY	atmometry
AEMMRSTYY	asymmetry
AEMNNOPST	Montespan
AEMNNORST	ornaments
AEMNNORTT	remontant
AEMNNOSWW	newswoman
AEMNOOPRT	monoptera
	protonema
AEMNOORST	anterooms
AEMNOORTX	taxonomer
AEMNORRSS	ransomers
AEMNORRTU	numerator
AEMNORSST	monsteras
	Sorenstam
AEMNORSTY	monastery
	oysterman
AEMNOSSTU	seamounts
AEMNPRTUY	prytaneum
AEMNQRRUY	quarrymen
AEMNRRSSU	surnamers
AEMNRSSST	smartness
AEMNRSSSU	Rasmussen
AEMNRSSUY	aneurysms
AEMNRSTTU	transmute
AEMNRSTVY	vestryman
AEMOORSTT	stateroom
AEMOOSSST	maestosos
AEMOOSSTU	autosomes
AEMOPRRTY	temporary
AEMOPRSTU	mousetrap
AEMOPRSTW	tapeworms
AEMOPSTTY	asymptote
AEMORRRSU	armourers
AEMORSTTU	tautomers
AEMOSTTZZ	mozzettas
AEMQRRTUY	marquetry
AENNOPRST	patronnes
AENNOPSST	pentosans
AENNORRST	resnatron
AENNORSSU	unreasons
AENNOSTTW	wantonest
AENNPSSTU	unaptness
AENNRSTTU	transeunt
AENNSSTUY	Sun Yat-sen
AENOOPSST	soapstone
	teaspoons
AENOORRST	resonator
AENOORRTV	renovator
AENOPRRST	prosterna
AENOPRSST	patroness
	transpose
AENOPRSTT	patentors
AENOPRSUV	supernova
AENORRSTW	narrowest
AENORRTWW	waterworn
AENORSSST	assentors
AENORSSTU	anestrous
	anoestrus
AENORSTTY	attorneys
AENPRSSTT	transepts
AENQRRSTU	quarterns
AENQSSSTU	squatness
AENRSSSTW	swartness
AEOOPPPSS	pappooses
AEOOPRRST	operators
AEOOPRSTU	autospore
AEOOPRSUX	auxospore
AEOOPRTTV	vaporetto
AEOORRSTV	overroast
AEOORRSTZ	Zoroaster
AEOORSTTT	tattooers
AEOORSTTV	rotovates
AEOORTTUU	autoroute
AEOPRRRTY	portrayer
AEOPRRSTT	prostrate
AEOPRRSTU	pterosaur
AEOPRRSTW	spearwort
AEOPRRSUV	vapourers
AEOPRRSVW	wrapovers
AEOPRSSSV	passovers
AEOPRSSTT	prostates
AEOPSTTUY	autotypes
AEOQRRSSU	squarrose
AEOQRSSTU	quaestors
AEORRSSST	assertors
	assorters
AEORRSTZZ	terrazzos
AEORSSSSS	assessors
AEORSSTTT	attestors
	testators
AEORSSTTU	outstares
AEORSSTUU	trousseau
AEORSSTVY	overstays
AEPPRRSST	strappers
AEPPRSSUY	papyruses
AEPPRSTUU	suppurate
AEPQRRTUY	parquetry
AEPRRSSTU	superstar
AEPRSSSSU	surpasses
AEPRSSSTT	tapstress
AEPRSSTTU	upstaters
AEQRSSTTU	squatters

AERRSSTUU susurrate
AFFGGINUW guffawing
AFFGHIRST affrights
AFFGIIMNR affirming
AFFGIINRT tariffing
AFFGIIRST sgraffiti
AFFGILNNS snaffling
AFFGILNSW wafflings
AFFGIORST sgraffito
AFFHILRSY raffishly
AFFIILNPT plaintiff
AFFIKLOOP Poliakoff
AFFILLMMS flimflams
AFFILNRUY ruffianly
AFFINOSSU affusions
AFFIPSSTT tipstaffs
AFFKNORRT Frankfort
AFFKNRRTU frankfurt
AFFLLOOST footfalls
AFFLLORUV flavorful
AFFLOOSTT flatfoots
AFFLOOTTU footfault
AFFLOPSTW plowstaff
AFGGGINOT faggoting
AFGGGINRS fraggings
AFGGIILNN finagling
AFGGIINSY gasifying
AFGGIINTU fatiguing
AFGGILOPS gigaflops
AFGGINRST graftings
AFGGINRUY argufying
AFGGLNNOU Falun Gong
AFGHIILNZ Fang Lizhi
AFGHIIMNS famishing
AFGHILLNT nightfall
AFGHILNST fanlights
AFGHILPSS flagships
AFGHILSTT lightfast
AFGHIMNOT fathoming
AFGHINRST farthings
AFGHINSST shaftings
AFGHMOORT homograft
AFGIIILNT filiating
AFGIILLNY failingly
AFGIILMNN inflaming
AFGIILNNT inflating
AFGIILNNU unfailing
AFGIILNOT foliating
AFGIILNSY salifying
AFGIILRTY fragility
AFGIIMNRY ramifying
AFGIINNYZ nazifying
AFGIINRTY ratifying
AFGIKNORS forsaking
AFGILLMNY flamingly
AFGILLNOW fallowing
AFGILLNST flatlings
AFGILLNUY gainfully
AFGILMNOS flamingos
AFGILNNTU flaunting
AFGILNNWY fawningly
AFGILNORV flavoring
AFGILNRZZ frazzling
AFGILRTUY frugality
AFGIMNSTU fumigants
AFGIMORTU fumigator
AFGINNOPR profaning
AFGINORRW farrowing
AFGINORUV favouring
AFGINRSTU figurants
AFGINSTTU fungistat
AFGIPRSTW giftwraps
AFGLLSSSU glassfuls
AFGLNNOOS gonfalons
AFGLNRTUU fulgurant
AFGNNNOOS gonfanons
AFGNOPRSW frogspawn
AFHIIKNOP kniphofia
AFHIILNSS snailfish
AFHIILNTU hifalutin
AFHIILSST fishtails
AFHIKMSUU Fukushima
AFHIKNRST rankshift
AFHINORTU thiofuran
AFHIORSTY forsythia
AFHLLMRUY harmfully
AFHLLORST shortfall
AFHLMNRUU unharmful
AFHOOPSTT footpaths
AFHOORRST hoarfrost
AFHOOSSTT soothfast
AFIIILNOT filiation
AFIILMNSU Flaminius
AFIILNNOT inflation
AFIILNOOT foliation
AFIILNSST finalists
AFIILORRT triforial
AFIIMNRRY infirmary
AFIINOSTX fixations
AFIIORRTU fioritura
AFIIORTVZ Fitzrovia
AFIJKRSTU jakfruits
AFIKLNNRS franklins
AFILLLOST flotillas
AFILLLUWY wailfully
AFILLNOUX fluxional
AFILLNPUY painfully
AFILLNRUV Furnivall
AFILLNTUY flauntily
AFILMMORS formalism
AFILMNNTU fulminant
AFILMOPRS salpiform
AFILMORST formalist
AFILMORTY formality
AFILNOOSV Alfonso VI
AFILNOOTT flotation
AFILNORST flatirons
inflators
AFILOORSS fossorial
AFILSSTTU flautists
AFIMNNORT informant
AFIMNOORT formation
AFINNOSTU fountains
AFINOOPRR rainproof
AFINOPRTY profanity
AFINRSTTX transfixt
AFIORRSST Froissart
AFIOSTTUU fatuitous
AFIRRSTTU starfruit
AFKLNOSTU outflanks
AFKLOOSTT footstalk
AFKMOORST footmarks
AFLLLPUYY playfully
AFLLNORTY frontally
AFLLNOSSW snowfalls
AFLLOOSTT footstall
AFLLOOSTW footwalls
AFLMNOPRS planforms
AFLMOPRST platforms
AFLMORRUY formulary
AFLMORSTW flatworms
AFLOOPSTY splayfoot
AFLOORSUV flavorous
AFLOPRRSU fluorspar
AFLOSTUUY fatuously
AFMNORRST transform
AFMOORSTY styrofoam
AFOORSSTZ sforzatos
AGGGILNNY naggingly
AGGGILNSS slaggings
AGGGLNOOO Goolagong
AGGHHILSY haggishly
AGGHIILNT alighting
AGGHILOOY hagiology
AGGHILSST gaslights
AGGHILSWY waggishly
AGGHINNRT thranging
AGGHLOOPR logograph
AGGHNOUUZ Guangzhou
AGGIIIMNN imagining
AGGIIJNNQ Jiang Qing
AGGIILLNP pillaging
AGGIILMNN maligning
AGGIILNNS signaling
AGGIILNVW lawgiving
AGGIIMNNR margining
AGGIIMNRT migrating
AGGIIMNST gigantism
AGGIINNOS agonising
AGGIINNOZ agonizing
AGGIINNSS assigning
AGGIINNTV vintaging
AGGIJNNOR jargoning
AGGIKNNSU Sungkiang
AGGILLLNY gallingly
AGGILLNOP galloping
AGGILLNRY glaringly
AGGILNNOS ganglions
singalong
AGGILNNPS spangling
AGGILNNRW wrangling
AGGILNNWY gnawingly
AGGILNOOY angiology
AGGILNPPR grappling
AGGILNPSY gaspingly
AGGILNRSY graylings

AGGILNRTY	gratingly
AGGILNRYZ	grazingly
AGGIMMNNO	gammoning
AGGIMMNRU	rummaging
AGGIMNPUZ	gazumping
AGGINNOOR	gorgonian
AGGINNORS	groanings
AGGINOPRT	portaging
AGGINORRS	grosgrain
AGGINORRT	garroting
AGGINORTT	garotting
AGGINORTU	outraging
	ragouting
AGGINPSTU	upstaging
AGGIRSTUZ	ziggurats
AGGKNNTUW	Kwangtung
AGGLLLOSY	lollygags
AGGLMOORS	logograms
AGGMOORRT	mortgagor
AGGMOSTYY	mystagogy
AGGNNOPYY	Pyongyang
AGGNSUWZZ	zugzwangs
AGHHIILST	hightails
AGHHIKNTW	nighthawk
AGHHILRTU	ultrahigh
AGHHILTUY	haughtily
AGHHINOOR	hoorahing
AGHHINRRU	hurrahing
AGHHINRST	thrashing
AGHHINUZZ	huzzahing
AGHHLOOPR	holograph
AGHHMOOPR	homograph
AGHHNOUZZ	Zhangzhou
AGHIIIKRZ	Kirghizia
AGHIILLTT	taillight
AGHIILNSV	lavishing
AGHIIMMMN	Immingham
AGHIINNRU	unhairing
AGHIINNSV	vanishing
AGHIINPRT	thraiping
AGHIINRSV	ravishing
AGHIINRTT	raintight
AGHIINRTU	Thuringia
AGHIINSSW	siwashing
AGHIIPRRS	hairgrips
AGHIJNRST	nightjars
AGHIKLSWY	gawkishly
AGHIKMNOW	Wokingham
AGHIKNOSU	Kaohsiung
AGHIKRRTW	Arkwright
AGHILLNOO	hallooing
	holloaing
AGHILLNOP	anglophil
AGHILLNOW	hallowing
AGHILLNRT	thralling
AGHILLNSY	lashingly
AGHILLNTY	haltingly
AGHILLORY	Holy Grail
AGHILMORT	algorithm
	logarithm
AGHILNNSU	unlashing
AGHILNOOS	hooligans
AGHILNORT	granolith
AGHILNOST	loathings
AGHILNPSS	splashing
AGHILNPTY	plaything
AGHILNTUY	naughtily
AGHILOOOR	horologia
AGHILOSTY	goatishly
AGHILRSTT	starlight
AGHIMNRST	hamstring
AGHIMOPRY	amphigory
AGHIMORST	histogram
AGHIMSTTU	mistaught
AGHINNOPR	orphaning
AGHINNOPT	phonating
AGHINNOST	gnathions
AGHINNRSY	grannyish
AGHINOORY	hooraying
AGHINORRW	harrowing
AGHINORTU	authoring
AGHINQSSU	squashing
AGHINRRUY	hurraying
AGHINRTTW	thwarting
AGHIOSTTU	outasight
AGHIPRRST	trigraphs
AGHIPRSUU	augurship
AGHIRSSTT	straights
AGHKMOPRY	kymograph
AGHKNOPST	pakthongs
AGHKOORSS	grasshook
AGHKOPRRU	Gorakhpur
AGHLLOOPY	haplology
AGHLMNOPU	ploughman
AGHLMOOPR	lagomorph
AGHLMOORS	holograms
AGHLMOOTU	goalmouth
AGHLNOOTY	anthology
AGHLNOSTU	onslaught
AGHLOOPTY	pathology
AGHLOPPRY	polygraph
AGHLOPRXY	xylograph
AGHLORSSU	hourglass
AGHLOSTUU	outlaughs
AGHMNOOPR	monograph
	nomograph
	phonogram
AGHMNOOPY	monophagy
AGHMNRSTU	hamstrung
AGHMOOPRT	photogram
AGHMOPRSY	myographs
AGHMOPRYY	myography
AGHNNSTUU	Hsüan T'ung
AGHNOORSS	shagroons
AGHNOPSSU	sphagnous
AGHNORSST	staghorns
AGHOOPRRY	orography
AGHOOPRYZ	zoography
AGHOPRRUY	urography
AGHORSTTY	hygrostat
AGIIIMNPR	impairing
AGIIIMNTT	imitating
AGIIINNRV	Virginian
AGIIINNSS	insignias
AGIIINSTV	vaginitis
AGIIINTTV	vitiating
AGIIKLMNR	grimalkin
AGIIKMNST	mistaking
AGIIKNNSY	kyanising
AGIIKNNYZ	kyanizing
AGIILLLOP	Gallipoli
AGIILLMMR	milligram
AGIILLNOR	gorillian
AGIILLNPR	pillaring
AGIILLNRT	trialling
AGIILLNRV	rivalling
AGIILLRSY	sigillary
AGIILMNSS	misaligns
AGIILMNSY	mislaying
AGIILMNTY	malignity
AGIILMSSV	Vigil Mass
AGIILNNSU	anilingus
AGIILNNWZ	Zwinglian
AGIILNORS	originals
AGIILNORT	tailoring
AGIILNOSS	assoiling
AGIILNOST	intaglios
	isolating
	ligations
AGIILNOSX	gloxinias
AGIILNOTV	violating
AGIILNPRS	spiraling
AGIILNQTU	liquating
AGIILNRST	ringtails
AGIILNRSV	virginals
AGIILNSSS	isinglass
AGIILNSTT	litigants
AGIILORTT	litigator
AGIILOTTT	Togliatti
AGIIMMNNS	misnaming
AGIIMMNRT	immigrant
AGIIMNNRT	inmigrant
AGIIMNORT	migration
AGIIMNOST	atomising
	sigmation
AGIIMNOTZ	atomizing
AGIIMNPRT	imparting
AGIIMNPST	impasting
AGIIMORTT	mitigator
AGIINNNOT	anointing
AGIINNNRS	insnaring
AGIINNORS	signorina
AGIINNORT	rationing
AGIINNPRS	spraining
AGIINNPST	paintings
AGIINNQTU	antiquing
AGIINNRST	straining
AGIINNRTT	intrigant
	nitrating
AGIINNRTU	urinating
AGIINNSTT	instating
AGIINORTV	grivation
AGIINOSTZ	azotising
AGIINOTZZ	azotizing
AGIINPPRS	apprising
AGIINPPRZ	apprizing

AGIINPRST	traipsing
AGIINPRSU	upraising
AGIINRSTT	striating
AGIINRTTT	titrating
AGIINSSST	assisting
AGIINSTTU	situating
AGIIORRRT	irrigator
AGIIRSSTT	gastritis
AGIIRSTTU	guitarist
AGIJLNOSU	jalousing
AGIJLNRRY	jarringly
AGIKLMORS	kilograms
AGIKLNPRS	sparkling
AGIKMNNSU	unmasking
AGIKNNPSS	spankings
AGIKNOSST	goatskins
AGIKNQSUW	squawking
AGILLLNUY	lingually
AGILLMNOS	slaloming
AGILLMNRU	Mullingar
AGILLMNSU	mulligans
AGILLNNNU	annulling
AGILLNOPW	walloping
AGILLNOSW	sallowing
AGILLNOTT	allotting
	totalling
AGILLNOTW	tallowing
AGILLNOWW	wallowing
AGILLNQSU	squalling
AGILLNSTY	lastingly
AGILLNTUU	ululating
AGILLOPST	gallipots
AGILMNNOO	mongolian
AGILMNNOT	lamington
AGILMNNOY	moaningly
AGILMNNST	mantlings
AGILMNOPY	Pygmalion
AGILMNPRT	trampling
AGILMNPSS	samplings
AGILMNSUY	amusingly
AGILMOORY	Mariology
AGILMOPRS	lipograms
AGILMORSS	algorisms
AGILMRSUV	vulgarism
AGILNNOPS	pangolins
	plainsong
AGILNNORT	Arlington
AGILNNRTY	rantingly
AGILNNRWY	warningly
AGILNNWYY	yawningly
AGILNOOSS	isogonals
AGILNORRY	roaringly
AGILNORVY	vainglory
AGILNOSTV	solvating
AGILNOTUV	ovulating
AGILNOTUW	outlawing
AGILNOTUY	outlaying
AGILNPRSS	sparlings
AGILNPRSW	sprawling
AGILNPRSY	sparingly
AGILNPRTT	prattling
AGILNPRTY	pratingly
AGILNPSTU	pulsating
AGILNRSST	starlings
AGILNRSSU	singulars
AGILNRSTT	startling
AGILNRSTW	warstling
AGILNRSUY	singulary
AGILNRVYY	varyingly
AGILNSTWY	wastingly
AGILOOPST	apologist
AGILOORSS	gloriosas
AGILOPRUY	uropygial
AGILRRTUY	garrulity
AGILRTUVY	vulgarity
AGIMMNSUY	gymnasium
AGIMNNNNU	unmanning
AGIMNNOOR	marooning
AGIMNNOPT	tamponing
AGIMNNORS	ransoming
AGIMNNOTU	amounting
AGIMNNRSU	surnaming
AGIMNOOSV	vamoosing
AGIMNORRT	mortaring
AGIMNORRU	armouring
AGIMNORSS	organisms
AGIMNORSU	ignoramus
AGIMNRRTY	martyring
AGIMOOSSU	isogamous
AGIMORRST	migrators
AGIMORRTY	migratory
AGINNNOPY	nonpaying
AGINNNOTW	wantoning
AGINNOORT	organotin
	ratooning
AGINNOPRT	pronating
AGINNORRW	narrowing
AGINNORTT	attorning
AGINNPRSU	unsparing
AGINNPSSW	wingspans
AGINNRTTU	truanting
AGINNRUVY	unvarying
AGINNSTUY	Tsingyuan
AGINOORST	rogations
AGINOOTTT	tattooing
AGINOPPRV	approving
AGINOPRRT	parroting
	prorating
AGINOPRTU	purgation
AGINOPRUV	vapouring
AGINORRSS	garrisons
AGINORSSS	assignors
AGINORSST	assorting
	organists
	roastings
AGINORSTV	gravitons
AGINORSTY	gyrations
	signatory
AGINORSUV	savouring
AGINOSSTT	tangoists
AGINOSTTU	gustation
AGINOTTTU	guttation
AGINPPRST	strapping
	trappings
AGINPPRSW	wrappings
AGINPRRTU	rapturing
AGINPRSTU	pasturing
AGINQRRUY	quarrying
AGINQSTTU	squatting
AGINRSSTY	stingrays
AGINRSTUX	surtaxing
AGINRSTVY	strayving
AGIOORSTU	autogiros
AGIOPRRSY	spirogyra
AGIQRSSTU	grassquit
AGISSTUUV	Gustavus I
AGJKNORRU	kurrajong
AGKLOORYY	karyology
AGKLORSSW	glasswork
AGKLPPRSU	sparkplug
AGKNORSST	knotgrass
AGLLNOOPY	polygonal
AGLMOORSU	glamorous
AGLMOORYY	Maryology
AGLMPRSUU	sugarplum
AGLOOPRTY	patrology
AGLOOPSST	goalposts
AGLOORSST	glossator
AGLOORSTY	astrology
AGLOOTTUY	tautology
AGLOPPRUY	playgroup
AGLORRSUU	garrulous
AGLORSSTW	glasswort
AGLRSTTUU	gutturals
AGMMNOORS	groomsman
	monograms
	nomograms
AGMMOSTUU	gummatous
AGMNNORST	strongman
AGMNOORSS	sonograms
AGMNORRST	Armstrong
	strongarm
AGMNORSST	angstroms
AGMNOSSUY	syngamous
AGMNSSTUY	nystagmus
AGNNOPPTU	oppugnant
AGNNOQSTU	quantongs
AGNOPTTUU	Tupungato
AGNRRSTUY	strangury
AGOORSTUY	autogyros
AGOPRRTUY	purgatory
AGORSSTTY	gyrostats
AGORSTTUY	gustatory
AGRSTTTTU	Stuttgart
AHHHOOSST	shahtoosh
AHHIIMORS	Hiroshima
AHHIKLSSS	shashliks
AHHMOSTUW	mouthwash
AHHMPRRSU	harrumphs
AHHNORRST	hartshorn
AHHNORSTV	Thorshavn
AHHNORSTW	hawthorns
AHIIILMNS	malihinis
AHIIILORT	Lothair II
AHIIILPST	philistia
AHIIILSST	lithiasis

AHIIJKNRS jinriksha
AHIILOOPZ zoophilia
AHIILOQSU Liu Shao Qi
AHIILORSU hilarious
AHIILOSST halitosis
AHIILRSTT shirttail
AHIIMMRST Mithraism
AHIIMPRSV vampirish
AHIINORST historian
AHIIPRSSZ sizarship
AHIIRRSTT arthritis
AHIIRSSTT Tsitsihar
AHIJLNOPU John Paul I
AHIJMOPRS majorship
AHIJNNOST Saint John
AHIKKNRSS sharkskin
AHIKKTTWY Kitty Hawk
AHIKLMSWY mawkishly
AHIKLNSVY knavishly
AHIKNOSTZ Zákinthos
AHILLOPRT prothalli
AHILLOSSW sallowish
AHILLOTTT tallitoth
AHILLPSST phallists
AHILLPSSY splashily
AHILLPSTW whipstall
AHILLQSSU squallish
AHILLSSVY slavishly
AHILMMRSY rammishly
AHILMNNSY mannishly
AHILMNNUY inhumanly
AHILMOPSY syphiloma
AHILMORST hailstorm
AHILMOSST mailshots
AHILMPRTU triumphal
AHILMPTTU multipath
AHILMRSTY lathyrism
AHILNORST horntails
AHILNORTT triathlon
AHILNPPUY unhappily
AHILOORST lotharios
AHILOPPTY Hippolyta
AHILOPSST hospitals
AHILORTTY throatily
AHILOSTTT statolith
AHILPSSWY waspishly
AHILQSSUY squashily
AHILRSTTY tartishly
AHILRSTWY swarthily
AHIMMMNOS mammonish
AHIMMMOSS shammosim
AHIMMNORU harmonium
AHIMMOPRS amorphism
AHIMNORST harmonist
AHIMNPSTY sympathin
AHIMNRTUU anthurium
AHIMNSSTU humanists
AHIMOOSTX homotaxis
AHIMOPRSS aphorisms
AHIMOPRSY mayorship
AHIMOPSST opsimaths
AHIMOPSTY opsimathy
AHIMOPSUX amphioxus
AHIMORRSW hairworms
AHINNOOPT phonation
AHINNOPST antiphons
AHINNOPTY antiphony
AHINOOPRR orpharion
AHINOORTT hortation
AHINOOSTU houstonia
AHINPRSST tranships
transship
AHIOPPRRY porphyria
AHIOPPSSY apophysis
AHIOPRSST aphorists
AHIOPRSUV vapourish
AHIOPSTXY hypotaxis
AHIORRTWY airworthy
AHIORTTUY authority
AHKLLMOWY mollyhawk
AHKMOORRS markhoors
AHKMOORSW Hawksmoor
AHKNPRSTU Pankhurst
AHKORSTUW Southwark
AHLLLOSWY shallowly
AHLLMOOPR allomorph
AHLLNOSUW unhallows
AHLLOPSUY aphyllous
AHLMMOPSY lymphomas
AHLMOOOPR homopolar
AHLMOOPSY homoplasy
AHLMOPSTY polymaths
AHLMOPTYY polymathy
AHLMORSTY solar myth
AHLNNORST lanthorns
AHLOPSSST slapshots
AHMNOOPTY taphonomy
AHMOOPPST photomaps
AHMOOPRSU amorphous
AHMOORSSW washrooms
AHMOPRTTU mouthpart
AHMORRSTW marshwort
AHMORSTTW tamworths
AHNNNOOTY hootnanny
AHNNORSTT Northants
AHNOOPRTY phonatory
AHNOPPSSW pawnshops
AHNOPSSST snapshots
AHNOPSTYY hyponasty
AHNORRSTY Strayhorn
AHNORRTTY thyratron
AHOOPRRTX prothorax
AHOOPRTTU autotroph
AHOOPRTUX auxotroph
AHOOPSTTT photostat
AHOOPTTXY phototaxy
AHOORRTTY hortatory
AHOOSSSTY soothsays
AHOPSSTUW southpaws
AHORSTTUW watthours
AIIIILLMW William II
AIIILLMVW William IV
AIIILLNTY initially
AIIILMNST laminitis
AIIIMNOTT imitation
AIIINNNOT inanition
AIIINNSTY asininity
AIIINORTT initiator
AIIINOTTV vitiation
AIIJLOTVY joviality
AIIKLNRRS larrikins
AIIKMNNNS mannikins
AIIKNNNPS pannikins
AIILLMMNY minimally
AIILLMRSY similarly
AIILLNOST illations
AIILLNSTY saintlily
AIILLPRRS spirillar
AIILLRSTT triallist
AIILLRTVY trivially
AIILLSWWW williwaws
AIILMMNUU aluminium
AIILMNORT trinomial
AIILMNSTT militants
AIILMOSST altissimo
AIILMPRRY primarily
AIILMRSST mistrials
AIILMRSTU ritualism
AIILNNORS rosanilin
AIILNOOST isolation
AIILNOOTV violation
AIILNOPSV pavilions
AIILNOQTU liquation
AIILNORSV livraison
AIILNORTT introital
AIILNOSTT siltation
AIILNOTTU tuitional
AIILNPRSU spirulina
AIILNPSST alpinists
tailspins
AIILNPSTY Ypsilanti
AIILNRSST sinistral
AIILPRSST spritsail
AIILPRSTU spiritual
AIILRSSTT trialists
AIILRSTTU ritualist
AIILSSTTV vitalists
AIIMMPRSV vampirism
AIIMNNOSS insomnias
AIIMNNTUY unanimity
AIIMNOPRS prosimian
AIIMNOPSS impassion
AIIMNOSTY animosity
AIIMNPSTT timpanist
AIIMOPRRS apriorism
AIIMORSTT imitators
AIIMPSSSV passivism
AIIMRSTUU Mauritius
AIIMRSUVV vivariums
AIINNNOOT Antonioni
AIINNNOPT pinnation
AIINNORTT nitration
AIINNORTU ruination
urination
AIINNOSSV invasions
AIINNOSTU sinuation

AIINNOSTV	nivations
AIINNOTTX	antitoxin
AIINNQSTU	quintains
AIINOPRTT	partition
AIINOPRTV	privation
AIINORSTT	striation
AIINORSVY	visionary
AIINORTTT	attrition
	titration
AIINOSTTU	situation
AIINQTTUY	antiquity
AIINRRSTT	irritants
AIINRSTUV	antivirus
AIINSSTTV	nativists
	visitants
AIIOPRRTY	apriority
AIIOPRSSS	psoriasis
AIIOPRSTT	parotitis
	topiarist
AIIOPRTVY	oviparity
AIIOPSSTT	pastitsio
AIIORRRTT	irritator
AIIORSTTV	vitiators
AIIORTTTV	titivator
AIIPRRSST	airstrips
AIIPRTTUY	pituitary
AIIPSSSTV	passivist
AIIPSSTVY	passivity
AIIRSSSTT	satirists
	sitarists
AIJKKNOSU	kinkajous
AIJLLOORS	jillaroos
AIJNOPPSY	popinjays
AIJNSSTTU	Saint-Just
AIKKLMNOS	Akmolinsk
AIKKRSTUZ	zikkurats
AIKLMOSTT	milktoast
AIKLMSTTU	multitask
AIKLNNPSS	snaplinks
AIKLNOSSY	ankylosis
AIKLOSTTW	kilowatts
AIKMNNOSW	kinswoman
AIKMRSSTZ	sitzmarks
AIKNNOOSS	nainsooks
AIKNNSSSW	swanskins
AIKNOPRTW	paintwork
AIKNSSUUY	San Suu Kyi
AIKPSTTUU	patutukis
AILLMMORY	immorally
AILLMNNOY	nominally
AILLMOPTY	optimally
AILLMPRSU	pluralism
AILLMSUUV	alluviums
AILLNOPPS	papillons
AILLNORST	tonsillar
AILLNORSU	lunisolar
AILLNOSST	stallions
AILLNOSSU	allusions
AILLNOSUV	alluvions
AILLNOTUU	ululation
AILLNPTUY	nuptially
AILLNRSUY	insularly
AILLOPPST	lipoplast
AILLOPTVY	pivotally
AILLORSTT	littorals
	tortillas
AILLORUXY	uxorially
AILLOSSTY	loyalists
AILLPPRUY	pupillary
AILLPRSTU	pluralist
AILLPRTUY	plurality
AILLPSSWY	spillways
AILLRTTUY	titularly
AILLRTUVY	virtually
AILMMNOOS	monomials
AILMMOORT	immolator
AILMMORST	immortals
AILMMRSUY	summarily
AILMMSTUU	mutualism
AILMMTTUU	ultimatum
AILMNNOTY	antimonyl
AILMNOOPS	palominos
AILMNOORS	monorails
AILMNOPSS	spoilsman
AILMNOPST	Platonism
AILMNOPSY	amylopsin
AILMNORST	mortal sin
AILMNORTY	normality
AILMNOSUU	aluminous
AILMNSTTU	stimulant
AILMORSST	moralists
AILMORSSU	solariums
AILMORSTU	simulator
AILMORTTU	mutilator
AILMORTTY	mortality
AILMOSSTY	atmolysis
AILMPRSTY	palmistry
AILMPSSST	psalmists
AILMRSSTU	muralists
	ultraisms
AILMSTTUU	mutualist
AILMTTUUY	mutuality
AILNNOPTU	plutonian
AILNNOSTU	lunations
AILNNSSTU	insulants
AILNNSTTY	instantly
AILNNSTUY	unsaintly
AILNOORST	tonsorial
	torsional
AILNOOSST	solations
AILNOOSTV	solvation
AILNOOTUV	ovulation
AILNOPSTU	platinous
	pulsation
AILNOPSTY	ponytails
AILNORSTU	insulator
AILNOSSUV	avulsions
AILNOSTUX	luxations
AILNOSTUY	autolysin
AILNOSUXY	anxiously
AILNPPSTU	suppliant
AILNPQTUY	piquantly
AILNRTUUX	luxuriant
AILNSSSTU	stunsails
AILNSSTTU	lutanists
AILOOPTTU	autopilot
AILOORSST	isolators
AILOORSTV	violators
AILOORSUV	variolous
AILOPRSTU	troupials
AILOPRSTV	postviral
AILORRSUV	rivalrous
AILORSSST	solarists
AILORSSTY	royalists
AILORSTTU	tutorials
AILORSTUV	outrivals
AILORSUVY	savourily
	variously
AILOSSTUY	autolysis
AILPRRSSU	surprisal
AILPSSTUY	playsuits
AILRRSSTU	ruralists
AILRSSTTU	altruists
	ultraists
AILRSSUVV	survivals
AIMMMMNOS	mammonism
AIMMMNOST	mammonist
AIMMNORTY	matrimony
AIMMNOSTU	summation
AIMMPRSUU	marsupium
AIMMRSSTU	summarist
AIMNNOORT	nominator
AIMNNOPST	pointsman
AIMNNORUV	mavournin
AIMNNOSTU	antimuons
	mountains
AIMNNOSUU	unanimous
AIMNNOTYY	anonymity
AIMNNRSTU	ruminants
AIMNOPRSY	parsimony
AIMNOPRTT	important
AIMNOPRTY	patrimony
AIMNORRST	rainstorm
AIMNORRTU	ruminator
AIMNORSUU	uniramous
AIMNOSTTU	mutations
AIMNPSTTY	tympanist
AIMNRSSTT	transmits
AIMNRSSTU	saturnism
AIMOOPRST	prostomia
AIMOPRSSS	prosaisms
AIMOPSSTU	potassium
AIMORRSST	armorists
AIMORRSSU	rosariums
AIMORRSUV	variorums
AIMPSSSTU	assumpsit
AINNNOSTU	Antoninus
	unisonant
AINNOOPRS	sopranino
AINNOOPRT	pronation
AINNOORTV	innovator
AINNOOSTT	notations
AINNOOSTV	novations
AINNOOSTZ	zonations
AINNORSTT	strontian
AINNOSTTU	nutations

AINOOPPRT appointor
apportion
AINOOPRRT proration
AINOOPSTT potations
AINOOQTTU quotation
AINOORSTT rotations
AINOOSSTT ostinatos
AINOOTTUX autotoxin
AINOPPSTU pupations
AINOPRSTU supinator
AINOPRSUU uniparous
AINOPSSTW swaptions
AINOQRRSU quarrions
AINORSSST arsonists
AINPSSTTU pantsuits
AINRSSTTU naturists
AINRSSTTY Tsaritsyn
AINRSTTTU antitrust
AIOOORRST oratorios
AIOOPPRST proposita
AIOOPPSST apoptosis
AIOOPRSUV apivorous
oviparous
AIOOSTTTT tattooist
AIOPRRSTT portraits
AIOPRSSST prosaists
AIOPRTTTY tyropitta
AIORRSSTU sartorius
AIORRSSTV varistors
AIORRSTUV rotavirus
AIORSSTTV votarists
AJMMNNOPU Panmunjom
AJMNORUWY jurywoman
AKKORSTVY Tarkovsky
AKKRSTVYY Syktyvkar
AKLLMMOWY mollymawk
AKLLMNOSU molluskan
AKLMNORWY workmanly
AKLNOSUVY Ulyanovsk
AKLOORSTT rootstalk
AKLOORSVZ Kolozsvár
AKLORSSTW saltworks
AKLPRRSSU larkspurs
AKMMNOORS monomarks
AKMNOOPSU mokopunas
AKMOPRSST postmarks
AKNNORSYY synkaryon
AKNOOPRRY prokaryon
AKNOPSSTW swankpots
ALLMNORUY unmorally
ALLMOOSSY lysosomal
ALLMOSUWY mulloways
ALLNOOPTY polytonal
ALLNOPTTU pollutant
ALLNSUUUY unusually
ALLOOPRTY allotropy
ALLOPPRUY popularly
ALLOPRSTY sallyport
ALLOPRSUY parlously
ALLOPSSUY spousally
ALLRSTUUY suturally
ALMMNSSUU Mussulman
ALMNNOOOS monsoonal
ALMNOORTY monolatry
ALMNOPRUY pulmonary
ALMOOPRSY playrooms
ALMOORSTU alumroots
ALMOORSUY amorously
ALMOPPSST lampposts
ALMPSSSTY symplasts
ALNOOPSTT tonoplast
ALNOOPSYZ polyzoans
ALNOPPRUU unpopular
ALNOPRSST plastrons
ALNOPSTTU postulant
ALNORTUVY voluntary
ALNPPSSTU supplants
ALNPSTTUU pustulant
ALOOPPRSS proposals
ALOOPRRTY Port Royal
ALOOPRSTV Stavropol
ALOOPSTYZ zooplasty
ALOPPRSSU prolapsus
ALOPRSSTU pulsators
ALOPRSTUY pulsatory
ALORSSTTW saltworts
AMMNPSTUY tympanums
AMMOOSTUY myomatous
AMNNOOSUY anonymous
AMNOOPSTW postwoman
AMNOORSTY astronomy
AMNOPRSST sportsman
AMNOSTTUY tautonyms
AMNOTTUYY tautonymy
AMOOORSTV vasomotor
AMOORRRWW arrowworm
AMOORSTWY motorways
AMOOSSTTU stomatous
AMOPRSSXY paroxysms
AMORRSTWW strawworm
AMORSSTTU outsmarts
AMPRSTUUY sumptuary
ANNOOPRSU nonparous
ANNOORSST sonorants
ANNORSTUY tyrannous
ANOOOPRSZ sporozoan
ANOOOPRTZ protozoan
ANOOPRRST pronators
ANOORSTWY Stornoway
ANOPRRSTT transport
ANOPRSTTU trapuntos
ANORSUUVY unsavoury
ANRRSSTUU susurrant
AOOORRRTW arrowroot
AOOORRTTV rotovator
AOOPRRSTT protostar
AOOPRSSTW soapworts
AOPPRSSST passports
AOPRRSTUU rapturous
AOPRSSTTY pyrostats
AORRRTWWY worrywart
AORRSSTTW starworts
AORSTTTUY statutory
BBBCDEEOW cobwebbed
BBBDEELRU blubbered
BBBDEHNOO hobnobbed
BBBEEELMU bumblebee
BBBEEELUZ Beelzebub
BBBEEIORS bobberies
BBBEELRRU blubberer
BBBEGLMUU bubblegum
BBBEIKORS skibobber
BBBEILOST blobbiest
BBBEILSTU bubbliest
BBBEINOST bobbinets
BBCDEELOR clobbered
BBCDEILRS scribbled
BBCDIMOSY bombycids
BBCEHISTU chubbiest
BBCEHLOUY cubbyhole
BBCEILRRS scribbler
BBCEILRSS scribbles
BBCEILSTU clubbiest
BBCEIRRSU scrubbier
BBCEIRSSU subscribe
BBCEKLSSU blesbucks
BBCEKTUUY buckytube
BBCERRSSU scrubbers
BBCGILNSU clubbings
BBCGINRSU scrubbing
BBCHILSUY cubbishly
BBCHKOOSS boschboks
BBCHKSSUU bushbucks
BBCIIILST biblicist
BBDEELORS slobbered
BBDEERSSU subbreeds
BBDEGIINR dibbering
BBDEGIMNO demobbing
BBDEHIRSU rubbished
BBDEIIRSU rubbidies
BBDEILLRS bellbirds
BBDEILRRS dribblers
BBDEILRST dribblets
BBDEILRSU bluebirds
BBDEIMOSV divebombs
BBDEIORRW bowerbird
BBDELLMSU dumbbells
BBDELMMOU bumbledom
BBDGIILNR dribbling
BBDGINRSU drubbings
BBDIIKKMU dibbukkim
BBDIKKMUY dybbukkim
BBDNOSTUU bundobust
BBEEEEINR bebeerine
BBEEEHLMU humblebee
BBEEEINRR berberine
BBEEIIRRS briberies
BBEEILPST plebbiest
BBEEINRTZ rebbetzin
BBEEIORRS robberies
BBEEIORSY yobberies
BBEEIRRSU rubberise
BBEEIRRUZ rubberize
BBEELLLSU bluebells
BBEELORRS slobberer
BBEELRRUY blueberry

BBEEOPPRS bebopper s
BBEFILRRS fribblers
BBEFILRST flibberts
BBEFIMORS firebombs
BBEGGIINR gibbering
BBEGGIINT gibbeting
BBEGGNOOW wobbegong
BBEGHIIRS gibberish
BBEGHILOS bobsleigh
BBEGHIOTW bobweight
BBEGIMNNU benumbing
BBEGINNOT Bebington
BBEGINSSU gubbinses
BBEGIRSTU grubbiest
BBEHILLOY Holy Bible
BBEHIOSTW bobwhites
BBEHIRRSU shrubbier
BBEHIRSSU rubbishes
BBEHLLMOS bombshell
BBEHRRSUY shrubbery
BBEIIRSTU rubbities
BBEIKLNOR knobblier
BBEIKNOST knobbiest
BBEILLLSU bluebills
BBEILOSTW wobbliest
BBEILQRSU quibblers
BBEINSSTU tubbiness
BBEIRSSTU subtribes
BBEISSTTU stubbiest
BBEKLOOSU bluebooks
BBEKNOOST bonteboks
BBELOORSW bobowlers
BBERRTTUU butterbur
BBFGIILNR fribbling
BBGHILLTU lightbulb
BBGHILNOO hobgoblin
BBGHIMOST bombsight
BBGHINORT throbbing
BBGIILNQU quibbling
BBGIINNOR ribboning
BBGIINQSU squibbing
BBGIIOSTY gibbosity
BBGILLNOO bobolling
BBGILMNSU bumblings
BBGILOSUY gibbously
BBHIOSSTY hobbyists
BBHRSSSUU subshrubs
BBIIILNRU bilirubin
BBIIKMTUZ kibbutzim
BBIKLNOOS bobolinks
BBILOSSTY lobbyists
BBLLNNSUU bulnbulns
BBLLOSUUY bulbously
BBLLOSUYY bullyboys
BCCCKMOOS cockscomb
BCCDEHKOY bodycheck
BCCDEMSUU succumbed
BCCEEILOR coercible
BCCEHIILO libecchio
BCCEHIKNP pinchbeck
BCCEHKKOO checkbook
BCCEIIILM imbecilic
BCCEIINOT cenobitic
BCCEILOSY biocycles
BCCEILRSU crucibles
BCCEILRSY bicyclers
BCCEINNOU concubine
BCCEKLORU cocklebur
BCCEMRSUU cucumbers
succumber
BCCGIILNY bicycling
BCCIILSTY bicyclist
BCCIKLLOY billycock
BCCILMUUU cubiculum
BCCINORRS corncribs
BCCIORSTU scorbutic
BCCIRSTUU cucurbits
BCCMOORXY coxcombry
BCCMORRUY currycomb
BCCOSSUUU succubous
BCDDEEHOU debouched
BCDDEEILU deducible
BCDDEEIRS described
BCDDEELOU beclouded
BCDDESTUU subducted
BCDDIIKRY dickybird
BCDEEEEHS beseeched
BCDEEEFIN beneficed
BCDEEEINO obedience
BCDEEGIKN bedecking
BCDEEHIIR herbicide
BCDEEHITW bewitched
BCDEEHOSU debouches
BCDEEHRTU butchered
BCDEEILRU reducible
BCDEEILSU seducible
BCDEEIORR cerebroid
BCDEEIRRS describer
BCDEEIRSS describes
BCDEEJSTU subjected
BCDEEKLLO bellocked
BCDEEKLRU bucklered
BCDEEKRSU reedbucks
BCDEELLOR corbelled
BCDEEMNTU decumbent
BCDEHINPT pitchbend
BCDEIILNU inducible
BCDEIINRS inscribed
BCDEIIRRS ricebirds
BCDEILOOR bicolored
BCDEILOSU Bois-le-Duc
BCDEILRUY reducibly
BCDEISTUU decubitus
BCDEKLLOU bullocked
BCDEKLNOU unblocked
BCDEKLNUU unbuckled
BCDEMOSTU combusted
BCDEOOTTY boycotted
BCDEORRSS crossbred
BCDGIKLOR goldbrick
BCDGOSYZZ Bydgoszcz
BCDHKNOUU buckhound
BCDIILOOS discoboli
BCDIIPSSU bicuspids
BCDIKLLSU duckbills
BCDILORSU colubrids
BCDIMOORS scombroid
BCDKLOOOW woodblock
BCDKNOOOS boondocks
BCDKNOORU rockbound
BCEEEEHRS beseecher
BCEEEEHSS beseeches
BCEEEFINS benefices
BCEEEHKNO cheekbone
BCEEELQRU becquerel
BCEEENQUW New Quebec
BCEEERSSU berceuses
BCEEFILNS fencibles
BCEEGHINR breeching
BCEEGIINR bigeneric
BCEEHINST Bechstein
benchiest
BCEEHISTW bewitches
BCEEHKLNU lebkuchen
BCEEHKOOR chokebore
BCEEHKTTU buckteeth
BCEEHNSTU beechnuts
BCEEHORTT brochette
BCEEHOSSU subechoes
BCEEHPRUY hypercube
BCEEHRTTU trebuchet
BCEEIIJTV bijective
BCEEIILMS imbeciles
BCEEIILNV evincible
BCEEIJOTV objective
BCEEIKLOR Lockerbie
BCEEIKNST Steinbeck
BCEEIKRRS bickerers
BCEEILLOR corbeille
BCEEILLOS bellicose
BCEEILMNY Cymbeline
BCEEILRTY celebrity
BCEEIMMOS misbecome
BCEEIMNOR recombine
BCEEINOOT coenobite
BCEEINOST cenobites
BCEEIORSX boxercise
BCEEIPRRS prescribe
BCEEJNORT jobcentre
BCEEKNORS beckoners
BCEEKRTTU trebucket
BCEELNOSY obscenely
BCEELOORS borecoles
BCEELOOSS obsolesce
BCEELRSTU tubercles
BCEELRUUY burleycue
BCEEMNRSU encumbers
BCEEMNRTU recumbent
BCEEMRRSU cerebrums
cumberers
BCEENPSTU pubescent
BCEENRSTU rubescent
BCEEPRSTY cyberpets
BCEFFIOSU suboffice
BCEFHISSU subchiefs
BCEFHISTT bitchfest

BCEFIIKRR firebrick
BCEFIIRTY febricity
BCEFIJOTY objectify
BCEFKLTUU bucketful
BCEGHILNN blenching
BCEGHNORS Schönberg
BCEGHORRU Cherbourg
BCEGIIKNR bickering
BCEGIINRS escribing
BCEGIINST bisecting
BCEGIJNOT objecting
BCEGIKNNO beckoning
BCEGIKNTU bucketing
BCEGILNOR corbeling
BCEGIMNOS becomings
BCEGIMNRU cumbering
BCEGKMSSU gemsbucks
BCEGKTTUU gutbucket
BCEHHORSS borshches
BCEHIILPT phlebitic
BCEHIINRU Cherubini
BCEHIIOST bioethics
BCEHIISTT bitchiest
BCEHILORT blotchier
BCEHIMORS chemisorb
BCEHINNOT benthonic
BCEHINOOP neophobic
BCEHINSTU bunchiest
BCEHIOQUU chibouque
BCEHIOSTT botchiest
BCEHIPSSU spicebush
BCEHIRSTT brichtest
BCEHKLMRU Lehmbruck
BCEHKMRUU humbucker
BCEHKNORW workbench
BCEHLNORY Chernobyl
BCEHLOSUU clubhouse
BCEHMNOOY honeycomb
BCEHMOORS chemosorb
BCEHOPSSU subepochs
BCEHORRSU brochures
BCEIIIOPT epibiotic
BCEIIJNOT bijection
BCEIIKLNS iceblinks
BCEIIKRST brickiest
BCEIILNOT bilection
BCEIILPSU publicise
BCEIILPUZ publicize
BCEIIMORT biometric
BCEIINNTY Benin City
BCEIINOST bisection
BCEIINRRS inscriber
BCEIINRSS inscribes
BCEIIRSTX bisectrix
BCEIJNOOT objection
BCEIKNOST steinbock
BCEILLMRU cribellum
BCEILMNOU columbine
BCEILMOTU columbite
BCEILMRRU crumblier
BCEILNOOT bolection
BCEILNORU colubrine
BCEILNRTU interclub
BCEILPRSU republics
BCEIMNNTU incumbent
BCEIMNORS combiners
BCEIMNORY embryonic
BCEIMNRSU incumbers
BCEIMRSTU crumbiest
BCEINOSTU bounciest
BCEINOSTY obscenity
BCEINSSUU incubuses
BCEIOOPSS bioscopes
BCEIOPRRS proscribe
BCEIORRSU Corbusier
BCEIORSST bisectors
BCEIORSTT obstetric
BCEIRSTUU București
BCEKLNSUU unbuckles
BCEKLRSSU subclerks
BCEKMRSUU bumsucker
BCEKNPRUY cyberpunk
BCEKORTUX tuckerbox
BCELMNOUW clubwomen
BCELMOOTY lobectomy
BCELOOSSU colobuses
lobscouse
BCELORSUY obscurely
BCEMOORSY corymbose
BCENOORRR cornborer
BCENORSTU curbstone
BCEORRRWY crowberry
BCEORSSTU obscurest
BCEORSTUX subcortex
BCEPRTTUU buttercup
BCFHILLNU bullfinch
BCGHILNOT blotching
BCGHILNTU nightclub
BCGIILOOS biologics
BCGIIMNNO combining
BCGIKLNSU bucklings
BCGIKRSUV Vicksburg
BCGILMNRU crumbling
BCGILMNSU scumbling
BCGINORSU obscuring
BCHIIMSTU bismuthic
BCHIIOPRS bishopric
BCHIIRSTU hubristic
BCHIIRSTY hybristic
BCHIKLSUY buckishly
BCHILLOTY blotchily
BCHILOOPY lyophobic
BCHIOORSY choirboys
BCHKNORSU buckhorns
BCHKNORTU buckthorn
BCHKOOTTU bucktooth
BCHKOSSTU buckshots
BCHLNOPUW punchbowl
BCHLOOOSY schoolboy
BCHLOORTW blowtorch
BCIILMSUU umbilicus
BCIILPSTU publicist
BCIILPTUY publicity
BCIILRTUY lubricity
BCIIMNOOS bionomics
BCIIMOSTY symbiotic
BCIIOOOTZ zoobiotic
BCIIOOPRT probiotic
BCIKKNOST knobstick
BCIKKNSSU buckskins
BCIKKORRW brickwork
BCIKLOOST bootlicks
BCIKNNRSU Innsbruck
BCIKNRSUW Brunswick
BCIKORRSW cribworks
BCIKOSSTT bitstocks
BCILLORSS crossbill
BCILMMOUU columbium
BCILORSUU lubricous
BCIMNOOTY mycobiont
BCINOSSTU subtonics
BCIOOPRSS proboscis
BCIOPSSTU subtopics
BCIORSTUY obscurity
BCIPRSSTU subscript
BCKKOOOOS cookbooks
BCKOOOPSY copybooks
BCLMOOSUU columbous
BCMNOOORR broomcorn
BCMOORSTU combustor
BCMOORSUY corymbous
BCOOORSTW crowboots
BCOORSSSW crossbows
BCORSSTTU obstructs
BDDDDEISU disbudded
BDDDEEFLU befuddled
BDDDEEINR bedridden
BDDDEGINU debudding
BDDEEEFIR debriefed
BDDEEEILV bedeviled
BDDEEEINZ bedizened
BDDEEFLSU befuddles
BDDEEFOOR foreboded
BDDEEGGRU begrudged
BDDEEGHIT bedighted
BDDEEGIMN embedding
BDDEEGIRR Redbridge
BDDEEINSW bindweeds
BDDEEIORR broidered
BDDEEIOSY disobeyed
BDDEEIRRS reedbirds
BDDEEISTU subedited
BDDEELNRU blundered
BDDEELORU redoubled
BDDEENORU rebounded
BDDEENRRU underbred
BDDEENSTU subtended
BDDEFINOR forbidden
BDDEFIORR forbidder
BDDEGIIMN imbedding
BDDEGIINR rebidding
BDDEGLOOU doodlebug
BDDEHINOU hidebound
BDDEHLOOS bloodshed
BDDEIILMR birdlimed
BDDEIILNS blindside

BDDEIIMOR dibromide
BDDEIISUV subdivide
BDDEILNRU unbridled
BDDEIMOSY disembody
BDDEINOTU outbidden
BDDEINRSU disburden
underbids
BDDEIRSSU disbursed
BDDEIRSTU disturbed
BDDEKNOSU deskbound
BDDELLOUZ bulldozed
BDDELNNUU unbundled
BDDELSUUY subduedly
BDDENNOUU unbounded
BDDENORUY underbody
BDDENOTUU undoubted
BDDENSUUU unsubdued
BDDFILLNO blindfold
BDDFMNOUU dumbfound
BDDGILNOR broddling
BDDHIIRSY dihybrids
BDDINNOUW windbound
BDDLOOOOW bloodwood
BDEEEEFLN enfeebled
BDEEEEJLW bejeweled
BDEEEELRV belvedere
BDEEEFILL Bielefeld
BDEEEFINT benefited
BDEEEGIRV Beveridge
BDEEEGLRR Lederberg
BDEEEGLUW bugleweed
BDEEEHLRT blethered
BDEEEHRSW beshrewed
BDEEEISTW dweebiest
BDEEEKNOT betokened
BDEEELMRS resembled
BDEEELMZZ embezzled
BDEEELNOS nosebleed
BDEEELSUW blueweeds
BDEEEMMNT embedment
BDEEEMORW embowered
BDEEENRTU debenture
BDEEERSTW bestrewed
BDEEERTTV brevetted
BDEEFIILS disbelief
BDEEFIIRV verbified
BDEEFINRS befriends
BDEEFLLOW bedfellow
BDEEFLORW flowerbed
BDEEFOORR foreboder
BDEEFOORS forebodes
BDEEFOOSW beefwoods
BDEEFOOTW webfooted
BDEEGGLOW bowlegged
BDEEGGORS Godesberg
BDEEGGRSU begrudges
BDEEGHINT benighted
BDEEGILOR de Broglie
BDEEGMRSU submerged
BDEEGNORU burgeoned
BDEEHIITX exhibited
BDEEHILMS blemished
BDEEHIORT Bodhi Tree
BDEEHLLSU bushelled
BDEEHLORS beholders
BDEEHORTT betrothed
BDEEHTUUX Buxtehude
BDEEIILLN indelible
BDEEIILOS biodiesel
BDEEIILRS derisible
BDEEIINNZ benzidine
BDEEIINRS binderies
BDEEIISTU dubieties
BDEEIKLNR blinkered
BDEEIKNRS briskened
BDEEILLRW bridewell
BDEEILLTT belittled
BDEEILMNO belemnoid
BDEEILMOR embroiled
BDEEILMOS embolised
BDEEILMOZ embolized
BDEEILMSS dissemble
BDEEILNNO nonedible
BDEEILNSU nebulised
BDEEILNSV vendibles
BDEEILNUZ nebulized
BDEEILOPR preboiled
BDEEILRST blistered
BDEEILRSW bewilders
BDEEIMMRS dismember
BDEEIMORR embroider
BDEEINRRT interbred
BDEEIORSY disobeyer
BDEEIQRTU briqueted
BDEEIRRST bestirred
BDEEIRSST bestrides
BDEEIRSSU suberised
BDEEIRSTT bedsitter
BDEEIRSUZ suberized
BDEEKNRSU debunkers
BDEEKNRUU unrebuked
BDEEKOORW brookweed
BDEELLNRU Brudenell
BDEELLSSY blessedly
BDEELMNOS emboldens
BDEELMRSU slumbered
BDEELMSUY bemusedly
BDEELNRRU blunderer
BDEELNSSU unblessed
BDEELORST bolstered
BDEELORSU redoubles
BDEELRSTU blustered
BDEEMMOOS embosomed
BDEEMNOST bodements
BDEEMRSSU submersed
BDEEOPRRV proverbed
BDEEORRRS borderers
BDEEORSTU outbreeds
BDEEORVYY everybody
BDEEPRRSU purebreds
BDEEPRRTU perturbed
BDEERSSUV subserved
BDEERSTUV subverted
BDEFHIRSU furbished
BDEFIILRR riflebird
BDEFIIRRS firebirds
BDEFIIRTU brutified
BDEFILLOO lifeblood
BDEFINORY boyfriend
BDEFINRRS fernbirds
BDEGGGINU debugging
BDEGGHMUU humbugged
BDEGGIINR begirding
BDEGGINTU budgeting
BDEGHILNO beholding
BDEGHILNR Lindbergh
BDEGHINRU Edinburgh
BDEGIIILR dirigible
BDEGIIINR birdieing
BDEGIILOS disoblige
BDEGIIMMN bedimming
BDEGIINNR rebinding
BDEGIKNNU debunking
BDEGIKOOU guidebook
BDEGIMNOY embodying
BDEGIMRUY Muybridge
BDEGINNNU unbending
BDEGINNRU burdening
BDEGINORR bordering
BDEGINORS desorbing
BDEGINORT Tonbridge
BDEGINRRU deburring
BDEGINSSU debussing
BDEGLNORU Oldenburg
BDEGLNOSU bludgeons
BDEHIIINT inhibited
BDEHIILMN Blindheim
BDEHIIRSY hybridise
BDEHIIRYZ hybridize
BDEHILPSU published
BDEHIMNOO Bohemond I
BDEHINRSU burnished
BDEHIORRS shorebird
BDEHIORSU birdhouse
BDEHLLOSY bodyshell
BDEHNOSTU South Bend
BDEHNRSUU unbrushed
underbush
BDEIIILSV divisible
BDEIIILTY edibility
BDEIIKLNS Libeskind
BDEIILLNY indelibly
BDEIILMOS mobilised
BDEIILMOZ mobilized
BDEIILMRS birdlimes
BDEIILNNO blennioid
BDEIIRTTU turbidite
BDEIISSSU subsidies
subsidise
BDEIISSTU subitised
BDEIISSUZ subsidize
BDEIISTUZ subitized
BDEIJMOSU jumboised
BDEIJMOUZ jumboized
BDEIJNOSU subjoined
BDEIKKORU duikerbok

BDEILLMSU bdelliums
BDEILLNOO bloodline
BDEILLNPS spellbind
BDEILMNOW Wimbledon
BDEILMOSS semibolds
BDEILNNSS blindness
BDEILNRSU unbridles
BDEILOOST bloodiest
BDEILOQTU quodlibet
BDEILORSV lovebirds
BDEILORUV overbuild
BDEILOSSU subsoiled
BDEILPRUU upbuilder
BDEILRRSY lyrebirds
BDEILSTTU subtitled
BDEIMNOST disentomb
BDEIMORSU mousebird
BDEIMSTTU submitted
BDEINNORW windborne
BDEINORSV ovenbirds
BDEINORTX tinderbox
BDEINORTZ Trebizond
BDEINOSTU soundbite
BDEINRSSU burnsides
sideburns
BDEINRSUU unbruised
BDEIOORRW brierwood
BDEIOORST broodiest
robotised
BDEIOORTZ robotized
BDEIORRSS disrobers
BDEIORSTU subeditor
BDEIOSSUX suboxides
BDEIPRSTU buprestid
BDEIRRSSU disburser
BDEIRRSTU disturber
BDEIRSSSU disburses
subsiders
BDEISSSTU subsisted
BDELLMOSY symbolled
BDELLOORS bordellos
BDELLOOSS bloodless
BDELLORUZ bulldozer
BDELLOSUZ bulldozes
BDELLRRUY blurredly
BDELMNNOO Ben Lomond
BDELMNPUU unplumbed
BDELMOOSS blossomed
BDELNNOSS blondness
BDELNNSUU unbundles
BDELNOOTU doubleton
BDELNOSSU boundless
BDELOORWW lowbrowed
BDELOPRSU superbold
BDELORSUU doublures
BDELOSSTU doubtless
BDEMMNOSU ombudsmen
BDEMNOOSU unbosomed
BDENNOOST bondstone
BDENNOSTU dubonnets
BDENNOTTU obtundent
BDENNRSUU sunburned
unburdens
BDENOORSU burnoosed
eurobonds
BDENOORTW Brentwood
BDENORSUU burnoused
BDENOSTUW westbound
BDENRSUUY underbuys
BDEOOORRW woodborer
BDEOPSSTU subdepots
BDEORRSSU suborders
BDEORRSTU obtruders
BDFFIPRSU puffbirds
BDFHIILNS blindfish
BDFHNOOOU hoofbound
BDFILLLOS billfolds
BDFILNOOS bloodfins
BDFIRRSSU surfbirds
BDFLNOOSY dobsonfly
BDFORSSUY bodysurfs
BDGHOOSUY doughboys
BDGIIKNRS kingbirds
BDGIILNNS blindings
BDGIILNSU buildings
BDGIINNNU unbinding
BDGIINORS disrobing
BDGIINSSU subsiding
BDGILNNOS blondings
BDGILNOOY bloodying
BDGINNORW bringdown
BDGINNOTU obtunding
BDGINOORS broodings
BDGINORSS birdsongs
songbirds
BDGINORTU obtruding
BDHIIMRSY hybridism
BDHIIRTYY hybridity
BDHIMOORS rhomboids
BDHINOOOR Robin Hood
BDHKOOORU Doukhobor
BDHLOOOST bloodshot
BDHOOORTY Boothroyd
BDHOORSUW brushwood
BDIIILSVY divisibly
BDIILLNSW windbills
BDIIMORTY morbidity
BDIIOSTUY dubiosity
BDIIRTTUY turbidity
BDIKNORUV Dubrovnik
BDILLORSW swordbill
BDILMNNOO moonblind
BDILMNORW blindworm
BDILNNOWW windblown
BDILOSUUY dubiously
BDIMOSSTU misdoubts
BDINNOORU ironbound
BDINNRTUW windburnt
BDINORSSW snowbirds
BDIORRSTU subtorrid
BDIORSUZZ burdizzos
BDIOSSTUY bodysuits
BDKOOORSW wordbooks
BDKOOSSTU studbooks
BDLMOOORW bloodworm
BDLMOOSUY molybdous
BDLNOOOSU doubloons
BDLNOOSWW blowdowns
BDLOOORT bloodroot
BDNNOOSUW snowbound
BDNORSTUW downburst
BEEEEKPR beekeeper
BEEEFLNR enfeebler
BEEEFLNS enfeebles
BEEEEKMRW Ember week
BEEEEMRRY Meyerbeer
BEEEFILST beetflies
BEEEFINSS beefiness
BEEEGGRUZ Zeebrugge
BEEEGIMNS beseeming
BEEEGIRSS besiegers
BEEEGLNRT greenbelt
BEEEGNNOR greenbone
BEEEGNOOW woebegone
BEEEGRSTT begetters
BEEEHHLMT Bethlehem
BEEEHISST bheesties
BEEEHLLOR hellebore
BEEEHLRTT Ethelbert
BEEEHLSWW webwheels
BEEEHNOSY honeybees
BEEEHNOTV Beethoven
BEEEILLLS Belle Isle
libellees
BEEEILLST billetees
BEEEILMMS emblemise
BEEEILMMZ emblemize
BEEEILMNT belemnite
BEEEILRSV believers
eversible
BEEEIMRSV semibreve
BEEEINRSS beeriness
BEEEIRRSW breweries
BEEEIRSTZ breeziest
BEEEKRRRS berserker
BEEELLRSV bevellers
BEEELMNSS ensembles
BEEELMRRS resembler
BEEELMRSS resembles
BEEELMRZZ embezzler
BEEELMSZZ embezzles
BEEELSSSU sublessee
BEEEMMRRS remembers
BEEENNOTV Benevento
BEEENOSSS obeseness
BEEERSSTT besetters
BEEFFGIRU febrifuge
BEEFFRSTU buffeters
BEEFIILMS misbelief
BEEFIILNR inferible
BEEFIIRSV verbifies
BEEFILRSS briefless
fiberless
fibreless
BEEFINRSS briefness
BEEFIORSX fireboxes

BEEFISTUX	tubifexes
BEEFLORSU	befoulers
BEEFOORST	freeboots
BEEGGIINS	besieging
BEEGGINNR	breenging
BEEGGINTT	begetting
BEEGGNRTU	Gutenberg
BEEGHIRTY	eyebright
BEEGHNRRU	Ehrenburg
BEEGIILLL	illegible
BEEGIILNV	believing
BEEGIINOT	Gibeonite
BEEGIKLLO	globelike
BEEGILLNR	rebelling
BEEGILLNV	bevelling
BEEGILLNW	wellbeing
BEEGILLRS	gerbilles
BEEGILNRS	inselberg
BEEGILNRY	berleying
BEEGILPRS	Spielberg
BEEGILRSU	beguilers
BEEGINNRR	Nirenberg
BEEGINNRS	beginners
BEEGINNRT	Tinbergen
BEEGINRTT	bettering
BEEGINRTV	breveting
BEEGINSST	beestings
BEEGINSSW	beeswings
BEEGINSTT	besetting
BEEGLNOOS	Bolognese
BEEGMNRRU	Nuremberg
BEEGMRRSU	Merseburg
BEEGMRSSU	submerges
BEEGNORRS	Rosenberg
BEEGNRRST	Sternberg
BEEGNRSSU	sungrebes
BEEGNRSUV	Venusberg
BEEGRSSSU	burgesses
BEEHHMOST	behemoths
BEEHIKRRS	Berkshire
BEEHILLMS	embellish
BEEHILMSS	blemishes
BEEHILTUZ	Buthelezi
BEEHINRTT	terebinth
BEEHIOPRS	biosphere
BEEHIORRV	herbivore
BEEHIRSTU	Buteshire
BEEHLLOSX	hellboxes
BEEHLLRSU	busheller
BEEHLMNSU	bushelmen
BEEHLNRSU	Shelburne
BEEHLOORS	boreholes
BEEHLOPRY	hyperbole
BEEHLRSSU	bushelers
BEEHNOOPS	neophobes
BEEHNOOPX	xenophobe
BEEHNORRS	Sherborne
BEEIIKNRZ	Berezniki
BEEIILLRV	Iberville
BEEIILNRT	libertine
BEEIILNSZ	zibelines
BEEIILOPS	epibolies
BEEIILRST	liberties
BEEIINRTY	inebriety
BEEIIRSTV	brevities
BEEIKLMRU	berkelium
BEEIKLMRY	Kimberley
BEEIKPRSU	superbike
BEEILLLRS	libellers
BEEILLMSU	emulsible
BEEILLNOR	rebellion
BEEILLNTU	ebullient
BEEILLRST	billeters
BEEILLRTT	belittler
BEEILLRTU	rubellite
BEEILLSTT	belittles
BEEILMORR	embroiler
BEEILMOSS	embolises
BEEILMOSZ	embolizes
BEEILMPRS	periblems
BEEILNOST	bilestone
BEEILNRSU	nebuliser
BEEILNRUZ	nebulizer
BEEILNSSS	sensibles
BEEILNSSU	nebulises
BEEILNSUZ	nebulizes
BEEILORTT	briolette
BEEILOSTV	lovebites
BEEILOTTU	oubliette
BEEILPRTU	eruptible
BEEILRSST	tribeless
BEEILRSTU	butleries
BEEILRSUZ	Berzelius
BEEILSSTU	bluesiest
BEEILSTUV	vestibule
BEEIMMNRT	timbermen
BEEIMMNTU	imbuement
BEEIMNRST	tenebrism
	tribesmen
BEEIMRRSU	reimburse
BEEIMRSTT	embitters
BEEINNOTT	bentonite
BEEINNRST	Bernstein
BEEINRRWY	wineberry
BEEINRSTT	tenebrist
BEEINRTTU	butterine
BEEIOQSSU	Essequibo
	obsequies
BEEIORSTV	overbites
BEEIOSSSV	obsessive
BEEIQRTTU	briquette
BEEIRSSSU	suberises
	subseries
BEEIRSSUZ	suberizes
BEEIRSTTT	bitterest
BEEIRSTTU	butteries
BEEIRTTTY	ytterbite
BEEJKOSUX	jukeboxes
BEEKNORST	kerbstone
BEEKNOSST	steenboks
BEEKOPRRY	pokeberry
BEELLLMUU	umbellule
BEELLORSU	resoluble
BEELLORSW	bellowers
	rebellows
BEELLRSUX	Bruxelles
BEELMNORU	Melbourne
BEELMOORT	bolometer
BEELMORST	temblores
BEELMRRST	tremblers
BEELMRRSU	lumberers
	slumberer
BEELNNORS	ennoblers
BEELNNOSS	nobleness
BEELNOSSU	bluenoses
BEELNOSTU	bluestone
BEELORRST	bolsterer
BEELORSVY	obversely
	verbosely
BEELORTTX	letterbox
BEELOSSTU	boletuses
BEELQRSUU	burlesque
BEELRRSTU	blusterer
BEELRSTUU	trueblues
BEEMMNNOR	nonmember
BEEMMNOTW	embowment
BEEMNNRTU	Number Ten
BEEMNRRSU	renumbers
BEEMOPRST	obtempers
BEEMORSSS	embossers
BEEMQSSUU	embusques
BEEMRSSSU	submerses
BEENOORRV	overborne
BEENOQSTU	obsequent
BEENORRST	resorbent
BEENORSSS	soberness
BEENORSTU	tenebrous
BEENRSTTU	brunettes
BEEOORRSW	boerewors
BEEOORSTT	beetroots
BEEORRSSV	observers
BEEORSSTU	tuberoses
BEEORSSTW	bestowers
BEEORSSUU	subereous
BEEORSTTU	soubrette
BEEPRRSTY	presbyter
BEERRSTTU	rebutters
BEERRSTUV	subverter
BEERSSSUV	subserves
BEERSSTTY	bystreets
BEFFGINRU	buffering
	rebuffing
BEFFGINTU	buffeting
BEFFIILLR	fiberfill
	fibrefill
BEFFLNSSU	bluffness
BEFGGGINO	befogging
BEFGHILOS	globefish
BEFGIILLS	fillibegs
BEFGIINRS	briefings
BEFGIINTT	befitting
BEFGILNOO	befooling
BEFGILNOU	befouling
BEFGILNSU	fungibles
BEFGINRUY	rubefying
BEFGLNRSU	Flensburg

BEFHILSSU bushflies
BEFHILSTU blueshift
BEFHIORRS Frobisher
BEFHIOSSX boxfishes
BEFHIRRSU brushfire
furbisher
refurbish
BEFHIRSSU bushfires
furbishes
BEFIILNSU infusible
BEFIILORT fibrolite
BEFIILRTY febrility
BEFIIRSTU brutifies
BEFILLOSW blowflies
BEFILMORS forelimbs
BEFINOPRU ibuprofen
BEFIORSTT frostbite
BEFLLLSUY bellyfuls
BEFLLOTTU bottleful
BEFLORSUW furbelows
BEFLRTTUY butterfly
BEGGGINRU buggering
BEGGGLOOX gogglebox
BEGGHMRUU humbugger
BEGGIILNU beguiling
BEGGIIMNR begriming
BEGGIINNN beginning
BEGGIINNR breinging
BEGGIINOO boogieing
BEGGILNNO belonging
BEGGINOSS bogginess
BEGGINSSU bugginess
BEGGNOORU Bourgogne
BEGGOOOSS goosegobs
BEGHHINOT thighbone
BEGHHOTTU bethought
BEGHIILPS philibegs
BEGHIILST blighties
BEGHILNSU busheling
BEGHILRST blighters
BEGHINOOV behooving
BEGHINORS neighbors
BEGHINORT bothering
BEGHINORU neighbour
BEGHINRST brightens
BEGHIORSU Brighouse
BEGHIOSST gobshites
BEGHIRSTT brightest
BEGHLNOSU bungholes
BEGHOSSUU bughouses
BEGIIILNT ignitible
BEGIILLLN libelling
BEGIILLLY illegibly
BEGIILLNT billeting
BEGIILMNR limbering
BEGIILNOR reboiling
BEGIILNOS obelising
BEGIILNOZ obelizing
BEGIILOOS biologies
BEGIIMNRT timbering
BEGIINNOS ebonising
BEGIINNOZ ebonizing
BEGIINNTY benignity
BEGIINRTT bittering
BEGIINSST biestings
BEGIIORST bigotries
BEGIJRTTU jitterbug
BEGIKNNRU bunkering
BEGIKNORR brokering
BEGILLLSU bluegills
BEGILLNOW bellowing
BEGILMNRT trembling
BEGILMNRU lumbering
BEGILMORY gorblimey
BEGILNNNO ennobling
BEGILNNTU unbelting
BEGILNRUY burleying
BEGILNSSS blessings
BEGILNSSU bulginess
BEGILRTTU litterbug
BEGIMNNOT entombing
BEGIMNNOW enwombing
BEGIMNNRU numbering
BEGIMNOSS embossing
BEGIMNPRU bumpering
BEGIMNSSU embussing
BEGINNNOS nonbeings
BEGINNORS ringbones
BEGINNORU Ben-Gurion
BEGINNSUV subvening
BEGINOORT rebooting
BEGINOOSU biogenous
BEGINORRS resorbing
BEGINORSU subregion
BEGINORSV observing
BEGINORTV obverting
BEGINOSSS obsessing
BEGINOSTT obtesting
BEGINOSTW bestowing
BEGINRRUY reburying
BEGINRTTU buttering
rebutting
BEGIOORSU bourgeois
BEGLLOOSY globosely
BEGLMRRSU grumblers
BEGLMRUUX Luxemburg
BEGMORRST Bergström
BEGNOORSU bourgeons
BEGNORSTU burgonets
BEGNOSSSU bogusness
BEGPRRSSU Pressburg
BEGPRSSUU superbugs
BEHHMOOOP homophobe
BEHIIINRT inhibiter
BEHIILPST phlebitis
BEHIIMNOY yohimbine
BEHIIORTX exhibitor
BEHIKLMTU thumblike
BEHIKLOSV bolshevik
BEHIKLRSU brushlike
shrublike
BEHIKLTUZ Kitzbühel
BEHIKSUVY Kuibyshev
BEHILLOSS shoebills
BEHILMRSW whimbrels
BEHILNNOR Heilbronn
BEHILNPSY biphenyls
BEHILOSST bolshiest
BEHILPRSU publisher
republish
BEHILPSSU publishes
BEHILRSTU thuribles
BEHINNOSS shinbones
BEHINOSSW wishbones
BEHINRRSU burnisher
BEHINRSSU burnishes
BEHINSSSU bushiness
BEHIORSTT theorbist
BEHIRSSTU brushiest
BEHKNOSUU bunkhouse
BEHLLOOSW blowholes
BEHLLRUVY Lévy-Bruhl
BEHLMSSTU thumbless
BEHLORRTY brotherly
BEHLRSSUU bulrushes
BEHMOORST thrombose
BEHMORSSU rhombuses
BEHNNRTUU unburthen
BEHNORSTU buhrstone
BEHOOPTTU phototube
BEHOOSSUY houseboys
BEHOPRTYY bryophyte
BEIIILNSV invisible
BEIIIOPSS epibiosis
BEIIIORRT Robert III
BEIIKRSTZ kibitzers
BEIILLNSY sibylline
BEIILLSST libelists
BEIILMNTW nimblewit
BEIILMOSS mobilises
omissible
BEIILMOSZ mobilizes
BEIILORTT trilobite
BEIILOTVZ Leibovitz
BEIILRRST bristlier
BEIILRSTU tilburies
BEIILSSTU subtilise
BEIILSTUZ subtilize
BEIIMNSSU minibuses
BEIIMORTU Umberto II
BEIINNRSS brininess
BEIINSSTT bittiness
BEIISSSTU subitises
BEIISSTUZ subitizes
BEIJMOSSU jumboises
BEIJMOSUZ jumboizes
BEIKLMOOR brooklime
BEIKLNSSU bulkiness
BEIKLOSTY kilobytes
BEIKMOORT motorbike
BEIKNOSST steinboks
BEIKNRSSS briskness
BEILLLOSU libellous
BEILLMRUY beryllium
BEILLMSUY sublimely
BEILLNORU Bernoulli

BEILLNOSU insoluble
BEILLNSTU bulletins
BEILLOPSX pillboxes
BEILLOQUY obliquely
BEILLRTTY brittlely
BEILLSSSS blissless
BEILLSTUY subtilely
BEILMMOSS embolisms
BEILMNRSU unlimbers
BEILMOOST bloomiest
BEILMOSSY symbolise
BEILMOSYZ symbolize
BEILNNSTU buntlines
BEILNOPSS bonspiels
BEILNPRTU blueprint
BEILNRSSU burliness
BEILOOPRT potboiler
BEILOOQSU obloquies
BEILOORSV boilovers
BEILOPPSW blowpipes
BEILOPSSS possibles
BEILORSST strobiles
BEILORSSU subsoiler
BEILORSTT librettos
BEILORTUV overbuilt
BEILOSSTW blowsiest
BEILOSTWZ blowziest
BEILPRSTV blipverts
BEILRRSTU blurriest
BEILRSTTT brittlest
BEILSSTTU subtilest
subtitles
BEIMMNORR merbromin
BEIMNOORS bromeosin
BEIMNORST brimstone
BEIMNOSSU omnibuses
BEIMNPSSU bumpiness
BEIMOORSS ribosomes
BEIMOORST biostrome
BEIMRSSTU resubmits
BEIMRSTTU submitter
BEIMRTTUY ytterbium
BEINNRSUW Swinburne
BEINOOPRT obreption
BEINOORSV obversion
BEINOOSSS obsession
BEINOOSSZ booziness
BEINOSSSS bossiness
BEINRRTWY twinberry
BEINRTTTU bitternut
BEINSSSUY businessy
BEIOOPRRU pourboire
BEIOORRRT brierroot
BEIOORSST robotises
BEIOORSTZ robotizes
BEIOQRSTU sobriquet
BEIOQSTUU boutiques
BEIORSTUV obtrusive
BEIORSTVY verbosity
BEIRSSSTU subsister
BEJORSTTU turbojets
BEKLOOOSU booklouse
BEKLOORST brooklets
BEKLOOSTY Byelostok
stylebook
BEKNNNOUW unbeknown
BEKNOOOST notebooks
BEKOOORSV overbooks
BEKOOSTTX textbooks
BELLNOSSU bullnoses
BELLORSTW bellworts
BELMOOORW elbowroom
BELMOORTY bolometry
BELMOPSUU plumbeous
BELMRSSTU stumblers
BELNNSSTU bluntness
BELNOORVW overblown
BELNRTTUU turbulent
BELOOPRST boltropes
BELOORSVW overblows
BELORRSTU troublers
BELORSSSU sublessor
BELQRSUUY brusquely
BEMNOORST trombones
BEMNOORSU unbosomer
BEMNOOSTT tombstone
BEMNORTUU outnumber
BEMNOSSUX buxomness
BEMOORRSS sombreros
BEMOOSTTT bottomset
BEMSSSTUY subsystem
BENNNOSTU sunbonnet
unbonnets
BENNOORSW brownnose
BENNOPSYY pennyboys
BENNORSSW brownness
BENOORRST Robertson
BENOORSSU burnooses
BENOOSTUU bounteous
BENORRSSU suborners
BENORRSTU burrstone
BENORRSWY snowberry
BENORRTTU Otterburn
BENORSSTU burstones
rubstones
BENORSSUU burnouses
BENORSTTU buttoners
obstruent
rebuttons
BENRTTTUU butternut
BEOOORSTV overboots
BEOOPSSTX postboxes
BEOORRRSW borrowers
BEOPSSSTU postbuses
BEORRRSUW burrowers
BFFHORSSU brushoffs
BFFIIMORR fibriform
BFFLOSTUU outbluffs
BFGHILLTU bullfight
BFGHINSTU bunfights
BFGLLORSU bullfrogs
BFGLORSUW Wolfsburg
BFHILOSST fishbolts
BFHILOSSW fishbowls
BFIILMORR libriform
BFIINORSU fibrinous
BFILNOTUU bountiful
BFILORSUY fibrously
BFIMORRSU bursiform
BFINORRST firstborn
BFLOORSSU subfloors
BFMMOOORR bromoform
BGGHIILNT blighting
BGGILLNUY bulgingly
BGGILMNRU grumbling
BGHHIORSW highbrows
BGHIIKNOS kiboshing
BGHIKLOOT booklight
BGHILMNSU humblings
BGHIMOSTU bigmouths
BGHINOOOO boohooing
BGHLOOPUY ploughboy
BGHMOOOOS Ogbomosho
BGHORRSUU Burroughs
BGIIIKNTZ kibitzing
BGIILLNOW billowing
BGIILLNOX bollixing
BGIILMNSU subliming
BGIILMOOR imbroglio
BGIILNOQU obliquing
BGIILNRSS brislings
BGIILNRST bristling
BGIILOOST biologist
BGIINRSSU bruisings
BGIKLNOST kingbolts
BGIKNOPRS springbok
BGILLNOSU globulins
BGILLNRSU bullrings
BGILMNOOY myoglobin
BGILMNOSY symboling
BGILMNSTU stumbling
BGILMOSTU gumbotils
BGILNNOTU unbolting
BGILNNRUY burningly
BGILNORST ringbolts
BGILNORTU troubling
BGILOORTY tribology
BGILOOSTY globosity
BGIMNOOTT bottoming
BGIMNSSUU subsuming
BGINNNOOT Bonington
BGINNORSU suborning
BGINNORSW brownings
BGINNORTU binturong
BGINNOTTU buttoning
BGINOORRW borrowing
BGINOOTUX outboxing
BGINOOWWW bowwowing
BGINORRUW burrowing
BGINORSTW bowstring
BGLLOOSUU globulous
BGLMOOSYY symbology
BGNOORSTX strongbox
BGOPRSSUU subgroups
BHHIIKKNU bhikkhuni
BHHIMORTY biorhythm

BHIIINORT inhibitor
BHIILLLLY hillbilly
BHIILLNOT billionth
BHIIMORUZ rhizobium
BHIIOPRST prohibits
BHIKLLOOS billhooks
BHIKLOOSY bookishly
BHILLNORS hornbills
BHILLNORT thornbill
BHILLPSUW bullwhips
BHILLSSTU bullshits
BHILMNOTY bimonthly
BHILOORSY boorishly
BHILRSTUY brutishly
BHIMOOSTY tomboyish
BHIOOPRST biotrophs
BHIOORRTT birthroot
BHIORRTTW birthwort
BHJOORSTW jobsworth
BHKNOOORS hornbooks
BHKORRSUW brushwork
BHLLNORSU bullhorns
BHLLOOOTT tollbooth
BHLMPSUUY subphylum
BHLOOOSTT tolbooths
BHMNOOOSU bonhomous
BHMNSTTUU thumbnuts
BHNOOOSST bosthoons
BHNOORSTX boxthorns
BIIILNSVY invisibly
BIIKNNOTV Botvinnik
BIILMSTUY sublimity
BIILNOOSV oblivions
BIILOOSUV oblivious
BIILOQTUY obliquity
BIILSTTUY subtility
BIIMMNORS brominism
BIIMMOSSZ zombiisms
BIIMNOORR Borromini
BIIMNOOST bionomist
BIIMOPRTY improbity
BIIMOSSSY symbiosis
BIKKORSYZ Korzybski
BIKLNNOSW snowblink
BIKOOSUUZ bouzoukis
BILLNOOPS spoonbill
BILLNOOSU bouillons
BILLNORST stillborn
BILLNOSUY insolubly
BILMMOSSY symbolism
BILMOORST Stromboli
BILMOSSTY symbolist
BILNOSTUU botulinus
BILOOPRTU politburo
BILOOSUVY obviously
BILORSSTU strobilus
BIMNOSSTY symbionts
BIMNRSUUV viburnums
BIMOPSTUU bumptious
BINOOOSUX obnoxious
BINOORSTU obtrusion
BIOPRSSTW bowsprits
BKKOOORSW workbooks
BKLLMNSUU numbskull
BKMOOORSW bookworms
BKOOORSTY storybook
BLLMOORSW bollworms
BLOORSTUU troublous
BNNOSTTUU unbuttons
BNOOOSSUY sonobuoys
BNOORSTUW brownouts
BNRSSSTUU sunbursts
BOOPPRRTU turboprop
BORSSTTUU outbursts
CCCDENOOT concocted
CCCEEINRT eccentric
CCCEIILPY epicyclic
CCCENOORT concocter
CCCFKOORT Cockcroft
CCCGINOOO gonococci
CCCHHIKOT Hitchcock
CCCHIINNO cinchonic
CCCHIKNOP pinchcock
CCCHILMOU colchicum
CCCHILOOT coccolith
CCCIILRTY tricyclic
CCCIKMMOR McCormick
CCCKOORSW cockcrows
CCCNOOORT concoctor
CCDDEEESU succeeded
CCDDEIINO coincided
CCDDEKLOU cuckolded
CCDDELNOU concluded
CCDDENOTU conducted
CCDEEEHKR checkered
rechecked
CCDEEEHRS screeched
CCDEEEINS decencies
CCDEEENRS credences
CCDEEERSU succeeder
CCDEEFNOT confected
CCDEEHIKW chickweed
CCDEEHIRS screiched
CCDEEHKNU unchecked
CCDEEHORT crocheted
CCDEEIINN incidence
CCDEEIKRT cricketed
CCDEEILNR encircled
CCDEEILOW colicweed
CCDEEINNY indecency
CCDEEINOT conceited
CCDEEINOV conceived
CCDEEINRS crescendi
CCDEEIOPS codpieces
CCDEELLOT collected
CCDEEMMNO commenced
CCDEENNOR concerned
CCDEENNOS ensconced
CCDEENNOT connected
CCDEENORS conceders
crescendo
CCDEENORT concerted
concreted
CCDEEORRT corrected
CCDEFIIRU crucified
CCDEGINNO conceding
CCDEGINOT decocting
CCDEHIPPU hiccupped
CCDEHNRSU scrunched
CCDEIIIPT epidictic
CCDEIIKNP picnicked
CCDEIINOS coincides
CCDEIIRTU circuited
CCDEILOOR crocodile
CCDEILRTY tricycled
CCDEILSTY dyslectic
CCDEINNOV convinced
CCDEINOOT decoction
CCDEINOTV convicted
CCDEINOUV conducive
CCDELNORU concluder
CCDELNOSU concludes
CCDELNOTU occludent
CCDENOORT Condorcet
CCDENORRU concurred
CCDENORSU conducers
CCDENOSSU concussed
CCDEORSUU succoured
CCDESSSUU succussed
CCDFKOORR Crockford
CCDGILNOU occluding
CCDGINNOU conducing
CCDHIILOR chloridic
CCDHIIMOR dichromic
CCDHIIOPT dichoptic
CCDHINOOS conchoids
CCDHKOOUW woodchuck
CCDIILNRY cylindric
CCDIILTYY cytidylic
CCDIINOSS scincoids
CCDIIOORT corticoid
CCDKLORUY cuckoldry
CCDKOOOSW woodcocks
CCDNOORTU conductor
CCDOOOSUW cocuswood
CCEEEFLNU feculence
CCEEEHHRR recherche
CCEEEHNOR coherence
CCEEEHRRS screecher
CCEEEHRSS screeches
CCEEEIKNP neckpiece
CCEEEINNS nescience
CCEEEINRT reticence
CCEEEIRSS secrecies
CCEEELORT rectocele
CCEEEMMOR ecommerce
CCEEGINOR concierge
CCEEGINOT ectogenic
CCEEHIKNR checkrein
CCEEHILMY hemicycle
CCEEHIRSS screiches
CCEEHKNNS schnecken
CCEEHKORV overcheck
CCEEHKPRS prechecks
CCEEHLORT cerecloth
CCEEHNORY coherency

CCEEHORRT crocheter
CCEEHOTTU couchette
CCEEIIPPR precipice
CCEEIKLST cleckiest
CCEEIKRRT cricketer
CCEEILNOR reconcile
CCEEILNRS encircles
CCEEILOST scolecite
CCEEILPRY pericycle
CCEEILPSY epicycles
CCEEILRST electrics
CCEEIMNOU oecumenic
CCEEIMORT ectomeric
CCEEINNNO innocence
CCEEINORS cicerones
CCEEINORT ectocrine
CCEEINORV conceiver
CCEEINOSV conceives
CCEEIOPST copesetic
CCEEIQRTU quercetic
CCEEIRRST rectrices
CCEEIRSTT tectrices
CCEEISTTU eutectics
CCEEKLLOR Cockerell
CCEEKLORS cockerels
CCEEKLORT cockleert
CCEELLORT recollect
CCEELOSTY cystocele
CCEELOTUY leucocyte
CCEEMMNOR commencer
CCEEMMNOS commences
CCEENNORT concenter
concentre
connecter
reconnect
CCEENNOSS ensconces
CCEENOOTY coenocyte
CCEENORST concretes
CCEENRSST crescents
CCEESSSSU successes
CCEFFHKOS checkoffs
CCEFFIIIL felicific
CCEFIIPSS specifics
CCEFIIRRU crucifier
CCEFIIRSU crucifies
CCEFIRRSU crucifers
CCEFKNOYY cockneyfy
CCEFLLOSU floccules
CCEGHHNOW Chengchow
CCEGHILNN clenching
CCEGHIMRU chemurgic
CCEGIKNOR cockering
CCEGILNRY recycling
CCEGINNOO oncogenic
CCEGINORY cryogenic
CCEHHIRRU churchier
CCEHHMNRU churchmen
CCEHHNRUW New Church
CCEHIILRS schlieric
CCEHIIORS chicories
CCEHIKLOO chokecoil
CCEHIKLST checklist
CCEHIKOSS cockshies
CCEHILNOR chronicle
CCEHILNRS clinchers
CCEHINORS corniches
CCEHINRRU crunchier
CCEHINRSU crunchies
scrunchie
CCEHIORST ricochets
CCEHKLNOT neckcloth
CCEHKLRSU chucklers
CCEHKMOOR checkroom
CCEHKOORS cockhorse
CCEHKORSW checkrows
CCEHKOSTU checkouts
CCEHLMORS cromlechs
CCEHLOSTY cholecyst
CCEHNNOSU scuncheon
CCEHNOSTU scutcheon
CCEHNRSSU scrunches
CCEHORRSS scorchers
CCEHORSTT crotchets
CCEHORTTY crotchety
CCEHOTTUZ zucchetto
CCEHRRTUY cutcherry
CCEHRSSTU scutchers
CCEIIIPRT epicritic
CCEIIIRST criticise
CCEIIIRTZ criticize
CCEIIKNPR picnicker
CCEIILNOT niccolite
CCEIILNST enclitics
CCEIILRST scleritic
CCEIIMOSS coseismic
CCEIINSTY cysteinic
CCEIIOPPR pericopic
CCEIKKLLO clocklike
CCEIKLLOY kilocycle
CCEIKLOSW clockwise
CCEIKNOSS cockiness
CCEILMOPS complices
CCEILNNOU nucleonic
CCEILNOSY concisely
CCEILNOTY cyclonite
CCEILNSUY unicycles
CCEILORST sclerotic
CCEILOSUV occlusive
CCEILRRSU curricles
CCEILRSTY tricycles
CCEILRSUU curlicues
CCEIMNOOS economics
CCEIMORTY microcyte
CCEIMOSST cosmetics
CCEIMRSUV cervicums
CCEINNNOY innocency
CCEINNORV convincer
CCEINNOSV convinces
CCEINOORS coercions
CCEINOOSS consocies
CCEINORRT incorrect
CCEINORTV reconvict
CCEINOSTT tectonics
CCEINPRST precincts
CCEINRSTU cinctures
CCEINRSTY syncretic
CCEINSSTY synectics
CCEIOORST creosotic
CCEIOPRSU occupiers
CCEIOPRTY precocity
CCEIORSSU succories
CCEKORRSS rockcress
CCEKORRSW corkscrew
CCELLMNNO McConnell
CCELLMRSU McCullers
CCELLNOOY colonelcy
CCELLOORT collector
CCELMNOOY monocycle
CCELMOOTY colectomy
CCELMOPST complects
CCELNSTUU succulent
CCELOPRSU corpuscle
CCELORRTY correctly
CCENNNORU unconcern
CCENNOORT connector
CCENOORST concertos
CCENOORSU concourse
CCENOORTV convector
CCENORRTU occurrent
CCENORSTU succentor
CCENOSSSU concusses
CCEOOPRSY cryoscope
CCEOOPRTT ectoproct
CCEOORRRT corrector
CCEOPPRUY preoccupy
CCEORRSSU succorers
CCEORRSUU succourer
CCEORSSSU successor
CCEORSSTU stuccoers
CCESSSSUU succusses
CCFGHIKOT cockfight
CCFHIINOO finocchio
CCFIILOOR colorific
CCFILNOST conflicts
CCFIMORRU cruciform
CCFINOSUU Confucius
CCFKLOOST cocklofts
CCFKOOOST cocksfoot
CCFLLOSUU flocculus
CCGHHINOU chincough
CCGHHINRU churching
CCGHHIOSU hiccoughs
CCGHIILNN clinching
CCGHIINPU hiccuping
CCGHIKLNU chuckling
CCGHILNTU clutching
CCGHILOOP choplogic
CCGHINNRU crunching
CCGHINOOT cootching
CCGHINORS scorching
CCGHINORU crouching
CCGHINOST scotching
CCGHINOSU couchings
CCGHINRTU crutching
CCGHINSTU scutching
CCGIINNOR cornicing

CCGIINOPP coppicing
CCGIKNOOU cuckooing
CCGILLLOY glycollic
CCGILMOOY mycologic
CCGILNOTU occulting
CCGILOORY cyclogiro
CCGINNOOO cocooning
CCGINOPUY occupying
CCGINORRU occurring
CCGINORSU succoring
CCGINOSTU stuccoing
CCHHILLRU Churchill
CCHHLORUW Low Church
CCHHOOPST hopscotch
CCHHOOSWW chowchows
CCHIIIRTT trichitic
CCHIILORT chloritic
CCHIIMOPR microchip
CCHIIMORT trichomic
CCHIINOOR chorionic
CCHIINSUZ zucchinis
CCHIIOORS isochoric
CCHIIORRT cirrhotic
trichroic
CCHILNRUY crunchily
CCHILOORT chlorotic
CCHINNOOR cornichon
CCHINRSTY strychnic
CCHIOPSTY psychotic
CCHKOOSST cockshots
CCHLNOOTY colocynth
CCIIILNOP picolinic
CCIIILNOS isoclinic
CCIIILNRT triclinic
CCIIIMRST criticism
CCIIINNOT nicotinic
CCIILLLOU colliculi
CCIILNOTY clonicity
CCIILOOST scoliotic
CCIILOPRT proclitic
CCIIMNSSY cynicisms
CCIINNOOS concision
CCIINOPSY isopycnic
CCIIORRTT tricrotic
CCIIRRTUY circuitry
CCIKKLOPS picklocks
CCIKKOSTT ticktocks
CCILMOSTU occultism
CCILNOOPY polyconic
CCILNOORU councilor
CCILNOOSU occlusion
CCILOOORT colicroot
CCILORSUU curculios
CCILOSTTU occultist
CCILOTTYY cytolytic
CCIMMOORS microcosm
CCIMNOOTY monocytic
CCIMOOPRY microcopy
CCINOOSSU conscious
CCINOPRST conscript
CCINORSTT constrict
CCIOOOPRZ coprozoic
CCIOOOPST otoscopic
CCIOOPRSU uroscopic
CCIOOSTTY otocystic
CCIOOSTXY oxytocics
CCIOOTTXY cytotoxic
CCJNNOSTU conjuncts
CCKKLOORW clockwork
CCKKLOOST stocklock
CCKMOOORS moorcocks
CCKNORSTU turncocks
CCKOOPPPY poppycock
CCKOOPSST stopcocks
CCKOPRSSU cockspurs
CCLNOORTY cyclotron
CCNORSTTU construct
CCOOPRSYY cryoscopy
CCOOSTTUU tucotucos
CCORSSSTU crosscuts
CCSTTUUUU tucutucus
CDDDEEENS descended
CDDDEEILY decidedly
CDDDEEINU undecided
CDDDEIORS discorded
CDDDIIOSY diddicoys
CDDEEEFLT deflected
CDDEEEINV evidenced
CDDEEENRS descender
redescend
CDDEEENST decedents
CDDEEEOPR proceeded
CDDEEFKOR defrocked
CDDEEGLLU cudgelled
CDDEEHLSU scheduled
CDDEEHNRU chundered
CDDEEHSSU duchessed
CDDEEIJST disjected
CDDEEIKRR derricked
CDDEEINRS discerned
rescinded
CDDEEINRU reinduced
CDDEEINSX exscinded
CDDEEIPRT predicted
CDDEEISST dissected
CDDEEITUV deductive
CDDEEKOST destocked
CDDEELNPU peduncled
CDDEELOPU decoupled
CDDEELPRU precluded
CDDEEMMNO commended
CDDEEMNNO condemned
CDDEEMNRU credendum
CDDEENNOS condensed
CDDEENNOT contended
CDDEENNOU denounced
CDDEENSUU unseduced
CDDEEPRTY decrypted
CDDEFIILU dulcified
CDDEGINTU deducting
CDDEGIOTY Dodge City
CDDEHORRT Dordrecht
CDDEIILMO domiciled
CDDEIILRU ridiculed
CDDEIINRT dendritic
CDDEIIOSV videodisc
CDDEIIRST discredit
CDDEILOSS disclosed
CDDEILOST cloddiest
CDDEIMOOU duodecimo
CDDEINOTU deduction
CDDEIOSUU deciduous
CDDEIRSTU cruddiest
CDDEISSSU discussed
CDDELNOUU unclouded
CDDELORWY crowdedly
CDDENORUW uncrowded
CDDEOORSW codewords
CDDHHILOO childhood
CDDHIIORY hydriodic
CDDHIIQTU quidditch
CDDIIILOP diploidic
CDDIISSTY dytiscids
CDDILNOOY condyloid
CDEEEEFNR deference
CDEEEELRT reelected
CDEEEERRT reerected
CDEEEERSX exceeders
CDEEEFITV defective
CDEEEFLRT reflected
CDEEEFPRT perfected
CDEEEGINR decreeing
CDEEEGINX exceeding
CDEEEGLNT neglected
CDEEEHKNP henpecked
CDEEEHLNO echeloned
CDEEEHQRU chequered
CDEEEIMRT decimeter
decimetre
CDEEEINNS desinence
CDEEEINPT centipede
CDEEEINRS residence
CDEEEINRT intercede
CDEEEINSV evidences
CDEEEINUV undeceive
CDEEEIPRT receipted
CDEEEIPRV perceived
CDEEEIPTV deceptive
CDEEEIRSV deceivers
CDEEEIRSX exercised
CDEEEITTV detective
CDEEELLOT decollete
CDEEELNOR redolence
CDEEELORT electrode
CDEEELPRT prelected
CDEEELSST deselects
CDEEEMNRT decrement
CDEEENNST sentenced
CDEEENPRT precedent
CDEEENQSU sequenced
CDEEEOPRR proceeder
CDEEEORRT retrocede
CDEEEORRV recovered
CDEEEPRSS precessed
CDEEEPRST respected
sceptered

CDEEEPRTX excerpted
CDEEERSTT detecters
CDEEFFIOR officered
CDEEFGINT defecting
CDEEFHLRS feldscher
CDEEFIILM fieldmice
CDEEFIINT deficient
CDEEFIIOT foeticide
CDEEFIIPS specified
CDEEFIIRT certified
rectified
CDEEFIIST feticides
CDEEFIKLR flickered
CDEEFILNT inflected
CDEEFILTU deceitful
CDEEFINOT defection
CDEEFIRTY decertify
CDEEFKORS foredecks
CDEEFKOST feedstock
CDEEFLORT deflector
CDEEFNORR conferred
CDEEFNOSS confessed
CDEEFORST defectors
CDEEFORSU refocused
CDEEGHIRS screighed
CDEEGIILN diligence
CDEEGIIMR germicide
CDEEGIINN indigence
CDEEGIINT digenetic
CDEEGIINV deceiving
CDEEGIIRS regicides
CDEEGIJNT dejecting
CDEEGILOR Coleridge
CDEEGILRY glyceride
CDEEGINNR decerning
CDEEGINOR endoergic
CDEEGINOS genocides
CDEEGINPR preceding
CDEEGINTT detecting
CDEEGIOSS geodesics
CDEEGIOST geodetics
CDEEGIRSU cudgeries
CDEEGLLRU cudgeller
CDEEGNORV converged
CDEEGNOST congested
CDEEHHIRS cherished
CDEEHIIST ethicised
CDEEHIITZ ethicized
CDEEHIKLS helidecks
CDEEHIKNT thickened
CDEEHIKRS shickered
CDEEHIKRW whickered
CDEEHILLS chiselled
CDEEHIMRS Remscheid
CDEEHINST dehiscent
CDEEHIPRS deciphers
CDEEHIRTT chittered
CDEEHITWW witchweed
CDEEHKOSU deckhouse
CDEEHLORT reclothed
CDEEHLORY hydrocele
CDEEHLPPS schlepped
CDEEHLQSU squelched
CDEEHLSSU schedules
CDEEHNRRS drenchers
CDEEHNRTU chuntered
CDEEHORTU retouched
CDEEHRSTT stretched
CDEEHSSSU duchesses
CDEEIILRT deciliter
decilitre
CDEEIILTV videlicet
CDEEIIMNS medicines
CDEEIIMPR epidermic
CDEEIIMPS epidemics
CDEEIIMPU epicedium
CDEEIIMRT cetrimide
CDEEIIMRV decemviri
vermicide
CDEEIINST indictees
CDEEIIPRR cirripede
CDEEIIPST pesticide
CDEEIIPTV depictive
CDEEIIRTV directive
CDEEIISTT dietetics
CDEEIJNOT dejection
CDEEIJPRU prejudice
CDEEIJRUV verjuiced
CDEEIKLLN nickelled
CDEEIKLNR clinkered
CDEEIKLNU duncelike
CDEEIKLRS slickered
CDEEIKNQU quickened
CDEEIKNRS snickered
CDEEIKSST stickseed
CDEEIKSTW stickweed
wickedest
CDEEILLNP pencilled
CDEEILNNO indolence
CDEEILNRS decliners
CDEEILNST denticles
stenciled
CDEEILORR Cordelier
CDEEILORS creolised
CDEEILORZ creolized
CDEEILQSU liquesced
CDEEILRST derelicts
CDEEILTXY excitedly
CDEEIMMXY myxedemic
CDEEIMNNU decennium
CDEEIMNOU eudemonic
CDEEIMNPU impudence
CDEEIMPRS premedics
CDEEIMRSV decemvirs
CDEEINNOR endocrine
CDEEINNSU secundine
CDEEINOPT deception
CDEEINORT recondite
CDEEINOST sectioned
CDEEINOTT detection
CDEEINPST inspected
CDEEINQUY De Quincey
CDEEINRRS discerner
rescinder
CDEEINRST stridence
CDEEINRSU reinduces
CDEEINRSY residency
CDEEINSTU inductees
CDEEINTUX unexcited
CDEEIORSV divorcees
CDEEIORSX exorcised
CDEEIORXZ exorcized
CDEEIOSTX coexisted
CDEEIOTTU eutectoid
CDEEIPRST depicters
CDEEIPRSU pedicures
CDEEIPRTU depicture
CDEEIRRSS descriers
CDEEIRRST redirects
CDEEIRRTU recruited
CDEEIRSTT trisected
CDEEIRTTU certitude
rectitude
CDEEIRTUV reductive
CDEEISTUV seductive
CDEEJOPRT projected
CDEEKOOPR precooked
CDEEKORST restocked
CDEEKORSW rockweeds
CDEELLMOP compelled
CDEELLNRU cullender
CDEELMNTU demulcent
CDEELMOPT completed
CDEELNORY redolency
CDEELNOSU counseled
CDEELNPSU peduncles
CDEELNPTU centupled
CDEELOPPY pelecypod
CDEELOPSU decouples
CDEELORSS sclerosed
CDEELPRSU precludes
CDEELRSTU clustered
CDEELRSUX excluders
CDEELRTTU cluttered
declutter
CDEEMMNOR recommend
CDEEMMNOT commented
CDEEMNNOR condemner
CDEEMNNOT contemned
CDEEMNOOS comedones
CDEEMOOPS decompose
CDEEMORST ectoderms
CDEENNORS condenser
CDEENNORT contender
CDEENNORU denouncer
renounced
CDEENNOSS condenses
CDEENNOST consented
CDEENNOSU denounces
CDEENNOTT contented
CDEENNRSU scunnered
CDEENNSTU unscented
CDEENOOPS endoscope
CDEENOORT coroneted
CDEENOQRU conquered
CDEENORRW recrowned

CDEENORSS seconders
CDEENORSV conserved
conversed
CDEENORTU countered
recounted
CDEENORTV converted
CDEENORUV uncovered
CDEENOSTT contested
CDEENOSTX coextends
CDEENPRTY encrypted
CDEENRRTU decurrent
CDEENRSSU crudeness
CDEENRSTU encrusted
CDEENRSUU unsecured
CDEENRSUW unscrewed
CDEENSUUX unexcused
CDEEOORST creosoted
CDEEOOSTV dovecotes
CDEEOPRRR prerecord
CDEEOPRRU procedure
reproduce
CDEEOPRSS processed
CDEEOPRTT protected
CDEEOQRTU croqueted
CDEEOQTTU coquetted
CDEEORRRS recorders
rerecords
CDEEORRSS recrossed
CDEEORSTT detectors
CDEEPPRSU scuppered
CDEEPRSSU percussed
CDEEPSSTU suspected
CDEERSTTU scuttered
CDEERSTUY curtseyed
CDEERTTUV curvetted
CDEFFIORU coiffured
CDEFGIINU fungicide
CDEFGINOR deforcing
CDEFHIILL Lichfield
CDEFHIIRR Friedrich
CDEFHIOSS codfishes
CDEFIIILS filicides
CDEFIIISS cissified
CDEFIIIST fideistic
CDEFIILNT inflicted
CDEFIILSU dulcifies
CDEFIINST disinfect
CDEFIIORS codifiers
scorified
CDEFIKLOR frolicked
CDEFIKOSS fossicked
CDEFILNOR cornfield
CDEFIMNOR confirmed
CDEFINNOT confident
CDEFINORS confiders
CDEFINTUY fecundity
CDEFKNORU unfrocked
CDEFMNOOR conformed
CDEFMOORT comforted
CDEFNOORW downforce
CDEGGILNU cudgeling
CDEGGLNOU unclogged
CDEGHIINS dehiscing
CDEGHINNO chignoned
CDEGHINNR drenching
CDEGHOSTT Gottsched
CDEGIIKNR dickering
CDEGIILNN declining
CDEGIILOO ideologic
CDEGIIMRU demiurgic
CDEGIINNR cindering
CDEGIINOT coediting
CDEGIINOV devoicing
CDEGIINPT depicting
CDEGIINRT crediting
directing
CDEGIKNOR redocking
CDEGIKNOT docketing
CDEGILNPU decupling
CDEGILNSU secluding
CDEGILNUX excluding
CDEGILOOP logopedic
CDEGILOSU glucoside
CDEGILOSY glycoside
CDEGINNOS consigned
seconding
CDEGINORR recording
CDEGINRSY descrying
CDEGINSSY dysgenics
CDEGLLOOU collogued
CDEGLORST goldcrest
CDEGNORSU scrounged
CDEHHINTU unhitched
CDEHIIKLL childlike
CDEHIILNO lichenoid
CDEHIILOS helicoids
CDEHIILRT Dirichlet
CDEHIIMOS homicides
CDEHIINOS echinoids
CDEHIIORT dichroite
CDEHIKLLO hillocked
CDEHIKOOY doohickey
CDEHIKPSY physicked
CDEHIKRSW herdwicks
CDEHILLSS childless
CDEHILOOR choleroid
CDEHILORS chlorides
CDEHILPST stepchild
CDEHILSST ditchless
CDEHINORT chondrite
threnodic
CDEHINOSU cushioned
CDEHIOORT Theodoric
CDEHIORRS cirrhosed
CDEHIORSW chordwise
CDEHIORTW dowitcher
CDEHKLSSU shelducks
CDEHKNOOR Rodchenko
CDEHKOSUV duckshove
CDEHLMOST Dolmetsch
CDEHLNORU chondrule
CDEHLNOTU unclothed
CDEHLOOSS deschools
CDEHMOOSZ schmoozed
CDEHNOOPS chenopods
CDEHNOOTT thecodont
CDEHNOTUU untouched
CDEHOOOPS hodoscope
CDEIIILSS silicides
CDEIIILSV civilised
CDEIIILVZ civilized
CDEIIIMST miticides
CDEIIIRST sideritic
CDEIIKKSS sidekicks
CDEIILLNO celloidin
decillion
CDEIILMOS domiciles
CDEIILMTU multicide
CDEIILNTU inductile
CDEIILORT doleritic
CDEIILOST idiolects
solicited
CDEIILOSU delicious
CDEIILPSS disciples
CDEIILRRU ridiculer
CDEIILRSU ridicules
CDEIILTVY declivity
CDEIIMNOS meniscoid
CDEIIMNTU ctenidium
CDEIIMNTY mendicity
CDEIIMOPS miscopied
CDEIIMRST misdirect
CDEIINNOT incondite
nicotined
CDEIINNST incidents
CDEIINOPT depiction
CDEIINORT cretinoid
direction
CDEIINOSS decisions
CDEIINRST indicters
CDEIINRTT interdict
CDEIINSTU cutinised
CDEIINTUV inductive
CDEIINTUZ cutinized
CDEIIOOSU dioecious
CDEIIORST siderotic
CDEIIORTY iridocyte
CDEIIORUX uxoricide
CDEIIORVV divorcive
CDEIIPRRS cirripeds
CDEIIRRTX directrix
CDEIIRSTU diuretics
CDEIJNNOO conjoined
CDEIKLLOR rollicked
CDEIKLLOU cloudlike
CDEIKLLRS drecksill
CDEIKLRST strickled
CDEIKLRSU ludericks
CDEIKOSST diestocks
CDEILLLOU celluloid
CDEILLORS colliders
CDEILLOSU lodicules
CDEILLTUY ductilely
CDEILMOPY polydemic
CDEILMRSU dulcimers
CDEILNOOS colonised

CDEILNOOZ colonized
CDEILNRSY cylinders
CDEILNSSU lucidness
CDEILOORZ colorized
CDEILOPSU clupeoids
CDEILORSS discloser
CDEILOSSS discloses
CDEILOSTU cloudiest
CDEILPRSU surpliced
CDEILRTUY credulity
CDEIMMNOO incommode
CDEIMMOTT committed
CDEIMNNOT condiment
CDEIMNOPR princedom
CDEIMNORS crimsoned
CDEIMNORU indecorum
CDEIMNOSU Nicodemus
CDEIMNPUY impudency
CDEIMNSSU mucidness
CDEIMOPRS comprised
CDEIMOSST domestics
CDEINNOTU continued
unnoticed
CDEINOOTX endotoxic
CDEINOPRS conspired
CDEINOPSY dyspnoeic
CDEINORSS considers
incrossed
CDEINORST centroids
doctrines
CDEINORSU coinsured
decurions
CDEINORTU introduce
reduction
CDEINORTV contrived
CDEINOSST consisted
CDEINOSTU eductions
seduction
CDEINPRSS prescinds
CDEINRSSU curdiness
CDEINRSTU incrusted
CDEINRSTY stridency
CDEINRTTU tinctured
CDEIOORRS corrodies
CDEIOORST coeditors
CDEIOPRRT predictor
CDEIOPRST depictors
CDEIOPSTY copyedits
CDEIORRST creditors
directors
CDEIORRSV codrivers
divorcers
CDEIORRTY directory
CDEIORSSS scissored
CDEIORSST dissector
CDEIORSSU discourse
CDEIORSSV discovers
CDEIORSTV discovert
CDEIORSVY discovery
CDEIOSSTU custodies
CDEIPPSTY dyspeptic
CDEIRSSSU discusser
CDEISSSSU discusses
CDEKLMORS clerkdoms
CDEKLNPUU unplucked
CDEKLOORY crookedly
CDEKNOORU undercook
CDEKOOPRU puckerood
CDELLOOPS clodpoles
scolloped
CDELLORSU colluders
CDELLOSSU cloudless
CDELLOSTU cloudlets
CDELMOOPU coupledom
CDELMPRSU scrumpled
CDELNOORS condolers
CDELNOORT decontrol
CDELNOORU undercool
CDELNOOSW closedown
CDELNOOTY cotyledon
CDELNOOVV convolved
CDELNOPUU uncoupled
CDELNORSU scoundrel
CDELNOSTU consulted
CDELNOSUV convulsed
CDELOORSU coloureds
decolours
CDELOORUV overcloud
CDELORSUU credulous
CDEMMOOOR commodore
CDEMMOORT dotcommer
CDEMNOORW downcomer
CDEMNOOSW comedowns
downcomes
CDEMNOSTU documents
CDEMOOPRT comported
CDEMOOPST composted
CDENNOORS condoners
CDENNORUW uncrowned
CDENNOTUU uncounted
CDENOOPSY endoscopy
CDENOORRT corrodent
CDENOORST consorted
creodonts
CDENOORTT contorted
CDENOORTU contoured
CDENORSSU uncrossed
CDENORSTU construed
CDENPRTUU punctured
CDENRSTUU undercuts
CDEOOPRRT proctored
CDEOOPSST postcodes
CDEOORRRS corroders
CDEOORRVW overcrowd
CDEOORSWW woodscrew
CDEOPRRSU producers
CDEOPRRTU corrupted
CDEORSTTU destructo
CDEORSTUV dustcover
CDERSSTTU destructs
CDFFIILTU difficult
CDFGHILNO goldfinch
CDFGIINNO confiding
CDFGIINOY codifying
CDFGIOOTY City of God
CDFHINORY chondrify
CDFIIMOST discomfit
CDFIIORSU sudorific
CDFIKORSS disfrocks
CDFIMOORR cordiform
CDFNNOOSU confounds
CDGHIILNY chidingly
CDGIIINNT indicting
CDGIIINOT indigotic
CDGIILLNO colliding
CDGIILNNU including
CDGIILOTT diglottic
CDGIINNTU inducting
CDGIINORV divorcing
CDGIKLNSU ducklings
CDGIKLORS gridlocks
CDGILLNOU colluding
CDGILNNOO condoling
CDGILNNOY condignly
CDGILNOSS scoldings
CDGILOOSY discology
CDGINNNOO condoning
CDGINNOOR cordoning
CDGINOORR corroding
CDGINOORT doctoring
CDGINOPRU producing
CDGNOOSTU gonoducts
CDHHIIOTY ichthyoid
CDHHILOST dishcloth
CDHIIINOT chitinoid
CDHIILLNW windchill
CDHIIMOPR dimorphic
CDHIIMORS dichroism
CDHIIOORS chorioids
CDHIIORRS scirrhoid
CDHIIORSY isohydric
CDHIIOSSZ schizoids
CDHIIRRTY trihydric
CDHILMNOO Moon Child
CDHILOOPS chilopods
CDHILOSTU dishclout
CDHIMNOOR monorchid
CDHIMOOTY dichotomy
CDHIMSTYY dysthymic
CDHINOPSY dysphonic
CDHIOOPRY chiropody
CDHIOOPSZ schizopod
CDHIOORST trochoids
CDHIOPRSW whipcords
CDHIOPRSY dysphoric
CDHLOOPSY copyholds
CDHMNOOOR monochord
CDHNNOOOU coonhound
CDHNOOORT notochord
CDHNOOTUW touchdown
CDHOOOPSW woodchops
CDHOOORTW torchwood
CDHOOOTUW touchwood
CDHOORRSU urochords
CDIIILMNS diclinism
CDIIIMNSS minidiscs

CDIIINNOT indiction
CDIIISTVY viscidity
CDIIJOSUU judicious
CDIIKNNOS Dickinson
CDIIKPSST dipsticks
CDIILMOOT dolomitic
CDIILNOPT diplontic
CDIILNOSU diclinous
CDIILOOPZ diplozoic
CDIILPTUY duplicity
CDIILTTUY ductility
CDIIMNPUY pycnidium
CDIIMORST dicrotism
CDIINNOOT condition
CDIINNOTU induction
CDIINOPRY cyprinoid
CDIINORST indictors
CDIINPRSY cyprinids
CDIINTWYY Windy City
CDIIOOPRS scorpioid
CDIIOPRST dioptrics
CDIIORRTT tortricid
CDIIPRSTU tricuspid
CDIIRSSTT districts
CDIJNOTUY jocundity
CDIJNSSTU disjuncts
CDIKKOPRS dropkicks
CDIKMRSTU drumstick
CDIKNOSSW windsocks
CDILLMOOU collodium
CDILLNOOO collodion
CDILOORSS discolors
CDILOORSU discolour
CDILOOSTY cotyloids
CDILORSUU ludicrous
CDIMMNOOS discommon
CDIMMOOTY commodity
CDIMNOORT microdont
CDIMNOORU doronicum
CDIMNORSY syndromic
CDIMOOPRR prodromic
CDIMOORST microdots
CDINNQSUU quidnuncs
CDINORSSW crosswind
CDINORSTU inductors
CDINOSSTU discounts
CDIOORRRS corridors
CDIOPRSSU cuspidors
CDIRRSTUU duricrust
CDKKNNOOW knockdown
CDKKNOOOR doorknock
CDKOOORSW corkwoods
CDKOOOSTW Stockwood
Woodstock
CDLOOSSTW Cotswolds
CDMNNORUU conundrum
CDMNOOPSU compounds
CDNNOOOST conodonts
CDNNOOTUW countdown
CDOORRSSW crossword
CDOORRSUY corduroys
CEEEEFFNR efference
CEEEEFNRR reference
CEEEEGMNR emergence
CEEEEHILP heelpiece
CEEEEHMNV vehemence
CEEEEIPSY eyepieces
CEEEELSST selectees
CEEEENRRV reverence
CEEEFFITV effective
CEEEFFLNU effluence
CEEEFFRST effecters
CEEEFHLTT flechette
CEEEFIKLN fencelike
CEEEFILST fleeciest
CEEEFINNR inference
CEEEFLNRU refluence
CEEEFLNSS fenceless
CEEEFNORR conferree
ferrocene
reenforce
CEEEFNORS conferees
CEEEFNQRU frequence
CEEEFPRRT perfecter
CEEEGILNT telegenic
CEEEGINRS regencies
CEEEGINRT energetic
CEEEGINSX exigences
CEEEGISTX exegetics
CEEEGLNRT neglecter
CEEEGMNRY emergency
CEEEGNRSV vergences
CEEEHIKLL leechlike
CEEEHIKST cheekiest
CEEEHILRS lecheries
CEEEHILST scheelite
CEEEHINNR inherence
CEEEHIRST cheeriest
CEEEHISST cheesiest
CEEEHKLSS cheekless
CEEEHLNTY entelechy
CEEEHLRSS cheerless
CEEEHOPRS ecosphere
CEEEHOPST sheepcote
CEEEHQRUX exchequer
CEEEHRSSW eschewers
CEEEHRTTV chevrette
CEEEIIMPT timepiece
CEEEIINRV vicereine
CEEEIJRTV rejective
CEEEIJSTV ejectives
CEEEILLNT clientele
CEEEILNRS relicense
CEEEILNSS licensees
CEEEILNST celestine
telecines
CEEEILPSS epicleses
CEEEILRST Leicester
CEEEILSTT celestite
CEEEILSTV electives
selective
CEEEIMNNS eminences
CEEEIMNSX excisemen
CEEEIMNTT cementite
CEEEIMRRS merceries
mercerise
CEEEIMRRZ mercerize
CEEEIMRST semierect
CEEEINNPT penitence
CEEEINNRT renitence
CEEEINNST enceintes
sentience
CEEEINOPS nosepiece
CEEEINPRT epicenter
epicentre
CEEEINRSS sceneries
CEEEINRSU esurience
CEEEINSTX existence
CEEEIPRRS creperies
CEEEIPRRV perceiver
CEEEIPRST creepiest
CEEEIPRSV perceives
CEEEIPRTV receptive
CEEEIPTVX exceptive
CEEEIRRSV receivers
CEEEIRRSX exerciser
CEEEIRSSV recessive
CEEEIRSSX exercises
sexercise
CEEEIRSTV secretive
CEEEIRTVX excretive
CEEEISSVX excessive
CEEEITUVX executive
CEEEJMNTT ejectment
CEEEJRRST rejecters
CEEEKKMST Kecskemét
CEEEKORRT rocketeer
CEEELLNRS crenelles
CEEELLNTX excellent
CEEELMNST selectmen
CEEELNOQU eloquence
CEEELNOSY Ceylonese
CEEELOPST telescope
CEEELPRST preelects
preselect
CEEELRSST reselects
CEEELRSTT electrets
CEEELRSTV cleverest
CEEEMNRRT recrement
CEEEMNRST cementers
cerements
CEEEMNRTX excrement
CEEEMORST ectomeres
CEEENNORV reconvene
CEEENNSST senescent
sentences
CEEENORTT entrecote
CEEENOSTY synoecete
CEEENPRSS presences
CEEENPRST pretences
CEEENQRSU sequencer
CEEENQSSU sequences
CEEENRRSS screeners
CEEENRSST erectness
CEEEOPRRU eurocreep
CEEEORRRV recoverer

CEEEPRRST respecter
CEEEPRSSS precesses
CEEEPRSTU persecute
CEEERRSTX excreters
CEEERSSST sesterces
CEEERSTUX executers
CEEFFGINT effecting
CEEFFIINT efficient
CEEFFIORS Escoffier
CEEFFIOSU coiffeuse
CEEFFOOPT coffeepot
CEEFFORST effectors
CEEFGLNTU genuflect
CEEFHIKRS kerchiefs
CEEFHIPSY speechify
CEEFHLNRS flenchers
CEEFHLRST fletchers
CEEFIINTV infective
CEEFIIPRS specifier
CEEFIIPSS specifies
CEEFIIRRT certifier
rectifier
CEEFIIRST certifies
rectifies
CEEFILNNU influence
CEEFILRTY electrify
CEEFIMPRT imperfect
CEEFINORR reinforce
CEEFINORT refection
CEEFINRST infecters
reinfects
CEEFINTTU fettucine
CEEFIRRST firecrest
CEEFLNRSU screenful
CEEFLNRSY flyscreen
CEEFLOORS foreclose
CEEFLORRT reflector
CEEFLORSS forceless
CEEFLORSU fluoresce
CEEFLPRTY perfectly
CEEFMOORT focometer
CEEFNOPRU fourpence
CEEFNORRR conferrer
CEEFNORRS confreres
enforcers
CEEFNOSSS confesses
CEEFNQRUY frequency
CEEFNRSTU rufescent
CEEFOOPST fetoscope
CEEFOPRRT perfector
CEEFOPRST perfectos
CEEFORRTY refectory
CEEFORSSU refocuses
CEEGHIMNO hegemonic
CEEGHINOR reechoing
CEEGHINRW Greenwich
CEEGHINSW eschewing
CEEGHLOSW cogwheels
CEEGIINRV receiving
CEEGIJNRT rejecting
CEEGIKNOT ketogenic
CEEGIKNRS greensick
CEEGILLNX excelling
CEEGILNOT telegonic
CEEGILNRY glycerine
CEEGILNST selecting
CEEGIMNNT cementing
CEEGIMNOP Compiègne
CEEGIMORT geometric
CEEGINNOS consignee
CEEGINNOX xenogenic
CEEGINNRS screening
secerning
CEEGINNRT centering
CEEGINNST ignescent
CEEGINOOR ecoregion
CEEGINOOT oogenetic
CEEGINORS congeries
recognise
CEEGINORX exergonic
CEEGINORZ recognize
CEEGINPTX excepting
expecting
CEEGINRSS recessing
CEEGINRST resecting
screeting
secreting
CEEGINRSU urgencies
CEEGINRTX excreting
CEEGINSTX exsecting
CEEGINTUX executing
CEEGIORRS groceries
CEEGKNOOS gooseneck
CEEGLMNRY clergymen
CEEGLNOOS Congolese
CEEGLNORT neglector
CEEGNNOOS oncogenes
CEEGNNORS congeners
CEEGNORSV converges
CEEGORRSU Courrèges
CEEGORTTU courgette
CEEHHIRRS cherisher
CEEHHIRSS cherishes
CEEHHIRVW whichever
CEEHIILLN helicline
CEEHIILRU Richelieu
CEEHIIPTT epithetic
CEEHIIRTT erethitic
CEEHIISST ethicises
CEEHIISTZ ethicizes
CEEHIKNRT kitchener
thickener
CEEHIKNTT kitchenet
CEEHIKPPR pikeperch
CEEHIKRST sketchier
CEEHILLMS schlemiel
CEEHILLNS chenilles
CEEHILLRS chiseller
CEEHILNOS lichenose
CEEHILNRS schlieren
CEEHILNSS Schlesien
CEEHILNTY ethylenic
CEEHILPRT telpheric
CEEHILRSV cleverish
CEEHILRSW clerihews
CEEHILSTT telestich
CEEHIMORT theoremic
CEEHIMPRY hyperemic
CEEHIMRSW shrewmice
CEEHINNRY inherency
CEEHINPRS enciphers
CEEHINPRT phrenetic
CEEHINPST phenetics
CEEHINQTU technique
CEEHINRRS enrichers
Schreiner
CEEHINSST techiness
CEEHINSTU euthenics
CEEHINSTZ Nietzsche
CEEHIOPSW showpiece
CEEHIORRT torchiere
CEEHIORSS coheiress
CEEHIORTT theoretic
CEEHIPRST herpetics
CEEHIRRST Streicher
CEEHISSTT chestiest
esthetics
CEEHISTTT tetchiest
CEEHKNNOR Chernenko
CEEHKNORV Cherenkov
CEEHKRSST sketchers
CEEHLLNOP cellphone
CEEHLMOOS hemocoels
CEEHLORST reclothes
CEEHLORSU lecherous
CEEHLPRSU sepulcher
sepulchre
CEEHLQRSU squelcher
CEEHLQSSU squelches
CEEHLRWYY Wycherley
CEEHMNORZ chernozem
CEEHMOSTY hemocytes
CEEHNOPRR percheron
CEEHNQRSU quenchers
CEEHNRRST trenchers
CEEHOPRSY corypheеs
CEEHOPSTT pochettes
CEEHOPTTY ectophyte
CEEHORRST Rochester
torcheres
CEEHORRTU retoucher
CEEHORSTU retouches
CEEHRRSTT stretcher
CEEHRSSTT stretches
CEEHRSTTU teuchters
CEEIIJNTV injective
CEEIIKLNN nickeline
CEEIILNPR pericline
CEEIILNRT lienteric
CEEIILNST insectile
CEEIILPPT epileptic
CEEIILPRX preexilic
CEEIILPSS epiclesis
CEEIIMMNN imminence
CEEIIMNPS epicenism
CEEIIMNRS reminisce

CEEIIMOST semeiotic
CEEIIMPRS imprecise
CEEIIMPST epistemic
CEEIINNOR eirenicon
CEEIINNRS insincere
CEEIINNRT encrinite
CEEIINNTV incentive
CEEIINPRT recipient
CEEIINPTV inceptive
CEEIINPTX excipient
CEEIINTVV invective
CEEIIOPST poeticise
CEEIIOPTZ poeticize
CEEIIORST eroticise
CEEIIORTZ eroticize
CEEIIOSST societies
CEEIIPRSS epicrises
spiceries
CEEIJLSSU juiceless
CEEIJNORT rejection
CEEIJNOST ejections
CEEIJNRTT interject
CEEIJORRS rejoicers
CEEIJRSUV verjuices
CEEIKLLRR clerklier
CEEIKLNNS necklines
CEEIKLNSW Sweelinck
CEEIKLPRS pickerels
CEEIKLRSW screwlike
CEEIKMORS mockeries
CEEIKNOPS kinescope
CEEIKNQRU requicken
CEEIKNRSS sickeners
CEEIKOORS cookeries
CEEIKOPRW piecework
workpiece
CEEIKORRS rockeries
CEEIKPRST picketers
CEEILLLPS pellicles
CEEILLLTU cellulite
CEEILLNOR Corneille
CEEILLNPR penciller
CEEILLNST lenticels
lenticles
CEEILLNTT intellect
CEEILMNNT inclement
CEEILMNOP policemen
CEEILMNSU luminesce
CEEILMOST comeliest
CEEILMRSS merciless
CEEILNNOS insolence
CEEILNORT centriole
CEEILNOST elections
selection
CEEILNPRS pencilers
CEEILNPRT princelet
CEEILNPST splenetic
CEEILNRRS recliners
CEEILNRSS licensers
silencers
CEEILNRSY sincerely
CEEILNRTV ventricle
CEEILNRUV virulence
CEEILORRS recoilers
CEEILORSX excelsior
CEEILOSSS isosceles
CEEILOSSV voiceless
CEEILPRSS eclipsers
priceless
CEEILPRSY precisely
CEEILQSSU liquesces
CEEILRSST sclerites
CEEILRSSV versicles
CEEILRSTU cruelties
reticules
CEEILRSTW crewelist
CEEILRSUV reclusive
CEEILSSTT testicles
CEEILSSUU Seleucus I
CEEILSSUV seclusive
CEEILSUVX exclusive
CEEIMMNSU ecumenism
CEEIMMORR micromere
CEEIMMOTT committee
CEEIMNNRT increment
CEEIMNOOS economies
economise
CEEIMNOOZ economize
CEEIMNOPT impotence
CEEIMNORR merocrine
CEEIMNOST centesimo
CEEIMNOWX New Mexico
CEEIMNPSS specimens
CEEIMNSTU intumesce
CEEIMOSTY meiocytes
CEEIMRRSU mercuries
CEEIMSSTT smectites
CEEINNNSV Vincennes
CEEINNORS recension
CEEINNRTY renitency
CEEINNSTY sentiency
CEEINOPRS preconise
CEEINOPRT reception
CEEINOPRZ preconize
CEEINOPST potencies
CEEINOPTX exception
CEEINORSS recession
CEEINORST erections
neoterics
resection
secretion
CEEINORSU cinereous
CEEINORSX exocrines
CEEINORTX excretion
CEEINOSSS secession
CEEINOSTX exsection
CEEINOTUX execution
CEEINPRRU prurience
CEEINPRST prentices
prescient
reinspect
CEEINPRTT intercept
CEEINPSSX sixpences
CEEINQRTU quercetin
CEEINQSTU quiescent
CEEINRRSV scrivener
CEEINRSSU sinecures
CEEINRSTT intersect
CEEINRSTU centuries
CEEINRSTV virescent
CEEINRSUY esuriency
CEEINSSTY necessity
CEEIOOPRS cooperies
CEEIOORTZ ozocerite
CEEIOPPRS pericopes
periscope
CEEIOPPSS episcopes
CEEIOPRRT receiptor
CEEIOPRRV overprice
CEEIOPSST cespitose
CEEIORRSS sorceries
CEEIORRST corsetier
rectories
CEEIORRSX exorciser
CEEIORRXZ exorcizer
CEEIORSSU sericeous
CEEIORSSX exorcises
CEEIORSXZ exorcizes
CEEIPRSST tricepses
CEEIPSTTU Epictetus
CEEIRRRTU recruiter
CEEIRRSUV recursive
CEEIRSSTU cerussite
CEEIRSSTW screwiest
CEEIRSUVX excursive
CEEIRTUXX executrix
CEEISSTTU cutesiest
CEEJORRST rejectors
CEEJORRTT retroject
CEEKLOTUY leukocyte
CEEKNORRS reckoners
CEEKOPRSX oxpeckers
CEELLLOSU cellulose
CEELLMNTY clemently
CEELLMOPR compeller
CEELLMOSU molecules
CEELLMOWY welcomely
CEELLNOSU nucleoles
CEELLPRSU cupellers
CEELLRSTU cruellest
CEELMMNSU musclemen
CEELMNOUW unwelcome
CEELMOPRT completer
CEELMOPST completes
CEELMOPSX complexes
CEELMORSW welcomers
CEELMOTYY myelocyte
CEELNORSS enclosers
CEELNORST electrons
CEELNORSU enclosure
CEELNOSSS closeness
CEELNPRUU purulence
CEELNPSTU centuples
CEELNRSSU cruelness
CEELNSSST scentless
CEELNSSUU nucleuses

CEELOOPRT coleopter
CEELOPRRT prelector
CEELOPSTY telescopy
CEELORSSS scleroses
CEELORSST corselets
selectors
CEELORSSV coverless
CEELORSTU Le Creusot
CEELORSTV coverlets
CEELORSUX exclosure
CEELRRSTU lecturers
CEELRSSST crestless
CEEMMNORT commenter
CEEMNNORT contemner
CEEMNOPTT competent
CEEMNORSW newcomers
CEEMNOSYZ coenzymes
CEEMNSTTU tumescent
CEEMOOPRS recompose
CEEMOORSV comeovers
overcomes
CEEMORRTY cryometer
CEEMOSSTY ecosystem
CEENNORRT rencontre
CEENNORRU renouncer
CEENNORST consenter
CEENNORSU renounces
CEENNORSV conveners
CEENNORTU encounter
CEENNRSSU sunscreen
CEENOOPST copestone
CEENOPRRS precensor
CEENOPRRT precentor
CEENOPSTT Pentecost
CEENOPSTW twopences
CEENOQRRU reconquer
CEENORRSV conserver
converser
CEENORRTV converter
reconvert
CEENORSSV conserves
converses
CEENORSTT contester
CEENORSTW sweetcorn
CEENORSVY conveyers
reconveys
CEENPPSTU tuppences
CEENRRRTU recurrent
CEENRRSSU censurers
CEENRRTUX excurrent
CEEOORRSV overscore
CEEOORSST creosotes
CEEOPPRRT preceptor
CEEOPRRSS reprocess
CEEOPRRST receptors
CEEOPRRTX excerptor
CEEOPRSSS processes
CEEOPRSTU prosecute
CEEOQRTTU croquette
CEEOQSTTU coquettes
CEEORRRSS sorcerers
CEEORRSSS recrosses
sorceress
CEEORRSST crosstree
secretors
CEEORRSSU recourses
resources
CEEORRSTW worcester
CEEORRSTY secretory
CEEORRSUV verrucose
CEEORRTUV coverture
CEEORRTXY excretory
CEEORSTTV corvettes
CEEORSTUX executors
CEEORTUXY executory
CEEPRSSSU percusses
CEEPRSSSY cypresses
CEEPRSSTU suspecter
CEERRRSTU resurrect
CEERSSSTW setscrews
CEFFHINRY frenchify
CEFFHISTU chuffiest
CEFFHNOOR forfochen
CEFFIIKLW Wickliffe
CEFFILSTU Sutcliffe
CEFFIORSU coiffeurs
coiffures
CEFFIRRSU scruffier
CEFFIRSSU sufficers
CEFGHILNN flenching
CEFGHILNT fletching
CEFGIINNT infecting
CEFGIKLNR freckling
CEFGINNOR enforcing
CEFHIIMSS mischiefs
CEFHIIMST fetichism
CEFHIISTT fetichist
CEFHIKRSW wreckfish
CEFHILMOR cheliform
CEFHILNRS flinchers
CEFHIOSSW cowfishes
CEFHKOORS forehocks
foreshock
CEFHLSSTU chestfuls
CEFHPRRSU surfperch
CEFIILNRT inflicter
CEFIILNRU luciferin
CEFIILTVY fictively
CEFIINNOT infection
CEFIINTTU fettucini
CEFIIORRS scorifier
CEFIIORSS scorifies
CEFIKLORR frolicker
CEFIKLORS firelocks
CEFIKORSS fossicker
CEFILLLOS follicles
CEFILNORT inflector
CEFILNOST flections
CEFIMNORR confirmer
reconfirm
CEFIMNORU cuneiform
CEFINNORS confiners
CEFINOORT confiteor
CEFINORSS forensics
CEFINORST infectors
CEFINORTU confiture
CEFIOORSU ferocious
CEFIORRSS crossfire
CEFIORSTU fruticose
CEFKLOORS forelocks
CEFKLOPTU pocketful
CEFKLPSSY flyspecks
CEFKOORRW workforce
CEFLNNOTU confluent
CEFLNOSUX confluxes
CEFLNRSUU furuncles
CEFMNOORR conformer
CEFMOORRT comforter
CEFNOORSS confessor
CEFNORSTU confuters
CEFOOPSTY fetoscopy
CEFOORRSU fourscore
CEFOORRTU forecourt
CEFOORSTV softcover
CEGGIINRZ grecizing
CEGGIOORR Correggio
CEGGLNOSY glycogens
CEGHIILNS chiseling
CEGHIINNR enriching
CEGHIINPR ciphering
CEGHIINSY hygienics
CEGHIIOST gothicise
CEGHIIOTZ gothicize
CEGHIKNST sketching
CEGHILLNS Schelling
CEGHILLOU guilloche
CEGHILMTU gemutlich
CEGHILNNU Ch'ien-lung
CEGHILNPU pleuching
CEGHILNTV vetchling
CEGHILSSW Schleswig
CEGHIMNSS schemings
CEGHINNQU quenching
CEGHINNRT trenching
CEGHINNRW wrenching
CEGHINOOT neogothic
theogonic
CEGHINOPY hypogenic
CEGHINORS coshering
CEGHINORT hectoring
tochering
CEGHINORV Chernigov
CEGHINPRY cyphering
CEGHIOPTY geophytic
CEGHIORRU grouchier
CEGHKNORU roughneck
CEGHMNOOR chromogen
CEGIIILNT eliciting
CEGIIJNNT injecting
CEGIIJNOR rejoicing
CEGIIKLNN nickeling
CEGIIKNNR nickering
CEGIIKNNS sickening
CEGIIKNPR Pickering
CEGIIKNPT picketing
CEGIIKNTT ticketing

CEGIILLNO	lignicole
CEGIILNNP	penciling
CEGIILNNR	reclining
CEGIILNNS	licensing
	silencing
CEGIILNOR	recoiling
CEGIILNPS	eclipsing
CEGIIMNOT	mitogenic
CEGIINNNS	incensing
CEGIINNOR	recoining
CEGIINNPT	incepting
CEGIINOOR	coorieing
CEGIINORU	courieing
CEGIINORV	revoicing
CEGIINOTV	cognitive
CEGIINPRR	repricing
CEGIINPRS	precising
CEGIINPST	pectising
CEGIINPTZ	pectizing
CEGIINRSV	servicing
CEGIIOSTT	egotistic
CEGIJKNOY	jockeying
CEGIKLNPS	speckling
CEGIKNNOR	reckoning
CEGIKNOPT	pocketing
CEGIKNORT	rocketing
CEGIKNOST	socketing
CEGIKNPRU	puckering
CEGIKNRSU	suckering
CEGIKNRTU	tuckering
CEGILLMOU	collegium
CEGILLNOT	colleting
CEGILLNPU	cupelling
CEGILMMNO	commingle
CEGILMNOW	welcoming
CEGILNNOS	enclosing
CEGILNOPY	polygenic
CEGILNOST	closeting
CEGILNOSY	lysogenic
CEGILNOTU	elocuting
CEGILNRSU	surcingle
CEGILNRTU	lecturing
	relucting
CEGILNSTU	cultigens
CEGILOORS	serologic
CEGILOOST	ecologist
CEGIMNNOO	monogenic
CEGIMNOOR	ergonomic
CEGIMNOPR	compering
CEGIMNOPT	competing
CEGIMNOUY	gynoecium
CEGIMNOYZ	zymogenic
CEGINNNOU	enouncing
CEGINNNOV	convening
CEGINNOOT	ontogenic
CEGINNORR	cornering
CEGINNORS	censoring
	consigner
	necrosing
CEGINNOVX	convexing
CEGINNOVY	conveying
CEGINNRST	centrings
CEGINNRSU	censuring
CEGINNSTY	encysting
CEGINOOPR	coopering
CEGINOOPS	geoponics
CEGINOPPR	coppering
CEGINOPRU	recouping
CEGINOPRY	pyrogenic
	recopying
CEGINOPTY	genotypic
CEGINORST	corseting
	escorting
CEGINORSV	coverings
CEGINORSW	escrowing
CEGINORTT	cottering
CEGINORTV	vectoring
CEGINOSST	cosseting
CEGINPRST	sceptring
CEGINRRRU	recurring
CEGINRRUV	recurving
CEGINRSST	crestings
CEGINRTTU	curetting
CEGINRTUV	curveting
CEGINSSTU	scungiest
CEGIOOPRT	geotropic
CEGISTYYZ	syzygetic
CEGKMRSUU	gumsucker
CEGLLOOSU	collogues
CEGLNOORY	necrology
CEGMNNOOS	cognomens
CEGNNORTU	congruent
CEGNOOSTY	gonocytes
CEGNORRSU	scrounger
CEGNORSSU	scrounges
CEGNORSUY	surgeoncy
CEGOOPRSY	gyroscope
CEGORRSSU	scourgers
CEHHHIIKT	hitchhike
CEHHIIMST	hemistich
CEHHIINNS	Chin-Hsien
CEHHILLMS	schlemihl
CEHHIMOST	shochetim
CEHHIMSTT	hemstitch
CEHHINSTU	unhitches
CEHHLOOTU	touchhole
CEHHNOSTU	Hutcheson
CEHHOOPSU	chophouse
CEHHOPSTY	hypothecs
CEHIIILPT	epilithic
CEHIIKLOR	choirlike
CEHIIKLRS	lickerish
CEHIIKLTW	witchlike
CEHIIKORS	hickories
CEHIILLST	chilliest
CEHIILMOT	homiletic
CEHIILNOT	ichnolite
	neolithic
CEHIILNST	lecithins
CEHIIMOSS	isocheims
	isochimes
CEHIIMSTY	mythicise
CEHIIMTYZ	mythicize
CEHIINPPT	pitchpine
CEHIINPRT	nephritic
	phrenitic
CEHIINRST	snitchier
CEHIINRTZ	chintzier
CEHIINSST	itchiness
CEHIINTTY	ethnicity
CEHIIPPPT	pitchpipe
CEHIIPPST	chippiest
	psephitic
CEHIIPPTY	epiphytic
CEHIIPRRT	peritrich
CEHIIPRST	chirpiest
CEHIIPRTT	tephritic
CEHIIPSTT	pitchiest
CEHIIRSST	christies
CEHIIRSTU	heuristic
CEHIISSTT	ethicists
CEHIISTTT	titchiest
CEHIKLORT	torchlike
CEHIKLPRS	clerkship
CEHIKLSTY	sketchily
CEHIKMRSU	muckerish
CEHIKNNOT	technikon
CEHIKNSST	thickness
CEHIKNSTT	Schnittke
CEHIKNSTU	chunkiest
CEHIKORTW	work ethic
CEHIKPRSW	shipwreck
CEHIKSSTT	thicksets
CEHILLNSS	chillness
CEHILLPRS	prechills
CEHILMNOS	Michelson
CEHILMNTU	lunchtime
CEHILMOSU	humicoles
CEHILMOTY	hemolytic
CEHILNOOR	holocrine
CEHILNORU	euchlorin
CEHILNOSU	lichenous
CEHILNOTU	touchline
CEHILNSTZ	schnitzel
CEHILOOSS	schoolies
CEHILOPRT	plethoric
CEHILORST	chlorites
	clothiers
CEHILRSTU	slutchier
CEHIMMOPR	morphemic
CEHIMMSTU	chummiest
CEHIMNNOU	ichneumon
CEHIMNOPS	phonemics
CEHIMNSTW	switchmen
CEHIMORST	trichomes
CEHIMPRUY	hypericum
CEHIMRRSS	smirchers
CEHIMRSTY	chemistry
CEHIMRTUY	eurythmic
CEHINOORS	isochrone
CEHINOPRT	nephrotic
CEHINOPRU	neurochip
CEHINOPST	Ctesiphon
	phonetics
CEHINOPTY	neophytic
CEHINORTY	Nictheroy

CEHINPRST	sphincter
CEHINPSTU	punchiest
CEHINQSSU	squinches
CEHINRSST	christens
	snitchers
CEHINSTTY	synthetic
CEHIOOPRT	orthoepic
CEHIOOPRX	exophoric
CEHIOORSS	isochores
CEHIOOSST	choosiest
CEHIOPPRT	prophetic
CEHIOPPRY	hyperopic
CEHIOPPST	choppiest
CEHIOPRRT	chiropter
CEHIOPRRY	pyorrheic
CEHIOPRTT	prothetic
CEHIOPRTU	eutrophic
CEHIOPRTV	overpitch
CEHIOPRTY	hypocrite
CEHIOPSST	postiches
CEHIOPSTY	sciophyte
CEHIORRST	chorister
	rhetorics
	torchiers
CEHIORSST	ostriches
CEHIORSUV	echovirus
CEHIOSSST	schistose
CEHIOSTTU	touchiest
CEHIPRRRU	chirruper
CEHIPRRSU	superrich
CEHIPRSTW	Prestwich
CEHIPRTTT	Pritchett
CEHIRSSTT	stitchers
CEHIRSSTW	switchers
CEHIRSSTY	hysterics
CEHIRSTTW	twitchers
CEHIRSTTY	stitchery
CEHITTTWY	witchetty
CEHKLNORS	schnorkel
CEHKLOOST	klootches
CEHKOOOSU	cookhouse
CEHKRSSTU	hucksters
CEHLLOOPT	photocell
CEHLMNOOS	schoolmen
CEHLMNOUU	homuncule
CEHLMOOPY	phocomely
CEHLNNOSU	luncheons
CEHLNOSTU	unclothes
CEHLNOSZZ	schnozzle
CEHLOOPRS	preschool
CEHLOOPSS	Sophocles
CEHLOPSST	splotches
CEHLORRST	chortlers
CEHLORSSU	slouchers
CEHLOSSTU	touchless
CEHMNOPRS	McPherson
CEHMOOPRT	ectomorph
CEHMOORRU	urochrome
CEHMOOSSZ	schmoozes
CEHMOTTYY	thymocyte
CEHMRSTTU	schmutter
CEHNNOPSU	puncheons
CEHNNORTU	truncheon
CEHNOOPPY	phenocopy
CEHNOORSS	schooners
CEHNOOTTU	touchtone
CEHNORRRS	schnorrer
CEHNSSTTU	chestnuts
CEHOOOPRS	horoscope
CEHOOORSZ	zoochores
CEHOPRTYY	cryophyte
CEHOPSSSY	psychoses
CEIIILRSV	civiliser
CEIIILRVZ	civilizer
CEIIILSSV	civilises
CEIIILSVZ	civilizes
CEIIIMMRS	mimicries
CEIIIMSTV	victimise
CEIIIMTVZ	victimize
CEIIINNPT	incipient
CEIIIPRSS	epicrisis
CEIIIPSTT	pietistic
CEIIJNNOT	injection
CEIIJNSSU	juiciness
CEIIJNSTU	injustice
CEIIKLMPS	mispickel
CEIIKLMQU	quicklime
CEIIKLMRS	limericks
CEIIKLNRS	crinklies
CEIIKLPRR	pricklier
CEIIKLSST	sickliest
CEIIKMMRS	mimickers
CEIIKNNPR	princekin
CEIIKNPRT	nitpicker
CEIIKNPSS	pickiness
CEIIKRRST	tricksier
CEIIKRSTT	trickiest
CEIIKSSTT	stickiest
CEIILLNNO	linolenic
CEIILLSSU	silicules
CEIILMORT	microlite
CEIILMOSV	Milošević
CEIILNNOR	crinoline
CEIILNNRS	incliners
CEIILNOSS	isoclines
	silicones
CEIILNPPR	principle
CEIILNSST	licitness
CEIILNSSV	civilness
CEIILNSUV	inclusive
CEIILNTYZ	citizenly
CEIILOQRU	liquorice
CEIILORST	elicitors
CEIILOSSU	siliceous
CEIILPRTU	pleuritic
CEIILRSST	scleritis
CEIILRSTV	verticils
CEIILSTTY	sectility
CEIILSTUV	Leviticus
CEIIMMNNY	imminency
CEIIMNOST	semitonic
CEIIMNRST	cretinism
CEIIMNSST	scientism
CEIIMOPSS	miscopies
CEIIMORST	eroticism
	isometric
	microsite
CEIIMOSST	semiotics
CEIIMOSTX	exoticism
CEIIMPRSU	epicurism
CEIIMRRTT	trimetric
CEIINNOPT	inception
CEIINNORS	irenicons
CEIINNORT	incretion
CEIINOPRS	precision
CEIINOPRT	proteinic
CEIINORRT	criterion
CEIINORSS	recisions
CEIINORTT	tricotine
CEIINOSSX	excisions
CEIINOSTV	evictions
CEIINPSSS	spiciness
CEIINQRTU	quercitin
CEIINRSSU	incisures
	sciurines
CEIINRSTX	extrinsic
CEIINRSTY	sincerity
CEIINRSUV	incursive
CEIINRTTY	intercity
CEIINRTYZ	citizenry
CEIINSSTT	scientist
CEIINSSTU	cutinises
CEIINSTUZ	cutinizes
CEIIOOPTZ	epizootic
CEIIORSST	isosteric
CEIIORSTU	triecious
CEIIORSTV	victories
CEIIPRSST	crispiest
CEIIPSTTY	septicity
CEIIQRSTU	critiques
CEIISSTVV	vivisects
CEIJNNOOR	conjoiner
CEIJNORST	injectors
CEIJNORTT	introject
CEIJNOSUV	cunjevois
CEIKKLMOS	smocklike
CEIKKLNRU	knucklier
CEIKKRRSS	skerricks
CEIKLLORS	sollicker
CEIKLNOOT	Cook Inlet
CEIKLNOPV	clovepink
CEIKLNORT	interlock
CEIKLNOSU	nickelous
CEIKLNRUU	unluckier
CEIKLNSSS	slickness
CEIKLNSSU	luckiness
CEIKLNSTU	clunkiest
CEIKLOPST	stockpile
CEIKLOSTV	livestock
CEIKLPSTU	pluckiest
CEIKLRSST	sticklers
	strickles
	trickless
CEIKMNORS	monickers
CEIKMNSSU	muckiness
CEIKNORSS	rockiness

CEIKNOSTT stockinet
CEIKNOSTY cytokines
CEIKNQSSU quickness
CEIKORRTV overtrick
CEIKOSSTT stockiest
CEIKPQSTU quickstep
CEIKPRSTW Prestwick
CEIKQSSTU quicksets
CEIKRRSTT trickster
CEILLLMTU clitellum
CEILLNOSS collinses
CEILLNOUV involucel
CEILLOPTU pollucite
CEILLOQSU coquilles
CEILLOSUV collusive
CEILLPSTY sylleptic
CEILMNNOO monocline
CEILMNOOS semicolon
CEILMNOTU monticule
CEILMNSSU lemniscus
CEILMNSUU minuscule
CEILMOPRS compilers
compliers
CEILMOPRY micropyle
polymeric
CEILMOSSS solecisms
CEILMOSSU coliseums
CEILMRTUU reticulum
CEILMSSTU clumsiest
CEILNNOOS cloisonne
CEILNNSSY synclines
CEILNOOPS scopoline
CEILNOORS coloniser
CEILNOORZ colonizer
CEILNOOSS colonises
CEILNOOSZ colonizes
CEILNOOTU elocution
CEILNOPRU pronuclei
CEILNOPSY Polynices
CEILNORSS inclosers
licensors
CEILNORST sclerotin
CEILNORSU inclosure
reclusion
CEILNORUV involucre
CEILNOSSU seclusion
CEILNOSUX exclusion
CEILNRSSU curliness
CEILNRSUV culverins
CEILNRUVY virulency
CEILNSSTU linctuses
CEILOOPRT coprolite
CEILOORSU colourise
CEILOORSZ colorizes
CEILOORUZ colourize
CEILOPPRT proleptic
CEILOPRSV coverslip
slipcover
CEILOPSTU poultices
CEILOPSTY epicotyls
CEILORRTU courtlier
CEILORSSS sclerosis
CEILORSST cloisters
CEILOSSST solecists
solstices
CEILOSSSU coulisses
CEILOSSTT costliest
CEILOSTVY costively
CEILPPRRS cripplers
CEILPPSUU Leucippus
CEILPRSSU surplices
CEILRSTUU Lucretius
CEILRSUVY cursively
CEIMMNNOS mnemonics
CEIMMNOOR monomeric
CEIMMNOOS economism
CEIMMNOSU communise
encomiums
CEIMMNOTU comminute
CEIMMNOTY metonymic
CEIMMNOUZ communize
CEIMMOORS microsome
CEIMMOORT microtome
CEIMMORST recommits
CEIMMORTT committer
CEIMMRSTU crummiest
CEIMMRSTY symmetric
CEIMNNOPU pneumonic
CEIMNNORT nonmetric
CEIMNNOST Mont Cenis
CEIMNOOPT coemption
CEIMNOORT microtone
CEIMNOOST economist
CEIMNOOSU monecious
CEIMNOPTY impotency
CEIMNORST intercoms
CEIMNRSST centrisms
CEIMOOPRR poromeric
CEIMOOPST composite
CEIMOORSS moriscoes
CEIMOORTZ zoometric
CEIMOOSTX exosmotic
CEIMOPRSS comprises
CEIMOPRSX proxemics
CEIMOPSUU pumiceous
CEIMORSSX exorcisms
CEIMORSTU costumier
CEIMORSTV Meštrović
CEIMOSSTU customise
CEIMOSTUV muscovite
CEIMOSTUZ customize
CEIMSSSTY systemics
CEINNNOOX connexion
CEINNNOST innocents
CEINNNOTT continent
CEINNNOTV connivent
CEINNOOTV connotive
CEINNOPRT Princeton
CEINNORSV connivers
CEINNORSY incensory
CEINNORTU centurion
continuer
CEINNOSTU continues
neustonic
CEINNRRTU incurrent
CEINOORST cortisone
CEINOOSSW Sosnowiec
CEINOPPRU porcupine
CEINOPRRS conspirer
CEINOPRRT intercrop
CEINOPRSS conspires
CEINOPRST inceptors
inspector
CEINOPRSV provinces
CEINOPRXY pyroxenic
CEINOPSTU pectinous
CEINORRST tricornes
CEINORRSU coinsurer
recursion
CEINORRTV contriver
CEINORRTY incretory
CEINORSSS incrosses
CEINORSSU coinsures
CEINORSTT cornetist
CEINORSTU countries
cretinous
neurotics
CEINORSTV contrives
CEINORSUX excursion
CEINOSSUY synecious
CEINOSTUV contusive
CEINOTVXY convexity
CEINPRSSS crispness
CEINRSSTT centrists
CEINRSTTU intercuts
tinctures
CEIOOPRSS coreopsis
CEIOOPRST porticoes
CEIOORRSV corrosive
CEIOORSTV vorticose
CEIOOSSTX toxicoses
CEIOPRRSU croupiers
CEIOPRTUY eurytopic
CEIORRSTT trisector
CEIORRSTU courtiers
CEIORRSUZ cruzeiros
CEIORRTUU couturier
CEIORSSSW crosswise
CEIORSSTX exorcists
CEIORSTTU toreutics
CEIPPRRST prescript
CEIPRRSST rescripts
CEIPRRSTU scripture
CEIRRSSTT restricts
CEIRRSTTU stricture
CEIRSSSSU scissures
CEIRSSTTT strictest
CEIRSSTTU crustiest
CEIRSSTUV scurviest
CEISSTUZZ scuzziest
CEJKOOTUY outjockey
CEJNORRSU conjurers
CEJNRSTUU junctures
CEJOOPRRT projector
CEKKORSTY skyrocket
CEKLLNORS rollnecks

CEKLLOOSV lovelocks
CEKLNNPUY luckpenny
CEKLRRSTU trucklers
CEKMNORTU mockernut
CEKNOORSV convokers
CEKNOPSST penstocks
CEKOOORSV overcooks
CEKOORRSS rockroses
CEKOORRSW coworkers
CEKOORSTV overstock
CEKOPRSST sprockets
CELLMOPXY complexly
CELLMSTUU scutellum
CELLNOSUU nucleolus
CELLOOPTY collotype
CELLOORSS colorless
CELMNOORU colourmen
CELMNOTUY contumely
CELMOOPRY copolymer
CELMOOSSU colosseum
CELMOOTUY leucotomy
CELMOPRUU operculum
CELMPRSSU scrumples
CELMPRSTU plectrums
CELMPSSUU speculums
CELNNOTTY contently
CELNOORSS consolers
CELNOORSU counselor
CELNOOSTU consolute
CELNOOSVV convolves
CELNOOTUV convolute
CELNOPRST plectrons
CELNOPRTU corpulent
CELNOPSUU uncouples
CELNORSSW crownless
CELNORSTU consulter
CELNOSSTU countless
CELNOSSUV convulses
CELNPRUUY purulency
CELNRRTUY currently
CELNRTTUU truculent
CELOOORSV overcools
CELOOPRSU supercool
CELOOPSSS cesspools
CELOORSTW coleworts
CELOPSSUU opuscules
CELORSSST crosslets
CELORSSUU surculose
CELPRSTUU sculpture
CEMMNOORS commoners
CEMMNOOST commonest
CEMMORSTU commuters
CEMNNOOPT component
CEMNOOOQU monocoque
CEMNOOORS monoceros
CEMNOORTY necrotomy
CEMNOOSTY monocytes
CEMNOPSTT contempts
CEMNORSSU consumers
CEMNORTUY emunctory
CEMOOPRSS composers
CEMOOPRSU composure
CEMOPRSTU computers
CEMORRSUU mercurous
CEMORRSWW screwworm
CEMORRTYY cryometry
CEMORSSTU costumers
customers
CENNOOPPY opponency
CENNOOPRU pronounce
CENNOORST cornstone
CENNOORSV convenors
CENNORSTU nocturnes
CENNOSSSU consensus
CENOOPRST stonecrop
CENOOQRRU conqueror
CENOORRST consorter
CENOORRTV convertor
CENOORSVY conveyors
CENOQSSTU conquests
CENORRSTU construer
CENORSSSS crossness
CENORSSSU uncrosses
CENORSSTU construes
CENORSSUY cynosures
CENORSTXY xenocryst
CENPRRTUU puncturer
CENPRSTUU punctures
CEOOOPSST otoscopes
CEOOPRRSS processor
CEOOPRRST prosector
CEOOPRRSV overcrops
CEOOPRRTT protector
CEOOPRSTY sporocyte
CEOOPSSTU octopuses
CEOORRSSU sorcerous
CEOORRSSV crossover
CEOORSTUU courteous
outsource
CEOPPRSST prospects
CEOPRRRSU precursor
procurers
CEOPRRRTU corrupter
CEOPRRSSU percussor
procuress
CEOPRSSTW screwtops
CEORRSUUV verrucous
CEPPRSTUU uppercuts
CEPRSSSUU cupressus
CEPRSSTUU cutpurses
CERRSTTUU structure
CFFGIINSU sufficing
CFFGILNSU scuffling
CFFHHIKOR Kirchhoff
CFFHIORST Christoff
CFFIIOOSU officious
CFFORRSSU crossruff
CFGHIILNN flinching
CFGHIILNS clingfish
CFGHIILNT flitching
CFGIIIKNN finicking
CFGIIINTY citifying
CFGIILLMN clingfilm
CFGIINNNO confining
CFGIINTYY cityfying
CFGILNNOU flouncing
CFGILNORY forcingly
CFGINNOSU confusing
CFGINNOTU confuting
CFGINOSSU focussing
CFHIINOOR honorific
CFHIKOPRT pitchfork
CFHIKOSST stockfish
CFHLOOOTT footcloth
CFHNOORRT Cornforth
CFIIKKLNS skinflick
CFIILMMOR microfilm
CFIILNORT inflictor
CFIILORST floristic
CFIINORST frictions
CFIIOOPRS soporific
CFIKLLNOT flintlock
CFIKLLOOR folkloric
CFIKLSSTU stickfuls
CFILNSUUU funiculus
CFIMMOORR microform
CFIMNORSU unciforms
CFIMORSTU scutiform
CFINNOOSU confusion
CFINNOSTU functions
CFKOOOSTT footstock
CFLLOORUU colourful
CFLNOORRU cornflour
CFLOOOSTT coltsfoot
CFLOOPSSU scoopfuls
CFNNOORST confronts
CFOOORSTW crowfoots
CFORSTUUU fructuous
CGGHIKNNU Chungking
CGGHINNOQ Chongqing
CGGHINORU grouching
CGGIINNOS cognising
CGGIINNOZ cognizing
CGGINORSS scroggins
CGGINORSU scourging
scrouging
CGHHINNOO honchoing
CGHIIKNST skitching
CGHIIKNTW wickthing
CGHIILLNS schilling
CGHIILNST chitlings
CGHIIMNRS smirching
CGHIIMOUZ Mizoguchi
CGHIINNST snitching
CGHIINPPS chippings
CGHIINSTT stitching
CGHIINSTW switching
witchings
CGHIINTTW twitching
CGHIINVVY chivvying
CGHIKNNSU chunkings
CGHILMOOO homologic
CGHILNNSY lynchings
CGHILNOOS schooling
CGHILNOOY ichnology
CGHILNORT chortling

CGHILNOSU slouching
CGHILOOOR horologic
CGHILORUY grouchily
CGHIMNOOS smooching
CGHIMNSTU smutching
CGHINNRSU churnings
CGHINOOSS scooshing
CGHINORSU chorusing
CGHINOSSU hocussing
CGHINSSSU schussing
CGHIOPRTY copyright
CGHLLNOOT longcloth
CGHLOOORY chorology
CGHLOOPYY phycology
CGIIIKMMN mimicking
CGIIILNNN inclining
CGIIINNOV invoicing
CGIIKLNNR crinkling
CGIIKLNPR prickling
CGIIKLNRT trickling
CGIIKLNST stickling
CGIIKMMRY gimmickry
CGIIKNNPU unpicking
CGIIKNSTY stickying
CGIIKPSST pigsticks
CGIILMNNY mincingly
CGIILMNOP compiling
CGIILMNPR crimpling
CGIILMNUU glucinium
CGIILNNOS inclosing
CGIILNNOU uncoiling
CGIILNPPR crippling
CGIILNPPS clippings
CGIILOSST glossitic
logistics
CGIILRSTU liturgics
CGIIMMNOX commixing
CGIIMNNOS incomings
CGIIMNORT morticing
CGIIMNPRS scrimping
CGIINNNOV conniving
CGIINNOOT cognition
incognito
CGIINNOUV unvoicing
CGIINNRRU incurring
CGIINNRUV incurving
CGIINOOSS isogonics
CGIINPRST scripting
CGIINPRTU picturing
CGIJNNORU conjuring
CGIKKLNNU knuckling
CGIKLMNOY mockingly
CGIKLNNOU unlocking
CGIKLNORS rocklings
CGIKLNRTU truckling
CGIKLNSSU sucklings
CGIKLOSTW glowstick
CGIKNNOOV convoking
CGIKNNORU uncorking
CGIKNNTUU untucking
CGIKNORSW corkwings
CGIKNOSST stockings
CGILLNOOY coolingly
CGILLNORS scrolling
CGILLNOYY cloyingly
CGILMNOOO monologic
CGILMNOPY complying
CGILMNPRU crumpling
CGILMOOYZ zymologic
CGILNNNUY cunningly
CGILNNOOR longicorn
CGILNNOOS consoling
CGILNNOSU unclosing
CGILNNRUU uncurling
CGILNOOOY coniology
iconology
CGILNOORS colorings
CGILNOORU colouring
CGILNOPSU couplings
CGILNOPTU octupling
CGILNORSU closuring
CGILNORTU cloturing
CGILNORWY crowingly
CGILNPRSU scrupling
CGILNPSTU sculpting
CGILNRTUU culturing
CGILNSTTU scuttling
CGILNTTUY cuttingly
CGILOOOPT topologic
CGILOOOSY sociology
CGILOOPTY typologic
CGIMMNNOU communing
CGIMMNOOV commoving
CGIMMNOTU commuting
CGIMMNRSU scrumming
CGIMNNOOS oncomings
CGIMNNOSU consuming
CGIMNOOPS composing
CGIMNOPTU computing
CGIMNOSTU costuming
CGIMNPRSU scrumping
CGINNNOOT connoting
CGINNOORS consignor
CGINNOOVY convoying
CGINNORSW crownings
CGINNORTU trouncing
CGINNOSTU contusing
CGINOOPRS scrooping
CGINOORTU Tourcoing
CGINOPRRU procuring
CGINORSSS crossings
CGINORSSU scourings
CGINORTUY congruity
outcrying
CGINRRSUY scurrying
CGINRSTUY curtsying
CGKNOSSTU gunstocks
CGLMOOOSY cosmology
CGLOOOPRY coprology
CGMNOOOSY cosmogony
CGNNOOTTU guncotton
CGNOORSUU congruous
CHHHIIMNO Ho Chi Minh
CHHIILLNS Chin Hills
CHHIMRSTY rhythmics
CHHINORTW Northwich
CHHKLLOOY hollyhock
CHIIILPPP philippic
CHIIILRTT trilithic
CHIIIMRRT Tirich Mir
CHIILLOPY lyophilic
CHIILLPTY phyllitic
CHIILMORT microlith
CHIILNNPS linchpins
CHIILOOPZ zoophilic
CHIILOOTT otolithic
CHIILORTU urolithic
CHIILORTY rhyolitic
CHIILPSTU sulphitic
CHIILPTTY typhlitic
CHIIMSTTY mythicist
CHIINOSTU chitinous
CHIIOPSST sophistic
CHIIORRSS cirrhosis
CHIIORSST trichosis
CHIIORTTY rhoticity
CHIIPSSTY physicist
CHIIRSSTT tristichs
CHIKLMOST locksmith
CHIKMNNSU munchkins
CHIKMNPSU chipmunks
CHIKMNSTU mutchkins
CHIKOOPTT toothpick
CHIKOPSTW whipstock
CHILLMOPY phyllomic
CHILLNOOT loincloth
CHILLOOST oilcloths
CHILLOSTY coltishly
CHILLOSUY slouchily
CHILLSTUY cultishly
CHILMNOUU homunculi
CHILMOOTY homolytic
CHILMUUUW Wu-lu-mu-ch'i
CHILNNOOS Nicholson
CHILNNPSY lynchpins
CHILNOPSU sulphonic
CHILOOPTY holotypic
CHILOORSS chlorosis
CHILORSTU trochilus
CHILORTUY ulotrichy
CHILOSTTY cystolith
CHILPRSUU sulphuric
CHILRRSUY currishly
CHIMMNOOY homonymic
CHIMNOOST monostich
CHIMNOPSY symphonic
CHIMNORSU Murchison
CHIMNORSW inchworms
CHIMOOPRT morphotic
CHIMPSTYY symphytic
CHINNOORT nonrhotic
CHINOOPST photonics
CHINOOPTY hypotonic
CHINOORST orthicons
CHINOPSTU countship
CHINOPSTY hypnotics

CHINOSSTZ schizonts
CHIOOPRTT orthoptic
CHIOOPTYZ zoophytic
CHIOORSTT orthotics
CHIOPRSTU courtship
CHIOPRSYY hypocrisy
CHIOPSSSY psychosis
CHIORRSSU scirrhous
CHIPRSTTY triptychs
CHKLMOOST Stockholm
CHKNORSSU cornhusks
CHLMNOORU lunchroom
CHLNOOOPS colophons
CHLNOOOPY colophony
CHLNOTUUY uncouthly
CHLOOPTYY hypocotyl
CHLOPPTYY polyptych
CHMNORRSU crumhorns
CHNNORSYY synchrony
CHNORSTUU cothurnus
CHOOOPPTY photocopy
CHOOOPRSY horoscopy
CHOOSTTTU Southcott
CHORSSTTU shortcuts
CIIILLLTY illicitly
CIIILMNOT limonitic
CIIILMOPT impolitic
CIIILMPTY implicity
CIIILOPST pisolitic
CIIILORTV vitriolic
CIIILOSSS silicosis
CIIILOSSU silicious
CIIIMSTTW witticism
CIIINNOSS incisions
CIIINNRST intrinsic
CIIKLPSST lipsticks
CIIKNNOPT nickpoint
CIIKNNOTY cytokinin
CIIKNPPRS pinpricks
CIILLMRUY Illyricum
CIILLMSTU tillicums
CIILLNOOS collision
CIILLNOOT cotillion
octillion
CIILLNUVY uncivilly
CIILLOPTY lipolytic
politicly
CIILMPRSY scrimpily
CIILMRSSY lyricisms
CIILNNOSU inclusion
CIILNOOST colonitis
CIILNOPTU punctilio
unpolitic
CIILOOPST politicos
CIILOORST solicitor
CIILOOSSS scoliosis
CIILOSSST sciolists
CIILOSUVY viciously
CIILRSSTY lyricists
CIILSSTTY stylistic
CIIMMSSTY mysticism
CIIMNORUZ zirconium
CIIMOOSST isosmotic
CIIMORSTV vorticism
CIINNNOTU inunction
CIINNORSU incursion
CIINNOSSW Wisconsin
CIINNOTUY innocuity
CIINNSSTT instincts
CIINOOPPR propionic
CIINOOPRT inotropic
CIINOPSSU suspicion
CIINORSTT striction
CIINORSUU incurious
CIINOSTVY synovitic
CIINPSSTU sinciputs
CIIOOPRST isotropic
CIIOOSSTX toxicosis
CIIOPRSTT tropistic
CIIORSTTU touristic
CIIORSTTV vorticist
CIIORSTUV virtuosic
CIIORSTUY curiosity
CIIOSSTVY viscosity
CIIRSTTUY rusticity
CIJKOSSTY joysticks
CIJNNOSTU junctions
CIKKOOSSU Kosciusko
CIKLLNUUY unluckily
CIKLNOSST linstocks
CIKLOORSU cokuloris
CIKLOPSSU liposucks
CIKLORSTW wristlock
CIKMOORSS sickrooms
CIKNNOOSS coonskins
CIKOSSSTT stockists
CILLMORUY collyrium
CILLMOUUV colluvium
CILLNOOST cotillons
CILLNOOSU collusion
CILLNOSSU scullions
CILLOOOST ocotillos
CILLOOOTY coyotillo
CILMNOPSU pulmonics
CILMNOSTU columnist
CILMOOPSY polysomic
CILMOTYYZ zymolytic
CILNOORUU unicolour
CILNOOSST colonists
CILNOOSTU locutions
CILNOSTYY cytolysin
CILOOPSUY copiously
CILOORRST tricolors
CILOORRTU tricolour
CILOORSST colorists
CILOORSTU colourist
CILOPPTYY polytypic
CILOPRTYY pyrolytic
CILORRSUY cursorily
CILORSUUY curiously
CILOSSTYY cytolysis
CILOSSUVY viscously
CILRSTTUU culturist
CILRSTUUU utriculus
CIMMMNOSU communism
CIMMNNOOU communion
CIMMNOOOS monosomic
CIMMNOOOT commotion
CIMMNOSTU communist
CIMMNOTUY community
CIMMOORTY microtomy
CIMNNOOOT monotonic
CIMNNOSYY synonymic
CIMNNOTUU continuum
CIMNOOOSU monoicous
CIMNOOPTY monotypic
toponymic
CIMNOOTXY mycotoxin
CIMNOSSTU miscounts
CIMNSTUYY syncytium
CINNOOSTU continuos
contusion
CINNOOSUU innocuous
CINOOOPST cooptions
CINOOORRS corrosion
CINOOPRSS scorpions
CINOOSSUY synoicous
CINOOTTXY cytotoxin
CINOPPRUY porcupiny
CINOPRRTU incorrupt
CINOPSSTY synoptics
CINOSSTUV viscounts
CINOSTUVY viscounty
CINRSSTTU instructs
CIOOOPRRT Porto Rico
CIOOOPRSZ zoosporic
CIOOOPRTZ protozoic
CIOOPPRSU Procopius
CIOOPSSTU posticous
CJNOORRSU conjurors
CKKLOOPST Klopstock
CKKNOOSTU knockouts
CKLMMOOSS slommocks
CKMMORSUW muckworms
CKMOOORST stockroom
CKNOOOSTW Cookstown
CKNOORRWW crownwork
CKOOORSTT rootstock
CKOOPRSTT Stockport
CKOOPSSTT stockpots
CLLOOOTTW Woollcott
CLMNNOOTU Montluçon
CLMOOOORT locomotor
CLMOOOPTY colpotomy
CLMOOOSTY colostomy
CLMOORSTU colostrum
CLNOOPRSU proconsul
CLNOORSTU consultor
CLNOOSUUY nocuously
CLNORTUUY uncourtly
CLOOOPRST protocols
CLOPRRTUY corruptly
CLOPRSSTU sculptors
CMMNOOORS Roscommon
CMNOOORST cosmotron
CMOOORRTU courtroom

CMOOORSST motocross
CMOOOSTTY costotomy
CMOOSTTYY cystotomy
CNNNOOTUU count noun
CNOOOORST octoroons
CNOORRSTY cryotrons
CNOORSSTW crosstown
CNOPRTUUY upcountry
COOPRRRTU corruptor
COOPRSSTY sporocyst
COORRSSTW crosswort
DDDEEEINX deindexed
DDDEEHRSU shuddered
DDDEEIIRV redivided
DDDEEINPS dispended
DDDEEINST distended
DDDEENOOS desnooded
DDDEENOPS desponded
DDDEENORU redounded
DDDEEORRS dodderers
DDDEGILOS dislodged
DDDEGINOR doddering
DDDEGOOTU outdodged
DDDEIILVY dividedly
DDDEIINSV dividends
DDDEIINUV undivided
DDDEILNRU unriddled
DDDEILOPS disploded
DDEEEEKNW weekended
DDEEEFINR redefined
DDEEEFNRS defenders
DDEEEFNRU underfeed
DDEEEGIPR pedigreed
DDEEEHLNR Den Helder
DDEEEILRV delivered
DDEEEINRW rewidened
DDEEEINSX deindexes
DDEEEIPTX expedited
DDEEEIRTU deuteride
DDEEELOPV developed
DDEEENNPT dependent
DDEEENORW reendowed
DDEEENPPR perpended
DDEEENPRT pretended
DDEEEORRR reordered
DDEEEPRSS depressed
DDEEERRSS redressed
DDEEESTUU desuetude
DDEEFFNOR forfended
DDEEFGINN defending
DDEEFGLNU unfledged
DDEEFILNU undefiled
DDEEFINNU undefined
DDEEFLOOR reflooded
DDEEFNORU foundered
DDEEFORST defrosted
DDEEGGGLO doglegged
DDEEGGNOU gudgeoned
DDEEGHILT delighted
DDEEGINNP depending
DDEEGINNR reddening
DDEEGIRSS digressed
DDEEGJPRU prejudged
DDEEGLNPU unpledged
DDEEGNORU guerdoned
DDEEGOSSS goddesses
DDEEHIINT hiddenite
DDEEHNORT dethroned
DDEEHNORU deerhound
DDEEHNRTU thundered
DDEEHRRSS shredders
DDEEIILMT delimited
DDEEIILNS sidelined
DDEEIIMRS dimerised
DDEEIIMRZ dimerized
DDEEIINOZ deionized
DDEEIIOSX deoxidise
DDEEIIOXZ deoxidize
DDEEIIPPT dipeptide
DDEEIIRSV redivides
DDEEIISSS disseised
DDEEIISSZ disseized
DDEEIKLLS deskilled
DDEEIKLNN enkindled
DDEEIKLNR rekindled
DDEEILLPS dispelled
DDEEILLRR redrilled
DDEEILLRV drivelled
DDEEILMMN middlemen
DDEEILMOS melodised
DDEEILMOZ melodized
DDEEILMSX Middlesex
DDEEILOPS despoiled
DDEEILORS soldiered
DDEEIMMNO demimonde
DDEEIMNOS demonised
DDEEIMNOZ demonized
DDEEIMNPU unimpeded
DDEEIMRST dermestid
DDEEINNST intendeds
DDEEINORW eiderdown
DDEEINOSV nosedived
DDEEINPSS dispensed
DDEEINRST dendrites
distender
DDEEINRSU underside
undesired
DDEEINSST dissented
DDEEIOORS deodorise
DDEEIOORZ deodorize
DDEEIOPRX peroxided
DDEEIOPST deposited
DDEEIPRSS dispersed
DDEEIPSTU deputised
DDEEIPTUZ deputized
DDEEIRSSS sidedress
DDEEIRSSV disserved
DDEELMORS smoldered
DDEELMORU mouldered
remoulded
DDEELNPRU plundered
DDEELOTVY devotedly
DDEEMNORS endoderms
DDEEMNOTU demounted
DDEEMOOPR predoomed
DDEEMOPUY Puy de Dôme
DDEENNORU underdone
DDEENNOUW unendowed
DDEENOPPR propended
DDEENOPRS responded
DDEENOPRT portended
DDEENOPUX expounded
DDEENORRT retrodden
DDEENORSU resounded
underdoes
DDEENOSSS oddnesses
DDEENPSSU suspended
DDEENRSSU undressed
DDEEOOPRT torpedoed
DDEEOORSV overdosed
DDEEORSTY destroyed
DDEFFIINT diffident
DDEFGIIIN dignified
DDEFGINOR foddering
DDEFGJORU forjudged
DDEFIILST fiddliest
DDEFIILSU fluidised
DDEFIILUZ fluidized
DDEFILNOP pinfolded
DDEFNNOUU unfounded
DDEGGHOOT hotdogged
DDEGGIORS disgorged
DDEGHINRS shredding
DDEGHINSS sheddings
DDEGIIIST digitised
DDEGIIITZ digitized
DDEGIIMSU misguided
DDEGIINNR niddering
DDEGIINSS giddiness
DDEGIISSU disguised
DDEGIJMSU misjudged
DDEGIJNRU juddering
DDEGILOSS dislodges
DDEGINNOR dondering
DDEGINNOS soddening
DDEGINNOT Eddington
DDEGINRRU undergird
DDEGINRTU detruding
DDEGISSTU disgusted
DDEGLMSUY smudgedly
DDEGLNOOR goldenrod
DDEGNOOOR godrooned
DDEGNORSU underdogs
DDEGOOSTU outdodges
DDEHHNRTU hundredth
DDEHIIRSY Yiddisher
DDEHILRSY reddishly
DDEHINORS dihedrons
DDEHIORXY hydroxide
DDEHIOSST shoddiest
DDEHOOSSW woodsheds
DDEIIINSV divinised
DDEIIINVZ divinized
DDEIIJNOS disjoined
DDEIIKOSV videodisk
DDEIILLST distilled

DDEIILMNS dislimned
DDEIILSTT tiddliest
DDEIIMSSS dismissed
DDEIINSST dissident
DDEIINSTU disunited
DDEIIOPSS diopsides
DDEIIPRSZ disprized
DDEIIRSUV reduviids
DDEIJNORY joyridden
DDEIKLNNU unkindled
DDEILMNOT Middleton
DDEILNRRU unriddler
DDEILNRSU unriddles
DDEILNTUU undiluted
DDEILOPSS displodes
DDEILORWW worldwide
DDEILOSSV dissolved
DDEILRSTW twiddlers
DDEILSTUY studiedly
DDEIMNOPU impounded
DDEIMNSSU muddiness
DDEIMOOSS sodomised
DDEIMOOSZ sodomized
DDEIMOSSU medusoids
DDEINORTU outridden
DDEINORWW windrowed
DDEINOSSW disendows
dowdiness
downsides
DDEINOSWZ downsized
DDEINRSSU ruddiness
DDEINSTUU unstudied
DDEIOPRST disported
DDEIOPRSV disproved
DDEIORRSS disorders
DDEIORSTT distorted
DDEIPRSTU disrupted
DDELMNOUU unmoulded
DDELNORSU undersold
DDELNORUY roundedly
DDEMNOSUU duodenums
DDENNORTU untrodden
DDENNORUU unrounded
DDENNORUW down under
DDENNOUUW unwounded
DDENOOPRS dropsonde
DDENOORUW underwood
DDENRSTTU Rundstedt
DDEOPRRTU protruded
DDFGILORU Guildford
DDFIOORTW driftwood
DDFMNOSUU dumfounds
DDGGIILNR griddling
DDGGINNOS dingdongs
DDGIIINOS indigoids
DDGIIKLNY kiddingly
DDGIILMNS middlings
DDGIILNNW dwindling
DDGIILNTW twiddling
DDGIINQSU squidding
DDGLORRSU druglords
DDHIOOOWW widowhood
DDIIIISVV dividivis
DDILOOPPS diplopods
DDILOOSWW wildwoods
DDINOPSUU dupondius
DDNOOORUW roundwood
DEEEEGKRS kedgerees
DEEEEGMRR reemerged
DEEEEGQSU squeegeed
DEEEEKNRW weekender
DEEEEMRRS redeemers
DEEEENPRS deepeners
DEEEENPST steepened
DEEEENRRT reentered
DEEEENSTW sweetened
DEEEFFFNO enfeoffed
DEEEFHNRS freshened
DEEEFHRRS refreshed
DEEEFINRS redefines
DEEEFINSV defensive
DEEEFLLNU needleful
DEEEFLLRU refuelled
DEEEFMNRT deferment
fermented
DEEEFNRST deferents
DEEEFORSV overfeeds
DEEEFPRRR preferred
DEEEFRRRS deferrers
DEEEGGHIR Heidegger
DEEEGHIRW reweighed
DEEEGIKLW wedgelike
DEEEGIMNR redeeming
DEEEGINNP deepening
DEEEGINRS energised
DEEEGINRZ energized
DEEEGINSS digeneses
DEEEGIPRS pedigrees
DEEEGIRRT ridgetree
DEEEGIRST greediest
DEEEGKLNT kentledge
DEEEGLNOY goldeneye
DEEEGLRSS greedless
DEEEGLSSV selvedges
DEEEGMNST segmented
DEEEGMRRS demergers
DEEEGNNRS engenders
DEEEGNRTT detergent
DEEEGRRSS regressed
DEEEGRRTT regretted
DEEEHHSTW wheeshted
DEEEHILRT Ethelred I
DEEEHILSW sidewheel
DEEEHIMPR ephemerid
DEEEHINPR ephedrine
DEEEHIRST etherised
DEEEHIRTZ etherized
DEEEHLPRT telphered
DEEEHLRST sheltered
DEEEHLRSW wheedlers
DEEEHNPRR reprehend
DEEEHNPRS ensphered
DEEEHNRRU hereunder
DEEEHORSW horseweed
shoreweed
DEEEILLMP millepede
DEEEILNNV enlivened
DEEEILPRV replevied
DEEEILPTV depletive
DEEEILRRV deliverer
redeliver
DEEEILRST leistered
DEEEILSSW edelweiss
DEEEILSTV televised
DEEEIMNRT determine
DEEEIMNSU Eumenides
DEEEIMPRR premiered
DEEEIMSST disesteem
DEEEINNSS neediness
DEEEINOPR pioneered
DEEEINPTX expedient
DEEEINQTU quietened
DEEEINRRS reindeers
DEEEINRSS reediness
DEEEINRST eternised
tenderise
teredines
DEEEINRTZ eternized
tenderize
DEEEINSSS seediness
DEEEINSSW weediness
DEEEIPRRV reprieved
DEEEIPRTX expediter
DEEEIPRVW previewed
DEEEIPSST speediest
DEEEIPSTX expedites
DEEEIRRRS derrieres
DEEEIRRTV retrieved
DEEEIRSTV detersive
DEEEIRUZZ Zuider Zee
DEEEISTTW tweediest
DEEEKLLNN kennelled
DEEEKLLNR kernelled
DEEEKNNTT kennetted
DEEELLPSW speedwell
DEEELNOPV enveloped
DEEELNSTU unsteeled
DEEELOPPR repeopled
DEEELOPRV developer
redevelop
DEEELPPRX perplexed
DEEELPSSS de Lesseps
DEEELRSTT resettled
DEEELRSTW sweltered
DEEEMNNOV envenomed
DEEEMNRTT determent
DEEEMOORT oedometer
DEEEMOPRT pedometer
DEEEMOPRW empowered
DEEEMORST dosemeter
DEEEMPPRT preempted
DEEEMPSTT tempested
DEEEMRSST deemsters
DEEENNRTU unentered
DEEENNRUW unrenewed
DEEENNSSS denseness

DEEENORSS endorsees
DEEENPRRT pretender
DEEENPRSS Despenser
DEEENPRST presented
repetends
DEEENPRSX expenders
DEEENPRTV prevented
DEEENRRRS renderers
DEEENRRST tenderers
DEEENRRSV reverends
DEEENRRTT deterrent
DEEENRSTT tenderest
DEEENRSTX extenders
DEEENSSVX vexedness
DEEEOPRST deportees
DEEEORRSS reredoses
DEEEORSTV stevedore
DEEEORSVW oversewed
DEEEORSVX oversexed
DEEEPRRSS repressed
DEEEPRRSV preserved
DEEEPRRTV perverted
DEEEPRSSS depresses
DEEEPRSST speedster
DEEEPRSSU supersede
DEEEPRSSX expressed
DEEEPRSTT pretested
DEEEPRSUW superweed
DEEEQRSTU requested
DEEERRRSS redresser
DEEERRRSV verderers
DEEERRSSS redresses
DEEERRSST deserters
DEEERRSSV deservers
DEEERSSTT detesters
DEEERUYZZ Zuyder Zee
DEEFFFSTU feedstuff
DEEFFHILS Sheffield
DEEFFINRT different
DEEFFINST stiffened
DEEFFIORT forfeited
DEEFFLOSU souffleed
DEEFFNORS forefends
offenders
DEEFFNORU unoffered
DEEFFOPRR proffered
DEEFGHIRT freighted
DEEFGIILR filigreed
DEEFGIIRS Siegfried
DEEFGILST fledgiest
DEEFGINNU unfeigned
DEEFGINRR deferring
DEEFGINRY redefying
DEEFGJORU forejudge
DEEFGLSUW gulfweeds
DEEFHIRSS redfishes
DEEFHLLUY heedfully
DEEFHLNUU unheedful
DEEFHLOPS sheepfold
DEEFHLORS freeholds
DEEFHLORT threefold
DEEFHLRSS feldshers
DEEFHRRTU furthered
DEEFIIJLL jellified
DEEFIIKLN fiendlike
DEEFIILMN minefield
DEEFIILNR infielder
DEEFIILQU liquefied
DEEFIIMNS feminised
misdefine
DEEFIIMNZ feminized
DEEFIIMRT metrified
DEEFIINNS definiens
DEEFIINRU reunified
DEEFIIPRS perfidies
DEEFIIPRT petrified
DEEFIIRRT terrified
DEEFIIRSS firesides
DEEFIIRSV versified
DEEFIISTT testified
DEEFILLRU fulleride
DEEFILMNS fieldsmen
DEEFILNOX deflexion
DEEFILORT trefoiled
DEEFILRTT flittered
DEEFIMRSU frusemide
DEEFINNRU unrefined
DEEFINRSU reinfused
DEEFINRTW winterfed
DEEFINSST fetidness
DEEFINSSX fixedness
DEEFIORRT torrefied
DEEFIORSS foresides
DEEFIPRRV perfervid
DEEFIPRST presifted
DEEFIPRTU putrefied
DEEFIPSTU stupefied
DEEFIRRTT frittered
DEEFIRSTU surfeited
DEEFLLNNU funnelled
DEEFLLNUY needfully
DEEFLNNUU unneedful
DEEFLNORS enfolders
DEEFLNOSV sevenfold
DEEFLNRTU underfelt
DEEFLOOTW Fleetwood
DEEFLORSW deflowers
DEEFLRSTU flustered
DEEFLRTTU fluttered
DEEFMOPRR performed
preformed
DEEFMORRS deformers
DEEFNOOST festooned
DEEFNRRSU refunders
DEEFOOPRR reproofed
DEEFOPRSS professed
DEEFORRST defroster
DEEFORSST deforests
DEEGGGILN legginged
DEEGGHHOS hedgehogs
DEEGGILNR ledgering
DEEGGIMNR demerging
DEEGGINRS sniggered
DEEGGINRT deterging
DEEGGIORS doggeries
DEEGGIRRT triggered
DEEGGIRST dreggiest
DEEGGIRSU ruggedise
DEEGGIRUZ ruggedize
DEEGGMNTU nutmegged
DEEGGNTTU nuggetted
DEEGGSSTU suggested
DEEGHHOPS hedgehops
DEEGHIINV inveighed
DEEGHILNT lightened
DEEGHILNW wheedling
DEEGHILRT delighter
relighted
DEEGHINNU unheeding
DEEGHINRT rightened
DEEGHINTT tightened
DEEGHINUW unweighed
DEEGHNORU roughened
DEEGHNOTU toughened
DEEGHOPSS sheepdogs
DEEGHORSW hedgerows
DEEGHORTW Edgeworth
DEEGIIKLR ridgelike
DEEGIILNU guideline
DEEGIILNV inveigled
DEEGIINNS indigenes
DEEGIINRT reediting
reignited
DEEGIINSS digenesis
DEEGIISTV digestive
DEEGIJKLU judgelike
DEEGILMMR glimmered
DEEGILNOU euglenoid
DEEGILNPT depleting
DEEGILNRS reedlings
DEEGILNRT ringleted
DEEGILNRW rewelding
DEEGILNSS gelidness
seedlings
DEEGILNST glistened
DEEGILOOU ideologue
DEEGILOPR ridgepole
DEEGILOSU eulogised
DEEGILOUZ eulogized
DEEGILQSU squilgeed
DEEGILRST glistered
DEEGILRSW weregilds
DEEGILRTT glittered
DEEGILSSU guideless
DEEGIMNNR remending
DEEGIMNNT dementing
DEEGIMNRY remedying
DEEGIMORT geometrid
DEEGIMRSU demiurges
DEEGINNPX expending
DEEGINNRR rendering
DEEGINNRT tendering
DEEGINNTX extending
DEEGINORT redingote
DEEGINPRS predesign
DEEGINRRR derringer

DEEGINRRS	deringers
DEEGINRRT	deterring
DEEGINRSS	designers
	redesigns
DEEGINRST	deserting
DEEGINRSV	deserving
DEEGINRTU	negritude
DEEGINRTV	divergent
DEEGINRUV	gerundive
DEEGINSTT	detesting
DEEGINSTV	devesting
DEEGINTTV	vignetted
DEEGIOSST	geodesist
DEEGIPRST	predigest
DEEGIRRSS	digresser
DEEGIRSSS	digresses
DEEGIRSST	digesters
	redigests
DEEGJLSSU	judgeless
DEEGJMNTU	judgement
DEEGJPRRU	prejudger
DEEGJPRSU	prejudges
DEEGKLNOW	knowledge
DEEGLLORV	grovelled
DEEGLMNOT	lodgement
DEEGLNORW	Glendower
DEEGLNTTU	englutted
DEEGLOPRS	pledgeors
DEEGMOORS	Sedgemoor
DEEGNNORU	undergone
DEEGNNSSU	Dungeness
DEEGNOORW	greenwood
DEEGNOPSU	geepounds
DEEGNORRU	guerdoner
	undergoer
DEEGNORSS	engrossed
DEEGNORSU	undergoes
DEEGOPRRU	regrouped
DEEHHIORS	horsehide
DEEHHPRSS	shepherds
DEEHIINPT	pethidine
DEEHIINRT	inherited
DEEHIKRSW	whiskered
DEEHILLRV	helldiver
DEEHILNPS	plenished
DEEHILOPP	pedophile
DEEHILORU	hierodule
DEEHILPRS	eldership
DEEHILRSS	shielders
DEEHILRST	slithered
DEEHILRSV	shriveled
DEEHILSSV	dishevels
DEEHIMMRS	shimmered
DEEHIMOPS	hemipodes
DEEHIMORT	moithered
DEEHIMOST	methodise
DEEHIMOTX	methoxide
DEEHIMOTZ	methodize
DEEHIMPRW	whimpered
DEEHIMSUX	humidexes
DEEHINNOV	Eindhoven
DEEHINNRS	enshrined
DEEHINOPX	phenoxide
DEEHINORT	dinothere
DEEHINPRS	insphered
	phrensied
DEEHINPRT	trephined
DEEHINRRS	hinderers
DEEHINRSS	drisheens
DEEHINRSW	swineherd
DEEHIOORT	Theodore I
DEEHIORST	theorised
DEEHIORTZ	theorized
DEEHIOSTX	ethoxides
DEEHIPPRS	reshipped
DEEHIPRSW	whispered
DEEHIRRST	ditherers
DEEHIRSSV	dervishes
DEEHIRSSW	shrewdies
DEEHIRSTW	swithered
DEEHIRTTW	whittered
DEEHKNOSS	keeshonds
DEEHLLNSU	unshelled
DEEHLLOSU	houselled
DEEHLLOSV	shovelled
DEEHLMORY	Meyerhold
DEEHLNOYY	honeyedly
DEEHLORST	holstered
DEEHMOORT	hodometer
DEEHMORST	smothered
DEEHMRRTU	murthered
DEEHNNORS	Henderson
DEEHNNORT	enthroned
DEEHNOPTY	endophyte
DEEHNORRS	dehorners
DEEHNORRT	dethroner
DEEHNORST	dethrones
	shortened
	threnodes
DEEHNOSWY	honeydews
DEEHNPRSU	unsphered
DEEHNRRTU	thunderer
DEEHOORTX	heterodox
DEEHOOSUW	Wodehouse
DEEHOPSTU	Deep South
DEEHORRSY	hydrosere
DEEHRSSTW	shrewdest
DEEHRSTTU	shuttered
DEEHSSTTU	dustsheet
DEEIIINPR	pieridine
DEEIILLMP	millipede
DEEIILMPR	imperiled
DEEIILNPP	pipelined
DEEIILNSS	sidelines
DEEIILRSV	devilries
DEEIILSTW	wieldiest
DEEIIMNTT	midinette
DEEIIMPRS	epidermis
DEEIIMRSS	dimerises
DEEIIMRSZ	dimerizes
DEEIINOSZ	deionizes
DEEIINRTV	reinvited
DEEIINSST	densities
	destinies
DEEIIPPPR	Pied Piper
DEEIIPRSU	Euripides
	priedieus
DEEIIPRUX	priedieux
DEEIIPSSW	sideswipe
DEEIIRRSV	riverside
DEEIIRSTV	revisited
DEEIIRTVV	divertive
DEEIISSSS	disseises
DEEIISSSZ	disseizes
DEEIJNORR	rejoinder
DEEIKLLRS	killdeers
	reskilled
DEEIKLMSW	milkweeds
DEEIKLMWY	midweekly
DEEIKLNNR	enkindler
DEEIKLNNS	enkindles
DEEIKLNRS	rekindles
DEEIKLNSX	sexlinked
DEEIKLSSW	silkweeds
DEEIKNORV	reinvoked
DEEIKNRSS	deerskins
DEEIKNSTW	stinkweed
DEEIKPPRS	skippered
DEEIKRSTT	skittered
DEEIKSSTT	diskettes
DEEILLMPS	millepeds
DEEILLNRW	indweller
DEEILLNST	tinselled
DEEILLNSV	snivelled
DEEILLPRS	dispeller
DEEILLRRV	driveller
DEEILLRST	trellised
DEEILLRTU	telluride
DEEILLSVW	swivelled
DEEILMNRU	relumined
DEEILMNSU	demilunes
DEEILMNTV	devilment
DEEILMORS	melodiser
DEEILMORZ	melodizer
DEEILMOSS	melodises
DEEILMOSZ	melodizes
DEEILMOTV	demivolte
DEEILMPTU	multipede
DEEILNNRU	underline
DEEILNNSS	Lindesnes
DEEILNOPT	depletion
	diplotene
DEEILNOST	deletions
DEEILNOSV	novelised
DEEILNOVZ	novelized
DEEILNPRT	interpled
DEEILNPTU	plenitude
DEEILNRRU	underlier
DEEILNRSU	underlies
DEEILNRTU	interlude
DEEILNSSX	indexless
DEEILNTVY	evidently
DEEILOPRS	despoiler
DEEILOPTX	exploited
DEEILORRS	orderlies
DEEILORST	dolerites

DEEILORSV evildoers
DEEILORVV overlived
DEEILOSVW vowelised
DEEILOVWZ vowelized
DEEILPPRS slippered
DEEILPRSX diplexers
DEEILRRSS riderless
DEEILRSVY diversely
DEEILRTUY eruditely
DEEIMMORS memorised
DEEIMMORZ memorized
DEEIMMOSS semidomes
DEEIMMRRT retrimmed
DEEIMMRST mistermed
DEEIMNNOT mentioned
DEEIMNNRU undermine
DEEIMNNTZ dizenment
DEEIMNORS domineers
modernise
DEEIMNORZ modernize
DEEIMNOSS demonises
Des Moines
DEEIMNOST moistened
monetised
DEEIMNOSU Idomeneus
DEEIMNOSZ demonizes
DEEIMNOTZ monetized
DEEIMNPRS spidermen
DEEIMNPST pediments
DEEIMNPTU unemptied
DEEIMNRRS reminders
DEEIMNRTT detriment
DEEIMNRTU undertime
unmerited
DEEIMNSST sediments
DEEIMNSSX mixedness
DEEIMOORT meteoroid
DEEIMOPRS reimposed
DEEIMOPRW impowered
DEEIMORST dosimeter
DEEIMORTV overtimed
DEEIMOSST modesties
DEEIMPRRS periderms
DEEIMPRSS impressed
DEEIMPRST distemper
DEEIMPRTT permitted
DEEIMRSST demisters
DEEIMRTUU deuterium
DEEINNOPS pensioned
DEEINNORT internode
DEEINNORV environed
DEEINNOTT detention
DEEINNPRU unripened
DEEINNRST indenters
intenders
DEEINNRTU indenture
DEEINNSSS snideness
DEEINOPRT repointed
DEEINOPTX pentoxide
DEEINORSS indorsees
DEEINORST desertion
DEEINORSW rosinweed

DEEINOSSV nosedives
DEEINPRRT reprinted
DEEINPRSS dispenser
DEEINPRST president
DEEINPRUX unexpired
DEEINPSSS dispenses
DEEINPSST tepidness
DEEINRRSU reinsured
DEEINRRSW rewinders
DEEINRSST dissenter
residents
tiredness
DEEINRSSW weirdness
DEEINRSTT trendiest
DEEINRSTX dextrines
DEEINRSUV unrevised
DEEINSSTW witnessed
DEEIOPRRT portiered
DEEIOPRST redeposit
reposited
DEEIOPRSX peroxides
DEEIOPRTX expeditor
DEEIORRRV overrider
DEEIORRST roistered
DEEIORRSV overrides
DEEIORRTV overtired
DEEIORRVV overdrive
DEEIORSVZ oversized
DEEIORTTX tetroxide
DEEIOTTVX videotext
DEEIPPRRS perspired
DEEIPRRSS disperser
presiders
DEEIPRRSV deprivers
DEEIPRSSS despisers
disperses
DEEIPRSST persisted
DEEIPRSTU disrepute
DEEIPSSST sidesteps
DEEIPSSTU deputises
DEEIPSTUZ deputizes
DEEIRRSST destriers
DEEIRRSTV diverters
DEEIRSSST dressiest
DEEIRSSSV disserves
dissevers
DEEIRSTTW retwisted
DEEIRSTUV divesture
servitude
DEEIRTTTW twittered
DEEIRTTXY dexterity
DEEISTTTU destitute
DEEJKNTTU junketted
DEEJNORUY journeyed
DEEJOORVY overjoyed
DEEKKNSUW skunkweed
DEEKKOOYY okeydokey
DEEKLNORS snorkeled
DEEKLNOSV veldskoen
DEEKNOORS snookered
DEEKNORST stonkered
DEEKNORUV unrevoked

DEEKNOSTW knotweeds
DEEKNQRUU Dunkerque
DEELLMMOP pommelled
DEELLMMPU pummelled
DEELLMORS modellers
DEELLNNTU tunnelled
DEELLNQUU unquelled
DEELLNRSU undersell
DEELLNRSY slenderly
DEELLNSSY endlessly
DEELLOPPR propelled
DEELLORSY yodellers
DEELLORTW trowelled
DEELLPSUW upswelled
DEELMMPTU plummeted
DEELMNOOS melodeons
DEELMOORV velodrome
DEELMOPRS empolders
DEELNNPST splendent
DEELNNPTY pendently
DEELNOOST lodestone
DEELNOPPU unpeopled
DEELNORST rondelets
DEELNPRRU plunderer
DEELNRSTU underlets
DEELNSTTU unsettled
DEELNSWWY newlyweds
DEELOPRRS deplorers
DEELOPRSX exploders
DEELOPRSY redeploys
DEELOPRTU ploutered
DEELOPRTW plowtered
DEELOPRTY depletory
DEELORRSS orderless
solderers
DEELORRUV overruled
DEELORSSW dowerless
DEELORSTT dotterels
DEELORTTU rouletted
DEELPPSTU septupled
DEELPRRSU preluders
DEELPRSTU drupelets
DEELPRTUY reputedly
DEEMMOOSS desmosome
DEEMNNOTW endowment
DEEMNNRUY Runnymede
DEEMNOPRS endosperm
DEEMNOPSU spodumene
DEEMNORST entoderms
DEEMNORTT tormented
DEEMNORTU remounted
DEEMNOSTU endosteum
DEEMNPTTU untempted
DEEMOORST odometers
DEEMORSSW wormseeds
DEEMORSTU udometers
DEEMPRSST dempsters
DEEMPRTTU trumpeted
DEEMRRRSU demurrers
murderers
DEEMRRSSU murderess
DEENNOPRS personned

DEENNOPST	deponents
DEENNORTU	undertone
DEENNRTUW	underwent
DEENOOPRS	endospore
DEENOPRRS	responder
DEENOPRRV	provender
DEENOPRSV	overspend
DEENOPRUX	expounder
DEENOPSUX	unexposed
DEENORRSS	endorsers
DEENORRSW	wonderers
DEENORSTT	snottered
DEENORSTU	deuterons
DEENORTUY	tourneyed
DEENPPSTU	unstepped
DEENPRSSU	suspender
	unpressed
DEENRRRSU	surrender
DEENRRSSU	sunderers
DEENRSSSU	undresses
DEENRSSTU	sederunts
	undersets
DEENRSTTU	entrusted
DEENRSTUV	undervest
DEENRSTYY	dysentery
DEENRTTUU	unuttered
DEEOOPRST	torpedoes
DEEOORRVV	overdrove
DEEOORSSV	overdoses
DEEOPPRRS	prospered
DEEOPPRSS	oppressed
DEEOPPRST	stoppered
DEEOPRRSS	depressor
DEEOPRRSW	powderers
DEEOPRSST	dopesters
DEEOPRSTT	protested
DEEOPRSUZ	douzepers
DEEOPSSSS	possessed
DEEORRRSS	redressor
DEEORRSSV	overdress
DEEORRSTU	trousered
DEEORRSTX	dextrorse
DEEORRSTY	destroyer
DEEORRSUV	devourers
DEEORRTUV	overtured
DEEORSTTT	stottered
DEEORSTUX	dexterous
DEEPRRSSU	pressured
DEEPRSTTU	sputtered
DEERRSSTU	tressured
DEERSTTTU	stuttered
DEFFGIINR	differing
DEFFGIJRU	Gurdjieff
DEFFGINNO	offending
DEFFIIORT	fortified
DEFFIISUV	diffusive
DEFFILLLU	fulfilled
DEFFILSUY	diffusely
DEFFIORSS	offsiders
DEFFIRSSU	diffusers
DEFFLMNUU	unmuffled
DEFFLNRUU	unruffled
DEFFNOPRU	Pufendorf
DEFFSSTUY	dyestuffs
DEFGGIINT	fidgeting
DEFGGILLN	fledgling
DEFGHILOT	eightfold
DEFGHIOSS	dogfishes
DEFGIIILN	lignified
DEFGIIINS	dignifies
	signified
DEFGIILOR	glorified
DEFGIINNR	friending
	infringed
DEFGIIRSU	disfigure
DEFGIISST	digestifs
DEFGILNNO	enfolding
DEFGILNOR	refolding
DEFGIMNOR	deforming
DEFGINNRU	refunding
DEFGINOOR	foredoing
DEFGJORSU	forjudges
DEFHIILSV	devilfish
DEFHIIORR	horrified
DEFHIMSSU	mudfishes
DEFHINRSU	furnished
DEFHLOOOW	wholefood
DEFHOOOTT	hotfooted
DEFIIINRT	nitrified
DEFIIIRTV	vitrified
DEFIIISSS	sissified
DEFIIJLLO	jollified
DEFIIJSTU	justified
DEFIILLMO	mollified
DEFIILLNU	nullified
DEFIILLOS	oilfields
DEFIILMSU	semifluid
DEFIILRSU	fluidiser
DEFIILRTU	Eid-ul-Fitr
DEFIILRUZ	fluidizer
DEFIILSSU	fluidises
DEFIILSUZ	fluidizes
DEFIIMMMU	mummified
DEFIIMNNY	indemnify
DEFIIMORS	modifiers
DEFIIMORT	mortified
DEFIIMRWY	midwifery
DEFIIMSTT	misfitted
DEFIIMSTY	mystified
DEFIINOPT	pontified
DEFIINRTY	denitrify
DEFIINSST	disinfest
DEFIIPPUY	yuppified
DEFIIPSSS	fissipeds
DEFIIRSSU	russified
DEFIIRSVY	diversify
DEFIIRTVY	devitrify
DEFIKLORW	fieldwork
DEFILLORV	frivolled
DEFILMNRU	remindful
DEFILMSUY	demulsify
DEFILNORS	infolders
DEFILNORT	interfold
DEFILNOSW	snowfield
DEFILNRSU	urnfields
DEFILNSSU	fluidness
DEFILORSU	fluorides
DEFILOSTU	outfields
DEFIMNORT	dentiform
DEFIMNORU	uniformed
DEFIMORTY	deformity
DEFIMSTYY	demystify
DEFINORSU	foundries
DEFINORSW	forewinds
DEFIOPSTX	postfixed
DEFIORSST	disforest
DEFIORTTU	fortitude
DEFIOTTTU	outfitted
DEFLLLOUY	dolefully
DEFLLOORS	folderols
DEFLLOOSS	floodless
DEFLMMOUX	flummoxed
DEFLNORSS	frondless
DEFLNORSU	flounders
	unfolders
DEFLNORUW	underflow
	wonderful
DEFLOORSV	overfolds
DEFMOOORS	foredooms
DEFNOOOTT	footnoted
DEFNOORTU	underfoot
DEFNRRSUU	underfurs
DEFOOOTTU	outfooted
DEFOORRSW	forewords
DEFORRSTT	Stretford
DEGGIILNR	regilding
	ridgeling
DEGGIINNS	designing
DEGGIINRV	diverging
DEGGIINST	digesting
DEGGIJNRU	rejudging
DEGGILQSU	squiggled
DEGGINORS	sodgering
DEGGINSTU	degusting
DEGGIORRS	disgorger
DEGGIORSS	disgorges
DEGGLNPUU	unplugged
DEGGLRSTU	struggled
DEGHIILNS	shielding
DEGHIILST	sidelight
DEGHIINNR	hindering
DEGHIINRT	dithering
DEGHIJPSU	judgeship
DEGHILMSU	gumshield
DEGHILNTU	unlighted
DEGHIMNRU	humdinger
DEGHINNOR	dehorning
DEGHINSTU	unsighted
DEGHIOPSS	dogeships
DEGHIORTU	doughtier
DEGHIOSTU	doughiest
DEGHIPRTU	uprighted
DEGHMOORT	godmother
DEGHNNRUU	underhung
DEGHNOORU	gorehound
DEGHNORUY	greyhound

DEGHOOSSU doghouses
DEGIIIMRS dirigisme
semirigid
DEGIIINST dignities
DEGIIIRST digitiser
dirigiste
DEGIIIRTZ digitizer
DEGIIISST digitises
DEGIIISTZ digitizes
DEGIILLNV devilling
DEGIILMMN immingled
DEGIILMNN mildening
DEGIILMNW mildewing
DEGIILNNR redlining
DEGIILNOV evildoing
DEGIILNRV driveling
DEGIILNRW wildering
DEGIILSTU digitules
DEGIIMNNP impending
DEGIIMNNR reminding
DEGIIMNOR moidering
DEGIIMNST demisting
DEGIIMNTT demitting
DEGIIMRSU misguider
DEGIIMSSU misguides
DEGIINNNT indenting
intending
DEGIINNNW enwinding
DEGIINNRS niderings
DEGIINNRW rewinding
DEGIINNSS dinginess
DEGIINNST destining
indigents
DEGIINOSS gneissoid
DEGIINOST digestion
DEGIINPRS presiding
DEGIINPRV depriving
DEGIINPSS despising
DEGIINPST despiting
DEGIINRSS rigidness
ringsides
DEGIINRTU intrigued
nigritude
DEGIINRTV diverting
DEGIINSST desisting
DEGIINSTU distingue
DEGIINSTV divesting
DEGIIOPRS prodigies
DEGIIQRSU squidgier
DEGIIRRSV verdigris
DEGIIRSSU disguiser
DEGIISSSU disguises
DEGIJMRSU misjudger
DEGIJMSSU misjudges
DEGIKLORU gourdlike
DEGIKNNOO de Kooning
DEGILLMNO modelling
DEGILLNOW dowelling
DEGILLNOY yodelling
DEGILLNSW dwellings
DEGILMNNU unmingled
DEGILMNOR goldminer
moldering
DEGILMNOS singledom
DEGILMNPU depluming
DEGILMNSU guildsmen
DEGILNNOU loudening
DEGILNNRU underling
DEGILNNTU indulgent
DEGILNOOR gondolier
DEGILNOPR deploring
DEGILNOPX exploding
DEGILNOPY deploying
DEGILNORS soldering
DEGILNORU ungodlier
DEGILNOSS godliness
DEGILNOSU delousing
DEGILNOTU longitude
DEGILNOVV devolving
DEGILNPRU preluding
DEGILNRSU indulgers
DEGILOOST goodliest
DEGILOSTT glottides
DEGILRSUV divulgers
DEGIMNRRU demurring
murdering
DEGINNOOW woodening
DEGINNOPR pondering
DEGINNORS endorsing
DEGINNORW wondering
DEGINNRSU sundering
DEGINNRUW underwing
DEGINOORV overdoing
DEGINOPRT deporting
DEGINOPRW powdering
DEGINOPSS podginess
DEGINORRW rewording
DEGINORSV ringdoves
DEGINORTU detouring
DEGINORUV devouring
DEGINPSSU pudginess
DEGINRRTU undergirt
DEGINRSSS dressings
DEGINRTUX extruding
DEGIOOSVW goodwives
DEGIOPRTY pterygoid
DEGIOPSTU guidepost
DEGIOSSTT stodgiest
DEGJMNSTU judgments
DEGLLLOOR logrolled
DEGLLOSSY godlessly
DEGLMNOST lodgments
DEGLMOPRU promulged
DEGLNOOPR prolonged
DEGLNOOST goldstone
DEGLNORSU groundsel
DEGLOOPRU prologued
DEGLOOSUU duologues
DEGNNOTUU outgunned
DEGNOORRW wrongdoer
DEGNOOSST stegodons
DEGNOOSTT stegodont
DEGNOPRUW gunpowder
DEGNORSYY gyrodynes
DEGOOPRRU prorogued
DEGORRSTU drugstore
DEHHIIMNT Hindemith
DEHHIINOS hoidenish
DEHHIKMOS sheikhdom
DEHHILNOS Holinshed
DEHHINOSY hoydenish
DEHHIOPPS phosphide
DEHHLLNOU hellhound
DEHHLOOSU household
DEHHLORST threshold
DEHHNOORU horehound
DEHIIINST histidine
DEHIIKLMR Kriemhild
DEHIILRSS disrelish
DEHIIMNTY thymidine
DEHIINNRS inshrined
DEHIINNRU hirundine
DEHIINOOP idiophone
DEHIIOSTY hideosity
DEHIISSTT ditheists
DEHIISTWW widthwise
DEHIJMNOS demijohns
DEHIKKOOZ Kozhikode
DEHIKMOSS sheikdoms
DEHIKNORT Thorndike
DEHIKORSS droshkies
DEHILLNOR Hölderlin
DEHILOORT rhodolite
DEHILOSTW dishtowel
DEHILOSTY holytides
DEHILOSUY hideously
DEHILPSSU sulphides
DEHILRRUY hurriedly
DEHIMMOST methodism
DEHIMNORT Trondheim
DEHIMNSSU humidness
DEHIMORRT thermidor
DEHIMOSTT methodist
DEHIMOSTU Methodius
DEHIMPRTU triumphed
DEHINNOPR endorphin
DEHINOORT rhodonite
DEHINOPSS sphenoids
DEHINORRT trihedron
DEHINORSU nourished
DEHINORVW windhover
DEHINOSST dishonest
hedonists
DEHINPPSU unshipped
DEHINRRUU unhurried
DEHIOORSW Isherwood
DEHIOOTWW howtowdie
whitewood
DEHIOPRSS spheroids
DEHIOPRSW worshiped
DEHIORSTY hysteroid
DEHIOSSSW sideshows
DEHKLNOSU elkhounds
DEHKLOOST stokehold
DEHKNOOOS hooknosed
DEHKNOOVZ Dovzhenko

DEHLLOOOP loopholed
DEHLLOPSY phyllodes
DEHLMNOPY endolymph
DEHLMOORU hordeolum
DEHLMOORW wormholed
DEHLOOPSS splooshed
DEHLOORSV holdovers
DEHLOOSSW woolsheds
DEHLOPRSU upholders
DEHLORSSU shoulders
DEHLORSYY hydrolyse
DEHLORTTT throttled
DEHLORTYY hydrolyte
DEHLORYYZ hydrolyze
DEHLOSSTU shouldest
DEHMNOOPR endomorph
DEHMOORSY hydrosome
DEHMOORTY hodometry
DEHNNOOPS sphenodon
DEHNNORTU unthroned
DEHNNOSTW Townshend
DEHNNOSUW newshound
DEHNOOSSW snowshoed
DEHNORSSU enshrouds
DEHNORSTU undershot
DEHNOSSSW snowsheds
DEHOOPRST theropods
DEHOORSTU Herodotus
DEHOOSSSU dosshouse
DEHOPRSST potsherds
DEHORSSTU studhorse
DEIIIKNTT identikit
DEIIILQSU liquidise
DEIIILQUZ liquidize
DEIIIMMNS minimised
DEIIIMMNZ minimized
DEIIINNQU quinidine
DEIIINSSS disseisin
DEIIINSSV divinises
DEIIINSSZ disseizin
DEIIINSVZ divinizes
DEIIKKLNR kilderkin
DEIIKLNST kindliest
DEIILLMNU illumined
DEIILLMPY impliedly
DEIILLMTY limitedly
DEIILLNST instilled
DEIILLOOP Leopold II
DEIILLOPR pilloried
DEIILLOPS ellipsoid
DEIILLRST distiller
DEIILMNTU unlimited
DEIILMOSS semisolid
DEIILMRSU deliriums
DEIILMSTT mistitled
DEIILNNSU indulines
DEIILNOTU toluidine
DEIILNPRS spindlier
DEIILNPSV vilipends
DEIILNSSV lividness
DEIILNTTU intituled
DEIILORSS idolisers
DEIILORSU delirious
DEIILORSZ idolizers
DEIILORTV vitrioled
DEIILPSSS sideslips
DEIILRRZZ drizzlier
DEIILSUVV divulsive
DEIIMMNSU immunised
DEIIMMNUZ immunized
DEIIMNNOS dimension
DEIIMNNTY indemnity
DEIIMNOSS demission
missioned
Simonides
DEIIMNPRT imprinted
DEIIMNRSS minidress
DEIIMNRTW midwinter
DEIIMNRUU uredinium
DEIIMNSST timidness
DEIIMOPST optimised
DEIIMOPTZ optimized
DEIIMPRSS misprised
DEIIMPRSU presidium
DEIIMPRSZ misprized
DEIIMSSSS dismisses
DEIINNNOT indention
DEIINNORT rendition
DEIINNOSU unionised
DEIINNOTT dentition
DEIINNOTV vendition
DEIINNOUZ unionized
DEIINNPPS pinnipeds
DEIINNRTW interwind
DEIINNSSW windiness
DEIINNTUV uninvited
DEIINOPRT perdition
DEIINOPSS indispose
DEIINORSS ironsides
resinoids
sironised
DEIINORST disorient
DEIINORSV diversion
DEIINORSZ sironized
DEIINORTT detrition
DEIINORTU erudition
DEIINOSST seditions
DEIINOTTZ Donizetti
DEIINPPSW windpipes
DEIINRSST dirtiness
disinters
DEIINRSTU disuniter
DEIINSSTU disunites
DEIINSSTV disinvest
DEIINSSVV vividness
DEIINSSZZ dizziness
DEIINSTTU untidiest
DEIINSTUV unvisited
DEIIOPRSS presidios
DEIIOPRST tripodies
DEIIORSSS disseisor
siderosis
DEIIORSSX oxidisers
DEIIORSSZ disseizor
DEIIORSTX trioxides
DEIIORSXZ oxidizers
DEIIOSSTU seditious
DEIIPPRST drippiest
DEIIPRSSZ disprizes
DEIIQSSTU disquiets
DEIIRSTVY diversity
DEIIRSUVV redivivus
DEIJLNOTY jointedly
DEIJNNOTU unjointed
DEIJNNRUU uninjured
DEIJORRSY joyriders
DEIKKLNOR klondiker
DEIKKNOOP pondokkie
DEIKLLNSU unskilled
DEIKLLOSV volkslied
DEIKLLPSU upskilled
DEIKLNPRS sprinkled
DEIKLORSW swordlike
DEIKNNSTU unkindest
DEIKNNTTU unknitted
DEIKNORRV overdrink
DEIKNSSSU duskiness
DEIKRSSVY skydivers
DEILLMNOU mullioned
DEILLNSUU unsullied
DEILLNUWY unwieldly
DEILLOOTT Doolittle
DEILLOOVW Woodville
DEILLOPST pistolled
postilled
DEILLORRW worldlier
DEILLORST lordliest
DEILLORSY soldierly
DEILLSSTU duellists
DEILLSTTY stiltedly
DEILMNOOS melodions
DEILMNOSS moldiness
DEILMOOST dolomites
DEILMOOSU melodious
DEILMOPRS impolders
DEILMORSU lemuroids
DEILMORTU turmoiled
DEILMOSST melodists
DEILMOSSU emulsoids
DEILMOSTU mouldiest
DEILMOSTV demivolts
DEILMPSTU multipeds
DEILMTTUU multitude
DEILNOOSS solenoids
DEILNOPRU purloined
DEILNOPSU unspoiled
DEILNOPTY pointedly
DEILNORSU undersoil
DEILNOSSS solidness
DEILNOSSU delusions
DEILNOTUV involuted
DEILNRSSU luridness
DEILNRSSW swindlers
DEILOOPSS podsolise
DEILOOPST topsoiled
DEILOOPSU duopolies

DEILOOPSW woodpiles
DEILOOPSZ podsolize
podzolise
DEILOOPZZ podzolize
DEILORRWY worriedly
DEILORSSV dissolver
DEILORVWW worldview
world-view
DEILOSSSV dissolves
DEILOSSTU dissolute
solitudes
DEILOSTUY tediously
DEILOSUVY deviously
DEILPRSSU serpulids
DEILPTUXY duplexity
DEIMMMRSU midsummer
DEIMMNORS modernism
DEIMMNOUY neodymium
DEIMMOSTY immodesty
DEIMNOORT monitored
DEIMNOOSS moodiness
DEIMNOOST demotions
DEIMNOOSX monoxides
DEIMNOPRU impounder
DEIMNORST modernist
DEIMNORTY modernity
DEIMNOSST demonists
DEIMNOSTW downtimes
DEIMNPRTU imprudent
DEIMNPSSS misspends
DEIMNPSSU dumpiness
DEIMNRSTU rudiments
DEIMNRTTU Tridentum
DEIMNSSTU tumidness
DEIMOOORT ideomotor
DEIMOORST motorised
DEIMOORTY iodometry
DEIMOORTZ motorized
DEIMOOSSS sodomises
DEIMOOSST sodomites
DEIMOOSSZ sodomizes
DEIMOPPUY yuppiedom
DEIMOPSST despotism
DEIMOQSTU misquoted
DEIMORSTY dosimetry
DEIMORSUX exordiums
DEIMOSSTT demotists
DEINNNOSU innuendos
DEINNOOST noontides
DEINNOOTX endotoxin
DEINNOPTU unpointed
DEINNORRV nondriver
DEINNORST indentors
DEINNOSSW downiness
DEINNOSTU nonsuited
tendinous
DEINNPRSU underpins
DEINNRSUU uninsured
DEINNRSUW unwinders
DEINNRTTU undertint
DEINNSTTU unstinted
DEINOOPRT portioned
DEINOOPSS opsonised
DEINOOPSZ opsonized
DEINOOSSW woodiness
DEINOOSTV devotions
DEINOPPRR properdin
DEINOPPSW downpipes
DEINOPRST dipterons
dripstone
DEINOPRSY pyrenoids
DEINOPRTV provident
DEINORRSS indorsers
DEINORRUW unworried
DEINORRWW windrower
DEINORSST dortiness
DEINORSSU sourdines
DEINORSSW disowners
rowdiness
wordiness
DEINORSTU detrusion
DEINORSVW overwinds
DEINOSSTT dottiness
DEINOSSWZ downsizes
DEINPRSTU unstriped
DEINPSTWW windswept
DEINRRSTU intruders
DEINRSTTU intrusted
DEINRSTTY dentistry
DEINSSSTU dustiness
DEINSTTUW untwisted
DEIOOPRST depositor
DEIOOPRTX protoxide
DEIOORRSU uredosori
DEIOOSSTW woodsiest
DEIOPRRST postrider
DEIOPRRSV providers
DEIOPRSSS disposers
DEIOPRSSU disposure
DEIOPRSSV disproves
DEIOPRSTU dipterous
DEIORRSTT distorter
DEIORRSTU outriders
DEIORSSTU dioestrus
outsiders
DEIORSSTW drowsiest
DEIORSTTX tetroxids
DEIOTTTUW outwitted
DEIPPTTTU tittupped
DEIPRRSSU surprised
DEIPRRSTU disrupter
DEIPRSSTU disputers
DEIPRTTUU turpitude
DEIPSSTTU stupidest
DEIRSSTTU sturdiest
DEISSTTTU duettists
DEJMOPTUU outjumped
DEJNOORSU sojourned
DEJOOPPPY joypopped
DEKKLNORY klondyker
DEKLNNRUY drunkenly
DEKNNOTTU unknotted
DEKNOORTU undertook
DEKNORRUV overdrunk
DEKOORTUW outworked
DELLNORSS drollness
DELMNOOOW lemonwood
DELMNOSTW meltdowns
DELMNPSUU pendulums
DELMNUUZZ unmuzzled
DELMORSSU smoulders
DELNNOOOS solenodon
DELNNOPSU nonplused
DELNOOOST dolostone
DELNOPRSS splendors
DELNOPRSU splendour
DELNOPRTU underplot
DELNOPSUU pendulous
DELNORSTU roundlets
DELNOSSSU soundless
DELNOSSUW woundless
DELNPRTUY prudently
DELNRRSTU trundlers
DELOOOSUW woodlouse
DELOORRSV overlords
DELOORSSU odourless
DELOPRSYY pyrolysed
DELOPRYYZ pyrolyzed
DELOPSSTU postludes
DELORSSSW swordless
DELORSTUY desultory
DELOSTUUY duteously
DEMMNOSSU summonsed
DEMMOOSTU stomodeum
DEMNNORSU roundsmen
DEMNNORUU unmourned
DEMNNOTUU unmounted
DEMNOOOPS monopodes
DEMNOPSUY pseudonym
DEMNORSSW swordsmen
DEMNORSSY syndromes
DEMNORSTU undermost
DEMOOPRRS prodromes
DEMOORSST doomsters
DEMORRSUU murderous
DENNORSSU roundness
DENNORSUW sundowner
DENNOSSSU soundness
DENNOSSTY syndetons
DENOOOPTW woodentop
DENOOOSTW woodnotes
DENOOPPST postponed
DENOOPPSU unopposed
DENOOPRSS sponsored
DENOOPRSU ponderous
DENOORRSS endorsors
DENOORSTU tournedos
DENOORUVW overwound
DENOPPRRU underprop
DENOPPSTU unstopped
DENOPRSSU proudness
DENOPSTTU unspotted
DENORSTUW undertows
DENORTTUU untutored
DENRSSTUU untrussed
DEOOORSSW rosewoods

DEOOORTTU outrooted
DEOOPPRST pteropods
DEOOPRRUV overproud
DEOOPRSST doorsteps
DEOOPRTUU outpoured
DEOORRSVW overwords
DEOPPRRTU purported
DEOPPRSTU supported
DEOPRRSTU protrudes
DEOPTTTUU outputted
DEORRSUUV verdurous
DFFFOOSTU foodstuff
DFFGIINSU diffusing
DFFIINOSU diffusion
DFFIORSSU diffusors
DFFOORSUW woodruffs
DFGGHIOST dogfights
DFGIIINNY nidifying
DFGIIIRTY frigidity
DFGIILNNO infolding
DFGIIMNOY modifying
DFGILNNOU foundling
unfolding
DFGILNNOY goldfinny
DFHHINOSU houndfish
DFHILOORY hydrofoil
DFHIORSSW swordfish
DFHLNOOUW wolfhound
DFHLOOOST footholds
DFHNOOSUX foxhounds
DFIILORTY floridity
DFIINPRST driftpins
spindrift
DFIKLNOPY Pink Floyd
DFIKOOPRS skidproof
DFILLMNUY mindfully
DFILLMOTU multifold
DFILLOSWW wildfowls
DFILLTUUY dutifully
DFILMNNUU unmindful
DFILNTUUU undutiful
DFINORSTW snowdrift
DFINRSSUW windsurfs
DFNOOPRSU profounds
DFOOOSSTW softwoods
DGGHILOSY doggishly
DGGHINOOT goodnight
DGGHNOORU groundhog
DGGIILLNY glidingly
DGGIILNNU indulging
DGGIILNRS ridglings
DGGIILNUV divulging
DGGIINNSW wingdings
DGGIJLNUY judgingly
DGGILNOPS splodging
DGGIMNOOS smoodging
DGGINNORU grounding
DGGIRSSTU druggists
DGHHIINST hindsight
DGHHINOPT diphthong
DGHHOORSU roughshod
DGHIKNOOS kinghoods

DGHILLNSU dunghills
DGHILMOST goldsmith
DGHILNOOP Godolphin
DGHILNOPU upholding
DGHILOPRT droplight
DGHILOTUY doughtily
DGHIMOPSY sphygmoid
DGHINOOOO hoodooing
DGHINORSU shrouding
DGHINORTW downright
DGHLOORYY hydrology
DGHNOSTUU doughnuts
DGHOORSUU sourdough
DGIIIKLNS disliking
DGIIILNOS idolising
DGIIILNOZ idolizing
DGIIINNOT indigotin
DGIIINNRT nitriding
DGIIINNTY indignity
DGIIINOSX oxidising
DGIIINOTX digitoxin
DGIIINOXZ oxidizing
DGIIJNORY joyriding
DGIIKNSVY skydiving
DGIILLNSW wildlings
DGIILLOOR gorilloid
DGIILMNOP imploding
DGIILNNPS spindling
DGIILNNSW swindling
DGIILNNWY windingly
DGIILNRZZ drizzling
DGIILOORY iridology
DGIIMNSSU Sigismund
DGIINNNUW unwinding
DGIINNORS indorsing
DGIINNOSW disowning
DGIINNOWW windowing
DGIINNRTU intruding
DGIINNTUY untidying
DGIINOPRV providing
DGIINOPSS disposing
DGIINORRS gridirons
DGIINORST digitrons
DGIINORTU outriding
DGIINPPRS drippings
DGIINPSTU disputing
DGIIRTTUY turgidity
DGIKNOOSW kingwoods
DGILLNOOP dolloping
DGILLNORS lordlings
DGILLNORW worldling
DGILLOOSW goodwills
DGILMNOOO mongoloid
DGILMNOSU mouldings
DGILMNPSU dumplings
DGILNNORY droningly
DGILNNOSY goldsinny
DGILNNRTU trundling
DGILNNUYY undyingly
DGIMNOSYZ Zsigmondy
DGINNOSSU soundings
DGINNOSUW swounding

DGINNOSWW downswing
DGINOOOOV voodooing
DGINOPPRS droppings
DGNNORTUU groundnut
DHHIKNSUU Hindu Kush
DHHILOSTW withholds
DHHLOORST shorthold
DHIIIPSTY hispidity
DHIILNRWW whirlwind
DHIILOPSY syphiloid
DHIIMNOOS hominoids
DHIINNNRY ninhydrin
DHIINOPTY typhoidin
DHIKNOOSW hoodwinks
DHIKORSSY hydroskis
DHILLLOSY dollishly
DHILLNOSW downhills
DHILLOSTY doltishly
DHILNNOSY donnishly
DHILOOPPY hypoploid
DHILOPRSS lordships
DHILPRSUY prudishly
DHIMNORUY hydronium
DHIMNOSTY hymnodist
DHIMOOOOS hoodooism
DHIMORSTW wordsmith
DHINNOTUW whodunnit
DHINNTUWY whydunnit
DHINOOPRS donorship
rhodopsin
DHINOORSS dishonors
DHINOORSU dishonour
DHINOSTUW whodunits
DHINSTUWY whydunits
DHIOOPRSZ rhizopods
DHIOOSTTW withstood
DHKMNOOOS monkshood
DHLLOOOWY Hollywood
DHLMOOTUU loudmouth
DHLNOORUW howlround
DHLNOOSYY holy synod
DHLOORSSY hydrosols
DHMNOOPWY wood nymph
DHNNOORTW North Down
DHNOORTWW downthrow
DHNOOSSWW showdowns
DHNOSSTUW shutdowns
DHOOORTXY orthodoxy
DHOOPPPUY puppyhood
DHOPRSTYY dystrophy
DIIILMPTY limpidity
DIIILNPSY insipidly
DIIILQTUY liquidity
DIIIMOSST idiotisms
DIIINOSSU insidious
DIIINOSSV divisions
DIIINOSUV invidious
DIIIPRSST dispirits
DIIJNOSST disjoints
DIIKLPSSU Piłsudski
DIILLMNOO modillion
DIILLMNRS millrinds

DIILLMNSW windmills
DIILLSSTY idyllists
DIILMOPPS pompilids
DIILNOSTU dilutions
DIILNOSUV divulsion
DIILOPRST triploids
DIILOSTTY stolidity
DIIMMNOSU dominiums
DIIMNNOOS dominions
DIIMNOPST midpoints
DIIMOORTV Dimitrovo
DIIMOORTY iridotomy
DIIMOPRSS prismoids
DIIMORSSY dimissory
DIINNOOQU quinonoid
DIINNOSSU disunions
DIINOSSSU sinusoids
DIINOSSUY Dionysius
DIIOPRTTY torpidity
DIIORRTTY torridity
DIIPRTTUY putridity
DIIPSTTUY stupidity
DIKNOOSTW stinkwood
DIKNORSTU outdrinks
DILLMNOPS millponds
DILLOOPPY polyploid
DILLOORSS doorsills
DILMNOOOP monoploid
DILMNOSSW slimdowns
DILMNPUUU impundulu
DILNOPSUX spondulix
DILOOPTUW tulipwood
DIMMNORSY myrmidons
DIMMOPSUY sympodium
DIMNOOSST monodists
DIMNOPRUU purdonium
DIMNORSTW windstorm
DIMNOSSTU dismounts
DIMOOOOSV voodooism
DIMOORRTY dormitory
DINOOORSU inodorous
DINOOORSW ironwoods
DINOOPRTW woodprint
DINOORRSS indorsors
DINORTTUY rotundity
DIOOOOSTV voodooist
DIOOOPSSU isopodous
DIOOORVWY ivorywood
DIOOPRSST prosodist
DIOPRRSTU disruptor
DIRSSSTTU distrusts
DJLLNRUUU Jullundur
DKMNOOORS komondors
DKORSSTUW studworks
DLLMORSSU slumlords
DLLNORUWY unworldly
DLMOOORXY loxodromy
DLNNOSUUY unsoundly
DLNOOSSWW slowdowns
DLOOORSUY odorously
DMNOORRUW roundworm
DMOOORSWW woodworms
DNNORRTUU turnround
DNNORSTUW downturns
DNOOPPRSU propounds
DNOOPRSSW snowdrops
DNOOPRSUW downpours
DNOOPSSTU soundpost
DNOOPSTUW downspout
DNOORTUWW woundwort
DNORRSSUU surrounds
DOOOPRSST doorposts
doorstops
DOOOPRSUU uropodous
DOOORSTUY outdoorsy
DOOPRRSTW dropworts
EEEEELRTY eyeleteer
EEEEFGNRS Genfersee
EEEEFHLRW freewheel
EEEEFHRST freesheet
EEEEFPRRZ prefreeze
EEEEFRRSZ refreezes
EEEEGGRRS greegrees
EEEEGINVV Geneviève
EEEEGINWW weeweeing
EEEEGISSS eisegeses
EEEEGLNRT genteeler
EEEEGMRRS reemerges
EEEEGNRRV evergreen
EEEEGQSSU squeegees
EEEEHLRSW elsewhere
EEEELLPSX expellees
EEEELMRTT telemeter
EEEELNOPT eleoptene
EEEELNSSV elevenses
sleeveens
EEEELNTVV velveteen
EEEENNSST Tennessee
EEEENNSTV seventeen
EEEENPRST presentee
EEEENRRSV veneerers
EEEENRSTW sweetener
EEEEPRRSV persevere
EEEEPRSSS peeresses
EEEEPSTTW peetweets
EEEERSSSS seeresses
EEEFFIJRS Jefferies
EEEFFRSVW feverfews
EEEFGKNRU fenugreek
EEEFHNOPR freephone
EEEFHNRRS freshener
EEEFHORRT therefore
EEEFHORRW wherefore
EEEFHORST foresheet
EEEFHORTT foreteeth
EEEFHRRRS refresher
EEEFHRRSS refreshes
EEEFILRVX reflexive
EEEFINRRS ferneries
EEEFINRRT interfere
EEEFLLNRU fullerene
EEEFLNSST fleetness
EEEFLRSSV feverless
EEEFLRSTY freestyle
EEEFLRTTU fleurette
EEEFMNRRT fermenter
EEEFNORST freestone
EEEFNORTT Nofretete
EEEFNRRST referents
EEEFNRSUZ unfreezes
EEEFORRSS foreseers
EEEFPRRRR preferrer
EEEFRRRRS referrers
EEEFRRRST ferreters
EEEFRRSTT fetterers
EEEGGILNS negligees
EEEGGORTT georgette
EEEGHILNR reheeling
EEEGHILNT gehlenite
EEEGHINST eighteens
EEEGHLRSS sheerlegs
EEEGHOPRS geosphere
EEEGIISSS eisegesis
EEEGILSTT gleetiest
EEEGIMNST esteeming
EEEGINNOT eigentone
EEEGINNRS engineers
EEEGINNRV veneering
EEEGINPRR peregrine
EEEGINRRS energiser
EEEGINRRZ energizer
EEEGINRSS energises
EEEGINRSZ energizes
EEEGINRTT teetering
EEEGINRUV Guinevere
EEEGIRSTY geyserite
EEEGISTTX exegetist
EEEGKLNRU Kerguelen
EEEGLLNTY genteelly
EEEGLLRWZ Zellweger
EEEGLMNNT gentlemen
EEEGLNRST greenlets
EEEGMNNRU energumen
EEEGMNORS greensome
EEEGMNRSS messenger
EEEGMNRSU merengues
EEEGMORRT ergometer
EEEGMORST geometers
EEEGNNRSS greenness
EEEGNOOSS oogeneses
EEEGNRRSU reneguers
EEEGNRRSV revengers
EEEGNRSSS negresses
EEEGOPRST protegees
EEEGRRRTT regretter
EEEGRRSSS regresses
EEEHIKLPS sheeplike
EEEHILLNS hellenise
EEEHILLNZ hellenize
EEEHILNNP nepheline
EEEHILNPT nephelite
EEEHILNST Heseltine
EEEHILRSW erewhiles
EEEHIMPRS ephemeris
EEEHIMPSU euphemise
EEEHIMPUZ euphemize

EEEHINNRS	henneries
EEEHIRRST	etheriser
EEEHIRRTZ	etherizer
EEEHIRSSS	heiresses
EEEHIRSST	etherises
EEEHIRSTZ	etherizes
EEEHISTWZ	wheeziest
EEEHKLNOS	kneeholes
EEEHKLOSU	houseleek
EEEHLLSSW	wheelless
EEEHLMNSW	wheelsmen
EEEHLMNTY	methylene
EEEHLMPST	helpmeets
EEEHLMSST	themeless
EEEHLNOPT	phenetole
	telephone
EEEHLNOSW	nosewheel
EEEHLNSTV	elevenths
EEEHLOPPS	peepholes
EEEHLRRST	shelterer
EEEHMMNTY	enthymeme
EEEHMNOPR	ephemeron
EEEHMORRT	rheometer
EEEHMORST	motherese
	threesome
EEEHMORSW	somewhere
EEEHMRTTT	thermette
EEEHNNPST	nepenthes
EEEHNNQSU	henequens
EEEHNPRSS	enspheres
EEEHNRSSS	sheerness
EEEHOPRSX	exosphere
EEEHORSST	shoetrees
EEEHRSTTU	usherette
EEEIIKLSV	sievelike
EEEIIKRST	kieserite
EEEIJKLLW	jewellike
EEEIKNNPR	innkeeper
EEEILLPRT	Pelletier
EEEILLRSV	reveilles
EEEILMSST	seemliest
EEEILNNRV	enlivener
EEEILNPRS	pelerines
	presenile
EEEILNQRU	queenlier
EEEILNRSS	leeriness
EEEILNRSY	eyeliners
EEEILNSTX	extensile
EEEILPRSV	replevies
EEEILPSST	sleepiest
EEEILPTVX	expletive
EEEILRRRV	Leverrier
EEEILRRSV	relievers
	revelries
EEEILRSTX	exsertile
EEEILRSVY	liveyeres
EEEILSSTV	televises
EEEIMMNNO	menominee
EEEIMMRSS	mesmerise
EEEIMMRSZ	mesmerize
EEEIMNNRT	nemertine
EEEIMNNRV	veniremen
EEEIMORTT	meteorite
EEEIMPRRS	premieres
EEEIMPRRT	perimeter
EEEIMRRSS	misereres
EEEIMRSTT	remittees
EEEIMSSTW	semisweet
EEEINNNST	nineteens
EEEINNRST	internees
EEEINNRTV	intervene
EEEINORRT	orienteer
EEEINPRRS	reserpine
EEEINPRST	perenties
EEEINPSSW	weepiness
EEEINPSVX	expensive
EEEINRRST	reentries
EEEINRRTW	wernerite
EEEINRSST	eternises
	sneeriest
EEEINRSTZ	eternizes
EEEINRTTV	retentive
EEEINSSTV	seventies
EEEINSSTW	weensiest
EEEINSTVX	extensive
EEEIPRRRV	repriever
EEEIPRRSV	reprieves
EEEIPRRTT	preterite
EEEIPRSTX	expertise
EEEIPRTXZ	expertize
EEEIQRRSU	equerries
EEEIQTTTU	etiquette
EEEIRRRTV	retriever
EEEIRRSTV	retrieves
EEEIRRSVW	reviewers
EEEIRSTTV	serviette
EEEJKNRTU	junketeer
EEEJLLRSW	jewellers
EEEJLLRWY	jewellery
EEEJNPRSS	Jespersen
EEEJNRSWY	New Jersey
EEEKLMPRR	Klemperer
EEEKLNSSS	sleekness
EEEKMORST	smoketree
EEEKMRSTU	musketeer
EEEKNOSTY	synoekete
EEELLLRSV	levellers
EEELLLSSW	sewellels
EEELLLSWY	Wellesley
EEELLNORS	enrollees
EEELLNPRT	repellent
EEELLNPTX	expellent
EEELLNQSU	quenelles
EEELLNSSV	levelness
EEELLPRRS	repellers
EEELLPRSX	expellers
EEELLPRTY	repletely
EEELLPSSS	sleepless
EEELLRRSV	revellers
EEELMMNOP	Melpomene
EEELMNOPR	perlemoen
EEELMNOPT	elopement
EEELMNRTV	revelment
EEELMOPSY	employees
EEELMOSTT	omelettes
EEELMRSTU	muleteers
EEELMRTTY	telemetry
EEELMRTXY	extremely
EEELNOPSV	envelopes
EEELNOPTT	leptotene
EEELNOSTT	solenette
EEELNOTTV	novelette
EEELNRRTY	terrenely
EEELNRSSV	nerveless
EEELNRSSW	newsreels
EEELNSSSS	senseless
EEELNSSST	tenseless
EEELOPPRS	repeoples
EEELOPRSV	oversleep
	sleepover
EEELPPRSX	perplexes
EEELRRSTT	letterers
EEELRRSVY	reversely
EEELRSSTT	resettles
EEELRSTTT	letterset
EEEMMNOST	mementoes
EEEMNNRTU	enurement
EEEMNNSTT	tenements
EEEMNOPRT	treponeme
EEEMNORRV	nevermore
EEEMNORSZ	mezereons
EEEMNOXYZ	exoenzyme
EEEMNRSST	steersmen
EEEMNRSTT	entremets
EEEMNRSTY	mesentery
EEEMNRTTV	revetment
EEEMOPRTX	extempore
EEEMORRSU	reremouse
EEEMORSST	stereomes
EEEMPRRST	temperers
EEEMPRSSS	empresses
EEEMRSSST	semesters
EEENNOPRS	neoprenes
EEENNORST	sonneteer
EEENNSSST	tenseness
EEENPRRST	presenter
	repenters
	represent
EEENPRRTV	preventer
EEENPRSST	pretenses
EEENPRSUV	supervene
EEENPSSST	steepness
EEENQRSSU	queerness
EEENRRSTU	returnees
EEENRRSTW	westerner
EEENRRSUV	revenuers
EEENRSSST	terseness
EEENSSSTW	sweetness
EEEOPSSST	poetesses
EEEORRSSV	overseers
EEEORRSSX	xeroseres
EEEORRSTV	oversteer
EEEORRTVX	overexert
EEEPPPRTU	puppeteer
EEEPRRRSS	represser
EEEPRRRSV	preserver

EEEPRRRTV perverter
EEEPRRSSS represses
EEEPRRSST pesterers
EEEPRRSSV preserves
EEEPRRSSX expresser
EEEPRRSTW pewterers
EEEPRSSSX expresses
EEEPRSTTU superette
EEEPSSTTT septettes
EEEQRRSTU requester
EEEQRSSTU sequester
EEEQRSSUZ squeezers
EEERRRSSV reservers
reversers
EEERRRSTV reverters
EEERRSSTT resetters
EEESSTTTX sextettes
EEFFFKLRU kerfuffle
EEFFFMNOT feoffment
EEFFGLNTU effulgent
EEFFHIKSY keffiyehs
EEFFHINTT fifteenth
EEFFHLRSU reshuffle
EEFFIILRS fireflies
EEFFINOSV offensive
EEFFINRST stiffener
EEFFIORRT forfeiter
EEFFIPRSU pufferies
EEFFJNORS Jefferson
EEFFLNSTU effluents
EEFFOPRRR profferer
EEFFRRSSU sufferers
EEFGHIMSS gemfishes
EEFGHIRRT freighter
EEFGIILRS filigrees
EEFGIINNR Feininger
EEFGIKLUU fuguelike
EEFGILLNY feelingly
EEFGILNNU unfeeling
EEFGILNRU refueling
EEFGILNRX reflexing
EEFGILRSS griefless
EEFGIMRUV vermifuge
EEFGINORR foreigner
EEFGINPTY tepefying
EEFGINRRR referring
EEFGINRRS fingerers
EEFGINRRT ferreting
EEFGINRST festering
EEFGINRTT fettering
EEFGIORRS forgeries
EEFGIPRRU prefigure
EEFGLLLUY gleefully
EEFGLLTUY Leyte Gulf
EEFGLNRTU refulgent
EEFGLRRTU regretful
EEFGOORRS foregoers
EEFGORRTT forgetter
EEFHIIRSS fisheries
EEFHIISST fetishise
EEFHIISTZ fetishize
EEFHIJLSW jewelfish
EEFHIJSSW jewfishes
EEFHIKLLS shelflike
EEFHILLRS fleshlier
shellfire
EEFHILSST fleshiest
EEFHIMNRS fishermen
EEFHINPRY hyperfine
EEFHINSST heftiness
EEFHIORSU firehouse
EEFHIOSUW housewife
EEFHLLSWY flywheels
EEFHLLTUW Ethelwulf
EEFHLMOTU mouthfeel
EEFHLSSTT theftless
EEFHMORRT therefrom
EEFHMORRW wherefrom
EEFHNRSSS freshness
EEFHOORRS foreshore
EEFHRRRTU furtherer
EEFIIJLLS jellifies
EEFIIKKLN knifelike
EEFIILLNS lifelines
EEFIILMST lifetimes
EEFIILMTX flexitime
EEFIILNRT infertile
interfile
EEFIILQRU liquefier
EEFIILQSU liquefies
EEFIILRST fertilise
EEFIILRTZ fertilize
EEFIIMNSS feminises
EEFIIMNSZ feminizes
EEFIIMNTY femineity
EEFIIMRRT metrifier
EEFIIMRST metrifies
EEFIINRSS fieriness
EEFIINRST Finistère
EEFIINRSU reunifies
EEFIINRTT Nefertiti
EEFIIPRRT petrifier
EEFIIPRST petrifies
EEFIIRRRT terrifier
EEFIIRRST terrifies
EEFIIRRSV verifiers
versifier
EEFIIRSSV versifies
EEFIIRSTT testifier
EEFIISSTT feistiest
testifies
EEFIKLLTU flutelike
EEFIKNRST kniferest
EEFIKNRSU refusenik
EEFILLLOS filoselle
EEFILLRST fillester
EEFILLRTU fullerite
EEFILLRTY fertilely
EEFILLSTY lifestyle
EEFILMPXY exemplify
EEFILMSST fistmeles
EEFILNORS felonries
EEFILNORX reflexion
EEFILNTUW wulfenite
EEFILOORS fooleries
EEFILORSV overflies
EEFILORTU outrelief
EEFILPRRS pilferers
EEFILRRST refilters
EEFILRSSU fusileers
EEFILSTVY festively
EEFIMNRTT refitment
EEFIMPRRU perfumier
EEFIMRSTU furmeties
EEFINNPVY fivepenny
EEFINORST firestone
EEFINPRSU superfine
EEFINRRRS inferrers
EEFINRSST infesters
EEFINRSSU reinfuses
EEFINRSTU interfuse
EEFIOPPRS fopperies
EEFIOPRRT profiteer
EEFIOPRRW firepower
EEFIORRRT retrofire
EEFIORRST torrefies
EEFIORRSU Soufrière
EEFIPRRTU putrefier
EEFIPRSTU putrefies
stupefier
EEFIPRSUV perfusive
EEFIPSSTU stupefies
EEFIRRRTT fritterer
EEFIRRRTU fruiterer
EEFIRRSTU surfeiter
EEFIRSSTT frisettes
EEFIRSTTZ frizettes
EEFKNOORT foretoken
EEFKOOPRS forespoke
EEFLLLNSU fluellens
EEFLLNPSU spleenful
EEFLLORST foretells
EEFLMORTW flowmeter
EEFLMRTUX fluxmeter
EEFLNOSST felstones
EEFLNRSTU resentful
EEFLNRTVY fervently
EEFLOPRSU reposeful
EEFLORRSW flowerers
reflowers
EEFLORRTX retroflex
EEFLORSTV leftovers
EEFLORSTW flowerets
EEFLRRTTU flutterer
EEFMNOORW forewomen
EEFMNORST fomenters
EEFMOPRRR performer
EEFMORRRS reformers
EEFMPRRSU perfumers
EEFMPRRUY perfumery
EEFNOPRRZ prefrozen
EEFNOPRST forespent
EEFNORSST softeners
EEFNORSTU fourteens
EEFNORSTW New Forest
EEFNQRSTU frequents

EEFNRSTTU unfetters
EEFOORRST rooftrees
EEFOPRRTY ferrotype
EEFOPRSSS professes
EEFORRSST foresters
fosterers
reforests
EEFORRTVW feverwort
EEFOSSSTT fossettes
EEFPRSSUU superfuse
EEGGHLLSS eggshells
EEGGHNORU Greenough
EEGGIIIOR George III
EEGGIILNS elegising
EEGGIILNT gelignite
EEGGIILNZ elegizing
EEGGIIPRS piggeries
EEGGIJRRS rejiggers
EEGGILNNR greenling
EEGGILNNT negligent
EEGGILNSS legginess
EEGGILOOS geologies
geologise
EEGGILOOZ geologize
EEGGINNRS greenings
EEGGINNRU reneguing
EEGGINNRV revenging
EEGGINRSS egressing
EEGGINRST greetings
EEGGINRTT gettering
EEGGIORSU egregious
EEGGLOORS geologers
EEGGRSSTU suggester
EEGHHIITT eightieth
EEGHHINST heightens
EEGHHINSW wheeshing
EEGHIIKLN hingelike
EEGHIINRV inveigher
EEGHIIRTW weightier
EEGHIKNTW weeknight
EEGHILMNT metheglin
EEGHILNNT enlighten
EEGHILNOR rhigolene
EEGHILNRT lengthier
EEGHILNSS hingeless
EEGHILRSS sleighers
EEGHIMMNR rehemming
EEGHIMNNS enmeshing
EEGHIMOST eightsome
EEGHINORS reshoeing
EEGHINPRT threeping
EEGHINRTT tethering
tightener
EEGHINSST sightseen
EEGHIORVW overweigh
EEGHIOSTT ghettoise
EEGHIOTTZ ghettoize
EEGHIRSST sightseer
EEGHIRSTU theurgies
EEGHIRSTW weighters
EEGHISSST sightsees
EEGHLLNOP phellogen

EEGHLMNNT lengthmen
EEGHLNNST lengthens
EEGHMNOSU hegumenos
EEGHMORST geotherms
EEGHNNORR greenhorn
EEGHNNOTY ethnogeny
EEGHNOOPT photogene
EEGHOPSTY geophytes
EEGIIKLRT tigerlike
EEGIILLPS Gillespie
EEGIILNRV inveigler
relieving
EEGIILNSV inveigles
EEGIILORS religiose
EEGIILPRV privilege
EEGIILRUX religieux
EEGIINPST epigenist
EEGIINRST reignites
EEGIINRVW reviewing
EEGIINSTV genitives
ingestive
EEGIISTTZ zeitgeist
EEGIJLLNW jewelling
EEGIJLNRY jeeringly
EEGIJOPRS jerepigos
EEGIKLLMU glumelike
EEGIKLNNN kenneling
EEGIKLNNR kerneling
EEGIKLNRY reekingly
EEGIKNRSW skewering
EEGIKNRTT Kettering
EEGILLLNV levelling
EEGILLMTU guillemet
EEGILLNPR repelling
EEGILLNPT pelleting
EEGILLNPX expelling
EEGILLNRS reselling
EEGILLNRT retelling
EEGILLNRV Grenville
revelling
EEGILLNRY leeringly
EEGILLSSU guileless
EEGILMMSU gelsemium
EEGILMNRT remelting
EEGILMNSY seemingly
EEGILMRSY Lyme Regis
EEGILNNRT relenting
EEGILNNRU unreeling
EEGILNNSS Esslingen
lessening
EEGILNNUY genuinely
EEGILNOOS neologies
neologise
EEGILNOOZ neologize
EEGILNORS eloigners
EEGILNPWY weepingly
EEGILNRRS lingerers
EEGILNRTT lettering
reletting
EEGILNRTW weltering
EEGILNTXY exigently
EEGILOPRS Pergolesi

EEGILOPSU epilogues
EEGILORST sortilege
EEGILORSU eulogiser
EEGILORUZ eulogizer
EEGILOSSU eulogises
EEGILOSUZ eulogizes
EEGILQSSU squilgees
EEGILRSTV verligtes
EEGIMNPRR Preminger
EEGIMNPRT tempering
EEGIMNPTX exempting
EEGIMNRST regiments
EEGIMNRSU meringues
EEGINNOPR reopening
EEGINNPRT repenting
EEGINNPSX expensing
EEGINNRST resenting
EEGINNRTT tentering
EEGINNRTU neutering
EEGINNRUV unreeving
EEGINOOSS oogenesis
EEGINOPRS progenies
EEGINOPRY epirogeny
EEGINOPSU epigenous
EEGINORRS erigerons
EEGINORSS egression
EEGINORSV sovereign
EEGINOSSS gneissose
EEGINOSST egestions
EEGINOSXY oxygenise
EEGINOXYZ oxygenize
EEGINPPPR peppering
EEGINPRST pestering
EEGINPSSW sweepings
EEGINQSUZ squeezing
EEGINRRSS resigners
EEGINRRSV reserving
reversing
EEGINRRTV reverting
EEGINRSSS ingresses
EEGINRSSU seigneurs
EEGINRSSY synergies
EEGINRSTT resetting
retesting
streeting
EEGINRSTV revesting
EEGINRSTW westering
EEGINRSTX exserting
EEGINRSUY seigneury
EEGINRTTV revetting
EEGINSSTU eugenists
EEGINSSTW sweetings
EEGINSTTV vignettes
EEGIORRSU rogueries
EEGIORSTV vertigoes
EEGIPRUUX Périgueux
EEGIRRSST registers
EEGIRRSSU regisseur
surgeries
EEGIRSSST tigresses
EEGIRSSTT grisettes
EEGLLMORU glomerule

EEGLLOOTY	teleology
EEGLLOPRS	gospeller
EEGLLORRV	groveller
EEGLLOSSV	gloveless
EEGLMNNOU	melungeon
EEGLMOORY	mereology
EEGLMOSSS	glossemes
EEGLNOPSY	polygenes
EEGLNORTT	lorgnette
EEGLNOSTU	Telegonus
EEGLPRSUU	superglue
EEGLRSSSU	surgeless
EEGLRSSUU	reguluses
EEGMNOORR	greenroom
EEGMNOSST	gemstones
EEGMNSTTU	teguments
EEGNNORST	roentgens
EEGNNOSSV	evensongs
EEGNOORST	oestrogen
EEGNOORSU	erogenous
EEGNOOSUX	exogenous
EEGNOPSTY	genotypes
EEGNORRSS	engrosser
EEGNORSSS	engrosses
EEGNORSSV	governess
EEGNOSTYZ	zygotenes
EEGNPRSUX	expungers
EEGNRRSTU	resurgent
EEGNRSSUY	guernseys
EEGOPRSSU	superegos
EEGOQRSTU	grotesque
EEGORRRSS	regressor
EEGRRSSTU	gesturers
EEHHHLNOO	Hohenlohe
EEHHILMOP	hemophile
EEHHINOPT	thiophene
EEHHINOSS	shoeshine
EEHHIRTTW	therewith
EEHHIRTWW	wherewith
EEHHLLLOS	hellholes
EEHHLOPTY	helophyte
EEHHNOPPS	phosphene
EEHHNOSSU	henhouses
EEHHOORSS	horseshoe
EEHHRRSST	threshers
EEHIIKRSS	Eskişehir
EEHIILNTW	White Nile
EEHIINNTT	ninetieth
EEHIIRTTW	witherite
EEHIJNOPS	Josephine
EEHIKLORS	horselike
EEHIKNPSS	sheepskin
EEHIKRRSS	shriekers
EEHILLLMW	millwheel
EEHILLNPS	helplines
EEHILMNSU	heleniums
EEHILMOPS	mesophile
EEHILMOST	homeliest
	lithesome
EEHILMRRT	Thirlmere
EEHILNOOP	oenophile
EEHILNOPX	xenophile
EEHILNORS	shoreline
EEHILNOSU	houseline
EEHILNPRS	plenisher
	replenish
EEHILNPSS	plenishes
	spleenish
EEHILNPSW	pinwheels
EEHILNSST	litheness
EEHILOPRX	xerophile
EEHILOPTY	heliotype
EEHILORST	helotries
	hoteliers
EEHILPSST	slipsheet
EEHILPSVY	peevishly
EEHILRSTW	erstwhile
EEHILSTUV	Helvétius
EEHIMMPSU	euphemism
EEHIMNRST	intermesh
EEHIMOPRT	hemitrope
EEHIMPRRW	whimperer
EEHIMRSTU	rheumiest
EEHINNORT	threonine
EEHINNOTV	Einthoven
EEHINNQSU	henequins
	heniquens
EEHINNRSS	enshrines
EEHINOPSU	euphonies
	euphonise
EEHINOPSX	phoenixes
EEHINOPUZ	euphonize
EEHINORRS	heronries
EEHINORTT	thereinto
EEHINORTW	whereinto
EEHINOSST	hessonite
	honesties
EEHINPRSS	inspheres
	phrensies
EEHINPRST	nephrites
	trephines
EEHINRSTT	thirteens
EEHINRSTW	whiteners
EEHINSSTW	whiteness
EEHINSTTU	euthenist
EEHINSTTX	sixteenth
EEHINTTTW	twentieth
EEHIORRST	theoriser
EEHIORRTZ	theorizer
EEHIORSST	heterosis
	isotheres
	theorises
EEHIORSTW	otherwise
EEHIORSTZ	theorizes
EEHIPPRRY	periphery
EEHIPPSST	psephites
EEHIPPSSY	epiphyses
EEHIPPSTY	epiphytes
EEHIPRRSW	whisperer
EEHIRRSST	heritress
EEHIRRSSV	shiverers
EEHIRRSTW	witherers
EEHIRRTTY	erythrite
EEHIRSSTT	Thersites
EEHIRTTTU	Hutterite
EEHKLOOST	stokehole
EEHKLORWW	wheelwork
EEHKORSTW	worksheet
EEHLLLNVY	Helvellyn
EEHLLORST	hosteller
EEHLLORSV	shoveller
EEHLMOOSW	wholesome
EEHLMORVW	overwhelm
EEHLMOSSY	hemolyses
EEHLMOSZZ	shemozzle
EEHLMRSSY	rhymeless
EEHLNOPTY	polythene
	telephony
EEHLNOSSW	wholeness
EEHLNOSTT	telethons
EEHLNSTVY	seventhly
EEHLOOPTT	telephoto
EEHLOPSST	heelposts
EEHLORSSS	horseless
	shoreless
EEHLORSST	hostelers
EEHLORSSV	shovelers
EEHLOSSSU	houseless
EEHLPRSSU	spherules
EEHMMOPRS	morphemes
EEHMMORST	ohmmeters
EEHMNOOPR	pheromone
EEHMNOORW	homeowner
EEHMNORTY	heteronym
EEHMNOSSY	homeyness
EEHMNPTTU	umpteenth
EEHMNRRWY	wherrymen
EEHMOPSTY	mesophyte
EEHMORRTY	rheometry
EEHMORSST	thermoses
EEHMRRRTU	murtherer
EEHMRRSTY	rhymester
EEHNNOOST	ethonones
EEHNNORST	enthrones
EEHNOOPRS	noosphere
EEHNOPPTY	phenotype
EEHNOPRTU	thereupon
EEHNOPRUW	whereupon
EEHNOPSTU	penthouse
EEHNOPSTY	neophytes
EEHNOPTTY	entophyte
EEHNORRST	shortener
EEHNORSST	otherness
EEHNORTUW	whereunto
EEHNOSTTW	whetstone
EEHNPPRSU	penpusher
EEHNPRSSU	unspheres
EEHNSSSTY	syntheses
EEHOOPRSS	oospheres
EEHOORSSV	overshoes
EEHOORSVW	howsoever
	whosoever
EEHOPPSSW	peepshows
EEHOPRRSU	superhero
EEHOPRTXY	xerophyte
EEHOPSSTU	pesthouse

EEHOPSSTW sweetshop
EEHORRSTX exhorters
EEHORRTVW overthrew
EEHORSTTY set theory
EEHOSSSST hostesses
EEHPRSSTU superhets
EEHPRSSTY hypesters
EEHPRTTXY hypertext
EEIIIKLMN Menelik II
EEIIIMNST nimieties
EEIIIMPST impieties
EEIIKKMSS Sikkimese
EEIIKLLST likeliest
EEIIKLNPS snipelike
EEIIKLNSW swinelike
EEIIKNNTZ zinkenite
EEIILLMMS milliemes
EEIILLMRT millerite
EEIILLMTW willemite
EEIILLNTV vitelline
EEIILLOPS eolipiles
EEIILLSTV liveliest
EEIILMRSS missileer
EEIILMSTT timeliest
EEIILNNRT interline
EEIILNOTV olivenite
EEIILNPPS pipelines
EEIILNQSU Esquiline
EEIILNRST resilient
EEIILNSTV lenitives
EEIILOPST sepiolite
EEIILRSST sterilise
EEIILRSTU Tuileries
EEIILRSTZ sterilize
EEIILRTUZ reutilize
EEIIMMPRS epimerism
EEIIMMPRT primetime
EEIIMMRST eremitism
EEIIMMRSV immersive
EEIIMOPST epitomise
EEIIMOPTZ epitomize
EEIIMORSS isomerise
EEIIMORSZ isomerize
EEIIMRSSV remissive
EEIIMRSTZ itemizers
EEIINNNPT penninite
EEIINNSTT intestine
EEIINNSTV intensive
EEIINNTVV inventive
EEIINQRSU enquiries
EEIINRRVV viverrine
EEIINRSTT enteritis
retinites
EEIINRSTV reinvites
EEIINRSTW winterise
EEIINRSVV inversive
EEIINRTVW interview
EEIINRTWZ winterize
EEIINSSST sensitise
EEIINSSTT tensities
EEIINSSTV sensitive
EEIINSSTZ sensitize
EEIINSSVW viewiness
EEIIOPQSU equipoise
EEIIOPSTZ epizoites
EEIIOSSTV sovietise
EEIIOSTVZ sovietize
EEIIQRSTU requisite
EEIIQSTUX exquisite
EEIIRSSTV resistive
EEIJKLLLY jellylike
EEIJKNRSS jerkiness
EEIJLNNSU juliennes
EEIJLNRST jetliners
EEIJLNSUV juveniles
EEIJNNORS enjoiners
EEIJNSSTT jettiness
EEIJPRRSU perjuries
EEIJQRTUY jequerity
EEIKLLMPU plumelike
EEIKLMORT kilometer
kilometre
EEIKLMOSU mouselike
EEIKLNOST stonelike
EEIKLOPRS proselike
EEIKLORST lorikeets
EEIKLPSST spikelets
EEIKLRSST triskeles
EEIKLRTWY triweekly
EEIKMNORS monkeries
EEIKMNORT konimeter
EEIKMOSTX ketoximes
EEIKNNPSV penknives
EEIKNORSV reinvokes
EEIKNPRSS perkiness
EEIKNPSSS peskiness
EEIKNRRST tinkerers
EEIKOORRS rookeries
EEIKOORTZ ozokerite
EEIKOQSUV equivokes
EEILLLNUV Lunéville
EEILLLNWY Llewelyn I
EEILLMNOR Niemöller
EEILLMNOT emollient
EEILLMNPT impellent
EEILLMOPR millepore
EEILLMPRS impellers
EEILLMSST smelliest
EEILLNNTY leniently
EEILLNOST loneliest
EEILLNRSV sniveller
EEILLNSSS illnesses
EEILLNSTY tensilely
EEILLOPTU petiolule
EEILLOSTV loveliest
EEILLPRUY puerilely
EEILLRSST trellises
EEILLRSSV liverless
EEILLRSTU tellurise
EEILLRSTY sterilely
EEILLRSUY leisurely
EEILLRSVY servilely
EEILLRTTU tellurite
EEILLRTUZ tellurize
EEILLSUVY elusively
EEILMMNPT implement
EEILMMNSY immensely
EEILMMORS sommelier
EEILMMORT milometer
EEILMNNOT eloinment
EEILMNNTY eminently
EEILMNOSS solemnise
EEILMNOST limestone
milestone
EEILMNOSZ solemnize
EEILMNPPR pimpernel
EEILMNRSU lemurines
relumines
EEILMNRVY liverymen
EEILMNSTU musteline
EEILMORTT tremolite
EEILMOSTT mistletoe
EEILMOSVW semivowel
EEILMOTVY emotively
EEILMPSSX simplexes
EEILMRSST meritless
EEILMRSTY lysimeter
EEILNNPSS penniless
EEILNNSST sentinels
EEILNNSTY intensely
EEILNOORS oleoresin
EEILNOPRT repletion
terpineol
EEILNOPTT telepoint
EEILNORVV reinvolve
EEILNORVW wolverine
EEILNOSSS lionesses
noiseless
EEILNOSSU selenious
EEILNOSSV novelises
EEILNOSTV novelties
EEILNOSVZ novelizes
Venizélos
EEILNPPSZ zeppelins
EEILNPRSU perilunes
EEILNPRSV replevins
EEILNPSSS spineless
EEILNPSTT pestilent
EEILNPSVY pensively
EEILNRSST enlisters
listeners
EEILNRSTU unsterile
EEILNRSVY inversely
EEILNSSSW sinewless
EEILOPRST epistoler
pistoleer
EEILOPSST politesse
EEILOPSVX explosive
EEILORRST loiterers
EEILORRTT Tortelier
EEILORSTT lotteries
EEILORSVV overlives
EEILOSSVW vowelises
EEILOSTTT toilettes
EEILOSVWZ vowelizes
EEILOTUVV evolutive

EEILPRSST epistlers
spirelets
EEILPRSTY peristyle
Priestley
EEILPRSUV prelusive
pulverise
repulsive
EEILPRUVZ pulverize
EEILPSSTY epistyles
EEILPSUVX expulsive
EEILRRSSV riverless
silverers
EEILRSTVY restively
EEILRSUVV revulsive
EEILSSSSU issueless
EEIMMMRSS mesmerism
EEIMMMRSU mummeries
EEIMMNNTU minutemen
EEIMMNRRT merriment
EEIMMORRS memoriser
EEIMMORRZ memorizer
EEIMMORSS memorises
EEIMMORST meteorism
EEIMMORSZ memorizes
EEIMMOSST sometimes
EEIMMRRSS immersers
EEIMMRSST meristems
mesmerist
EEIMMRSTU summiteer
EEIMMRSTW swimmeret
EEIMMRSTX extremism
EEIMNNNOT Mennonite
EEIMNNORT mentioner
EEIMNNRTT interment
EEIMNNRTU inurement
EEIMNNSTT sentiment
EEIMNOPTX exemption
EEIMNORSS emersions
sermonise
EEIMNORST moistener
EEIMNORSZ sermonize
EEIMNORTW tirewomen
EEIMNOSST monetises
semitones
EEIMNOSTX sixteenmo
EEIMNOSTZ monetizes
zonetimes
EEIMNOSYZ isoenzyme
EEIMNPQTU equipment
EEIMNPRSS primeness
EEIMNPSST emptiness
EEIMNRRSS merriness
EEIMNRSTU mutineers
EEIMNRSTV virements
EEIMNRTTT remittent
EEIMNSSSS messiness
EEIMOOPRS meiospore
EEIMOORTZ merozoite
EEIMOPRSS promisees
reimposes
EEIMOPRST peristome
temporise
EEIMOPRTZ temporize
EEIMORRSW wormeries
EEIMORSTV overtimes
EEIMOSSTZ mestizoes
EEIMPPRRS perisperm
EEIMPRRSS impresser
simperers
EEIMPRRTT permitter
pretermit
EEIMPRRTY perimetry
EEIMPRSSS impresses
EEIMPSSTU impetuses
EEIMQSSTU mesquites
EEIMQSTUU equisetum
EEIMRRSST rimesters
EEIMRRSTT remitters
trimester
trimeters
EEIMRSSSU messieurs
EEIMRSSTY mysteries
EEIMRSTTX extremist
EEIMRTTXY extremity
EEIMSSSTY systemise
EEIMSSTTU sutteeism
EEIMSSTYZ systemize
EEINNNRSS innerness
EEINNNRSU nunneries
EEINNOPPS Nipponese
EEINNOPRS pensioner
EEINNORTT retention
EEINNOSTV veinstone
EEINNOSTX extension
EEINNPRST spinneret
EEINNPRTT pertinent
EEINNPSST ineptness
EEINNPSTT penitents
EEINNRSST inertness
EEINNRSSV inverness
nerviness
EEINNRSTV reinvents
EEINNSSSW newsiness
EEINNSSTT intensest
sentients
EEINOPPPR pepperoni
EEINOPPRS ronepipes
EEINOPPST peptonise
pipestone
EEINOPPTZ peptonize
EEINOPRST entropies
interpose
EEINOQSUX equinoxes
EEINORRST reorients
EEINORRSV reversion
EEINORSSV eversions
EEINORSTX exertions
exsertion
EEINORTVW interwove
EEINOSSTT noisettes
EEINOSSTV ostensive
EEINOTTUZ teutonize
EEINPPPSS peppiness
EEINPRRRT reprinter
EEINPRRTT interpret
EEINPRSSW winepress
EEINPSSTT pettiness
EEINQRRSU enquirers
EEINQRSSU squireens
EEINQSSTU quietness
EEINQTTTU quintette
EEINRRRSU reinsurer
EEINRRSST inserters
reinserts
EEINRRSSU nurseries
reinsures
EEINRRSTU reuniters
turneries
EEINRRSTV inverters
EEINRRSTW winterers
EEINRRTTW rewritten
EEINRSSSY syneresis
EEINRSSTT insetters
interests
triteness
EEINRSSTV sirventes
EEINRSSTW witnesser
EEINRSSUV universes
EEINSSSTT testiness
EEINSSSTW witnesses
EEINSSTTX existents
EEINSTTXY extensity
EEIOPPSTV stovepipe
EEIOPRRST portieres
EEIOPRSTT potteries
EEIOPRTTU pirouette
EEIOPSTTT pettitoes
EEIOQQUUV equivoque
EEIORRRST roisterer
terrorise
EEIORRRSV reservoir
EEIORRRTZ terrorize
EEIORRSTV overtires
EEIORRSTX exteriors
EEIORRTTU tourtiere
EEIORRTVW overwrite
EEIORSSUV overissue
EEIORSSVZ oversizes
EEIORTTVX extortive
EEIPPQRSU equippers
EEIPPRRSS perspires
EEIPPRSST peptisers
EEIPPRSTZ peptizers
EEIPRRSST persister
EEIPRRSTT preterits
EEIPRSSST priestess
EEIPRSSTX preexists
EEIPRSSUV supervise
EEIPRSTTT prettiest
EEIPRTTWY typewrite
EEIQRRRSU requirers
EEIQRRSTU requiters
EEIQRRSUV quiverers
EEIQSSTUU quietuses
EEIRRSSST resisters
EEIRRSSTV reservist

EEIRRSTTT	titterers
EEIRRTTTW	twitterer
EEIRSTUVX	extrusive
EEJKNRSTU	junketers
EEJKNRTTU	junketter
EEJLNOSST	Jesselton
EEJLPSSTU	pulsejets
EEJMNNOTY	enjoyment
EEJNOQSUU	Junoesque
EEJNORRUY	journeyer
EEJPRRRSU	perjurers
EEKKORSTY	keystroke
EEKKORSWW	workweeks
EEKLLNNOS	Nollekens
EEKLMOSSS	smokeless
EEKLNNNSU	unkennels
EEKLNOSST	skeletons
EEKLNPRSU	spelunker
EEKLORSTW	steelwork
EEKMNOPSS	spokesmen
EEKNORRTW	networker
EEKNORRWY	New Yorker
EEKNOSSTY	keystones
EEKRRSTUZ	kreutzers
EELLLLNWY	Llewellyn
EELLMOSTW	mellowest
EELLMPSSU	plumeless
EELLNNRTU	tunneller
EELLNORRS	enrollers
EELLOPPRR	propeller
EELLORRTW	troweller
EELLORSST	sollerets
EELLORSSV	oversells
EELLORSTX	extollers
EELLORSVY	volleyers
EELLOSSVW	vowelless
EELLOSTWY	yellowest
EELLPSSSU	pulseless
EELLPSSSY	syllepses
EELLSSSUY	uselessly
EELLSSSXY	sexlessly
EELMMNOTU	emolument
EELMNNORT	enrolment
EELMNOSSS	solemness
EELMNOSSV	venomless
EELMNOTTX	extolment
EELMOOPST	leptosome
EELMOPRSY	employers
	reemploys
EELMOPRTU	petroleum
EELMORSST	molesters
EELMORTTV	voltmeter
EELMORTUV	volumeter
EELMOSTVW	twelvemos
EELMPRSUY	supremely
EELMRRSTU	murrelets
EELNNOOUV	Nuevo León
EELNNOPRS	personnel
EELNNOSSY	Lyonnesse
EELNNRSTU	tunnelers
EELNOORSS	looseners
EELNOOSSS	looseness
EELNOPPRY	propylene
EELNOPPSU	unpeoples
EELNOPRST	petronels
EELNOPSTU	plenteous
EELNORSST	entresols
	tenorless
EELNORSTV	resolvent
EELNORTUV	volunteer
EELNOSSST	stoneless
EELNPRSTY	presently
EELNQSTUY	sequently
EELNSSTTU	unsettles
EELOOPRSY	operosely
EELOORSTV	Roosevelt
EELOPPRSS	prolepses
EELOPRRSX	explorers
EELOPRRTU	poulterer
EELOPRSSU	peloruses
EELOPRSSW	powerless
EELOPRSTT	teleports
EELOPRSTV	overslept
EELOPRSTY	polyester
	proselyte
EELOPRTXY	expletory
EELOPSSTU	sleepouts
EELORRSSV	resolvers
EELORRSTV	revolters
EELORRSTW	trowelers
EELORRSUV	overrules
EELORRSVV	revolvers
EELORSSUV	ourselves
EELORSTTU	roulettes
EELORSTUV	trueloves
EELPPSSTU	septuples
EELPPSTTU	septuplet
EELPRRSSU	repulsers
EELPRSSXY	expressly
EELPRSTUU	sepulture
EELPSSTUX	sextuples
EELPSTTUX	sextuplet
EELRRSSTW	wrestlers
EELRSSTTU	utterless
EEMMNNOSY	Mnemosyne
EEMMNOORT	metronome
	monometer
	monotreme
EEMMNOSTV	movements
EEMMOORST	osmometer
EEMMORTYZ	zymometer
EEMNNOPRS	prenomens
EEMNNOPST	penstemon
EEMNNORWY	New Romney
EEMNOORTT	tonometer
EEMNOOSTT	tomentose
EEMNOPRYZ	proenzyme
EEMNORRTT	tormenter
EEMNORRTV	Vermonter
EEMNORRTY	Monterrey
EEMNORSTY	oystermen
EEMNRSTVY	vestrymen
EEMNSSTTV	vestments
EEMOOOSTT	osteotome
EEMOOPRST	proteomes
EEMOOPRTT	optometer
	potometer
EEMOORRST	orometers
EEMOORSTT	roomettes
EEMOPPRRT	preemptor
EEMOPRRTY	pyrometer
EEMOQRSSU	moresques
EEMOSTTTU	teetotums
EEMPRRSSU	presumers
EEMPRRTTU	trumpeter
EEMPRSSTT	temptress
EEMRRSTTU	mutterers
EEMRSSTTU	metestrus
EENNNOSTV	nonevents
EENNOOSTU	neotenous
EENNOPRSS	proneness
EENNOPSTX	exponents
EENNOSSTV	Stevenson
EENNRSSST	sternness
EENOORRSU	erroneous
EENOORSTU	euronotes
EENOORSTV	overtones
EENOPPRTT	prepotent
EENOPRRSS	responser
EENOPRSSS	responses
EENOPRSTT	entrepots
EENOPRSTV	overspent
EENOPRSXY	pyroxenes
EENOPSTTY	stenotype
EENORRTUY	tourneyer
EENORSSTV	overtness
EENORSSTX	extensors
EENORTTTU	neutretto
EENOSSTUV	ventouses
EENPRSSSU	suspenser
EENRRRSTU	returners
EENRRSTUV	venturers
EEOOPRRVW	overpower
EEOOPRSST	proteoses
EEOOPRSSX	exospores
EEOOPRSTZ	zoetropes
EEOORRTVW	overwrote
EEOOSSSTX	exostoses
EEOOSSTTV	ovotestes
EEOPPRSSS	oppresses
EEOPPRSSU	superpose
EEOPRRRSS	repressor
EEOPRRRST	reporters
EEOPRRRSV	reprovers
EEOPRRRTY	repertory
EEOPRRSTT	potterers
	protester
EEOPRRSTX	exporters
	reexports
EEOPRSSSS	espressos
	repossess
EEOPRSSSU	espousers
	repousses
EEOPRSSSX	expressos
EEOPRSSTV	oversteps
EEOPRSSUX	exposures

EEOPRTTWY	typewrote
EEOPSSSSS	possesses
EEOPSSSTW	sweetsops
EEOPSSTTU	poussette
EEOQRSSTU	torqueses
EEORRRSST	resorters
	restorers
EEORRRSTT	retorters
EEORRSSTU	retrousse
EEORRSTTT	totterers
EEORRSTTX	extorters
EEORRSTUV	overtures
	trouveres
EEORRTTVX	extrovert
EEORSSSTV	votresses
EEORSTTTZ	terzettos
EEPRRSSST	prestress
EEPRRSSSU	pressures
EEPRRSTTU	putterers
	sputterer
EEPRSSTTU	upsetters
EERRSSSTU	tressures
EERRSSUVY	resurveys
EERRSTTTU	stutterer
EFFFILSTU	fluffiest
EFFFKLRUU	kurfuffle
EFFFLORTU	effortful
EFFGGINOR	goffering
EFFGHIIRT	firefight
EFFGINORS	offerings
EFFGINRSU	suffering
EFFGLORTU	forgetful
EFFGNRSSU	gruffness
EFFHIISTT	fiftieths
EFFHIISTW	whiffiest
EFFHIKSWW	skewwhiff
EFFHILRSW	whifflers
EFFHINSSU	huffiness
EFFHLRSSU	shufflers
EFFIIMNSS	miffiness
EFFIINSST	sniffiest
EFFIIORRT	fortifier
EFFIIORST	fortifies
EFFIIPSST	spiffiest
EFFIIQRSU	squiffier
EFFILLLRU	fulfiller
EFFILMUUV	effluvium
EFFILNRSS	snifflers
EFFINOSSU	effusions
EFFINPSSU	puffiness
EFFINSSST	stiffness
EFFINSSTU	snuffiest
EFFIOOPRR	fireproof
EFFIORRTY	refortify
EFFISSTTU	stuffiest
EFFISSUUV	suffusive
EFFLLRTUY	fretfully
EFFLMNSUU	unmuffles
EFFLNRSSU	snufflers
EFFNOORRT	forefront
EFFOORRTY	offertory
EFFORSTUV	overstuff
EFGGIINNR	fingering
EFGGILNNU	engulfing
EFGGILOOS	solfeggio
EFGGINOOR	foregoing
EFGGINORR	reforging
EFGGINOSS	fogginess
EFGHHIILR	highflier
EFGHHILRY	highflyer
EFGHHIOSS	hogfishes
EFGHIILNT	nightlife
EFGHIILRT	flightier
EFGHIINRT	infighter
EFGHIIPSS	pigfishes
EFGHILNSS	fleshings
EFGHILPRT	preflight
EFGHILTWY	flyweight
EFGHINRST	frightens
EFGHIOOSS	goosefish
EFGHIORST	foresight
EFGIIILNS	lignifies
EFGIIINRS	signifier
EFGIIINSS	signifies
EFGIILLNR	refilling
EFGIILLNT	filleting
EFGIILMNR	refilming
EFGIILNPR	pilfering
EFGIILNRT	filtering
EFGIILNSU	figulines
EFGIILORR	glorifier
EFGIILORS	glorifies
EFGIILRSU	uglifiers
EFGIINNRR	inferring
	infringer
EFGIINNRS	infringes
EFGIINNSS	finessing
EFGIINNST	infesting
EFGIINPRT	fingertip
EFGIINPRX	prefixing
EFGIINRSU	figurines
EFGIINRTT	refitting
EFGIINRVY	verifying
EFGIISTUV	fugitives
EFGILLNOW	fellowing
EFGILLNRU	fullering
EFGILNNNU	funneling
EFGILNORW	flowering
EFGILNORY	foreignly
EFGILNRRU	ferruling
EFGILNRUX	refluxing
EFGILPRSU	fireplugs
EFGILRTUU	fulgurite
EFGIMNNOT	fomenting
EFGIMNORR	reforming
EFGIMNPRU	perfuming
EFGIMNTUY	tumefying
EFGINNOST	softening
EFGINNRYZ	frenzying
EFGINOORR	reroofing
EFGINOORT	footering
EFGINOOSS	goofiness
EFGINORST	foresting
	fostering
EFGINORSW	forewings
EFGINORTU	foutering
EFGINPRSU	perfusing
EFGINRRTU	returfing
EFGIOPSTT	pettifogs
EFGIORRSV	forgivers
EFGKNSTUU	K'ung Fu-tse
EFGLLNTUY	fulgently
EFGLOOSVX	foxgloves
EFGNOORTT	forgotten
EFGOOOOST	goosefoot
EFHHIISTW	whitefish
EFHHILLSS	shellfish
EFHIILSTT	filthiest
EFHIIMSST	fetishism
EFHIINPSS	pinfishes
	snipefish
EFHIINRSS	finishers
EFHIINSSS	fishiness
EFHIIORRS	horrifies
EFHIIRRTT	thriftier
EFHIISSTT	fetishist
	shiftiest
EFHIISSVW	fishwives
EFHIJLLSY	jellyfish
EFHILLSSW	swellfish
EFHILLSSY	selfishly
EFHILMNOS	lemonfish
EFHILNSSU	unselfish
EFHILSSST	shiftless
EFHIMOPRZ	Pforzheim
EFHINORRT	firethorn
EFHINOSST	stonefish
EFHINRRSU	furnisher
	refurnish
EFHINRSSU	furnishes
EFHINSSSU	sunfishes
EFHIORSTT	fortieths
	frothiest
EFHIRRSTU	thurifers
EFHLLLPUY	helpfully
EFHLLNPUU	unhelpful
EFHLLOPUY	hopefully
EFHLLOSST	softshell
EFHLLOSUV	shovelful
EFHLNSSSU	flushness
EFHLOOPSU	flophouse
EFHLOPSST	fleshpots
EFHNOORSW	foreshown
EFHNORTUX	foxhunter
EFHOOORTT	foretooth
EFHOORSSW	foreshows
EFIIILRSV	vilifiers
EFIIINRST	nitrifies
EFIIIRSTV	vitrifies
EFIIIRSVV	vivifiers
EFIIJLLOS	jollifies
EFIIJRSTU	justifier
EFIIJSSTU	justifies
EFIIKLRTU	fruitlike
EFIIKRSST	friskiest
EFIILLMOR	mollifier

EFIILLMOS mollifies
EFIILLNRU nullifier
EFIILLNSU nullifies
EFIILLRST fillister
EFIILMNSS filminess
EFIILMOTT leitmotif
EFIILMSST flimsiest
EFIILNNOX inflexion
EFIILNSTT flintiest
EFIILOPSV spoilfive
EFIILOSSS fossilise
EFIILOSSZ fossilize
EFIILRRZZ frizzlier
EFIILRSST filisters
EFIILRSSU fusiliers
EFIILRTTY fertility
EFIIMMMSU mummifies
EFIIMNSST feminists
EFIIMORRT mortifier
EFIIMORST mortifies
EFIIMRSTY mystifier
EFIIMSSTY mystifies
EFIINNNOT nonfinite
EFIINNSST niftiness
EFIINNSTY intensify
EFIINOPRX prefixion
EFIINOPST pontifies
EFIINORRS inferiors
EFIINORST notifiers
EFIINSSZZ fizziness
EFIIORRTU fioriture
EFIIORSSS ossifiers
EFIIPPSUY yuppifies
EFIIPRRSU purifiers
EFIIPRSST spitfires
EFIIPRSTY typifiers
EFIIRSSSU russifies
EFIIRSTTU fruitiest
EFIIRSTZZ frizziest
EFIISTTVY festivity
EFIKLNSSU flukiness
EFIKLORST frostlike
EFIKLOSST folksiest
EFIKLRSTY flystrike
EFIKNORSS foreskins
EFIKNRSSU refusniks
EFIKOOPRV Prokofiev
EFIKORRSW fireworks
EFILLLNSU fluellins
EFILLMOPU filoplume
EFILLNPTU plentiful
EFILLORRV frivoller
EFILLORSV overfills
EFILMNORT lentiform
EFILMNOSY solemnify
EFILMOPRX plexiform
EFILMORSW wormflies
EFILNNORT frontline
EFILNNSTU influents
EFILNOORS solferino
EFILNOOSU felonious
EFILNORTW interflow
EFILNOSST loftiness
EFILOPPST floppiest
EFILOPRRS profilers
EFILORRSV frivolers
EFILOSSST flossiest
EFILPRSTU uplifters
EFILQRUUV quiverful
EFILRRSZZ frizzlers
EFILRSSTU fruitless
EFILRTUVY furtively
EFILSSTTW swiftlets
EFIMMORRS reformism
EFIMMORRV vermiform
EFIMNORRS informers
reinforms
EFIMORRRS serriform
EFIMORRST firestorm
reformist
restiform
EFINNNSSU funniness
EFINNSSTU unfitness
EFINOPRSU perfusion
EFINOPRSY personify
EFINORRST frontiers
EFINOSTVW Five Towns
EFINRRSSU furriness
EFINRRTUU furniture
EFINRSSTU turfiness
EFINRSSUU unfussier
EFINSSSSU fussiness
EFINSSSTU fustiness
EFINSSSTW swiftness
EFINSSUZZ fuzziness
EFIOORSUV oviferous
EFIOPRRST portfires
profiters
EFIOPSSTX postfixes
EFIORRSTT retrofits
EFIORRSTW frowstier
EFIORSSTT frostiest
EFIORSSTW frowsiest
EFIORSTUZ frouziest
EFIORSTWZ frowziest
EFIORTTTU outfitter
EFKLMNOOW womenfolk
EFKLMOOST folkmotes
EFKNNOORW foreknown
EFKNOOPRS forspoken
EFKNOORSW foreknows
EFKNRSSTU funksters
EFLLLOOSW woolfells
EFLLMOSUY fulsomely
EFLLMSUUY musefully
EFLLNTUUY tunefully
EFLLOORSW followers
EFLLRSTUY restfully
EFLLSTUYZ zestfully
EFLMMOSUX flummoxes
EFLNNTUUU untuneful
EFLNOORVW overflown
EFLNOPRTU profluent
EFLNORSST frontless
EFLNORSTT frontlets
EFLNORSUW sunflower
EFLOOOOST footloose
EFLOOPRTW flowerpot
EFLOORSVW overflows
EFLOOSTTW Lowestoft
EFLOPRSUY profusely
EFLORRRTU terrorful
EFLRSSSTU stressful
EFLRSSTUU frustules
EFMOOPRRR proreform
EFMOORSSU foursomes
EFNNOOORS forenoons
EFNNOPRUY fourpenny
EFNOOOSTT footnotes
EFOOOPRST footropes
EFOOPRRSS professor
EFOOPSSTT footsteps
EFOORSSTT footrests
EFORRRSUW furrowers
EGGGIIJNR rejigging
EGGGIILST giggliest
EGGGIINNR gingering
EGGGINNOR engorging
EGGGINNPU unpegging
EGGGINORR regorging
EGGGIORST groggiest
EGGGOOOSS goosegogs
EGGHIILNS sleighing
EGGHIINNR rehinging
EGGHIINNW whingeing
EGGHIINTW weighting
EGGHIKSSW eggwhisks
EGGHILNPU pleughing
EGGHINNRU hungering
EGGIIJLST jiggliest
EGGIILMNT gimleting
EGGIILNNO eloigning
EGGIILNNR lingering
EGGIILNST niggliest
EGGIILSTW wiggliest
EGGIIMMNR immerging
EGGIINNRS resigning
EGGIINNST ingesting
signeting
EGGIINNSW swingeing
EGGIINOOR Giorgione
EGGIINOPR Prigogine
EGGIINRSV grievings
EGGIISTTW twiggiest
EGGIJNSSU jugginses
EGGILLNRU gruelling
EGGILLNUY gulleying
EGGILNORV groveling
EGGILNORW glowering
EGGILNRSS snigglers
EGGILNRSU gruelings
EGGILOOST geologist
EGGILQRSU squiggler
EGGILQSSU squiggles
EGGILRRSW wrigglers
EGGIMNNOR mongering

EGGIMNSSU mugginess
EGGINNNOR Groningen
EGGINNORV governing
EGGINNOTT Göttingen
EGGINNPRU repugning
EGGINNPUX expunging
EGGINORRS gorgerins
EGGINORRW regrowing
EGGINORST gostering
EGGINOSSS sogginess
EGGINRRSU resurging
EGGINRSTU gesturing
grungiest
EGGINRTTU guttering
EGGINSSTU gusseting
EGGIORRTU outrigger
EGGIORRXY Gregory IX
EGGIPRRSS spriggers
EGGLMMOOY gemmology
EGGLMRSSU smugglers
EGGLRRSTU struggler
EGGLRSSTU struggles
EGHHIIORS Hiroshige
EGHHINNPY hyphening
EGHHINRST threshing
EGHHIPRSU superhigh
EGHHMOTTU methought
EGHHNORUW roughhewn
EGHHNOUZZ Zhengzhou
EGHHOPPYY hypophyge
EGHHORSUW roughhews
EGHHORTTU rethought
EGHIIKLNT nightlike
EGHIIKNRS shrieking
EGHIILLMT limelight
EGHIILNRS hirelings
relishing
EGHIILNSS shielings
EGHIILNST sightline
EGHIILRST sightlier
EGHIILTWY weightily
EGHIIMMNS immeshing
EGHIIMNNS inmeshing
EGHIIMNTT nighttime
EGHIIMSTT mightiest
EGHIINNTW whitening
EGHIINPRS perishing
EGHIINRSV shivering
EGHIINRTW withering
EGHIINSTY hygienist
EGHIIRSTZ rightsize
EGHIISSTY hygieists
EGHIKLOST ghostlike
EGHIKNNRU hunkering
EGHILLMOT megilloth
EGHILLNOR hollering
EGHILLNOV hovelling
EGHILLNTY lengthily
EGHILLSST lightless
EGHILMNNU unhelming
EGHILMORS homegirls
EGHILMOST lightsome
EGHILNNOR Lohengrin
EGHILNOPR negrophil
EGHILNORS Helsingør
EGHILNOST hosteling
EGHILNOSU houseling
EGHILNOSV shoveling
EGHILNRSS shinglers
EGHILNSST lightness
nightless
EGHILNSTU sleuthing
EGHILNSUW gluhweins
EGHILOORS shooglier
EGHILOORY hierology
EGHILORST ghostlier
EGHILPRST plighters
EGHILPRTU uplighter
EGHILSSST sightless
EGHILSSTT slightest
EGHIMNORT mothering
EGHIMNOST something
EGHIMPPSU pemphigus
EGHINNSST sennights
EGHINNSTU enthusing
EGHINOORV hoovering
EGHINOPRT pothering
EGHINORSU rehousing
EGHINORSW showering
EGHINORTV overnight
EGHINORTX exhorting
EGHINOSST histogens
EGHINOSTU noughties
EGHINOSTY histogeny
EGHINPRSY syphering
EGHINRSST rightness
EGHINRSTU hungriest
EGHINRTUW wuthering
EGHINSSSU gushiness
EGHINSSTT tightness
EGHIOPRTT tightrope
EGHIORSTU righteous
EGHIORSTV oversight
EGHIOSTUW outweighs
EGHIRSTTU theurgist
EGHLLOPSU plugholes
EGHLMNOPU ploughmen
EGHLMOOOU homologue
EGHLNOOPY nephology
phenology
EGHLNOORS longshore
EGHLNOOSU longhouse
EGHLNOOTY ethnology
EGHLNOPYY phylogeny
EGHLOOORR horologer
EGHLOOORS horologes
EGHLOPRSU ploughers
EGHLORSTU Gütersloh
EGHMNOORW homegrown
EGHMOOPSS gomphoses
EGHNOOOPR gonophore
EGHNOOPRY gynophore
EGHNOPTYY phytogeny
EGHNORSSU roughness
EGHNOSSTU toughness
EGHNRSSTT strengths
EGHOOOSSW hoosegows
EGHOOPSUY hypogeous
EGHOPTYYZ zygophyte
EGHORRSTW regrowths
EGIIIMNST itemising
EGIIIMNTZ itemizing
EGIIJLNST jingliest
EGIIJNNNO enjoining
EGIIJNNOR rejoining
EGIIJNRTT jittering
EGIIKLNST kingliest
EGIIKNNRT tinkering
EGIIKNPPR kippering
EGIIKNRSS Kissinger
EGIIKRSTZ sitzkrieg
EGIILLMNP impelling
EGIILLNNO nielloing
EGIILLNOR gorilline
EGIILLNRT tillering
EGIILMMNS immingles
EGIILNNOT entoiling
EGIILNNST enlisting
listening
tinseling
EGIILNNSV sniveling
EGIILNNTT entitling
inletting
EGIILNNUV unveiling
EGIILNORS religions
EGIILNORT loitering
EGIILNOST gilsonite
EGIILNPSS singspiel
EGIILNRSS rieslings
EGIILNRST relisting
EGIILNRSV silvering
slivering
EGIILNRTT littering
retitling
EGIILNSVW swiveling
EGIILNTTY gentility
EGIILOPST epilogist
EGIILORST trilogies
EGIILORSU religious
EGIILRRST gristlier
EGIILRRZZ grizzlier
EGIILRSST grisliest
EGIILRSTU liturgies
EGIILRSZZ grizzlies
EGIILSTTU guiltiest
EGIILSTTZ glitziest
Stieglitz
EGIIMMNRS immersing
simmering
EGIIMNNRT reminting
EGIIMNPRS impingers
premising
simpering
EGIIMNPRX premixing
EGIIMNRSS griminess
EGIIMNRST mistering

EGIIMNRTT	remitting
EGIIMNSTY	stymieing
EGIIMOPST	impetigos
EGIIMORRS	grimoires
EGIINNNPR	repinning
EGIINNNRT	interning
EGIINNNRV	innerving
EGIINNNTV	inventing
EGIINNNTW	entwining
EGIINNORS	nigrosine
	signorine
EGIINNORT	orienting
EGIINNOST	ingestion
EGIINNOSU	ingenious
EGIINNQRU	enquiring
EGIINNRRT	interring
EGIINNRST	inserting
	sintering
EGIINNRSW	inswinger
EGIINNRTU	reuniting
EGIINNRTV	inverting
EGIINNRTW	wintering
EGIINNSTT	insetting
EGIINNSTV	investing
EGIINNTUY	ingenuity
EGIINOPRS	peignoirs
EGIINOPST	poetising
EGIINOPTT	tiptoeing
EGIINOPTZ	poetizing
EGIINORSS	seigniors
	signories
EGIINORST	sortieing
EGIINORSY	seigniory
EGIINPPQU	equipping
EGIINPPST	peptising
EGIINPPTT	pipetting
EGIINPPTZ	peptizing
EGIINPQRU	repiquing
EGIINPRRS	reprising
	respiring
	springier
EGIINPRST	priesting
	respiting
EGIINPRSV	prevising
EGIINQRRU	requiring
EGIINQRSU	esquiring
EGIINQRTU	requiting
EGIINQRUV	quivering
EGIINRRST	stringier
EGIINRRTU	intriguer
EGIINRRTW	rewriting
EGIINRSST	resisting
EGIINRSTT	resitting
EGIINRSTU	intrigues
EGIINRTTT	tittering
EGIINRTTW	wittering
EGIINRTTY	integrity
EGIINSSTT	stingiest
EGIINSSTW	swingiest
EGIIRSTTT	grittiest
EGIJKNNTU	junketing
EGIJLNSTU	jungliest
EGIJLNSTY	jestingly
EGIJNPRRU	perjuring
EGIKLLNSY	skellying
EGIKLNNOO	inglenook
EGIKMNNOY	monkeying
EGIKNNOTY	keynoting
EGIKNORRW	reworking
EGILLLNTY	tellingly
EGILLMNOW	mellowing
EGILLMNTY	meltingly
EGILLMORU	glomeruli
EGILLMOTU	guillemot
EGILLNNOR	enrolling
EGILLNNOT	Ellington
EGILLNORW	rowelling
EGILLNOTW	towelling
EGILLNOTX	extolling
EGILLNOUU	Longueuil
EGILLNOVY	volleying
EGILLNOWY	yellowing
EGILLNPSS	spellings
EGILLNSSW	swellings
EGILLNSTU	glutelins
EGILLOORS	glorioles
EGILLOSSY	syllogise
EGILLOSYZ	syllogize
EGILLSSTU	guiltless
EGILMMNOP	pommeling
EGILMMNPU	pummeling
EGILMNOOS	neologism
EGILMNOPY	employing
EGILMNOST	molesting
EGILMOORS	oligomers
EGILMOOST	gloomiest
EGILMOOSY	myologies
	semiology
EGILMOSUU	eulogiums
EGILMPRSS	glimpsers
EGILNNNTU	tunneling
EGILNNOOS	loosening
EGILNNOSS	lessoning
EGILNNOST	singleton
EGILNNOSU	ensouling
EGILNNOSW	lowsening
EGILNNOTX	Lexington
EGILNNRSU	nurseling
EGILNNSST	nestlings
EGILNNVYY	envyingly
EGILNOORT	retooling
EGILNOOST	enologist
	neologist
EGILNOOSU	sinologue
EGILNOPRX	exploring
EGILNORSV	resolving
EGILNORTV	revolting
EGILNORTW	troweling
EGILNORVV	revolving
EGILNORVY	overlying
EGILNOTVY	longevity
EGILNPRST	springlet
EGILNPRSU	repulsing
EGILNRSSW	newsgirls
EGILNRSTU	lustering
	resulting
EGILNRSTW	wrestling
EGILNRSTY	restyling
EGILNSSTT	settlings
EGILOOOSZ	zoologies
EGILOOSSU	isologues
EGILOSSST	glossiest
EGILOSSTT	glottises
EGILOSSTU	eulogists
EGILRRSZZ	grizzlers
EGILRSSTY	greylists
EGIMMNNOU	immunogen
EGIMMNRSU	summering
EGIMMNSSU	gumminess
EGIMNNORT	mentoring
EGIMNORRT	tremoring
EGIMNORST	Germiston
EGIMNORSV	misgovern
EGIMNPRSU	impugners
	presuming
EGIMNPRTU	permuting
EGIMNRSSY	synergism
EGIMNRSTU	mustering
EGIMNRSUY	eryngiums
EGIMNRTTU	muttering
EGIMPRSTU	grumpiest
EGINNNOST	sonneting
EGINNNRRU	rerunning
EGINNNRUV	unnerving
EGINNOORT	enrooting
EGINNORRT	Tengri Nor
EGINNORSV	vignerons
EGINNORSW	worsening
EGINNOSUU	ingenuous
EGINNRRTU	returning
EGINNRSTT	stringent
EGINNRSTU	insurgent
EGINNRTUV	venturing
EGINOOSSS	goosiness
EGINOOSSU	isogenous
EGINOPPST	estopping
EGINOPRRR	porringer
EGINOPRRT	reporting
EGINOPRRV	reproving
EGINOPRST	progestin
EGINOPRTT	pottering
	repotting
EGINOPRTX	exporting
EGINOPSST	spongiest
EGINOPSSU	espousing
EGINOPSUY	epigynous
EGINOQRTU	roqueting
EGINORRST	resorting
	restoring
	rostering
EGINORRTT	retorting
EGINORRTU	rerouting
EGINORSTT	gritstone
EGINORSTY	oystering
EGINORSUV	overusing
EGINORSVW	wingovers

EGINORTTT tottering
EGINORTTX extorting
EGINOSSTU goutiness
EGINPPRSU suppering
EGINPRRSS springers
EGINPRSSS pressings
EGINPRTTU puttering
EGINPRTTY prettying
EGINPRUVY purveying
EGINPSTTU upsetting
EGINPSTWW sweptwing
EGINRRSST restrings
ringsters
stringers
EGINRSSST stressing
EGINRSSTY synergist
EGINRSTUV vesturing
EGINRSUVY surveying
EGINRTTUX texturing
EGINSSSTU gustiness
EGINSTTTU tungstite
EGIOORSTV grooviest
EGIOORSUV ovigerous
EGIOPRSSS gossipers
EGIORSTTT grottiest
EGIORSTTU groutiest
EGIPPRTTU gruppetti
EGIPSTUZZ Zugspitze
EGJLNORSU jongleurs
EGJLNOSTU jelutongs
EGKORSSUW guesswork
EGLLLOORR logroller
EGLLMNORY mongrelly
EGLLMOOSS gloomless
EGLLMORSW gromwells
EGLLOOPRS gollopers
EGLLOSSSS glossless
EGLMNOOOU monologue
EGLMOORTY metrology
EGLMOOSUY museology
EGLMOOTYY etymology
EGLMOPRSU promulges
EGLNNOORS longerons
EGLNNPTUY pungently
EGLNOOOPY poenology
EGLNOOPRR prolonger
EGLNOOPRS prolonges
EGLNOORUY neurology
EGLNOOSUV longevous
EGLNORSTY strongyle
EGLNORSUU longueurs
EGLNOSTUU glutenous
EGLNRTTUY turgently
EGLOOORTY erotology
EGLOOOSTY osteology
EGLOOPRSU prologues
EGLOOPRTY petrology
EGLOOPSTY logotypes
EGMMNOORS groomsmen
EGMNNORST strongmen
EGMNOOOSS gonosomes
mongooses
EGNNNRRUU gunrunner
EGNNOOPRT Negropont
EGNNORSSW wrongness
EGNOOOPRS gonopores
EGNOOPRSS prognoses
EGNOORRSV governors
EGNOORRVW overgrown
EGNOORSUU urogenous
EGNOOSTUX oxtongues
EGNOOSUXY oxygenous
EGNOPPRSU oppugners
EGNOPRSUW newsgroup
EGNORSSSS grossness
EGNORSSST songsters
EGNORSSTT strongest
EGNORSSTU sturgeons
EGNORSTUY youngster
EGOOPRRSU prorogues
EGOOPRSYZ zygospore
EGOORRSVW overgrows
EGOPPRTTU gruppetto
EHHIIPRSS heirships
EHHIIRTTT thirtieth
EHHILLLSY hellishly
EHHILMNST helminths
EHHILMOOP homophile
EHHIMPRSU Humphries
EHHINOPPS phosphine
EHHINORTW nowhither
EHHIOPPST phosphite
EHHIOPRSW horsewhip
EHHIORSST horseshit
EHHIORTTT thitherto
EHHIOSTVY yeshivoth
EHHLLMOTZ Helmholtz
EHHLOOPTY holophyte
EHHMNNOPP Phnom Penh
EHHMNOOOP homophone
EHHMRTUYY eurhythmy
EHHNOORSS shoehorns
EHHOOPSTY theosophy
EHHOOSSTU hothouses
EHIIILLMW Wilhelm II
EHIIINRVY Henry VIII
EHIIKNSTT kittenish
EHIILNTTW lintwhite
EHIILRSTW Wiltshire
EHIIMRSTT tritheism
EHIIMSSTW whimsiest
EHIINNORT ornithine
EHIINNRSS inshrines
EHIINNSSS shininess
EHIINOPST Tisiphone
EHIINORRT inheritor
EHIINPRST nephritis
phrenitis
EHIINPSST pithiness
EHIINRSTW winterish
EHIIORSST histories
EHIIPPSSY epiphysis
EHIIRRSTT thirstier
EHIIRSSTT shirtiest
EHIIRSTTT tritheist
EHIIRSTTZ zitherist
EHIISSTTT shittiest
EHIISSTTX sixtieths
EHIISTWZZ whizziest
EHIJMNOTU Jotunheim
EHIKLLPSY sylphlike
EHIKLMNPY nymphlike
EHIKLNOSS sinkholes
EHIKLNPRY hyperlink
EHIKLOOST tikoloshe
EHIKLOOTT toothlike
EHIKLORTZ kilohertz
EHIKNOSST shonkiest
EHIKNPRRS preshrink
EHIKNRRSS shrinkers
EHIKNSSSU huskiness
EHIKORRSY Yorkshire
EHILLLMOS molehills
EHILLMOPS philomels
EHILLOSTY hostilely
EHILLOSWY yellowish
EHILLRRST thrillers
EHILLRSST shrillest
EHILMNOST monthlies
EHILMNOSY hemolysin
EHILMOORS heirlooms
EHILMOSSY hemolysis
EHILMPPRY perilymph
EHILMPSSY symphiles
EHILMRSST mirthless
EHILMRSTU Lutherism
EHILMRSUV Hilversum
EHILNOOPT lithopone
phonolite
EHILNOPST tholepins
EHILNOSST holsteins
EHILNOSTU unholiest
EHILNOSTX xenoliths
EHILNOSUY heinously
EHILOOPSZ zoophiles
EHILOPRSS polishers
EHILOPRST heliports
EHILOPRXY xerophily
EHILOPSST isopleths
EHILOPTYY heliotypy
EHILPSSTU sulphites
EHILPSTTY pettishly
EHILRSSTW whistlers
EHILRSTTW whittlers
EHILSSSTU slushiest
EHIMMNSUY hymeniums
EHIMNNOOS moonshine
EHIMNOPRS premonish
EHIMNOPUU euphonium
EHIMNORST horsemint
thermions
EHIMNOSTT monteiths
EHIMNPSST shipments
EHIMNPSSU humpiness
EHIMNRTUU ruthenium
EHIMNSSSU mushiness

EHIMNSTTU tunesmith
EHIMOOSST smoothies
EHIMOPPRR perimorph
EHIMOPRTY hemitropy
EHIMORSST isotherms
EHIMOSTTU mouthiest
Thutmose I
EHIMPRRSS shrimpers
EHIMPRRTU triumpher
EHIMPSSUU euphuisms
EHIMRRSTY erythrism
EHIMSSSTU isthmuses
EHINNOPSS phoniness
EHINNOPTY phenytoin
EHINNORSS horniness
EHINNOSTW whinstone
EHINNSSSU sunshines
EHINOOOPR ionophore
EHINOOPSS isophones
EHINOPPRS hornpipes
EHINOPRSS nephrosis
EHINOPRSW ownership
shipowner
EHINOPSTT phonetist
EHINOPSTY hypnotise
EHINOPSVY envoyship
EHINOPTYZ hypnotize
EHINORRSU nourisher
EHINORSSS horsiness
EHINORSSU nourishes
EHINORSSW Weisshorn
EHINORSTT thorniest
EHINORTXY thyroxine
EHINOSSSW showiness
EHINOSSTU outshines
EHINPPSTU unhippest
EHINPRRTY pyrethrin
EHINPRSSU punishers
EHINPSSSU pushiness
EHINRSSSU rushiness
EHINSSSTY synthesis
EHIOOPRTW wirephoto
EHIOOSTTT toothiest
EHIOPRSST prothesis
sophister
EHIORSSTT theorists
EHIORSTTW worthiest
EHIORSTWZ howitzers
EHIOSSSTU stoushies
EHIOSSTTU shoutiest
EHIOSTTUW whiteouts
EHIPQSSUY physiques
EHIPRSSTW whipsters
EHIPSSTUU euphuists
EHIRRSSTT thirsters
EHIRSTTTW whittrets
EHJOOSSSU joss house
EHKKLOOSS kolkhoses
EHKKLOOSZ kolkhozes
EHKLNOOST knotholes
EHKLOOOST tokoloshe
EHKNNOORS nonkosher
EHKNOOOSS hooknoses
EHKNPRRSU preshrunk
EHKOORRSW workhorse
EHKOORSUW housework
workhouse
EHLLMOPSY mesophyll
phyllomes
EHLLNSSTU nutshells
EHLLOOOPS loopholes
EHLLOOSTU tollhouse
EHLLOSTUW Southwell
EHLMOORSW wormholes
EHLMORSSU humorless
EHLNOOPPY polyphone
EHLNOOPXY xylophone
EHLNOORSS honorless
EHLNOOSTY holystone
EHLNOPSSU sulphones
EHLNORRTY northerly
EHLNORSST thornless
EHLNPSSSU plushness
EHLOOPRST portholes
potholers
EHLOOPSSS splooshes
EHLOOPSTU South Pole
EHLOOPSTY holotypes
EHLOOSSTT toothless
EHLOPRSTU upholster
EHLOPSTYY hypostyle
EHLORRTTT throttler
EHLORSSTT throstles
EHLORSSTW worthless
EHLORSTTT throttles
EHLORSTUY southerly
EHLORTTUW Lower Hutt
EHLOSSTUY youthless
EHLPRSTUU sulphuret
EHLRSSTTU truthless
EHMMOOPRS mesomorph
EHMMOORSU humorsome
EHMMRRSTU thrummers
EHMNNOOOY honeymoon
EHMNOOSST smoothens
EHMNOTTUY Tynemouth
EHMOOOPRS sophomore
EHMOOORSU houseroom
EHMOOOSTT toothsome
EHMOOPRSS morphoses
EHMOORSST smoothers
EHMOOSSTT smoothest
EHMOOSSUU houmouses
EHMORSTUV vermouths
EHMPRRTUY pyrethrum
EHMPSSSYY symphyses
EHNNOORST hornstone
EHNNORSTU unthrones
EHNNPRTUY thrupenny
EHNOOOPPT optophone
EHNOOORTT orthotone
EHNOOPPTY phonotype
EHNOORRSU honourers
EHNOORSSW snowshoer
whoresons
EHNOORSTW honeworts
EHNOOSSSW snowshoes
EHNOOSSUY Syon House
EHNOOSTUW townhouse
EHNOOTTTT hottentot
EHNOPRTTU pothunter
EHNOPSSTY pythoness
EHNORSSST shortness
EHNORSTTW northwest
North West
EHNORTTWW Wentworth
EHNOSSTUU nuthouses
EHOOOPRSU poorhouse
EHOOORSTV overshoot
EHOOPPTTY phototype
EHOOPRRTT orthopter
EHOOPRRTV hoverport
EHOOPRSST posthorse
EHOOPSSTT photosets
EHOOPSSTU housetops
posthouse
pothouses
EHOOPSTYZ zoophytes
EHOORRTVW overthrow
EHOOSSTUU outhouses
EHOPRSSUV pushovers
EHOPRSTXY exstrophy
EHORRSTTW throwster
EHORSSTUU outrushes
EHOSSTTUW southwest
EHRRSSTTU thrusters
EIIILNNQU inquiline
EIIILPPRS liripipes
EIIILSTTU utilities
EIIIMMNRS minimiser
EIIIMMNRZ minimizer
EIIIMMNSS minimises
EIIIMMNSZ minimizes
EIIIMPRTV primitive
EIIINNPST insipient
EIIINNRTU Niu Tireni
EIIINQRSU inquiries
EIIINRSTT retinitis
trinities
EIIINTTUV intuitive
EIIIPRSTV privities
EIIJLLNOV Joinville
EIIJLLOST jollities
EIIJMSSTU jesuitism
EIIJQRTUY jequirity
EIIKKNNSS kinkiness
EIIKLLMNS limekilns
EIIKLMNSS milkiness
EIIKLMRSS mislikers
EIIKLNNRT interlink
EIIKLNRRW wrinklier
EIIKLNRSW wrinklies
EIIKLNSSS silkiness
EIIKLNSST slinkiest
EIIKMNRSS mirkiness
EIIKMPSST skimpiest

EIIKNNOSS noiseniks
EIIKNNRTT interknit
EIIKNNSST skinniest
EIIKNNSSW wineskins
EIIKNPSSS spikiness
EIIKNRSSS riskiness
EIIKQRSTU quirkiest
EIILLMNRS milliners
EIILLMNRY millinery
EIILLMNSU illumines
EIILLMSST limitless
EIILLNNOP penillion
EIILLNRST instiller
EIILLNSSS silliness
EIILLNSST niellists
EIILLNSTU nullities
EIILLNSTV vitellins
EIILLNTUY inutilely
EIILLOPRS pillories
EIILMMORS meliorism
EIILMNNST liniments
EIILMNORV vermilion
EIILMNOST limonites
EIILMNOSU limousine
EIILMNSSS sliminess
EIILMOPSV implosive
EIILMOPTY Ptolemy II
EIILMORST meliorist
EIILMOTTV leitmotiv
EIILMPRSU puerilism
EIILMPSUV impulsive
EIILMRSSY missilery
EIILMSSST slimsiest
EIILMSSTT mistitles
EIILNNOQU quinoline
EIILNORSS lionisers
EIILNORSZ lionizers
EIILNPSST splenitis
EIILNPSTY pensility
EIILNQSTU quintiles
EIILNQTUY inquietly
EIILNSTTU intitules
EIILNSTTY tensility
EIILNTUVY unitively
EIILOPSST pisolites
EIILOQSSU siliquose
EIILORRSV Oil Rivers
EIILPPSST slippiest
EIILPRSTU spirituel
EIILPRTUY puerility
EIILRSSTU utilisers
EIILRSTTY sterility
EIILRSTUZ utilizers
EIILRSTVY servility
EIILSSSTY sessility
EIIMMNNOS menominis
EIIMMNORS immersion
EIIMMNOSS misoneism
EIIMMNRSU immuniser
EIIMMNRUZ immunizer
EIIMMNSSU immunises
EIIMMNSTY immensity
EIIMMNSUZ immunizes
EIIMMORSS isomerism
EIIMMORST memoirist
EIIMMOSTV emotivism
EIIMMPSSS pessimism
EIIMMPSUY epimysium
EIIMMRTUX immixture
EIIMNNRTU triennium
EIIMNOPST pimientos
EIIMNORSS missioner
remission
EIIMNOSSS emissions
EIIMNOSST misoneist
EIIMNOSUV vimineous
EIIMNPRRT imprinter
EIIMNPRSU supermini
EIIMNRSST ministers
EIIMNRSTT intermits
EIIMNSSST mistiness
EIIMOPRSU imperious
EIIMOPRSV improvise
EIIMOPSST optimises
EIIMOPSTT epitomist
EIIMOPSTZ optimizes
EIIMOSSTV sovietism
EIIMOSTVV vomitives
EIIMOTTVY emotivity
EIIMPRSSS misprises
EIIMPRSSZ misprizes
EIIMPSSST pessimist
EIIMSSSTT semitists
EIINNNOST intension
EIINNNOTT intention
EIINNNOTV invention
EIINNNSST tinniness
EIINNORST insertion
EIINNORSV inversion
EIINNOSSS noisiness
EIINNOSSU unionises
EIINNOSSV envisions
EIINNOSUZ unionizes
EIINNPPSS nippiness
EIINNPSSS spininess
EIINNRSTT internist
EIINNSSTT insistent
EIINNSTTY intensity
EIINOPRST poitrines
EIINOPRSV prevision
EIINOPSTT petitions
pointiest
EIINOPTVW viewpoint
EIINORRST interiors
EIINORSSS sironises
EIINORSSV revisions
EIINORSSZ sironizes
EIINORSTY seniority
EIINPPRST pinstripe
EIINPPSST snippiest
EIINPRRSS inspirers
EIINPSSST tipsiness
EIINPSSSW wispiness
EIINQRRSU inquirers
EIINRSSST insisters
EIINRSSTZ ritziness
EIINRSTTW wintriest
EIINRSTUV intrusive
EIINRTTUV nutritive
EIINSSSYZ synizesis
EIINSSTTW wittiness
EIINSTTTU institute
EIIOOPSST isotopies
EIIOPSSTV positives
EIIOQRSSU Siqueiros
EIIOSSTTV sovietist
EIIPRRSTW tripwires
EIIPRRTUV irruptive
EIIPRSSST prissiest
EIIPRSSTT stripiest
EIIQSSTTU quietists
EIIRSSTTW wristiest
EIJKORRSS skijorers
EIJLLNOSS jolliness
EIJMNPSSU jumpiness
EIJNORSST jointress
EIJNORSTU jointures
EIJNOSSTT jettisons
EIKLLNOVX Knoxville
EIKLMNOSS moleskins
EIKLMNSYZ Zemlinsky
EIKLMORST stormlike
EIKLMORSY irksomely
EIKLNOSTU snoutlike
EIKLNPRRS sprinkler
EIKLNPRSS sprinkles
EIKLNRSTU knurliest
EIKLNRSTW twinklers
EIKLNSSSU sulkiness
EIKLSTTUZ klutziest
EIKMNNOSW kinswomen
EIKMNOORS monoskier
EIKMNOSSS smokiness
EIKMNRSSU murkiness
EIKMNSSSU muskiness
EIKNNOPRT pinkerton
EIKNOPRSS porkiness
EIKNORRTW interwork
EIKNOSTTT knottiest
EIKNPRSTU turnpikes
EIKNPSSTU spunkiest
EIKNRRTTY trinketry
EIKOOPSST spookiest
EIKORRSTV overskirt
EIKORRSWW wireworks
EIKORSTTU strikeout
EIKOSSTYZ Ossietzky
EIKPRRSSU spruikers
EIKRRSTWY skywriter
EILLMNOST millstone
EILLMNSSU sensillum
EILLMOOPT Melitopol
EILLMOPSS plimsoles
EILLMORTU multirole
EILLMOSSY lissomely
EILLMPSSS misspells

EILLMPSTU	multiples
EILLMPTTU	multiplet
EILLMPTUX	multiplex
EILLMRTUU	tellurium
EILLNOPRU	nullipore
EILLNORTU	tellurion
EILLNOSSW	lowliness
EILLNOTVY	violently
EILLNPSSW	pinswells
EILLNSSST	stillness
EILLNSSSY	sinlessly
EILLOOPRV	Liverpool
EILLOOSTW	woolliest
EILLOPRSV	overspill
	spillover
EILLOPRTY	pellitory
EILLOPRWW	willpower
EILLOSTTY	stylolite
EILLPSSSY	syllepsis
EILLSSTWY	witlessly
EILMMNTUU	nummulite
EILMMOPSY	misemploy
EILMMPSTU	plummiest
EILMNOOSY	noisomely
EILMNOPSS	spoilsmen
EILMNOPST	simpleton
EILMNORTT	tormentil
EILMNORTU	Montreuil
EILMNOSSU	emulsions
EILMNOSTY	solemnity
EILMNOSWY	winsomely
EILMNPSSU	lumpiness
EILMNPSTU	tumplines
EILMNRSST	minstrels
EILMOOPSS	liposomes
EILMOOSTY	ileostomy
EILMOPRRS	implorers
EILMOPSST	mileposts
	polemists
EILMOSSSU	semisolus
EILMOSTUY	timeously
EILMRSTUU	multiuser
EILNNOOQU	quinolone
EILNNOOSS	looniness
EILNNOSTV	insolvent
EILNOOPSS	slipnoose
EILNOOPSX	explosion
EILNOOSST	oilstones
EILNOOTUV	evolution
EILNOPRRU	purloiner
EILNOPRSU	neuropils
	prelusion
	repulsion
EILNOPSST	pointless
EILNOPSSU	spinulose
EILNOPSSY	spinosely
EILNOPSUX	expulsion
EILNORSTT	trotlines
EILNORSTY	storyline
EILNORSUV	revulsion
EILNORSVV	involvers
EILNORTUY	routinely
EILNOSSSU	lousiness
EILNOSSSW	lewissons
EILNOSSTT	siltstone
EILNOSSTV	novelists
EILNOSSUV	evulsions
EILNOSTUV	involutes
EILNOSUVY	enviously
EILNPPSSU	pulpiness
EILNPQTUU	quintuple
EILNPRSST	splinters
EILNPRSTU	Nelspruit
EILNPRSTY	splintery
EILNQTUUY	unquietly
EILNRSSSU	surliness
EILNRSSTU	insulters
EILNRSTTU	turnstile
EILNRSTUU	unruliest
EILNRTUUV	vulturine
EILNSSSTU	lustiness
EILNSSTTU	lutenists
EILOPPRSS	prolepsis
EILOPPRTY	propylite
EILOPPSST	sloppiest
EILOPRSSV	slipovers
EILOPRSTT	portliest
EILOPRSTV	overspilt
EILOPRSTW	pileworts
EILOPSSTY	stylopise
EILOPSTUY	piteously
EILOPSTYZ	stylopize
EILORRTVW	liverwort
EILORSSSV	visorless
EILORSSUY	seriously
EILORSSVZ	vizorless
EILOSSTTT	stilettos
EILPPRSST	stipplers
EILPPRSSU	suppliers
EILPRSSTT	splitters
EILQRRSSU	squirrels
EILRSSSTY	stylisers
EILRSSTTU	sultriest
	surtitles
EILRSSTTW	wristlets
EILRSSTYZ	stylizers
EIMMNNSTU	muniments
EIMMNOPRS	persimmon
EIMMNORRT	minor term
EIMMNORSS	misnomers
EIMMOPRSU	emporiums
EIMMOPSTU	impostume
EIMNNNRTU	inurnment
EIMNNOOSS	mooniness
EIMNNOOST	noontimes
EIMNNOOTZ	monzonite
EIMNNOPRT	prominent
EIMNNOPST	imponents
	pointsmen
EIMNNORST	innermost
EIMNNOSTT	ointments
EIMNNPTUU	neptunium
EIMNNRTTU	nutriment
EIMNOOPSS	empoisons
EIMNOORRT	remontoir
EIMNOORSS	roominess
EIMNOORSV	omnivores
EIMNOPRTU	importune
EIMNOPSST	nepotisms
EIMNORRTW	worriment
EIMNORSST	monitress
EIMNORSSU	sensorium
EIMNORSSW	worminess
EIMNORSUV	verminous
EIMNOSSSS	mossiness
EIMNOSSST	moistness
EIMNOSSSU	mousiness
EIMNOSTTY	testimony
EIMNOTTZZ	mezzotint
EIMNSSSSU	mussiness
EIMNSSSTU	mustiness
EIMNSSUZZ	muzziness
EIMOOPRTV	promotive
EIMOORRSW	worrisome
EIMOORSST	motorises
EIMOORSSU	isomerous
EIMOORSTZ	motorizes
EIMOOSSSX	exosmosis
EIMOPRRSS	primroses
	promisers
EIMOPRRST	importers
	misreport
	reimports
EIMOPRRSV	improvers
EIMOPRSST	imposters
EIMOPRSTU	imposture
EIMOPSTUU	impetuous
EIMOQSSTU	misquotes
EIMORRRST	terrorism
EIMORRSST	mortisers
EIMORRSTT	remittors
EIMORRSTU	trimerous
EIMORRSWW	wireworms
EIMORRTTW	miterwort
	mitrewort
EIMORSSTT	stormiest
EIMORSUVY	voyeurism
EIMOSSTTT	totemists
EIMOSSTUV	vomituses
EIMPSSTTU	stumpiest
EIMQRRSSU	squirmers
EIMQSSTUY	mystiques
EIMRRSSSU	surmisers
EIMSSTTTU	smuttiest
EINNNOTTY	nonentity
EINNNSSSU	sunniness
EINNOOPRT	pontonier
	prenotion
EINNOORST	ironstone
	serotonin
EINNORSTU	neutrinos
EINNORSTV	inventors
EINNORSWW	winnowers
EINNORTVY	inventory
EINNOSSST	stoniness
EINNOSSSW	snowiness

EINNOSSTX	nonsexist
EINNPRSTW	newsprint
EINNRSSTU	runtiness
EINNRSTTU	nutrients
EINNRTTUW	unwritten
EINNSSTTU	nuttiness
EINOOPRSS	poisoners
EINOOPSSS	opsonises
EINOOPSST	spooniest
EINOOPSSZ	opsonizes
EINOORRST	retorsion
EINOORRTT	retortion
EINOORSST	rootiness
EINOORSSZ	ozonisers
EINOORSZZ	ozonizers
EINOORTTX	extortion
EINOORTTY	notoriety
EINOOSSST	sootiness
EINOOSSTT	snootiest
EINOOSSWZ	wooziness
EINOOSTXX	exotoxins
EINOPPSSS	soppiness
EINOPRRSS	prisoners
EINOPRRTV	overprint
EINOPRSSS	prosiness
EINOPRSTU	eruptions
	Petronius
EINOPRSUU	penurious
EINOPSSSU	piousness
EINOPSSSY	synopsise
EINOPSSTT	nepotists
	pottiness
EINOPSSYZ	synopsize
EINOQSSTU	questions
EINOQSTTU	quotients
EINORRSSS	sorriness
EINORRSTV	invertors
EINORRTTV	introvert
EINORRUWZ	Ruwenzori
EINORSSTU	Nestorius
EINORSSTV	investors
EINORSSUV	souvenirs
EINORSTUX	extrusion
EINOSSTTT	snottiest
EINOSSTUU	Suetonius
EINPRRSST	sprinters
EINPRRTTU	interrupt
EINPRSSST	spinsters
EINQRSSTU	squinters
EINQRSTTU	quitrents
EINRSSSTU	rustiness
EINRSSTTU	ruttiness
EINRSSTTY	entryists
EIOOPPRSS	porpoises
EIOOPPSST	opposites
EIOOPRRST	posterior
EIOOPRSSV	provisoes
EIOOPRSTX	expositor
EIOORSSTT	tortoises
EIOORSTTT	troostite
EIOOSSSTX	exostosis
EIOOSSTTV	ovotestis
EIOPPRRST	stroppier
EIOPPRRTY	propriety
EIOPPRSUV	purposive
EIOPRRSSU	superiors
EIOPRRSTU	Pretorius
EIOPRSSTT	sportiest
EIOPRSSTU	posturise
EIOPRSTTU	proustite
EIOPRSTTY	posterity
EIOPRSTUZ	posturize
EIOPSSTTT	spottiest
EIOQRSTUU	turquoise
EIORRRSTT	terrorist
EIORRRTTY	territory
EIORRSSST	resistors
EIORRSSTU	Sertorius
EIORRSSTV	servitors
EIORSSTTU	out sister
EIOSSTTTW	swottiest
EIPPRRSST	strippers
EIPQRSSTU	quipsters
EIPQRTTUY	triptyque
EIPRRRSSU	spurriers
	surpriser
EIPRRSSSU	surprises
EIPRRSSTZ	spritzers
EIPRSSSTU	pertussis
EIQRRSSTU	squirters
EIRSSTTTU	trustiest
EJLLOSSYY	joylessly
EJLOPSSTU	pulsojets
EJMNORUWY	jurywomen
EJNOORRSU	sojourner
EKKOOPRRW	pokerwork
EKLMMNOSU	muskmelon
EKLMNPTUY	unkemptly
EKLNOOORS	onlookers
EKLNRSSTU	trunkless
EKLOOORSV	lookovers
	overlooks
EKLOOPSSW	slowpokes
EKMNNOORS	nonsmoker
EKMNOOPTY	monkeypot
EKMOOPRRS	moreporks
EKNOOPSTU	outspoken
EKNOORSTW	stonework
EKNORSSTU	sunstroke
EKOORRSVW	overworks
EKOORRTUW	outworker
EKOORSTTW	twostroke
EKOORSTWW	kowtowers
EKOPRRSSW	presswork
EKOPRSSTU	upstrokes
ELLLNOSWY	swollenly
ELLMOOSUV	Sullom Voe
ELLMOPSUY	plumosely
ELLMORSTU	rostellum
ELLMOSUUY	emulously
ELLMRSTUU	surmullet
ELLNOPSUW	upswollen
ELLNOPTUY	opulently
ELLNOSTVY	solvently
ELLNOTTTY	Lyttelton
ELLNSSSUY	sunlessly
ELLOORRSV	rollovers
ELLOPRSST	pollsters
ELLOPRSTU	polluters
ELLOPRSUV	pullovers
ELLOPRSUY	leprously
ELLORRSST	strollers
ELLORSTUU	tellurous
ELMNNOOST	somnolent
ELMNOOOPS	monopoles
ELMNOORTV	Lermontov
ELMNPPSSU	plumpness
ELMNSUUZZ	unmuzzles
ELMOOPSSY	polysomes
ELMOORSTW	lowermost
ELMOOSSSY	lysosomes
ELMORSTUU	tremulous
ELMORTUVY	volumetry
ELMPRSSTU	trumpless
ELNNOOSSU	unloosens
ELNNOPSSU	nonpluses
ELNOOOPRV	provolone
ELNOORSUY	onerously
ELNORSSTU	turnsoles
ELNORSUVY	nervously
ELNOSSSTU	snoutless
ELNOSTUUY	tenuously
ELOOORSTZ	zoosterol
ELOORSTUW	lousewort
ELOOSSSUY	osseously
ELOPPRSUY	purposely
ELOPRRSUY	prelusory
ELOPRRSYY	pyrolyser
ELOPRRYYZ	pyrolyzer
ELOPRSSTY	prostyles
ELOPRSSYY	pyrolyses
ELOPRSYYZ	pyrolyzes
ELOQRSUUU	querulous
ELORSSTUY	urostyles
ELPRSSSUU	surpluses
ELPRSSTTU	splutters
ELRSSSTTU	trustless
EMMMNOSTU	momentums
EMMNNOSTU	monuments
EMMNOOOSS	monosomes
EMMNOOOST	monostome
EMMNOOSTU	momentous
EMMNORSSU	resummons
EMMNOSSSU	summonses
EMMNRSTUU	menstruum
EMMOORSTY	osmometry
EMMRRRSUU	murmurers
EMMRRSSTU	strummers
EMNNOOOST	monotones
	moonstone
EMNOOPSTW	postwomen
EMNOOPSTY	monotypes
EMNOOPSUY	eponymous
EMNOORRTT	tormentor
EMNOORSST	mesotrons
EMNOORSSW	newsrooms

EMNOORTTY tonometry
EMNOORTUY neurotomy
EMNOORTWY moneywort
EMNOPRSST sportsmen
EMNOPRSSU responsum
EMNORSSTT sternmost
EMNRSTUUV Vertumnus
EMOOORRST storeroom
EMOOOSTTY osteotomy
EMOOPRRSS pressroom
EMOOPRRST promoters
EMOOPRSSZ zoosperms
EMOOPRTTY optometry
EMOORRSTU tremorous
EMOORSTTU outermost
EMOPPRRST prompters
EMOPPRSTU uppermost
EMOPRRTUV overtrump
EMOPRRTYY pyrometry
EMORSTTTU uttermost
EMPRSSTTU strumpets
ENNNOOPRS nonperson
ENNNORRTU nonreturn
ENNOOPPRT proponent
ENNOOPPST opponents
ENNOORSTV nonvoters
ENNOPRSSU unpersons
ENNOPRTWY pennywort
ENNORRTUU outrunner
ENNORSSST sternsons
ENNORSTTU turnstone
ENOOPPRST postponer
ENOOPPRTU opportune
ENOOPPSST postpones
ENOOPRRSS responsor
ENOORSSTY ostensory
ENOORSTTW stonewort
ENOOSSTTU sostenuto
ENOPRSSSU suspensor
ENOPRSSTT sternpost
ENOPRSTUW uptowners
ENOPSTTYY stenotypy
ENORRSTUV overturns
turnovers
ENORSSTUU strenuous
ENORSTUUV venturous
ENOSSSTTU stoutness
ENRRRSTUU nurturers
ENRSSSTUU untrusses
EOOOPRRTU Europoort
EOOOPRSSZ zoospores
EOOORRSST roseroots
EOOPPRRRT propretor
EOOPPRRSS oppressor
proposers
EOOPPRRST prepostor
EOOPPRSST proptoses
EOOPPRTTY prototype
EOOPPSTTY topotypes
EOOPRRSTT protestor
EOOPRRSTU uprooters
EOOPRRTTU outporter
EOOPRSSSS possessor
EOOPRSSTV stopovers
EOOPSSTTV stovetops
EOORRRSSW sorrowers
EOPPRRSTU supporter
EOPPRSSSU supposers
EOPRRSSTU posturers
proestrus
EOPRRSUVY purveyors
EORRRSTTU torturers
EORRSSSST stressors
EORRSSUVY surveyors
EORRSTUUV trouveurs
ERRSSTTTU strutters
FFGHIILNW whiffling
FFGHILNSU shuffling
FFGHILRTU frightful
FFGHINORS shroffing
FFGIILNNS sniffling
FFGIINSUX suffixing
FFGILNNSU snuffling
FFGIMNORU fungiform
FFGINOPRS offspring
FFGINSSTU stuffings
FFGINSSUU suffusing
FFHHILSUY huffishly
FFHOOOSST offshoots
FFIINOSUX suffixion
FFIKLORST forklifts
FFINOPRST offprints
FFINOSSUU suffusion
FFLMNOOSU moufflons
FFLOOOOPR foolproof
FGGHIILNT flighting
FGGHIINRT frighting
FGGHINSTU gunfights
FGGIILNNU ingulfing
FGGIILNUY uglifying
FGGIINORV forgiving
FGHIIINNS finishing
FGHIILLTY flightily
FGHIIMNUY humifying
FGHILNSSU flushings
FGHILOPTT topflight
FGHINORTT fortnight
FGHIOSTTU outfights
FGHLORSUU furloughs
FGHMOORTU frogmouth
FGHOOTTUU outfought
FGIIILLNN infilling
FGIIILLNP filliping
FGIIILMNS misfiling
FGIIILNVY vilifying
FGIIIMNNY minifying
FGIIIMNRS misfiring
FGIIINVVY vivifying
FGIILMNOR ligniform
FGIILNNOW inflowing
FGIILNOPR profiling
FGIILNORV frivoling
FGIILNPTU uplifting
FGIILNRST firstling
FGIILNRZZ frizzling
FGIILNTTY fittingly
FGIIMNNOR informing
FGIINNOTY notifying
FGIINNTTU unfitting
FGIINOPRT profiting
FGIINOSSY ossifying
FGIINPRUY purifying
FGIINPTYY typifying
FGIINRSSU fissuring
FGILLNOOW following
FGILNNRUU unfurling
FGILNNSTU gunflints
FGILNOTUY outflying
FGILNPRSU purflings
FGILNRRUY flurrying
FGILOOSTU ufologist
FGINNORTU fortuning
FGINOOTUX outfoxing
FGINORRUW furrowing
FGINORSST frostings
FGLLNOSUY songfully
FGLOOOSST footslogs
FGLORSUUU fulgurous
FHHIKOOSS fishhooks
FHHIORTTW forthwith
FHIIIKLLS killifish
FHIILRTTY thriftily
FHIKNRSTU trunkfish
FHIKORSTW shiftwork
FHILLOOST foothills
FHILLOOSY foolishly
FHILLORST hillforts
FHILLSUWY wishfully
FHILOPPSY foppishly
FHKLORSUW flushwork
FHLLRTUUY hurtfully
ruthfully
FHLMORUUU humourful
FHLMOSTUU mouthfuls
FHMOOOPRT mothproof
FHOORRTTW Fort Worth
FIIIKRTUW kiwifruit
FIIILSSTY fissility
FIIIMNRTY infirmity
FIIINNOSX infixions
FIIKLNNST skinflint
FIILLMORV villiform
FIILLMOTU multifoil
FIILLPTUY pitifully
FIILMORTU trifolium
FIILMPRST filmstrip
FIILOPRST profilist
FIILORSUV filovirus
FIILORTVY frivolity
FIIMMNORS misinform
FIIMNOSSU fusionism
FIIMOPRSS pisiforms
FIIMOPRST stipiform
FIIMORRTU triforium
FIIMORRTV vitriform
FIINNOSSU infusions

FIINOSSTU fusionist
FIKLLLSUY skilfully
FIKLLNSUU unskilful
FILLLLUWY willfully
FILLSTUWY wistfully
FILMMORSU formulism
FILMMORTU multiform
FILMNORUY uniformly
FILMNOSUU fulminous
FILMORSTU formulist
FILMORSTY styliform
FILMORUVV vulviform
FILOOOPRT portfolio
FILOORSSU fluorosis
FILOORSUV frivolous
FILORSUUY furiously
FILOSSTUU fistulous
FINNOOPRT nonprofit
FINOOPRSU profusion
FINOOPRTT footprint
FIRSSTTUU futurists
FKKLOORSW workfolks
FKLMOOOST folkmoots
FKLNOOSTW townsfolk
FKLNRSTUU trunkfuls
FKMOORRSW formworks
FKOORRSTW frostwork
FLLLOSUUY soulfully
FLLLSTUUY lustfully
FLLNOORRY forlornly
FLNOOPSSU spoonfuls
FLOOOOSTT footstool
FLOORRSUW sorrowful
FOOPRRSTU rustproof
FOOPSSTUY pussyfoot
GGGGIILNS gigglings
GGGHINRSU shrugging
GGGIILNNS nigglings
sniggling
GGGIILNRW wriggling
GGGIINNRU unrigging
GGGIINPRS sprigging
GGGILLOOW golliwogg
GGGILMNSU smuggling
GGGILNNSU snuggling
GGHHHIILT highlight
GGHHILOSY hoggishly
GGHIIILRW whirligig
GGHIIKNNT knighting
GGHIILNNS shingling
GGHIILNNT lightning
GGHIILNPT plighting
GGHIILNST slighting
GGHIILPSY piggishly
GGHIINNNU unhinging
GGHILNNOT nightlong
GGHILNOOS shoogling
GGHILNOPU ploughing
GGHILNOSU sloughing
GGHILNSUY gushingly
GGHILOOPR logogriph
GGHINNORT thronging
GGHINNOTW nightgown
GGHOOPRSS grogshops
GGIIIMNNP impinging
GGIIIMNSV misgiving
GGIILMNPS glimpsing
GGIILNNSW swingling
GGIILNPRY gripingly
GGIILNRZZ grizzling
GGIIMNNPU impugning
GGIIMPRSS priggisms
GGIINNORW ingrowing
GGIINNPRS springing
GGIINNRST stringing
GGIINNRSY syringing
GGIINOPSS gossiping
GGILLNNOY longingly
GGILLNOOP golloping
GGILLNOWY glowingly
GGILLNPUY gulpingly
GGILLOOSW golliwogs
GGILMNSUY ginglymus
GGILNNOUY youngling
GGILNOOPR prologing
GGILNOPRY gropingly
GGILNPRSU splurging
GGIMNOORS groomings
GGINNOPPU oppugning
GGINNOSSS singsongs
GGINOOSTU outgoings
GGINOPRSU groupings
GGINPRSUU upsurging
GGKNNOOSY Kyongsong
GHHHIIMST Highsmith
GHHIILPST lightship
GHHIINSTW whishting
GHHILRSTU rushlight
GHHINOOSW whooshing
GHHLOOSTY Holy Ghost
GHHLORTUY throughly
GHHNOTTUU unthought
GHIIKMNST King-Smith
GHIIKNNRS shrinking
GHIIKNPSS kingships
GHIIKNSTT skintight
GHIIKNTTT tightknit
GHIILLNRS shrilling
GHIILLNRT thrilling
GHIILLNSS shillings
GHIILLRSY girlishly
GHIILNNTY hintingly
GHIILNNWY whiningly
GHIILNOPS polishing
GHIILNSTW whistling
GHIILNTTW whittling
GHIIMMNSY shimmying
GHIIMNPRS shrimping
GHIINNNSY shinnying
GHIINNNWY whinnying
GHIINNOPS siphoning
GHIINNPSU punishing
GHIINNRSU inrushing
GHIINNSTY shintying
GHIINNSUW unwishing
GHIINPPSW whippings
GHIINQSSU squishing
GHIINRRSS shirrings
GHIINRSST shirtings
GHIINRSTT thirsting
GHIINSTTY stithying
GHIIRSSTT rightists
GHIKLSSTY skylights
GHIKNNOOU unhooking
GHILLNOOW hollowing
GHILLNOWY howlingly
GHILLOOPY philology
GHILLOOTY lithology
GHILLOSTW lowlights
GHILMNOOT moonlight
GHILNOOPT potholing
GHILNOORY rhinology
GHILNOPSS longships
sploshing
GHILNOPYY philogyny
GHILNOSST slingshot
GHILNPSUY pushingly
GHILNSTTU shuttling
GHILNSTUY unsightly
GHILOOOPY ophiology
GHILOOSTY histology
GHILOPRTW Plowright
GHILOPSTT spotlight
stoplight
GHILORSSW showgirls
GHILORSUY roguishly
GHILPRSTY sprightly
triglyphs
GHILPRTUY uprightly
GHIMMNRTU thrumming
GHIMMNTUY thingummy
GHIMNOOST smoothing
GHIMNORUU humouring
GHIMNOSST songsmith
GHIMNSSTU gunsmiths
GHIMOOPSS gomphosis
GHINNOORU honouring
GHINNOPSY syphoning
GHINNORST northings
GHINNORSU unhorsing
GHINOOSSW swooshing
GHINOPSTT nightspot
GHINORSST strongish
GHINORSTW ingrowths
GHINORTUW inwrought
GHINOSSTU southings
stoushing
GHINRSTTU thrusting
GHIORRSTY hygristor
GHLLOOOPY hoplology
GHLMNOOYY hymnology
GHLMOOTYY mythology
GHLNNOORS longhorns
GHLNOOOPY phonology
GHLNOOPYY hypnology
GHLNOSSTU slungshot

GHLOOPTYY	phytology
GHLORSTUU	turloughs
GHMNOOSUU	humongous
GHMNOSUUU	humungous
GHNNOOOSZ	gohonzons
GHNNOOPRR	pronghorn
GHOORSTUY	yoghourts
GHOORTTUW	outgrowth
GHOPRSTUW	upgrowths
GIIIKLMNS	misliking
GIIILNNOS	lionising
GIIILNNOZ	lionizing
GIIILNSTU	utilising
GIIILNTUZ	utilizing
GIIILOSTU	litigious
GIIIMMNST	mistiming
GIIIMNRUV	virginium
GIIIMRSST	mistigris
GIIINNNOP	pinioning
GIIINNNTW	intwining
GIIINNORS	ironising
GIIINNORZ	ironizing
GIIINNOST	ignitions
GIIINNOSV	visioning
GIIINNPRS	inspiring
GIIINNPSS	Nipissing
GIIINNQRU	inquiring
GIIINNSST	insisting
GIIINNSTU	unitising
GIIINNTTU	intuiting
GIIINNTUZ	unitizing
GIIINOSSS	Issigonis
GIIINPRST	spiriting
GIIINRTVY	virginity
GIIJKLMNO	Kim Jong Il
GIIJKNORS	skijoring
GIIJNOSST	jingoists
GIIKKLNPS	kingklips
GIIKLLLNY	killingly
GIIKLLNSS	skillings
GIIKLMNSU	Kim Il Sung
GIIKLNNNU	unlinking
GIIKLNNOP	Linköping
GIIKLNNRW	wrinkling
GIIKLNNST	tinklings
GIIKLNNTW	twinkling
GIIKMMNSS	skimmings
GIIKNNNUW	unwinking
GIIKNPRSU	prusiking
	spruiking
GIIKNRSST	skirtings
GIIKNSVVY	skivvying
GIILLLNWY	willingly
GIILLMNPY	limpingly
GIILLMNSY	smilingly
GIILLMRST	gristmill
GIILLNNUW	unwilling
GIILLNOPW	pillowing
GIILLNORS	grillions
GIILLNPSY	lispingly
GIILMNNSU	unsmiling
GIILMNOPR	imploring
GIILMNRSU	misruling
GIILMRSTU	liturgism
GIILNNNWY	winningly
GIILNNOST	Islington
GIILNNOSU	insouling
GIILNNOTU	outlining
GIILNNOVV	involving
GIILNNPPY	nippingly
GIILNNPST	splinting
GIILNNSTU	insulting
GIILNOPST	pistoling
	postiling
GIILNOQRU	liquoring
GIILNOTUV	outliving
GIILNPPRY	rippingly
GIILNPPST	stippling
GIILNPRST	stripling
GIILNPRSY	springily
GIILNPSTT	splitting
GIILNPTTU	uptilting
	uptitling
GIILNPTYY	pityingly
GIILNQSSU	quislings
GIILNQSTU	quiltings
GIILNRSTY	stringily
GIILNSSTU	linguists
GIILNSSTY	stylising
GIILNSTYZ	stylizing
GIILNSWZZ	swizzling
GIILNTTWY	wittingly
GIILOSSST	glossitis
GIILPSSTU	pugilists
GIILRSTTU	liturgist
GIIMMNRST	trimmings
GIIMNNOOT	motioning
GIIMNNTUY	mutinying
GIIMNOPRS	promising
GIIMNOPRT	importing
GIIMNOPRV	improving
GIIMNOPST	imposting
GIIMNORRR	mirroring
GIIMNORST	mortising
GIIMNPSTY	mistyping
GIIMNQRSU	squirming
GIIMNRSSU	surmising
GIINNNNPU	unpinning
GIINNNOWW	winnowing
GIINNNTUW	untwining
GIINNOOPS	poisoning
GIINNOOPT	optioning
GIINNOOSZ	ozonising
GIINNOOZZ	ozonizing
GIINNORSS	nigrosins
GIINNORST	ignitrons
GIINNPPRU	unripping
GIINNPPSS	snippings
GIINNPPUZ	unzipping
GIINNPRST	printings
	sprinting
GIINNPTTU	inputting
GIINNPTUY	unpitying
GIINNQSTU	squinting
GIINNTTUW	unwitting
GIINOPRST	riposting
GIINORRTW	worriting
GIINPPRST	stripping
GIINPRRTU	irrupting
GIINPRSSU	suspiring
	uprisings
GIINQRSTU	squirting
GIINRSUVV	surviving
GIIORRSST	rigorists
GIIORRSUU	irriguous
GIJKNNOOP	Jönköping
GIJLLNOTY	joltingly
GIJLMNPUY	jumpingly
GIKLLORRW	grillwork
GIKLNNNSY	King's Lynn
GIKLNNOOO	onlooking
GIKLNNOWY	knowingly
GIKLNOOOY	koniology
GIKNNNOUW	unknowing
GIKNNOSTW	Kingstown
GIKNOOPRV	provoking
GIKNOOTWW	kowtowing
GIKOORRVY	Krivoy Rog
GILLLNOOP	lolloping
GILLMNOOY	limnology
GILLMOORR	grillroom
GILLMOSSY	syllogism
GILLNNORU	unrolling
GILLNOPSY	slopingly
GILLNOPTU	polluting
GILLNORST	strolling
GILLNORUY	louringly
GILLOOOPY	oligopoly
GILLOOPSW	polliwogs
GILMMNOOS	mongolism
GILMMSTUY	multigyms
GILMNNOTY	Lymington
GILMOOSTY	myologist
GILNNOOSU	unloosing
GILNNRSSU	nurslings
GILNOPPST	stoppling
GILNOPTUY	poutingly
GILNORSUY	rousingly
GILNOSTUU	glutinous
GILNPPSUY	supplying
GILNRSSTU	lustrings
	rustlings
GILNSSTUU	singultus
GILOOORST	orologist
GILOOOSST	oologists
GILOOOSSU	isologous
GILOOOSTT	otologist
GILOOOSTZ	zoologist
GILOORSTU	urologist
GILOSSSST	glossists
GIMMNNOSU	summoning
GIMMNRRUU	murmuring
GIMMNRSTU	strumming
GIMNNOORS	monsignor
GIMNNOORU	unmooring
GIMNNOSTU	mountings

GIMNOOOSU	oogoniums
GIMNOOPRT	promoting
GIMNOORSU	ginormous
GIMNOPPRT	prompting
GIMNORRSW	ringworms
GIMNORRUU	rumouring
GIMOPRUUY	uropygium
GINNNOOTV	nonvoting
GINNOOPPR	proponing
GINNOOPRT	Orpington
GINNOORTU	unrooting
GINNOQTUU	unquoting
GINNORSTU	tonsuring
GINNOSUUU	unguinous
GINNPRTUU	upturning
GINNRRTUU	nurturing
GINNRSSTU	unstrings
GINOOPPRS	proposing
GINOOPRSS	prognosis
GINOOPRTU	uprooting
GINOOPWWW	powwowing
GINOORRSW	sorrowing
GINOORSTU	trigonous
GINOOTTUV	outvoting
GINOPPRST	stropping
GINOPPRSU	purposing
GINOPPSST	stoppings
GINOPPSSU	supposing
GINOPRSTU	posturing
	sprouting
GINOPRSUU	uprousing
GINOPSSST	signposts
GINORRTTU	torturing
GINPPRSSU	upsprings
GINPRRTUU	rupturing
GINRSTTTU	strutting
GIOPRSTWY	gipsywort
GLLNOOOOS	songololo
GLLOOPSTY	polyglots
GLLOOPSWY	pollywogs
GLMNOOPUY	polygonum
GLMNORSUW	lungworms
GLMNRSTUU	ngultrums
GLMOORSWW	glowworms
GLNOOOSTY	nostology
GLNOPRSSU	longspurs
GLNORSSTY	strongyls
GLNORSTUW	lungworts
GLOOOPRTY	tropology
GNOOOPRSY	sporogony
GNOOPRTYY	protogyny
GNOSSTTUU	tungstous
GOOPRSTUU	outgroups
GORRSTUWY	worryguts
HHHOOPRST	shophroth
HHIIOOSTY	Yoshihito
HHILLNORT	Thornhill
HHILMOSSS	shloshims
HHILORSWY	whorishly
HHIMRSTTY	rhythmist
HHKLOOOSV	Sholokhov
HHLMOOPYY	homophyly
HHMNOOOPY	homophony
HHNOORRST	shorthorn
HHOOPPRSS	phosphors
HIIIJNOXX	John XXIII
HIIILNSST	nihilists
HIIJLLNOT	jillionth
HIIKNSSVY	Vishinsky
HIILLMNOT	millionth
HIILLOSWW	willowish
HIILMOPYY	myiophily
HIILMOSST	homilists
HIILNORTT	trilithon
HIILNSSWY	swinishly
HIILOPSST	pisoliths
HIILOQRSU	liquorish
HIILOSTTY	hostility
HIILPSTTY	typhlitis
HIILRSTTY	thirstily
HIIMNSSTT	tinsmiths
HIIMOPSTU	hospitium
HIIOPRSTU	Pirithoüs
HIKKNSSUU	inukshuks
HIKLMNOSY	monkishly
HIKNNORST	stinkhorn
HIKNNORWY	hornywink
HIKNOORST	Kórinthos
HIKNOSTTU	outthinks
HIKNSSVYY	Vyshinsky
HILLLMTUU	multihull
HILLMPSUY	lumpishly
HILLNPSUY	sulphinyl
HILLOOPRW	whirlpool
HILLOOPST	lopoliths
HILLOSTUY	loutishly
HILLSSTYY	stylishly
HILMNOOST	monoliths
HILMOOSSY	homolysis
HILMOOSYZ	hylozoism
HILMOOTTY	lithotomy
HILOOPTXY	toxophily
HILOOSTYZ	hylozoist
HILORSSTT	shortlist
HILRSTTUY	ruttishly
HIMMOPRSU	phormiums
HIMNOPSTY	hypnotism
HIMOOPRSS	isomorphs
	morphosis
HIMOORTYZ	rhizotomy
HIMOPRRST	trimorphs
HIMOPRSSW	shipworms
HIMOPRSWW	whipworms
HIMORSSTU	humorists
HIMOSTTUU	Mutsuhito
HIMPSSSYY	symphysis
HINOPPRRY	porphyrin
HINOPSSTW	townships
HINOPSTTY	hypnotist
HIOOPPRST	troopship
HIOORSTTT	orthotist
HIOPRSSTY	sophistry
HIOPRSTTU	tutorship
HIORRSTTY	thyristor
HKLMMORUZ	krummholz
HKMMNORRU	krummhorn
HKMOOORSW	hookworms
HKOOPRSSW	workshops
HLLMNOOSU	monohulls
HLLNOPSUY	sulphonyl
HLLPRSUUY	sulphuryl
HLMOOPPRY	polymorph
HLNOOPPYY	polyphony
HLNOORSTU	Solothurn
HLOOORTWW	Woolworth
HLOOPPRSY	sporophyl
HMMOORSSU	mushrooms
HMNNOOOPY	monophony
HMNOOOSST	moonshots
HMOOOPRSY	homospory
HMOOORSSW	showrooms
HNOOOSTTU	Sutton Hoo
HNOOPPTYY	phonotypy
HNOOPRTTY	phytotron
HNOORRSTW	hornworts
HNOORSSTU	southrons
HOOORTTTW	toothwort
HOOOSSTTU	outshoots
	shootouts
HOOPRSSTT	shortstop
HOOPRSTTU	Southport
HPRSSTTUU	upthrusts
IIIILOSUV	Louis VIII
IIIILOSUX	Louis XIII
IIIKLLNPS	spillikin
IIIKLNPSS	spilikins
IIIKMNRST	miniskirt
IIILLMNPS	minipills
IIILMSUVX	lixiviums
IIILNOSTV	violinist
IIILNTTUY	inutility
IIILOSUVX	Louis XVII
IIIMPRSST	spiritism
IIIMRRTUV	triumviri
IIINNOTTU	intuition
IIINPRSST	inspirits
IIINSSSTU	sinusitis
IIIPRSSTT	spiritist
IIJNORSUU	injurious
IIKKMNOSW	Minkowski
IIKLLNOSS	skillions
IIKLNNOSW	Wilkinson
IIKNNNOOS	onionskin
IILLMNOPU	pollinium
IILLMPRSU	spirillum
IILLMRSTU	trilliums
IILLNNNOO	nonillion
IILLNOQSU	squillion
IILLNORST	trillions
IILLNOSSU	illusions
IILLOPSSY	lipolysis
IILLOSTVY	villosity
IILMNOOPS	implosion
IILMNOPSU	impulsion
IILMNOSSU	Mussolini
IILMOPSSS	solipsism

IILMOPSUY	impiously
IILNOOPST	postilion
IILNOOSTV	volitions
IILOOPPRS	liripoops
IILOPRTXY	prolixity
IILOPSSST	solipsist
IILOQSSUU	siliquous
IILORSSTT	troilists
IILORTTTY	tortility
IILOSTVVZ	slivovitz
IIMNNOOST	monitions
IIMNNOSTU	munitions
IIMNOOSSS	omissions
IIMNOPRSS	imprisons
IIMNOPSSZ	Spinozism
IIMNORSTT	intromits
IIMNOSSST	simonists
IIMNPRSST	misprints
IIMOPRTXY	proximity
IIMOPSSTT	optimists
IIMOQSTUX	quixotism
IIMORSTTU	tutiorism
IIMRRSTUV	triumvirs
IIMSSSTUW	swimsuits
IINNOORST	intorsion
IINNOOSUX	innoxious
IINNOPPST	pinpoints
IINNORSTU	intrusion
IINNORTTU	nutrition
IINNOSSTU	unionists
IINOOPRSV	provision
IINOOPSST	positions
IINOORSTT	sortition
IINOPRRTU	irruption
IINOPSSTY	spinosity
IINOSSTUY	sinuosity
IINOSSTVY	synovitis
IIOOPPRST	propositi
IIOOPRSST	spiritoso
IIOOPSSTV	oviposits
IIOORRRRS	riroriros
IIOPRSSTU	spiritous
IIORSTTTU	tutiorist
IJMNOORTW	jointworm
IKKKMOSUW	Kuskokwim
IKKLNORSW	linkworks
IKKNOOPRT	Kropotkin
IKKOOSSTW	Stokowski
IKLLOOSTV	kilovolts
IKLMOPPSY	milksoppy
IKLMORSSW	silkworms
IKLMORSTW	milkworts
IKLNOPSST	slipknots
IKMNOOPTY	Potyomkin
IKMOPPRUY	Yom Kippur
IKNOOPRST	pinkroots
IKNOORRSW	ironworks
IKNOPSSTT	stinkpots
IKORSSTTU	outskirts
ILLLMOPSS	plimsolls
ILLLOOPPS	lollipops
ILLLOSUVY	villously
ILLLPSUUV	pulvillus
ILLMOORST	stillroom
ILLNOOPTU	pollution
ILLNOORTT	tortillon
ILLNOPVYY	polyvinyl
ILLOOQSUY	soliloquy
ILLOPPSSS	slipslops
ILLOQRTUW	quillwort
ILMNOOSUY	ominously
ILMNOPTUU	plutonium
ILMNOPXYY	polymyxin
ILMOOOPRT	pilomotor
ILMOPSTUY	plumosity
ILMOSSYYZ	zymolysis
ILNOOPRSU	prolusion
ILNOOSSTU	solutions
ILNOOSTUV	volutions
ILNOOSUXY	noxiously
ILNOPRXYY	pyroxylin
ILNORSUUY	ruinously
ILNOSSUUY	sinuously
ILOOPPRSY	isopropyl
ILOOPRSTU	Port Louis
ILOORSTUY	riotously
ILOPPRSTY	stroppily
ILOPPSSTU	populists
ILOPRSSYY	pyrolysis
ILORSUUUX	luxurious
IMMOPPRTU	impromptu
IMMOPSSUY	symposium
IMNNOOPTW	topminnow
IMNNOOSTT	monotints
IMNOOOPRT	promotion
IMNOOOSSU	isonomous
IMNORSTTU	strontium
IMOOOSTTZ	zootomist
IMOOPPSTY	pomposity
IMOOPRRSS	promisors
IMOOPRSST	impostors
IMOOQSSTU	mosquitos
IMOORSSTT	motorists
IMORSUVXY	myxovirus
IMRSSSTTU	mistrusts
INNNNOOSU	nonunions
INNNORSTU	trunnions
INNOOPSSS	sponsions
INNOOSSUU	unisonous
INOOOPRTY	ionotropy
INOOOPSSU	poisonous
INOOORSTU	notorious
INOOOSTXZ	zootoxins
INOOPPRST	Propontis
INOOPPRTU	pourpoint
INOOPRSST	positrons
INOOPSSTT	spittoons
INOOPSTTU	outpoints
INOPRSTTU	outsprint
	printouts
INOPSSTTY	synoptist
INPRRSSTU	surprints
INPRSSTTU	turnspits
IOOORRRST	orrisroot
IOOPPRRTU	potpourri
IOOPPRSST	proptosis
IOOPRRSVY	provisory
IOORSSSUV	voussoirs
IOORSSTUV	virtuosos
IOPRSSTTU	outstrips
IORRSSUVV	survivors
JNNOORRSU	nonjurors
KLLMNSSUU	numskulls
KLNORSSTY	klystrons
KMOOORRSW	workrooms
KMOPRSTUW	stumpwork
KOOORSSTV	voorskots
KOORSSTVY	Ostrovsky
LMOOOOPRS	poolrooms
LMOOOORST	toolrooms
LMOOPPSUY	pompously
LMOOPRSTU	pulmotors
LMOORSSWW	slowworms
LNOOOPPTY	Pontypool
LNOOOPRST	poltroons
LNOOPPRSY	propylons
LOOPRRSUY	prolusory
LORSTUUUV	vulturous
MMORRSUUU	murmurous
MNNOOOPSY	monopsony
MNOORSSTU	monstrous
MNOORSSTW	snowstorm
MNORSSTUU	surmounts
MNORSTUUV	Vortumnus
MOOORRSTW	tomorrows
MOPSSTUUU	sumptuous
NNOOOPRSU	nonporous
NNOOOPSST	spontoons
NOOOOPRTV	Porto Novo
NOOOOPRTZ	protozoon
OOOOPRSSU	oosporous
OOPRSSTUU	stuporous
OOPRTTTUY	puttyroot
OORRSTTUU	torturous

Ten Letters

AAAAABCCRS asarabacca
AAAABBDDIS Addis Ababa
AAAABCCLNP Capablanca
AAAABCCLNS Casablanca
AAAABCENRS scarabaean
AAAABCLLSV balaclavas
AAAABCLMNS balmacaans
AAAABDFILS Faisalabad
AAAABEINRS Arabian Sea
AAAABGKORY kabaragoya
AAAABIKLLS balalaikas
AAAABJLMSY jambalayas
AAAABLRSTU tabula rasa
AAAACCHMST tacamahacs
AAAACCINRT Tacna-Arica
AAAACDGMNS Madagascan
AAAACDGMRS Madagascar
AAAACDIMMS macadamias
AAAACDJNRS jacarandas
AAAACDMMRT tarmacadam
AAAACHILPP Appalachia
AAAACHKKLS chakalakas
AAAACHSSUY ayahuascas
AAAACILPST cataplasia
AAAACIRRSU araucarias
AAAACLMNRT almacantar
AAAACLNRST Santa Clara
AAAACMNRST catamarans
AAAADDLMNR Damaraland
AAAADEGPRS Pasargadae
AAAADELLLN Allan-a-Dale
AAAADELMMT Alma-Tadema
AAAADEMNNS Andaman Sea
AAAADHMNRV Vardhamana
AAAADHMRUZ Ahura Mazda
AAAADIJVWY Vijayawada
AAAAEFRRSU Arafura Sea
AAAAEGLMMT amalgamate
AAAAEHMNNV Ahvenanmaa
AAAAELMMNT analemmata
AAAAGGGGWW Wagga Wagga
AAAAGHMRST Sagarmatha
AAAAGHRSTY satyagraha
AAAAGMSSSU massasauga
AAAAGNORSX Anaxagoras
AAAAGNPRUY Paraguayan
AAAAHHJMRS maharajahs
AAAAHINNST Athanasian
AAAAHIPPRS paraphasia
AAAAHKPPSW whakapapas
AAAAILLPRS paralalias
AAAAIMNNNP Panamanian
AAAAIMNRST Santa Maria
AAAAKMNORY Arakan Yoma
AAAALMNRSZ salmanazar
AAAALPRSTT parastatal
AAAAMNRSTT Santa Marta
AAAAMNRSTU Santa Maura
AAAAMPRRTT parramatta
AAABBCCHMO Cochabamba
AAABBCILST sabbatical
AAABBEILMT baalebatim
AAABBEIRSS Bessarabia
AAABBIILNR ibn-al-Arabi
AAABBINRRS barbarians
AAABBORRSS Barbarossa
AAABCCHLNS bacchanals
AAABCCHNRS charabancs
AAABCCKNSV canvasback
AAABCDEIRS scarabaeid
AAABCDELNR candelabra
AAABCDIIST adiabatics
AAABCDRRSU barracudas
AAABCEGILN Balenciaga
AAABCEHLSS calabashes
AAABCEHLTT attachable
AAABCEKLTT attackable
AAABCELLLR clarabella
AAABCEMRST carbamates
AAABCERSSU scarabaeus
AAABCHILNR abranchial
AAABCHINRT batrachian
AAABCIILST Basilicata
AAABCLLMRU ambulacral
AAABCLMORS carambolas
AAABCORRTU barracouta
AAABCORSTV Costa Brava
AAABDEEGLM damageable
AAABDEEHHY dahabeeyah
AAABDEGLOY Delagoa Bay
AAABDEHLRZ hazardable
AAABDENRSS sarabandes
AAABDILNST Stalinabad
AAABDINNST anabantids
AAABDMNRRU barramunda
AAABDMORSS ambassador
AAABEEGLMN manageable
AAABEELLPP appealable
AAABEELPPS appeasable
AAABEGLLSU Elagabalus
AAABEGLMNY manageably
AAABEIJNRZ Azerbaijan
AAABEILLSS assailable
AAABEILNTT attainable
AAABEKPRRS parabrakes
AAABEKRSWY breakaways
AAABELLNSY analysable
AAABELLNYZ analyzable
AAABELMSTT blastemata
AAABELNRRT narratable
AAABELRSTW basaltware
AAABFHHIIT Baha'í Faith
AAABFHHINU Abu Hanifah
AAABGLORRS algarrobas
AAABHIOPQU aquaphobia
AAABHLMQTU Quathlamba
AAABHLPRUW Bahawalpur
AAABHLRSTZ balthazars
AAABHNRSSU sub-Saharan
AAABIILRRT atrabiliar
AAABIINRRT Irian Barat
AAABIKLNPP Balikpapan
AAABILLNOS labionasal
AAABILRSTV Bratislava
AAABIMNPST anabaptism
AAABIMOPRR Paramaribo
AAABINPSTT anabaptist
AAABLMOSTT blastomata
AAABLPRSST parablasts
AAABMNRSTU marabuntas
AAACCCIORT cacciatora
AAACCCRSTU Caractacus
AAACCDELSV cavalcades
AAACCDIOPP Cappadocia
AAACCEHNNT catananche
AAACCEHRSS saccharase
AAACCEHRST saccharate
AAACCEIPTT capacitate
AAACCELSST cataclases
AAACCENRUV Cuernavaca
AAACCHILNR anarchical

AAACCHKMST tacmahacks
AAACCILLNT cataclinal
AAACCILLRS cascarilla
AAACCILNTV Cavalcanti
AAACCILSST cataclasis
AAACCINRTT Antarctica
AAACCIPRTT paratactic
AAACCIRSTT ataractics
AAACCMOPRR macrocarpa
AAACDDELRW Cadwalader
AAACDEHLNV avalanched
AAACDEHRSZ azedarachs
AAACDEIMMS macadamise
AAACDEIMMZ macadamize
AAACDEKNPY Pancake Day
AAACDELMNR calamander
AAACDENNRV caravanned
AAACDGGHIL haggadical
AAACDGIILR cardialgia
AAACDGLNNR Grand Canal
AAACDHIKST kadaitchas
AAACDHINNR arachnidan
AAACDHNRSS sandarachs
AAACDIIPRS paradisiac
AAACDILNRS calandrias
AAACDILRTY caryatidal
AAACEEGNNR carageenan
AAACEENPPR appearance
AAACEFIRST East Africa
AAACEFLQTU catafalque
AAACEGNORT Arctogaean
AAACEHIMNN Manichaean
AAACEHIMNU naumachiae
AAACEHLNSV avalanches
AAACEIINRS Icarian Sea
AAACEILMNT catamenial
AAACEINNRT catenarian
AAACEINPRS paracasein
AAACEINPSS Caspian Sea
AAACEINPST anapaestic
AAACEINRRS sarracenia
AAACEJKNPS jackanapes
AAACELLMNP Campanella
AAACELLNPT aplacental
AAACELMPRT metacarpal
AAACGGILNO anagogical
AAACGGIORV Caravaggio
AAACGHNRTT tragacanth
AAACGILLMY agamically
AAACGILLNO analogical
AAACGILLNV galvanical
AAACGINNRU Nicaraguan
AAACGLLSSW scallawags
AAACHHOPRY Chao Phraya
AAACHILLNW Wallachian
AAACHIMNSU naumachias
AAACHJOPRS chaparajos
AAACHKKMNT Kamchatkan
AAACHKPRRS pracharaks
AAACHLMOST chloasmata
AAACHLNOTU anacolutha
Talcahuano
AAACHLNRST charlatans
AAACHLPRRS chaparrals
AAACHNPRTY pyracantha
AAACHNPSTY panchayats
AAACHOPRST cataphoras
AAACHQTUUU chautauqua
AAACIIRSSS ascariasis
AAACILLMNU animalcula
AAACILLMNY maniacally
AAACILLMRS camarillas
AAACILLNTY analytical
AAACILMMNO ammoniacal
AAACILMNOT anatomical
AAACILNPST anaplastic
AAACILNRSS carnassial
AAACILNRST scarlatina
AAACIMNPTY Panama City
AAACINOPRS paranoiacs
AAACINRRTT tractarian
AAACINRSSU casuarinas
AAACLMNPSU campanulas
AAACLMNRTU almucantar
AAACLMNRVY cavalryman
AAACLMPSST cataplasms
AAACLNSSTU Santa Claus
AAACMRSTUX taraxacums
AAACNORSSU anasarcous
AAACNRTTTT attractant
AAADDEGNTV advantaged
AAADDELMPT maladapted
AAADDELPSY dasypaedal
AAADDHMRSY hamadryads
AAADEEGHNP phagedaena
AAADEELLNV Avellaneda
AAADEELNRW Delawarean
AAADEFIOST asafoetida
AAADEGGRTV aggravated
AAADEGHMNR Ahmednagar
AAADEGINRV devanagari
AAADEGLMTY amygdalate
AAADEGLNTV galavanted
AAADEGNNRW New Granada
AAADEGNSTV advantages
AAADEHLNPR aphelandra
AAADEILNRX Alexandria
AAADEIMNNT adamantine
AAADEIMSTT diastemata
AAADELMMRS marmalades
AAADELMNRS salamander
AAADELNPQU aquaplaned
AAADEOPSTZ zapateados
AAADGHLMNR Graham Land
AAADGHNQRY Qaraghandy
AAADGIILLR gaillardia
AAADGILLNR granadilla
AAADGLLNOR allargando
AAADGMMMNR grandmamma
AAADGMMNRS grandmamas
AAADGMNNNR Grand Manan
AAADGMNORR mandragora
AAADGNOPPR propaganda
AAADGNPPRS grandpapas
AAADHHIMYY Ahmadiyyah
AAADHHMRTU Hadhramaut
AAADHMMMNU Muhammadan
AAADIILNPR lapidarian
AAADIIMMNR Maid Marian
AAADILMNST dalmatians
AAADILNOPS diapasonal
AAADINOPTT adaptation
AAADKLRSSU Ruda Sląska
AAADLMMNNN landammann
AAADLNNSSY analysands
AAADLNQRTU quadrantal
AAADORSTTU autostrada
AAAEEHMNRS maharanees
AAAEEKLPRY parakeelya
AAAEELPRST palaestrae
AAAEFLMNST malfeasant
AAAEGGIMNT gametangia
AAAEGGRSTV aggravates
AAAEGHIOPR aerophagia
AAAEGHLLNP phalangeal
AAAEGILMNR managerial
AAAEGILNST East Anglia
AAAEGILPPR paraplegia
AAAEGINPRS asparagine
AAAEGLLMNS Magallanes
AAAEGLMNSU malaguenas
AAAEGLMNTU Guatemalan
AAAEGLMTXY metagalaxy
AAAEGMMNRR anagrammer
AAAEGMNNST manganates
AAAEGMRRTV margravate
AAAEGPSSWY passageway
AAAEHHSSTT tatahashes
AAAEHIKKST kahikateas
AAAEHIMRTU haematuria
AAAEHINSTU euthanasia
AAAEHMMOST haematomas
AAAEHMMOTT hematomata
AAAEHMOOTZ haematozoa
AAAEHMORTT atheromata
AAAEHNOPPR epanaphora
AAAEHPPRRS paraphrase
AAAEIILNTT italianate
AAAEIKLPRS parakelias
AAAEILLPST palatalise
AAAEILLPTZ palatalize
AAAEILMPST metaplasia
AAAEILMRTU tularaemia
AAAEILNPRT planetaria
AAAEILNPTT palatinate
AAAEIMNPRS paramnesia
AAAEIMNQRU aquamarine
AAAEIMNRTU Mauretania
AAAEINNRTV Tananarive
AAAELLNPST panatellas
AAAELLNRTT tarantella
AAAELLPRSX parallaxes
AAAELMMNOT melanomata
AAAELMRSTT metatarsal
AAAELNNSTT antenatals
AAAELNPQSU aquaplanes

AAAELNRTTU tarantulae
AAAELNSTTT tantalates
AAAELPRSST palaestras
AAAEMORTTT teratomata
AAAEPPRRSX parapraxes
AAAFFIKNRR Kaffrarian
AAAFIILLRS alfilarias
AAAFIJNNRS Rafsanjani
AAAFLORSST solfataras
AAAGGILLNO algolagnia
AAAGGILRST gastralgia
AAAGGNNRTU gargantuan
AAAGHILRRT arthralgia
AAAGHIMNOP phagomania
AAAGHIRSTY satyagrahi
AAAGHNPSTU agapanthus
AAAGHPPRRS paragraphs
AAAGIILMNR marginalia
AAAGIILMST galimatias
AAAGIKNNTY Tanganyika
AAAGILMNNO anglomania
AAAGILNPRS Graian Alps
AAAGIMMNRR grammarian
AAAGIMNSTT anastigmat
AAAGIMRRST margaritas
AAAGINNOPT Patagonian
AAAGINRRST rangatiras
AAAGJJKORT Jogjakarta
AAAGJLNRUW Gujranwala
AAAGJNOTUU Guanajuato
AAAGKORTYY Yogyakarta
AAAGLMMNPU Mpumalanga
AAAGLRSSTU astragalus
AAAGMNNOTU Guantánamo
AAAGMNSTTY syntagmata
AAAHIILPPR paraphilia
AAAHIKKLST kathakalis
AAAHIMMMST mahatmaism
AAAHINSSTU Athanasius
AAAHKKNSTZ Kazakhstan
AAAHKNRSST astrakhans
AAAHLLOSTY ayatollahs
AAAHLMNPST phantasmal
AAAHLMNRSU Al Mansûrah
AAAIIMNRTU Mauritania
AAAIINNRST sanitarian
AAAIINOPRS Pasionaria
AAAIKLLNST antalkalis
AAAIKLMNNT Kalimantan
AAAIKLMNRS Karamanlis
AAAIKMMRSW Wasim Akram
AAAIKRRTTU titarakura
AAAIKSSTVY Savitskaya
AAAILLLPTY palatially
AAAILLMNNZ manzanilla
AAAILLNOTV lavational
AAAILLORTV lavatorial
AAAILMMMNS mammalians
AAAILMNRWY railwayman
AAAILMPSTU Tamaulipas
AAAILNNOTT natational
AAAILNNPRS planarians
AAAILNORTT natatorial
AAAILNOTTX taxational
AAAILNRSTU Australian
saturnalia
AAAILNSSST assailants
AAAILOPRSV Valparaíso
AAAILPPRSS appraisals
AAAIMNORST inamoratas
AAAIMNRSST samaritans
AAAINNPRSS Parnassian
AAAINOPRSS saponarias
AAAINPSSTV vanaspatis
AAAIPPRRSX parapraxis
AAAJJKKORT Jokjakarta
AAALLNRTUW natural law
AAALMNOPRR paranormal
AAALNNOSST assonantal
AAALNOORSV Savonarola
AAALNRSTTU tarantulas
AAAMNNORTT tramontana
AAAMNPSSTU Maupassant
AAAMRTZZZZ razzmatazz
AABBBEJNOS bobbejaans
AABBBELORS absorbable
AABBCDEEKR barebacked
AABBCDEKLR Blackbeard
AABBCDKLOR blackboard
AABBCDKORS backboards
AABBCEEHLL bleachable
AABBCEILRS ascribable
AABBCELMOT combatable
AABBCENORS absorbance
AABBCIILNR rabbinical
AABBCIJKRT jackrabbit
AABBCILSST cabbalists
AABBCKLLLS blackballs
AABBCKMRRS barmbracks
AABBCKNRRS barnbracks
AABBDDEENN Baden-Baden
AABBDDEORR breadboard
AABBDEEELT debateable
AABBDEGILR abridgable
AABBDEGORR bargeboard
AABBDEIRRS barbarised
AABBDEIRRZ barbarized
AABBDELORS adsorbable
AABBDELSST beadblasts
AABBDEOORV aboveboard
AABBDEORSS baseboards
bosberaads
AABBEEELRT rebateable
AABBEEHLRT breathable
AABBEEIRTV abbreviate
AABBEEKLRS breakables
AABBEELLRT barbellate
AABBEELNRU unbearable
AABBEELNTU unbeatable
AABBEILMNO abominable
AABBEILNOT obtainable
AABBEILRRT arbitrable
AABBEIMNWZ Zimbabwean
AABBEINRST rabbinates
AABBEIRRSS barbarises
AABBEIRRSZ barbarizes
AABBEKLLST basketball
AABBELLOSV absolvable
AABBELNRUY unbearably
AABBGGILNR balbriggan
AABBIKLSST kabbalists
AABBIKORUY Aboukir Bay
AABBILLNTU balibuntal
AABBILLOOS boobiallas
AABBILMNOY abominably
AABBIMRRSS barbarisms
AABBLLMTTU albumblatt
AABCCDEKKP backpacked
AABCCDEKPS backspaced
AABCCDELOR accordable
AABCCEELPT acceptable
AABCCEFKLS blackfaces
AABCCEHNST bacchantes
AABCCEKKPR backpacker
AABCCEKPSS backspaces
AABCCELLLU calculable
AABCCELOST accostable
AABCCELPTY acceptably
AABCCGIKLM black magic
AABCCHHKST hatchbacks
AABCCIILOU coulibiaca
AABCCIILST cabalistic
AABCCIINRT bacitracin
AABCCIKKPS pickabacks
AABCCIKNRR crackbrain
AABCCIORST acrobatics
AABCCJKKLS blackjacks
AABCCKKRST backtracks
AABCCKRRSY carrybacks
AABCCLLLUY calculably
AABCDDEELU adduceable
AABCDDEHKN backhanded
AABCDDEIRR barricaded
AABCDDEKLS saddleback
AABCDDEMSU ambuscaded
AABCDDORRY cardboardy
AABCDEEEFL defaceable
AABCDEEHHS beachheads
AABCDEEHHY Beachy Head
AABCDEEHLT detachable
AABCDEEILR eradicable
AABCDEEKNR breakdance
AABCDEELLR declarable
AABCDEELTU educatable
AABCDEFIRT fabricated
AABCDEHIRT brachiated
AABCDEHKLS blackheads
AABCDEHKNR backhander
AABCDEHKSW backwashed
AABCDEIILS Alcibiades
AABCDEIITV abdicative
AABCDEILRT calibrated
AABCDEILRY eradicably
AABCDEIRRR barricader
AABCDEIRRS barricades
AABCDEKLPS backpedals

AABCDEKSWY	swaybacked
AABCDELNNU	unbalanced
AABCDELORS	scaleboard
AABCDELORT	carbolated
AABCDEMSSU	ambuscades
AABCDENNOS	abondances
AABCDENNSU	abundances
AABCDENORS	carbonades
AABCDENORT	carbonated
AABCDENPSS	spacebands
AABCDERSTT	abstracted
AABCDGIINT	abdicating
AABCDGIKNT	backdating
AABCDGKLRU	blackguard
AABCDHILNO	baldachino
AABCDHILNS	baldachins
AABCDHKLOR	chalkboard
AABCDHMORT	matchboard
AABCDHNSTW	watchbands
AABCDHOPRT	patchboard
AABCDIILLO	diabolical
AABCDIINOT	abdication
AABCDILMMS	lambdacism
AABCDIORST	abdicators
AABCDKLMPS	blackdamps
AABCDKLRWY	backwardly
AABCDLOPRS	clapboards
AABCDNNORT	contraband
AABCDNOORS	carbonados
AABCDORSST	broadcasts
AABCEEEFFL	effaceable
AABCEEELMR	amerceable
AABCEEEMRR	macebearer
AABCEEERTT	ebracteate
AABCEEERTX	exacerbate
AABCEEFNRR	Benacerraf
AABCEEGHLN	changeable
AABCEEGHLR	chargeable
AABCEEHILV	achievable
AABCEEHLNS	encashable
AABCEEHLPR	preachable
AABCEEHLRS	searchable
AABCEEHLTY	chalybeate
AABCEEHRST	sabretache
AABCEEIMRT	bacteremia
AABCEEINRR	carabineer
AABCEEIRTU	eubacteria
AABCEEKLSS	leasebacks
AABCEEKNRS	canebrakes
AABCEELLLR	recallable
AABCEELLNS	cleansable
AABCEELNRT	tabernacle
AABCEELPPR	recappable
AABCEELRTU	trabeculae
AABCEERSTT	bracteates
AABCEESTTU	subacetate
AABCEFIILP	pacifiable
AABCEFIRST	fabricates
AABCEFLORT	factorable
AABCEGHLNY	changeably
AABCEGHLRY	chargeably
AABCEGINRT	abreacting
	acerbating
AABCEGLLOU	coagulable
AABCEGLMNN	blancmange
AABCEGLMRS	cablegrams
AABCEGPRST	carpetbags
AABCEHHKLT	Blackheath
AABCEHIIMM	Miami Beach
AABCEHILMN	machinable
AABCEHILNN	Balanchine
AABCEHILPT	alphabetic
AABCEHILRT	charitable
AABCEHINRT	branchiate
AABCEHIRST	brachiates
AABCEHKLRT	blackheart
AABCEHKLSS	backlashes
AABCEHKLSW	whalebacks
AABCEHKSSW	backwashes
AABCEHLNST	stanchable
AABCEHPSTY	bathyscape
AABCEHRRTT	tetrabrach
AABCEIILLM	bacillemia
AABCEIINRR	carabinier
AABCEIINTU	beautician
AABCEILLLR	claribella
AABCEILLMP	implacable
AABCEILLPP	applicable
AABCEILMNS	imbalances
AABCEILMOT	ametabolic
AABCEILMST	masticable
AABCEILNOT	actionable
AABCEILNST	cantabiles
AABCEILOSS	associable
AABCEILOTT	catabolite
AABCEILQRU	acquirable
AABCEILRRT	calibrater
AABCEILRST	calibrates
AABCEIMNRS	mainbraces
AABCEINNTY	betacyanin
AABCEINORT	abreaction
AABCEINRRS	carabiners
AABCEIORST	aerobatics
AABCEIRRTU	bacteruria
AABCEIRSTT	tetrabasic
AABCEJKMRS	amberjacks
AABCEKKLNS	blacksnake
AABCEKKMRR	backmarker
AABCEKLRTW	blackwater
AABCEKPPRS	paperbacks
AABCEKPRRT	bratpacker
AABCEKRRRS	barrackers
AABCEKRSTW	backwaters
AABCELLNSU	unscalable
AABCELLORR	barcarolle
AABCELLORS	caballeros
AABCELMNSU	ambulances
AABCELMOPR	comparable
AABCELMTUU	acetabulum
AABCELNNSU	unbalances
AABCELNOTU	outbalance
AABCELOOSS	calabooses
AABCELORRS	barcaroles
AABCELRRTU	trabecular
AABCENORST	carbonates
AABCERRTUU	bureaucrat
AABCFHKLSS	flashbacks
AABCFIKLRR	Black Friar
AABCFINRST	fabricants
AABCFIORRT	fabricator
AABCGIILLM	galliambic
AABCGIKNRR	barracking
AABCGILLSU	subglacial
AABCGKMMNO	backgammon
AABCHHIMPR	amphibrach
AABCHHPSTY	bathyscaph
AABCHIKRSY	hairybacks
AABCHILRTY	charitably
AABCHINOTT	cohabitant
AABCHIOOPR	acrophobia
AABCHKLPSS	splashback
AABCHNRRUY	brachyuran
AABCIIKLOU	koulibiaca
AABCIIKLST	kabalistic
AABCIILLMY	iambically
AABCIILLRU	bacilluria
AABCIILLRY	biracially
AABCIILNOT	anabolitic
AABCIILPTY	capability
AABCIILTTY	actability
AABCIIOPRT	parabiotic
AABCIKLLMS	blackmails
AABCIKLLST	blacktails
AABCIKRSST	backstairs
AABCILLMPY	implacably
AABCILLPPY	applicably
AABCILMOPR	procambial
AABCILMORU	columbaria
AABCILMOST	catabolism
AABCILNNUU	incunabula
AABCILNOST	botanicals
AABCILNOTY	actionably
AABCILNRSU	subcranial
AABCILNSUV	subclavian
AABCILORRT	calibrator
AABCILPRSU	bicapsular
AABCILRRUV	vibracular
AABCILRSTU	ultrabasic
AABCIMMNOZ	Mozambican
AABCINNORS	carbanions
AABCIOQRSU	aquarobics
AABCIQSTUU	subaquatic
AABCKLLOTV	Black Volta
AABCKLLRST	trackballs
AABCKLMOOR	blackamoor
AABCKLPRST	blackstrap
AABCKORRSZ	razorbacks
AABCLLNNNO	cannonball
AABCLMMRUU	ambulacrum
AABCLMOPRY	comparably
AABCLORUVY	vocabulary
AABCMNOSTT	combatants
AABCNOORRS	barracoons
AABCNORSST	contrabass
AABDDDEEHL	baldheaded
AABDDEEEHR	bareheaded

AABDDEEGHN	headbanged
AABDDEEGLR	degradable
AABDDEEHNR	barehanded
AABDDEEKLR	Abdelkader
AABDDEELMN	demandable
AABDDEGGNS	sandbagged
AABDDEGLSS	saddlebags
AABDDEHLLN	handballed
AABDDEHLMO	hebdomadal
AABDDEHLRS	balderdash
AABDDEHORS	headboards
AABDDEMRTU	adumbrated
AABDDHORSS	dashboards
AABDDILLMO	lambdoidal
AABDDLNORS	Broadlands
AABDDNNSST	bandstands
AABDDORRST	dartboards
AABDEEEMNO	endamoebae
AABDEEFLRY	defrayable
AABDEEGLRR	regardable
AABDEEHLLN	handleable
AABDEEHRRT	threadbare
AABDEEILNT	detainable
AABDEEILRU	Baudelaire
AABDEELLRS	balladeers
AABDEELNPX	expandable
AABDEELNRU	unreadable
AABDEELORT	elaborated
AABDEELPRS	spreadable
AABDEELPTU	updateable
AABDEELRRV	laverbread
AABDEELRRW	rewardable
AABDEEMNOS	endamoebas
AABDEENNOS	abandonees
AABDEFFLOR	affordable
AABDEFLRST	flatbreads
AABDEGGGNN	gangbanged
AABDEGGINR	brigandage
AABDEGGNRS	sandbagger
AABDEGHLNS	Bangladesh
AABDEGINNO	gabionnade
AABDEGINOS	gabionades
AABDEGINRS	gabardines
AABDEGORST	goatsbeard
AABDEGRRSY	graybeards
AABDEHITTU	habituated
AABDEHKNRS	handbrakes
AABDEHKRSW	hawksbeard
AABDEHLLNR	handballer
AABDEHLNRS	handlebars
AABDEIILLS	labialised
AABDEIILLZ	labialized
AABDEIKLNS	balkanised
AABDEIKLNZ	balkanized
AABDEILLNR	banderilla
AABDEILLSY	dialysable
AABDEILLYZ	dialyzable
AABDEILRSV	adverbials
AABDEIMNOT	abominated
AABDEINNOR	Aberdonian
AABDEINRTZ	bartizaned
AABDEIOSSY	bioassayed
AABDEIQRTU	biquadrate
AABDEIRRTT	arbitrated
AABDEIRSST	bastardise
AABDEIRSTZ	bastardize
AABDEJLSTU	adjustable
AABDEKORST	skateboard
AABDELLNNO	belladonna
AABDELLNST	tablelands
AABDELNOPR	pardonable
AABDELNRUY	unreadably
AABDELNTUY	unabatedly
AABDELRSTU	balustrade
AABDELSTWY	twayblades
AABDEMNRST	bandmaster
AABDEMORST	dreamboats
AABDEMRSTU	adumbrates
AABDENSSTW	sweatbands
AABDEOPPRR	paperboard
AABDEOPPRT	approbated
AABDEOPRST	pasteboard
AABDEORSST	adsorbates
AABDFHLORS	flashboard
AABDGIILRS	garibaldis
AABDGINNNO	abandoning
AABDGKNNRS	Grand Banks
AABDGNNOSW	bandwagons
AABDHIILLU	Abdullah II
AABDHIORSZ	biohazards
AABDHMNNSU	husbandman
AABDHNORRW	handbarrow
AABDHORSSW	washboards
AABDIIKRRY	Diyarbakir
AABDIJNORS	jaborandis
AABDIJOORU	Ouija board
AABDILMNRU	mandibular
AABDILNQSU	baldaquins
AABDILOOPR	paraboloid
AABDILORSS	sailboards
AABDILORST	broadtails
	tailboards
AABDILSSSU	disabusals
AABDIMNRRU	barramundi
AABDINNRST	trainbands
AABDINSSTW	waistbands
AABDJLSTUY	adjustably
AABDKLORSW	boardwalks
AABDLNNTUY	abundantly
AABDLNOPRY	pardonably
AABDLNOSTU	Basutoland
AABDLNSSST	sandblasts
AABDLORRTY	bardolatry
AABDORRSST	starboards
AABDORRSTW	strawboard
AABEEELLPR	repealable
AABEEELLRS	resaleable
	resealable
AABEEELLRV	revealable
AABEEELPRT	repeatable
AABEEEMNOT	entamoebae
AABEEFILRR	rarefiable
AABEEFLLLT	flabellate
AABEEFLNTT	fattenable
AABEEFNSST	beanfeasts
AABEEGHLRT	gatherable
AABEEGILNR	regainable
AABEEGIMNS	Senegambia
AABEEGLLST	bagatelles
AABEEGLMSS	assemblage
AABEEGLNST	East Bengal
AABEEGNORT	baronetage
AABEEGRSUV	subaverage
AABEEHKRRT	heartbreak
AABEEHLSTW	swatheable
AABEEHRRSS	earbashers
AABEEHRSTT	heartbeats
AABEEILLRS	realisable
AABEEILLRZ	realizable
AABEEILMNX	examinable
AABEEILNRT	retainable
AABEEILPRR	repairable
AABEEIMOSS	amoebiases
AABEEJKRRW	jawbreaker
AABEEKLMRR	remarkable
AABEEKLMRT	marketable
AABEEKLPPS	bakeapples
AABEEKLRRW	lawbreaker
AABEEKRRTW	breakwater
AABEELLLSZ	sleazeball
AABEELLMNT	lamentable
AABEELLNSU	unsaleable
	unsealable
AABEELLPRR	pallbearer
AABEELMNNU	unnameable
AABEELMNTU	untameable
AABEELMRSU	measurable
AABEELMSTT	metastable
AABEELNNTT	tenantable
AABEELNORS	reasonable
AABEELNOSS	seasonable
AABEELNPTT	patentable
AABEELNRSW	answerable
AABEELOPRV	evaporable
AABEELORST	elaborates
AABEELPPRT	palpebrate
AABEELPPRY	prepayable
AABEELRRST	arrestable
AABEELSSSS	assessable
AABEELSTTT	attestable
AABEEMNOST	entamoebas
AABEEMNSTT	abatements
AABEENRSST	Barents Sea
AABEEQRSSU	arabesques
AABEFGIILS	gasifiable
AABEFGKLNR	klangfarbe
AABEFHLMOT	fathomable
AABEFIILLS	salifiable
AABEFIILRT	ratifiable
AABEFILLNT	inflatable
AABEFIMORS	framboesia
AABEFINRRT	afterbrain
AABEFKRSST	breakfasts
AABEFLORUV	favourable
AABEGGGNNR	gangbanger
AABEGGINNT	abnegating

AABEGGRRTY ratbaggery
AABEGHINRS earbashing
AABEGHORRS harborages
AABEGHORRU harbourage
AABEGIILMN imaginable
AABEGILNOZ zabaglione
AABEGILNSS assignable
AABEGILRST algebraist
AABEGINNOT abnegation
AABEGINNPT gabapentin
AABEGINNRT interabang
AABEGINRRS bargainers
AABEGINRST Great Basin
AABEGIRRST arbitrages
AABEGIRRSU bigarreaus
AABEGKLORS gaolbreaks
AABEGLNRUU unarguable
AABEGLOPPR propagable
AABEGMNRSU submanager
AABEGMNRTU Baumgarten
AABEGNORST abnegators
AABEHIILTT habilitate
AABEHILORV behavioral
AABEHIOOPR aerophobia
AABEHISTTU habituates
AABEHKLNSU unshakable
AABEHKNRSU Barkhausen
AABEHLOSTW whaleboats
AABEHLQSSU squashable
AABEHLRSZZ belshazzar
AABEIIILLS Isabella II
AABEIILLSS labialises
AABEIILLSZ labializes
AABEIILMPR impairable
AABEIILNRV invariable
AABEIILNST banalities
insatiable
AABEIILPRT biparietal
AABEIILRSV braaivleis
AABEIILSST assibilate
AABEIIMOSS amoebiasis
AABEIIRRTT abirritate
AABEIIRSTU aubrietias
AABEIJKLRS jailbreaks
AABEIJLOSU beaujolais
AABEIKLMST mistakable
AABEIKLNSS balkanises
AABEIKLNSZ balkanizes
AABEIKNNRT barkantine
AABEIKNRRS karabiners
AABEILLMPP impalpable
AABEILLNRS ballerinas
AABEILLNUV invaluable
AABEILLORV labiovelar
AABEILLRSY realisably
AABEILLRYZ realizably
AABEILMNRS lamebrains
AABEILMNTU albuminate
AABEILMNTV ambivalent
AABEILMPRT impartable
AABEILMPSS impassable
AABEILMSUX ambisexual
AABEILNNTU biannulate
AABEILNOST anabolites
AABEILOPRS parabolise
AABEILOPRZ parabolize
AABEILRSTU tabularise
AABEILRTTT titratable
AABEILRTUZ tabularize
AABEIMNORU anaerobium
AABEIMNOST abominates
AABEINORRT aberration
AABEINORTT trabeation
AABEINRRTW waterbrain
AABEINRSST abstainers
AABEINRSVW brainwaves
AABEINSSTT bastnasite
AABEINSTUV Buena Vista
AABEIORRTV arborvitae
AABEIRRRST barratries
AABEIRRSTT arbitrates
AABEIRRTTT bitartrate
AABEKLMRRY remarkably
AABEKLMRTY marketably
AABEKLNOOR Alanbrooke
AABEKLNSST beanstalks
AABEKPPRRS paperbarks
AABELLLNNU annullable
AABELLLPRY ballplayer
AABELLMNTY lamentably
AABELLMOST ameloblast
AABELLNNTY Ballantyne
AABELLNPUY unplayable
AABELMOSUX ambosexual
AABELMRSUY measurably
AABELNNOTX nontaxable
AABELNORSY reasonably
AABELNOSSY seasonably
AABELNPRST Barnstaple
AABELNRSWY answerably
AABELOORRT elaborator
AABELOPRRT proratable
AABELOPRUV vapourable
AABELORSST astrolabes
AABELRSTTU tablatures
AABELSTTTU statutable
AABEMOSSTT steamboats
AABEMRSTTU masturbate
AABENOPRTU Buonaparte
AABEOPPRST approbates
AABEPRRSUZ superbazar
AABEQRRSTU Quatre Bras
AABFFIILTY affability
AABFHILSWY Walfish Bay
AABFLMNOTY flamboyant
AABFLORUVY favourably
AABGGGGINS gasbagging
AABGGIINNR bargaining
AABGGINORT abrogating
AABGGINOST sabotaging
AABGHILOOP algophobia
AABGHOPRRS barographs
AABGIILMNY imaginably
AABGIILNOR aboriginal
AABGIINNST abstaining
AABGILLNST ballasting
AABGILMNST lambasting
AABGILMNTU ambulating
AABGILNSSY assignably
AABGILNTTU tabulating
AABGIMNRSU brugmansia
AABGINNOOT Tobagonian
AABGINNOTW angwantibo
AABGINOORT abrogation
AABGINORTU outbargain
AABGIOSSSS bagassosis
AABGLNRUUY unarguably
AABGNRRSUW burrawangs
AABGOORRST abrogators
AABHHIKSSU hibakushas
AABHIILOPS basophilia
AABHIILRSZ bilharzias
AABHIIMNPS amphibians
AABHIINNTT inhabitant
AABHIINOTT habitation
AABHIKKLNU Kublai Khan
AABHIKLLRU Rub' al Khali
AABHILLTUY habitually
AABHIMMNRS Brahmanism
AABHIMRTVZ Bar Mitzvah
AABHIMSTVZ Bas Mitzvah
AABHIMTTVZ Bat Mitzvah
AABHINSSSW washbasins
AABHIPRRSV vibraharps
AABHKKORSV Khabarovsk
AABHKLNSUY unshakably
AABHLLLOOU hullabaloo
AABHLPSSYY hypabyssal
AABIIILMTY amiability
AABIILLNOT libational
AABIILLSTY salability
AABIILMTTY tamability
AABIILNRRS librarians
AABIILNRVY invariably
AABIILNSTY insatiably
AABIILRTTY ratability
AABIILTTXY taxability
AABIIMNNSS Minas Basin
AABIINNSSY Abyssinian
AABIINPRST bipartisan
AABIINRRTT abirritant
AABIIOPRSS parabiosis
AABIJNORTU abjuration
AABIKLMOST katabolism
AABIKLMSTY mistakably
AABILLMNUY bimanually
AABILLMPPY impalpably
AABILLNNUY biannually
AABILLNOOT oblational
AABILLNRUY binaurally
AABILLNUVY invaluably
AABILLORSS isallobars
AABILLRUVV bivalvular
AABILMNOSS anabolisms
AABILMNOTU ambulation
AABILMPSSY impassably

AABILMRSST strabismal
AABILNOORT abortional
AABILNOOSV Nova Lisboa
AABILNOSTT battalions
AABILNOTTU tabulation
AABILOPRST parabolist
AABIMNOORT abominator
AABINNORTY antibaryon
AABINOSSTW boatswains
AABIORRRTT arbitrator
AABIRSSSTT Bass Strait
AABKKOORRU kookaburra
AABKLOSTUW walkabouts
AABLLMNORY abnormally
AABLMNORSY myrobalans
AABLMORTUY ambulatory
AABLOORRTY laboratory
AABLORSTTU tabulators
AABLOSSTTT statoblast
AABLRSSTTU substratal
AABLSTTTUY statutably
AABORRRSTU barratrous
AACCCDENOR accordance
AACCCEENPT acceptance
AACCCEILTT catalectic
AACCCEINOT catenaccio
AACCCEIORT cacciatore
AACCCEIRSU accuracies
AACCCEOSTU cactaceous
AACCCINRUY inaccuracy
AACCDEENNS ascendance
AACCDEENSU succedanea
AACCDEHIRS saccharide
AACCDEHKRS crackheads
AACCDEHLOR charcoaled
AACCDEHNOR archdeacon
AACCDEIIPR epicardiac
AACCDEIIRS acaricides
AACCDEILMT acclimated
AACCDEILNT accidental
AACCDEILTU aciculated
AACCDEIMNU unacademic
AACCDEINTV vaccinated
AACCDEIOSV advocacies
AACCDELLTU calculated
AACCDELNOR cladoceran
AACCDELSTU sacculated
AACCDEMNOO cacodaemon
AACCDENNSY ascendancy
AACCDEORTT coarctated
AACCDGIILR cardialgic
AACCDHIILR diarchical
AACCDHILOT cathodical
AACCDHILRY dyarchical
AACCDHIORS saccharoid
AACCDIIINT adiactinic
AACCDIIRTY caryatidic
AACCDIISTU diacaustic
AACCDIORST Caird Coast
AACCEEELRT accelerate
AACCEEGPRS scapegrace
AACCEELLNT cancellate
AACCEELLOT calceolate
AACCEELNRS clearances
AACCEELNRT accelerant
AACCEENTTU accentuate
AACCEEORTV coacervate
AACCEFHKLS chalkfaces
AACCEFPRST spacecraft
AACCEGHOST stagecoach
AACCEHILLM alchemical
AACCEHILLS cailleachs
AACCEHILMN mechanical
AACCEHILMR Carmichael
AACCEHINNT cachinnate
AACCEHINRS saccharine
AACCEHIRSS saccharise
AACCEHIRSZ saccharize
AACCEHJKPS cheapjacks
AACCEHLNOT coelacanth
AACCEHORSS saccharose
AACCEHRRST characters
AACCEHRRTY charactery
AACCEHRTTW catchwater
AACCEHSSTW watchcases
AACCEIILNS caecilians
AACCEIINRV vicariance
AACCEIIPST capacities
AACCEIIPTV capacitive
AACCEIKMMO cockamamie
AACCEILMRS acclaimers
AACCEILMST acclimates
AACCEILPTT cataleptic
AACCEINNOT canonicate
AACCEINORV covariance
AACCEINPRT pancreatic
AACCEINRRS cercarians
AACCEINRTT cantatrice
AACCEINRTU inaccurate
AACCEINSTV vaccinates
AACCEIRRTU caricature
AACCEISTUV accusative
AACCEJKLNS lancejacks
AACCEJKRRS carjackers
AACCEKNRSS crankcases
AACCEKRRST racetracks
AACCELLRST catcallers
AACCELLSTU calculates
AACCELMSTY cyclamates
AACCELMTUU accumulate
AACCELORSU calcareous
AACCELRTUY accurately
AACCENRSTU crustacean
AACCEORSTT coarctates
AACCFGILLU calcifugal
AACCFHIRSY saccharify
AACCFILLRY farcically
AACCFILRSU fascicular
AACCFINNRS Franciscan
AACCGHIORY hagiocracy
AACCGHIPRY graphicacy
AACCGHOPRY cacography
AACCGIILMN acclaiming
AACCGILLNT catcalling
AACCGILNOR caracoling
AACCHIIRST archaistic
AACCHILNPY chaplaincy
AACCHIMORT achromatic
AACCHINNOR anachronic
AACCHINRSS saccharins
AACCHIOPRT cataphoric
AACCHIPRRS archicarps
AACCHIQSUU Chuquisaca
AACCHIRSTT cathartics
AACCHKLLUW chuckwalla
AACCHLNORY acronychal
AACCHMORSU scaramouch
AACCHNOTYY chatoyancy
AACCIILLMT climatical
AACCIILLNU canaliculi
AACCIILORS sacroiliac
AACCIILPRT accipitral
AACCIINPTY incapacity
AACCIINRSS circassian
AACCIINSTT tacticians
AACCILLRUV clavicular
AACCILLTTY tactically
AACCILMMUY immaculacy
AACCILMNSU cacuminals
AACCILNNOS canonicals
AACCILNOOS occasional
AACCILOSTU acoustical
AACCILPRST practicals
AACCILRTUY articulacy
AACCIMNORS carcinomas
macaronics
maccaronis
AACCINNRSZ cancrizans
AACCINORST Costa Rican
AACCINORTV vaccinator
AACCINOSTU accusation
anacoustic
AACCINPTTY anaptyctic
AACCINRSTU anacrustic
AACCIOPRST capacitors
AACCIORTTU autocratic
AACCLLORTU calculator
AACCLMORSY cycloramas
AACCLMSSTY cataclysms
AACCLNOTTU contactual
AACCLNRRUU caruncular
AACCLORSVY slavocracy
AACCMNORTY cartomancy
AACCNNOTTU accountant
AACCNORSST sacrosanct
AACCOPRRSS sarcocarps
AACCORSTUY accusatory
AACDDEEEFT defaecated
AACDDEEFLT defalcated
AACDDEEHLR decahedral
AACDDEEIRT eradicated
AACDDEELLR Calderdale
AACDDEELNR calendared
AACDDEEMNS damascened
AACDDEEMRT demarcated
AACDDEGNOS gasconaded

AACDDEIJTU adjudicate
AACDDEILRU Ciudad Real
AACDDEILTU acidulated
AACDDEINOR endocardia
AACDDEINST candidates
AACDDEKLPS packsaddle
AACDDELNPS landscaped
AACDDEMNTU manducated
AACDDENNNO cannonaded
AACDDHKPWY paddywhack
AACDDIIMMR MacDiarmid
AACDDIOTTU autodidact
AACDDKPSWY paddywacks
AACDDMORSU docudramas
AACDEEEFNS defeasance
AACDEEEFST defaecates
AACDEEEHNX hexadecane
AACDEEFHMS shamefaced
AACDEEFLST defalcates
AACDEEFORT defaecator
AACDEEGKPR repackaged
AACDEEGNOT anecdotage
AACDEEHRTT reattached
AACDEEHRTX ex cathedra
AACDEEIINT taeniacide
AACDEEINRT deracinate
AACDEEINRV cadaverine
AACDEEIPTT decapitate
AACDEEIRST eradicates
AACDEEITTV deactivate
AACDEEJLTU ejaculated
AACDEEJNNR Jeanne d'Arc
AACDEEKKLW cakewalked
AACDEELMNO Lacedaemon
AACDEELRSS escaladers
AACDEELRTT altercated
AACDEELTTY acetylated
AACDEEMNSS damascenes
AACDEEMRST demarcates
AACDEENNTT attendance
AACDEENORU Ecuadorean
AACDEFINRU fricandeau
AACDEFINST fascinated
AACDEFJNUU Juan de Fuca
AACDEFLORT defalcator
AACDEGHHMU gamahuched
AACDEGHHNR chargehand
AACDEGHMRU gamaruched
AACDEGILNS escalading
AACDEGIMNP campaigned
AACDEGISTT castigated
AACDEGLOTU catalogued
coagulated
AACDEGNORS gasconader
AACDEGNOSS gasconades
AACDEHHTTW deathwatch
AACDEHILNS enchiladas
AACDEHILRS charladies
AACDEHILRT tracheidal
AACDEHIMNT machinated
AACDEHIORS icosahedra
AACDEHKMSS smackheads

AACDEHKPRT packthread
AACDEHLLNS dancehalls
AACDEHLMTY chlamydate
AACDEHLORT octahedral
AACDEHLRST cathedrals
clartheads
AACDEHMNOR Andromache
AACDEHNTTU unattached
AACDEHOPPR approached
AACDEHPRTU parachuted
AACDEIILNT acetanilid
laciniated
AACDEIILPR epicardial
AACDEIINRR irradiance
AACDEIINRS radiancies
AACDEIIPRR pericardia
AACDEIIPRT paediatric
AACDEIIRTV divaricate
AACDEIISTU audacities
AACDEIJLTV adjectival
AACDEILLNS dalliances
AACDEILLTV vacillated
AACDEILMNO demoniacal
AACDEILMNR aldermanic
AACDEILNOR androecial
AACDEILNOS laodiceans
AACDEILNSS scandalise
AACDEILNSZ scandalize
AACDEILPSS asclepiads
AACDEILSTU acidulates
actualised
AACDEILTUZ actualized
AACDEIMNNO Macedonian
AACDEIMNTT admittance
AACDEIMNTU acuminated
AACDEIMPRS paramedics
AACDEIMSST steadicams
AACDEIMSTT masticated
AACDEINNOR endocrania
AACDEINNRT incarnated
AACDEINOST diaconates
AACDEINOTV vacationed
AACDEINQTU acquainted
AACDEINQUY inadequacy
AACDEIORRT eradicator
AACDEIOSST associated
AACDEIPSTU auspicated
AACDEIPTTV captivated
AACDEIRSTY caryatides
AACDEJLNTY adjacently
AACDELLNOW allowanced
AACDELLNSU calendulas
AACDELMOPR camelopard
AACDELNNTU cannulated
AACDELNOPR endocarpal
AACDELNPSS landscapes
AACDELNRST declarants
AACDELNSST sandcastle
AACDELOPSS loadspaces
AACDELORRT declarator
AACDELORST sacerdotal
AACDELOTUV autoclaved

AACDELPSTU capsulated
AACDELPTTU catapulted
AACDEMNSTU manducates
AACDEMORRT demarcator
AACDENNNOS cannonades
AACDENNSST ascendants
AACDENORRS carronades
AACDENRSTT Tradescant
transacted
AACDENTTUU unactuated
AACDEOOPPT apocopated
AACDEOPRRS radarscope
AACDEORSUV cadaverous
AACDFHINRT handicraft
AACDFHNRST handcrafts
AACDFIINOO aficionado
AACDFIMORR microfarad
AACDFIOPRS picofarads
AACDGHHINR Chandigarh
AACDGILMOT dogmatical
AACDGILNNS scandaling
AACDGILNPR placarding
AACDGILOPR podagrical
AACDGIMORR cardiogram
AACDGINORS carangoids
AACDGINOTV advocating
AACDGLMORS cladograms
AACDGORSTU coastguard
AACDHHIILR rhachidial
AACDHHIMNS shadchanim
AACDHIKRTU kurdaitcha
AACDHILMSY chlamydias
AACDHINORS arachnoids
AACDHINORT anthracoid
AACDHINRST cantharids
AACDHLMNRS marchlands
AACDHLNPSS handclasps
AACDHLNRSS crashlands
AACDHMNORR orchardman
AACDHNNORY chardonnay
AACDHPRRSS cardsharps
AACDIIILMR miracidial
AACDIILLRV larvicidal
AACDIILMRS radicalism
AACDIILMRT matricidal
AACDIILNNR clinandria
AACDIILPRR parricidal
AACDIILPRT patricidal
AACDIILSTT diastaltic
AACDIINNRS cnidarians
AACDIINOPS diapasonic
AACDILLNRY cardinally
AACDILMNNO calamondin
AACDILMORY myocardial
AACDILNSTY dynastical
AACDIMNRTU undramatic
AACDINOOTV advocation
AACDINOSTU caudations
AACDINRSTU traducians
AACDIQRSTU quadratics
AACDJNOTTU coadjutant
AACDLNOSSU scandalous

AACDLOSTUY adactylous
AACDMMNNOT commandant
AACDMOSSUV muscavados
AACDNOORST ostracodan
AACDNORRSS crossandra
AACDOORTVY advocatory
AACEEEGHST escheatage
AACEEEGNRS careenages
AACEEEKMPR peacemaker
AACEEELMNP elecampane
AACEEFIRST cafeterias
AACEEFLPST faceplates
AACEEFMRST farcemeats
AACEEGHNRR carragheen
AACEEGHRUV Che Guevara
AACEEGILLN allegiance
AACEEGKPPR prepackage
AACEEGKPRS repackages
AACEEHHRST heartaches
AACEEHILNT chatelaine
AACEEHINNP phenacaine
AACEEHIPRT aphaeretic
AACEEHKPST cheapskate
AACEEHLMNO chamaeleon
AACEEHLMNR menarcheal
AACEEHMNRY aerenchyma
AACEEHNNRT anthracene
AACEEHPRST eparchates
AACEEHRSTT reattaches
AACEEHRSTX exarchates
AACEEILMRS caramelise
AACEEILMRZ caramelize
AACEEILPRT altarpiece
AACEEILRTV calaverite
lacerative
AACEEILSTT elasticate
AACEEIMNOT acetonemia
AACEEIMNPT emancipate
AACEEIMRTV macerative
AACEEINRST catenaries
AACEEIPPRT appreciate
AACEEIRTTV reactivate
AACEEITUVV evacuative
AACEEJLSTU ejaculates
AACEEKKLRW cakewalker
AACEEKMPRS pacemakers
AACEEKRRST caretakers
AACEELLLUV valleculae
AACEELLMSU melaleucas
AACEELLNOT lanceolate
AACEELLORT reallocate
AACEELLPRT carpellate
AACEELMSTU emasculate
AACEELNPSS pleasances
AACEELNPTT placentate
AACEELNSST elastances
AACEELNTTU catenulate
AACEELOPRT capreolate
AACEELOPSU paleaceous
AACEELPPSU applesauce
AACEELPRST paracletes
AACEELRSTT altercates
AACEELRTVY acervately
AACEELSTTY acetylates
AACEEMPSST meatspaces
AACEEMRRST maceraters
AACEENNRSS arcaneness
AACEENORSU arenaceous
AACEENPRSS pancreases
AACEENRSTU centaureas
AACEEPRSTW waterscape
AACEERSSTV stavesacre
AACEFFIRST affricates
AACEFGLMOU camouflage
AACEFGNRRS fragrances
AACEFGRSTT stagecraft
AACEFHLLNP chapfallen
AACEFIILTT facilitate
AACEFIINST fanaticise
AACEFIINTZ fanaticize
AACEFILNSU final cause
AACEFILSTY fasciately
AACEFINSST fascinates
AACEFKMPRS packframes
AACEFLMORT malefactor
AACEFNNORR Caernarfon
AACEFRRTTW watercraft
AACEFRSTTT statecraft
AACEGHHMSU gamahuches
AACEGHILNR alcheringa
AACEGHIMNP Champaigne
AACEGHIMRS archimages
AACEGHINOR archegonia
AACEGHLMOU guachamole
AACEGHLNRS archangels
AACEGHLOPS phascogale
AACEGHMNPS champagnes
AACEGHMOPR macrophage
AACEGHMRSU gamaruches
AACEGHNORS anchorages
AACEGIIMNT emaciating
AACEGIINRT acierating
AACEGIKNRT caretaking
AACEGILLNS galenicals
AACEGILLPR preglacial
AACEGILNRT lacerating
AACEGILNSS analgesics
AACEGILNST escalating
AACEGILORT categorial
AACEGILPPR paraplegic
AACEGILTUV victualage
AACEGIMNOS egomaniacs
AACEGIMNPR campaigner
AACEGIMNRT macerating
AACEGINNTT catenating
AACEGINRSV vagrancies
AACEGINTUV evacuating
AACEGINTVX excavating
AACEGISSTT castigates
AACEGJKRUV Kragujevac
AACEGKRSWY graywackes
AACEGLMNOR carmagnole
AACEGLMORY acromegaly
AACEGLMOSU guacamoles
AACEGLORTU cataloguer
AACEGLOSSU coagulases
AACEGLOSTU catalogues
coagulates
AACEGMNRTY termagancy
AACEGOPSST scapegoats
AACEGORSTT greatcoats
AACEHHILRR hierarchal
AACEHHKLMS hamshackle
AACEHHLPRT heptarchal
AACEHIILRT hieratical
AACEHIIMNT haematinic
AACEHIIMSS ischaemias
AACEHIIMTT haematitic
AACEHIINPT Cap-Haitien
AACEHILMNR menarchial
AACEHILMPR alphameric
AACEHILNOP Cephalonia
AACEHILNPT chainplate
AACEHILNRS Lancashire
AACEHILNSS selachians
AACEHILNST chatelains
AACEHILOPT apothecial
AACEHILPRS seraphical
AACEHILPRX hexaplaric
AACEHILPST caliphates
chaptalise
AACEHILPTZ chaptalize
AACEHILRTT theatrical
AACEHIMMPR amphimacer
AACEHIMMTT mathematic
AACEHIMNOT theomaniac
AACEHIMNST machinates
AACEHIMNSU Manichaeus
naumachies
AACEHIMPRS pharmacies
AACEHIMRTU haematuric
AACEHINNOU ouananiche
AACEHINRRT catarrhine
AACEHINRTT anthracite
AACEHIOPRX echopraxia
AACEHIPSTT chapatties
AACEHIRRSS archaisers
AACEHIRRSZ archaizers
AACEHIRRTV architrave
AACEHIRSTU autarchies
AACEHIRTTT chatterati
AACEHJKMMR jackhammer
AACEHJOPRS chaparejos
AACEHKLMRS ramshackle
AACEHKLNOS kalanchoes
AACEHKMMRT matchmaker
AACEHKMNPU Kampuchean
AACEHKMORS hackamores
AACEHKMRTW watchmaker
AACEHKRSSV haversacks
AACEHLMMRW clawhammer
AACEHLNPTY phlyctaena
AACEHLOPSU acephalous
AACEHLPRTY archetypal
AACEHLRSTT clathrates
scarlet hat

AACEHMNPRY	parenchyma
AACEHMNRRT	Carmarthen
AACEHMNRTY	athermancy
AACEHMNTTT	attachment
AACEHMOPRT	camphorate
AACEHMORST	Samothrace
AACEHNOPTY	tachypnoea
AACEHNOSTV	anchovetas
AACEHNPRSS	sarpanches
AACEHNSSTU	acanthuses
AACEHOPPRS	approaches
AACEHOPRTY	apothecary
AACEHPPRSS	scrapheaps
AACEHPRSTU	parachutes
AACEIILMST	calamities
AACEIILMTU	maieutical
AACEIILPST	capitalise
AACEIILPTZ	capitalize
AACEIIMNOT	emaciation
AACEIINNRV	invariance
AACEIINORT	acieration
AACEIINPRR	pericrania
AACEIINPTT	anticipate
AACEIINRRS	cinerarias
AACEIINRST	insectaria
AACEIINTTV	inactivate
	vaticinate
AACEIIOPSS	Cassiopeia
AACEIIPRRS	persicaria
AACEIIPRTT	patriciate
AACEIIPTTV	capitative
AACEIIRSTV	vicariates
AACEIJLMST	majestical
AACEILLMNU	animalcule
AACEILLNOS	escallonia
AACEILLNRT	carnallite
AACEILLNTT	cantillate
AACEILLOSU	alliaceous
AACEILLPRT	prelatical
AACEILLRRV	varicellar
AACEILLRVY	cavalierly
AACEILLSTV	vacillates
AACEILLSTY	salicylate
AACEILMMTU	immaculate
AACEILMNPS	campaniles
AACEILMNRT	reclaimant
AACEILMNRU	unicameral
AACEILMNTU	calumniate
AACEILMRTU	tularaemic
AACEILMSTV	calmatives
AACEILNNRS	carnelians
AACEILNORT	creational
	laceration
	reactional
AACEILNOST	escalation
AACEILNPPS	appliances
AACEILNPST	analeptics
AACEILNPTU	paniculate
AACEILNRSS	arsenicals
AACEILNRST	lacertians
AACEILNRTU	retinacula
AACEILNRUV	naviculare
AACEILPRRS	perisarcal
AACEILPTTU	capitulate
AACEILRTTU	articulate
AACEILRTUU	auriculate
AACEILSSTU	actualises
	casualties
AACEILSTTT	stalactite
AACEILSTUZ	actualizes
AACEIMMPRU	paramecium
AACEIMNNOR	necromania
AACEIMNNST	anamnestic
AACEIMNORS	macaronies
AACEIMNORT	maceration
AACEIMNORU	oceanarium
AACEIMNSTU	acuminates
AACEIMOPST	aposematic
AACEIMORRT	crematoria
AACEIMPRRT	parametric
AACEIMSSTT	masticates
AACEIMSTTT	metastatic
AACEINNNTU	annunciate
AACEINNOTT	catenation
AACEINNPRT	pancreatin
AACEINNRST	incarnates
AACEINORTU	acetonuria
AACEINORTV	vacationer
AACEINOTUV	evacuation
AACEINOTVX	excavation
AACEINQRTU	reacquaint
AACEINRRST	tarriances
AACEINRSST	ascertains
	incrassate
	sectarians
AACEINSSST	assistance
AACEIORSTT	aerostatic
AACEIOSSST	associates
AACEIOSTVV	vasoactive
AACEIPSSTU	auspicates
AACEIPSTTV	captivates
AACEIRSSST	staircases
AACEIRTTTV	attractive
AACEISSTUV	causatives
AACEJKNRTT	natterjack
AACEJLORTU	ejaculator
AACEKLPSSW	spacewalks
AACEKNRRSS	ransackers
AACELLLORT	collateral
AACELLLRST	saltcellar
AACELLLRUV	vallecular
AACELLNOSW	allowances
AACELLNSST	castellans
AACELLPRRY	carpellary
AACELMMORS	sarcolemma
AACELMNOPT	complanate
AACELMNRVY	cavalrymen
AACELMOPSU	palmaceous
AACELMORST	scleromata
AACELMOSUV	malvaceous
AACELMOSUY	amylaceous
AACELMPRST	campestral
AACELMSSST	classmates
AACELNNOTV	covenantal
AACELNNSTU	cannulates
AACELNOPTU	cantaloupe
AACELNOTTV	octavalent
AACELNRRUV	vernacular
AACELNRTTU	tentacular
AACELNSSSU	casualness
AACELNTUUV	avunculate
AACELOPPSY	apocalypse
AACELOPRST	cleopatras
AACELOPRSU	acarpelous
AACELORSST	escalators
AACELORSUU	lauraceous
AACELOSSTV	Slave Coast
AACELOSTUV	autoclaves
AACELPPRST	applecarts
AACELPRSSU	Paracelsus
AACELPRTTY	calyptrate
AACELRSSTY	catalysers
AACELRSTUW	caterwauls
AACELRSTYZ	catalyzers
AACELSTTUU	auscultate
AACEMMOTTY	mycetomata
AACEMNOPRS	mascarpone
AACEMNOPSW	spacewoman
AACEMNORST	Sacramento
AACEMNRSST	sacraments
AACEMORRST	macerators
AACEMPRSTU	metacarpus
AACEMRRSSS	massacrers
AACENNNOSY	annoyances
AACENNOTTZ	canzonetta
AACENNSSTV	vacantness
AACENORRTV	Travancore
AACENRSSSU	assurances
AACENRSSSV	canvassers
AACENRSTTU	cauterants
AACEOOPPST	apocopates
AACEORRTTT	terracotta
AACEORSTUV	evacuators
AACEORSTVX	excavators
AACERRSTTT	attracters
AACFFGIINN	affiancing
AACFFHIOTT	act of faith
AACFGIILMN	magnifical
AACFGIIMNT	magnificat
AACFHIMNRS	chamfrains
AACFHJKSST	jackshafts
AACFHKNRST	crankshaft
AACFIIILRT	artificial
AACFIILNOR	California
AACFIILSTT	fatalistic
AACFIIMNST	fanaticism
AACFIIMORR	formicaria
AACFIINOST	fasciation
AACFILLOSU	fallacious
AACFILMSTU	factualism
AACFILNORT	fractional
AACFILORST	solfataric
AACFILORSV	varifocals
AACFILSTTU	factualist
AACFILTTUY	factuality
AACFINNNOR	Franconian

AACFINORST fascinator
AACFINSSTT fantastics
AACFLNNOTU nonfactual
AACFNRSTTU surfactant
AACGGGGIMN cagmagging
AACGGIILNT glaciating
AACGGIILOS sialagogic
AACGGIKNPS packagings
AACGGILLNO algolagnic
AACGGILNOT cataloging
AACGGILRST gastralgic
AACGGLLMNO McGonagall
AACGHHOPRT tachograph
AACGHIINRS archaising
AACGHIINRZ archaizing
AACGHIKNSW hacksawing
AACGHILNPY anaglyphic
AACGHILRRT arthralgic
AACGHIMNPS champaigns
AACGHIOPRS sarcophagi
AACGHISSTT shagtastic
AACGHLSSTW watchglass
AACGHMMOSY chasmogamy
AACGHMOPRR macrograph
AACGHMORST tachograms
AACGHOPRRS arcographs
AACGIILLST glacialist
AACGIILNNS canalising
AACGIILNNZ canalizing
AACGIILNOT glaciation
AACGIIMRRT margaritic
AACGIIMSTT astigmatic
AACGIINNPT captaining
AACGIINPST paganistic
AACGIINTTV activating
AACGIKMNRT tarmacking
AACGIKMORY karyogamic
AACGIKNNRS ransacking
AACGILLNOT allocating
AACGILLOSS scagliolas
AACGILLRTY tragically
AACGILMNNY malignancy
AACGILMNTU maculating
AACGILNNTU canulating
AACGILNPTY anaglyptic
playacting
AACGILNSTY catalysing
AACGILNTYZ catalyzing
AACGILPRSY spagyrical
AACGIMNORT morganatic
AACGIMNRSS massacring
AACGIMPRST pragmatics
AACGIMRSTY magistracy
AACGINNPPT catnapping
AACGINNSSV canvassing
AACGINOOPR carpogonia
AACGINORTU argonautic
AACGINRSTT castrating
AACGINRTTT attracting
AACGIORSTT castigator
AACGLLMOOY malacology
AACGLLSSWY scallywags
AACGLNORTU octangular
AACGLNOSTU coagulants
AACGLOORTU coagulator
AACGMORRST cartograms
AACGORSSTU sugarcoats
AACHHHISUU chihuahuas
AACHHILLRS rhachillas
AACHHILNPT naphthalic
AACHIIRRSV charivaris
AACHILLOPT allopathic
AACHILMNOR monarchial
AACHILMNRT Altrincham
AACHILNNOY halcyonian
AACHILNNPT plainchant
AACHILNOSZ chalazions
AACHILNPRY chaplainry
AACHILOPST chipolatas
AACHILOPSY polychasia
AACHILPRSU haruspical
AACHIMNNOR anharmonic
AACHIMNNRU Manchurian
AACHIMNOOS monochasia
AACHIMNOPR anamorphic
AACHIMNORS anachorism
harmonicas
maraschino
AACHIMNORT achromatin
machinator
AACHIMNORW chairwoman
AACHIMNPST phantasmic
AACHIMPRST pharmacist
AACHIMRRST matriarchs
AACHIMRRTY matriarchy
AACHIMRSTT Maastricht
AACHIMSSTT asthmatics
AACHINRSST anarchists
AACHINRSTU Carthusian
AACHIPRRST patriarchs
AACHIPRRTY patriarchy
AACHIPRSTY parastichy
AACHKMMRST matchmarks
AACHLLORTT altar cloth
AACHLLPSTY cataphylls
AACHLNNNOT nonchalant
AACHLOPPRY apocryphal
AACHLRRTUY chartulary
AACHMOOPRT apochromat
AACHMORTUY tauromachy
AACHNOOPST Pocahontas
AACHNOSTTY chatoyants
AACHORRSTU catarrhous
AACHPRSTTW watchstrap
AACIILLNNT anticlinal
AACIILLNOS salicional
AACIILLOPT apolitical
AACIILLRST altricials
AACIILMNOS simoniacal
AACIILMNST talismanic
AACIILMNTX anticlimax
AACIILMPST capitalism
AACIILMRSS racialisms
AACIILNNOR Carolinian
AACIILNNST annalistic
AACIILNORS salicornia
AACIILNOST antisocial
AACIILNRST Saint Clair
AACIILNSTU Saint Lucia
AACIILPPST papistical
AACIILPSTT capitalist
AACIILRRTU urticarial
AACIILRSST racialists
AACIIMNNOT anamniotic
AACIIMNNRT Martinican
AACIIMNRST antiracism
AACIIMNSTV Vaticanism
AACIIMSSTT astaticism
AACIINNOPS poincianas
AACIINNPTT anticipant
AACIINNRRT trinacrian
AACIINNRVY invariancy
AACIINOPTT capitation
AACIINORTV victoriana
AACIINOTTV activation
cavitation
AACIINPRST patricians
AACIINRSTT antiracist
AACIINSTTT antistatic
AACIIORSUV avaricious
AACIJNOSTT jactations
AACIKNSSTY Kansas City
AACILLMNTY mantically
AACILLMORT matrilocal
AACILLMOTY atomically
AACILLNOOT allocation
AACILLNTUY nautically
AACILLOOPR coprolalia
AACILLOPRT allopatric
patrilocal
AACILLORTV vacillator
AACILLPTYY atypically
AACILLSTTY statically
AACILMNOST monastical
AACILMNOTU maculation
AACILMNOTY claymation
AACILMORRT lacrimator
AACILMORSU marlacious
AACILMOSTU calamitous
AACILMPPRY paralympic
AACILNNOOT conational
AACILNNOTU canulation
AACILNNRTY tyrannical
AACILNOOTV vocational
AACILNOPPT panoptical
AACILNOPRS parsonical
AACILNOPST placations
AACILNOPTY nyctalopia
AACILNORSS scansorial
AACILNORTT tractional
AACILNOSTY claytonias
AACILNPPST applicants
AACILNPSTY synaptical
AACILNRSST carnalists
AACILNRSUV naviculars
AACILOORRT oratorical

AACILOPPRT	applicator
AACILORRTU	curatorial
AACILORSTU	alacritous
	lactosuria
AACILPRRSU	spiracular
AACILPRRTU	particular
AACILPRSTY	paralytics
AACILPRTUY	capitulary
AACILQSTTU	acquittals
AACILRRSUU	auriculars
AACIMMNNOO	monomaniac
AACIMNOPRY	pyromaniac
AACIMNPRTU	pancratium
AACIMORSTT	masticator
AACIMOSTTU	automatics
AACINNOOTZ	actinozoan
AACINNORRT	contrarian
AACINNORST	carnations
AACINNOSTT	Constantia
AACINOOPTT	coaptation
AACINOOSTV	avocations
	Nova Scotia
AACINOPRSS	caparisons
AACINORSTT	castration
AACINORSTU	arcuations
AACINORTTT	attraction
AACINORTUY	cautionary
AACINOSSST	cassations
AACINOSSTU	causations
AACINOSTTU	actuations
AACINRSSST	sacristans
AACIOOPPRT	apotropaic
AACIOORSST	associator
AACIOPRTTV	captivator
AACIORRSTT	aristocrat
AACIORSTTV	activators
AACIOSSTTW	waistcoats
AACJKRSSTW	jackstraws
AACJLMRSUU	majuscular
AACJLNORSU	Juan Carlos
AACLLOPRSS	collapsars
AACLLORRUY	oracularly
AACLLRSUVY	vascularly
AACLMMOPSY	mycoplasma
AACLMNNOSW	clanswoman
AACLMOPRSS	sarcoplasm
AACLMORRTY	lacrymator
AACLNNORTU	connatural
AACLNOPSTU	cantaloups
AACLOORRTU	coloratura
AACLOPPRSS	papal cross
AACLOPRSTU	portulacas
AACMNOSTTU	catamounts
AACMOOPRRT	comparator
AACNNNOSTT	constantan
AACNORRSTT	transactor
AACNORRSTW	narrowcast
AACOOPPRSU	apocarpous
AACOOPSSTT	capotastos
AACORRSSTT	castrators
AACORRSTTT	attractors
	stratocrat
AADDDDEEEH	deadheaded
AADDDDGNRY	granddaddy
AADDDEEHHR	hardheaded
AADDDEEMRY	daydreamed
AADDDEILPR	paradiddle
AADDDEILRT	taradiddle
AADDEEHIMN	maidenhead
AADDEEHMST	mastheaded
AADDEEHNRV	verandahed
AADDEEILLN	Adélie Land
AADDEEIMNT	deaminated
AADDEEIRST	desiderata
AADDEELTUV	devaluated
AADDEEMRRY	daydreamer
AADDEEMRSU	admeasured
AADDEEMRSY	readymades
AADDEEPPRT	preadapted
AADDEESTTV	devastated
AADDEFHNST	handfasted
AADDEGHNOR	dragonhead
AADDEGIMMR	diagrammed
AADDEGIMNV	Magen David
AADDEGINRR	darraigned
AADDEGIPRS	disparaged
AADDEGIRRT	tardigrade
AADDEGMNOR	Armageddon
AADDEGNNOR	dragonnade
AADDEHIMNN	handmaiden
AADDEHLMNN	manhandled
AADDEHLNNP	panhandled
AADDEHNSST	headstands
AADDEIILPT	dilapidate
AADDEIIRRT	irradiated
AADDEILLNS	landladies
AADDEILNSV	vandalised
AADDEILNVZ	vandalized
AADDEILORR	railroaded
AADDEIMPST	misadapted
AADDEIMRST	dramatised
AADDEIMRTZ	dramatized
AADDEIRRSY	disarrayed
AADDELMRSS	maladdress
AADDEMNNST	demandants
AADDEORSST	roadsteads
AADDGILMOY	amygdaloid
AADDGNNRST	grandstand
AADDHHIRST	Siddhartha
AADDHNNRSY	shandrydan
AADDHNNSST	handstands
AADDIILNOT	additional
AADDIIMRSY	dairymaids
AADDILLLOV	Valladolid
AADDINORRT	ritardando
AADDINPRST	dandiprats
AADDLNOOSW	sandalwood
AADEEEHNNR	enneahedra
AADEEEKNRW	reawakened
AADEEEPPRR	reappeared
AADEEFGLRT	deflagrate
AADEEFHRST	fatshedera
AADEEFILRR	fairleader
AADEEGGGRT	aggregated
AADEEGHMST	megadeaths
AADEEGHNPS	phagedenas
AADEEGINTV	evaginated
AADEEGIRTV	variegated
AADEEGLMNS	magdalenes
AADEEGNORS	orangeades
AADEEGNPPS	appendages
AADEEGNRRR	rearranged
AADEEGNRTU	guaranteed
AADEEHHLRX	hexahedral
AADEEHHMMR	hammerhead
AADEEHHPRT	heptahedra
AADEEHIRTW	headwaiter
AADEEHKNSS	snakeheads
AADEEHMRST	headmaster
	headstream
AADEEHNPRT	pentahedra
AADEEHNRVW	heavenward
AADEEHPRSS	spearheads
AADEEHQRSU	headsquare
AADEEHRRTT	tetrahedra
AADEEHRSTW	headwaters
AADEEIKSWW	wideawakes
AADEEILLTV	alleviated
AADEEILMNT	delaminate
AADEEILNNR	adrenaline
AADEEILNRX	Aleixandre
	Alexander I
AADEEILNST	desalinate
AADEEILRTT	retaliated
AADEEIMNOU	eudaemonia
AADEEIMNRT	reanimated
AADEEIMNST	deaminates
AADEEIMPRT	preadamite
AADEEINNPT	antependia
AADEEINQTU	inadequate
AADEEINRTT	reattained
AADEEIPRTU	eupatridae
AADEEIPTTX	expatiated
AADEEIRSTT	asteriated
AADEEISTTV	aestivated
AADEELLLMT	lamellated
AADEELLLPR	paralleled
AADEELLMNS	allemandes
AADEELLPPR	apparelled
AADEELMNRV	Val-de-Marne
AADEELMRTT	maltreated
AADEELMSTT	stalemated
AADEELNNWZ	New Zealand
AADEELNPSS	esplanades
AADEELNRSX	alexanders
AADEELNRTT	alternated
AADEELQTUY	adequately
AADEELRTTU	adulterate
AADEELRTUV	revaluated
AADEELSTUV	devaluates
AADEEMQRSU	masquerade
AADEEMQSTU	desquamate
AADEEMRSSU	admeasures
AADEENSTVZ	Zend-Avesta
AADEENTTTU	attenuated
AADEEOPRTV	evaporated

AADEEORSTT toadeaters
AADEEPRSST paederasts
AADEEPRSTY paederasty
AADEERRSTT retardates
AADEESSTTV devastates
AADEFFIILT affiliated
AADEFGLNNS fandangles
AADEFGRSSU safeguards
AADEFHLNRT fatherland
AADEFIIKLL alkalified
AADEFIMNOT defamation
AADEFINSST fantasised
AADEFINSTZ fantasized
AADEFINTTU infatuated
AADEFIRRSS faradisers
AADEFIRRSZ faradizers
AADEFLNORS farandoles
AADEFLOSTX toadflaxes
AADEFMORTY defamatory
AADEFMRSST farmsteads
AADEFRRSTW afterwards
AADEGGILNT gangliated
AADEGGIMNN endamaging
AADEGGINRS aggrandise
AADEGGINRZ aggrandize
AADEGGNOOR dragoonage
AADEGHHINS shanghaied
AADEGHLNNR handlanger
AADEGHNRSY hydrangeas
AADEGHNSST stagehands
AADEGIINRT eradiating
AADEGILMNY amygdaline
AADEGILNOS analogised
AADEGILNOZ analogized
AADEGILNSV galvanised
AADEGILNTV galivanted
AADEGILNVZ galvanized
AADEGILPRR paraglider
AADEGILRST saltigrade
AADEGILTTY agitatedly
AADEGIMMNS mismanaged
AADEGIMNRS smaragdine
AADEGIMNRT marginated
AADEGIMNST diamagnets
AADEGIMRST smaragdite
AADEGINNTT antedating
AADEGINPRT readapting
AADEGINRRS disarrange
AADEGINRST tragedians
AADEGINRTU guarantied
AADEGIOPRR radiopager
AADEGIORST Deo gratias
AADEGIPRRS disparager
AADEGIPRSS disparages
AADEGIRSTV stravaiged
AADEGIRTTV gravitated
AADEGKNOOR kangarooed
AADEGLLNRU eglandular
AADEGLLOPS gallopades
AADEGLMNTU mangulated
AADEGLNNRS rangelands
AADEGLNQRU quadrangle
AADEGLNRSV landgraves
AADEGLNRTU granulated
AADEGLRSVW waldgraves
AADEGLRTTU gratulated
AADEGMRRTU dramaturge
AADEGOPPRT propagated
AADEGRRRSU rearguards
AADEGRRSVY graveyards
AADEHHKNSS handshakes
AADEHIIMNR maidenhair
AADEHIIMRT diathermia
AADEHIINRT antheridia
AADEHIKMNO Makedhonia
AADEHILNNT lanthanide
AADEHILORR diarrhoeal
AADEHIORRT arthrodiae
AADEHIRSST stairheads
AADEHKLLMR hallmarked
AADEHKMOTW tomahawked
AADEHLLMRS marshalled
AADEHLLSST headstalls
AADEHLMNNR Arnhem Land
AADEHLMNNS manhandles
AADEHLNNPR panhandler
AADEHLNNPS panhandles
AADEHLNRST heartlands
AADEHMMMNO Mohammedan
AADEHMRSST stramashed
AADEHNOPTY adenopathy
AADEHORRSW arrowheads
AADEHPRSTT deathtraps
AADEHRRSTW earthwards
AADEHRSSVW drawshaves
AADEIILMNS animalised
AADEIILMNZ animalized
AADEIILMRW Waldemar II
AADEIILNTV invalidate
AADEIILPRS lapidaries
AADEIIMNNT diamantine
maintained
AADEIIMNST mediastina
AADEIIMPRS imparadise
AADEIINNTV vanadinite
AADEIINORT eradiation
AADEIINTTV adventitia
AADEIIRRST irradiates
AADEIIRRTT triradiate
AADEIKLNSW Wake Island
AADEILLMMT mamillated
AADEILMMST Lammastide
AADEILMNNR mainlander
AADEILMNNS almandines
AADEILMNRV Viña del Mar
AADEILMNTY animatedly
AADEILMORT tailormade
AADEILMRTX taxidermal
AADEILMRVW Waldemar IV
AADEILNNNS annelidans
AADEILNNSU annualised
AADEILNNUZ annualized
AADEILNOPR Adrianople
AADEILNOST dealations
AADEILNPPR appledrain
AADEILNRRY drainlayer
AADEILNRSU unsalaried
AADEILNRTW landwaiter
AADEILNSSS Sea Islands
AADEILNSSU unassailed
AADEILNSSV vandalises
AADEILNSTT tantalised
AADEILNSTU andalusite
AADEILNSVZ vandalizes
AADEILNTTZ tantalized
AADEILNTZZ antidazzle
AADEILORST asteroidal
AADEILORTV variolated
AADEILPPTT palpitated
AADEILSSST diastalses
AADEILSSSV vassalised
AADEILSSVZ vassalized
AADEIMMNOT ammoniated
AADEIMNNSW swan maiden
AADEIMNNTU unanimated
AADEIMNOST anatomised
AADEIMNOTZ anatomized
AADEIMNRTV animadvert
AADEIMORST aromatised
AADEIMORTZ aromatized
AADEIMRRST dramatiser
AADEIMRRTZ dramatizer
AADEIMRSST dramatises
AADEIMRSTZ dramatizes
AADEINNOPT antipodean
AADEINNQRU quadrennia
AADEINORTY arytaenoid
AADEINPQSU pasquinade
AADEINPRST pintaderas
AADEINQRSU quandaries
AADEINQTTU antiquated
aquatinted
AADEINRSST steradians
AADEINRSTT antitrades
attainders
AADEIOPQRU radiopaque
AADEIPPRSS disappears
AADEIPPTTT pitapatted
AADEIPRSST disparates
AADEIPSSTV passivated
AADEIRRSTT tartarised
AADEIRRTTZ tartarized
AADEKLMORW meadowlark
AADEKMRRST trademarks
AADELLMNPR Palmer Land
AADELLMNRS mallanders
AADELLNPTT platteland
AADELLNSTU landaulets
AADELLORSV El Salvador
AADELLQRSU quadrellas
AADELMMNST Mandelstam
AADELMMORS melodramas
AADELMNRRY aldermanry
AADELMNSSS landmasses
AADELMOOST stomodaeal
AADELMOPRR madreporal

AADELNRSTT	translated
AADELNRTTU	adulterant
AADELNSSTW	wastelands
AADELOPRST	pardalotes
AADELORSVW	aardwolves
AADELPPRSU	applauders
AADELPRSTW	drawplates
AADELRRTUX	extradural
AADELRSTWY	eastwardly
AADEMMNSSU	mandamuses
AADEMNORTY	amendatory
AADEMNPRSS	ampersands
AADEMOQRTU	Torquemada
AADEMRRSST	smartarsed
AADENNPPST	appendants
AADENNPSSU	pandanuses
AADENNRTTU	denaturant
AADENNSTTT	attendants
AADENOPPRU	Papandreou
AADENOPRSU	andropause
AADENOSWWX	woadwaxens
AADENPPRSS	sandpapers
AADENRRSTT	retardants
AADENRSTTU	transudate
AADEORSTTV	devastator
AADEQRRTUU	quadrature
AADFFGHNSY	shandygaff
AADFFIISTV	affidavits
AADFGIINRS	faradising
AADFGIINRZ	faradizing
AADFGLLNRS	Grand Falls
AADFIILNTU	latifundia
AADGGHISST	haggadists
AADGGIIMNR	diagraming
AADGGIINTV	divagating
AADGGILMNY	damagingly
AADGGILNNR	garlanding
AADGGINRTU	graduating
AADGGLNOOW	waggonload
AADGHHLNSU	Lughnasadh
AADGHIILRU	Dhaulagiri
AADGHIMPRS	diaphragms
AADGHIOPRR	radiograph
AADGHIPRSY	dysgraphia
AADGIIIRSS	giardiasis
AADGIILNPS	palisading
AADGIILNPT	lapidating
AADGIILNTV	validating
AADGIIMNNR	marinading
AADGIINOTV	divagation
AADGIJNORU	jaguarondi
AADGIJNRUU	jaguarundi
AADGILLNOY	diagonally
AADGILMNSU	salmagundi
AADGILMRSU	gradualism
AADGILNOOT	odontalgia
AADGILNORS	girandolas
AADGILNPPU	applauding
AADGILNRST	Stalingrad
AADGILORST	gladiators
AADGILPSUV	Daugavpils
AADGILRRSU	guardrails
AADGILRSTU	gradualist
AADGIMORRS	radiograms
AADGIMORSU	audiograms
AADGINNNYY	Yin and Yang
AADGINORST	gradations
AADGINORTU	graduation
AADGINQRTU	quadrating
AADGLMNSUY	salmagundy
AADGLNOOSW	wagonloads
AADGLNRSSS	grasslands
AADGMNNORT	montagnard
AADGMRRSTU	dramaturgs
AADGMRRTUY	dramaturgy
AADGNNOPRS	snapdragon
AADGNNRSTU	grandaunts
AADGORRSTU	graduators
AADHIILPSY	diaphysial
AADHIIMNOT	amianthoid
AADHILORRT	arthrodial
AADHILRSST	tahsildars
AADHILRTWW	withdrawal
AADHINNOST	danthonias
AADHINOPSU	diaphanous
AADHIRRSTY	dysarthria
AADHKLNRSS	landsharks
AADHLMNRSS	marshlands
AADHNSSSTW	washstands
AADHORRSSU	hadrosaurs
AADIIKLNST	Saint Kilda
AADIILLNST	tillandsia
AADIILLSSU	Ladislaus I
AADIILMMOT	ommatidial
AADIILNOPT	lapidation
AADIILNOTT	dilatation
AADIILNOTV	validation
AADIILNPRW	Rawalpindi
AADIILORTU	auditorial
AADIILQRUV	quadrivial
AADIILSSST	diastalsis
AADIIMNOPS	dipsomania
AADIIMNORT	admiration
AADIIMNOST	staminodia
AADIIMNRSZ	zamindaris
AADIINORST	radiations
AADIINRSSU	Nuri as-Said
AADIIOPRST	parasitoid
AADIIORRRT	irradiator
AADIIPRSST	aspidistra
AADIIRRSTV	Stradivari
AADIJNORTU	adjuration
AADILLMNOS	Somaliland
AADILLMOPS	plasmodial
AADILLMORS	armadillos
AADILLMPSU	palladiums
AADILLNOST	allantoids
AADILLNPRY	prandially
AADILLOPSS	sapodillas
AADILMNNOS	adnominals
AADILNORTU	durational
AADILNRSSU	Aru Islands
AADILNSSUW	duniwassal
AADILORSTT	dilatators
AADILORTVY	validatory
AADILOSSVW	disavowals
AADIMNNOST	damnations
AADIMNOPRY	myriapodan
AADIMNSUVZ	avizandums
AADIMOPPRU	parapodium
AADIMRSSTT	dramatists
AADINNNOST	andantinos
AADINOORST	adorations
AADIOQRSUY	Quai d'Orsay
AADJMNNPRU	panjandrum
AADJORRTUY	adjuratory
AADLMNNRUY	laundryman
AADLMNPSSW	swamplands
AADLMNPSUY	Palm Sunday
AADMMNOORS	monodramas
AADMNOORSU	anadromous
AADNOOPPSW	sappanwood
AADNOPRRUW	wraparound
AAEEEFLMMT	metafemale
AAEEEGGMMT	megagamete
AAEEEGGRTX	exaggerate
AAEEEHNNST	Asantehene
AAEEEHRSST	heartsease
AAEEELNPRS	paraselene
AAEEELRTUV	reevaluate
AAEEEPRSTX	exasperate
AAEEERSSTV	asseverate
AAEEFGIMRT	afterimage
AAEEFGINTU	taeniafuge
AAEEFGLLLT	flagellate
AAEEFHRSTV	aftershave
AAEEFKLMRT	fleamarket
AAEEFKPRST	afterpeaks
AAEEFNRRST	Far Eastern
AAEEFRSTTT	aftertaste
AAEEGGGRST	aggregates
AAEEGGHMOU	haemagogue
AAEEGGHNRV	Gravenhage
AAEEGHLNOT	halogenate
AAEEGHLOPS	esophageal
AAEEGHRRSV	Hargreaves
AAEEGILMNN	emalangeni
AAEEGIMNRT	emarginate
AAEEGIMRRR	remarriage
AAEEGIMSSX	Sexagesima
AAEEGINRTV	vegetarian
AAEEGINSTV	evaginates
AAEEGIRSSV	savageries
AAEEGIRSTV	variegates
AAEEGKLRST	Great Lakes
AAEEGLLSSS	galleasses
AAEEGLMNPS	plasmagene
AAEEGMMNNT	management
AAEEGMMORR	aerogramme
AAEEGMNORV	overmanage
AAEEGMNRSS	manageress
AAEEGMNRST	East German
AAEEGMNRTV	ravagement
AAEEGNPRRR	prearrange
AAEEGNRRRR	rearranger
AAEEGNRRRS	rearranges

AAEEGNRSTU guarantees
AAEEGNRSXY sexagenary
AAEEGNSSSV savageness
AAEEGQRRTU quarterage
AAEEHILRTX exhilarate
AAEEHIMNST haemateins
AAEEHIMPRY hyperaemia
AAEEHINSST anesthesia
AAEEHIPRSS aphaeresis
AAEEHKNPRY Harney Peak
AAEEHKQRTU earthquake
AAEEHLMRTX hexametral
AAEEHLNTVX hexavalent
AAEEHLRRSS rehearsals
AAEEHMNORR amenorrhea
AAEEHMNRTU Haute-Marne
AAEEHMNRTW weatherman
AAEEHMNSTU athenaeums
AAEEHMNSTX exanthemas
AAEEHMPRST metaphrase
AAEEHNOSTU Haute-Saône
AAEEHNPRSV Enver Pasha
AAEEHRRSTW shearwater
AAEEHRRTTW heartwater
AAEEHRSTWW Hawes Water
AAEEIILNRS Eilean Siar
AAEEIKLMNS seamanlike
AAEEIKMNOT ketonaemia
AAEEILLMMT Tamil Eelam
AAEEILLRTT alliterate
AAEEILLSTV alleviates
AAEEILMORT ameliorate
AAEEILMRSS lamaseries
AAEEILNPRT penetralia
AAEEILRSTT aliterates
retaliates
AAEEILRTTV alterative
AAEEILTUVV evaluative
AAEEIMNNSX Anaximenes
AAEEIMNRRW weimaraner
AAEEIMNRST reanimates
AAEEINPPRV papaverine
AAEEIPPRRS reappraise
AAEEIPRRTT repatriate
AAEEIPRRTV reparative
AAEEIPRSTV separative
AAEEIPRTTX expatriate
AAEEIPSTTX expatiates
AAEEISSTTV aestivates
AAEEJPRRSW jasperware
AAEEKLNNPS palankeens
AAEEKLNPSS Lassen Peak
AAEEKMRSTT tastemaker
AAEEKNPSTW wapentakes
AAEEKPRRST parrakeets
AAEELLPRTY platelayer
AAEELLQRSU aquarelles
AAEELLTTTT tattletale
AAEELMNPST nameplates
AAEELMPRRT marprelate
AAEELMRRTT maltreater
AAEELMSSTT stalemates
AAEELNOPRS aeroplanes
AAEELNPRRT parenteral
AAEELNRSTT alternates
AAEELNSTVX sexavalent
AAEELPRSTY separately
AAEELRSTTZ lazarettes
AAEELRSTUV revaluates
AAEEMMNRRT rearmament
AAEEMPRRST parameters
AAEEMSSSTT metastases
AAEENPPRST parapentes
AAEENRRSTW warrantees
AAEENSTTTU attenuates
AAEEOPRSSU aeropauses
AAEEOPRSTV evaporates
AAEEPPRSTW wastepaper
AAEEPRRSTY ratepayers
AAEFFHRSTT aftershaft
AAEFFIILST affiliates
AAEFFILRSS rafflesias
AAEFFINPRS paraffines
AAEFFINRST raffinates
AAEFGHNRTU fearnaught
AAEFGIISTT fastigiate
AAEFGINNPR frangipane
AAEFGIRSSX saxifrages
AAEFGLLLNS Angel Falls
AAEFGLLLNT flagellant
AAEFGLLNRU langlaufer
AAEFGLMNRT fragmental
AAEFGLSSTV flagstaves
AAEFHNRSUU hausfrauen
AAEFIIKLLS alkalifies
AAEFIILLRS alfilerias
AAEFIILSTT fatalities
AAEFILLNRX fraxinella
AAEFILMNOU meiofaunal
AAEFILNNOT La Fontaine
AAEFIMMNRS mainframes
AAEFINNRSS safranines
AAEFINPRST afterpains
AAEFINSSST fantasises
AAEFINSSTZ fantasizes
AAEFINSTTU infatuates
AAEFKLLSST leafstalks
AAEFKLNRRS farnarkels
AAEFLLNSTU fustanella
AAEFLLRSTW waterfalls
AAEFLNRRST transferal
AAEFNNOSST San Stefano
AAEGGGORRT aggregator
AAEGGILLNS galingales
AAEGGILNSW Glaswegian
AAEGGILOSU sialagogue
AAEGGLLNOS gallonages
AAEGGLMOSU magalogues
AAEGGOPRSU paragogues
AAEGHILLSS Galashiels
AAEGHILNPR nephralgia
AAEGHILORT hagiolater
AAEGHILPSY hypalgesia
AAEGHILRTU gaultheria
AAEGHIMMNO hemangioma
AAEGHIMNOS mahoganies
AAEGHINNNS shenanigan
AAEGHLNOPT heptagonal
AAEGHLNPRS phalangers
AAEGHLNPRY pharyngeal
AAEGHLNRUX hexangular
AAEGHMNOPR anemograph
phanerogam
AAEGHNOPRS orphanages
AAEGHNORSS angashores
AAEGHNRRSU haranguers
AAEGHOPRRY aerography
areography
AAEGHRSSTW wheatgrass
AAEGIILLNV villainage
AAEGIILNNT alienating
AAEGIILPRS plagiaries
plagiarise
AAEGIILPRZ plagiarize
AAEGIINNTV invaginate
AAEGIINRTT ingratiate
AAEGIIPRST epigastria
AAEGIKMNRR earmarking
AAEGILLMNT ligamental
AAEGILLMOS allogamies
AAEGILLMQU maquillage
AAEGILLNOT allegation
AAEGILLORT legatorial
AAEGILLPRS aspergilla
AAEGILLRSU sugarallie
AAEGILLSSS galliasses
AAEGILMNRT martingale
AAEGILMORR rigamarole
AAEGILMSTT stalagmite
AAEGILNNST galantines
AAEGILNNTT tangential
AAEGILNOSS analogises
AAEGILNOSZ analogizes
AAEGILNPPR appareling
AAEGILNPPS lagniappes
AAEGILNPRV palavering
AAEGILNRSV galvaniser
AAEGILNRVZ galvanizer
AAEGILNSSV galvanises
AAEGILNSVZ galvanizes
AAEGILNTUV evaluating
AAEGILPRTY apterygial
AAEGILRSTT tailgaters
AAEGIMMNRS mismanager
AAEGIMMNSS mismanages
AAEGIMNRRS margarines
misarrange
AAEGIMNRRV margravine
AAEGIMNRST marginates
AAEGIMRSTT magistrate
AAEGINNOST antagonise
AAEGINNOTZ antagonize
AAEGINNSTU nauseating
AAEGINPRSS paganisers
AAEGINPRST separating
AAEGINPRSZ paganizers

AAEGINRRRS	arraigners
AAEGINRSSY	gainsayers
AAEGINRSTU	guaranties
AAEGINRTUU	inaugurate
AAEGIORRTV	arrogative
AAEGIRRTTV	gravitater
AAEGIRSTTV	gravitates
AAEGKLMNOS	maskalonge
AAEGKLMRSS	glassmaker
AAEGKLNOPY	Poyang Lake
AAEGKMNNOS	maskanonge
AAEGLLPSST	plateglass
AAEGLLRRTU	ultralarge
AAEGLMNSTU	mangulates
AAEGLMORSU	megalosaur
AAEGLMSTTU	glutamates
AAEGLNNOPT	pentagonal
AAEGLNORTT	tetragonal
AAEGLNRRTU	granulater
AAEGLNRSTU	granulates
AAEGLNRSUX	sexangular
AAEGLPPRSS	glasspaper
AAEGLPRSSV	palsgraves
AAEGLRSSTW	waterglass
AAEGLRSTTU	gratulates
AAEGMMNOST	Mostaganem
AAEGMMORST	agrostemma
AAEGMNPRST	pentagrams
AAEGMNRSTT	termagants
AAEGMOPRSU	rampageous
AAEGMRRSTT	tetragrams
AAEGMRSSTT	stratagems
AAEGNOPRSS	parsonages
AAEGOPPRST	propagates
AAEGOPSTTY	steatopyga
AAEGRRSSTZ	stargazers
AAEHHILLLU	halleluiah
AAEHHJLLLU	hallelujah
AAEHHKMNRS	Kermanshah
AAEHHLPRTY	hypaethral
AAEHHMNRSV	Marheshvan
AAEHIILMNS	leishmania
AAEHIILNNT	annihilate
AAEHIILRSV	Rhea Silvia
AAEHIIMNNT	amianthine
AAEHIIMNOP	hemianopia
AAEHIKRRST	hairstreak
AAEHILLOPT	palaeolith
AAEHILNOTX	exhalation
AAEHILNRTX	exhilarant
AAEHILNSST	Thessalian
AAEHILNSTV	leviathans
AAEHILPSTT	asphaltite
AAEHILPSTW	Westphalia
AAEHILRSST	harestails
AAEHIMNPRY	hypermania
AAEHIMNPSS	seamanship
AAEHIMNSTY	myasthenia
AAEHIMOSST	haematosis
	hemostasia
AAEHIMRSTU	amateurish
AAEHINNORV	Hanoverian
AAEHINOPST	asthenopia
AAEHINPSST	phantasies
AAEHIPSTXY	asphyxiate
AAEHLLMRRS	marshaller
AAEHLMRRSS	marshalers
AAEHLNOPSY	synaloepha
AAEHLNPSSY	synalephas
AAEHLOPPRS	phalaropes
AAEHLPSTTU	spathulate
AAEHMNRSST	harassment
AAEHMNRSTV	harvestman
AAEHMORTTX	metathorax
AAEHMOSSTT	haemostats
AAEHMPRSTT	metaphrast
AAEHMRSSST	stramashes
AAEHMRSSTU	shamateurs
AAEHNNRSTU	Tannhäuser
AAEHNOPRST	anastrophe
AAEHNPPSWW	wappenshaw
AAEHOPPSTY	apophysate
AAEHPPRSSY	paraphyses
AAEIIILNST	italianise
AAEIIILNTZ	italianize
AAEIIJNRSZ	janizaries
AAEIIKNOST	Seto Naikai
AAEIILLPTV	palliative
AAEIILLRSX	axillaries
AAEIILMMRT	immaterial
AAEIILMNRS	animaliers
	seminarial
AAEIILMNSS	animalises
AAEIILMNSZ	animalizes
AAEIILMRST	latimerias
AAEIILMSST	assimilate
AAEIILNNOT	alienation
AAEIILNNST	salientian
AAEIILNPST	sapiential
AAEIILNSST	nasalities
AAEIILNSTT	natalities
AAEIILNSTV	insalivate
AAEIILRSST	aerialists
AAEIIMNNRS	seminarian
AAEIIMNNRT	maintainer
AAEIIMPPRR	primiparae
AAEIIMRRTT	termitaria
AAEIIPPRSV	appraisive
AAEIIPRSST	parasitise
AAEIIPRSTZ	parasitize
AAEIIRSTVX	aviatrixes
AAEIKLNPST	Stalin Peak
AAEIKMNRRS	rainmakers
AAEIKMRSST	samarskite
AAEIKNNRST	Transkeian
AAEIKOSSTU	Sato Eisaku
AAEILLLLNV	villanella
AAEILLLRST	saltarelli
AAEILLMMMT	mammillate
AAEILLMPRX	premaxilla
AAEILLMRTY	materially
AAEILLNORT	relational
AAEILLNPRS	enalaprils
AAEILLNPRU	nulliparae
AAEILLNPSS	sailplanes
AAEILLNPST	tailplanes
AAEILLNRTU	unilateral
AAEILLORTV	alleviator
AAEILLPRXY	preaxially
AAEILLPSSS	paillasses
	palliasses
AAEILLRRTT	trilateral
AAEILLRRTY	arterially
AAEILLRTTY	laterality
AAEILLRTVY	varietally
AAEILMNNSU	semiannual
AAEILMNORT	ameliorant
AAEILMNPRT	parliament
AAEILMNPTU	manipulate
AAEILMNRSU	aneurismal
AAEILMNRTY	alimentary
AAEILMNRWY	railwaymen
AAEILMNSST	assailment
AAEILMNSTU	aluminates
AAEILMPRRT	premarital
AAEILMPRTU	multiparae
AAEILMPSTT	palmitates
AAEILNNOPT	neapolitan
AAEILNNOTV	venational
AAEILNNRTU	Laurentian
AAEILNNSSU	annualises
AAEILNNSUZ	annualizes
AAEILNOORT	areolation
AAEILNOQTU	equational
AAEILNORST	alienators
	rationales
	senatorial
AAEILNORTT	alteration
AAEILNORTU	laureation
AAEILNORTX	relaxation
AAEILNOTTX	exaltation
AAEILNOTUV	evaluation
AAEILNPRST	Palestrina
AAEILNPSTX	taxiplanes
AAEILNRSSY	reanalysis
AAEILNRSTT	tantaliser
AAEILNRSTU	naturalise
AAEILNRTTZ	tantalizer
AAEILNRTUZ	naturalize
AAEILNSSTT	tantalises
AAEILNSTTZ	tantalizes
AAEILOPRRS	leprosaria
AAEILOPRRT	praetorial
AAEILOQRTU	equatorial
AAEILORRTT	retaliator
AAEILORSTV	lavatories
	variolates
AAEILPPRSS	paralipses
AAEILPPSTT	palpitates
AAEILRSSSW	wassailers
AAEILSSSSV	vassalises
AAEILSSSVZ	vassalizes
AAEILSSTUV	assaultive
AAEILSTUXY	asexuality
AAEIMMNOST	ammoniates
AAEIMMNRST	mainstream

AAEIMMRSTU	amateurism
AAEIMNNOPR	praenomina
AAEIMNNOST	anamniotes
	emanations
AAEIMNNOSY	mayonnaise
AAEIMNNSSU	amanuensis
AAEIMNNTTT	attainment
AAEIMNOORT	erotomania
AAEIMNORST	anatomiser
AAEIMNORTZ	anatomizer
AAEIMNOSST	anatomises
AAEIMNOSTZ	anatomizes
AAEIMNPRTZ	nitrazepam
AAEIMNQSTU	antimasque
AAEIMNRTTT	antimatter
AAEIMORSST	aromatises
AAEIMORSTZ	aromatizes
AAEIMOSSTT	Metastasio
AAEIMOSTTU	automatise
AAEIMOTTUZ	automatize
AAEIMPRSST	separatism
AAEIMQRSTU	marquisate
AAEIMRRSST	airstreams
AAEIMRSTTU	traumatise
AAEIMRTTUV	maturative
AAEIMRTTUZ	traumatize
AAEIMSSSTT	metastasis
AAEINNNOTX	annexation
AAEINNOSTU	nauseation
AAEINNOTTV	annotative
AAEINNQRTU	quarantine
AAEINNRSST	stannaries
AAEINNRTUV	avanturine
AAEINNSSST	Saint-Saëns
AAEINOPRRT	praetorian
	reparation
AAEINOPRST	separation
AAEINOPSST	passionate
AAEINPPRST	appertains
AAEINQSTTU	antiquates
AAEINRRSTV	narratives
AAEINRRSTW	warranties
AAEINRRTTZ	tartrazine
AAEINRSTTT	intrastate
AAEINRTTTU	attainture
AAEIOPRRSS	aspersoria
AAEIOPRTTX	expatiator
AAEIOPSSST	apostasies
AAEIOPSSTT	apostatise
AAEIOPSTTZ	apostatize
AAEIORSTTV	aestivator
AAEIPPRRSS	appraisers
AAEIPRRSTX	separatrix
AAEIPRSSTT	separatist
AAEIPSSSTV	passivates
AAEIRRRRVY	Yarra River
AAEIRRSSTT	tartarises
AAEIRRSTTZ	tartarizes
AAEJKLRSWY	jaywalkers
AAEJNNORTU	Juantorena
AAEJOOOPSS	João Pessoa
AAEKLMPRST	platemarks
AAEKLMPRSY	playmakers
AAEKLPRSST	lapstrakes
	lapstreaks
AAEKMRRSTW	watermarks
AAEKMRSSTT	taskmaster
AAEKNORTTZ	Kazan Retto
AAEKRRSTUU	sauerkraut
AAELLLLMRY	lamellarly
AAELLLMNOS	salmonella
AAELLLORST	saltarello
AAELLMNRTY	maternally
AAELLMORTT	martellato
AAELLMORZZ	mozzarella
AAELLMPRTY	malapertly
AAELLNNOTY	neonatally
AAELLNOSSY	seasonally
AAELLNPPST	appellants
AAELLNPRTY	parentally
	paternally
	prenatally
AAELLNPSTY	pleasantly
AAELLPPRSW	wallpapers
AAELLRSTTT	tattersall
AAELMMPSST	metaplasms
AAELMNNORT	ornamental
AAELMNOPSU	menopausal
AAELMNOSSW	saleswoman
AAELMNRSUY	aneurysmal
AAELMORSSU	elasmosaur
AAELMRRTUX	extramural
AAELNNNPRU	penannular
AAELNNPSTU	unpleasant
AAELNOPRST	rotaplanes
AAELNORRTT	alternator
AAELNPPRTY	apparently
AAELNPRRSU	suprarenal
AAELNPRSTT	transeptal
AAELNPRSTY	pleasantry
AAELNRSSTT	translates
AAELNRSSUY	uranalyses
AAELNRSTUV	transvalue
AAELNRSTUX	transexual
AAELNSSTTU	sultanates
	tantaluses
AAELOOPSTT	apostolate
AAELOPRSST	pastorales
AAELORRSSU	rearousals
AAELORRSTX	extrasolar
AAELORRTTV	travelator
AAELORSSTT	attolasers
AAELORSTTZ	lazarettos
AAELORSTUV	evaluators
AAELPRRSTU	superaltar
AAELPRRTTT	rattletrap
AAELRRSSTV	traversals
AAELRSSSTU	assaulters
AAEMMORSTT	mattamores
AAEMNNORTT	tramontane
AAEMNNRSTV	manservant
AAEMNOOSST	anastomose
AAEMNPRSTT	apartments
AAEMPRSSTT	pastmaster
AAEMPRSSTY	paymasters
AAEMRRSSST	smartarses
AAEMRSSSTT	mattrasses
AAEMRSSTTU	metatarsus
AAENNPPRTU	unapparent
AAENNPRRST	trapanners
AAENNSTTTU	attenuants
AAENORTTTU	attenuator
AAENPSSTTW	sweatpants
AAENQRRTUY	quaternary
AAENRRRSTW	warranters
AAENRRSTTU	restaurant
AAENSSTTTT	attestants
AAEOOPRRTV	evaporator
AAEOPRRRTY	reparatory
AAEOPRRSST	separators
AAEOPRRSTY	separatory
AAEOPRSSTT	pastorates
AAEORSTTTT	attestator
AAEQRRSTUW	quartersaw
AAERRSSTTU	saturaters
AAFFFGLSST	flagstaffs
AAFFGIMNRU	ragamuffin
AAFFGNRSSU	suffragans
AAFFIINOTX	affixation
AAFFIMNRST	affirmants
AAFGIINNPR	frangipani
AAFGILNNTU	antifungal
AAFGILNSST	falangists
AAFGINNSTY	fantasying
AAFGINRSWY	wayfarings
AAFGLLNRTY	flagrantly
AAFGLLORST	allografts
AAFGLNRRTY	fragrantly
AAFGORSTTU	autografts
AAFHHINORS	Shah of Iran
AAFIIILRSS	filariasis
AAFIIKNRST	Kafiristan
AAFIILLMRY	familiarly
AAFIILMNRU	unfamiliar
AAFIINRRTU	fruitarian
AAFILNOOTT	floatation
AAFILNOSTX	aflatoxins
AAFILORSUW	rauwolfias
AAFIMMORRS	samariform
AAFIMOORRS	afrormosia
AAFIOQRSTU	aquafortis
AAGGHINNRU	haranguing
AAGGIILNTT	tailgating
AAGGIINNPS	paganising
AAGGIINNPT	paginating
AAGGIINNPZ	paganizing
AAGGIINNRR	arraigning
AAGGIINNSY	gainsaying
AAGGIINNTV	navigating
AAGGILLNNT	gallanting
AAGGILNNTU	angulating
AAGGIMMNUY	mamaguying
AAGGIMNORS	angiograms
AAGGINNOPR	paragoning
AAGGINNSTT	stagnating
AAGGINORRT	arrogating

AAGGINRSTZ stargazing
AAGGKLNNPS gangplanks
AAGGLLLOSS galloglass
AAGGNNOOPP Pango Pango
AAGHHIMNWY highwayman
AAGHILLLLN hallalling
AAGHILMNRS marshaling
AAGHILMNSW Walsingham
AAGHILNPST asphalting
phalangist
AAGHILOPPY polyphagia
AAGHILORTY hagiolatry
AAGHILPSSU ispaghulas
AAGHIMPRRS marigraphs
AAGHINPRSS springhaas
AAGHINRSSS harassings
AAGHLLOPRS allographs
AAGHMMMOPR mammograph
AAGHNNSSTU Hsüan-tsang
AAGHNOPPRT pantograph
AAGHOPRSTU autographs
AAGHOPRSTY Pythagoras
AAGHOPRTUY autography
AAGIIILMNR airmailing
AAGIIKLLNS alkalising
AAGIIKLLNZ alkalizing
AAGIIKMNNR rainmaking
AAGIIKNPRS paraskiing
AAGIILLNPT palliating
AAGIILLNVY availingly
AAGIILMNNT laminating
AAGIILMPRS plagiarism
AAGIILNNPS salpingian
AAGIILNNSS nasalising
AAGIILNNSZ nasalizing
AAGIILNNUV unavailing
AAGIILNRTV travailing
AAGIILNSSW wassailing
AAGIILNSTV salivating
AAGIILPRST plagiarist
AAGIIMNNRT marinating
AAGIIMNOPR parmigiano
AAGIINNOPT pagination
AAGIINNOTV navigation
AAGIINNTTT attainting
AAGIINOSTT agitations
AAGIINPPRS appraising
AAGIINPRST aspirating
AAGIINRSTV Tsvangirai
AAGIJKLNWY jaywalking
AAGIJLOSUV Jugoslavia
AAGIKLLNTY alkylating
AAGIKMRSSS kissagrams
AAGILLMNRY alarmingly
marginally
AAGILLNSTV gallivants
AAGILLORSS glossarial
AAGILLORST alligators
AAGILLPSSW galliwasps
AAGILLSTTY sagittally
AAGILMNNST malignants
AAGILMNORS organismal
AAGILMOPRS paralogism
AAGILMRSST magistrals
AAGILNNOTU angulation
AAGILNOPRS sporangial
AAGILNOSST analogists
AAGILNPRSY paralysing
AAGILNPRYZ paralyzing
AAGILNRRTU triangular
AAGILNRSUU inaugurals
AAGILNRSUV vulgarians
AAGILNRTUY angularity
AAGILNSSTU assaulting
AAGILOPRST paralogist
AAGILOSUVY Yugoslavia
AAGIMMPRST pragmatism
AAGIMNNOST antagonism
AAGIMNOTTU automating
AAGIMNPRRT ramparting
AAGIMNPRST ptarmigans
AAGIMNPTTU amputating
AAGIMNRTTU maturating
AAGIMNSSTY gymnasiast
AAGIMORSTU matagouris
AAGIMPRSTT pragmatist
AAGIMSSSST massagists
AAGINNNOTT annotating
AAGINNNPRT trapanning
AAGINNOSTT antagonist
stagnation
AAGINNRRTW warranting
AAGINNRSUY sanguinary
AAGINOOPST topagnosia
AAGINOORRT arrogation
AAGINOOSTV vagotonias
AAGINORSTV navigators
AAGINORTTV rotavating
AAGINRSTTU antitragus
saturating
AAGINSSTTU sitatungas
AAGKMORRSY karyograms
AAGLLMOOSU allogamous
AAGLLNOPTT topgallant
AAGLLNRRUY granularly
AAGLMMNOOQ Qomolangma
AAGLMNORSU granulomas
AAGLMOOPRR polarogram
AAGLNNSTTY stagnantly
AAGLNORRTU granulator
AAGLNORRTY arrogantly
AAGMMMMORS mammograms
AAGMOOSTUU autogamous
AAGNNORSTU orangutans
AAGNORRSTU guarantors
AAGOOPPRRT propagator
AAGOOPRRST Protagoras
AAGOORRRST arrogators
AAGORRRSSW arrowgrass
AAHHHOPRTT haphtaroth
AAHHIIMRSS maharishis
AAHHILMOPT ophthalmia
AAHHILNNPT naphthalin
AAHHILNPTY hypanthial
AAHHIMMMSS shammashim
AAHHIMRRTY arrhythmia
AAHHLORSTT throatlash
AAHIIKMNRS Kashmirian
AAHIIKNSUY Yuan Shi Kai
AAHIILNNOT inhalation
AAHIILNOPS Hispaniola
AAHIIMPRSS pharisaism
AAHIKMORST matrioshka
AAHIKPPSSS Shipka Pass
AAHILLOPRT prothallia
AAHILMOOTX homotaxial
AAHILMTTUZ altazimuth
AAHILNNOPT antiphonal
AAHILNORST inhalators
AAHILOPPSY apophysial
hypoplasia
AAHILORSTU haustorial
AAHIMMNOTY mythomania
AAHIMNSSST shamanists
AAHINNOTTX xanthation
AAHINPSTXY asphyxiant
AAHINRSTUV hantavirus
AAHIPPRSSY paraphysis
AAHIPRRSSY hairsprays
AAHKLOORSY Yoshkar-Ola
AAHKMORSTY matryoshka
AAHKOPTUUW pohutukawa
AAHLLLLOSW Allhallows
AAHLLMOPSY hyaloplasm
AAHLMMOPTY lymphomata
AAHLNNNOST lanthanons
AAHMNPPRSY paranymphs
AAHMOPPRRS paramorphs
AAHNNOOSTZ anthozoans
AAHNNRSTUY thysanuran
AAHNOPRTTU naturopath
AAHNORRSTU anarthrous
AAHORSTWWY throwaways
AAIIIKNRST Kristiania
AAIIILMMNT militiaman
AAIIILMMNX Maximilian
AAIIILMNRT limitarian
AAIIJKNSTT Tajikistan
AAIIJLNORT janitorial
AAIIKLLNTY alkalinity
AAIILLNOPT palliation
AAIILLNUXY uniaxially
AAIILMMNSS animalisms
AAIILMMRST martialism
AAIILMMSTX maximalist
AAIILMNNOT antimonial
lamination
AAIILMNORT minatorial
AAIILMNSST animalists
AAIILMRSTT martialist
AAIILNNSTU Lusitanian
AAIILNOPPS palinopsia
AAIILNORRT irrational
AAIILNOSTV salivation
AAIILNRSTY sanitarily
AAIILPPRSS paralipsis

AAIILPRTTY partiality
AAIILPSTTY spatiality
AAIIMMNOTX maximation
AAIIMNNNOT antinomian
AAIIMNNOPT impanation
AAIIMNNORT marination
AAIIMNNOST animations
AAIIMNRSTU sanitarium
AAIIMNSSSS Massinissa
AAIIMPPRRS primiparas
AAIIMPRSST parasitism
AAIINNOSTT sanitation
AAIINNRRTU Ruritanian
AAIINNRSTU unitarians
AAIINNRSTV invariants
AAIINNRSTY insanitary
AAIINOPPRT apparition
AAIINOPRST aspiration
AAIINOPRTT patriation
tritanopia
AAIINORSTV variations
AAIINRSTWZ Waziristan
AAIIRSSSTY satyriasis
AAIJLLNPSU Julian Alps
AAIJRSSSTW swarajists
AAIKKMOSVY Mayakovski
AAIKLLNOTY alkylation
AAIKLPRSTT Palk Strait
AAIKNNOPST pontianaks
AAIKNOSTTU taikonauts
AAIKNQRSTU antiquarks
AAIKRSSTTU autarkists
AAILLLPSTU pulsatilla
AAILLMMMRY mammillary
AAILLMOPPS papillomas
AAILLMORST tamarillos
AAILLNNOOP Apollonian
AAILLNNOTY nationally
AAILLNNSTT installant
AAILLNOPST spallation
AAILLNORSY orinasally
AAILLNORTY notarially
rationally
AAILLNOSTV vallations
AAILLOPRST palliators
AAILLRSTUY salutarily
AAILMNOPST palmations
AAILMNORST laminators
AAILMNOTTU mutational
AAILMNRRTU intramural
AAILMNRSTU naturalism
AAILMOPPRX approximal
AAILMORRTY Mariolatry
AAILMPRSSU marsupials
AAILNNNOTU annulation
AAILNNOOTT notational
AAILNNOPTT plantation
AAILNNORTZ intrazonal
AAILNNOTTU nutational
AAILNNPQSU palanquins
AAILNNRTUY annularity
AAILNOORTT rotational
AAILNOPPST palpations
AAILNOPSSS passionals
AAILNOPSUW paulownias
AAILNOSSTT saltations
AAILNOSSTV salvations
AAILNOSTTU salutation
AAILNOSTUV valuations
AAILNPRSTU tarpaulins
AAILNPSSTU Saint Paul's
AAILNRSSUY uranalysis
AAILNRSTTU naturalist
AAILOOPRYZ polyzoaria
AAILORSTTT altostrati
AAILOSSTTT tsotsitaal
AAIMMOSTTU automatism
AAIMMRSTTU traumatism
AAIMNOORST inamoratos
AAIMNOOTTU automation
AAIMNOPTTU amputation
AAIMNOQSTU squamation
AAIMNORSTU sanatorium
AAIMNORTTU maturation
natatorium
AAIMNOSSTT anatomists
AAIMNPRSSU marsupians
AAIMOSTTTU automatist
AAINNNOOST San Antonio
AAINNNOOTT annotation
AAINNNSSSY sannyasins
AAINNNSTTU annuitants
AAINNORRST narrations
AAINNRSTUY unsanitary
AAINOOPPRT protanopia
AAINOORRST oratorians
AAINOPSSTT antipastos
AAINORSTTU saturation
titanosaur
AAINORSTTV starvation
AAINORSTTY stationary
AAINPSTTWY pantywaist
AAINRSTTTV Vansittart
AAINSSSSTT assistants
AAIOPPRRST apparitors
AAIOPRRSST aspirators
AAIOPRRSTY aspiratory
AAIOPSSTTU autopistas
AAIORRSTTT trattorias
AAKKLNORRS Karlskrona
AAKKMORRST Kramatorsk
AAKLMOPRSY karyoplasm
AAKLNORSUY ankylosaur
AAKMMNORSW markswoman
AAKMNNORTY Mark Antony
AAKNOOSSST saskatoons
AALLMNORUY monaurally
AALLMNOTWY tallywoman
AALLMNTUUY autumnally
AALLNNOPSY pollyannas
AALLOPRSTY pastorally
AALLORSSUU allosaurus
AALLRSTTWY stalwartly
AALMOOPPRS malapropos
AALMOOPRTY laparotomy
AALMOPRSXY paroxysmal
AALMOQSSSU squamosals
AALMORRTYY Maryolatry
AALNNNORTU nonnatural
AALNNOOPST pantaloons
AALNNPRSTT transplant
AALNNRRSTU translunar
AALNOOPSZZ pozzolanas
AALNOOPUZZ pozzuolana
AALNOPRRST transpolar
AALNOPRSST transposal
AALNOPSUZZ puzzolanas
AALNORRSTT translator
AALOORRTTV travolator
AALOPRRSTY portrayals
AALOPSTTUY autoplasty
AALORSTTTY statolatry
AALORSTTUY salutatory
AAMNNOTTTU tantamount
AAMNOOSTTU automatons
AAMNOPRSTU paramounts
AAMOOPPTTX Appomattox
AAMOOSSTTU astomatous
AAMOOSTTUU automatous
AAMOPRSTTU amputators
AAMORSSSUU mosasaurus
AANNOORSTT annotators
AANOOPRSTU anatropous
AANORRRSTW warrantors
AANORSSTTU astronauts
AANOSTTTWW Watson-Watt
AAOOPPRRST paratroops
AAOORRSTTV rotavators
AAORRSSTTU saturators
ABBBEELMNT babblement
ABBBEGILNR blabbering
ABBBEHISSU bushbabies
ABBBEILNRU unbribable
ABBBGIINTT babbitting
ABBCCDEKMO backcombed
ABBCCKKLOS backblocks
ABBCCKKLSU blackbucks
ABBCDEEHMR bedchamber
ABBCDEHINO Bondi Beach
ABBCDEKNRU backburned
ABBCDEMRRU breadcrumb
ABBCDIKLRS blackbirds
ABBCDKLOOR blockboard
ABBCDKORSU buckboards
ABBCEFHIIR Chief Rabbi
ABBCEGINRU barbecuing
ABBCEIKNTT backbitten
ABBCEIKRST backbiters
ABBCEILMNO combinable
ABBCEILRSU subcaliber
subcalibre
ABBCEINSSS scabbiness
ABBCEKLRRY blackberry
ABBCELRRSS scrabblers
ABBCENORSY absorbency
ABBCFGINNO confabbing

ABBCGIIKNT	backbiting
ABBCGIIORT	gabbroitic
ABBCGILNRS	scrabbling
ABBCIILLLY	biblically
ABBCIIRRTU	barbituric
ABBCKLLSUY	buckyballs
ABBCKLOOST	bootblacks
ABBCKLSTTU	blackbutts
ABBCLMOOSU	abcoulombs
ABBDDOORSY	bodyboards
ABBDEEGILR	bridgeable
ABBDEEHLPS	pebbledash
ABBDEELNNU	unbendable
ABBDEELORU	belaboured
ABBDEELRSU	bluebeards
ABBDEEORRS	reabsorbed
ABBDEFIORR	fiberboard
	fibreboard
ABBDEGIINR	Bainbridge
ABBDEILMOT	bombilated
ABBDEILOUY	Douay Bible
ABBDEIMNOT	bombinated
ABBDEIMORR	bombardier
ABBDELLNRU	landlubber
ABBDELLNSY	bellybands
ABBDELMOOZ	bamboozled
ABBDELORSY	absorbedly
ABBDENORSU	unabsorbed
ABBDGIMNOR	bombarding
ABBDHORRSU	broadbrush
ABBDILLORS	billboards
	broadbills
ABBDIMORRS	broadbrims
ABBDMNOORS	bombardons
ABBDNORSSU	brassbound
ABBDNOSSTU	bandobusts
ABBEEEILLV	believable
ABBEEILLVY	believably
ABBEEIRRRS	barberries
ABBEEIRRSY	bayberries
ABBEELLMSS	semblables
ABBEELORSV	observable
ABBEELRRSS	slabberers
ABBEELRTTU	rebuttable
ABBEENORST	breastbone
ABBEENORTW	browbeaten
ABBEENRRSU	baseburner
ABBEEORRTW	browbeater
ABBEFILNSS	flabbiness
ABBEGHINSU	Ebbinghaus
ABBEGILNOR	belaboring
ABBEGILNRS	slabbering
ABBEGJLSUU	subjugable
ABBEHINSSS	shabbiness
ABBEHOPRRS	barbershop
ABBEIIOSSS	babesiosis
ABBEIIRRST	rabbitries
ABBEIKRRTT	bitterbark
ABBEILLMSU	sublimable
ABBEILMOPR	improbable
ABBEILMOST	bombilates
ABBEILMRST	brambliest
ABBEILNOTU	obnubilate
ABBEIMNOST	bombinates
ABBEINORSX	brainboxes
ABBELLRTTU	butterball
ABBELMOORZ	bamboozler
ABBELMOOSZ	bamboozles
ABBELMSSUU	subsumable
ABBELORSVY	observably
ABBELOSSTY	stableboys
ABBELQRSSU	squabblers
ABBENORSST	absorbents
ABBERSSUUU	subbureaus
ABBERSUUUX	subbureaux
ABBFFIILMU	bumbailiff
ABBFHIIRST	rabbitfish
ABBFHLLSSU	flashbulbs
ABBFILORST	fibroblast
ABBGHINRRU	rhubarbing
ABBGIILNOR	ibn-Gabirol
ABBGIILNOT	bobtailing
ABBGILLNOS	billabongs
ABBGILMNRS	bramblings
ABBGILNQSU	squabbling
ABBGILOOST	obbligatos
ABBHILMSUU	Lubumbashi
ABBHIOPSST	abbotships
ABBIILLORR	Barbirolli
ABBIINRSST	rabbinists
ABBILMOPRY	improbably
ABBILORSTU	suborbital
ABBLLNOTTU	buttonball
ABCCCEFIOS	beccaficos
ABCCCEMNUY	accumbency
ABCCCIILLY	bicyclical
ABCCCKKLOS	blackcocks
ABCCDEEIRT	brecciated
ABCCDELNRU	carbuncled
ABCCEEELNS	albescence
ABCCEEENST	tabescence
ABCCEEFRSY	cybercafes
ABCCEEILMP	impeccable
ABCCEEILSS	accessible
ABCCEELLRY	recyclable
ABCCEENRSU	buccaneers
ABCCEEPRSY	cyberspace
ABCCEGHINN	bechancing
ABCCEHHOOR	Cooch Behar
ABCCEHILRU	cherubical
ABCCEHLNRU	crunchable
ABCCEILMPY	impeccably
ABCCEILORU	corbiculae
ABCCEILSSY	accessibly
ABCCEINOSU	suboceanic
ABCCEJNSUY	subjacency
ABCCEKLOOT	cockleboat
ABCCEKNORR	cornerback
ABCCELNRSU	carbuncles
ABCCELORSU	succorable
ABCCELORSY	cryocables
ABCCELRTUU	Culebra Cut
ABCCEMNRSU	cumbrances
ABCCHHKNSU	hunchbacks
ABCCHIIMOR	choriambic
ABCCHIIRRT	tribrachic
ABCCHIKSTT	backstitch
ABCCHIKSTW	switchback
ABCCHILOTU	coachbuilt
ABCCHIOOPR	acrophobic
ABCCHKLOST	backcloths
ABCCHKOSTU	touchbacks
ABCCIILOST	bioclastic
ABCCIKRSST	crabsticks
ABCCILNORY	carbonylic
ABCCILORXY	carboxylic
ABCCILOTUU	Boucicault
ABCCIMOORT	mobocratic
ABCCINORTU	buccinator
ABCCINORTY	corybantic
ABCCIOOPRS	baroscopic
ABCCKKOORS	crookbacks
ABCCKLLOUY	cockabully
ABCCKNOSTU	countbacks
ABCCKORSTU	backcourts
ABCDDEFIKL	fiddleback
	fiddle-back
ABCDDKORSU	duckboards
ABCDEEEELR	decreeable
ABCDEEEELX	exceedable
ABCDEEEHSU	debauchees
ABCDEEEILV	deceivable
ABCDEEELLT	delectable
ABCDEEELRT	celebrated
ABCDEEELSU	seduceable
ABCDEEELTT	detectable
ABCDEEERRT	cerebrated
ABCDEEGNRS	Scanderbeg
ABCDEEHLLY	bellyached
ABCDEEHLNU	unbleached
ABCDEEHRSU	debauchers
ABCDEEHRUY	debauchery
ABCDEEILLN	declinable
ABCDEEILNU	ineducable
ABCDEEILPR	predicable
ABCDEEILPS	despicable
ABCDEEILRT	creditable
ABCDEEILVY	deceivably
ABCDEEKKSW	skewbacked
ABCDEEKLRV	backvelder
ABCDEELLTY	delectably
ABCDEELLUX	excludable
ABCDEELMRS	descramble
ABCDEELNUU	uneducable
ABCDEELORR	recordable
ABCDEEMORT	embrocated
ABCDEENRTY	cybernated
ABCDEENSTU	abducentes
ABCDEEORST	obsecrated
ABCDEFIKLL	backfilled
ABCDEFIKLS	backfields
ABCDEFIRTU	bifurcated
ABCDEFOSTU	obfuscated
ABCDEGHINU	debauching
ABCDEGIKRS	ridgebacks
ABCDEGIORT	Coatbridge

ABCDEGKMOS	gobsmacked
ABCDEHIILR	herbicidal
ABCDEHKLOS	blockheads
ABCDEHKMPU	humpbacked
ABCDEHLLUU	clubhauled
ABCDEHLNUW	Buchenwald
ABCDEHORSS	chessboard
ABCDEIILMO	biomedical
ABCDEIILNT	indictable
ABCDEIILNV	vindicable
ABCDEIIMRT	imbricated
ABCDEIKLRS	backslider
ABCDEIKLSS	backslides
ABCDEIKOUV	bivouacked
ABCDEIKRSU	rudbeckias
ABCDEILLNU	includable
ABCDEILLPU	duplicable
ABCDEILORS	carbolised
ABCDEILORZ	carbolized
ABCDEILPSY	despicably
ABCDEILRTU	lubricated
	traducible
ABCDEILRTY	creditably
ABCDEILSTU	subdialect
ABCDEINORS	carbonised
ABCDEINORZ	carbonized
ABCDEIORST	bacteroids
ABCDEIPRRS	crispbread
ABCDEIRRSU	carburised
ABCDEIRRTU	rubricated
ABCDEIRRUZ	carburized
ABCDEJKOOT	jackbooted
ABCDEKLLOS	ballocksed
ABCDEKLORS	blockaders
ABCDEKLPRU	parbuckled
ABCDEKMOSS	mossbacked
ABCDELMNRU	Cumberland
ABCDELNNOO	condonable
ABCDELRTUU	lucubrated
ABCDELSSSU	subclassed
ABCDENORSS	absconders
ABCDENOSSU	subdeacons
ABCDEOORRS	scoreboard
ABCDERSTTU	subtracted
ABCDGIKLNO	blockading
ABCDGINNOS	absconding
ABCDGKNORU	background
ABCDHIILNR	brainchild
ABCDHINNRU	nudibranch
ABCDHINORU	chairbound
ABCDHIOOPR	brachiopod
ABCDHKRRTU	Burckhardt
ABCDHLOORT	broadcloth
ABCDHNOPRU	punchboard
ABCDIIISTY	dibasicity
ABCDIILLSY	disyllabic
ABCDIILNTY	indictably
ABCDIIMNOY	biodynamic
ABCDIIRSTY	scabridity
ABCDIISTUY	subacidity
ABCDIKRRSY	brickyards
ABCDILMOOR	Arcimboldo
ABCDILNOST	cnidoblast
ABCDILOPRS	clipboards
ABCDILOSST	blastodisc
ABCDINOOST	bandicoots
ABCDINOSTU	abductions
ABCDKLOORS	roadblocks
ABCDKLOOSW	blackwoods
ABCDKORSSW	backswords
ABCDLNRSSU	scrublands
ABCEEEELSS	Celebes Sea
ABCEEEHKRS	Schaerbeek
ABCEEEIKRR	icebreaker
ABCEEEILPR	pierceable
ABCEEEILRV	receivable
ABCEEEJLRT	rejectable
ABCEEELLRR	cerebellar
ABCEEELNRS	screenable
ABCEEELPTX	expectable
ABCEEELRST	celebrates
ABCEEELTUX	executable
ABCEEENRUX	exuberance
ABCEEERRST	cerebrates
ABCEEFIILN	beneficial
ABCEEFIRSS	briefcases
ABCEEFNORT	benefactor
ABCEEGKNRS	greenbacks
ABCEEHHKSS	backsheesh
ABCEEHILNR	hibernacle
ABCEEHIOST	cohabitees
ABCEEHKLST	sketchable
ABCEEHKRTU	hackbuteer
ABCEEHLLRY	bellyacher
ABCEEHLLSY	bellyaches
ABCEEHLNQU	quenchable
ABCEEHNORR	abhorrence
ABCEEHORSU	herbaceous
ABCEEIILLT	elicitable
ABCEEIIRST	acerbities
ABCEEIJLNT	injectable
ABCEEIKLNR	linebacker
ABCEEILLNR	reclinable
ABCEEILLNS	licensable
ABCEEILLOT	biocellate
ABCEEILLPX	explicable
ABCEEILMMT	emblematic
ABCEEILMNS	lambencies
ABCEEILNNU	enunciable
ABCEEILNOT	noticeable
ABCEEILNSV	bivalences
ABCEEILNTU	binucleate
ABCEEILPST	pectisable
ABCEEILRTX	extricable
ABCEEINNOZ	benzocaine
ABCEEINNST	abstinence
ABCEEINOSS	obeisances
ABCEEINRRS	carbineers
ABCEEJKLTU	bluejacket
ABCEEJNSST	abjectness
ABCEEKLOPT	pocketable
ABCEEKRSTT	backstreet
ABCEELLNOS	enclosable
ABCEELLOPR	percolable
ABCEELLORT	brocatelle
ABCEELLPUX	exculpable
ABCEELLRRY	cerebrally
ABCEELMNSS	semblances
ABCEELMRRS	clamberers
ABCEELMRSY	cymbaleers
ABCEELNORS	censorable
ABCEELNOTT	balconette
ABCEELNOTU	Canteloube
ABCEELNOVY	conveyable
ABCEELNRST	celebrants
ABCEELNRSU	censurable
ABCEELOPRU	recoupable
ABCEELORRT	celebrator
ABCEELORST	bracteoles
ABCEELPTXY	expectably
ABCEEMOOTY	amoebocyte
ABCEEMORRS	embraceors
ABCEEMORST	embrocates
ABCEEMOSTY	amebocytes
ABCEENORSV	observance
ABCEENORTT	carbonette
ABCEENRRTY	barycentre
ABCEENRSTY	cybernates
ABCEEORSST	obsecrates
ABCEEOSSUX	sauceboxes
ABCEEPRRSU	cupbearers
ABCEFHLSSU	flashcubes
ABCEFIKLLS	blackflies
ABCEFILNNO	confinable
ABCEFIRSTU	bifurcates
ABCEFLNOSU	confusable
ABCEFLNOTU	confutable
ABCEFOSSTU	obfuscates
ABCEFRSSUU	subsurface
ABCEGHIMNR	chambering
ABCEGIKLNN	blackening
ABCEGIKNRT	bracketing
ABCEGILMNR	clambering
ABCEGILNOS	cognisable
ABCEGILNOZ	cognizable
ABCEGILORS	bricolages
ABCEGINNNY	benignancy
ABCEGINSSS	abscessing
ABCEGJLNOU	conjugable
ABCEGKRSTU	tuckerbags
ABCEGLNOOT	conglobate
ABCEHIILOT	bioethical
ABCEHIKLNR	branchlike
ABCEHIKRRT	brickearth
ABCEHILNNR	branchline
ABCEHILPRT	birthplace
ABCEHIMORT	bichromate
ABCEHINORR	chairborne
ABCEHINOST	aitchbones
ABCEHINRRY	chinaberry
ABCEHIOOPR	aerophobic
ABCEHIORST	cohabiters
ABCEHIPRRY	hyperbaric
ABCEHKLLSS	shellbacks
ABCEHKLOSS	shoeblacks
ABCEHKMNRS	benchmarks

ABCEHKORSY	Cheboksary
ABCEHKRTTU	hackbutter
ABCEHLLOTT	tablecloth
ABCEHLNRSS	branchless
ABCEHMOPRT	chamberpot
ABCEHMOSTX	matchboxes
ABCEHNNOOR	Baron-Cohen
ABCEHOQRSU	quebrachos
ABCEHORSTU	tarbouches
ABCEHORTTX	chatterbox
ABCEHPRSTU	subchapter
ABCEHRSTTU	bruschetta
ABCEIIISST	basicities
ABCEIILLMT	bimetallic
ABCEIILLNN	inclinable
ABCEIILLNR	brilliance
ABCEIILMTU	umbilicate
ABCEIILPST	epiblastic
ABCEIIMRST	imbricates
ABCEIINRSV	vibrancies
ABCEIINTUV	incubative
ABCEIIOORT	aerobiotic
ABCEIIORST	aerobicist
ABCEIJLOTV	objectival
ABCEIKKSTY	stickybeak
ABCEIKLRRY	bricklayer
ABCEIKLRSV	silverback
ABCEILLMOP	compliable
ABCEILLNOS	inclosable
ABCEILLNOU	inoculable
ABCEILLNPU	inculpable
ABCEILLNRS	cranesbill
ABCEILLTUV	cultivable
ABCEILMOPT	compatible
ABCEILMSST	cembalists
ABCEILNOSU	unsociable
ABCEILNOTY	noticeably
ABCEILNPRU	republican
ABCEILNRRU	incurrable
ABCEILNRSU	incurables
ABCEILORSS	carbolises
ABCEILORST	cabriolets
ABCEILORSZ	carbolizes
ABCEILORTU	orbiculate
ABCEILRSTU	lubricates
	subarticle
ABCEIMMOQU	Moçambique
ABCEIMOORT	Coimbatore
ABCEIMORRT	barometric
ABCEINORRS	carboniser
ABCEINORRZ	carbonizer
ABCEINORSS	carbonises
ABCEINORSZ	carbonizes
ABCEINORTU	bicornuate
ABCEINOSUY	buoyancies
ABCEINRRST	transcribe
ABCEIORSUU	rubiaceous
ABCEIOSSSU	scabiouses
ABCEIRRRSU	subcarrier
ABCEIRRSSU	carburises
ABCEIRRSTU	rubricates
ABCEIRRSUZ	carburizes
ABCEJKLMRU	lumberjack
ABCEKKORST	backstroke
ABCEKLLNOU	unlockable
ABCEKLLOSS	ballockses
ABCEKLNOST	Blackstone
ABCEKLPRSU	parbuckles
ABCEKLRTTU	turtleback
ABCEKRSTUW	waterbucks
ABCELLMOOP	Campobello
ABCELLNOOR	collarbone
ABCELLNOOS	consolable
ABCELLOORU	colourable
ABCELLOOST	blastocoel
ABCELLOSTU	leucoblast
ABCELLRSSU	subcellars
ABCELLRSSW	screwballs
ABCELMMNOO	commonable
ABCELMMOTU	commutable
ABCELMNOSU	consumable
ABCELMNRSU	unscramble
ABCELMOPTU	computable
ABCELMOSTU	customable
ABCELMRRSS	scramblers
ABCELNORRY	barleycorn
ABCELNOSST	constables
ABCELNRSUU	subnuclear
ABCELNRSUY	censurably
ABCELOPRRU	procurable
ABCELOSSTT	ectoblasts
ABCELRRTUU	tubercular
ABCELRSTUU	lucubrates
ABCELSSSSU	subclasses
ABCELSSSUU	subclauses
ABCEMNOPRU	Pernambuco
ABCEMOOPRT	amboceptor
ABCEMORSSS	crossbeams
ABCEMOSSUU	submucosae
ABCEMRSSUV	verbascums
ABCENNSTUY	subtenancy
ABCENORSTY	corybantes
ABCENRRTUY	canterbury
ABCENRSTUU	bucentaurs
ABCENSSSTU	substances
ABCEOOPRRT	baroceptor
ABCEOOPRSS	baroscopes
ABCEORRRTU	carburetor
ABCERRSTTU	subtracter
ABCFGHIKST	fightbacks
ABCFGIIKNR	backfiring
ABCFILMORU	baculiform
ABCGGIKPSY	piggybacks
ABCGHIINOT	cohabiting
ABCGHIIOPR	biographic
ABCGHIKMNU	Buckingham
ABCGHIKSST	backsights
ABCGHINNRS	branchings
ABCGHINOOT	cohobating
ABCGHLORYY	brachylogy
ABCGIILLOO	biological
ABCGIINNTU	incubating
ABCGIINRTT	bratticing
ABCGIKLNSS	slingbacks
ABCGIKMNRU	buckraming
ABCGILMNRS	scrambling
ABCGILNOSY	cognisably
ABCGILNOYZ	cognizably
ABCHHIOPRS	archbishop
ABCHHKSSUW	bushwhacks
ABCHIILLNS	chilblains
ABCHIILMOP	amphibolic
ABCHIILOPR	barophilic
ABCHIILOPS	basophilic
ABCHIILOTT	batholitic
ABCHIKLLLS	Black Hills
ABCHIKLLSY	blackishly
ABCHIKLMST	blacksmith
ABCHIMMNSU	Buchmanism
ABCHIMOORZ	Chimborazo
ABCHIMORSU	choriambus
ABCHINOOPY	cynophobia
ABCHKLNORT	blackthorn
ABCHKMRSSU	marshbucks
ABCHKMSTTU	thumbtacks
ABCHKNORST	thornbacks
ABCHKORSSV	boschvarks
ABCHKORSTW	throwbacks
ABCHLLNPSU	punchballs
ABCIIIKLSW	bailiwicks
ABCIIILNST	albinistic
ABCIIINOTT	antibiotic
ABCIILLMSU	umbilicals
ABCIILLNRY	brilliancy
ABCIILLSST	ballistics
ABCIILMOPS	bioplasmic
ABCIILRTUY	curability
ABCIIMNOSS	ambisonics
ABCIIMRSST	strabismic
ABCIINNOTU	incubation
ABCIINOSSS	abscission
ABCIINRRSU	rubricians
ABCIIOSSTT	biostatics
ABCIKLLORY	rockabilly
ABCIKLLSST	blacklists
ABCILLMOPY	compliably
ABCILLMOSY	symbolical
ABCILLNPUY	inculpably
ABCILLRRUY	rubrically
ABCILMOPTY	compatibly
ABCILMRUUV	vibraculum
ABCILMSSTY	cymbalists
ABCILNORSU	binoculars
ABCILNOSUY	unsociably
ABCILNRSTU	lubricants
ABCILORRSU	courbarils
ABCILORRTU	lubricator
ABCILPSTUY	subtypical
ABCIMMOPRU	procambium
ABCINORSTU	incubators
ABCINORTUY	incubatory
ABCIORRRTU	rubricator
ABCKKNOOTU	knockabout
ABCKLLLOPS	blackpolls
ABCKNPRTUY	bankruptcy
ABCKOOPRSS	scrapbooks

ABCLLOORUY colourably
ABCLORRTUU lucubrator
ABCLORSSUY scabrously
ABCLOSSTTY blastocyst
ABCNORSSTU obscurants
ABDDEEEFLN defendable
ABDDEEEHNO boneheaded
ABDDEEELNP dependable
ABDDEEGGLR bedraggled
ABDDEEGHIR bridgehead
ABDDEEHLLU bullheaded
ABDDEEILNS disenabled
ABDDEEKORY keyboarded
ABDDEELNPY dependably
ABDDEENNOS nosebanded
ABDDEEPRSS bedspreads
ABDDEGINRU unabridged
ABDDEGIRRW drawbridge
ABDDEHHINN behindhand
ABDDEHILNR Hildebrand
ABDDEHILNS blandished
ABDDEHINRS brandished
ABDDEHMOTU badmouthed
ABDDEIILOS diabolised
ABDDEIILOZ diabolized
ABDDEIIMRS bridesmaid
ABDDEILLLS saddlebill
ABDDEILLUW bullwaddie
ABDDEIORSS broadsides
sideboards
ABDDELMORU Boulder Dam
ABDDELNORR borderland
ABDDELNRTU bladdernut
ABDDELOSSW saddlebows
ABDDGIINNS disbanding
ABDDGORSUY bodyguards
ABDDHINSTW bandwidths
ABDDILLORR dollarbird
ABDDLMOORS moldboards
ABDDLMOORU mouldboard
ABDDNOORSU soundboard
ABDDOORRSW broadsword
ABDEEEELMR redeemable
ABDEEEFHRT featherbed
ABDEEEFILS defeasible
ABDEEEFLRR deferrable
ABDEEEGGRW beggarweed
ABDEEEHQTU bequeathed
ABDEEEILLN delineable
ABDEEEILMR remediable
ABDEEEILRT deliberate
ABDEEEINRV aberdevine
ABDEEEKMRR reembarked
ABDEEELLLR relabelled
ABDEEELLPT depletable
ABDEEELMRY redeemably
ABDEEELNPX expendable
ABDEEELNRR renderable
ABDEEELNRT tenderable
ABDEEELNTX extendable
ABDEEELSTT detestable
ABDEEEMNST debasement
ABDEEERSTW sweetbread
ABDEEERTUX exuberated
ABDEEFFHLU bufflehead
ABDEEFHNOR beforehand
ABDEEFIITU beautified
ABDEEFLMOR deformable
ABDEEFLNRU refundable
ABDEEFOORT barefooted
ABDEEGGLRS bedraggles
ABDEEGHIRT bighearted
ABDEEGHNRR Hardenberg
ABDEEGILNS designable
ABDEEGINRS gaberdines
ABDEEGINST besteading
ABDEEGLMNR embrangled
ABDEEGLNPS bespangled
ABDEEGORRS garderobes
ABDEEGORRV vergeboard
ABDEEGRRSY greybeards
ABDEEHIKNR Birkenhead
ABDEEHILLS deshabille
ABDEEHILPS beadleship
ABDEEHILRR halberdier
ABDEEHIMRT timberhead
ABDEEHIMSV misbehaved
ABDEEHINRT hibernated
inbreathed
ABDEEHLMPS blasphemed
ABDEEHORST broadsheet
ABDEEIILTT debilitate
ABDEEIINRS badineries
ABDEEIINRT inebriated
ABDEEILMRY remediably
ABDEEILMST bedlamites
ABDEEILMTT timetabled
ABDEEILNNU undeniable
ABDEEILNRS breadlines
ABDEEILNSS disenables
ABDEEILPRU repudiable
ABDEEILPRV deprivable
ABDEEILRSS desirables
ABDEEILRSV verbalised
ABDEEILRVZ verbalized
ABDEEINNOR debonnaire
ABDEEINNRR Bernardine
ABDEEIORUV de Beauvoir
ABDEEIPRST rebaptised
ABDEEIPRTZ rebaptized
ABDEEIRRVW weaverbird
ABDEEISTTU beatitudes
ABDEEKORRY keyboarder
rekeyboard
ABDEELLLNU unlabelled
ABDEELLMTU umbellated
ABDEELLOPR deplorable
ABDEELLORS solderable
ABDEELLPSS speedballs
ABDEELMNOZ emblazoned
ABDEELMRRU demurrable
ABDEELNOPR ponderable
ABDEELNORS banderoles
bandoleers
endorsable
ABDEELNRSU sunderable
ABDEELOPRT deportable
ABDEELORTT battledore
ABDEELPRRU perdurable
ABDEELSTTY detestably
ABDEEMNRST debarments
ABDEEMRRSU embrasured
ABDEEMRRSW bedwarmers
ABDEENOPSU subpoenaed
ABDEENORTT Bernadotte
ABDEENOTTY bayonetted
ABDEENPRRY prebendary
ABDEENRRST bartenders
ABDEENSTTU debutantes
ABDEEOPRRT reprobated
ABDEEOPSST speedboats
ABDEEORRUX bordereaux
ABDEERRSST redbreasts
ABDEERRSTT Bradstreet
ABDEFIILMO modifiable
ABDEFIIMRT fimbriated
ABDEFILMOR formidable
ABDEFINRRS firebrands
ABDEFINRSS Fassbinder
ABDEFIRRTU breadfruit
ABDEFORRST fretboards
ABDEGGHOOR beggarhood
ABDEGGIRRU budgerigar
ABDEGGKNOR Dogger Bank
ABDEGGNOOT tobogganed
ABDEGHHILL highballed
ABDEGHINSU subheading
ABDEGHNRRU Hardenburg
ABDEGIINNR brigandine
ABDEGIINSU biguanides
ABDEGIIRRS brigadiers
ABDEGIKNRR ringbarked
ABDEGILLOS globalised
ABDEGILNSY debasingly
ABDEGILNZZ bedazzling
ABDEGIMNRT abridgment
ABDEGINNOR broadening
ABDEGINNRR rebranding
ABDEGIRRTW Bridgwater
ABDEGJORTU objurgated
ABDEGJSTUU subjugated
ABDEGKRSTU grubstaked
ABDEGLNNRU Burgenland
ABDEGLNRUW Waldenburg
ABDEGNNRUU Graubünden
ABDEGORSTU subrogated
ABDEHHSSSU shadbushes
ABDEHIILLS dishabille
ABDEHILNSS blandishes
ABDEHILSST stablished
ABDEHINRRS brandisher
ABDEHINRSS brandishes
ABDEHIORTW whiteboard
ABDEHIRRSU airbrushed
ABDEHLLMOT mothballed
ABDEHLLOOY ballyhooed

ABDEHLOSTW	deathblows
ABDEHMNNSU	husbandmen
ABDEHNORTU	earthbound
ABDEHNRSSU	husbanders
ABDEHNRSTU	subtrahend
ABDEHNRTUY	Thunder Bay
ABDEHORRST	shortbread
ABDEHOSUWY	bawdyhouse
ABDEIIKLLS	dislikable
ABDEIILMSS	admissible
ABDEIILOSS	diabolises
ABDEIILOSZ	diabolizes
ABDEIILRRS	ribaldries
ABDEIILRSU	subdeliria
ABDEIILSST	stabilised
ABDEIILSTZ	stabilized
ABDEIINOST	antibodies
ABDEIKMRSS	disembarks
ABDEIKNRSS	snakebirds
ABDEIKNRSW	windbreaks
ABDEILLLSY	disyllable
ABDEILMNRT	timberland
ABDEILMORS	bromeliads
ABDEILMSTU	sublimated
ABDEILNNUW	unwindable
ABDEILNNUY	undeniably
ABDEILNORS	bandoliers
	indorsable
ABDEILNORY	debonairly
ABDEILNRTV	Vanderbilt
ABDEILNSUY	unbiasedly
ABDEILOPSS	disposable
ABDEILPSTU	disputable
ABDEILRSTU	brutalised
ABDEILRTTW	wattlebird
ABDEILRTUZ	brutalized
ABDEIMNORT	brominated
ABDEIMNRST	disbarment
ABDEIMNSTU	submediant
ABDEIMRRTY	timberyard
ABDEIMRTUW	dumbwaiter
ABDEINNOTU	unobtained
ABDEINORSU	boundaries
ABDEINPSTU	unbaptised
ABDEINPTUZ	unbaptized
ABDEINRTTU	turbinated
ABDEIPRRSU	upbraiders
ABDEIRTTTU	attributed
ABDEJKKMOS	sjambokked
ABDEKLLNOR	bankrolled
ABDEKNORSW	breakdowns
ABDEKNPRTU	bankrupted
ABDEKORRSW	wordbreaks
ABDELLNOSW	snowballed
ABDELLOPRY	deplorably
ABDELLORST	Lord's table
ABDELLORUY	labouredly
ABDELMOORW	marblewood
ABDELMORST	blastoderm
ABDELMOSTY	molybdates
ABDELMRRUY	lumberyard
ABDELNNORU	nondurable

ABDELNOPRY	ponderably
ABDELNORTU	roundtable
	Round Table
ABDELNORUU	unlaboured
ABDELNOSST	endoblasts
ABDELOOORT	bootloader
ABDELORSUV	boulevards
ABDELORTUY	obdurately
ABDELOSTTU	subtotaled
ABDELPRRUY	perdurably
ABDELSTUUX	subluxated
ABDENOORUV	overabound
ABDENOPPRU	paperbound
ABDENORSST	adsorbents
ABDENRSSSU	absurdness
ABDENRSSTY	bystanders
ABDEOORRST	breadroots
ABDEOORSWZ	zebrawoods
ABDEOOSTTU	outboasted
ABDFIIRRRS	friarbirds
ABDFILMORY	formidably
ABDFILNORU	floribunda
ABDFLOOORR	floorboard
ABDFOOORST	footboards
ABDFORRSSU	surfboards
ABDGHIIINT	adhibiting
ABDGHINNSU	husbanding
ABDGIINPRU	upbraiding
ABDGIINRRS	disbarring
ABDGIINSSU	disabusing
ABDGILNNRS	brandlings
ABDGINNRUU	Burgundian
ABDGINORSS	signboards
ABDGINORTU	groundbait
ABDGLOPRSU	plugboards
ABDHIIINOT	adhibition
ABDHIKLNNU	ibn-Khaldun
ABDHILMOOR	rhomboidal
ABDHIMORSY	hybridomas
ABDHIMRSTY	dithyrambs
ABDHINRTUY	unbirthday
ABDHKNOSYZ	Dobzhansky
ABDIIILSTY	disability
ABDIIILTUY	audibility
ABDIIKNNRY	bradykinin
ABDIILMNOU	albuminoid
ABDIILORRT	tailorbird
ABDIILOSST	diabolists
	idioblasts
ABDIILPTUY	dupability
ABDIILRTUY	durability
ABDIIMPRSY	bipyramids
ABDIINOTTU	dubitation
ABDIIRSSUY	subsidiary
ABDIKMORSS	skimboards
ABDILNOOST	bloodstain
ABDILNORSU	subordinal
ABDILOORTY	botryoidal
ABDILOORWZ	brazilwood
ABDILPSTUY	disputably
ABDIMNNOST	badmintons
ABDIMNOOSU	abdominous

ABDINRSSTW	wristbands
ABDLMOOORS	broadlooms
ABDMOOORRS	boardrooms
ABDNOORSSW	snowboards
ABDNOORTUU	roundabout
ABDOORRSTY	storyboard
ABDOORRTUU	troubadour
ABEEEEFRST	beefeaters
ABEEEFKSST	beefsteaks
ABEEEFLPRR	preferable
ABEEEFLRRR	referrable
ABEEEGGLRS	segregable
ABEEEGGRST	eggbeaters
ABEEEGHLLO	Beaglehole
ABEEEGLRSU	beleaguers
ABEEEGLSTV	vegetables
ABEEEHITTV	hebetative
ABEEEHLSSW	wheelbases
ABEEEHQRTU	bequeather
ABEEEHRSTT	hartebeest
ABEEEIKLNR	Berkeleian
ABEEEIKRRT	tiebreaker
ABEEEILLRV	relievable
ABEEEILMRR	irremeable
ABEEEILRVW	reviewable
ABEEEIRRST	teaberries
ABEEEKPRRS	barkeepers
ABEEELLLPX	expellable
ABEEELLSTT	settleable
ABEEELMNNT	enablement
ABEEELMNRU	enumerable
ABEEELMPRT	temperable
ABEEELMRSS	reassemble
ABEEELNPRT	penetrable
ABEEELNRSW	renewables
ABEEELQSUZ	squeezable
ABEEELRRSV	reservable
ABEEENNOZZ	azobenzene
ABEEENNRTT	bannerette
ABEEEORSTT	stereobate
ABEEERRSST	Basseterre
	Basse-Terre
ABEEERRTTV	vertebrate
ABEEERSTUX	exuberates
ABEEERSWYZ	breezeways
ABEEFFLMNT	bafflement
ABEEFFLRSU	sufferable
ABEEFGILMN	flambeeing
ABEEFGINRS	freebasing
ABEEFGKNPR	Kapfenberg
ABEEFIILNS	infeasible
ABEEFIILRV	verifiable
ABEEFIIRTU	beautifier
ABEEFIISTU	beautifies
ABEEFIKRRS	firebreaks
ABEEFILLLR	refillable
ABEEFILLRT	filterable
ABEEFILNRR	inferrable
ABEEFILNSU	unfeasible
ABEEFLMORR	reformable
ABEEFLOPRR	perforable
ABEEFLPRRY	preferably

ABEEFORRRS forbearers
ABEEGHINTT hebetating
ABEEGHNORS habergeons
ABEEGHNORU haubergeon
ABEEGHRSTU hagbuteers
ABEEGIKNPS bespeaking
ABEEGILLNR relabeling
ABEEGILMNR germinable
ABEEGILNOT negotiable
ABEEGILNRT integrable
ABEEGILNSS Albigenses
ABEEGILRTW bilgewater
ABEEGIMNRS besmearing
ABEEGINORT bioreagent
ABEEGINRSU aubergines
ABEEGINSWX beeswaxing
ABEEGKORRS brokerages
ABEEGLLNRW Wallenberg
ABEEGLMNRS embrangles
ABEEGLNORV governable
ABEEGLNPSS bespangles
ABEEGLNSTW West Bengal
ABEEGLOPRS bargepoles
porbeagles
ABEEGMNRSW wambengers
ABEEGNNNRT Tannenberg
ABEEGNNSYZ Nagyszeben
ABEEGNRSTT abstergent
ABEEHHRRTY heathberry
ABEEHIILTZ Elizabeth I
ABEEHILLRS relishable
ABEEHILPRS perishable
ABEEHIMRSV misbehaver
ABEEHIMSSV misbehaves
ABEEHIMSTW whitebeams
ABEEHINOTT hebetation
ABEEHINRST hibernates
inbreathes
ABEEHIRSTT breathiest
ABEEHKNORS boneshaker
ABEEHKOSSU bakehouses
ABEEHLMPRS blasphemer
ABEEHLMPSS blasphemes
ABEEHLNOSW whalebones
ABEEHLORRS seborrheal
ABEEHLRSST breathless
ABEEHMORTT bathometer
ABEEHNORSU Oberhausen
ABEEHOORRS seborrhoea
ABEEHORSTU hereabouts
ABEEHORTTU thereabout
ABEEHORTUW whereabout
ABEEHPRRSY barysphere
ABEEHRSSTT hartbeests
ABEEIILLMN eliminable
ABEEIILLNS isabelline
ABEEIILLRS liberalise
ABEEIILLRZ liberalize
ABEEIILNPX inexpiable
ABEEIILNTV inevitable
ABEEIILSST bestialise
ABEEIILSTZ bestialize
ABEEIINRST inebriates
ABEEIIRRRZ bizarrerie
ABEEIIRRSV breviaries
ABEEIIRRSZ brazieries
ABEEIIRSST bestiaries
ABEEIKLLNU unlikeable
ABEEIKLMRT Timberlake
ABEEIKNNRT barkentine
ABEEIKNSST snakebites
ABEEILLLLT Lille Bælt
ABEEILLMNR bellarmine
ABEEILLMOR meliorable
ABEEILLNOR neoliberal
ABEEILLNRU unreliable
ABEEILLNSS liableness
ABEEILLNST listenable
ABEEILLNTV ventilable
ABEEILLNUV unliveable
ABEEILMMOR memorabile
ABEEILMMOV immoveable
ABEEILMNRT terminable
ABEEILMNSU albumenise
ABEEILMNUZ albumenize
ABEEILMOST metabolise
ABEEILMOTT metabolite
ABEEILMOTZ metabolize
ABEEILMRRY irremeably
ABEEILMRTT remittable
ABEEILMSSS assemblies
ABEEILMSTT timetables
ABEEILNNTV inventable
ABEEILNNUV unenviable
ABEEILNOPR inoperable
ABEEILNORX inexorable
ABEEILNPSX expansible
ABEEILNRSS bleariness
ABEEILNRST East Berlin
insertable
ABEEILNRTU reunitable
ABEEILNSTV investable
ABEEILORTT obliterate
ABEEILPPST peptisable
ABEEILPPTZ peptizable
ABEEILPRRS respirable
ABEEILQRRU requirable
ABEEILQRTU requitable
ABEEILRRSV verbaliser
ABEEILRRTX Liber Extra
ABEEILRRVZ verbalizer
ABEEILRSST assertible
ABEEILRSSV verbalises
ABEEILRSVZ verbalizes
ABEEILSSTT beastliest
ABEEIOORSS aerobioses
ABEEIPRSST rebaptises
ABEEIPRSTZ rebaptizes
ABEEIRRRST barretries
ABEEIRRSSS brasseries
brassieres
ABEEIRRSTY tayberries
ABEEIRRSWX waxberries
ABEEJLLNSY jellybeans
ABEEJMMNNT enjambment
ABEEKLNNOS anklebones
ABEEKMMNNT embankment
ABEEKMMNRT embarkment
ABEELLMNTU antebellum
ABEELLMOPY employable
ABEELLNOUV unloveable
ABEELLNRST netballers
ABEELLNRUV vulnerable
ABEELLORSV resolvable
ABEELLORVV revolvable
ABEELLPRUV pulverable
ABEELLSSSY baselessly
ABEELMMMNT embalmment
ABEELMMOOT metabolome
ABEELMNOUV unmoveable
ABEELMNRST resemblant
ABEELMNRSU lebensraum
mensurable
ABEELMNTTT battlement
ABEELMORST astrobleme
blastomere
ABEELMPRSU presumable
ABEELMPRTU permutable
ABEELMRSSS assemblers
ABEELMRSSY reassembly
ABEELNNNOY Anne Boleyn
ABEELNOPRS personable
ABEELNPRTY penetrably
ABEELNQTTU blanquette
ABEELNRRTU returnable
ABEELNSSST stableness
ABEELNSSSU usableness
ABEELOPRRT reportable
ABEELOPRRV reprovable
ABEELOPRTX exportable
ABEELORRST restorable
ABEELORSTT Store Bælt
ABEELPSTTU upsettable
ABEELRSUVY surveyable
ABEEMMNSTY embayments
ABEEMNSTTT battements
ABEEMORRST barometers
ABEEMRRSSU embrasures
ABEEMRSSTW webmasters
ABEENNRRSS barrenness
ABEENNRSSU urbaneness
ABEENNRSSZ brazenness
ABEENORRTW waterborne
ABEENORSSS baronesses
ABEENORSTU Eastbourne
ABEENOSSSW sawboneses
ABEENQRSTU banqueters
ABEENQSTTU banquettes
ABEEOPRRRT reprobater
ABEEOPRRST perborates
reprobates
ABEEOSSTWX sweatboxes
ABEEPRSSTT bespatters
ABEEQRSSUU arquebuses
ABEFFGILRU febrifugal
ABEFFHINRS Banffshire

ABEFFLRSUV	sufferably
ABEFGIINTY	beatifying
ABEFGILORV	forgivable
ABEFGILRSS	fiberglass
	fibreglass
ABEFGINORR	forbearing
ABEFHIORSS	boarfishes
ABEFHIRRTT	afterbirth
ABEFIILLLN	infallible
ABEFIILNOT	notifiable
ABEFIILNTU	infibulate
ABEFIILRVY	verifiably
ABEFILMNOR	informable
ABEFILOPRT	profitable
ABEFINORRS	forebrains
ABEFKLSSTU	basketfuls
ABEFKNORRT	breakfront
ABEFLLLMUY	blamefully
ABEFLLLOOW	followable
ABEFLLLORW	ballflower
ABEFLLOORT	footballer
ABEFLLRRSU	barrelfuls
ABEFLORSTW	batfowlers
ABEFNNORUZ	benzofuran
ABEFNORSTY	Fray Bentos
ABEFORRSTY	ferryboats
ABEGGIMNOR	embargoing
ABEGGINRSW	bagswinger
ABEGGKLOUZ	Gülek Bogaz
ABEGGNOORT	tobogganer
ABEGHIINRZ	hebraizing
ABEGHILNRT	blathering
ABEGHINRRS	harbingers
ABEGHINRST	breathings
ABEGHINRTU	thunbergia
ABEGHIOPRR	biographer
ABEGHLNOOP	anglophobe
ABEGHMRRSU	hamburgers
ABEGHNRRSU	bushranger
ABEGHQSUUU	usquebaugh
ABEGHRSTTU	hagbutters
ABEGIILNNT	intangible
ABEGIILNRT	liberating
ABEGIILNSW	bewailings
ABEGIILOTV	obligative
ABEGIINNRT	brigantine
ABEGIINORS	aborigines
ABEGIINOST	abiogenist
ABEGIKLNNU	Gulbenkian
ABEGILLNRR	barrelling
ABEGILLNRV	verballing
ABEGILLOSS	globalises
ABEGILMNPU	impugnable
ABEGILMNSS	assembling
ABEGILMNTT	embattling
ABEGILNNRY	blarneying
ABEGILNSSU	subleasing
ABEGILRRSU	burglaries
	burglarise
ABEGILRRUZ	burglarize
ABEGIMORSU	seaborgium
ABEGIMOSSU	subimagoes

ABEGINNORS	Bergsonian
ABEGINNOTY	bayoneting
ABEGINNQTU	banqueting
ABEGINNSTT	battenings
ABEGINOORS	boongaries
ABEGINRSTT	batterings
ABEGINRSUY	guberniyas
ABEGJORSTU	objurgates
ABEGJSSTUU	subjugates
ABEGKRRSTU	grubstaker
ABEGKRSSTU	grubstakes
ABEGLLNOOY	balneology
ABEGLNORRY	loganberry
ABEGLORRRV	Vorarlberg
ABEGMNOORS	boomerangs
ABEGMNOOTY	Montego Bay
ABEGMORRSS	bromegrass
ABEGMORSUU	umbrageous
ABEGNNSTTU	subtangent
ABEGNOORTU	Baton Rouge
ABEGORSSTU	subrogates
ABEHHILLST	sheathbill
ABEHHIOOPT	theophobia
ABEHHMMRSU	bushhammer
ABEHHORRTT	heartthrob
ABEHHOSSTU	bathhouses
ABEHIILMNT	habiliment
ABEHIKLNRS	shrinkable
ABEHIKLORS	kohlrabies
ABEHILLOPS	polishable
ABEHILMOPS	amphiboles
ABEHILMPRS	blepharism
ABEHILNPSU	punishable
ABEHILOPRS	barophiles
ABEHILOPSS	basophiles
ABEHILOPST	hospitable
ABEHILORSS	abolishers
ABEHILOSTT	batholites
ABEHILPRSY	perishably
ABEHILPSTT	battleship
ABEHILPSTU	bisulphate
ABEHILRSST	herbalists
ABEHILSSST	stablishes
ABEHILTWYY	Whitley Bay
ABEHIMMNST	Benthamism
ABEHIMNNST	banishment
ABEHIMRRSU	herbariums
ABEHINOOPX	xenophobia
ABEHINOPRV	vibraphone
ABEHINORRT	hibernator
ABEHINRSSS	brashiness
ABEHIOPRSU	euphorbias
ABEHIORSUV	behaviours
ABEHIRRSSU	airbrushes
ABEHKLLRSS	shellbarks
ABEHKPRSSY	Khyber Pass
ABEHLMOOST	smoothable
ABEHLMOTTU	ethambutol
ABEHLNOORU	honourable
ABEHLOPRSY	hyperbolas
ABEHLORRSS	harborless
ABEHLORRTY	lay brother

ABEHLORSTT	betrothals
ABEHLORTTU	bluethroat
ABEHLRTTTU	truth table
ABEHLSSSTU	saltbushes
ABEHMMRRSU	Masherbrum
ABEHMORTTY	bathometry
ABEHMRSSTU	bushmaster
ABEHMRTTYY	bathymetry
ABEHNOPRTY	hyperbaton
ABEHNRSSTU	sunbathers
ABEHOORSST	tarbooshes
ABEHOOSSTU	boathouses
	houseboats
ABEHORRRSU	harbourers
ABEIIILMNT	inimitable
ABEIIILNNZ	Leibnizian
ABEIIILNSS	sensibilia
ABEIIILQRU	equilibria
ABEIILLMRS	liberalism
ABEIILLNNY	biennially
ABEIILLNOV	inviolable
ABEIILLNRT	brilliante
ABEIILLRST	liberalist
ABEIILLRTY	liberality
ABEIILLSTU	utilisable
ABEIILLTUZ	utilizable
ABEIILMNSS	lesbianism
ABEIILMPRT	impartible
ABEIILMPSS	impassible
ABEIILMRST	bimestrial
ABEIILNORT	liberation
ABEIILNPRS	inspirable
ABEIILNPXY	inexpiably
ABEIILNRST	nailbiters
ABEIILNTTU	intuitable
ABEIILNTTY	tenability
ABEIILNTVY	inevitably
ABEIILQTUY	equability
ABEIILRSST	stabiliser
ABEIILRSSU	Belisarius
ABEIILRSTZ	stabilizer
ABEIILSSST	stabilises
ABEIILSSTZ	stabilizes
ABEIILSTTY	bestiality
ABEIILSTUY	useability
ABEIINNRRT	interbrain
ABEIINNRSS	braininess
ABEIINNRST	inebriants
ABEIINNRTW	New Britain
ABEIINRSTU	urbanities
ABEIIOORSS	aerobiosis
ABEIIORSTU	obituaries
ABEIKLNNSU	unsinkable
ABEIKLNSSU	baulkiness
ABEIKMORRS	biomarkers
ABEIKNOPRT	breakpoint
ABEIKNSTUZ	Uzbekistan
ABEILLLNST	libellants
ABEILLLNTU	untillable
ABEILLMSTU	stimulable
ABEILLNNOZ	Bellinzona
ABEILLNOSV	insolvable

ABEILLPPSU	suppliable
ABEILLPSTU	stipulable
ABEILLSUXY	bisexually
ABEILMMOST	metabolism
ABEILMMOVY	immoveably
ABEILMNNRU	Melburnian
ABEILMNQRU	lambrequin
ABEILMNRTY	terminably
ABEILMNSSU	unmissable
ABEILMNSSW	wambliness
ABEILMOOTU	automobile
ABEILMOPRT	importable
ABEILMOPRV	improvable
ABEILMORTY	traymobile
ABEILMRSSU	surmisable
ABEILMRSSV	verbalisms
ABEILMSSTU	sublimates
ABEILNNNUW	unwinnable
ABEILNNRUY	inurbanely
ABEILNOPRY	inoperably
ABEILNORSZ	blazonries
ABEILNORXY	inexorably
ABEILNOSTY	obeisantly
ABEILNSTUU	unsuitable
ABEILOPRRV	proverbial
ABEILOPSTU	bipetalous
ABEILOPSTY	polybasite
ABEILORRST	liberators
ABEILORSSU	Belorussia
ABEILRRTTU	triturable
ABEILRSSTU	brutalises
ABEILRSSTV	verbalists
ABEILRSTUV	vestibular
ABEILRSTUZ	brutalizes
ABEILRSUVV	survivable
ABEIMMOQUZ	Mozambique
ABEIMNNOTT	obtainment
ABEIMNORST	brominates
ABEIMNORTT	montbretia
ABEIMNORTU	tambourine
ABEIMNRRSU	submariner
ABEIMNRSST	brainstems
ABEIMNRSSU	submarines
ABEIMOSSTU	abstemious
ABEIMPRSST	rebaptisms
ABEINNORTU	eburnation
ABEINNOSST	sanbenitos
ABEINNOSTT	abstention
ABEINNRRTU	interurban
ABEINNRSST	bannisters
ABEINNRSSW	brawniness
ABEINOOPSW	bioweapons
ABEINOPRRW	brainpower
ABEINOPSTX	paintboxes
ABEINORTTX	exorbitant
ABEINPRSST	breastpins
ABEINRSSSS	brassiness
ABEINRSTTU	turbinates
ABEIOPPRSY	presbyopia
ABEIOPRSTV	absorptive
ABEIOSSSST	asbestosis
ABEIPRSTTY	baptistery
ABEIRRRSST	barristers
ABEIRRTTTU	attributer
ABEIRSTTTU	attributes
ABEIRSTUVY	subvariety
ABEJLMOTUU	autojumble
ABEKKMOORR	bookmarker
ABEKKMOORS	bookmakers
ABEKKORSTW	basketwork
	workbasket
ABEKLLNORR	bankroller
ABEKLLORWY	yellowbark
ABEKLLOSTU	leukoblast
ABEKLNNOUW	unknowable
ABEKLNORUW	unworkable
ABEKLOOPST	bookplates
ABEKLORSTW	worktables
ABEKMNNOTU	mountebank
ABEKNOPRRW	pawnbroker
ABEKNORWYY	New York Bay
ABEKOOPRRY	prayer book
ABEKORRSTW	breastwork
ABELLLLORR	rollerball
ABELLLLOVY	volleyball
ABELLMNOYY	Ballymoney
ABELLMOOOP	Pool Malebo
ABELLMOSTY	myeloblast
ABELLNOSUV	unsolvable
ABELLNRUVY	vulnerably
ABELLORRRU	bullroarer
ABELLORVVY	revolvably
ABELLOSTUY	absolutely
ABELLSSSUY	syllabuses
ABELMMNOSU	summonable
ABELMNNOOW	noblewoman
ABELMNOOST	monostable
ABELMNORYZ	emblazonry
ABELMOOPRT	promotable
ABELMOSSST	mesoblasts
ABELMPRSUY	presumably
ABELMPRTUY	permutably
ABELNOOPST	tablespoon
ABELNOPRSY	personably
ABELNOQTUU	unquotable
ABELNORSTU	neuroblast
ABELNOSSTT	entoblasts
ABELNRRTUU	nurturable
ABELNRSSTU	subalterns
ABELNRSTTU	turntables
ABELOOPPRS	proposable
ABELOOPRST	blastopore
ABELOOPSST	Sebastopol
ABELOOSSTT	osteoblast
ABELOPPSSU	supposable
ABELOSSTTY	stylobates
ABELPRRTUU	rupturable
ABELPRSTTU	prebuttals
ABELRSSTUY	abstrusely
ABELSSTUUX	subluxates
ABEMMNORSU	membranous
ABEMNNOSTU	submontane
ABEMNOORRW	marrowbone
ABEMOPRSTY	ambrotypes
ABEMORRSTU	arboretums
ABEMRRSSUY	burramyses
ABENNSSTTU	subtenants
ABENOOSSTT	stoneboats
ABENOPRRSS	barpersons
ABENORRRTW	barrenwort
ABENPRSSTU	abruptness
ABEOOPRSTW	powerboats
ABEOORSTUU	rouseabout
ABEOQSSUUU	subaqueous
ABEORRRSTU	barretrous
ABERRRSTWY	strawberry
ABERSSSTTU	substrates
ABFFGILLNY	bafflingly
ABFFGILNOU	buffaloing
ABFFIKMOOR	kaffirboom
ABFGILNOTW	batfowling
ABFGILORVY	forgivably
ABFIIILRTY	friability
ABFIILLLNY	infallibly
ABFIILNORV	riboflavin
ABFILOPRTY	profitably
ABFLLOSTUY	boastfully
ABFLLOSUUY	fabulously
ABFLORRSUW	barrowfuls
ABGGGILNRY	braggingly
ABGGIILNOT	obligating
ABGGILLMNO	gambolling
ABGHIIINNT	inhabiting
ABGHIILNOS	abolishing
ABGHIIMMNR	Birmingham
ABGHILMNSS	shamblings
ABGHILNOUX	boxhauling
ABGHINNSTU	sunbathing
ABGHINORRU	harbouring
ABGHINSWZZ	whizzbangs
ABGHIRRRSU	Harrisburg
ABGHOORRUY	yarborough
ABGIIILNST	sibilating
ABGIIJLNTU	jubilating
ABGIILLNSU	bilinguals
ABGIILNNTY	intangibly
ABGIILNOOT	obligation
ABGIILNOPR	parboiling
ABGIIMNNOO	Mabinogion
ABGIINNOST	botanising
ABGIINNOTZ	botanizing
ABGIINNRSU	urbanising
ABGIINNRUZ	urbanizing
ABGIINNTTU	intubating
ABGIKKMNOO	bookmaking
ABGIKLNRUW	bulwarking
ABGILLLNSY	syllabling
ABGILLLNUY	lullabying
ABGILLNNOO	ballooning
ABGILLNORY	laboringly
ABGILLNSUU	sublingual
ABGILMOSUY	bigamously
ABGILNOSTY	boastingly
ABGILNTTUU	tubulating
ABGILOORST	obligators
ABGILOORTY	obligatory

ABGIMNORTU	tambouring
ABGINNORRT	Barrington
ABGINOORSS	barognosis
ABGINORTTU	obturating
ABGINORTUV	outbraving
ABGINOSSTW	swingboats
ABGJOORRTU	objurgator
ABGJORSTUU	subjugator
ABGLLLORUY	globularly
ABGLLORUUU	Luluabourg
ABGLMNOOSS	boomslangs
ABGMOPRRSU	subprogram
ABGORRSSTU	Strasbourg
ABHHIIRSUV	bahuvrihis
ABHHILOSTT	batholiths
ABHHIMOOOP	homophobia
ABHIIMNSST	absinthism
ABHIIMOPSU	amphibious
ABHIKLLSSW	hawksbills
ABHIKMRRST	birthmarks
ABHILMNSTU	thumbnails
ABHILNOOPT	haplobiont
ABHILNOOST	halobionts
ABHILNRSTY	labyrinths
ABHILOPSTY	hospitably
ABHILORTUW	whirlabout
ABHIMNOOOP	monophobia
ABHIMNOOPY	ambiophony
ABHINOOOPS	nosophobia
ABHINPRSTU	paintbrush
ABHIPRRSSU	bursarship
ABHKMRRSSU	brushmarks
ABHLLMSTTU	thumbstall
ABHLNOORUY	honourably
ABHLOPSSTY	hypoblasts
ABHMNORRTU	rhumbatron
ABIIILLPTY	pliability
ABIIILLTVY	livability
ABIIILMNTY	inimitably
ABIIILMTXY	mixability
ABIIILNOST	sibilation
ABIIINOSST	antibiosis
ABIIJLNOTU	jubilation
ABIILLMNOY	binomially
ABIILLMNSU	subliminal
ABIILLNOVY	inviolably
ABIILLNRST	brilliants
ABIILLNSTY	sibilantly
ABIILLOTVY	lovability
ABIILMNNOS	binominals
ABIILMOTVY	movability
ABIILMPRTY	impartibly
ABIILMPSSY	impassibly
ABIILMTTUY	mutability
ABIILNOOSV	bolivianos
ABIILNORST	librations
ABIILNOTTY	notability
ABIILOPRTY	bipolarity
ABIILOPTTY	potability
ABIILORRTU	lubritoria
ABIILRSSTT	tribalists
ABIIMORSSV	bravissimo
ABIIMRSSTY	sybaritism
ABIINNOTTU	intubation
ABIINNRTUY	inurbanity
ABIINOOSTV	obviations
ABIINORSTV	vibrations
ABIINOTTTU	titubation
ABIIORSTTU	obituarist
ABIJLLNTUY	jubilantly
ABIJNOORTU	objuration
ABIKKNSTUY	Aktyubinsk
ABILLLOOSV	Villa-Lobos
ABILLNOOST	balloonist
ABILLNOOTU	lobulation
ABILLNOPST	ballpoints
ABILLNOSVY	insolvably
ABILLORRSZ	razorbills
ABILMNOSUU	albuminous
ABILMNOTUX	toxalbumin
ABILMOPRVY	improvably
ABILMORSXY	xylorimbas
ABILMOSSTU	absolutism
ABILMSSTTU	submittals
ABILNOOSTU	absolution
ABILNOTTUU	tubulation
ABILORSSTU	labourists
ABILORSSUU	salubrious
ABILOSSTTU	absolutist
ABILOSSTUY	sabulosity
ABILRSSTTU	brutalists
ABILRSTTUU	subtitular
ABILRTTUUY	tubularity
ABIMMNRSUU	manubriums
ABIMNORRST	brainstorm
ABIMNORSTU	tambourins
ABIMRSSSTU	strabismus
ABINOOPRST	absorption
	probations
	saprobiont
ABINOOPSST	spoonbaits
ABINOORRTU	Buonarroti
ABINOORTTU	obturation
ABINOOSSST	bassoonist
ABINOSSTTU	substation
ABINRSSTUY	Saintsbury
ABIORRTTTU	attributor
ABKLLOOSST	bookstalls
ABKLNNOUWY	unknowably
ABKMORSSYZ	Szymborska
ABLMNORSSU	subnormals
ABLOOPRSST	blastopors
ABLOOPRTTT	Port Talbot
ABLOORSTUY	absolutory
ABLORSTTUU	tubulators
ABMNORRSST	barnstorms
ABMOOORSTT	motorboats
ABMOORSTTY	strabotomy
ABMRSSTTUU	substratum
ABNOORRSTU	brontosaur
ABNOORSTUZ	zorbonauts
ABNORSTTUU	turnabouts
ABOOPRSSTT	bootstraps
ABOORRSTTU	obturators
ABOORSTTUU	roustabout
ABRRSSSTTU	starbursts
ABRRSSTTUW	bratwursts
ACCCDEHIIL	Chalcidice
ACCCEEENNS	canescence
ACCCEEHITT	catechetic
ACCCEENRST	accrescent
ACCCEFHKOR	cockchafer
ACCCEGINOS	cacogenics
ACCCEHILOT	chalcocite
ACCCEHORTW	cowcatcher
ACCCEHORUU	accoucheur
ACCCEIILRT	cicatricle
ACCCEIIRST	cicatrices
ACCCEIKORT	cockatrice
ACCCEILLNY	encyclical
ACCCEILLOS	calcicoles
ACCCEILMOP	accomplice
ACCCEIMNPY	impeccancy
ACCCGLNOOO	gonococcal
ACCCHHILOO	chocaholic
ACCCHINOOP	cacophonic
ACCCHKOPST	spatchcock
ACCCHLOORY	ochlocracy
ACCCHOOTUU	caoutchouc
ACCCIILLOT	laccolitic
ACCCIIOPRS	capriccios
ACCCILLLYY	cyclically
ACCCILLNOY	cyclonical
ACCCILMOPY	complicacy
ACCCILMORY	cycloramic
ACCCIMORTY	macrocytic
ACCCINOPPU	cappuccino
ACCDDEEENS	decadences
ACCDDEEIRT	accredited
ACCDDEEIST	desiccated
ACCDDEINOO	dodecanoic
ACCDDIORSS	disaccords
ACCDEEELRS	recalesced
ACCDEEENNS	ascendence
ACCDEEENRT	reaccented
ACCDEEEPRT	reaccepted
ACCDEEGINR	reacceding
ACCDEEHIKS	chickadees
ACCDEEHIST	catechised
ACCDEEHITZ	catechized
ACCDEEHKMT	checkmated
ACCDEEHLOT	cochleated
ACCDEEHNOR	encroached
ACCDEEIILS	delicacies
ACCDEEINNS	incandesce
ACCDEEIQSU	acquiesced
ACCDEEIRRT	reaccredit
ACCDEEISST	desiccates
ACCDEEISTX	exsiccated
ACCDEELLOR	clearcoled
ACCDEELPST	spectacled
ACCDEELPTY	acceptedly
ACCDEENNST	candescent
ACCDEENNSY	ascendency
ACCDEENNTU	unaccented
ACCDEEORTU	accoutered

ACCDEFIIRS	sacrificed
ACCDEGHORT	dogcatcher
ACCDEHLNOY	chalcedony
ACCDEIILMN	calcimined
ACCDEIILNY	indelicacy
ACCDEIILST	dialectics
ACCDEIINOS	cocainised
ACCDEIINOZ	cocainized
ACCDEIIOPT	apodeictic
ACCDEIIRST	cicatrised
ACCDEIIRTZ	cicatrized
ACCDEIKLNW	candlewick
ACCDEILLOP	peccadillo
ACCDEILNOT	occidental
ACCDEILNTU	inculcated
ACCDEILOPY	cyclopedia
ACCDEILRTU	circulated
ACCDEIMNNY	mendicancy
ACCDEIMORT	democratic
ACCDEINNTU	inductance
ACCDEINOOS	occasioned
ACCDEINOPR	endocarpic
ACCDEINSST	desiccants
ACCDEIORST	desiccator
ACCDEIORTT	corticated
ACCDELLOOT	collocated
ACCDELOPSU	cloudscape
ACCDELRSUY	accursedly
ACCDEMNOOS	cacodemons
ACCDEMORRS	camcorders
ACCDEMOSTU	accustomed
ACCDENORTT	contracted
ACCDEORRSS	scorecards
ACCDEORSTU	coruscated
ACCDFIILTY	flaccidity
ACCDGHIIMO	dichogamic
ACCDHHRRUY	churchyard
ACCDHIINOR	diachronic
ACCDHIIORS	radicchios
ACCDHILNOO	conchoidal
ACCDHILORV	clavichord
ACCDHINORS	chancroids
ACCDHOOOSW	coachwoods
ACCDHOORST	octachords
ACCDHORSTW	catchwords
ACCDIIIRST	diacritics
ACCDIILLPY	piccadilly
ACCDIILSST	cladistics
ACCDIIMNOO	monoacidic
ACCDINOORS	accordions
ACCDINORTT	contradict
ACCDKNORSW	crackdowns
ACCDNNOORT	concordant
ACCDNOORST	concordats
ACCEEEEHKS	cheesecake
ACCEEEHILR	chelicerae
ACCEEELMNU	Clemenceau
ACCEEELPRT	receptacle
ACCEEELRSS	recalesces
ACCEEENNRS	renascence
ACCEEENPTX	expectance
ACCEEGLMSY	megacycles
ACCEEHIKRS	chickarees
ACCEEHILLR	cheliceral
ACCEEHILNP	encephalic
ACCEEHINRS	chanceries
ACCEEHIRST	catechiser
ACCEEHIRTZ	catechizer
ACCEEHISST	catechises
ACCEEHISTZ	catechizes
ACCEEHKMNS	namechecks
ACCEEHKMST	checkmates
ACCEEHLNRT	chantecler
ACCEEHLNSS	chanceless
ACCEEHMNTU	catechumen
ACCEEHNORR	encroacher
ACCEEHNORS	encroaches
ACCEEILLRT	electrical
ACCEEILMNU	ecumenical
ACCEEILNTY	acetylenic
ACCEEILORV	varicocele
ACCEEILPSY	epicalyces
ACCEEIMNRS	miscreance
ACCEEINNSS	nascencies
ACCEEIORSU	ericaceous
ACCEEIQSSU	acquiesces
ACCEEIRTUX	excruciate
ACCEEISSTX	exsiccates
ACCEEKLOST	cockateels
ACCEELLNRS	cancellers
ACCEELLORS	clearcoles
ACCEELNORS	concealers
ACCEELNOST	coalescent
ACCEELNOSV	convalesce
	covalences
ACCEELNPRS	precancels
ACCEELNPRU	crapulence
ACCEELNRTU	reluctance
ACCEELNSTT	lactescent
ACCEELNSTU	caulescent
ACCEELPSST	spectacles
ACCEEMNRST	marcescent
	scarcement
ACCEEMOSTY	ascomycete
ACCEENNNOV	convenance
ACCEENNOVY	conveyance
ACCEENOPRR	coparcener
ACCEENORST	consecrate
ACCEENPTXY	expectancy
ACCEENRSSS	scarceness
ACCEEORRSU	racecourse
ACCEEORSTU	cretaceous
ACCEFFIINY	inefficacy
ACCEFGILSU	calcifuges
ACCEFHILST	catchflies
ACCEFHLRTY	flycatcher
ACCEFIILPS	specifical
ACCEFIIRRS	sacrificer
ACCEFIIRSS	sacrifices
ACCEFILLOR	calciferol
ACCEFILMOR	calceiform
ACCEFILSSU	fascicules
ACCEFINOST	confiscate
ACCEFLLOTU	flocculate
ACCEGHLNOS	chalcogens
ACCEGIINOR	cariogenic
ACCEGIKNOP	peacocking
ACCEGILLNN	cancelling
ACCEGILLNO	collagenic
ACCEGILLOO	ecological
ACCEGILNNO	concealing
ACCEGILNOS	coalescing
ACCEGILNOT	lactogenic
ACCEGILOOS	cacologies
ACCEGIMOPS	megascopic
ACCEGINNOR	carcinogen
ACCEGINNOS	cognisance
ACCEGINNOZ	cognizance
ACCEHHIIRR	hierarchic
ACCEHHIKSU	Chukchi Sea
ACCEHHIMRS	Carchemish
ACCEHHIPRT	heptarchic
ACCEHHMRSU	Schumacher
ACCEHIILMR	chimerical
ACCEHIINNT	technician
ACCEHIINPT	epicanthic
ACCEHIKLRS	checkrails
ACCEHIKOPS	peacockish
ACCEHILLMY	chemically
ACCEHILLRU	cleruchial
ACCEHILLTY	hectically
ACCEHILNOS	cochineals
ACCEHILOST	chicalotes
ACCEHIMSST	schematics
ACCEHINNSS	chanciness
ACCEHINOPT	cenotaphic
ACCEHINRRU	craunchier
ACCEHINSST	catchiness
ACCEHIORRY	hierocracy
ACCEHIORST	escharotic
	octarchies
ACCEHIORTT	rheotactic
	theocratic
ACCEHIRRTT	tetrarchic
ACCEHIRSST	scratchies
ACCEHIRSTT	architects
ACCEHIRTVZ	czarevitch
ACCEHISSTT	catechists
ACCEHLLNOR	chancellor
ACCEHLMOOR	homocercal
ACCEHLOOST	chocolates
ACCEHLOPST	catchpoles
ACCEHLOSUY	chylaceous
ACCEHMNSTT	catchments
ACCEHNNPTY	catchpenny
ACCEHNNRTY	trenchancy
ACCEHNOOTY	choanocyte
ACCEHNORTT	technocrat
ACCEHORSTU	cartouches
ACCEHRRSST	scratchers
ACCEIILMNS	calcimines
ACCEIILNOT	conciliate
ACCEIILRRT	rectricial
ACCEIILRTT	tectricial
ACCEIILSSS	classicise
ACCEIILSSZ	classicize

ACCEIIMRST	ceramicist
ACCEIIMSST	asceticism
ACCEIINOSS	cocainises
ACCEIINOSZ	cocainizes
ACCEIINRST	Cistercian
ACCEIIORSS	accessorii
	isocracies
ACCEIIPPRR	pericarpic
ACCEIIPRST	accipiters
ACCEIIRRST	cicatriser
ACCEIIRRTZ	cicatrizer
ACCEIIRSST	cicatrises
	scarcities
ACCEIIRSTZ	cicatrizes
ACCEIISSTV	siccatives
ACCEIKKLPS	placekicks
ACCEIKLOST	cockatiels
ACCEIKRSSW	wisecracks
ACCEILLLPS	scalpellic
ACCEILLLRY	clerically
ACCEILLNSY	scenically
ACCEILLOST	laccolites
ACCEILMMOR	commercial
ACCEILMNOO	economical
ACCEILMNOP	compliance
ACCEILMOPT	complicate
ACCEILMOST	cacomistle
ACCEILMOSX	cacomixles
ACCEILNOSS	neoclassic
ACCEILNOTU	noctilucae
ACCEILNRST	calcsinter
ACCEILNSTU	inculcates
ACCEILOPPT	apoplectic
ACCEILOPRR	reciprocal
ACCEILOPRS	precocials
ACCEILOPRV	prevocalic
ACCEILOTVY	coactively
ACCEILRSTU	circulates
ACCEILRTUY	cruciately
ACCEIMNORS	sciomancer
ACCEIMNRSY	miscreancy
ACCEIMORST	mesocratic
ACCEINNNOV	connivance
ACCEINNORT	concertina
ACCEINNSSY	incessancy
ACCEINOOST	consociate
ACCEINORST	accretions
	anorectics
ACCEINOSSS	accessions
ACCEINOSST	oscitances
ACCEINSSTU	encaustics
	succinates
ACCEINTTUV	cunctative
ACCEIOORSU	coriaceous
ACCEIOPPSY	episcopacy
ACCEIORSTX	exsiccator
ACCEIORTUY	eucaryotic
ACCEIOSSTU	cistaceous
ACCEIPSSTY	cityscapes
ACCEJKRSSW	jackscrews
ACCEJNOSUU	juncaceous
ACCEKKLMOR	clockmaker
ACCEKNORRS	corncrakes
ACCEKNRRTU	nutcracker
ACCELLNOSU	cancellous
ACCELLOORT	colorectal
ACCELLOOST	collocates
ACCELLSSUU	calculuses
ACCELMNOPT	complacent
ACCELNOOPY	Cape Colony
ACCELNOPTU	conceptual
ACCELNRTUY	reluctancy
ACCELOOPST	lactoscope
ACCELOSTUY	autocycles
ACCEMNNORY	necromancy
ACCEMOPRST	compacters
ACCEMORSTU	reaccustom
ACCEMORSTY	macrocytes
ACCENNNOOS	consonance
ACCENOORSS	coenosarcs
ACCENOORSU	cornaceous
ACCENOPRRU	procurance
ACCENORTTU	counteract
ACCEORRSSW	scarecrows
ACCEORRSTU	securocrat
ACCEORSSTU	coruscates
ACCEORSUUV	curvaceous
ACCFFFFHHI	chiffchaff
ACCFGIILNY	calcifying
ACCFHIRTTW	witchcraft
ACCFIINNOT	fantoccini
ACCFILSSUU	fasciculus
ACCFIMOPTY	compactify
ACCFLLNOTU	flocculant
ACCGGHILOO	cholagogic
ACCGHHIIRT	High Arctic
ACCGHIILOR	oligarchic
ACCGHINNRU	craunching
ACCGHINRST	scratching
ACCGHIOPTY	phagocytic
ACCGHLOPRY	cyclograph
ACCGIIMORT	tragicomic
ACCGIINPRT	practicing
ACCGIKLNRS	cracklings
ACCGILNSUY	accusingly
ACCGILOOST	scatologic
ACCGIMNOPT	compacting
ACCGINNORT	Accrington
ACCGINNOTT	contacting
ACCGINNOTU	accounting
ACCGINORTU	accoutring
ACCHHIILLN	chinchilla
ACCHHIIPUU	Ch'ü Ch'iu-pai
ACCHHINRTU	antichurch
ACCHHMRRUY	Church Army
ACCHHORSST	crosshatch
ACCHIIILST	chiliastic
ACCHIILORT	acrolithic
ACCHIILTTY	tachylitic
ACCHIIMSST	schismatic
ACCHIINNPS	chincapins
ACCHIINOTY	thiocyanic
ACCHIKMSTT	matchstick
ACCHIKPSST	chapsticks
ACCHILLOOS	alcoholics
ACCHILLOST	laccoliths
ACCHILLOTY	catholicly
ACCHILMOPS	accomplish
ACCHILNNPS	splanchnic
ACCHILNOOT	catholicon
ACCHILNOTY	anchylotic
ACCHILOOST	Catholicos
ACCHILOSST	scholastic
ACCHILRSTY	scratchily
ACCHILTTYY	tachylytic
ACCHIMNORY	chiromancy
ACCHIMORST	chromatics
ACCHIMOSST	stomachics
ACCHIOPRSZ	schizocarp
ACCHIOPTTY	hypotactic
ACCHIOSSTT	stochastic
ACCHKLMOST	matchlocks
ACCHKLSSTU	saltchucks
ACCHKOORSW	coachworks
ACCHLLOPST	catchpolls
ACCHLOORST	ochlocrats
ACCHMOOORT	motorcoach
ACCHNOPSYY	sycophancy
ACCHNORRST	cornstarch
ACCHOPRSST	crosspatch
ACCIIILLLP	piccalilli
ACCIIILNNS	clinicians
ACCIIINNNT	Cincinnati
ACCIIKKMNS	camiknicks
ACCIILLLNY	clinically
ACCIILLOST	localistic
ACCIILLRTY	critically
ACCIILMNOS	laconicism
ACCIILMSSS	classicism
ACCIILNNOT	calcitonin
ACCIILNOSS	calcinosis
ACCIILNRTU	uncritical
ACCIILOPST	occipitals
ACCIILORTY	caloricity
ACCIILSSST	classicist
ACCIIMNNNO	cinnamonic
ACCIIMNOOT	iconomatic
ACCIIMNOST	sciomantic
ACCIIMORTT	timocratic
ACCIINNNPY	piccaninny
ACCIINNOTY	canonicity
ACCIINORSS	carcinosis
ACCIIOPRSU	auriscopic
	capricious
ACCIIOPSST	pasticcios
ACCIIOTTVY	coactivity
ACCIISTTUY	causticity
ACCIKKKKNN	knickknack
ACCIKKRRTT	tricktrack
ACCIKNOSSW	cockswains
ACCILLMOSY	cosmically
ACCILLORTY	cortically
ACCILLRRUY	circularly
ACCILMNNOU	councilman
ACCILMNOOS	iconoclasm

ACCILMNOPY compliancy
ACCILNOOST iconoclast
ACCILNORSV clavicorns
ACCILNORTU inculcator
ACCILNOSTV conclavist
ACCILNSSTY synclastic
ACCILOPPRY polycarpic
ACCILORRTU circulator
ACCILRRRUU curricular
ACCIMNNOVY vancomycin
ACCIMNOOPR monocarpic
ACCIMNOOPT compaction
ACCIMNOORT monocratic
ACCIMOORSS crocosmias
ACCINNOTTU cunctation
ACCINOOPRU cornucopia
ACCINOOPTU occupation
ACCINOPRSY conspiracy
ACCINORSTY Carson City
ACCINSSTTY syntactics
ACCIOPRSTT catoptrics
ACCJKORSSS crossjacks
ACCKKMMSUU muckamucks
ACCKLMOORU cockalorum
ACCLOPRTUY plutocracy
ACCLRSSSUU succursals
ACCMMOORSS macrocosms
ACCMORSSTY macrocysts
ACCNNNOOSY consonancy
ACCNOOORTV convocator
ACCNOOPRRY pornocracy
ACCNOORRTT contractor
ACCNOORSTT contactors
ACCNORSTTU cunctators
ACCOPRSSTY cystocarps
ACDDDEEKLO deadlocked
ACDDEEEIRT rededicate
ACDDEEEIST dedicatees
ACDDEEELNR calendered
ACDDEEENNP dependance
ACDDEEENOS Dodecanese
ACDDEEENRS reascended
ACDDEEEPRT deprecated
ACDDEEERST desecrated
ACDDEEERTU reeducated
ACDDEEFNTU fecundated
ACDDEEHLLN chandelled
ACDDEEHNOR decahedron
ACDDEEHPST despatched
ACDDEEIIPT diapedetic
ACDDEEIITV dedicative
ACDDEEIKMV medivacked
ACDDEEILMT maledicted
ACDDEEILTU elucidated
ACDDEEIPRT predicated
ACDDEELLOT decollated
ACDDEELNRU undeclared
ACDDEELNTY decadently
ACDDEENNPY dependancy
ACDDEENNST descendant
ACDDEENRTU underacted
ACDDEENTUU uneducated
ACDDEESSTU decussated
ACDDEFFHNU handcuffed
ACDDEFFIRT diffracted
ACDDEFFLOS scaffolded
ACDDEGHIRS discharged
ACDDEGHNNY cynghanedd
ACDDEGIINT dedicating
ACDDEGNOOS dodecagons
ACDDEHIIOS diadochies
ACDDEHIKNP handpicked
ACDDEHINSW sandwiched
ACDDEHIPST dispatched
ACDDEHNNOS secondhand
ACDDEHNORT Chadderton
ACDDEIILMS disclaimed
ACDDEIINOT dedication
ACDDEIINTV vindicated
ACDDEILMOU duodecimal
ACDDEILOST dislocated
ACDDEILPTU duplicated
ACDDEILTTW wildcatted
ACDDEINNSS candidness
ACDDEINSTY syndicated
ACDDEIORST dedicators
ACDDEIORTY dedicatory
ACDDEIPSTU cuspidated
ACDDEIRRSS discarders
ACDDEIRSTT distracted
ACDDEKLLNO landlocked
ACDDEKLORS dreadlocks
ACDDELNNOO colonnaded
ACDDELNOOW candlewood
ACDDENNRUY redundancy
ACDDEOOPSU decapodous
ACDDFHIORU chaudfroid
ACDDGHILNR grandchild
ACDDGIINRS discarding
ACDDGIKNOP paddocking
ACDDHHNSSU dachshunds
ACDDIINOST addictions
ACDDIMORSW caddisworm
ACDDINORST discordant
ACDEEEEHHS headcheese
ACDEEEELRT decelerate
ACDEEEEPRS predecease
ACDEEEFLNR freelanced
ACDEEEFMNT defacement
ACDEEEGILS delegacies
ACDEEEGNRY degeneracy
ACDEEEHIPS headpieces
ACDEEEHLTT decathlete
ACDEEEHNRS adherences
ACDEEEHRRS researched
ACDEEEIPRT depreciate
ACDEEEKNPP kneecapped
ACDEEELNPR precleaned
ACDEEELNRT crenelated
ACDEEELNTU enucleated
ACDEEELSTT telecasted
ACDEEEMRST decameters
decametres
ACDEEENNTT antecedent
ACDEEENRTV advertence
ACDEEEORRT redecorate
ACDEEEPRST deprecates
ACDEEERRST desecrater
ACDEEERSST desecrates
ACDEEERSTU reeducates
ACDEEFFLTY affectedly
ACDEEFFNTU unaffected
ACDEEFGINT defecating
ACDEEFIIRR Fredericia
ACDEEFINOT defecation
ACDEEFINRT interfaced
ACDEEFIRSS fricasseed
ACDEEFKRST afterdecks
ACDEEFLNOR confederal
ACDEEFNSTU fecundates
ACDEEFORST defecators
forecasted
ACDEEFRRSU resurfaced
ACDEEGHLLN challenged
ACDEEGHNNO hendecagon
ACDEEGIIMN mediagenic
ACDEEGIINT diagenetic
ACDEEGIKLR girdlecake
ACDEEGILOS geodesical
ACDEEGINNR grandniece
ACDEEGINNT anteceding
ACDEEGINOP paedogenic
ACDEEGINRR adrenergic
ACDEEGINRS decreasing
ACDEEGINRT centigrade
ACDEEGNORU encouraged
ACDEEHHLLT hatchelled
ACDEEHILMS alchemised
ACDEEHILMZ alchemized
ACDEEHILNR chandelier
ACDEEHIMNS mechanised
ACDEEHIMNZ mechanized
ACDEEHIMRS Archimedes
ACDEEHINOT endothecia
theodicean
ACDEEHIRST tracheides
ACDEEHKLLS shellacked
ACDEEHLLNN channelled
ACDEEHLLNS chandelles
ACDEEHLLST satchelled
ACDEEHLNRT Anderlecht
ACDEEHMNRT merchanted
ACDEEHMNTT detachment
ACDEEHNOPR chaperoned
ACDEEHOPPR copperhead
ACDEEHOPRR reproached
ACDEEHORRV overarched
ACDEEHORTU outreached
ACDEEHPRST despatcher
ACDEEHPSST despatches
ACDEEIILMS decimalise
ACDEEIILMZ decimalize
ACDEEIILNT indelicate
ACDEEIILTT dietetical
ACDEEIIMRT acidimeter
ACDEEIIMTV medicative

ACDEEIINST teniacides
ACDEEIINSV deviancies
ACDEEIJSTV adjectives
ACDEEILLOS delocalise
ACDEEILLOZ delocalize
ACDEEILLPR callipered
ACDEEILLPS specialled
ACDEEILLRS escadrille
ACDEEILLTV vellicated
ACDEEILLTY delicately
ACDEEILMPR premedical
ACDEEILMRS declaimers
ACDEEILMRV decemviral
ACDEEILNNS celandines
decennials
ACDEEILNPP appendicle
ACDEEILNRT credential
interlaced
ACDEEILOSV devocalise
ACDEEILOVZ devocalize
ACDEEILPPY pipeclayed
ACDEEILPRT replicated
ACDEEILPTU pediculate
ACDEEILPTX explicated
ACDEEILRST cartelised
decaliters
decalitres
ACDEEILRTZ cartelized
ACDEEILSTU elucidates
ACDEEILSTY acetylides
ACDEEIMMNT medicament
ACDEEIMNOS macedoines
ACDEEIMNOU eudaemonic
ACDEEIMNPS impedances
ACDEEIMORT acidometer
ACDEEIMPRT imprecated
mercaptide
ACDEEIMRSS semisacred
ACDEEIMRST miscreated
ACDEEIMRTT metricated
ACDEEIMSTU miseducate
ACDEEINNNT intendance
ACDEEINNTU denunciate
enunciated
ACDEEINOPR percoidean
ACDEEINORS deaconries
ACDEEINPPS appendices
ACDEEINPTT pectinated
ACDEEINRTT interacted
ACDEEINSST desistance
ACDEEIORTV decorative
ACDEEIORTX excoriated
ACDEEIOTTX detoxicate
ACDEEIPRST pederastic
predicates
ACDEEIPRTT crepitated
ACDEEIQRRU reacquired
ACDEEIRSTU cauterised
ACDEEIRTTV detractive
ACDEEIRTTX extricated
ACDEEIRTUZ cauterized
ACDEEITTUX exactitude

ACDEELLMSU muscadelle
ACDEELLNPS spancelled
ACDEELLORV overcalled
ACDEELLOST decollates
ACDEELLOTT dolcelatte
ACDEELMORT ectodermal
ACDEELMORU leucoderma
ACDEELNOST adolescent
ACDEELNRTU crenulated
ACDEELOPRT percolated
ACDEELORRT correlated
ACDEELORSS casseroled
ACDEELORSW lowercased
ACDEELORTU edulcorate
ACDEELPRSY clepsydrae
ACDEELPSTU speculated
ACDEELPTUX exculpated
ACDEELSSTY decastyles
ACDEEMMNOR commandeer
ACDEEMMNPT decampment
ACDEEMNOTY adenectomy
ACDEEMRRTU mercurated
ACDEENNOST condensate
ACDEENNOTV covenanted
ACDEENNRSU sunderance
ACDEENNSST ascendents
ACDEENOPRR ropedancer
ACDEENRSSS sacredness
ACDEENRSST descanters
ACDEENRSSU ascendeurs
ACDEENRSTT transected
ACDEENRSTY daycentres
ACDEENRTTU detruncate
ACDEENRTVY advertency
ACDEEOOPRT cooperated
ACDEEOPRRT deprecator
procreated
ACDEEOPRRY copyreader
ACDEEOPRSS Pescadores
ACDEEOPRSU predaceous
ACDEEORRST desecrator
ACDEEORRTT retroacted
ACDEEPPRSU uppercased
ACDEEPRRTU recaptured
ACDEERSSTU reductases
ACDEESSSTU decussates
ACDEFFFLRU carfuffled
ACDEFFHINO chiffonade
ACDEFFIIOT officiated
ACDEFFIKRT trafficked
ACDEFFILRT fieldcraft
ACDEFFISST disaffects
ACDEFFLORS scaffolder
ACDEFFMORS cofferdams
ACDEFFOSTU suffocated
ACDEFGHILT lightfaced
ACDEFGLLNO golden calf
ACDEFHILNS candlefish
ACDEFHINRS archfiends
franchised
ACDEFHLRSS feldschars
ACDEFHOSUV vouchsafed

ACDEFIIINT nidificate
ACDEFIIIRS acidifiers
ACDEFIILMS facsimiled
ACDEFIILOT foeticidal
ACDEFIILSS classified
ACDEFIINPU unpacified
ACDEFIINST sanctified
ACDEFIIRRT fratricide
ACDEFIISST satisficed
ACDEFIJKKN jackknifed
ACDEFIKRTU fruitcaked
ACDEFILLOS coalfields
ACDEFILSSY declassify
ACDEFIMORT formicated
ACDEFINNOT confidante
ACDEFINORS fricandoes
ACDEFINORT fornicated
fractioned
ACDEFINSTU infuscated
ACDEFIORST factorised
ACDEFIORTZ factorized
ACDEFLNORS landforces
ACDEFLORST Castleford
ACDEFLTTUU fluctuated
ACDEFNORTU fecundator
ACDEGGIOPS pedagogics
ACDEGHHIJK highjacked
ACDEGHIRRS discharger
ACDEGHIRSS discharges
ACDEGHLLOR gralloched
ACDEGHOSTW dogwatches
ACDEGHRRSU surcharged
ACDEGIILLS gallicised
ACDEGIILLZ gallicized
ACDEGIILMN declaiming
ACDEGIILMR germicidal
ACDEGIILNS anglicised
ACDEGIILNZ anglicized
ACDEGIIMNT decimating
medicating
ACDEGIINOR radiogenic
ACDEGIINOU audiogenic
ACDEGILLOT colligated
ACDEGILNSS declassing
ACDEGILNTU cingulated
ACDEGILOOP logopaedic
ACDEGILOOS logaoedics
ACDEGIMMRS scrimmaged
ACDEGIMNOY geodynamic
ACDEGINNOR androgenic
ACDEGINORR corrigenda
ACDEGINORT decorating
ACDEGINRTT detracting
ACDEGIORSU discourage
ACDEGIRRSS disgracers
ACDEGIRRST cartridges
ACDEGJNOTU conjugated
ACDEGLNNRU granduncle
ACDEGLNORS cradlesong
ACDEGLNORU clangoured
ACDEGMMRSU scrummaged
ACDEGNNOOT contangoed

ACDEGNNOSU undecagons
ACDEGORRTU corrugated
ACDEHHIKST thickheads
ACDEHHILRT Leichhardt
ACDEHHLMOO Chol Hamoed
ACDEHHORSX hexachords
ACDEHIIINR enchiridia
ACDEHIILLO helicoidal
ACDEHIILOP acidophile
ACDEHIIMRT diathermic
ACDEHIIORR diarrhoeic
ACDEHILMOT methodical
ACDEHILMRS childermas
ACDEHIMMST mismatched
ACDEHIMNOP championed
ACDEHIMORT dichromate
ACDEHINNRS hindrances
ACDEHINNST disenchant
ACDEHINOPS deaconship
ACDEHINORT achondrite
ACDEHINRSZ scherzandi
ACDEHINSSW sandwiches
ACDEHIPRST dispatcher
ACDEHIPSST cadetships
dispatches
ACDEHIRTTW ditchwater
ACDEHKMPSU chempaduks
ACDEHKOSST headstocks
ACDEHLNOST decathlons
ACDEHLNOSY anchylosed
ACDEHLOOPP cephalopod
ACDEHMNORR orchardmen
ACDEHMOSTU moustached
ACDEHMOTTU outmatched
ACDEHMPRSY pachyderms
ACDEHNNORT Chardonnet
ACDEHNOORT octahedron
ACDEHNOPRS cardphones
phonecards
ACDEHNORSZ scherzando
ACDEHOOPST chaetopods
ACDEHOORTU coauthored
ACDEHORRSW wordsearch
ACDEHORRTT tetrachord
ACDEHORSSS crossheads
ACDEIIILST idealistic
italicised
ACDEIIILTZ italicized
ACDEIIINST dieticians
ACDEIIINTV indicative
ACDEIIJTUV judicative
ACDEIILLOT idiolectal
ACDEIILMMT dilemmatic
ACDEIILMNS adminicles
medicinals
ACDEIILMPT implicated
ACDEIILMRS disclaimer
ACDEIILMRV vermicidal
ACDEIILNNT incidental
ACDEIILNOS decisional
ACDEIILNOT Diocletian
ACDEIILNSX indexicals
ACDEIILOPR periodical
ACDEIILOPS episodical
ACDEIILOSS socialised
ACDEIILOSZ socialized
ACDEIILPST pesticidal
septicidal
ACDEIILRSV larvicides
ACDEIIMNOT decimation
medication
ACDEIIMNRT criminated
ACDEIIMPRU epicardium
ACDEIIMRRS miscarried
ACDEIIMRST matricides
ACDEIIMRTX taxidermic
ACDEIIMRTY acidimetry
ACDEIINNRY incendiary
ACDEIINOSS sciaenoids
ACDEIINOSY isocyanide
ACDEIINSTV vindicates
ACDEIINTTT nictitated
ACDEIIORSU iridaceous
ACDEIIOSST dissociate
ACDEIIPRRS parricides
ACDEIIPRST patricides
pediatrics
ACDEIIPRTY peracidity
ACDEIJNTUV adjunctive
ACDEIJRTUU judicature
ACDEIKRSST sidetracks
ACDEILLMOT collimated
ACDEILLORR cordillera
ACDEILLOST Old Castile
oscillated
ACDEILLTUV victualled
ACDEILMNNO nonmedical
ACDEILMNOP complained
ACDEILMNTU culminated
ACDEILMOPR proclaimed
ACDEILNNOR endocrinal
ACDEILNNPS candlepins
ACDEILNOSV volcanised
ACDEILNOTU inoculated
ACDEILNOVZ volcanized
ACDEILNPSS placidness
ACDEILNPTU inculpated
ACDEILNSUV vulcanised
ACDEILNUVZ vulcanized
ACDEILOPST despotical
ACDEILORTU elucidator
ACDEILOSST dislocates
ACDEILOSUY edaciously
ACDEILOTTU colatitude
ACDEILPRSS displacers
ACDEILPSSU capsulised
ACDEILPSTU duplicates
ACDEILPSUZ capsulized
ACDEILRSSS laserdiscs
ACDEILRTTW wildcatter
ACDEILTTUV cultivated
ACDEIMMORT dermatomic
ACDEIMNNOP pandemonic
ACDEIMNNOT demicanton
ACDEIMNNST mendicants
ACDEIMNORU androecium
ACDEIMNOSU mendacious
ACDEIMNSSU muscadines
ACDEIMOPRR madreporic
ACDEIMORST decimators
ACDEIMORVW microwaved
ACDEIMRTTU micturated
ACDEINNNTY intendancy
ACDEINNORS ordinances
ACDEINNOSS dissonance
ACDEINNOST sanctioned
ACDEINNRSS rancidness
ACDEINOORT carotenoid
coordinate
decoration
ACDEINOPRS scorpaenid
ACDEINORRW cordwainer
ACDEINORST narcotised
redactions
ACDEINORTT detraction
ACDEINORTZ narcotized
ACDEINOSTT anecdotist
ACDEINOSTU educations
ACDEINOSTV advections
ACDEINOSTW wainscoted
ACDEINOTTX detoxicant
ACDEINPRST discrepant
predicants
ACDEINRSST discanters
ACDEINRTUV incurvated
ACDEINSSTY syndicates
ACDEINSTTU sanctitude
ACDEIOOPRS radioscope
ACDEIOPRRT predicator
ACDEIOPRSU predacious
ACDEIOPRTT tetrapodic
ACDEIOPSSU spadiceous
ACDEIOPSTY adipocytes
ACDEIORSST ostracised
ACDEIORSTZ ostracized
ACDEIPQRSU quadriceps
ACDEIQRSTU quadrisect
ACDEIRRSTT distracter
ACDEIRSSTT dictatress
ACDEIRSSTU crassitude
ACDEIRSTTU rusticated
ACDEISSSTY ecdysiasts
ACDEKKMOPR pockmarked
ACDEKORSTY rocksteady
ACDELLOORT decollator
ACDELMNOOR coromandel
ACDELMNOTU columnated
documental
ACDELMOPRR palmcorder
ACDELMOPRS placoderms
ACDELMORST Coldstream
ACDELNNOOS colonnades
ACDELNNOOY Conan Doyle
ACDELNNSTU candlenuts
ACDELNOORS canoodlers
ACDELNOORT decolorant

ACDELNOOSW lancewoods
ACDELNOOTY acotyledon
ACDELNPRUU peduncular
ACDELNRSSU underclass
ACDELOPRRU procedural
ACDELORTYY D'Oyly Carte
ACDELOSSTU outclassed
ACDELPRSSY clepsydras
ACDEMMMNOS commendams
ACDEMMNOOS commandoes
ACDEMMNORS commanders
ACDEMMOTTU commutated
ACDEMNOPRS companders
ACDEMNORTU mucronated
ACDEMOOPRR compradore
ACDEMOORST motorcades
ACDEMOPRSU dampcourse
ACDENNNOOR ordonnance
ACDENNNOOS nanosecond
ACDENNRSST transcends
ACDENOOOSW canoewoods
ACDENOPPSW snowcapped
ACDENOPSTY syncopated
ACDENORSTT contrasted
ACDENORSTU undercoats
ACDENPSUYY Puy de Sancy
ACDENPTTUU punctuated
ACDENRRRTU redcurrant
ACDENRRSTU transducer
undercarts
ACDEOORRST decorators
ACDEOORRVW woodcarver
ACDEOORSTT doctorates
ACDEOPPRSU pseudocarp
ACDEOPRRTT protracted
ACDEOPRSUU drupaceous
ACDEORRSTT detractors
ACDEORRTTY detractory
ACDFGIIINY acidifying
ACDFGIILNU fungicidal
ACDFIILLUY fiducially
ACDFIMNNOR confirmand
ACDFINNOST confidants
ACDFLNOSSY candyfloss
ACDFNSTTUY candytufts
ACDFORRSTW swordcraft
ACDGGIINRS disgracing
ACDGHIINNS Ding an sich
ACDGIIIMNR gramicidin
ACDGIIINNT indicating
ACDGIIJNNU jaundicing
ACDGIILNPS displacing
ACDGIINNST discanting
distancing
ACDGIINOST diagnostic
ACDGIIRSST digastrics
ACDGIKLNOP padlocking
ACDGIKNOST stockading
ACDGILLMOO modal logic
ACDGILLOSU glucosidal
ACDGILNNOO canoodling
ACDGILNOOT odontalgic
ACDGILOORY cardiology
ACDGIMMNNO commanding
ACDGINNOTU outdancing
ACDGLOTYYZ zygodactyl
ACDHIIIIRR Richard III
ACDHIIIOPT idiopathic
ACDHIINORT anhidrotic
ACDHILMNOY hymnodical
ACDHILMOOR harmolodic
ACDHILNOOP chilopodan
ACDHILOORT trochoidal
ACDHILRSSY chrysalids
ACDHILRSUY hydraulics
ACDHIMOORT chromatoid
ACDHIMORST chromatids
ACDHINOOOX chionodoxa
ACDHINORRS Richardson
ACDHIORTTY trachytoid
ACDHIRSTWY switchyard
ACDHLLLOPY cladophyll
phylloclad
ACDHLOORRU urochordal
ACDHLOORRY hydrocoral
ACDHMNOORS chondromas
ACDHMNORYY hydromancy
ACDHOOPPSS scaphopods
ACDHORSTWW watchwords
ACDIIILSUU Claudius II
ACDIIIMMRU miracidium
ACDIIIMNST diactinism
ACDIIINNOT indication
ACDIIJLLUY judicially
ACDIILLSUY suicidally
ACDIILMOPT diplomatic
ACDIILOPRT dioptrical
ACDIILORST clostridia
ACDIILORTY cordiality
radiolytic
ACDIILORUX uxoricidal
ACDIILPRSU discipular
ACDIIMNORT antidromic
ACDIIMNOST monadistic
ACDIIMNOSY isodynamic
ACDIIMNOTU coatimundi
ACDIIMNSTY dynamistic
ACDIIMRSTY mydriatics
ACDIINNORY inordinacy
ACDIINOORT carotinoid
ACDIINORST indicators
ACDIINORTV vindicator
ACDIINORTY dictionary
indicatory
ACDIINOSTT dictations
ACDIINRTUY iracundity
ACDIIOORTX radiotoxic
ACDIIOSSSU Dio Cassius
ACDIJNNOTU adjunction
ACDIJORSTU judicators
ACDIJORTUX coadjutrix
ACDIJORTUY judicatory
ACDIKKNSST kickstands
ACDIKNQSSU quicksands
ACDIKRSSTY yardsticks
ACDILLMNOU calmodulin
ACDILLNOOY conoidally
ACDILLOOTY cotyloidal
ACDILMOSTU comatulids
ACDILNOSTU Saint-Cloud
ACDILOPRTU duplicator
ACDILPSSTY dysplastic
ACDIMMORUY myocardium
ACDIMNNOOT codominant
ACDIMOORSU mordacious
ACDINNOSSY dissonancy
ACDINOOPST actinopods
ACDINOSSTU custodians
ACDINPSSSU scindapsus
ACDINSSSTU discussant
ACDIOOPRSY radioscopy
ACDJOORSTU coadjutors
ACDKLORSTU truckloads
ACDKMNNOOS monadnocks
ACDKNORSTU soundtrack
ACDKORSSTY stockyards
ACDLLOOPSW codswallop
ACDLLOPTYY polydactyl
ACDLMNOOSY condylomas
ACDLMNOPSW clampdowns
ACDLNSSTYY syndactyls
ACDMMNORSU communards
ACDMOOPRRS compradors
ACDNOORRST corrodants
ACDOORRSSS crossroads
ACDORRSTUY courtyards
ACEEEFFMNT effacement
ACEEEFFTTU effectuate
ACEEEFIPRT afterpiece
ACEEEFIRST cafetieres
ACEEEFLNRR freelancer
ACEEEFLNRS freelances
ACEEEFMNNT enfacement
ACEEEGHPRS repechages
ACEEEGILNN inelegance
ACEEEGILNS elegancies
ACEEEGILTX exegetical
ACEEEGNPRT percentage
ACEEEGNRRS screenager
ACEEEGNRRY regeneracy
ACEEEHIMRX hexaemeric
ACEEEHIRSV echeverias
ACEEEHLMOT hematocele
ACEEEHLPSW scapewheel
ACEEEHNPRS cheapeners
ACEEEHRRRS researcher
ACEEEHRRSS researches
ACEEEIMRRS creameries
ACEEEIPPRV apperceive
ACEEEIPRRV Peace River
ACEEEIRRST secretaire
ACEEEIRRTV recreative
ACEEEIRSTV eviscerate
ACEEEIRTVX execrative
ACEEEKNQSU queencakes
ACEEEKRRST racketeers

ACEEELLNRT crenellate
ACEEELMNNT enlacement
ACEEELNORT coelentera
ACEEELNPRV prevalence
ACEEELNRST crenelates
ACEEELNSTU enucleates
ACEEELORTT electorate
ACEEELPRVY everyplace
ACEEELRSSS creaseless
ACEEELRSTT telecaster
ACEEEMMNRT amercement
ACEEEMNNPR permanence
ACEEEMNNST encasement
ACEEEMNPRT temperance
ACEEEMNPST escapement
ACEEEMNRTT metacenter
metacentre
ACEEEMORTT acetometer
ACEEENNOTV covenantee
ACEEENNPRT penetrance
repentance
ACEEENNRRT reentrance
ACEEENNSTV evanescent
ACEEENPPST appetences
ACEEENPRSS esperances
ACEEENRSSV severances
ACEEEPRRTU recuperate
ACEEEPRSTT pacesetter
ACEEFFHRRS chafferers
ACEEFFHSUU chauffeuse
ACEEFFIMNY effeminacy
ACEEFFLSST affectless
ACEEFFNRSU sufferance
ACEEFHISSV cavefishes
ACEEFHLPRS parfleches
ACEEFHMRRS chamferers
ACEEFHNORT technofear
ACEEFHSSTT factsheets
ACEEFIILTT felicitate
ACEEFIIRST acetifiers
ACEEFILMNT maleficent
ACEEFILNSS facileness
ACEEFILORV overfacile
ACEEFILPRS fireplaces
ACEEFINRST interfaces
ACEEFIORTV vociferate
ACEEFIORTW cowfeteria
ACEEFIRRTV refractive
ACEEFIRSSS fricassees
ACEEFLLNTU flatulence
ACEEFLLORV cloverleaf
ACEEFLLPUY peacefully
ACEEFLNPUU unpeaceful
ACEEFLNSTV flavescent
ACEEFLORST forecastle
ACEEFLRTTU leafcutter
ACEEFORRST forecaster
ACEEFRRSSU resurfaces
ACEEGGILNO genealogic
ACEEGGNORT congregate
ACEEGHINNP cheapening
ACEEGHINRT reteaching
ACEEGHINST escheating
ACEEGHIRSU gaucheries
ACEEGHLLNR challenger
ACEEGHLLNS challenges
ACEEGHLNSS changeless
ACEEGHNNOP Copenhagen
ACEEGHNORV changeover
ACEEGHNRSX exchangers
ACEEGHNSSU gaucheness
ACEEGHORRV overcharge
ACEEGIILPP epipelagic
ACEEGILLNR allergenic
ACEEGILLOT collegiate
ACEEGILNNY inelegancy
ACEEGILNTU geniculate
ACEEGILSTU sluicegate
ACEEGIMNOS geomancies
ACEEGINNOS caseinogen
ACEEGINNPT pangenetic
ACEEGINNRT reenacting
ACEEGINNST tangencies
ACEEGINNSV evanescing
ACEEGINRRT recreating
ACEEGINRSV grievances
ACEEGINRTX execrating
ACEEGIOPRS geocarpies
ACEEGIORST categories
categorise
ACEEGIORTZ categorize
ACEEGIOTTX excogitate
ACEEGIRRSV caregivers
ACEEGIRSTT cigarettes
ACEEGKRSWY greywackes
ACEEGLLOSU colleagues
ACEEGLMNOR camerlengo
ACEEGLNORS congealers
ACEEGLNRST rectangles
ACEEGMMOSU gemmaceous
ACEEGMNORS geomancers
ACEEGMOTTY gametocyte
ACEEGNNORV governance
ACEEGNNPRU repugnance
ACEEGNNSWY newsagency
ACEEGNORRU encourager
ACEEGNORSU encourages
ACEEGNRSSV scavengers
ACEEGNRSVY scavengery
ACEEGOOPRS cooperages
ACEEHHILNW chainwheel
ACEEHHILRW wheelchair
ACEEHHIRRS heresiarch
ACEEHHIRST hatcheries
thearchies
ACEEHHLLRT hatcheller
ACEEHHLMNT Cheltenham
ACEEHHMMOR hemachrome
ACEEHHOPTY hypothecae
ACEEHHPTTU Heptateuch
ACEEHHRRTY heterarchy
ACEEHIINRT Catherine I
ACEEHIIPRS hairpieces
ACEEHIIPRT perithecia
ACEEHILMNN manchineel
ACEEHILMRT hermetical
ACEEHILMSS alchemises
ACEEHILMSZ alchemizes
ACEEHILNNP encephalin
ACEEHILNNS channelise
ACEEHILNNZ channelize
ACEEHILNST anthelices
ACEEHILPTT telepathic
ACEEHILRSV chevaliers
ACEEHILSTT esthetical
ACEEHIMNPZ chimpanzee
ACEEHIMNRS mechaniser
ACEEHIMNRZ mechanizer
ACEEHIMNSS mechanises
ACEEHIMNSZ mechanizes
ACEEHIMPRS impeachers
ACEEHIMPRY hyperaemic
ACEEHIMPTT empathetic
ACEEHIMRTX hexametric
ACEEHIMSST misteaches
schematise
ACEEHIMSTT metaethics
meta-ethics
ACEEHIMSTZ schematize
ACEEHIMTTT metathetic
ACEEHINNPT phenacetin
ACEEHINPSS peachiness
ACEEHINRRS rancheries
ACEEHINSTT anesthetic
ACEEHIORRT charioteer
ACEEHIPRST preachiest
ACEEHIRSSU eucharises
ACEEHISSTT aesthetics
ACEEHKLLRS shellacker
ACEEHKLNRT halterneck
ACEEHLLLOR La Rochelle
ACEEHLLNNR channeller
ACEEHLLNOP cellophane
ACEEHLMNOS chameleons
ACEEHLMOOS haemocoels
ACEEHLMSTU Telemachus
ACEEHLNNOP encephalon
ACEEHLNPRU leprechaun
ACEEHLNPTT planchette
ACEEHLNPTY phlyctenae
ACEEHLNSSS seneschals
ACEEHLOPTY polychaete
ACEEHLRSTW cartwheels
ACEEHLSSST scatheless
ACEEHMMRST machmeters
ACEEHMMRSU meerschaum
ACEEHMNNST encashment
ACEEHMNOOR anemochore
ACEEHMNPRT preachment
ACEEHMNRST manchester
ACEEHMORTT tachometer
ACEEHMOSTY haemocytes
ACEEHMRTTY tachymeter
ACEEHNNRST enchanters
ACEEHNOPRS chaperones
ACEEHNORTT anchorette

ACEEHNPTTU Pentateuch
ACEEHNRSST chasteners
ACEEHNRSTT entrechats
ACEEHNSSST chasteness
ACEEHNSSTU chanteuses
ACEEHOPRRR reproacher
ACEEHOPRRS archespore
reproaches
ACEEHORRSS racehorses
ACEEHORRSV overarches
ACEEHORSTU outreaches
ACEEHPPRSY hyperspace
ACEEHPRRSU repurchase
ACEEHPRSTY archetypes
ACEEHPRTUY hyperacute
ACEEHRRRST charterers
recharters
ACEEHRRSTT chatterers
ACEEHRRSTU chartreuse
ACEEIILLSX lexicalise
ACEEIILLXZ lexicalize
ACEEIILMRT eremitical
ACEEIILNTT licentiate
ACEEIILPSS specialise
ACEEIILPST tailpieces
ACEEIILPSZ specialize
ACEEIILSST elasticise
ACEEIILSTZ elasticize
ACEEIIMNPT impatience
ACEEIIMNTT antiemetic
ACEEIIMPST episematic
septicemia
ACEEIINNRT creatinine
incinerate
ACEEIIRSTV veracities
ACEEIIRTTV recitative
ACEEIITTVX excitative
ACEEIJLORS cajoleries
ACEEIJLRTT trajectile
ACEEIKKNRS knackeries
ACEEIKLNRT trancelike
ACEEIKLRRT craterlike
ACEEIKNRSS creakiness
ACEEIKQRSU quackeries
ACEEILLMTY emetically
ACEEILLNNT cellentani
ACEEILLNST cleanliest
ACEEILLPRX prelexical
ACEEILLPSY especially
ACEEILLSTV vellicates
ACEEILMNOR ceremonial
ACEEILMNOT colemanite
ACEEILMNOU leucomaine
ACEEILMNRT mercantile
ACEEILMNST centesimal
lemniscate
ACEEILMOSU meliaceous
ACEEILMRRS reclaimers
ACEEILMRST carmelites
ACEEILMRSX exclaimers
ACEEILMSST timescales
ACEEILMSTT telematics

ACEEILNNNT centennial
ACEEILNOPU leucopenia
ACEEILNOTV evectional
ACEEILNPRT epicentral
ACEEILNRST centralise
interlaces
linecaster
ACEEILNRTV cantilever
ACEEILNRTY increately
ACEEILNRTZ centralize
ACEEILNSTW New Castile
ACEEILPRST replicates
ACEEILPSTX explicates
ACEEILPSXY epicalyxes
ACEEILRRTT retractile
ACEEILRSST cartelises
ACEEILRSSU secularise
ACEEILRSTZ cartelizes
ACEEILRSUZ secularize
ACEEILRTTU reticulate
ACEEILRTUV ulcerative
ACEEILRTVY creatively
reactively
ACEEILSTUV vesiculate
ACEEIMNNST incasement
ACEEIMNNWX New Mexican
ACEEIMNORT actinomere
ACEEIMNRSS creaminess
ACEEIMNRSV serviceman
ACEEIMNRTT remittance
ACEEIMORRT aerometric
ACEEIMPRST imprecates
spermaceti
ACEEIMRSST masseteric
miscreates
ACEEIMRSTT metricates
ACEEIMRSVW crimewaves
ACEEINNRST nectarines
transience
ACEEINNRTU renunciate
ACEEINNSTU enunciates
ACEEINORRT recreation
ACEEINORSU erinaceous
ACEEINORTU auctioneer
ACEEINORTX execration
ACEEINPPRT apprentice
ACEEINPRRT Carpentier
ACEEINPRST interspace
ACEEINPRSU epicureans
ACEEINRRSS increasers
ACEEINRSST ancestries
resistance
ACEEINRSTT intercaste
ACEEINRSTU centauries
ACEEINRTUV uncreative
unreactive
ACEEINRTVY inveteracy
ACEEINSSTV activeness
ACEEIOOPRS aeciospore
ACEEIOPPST episcopate
ACEEIOPSST caespitose
ACEEIOQTUV equivocate

ACEEIORSTX excoriates
ACEEIORTVV overactive
ACEEIPQRSU picaresque
ACEEIPRSTT crepitates
ACEEIQRRSU reacquires
ACEEIQRSTU requiescat
ACEEIRRSST careerists
ACEEIRRSTX creatrixes
ACEEIRRTTV retractive
ACEEIRSSTU cauterises
ACEEIRSTTX extricates
ACEEIRSTUZ cauterizes
ACEEIRTTUV eructative
ACEEIRTTVX extractive
ACEEJLMNOT cajolement
ACEEKLLOWY yellowcake
ACEEKLLRSS salesclerk
ACEEKNSSTT snackettes
ACEEKORRSW caseworker
ACEELLLMOU columellae
ACEELLMRRS marcellers
ACEELLNOTU nucleolate
ACEELLNPST pallescent
ACEELLORTT collarette
ACEELLRSSY carelessly
ACEELLSTTU scutellate
ACEELMNOTY melanocyte
ACEELMNPST placements
ACEELMOPRT clapometer
ACEELMORST latecomers
ACEELMORSY racemosely
ACEELMORTT lactometer
ACEELNNRSU cannelures
ACEELNOPST opalescent
ACEELNORST tolerances
ACEELNPRSY screenplay
ACEELNRRTY recreantly
ACEELNRTVY tervalency
ACEELNSSUW Wenceslaus
ACEELOPRST percolates
ACEELOPRTU operculate
ACEELORRST correlates
ACEELORSSS casseroles
ACEELORSSW lowercases
ACEELORSTT lectorates
ACEELPPRTU perceptual
ACEELPSSTU speculates
ACEELPSTUX exculpates
ACEELQRRSU lacquerers
ACEELQRRUU craquelure
ACEELRRSST craterless
ACEELRRSTT clatterers
ACEELRRTUY creaturely
ACEELRSSSU saucerless
ACEEMMNNPT encampment
ACEEMMNOTT commentate
ACEEMMORRS macromeres
ACEEMMORSU commeasure
ACEEMNNORR amen corner
ACEEMNNPRY permanency
ACEEMNNSTT enactments
ACEEMNOOPS anemoscope

ACEEMNOPST compensate
ACEEMNOPSW spacewomen
ACEEMNPRST escarpment
ACEEMOPRSS capsomeres
ACEEMORRSS sarcomeres
ACEEMORSTT octameters
ACEEMOSTUZ eczematous
ACEEMPRRSS scamperers
ACEEMRRSTU mercurates
ACEENNNORS cannoneers
ACEENNOPRV provenance
ACEENNOPSU pennaceous
ACEENNORSS resonances
ACEENNORTV contravene
covenanter
ACEENNOSSS canonesses
ACEENNPRTU purtenance
ACEENNRSSV cravenness
ACEENNSSTU sustenance
ACEENOOSTU coetaneous
ACEENORSSS coarseness
ACEENORSTU nectareous
ACEENORSTX Xenocrates
ACEENPRRST carpenters
ACEENPRUVY purveyance
ACEENPSTTX expectants
ACEENRRSTU crenatures
ACEENRSSST ancestress
ACEENRSSTW newscaster
ACEENRSTTU utterances
ACEENSTTUX executants
ACEEOOPRST cooperates
ACEEOPRRST procreates
ACEEORRRST recreators
ACEEORRSTT rectorates
ACEEORRSTV overreacts
ACEEORRTXY execratory
ACEEORSTUY eucaryotes
ACEEOSSTTU testaceous
ACEEPPRSSU uppercases
ACEEPRRSTU recaptures
ACEEPRSTTY typecaster
ACEERRSSTT scatterers
streetcars
ACEERRSSTW watercress
ACEFFFLRSU carfuffles
ACEFFGHINR chaffering
ACEFFHRSUU chauffeurs
ACEFFIILTV afflictive
ACEFFIIOST officiates
ACEFFIKMRS maffickers
ACEFFIKRRT trafficker
ACEFFILOOV Oval Office
ACEFFINOST affections
ACEFFOSSTU suffocates
ACEFFOSTUU tuffaceous
ACEFGHIMNR chamfering
ACEFGIINTY acetifying
ACEFGINRRT refracting
ACEFGLLRUY gracefully
ACEFGLNORS gerfalcons
ACEFGLNRUU ungraceful

ACEFHHINSW hawfinches
ACEFHHIRRS archerfish
ACEFHIINST chieftains
ACEFHIINTT fianchetti
ACEFHIJKSS jackfishes
ACEFHILOSS coalfishes
ACEFHILPST felspathic
ACEFHILRTU ultrafiche
ACEFHINOTT fianchetto
ACEFHINRSS franchises
ACEFHIRSSW crawfishes
ACEFHIRSSY crayfishes
ACEFHIRSTT fratchiest
ACEFHKORST aftershock
ACEFHLLNOP chopfallen
ACEFHLOPRY hyperfocal
ACEFHORRTV hovercraft
ACEFHORSTU housecraft
ACEFHOSSUV vouchsafes
ACEFIIILST facilities
ACEFIILMSS facsimiles
ACEFIILPST spiflicate
ACEFIILRRS clarifiers
ACEFIILRSS classifier
ACEFIILRST laticifers
ACEFIILSSS classifies
ACEFIINNRS financiers
ACEFIINRST sanctifier
ACEFIINSST sanctifies
ACEFIIRRSS scarifiers
ACEFIIRRST artificers
ACEFIIRSST satisficer
ACEFIIRSTV fricatives
ACEFIISSST satisfices
ACEFIJKKNS jackknifes
ACEFIKRSTU fruitcakes
ACEFILLNOT flectional
ACEFILNTUU funiculate
ACEFILOOSU foliaceous
ACEFILORST fortalices
ACEFILRSSY reclassify
ACEFIMORST formicates
ACEFINORRT refraction
ACEFINORST fornicates
ACEFINORTV vociferant
ACEFINPRST faceprints
ACEFINRSST craftiness
ACEFINSTTV ventifacts
ACEFIORSST factorises
ACEFIORSTZ factorizes
ACEFIRRTTU trifurcate
ACEFIRSSTU first cause
ACEFKLNORS cornflakes
ACEFKRRSTU starfucker
ACEFLLNTUY flatulency
ACEFLNORRS conferrals
ACEFLPSTUU teacupfuls
ACEFLRSSUU saucerfuls
ACEFLSTTUU fluctuates
ACEFMNOORT canto fermo
ACEFNNOSST confessant
ACEFNOPRTT Pontefract

ACEFNRSSTT transfects
ACEFORRRST refractors
ACEFORRRSU carrefours
ACEFORRRTY refractory
ACEFRRSSTU surfcaster
ACEGGHILNN changeling
ACEGGHINNX exchanging
ACEGGHINRR recharging
ACEGGHIOPR geographic
ACEGGHLOOU cholagogue
ACEGGIINRZ graecizing
ACEGGILLOO geological
ACEGGILNNO congealing
ACEGGILRRS scragglier
ACEGGINNOO oceangoing
ACEGGINNSV scavenging
ACEGGINRSS cragginess
ACEGGIRSST scraggiest
ACEGGNNORT congregant
ACEGHHIJKR highjacker
ACEGHHILNT hatcheling
ACEGHHOPRT hectograph
ACEGHHOPRY echography
ACEGHIILMT megalithic
ACEGHIIMNP impeaching
ACEGHIINNN enchaining
ACEGHIINRS cashiering
ACEGHIINTU authigenic
ACEGHIIPPR epigraphic
ACEGHIKNNY hackneying
ACEGHILMPT phlegmatic
ACEGHILNNN channeling
ACEGHILNPR nephralgic
ACEGHILNTY cheatingly
ACEGHILPSY hypalgesic
ACEGHILRTU theurgical
ACEGHIMNNU machinegun
ACEGHIMNOP megaphonic
ACEGHIMNRT rematching
ACEGHINNNT enchanting
ACEGHINNST chastening
ACEGHINNTU unteaching
ACEGHINOPT pathogenic
ACEGHINRRT chartering
recharting
ACEGHINRSY gynarchies
ACEGHINRTT chattering
ACEGHIOOPS hagioscope
ACEGHIRSTW switchgear
ACEGHLOORY archeology
ACEGHMNOSS cheongsams
ACEGHMORST hectograms
ACEGHNORSU Schongauer
ACEGHOPRRY cerography
ACEGHOPSTY phagocytes
ACEGHORSSU choraguses
ACEGHRRRSU surcharger
ACEGHRRSSU surcharges
ACEGIILLSS gallicises
ACEGIILLST legalistic
ACEGIILLSZ gallicizes
ACEGIILMNR reclaiming

ACEGIILMNX exclaiming
ACEGIILMTY legitimacy
ACEGIILNNO lignocaine
ACEGIILNPR calipering
ACEGIILNSS anglicises
ACEGIILNSZ anglicizes
ACEGIILOST egoistical
ACEGIIMNRS racemising
ACEGIIMNRZ racemizing
ACEGIIMNTT magnetitic
ACEGIIMOST isogametic
ACEGIIMOTT Giacometti
ACEGIIMPTT pegmatitic
ACEGIINNRS increasing
ACEGIINORT iatrogenic
ACEGIINPST speciating
ACEGIINSTV vesicating
ACEGIIOTTV cogitative
ACEGIIPRST epigastric
ACEGIIRRST geriatrics
ACEGIJNRTT trajecting
ACEGIKKNNR knackering
ACEGIKLNNS slackening
ACEGIKLNRY creakingly
ACEGIKNPPR prepacking
ACEGIKNRST restacking
ACEGIKPRRS ragpickers
ACEGILLMNR marcelling
ACEGILLNOO enological
neological
ACEGILLNOS collegians
ACEGILLNPR parcelling
ACEGILLOOS oligoclase
ACEGILLOST colligates
ACEGILMNNY menacingly
ACEGILMNOR camerlingo
ACEGILNNOT congenital
ACEGILNNPS enclasping
spanceling
ACEGILNNTU nucleating
ACEGILNOPR pelargonic
ACEGILNOPS opalescing
ACEGILNORT relocating
ACEGILNOTU glauconite
ACEGILNPRY caperingly
ACEGILNPTU peculating
ACEGILNQRU lacquering
ACEGILNRSW clearwings
ACEGILNRTT clattering
ACEGILNRTU ulcerating
ACEGILNTXY exactingly
ACEGILOOPT apologetic
ACEGILRSTU graticules
ACEGIMMRRS scrimmager
ACEGIMMRSS scrimmages
ACEGIMNPRS scampering
ACEGIMNRST centigrams
ACEGIMOPRS megasporic
ACEGIMORST gasometric
ACEGINNNRT entrancing
ACEGINNORS coarsening
ignorances
ACEGINNRST transgenic
ACEGINOPRS saprogenic
ACEGINORTV overacting
ACEGINOSTU autogenics
ACEGINPRRS scarpering
ACEGINPRST precasting
ACEGINPRSY panegyrics
ACEGINPSTT spectating
ACEGINQRTU racqueting
ACEGINRRST terracings
ACEGINRRTT retracting
ACEGINRSSU surceasing
ACEGINRSSV crevassing
ACEGINRSTT scattering
ACEGINRTTU eructating
ACEGINRTTX extracting
ACEGIOSSTT geostatics
ACEGIRSSTT strategics
ACEGJNOSTU conjugates
ACEGKORSTU goatsucker
ACEGLMOSUU glumaceous
ACEGLNOOOY oceanology
ACEGLOOPRT colportage
ACEGLOOPSY escapology
ACEGLOOTUY autecology
ACEGMMRRSU scrummager
ACEGMMRSSU scrummages
ACEGNNOOST contangoes
ACEGNNOSTT cotangents
ACEGNNPRUY repugnancy
ACEGNOORSU acrogenous
ACEGNOORTY octogenary
ACEGNRSSUY assurgency
ACEGNRSTTU scattergun
ACEGOORSUU courageous
ACEGOPRRSU supercargo
ACEGORRSTU corrugates
ACEHHILOPT Achitophel
ACEHHILORS holarchies
ACEHHILPSS chelaships
ACEHHINOPT theophanic
ACEHHIOPTT theopathic
ACEHHIPSTT heptastich
ACEHHISSTX hexastichs
ACEHHLSSTT thatchless
ACEHHMNSTT hatchments
ACEHHNSTTU nuthatches
ACEHHOOSTT toothaches
ACEHIIILRS Charles III
ACEHIILLPT philatelic
ACEHIILMNS Sanmicheli
ACEHIILMOS isocheimal
ACEHIILMPT mephitical
ACEHIILMRT hermitical
ACEHIILNOP neophiliac
ACEHIILRSV Charles VII
chivalries
ACEHIILRSX Charles XII
ACEHIILSTT theistical
ACEHIILTTY ethicality
ACEHIIMNST hematinics
ACEHIIMRTT arithmetic
ACEHIINOTV inchoative
ACEHIINTTT antithetic
ACEHIIPRRT peritricha
ACEHIIRRST triarchies
ACEHIIRSTT tracheitis
ACEHIKLNSS chalkiness
ACEHIKLRST starchlike
ACEHIKMNSY hackneyism
ACEHIKMNTW Twickenham
ACEHIKMRRS reichsmark
ACEHIKNOPR Archipenko
ACEHIKORST artichokes
ACEHILLNTY ethnically
ACEHILLOOS alcoholise
ACEHILLOOZ alcoholize
ACEHILLORY heroically
ACEHILLOSU hellacious
ACEHILLPRY Caerphilly
ACEHILLTTY thetically
ACEHILMMOS chamomiles
ACEHILMMST mischmetal
ACEHILMNNS Schliemann
ACEHILMNOR chloramine
ACEHILMOOP phocomelia
ACEHILMOTY haemolytic
ACEHILMSST alchemists
ACEHILNNOS chelonians
ACEHILNNOT nonethical
ACEHILNORT chlorinate
ACEHILNOST chelations
ACEHILNOTY inchoately
ACEHILNSTY thylacines
ACEHILOORZ coleorhiza
ACEHILOPRT arctophile
ACEHILOPST telophasic
ACEHILORRT rhetorical
ACEHILPRSS clipshears
ACEHILRSTU Heraclitus
ACEHILRSTY hysterical
ACEHILRSVX Charles XIV
ACEHIMMNSS mechanisms
ACEHIMMSST mismatches
schematism
ACEHIMNNOR enharmonic
ACEHIMNNOY hemocyanin
ACEHIMNORS monarchies
nomarchies
ACEHIMNORW chairwomen
ACEHIMNPTU unemphatic
ACEHIMNRSV revanchism
ACEHIMNSST mechanists
ACEHIMNSSU Ssu-ma Ch'ien
ACEHIMNSTY myasthenic
ACEHIMOPRS semaphoric
ACEHIMOPRT amphoteric
metaphoric
ACEHIMOPTU apothecium
ACEHIMORTT hematocrit
ACEHIMOSTT hemostatic
ACEHIMOSTX chemotaxis
ACEHIMPSTY metaphysic
ACEHIMRSTT Maestricht

ACEHIMRSTU rheumatics
ACEHINOPST asthenopic
ACEHINORRT chitarrone
ACEHINORST anchorites
antechoirs
ACEHINORSX chronaxies
ACEHINORTV chevrotain
ACEHINPSST patchiness
ACEHINPSTT pentastich
ACEHINPSTU epicanthus
ACEHINRRSU hurricanes
ACEHINRSSY synarchies
ACEHINRSTU raunchiest
ACEHINRSTV revanchist
ACEHINSSTT chattiness
snatchiest
ACEHIOPRST toparchies
ACEHIOPRSX echopraxis
ACEHIOPSTY isopachyte
ACEHIORSTT rheostatic
ACEHIORSTV tovariches
ACEHIPPSSS spaceships
ACEHIPRRST archpriest
ACEHIPRSSU haruspices
ACEHIPRSTU pasticheur
ACEHIPRSUY eucryphias
ACEHIPSTTU chupatties
ACEHIRRRST trierarchs
ACEHIRRRTY trierarchy
ACEHIRSSST chastisers
ACEHIRSSTT starchiest
ACEHIRSTTT tetrastich
ACEHIRSTTV tsarevitch
ACEHIRTTWW water witch
ACEHJKNNOY johnnycake
ACEHJRRSUW jawcrusher
ACEHKLMMOR hammerlock
ACEHKLNOST chalkstone
Shackleton
ACEHKMORSY chromakeys
ACEHKOPRSS packhorses
ACEHKORSST shortcakes
ACEHLLLMSS clamshells
ACEHLLLORS chlorellas
ACEHLLMNOY melancholy
ACEHLLPRSU sepulchral
ACEHLMOOST schoolmate
ACEHLMORSY lachrymose
ACEHLMOSST moschatels
ACEHLNORST charleston
ACEHLNOSSY anchyloses
ACEHLOORST orthoclase
ACEHLOPSSW showplaces
ACEHLOPSTT potlatches
ACEHLOPXYY oxycephaly
ACEHLORRST orchestral
trochlears
ACEHLORSSU housecarls
ACEHLORSTT charlottes
ACEHLOSTTY catholytes
ACEHLPRTYY phylactery
ACEHMMNOOR chromonema

ACEHMNOPRS Macpherson
ACEHMNORST metarchons
ACEHMNOSTY chemonasty
ACEHMNOTUV avouchment
ACEHMNPRST parchments
ACEHMNPRTY parchmenty
ACEHMNSTTU humectants
ACEHMOORUX auxochrome
ACEHMORRTU routemarch
ACEHMORSST stomachers
ACEHMORTTY tachometry
ACEHMOSSTT chemostats
ACEHMOSSTU moustaches
ACEHMOSTTU outmatches
ACEHMRTTYY tachymetry
ACEHNOPTYY cyanophyte
ACEHNORRTT trochanter
ACEHNORTTT Chatterton
ACEHNOSSTT stonechats
ACEHNPPRSS schnappers
ACEHNRSSTU staunchers
ACEHNRSSUZ schnauzers
ACEHNSSTTU staunchest
ACEHOOPPRR carpophore
ACEHOOPSTU tophaceous
ACEHOOSSTU housecoats
ACEHOPPRRS hoppercars
ACEHOPPRTU touchpaper
ACEHOPRRSS sharecrops
ACEHOPRSUY coryphaeus
ACEHOPSSST chassepots
ACEHORRSST carthorses
orchestras
ACEHORRSYZ Crazy Horse
ACEHORSTTU rotachutes
ACEHORTTWW watchtower
ACEHPRRSSU purchasers
ACEIIIKNST ekistician
ACEIIILLNP penicillia
ACEIIILSST italicises
ACEIIILSTZ italicizes
ACEIIIMNST intimacies
ACEIIISTTV activities
ACEIIISTVV vivacities
ACEIIJLSTU jesuitical
ACEIIKMNST kinematics
ACEIIKMRWZ Markiewicz
ACEIIKRSTT rickettsia
ACEIILLLPT elliptical
ACEIILLNPR periclinal
ACEIILLNRY irenically
ACEIILLOST localities
ACEIILLOSU liliaceous
ACEIILLRTY illiteracy
ACEIILLTXY lexicality
ACEIILMMST melismatic
ACEIILMNST melanistic
ACEIILMOPT epitomical
ACEIILMPSS specialism
ACEIILMPST implicates
ACEIILMRST salimetric
ACEIILNNST anticlines

ACEIILNOPT capitoline
ACEIILNOTT actinolite
ACEIILNPST plasticine
ACEIILNTVY inactively
ACEIILORSS socialiser
ACEIILORSZ socializer
ACEIILOSSS socialises
ACEIILOSST socialites
ACEIILOSSZ socializes
ACEIILOSTU tiliaceous
ACEIILOSTV vocalities
ACEIILPPRT participle
ACEIILPRTT triplicate
ACEIILPSST plasticise
specialist
ACEIILPSTY speciality
ACEIILPSTZ plasticize
ACEIILRSSS scleriasis
ACEIILRSTT recitalist
ACEIILSTTY elasticity
ACEIIMNORS acrimonies
anisomeric
Micronesia
ACEIIMNORT romanicite
ACEIIMNPST emancipist
ACEIIMNRRU cinerarium
ACEIIMNRST criminates
ACEIIMRRSS miscarries
ACEIIMRSST armistices
ACEIIMRSTT tasimetric
ACEIINNORT cineration
ACEIINNQRU quinacrine
ACEIINNRTY itinerancy
ACEIINOPST speciation
ACEIINORTT recitation
ACEIINOSTV noviciates
vesication
ACEIINOTTX excitation
intoxicate
ACEIINOTVV invocative
ACEIINPPRT principate
ACEIINPRSS precisians
ACEIINPSTT antiseptic
psittacine
ACEIINRTVY inveracity
ACEIINSSTT sanctities
ACEIINSTTT nictitates
ACEIINSTTU austenitic
ACEIIORRRT certiorari
ACEIIORSTT atrocities
ACEIIPPSST epispastic
ACEIIRRSSU cuirassier
ACEIIRSSST sacristies
ACEIIRSTTV astrictive
ACEIIRTTVY creativity
reactivity
ACEIJKKNSV jackknives
ACEIJKNPSS jacksnipes
ACEIJNORTT trajection
ACEIKKNNTU Kentuckian
ACEIKLNNSS cleanskins
ACEIKNNRSS crankiness

ACEIKNORSS	croakiness
ACEIKNPTTW	pawnticket
ACEIKOPSSS	skiascopes
ACEIKORTUY	eukaryotic
ACEIKPRRST	peritracks
ACEILLLPRU	pellicular
ACEILLLTUY	luetically
ACEILLMNSY	miscellany
ACEILLMORT	allometric
ACEILLMOST	collimates
ACEILLMPTU	capitellum
ACEILLMRSS	miscallers
ACEILLMRTY	metrically
ACEILLNNNO	cannelloni
ACEILLNOOT	ocellation
ACEILLNORS	corallines
ACEILLNORT	citronella
ACEILLNPSS	spellicans
ACEILLNRTU	lenticular
ACEILLOPSW	pillowcase
ACEILLOPTY	poetically
ACEILLORSS	localisers
ACEILLORST	allosteric
	corallites
	sclerotial
ACEILLORSZ	localizers
ACEILLORTV	vorticella
ACEILLORTY	erotically
ACEILLOSST	oscillates
ACEILLOSTY	societally
ACEILLOTXY	exotically
ACEILLPRUY	peculiarly
ACEILLPSTY	septically
ACEILLRSTY	sterically
ACEILLRSVY	viscerally
ACEILLRTUV	victualler
ACEILLRTVY	vertically
ACEILMMNSS	clamminess
ACEILMNOPR	complainer
ACEILMNORS	normalcies
	sermonical
ACEILMNRST	centralism
ACEILMNRTU	unmetrical
ACEILMNRUW	lawrencium
ACEILMNSTU	culminates
ACEILMOPRR	proclaimer
ACEILMOPRY	promycelia
ACEILMOSSS	coseismals
ACEILMRRSU	mercurials
ACEILMRRUV	vermicular
ACEILMRSSU	secularism
ACEILMTUUV	cumulative
ACEILNNORS	cornelians
ACEILNNOST	nonelastic
ACEILNNOTU	nucleation
ACEILNNUVY	univalency
ACEILNOORT	iconolater
	relocation
ACEILNOPPS	scaloppine
ACEILNOPRT	pratincole
ACEILNOPST	neoplastic
	pleonastic
ACEILNOPTU	peculation
ACEILNORRS	resorcinal
ACEILNORST	clarionets
ACEILNORTU	ulceration
ACEILNORTY	lectionary
ACEILNOSSS	socialness
ACEILNOSST	coastlines
ACEILNOSSV	volcanises
ACEILNOSTU	inoculates
	inosculate
ACEILNOSVZ	volcanizes
ACEILNOTUV	novaculite
ACEILNPPSU	suppliance
ACEILNPSTU	inculpates
ACEILNRSST	interclass
	larcenists
ACEILNRSTT	centralist
ACEILNRSTU	lacustrine
ACEILNRSUV	vulcaniser
ACEILNRTTY	centrality
ACEILNRTVY	trivalency
ACEILNRUUX	luxuriance
ACEILNRUVZ	vulcanizer
ACEILNSSSS	classiness
ACEILNSSUV	vulcanises
ACEILNSUVZ	vulcanizes
ACEILOOSUV	olivaceous
	violaceous
ACEILOPPRS	sapropelic
ACEILOPRTX	explicator
ACEILOPSST	scapolites
ACEILOPTUV	copulative
ACEILOQTUY	coequality
ACEILORSSV	vocalisers
ACEILORSVZ	vocalizers
ACEILOTVVY	vocatively
ACEILPPPRS	paperclips
ACEILPPSTU	supplicate
ACEILPRSTU	plicatures
ACEILPRTUU	apiculture
ACEILPSSSU	capsulises
ACEILPSSUZ	capsulizes
ACEILRRSTU	curtailers
ACEILRRSUV	versicular
ACEILRSSTU	secularist
ACEILRSSTY	crystalise
ACEILRSTTU	testicular
ACEILRSTUV	revictuals
ACEILRSTUY	secularity
ACEILRSTYZ	crystalize
ACEILRTTUU	utriculate
ACEILRTUUV	aviculture
ACEILRTUVY	curatively
ACEILSSUWY	sluiceways
ACEILSTTUV	cultivates
ACEILSTUWZ	Clausewitz
ACEIMMNORT	manometric
ACEIMMNOSS	scammonies
ACEIMMPRTY	campimetry
ACEIMMRSTY	asymmetric
ACEIMNNOST	cismontane
ACEIMNNRUY	innumeracy
ACEIMNOPRT	importance
ACEIMNOPSU	menopausic
ACEIMNOPTT	pentatomic
ACEIMNORST	cremations
ACEIMNOSST	encomiasts
ACEIMNPSTU	pneumatics
ACEIMNRSST	miscreants
ACEIMOPPPT	apopemptic
ACEIMORRTT	meritocrat
ACEIMORSST	costmaries
ACEIMORSVW	microwaves
ACEIMORTTT	tetratomic
ACEIMORTTU	tautomeric
ACEIMRSTTU	micturates
ACEIMSSTTY	systematic
ACEINNNORS	cannonries
ACEINNNSTU	uncanniest
ACEINNOPTT	pentatonic
ACEINNORST	containers
	crenations
	sanctioner
ACEINNORTU	enunciator
ACEINNOSSS	ascensions
ACEINNRSSU	insurances
ACEINNRSTY	transiency
ACEINNRTUU	nunciature
ACEINNSSST	scantiness
ACEINNSSTT	intactness
ACEINOORRS	coronaries
ACEINOORST	octonaries
ACEINOORTV	revocation
ACEINOOSST	isooctanes
ACEINOOSTV	evocations
ACEINOPRTU	precaution
ACEINOPSTT	constipate
ACEINORRST	cinerators
	contraries
ACEINORRSV	carnivores
ACEINORRTT	retraction
ACEINORSST	narcotises
ACEINORSSY	cessionary
ACEINORSTU	cautioners
ACEINORSTZ	narcotizes
ACEINORTTU	eructation
ACEINORTTX	extraction
ACEINOSSST	cessations
ACEINOSTTU	unicostate
ACEINQSTTU	quittances
ACEINRSSST	scenarists
ACEINRSSTW	scrawniest
ACEINRSTUV	incurvates
ACEINSSSTT	scattiness
ACEIOOPRSU	paroecious
ACEIOOPRTZ	azeotropic
ACEIOOPTTV	cooptative
ACEIOORTTU	autoerotic
ACEIOOSTUU	autoecious
ACEIOPRRSS	acrospires
ACEIOPRRSU	precarious
ACEIOPSSTV	vitascopes
ACEIOPSTTT	petticoats
ACEIOQSSUU	sequacious

ACEIORRSST	assertoric
	ostraciser
ACEIORRSTZ	ostracizer
ACEIORSSST	ostracises
ACEIORSSTZ	ostracizes
ACEIORSTTT	tricostate
ACEIORSTVY	vesicatory
ACEIORTTXY	excitatory
ACEIOSTTUU	autocuties
ACEIPPRSST	scrappiest
ACEIPSSSTU	spacesuits
ACEIQRSTTU	acquitters
ACEIRSSTTU	rusticates
ACEIRSSUWY	cruiseways
ACEJKKMOSS	smokejacks
ACEJKKRSSY	skyjackers
ACEJKLMSST	jacksmelts
ACEJKLPPSU	supplejack
ACEJKNOSST	jackstones
ACEJLMSSUU	majuscules
ACEJORRTTY	trajectory
ACEKKMOSST	smokestack
ACEKKMRRSU	muckrakers
ACEKLLMMSU	mallemucks
ACEKLLRSTU	lackluster
	lacklustre
ACEKLNOPST	alpenstock
ACEKLOPRSW	workplaces
ACEKMNORRW	cankerworm
ACEKMSSTUW	mucksweats
ACEKOPRRST	retropacks
ACEKOPRSTY	copytakers
ACEKPRRSSY	skyscraper
ACEKPRSSSU	sapsuckers
ACELLLMORU	columellar
ACELLMTUUY	cumulately
ACELLNOSSW	callowness
ACELLNOTVY	covalently
ACELLOPRSS	scallopers
ACELLOPRTY	pectorally
ACELLOPSTU	leucoplast
ACELLOPTUY	eucalyptol
ACELLPRSTY	spectrally
ACELLPRSUY	specularly
ACELLPRUUV	vulpecular
ACELLSSTTY	tactlessly
ACELMMNOOW	commonweal
ACELMMNOSS	commensals
ACELMNNOSW	clanswomen
ACELMNNOTT	malcontent
ACELMNOORT	Monte Carlo
ACELMNOOSV	mooncalves
ACELMOOPST	Compostela
ACELMOOSTY	comatosely
ACELMORRSU	clamourers
ACELMORSUY	racemously
ACELNNNORT	noncentral
ACELNNNORU	nonnuclear
ACELNNOORS	olecranons
ACELNNOSSU	consensual
ACELNNOSTU	Launceston
ACELNNOTUV	conventual
ACELNOPRRU	pronuclear
ACELNOPRSY	narcolepsy
ACELNORRTY	necrolatry
ACELNORSTU	nucleators
	recountals
ACELNOSSTU	consulates
ACELNOSSTY	claystones
ACELNOTTUX	contextual
ACELNRTTUY	truncately
ACELOOPRRS	corporales
ACELOOPRRT	percolator
ACELOORRTU	colorature
ACELOORRTW	watercolor
ACELOOSSTT	coelostats
	osteoclast
ACELOPRSTU	peculators
	speculator
ACELOPRSTY	Polycrates
ACELOPRSUY	pelycosaur
ACELORRSSU	carrousels
ACELORRSTY	clearstory
ACELOSSSTU	cassoulets
	outclasses
ACELPPRRSU	curlpapers
ACELPRSSSU	superclass
ACELPSTUUY	eucalyptus
ACEMMNORTY	commentary
ACEMMNOSTU	consummate
ACEMMOSTTU	commutates
ACEMMOSTTY	mastectomy
ACEMNNNOTT	cantonment
ACEMNNORST	monstrance
ACEMNOOPSS	moonscapes
ACEMNOOTYZ	mycetozoan
ACEMNOPRRY	pyromancer
ACEMNOSTTY	nematocyst
ACEMOOPRRS	macrospore
ACEMOORSTU	octamerous
ACEMORSTUY	myrtaceous
ACENNNORSU	announcers
ACENNOORTV	covenantor
ACENNORSTV	conversant
ACENNORTUY	Courantyne
ACENNOSTTT	contestant
ACENOPRRST	copartners
ACENOPRTTT	protectant
ACENOPSSTW	townscapes
ACENOPSSTY	syncopates
ACENOPSTYY	cyanotypes
ACENORRSTU	raconteurs
ACENORRSWY	cornerways
ACENORSSTU	courtesans
ACENORSTUZ	courtezans
ACENPSTTUU	punctuates
ACEOOOPRRT	cooperator
ACEOOPPRRS	carpospore
ACEOOPRRRT	procreator
ACEOOPRRTY	procaryote
ACEOOPRSSS	ascospores
ACEOOPSSTT	statoscope
ACEOORRTVY	revocatory
ACEOPPRSST	spaceports
ACEOPRSSTT	spectators
ACEORRRSTT	retractors
ACEORRRSVY	carryovers
ACEORRSTTX	extractors
ACEORSSTTY	astrocytes
ACEORSTUXY	excusatory
ACERRSTUUV	curvatures
ACFFGIIKMN	mafficking
ACFFGIILNT	afflicting
ACFFIILLOY	officially
ACFFIILNOS	officinals
ACFFIILNOT	affliction
ACFFIILNOU	unofficial
ACFFIINOST	officiants
ACFFIIOORT	officiator
ACFFILLNUY	fancifully
ACFGHILNNU	flaunching
ACFGHINRSS	grassfinch
ACFGIILNOS	focalising
ACFGIILNOZ	focalizing
ACFGIILNRY	clarifying
ACFGIINNRT	infracting
ACFGIINNRY	carnifying
ACFGIINRSY	scarifying
ACFGILNNOT	conflating
ACFGILOPRY	profligacy
ACFGINORST	factorings
ACFGINRRTU	fracturing
ACFGLNORSY	gyrfalcons
ACFHIILRST	chairlifts
ACFHILNOPR	francophil
ACFHIOPRST	factorship
ACFHKORSST	rockshafts
ACFHLLTUWY	watchfully
ACFIIILNST	finalistic
ACFIIILNTY	finicality
ACFIIIMNPR	rifampicin
ACFIILLLMY	filmically
ACFIILMMOR	limaciform
ACFIILNOPT	pontifical
ACFIILNORT	frictional
ACFIIMNORT	actiniform
ACFIINNORS	infrasonic
ACFIINNORT	infarction
	infraction
ACFIIOSTTU	factitious
ACFIJKRSTU	jackfruits
ACFIKNRSSS	scarfskins
ACFILLLORU	follicular
ACFILLORUY	cauliflory
ACFILNNOOT	conflation
ACFILNNORS	francolins
ACFILNNOTU	functional
ACFILNRSUU	funiculars
ACFILOSTUY	factiously
ACFINOORRT	fornicator
ACFINORRST	infractors
ACFINORSTU	furcations
ACFIOPRSST	profascist
ACFLNOORTW	contraflow
ACFLNRRUUU	furuncular
ACFLOORSTU	colourfast

ACGGHIILOO	hagiologic
ACGGHIINNR	chagrining
ACGGHINNNU	unchanging
ACGGHINNRU	graunching
ACGGHINOPY	hypnagogic
ACGGHINOTT	chittagong
ACGGIILNNO	ganglionic
ACGGIILOOS	sialogogic
ACGGIINOTT	cogitating
ACGGILLNNY	glancingly
ACGGILLOOY	glaciology
ACGGILNNOR	clangoring
ACGGIMOSTY	mystagogic
ACGHHHIIRS	highchairs
ACGHHILNST	hatchlings
ACGHHINTTW	watch night
ACGHIIMOPR	amphigoric
ACGHIINNNU	unchaining
ACGHIINNOT	inchoating
ACGHIINSST	chastising
ACGHIIPRRT	trigraphic
ACGHIJKLST	jacklights
ACGHIKMNOR	Rockingham
ACGHIKNOPS	hopsacking
ACGHILLNSY	clashingly
ACGHILLOOP	haplologic
ACGHILLOTY	gothically
ACGHILMNRY	charmingly
ACGHILNNTU	unlatching
ACGHILNNTY	chantingly
ACGHILNSTY	scathingly
ACGHILOOPT	pathologic
ACGHILOOST	chaologist
ACGHIMNNNU	Cunningham
ACGHIMNNOP	champignon
ACGHIMNOOR	homorganic
ACGHIMNOST	stomaching
ACGHIMOPRR	micrograph
ACGHIMOPRY	myographic
ACGHINNSTU	staunching
ACGHINOPRT	prognathic
ACGHINOPRZ	zincograph
ACGHINOSSW	showcasing
ACGHINPRSU	purchasing
ACGHIOOPRR	orographic
ACGHIOOPRZ	zoographic
ACGHIOPPRT	pictograph
ACGHIRRTTW	cartwright
ACGHMNOORR	chronogram
ACGHMOPRSY	cymographs
ACGHOOPPRY	coprophagy
ACGHOPPRSY	copygraphs
ACGHORSSTU	roughcasts
ACGIIILLRT	argillitic
ACGIIKLNNN	calkinning
ACGIIKMNNN	nicknaming
ACGIILLMNS	miscalling
ACGIILLMSS	gallicisms
ACGIILLNOS	localising
ACGIILLNOZ	localizing
ACGIILLORS	cigarillos
ACGIILLOST	logistical
ACGIILLOTY	logicality
ACGIILLPRS	pilgarlics
ACGIILLRTU	liturgical
ACGIILMNPS	misplacing
ACGIILMNSS	anglicisms
ACGIILMNTU	glutaminic
ACGIILMORS	algorismic
	microglias
ACGIILNNNP	pinnacling
ACGIILNNOR	clarioning
ACGIILNOPR	caprioling
ACGIILNORZ	calorizing
ACGIILNOSU	caliginous
ACGIILNOSV	vocalising
ACGIILNOVZ	vocalizing
ACGIILNRTU	curtailing
	granulitic
ACGIILNRTY	laryngitic
ACGIILNSST	anglicists
ACGIILNTUV	victualing
ACGIIMNNRU	manicuring
ACGIIMNORS	organicism
	organismic
ACGIIMNSST	miscasting
ACGIIMSSTT	stigmatics
ACGIINNNOS	canonising
ACGIINNNOT	containing
ACGIINNNOZ	canonizing
ACGIINNNST	instancing
ACGIINNOPS	caponising
ACGIINNOPT	captioning
ACGIINNOPZ	caponizing
ACGIINNOST	incognitas
ACGIINNOTT	incogitant
ACGIINNOTU	auctioning
	cautioning
ACGIINNOTV	invocating
ACGIINNRTU	curtaining
ACGIINOOTT	cogitation
ACGIINORST	organicist
ACGIINPRST	practising
ACGIINQTTU	acquitting
ACGIINRRSU	curarising
ACGIINRRUZ	curarizing
ACGIINRSSU	cuirassing
ACGIINRSTT	astricting
ACGIINRSTY	gyniatrics
ACGIINRTTU	urticating
ACGIJKKNSY	skyjacking
ACGIJLLNOY	cajolingly
ACGIKKMNRU	muckraking
ACGIKLLNNY	clankingly
ACGIKMMMNO	mammocking
ACGILLMNOY	gnomically
ACGILLMOOY	myological
ACGILLMOSU	logical sum
ACGILLNNOO	nonlogical
ACGILLNOPS	collapsing
	scalloping
ACGILLNORR	corralling
ACGILLNORS	carollings
ACGILLNOSU	callousing
ACGILLNRWY	crawlingly
ACGILLOOOR	orological
ACGILLOOOT	otological
ACGILLOOOZ	zoological
ACGILLOORU	urological
ACGILLOPRY	pyrogallic
ACGILLOSST	collagists
ACGILLRSUY	surgically
ACGILMNNOO	cognominal
ACGILMNORU	clamouring
ACGILMNTUU	cumulating
ACGILNNPRY	prancingly
ACGILNNPSU	unclasping
ACGILNNSST	scantlings
ACGILNOORY	craniology
ACGILNOPTU	copulating
ACGILNOSTU	osculating
ACGILOORST	Cagliostro
ACGILOOTTU	tautologic
ACGILORSUU	glucosuria
ACGILORSUY	glycosuria
	graciously
ACGIMNNOPR	cramponing
ACGIMNNOPY	companying
ACGIMNOORS	agronomics
ACGIMNOOSU	ascogonium
ACGIMNOPSS	compassing
ACGIMNORRS	cairngorms
ACGIMNSSTY	gymnastics
ACGIMOPRST	pictograms
ACGINNNNOU	announcing
ACGINNNOOR	nonorganic
ACGINNOOST	cognations
	contagions
ACGINNORRT	Carrington
ACGINNRTTU	truncating
ACGINOOSTU	contagious
ACGINOPRTY	agrypnotic
ACGINOPSUU	pugnacious
ACGINORRST	costarring
ACGINORSUU	ungracious
ACGINOSTTU	outcasting
ACGIOOPRTV	vagotropic
ACGIOORSTT	cogitators
ACGIORSTTY	gyrostatic
ACGJLLNOUY	conjugally
ACGJNNOSTU	conjugants
ACGJNOORTU	conjugator
ACGJNORRSU	currajongs
ACGLLOSUUY	glaucously
ACGLMNOOOS	cosmogonal
ACGLNOORSU	clangorous
ACGMOPRSTY	cryptogams
ACGNNOPPUY	oppugnancy
ACGNORRSUW	currawongs
ACGOORRRTU	corrugator
ACHHIILLOP	halophilic
ACHHIILPST	phthisical
ACHHIKLSSS	shashlicks
ACHHILMOPT	ophthalmic
ACHHILMRTY	rhythmical
ACHHILOOPS	shopaholic

ACHHILOPTY halophytic
ACHHINOPRS archonship
ACHHINSTUY Hyacinthus
ACHHIOPPST phosphatic
ACHHIPPRSU Hipparchus
ACHHIPRSSU pushchairs
ACHHLOSSTW washcloths
ACHHNOOTTU autochthon
ACHHOPPSTY psychopath
ACHIIILNOS Nicholas II
ACHIIIMNST histaminic
ACHIIIRSST trichiasis
ACHIIJKNRS jinricksha
ACHIIKNNPS chinkapins
ACHIILLMPS phallicism
ACHIILLPST phallicist
ACHIILORST historical
ACHIILORTU thiouracil
ACHIIMNNOR inharmonic
ACHIIMNSST machinists
ACHIIMNSTU humanistic
ACHIIMNSUV chauvinism
ACHIIMOPPP hippocampi
ACHIINNOOT inchoation
ACHIINNORT Corinthian
ACHIINNPQU chinquapin
ACHIINORRT chitarroni
ACHIINORTT anorthitic
ACHIINPSSY physicians
ACHIINPSUY picayunish
ACHIINRSTT Antichrist
ACHIINRSTX Christian X
ACHIINSTUV chauvinist
ACHIIOPRST aphoristic
ACHIIOPSST pistachios
ACHIIPRSSV vicarships
ACHIIPRSTY physiatric
ACHIIRRSTT arthritics
ACHIIRSSTV archivists
ACHIKKNRSU Cruikshank
ACHIKLMSST mahlsticks
ACHIKLOORW workaholic
ACHIKMNOST mackintosh
ACHIKMNRSS scrimshank
ACHILLMOOS alcoholism
ACHILLMTYY mythically
ACHILLNNSY clannishly
ACHILLNOOP allophonic
ACHILLNOPY phonically
ACHILLOPRT prothallic
ACHILLOPRY orphically
ACHILLPSYY physically
ACHILMOOOS homosocial
ACHILMOPTY polymathic
ACHILMORYZ mycorhizal
ACHILMPSTY lymphatics
ACHILMSSUY Lysimachus
ACHILNOORS isochronal
ACHILNORUY hyaluronic
ACHILNOSSY anchylosis
ACHILOPRST strophical
ACHILOPRTY cartophily
ACHILORSTV archivolts
ACHILORSUV chivalrous
ACHILOSSST scholiasts
ACHILOSTTW waistcloth
ACHIMMNORS monarchism
ACHIMNNORS Cornishman
ACHIMNOOPT taphonomic
ACHIMNOPTY amphictyon
ACHIMNORST chromatins
monarchist
ACHIMNOSST monachists
ACHIMNSSTU miscanthus
ACHIMOORTY rachiotomy
ACHIMORRTT trichromat
ACHIMORRYZ mycorrhiza
ACHIMORSTT chromatist
ACHIMORSYZ mycorhizas
ACHIMOSSST masochists
ACHIMOSSTU mustachios
ACHIMRSSSW scrimshaws
ACHINNOSST stanchions
ACHINOOPSX saxophonic
ACHINOORST cartoonish
ACHINOPSST cashpoints
ACHINOPSTY hyponastic
ACHIOOPSST sociopaths
ACHIOOPSTY sociopathy
ACHIOPRSTY physiocrat
ACHIOPSTTY hypostatic
ACHIOPTTUY autophytic
ACHIORRSSS crosshairs
ACHIORSSTT rhotacists
ACHIPRSTYY psychiatry
ACHIQRRSUY squirarchy
ACHIRSTTWW wristwatch
ACHKLLOSST shockstall
ACHKLMNOOT klootchman
ACHKMORSTU touchmarks
ACHKNOOTTU Nouakchott
ACHLLOOPSY playschool
ACHLMMOORS schoolmarm
ACHLMNORUU homuncular
ACHLOORSUW colourwash
ACHLOOSSTU holocausts
ACHMOSSUYY hyoscyamus
ACHNOOPSYZ scyphozoan
ACHNOPSSTY sycophants
ACHOPSSTUY hypocausts
ACHORSTTTU cutthroats
ACIIIIIMRS Casimir III
ACIIILLMMO Malcolm III
ACIIILLMNP ampicillin
ACIIILLMNY inimically
ACIIILNOPT politician
ACIIILNOSS sicilianos
ACIIILNOST ciliations
ACIIILNPST sincipital
ACIIILORTV variolitic
ACIIILSTTV vitalistic
ACIIINNOTT incitation
ACIIINRSTT inartistic
ACIIINSTTV nativistic
ACIIINTTVY inactivity
ACIIJLRSTU juristical
ACIIJRSSTU justiciars
ACIIJRSTUY justiciary
ACIIKNNNPY pickaninny
ACIILLMNRY criminally
ACIILLNNOS Scillonian
ACIILLNORY ironically
ACIILLNOSS isoclinals
ACIILLNRUY culinarily
ACIILLNSST scintillas
ACIILLOPSS calliopsis
ACIILMNSUY musicianly
ACIILMORST moralistic
ACIILMQSTU quitclaims
ACIILMSTUY musicality
ACIILNNOST clintonias
ACIILNOOST coalitions
ACIILNOPPR pilocarpin
ACIILNOPPS scaloppini
ACIILNOPRV provincial
ACIILNOPST plications
ACIILNORTT tinctorial
ACIILNOTXY anxiolytic
ACIILNPPRS principals
ACIILOPRST pictorials
saprolitic
ACIILOPTTY topicality
ACIILORSTY royalistic
ACIILOSSST socialists
ACIILOSSUV lascivious
ACIILPSTTY plasticity
ACIILPTTYY typicality
ACIILRSTTU altruistic
ultraistic
ACIILRTTTY tractility
ACIILSSTUV vasculitis
ACIIMMNOPT pantomimic
ACIIMMNORS Marcionism
ACIIMMNSTU numismatic
ACIIMNNOSS insomniacs
ACIIMNORRT criminator
ACIIMNORST morticians
ACIIMNPTTY tympanitic
ACIIMNRSSS narcissism
ACIIMNRSTU manicurist
ACIIMOPRSS prosaicism
ACIIMOPRST porismatic
ACIIMOSSST mosaicists
ACIIMOSTTT stomatitic
ACIINNOOTV invocation
ACIINNOSTT nictations
ACIINNOSTU incautions
insouciant
ACIINNOTTX intoxicant
ACIINOOSTT oscitation
ACIINOPRST ascription
crispation
ACIINOPRTT tritanopic
ACIINOPSTU ancipitous
ACIINORSTT astriction
ACIINORSTX Saint Croix

ACIINORTTU urtication
ACIINOSTUU incautious
ACIINRSSST narcissist
ACIINRSTTU unartistic
ACIIOPRRST scriptoria
ACIIOPSSUU auspicious
ACIIORSTVY varicosity
ACIIPRSSTT patristics
ACIIPSSTTY spasticity
ACIISSSTTT statistics
ACIJLNNOTU junctional
ACIJLORTUY jocularity
ACIKKLMNOR Kilmarnock
ACIKKNNOST antiknocks
ACIKLMPSTU multipacks
ACIKLMRTTU multitrack
ACIKLMSSTU maulsticks
ACIKLNNOPT planktonic
ACIKLORTYY karyolytic
ACIKLOSSTT tailstocks
ACIKLPSSST slapsticks
ACIKNOOPRS pickaroons
ACIKOORSTT Cook Strait
ACIKOPRTYY karyotypic
ACIKRSSTTU tracksuits
ACILLLNOOY colonially
ACILLLOOQU colloquial
ACILLMNNOO monoclinal
ACILLMOORT collimator
ACILLMOPYY myopically
ACILLMOTUU altocumuli
ACILLMOTUV multivocal
ACILLMOTYY amylolytic
ACILLMSTYY mystically
ACILLNOOST collations
ACILLNOOTU allocution
loculation
ACILLNORSW Cornwallis
ACILLNORUU unilocular
ACILLNORUV involucral
ACILLNOUVY univocally
ACILLOOPRT allotropic
ACILLOORST oscillator
ACILLOPRTY tropically
ACILLOPSTY postically
ACILLORRTU trilocular
ACILLORSYZ zircalloys
ACILLORTVY vortically
ACILLRSTUY rustically
ACILMMOORS microsomal
ACILMMOSTT committals
ACILMMRSUU simulacrum
ACILMNOOOS nosocomial
ACILMNOORT microtonal
ACILMNOPST complaints
ACILMNOSUU calumnious
ACILMNOTUU cumulation
ACILMNRSUU minuscular
ACILMOOOTZ zootomical
ACILMOOPTY polyatomic
ACILMOPRRY micropylar
ACILMOPRSS comprisals
ACILMORSUU miraculous
ACILMPSSTY symplastic
ACILMSSSTU masculists
simulcasts
ACILNNOPTY nontypical
ACILNNOSTU inoculants
ACILNOOORT coloration
ACILNOOPTU copulation
ACILNOORST consortial
ACILNOORSU Coriolanus
ACILNOORTU inoculator
ACILNOORTY iconolatry
ACILNOOSSS Colossians
ACILNOOSTU osculation
ACILNOOTTT cottontail
ACILNORRTU trinocular
ACILNORRTY contrarily
ACILNORSTU ultrasonic
ACILNOSSTT clinostats
ACILNOSSTU sulcations
ACILNOSTUY lacunosity
ACILNPPSTU supplicant
ACILNRTTUY taciturnly
ACILOOPRRT proctorial
ACILOOPSTT postcoital
ACILOOPSTZ zooplastic
ACILOOQSUU loquacious
ACILOOSSUX saxicolous
ACILOPPRST captoprils
ACILOPSSUY spaciously
ACILOPSTUY captiously
ACILORRRVY corrivalry
ACILORSSTU ocularists
ACILORTTUV cultivator
ACILOSTUUY cautiously
ACILPRRSTU scriptural
ACIMMNOOOT monoatomic
ACIMMNOPSS pancosmism
ACIMMNORTY matronymic
ACIMMORSSS commissars
ACIMMORSSY commissary
ACIMNNNOOR minor canon
ACIMNNOOPS companions
ACIMNNORTU unromantic
ACIMNNOSTY sanctimony
ACIMNOOPRS comparison
ACIMNOOPSS compassion
ACIMNOORST astronomic
ACIMNOORTY craniotomy
ACIMNOOSST onomastics
ACIMNOOSTU autonomics
ACIMNOOSTY actomyosin
ACIMNOPRTY patronymic
pyromantic
ACIMNOTTUY tautonymic
ACIMNPRSTU manuscript
ACIMOOPRTT compatriot
ACIMOORTVY varicotomy
ACIMOPRSXY paroxysmic
ACIMOPSSSY symposiacs
ACIMOPSTTY asymptotic
ACIMORSSST ostracisms
ACINNNOSTT inconstant
ACINNNOTTU continuant
ACINNOOORT coronation
ACINNOPTTU punctation
ACINNORSST constrains
ACINNORSTT constraint
ACINNORTTU truncation
ACINNRSTTU incrustant
ACINNSTTYY nyctinasty
ACINOOOPTT cooptation
ACINOOPPRT protanopic
ACINOOPRRT Porto Rican
ACINOORRSS corrasions
ACINOORSTT cartoonist
ACINOORSTV invocators
ACINOORTVY invocatory
ACINORSSST croissants
ACINORSSTY crayonists
ACINPRRSTT transcript
ACIOORSTVY Ivory Coast
ACIOPRSTTY pyrostatic
ACIORRSTTU rusticator
ACJKOPRSST jockstraps
ACKKNRSTUW knackwurst
ACKLMOOORS cloakrooms
ACKLNORSST cornstalks
ACKLORSSSW crosswalks
ACKRRSSTTU starstruck
ACLLLOOSSY colossally
ACLLLRTUUY culturally
ACLLMMNOUY communally
ACLLMNNOOO monoclonal
ACLLMRSUUY muscularly
ACLLNPTUUY punctually
ACLLOOPRRY corporally
ACLLORRSSY rallycross
ACLLPRSTUU sculptural
ACLMMNOOTY commonalty
ACLMNOORSU monoculars
ACLMOORSSS classrooms
ACLNNOSTTU consultant
ACLNNOSTTY constantly
ACLNNOSTUV convulsant
ACLNNPTUUU unpunctual
ACLNNRSUUU ranunculus
ACLNOORSTT contraltos
ACLNOORSUY canorously
ACLNOPSTUY postulancy
ACLOOORRST coralroots
ACLOOPRTUY copulatory
ACLOORSTUY osculatory
ACLOORSUWY colourways
ACLOPRSTTU plutocrats
ACLRRSTTUU structural
ACMMOORTTU commutator
ACMNNORTUY countryman
ACMNOORRST cormorants
ACMNOORSUY acronymous
ACMNOOSSTU cosmonauts
ACMOOOPRTT compotator
ACNNNOOSST consonants
ACNOOPRSST corposants

ACNOOPRSTY syncopator
ACNOPRSSUY syncarpous
ACNOPRTTUU punctuator
ACOOOPRRRT corporator
ACOOPPRRSS sporocarps
ACOOPRRRTT protractor
ACOOPRRRTU procurator
ACOPRSSSTT sportscast
ACORRSSTTU scrutators
ACOSSSTTTY statocysts
ADDDDEEKLS skedaddled
ADDDEEEMNR redemanded
ADDDEEEPRT depredated
ADDDEEFHIL fiddlehead
ADDDEEHNRU dunderhead
ADDDEEHRRU rudderhead
ADDDEEHRTY dehydrated
ADDDEEILSS sidesaddle
ADDDEEKLSS skedaddles
ADDDEEPRSU superadded
ADDDEGNORW downgraded
ADDDEIIIMT dimidiated
ADDDEILNOR dendroidal
ADDDELNOOW downloaded
ADDEEEFHNR freehanded
ADDEEEFLOR freeloaded
ADDEEEFNTU undefeated
ADDEEEGNNR endangered
ADDEEEHNNV evenhanded
ADDEEEHNRR rehardened
ADDEEEHRRT rethreaded
ADDEEEILNT delineated
ADDEEEIRST desiderate
ADDEEEKMRT demarketed
ADDEEELLSW Weddell Sea
ADDEEELNVV van de Velde
ADDEEELRST saddletree
ADDEEENORV endeavored
ADDEEENRTV denervated
ADDEEEPRST depredates
ADDEEERSSS addressees
ADDEEERTTU deuterated
ADDEEFHNOR forehanded
ADDEEFHOST softheaded
ADDEEFIINN definienda
ADDEEFIINZ denazified
ADDEEFILOT defoliated
ADDEEFILSU feudalised
ADDEEFILUZ feudalized
ADDEEFNNST defendants
ADDEEFRRSU defrauders
ADDEEGGINS disengaged
ADDEEGHITW deadweight
ADDEEGHLNO longheaded
ADDEEGINRT denigrated
ADDEEGINST designated
ADDEEGLLNR Gelderland
ADDEEGLNRS gladdeners
ADDEEGNRUZ gazundered
ADDEEGSTTU degustated
ADDEEHLLNS handselled
ADDEEHLMMU dummelhead
ADDEEHLNRU unheralded
ADDEEHNNOP openhanded
ADDEEHNNRU unhardened
ADDEEHNNSS handedness
ADDEEHNOOW woodenhead
ADDEEHNORV overhanded
ADDEEHNRTU unthreaded
ADDEEHRSTY dehydrates
ADDEEIIMNS deaminised
ADDEEIIMNZ deaminized
ADDEEIIMST mediatised
ADDEEIIMTZ mediatized
ADDEEIIPSS diapedesis
ADDEEILMPS mispleaded
ADDEEILMST Middle East
ADDEEILNSS deadliness
ADDEEILPSS displeased
ADDEEILRSS saddleries
ADDEEILRSV daredevils
ADDEEIMRTT readmitted
ADDEEINORT derationed
ADDEEINRTT denitrated
ADDEEINSTU unsteadied
ADDEEIOPTV videotaped
ADDEEIPRSW widespread
ADDEEIPRTU repudiated
ADDEEIRSTV advertised
ADDEEIRTTX extradited
ADDEEIRTVZ advertized
ADDEEJRSTU readjusted
ADDEELLMTU medullated
ADDEELLSSS saddleless
ADDEELMNOR endodermal
ADDEELMOTU demodulate
ADDEELNORV overlanded
ADDEELOORV overloaded
ADDEELPRST stepladder
ADDEEMNNRU undernamed
ADDEEMNOPR promenaded
ADDEEMPSTU despumated
ADDEENNPST dependants
ADDEENNTTU unattended
ADDEENPRTU dunderpate
ADDEENQRSU squandered
ADDEENRRTU underrated
ADDEENRRUW unrewarded
ADDEENRTUV adventured
ADDEEOPRRT depredator
ADDEEOPRSS desperados
ADDEEORRTV overtraded
ADDEEPRSTU depastured
ADDEERRSSS addressers
ADDEFGIILN defilading
ADDEFGINRU defrauding
ADDEFGLLNO oldfangled
ADDEFHILPS paddlefish
ADDEFIIILP lapidified
ADDEFIINNR Ferdinand I
ADDEFILLSU fusilladed
ADDEFILMNO manifolded
ADDEFINNRV Ferdinand V
ADDEFINRSU fundraised
ADDEFIORSV disfavored
ADDEFLLOOP flapdoodle
ADDEFLLRUY dreadfully
ADDEGGILNN gladdening
ADDEGHILST deadlights
ADDEGHLORT goldthread
ADDEGIILOS dialogised
ADDEGIILOZ dialogized
ADDEGILLNW windgalled
ADDEGILTUV divulgated
ADDEGIMNOV Mogen David
ADDEGIMOST dogmatised
ADDEGIMOTZ dogmatized
ADDEGINNTU denudating
ADDEGINRSS addressing
ADDEGINUUV Du Vigneaud
ADDEGIORRS dorsigrade
ADDEGIRRSS disregards
ADDEGMNORR dendrogram
ADDEGNORSW downgrades
ADDEGNRRSU undergrads
ADDEHHOSTY hydathodes
ADDEHIJMNU mujaheddin
ADDEHILMNS mishandled
ADDEHIMNOO maidenhood
ADDEHIMNOS admonished
ADDEHINRSY anhydrides
ADDEHIRSYZ hydrazides
ADDEHKNORW handworked
ADDEHLLNOR landholder
ADDEHLORST stadholder
ADDEHNOSUW unshadowed
ADDEHORRTY dehydrator
ADDEIIIMST dimidiates
ADDEIIIRVW Edward VIII
ADDEIILMPY epididymal
ADDEIILQTU liquidated
ADDEIINOTU auditioned
ADDEIINRST distrained
ADDEIIOSTZ diazotised
ADDEIIOTZZ diazotized
ADDEIIPRSS dispraised
ADDEIIPSST dissipated
ADDEILLNSS landslides
ADDEILLOSW disallowed
ADDEILMNST dismantled
ADDEILMTTY admittedly
ADDEILNNOS dandelions
ADDEILNNSY Disneyland
ADDEILNPST displanted
ADDEILNSSW windlassed
ADDEILNSSY deadly sins
ADDEIMNORS randomised
ADDEIMNORZ randomized
ADDEIMNOST demantoids
ADDEIMNSUY undismayed
ADDEIMRSSS misaddress
ADDEINNORU unordained
ADDEINNOTU denudation
ADDEINNRRU underdrain
ADDEINOORS radiosonde
ADDEINOPSW pandowdies

ADDEINRSTT	dittanders
ADDEIOPPRR	airdropped
ADDEIRSSSU	dissuaders
ADDELMNOPY	paddymelon
ADDELNNOOT	endodontal
ADDELNNORW	wonderland
ADDELNNRSU	Sunderland
ADDELNOORW	woodlander
ADDELNOPWY	downplayed
ADDELPQRUU	quadrupled
ADDELRRSST	straddlers
ADDENNRSTU	understand
ADDENOORST	deodorants
ADDEORRSSS	addressors
ADDEPQRSUU	quadrupeds
ADDFGIINNY	dandifying
ADDFGIOORY	Good Friday
ADDFIILNSU	disdainful
ADDGHNORSU	draghounds
ADDGIIINNS	disdaining
ADDGIIMNNO	diamonding
ADDGIINSSU	dissuading
ADDGILLNWY	dawdlingly
ADDGILNNSU	unsaddling
ADDGILNRST	straddling
ADDGINNOTW	Waddington
ADDHLOOSTU	adulthoods
ADDIIILNUV	individual
ADDILLLLYY	dillydally
ADDILNPSSU	Spud Island
ADDIMNOSUY	didynamous
ADDIMOORSU	diadromous
ADDLNORSST	landdrosts
ADDLNORWWY	downwardly
ADEEEEGNRT	degenerate
ADEEEFILRS	federalise
ADEEEFILRZ	federalize
ADEEEFIRTV	federative
ADEEEFKPRS	speedfreak
ADEEEFLLRW	farewelled
ADEEEFLORR	freeloader
ADEEEFNRST	refastened
ADEEEGGRST	gadgeteers
	segregated
ADEEEGHNRS	greenheads
ADEEEGHRRT	regathered
ADEEEGLNTW	tangleweed
ADEEEGLOPV	Lope de Vega
ADEEEGLRSV	everglades
ADEEEGLRTU	deregulate
ADEEEGORRV	overgeared
ADEEEHHPSS	sheepshead
ADEEEHJMNU	mujahedeen
ADEEEHKLLU	keelhauled
ADEEEHLPSY	sleepyhead
ADEEEHLPTT	telepathed
ADEEEHLRTT	letterhead
ADEEEHLRTW	treadwheel
ADEEEHLSST	steelheads
ADEEEHNRTT	threatened
ADEEEHNRTW	enwreathed
ADEEEHNSST	heatedness
ADEEEHORTV	overheated
ADEEEIKLRU	Auld Reekie
ADEEEILMNS	madeleines
ADEEEILNST	delineates
ADEEEILPRS	espaliered
ADEEEIMNRX	reexamined
ADEEEIRRTT	reiterated
ADEEEKNSSW	snakeweeds
ADEEELLMNP	empanelled
ADEEELLRSS	leaderless
ADEEELNNSS	leadenness
ADEEELNNUV	unleavened
ADEEELNPRU	unrepealed
ADEEELNRSW	newsdealer
ADEEELNRUV	unrevealed
ADEEELNRUW	Leeuwarden
ADEEELNSST	elatedness
ADEEELNTTU	edentulate
ADEEELOPRV	overleaped
ADEEELPRTY	repeatedly
ADEEEMNNRT	endearment
ADEEEMNRRS	meanderers
ADEEEMNRTU	enumerated
ADEEEMNRUV	maneuvered
ADEEEMOOST	oedematose
ADEEEMPRTT	attempered
ADEEEMRRST	remastered
ADEEEMRRSU	remeasured
ADEEENNPRT	perennated
ADEEENNRTU	undereaten
ADEEENORRV	endeavorer
ADEEENORTX	exonerated
ADEEENPRTT	penetrated
ADEEENRRSS	serenaders
ADEEENRRSW	newsreader
ADEEENRSTV	denervates
ADEEENRTTV	anteverted
ADEEENSSST	sedateness
ADEEENTTUV	eventuated
ADEEENTTUX	extenuated
ADEEERRRST	rearrested
ADEEERRSST	reasserted
ADEEERSSSS	reassessed
ADEEERSTTU	deuterates
ADEEERSTWW	waterweeds
ADEEFFILRS	fieldfares
ADEEFFIMRR	reaffirmed
ADEEFFLNRU	Frauenfeld
ADEEFFORST	afforested
ADEEFGHIRU	figurehead
ADEEFGILLR	fillagreed
ADEEFGINRT	federating
ADEEFGLNNW	newfangled
ADEEFGMNRT	fragmented
ADEEFHILSS	dealfishes
ADEEFHNRTU	unfathered
ADEEFIINSZ	denazifies
ADEEFIKRRS	firedrakes
ADEEFILLLS	Sellafield
ADEEFILMRS	federalism
ADEEFILOST	defoliates
ADEEFILOTX	exfoliated
ADEEFILRST	federalist
ADEEFILSSU	feudalises
ADEEFILSUZ	feudalizes
ADEEFIMNST	manifested
ADEEFINORT	federation
ADEEFINRRW	firewarden
ADEEFIRSTU	disfeature
ADEEFISSTT	defeatists
ADEEFKNPRR	prefranked
ADEEFLLLNN	flannelled
ADEEFLNNOR	nonfederal
ADEEFLOOTV	foveolated
ADEEFLRSTU	defaulters
ADEEFMNORW	freedwoman
ADEEFMNRTY	defrayment
ADEEFMORST	fadometers
ADEEFNNSTU	unfastened
ADEEFNORRW	forewarned
ADEEFNRTUU	unfeatured
ADEEFOPRRT	perforated
ADEEFORSTT	foretasted
ADEEGGHLOR	loggerhead
ADEEGGILNT	delegating
ADEEGGIMOS	demagogies
ADEEGGINRS	degreasing
ADEEGGINSS	disengages
ADEEGGJNSS	jaggedness
ADEEGGLNOT	Golden Gate
ADEEGGMOSU	demagogues
ADEEGGNRSS	raggedness
ADEEGGOPSU	pedagogues
ADEEGHINRS	garnisheed
ADEEGHINRT	ingathered
ADEEGHNRTU	ungathered
ADEEGIINSS	diagenesis
ADEEGIJLNR	Darjeeling
ADEEGILLST	legislated
ADEEGILMNR	malingered
ADEEGILNOT	delegation
ADEEGILNRR	ringleader
ADEEGILNRY	delayering
ADEEGILRST	gradeliest
ADEEGIMNNR	meandering
ADEEGIMNOS	endogamies
ADEEGIMNRT	germinated
ADEEGIMNRZ	germanized
ADEEGIMNST	magnetised
ADEEGIMNTZ	magnetized
ADEEGIMRRT	remigrated
ADEEGINNOT	denegation
ADEEGINNRS	grenadines
	serenading
ADEEGINOTT	negotiated
ADEEGINPRR	prereading
ADEEGINPRT	interpaged
ADEEGINRRS	grenadiers
ADEEGINRRT	intergrade
	retreading
ADEEGINRSS	reassigned
ADEEGINRST	denigrates
ADEEGINRTT	integrated
ADEEGINSST	designates

ADEEGIORTV derogative
ADEEGISUVW waveguides
ADEEGLLNOS goldenseal
ADEEGLNNNW New England
ADEEGLNPRU plunderage
ADEEGLNRSS dangerless
gardenless
ADEEGLNRUZ underglaze
ADEEGLOOSW eaglewoods
ADEEGLOPUU Guadeloupe
ADEEGLORTY derogately
ADEEGLRRSS regardless
ADEEGMNORT dermatogen
ADEEGMNRRS germanders
ADEEGMNRRY gendarmery
ADEEGMRRSU demurrages
ADEEGNOTXY oxygenated
ADEEGNRRSW greensward
ADEEGNRRUZ gazunderer
ADEEGOORSV overdosage
ADEEGOORSW greasewood
ADEEGORRRT retrograde
ADEEGORRVZ overgrazed
ADEEGPRTUX expurgated
ADEEGSSTTU degustates
ADEEHHILMR hemihedral
ADEEHHLOSV shovelhead
ADEEHHMNOT heathendom
ADEEHHNOPS headphones
ADEEHHNORX hexahedron
ADEEHHNPTY hyphenated
ADEEHHNRTU headhunter
ADEEHHNSTU unsheathed
ADEEHIIKTV khediviate
ADEEHIIRRW wirehaired
ADEEHIJMNU mujahideen
ADEEHIKLRT threadlike
ADEEHILNOT endothelia
ethanediol
ADEEHILNRS headliners
ADEEHILNTU heulandite
ADEEHILOPP paedophile
ADEEHILPPR harelipped
ADEEHILPRS dealership
leadership
ADEEHILRRS heraldries
ADEEHILSVY adhesively
ADEEHILSWY daisywheel
ADEEHIMNSU dehumanise
ADEEHIMNUZ dehumanize
ADEEHIMPRY hypermedia
ADEEHIMPSS emphasised
ADEEHIMPST empathised
ADEEHIMPSZ emphasized
ADEEHIMPTZ empathized
ADEEHINRST dishearten
ADEEHINRTT thenardite
ADEEHIOPSX hexapodies
ADEEHIPRRS readership
ADEEHIRRSS sherardise
ADEEHIRRSZ sherardize
ADEEHIRRTY hereditary
ADEEHIRSTT threadiest
ADEEHKLRSS sheldrakes
ADEEHKORRW headworker
ADEEHLLNRT enthralled
ADEEHLLNSS handleless
ADEEHLLOSS leaseholds
ADEEHLLOSW wholesaled
ADEEHLLOWY yellowhead
ADEEHLMTTY methylated
ADEEHLNOPT phenolated
ADEEHLOOSX aldohexose
ADEEHLOPRT petrolhead
ADEEHLORUV overhauled
ADEEHLRSST threadless
ADEEHMNPRU unhampered
ADEEHMOPRS semaphored
ADEEHMOSST homesteads
ADEEHNNRTU underneath
ADEEHNOSST headstones
ADEEHNPPRS apprehends
ADEEHORSUW warehoused
ADEEHRRSTT Thar Desert
ADEEHRSSTW watersheds
ADEEIIILST idealities
ADEEIIJNRR jardiniere
ADEEIIKLMN maidenlike
ADEEIILMNT eliminated
ADEEIILMTT delimitate
ADEEIILNSS desalinise
ADEEIILNSZ desalinize
ADEEIILNTV evidential
ADEEIILRSS idealisers
serialised
ADEEIILRSZ idealizers
serialized
ADEEIILSTV devitalise
ADEEIILTVZ devitalize
ADEEIIMNSS deaminises
ADEEIIMNSZ deaminizes
ADEEIIMSST mediatises
ADEEIIMSTZ mediatizes
ADEEIIMTTV meditative
ADEEIINRST distrainee
ADEEIINRTT itinerated
ADEEIINRVV vivandiere
ADEEIINSST dessiatine
East Indies
ADEEIIRTTW tidewaiter
ADEEIIRTVV derivative
ADEEIJOPRS jeopardise
ADEEIJOPRZ jeopardize
ADEEIKNRRT dreikanter
ADEEIKPRSW Paderewski
ADEEIKRSST asterisked
ADEEILLMNP impanelled
ADEEILLMNV Mandeville
ADEEILLMOS damoiselle
ADEEILLMRY remedially
ADEEILLMST metallised
ADEEILLMTZ metallized
ADEEILLMVY medievally
ADEEILLNOT lineolated
ADEEILLPRS espadrille
ADEEILLPST palletised
ADEEILLPTZ palletized
ADEEILLRRU derailleur
ADEEILLRSY sidereally
ADEEILLSTT satellited
ADEEILLUVV vaudeville
ADEEILMMST lemmatised
ADEEILMMTZ lemmatized
ADEEILMNPT pedimental
ADEEILMNRS madrilenes
ADEEILMNRT derailment
ADEEILMNTY myelinated
ADEEILMORS demoralise
ADEEILMORT meliorated
ADEEILMORZ demoralize
ADEEILMPRR peridermal
ADEEILMPRS impleaders
ADEEILMRSS misdealers
misleaders
ADEEILMRST misrelated
ADEEILNNRW New Ireland
ADEEILNORT delineator
ADEEILNPRT interplead
ADEEILNRSU unrealised
ADEEILNRSV vernalised
ADEEILNRTU adulterine
ADEEILNRUZ unrealized
ADEEILNRVZ vernalized
ADEEILNSSS Dessalines
ADEEILNTTT dilettante
ADEEILNTTV ventilated
ADEEILOPRS depolarise
ADEEILOPRZ depolarize
ADEEILOPTT petiolated
ADEEILPRST pilastered
ADEEILPSSS displeases
ADEEILRSST slaistered
ADEEILRSTU adulteries
ADEEILRTTU elutriated
ADEEILSSUX sexualised
ADEEILSUXZ sexualized
ADEEIMMNSS maimedness
misdemeans
ADEEIMMORT immoderate
ADEEIMNNOT denominate
emendation
ADEEIMNNTT detainment
ADEEIMNORT endometria
ADEEIMNPRS Parmenides
ADEEIMNRRS remainders
ADEEIMNRSS dreaminess
ADEEIMNRTT terminated
ADEEIMNSTV advisement
ADEEIMORRT radiometer
ADEEIMORRX xerodermia
ADEEIMORTU audiometer
ADEEIMPRTT impetrated
ADEEIMRSTT mistreated
ADEEIMSSST demitasses
ADEEINNRTV innervated
ADEEINOPSW weaponised

ADEEINOPWZ	weaponized
ADEEINORTT	orientated
ADEEINOTTV	denotative
	detonative
ADEEINPPST	pepsinated
ADEEINPPSX	appendixes
ADEEINPRRU	unrepaired
ADEEINPRST	pedantries
	pedestrian
ADEEINPTUX	unexpiated
ADEEINRRSS	dreariness
ADEEINRRST	restrained
ADEEINRSSV	variedness
ADEEINRSTT	denitrates
	reinstated
	straitened
ADEEINRSTU	denaturise
ADEEINRTTT	tridentate
ADEEINRTUZ	denaturize
ADEEINSSST	steadiness
ADEEINSSTT	Eisenstadt
ADEEINSSTU	unsteadies
ADEEINSTVV	adventives
ADEEIOPRST	operatised
	periodates
ADEEIOPRSX	peroxidase
ADEEIOPRTZ	operatized
ADEEIOPSTV	videotapes
ADEEIPPRSU	pauperised
ADEEIPPRTW	wiretapped
ADEEIPPRUZ	pauperized
ADEEIPPSSS	passepieds
ADEEIPPSST	peptidases
ADEEIPRSTT	tapestried
ADEEIPRSTU	repudiates
ADEEIPRTTX	extirpated
ADEEIPRTUV	depurative
ADEEIRRSTV	advertiser
ADEEIRRSTW	watersider
ADEEIRRTVZ	advertizer
ADEEIRSSTT	dissertate
ADEEIRSSTV	advertises
ADEEIRSSTW	waitressed
ADEEIRSTTV	travestied
ADEEIRSTTW	tidewaters
ADEEIRSTTX	extradites
ADEEIRSTVZ	advertizes
ADEEJRRSTU	readjuster
ADEEKLMORU	leukoderma
ADEEKMNRSS	markedness
ADEEKMRRSS	dressmaker
ADEEKNNRTU	undertaken
ADEEKNRRTU	undertaker
ADEEKNRSTU	undertakes
ADEEKORSTV	overtasked
ADEELLMMRT	trammelled
ADEELLMNRS	mallenders
ADEELLMNTY	lamentedly
ADEELLNQUU	unequalled
ADEELLNRSS	sallenders
ADEELLNRUV	unravelled
ADEELLOPST	sellotaped
ADEELLORTT	reallotted
ADEELLOSTY	desolately
ADEELLQRRU	quarrelled
ADEELMMORS	mesodermal
ADEELMNNTU	unlamented
ADEELMNOPS	pademelons
ADEELMNORT	entodermal
ADEELMNPUX	unexampled
ADEELMORTY	moderately
ADEELMRSUY	measuredly
ADEELNNPPR	preplanned
ADEELNNQSU	Queensland
ADEELNNTTU	untalented
ADEELNORRV	overlander
ADEELNORSY	reasonedly
ADEELNRRSS	slanderers
ADEELNRRSU	launderers
ADEELNRRUY	underlayer
ADEELNRSSU	underseals
ADEELNRTTU	laundrette
ADEELNRTUV	untraveled
ADEELNRUUV	undervalue
ADEELOPPRV	overlapped
ADEELOPPTU	depopulate
ADEELOPRSS	leopardess
ADEELOPRVY	overplayed
ADEELORSST	desolaters
ADEELORUVV	overvalued
ADEELPPRRY	preparedly
ADEELPRSTT	splattered
ADEELRRSSW	rewardless
ADEELRRSTU	adulterers
	serrulated
ADEELRSSTU	adulteress
ADEELRSSTY	steelyards
ADEEMMNNRT	remandment
ADEEMMNNST	amendments
ADEEMMORST	dermatomes
ADEEMNNNRU	unmannered
ADEEMNNORT	ornamented
ADEEMNNORV	overmanned
ADEEMNOPRR	promenader
ADEEMNOPRS	promenades
ADEEMNORST	emendators
ADEEMNORSU	demeanours
ADEEMNORTY	emendatory
ADEEMNORUV	manoeuvred
ADEEMNPRTT	department
ADEEMNRRSU	maunderers
ADEEMNRRTT	retardment
ADEEMNRSTU	unmastered
	unstreamed
ADEEMNRSTY	dynameters
ADEEMNRSUU	unmeasured
ADEEMNSTUU	mansuetude
ADEEMOORRS	aerodromes
ADEEMOOSTU	oedematous
ADEEMOPRRS	madrepores
ADEEMORSST	dermatoses
ADEEMORSTT	trematodes
ADEEMPRSST	stampeders
ADEEMPRTTU	permutated
ADEEMPSSTU	despumates
ADEENNNTTU	untenanted
ADEENNORRS	nonreaders
ADEENNORSU	unreasoned
ADEENNOSSU	unseasoned
ADEENNPRSU	depanneurs
ADEENNPTTU	unpatented
ADEENNRSUW	unanswered
ADEENOPRST	personated
ADEENOPRTV	Pontevedra
ADEENOPRVX	overexpand
ADEENORSUV	endeavours
ADEENPPRRU	unprepared
ADEENPPRSS	dapperness
ADEENPRRTU	enraptured
ADEENPRSST	depressant
ADEENQRRSU	squanderer
ADEENRRSTU	underrates
ADEENRRTUV	adventurer
ADEENRRTUW	underwater
ADEENRSTTU	understate
ADEENRSTUV	adventures
ADEENSTTTU	unattested
ADEEOPRRSV	overspread
ADEEOPRRTV	overparted
ADEEOPRSSV	eavesdrops
	overpassed
ADEEORRSTV	overtrades
ADEEORSSTX	extradoses
ADEEORSTTV	overstated
ADEEORSTVY	overstayed
ADEEPRRSSU	persuaders
ADEEPRRSTU	departures
ADEEPRSSST	trespassed
ADEEPRSSTU	depastures
ADEERRSSSW	wardresses
ADEERSSSTW	stewardess
ADEERSSTYY	yesterdays
ADEFFGHIRT	affrighted
ADEFFLOOTT	flatfooted
ADEFGHIRST	farsighted
ADEFGHORST	godfathers
ADEFGIILNN	enfilading
ADEFGILNRY	ladyfinger
ADEFGILNTU	defaulting
ADEFGILRSU	lifeguards
ADEFGILRTZ	Fitzgerald
ADEFGINORR	firedragon
ADEFGINRRT	redrafting
ADEFGIRRSU	fireguards
ADEFGISTTU	fustigated
ADEFGLOOST	floodgates
ADEFGLRTUU	fulgurated
ADEFHHOORT	fatherhood
ADEFHIILST	fishtailed
ADEFHILMSS	damselfish
ADEFHILTTW	halfwitted
ADEFHINPRT	pathfinder
ADEFHINRST	threadfins
ADEFHIOSST	toadfishes
ADEFHIRSST	starfished
ADEFHIRSTV	driveshaft

ADEFHLOOSS	falsehoods
ADEFHLTTWY	Twelfth Day
ADEFHMNOTU	unfathomed
ADEFHOORSW	foreshadow
ADEFIIILPS	lapidifies
ADEFIILPSS	fissipedal
ADEFIIMMNO	ammonified
ADEFIINOPS	saponified
ADEFIINQTU	quantified
ADEFIINRTU	infuriated
ADEFIIRSTT	stratified
ADEFIJORUZ	Juiz de Fora
ADEFILLNTY	inflatedly
ADEFILLSSU	fusillades
ADEFILMNOR	manifolder
ADEFILMNTU	fulminated
ADEFILMORS	formalised
ADEFILMORZ	formalized
ADEFILNNSZ	zinfandels
ADEFILNOST	deflations
	defoliants
ADEFILOORT	defoliator
ADEFILORTU	fluoridate
ADEFILSSTU	feudalists
ADEFINNOTU	fountained
ADEFINOORR	foreordain
ADEFINRRSU	fundraiser
ADEFINRSST	draftiness
ADEFINRSSU	fundraises
ADEFINRSTX	transfixed
ADEFKLNOTU	outflanked
ADEFKLORST	tradesfolk
ADEFLLMRUY	dreamfully
ADEFLLNNOW	downfallen
ADEFLMMOOR	formal mode
ADEFLMORTU	formulated
ADEFLNRTUU	fraudulent
ADEFLORRTW	afterworld
ADEFLORSWY	dayflowers
ADEFLSSTTY	stedfastly
ADEFMNNSTU	fundaments
ADEFMOORRS	doorframes
ADEFNNOOPR	Fernando Po
ADEFNORUUV	unfavoured
ADEFNRSSTU	transfused
ADEFOOPRRS	proofreads
ADEFORRRSW	forwarders
ADEFORRSTV	overdrafts
ADEFORRSTW	afterwords
ADEFRRSSTU	fraudsters
ADEFRRSTTU	frustrated
ADEGGHORUY	hydragogue
ADEGGIINNR	deraigning
ADEGGIISTZ	dziggetais
ADEGGIMOPS	pedagogism
ADEGGINORT	derogating
ADEGGINSSU	degaussing
ADEGGNORSU	groundages
ADEGGNUWZZ	zugzwanged
ADEGHHIILT	hightailed
ADEGHHIKNT	knighthead
ADEGHHILNR	highlander
ADEGHHILST	headlights
ADEGHHINST	nightshade
ADEGHILLNO	Heligoland
ADEGHILNNR	rehandling
ADEGHILNNS	handseling
ADEGHILNOO	halogenoid
ADEGHILNSU	languished
ADEGHINNRS	hardenings
ADEGHINPRS	headspring
	springhead
ADEGHIOPRS	ideographs
ADEGHIOPRY	ideography
ADEGHIRRTU	draughtier
ADEGHISSTT	tightassed
ADEGHLORSS	gasholders
ADEGHLOTUU	outlaughed
ADEGHLRTUY	daughterly
ADEGHMOPRY	demography
ADEGHNORST	headstrong
ADEGHNOSUZ	gazehounds
ADEGHORSUU	guardhouse
ADEGHRRSTU	draughters
ADEGIIILNS	idealising
ADEGIIILNZ	idealizing
ADEGIIILST	digitalise
ADEGIIILTZ	digitalize
ADEGIILLNR	redialling
ADEGIILLSU	seguidilla
ADEGIILMNP	impleading
ADEGIILMNS	misaligned
	misdealing
	misleading
ADEGIILNOT	gadolinite
	gelatinoid
ADEGIILNPR	lipreading
ADEGIILNPT	depilating
ADEGIILNRS	grindelias
ADEGIILNSS	signalised
ADEGIILNSZ	signalized
ADEGIILOSS	dialogises
ADEGIILOSZ	dialogizes
ADEGIILTTY	digitately
ADEGIIMMRT	immigrated
ADEGIIMNNU	unimagined
ADEGIIMNRS	misreading
ADEGIIMNTT	meditating
ADEGIINNRT	detraining
ADEGIINNRV	reinvading
ADEGIINORT	originated
ADEGIINPRS	despairing
ADEGIINSTT	instigated
ADEGIJNORS	jargonised
ADEGIJNORZ	jargonized
ADEGIKLNSV	gavelkinds
ADEGILLNTU	lingulated
ADEGILMNRY	dreamingly
ADEGILMORS	glamorised
ADEGILMORZ	glamorized
ADEGILNNNO	nonaligned
ADEGILNNPY	endplaying
ADEGILNNRS	sanderling
	slandering
ADEGILNNRU	laundering
ADEGILNORS	girandoles
ADEGILNOST	desolating
ADEGILNOTT	glottidean
ADEGILNRUV	gerundival
ADEGILOOPS	apologised
ADEGILOOPZ	apologized
ADEGILORRY	goliardery
ADEGILORSU	dialoguers
ADEGILRRSS	rigsdalers
ADEGILRSSS	glissaders
ADEGILRSUV	vulgarised
ADEGILRTUV	divulgater
ADEGILRUVZ	vulgarized
ADEGILSTUV	divulgates
ADEGIMNNRU	maundering
ADEGIMNOPU	impoundage
ADEGIMNORS	gormandise
ADEGIMNORT	moderating
ADEGIMNORZ	gormandize
ADEGIMNPST	stampeding
ADEGIMNSTU	magnitudes
ADEGIMORST	dogmatiser
ADEGIMORTZ	dogmatizer
ADEGIMOSST	dogmatises
ADEGIMOSTZ	dogmatizes
ADEGINNOTT	detonating
ADEGINNRST	integrands
ADEGINNRSW	wanderings
ADEGINNRTU	denaturing
	untreading
ADEGINNSSU	unassigned
ADEGINOORT	derogation
ADEGINOPRT	readopting
ADEGINORRS	garrisoned
ADEGINORRT	denigrator
ADEGINORST	designator
ADEGINPRSU	persuading
ADEGINPRSW	wingspread
ADEGINPRTU	depurating
ADEGINRRSS	grandsires
ADEGINRSSV	gravidness
ADEGINRSTW	stewarding
ADEGINSSTT	digestants
ADEGINSTTW	wadsetting
ADEGIPRRST	partridges
ADEGJLMNTU	judgmental
ADEGKNRRRU	krugerrand
ADEGLLMOSY	gladsomely
ADEGLNOORT	Togolander
ADEGLNORSU	glanderous
ADEGLNOSST	gladstones
ADEGMMOPRR	programmed
ADEGMNOOSU	endogamous
ADEGMOPRRS	deprograms
ADEGNNOPRS	pendragons
ADEGNNORSY	androgynes
ADEGNOOORW	orangewood
ADEGNOORSS	goosanders
ADEGNOPRST	godparents
ADEGNORSSU	sandgrouse
ADEGNOSSTU	soundstage

ADEGOOPRST	gasteropod
ADEGOORRTY	derogatory
ADEGORRSTU	surrogated
ADEHHIIPRT	diphtheria
ADEHHIRRTW	hitherward
ADEHHIRSSW	dishwasher
ADEHHLLOOR	holohedral
ADEHHMPRRU	harrumphed
ADEHHNOPRY	hydrophane
ADEHIILMTU	humiliated
ADEHIILNPR	nephridial
ADEHIILOPP	pedophilia
ADEHIILOPU	audiophile
ADEHIIMMMO	Mohammed II
ADEHIIMRTT	mithridate
ADEHIINOPR	heparinoid
ADEHIIPSUU	euphausiid
ADEHIIRRRS	hairdriers
ADEHIJNSSS	jadishness
ADEHIKNPSS	handspikes
ADEHILLORU	loudhailer
ADEHILMNSS	mishandles
ADEHILNNRT	hinterland
ADEHILNOPS	sphenoidal
ADEHILNORT	threnodial
ADEHILNPRS	philanders
ADEHILNRRS	hardliners
ADEHILNRST	disenthral
ADEHILOPRS	spheroidal
ADEHILPRUY	hyperdulia
ADEHILPSTU	disulphate
ADEHILRRST	trihedrals
ADEHILRSST	heraldists
ADEHIMNORS	admonisher
	harmonised
	rhodamines
ADEHIMNORZ	harmonized
ADEHIMNOSS	admonishes
ADEHIMNRSS	mindshares
ADEHIMORTU	rheumatoid
ADEHIMOSSU	housemaids
ADEHINOOPR	radiophone
ADEHINOPSU	audiphones
ADEHINOSST	astonished
ADEHINPRST	printheads
ADEHINPSSU	dauphiness
ADEHINQSUV	vanquished
ADEHINRSTY	anhydrites
	hydrastine
ADEHINSSTU	dianthuses
ADEHIOPRSS	rhapsodies
	rhapsodise
ADEHIOPRSZ	rhapsodize
ADEHIORSTU	authorised
ADEHIORTUZ	authorized
ADEHIPRRST	tradership
ADEHIPRRSW	wardership
ADEHIPRSST	therapsids
ADEHIRRRSY	hairdryers
ADEHIRRTTY	trihydrate
ADEHIRRTWW	withdrawer
ADEHJMPRSU	Jamshedpur
ADEHKNORST	handstroke
ADEHKNOSSW	shakedowns
ADEHLLNOUW	unhallowed
ADEHLLOPRY	polyhedral
ADEHLMNORT	motherland
ADEHLMNOSY	handsomely
ADEHLMOPRY	hypodermal
ADEHLMOPTY	methyldopa
ADEHLNOPRY	hydroplane
ADEHLNRSTU	Sutherland
ADEHLORSSY	hydrolases
ADEHLOSSSW	shadowless
ADEHLRTTWY	thwartedly
ADEHMNOSST	handsomest
ADEHMNOTTU	muttonhead
ADEHMOORST	masterhood
ADEHMORRTW	threadworm
ADEHMORSTY	Mother's Day
ADEHNOOPRR	androphore
ADEHNOOPRT	parenthood
	theropodan
ADEHNORSVY	hydrovanes
ADEHNOSSWW	downwashes
ADEHOORSSU	roadhouses
ADEHOORSVW	overshadow
ADEHOPPPSY	poppyheads
ADEHORRSSW	shorewards
ADEHORRSSY	drayhorses
ADEIIIKNSS	diakinesis
ADEIIILLNT	initialled
ADEIIILTVX	lixiviated
ADEIIIMNTT	intimidate
ADEIIINSTT	dietitians
ADEIIIPSTV	vapidities
ADEIIKLNOZ	kaolinized
ADEIIKNSSY	dyskinesia
ADEIILLMPX	maxilliped
ADEIILLPTX	pixillated
ADEIILLSTT	distillate
ADEIILLTTT	titillated
ADEIILMMTU	multimedia
ADEIILMNOR	meridional
ADEIILMNSU	aluminised
ADEIILMNUZ	aluminized
ADEIILMOST	modalities
ADEIILMOSZ	imidazoles
ADEIILMPPS	misapplied
ADEIILNOPT	depilation
ADEIILNOPV	pavilioned
ADEIILNPST	platinised
ADEIILNPTZ	platinized
ADEIILNRTT	intertidal
ADEIILNSST	disentails
ADEIILNTTT	dilettanti
ADEIILORST	editorials
	idolatries
	idolatrise
ADEIILORTZ	idolatrize
ADEIILOSST	sodalities
ADEIILPRTY	prediality
ADEIILQSTU	liquidates
ADEIILRSTU	ritualised
ADEIILRTUZ	ritualized
ADEIILSSUV	visualised
ADEIILSUVZ	visualized
ADEIIMMNOS	Maimonides
ADEIIMNOST	mediations
ADEIIMNOTT	meditation
ADEIIMNOTV	dominative
ADEIIMNPRU	unimpaired
ADEIIMNRST	administer
ADEIIMNRSZ	zemindaris
ADEIIMOSTT	diatomites
ADEIIMPRSU	praesidium
ADEIIMRSTT	dermatitis
ADEIINNNOS	Indonesian
ADEIINNORT	inordinate
ADEIINNOTW	nationwide
ADEIINNOTX	indexation
ADEIINNPPT	pinnatiped
ADEIINNSST	daintiness
	Saint-Denis
ADEIINNSTU	insinuated
ADEIINNSTW	West Indian
ADEIINORRS	ordinaries
ADEIINORTU	auditioner
ADEIINORTV	derivation
ADEIINOSTV	deviations
ADEIINPPRS	drainpipes
ADEIINPTTU	inaptitude
ADEIINRRST	distrainer
ADEIINRTUV	indurative
ADEIIORSSV	advisories
ADEIIORSTU	auditories
ADEIIOSSTZ	diazotises
ADEIIOSTZZ	diazotizes
ADEIIPRRSS	dispraiser
ADEIIPRSSS	dispraises
ADEIIPRSST	dissipater
ADEIIPRSTV	privatised
ADEIIPRTVZ	privatized
ADEIIPSSST	dissipates
ADEIISSSUV	dissuasive
ADEIITTTTV	tittivated
ADEIJLLOTV	Jadotville
ADEIJMMNRW	windjammer
ADEIKLLNSW	Wilkes Land
ADEIKLLNUY	unladylike
ADEIKLMNOS	kalsomined
ADEIKLNOSU	soundalike
ADEIKLRSSS	laserdisks
ADEIKNPPRS	kidnappers
ADEIKNPRST	predikants
ADEIKNRRTW	Drinkwater
ADEIKNRSVW	drawknives
ADEILLMNOS	medaillons
	medallions
ADEILLMOST	metalloids
ADEILLMRST	treadmills
ADEILLMSST	medallists
ADEILLMSTW	Willemstad
ADEILLNOOS	solenoidal
ADEILLNOPR	Pirandello
ADEILLNOPT	pollinated

ADEILLNOSU	delusional
ADEILLNPSS	pallidness
ADEILLNRRT	tendrillar
ADEILLNRUV	unrivalled
ADEILLPQSU	pasquilled
ADEILLPRSU	pluralised
ADEILLPRUZ	pluralized
ADEILLQRSU	quadrilles
ADEILLRSUY	residually
ADEILMNNOS	mandolines
ADEILMNOPR	palindrome
ADEILMNORS	normalised
ADEILMNORT	intermodal
ADEILMNORZ	normalized
ADEILMNRST	dismantler
ADEILMNRTU	rudimental
ADEILMNSSS	dismalness
ADEILMNSST	dismantles
ADEILMNSTU	dentaliums
ADEILMOPSS	psalmodies
ADEILMOPST	diplomates
ADEILMOPSY	polyamides
ADEILMOTUV	modulative
ADEILMPSTU	amplitudes
ADEILMSTTU	stimulated
ADEILMSTUU	mutualised
ADEILMTUUZ	mutualized
ADEILNNORT	internodal
ADEILNOOST	desolation
ADEILNOOTV	devotional
ADEILNOPST	planetoids
ADEILNOPSU	aneuploids
ADEILNOPUY	aneuploidy
ADEILNPRTU	prudential
ADEILNPTUV	pulvinated
ADEILNRRST	interlards
ADEILNRSTU	uitlanders
ADEILNSSSW	windlasses
ADEILNSTTU	testudinal
ADEILNSTUY	unsteadily
ADEILOORST	oestradiol
ADEILOPQRU	quadripole
ADEILOPRST	depilators
ADEILOPRTT	tetraploid
ADEILOPRTY	depilatory
ADEILOPSSU	disepalous
ADEILOPSTU	dipetalous
ADEILOQSSU	odalisques
ADEILORSST	idolatress
ADEILORTUV	outrivaled
ADEILPRSSS	dispersals
ADEILPRSSY	displayers
ADEILPSTTU	platitudes
	stipulated
ADEILRSTTU	stridulate
ADEILRTTXY	dextrality
ADEILRTUUX	luxuriated
ADEIMMNOPT	pantomimed
ADEIMMNRST	mastermind
ADEIMMNTTU	manumitted
ADEIMMORST	moderatism
ADEIMMRSSU	summarised
ADEIMMRSUZ	summarized
ADEIMNNORT	ordainment
ADEIMNOORT	moderation
ADEIMNORRS	randomiser
ADEIMNORRZ	randomizer
ADEIMNORSS	randomises
ADEIMNORSZ	randomizes
ADEIMNOSST	staminodes
ADEIMNPRRS	reprimands
ADEIMNQRUU	Marinduque
ADEIMNRRTT	Mitterrand
ADEIMNRSSU	nursemaids
ADEIMNRSTY	dynamiters
ADEIMORRTY	radiometry
ADEIMORSST	dermatosis
ADEIMORSTT	meditators
ADEIMORTUY	audiometry
ADEIMORTWW	mowdiewart
ADEIMPRSST	spermatids
ADEIMRRSTY	martyrised
ADEIMRRTYZ	martyrized
ADEIMRSTUX	admixtures
ADEIMRTUUV	duumvirate
ADEINNNSTT	intendants
ADEINNOOTT	denotation
	detonation
ADEINNOPWW	windowpane
ADEINNORSW	rawinsonde
ADEINNOSTT	dentations
ADEINNRSSW	inwardness
ADEINNRSTU	unstrained
ADEINNRSTY	tyrannised
ADEINNRTYZ	tyrannized
ADEINOPRRS	preordains
ADEINOPRST	patronised
	predations
ADEINOPRTU	depuration
ADEINOPRTZ	patronized
ADEINOPTTU	deputation
ADEINORRSS	serranoids
ADEINORSST	adroitness
	intradoses
ADEINORSTY	arytenoids
ADEINORSUV	adenovirus
ADEINORTUW	autowinder
ADEINOSTUX	exudations
ADEINPPRSS	sandpipers
ADEINPPSST	standpipes
ADEINPRRST	transpired
ADEINPRSST	dispersant
ADEINPRSSY	dispensary
ADEINRSSTW	tawdriness
ADEINRSTTU	unstriated
ADEINSSSTU	unassisted
ADEIOPPRSV	disapprove
ADEIOPRRTU	repudiator
ADEIOPRSTY	depositary
ADEIOPRSTZ	trapezoids
ADEIORRSTT	traditores
ADEIORSSTT	siderostat
ADEIORSSTU	sudatories
ADEIORSSVW	disavowers
ADEIRRTTTU	triturated
ADEJMNSTTU	adjustment
ADEJOPSTUX	juxtaposed
ADEKMOPRST	postmarked
ADEKOPRTYY	karyotyped
ADELLLPTUU	pullulated
ADELLNNSUY	Lundy's Lane
ADELLNOPRS	landlopers
ADELLNORSW	lowlanders
ADELLOORRR	roadroller
ADELLOORRU	eurodollar
ADELMMOPSS	plasmodesm
ADELMNNRUY	laundrymen
ADELMOPSTU	deutoplasm
ADELNNNOOR	nandrolone
ADELNNOOST	East London
ADELNNORSW	landowners
ADELNOOSST	loadstones
ADELNOPRSS	pardonless
ADELNORSSU	slanderous
ADELNORSTU	outlanders
ADELNORSUY	roundelays
ADELNPPSTU	supplanted
ADELNPRSUY	underplays
ADELNRSTUW	wanderlust
ADELOORSST	desolators
ADELOPQRUU	quadrupole
ADELOPRSSU	superloads
ADELOPRSTU	sporulated
ADELOPSTTU	postulated
ADELORRSTX	dextrorsal
ADELORSTUU	adulterous
ADELPQRSUU	quadruples
ADELPQRTUU	quadruplet
ADELPQRUUX	quadruplex
ADELPSTTUU	pustulated
ADELRRSSTY	drysalters
ADELRSTWWY	westwardly
ADEMMMNORU	memorandum
ADEMMOOSTU	stomodaeum
ADEMNNORSS	randomness
ADEMNNORST	adornments
ADEMNORSTW	downstream
ADEMNRRTTU	Dürrenmatt
ADEMNRSTTU	transmuted
ADEMOORRST	moderators
ADEMOORSST	astrodomes
ADEMORSTTU	outsmarted
ADENNOPSTU	outspanned
ADENNORRRU	roadrunner
ADENNOSSST	sandstones
ADENNPRSTU	underpants
ADENNSSSTW	newsstands
ADENOORSTT	detonators
ADENOOSWWX	woodwaxens
ADENOPPRUV	unapproved
ADENOPRSST	transposed
ADENOPRSTV	davenports
	Van der Post
ADENORSSTV	standovers
ADENORSSTW	towardness
ADENOSSTTW	downstates

ADENOSTTWY wyandottes
ADENPPRSTU unstrapped
ADENPRRSTU underparts
ADENPRSSUW upwardness
ADENRRSSTW sternwards
ADEOPRRSTT prostrated
ADEOPRRSTU depurators
ADEOPRSSTU outspreads
ADEORRSSWW swearwords
ADEPPRSTUU suppurated
ADERRSSTUU susurrated
ADFFGILNOO offloading
ADFFIIMRSS disaffirms
ADFGIIMNNY damnifying
ADFGIMNRTU Grand Mufti
ADFGINORRU fairground
ADFGINORRW forwarding
ADFHILLORS dollarfish
ADFHILRSWY dwarfishly
ADFHINNOOT infanthood
ADFIIILNOS solifidian
ADFIIILPTT Fittipaldi
ADFIIINNPT pinnatifid
ADFIILMRSU disulfiram
ADFIILQSUY disqualify
ADFIIOSSTU fastidious
ADFIISSSTY dissatisfy
ADFILLMNOY manifoldly
ADFILLNOOP floodplain
ADFILNOOSV flavonoids
ADFINNOOTU foundation
ADFINNORSU infrasound
ADFINRSSTT standfirst
ADFIORSSUV disfavours
ADFLLOOSST faldstools
ADFLNORSTW strandwolf
ADFNOORSSZ sforzandos
ADFNOORTUY foudroyant
ADFNORRSTW frontwards
ADGGIILNOU dialoguing
ADGGIILNSS glissading
ADGGIINNOS diagnosing
ADGGILLNNY danglingly
ADGGINNOOR dragooning
ADGGINNOPP dognapping
ADGGLLRSUY sluggardly
ADGHHOOPRS hodographs
ADGHHOPRRY hydrograph
ADGHIILNOY holidaying
ADGHILLLSU guildhalls
ADGHILRTUY draughtily
ADGHINNPRS handspring
ADGHINRSTU indraughts
ADGHIRRSTW rightwards
ADGHIRSTTU distraught
ADGHNOOPRS ondographs
ADGHNOSSTU staghounds
ADGHOOPRXY doxography
ADGHPRSTUU updraughts
ADGIIILMNO Modigliani
ADGIIILMST digitalism
ADGIIILNNV invaliding
ADGIIINOTT digitation
ADGIIKNNPP kidnapping
ADGIIKNNPS kidnapings
ADGIILMNOU gadolinium
ADGIILMNRY admiringly
ADGIILNPSY displaying
ADGIILOSST dialogists
ADGIIMNNOS nomadising
ADGIIMNNOT dominating
ADGIIMNNOZ nomadizing
ADGIIMNNTY dynamiting
ADGIIMNPRY pyramiding
ADGIIMNSST dismasting
ADGIINNNTU inundating
ADGIINNOPR poniarding
ADGIINNRTU indurating
ADGIINOSVW disavowing
ADGIINRSST distringas
ADGIINSSTT distasting
ADGIJNNORU adjourning
ADGIKLORTU Utgard-Loki
ADGIKOORRV Kirovograd
ADGILLNNOS Long Island
ADGILLNOPR pollarding
ADGILLNYZZ dazzlingly
ADGILLOPRY prodigally
ADGILMNOSW gildswoman
ADGILMNOTU modulating
ADGILNNNOW landowning
ADGILNNORT Darlington
ADGILNNTUU undulating
ADGILNNTUY dauntingly
ADGILNOSSS glissandos
ADGILNOSTT Ingolstadt
ADGILORTUV divulgator
ADGIMNNORT mordanting
ADGIMNNRSY gynandrism
ADGIMOSSTT dogmatists
ADGINNOOSU iguanodons
ADGINNOSTU astounding
ADGINNPSTU upstanding
ADGINNRSTU transuding
ADGINOPSTT postdating
ADGINRRSTW drawstring
ADGLLNOSUU glandulous
ADGLMNOOOY monadology
ADGLNOPRUY playground
ADGMNNORSU groundsman
ADGMNORSSU groundmass
ADGMOORRSU guardrooms
ADGNNORSUY gynandrous
ADGNOOORRT dragonroot
ADGOOPRSST gastropods
ADHHNOORSU hoarhounds
ADHHNOSTTU thousandth
ADHHOPRSTY hydropaths
ADHHOPRTYY hydropathy
ADHIIIKKKL Khalkidíki
ADHIILLNOP phalloidin
ADHIILMNOT Midlothian
ADHIIMMNPS midshipman
ADHIIMSTTU humidistat
ADHIINNSTU Hindustani
ADHIINORSS anhidrosis
ADHILLLOPY phyllodial
ADHILLNOSY Holy Island
ADHILMNPSY nymphalids
ADHILNOPYY hypolydian
ADHILNOSTU outlandish
ADHILOOPRS drosophila
ADHIMNORSY disharmony
ADHIMNOTWY Whit Monday
ADHINNOOOT nationhood
ADHINNOSTY hydantoins
ADHINOOPRT anthropoid
ADHINOOPRY hypodorian
radiophony
ADHINOOPRZ rhizopodan
ADHINOPSTU Diophantus
ADHINORSTY hydrations
ADHINSSTTW withstands
ADHINSTUWY Whitsunday
Whit Sunday
ADHIOPRSST rhapsodist
ADHIOPRSTY dystrophia
ADHIORSTXY hydrotaxis
ADHKNNORTU drunkathon
ADHLNOPSSW splashdown
ADHMNOOORT matronhood
ADHNOORSYZ hydrozoans
ADHNORRSTW northwards
ADHNORSTUY hydronauts
ADHNORSTWW Wandsworth
ADHOOPRRST arthropods
ADHOORRTWY roadworthy
ADHORSSTTY hydrostats
ADHORSSTUW southwards
ADIIILMNSV invalidism
ADIIILMRSS dissimilar
ADIIILNOSV divisional
ADIIILNTVY invalidity
ADIIINNOTV divination
ADIIINOOST iodisation
ADIIINOOTZ iodization
ADIILLORTY dilatorily
ADIILMMNSU maudlinism
ADIILMNOXY mixolydian
ADIILMOPRR primordial
ADIILMOPRS prismoidal
ADIILMSSSS dismissals
ADIILNORRY ordinarily
ADIILNOSSU sinusoidal
ADIILNOSTU nautiloids
ADIILNRSTU industrial
ADIILOPPSY polydipsia
ADIILOQRTU liquidator
ADIILORSSY radiolysis
ADIILORSTY solidarity
ADIILQSTUY squalidity
ADIIMMMOTU ommatidium
ADIIMNNOOT admonition
domination
ADIIMNORTX dominatrix
ADIIMNOSSS admissions

ADIIMNRSST misandrist
ADIIMOPRST diatropism
prismatoid
ADIIMORTUU auditorium
ADIIMQRUUV quadrivium
ADIINNNOTU inundation
ADIINNOORT ordination
ADIINNORTU induration
ADIINOPPST disappoint
ADIINOPSSS dispassion
ADIINOQSTU quotidians
ADIINORRST distrainor
ADIINORSTT traditions
ADIINORTVY divinatory
ADIINOSSSU dissuasion
ADIINRSSTT distraints
ADIINRSSTU saturniids
ADIIOPRSST dissipator
ADIIOPRSTT podiatrist
ADILLLOSVY disloyally
ADILLNSSTT standstill
ADILLOSTYY disloyalty
ADILMMOPSU plasmodium
ADILMNNOTY dominantly
ADILMNOOOP monopodial
ADILMNOOSS salmonoids
ADILMNOOTU modulation
ADILMOPSST psalmodist
ADILMORTUY modularity
ADILNNOTUU undulation
ADILNORSSS Ross Island
ADILNORSTW antiworlds
ADILNRSTTU stridulant
ADILOOPSTY stylopodia
ADILOORSTU idolatrous
ADILORSSTW swordtails
ADIMNOORST admonitors
dominators
ADIMNOORTY admonitory
ADIMNORSSU misandrous
ADIMNRRTUV Trivandrum
ADIMORSTUU sudatorium
ADINNOPSTT standpoint
ADINNORSTU inundators
ADINNORTUY inundatory
ADINOOPRST adsorption
ADINOPSSTY dystopians
ADINORSSTW downstairs
ADINPSSTTU disputants
ADIORSSSTU disastrous
ADJMMOOORS majordomos
ADKNOORRUW workaround
ADLLMORSSW smallsword
ADLMOOORSU malodorous
ADLMOORSTU modulators
ADLMOORTUY modulatory
ADLMOPRSUW mouldwarps
ADLMOPRUWY mouldywarp
ADLNNOORSW nanoworlds
Rowlandson
ADLNORSTUU ultrasound
undulators
ADLNORTUUY undulatory
ADLNORTUWY untowardly
ADLOOOSSTT toadstools
ADMNNOORSU monandrous
ADMNOORSTY dynamotors
ADMNORSSST sandstorms
ADMOOOPSTT stomatopod
ADMOOPPRSU pompadours
ADNNORRTUU turnaround
ADNOPRRSUW wraprounds
ADOOORRSWW arrowwoods
AEEEEGKMPR gamekeeper
AEEEEGKPRT gatekeeper
AEEEEGLNSS Senegalese
AEEEEGNRRT regenerate
AEEEEGRTTV revegetate
AEEEELNOPT elaeoptene
AEEEENRTTX exenterate
AEEEFFGLRU effleurage
AEEEFFIMNT effeminate
AEEEFGLNRU enfleurage
AEEEFHRRTT thereafter
AEEEFHRRTW whereafter
AEEEFINRTZ antifreeze
AEEEFLLNST fenestella
AEEEFLLRST leafleters
AEEEFLMNSS femaleness
AEEEFLNOOZ Zeno of Elea
AEEEFNRRST transferee
AEEEFNRSTT fenestrate
AEEEGGGNRS greengages
AEEEGGMNNT engagement
AEEEGGRSST segregates
AEEEGHLPRT telpherage
AEEEGHLRSW gearwheels
AEEEGHMNST Gethsemane
AEEEGHMRST megatheres
AEEEGHNRRT greenheart
AEEEGILNRS generalise
AEEEGILNRZ generalize
AEEEGILNSV evangelise
AEEEGILNUV eigenvalue
AEEEGILNVZ evangelize
AEEEGIMNRS menageries
AEEEGINNRT ingenerate
AEEEGINRTV generative
AEEEGITTVV vegetative
AEEEGKLOPR goalkeeper
AEEEGLMNRT regalement
AEEEGLMPSX megaplexes
AEEEGLNOST eaglestone
AEEEGLRSSS eelgrasses
greaseless
AEEEGLSSSY eyeglasses
AEEEGMNNPS empennages
AEEEGMNNRT enragement
AEEEGMNRSS meagerness
meagreness
AEEEGMNRST agreements
AEEEGNRSTW tweenagers
AEEEGPRSSX expressage
AEEEGQSTUU squeteague
AEEEGRSTTZ gazetteers
AEEEHHINST heathenise
AEEEHHINTZ heathenize
AEEEHILMMT Mehemet Ali
AEEEHKNRRS hearkeners
AEEEHLLRTY ethereally
AEEEHLMPRS ephemerals
AEEEHLRTWW waterwheel
AEEEHMNORX hexaemeron
AEEEHMNRTW weathermen
AEEEHMPRTT heptameter
AEEEHMRSTX hexameters
AEEEHMSSTT metatheses
AEEEHNNNPT nepenthean
AEEEHNORTY honeyeater
AEEEHNRRTT threatener
AEEEHOPRRS aerosphere
AEEEHRRRSS rehearsers
AEEEHRRSTW weatherers
AEEEHRSTTW sweetheart
AEEEIIPPRT peripeteia
AEEEILNRST eternalise
AEEEILNRTV interleave
AEEEILNRTZ eternalize
AEEEILRSST easterlies
AEEEIMNRSX reexamines
AEEEIMNRTT intemerate
AEEEIMNSTV Vietnamese
AEEEIMPRTV permeative
AEEEINNNTV antivenene
AEEEINNRTT intenerate
AEEEINRSTT entreaties
AEEEINRTTV inveterate
AEEEINRTVV enervative
AEEEINRTVW interweave
AEEEIPPRST papeteries
AEEEIRRSTT reiterates
AEEEJKRRRT tearjerker
AEEEJNRTUV rejuvenate
AEEEKLSTTT teakettles
AEEEKNSSSW weaknesses
AEEEKPSSTW sweepstake
AEEELLMNRS enamellers
AEEELLRSST teasellers
AEEELLSSTT tessellate
AEEELMMNPT empalement
AEEELMNNTT lentamente
tenemental
AEEELMNRTT manteltree
mantletree
AEEELMNRTV revealment
AEEELMNRTY elementary
AEEELNNPPS peneplanes
AEEELNNUVZ Venezuelan
AEEELNPRTT terneplate
AEEELPSTTU epaulettes
AEEEMMNORT anemometer
AEEEMMNSST semantemes
AEEEMNNRST nemerteans
AEEEMNPRTT pentameter
AEEEMNRRTU remunerate
AEEEMNRRUV maneuverer

AEEEMNRSTU	enumerates
AEEEMORRST	aerometers
AEEEMRRSSU	remeasures
AEEEMRRTTT	tetrameter
AEEEMRSTVW	wavemeters
AEEEMSSTTW	sweetmeats
AEEENNNSST	Tennessean
AEEENNPRST	perennates
AEEENOPRSW	weaponeers
AEEENORSTX	exonerates
AEEENPRSST	sea serpent
AEEENPRSTT	penetrates
AEEENRRSST	easterners
AEEENRSSSV	averseness
AEEENSTTUV	eventuates
AEEENSTTUX	extenuates
AEEEPPRRTT	perpetrate
AEEEPPRTTU	perpetuate
AEEERRSTTW	streetwear
AEEERRSTYY	yesteryear
AEEERSSSSS	reassesses
AEEFFHORRT	forefather
AEEFFORRST	reafforest
AEEFGGHIRT	freightage
AEEFGHINRT	feathering
AEEFGHORRT	foregather
AEEFGILLNT	leafleting
AEEFGILLRS	fillagrees
AEEFGILPRS	persiflage
AEEFGINSTU	teniafuges
AEEFGLLNSS	flangeless
AEEFGLLOST	flageolets
AEEFGLPRSU	presageful
AEEFGORRRU	fourragere
AEEFHHINRT	Fahrenheit
AEEFHIKLRT	fatherlike
AEEFHIKSSW	weakfishes
AEEFHINPRT	pinfeather
AEEFHLOPPR	leafhopper
AEEFHLRSST	fatherless
AEEFHMMRST	Hammerfest
AEEFHMORTT	fathometer
AEEFHPRSTT	stepfather
AEEFHRRSTW	freshwater
AEEFIIRRRS	farrieries
AEEFIKNPPR	paperknife
AEEFIKNRSS	freakiness
AEEFILNSST	featliness
AEEFILOPRT	perfoliate
AEEFILOSTX	exfoliates
AEEFILRSSV	lifesavers
AEEFILRSTT	flatteries
AEEFILRSTV	afterlives
AEEFIMNRRT	freemartin
AEEFINRRRS	refrainers
AEEFINRRST	fraternise
AEEFINRRTZ	fraternize
AEEFKOPRSS	forespeaks
AEEFLLNNOT	fontanelle
AEEFLLNRUY	funereally
AEEFLLNSTU	fustanelle
AEEFLLRSSY	fearlessly
AEEFLMORSY	fearsomely
AEEFLNRSTT	flatteners
AEEFLRRSTT	flatterers
AEEFMNORSS	freemasons
AEEFNORRRW	forewarner
AEEFNRRRST	retransfer
AEEFOPRRST	perforates
AEEFORRRSW	forswearer
AEEFORSSTT	foretastes
AEEGGGINNR	reengaging
AEEGGHILRT	lighterage
AEEGGHMOSU	hemagogues
AEEGGHOPRR	geographer
AEEGGILNRT	regelating
	relegating
AEEGGINNRT	generating
	greatening
AEEGGINORW	New Georgia
AEEGGINRRS	grangerise
	gregarines
AEEGGINRRZ	grangerize
AEEGGINTTV	vegetating
AEEGGIRSSV	aggressive
AEEGGMNOTY	gametogeny
AEEGGMORRT	remortgage
AEEGGMORST	mortgagees
AEEGGNNRTU	Terengganu
AEEGGNOTTW	waggonette
AEEGGORRST	segregator
AEEGGRRSST	staggerers
AEEGGRRSSW	swaggerers
AEEGHHMORR	hemorrhage
AEEGHIILMP	hemiplegia
AEEGHIKMTW	makeweight
AEEGHIKNNR	hearkening
AEEGHILNRT	leathering
AEEGHILPST	legateship
AEEGHILRST	lethargies
AEEGHIMRST	hermitages
AEEGHINNRT	heartening
AEEGHINPRT	preheating
AEEGHINRRS	rehearsing
AEEGHINRRT	ingatherer
AEEGHINRSS	garnishees
AEEGHINRST	reheatings
AEEGHINRTW	weathering
AEEGHIPPRR	epigrapher
AEEGHKNNRS	greenshank
AEEGHLMORT	geothermal
AEEGHLNTVW	wavelength
AEEGHLORTT	altogether
AEEGHLPRST	telegraphs
AEEGHLPRTY	telegraphy
AEEGHMNOOT	homogenate
AEEGHMNOPS	megaphones
AEEGHMORTY	heterogamy
AEEGHNOPST	pathogenes
AEEGHORSTT	othergates
AEEGHOSSTU	gatehouses
AEEGIILLLS	illegalise
AEEGIILLLZ	illegalize
AEEGIILLNV	villeinage
AEEGIILLST	legalities
AEEGIILMTT	legitimate
AEEGIILNST	gelatinise
AEEGIILNTZ	gelatinize
AEEGIILRST	regalities
AEEGIILRSZ	glazieries
AEEGIIMNNT	ingeminate
AEEGIIMNST	enigmatise
AEEGIIMNTZ	enigmatize
AEEGIINRRT	garnierite
AEEGIKNNRW	rewakening
AEEGILLMNN	enamelling
AEEGILLNST	teaselling
AEEGILLNSW	weaselling
AEEGILLNTZ	teazelling
AEEGILLORS	allegories
	allegorise
AEEGILLORZ	allegorize
AEEGILLRSV	grevilleas
AEEGILLSST	legislates
AEEGILMNNP	empaneling
AEEGILMNRR	malingerer
AEEGILMNRT	regimental
AEEGILMNSV	evangelism
AEEGILMNTY	geminately
AEEGILNNRR	relearning
AEEGILNNSS	genialness
AEEGILNNST	eglantines
AEEGILNNSV	leavenings
AEEGILNORT	regelation
	relegation
AEEGILNRRT	realtering
AEEGILNRST	generalist
AEEGILNRTU	Argenteuil
AEEGILNRTY	generality
AEEGILNSTV	evangelist
AEEGILNTVY	negatively
AEEGILRRSU	regularise
AEEGILRRUZ	regularize
AEEGILRSST	gaiterless
AEEGILRSTU	gauleiters
AEEGILRTUV	regulative
AEEGIMNOSX	xenogamies
AEEGIMNPRT	impregnate
	permeating
AEEGIMNRST	germanites
	germinates
	magnetiser
AEEGIMNRSZ	germanizes
AEEGIMNRTZ	magnetizer
AEEGIMNSST	magnetises
AEEGIMNSTU	mutagenise
AEEGIMNSTZ	magnetizes
AEEGIMNTUZ	mutagenize
AEEGIMOSST	isogametes
AEEGIMPSTT	pegmatites
AEEGIMRRST	remigrates
AEEGIMRRTU	marguerite
AEEGIMRRTV	gravimeter
AEEGIMSTTU	guestimate
AEEGINNNSU	ensanguine
AEEGINNORT	generation

AEEGINNPSS pangenesis
AEEGINNRRT interregna
AEEGINNRST argentines
tangerines
AEEGINNRTT entreating
AEEGINNRTV enervating
venerating
AEEGINNSUX exsanguine
AEEGINORRS orangeries
reorganise
AEEGINORRZ reorganize
AEEGINORTV overeating
AEEGINOSTT negotiates
AEEGINOTTV vegetation
AEEGINPPRR repapering
AEEGINPRST interpages
AEEGINPRSV grapevines
AEEGINPRSY panegyrise
AEEGINPRYZ panegyrize
AEEGINRRTT retreating
AEEGINRRTX generatrix
AEEGINRSSS greasiness
AEEGINRSST stingarees
AEEGINRSSV vernissage
AEEGINRSTT estreating
integrates
AEEGINSSST giantesses
AEEGIRSSTT strategies
AEEGKORRWW wageworker
AEEGLLNORS organelles
AEEGLLNOSS los Angeles
AEEGLLORTT allegretto
AEEGLMMOSY gamesomely
AEEGLMNNTT tanglement
AEEGLMNTTU tegumental
AEEGLMORST algometers
AEEGLMRRSW legwarmers
AEEGLNNPST pentangles
AEEGLNNRST entanglers
AEEGLNORSS sloganeers
AEEGLNORTU outgeneral
AEEGLNORTV graveolent
AEEGLORTUV travelogue
AEEGLRSSTT targetless
AEEGMNNOST mangosteen
AEEGMNOQSU Monegasque
AEEGMNRRSS mergansers
AEEGMNRSTU augmenters
AEEGMNRSTW West German
AEEGMNRSTY segmentary
AEEGMOPRSS megaspores
AEEGMORRST stereogram
AEEGMORSST gasometers
AEEGMRSSTU gaussmeter
AEEGNNORTT Teton Range
AEEGNNSSTW newsagents
AEEGNOPRSS personages
AEEGNORRST generators
AEEGNORSTT teratogens
AEEGNORSTU entourages
AEEGNORSTV gravestone
AEEGNOSTTW wagonettes
AEEGNOSTXY oxygenates
AEEGNPRSSS passengers
AEEGNRRSST estrangers
AEEGOPRRST reportages
AEEGORRSVZ overgrazes
AEEGPRSTUX expurgates
AEEGRRSSSY ryegrasses
AEEHHHINST heathenish
AEEHHILMOP haemophile
AEEHHILSTT healthiest
AEEHHIMNST heathenism
AEEHHINRST earthshine
AEEHHKNPSS sheepshank
AEEHHLMSTU Methuselah
AEEHHLOSSW hawseholes
AEEHHLOTWW wholewheat
AEEHHNNPST naphthenes
AEEHHNPSTY hyphenates
AEEHHNSSTU unsheathes
AEEHHPSSTU Hephaestus
AEEHIILLPT epithelial
AEEHIILMST Ishmaelite
AEEHIIMPRT Ephraimite
AEEHIINPPS epiphanies
AEEHIISTTV hesitative
AEEHIKLNNP enkephalin
AEEHIKLNOR Herakleion
AEEHIKLRTW wreathlike
AEEHILLORT heliolater
AEEHILMOST mesothelia
AEEHILMRST thermalise
AEEHILMRTY hemielytra
AEEHILMRTZ thermalize
AEEHILNRUY euryhaline
AEEHILNSSV shinleaves
AEEHILNSTW Wiesenthal
AEEHILNSTX anthelixes
AEEHILOPSU heliopause
AEEHILORTU Haute-Loire
AEEHILPPRR peripheral
AEEHILPPSY epiphyseal
AEEHILPRST sphalerite
AEEHILPSST shapeliest
AEEHILRSTT earthliest
stealthier
AEEHILRTTT triathlete
AEEHILSTTW wealthiest
AEEHIMMNNR Mannerheim
AEEHIMMRSX hexamerism
AEEHIMNPRT hemipteran
AEEHIMNRUZ rehumanize
AEEHIMNSST mainsheets
AEEHIMPSSS emphasises
AEEHIMPSST empathises
AEEHIMPSSZ emphasizes
AEEHIMPSTZ empathizes
AEEHIMRRTY erythremia
AEEHIMRSST hetaerisms
AEEHIMSSTT metathesis
AEEHINORST antiheroes
AEEHINPRST interphase
AEEHINRSST earthiness
heartiness
AEEHINRSSV haversines
AEEHINRSTU eutherians
AEEHINRTTU uintathere
AEEHINSSTT antitheses
AEEHIPPSSW hawsepipes
AEEHIPRSSU euphrasies
AEEHIRRSST earthrises
trasheries
AEEHIRSSTT hesitaters
hetaerists
AEEHISTUVX exhaustive
AEEHKLORRU leukorrhea
AEEHKLPSSW sheepwalks
AEEHKMMORS homemakers
AEEHKMORSS shoemakers
AEEHKOPSSV spokeshave
AEEHKORSTT heatstroke
AEEHKORSTV Tereshkova
AEEHKOSSTU steakhouse
AEEHLLMRTY hemelytral
AEEHLLNRRT enthraller
AEEHLLORSW wholesaler
AEEHLLOSSW wholesales
AEEHLLSSTW wealthless
AEEHLMMRSS hammerless
AEEHLMNNOP phenomenal
AEEHLMORTX exothermal
AEEHLMOSSY haemolyses
AEEHLMSTTY methylates
AEEHLNOPRS Rhône-Alpes
AEEHLNOPST phenolates
AEEHLNPPRY hyperplane
AEEHLRSSTW wreathless
AEEHLRSTTY Hattersley
AEEHLRTTTY tetraethyl
AEEHLSSTXY hexastyles
AEEHMMORST hammertoes
AEEHMNNSSU humaneness
AEEHMNOORR menorrhoea
AEEHMNOPRT Promethean
AEEHMNRSTV harvestmen
AEEHMOPRSS semaphores
AEEHMOPRST atmosphere
AEEHMORRRT arthromere
AEEHMORRTV earthmover
AEEHMORSUX hexamerous
AEEHMORTTY metatheory
AEEHMPRSST petershams
AEEHNNOPSX Xenophanes
AEEHNOOPRR harpooneer
AEEHNOORST oenotheras
AEEHNOPPRT Parthenope
AEEHNOPPRY hyperpnoea
AEEHNORSSS hoarseness
AEEHNPRRSS sharpeners
AEEHNRRSSS harnessers
AEEHOOPRST peashooter
AEEHOOPSST apotheoses
AEEHOPRSTY aerophytes
AEEHOPTTTY typothetae
AEEHORSSUW warehouses

AEEHORSTUW	Waterhouse
AEEHORSTVW	whatsoever
AEEHORTTXY	heterotaxy
AEEHOSSTTU	statehouse
AEEHPRSSTU	superheats
AEEHPRSUVY	superheavy
AEEHRRSSTT	shatterers
AEEHRRSSTV	harvesters
AEEHRSSTUX	exhausters
AEEIIKNRST	keratinise
AEEIIKNRTZ	keratinize
AEEIILLOPS	aeolipiles
AEEIILLRRS	railleries
AEEIILLRTT	illiterate
AEEIILMNRS	mineralise
AEEIILMNRZ	mineralize
AEEIILMNST	eliminates
AEEIILNPRU	epineurial
AEEIILNPRX	pre-exilian
AEEIILNSTV	venalities
AEEIILQSTU	equalities
AEEIILRRTV	irrelative
AEEIILRSSS	serialises
AEEIILRSSZ	serializes
AEEIILRSTV	relativise
	revitalise
AEEIILRTVZ	relativize
	revitalize
AEEIIMNNST	inseminate
AEEIIMNNTT	tiemannite
AEEIIMNRSS	seminaries
AEEIIMPRTV	imperative
AEEIIMRSSS	emissaries
AEEIIMSTTV	estimative
AEEIINPPRT	peripetian
AEEIINPPRZ	piperazine
AEEIINPSST	epinasties
AEEIINRSTT	itinerates
AEEIINRSTU	uniseriate
AEEIINTTTV	entitative
AEEIIPPRST	peripetias
AEEIIPPTTV	appetitive
AEEIIPRSST	asperities
	patisserie
AEEIIPRSSV	vespiaries
AEEIIRRSTT	tertiaries
AEEIIRSSTV	vestiaries
AEEIIRSTVZ	vizierates
AEEIJLOSSU	jealousies
AEEIJMNSSS	jessamines
AEEIJOPRTV	pejorative
AEEIKKLRST	streaklike
AEEIKLLNSS	silkalenes
AEEIKLMRST	streamlike
AEEIKLNNRT	Interlaken
AEEIKLNOPU	leukopenia
AEEIKLNSSW	weakliness
AEEIKLPRSS	sprekelias
AEEIKLRRWW	wirewalker
AEEIKMNORS	noisemaker
AEEIKMRRST	Steiermark
AEEIKNNSSS	sneakiness
AEEIKNRRSV	Snake River
AEEIKQSSTU	squeakiest
AEEIKRSSTT	streakiest
AEEILLLLNV	villanelle
AEEILLMNST	enamellist
AEEILLMRSS	marseilles
AEEILLMSST	metallises
AEEILLMSTZ	metallizes
AEEILLNOST	linoleates
AEEILLNSVV	Evansville
AEEILLORSY	Isle Royale
AEEILLPSST	palletises
AEEILLPSTT	paillettes
	stipellate
AEEILLPSTZ	palletizes
AEEILLRSSV	Versailles
AEEILLRSTV	trevallies
AEEILLRTTY	literately
AEEILLRTVY	relatively
AEEILLSSTT	satellites
AEEILLSTUV	televisual
AEEILMMNPT	impalement
AEEILMMNRU	neurilemma
AEEILMMSST	lemmatises
AEEILMMSTZ	lemmatizes
AEEILMNNNO	Nemean lion
AEEILMNNST	alinements
	lineaments
AEEILMNNTT	entailment
AEEILMNORS	neorealism
AEEILMNPRT	planimeter
AEEILMNRST	streamline
AEEILMNRSY	minelayers
AEEILMNSST	enamelists
	mesnalties
AEEILMOOSS	elaiosomes
AEEILMORST	meliorates
AEEILMRSST	misrelates
	salimeters
AEEILMRSTT	altimeters
AEEILMRSYY	semiyearly
AEEILNNPPS	peneplains
AEEILNNPRS	perennials
AEEILNNPST	septennial
AEEILNNSSX	sexennials
AEEILNNSTT	sentential
AEEILNNSTV	levantines
	valentines
AEEILNNTTU	lieutenant
AEEILNOPRT	peritoneal
AEEILNORST	neorealist
AEEILNORTV	revelation
AEEILNOSTV	elevations
AEEILNPPPS	pineapples
AEEILNPRSS	pearliness
AEEILNPRST	alpestrine
	episternal
AEEILNPRSX	explainers
AEEILNQSTU	sequential
AEEILNQTUV	equivalent
AEEILNRRTV	irrelevant
AEEILNRSSV	vernalises
AEEILNRSTU	neutralise
AEEILNRSVZ	vernalizes
AEEILNRTTY	eternality
AEEILNRTUZ	neutralize
AEEILNSSST	essentials
AEEILNSSSZ	sleaziness
AEEILNSTTV	ventilates
AEEILNSTVX	sexivalent
AEEILOPRST	periosteal
AEEILORRST	arterioles
AEEILORRSV	revalorise
AEEILORRVZ	revalorize
AEEILORTTV	tolerative
AEEILPPRRT	peripteral
AEEILPRRRV	Pearl River
AEEILPRRSV	prevailers
AEEILPRSST	psalteries
AEEILPRSSY	erysipelas
AEEILPRSTX	Praxiteles
AEEILPSTTU	estipulate
AEEILQRSSU	equalisers
AEEILQRSUZ	equalizers
AEEILRRSTV	retrievals
AEEILRRSVV	Slave River
AEEILRRSVW	silverware
AEEILRRTTU	literature
AEEILRSTTU	elutriates
	tutelaries
AEEILRSVVY	aversively
AEEILSSSUX	sexualises
AEEILSSTTT	stateliest
AEEILSSUXZ	sexualizes
AEEIMMMRST	metamerism
AEEIMMOPRT	emmetropia
AEEIMMRSSU	mismeasure
AEEIMNNORT	enantiomer
	renominate
AEEIMNNRTT	retainment
AEEIMNNRTU	innumerate
AEEIMNNSZZ	mezzanines
AEEIMNOPRT	permeation
AEEIMNORTT	marionette
AEEIMNOSTT	maisonette
AEEIMNPRRU	praemunire
AEEIMNRSSS	smeariness
AEEIMNRSTT	martensite
	terminates
AEEIMNRTUV	numerative
AEEIMNSSST	steaminess
AEEIMNSSTT	estaminets
AEEIMOPPRS	peperomias
AEEIMOPQSU	semiopaque
AEEIMORRSS	rosemaries
AEEIMORRTV	variometer
AEEIMORSSS	isomerases
AEEIMPRRSS	spermaries
AEEIMPRSTT	impetrates
AEEIMQRSUV	semiquaver
AEEIMRSSTT	streamiest
	tasimeters
AEEIMRSTTX	taximeters
AEEINNNPWY	Pennine Way

AEEINNNSSS insaneness
AEEINNNSST innateness
AEEINNORTV enervation
veneration
AEEINNOTTT Antoinette
AEEINNPPTT inappetent
AEEINNRSSW swanneries
AEEINNRSTT entertains
tenantries
AEEINNRSTV innervates
AEEINNRTUV aventurine
AEEINNSSSU uneasiness
AEEINNSSTT assentient
AEEINNSSTV nativeness
AEEINOPPST appointees
AEEINOPRST proteinase
AEEINOPRTX paroxetine
AEEINOPSSW weaponises
AEEINOPSWZ weaponizes
AEEINOPTTT potentiate
AEEINORSTT orientates
AEEINORTVV renovative
AEEINPPRSS paperiness
AEEINPPSST pepsinates
AEEINPRSSS passerines
AEEINPRSST pistareens
AEEINPRSTU resupinate
AEEINPSTTU uniseptate
AEEINQRSTU equestrian
AEEINQSSSU queasiness
AEEINRRRST errantries
restrainer
AEEINRRTTV travertine
AEEINRRTVY veterinary
AEEINRSSSY synaeresis
AEEINRSSTT reinstates
AEEINRSSTW wateriness
AEEINRSTTT interstate
AEEINSSSTT titanesses
AEEINSSSTW sweatiness
AEEINSSSTY yeastiness
AEEINSSTTT intestates
AEEIOPRRSV overpraise
AEEIOPRSST operatises
AEEIOPRSTV evaporites
operatives
AEEIOPRSTZ operatizes
AEEIPPRRTW wiretapper
AEEIPPRSST appetisers
AEEIPPRSSU pauperises
AEEIPPRSTZ appetizers
AEEIPPRSUZ pauperizes
AEEIPRRSTV privateers
AEEIPRSSTT striptease
tapestries
AEEIPRSSTU pasteurise
AEEIPRSSUV persuasive
AEEIPRSTTX extirpates
sexpartite
AEEIPRSTUZ pasteurize
AEEIPRTTUV vituperate
AEEIRRSSTU treasuries
AEEIRSSSTW waitresses
AEEIRSSTTV travesties
AEEIRSSTWW wasteweirs
AEEIRSTTUX textuaries
AEEJLNORSU journalese
AEEJMORSTT majorettes
AEEKLLLSTY skeletally
AEEKLLORSW Lower Lakes
AEEKLLPSSW sleepwalks
AEEKLMNNRT kernmantel
AEEKLMNORW enamelwork
AEEKMMNORY moneymaker
AEEKMMRRRY merrymaker
AEEKMNRSTW newmarkets
AEEKMORRTU euromarket
AEEKMPRRTV verkrampte
AEEKORSTUY eukaryotes
AEELLLSTTY stellately
AEELLMMRRT trammeller
AEELLMNOTV malevolent
AEELLMNRTU allurement
AEELLMNSSY namelessly
AEELLNPRST repellants
AEELLNPSTX expellants
AEELLNRRUV unraveller
AEELLNRTVY relevantly
AEELLNRTXY externally
AEELLNTUVY eventually
AEELLOPSST sellotapes
soleplates
AEELLORSTT rostellate
AEELLOTTTY teetotally
AEELLQRRRU quarreller
AEELLRRSTV travellers
AEELLRSTTU tellurates
AEELLRSTTW Wall Street
AEELMMNORU neurolemma
AEELMMNRST entrammels
AEELMMRRST trammelers
AEELMNNRSS mannerless
AEELMNOPRT planometer
AEELMNORTV overmantel
AEELMNORTW watermelon
AEELMNOSSW saleswomen
AEELMNPRST parlements
AEELMNRSTV ravelments
AEELMNSTTV vestmental
AEELMOPRSY polymerase
AEELMOPSTT palmettoes
AEELMORSST elastomers
AEELMORTTV voltameter
AEELMOSTTT matelottes
AEELMPRSSU supermales
AEELMPRSTT streetlamp
AEELMRSSST masterless
AEELMRSSTT streamlets
AEELNNNSTU antennules
AEELNNORSW New Orleans
AEELNNPSTW new planets
AEELNNPTTU antepenult
AEELNNQSTU lansquenet
AEELNNSSTT tenantless
AEELNOPSSW weaponless
AEELNOPSTX exoplanets
AEELNOSSSS seasonless
AEELNPRSST parentless
AEELNPRTTW wentletrap
AEELOPPRTU repopulate
AEELOPSSTT salopettes
AEELOQRRUU roquelaure
AEELORSTTU lotus-eater
AEELORSUVV overvalues
AEELPPRSTU perpetuals
AEELPRRSST plasterers
AEELPRRSSY prayerless
AEELPRRSTU prelatures
AEELQRRRSU quarrelers
AEELQRSSTU sequestral
AEELRRSTUW lusterware
lustreware
AEELRSSTTY treatyless
AEEMMNORST manometers
AEEMMNORTT antemortem
AEEMMNORTY anemometry
AEEMMNSSTU amusements
AEEMMORSTT atmometers
AEEMMRRSST stammerers
AEEMNNOPRS praenomens
AEEMNNORST nanometres
AEEMNNORUV mavourneen
AEEMNNOSTT atonements
AEEMNNPRTT entrapment
AEEMNNRSST Stresemann
AEEMNOPRST treponemas
AEEMNOPSYZ apoenzymes
AEEMNORRTU enumerator
AEEMNORRUV manoeuvrer
AEEMNORSST sarmentose
AEEMNORSUV manoeuvres
AEEMNPPRTY prepayment
AEEMNPRSTY repayments
AEEMNRRSTT arrestment
AEEMNRSSTU matureness
AEEMNRSTTT treatments
AEEMNRSTTU menstruate
AEEMNSSSST assessment
AEEMNSSTTT statements
testaments
AEEMORRSTT rotameters
AEEMORRSTV overmaster
AEEMORRTTV overmatter
AEEMORSSSY mayoresses
AEEMORSTTU autometers
AEEMPRSTTT attempters
reattempts
AEEMPRSTTU permutates
AEEMQRSSSU marquesses
AEEMRRSSTT smatterers
AEEMRSSSST seamstress
AEEMRSSSTT mattresses
AEEMRSTTTW wattmeters
AEENNOPSTT panettones
AEENNORSST ornateness
AEENNPRRST trepanners

AEENNPRSTT	penetrants
AEENNRRSTT	reentrants
AEENOORRTX	exonerator
AEENOPPRST	notepapers
AEENOPQSSU	opaqueness
AEENOPRRTT	penetrator
AEENOPRRTU	neuroptera
AEENOPRSST	personates
AEENOPRSUV	supernovae
AEENOPSTTT	potentates
AEENORRSTV	enervators
	veneraters
AEENORSTUX	extraneous
AEENORTTUX	extenuator
AEENPPRRST	entrappers
AEENPPRSSW	newspapers
AEENPPRSTT	stepparent
AEENPRRSTU	enraptures
AEENPRSSSS	sparseness
AEENQRSSSU	squareness
AEENRRSSTU	saunterers
AEENRRSSTV	transverse
AEENRRSTUV	nervatures
AEENSSSTTU	astuteness
AEEOOPRSTZ	azeotropes
AEEOPPRSSU	peasoupers
AEEOPRRSTT	tetraspore
AEEOPRRTWW	waterpower
AEEOPRSSSV	overpasses
AEEOPRSSTT	poetasters
AEEORRSSTV	overassert
AEEORRSTVW	overwaters
AEEORRSTVY	overstayer
AEEORSSSTV	votaresses
AEEORSSTTV	overstates
AEEORSSTTW	twoseaters
AEEPRRSSST	trespasser
AEEPRSSSST	trespasses
AEEPRSSTTU	superstate
AEEPRSSTUX	supertaxes
AEEPRSSWXY	expressway
AEEQRSTTTU	quartettes
AEEQRSTUUX	exequaturs
AEEQSSTTUU	statuesque
AEERRRSSSU	reassurers
AEERRRSSTU	serratures
	treasurers
AEERRRSSTV	traversers
AEERRSTTVX	extraverts
AEESSSSTUX	East Sussex
AEESSTTTTU	statuettes
AEFFGGINRU	gauffering
AEFFGINRST	restaffing
AEFFHILLSS	fallfishes
AEFFHILSST	flatfishes
AEFFHNORRU	Fraunhofer
AEFFIIINST	affinities
AEFFIIINTV	affinitive
AEFFIILRSS	falsifiers
AEFFIKPSST	pikestaffs
AEFFILNSTU	insufflate
AEFFILRSST	tariffless
AEFFIRSTUX	affixtures
AEFFLMOOPR	flameproof
AEFFLMOORW	foamflower
AEFFLNOPST	pantoffles
AEFFOOSTTU	affettuoso
AEFFORSSTV	overstaffs
AEFGGHNOUU	Hua Guo Feng
AEFGGINNRT	engrafting
AEFGHIIRRT	airfreight
AEFGHILNRS	anglerfish
AEFGHILSST	safelights
AEFGHINRRW	wharfinger
AEFGHIOSST	goatfishes
AEFGHIRSST	gearshifts
AEFGHNORTU	fearnought
AEFGHORRST	forgathers
AEFGIILLOR	florilegia
AEFGIILNNR	fingernail
AEFGIILNSV	lifesaving
AEFGIIMNRS	magnifiers
AEFGIINNRR	refraining
AEFGIIRRST	gratifiers
AEFGIIRTUV	figurative
AEFGIKMNRR	fingermark
AEFGILLNNN	flanneling
AEFGILMNNU	meaningful
AEFGILMNOS	flamingoes
AEFGILMRUV	vermifugal
AEFGILNNTT	flattening
AEFGILNORT	refloating
AEFGILNRTT	flattering
AEFGILOPRT	profligate
AEFGILRTUY	figurately
AEFGIMNORR	forearming
AEFGINNSST	fastenings
AEFGINRSTU	figurantes
AEFGIORSSS	ossifrages
AEFGIPRRTU	grapefruit
AEFGISSTTU	fustigates
AEFGKLNRTU	Klagenfurt
AEFGLLLMSU	flagellums
AEFGLLRTUY	gratefully
AEFGLNOSST	flagstones
AEFGLNRSSU	frugalness
AEFGLNRTUU	ungrateful
AEFGLRSTUU	fulgurates
AEFGLSSTTU	Gulf States
AEFGNORSTX	xenografts
AEFHHLORTY	Holy Father
AEFHHLOSTW	heathfowls
AEFHIILSSS	sailfishes
AEFHIINRTT	interfaith
AEFHIIRRTW	white friar
AEFHIKLRSY	freakishly
AEFHIKMSST	makeshifts
AEFHILNSSS	flashiness
AEFHILPSST	fishplates
AEFHIMMNST	famishment
AEFHINORSS	fashioners
	refashions
AEFHINOSSS	oafishness
AEFHIRSSST	starfishes
AEFHKNORSS	foreshanks
AEFHLLMSUY	shamefully
AEFHLLSTTU	stealthful
AEFHLLSTUY	hastefully
AEFHLMOSST	fathomless
AEFHLORSSV	flashovers
AEFHMORSSU	farmhouses
AEFHORSSTW	aftershows
AEFIIILNST	finalities
AEFIILLNSS	filialness
AEFIILLTUV	fluviatile
AEFIILMNSS	semifinals
AEFIILMPRS	amplifiers
AEFIILNOTU	unifoliate
AEFIILNRTT	infiltrate
AEFIILORTT	trifoliate
AEFIILQRSU	qualifiers
AEFIIMMNOS	ammonifies
AEFIINNRST	infantries
AEFIINOPRS	saponifier
AEFIINOPSS	saponifies
AEFIINQRTU	quantifier
AEFIINQSTU	quantifies
AEFIINRSTU	infuriates
AEFIIRSSST	satisfiers
AEFIIRSSTT	stratifies
AEFIJLRSTT	rijsttafel
AEFILLNNRY	infernally
AEFILLNNUZ	influenzal
AEFILLNOST	fellations
AEFILLPRXY	prefixally
AEFILLRUWY	wearifully
AEFILMNSTU	fulminates
AEFILMNSTY	manifestly
AEFILMORRS	formaliser
	Miraflores
AEFILMORRZ	formalizer
AEFILMORSS	formalises
AEFILMORSZ	formalizes
AEFILMORTW	wolframite
AEFILNNSUZ	influenzas
AEFILNORST	reflations
AEFILNORSU	laniferous
AEFILNORSY	farinosely
AEFILNORTU	fluorinate
AEFILNSSTU	faultiness
AEFILNSTTU	flauntiest
AEFILOQRTU	quatrefoil
AEFILORSSU	saliferous
AEFILRSSTW	welfarists
AEFIMNOSST	manifestos
AEFIMORSSS	misfeasors
AEFIMORSTU	fumatories
AEFINNRSSU	unfairness
AEFINOOPRT	fortepiano
	pianoforte
AEFINOPRRS	poriferans
AEFINORRST	rainforest
AEFINORTTU	refutation
AEFINRRTTY	fraternity
AEFINRSSTX	transfixes
AEFIOPRSTU	fetiparous

AEFIORRSUU	auriferous
AEFIORSTUV	favourites
AEFKLNORSY	forsakenly
AEFKLNOSSW	snowflakes
AEFKLORSSW	falseworks
AEFKMORRSW	frameworks
AEFKNNORSU	unforsaken
AEFLLLOPWY	playfellow
AEFLLLORWW	wallflower
AEFLLLSSWY	flawlessly
AEFLLNOSSW	fallowness
AEFLLNSSUW	lawfulness
AEFLLORSST	forestalls
AEFLLORSSV	flavorless
AEFLLSTTUY	tastefully
AEFLLSTUWY	wastefully
AEFLMNNSSU	manfulness
AEFLMNORSS	formalness
AEFLMOORSV	flavorsome
AEFLMOOSSW	Law of Moses
AEFLMORRSV	salverform
AEFLMORSTU	formulates
AEFLMORSWY	mayflowers
AEFLNOPRRT	prefrontal
AEFLNOPSTU	pantoufles
AEFLNRSSTU	artfulness
AEFLOOPSTT	footplates
AEFLORRSTW	starflower
AEFLORRSUV	flavourers
AEFLORSTWW	waterfowls
AEFMMORRST	Tammerfors
AEFMNOSSSU	famousness
AEFMOORRST	Amersfoort
AEFMOPRRST	permafrost
AEFNNOORST	afternoons
AEFNNOSSST	Stefansson
AEFNORRRST	transferor
AEFNORRTTW	waterfront
AEFNORSTVW	wavefronts
AEFNRRSSTU	transfuser
AEFNRSSSTU	transfuses
AEFOOPRRRT	perforator
AEFOOPRRTW	waterproof
AEFOORRSTT	tortfeasor
AEFOQRRSUU	foursquare
AEFRRRSTTU	frustrater
AEFRRSSTTU	frustrates
AEGGGIINRV	aggrieving
AEGGGIINRW	earwigging
AEGGGILNNY	engagingly
AEGGGINNNR	gangrening
AEGGGINRSS	aggressing
AEGGGINRST	staggering
AEGGGINRSW	swaggering
AEGGGIRSWW	wigwaggers
AEGGHIMOPS	geophagism
AEGGHINRST	gatherings
AEGGHINSSS	shagginess
AEGGHIOPST	geophagist
AEGGHOOPSU	geophagous
AEGGHOPRRS	ergographs
AEGGIILLNS	legalising
AEGGIILLNZ	legalizing
AEGGIILMPR	pilgrimage
AEGGIILNNR	engrailing
	realigning
AEGGIILNTV	levigating
AEGGIIMNNT	geminating
AEGGIIMNRT	emigrating
AEGGIINNNR	engraining
AEGGIINNSV	envisaging
AEGGIINNTV	negativing
AEGGIJMRST	jiggermast
AEGGILLNRV	gravelling
AEGGILNNNT	entangling
AEGGILNNOT	elongating
AEGGILNRTU	regulating
AEGGILOOSU	sialogogue
AEGGIMNNRT	garmenting
	margenting
AEGGIMNNTU	augmenting
AEGGIMNRRS	grangerism
AEGGIMNRRT	triggerman
AEGGINNRST	estranging
AEGGINNRSV	engravings
AEGGINORSS	aggression
AEGGINQSSU	quagginess
AEGGIORRSU	gregarious
AEGGJNRTUU	juggernaut
AEGGLLNOOY	angelology
AEGGLNOSSW	waggonless
AEGGLOORTY	geratology
AEGGLRRSST	stragglers
AEGGMORRST	mortgagers
AEGGMOSTUY	mystagogue
AEGGNNOORY	organogeny
AEGGNNORSU	gangrenous
AEGGNOSSUY	synagogues
AEGGOORSSS	goosegrass
AEGGORRSSS	aggressors
AEGHHILLLS	shillelagh
AEGHHILOPR	heliograph
AEGHHILRTT	earthlight
AEGHHIMNWY	highwaymen
AEGHHINSST	sheathings
AEGHHISTTU	haughtiest
AEGHHLORSU	horselaugh
AEGHHMOPPT	apophthegm
AEGHHNOPPR	nephograph
AEGHHOPRTY	hyetograph
AEGHIIMNRS	mishearing
AEGHIINNRT	inearthing
AEGHIINNSV	evanishing
AEGHIINRSV	vinegarish
AEGHIINSTT	hesitating
AEGHIIPRST	graphitise
AEGHIIPRTZ	graphitize
AEGHIKMMNO	homemaking
AEGHIKMNOS	shoemaking
AEGHIKNNRS	hankerings
AEGHIKNNRT	Tengri Khan
AEGHIKNRSS	shrinkages
AEGHILLNNS	hanselling
AEGHILLNOP	anglophile
AEGHILLNRT	allnighter
AEGHILMORT	lithomarge
AEGHILNNSU	unleashing
AEGHILNOOT	theologian
AEGHILNRSS	ringhalses
	shearlings
AEGHILNRST	earthlings
	slathering
AEGHILNSSU	languishes
AEGHILNSSV	shavelings
AEGHILNTTY	ethylating
AEGHILPRXY	lexigraphy
AEGHILSSTT	ghastliest
AEGHIMMOPR	mimeograph
AEGHIMNRST	nightmares
AEGHIMORRS	hierograms
AEGHIMPPRS	epiphragms
AEGHIMSTTT	steamtight
AEGHINNORS	hoarsening
AEGHINNPPS	happenings
AEGHINNPRS	sharpening
AEGHINNRSS	harnessing
AEGHINNRTU	unearthing
AEGHINNSTW	enswathing
AEGHINPPRS	preshaping
AEGHINPRRS	rephrasing
AEGHINPRSS	springhase
AEGHINPRSW	prewashing
AEGHINRRSS	garnishers
AEGHINRSSS	garishness
AEGHINRSTT	shattering
	straighten
AEGHINRSTV	harvesting
AEGHINSTTU	naughtiest
AEGHINSTUX	exhausting
AEGHIPRRSS	serigraphs
AEGHIPRRSY	serigraphy
AEGHIRRSTT	straighter
AEGHIRTTTW	watertight
AEGHISSSTT	tightasses
AEGHLLMPSY	megaphylls
AEGHLMOOOT	homologate
AEGHLMOOTY	hematology
AEGHLMORTU	largemouth
AEGHLNNOOP	anglophone
AEGHLNOORR	gonorrheal
AEGHLNOORS	alongshore
AEGHLNOOSU	halogenous
AEGHLNSTWY	lengthways
AEGHLOOORR	logorrhoea
AEGHLOOPRS	oleographs
AEGHLOOPRY	oleography
AEGHLOOPST	gospel oath
AEGHLORSTT	larghettos
AEGHLORSUV	overslaugh
AEGHLOSSSU	glasshouse
AEGHLRSSTU	slaughters
AEGHMMORRT	thermogram
AEGHMNOOPR	gramophone
AEGHMNOPRS	nephograms
	sphenogram
AEGHMNOSTY	mesognathy

AEGHNOOORR	gonorrhoea
AEGHNOPRRY	granophyre
AEGHNOPRST	stenograph
AEGHNOPRVY	venography
AEGHNOSSTU	shogunates
AEGHOOPRRR	orographer
AEGHOOPRRZ	zoographer
AEGHOOPSSU	oesophagus
AEGHOPRRXY	xerography
AEGIIILNTV	invigilate
AEGIIIMTTV	mitigative
AEGIIIRRTV	irrigative
AEGIIJMNNZ	Jiang Zemin
AEGIILLLTY	illegality
AEGIILLPRS	aspergilli
AEGIILLRSS	grisailles
AEGIILLRST	argillites
AEGIILMNNP	impaneling
AEGIILMNNT	alimenting
AEGIILMNPR	impearling
AEGIILMNRT	trigeminal
AEGIILMNTZ	metalizing
AEGIILNNOT	toenailing
AEGIILNNPS	penalising
AEGIILNNPX	explaining
AEGIILNNPZ	penalizing
AEGIILNNRU	ungainlier
AEGIILNNSS	gainliness
AEGIILNOST	antilogies
AEGIILNOTT	etiolating
AEGIILNOTV	levigation
AEGIILNPRV	prevailing
AEGIILNQSU	equalising
AEGIILNQUZ	equalizing
AEGIILNRSS	glairiness
AEGIILNRSV	velarising
AEGIILNRVZ	velarizing
AEGIILNSSS	signalises
AEGIILNSSZ	signalizes
AEGIILNSTV	vigilantes
AEGIILNTTV	levitating
AEGIILRTTT	glitterati
AEGIIMMRST	immigrates
AEGIIMMSTT	migmatites
AEGIIMNNOT	gemination
AEGIIMNORS	agrimonies
AEGIIMNORT	emigration
AEGIIMNSTT	estimating
AEGIIMNSTV	negativism
	timesaving
AEGIIMSSTT	stigmatise
AEGIIMSTTZ	stigmatize
AEGIINNNRT	entraining
AEGIINNOST	isoantigen
AEGIINNPRT	pertaining
	repainting
AEGIINNRRT	retraining
AEGIINNRSS	graininess
AEGIINNRST	resinating
AEGIINNRTT	intreating
	intrigante
AEGIINNSTT	tetanising
AEGIINNTTZ	tetanizing
AEGIINORST	originates
AEGIINORTV	invigorate
AEGIINOSTT	goniatites
AEGIINPPST	appetising
AEGIINPPTZ	appetizing
AEGIINSSTT	instigates
AEGIINSTTV	estivating
	negativist
AEGIINTTVY	negativity
AEGIINTUVX	exuviating
AEGIIRRSTT	geriatrist
AEGIIRSTTT	targetitis
AEGIIRSTTU	gratuities
AEGIISSSTV	visagistes
AEGIJNORSS	jargonises
AEGIJNORSZ	jargonizes
AEGIKKMNRS	kingmakers
AEGIKLLOOR	Kalgoorlie
AEGIKLMMOR	kilogramme
AEGIKLMNOV	lovemaking
AEGIKLNNSY	sneakingly
AEGIKLRSTV	Lagerkvist
AEGIKMNNOS	maskinonge
AEGIKNNPSU	unspeaking
AEGIKNNSST	takingness
AEGIKNOPRS	presoaking
AEGIKNORTV	overtaking
AEGILLLNRU	laurelling
AEGILLLNSU	gallinules
AEGILLMNRV	marvelling
AEGILLMNRY	germinally
AEGILLNORY	regionally
AEGILLNOXY	glyoxaline
AEGILLNPPR	rappelling
AEGILLNPSY	pleasingly
AEGILLNRSS	signallers
AEGILLNRTV	travelling
AEGILLNRTY	integrally
AEGILLNSST	tasselling
AEGILLOPTT	epiglottal
AEGILLORST	allegorist
	legislator
AEGILLPRSS	aspergills
AEGILLRRSU	guerrillas
AEGILLRSSS	salesgirls
AEGILLRSST	allergists
	gallerists
AEGILMMNRT	trammeling
AEGILMNNST	alignments
	signalment
AEGILMNOOP	monoplegia
AEGILMNORS	rosemaling
AEGILMNORY	mineralogy
AEGILMORRS	glamoriser
	rigmaroles
AEGILMORRZ	glamorizer
AEGILMORSS	glamorises
AEGILMORSZ	glamorizes
AEGILMORUZ	glamourize
AEGILMSTTU	multistage
AEGILNNNPR	replanning
AEGILNNNRU	unlearning
AEGILNNOOT	elongation
AEGILNNOSU	lanuginose
AEGILNNPRT	replanting
AEGILNNPSU	unpleasing
AEGILNNPTX	explanting
AEGILNNRUV	unraveling
AEGILNNRVY	raveningly
AEGILNNRYY	yearningly
AEGILNNSSS	slanginess
AEGILNNSUY	sanguinely
AEGILNOOSU	oleaginous
AEGILNOPTU	outleaping
AEGILNORSU	lanigerous
	neuroglias
AEGILNORTT	tolerating
AEGILNORTU	regulation
	urogenital
AEGILNORVY	overlaying
AEGILNOSTU	gelatinous
AEGILNPPRY	reapplying
AEGILNPRST	plastering
AEGILNPRSU	pleasuring
AEGILNPRTY	taperingly
AEGILNQRRU	quarreling
AEGILNRSTU	granulites
AEGILNRSTV	starveling
AEGILNRVWY	waveringly
AEGILNRWYY	wearyingly
AEGILNSSSS	glassiness
AEGILOOPRS	apologiser
AEGILOOPRZ	apologizer
AEGILOOPSS	apologises
AEGILOOPSZ	apologizes
AEGILOORST	aerologist
AEGILOPRTT	graptolite
AEGILORRSS	gressorial
AEGILORSSS	glossaries
AEGILORSTV	levigators
AEGILPPRRS	papergirls
AEGILRRRSU	irregulars
AEGILRRSUV	vulgariser
AEGILRRTUY	regularity
AEGILRRUVZ	vulgarizer
AEGILRSSUV	vulgarises
AEGILRSTTZ	Salzgitter
AEGILRSUVZ	vulgarizes
AEGIMMNOST	gemmations
AEGIMMNRST	stammering
AEGIMNNORS	omniranges
AEGIMNNORU	enamouring
AEGIMNNRST	smartening
AEGIMNNRTU	numerating
AEGIMNNSST	assignment
AEGIMNNSTY	amnestying
AEGIMNOPRS	angiosperm
AEGIMNORRT	germinator
AEGIMNORSU	gramineous
AEGIMNPRRW	prewarming
AEGIMNPRSV	revampings
AEGIMNPRTY	pigmentary
AEGIMNPTTT	attempting

AEGIMNRRRY remarrying
AEGIMNRRST ringmaster
AEGIMNRSSU reassuming
AEGIMNRSTT smattering
AEGIMNSSTT magnetists
AEGIMOOSTV vagotomies
AEGIMORRSU armigerous
AEGIMORRTY emigratory
AEGIMOSSTY stegomyias
AEGIMRRTVY gravimetry
AEGINNNNOR nonearning
AEGINNNOTV nonvintage
AEGINNNPRT trepanning
AEGINNORST resonating
AEGINNORSZ organzines
AEGINNORTV renovating
AEGINNOSSS seasonings
AEGINNOSTT negotiants
AEGINNPPRT entrapping
AEGINNPPRW enwrapping
AEGINNPRRT partnering
AEGINNPRTT patterning
AEGINNRSTT astringent
integrants
AEGINNRSTU sauntering
AEGINNRSUW unswearing
AEGINNRUVW unwavering
AEGINNRUWY unwearying
AEGINOORTT negotiator
AEGINOPRRT perorating
AEGINOPRVY overpaying
AEGINORRSS organisers
AEGINORRSU rearousing
AEGINORRSV granivores
AEGINORRSZ organizers
AEGINORRTT integrator
AEGINORRTV overrating
AEGINORSTT gittarones
AEGINORSUU aeruginous
AEGINORTUW outwearing
AEGINORTVX overtaxing
AEGINOSSTT gestations
AEGINPPRRW rewrapping
AEGINPQRTU parqueting
AEGINPRRSY respraying
AEGINPRSSS preassigns
AEGINPRSTT spattering
AEGINPRSTU supergiant
AEGINPRSTY panegyrist
AEGINPSTTU Septuagint
AEGINQRRTU quartering
AEGINRRSSU reassuring
AEGINRRSTT registrant
restarting
AEGINRRSTU garnitures
treasuring
AEGINRRSTV traversing
AEGINRSSSS grassiness
AEGINRSSSU sugariness
AEGINRSSTU signatures
AEGIPRSTUV purgatives
AEGIRRRSST registrars
AEGIRSSTTT strategist
AEGKLNOOPS pokelogans
AEGKORSSTT agterskots
AEGLLLLNNO Llangollen
AEGLLMORRU glomerular
AEGLLMRTUY metallurgy
AEGLLNNPTY plangently
AEGLLNOPSW alpenglows
AEGLLNOSST gallstones
AEGLLOPRSU pellagrous
AEGLMMORSY myelograms
AEGLMNOOOV avgolemono
AEGLMNORSS lemongrass
AEGLMNORSW angleworms
AEGLMOOSTY sematology
AEGLMOPRTU promulgate
AEGLNNPRTY pregnantly
AEGLNOPRSY gyroplanes
AEGLNOSSTU langoustes
AEGLNRRSST stranglers
AEGLNSSSSU sunglasses
AEGLOORRST astrologer
AEGLOORTTY teratology
AEGLOPPRSU propagules
AEGLORRSTU regulators
AEGLORRTUY regulatory
AEGLPRSSUU surplusage
AEGLPSSSSY spyglasses
AEGMMNOPRU pneumogram
AEGMMOPRRR programmer
AEGMMOPRRS programmes
AEGMNNORST magnetrons
AEGMNOORST gastronome
AEGMNOOSUX xenogamous
AEGMNORRSW warmongers
AEGMNORSTU augmentors
AEGMNOSTTU mangetouts
Mao Tse-tung
AEGNNOOSSU nongaseous
AEGNNRTUUY unguentary
AEGNOORTXY oxygenator
AEGNOOSTUU autogenous
AEGNORRSWY garryowens
AEGNRRSSST transgress
AEGNSSSTUU augustness
AEGOOPRSYZ azygospore
AEGOORSTUU outrageous
AEGOOSSWYZ wayzgooses
AEGOPRRSUW groupwares
AEGOPRRTUX expurgator
AEGORRRSTT garrotters
AEGORRSSTU surrogates
AEGORRSTTU Great Stour
AEGORSSSTU stegosaurs
AEGPRRSSSU supergrass
AEHHHILOPT Ahithophel
AEHHIILMOP hemophilia
AEHHILLOPS halophiles
AEHHILNPST phthaleins
AEHHILNSTU helianthus
AEHHILPSSW whiplashes
AEHHIMMSSS mishmashes
AEHHIMNOPV Phomvihane
AEHHINOPRT hierophant
AEHHLMNSUU Mühlhausen
AEHHLNOPTT heptathlon
AEHHLOPSTY halophytes
AEHHMOOOPT homoeopath
AEHHMOOPST homeopaths
AEHHMOOPTY homeopathy
AEHHNOOPRT anthophore
AEHHOPPSST phosphates
AEHHPSSTTU Hatshepsut
AEHIIILNNS Sinhailien
AEHIIKLRTW wraithlike
AEHIILLLNT Lilienthal
AEHIILMSTU humiliates
AEHIILOSTX heliotaxis
AEHIILPPSY epiphysial
AEHIIMMPSX amphimixes
AEHIIMNSTT antitheism
AEHIIMNSTU humanities
AEHIIMPRTT Amphitrite
AEHIIMRSST hetairisms
AEHIINNRRS Nairnshire
AEHIINORTT thorianite
AEHIINOSTT hesitation
AEHIINPPRS sapphirine
AEHIINSSTT antithesis
AEHIINSTTT antitheist
AEHIIPPSTT epitaphist
AEHIIRSSTT hetairists
AEHIJLOSSU jailhouses
AEHIKLNRSS rinkhalses
AEHIKNRSSS rakishness
AEHILLMOPS philomelas
AEHILLORTY heliolatry
AEHILLSTTY stealthily
AEHILLSTWW whitewalls
AEHILMNNUY inhumanely
AEHILMNOPY anemophily
AEHILMNOSY haemolysin
AEHILMNSTV lavishment
AEHILMORST isothermal
thimerosal
AEHILMOSSY haemolysis
AEHILMPSTU multiphase
AEHILNOOSZ heliozoans
AEHILNOPTT thiopental
AEHILNOSSS shoaliness
AEHILNOSST hailstones
AEHILNOTTY ethylation
AEHILNPRSS planishers
AEHILNQRSU harlequins
AEHILNSSSV lavishness
AEHILNSTTY hesitantly
AEHILOPRST hospitaler
AEHILOPSTT Hospitalet
AEHILORSST horsetails
AEHILORSVV overlavish
AEHILOSSTT heliostats
AEHILOTTVW White Volta
AEHILPSSST splashiest
AEHILRSSTY hairstyles

AEHILRSTVY	shrievalty
AEHIMMPRRT	triphammer
AEHIMMRSTU	rheumatism
AEHIMNNPPS	penmanship
AEHIMNORRS	harmoniser
AEHIMNORRZ	harmonizer
AEHIMNORSS	harmonises
AEHIMNORSZ	harmonizes
AEHIMNOTUX	exhumation
AEHIMNRSSS	marshiness
AEHIMNRSSU	humanisers
AEHIMNRSTV	ravishment
AEHIMNRSUZ	humanizers
AEHIMNSSTU	enthusiasm
AEHIMOOPTY	mythopoeia
AEHIMOPRSY	hyperosmia
AEHIMOPSTY	myopathies
AEHIMOSSST	hemostasis
AEHIMPRSST	mastership
	shipmaster
AEHIMPSSST	steamships
AEHIMPSSTT	empathists
AEHIMPSSTY	sympathies
	sympathise
AEHIMPSTYZ	sympathize
AEHINOPRTU	euphoriant
AEHINORRTV	hovertrain
AEHINOSSST	astonishes
AEHINOSTUX	exhaustion
AEHINPPSTU	unhappiest
AEHINPRSUW	wharepunis
AEHINPSSTT	pantheists
AEHINQRSUV	vanquisher
AEHINQSSUV	vanquishes
AEHINRRSST	tarnishers
AEHINRRSSV	varnishers
AEHINRSSST	trashiness
AEHINSSTTU	enthusiast
AEHIOOPSST	apotheosis
AEHIORRSTU	authoriser
AEHIORRTUZ	authorizer
AEHIORSSTT	hesitators
AEHIORSSTU	authorises
AEHIORSSTV	tovarishes
AEHIORSTTT	throatiest
AEHIORSTUZ	authorizes
AEHIPRSSTT	therapists
AEHIQSSSTU	squashiest
AEHIRSSTTW	swarthiest
	sweatshirt
AEHKLOPRSW	shopwalker
AEHKMNOSTU	snakemouth
AEHKNOORRT	North Korea
AEHKOORSTU	South Korea
AEHKORRSTW	earthworks
AEHLLMRSSY	harmlessly
AEHLLMSTUU	haustellum
AEHLLNOOPS	allophones
AEHLLOOPRT	Hartlepool
AEHLLOORWW	hollowware
AEHLLOPRXY	phylloxera
AEHLLOSSTW	shallowest
AEHLMOOSUX	homosexual
AEHLMORTTY	methylator
AEHLMOSSSU	almshouses
AEHLMPSSYY	symphyseal
AEHLNNOPRS	alpenhorns
AEHLNNOPTT	pentathlon
AEHLNOPSTU	houseplant
	sulphonate
AEHLOOPRRY	pyorrhoeal
AEHLOPRSSW	plowshares
AEHLOPSSUY	playhouses
AEHLORSTUU	outhaulers
AEHLPRSTUU	sulphurate
AEHLRTTUUV	truth-value
AEHMNNORWY	New Harmony
AEHMNNRSTU	manhunters
AEHMNOOOTZ	hematozoon
AEHMNOOPRT	homopteran
AEHMNOORSW	horsewoman
AEHMNORRTT	Matterhorn
AEHMNORRTW	harrowment
AEHMNPRSUU	superhuman
AEHMNPRTWY	water nymph
AEHMNRSTUY	Erymanthus
AEHMOOPRSS	shampooers
AEHMOORSTX	mesothorax
AEHMORRSTW	earthworms
	heartworms
AEHMORSTTT	thermostat
AEHMORSTWW	wheatworms
AEHMQSSSUU	musquashes
AEHNNNOOTY	hootenanny
AEHNOOPRRS	harpooners
AEHNOOPSSU	sousaphone
AEHNOOPSSX	saxophones
AEHNOPRSTU	neuropaths
AEHNOPRSTY	honeytraps
AEHNOPRTUY	neuropathy
AEHNORRSTW	Rawsthorne
AEHNRSSSTW	swarthness
AEHOOPPRST	apostrophe
AEHOOPRRTT	orthoptera
AEHOOPRYZZ	Zaporozhye
AEHOOPSSTT	osteopaths
AEHOOPSTTT	toothpaste
AEHOOPSTTY	osteopathy
AEHOORSSTY	soothsayer
AEHOPPRSTY	saprophyte
AEHOPSSSTW	sweatshops
AEHOPSSSTY	hypostases
AEHOPSTTUY	autophytes
AEHORRRSTW	restharrow
AEHPRSSTTY	strathspey
AEIIIIINRR	Rainier III
AEIIIILNST	initialise
AEIIIILNTZ	initialize
AEIIIINTTV	initiative
AEIIILLNRT	initialler
AEIIILLNSV	villainies
AEIIILMMNT	militiamen
AEIIILMRST	militaries
	militarise
AEIIILMRTZ	militarize
AEIIILNRST	initialers
AEIIILRSTV	trivialise
AEIIILRTVZ	trivialize
AEIIILSTTV	vitalities
AEIIILSTVX	lixiviates
AEIIIMMNPR	imipramine
AEIIIMNRST	ministeria
AEIIIMPRST	imparities
AEIIINNSST	insanities
AEIIINSTTV	nativities
AEIIIPRSVV	viviparies
AEIIIRRTTV	irritative
AEIIJMORST	majorities
AEIIKKSTTW	kittiwakes
AEIIKLLNPR	painkiller
AEIIKLMRSY	Yeşil Irmak
AEIIKLNOSZ	kaolinizes
AEIILLLMMS	millesimal
AEIILLLMNN	millennial
AEIILLLTVY	illatively
AEIILLMNSS	sinsemilla
AEIILLMNTU	illuminate
AEIILLMOST	molalities
AEIILLMPRY	imperially
AEIILLMRST	literalism
AEIILLNRTU	uniliteral
AEIILLNSSV	villainess
AEIILLOSTV	volatilise
AEIILLOTVZ	volatilize
AEIILLPRTT	tripletail
AEIILLPSTT	pistillate
AEIILLRRTT	triliteral
AEIILLRRTY	literarily
AEIILLRSTT	literalist
AEIILLRSTV	silvertail
AEIILLRTTY	literality
AEIILLSTTT	titillates
AEIILMMMOR	immemorial
AEIILMNNRS	mainliners
AEIILMNNST	eliminants
AEIILMNORT	eliminator
AEIILMNOSZ	iminazoles
AEIILMNRSU	luminaries
AEIILMNSSU	aluminises
AEIILMNSTY	seminality
AEIILMNSUZ	aluminizes
AEIILMNTTY	intimately
AEIILMORST	molarities
	moralities
AEIILMOSSS	isoseismal
AEIILMPPSS	misapplies
AEIILMRSTV	relativism
AEIILMRSVV	revivalism
AEIILMSTUV	simulative
AEIILMTTUV	mutilative
AEIILMTTUZ	Mutazilite
AEIILNNOOP	Napoleon II
AEIILNNORS	rosaniline
AEIILNNOST	lineations
AEIILNNRST	triennials
AEIILNNSTT	intestinal

AEIILNOOTT	etiolation
AEIILNOPST	epilations
AEIILNOPTX	pixelation
AEIILNORTT	literation
AEIILNOSTT	tonalities
AEIILNOTTV	levitation
AEIILNOTUV	eluviation
AEIILNPRST	reptilians
AEIILNPSST	platinises
AEIILNPSTZ	platinizes
AEIILNQTUY	inequality
AEIILNSSTT	saintliest
AEIILNSSTW	waistlines
AEIILOPRST	polarities
AEIILORSST	solitaires
	solitaries
AEIILORSTV	variolites
AEIILOSTTT	totalities
AEIILRSSTU	ritualises
AEIILRSSTV	vitalisers
AEIILRSSUV	visualiser
AEIILRSTTU	titularies
AEIILRSTTV	relativist
AEIILRSTTZ	strelitzia
AEIILRSTUZ	ritualizes
AEIILRSTVV	revivalist
AEIILRSTVZ	vitalizers
AEIILRSUVZ	visualizer
AEIILRTTVY	relativity
AEIILSSSUV	visualises
AEIILSSUVZ	visualizes
AEIIMMNPRT	impairment
AEIIMMNRST	antimerism
AEIIMMNSSS	messianism
AEIIMMRSSX	maximisers
AEIIMMRSXZ	maximizers
AEIIMNNNOT	innominate
AEIIMNNOST	antinomies
	semination
AEIIMNNOTV	nominative
AEIIMNORSU	iminoureas
AEIIMNOSTT	estimation
AEIIMNPQRU	primaquine
AEIIMNQRTU	Martinique
AEIIMNQTUY	equanimity
AEIIMNRSTT	intimaters
AEIIMNRSTU	miniatures
AEIIMNRTUV	ruminative
AEIIMOPRRS	impresario
AEIIMOTTVV	motivative
AEIIMPTTUV	imputative
AEIIMRSTTU	maturities
AEIINNNSTV	antivenins
AEIINNORSV	reinvasion
AEIINNOTVV	innovative
AEIINNPRTT	tripinnate
AEIINNPRTY	antipyrine
AEIINNPSTT	inpatients
AEIINNRSTT	itinerants
AEIINNRSTU	uraninites
AEIINNSSTU	insinuates
AEIINOPPST	inapposite
AEIINOPPTV	appointive
AEIINOPRTX	expiration
AEIINOPSTT	poinsettia
AEIINOPSTX	expiations
AEIINOQTTU	equitation
AEIINORSTT	iterations
AEIINOSTTV	estivation
	novitiates
AEIINOTUVX	exuviation
AEIINPSSST	antisepsis
	inspissate
AEIINQSTTU	quantities
AEIINQTTUV	quantitive
AEIINRRSTT	tristearin
AEIINRSTTV	transitive
AEIINRTTZZ	tetrazzini
AEIIOPPRTT	propitiate
AEIIOPPSTV	appositive
AEIIPPSSSW	pipsissewa
AEIIPRRTTT	tripartite
AEIIPRSSTV	privatises
AEIIPRSTTV	partitives
AEIIPRSTVZ	privatizes
AEIIRRSSST	satirisers
AEIIRRSSTV	arrivistes
AEIIRRSSTZ	satirizers
AEIISTTTTV	tittivates
AEIJKLRSUZ	Jaruzelski
AEIJLNORSU	journalise
AEIJLNORUZ	journalize
AEIJLNOSSV	jovialness
AEIJNNSSTU	jauntiness
AEIJNOOPRT	pejoration
AEIKKLLOOS	lookalikes
AEIKKNNSSS	snakeskins
AEIKLMNOSS	kalsomines
AEIKLMNSTY	mistakenly
AEIKLNSSST	stalkiness
AEIKLNSSTU	Eskilstuna
AEIKMNPRRT	printmaker
AEIKNNPRSS	spinnakers
AEIKNNSSSW	swankiness
AEIKNRSTTU	Turkestani
AEIKPPQSSU	pipsqueaks
AEILLLOTWY	yellowtail
AEILLLSSTY	taillessly
AEILLLSUVY	allusively
AEILLMMORS	allomerism
AEILLMMORY	memorially
AEILLMMRST	millstream
AEILLMNPTU	multiplane
AEILLMNRTY	terminally
AEILLMPRVY	primevally
AEILLMSSTT	metallists
AEILLMTTUY	ultimately
AEILLNNRTY	internally
AEILLNOPST	pollinates
AEILLNOPTT	potentilla
AEILLNPSST	panellists
AEILLNPSSY	painlessly
AEILLNRSST	installers
	reinstalls
AEILLNRSTU	tellurians
AEILLNRTTU	Tertullian
AEILLNRTUY	tenurially
AEILLOPPST	papillotes
AEILLPRRSU	pluraliser
AEILLPRRUZ	pluralizer
AEILLPRSSU	pluralises
AEILLPRSUZ	pluralizes
AEILLPSSTT	pastellist
AEILLRSSTW	stairwells
AEILLRSTTU	illustrate
AEILMMNNTY	immanently
AEILMMRTUY	immaturely
AEILMMRUUV	Verulamium
AEILMNNOPR	prenominal
AEILMNNSTT	instalment
AEILMNOPRS	impersonal
	prolamines
AEILMNOPRT	trampoline
AEILMNORSS	normalises
AEILMNORSZ	normalizes
AEILMNORTU	tourmaline
AEILMNORTY	monetarily
AEILMNOSTU	emulations
AEILMNOSTY	melanosity
AEILMNPRST	implanters
AEILMNPRTY	planimetry
AEILMNPSSU	aspleniums
AEILMNPSTU	penultimas
AEILMNRSTU	neutralism
AEILMNSSSU	sensualism
AEILMNSSTT	mentalists
AEILMOORRT	meliorator
AEILMOPPSS	ampelopsis
AEILMOPRST	peristomal
AEILMOPSST	semipostal
AEILMORRSS	moralisers
AEILMORRSZ	moralizers
AEILMORSTV	removalist
AEILMOSSTU	mousetails
AEILMPPSST	palimpsest
AEILMPRSST	slipstream
AEILMPRSTU	psalterium
AEILMRRSSU	surrealism
AEILMRRSTT	trimestral
AEILMRSTTU	stimulater
AEILMSSTTU	stimulates
AEILMSSTUU	mutualises
AEILMSTTUX	textualism
AEILMSTUUZ	mutualizes
AEILNNOPRS	nonpareils
AEILNNOPTT	antilepton
AEILNNORTT	intolerant
AEILNNOSST	nationless
AEILNNOSTV	antinovels
AEILNNPRSU	peninsular
AEILNNPSST	pliantness
AEILNNPSSU	peninsulas
AEILNNRRTU	interlunar
AEILNNSTWY	Winstanley
AEILNOOPRT	tropaeolin
AEILNOOPSS	polonaises

AEILNOORTT	toleration
AEILNOPRRT	interpolar
AEILNOPRST	interposal
AEILNOPSST	sealpoints
AEILNOPSTT	peltations
	potentials
AEILNORRTT	torrential
AEILNORTTV	ventilator
AEILNOTTUX	exultation
AEILNPPRTU	prenuptial
AEILNPRSST	paltriness
	straplines
AEILNPRSTY	interplays
AEILNRSSTT	sterilants
AEILNRSSUV	universals
AEILNRSSUY	urinalyses
AEILNRSTTU	neutralist
AEILNRTTUY	neutrality
AEILNRTTWW	Written Law
AEILNSSSTU	sensualist
AEILNSSTUU	nautiluses
AEILNSSTUY	sensuality
AEILOOPRST	Portlaoise
AEILOOPTTZ	topazolite
AEILOPPRSU	popularise
AEILOPPRSY	polyparies
AEILOPPRUZ	popularize
AEILOPPSTY	appositely
AEILOPRRSS	polarisers
AEILOPRRSZ	polarizers
AEILOPRSST	saprolites
AEILOPRSSU	plesiosaur
AEILOPRSTY	epistolary
AEILOPSTZZ	Pestalozzi
AEILOQRSTU	questorial
AEILORRRTV	retroviral
AEILORRSTT	literators
AEILORRTTU	elutriator
AEILORSSTT	aristotles
	totalisers
AEILORSTTU	staurolite
AEILORSTTV	levitators
AEILORSTTZ	totalizers
AEILORSTUW	outlawries
AEILORTTVY	rotatively
AEILPRRSTY	peristylar
AEILPRSSTT	prelatists
AEILPSSSTT	pastelists
AEILPSSTTU	stipulates
AEILPTTUVY	putatively
AEILRRSSTU	surrealist
AEILRSTTUV	lustrative
AEILRSTTUZ	Austerlitz
AEILRSTUUX	luxuriates
AEILSTTTUX	textualist
AEIMMMNOST	mammonites
AEIMMNNOOS	monoamines
AEIMMNNRSS	mannerisms
AEIMMNOPST	pantomimes
AEIMMNORST	monetarism
AEIMMNOTUU	autoimmune
AEIMMNPRTT	impartment
AEIMMNRSSS	smarminess
AEIMMNRTTU	manumitter
AEIMMNSSTZ	mizenmasts
AEIMMNSTZZ	mizzenmast
AEIMMPRSTU	spermatium
AEIMMRRSSU	summariser
AEIMMRRSUZ	summarizer
AEIMMRSSSU	summarises
AEIMMRSSUZ	summarizes
AEIMNNNOST	Minnesotan
AEIMNNNOTT	anointment
AEIMNNNQSU	mannequins
AEIMNNORTU	numeration
AEIMNNOSTT	mentations
AEIMNNRSST	mannerists
AEIMNOOSTU	autonomies
AEIMNOOSTX	taxonomies
AEIMNOPRST	protamines
AEIMNOPRTT	armipotent
	portamenti
AEIMNOPTTT	temptation
AEIMNOQSUU	equanimous
AEIMNORRST	ironmaster
AEIMNORRTT	terminator
AEIMNORSSW	womanisers
AEIMNORSTT	monetarist
AEIMNORSWZ	womanizers
AEIMNPPRST	pentaprism
AEIMNPSTTY	tympanites
AEIMNRRRTY	intermarry
AEIMNRRSTT	retransmit
AEIMNRSSTU	antiserums
AEIMOOPPST	pampooties
AEIMOORSTX	xerostomia
AEIMOOSTTU	autotomies
	autotomise
AEIMOOTTUV	automotive
AEIMOOTTUZ	autotomize
AEIMOPRRST	imperators
AEIMOPRRTT	impetrator
AEIMOPRTUU	eupatorium
AEIMORRSTU	mortuaries
AEIMORSSTT	estimators
AEIMORSTTU	autotimers
AEIMPRSSTU	pasteurism
AEIMPRSTUU	Maupertuis
AEIMPRSTUZ	trapeziums
AEIMPSSTUV	assumptive
AEIMQRSTUZ	quizmaster
AEIMRRRSTU	terrariums
AEIMRRSSTY	martyrises
AEIMRRSTYZ	martyrizes
AEINNOORST	resonation
AEINNOORTV	renovation
AEINNOPRSY	pensionary
AEINNOPSSX	expansions
AEINNOQRTU	quaternion
AEINNORSTT	stentorian
AEINNORSTV	nervations
	vernations
AEINNOSSST	sensations
AEINNOSTTT	attentions
AEINNOSTTV	nonstative
AEINNPPSSS	snappiness
AEINNQSSTU	quaintness
AEINNRRSTY	tyranniser
AEINNRRTYZ	tyrannizer
AEINNRSSTT	transients
AEINNRSSTY	tyrannises
AEINNRSSUW	unwariness
AEINNRSTUV	aventurins
AEINNRSTYZ	tyrannizes
AEINNSSSZZ	snazziness
AEINOOPPRT	apoprotein
	propionate
AEINOOPRRT	peroration
AEINOOPRST	operations
AEINOPPPRT	preappoint
AEINOPPRRS	Proserpina
AEINOPPRST	appointers
	reappoints
AEINOPRRST	patroniser
	periastron
AEINOPRRTZ	patronizer
AEINOPRSSS	aspersions
AEINOPRSST	patronises
AEINOPRSSU	persuasion
AEINOPRSSV	pervasions
AEINOPRSTZ	patronizes
AEINOPRTTU	reputation
AEINOPTTTU	outpatient
AEINOQRSTU	ortaniques
AEINORRSST	serrations
AEINORRSTT	reinstator
AEINORRSTU	souterrain
AEINORRSTV	overstrain
	overtrains
AEINORSSST	assertions
AEINORSSSV	savoriness
AEINORSSTT	stationers
AEINORSSTV	sovranties
AEINORSSTY	tyrosinase
AEINORSTTY	stationery
AEINPRRSST	transpires
AEINPRRTTU	parturient
AEINPRSTTT	strepitant
AEINQRTTUY	quaternity
AEINRRSSST	starriness
AEINRRSSTT	restraints
AEINRSSSTT	resistants
	straitness
AEINRSSSTU	sustainers
AEINRSTUYZ	suzerainty
AEIOOPPRST	propositae
AEIOPRRRST	respirator
AEIOPRRSSV	vaporisers
AEIOPRRSTU	Praetorius
AEIOPRRSVZ	vaporizers
AEIOPRRTTX	extirpator
AEIOPRRTXY	expiratory
AEIORSSTTV	estivators
AEIORSTUVV	uvarovites
AEIPRSSSTU	prussiates
AEIPRSSTTU	petaurists

AEIPRSTUUV usurpative
AEIQRSTTUZ quartzites
AEIRRSTTTU triturates
AEJMNNORUY journeyman
AEJOPSSTUX juxtaposes
AEKKLRRSSY skylarkers
AEKLLMRUWY lukewarmly
AEKLMOORST toolmakers
AEKLMORSSS lossmakers
AEKMMNORSW markswomen
AEKMNOOQSU moonquakes
AEKMNOORRS moonrakers
AEKMOORRSV voorkamers
AEKMOORSSY karyosomes
AEKMOORTTY keratotomy
AEKMORRSTW masterwork
AEKMPRRSSS pressmarks
AEKNOORSST snakeroots
AEKNPRRSST pranksters
AEKOOPRRTY prokaryote
AEKOPRSTYY karyotypes
AEKORRSTWW waterworks
AEKORRSWWX waxworkers
AELLLPSTUU pullulates
AELLMNNOUY noumenally
AELLMNOSTT allotments
AELLMNOTWY tallywomen
AELLMOORSU allomerous
AELLMOPRSY permalloys
AELLMOPRTY temporally
AELLMOPSSY plasmolyse
AELLMOPSYZ plasmolyze
AELLMORSUV marvellous
AELLMOSSYY amylolyses
AELLNOPPRT propellant
AELLNOPRSY personally
AELLNOPTVY polyvalent
AELLNORTTY tolerantly
AELLNOSSSW sallowness
AELLNOSSTW stonewalls
AELLNPRSUY supernally
AELLNPTTUY petulantly
AELLNRSTTY slatternly
AELLNTTUXY exultantly
AELLOOPRST allotropes
AELLOPRRST patrollers
AELLOPRSTW potwallers
wallposter
AELLORSSWW swallowers
AELLRSSTVY sylvestral
AELLRTTUXY texturally
AELMMNNOTU monumental
AELMMOOPSS plasmosome
AELMMOPRRW palmerworm
AELMMORSST maelstroms
AELMMOSSUU mausoleums
AELMNNNRUY unmannerly
AELMNNNSTU annulments
AELMNNOOPS monoplanes
AELMNNOOTV monovalent
AELMNOOPRS lampooners
AELMNOOPRT monopteral
protonemal
AELMNOOPRY lampoonery
AELMNOORST monolaters
AELMNOORSY monolayers
AELMNOPRST Palmerston
AELMNOPRTY planometry
AELMNOPSTU pulmonates
AELMNRSTTU tremulants
AELMNSSTUU mutualness
AELMOOPRTU tropaeolum
AELMOORSSS salesrooms
AELMOPPRUY propylaeum
AELMOPRTTU petrolatum
AELMOQSSUU squamulose
AELMOQSSUY squamosely
AELMORSSTU somersault
AELMORSTTT lattermost
AELNNOPRYY pennyroyal
AELNNORSTY resonantly
AELNOPRSTY personalty
AELNORRSTY antrorsely
AELNORSTVW navelworts
AELNORSUVY ravenously
AELNOSSUUY nauseously
AELNPPRSTU supplanter
AELNPRRSUU superlunar
AELNRSSTTU resultants
AELOOPRSVY parleyvoos
AELOOPSSTV Sevastopol
AELOORRSTT tolerators
AELOPPRRRU pourparler
AELOPPRTUV Upper Volta
AELOPRRSTW pearlworts
AELOPRRSVY proslavery
AELOPRSSTU sporulates
AELOPRSSUV vapourless
AELOPSSTTU postulates
AELORSSSUV savourless
AELPPRSSTU Last Supper
AELPPSSTUY platypuses
AELPSSTTUU pustulates
AEMMNORRTT Montmartre
AEMNNNNOUV von Neumann
AEMNNNOPTY nonpayment
AEMNNOOSST stonemason
AEMNNORSTT remontants
AEMNNORTTT attornment
AEMNNORTTU tournament
AEMNNRRSUY nurseryman
AEMNOOPRTT portamento
AEMNOORRST astronomer
AEMNOORSTX taxonomers
AEMNOORTXY axonometry
AEMNOPRSUW superwoman
AEMNORRSTT Montserrat
AEMNORRSTU numerators
AEMNORSSTT assortment
AEMNORSSTU sarmentous
AEMNRRSTTU transmuter
AEMNRSSTTU transmutes
AEMOOPSTTY somatotype
AEMOORSSTT staterooms
AEMOPRSSTT postmaster
AEMOPRSSTU mousetraps
AEMOPSSTTY asymptotes
AEMORRSTTY astrometry
AENNNOSSTW wantonness
AENNORRSST resnatrons
AENNORRSSW narrowness
AENNORRSTT nonstarter
AENOOPRRST personator
AENOOPRTXY paroxytone
AENOOPSSST postseason
AENOORRSST resonators
AENOORRSTV renovators
AENOORSSTU anoestrous
treasonous
AENOPRRSST transposer
AENOPRSSST transposes
AENOPRSSUV supernovas
AENOPRSTTT protestant
AENPRRSTTU transputer
AENSSTTUVY Stuyvesant
AEOOPPRRRT propraetor
AEOOPPRSTU tropopause
AEOOPRSSTU autospores
AEOOPRSSUX auxospores
AEOOPRSTTV vaporettos
AEOORRSSTV overroasts
AEOORSTTUU autoroutes
AEOPPRRRTU rapporteur
AEOPRRRSTY portrayers
AEOPRRSSTT prostrates
AEOPRRSSTU pterosaurs
AEOPRRSSTW spearworts
sportswear
AEOPRSTTUW waterspout
AEORSSSTUU trousseaus
AEORSSTUUX trousseaux
AEPPRSSTUU suppurates
AEPRRSSSTU superstars
AERRSSSTUU susurrates
AFFGIILNSY falsifying
AFFGIINORT forfaiting
AFFGIIRSTT graffitist
AFFGILNSTU sufflating
AFFGIMRSSU suffragism
AFFGINNORT affronting
AFFGIRSSTU suffragist
AFFGNOORST stroganoff
AFFHILLTUY faithfully
AFFHILNTUU unfaithful
AFFIILNPST plaintiffs
AFFIIMNRSU ruffianism
AFFILNOSTU sufflation
AFFILORSSY fairyfloss
AFFLLMOPUW mallowpuff
AFFLLORUUV flavourful
AFFLOPSSTW plowstaffs
AFGGGILNNU unflagging
AFGGIILNNY anglifying
AFGGIIMNNY magnifying
AFGGIIMNTU fumigating
AFGGIINNRT ingrafting

AFGGIINRTY	gratifying
AFGHHILLST	flashlight
AFGHIINNOS	fashioning
AFGHIIRSTU	guitarfish
AFGHILLNST	nightfalls
AFGHMOORST	homografts
AFGIIILNNS	finalising
AFGIIILNNZ	finalizing
AFGIIILNRT	airlifting
AFGIIIMNNS	infamising
AFGIIIMNNZ	infamizing
AFGIILLNNT	flatlining
AFGIILMNPY	amplifying
AFGIILNNTY	faintingly
AFGIILNQUY	qualifying
AFGIILNRTT	filtrating
AFGIILOSTU	flagitious
AFGIIMNOTU	fumigation
AFGIIMNTTY	mattifying
AFGIINORTU	figuration
AFGIINSSTY	satisfying
AFGILLNOTY	floatingly
AFGILNORSV	flavorings
AFGILNORUV	flavouring
AFGILNORVY	favoringly
AFGIMNORSU	ausforming
AFGIMNORTT	formatting
AFGIMORSTU	fumigators
AFGINSSTTU	fungistats
AFGIORSTTU	fustigator
AFGNOPRSSW	frogspawns
AFHHLOOPST	photoflash
AFHIIKNOPS	kniphofias
AFHIKNRSST	rankshifts
AFHILLMOYY	Holy Family
AFHIMORRTY	Moray Firth
AFHIOPRRST	parrotfish
AFHIORSSTY	forsythias
AFHKLLNTUY	thankfully
AFHKLNNTUU	unthankful
AFHLLORSST	shortfalls
AFHLLRTUWY	wrathfully
AFIIILNOST	filiations
AFIIINNOTX	infixation
AFIILLRRTY	fritillary
AFIILMNNSU	Flamininus
AFIILNNOST	inflations
AFIILNOOST	foliations
AFIILNORSU	infusorial
AFIILNORTT	filtration
	flirtation
AFIILRSUVV	flavivirus
AFIIMNORRR	Friar Minor
AFIIMORSTV	favoritism
AFIINNORSU	infusorian
AFILLMNORY	informally
AFILLMORTU	multiflora
AFILLNPPTY	flippantly
AFILMNORTU	fulminator
AFILMNOSUY	infamously
AFILMORRVY	variformly
AFILMORSST	formalists
AFILNOOSTT	flotations
AFILNORTTY	frontality
AFILNORUXY	fluxionary
AFIMMOQRSU	squamiform
AFIMMORTUU	fumatorium
AFIMNNORST	informants
AFIMNOORST	formations
AFIMORRSTT	stratiform
AFINOOPRRS	rainproofs
AFKLOOSSTT	footstalks
AFLLLNUUWY	unlawfully
AFLLOOSSTT	footstalls
AFLMOORRTU	formulator
AFMNORRSST	transforms
AGGGGIINWW	wigwagging
AGGGGIINZZ	zigzagging
AGGGIIMNSU	misgauging
AGGGILLNWY	wagglingly
AGGGILNRST	straggling
AGGGIMNORT	mortgaging
AGGHHOPRRY	hygrograph
AGGHIILLMN	Gillingham
AGGHIINNRS	garnishing
AGGHIINNSU	anguishing
AGGHILLNUY	laughingly
AGGHILMNPU	galumphing
AGGHILNNSY	gnashingly
AGGHLOOPRS	logographs
AGGHLOOPRY	graphology
	logography
AGGHNRRTUU	Guru Granth
AGGIIILNTT	litigating
AGGIIIMNTT	mitigating
AGGIIINNNR	ingraining
AGGIIINRRT	irrigating
AGGIILLNNS	signalling
AGGIILNNTU	agglutinin
AGGIILNRTU	ligaturing
AGGIINNORS	organising
AGGIINNORZ	organizing
AGGIJLNTUU	jugulating
AGGIKNORTZ	Königgrätz
AGGILLNOTY	gloatingly
AGGILLOOST	algologist
AGGILNNNTU	untangling
AGGILNNOOO	ologoaning
AGGILNNORY	groaningly
AGGILNNOSS	singalongs
AGGILNNRST	strangling
AGGILNOOOY	agnoiology
AGGILNPPRS	grapplings
AGGILNPRSY	graspingly
AGGINNOORS	gorgonians
AGGINNORTU	outranging
AGGINORRSS	grosgrains
AGGINORRTT	garrotting
AGGINOSSTU	outgassing
AGGLNOOORY	organology
AGGLOORSTY	gastrology
AGGMOORRST	mortgagors
AGHHIKNSTW	nighthawks
AGHHILOPRT	lithograph
AGHHIMRRTT	Mithgarthr
AGHHINRSST	thrashings
AGHHLOOPRS	holographs
AGHHLOOPRY	holography
AGHHMOOPRS	homographs
AGHHNOOPPR	phonograph
AGHHOOPPRT	photograph
AGHHOPPTYY	phytophagy
AGHHORTUWY	throughway
AGHIIKNRRS	shikarring
AGHIILLMTY	almightily
AGHIILLSTT	taillights
AGHIILNNPS	planishing
AGHIIMNNSU	humanising
AGHIIMNNUZ	humanizing
AGHIIMNPSS	misshaping
AGHIIMOPRU	amphigouri
AGHIINNRST	tarnishing
AGHIINNRSV	varnishing
AGHIINNRTU	Thuringian
AGHIINOPRS	aphorising
AGHIINOPRZ	aphorizing
AGHIINPRRS	hairspring
AGHIINPRST	thraipings
AGHIINPSWW	whipsawing
AGHIINRTWW	wainwright
AGHILLNOPS	anglophils
AGHILLNOSW	shallowing
AGHILLNOTY	loathingly
	tallyhoing
AGHILLNSSY	slashingly
AGHILMORST	algorithms
	logarithms
AGHILNNTUY	hauntingly
AGHILNPPRT	thrappling
AGHILNPRST	springhalt
AGHILNPSTU	sulphating
AGHILNPSTY	playthings
AGHILNRSTT	stringhalt
AGHILOPPRY	lipography
AGHILOPPSY	gypsophila
AGHILORSTT	gastrolith
AGHILPRTWY	playwright
AGHILRSTTY	straightly
AGHIMNNOTT	Nottingham
AGHIMNNPSU	gunmanship
AGHIMNOOPS	shampooing
AGHIMNRSST	hamstrings
AGHIMORSST	histograms
AGHINNOOPR	harpooning
AGHINNORRT	Harrington
AGHINNORTT	Hartington
AGHINNOSTW	Washington
AGHINNSTUW	unswathing
AGHINOPRTY	atrophying
AGHIOPPRRS	spirograph
AGHKMOPRSY	kymographs
AGHKNNORSU	Kongur Shan
AGHKOORSSS	grasshooks
AGHLMNOOYY	Moholy-Nagy
AGHLMOOPRS	lagomorphs
AGHLMOOSTU	goalmouths

AGHLNOOORT	orthogonal
AGHLNOSSTU	onslaughts
AGHLOPPRSY	polygraphs
AGHLOPRSTY	stylograph
AGHLOPRSXY	xylographs
AGHLOPRXYY	xylography
AGHLORSTWY	Galsworthy
AGHMMOOOSU	homogamous
AGHMNOOPRS	monographs
	nomographs
	phonograms
AGHMNOOPRY	nomography
AGHMNOOPTY	pathognomy
AGHMOOOPSU	omophagous
AGHMOOPRST	photograms
AGHMOOPRTY	tomography
AGHNNSSTUU	Hsüan-tsung
AGHNOOPRSY	nosography
AGHOOOPSUZ	zoophagous
AGHOOPPRTY	topography
AGHOPPRRYY	pyrography
AGHOPPRTYY	typography
AGHORSSTTY	hygrostats
AGIIIILNNT	initialing
AGIIIINNTT	initiating
AGIIILMNNN	mainlining
AGIIILMNTT	militating
AGIIILNNTZ	latinizing
AGIIILNOTT	litigation
AGIIILNSTV	vitalising
AGIIILNTVZ	vitalizing
AGIIIMMNSX	maximising
AGIIIMMNXZ	maximizing
AGIIIMNNTT	intimating
AGIIIMNOTT	mitigation
AGIIINNSST	sanitising
AGIIINNSTZ	sanitizing
AGIIINORRT	irrigation
AGIIINRRTT	irritating
AGIIINRSST	satirising
AGIIINRSTZ	satirizing
AGIIINRTTT	tritiating
AGIIINTTTV	titivating
AGIIKLMNRS	grimalkins
AGIILLMMRS	milligrams
AGIILLNNST	installing
AGIILLNNUU	unilingual
AGIILLNORY	originally
AGIILLNPRS	spiralling
AGIILLNRTU	trilingual
AGIILLNRTY	trailingly
AGIILLNRVY	virginally
AGIILLNTVY	vigilantly
AGIILMMNOT	immolating
AGIILMNNPT	implanting
AGIILMNORS	moralising
AGIILMNORZ	moralizing
AGIILMNPSY	misplaying
AGIILMNSTU	simulating
AGIILMNSUV	misvaluing
AGIILMNTTU	mutilating
AGIILNNORU	unoriginal
AGIILNNOST	insolating
AGIILNNPTT	tinplating
AGIILNNSTU	insulating
AGIILNOPPT	oppilating
AGIILNOPRS	polarising
AGIILNOPRZ	polarizing
AGIILNOPST	spoliating
AGIILNORSS	solarising
AGIILNORSV	valorising
AGIILNORSZ	solarizing
AGIILNORVZ	valorizing
AGIILNOSTT	totalising
AGIILNOTTZ	totalizing
AGIILNPRST	springtail
AGIILNRRSU	ruralising
AGIILNRRUZ	ruralizing
AGIILNRSTY	laryngitis
AGIILOOSTX	axiologist
AGIILORSTT	litigators
AGIIMMNRST	immigrants
AGIIMMORRT	immigrator
AGIIMMOSST	misogamist
AGIIMMSSTT	stigmatism
AGIIMNNNOT	nominating
AGIIMNNORS	romanising
AGIIMNNORZ	romanizing
AGIIMNNOSW	womanising
AGIIMNNOWZ	womanizing
AGIIMNNPRS	mainspring
AGIIMNNRST	inmigrants
AGIIMNNRTU	ruminating
AGIIMNORST	amortising
	migrations
AGIIMNORSU	migrainous
AGIIMNORTZ	amortizing
AGIIMNOTTV	motivating
AGIIMNRRVY	Virgin Mary
AGIIMNSSTT	misstating
AGIIMNSSUV	vaginismus
AGIIMORSTT	mitigators
AGIIMORTTY	mitigatory
AGIIMSSTTT	stigmatist
AGIINNNNPS	inspanning
AGIINNNOTT	intonating
AGIINNNOTV	innovating
AGIINNOPPT	appointing
AGIINNORSS	signorinas
AGIINNORST	notarising
AGIINNORTZ	notarizing
AGIINNOSTT	stationing
AGIINNOSTU	Antigonus I
AGIINNPPRW	inwrapping
AGIINNPRSU	unaspiring
AGIINNPSTU	supinating
AGIINNQSTU	quantising
AGIINNQTUZ	quantizing
AGIINNRSTT	intrigants
	transiting
AGIINNRTTU	intriguant
AGIINNSSTU	sustaining
AGIINNSTUY	sanguinity
AGIINOORRT	originator
AGIINOPRSV	vaporising
AGIINOPRVZ	vaporizing
AGIINORSTT	instigator
AGIINORSTV	grivations
AGIINORSUV	viraginous
AGIINPRTVY	varityping
AGIINRTTTT	attritting
AGIIORRRST	irrigators
AGIIRSSTTU	guitarists
AGIISSTUUV	Gustavus II
AGIJLNNTUY	jauntingly
AGIJLNOTUU	jugulation
AGIKKLNRSY	skylarking
AGIKLMNOOT	toolmaking
AGIKLMNOSS	lossmaking
AGIKLNNOSY	ankylosing
AGIKLNOTTU	outtalking
AGIKLNOTUW	outwalking
AGIKNNORTT	Tarkington
AGIKNNORTU	outranking
AGILLLNRUY	alluringly
AGILLNNRSY	snarlingly
AGILLNNSTY	slantingly
AGILLNOPRT	patrolling
AGILLNOPSW	wallopings
AGILLNOSWW	swallowing
AGILLNRSUY	singularly
AGILLOOSSS	isoglossal
AGILMNNOOP	lampooning
AGILMNNOST	lamingtons
AGILMOOSTU	gliomatous
AGILMOPSTY	polygamist
AGILMRSSUV	vulgarisms
AGILNNNOPY	nonplaying
AGILNNNOYY	annoyingly
AGILNNNRSU	unsnarling
AGILNNOPTY	poignantly
AGILNNORTY	ignorantly
AGILNNOSUU	lanuginous
AGILNNTTUY	tauntingly
AGILNOPPRS	prolapsing
AGILNOPPTU	populating
AGILNOPTUY	outplaying
AGILNOSSTT	nostalgist
AGILNOSTTU	outlasting
AGILNOSTUY	autolysing
AGILNOTUUV	outvaluing
AGILNOTUYZ	autolyzing
AGILNPPRRU	larrupping
AGILNRSTTU	lustrating
AGILOOPSST	apologists
AGILORSSST	glossarist
AGIMMNOOST	monogamist
AGIMMNOSSU	Simon Magus
AGIMMNSSUY	gymnasiums
AGIMNNNOTU	outmanning
AGIMNNSSUU	unassuming
AGIMNOORST	agronomist
AGIMNOPRSU	sporangium
AGINNNPPSU	unsnapping
AGINNOORTT	rattooning
AGINNORRTW	Warrington

AGINNPPRUW	unwrapping
AGINOOOPRS	sporogonia
AGINOOPSST	topagnosis
AGINOORTTV	rotovating
AGINOPRRTY	portraying
AGINORSTTU	outstaring
AGINOSSTTU	gustations
AGINOSTTUY	outstaying
AGINPRSSSU	surpassing
AGINPRSTTU	upstarting
AGIORSTTUU	gratuitous
AGIQRSSSTU	grassquits
AGISSTUUVV	Gustavus VI
AGJKNORRSU	kurrajongs
AGKLORSSSW	glassworks
AGKNRSTYYZ	Kyrgyzstan
AGLLLOOPRY	pyrogallol
AGLLNOOPYY	palynology
AGLLRTTUUY	gutturally
AGLMOOOPTY	potamology
AGLMOOOSTY	somatology
AGLMOOPSUY	polygamous
AGLMOORSUU	glamourous
AGLMOPPRUU	propagulum
AGLMPRSSUU	sugarplums
AGLNOORSUU	languorous
AGLOOOSTUU	autologous
AGLOOPPRYY	papyrology
AGLOORSSST	glossators
AGLOPPRSUY	playgroups
AGLORSSSTW	glassworts
AGMMNOOOSU	monogamous
AGMNOORSTY	gastronomy
AGMNORRSST	strongarms
AGMOOORSST	Mato Grosso
AGMOORSTTY	gastrotomy
AGOORRSSST	grassroots
AHHIMNPTUY	hypanthium
AHHIMOPTYY	hypothymia
AHHIOPRSTU	authorship
AHHLNOPTXY	xanthophyl
AHHMORRSTW	Harmsworth
AHIIIJKNRS	jinrikisha
AHIIILNPPP	Philippian
AHIIILNPST	Philistian
AHIIIMMPSX	amphimixis
AHIIJKNRSS	jinrikshas
AHIIJLNOPU	John Paul II
AHIIKLNSTV	Tskhinvali
AHIILMORTU	humiliator
AHIILRSSTT	shirttails
AHIIMNNOTU	inhumation
AHIIMNNTUY	inhumanity
AHIINORSST	historians
AHIIPRSSSZ	sizarships
AHIIRSSTTW	shirtwaist
AHIJNNOSST	Saint John's
AHIKKSTUUY	Kitakyushu
AHILLMQSUY	qualmishly
AHILLPSSTW	whipstalls
AHILMNOPYY	Polyhymnia
AHILMNOSWY	womanishly
AHILMOPSSY	syphilomas
AHILMORSST	hailstorms
AHILMPSSYY	symphysial
AHILNOORTZ	horizontal
AHILNOPSTU	sulphation
AHILNORSTT	triathlons
AHILNPSSTU	sultanship
AHILOSSTTT	statoliths
AHIMMNORSU	harmoniums
AHIMMOPRSS	amorphisms
AHIMNOOOSU	homoousian
AHIMNOORRU	honorarium
AHIMNOORSU	harmonious
AHIMNOOSST	Matosinhos
AHIMNOPRST	matronship
AHIMNOPRTY	Amphitryon
AHIMNORSST	harmonists
AHIMNPRTTU	triumphant
AHIMORSTUU	haustorium
AHINOOPRRS	orpharions
AHINOORSTT	hortations
AHINOOSSTU	houstonias
AHINOPRSTY	notaryship
AHINOPRSUX	xiphosuran
AHINPRSSST	transships
AHIOOPSTTX	phototaxis
AHIOPPRSST	pastorship
AHIOPSSSTY	hypostasis
AHKLLMOSWY	mollyhawks
AHKLMOPRYY	karyolymph
AHKLORSSTW	walkshorts
AHLLMMOSTU	smallmouth
AHLLMOOPRS	allomorphs
AHLLOPRSTU	prothallus
AHLLOPTXYY	phyllotaxy
AHLMOOPRTU	photomural
AHLMOOPSTY	homoplasty
AHLNOPSTUY	polyanthus
AHLOPPSTYY	hypoplasty
AHLORRSTTU	ultrashort
AHMMORSTTU	smartmouth
AHMNNOOSTU	monanthous
AHMNOOPRTU	protohuman
AHMOOPRTYY	amyotrophy
AHMOPRSTTU	mouthparts
AHNNOSTTWY	shantytown
AHNOOPSTTY	photonasty
AHNOPPRTTY	tryptophan
AHNORRSTTY	thyratrons
AHOOPPRRST	saprotroph
AHOOPPRTTY	protopathy
AHOOPRRTXY	orthopraxy
AHOOPRSTTU	autotrophs
AHOOPRSTUX	auxotrophs
AHOOPSSTTT	photostats
AHOPRRRTTU	Port Arthur
AIIIIILLMW	William III
AIIIIKKPRR	pakirikiri
AIIIIKMRTT	Kiritimati
AIIIINNOTT	initiation
AIIIINRTTX	initiatrix
AIIIJNNSTU	Justinian I
AIIIKKLMRZ	Kizil Irmak
AIIILLMNTU	illuminati
AIIILLMRTY	militarily
AIIILLNNOS	Illinoisan
AIIILMMMNS	minimalism
AIIILMMNST	minimalist
AIIILMMRST	militarism
AIIILMNOTT	limitation
	militation
AIIILMRSTT	militarist
AIIILMRSTV	trivialism
AIIILMRSTY	similarity
AIIILNNQTU	Quintilian
AIIILNOPTX	pixilation
AIIILORSTV	visitorial
AIIILRTTVY	triviality
AIIIMNNOTT	intimation
AIIIMNOPSS	pianissimo
AIIIMNOSTT	imitations
AIIIMNSSST	Mistassini
AIIIMPRSVV	viviparism
AIIINNOOST	ionisation
AIIINNOOTZ	ionization
AIIINNOTTV	invitation
AIIINORRTT	irritation
AIIINORSTT	initiators
AIIINORTTT	tritiation
AIIINORTTY	initiatory
AIIINOSTTV	visitation
	vitiations
AIIINOTTTV	titivation
AIIIPRSSTY	pityriasis
AIIIPRTVVY	viviparity
AIIKLMNOSW	Malinowski
AIIKNSSTTT	Saint Kitts
AIILLLNOSU	illusional
AIILLMNNTU	illuminant
AIILLMNOSW	Williamson
AIILLMNOTU	illuminato
AIILLMNTTY	militantly
AIILLNOOTV	volitional
AIILLNOSUV	villainous
AIILLNOSVY	visionally
AIILLORSTY	solitarily
AIILLOSSTT	solstitial
AIILLOTTVY	volatility
AIILLRSSTT	triallists
AIILLSTUVV	valvulitis
AIILMMNNOS	nominalism
AIILMMNOOT	immolation
AIILMMORST	immoralist
AIILMMORTY	immorality
AIILMNNOST	nominalist
AIILMNOORT	monitorial
AIILMNORST	trinomials
AIILMNORTY	minatorily
AIILMNOSTU	simulation
AIILMNOTTU	mutilation
AIILMNRSSU	insularism
AIILMNRTUY	unmilitary
AIILMOPTTY	optimality
AIILMRRTUV	triumviral

AIILNNOOST	insolation
AIILNNOSTU	insulation
AIILNOOPPT	oppilation
AIILNOOPST	positional
	spoliation
AIILNOOSTV	violations
AIILNOQSTU	liquations
AIILNORSSV	livraisons
AIILNOSSTU	Saint Louis
	Saint-Louis
AIILNPRSSU	spirulinas
AIILNRSSUY	urinalysis
AIILNRSTUY	insularity
AIILPPRTUY	pupilarity
AIILPRSSST	spritsails
AIILPRSSTU	spirituals
AIILRSSTTU	ritualists
AIILRTTUVY	virtuality
AIIMMNNOTU	ammunition
AIIMMPRRTU	imprimatur
AIIMMRTTUY	immaturity
AIIMNNNOOT	nomination
AIIMNNORTU	rumination
AIIMNNOSST	Saint-Simon
AIIMNNRSTT	ministrant
AIIMNOOTTV	motivation
AIIMNOPRSS	prosimians
AIIMNOPRTV	provitamin
AIIMNOPSSS	impassions
AIIMNOPSTU	utopianism
AIIMNOPTTU	imputation
AIIMNORSSU	Missourian
AIIMNORSSY	missionary
AIIMNPRSTU	puritanism
AIIMNPSSTT	timpanists
AIIMNPSSTU	impuissant
AIIMNPSTTY	tympanitis
AIIMNQRSSU	sinarquism
AIIMOPRSTT	patriotism
AIIMOSSTTT	stomatitis
AIINNNOOTT	intonation
AIINNNOOTV	innovation
AIINNNOPST	pinnations
AIINNOPSTU	supination
AIINNORSTT	nitrations
	transition
AIINNORSTU	insinuator
	ruinations
	urinations
AIINNOSSTU	sinuations
AIINNOSSTX	Six Nations
AIINNOSTTX	antitoxins
AIINOOPPST	apposition
AIINOPRRST	inspirator
AIINOPRSTT	partitions
AIINOPRSTV	privations
AIINORSSTT	striations
AIINORSTTT	titrations
AIINORTTVY	invitatory
AIINOSSTTU	situations
AIINQRSSTU	sinarquist
AIIOPRSSTT	topiarists
AIIOPRSUVV	viviparous
AIIOPSSSTT	pastitsios
AIIORRRSTT	irritators
AIIORSTTTV	titivators
AIIORTTTTV	tittivator
AIIPPRSSTU	Aristippus
AIIPRSTTVY	varitypist
AIIPSSSSTV	passivists
AIJLMNORSU	journalism
AIJLNORSTU	journalist
AIKLMOSSTT	milktoasts
AIKLMSSTTU	multitasks
AIKLORSSYY	karyolysis
AIKNRSSTVY	Stravinsky
AILLLOOOPU	Pollaiuolo
AILLMMORTY	immortally
AILLMNOOPY	polynomial
AILLMOPRXY	proximally
AILLMOSSVY	amylolysis
AILLNNOOTY	notionally
AILLNOOPRT	pollinator
AILLNOOPTY	optionally
AILLNORSTY	tonsillary
AILLNOSTUU	ululations
AILLNOSVYY	synovially
AILLNQRTUY	tranquilly
AILLOPPSST	lipoplasts
AILLPRSSTU	pluralists
AILMMOORST	immolators
AILMMSTTUU	ultimatums
AILMNNOOPR	pronominal
AILMNNOSTY	antimonyls
AILMNOOPST	lampoonist
AILMNORTUY	unmorality
AILMNSSTTU	stimulants
AILMOOPRST	prostomial
AILMOOPSTU	lipomatous
AILMOPPRUY	polyparium
AILMORSSTU	simulators
AILMORSTTU	mutilators
	stimulator
AILMPRTTUY	multiparty
AILMSSTTUU	mutualists
AILNOOPPTU	population
AILNOOPRSS	sponsorial
AILNOOSTUV	ovulations
AILNOPSSTU	pulsations
AILNORSSTU	insulators
AILNORSTTU	lustration
AILNORSUVY	unsavorily
AILNOSSTUY	autolysins
AILNOSTTUU	ustulation
AILNPPSSTU	suppliants
AILNPSSTUY	puissantly
AILOOPRSTY	spoliatory
AILOOPSTTU	autopilots
AILOPPRTUY	popularity
AILOPRSTTU	stipulator
AILRRSTUUV	ultravirus
AIMMMNOSST	mammonists
AIMMNORSTU	stramonium
AIMMNOSSTU	summations
AIMMOORRTU	moratorium
AIMMRSSSTU	summarists
AIMNNOORST	nominators
AIMNNOOSTU	antimonous
AIMNOOSTTU	autonomist
AIMNOOSTTX	taxonomist
AIMNOPSSTU	assumption
AIMNORRSST	rainstorms
AIMNORRSTU	ruminators
AIMNPSSTTY	tympanists
AIMNRSTTUU	nasturtium
AIMOOORTVY	ovariotomy
AIMOPSSSTY	symposiast
AIMPSSSSTU	assumpsits
AINNOOPRSS	sopraninos
AINNOOPRTT	antiproton
AINNOORSTV	innovators
AINNOORTVY	innovatory
AINOOPPRST	appointors
	apportions
AINOOPRRST	prorations
AINOOPRSTY	anisotropy
AINOOQSTTU	quotations
AINOOSTTTU	outstation
AINOOSTTUX	autotoxins
AINOPRSSTU	supinators
AINOPRSTUU	usurpation
AINORRSSTT	transistor
AINORRSTTY	transitory
AINPRSTUUV	pursuivant
AIOOPRRSUU	uproarious
AIOOPRSTVY	vaporosity
AIOORRSTTU	traitorous
AIOOSSTTTT	tattooists
AIOPPPRSUU	pupiparous
AIOPRRSUVV	parvovirus
AIOPRSTTTY	tyropittas
AIORRRTTTU	triturator
AKKMMNORSU	Kommunarsk
AKLLMMOSWY	mollymawks
AKLOORSSTT	rootstalks
AKNNORSSYY	synkaryons
AKNOOPRRSY	prokaryons
ALLNOPSTTU	pollutants
ALLOORSUVY	valorously
ALLOPRSSTY	sallyports
ALLOPSTUUY	patulously
ALMNOPRTUY	poultryman
ALMOOPPRST	protoplasm
ALMOQSSUUY	squamously
ALNOOPSSTT	tonoplasts
ALNOPSSTTU	postulants
ALNPRSTUUY	pursuantly
ALNPSSTTUU	pustulants
ALOOORSTUZ	zoolatrous
ALOOPPRSTT	protoplast
ALOOPPRTTY	prototypal
ALOOPRSTTU	postulator
ALOOPRSUVY	vaporously
ALOPRTUUVY	voluptuary
ALORSSTTUU	Lotus Sutra
AMMOOSTUXY	myxomatous

AMNNOOSTUY	antonymous
AMNNOOSTWW	townswoman
AMNNOSTTUW	stuntwoman
AMNOOOSTUU	autonomous
AMNOOPRSUY	paronymous
AMOORRRSWW	arrowworms
AMOORSSTTU	stromatous
AMOPPRSTTU	postpartum
AMORRSSTWW	strawworms
ANNOOPRSST	transposon
ANOOOPRSSZ	sporozoans
ANOOOPRSTZ	protozoans
ANOPRRSSTT	transports
AOOORRSTTV	rotovators
AOOPRRSSTT	protostars
AOPRRSTUUY	usurpatory
AORRRSTWWY	worrywarts
BBBCKOOSSY	bobbysocks
BBBEEELMSU	bumblebees
BBBEEIINRW	winebibber
BBBEELRRSU	blubberers
BBBEGILNRU	blubbering
BBBEIKORSS	skibobbers
BBBEOORSXY	bobbysoxer
BBBGHINNOO	hobnobbing
BBBGIIKNOS	skibobbing
BBBHRSSUUY	subshrubby
BBCDEIRSSU	subscribed
BBCEEKNRRU	rubberneck
BBCEELNOOU	bubonocele
BBCEGILNOR	clobbering
BBCEHINSSU	chubbiness
BBCEHLOSUY	cubbyholes
BBCEHNRRUY	bunchberry
BBCEILRRSS	scribblers
BBCEIRRSSU	subscriber
BBCEIRSSSU	subscribes
BBCEIRSSTU	scrubbiest
BBCEKSTUUY	buckytubes
BBCGIILNRS	scribbling
BBCIIILSST	biblicists
BBDDDEELOS	bobsledded
BBDDEEIMOV	divebombed
BBDDEEORUV	overdubbed
BBDEEIRRSU	rubberised
BBDEEIRRUZ	rubberized
BBDEIKNOOR	bookbinder
BBDEIORRSW	bowerbirds
BBDEIOSSUY	busybodies
BBDHIIOPRS	bishopbird
BBDINOOORW	ribbonwood
BBDNOSSTUU	bundobusts
BBEEEFGRRU	beefburger
BBEEEHLMSU	humblebees
BBEEHLSSUU	bluebushes
BBEEIILRRS	bilberries
BBEEINRSTZ	rebbetzins
BBEEIORRSX	boxberries
BBEEIRRSSU	rubberises
BBEEIRRSUZ	rubberizes
BBEELLOTTU	bluebottle
BBEELNNOTU	bluebonnet
BBEELORRSS	slobberers
BBEGGNOOSW	wobbegongs
BBEGHILOSS	bobsleighs
BBEGHIOSTW	bobweights
BBEGILNORS	slobbering
BBEGINRSSU	grubbiness
BBEGJNOORR	Björneborg
BBEHHILOST	shibboleth
BBEHHOORSY	hobbyhorse
BBEHIRSSTU	shrubbiest
BBEHLLMOSS	bombshells
BBEIIKLNOR	ribbonlike
BBEIILLOOP	bibliopole
BBEIIORRTU	urbi et orbi
BBEIKLMOOO	bookmobile
BBEIKLNOST	knobbliest
BBEILNOSSW	wobbliness
BBEINOPRRT	Ribbentrop
BBEINSSSTU	stubbiness
BBEJLOPRUU	Jubbulpore
BBEKLORRUW	rubblework
BBEKNORSTU	bonkbuster
BBERRSTTUU	butterburs
BBFHIINORS	ribbonfish
BBGHIINRSU	rubbishing
BBGHILNOOS	hobgoblins
BBGHIMOSST	bombsights
BBGIILNQSU	quibblings
BBGIMOORRY	borborygmi
BBHIIILLOP	bibliophil
BBHILNOSSY	snobbishly
BBIIIIMNOT	imbibition
BBIILLOOPY	bibliopoly
BBILLOSUUY	bibulously
BBIMNOORSU	bourbonism
BBJMMMOOUU	mumbo jumbo
BBLMOORSUY	Bloomsbury
BBLNORSTUY	stubbornly
BCCCKMOOSS	cockscombs
BCCDEEEMNU	decumbence
BCCDEEMNUY	decumbency
BCCDEHKOSY	bodychecks
BCCDEILNOU	conducible
BCCEEEMNRU	recumbence
BCCEEENPSU	pubescence
BCCEEENRSU	rubescence
BCCEEIINOS	bioscience
BCCEEIMRRY	cybercrime
BCCEEINRTY	cybernetic
BCCEEMNRUY	recumbency
BCCEHIINOR	Boccherini
BCCEHIKNPS	pinchbecks
BCCEHKKOOS	checkbooks
BCCEHNORSS	crossbench
BCCEIINOOT	biocenotic
	coenobitic
BCCEILORTU	Bertolucci
BCCEIMNNUY	incumbency
BCCEINNOSU	concubines
BCCEKLORSU	cockleburs
BCCEMRSSUU	succumbers
BCCGIMNSUU	succumbing
BCCHIINORT	bronchitic
BCCIILSSTY	bicyclists
BCCIKLLOSY	billycocks
BCCMORRSUY	currycombs
BCDDEEILTU	deductible
BCDDEIIKRY	dickeybird
BCDDIIKRSY	dickybirds
BCDEEEIINT	benedicite
BCDEEEILTT	detectible
BCDEEEIRRS	redescribe
BCDEEEMNRU	encumbered
BCDEEHIIRS	herbicides
BCDEEHIMRS	besmirched
BCDEEHLNNU	unblenched
BCDEEHLOST	bedclothes
BCDEEHORUU	debouchure
BCDEEIILNR	incredible
BCDEEILLUX	excludible
BCDEEIMNOR	recombined
BCDEEIMNRU	incumbered
BCDEEINSSU	subsidence
BCDEEINSTU	Benedictus
BCDEEINTVX	Benedict XV
BCDEEIPRRS	prescribed
BCDEEIRRSS	describers
BCDEEKLLNU	bullnecked
BCDEELOOSS	obsolesced
BCDEEORRSS	crossbreed
BCDEEOSTWY	Betws-y-Coed
BCDEFLOOTU	clubfooted
BCDEGHINOU	debouching
BCDEGIINRS	describing
BCDEGILNOU	beclouding
BCDEHIILOR	bichloride
BCDEHINPST	pitchbends
BCDEIILLNU	includible
BCDEIILNRY	incredibly
BCDEIILPSU	publicised
BCDEIILPUZ	publicized
BCDEIINOOT	endobiotic
BCDEIINSSU	subindices
BCDEIKLOOT	bootlicked
BCDEILOORR	corrodible
BCDEILOORU	bicoloured
BCDEILOPRU	producible
BCDEIMNNOU	uncombined
BCDEIOPRRS	proscribed
BCDEKLLOOS	bollocksed
BCDELORRUY	cloudberry
BCDEMMNRUU	cummerbund
BCDENORSUU	unobscured
BCDEORRSSS	crossbreds
BCDEORSTTU	obstructed
BCDGINSTUU	subducting
BCDHHIILRT	childbirth
BCDHKNOSUU	buckhounds
BCDHLNOOTU	clothbound
BCDIILMORU	lumbricoid
BCDIIOPRRT	tropicbird
BCDILOOOSS	discobolos
BCDILOOSSU	discobolus
BCDIMOORSS	scombroids

BCDINOSTUU	subduction
BCDKLOOOST	bloodstock
BCDKMRSTUU	dumbstruck
BCDLORSTUU	cloudburst
BCEEEEHKOO	Okeechobee
BCEEEEHRSS	beseechers
BCEEEFFILT	effectible
BCEEEFINNT	beneficent
BCEEEGHINS	beseeching
BCEEEHKNOS	cheekbones
BCEEEILLNU	ebullience
BCEEEIRSTV	brevetcies
BCEEELLMRU	cerebellum
BCEEELQRSU	becquerels
BCEEENRSTU	erubescent
BCEEFGIINN	beneficing
BCEEFIOPRS	fiberscope
	fibrescope
BCEEGHINRS	breechings
BCEEGHNORS	Schoenberg
BCEEGIINOT	biogenetic
BCEEGINRSU	subgeneric
BCEEHIKLNT	Liebknecht
BCEEHIMRSS	besmirches
BCEEHIORRS	seborrheic
BCEEHIRSTU	butcheries
BCEEHKLNOU	hucklebone
BCEEHKOOQU	chequebook
BCEEHKOORS	chokebores
BCEEHKORRY	chokeberry
BCEEHMNRSU	Übermensch
BCEEHMORUU	embouchure
BCEEHNOOPR	necrophobe
BCEEHORSTT	brochettes
BCEEHPRSUY	hypercubes
BCEEHRSTTU	trebuchets
BCEEIILLMY	imbecilely
BCEEIILPST	plebiscite
BCEEIILTYZ	Belize City
BCEEIJOSTV	objectives
BCEEIJSTUV	subjective
BCEEILLNUY	ebulliency
BCEEILLOOS	cellobiose
BCEEILLORS	corbeilles
BCEEILMOST	comestible
BCEEIMMOSS	misbecomes
BCEEIMNORS	recombines
BCEEINOOST	coenobites
BCEEIOORUV	Courbevoie
BCEEIORRSW	cowberries
BCEEIPRRRS	prescriber
BCEEIPRRSS	prescribes
BCEEIPRRSY	spiceberry
BCEEIPSSSU	subspecies
BCEEJNORST	jobcentres
BCEEKLNOTT	bottleneck
BCEEKRSTTU	trebuckets
BCEELNOTTU	cuttlebone
BCEELNRTUU	turbulence
BCEELOOSSS	obsolesces
BCEELOPPRT	Copper Belt
BCEELORSTU	beltcourse
BCEELRSUUY	burleycues
BCEEMMORSU	cumbersome
BCEEOOORRR	corroboree
BCEFFIORSU	subofficer
BCEFFIOSSU	suboffices
BCEFHISSTT	bitchfests
BCEFIIKRRS	firebricks
BCEFIIMORR	microfiber
	microfibre
BCEFIIOPRT	fibreoptic
BCEFIJSTUY	subjectify
BCEFKLSTUU	bucketfuls
BCEGHIINTW	bewitching
BCEGHINRTU	butchering
BCEGIIKNRS	bickerings
BCEGIILORR	corrigible
BCEGIJNSTU	subjecting
BCEGIKLLNO	bellocking
BCEGIKLNRU	bucklering
BCEGILLNOR	corbelling
BCEGILMNOY	becomingly
BCEGILOOOY	bioecology
BCEGIMNNOU	unbecoming
BCEHHNNOUY	honeybunch
BCEHIIMOST	biochemist
BCEHIINSST	bitchiness
BCEHIISSSU	hibiscuses
BCEHILNOOR	bronchiole
BCEHILOPRY	hyperbolic
BCEHILOSTT	blotchiest
BCEHIMORSS	chemisorbs
BCEHINNSSU	bunchiness
BCEHINOOPX	xenophobic
BCEHINOSST	botchiness
BCEHIOQSUU	chibouques
BCEHKKOOST	sketchbook
BCEHKLOOSU	blockhouse
BCEHKMRSUU	humbuckers
BCEHLNOSUX	lunchboxes
BCEHLOSSUU	clubhouses
BCEHMNOOSY	honeycombs
BCEHMOORSS	chemosorbs
BCEHMRSTUW	thumbscrew
BCEIIILMMS	immiscible
BCEIIILMTY	imbecility
BCEIIILNNV	invincible
BCEIIIMMOT	biomimetic
BCEIIJNOST	bijections
BCEIIKLLLS	sicklebill
BCEIILLOTT	Botticelli
BCEIILMMOS	embolismic
BCEIILMPSU	semipublic
BCEIILNOST	bilections
BCEIILPSSU	publicises
BCEIILPSUZ	publicizes
BCEIIMOQTU	coquimbite
BCEIIMORST	biometrics
BCEIINOOSS	biocenosis
BCEIINOSST	bisections
BCEIINRRSS	inscribers
BCEIIOOPSS	bioscopies
BCEIJNOOST	objections
BCEIJNOSTU	subjection
BCEIKLLOSU	bullockies
BCEIKLOORT	bootlicker
BCEIKNOSST	steinbocks
BCEILMNOSU	columbines
BCEILMOORT	bolometric
BCEILMRSTU	crumbliest
BCEILNOOST	bolections
BCEILNORSU	Berlusconi
BCEILNRTUU	tuberculin
BCEIMNNSTU	incumbents
BCEIMOSTUV	combustive
BCEINNOSSU	bounciness
BCEINOPSTU	subception
BCEINORTTU	contribute
BCEINOSSTU	subsection
BCEIOPPRSY	presbyopic
BCEIOPRRRS	proscriber
BCEIOPRRSS	proscribes
BCEIORSSTT	obstetrics
BCEJKMPRUU	buckjumper
BCEKKOOOPT	pocketbook
BCEKLLOOSS	bollockses
BCEKLNRTUU	turnbuckle
BCEKMRSSUU	bumsuckers
BCEKNPRSUY	cyberpunks
BCEKRSTTUU	rustbucket
BCELNORSTU	Culbertson
BCELNRTUUY	turbulency
BCELRSTUUU	subculture
BCEMNOPRTU	procumbent
BCENOORSSS	crossbones
BCENORSSTU	curbstones
BCEPRSTTUU	buttercups
BCFIIMORRR	cribriform
BCGHILNSTU	nightclubs
BCGIIINNRS	inscribing
BCGIIKKNOX	kickboxing
BCGIILORRY	corrigibly
BCGIKLLNOO	bollocking
BCGIKLLNOU	bullocking
BCGIKLNNOU	unblocking
BCGIKLNNUU	unbuckling
BCGIKMNSUU	bumsucking
BCGIKNPRSU	springbuck
BCGIMNOSTU	combusting
BCGINOOTTY	boycotting
BCHHIMOOOP	homophobic
BCHIILNOPY	phycobilin
BCHIINORST	bronchitis
BCHIIOPRSS	bishoprics
BCHIIOPSSY	biophysics
BCHIKLLOSY	blockishly
BCHIMNOOOP	monophobic
BCHIMOORTT	thrombotic
BCHIMOORTW	witchbroom
BCHINOOPTY	phycobiont
BCHIOOORRT	orthoboric
BCHIOPRTYY	bryophytic
BCHKNORSTU	buckthorns
BCHLNOPSUW	punchbowls
BCHLOOOSSY	schoolboys

BCIIILMMSY immiscibly
BCIIILNNVY invincibly
BCIIILORTT trilobitic
BCIIIMMORY biomimicry
BCIILNOPSY psilocybin
BCIILORSUU lubricious
BCIILPSSTU publicists
BCIIMNOSTY symbiontic
BCIKKNOSST knobsticks
BCIKKORRSW brickworks
BCIKMOORST broomstick
BCILLORSSS crossbills
BCILOOSTUU tubicolous
BCIMNOOSTU combustion
BCIMNOOSTY mycobionts
BCIMORRSTU microburst
BCIOPRSSTU subtropics
BCIPRSSSTU subscripts
BCLMORSUUY cumbrously
BCMOOOTTUU Tombouctou
BCMOORSSTU combustors
BCOORRSTTU obstructor
BDDDEGIOOS dogsbodied
BDDDEIISUV subdivided
BDDDGIINSU disbudding
BDDEEEFINR befriended
BDDEEEILLV bedevilled
BDDEEEILRW bewildered
BDDEEELMNO emboldened
BDDEEENRTU debentured
BDDEEFNORW New Bedford
BDDEEGLNOU bludgeoned
BDDEEGNTUU unbudgeted
BDDEEILMSS dissembled
BDDEEINORV overbidden
BDDEEINRST bestridden
BDDEEIORSS sobersided
BDDEELMORU dumbledore
BDDEENNRUU unburdened
BDDEFGILNU befuddling
BDDEFIORRS forbidders
BDDEFORSUY bodysurfed
BDDEGIILOS disobliged
BDDEGILMRU Middelburg
BDDEGIOOSS dogsbodies
BDDEGLOOSU doodlebugs
BDDEHIIRSY hybridised
BDDEHIIRYZ hybridized
BDDEHLNOOR bondholder
BDDEIIMORS dibromides
BDDEIIRSUV subdivider
BDDEIISSSU subsidised
BDDEIISSUV subdivides
BDDEIISSUZ subsidized
BDDEILMORW middlebrow
BDDEIMOSTU misdoubted
BDDEINNRUW windburned
BDDEINRSSU disburdens
BDDELOOORW Boldrewood
BDDFGIINOR forbidding
BDDFILLNOS blindfolds
BDDFMNOSUU dumbfounds
BDDGIINOTU outbidding
BDDHLNOOOU bloodhound
BDDLOOOOSW bloodwoods
BDEEEEJLLW bejewelled
BDEEEELRSV belvederes
BDEEEEMMRR remembered
BDEEEFILNS defensible
BDEEEFINTT benefitted
BDEEEFOORT freebooted
BDEEEGHILR Heidelberg
BDEEEHLLNR hellbender
BDEEEIILSV disbelieve
BDEEEILMMS emblemised
BDEEEILMMZ emblemized
BDEEEILNSS edibleness
BDEEEILNTX extendible
BDEEEILSTW wildebeest
BDEEEIMRTT embittered
BDEEEINRRT interbreed
BDEEEIRRSW dewberries
BDEEEIRTTW bitterweed
BDEEELLMOW embowelled
BDEEELLORW rebellowed
BDEEELMTUW tumbleweed
BDEEELNOSS nosebleeds
BDEEELORTU doubletree
BDEEELRRRY elderberry
BDEEEMMNST embedments
BDEEEMNRRU renumbered
BDEEEMOPRT obtempered
BDEEENRSTU debentures
BDEEFGIINR debriefing
BDEEFIILSS disbeliefs
BDEEFILNSY defensibly
BDEEFLLOSW bedfellows
BDEEFLORSW flowerbeds
BDEEFLORUW furbelowed
BDEEFOORRS foreboders
BDEEGGLOOT bootlegged
BDEEGHILRT Lethbridge
BDEEGHINOR neighbored
BDEEGHINRT brightened
BDEEGIILNV bedeviling
BDEEGIILST digestible
BDEEGIINNR inbreeding
BDEEGIINNZ bedizening
BDEEGILRSS bridgeless
BDEEGIMOSU disembogue
BDEEGINRSU Duisenberg
BDEEGIORRS dogberries
BDEEGLNORU bludgeoner
BDEEGNOORU bourgeoned
BDEEGNORSW Swedenborg
BDEEHILLRS Breed's Hill
BDEEHIMOOS homebodies
BDEEHIMRSU Humberside
BDEEHIRRSY Derbyshire
BDEEHLNNOR hornblende
BDEEHLNNOU unbeholden
BDEEIIILST debilities
BDEEIILLNU ineludible
BDEEIILMOS demobilise
BDEEIILMOZ demobilize
BDEEIILOSS biodiesels
BDEEIILRSW bridlewise
BDEEIILRTV divertible
BDEEIILSTV divestible
BDEEILLNTU bulletined
BDEEILLOPT potbellied
BDEEILLRSW bridewells
BDEEILMNRU unlimbered
BDEEILMOSW disembowel
BDEEILMRSS dissembler
BDEEILMSSS dissembles
BDEEILNORR borderline
BDEEILNOTY obediently
BDEEILORSW bowdlerise
BDEEILORWZ bowdlerize
BDEEIMMNOT embodiment
BDEEIMMRSS dismembers
BDEEIMOOSS somebodies
BDEEIMORRS embroiders
BDEEIMORRY embroidery
BDEEIMRRSU reimbursed
BDEEINSSUX subindexes
BDEEIORSSS sobersides
BDEEIORSSY disobeyers
BDEEIQRTTU briquetted
BDEEIRSSTT bedsitters
BDEEKOOORV overbooked
BDEEKOORSW brookweeds
BDEELLNRUY underbelly
BDEELNNOSS blondeness
BDEELNOSSU doubleness
BDEELNRRSU blunderers
BDEELQRSUU burlesqued
BDEEMNNRUU unnumbered
BDEEMNORSU burdensome
BDEENNNOTU unbonneted
BDEENORRUV overburden
BDEENORSUV unobserved
BDEENORTTU rebuttoned
BDEERSSTTU buttressed
BDEFFIILSU diffusible
BDEFFLOTUU outbluffed
BDEFGINOOR foreboding
BDEFGIOORT footbridge
BDEFGSSTUU fussbudget
BDEFIILRRS riflebirds
BDEFILLMOO Bloomfield
BDEFILNORW brownfield
BDEFINORSY boyfriends
BDEFORRSUY bodysurfer
BDEGGGINRU begrudging
BDEGGHIINT bedighting
BDEGGLNOOO boondoggle
BDEGHHIINR highbinder
BDEGHHIORW highbrowed
BDEGHIMOTU bigmouthed
BDEGHINNRU Hindenburg
BDEGIIILRS dirigibles
BDEGIILNRU rebuilding
BDEGIILOSS disobliges
BDEGIILSTY digestibly

BDEGIINORR broidering
BDEGIINOSY disobeying
BDEGIINRST bestriding
BDEGIINSTT bedsitting
BDEGIINSTU subediting
BDEGIKOOSU guidebooks
BDEGIKORRW bridgework
BDEGILNNRU blundering
BDEGILNORU bouldering
redoubling
BDEGIMOORR bridegroom
BDEGINNORU rebounding
BDEGINNSTU subtending
BDEGINOORY gooneybird
BDEGINORTW Bridgetown
BDEGINRRST Strindberg
BDEGINRSUU burgundies
BDEGIOPRRT Bridgeport
BDEGIORRTW Trowbridge
BDEHIILPSU bisulphide
BDEHIIMOOR rhomboidei
BDEHIIOPRT prohibited
BDEHIIRRSY hybridiser
BDEHIIRRYZ hybridizer
BDEHIIRSSY hybridises
BDEHIIRSYZ hybridizes
BDEHIORSSU birdhouses
BDEHMOORST thrombosed
BDEHNOOSUU housebound
BDEHNORTUX thunderbox
BDEHNRRSUU underbrush
undershrub
BDEIIILNRV biliverdin
BDEIIKLOOS obeliskoid
BDEIILLNUY ineludibly
BDEIILMORS disembroil
BDEIILNNOS blennioids
BDEIILSSTU subtilised
BDEIILSTUZ subtilized
BDEIIRSSSU subsidiser
BDEIIRSSUZ subsidizer
BDEIIRSTTU distribute
turbidites
BDEIISSSSU subsidises
BDEIISSSUZ subsidizes
BDEIJNORSU subjoinder
BDEIKKORSU duikerboks
BDEILLNOOS bloodlines
BDEILLNPSS spellbinds
BDEILLORWY yellowbird
BDEILLOSSU dissoluble
BDEILMOOSS disselboom
BDEILMORSW bowdlerism
BDEILMOSSY symbolised
BDEILMOSYZ symbolized
BDEILNOOSS bloodiness
BDEILOQSTU quodlibets
BDEILORSUV overbuilds
BDEILPRSUU upbuilders
BDEIMNORSS morbidness
BDEIMNOSST disentombs
BDEIMORSSU mousebirds
BDEINOORSS broodiness
BDEINRSSTU turbidness
BDEIOORTTW bitterwood
BDEIORSSTU subeditors
BDEIPRSSTU buprestids
BDEIRRSSSU disbursers
BDEIRRSSTU disturbers
BDEKMMNRUU kummerbund
BDELLNOPSU spellbound
BDELLOOTUW bulletwood
BDELLORSUZ bulldozers
BDELMMNOUY molybdenum
BDELMNOTUW tumbledown
BDELNOOOST bloodstone
BDELNOOSTU doubletons
BDELNORTUU untroubled
BDEMOORRRS smorrebrod
BDENNOORSW brownnosed
BDENNOOSST bondstones
BDENNOTTUU unbuttoned
BDENOOSSUX soundboxes
BDEOOORRSW woodborers
BDFLLOTUUY doubtfully
BDGHIILNNT nightblind
BDGHIILNST blindsight
BDGIIILMNR birdliming
BDGIILLNNY blindingly
BDGIILNNRU unbridling
BDGIILNPUU upbuilding
BDGIINRSSU disbursing
BDGIINRSTU disturbing
BDGIKMNOSU subkingdom
BDGILLNOUZ bulldozing
BDGILLOOTU bloodguilt
BDGILNNNUU unbundling
BDGILNOORY broodingly
BDGILNOTUY doubtingly
BDHIILRRWY whirlybird
BDHIMNOORY monohybrid
BDHNNOORTU northbound
BDHNOOSTUU southbound
BDIIILNOSU libidinous
BDIILNOOPT diplobiont
BDIIMNRSUU Brundisium
BDILLORSSW swordbills
BDILMNORSW blindworms
BDILMNORUY moribundly
BDILNORSTY blindstory
BDKNNOOORY donnybrook
BDLMOOORSW bloodworms
BDLOOOORST bloodroots
BDMNOORSTU stormbound
BDNOOOTTUW buttonwood
BDNORSSTUW downbursts
BEEEEEKPRS beekeepers
BEEEEFLNRS enfeeblers
BEEEEFLNSS feebleness
BEEEEGIKNP beekeeping
BEEEELNRRS Berners-Lee
BEEEEMMRRR rememberer
BEEEFGILNN enfeebling
BEEEFILLRX reflexible
BEEEFIMORT beforetime
BEEEFMRRUZ bumfreezer
BEEEFOORRT freebooter
BEEEGGIRRZ Erzgebirge
BEEEGGLMNR Mengelberg
BEEEGGRRUV vegeburger
BEEEGHINRS Heisenberg
BEEEGIILLR reeligible
BEEEGIJLNW bejeweling
BEEEGINRRR greenbrier
BEEEGNNORS greenbones
BEEEHLLORS hellebores
BEEEHLLRTW bellwether
BEEEIIKLSW biweeklies
BEEEIKLLRR bierkeller
BEEEILMMSS emblemises
BEEEILMMSZ emblemizes
BEEEILMNST belemnites
BEEEILNRUV unbeliever
BEEEILNSTX extensible
BEEEILRRSV reversible
BEEEILRRTV revertible
BEEEIMRRTT embitterer
BEEEIMRSSV semibreves
BEEEINRSSZ breeziness
BEEEIRRSTW sweetbrier
BEEEKKOOPR bookkeeper
BEEEKRRRSS berserkers
BEEELLRSST bestseller
BEEELMMNST emblements
BEEELMMRSS memberless
BEEELMRRSS resemblers
BEEELMRSZZ embezzlers
BEEELNNOTV benevolent
BEEELNRSST trebleness
BEEELSSSSU sublessees
BEEEMMNRTU embruement
BEEEMMNSTU bemusement
BEEEMNRTTT betterment
BEEEMRRTTU Buttermere
BEEENORSTT bonesetter
BEEFFGIRSU febrifuges
BEEFFHNOOR Bonhoeffer
BEEFGIINNT benefiting
BEEFGRSTUU subterfuge
BEEFHILSSU bluefishes
BEEFHINOSS bonefishes
BEEFIILLNX inflexible
BEEFIILMSS misbeliefs
BEEFIILNRR inferrible
BEEFILLMRU umbellifer
BEEFILRSTU subfertile
BEEFIORSSU sebiferous
BEEFLLLORW bellflower
BEEFLMNOTU befoulment
BEEGGIILLN negligible
BEEGGLOORT bootlegger
BEEGGNRRSU Regensburg
BEEGHILNRT blethering
BEEGHINRRT brightener
BEEGHINRSW beshrewing
BEEGHIRSTY eyebrights

BEEGHNOOPR	negrophobe
BEEGIIILLN	ineligible
BEEGIILNRT	Gilbertine
BEEGIILNST	ingestible
BEEGIINOSS	biogenesis
BEEGIKNNOT	betokening
BEEGILMNOT	obligement
BEEGILMNRS	resembling
BEEGILMNZZ	embezzling
BEEGILNRSS	inselbergs
BEEGIMMNOS	gombeenism
BEEGIMNORW	embowering
BEEGINRSTW	bestrewing
BEEGINRTTV	brevetting
BEEGINRTTW	Wittenberg
BEEGIOORSU	bourgeoise
BEEGLNOTUU	bluetongue
BEEGMNORYY	embryogeny
BEEGMNSSTU	subsegment
BEEGNNOTTU	unbegotten
BEEGNOORRS	Greensboro
BEEGNSSSUU	subgenuses
BEEGOORRSY	gooseberry
BEEGPRRSTU	Petersburg
BEEHIIITVX	exhibitive
BEEHILMOST	blithesome
BEEHILNSST	blitheness
BEEHIMMPRS	membership
BEEHINRSTT	terebinths
BEEHIORRSV	herbivores
BEEHKOORRS	Sherbrooke
BEEHLLRSSU	bushellers
BEEHLMMOTU	tumblehome
BEEHLMNSSU	humbleness
BEEHMOORST	bothersome
BEEHNOOPSX	xenophobes
BEEHOORSSX	horseboxes
BEEIIJORTU	bijouterie
BEEIIKLMRT	kimberlite
BEEIIKNRRS	inkberries
BEEIILLLRV	Libreville
BEEIILMMRS	immersible
BEEIILMNRT	timberline
BEEIILMRSS	remissible
BEEIILNNSS	insensible
BEEIILNNTV	inventible
BEEIILNRST	libertines
BEEIILNRTV	invertible
BEEIILNSTV	investible
BEEIILRSST	resistible
BEEIILSSTX	bissextile
BEEIKKNORR	knobkerrie
BEEIKLNPRS	besprinkle
BEEIKPRSSU	superbikes
BEEILLLTTT	Little Belt
BEEILLMRST	belletrism
BEEILLNORS	rebellions
BEEILLOPST	potbellies
BEEILLORSU	rebellious
BEEILLRSTT	belittlers
	belletrist
BEEILMNNSS	nimbleness
BEEILMNRSS	limberness
BEEILMOORS	bloomeries
BEEILMORRS	embroilers
BEEILMPRSU	plumberies
BEEILMRRSU	mulberries
BEEILNOSST	bilestones
	ostensible
BEEILNRSSU	nebulisers
BEEILNRSTW	West Berlin
BEEILNRSUZ	nebulizers
BEEILORSTT	briolettes
BEEILOSTTU	oubliettes
BEEILRRSVY	reversibly
BEEILRSTUX	extrusible
BEEILSSTTU	subtleties
BEEILSSTUV	vestibules
BEEIMMNRTU	imbruement
BEEIMRRRSU	reimburser
BEEIMRRSSU	reimburses
BEEINORRTT	torbernite
BEEINORSTU	tenebrious
BEEINRSSTT	bitterness
	tenebrists
BEEINRSSTU	subentries
BEEINSSSSU	businesses
BEEIQRRSUU	brusquerie
BEEIQRSTTU	briquettes
BEEIRSSUVV	subversive
BEEJNNORSU	Burne-Jones
BEEKNORSST	kerbstones
BEEKRSTUWY	Tewkesbury
BEELLLMSUU	umbellules
BEELLOOSTY	obsoletely
BEELMNNOOW	noblewomen
BEELMNRSSU	numberless
BEELMOORST	bolometers
BEELMRRSSU	slumberers
BEELNOOSTT	bottlenose
BEELNOSSTU	bluestones
BEELNPRTUU	puberulent
BEELNSSSTU	subtleness
BEELOOOSSX	looseboxes
BEELOORSUV	overblouse
BEELORRSST	bolsterers
BEELORSTUV	oversubtle
BEELQRRSUU	burlesquer
BEELQRSSUU	burlesques
BEELRRSSTU	blusterers
BEEMMNNORS	nonmembers
BEEMMNNOTT	entombment
BEEMMNOSST	embossment
BEEMMNOSTW	embowments
BEEMNORSSS	somberness
	sombreness
BEEMNOSTTW	bestowment
BEENOSSSTU	obtuseness
BEENPRSSSU	superbness
BEENQSSTUU	subsequent
BEEORSSTTU	soubrettes
BEEPRRSSTY	presbyters
BEEPRRSTYY	presbytery
BEERRSSTUV	subverters
BEERSSSTTU	buttresses
BEFFGINSTU	buffetings
BEFFNOORUY	buffoonery
BEFFNOSSUX	snuffboxes
BEFGIINNOR	fibrinogen
BEFGIINRVY	verbifying
BEFGILNORW	fingerbowl
BEFHIILLSS	billfishes
BEFHILLMTU	thimbleful
BEFHILOSSW	blowfishes
BEFHIMNSSU	numbfishes
BEFHIRRSSU	furbishers
BEFHIRSTTU	butterfish
BEFIILLNXY	inflexibly
BEFIILLORS	fibrillose
BEFIILRSTU	filibuster
BEFIORSSTT	frostbites
BEFLLMRTUU	tumblerful
BEFLLOSTTU	bottlefuls
BEGGHILORT	Toghril Beg
BEGGHMRSUU	humbuggers
BEGGHMRUUY	humbuggery
BEGGHNORTU	Gothenburg
BEGGIILLNY	negligibly
BEGGIINNNS	beginnings
BEGGIKNORS	Königsberg
BEGGILNNOS	belongings
BEGGIMNRSU	submerging
BEGGINNORU	burgeoning
BEGGRSTTUY	Gettysburg
BEGHHINOST	thighbones
BEGHIIINTX	exhibiting
BEGHIIKNNT	bethinking
BEGHIILMNS	blemishing
BEGHIILMRT	thimblerig
BEGHIILNRT	blithering
BEGHIINRRT	rebirthing
BEGHILLNSU	bushelling
BEGHILMNOO	hemoglobin
BEGHILNORY	neighborly
BEGHINORSU	neighbours
BEGHINORTT	betrothing
BEGHINRSST	brightness
BEGHMNOORT	thrombogen
BEGHOORRTU	Borgerhout
BEGHOORTUV	overbought
BEGIIILLNY	ineligibly
BEGIIILLTY	legibility
BEGIIIMNRT	ignimbrite
BEGIIKLNNR	blinkering
BEGIIKLRTZ	blitzkrieg
BEGIIKNNRS	briskening
BEGIILLNNR	brinelling
BEGIILLNTT	belittling
BEGIILMNOR	embroiling
BEGIILMNOS	embolising
BEGIILMNOZ	embolizing
BEGIILNNSU	nebulising
BEGIILNNUZ	nebulizing
BEGIILNOPR	preboiling
BEGIILNRST	blistering
BEGIILNRTT	bitterling

BEGIINQRTU briqueting
BEGIINRRST bestirring
BEGIINRSSU suberising
BEGIINRSUZ suberizing
BEGIJRSTTU jitterbugs
BEGILMNRSU lumberings
slumbering
BEGILNORST bolstering
BEGILNORSY soberingly
BEGILNRSTU blustering
BEGILNSTTU subletting
BEGILOOOXY exobiology
BEGILPSTTU spittlebug
BEGILRSTTU litterbugs
BEGIMMNOOS embosoming
BEGIMNORSS Bergsonism
BEGIMNRSSU submersing
BEGINNNNOT Bennington
BEGINOPRRV proverbing
BEGINORSSU subregions
BEGINORTUZ Buitenzorg
BEGINORUVY overbuying
BEGINPRRTU perturbing
BEGINRSSUV subserving
BEGINRSTUV subverting
BEGIORRSUY biosurgery
BEGLMOORYY embryology
BEGLMORUUX Luxembourg
BEGLNNNOOT Longbenton
BEGMOORRSV Bromsgrove
BEGNORRUYY youngberry
BEGOOPPRST gobstopper
BEGOORRTTT bogtrotter
BEHHMOOOPS homophobes
BEHIIIINTV inhibitive
BEHIIINOTX exhibition
BEHIIINRST inhibiters
BEHIILMTTW thimblewit
BEHIILPSTU bisulphite
BEHIIOPRRT prohibiter
BEHIIORSTX exhibitors
BEHIIORTXY exhibitory
BEHIKLLNOR Broken Hill
BEHIKLOSSV bolsheviks
BEHIKOPRRS shipbroker
BEHILLORWW willowherb
BEHILMOSSV bolshevism
BEHILNSSSU bluishness
BEHILOSSTV bolshevist
BEHILPRSSU publishers
BEHIMMORTU embothrium
BEHINORSTT birthstone
BEHINOSSSY boyishness
BEHINRRSSU burnishers
BEHIOORSST boosterish
BEHIORSSTT theorbists
BEHKNOSSUU bunkhouses
BEHLMOOPTY phlebotomy
BEHLNOOTTU buttonhole
BEHMOOORST smoothbore
BEHMOORSST thromboses
BEHNNRSTUU unburthens
BEHNORSSTU buhrstones
BEHOOPSTTU phototubes
BEHOPRSTYY bryophytes
BEHRRSSUWY Shrewsbury
BEIIILMMOS immobilise
BEIIILMMOZ immobilize
BEIIILNOST nobilities
BEIIILNSSV invisibles
BEIIIMNSTU bituminise
BEIIIMNTUZ bituminize
BEIIIOOPSS biopoiesis
BEIILLNOTU ebullition
BEIILLOSSU solubilise
BEIILLOSUZ solubilize
BEIILMNSTW nimblewits
BEIILMOPSS impossible
BEIILMRTUY muliebrity
BEIILNNSSY insensibly
BEIILORSTT trilobites
BEIILORSTU boilersuit
BEIILRSSTT bristliest
BEIILRSSTU subtiliser
BEIILRSSTY resistibly
BEIILRSTTT librettist
BEIILRSTTW Birtwistle
BEIILRSTUZ subtilizer
BEIILSSSTU subtilises
BEIILSSTTU subtilties
BEIILSSTUZ subtilizes
BEIIMSSSUV submissive
BEIINNOQUU ubiquinone
BEIINNRSTU Rubinstein
BEIINORSTY insobriety
BEIIORSSTU bistouries
BEIKLMOORS brooklimes
BEIKLMRTTU buttermilk
BEIKMOORST motorbikes
BEIKMORRTW timberwork
BEILLLLOOS loblollies
BEILLMSSUU subsellium
BEILLOPRST billposter
BEILMNOOSW snowmobile
BEILMOOOST lobotomies
BEILMOSSSY symbolises
BEILMOSSYZ symbolizes
BEILNOSSSW blowsiness
BEILNOSSTY ostensibly
BEILNOSSWZ blowziness
BEILNOSTUY nebulosity
BEILNPRSTU blueprints
BEILNRRSSU blurriness
BEILOOPRST potboilers
BEILOOTUVV obvolutive
BEILORSSSU subsoilers
BEILORSSTT lost tribes
BEIMMRSTYY bisymmetry
BEIMNNOOPT embonpoint
BEIMNORSST brimstones
BEIMNORSSU submersion
BEIMOORSST biostromes
boosterism
BEIMOORSTT bottomries
BEIMRSSTTU submitters
BEINNOSTUV subvention
BEINOOPRST obreptions
BEINOORSSV obversions
BEINOOSSSS obsessions
BEINOPRSTU subreption
BEINORSSUV subversion
BEINORSTUU subroutine
BEINRSTTTU bitternuts
BEINSSSTTU subsistent
BEIOOPRRSU pourboires
BEIOOQSSUU obsequious
BEIOORSSTU boisterous
BEIOQRSSTU sobriquets
BEIOQRSTUU soubriquet
BEIORSTTUY tuberosity
BEIRSSSSTU subsisters
BEISSTTTUU substitute
BEKLLOORUW boullework
BEKLNNORUY unbrokenly
BEKLOOSSTY stylebooks
BEKMNORSSU mossbunker
BELLMOPSTU postbellum
BELLNOSUUY nebulously
BELLOOOPRT portobello
BELLOOSSTY bootlessly
BELLORSTUY trolleybus
BELMOOSSTT bottomless
BELMORSSUU slumberous
BELNOORSWW snowblower
BELNOSSTTU buttonless
BELORSSSSU sublessors
BELORSSTUU blusterous
BEMNOORSSU unbosomers
BEMNOOSSTT tombstones
BEMNOPRSUU penumbrous
BEMNORSTUU outnumbers
BEMOORSSTU motorbuses
BEMSSSSTUY subsystems
BENNNOSSTU sunbonnets
BENNOORSSW brownnoses
BENNOORSTW brownstone
BENORRSSTU burrstones
BENORSSSTU robustness
BENORSSTTU obstruents
BENRSTTTUU butternuts
BEORRTTTUW butterwort
BFGHIINRSU furbishing
BFGHILLSTU bullfights
BFGIINRTUY brutifying
BFGILLMNUY fumblingly
BFGILLNOWY flyblowing
BFIIILSTUY fusibility
BFIIIORSST fibrositis
BFIILMMORU umbiliform
BFILLLSSUY blissfully
BFINORRSST firstborns
BGGGHIMNUU humbugging
BGGIILLNOY obligingly
BGGIINNPRU upbringing
BGHHIIRRTT birthright
BGHIIIINNT inhibiting

BGHIILNPSU publishing
BGHIINNRSU burnishing
BGHIKLOOST booklights
BGHIKORRTW brightwork
BGHILLMNUY humblingly
BGHILLNSUY blushingly
BGHILNNSUU unblushing
BGHIPRSTTU Pittsburgh
BGHLOOPSUY ploughboys
BGIIILMNOS mobilising
BGIIILMNOZ mobilizing
BGIIILNOTY ignobility
BGIIINSSTU subitising
BGIIINSTUZ subitizing
BGIIJMNOSU jumboising
BGIIJMNOUZ jumboizing
BGIIJNNOSU subjoining
BGIIKLNNNU unblinking
BGIILMOORS imbroglios
BGIILNOSSU subsoiling
BGIILNSTTU subtitling
BGIILOOSST biologists
BGIIMNSTTU submitting
BGIINOORST robotising
BGIINOORTZ robotizing
BGIINORSUU rubiginous
BGIINSSSTU subsisting
BGIKNOPRSS springboks
BGILLMMNUY mumblingly
BGILLMNOSY symbolling
BGILLMNRUY rumblingly
BGILMNOOSS blossoming
BGILNNORTU Burlington
BGILOORSTY bryologist
BGILOORSUU Louisbourg
BGILORSUUU lugubrious
BGIMNNOOSU unbosoming
BGINNORSTU binturongs
BGINNOSTUW snowtubing
BGINORSSTW bowstrings
BHHIMORSTY biorhythms
BHHOORSTTU toothbrush
BHIIIINNOT inhibition
BHIIINORST inhibitors
BHIIINORTY inhibitory
BHIILLNOST billionths
BHIILLRSTT stillbirth
BHIIOOPRRT prohibitor
BHILLNORST thornbills
BHIMNPRTTU thumbprint
BHIMOORSST thrombosis
BHIMOSSTUU bismuthous
BHIOORRSTT birthroots
BHIORRSTTW birthworts
BHJOORSSTW jobsworths
BHKNOOOTTU buttonhook
BHLLOOOSTT tollbooths
BHOOOOPSUZ zoophobous
BIIIILRSTY risibility
BIIIILSTVY visibility
BIIILMMMOS immobilism
BIIILMMOTY immobility
BIILLOSTUY solubility
BIILLOTUVY volubility
BIILMOPSSY impossibly
BIIMNOOSST bionomists
BIIMNOSSSU submission
BIIMNOSTUU bituminous
BIINOSSSSY byssinosis
BIIOQSTUUU ubiquitous
BIKLLORSST storksbill
BILLNOOPSS spoonbills
BILLNORSST stillborns
BILMMOSSSY symbolisms
BILMOORSWW lowbrowism
BILMOSSSTY symbolists
BILNOOOTUV obvolution
BILOOPRSTU politburos
BIMNOORSTT trombonist
BIMOOPPRRU opprobrium
BINOORSSTU obtrusions
BIOORSSTUU robustious
BKLLMNSSUU numbskulls
BKMOOOPPRT promptbook
BKOOORSSTY storybooks
BLLOOTTUWY woollybutt
BLLOSTUUUY tubulously
BMMOOOSTTT bottommost
BOOPPRRSTU turboprops
CCCCGINOOO gonococcic
CCCCIIMOOR micrococci
CCCDEILOPY cyclopedic
CCCDIILOOP diplococci
CCCEEINNOS conscience
CCCEEINORT ecocentric
CCCEEINRST crescentic
eccentrics
CCCEELNSUU succulence
CCCEENORRU occurrence
CCCEHIILMY hemicyclic
CCCEHIILNO colchicine
CCCEHIIORS chiccories
CCCEHIMOTY ecchymotic
CCCEHKORSS crosscheck
CCCEIILPRY pericyclic
CCCEIIMRSU circumcise
CCCEIIRSTY cysticerci
CCCEILOTUY leucocytic
CCCEINNOOP Concepción
CCCEINNORT concentric
CCCEINOOTV concoctive
CCCEINOOTY coenocytic
CCCEKLNOOR corncockle
CCCELNSUUY succulency
CCCENOORST concocters
CCCGINNOOT concocting
CCCGNOOOSU gonococcus
CCCHHILOOO chocoholic
CCCHIKNOPS pinchcocks
CCCHIKOPST spitchcock
CCCHILMOOY homocyclic
CCCHILMOSU colchicums
CCCHILOOST coccoliths
CCCIILRSTY tricyclics
CCCIIMORTY microcytic
CCCILLOPYY polycyclic
CCCILMNOOY monocyclic
CCCILNSTUY succinctly
CCCINNOOOT concoction
CCCIOOPRSY cryoscopic
CCCNOOORST concoctors
CCDDEEHLTU declutched
CCDDEELNOY concededly
CCDDEENNOS condescend
CCDEEEENPR precedence
CCDEEEHINS dehiscence
CCDEEEHKPR prechecked
CCDEEENPRY precedency
CCDEEENRST decrescent
CCDEEERRSU recrudesce
CCDEEERSSU succeeders
CCDEEFIINY deficiency
CCDEEFINNO confidence
CCDEEGINSU succeeding
CCDEEHIKSW chickweeds
CCDEEHIORT ricocheted
CCDEEHKORW checkrowed
CCDEEHLSTU declutches
CCDEEHMOSY ecchymosed
CCDEEHNOSY synecdoche
CCDEEIIIPT epideictic
CCDEEIILRT dielectric
CCDEEIIMRT decimetric
CCDEEIINNS incidences
CCDEEIIPPR precipiced
CCDEEIKLRV cleverdick
CCDEEILNOR reconciled
CCDEEILOSW colicweeds
CCDEEIMORT ectodermic
CCDEEIOPRU reoccupied
CCDEELMOPT complected
CCDEELNNOO condolence
CCDEENNORT concentred
CCDEENORSS crescendos
CCDEEORRRU reoccurred
CCDEFIIKNO cocknified
CCDEFILNOT conflicted
CCDEGHHIOU hiccoughed
CCDEHHNRUU unchurched
CCDEHILNOR chronicled
CCDEIIILOT idiolectic
CCDEIIIRST criticised
CCDEIIIRTZ criticized
CCDEIILOPY epicycloid
CCDEIINNOR endocrinic
CCDEIINNOT coincident
CCDEIKKOTT ticktocked
CCDEILOORS crocodiles
CCDEIMOOOT octodecimo
CCDEINNOST disconnect
CCDEINOOPS endoscopic
picosecond
CCDEINOOST decoctions
CCDEINOPUU unoccupied
CCDEINORST disconcert
CCDEINOTUV conductive

CCDELNORSU	concluders
CCDGIIINNO	coinciding
CCDGIILOSU	glucosidic
CCDGIILOSY	glycosidic
CCDGIKLNOU	cuckolding
CCDGILNNOU	concluding
CCDGILOOOY	codicology
CCDGINNOTU	conducting
CCDHIIIORT	dichroitic
CCDHIIMOOT	dichotomic
CCDHIINORT	chondritic
CCDHKOOSUW	woodchucks
CCDIIOORST	corticoids
CCDIMNOSTU	misconduct
CCDINNOOTU	conduction
CCDNOORSTU	conductors
CCDOOOSSUW	cocuswoods
CCEEEEHIKP	cheekpiece
CCEEEELLNX	excellence
CCEEEENNSS	senescence
CCEEEFNNOR	conference
CCEEEFNRSU	rufescence
CCEEEGINOS	geoscience
CCEEEHIPSS	chesspiece
CCEEEHRRSS	screechers
CCEEEIINPR	recipience
CCEEEIKNPS	neckpieces
CCEEEILMNS	clemencies
CCEEEINPRS	prescience
CCEEEINQSU	quiescence
CCEEEINRSV	virescence
CCEEEIOPSS	ecospecies
CCEEELLNXY	excellency
CCEEELNOST	Ecclestone
CCEEELORST	rectoceles
CCEEEMMNOR	recommence
CCEEEMNOPT	competence
CCEEEMNSTU	tumescence
CCEEENRRRU	recurrence
CCEEENRSTX	excrescent
CCEEFFIINY	efficiency
CCEEFHHRRU	Free Church
CCEEFINTTU	fettuccine
CCEEFLNNOU	confluence
CCEEGHIKNR	checkering
	rechecking
CCEEGHINRS	screeching
CCEEGINNOR	congeneric
CCEEGINORS	concierges
CCEEGINORT	egocentric
	geocentric
CCEEGNNORU	congruence
CCEEHHIRST	Chichester
CCEEHHKOPU	cheekpouch
CCEEHIKNRS	checkreins
CCEEHILMSY	hemicycles
CCEEHILRSU	cleruchies
CCEEHINOSS	choiceness
CCEEHIRSTU	cutcheries
CCEEHKORSV	overchecks
CCEEHLORST	cerecloths
	Colchester
CCEEHMOSSY	ecchymoses
CCEEHNOSTU	escutcheon
CCEEHORRST	crocheters
CCEEHOSTTU	couchettes
CCEEIIINNP	incipience
CCEEIILMRS	semicircle
CCEEIILPTU	epicuticle
CCEEIIMPST	septicemic
CCEEIIPPRS	precipices
CCEEIKRRST	cricketers
CCEEILLOTV	collective
CCEEILMNNY	inclemency
CCEEILNOPU	leucopenic
CCEEILNORR	reconciler
CCEEILNORS	reconciles
CCEEILNORT	electronic
CCEEILOPST	telescopic
CCEEILORVY	coercively
CCEEILOTUX	exocuticle
CCEEILPRSY	pericycles
CCEEINNNOT	continence
CCEEINNOTV	connective
CCEEINNRRU	incurrence
CCEEINNRST	increscent
CCEEINOPRT	encopretic
CCEEINOPRW	crownpiece
CCEEINOPTV	conceptive
CCEEINORST	concertise
	concretise
	cornetcies
	ectocrines
CCEEINORSV	conceivers
CCEEINORTV	concretive
CCEEINORTX	exocentric
CCEEINORTZ	concertize
	concretize
CCEEINOSSV	concessive
CCEEINOTVV	convective
CCEEINQSUY	quiescency
CCEEINRRSU	currencies
CCEEIOPRSS	crosspiece
CCEEIOPRSU	reoccupies
CCEEIOPSTT	copesettic
CCEEIORRTV	corrective
CCEEISSSUV	successive
CCEEJNORTU	conjecture
CCEEKKLOYY	cockyleeky
CCEEKLORST	cockleerts
CCEELLORST	recollects
CCEELMORTY	cyclometer
CCEELNOPRU	corpulence
CCEELNORTY	concretely
CCEELNRTUU	truculence
CCEELOSSTY	cystoceles
CCEELOSTUY	leucocytes
CCEEMMNORS	commencers
CCEEMNOPTY	competency
CCEENNOOST	conoscente
CCEENNORST	concentres
	connecters
	reconnects
CCEENOOSTY	coenocytes
CCEENOPRRT	preconcert
CCEEOORTUX	coexecutor
CCEFGINNOT	confecting
CCEFHIIMOR	microfiche
CCEFIIINST	scientific
CCEFIIKNOS	cocknifies
CCEFIINPSU	unspecific
CCEFIIRRSU	crucifiers
CCEFIIRSUX	crucifixes
CCEFILMRUX	circumflex
CCEFIMRSUU	circumfuse
CCEFINNOOT	confection
CCEFLLNOTU	flocculent
CCEFLSSSUU	successful
CCEGGILNOY	glycogenic
CCEGHHORRU	churchgoer
CCEGHIIIOP	pichiciego
CCEGHIILNO	conchiglie
CCEGHIINRS	screiching
CCEGHINORT	crocheting
CCEGIIKNRT	cricketing
CCEGIILNNR	encircling
CCEGIINNOT	conceiting
CCEGIINNOV	conceiving
CCEGILLNOT	collecting
CCEGIMMNNO	commencing
CCEGINNNOR	concerning
CCEGINNNOS	ensconcing
CCEGINNNOT	connecting
CCEGINNORT	concerting
	concreting
CCEGINORRT	correcting
CCEGINORSY	cryogenics
CCEGNNORUY	congruency
CCEHHIRSTU	churchiest
CCEHHNRSUU	unchurches
CCEHIINNNO	cinchonine
CCEHIINNOS	cinchonise
CCEHIINNOZ	cinchonize
CCEHIKNOPT	checkpoint
CCEHIKNOPX	chickenpox
CCEHIKNOSY	cockneyish
CCEHILLORY	cholericly
CCEHILMOOP	phocomelic
CCEHILNORR	chronicler
CCEHILNORS	chronicles
CCEHILOOPR	pleochroic
CCEHILOPRR	perchloric
CCEHIMOSSY	ecchymosis
CCEHINRSSU	scrunchies
CCEHINRSTU	crunchiest
CCEHIOORRV	Verrocchio
CCEHIOPTTY	ectophytic
CCEHKLNOST	neckcloths
CCEHKMOORS	checkrooms
CCEHKNOOST	chockstone
CCEHKOORSS	cockhorses
CCEHLOSSTY	cholecysts
CCEHMOORTY	cytochrome
CCEHNNORSU	scruncheon
CCEHNNOSSU	scuncheons
CCEHNOPRUW	cowpuncher

CCEHNOSSTU scutcheons
CCEHOSTTUZ zucchettos
CCEIIIKMWZ Mickiewicz
CCEIIILNOR ricinoleic
CCEIIINNPY incipiency
CCEIIIRRST criticiser
CCEIIIRRTZ criticizer
CCEIIIRSST criticises
CCEIIIRSTU circuities
CCEIIIRSTV cervicitis
CCEIIIRSTZ criticizes
CCEIIKNPRS picnickers
CCEIILMNOR microcline
CCEIILMORT cliometric
CCEIILNOST niccolites
CCEIILOSST solecistic
CCEIIMOORS seriocomic
CCEIIMOSSS coseismics
CCEIIMOTXY Mexico City
CCEIIMPSST scepticism
CCEIINNORT concertini
CCEIINOTVV convictive
CCEIINRTTY centricity
CCEIIOORST crocoisite
CCEIIOPPRS periscopic
CCEIIORTVY coercivity
CCEIKKOPPT pickpocket
CCEIKLLOSY kilocycles
CCEIKLOTUY leukocytic
CCEIKMNOSY cockneyism
CCEILLLOSU cellulosic
CCEILLNOOT collection
CCEILMNNOU councilmen
CCEILMOTYY myelocytic
CCEILNNOSU nucleonics
CCEILNOSUV conclusive
CCEILOOQTU coquelicot
CCEILORSST sclerotics
CCEILOSSUV occlusives
CCEIMNNOOU uneconomic
CCEIMNRTUV circumvent
CCEIMOOPRS microscope
CCEIMORSTY microcytes
CCEINNNOOT connection
CCEINNNOTY continency
CCEINNOOPT conception
CCEINNOORT concertino
concretion
CCEINNOOSS concession
CCEINNOOST conoscenti
CCEINNOOTV convection
CCEINNORSV convincers
CCEINOOOPS iconoscope
CCEINOOPRT nociceptor
CCEINOORRT correction
CCEINOPRSU Copernicus
CCEINORSTV reconvicts
CCEINOSSSU succession
CCEINOSSUV concussive
CCEIOOPRSU precocious
CCEISSSUUV successive
CCEKLORSUY cocksurely
CCEKORRSSW corkscrews
CCELLOORST collectors
CCELLOSTYY cyclostyle
CCELMNOOSY monocycles
CCELMOORTY motorcycle
CCELMOOSTY cyclostome
CCELMORTYY cyclometry
CCELNOPRUY corpulency
CCELNOSSTU occultness
CCELNRTUUY truculency
CCELNSSTUU succulents
CCELOOOPPS colposcope
CCELOPRSSU corpuscles
CCELOPRSUU corpuscule
CCELORSSSU succorless
CCEMOSTTYY cystectomy
CCENNOORST connectors
CCENNORRTU concurrent
CCENOOPRSY necroscopy
CCENOORSSU concourses
CCENOORSTV convectors
CCENOPSSTU conspectus
CCENORSSTU succentors
CCEOOPRSSY cryoscopes
CCEOOPRSTT ectoprocts
CCEOOPSSTY cystoscope
CCEOORRRST correctors
CCEORRSSUU succourers
CCEORSSSSU successors
CCFGHIKOST cockfights
CCFGIINRUY crucifying
CCFILMORUU cuculiform
CCFIMORRSU cruciforms
CCFKOOOSST cocksfoots
CCGHHHHIRU High Church
CCGHIINPPU hiccupping
CCGHINNRSU scrunching
CCGHINRSTU crutchings
CCGHLNOOOY conchology
CCGIIIKNNP picnicking
CCGIIINRTU circuiting
CCGIILNRTY tricycling
CCGIINNNOV convincing
CCGIINNOTV convicting
CCGILMOOOS cosmologic
CCGILOORSY cyclogiros
CCGILORSUU glucosuric
CCGILORSUY glycosuric
CCGIMNOOOS cosmogonic
CCGINNORRU concurring
CCGINNOSSU concussing
CCGINORSUU succouring
CCGINSSSUU succussing
CCGIOOPRSY gyroscopic
CCHHHOOPTT hotchpotch
CCHHIIOTTY ichthyotic
CCHIIIRSTT tristichic
CCHIILMOOX Xochimilco
CCHIILNNOO conchiolin
CCHIILOPRY cryophilic
CCHIIMNNOS cinchonism
CCHIIMOPRS microchips
CCHIIMORRT trichromic
CCHIINORTY chronicity
CCHIIOPSTY sciophytic
CCHIKLOSTT lockstitch
CCHIKOPSST chopsticks
CCHIMNOOOR monochroic
CCHINNOORS cornichons
CCHINNORSU scrunchion
CCHINNORSY synchronic
CCHIOOOPRS horoscopic
CCHIOPSSTY psychotics
CCHIORSTTY trichocyst
CCHLNOOSTY colocynths
CCIIILNOSS isoclinics
CCIIILOSST sciolistic
CCIIIMRSST criticisms
CCIILLNOPY polyclinic
CCIILMNNOO monoclinic
CCIILMOPTY complicity
CCIILNSTUY unicyclist
CCIILOOPRT coprolitic
CCIILOPRST proclitics
CCIILRSTTY tricyclist
CCIIMMOORT microtomic
CCIINNNOTY concinnity
CCIINNOOSS concisions
CCIINNOOTV conviction
CCIINOOPRS scorpionic
CCIINOPSSY isopycnics
CCIIORSTUU circuitous
CCIKNOOPTU cuckoopint
CCILLLOSUU colliculus
CCILLNOORU councillor
CCILLOOPTY collotypic
CCILMRRUUU curriculum
CCILNNOOSU conclusion
CCILNOORSU councilors
CCILNOOSSU occlusions
CCILOOORST colicroots
CCILOPSTYY polycystic
CCILOSSTTU occultists
CCIMMOORSS microcosms
CCIMOOPRSY microscopy
CCINNNOOSU concinnous
CCINNOOSSU concussion
CCINOPRSST conscripts
CCINORSSTT constricts
CCINOSSSUU succussion
CCINOSTUVY viscountcy
CCIOOPRTYZ cryptozoic
CCIOPPRRTY procryptic
CCIORRSSSS crisscross
CCJLNNOTUY conjunctly
CCKKLOORSW clockworks
CCKOORSTUW stuccowork
CCLLOOORTU collocutor
CCLNOORSTY cyclotrons
CCNORSSTTU constructs
CCOOPSSTYY cystoscopy
CDDEEEELST deselected
CDDEEEENNP dependence
CDDEEEHIPR deciphered

CDDEEEINRT interceded
CDDEEEINUV undeceived
CDDEEEIRRT redirected
CDDEEEJLTY dejectedly
CDDEEELNOR needlecord
CDDEEENNPY dependency
CDDEEENNST descendent
CDDEEENOTX coextended
CDDEEENRSS descenders
redescends
CDDEEENRSU descendeur
CDDEEENTTU undetected
CDDEEEORRR rerecorded
CDDEEEORRT retroceded
CDDEEFFIIN diffidence
CDDEEFIIOR recodified
CDDEEFIKLN fiddleneck
CDDEEGINNS descending
CDDEEHLOOS deschooled
CDDEEIINSS dissidence
CDDEEIJPRU prejudiced
CDDEEILNRY cylindered
CDDEEIMNOR endodermic
CDDEEINORS considered
CDDEEINPRS prescinded
CDDEEINRTU undirected
CDDEEIOPTY copyedited
CDDEEIORSV discovered
CDDEEIPRTU depictured
CDDEELLSUY secludedly
CDDEELMOSU cuddlesome
CDDEELOORU decoloured
CDDEEMNOTU documented
CDDEEMOOPS decomposed
CDDEENNOSU unseconded
CDDEENORRU unrecorded
CDDEEOPRRU reproduced
CDDEERSTTU destructed
CDDEFIKORS disfrocked
CDDEFNNOOU confounded
CDDEGIKLOR gridlocked
CDDEHIILOR dichloride
CDDEHISTUY Thucydides
CDDEIIRSST discredits
CDDEIIRSTT districted
CDDEILOORS discolored
CDDEIMMNOO incommoded
CDDEIMMNOS discommend
CDDEIMMOOS discommode
CDDEIMOOSU duodecimos
CDDEINNOOT endodontic
CDDEINORTU introduced
CDDEINOSTU deductions
discounted
CDDEIORSSU discoursed
CDDEMNOOPU compounded
decompound
CDDGIINORS discording
CDDHHIIMSU shidduchim
CDDHHILOOS childhoods
CDDHILLOSY cloddishly
CDDIILNORY cylindroid
CDDILOOPSU diplodocus
CDDINNOOTY dicynodont
CDEEEEFNRR referenced
CDEEEEGNRT detergence
CDEEEEINPX expedience
CDEEEELPRT preelected
CDEEEELRST reselected
CDEEEENRRT deterrence
CDEEEENRRV reverenced
CDEEEFFINR difference
CDEEEFHIKR kerchiefed
CDEEEFIILP fieldpiece
CDEEEFILTV deflective
CDEEEFINRT reinfected
CDEEEFNORR reenforced
CDEEEGINRV divergence
CDEEEGNRTY detergency
CDEEEHINPR enciphered
CDEEEHIPRR decipherer
CDEEEHIRRT Eric the Red
CDEEEHLRSU reschedule
CDEEEHNNRT entrenched
CDEEEHNRRT retrenched
CDEEEHOOSW cheesewood
CDEEEIKNPR Penderecki
CDEEEILNRS relicensed
CDEEEILOPV velocipede
CDEEEILQSU deliquesce
CDEEEIMNNO comedienne
CDEEEIMNNP impendence
CDEEEIMRRS mercerised
CDEEEIMRRZ mercerized
CDEEEIMRST decimeters
decimetres
CDEEEINNSS desinences
CDEEEINNST tendencies
CDEEEINPST centipedes
CDEEEINPXY expediency
CDEEEINRRT interceder
CDEEEINRSS residences
CDEEEINRST intercedes
CDEEEINRSW widescreen
CDEEEINRUV undeceiver
CDEEEINSST desistence
CDEEEINSUV undeceives
CDEEEISTTV detectives
CDEEELLNUX unexcelled
CDEEELMOPS Empedocles
CDEEELNSTU unselected
CDEEELOPST telescoped
CDEEELORST electrodes
CDEEEMNNOT encodement
CDEEEMNRST decrements
CDEEEMSSTY metecdyses
CDEEENNORS recondense
CDEEENNORV reconvened
CDEEENNRSU unscreened
CDEEENNSST decentness
CDEEENORVY reconveyed
CDEEENPRST precedents
CDEEENPTUX unexpected
CDEEENTUUX unexecuted
CDEEEOPRRS proceeders
CDEEEORRST retrocedes
CDEEEPRSTU persecuted
CDEEFGILNT deflecting
CDEEFHLRSS feldschers
CDEEFIIKRR Frederick I
CDEEFIINRT dentifrice
CDEEFIIORS recodifies
CDEEFIIOST foeticides
CDEEFIKRRV Frederick V
CDEEFILNNU influenced
CDEEFILNOT deflection
CDEEFINNTU uninfected
CDEEFINORR reinforced
CDEEFINOST defections
CDEEFINTUV defunctive
CDEEFKLOOR forelocked
CDEEFKLPSY flyspecked
CDEEFKOSST feedstocks
CDEEFLNORT centerfold
centrefold
CDEEFLNORY enforcedly
CDEEFLOORS foreclosed
CDEEFLORST deflectors
CDEEFLORSU fluoresced
CDEEFNNORU unenforced
CDEEFNORSS forcedness
CDEEFORSSU refocussed
CDEEGIILNS diligences
CDEEGIIMRS germicides
CDEEGIINNV evidencing
CDEEGIINOR Ceredigion
CDEEGILNNU indulgence
CDEEGILNUV divulgence
CDEEGILRSY glycerides
CDEEGINNOR endergonic
CDEEGINOPR proceeding
CDEEGINORS recognised
CDEEGINORZ recognized
CDEEGINRVY divergency
CDEEGLLRSU cudgellers
CDEEHIILOP ophicleide
CDEEHIIOST theodicies
CDEEHILLPR prechilled
CDEEHIMNOR echinoderm
CDEEHINNRT intrenched
CDEEHINRST christened
CDEEHKNPUY keypunched
CDEEHKOSSU deckhouses
CDEEHKRSTU huckstered
CDEEHLORSY hydroceles
CDEEHLPRSU sepulchred
CDEEHLRTWY wretchedly
CDEEHMNOPR comprehend
CDEEHNNQUU unquenched
CDEEHORRST Dorchester
CDEEIIIMNT cimetidine
CDEEIIINSV indecisive
CDEEIILRST deciliters
decilitres
CDEEIILSVY decisively
CDEEIIMNRS reminisced

CDEEIIMNTY	endemicity
CDEEIIMPRR	peridermic
CDEEIIMPRS	spermicide
CDEEIIMRSV	vermicides
CDEEIINRST	indiscreet
	indiscrete
	iridescent
CDEEIIOPST	poeticised
CDEEIIOPTZ	poeticized
CDEEIIORRT	cordierite
CDEEIIORST	eroticised
CDEEIIORTZ	eroticized
CDEEIIPRRS	cirripedes
CDEEIIPRTV	predictive
CDEEIIPSST	pesticides
CDEEIIRSSV	disservice
CDEEIIRSTV	directives
CDEEIISTVV	vivisected
CDEEIJPRSU	prejudices
CDEEIKNSSW	wickedness
CDEEILLNST	stencilled
CDEEILMNSU	luminesced
CDEEILNNOS	declension
CDEEILNNSU	unlicensed
CDEEILNNTY	indecently
CDEEILNOOS	decolonise
CDEEILNOOZ	decolonize
CDEEILNOSU	nucleoside
CDEEILNOTU	nucleotide
CDEEILNRVY	Inverclyde
CDEEILOORS	decolorise
CDEEILOORZ	decolorize
CDEEILORST	cloistered
CDEEILPRTY	decrepitly
CDEEILRSST	creditless
CDEEILRSTY	discreetly
	discretely
CDEEIMMORS	mesodermic
CDEEIMMOXY	myxoedemic
CDEEIMNNPY	impendency
CDEEIMNNSU	decenniums
CDEEIMNNTU	inducement
CDEEIMNOOS	economised
CDEEIMNOOZ	economized
CDEEIMNORT	entodermic
CDEEIMNOSU	eudemonics
CDEEIMNPRU	imprudence
CDEEIMNPSU	impudences
CDEEIMNSTU	intumesced
CDEEIMSSTY	metecdysis
CDEEINNORS	endocrines
CDEEINNRSW	windscreen
CDEEINNSSU	secundines
CDEEINOPRS	preconised
CDEEINOPRV	providence
CDEEINOPRZ	preconized
CDEEINOPST	deceptions
CDEEINORRS	considerer
	reconsider
CDEEINPRRU	underprice
CDEEINPRSY	presidency
CDEEINRRRU	reincurred
CDEEINRRSS	discerners
	rescinders
CDEEINRSST	directness
CDEEINRSTY	dysenteric
CDEEIOPRRV	overpriced
CDEEIORRSV	discoverer
	rediscover
CDEEIOSTTU	eutectoids
CDEEIPRSST	disrespect
CDEEIPRSTU	depictures
CDEEIRRSST	directress
CDEEIRRSTT	derestrict
	restricted
CDEEIRSTTU	certitudes
CDEEKNNORU	unreckoned
CDEEKOOORV	overcooked
CDEEKOOPRW	woodpecker
CDEELLNOSU	counselled
CDEELLNRSU	cullenders
CDEELMNSTU	demulcents
CDEELNNOSU	unenclosed
CDEELNSSTU	dulcetness
CDEELOOORV	overcooled
CDEELOPPSY	pelecypods
CDEELOPSUY	Polydeuces
CDEELRSTTU	declutters
CDEEMMNORS	recommends
CDEEMNNOPR	precondemn
CDEEMNNORS	condemners
CDEEMNNOST	secondment
CDEEMOOPRS	decomposer
	recomposed
CDEEMOOPSS	decomposes
CDEEMOPRSS	compressed
	decompress
CDEENNORSS	condensers
CDEENNORST	contenders
CDEENNORSU	denouncers
	uncensored
CDEENNRSUU	uncensured
CDEENOOPSS	endoscopes
CDEENOOSTT	cottonseed
CDEENOOTTW	cottonweed
CDEENORRSU	underscore
CDEENORRUV	undercover
CDEENORSTU	unescorted
CDEENOSTUU	consuetude
CDEENRSSSU	cursedness
CDEENRSSUV	curvedness
CDEENSSSSU	cussedness
CDEEOORRSV	overscored
CDEEOPPRST	prospected
CDEEOPRRRS	prerecords
CDEEOPRRRU	reproducer
CDEEOPRRSU	procedures
	reproduces
CDEEOPRSTU	prosecuted
CDEERSSSTU	seductress
CDEFFIIRTU	fructified
CDEFGIINSU	fungicides
CDEFGIKNOR	defrocking
CDEFHLMORS	Chelmsford
CDEFIIIILS	silicified
CDEFIINSST	disinfects
CDEFILNNOY	confinedly
CDEFILNORS	cornfields
CDEFINNNOU	unconfined
CDEFINNOTU	functioned
CDEFINOORV	confervoid
CDEFLNOSUY	confusedly
CDEFNNOORT	confronted
CDEFNNOORU	confounder
CDEFNNOSUU	unconfused
CDEFNORRTU	undercroft
CDEGGILLNU	cudgelling
CDEGHIIOST	gothicised
CDEGHIIOTZ	gothicized
CDEGHILNSU	scheduling
CDEGHINNRS	drenchings
CDEGHINNRU	chundering
CDEGHINSSU	duchessing
CDEGIIJNST	disjecting
CDEGIIKNRR	derricking
CDEGIINNRS	discerning
	rescinding
CDEGIINNRU	reinducing
CDEGIINNSX	exscinding
CDEGIINOTU	digoneutic
CDEGIINPRT	predicting
CDEGIINSST	dissecting
CDEGIKNOST	destocking
	stockinged
CDEGILMMNO	commingled
CDEGILNOPU	decoupling
CDEGILNPRU	precluding
CDEGILNRSU	surcingled
CDEGILNSUU	Du Guesclin
CDEGILOOPS	logopedics
CDEGILOSSU	glucosides
CDEGILOSSY	glycosides
CDEGIMMNNO	commending
CDEGIMNNNO	condemning
CDEGINNNOS	condensing
CDEGINNNOT	contending
CDEGINNNOU	denouncing
CDEGINORRS	recordings
CDEGINPRTY	decrypting
CDEGIOORRR	corregidor
CDEGLORSST	goldcrests
CDEGMNORUU	curmudgeon
CDEGOOORRR	Cerro Gordo
CDEHHHIIKT	hitchhiked
CDEHHIIPRT	diphtheric
CDEHIIISTT	ditheistic
CDEHIIKOOS	doohickies
CDEHIILNOT	endolithic
CDEHIILOPS	discophile
CDEHIILORU	hierodulic
CDEHIILPTY	diphyletic
CDEHIIMSTY	mythicised
CDEHIIMTYZ	mythicized
CDEHIINOST	hedonistic
CDEHILPRUY	hyperdulic
CDEHIMOPRY	hypodermic

CDEHINOPST docentship
CDEHINOPTY endophytic
CDEHINORST chondrites
CDEHINPRTU underpitch
CDEHIOOPRT orthopedic
CDEHIORSTW dowitchers
CDEHIPPRRU chirrupped
CDEHKORSUV duckshover
CDEHLNOOSU unschooled
CDEHLNORSU chondrules
CDEHLOOPPR clodhopper
CDEHLOOPRY copyholder
CDEHNOOSTT thecodonts
CDEHNORSUU chunderous
CDEHOOOPSS hodoscopes
CDEHOOPRSY hydroscope
CDEIIILLST stillicide
CDEIIILNNS disincline
CDEIIILNOT indicolite
CDEIIILNPS discipline
CDEIIIMRSV recidivism
CDEIIIMSTV victimised
CDEIIIMTVZ victimized
CDEIIINNOS indecision
CDEIIINTVV vindictive
CDEIIIRSTV recidivist
CDEIIKNPPR pinpricked
CDEIILLNOS decillions
CDEIILMSTU multicides
CDEIILNPPR principled
CDEIILNRTY indirectly
CDEIILOSTU solicitude
CDEIILOSUY dieciously
CDEIILRRSU ridiculers
CDEIIMNNTT indictment
CDEIIMNOST midsection
CDEIIMOORT iodometric
CDEIIMORRS misericord
CDEIIMORST dosimetric
CDEIIMORTY iridectomy
mediocrity
CDEIIMRSST misdirects
CDEIINOPRT prediction
CDEIINOPST depictions
CDEIINORST directions
discretion
CDEIINORTY tyrocidine
CDEIINOSST dissection
CDEIINRSTT interdicts
CDEIINSSSV viscidness
CDEIIOORRS sororicide
CDEIIORSTY iridocytes
CDEIIORSUV recidivous
CDEIIORSUX uxoricides
CDEIIRSSUV discursive
CDEIKLLRSS drecksills
CDEIKLOPST stockpiled
CDEIKLOPSU liposucked
CDEIKNRRTU undertrick
CDEIKNRSUW windsucker
CDEILLLOSU celluloids
CDEILLLPUY pellucidly
CDEILNNOSU uninclosed
CDEILNOSSU cloudiness
CDEILOORRT tricolored
CDEILOORSU colourised
CDEILOORUZ colourized
CDEILOPSUU pediculous
CDEILORSSS disclosers
CDEILORSSU disclosure
CDEIMMNOOS incommodes
CDEIMMNOPU compendium
CDEIMMNOSU communised
CDEIMMNOTU comminuted
CDEIMMNOUZ communized
CDEIMNNOST condiments
CDEIMNOOST endosmotic
CDEIMNOOSY diseconomy
CDEIMNOPRS princedoms
CDEIMNOSTU miscounted
CDEIMOOPSS discompose
CDEIMOOPST composited
CDEIMORSTU Democritus
CDEIMOSSTU customised
CDEIMOSTUZ customized
CDEINNOSTT discontent
CDEINOORSU indecorous
CDEINOOSTX exodontics
CDEINOPRTY decryption
CDEINORRTU introducer
CDEINORSTU discounter
introduces
rediscount
reductions
CDEINOSSTU seductions
CDEINPRSTU unscripted
CDEINRSTTU instructed
CDEIOPRRST predictors
CDEIOPRTUV productive
CDEIORRSSU discourser
CDEIORSSST dissectors
CDEIORSSSU discourses
CDEIPPSSTY dyspeptics
CDEIRRSTTU strictured
CDEIRSSSSU discussers
CDEJNNOSSU jocundness
CDEKLMMOOS slommocked
CDEKNOORSU undercooks
CDELLNOORT controlled
CDELMNOSUY consumedly
CDELMOOPSY composedly
CDELMOOPTT complotted
CDELNNOOSU unconsoled
CDELNOORST decontrols
CDELNOORSU undercools
CDELNOORUU uncoloured
CDELNOORUY Euroclydon
CDELNOOSSW closedowns
CDELNOOSTY cotyledons
CDELNOOTUV convoluted
CDELNORSSU scoundrels
CDELNRTUUU uncultured
CDELOORSUV overclouds
CDELOORSUY decorously
CDELPRSTUU sculptured
CDEMMOOORS commodores
cosmodrome
CDEMNOOPRU compounder
CDEMNOORSW downcomers
CDENNOOPRU pronounced
CDENOOPRRS correspond
CDENOORRST corrodents
CDEOOPPRTU outcropped
CDEOOPRTUU outproduce
CDEOORRSVW overcrowds
CDEOORSSTU outcrossed
CDEOORSSWW woodscrews
CDEOORSTUU outsourced
CDEOORTTUW woodcutter
CDEORRSTTU destructor
CDEORSSTTU destructos
CDERRSTTUU structured
CDFFIILTUY difficulty
CDFGIILNUY dulcifying
CDFIIMNORS disconfirm
CDFIIMOSST discomfits
CDFIIORSSU sudorifics
CDFIMOORST discomfort
CDGHIILMOU glochidium
CDGHILOORY hydrologic
CDGIIILMNO domiciling
CDGIIILNRU ridiculing
CDGIILLOPY glycolipid
CDGIILNOSS disclosing
CDGIINSSSU discussing
CDGIKLLOOS goldilocks
CDGILLNOSY scoldingly
CDHHIILLSY childishly
CDHHIIOSTY ichthyoids
CDHHILORST Rothschild
CDHHILOSST dishcloths
CDHHIOORST Christhood
CDHIIINOOP idiophonic
CDHIILMTYY thymidylic
CDHIIMNOOR chironomid
CDHIINPSSY syndicship
CDHIIOSSTU distichous
CDHILOPRYY polyhydric
CDHILORTYY hydrolytic
CDHILORXYY hydroxylic
CDHILOSSTU dishclouts
CDHIMNOORY monohydric
CDHINOOOSU cousinhood
CDHINOOPRY hydroponic
CDHIOOPSSZ schizopods
CDHIOPRSTY dystrophic
CDHLMMNOOO commonhold
CDHMNOOORS monochords
CDHNNOOOSU coonhounds
CDHNOOORST notochords
CDHNOOSTUW touchdowns
CDIIILNOTY indocility
CDIIIMPTUY impudicity
CDIIINNOST indictions
CDIIINNSTT indistinct
CDIIINOSSS discission

CDIILNOOSU	nidicolous
CDIILNSTTY	distinctly
CDIILOOSUY	dioicously
CDIILOPPSY	polydipsic
CDIILORSUU	ridiculous
CDIIMNORST	doctrinism
CDIINNOOST	conditions
CDIINNOSTU	inductions
CDIINOPRSY	cyprinoids
CDIINORSTT	doctrinist
CDIINOSSSU	discussion
CDIIORRSTT	tortricids
CDIIPRSSTU	tricuspids
CDIKLLORST	drillstock
CDIKMRSSTU	drumsticks
CDIKORSSTW	swordstick
CDILLMOOSU	molluscoid
CDILMOOORX	loxodromic
CDILMOOPUY	lycopodium
CDILOORSSU	discolours
CDIMMNOOSS	discommons
CDIMMOOOSU	commodious
CDIMNOOOTY	monocytoid
CDINOOPRTU	production
CDINORSSSW	crosswinds
CDIRRSSTUU	duricrusts
CDKKNNOOSW	knockdowns
CDKKNOOORS	doorknocks
CDMNNORSUU	conundrums
CDNNOOSTUW	countdowns
CDNOOOOTTW	cottonwood
CDNOOOPSUY	cynopodous
CDNOSSSTUU	Duns Scotus
CDOORRSSSW	crosswords
CEEEEFFRSV	effervesce
CEEEEFNPRR	preference
CEEEEFNRRR	referencer
CEEEEFNRRS	references
CEEEEGIPTX	epexegetic
CEEEEGMNRS	emergences
CEEEEHILPS	heelpieces
CEEEEHIMST	cheesemite
CEEEEIMRST	cemeteries
CEEEEINPRX	experience
CEEEELLNPR	repellence
CEEEENRRRV	reverencer
CEEEENRRSV	reverences
CEEEFFGLNU	effulgence
CEEEFFLNSU	effluences
CEEEFFLORS	effloresce
CEEEFGLNRU	refulgence
CEEEFHLSTT	flechettes
CEEEFILNSS	fleeciness
CEEEFILRTV	reflective
CEEEFINNNS	fescennine
CEEEFINNRS	inferences
CEEEFINRRS	firescreen
CEEEFINRSS	fierceness
CEEEFINRSV	fervencies
CEEEFIPRTV	perfective
CEEEFNORRS	conferrees
	reenforces
CEEEFNQRSU	frequences
CEEEFPRRST	perfecters
CEEEFPRRTU	prefecture
CEEEGGILNN	negligence
CEEEGIINPT	epigenetic
CEEEGIINSX	exigencies
CEEEGILNRT	reelecting
CEEEGIMMNR	immergence
CEEEGINNOX	xenogeneic
CEEEGINORS	recognisee
CEEEGINORZ	recognizee
CEEEGINRRT	reerecting
CEEEGINRST	energetics
CEEEGINRTV	vicegerent
	viceregent
CEEEGLLOPR	precollege
CEEEGLNORT	electrogen
CEEEGLNRST	neglecters
CEEEGNRRSU	resurgence
CEEEHHLORS	horseleech
CEEEHHMRTU	Erechtheum
CEEEHHRSTU	Erechtheus
CEEEHIKNSS	cheekiness
CEEEHIMSTT	chemisette
CEEEHINPRR	encipherer
CEEEHINPTT	epenthetic
CEEEHINRSS	cheeriness
CEEEHINSSS	cheesiness
CEEEHIPRRS	percheries
CEEEHLLSSY	Seychelles
CEEEHLPSSS	speechless
CEEEHMMNSY	mesenchyme
CEEEHMORTT	hectometer
	hectometre
CEEEHNNRRT	entrencher
CEEEHNNRST	entrenches
CEEEHNORSS	chersonese
CEEEHNRRST	retrenches
CEEEHOPSST	sheepcotes
CEEEHOQRUU	eurocheque
CEEEHORRST	threescore
CEEEHQRSUX	exchequers
CEEEHRSTTV	chevrettes
CEEEIILNRS	resilience
CEEEIIMNNS	eminencies
CEEEIIMPST	timepieces
CEEEIINRSV	vicereines
CEEEIJLTVY	ejectively
CEEEIKLNRS	screenlike
CEEEILLMNO	emollience
CEEEILLTVY	electively
CEEEILMNNT	clementine
CEEEILMORT	ceilometer
CEEEILMRTT	telemetric
CEEEILNORT	reelection
CEEEILNPRT	percentile
CEEEILNPST	pestilence
CEEEILNRSS	relicenses
CEEEIMNNTT	enticement
CEEEIMNORS	ceremonies
CEEEIMNRST	mesenteric
CEEEIMNRSV	servicemen
CEEEIMNRTT	centimeter
	centimetre
	remittence
CEEEIMNTTX	excitement
CEEEIMRRSS	mercerises
CEEEIMRRSZ	mercerizes
CEEEINNPRT	pertinence
CEEEINOPSS	nosepieces
CEEEINPRRT	pericenter
	pericentre
CEEEINPRSS	creepiness
CEEEINPRST	epicenters
	epicentres
CEEEINSSTX	existences
CEEEINTTWY	winceyette
CEEEIORRST	corsetiere
CEEEIORRSV	recoveries
CEEEIORTVX	overexcite
CEEEIPPRTV	perceptive
	preceptive
CEEEIPRRSV	perceivers
CEEEIPRSTV	respective
CEEEIRRSSX	exercisers
CEEEIRSSSV	recessives
CEEEISTUVX	executives
CEEEJLORTT	electrojet
CEEEJMNSTT	ejectments
CEEEKKLNPS	kenspeckle
CEEEKLRSSS	clerkesses
CEEEKORRST	rocketeers
CEEEKRRSSU	seersucker
CEEELLNPRY	repellency
CEEELMORRT	electromer
CEEELNOORU	neurocoele
CEEELNRSSV	cleverness
CEEELNSSST	selectness
CEEELOPSST	telescopes
CEEELPRSST	preselects
CEEEMNNRST	secernment
CEEEMNOPRS	recompense
CEEEMNORRT	centromere
CEEEMNOTYZ	ectoenzyme
CEEEMNRSTU	securement
CEEENNORSV	reconvenes
CEEENNRSST	recentness
CEEENOPRSS	encopreses
CEEENORSTT	entrecotes
CEEENOSSTY	synoecetes
CEEENQRSSU	sequencers
CEEENRSSSU	secureness
CEEEORRRSV	recoverers
CEEEPRRSST	respecters
CEEEPRSSTU	persecutes
CEEFFHILNS	Schlieffen
CEEFFIOSSU	coiffeuses
CEEFFOOPST	coffeepots
CEEFGHINNR	greenfinch
CEEFGILNRT	reflecting
CEEFGINOSU	Cienfuegos
CEEFGINPRT	perfecting
CEEFGINRTU	centrifuge
CEEFGLLNTU	neglectful

CEEFGLNRUY refulgency
CEEFGLNSTU genuflects
CEEFHHNORT henceforth
CEEFHLLRUY cheerfully
CEEFHORTTU fourchette
CEEFIIILST felicities
CEEFIILNTV inflective
CEEFIINORT fictioneer
CEEFIIPRSS specifiers
CEEFIIRRST certifiers
rectifiers
CEEFIKLNSS fickleness
CEEFILNNRU influencer
CEEFILNNSU influences
CEEFILNORT reflection
CEEFIMPRST imperfects
CEEFINOPRT perfection
CEEFINORRS reinforces
CEEFIORRSU ceriferous
CEEFIRRSST firecrests
CEEFKLLSSY fecklessly
CEEFKLORTT fetterlock
CEEFLNOORW coneflower
CEEFLNRSSU screenfuls
CEEFLNRSSY flyscreens
CEEFLOORSS forecloses
CEEFLORRST reflectors
CEEFLORSSU fluoresces
CEEFLPPRTU pluperfect
CEEFLPRSTU respectful
CEEFMNNORT conferment
CEEFMOORST focometers
CEEFNOPRSU fourpences
CEEFNORRRS conferrers
CEEFNRSTTU frutescent
CEEFOOPSST fetoscopes
CEEFOORRSU forecourse
CEEFOPRRST perfectors
CEEFORSSSU refocusses
CEEGGILNNT neglecting
CEEGGLNOOY genecology
CEEGHIILMP hemiplegic
CEEGHIKNNP henpecking
CEEGHILNNO echeloning
CEEGHILNRY cheeringly
CEEGHIMORT geothermic
CEEGHIMOST geochemist
CEEGHINNOT ethnogenic
CEEGHINQRU chequering
CEEGHKMNRU Kremenchug
CEEGIINNSS ensigncies
CEEGIINOPR epirogenic
CEEGIINPRT receipting
CEEGIINPRV perceiving
CEEGIINRSX exercising
CEEGIINSTT geneticist
CEEGIINSTU eugenicist
CEEGIKNRST greenstick
CEEGILLOOT teleologic
CEEGILNOST tense logic
CEEGILNPRT prelecting
CEEGINNNST sentencing
CEEGINNORU neurogenic
CEEGINNOSS consignees
CEEGINNQSU sequencing
CEEGINNRSS screenings
CEEGINNRST centerings
nigrescent
CEEGINNRSU insurgence
CEEGINNSST ignescents
CEEGINOORS ecoregions
CEEGINOORT erotogenic
orogenetic
CEEGINOOST osteogenic
CEEGINORRS recogniser
CEEGINORRV recovering
CEEGINORRZ recognizer
CEEGINORSS recognises
CEEGINORST estrogenic
CEEGINORSZ recognizes
CEEGINOSTV congestive
CEEGINPRSS precessing
CEEGINPRST respecting
sceptering
CEEGINPRTX excerpting
CEEGINRSTY synergetic
CEEGKNOOSS goosenecks
CEEGLNORST neglectors
CEEGLORSTU Gloucester
CEEGMOTYYZ zygomycete
CEEGNNORTV convergent
CEEGNOOSTU ectogenous
CEEGNORSSS congresses
CEEGNRSTTU turgescent
CEEGORSTTU courgettes
CEEHHIRRSS cherishers
CEEHHMMOOR hemochrome
CEEHIIILST helicities
CEEHIIKNPT thinkpiece
CEEHIILLNS heliclines
CEEHIIMRST erethismic
CEEHIIRRST heritrices
CEEHIIRSTT erethistic
CEEHIIRSTW witcheries
CEEHIKLRRY cherrylike
CEEHIKLSTY scythelike
CEEHIKNRST thickeners
CEEHIKNSTT kitchenets
CEEHIKPPRS schipperke
CEEHIKRSTT Treitschke
CEEHIKSSTT sketchiest
CEEHILLMSS schlemiels
CEEHILLRSS chisellers
CEEHILMNOP clomiphene
CEEHILNOPR necrophile
CEEHILNOPT telephonic
CEEHILNORU euchlorine
CEEHILNSST Clisthenes
CEEHILOPRT helicopter
CEEHILORRT Loir-et-Cher
CEEHILORTT hectoliter
hectolitre
CEEHILOSVY cohesively
CEEHILSSTT telestichs
CEEHIMNNRT enrichment
CEEHIMNRTT Metternich
CEEHIMNTTU technetium
CEEHIMOPTU mouthpiece
CEEHIMORRT rheometric
CEEHIMORTX exothermic
CEEHINNORT incoherent
CEEHINNRRT intrencher
CEEHINNRST intrenches
CEEHINOPPR Hippocrene
CEEHINORSS heroicness
CEEHINQSTU techniques
CEEHINRRST christener
rechristen
CEEHINRSTW winchester
CEEHINSSST chestiness
CEEHINSSTT tetchiness
CEEHIOPPRS prophecies
CEEHIOPRST spirochete
CEEHIOPSSW showpieces
CEEHIORRST Österreich
torchieres
CEEHIORSTT theoretics
CEEHIRRSTT stretchier
CEEHIRSTTY hysteretic
CEEHIRSTWZ Schweitzer
CEEHKNPSUY keypunches
CEEHLLNOPS cellphones
CEEHLNORTY coherently
CEEHLNQSSU quenchless
CEEHLPRSSU sepulchers
sepulchres
CEEHLQRSSU squelchers
CEEHMMOORR chromomere
CEEHNOOPPS nephoscope
CEEHNOOPRT ctenophore
CEEHNOPRRS percherons
CEEHNOPRTY hypocentre
CEEHNORSTT Chesterton
CEEHNORSTV chervonets
CEEHOPSTTY ectophytes
CEEHORRSTU retouchers
CEEHRRSSTT stretchers
CEEIIINNPS insipience
CEEIIKLLSU sluicelike
CEEIIKLNPR princelike
CEEIIKNNTZ zinckenite
CEEIIKRRST trickeries
CEEIILLMRV vermicelli
CEEIILLORS collieries
CEEIILMNTV Clement VII
CEEIILNOSU isoleucine
CEEIILNPRR princelier
CEEIILNPRS periclines
CEEIILNRSY resiliency
CEEIILNRTT centiliter
centilitre
CEEIILOSTV velocities
CEEIILPPST epileptics
CEEIILRTTY erectility
CEEIILTTVY electivity
CEEIIMMPRT metempiric

CEEIIMNNTT	incitement
CEEIIMNRSS	reminisces
CEEIIMNRTV	ivermectin
CEEIIMORTT	meteoritic
CEEIIMOSST	semeiotics
CEEIIMPRRT	perimetric
CEEIIMPSSS	speciesism
CEEIIMPSST	epistemics
CEEIINNORS	eirenicons
CEEIINNRST	encrinites
CEEIINNSST	insistence
CEEIINNSTV	incentives
CEEIINOPST	centipoise
CEEIINPPRT	percipient
CEEIINPRST	recipients
CEEIINPSTV	inceptives
	inspective
CEEIINPSTX	excipients
CEEIINRSTT	interstice
CEEIINSSTZ	citizeness
CEEIINSTVV	invectives
CEEIINTTVX	extinctive
CEEIIOPSST	poeticises
CEEIIOPSTZ	poeticizes
CEEIIORRST	escritoire
CEEIIORSST	eroticises
CEEIIORSTZ	eroticizes
CEEIIPSSST	speciesist
CEEIIRRRSU	currieries
CEEIIRSSTU	securities
CEEIJLOPRT	projectile
CEEIJNORST	rejections
CEEIJNRSTT	interjects
CEEIJOPRTV	projective
CEEIJRSTUV	surjective
CEEIJRSTYY	Jersey City
CEEIKLLRST	clerkliest
CEEIKLNOPU	leukopenic
CEEIKLNRSS	silkscreen
CEEIKNOPSS	kinescopes
CEEIKNPRTY	pernickety
CEEIKNQRSU	requickens
CEEIKNSSSS	sicknesses
CEEIKOPRSW	workpieces
CEEILLNPRS	pencillers
CEEILLNRST	stenciller
CEEILLNSTT	intellects
CEEILLOOPT	coleoptile
CEEILLORSS	recoilless
CEEILLRSSU	sculleries
CEEILMNOPT	incomplete
CEEILMNORT	clinometer
CEEILMNOSS	comeliness
CEEILMNSSU	luminesces
CEEILMOPRS	microsleep
CEEILMOPTV	completive
CEEILNOORS	recolonise
CEEILNOORZ	recolonize
CEEILNOPRT	prelection
CEEILNORST	centrioles
CEEILNOSST	selections
CEEILNPRST	princelets
CEEILNPSST	splenetics
CEEILNQSTU	liquescent
CEEILNRSTV	ventricles
CEEILNRSUY	insecurely
CEEILNRTTY	reticently
CEEILORSST	sclerotise
CEEILORSTZ	sclerotize
CEEILPRSUV	preclusive
CEEILRSSTW	crewelists
CEEILSSUVX	exclusives
CEEIMMOPRT	emmetropic
CEEIMMORRS	micromeres
CEEIMMORRT	micrometer
	micrometre
CEEIMMOSTT	committees
CEEIMNNOPR	prominence
CEEIMNNRST	increments
CEEIMNOORS	economiser
CEEIMNOORZ	economizer
CEEIMNOOSS	economises
CEEIMNOOSZ	economizes
CEEIMNOSST	centesimos
CEEIMNRTTY	remittency
CEEIMNSSSU	meniscuses
CEEIMNSSTU	intumesces
CEEIMORSTV	viscometer
CEEIMOSSTV	vicomtesse
CEEINNNOTV	convenient
CEEINNORSS	recensions
CEEINNPSST	spinescent
CEEINOPPRT	perception
CEEINOPRSS	encopresis
	necropsies
	precession
	preconises
CEEINOPRST	receptions
CEEINOPRSZ	preconizes
CEEINOPRTX	excerption
CEEINOPSTX	exceptions
CEEINORRST	Corrientes
CEEINORRSW	cornerwise
CEEINORSSS	recessions
CEEINORSST	resections
	secretions
CEEINORSTV	ventricose
CEEINORTTV	convertite
CEEINORTTY	coeternity
CEEINORTVV	convertive
CEEINOSSSS	secessions
CEEINOSSTX	exoticness
CEEINOSTTX	coexistent
CEEINOSTUX	executions
CEEINPRSSS	princesses
CEEINPRSST	reinspects
CEEINPRSTT	intercepts
CEEINPRSTU	putrescine
CEEINRRSSV	scriveners
CEEINRRSTU	scrutineer
CEEINRSSTT	intersects
CEEINRSSTY	syncretise
CEEINRSTTT	trecentist
CEEINRSTTV	vitrescent
CEEINRSTYZ	syncretize
CEEIOPPRSS	periscopes
CEEIOPRRST	receiptors
CEEIOPRRSV	overprices
CEEIOPRTTV	protective
CEEIOQRSTU	coquetries
CEEIORRSST	corsetiers
CEEIORRSSX	exorcisers
CEEIORRSXZ	exorcizers
CEEIORRTUU	couturiere
CEEIORSSTU	courtesies
CEEIPRRSUV	precursive
CEEIPRSSUV	percussive
CEEIPSSTUV	susceptive
CEEIRRRSTU	recruiters
CEEJNOOSSS	jocoseness
CEEJORRSTT	retrojects
CEEKLLRSSY	recklessly
CEEKLNRTTU	turtleneck
CEEKLOPSST	pocketless
CEEKLORRWW	crewelwork
CEEKLOSTUY	leukocytes
CEELLMOPRS	compellers
CEELLMOPTY	completely
CEELMMNOPT	complement
CEELMNNOOS	somnolence
CEELMNOOPX	complexone
CEELMNOOSU	nucleosome
CEELMOORTU	coulometer
CEELMOPRST	completers
CEELMOSTYY	myelocytes
CEELNORSSU	enclosures
CEELNORSVY	conversely
CEELOOPRST	coleopters
CEELOPRRST	prelectors
CEELORRSTY	clerestory
CEELORSSUX	exclosures
CEEMMNORST	commenters
CEEMMOTXYY	myxomycete
CEEMNNORST	contemners
CEEMNNSTTY	encystment
CEEMNOORST	centrosome
CEEMNOOSTU	coenosteum
CEEMNOPRTU	recoupment
CEEMNOPRTY	pycnometer
CEEMNORTUY	neurectomy
CEEMNPSSTU	spumescent
CEEMOOPRSS	recomposes
CEEMOPRSSS	compresses
CEEMORRSTY	cryometers
CEEMOSSSTY	ecosystems
CEENNOQSTU	consequent
CEENNORRST	rencontres
CEENNORRSU	renouncers
CEENNORRTU	rencounter
CEENNORSST	consenters
CEENNORSTU	encounters
CEENNPRSSY	pennycress
CEENOOPSST	copestones
CEENOPPPRR	peppercorn
CEENOPPRTY	prepotency
CEENOPRRSS	precensors

CEENOPRRST	precentors
CEENOQRRSU	reconquers
CEENOQRSTU	reconquest
CEENORRSSV	conservers
	conversers
CEENORRSTV	converters
	reconverts
CEENORSSTT	contesters
CEENORSSTV	covertness
CEENORTTUX	contexture
CEENOSSSTU	countesses
CEENPRSSSU	spruceness
CEENPRSTTU	putrescent
CEEOORRSSV	overscores
CEEOPPRRST	preceptors
CEEOPPRRTY	preceptory
CEEOPRRSTT	retrospect
CEEOPRRSTU	persecutor
CEEOPRRSTX	excerptors
CEEOPRSSTU	prosecutes
CEEOQRSTTU	croquettes
CEEORRSSST	crosstrees
CEEPRSSSTU	suspecters
CEERRRSSTU	resurrects
CEERSSSUUX	excursuses
CEFFGIINOR	officering
CEFFHIINOR	chiffonier
CEFFHILOOY	Holy Office
CEFFIINSTU	sufficient
CEFFIIRRTU	fructifier
CEFFIIRSTU	fructifies
CEFFIRSSTU	scruffiest
CEFFLLORUY	forcefully
CEFGHILNST	fletchings
CEFGHILNTY	fetchingly
CEFGIIKLNR	flickering
CEFGIILNNT	inflecting
CEFGIINPSY	specifying
CEFGIINRTY	certifying
	rectifying
CEFGINNORR	conferring
CEFGINNOSS	confessing
CEFGINORSU	refocusing
CEFHHINORT	Richthofen
CEFHIISSTT	fetichists
CEFHIKORSS	rockfishes
CEFHIKRSSU	suckerfish
CEFHIKSSSU	suckfishes
CEFHILSTTU	cuttlefish
CEFHKOORSS	foreshocks
CEFIIIILSS	silicifies
CEFIIILNTV	inflictive
CEFIIILNTY	infelicity
CEFIILNNOT	inflection
CEFIILNOQU	cinquefoil
CEFIILNRST	inflicters
CEFIILOSTU	felicitous
CEFIIMNNOT	omnificent
CEFIIMNNTU	munificent
CEFIINNOST	infections
CEFIINOPRT	proficient
CEFIINOPST	pontifices
CEFIINOSTU	infectious
CEFIIORRSS	scorifiers
CEFIKLORRS	frolickers
CEFIKORSSS	fossickers
CEFILLMRUY	mercifully
CEFILMNRUU	unmerciful
CEFILMOORS	frolicsome
CEFILNORST	inflectors
CEFILORSUU	luciferous
CEFIMNORRS	confirmers
	reconfirms
CEFIMORSUY	cymiferous
CEFINNOOSS	confession
CEFINOORSU	coniferous
CEFINORSTU	confitures
CEFIOORSUV	vociferous
CEFKLOPSTU	pocketfuls
CEFKOORRSW	workforces
CEFLNNOSTU	confluents
CEFLNOORRW	cornflower
CEFMNOORRS	conformers
CEFMOORRST	comforters
CEFNNOORRT	confronter
CEFNOORSSS	confessors
CEFOORRSTU	forecourts
CEGGHIINRS	screighing
CEGGILNOSS	clogginess
CEGGINNORV	converging
CEGGINNOST	congesting
CEGGINOOST	geognostic
CEGGLNOOYY	gynecology
CEGHHIINRS	cherishing
CEGHIIINST	ethicising
CEGHIIINTZ	ethicizing
CEGHIIKNNT	thickening
CEGHIIKNRW	whickering
CEGHIILLNS	chiselling
CEGHIILOOR	hierologic
CEGHIINNUY	unhygienic
CEGHIINORZ	rhizogenic
CEGHIINOST	histogenic
CEGHIINRTT	chittering
CEGHIIOSST	gothicises
CEGHIIOSTZ	gothicizes
CEGHILLOSU	guilloches
CEGHILMNSY	schemingly
CEGHILNOOT	ethnologic
CEGHILNOPY	phylogenic
CEGHILNORT	reclothing
CEGHILNPPS	schlepping
CEGHILNQSU	squelching
CEGHILNSTV	vetchlings
CEGHILOPRY	hypergolic
CEGHIMMNOO	homecoming
CEGHIMOOPR	geomorphic
CEGHINNRTU	chuntering
CEGHINOOPT	photogenic
CEGHINOORR	gonorrheic
CEGHINOORT	orthogenic
CEGHINOPTY	phytogenic
	typhogenic
CEGHINORRU	chirurgeon
CEGHINORTU	retouching
CEGHINORTY	trichogyne
CEGHINRSTT	stretching
CEGHIOPSSY	geophysics
CEGHIORSTU	grouchiest
CEGHIRRRUY	chirurgery
CEGHKNORSU	roughnecks
CEGHLNOOTY	technology
CEGHLOOPRU	glucophore
CEGHLOPTYY	glycophyte
CEGHMNOORS	chromogens
CEGHOOPRSY	hygroscope
CEGIIIMNNT	meningitic
CEGIIJNRUV	verjuicing
CEGIIKLLNN	nickelling
CEGIIKLNNR	clinkering
CEGIIKNNQU	quickening
CEGIIKNNRS	snickering
CEGIIKPRST	pigsticker
CEGIILLNNP	pencilling
CEGIILMOOS	semiologic
CEGIILNNPR	princeling
CEGIILNNSS	clinginess
CEGIILNNST	stenciling
CEGIILNNTY	enticingly
CEGIILNPRY	piercingly
CEGIILNQSU	liquescing
CEGIILNTXY	excitingly
CEGIILOPTT	epiglottic
CEGIILORTU	oliguretic
CEGIILOSTU	eulogistic
CEGIINNOST	sectioning
CEGIINNPST	inspecting
CEGIINNTUX	unexciting
CEGIINORSX	exorcising
CEGIINORXZ	exorcizing
CEGIINOSTX	coexisting
CEGIINOSTZ	Gnosticize
CEGIINRRTU	recruiting
CEGIINRSTT	trisecting
CEGIJNOPRT	projecting
CEGIKNNORS	reckonings
CEGIKNOOPR	precooking
CEGIKNORST	restocking
	stockinger
CEGILLMNOP	compelling
CEGILLMOSU	collegiums
CEGILLOOXY	lexicology
CEGILMMNOS	commingles
CEGILMNOOP	monoplegic
CEGILMNOPT	completing
CEGILMOOSY	mycologies
CEGILNNOST	clingstone
CEGILNNOSU	counseling
CEGILNNPTU	centupling
CEGILNRSSU	surcingles
CEGILNRSTU	clustering
CEGILNRTTU	cluttering
CEGILOOOST	oecologist
CEGILOOSST	ecologists
CEGILOOSTT	cetologist
CEGILOOSTY	cytologies

CEGIMMNNOT	commenting
CEGIMNNNOT	contemning
CEGIMNOORS	ergonomics
CEGIMNOORV	overcoming
CEGINNNORU	renouncing
CEGINNNOST	consenting
CEGINNNOTT	contenting
	contingent
CEGINNNRSU	scunnering
CEGINNOOST	congestion
CEGINNOQRU	conquering
CEGINNORRW	recrowning
CEGINNORSS	consigners
CEGINNORST	constringe
CEGINNORSV	conserving
	conversing
CEGINNORTU	countering
	recounting
CEGINNORTV	converting
CEGINNORUV	uncovering
CEGINNOSTT	contesting
CEGINNPRTY	encrypting
CEGINNRSTU	encrusting
CEGINNRSTY	stringency
CEGINNRSUW	unscrewing
CEGINNRSUY	insurgency
CEGINOOOPS	gonioscope
CEGINOOPRT	protogenic
CEGINOORRS	recognisor
CEGINOORRZ	recognizor
CEGINOORST	creosoting
CEGINOPRSS	processing
CEGINOPRTT	protecting
CEGINOQRTU	croqueting
CEGINOQTTU	coquetting
CEGINORRSS	recrossing
CEGINPPRSU	scuppering
CEGINPRSSU	percussing
CEGINPSSTU	suspecting
CEGINRSTTU	scuttering
CEGINRSTUY	curtseying
CEGINRTTUV	curvetting
CEGKMRSSUU	gumsuckers
CEGLNOOSYY	synecology
CEGNNOOOSU	oncogenous
CEGNORRSSU	scroungers
CEGOOPRSSY	gyroscopes
CEHHHIIKRT	hitchhiker
CEHHHIIKST	hitchhikes
CEHHHKRSUV	Khrushchev
CEHHIILMNT	helminthic
CEHHIILMOP	hemophilic
CEHHIIMSST	hemistichs
CEHHILLMSS	schlemihls
CEHHIMRTUY	eurhythmic
CEHHIOOPST	theosophic
CEHHIOPRST	Christophe
CEHHIOPTTY	hypothetic
CEHHKLLOSS	shellshock
CEHHLMOOOS	homeschool
CEHHLOOPRT	choropleth
CEHHLOOSTU	touchholes
CEHHLORTTW	Letchworth
CEHHMOOPTY	chomophyte
CEHHOOPSSU	chophouses
CEHIIINRST	trichinise
CEHIIINRTZ	trichinize
CEHIIKLPTY	kelyphitic
CEHIIKLRST	Christlike
CEHIIKLSTW	switchlike
CEHIIKRTTV	Trevithick
CEHIILLNSS	chilliness
CEHIILMOPS	mesophilic
CEHIILMOST	homiletics
CEHIILNOST	ichnolites
CEHIILNOTX	xenolithic
CEHIILOPTY	heliotypic
CEHIIMNORT	thermionic
CEHIIMOPPR	epimorphic
CEHIIMOPRT	hemitropic
CEHIIMRSTY	mythiciser
CEHIIMRTYZ	mythicizer
CEHIIMSSTY	mythicises
CEHIIMSTYZ	mythicizes
CEHIINPRSS	chirpiness
CEHIINPSST	pitchiness
CEHIINSSTT	snitchiest
CEHIINSTTZ	chintziest
CEHIIOSTTY	histiocyte
CEHIIPRSTY	sphericity
CEHIIPSTUU	euphuistic
CEHIIRRTTU	urethritic
CEHIIRSSTU	heuristics
CEHIKLNSUY	Chelyuskin
CEHIKLPRSS	clerkships
CEHIKNNOST	technikons
CEHIKNNSSU	chunkiness
CEHIKNSSST	kitschness
CEHIKPRSSW	shipwrecks
CEHILMOOZZ	Michelozzo
CEHILNOPST	clothespin
CEHILNOSTU	touchlines
CEHILNRSTZ	Schnitzler
CEHILNSSTZ	schnitzels
CEHILOPRST	lectorship
CEHILORSTY	chrysolite
	chrysotile
CEHILSSTTU	slutchiest
CEHIMMNSSU	chumminess
CEHIMNNOSU	ichneumons
CEHIMNOOPR	microphone
CEHIMNOOTT	nomothetic
CEHIMNOPTY	chimneypot
CEHIMOOORT	homoerotic
CEHIMOOPTY	homeotypic
	mythopoeic
CEHIMOPRTY	microphyte
CEHIMOPSTY	mesophytic
CEHIMPRSUY	hypericums
CEHIMRSTUY	eurythmics
CEHINNNPPY	pinchpenny
CEHINNPSSU	punchiness
CEHINNRSTY	strychnine
CEHINOORRS	rhinoceros
CEHINOORSS	isochrones
CEHINOPPRR	pronephric
CEHINOPPSS	choppiness
CEHINOPPTY	phenotypic
CEHINOPRSS	censorship
CEHINOPRSU	neurochips
CEHINOPRSY	hypersonic
CEHINOPRTY	hypertonic
CEHINOPSTT	pitchstone
CEHINOPTTY	enphytotic
	entophytic
CEHINOSSTU	touchiness
CEHINPRSST	sphincters
CEHINSSTTY	synthetics
CEHIOOPRRT	rheotropic
CEHIOOPRRY	pyorrhoeic
CEHIOORRRT	retrochoir
CEHIOORSTW	switcheroo
CEHIOPRRST	chiropters
	rectorship
CEHIOPRSTT	prosthetic
CEHIOPRSTY	hypocrites
CEHIOPRTXY	xerophytic
CEHIOPSSTY	sciophytes
CEHIOQSTTU	coquettish
CEHIORRSST	choristers
CEHIORSTTU	Theocritus
CEHIPRRRSU	chirrupers
CEHIRRSSSU	scirrhuses
CEHIRSSTTW	Schwitters
CEHKLMNOOT	klootchmen
CEHKLNORSS	schnorkels
CEHKOOOSSU	cookhouses
CEHKOOPPRR	rockhopper
CEHKOORSST	stockhorse
CEHLLOOPST	photocells
CEHLMNOSUU	homuncules
CEHLMOOPRY	polychrome
CEHLMOPTYY	lymphocyte
CEHLNOSSZZ	schnozzles
CEHLOOOPRT	tocopherol
CEHMMNOOOR	monochrome
CEHMMOOORS	chromosome
CEHMMOTTYY	thymectomy
CEHMOOPRST	ectomorphs
CEHMOOPRTY	cormophyte
	ectomorphy
CEHMOSTTYY	thymocytes
CEHNNORSTU	truncheons
CEHNOOOPPS	phonoscope
CEHNOOPRRT	necrotroph
CEHNOOPRTT	topnotcher
CEHNOOSTTU	touchstone
CEHNOPRSTU	Scunthorpe
CEHNOPRSTY	phenocryst
CEHNOPRTYY	pyrotechny
CEHNORRRSS	schnorrers
CEHNORSTVY	Chernovtsy
CEHOOOPRSS	horoscopes
CEHOOOPRST	orthoscope
CEHOORSTUU	courthouse
CEHOPRSTYY	cryophytes

CEHORSTTTU	outstretch
CEIIIILSTV	civilities
CEIIIINSTV	vicinities
CEIIILLMNO	limicoline
CEIIILLNNP	penicillin
CEIIILMOPS	impolicies
CEIIILNPTX	inexplicit
CEIIILNSVY	incisively
CEIIILOPST	politicise
CEIIILOPTZ	politicize
CEIIILRSSV	civilisers
CEIIILRSVZ	civilizers
CEIIIMMPRS	empiricism
CEIIIMOSSS	isoseismic
CEIIIMPRST	empiricist
CEIIIMRSTV	victimiser
CEIIIMRTVZ	victimizer
CEIIIMSSTV	victimises
CEIIIMSSTY	seismicity
CEIIIMSTVZ	victimizes
CEIIINNNOT	Innocent II
CEIIINNORT	interionic
CEIIINOSTT	tonicities
CEIIINPPRT	precipitin
CEIIIOPSST	isopiestic
CEIIIOSTTX	toxicities
CEIIJNNOST	injections
CEIIJNNTUV	injunctive
CEIIJNSSTU	injustices
CEIIJOOSST	jocosities
CEIIKLMORT	kilometric
CEIIKLNSSS	sickliness
CEIIKLOPRT	politicker
CEIIKLPRST	prickliest
CEIIKMPSST	skepticism
CEIIKNNPRS	princekins
CEIIKNOSTT	tokenistic
CEIIKNPRST	nitpickers
CEIIKNRSST	trickiness
CEIIKNSSST	stickiness
CEIIKRSSTT	tricksiest
CEIILLLSTU	cellulitis
CEIILLNNOT	centillion
CEIILLNRTU	citrulline
CEIILLORRT	Torricelli
CEIILLOSSU	siliculose
CEIILLPTXY	explicitly
CEIILMOPST	polemicist
CEIILMORST	microlites
CEIILNNORS	crinolines
CEIILNOSTU	licentious
CEIILNOSTV	novelistic
CEIILNPPRS	principles
CEIILNRTUV	ventriculi
CEIILOPSTX	postexilic
CEIILORSST	clitorises
CEIIMMORSS	microseism
CEIIMNNOST	omniscient
CEIIMNOSYZ	isoenzymic
CEIIMNRSSU	sinecurism
CEIIMORSST	isometrics
	microsites
CEIIMOSSTX	exoticisms
CEIIMOSTTT	totemistic
CEIIMPRSSU	epicurisms
CEIINNNOTV	Innocent IV
CEIINNOPST	inceptions
	inspection
CEIINNORST	incretions
CEIINNOTTX	extinction
CEIINNSSTY	insistency
CEIINOPRST	isentropic
CEIINOPRSU	pernicious
CEIINOPRTV	voiceprint
CEIINOPSTT	nepotistic
CEIINORRST	criterions
CEIINORSSS	rescission
CEIINORSTT	trisection
CEIINPRSSS	crispiness
CEIINRSSTU	scrutinies
	scrutinise
	sinecurist
CEIINRSTUY	insecurity
CEIINRSTUZ	scrutinize
CEIINSSSTT	scientists
CEIIOOPSTZ	epizootics
CEIIOORSTU	trioecious
CEIIOPRSTY	preciosity
CEIIOPSSTY	speciosity
CEIIORSTVV	vivisector
CEIJNNOORS	conjoiners
CEIJNOOPRT	projection
CEIJNORSTT	introjects
CEIJNORSTU	surjection
CEIKKLNSTU	knuckliest
CEIKKORRST	kicksorter
CEIKKORRWW	wickerwork
CEIKLLORSS	sollickers
CEIKLLORTT	Little Rock
CEIKLNNOST	clinkstone
CEIKLNORST	interlocks
CEIKLNPSSU	pluckiness
CEIKLNRSTY	strickenly
CEIKLNSTUU	unluckiest
CEIKLOPRST	stockpiler
CEIKLOPSST	stockpiles
CEIKLPRSSU	superslick
CEIKMORSTU	mesokurtic
CEIKNOSSST	stockiness
CEIKNOSSTT	stockinets
CEIKORRSTV	overtricks
CEIKPQSSTU	quicksteps
CEIKRRSSTT	tricksters
CEILLNOSUV	involucels
CEILLOOPST	colestipol
CEILLOOQSU	colloquies
CEILMMNOPT	compliment
CEILMNNOOS	monoclines
CEILMNOOPT	completion
CEILMNOOPX	complexion
CEILMNOOSS	semicolons
CEILMNORTY	clinometry
CEILMNOSTU	monticules
CEILMNPSSU	clumpiness
CEILMNSSSU	clumsiness
CEILMNSSUU	minuscules
CEILMOOOST	colotomies
CEILMOOOTV	locomotive
CEILMOOPST	leptosomic
CEILMOPRSY	micropyles
CEILMOPSTT	completist
CEILMOPSUV	compulsive
CEILMOPTXY	complexity
CEILMORSTU	sclerotium
CEILMORTUV	volumetric
CEILMOSTUU	meticulous
CEILNNNOTY	innocently
CEILNNOOSS	cloisonnes
CEILNNOSVY	insolvency
CEILNOOPRS	necropolis
CEILNOORRS	resorcinol
CEILNOORSS	colonisers
CEILNOORSZ	colonizers
CEILNOPRSU	preclusion
CEILNOPSTU	pleustonic
CEILNORSSU	inclosures
CEILNORSUV	involucres
CEILNORTTY	contritely
CEILNOSSST	costliness
CEILNOSSUX	exclusions
CEILNOSTUV	consultive
CEILNOSUVV	convulsive
CEILOOPRST	coprolites
CEILOORRSV	versicolor
CEILOORSSU	colourises
CEILOORSUZ	colourizes
CEILOPRSSV	slipcovers
CEILOPRSTY	proselytic
CEILOPRSUY	preciously
CEILOPSSUY	speciously
CEILORSTTU	courtliest
CEIMMMNOTT	commitment
CEIMMNOORT	metronomic
	monometric
CEIMMNOQUU	communique
CEIMMNORTY	metronymic
CEIMMNOSSU	communises
CEIMMNOSTU	comminutes
CEIMMNOSUZ	communizes
CEIMMOOPRS	compromise
CEIMMOORSS	microsomes
CEIMMOORST	microtomes
	osmometric
CEIMMOORTV	overcommit
CEIMMORRTY	micrometry
CEIMMORSSU	commissure
CEIMMORSTT	committers
CEIMMORTUX	commixture
CEIMNNORTV	Mont Cervin
CEIMNOOOSU	monoecious
CEIMNOOPSS	meconopsis
CEIMNOOPST	coemptions
CEIMNOORST	microtones
CEIMNOORTT	tonometric
CEIMNOOSST	economists
CEIMNOPRSU	proscenium

CEIMNORSUU ceruminous
CEIMNRSSTY syncretism
CEIMOOPRRS microspore
poromerics
CEIMOOPRRW micropower
CEIMOOPRST proteomics
CEIMOOPRTT competitor
optometric
CEIMOOPSST composites
CEIMOORSTU ecotourism
CEIMOORSTY sociometry
CEIMOPRRTY pyrometric
CEIMORSSTU costumiers
CEIMORSTVY viscometry
CEIMOSSSTU customises
CEIMOSSTUV muscovites
CEIMOSSTUZ customizes
CEINNNOOSX connexions
CEINNNOOTT contention
CEINNNOOTV convention
CEINNNOSTT continents
CEINNOORSV conversion
CEINNOPRTY encryption
CEINNOPTUX expunction
CEINNORSTU centurions
continuers
CEINNOSSTT consistent
CEINNQSUUX quincunxes
CEINOOPRSS procession
CEINOOPRTT protection
CEINOOPSTT stenotopic
CEINOORSSU censorious
CEINOORTTV contortive
CEINOORTUX neurotoxic
CEINOOSSUY synoecious
CEINOPPRSU porcupines
CEINOPRRSS conspirers
CEINOPRRST intercrops
CEINOPRSST inspectors
CEINOPRSSU percussion
supersonic
CEINOPRSTT introspect
CEINOPRSTU supertonic
CEINOPSTTY stenotypic
CEINOQTUYZ Quezon City
CEINORRSST intercross
CEINORRSSU coinsurers
recursions
CEINORRSTV contrivers
CEINORSSTT cornetists
CEINORSSUX excursions
CEINORSTTT cornettist
CEINORTWZZ Czernowitz
CEINOSSTUU incestuous
CEINOSTTTU constitute
CEINRSSSTT strictness
CEINRSSSTU crustiness
CEINRSSSUV scurviness
CEINRSSTTY syncretist
CEIOOPRRTU Puerto Rico
CEIOOPRRTY corporeity
CEIOORRSSV corrosives
CEIOORSSTT scooterist
CEIOORSTTU ecotourist
CEIOOSSTXY exocytosis
CEIOPRRTUV corruptive
CEIOPRRTWY copywriter
CEIORRRSSV Cross River
CEIORRSSSY rescissory
CEIORRSSTT trisectors
CEIORRSTUU couturiers
CEIPPRRSST prescripts
CEIPPRSTTY typescript
CEIPRRSSTU scriptures
CEIRRSSTTU strictures
CEJKOOSTUY outjockeys
CEJOOPRRST projectors
CEKKORSSTY skyrockets
CEKLLLSSUY lucklessly
CEKLMPRSUU lumpsucker
CEKOORRSUW coursework
CEKOORSSTV overstocks
CEKOORSTTU stockroute
CELLLNTUUY luculently
CELLNOORRT controller
CELLNOORSU counsellor
CELLOOOSST closestool
CELLOOPSTY collotypes
CELLOORSSU colourless
CELLORSUUY ulcerously
CELMMOPTUY lumpectomy
CELMNNOOSY somnolency
CELMOOPRSY copolymers
CELMOOPRTT complotter
CELMOORSTY sclerotomy
CELMOORTUY coulometry
CELMOOSSSU colosseums
CELMOPRSUU operculums
CELNOORSSU counselors
CELNOOSTUV convolutes
CELNOPRSUU pronucleus
CELNORSSTU consulters
CELOOPRRTU colporteur
CELOOPRSSU supercools
CELOOSSSSU colossuses
CELOOSTUVY covetously
CELPRSSSTU sculptress
CELPRSSTUU sculptures
CEMMMOOTYY myomectomy
CEMMNNOOSS commonness
CEMNNOOORT Monte Corno
CEMNNOOPST components
CEMNNORTUY countrymen
CEMNOOOQSU monocoques
CEMNOORTUV covermount
CEMOOPRRSS compressor
CEMORRSSWW screwworms
CENNNORRTU noncurrent
CENNOOPRRU pronouncer
CENNOOPRSU pronounces
CENOOPRSST stonecrops
CENOOQRRSU conquerors
CENOORRSST consorters
CENOORRSTV convertors
CENOORRTTV controvert
CENOPRSTUY counterspy
CENORRSSTU construers
CENORSSTXY xenocrysts
CENPRRSTUU puncturers
CEOOPPRRST prospector
CEOOPRRSSS processors
CEOOPRRSST prosectors
CEOOPRRSTT protectors
CEOOPRRSTU prosecutor
CEOOPRRTTY protectory
CEOOPRSSTY sporocytes
CEOORRSSSV crossovers
CEOORSSSTU outcrosses
CEOORSSTUU outsources
CEOPPRSSTU prospectus
CEOPRRRSSU precursors
CEOPRRRSTU corrupters
CEOPRRRSUY precursory
CEOPRRSSSU percussors
CEOPRRSSTU Procrustes
CERRSSTTUU structures
CFFFIISSTU fisticuffs
CFFGIIIORR frigorific
CFFGIINORU coiffuring
CFFGILNOSY scoffingly
CFFORRSSSU crossruffs
CFGIIILNNT inflicting
CFGIIKLNOR frolicking
CFGIIKNOSS fossicking
CFGIIMNNOR confirming
CFGIINORSY scorifying
CFGIKNNORU unfrocking
CFGILOSUUU lucifugous
CFGILOUYZZ fuzzy logic
CFGIMNNOOR conforming
CFGIMNOORT comforting
CFHIKOPRST pitchforks
CFHIMOPRSY scyphiform
CFHKOOOPRS shockproof
CFHLMOOORR chloroform
CFHLOOOSTT footcloths
CFIIILNNOT infliction
CFIIIMNORS incisiform
CFIIINOSTT fictionist
CFIIIOSTTU fictitious
CFIILLLNOU folliculin
CFIILMMORS microfilms
CFIILMOOSU fimicolous
CFIILNORST inflictors
CFIILORSST floristics
CFIINNNOOT nonfiction
CFIIOOPRRT torporific
CFIIOOPRSS soporifics
CFIIRSTTUU futuristic
CFIKLLNOST flintlocks
CFILMMORUU cumuliform
CFIMNOORST conformist
CFIMNOORTY conformity
CFINNOOSSU confusions
CFIOORSUUV fucivorous
CFKOOOSSTT footstocks

CFLLNORSUY scornfully
CFLOOOSSTT coltsfoots
CFLOORSSUU scrofulous
CFNOORRTTU frontcourt
CGGGILNNOU unclogging
CGGHINOOPY hypnogogic
CGGIILLNNY clingingly
CGGIILNNRY cringingly
CGGIINNNOS consigning
CGGILLNOOU colloguing
CGGINNORSU scrounging
CGHHIINNTU unhitching
CGHIIKNPSY physicking
CGHIIKNSTT nightstick
CGHIIKNSTW wickthings
CGHIIKSTTT sticktight
CGHIILLLNY chillingly
CGHIILLNSS schillings
CGHIILLOOT lithologic
CGHIILMORT microlight
CGHIILNTWY witchingly
CGHIILOOST histologic
CGHIILOPST phlogistic
CGHIILPRTY triglyphic
CGHIILRSTW switchgirl
CGHIINNOSU cushioning
CGHIKLNOSY shockingly
CGHILLOORS schoolgirl
CGHILMNOOY hymnologic
CGHILNNOTU unclothing
CGHILNOOPY hypnologic
CGHILNOOSS schoolings
CGHILNOTUY touchingly
CGHILOORTY trichology
CGHIMNOOSZ schmoozing
CGHINOOOPR gonophoric
CGHINOOPRY gynophoric
CGHINOOSYZ schizogony
CGHIOPRSTY copyrights
CGHLNOOORY chronology
CGHLOOPSYY psychology
CGIIIILNSV civilising
CGIIIILNVZ civilizing
CGIIIJNOST jingoistic
CGIIIKNNPT nitpicking
CGIIILNNTY incitingly
CGIIILNOST soliciting
CGIIILNSTU linguistic
CGIIILPSTU pugilistic
CGIIINNSTU cutinising
CGIIINNTUZ cutinizing
CGIIIORRST rigoristic
CGIIJNNNOO conjoining
CGIIKLLNOR rollicking
CGIIKLNRST strickling
CGIIKNNSTU unsticking
CGIILLMNOO limnologic
CGIILNNOOS colonising
CGIILNNOOZ colonizing
CGIILNOORZ colorizing
CGIILNOPRY pyrolignic
CGIILOOSTT isoglottic
CGIIMMNOTT committing
CGIIMMNNORS crimsoning
CGIIMNOPRS comprising
CGIIMNOPSY miscopying
CGIIMNOSST gnosticism
CGIINNNOTU continuing
CGIINNOOST cognitions
incognitos
CGIINNOPRS conspiring
CGIINNORSS incrossing
CGIINNORSU coinsuring
CGIINNORTV contriving
CGIINNOSST consisting
CGIINNRSTU incrusting
CGIINNRTTU tincturing
CGIINORSSS scissoring
CGIINOTTUY contiguity
CGIJNNORSU conjurings
CGIKLOSSTW glowsticks
CGILLNOOPS scolloping
CGILLOSSYY glycolysis
CGILMNPRSU scrumpling
CGILMOOSTY mycologist
CGILMOOSUY musicology
CGILNNOORS longicorns
CGILNNOOVV convolving
CGILNNOPUU uncoupling
CGILNNOSTU consulting
CGILNNOSUV convulsing
CGILNOOOST nostologic
oncologist
CGILNOORSU colourings
CGILOOOPRT tropologic
CGILOOOTXY toxicology
CGILOOPRTT proglottic
CGILOOSTTY cytologist
CGIMNOOPRT comporting
CGIMNOOPST composting
CGINNNORUW uncrowning
CGINNOORSS consignors
CGINNOORST consorting
CGINNOORTT contorting
CGINNOORTU contouring
CGINNORSSU uncrossing
CGINNORSTU construing
CGINNPRTUU puncturing
CGINOOPRRT proctoring
CGINOOPRST prognostic
CGINOOSTUU contiguous
CGINOPRRTU corrupting
CGIOOPRSYZ zygosporic
CGLOOOPRTY proctology
CGLOOPRTYY cryptology
CHHIIOSSTY ichthyosis
CHHIIPSTTW whipstitch
CHHILLRSUY churlishly
CHHILOOPTY holophytic
CHHIMNOOOP homophonic
CHHIMNRTUY unrhythmic
CHHINOOPPS phosphonic
CHHIOOPPRS phosphoric
CHHKLLOOSY hollyhocks
CHHLLOOPRY chlorophyl
CHIIIILNST nihilistic
CHIIILLOPP lipophilic
CHIIILPPPS philippics
CHIIILPSTY syphilitic
CHIIINORST histrionic
CHIIKLLSTY ticklishly
CHIILLQSUY cliquishly
CHIILMNOOT monolithic
CHIILMOOTT lithotomic
CHIILMORST microliths
CHIILNOOPT phonolitic
CHIILOSTTY histolytic
CHIIMOOPRS isomorphic
CHIIMOPRRT trimorphic
CHIIMORRST trichroism
CHIIMORSTU humoristic
CHIIMSSTTY mythicists
CHIINNOPPT pinchpoint
CHIINNOPSU pincushion
CHIINOPSSU cousinship
CHIINORSTU trichinous
CHIIOOOPRT oophoritic
CHIIORSSSU rhoicissus
CHIIPSSSTY physicists
CHIKLMOSST locksmiths
CHIKLOSSTY stockishly
CHIKNOQRTU quickthorn
CHIKOOPSTT toothpicks
CHIKOPSSTW whipstocks
CHILLMOPRY microphyll
CHILLNOOST loincloths
CHILLNOSWY clownishly
CHILMOOSUU humicolous
CHILNOOPPY polyphonic
CHILNOOPXY xylophonic
CHILNOPSSU consulship
CHILOOPTTY photolytic
CHILOSSTTY cystoliths
CHIMNNOOOP monophonic
CHIMNOOSST monostichs
CHIMOOOPRZ zoomorphic
CHIMOOPRSY hypocorism
CHIMOORTTY trichotomy
CHIMPSSTYY symphystic
CHINOOOPTT phototonic
CHINOOPPTY phonotypic
CHINOOPRSY rhinoscopy
CHINOPSSTU countships
CHIOOOPTTX phototoxic
CHIOOORSSU isochroous
CHIOOPPRRY pyrophoric
CHIOOPPTTY phototypic
CHIOOPRSTT orthoptics
CHIOOPTTXY phytotoxic
CHIOPRSSTU courtships
CHIORSTTTW stitchwort
CHLMNOORSU lunchrooms
CHLMNOSUUU homunculus
CHLMOOPRYY polychromy
CHLOOPSTYY hypocotyls
CHLOPPSTYY polyptychs

CHMOORSSTY Chrysostom
CHOOOORSUZ zoochorous
CHORRSSTTU shortcrust
CIIIIKKNNN kinnikinic
CIIIILNTVY incivility
CIIILLMORV microvilli
CIIILLMPTY implicitly
CIIILMNRTU triclinium
CIIILMPSST simplistic
CIIILMPSTY simplicity
CIIILNTUVY uncivility
CIIILPRTTY triplicity
CIIIMNNOST nicotinism
CIIIMNPPRU principium
CIIIMOPSTT optimistic
CIIIMSSTTW witticisms
CIIINNNOTT intinction
CIIINNOSTU unionistic
CIIJNNNOTU injunction
CIIKKNNOPT knickpoint
CIIKNNOPST nickpoints
CIIKNNOSTY cytokinins
CIILLMOOSU limicolous
CIILLNNOST scintillon
CIILLNOOSS collisions
CIILLNOOST cotillions
octillions
CIILLNOOTU illocution
CIILLOSTTY stylolitic
CIILMMNTUU nummulitic
CIILNNOSSU inclusions
CIILNOPSTU punctilios
CIILOOPPRT lipotropic
CIILOORSST solicitors
CIILOOSSTU solicitous
CIILOPPSTU populistic
CIILOPRTVY proclivity
CIILRRSTUY scurrility
CIILSSSTTY stylistics
CIIMMNOOSS commission
CIIMMOPRRS microprism
CIIMNNOOTZ monzonitic
CIIMNOPRRT microprint
CIIMORRSTT tricrotism
CIINNNOOPT conniption
CIINNNOSTU inunctions
CIINNOORTT contrition
CIINNORSSU incursions
CIINNOTTUY continuity
CIINOOPRTX picrotoxin
CIINOPSSSU suspicions
CIIOORSTUV victorious
CIIOPSSSUU suspicious
CIIORSSTTV vorticists
CIIPSTTTYY stypticity
CIJLNNOOTY conjointly
CIKKOOSSUZ Kosciuszko
CIKLORSSTW wristlocks
CIKORRSTUW rusticwork
CILLMOOQUU colloquium
CILLMORSUY collyriums
CILLMOSUUV colluviums
CILLNOOSSU collusions
CILLNOOUVV convolvuli
CILLOOOSTY coyotillos
CILLOOQSTU colloquist
CILLOPRSTU portcullis
CILLOPSTUY Polyclitus
CILLOSSUUY lusciously
CILMNOOOOT locomotion
CILMNOOPSU compulsion
CILMNORUUV involucrum
CILMNOSSTU columnists
CILMOOOPSS cosmopolis
CILNNOOSUV convulsion
CILNOSSTYY cytolysins
CILOOPRSUU rupicolous
CILOORRSTU tricolours
CILOORSSTU colourists
CILORRSSUU scurrilous
CILRSSTTUU culturists
CIMMNNOOSU communions
CIMMNOOOST commotions
CIMMNOSSTU communists
CIMNNOOOPP nincompoop
CIMNNOSTUU continuums
CIMNOORSTU consortium
CIMNOOSTXY mycotoxins
CIMOOOPRST compositor
CINNOOORTT contortion
CINNOOSSTU contusions
CINNOOSTUU continuous
CINOOPRRTU corruption
CINOORSSTY consistory
CINOORSUUV nucivorous
CINOOSTTXY cytotoxins
CINORRSTTU instructor
CINOSTTUUY unctuosity
CIOOPPRTTY prototypic
CIOOPRSSTU uroscopist
CIOOPRSTTT protoctist
CIOOPRSTTU prosciutto
CIOPPRSSTT postscript
CKKNORSTUW knockwurst
CKLLOORRSW scrollwork
CKMNOORSTU moonstruck
CKMOOORSST stockrooms
CKOOORSSTT rootstocks
CLMMNNOOUY uncommonly
CLMOOOORTU oculomotor
CLMOOPRSUY compulsory
CLNOOOPTTY polycotton
CLNOOPRSSU proconsuls
CLNOORSSTU consultors
CLNOSTUUUY unctuously
CLOOOPRRTU prolocutor
CLOPRSSUUU scrupulous
CMNOOOOSTU monotocous
CMNOOORSST cosmotrons
CMOOORRSTU courtrooms
COOPRRRSTU corruptors
COOPRSSSTY sporocysts
DDDEEEFNNU undefended
DDDEEFIOST eisteddfod
DDDEEIIOSX deoxidised
DDDEEIIOXZ deoxidized
DDDEEINOSW disendowed
DDDEEIOORS deodorised
DDDEEIOORZ deodorized
DDDEEIORRS disordered
DDDEFILOOW fiddlewood
DDDEFMNOUU dumfounded
DDDEGIIOOR didgeridoo
DDEEEEELTW tweedledee
DDEEEEGNNR engendered
DDEEEEMNRU unredeemed
DDEEEFFNOR forefended
DDEEEFLORW deflowered
DDEEEFNRSU underfeeds
DDEEEFORST deforested
DDEEEGINRS redesigned
DDEEEGIRST redigested
DDEEEHHPRS shepherded
DDEEEHILSV disheveled
DDEEEHLNUY unheededly
DDEEEHNOWY honeydewed
DDEEEIMNOR domineered
DDEEEIMNRT determined
DDEEEIMNRU unremedied
DDEEEINRST tenderised
DDEEEINRTZ tenderized
DDEEEIRSSV dissevered
DDEEEIRSTU deuterides
DDEEELLMOR remodelled
DDEEELMMOS meddlesome
DDEEELMNTY dementedly
DDEEELMOPR empoldered
DDEEELNTXY extendedly
DDEEELOPRY redeployed
DDEEELRSVY deservedly
DDEEENNPST dependents
DDEEENNRRU unrendered
DDEEENNTUX unextended
DDEEENRRTU undeterred
DDEEENRSUV undeserved
DDEEENRSUX undersexed
DDEEEORRST ordered set
DDEEEORSTV stevedored
DDEEEPRSSU superseded
DDEEFFNNOU unoffended
DDEEFGJORU forejudged
DDEEFIIINT identified
DDEEFIIMNS misdefined
DDEEFIIMOR remodified
DDEEFIINRT trendified
DDEEFIINTU definitude
DDEEFIIOTX detoxified
DDEEFIMORS semifreddo
DDEEFINNRU unfriended
DDEEFLMORY deformedly
DDEEFLNORU floundered
DDEEFMOOOR foredoomed
DDEEGGHOOP hodgepodge
DDEEGGIRSU ruggedised
DDEEGGIRUZ ruggedized
DDEEGGNOSS doggedness

DDEEGIINNX deindexing
DDEEGIINST indigested
DDEEGILNSY designedly
DDEEGINNSU undesigned
DDEEGINSTU undigested
DDEEGIRRSU drudgeries
DDEEHIINST hiddenites
DDEEHILMOS demolished
DDEEHILNSU unshielded
DDEEHIMOST methodised
DDEEHIMOTZ methodized
DDEEHINNRU unhindered
DDEEHINNSS hiddenness
DDEEHLORSU shouldered
DDEEHNORSU deerhounds
enshrouded
DDEEIILNPV vilipended
DDEEIIMOPR epidermoid
DDEEIINRSW sidewinder
DDEEIIORSX deoxidiser
DDEEIIORXZ deoxidizer
DDEEIIOSSX deoxidises
DDEEIIOSXZ deoxidizes
DDEEIIPPST dipeptides
DDEEIIPSSW sideswiped
DDEEIIQSTU disquieted
DDEEILMMRT middle term
DDEEILMOPR impoldered
DDEEILMSTW Middle West
DDEEILNNRU underlined
DDEEIMNNRU undermined
DDEEIMNORS endodermis
modernised
DDEEIMNORZ modernized
DDEEINNNTU unintended
DDEEINNRTU indentured
DDEEINORRV overridden
DDEEINORSW disendower
eiderdowns
DDEEINRSST distenders
DDEEINRSSU undersides
DDEEINRSUZ undersized
DDEEIOORRS deodoriser
DDEEIOORRZ deodorizer
DDEEIOORSS deodorises
DDEEIOORSZ deodorizes
DDEEIRSSST distressed
DDEEIRSSSU druidesses
DDEELMMNTU muddlement
DDEELMORSU smouldered
DDEELRRSSU rudderless
DDEENNOPST despondent
DDEENNOSSS soddenness
DDEENNPRSU underspend
DDEENNSSSU suddenness
DDEFFLNORU Ludendorff
DDEFGIIIIR rigidified
DDEFGIIRSU disfigured
DDEFHIIIMU humidified
DDEFHIIMUY dehumidify
DDEFHLNORU fundholder
DDEFIIILOS solidified
DDEFIIMNOU unmodified
DDEFIMNORR dendriform
DDEFINRSUW windsurfed
DDEFLORSSU Düsseldorf
DDEGHINRSU shuddering
DDEGHIORRU roughdried
DDEGIIINRV redividing
DDEGIILNRY deridingly
DDEGIINNPS dispending
DDEGIINNRS nidderings
DDEGIINNST distending
DDEGILLMNY meddlingly
DDEGILLNUY deludingly
DDEGINNOOS desnooding
DDEGINNOPS desponding
DDEGINNORU redounding
underdoing
DDEGINRRSU undergirds
DDEGLNOORS goldenrods
DDEGLNOORY dendrology
DDEGNNORUU ungrounded
DDEHHNRSTU hundredths
DDEHIIIMNS diminished
DDEHIILNSW windshield
DDEHIILPSU disulphide
DDEHIKNOOW hoodwinked
DDEHINOORS dishonored
DDEHINOSSS shoddiness
DDEHIOOOPT photodiode
DDEHIORRRT Third Order
DDEHIORSXY hydroxides
DDEHLNOSTU Huddleston
DDEHLORSYY hydrolysed
DDEHLORYYZ hydrolyzed
DDEIIILQSU liquidised
DDEIIILQUZ liquidized
DDEIIIMPSY epididymis
DDEIIIPRST dispirited
DDEIIIQSTU quiddities
DDEIIJNOST disjointed
DDEIIKOSSV videodisks
DDEIILLMNW windmilled
DDEIIMNNOU diminuendo
DDEIINOPSS indisposed
DDEIINOSTU duodenitis
DDEIINOUVZ zidovudine
DDEIINSSST dissidents
DDEIIOPRSS dispersoid
DDEIKNNRUW wunderkind
DDEILLNPSY splendidly
DDEILLOPSY lopsidedly
DDEILMMOST middlemost
DDEILNRRSU unriddlers
DDEILOOPSS podsolised
DDEILOOPSZ podsolized
podzolised
DDEILOOPZZ podzolized
DDEILORRSY disorderly
DDEIMNOSTU dismounted
DDEINOPRUV unprovided
DDEINOPSSU undisposed
DDEINORSSS sordidness
DDEINPSTUU undisputed
DDEIRSSTTU distrusted
DDELMOOTUY outmodedly
DDELNORRUW underworld
DDENOOPPRU propounded
DDENOOPRSS dropsondes
DDENOORSTU understood
DDENORRSUU surrounded
DDENRSTUUY understudy
DDEOPRRSTU rudderpost
DDGGIILNOS dislodging
DDGGILNRUY drudgingly
DDGGINOOTU outdodging
DDGIILLMNY middlingly
DDGIILLNPY piddlingly
DDGIILNNRU unriddling
DDGIILNOPS disploding
DDGILLMNUY muddlingly
DDGILLNOPY ploddingly
DDHINOOPTY diphyodont
DDIIKLNTWY tiddlywink
DDINOOOPRT diprotodon
DDINOPPRTY Pontypridd
DEEEEEFPRZ deepfreeze
DEEEEFLNRS Senefelder
DEEEEFNRTT tenderfeet
DEEEEGINNR engineered
DEEEEGLRSS degreeless
DEEEEGNNRR engenderer
DEEEEKNRSW weekenders
DEEEELMNVY Mendeleyev
DEEEEMNNPU Peenemünde
DEEEEMNNTT tenemented
DEEEEPRRSV persevered
DEEEFGILNR greenfield
DEEEFHIIRT etherified
DEEEFHILNS needlefish
DEEEFHLORR freeholder
DEEEFIILMR demirelief
DEEEFIIRRV reverified
DEEEFIIRST esterified
DEEEFILMNT defilement
DEEEFILRRT refiltered
DEEEFIMRSW swimfeeder
DEEEFINRRT interfered
DEEEFINRTW winterfeed
DEEEFLLNSU needlefuls
DEEEFLORRW deflowerer
reflowered
DEEEFMNRRU referendum
DEEEFMNRST deferments
DEEEFNQRTU frequented
DEEEFNRTTU unfettered
DEEEFORRST deforester
reforested
DEEEGHHINT heightened
DEEEGHLNNT lengthened
DEEEGIIMRV demivierge
DEEEGIKNNW weekending
DEEEGILNRS legendries
DEEEGILOVW Vogelweide
DEEEGIMNRT regimented

DEEEGINRSS greediness
DEEEGIRRST deregister
registered
ridgetrees
DEEEGLNOSY goldeneyes
DEEEGLNRSS genderless
DEEEGMNNOR mondegreen
DEEEGNRSTT detergents
DEEEHIILRT Ethelred II
DEEEHIIRST heredities
DEEEHILLNS hellenised
DEEEHILLNZ hellenized
DEEEHILNTY diethylene
DEEEHILSSW sidewheels
DEEEHIMPRS ephemerids
DEEEHIMPSU euphemised
DEEEHIMPUZ euphemized
DEEEHIPRSS Hesperides
DEEEHKNNOS keeshonden
DEEEHLLSSY heedlessly
DEEEHLNOPT telephoned
DEEEHLNORS lederhosen
DEEEHNORTY heterodyne
DEEEHNPRRS reprehends
DEEEHNRRTU thereunder
DEEEHNRTTU untethered
DEEEIILRSV deliveries
DEEEIIMNPR meperidine
DEEEIKLLRW weedkiller
DEEEILLMOS demoiselle
DEEEILLMPS millepedes
DEEEILMRSS remediless
DEEEILNNST sentineled
DEEEILNPRV replevined
DEEEILNRSS slenderise
DEEEILNRSZ slenderize
DEEEILNRUV unrelieved
DEEEILRRSV deliverers
redelivers
DEEEILRRVY redelivery
DEEEILRSSW wirelessed
DEEEILRSVW silverweed
DEEEIMMRSS mesmerised
DEEEIMMRSZ mesmerized
DEEEIMNOST demonetise
DEEEIMNOTZ demonetize
DEEEIMNRRT determiner
DEEEIMNRRW Windermere
DEEEIMNRST densimeter
determines
DEEEIMORTU eudiometer
DEEEIMPRTV redemptive
DEEEIMRSSY Merseyside
DEEEIMSSST disesteems
DEEEINNPTV pendentive
DEEEINNRTV intervened
reinvented
DEEEINORRT reoriented
DEEEINPRST predestine
DEEEINPSSS speediness
DEEEINPSTX expedients
DEEEINRRRT reinterred

DEEEINRRST reinserted
tenderiser
DEEEINRRTZ tenderizer
DEEEINRSST tenderises
DEEEINRSTT interested
DEEEINRSTZ tenderizes
DEEEINSSTW tweediness
DEEEIPPQRU reequipped
DEEEIPRSSV depressive
DEEEIPRSTX expediters
expertised
preexisted
DEEEIPRTXZ expertized
DEEEIRSSTT sidestreet
DEEEKLNNNU unkenneled
DEEEKLNORW needlework
DEEEKOOPRR doorkeeper
DEEELLNSSY needlessly
DEEELLOWWY yellowweed
DEEELLPSSW speedwells
DEEELMOPRY reemployed
DEEELNOOTV Deo volente
DEEELNORSS nesselrode
DEEELNRTTU unlettered
DEEELOPRSV developers
redevelops
DEEELOPRTT teleported
DEEELRRSVY reservedly
DEEEMNNOTT denotement
DEEEMNNOTU denouement
DEEEMNNOYZ endoenzyme
DEEEMNOTTV devotement
DEEEMNPRTU untempered
DEEEMNRSSU demureness
DEEEMNRSTT determents
DEEEMNRSUW Wesermünde
DEEEMNSTTV vestmented
DEEEMOORST oedometers
DEEEMOPRST pedometers
DEEEMORSST dosemeters
DEEENNRSST tenderness
DEEENNRSSU enuredness
DEEENOOSWZ sneezewood
DEEENORTVX overextend
DEEENPPPRU unpeppered
DEEENPRRST pretenders
DEEENPRSSU superdense
DEEENPRSUV supervened
DEEENRRSTT deterrents
DEEENRRSTU understeer
DEEENRRSUV unreserved
DEEEOPRRTX reexported
DEEEORRRRT reredorter
DEEEORSSTV stevedores
DEEEPRRSSU superseder
DEEEPRSSST speedsters
DEEEPRSSSU supersedes
DEEEPRSSUW superweeds
DEEERRRSSS redressers
DEEERRSUVY resurveyed
DEEERSSUVX Deux-Sèvres
DEEFFFKLRU kerfuffled

DEEFFHLRSU reshuffled
DEEFGGILLN fledgeling
DEEFGHINRT frightened
DEEFGIINNR redefining
DEEFGINSST giftedness
DEEFGIPRRU prefigured
DEEFGJORSU forejudges
DEEFHIILTW Whitefield
DEEFHIINRS refinished
DEEFHIORSV overfished
DEEFHLOPSS sheepfolds
DEEFHOORSW foreshowed
DEEFIIILST fidelities
DEEFIIINNP nifedipine
DEEFIIINNT indefinite
DEEFIIINRT identifier
DEEFIIINST identifies
DEEFIIINTV definitive
DEEFIIIRVV revivified
DEEFIILLST stellified
DEEFIILMNS minefields
DEEFIILMSU emulsified
DEEFIILNRR friendlier
DEEFIILNRS friendlies
infielders
DEEFIILNRT interfiled
DEEFIILNTY definitely
DEEFIILRST fertilised
DEEFIILRTZ fertilized
DEEFIIMNSS misdefines
DEEFIIMORS remodifies
DEEFIINORT renotified
DEEFIINRST trendifies
DEEFIINRUV unverified
DEEFIINRVW viewfinder
DEEFIIOSTX detoxifies
DEEFIIPRRU repurified
DEEFIIPRTT prettified
DEEFILLORV overfilled
DEEFILLRSU fullerides
DEEFILMOSU fieldmouse
DEEFILNOST fieldstone
DEEFILNOSX deflexions
DEEFILNRSS friendless
DEEFILNRTU unfiltered
DEEFILNRYZ frenziedly
DEEFILORTU outfielder
DEEFILPSTU despiteful
DEEFIMNORR reinformed
DEEFIMORSU furosemide
DEEFINORRX ferredoxin
DEEFINOSST foetidness
DEEFINRSSV fervidness
DEEFINRSTU interfused
DEEFKNORSS forkedness
DEEFLLMORW well-formed
DEEFLMNNOT enfoldment
DEEFLNRSTU underfelts
DEEFLOORVW overflowed
DEEFNOORTT tenderfoot
DEEFNORSTU unforested
DEEFOORSTU surefooted

DEEFORRSST defrosters
fortressed
DEEFPRSSUU superfused
DEEGGILOOS geologised
DEEGGILOOZ geologized
DEEGGIRSSU ruggedises
DEEGGIRSUZ ruggedizes
DEEGGLRSSU grudgeless
DEEGGNRSSU ruggedness
DEEGHHORUW roughhewed
DEEGHIJNNZ Jingdezhen
DEEGHILRST delighters
DEEGHINOPS diphosgene
DEEGHINOUY honeyguide
DEEGHINSTU gesundheit
DEEGHIOSTT ghettoised
DEEGHIOTTZ ghettoized
DEEGHIOTUW outweighed
DEEGIILNRV delivering
DEEGIILNSU guidelines
DEEGIILOOS ideologies
DEEGIILPRV privileged
DEEGIINNRT ingredient
DEEGIINNRW rewidening
DEEGIINPTX expediting
DEEGIINRRS grinderies
DEEGIIRSSV digressive
DEEGIISSTV digestives
DEEGILNOOS neologised
DEEGILNOOZ neologized
DEEGILNOPV developing
DEEGILNRSY resignedly
DEEGILOOSU ideologues
DEEGILOPRS ridgepoles
DEEGILRSTY greylisted
DEEGIMORST geometrids
DEEGINNORW reendowing
DEEGINNPPR perpending
DEEGINNPRT pretending
DEEGINNRRS renderings
DEEGINORRR reordering
DEEGINORSS degression
DEEGINORST redingotes
DEEGINORVY overdyeing
DEEGINOSXY oxygenised
DEEGINOXYZ oxygenized
DEEGINPRSS depressing
predesigns
DEEGINRRRS derringers
DEEGINRRSS redressing
DEEGINRSUV gerundives
DEEGIOSSST geodesists
DEEGIPRSST predigests
DEEGIRRSSS digressers
DEEGJMNSTU judgements
DEEGJPRRSU prejudgers
DEEGLLNORU golden rule
DEEGLMNOST lodgements
DEEGLMSSSU smudgeless
DEEGLNNOSS goldenness
DEEGLOOOPP good people
DEEGNNOOSU endogenous
DEEGNNORUV ungoverned
DEEGNOORSW greenwoods
DEEGNORRSU guerdoners
undergoers
DEEGOPRRSS progressed
DEEGORRTXY dextrogyre
DEEGOSSTUU outguessed
DEEHHIILMS Hildesheim
DEEHHIORSS horsehides
DEEHHOORSS horseshoed
DEEHIIKLLS shieldlike
DEEHIINPRS hesperidin
DEEHIIRSTT hereditist
DEEHILLRSV helldivers
shrivelled
DEEHILMORS demolisher
DEEHILMOSS demolishes
DEEHILOOTT theodolite
DEEHILOPPS pedophiles
DEEHILOPRS repolished
DEEHILORSU hierodules
DEEHILPRSS elderships
DEEHIMORST methodiser
DEEHIMORTZ methodizer
DEEHIMOSST methodises
DEEHIMOSTX methoxides
DEEHIMOSTZ methodizes
DEEHINOOPV videophone
DEEHINOPSU euphonised
DEEHINOPSX phenoxides
DEEHINOPUZ euphonized
DEEHINORST dinotheres
threnodies
DEEHINORSV Devonshire
DEEHINRSSW swineherds
DEEHINRTUW unwithered
DEEHIOPPRS prophesied
DEEHIORSTV Shrovetide
DEEHKNOOSS hookedness
DEEHLLMOPR phelloderm
DEEHLMNRUW underwhelm
DEEHLNOSUU unhouseled
DEEHMNOOST smoothened
DEEHMOORST hodometers
DEEHMORRTY hydrometer
DEEHNNORSS hornedness
DEEHNOORTT heterodont
DEEHNOPSTY endophytes
DEEHNORRST dethroners
DEEHNRRSTU thunderers
DEEHNRSSSW shrewdness
DEEHOORTXY heterodoxy
DEEHOPRSST hotpressed
DEEHORRSSY hydroseres
DEEHSSSTTU dustsheets
DEEIIIMNSV semidivine
DEEIIINPPR piperidine
DEEIIINSTT identities
DEEIIKKLNY kidneylike
DEEIIKLNRW Winkelried
DEEIILLMPR imperilled
DEEIILLMPS millipedes
DEEIILLOPT lepidolite
DEEIILNNRT interlined
DEEIILNNVY vinylidene
DEEIILNPRV vilipender
DEEIILNSTT disentitle
DEEIILOPPT epileptoid
DEEIILORSS soldieries
DEEIILORST siderolite
DEEIILRSST sterilised
DEEIILRSSV silverside
DEEIILRSTV deviltries
DEEIILRSTZ sterilized
DEEIILRSVY derisively
DEEIILRTUZ reutilized
DEEIIMMNPT impediment
DEEIIMNNTT inditement
DEEIIMNRST ministered
DEEIIMNRTX intermixed
DEEIIMNSTT midinettes
DEEIIMOPST epitomised
DEEIIMOPTZ epitomized
DEEIIMORSS isomerised
DEEIIMORSZ isomerized
DEEIINNOSV envisioned
DEEIINNRTT Tridentine
DEEIINNSSV divineness
DEEIINNSTW disentwine
DEEIINOPTT petitioned
DEEIINOPTX expedition
DEEIINPTTU ineptitude
DEEIINQTUU inquietude
DEEIINRSTW winterised
DEEIINRTTW wintertide
DEEIINRTWZ winterized
DEEIINSSST sensitised
DEEIINSSTW West Indies
DEEIINSSTZ sensitized
DEEIIOPQSU equipoised
DEEIIOPRTT peridotite
DEEIIOSSTV sovietised
DEEIIOSTVZ sovietized
DEEIIPRSSV dispersive
DEEIIPRSSW sideswiper
DEEIIPSSSW sideswipes
DEEIJMNOSW jimsonweed
DEEIJNORRS rejoinders
DEEIJNOSTT jettisoned
DEEIKLNNRS enkindlers
DEEIKNNRSU Iskenderun
DEEIKNNSSS kindnesses
DEEIKORSST sidestroke
DEEILLMPSS misspelled
DEEILLNRSW indwellers
DEEILLORRS drolleries
DEEILLPRSS dispellers
DEEILLRRSV drivellers
DEEILLRSTU tellurides
tellurised
DEEILLRTUZ tellurized
DEEILLSUVY delusively
DEEILMNOSS solemnised
DEEILMNOSZ solemnized

DEEILMNRTW	wilderment
DEEILMNSTV	devilments
DEEILMORSS	melodisers
DEEILMORSZ	melodizers
DEEILMOSTV	demivoltes
DEEILMPSTU	multipedes
DEEILNNNRU	underlinen
DEEILNNORT	tenderloin
DEEILNNQTU	delinquent
DEEILNNRSU	underlines
DEEILNOPST	depletions
DEEILNORVV	reinvolved
DEEILNPRST	splintered
DEEILNRRSU	underliers
DEEILNRSSW	wilderness
DEEILNRSTU	interludes
DEEILOPRSS	despoilers
DEEILORSSV	redissolve
DEEILOSTTT	stilettoed
DEEILPPRSU	resupplied
DEEILPRSUV	pulverised
DEEILPRUVZ	pulverized
DEEILQRRSU	squirreled
DEEILRRSSV	driverless
DEEIMMNOSU	eudemonism
DEEIMNNNTT	intendment
DEEIMNNRRU	underminer
DEEIMNNRSU	undermines
DEEIMNNSTZ	dizenments
DEEIMNOOPS	empoisoned
DEEIMNOOTV	Montevideo
DEEIMNOPRT	redemption
DEEIMNOPTT	idempotent
DEEIMNORRS	moderniser
DEEIMNORRZ	modernizer
DEEIMNORSS	modernises
	sermonised
DEEIMNORSZ	modernizes
	sermonized
DEEIMNORTV	Monteverdi
DEEIMNOSTU	eudemonist
DEEIMNPRSS	misspender
DEEIMNRSTW	Midwestern
	stemwinder
DEEIMNRSTY	densimetry
DEEIMNRTTU	unremitted
DEEIMNSTTV	divestment
DEEIMOORST	meteoroids
DEEIMOPRRT	reimported
DEEIMOPRST	temporised
DEEIMOPRSW	disempower
DEEIMOPRTZ	temporized
DEEIMORSST	dosimeters
DEEIMORTUY	eudiometry
DEEIMPRSST	distempers
DEEIMRSTUW	Tweedsmuir
DEEIMSSSTY	systemised
DEEIMSSTYZ	systemized
DEEINNNOSU	innuendoes
DEEINNOPRS	prednisone
DEEINNORST	internodes
DEEINNOSTT	detentions
DEEINNRSST	trendiness
DEEINNRSSU	inuredness
DEEINNRSTU	indentures
DEEINNSSTU	unitedness
DEEINNSTUV	uninvested
DEEINOPPST	peptonised
DEEINOPPTZ	peptonized
DEEINOPRSS	depression
DEEINOPRST	interposed
DEEINOPSTX	pentoxides
DEEINOQSTU	questioned
DEEINORRVV	overdriven
DEEINORSST	desertions
DEEINORSSW	rosinweeds
DEEINORSUV	souvenired
DEEINOTTUZ	teutonized
DEEINPPQUU	unequipped
DEEINPRRST	rinderpest
DEEINPRSSS	dispensers
DEEINPRSST	presidents
DEEINQRTUU	unrequited
DEEINRRTUW	underwrite
DEEINRSSSS	dressiness
DEEINRSSST	dissenters
DEEINRSSTU	unresisted
DEEINSSTTU	testudines
DEEINSTTTV	vendettist
DEEIOPPRRT	propertied
DEEIOPPRSS	predispose
DEEIOPPRST	predeposit
DEEIOPRSST	redeposits
DEEIOPRSTX	expeditors
DEEIOPRSUX	superoxide
DEEIOPRTTU	pirouetted
DEEIOPSSTU	despiteous
DEEIORRRST	terrorised
DEEIORRRSV	overriders
DEEIORRRTZ	terrorized
DEEIORRSTV	overstride
DEEIORRSVV	overdrives
DEEIORSSUV	overissued
DEEIORSTTX	tetroxides
DEEIPRRSSS	dispersers
DEEIPRRTUY	eurypterid
DEEIPRSSUV	supervised
DEEIRSSSST	distresses
DEEIRSSTUV	divestures
DEEKKNSSUW	skunkweeds
DEEKLLNORS	snorkelled
DEEKLMRTTU	kettledrum
DEEKLNOSSV	veldskoens
DEEKLOOORV	overlooked
DEEKOORRVW	overworked
DEELLNORTY	redolently
DEELLNRSSU	undersells
DEELLORSVY	resolvedly
DEELMNOPTY	deployment
DEELMNOPUY	unemployed
DEELMNOSTU	unmolested
DEELMOORSV	velodromes
DEELMOPRSU	supermodel
DEELMPRSUY	presumedly
DEELNNOOST	selenodont
DEELNNOOSU	unloosened
DEELNOOSST	lodestones
DEELNOPRUX	unexplored
DEELNORSSW	wonderless
DEELNORSUV	unresolved
DEELNOSTUU	edentulous
DEELNPRRSU	plunderers
DEELOPRRTY	reportedly
DEELOPRSTY	proselyted
DEELORTTUV	turtledove
DEELPRSTTU	spluttered
DEEMMNORSU	resummoned
DEEMMOOSSS	desmosomes
DEEMNNORSS	modernness
DEEMNNORTW	wonderment
DEEMNNOSTW	endowments
DEEMNOPRTT	deportment
DEEMNORSTU	tremendous
DEEMOORRST	drosometer
DEEMOORSTV	overmodest
DEEMOPRRTY	redemptory
DEENNOOSSW	woodenness
DEENNOPRST	respondent
DEENNORSTU	undertones
DEENNPRSTU	underspent
DEENNRRTUU	unreturned
DEENOOPRSS	endospores
DEENOOSSST	endostoses
DEENOPRRSS	responders
DEENOPRRTU	unreported
DEENOPRRUV	unreproved
DEENOPRSSV	overspends
DEENOPRSUX	expounders
DEENOQRTUU	underquote
DEENORRTUV	overturned
DEENORRTUW	underwrote
DEENORSSSU	rousedness
DEENORSUVZ	rendezvous
DEENOSSTUV	devoutness
DEENPRSSSU	suspenders
DEENRRRSSU	surrenders
DEENRSSSSU	sundresses
DEENRSSSTU	unstressed
DEENRSSTUV	undervests
DEEOOPPRTV	overtopped
DEEOOPRRSU	uredospore
DEEOORRSTV	overstrode
DEEOPPRSSU	superposed
DEEOPPSTTU	outstepped
DEEOPRRRSU	superorder
DEEOPRRSSS	depressors
DEEOPSSTTU	poussetted
DEEORRRSSS	redressors
DEEORRSSTY	destroyers
DEEPPRSSSU	suppressed
DEFFFKLRUU	kurfuffled
DEFFGINNOR	forfending
DEFFHIMORS	sheriffdom
DEFFINOPRT	offprinted
DEFGGILLNS	fledglings
DEFGHILLTU	delightful

DEFGHILOSS goldfishes
DEFGHLORUU furloughed
DEFGHOOOSU house of God
DEFGIIIIRS rigidifies
DEFGIILNRR girlfriend
DEFGIILNYY edifyingly
DEFGIINNUY unedifying
DEFGIINRSS frigidness
DEFGIIRRSU disfigurer
DEFGIIRSSU disfigures
DEFGILNOOR reflooding
DEFGILOOSS Isle of Dogs
DEFGINNORU foundering
DEFGINORST defrosting
DEFGNOORRU foreground
DEFHIIIMRU humidifier
DEFHIIIMSU humidifies
DEFHIILNSY fiendishly
DEFHIINNSU unfinished
DEFHIINPRS friendship
DEFHILORSU flourished
DEFHIMRSSU drumfishes
DEFHLOOOSW wholefoods
DEFHORRRTU rutherford
DEFIIILMPS simplified
DEFIIILNTY infidelity
DEFIIILORS solidifier
DEFIIILOSS solidifies
DEFIIINNOT definition
DEFIIINNTU infinitude
DEFIILLNRY friendlily
DEFIILMSSU semifluids
DEFIILOSSS fossilised
DEFIILOSSZ fossilized
DEFIILRSSU fluidisers
DEFIILRSUZ fluidizers
DEFIILSTTU stultified
DEFIINOOPS opsonified
DEFIINPRUU unpurified
DEFIINSSST disinfests
DEFIIOPRSU perfidious
DEFIKLORSW fieldworks
DEFILLORWW wildflower
wildfowler
DEFILLPRUY pridefully
DEFILMNNOT infoldment
DEFILMNORY informedly
DEFILNNRUY unfriendly
DEFILNORSS floridness
DEFILNORST interfolds
DEFILNORWW windflower
DEFILNOSSW snowfields
DEFILPRSUU superfluid
DEFIMNNORU uninformed
DEFINNORZZ Zinzendorf
DEFINRRSUW windsurfer
DEFIORRRST first-order
DEFIORSSST disforests
DEFLNOORRU underfloor
DEFLNOORTU unforetold
DEFLNORSUW underflows
DEFNOOPRRU underproof
DEFNORRUUW unfurrowed
DEFOORTTTX foxtrotted
DEGGGGILNO doglegging
DEGGGINNOU gudgeoning
DEGGHIILNT delighting
DEGGIILNRS ridgelings
DEGGIINRSS digressing
DEGGIJNPRU prejudging
DEGGINNORU guerdoning
undergoing
DEGGIORRSS disgorgers
DEGGMNOOOR Demogorgon
DEGHIILSST sidelights
DEGHIINRRT nightrider
DEGHIIRSTZ rightsized
DEGHIJPSSU judgeships
DEGHILMSSU gumshields
DEGHIMNRSU humdingers
DEGHINNORT dethroning
DEGHINNRTU thundering
DEGHINRSST nightdress
DEGHIORRRU roughrider
DEGHIORRSU roughdries
DEGHIOSTTU doughtiest
DEGHLNNOOR Golden Horn
DEGHLNOPUU unploughed
DEGHMOORST godmothers
DEGHNNOSTU shotgunned
DEGHNOORSU gorehounds
DEGHNORSUY greyhounds
DEGHOOOPRW gopher wood
gopherwood
DEGIIILMNT delimiting
DEGIIILNNS sidelining
DEGIIILNOT indigolite
DEGIIIMNRS dimerising
DEGIIIMNRZ dimerizing
DEGIIINNOZ deionizing
DEGIIINNTY indigenity
DEGIIINSSS disseising
DEGIIINSSZ disseizing
DEGIIIRSST digitisers
DEGIIIRSTZ digitizers
DEGIIKLLNS deskilling
DEGIIKLNNN enkindling
DEGIIKLNNR rekindling
DEGIILLNNW indwelling
DEGIILLNPS dispelling
DEGIILLNRR redrilling
DEGIILLNRV drivelling
DEGIILLNTY diligently
DEGIILLNYY yieldingly
DEGIILMNOS melodising
DEGIILMNOZ melodizing
DEGIILMNPY impedingly
DEGIILNNTY indigently
DEGIILNNUY unyielding
DEGIILNOPS despoiling
DEGIILNORS soldiering
DEGIILNOSV evildoings
DEGIILOOST ideologist
DEGIIMNNOS demonising
DEGIIMNNOZ demonizing
DEGIIMRSSU misguiders
DEGIINNORT dinitrogen
DEGIINNOSU indigenous
DEGIINNOSV nosediving
DEGIINNPSS dispensing
DEGIINNSST dissenting
DEGIINOPRX peroxiding
DEGIINOPST depositing
DEGIINORRV overriding
DEGIINORSS digression
DEGIINPRSS dispersing
DEGIINPRST springtide
DEGIINPSTU deputising
DEGIINPTUZ deputizing
DEGIINRSSV disserving
DEGIINRSTU nigritudes
DEGIINRSTW West Riding
DEGIIQSSTU squidgiest
DEGIIRSSSU disguisers
DEGIJMRSSU misjudgers
DEGILLOOTY deltiology
DEGILLOSSY syllogised
DEGILLOSYZ syllogized
DEGILMNORS goldminers
smoldering
DEGILMNORU mouldering
remoulding
DEGILMNOSW gildswomen
DEGILMNRSU mudslinger
DEGILNNPRU plundering
DEGILNNRSU underlings
DEGILNNRUY enduringly
underlying
DEGILNOORS gondoliers
DEGILNOOSS goodliness
DEGILNOSTU longitudes
ungodliest
DEGILNRSTU disgruntle
DEGILOOOSX doxologies
DEGILOOPST pedologist
DEGIMNNOTU demounting
DEGIMNOOPR predooming
DEGIMNSSSU smudginess
DEGINNOPPR propending
DEGINNOPRS responding
DEGINNOPRT portending
DEGINNOPUX expounding
DEGINNORST grindstone
stringendo
DEGINNORSU resounding
DEGINNPSSU suspending
DEGINNRSSU undressing
DEGINNRSUW underwings
DEGINOOOPW woodpigeon
DEGINOOPRT torpedoing
DEGINOORSV overdosing
DEGINOPSST signposted
DEGINORSTY destroying
DEGINOSSST stodginess
DEGINRSSTU turgidness
DEGIOPSSTU guideposts

DEGLMNOOOY	demonology
DEGLNNRSUU	underslung
DEGLNOOOTY	deontology
DEGLNORSSU	groundless
	groundsels
DEGLOORTTY	troglodyte
DEGMNNORSU	groundsmen
DEGNNORRUW	undergrown
DEGNOORRSW	wrongdoers
DEGNOORRUV	overground
DEGNOORRUZ	ground zero
DEGNOOSSTT	stegodonts
DEGNOPRSUW	gunpowders
DEGNOPRUWY	gunpowdery
DEGNOPSTUU	Puget Sound
DEGOOORSUW	woodgrouse
DEGORRSSTU	drugstores
DEHHIKMOSS	sheikhdoms
DEHHILOPRS	holdership
DEHHILOPRY	hydrophile
DEHHILORTW	withholder
DEHHIOPPSS	phosphides
DEHHLLNOSU	hellhounds
DEHHLOOSSU	households
DEHHLORSST	thresholds
DEHHMOOORT	motherhood
DEHHNOOPRY	hydrophone
DEHHNOORSU	horehounds
DEHHOPRTYY	hydrophyte
DEHIIIMNSS	diminishes
	minidishes
DEHIIINOTT	dithionite
DEHIIINRST	disinherit
DEHIIKLLOO	likelihood
DEHIIKMRSS	skirmished
DEHIILLOOV	livelihood
DEHIILLSVY	devilishly
DEHIILMNPU	delphinium
DEHIIMMNPS	midshipmen
DEHIIMNOPR	prehominid
DEHIIMNPRU	nephridium
DEHIINOOPS	idiophones
DEHIIOPRST	editorship
DEHIKNOORW	hoodwinker
DEHIKNRSZZ	Dzerzhinsk
DEHILNNOOP	indophenol
DEHILNOPSU	unpolished
DEHILOOPSS	shopsoiled
DEHILOPPRY	hyperploid
DEHILOSSTW	dishtowels
DEHIMMPSSY	dysphemism
DEHIMNORST	hindermost
DEHIMNOSSS	modishness
DEHIMOOPPR	hippodrome
DEHIMOPRSY	hypodermis
DEHIMOSSTT	methodists
DEHINNOPRS	endorphins
DEHINNPSUU	unpunished
DEHINOORRS	dishonorer
DEHINOPSTY	hypnotised
DEHINOPTYZ	hypnotized
DEHINORRSS	horridness
DEHINORRST	trihedrons
DEHINORSTT	threnodist
DEHINORSVW	windhovers
DEHINOSSTY	dishonesty
DEHINRRSTU	undershirt
DEHIOOOPRR	odoriphore
DEHIOOPRST	priesthood
DEHIOORSST	sisterhood
DEHIOOSTWW	whitewoods
DEHIOPPRSW	worshipped
DEHIOPRRTY	pyrethroid
DEHIRRSSST	shirtdress
DEHKLOOSST	stokeholds
DEHLNOOPRY	polyhedron
DEHLNOOSTY	holystoned
DEHLOORRSY	holy orders
DEHLOORRTW	otherworld
DEHLORRSYY	hydrolyser
DEHLORRYYZ	hydrolyzer
DEHLORSSSU	shroudless
DEHLORSSYY	hydrolyses
DEHLORSTYY	hydrolytes
DEHLORSYYZ	hydrolyzes
DEHMMOORSU	mushroomed
DEHMNOOPRS	endomorphs
DEHMNOOPRY	endomorphy
DEHMORRTYY	hydrometry
DEHNNOOPSS	sphenodons
DEHNNOORUU	unhonoured
DEHNNORSUU	nursehound
DEHNNOSSUW	newshounds
DEHNOORRSU	horrendous
DEHNOORSTU	undershoot
DEHNOORSUU	roundhouse
DEHNORSTUU	thunderous
DEHOOPPTTY	phototyped
DEHOOPRRWY	hydropower
DEHOORSSUW	woodrushes
DEHOOSSSSU	dosshouses
DEHORSSSTU	studhorses
DEIIIINSTV	divinities
DEIIILLOOP	Leopold III
DEIIILMQSU	semiliquid
DEIIILMSTU	similitude
DEIIILQRSU	liquidiser
DEIIILQRUZ	liquidizer
DEIIILQSSU	liquidises
DEIIILQSUZ	liquidizes
DEIIILSVVY	divisively
DEIIIMNORS	iridosmine
DEIIIMNPRY	pyrimidine
DEIIIMNTUV	diminutive
DEIIIMSSSV	dismissive
DEIIINORSV	redivision
DEIIINPRST	inspirited
DEIIINSSSS	disseisins
DEIIINSSSZ	disseizins
DEIIINSSTU	disunities
DEIIJMNORS	misjoinder
DEIIKKLNRS	kilderkins
DEIIKLNNSS	kindliness
DEIILLMPTU	multiplied
DEIILLNOSU	illusioned
DEIILLNUWY	unwieldily
DEIILLOPSS	ellipsoids
DEIILLORTV	vitriolled
DEIILLRSST	distillers
DEIILLRSTY	distillery
DEIILMNOOT	demolition
DEIILMNPSS	limpidness
DEIILMOSSS	semisolids
DEIILNPRTY	intrepidly
DEIILNPSST	spindliest
DEIILNQSSU	liquidness
DEIILPRSTY	spiritedly
DEIILQSTUY	disquietly
DEIILRSTZZ	drizzliest
DEIIMNNOSS	dimensions
DEIIMNNOTU	munitioned
DEIIMNOPRS	imprisoned
DEIIMNOSSS	demissions
DEIIMNPRST	misprinted
DEIIMNRSTW	midwinters
DEIIMNSTUY	seminudity
DEIIMOPRSV	improvised
DEIIMORTXY	oxidimetry
DEIIMPRSSU	presidiums
DEIINNNOST	indentions
DEIINNOPPT	pinpointed
DEIINNORST	renditions
DEIINNOSSS	dissension
DEIINNOSST	distension
DEIINNOSTT	dentitions
	distention
DEIINNOSTV	venditions
DEIINNPRSU	uninspired
DEIINNRSTW	interwinds
DEIINNSSTU	untidiness
DEIINOOPST	deposition
	positioned
DEIINOPRSS	dispersion
DEIINOPRXY	pyridoxine
DEIINOPSSS	indisposes
DEIINORSST	disorients
DEIINORSSV	diversions
DEIINORSTT	detritions
DEIINRSSTU	disuniters
	industries
DEIINSSSTV	disinvests
DEIINSTTTU	instituted
DEIIOOPSTV	oviposited
DEIIORSSSS	disseisors
DEIIORSSSZ	disseizors
DEIIORSTTV	distortive
DEIIPRSTUV	disruptive
DEIJNNNOOR	nonjoinder
DEIKKLNORS	klondikers
DEIKKNOOPS	pondokkies
DEIKLLNSSY	kindlessly
DEIKMPPRSU	mudskipper
DEIKNNNORR	nondrinker
DEIKNNNSSU	unkindness
DEIKNORRSV	overdrinks
DEIKNRRSTU	underskirt

DEILLLLSUV dullsville
DEILLMNSSY mindlessly
DEILLNNOTY indolently
DEILLNORSS lordliness
DEILLNSSWY windlessly
DEILLOOTTW Littlewood
DEILLORSTW worldliest
DEILMMOSTY immodestly
DEILMNOSSU Desmoulins
mouldiness
DEILMNPTUY impudently
DEILMSTTUU multitudes
DEILNNOUVV uninvolved
DEILNOOOTT odontolite
DEILNOOTUV devolution
DEILNORSTU tendrilous
DEILNOSSST stolidness
DEILNOSSTV dissolvent
DEILNPQTUU quintupled
DEILNRSTTY stridently
DEILOOPPSY polypodies
DEILOOPSSS podsolises
DEILOOPSSZ podsolizes
podzolises
DEILOOPSZZ podzolizes
DEILOPSSTY stylopised
DEILOPSTYZ stylopized
DEILORSSSV dissolvers
DEILORSSUY desirously
DEILORSVWW worldviews
DEIMMMRSSU midsummers
DEIMMNNTUU indumentum
DEIMNNOSTW disownment
DEIMNNSTYZ Mindszenty
DEIMNOOSSS endosmosis
DEIMNOPRSU impounders
DEIMNOPRTU importuned
DEIMNOPRUV unimproved
DEIMNORSST modernists
DEIMOORRTY odorimetry
DEIMOPRSSU dispermous
DEIMRSSTTU mistrusted
DEINNNORTU trunnioned
DEINNOOSTX endotoxins
DEINNORRSV nondrivers
DEINNORSWW New Windsor
DEINNORTUW interwound
DEINNRSTTU undertints
DEINOOPRSS droopiness
DEINOOPRST desorption
DEINOOPTTU outpointed
DEINOOSSST endostosis
DEINOOSSSU odiousness
DEINOOSTTX exodontist
DEINOPRSST dripstones
DEINOPSSSU suspensoid
DEINOPSSSY synopsised
DEINOPSSYZ synopsized
DEINORRSST torridness
DEINORRSWW windrowers
DEINORSSSS drossiness
DEINORSSSW drowsiness

DEINORSSTU detrusions
DEINPRRSTU surprinted
DEINPRSSTU putridness
DEINPRSTUU Prudentius
DEINPSSSTU stupidness
DEINRSSSTU sturdiness
DEIOOPRSST depositors
DEIOOPRSTX protoxides
DEIOOPRSTY depository
DEIOPRRSST postriders
DEIOPRRSTW spiderwort
DEIOPRSSSU disposures
DEIOPRSSTU posturised
DEIOPRSTUZ posturized
DEIOPSSSSS dispossess
DEIORRSSTT distorters
DEIPRRSSTU disrupters
DEIRRSSTTU distruster
DEKKLNORSY klondykers
DEKKNOORWY donkeywork
DEKLORSSVV Sverdlovsk
DEKNOOPRUV unprovoked
DEKNOORRWW wonderwork
DEKOOORRWW woodworker
DEKOOSSTVY Dostoevsky
DELLNOPTUU unpolluted
DELLOOOWWY yellowwood
DELLOORRWW lower world
DELLORSSWY wordlessly
DELLOSSUUY sedulously
DELMNOOOSW lemonwoods
DELNNOOOSS solenodons
DELNNOPSSU nonplussed
DELNNOTUWY unwontedly
DELNOOOSST dolostones
DELNOOPRTU pleurodont
DELNOPRSSU splendours
splendrous
DELNOPRSTU underplots
DELNOPRSUU plunderous
DELOPPSSUY supposedly
DELORRTTUY torturedly
DELORSTUXY dextrously
DEMMOORSUW summerwood
DEMNOOPRST postmodern
DEMNOPPRTU unprompted
DEMNOPSSUY pseudonyms
DEMNORSTUU surmounted
DEMNPRRTUU undertrump
DENNOOPRSS nonprossed
DENNOORTWW downtowner
DENNORSSTU rotundness
DENNORSSUW sundowners
DENNRRTUUU unnurtured
DENOOPPRRU propounder
DENOOPPRSU unproposed
DENOPPRRSU underprops
DENOPRRTTU protrudent
DENOPSSTTU sunspotted
DENOPSSTUU stupendous
DEOOOOPRRT Roodepoort
DEOORRSSUU uredosorus

DFFFOOSSTU foodstuffs
DFFIINOSSU diffusions
DFGGIIINNY dignifying
DFGGIJNORU forjudging
DFGHILLOOT floodlight
DFGIIILLNR fringillid
DFGIIILNSU fluidising
DFGIIILNUZ fluidizing
DFGIIIMORT digitiform
DFGIILNNOP pinfolding
DFGIINOSUU nidifugous
DFGILLNNOY fondlingly
DFGILNNOSU foundlings
DFGILSSTUU disgustful
DFHILOORSY hydrofoils
DFHLNOOSUW wolfhounds
DFHLOOOOPT photoflood
DFIILLMTUY multifidly
DFINOOPRST spoondrift
DFINOPRTUY profundity
DFINORSSTW snowdrifts
DFLNOOPRUY profoundly
DFNOOOPRSU soundproof
DGGGHINOOT hotdogging
DGGGIINORS disgorging
DGGGILNRUY grudgingly
DGGGINNRUU ungrudging
DGGHNOORSU groundhogs
DGGIIIINST digitising
DGGIIIINTZ digitizing
DGGIIIMNSU misguiding
DGGIIINSSU disguising
DGGIIJMNSU misjudging
DGGIILNNRY grindingly
DGGIINSSTU disgusting
DGGILNNORU groundling
DGGINNOORW wrongdoing
DGGINNORSU groundings
DGHHIINSST hindsights
DGHHIKNOOT knighthood
DGHHINOPST diphthongs
DGHIILLNNO Hillingdon
DGHIILMNTY midnightly
DGHILMOSST goldsmiths
DGHILOPRST droplights
DGHINNNOTU Huntingdon
DGHLNOORST stronghold
DGHNOORSUW showground
DGHOORSSUU sourdoughs
DGIIIINNSV divinising
DGIIIINNVZ divinizing
DGIIIJNNOS disjoining
DGIIILLNST distilling
DGIIILMNNS dislimning
DGIIIMNSSS dismissing
DGIIINNSTU disuniting
DGIIINOSTX digitoxins
DGIIINPRSZ disprizing
DGIIINPTUY pinguidity
DGIILNNPSS spindlings
DGIILNOSSV dissolving
DGIIMNNOPU impounding

DGIIMNOOSS sodomising
DGIIMNOOSZ sodomizing
DGIINNORWW windrowing
DGIINNOSWZ downsizing
DGIINOPRST disporting
DGIINOPRSV disproving
DGIINORSTT distorting
DGIINPRSTU disrupting
DGIIOOPRSU prodigious
DGILLNORSU groundsill
DGILLNORSW worldlings
DGILMNOOOS mongoloids
DGILNNOSUY soundingly
DGILNNOUWY woundingly
DGILNOOPRY droopingly
DGILOOPRTT proglottid
DGINNOSSWW downswings
DGINOOPRSW springwood
DGINOPRRTU protruding
DGKNOORRUW groundwork
DGLNOOOOTY odontology
DGLNOOPTTY glyptodont
DGNNORSTUU groundnuts
DHHILOPRYY hydrophily
DHIILNRSWW whirlwinds
DHIIMMOPRS dimorphism
DHIINNNRSY ninhydrins
DHIINOOSTU dithionous
DHILLOPSUY diphyllous
DHILMMOOSU hoodlumism
DHILNOOPPY podophylin
DHILOOPPYY hypoploidy
DHILORSSYY hydrolysis
DHIMMNNOST month's mind
DHIMNOSSTY hymnodists
DHIMOOPRSU dimorphous
DHIMORSSTW wordsmiths
DHINNOSTUW whodunnits
DHINNSTUWY whydunnits
DHINOOOPRT ornithopod
DHINOOPRSS donorships
DHINOORSSU dishonours
DHINOPRSTY dystrophin
DHIOOPPRRY porphyroid
DHIORRTXYY trihydroxy
DHLMOOSTUU loudmouths
DHLNOORSUW howlrounds
DHLOOORTXY orthodoxly
DHNOOORTUX unorthodox
DHNOORSTWW downthrows
DHNOOSSTUW South Downs
DHOORRSTWW Wordsworth
DIIIINPSTY insipidity
DIIILSTTUY disutility
DIIIMMORSU iridosmium
osmiridium
DIIIMNNOTU diminution
DIILLMNOOS modillions
DIILLNOSWW windowsill
DIILNOSSUV divulsions
DIIMMOPRRU primordium
DIINOORSTT distortion
DIINOPRSTU disruption
DILLOOPPSY polyploids
DILLOOPPYY polyploidy
DILMNPSUUU impundulus
DILORSSTUU stridulous
DILOSSTUUY studiously
DIMMNOOOPU monopodium
DIMMNOOOSU monosodium
DIMNOPRSUU purdoniums
DIMNORSSTW windstorms
DIMOPRSSUY dysprosium
DINOOPRSTW woodprints
DIOOOOSSTV voodooists
DIOOORSVWY ivorywoods
DIOOPRSSST prosodists
DIOPRRSSTU disruptors
DLLOOORSUY dolorously
DLNOORSUWY wondrously
DLOOOPPSUY polypodous
DMNOORRSUW roundworms
DNNORRSTUU turnrounds
DNOOPSSSTU soundposts
DNOOPSSTUW downspouts
DNOORSTUWW woundworts
EEEEEGPSSX epexegeses
EEEEELRSTY eyeleteers
EEEEFFNSST effeteness
EEEEFGINRR refereeing
EEEEFHLRSW freewheels
EEEEFHRSST freesheets
EEEEFPRRSZ prefreezes
EEEEGINRRS greeneries
EEEEGIPSSX epexegesis
EEEEGLNSTT genteelest
EEEEGNRRSV evergreens
EEEEHIMRSU euhemerise
EEEEHIMRUZ euhemerize
EEEEHNPSST epentheses
EEEEHRRVWY everywhere
EEEEIJLRTZ Jezreelite
EEEEIKLLSV sleevelike
EEEEIKMPRT timekeeper
EEEEKLPRSS keeperless
EEEEKMRRSY kerseymere
EEEELLSSSV sleeveless
EEEELMRSTT telemeters
EEEELNOPST eleoptenes
EEEELNSSSZ sneezeless
EEEELNSTVV velveteens
EEEELORSVV oversleeve
EEEENNRSSS sereneness
EEEENNSSTV seventeens
EEEENPRSST presentees
EEEENRSSSV severeness
EEEENRSSTW sweeteners
EEEEPPPRRT peppertree
EEEEPRRSSV perseveres
EEEFFILORT tree of life
EEEFFLNRTY efferently
EEEFGILNRS greenflies
EEEFGIMRSU refugeeism
EEEFGINORS foreseeing
EEEFGINRRZ refreezing
EEEFGLNRUV revengeful
EEEFHIIRST etherifies
EEEFHNRRSS fresheners
EEEFHOORRT heretofore
EEEFHORRSW wherefores
EEEFHORSST foresheets
EEEFHRRRSS refreshers
EEEFIINRRS refineries
EEEFIIRRSV reverifies
EEEFIIRSST esterifies
EEEFILNNSS felineness
EEEFILRSVX reflexives
EEEFIMNNRT refinement
EEEFINORRV overrefine
EEEFINRRRT interferer
EEEFINRRST interferes
EEEFIORRST feretories
EEEFLLNNOT Fontenelle
EEEFLLNRSU fullerenes
EEEFLLORRT foreteller
EEEFLRSSTT fetterless
EEEFLRSTTU fleurettes
EEEFMNPRRT preferment
EEEFMNRRST fermenters
EEEFNNORSU unforeseen
EEEFNORSST freestones
EEEFNQRRTU frequenter
EEEFPRRRRS preferrers
EEEGGIMNRR reemerging
EEEGHHINRT heightener
EEEGHHINTT eighteenth
EEEGHILNST gehlenites
EEEGHIMNOS hegemonies
EEEGHIMNOT eighteenmo
EEEGHLNNRT lengthener
EEEGHNNOST Stonehenge
EEEGHNORSU greenhouse
EEEGHRRTWY greywether
EEEGIILRSU religieuse
EEEGIINNRS engineries
EEEGIINPSS epigenesis
EEEGILMNST genteelism
EEEGILNOST telegonies
EEEGILNRST singletree
EEEGILNSST gentilesse
EEEGILOTTX geotextile
EEEGIMORST geometries
geometrise
EEEGIMORTZ geometrize
EEEGINNOST eigentones
EEEGINNPST steepening
EEEGINNRRT reentering
EEEGINNSTW sweetening
EEEGINOPRY epeirogeny
EEEGINORSV overseeing
EEEGINORTY erogeneity
EEEGINRRRV Green River
EEEGINRRSS energisers
EEEGINRRST interreges
EEEGINRRSZ energizers
EEEGIRRRST registerer

EEEGIRRSSV	regressive
EEEGISSTTX	exegetists
EEEGLMNRTY	emergently
EEEGLNNSST	gentleness
EEEGMNNRSU	energumens
EEEGMNORSS	greensomes
EEEGMNRSSS	messengers
EEEGMORRST	ergometers
EEEGNNORST	greenstone
EEEGRRRSTT	regretters
EEEHHIMPRS	hemisphere
EEEHHLORSW	wheelhorse
EEEHHLOSUW	wheelhouse
EEEHHORRTW	otherwhere
EEEHIKPPRS	keepership
EEEHILLNSS	hellenises
EEEHILLNSZ	hellenizes
EEEHILMORT	heliometer
EEEHILNPRS	prehensile
EEEHILPSSS	lesseeship
EEEHIMMRSU	euhemerism
EEEHIMPRSU	euphemiser
EEEHIMPRUZ	euphemizer
EEEHIMPSSU	euphemises
EEEHIMPSUZ	euphemizes
EEEHIMRSTU	euhemerist
EEEHINNNTT	nineteenth
EEEHINORSW	Eisenhower
EEEHINPSST	epenthesis
EEEHINSSWZ	wheeziness
EEEHINSTTV	seventieth
EEEHIRRSST	etherisers
EEEHIRRSTZ	etherizers
EEEHKLOSSU	houseleeks
EEEHKOPPRS	shopkeeper
EEEHLLMRUV	Leverhulme
EEEHLMNTVY	vehemently
EEEHLMSSTV	themselves
EEEHLNOPRT	telephoner
EEEHLNOPST	telephones
EEEHLNOPTY	polyethene
EEEHLRRSST	shelterers
EEEHMMNNST	enmeshment
EEEHMMNSTY	enthymemes
EEEHMNOPRS	ephemerons
EEEHMOPRSS	mesosphere
EEEHMORRRT	Rothermere
EEEHMORRST	rheometers
EEEHMORSST	threesomes
EEEHMPRRTY	hypermeter
EEEHMRSTTT	thermettes
EEEHNNPRTY	threepenny
EEEHNOPPRS	Persephone
EEEHNORSVW	whensoever
EEEHOPPRRT	treehopper
EEEHRSSTTU	usherettes
EEEIILLSTV	velleities
EEEIINNSST	Eisenstein
EEEIINRSST	serenities
EEEIINRSTT	entireties
	eternities
EEEIIPPRST	peripeties
EEEIIPRTTV	repetitive
EEEIIRSSTV	severities
EEEIJLMRSS	IJsselmeer
EEEIKLLNTT	nettlelike
EEEIKLLTVV	velvetlike
EEEIKLMSWY	semiweekly
EEEIKLNSSS	likenesses
EEEIKNNPRS	innkeepers
EEEILLNUVV	Villeneuve
EEEILMMORT	mileometer
EEEILMMSSW	Semmelweis
EEEILMNRST	resilement
EEEILMNRTV	revilement
EEEILMNSSS	seemliness
EEEILMNSTY	mesitylene
EEEILMRSST	smelteries
EEEILNNRSV	enliveners
EEEILNPRRT	terreplein
EEEILNPSSS	sleepiness
EEEILNQSTU	queenliest
EEEILNSSST	steeliness
EEEILORRTU	Eure-et-Loir
EEEILPSTVX	expletives
EEEILRRTTW	telewriter
EEEILRSSSW	wirelesses
EEEILRSSTW	westerlies
EEEIMMNNOS	menominees
EEEIMMRRSS	mesmeriser
EEEIMMRRSZ	mesmerizer
EEEIMMRSSS	mesmerises
EEEIMMRSSZ	mesmerizes
EEEIMNNPRT	preeminent
EEEIMNNRST	nemertines
EEEIMNORST	remonetise
EEEIMNORTZ	remonetize
EEEIMNPRTX	experiment
EEEIMNRRTT	retirement
EEEIMNRSTT	tensimeter
EEEIMOPRTZ	piezometer
EEEIMORSTT	meteorites
EEEIMPPRTV	preemptive
EEEIMPRRST	perimeters
EEEIMRRSTV	timeserver
EEEINNOPRS	pensioneer
EEEINNPRSS	persiennes
EEEINNPRST	serpentine
EEEINNPRTV	prevenient
EEEINNRRTV	intervener
EEEINNRSST	entireness
EEEINNRSTV	intervenes
EEEINORRST	orienteers
EEEINPRRST	enterprise
EEEINPRSTV	pretensive
	vespertine
EEEINPRTVV	preventive
EEEINQTTTU	netiquette
EEEINRRRTV	irreverent
EEEINRSSTW	westernise
EEEINRSSTX	intersexes
EEEINRSTWZ	westernize
EEEINSSTWY	eyewitness
EEEIOPRRRT	repertoire
EEEIPRRRSV	reprievers
EEEIPRRSSV	repressive
EEEIPRRSTT	preterites
EEEIPRRSVV	perversive
EEEIPRRTTU	repetiteur
EEEIPRSSTX	expertises
EEEIPRSSVX	expressive
EEEIPRSTXZ	expertizes
EEEIQSTTTU	etiquettes
EEEIRRRSTV	retrievers
EEEIRSSTTV	serviettes
EEEIRSSTTW	streetwise
EEEJJNNSSU	jejuneness
EEEJKNRSTU	junketeers
EEEKLNRSUV	Leverkusen
EEEKLORRTW	teleworker
EEEKMRSSTU	musketeers
EEEKNOSSTY	synoeketes
EEELLNPRST	repellents
EEELLNPSTX	expellents
EEELLNRSST	relentless
EEELLNSSTU	entelluses
EEELMMOSTT	mettlesome
EEELMNOPRS	perlemoens
EEELMNOPST	elopements
EEELMNOSTT	nettlesome
EEELMNOTVV	evolvement
EEELMNRSTV	revelments
EEELMNSTTT	settlement
EEELNOSSTT	solenettes
EEELNOSTTV	novelettes
EEELNRRTVY	reverently
EEELNRSTTW	newsletter
EEELOPRSSV	oversleeps
EEELORSVWW	werewolves
EEELPRRSVY	perversely
EEEMNNORST	mesenteron
EEEMNNRSTT	resentment
EEEMNNRSTU	enurements
EEEMNNSSTU	unmeetness
EEEMNOPRST	treponemes
EEEMNORSST	remoteness
EEEMNOSXYZ	exoenzymes
EEEMNRSTTV	revetments
EEENNNSSUV	unevenness
EEENNORSST	sonneteers
EEENORSTWZ	sneezewort
EEENPRRSST	presenters
	represents
EEENPRRSTV	preventers
EEENPRSSTX	expertness
EEENPRSSUV	supervenes
EEENRRSSTW	westerners
EEEOOPRSVX	overexpose
EEEOPRSTTY	stereotype
EEEORRRSTV	retroverse
EEEORRSSTV	oversteers
EEEORRSTVX	overexerts
EEEPPPRSTU	puppeteers
EEEPRRRSSS	repressers
EEEPRRRSSV	preservers
EEEPRRRSTV	perverters

EEEPRRSSSX	expressers
EEEPRSSSUX	supersexes
EEEPRSSTTU	superettes
EEEPRSSTUW	supersweet
EEEPRSTTTY	typesetter
EEEQRRSSTU	requesters
EEEQRSSSTU	sequesters
EEFFFGINNO	enfeoffing
EEFFFKLRSU	kerfuffles
EEFFFMNOST	feoffments
EEFFGIINRV	fivefinger
EEFFGINORR	forefinger
EEFFGNRSTU	greenstuff
EEFFHIILSS	filefishes
EEFFHINSTT	fifteenths
EEFFHLRRSU	refreshful
EEFFHLRSSU	reshuffles
EEFFIILLRZ	Zeffirelli
EEFFILSUVY	effusively
EEFFINOSSV	offensives
EEFFINRSST	stiffeners
EEFFIORRST	forfeiters
EEFFIORRTU	forfeiture
EEFFLOORTT	left-footer
EEFFLORSST	effortless
EEFFNORRTY	effrontery
EEFFOPRRRS	profferers
EEFGHHILRS	higher self
EEFGHINNRS	freshening
EEFGHINRRS	refreshing
EEFGHINRRT	frightener
EEFGHIRRST	freighters
EEFGHLOOSS	gooseflesh
EEFGIINRRT	gentrifier
EEFGILLNRU	refuelling
EEFGILLNRY	fleeringly
EEFGILLNTY	fleetingly
EEFGILNRSS	fingerless
	fringeless
EEFGILRSSU	figureless
EEFGIMNNRT	fermenting
EEFGIMRSUV	vermifuges
EEFGINNRRT	refringent
EEFGINNRUZ	unfreezing
EEFGINORRS	foreigners
EEFGINPRRR	preferring
EEFGIPRRSU	prefigures
EEFGKLLNOT	gentlefolk
EEFGLLMNOR	fellmonger
EEFGLLNUVY	vengefully
EEFGLMNNTU	engulfment
EEFGORRSTT	forgetters
EEFHHLORSS	horseflesh
EEFHIILSST	tilefishes
EEFHIILSTW	whiteflies
EEFHIINRRS	refinisher
EEFHIINRSS	refinishes
EEFHIIPPSS	pipefishes
EEFHILLSST	fleshliest
EEFHILNSSS	elfishness
	fleshiness
EEFHILORSS	horseflies
EEFHILOSSU	houseflies
EEFHILRSVY	feverishly
EEFHIORSSS	rosefishes
EEFHIORSSU	firehouses
EEFHIORSSV	overfishes
EEFHIOSUWY	housewifey
EEFHLNOORS	Holofernes
EEFHMOORRT	foremother
EEFHNORTTU	fourteenth
EEFHOORRSS	foreshores
EEFHRRRSTU	furtherers
EEFIIIRSVV	revivifies
EEFIIKLLNU	unlifelike
EEFIILLSST	stellifies
EEFIILMNNY	femininely
EEFIILMRSU	emulsifier
EEFIILMSSU	emulsifies
EEFIILNRST	interfiles
EEFIILNSSW	wifeliness
EEFIILQRSU	liquefiers
EEFIILRRST	fertiliser
EEFIILRRTZ	fertilizer
EEFIILRSST	fertilises
EEFIILRSTZ	fertilizes
EEFIIMNNNU	unfeminine
EEFIIMRRST	metrifiers
EEFIINNSST	finiteness
EEFIINORST	renotifies
EEFIINRRST	Finisterre
EEFIIPPRRS	fripperies
EEFIIPPRTT	pipefitter
EEFIIPRRST	petrifiers
EEFIIPRRSU	repurifies
EEFIIPRRTT	prettifier
EEFIIPRSTT	prettifies
EEFIIRRRST	terrifiers
EEFIIRRRSU	furrieries
EEFIIRRSSV	versifiers
EEFIIRSSTT	testifiers
EEFIKLLORW	flowerlike
EEFIKNRSST	kniferests
EEFIKNRSSU	refuseniks
EEFILLLOSS	filoselles
EEFILLLSSY	lifelessly
EEFILLNOTU	feuilleton
EEFILLRSST	fillesters
EEFILLRSTU	fullerites
EEFILLRSTY	lifestyler
EEFILLSSTY	lifestyles
EEFILMMRSU	flummeries
EEFILMNOQU	mefloquine
EEFILMRSTT	filmsetter
EEFILNNORT	florentine
EEFILNORSX	reflexions
EEFILNOSST	stoneflies
EEFILNOTUX	fluoxetine
EEFILNRSSU	irefulness
EEFILNRTUV	interfluve
EEFILNSSTU	futileness
EEFILOSTWX	Felixstowe
EEFIMNORST	fromenties
EEFIMNOSTT	oftentimes
EEFIMNRSTT	refitments
EEFIMNRSTU	frumenties
	furmenties
EEFIMPRRSU	perfumiers
EEFINNORRT	interferon
EEFINNQRTU	infrequent
EEFINORSST	firestones
EEFINRSSTU	interfuses
EEFIOPRRST	profiteers
EEFIORRRST	retrofires
EEFIORRSST	forestries
EEFIORRSTT	forsterite
EEFIORSSTU	setiferous
EEFIPRRSTU	putrefiers
EEFIPRSSTU	stupefiers
EEFIPRSSUX	superfixes
EEFIRRRSTT	fritterers
EEFIRRRSTU	fruiterers
EEFIRRSSTU	surfeiters
EEFKLLOOWY	yokefellow
EEFKLNOOST	Folkestone
EEFKNOOPRS	forespoken
EEFKNOORST	foretokens
EEFLLLSSSY	selflessly
EEFLLNTUVY	eventfully
EEFLLORSSW	flowerless
EEFLMORRSU	remorseful
EEFLMORSTW	flowmeters
EEFLMRSTUX	fluxmeters
EEFLNNTUUV	uneventful
EEFLNOSSUW	woefulness
EEFLNQRTUY	frequently
EEFLNRSSUU	ruefulness
EEFLNSSSUU	usefulness
EEFLORSSST	forestless
EEFLORSUVY	feverously
EEFLRRSTTU	flutterers
EEFLRSSTUU	futureless
EEFMOPRRRS	performers
EEFNNORRRU	forerunner
EEFNNORSSZ	frozenness
EEFNOORSTY	festoonery
EEFOPRRSTY	ferrotypes
EEFORRSSST	fortresses
EEFPRSSSUU	superfuses
EEGGHIINRW	reweighing
EEGGHILNRT	greenlight
EEGGIINNRS	energising
EEGGIINNRZ	energizing
EEGGILNNRS	greenlings
EEGGILOOSS	geologises
EEGGILOOSZ	geologizes
EEGGIMNNST	segmenting
EEGGINRRSS	regressing
EEGGINRRTT	regretting
EEGGINRSSU	snuggeries
EEGGISSTUV	suggestive
EEGGNOORTW	Georgetown
	George Town
EEGGRSSSTU	suggesters
EEGHHIISTT	eightieths
EEGHHINSSS	highnesses

EEGHHINSTW wheeshting
EEGHHIRSTT High Street
EEGHHLNOPT Phlegethon
EEGHIINRST etherising
EEGHIINRSV inveighers
EEGHIINRTZ etherizing
EEGHIISTTW weightiest
EEGHIKLRSU kieselguhr
EEGHIKNSTW weeknights
EEGHILNNST enlightens
EEGHILNOOP pigeonhole
EEGHILNOPR negrophile
EEGHILNPRT telphering
EEGHILNRST sheltering
EEGHILNSTT lengthiest
EEGHILNSTW lengthwise
EEGHILNSTY seethingly
EEGHILOOST theologies
theologise
EEGHILOOTZ theologize
EEGHILSSTW weightless
EEGHIMNOOS homogenise
EEGHIMNOOZ homogenize
EEGHIMOSST eightsomes
EEGHINNPRS ensphering
EEGHINOOST theogonies
EEGHINOPST phosgenite
EEGHINPRST regentship
EEGHINRSTT tighteners
EEGHINRTVY everything
EEGHIORSVW overweighs
EEGHIORTVW overweight
EEGHIOSSTT ghettoises
EEGHIOSTTZ ghettoizes
EEGHIRSSST sightseers
EEGHLLNOPS phellogens
EEGHLNORST Glenrothes
EEGHLOOPRT Oglethorpe
EEGHLOORTY heterology
EEGHMORRTY hygrometer
EEGHNNORRS greenhorns
EEGHNNRSTT strengthen
EEGHNOOPST photogenes
EEGHNOORTY heterogony
EEGHNOPTTY gnetophyte
EEGHNORTTU untogether
EEGHORSSTU otherguess
EEGHOSSTUU guesthouse
houseguest
EEGIIILMST legitimise
EEGIIILMTZ legitimize
EEGIIKLPRS kriegspiel
EEGIILNNNV enlivening
EEGIILNNST lentigines
EEGIILNRST leistering
EEGIILNRSV inveiglers
EEGIILNSTV televising
EEGIILOOST etiologies
EEGIILPRSV privileges
EEGIIMNPRR premiering
EEGIINNOPR pioneering
EEGIINNQTU quietening
EEGIINNRST eternising
EEGIINNRTZ eternizing
EEGIINPRRV reprieving
EEGIINPRVW previewing
EEGIINPSST epigenists
EEGIINRRTV retrieving
EEGIINRSSV ingressive
EEGIINRSTV vertigines
EEGIIRRSST registries
EEGIISSTTZ zeitgeists
EEGIKLLNNN kennelling
EEGIKLLNNR kernelling
EEGIKLNOPS spongelike
EEGIKLNOTU tonguelike
EEGIKLNRSS Kesselring
EEGIKLOORV groovelike
EEGIKLORSU grouselike
EEGIKNNNTT kennetting
EEGILLMSTU guillemets
EEGILLNPRS preselling
EEGILMMSSU gelsemiums
EEGILMNNOT eloignment
EEGILMNOOS menologies
EEGILMNORS mongrelise
EEGILMNORZ mongrelize
EEGILMOOSY semeiology
EEGILNNOPV enveloping
EEGILNNRSY sneeringly
EEGILNNRTU Reutlingen
EEGILNNSSS singleness
EEGILNNSTU unsteeling
EEGILNOOSS neologises
EEGILNOOSZ neologizes
EEGILNOPPR repeopling
EEGILNOSST telegnosis
EEGILNPPRX perplexing
EEGILNPRVY replevying
EEGILNPSWY sweepingly
EEGILNRSTT resettling
EEGILNRSTW sweltering
EEGILORSST sortileges
EEGILORSSU eulogisers
EEGILORSUZ eulogizers
EEGIMNNNOV envenoming
EEGIMNNOTT mignonette
EEGIMNNTTU integument
EEGIMNOORT goniometer
EEGIMNOPRW empowering
EEGIMNPPRT preempting
EEGIMNPSTT tempesting
EEGINNOPPS pepsinogen
EEGINNORST rontgenise
EEGINNORTZ rontgenize
EEGINNPRST presenting
EEGINNPRTV preventing
EEGINNSSSY syngenesis
EEGINOORSS orogenesis
EEGINOPSSY pyogenesis
EEGINORRSS regression
EEGINORRWW winegrower
EEGINORSSV sovereigns
EEGINORSTY generosity
EEGINORSVW oversewing
EEGINORSXY oxygeniser
EEGINORXYZ oxygenizer
EEGINOSSXY oxygenises
EEGINOSXYZ oxygenizes
EEGINPPSUW upsweeping
EEGINPRRSS repressing
EEGINPRRSV preserving
EEGINPRRTV perverting
EEGINPRSSX expressing
EEGINPRSTT presetting
pretesting
EEGINQRSTU requesting
EEGIORSSTU setigerous
EEGIRRSSSU regisseurs
EEGLLLOSWY yellowlegs
EEGLLMORSU glomerules
EEGLLNOOSY selenology
EEGLLOOPSY speleology
EEGLLOPRSS gospellers
EEGLLORRSV grovellers
EEGLMNNOSU melungeons
EEGLMORSUY gruesomely
EEGLNOOSTU telegonous
EEGLNORSTT lorgnettes
EEGLNORSUY generously
EEGLNOSSTU tongueless
EEGLOORRST ergosterol
EEGLOORSSV grooveless
EEGLOPRTWY Lower Egypt
EEGMNNOORT Montenegro
EEGMNNORSW newsmonger
EEGMNNORTV government
EEGMNOORRS greenrooms
EEGNNORSUU ungenerous
EEGNOORSST oestrogens
EEGNORRSSS engrossers
EEGOPRRSSS progresses
EEGOQRSSTU grotesques
EEGORRRSSS regressors
EEGORRRSST retrogress
EEGOSSSTUU outguesses
EEGPPPRTUY Upper Egypt
EEHHIKMORR Horkheimer
EEHHILMOPS hemophiles
EEHHILOPTY heliophyte
EEHHILPSSY sheepishly
EEHHIMNOST henotheism
EEHHINOSTT henotheist
EEHHINRTTT thirteenth
EEHHIORSTW Whitehorse
EEHHIPRRST Perthshire
EEHHLOPSTY helophytes
EEHHNOPPSS phosphenes
EEHHOORSSS horseshoes
EEHHOORSUW whorehouse
EEHHOPRTTY therophyte
EEHHOPSSTY hypotheses
EEHIIKLNRS shrinelike
EEHIILMPTU epithelium
EEHIILNOPR perihelion
EEHIIMNNOT methionine

EEHIIMRSST	smitheries
EEHIINNPPR	epinephrin
EEHIINNSTT	ninetieths
EEHIIPRSVW	viewership
EEHIIRRSTX	heritrixes
EEHIKNPSSS	sheepskins
EEHILLLMSW	millwheels
EEHILLPRST	tellership
EEHILMNOSS	homeliness
EEHILMOPRT	thermopile
EEHILMOPSS	mesophiles
EEHILMORTY	heliometry
EEHILNNRTY	inherently
EEHILNOOPS	oenophiles
EEHILNOPSX	xenophiles
EEHILNORSS	shorelines
EEHILNOSSS	holinesses
EEHILNOSSU	houselines
EEHILNPRSS	plenishers
EEHILNPRTW	printwheel
EEHILNSSSV	elvishness
EEHILOOPRT	heliotrope
EEHILOPRSS	repolishes
EEHILOPRSX	xerophiles
EEHILOPSTY	heliotypes
EEHILORSST	hostelries
EEHILOSTTU	silhouette
EEHILPPRSY	Lippershey
EEHILPRSTU	spherulite
EEHILPSSST	slipsheets
EEHIMMPSSU	euphemisms
EEHIMNNRTU	minehunter
EEHIMNOPPS	Hippomenes
EEHIMNOPRT	hemipteron
EEHIMOPRST	hemitropes
EEHIMOPRSV	empoverish
EEHIMPRRSW	whimperers
EEHINNOPRS	prehension
EEHINNOPRT	interphone
EEHINNORST	rhinestone
EEHINNSSSW	newishness
EEHINOOPRS	ionosphere
EEHINOPSSU	euphonises
EEHINOPSUZ	euphonizes
EEHINSSSTX	sixth sense
EEHINSSSTY	synthesise
EEHINSSTTU	euthenists
EEHINSSTTX	sixteenths
EEHINSSTTY	synthetise
EEHINSSTYZ	synthesize
EEHINSTTTW	twentieths
EEHINSTTYZ	synthetize
EEHIOPPRRS	prophesier
EEHIOPPRSS	prophesies
EEHIOPPRST	epistrophe
EEHIOPPSSU	eohippuses
EEHIORRSST	theorisers
EEHIORRSTZ	theorizers
EEHIOSSUVW	housewives
EEHIPRRSSW	whisperers
EEHIRSSSTY	hysteresis
EEHKKOOPYY	hokeypokey
EEHKLLORRW	Hellerwork
EEHKLNORRV	herrenvolk
EEHKLOOOWY	Wookey Hole
EEHKLOOSST	stokeholes
EEHKLORSWW	wheelworks
EEHKMOORRW	homeworker
EEHKMOOSSU	smokehouse
EEHKNOORTT	heterokont
	tenterhook
EEHKORSSTW	worksheets
EEHLLLPSSY	helplessly
EEHLLMNOOP	mellophone
EEHLLMORTW	Motherwell
EEHLLNOPST	Hellespont
EEHLLOPSSY	hopelessly
EEHLLORSST	hostellers
EEHLLORSSV	shovellers
EEHLMNOOYZ	holoenzyme
EEHLMNORTY	hemelytron
EEHLMORSST	motherless
EEHLMORSVW	overwhelms
EEHLNOOSSV	shovelnose
EEHLNOPSTY	polythenes
EEHLNORSST	throneless
EEHMNNNOOP	phenomenon
EEHMNNORTY	North Yemen
EEHMNOOPRS	pheromones
EEHMNOOPRT	phonometer
EEHMNOORSW	homeowners
	horsewomen
EEHMNOORTY	heteronomy
EEHMNORSTT	nethermost
EEHMNORSTY	heteronyms
EEHMNOSTUY	South Yemen
EEHMOOPRTT	photometer
EEHMOORSVW	whomsoever
EEHMOPRSTT	stepmother
EEHMOPRSTU	Prometheus
EEHMOPRSTY	hypsometer
EEHMOPSSTY	hemoptyses
	mesophytes
EEHMOQRSUU	humoresque
EEHMORSSUW	shrewmouse
EEHMRRRSTU	murtherers
EEHMRRSSTY	rhymesters
EEHNNOPSST	Stephenson
EEHNNOPSSY	phoneyness
EEHNNORRRT	northerner
EEHNNOSSST	honestness
EEHNOPPSTY	phenotypes
EEHNOPRSUY	Euphrosyne
EEHNOPSSTU	penthouses
EEHNOPSTTY	entophytes
EEHNOPSTUY	hypotenuse
EEHNORRSST	shorteners
EEHNORRSTU	southerner
EEHNORRTTW	Wetterhorn
EEHNOSSTTW	whetstones
EEHNPPRSSU	penpushers
EEHNRSSSTU	huntresses
EEHOOPRRSW	horsepower
EEHOOPRSUW	powerhouse
EEHOOPRTTY	heterotopy
EEHOOPSTTY	osteophyte
EEHOORSSTU	storehouse
EEHOPPRRWY	hyperpower
EEHOPPRSST	prophetess
EEHOPRRSTV	Shreveport
EEHOPRSSST	hotpresses
	prostheses
EEHOPRSTXY	xerophytes
EEHOPSSSTU	pesthouses
EEHPRSTTXY	hypertexts
EEHRSSTUUY	Eurystheus
EEIIIMNRSS	miniseries
EEIIINQSTU	inequities
EEIIKLLNRU	unlikelier
EEIIKLLNSS	likeliness
EEIIKLNPRW	periwinkle
EEIIKLPRST	priestlike
EEIIKNNSTZ	zinkenites
EEIILLLNWY	Llewelyn II
EEIILLMMRT	millimeter
	millimetre
EEIILLNSSV	liveliness
EEIILMNSST	timeliness
EEIILNNRRT	interliner
EEIILNNRST	interlines
EEIILNOSTV	olivenites
	television
EEIILNSSSW	wilinesses
EEIILOPSST	sepiolites
EEIILOPTVX	exploitive
EEIILORSTT	toiletries
EEIILPRRST	priestlier
EEIILRRSST	steriliser
EEIILRRSTZ	sterilizer
EEIILRSSST	sterilises
EEIILRSSTZ	sterilizes
EEIILRSTUZ	reutilizes
EEIIMMNRTU	meitnerium
EEIIMNNPTT	impenitent
	pentimenti
EEIIMNORST	enormities
EEIIMNPRUU	epineurium
EEIIMNRSTX	intermixes
EEIIMNRTTW	wintertime
EEIIMNRTZZ	intermezzi
EEIIMOPRST	epitomiser
EEIIMOPRTZ	epitomizer
EEIIMOPSST	epitomises
EEIIMOPSTZ	epitomizes
EEIIMORSSS	isomerises
EEIIMORSSZ	isomerizes
EEIIMPRSSV	impressive
	permissive
EEIINNNSTT	insentient
EEIINNRTTW	intertwine
EEIINNSSSW	sinewiness
EEIINNSSTT	intestines
EEIINNSSTV	intensives
EEIINNSTTX	inexistent
EEIINOPRTT	petitioner
	repetition

EEIINPRRST printeries
EEIINRRSVV viverrines
EEIINRSSST sensitiser
EEIINRSSTW winterises
EEIINRSSTZ sensitizer
EEIINRSTVW interviews
EEIINRSTWZ winterizes
EEIINSSSST sensitises
EEIINSSSTZ sensitizes
EEIIOPQSSU equipoises
EEIIOPSTVX expositive
EEIIORRSST rotisserie
EEIIOSSSTV sovietises
EEIIOSSTVZ sovietizes
EEIIPQRSTU perquisite
EEIIQRSSTU requisites
EEIIQSSTUX exquisites
EEIJLLNUVY juvenilely
EEIJLORSSV Overijssel
EEIJMNNNOT enjoinment
EEIKKMORSS kromeskies
EEIKKORSST koeksister
EEIKLMMRSU summerlike
EEIKLMORST kilometers
kilometres
EEIKLNNOPT Pentelikon
EEIKLNNSSU unlikeness
EEIKLRSSST strikeless
EEIKMNORST konimeters
EEIKMORRTW timeworker
EEIKOPRSTV perovskite
EEILLLRSST tillerless
EEILLMMORT immortelle
EEILLMNOST emollients
EEILLMNPST impellents
EEILLMNSSS smelliness
EEILLMOPRS millepores
EEILLMORSV Somerville
EEILLMPPPR peppermill
EEILLMSSTY timelessly
EEILLNNOSS loneliness
EEILLNOSSV loveliness
EEILLNRSSV snivellers
EEILLOPSTU petiolules
EEILLPRRUW wirepuller
EEILLRSSTU tellurises
EEILLRSSTY tirelessly
EEILLRSTTU tellurites
EEILLRSTUZ tellurizes
EEILLSSTUV vitelluses
EEILMMNPST implements
EEILMMORSS sommeliers
EEILMMORST milometers
EEILMMRTTU multimeter
EEILMNNOTT entoilment
EEILMNNSTT enlistment
EEILMNOPRT Montpelier
EEILMNORSS solemniser
EEILMNORSZ solemnizer
EEILMNOSSS solemnises
EEILMNOSST milestones
EEILMNOSSU mousseline
EEILMNOSSZ solemnizes
EEILMNPPRS pimpernels
EEILMNPSSS simpleness
EEILMNSSTU mustelines
EEILMOPRSY polymerise
EEILMOPRYZ polymerize
EEILMORSTT Timor-Leste
EEILMORSTY tiresomely
EEILMOSSTV motiveless
EEILMOSSVW semivowels
EEILMPRSTU pulsimeter
EEILMPRTVY pelvimetry
EEILMRSSTY lysimeters
EEILNNOQTU ineloquent
EEILNNPTTY penitently
EEILNNSSST silentness
EEILNNSTTY sentiently
EEILNOORSS oleoresins
EEILNOPRRT interloper
EEILNOPSST politeness
EEILNORSVV reinvolves
EEILNORSVW wolverines
EEILNORTVV intervolve
EEILNPRTXY inexpertly
EEILNRSSTW winterless
EEILNRSTUY esuriently
EEILOOPRST teliospore
EEILOPPRSS Persepolis
EEILOPRSST epistolers
pistoleers
EEILOPSSVX explosives
EEILORRSTU irresolute
EEILORRTTW rottweiler
EEILORRTXY exteriorly
EEILORSTUV resolutive
EEILOSSTTT stilettoes
EEILPPRSSU resupplies
EEILPPRTXY perplexity
EEILPPSTUV suppletive
EEILPRRSTY sperrylite
EEILPRRSUV pulveriser
EEILPRRUVZ pulverizer
EEILPRSSTY peristyles
EEILPRSSUV pulverises
EEILPRSUVZ pulverizes
EEILPRTUVY eruptively
EEILRSSSST resistless
EEILRSSTUV virtueless
EEILRSSUVV revulsives
EEIMMMNRTU immurement
EEIMMMRSTU summertime
EEIMMNOSTY metonymies
EEIMMOPRRV prime mover
Prime Mover
EEIMMORRSS memorisers
EEIMMORRSZ memorizers
EEIMMRSSST mesmerists
EEIMMRSSTW swimmerets
EEIMMRSSTY symmetries
symmetrise
EEIMMRSTYZ symmetrize
EEIMNNNRTT internment
EEIMNNOPTT pentimento
EEIMNNORST mentioners
minestrone
EEIMNNPSTU septennium
EEIMNNRSTT interments
EEIMNNRSTU inurements
EEIMNNSSTT sentiments
EEIMNNSSTU minuteness
EEIMNNSTTV investment
EEIMNOORRT remontoire
EEIMNOORST eriostemon
EEIMNOOSTT tenotomies
EEIMNOPPRT preemption
EEIMNOPRST Simon Peter
EEIMNOPRTU peritoneum
EEIMNOPSTX exemptions
EEIMNORRSS sermoniser
EEIMNORRSZ sermonizer
EEIMNORRTT nitrometer
EEIMNORRTU urinometer
EEIMNORSSS sermonises
EEIMNORSST moisteners
EEIMNORSSZ sermonizes
EEIMNORTTT tintometer
EEIMNORTZZ intermezzo
EEIMNOSSTX sixteenmos
EEIMNOSSYZ isoenzymes
EEIMNPPPRT peppermint
EEIMNPRSSU impureness
EEIMNPRSTU episternum
EEIMNRSSSS remissness
EEIMNRSSTU terminuses
EEIMNRSSTW westernism
EEIMOOPRSS meiospores
EEIMOOPRSX peroxisome
EEIMOORSTZ merozoites
EEIMOPRRRT reimporter
EEIMOPRRST spirometer
temporiser
EEIMOPRRTZ temporizer
EEIMOPRSST peristomes
temporises
EEIMOPRSTU periosteum
EEIMOPRSTZ temporizes
EEIMOPRTYZ piezometry
EEIMPPRRUU puerperium
EEIMPRRSSS impressers
EEIMPRRSSU impressure
EEIMPRRSTT permitters
pretermits
EEIMPRRSTU trumperies
EEIMPRSTUV resumptive
EEIMQSSTUU equisetums
EEIMRRSSTT trimesters
EEIMRSSSST mistresses
EEIMRSSSTY systemiser
EEIMRSSTTU sestertium
EEIMRSSTTX extremists
EEIMRSSTYZ systemizer
EEIMSSSSTY systemises
EEIMSSSTYZ systemizes
EEINNNSSTT intentness

EEINNOPRSS pensioners
EEINNOPRST pretension
EEINNOPRTV prevention
EEINNORRSS orneriness
EEINNORRTV intervenor
EEINNORSTT retentions
EEINNORTVW interwoven
EEINNOSSTV veinstones
EEINNOSSTX extensions
EEINNPRSST spinnerets
EEINNPRSSU unripeness
EEINNPRTTU turpentine
EEINNPSSSU supineness
EEINNQSSUU uniqueness
EEINNRSSTV inventress
EEINNSSSUW unwiseness
EEINOOSSST otioseness
EEINOOSTVZ Soviet Zone
EEINOPPRST peptoniser
EEINOPPRTZ peptonizer
EEINOPPSST peptonises
EEINOPPSTZ peptonizes
EEINOPQTTU equipotent
EEINOPRRSS repression
EEINOPRRST interposer
EEINOPRRSV perversion
EEINOPRSST interposes
EEINOPRSSV responsive
EEINOPRSSX expression
EEINOPRTXY pyroxenite
EEINOQRSTU questioner
EEINORRSSV reversions
EEINORRSUV overinsure
EEINORRTVW overwinter
EEINOSSTVV votiveness
EEINOSTTUZ teutonizes
EEINPRRRST reprinters
EEINPRRSTT interprets
EEINPRSSTT persistent
prettiness
EEINPSSSUV suspensive
EEINQSTTTU quintettes
EEINRRRSSU reinsurers
EEINRSSSTW witnessers
EEIOPPRRST properties
EEIOPPRSSV oppressive
EEIOPPSSTV stovepipes
EEIOPRRSSS prioresses
EEIOPRRSTV resorptive
EEIOPRSSST stereopsis
EEIOPRSSSV espressivo
EEIOPRSTTT operettist
EEIOPRSTTU pirouettes
EEIOPSSSSV possessive
EEIOQQSUUV equivoques
EEIORRRRST terroriser
EEIORRRRTZ terrorizer
EEIORRRSST roisterers
terrorises
EEIORRRSSV reservoirs
EEIORRRSTZ terrorizes
EEIORRSTTU tourtieres
EEIORRSTVW overwrites
EEIORSSSUV overissues
EEIPPRTTUY perpetuity
EEIPRRSSST persisters
EEIPRRSSSU pressurise
EEIPRRSSUZ pressurize
EEIPRRSTVY perversity
EEIPRRTTWY typewriter
EEIPRSSSTT stepsister
EEIPRSSSUV supervises
EEIPRSTTWY typewrites
EEIRRSSSTV reservists
EEIRRSTTTW twitterers
EEIRSSSTTU sestertius
EEJKNRSTTU junketters
EEJLMNOSTT jostlement
EEJMNNORUY journeymen
EEJMNNOSTY enjoyments
EEJNORRSUY journeyers
EEKKORSSTY keystrokes
EEKLNPRSSU spelunkers
EEKLOOORRV overlooker
EEKLOOPPRW workpeople
EEKLORRSSW workerless
EEKLORSSTW steelworks
EEKNORRSTW networkers
EELLLOSSVY lovelessly
EELLMNNORT enrollment
EELLMNOOSY lonesomely
EELLMNOSSW mellowness
EELLNNRSTU tunnellers
EELLNNSSSU sullenness
EELLNOPPRT propellent
EELLNOQTUY eloquently
EELLNOSSTY tonelessly
EELLNOSSWY yellowness
EELLNSSTUY tunelessly
EELLOPPRRS propellers
EELLORRSTW trowellers
EELLORSTUY resolutely
EELLRSSSTU lusterless
lustreless
EELLRSSSTY restlessly
EELMMNOPTY employment
EELMMNOSTU emoluments
EELMMRSSSU summerless
EELMNNORST enrolments
EELMNNOSSS solemnness
EELMNNOSTU ensoulment
EELMNOSTTX extolments
EELMNPPSTU supplement
EELMNPTUZZ puzzlement
EELMOOPSST leptosomes
EELMOPRSTU pulsometer
EELMORRSST tremorless
EELMORSTTV voltmeters
EELMORSTUV volumeters
EELMSSSSTY systemless
EELNOPRSTW spleenwort
EELNORSSTV resolvents
EELNORSTUV volunteers
EELNPPRSSU purpleness
EELNPPSSSU suppleness
EELOOPRSTT protostele
EELOPRRSTU poulterers
EELOPRSSTY polyesters
proselytes
EELORRRSST terrorless
EELORRRSTY retrorsely
EELORSSUVY yourselves
EELPPRSSSU supperless
EELPPSSTTU septuplets
EELPRRSTTU splutterer
EELPRSSTUU sepultures
EELPSSTTUX sextuplets
EEMMNOORST metronomes
monometers
monotremes
EEMMOORSST osmometers
EEMMORSTYZ zymometers
EEMNNOPSST penstemons
EEMNNOPSTT pentstemon
EEMNNRRSUY nurserymen
EEMNNRSTUU Neumünster
EEMNOORSSS moroseness
EEMNOORSTT tonometers
EEMNOORTTY enterotomy
EEMNOPRSUW superwomen
EEMNOPRSYZ proenzymes
EEMNORRSTT tormenters
EEMNOSSUUY euonymuses
EEMNOSSUVY evonymuses
EEMOOOSSTT osteotomes
EEMOOPRSTT optometers
potometers
EEMOORSTTY stereotomy
EEMOPPRRST preemptors
EEMOPPRRTY peremptory
EEMOPRRSTY pyrometers
EEMORSSTTU metestrous
metoestrus
EEMPRRSTTU trumpeters
EEMPRSSSST sempstress
EEMQRSSTUU sequestrum
EENNOPSSTT potentness
EENNOQRSTU quernstone
EENNOQSTUW Queenstown
EENNORSSTT rottenness
EENNOSSSUV venousness
EENNRSSTUU untrueness
EENOPPRRSS properness
EENOPRRSSS responsers
EENOPSSTTY stenotypes
EENORRSSST Stroessner
EENORRSTUY tourneyers
EENORSSSSU serousness
EENORSTTTU neutrettos
EENPRRSSUU supernurse
EEOOPRRSVW overpowers
EEOORRRSTV rootserver
EEOOSSTTTV voetstoets
EEOPPPRRTW pepperwort
EEOPPPRSSU presuppose
EEOPPRRSUW superpower

EEOPPRSSSS	prepossess
EEOPPRSSSU	superposes
EEOPRRRSSS	repressors
EEOPRRSSST	portresses
EEOPRRSSTT	protesters
EEOPRRSSTU	superstore
EEOPRSTTYY	stereotypy
EEOPSSSTTU	poussettes
EEORRSTTVX	extroverts
EEPPRRSSSU	suppresser
EEPPRSSSSU	suppresses
EEPRRSSTTU	sputterers
EERRSSTTTU	stutterers
EESSSSTUWX	West Sussex
EFFFILNSSU	fluffiness
EFFFKLRSUU	kurfuffles
EFFGHIINRS	fishfinger
EFFGHIIRST	firefights
EFFGHIORSS	frogfishes
EFFGIINNST	stiffening
EFFGIINORT	forfeiting
EFFGIINOST	Ffestiniog
EFFGINOPRR	proffering
EFFGINOSTT	offsetting
EFFGINRSSU	sufferings
EFFHILOSSW	wolffishes
EFFHINOSSS	offishness
EFFIINNSSS	sniffiness
EFFIINPSSS	spiffiness
EFFIIORRST	fortifiers
EFFIIQSSTU	squiffiest
EFFILLLRSU	fulfillers
EFFILLMNTU	fulfilment
EFFILMSUUV	effluviums
EFFILNSSTU	fitfulness
EFFINNSSSU	snuffiness
EFFINSSSTU	stuffiness
EFFIOOPRRS	fireproofs
EFFORSSTUV	overstuffs
EFGGHIINRT	freighting
EFGGHINRTU	gunfighter
EFGGIILNNR	fingerling
EFGGIILNNY	feigningly
EFGGILOOSS	solfeggios
EFGGINORTT	forgetting
EFGHHIILRS	highfliers
EFGHHILRSY	highflyers
EFGHIIKNRS	kingfisher
EFGHIIKNSS	kingfishes
EFGHIILNST	nightlifes
EFGHIILSTT	flightiest
EFGHIINRST	infighters
EFGHIIPRTZ	prizefight
EFGHILLSST	flightless
EFGHILNSSU	lungfishes
EFGHILORTV	overflight
EFGHILSTWY	flyweights
EFGHIMNORS	fishmonger
EFGHINRRTU	furthering
EFGHLLNORU	flugelhorn
EFGHOOPPRR	froghopper
EFGIIIMNNS	feminising
EFGIIIMNNZ	feminizing
EFGIIINRSS	signifiers
EFGIIJLLNY	jellifying
EFGIILNQUY	liquefying
EFGIILNRTT	flittering
EFGIILORRS	glorifiers
EFGIILTUVY	fugitively
EFGIIMNORS	foreignism
EFGIIMNRTY	metrifying
EFGIINNRRS	infringers
EFGIINNRSU	reinfusing
EFGIINNRUY	reunifying
EFGIINPRST	fingertips
	presifting
EFGIINPRSY	presignify
EFGIINPRTY	petrifying
EFGIINRRTT	frittering
EFGIINRRTY	terrifying
EFGIINRSTU	surfeiting
EFGIINRSVY	versifying
EFGIINSTTY	testifying
EFGIKLNORS	folksinger
EFGILLLUUY	guilefully
EFGILLNNNU	funnelling
EFGILMNNTU	ingulfment
EFGILNORST	fosterling
EFGILNORVY	overflying
EFGILNRSTU	flustering
EFGILNRTTU	fluttering
EFGILRSTUU	fulgurites
EFGIMNOPRR	performing
	preforming
EFGINNOOST	festooning
EFGINNORUV	unforgiven
EFGINOOPRR	reproofing
EFGINOPRSS	professing
EFGINOPRST	fingerpost
EFGINORRTY	torrefying
EFGINPRTUY	putrefying
EFGINPSTUY	stupefying
EFGLLLNOOW	Longfellow
EFGOOOOSST	goosefoots
EFHIIKLMSS	milkfishes
EFHIILNOSS	lionfishes
EFHIILNRST	Flintshire
EFHIILNSST	filthiness
EFHIILRSSV	silverfish
EFHIINSSST	shiftiness
EFHIIRSTTT	thriftiest
EFHIISSSTT	fetishists
EFHIKMNOSS	monkfishes
EFHILLOPSW	fellowship
EFHILMPSSU	lumpfishes
EFHILOPRST	shoplifter
EFHILORRSU	flourisher
EFHILORSSU	flourishes
EFHILRSSTT	thriftless
EFHIMNNOPR	phenformin
EFHIMNOOSS	moonfishes
EFHINORRST	firethorns
EFHINORSST	frothiness
EFHINRRSSU	furnishers
EFHLLOOPRS	shellproof
EFHLLOSSUV	shovelfuls
	shovelsful
EFHLNNOOSW	Wolfensohn
EFHLOOPSSU	flophouses
EFHNORSTUX	foxhunters
EFIIIINNST	infinities
EFIIIINNTV	infinitive
EFIIILLMOR	millefiori
EFIIILMPRS	simplifier
EFIIILMPSS	simplifies
EFIIILNNTY	infinitely
EFIIILSTTU	futilities
EFIIIMNNTY	femininity
EFIIJRSSTU	justifiers
EFIIKNNOPT	knifepoint
EFIIKNRSSS	friskiness
EFIILLMORS	mollifiers
EFIILLNRSS	frilliness
EFIILLNRSU	nullifiers
EFIILLRSST	fillisters
EFIILMNSSS	flimsiness
EFIILMOSTT	leitmotifs
EFIILNNOSX	inflexions
EFIILNNSST	flintiness
EFIILNORRY	inferiorly
EFIILOPRSU	piliferous
EFIILOSSSS	fossilises
EFIILOSSSZ	fossilizes
EFIILRSTTU	stultifier
EFIILRSTZZ	frizzliest
EFIILSSTTU	stultifies
EFIIMNNRSS	infirmness
EFIIMORRST	mortifiers
EFIIMORSTU	fumitories
EFIIMRSSTY	mystifiers
EFIINOOPSS	opsonifies
EFIINORSUV	viniferous
EFIINRSSTU	fruitiness
EFIINRSSZZ	frizziness
EFIIORSTTU	fortuities
EFIIRSTTUU	futurities
EFIKLNOSSS	folksiness
EFIKLRSSTY	flystrikes
EFILLMOPSU	filoplumes
EFILLMORST	stelliform
EFILLNSSUW	wilfulness
EFILLORRSV	frivollers
EFILLPSTUY	spitefully
EFILMOOPRS	Simferopol
EFILNNSSSU	sinfulness
EFILNOPPSS	floppiness
EFILNORSTW	interflows
EFILNORTWW	twinflower
EFILOPRSST	profitless
EFILQRSUUV	quiverfuls
EFIMMORRSS	reformisms
EFIMNORSTU	misfortune
EFIMNPRSSU	frumpiness
EFIMOOPRSU	pomiferous
EFIMORRSST	firestorms
	reformists

EFIMORRSTV First Mover
EFINOOPRSS profession
EFINOORSSU soniferous
EFINOPRSSU perfusions
EFINORSSST frostiness
EFINORSSSW frowsiness
EFINORSSUZ frouziness
EFINORSSWZ frowziness
EFINSSSTUU unfussiest
EFIOOPRRSU poriferous
EFIOORRSTU rotiferous
EFIOORSSSU ossiferous
EFIORSSTTW frowstiest
EFIORSTTTU outfitters
EFJLNOSSUY joyfulness
EFKLMNOOSW womenfolks
EFLLMORSSY formlessly
EFLLOPRUWY powerfully
EFLLOSUUXY flexuously
EFLMNOOORW moonflower
EFLMOOORTY tomfoolery
EFLNORSSUW sunflowers
EFLOOPRSTW flowerpots
EFLOPPRSUU purposeful
EFLORRSSUW furrowless
EFMOOPRRTU outperform
EFMORRSTTU Fort Sumter
EFNNOORRSU nonferrous
EFOOPRRSSS professors
EGGGIINNRS sniggering
EGGGIINRRT triggering
EGGGIMNNTU nutmegging
EGGGINNTTU nuggetting
EGGGINORSS grogginess
EGGGINSSTU suggesting
EGGHIIINNV inveighing
EGGHIILNNT lightening
EGGHIILNRT relighting
EGGHIINNRT rightening
EGGHIINNSW whingeings
EGGHIINNTT tightening
EGGHIINSTW weightings
EGGHIMNOSU gumshoeing
EGGHINNORU roughening
EGGHINNOTU toughening
EGGIIILNNV inveigling
EGGIIINNRT reigniting
EGGIILMMNR glimmering
EGGIILNNST glistening
EGGIILNOSU eulogising
EGGIILNOUZ eulogizing
EGGIILNRST glistering
EGGIILNRTT glittering
EGGIILNRVY grievingly
EGGIINNOPW pigeonwing
EGGIINNTTV vignetting
EGGIIORRVY Gregory VII
EGGILLNORV grovelling
EGGILLNRSU gruellings
EGGILLPSUU pluguglies
EGGILMOOST gemologist
EGGILNNRSU gunslinger
EGGILNNTTU englutting
EGGILNSSUY guessingly
EGGILQRSSU squigglers
EGGINNOOOR gorgoneion
EGGINNORSS engrossing
EGGINOPRRU regrouping
EGGINOSSTU suggestion
EGGIORRSTU outriggers
EGGLLOOOPX googolplex
EGGLOORSUY gorgeously
EGGLRRSSTU strugglers
EGHHIIPRST high priest
EGHHILOPRY hieroglyph
hygrophile
EGHHILOSTU lighthouse
EGHHNOTTUW New Thought
EGHHOORSUU roughhouse
EGHHOPPSYY hypophyges
EGHHOPRTYY hygrophyte
EGHIIINNRT inheriting
EGHIIKNNRT rethinking
EGHIILNNPS plenishing
EGHIILNNRT Inner Light
EGHIILNRST slithering
EGHIILNRSV shriveling
EGHIILNSST sightlines
EGHIILRSTY tigerishly
EGHIILSSTT sightliest
EGHIIMMNRS shimmering
EGHIIMNORT moithering
EGHIIMNPRW whimpering
EGHIIMNSST mightiness
EGHIIMNSTT nighttimes
EGHIINNNRS enshrining
EGHIINNPRS insphering
EGHIINNPRT trephining
EGHIINNPSS ensignship
EGHIINORST theorising
EGHIINORTZ theorizing
EGHIINPPRS reshipping
EGHIINPRSW whispering
EGHIINRSTW swithering
EGHIINRTTW whittering
EGHIINSSTY hygienists
EGHIINSTUX extinguish
EGHIIRSSTZ rightsizes
EGHIKLORTU troughlike
EGHILLNOST hostelling
EGHILLNOSU houselling
EGHILLNOSV shovelling
EGHILLOOPR philologer
EGHILMNOOS Mesolonghi
EGHILMOOOS homologies
homologise
EGHILMOOOZ homologize
EGHILNNORT Lothringen
EGHILNOPRS negrophils
EGHILNORVY hoveringly
EGHILNSSST slightness
EGHILOOPPT phlogopite
EGHILOORST rheologist
EGHILOOSST shoogliest
EGHILOOSTT ethologist
theologist
EGHILOSSTT ghostliest
EGHILPRSTU uplighters
EGHIMNORST smothering
EGHIMNRRTU murthering
EGHIMOSUYZ hemizygous
EGHINNNORT enthroning
EGHINNORST shortening
EGHINNOSUZ Ingenhousz
EGHINNPPSU penpushing
EGHINNPRSU gunnership
unsphering
EGHINNPRSY phrensying
EGHINNRSSU hungriness
EGHINOOSTT theogonist
EGHINORSST shoestring
EGHINORSTV overnights
EGHINRSTTU shuttering
EGHIOPRSTT tightropes
EGHIORSSTV oversights
EGHIORSTTW ghostwrite
EGHIRSSTTU theurgists
EGHLMOOOSU homologues
EGHLMOORTY mythologer
EGHLNOOPRY nephrology
phrenology
EGHLOOORRS horologers
EGHLOOPPSY psephology
EGHLOPPRTY petroglyph
EGHMNOOOSU homogenous
EGHMOOOTYZ homozygote
EGHMORRTYY hygrometry
EGHNOOOPRS gonophores
EGHNOOPRSY gynophores
EGHNOOPSUY hypogenous
EGHOOPRSUU house group
EGHOORRTVW overgrowth
EGHOORSTTW ghostwrote
EGHOPSTYYZ zygophytes
EGIIILMMST legitimism
EGIIILMNPR imperiling
EGIIILMSTT legitimist
EGIIILNNPP pipelining
EGIIILNORR irreligion
EGIIIMNNOS ignominies
EGIIIMNNST meningitis
EGIIINNRTV reinviting
EGIIINRSTV revisiting
EGIIKLLNRS reskilling
EGIIKLNNSS kingliness
EGIIKLNPRS springlike
EGIIKLNRST stringlike
EGIIKNNORV reinvoking
EGIIKNPPRS skippering
EGIIKNRSTT skittering
EGIIKRSSTZ sitzkriegs
EGIILLNNST tinselling
EGIILLNNSV snivelling
EGIILLNORS Signorelli
EGIILLNOTU guillotine
EGIILLNRST trellising

EGIILLNSVW	swivelling
EGIILMNNRU	relumining
EGIILNNOSV	novelising
EGIILNNOVZ	novelizing
EGIILNNSSV	Vlissingen
EGIILNNSUV	unveilings
EGIILNOPTX	exploiting
EGIILNORST	loiterings
EGIILNORVV	overliving
EGIILNOSVW	vowelising
EGIILNOVWZ	vowelizing
EGIILNPPRS	slippering
EGIILNPSSS	singspiels
EGIILNQRSU	squireling
EGIILNRRTY	retiringly
EGIILNRSSS	grisliness
EGIILNRVVY	revivingly
EGIILNSSTU	guiltiness
EGIILOORSV	virologies
EGIILOOSTT	etiologist
EGIILOPSST	epilogists
EGIILOPSTT	epiglottis
EGIILORSSU	oliguresis
EGIILRSSTT	gristliest
EGIILRSTZZ	grizzliest
EGIIMMNORS	memorising
EGIIMMNORZ	memorizing
EGIIMMNRRT	retrimming
EGIIMMNRST	misterming
EGIIMNNNOT	mentioning
EGIIMNNOST	moistening
	monetising
EGIIMNNOTZ	monetizing
EGIIMNOPRS	reimposing
EGIIMNOPRW	impowering
EGIIMNORTV	overtiming
EGIIMNOTWY	Wyomingite
EGIIMNPRSS	impressing
EGIIMNPRST	springtime
EGIIMNPRTT	permitting
EGIINNNOPS	pensioning
EGIINNNORV	environing
EGIINNOPRT	repointing
EGIINNORSS	ingression
	nigrosines
EGIINNORSV	versioning
EGIINNPRRT	reprinting
EGIINNRRSU	reinsuring
EGIINNRSSW	inswingers
EGIINNSSST	stinginess
EGIINNSSTW	witnessing
EGIINOPRST	repositing
EGIINORRST	roistering
EGIINORRTT	intertrigo
EGIINORRTV	overtiring
EGIINPPRRS	perspiring
EGIINPRSST	persisting
	springiest
EGIINRRSTU	intriguers
EGIINRSSTT	grittiness
	stringiest
EGIINRSTTW	retwisting
EGIINRTTTW	twittering
EGIINSTTTV	vignettist
EGIJKNNTTU	junketting
EGIJNNORUY	journeying
EGIJNOORVY	overjoying
EGIKLNNOOS	inglenooks
EGIKLNNORS	snorkeling
EGIKLNNPSU	spelunking
EGIKNNOORS	snookering
EGIKNNORTW	networking
EGILLMMNOP	pommelling
EGILLMMNPU	pummelling
EGILLMOSTU	guillemots
EGILLNNNTU	tunnelling
EGILLNNOTW	wellington
EGILLNOPPR	propelling
EGILLNORTW	trowelling
EGILLNORWY	loweringly
EGILLNOSTU	outselling
EGILLNPRSW	wellspring
EGILLNPSUW	upswelling
EGILLNTUXY	exultingly
EGILLORSSY	syllogiser
EGILLORSYZ	syllogizer
EGILLOSSSY	syllogises
EGILLOSSYZ	syllogizes
EGILMMNORS	mongrelism
EGILMMNPTU	plummeting
EGILMNOOSS	gloominess
	neologisms
EGILMNOPRR	longprimer
EGILMNOSUU	leguminous
EGILMNPTTY	temptingly
EGILMOOSSY	seismology
EGILNNOPPU	unpeopling
EGILNNOSST	singletons
EGILNNOSSV	lovingness
EGILNNOSSW	lowsenings
EGILNNRRUY	unerringly
EGILNNRSSU	nurselings
EGILNNSTTU	unsettling
EGILNOOOST	oenologist
	ontologies
EGILNOOPST	penologist
EGILNOOSST	neologists
EGILNOOSSU	sinologues
EGILNOPRTT	Port-Gentil
EGILNOPRTU	ploutering
EGILNOPRTW	plowtering
EGILNORRUV	overruling
EGILNORTTU	rouletting
EGILNORTWY	toweringly
EGILNOSSSS	glossiness
EGILNPPSTU	septupling
EGILNPRSSS	springless
EGILNPRSST	springlets
EGILNPRSSY	pressingly
EGILNQSTUY	questingly
EGILNRSTTU	lutestring
EGILOOOPST	topologies
EGILOOPSTY	typologies
EGILOORSST	serologist
EGILOOSSSS	isoglosses
EGILOOSSTX	sexologist
EGILORSUVY	grievously
EGILOSUUXY	exiguously
EGIMMNNOSU	immunogens
EGIMMNNPTU	impugnment
EGIMNNOORR	ironmonger
EGIMNNORST	monstering
EGIMNNORTT	tormenting
EGIMNNORTU	remounting
EGIMNOORST	ergonomist
EGIMNOORTY	goniometry
EGIMNORSSV	misgoverns
EGIMNPRSSU	grumpiness
EGIMNPRTTU	trumpeting
EGIMNRSSSY	synergisms
EGIMNRSTTU	mutterings
EGIMOOPRST	geotropism
EGIMRRSTUU	Tîrgu Mureş
EGINNOPSSS	sponginess
EGINNORSTT	snottering
EGINNORTUY	tourneying
EGINNPPSTU	unstepping
EGINNRSSTU	insurgents
EGINNRSSTY	tryingness
EGINNRSTTU	entrusting
EGINNRSUVW	unswerving
EGINOOPRRT	progenitor
EGINOPPRRS	prospering
EGINOPPRSS	oppressing
EGINOPPRST	stoppering
EGINOPRRRS	porringers
EGINOPRRTU	intergroup
EGINOPRSST	progestins
EGINOPRSTT	protesting
EGINOPRSUY	perigynous
EGINOPSSSS	possessing
EGINORRSTW	songwriter
EGINORRTUV	overturing
EGINORSTTT	stottering
EGINORSTUW	outswinger
EGINPRRSSU	pressuring
EGINPRSTTU	sputtering
EGINRSSSTY	synergists
EGINRSTTTU	stuttering
	Turing test
EGKORSSSUW	guessworks
EGLLLOORRS	logrollers
EGLLMORSUU	glomerulus
EGLMNOOOSU	monologues
EGLMNOOOTY	entomology
EGLMNOORUY	numerology
EGLMNOOYYZ	enzymology
EGLNOOPRRS	prolongers
EGLNOOSSXY	xenoglossy
EGLNOOSUXY	xylogenous
EGLNORSSTY	strongyles
EGLOOORRWW	woolgrower
EGMMNOORTY	Montgomery
EGMMNOPRSY	gymnosperm
EGMMPRUUWY	mugwumpery
EGMNNOOOSU	monogenous

EGNNNRRSUU	gunrunners
EGNNORSSST	strongness
EGNOOPRSUY	pyrogenous
EGNORRSTUV	overstrung
EGNORSSSST	songstress
EGNORSSTUY	youngsters
EGOOPRSSYZ	zygospores
EGOPPRRSUU	supergroup
EHHIILSTVY	thievishly
EHHIIMSTTW	whitesmith
EHHIIRSTTT	thirtieths
EHHILMOOPS	homophiles
EHHILMOPRT	thermophil
EHHILMOSTY	hylotheism
EHHILOPRSU	Herophilus
EHHILOPSTU	Theophilus
EHHILOPTTY	lithophyte
EHHILORTWW	worthwhile
EHHILRSSWY	shrewishly
EHHIMMOPRY	hemimorphy
EHHIMORSTT	hithermost
EHHINORTTW	whitethorn
EHHIOPPSST	phosphites
EHHIOPRRSS	Shropshire
EHHIOPRSSW	horsewhips
EHHIOPSSTY	hypothesis
EHHLLOOSTT	toothshell
EHHLMRSSTY	rhythmless
EHHLOOOPPR	lophophore
EHHLOOPSTY	holophytes
EHHMMOORTY	homothermy
EHHMNOOOPS	homophones
EHHOOOPPRT	photophore
EHHOPPSSYY	hypophyses
EHIIILMSTU	humilities
EHIIILNPPP	philippine
EHIIILNPST	philistine
EHIIINRRTX	inheritrix
EHIIIPRSVZ	viziership
EHIIKLNPSX	sphinxlike
EHIIKMRRSS	skirmisher
EHIIKMRSSS	skirmishes
EHIILLOOPS	Heliopolis
EHIILLOPSY	lyophilise
EHIILLOPYZ	lyophilize
EHIILMOPRT	limitrophe
EHIILNOOPS	eosinophil
EHIILNQRSU	relinquish
EHIILNSTTW	lintwhites
EHIILNSVXY	vixenishly
EHIILORTTT	lithotrite
EHIILPRSVY	viperishly
EHIILPRTTY	triphylite
EHIIMNPSSS	impishness
EHIIMOPRSV	impoverish
EHIIMPPRSU	umpireship
EHIINNPRST	internship
EHIINORRST	inheritors
EHIINRSSST	shirtiness
EHIINSSSTT	shittiness
EHIIRRSTTU	urethritis
EHIIRSSTTT	thirstiest
	tritheists
EHIIRSSTTZ	zitherists
EHIJLLNOTT	Little John
EHIKLMNOPY	lymphokine
EHIKLNORTW	Kenilworth
EHIKLOOSST	tikoloshes
EHIKMNOOST	Timoshenko
EHIKNPRRSS	preshrinks
EHILLMNPUY	phillumeny
EHILLMOORS	Hermosillo
EHILLNRSSS	shrillness
EHILLNSTUV	Huntsville
EHILMNOOOS	homolosine
EHILMNOSSY	hemolysins
EHILMNSSSU	mulishness
EHILMOPSTY	polytheism
EHILNNOSSU	unholiness
EHILNOOPST	lithopones
EHILNOPRTU	neutrophil
EHILNORRSV	silverhorn
EHILNOSSSW	owlishness
EHILNSSSSU	slushiness
EHILOOPSTU	pilothouse
EHILOPSTTY	polytheist
EHILORRTTY	erythritol
EHILPRSSTU	sutlership
EHILPRSSUU	sulphurise
EHILPRSUUZ	sulphurize
EHIMMNOOST	monotheism
EHIMMOPRTU	promethium
EHIMMOPSTU	imposthume
EHIMNNOORS	moonshiner
EHIMNNPSTU	punishment
EHIMNOOSTT	monotheist
EHIMNOPSSY	symphonies
EHIMNOPSUU	euphoniums
EHIMNORSST	horsemints
EHIMNORSUY	Hieronymus
EHIMNSSTTU	tunesmiths
EHIMNSSTTY	synthetism
EHIMOPPRRS	perimorphs
EHIMOPSSTY	hemoptysis
EHIMORRSTT	thermistor
EHIMPRRSTU	triumphers
EHINNORSST	thorniness
EHINOOOPRS	ionophores
EHINOOPPRR	pronephroi
EHINOOPSUU	euphonious
EHINOOSSTT	toothiness
EHINOPPRTY	periphyton
EHINOPRRTY	pyrrhotine
EHINOPRSSW	shipowners
EHINOPRSTY	hypnotiser
EHINOPRTYZ	hypnotizer
EHINOPSSTT	phonetists
EHINOPSSTY	hypnotises
EHINOPSSVY	envoyships
EHINOPSTYZ	hypnotizes
EHINORRSSU	nourishers
EHINORSSTW	worthiness
EHINORSTUU	ruthenious
EHINPPSSSU	uppishness
EHINRRTTUW	Winterthur
EHINSSSTTY	synthesist
EHINSSTTTY	synthetist
EHIOOPRSTW	wirephotos
EHIOOPRTTX	thixotrope
EHIOPPRRST	pretorship
EHIOPPRRSW	worshipper
EHIOPPRRSY	porphyries
EHIOPRRSTY	prehistory
EHIOPRRTTY	pyrrhotite
EHIOPRSSST	prosthesis
	sophisters
EHIOPRSSUZ	rhizopuses
EHIPRSSTUY	suretyship
EHJMOPRSUW	showjumper
EHKLOOOSST	tokoloshes
EHKNORRSUY	Krušné Hory
EHKOORRSSW	workhorses
EHKOORSSUW	workhouses
EHLLLOORRY	Holy Roller
EHLLMOPSSY	mesophylls
EHLLNOOSSW	hollowness
EHLLOOSSTU	tollhouses
EHLLRSSTUY	ruthlessly
EHLMNOPPTY	nympholept
EHLMOOPPRY	pleomorphy
EHLMOPPSUY	Polyphemus
EHLMORSSUU	humourless
EHLNOOPPSY	polyphones
EHLNOOPSTY	stylophone
EHLNOOPSXY	xylophones
EHLNOORSSU	honourless
EHLNOOSSTY	holystones
EHLNORSTUY	southernly
EHLOOOPRTV	Porto Velho
EHLOOPRSTU	toolpusher
EHLOPRSSTU	upholsters
EHLOPRSTUY	upholstery
EHLOPSSTYY	hypostyles
EHLORRSTTT	throttlers
EHLPRSSTUU	sulphurets
EHMMOOPRSS	mesomorphs
EHMMOOPRSY	mesomorphy
EHMMOORSUU	humoursome
EHMNNOOOSY	honeymoons
EHMNOOPRTY	nephrotomy
EHMNOOSSST	smoothness
EHMOOOPRSS	sophomores
EHMOOPRTTY	photometry
EHMOORRTTW	motherwort
EHMOPRSTYY	hypsometry
EHMPRRSTUY	pyrethrums
EHNNOPRTWY	pennyworth
EHNOOOPPST	optophones
EHNOOORSTT	orthotones
EHNOOPPRRS	pronephros
EHNOOPPRTY	phonotyper
EHNOOPPSTY	phonotypes
EHNOORRTVW	overthrown
EHNOORSSSW	snowshoers
EHNOORTTWY	noteworthy
EHNOOSTTTT	hottentots

EHNOPRSTTU pothunters
EHNORSTWWY newsworthy
EHOOOPPRRS sporophore
EHOOOPRSSU poorhouses
EHOOORSSTV overshoots
EHOOPPRSTY sporophyte
EHOOPPRTTY tropophyte
EHOOPPSTTY phototypes
EHOOPRRSTT orthopters
EHOOPRRSTV hoverports
EHOORRSTVW overthrows
EHORRSSTTW throwsters
EHORRSTTUV overthrust
EIIIINQSTU iniquities
EIIILLLMRT milliliter
millilitre
EIIILMNNOP epilimnion
EIIILNNQSU inquilines
EIIILORSTV vitriolise
EIIILORTVZ vitriolize
EIIIMMNRSS minimisers
EIIIMMNRSZ minimizers
EIIIMMNSTU immunities
EIIIMNORST minorities
EIIIMNPSTU impunities
EIIIMNRSST ministries
EIIIMPRSTU impurities
EIIIMPRSTV primitives
EIIIMSSTVY emissivity
EIIINPRRST inspiriter
EIIIOPRRST priorities
prioritise
EIIIOPRRTZ prioritize
EIIJLNTUVY juvenility
EIIKKLNOSS kolinskies
EIIKKLOSSW Kieślowski
EIIKLLLOWW willowlike
EIIKLLNPST splintlike
EIIKLLNRTW winterkill
EIIKLMORRR mirrorlike
EIIKLNNRST interlinks
EIIKLNNSSS slinkiness
EIIKLNORST triskelion
EIIKLNRSTW wrinkliest
EIIKMNORST ministroke
EIIKMNPSSS skimpiness
EIIKNNNSSS skinniness
EIIKNNRSTT interknits
EIIKNOSVVZ Zinovievsk
EIIKNQRSSU quirkiness
EIILLLOSUV Louisville
EIILLLSUVY illusively
EIILLMMNNU millennium
EIILLMNORV vermillion
EIILLMOPTY impolitely
EIILLMPRTU multiplier
EIILLMPSTU multiplies
EIILLNNNOP pennillion
EIILLNOPST septillion
EIILLNORRT ritornelli
EIILLNORSS Rossellini
EIILLNORTT tortellini
EIILLNOSTX sextillion
EIILLNRSST instillers
EIILLPPRSY slipperily
EIILLPSSTY pitilessly
EIILMMNNTY imminently
EIILMNNSTT instilment
EIILMNORSV vermilions
EIILMNOSST lentissimo
EIILMNOSSU limousines
EIILMNPPSS pimpliness
EIILMOPSSV implosives
EIILMORSST meliorists
EIILMOSTTV leitmotivs
EIILMOSUXY eximiously
EIILNNOQSU quinolines
EIILNORRTY interiorly
EIILNOSSSV visionless
EIILNPPSSS slippiness
EIILNPTUVY punitively
EIILNRSSTY sinisterly
EIILNRSTUV lentivirus
EIILOPSTVY positively
EIILPRSSST spiritless
EIIMMNORSS immersions
EIIMMNRSSU immunisers
EIIMMNRSUZ immunizers
EIIMMORSSS isomerisms
EIIMMORSST memoirists
EIIMMPRSUY perimysium
EIIMMSSTTU mittimuses
EIIMNNORSU reunionism
EIIMNNORTU munitioner
EIIMNNRSTU trienniums
EIIMNOORST monitories
EIIMNOPRRS imprisoner
EIIMNOPRSS impression
permission
EIIMNORSSS missioners
remissions
EIIMNOSSST misoneists
EIIMNPRRST imprinters
EIIMOOPSTY episiotomy
EIIMOORSTV vomitories
EIIMOPRRSV improviser
EIIMOPRSSV improvises
EIIMOPRSUV impervious
EIIMOPSSTT epitomists
EIIMORSSTU moisturise
EIIMORSTUZ moisturize
EIIMOSSSTV sovietisms
EIIMPSSSST pessimists
EIINNNOSST intensions
EIINNNOSTT intentions
EIINNNOSTV inventions
EIINNORSST insertions
EIINNORSSV inversions
EIINNORSTU reunionist
EIINNPPSSS snippiness
EIINNRSSTT internists
EIINNRSSTW wintriness
EIINOOPRST reposition
EIINOOPSTX exposition
EIINOORSST sonorities
EIINOPRSSV previsions
EIINOPSTVW viewpoints
EIINORTTWZ zwitterion
EIINPPRSST pinstripes
EIINPRSSSS prissiness
EIINRSTTTU instituter
EIINRSTTTW intertwist
EIINRSTTUV nutritives
EIINRSTUVY university
EIINSSTTTU institutes
EIIOOPPSTV oppositive
EIIOOPRSST porosities
EIIOORRSST sororities
EIIOORSSTT torosities
EIIORSSSST Sesostris I
EIIORSTTVY vitreosity
EIIOSSSTTV sovietists
EIIPRRSTTV Pitt-Rivers
EIIPRTTUVY eruptivity
EIJOPRRSUU perjurious
EIKLNPRRSS sprinklers
EIKMNOORSS monoskiers
EIKNNOSSTT knottiness
stinkstone
EIKNOOPSSS spookiness
EIKNOORRRW ironworker
EIKNORRSTW interworks
EIKNORRUVY Yukon River
EIKORRSSTV overskirts
EIKRRSSTWY skywriters
EILLLSSSTY listlessly
EILLMNOSST millstones
EILLMOOSTY toilsomely
EILLMORSTU lumisterol
EILLMPSTTU multiplets
EILLNNOSTY insolently
EILLNOOPSS pollenosis
EILLNOORRT ritornello
EILLNOOSSW woolliness
EILLNOPRSU nullipores
EILLNORSTU tellurions
EILLNOSTVW Townsville
EILLNOTUVY involutely
EILLNRTUVY virulently
EILLOPRSSV overspills
spillovers
EILLOPRSUY perilously
EILLORRTUY ulteriorly
EILLORSSTU trolliuses
EILLOSSTTY stylolites
EILMMNSTUU nummulites
EILMMOPRSY polymerism
EILMMOPSSY misemploys
EILMMSSSTU summitless
EILMNNOSTU insoulment
EILMNOOOPS monopolies
monopolise
EILMNOOOPZ monopolize
EILMNOOSST motionless
EILMNOPSST simpletons
EILMNOPTTY impotently

EILMNORSTT	tormentils
EILMNOSSSS	lissomness
EILMNRSSTY	minstrelsy
EILMOOPRST	metropolis
EILMOPPRRY	improperly
EILNNNOOTV	nonviolent
EILNNOSSTV	insolvents
EILNNOSTTW	Tinseltown
EILNNRSSUU	unruliness
EILNOOPSSS	slipnooses
EILNOOPSSX	explosions
EILNOORSTU	resolution
EILNOORTUV	revolution
EILNOOSTUV	evolutions
EILNOPPRTW	nipplewort
EILNOPPSSS	sloppiness
EILNOPPSTU	suppletion
EILNOPRRSU	purloiners
EILNOPRSST	portliness
EILNOPRSSU	repulsions
EILNOPRSSX	prolixness
EILNOPSSUX	expulsions
EILNORRSTY	introrsely
EILNORSSUV	revulsions
EILNORSSUY	resinously
EILNOSTUUV	velutinous
EILNPQSTUU	quintuples
EILNPQTTUU	quintuplet
EILNPRRTUY	pruriently
EILNRSSSTU	sultriness
EILNRSSTTU	turnstiles
EILOOPPRST	Petrópolis
EILOOPPSTY	oppositely
EILOORSSTT	sitosterol
EILOPPRSTY	propylites
EILOPPRSUV	propulsive
EILOPRRSTU	protrusile
EILOPRRSUY	superiorly
EILOPRSTUY	pyrolusite
EILOPRSTVY	sportively
EILOPRSUVY	perviously
	previously
	viperously
EILOPSSSTY	stylopises
EILOPSSTYZ	stylopizes
EILORRSTVW	liverworts
EILORSTUVY	vitreously
EILRRSTUVW	liverwurst
EIMMNNORSW	nonswimmer
EIMMOPSSTU	impostumes
EIMNNNRSTU	inurnments
EIMNNOOOST	monotonies
	monotonise
EIMNNOOOTZ	monotonize
EIMNNOOPTT	omnipotent
EIMNNORSUU	innumerous
EIMNNOSSYY	synonymies
	synonymise
EIMNNOSYYZ	synonymize
EIMNNRSTTU	instrument
	nutriments
EIMNOOOPRT	monopteroi
EIMNOOPRSS	spoonerism
EIMNOORRST	remontoirs
EIMNOORSST	Montessori
EIMNOOSTTT	tenotomist
EIMNOPRRTU	importuner
EIMNOPRSTU	importunes
	resumption
EIMNORRSTW	worriments
EIMNORSSST	storminess
EIMNORSSSU	sensoriums
EIMNOSTTZZ	mezzotints
EIMNPSSSTU	stumpiness
EIMNSSSTTU	smuttiness
EIMOOQSSTU	mosquitoes
EIMOPRRSST	misreports
EIMOPRRSTY	spirometry
EIMOPRSSTU	impostures
EIMORRSTTW	miterworts
	mitreworts
EIMORSSTUY	mysterious
EIMRRSSTTU	mistruster
EINNNOORTU	nonroutine
EINNOOPRST	pontoniers
	prenotions
EINNOORSST	ironstones
	notornises
EINNOORTUX	neurotoxin
EINNOOSSST	snootiness
EINNOPSSSU	suspension
EINNOSSSTT	snottiness
EINNOSSTTU	sustention
EINOOPPRSS	oppression
EINOOPRRST	resorption
EINOOPRSTU	proteinous
EINOOPSSSS	possession
EINOOPTTTT	totipotent
EINOORRSST	retorsions
EINOORRSTT	retortions
EINOORSSTU	serotinous
EINOORSTTX	extortions
EINOORTTTT	Tintoretto
EINOPPRSTY	propensity
EINOPRRRST	ripsnorter
EINOPRRSTV	overprints
EINOPRSSST	sportiness
EINOPSSSSY	synopsises
EINOPSSSTT	spottiness
EINOPSSSYZ	synopsizes
EINOQRTTUU	tourniquet
EINORRSTTV	introverts
EINORRSVWY	Snowy River
EINORSSTUX	extrusions
EINPRRSTTU	interrupts
EINRSSSTTU	trustiness
EIOOOPRSTZ	sporozoite
EIOOPPRRRT	proprietor
EIOOPPRRST	prepositor
EIOOPRRSST	posteriors
EIOOPRRSTY	repository
EIOOPRSSTT	strepitoso
EIOOPRSSTX	expositors
EIOOPRSTXY	expository
EIOORRSSTU	roisterous
EIOORSTTUZ	zootsuiter
EIOPPRRSTU	Propertius
EIOPPRRSTY	prosperity
EIOPPRSSTT	stroppiest
EIOPPRSTUV	supportive
EIOPRRSSUV	proviruses
	supervisor
EIOPRRSTTU	tripterous
EIOPRRSTUV	protrusive
EIOPRSSSTU	posturises
EIOPRSSTTU	strepitous
EIOPRSSTUZ	posturizes
EIOPRSTTTU	prostitute
EIORRRSSTT	terrorists
EIORRRSTUV	retrovirus
EIPQRSTTUY	triptyques
EIPRRRSSSU	surprisers
EJNNSSSTUU	unjustness
EJNOORRSSU	sojourners
EJNOOSSSUY	joyousness
EKLMMNOSSU	muskmelons
EKLOOPRRSW	slopworker
EKMNNOORSS	nonsmokers
EKMNOOPSTY	monkeypots
EKOORRSTUW	outworkers
EKOPPRRSUW	upperworks
ELLLOSSSUY	soullessly
ELLMRSSTUU	surmullets
ELLNNOPTUY	polytunnel
ELLNPRTUUY	purulently
ELLOORTWWY	yellowwort
ELLOPSSSTY	spotlessly
ELLOSSUUVV	volvuluses
ELMNOORSUY	enormously
ELMNOOSUVY	venomously
ELMNOPRTUY	poultrymen
ELMNORSUUY	numerously
ELMOOPRSUY	polymerous
ELMOOPRTUY	pleurotomy
ELMOOPRTXY	protoxylem
ELMOOPSSUY	polysemous
ELNNOPSSSU	nonplusses
ELNOSSSUUY	sensuously
ELOOORRSTW	woolsorter
ELOOORSSTZ	zoosterols
ELOORSSTUW	louseworts
ELOPPRSTUY	suppletory
ELOPPRSUVY	oversupply
ELOPRRSSYY	pyrolysers
ELOPRRSYYZ	pyrolyzers
EMMNOOORSU	monomerous
EMMNRSSTUU	menstruums
EMMOOPRSTT	postmortem
EMNNOOOPRT	monopteron
EMNNOOORTU	motoneuron
EMNNOOOSST	moonstones
EMNNOOSTWW	townswomen
EMNNOSTTUW	stuntwomen
EMNOOOPRST	monopteros
EMNOOORSST	sensomotor
EMNOORRSTT	tormentors

EMNOPPRSST promptness
EMNOPRRSTU prosternum
EMNORRSTUU surmounter
EMNORSSTUU menstruous
EMOOORRSST storerooms
EMOOORRSTV servomotor
EMOOPRRSSS pressrooms
EMOPRRSTUV overtrumps
ENNNOOPRSS nonpersons
ENNOOPPRST proponents
ENNOOPRSSS nonprosses
ENNOPRSTWY pennyworts
ENNORRSTUU outrunners
ENNORSSTTU turnstones
ENOOPPRSST postponers
ENOOPRRSSS responsors
ENOOPRRSSY responsory
ENOOPRSSSU porousness
ENOOPRSTTU portentous
ENOORSSTTW stoneworts
ENOPRSSSSU suspensors
ENOPRSSSTT sternposts
ENOPRSSSUY suspensory
EOOOPRSSUX exosporous
EOOOSSTTTV voetstoots
EOOPPRRRST propretors
EOOPPRRSSS oppressors
EOOPPRRSST prepostors
EOOPPRRSSU prosperous
EOOPPRSTTY prototypes
EOOPRRSSTT protestors
EOOPRRSTTU outporters
EOOPRSSSSS possessors
EOOPRSSSSY possessory
EOORRSSTTU stertorous
EOPPRRSSSU suppressor
EOPPRRSSTU supporters
EOPRSSSSUU sourpusses
FFGHIIOPPR hippogriff
FFGIILLLNU fulfilling
FFGIINORTY fortifying
FFGILMNNUU unmuffling
FFGINNOOTW Woffington
FFGINOPRSS offsprings
FFILLRTUUY fruitfully
FFILNRTUUU unfruitful
FFINOSSSUU suffusions
FGGHIIINNT infighting
FGGIIILNNY lignifying
FGGIIINNNR infringing
FGGIIINNSY signifying
FGGIILNORY glorifying
FGHHIORRTT forthright
FGHHLOTTUU thoughtful
FGHIILNSTU insightful
FGHIINNRSU furnishing
FGHIINORRY horrifying
FGHILLRTUY rightfully
FGHILOOSTT footlights
FGHINNOTUX foxhunting
FGHINOOOTT hotfooting
FGHINORSTT fortnights
FGHMOORSTU frogmouths
FGIIILLNNS infillings
FGIIIMNSTT misfitting
FGIIINNRTY nitrifying
FGIIINRTVY vitrifying
FGIIJLLNOY jollifying
FGIIJNSTUY justifying
FGIIKLNRSY friskingly
FGIILLMNOY mollifying
FGIILLNNUY nullifying
FGIILLNORV frivolling
FGIILLNRTY flirtingly
triflingly
FGIILLNSTY stiflingly
FGIILMNORU linguiform
FGIILNNOSW inflowings
FGIILNOSUU fuliginous
FGIILNRSST firstlings
FGIIMMMNUY mummifying
FGIIMNNORU uniforming
FGIIMNORTY mortifying
FGIIMNSTYY mystifying
FGIIMORRST strigiform
FGIINNOPTY pontifying
FGIINOPSTX postfixing
FGIINOTTTU outfitting
FGIINPPUYY yuppifying
FGIINRSSUY russifying
FGILLNOOSW followings
FGILLNOTUY floutingly
FGILMMNOUX flummoxing
FGILNNORWY frowningly
FGILNOPSTY flyposting
FGILOOSSTU ufologists
FGIMNOOPRS spongiform
FGINNOOOTT footnoting
FGINOOOTTU outfooting
FGLLLMOOUY gloomfully
FGLLNORUWY wrongfully
FGLOORTUUY futurology
FHILLMRTUY mirthfully
FHILLNOOWW Howlin' Wolf
FHILLOOPSW followship
FHILMOOOST tomfoolish
FHILMPRSUY frumpishly
FHILOPRSUW worshipful
FHLLLOSTUY slothfully
FHLLOTUUYY youthfully
FHLLRTTUUY truthfully
FHLNRTTUUU untruthful
FHMOOOPRST mothproofs
FIIKLNNSST skinflints
FIIKLNNSTY skinflinty
FIILLMORST stilliform
FIILLMOSTU multifoils
FIILMMNOOR moniliform
FIILMORSTU trifoliums
FIILOPRSST profilists
FIIMMNORSS misinforms
FIIMNORTUY uniformity
FIIMOORSST fortissimo
FIIMORSTTU fortuitism
FIINOSSSTU fusionists
FIIORSTTTU fortuitist
FIKLLLLSUY skillfully
FIKLLLNSUU unskillful
FIKLLOORST folklorist
FILLOOPTTY toploftily
FILLRSTTUY tristfully
FILMORSSTU formulists
FILOOOPRST portfolios
FIMNNNOORU nonuniform
FINOOPRSSU profusions
FINOOPRSTT footprints
FIOORSTTUU fortuitous
FLLMNORUUY mournfully
FLLOPRSTUY sportfully
FLLRSTTUUY trustfully
FLOOOOSSTT footstools
FMOOOPRRST stormproof
FOOPSSSTUY pussyfoots
GGGGIILLNY gigglingly
GGGIILLNNY nigglingly
GGGIILNQSU squiggling
GGGILLOOSW golliwoggs
GGGILNNPUU unplugging
GGGILNRSTU struggling
GGHHHIILST highlights
GGHIIILLTV vigil light
GGHIIILRSW whirligigs
GGHIILPRSY priggishly
GGHIINPRTU uprighting
GGHILLSSUY sluggishly
GGHILOOPRS logogriphs
GGHINNOSTW nightgowns
GGIIIINSTV gingivitis
GGIIILMMNN immingling
GGIIIMNSSV misgivings
GGIIINNRTU intriguing
GGIILLNNTY tinglingly
GGIILNNNSU unslinging
GGIILNNSTY stingingly
GGIILNNSWY swingingly
GGIILNPPRY grippingly
GGIINNOSTU outsinging
GGIINNPRSS springings
GGIINNPSUW upswinging
GGILLLNOOR logrolling
GGILLNORWY growlingly
GGILLNOSSY glossingly
GGILLNTTUY gluttingly
GGILMNOPRU promulging
GGILNNOOPR prolonging
GGILNNOSUY younglings
GGILNNRTUY gruntingly
GGILNOOPRU prologuing
GGINNNNRUU gunrunning
GGINNNOTUU outgunning
GGINOOPRRU proroguing
GGINOORTUW outgrowing
GGLLNNOOOW Wollongong
GGLLOOOSSY glossology
GHHIILPSST lightships
GHHIINRSTT nightshirt

GHHIIPRSTW	shipwright
GHHILLOSUY	ghoulishly
GHHINOPRTT	triphthong
GHHIOPPPRY	hippogryph
GHHLOORTUY	thoroughly
GHHOORTTUU	throughout
GHHOOTTTUU	outthought
GHHOPRTTUU	throughput
GHIIIMNSTT	mishitting
GHIIINNNRS	inshrining
GHIIKNNNTU	unthinking
GHIILLMRTW	millwright
GHIILLNOTW	Linlithgow
GHIILLNRWY	whirlingly
GHIILNRTVY	thrivingly
GHIILNSSWY	swishingly
GHIILNSTTW	whittlings
GHIIMNPRTU	triumphing
GHIINNORSU	nourishing
GHIINNOSTU	outshining
GHIINNPPSU	unshipping
GHIINNRSSU	inrushings
GHIINOPRSW	worshiping
GHIINOTTTU	outhitting
GHIKNOPRTU	groupthink
GHILLNOOOP	loopholing
GHILMNOOST	moonlights
GHILMNPTUY	thumpingly
GHILMOOORU	horologium
GHILMPRSUY	grumpishly
GHILNOOOOR	horologion
GHILNOOPSS	splooshing
GHILNOOPST	phlogiston
GHILNOOSTY	soothingly
GHILNORTTT	throttling
GHILNOSSST	slingshots
GHILNRRUYY	hurryingly
GHILOOORST	horologist
GHILOOPSYY	physiology
GHILOPSSTT	spotlights
	stoplights
GHIMMPSUUW	mugwumpish
GHIMNOSSST	songsmiths
GHINNNORTU	unthroning
GHINNOPTTU	pothunting
GHINOPSSTT	nightspots
GHIORRSSTY	hygristors
GHLLOOPTYY	typhlology
GHLMOOOOSU	homologous
GHLMOOOPRY	morphology
GHLNOOPSUW	snowplough
GHMNOOOOSU	homogonous
GHMNOOPSYY	gymnosophy
GHMOOOSUYZ	homozygous
GHMOOPRYYZ	zygomorphy
GHNNOOPRRS	pronghorns
GHNOOPSUYY	hypogynous
GHOORSTTUW	outgrowths
GHOORTTUUW	outwrought
GIIIIMMNNS	minimising
GIIIIMMNNZ	minimizing
GIIIKLMNSS	mislikings
GIIILLMNNU	illumining
GIIILLNNST	instilling
GIIILMNSTT	mistitling
GIIILNNTTU	intituling
GIIILNNTVY	invitingly
GIIILNORTV	vitrioling
GIIIMMNNSU	immunising
GIIIMMNNUZ	immunizing
GIIIMNNOSS	missioning
GIIIMNNPRT	imprinting
GIIIMNOPST	optimising
GIIIMNOPTZ	optimizing
GIIIMNPRSS	misprising
GIIIMNPRSZ	misprizing
GIIINNNOSU	unionising
GIIINNNOUZ	unionizing
GIIINNNTUV	uninviting
GIIINNORSS	sironising
GIIINNORSZ	sironizing
GIIKLLNPSU	upskilling
GIIKLMNRSY	smirkingly
GIIKLNNPRS	sprinkling
GIIKLNNSTW	twinklings
GIIKLNNSTY	stinkingly
GIIKLNRSTY	strikingly
GIIKMNNOOS	monoskiing
GIIKNNNTTU	unknitting
GIIKNRSTWY	skywriting
GIILLMNNOU	mullioning
GIILLMRSST	gristmills
GIILLNOPRY	pillorying
GIILLNOPST	pistolling
	postilling
GIILLNPPRY	ripplingly
GIILLNRSWY	swirlingly
GIILMMNSWY	swimmingly
GIILMNNOTW	Wilmington
GIILMNOPSY	imposingly
GIILMNORTU	turmoiling
GIILMOOSST	misologist
GIILMOOSSY	missiology
GIILMOOSTX	mixologist
GIILNNOPRU	purloining
GIILNNOSTV	Livingston
GIILNNOTUV	involuting
GIILNOOPST	topsoiling
GIILNOORSU	inglorious
GIILNOOSST	sinologist
GIILNPPRTY	trippingly
GIILNPRSST	striplings
GIILNRRSTY	stirringly
GIILOORSTV	virologist
GIILRSSTTU	liturgists
GIIMNNOORS	monsignori
GIIMNNOORT	monitoring
GIIMNNOPSU	unimposing
GIIMNOORST	motorising
GIIMNOORTZ	motorizing
GIIMNOQSTU	misquoting
GIIMNOSSTY	misogynist
GIINNNOSTU	nonsuiting
GIINNNSTTU	unstinting
GIINNOOPRT	portioning
GIINNOOPSS	opsonising
GIINNOOPSZ	opsonizing
GIINNRSTTU	intrusting
GIINNSTTUW	untwisting
GIINOSTTTU	outsitting
GIINOTTTUW	outwitting
GIINPPTTTU	tittupping
GIINPRRSSU	surprising
GIJMNOPTUU	outjumping
GIJNNOORSU	sojourning
GIJNOOPPPY	joypopping
GIKLLORRSW	grillworks
GIKMNNNOOS	nonsmoking
GIKNNNOORW	nonworking
GIKNNNOTTU	unknotting
GIKNNOOPRR	Norrköping
GIKNOORTUW	outworking
GILLMOORRS	grillrooms
GILLMOSSSY	syllogisms
GILLNRSTUY	rustlingly
GILLOORSUY	gloriously
GILMMNOOUY	immunology
GILMNNORUY	mourningly
GILMNNUUZZ	unmuzzling
GILMNOOOST	monologist
	nomologist
GILMOOOPST	pomologist
GILMOOSSTY	myologists
GILMOOSTYZ	zymologist
GILNNNOPSU	nonplusing
GILNNNSTUY	stunningly
GILNNOOSWY	swooningly
GILNNORSTY	snortingly
GILNOOOPSY	oligopsony
GILNOOOSST	nosologist
GILNOOPPSY	opposingly
GILNOOPSTY	stoopingly
GILNOPRSTY	sportingly
GILNOPRSYY	pyrolysing
GILNOPRYYZ	pyrolyzing
GILNOPSTYY	polygynist
GILNORRWYY	worryingly
GILNRSTTUY	trustingly
GILOOOPSTT	topologist
GILOOORSST	orologists
GILOOOSSTT	otologists
GILOOOSSTZ	zoologists
GILOOPRSTT	proglottis
GILOOPSTTY	typologist
GILOORRSUY	rigorously
GILOORSSTU	urologists
GILOORSUVY	vigorously
GIMMMPSUUW	mugwumpism
GIMMNNOSSU	summonsing
GIMMNRRSUU	murmurings
GIMNNOORSS	monsignors
GIMNNOOSTY	monogynist
GIMNOOSSUY	misogynous
GIMOPRSUUY	uropygiums
GINNNOORRT	Norrington
GINNNORTUU	outrunning

GINNOOPPST postponing
GINNOOPRSS sponsoring
GINNOPPSTU unstopping
GINNOPRSTU unsporting
GINNRSSTUU untrussing
GINOOORTTU outrooting
GINOOPRTUU outpouring
GINOPPRRTU purporting
GINOPPRSTU supporting
GINOPTTTUU outputting
GIOPRSSTWY gipsyworts
GKLMOOOORV Kolmogorov
GKMORSSSUY Mussorgsky
GLLNOOOOSS songololos
GLMNOOPSUY polygonums
GLNOOPSTUY Polygnotus
GLNOOPSUYY polygynous
GLNOOSTTUU gluttonous
GMNNOOOSUY monogynous
GMNOOORRST strongroom
GNNOOSTUWY Youngstown
HHILOOOPTT photolitho
HHILOOPPSY philosophy
HHILOOPPTY photophily
HHIMOOPRRZ rhizomorph
HHIMRSSTTY rhythmists
HHIOPPSSYY hypophysis
HHLMOPRTYY polyrhythm
HHMMOOOPRY homomorphy
HHNOORRSST shorthorns
HHOOOPPRTT phototroph
HHOOPPRSSU phosphorus
HIIKLSSTTY skittishly
HIILLMNOST millionths
HIILLNORTT trillionth
HIILMOOPSZ zoophilism
HIILNORSTT trilithons
HIILOPRSTY Holy Spirit
HIILORTTTY lithotrity
HIILOSSSTY histolysis
HIIMMNOPRS morphinism
HIINOORSST ornithosis
HIIOOOPRST oophoritis
HIKNNORSST stinkhorns
HIKNNORSWY hornywinks
HILLLMSTUU multihulls
HILLNPSSUY sulphinyls
HILLOOPRSW whirlpools
HILLSSTTUY sluttishly
HILMNOPSUU sulphonium
HILMNORTTY trimonthly
HILMOOPSUY myophilous
HILNORTUWY unworthily
HILOOOPSUZ zoophilous
HILOOORSVV Voroshilov
HILOOPSSTY photolysis
HILOOSSTYZ hylozoists
HILOPPSTUY Hippolytus
HILORSSSTT shortlists
HIMMNOOTYY homonymity
HIMNOPRRSY Pyrrhonism
HIMNOPSSTY hypnotisms
symphonist
HINOOPTTXY phytotoxin
HINOPPRRSY porphyrins
HINOPSSTTY hypnotists
HIOOPPRSST troopships
HIOOPRSTTT orthoptist
HIOOPRTTXY thixotropy
HIOORSSTTT orthotists
HIORRSSTTY thyristors
HIORSSTTUU struthious
HKMMNORRSU krummhorns
HLLOOPPRSY sporophyll
HLMOOPPRSY polymorphs
HLMOORSUUY humorously
HLOOPPRSSY sporophyls
HLOORSTTUY South Tyrol
HLOPRSSUUU sulphurous
HMMNOOOSUY homonymous
HMOOPRSTTU Portsmouth
HMOOPSSTUU posthumous
HMOOPTTTUY pottymouth
HNOOOPSTTU phototonus
HNOOPRSTTY phytotrons
HOOOPPRTTY phototropy
HOOORSTTTW toothworts
HOOPRSSSTT shortstops
IIIILOSUVX Louis XVIII
IIIKLLNPSS spillikins
IIIKLLNPSW pilliwinks
IIIKMNRSST miniskirts
IIILLMMNSU illuminism
IIILLMNSTU illuminist
IIILMMOTTY immotility
IIILNOSSTV violinists
IIIMNOOPST imposition
IIIMNOPRSS misprision
IIIMOPSSTV positivism
IIINNOSTTU intuitions
IIINOQRSTU inquisitor
IIINOQSTUU iniquitous
IIIOPSSTTV positivist
IIIOPSTTVY positivity
IIIPRSSSTT spiritists
IIKLMMOPSS milksopism
IIKNNNOOSS onionskins
IIKOPRSSTW kiwisports
IILLLOPPSW pillowslip
IILLLORSUY illusorily
IILLNNNOOS nonillions
IILLNOOPSS pollinosis
IILLNOOPST postillion
IILLNOQSSU squillions
IILMNOOPSS implosions
IILMNOPSSU impulsions
IILMNOPSTY postliminy
IILMNOSTUY luminosity
IILMOORSUV limivorous
IILNNOOTUV involution
IILNOOPSST postilions
IILOPSSSST solipsists
IIMMOORTUV vomitorium
IIMNNOOSSU insomnious
IINNOORSST intorsions
IINNORSSTU intrusions
IINOOOPPST opposition
IINOOPRSSV provisions
IINOORSSTT sortitions
IINOPRRSTU irruptions
IINORSSSTU sinistrous
IINORSTTTU institutor
IINORSTTUU nutritious
IIOOOPRSTV ovipositor
IIOOPPRSTU propitious
IIOPRSSTUU spirituous
IIORSSTTTU tutiorists
IIORSTTUVY virtuosity
IJMNOORSTW jointworms
ILLMNOSUUY luminously
ILLNOOPSTU pollutions
ILLNOORSSU Roussillon
ILLNOORSTT tortillons
ILLOOSSSVY solvolysis
ILLOQRSTUW quillworts
ILMMNOOOPS monopolism
ILMNOOOPST monopolist
ILMNOOQSUY somniloquy
ILMNOOSUUV voluminous
ILMNOPSXYY polymyxins
ILMNOSTUUY mutinously
ILMOORSTUY timorously
ILMOOSTTXY xylotomist
ILMOSTTUUY tumulosity
ILNOOOSSYZ ozonolysis
ILNOOPPRSU propulsion
ILNOOPRSSU prolusions
ILOOPPRSST spoilsport
ILOORSTTUY tortiously
ILOORSUUXY uxoriously
ILOPRSSUUY spuriously
ILORSTUUVY virtuously
IMMOOPRSTU prostomium
IMMOPPRSTU impromptus
IMMOPSSSUY symposiums
IMNNOOPSTW topminnows
IMNNOSTYYY synonymity
IMNOOOPRST promotions
IMNOOORSUV omnivorous
IMOOOSSTTZ zootomists
IMOOPRRSSY promissory
IMOOPRSSTU impostrous
INOOOPPRRT proportion
INOOPPRSTU pourpoints
INOOPRRSTU protrusion
INOPRSSTTU outsprints
INOPSSSTTY synoptists
IOOOPRSSTU isotropous
IOOPPRRSTU potpourris
IOOPPRSSTU propositus
IOORSTTTUY tortuosity
KKLMMOOOSS Komsomolsk
LLOOPPSUUY populously
LMOOOSTUXY xylotomous
LMOSTTUUUU tumultuous
LNOOORSSUY sonorously

LOOPPRRSUY propulsory
LOOPSTUUUV voluptuous
LOORSTTUUY tortuously
MNNOOOOSTU monotonous
MNNOOSSUYY synonymous
MNOOOPRRTY promontory
MNOORSSSTW snowstorms
OOOOPRSSUZ zoosporous

Eleven Letters

AAAAABBCDRR	abracadabra
AAAAABHHMRT	Mahabharata
AAAAACLMNNP	Panama Canal
AAAAADGJLRU	Guadalajara
AAAABBCHILN	Bahía Blanca
AAAABBCORSS	Cabora Bassa
AAAABBINRST	sabbatarian
AAAABCCHILN	bacchanalia
AAAABCEELTT	Cetatea Albă
AAAABCENRSS	scarabaeans
AAAABCGMNRU	Bucaramanga
AAAABDGHMNR	Grand Bahama
AAAABDIIRSU	Saudi Arabia
AAAABGKORSY	kabaragoyas
AAAABGNNPRT	Nanga Parbat
AAAABHKLLRU	Allahu Akbar
AAAABHLRSTT	Shatt-al-Arab
AAAACDGLLNU	Guadalcanal
AAAACDGMOSV	Vasco da Gama
AAAACDHMNRR	Ramachandra
AAAACGILPSS	passacaglia
AAAACGINNRR	Gran Canaria
AAAACHHKKLM	Makhachkala
AAAACHILNPP	Appalachian
AAAACLMNRST	almacantars
AAAACNRRSVY	caravansary
AAAADEGLMMT	amalgamated
AAAADEHRTVV	Atharva-Veda
AAAADELMRSS	Dar es Salaam
AAAADLMNNQU	Namaqualand
AAAAEGKLNRS	Alaska Range
AAAAEGLMMST	amalgamates
AAAAEHMMOTT	haematomata
AAAAEJKLSTT	Jataka Tales
AAAAENNNRST	Antseranana
AAAAFGNOSTT	Antofagasta
AAAAFINRRST	rastafarian
AAAAGGNOSTY	Astanga yoga
AAAAGHIPPRR	paragraphia
AAAAGIMPTVZ	Vizagapatam
AAAAGJNNNRY	Narayanganj
AAAAGMSSSSU	massasaugas
AAAAGORRSTZ	Stara Zagora
AAAAHHMRRST	Maharashtra
AAAAILRSSTU	Australasia
AAAALLLOOPZ	lalapalooza
AAAALPRSSTT	parastatals
AAABBCEELLN	balanceable
AAABBCILSST	sabbaticals
AAABCCKNSSV	canvasbacks
AAABCDDIRRY	bradycardia
AAABCDEEINR	abecedarian
AAABCDEIORS	scarabaeoid
AAABCDEIRSS	scarabaeids
AAABCDELNRS	candelabras
AAABCDGINRY	Cardigan Bay
AAABCEEIMRT	bacteraemia
AAABCEGILLR	algebraical
AAABCEHINRT	abranchiate
AAABCEHNNRS	anabranches
AAABCEIILLM	bacillaemia
AAABCELLLOT	allocatable
AAABCELLLRS	clarabellas
AAABCELRTTT	attractable
AAABCHINRST	batrachians
AAABCHLLMPS	Paschal Lamb
AAABCIILNRS	basicranial
AAABCILLNTY	abactinally
AAABCILLOPR	parabolical
AAABCILNOTT	ablactation
AAABCILPRST	parablastic
AAABCORRSTU	barracoutas
AAABDEEHHSY	dahabeeyahs
AAABDEGGNOV	vagabondage
AAABDELNPTU	unadaptable
AAABDGNNOOU	Oda Nobunaga
AAABDHLMNRU	Abdul Rahman
AAABDMNRRSU	barramundas
AAABDMORSSS	ambassadors
AAABEEGLLSV	salvageable
AAABEEGLNRR	arrangeable
AAABEHIMNPS	amphisbaena
AAABEHINRRT	breatharian
AAABEHINRSU	Beauharnais
AAABEIKLLLS	alkalisable
AAABEIKLLLZ	alkalizable
AAABEILLNUV	unavailable
AAABEILNRST	alabastrine
AAABEILNSST	Santa Isabel
AAABEILPPRS	appraisable
AAABEJLOTUV	Vuelta Abajo
AAABELLNPTU	unpalatable
AAABELNNOTT	annotatable
AAABELNRRTW	warrantable
AAABEMRSTTT	Stabat Mater
AAABEPRRSUZ	superbazaar
AAABGHIOOPR	agoraphobia
AAABHIOPRST	astraphobia
AAABHIORSTU	South Arabia
AAABHMPRRTU	Brahmaputra
AAABIJMNNRS	Banjarmasin
AAABILLNOSS	labionasals
AAABILNNSST	Saint Albans
AAABINPSSTT	anabaptists
AAABLNRRTWY	warrantably
AAACCCEILTT	acatalectic
AAACCCEINPT	capacitance
AAACCCIISSU	Ciscaucasia
AAACCCILSTT	cataclastic
AAACCCISTTU	catacaustic
AAACCDEIIMN	academician
AAACCDEILMS	academicals
AAACCDEIPTT	capacitated
AAACCDEOPRU	Pão de Açúcar
AAACCDHIRTY	tachycardia
AAACCDINOPP	Cappadocian
AAACCEHINPU	ipecacuanha
AAACCEHNNST	catananches
AAACCEHRSST	saccharates
AAACCEILLOR	calceolaria
AAACCEIPSTT	capacitates
AAACCGILORR	García Lorca
AAACCHILLRY	archaically
AAACCHILRTU	autarchical
AAACCILLNRU	canalicular
AAACCILLPRT	parallactic
AAACCILLRSS	cascarillas
AAACCILMNOT	acclamation
AAACCILOSVV	Cavaco Silva
AAACCILPSTT	cataplastic
AAACCILRRTU	caricatural
AAACCILSTUV	accusatival
AAACCIMNORT	carcinomata
AAACCKLMNNN	Clackmannan

AAACCLLMSTY	cataclysmal
AAACCLMOPRT	caprolactam
AAACCLMORTY	acclamatory
AAACDDEIMMS	macadamised
AAACDDEIMMZ	macadamized
AAACDEEIMRR	camaraderie
AAACDEHINRT	acidanthera
AAACDEIIRST	Adriatic Sea
AAACDEILMPR	paramedical
AAACDEILNRT	cardinalate
AAACDEILPSS	Pas-de-Calais
AAACDEIMMRS	macadamiser
AAACDEIMMRZ	macadamizer
AAACDEIMMSS	macadamises
AAACDEIMMSZ	macadamizes
AAACDEINRTY	caryatidean
AAACDELNORW	Lower Canada
AAACDENPPRU	Upper Canada
AAACDGIILRS	cardialgias
AAACDGNNRRY	Grand Canary
AAACDHINNRS	arachnidans
AAACDIINNSV	Scandinavia
AAACDILOPRX	paradoxical
AAACEEFLMNS	malfeasance
AAACEEGNNRR	carrageenan
AAACEEGNNRS	carageenans
AAACEEIMNOT	acetonaemia
AAACEENPPRS	appearances
AAACEFINRST	East African
AAACEFLQSTU	catafalques
AAACEGHILLP	cephalalgia
AAACEGILLNN	gallinacean
AAACEGILMNO	egomaniacal
AAACEGIRRWY	carriageway
AAACEHILLPR	parheliacal
AAACEHLMNNP	Panchen Lama
AAACEILMMNT	analemmatic
AAACEILORSU	araliaceous
AAACEINPRRT	carpentaria
AAACEINRRSS	sarracenias
AAACEIPPRRT	paraparetic
AAACELLLMPU	ampullaceal
AAACELMNPTU	campanulate
AAACELMNRST	sacramental
AAACELMOPRT	paracetamol
AAACELMPRST	metacarpals
AAACFILLNTY	fanatically
AAACFILNSTT	fantastical
AAACFIMNRRT	aircraftman
AAACGGILOPR	paragogical
AAACGHILNNV	avalanching
AAACGHIMNOP	phagomaniac
AAACGHIPPRR	paragraphic
AAACGHNOOTT	Chattanooga
AAACGHNRSTT	tragacanths
AAACGILMMRT	grammatical
AAACGILMNNO	anglomaniac
AAACGILMPRT	pragmatical
AAACGINNNRV	caravanning
AAACHHINPTX	hapaxanthic
AAACHIILPRS	pharisaical
AAACHIKPPRT	apparatchik
AAACHILMRRT	matriarchal
AAACHILNOTU	anacoluthia
AAACHILPRRT	patriarchal
AAACHLNRRTY	charlatanry
AAACHLNRTTU	Uttaranchal
AAACHNPRSTY	pyracanthas
AAACHQSTUUU	chautauquas
AAACIILMMST	miasmatical
AAACIILMOTX	axiomatical
AAACIILPRST	parasitical
AAACILLMNRU	animalcular
AAACILLMORT	clamatorial
AAACILLNOTT	lactational
AAACILLNRST	scarlatinal
AAACILLNSTY	satanically
AAACILLSTTY	astatically
AAACILNNRST	Lancastrian
AAACILNOSTU	causational
AAACILNRSSS	carnassials
AAACILOPSTT	apostatical
AAACINRRSTT	tractarians
AAACLMNRSTU	almucantars
AAACNORSUXY	Roxas y Acuña
AAACNRSTTTT	attractants
AAADDDIMNNU	Daman and Diu
AAADEEGHNPS	phagedaenas
AAADEEJNRWY	Jayawardene
AAADEFFNNOR	fanfaronade
AAADEGHPPRR	paragraphed
AAADEGLNRTV	landgravate
AAADEHLNPRS	aphelandras
AAADEHMRSSY	hamadryases
AAADEHPPRRS	paraphrased
AAADEIKNNVV	Vivekananda
AAADEILLPST	palatalised
AAADEILLPTZ	palatalized
AAADEILMPTV	maladaptive
AAADEILNNRX	Alexandrian
AAADEILNRSS	Alessandria
AAADEILRRSV	adversarial
AAADEIMNNRT	mandarinate
AAADEIMNNRX	Anaximander
AAADEIMNRST	mandataries
AAADELLMPRT	Mar del Plata
AAADELLOSTV	Valle d'Aosta
AAADELMNRSS	salamanders
AAADELNRSVW	van der Waals
AAADENNPRST	transpadane
AAADGGINNTV	advantaging
AAADGGINORT	aggradation
AAADGIILLRS	gaillardias
AAADGIILMNR	madrigalian
AAADGILLNRS	granadillas
AAADGILNORT	gradational
AAADGMMMNRS	grandmammas
AAADGMNORRS	mandragoras
AAADGNOPPRS	propagandas
AAADHHIJNSU	Judah ha-Nasi
AAADHHLPRYZ	haphazardly
AAADHILMMMU	Muhammad Ali
AAADIILNORR	radiolarian
AAADIILNORT	radiational
AAADIKKLVVZ	Vladikavkaz
AAADILLLNOT	allantoidal
AAADILNNRSS	Aran Islands
AAADILNORSV	Salvadorian
AAADILOPRRX	liar paradox
AAADINOPSTT	adaptations
AAADLMMNNNS	landammanns
AAADLNORSSV	San Salvador
AAADLOORSSV	São Salvador
AAADORSSTTU	autostradas
AAAEEELNPRS	paraselenae
AAAEEGINPRS	paragenesia
AAAEEGRTTVX	extravagate
AAAEEHINSST	anaesthesia
AAAEEHLLSST	Tallahassee
AAAEEHMNTTX	exanthemata
AAAEEKLPRSY	parakeelyas
AAAEERSTTVX	extravasate
AAAEFLMNSST	malfeasants
AAAEFRSSSSS	sassafrases
AAAEGGILMNT	gametangial
AAAEGHIMMNO	haemangioma
AAAEGIILNRT	egalitarian
AAAEGILMMNO	megalomania
AAAEGILMNNT	galantamine
AAAEGILNNST	East Anglian
AAAEGIMRRTV	margraviate
AAAEGMMNRRS	anagrammers
AAAEGMNOPSS	Mona Passage
AAAEGMRRSTV	margravates
AAAEGNRTTVX	extravagant
AAAEGORSSSS	Sargasso Sea
AAAEGPSSSWY	passageways
AAAEHIILMPT	epithalamia
AAAEHILMSST	thalassemia
AAAEHILNPRX	hexaplarian
AAAEHIMNNRT	amaranthine
AAAEHIMOSST	haemostasia
AAAEHLNOPPR	epanaphoral
AAAEHPPRRSS	paraphrases
AAAEHPPRSTY	paraphysate
AAAEIKLLNNT	antalkaline
AAAEIKLLNST	antalkalies
AAAEILLPSST	palatalises
AAAEILLPSTZ	palatalizes
AAAEILMNNOT	emanational
AAAEILNPRTU	Telanaipura
AAAEILNPSST	anaplasties
AAAEILNPSTT	palatinates
AAAEILPPRRS	reappraisal
AAAEIMNNRTU	Mauretanian
AAAEIMNQRSU	aquamarines
AAAEINSSSST	assassinate
AAAEIPPRRSS	paraparesis
AAAELLMMMPS	plasmalemma

AAAELLNNTTY antenatally
AAAELLNRSTT tarantellas
AAAELMRSSTT metatarsals
AAAELMSSTTY Malay States
AAAENNPRSTU Punta Arenas
AAAENRSSSTT tarantasses
AAAEPPRSSTU apparatuses
AAAFGHINNST Afghanistan
AAAFLLMNSTY fantasmally
AAAGGGINRTV aggravating
AAAGGHHIOPR Hagiographa
AAAGGHILOPR logagraphia
AAAGGILNNTV galavanting
AAAGGILRSST gastralgias
AAAGGINORTV aggravation
AAAGHILNOPP Paphlagonia
AAAGHIRSSTY satyagrahis
AAAGIILNOTT agitational
AAAGIILNPRS parasailing
AAAGIIMNRRS agrarianism
AAAGIINNRSU sanguinaria
AAAGIINRSTT sagittarian
AAAGIKNNNTY Tanganyikan
AAAGILNNPQU aquaplaning
AAAGIMMNRRS grammarians
AAAGIMNSSTT anastigmats
AAAGLLORSSV Vargas Llosa
AAAGLMNORTU granulomata
AAAHIILMPSS Ismail Pasha
AAAHIILPPRS paraphilias
AAAHIKMNRRS Ramakrishna
AAAHILMOPRT prothalamia
AAAHILNPSXY anaphylaxis
AAAHIMMMSST mahatmaisms
AAAHKMMORYY Omar Khayyám
AAAHRRSTTUZ Zarathustra
AAAIILNORTV variational
AAAIILNPSTU saintpaulia
AAAIIMNNRTU Mauritanian
AAAIINNQRTU antiquarian
AAAIINNRSST sanitarians
AAAIKKNSTZZ Kazantzakis
AAAIKRRSTTU titarakuras
AAAILLMNNSZ manzanillas
AAAILLMOPPT papillomata
AAAILLNNPSZ Spallanzani
AAAILLNOSTV salvational
AAAILLNOTUV valuational
AAAILLORSTT saltatorial
AAAILMNOPPR malapropian
AAAILNNOSTY analysation
AAAILNNOTYZ analyzation
AAAILNNRSTU saturnalian
AAAILNORTVV Navratilova
AAAILNRSSTU saturnalias
AAAIMNNOOST antonomasia
AAAIMNOOPRS paronomasia
AAAINNNNOST San Antonian
AAAIRRSTTTT Tatar Strait
AAAKNPRRSUU Sukarnapura
AABBBDEELMN Bab el Mandeb
AABBCCIILST cabbalistic
AABBCDEKLLL blackballed
AABBCDKLORS blackboards
AABBCEEELMR embraceable
AABBCEEKKRR backbreaker
AABBCEGMORW cabbageworm
AABBCEGNOTW cabbagetown
AABBCEINORT bicarbonate
AABBCIIKLST kabbalistic
AABBDDEELST beadblasted
AABBDDEORRS breadboards
AABBDEEGILR abridgeable
AABBDEEIRTV abbreviated
AABBDEEKRST breadbasket
AABBDEELNTU undebatable
AABBDEELRST beadblaster
AABBDEEORRV beaverboard
AABBDEGORRS bargeboards
AABBDEILLOR della Robbia
AABBEEIRRTV rebarbative
AABBEEIRSTV abbreviates
AABBEEKLLRR ballbreaker
AABBEEKLNRU unbreakable
AABBEELLRST barbastelle
AABBEFGLRST flabbergast
AABBEGIINRT bearbaiting
AABBEHIILNT inhabitable
AABBEHILLOS abolishable
AABBEHNRSUW Bhubaneswar
AABBEIIRRST barbarities
AABBEIORRTV abbreviator
AABBEIRRTTU barbiturate
AABBEKLLSST basketballs
AABBGGILNRS balbriggans
AABBGHIMNOT thingamabob
AABBGIINRRS barbarising
AABBGIINRRZ barbarizing
AABBHIKOSUZ bashibazouk
AABBIIILMNO bibliomania
AABBIIKLNTY bankability
AABBILLNSTU balibuntals
AABBKKMOOOO amabokoboko
AABBLLMSTTU albumblatts
AABBLORRSUY barbarously
AABCCDEIKKP pickabacked
AABCCDEJKKL blackjacked
AABCCDEKKRT backtracked
AABCCEEELLR accelerable
AABCCEELLNO concealable
AABCCEHLNRU craunchable
AABCCEILPRT practicable
AABCCEKKPRS backpackers
AABCCEKRSTT backscatter
AABCCELLMUU accumulable
AABCCELNOTT contactable
AABCCELNOTU accountable
AABCCERRUUY bureaucracy
AABCCGIKKNP backpacking
AABCCGIKNPS backspacing
AABCCIILOSU coulibiacas
AABCCIKNRRS crackbrains
AABCCILPRTY practicably
AABCCLNOTUY accountably
AABCCLNRRUU carbuncular
AABCDDEEKLP backpedaled
AABCDDEEKNR breakdanced
AABCDDEKLSS saddlebacks
AABCDDELOPR clapboarded
AABCDDENOOR carbonadoed
AABCDDEORST broadcasted
AABCDDIKMNO diamondback
AABCDEEERTX exacerbated
AABCDEEFLRY barefacedly
AABCDEEILMT alembicated
AABCDEEKNRR breakdancer
AABCDEEKNRS breakdances
AABCDEEKPPR paperbacked
AABCDEENORT decarbonate
AABCDEFIIIL acidifiable
AABCDEHHMNR chamberhand
AABCDEHIMMR chambermaid
AABCDEHKNRS backhanders
AABCDEIILNT indicatable
AABCDEIIMNR carbamidine
AABCDEIKLLM blackmailed
AABCDEIRRRS barricaders
AABCDELMNRU candelabrum
AABCDELNOTU outbalanced
AABCDELORSS scaleboards
AABCDENOORS carbonadoes
AABCDEORRST broadcaster
rebroadcast
AABCDGGIOOR braggadocio
AABCDGHIKNN backhanding
AABCDGIINRR barricading
AABCDGIMNSU ambuscading
AABCDGKLRSU blackguards
AABCDHILNOS baldachinos
AABCDHKLORS chalkboards
AABCDHMNORY rhabdomancy
AABCDHMORST matchboards
AABCDIINNNO cannabinoid
AABCDIINOST abdications
AABCDIIOPRS basidiocarp
AABCDIIQRTU biquadratic
AABCDILNOSU subdiaconal
AABCDINOORR radiocarbon
AABCEEEHLST escheatable
AABCEEELLPR replaceable
AABCEEELRRT retraceable
AABCEEEMRRS macebearers
AABCEEERSTX exacerbates
AABCEEFLRRT refractable
AABCEEFNORR forbearance
AABCEEGLLNO congealable
AABCEEHILMN machineable
AABCEEHILMP impeachable
AABCEEHKLRT leatherback
AABCEEHLMNR Malebranche
AABCEEHLNTU unteachable
AABCEEHLSTY chalybeates
AABCEEHMNRT antechamber
AABCEEHRSST sabretaches
AABCEEIINRR carabiniere

AABCEEILLMR reclaimable
AABCEEILMNV ambivalence
AABCEEILNPS inescapable
AABCEEILNRS increasable
AABCEEILPPR appreciable
AABCEEINRRS aberrancies
carabineers
AABCEEKPPRR paperbacker
AABCEELNORV overbalance
AABCEELNPSS capableness
AABCEELNPSU unescapable
AABCEELNRST tabernacles
AABCEELNRTU untraceable
AABCEELORTT bracteolate
AABCEELRRTT retractable
AABCEELRSTT scatterable
AABCEELRTTU trabeculate
AABCEELRTTX extractable
AABCEESSTTU subacetates
AABCEFIIRTV fabricative
AABCEFILNOT labefaction
AABCEFLMNOY flamboyance
AABCEFLNOTU confabulate
AABCEFLRRTU fracturable
AABCEGLMNNS blancmanges
AABCEHHPSTY bathyscaphe
AABCEHIINNT inhabitance
AABCEHILMNR chamberlain
AABCEHILNRU hibernacula
AABCEHILSST chastisable
AABCEHIPRRY hypercarbia
AABCEHKLRST blackhearts
AABCEHLNSTU staunchable
AABCEHLPRSU purchasable
AABCEHPSSTY bathyscapes
AABCEHRRSTT tetrabrachs
AABCEIIINRR carabinieri
AABCEIILNNS cannibalise
AABCEIILNNZ cannibalize
AABCEIINPUV bupivacaine
AABCEIINRRS carabiniers
AABCEIINSTU beauticians
AABCEIIRRTU bacteriuria
AABCEIKLLMR blackmailer
AABCEILLLOS localisable
AABCEILLLOZ localizable
AABCEILLLRS claribellas
AABCEILLMNU calumniable
AABCEILLNSU suballiance
AABCEILLRTT ballicatter
AABCEILLRTY bacterially
AABCEILLSTY syllabicate
AABCEILMNRY carbylamine
AABCEILMNVY ambivalency
AABCEILMORZ carbimazole
AABCEILNNOT containable
AABCEILNPSY inescapably
AABCEILNRTT intractable
AABCEILPPRY appreciably
AABCEILRRST calibraters
AABCEINNSTY betacyanins
AABCEINORST abreactions
AABCEIOQRSU aquaerobics
AABCEIRSTTV abstractive
AABCEKKLNSS blacksnakes
AABCEKLLRRT trackerball
AABCEKNRRSU Saarbrücken
AABCEKPRRST bratpackers
AABCEKQRRTU quarterback
AABCELLLOPS collapsable
AABCELLOORT collaborate
AABCELLORRS barcarolles
AABCELMOPSS compassable
AABCELNOSTU outbalances
AABCELNRTTU untractable
AABCELORSXY carboxylase
AABCELORTXY carboxylate
AABCENOPRST absorptance
AABCEOORRSU arboraceous
AABCEOORTTZ azotobacter
AABCERRSTUU bureaucrats
AABCFGIINRT fabricating
AABCFIINORT fabrication
AABCFIORRST fabricators
AABCFIORRVY Vicar of Bray
AABCFLMNOYY flamboyancy
AABCGHIINRT brachiating
AABCGHIKNSW backwashing
AABCGHIOOPR agoraphobic
AABCGHIOPRR barographic
AABCGIILLMS galliambics
AABCGIILNRT calibrating
AABCGILNNNU unbalancing
AABCGINNORT carbonating
AABCGINRSTT abstracting
AABCGKMMNOS backgammons
AABCHHIMPRS amphibrachs
AABCHHPSSTY bathyscaphs
AABCHIILRRT tribrachial
AABCHIINNTY inhabitancy
AABCHIINORT brachiation
AABCHILNSTU Baluchistan
AABCHINOSTT cohabitants
AABCHIOPRST astraphobic
AABCHKLPSSS splashbacks
AABCHNRRSUY brachyurans
AABCIIILMRS biracialism
AABCIIILMTY amicability
AABCIIKLOSU koulibiacas
AABCIILLPTY placability
AABCIILMNNS cannibalism
AABCIILNORT calibration
AABCIILRRUU biauricular
AABCIILRSTY sybaritical
AABCIILSTUY causability
AABCILLMNTU lactalbumin
AABCILLNOTY botanically
AABCILMOSST catabolisms
AABCILNNRUU incunabular
AABCILNRTTY intractably
AABCILORRST calibrators
AABCILOSTTY biocatalyst
AABCINNOORT carbonation
AABCINORRTU carburation
AABCINORSTT abstraction
AABCKLMOORS blackamoors
AABCLLLRSTY crystal ball
AABCLLNNNOS cannonballs
AABCLPRSSUU subscapular
AABDDEEGRRY graybearded
AABDDEELORR leaderboard
AABDDEELRSS addressable
AABDDEGGORR daggerboard
AABDDEGLLLR gallbladder
AABDDEHHNRT handbreadth
AABDDEHMORY hebdomadary
AABDDEILSSU dissuadable
AABDDEINOST bastinadoed
AABDDEIRSST bastardised
AABDDEIRSTZ bastardized
AABDDELNSST sandblasted
AABDDEORRST starboarded
AABDDHHIMOR Bodhidharma
AABDDILLRRU Baudrillard
AABDDNRSSTU substandard
AABDEEFKRST breakfasted
AABDEEHHRRS haberdasher
AABDEEHINRR harebrained
AABDEEILLMP impleadable
AABDEEIMNTT ambidentate
AABDEELORSV broadleaves
AABDEELPPRT palpebrated
AABDEELPRSU persuadable
AABDEEMRRSS embarrassed
AABDEEPRRSY prayer beads
AABDEGGHINN headbanging
AABDEGGINRS brigandages
AABDEGGLLRY ballyragged
AABDEGGNRSS sandbaggers
AABDEGHILNS Bangladeshi
AABDEGILNOS diagnosable
AABDEGINNOS gabionnades
AABDEGORSST goatsbeards
AABDEHIILTT habilitated
AABDEHIINRR hairbrained
AABDEHINRSW brainwashed
AABDEHLLNRS handballers
AABDEHLRSTT Halberstadt
AABDEHRSTWY breadthways
AABDEIILLNT dentilabial
AABDEIILNSV inadvisable
AABDEIILRTY readability
AABDEIILSST assibilated
AABDEIIRRTT abirritated
AABDEIKNORT debarkation
AABDEILLNOT labiodental
AABDEILLNRS banderillas
AABDEILLRVY adverbially
AABDEILMNTU mandibulate
AABDEILNOUV unavoidable
AABDEILNSUV unadvisable
AABDEILOPRS parabolised
AABDEILOPRZ parabolized
AABDEILORRT labradorite
AABDEILRSTU tabularised

AABDEILRTUZ	tabularized
AABDEIMRTUV	adumbrative
AABDEINOSST	bastinadoes
AABDEIQRSTU	biquadrates
AABDEIRSSST	bastardises
AABDEIRSSTZ	bastardizes
AABDEKORSST	skateboards
AABDELLNNOS	belladonnas
AABDELNNRRS	Barren Lands
AABDELNRSST	sandblaster
AABDELRSSTU	balustrades
AABDEMNNNOT	abandonment
AABDEMNRSST	bandmasters
AABDEMRSTTU	masturbated
AABDEOPRSST	pasteboards
AABDFHLORSS	flashboards
AABDGGGINNS	sandbagging
AABDGHILLNN	handballing
AABDGHINOSV	vagabondish
AABDGIILRTY	gradability
AABDGIMNOSV	vagabondism
AABDGIMNRTU	adumbrating
AABDHIILNTU	habitudinal
AABDHIOSTTV	bodhisattva
AABDHLOPRSS	splashboard
AABDHMMOORY	rhabdomyoma
AABDHNORRSW	handbarrows
AABDIILLTUY	laudability
AABDIILMNTY	damnability
AABDIILMQRU	liquidambar
AABDIILNSVY	inadvisably
AABDIKLNNSS	Banks Island
AABDILLMNOY	abdominally
AABDILNOUVY	unavoidably
AABDILOOPRS	paraboloids
AABDILOORRS	boardsailor
AABDIMNORTU	adumbration
AABDIMNRRSU	barramundis
AABDINRSSSU	Buridan's ass
AABDMOORRRT	mortarboard
AABEEEGKMRR	gamebreaker
AABEEEGLLNR	enlargeable
AABEEEGLLRT	relegatable
AABEEEKSTVW	basketweave
AABEEFKRRST	breakfaster
AABEEFLLRTT	flatterable
AABEEFORSTU	Beaufort Sea
AABEEGILNST	East Bengali
AABEEGINNRT	annabergite
AABEEGLMNTU	augmentable
AABEEGLMSSS	assemblages
AABEEGNORST	baronetages
AABEEHILPST	alphabetise
AABEEHILPTZ	alphabetize
AABEEHIRSST	baresthesia
AABEEHKLNSU	unshakeable
AABEEHLRSTY	breathalyse
AABEEHLRTYZ	breathalyze
AABEEIILLNN	inalienable
AABEEIKLMST	mistakeable
AABEEILLMOR	ameliorable
AABEEILLNNU	unalienable
AABEEILLNPX	explainable
AABEEILLNRT	inalterable
AABEEILMNSS	amiableness
AABEEILNPRS	inseparable
AABEEILORTV	elaborative
AABEEILPRRR	irreparable
AABEEINRRRT	trainbearer
AABEEINRRST	brainteaser
AABEEINSSTT	bastnaesite
AABEEJKRRSW	jawbreakers
AABEEKLNPSU	unspeakable
AABEEKLRRSW	lawbreakers
AABEEKRRSTW	breakwaters
AABEEKSSTTW	wastebasket
AABEELLLSSZ	sleazeballs
AABEELLMNOT	balletomane
AABEELLNPTT	battleplane
AABEELLNRTU	unalterable
AABEELLNSSS	salableness
AABEELLORTY	elaborately
AABEELLPRRS	pallbearers
AABEELLPRSU	pleasurable
AABEELMNSST	tamableness
AABEELMPRTU	perambulate
AABEELMPTTT	attemptable
AABEELMSSTT	metastables
AABEELNORST	treasonable
AABEELNRSST	ratableness
AABEELNRTTU	entablature
AABEELNSSSV	savableness
AABEELNSSTX	taxableness
AABEELPPRST	palpebrates
AABEELPRSTT	breastplate
AABEELPSSSS	Basses-Alpes
AABEELRRSTU	treasurable
AABEELRRSTV	traversable
AABEEMMOPRT	meprobamate
AABEEMRRSSS	embarrasses
AABEENRRSTU	sauerbraten
AABEFFIILLS	falsifiable
AABEFGIILMN	magnifiable
AABEFHILNOS	fashionable
AABEFIILLMP	amplifiable
AABEFIILLQU	qualifiable
AABEFIILSST	satisfiable
AABEFILLMMN	inflammable
AABEFILLNST	inflatables
AABEFILLRTT	filtratable
AABEFINRRST	afterbrains
AABEFLLNPPU	unflappable
AABEFLNORUV	unfavorable
AABEGGGNNRS	gangbangers
AABEGGINORY	Georgian Bay
AABEGHINRSS	earbashings
AABEGHORRSU	harbourages
AABEGIILNNV	invaginable
AABEGIJKNRW	jawbreaking
AABEGIKLNRW	lawbreaking
AABEGIKNORR	aerobraking
AABEGILNNUV	unnavigable
AABEGILNORT	elaborating
AABEGILNOSZ	zabagliones
AABEGILRSST	algebraists
AABEGINNPST	gabapentins
AABEGINNRST	interabangs
AABEGIRRRTU	arbitrageur
AABEGLLMOST	megaloblast
AABEGLMOPRR	programable
AABEGMNRSSU	submanagers
AABEHHIOPPT	taphephobia
AABEHIILLNN	annihilable
AABEHIILSTT	habilitates
AABEHILNRST	tarnishable
AABEHILORUV	behavioural
AABEHINRRSW	brainwasher
AABEHINRSSW	brainwashes
AABEHKLNSUY	unshakeably
AABEHLMOSTT	hematoblast
AABEHLMOSTV	Baal Shem Tov
AABEHLOPRRR	Pearl Harbor
AABEIILLMSS	assimilable
AABEIILLNNY	inalienably
AABEIILLSTY	saleability
AABEIILMMOR	memorabilia
AABEIILMNTY	amenability
AABEIILMTTY	tameability
AABEIILNRRT	libertarian
AABEIILNRSV	invariables
AABEIILNSSX	Aix-les-Bains
AABEIILRTTY	rateability
AABEIILRTWY	wearability
AABEIILSSST	assibilates
AABEIINOORT	bioaeration
AABEIIRRSTT	abirritates
AABEIKLMSTY	mistakeably
AABEIKMNORT	embarkation
AABEIKNNRST	barkantines
AABEILLLRTY	bilaterally
AABEILLMNPU	manipulable
AABEILLNRTY	inalterably
AABEILLOPRS	polarisable
AABEILLOPRZ	polarizable
AABEILLORSV	labiovelars
AABEILLRRTZ	trailblazer
AABEILLRSSY	syllabaries
AABEILLRVZZ	Brazzaville
AABEILMNRTU	Tamburlaine
AABEILMNSTU	albuminates
AABEILMORST	amortisable
AABEILMORTZ	amortizable
AABEILNNNOT	Anti-Lebanon
AABEILNOORT	elaboration
AABEILNPRSY	inseparably
AABEILNRRTT	rattlebrain
AABEILNRSSU	Belarussian
AABEILNRSTT	transitable
AABEILNSSTU	sustainable
AABEILOPRSS	parabolises
AABEILOPRSV	vaporisable
AABEILOPRSZ	parabolizes
AABEILOPRVZ	vaporizable

AABEILPRRRY	irreparably
AABEIMNRRTT	arbitrament
AABEINNPRSS	Bernina Pass
AABEINNQRTU	barquantine
AABEINORRST	aberrations
AABEINRRSTW	waterbrains
AABEIOPPRTV	approbative
AABEIRRSTTT	bitartrates
AABEKLNPSUY	unspeakably
AABELLLNOUW	unallowable
AABELLLOSWW	swallowable
AABELLLPRSY	ballplayers
AABELLMOSST	ameloblasts
AABELLPRSUY	pleasurably
AABELMMNSSY	assemblyman
AABELNORSTY	treasonably
AABELOORRST	elaborators
AABELOPRRTY	portrayable
AABELORSSST	albatrosses
AABELPRSSSU	surpassable
AABEMRSSTTU	masturbates
AABENNORTUV	Bonaventura
AABEPRRSSUZ	superbazars
AABFHILNOSY	fashionably
AABFIKNORSU	Burkina-Faso
AABFILLMMNY	inflammably
AABFLLMOOSY	Boyoma Falls
AABFLLNPPUY	unflappably
AABFLMNOSTY	flamboyants
AABFLNORUVY	unfavorably
AABGGGGINNN	gangbanging
AABGGIINNRS	bargainings
AABGGILMNOO	Giambologna
AABGHIINRSU	Ubangi-Shari
AABGHIINTTU	habituating
AABGHILNOOP	anglophobia
AABGIIILLNS	labialising
AABGIIILLNZ	labializing
AABGIIKLNNS	balkanising
AABGIIKLNNZ	balkanizing
AABGIILNORS	aboriginals
AABGIIMNNOT	abominating
AABGIINOSSY	bioassaying
AABGIINRRTT	arbitrating
AABGILMNRSU	submarginal
AABGINNOSTW	angwantibos
AABGINOPPRT	approbating
AABGINORSTU	outbargains
AABGLLMORSY	syllabogram
AABHIILORTT	habilitator
AABHIILSTWY	washability
AABHIINNSTT	inhabitants
AABHIINOSTT	habitations
AABHIINOTTU	habituation
AABHIMNPSST	batsmanship
AABHIOOPRST	astrophobia
AABHLLLLOOU	hullaballoo
AABHLLLOOSU	hullabaloos
AABHMOOSSTU	Matsuo Basho
AABIIILLMTY	mailability
AABIIILRTVY	variability
AABIIILSTTY	satiability
AABIIKLLTTY	talkability
AABIILLMSSY	assimilably
AABIILLNORT	librational
AABIILLPPTY	palpability
AABIILLPTYY	playability
AABIILLSTVY	salvability
AABIILMNRUU	albuminuria
AABIILMOOTU	automobilia
AABIILNORTV	vibrational
AABIILNORTY	libationary
AABIILORSTU	atrabilious
AABIILRRRTY	arbitrarily
AABIIMNNOOT	abomination
AABIINORRTT	arbitration
AABIINRRSTT	abirritants
AABIKLMOSST	katabolisms
AABILLMORSY	ambrosially
AABILLMPSTY	baptismally
AABILLRSUXY	subaxillary
AABILMNORTY	abnormality
AABILMNOSTU	ambulations
AABILNOOPRT	probational
AABILNORTUY	ablutionary
AABILNOSTTU	tabulations
AABILNSSTTU	substantial
AABILOPRSST	parabolists
AABIMMNOQUZ	Mozambiquan
AABIMNOORST	abominators
AABINNORSTY	antibaryons
AABINOOPPRT	approbation
AABIORRRSTT	arbitrators
AABKKOORRSU	kookaburras
AABLLMOORSV	Vallombrosa
AABLLOOPRST	blastoporal
AABLOSSSTTT	statoblasts
AABMORRSTTU	masturbator
AABNOORSTTY	astrobotany
AABOOPPRRTY	approbatory
AACCCDEOSUY	cycadaceous
AACCCDHRRST	scratchcard
AACCCEENPST	acceptances
AACCCEILPTT	cataplectic
AACCCEINORT	Arctic Ocean
AACCCEJKKRR	crackerjack
AACCCGHIOPR	cacographic
AACCCIIILRT	cicatricial
AACCCIILLMT	climactical
AACCCILMSTY	cataclysmic
AACCCNNOTUY	accountancy
AACCDDEIINS	candidacies
AACCDDEINOR	endocardiac
AACCDDHIIRS	disaccharid
AACCDEEELRT	accelerated
AACCDEELLNT	cancellated
AACCDEELNOR	accelerando
AACCDEENTTU	accentuated
AACCDEHINNT	cachinnated
AACCDEHIORS	adhocracies
AACCDEHIRSS	saccharides
	saccharised
AACCDEHIRSZ	saccharized
AACCDEHNORS	archdeacons
AACCDEIILLT	dialectical
AACCDEIIMMS	academicism
AACCDEIIPRR	pericardiac
AACCDEILLNR	calendrical
AACCDEILLNY	decanically
AACCDEILNST	accidentals
AACCDEILOPY	cyclopaedia
AACCDEIMNNO	nonacademic
AACCDEIMNOP	accompanied
AACCDEIRRTU	caricatured
AACCDELMTUU	accumulated
AACCDELNORS	cladocerans
AACCDEMMOOT	accommodate
AACCDEMNOOS	cacodaemons
AACCDENNORT	contradance
AACCDHIINOR	arachidonic
AACCDHILNOR	chancroidal
AACCDHIORSS	saccharoids
AACCDIIILRT	diacritical
AACCDIISSTU	diacaustics
AACCDILLSUY	dyscalculia
AACCDLNORTY	accordantly
AACCEEELRST	accelerates
AACCEEFILNT	calefacient
AACCEEFKRRS	safecracker
AACCEEGPRSS	scapegraces
AACCEEINPRS	parascience
AACCEEINRRT	incarcerate
AACCEEINRTV	revaccinate
AACCEEIRSSS	accessaries
AACCEEKLRRW	crackleware
AACCEELLNOT	collectanea
AACCEELLRTU	recalculate
AACCEELNRST	accelerants
AACCEELNSTU	acaulescent
AACCEELORRT	accelerator
AACCEENNOTT	concatenate
AACCEENSTTU	accentuates
AACCEEORSTV	coacervates
AACCEFILNOT	calefaction
AACCEFILSTU	fasciculate
AACCEFLORTY	calefactory
AACCEFPRSST	spacecrafts
AACCEGHILNR	archangelic
AACCEGHNRTT	gnatcatcher
AACCEGHOPRR	cacographer
AACCEGILMOR	acromegalic
AACCEGILORT	categorical
AACCEGORRTY	ergatocracy
AACCEHHMOST	stomachache
AACCEHHPRST	catchphrase
AACCEHIIMNN	mechanician
AACCEHIIMSS	sciamachies
AACCEHILMNS	mechanicals
AACCEHILMOS	mailcoaches
AACCEHILMOT	machicolate
AACCEHILMST	catechismal
AACCEHINNST	cachinnates
AACCEHIRSSS	saccharises
AACCEHIRSST	catachresis
AACCEHIRSSZ	saccharizes
AACCEHLNNNO	nonchalance

AACCEHLNOST	coelacanths
AACCEHMORSU	scaramouche
AACCEHRSTTW	catchwaters
AACCEIILMST	acclimatise
AACCEIILMTZ	acclimatize
AACCEIINPST	captaincies
AACCEILLRST	Callicrates
AACCEILLSTY	ascetically
AACCEILLTUV	calculative
	claviculate
AACCEILMPRT	malpractice
AACCEILNORS	anisocercal
AACCEILNOSS	accessional
AACCEILORSS	accessorial
AACCEILOSSU	salicaceous
AACCEILRSSY	accessarily
AACCEIMNNOR	necromaniac
AACCEIMNOPR	accompanier
AACCEIMNOPS	accompanies
AACCEIMNORS	maccaronies
AACCEINNORT	anacreontic
AACCEINNOST	canonicates
AACCEINOPTT	acceptation
AACCEINQTTU	acquittance
AACCEINRSTT	cantatrices
AACCEIORSTU	autocracies
AACCEIRRSTU	caricatures
AACCEISSTUV	accusatives
AACCEKLLNOY	cycloalkane
AACCELLNTUY	accentually
AACCELLPPRW	clapperclaw
AACCELMSTUU	accumulates
AACCELNRTUU	caruncalate
AACCELPRSTU	spectacular
AACCELRTTUU	acculturate
AACCENNORSS	Carcassonne
AACCENOPRRY	coparcenary
AACCENRSSTU	crustaceans
AACCFIIILRS	sacrificial
AACCFIILLPY	pacifically
AACCFIILRTY	farcicality
AACCFIIMNOR	acinaciform
AACCGHILNOR	charcoaling
AACCGHIMOPR	macrophagic
AACCGIILMNT	acclimating
AACCGIINNTV	vaccinating
AACCGILLNTU	calculating
AACCGINORTT	coarctating
AACCGNOQRUY	quangocracy
AACCHIIMRRT	matriarchic
AACCHIIMRST	charismatic
AACCHIINRST	anarchistic
AACCHIINRTT	anthracitic
AACCHILLMSU	Callimachus
AACCHILLOTY	chaotically
AACCHILMNOR	monarchical
AACCHILMOST	stomachical
AACCHILNNPS	asplanchnic
AACCHILNOTU	anacoluthic
AACCHKLLSUW	chuckwallas
AACCIILLNTY	actinically
AACCIILMNOT	acclimation
AACCIILMPRT	impractical
AACCIILNNOT	calcination
AACCIILNSTT	anticlastic
AACCIILSSTU	casuistical
AACCIILSTTT	stalactitic
AACCIINNOTV	vaccination
AACCIINOPRR	Capricornia
AACCIINOSTU	acoustician
AACCIINRSSS	circassians
AACCIINRSTT	cicatrisant
AACCIINRTTZ	cicatrizant
AACCIINTTVY	Vatican City
AACCILLLNOY	laconically
AACCILLLSSY	classically
AACCILLNNOY	canonically
AACCILLNORY	acronically
AACCILLNOTU	calculation
AACCILLNSUU	canaliculus
AACCILLPRTY	practically
AACCILLSTUY	caustically
AACCILNOSTU	sacculation
AACCILNPRTU	unpractical
AACCILNSTTY	syntactical
AACCILOPPTY	apocalyptic
AACCILOPRTT	catoptrical
AACCILOPSUY	capaciously
AACCIMNOPST	accompanist
AACCINOORTT	coarctation
AACCINORSTV	vaccinators
AACCINOSSTU	accusations
AACCIORRSTY	aristocracy
AACCLLNORYY	acronycally
AACCLLORSTU	calculators
AACCLMORTUU	accumulator
AACCLNOPRTY	plantocracy
AACCLNORTTU	contractual
AACCMOORRSZ	Occam's razor
AACCNNOSTTU	accountants
AACCOOPRRSU	acrocarpous
AACCORRSTTY	stratocracy
AACDDDEIJTU	adjudicated
AACDDEEEHHR	headreached
AACDDEEEHLR	clearheaded
AACDDEEINRT	deracinated
AACDDEEIPTT	decapitated
AACDDEEITTV	deactivated
AACDDEFHNRT	handcrafted
AACDDEGLNOO	dodecagonal
AACDDEHINPP	handicapped
AACDDEHLNRS	crashlanded
AACDDEIIRTV	divaricated
AACDDEIJSTU	adjudicates
AACDDEILNOR	endocardial
AACDDEILNSS	scandalised
AACDDEILNSZ	scandalized
AACDDEINRTU	candidature
AACDDEINTUU	nudicaudate
AACDDEIPRRS	Cedar Rapids
AACDDEKLPSS	packsaddles
AACDDHKPSWY	paddywhacks
AACDDIIINSS	candidiasis
AACDDIJORTU	adjudicator
AACDDIOSTTU	autodidacts
AACDEEEFNSS	defeasances
AACDEEEHHRS	headreaches
AACDEEENPRV	Cape Verdean
AACDEEFFINT	caffeinated
AACDEEFGINT	defaecating
AACDEEFINOT	defaecation
AACDEEFORST	defaecators
AACDEEGHRST	gatecrashed
AACDEEGKPPR	prepackaged
AACDEEGORTT	greatcoated
AACDEEHILMX	hexadecimal
AACDEEHNRTU	Hardecanute
AACDEEHRRST	Sacred Heart
AACDEEHRSSV	headscarves
AACDEEIILNT	acetanilide
AACDEEIINST	taeniacides
AACDEEIIRTV	eradicative
AACDEEILMRS	caramelised
AACDEEILMRZ	caramelized
AACDEEILRTV	declarative
AACDEEILSTT	elasticated
AACDEEIMNPT	emancipated
AACDEEINRST	ascertained
	deracinates
AACDEEIPPRT	appreciated
AACDEEIPRST	paederastic
AACDEEIPSTT	decapitates
AACDEEIRTTV	reactivated
AACDEEISTTV	deactivates
AACDEEKLPSW	spacewalked
AACDEELLORT	reallocated
AACDEELLSTT	castellated
AACDEELMSTU	emasculated
AACDEELPSTU	decapsulate
AACDEELRTUW	caterwauled
AACDEEMNNTV	advancement
AACDEENNSTT	attendances
AACDEFGILNT	defalcating
AACDEFGLMOU	camouflaged
AACDEFIILTT	facilitated
AACDEFIINST	fanaticised
AACDEFIINTZ	fanaticized
AACDEFILNOT	defalcation
AACDEFINRSU	fricandeaus
AACDEFINRUX	fricandeaux
AACDEFLORST	defalcators
AACDEGGILMO	demagogical
AACDEGGILOP	pedagogical
AACDEGIIMNT	diamagnetic
AACDEGIINRT	eradicating
AACDEGIIRSY	Erciyas Daği
AACDEGILNNR	calendaring
AACDEGIMNNS	damascening
AACDEGIMNRT	demarcating
AACDEGLLNOY	decagonally
AACDEGMNOPR	Campo Grande
AACDEGNORSS	gasconaders
AACDEGORSTU	sugarcoated
AACDEHHKLMS	hamshackled
AACDEHILLPY	edaphically

AACDEHILORS	icosahedral
AACDEHILPST	chaptalised
AACDEHILPTZ	chaptalized
AACDEHINORY	hyracoidean
AACDEHINOTT	anticathode
AACDEHINPPR	handicapper
AACDEHINRST	cantharides
AACDEHINRTU	Hardicanute
AACDEHKLNNR	crankhandle
AACDEHKMMRT	matchmarked
AACDEHMOORR	choreodrama
AACDEHMOPRT	camphorated
AACDEHPRRRS	cardsharper
AACDEIILMRT	diametrical
AACDEIILPRR	pericardial
AACDEIILPST	capitalised
AACDEIILPTZ	capitalized
AACDEIINNNO	Indian Ocean
AACDEIINNNR	incarnadine
AACDEIINNRT	incardinate
AACDEIINORT	eradication
AACDEIINPTT	anticipated
AACDEIINRRS	irradiances
AACDEIINTTV	inactivated
	vaticinated
AACDEIIORTV	radioactive
AACDEIIPRST	paediatrics
AACDEIIPRSU	parasuicide
AACDEIIRSTV	divaricates
AACDEIJNSTU	adjutancies
AACDEILLNTT	cantillated
AACDEILMNOT	declamation
AACDEILMNTU	calumniated
AACDEILNNOR	endocranial
AACDEILNORT	declaration
	redactional
AACDEILNOTU	educational
AACDEILNPTU	paniculated
AACDEILNRSS	radicalness
	scandaliser
AACDEILNRSZ	scandalizer
AACDEILNSSS	scandalises
AACDEILNSSZ	scandalizes
AACDEILPTTU	capitulated
AACDEILRSTT	straitlaced
AACDEILRTTU	articulated
AACDEILRTUU	auriculated
AACDEIMNNOP	pandemoniac
AACDEIMNORT	demarcation
AACDEIMNORY	aerodynamic
AACDEINNNTU	annunciated
AACDEINOPRS	caparisoned
AACDEINOTUV	coadunative
AACDEINRSST	incrassated
AACDEIOPRTT	decapitator
AACDEIORRST	eradicators
AACDEIORTTV	deactivator
AACDEIOSTTW	waistcoated
AACDELMOPRS	camelopards
AACDELMORTY	declamatory
AACDELNPTTY	pentadactyl
AACDELORRST	declarators
AACDELORRTY	declaratory
AACDELRTTTY	tetradactyl
AACDELSTTUU	auscultated
AACDEMORRST	demarcators
AACDEOPRRSS	radarscopes
AACDFHINRST	handicrafts
AACDFIILLTY	fatidically
AACDFIILRRT	fratricidal
AACDFIINOOS	aficionados
AACDFIMORRS	microfarads
AACDGGHIIST	haggadistic
AACDGGINNOS	gasconading
AACDGHHMNOY	hochmagandy
AACDGHINTUU	Dutch Guiana
AACDGHIOPRR	cardiograph
AACDGIILNTU	acidulating
AACDGILLRTU	Gaillard Cut
AACDGILNNPS	landscaping
AACDGILNNVY	advancingly
AACDGIMNNTU	manducating
AACDGIMORRS	cardiograms
AACDGIMRRTU	dramaturgic
AACDGINNNNO	cannonading
AACDGLMORTY	dactylogram
AACDGNNNORY	Grand Canyon
AACDGORSSTU	coastguards
AACDHIILLSY	dichasially
AACDHIIOPRS	aphrodisiac
AACDHIKRSTU	kurdaitchas
AACDHILLRSY	chrysalidal
AACDHLRSWWZ	Schwarzwald
AACDHMNOORT	chondromata
AACDHMOPRSY	psychodrama
AACDHNNORSY	chardonnays
AACDIIILMOT	idiomatical
AACDIILMPRY	pyramidical
AACDIILMRSS	radicalisms
AACDIILNNOR	androclinia
AACDIILNOTT	dictational
AACDIILNOTU	acidulation
AACDIILNPRS	Dinaric Alps
AACDIILNRTY	cardinality
AACDIILNSTV	vandalistic
AACDIILORTT	dictatorial
AACDIIMNOPS	dipsomaniac
AACDIINNOTY	cyanidation
AACDIIOPRTY	radiopacity
AACDIIORRTV	divaricator
AACDILLMNOY	monadically
	nomadically
AACDILLMNYY	dynamically
AACDILLRSTY	drastically
AACDILMNNOS	calamondins
AACDILMOPSS	spasmodical
AACDILNOSTY	anisodactyl
AACDILNPSST	landscapist
AACDILORTTY	artiodactyl
AACDILOSUUY	audaciously
AACDIMNNORT	nondramatic
AACDIMNNOTU	manducation
AACDIMOORST	sarcomatoid
AACDINNOOTU	coadunation
AACDINOOSTV	advocations
AACDJNOSTTU	coadjutants
AACDLMNOOTY	condylomata
AACDMMNNOST	commandants
AACDMNORTUY	manducatory
AACDMOORSTU	catadromous
AACDNORRSSS	crossandras
AACEEEHLMOT	haematocele
AACEEEHLNPP	epencephala
AACEEEKMPRS	peacemakers
AACEEENPRST	Eastern Cape
AACEEFGORRY	year of grace
AACEEFIMNSS	misfeasance
AACEEFIRRTV	rarefactive
AACEEFNNNOS	nonfeasance
AACEEGHLMNR	Charlemagne
AACEEGHLMPY	megacephaly
AACEEGHLRST	Castlereagh
AACEEGHNOPR	chaperonage
AACEEGHRRST	gatecrasher
AACEEGHRSST	gatecrashes
AACEEGIKMNP	peacemaking
AACEEGILLLY	elegiacally
AACEEGILLNS	allegiances
AACEEGILLNV	evangelical
AACEEGINPRT	paragenetic
AACEEGKPPRS	prepackages
AACEEGMMORT	macrogamete
AACEEGMNNOR	German Ocean
AACEEHHLTUX	hexateuchal
AACEEHHMMOR	haemachrome
AACEEHHMPTY	chamaephyte
AACEEHILMTT	metaethical
AACEEHILNST	chatelaines
AACEEHILSTT	aesthetical
AACEEHINSTT	anaesthetic
AACEEHKPSST	cheapskates
AACEEHLMNOP	encephaloma
AACEEHLNNPY	anencephaly
AACEEHLNPTY	phlyctaenae
AACEEHMPRST	spermatheca
AACEEHRRTTT	tetrarchate
AACEEIIMPST	septicaemia
AACEEIJLTUV	ejaculative
AACEEILLMNS	mesalliance
	miscellanea
AACEEILLRTV	varicellate
AACEEILMRSS	caramelises
AACEEILMRSZ	caramelizes
AACEEILNNRS	encarnalise
AACEEILNNRZ	encarnalize
AACEEILNPPT	epanaleptic
AACEEILNPRS	paraselenic
AACEEILNRTT	intercalate
AACEEILPRST	altarpieces
AACEEILRRST	secretarial
AACEEILSSTT	atelectasis
	elasticates
AACEEIMMORS	Mesoamerica
AACEEIMNNNT	maintenance
AACEEIMNPST	emancipates

AACEEINNNRT	centenarian
AACEEINNRRT	reincarnate
AACEEINNRSS	necessarian
	renaissance
AACEEIPPRST	appreciates
AACEEIPRRTV	prevaricate
AACEEIRRSST	tracasserie
AACEEIRRSTT	secretariat
AACEEIRSTTV	reactivates
AACEEKKLRSW	cakewalkers
AACEEKLMPRT	marketplace
AACEELLLTUV	valleculate
AACEELLORST	reallocates
AACEELMSSTU	emasculates
AACEELNPSTU	encapsulate
AACEELRRTUW	caterwauler
AACEEMNOSTU	amentaceous
AACEENRRSSU	reassurance
AACEEPRSSTW	waterscapes
AACEERSSSTV	stavesacres
AACEFFHINRS	affranchise
AACEFFIIRTV	affricative
AACEFFILNOT	affectional
AACEFFINOTT	affectation
AACEFGILNSV	Fingal's Cave
AACEFGINRRS	fragrancies
AACEFGLMOSU	camouflages
AACEFIILNRT	interfacial
AACEFIILNRV	acriflavine
AACEFIILSTT	facilitates
AACEFIINSST	fanaticises
AACEFIINSTV	fascinative
AACEFIINSTZ	fanaticizes
AACEFILMNOT	malefaction
AACEFILTTUV	facultative
AACEFIMNRRT	aircraftmen
AACEFINORRT	rarefaction
AACEFINORRV	vicar forane
AACEFINORSU	farinaceous
AACEFINORTT	fractionate
AACEFLMORST	malefactors
AACEFLNSSTU	factualness
AACEFMNRTUU	manufacture
AACEGGIKNPR	repackaging
AACEGGILPTU	Tegucigalpa
AACEGHHIIRS	hagiarchies
AACEGHHNOTT	chaetognath
AACEGHILLRT	lethargical
AACEGHILOPR	archipelago
AACEGHINRTT	reattaching
AACEGHKLORV	Gerlachovka
AACEGHLMOSU	guachamoles
AACEGHLOORY	archaeology
AACEGHLOPSS	phascogales
AACEGHMOPRS	macrophages
AACEGHNORTU	autochanger
AACEGIILLPR	periglacial
AACEGIILMNT	enigmatical
AACEGIIMRRS	miscarriage
AACEGIJLNTU	ejaculating
AACEGIKKLNW	cakewalking
AACEGILLLNY	angelically
	englacially
AACEGILLLOR	allegorical
AACEGILLOOR	aerological
AACEGILLOPS	plagioclase
AACEGILMNPS	plasmagenic
AACEGILNPRY	panegyrical
AACEGILNRTT	altercating
AACEGILNTTY	acetylating
AACEGILOTUV	coagulative
AACEGILPPRS	paraplegics
AACEGILRSTT	strategical
AACEGIMMNOR	micromanage
AACEGIMMNRT	engrammatic
AACEGIMNNPR	permanganic
AACEGIMNPRS	campaigners
AACEGLMNORS	carmagnoles
AACEGLNRRTU	rectangular
AACEGLORSTU	cataloguers
AACEGNOORSU	onagraceous
AACEHHIIMPT	amphithecia
AACEHHIKNNV	Nakhichevan
AACEHHKLMSS	hamshackles
AACEHHMNRSV	Marcheshvan
AACEHIIKLNT	kitchenalia
AACEHIIKMSS	skiamachies
AACEHIILLMV	Machiavelli
AACEHIILMPT	epithalamic
AACEHIILSTT	atheistical
AACEHIIMMNS	Manichaeism
AACEHIIMNST	haematinics
AACEHILLMNO	melancholia
AACEHILLNTU	hallucinate
AACEHILLPSS	callipashes
AACEHILLPTY	aphetically
AACEHILNPST	chainplates
AACEHILPSST	chaptalises
AACEHILPSTZ	chaptalizes
AACEHILRSTT	theatricals
AACEHIMMPRS	amphimacers
AACEHIMMSTT	mathematics
AACEHIMNNOY	haemocyanin
AACEHIMNOST	theomaniacs
AACEHIMORST	achromatise
AACEHIMORTT	haematocrit
AACEHIMORTZ	achromatize
AACEHIMOSTT	haemostatic
AACEHINNOSU	ouananiches
AACEHINORRS	archaeornis
AACEHINOTTY	thiocyanate
AACEHINPPRY	hypercapnia
AACEHINRRST	catarrhines
AACEHIOPRRS	archesporia
AACEHIRRSTV	architraves
AACEHJKMMRS	jackhammers
AACEHKMMRST	matchmakers
AACEHKMRSTW	watchmakers
AACEHLMORTY	hematocryal
AACEHLOPTUY	autocephaly
AACEHMMNNRT	merchantman
AACEHMNORSU	rhamnaceous
AACEHMNSTTT	attachments
AACEHMOPRST	camphorates
AACEHNNORST	anthracnose
AACEHOPRSTT	catastrophe
AACEHOPSSTU	spathaceous
AACEHORTUUX	Châteauroux
AACEIILLMNS	misalliance
AACEIILLNRS	ancillaries
AACEIILLNRT	lacertilian
AACEIILLNRV	incarvillea
AACEIILLPRS	capillaries
AACEIILLRTV	leviratical
AACEIILNPRR	pericranial
AACEIILNRRT	interracial
AACEIILNRST	carnalities
AACEIILPPRR	pericarpial
AACEIILPPTV	applicative
AACEIILPSST	capitalises
AACEIILPSTZ	capitalizes
AACEIILRSST	rascalities
AACEIILSSTU	causalities
AACEIILSTTU	actualities
AACEIIMNRTV	carminative
AACEIIMQSTU	semiaquatic
AACEIINORTT	ratiocinate
AACEIINPSTT	anticipates
AACEIINSTTV	inactivates
	vaticinates
AACEIIOSSTV	associative
AACEIIPPRTT	participate
AACEIJLNOTU	ejaculation
AACEILLLNNV	Valle-Inclán
AACEILLLSTY	elastically
AACEILLMNPT	implacental
AACEILLMNSU	animalcules
AACEILLMPUX	amplexicaul
AACEILLNOSS	escallonias
AACEILLNSTT	cantillates
AACEILLNTTY	tetanically
AACEILLNTVY	venatically
AACEILLPRRT	caterpillar
AACEILLRRTY	erratically
AACEILLSSTY	salicylates
AACEILMMPST	metaplasmic
AACEILMNOPT	cleptomania
AACEILMNORT	reclamation
AACEILMNOTX	exclamation
AACEILMNRST	reclaimants
AACEILMNSTU	calumniates
AACEILMRTTU	matriculate
AACEILNNOSS	ascensional
AACEILNNRTU	antinuclear
AACEILNORST	lacerations
AACEILNORTT	altercation
AACEILNOSST	escalations
AACEILNOTTY	acetylation
AACEILNPSTU	incapsulate
AACEILNRRTU	retinacular
AACEILNRRTY	intercalary
AACEILNRSUV	naviculares
AACEILPRSSU	scapularies
AACEILPRSTU	spiraculate
AACEILPRTTU	particulate

AACEILPSSUU Aesculapius
AACEILPSTTU capitulates
AACEILRRSTU cartularies
AACEILRSTTU articulates
AACEILSSTTT stalactites
AACEILSTUVY causatively
AACEIMMNOST scammoniate
AACEIMNNOTT contaminate
AACEIMNOORT erotomaniac
AACEIMNOPRT emancipator
AACEIMNORST macerations
AACEIMNORSU oceanariums
AACEIMOPRTV comparative
AACEINNNSTU annunciates
AACEINNORTT recantation
AACEINNOSTT catenations
AACEINORRTY reactionary
AACEINORSTU aeronautics
AACEINORSTV vacationers
AACEINOSTUV evacuations
AACEINOSTVX excavations
AACEINPQRTU preacquaint
AACEINQRSTU reacquaints
AACEINRSSST incrassates
AACEINRSSTU sanctuaries
AACEIOPPRRT appreciator
AACEIORSSSW cassowaries
AACEIORSSTT aerostatics
AACEJKNRSTT natterjacks
AACEJLORSTU ejaculators
AACEJLORTUY ejaculatory
AACEKLQRSUV quacksalver
AACELLLNOOV Leoncavallo
AACELLLORST collaterals
AACELLLRSST saltcellars
AACELLNRSTY ancestrally
AACELLOPRSU acarpellous
AACELMMORSS sarcolemmas
AACELMORSTU emasculator
AACELMORTXY exclamatory
AACELMRSSST masterclass
AACELNNRSTT transcalent
AACELNOOSSU solanaceous
AACELNOPSTU cantaloupes
AACELNORSTT translocate
AACELNRRSUV vernaculars
AACELOOPPRS laparoscope
AACELOPPSSY apocalypses
AACELQRTUUU aquaculture
AACELSSTTUU auscultates
AACENNOSTTZ canzonettas
AACENOOPSSU saponaceous
AACENORRTVY contrayerva
AACEOOPSSTU sapotaceous
AACEOPPRSUY papyraceous
AACEORRSTTT terracottas
AACFFIORRTT trafficator
AACFGIIMNST magnificats
AACFGIINNST fascinating
AACFGILLSUU Iguaçú Falls
AACFGLNNORT conflagrant
AACFHINORRT North Africa
AACFHIORSTU South Africa
AACFHKNRSST crankshafts
AACFIILLNNY financially
AACFIILNNOR Californian
AACFIILORTT facilitator
AACFIINNOST fascination
AACFIINSSTT antifascist
AACFILLNOTV lactoflavin
AACFILLNRTY frantically
AACFILLORTY factorially
AACFILMORRS scalariform
AACFILNORST infracostal
AACFILSSTTU factualists
AACFINORRTY fractionary
AACFINORSST fascinators
AACFLMNRSTY craftsmanly
AACFMNORSTW craftswoman
AACFMNORTUY manufactory
AACFNORSTUU anfractuous
AACFNRSSTTU surfactants
AACGGHHIMNU gamahuching
AACGGHIMNRU gamaruching
AACGGIIMNNP campaigning
AACGGIINSTT castigating
AACGGILLLOO algological
AACGGILLOOR agrological
AACGGILNOSY synagogical
AACGGILNOTU cataloguing
coagulating
AACGHHOPRST tachographs
AACGHHPRTYY tachygraphy
AACGHIIMNNT machinating
AACGHIKLNRW warchalking
AACGHIKMMNT matchmaking
AACGHIKMNTW watchmaking
AACGHILLOPR allographic
AACGHILLPRY calligraphy
graphically
AACGHIMNRSY gymnasiarch
AACGHINOPPR approaching
AACGHINPRTU parachuting
AACGHIOPRTU autographic
AACGHKNNOWW Kwangchowan
AACGHLMMNOO Chomolangma
AACGHLMOORU chaulmoogra
AACGHLNOORY arachnology
AACGHMOPRRS macrographs
AACGHNOOPRR coronagraph
AACGHNOPRTU Chota Nagpur
AACGHOPRRTY cartography
AACGHOPRSSU sarcophagus
AACGIILLMNS Gallicanism
AACGIILLNPY callipygian
AACGIILLNTV vacillating
AACGIILLOOX axiological
AACGIILLSST glacialists
AACGIILMNNS Anglicanism
AACGIILMSTT stalagmitic
AACGIILNSTU actualising
AACGIILNTUZ actualizing
AACGIIMNNTU acuminating
AACGIIMNSTT masticating
AACGIIMSSTT astigmatics
AACGIINNNRT incarnating
AACGIINNOTV vacationing
AACGIINNQTU acquainting
AACGIINOSST associating
AACGIINOSTT castigation
AACGIINPSTU auspicating
AACGIINPTTV captivating
AACGIKLNRTY tracklaying
AACGILLNNOW allowancing
AACGILLNORY organically
AACGILLOPST postglacial
AACGILMNOOR agronomical
AACGILNNNTU cannulating
AACGILNOOPR carpogonial
AACGILNOOTU coagulation
AACGILNOTUV autoclaving
AACGILNPTTU catapulting
AACGILOSSUY sagaciously
AACGILOSTTU cataloguist
AACGIMNSTTY syntagmatic
AACGINNRSTT transacting
AACGINOOPPT apocopating
AACGINOPRSU craniopagus
AACGINORSST nasogastric
AACGIORSSTT castigators
AACGIORSTTY castigatory
AACGLLNOOTY octagonally
AACGLMNOOPY campanology
AACGLOORSTU coagulators
AACHHIIMPPT amphipathic
AACHHIIMPRT amphitricha
AACHHIMNPPS chapmanship
AACHHLORTTT throatlatch
AACHIIINRST christiania
AACHIILORST ahistorical
AACHIIMNNOT machination
AACHIIMNSST shamanistic
AACHIINPPST captainship
AACHIINRSSU saurischian
AACHIKMNPRU Kanchipuram
AACHILLMOPY malacophily
AACHILLOPRY parochially
AACHILMNOOS monochasial
AACHILMOPPP hippocampal
AACHILNOPPS pansophical
AACHILNORST thrasonical
AACHILQRRSU squirarchal
AACHIMMNOTY mythomaniac
AACHIMMORST achromatism
AACHIMNNORS anachronism
AACHIMNORSS anachorisms
maraschinos
AACHIMNORST machinators
AACHIMNOTTY Titanomachy
AACHIMOPPRR paramorphic
AACHIMPRSST pharmacists
AACHINNNOTY anthocyanin
AACHINORSST anthracosis
AACHIPRSTTU parachutist
AACHLLMNORY monarchally
AACHLLOOSTU holocaustal

AACHLMORRTY lachrymator
AACHLNNOOTU anacoluthon
AACHLPPPPYY happy-clappy
AACHMNNOORW anchorwoman
AACHMNOSTWY yachtswoman
AACHMOOPRST apochromats
AACHMOORSTU achromatous
AACHPRSSTTW watchstraps
AACIIILNNOT laciniation
AACIIILNOST laicisation
AACIIILNOTZ laicization
AACIIILPPRT participial
AACIIJNOTTT jactitation
AACIILLMRTU multiracial
AACIILLNOOT coalitional
AACIILLNOSS salicionals
AACIILLNOTV vacillation
AACIILLNTTY titanically
AACIILLPRTY capillarity
piratically
AACIILLRSTY satirically
AACIILMNORT lacrimation
AACIILMNOST anomalistic
AACIILMOSTT atomistical
AACIILNNNOT lancination
AACIILNOPPT application
AACIILNPRTU puritanical
AACIILNPTTY antitypical
AACIILOPRST piscatorial
AACIILPRSTT patristical
AACIILPSSTT capitalists
AACIILSSTTT statistical
AACIIMNNORT animatronic
AACIIMNNOTU acumination
AACIIMNOSTT mastication
AACIIMORTTY aromaticity
AACIINNNORT incarnation
AACIINNNOTT incantation
AACIINNPSTT anticipants
AACIINOOSST association
AACIINOPRTT anticipator
AACIINOPSTT capitations
AACIINOPTTV captivation
AACIINORTTV vaticinator
AACIINOSTTV activations
vacationist
AACIINPPRTT participant
AACIINRSSTT antiracists
AACILLLNTUY lunatically
AACILLLPSTY plastically
AACILLMMNUU animalculum
AACILLMNORT matroclinal
AACILLMNOSY masonically
AACILLMOSTY somatically
AACILLNOOST allocations
AACILLNOPRS rapscallion
AACILLOOPST apostolical
AACILLOPRSY prosaically
AACILLORSTV vacillators
AACILLOSSUY salaciously
AACILLPRTUU apicultural
AACILLPRTUY capitularly
AACILLPSSTY spastically
AACILLRRUUY auricularly
AACILMNNOPT complainant
AACILMNOOTX taxonomical
AACILMNOPST complaisant
AACILMNORTU calumniator
AACILMNOSTU maculations
AACILMNRTTU matriculant
AACILMORRST lacrimators
AACILMORRTY lacrimatory
AACILMPPRSY paralympics
AACILNNNOTU cannulation
AACILNNOPSY calypsonian
AACILNNOSTU canulations
AACILNOOTUV vacuolation
AACILNOPRTY coplanarity
AACILNOPSTT Cottian Alps
AACILNOPSTU capsulation
AACILNORRTU intraocular
AACILNORTVY clairvoyant
AACILOPPRST applicators
AACILOPPRTY applicatory
AACILOPRSUY rapaciously
AACILOPRTTU capitulator
AACILOPSTTU autoplastic
AACILORRTTU articulator
AACILPRRSTU particulars
AACILRSTUVY vascularity
AACIMMNNOOS monomaniacs
AACIMNNNOTT contaminant
AACIMNOOSTT anastomotic
AACIMNOPRSY pyromaniacs
AACIMORSSTT masticators
AACIMORSTTY masticatory
AACINNNORTU annunciator
AACINNOOSTV Nova Scotian
AACINNOOSTZ actinozoans
AACINNORSTT transaction
AACINNORTTY incantatory
AACINNRRSTU transuranic
AACINOOOPPT apocopation
AACINOOPSTT coaptations
AACINORSSTT castrations
AACINORSTTT attractions
AACINORSTTU astronautic
AACIOORSSST associators
AACIOORSSTY associatory
AACIOPPPRRY appropriacy
AACIOPRSTTV captivators
AACIORRSSTT aristocrats
AACLMORRSTY lacrymators
AACLMORRTYY lacrymatory
AACLNNNOOST consonantal
AACLOOPPRSY laparoscopy
AACLOORRSTU coloraturas
AACLORSTTUU auscultator
AACMMNORSTU Murman Coast
AACMNOPRTUY paramountcy
AACMOOPRRST comparators
AACMOORSSTU sarcomatous
AACNORRSSTT transactors
AACNORRSSTW narrowcasts
AACORRSSTTT stratocrats
AADDDEEGHIN deadheading
AADDDEGINRS grandaddies
AADDDEGNNOR dragonnaded
AADDDEIILPT dilapidated
AADDDEILPRS paradiddles
AADDDEILRRT tarradiddle
AADDDEILRST taradiddles
AADDEEEHPRS spearheaded
AADDEEFGLRT deflagrated
AADDEEFGRSU safeguarded
AADDEEHHRRT hardhearted
AADDEEHIMNS maidenheads
AADDEEHLPRY paraldehyde
AADDEEILMNT delaminated
AADDEEILNRS adrenalised
AADDEEILNRZ adrenalized
AADDEEILNST desalinated
AADDEEIPPRS disappeared
AADDEEKMRRT trademarked
AADDEELLNRS Dardanelles
AADDEELRTTU adulterated
AADDEEMQRSU masqueraded
AADDEEMQSTU desquamated
AADDEEMRRSY daydreamers
AADDEENPPRS sandpapered
AADDEGGINRS aggrandised
AADDEGGINRZ aggrandized
AADDEGHNORS dragonheads
AADDEGHNRTU dreadnaught
AADDEGIMNRY daydreaming
AADDEGINORT degradation
AADDEGINRRS disarranged
AADDEGIRRST tardigrades
AADDEGNNORS dragonnades
AADDEHILLNV de Havilland
AADDEHIMNNS handmaidens
AADDEIILNTV invalidated
AADDEIILPST dilapidates
AADDEIIMPRS imparadised
AADDEIIRVVZ Díaz de Vivar
AADDEINPQSU pasquinaded
AADDEINRSST standardise
AADDEINRSTZ standardize
AADDEJLMSTU maladjusted
AADDELPQRUU quadrupedal
AADDFIORSTV Star of David
AADDGILMOSY amygdaloids
AADDGINPRRS Grand Rapids
AADDGNNRSST grandstands
AADDHIKUUZZ Dzaudzhikau
AADDHNNRSSY shandrydans
AADDIIINNRT Trinidadian
AADDIILOPRT dilapidator
AADDIINSSTV Saint David's
AADDNNNORST nonstandard
AADEEEFHHRT featherhead
AADEEEGGRTX exaggerated
AADEEEHHLRT leatherhead

AADEEEHLNNR enneahedral
AADEEELRTUV reevaluated
AADEEEPRSTX exasperated
AADEEERSSTV asseverated
AADEEFGLLLT flagellated
AADEEFGLRST deflagrates
AADEEFHHLRT halfhearted
AADEEFHRSST fatshederas
AADEEFILRRS fairleaders
AADEEFKLNRR farnarkeled
AADEEGHLNOT halogenated
AADEEGHLNPY Handley Page
AADEEGIKKRR Kierkegaard
AADEEGILRRT laterigrade
AADEEGIMNRT emarginated
AADEEGINRTU aguardiente
AADEEGMNORV overmanaged
AADEEGNORRT anterograde
AADEEGNPRRR prearranged
AADEEHHLPRT heptahedral
AADEEHHMMRS hammerheads
AADEEHHRTXY hexahydrate
AADEEHILRTX exhilarated
AADEEHLLTVY Death Valley
AADEEHLNNRT neanderthal
AADEEHLNPRT pentahedral
AADEEHLRRTT tetrahedral
AADEEHMPRST metaphrased
AADEEHMRRTW warmhearted
AADEEHMRSST headmasters
headstreams
AADEEHNRSVW heavenwards
AADEEHQRRTU headquarter
AADEEHQRSSU headsquares
AADEEIILNRX Alexander II
AADEEILLMVY mediaevally
AADEEILLRTT alliterated
AADEEILLSSS salesladies
AADEEILMNST delaminates
AADEEILMORT ameliorated
AADEEILNNRX alexandrine
AADEEILNRTX alexandrite
AADEEILNRVX Alexander VI
AADEEILNSST desalinates
AADEEIMPRST preadamites
AADEEIMRRRS Sierra Madre
AADEEINORST asteroidean
AADEEINPPRT appertained
AADEEIPPRRS reappraised
AADEEIPRRTT repatriated
AADEEIPRTTX expatriated
AADEEIRRSSV adversaries
AADEEIRRTTV retardative
AADEEIRSTVV adversative
AADEEISTTVV devastative
AADEEKMRRTW watermarked
AADEELLNTTU landaulette
AADEELLPPRW wallpapered
AADEELRSTTU adulterates
AADEEMNNSSU Amundsen Sea
AADEEMNPRRT dermapteran
AADEEMQRRSU masquerader
AADEEMQRSSU masquerades
AADEEMQSSTU desquamates
AADEEMRRSTU Estremadura
AADEEMRRTUX Extremadura
AADEENNRTWY Tyne and Wear
AADEENPRSTU unseparated
AADEFGHNRRT grandfather
AADEFGIISTT fastigiated
AADEFHLNRST fatherlands
AADEFIMNOST defamations
AADEFLMNNTU fundamental
AADEFLSSTTY steadfastly
AADEFNNNORS San Fernando
AADEFNNSSTU Stefan Dušan
AADEGGGLLLY lallygagged
AADEGGHNRSS haggardness
AADEGGINRRS aggrandiser
AADEGGINRRZ aggrandizer
AADEGGINRSS aggrandises
AADEGGINRSZ aggrandizes
AADEGGLNRSS laggardness
AADEGHIMNST mastheading
AADEGHLNNRS handlangers
AADEGHOPRTU autographed
AADEGIILNTT intagliated
AADEGIILPRS plagiarised
AADEGIILPRZ plagiarized
AADEGIIMNNT deaminating
AADEGIINNTV invaginated
AADEGIINRTT ingratiated
AADEGILLNTV gallivanted
AADEGILNNRV landgravine
Vlaardingen
AADEGILNPRT plantigrade
AADEGILNTUV devaluating
AADEGILPRRS paragliders
AADEGIMNNRV Venn diagram
AADEGIMNRRS misarranged
AADEGIMNRSU admeasuring
AADEGINNOST antagonised
AADEGINNOTZ antagonized
AADEGINNTUV unnavigated
AADEGINPPRT preadapting
AADEGINRRSS disarranges
AADEGINRTUU inaugurated
AADEGINSTTV devastating
AADEGIOPRRS radiopagers
AADEGIPRRSS disparagers
AADEGLNQRSU quadrangles
AADEGLNRSSU gradualness
AADEGLNSSSS sandglasses
AADEGMNRRST grandmaster
AADEGMRRSTU dramaturges
AADEGNNPRRT grandparent
AADEHHIJLUV Judah ha-Levi
AADEHIILNNT annihilated
AADEHIILNRT antheridial
AADEHIILOPP paedophilia
AADEHIINPTY diaphaneity
AADEHILLNOS hollandaise
AADEHILMMMO Mohammed Ali
AADEHILNNST lanthanides
AADEHILNOSW Noahide Laws
AADEHINOPPY hypnopaedia
AADEHIPSTXY asphyxiated
AADEHLMNSUY unashamedly
AADEHLNNPRS panhandlers
AADEHPRSSTT spatterdash
AADEIIILNST italianised
AADEIIILNTZ italianized
AADEIIIRRTV irradiative
AADEIILMNST mediastinal
AADEIILMORT mediatorial
AADEIILMRST admiralties
AADEIILMSST assimilated
AADEIILNRRT interradial
AADEIILNSTV insalivated
invalidates
AADEIILPRTY praediality
AADEIIMNNOT deamination
AADEIIMPRSS imparadises
AADEIINORRT reradiation
AADEIINORST eradiations
AADEIINSTTV adventitias
AADEIIPRSST parasitised
AADEIIPRSTZ parasitized
AADEIJKLRRS rijksdaaler
AADEIKLNPST Staked Plain
AADEIKMNORT demarkation
AADEILLLMOT metalloidal
AADEILLMMMT mammillated
AADEILLMRTY diametrally
AADEILLNOPT planetoidal
AADEILLNOST allantoides
AADEILMNNRS mainlanders
AADEILMNORR Māorilander
AADEILMNPTU manipulated
AADEILMNRRT intradermal
AADEILNNQRU quadrennial
AADEILNOPSS anadiploses
AADEILNORTY arytenoidal
AADEILNOTUV devaluation
AADEILNPPRR preprandial
AADEILNPPRS appledrains
AADEILNRRSY drainlayers
AADEILNRSTU naturalised
AADEILNRSTW landwaiters
AADEILNRTUZ naturalized
AADEILORRTV advertorial
AADEILPRSTY disparately
AADEIMMNRST disarmament
AADEIMNNNOV Vandemonian
AADEIMNNOPS Epaminondas
AADEIMNOPRR madreporian
AADEIMNORST mandatories
AADEIMNRSTV animadverts
maidservant
AADEIMOSTTU automatised
AADEIMOTTUZ automatized
AADEIMRRSST dramatisers
AADEIMRRSTZ dramatizers
AADEIMRSTTU traumatised

AADEIMRTTUZ	traumatized
AADEINNQRTU	quarantined
AADEINOPRTV	depravation
AADEINORRTT	retardation
AADEINORSST	diatessaron
AADEINORSTY	arytaenoids
AADEINOSTTV	devastation
AADEINPQRSU	pasquinader
AADEINPQSSU	pasquinades
AADEINPRSTU	unaspirated
AADEIOPSSTT	apostatised
AADEIOPSTTZ	apostatized
AADEKLMORSW	meadowlarks
AADEKNRSSWW	awkwardness
AADELLMNORT	martellando
AADELLNNORT	rallentando
AADELMMOPSS	plasmodesma
AADELMNORST	Aldermaston
AADELMNRRST	transdermal
AADELNRSTTU	adulterants
AADELNRSTUV	transvalued
AADELORRTTU	adulterator
AADEMNOOSST	anastomosed
AADEMNORSTW	tradeswoman
AADENNRRTUW	unwarranted
AADENNRSTTU	denaturants
AADENOPRSSU	andropauses
AADENPRSTTT	standpatter
AADENRSSTTU	transudates
AADENRSSWWY	waywardness
AADENRSTTUU	unsaturated
AADEOPPRSST	strappadoes
AADEORRRTTY	retardatory
AADEORSSTTV	devastators
AADEQRRSTUU	quadratures
AADFFGHNSSY	shandygaffs
AADFGHINNST	handfasting
AADFIKNNOOR	Kordofanian
AADFMNORSTW	draftswoman
AADGGGGMNOO	Gog and Magog
AADGGIILNPR	paragliding
AADGGIIMMNR	diagramming
AADGGIINNRR	darraigning
AADGGIINOPR	radiopaging
AADGGIINPRS	disparaging
AADGGLNOOSW	waggonloads
AADGGOOOUUU	Ouagadougou
AADGHHIKNNS	handshaking
AADGHHOPRSW	shadowgraph
AADGHIILNOR	Ghirlandaio
AADGHILMNNN	manhandling
AADGHILNNNP	panhandling
AADGHIMNNRS	Sandringham
AADGHIOPRRS	radiographs
AADGHIOPRRY	radiography
AADGHIRRRYY	hydrargyria
AADGHMNRSTU	draughtsman
AADGIIINRRT	irradiating
AADGIIKLNNR	Kaliningrad
AADGIILLNOV	Gallovidian
AADGIILMRST	madrigalist
AADGIILNNSV	vandalising
AADGIILNNVZ	vandalizing
AADGIILNORR	railroading
AADGIIMNPST	misadapting
AADGIIMNRST	dramatising
AADGIIMNRTZ	dramatizing
AADGIINOSTV	divagations
AADGIINRRSY	disarraying
AADGIJNORSU	jaguarondis
AADGIJNRSUU	jaguarundis
AADGILMNSSU	salmagundis
AADGILNOOTU	autoloading
AADGILRSSTU	gradualists
AADGINORSTU	graduations
AADGLLLNRUY	glandularly
AADGMNNORST	montagnards
AADGNNOPRSS	snapdragons
AADGNOOPRST	gastropodan
AADHIIKRSTV	Dasht-i-Kavir
AADHIILLLSV	Valdai Hills
AADHIILMPRS	admiralship
AADHIIMOPRS	adiaphorism
AADHIIOPRST	adiaphorist
AADHILRSTWW	withdrawals
AADHIOOPRSU	adiaphorous
AADHIOPPRTY	paratyphoid
AADHIOPPSSY	hypospadias
AADHIOPRRTY	parathyroid
AADHKNOORTT	North Dakota
AADHKOOSTTU	South Dakota
AADHLOOPRRT	arthropodal
AADHLORSUYZ	hazardously
AADHNOPQRUY	quadraphony
AADHORRSSUU	hadrosaurus
AADIIINORRT	irradiation
AADIILLNTTU	altitudinal
	latitudinal
AADIILLSWWY	Władysław II
AADIILNOOTX	oxidational
AADIILNOPSS	anadiplosis
AADIILNOPST	lapidations
AADIILNORTT	traditional
AADIILNORTV	invalidator
AADIILNOSTT	dilatations
AADIILNOSTV	validations
AADIILNOSTY	dialysation
AADIILNOTYZ	dialyzation
AADIILNTTTU	attitudinal
AADIILOSUUV	audiovisual
AADIIMNORST	admirations
AADIINNORSU	dinosaurian
AADIINNOTTX	antioxidant
AADIIOPRSST	parasitoids
AADIIORRRST	irradiators
AADIIPRSSST	aspidistras
AADIIRSSTTV	Davis Strait
AADIJNORSTU	adjurations
AADILLMNOOT	amontillado
AADILLMORTY	maladroitly
AADILLMPRYY	pyramidally
AADILLSVWWY	Władysław IV
AADILMMPSSW	Dismal Swamp
AADILMNORTY	mandatorily
AADILNRRSSU	Arru Islands
AADILNSSSUW	duniwassals
AADILOOORSV	Via Dolorosa
AADILOORSTV	vasodilator
AADILOPPRSV	disapproval
AADINRSSTTU	Sunda Strait
AADJMNNPRSU	panjandrums
AADJNNORRST	Trans-Jordan
AADLLLOSSUY	All Souls' Day
AADMNORSSTU	Nostradamus
AADNOPRRSUW	wraparounds
AAEEEFLMMST	metafemales
AAEEEGGMMST	megagametes
AAEEEGGRSTX	exaggerates
AAEEEGRSTWY	steerageway
AAEEEHKPRSS	Shakespeare
AAEEEHLLRTY	aethereally
AAEEEHNRRTW	earthenware
AAEEEIKPSSS	speakeasies
AAEEELRSTUV	reevaluates
AAEEEMNPPST	appeasement
AAEEENRSSTU	aureateness
AAEEEPRRSTX	exasperater
AAEEEPRSSTX	exasperates
AAEEERSSSTV	asseverates
AAEEFGHLMRT	Magherafelt
AAEEFGIMRST	afterimages
AAEEFGINSTU	taeniafuges
AAEEFGLLLST	flagellates
AAEEFHIRRTW	Fairweather
AAEEFHMRRRS	sharefarmer
AAEEFHRSSTV	aftershaves
AAEEFNRRSST	transferase
AAEEFRSSTTT	aftertastes
AAEEGGGIRTV	aggregative
AAEEGGGLRTY	aggregately
AAEEGGHMOSU	haemagogues
AAEEGGIMNRV	graven image
AAEEGGLMORT	agglomerate
AAEEGGORRTX	exaggerator
AAEEGHHMORR	haemorrhage
AAEEGHIMNRT	megatherian
AAEEGHLNOST	halogenates
AAEEGHLOOPS	oesophageal
AAEEGHNPPRR	paperhanger
AAEEGIKNNRW	reawakening
AAEEGILLLNS	selaginella
AAEEGILLLTT	tagliatelle
AAEEGILLNNT	gentianella
AAEEGILMSSX	sexagesimal
AAEEGILPRTT	tetraplegia
AAEEGIMRRRS	remarriages
AAEEGINPPRR	reappearing
AAEEGINPRSS	paragenesis
AAEEGINPRST	greasepaint
	pageantries
AAEEGINRRTW	graniteware
AAEEGINRSTV	vegetarians
AAEEGLMNOPT	planogamete

AAEEGLMNPSS	plasmagenes
AAEEGLNNPTT	Plantagenet
AAEEGLNSSTV	vantageless
AAEEGLORTVY	laevogyrate
AAEEGMMNNST	managements
AAEEGMMORRS	aerogrammes
AAEEGMNNRRT	arrangement
AAEEGMNOPRT	pomegranate
AAEEGMNORSV	overmanages
AAEEGMNRSTV	ravagements
AAEEGMNRSTY	East Germany
AAEEGMNSSTU	assuagement
AAEEGNPRRRS	prearranges
AAEEGNRRRRS	rearrangers
AAEEGQRRSTU	quarterages
AAEEHHKRRST	earthshaker
AAEEHHLNNPT	naphthalene
AAEEHILMOPR	hemeralopia
AAEEHILNNST	Saint Helena
AAEEHILRSTX	exhilarates
AAEEHIMMNPT	amphetamine
AAEEHIMNRTT	metatherian
AAEEHIMRRTY	erythraemia
AAEEHIORTTX	heterotaxia
AAEEHIOSTUV	Haute-Savoie
AAEEHIPRSST	paresthesia
AAEEHKQRSTU	earthquakes
AAEEHLLSTTU	haustellate
AAEEHLNPTTV	heptavalent
AAEEHLPSSTU	Hautes-Alpes
AAEEHMNOORR	amenorrhoea
AAEEHMPRSST	metaphrases
AAEEHNOPRSS	anaphoreses
AAEEHNSSSSU	Hesse-Nassau
AAEEHORRSTT	steatorrhea
AAEEHRRSSTW	shearwaters
AAEEIILLTVV	alleviative
AAEEIILMRST	materialise
AAEEIILMRTZ	materialize
AAEEIILRRST	arterialise
AAEEIILRRTZ	arterialize
AAEEIILRTTV	retaliative
AAEEIINRSSV	sansevieria
AAEEIKLLMRT	alkalimeter
AAEEIKLMNUW	Milwaukeean
AAEEILLMNNT	lineamental
AAEEILLMPRX	premaxillae
AAEEILLNOTV	elevational
AAEEILLNPRT	Pantelleria
AAEEILLPPTV	appellative
AAEEILLQRTU	equilateral
AAEEILLRSTT	alliterates
AAEEILMMPST	semipalmate
AAEEILMORST	ameliorates
AAEEILNNPRT	penetralian
AAEEILNPPSS	epanalepsis
AAEEILNPRST	planetaries
AAEEILNPTVX	explanative
AAEEILNRTTV	alternative
AAEEILPPRSS	paraleipses
AAEEILRSTTV	alteratives
AAEEIMMNRSS	Sammarinese
AAEEIMNNRSS	San Marinese
AAEEIMNNRSW	weimaraners
AAEEIMNSSTV	amativeness
AAEEIMSSSTT	metastasise
AAEEIMSSTTZ	metastasize
AAEEIOPRSTX	exoparasite
AAEEIOPRTVV	evaporative
AAEEIPPRRSS	reappraises
AAEEIPPRRTV	preparative
AAEEIPRRSTT	repatriates
AAEEIPRSTTX	expatriates
AAEEIRRSTXX	Artaxerxes I
AAEEIRSSSTV	aviatresses
AAEEKLNRSTT	rattlesnake
AAEELLLLMTY	lamellately
AAEELLLMNOS	salmonellae
AAEELLMNTTT	mantelletta
AAEELLNRTTY	alternately
AAEELLPRSTY	platelayers
AAEELLSTTTT	tattletales
AAEELMNSTTT	testamental
AAEELMRRSTT	maltreaters
AAEELNNPTTV	pentavalent
AAEELNPSTTT	pantalettes
AAEELNPSTTV	septavalent
AAEELNRRSTT	retranslate
AAEELNRTTTV	tetravalent
AAEELOPRTTX	extrapolate
AAEEMMNRRST	rearmaments
AAEEMMPRTUY	empyreumata
AAEEMNOPRTT	treponemata
AAEEMNORTUX	auxanometer
AAEEMQRSSTU	marquessate
AAEENNRSSUW	unawareness
AAEFFHRSSTT	aftershafts
AAEFFIIMRTV	affirmative
AAEFFILLNTU	affluential
AAEFGHILNRT	farthingale
AAEFGHNRSTU	fearnaughts
AAEFGILPRST	septifragal
AAEFGINNPRS	frangipanes
AAEFGLLLNST	flagellants
AAEFGLLLORT	flagellator
AAEFGLLNRSU	langlaufers
AAEFGLMNORY	Morgan le Fay
AAEFGMNRRTY	fragmentary
AAEFIIILMRS	familiarise
AAEFIIILMRZ	familiarize
AAEFIIMOSUV	mauvaise foi
AAEFILMMNRT	firmamental
AAEFILMNRTY	filamentary
AAEFILOPRRT	prefatorial
AAEFLLNRRTY	fraternally
AAEFLLNSSTU	fustanellas
AAEFLLORRTX	extrafloral
AAEFLNORTUW	law of nature
AAEFLNRRRST	transferral
AAEGGGGINRT	aggregating
AAEGGGINORT	aggregation
AAEGGGORRST	aggregators
AAEGGIINNRR	gregarinian
AAEGGIINNTV	evaginating
AAEGGIINRTV	variegating
AAEGGILNTTU	agglutinate
AAEGGILOSSU	sialagogues
AAEGGIMMNTU	gametangium
AAEGGIMNOOS	agamogonies
AAEGGINNRRR	rearranging
AAEGGLMMORU	grammalogue
AAEGHHIPPRY	hyperphagia
AAEGHIINRVW	hairweaving
AAEGHILNPRS	nephralgias
AAEGHILORST	hagiolaters
AAEGHILRSTU	gaultherias
AAEGHIMMNOS	hemangiomas
AAEGHIMNORR	menorrhagia
AAEGHIMNPRS	managership
AAEGHINNNSS	shenanigans
AAEGHINRYYZ	Nyíregyháza
AAEGHKKLNRS	Arkhangelsk
AAEGHLLNOXY	hexagonally
AAEGHLMNNOO	Monongahela
AAEGHLMOOTY	haematology
AAEGHLNPRTU	heptangular
AAEGHMNOPRS	anemographs phanerogams
AAEGHMNOPRY	anemography
AAEGHMOPRRS	phraseogram
AAEGHMRTTUU	thaumaturge
AAEGHNPRRST	straphanger
AAEGIIIMNTV	imaginative
AAEGIILLNTV	alleviating
AAEGIILMNPS	Pelagianism
AAEGIILMNRS	marginalise
AAEGIILMNRZ	marginalize
AAEGIILMRST	magisterial
AAEGIILNRTT	retaliating
AAEGIILPRRS	plagiariser
AAEGIILPRRZ	plagiarizer
AAEGIILPRSS	plagiarises
AAEGIILPRST	epigastrial
AAEGIILPRSZ	plagiarizes
AAEGIIMMRRS	mismarriage
AAEGIIMNNRT	reanimating
AAEGIIMNRSS	Minas Gerais
AAEGIINNOTV	evagination
AAEGIINNRTT	reattaining
AAEGIINNSTV	invaginates
AAEGIINORTV	variegation
AAEGIINPTTX	expatiating
AAEGIINRSTT	ingratiates
AAEGIINSTTV	aestivating
AAEGIIRTTVV	gravitative
AAEGILLLNPR	paralleling
AAEGILLNOST	allegations
AAEGILLNPPR	apparelling
AAEGILLNPPY	appealingly
AAEGILLNRST	gallantries
AAEGILMNRST	martingales
AAEGILMNRTT	maltreating
AAEGILMNRTY	ligamentary
AAEGILMNSTT	stalemating

AAEGILMORRS rigamaroles
AAEGILMSSTT stalagmites
AAEGILNNPPU unappealing
AAEGILNNRTT alternating
AAEGILNORTY legationary
AAEGILNOSTT gestational
AAEGILNPRST Great Plains
AAEGILNPRSV palsgravine
AAEGILNQRUU equiangular
AAEGILNRSSV galvanisers
AAEGILNRSVZ galvanizers
AAEGILNRTTU triangulate
AAEGILNRTUV granulative
revaluating
AAEGILORSTT gestatorial
AAEGIMMNRSS mismanagers
AAEGIMNNRRT arraignment
AAEGIMNNTTU antimutagen
AAEGIMNRRSS misarranges
AAEGIMNRRSV margravines
AAEGIMOOPST Aegospotami
AAEGIMRSSTT magistrates
AAEGINNOPRS Singaporean
AAEGINNORSS anagnorises
AAEGINNOSST antagonises
AAEGINNOSTZ antagonizes
AAEGINNTTTU attenuating
AAEGINOPRTV evaporating
AAEGINRSTUU inaugurates
AAEGIOPPRTV propagative
AAEGIOPSTTY steatopygia
AAEGIRRSTTV gravitaters
AAEGKLMNORY Kolyma Range
AAEGKLMNOSS maskalonges
AAEGKLMRSSS glassmakers
AAEGKMNNOSS maskanonges
AAEGKMNRTUU Kumaratunge
AAEGKOPRSSW passagework
AAEGLLLNRYY laryngeally
AAEGLLNNSST gallantness
AAEGLLNNTTY tangentally
AAEGLLOPRTY pyrogallate
AAEGLMMRRSS grammarless
AAEGLMNRTTY termagantly
AAEGLMORSSU megalosaurs
AAEGLNNPRTU pentangular
AAEGLNNRSSU angularness
AAEGLNRRSTU granulaters
AAEGLNRSTTU strangulate
AAEGLPPRSSS glasspapers
AAEGMMOPRSY agamospermy
AAEGMMORSST agrostemmas
AAEGNNRSSTV vagrantness
AAEGOPSSTTY steatopygas
AAEHHHJOPST Jehoshaphat
AAEHHIILMOP haemophilia
AAEHHIKNRRS Hare Krishna
AAEHHILLLSU halleluiahs
AAEHHILNNPT naphthaline
AAEHHJLLLSU hallelujahs
AAEHHOPPSST phosphatase
AAEHIIKLLNP Kephallinía
AAEHIILMNSS leishmanias
AAEHIILNNST annihilates
AAEHIIMNOPS hemianopsia
AAEHIIMNSST histaminase
AAEHIINPSTT antipathies
AAEHIKLNRRS Lanarkshire
AAEHIKRRSST hairstreaks
AAEHILLOPST palaeoliths
AAEHILNOSTT East Lothian
AAEHILNOSTX exhalations
AAEHILNPSTW Westphalian
AAEHILNRSTX exhilarants
AAEHILNSSTU ailanthuses
AAEHILORRTX exhilarator
AAEHILPPPRS slaphappier
AAEHILPPRSY hyperplasia
AAEHILPSSTT asphaltites
AAEHIMNPRSY hypermanias
AAEHIMNSSTU amianthuses
AAEHIMNSSTY myasthenias
AAEHIMOSSST haemostasis
AAEHINOPRSS anaphoresis
AAEHIPSSTXY asphyxiates
AAEHKLORSTT Holkar State
AAEHKMNNTTU Tutankhamen
AAEHLLLOPTY allelopathy
AAEHLLMRRSS marshallers
AAEHLNOPSSY synaloephas
AAEHLNPRSTY phalanstery
AAEHLPRRSWY prayer shawl
AAEHMNOOOTZ haematozoon
AAEHMNORSTU athermanous
AAEHMNORSWW washerwoman
AAEHMNRSSST harassments
AAEHMOPRTTU thaumatrope
AAEHMPRSSTT metaphrasts
AAEHNNQSSUU Susquehanna
AAEHNOPRSST anastrophes
AAEHNOPSSTT thanatopses
AAEHNPPSSWW wappenshaws
AAEIIIKNNOS aniseikonia
AAEIIILNSST italianises
AAEIIILNSTZ italianizes
AAEIIILRSUX auxiliaries
AAEIIJNRSSS janissaries
AAEIILLMNNR millenarian
AAEIILLMNRT matrilineal
AAEIILLNOPR Apollinaire
AAEIILLNOTV alleviation
AAEIILLNPRT patrilineal
AAEIILLPRST ipsilateral
AAEIILLPSTV palliatives
AAEIILMMRST materialism
AAEIILMNNTY inanimately
AAEIILMPRTV imperatival
AAEIILMRSTT materialist
AAEIILMRTTY materiality
AAEIILMSSST assimilates
AAEIILNNOST alienations
nationalise
AAEIILNNOTZ nationalize
AAEIILNNPST Palestinian
AAEIILNNSST salientians
AAEIILNORST rationalise
realisation
AAEIILNORTT retaliation
AAEIILNORTZ rationalize
realization
AAEIILNPRRT patrilinear
AAEIILNSSTV insalivates
AAEIILNSTTY insatiately
AAEIILPPRSS paraleipsis
AAEIILQTTUV qualitative
AAEIIMNNORT reanimation
AAEIIMNNOTX examination
exanimation
AAEIIMNNRSS seminarians
AAEIIMNNRST maintainers
AAEIIMNRSTT Menai Strait
AAEIINNPPRT paripinnate
AAEIINNSTTT instantiate
AAEIINOPTTX expatiation
AAEIINOSTTV aestivation
AAEIINQRSTU antiquaries
AAEIIPRSSST parasitises
AAEIIPRSSTZ parasitizes
AAEIKLLMRTY alkalimetry
AAEIKLLTTVY talkatively
AAEIKLMNOPT kleptomania
AAEIKLMRSTT Sterlitamak
AAEIKORRSTT Korea Strait
AAEILLLLNSV villanellas
AAEILLLMNOT lamellation
AAEILLLMPRS parallelism
AAEILLLOOPS soapolallie
AAEILLLPRST parallelist
AAEILLMPRVY primaevally
AAEILLMRSSY amaryllises
AAEILLNOOTV alveolation
AAEILLNOPPT appellation
AAEILLORSTV alleviators
AAEILLORTTU ratatouille
AAEILLQRSTU aquarellist
AAEILMMNRST maternalism
AAEILMNNOPR praenominal
AAEILMNNOTT lamentation
AAEILMNORST ameliorants
monasterial
AAEILMNPRST parliaments
paternalism
AAEILMNPRTU planetarium
AAEILMNPSTU manipulates
AAEILMNRRTU ultramarine
AAEILMNRSST martialness
AAEILMOORRT ameliorator
AAEILMOPTTT totipalmate
AAEILMORSTY mayoralties
AAEILNNOPST neapolitans
AAEILNNOPTX explanation
AAEILNNORTT alternation
AAEILNNOSST sensational
AAEILNNPRST transalpine
AAEILNNPTTU antenuptial
AAEILNOOPRT operational

AAEILNOPRRT proletarian
AAEILNORSTT alterations
AAEILNORSTU laureations
AAEILNORSTX relaxations
AAEILNORTUV revaluation
AAEILNOSTTX exaltations
AAEILNOSTUV evaluations
AAEILNPRSST partialness
AAEILNPRSTT paternalist
AAEILNRRSTU sertularian
AAEILNRRTVY narratively
AAEILNRSSTT tantalisers
AAEILNRSSTU naturalises
AAEILNRSTTZ tantalizers
AAEILNRSTUZ naturalizes
AAEILNRSTVY antislavery
AAEILOPRRTT proletariat
AAEILOQRSTU quaestorial
AAEILORRSTT retaliators
AAEILORRTTY retaliatory
AAEILORSSSS assessorial
AAEIMMOOPST Mesopotamia
AAEIMNNOSSY mayonnaises
AAEIMNNRRST transmarine
AAEIMNNRSTT Sint Maarten
AAEIMNNSTTT attainments
AAEIMNORSST anatomisers
AAEIMNORSTZ anatomizers
AAEIMNQSSTU antimasques
AAEIMOOPRSZ azoospermia
AAEIMOOTTUX autotoxemia
AAEIMOPPRTX approximate
AAEIMOSSTTU automatises
AAEIMOSTTUZ automatizes
AAEIMQRSSTU marquisates
AAEIMRSSTTU traumatises
AAEIMRSTTUZ traumatizes
AAEINNNOSTX annexations
AAEINNOPRTT trepanation
AAEINNOSSTT assentation
AAEINNOTTTU attenuation
AAEINNQRSTU quarantines
AAEINNRRSVY anniversary
AAEINOOPRTV evaporation
AAEINOORSTT aerostation
AAEINOPPRRT preparation
AAEINOPRRST praetorians
reparations
AAEINOPRSST separations
AAEINORRSTT arrestation
AAEINORSSTU Austronesia
AAEINOSTTTT attestation
AAEIOPPPRRT appropriate
AAEIOPPRRSS appressoria
AAEIOPRRSST raspatories
AAEIOPRSTTX expatiators
AAEIOPSSSTT apostatises
AAEIOPSSTTZ apostatizes
AAEIORSSTTV aestivators
assortative
AAEIPRSSSTT separatists
AAEIPRSSSTU East Prussia

AAEKKNOPRSU Sukarno Peak
AAEKMRSSSTT taskmasters
AAELLLNNOPR nonparallel
AAELLLORSST saltarellos
AAELLMMORRY marmoreally
AAELLMNORUY malonylurea
AAELLORRSTT stellarator
AAELLRSSTTT Tattersall's
AAELMNNORST ornamentals
AAELMNSSTTY statesmanly
AAELMORSSSU elasmosaurs
AAELNNNOOSS nonseasonal
AAELNNRSSTU naturalness
AAELNOOPPRS aplanospore
AAELNOPRTXY explanatory
AAELNORRSTT alternators
AAELNRRSSTV transversal
AAELNRRSSTW warrantless
AAELNRRSTUV transvaluer
AAELNRSSTUV transvalues
AAELNRSSTUX transexuals
transsexual
AAELOOPSSTT apostolates
AAELOORRTVY laevorotary
AAELORRSTTV travelators
AAELPRRSSTU superaltars
AAELPRRSTTT rattletraps
AAEMNNORSTT tramontanes
AAEMNOOPRTT protonemata
AAEMNOOSSST anastomoses
AAEMNOPRTTU portmanteau
AAEMNOSSTTW stateswoman
AAEMOOPRSTZ spermatozoa
AAEMORSSTTT toastmaster
AAENNPPRTTU appurtenant
AAENNPRRSTT transparent
AAENNPRSTTU supernatant
AAENORSTTTU attenuators
AAENQRRSTUW quartersawn
AAENRRSSTTU restaurants
AAEOOPRRSTV evaporators
AAEOPPRRRTY preparatory
AAEOPRSSTTU stratopause
AAEORSSTTTT attestators
AAEPRRSSTTU superstrata
AAEQRRSSTUW quartersaws
AAFFGIIILNT affiliating
AAFFGIMNRSU ragamuffins
AAFFIIILNOT affiliation
AAFFIIMNORT affirmation
AAFFIINOSTX affixations
AAFGHIKLRUU Hauraki Gulf
AAFGIIKLLNY alkalifying
AAFGIINNPRS frangipanis
AAFGIINNSST fantasising
AAFGIINNSTZ fantasizing
AAFGIINNTTU infatuating
AAFGILLMRUY gallimaufry
AAFGILNOSTT stagflation
AAFGINORRSU farraginous
AAFHIINOSST fashionista
AAFIIILMRTY familiarity

AAFIINNOTTU infatuation
AAFIINRRSTU fruitarians
AAFILMNOORT formational
AAFILNOOSTT floatations
AAFIMNNNRTY infantryman
AAFINNOOPRT profanation
AAFLNNOORST nasofrontal
AAFNOOPRRTY profanatory
AAFOPRRRSTW sparrowfart
AAGGHHIINNS shanghaiing
AAGGHHIOPRY hagiography
AAGGHIIJMNT thingamajig
AAGGHINOPRY angiography
AAGGIIJNNOX Gao Xingjian
AAGGIILNNOS analogising
AAGGIILNNOZ analogizing
AAGGIILNNSV galvanising
AAGGIILNNTV galivanting
AAGGIILNNVZ galvanizing
AAGGIIMMNNS mismanaging
AAGGIIMNNRT marginating
AAGGIINRSTV stravaiging
AAGGIINRTTV gravitating
AAGGIKLMNSS glassmaking
AAGGIKNNOOR kangarooing
AAGGILLMORR gorillagram
AAGGILLNOST algolagnist
AAGGILMNNTU mangulating
AAGGILNNNUY Lianyungang
AAGGILNNRTU granulating
AAGGILNNTTU agglutinant
AAGGILNRTTU gratulating
AAGGINNRTUY guarantying
AAGGINOPPRT propagating
AAGGLLLOSSW gallowglass
AAGHHLOPPRY haplography
AAGHIILLNOP anglophilia
AAGHIJKNOUZ Zhangjiakou
AAGHIKLLMNR hallmarking
AAGHIKMNOTW tomahawking
AAGHILLMNPY lymphangial
AAGHILLMNRS marshalling
AAGHILNPSST phalangists
AAGHIMNRSST stramashing
AAGHIOPRSTY hypogastria
AAGHIRSTTWY straightway
AAGHLNOOTTY thanatology
AAGHLNOPPRY planography
AAGHLOOPPRR polarograph
AAGHMMMOPRS mammographs
AAGHMMMOPRY mammography
AAGHMRTTUUY thaumaturgy
AAGHNOPPRST pantographs
AAGHNOPPRTY pantography
AAGHNOPRRUY uranography
AAGIIILMNNS animalising
AAGIIILMNNZ animalizing
AAGIIILMNRY imaginarily
AAGIIIMNNNT maintaining
AAGIIIMNNOT imagination
AAGIIKNNPST painstaking
AAGIILLLNWW Wailing Wall

AAGIILMNORT	migrational
AAGIILMNRTY	marginality
AAGIILMPRSS	plagiarisms
AAGIILNNNSU	annualising
AAGIILNNNUZ	annualizing
AAGIILNNSTT	tantalising
AAGIILNNTTZ	tantalizing
AAGIILNORTV	variolating
AAGIILNPPTT	palpitating
AAGIILNSSSV	vassalising
AAGIILNSSVZ	vassalizing
AAGIILOPRRT	Gloria Patri
AAGIILPRSST	plagiarists
AAGIIMMNNOT	ammoniating
AAGIIMMNNTY	magnanimity
AAGIIMMSSTT	astigmatism
AAGIIMNNORT	margination
AAGIIMNNOST	anatomising
AAGIIMNNOTZ	anatomizing
AAGIIMNORST	aromatising
AAGIIMNORTZ	aromatizing
AAGIIMSSSSU	Mississauga
AAGIINNOPST	paginations
AAGIINNORSS	anagnorisis
AAGIINNOSST	assignation
AAGIINNOSTV	navigations
AAGIINNQTTU	antiquating
	aquatinting
AAGIINNSTUU	Augustinian
AAGIINORTTV	gravitation
AAGIINPPTTT	pitapatting
AAGIINPSSTV	passivating
AAGIINRRSTT	tartarising
AAGIINRRTTZ	tartarizing
AAGIIRSSTTU	Sagittarius
AAGILLLNPPY	appallingly
AAGILLLOOSS	glossolalia
AAGILLMNNTY	malignantly
AAGILLMOORY	malariology
AAGILMMMOST	mammalogist
AAGILMOPRSS	paralogisms
AAGILNNORTU	granulation
AAGILNNOSTU	angulations
AAGILNNPPUU	Pulau Pinang
AAGILNNRSTT	translating
AAGILNOPSTY	angioplasty
AAGILNORTTU	gratulation
AAGILNOSUVY	Yugoslavian
AAGILNRRTUY	granularity
AAGILOPRRTU	purgatorial
AAGILOPRSST	paralogists
AAGILORSUVY	vagariously
AAGIMMNNOSU	magnanimous
AAGIMNNOSST	antagonisms
AAGIMNOOSSU	anisogamous
AAGIMNOOSTU	angiomatous
AAGIMNSSSTY	gymnasiasts
AAGIMPRSSTT	pragmatists
AAGINNOSSTT	antagonists
AAGINOOPPRT	propagation
AAGINOORRST	arrogations
AAGINORRTUU	inaugurator
AAGLLMNRTUU	multangular
AAGLLNOOSUY	analogously
AAGLLNOPSTT	topgallants
AAGLMOOPRRS	polarograms
AAGLNORRSTU	granulators
AAGLOOPRTXY	protogalaxy
AAGLORRTTUY	gratulatory
AAGOOPPRRST	propagators
AAHHHKLLLMO	Holkham Hall
AAHHIIKOSWW	kowhaiwhais
AAHHILMOPTY	hypothalami
AAHHILMPRSS	marshalship
AAHIIJNNOOU	Haji-Ioannou
AAHIILNNORT	annihilator
AAHIILNNOST	inhalations
AAHIINPRSST	antiphrasis
AAHIKKLNOSV	kalashnikov
AAHILLLOPRT	prothallial
AAHILLMTUYZ	azimuthally
AAHILLOPSTT	allopathist
AAHILMOPSTY	syphilomata
AAHILMPRSTY	amphistylar
AAHILMSTTUZ	altazimuths
AAHILNNOPST	antiphonals
AAHIMMNNOPY	nymphomania
AAHIMMNOPRS	anamorphism
AAHIMNOPRSS	oarsmanship
AAHIMNOSSTT	Saint Thomas
AAHINNOPRTY	antiphonary
AAHINNOSTTX	xanthations
AAHINOPSSTT	thanatopsis
AAHINPSSTXY	asphyxiants
AAHIOPRSTXY	asphyxiator
AAHKOPRRSWW	sparrowhawk
AAHKOPSTUUW	pohutukawas
AAHLLMMORSW	marshmallow
AAHMNNRSTTU	transhumant
AAHNNOPRSXY	nasopharynx
AAHNNRSSTUY	thysanurans
AAHNOPRSTTU	naturopaths
AAHNOPRTTUY	naturopathy
AAIIIIKMORS	Makarios III
AAIIIILMMNX	Maximilian I
AAIIILMNOTT	imitational
AAIIILMNRST	limitarians
AAIIILNRTTU	utilitarian
AAIIILNSSTW	Stanisław II
AAIIIMNNNOT	inanimation
AAIIINNRRTT	trinitarian
AAIIJKLMNOR	Kilimanjaro
AAIIKNNOSTY	kyanisation
AAIIKNNOTYZ	kyanization
AAIILLMPRTY	impartially
AAIILLNOPST	palliations
AAIILMMNORT	matrimonial
AAIILMMSSTX	maximalists
AAIILMNNOPR	paralimnion
AAIILMNNOST	antimonials
	laminations
	nationalism
AAIILMNNOTV	nominatival
AAIILMNOPRT	patrimonial
AAIILMNOPST	maintopsail
AAIILMNORST	rationalism
AAIILMORSST	assimilator
AAIILMRSSTT	martialists
AAIILNNOSTT	nationalist
AAIILNNOTTY	nationality
AAIILNOORTV	variolation
AAIILNOPPTT	palpitation
AAIILNORSTT	rationalist
AAIILNORTTT	attritional
AAIILNORTTY	rationality
AAIILNOSTTU	situational
AAIIMMMNORY	Yamim Nora'im
AAIIMMNNOOT	ammoniation
AAIIMMNOSTX	maximations
AAIIMNNNOST	antinomians
AAIIMNNORST	marinations
	Mastroianni
AAIIMNNRSTT	Saint Martin
AAIIMNOOSTT	atomisation
AAIIMNOOTTZ	atomization
AAIIMNOPRTT	impartation
AAIIMNOPSTT	impastation
AAIIMNRSSTU	sanitariums
AAIINOPPRST	apparitions
AAIINOPRSST	aspirations
AAIKLLMMNUZ	Nizam al-Mulk
AAIKLLNOSTY	alkylations
AAILLLOSTWW	swallowtail
AAILLLPSSTU	pulsatillas
AAILLMNTTUY	matutinally
AAILLNNSSTT	installants
AAILLNOPSST	spallations
AAILLOOPRYZ	polyzoarial
AAILLORRSTY	sartorially
AAILMMNOSTU	summational
AAILMMOPPRS	malapropism
AAILMNOPRTU	manipulator
AAILMNRSTTT	transmittal
AAILMOPRSST	pastoralism
AAILNNNNOOT	nonnational
AAILNNNOORT	nonrational
AAILNNNOSTU	annulations
AAILNNOPSTT	plantations
AAILNNORSTT	translation
AAILNOSSTTU	salutations
AAILNRSSTTU	naturalists
AAILOORSTTT	totalisator
AAILOORTTTZ	totalizator
AAILOPRSSTT	pastoralist
AAIMMNOPSTT	maintopmast
AAIMMNOSSUY	immunoassay
AAIMMRSSTTU	traumatisms
AAIMNOOOSTT	somatotonia
AAIMNOOSSST	anastomosis
AAIMNOPSTTU	amputations
AAIMNOQSSTU	squamations
AAIMNORSSTU	sanatoriums
AAIMNORSTTU	maturations
	natatoriums

AAIMNPRRTTU	intrapartum
AAIMOSSTTTU	automatists
AAINNNOOSTT	annotations
AAINNNOPRST	nonpartisan
AAINNNOPRTZ	nonpartizan
AAINNOOQRTU	Quintana Roo
AAINNOPRSTT	patron saint
AAINOORRSTZ	Zoroastrian
AAINORRSTTU	instaurator
AAINORSSTTU	titanosaurs
AAINPSSTTWY	pantywaists
AAKKNORRSSY	Krasnoyarsk
AAKLLMPRUUU	Kuala Lumpur
AAKLNORSSUY	ankylosaurs
AAKLORRVVYY	Karlovy Vary
AALLMNOOSUY	anomalously
AALLNNRTUUY	unnaturally
AALMMOOPSST	somatoplasm
AALMNNOPSTW	plantswoman
AALMNOPRTUY	paramountly
AALNNPRSSTT	transplants
AALNNRRSTUY	translunary
AALNOOPSUZZ	pozzuolanas
AALNOPRSSST	transposals
AALNORRSSTT	translators
AALOORRSTTV	travolators
AALORSSTTTU	altostratus
AAMNPRSSTTY	smartypants
AANNORRSTUY	tyrannosaur
ABBBEELMNST	babblements
ABBBENORUWY	Woburn Abbey
ABBCCEEHKNR	backbencher
ABBCCEEHMOR	beachcomber
ABBCCEKKLOR	backblocker
ABBCCGIKMNO	backcombing
ABBCDDEIKLR	blackbirded
ABBCDEEFIKO	biofeedback
ABBCDEEHMRS	bedchambers
ABBCDEEILRS	describable
ABBCDEENRSS	crabbedness
ABBCDEMRRSU	breadcrumbs
ABBCDKLOORS	blockboards
ABBCEEEKNRU	Beckenbauer
ABBCEEIMORR	Abercrombie
ABBCEEJLSTU	subjectable
ABBCEHIILOT	bibliotheca
ABBCEHIOPRY	cyberphobia
ABBCEHNRSSU	subbranches
ABBCEIILNRS	inscribable
ABBCEJKORWY	jabberwocky
ABBCGIKNNRU	backburning
ABBCIIINRST	rabbinistic
ABBCIILLTUY	clubability
ABBCIILMNOY	bibliomancy
ABBCKNNNORU	Bannockburn
ABBDDEGIORR	bridgeboard
ABBDDEIINRR	birdbrained
ABBDEELORTU	redoubtable
ABBDEGNNRRU	Brandenburg
ABBDEIILNTU	indubitable
ABBDEILNOTU	obnubilated
ABBDEILRSSU	disbursable
ABBDEIMORRS	bombardiers
ABBDELLNRSU	landlubbers
ABBDELNOTUU	undoubtable
ABBDELORTUY	redoubtably
ABBDEMMNORT	bombardment
ABBDHIINORZ	Birobidzhan
ABBDIILNTUY	indubitably
ABBEEEILRRS	blaeberries
ABBEEEINRRS	baneberries
ABBEEEIRRRS	bearberries
ABBEEKOORRV	Beaverbrook
ABBEELPRRTU	perturbable
ABBEELSSTTU	battlebuses
ABBEEMNSSTU	subbasement
ABBEENORSST	breastbones
ABBEENRRSSU	baseburners
ABBEEORRSTW	browbeaters
ABBEGILNORU	belabouring
ABBEGINORRS	reabsorbing
ABBEGINORTW	browbeating
ABBEHIIILNT	inhibitable
ABBEHILLPSU	publishable
ABBEHILNRSU	burnishable
ABBEHOPRRSS	barbershops
ABBEIILLMOS	mobilisable
ABBEIILLMOZ	mobilizable
ABBEIKRRSTT	bitterbarks
ABBEILMSTTU	submittable
ABBEILNOSTU	obnubilates
ABBEINRSSUU	suburbanise
ABBEINRSTUU	suburbanite
ABBEINRSUUZ	suburbanize
ABBELLRSTTU	butterballs
ABBELMOORSZ	bamboozlers
ABBELMSSSUY	subassembly
ABBELPRRTUY	perturbably
ABBFFIILMSU	bumbailiffs
ABBFFILLLOU	Buffalo Bill
ABBFILORSST	fibroblasts
ABBGHHINSSU	bushbashing
ABBGHIMNOTU	thingumabob
ABBGIILMNOT	bombilating
ABBGIIMNNOT	bombinating
ABBGILMNOOZ	bamboozling
ABBGILNORSY	absorbingly
ABBGLMOORRY	borborygmal
ABBHILLMOSY	Bombay Hills
ABBIILLORTY	bibliolatry
ABBIILMOPRS	probabilism
ABBIILOPRST	probabilist
ABBIILOPRTY	probability
ABBIIMNNOOT	bombination
ABBLLNOSTTU	buttonballs
ABCCCCILORY	carbocyclic
ABCCCHKKLOO	chockablock
ABCCDDHIIKY	chickabiddy
ABCCDEEELSU	succeedable
ABCCDEEENRU	buccaneered
ABCCDEEIIRT	bactericide
ABCCDEHHKNU	hunchbacked
ABCCDEKKOOR	crookbacked
ABCCDEKORSS	backcrossed
ABCCDHHORRU	Broad Church
ABCCEEELLRY	recycleable
ABCCEEILNOV	conceivable
ABCCEELLLOT	collectable
ABCCEELNNOT	connectable
ABCCEELORRT	correctable
ABCCEEMNNRU	encumbrance
ABCCEFILNOS	confiscable
ABCCEFIORSU	bacciferous
ABCCEGINNOU	concubinage
ABCCEHIILMO	biochemical
ABCCEHINRTT	tectibranch
ABCCEHKRSTT	backstretch
ABCCEIILLNO	conciliable
ABCCEIILNOT	cenobitical
ABCCEIILPTY	peccability
ABCCEIKKLST	stickleback
ABCCEIKLNPR	Black Prince
ABCCEILNOTV	convictable
ABCCEILNOVY	conceivably
ABCCEILNSSU	cubicalness
ABCCEILOSTT	ectoblastic
ABCCEIMNNRU	incumbrance
ABCCEIMOORS	mobocracies
ABCCEINORRT	centrobaric
ABCCEINRRTY	barycentric
ABCCEKLOOST	cockleboats
ABCCEKNORRS	cornerbacks
ABCCEKORSSS	backcrosses
ABCCELOOSST	tobaccoless
ABCCELORSUU	succourable
ABCCHIKSSTW	switchbacks
ABCCIILLNSU	subclinical
ABCCIILRSTU	subcritical
ABCCIIMOORT	macrobiotic
ABCCIINOTVY	biconcavity
ABCCILLLOUY	bucolically
ABCCILORSTU	subcortical
ABCCINNORUY	concubinary
ABCCINOOSTT	tobacconist
ABCCINORSTU	buccinators
ABCCIOORSUV	baccivorous
ABCCKNORTUY	backcountry
ABCCNORSTTU	subcontract
ABCDDEEELNS	descendable
ABCDDEEHKLO	blockheaded
ABCDDEEHLUY	debauchedly
ABCDDEELMRS	descrambled
ABCDDEFIKLS	fiddlebacks
ABCDDEFINOR	forbiddance
ABCDDEHINRS	disbranched
ABCDDEIKLNS	backslidden
ABCDDEINOOT	bandicooted
ABCDDEKLORS	badderlocks
ABCDEEEERRT	decerebrate
ABCDEEEHORS	cheeseboard
ABCDEEEILPR	depreciable
ABCDEEGGKLL	blacklegged
ABCDEEHMNTU	debauchment
ABCDEEIILMM	immedicable
ABCDEEILNRS	discernable
	rescindable

ABCDEEILNTU	binucleated
ABCDEEILORV	divorceable
ABCDEEILPRS	predicables
ABCDEEILPRT	predictable
ABCDEEINORS	decarbonise
ABCDEEINORZ	decarbonize
ABCDEEIRRSU	decarburise
ABCDEEIRRUZ	decarburize
ABCDEEKLRSV	backvelders
ABCDEELLPRU	precludable
ABCDEELMMNO	commendable
ABCDEELMNNO	condemnable
ABCDEELMRRS	descrambler
ABCDEELMRSS	descrambles
ABCDEELNNOS	condensable
ABCDEELNRRY	candleberry
ABCDEENORRT	centreboard
ABCDEERRTTU	carburetted
ABCDEFILORS	Frescobaldi
ABCDEGGIKPY	piggybacked
ABCDEGLNOOT	conglobated
ABCDEHHKSUW	bushwhacked
ABCDEHIILLN	chilblained
ABCDEHILSTW	switchblade
ABCDEHINRSS	disbranches
ABCDEHIRRTW	birdwatcher
ABCDEHORSSS	chessboards
ABCDEIILMMY	immedicably
ABCDEIILOSS	dissociable
ABCDEIILTUY	educability
ABCDEIIPSTU	bicuspidate
ABCDEIKLLST	blacklisted
ABCDEIKLRSS	backsliders
ABCDEILNOST	endoblastic
ABCDEILNRSY	discernably
ABCDEILORTU	orbiculated
ABCDEILPRTY	predictably
ABCDEILSSSU	discussable
ABCDEILSSTU	subdialects
ABCDEINRRST	transcribed
ABCDEINRSTU	disturbance
ABCDEINSSSU	subacidness
ABCDEIPRRSS	crispbreads
ABCDEKOPPST	backstopped
ABCDELMMNOY	commendably
ABCDELMNNOY	condemnably
ABCDELMNRSU	unscrambled
ABCDELMNRUU	Cumbernauld
ABCDEOORRSS	scoreboards
ABCDGIIKLNS	backsliding
ABCDGKNORSU	backgrounds
ABCDHIIMRTY	dithyrambic
ABCDHIIRSTU	hudibrastic
ABCDHINNRSU	nudibranchs
ABCDHINOOPR	branchiopod
ABCDHIOOPRS	brachiopods
ABCDHIORSTW	switchboard
ABCDHLOORST	broadcloths
ABCDHNOORRY	hydrocarbon
ABCDHNOORTY	brachyodont
ABCDHNOPRSU	punchboards
ABCDIIILOST	idioblastic

ABCDIILLSSY	dissyllabic
ABCDIILORUV	vibraculoid
ABCDIILOSSY	dissociably
ABCDIIMNOSY	biodynamics
ABCDILNOSST	cnidoblasts
ABCEEEFLNOR	enforceable
ABCEEEGKNRR	greenbacker
ABCEEEIKRRS	icebreakers
ABCEEEILPRV	perceivable
ABCEEEILPTT	battlepiece
ABCEEEILRSV	receivables
	serviceable
ABCEEEILRSX	exercisable
ABCEEEILRTV	celebrative
ABCEEEIMRRS	embraceries
ABCEEELLNTU	unelectable
ABCEEELMNRS	resemblance
ABCEEELORRV	recoverable
ABCEEELPRST	respectable
ABCEEEMMNRR	remembrance
ABCEEEMMNRT	embracement
ABCEEENRSUX	exuberances
ABCEEFIILPS	specifiable
ABCEEFIILRT	certifiable
	rectifiable
ABCEEFIINRY	beneficiary
ABCEEFILNNO	confineable
ABCEEFINNOT	benefaction
ABCEEFINRTU	rubefacient
ABCEEFLNORR	conferrable
ABCEEFLNOSS	confessable
ABCEEFNORST	benefactors
ABCEEGIINOT	abiogenetic
ABCEEGILNRT	celebrating
ABCEEGILOTX	excogitable
ABCEEGINRRT	cerebrating
ABCEEGLNRST	glabrescent
ABCEEHHILRS	cherishable
ABCEEHIKRRS	hackberries
ABCEEHILNRS	hibernacles
ABCEEHINNRS	Sennacherib
ABCEEHKRSTU	hackbuteers
ABCEEHLLRSY	bellyachers
ABCEEHLORTU	retouchable
ABCEEHLRSTT	stretchable
ABCEEHNORRS	abhorrences
ABCEEHORRRT	torchbearer
ABCEEIILNSV	bivalencies
ABCEEIKLNRS	linebackers
ABCEEILLNTU	ineluctable
ABCEEILNORT	celebration
ABCEEILNPST	inspectable
ABCEEILNSUX	inexcusable
ABCEEILORRV	irrevocable
ABCEEILPRVY	perceivably
ABCEEILRRSU	irrecusable
ABCEEILRRTT	retractible
ABCEEILRRTU	recruitable
ABCEEILRSVY	serviceably
ABCEEIMRTUU	eubacterium
ABCEEINNRTY	bicentenary
ABCEEINORRT	cerebration

ABCEEINORST	baronetcies
ABCEEINORTX	exorbitance
ABCEEINRRRS	cranberries
ABCEEJKLSTU	bluejackets
ABCEEKRSSTT	backstreets
ABCEELLLMOP	compellable
ABCEELLNOSU	counselable
ABCEELLOOST	blastocoele
ABCEELMNOPS	compensable
ABCEELNOQRU	conquerable
ABCEELNORSV	conservable
	conversable
ABCEELNOSTT	contestable
ABCEELNRSSU	curableness
ABCEELORRST	celebrators
ABCEELORRTY	celebratory
ABCEELOSTUU	betulaceous
ABCEELPRSTY	respectably
ABCEELRTTUU	tuberculate
ABCEEMOOSTY	amoebocytes
ABCEENORRST	arborescent
ABCEENORSSV	observances
ABCEENORSTT	carbonettes
ABCEENRRSTY	barycentres
ABCEERRRTTU	carburetter
ABCEFHIKLSS	blackfishes
ABCEFHNOOPR	francophobe
ABCEFIILLNT	inflictable
ABCEFIILRTY	certifiably
ABCEFILMNOR	confirmable
ABCEFINORTU	rubefaction
ABCEFKLORST	Black Forest
ABCEFLMNOOR	conformable
ABCEFLMOORT	comfortable
ABCEGHILLNY	bellyaching
ABCEGIILNOT	incogitable
ABCEGIKNRST	bracketings
ABCEGILLNRS	sacring bell
ABCEGILNNOS	consignable
ABCEGILNOST	blastogenic
ABCEGIMNORT	embrocating
ABCEGINNRTY	cybernating
ABCEGINORST	obsecrating
ABCEGLNOOST	conglobates
ABCEGORSTUY	subcategory
ABCEHHIOOPT	theophobiac
ABCEHHIOPPT	taphephobic
ABCEHHKORSV	Shcherbakov
ABCEHHKRSUW	bushwhacker
ABCEHHMOORT	bathochrome
ABCEHIILPRT	blepharitic
ABCEHIKLNSY	Chelyabinsk
ABCEHIKRRST	brickearths
ABCEHILOPSU	bicephalous
ABCEHILPRST	birthplaces
ABCEHIMORST	bichromates
ABCEHIMORTT	bathometric
ABCEHIMRTTY	bathymetric
ABCEHINNRRT	interbranch
ABCEHINOOPR	necrophobia
ABCEHKLNOSU	unshockable
ABCEHKLOSVY	Lobachevsky

ABCEHKRSTTU hackbutters
ABCEHLLOSTT tablecloths
ABCEHLNOTUU untouchable
ABCEHPRSSTU subchapters
ABCEHRSSTTU bruschettas
ABCEIIILLSV civilisable
ABCEIIILLVZ civilizable
ABCEIIJLSTU justiciable
ABCEIILMRTY imbricately
ABCEIILNOTX intoxicable
ABCEIILRTUV lubricative
ABCEIIMNOTV combinative
ABCEIINOSST obstinacies
ABCEIINRSTU Saint-Brieuc
ABCEIIORSST aerobicists
ABCEIKKSSTY stickybeaks
ABCEIKLRRSY bricklayers
ABCEIKLRSSV silverbacks
ABCEIKNORTW cabinetwork
ABCEILLLOPS collapsible
ABCEILLMORU bimolecular
ABCEILLMRSU lumbricales
ABCEILLNOOS colonisable
ABCEILLNOOZ colonizable
ABCEILLNRSS cranesbills
ABCEILLNTUY ineluctably
ABCEILMMOTT committable
ABCEILMOPRS comprisable
ABCEILMOPRT problematic
ABCEILMORST blastomeric
meroblastic
ABCEILMOSST mesoblastic
ABCEILMOTVY combatively
ABCEILMSSUX subclimaxes
ABCEILNNOTU continuable
ABCEILNORTV contrivable
ABCEILNOSTT entoblastic
ABCEILNPRSU republicans
ABCEILNRSTU inscrutable
ABCEILNSUXY inexcusably
ABCEILORRVY irrevocably
ABCEILORSTT obstetrical
ABCEILRRSUY irrecusably
ABCEILRSSTU subarticles
ABCEIMNNORT recombinant
ABCEIMNOORT embrocation
ABCEINNORTY cybernation
ABCEINOORST obsecration
ABCEINORRSS carbonisers
ABCEINORRSZ carbonizers
ABCEINRRRST transcriber
ABCEINRRSST transcribes
ABCEIOORRRV Barcoo River
ABCEIRRRSSU subcarriers
ABCEIRSTTUV subtractive
ABCEJKLMRSU lumberjacks
ABCEJLNSTUY subjacently
ABCEKKORSST backstrokes
ABCEKLRSTTU turtlebacks
ABCELLLMNOO collembolan
ABCELLLMOPY compellably
ABCELLNOORS collarbones
ABCELLNOSTU consultable
ABCELLNSSTU Sanctus bell
ABCELLOOSST blastocoels
ABCELLOSSTU leucoblasts
ABCELMNOSSU consumables
ABCELMNRRSU unscrambler
ABCELMNRSSU unscrambles
ABCELMOOPST compostable
ABCELNNOTUU uncountable
ABCELNOORST consortable
ABCELNORRSY barleycorns
ABCELNORSTU construable
ABCELNORSVY conversably
ABCELNOSTTY contestably
ABCELNPRTUU puncturable
ABCELRRSTUU tuberculars
ABCEMOOPRST amboceptors
ABCEOOORRRT corroborate
ABCEOOPRRST baroceptors
ABCEORRRSTU carburetors
ABCEORRRTTU carburettor
ABCEORSTUUY butyraceous
ABCERRSSTTU subtracters
ABCFGIIKLLN backfilling
ABCFGIINRTU bifurcating
ABCFGINOSTU obfuscating
ABCFHINOOST sonofabitch
ABCFIILLMOR bacilliform
ABCFIINORTU bifurcation
ABCFILSSSUY subclassify
ABCFINOOSTU obfuscation
ABCFLMNOORY conformably
ABCFLMOORTY comfortably
ABCFOORSTUY obfuscatory
ABCGHILLNUU clubhauling
ABCGHOORRSU Scarborough
ABCGIIIMNRT imbricating
ABCGIIKLNRY bricklaying
ABCGIIKNOUV bivouacking
ABCGIILLOOS biologicals
ABCGIILNORS carbolising
ABCGIILNORZ carbolizing
ABCGIILNRTU lubricating
ABCGIINNORS carbonising
ABCGIINNORZ carbonizing
ABCGIINRRSU carburising
ABCGIINRRTU rubricating
ABCGIINRRUZ carburizing
ABCGIKLLNOS ballocksing
ABCGIKLNPRU parbuckling
ABCGILLOORY bryological
ABCGILNRTUU lucubrating
ABCGILNSSSU subclassing
ABCGINRSTTU subtracting
ABCHHIILOTT batholithic
ABCHHILOOOP ochlophobia
ABCHHIOOPTT photobathic
ABCHHIOPRSS archbishops
ABCHHLNOOPR lophobranch
ABCHIIIMOPT amphibiotic
ABCHIILNOOT halobiontic
ABCHIILNRTY labyrinthic
ABCHIILOPSY biophysical
ABCHIKLMSST blacksmiths
ABCHILLNORY bronchially
ABCHILLOOST holoblastic
ABCHILMOOST homoblastic
ABCHILNOORR bronchiolar
ABCHILOPSTY hypoblastic
ABCHIMNORSU subharmonic
ABCHINOOPTY nyctophobia
ABCHINORRSY chrysarobin
ABCHIOOPRST astrophobic
ABCHKLNORST blackthorns
ABCIIILOSTY sociability
ABCIIILRSTT tribalistic
ABCIIIMNORT imbrication
ABCIIINOSTT antibiotics
ABCIIKLNRSY brainsickly
ABCIILLLMUY umbilically
ABCIILLMRSU lumbricalis
ABCIILLPTUY culpability
ABCIILLRSTY trisyllabic
ABCIILMOSTY symbiotical
ABCIILNOPTU publication
ABCIILNORTU lubrication
ABCIIMNNOOT combination
ABCIINNOSTU incubations
ABCIINORRTU rubrication
ABCIINORSTT abstriction
ABCIKLLMMSU Black Muslim
ABCILLNNOUY connubially
ABCILLORRUY orbicularly
ABCILLOSSUY subsocially
ABCILMMORUU columbarium
ABCILMNNUUU incunabulum
ABCILNORTUU lucubration
ABCILNRSTUY inscrutably
ABCILOOPRST blastoporic
ABCILOPRSTU subtropical
ABCILORRSTU lubricators
ABCIMNOORTY combinatory
ABCIMOPSUVX pax vobiscum
ABCINNOORTU conurbation
ABCINOORSTU obscuration
ABCINORSTTU subtraction
ABCIORRRSTU rubricators
ABCKKNOOSTU knockabouts
ABCLLRSTUUU subcultural
ABCLORRSTUU lucubrators
ABCLOSSSTTY blastocysts
ABCMNOORSSW crossbowman
ABCNOOORRRT corroborant
ABCNORRSTUY subcontrary
ABDDDEIMNOR broadminded
ABDDEEEGRRY greybearded
ABDDEEEILRT deliberated
ABDDEEEILTY baddeleyite
ABDDEEENSSS debasedness
ABDDEEGHILY bigheadedly
ABDDEEGHIRS bridgeheads
ABDDEEIILLU Île du Diable
ABDDEEIILTT debilitated

ABDDEEIKMRS	disembarked
ABDDEELNNRY	Enderby Land
ABDDEELNORS	bladdernose
ABDDEGIRRSW	drawbridges
ABDDEHKLNNU	Bundelkhand
ABDDEHOOSWX	shadowboxed
ABDDEIIMRSS	bridesmaids
ABDDEILLLSS	saddlebills
ABDDEIMNNST	disbandment
ABDDELNORRS	borderlands
ABDDELNRSTU	bladdernuts
ABDDELORRTW	bladderwort
ABDDILLORRS	dollarbirds
ABDDLMOORSU	mouldboards
ABDDOORRSSW	broadswords
ABDEEEEGLRU	beleaguered
ABDEEEFHRST	featherbeds
ABDEEEFIKNR	Diefenbaker
ABDEEEGGRSW	beggarweeds
ABDEEEHHKSS	baksheeshed
ABDEEEHILRT	hereditable
ABDEEEILLRV	deliverable
ABDEEEILRST	deliberates
ABDEEEINRSV	aberdevines
ABDEEELLOPV	developable
ABDEEELMNRU	denumerable
ABDEEELMRSS	reassembled
ABDEEELNPSX	expendables
ABDEEELNSST	belatedness
ABDEEELRRSS	redressable
ABDEEEMNSST	debasements
ABDEEEPRSTT	bespattered
ABDEEERSSTW	sweetbreads
ABDEEFFHLSU	buffleheads
ABDEEFIILNN	indefinable
ABDEEFILLTT	battlefield
ABDEEFILNNU	undefinable
ABDEEFIORST	afterbodies
ABDEEGGINRR	gingerbread
ABDEEGHINRR	harbingered
ABDEEGIMNRT	abridgement
ABDEEGINPRS	bespreading
ABDEEGKNRRS	Drakensberg
ABDEEGMNOOR	boomeranged
ABDEEGORRSV	vergeboards
ABDEEHILLSS	deshabilles
ABDEEHILPSS	beadleships
ABDEEHILRRS	halberdiers
ABDEEHILRTY	hereditably
ABDEEHILSST	established
ABDEEHIMRST	timberheads
ABDEEHIRRSS	shadberries
ABDEEHIRSTW	breadthwise
ABDEEHNPRRS	sharpbender
ABDEEHORSST	broadsheets
ABDEEIIKLLS	dislikeable
ABDEEIILLRS	liberalised
ABDEEIILLRZ	liberalized
ABDEEIILRST	detribalise
ABDEEIILRTZ	detribalize
ABDEEIILSST	bestialised
	destabilise
ABDEEIILSTT	debilitates
ABDEEIILSTZ	bestialized
	destabilize
ABDEEIKNRRW	windbreaker
ABDEEIKNRSY	Iskander Bey
ABDEEILLLMS	mislabelled
ABDEEILMNNO	denominable
ABDEEILMNST	disablement
ABDEEILMNSU	albumenised
ABDEEILMNUZ	albumenized
ABDEEILMOST	metabolised
ABDEEILMOTZ	metabolized
ABDEEILMSSS	disassemble
ABDEEILNPSS	dispensable
ABDEEILNRSU	undesirable
ABDEEILNRTU	unliberated
ABDEEILNSSU	audibleness
ABDEEILORRT	deliberator
ABDEEILORTT	obliterated
ABDEEINNRRW	breadwinner
ABDEEIRRSVW	weaverbirds
ABDEEKORRSY	keyboarders
	rekeyboards
ABDEELLLORR	rollerblade
ABDEELLNOPW	Baden-Powell
ABDEELLNPRU	plunderable
ABDEELLOOUW	Belleau Wood
ABDEELMNOTU	demountable
ABDEELMNRUY	denumerably
ABDEELNNRUU	unendurable
ABDEELNOPRS	ponderables
ABDEELNORSS	laboredness
ABDEELNRSSU	durableness
ABDEELNRSTW	waldsterben
ABDEELORSTT	battledores
ABDEELORSTY	destroyable
ABDEELRSSTT	battledress
ABDEEORRRSW	swordbearer
ABDEFGINORR	fingerboard
ABDEFIILLSY	syllabified
ABDEFIILNNY	indefinably
ABDEFIILNTU	infibulated
ABDEFIRRSTU	breadfruits
ABDEGGGILNR	bedraggling
ABDEGGINRWY	windbaggery
ABDEGGIRRSU	budgerigars
ABDEGGLLRUY	bullyragged
ABDEGHINSSU	subheadings
ABDEGIILNNS	disenabling
ABDEGIILSSU	disguisable
ABDEGIINNRS	brigandines
ABDEGIINRRS	brigandries
ABDEGIKNORY	keyboarding
ABDEGILRRSU	burglarised
ABDEGILRRUZ	burglarized
ABDEGIMNRST	abridgments
ABDEHHMOORR	rhombohedra
ABDEHIILLSS	dishabilles
ABDEHIINNTU	uninhabited
ABDEHINRRSS	brandishers
ABDEHIORSTW	whiteboards
ABDEHLNSSSU	husbandless
ABDEHMOORRT	motherboard
ABDEHNRSSTU	subtrahends
ABDEHOOSSWX	shadowboxes
ABDEHORRSST	shortbreads
ABDEHOSSUWY	bawdyhouses
ABDEIIIJLNOS	disjoinable
ABDEIIILLLST	distillable
ABDEIILLTWY	weldability
ABDEIILMNOT	indomitable
ABDEIIMNOST	demibastion
ABDEIIRSSTU	absurdities
ABDEIKLNNRU	undrinkable
ABDEIKORSTY	keyboardist
ABDEILLLSSY	dissyllable
	disyllables
ABDEILLOSSV	dissolvable
ABDEILMNOPU	impoundable
ABDEILMNORT	Montbéliard
ABDEILMNRST	timberlands
ABDEILMOTTU	tolbutamide
ABDEILMSSSY	disassembly
ABDEILNRSUY	undesirably
ABDEILNSSUY	unbiassedly
ABDEILOPRSV	disprovable
ABDEILOPSSS	disposables
ABDEILRSTTW	wattlebirds
ABDEIMNRSST	disbarments
ABDEIMNSSTU	submediants
ABDEIMRRSTY	timberyards
ABDEIMRSTUW	dumbwaiters
ABDEINNOSST	Donets Basin
ABDEINORSTU	subordinate
ABDEJKLLNOR	Jodrell Bank
ABDELLOSTTU	subtotalled
ABDELMOORST	bloodstream
ABDELMOORSW	marblewoods
ABDELMORSST	blastoderms
ABDELMRRSUY	lumberyards
ABDELOOORST	bootloaders
ABDELOPRRTU	protrudable
ABDEMNORRST	barnstormed
ABDENNORSTV	bondservant
ABDENOORSUV	overabounds
ABDENOPRSUU	superabound
ABDFIILNNUU	infundibula
ABDFILMOORR	dolabriform
ABDFILNORSU	floribundas
ABDFLOOORRS	floorboards
ABDGHIILNNS	blandishing
ABDGHIINNRS	brandishing
ABDGHIMNOTU	badmouthing
ABDGIIILNOS	diabolising
ABDGIIILNOZ	diabolizing
ABDGIINPRSU	upbraidings
ABDGINOPRRS	springboard
ABDGINORRST	stringboard
ABDGINORSTU	groundbaits
ABDGMOORRSS	smorgasbord
ABDHHIOOPRY	hydrophobia
ABDHIIINOST	adhibitions
ABDHINRSTUY	unbirthdays
ABDIIILLLNY	libidinally

ABDIIILRTVY	drivability
ABDIIILTTUY	dutiability
ABDIILLMOTY	moldability
ABDIILMNOSU	albuminoids
ABDIILMNOTY	indomitably
ABDIILORRST	tailorbirds
ABDIINOSTUU	subaudition
ABDILNOOSST	bloodstains
ABDIMNNOSTU	subdominant
ABDINORRSUY	subordinary
ABDLNOOOSTT	odontoblast
ABDNOORSTUU	roundabouts
ABDOORRSSTY	storyboards
ABDOORRSTUU	troubadours
ABEEEEFLORS	foreseeable
ABEEEEGLNRR	regenerable
ABEEEEMNRTV	bereavement
ABEEEERRRTV	reverberate
ABEEEFLMNRT	fermentable
ABEEEGILRRS	bersagliere
ABEEEGLRRTT	regrettable
ABEEEHHINPR	hebephrenia
ABEEEHHKSSS	baksheeshes
ABEEEHINRST	abernethies
ABEEEHMNRRV	Bremerhaven
ABEEEHQRSTU	bequeathers
ABEEEHRSSTT	hartebeests
ABEEEIKRRST	tiebreakers
ABEEEILLPRV	repleviable
ABEEEILMMPR	impermeable
ABEEEILMMST	emblematise
ABEEEILMMTZ	emblematize
ABEEEILPRRV	reprievable
ABEEEILRRTV	retrievable
ABEEEIMNSST	absenteeism
ABEEEINRRSS	naseberries
ABEEEINSTUV	Sainte-Beuve
ABEEEJMMNNT	enjambement
ABEEELMNNST	enablements
ABEEELMNNTT	entablement
ABEEELMNRRU	remunerable
ABEEELMRSSS	reassembles
ABEEELNNSST	tenableness
ABEEELNPRSS	Bernese Alps
ABEEELNPRST	presentable
ABEEELNPRTV	preventable
ABEEELNQSSU	equableness
ABEEELNSSSU	useableness
ABEEELPRRSV	preservable
ABEEENNRSTT	bannerettes
ABEEENRRRTV	reverberant
ABEEEORSSTT	stereobates
ABEEERRSTTV	vertebrates
ABEEFFILORT	forfeitable
ABEEFGILNRR	refrangible
ABEEFGLORTT	forgettable
ABEEFIILLQU	liquefiable
ABEEFIILNRT	antifebrile
ABEEFIIRSTU	beautifiers
ABEEFILNNSS	finableness
ABEEFILNRSS	friableness
ABEEFILPRTU	putrefiable
ABEEFILRRTU	irrefutable
ABEEFLLNSSU	balefulness
ABEEFLMOPRR	performable
ABEEFLNNSSU	banefulness
ABEEFNRRRTU	afterburner
ABEEGHINQTU	bequeathing
ABEEGHNORSU	haubergeons
ABEEGIILLRT	belligerati
ABEEGIILNRT	libertinage
ABEEGIILRRS	bersaglieri
ABEEGIINOSS	abiogenesis
ABEEGIKMNRR	reembarking
ABEEGILLLNR	relabelling
ABEEGILMNPR	impregnable
ABEEGILNRUZ	gaberlunzie
ABEEGILRRST	registrable
ABEEGINORRV	overbearing
ABEEGINORST	bioreagents
ABEEGINRTUX	exuberating
ABEEGLRRTTY	regrettably
ABEEGLRSSSU	bluegrasses
ABEEHHPRSTY	bathysphere
ABEEHIIILTZ	Elizabeth II
ABEEHIILNRT	inheritable
ABEEHILMPSS	blasphemies
ABEEHILPRSS	perishables
ABEEHILRSST	establisher reestablish
ABEEHILSSST	establishes
ABEEHILSTUX	exhaustible
ABEEHIMRSSV	misbehavers
ABEEHINRSSS	bearishness
ABEEHINRSST	breathiness
ABEEHKNORRT	heartbroken
ABEEHKNORSS	boneshakers
ABEEHLMPRSS	blasphemers
ABEEHLNNORR	blennorrhea
ABEEHLOORRS	seborrhoeal
ABEEHLORRSU	barrelhouse
ABEEHLORRWW	wheelbarrow
ABEEHMORSTT	bathometers
ABEEHNOPRRY	hyperborean
ABEEHORSTTU	thereabouts
ABEEHORSTUW	whereabouts
ABEEHPRRSSY	baryspheres
ABEEHQRSSUU	harquebuses
ABEEIIKKMOR	bokmakierie
ABEEIILLRRS	liberaliser
ABEEIILLRRZ	liberalizer
ABEEIILLRSS	liberalises
ABEEIILLRSZ	liberalizes
ABEEIILMNPS	plebeianism
ABEEIILMNST	inestimable
ABEEIILMPRV	imperviable
ABEEIILNQTU	inequitable
ABEEIILQRTU	equilibrate
ABEEIILSSST	bestialises
ABEEIILSSTZ	bestializes
ABEEIIRRRSZ	bizarreries
ABEEIKLLNSS	likableness
ABEEIKLMORR	boilermaker
ABEEIKLRSTT	Bitter Lakes
ABEEIKNNRST	barkentines
ABEEILLMNRS	bellarmines
ABEEILLMOPT	tempolabile
ABEEILLNORT	intolerable
ABEEILLNPSS	pliableness
ABEEILLNRSS	liberalness
ABEEILLNSSV	livableness
ABEEILLOPRT	boilerplate
ABEEILLOPTX	exploitable
ABEEILMMORS	memorisable
ABEEILMMORZ	memorizable
ABEEILMMOSV	immoveables
ABEEILMMPRY	impermeably
ABEEILMNNOT	mentionable
ABEEILMNNRU	innumerable
ABEEILMNSSU	albumenises
ABEEILMNSUZ	albumenizes
ABEEILMORRV	irremovable
ABEEILMOSST	metabolises
ABEEILMOSTT	metabolites
ABEEILMOSTZ	metabolizes
ABEEILNNOPS	pensionable
ABEEILNPRSU	insuperable
ABEEILNRRTV	invertebral
ABEEILNRSST	triableness
ABEEILNSSST	beastliness
ABEEILNSSSZ	sizableness
ABEEILNSSTW	witnessable
ABEEILORSTT	obliterates
ABEEILPRSSU	persuasible
ABEEILRRSSV	verbalisers
ABEEILRRSVZ	verbalizers
ABEEILRRTVY	retrievably
ABEEINNQRTU	barquentine
ABEEINORSSU	Buenos Aires
ABEEINRRSSZ	bizarreness
ABEEINRSTUX	exurbanites
ABEEINSSSUV	abusiveness
ABEEIOPRRSS	soapberries
ABEEIOPRRTV	reprobative
ABEEIPRRRSS	raspberries
ABEEIQRRSUU	arquebusier
ABEEIRRSSST	arbitresses
ABEEJLNNOUY	unenjoyable
ABEEJMMNNST	enjambments
ABEEKMMNNST	embankments
ABEEKMMNRST	embarkments
ABEELLLMSSY	blamelessly
ABEELLLMTUU	umbellulate
ABEELLLMTUY	umbellately
ABEELLNOSSS	losableness
ABEELLNOSSV	lovableness
ABEELLORSST	Ballesteros
ABEELLRRTVY	vertebrally
ABEELMMNORU	unmemorable
ABEELMMNSSY	assemblymen
ABEELMNOSSV	movableness
ABEELMNPRTU	numberplate
ABEELMNRSSU	lebensraums
ABEELMNSSTU	mutableness
ABEELMNSTTT	battlements
ABEELMORSST	astroblemes

	blastomeres
ABEELNNOSST	notableness
ABEELNPRSTY	presentably
ABEELNPRTVY	preventably
ABEELNQSTTU	blanquettes
ABEELNRTTUU	unutterable
ABEELNRTUXY	exuberantly
ABEELORSTTX	rattleboxes
ABEELOSTUUY	beauteously
ABEELPRRSTY	presbyteral
ABEELPRRSVY	preservably
ABEELQQRUUU	Albuquerque
ABEEMMNORSU	membraneous
ABEEMNRSSTU	surbasement
ABEENNPRRSS	Brenner Pass
ABEEOPRRRST	reprobaters
ABEEOPRRTTU	protuberate
ABEFFGIKNRT	Krafft-Ebing
ABEFFIILORT	fortifiable
ABEFGIIILNS	signifiable
ABEFGIILLOR	glorifiable
ABEFGIILNNR	infrangible
ABEFGIINTUY	beautifying
ABEFHIRRSTT	afterbirths
ABEFHLNSSSU	bashfulness
ABEFHRSSTUY	Shaftesbury
ABEFIIILNRT	nitrifiable
ABEFIIILRTV	vitrifiable
ABEFIIILSTY	feasibility
ABEFIIJLSTU	justifiable
ABEFIILLLMO	mollifiable
ABEFIILLLNS	infallibles
ABEFIILLMRT	fimbrillate
ABEFIILLOOT	bifoliolate
ABEFIILLSSY	syllabifies
ABEFIILMSSU	subfamilies
ABEFIILNORV	riboflavine
ABEFIILNOSS	fissionable
ABEFIILNSTU	infibulates
ABEFILLTUUY	beautifully
ABEFILRRTUY	irrefutably
ABEFLLLORSW	ballflowers
ABEFLLOORST	footballers
ABEFLMOORTT	footlambert
ABEGGHRSSTU	staggerbush
ABEGGIILNOR	globigerina
ABEGGILMNNR	embrangling
ABEGGILNNPS	bespangling
ABEGGINRSSW	bagswingers
ABEGGNOORST	tobogganers
ABEGHIIMNSV	misbehaving
ABEGHIINNRT	hibernating
	inbreathing
ABEGHIIOPRS	biographies
	biographise
ABEGHIIOPRZ	biographize
ABEGHILMNOO	haemoglobin
ABEGHILMNPS	blaspheming
ABEGHINOOPR	negrophobia
ABEGHINRSTU	thunbergias
ABEGHIOPRRS	biographers
ABEGHLNOOPS	anglophobes
ABEGHNRRSSU	bushrangers
ABEGHORSSTU	broughtases
ABEGHQSSUUU	usquebaughs
ABEGIIILMMT	immitigable
ABEGIIIMSTU	ambiguities
ABEGIIINNRT	inebriating
ABEGIILLNWY	bewailingly
ABEGIILMNTT	timetabling
ABEGIILNNST	intangibles
ABEGIILNRSV	verbalising
ABEGIILNRVZ	verbalizing
ABEGIIMNSSU	subimagines
ABEGIINNRST	brigantines
ABEGIINOSST	abiogenists
ABEGIINPRST	rebaptising
ABEGIINPRTZ	rebaptizing
ABEGIIRRSTU	subirrigate
ABEGIJORTUV	objurgative
ABEGIKNOSST	Basingstoke
ABEGILMNNOZ	emblazoning
ABEGILMNOTY	amblygonite
ABEGILMNPRY	impregnably
ABEGILNNNTY	benignantly
ABEGILNORSU	subregional
ABEGILOOORY	aerobiology
ABEGILRRSSU	burglarises
ABEGILRRSUZ	burglarizes
ABEGINNOPSU	subpoenaing
ABEGINNORRT	interrobang
ABEGINNOTTY	bayonetting
ABEGINOPRRT	reprobating
ABEGKLNRSUU	Klausenburg
ABEGKNOORRS	Brooks Range
ABEGKRRSSTU	grubstakers
ABEGLLORSSW	glassblower
ABEGMORRSTU	burgomaster
ABEGNNSSTTU	subtangents
ABEHHILLSST	sheathbills
ABEHHIRRSSU	hairbrushes
ABEHHJOORRU	Johore Bahru
ABEHHMMRSSU	bushhammers
ABEHHORRSTT	heartthrobs
ABEHIILMNST	habiliments
ABEHIILMOPS	amphibolies
ABEHIILMOPT	amphibolite
ABEHIILNRTY	inheritably
ABEHIILPRST	blepharitis
ABEHIIMMNOS	bohemianism
ABEHIIMORSV	behaviorism
ABEHIINNORT	hibernation
ABEHIIORSTV	behaviorist
ABEHIKLNNTU	unthinkable
ABEHILMNOST	abolishment
ABEHILMPRSS	blepharisms
ABEHILNRSSU	nailbrushes
ABEHILOOPRU	ailurophobe
ABEHILOPRSW	worshipable
ABEHILPSSTT	battleships
ABEHILPSSTU	bisulphates
ABEHIMNNSST	banishments
ABEHINOORTT	botheration
ABEHINOPRSV	vibraphones
ABEHINORRST	hibernators
ABEHINORSSS	boarishness
ABEHLMOORTW	Bartholomew
ABEHLMOPSSU	blasphemous
ABEHLMORTWY	blameworthy
ABEHLMOSTYZ	Szombathely
ABEHLNORRTY	abhorrently
ABEHLORRSSU	harbourless
ABEHLORSTTU	bluethroats
ABEHMRSSSTU	bushmasters
ABEHNNOOTTY	ethnobotany
ABEHRSTTWYY	Aberystwyth
ABEIIIILLST	liabilities
ABEIIIILNST	inabilities
ABEIIIILSTV	viabilities
ABEIIILLLMT	illimitable
ABEIIILLNOR	billionaire
ABEIIILLRTY	reliability
ABEIIILLTVY	liveability
ABEIIILSSTT	stabilities
ABEIIINNORT	inebriation
ABEIIINNOSS	Assiniboine
ABEIILLLLRY	illiberally
ABEIILLLMNU	illuminable
ABEIILLMMST	bimetallism
ABEIILLMNRY	bimillenary
ABEIILLMPSU	implausible
ABEIILLMSTT	bimetallist
ABEIILLMTTY	meltability
ABEIILLNSWZ	Leibniz's law
ABEIILLOTVY	loveability
ABEIILLRSST	liberalists
ABEIILLRSTT	bristletail
ABEIILMMRSS	miserablism
ABEIILMNSTY	inestimably
ABEIILMSSUX	bisexualism
ABEIILNNPTY	bipinnately
ABEIILNNSTV	vinblastine
ABEIILNOPRT	prelibation
ABEIILNQRTU	equilibrant
ABEIILNQTUY	inequitably
ABEIILNRRTT	intertribal
ABEIILNRTTY	rentability
ABEIILOPPRT	propitiable
ABEIILOPRTY	operability
ABEIILORTXY	exorability
ABEIILPRTTY	bipartitely
ABEIILRSSST	stabilisers
ABEIILRSSTZ	stabilizers
ABEIILRSTTU	brutalities
ABEIILRSTUY	reusability
ABEIILSTTTY	testability
ABEIILSTUXY	bisexuality
ABEIILTTTWY	wettability
ABEIIMNORSV	ambiversion
ABEIINNRRST	interbrains
ABEIIPRSSTT	baptistries
ABEIIRRSTTU	tributaries
ABEIIRTTTUV	attributive
ABEIKLNNNOS	nonsinkable
ABEIKNOPRST	breakpoints

ABEILLLRSTY	trisyllable
ABEILLMORTU	rambouillet
ABEILLNORTY	intolerably
ABEILLNRSSY	brainlessly
ABEILMMOSST	metabolisms
ABEILMNNRUY	innumerably
ABEILMNQRSU	lambrequins
ABEILMNRSTU	subterminal
ABEILMOOSTU	automobiles
ABEILMORRVY	irremovably
ABEILMORSTY	traymobiles
ABEILNNPRTU	unprintable
ABEILNNRSUU	uninsurable
ABEILNOOSSS	obsessional
ABEILNORSSU	Belorussian
ABEILNOSTTY	obstinately
ABEILNPRSUY	insuperably
ABEILOORRTT	obliterator
ABEILOPRTVY	probatively
ABEILORSSTW	belowstairs
ABEILORSSUY	Byelorussia
ABEILQRRTUY	biquarterly
ABEIMNNSSSU	businessman
ABEIMNORSTT	montbretias
ABEIMNORSTU	tambourines
ABEIMNRRSSU	submariners
ABEINNORSTV	inobservant
ABEINNOSSTT	abstentions
ABEINOOPRRT	probationer
	reprobation
ABEINOORSTV	observation
ABEINOOSTTT	obtestation
ABEINORSTUV	subornative
ABEINOSSTTU	abstentious
ABEINSSTTUV	substantive
ABEIORRSSUV	arboviruses
ABEIRRSTTTU	attributers
ABEIRSSTTUV	substrative
ABEJLMOSTUU	autojumbles
ABEKKMOORRS	bookmarkers
ABEKLLORSWY	yellowbarks
ABEKLLOSSTU	leukoblasts
ABEKMNNOSTU	mountebanks
ABEKNOPRRSW	pawnbrokers
ABEKORRSSTW	breastworks
ABELLLLORRS	rollerballs
ABELLLLOSVY	volleyballs
ABELLMOSSTY	myeloblasts
ABELLORRRSU	bullroarers
ABELMMOOORT	Bartolommeo
ABELMNORRSY	salmonberry
ABELNOOPPST	postponable
ABELNOOPSST	tablespoons
ABELNOPPSTU	unstoppable
ABELNORSSTU	neuroblasts
ABELNORSTVY	observantly
ABELNRTTUUY	unutterably
ABELOOPRSST	blastopores
	blastospore
ABELOOSSSTT	osteoblasts
ABELOPPRSTU	supportable
ABELRRSTTUU	surrebuttal
ABEMNNOTTTU	Mountbatten
ABEMNOORRSW	marrowbones
ABEMNORRRST	barnstormer
ABENNORSTUV	unobservant
ABENOPRRTTU	protuberant
ABEOORRSTVY	observatory
ABEOORSSTUU	rouseabouts
ABERRSSTUUY	subtreasury
ABFFFHILOSU	buffalofish
ABFFIKMOORS	kaffirbooms
ABFFILLMSTU	bullmastiff
ABFGHNOORRU	Farnborough
ABFGIILNNRY	infrangibly
ABFIIILLLTY	fallibility
ABFIIIMNORT	fimbriation
ABFIIJLSTUY	justifiably
ABFIILORSUY	bifariously
ABFILMMNSUU	funambulism
ABFILMNSTUU	funambulist
ABFIMOORSTU	fibromatous
ABGGGINNOOT	tobogganing
ABGGHHIILLN	highballing
ABGGHILNORS	Hälsingborg
ABGGIIKNNRR	ringbarking
ABGGIILLNOS	globalising
ABGGIJNORTU	objurgating
ABGGIJNSTUU	subjugating
ABGGIKNRSTU	grubstaking
ABGGILOOORY	agrobiology
ABGGILOORST	garbologist
ABGGINOOSTT	tobogganist
ABGGINORSTU	subrogating
ABGHIILNSST	stablishing
ABGHIINRRSU	airbrushing
ABGHIINRSTT	brattishing
ABGHIKLNSUW	bushwalking
ABGHILLMNOT	mothballing
ABGHILLNOOY	ballyhooing
ABGHILMOOPY	amphibology
ABGHLMOORRU	Marlborough
ABGHOORRSUY	yarboroughs
ABGIIILMMTY	immitigably
ABGIIILNSST	stabilising
ABGIIILNSTZ	stabilizing
ABGIIILNTTY	tangibility
ABGIILLLNUY	bilingually
ABGIILMNSTU	sublimating
ABGIILNOOST	obligations
ABGIILNRSTU	brutalising
ABGIILNRTUZ	brutalizing
ABGIILNRTVY	vibratingly
ABGIIMNNORT	brominating
ABGIINRTTTU	attributing
ABGIJKKMNOS	sjambokking
ABGIJNOORTU	objurgation
ABGIJNOSTUU	subjugation
ABGIKLLNNOR	bankrolling
ABGIKNNOPRW	pawnbroking
ABGIKNNPRTU	bankrupting
ABGIKNRRSTY	stringybark
ABGILLNNOOS	balloonings
ABGILLNNOSW	snowballing
ABGILLNORUY	labouringly
ABGILLORTUY	globularity
ABGILMOSUUY	ambiguously
ABGILNOSTTU	subtotaling
ABGILNSTUUX	subluxating
ABGILORRSUU	burglarious
ABGIMNOSUUU	unambiguous
ABGINOORSTU	subrogation
ABGINOOSTTU	outboasting
ABGJOORRSTU	objurgators
ABGJOORRTUY	objurgatory
ABGJORSSTUU	subjugators
ABGLNORSTUY	Glastonbury
ABGMOPRRSSU	subprograms
ABHHIOOOPPT	photophobia
ABHIILNOSTT	nihil obstat
ABHIKLNNTUY	unthinkably
ABHIKNORSVY	Baryshnikov
ABHILMOOPSU	amphibolous
ABHILNOOPST	haplobionts
ABHILORSTUW	whirlabouts
ABHIMNORRTU	Northumbria
ABHIPRRSSSU	bursarships
ABHLLMOPSTY	lymphoblast
ABHLLMSSTTU	thumbstalls
ABHLOOPRSTT	trophoblast
ABHMNORRSTU	rhumbatrons
ABIIIILMTTY	imitability
ABIIIILNTVY	inviability
ABIIILLLMTY	illimitably
ABIIILLOSTY	isolability
ABIIILLOTVY	violability
ABIIILNOSST	sibilations
ABIIILNRSTY	rinsability
ABIIILNSTTY	instability
ABIIILPSSTY	passibility
ABIIILRTTVY	vibratility
ABIIILSTTUY	suitability
ABIIINOPRTT	bipartition
ABIIJLNOSTU	jubilations
ABIIKLORTWY	workability
ABIILLLNRTY	brilliantly
ABIILLMPSUY	implausibly
ABIILLOSTVY	solvability
ABIILMNOSTU	sublimation
ABIILMOSTUY	ambitiously
ABIILNORTTU	tribulation
ABIILNRSTUY	insalubrity
ABIILOPRTTY	portability
ABIILOQTTUY	quotability
ABIILRRTTUY	tributarily
ABIIMNNOORT	bromination
ABIIMNORSTT	nimbostrati
ABIIMNOSTUU	unambitious
ABIINNORTTU	turbination
ABIINNOSTTU	intubations
ABIINOOPSTT	obstipation
ABIINOORSTT	abortionist
ABIINORTTTU	attribution
ABIIORSSTTU	obituarists
	tibiotarsus
ABIJNOORSTU	objurations

ABILLNOOSST balloonists
ABILLOORSUY laboriously
ABILLORSTTU sublittoral
ABILMNOSTUX toxalbumins
ABILNNPRTUY unprintably
ABILNOOSSTU absolutions
ABILNOSTTUU tubulations
ABILNOSTUUX subluxation
ABILOOPRSTT postorbital
ABILOSSSTTU absolutists
ABIMNORRSST brainstorms
ABINNOORSTU subornation
ABINOOOPRRT proabortion
ABINOOPRRTW Barrow Point
ABINOOPRSST saprobionts
ABINOORSTTU obturations
ABINOOSSSST bassoonists
ABINOSSSTTU substations
ABIORRSTTTU attributors
ABLLMNORSUY subnormally
ABLNOPPSTUY unstoppably
ABLOPPRSTUY supportably
ABNOORRSSTU brontosaurs
ABOORSSTTUU roustabouts
ACCCDEEENNS candescence
ACCCDEHILNO chalcedonic
ACCCDEILOPY cyclopaedic
ACCCDENNOOR concordance
ACCCDENNOTU conductance
ACCCDILLOOP diplococcal
ACCCEEELNOS coalescence
ACCCEEELNST lactescence
ACCCEEEMNRS marcescence
ACCCEEHOSUU accoucheuse
ACCCEELMNOP complacence
ACCCEELNOPT conceptacle
ACCCEFHKORS cockchafers
ACCCEGNORYY gynecocracy
ACCCEHIISTT catechistic
ACCCEHILORT chloracetic
ACCCEHIMOTT chemotactic
ACCCEHKOORS cockroaches
ACCCEHNORTY technocracy
ACCCEHORSTW cowcatchers
ACCCEHORSUU accoucheurs
ACCCEIILLPY epicyclical
ACCCEIILMRT climacteric
ACCCEIILRST cicatricles
ACCCEIIOPST cacoepistic
ACCCEIIORST cicatricose
ACCCEIKORST cockatrices
ACCCEILLNSY encyclicals
ACCCEILMOPS accomplices
ACCCEILORTU leucocratic
ACCCEILRTTY tetracyclic
ACCCEINOPSU occupancies
ACCCEINORRT acrocentric
ACCCELMNOPY complacency
ACCCHHIINNO Cochin China
ACCCHHILOOS chocaholics
ACCCHHIMPUU Machu Picchu
ACCCHIILLOT laccolithic
ACCCHILOORT ochlocratic
ACCCHKOPSST spatchcocks
ACCCHOOPRTY ptochocracy
ACCCIIOOPRS capriccioso
ACCCILLOOSU calcicolous
ACCCIMMOORS macrocosmic
ACCCIMOOPRS macroscopic
ACCCINOPPSU cappuccinos
ACCCIOPRSTY cystocarpic
ACCDDDEIORS disaccorded
ACCDDEEEINS decadencies
ACCDDEEFIIL decalcified
ACCDDEEIINO decanedioic
ACCDDEEINNS incandesced
ACCDDEIIRST disaccredit
ACCDDEINORS discordance
ACCDDELLMOU maloccluded
ACCDDIIIMST didacticism
ACCDDINORSY discordancy
ACCDEEEENNT antecedence
ACCDEEEHKMN namechecked
ACCDEEELNOS adolescence
ACCDEEELNPR precanceled
ACCDEEELNST decalescent
ACCDEEFIILR decalcifier
ACCDEEFIILS decalcifies
ACCDEEFNORY confederacy
ACCDEEHHKLU chucklehead
ACCDEEHIORS archdiocese
ACCDEEIISTV desiccative
ACCDEEIKKLP placekicked
ACCDEEIKRSW wisecracked
ACCDEEIMORS democracies
ACCDEEINNSS incandesces
ACCDEEIORTT decorticate
ACCDEEIRRST reaccredits
ACCDEEIRTUX excruciated
ACCDEELNNOU unconcealed
ACCDEELNOSV convalesced
ACCDEEMNSUU succedaneum
ACCDEENORST consecrated
ACCDEFILNSS flaccidness
ACCDEFINOST confiscated
ACCDEFLLOTU flocculated
ACCDEGHORST dogcatchers
ACCDEGIINRT accrediting
ACCDEGIINST desiccating
ACCDEHHIRSU archduchies
ACCDEHHITTT chitchatted
ACCDEHHRSSU archduchess
ACCDEHILPRY diphycercal
ACCDEHNRSTU unscratched
ACCDEIIIMRT acidimetric
ACCDEIILLTY deictically
ACCDEIILNOT conciliated
ACCDEIILSSS classicised
ACCDEIILSSZ classicized
ACCDEIINOOT octanedioic
ACCDEIINOST desiccation
ACCDEIIRSTT dictatrices
ACCDEIKLNST candlestick
ACCDEIKLNSW candlewicks
ACCDEILLOPS peccadillos
ACCDEILMOPT complicated
ACCDEILNOST occidentals
ACCDEILOPSY cyclopedias
ACCDEIMNNOO codominance
ACCDEINNSTU inductances
ACCDEINOOST consociated
ACCDEINOOTU coeducation
ACCDEINPRSY discrepancy
ACCDEINPRTU unpracticed
ACCDEIORSST desiccators
ACCDEKKMMUU muckamucked
ACCDELOPSSU cloudscapes
ACCDENNOTUU unaccounted
ACCDGILNORY accordingly
ACCDHHRRSUY churchyards
ACCDHIIILOP acidophilic
ACCDHIIMORT dichromatic
ACCDHIINORT achondritic
ACCDHILLOOT Old Catholic
ACCDHILORSV clavichords
ACCDHINOPRY hydnocarpic
ACCDHINORYY hydrocyanic
ACCDHIORTTY hydrotactic
ACCDIIINNOS scincoidian
ACCDIILLNRY cylindrical
ACCDIILLORY codicillary
ACCDIILNOOR crocodilian
ACCDIIOOPRS radioscopic
ACCDILLLOYY cycloidally
ACCDIMOSSTU disaccustom
ACCDINORSTT contradicts
ACCEEEEHKSS cheesecakes
ACCEEEENNSV evanescence
ACCEEEFILMN maleficence
ACCEEEFLNRT reflectance
ACCEEEHIIST haecceities
ACCEEEHILRT chelicerate
ACCEEEIKKLO cockaleekie
ACCEEELNOPS opalescence
ACCEEELNRST recalescent
ACCEEELPRST receptacles
ACCEEENNRSS renascences
ACCEEENPSTX expectances
ACCEEFIIRTT certificate
ACCEEFIKRRR firecracker
ACCEEFINORV vociferance
ACCEEGHILMO geochemical
ACCEEGILNRS recalescing
ACCEEGINNRT reaccenting
ACCEEGINPRT reaccepting
ACCEEHIINRS chicaneries
ACCEEHILMNO chameleonic
ACCEEHILNRT chanticleer
ACCEEHINRRT archenteric
ACCEEHIORST theocracies
ACCEEHIRRTU charcuterie
ACCEEHIRSST catechisers
ACCEEHIRSTZ catechizers
ACCEEHKORTW weathercock
ACCEEHLLNRY chancellery
ACCEEHLNOXY cyclohexane

ACCEEHLNRST chanteclers
ACCEEHMNSTU catechumens
ACCEEHNORRS encroachers
ACCEEIILNRT electrician
ACCEEIIMPST septicaemic
ACCEEIISTVX exsiccative
ACCEEIKRRSW wisecracker
ACCEEILMNOU oecumenical
ACCEEILNNST incalescent
ACCEEILNORT electronica
ACCEEILNOSV covalencies
ACCEEILRRTU recirculate
ACCEEIMNRTT metacentric
ACCEEINNOST cotenancies
ACCEEINQSTU acquiescent
ACCEEIOPRRT reciprocate
ACCEEIORSSS accessories
accessorise
ACCEEIORSSZ accessorize
ACCEEIRSTUX excruciates
ACCEEKLSSSU Lake Success
ACCEELLOPRT leptocercal
ACCEELMNNOT concealment
ACCEELNORST calorescent
ACCEELNOSSV convalesces
ACCEEMNNORR necromancer
ACCEEMNOPPU comeuppance
ACCEEMOSSTY ascomycetes
ACCEENNNOTU countenance
ACCEENNORSV conversance
ACCEENNORTT concentrate
concertante
ACCEENNORVY conveyancer
ACCEENNOSSV concaveness
ACCEENNOSVY conveyances
ACCEENOPRRS coparceners
ACCEENORSST consecrates
ACCEENPSSTU susceptance
ACCEEOPRSUY cyperaceous
ACCEEORRSSU racecourses
ACCEFFHHINS chaffinches
ACCEFFIIOSU efficacious
ACCEFHIINTY chieftaincy
ACCEFHLRSTY flycatchers
ACCEFIINRRY ferricyanic
ACCEFIIRRSS sacrificers
ACCEFILORSU calciferous
ACCEFINORRY ferrocyanic
ACCEFINOSST confiscates
ACCEFLLOSTU flocculates
ACCEFMNNOOR conformance
ACCEGGHHINN Cheng-chiang
ACCEGHHITTW catchweight
ACCEGHIINST catechising
ACCEGHIINTZ catechizing
ACCEGHIKMNT checkmating
ACCEGHILMRU chemurgical
ACCEGHINNOR encroaching
ACCEGHIOPRR cerographic
ACCEGIINQSU acquiescing
ACCEGIINSTX exsiccating
ACCEGIKMRRY gimcrackery

ACCEGILLNOR clearcoling
ACCEGILLOOO oecological
ACCEGILLOOT cetological
ACCEGILLOPY cycloplegia
ACCEGINNORS carcinogens
ACCEGINORTU accoutering
ACCEHHHHIIR Chichihaerh
ACCEHHIINTZ Chichen Itzá
ACCEHHIISTX hexastichic
ACCEHIILMST alchemistic
ACCEHIILNST calisthenic
ACCEHIILOST catholicise
ACCEHIILOTT heliotactic
ACCEHIILOTZ catholicize
ACCEHIIMNST mechanistic
ACCEHIIMOSS sciomachies
ACCEHIINNST technicians
ACCEHIIORRT hierocratic
ACCEHIIRSTU eucharistic
ACCEHILLMNO melancholic
ACCEHILLNTY technically
ACCEHILMOOZ zoochemical
ACCEHILMRTY methacrylic
ACCEHILOORT chocolatier
ACCEHILOPPR procephalic
ACCEHILOPXY oxycephalic
ACCEHIMNNOR chrominance
ACCEHIMNORR chiromancer
ACCEHIMORTT tachometric
ACCEHIMORTU euchromatic
ACCEHIMRTTY tachymetric
ACCEHINOOPS cacophonies
ACCEHINPPRY hypercapnic
ACCEHINRSTU craunchiest
ACCEHIORSST escharotics
ACCEHKLRSTU saltchucker
ACCEHLLMNOY collenchyma
ACCEHLLNORS chancellors
ACCEHLLNORY chancellory
ACCEHLOOSSW slowcoaches
ACCEHNOOSTY choanocytes
ACCEHNORSTT technocrats
ACCEHOOSTWZ Częstochowa
ACCEIIILSTV acclivities
ACCEIIINPRT accipitrine
ACCEIIINRST intricacies
ACCEIILLMRS clericalism
ACCEIILLNPR preclinical
ACCEIILLRST clericalist
ACCEIILMOSV semivocalic
ACCEIILNOST conciliates
ACCEIILNRTY circinately
ACCEIILPRRT precritical
ACCEIILPRST periclastic
ACCEIILRRSU circularise
ACCEIILRRUZ circularize
ACCEIILRTUV circulative
ACCEIILSSSS classicises
ACCEIILSSSZ classicizes
ACCEIIMNOST cosmetician
encomiastic
ACCEIIMORST timocracies

ACCEIIMRSST ceramicists
ACCEIINNOSU insouciance
ACCEIINOSST oscitancies
ACCEIINOSTV concavities
ACCEIINOSTX exsiccation
ACCEIIRRSST cicatrisers
ACCEIIRRSTZ cicatrizers
ACCEIKKOTTT ticktacktoe
ACCEIKLMRST clickstream
ACCEIKNRSSS carsickness
ACCEILLNNOR nonclerical
ACCEILLNRTY centrically
ACCEILLPSTY sceptically
ACCEILMMORS commercials
ACCEILMNOPS compliances
ACCEILMNORU macronuclei
ACCEILMNOSS comicalness
ACCEILMOPST complicates
ectoplasmic
ACCEILMOSST cacomistles
ACCEILMSSTU multiaccess
ACCEILNNOTY anticyclone
ACCEILNNSSY cynicalness
ACCEILNOPRT narcoleptic
ACCEILNORTT contractile
ACCEILNORTU corniculate
ACCEILOPPST apoplectics
ACCEILOPRRS reciprocals
ACCEILOPRST ceroplastic
ACCEILORSSY accessorily
ACCEIMMNOTU communicate
ACCEIMNNORT necromantic
ACCEIMNOORS monocracies
nomocracies
ACCEIMNORSS sciomancers
ACCEIMNOSTU contumacies
ACCEIMORRTY meritocracy
ACCEINNNOSV connivances
ACCEINNNOTU continuance
ACCEINNORST concertinas
ACCEINNORSU coinsurance
ACCEINNORTT concertanti
ACCEINNORTV contrivance
ACCEINOOSST consociates
ACCEINOOTVV convocative
ACCEINORTTV contractive
ACCEINSSSTU causticness
ACCEIOORSSU scoriaceous
ACCEIOPRRSU procuracies
ACCEIORSSSU accessorius
ACCEIORSSTX exsiccators
ACCEIORSTUU urticaceous
ACCEJLNORTU conjectural
ACCEKKLMORS clockmakers
ACCEKNRRSTU nutcrackers
ACCELLLTUUY cucullately
ACCELMMNOOP commonplace
ACCELNORSUY cancerously
ACCELOOPSST lactoscopes
ACCELORSSSU successoral
ACCELPRRSUU crepuscular
ACCEMNOPSST compactness

ACCEMORSSTU reaccustoms
ACCENNNOOSS consonances
ACCENNORSVY conservancy
conversancy
ACCENOOPRTU pococurante
ACCENOORRST consecrator
ACCENOPRRSU procurances
ACCENOPRRTT precontract
ACCENORRTTU contracture
ACCENORSTTU counteracts
ACCENPRTUUU acupuncture
ACCEOORSSTU ectosarcous
ACCEORRSSTU securocrats
ACCEORSSTUU crustaceous
ACCFFFFHHIS chiffchaffs
ACCFGIIINRS sacrificing
ACCFGILOSUU calcifugous
ACCFIILOPRY prolificacy
ACCFIIMOORR coraciiform
ACCFILMORSU sacculiform
ACCFINOORST confiscator
ACCGGHHIINN Chiang Ch'ing
ACCGGIILLOO glaciologic
ACCGHIIOOPS hagioscopic
ACCGHIMOPRY cymographic
ACCGHINRSST scratchings
ACCGHLOPRSY cyclographs
ACCGIIILMNN calcimining
ACCGIIINNOS cocainising
ACCGIIINNOZ cocainizing
ACCGIIINRST cicatrising
ACCGIIINRTZ cicatrizing
ACCGIILNNTU inculcating
ACCGIILNOTU glauconitic
ACCGIILNRTU circulating
ACCGIINNOOS occasioning
ACCGILLMOOY mycological
ACCGILLNOOO oncological
ACCGILLNOOT collocating
ACCGILLOOTY cytological
ACCGILOORST gastrocolic
ACCGIMNOSTU accustoming
ACCGIMOPRTY cryptogamic
ACCGINNORTT contracting
ACCGINORSTU coruscating
ACCHHIILLNS chinchillas
ACCHHIIMOPR amphichroic
ACCHHIINSTT chainstitch
ACCHHILNRTU Latin Church
ACCHHILORSU Archilochus
ACCHHLMNRUY churchmanly
ACCHHMNORUW churchwoman
ACCHHMOPSYY psychomachy
ACCHIIIMMPT amphimictic
ACCHIILLSTY stichically
ACCHIILMOST catholicism
ACCHIILOSST scholiastic
ACCHIILOTTY catholicity
ACCHIIMNORT chromatinic
ACCHIIMOSST masochistic
ACCHIIMSSST schismatics
ACCHIIOOPST sociopathic
ACCHIIORSTT rhotacistic
ACCHIIPRSTY psychiatric
ACCHIKMSSTT matchsticks
ACCHILLNORY chronically
ACCHILLPSYY psychically
ACCHILMOTYY cyclothymia
ACCHILNNOOT non-Catholic
ACCHILNOOST catholicons
ACCHILOOSTU holocaustic
ACCHINOPSTY sycophantic
ACCHIOOPTTT phototactic
ACCHIOORRSU chiaroscuro
ACCHIOPRSSZ schizocarps
ACCHIOPRSYY physiocracy
ACCHNOOOPSU cacophonous
ACCIIILOSST socialistic
ACCIIILRTTY criticality
ACCIILLLNOX cloxacillin
ACCIILLNNNO nonclinical
ACCIILLNORY conciliarly
ACCIILMNOSS laconicisms
ACCIILMSSSS classicisms
ACCIILNNORT noncritical
ACCIILNNOTU inculcation
ACCIILNNQUU quincuncial
ACCIILNOORT conciliator
ACCIILNORTU circulation
ACCIILNOTVY volcanicity
ACCIILOSTUV acclivitous
ACCIILRRTUY circularity
ACCIILSSSST classicists
ACCIIMMORST microsmatic
ACCIIMNNOTY actinomycin
ACCIIMNOTTY antimycotic
ACCIINNNSTU Cincinnatus
ACCIINNSTTY nyctinastic
ACCIINOORTT cortication
ACCIINORRSU Rosicrucian
ACCIJNNOTUV conjunctiva
ACCIKKKKNNS knickknacks
ACCILLNOOOT collocation
ACCILLPRTYY cryptically
ACCILMNRRUU circumlunar
ACCILMOPRRU circumpolar
ACCILMOPSTY cytoplasmic
ACCILMORRSU circumsolar
ACCILNOOSST iconoclasts
ACCILNOOTTU occultation
ACCILNORSTU inculcators
ACCILNOSSTV conclavists
ACCILOOPSTV postvocalic
ACCILOPRSTY pyroclastic
ACCILOPRTTU plutocratic
ACCILORRSTU circulators
ACCILORRTUY circulatory
ACCIMMNNOTU communicant
ACCIMNNOOTT concomitant
ACCINNNOSTY inconstancy
ACCINNOOOTV convocation
ACCINNOOPRU cornucopian
ACCINNOORTT contraction
ACCINNOSTTU cunctations
ACCINOOPRSU cornucopias
ACCINOOPSTU occupations
ACCINOORSTU coruscation
ACCIOOPRRTY procaryotic
ACCIORSSSTY syssarcotic
ACCKLMOORSU cockalorums
ACCLNNOSTUY consultancy
ACCLNORSUUU carunculous
ACCLOPRRSUU corpuscular
ACCNOOORSTV convocators
ACCNOORRSTT contractors
ACDDDEEEIRT rededicated
ACDDEEEELRT decelerated
ACDDEEEEPRS predeceased
ACDDEEEIPRT depreciated
ACDDEEEIRST rededicates
ACDDEEEORRT redecorated
ACDDEEFFIST disaffected
ACDDEEGIKLR griddlecake
ACDDEEHHIKT thickheaded
ACDDEEHHKOS shockheaded
ACDDEEHLORT coldhearted
ACDDEEHNORS decahedrons
ACDDEEIILMS decimalised
ACDDEEIILMZ decimalized
ACDDEEIKRST sidetracked
ACDDEEILLOS delocalised
ACDDEEILLOZ delocalized
ACDDEEILOSV devocalised
ACDDEEILOVZ devocalized
ACDDEEIMNTU unmedicated
ACDDEEIMSTU miseducated
ACDDEEINNTU denunciated
ACDDEEIOTTX detoxicated
ACDDEELORTU edulcorated
ACDDEENNRST transcended
ACDDEENNSST descendants
ACDDEENORTU undecorated
undercoated
ACDDEENRTTU detruncated
ACDDEFIIINT nidificated
ACDDEGIKLNO deadlocking
ACDDEGIORSU discouraged
ACDDEHLLOST saddlecloth
ACDDEHLNSTU Deutschland
ACDDEHNOOPY dodecaphony
ACDDEIILNRT dendritical
ACDDEIINOST dedications
ACDDEIIOSST dissociated
ACDDEILMOSU duodecimals
ACDDEIMNORU endocardium
ACDDEINOORT coordinated
ACDDELNOOSW candlewoods
ACDDFHIORSU chaudfroids
ACDDIILMSTY didactylism
ACDEEEEHLRR cheerleader
ACDEEEEKRRT racketeered
ACDEEEELRST decelerates
ACDEEEEPRSS predeceases
ACDEEEFFTTU effectuated
ACDEEEFHORR forereached

ACDEEEFILNR Île-de-France
ACDEEEFLNRT needlecraft
ACDEEEFMNST defacements
ACDEEEFNORT confederate
ACDEEEGLLOT decolletage
ACDEEEHILRS Heracleides
ACDEEEHLSTT decathletes
ACDEEEHORRV overreached
ACDEEEHRRRT rechartered
ACDEEEILLPT pedicellate
ACDEEEILNRV deliverance
ACDEEEIMRTV decemvirate
ACDEEEINNRS decennaries
ACDEEEIPPRV apperceived
ACDEEEIPRST depreciates
ACDEEEIPRTT decrepitate
ACDEEEIPRTV deprecative
ACDEEEIRSTV eviscerated
ACDEEELLNRT crenellated
ACDEEELLSST Leeds Castle
ACDEEELORRT decelerator
ACDEEENNSTT antecedents
ACDEEENOSSS deaconesses
ACDEEENPRRT carpentered
ACDEEENRSTV advertences
ACDEEEORRST redecorates
ACDEEEORRTV overreacted
ACDEEEORTUV overeducate
ACDEEEPRRTU recuperated
ACDEEERRSST desecraters
ACDEEFFHRUU chauffeured
ACDEEFHIIPR preachified
ACDEEFIILTT felicitated
ACDEEFINOST defecations
ACDEEFIORTV vociferated
ACDEEFLNRUU fraudulence
ACDEEFNRSTT transfected
ACDEEFORRTT tractorfeed
ACDEEGGNORT congregated
ACDEEGHNNOS hendecagons
ACDEEGHNRRU undercharge
ACDEEGHORRV overcharged
ACDEEGIKLRS girdlecakes
ACDEEGILNNR calendering
Greenlandic
ACDEEGINNRS grandnieces
reascending
ACDEEGINPRT deprecating
ACDEEGINRST desecrating
ACDEEGINRTU reeducating
ACDEEGIORST categorised
ACDEEGIORTZ categorized
ACDEEGIOTTX excogitated
ACDEEGKLNOW acknowledge
ACDEEGLNORU Grand Coulee
ACDEEHIINOT ethanedioic
ACDEEHILNNS channelised
ACDEEHILNNZ channelized
ACDEEHILNOT endothecial
ACDEEHILNPP Chippendale
ACDEEHILNRS chandeliers
chandleries
ACDEEHILPSY psychedelia
ACDEEHIMNRS merchandise
ACDEEHIMSST schematised
ACDEEHIMSTZ schematized
ACDEEHINRTW windcheater
ACDEEHIORTT octahedrite
ACDEEHKKLNU knucklehead
ACDEEHKNNUY unhackneyed
ACDEEHMNSTT detachments
ACDEEHMORTV overmatched
ACDEEHNRRTU unchartered
ACDEEHOPPRS copperheads
ACDEEHORTVW overwatched
ACDEEHPRRSU repurchased
ACDEEHPRSST despatchers
ACDEEIILLSX lexicalised
ACDEEIILLTY eidetically
ACDEEIILLXZ lexicalized
ACDEEIILMSS decimalises
ACDEEIILMSZ decimalizes
ACDEEIILMTV maledictive
ACDEEIILNSV divalencies
ACDEEIILPSS specialised
ACDEEIILPSZ specialized
ACDEEIILSST elasticised
ACDEEIILSTZ elasticized
ACDEEIILTUV elucidative
ACDEEIIMNST mendacities
ACDEEIIMRST acidimeters
ACDEEIINNOT neonaticide
ACDEEIINNRT incinerated
ACDEEIIOPPS epidiascope
ACDEEIIPRTV predicative
ACDEEIIRRRV arrivederci
ACDEEILLMNY endemically
ACDEEILLNNY decennially
ACDEEILLOSS delocalises
ACDEEILLOSZ delocalizes
ACDEEILLRSS escadrilles
ACDEEILNNST clandestine
ACDEEILNOTT delectation
ACDEEILNPPS appendicles
ACDEEILNRST centralised
credentials
ACDEEILNRSY increasedly
ACDEEILNRTZ centralized
ACDEEILNTTU denticulate
ACDEEILOSSV devocalises
ACDEEILOSVZ devocalizes
ACDEEILPRTU reduplicate
ACDEEILPSTU pediculates
ACDEEILRSSU secularised
ACDEEILRSTT decretalist
ACDEEILRSUZ secularized
ACDEEILRTTU reticulated
ACDEEILSTUV vesiculated
ACDEEIMMNST medicaments
ACDEEIMNOSU eudaemonics
ACDEEIMNPRT predicament
ACDEEIMORRR microreader
ACDEEIMORST acidometers
democratise
ACDEEIMORTZ democratize
ACDEEIMOSTT domesticate
ACDEEIMPRST mercaptides
ACDEEIMSSTU miseducates
ACDEEINNNST intendances
ACDEEINNSTU denunciates
ACDEEINOOPT Pico de Aneto
ACDEEINOPRS percoideans
ACDEEINOPRT deprecation
ACDEEINORSS dinocerases
secondaries
ACDEEINORST considerate
desecration
ACDEEINORTU reeducation
ACDEEINPPRT apprenticed
ACDEEINPRST interspaced
ACDEEINRTUV underactive
ACDEEIOOPRS aecidospore
ACDEEIOPRRT depreciator
ACDEEIOQTUV equivocated
ACDEEIORRTT directorate
ACDEEIOSTTX detoxicates
ACDEEKNORSW Dawson Creek
ACDEEKQRRTU quarterdeck
ACDEELLMORU leucodermal
ACDEELLMSSU muscadelles
ACDEELLNOTU nucleolated
ACDEELMORRS scleroderma
ACDEELMORSU leucodermas
ACDEELNOPRW candlepower
ACDEELNOSST adolescents
ACDEELNPTUU pedunculate
ACDEELORSTU edulcorates
ACDEELSSTUY decussately
ACDEEMMNORS commandeers
ACDEEMMNOTT commentated
ACDEEMMNPST decampments
ACDEEMMORSU commeasured
ACDEEMNOPSS encompassed
ACDEEMNOPST compensated
ACDEEMNRTTU traducement
ACDEENNORST contredanse
ACDEENNORTV contravened
ACDEENNOSST condensates
ACDEENRSTTU detruncates
ACDEEOPRRST deprecators
ACDEEOPRRSY copyreaders
ACDEEOPRRTY deprecatory
ACDEEORRSST desecrators
ACDEEORSSTU ceratoduses
ACDEFFIIRTV diffractive
ACDEFFLORSS scaffolders
ACDEFGHMORR frogmarched
ACDEFGILRSU disgraceful
ACDEFGINNTU fecundating
ACDEFHIINNR French India
ACDEFHILPST feldspathic
ACDEFHILSSS scaldfishes
ACDEFHNNRSU French Sudan
ACDEFIIINNT infanticide

ACDEFIIINOT	deification
	edification
ACDEFIIINST	nidificates
ACDEFIIIRSU	fiduciaries
ACDEFIILNRU	unclarified
ACDEFIILPST	spiflicated
ACDEFIILSTU	feudalistic
ACDEFIIORTY	edificatory
ACDEFIIRRST	fratricides
ACDEFINNOST	confidantes
ACDEFINNOTU	fecundation
ACDEFIRRTTU	trifurcated
ACDEFLNRUUY	fraudulency
ACDEFNORSTU	fecundators
ACDEFNORTUY	fecundatory
ACDEGHIILOT	glochidiate
ACDEGHIIMNR	Michigander
ACDEGHILLNN	chandelling
ACDEGHILLNT	candlelight
ACDEGHILLRR	chargrilled
ACDEGHIMOPR	demographic
ACDEGHINNRT	night dancer
ACDEGHINPST	despatching
ACDEGHIRRSS	dischargers
ACDEGHNNORU	changeround
ACDEGIILLOO	ideological
ACDEGIILMNT	maledicting
ACDEGIILMRU	demiurgical
ACDEGIILNTU	elucidating
ACDEGIIMNSU	misguidance
ACDEGIINPRT	predicating
ACDEGILLNOT	decollating
ACDEGILLOOP	pedological
ACDEGILOOPS	logopaedics
ACDEGIMNOSY	geodynamics
ACDEGIMORTY	tragicomedy
ACDEGINNOQU	quindecagon
ACDEGINNRTU	underacting
ACDEGINOORT	Ticonderoga
ACDEGINOPRY	copyreading
ACDEGINSSTU	decussating
ACDEGIORRSU	discourager
ACDEGIORSSU	discourages
ACDEGKLOORS	sockdolager
ACDEGLNNRSU	granduncles
ACDEGLNORSS	cradlesongs
ACDEHIILMPS	dicephalism
ACDEHIILOPP	pedophiliac
ACDEHIIOPRT	diaphoretic
ACDEHIKLNST	stickhandle
ACDEHILLOOS	alcoholised
ACDEHILLOOZ	alcoholized
ACDEHILNORT	chlorinated
ACDEHILOPSU	dicephalous
ACDEHILRSSY	chrysalides
ACDEHIMOPRS	comradeship
ACDEHIMORST	dichromates
ACDEHIMOSTU	mustachioed
ACDEHIMRSSW	scrimshawed
ACDEHINNOST	stanchioned
ACDEHINNSST	disenchants
ACDEHINOORS	icosahedron
ACDEHINOPSS	deaconships
ACDEHINORST	achondrites
ACDEHIOOPRT	orthopaedic
ACDEHIPRSST	dispatchers
ACDEHKLNNST	landsknecht
ACDEHLLLOPY	phylloclade
ACDEHLMOSUY	chlamydeous
ACDEHLNPRTU	thunderclap
ACDEHLOOPPS	cephalopods
ACDEHMNNOOR	enchondroma
ACDEHMNORRY	hydromancer
ACDEHMOORTW	doomwatcher
ACDEHNOORST	octahedrons
ACDEHNORSSZ	scherzandos
ACDEHOORRTU	urochordate
ACDEHORRSTT	tetrachords
ACDEHORRTYY	cryohydrate
ACDEIIIJRSU	judiciaries
ACDEIIILMOT	domiciliate
ACDEIIINSTV	indicatives
ACDEIIJLPRU	prejudicial
ACDEIILLMNY	medicinally
ACDEIILLNTY	identically
ACDEIILLORV	varicelloid
ACDEIILLRVY	veridically
ACDEIILLSTY	deistically
ACDEIILMNOT	malediction
ACDEIILMOPS	diplomacies
ACDEIILMPRS	spermicidal
ACDEIILMQTU	quitclaimed
ACDEIILMRSS	disclaimers
ACDEIILMSSX	disclimaxes
ACDEIILNNOT	declination
ACDEIILNNST	incidentals
ACDEIILNORT	directional
ACDEIILNOTU	elucidation
ACDEIILNOTV	valediction
ACDEIILNPTU	induplicate
ACDEIILOPRS	periodicals
ACDEIILORRT	directorial
ACDEIILPRTT	triplicated
ACDEIILPSST	plasticised
ACDEIILPSTZ	plasticized
ACDEIILPTUV	duplicative
ACDEIILRTUV	diverticula
ACDEIIMNOST	medications
ACDEIIMNRRT	intradermic
ACDEIIMORRT	radiometric
ACDEIIMORTU	audiometric
ACDEIIMPRRU	pericardium
ACDEIINNRTY	tyrannicide
ACDEIINOPRT	predication
ACDEIINORRT	doctrinaire
ACDEIINOSSY	isocyanides
ACDEIINOTTX	intoxicated
ACDEIIOSSST	dissociates
ACDEIIRSTTV	distractive
ACDEIJRSTUU	judicatures
ACDEILLLMOY	melodically
ACDEILLMNOY	demonically
ACDEILLNNOR	carillonned
ACDEILLNOOT	decollation
ACDEILLNORR	cordilleran
ACDEILLORRS	cordilleras
ACDEILLPTUY	duplicately
ACDEILMNOPS	endoplasmic
ACDEILMOPRR	dimercaprol
ACDEILMORTY	maledictory
ACDEILMSSTU	simulcasted
ACDEILNNOSY	Coney Island
ACDEILNOOST	consolidate
ACDEILNORSS	cordialness
ACDEILNORSY	secondarily
ACDEILNORTU	radiolucent
ACDEILNOSTU	inosculated
ACDEILNOTTU	tentaculoid
ACDEILNRSTU	stridulance
ACDEILOORRV	varicolored
ACDEILORSTU	elucidators
ACDEILORTUY	elucidatory
ACDEILORTVY	valedictory
ACDEILPPSTU	supplicated
ACDEILPPSTY	dyspeptical
ACDEILRSSTY	crystalised
ACDEILRSTTW	wildcatters
ACDEILRSTYZ	crystalized
ACDEIMNNOOP	companioned
ACDEIMNNORU	endocranium
ACDEIMNNOST	demicantons
ACDEINNORST	constrained
ACDEINNORTU	denunciator
ACDEINOOPRS	scorpaenoid
ACDEINOORST	carotenoids
	coordinates
	decorations
ACDEINOPRSS	scorpaenids
ACDEINOPSTT	constipated
ACDEINORRSW	cordwainers
ACDEINORRWY	cordwainery
ACDEINORSTT	detractions
ACDEINOSSTU	decussation
ACDEINOSTTU	outdistance
ACDEINOSTTW	wainscotted
ACDEINOSTTX	detoxicants
ACDEINPRSTU	unpractised
ACDEINPRSTY	predynastic
ACDEIOOPRSS	radioscopes
ACDEIOOPRSU	adipocerous
ACDEIOPRRST	predicators
ACDEIOPRRTY	predicatory
ACDEIOPRSSY	caryopsides
ACDEIQRSSTU	quadrisects
ACDEIRRSSTT	distracters
ACDEJORSSTU	coadjutress
ACDEKNNOPRY	Nordkyn Cape
ACDELLNOOTY	cotyledonal
ACDELLOORST	decollators
ACDELMOPRRS	palmcorders
ACDELNOORST	decolorants
ACDELNOOSTY	acotyledons
ACDELOPRTTY	pterodactyl
ACDEMMMNNOT	commandment
ACDEMMNOSTU	consummated
ACDEMNNORTU	countermand

ACDEMNORTUY	documentary
ACDEMOOPRRS	compradores
ACDEMOORRST	Côtes-d'Armor
	ostracoderm
ACDEMOPRSSU	dampcourses
ACDENNNNOUU	unannounced
ACDENNNOORS	ordonnances
ACDENNNOOSS	nanoseconds
ACDENRRRSTU	redcurrants
ACDENRRSSTU	transducers
ACDEOORRSVW	woodcarvers
ACDEOPPRSSU	pseudocarps
ACDFFGHINNU	handcuffing
ACDFFGIINRT	diffracting
ACDFFGILNOS	scaffolding
ACDFFIILMOO	officialdom
ACDFFIINORT	diffraction
ACDFIIILRUY	fiduciarily
ACDFIMNNORS	confirmands
ACDGGHIINRS	discharging
ACDGHHIOOPR	hodographic
ACDGHIIIOPR	idiographic
ACDGHIIKNNP	handpicking
ACDGHIINNSW	sandwiching
ACDGHIINPST	dispatching
ACDGHIMOOSU	dichogamous
ACDGHIOOPRX	doxographic
ACDGHIOPRSY	discography
ACDGHIRRRYY	hydrargyric
ACDGIIILMNS	disclaiming
ACDGIIILOST	dialogistic
ACDGIIINNTV	vindicating
ACDGIILNOST	dislocating
ACDGIILNPTU	duplicating
ACDGIILNTTW	wildcatting
ACDGIINNSTY	syndicating
ACDGIINOSST	diagnostics
ACDGIINRSTT	distracting
ACDGILLOOOX	doxological
ACDGIMNNOOT	nondogmatic
ACDGINOORVW	woodcarving
ACDGLLOOTYY	dactylology
ACDGLOSTYYZ	zygodactyls
ACDHHIILOTY	ichthyoidal
ACDHHIOPRRS	harpsichord
ACDHHIOPRTY	hydropathic
ACDHIIIMRTT	mithridatic
ACDHIILLMOY	homicidally
ACDHIILOOPR	chiropodial
ACDHIIMNORS	diachronism
ACDHIINOOPR	radiophonic
ACDHIINORST	anhidrotics
ACDHIIOPRST	diastrophic
ACDHIIOPTYY	hypoacidity
ACDHILMOORS	harmolodics
ACDHILNOOPS	chilopodans
ACDHIMNNSTU	Duncan Smith
ACDHIMNOORT	trichomonad
ACDHIMNORTY	hydromantic
ACDHINNORYY	cyanohydrin
ACDHINOOOSX	chionodoxas
ACDHINOORSU	diachronous
ACDHIORSTTY	hydrostatic
ACDHLLLOPSY	cladophylls
	phylloclads
ACDHLNOOORT	notochordal
ACDHLOORRSY	hydrocorals
ACDIIIILLNPS	disciplinal
ACDIIILLOTY	idiotically
ACDIIILMOPS	idioplasmic
ACDIIILMORY	domiciliary
ACDIIILNNOT	indictional
ACDIIIMNOST	diatonicism
ACDIIIMNOTU	unidiomatic
ACDIIIMOTTY	diatomicity
ACDIIINNOST	indications
ACDIIINNOTV	vindication
ACDIIIOPRTT	parotiditic
ACDIIJLLRUY	juridically
ACDIILLLLYY	idyllically
ACDIILLORST	clostridial
ACDIILMNNRU	clinandrium
ACDIILMNOPR	palindromic
ACDIILMNSSY	syndicalism
ACDIILMOPST	diplomatics
ACDIILNNOOT	conditional
ACDIILNNOTU	inductional
ACDIILNOOST	dislocation
ACDIILNOPTU	duplication
ACDIILNORST	clostridian
ACDIILNSSTY	syndicalist
ACDIILOORRS	sororicidal
ACDIILPRSTU	tricuspidal
ACDIIMNORSS	sardonicism
ACDIIMNOSTU	coatimundis
ACDIIMORSTY	myocarditis
ACDIINNOSTY	syndication
ACDIINOORST	carotinoids
ACDIINOPRST	adscription
ACDIINOPSTU	cuspidation
ACDIINORSTT	distraction
ACDIINORSTV	vindicators
ACDIINORTVY	vindicatory
ACDIJNNOSTU	adjunctions
ACDIKLNOOSS	Cook Islands
ACDIKNOPRTW	Downpatrick
ACDILLMNOOY	monodically
ACDILLNORTY	doctrinally
ACDILLOOSTY	cotyloidals
ACDILLOPRSY	dropsically
ACDILLORSTY	crystalloid
ACDILNOSUUU	nudicaulous
ACDILOPRSTU	duplicators
ACDIMNOOSTT	mastodontic
ACDIMNORSUY	urodynamics
ACDINNNOOOT	condonation
ACDINOOORRT	coordinator
ACDIOORSSSU	Cassiodorus
ACDKNORSSTU	soundtracks
ACDLLOPSTYY	polydactyls
ACDLNOOORTY	condolatory
ACDMOOORRSU	acrodromous
ACDMORRSSUU	sursum corda
ACDOOORSSTU	ostracodous
ACEEEEEKPPR	peacekeeper
ACEEEFFFRTT	aftereffect
ACEEEFFMNST	effacements
ACEEEFFSTTU	effectuates
ACEEEFHORRS	forereaches
ACEEEFIPRST	afterpieces
ACEEEFLNRRS	freelancers
ACEEEFMNNST	enfacements
ACEEEGHHRST	chargesheet
ACEEEGHLLNR	rechallenge
ACEEEGIMNTT	metagenetic
ACEEEGLOTTT	telecottage
ACEEEGNPRST	percentages
ACEEEGNRRSS	screenagers
ACEEEHHIMRX	hexahemeric
ACEEEHIMNRS	archenemies
ACEEEHIMNTV	achievement
ACEEEHINSST	cenesthesia
ACEEEHIORVV	overachieve
ACEEEHIRRST	treacheries
ACEEEHIRSTT	catheterise
ACEEEHIRTTZ	catheterize
ACEEEHKLNRT	leatherneck
ACEEEHLLNRT	chanterelle
ACEEEHLMOST	hematoceles
ACEEEHLPSSW	scapewheels
ACEEEHLRSST	teacherless
ACEEEHLRSTV	Hever Castle
ACEEEHMNNNT	enhancement
ACEEEHMORTT	tacheometer
ACEEEHNPTTU	Tehuantepec
ACEEEHORRSV	overreaches
ACEEEHRRRSS	researchers
ACEEEIKLNNW	Wanne-Eickel
ACEEEILMNPT	mantelpiece
ACEEEILNQUV	equivalence
ACEEEILNRRV	irrelevance
ACEEEILRSTU	electuaries
ACEEEIMNRRS	mercenaries
ACEEEIMPRST	masterpiece
ACEEEINNPPT	inappetence
ACEEEINNRST	centenaries
ACEEEINPPST	appetencies
ACEEEINRSSS	necessaries
ACEEEINSSTT	necessitate
ACEEEIPPRSV	apperceives
ACEEEIPTTVX	expectative
ACEEEIRRSST	secretaires
	secretaries
ACEEEIRSSTV	eviscerates
ACEEEJKLPST	steeplejack
ACEEEKLORTW	electroweak
ACEEELLMNOT	metallocene
ACEEELLMNOV	malevolence
ACEEELLNRST	crenellates
ACEEELLSSSY	ceaselessly
ACEEELMMNPT	emplacement
ACEEELMNNST	enlacements
ACEEELMNPRT	replacement
ACEEELMNRRT	recremental
ACEEELMNRTX	excremental

ACEEELNOSUX exonuclease
ACEEELORSTT electorates
selectorate
ACEEELRRSST terraceless
ACEEELRSSTT telecasters
ACEEEMMNRST amercements
ACEEEMNNRTT reenactment
ACEEEMNNSST encasements
ACEEEMNPSST escapements
ACEEEMNRRTT retracement
ACEEEMNRSTT metacenters
metacentres
ACEEEMORSTT acetometers
ACEEENNOSTV covenantees
ACEEENNPRST repentances
ACEEENNRRST reentrances
ACEEENPRSTW Western Cape
ACEEENRRSSV screensaver
ACEEEOPRTTX expectorate
ACEEEPRRSTU recuperates
ACEEEPRSSTT pacesetters
ACEEERRSSST creatresses
ACEEERRSTTY Carey Street
ACEEFFHSSUU chauffeuses
ACEEFFIILOS officialese
ACEEFFILNTU ineffectual
ACEEFFLLTUY effectually
ACEEFGILNNR freelancing
ACEEFHIIPRS preachifies
ACEEFHINNRS enfranchise
ACEEFHNRRTU furtherance
ACEEFIILSTT felicitates
ACEEFIKLLPS Scafell Pike
ACEEFILLRST fellatrices
ACEEFIMNORS freemasonic
ACEEFIMNTTU tumefacient
ACEEFINOPTT tepefaction
ACEEFIORSTV vociferates
ACEEFIORSTW cowfeterias
ACEEFLLNRST crestfallen
ACEEFLNRSSU carefulness
ACEEFLORRUV overcareful
ACEEFLORSST forecastles
ACEEFLORSUU ferulaceous
ACEEFLPRRTU prefectural
ACEEFLRSSSU surfaceless
ACEEFLRSTTU leafcutters
ACEEFMNOPRR performance
ACEEFORRSST forecasters
ACEEGGIMMNO emmenagogic
ACEEGGIMNOT gametogenic
gamogenetic
geomagnetic
ACEEGGNORST congregates
ACEEGHHPRRY hypercharge
ACEEGHILOOT oligochaete
ACEEGHILPRT telegraphic
ACEEGHIMNOT hematogenic
ACEEGHINNRT interchange
ACEEGHINORT atherogenic
ACEEGHINORV Hercegovina
ACEEGHINRRS researching
ACEEGHLLNRS challengers
ACEEGHMMORT hectogramme
ACEEGHNORSV changeovers
ACEEGHNRRSU chargenurse
ACEEGHORRSV overcharges
ACEEGHPRRSU supercharge
ACEEGIILNNT geanticline
ACEEGIKNNPP kneecapping
ACEEGILLNRY generically
ACEEGILLNTY genetically
ACEEGILLNUY eugenically
ACEEGILLRVY viceregally
ACEEGILMMRT telegrammic
ACEEGILMOPS mesopelagic
ACEEGILMORT geometrical
ACEEGILNNPR precleaning
ACEEGILNNRT crenelating
ACEEGILNNTU enucleating
ACEEGILNRSS gracileness
ACEEGILNSTT telecasting
ACEEGILPRTT tetraplegic
ACEEGILSSTU sluicegates
ACEEGILSTTU gesticulate
ACEEGIMMNPT camp meeting
ACEEGIMMNRT centigramme
ACEEGIMMORT microgamete
ACEEGINNPRS pregnancies
ACEEGINNRST astringence
ACEEGINORTT teratogenic
ACEEGINOTTU autogenetic
ACEEGIORSST categorises
ACEEGIORSTZ categorizes
ACEEGIOSTTX excogitates
ACEEGIRRRTY cerargyrite
ACEEGLLRSSY gracelessly
ACEEGLMNNOT congealment
ACEEGLMNORS camerlengos
ACEEGMNORRS scaremonger
ACEEGMOSTTY gametocytes
ACEEGNNOSST cognateness
ACEEGNORRSU encouragers
ACEEHHIIRRS hierarchies
ACEEHHILRSW wheelchairs
ACEEHHIMOST theomachies
ACEEHHINRST ethnarchies
ACEEHHIPRST heptarchies
ACEEHHIRRSS heresiarchs
ACEEHHLLRST hatchellers
ACEEHHMMOOR haemochrome
ACEEHHMMORS hemachromes
ACEEHHOPTTY hypothecate
ACEEHIIINRT Catherine II
ACEEHIIKLMN machinelike
ACEEHIILNST antihelices
lecithinase
ACEEHIILPTT epithetical
ACEEHIIMNRS machineries
ACEEHIINNRT inheritance
ACEEHIINSTT esthetician
ACEEHIIRSTT hetaeristic
ACEEHIKLSTV thickleaves
ACEEHIKNRTW kitchenware
ACEEHILLNNP panhellenic
ACEEHILLRTY heretically
ACEEHILMNNS manchineels
ACEEHILMNSS machineless
ACEEHILMOPR hemeralopic
ACEEHILNNSS channelises
ACEEHILNNSZ channelizes
ACEEHILNSST ethicalness
ACEEHILOORZ coleorhizae
ACEEHILORTT theoretical
ACEEHIMMNPT impeachment
ACEEHIMNNNT enchainment
ACEEHIMNPSZ chimpanzees
ACEEHIMNRSS mechanisers
ACEEHIMNRSZ mechanizers
ACEEHIMORTT theorematic
ACEEHIMPRST champerties
ACEEHIMRTTY erythematic
ACEEHIMSSST schematises
ACEEHIMSSTZ schematizes
ACEEHINNSTZ Nietzschean
ACEEHINPRRT Charpentier
ACEEHINPRST pentarchies
ACEEHINPRTT parenthetic
ACEEHINSSTT anesthetics
ACEEHIOPRST pothecaries
spirochaete
ACEEHIORRST charioteers
ACEEHIORSST theocrasies
ACEEHIORTTX heterotaxic
ACEEHIPRSTT paresthetic
ACEEHIPRTTU therapeutic
ACEEHIPRTVY hyperactive
ACEEHIRRSTT tetrarchies
ACEEHKLLRSS shellackers
ACEEHKLNRST halternecks
ACEEHLLNNRS channellers
ACEEHLMMNSY mesenchymal
ACEEHLMNRUU Herculaneum
ACEEHLMOPRS polemarches
ACEEHLMOPSY mesocephaly
ACEEHLNOPSU encephalous
ACEEHLNPRSU leprechauns
ACEEHLNPSTT planchettes
ACEEHLOORRU leucorrhoea
ACEEHLOPRRT perchlorate
ACEEHLOPSTY polychaetes
ACEEHMMNNRT merchantmen
ACEEHMMRSSU meerschaums
ACEEHMNNNTT enchantment
ACEEHMNNRRT trencherman
ACEEHMNNSST encashments
ACEEHMNOORS anemochores
ACEEHMNOSTU menthaceous
ACEEHMNPRST preachments
ACEEHMNRSST manchesters
ACEEHMORSTT tachometers
ACEEHMORSTV overmatches
ACEEHMORTTY tacheometry
ACEEHMRSTTY tachymeters
ACEEHNNORRT archenteron
ACEEHNNRSST enchantress

ACEEHNORSSS	anchoresses
ACEEHNORSTT	anchorettes
ACEEHOPRRRS	reproachers
ACEEHOPRRSS	archespores
ACEEHORRSTT	orchestrate
ACEEHORRSTU	treacherous
ACEEHORSTVW	overwatches
ACEEHPRRSSU	repurchases
ACEEIIINRST	itineracies
ACEEIIKRSTT	rickettsiae
ACEEIILLNPT	penicillate
ACEEIILLNRT	rectilineal
ACEEIILLNRY	eirenically
ACEEIILLSSX	lexicalises
ACEEIILLSXZ	lexicalizes
ACEEIILLTVV	vellicative
ACEEIILNRRT	rectilinear
ACEEIILNSTT	licentiates
ACEEIILPRTV	replicative
ACEEIILPSSS	specialises
ACEEIILPSST	specialties
ACEEIILPSSZ	specializes
ACEEIILPTVX	explicative
ACEEIILSSST	elasticises
ACEEIILSSTZ	elasticizes
ACEEIIMNRRT	recriminate
ACEEIIMNSTT	antiemetics
ACEEIINNRST	incinerates
ACEEIINNTUV	enunciative
ACEEIINRSST	insectaries
	Resistencia
ACEEIINRSTT	certainties
ACEEIINRTTV	interactive
ACEEIINSSTT	intestacies
ACEEIIPPRTT	peripatetic
	precipitate
ACEEIIRSSTT	cassiterite
ACEEIIRSTTV	recitatives
ACEEIJNNRTT	interjacent
ACEEIKLMNRT	Maeterlinck
ACEEIKNRSTW	awestricken
ACEEIKNSSSS	seasickness
ACEEILLLORT	colleterial
ACEEILLLSTY	celestially
ACEEILLNNSS	cleanliness
ACEEILLORTV	vorticellae
ACEEILLPPTT	cappelletti
ACEEILMNNRT	incremental
ACEEILMNORS	ceremonials
ACEEILMNORT	Trincomalee
ACEEILMNOSU	leucomaines
ACEEILMNRRY	mercenarily
ACEEILMNSST	centesimals
	lemniscates
ACEEILMORRT	calorimeter
ACEEILMORST	elastomeric
ACEEILMPSST	esemplastic
ACEEILMRTUV	vermiculate
ACEEILNNNST	centennials
ACEEILNNORT	crenelation
	intolerance
ACEEILNNOTU	enucleation
ACEEILNNRST	intercensal
ACEEILNNTUY	lieutenancy
ACEEILNOPTX	exceptional
ACEEILNORSS	recessional
ACEEILNORST	resectional
ACEEILNORTU	reinoculate
ACEEILNOSSS	secessional
ACEEILNOSST	coessential
ACEEILNPRTT	centripetal
ACEEILNPSSS	specialness
ACEEILNPSST	plicateness
ACEEILNQUVY	equivalency
ACEEILNRRST	centraliser
ACEEILNRRTZ	centralizer
ACEEILNRRVY	irrelevancy
ACEEILNRSST	centralises
	linecasters
	treacliness
ACEEILNRSSY	necessarily
ACEEILNRSTV	cantilevers
ACEEILNRSTZ	centralizes
ACEEILNRTTY	Eternal City
ACEEILOPRTV	percolative
ACEEILORRTV	correlative
ACEEILORTUX	executorial
ACEEILOTVVY	evocatively
ACEEILPRRTY	preliteracy
ACEEILPSTUV	speculative
ACEEILRRSSU	seculariser
ACEEILRRSUZ	secularizer
ACEEILRSSSU	secularises
ACEEILRSSUZ	secularizes
ACEEILRSTTU	reticulates
ACEEILSSTUV	vesiculates
ACEEILSTTTU	testiculate
ACEEIMMNORT	anemometric
ACEEIMMORST	commiserate
ACEEIMNNOTT	cementation
ACEEIMNNSST	incasements
ACEEIMNOPRT	armipotence
ACEEIMNORRT	craniometer
ACEEIMNORST	actinomeres
ACEEIMNORTT	actinometer
ACEEIMNQRTU	acquirement
ACEEIMNRSTT	remittances
ACEEIMORRST	crematories
ACEEIMOSSTV	vasectomies
ACEEINNNSST	ancientness
ACEEINNOPTZ	pentazocine
ACEEINNORTV	noncreative
ACEEINNPPTY	inappetency
ACEEINNRRSU	reinsurance
ACEEINNSSTX	inexactness
ACEEINOPTTX	expectation
ACEEINORRST	recreations
ACEEINORSTU	auctioneers
ACEEINORSTX	execrations
ACEEINPPRST	apprentices
ACEEINPRRST	transpierce
ACEEINPRSST	interspaces
ACEEINRRSTV	transceiver
ACEEINRSSST	resistances
ACEEIOOPRSS	aeciospores
ACEEIOOPRTV	cooperative
ACEEIOPPRSU	piperaceous
ACEEIOPPSST	episcopates
ACEEIOPRRTV	procreative
ACEEIOQSTUV	equivocates
ACEEIORRSTV	eviscerator
ACEEIORRTTV	retroactive
ACEEIPRSTUV	superactive
ACEEIQRSSTU	requiescats
ACEEIRSSTTU	resuscitate
ACEEJLMNOST	cajolements
ACEEJNPRSTU	superjacent
ACEEKLLRSSS	salesclerks
ACEEKORRSSW	caseworkers
ACEELLLORTY	electorally
ACEELLNORTY	coeternally
ACEELLNOSTT	constellate
ACEELLOPTUY	eucalyptole
ACEELLORSTT	collarettes
ACEELLRSSTY	tracelessly
ACEELMNNOOV	monovalence
ACEELMNOPTT	contemplate
ACEELMNOSTY	melanocytes
ACEELMORSTT	lactometers
ACEELNNNSSU	uncleanness
ACEELNNRSSU	unclearness
ACEELNOOPRT	coleopteran
ACEELNOPSTT	Pentecostal
ACEELNOQSSU	coequalness
ACEELNPRSSY	screenplays
ACEELNPTTXY	expectantly
ACEELOORRTW	watercooler
ACEELOPPPRT	copperplate
ACEELOPPRRT	preceptoral
ACEELOSSTUY	setaceously
ACEEMMMOORT	commemorate
ACEEMMNNPST	encampments
ACEEMMNOSTT	commentates
ACEEMMORSSU	commeasures
ACEEMNOOPSS	anemoscopes
ACEEMNOPSSS	encompasses
ACEEMNOPSST	compensates
ACEEMNPRSST	escarpments
ACEEMOPRTTU	computerate
ACEENNNOPRU	preannounce
ACEENNNOSST	connateness
ACEENNOPRTU	counterpane
ACEENNORRTV	contravener
ACEENNORSTT	consternate
ACEENNORSTV	contravenes
	covenanters
ACEENNPRSTU	purtenances
ACEENNRSSUY	unnecessary
ACEENOORSTT	cotoneaster
ACEENOPRSTV	vaporescent
ACEENOPRTTX	expectorant
ACEENRSSSTW	newscasters
ACEEOOPRSTU	proteaceous
ACEEOPRRRTU	recuperator
ACEEORRSTUW	watercourse
ACEEPRRSSUU	acupressure

ACEEPRSSTTY typecasters
ACEFFGHILNR cliffhanger
ACEFFGILNTY affectingly
ACEFFIIIORS officiaries
ACEFFIILPST spifflicate
ACEFFIITTVY affectivity
ACEFFIKRRST traffickers
ACEFFILRSST trafficless
ACEFFIOSTUV suffocative
ACEFGHLLNUY changefully
ACEFGHMORRS frogmarches
ACEFGIIMNNT magnificent
ACEFGIIMNOS magnificoes
ACEFGIINNNR refinancing
ACEFGIINNRT interfacing
ACEFGILNRTU centrifugal
ACEFGINORST forecasting
ACEFGINRRSU resurfacing
ACEFHILNOPR francophile
ACEFHILRSTU ultrafiches
ACEFHINOSTT fianchettos
ACEFHKORSST aftershocks
ACEFHLOPRRU reproachful
ACEFHNNOOPR francophone
ACEFHORRSTV hovercrafts
ACEFIIINORT reification
ACEFIILMNOR infomercial
ACEFIILNNSS finicalness
ACEFIILORTT felicitator
ACEFIILPRSU superficial
ACEFIILPSST spiflicates
ACEFIILRSSS classifiers
ACEFIILTTVY factitively
ACEFIIMORRS formicaries
ACEFIINOPTT pontificate
ACEFIINORST fractionise
ACEFIINORTZ fractionize
ACEFIINRSST sanctifiers
ACEFIIORRTY reificatory
ACEFIIRSSST satisficers
ACEFIKLORTY factorylike
ACEFILLLOTU folliculate
ACEFILLORUW cauliflower
ACEFILOORST olfactories
ACEFILORSTU lactiferous
ACEFILOSTUY facetiously
ACEFIMNOTTU tumefaction
ACEFINNRSST franticness
ACEFINORRST refractions
ACEFINORSTV vociferants
ACEFINOTTUV confutative
ACEFIOORRTV vociferator
ACEFIPRRSTT priestcraft
ACEFKRRSSTU starfuckers
ACEFLNSSTTU tactfulness
ACEFMNORSTW craftswomen
ACEFNNOSSST confessants
ACEFRRSSSTU surfcasters
ACEGGHILLNN challenging
ACEGGHILNNS changelings
ACEGGHLOOSU cholagogues
ACEGGILLMOO gemological
ACEGGILRSST scraggliest
ACEGGINNORU encouraging
ACEGGINRSSS scragginess
ACEGGLNOOYY gynaecology
ACEGGNNORST congregants
ACEGGNOORRT congregator
ACEGHHIJKRS highjackers
ACEGHHILLNT hatchelling
ACEGHHILOPR helicograph
ACEGHHILRST searchlight
ACEGHHIMORR hemorrhagic
ACEGHHNORST shortchange
ACEGHHOOPRR choreograph
ACEGHHOPRRY choregraphy
ACEGHHOPRST hectographs
ACEGHHOPRTY hectography
ACEGHIIIMNT Michiganite
ACEGHIILMNS alchemising
ACEGHIILMNZ alchemizing
ACEGHIILORS oligarchies
ACEGHIIMNNS mechanising
ACEGHIIMNNZ mechanizing
ACEGHIIMNST misteaching
ACEGHIKLLNS shellacking
ACEGHILLNNN channelling
ACEGHILLOOR rheological
ACEGHILLOOT ethological
theological
ACEGHILMOOS logomachies
ACEGHILMOOT hematologic
ACEGHILNRSY searchingly
ACEGHILNTTW angletwitch
ACEGHILOOPR oleographic
ACEGHILOPSY geophysical
ACEGHIMMOOT homogametic
ACEGHIMNNRT merchanting
ACEGHIMNNSU machineguns
ACEGHIMNORR menorrhagic
ACEGHIMNORU archegonium
ACEGHIMRSST Great Schism
ACEGHINNNOT nonteaching
ACEGHINNOPR chaperoning
ACEGHINOPRR reproaching
ACEGHINORRV overarching
ACEGHINORTU outreaching
ACEGHINPRSS graphicness
ACEGHINRSTT chatterings
ACEGHIOOPSS hagioscopes
ACEGHIOPRRX xerographic
ACEGHIRSSTW switchgears
ACEGHLNOPTT plectognath
ACEGHLOOSTY eschatology
ACEGHNOPRSY scenography
ACEGHOOPRSU creophagous
ACEGHORRSTU roughcaster
ACEGHRRRSSU surchargers
ACEGIILLNPR callipering
ACEGIILLNPS specialling
ACEGIILLNTV vellicating
ACEGIILLOOT etiological
ACEGIILLOTV colligative
ACEGIILMNOR mineralogic
ACEGIILMRRU Muir Glacier
ACEGIILNNRT interlacing
ACEGIILNOST Castiglione
ACEGIILNPPY pipeclaying
ACEGIILNPRT replicating
ACEGIILNPTX explicating
ACEGIILNRST cartelising
ACEGIILNRTZ cartelizing
ACEGIILOSTT egotistical
ACEGIILRSST sacrilegist
ACEGIIMNOST isomagnetic
ACEGIIMNPRT imprecating
ACEGIIMNRST miscreating
ACEGIIMNRTT metricating
ACEGIIMRRTV gravimetric
ACEGIINNNTU enunciating
ACEGIINNRTT interacting
ACEGIINORTX excoriating
ACEGIINPRTT crepitating
ACEGIINQRRU reacquiring
ACEGIINRSTU cauterising
ACEGIINRTTX extricating
ACEGIINRTUZ cauterizing
ACEGIJNOTUV conjugative
ACEGILLLLOY collegially
ACEGILLMRTU metallurgic
ACEGILLNNOY congenially
ACEGILLNNPS spancelling
ACEGILLNOOO oenological
ACEGILLNOOP penological
ACEGILLNORV overcalling
ACEGILLNOSS logicalness
ACEGILLOORS serological
ACEGILLOOSS oligoclases
ACEGILLOOSX sexological
ACEGILMNORS camerlingos
ACEGILMNOSU glucosamine
ACEGILMOSTY cleistogamy
ACEGILNNNOU uncongenial
ACEGILNNOOT congelation
ACEGILNNSUY unceasingly
ACEGILNOPRT percolating
ACEGILNOPTY genotypical
ACEGILNORRT correlating
ACEGILNORSS casseroling
ACEGILNORSW lowercasing
ACEGILNPSTU speculating
ACEGILNPTUX exculpating
ACEGILNRSSY caressingly
ACEGILNTUUU unguiculate
ACEGILOOPST apologetics
ACEGILOORTT teratologic
ACEGILRRTUU agriculture
ACEGIMMRRSS scrimmagers
ACEGIMNNNOT nonmagnetic
ACEGIMNNOPR panicmonger
ACEGIMNNORT centimorgan
ACEGIMNOOST somatogenic
ACEGIMNOTVY vaginectomy
ACEGIMNRRTU mercurating
ACEGIMORSST mesogastric
ACEGINNNOSU consanguine

ACEGINNNOTV covenanting
ACEGINNORST recognisant
ACEGINNORTZ recognizant
ACEGINNRSTT transecting
ACEGINNRSTY astringency
ACEGINOOPRT cooperating
ACEGINOPRRT procreating
ACEGINORRTT retroacting
ACEGINORSTV overcasting
ACEGINPPRSU uppercasing
ACEGINPRRTU recapturing
ACEGINPSTTY typecasting
ACEGINRSSTT scatterings
ACEGIOORTTX excogitator
ACEGIOPSTTY steatopygic
ACEGJLNOTUY conjugately
ACEGKORSSTU goatsuckers
ACEGKRSSTTU stagestruck
ACEGLLNOOSU collagenous
ACEGLNOPRTY calyptrogen
ACEGLNORTUY granulocyte
ACEGMMRRSSU scrummagers
ACEGMNNORSS congressman
ACEGMOPRRST spectrogram
ACEGMORSTTY gastrectomy
ACEGNOORRTT gerontocrat
ACEGNORRSTT congratters
ACEGNRSSTTU scatterguns
ACEGOOPRSST gastroscope
ACEHHIILMOP haemophilic
hemophiliac
ACEHHIIMRRS hierarchism
ACEHHIINNTY hyacinthine
ACEHHILNOTT chloanthite
ACEHHIMOOPT homeopathic
ACEHHINOSTX hexastichon
ACEHHIPSSTT heptastichs
ACEHHIRSTUV Turishcheva
ACEHHLMNNOT Melanchthon
ACEHIIIILMV Michael VIII
ACEHIIINPSS hispanicise
ACEHIIINPSZ hispanicize
ACEHIIIRSTT hetairistic
ACEHIILLMOT homiletical
ACEHIILLOST isolecithal
ACEHIILMSTT athleticism
ACEHIILNOPR necrophilia
ACEHIILNOPS neophiliacs
ACEHIILOSTT chiastolite
heliostatic
ACEHIILPPTY epiphytical
ACEHIILRSTT thersitical
ACEHIILSTWW welwitschia
ACEHIINNOPT phonetician
ACEHIINOPRY perionychia
ACEHIINORRT rhetorician
ACEHIINPSTT pantheistic
ACEHIIPRSSU haruspicies
ACEHIKLPRRS parish clerk
ACEHIKMRRSS reichsmarks
ACEHILLOOSS alcoholises
ACEHILLOOSZ alcoholizes
ACEHILLPRSY spherically
ACEHILMNOOR melanochroi
ACEHILMNORS chloramines
ACEHILMOPSU mailpouches
ACEHILMRTUY eurythmical
ACEHILNORST chlorinates
ACEHILNPRST sphincteral
ACEHILNSSTU clianthuses
ACEHILNSTTY synthetical
ACEHILOPRST arctophiles
ACEHILOPRSY polyarchies
ACEHILRSSSY chrysalises
ACEHIMMOPRT metamorphic
ACEHIMNORSS marchioness
ACEHIMNORTU euchromatin
ACEHIMNOSST macintoshes
ACEHIMNOSYY hyoscyamine
ACEHIMNRSSV revanchisms
ACEHIMOOSTT homeostatic
ACEHIMOPRST atmospheric
ACEHIMORRRT arthromeric
ACEHIMORRST choirmaster
ACEHIMORRYZ mycorrhizae
ACEHIMORSST metachrosis
ACEHIMORSTT hematocrits
ACEHIMORTTX thermotaxic
ACEHIMOSSTT hemostatics
ACEHIMPSSTY metaphysics
ACEHIMPSTTY sympathetic
ACEHINNOPTT pantothenic
ACEHINNPSSU paunchiness
ACEHINNRSSU raunchiness
ACEHINNTTUU unauthentic
ACEHINOPRRS chairperson
ACEHINOPRRT chiropteran
ACEHINOPRTU neuropathic
ACEHINOPRTY hyperaction
ACEHINORRST orchestrina
ACEHINORSTV chevrotains
ACEHINRSSST starchiness
ACEHINRSSTV revanchists
ACEHINSSSTT cattishness
ACEHIOOPSTT osteopathic
ACEHIOOPTTV photoactive
ACEHIOPPRST Hippocrates
ACEHIOPRRST creatorship
ACEHIOPSSTY isopachytes
ACEHIORSSTV tovarisches
ACEHIPRRSST archpriests
ACEHIQRRSUY squirearchy
ACEHIRSSTTT tetrastichs
ACEHJKNNOSY johnnycakes
ACEHJRRSSUW jawcrushers
ACEHKKRRSSU sharksucker
ACEHKLMMORS hammerlocks
ACEHKLNOSST chalkstones
ACEHKNOSSTU Stockhausen
ACEHLLMSSTY matchlessly
ACEHLMMNOOR chromonemal
ACEHLMOOSST schoolmates
ACEHLNNRTTY trenchantly
ACEHLNOPRTY lycanthrope
ACEHLNORSST charlestons
ACEHLORSTUY lythraceous
ACEHMNNOORW anchorwomen
ACEHMNOPRSY prosenchyma
ACEHMNOSTWY yachtswomen
ACEHMOORSUX auxochromes
ACEHMOORTTY tracheotomy
ACEHMOPRSTU champertous
ACEHMORRTTY arthrectomy
ACEHNNOOPRT ctenophoran
ACEHNNSSSTU staunchness
ACEHNOPSTYY cyanophytes
ACEHNORRSTT trochanters
ACEHOOPPRRS carpophores
ACEHOOPRRST arthroscope
crapshooter
prothoraces
ACEHOPPRSTU touchpapers
ACEHOPRRSSY chrysoprase
ACEHOPRRTYY cryotherapy
ACEHOPSSTTW stopwatches
ACEHORSTTWW watchtowers
ACEIIIILNSV civilianise
ACEIIIILNVZ civilianize
ACEIIIKNNOS aniseikonic
ACEIIIKNSST ekisticians
ACEIIILMNRS criminalise
ACEIIILMNRZ criminalize
ACEIIILMPTV implicative
ACEIIILNOTT elicitation
ACEIIILOSST socialities
ACEIIILPSTT pietistical
ACEIIIMNNRT incriminate
ACEIIIMNOST semiotician
ACEIIIMNRTV criminative
ACEIIIPSTTV captivities
ACEIIIQSTUV acquisitive
ACEIIKLLNTY kinetically
ACEIIKLLOOR kilocalorie
ACEIIKLRSTT rickettsial
ACEIIKNOTTU autokinetic
ACEIIKNRSSS airsickness
ACEIIKRSSTT rickettsias
ACEIILLLTVY levitically
ACEIILLMMTY mimetically
ACEIILLMNNU illuminance
ACEIILLMOTY meiotically
ACEIILLMPRY empirically
ACEIILLMSSY seismically
ACEIILLNOTV vellication
ACEIILLNRTV intervallic
ACEIILLNRUV curvilineal
ACEIILLNSTT scintillate
ACEIILLOSST callosities
ACEIILMNPRT planimetric
ACEIILMNSSU masculinise
ACEIILMNSTT mentalistic
ACEIILMNSUZ masculinize
ACEIILMORST isometrical
ACEIILMOTTU itacolumite
ACEIILMPRTU implicature
ACEIILMRRTT trimetrical

ACEIILNNORT	reclination
ACEIILNOORT	coalitioner
ACEIILNOPPR	pilocarpine
ACEIILNOPRT	replication
ACEIILNOPTX	explication
ACEIILNOQTU	equinoctial
ACEIILNOTUV	inoculative
ACEIILNPRUY	pecuniarily
ACEIILNPTUV	inculpative
ACEIILNRRUV	curvilinear
ACEIILNRSTT	clarinetist
ACEIILNRSTU	unrealistic
ACEIILNRTTY	intricately
ACEIILOPRST	tropicalise
ACEIILOPRTZ	tropicalize
ACEIILORSSS	socialisers
ACEIILORSSZ	socializers
ACEIILPPRST	participles
ACEIILPRSST	plasticiser
ACEIILPRSTT	peristaltic
	triplicates
ACEIILPRSTZ	plasticizer
ACEIILPRTUY	peculiarity
ACEIILPSSST	plasticises
	specialists
ACEIILPSSTZ	plasticizes
ACEIILRSSTT	recitalists
ACEIILRTTVY	verticality
ACEIIMMORSS	commissaire
ACEIIMNNRST	manneristic
ACEIIMNOPRT	imprecation
ACEIIMNORST	anisometric
	creationism
	miscreation
	reactionism
	romanticise
ACEIIMNORTT	interatomic
	metrication
ACEIIMNORTZ	romanticize
ACEIIMNPRRU	pericranium
ACEIIMNPSST	emancipists
ACEIIMNPSSU	impuissance
ACEIIMNRSTT	martensitic
ACEIIMNRSTU	insectarium
ACEIIMNSSTT	semanticist
ACEIINNNOST	incensation
ACEIINNNOTU	enunciation
ACEIINNOPTT	pectination
ACEIINNORRT	incinerator
ACEIINNORST	cinerations
ACEIINNORTT	interaction
ACEIINNPSTT	pinnatisect
ACEIINOORTX	excoriation
ACEIINOPRTT	crepitation
ACEIINOPSTT	pectisation
ACEIINOPTTZ	pectization
ACEIINORSTT	creationist
	reactionist
	recitations
ACEIINORTTX	extrication
ACEIINOSSTV	vesications
ACEIINOSTTX	excitations
	intoxicates
ACEIINPPRST	principates
ACEIINPPRTT	precipitant
ACEIINPRTTY	antipyretic
	pertinacity
ACEIINPSSTT	antiseptics
ACEIIOOPPST	aposiopetic
ACEIIORRRST	certioraris
ACEIIPPSSST	epispastics
ACEIIRRSSSU	cuirassiers
ACEIIRSSSTU	casuistries
ACEIJNORSTT	trajections
ACEIKLLPSTY	skeptically
ACEIKLMNNNW	Winckelmann
ACEIKLORTTW	latticework
ACEILLLMNOR	lamellicorn
ACEILLLMOPY	polemically
ACEILLLNORT	citronellal
ACEILLLNORY	collinearly
ACEILLLNOUV	involucella
ACEILLLNRUU	unicellular
ACEILLLRTUY	cellularity
ACEILLMMSTY	symmetallic
ACEILLMNNOT	nonmetallic
ACEILLMNOST	callistemon
ACEILLMNRUY	numerically
ACEILLMNSUY	masculinely
ACEILLMOPRY	promycelial
ACEILLMOTTY	totemically
ACEILLMRRUY	mercurially
ACEILLNNOOO	neocolonial
ACEILLNNOTY	octennially
ACEILLNOOST	ocellations
ACEILLNOPTU	cupellation
ACEILLNOSTY	sectionally
ACEILLNOTTY	tonetically
ACEILLNRSSY	lyricalness
ACEILLNRSTY	crystalline
ACEILLOORRS	corollaries
ACEILLOPPSY	episcopally
ACEILLOPSSW	pillowcases
ACEILLOQUVY	equivocally
ACEILLORTVY	vectorially
ACEILLRSSTY	crystallise
ACEILLRSTTY	crystallite
ACEILLRSTUV	victuallers
ACEILLRSTYZ	crystallize
ACEILLRSUVY	vesicularly
ACEILLRTUVY	lucratively
ACEILLSSTUV	victualless
ACEILMMNOSU	communalise
ACEILMMNOTY	laminectomy
	metonymical
ACEILMMNOUZ	communalize
ACEILMMORTT	recommittal
ACEILMMRSTY	symmetrical
ACEILMNNORT	conterminal
ACEILMNOOPS	scopolamine
ACEILMNOOPW	policewoman
ACEILMNOPRS	complainers
ACEILMNOPRT	planometric
ACEILMNOPTY	amylopectin
ACEILMNRTTU	curtailment
ACEILMNRTUU	retinaculum
ACEILMNSSSU	musicalness
ACEILMOORTZ	zoometrical
ACEILMOPRRS	proclaimers
ACEILMORRTY	calorimetry
ACEILMORTTV	voltametric
ACEILMRRTUU	mariculture
ACEILNNNOOX	connexional
ACEILNNNOSS	nonsensical
ACEILNNNOTT	continental
ACEILNNNOTU	antinucleon
ACEILNNORTU	crenulation
ACEILNNOSTU	nucleations
ACEILNNRTUY	uncertainly
ACEILNNSSTY	incessantly
ACEILNOOPRR	incorporeal
ACEILNOOPRT	percolation
ACEILNOORRT	correlation
ACEILNOORST	iconolaters
	relocations
ACEILNOORSU	arenicolous
ACEILNOPRST	inspectoral
	pratincoles
ACEILNOPSTU	peculations
	speculation
ACEILNOPTUX	exculpation
ACEILNOQUUV	unequivocal
ACEILNORSTT	intercostal
ACEILNORSTU	ulcerations
ACEILNORTUV	countervail
	involucrate
ACEILNOSSST	stoicalness
ACEILNOSSTU	inosculates
ACEILNOSTUV	novaculites
ACEILNOSTUY	tenaciously
ACEILNPSSTY	typicalness
ACEILNRRRTU	intercrural
ACEILNRRTUV	ventricular
ACEILNRSSTT	centralists
ACEILNRSSUV	vulcanisers
ACEILNRSUUX	luxuriances
ACEILNRSUVZ	vulcanizers
ACEILOOOPRT	aeolotropic
ACEILOOPPRS	polariscope
ACEILOOPRSS	acropolises
ACEILOOSSST	osteoclasis
ACEILOPRRTT	protractile
ACEILOPRSTX	explicators
ACEILOPRTXY	explicatory
ACEILORSUVY	veraciously
ACEILORTVYY	viceroyalty
ACEILPPSSTU	supplicates
ACEILPRSTTY	spectrality
ACEILQRTUUU	aquiculture
ACEILRRSSTY	crystaliser
ACEILRRSTYZ	crystalizer
ACEILRRTTUU	turriculate
ACEILRSSSTU	secularists
ACEILRSSSTY	crystalises
ACEILRSSTYZ	crystalizes
ACEIMMOOSSU	mimosaceous

ACEIMMORRTU crematorium
ACEIMMOTTUV commutative
ACEIMMPRSSU supremacism
ACEIMNNNOTT containment
ACEIMNNOORY oneiromancy
ACEIMNOORTX axonometric
ACEIMNOPRST importances
ACEIMNORRTU mercuration
ACEIMNORRTY craniometry
ACEIMNORTTY actinometry
ACEIMOOPRSZ azoospermic
ACEIMOORTVY ovariectomy
ACEIMOPRRTY cryptomeria
imprecatory
ACEIMORRSTT astrometric
meritocrats
ACEIMORSSTU customaries
ACEIMPRSSTU supremacist
ACEIMSSSTTY systematics
ACEINNNNSSU uncanniness
ACEINNNOSTT Constantine
ACEINNOOTTV connotative
ACEINNORRST constrainer
ACEINNORRTV Canton River
ACEINNORSST sanctioners
ACEINNORSTT transection
ACEINNORSTU enunciators
ACEINNORTUY enunciatory
ACEINNOSTTY encystation
ACEINNPTUUV nuncupative
ACEINNRSSSW scrawniness
ACEINNRSTUU nunciatures
ACEINNRTTUY uncertainty
ACEINOOOPRT cooperation
ACEINOOPRRT incorporate
procreation
ACEINOOPRTU aponeurotic
ACEINOORRTT retroaction
ACEINOORSTV revocations
ACEINOOSSST iconostases
ACEINOPRRTU Puerto Rican
ACEINOPRSSS prosaicness
ACEINOPRSTU precautions
ACEINOPSSTT constipates
ACEINORRSTT retractions
ACEINORRTTY contrariety
ACEINORSSSU cariousness
ACEINORSTTU eructations
ACEINORSTTV contrastive
ACEINORSTTX extractions
ACEINPPRSSS scrappiness
ACEINPRRTUY parturiency
ACEINRRTUUV incurvature
ACEINRSSSSU narcissuses
ACEIOOPRRST corporatise
ACEIOOPRRTV corporative
ACEIOOPRRTZ corporatize
ACEIOOPRTVV provocative
ACEIOOQRTUV equivocator
ACEIOPRRSSU perisarcous
ACEIOPRRSTT tetrasporic
triceratops

ACEIOPRRTTV protractive
ACEIOPRSTUU precautious
ACEIORRSSST ostracisers
ACEIORRSSTZ ostracizers
ACEJKLPPSSU supplejacks
ACEKKMOSSST smokestacks
ACEKLLRSSTY tracklessly
ACEKLNOPSST alpenstocks
ACEKMNORRSW cankerworms
ACEKNNORSTU countersank
ACEKPRRSSSY skyscrapers
ACELLLMORUY molecularly
ACELLLNNORU noncellular
ACELLMMNOSY commensally
ACELLMNOPSU nucleoplasm
ACELLNOPRUY polynuclear
ACELLNOPVYY polyvalency
ACELLNORSUY larcenously
ACELLNOSSSU callousness
ACELLNPRTUY crapulently
ACELLNRTTUY reluctantly
ACELLOOPRRY corporeally
ACELLOPSSTU leucoplasts
ACELMNNOORT nomenclator
ACELMNNOORU mononuclear
ACELMNNOOVY monovalency
ACELMNNOSTT malcontents
ACELMRSTUUU musculature
ACELNNOPRSU nonspecular
ACELNNOSTUV conventuals
ACELNNRSTTU translucent
ACELNORSUVY cavernously
ACELNORTTUX contextural
ACELNOSSTTU sansculotte
ACELNOSTUUY cutaneously
ACELOOPRRST percolators
ACELOOPRRTT protectoral
ACELOOPRRTY corporately
ACELOORRSTU coloratures
ACELOORRSTW watercolors
ACELOORRSUU coelurosaur
ACELOORRTUW watercolour
ACELOOSSSTT osteoclasts
ACELOPRSSTU speculators
ACELOPRSSUY pelycosaurs
ACELOPRTUXY exculpatory
ACEMMNOORTT commentator
ACEMMNOPRTT compartment
ACEMMNOSSTU consummates
ACEMNNNOSTT cantonments
ACEMNNORSST monstrances
ACEMNOOPRST compensator
ACEMNOOSTYZ mycetozoans
ACEMNOPRRSY pyromancers
ACEMNOSSTTY nematocysts
ACEMOOPRRSS macrospores
ACEMOOPRRTY cotemporary
ACEMORSSTTU scoutmaster
ACENNOORSTV covenantors
ACENNOSSTTT contestants
ACENOORRSTV conservator
ACENOPRRSTU procrustean

ACENOPRRTTU counterpart
ACENOPRSTTT protectants
ACENORSSSUU raucousness
ACENORSTTUY countryseat
ACENOSSSUUV vacuousness
ACEOOOPRRST cooperators
ACEOOPPRRSS carpospores
ACEOOPRRRST procreators
ACEOOPRRSTY procaryotes
ACEOOPRSSTU stauroscope
ACEOOPSSSTT statoscopes
ACEORSSSSSY syssarcoses
ACFFFGILNRU carfuffling
ACFFGIIINOT officiating
ACFFGIIKNRT trafficking
ACFFGINOSTU suffocating
ACFFIIINOOT officiation
ACFFIILLNOY officinally
ACFFIILNNOO nonofficial
ACFFIILNOST afflictions
ACFFIIOORST officiators
ACFFILMNOOR falconiform
ACFFINOOSTU suffocation
ACFGHIINNRS franchising
ACFGHILNNSU flaunchings
ACFGHINOSUV vouchsafing
ACFGIIINNST significant
ACFGIIINSST satisficing
ACFGIIJKKNN jackknifing
ACFGIILNSSY classifying
ACFGIIMNORT formicating
ACFGIINNORT fornicating
fractioning
ACFGIINNSTY sanctifying
ACFGIINORST factorising
ACFGIINORTZ factorizing
ACFGIINSTTU fungistatic
ACFGIKNRSTU starfucking
ACFGILLMOOR formal logic
logical form
ACFGILNORSU Saronic Gulf
ACFGILNTTUU fluctuating
ACFGILOSUUY fugaciously
ACFGINRSSTU surfcasting
ACFHILNOPRS francophils
ACFHINNOTUX fucoxanthin
ACFHKOPRSWZ Schwarzkopf
ACFIIINNOTU unification
ACFIIINORTV vinificator
ACFIIKPRTTZ Fitzpatrick
ACFIILLNOTY fictionally
ACFIILMNORU californium
ACFIILMORST formalistic
ACFIILMSSSY misclassify
ACFIILNOPST pontificals
ACFIIMMORRU formicarium
ACFIIMNOORT formication
ACFIIMNORST informatics
ACFIINNOORT fornication
ACFIINNORST infarctions
infractions
ACFIIOPRRTU purificator

ACFILMNNOTU	malfunction
ACFILNNOOST	conflations
ACFILNNOOSU	confusional
ACFILNNOSTU	functionals
ACFILNOTTUU	fluctuation
ACFILORSTUY	fractiously
ACFIMMOOOPR	Campo Formio
ACFINNOOTTU	confutation
ACFINNORTUY	functionary
ACFINOORRST	fornicators
ACFLNOORSTW	contraflows
ACGGHHIIJKN	highjacking
ACGGHILLNOR	gralloching
ACGGHILOOPR	graphologic
	logographic
ACGGHINRRSU	surcharging
ACGGIIILLNS	gallicising
ACGGIIILLNZ	gallicizing
ACGGIIILNNS	anglicising
ACGGIIILNNZ	anglicizing
ACGGIILLNOT	colligating
ACGGIILMNRY	grimacingly
ACGGIIMMNRS	scrimmaging
ACGGIJNNOTU	conjugating
ACGGILNNORU	clangouring
ACGGIMMNRSU	scrummaging
ACGGINNNOOT	contangoing
ACGGINORRTU	corrugating
ACGHHILOOPR	holographic
ACGHHIMOOPR	homographic
ACGHHINOPRY	ichnography
ACGHHIOPRRY	chirography
ACGHHNOOPRR	chronograph
ACGHHOOPRRY	chorography
ACGHIILLNOP	anglophilic
ACGHIILMORT	algorithmic
	logarithmic
ACGHIILNORT	granolithic
ACGHIIMMNST	mismatching
ACGHIIMNNOP	championing
ACGHIIPRSST	sphragistic
ACGHIKMOPRY	kymographic
ACGHILLMOOO	homological
ACGHILLOOOR	horological
ACGHILMOOPR	lagomorphic
ACGHILMOORT	cologarithm
ACGHILMOOST	logomachist
ACGHILNNOSY	anchylosing
ACGHILNRSTT	latchstring
ACGHILOOSST	chaologists
ACGHILOPPRY	polygraphic
ACGHILOPRXY	xylographic
ACGHIMNNOPS	champignons
ACGHIMNOOPR	gramophonic
	monographic
	nomographic
	phonogramic
ACGHIMNOTTU	outmatching
ACGHIMOPRRS	micrographs
ACGHIMOPRRY	micrography
ACGHINOOPRS	nosographic
ACGHINOOPRY	iconography
ACGHINOORTU	coauthoring
ACGHINOPRRY	granophyric
ACGHINOPRSZ	zincographs
ACGHINOPRYZ	zincography
ACGHIOOPPRT	topographic
ACGHIOPPRRY	pyrographic
ACGHIOPPRST	pictographs
ACGHIOPPRTY	pictography
	typographic
ACGHIOPRSTY	hypogastric
ACGHIORRSTT	gastrotrich
ACGHIRRSTTW	cartwrights
ACGHMNOORRS	chronograms
ACGHMOOPRSY	cosmography
ACGHNOOOPRR	coronograph
ACGHOPPRRTY	cryptograph
ACGHOPRSTYY	cystography
ACGIIIILNST	italicising
ACGIIIILNTZ	italicizing
ACGIIILMNPT	implicating
ACGIIILNOSS	socialising
ACGIIILNOST	logistician
ACGIIILNOSZ	socializing
ACGIIILNPST	salpingitic
ACGIIIMNNRT	criminating
ACGIIINNTTT	nictitating
ACGIILLLLOY	illogically
ACGIILLMNOT	collimating
ACGIILLNOOS	sinological
ACGIILLNOOT	colligation
ACGIILLNOST	oscillating
ACGIILLNTUV	victualling
ACGIILLOORV	virological
ACGIILMNNOP	complaining
ACGIILMNNTU	culminating
ACGIILMNOPR	proclaiming
ACGIILNNOOT	cognitional
ACGIILNNOSV	volcanising
ACGIILNNOTU	inoculating
ACGIILNNOVZ	volcanizing
ACGIILNNPTU	inculpating
ACGIILNNSUV	vulcanising
ACGIILNNUVZ	vulcanizing
ACGIILNPSSU	capsulising
ACGIILNPSUZ	capsulizing
ACGIILNTTUV	cultivating
ACGIIMNORVW	microwaving
ACGIIMNOSST	agnosticism
ACGIIMNRRSY	miscarrying
ACGIIMNRSST	scintigrams
ACGIIMNRTTU	micturating
ACGIINNNOST	sanctioning
ACGIINNNOTZ	incognizant
ACGIINNORST	narcotising
ACGIINNORTZ	narcotizing
ACGIINNOSTW	wainscoting
ACGIINNRTUV	incurvating
ACGIINOOSTT	cogitations
ACGIINORSST	organicists
	ostracising
ACGIINORSTZ	ostracizing
ACGIINRSTTU	rusticating
ACGIJLNOTUY	conjugality
ACGIJNNOOTU	conjugation
ACGIKKMNOPR	pockmarking
ACGIKKNOSTT	stocktaking
ACGILLMNOOO	monological
	nomological
ACGILLMOOOP	pomological
ACGILLMOORS	oscillogram
ACGILLMOOTY	climatology
ACGILLMOOYZ	zymological
ACGILLNOOOS	nosological
ACGILLNOOOT	ontological
ACGILLNOSTY	gnostically
ACGILLOOOPS	posological
ACGILLOOOPT	topological
ACGILLOOPTY	typological
ACGILLOPSUY	callipygous
ACGILLOTYYZ	zygotically
ACGILMOOOST	somatologic
ACGILNNORSU	nonsurgical
ACGILNOSSTU	outclassing
ACGILOOPRST	carpologist
ACGILOOSSTT	scatologist
ACGIMMNOTTU	commutating
ACGIMNOOPRU	carpogonium
ACGIMNOORST	gastronomic
ACGINNOPSTY	syncopating
ACGINNORSTT	contrasting
ACGINNPTTUU	punctuating
ACGINOORRTU	corrugation
ACGINOORSTY	cosignatory
ACGINOPRRTT	protracting
ACGINOPRSTY	agrypnotics
ACGIORSSTTY	gyrostatics
ACGJNOORSTU	conjugators
ACGLLNOOOVY	volcanology
ACGLLNOOUVY	vulcanology
ACGMOOPRRTU	compurgator
ACGMOOPRSSY	gyrocompass
ACGMOPRRSTY	cryptograms
ACGOOPRSSTY	gastroscopy
ACGOORRRSTU	corrugators
ACHHIILLPTY	ithyphallic
ACHHILLMOOT	homothallic
ACHHILLOOOT	thioalcohol
ACHHILOOPSS	shopaholics
ACHHILOPRSS	scholarship
ACHHINOPRSS	archonships
ACHHINSSTUZ	schizanthus
ACHHIORSTUY	ichthyosaur
ACHHNOOSTTU	autochthons
ACHHNOOTTUY	autochthony
ACHHOPPSSTY	psychopaths
ACHHOPPSTYY	psychopathy
ACHHORRSTWY	crashworthy
ACHIIIMNPSS	hispanicism
ACHIIINRSTV	Christian IV
ACHIIJKNRSS	jinrickshas
ACHIIJKNRSW	jinrickshaw
ACHIILLMSWY	whimsically
ACHIILLPSST	phallicists
ACHIILMPSSY	physicalism

ACHIILNRSTY christianly
ACHIILOOPPR coprophilia
ACHIILOPSST sophistical
ACHIILOSTTT lithostatic
statolithic
ACHIILPSSTY physicalist
ACHIILPSTYY physicality
ACHIIMNORST chrismation
harmonistic
ACHIIMNSSUV chauvinisms
ACHIIMOPPRT amphiprotic
ACHIINNORST Corinthians
ACHIINNPQSU chinquapins
ACHIINNRSTU unchristian
ACHIINOSTUV Antiochus IV
ACHIINSSTUV chauvinists
ACHIIPRSSTY physiatrics
ACHIKKOSTVY Tchaikovsky
ACHIKLOORSW workaholics
ACHIKMNRSSS scrimshanks
ACHILLMNOOP Champollion
ACHILLMOOPR allomorphic
ACHILLOPRTY trophically
ACHILMNOORT trichomonal
ACHILMOOPST homoplastic
ACHILMOPSUY polychasium
ACHILMORRYZ mycorrhizal
ACHILNNOPSY nonphysical
ACHILNOORRT chlorinator
ACHILOOPTYZ zoophytical
ACHILOPPSTY hypoplastic
ACHILOSSTTW waistcloths
ACHIMMNOOSU monochasium
ACHIMNNNOOR nonharmonic
ACHIMNOPSTY amphictyons
ACHIMNOPTYY amphictyony
ACHIMNORSST monarchists
ACHIMOOOPST photomosaic
ACHIMOPPPSU hippocampus
ACHIMOPRSSY symposiarch
ACHIMOPSSTY scyphistoma
ACHIMORRSTT trichromats
ACHIMORRSTY chrismatory
ACHIMORSSTT chromatists
ACHINNOOPTY apocynthion
ACHINNOPSSY nanophysics
ACHINOOPSTT photonastic
ACHIOOPPRST apostrophic
ACHIOOPPRTT protopathic
ACHIOOPRTTU autotrophic
ACHIOOPRTUX auxotrophic
ACHIOOPSTTT photostatic
ACHIOPPRSTY saprophytic
ACHIOPRRSTU curatorship
ACHIOPRSSTY physiocrats
ACHIOPSSTTY attophysics
ACHKLMNOOST klootchmans
ACHKMNOOPRT Rockhampton
ACHLLNORSUY unscholarly
ACHLLOOPRST chloroplast
ACHLLOOPSSY playschools
ACHLMMOOORS chromosomal
ACHLMMOORSS schoolmarms
ACHLMOOPRST chromoplast
ACHLNOPRTYY lycanthropy
ACHMMNOOORT monochromat
ACHMOOORTTY thoracotomy
ACHNNOORRTU Harnoncourt
ACHNNOSTTUY nyctanthous
ACHNOOPSSYZ scyphozoans
ACHOOPRRSTY arthroscopy
ACIIIILMNTY inimicality
ACIIILMNOPT implication
ACIIILMNRTY criminality
ACIIILNNNOT inclination
ACIIILNNRST intrinsical
ACIIILNOPST politicians
ACIIILRSTTU ritualistic
ACIIIMNNORT crimination
ACIIINNOTTT nictitation
ACIIINOQSTU acquisition
ACIIKKKPRRT Kirkpatrick
ACIILLLOPTY politically
ACIILLMNOOS colonialism
ACIILLMNOOT collimation
ACIILLMNPUY municipally
ACIILLMOSUY maliciously
ACIILLMOTTY mitotically
ACIILLNNSTT scintillant
ACIILLNOOST colonialist
oscillation
ACIILLNOVVY convivially
ACIILLNPPRY principally
ACIILLOPRTY pictorially
ACIILLPRSTU pluralistic
ACIILLQUYZZ quizzically
ACIILMNNNOR noncriminal
ACIILMNNOPT incompliant
ACIILMNNOTU culmination
ACIILMNOOPT compilation
ACIILMNORTU tourmalinic
ACIILMNOSUY minaciously
ACIILMNSSTU masculinist
ACIILMNSTUY masculinity
ACIILMSTTUU mutualistic
ACIILNNOOTU inoculation
ACIILNNOPTU inculpation
ACIILNNORSY synclinoria
ACIILNNSTTU instinctual
ACIILNOPRSV provincials
ACIILNOPSSU suspicional
ACIILNOSTXY anxiolytics
ACIILNOTTUV cultivation
ACIILOPRTTY tropicality
ACIILORSTTU staurolitic
ACIILORSUVY vicariously
ACIILOSUVVY vivaciously
ACIIMMMNOST mammonistic
ACIIMMNNOOT commination
ACIIMMNORST romanticism
ACIIMMNOSST monasticism
ACIIMMNSSTU numismatics
ACIIMNOORSU acrimonious
ACIIMNORRST criminators
ACIIMNORRTY criminatory
ACIIMNORSTT romanticist
ACIIMNRSSTU manicurists
ACIIMOPRSSS prosaicisms
ACIIMOPRSTT tropismatic
ACIINNOOSTV invocations
ACIINNORTUV incurvation
ACIINNOSTTX intoxicants
ACIINOOPRST anisotropic
ACIINOORTTX intoxicator
ACIINOOSSST iconostasis
ACIINOOSSTT oscitations
ACIINOPRSST ascriptions
crispations
ACIINOPRTTU unpatriotic
ACIINORSSTT astrictions
ACIINORSTTU rustication
urtications
ACIINRSSSST narcissists
ACIINRTTTUY taciturnity
ACIIOPSSSTT psittacosis
ACIIORRRSTT cirrostrati
ACIIORRSTUU urticarious
ACIJNNOORTU conjuration
ACIKLPRTTUY platykurtic
ACIKNNORSYY synkaryonic
ACIKOOPRRTY prokaryotic
ACILLMNOORY moronically
ACILLMNOPTY compliantly
ACILLMNSUUY unmusically
ACILLMOORST collimators
ACILLMOOSTY osmotically
ACILLMOPSTY plasmolytic
ACILLMOTYYZ zymotically
ACILLNNOTUY continually
ACILLNOOSTU allocutions
ACILLOORRTT torticollar
ACILLOORSST oscillators
ACILLOORSTY oscillatory
ACILLOPPTYY polytypical
ACILMMMNOSU communalism
ACILMMNNOOU communional
ACILMMNOOOT commotional
ACILMMNOOTY commonality
ACILMMNOSTU communalist
ACILMMNOTUY communality
ACILMMORSSU commissural
ACILMNNOPTU uncompliant
ACILMNNOSTY nonmystical
ACILMNNOSYY synonymical
ACILMNOOPTY toponymical
ACILMNOSTUU cumulations
ACILMOOPSTX toxoplasmic
ACILMORSTUY customarily
ACILMRSTUUY muscularity
ACILNNOOOST consolation
ACILNNOOPRT nontropical
ACILNOOORST colorations
ACILNOOORTU colouration
ACILNOOPSTU copulations
ACILNOORSTU inoculators
ACILNOORTUY locutionary

ACILNOOSSTU	osculations
ACILNOOSTTT	cottontails
ACILNOPRTUY	inculpatory
ACILNORSSTU	ultrasonics
ACILNPPSSTU	supplicants
ACILNPTTUUY	punctuality
ACILOOPRRTY	corporality
ACILOORSTUY	atrociously
ACILOORSUVY	voraciously
ACILORSTTUV	cultivators
ACIMMNOORTY	comminatory
ACIMMNOOTTU	commutation
ACIMMOPSTTY	symptomatic
ACIMNNOORTU	mucronation
ACIMNOOOPTT	compotation
ACIMNOOPRSS	comparisons
ACIMNOOPTTU	computation
ACIMNOPRSTY	patronymics
ACIMNOPRTUY	importunacy
ACIMNPRSSTU	manuscripts
ACIMOOPRRST	corporatism
ACIMOOPRSTT	compatriots
ACINNNNOOST	inconsonant
ACINNNOOOTT	connotation
ACINNNOSTTU	continuants
ACINNOOORST	coronations
ACINNOOPRTT	contraption
ACINNOOPSTY	syncopation
ACINNOORTTU	continuator
ACINNOPSTTU	punctations
ACINNOPTTUU	punctuation
ACINNORSSTT	constraints
ACINNORSTTU	truncations
ACINNRSSTTU	incrustants
ACINOOOPRRT	corporation
ACINOOOPRTV	provocation
ACINOOOPSTT	cooptations
ACINOOPRRST	conspirator
ACINOOPRRTT	protraction
ACINOOPRRTU	procuration
ACINOOPRTXY	paroxytonic
ACINOORRSTU	contrarious
ACINOORRSUV	carnivorous
ACINOORSSTT	cartoonists
ACINPRRSSTT	transcripts
ACIOOPRRSTT	corporatist
ACIORRSSTTU	rusticators
ACIORSSSSSY	syssarcosis
ACJKNOOPRST	Port Jackson
ACKKNRSSTUW	knackwursts
ACLLMNOORUY	monocularly
ACLLMOORSUY	clamorously
ACLLMOSTUUU	altocumulus
ACLLNNORTUY	nocturnally
ACLLOPRSTYY	polycrystal
ACLLOPRSUUY	crapulously
ACLNNNOOSTY	consonantly
ACLNNOSSTTU	consultants
ACLNNOSSTUV	convulsants
ACLNOOORSTY	consolatory
ACLNOOPRRSU	proconsular
ACLNOORRSUY	rancorously
ACLOOPPRSUY	polycarpous
ACLOOPRSUXY	xylocarpous
ACMMNOORSTU	consummator
ACMMOORSTTU	commutators
ACMNOOOPRSU	monocarpous
ACMNORSTUUY	uncustomary
ACMOOOPRSTT	compotators
ACMOOOSSTTU	scotomatous
ACNOOPRRSTT	cotransport
ACNOOPRSSTY	syncopators
ACNOPRSTTUU	punctuators
ACOOOPRRRST	corporators
ACOOPRRRSTT	protractors
ACOOPRRRSTU	procurators
ACOOPRRRTUY	procuratory
ACOPRSSSSTT	sportscasts
ADDDEEEIRST	desiderated
ADDDEEERRSS	readdressed
ADDDEEFHILS	fiddleheads
ADDDEEGIRRS	disregarded
ADDDEEHNNRU	underhanded
ADDDEEHNRSU	dunderheads
ADDDEEHRRSU	rudderheads
ADDDEEILSSS	sidesaddles
ADDDEEIMORS	Madre de Dios
ADDDEELMOTU	demodulated
ADDDEENRSSU	unaddressed
ADDDEGIKLNS	skedaddling
ADDEEEEGNRT	degenerated
ADDEEEEHLLV	levelheaded
ADDEEEFILRS	federalised
ADDEEEFILRZ	federalized
ADDEEEFNRTU	unfederated
ADDEEEGLRTU	deregulated
ADDEEEHLLSW	swellheaded
ADDEEEHNPPR	apprehended
ADDEEEHRSSS	headdresses
ADDEEEIMMNS	misdemeaned
ADDEEEIMNRR	remaindered
ADDEEEIRSST	desiderates
ADDEEELNRSU	undersealed
ADDEEELRSST	saddletrees
ADDEEENORUV	endeavoured
ADDEEEOPRSS	desperadoes
ADDEEERRSSS	readdresses
ADDEEFGHINN	handfeeding
ADDEEFHLRUY	furaldehyde
ADDEEFIRSTU	disfeatured
ADDEEFMNRTU	defraudment
ADDEEGHILPY	pigheadedly
ADDEEGHNORW	wrongheaded
ADDEEGIMNNR	redemanding
ADDEEGINPRT	depredating
ADDEEGINRRT	intergraded
ADDEEGIRRRS	disregarder
ADDEEGNRSSU	guardedness
ADDEEGORRRT	retrograded
ADDEEHHLOTY	hotheadedly
ADDEEHHNRTU	thunderhead
ADDEEHIKNRT	kindhearted
ADDEEHILNPR	philandered
ADDEEHIMNSU	dehumanised
ADDEEHIMNUZ	dehumanized
ADDEEHIRRSS	sherardised
ADDEEHIRRSZ	sherardized
ADDEEHLMMSU	dummelheads
ADDEEHNOOSW	woodenheads
ADDEEHNORTW	downhearted
ADDEEIILMTT	delimitated
ADDEEIILNSS	desalinised
ADDEEIILNST	disentailed
ADDEEIILNSZ	desalinized
ADDEEIILSTV	devitalised
ADDEEIILTVZ	devitalized
ADDEEIJOPRS	jeopardised
ADDEEIJOPRZ	jeopardized
ADDEEILMORS	demoralised
ADDEEILMORZ	demoralized
ADDEEILNRRT	interlarded
ADDEEILOPRS	depolarised
ADDEEILOPRZ	depolarized
ADDEEILRRVY	daredevilry
ADDEEIMNNOT	denominated
ADDEEIMNPRR	reprimanded
ADDEEIMORRS	dromedaries
ADDEEIMRSTU	desideratum
ADDEEINOPRR	preordained
ADDEEINOPRT	depredation
ADDEEINRSTU	denaturised
ADDEEINRTUZ	denaturized
ADDEEIRSSTT	dissertated
ADDEELMOSTU	demodulates
ADDEELNNSTU	Sudetenland
ADDEELNPRUY	underplayed
ADDEELNRUUV	undervalued
ADDEELOPPTU	depopulated
ADDEELPRSST	stepladders
ADDEEMNNNRU	undermanned
ADDEENPRSTU	dunderpates
ADDEENPRSUU	unpersuaded
ADDEENRSTTU	understated
ADDEEOPRRST	depredators
ADDEEOPRRTY	depredatory
ADDEFFHLNOY	offhandedly
ADDEFFIIMRS	disaffirmed
ADDEFHINSSS	faddishness
ADDEFIIINNR	Ferdinand II
ADDEFIKRRST	Fredrikstad
ADDEFILORTU	fluoridated
ADDEFIORSUV	disfavoured
ADDEGGHORTU	goddaughter
ADDEGGIIIRT	digitigrade
ADDEGGILNRY	degradingly
ADDEGHINRTY	dehydrating
ADDEGHLORST	goldthreads
ADDEGHNORTU	dreadnought
ADDEGIIILST	digitalised
ADDEGIIILTZ	digitalized
ADDEGILLNRW	Grindelwald
ADDEGILMNNY	demandingly maddeningly
ADDEGIMNNNU	undemanding
ADDEGIMNORS	gormandised

ADDEGIMNORZ	gormandized
ADDEGINNOSU	undiagnosed
ADDEGINPRSU	superadding
ADDEGJMNTUY	Judgment Day
ADDEGLNRUUY	unguardedly
ADDEGMNORRS	dendrograms
ADDEHHMORTU	hardmouthed
ADDEHHNORST	shorthanded
ADDEHIILMOT	thalidomide
ADDEHILLLRT	Liddell Hart
ADDEHILNOPR	philodendra
ADDEHILNORS	Rhode Island
ADDEHILNSSS	laddishness
ADDEHILOPSU	diadelphous
ADDEHINORTY	dehydration
ADDEHIOPRSS	rhapsodised
ADDEHIOPRSZ	rhapsodized
ADDEHIRRTTY	trihydrated
ADDEHLLNORS	landholders
ADDEHLNOPRY	hydroplaned
ADDEHLORSST	stadholders
ADDEHLORSTT	stadtholder
ADDEHMORSUY	hydromedusa
ADDEHORRSTY	dehydrators
ADDEIIIMNTT	intimidated
ADDEIIINTUV	individuate
ADDEIILNORR	liriodendra
ADDEIILORST	idolatrised
ADDEIILORTZ	idolatrized
ADDEILLNNSU	disannulled
ADDEILNSUVY	unadvisedly
ADDEILOSVWY	disavowedly
ADDEILRSTTU	stridulated
ADDEINNOSTU	denudations
ADDEINNRRSU	underdrains
ADDEINOORSS	radiosondes
ADDEIOOPPSU	pseudopodia
ADDEIOPPRSV	disapproved
ADDELMNOPSY	paddymelons
ADDELMNOTUU	unmodulated
ADDELMOORTU	demodulator
ADDELNNORSW	wonderlands
ADDELNNRTUY	redundantly
ADDELNNTUUY	undauntedly
ADDELNOORSW	woodlanders
ADDEMNOOORT	rodomontade
ADDENNRSSTU	understands
ADDGGINNORW	downgrading
ADDGHILLNNO	landholding
ADDGHILNOOR	roadholding
ADDGHNORTUW	downdraught
ADDGIIIIMNT	dimidiating
ADDGILNNOOW	downloading
ADDHILLNOUZ	Zuidholland
ADDIIIIMNOT	dimidiation
ADDIIILNSUV	individuals
ADDILLMNORS	landlordism
ADEEEEFGHRT	featheredge
ADEEEEFHRRT	freehearted
ADEEEEGGRST	desegregate
ADEEEEGNRRT	regenerated
ADEEEEGNRST	degenerates
ADEEEEGRTTV	revegetated
ADEEEEILRRT	Terre Adélie
ADEEEENRTTX	exenterated
ADEEEFILNRT	deferential
ADEEEFILRSS	federalises
ADEEEFILRSZ	federalizes
ADEEEFKPRSS	speedfreaks
ADEEEFLORRS	freeloaders
ADEEEFNRSTT	fenestrated
ADEEEGHLPRT	telegraphed
ADEEEGILMNR	legerdemain
ADEEEGILNRS	generalised
ADEEEGILNRZ	generalized
ADEEEGILNSV	evangelised
ADEEEGILNVZ	evangelized
ADEEEGIMNRR	gendarmerie
ADEEEGIMNST	demagnetise
ADEEEGIMNTZ	demagnetize
ADEEEGINNRT	ingenerated tragedienne
ADEEEGJMNNU	Jean de Meung
ADEEEGLNNRR	Greenlander
ADEEEGLNORS	sloganeered
ADEEEGLRSTU	deregulates
ADEEEGMNNRT	derangement
ADEEEGNOTXY	deoxygenate
ADEEEGNRRRT	Grande-Terre
ADEEEGRRSSS	deergrasses
ADEEEHHINST	heathenised
ADEEEHHINTZ	heathenized
ADEEEHHPSSS	sheepsheads
ADEEEHLLORS	leaseholder
ADEEEHLPSSY	sleepyheads
ADEEEHLRSTT	letterheads
ADEEEHLRSTW	treadwheels
ADEEEHMORST	homesteader
ADEEEHNNNOR	enneahedron
ADEEEHNOPRT	openhearted
ADEEEHNRRSU	unrehearsed
ADEEEHPRSST	spreadsheet
ADEEEHPRSTU	superheated
ADEEEIILNTV	delineative
ADEEEILLMRS	Emerald Isle
ADEEEILNRST	eternalised
ADEEEILNRTV	interleaved
ADEEEILNRTZ	eternalized
ADEEEILSSUX	desexualise
ADEEEILSUXZ	desexualize
ADEEEIMNRTT	determinate
ADEEEIMNSST	mediateness
ADEEEIMPRTT	premeditate
ADEEEINNRTT	entertained intenerated
ADEEEINRTVW	interweaved
ADEEEINSSTT	Eisenstaedt
ADEEEIORRTT	deteriorate
ADEEEIORTVV	overdeviate
ADEEEIPRRTV	privateered
ADEEEJNRTUV	rejuvenated
ADEEEKLLPSW	sleepwalked
ADEEEKLRRST	deerstalker
ADEEELLNSWY	wensleydale
ADEEELLSSTT	tessellated
ADEEELMNNOW	needlewoman
ADEEELNNRSS	learnedness
ADEEELNRSST	relatedness
ADEEELNRSSW	newsdealers
ADEEELNRSUV	underleaves
ADEEELNRTTU	launderette
ADEEELNSSTX	exaltedness
ADEEELPRSTY	desperately
ADEEEMNNRST	endearments
ADEEEMNPRTT	departement
ADEEEMNRRTU	remunerated
ADEEEMOSTWW	meadowsweet
ADEEEMPRTTT	reattempted
ADEEENORRSV	endeavorers
ADEEENORRUV	endeavourer
ADEEENRRSSW	newsreaders
ADEEENRSSSV	adverseness
ADEEEORRTVW	overwatered
ADEEEPPRRTT	perpetrated
ADEEEPPRTTU	perpetuated
ADEEERRTTVX	extraverted
ADEEFFIINRT	differentia
ADEEFFORSTV	overstaffed
ADEEFGGLOPR	leapfrogged
ADEEFGHIRSU	figureheads
ADEEFGHORRT	forgathered
ADEEFGILNNY	deafeningly
ADEEFGILNOR	freeloading
ADEEFGINNRR	rangefinder
ADEEFGKLNPR	frankpledge
ADEEFHINORS	refashioned
ADEEFHIPSSS	spadefishes
ADEEFHORSTT	softhearted
ADEEFIIINNT	definientia
ADEEFIILSTU	feudalities
ADEEFILLMSS	damselflies
ADEEFILRSST	federalists
ADEEFINORST	federations
ADEEFINRRST	fraternised
ADEEFINRRSW	firewardens
ADEEFINRRTZ	fraternized
ADEEFIORSTU	feudatories
ADEEFIRSSTU	disfeatures
ADEEFLLORST	forestalled
ADEEFMNRSTY	defrayments
ADEEFNRRRST	transferred
ADEEFOOPRRR	proofreader
ADEEGGHLORS	loggerheads
ADEEGGIINRS	disagreeing
ADEEGGILRVY	aggrievedly
ADEEGGINNNR	endangering
ADEEGGINRRS	grangerised
ADEEGGINRRZ	grangerized
ADEEGGLORTW	waterlogged
ADEEGGMORRT	remortgaged
ADEEGGMORUY	demagoguery
ADEEGHHMORR	hemorrhaged
ADEEGHINNRR	rehardening
ADEEGHINPRS	grandeeship
ADEEGHINRRT	rethreading

ADEEGHINRST nearsighted
ADEEGHLRSTU slaughtered
ADEEGHMOPRR demographer
ADEEGHNNPRW grandnephew
ADEEGHNORTY hydrogenate
ADEEGIILLLS illegalised
ADEEGIILLLZ illegalized
ADEEGIILMTT legitimated
ADEEGIILNNT delineating
ADEEGIILNST gelatinised
ADEEGIILNTZ gelatinized
ADEEGIIMNNT ingeminated
ADEEGIIMNST enigmatised
ADEEGIIMNTZ enigmatized
ADEEGIINSTV designative
ADEEGIKMNRT demarketing
ADEEGILLORS allegorised
ADEEGILLORZ allegorized
ADEEGILNNRY endearingly
engrainedly
ADEEGILNNST disentangle
ADEEGILNOST delegations
ADEEGILNRRS ringleaders
ADEEGILNRSY delayerings
ADEEGILNTTU deglutinate
ADEEGILRRSU regularised
ADEEGILRRUZ regularized
ADEEGIMNNRT deraignment
ADEEGIMNPRT impregnated
ADEEGIMORRT gradiometer
ADEEGIMSTTU guestimated
ADEEGINNNSU ensanguined
ADEEGINNORV endeavoring
ADEEGINNOST denegations
ADEEGINNRTU undereating
ADEEGINNRTV denervating
ADEEGINORRS reorganised
ADEEGINORRZ reorganized
ADEEGINPRSS preassigned
ADEEGINPRSY panegyrised
ADEEGINPRYZ panegyrized
ADEEGINRRST intergrades
ADEEGINRTTU deuterating
ADEEGIORSUZ Diégo-Suarez
ADEEGJLMNTU judgemental
ADEEGLLNOSS goldenseals
ADEEGLNRSUZ underglazes
ADEEGLNRTUU unregulated
ADEEGLOPRSZ Pérez Galdós
ADEEGLORRTU deregulator
ADEEGMMOPRR deprogramme
ADEEGMNRRRY gerrymander
ADEEGMORTUY deuterogamy
ADEEGNNRRST transgender
ADEEGNORSSS dragonesses
ADEEGNRRSUZ gazunderers
ADEEGOORSSV overdosages
ADEEGOORSSW greasewoods
ADEEGORRRST retrogrades
ADEEHHIMRTY hemihydrate
ADEEHHISTWW whitewashed
ADEEHHLORRS shareholder
ADEEHHLOSSV shovelheads
ADEEHHNOPRT heptahedron
ADEEHHNORSX hexahedrons
ADEEHHNRSTU headhunters
ADEEHIIOPRS isodiaphere
ADEEHILLNOT endothelial
ADEEHILMRST thermalised
ADEEHILMRTZ thermalized
ADEEHILNOPT elephantoid
ADEEHILNORT lionhearted
ADEEHILNPRR philanderer
ADEEHILNSST deathliness
ADEEHILOPPS paedophiles
ADEEHILSSWY daisywheels
ADEEHIMNRUZ rehumanized
ADEEHIMNSSU dehumanises
ADEEHIMNSUZ dehumanizes
ADEEHINRSST disheartens
threadiness
ADEEHIPRRSS readerships
ADEEHIRRRSS hairdresser
ADEEHIRRSSS sherardises
ADEEHIRRSSZ sherardizes
ADEEHKLORST stakeholder
ADEEHKORRSW headworkers
ADEEHLLORSV slaveholder
ADEEHLLOSWY yellowheads
ADEEHLLSSTY deathlessly
ADEEHLMNORT endothermal
ADEEHLMNOTT mentholated
ADEEHLNNRST Netherlands
ADEEHLNORTY theory-laden
ADEEHLOORTW leatherwood
ADEEHLOOSSX aldohexoses
ADEEHLOPRST petrolheads
ADEEHNNOPRT pentahedron
ADEEHNNRSSU unharnessed
ADEEHNORRTT tetrahedron
ADEEHNOSSTW stonewashed
ADEEHNRSTUV unharvested
ADEEIIJNRRS jardinieres
ADEEIIKNRST keratinised
ADEEIIKNRTZ keratinized
ADEEIILLNRT interallied
ADEEIILMMSV medievalism
ADEEIILMMTY immediately
ADEEIILMNRS mineralised
ADEEIILMNRZ mineralized
ADEEIILMSTT delimitates
ADEEIILMSTV medievalist
ADEEIILNNOT delineation
ADEEIILNNST desinential
ADEEIILNRST residential
ADEEIILNSSS desalinises
ADEEIILNSSZ desalinizes
ADEEIILRSTV relativised
revitalised
ADEEIILRTVZ relativized
revitalized
ADEEIILSSTV devitalises
ADEEIILSTVZ devitalizes
ADEEIIMMNPT impedimenta
ADEEIIMNNPT pentamidine
ADEEIIMNNST inseminated
ADEEIIMNORT remediation
ADEEIIMNSST disseminate
ADEEIINRRTV veratridine
ADEEIINRSST distrainees
ADEEIINRSVV vivandieres
ADEEIINSSST dessiatines
ADEEIIPRSTV depravities
ADEEIIPRTUV repudiative
ADEEIIRSSTV adversities
ADEEIIRSTTW tidewaiters
ADEEIIRSTVV derivatives
ADEEIJOPRSS jeopardises
ADEEIJOPRSZ jeopardizes
ADEEIKNRRST dreikanters
ADEEIKRRSTV Kavir Desert
ADEEILLMOSS damoiselles
ADEEILLNRST reinstalled
ADEEILLPRSS espadrilles
ADEEILLRRSU derailleurs
ADEEILLSUVV vaudevilles
ADEEILMNORT endometrial
ADEEILMNRST derailments
streamlined
ADEEILMNRTT detrimental
ADEEILMOORT meteoroidal
ADEEILMORRS demoraliser
ADEEILMORRZ demoralizer
ADEEILMORSS demoralises
ADEEILMORSZ demoralizes
ADEEILMORTT dilatometer
ADEEILMSTUU demutualise
ADEEILMTUUZ demutualize
ADEEILNNPTT pentlandite
ADEEILNNPUX unexplained
ADEEILNNRST Landsteiner
ADEEILNNRTT interdental
ADEEILNORST delineators
ADEEILNPPRT interlapped
ADEEILNPRST interpleads
ADEEILNRSTU neutralised
ADEEILNRSTY sedentarily
ADEEILNRTUZ neutralized
ADEEILNRUWY unweariedly
ADEEILNSTTT dilettantes
ADEEILOPPRT lepidoptera
ADEEILOPRRS depolariser
ADEEILOPRRZ depolarizer
ADEEILOPRSS depolarises
ADEEILOPRSZ depolarizes
ADEEILORRSV revalorised
ADEEILORRVZ revalorized
ADEEILPPRTV livetrapped
ADEEILPQSSU sesquipedal
ADEEILPRSSU displeasure
ADEEIMMNORS misdemeanor
ADEEIMMNOSU eudaemonism
ADEEIMMRSSU mismeasured
ADEEIMNNORT renominated
ADEEIMNNOST denominates
emendations

ADEEIMNNPTU	antependium
ADEEIMNNRTT	determinant
	detrainment
ADEEIMNNTTU	edutainment
ADEEIMNOPRT	predominate
ADEEIMNOSTU	eudaemonist
ADEEIMNRSTY	sedimentary
ADEEIMORRST	radiometers
ADEEIMORSTT	stadiometer
ADEEIMORSTU	audiometers
ADEEIMRTTTY	tetradymite
ADEEINNORTV	denervation
ADEEINNRSSU	unreadiness
ADEEINNRTTV	inadvertent
ADEEINOPPRT	reappointed
ADEEINOPRST	desperation
ADEEINOPTTT	potentiated
ADEEINORRTV	overtrained
ADEEINOSTTT	detestation
ADEEINPRRSU	underpraise
ADEEINPRSST	pedestrians
ADEEINRSSTU	denaturises
ADEEINRSTUZ	denaturizes
ADEEIOPRRSV	overpraised
ADEEIOPRSSX	peroxidases
ADEEIOPRSTT	tetrapodies
ADEEIPRSSTU	pasteurised
ADEEIPRSTUV	depuratives
ADEEIPRSTUZ	pasteurized
ADEEIPRTTUV	vituperated
ADEEIRRSSTV	advertisers
ADEEIRRSSTW	watersiders
ADEEIRRSTVZ	advertizers
ADEEIRSSSTT	dissertates
ADEEJRRSSTU	readjusters
ADEEKLLMORU	leukodermal
ADEEKLMORSU	leukodermas
ADEEKLOPRSU	loudspeaker
ADEEKMRRSSS	dressmakers
ADEEKNRRSTU	undertakers
ADEELLMRSSY	dreamlessly
ADEELLNNRUY	unlearnedly
ADEELLNOSTW	stonewalled
ADEELLNRTUV	untravelled
ADEELLOPRTT	preallotted
ADEELMMNRTU	untrammeled
ADEELMNOORT	demonolater
ADEELNNRTUW	Unterwalden
ADEELNOORST	aldosterone
ADEELNOORUV	Nuevo Laredo
ADEELNORRSV	overlanders
ADEELNRRSUY	underlayers
ADEELNRRUUV	undervaluer
ADEELNRSSSU	laundresses
ADEELNRSTTU	laundrettes
ADEELNRSUUV	undervalues
ADEELNRTTVY	advertently
ADEELOOPRVY	parleyvooed
ADEELOPPRTU	repopulated
ADEELOPPSTU	depopulates
ADEEMMNNRST	remandments
ADEEMMNORTY	dynamometer
ADEEMNNNSSU	mundaneness
ADEEMNOPRRS	promenaders
ADEEMNORSTT	demonstrate
ADEEMNORSTW	tradeswomen
ADEEMNPRSTT	departments
ADEEMNPTTTU	unattempted
ADEEMNRRSTT	retardments
ADEEMNRSTTU	menstruated
ADEENOPRSVX	overexpands
ADEENPRSSST	depressants
ADEENPRSSSU	underpasses
ADEENQRRSSU	squanderers
ADEENRRSTUV	adventurers
ADEENRSSSSU	assuredness
ADEENRSSTTU	understates
ADEENRSSTUV	adventuress
ADEEOORRSTV	overroasted
ADEEOPRRSSV	overspreads
ADEFFILLMMM	flimflammed
ADEFFILNRTU	faultfinder
ADEFFILNSTU	insufflated
ADEFFIORSST	disafforest
ADEFGHINNOR	forehanding
ADEFGIILNOT	defoliating
ADEFGIILNSU	feudalising
ADEFGIILNUZ	feudalizing
ADEFGIIMNNU	unmagnified
ADEFGIINNYZ	denazifying
ADEFGILNORS	dragonflies
ADEFGILNRSY	ladyfingers
ADEFGINORRS	firedragons
ADEFGIPPRTW	giftwrapped
ADEFGKNOORS	godforsaken
ADEFGLLRRUY	regardfully
ADEFHIKNRST	rankshifted
ADEFHILOORR	foolhardier
ADEFHINPRST	pathfinders
ADEFHOORSSW	foreshadows
ADEFIILMNNS	infieldsman
ADEFIILMNPU	unamplified
ADEFIILNNRS	Lindisfarne
ADEFIILNOOT	defoliation
ADEFIILNQUU	unqualified
ADEFIILNRTT	infiltrated
ADEFIILORTT	trifoliated
ADEFIINNOTU	infeudation
ADEFIINSSTU	unsatisfied
ADEFILMNORS	manifolders
ADEFILNOORT	defloration
ADEFILNORTU	fluorinated
ADEFILOORST	defoliators
ADEFILORSTU	fluoridates
ADEFILSSTTU	distasteful
ADEFIMNOORT	deformation
ADEFINOOPRR	rainproofed
ADEFINOORRS	foreordains
ADEFINRRSSU	fundraisers
ADEFLNORUUV	unflavoured
ADEFLOOPSTY	splayfooted
ADEFLORRSTW	afterworlds
ADEFMNORRST	transformed
ADEFMNORSTW	draftswomen
ADEFNORRSSW	forwardness
	frowardness
ADEGGGIINNS	disengaging
ADEGGGLLLOY	lollygagged
ADEGGHORSUY	hydragogues
ADEGGIILMPR	pilgrimaged
ADEGGIINNRT	denigrating
ADEGGIINNST	designating
ADEGGILNRUU	unguligrade
ADEGGIMMOSU	demagoguism
ADEGGIMOPSU	pedagoguism
ADEGGINNRUZ	gazundering
ADEGGINSTTU	degustating
ADEGHHIKNST	knightheads
ADEGHHILNRS	highlanders
ADEGHHINNTU	headhunting
ADEGHIIPRST	graphitised
ADEGHIIPRTZ	graphitized
ADEGHILLNNS	handselling
ADEGHILRSTT	starlighted
ADEGHINNORV	overhanding
ADEGHINNRTU	unthreading
ADEGHINPRSS	headsprings
	springheads
ADEGHIOPRVY	videography
ADEGHIRSTTU	draughtiest
ADEGHLMOOOT	homologated
ADEGHLMOOSU	Douglas-Home
ADEGHLOPRXY	xylographed
ADEGHMNOOPR	monographed
ADEGHMNORRT	grandmother
ADEGHMNRSTU	draughtsmen
ADEGHOOPRRX	doxographer
ADEGHORRSSU	Horse Guards
ADEGHORRTUV	overdraught
ADEGHORSSUU	guardhouses
ADEGIIILNTV	invigilated
ADEGIIILSST	digitalises
ADEGIIILSTZ	digitalizes
ADEGIIIMNNS	deaminising
ADEGIIIMNNZ	deaminizing
ADEGIIIMNST	mediatising
ADEGIIIMNTZ	mediatizing
ADEGIIINRST	dignitaries
ADEGIILLSSU	seguidillas
ADEGIILMNPS	mispleading
ADEGIILNNRY	ingrainedly
ADEGIILNOST	digestional
	gelatinoids
ADEGIILNPSS	displeasing
ADEGIIMNOSS	misdiagnose
ADEGIIMNRTT	readmitting
ADEGIIMNTTU	unmitigated
ADEGIIMSSTT	stigmatised
ADEGIIMSTTZ	stigmatized
ADEGIINNORT	denigration
	derationing
ADEGIINNOST	designation
ADEGIINNRTT	denitrating
ADEGIINOPTV	videotaping
ADEGIINORSS	disorganise
ADEGIINORSZ	disorganize

ADEGIINORTV invigorated
ADEGIINPRTU repudiating
ADEGIINRRWW wiredrawing
ADEGIINRSTV advertising
ADEGIINRTTU ingratitude
ADEGIINRTTX extraditing
ADEGIINRTVZ advertizing
ADEGIJNRSTU readjusting
ADEGIKMNRSS dressmaking
ADEGIKNNRTU undertaking
ADEGILLOSSU gladioluses
ADEGILMORUZ glamourized
ADEGILNNORV overlanding
ADEGILNNRSS sanderlings
ADEGILNNRUY underlaying
ADEGILNNRWY wanderingly
ADEGILNNSSU languidness
ADEGILNOORV overloading
ADEGILNORST Tselinograd
ADEGILNORSY grandiosely
ADEGILOOPST paedologist
ADEGILRSTUV divulgaters
ADEGIMNNOPR promenading
ADEGIMNORRS gormandiser
ADEGIMNORRZ gormandizer
ADEGIMNORSS gormandises
ADEGIMNORSU gourmandise
ADEGIMNORSZ gormandizes
ADEGIMNPSTU despumating
ADEGIMORSST dogmatisers
ADEGIMORSTZ dogmatizers
ADEGINNORSU unorganised
ADEGINNORUZ unorganized
ADEGINNPRUY underpaying
ADEGINNQRSU squandering
ADEGINNRRTU underrating
ADEGINNRRUW unrewarding
ADEGINNRTUV adventuring
ADEGINNSTUY unsteadying
ADEGINORRST denigrators
ADEGINORRTV overtrading
ADEGINORRVW overdrawing
ADEGINORSST designators
ADEGINORSTY designatory
ADEGINOSTTU degustation
ADEGINPRSSW wingspreads
ADEGINPRSTU depasturing
ADEGINRSSYY dyssynergia
ADEGKNRRRSU krugerrands
ADEGLMOORTY dermatology
ADEGLMOPRTU promulgated
ADEGLNORSUY dangerously
ADEGMMMNOOR monogrammed
ADEGMNORRST strongarmed
ADEGNNOORSU androgenous
ADEGNORRTUW groundwater
ADEGOOPRSST gasteropods
ADEHHIILPRT diphtherial
ADEHHIOPPST phosphatide
ADEHHIORRSS horseradish
ADEHHIRRSTW hitherwards
ADEHHIRRTTW thitherward
ADEHHIRRTWW whitherward
ADEHHIRSSSW dishwashers
ADEHIIIOPST idiopathies
ADEHIILOPSU audiophiles
ADEHIIMNOPR diamorphine
ADEHIIMNRTU antheridium
ADEHIIMNSSS maidishness
ADEHIIMRSTT mithridates
ADEHIIOPRSS diaphoresis
ADEHIIORSTT historiated
ADEHIIPSSUU euphausiids
ADEHIKOORST Theodorakis
ADEHILLNRST disenthrall
ADEHILLORSU loudhailers
ADEHILNNRST hinterlands
ADEHILNRSST disenthrals
ADEHILOOPRS drosophilae
ADEHILORSTY hysteroidal
ADEHILPSSTU disulphates
ADEHIMNORSS admonishers
ADEHIMORRTY radiothermy
ADEHIMPSSTY sympathised
ADEHIMPSTYZ sympathized
ADEHIMRRSTT thirdstream
ADEHINNRSTU untarnished
ADEHINNRSUV unvarnished
ADEHINNRTTW handwritten
ADEHINOOPRS radiophones
ADEHINOORTZ antherozoid
ADEHINORRRS Radnorshire
ADEHINOSSSW shadowiness
ADEHINPPRST transhipped
ADEHINQRRTU hindquarter
ADEHINRSSTY hydrastines
ADEHINRSTTW withstander
ADEHIOPPSSY diapophyses
ADEHIOPRSSS rhapsodises
ADEHIOPRSSZ rhapsodizes
ADEHIORRSST diarthroses
ADEHIPRRSST traderships
ADEHIPRRSSW wardерships
ADEHIPRSSTW stewardship
ADEHIRRSTTY trihydrates
ADEHIRRSTWW withdrawers
ADEHIRSSSTY hydrastises
ADEHJMNOOOR Mohenjo-Daro
ADEHKNORSST handstrokes
ADEHLLLMORS smallholder
ADEHLLLORST stallholder
ADEHLMNORST motherlands
ADEHLNNORRT Northlander
ADEHLNOPRSY hydroplanes
ADEHLNOPSTU sulphonated
ADEHLNORSTV Thorvaldsen
ADEHLORSTYY hydrolysate
ADEHLPRSTUU sulphurated
ADEHMNOORTY monohydrate
ADEHMNOSTTU muttonheads
ADEHMOOPPPT photomapped
ADEHMORRSTW threadworms
ADEHNOOPRRS androphores
ADEHNOOPRST theropodans
ADEHOOPSTTT photostated
ADEHOORSSVW overshadows
ADEIIIILNST initialised
ADEIIIILNTZ initialized
ADEIIILMRST militarised
ADEIIILMRTZ militarized
ADEIIILMSST dissimilate
ADEIIILRSTV trivialised
ADEIIILRTVZ trivialized
ADEIIIMNSTT intimidates
ADEIIIMRSTY semiaridity
ADEIIINNNPP pinnipedian
ADEIIINNTTU uninitiated
ADEIIIOPSTV diapositive
ADEIIIPRSST disparities
ADEIIIPSSTV dissipative
ADEIIISSSTU assiduities
ADEIILLLOPS ellipsoidal
ADEIILLMNTU illuminated
ADEIILLMPSX maxillipeds
ADEIILLNNSS Line Islands
ADEIILLORTY editorially
ADEIILLOSTV volatilised
ADEIILLOTVZ volatilized
ADEIILLSSTT distillates
ADEIILMNNOS dimensional
ADEIILMNORS meridionals
ADEIILMNRSU semidiurnal
ADEIILMSSTU dissimulate
ADEIILNNSSV invalidness
ADEIILNOPRR Pinar del Río
ADEIILNOPST depilations
ADEIILNORSV diversional
ADEIILORRST idolatriser
ADEIILORRTZ idolatrizer
ADEIILORSST idolatrises
ADEIILORSTZ idolatrizes
ADEIIMMNSTU mediastinum
ADEIIMNNSTU mundanities
ADEIIMNOPSS impassioned
ADEIIMNORSS readmission
ADEIIMNOSST staminodies
ADEIIMNOSTT meditations
ADEIIMNRSST administers
ADEIIMPRSSU praesidiums
ADEIIMRSTTX taxidermist
ADEIINNNOTT indentation
ADEIINNOOPT opinionated
ADEIINNORTT denitration
ADEIINNOSTT destination
ADEIINNOSTX indexations
ADEIINOPRTT partitioned, trepidation
ADEIINOPRTU repudiation
ADEIINOPRTV deprivation
ADEIINOPSST Passiontide
ADEIINORSTU auditioners
ADEIINORSTV derivations
ADEIINORSTY seditionary
ADEIINORTTX extradition
ADEIINPRSTY stipendiary

ADEIINPSSST	inspissated
ADEIINQSTTU	equidistant
ADEIINRRSST	distrainers
ADEIINRSTVY	vineyardist
ADEIIOPPRTT	propitiated
ADEIIPRRSSS	dispraisers
ADEIIPRSSST	dissipaters
ADEIIPSTTUV	disputative
ADEIJLNORSU	journalised
ADEIJLNORUZ	journalized
ADEIJMMNRSW	windjammers
ADEIKLMSTTU	multitasked
ADEIKLNOSSU	soundalikes
ADEILLMRRST	drillmaster
ADEILLORTUV	outrivalled
ADEILLRSTTU	illustrated
ADEILLSSTUU	Îles du Salut
ADEILMMOOTY	myelomatoid
ADEILMNNSSU	maudlinness
ADEILMNOPRS	palindromes
ADEILMNOPRT	trampolined
ADEILMNOPTU	deplumation
ADEILMNRSST	dismantlers
ADEILMOOSSY	amyloidoses
ADEILMORTTY	dilatometry
ADEILNOOPRT	periodontal
ADEILNOOSTV	devotionals
ADEILNOPRSU	unpolarised
ADEILNOPRUY	pleurodynia
ADEILNOPRUZ	unpolarized
ADEILNQSSSU	squalidness
ADEILNRSTWW	windlestraw
ADEILNRSTWZ	Switzerland
ADEILNSSTUY	sustainedly
ADEILOPPRSS	predisposal
ADEILOPPRSU	popularised
ADEILOPPRUZ	popularized
ADEILOPQRSU	quadripoles
ADEILOPRRTY	predatorily
ADEILOPRSTT	tetraploids
ADEILRSSTTU	stridulates
ADEIMMNNOPU	pandemonium
ADEIMMNOOST	somatomedin
ADEIMMNRSST	masterminds
ADEIMMNSSTT	dismastment
ADEIMNNOORT	denominator
ADEIMNNOPRT	predominant
ADEIMNNORST	ordainments
ADEIMNNQRUU	quadrennium
ADEIMNOORST	moderations
ADEIMNOPSTU	despumation
ADEIMNORRSS	randomisers
ADEIMNORRSZ	randomizers
ADEIMNOTTUV	unmotivated
ADEIMNRRSUY	nurserymaid
ADEIMNRRTUY	rudimentary
ADEIMNRSTTT	transmitted
ADEIMNRSTUV	adventurism
ADEIMOOSTTU	autotomised
ADEIMOOTTUZ	autotomized
ADEIMORSTWW	mowdiewarts
ADEIMRSTUUV	duumvirates
ADEINNOOSTT	denotations detonations
ADEINNOPPTU	unappointed
ADEINNOPSWW	windowpanes
ADEINNORSSW	rawinsondes
ADEINNORSTT	nonstriated
ADEINNSSSTT	distantness
ADEINNSSTUU	unsustained
ADEINOOPPRT	apportioned
ADEINOOPRTT	deportation
ADEINOPRSTU	depurations
ADEINOPSTTU	deputations
ADEINORSTUW	autowinders
ADEINPRSSST	dispersants
ADEINRSTTUV	adventurist
ADEINRSTTUY	testudinary
ADEIOPPRSSV	disapproves
ADEIOPRRSTU	repudiators
ADEIORRSSTT	dissertator
ADEIORSSSTT	siderostats
ADEJMNNORTU	adjournment
ADEJMNSSTTU	adjustments
ADEJMOORRRS	major orders
ADELLMOPSSY	plasmolysed
ADELLMOPSYZ	plasmolyzed
ADELLNSSTUY	dauntlessly
ADELLOOPRRT	petrodollar
ADELLOORRRS	roadrollers
ADELLOORRSU	eurodollars
ADELMMOPSSS	plasmodesms
ADELMNOORTY	demonolatry
ADELMNORRTU	ultramodern
ADELMNORSTW	Westmorland
ADELMOPSSTU	deutoplasms
ADELNOPPTUU	unpopulated
ADELNPRRSTU	Rupert's Land
ADELOPQRSUU	quadrupoles
ADELOPRRRSY	Lord's Prayer
ADELOPRRSWY	swordplayer
ADELPQRSTUU	quadruplets
ADEMMMNORSU	memorandums
ADEMMNNOUYY	Maundy money
ADEMMNORTYY	dynamometry
ADEMNOOPSSU	pseudomonas
ADENNOPRRST	transponder
ADENNORRRSU	roadrunners
ADENOPRRSTT	transported
ADENORSSSUU	arduousness
ADENORSSTUW	outwardness
ADENORSTUUV	adventurous
ADENPRSSSUU	unsurpassed
ADFFHINOSST	standoffish
ADFGHIINNPT	pathfinding
ADFGIIILNPY	lapidifying
ADFGIILLNSU	fusillading
ADFGIILMNNO	manifolding
ADFGIINORSV	disfavoring
ADFGINORRSU	fairgrounds
ADFHILLOORY	foolhardily
ADFHINNOOST	infanthoods
ADFIIILLNNU	nullifidian
ADFIIILNOSS	solifidians
ADFIILMNTUU	latifundium
ADFIMNOPRRU	panduriform
ADFINNOORRZ	rinforzando
ADFINNOOSTU	foundations
ADFINRSSSTT	standfirsts
ADGGIIILNOS	dialogising
ADGGIIILNOZ	dialogizing
ADGGIILNTUV	divulgating
ADGGIIMNOST	dogmatising
ADGGIIMNOTZ	dogmatizing
ADGHHILNOPT	diphthongal
ADGHHOPRRSY	hydrographs
ADGHHOPRRYY	hydrography
ADGHIILMNNS	mishandling
ADGHIIMNNOS	admonishing
ADGHIINNRTW	handwriting
ADGHIINRTWW	withdrawing
ADGHIKNORRW	hardworking
ADGHINNPRSS	handsprings
ADGHIOPRTTY	dittography
ADGHMRRRUYY	hydrargyrum
ADGIIILNQTU	liquidating
ADGIIILOOSS	idioglossia
ADGIIINNNOT	indignation
ADGIIINNOTU	auditioning
ADGIIINNRST	distraining
ADGIIINOSTZ	diazotising
ADGIIINOTZZ	diazotizing
ADGIIINPRSS	dispraising
ADGIIINPSST	dissipating
ADGIIKNNPPS	kidnappings
ADGIILLNOSW	disallowing
ADGIILMNNST	dismantling
ADGIILMNRSY	disarmingly
ADGIILNNNTY	indignantly
ADGIILNNPST	displanting
ADGIILNNSSW	windlassing
ADGIILNOTUV	divulgation
ADGIILOORST	radiologist
ADGIILOOSTU	audiologist
ADGIILOPRTY	prodigality
ADGIIMNNORS	randomising
ADGIIMNNORZ	randomizing
ADGIINOPPRR	airdropping
ADGIINOPTUY	audiotyping
ADGIINORSTY	grandiosity
ADGIKNNOORT	Gordian knot
ADGILMNOSUW	guildswoman
ADGILNNOPWY	downplaying
ADGILNOORST	andrologist Stalinogrod
ADGILNPQRUU	quadrupling
ADGILORSTUV	divulgators
ADGIMMNORSU	gourmandism
ADGINNOSTTU	outstanding
ADGINRRSSTW	drawstrings
ADGLNOPRSUY	playgrounds
ADGNNOORSUY	androgynous
ADGNOOORRST	dragonroots

ADGORRSTTUY	Dry Tortugas
ADHHNOSSTTU	thousandths
ADHHOORRTXY	hydrothorax
ADHIIMSSTTU	humidistats
ADHIIOPPSSY	diapophysis
ADHIIORRSST	diarthrosis
ADHILNNORST	North Island
ADHILNOSSTU	South Island
ADHILOOPRSS	drosophilas
ADHIMOOPPSU	amphipodous
ADHINNOOOST	nationhoods
ADHINNOPRSX	androsphinx
ADHINOOORTT	orthodontia
ADHINOOPRST	anthropoids
ADHINOOPRSZ	rhizopodans
ADHIOPRSSST	rhapsodists
ADHKNNORSTU	drunkathons
ADHLNOPSSSW	splashdowns
ADHLNORRTWY	northwardly
ADHLORSTUWY	southwardly
ADHNOOPQRUY	quadrophony
ADIIILLMSUV	diluvialism
ADIIILMNTUV	diminutival
ADIIILNOOST	idolisation
ADIIILNOOTZ	idolization
ADIIILNOQTU	liquidation
ADIIIMNORTT	intimidator
ADIIIMOSSTT	mastoiditis
ADIIINNOSTV	divinations
ADIIINOOSST	iodisations
ADIIINOOSTX	oxidisation
ADIIINOOSTZ	iodizations
ADIIINOOTXZ	oxidization
ADIIINOPSST	dissipation
ADIIINORSVY	divisionary
ADIIIOPRSTT	parotiditis
ADIILLNOQRU	quadrillion
ADIILLOPPST	lipidoplast
ADIILMNNOST	mandolinist
ADIILMOOSSY	amyloidosis
ADIILMOPRRS	primordials
ADIILMOPSTT	diplomatist
ADIILNRSSTU	industrials
ADIILOQRSTU	liquidators
ADIIMMNOSTU	staminodium
ADIIMNNOOST	admonitions
	dominations
ADIIMNRSSST	misandrists
ADIIMOPRSST	prismatoids
ADIIMORSTUU	auditoriums
ADIINNNOSTU	inundations
ADIINNOORST	ordinations
ADIINNORSTU	indurations
ADIINOPPSST	disappoints
ADIINOPSTTU	disputation
ADIINORRSST	distrainors
ADIINOSSSSU	dissuasions
ADIIOOPRSUV	avoirdupois
ADIIOPRSSST	dissipators
ADIIOPRSSTT	podiatrists
ADIIOPSTTUY	audiotypist
ADIKLNRSSTU	Truk Islands
ADIKLOOSTVV	Vladivostok
ADILLLOOPPY	polyploidal
ADILLMOPSYY	sympodially
ADILLNSSSTT	standstills
ADILMNOOSTU	modulations
ADILMOPSSST	psalmodists
ADILNNOSSTY	dissonantly
ADILNNOSTUU	undulations
ADILORRSTTU	stridulator
ADILOSSSUUY	assiduously
ADIMOOPRSUY	myriapodous
ADINNOOPPPT	Pontoppidan
ADINNOPSSTT	standpoints
ADLLMORSSSW	smallswords
ADLLOOOSWWW	woodswallow
ADLMOPRSUWY	mouldywarps
ADLNOOPRSUY	polyandrous
ADMOOOPSSTT	stomatopods
ADNNOOPRRST	transpondor
ADNNORRSTUU	turnarounds
ADNOOPRRSTU	protandrous
ADOOOPRSSUU	sauropodous
AEEEEFLLNST	fenestellae
AEEEEGKMPRS	gamekeepers
AEEEEGKPRST	gatekeepers
AEEEEGNRRST	regenerates
AEEEEGRSTTV	revegetates
AEEEEHILRST	etherealise
AEEEEHILRTZ	etherealize
AEEEEHLRTTT	leatherette
AEEEELNOPST	elaeoptenes
AEEEENRSTTX	exenterates
AEEEFGIKNPS	safekeeping
AEEEFGIRRRT	refrigerate
AEEEFGLNRSU	enfleurages
AEEEFHINRRT	hereinafter
AEEEFHLRSST	featherless
AEEEFILNRRT	referential
AEEEFLLNNTT	flannelette
AEEEFLMPRSU	superfemale
AEEEFLNSSSU	easefulness
AEEEFLRSSTU	featureless
AEEEFNRRSST	transferees
AEEEFPRSTTU	superfetate
AEEEGGIKMNP	gamekeeping
AEEEGGILNOS	genealogies
AEEEGGIRSTV	segregative
AEEEGGMMNOU	emmenagogue
AEEEGGMNNST	engagements
AEEEGGNNRRT	Gretna Green
AEEEGHLPRRT	telegrapher
AEEEGHNRRST	greenhearts
AEEEGILMMRR	lammergeier
AEEEGILNRRS	generaliser
AEEEGILNRRZ	generalizer
AEEEGILNRSS	generalises
AEEEGILNRSV	evangeliser
AEEEGILNRSZ	generalizes
AEEEGILNRVZ	evangelizer
AEEEGILNSSV	evangelises
AEEEGILNSUV	eigenvalues
AEEEGILNSVZ	evangelizes
AEEEGIMNSST	metagenesis
AEEEGINNRST	ingenerates
AEEEGINORTT	renegotiate
AEEEGINPRRT	peregrinate
AEEEGINRRTT	reintegrate
AEEEGINRTTV	vinegarette
AEEEGKLOPRS	goalkeepers
AEEEGLMMRRY	lammergeyer
AEEEGLMNNRT	enlargement
AEEEGLMNRST	regalements
AEEEGLNNRSS	generalness
AEEEGLNOSST	eaglestones
AEEEGLNSSSS	agelessness
AEEEGMNNRSS	germaneness
AEEEGMNNRST	enragements
AEEEGNORRRT	regenerator
AEEEGPRSSSX	expressages
AEEEGQSSTUU	squeteagues
AEEEHHINSST	heathenises
AEEEHHINSTZ	heathenizes
AEEEHHLPTTT	heptathlete
AEEEHHMNORX	hexahemeron
AEEEHHNNSST	heathenness
AEEEHILNNPT	elephantine
AEEEHILPSTT	telepathise
AEEEHILPTTZ	telepathize
AEEEHILRTTY	ethereality
AEEEHILSSTT	telesthesia
AEEEHIMMNNT	methenamine
AEEEHIMMSST	hematemesis
AEEEHIMPRSZ	reemphasize
AEEEHIMSSTT	metathesise
AEEEHIMSTTZ	metathesize
AEEEHINNTUV	Haute-Vienne
AEEEHINSTTZ	anesthetize
AEEEHLLMPRY	ephemerally
AEEEHLMPPRT	pamphleteer
AEEEHLNPTTT	pentathlete
AEEEHLPRRWY	prayer wheel
AEEEHMPRSTT	heptameters
AEEEHNORSTY	honeyeaters
AEEEHNPRSST	parentheses
AEEEHNRRSTT	threateners
AEEEHOPRRSS	aerospheres
AEEEHPRRSTU	superheater
AEEEHRSSTTW	sweethearts
AEEEIINPPRT	peripeteian
AEEEIIPPRST	peripeteias
AEEEIIRRTTV	reiterative
AEEEILNORRS	Sierra Leone
AEEEILNRRTT	interrelate
AEEEILNRRTV	reverential
AEEEILNRSST	eternalises
AEEEILNRSTV	interleaves
AEEEILNRSTX	externalise
AEEEILNRSTZ	eternalizes
AEEEILNRTXZ	externalize
AEEEILPRRTT	preliterate
AEEEILRSSTV	severalties
AEEEIMNPRTT	intemperate
AEEEIMNRRST	Armentières
AEEEIMNRTTX	exterminate

AEEEIMNRTUV enumerative
AEEEIMPRSTT Empire State
AEEEIMQRRTU marqueterie
AEEEINNNSTV antivenenes
AEEEINNRRTT entertainer
AEEEINNRSTT intenerates
AEEEINOPRSU europeanise
AEEEINOPRUZ europeanize
AEEEINORTVX exonerative
AEEEINPRSST septenaries
AEEEINPRTTV penetrative
AEEEINRRSTT Eastern rite
AEEEINRRTVW interweaver
AEEEINRSTVW interweaves
AEEEINSSSVV evasiveness
AEEEJKRRRST tearjerkers
AEEEJNRSTUV rejuvenates
AEEEKLLOSTX exoskeletal
AEEEKLLPRSW sleepwalker
AEEEKPSSSTW sweepstakes
AEEELLLMNTY elementally
AEEELLORTTT teetotaller
AEEELLSSSTT tessellates
AEEELMMNNPT empanelment
AEEELMMNPST empalements
AEEELMNNSTV enslavement
AEEELMNRSTT manteltrees
mantletrees
AEEELMPRTTY temperately
AEEELMRSSSU measureless
AEEELNNRSST eternalness
AEEEMMNORST anemometers
AEEEMMNPRTT temperament
AEEEMMNRSTU measurement
AEEEMNNNRST ensnarement
AEEEMNNRTTT entreatment
AEEEMNNRTTY tenementary
AEEEMNOSSSW awesomeness
AEEEMNPRSTT pentameters
AEEEMNRRSTU remunerates
AEEEMNRRSUV maneuverers
AEEEMNRSTTT restatement
AEEEMORRSUV overmeasure
AEEEMPRRTTU temperature
AEEEMRRSTTT tetrameters
AEEENNRSSST earnestness
AEEENOPRSTT stearoptene
AEEENORRSTV overearnest
AEEENPRRSTV perseverant
AEEENRSSSTU austereness
AEEEPPRRSTT perpetrates
AEEEPPRSTTU perpetuates
AEEEQRSSTTU sequestrate
AEEERRSSTYY yesteryears
AEEFFGRSTTU suffragette
AEEFFHORRST forefathers
AEEFFLNRSSU fearfulness
AEEFFLNSSTU fatefulness
AEEFFORRSST reafforests
AEEFGGIILNR filagreeing
AEEFGHILNSS angelfishes
AEEFGHINRST featherings
AEEFGHORRST foregathers
AEEFGHORRTT heterograft
AEEFGILLNRW farewelling
AEEFGILNRSS fragileness
AEEFGILSSTU fatigueless
AEEFGIMNRTZ fragmentize
AEEFGINNRST refastening
AEEFGINRRRT refrigerant
AEEFGLLORVY Valley Forge
AEEFGMNNRTT engraftment
AEEFGORRRSU fourrageres
AEEFHHISSST sheatfishes
AEEFHHORSTU housefather
AEEFHILNNPS halfpennies
AEEFHILNRST Riefenstahl
AEEFHINPRST pinfeathers
AEEFHIPRSSS spearfishes
AEEFHLLMNST mantelshelf
AEEFHLNSSSW newsflashes
AEEFHLNSSTU hatefulness
AEEFHLOPPRS leafhoppers
AEEFHLOPSST felspathose
AEEFHMORSTT fathometers
AEEFHPRSSTT stepfathers
AEEFIILNNRT inferential
AEEFIILOTVX exfoliative
AEEFILLNORX reflexional
AEEFILNORTV overinflate
AEEFILOPRRT proliferate
AEEFIMNNRRT refrainment
AEEFIMNOSST manifestoes
AEEFIMNRRST freemartins
AEEFIMOPRRT imperforate
AEEFIMORRTV reformative
AEEFINRRRST fraterniser
AEEFINRRRTZ fraternizer
AEEFINRRSST fraternises
AEEFINRRSTZ fraternizes
AEEFIOPRRTV perforative
AEEFKLNSSUW wakefulness
AEEFLLNNOST fontanelles
AEEFLLNSSTU fustanelles
AEEFLLORRST forestaller
AEEFLLPRSUU pleasureful
AEEFLMORRTU reformulate
AEEFLNRSSTU tearfulness
AEEFMNORRSY freemasonry
AEEFNNOPRSS profaneness
AEEFNORRRSW forewarners
AEEFNRRRRST transferrer
AEEFNRRRSST retransfers
AEEFOQRRRTU forequarter
AEEFORRRSSW forswearers
AEEGGGINRST segregating
AEEGGHINRRT regathering
AEEGGHIOPRS geographies
AEEGGHOPRRS geographers
AEEGGIINORS seigniorage
AEEGGIKLNOP goalkeeping
AEEGGILNOST genealogist
AEEGGILNRRS glengarries
AEEGGIMNOSS gamogenesis
AEEGGINORRV overgearing
AEEGGINORST segregation
AEEGGINQSTU gigantesque
AEEGGINRRRS grangeriser
AEEGGINRRRZ grangerizer
AEEGGINRRSS grangerises
AEEGGINRRSZ grangerizes
AEEGGIRRTTU regurgitate
AEEGGMORRST remortgages
AEEGGNOSTTW waggonettes
AEEGGORRSST segregators
AEEGGORSTTY geostrategy
AEEGHHIOPST theophagies
AEEGHHITVWY heavyweight
AEEGHHMORRS hemorrhages
AEEGHIIMRRT Margrethe II
AEEGHIKLLNU keelhauling
AEEGHIKMSTW makeweights
AEEGHILNPRS generalship
AEEGHILNPTT telepathing
AEEGHILPSST legateships
AEEGHIMPRSY hypergamies
AEEGHINNRTT threatening
AEEGHINNRTW enwreathing
AEEGHINORRV overhearing
AEEGHINORTV overheating
AEEGHINORVZ Herzegovina
AEEGHINRRST ingatherers
AEEGHIPPRRS epigraphers
AEEGHIPPRTW paperweight
AEEGHKNNRSS greenshanks
AEEGHLNOPRS selenograph
AEEGHLNSTVW wavelengths
AEEGHLRRSTU slaughterer
AEEGHMNOOST homogenates
AEEGHMOOPRT gametophore
AEEGHMOPTTY gametophyte
AEEGHNPRSTV stevengraph
AEEGHOPRRRX xerographer
AEEGHOPRRST stereograph
AEEGHOPSSSU esophaguses
AEEGIIKLNRT granitelike
AEEGIILLLSS illegalises
AEEGIILLLSZ illegalizes
AEEGIILLSTV legislative
AEEGIILLTTU aiguillette
AEEGIILMSTT legitimates
AEEGIILNNOR legionnaire
AEEGIILNORS legionaries
AEEGIILNPRS espaliering
AEEGIILNRST gelatiniser
AEEGIILNRSU seigneurial
AEEGIILNRTZ gelatinizer
AEEGIILNSST gelatinises
AEEGIILNSTZ gelatinizes
AEEGIILOOST aetiologies
AEEGIIMNNRX reexamining
AEEGIIMNNST ingeminates
AEEGIIMNRTV germinative
AEEGIIMNSST enigmatises
AEEGIIMNSTZ enigmatizes
AEEGIIMRSST magisteries

AEEGIINRRTT reiterating
AEEGIINRTTV integrative
vinaigrette
AEEGIINSTTV investigate
AEEGIKLNSST glaiketness
AEEGILLLNRW general will
AEEGILLMNNP empanelling
AEEGILLNNTY inelegantly
AEEGILLNRVY revealingly
AEEGILLORSS allegorises
AEEGILLORSZ allegorizes
AEEGILLRSTU legislature
AEEGILMNNRT engrailment
realignment
AEEGILMNNSS meaningless
AEEGILMNRRS malingerers
AEEGILMNRST regimentals
AEEGILNNRRT interregnal
AEEGILNNRUV unrevealing
AEEGILNOPRV overleaping
AEEGILNORST regelations
relegations
AEEGILNRSST generalists
AEEGILNRSTV everlasting
AEEGILNSSSW wineglasses
AEEGILNSSTV evangelists
AEEGILORSTT tetralogies
AEEGILRRSSU regularises
AEEGILRRSUZ regularizes
AEEGIMNNRTU enumerating
AEEGIMNNRUV maneuvering
AEEGIMNOTTW witenagemot
AEEGIMNPRST impregnates
AEEGIMNPRTT attempering
AEEGIMNRRST remastering
AEEGIMNRRSU remeasuring
AEEGIMNRSST magnetisers
AEEGIMNRSTZ magnetizers
AEEGIMNSSTU mutagenesis
AEEGIMRRSTU marguerites
AEEGIMRRSTV gravimeters
AEEGIMSSTTU guesstimate
guestimates
AEEGINNNPRT perennating
AEEGINNNSSU ensanguines
AEEGINNORST generations
AEEGINNORTX exonerating
AEEGINNPRTT penetrating
AEEGINNRTTV anteverting
AEEGINNTTUV eventuating
AEEGINNTTUX extenuating
AEEGINORRRZ reorganizer
AEEGINORRSS reorganises
AEEGINORRSZ reorganizes
AEEGINORRTT interrogate
AEEGINOSSTU autogenesis
AEEGINOSTTV vegetations
AEEGINPRSSY panegyrises
AEEGINPRSYZ panegyrizes
AEEGINRRRST rearresting
AEEGINRRSST reasserting
AEEGINRSSSS reassessing
AEEGINRSSSV vernissages
AEEGIOPRRTV prerogative
AEEGIOSTTUV vegetatious
AEEGKNPRRST Regent's Park
AEEGLLMNNTY gentlemanly
AEEGLLMNSTY segmentally
AEEGLLMORTU glomerulate
AEEGLLOOPSY spelaeology
AEEGLLORSTT allegrettos
AEEGLMNNOTW gentlewoman
AEEGLMNNSTT tanglements
AEEGLMNOOPR prolegomena
AEEGLMNRSST garmentless
AEEGLNORSTU outgenerals
AEEGLOOPRRT Porto Alegre
AEEGLOORTVV overvoltage
AEEGLORSTUV travelogues
AEEGMNNOSST mangosteens
AEEGMNORRTV overgarment
AEEGMNRSTWY West Germany
AEEGMNRTTUY tegumentary
AEEGMORRSST stereograms
AEEGMRSSSTU gaussmeters
AEEGNNRSSST strangeness
AEEGNORSSTV gravestones
AEEGNOSSSSU gaseousness
AEEGPPPRRSS peppergrass
AEEHHILMOPS haemophiles
AEEHHILNRTU unhealthier
AEEHHILNSST healthiness
AEEHHILRTTW therewithal
whitleather
AEEHHILRTWW wherewithal
AEEHHINOPST theophanies
AEEHHIPSSTY hypesthesia
AEEHHIRSTWW whitewasher
AEEHHISSTWW whitewashes
AEEHHKNPSSS sheepshanks
AEEHHMORRTT earth mother
AEEHHNORSTT hearthstone
AEEHIIKNSST kinesthesia
AEEHIILLSTT lethalities
AEEHIILMOPT epithelioma
AEEHIILNRST Saint Helier
AEEHIILNSTX antihelixes
AEEHIIMPRSS phariseeism
AEEHIINPPRR perinephria
AEEHIKLMRRS sharemilker
AEEHIKNSSSW weakishness
AEEHIKPPRSS speakership
AEEHILLMOST mesothelial
AEEHILLMRTY hemielytral
AEEHILLMRUV humeral veil
AEEHILLORST heliolaters
AEEHILLPRSV Sharpeville
AEEHILMMNTY methylamine
AEEHILMNNPY phenylamine
AEEHILMRSST thermalises
AEEHILMRSTZ thermalizes
AEEHILNNOST stenohaline
AEEHILNNSST Saint Helens
AEEHILNPPRS planisphere
AEEHILNPSSS shapeliness
AEEHILNRSST earthliness
AEEHILNSSTW wealthiness
AEEHILPSTTT telepathist
AEEHILRSTTT triathletes
AEEHILSSTTT stealthiest
AEEHIMNNSTV evanishment
AEEHIMNOPRT metanephroi
AEEHIMNOPTV Amenhotep IV
AEEHIMNPRST hemipterans
AEEHIMNPRSY hypermnesia
AEEHIMNRSUZ rehumanizes
AEEHIMNSTTY amethystine
AEEHIMOSSST somesthesia
AEEHINNSSTT Antisthenes
AEEHINORTTT titanothere
AEEHINPRSST interphases
parenthesis
AEEHINRSTTU uintatheres
AEEHINSSSTY synesthesia
AEEHINSSTTT anesthetist
AEEHIOOPRTT heterotopia
AEEHIOOPSST apotheosise
AEEHIOOPSTZ apotheosize
AEEHIOPRRXY hyperorexia
AEEHIORSTTX heterotaxis
AEEHIORTTVX exhortative
AEEHIPPRRSS periphrases
AEEHKLLORRU leukorrheal
AEEHKMPRRTY hypermarket
AEEHKOPSSSV spokeshaves
AEEHKOSSSTU steakhouses
AEEHLLMSSSY shamelessly
AEEHLLNRRST enthrallers
AEEHLLOPRXY phylloxerae
AEEHLLORSSW wholesalers
AEEHLLPSSSY shapelessly
AEEHLLRSSTY heartlessly
AEEHLMNNRTT enthralment
AEEHLMOPRTY Thermopylae
AEEHLMORSTY heartsomely
AEEHLMOSSTY hematolyses
AEEHLMRRTUY eurythermal
AEEHLNORTVW Leavenworth
AEEHLNPPRSY hyperplanes
AEEHLNPSSSS haplessness
AEEHLNRSSSS harnessless
AEEHLOOPRRT heteropolar
AEEHLPPRRTU purpleheart
AEEHLRSSSTV harvestless
AEEHMMNORST hammerstone
AEEHMMNRTUX xeranthemum
AEEHMNOPRST metanephros
AEEHMNOPRTY hymenoptera
AEEHMNORSWW washerwomen
AEEHMNPRRTU preterhuman
AEEHMOPRSST atmospheres
AEEHMOPRSTU heptamerous
AEEHMOPSSTY haemoptyses
AEEHMORRRST arthromeres
AEEHMORRSTW whoremaster

AEEHMORSSTU	housemaster
AEEHNNOPRSW	answerphone
AEEHNNRSSSU	unharnesses
AEEHNOOPRRS	harpooneers
AEEHNORRSST	enarthroses
	nearthroses
AEEHNORRSTT	northeaster
AEEHNORRTWW	weatherworn
AEEHOOPRSST	peashooters
AEEHOPRRSTY	serotherapy
AEEHORSSSTU	authoresses
AEEHORSSTTU	southeaster
AEEHOSSSTTU	statehouses
AEEHRSSSTUU	thesauruses
AEEIIILMNTV	eliminative
AEEIIILNSTV	venialities
AEEIIINRRST	itineraries
AEEIIKNRSST	keratinises
AEEIIKNRSTZ	keratinizes
AEEIILLMNRS	millenaries
AEEIILLNNRT	interlineal
AEEIILLRSTT	illiterates
AEEIILMMORS	memorialise
AEEIILMMORZ	memorialize
AEEIILMNRRS	mineraliser
AEEIILMNRRZ	mineralizer
AEEIILMNRSS	mineralises
AEEIILMNRSZ	mineralizes
AEEIILMNSTT	mentalities
AEEIILMORSU	Marie Louise
AEEIILMORTV	meliorative
AEEIILMRRST	semitrailer
AEEIILNNPTT	penitential
AEEIILNNRRT	interlinear
AEEIILNNRST	internalise
AEEIILNNRTZ	internalize
AEEIILNNSST	inessential
AEEIILNORST	orientalise
AEEIILNORTZ	orientalize
AEEIILNPRRU	perineurial
AEEIILNRSTU	unrealities
AEEIILNSTTX	existential
AEEIILNTTVV	ventilative
AEEIILQRRSU	reliquaries
AEEIILRSSTV	relativises
	revitalises
AEEIILRSTVZ	relativizes
	revitalizes
AEEIILRTTVY	iteratively
AEEIILSSTUX	sexualities
AEEIIMMSSTT	misestimate
AEEIIMNNSST	inseminates
AEEIIMNRTTV	terminative
AEEIIMPRSTV	imperatives
	semiprivate
AEEIIMPRTTV	impetrative
AEEIINNTTTV	inattentive
AEEIINOPRTV	inoperative
AEEIINORRTT	reiteration
AEEIINPRRST	Saint-Pierre
AEEIINSTUVV	vesuvianite
AEEIIPRSSST	patisseries
AEEIIPRTTVX	extirpative
AEEIIRSSTTU	austerities
AEEIJNRSSST	janitresses
AEEIJOPRSTV	pejoratives
AEEIKLRRSWW	wirewalkers
AEEIKMNORSS	noisemakers
AEEIKNOPSSW	Passion Week
AEEIKNPPRSV	paperknives
AEEIKNQSSSU	squeakiness
AEEIKNRSSST	streakiness
AEEIKOPRRST	perestroika
AEEILLLLNSV	villanelles
AEEILLMMNPT	implemental
AEEILLMNOPS	psilomelane
AEEILLMNSST	enamellists
AEEILLMPRXY	exemplarily
AEEILLMTUVY	emulatively
AEEILLNNPRY	perennially
AEEILLNNSTW	Wallenstein
AEEILLNNSXY	sexennially
AEEILLNRSST	literalness
AEEILLNSSTY	essentially
AEEILLOPSTV	Elisavetpol
AEEILLRSSWY	wearilessly
AEEILLRSTVY	versatilely
AEEILMMNNPT	impanelment
AEEILMMNPST	impalements
AEEILMMNRSU	neurilemmas
AEEILMNNSTT	entailments
	sentimental
AEEILMNORST	salinometer
AEEILMNPRST	planimeters
	sempiternal
AEEILMNPTTU	penultimate
AEEILMNRSST	streamlines
AEEILMNRSTX	externalism
AEEILMNSSSS	aimlessness
AEEILMOPRRT	polarimeter
AEEILMORRST	solarimeter
AEEILMORSWY	wearisomely
AEEILMOSTTT	teetotalism
AEEILMPPRRS	perispermal
AEEILMPRSTY	semelparity
AEEILNNNPPS	Pennine Alps
AEEILNNOPTX	exponential
AEEILNNOSTX	extensional
AEEILNNPSTU	peninsulate
AEEILNNSSTU	unessential
AEEILNNSSTY	insensately
AEEILNNSTTU	lieutenants
AEEILNOPRSS	personalise
AEEILNOPRSZ	personalize
AEEILNOPRTT	interpolate
AEEILNOPSST	neoplasties
AEEILNORRSV	reversional
AEEILNORSST	neorealists
AEEILNORSTV	revelations
AEEILNPRSTT	interseptal
AEEILNPSTTV	septivalent
AEEILNPSVXY	expansively
AEEILNQSTUV	equivalents
AEEILNRRSTU	neutraliser
AEEILNRRSUV	vulneraries
AEEILNRRTUZ	neutralizer
AEEILNRSSSS	airlessness
AEEILNRSSTU	neutralises
AEEILNRSTTX	externalist
AEEILNRSTUX	intersexual
AEEILNRSTUZ	neutralizes
AEEILNRTTXY	externality
AEEILNSSSTT	stateliness
AEEILNTTTVY	attentively
	tentatively
AEEILNTTUVY	eventuality
AEEILOPPSTU	epipetalous
AEEILOPRRRT	repertorial
AEEILOPRRST	proletaries
AEEILOPRTVX	explorative
AEEILOPRTVY	operatively
AEEILORRSSV	revalorises
AEEILORRSVZ	revalorizes
AEEILPRSSST	peristalses
AEEILPRSSVY	aspersively
AEEILPRSTUV	superlative
AEEILPRSVVY	pervasively
AEEILPSTTUX	exstipulate
AEEILQRRSTU	quarterlies
AEEILRRRSTT	terrestrial
AEEILRRTTTU	litterateur
AEEILRSSTVY	assertively
AEEIMMNNPRT	impermanent
AEEIMMNPRST	pentamerism
AEEIMMRRSTT	tetramerism
AEEIMMRSSSU	mismeasures
AEEIMNNNOQU	menaquinone
AEEIMNNNRST	insnarement
AEEIMNNNRTT	entrainment
AEEIMNNORST	enantiomers
	renominates
AEEIMNNORTU	enumeration
	mountaineer
AEEIMNNOSTT	maisonnette
AEEIMNNRSTU	innumerates
AEEIMNNRTTT	intreatment
AEEIMNNSTTT	instatement
AEEIMNOPRST	impersonate
AEEIMNORSST	monasteries
AEEIMNORSTT	marionettes
AEEIMNOSSTT	maisonettes
AEEIMNPRRSU	praemunires
AEEIMNRSSST	streaminess
AEEIMNRSTUV	mensurative
AEEIMNSSSSV	massiveness
AEEIMOPRRST	temporaries
AEEIMOPRRTV	vaporimeter
AEEIMORRSTU	temerarious
AEEIMORRSTV	variometers
AEEIMQRRSTU	marquetries
AEEIMQRSSTU	Times Square
AEEIMQRSSUV	semiquavers
AEEIMQRSTTU	marquisette
AEEIMSSSTTY	systematise
AEEIMSSTTYZ	systematize
AEEINNOORTX	exoneration

AEEINNOPRTT	penetration
AEEINNOPRTU	neutropenia
AEEINNORSTV	anteversion
AEEINNORSTX	Oxenstierna
AEEINNORTTV	eventration
AEEINNOTTUV	eventuation
AEEINNOTTUX	extenuation
AEEINNSSSTT	assentients
AEEINOPRSST	proteinases
AEEINOPRSSY	aepyornises
AEEINOPRSTV	personative
AEEINOPRSTX	paroxetines
AEEINOPSTTT	potentiates
AEEINORRSST	reassertion
AEEINORRSTV	reservation
AEEINPRSSST	spessartine
AEEINPRSSTT	Saint Peter's
AEEINPRSSTY	antipyreses
AEEINPSSSSV	passiveness
AEEINQRSSTU	equestrians
AEEINRRRSST	restrainers
AEEINRSSTUV	unassertive
AEEIOOPPSSS	aposiopeses
AEEIOPPRRTX	expropriate
AEEIOPRRSSV	overpraises
AEEIORRSTTV	restorative
AEEIORSSTTX	stereotaxis
AEEIPPRRSTW	wiretappers
AEEIPRRSSTT	stripteaser
AEEIPRRSSTU	pasteuriser
AEEIPRRSTUZ	pasteurizer
AEEIPRSSSTT	spessartite
AEEIPRSSSTU	pasteurises
AEEIPRSSTUZ	pasteurizes
	trapeziuses
AEEIPRSTTUV	vituperates
AEEIRRSSSTT	traitresses
AEEIRSSTTTX	testatrixes
AEEJLNOSSSU	jealousness
AEEJNORRTUV	rejuvenator
AEEKLMNNRST	kernmantels
AEEKLMORRTW	metalworker
AEEKMMNORSY	moneymakers
AEEKMMRRRSY	merrymakers
AEEKMORRSTU	euromarkets
AEEKMPRRSTU	supermarket
AEEKMPRRSTV	verkramptes
AEEKNPRRSTU	supertanker
AEELLMMRRST	trammellers
AEELLMNORTT	reallotment
AEELLMNRSTU	allurements
AEELLMORRST	steamroller
AEELLNORRTT	retrolental
AEELLNORSTW	stonewaller
AEELLNPRTVY	prevalently
AEELLNRRSUV	unravellers
AEELLNRSTWW	Western Wall
AEELLNSSSSW	lawlessness
AEELLPPRTUY	perpetually
AEELLQRRRSU	quarrellers
AEELLSSSTTY	tastelessly
AEELMMNORSU	neurolemmas
AEELMMORTTV	voltammeter
AEELMNNPRTY	permanently
AEELMNNRTUV	unravelment
AEELMNOPRST	planometers
AEELMNORSTV	overmantels
AEELMNORSTW	watermelons
AEELMOPRSSU	semelparous
AEELMOPRSSY	polymerases
AEELMOPRSTT	plastometer
AEELMOQRRSU	quarrelsome
AEELMORSTTV	voltameters
AEELMPRRTUY	prematurely
AEELMPRSSTT	streetlamps
AEELNNPRTTY	repentantly
AEELNNPSTTU	antepenults
AEELNNQSSTU	lansquenets
AEELNNSSSSU	sensualness
AEELNOPRSSS	salesperson
AEELNOPRSST	prolateness
AEELNOSSSUZ	zealousness
AEELNPRRSST	partnerless
AEELNPRSTTW	wentletraps
AEELNRSSSST	artlessness
AEELNRSSSSY	raylessness
AEELNSSSSTU	sultanesses
AEELOORSUVZ	overzealous
AEELOPPRSTU	repopulates
AEELOPSTTUX	expostulate
AEELOQRRSUU	roquelaures
AEEMNNPRSTT	entrapments
AEEMNNRSSTV	menservants
AEEMNOPRRTY	pyranometer
AEEMNOPRSTU	pentamerous
AEEMNOQRTTU	quantometer
AEEMNORRRTU	remunerator
AEEMNORRSTT	remonstrate
AEEMNORRSTU	enumerators
AEEMNORRSUV	manoeuvrers
AEEMNORSSTT	easternmost
AEEMNORTUUV	outmaneuver
AEEMNOSSTTW	stateswomen
AEEMNPPRSTY	prepayments
AEEMNRRSSTT	arrestments
AEEMNRSSTTU	menstruates
AEEMNSSSSST	assessments
AEEMOPRRTXY	extemporary
AEEMORRSSTV	overmasters
AEEMORRSTTU	tetramerous
AEEMRRSSTTT	streetsmart
AEENNNPRTTU	unrepentant
AEENNOPRRTU	neuropteran
AEENOOPRSSU	aponeuroses
AEENOORRSTX	exonerators
AEENOPRRSTT	paternoster
	penetrators
AEENOPRSSST	patronesses
AEENORSTTUX	extenuators
AEENORTTUXY	extenuatory
AEENPPRSSTT	stepparents
AEENQRSSTTU	sequestrant
AEENRRRSTTV	transverter
AEENRRSSSTV	transverses
AEEOPPRRRTT	perpetrator
AEEOPRRSSTT	tetraspores
AEEORRSSSTV	overasserts
AEEORRSSTVY	overstayers
AEEPRRSSSST	trespassers
AEEPRSSSSTT	tapstresses
AEEPRSSSTTU	superstates
AEEPRSSSWXY	expressways
AEFFGIIMNRR	reaffirming
AEFFGIMSTUU	suffumigate
AEFFGINORST	afforesting
AEFFHINRSSS	raffishness
AEFFIIMNORR	foraminifer
AEFFIJNORSZ	Franz Josef I
AEFFILLMMMR	flimflammer
AEFFILNSSTU	insufflates
AEFFILORRRW	Wolf-Ferrari
AEFFKNRRRTU	frankfurter
AEFFLMOORSW	foamflowers
AEFGGIMNNRT	fragmenting
AEFGHIIRRST	airfreights
AEFGHINRRSW	wharfingers
AEFGHLOPRXY	flexography
AEFGHNORSTU	fearnoughts
AEFGIIKLNRW	fire walking
AEFGIILNNRS	fingernails
AEFGIILNOTX	exfoliating
AEFGIIMNNST	manifesting
AEFGIKMNRRS	fingermarks
AEFGIKNOPRS	forspeaking
AEFGILLLNNN	flannelling
AEFGILLNRST	fingerstall
AEFGILLNRTY	falteringly
AEFGILNNOOR	gonfalonier
AEFGILNNSSU	gainfulness
AEFGILNPRSU	Persian Gulf
AEFGILOPRST	profligates
AEFGIMNNRTT	ingraftment
AEFGINNNSSW	fawningness
AEFGINNNSTU	unfastening
AEFGINNORRW	forewarning
AEFGINOPRRT	perforating
AEFGINORRSW	forswearing
AEFGINORSTT	foretasting
AEFGINRRSTU	transfigure
AEFGIPRRSTU	grapefruits
AEFGLNRRTUW	Furtwängler
AEFHHLLLTUY	healthfully
AEFHIILNSSS	snailfishes
AEFHILLSSTY	faithlessly
AEFHIMNOPRS	foremanship
AEFHLMNRSSU	harmfulness
AEFHMORRSTT	farthermost
AEFIIIMNRRS	infirmaries
AEFIIKLNNRT	franklinite
AEFIILLNNOX	inflexional
AEFIILLNNTU	influential
AEFIILMORST	formalities
AEFIILNNRTY	infernality
AEFIILNOOTX	exfoliation

AEFIILNRSTT	infiltrates
AEFIILNRTUY	infuriately
AEFIIMNORTV	informative
AEFIINNORTV	infantivore
AEFIINNOSTT	festination
	infestation
	sinfonietta
AEFIINNRSTT	transfinite
AEFIINOPRSS	saponifiers
AEFIINOPRST	profanities
AEFIINQRSTU	quantifiers
AEFILLLMMOR	lamelliform
AEFILLMOPRT	patelliform
AEFILLRRTTU	ultrafilter
AEFILMNOSTU	filamentous
AEFILMNOUVX	fluvoxamine
AEFILMORRSS	formalisers
AEFILMORRSU	formularies
	formularise
AEFILMORRSZ	formalizers
AEFILMORRUZ	formularize
AEFILMORTVY	formatively
AEFILMPRSUY	superfamily
AEFILNNPSSU	painfulness
AEFILNNSSTU	flauntiness
AEFILNORSTU	fluorinates
AEFILNORSTW	satinflower
AEFILNORSUY	nefariously
AEFILOPRRTY	prefatorily
AEFILOQRSTU	quatrefoils
AEFIMMMORSU	mammiferous
AEFIMNNNRTY	infantrymen
AEFIMNNOOTT	fomentation
AEFIMNOORRT	reformation
AEFIMOPRRTZ	trapeziform
AEFINNRRRST	transferrin
AEFINOOPRRT	perforation
AEFINOOPRST	fortepianos
	pianofortes
AEFINOORSTT	forestation
AEFINORRSST	rainforests
AEFINORSTTU	refutations
AEFINRSSTUV	transfusive
AEFIOOPRSTU	foetiparous
AEFKLLOORRW	floorwalker
AEFLLLNTTUY	flatulently
AEFLLLOPSWY	playfellows
AEFLLLORSWW	wallflowers
AEFLLLSSTUY	faultlessly
AEFLLMRSTUY	masterfully
AEFLLNPSSUY	playfulness
AEFLLORSSUV	flavourless
AEFLLPRRUYY	prayerfully
AEFLMOORSUV	flavoursome
AEFLNOOPSTU	teaspoonful
AEFLNORTTUY	fortunately
AEFLORRSSTW	starflowers
AEFLORRSTWW	strawflower
AEFMNORRRST	transformer
AEFMOOPRSTT	foretopmast
AEFMOORRRTY	reformatory
AEFNNORTTUU	unfortunate
AEFNORRRSST	transferors
AEFNORRSTTW	waterfronts
AEFNOSSSTUU	fatuousness
AEFNRRSSSTU	transfusers
AEFOOPRRRST	perforators
AEFOOPRRRTY	perforatory
AEFOOPRRSTW	waterproofs
AEFOORRSSTT	tortfeasors
AEFRRRSSTTU	frustraters
AEGGGIINRSW	earwiggings
AEGGHHIKNNS	Genghis Khan
AEGGHHINSSS	haggishness
AEGGHIILNNT	nightingale
AEGGHIILOOS	hagiologies
AEGGHIINNRT	ingathering
AEGGHINNORV	overhanging
AEGGHINSSSW	waggishness
AEGGHIOPSST	geophagists
AEGGHLOOPRR	logographer
AEGGHMNORTU	Grangemouth
AEGGIIJNNWW	Wang Jing Wei
AEGGIILLNST	legislating
AEGGIILMMNR	mailmerging
AEGGIILMNNR	malingering
AEGGIILMPRS	pilgrimages
AEGGIIMNNRT	germinating
AEGGIIMNNRZ	germanizing
AEGGIIMNNST	magnetising
AEGGIIMNNTZ	magnetizing
AEGGIIMNRRT	remigrating
AEGGIINNOTT	negotiating
AEGGIINNPRT	interpaging
AEGGIINNRSS	reassigning
AEGGIINNRTT	integrating
AEGGIINRTTU	ingurgitate
AEGGIJMRSST	jiggermasts
AEGGILNNRSS	glaringness
AEGGILOOSSU	sialogogues
AEGGIMNOOTY	geitonogamy
AEGGIMNRRSS	grangerisms
AEGGIMNRSST	gangsterism
AEGGINNOTXY	oxygenating
AEGGINORRVZ	overgrazing
AEGGINORSSS	aggressions
AEGGINPRTUX	expurgating
AEGGINRRTTU	regurgitant
AEGGJNRSTUU	juggernauts
AEGGMOSSTUY	mystagogues
AEGHHIJKNNS	Jenghis Khan
AEGHHILLLSS	shillelaghs
AEGHHILOPRS	heliographs
AEGHHILOPRY	heliography
AEGHHINNPTY	hyphenating
AEGHHINNSTU	unsheathing
AEGHHINSSTU	haughtiness
AEGHHLOPRSU	ploughshare
AEGHHMOPPST	apophthegms
AEGHHMOPRRT	thermograph
AEGHHNOPPRS	nephographs
AEGHHNOPRTY	ethnography
AEGHHOPRSTY	hyetographs
AEGHHOPRTYY	hyetography
AEGHIIIJJNS	Jiang Jie Shi
AEGHIIMNPSS	emphasising
AEGHIIMNPST	empathising
AEGHIIMNPSZ	emphasizing
AEGHIIMNPTZ	empathizing
AEGHIIMOPRS	amphigories
AEGHIINPSTT	spaghettini
AEGHIIPPRST	epigraphist
AEGHIIPRSST	graphitises
AEGHIIPRSTZ	graphitizes
AEGHIKNSSSW	gawkishness
AEGHILLMPRT	lamplighter
AEGHILLNNRT	enthralling
AEGHILLNOPS	anglophiles
AEGHILLNOSW	wholesaling
AEGHILLNRST	allnighters
AEGHILLRRSY	Argyllshire
AEGHILMNTTY	methylating
AEGHILNNOPT	phenolating
AEGHILNNSST	haltingness
AEGHILNOOST	anthologies
	anthologise
	theologians
AEGHILNOOTZ	anthologize
AEGHILNORUV	overhauling
AEGHILNOTTU	glutathione
AEGHILNSSST	ghastliness
AEGHILOOPST	pathologies
	pathologise
AEGHILOOPTZ	pathologize
AEGHIMMOPRS	mimeographs
AEGHIMNNRST	garnishment
AEGHIMNOPRS	semaphoring
AEGHIMOPRSS	seismograph
AEGHINNSSTU	naughtiness
AEGHINOPSTU	epignathous
AEGHINORSUW	warehousing
AEGHINOSSST	goatishness
AEGHINRSSTT	straightens
AEGHINRSSTV	harvestings
AEGHIRSSTTT	straightest
AEGHIRSTTWW	strawweight
AEGHLMOOOST	homologates
AEGHLMOPRYY	myelography
AEGHLNNOOPS	anglophones
AEGHLNOOORR	gonorrhoeal
AEGHLOOPRSY	phraseology
AEGHLOPPRYY	pyelography
AEGHLOPRRXY	xylographer
AEGHLORSSSU	hourglasses
AEGHLORSSUV	overslaughs
AEGHLOSSSSU	glasshouses
AEGHMMORRST	thermograms
AEGHMNOOPRR	monographer
	nomographer
AEGHMNOOPRS	gramophones
AEGHMNOOSTT	gnathostome
AEGHMNOPPRU	pneumograph
AEGHMNOPRSS	sphenograms
AEGHMOPRSUY	hypergamous

AEGHNOOPRRS	nosographer
AEGHNOPRSST	stenographs
AEGHNOPRSTY	stenography
AEGHOOPPRRT	topographer
AEGHOOPRRRS	orographers
AEGHOOPRRSZ	zoographers
AEGHOPPRRRY	pyrographer
	reprography
AEGHOPPRRSS	grasshopper
AEGHOPPRRTY	petrography
	typographer
AEGIIILMNNT	eliminating
AEGIIILMNST	malignities
AEGIIILNORS	seigniorial
AEGIIILNRSS	serialising
AEGIIILNRSZ	serializing
AEGIIILNSTV	invigilates
AEGIIINNRTT	itinerating
AEGIIINSTTV	instigative
AEGIIKLNSST	glaikitness
AEGIIKMNNOS	noisemaking
AEGIIKNRSST	asterisking
AEGIIKNRSTW	waterskiing
AEGIILLMMMR	milligramme
AEGIILLMNNP	impanelling
AEGIILLMNST	metallising
AEGIILLMNTZ	metallizing
AEGIILLMRSU	guerillaism
AEGIILLNOST	legislation
AEGIILLNPST	palletising
AEGIILLNPTZ	palletizing
AEGIILLNSTT	satelliting
AEGIILLNTVY	genitivally
AEGIILLSTVY	vestigially
AEGIILMMNST	lemmatising
AEGIILMMNTZ	lemmatizing
AEGIILMNORS	regionalism
AEGIILMNORT	meliorating
AEGIILMNRST	misrelating
AEGIILNNRSV	vernalising
AEGIILNNRTU	interlingua
AEGIILNNRTY	interlaying
AEGIILNNRVZ	vernalizing
AEGIILNNSTU	ungainliest
AEGIILNNTTV	ventilating
AEGIILNORST	regionalist
AEGIILNORSV	vainglories
AEGIILNPPQU	appliqueing
AEGIILNRSST	slaistering
AEGIILNRSSU	singularise
AEGIILNRSUZ	singularize
AEGIILNRTTU	elutriating
AEGIILNRTTY	integrality
AEGIILNSUXZ	sexualizing
AEGIILOOSTT	aetiologist
AEGIILRSTUV	vulgarities
AEGIIMMRSTU	magisterium
AEGIIMNNORT	germination
AEGIIMNNOST	geminations
AEGIIMNNRTT	terminating
AEGIIMNORST	emigrations
AEGIIMNPRTT	impetrating
AEGIIMNRSTT	mistreating
AEGIIMPRSTU	epigastrium
AEGIIMRSSTT	stigmatiser
AEGIIMRSTTZ	stigmatizer
AEGIIMSSSTT	stigmatises
AEGIIMSSTTZ	stigmatizes
AEGIINNNOST	angiotensin
AEGIINNNRTV	innervating
AEGIINNOOTT	negotiation
AEGIINNOPSW	weaponising
AEGIINNOPWZ	weaponizing
AEGIINNORST	resignation
AEGIINNORTT	integration
	orientating
AEGIINNOSST	isoantigens
AEGIINNPPST	pepsinating
AEGIINNRRST	restraining
AEGIINNRSTT	intrigantes
	reinstating
	straitening
AEGIINNRTTU	intriguante
AEGIINOPRST	operatising
AEGIINOPRTZ	operatizing
AEGIINORSST	signatories
AEGIINORSTV	invigorates
AEGIINPPRSU	pauperising
AEGIINPPRTW	wiretapping
AEGIINPPRUZ	pauperizing
AEGIINPRTTX	extirpating
AEGIINRSSTW	waitressing
AEGIINSSTTV	negativists
AEGIIRRSSTT	geriatrists
AEGIKLMMORS	kilogrammes
AEGIKMMNNOY	moneymaking
AEGIKMMNRRY	merrymaking
AEGIKMNNOSS	maskinonges
AEGIKNNNOPS	nonspeaking
AEGIKNOPSTU	outspeaking
AEGIKNORSTV	overtasking
AEGILLMMNRT	trammelling
AEGILLMNNTY	lamentingly
AEGILLMOOPS	megalopolis
AEGILLMPRSU	aspergillum
AEGILLNNRUV	unravelling
AEGILLNOPST	sellotaping
AEGILLNORTT	reallotting
AEGILLNQRRU	quarrelling
AEGILLORSST	allegorists
	legislators
AEGILLPRRRZ	Grillparzer
AEGILLPRSSU	aspergillus
AEGILLRRRUY	irregularly
AEGILMMNOTU	gemmulation
AEGILMNNNUY	unmeaningly
AEGILMNNOPS	plasminogen
AEGILMNNSST	signalments
AEGILMNOORT	glomeration
AEGILMNOPRU	pelargonium
AEGILMNORSS	rosemalings
AEGILMNOSTU	ligamentous
AEGILMOOSSY	semasiology
AEGILMORRSS	glamorisers
AEGILMORRSZ	glamorizers
AEGILMORSUZ	glamourizes
AEGILNNNPPR	preplanning
AEGILNNOOST	elongations
AEGILNNOSTU	langoustine
AEGILNNSSST	lastingness
AEGILNOORRT	Oregon trail
AEGILNOOSSX	xenoglossia
AEGILNOPPRV	overlapping
AEGILNOPRVY	overplaying
AEGILNORSTU	regulations
AEGILNORUVV	overvaluing
AEGILNPRSST	plasterings
AEGILNPRSTT	splattering
AEGILNQRUVY	quaveringly
AEGILNRRSTY	arrestingly
AEGILNRSSTV	starvelings
AEGILOOPRSS	apologisers
AEGILOOPRSZ	apologizers
AEGILOORSST	aerologists
AEGILOOSTTU	tautologies
	tautologise
AEGILOOTTUZ	tautologize
AEGILOPRSTT	graptolites
AEGILPRTUVY	purgatively
AEGILRRSSUV	vulgarisers
AEGILRRSUVZ	vulgarizers
AEGILRSTTUU	gutturalise
AEGILRTTUUZ	gutturalize
AEGIMMNRSST	stammerings
AEGIMMOPRSU	gemmiparous
AEGIMNNNORT	ornamenting
AEGIMNNNORV	overmanning
AEGIMNNORUV	manoeuvring
AEGIMNNSSST	assignments
AEGIMNOOPRS	spermogonia
AEGIMNOPRRT	impregnator
AEGIMNOPRSS	angiosperms
AEGIMNORRST	germinators
AEGIMNORSSU	ignoramuses
AEGIMNPRTTU	permutating
AEGIMNRRSST	ringmasters
AEGIMNRSSTT	smatterings
AEGINNNORSU	unreasoning
AEGINNOORRV	vinegarroon
AEGINNOOTXY	oxygenation
AEGINNOPRST	personating
AEGINNOSSUU	sanguineous
AEGINNPRRTU	enrapturing
AEGINNPRSSS	sparingness
AEGINNRSSTT	astringents
AEGINOORSTT	negotiators
AEGINOPRSSV	overpassing
AEGINOPRTUX	expurgation
AEGINORRSTT	integrators
AEGINORSTTV	overstating
AEGINORSTVY	overstaying
AEGINPRSSST	trespassing
AEGINPRSSTU	supergiants
AEGINPRSSTY	panegyrists
AEGINQRRSTU	quarterings
AEGINRRSSTT	registrants

AEGINRSTTVY travestying
AEGIOPRRSTU purgatories
AEGIPRRRTYY pyrargyrite
AEGIRSSSTTT strategists
AEGKKNNOUYY Nguyen Kao Ky
AEGKLORRSSW glassworker
AEGLLNOOPTY planetology
AEGLMOPRSTU promulgates
AEGLNNOOOTY neonatology
AEGLNNPRTUY repugnantly
AEGLOORRSST astrologers
AEGLPRSSSUU surplusages
AEGMMNOPRSU pneumograms
AEGMMOPRRRS programmers
AEGMNOORRST gastronomer
AEGMNOORSST gastronomes
AEGMNSSSTUY nystagmuses
AEGNOOPRSSU saprogenous
AEGNOORSTXY oxygenators
AEGOOPRSSYZ azygospores
AEGOORRRTUV rotogravure
AEGOPRRSTUX expurgators
AEGOPRRTUXY expurgatory
AEGORSSSTUU stegosaurus
AEHHIIILNNS Hsin-hai-lien
AEHHIIMPSSS messiahship
AEHHILLNTUY unhealthily
AEHHIMOPRTY hypothermia
AEHHIMPRTYY hyperthymia
AEHHINNOPTY hyphenation
AEHHINOPRST hierophants
AEHHINOPSTY hyposthenia
AEHHIOPPSST phosphatise
AEHHIOPPSTZ phosphatize
AEHHIORTTTW whitethroat
AEHHLLOPTTY thallophyte
AEHHLMMOORT homothermal
AEHHLMOPRTY hypothermal
AEHHLNOPSTT heptathlons
AEHHLOPPSYY hypophyseal
AEHHMOOOPST homoeopaths
AEHHMOOOPTY homoeopathy
AEHHMOSSTUW mouthwashes
AEHHNOOPRST anthophores
AEHHNOOPSTU theophanous
AEHHNOPRRTY tenorrhaphy
AEHHOOPPRST phosphorate
AEHHRRSTTUW waterthrush
AEHIIILLMNW Wilhelmina I
AEHIIILMNST Saint-Mihiel
AEHIIILMTUV humiliative
AEHIILLOPRU ailurophile
AEHIILLPSTT philatelist
AEHIILOPSST hospitalise
AEHIILOPSTZ hospitalize
AEHIIMNRSTT martinetish
AEHIINNOPST antiphonies
AEHIINOPRRS parishioner
AEHIINOSSTT hesitations
AEHIINPRSTX xiphisterna
AEHIINSSTTT antitheists
AEHIIORSTTU authorities
AEHIIPPRRSS periphrasis
AEHIIPPSSTT epitaphists
AEHIIRSSTUW White Russia
AEHIKLNRSSS larkishness
AEHIKMNSSSW mawkishness
AEHIKNNSSSV knavishness
AEHILLMTTUU ultima Thule
AEHILLOPPTY apophyllite
AEHILLOPRST hospitaller
AEHILMNNOOP aminophenol
AEHILMNOPPY lymphopenia
AEHILMNOSSY haemolysins
AEHILMNOTTY methylation
AEHILMNOTXY hematoxylin
AEHILMNPSSY misshapenly
AEHILMNSSTV lavishments
AEHILMORSST isothermals
AEHILMOSSTY hematolysis
AEHILMQSSUY squeamishly
AEHILMRRSTY erythrismal
AEHILNOPTXY phytoalexin
AEHILNOSTTW West Lothian
AEHILNOSTTY ethylations
AEHILNPRRTY platyrrhine
AEHILNPRSST shinplaster
AEHILNPSSSS splashiness
AEHILNSSSSV slavishness
AEHILOPRSST hospitalers
AEHILORSTVY overhastily
AEHILORTTVY hortatively
AEHIMMNRSSS rammishness
AEHIMMPRRST triphammers
AEHIMMRSSTU rheumatisms
AEHIMNNNSSS mannishness
AEHIMNNNSSU inhumanness
AEHIMNOOPPR apomorphine
AEHIMNOPRST misanthrope
AEHIMNORRSS harmonisers
AEHIMNORRSZ harmonizers
AEHIMNOSTUX exhumations
AEHIMNRSSTV ravishments
AEHIMNSSSTU enthusiasms
AEHIMOOSSST homeostasis
AEHIMOPSSTY haemoptysis
AEHIMORSTTX thermotaxis
AEHIMPPRSTU hippeastrum
AEHIMPRSSST shipmasters
AEHIMPRSSTY sympathiser
AEHIMPRSTYZ sympathizer
AEHIMPSSSTY sympathises
AEHIMPSSTYZ sympathizes
AEHINNNOOST hootnannies
AEHINNPPSSU unhappiness
AEHINNPSSTY synthespian
AEHINOORSTT anorthosite
AEHINOORTTX exhortation
AEHINOPRSTT antistrophe
AEHINOPRSTU euphoriants
AEHINOPSSTT stephanotis
AEHINORRSST enarthrosis
nearthrosis
AEHINORRSTV hovertrains
AEHINORSSTT throatiness
AEHINPPRRST partnership
AEHINPSSSSW waspishness
AEHINQRSSUV vanquishers
AEHINQSSSSU squashiness
AEHINRSSSTW swarthiness
AEHINSSSTTU enthusiasts
AEHIOPPRRST praetorship
AEHIOPRRSTY erythropsia
AEHIOPSSSTY hypostasise
AEHIOPSSTTY hypostatise
AEHIOPSSTYZ hypostasize
AEHIOPSTTYZ hypostatize
AEHIORRSSTU authorisers
AEHIORRSTUZ authorizers
AEHIRSSSTTW sweatshirts
AEHJNOORRST Trojan Horse
AEHKLLNSSTY thanklessly
AEHKLOPRSSW shopwalkers
AEHKMNOSSTU snakemouths
AEHKNNOORRT North Korean
AEHKNOORSTU South Korean
AEHLLLMOOPR allelomorph
AEHLLLNOPPY phylloplane
AEHLLMOOSTY loathsomely
AEHLLNOSSSW shallowness
AEHLLOPRSXY phylloxeras
AEHLLOPSTXY phyllotaxes
AEHLMNNORTT Montherlant
AEHLMOOSSUX homosexuals
AEHLMOPPRRY lamprophyre
AEHLMORSTTY methylators
AEHLNNOPSTT pentathlons
AEHLNOPRTUY polyurethan
AEHLNOPSSTU sulphonates
AEHLPRSSTUU sulphurates
AEHMMNORRSY Romney Marsh
AEHMMOOOPRT ommatophore
AEHMNORRSTW harrowments
AEHMNORSTTY thermonasty
AEHMORSSTTT thermostats
AEHNOOPRRTT orthopteran
AEHNOOPSSSU sousaphones
AEHNORSTUWY unseaworthy
AEHOOPPRSST apostrophes
AEHOOPRRRST arthrospore
AEHOOPRRSTT trapshooter
AEHOOPRRSTX prothoraxes
AEHOOPSSTTT toothpastes
AEHOORRTTXY exhortatory
AEHOORSSSTY soothsayers
AEHOPPRSSTY saprophytes
AEHORRRSSTW restharrows
AEHPRSSSTTY strathspeys
AEIIIILNSST initialises
AEIIIILNSTZ initializes
AEIIIINSTTV initiatives
AEIIILLMNOR millionaire
AEIIILLMNST sillimanite
AEIIILLNRST initiallers

AEIIILLTTTV	titillative
AEIIILMMPRS	imperialism
AEIIILMNNOT	elimination
AEIIILMNRST	ministerial
AEIIILMNSST	antimissile
AEIIILMPRST	imperialist
AEIIILMRRSV	verisimilar
AEIIILMRSST	militarises
AEIIILMRSTZ	militarizes
AEIIILMTTVY	imitatively
AEIIILNNOOP	Napoleon III
AEIIILNPRST	pleinairist
AEIIILRSSTV	trivialises
AEIIILRSTVZ	trivializes
AEIIIMNOSST	animosities
AEIIIMNOSTT	itemisation
AEIIIMNOTTZ	itemization
AEIIIMNRSTU	miniaturise
AEIIIMNRTUZ	miniaturize
AEIIINNORTT	itineration
AEIIINNSTUV	insinuative
AEIIINORSSV	visionaries
AEIIINPRSTV	inspirative
AEIIINQSTTU	antiquities
AEIIINRSSTT	initiatress
AEIIIPRSTTU	pituitaries
AEIIKLLNPRS	painkillers
AEIIKLLOPRT	realpolitik
AEIIKLMNPRS	marlinspike
AEIIKNNRSST	Kristiansen
AEIILLMNSTU	illuminates
AEIILLMSTTU	satellitium
AEIILLNNRTY	triennially
AEIILLNOTVY	inviolately
AEIILLNPTVY	plaintively
AEIILLNTUUX	luxulianite
AEIILLOSSTV	volatilises
AEIILLOSTVZ	volatilizes
AEIILLPRSTT	tripletails
AEIILLPRSTU	pluralities
AEIILLRRSTT	triliterals
AEIILLRSSTT	literalists
AEIILLRSSTV	silvertails
AEIILMMORST	immortalise
	memorialist
AEIILMMORTZ	immortalize
AEIILMNNOPS	Minneapolis
AEIILMNOORT	melioration
AEIILMNORST	eliminators
	misrelation
	normalities
	orientalism
AEIILMNORTY	eliminatory
AEIILMNOSTT	testimonial
AEIILMNPRRY	preliminary
AEIILMNPTTY	impatiently
AEIILMOPRST	peristomial
AEIILMORSTT	mortalities
AEIILMOSSSS	isoseismals
AEIILMPSSVY	impassively
AEIILMRRSTT	trimestrial
AEIILMRSSVV	revivalisms
AEIILMSTTUV	stimulative
AEIILNNNOST	intensional
AEIILNNNOTT	intentional
AEIILNNNOTV	inventional
AEIILNNORST	insertional
AEIILNNORTV	inventorial
AEIILNNOTTV	ventilation
AEIILNNPRST	interspinal
AEIILNNRSTT	transilient
AEIILNNRTTY	internality
	itinerantly
AEIILNNSSST	saintliness
AEIILNOPSTX	pixelations
	postexilian
AEIILNORSSS	insessorial
AEIILNORSTT	orientalist
AEIILNORTTU	elutriation
AEIILNOSTTV	levitations
AEIILNQRTUZ	tranquilize
AEIILNRSSTV	trivialness
AEIILORRRTT	territorial
AEIILPRSSST	peristalsis
AEIILPRTTVY	partitively
AEIILPRTVVY	privatively
AEIILRSSSUV	visualisers
AEIILRSSTTV	relativists
AEIILRSSTTZ	strelitzias
AEIILRSSTVV	revivalists
AEIILRSSUVZ	visualizers
AEIILRSTTVY	versatility
AEIIMMMNNST	immanentism
AEIIMMNNSTT	immanentist
AEIIMMNORST	matrimonies
AEIIMMNOTUZ	Montezuma II
AEIIMMNRSTT	martinetism
AEIIMMRRTTU	termitarium
AEIIMNNOPRY	aminopyrine
AEIIMNNORST	inseminator
	nitrosamine
AEIIMNNORTT	termination
AEIIMNNORTV	vermination
AEIIMNNOSST	seminations
AEIIMNNOSTV	nominatives
AEIIMNOPRST	patrimonies
AEIIMNOPRTT	impetration
AEIIMNOSSTT	estimations
AEIIMOOPRST	isometropia
AEIIMOPPRRT	impropriate
AEIIMOPRRSS	impresarios
AEIIMRRTTUV	triumvirate
AEIINNNORTV	innervation
AEIINNNOSVV	noninvasive
AEIINNNOTTT	inattention
AEIINNNQQUU	quinquennia
AEIINNOORTT	orientation
AEIINNORSSV	reinvasions
AEIINOPPSTT	peptisation
AEIINOPPTTZ	peptization
AEIINOPRRST	respiration
AEIINOPRRTT	partitioner
	repartition
AEIINOPRRTU	proteinuria
AEIINOPRSTX	expirations
AEIINOPRTTX	extirpation
AEIINOPRTTY	petitionary
AEIINOPSSTT	poinsettias
AEIINOQSTTU	equitations
AEIINORRSVY	revisionary
AEIINORRTTY	anteriority
AEIINPRSSSU	prussianise
AEIINPRSSTY	antipyresis
AEIINPRSSUZ	prussianize
AEIINPSSSST	inspissates
AEIINPSTVXY	expansivity
AEIINRSSTTV	transitives
AEIINSSTTUV	antitussive
AEIIOOPPSSS	aposiopesis
AEIIOOPRRST	a posteriori
AEIIOPPRSTT	propitiates
AEIIOPRTTVY	operativity
AEIIPPSSSSW	pipsissewas
AEIJLNORRSU	journaliser
AEIJLNORRUZ	journalizer
AEIJLNORSSU	journalises
AEIJLNORSUZ	journalizes
AEIKKLMNORW	workmanlike
AEIKLNNOPPS	plainspoken
AEIKLNOPSTT	kinetoplast
AEIKLOPRRSW	sparrowlike
AEIKMNPRRST	printmakers
AEILLLMOSTY	lamellosity
AEILLLOSTWY	yellowtails
AEILLMMORSS	allomerisms
AEILLMMRSST	millstreams
AEILLMNNSTT	installment
AEILLMNOOTY	emotionally
AEILLMNOSTY	semitonally
AEILLMNPSTU	multiplanes
AEILLMNTTUV	multivalent
AEILLNNOOTV	nonvolatile
AEILLNOOTUV	evolutional
AEILLNOPSTT	potentillas
AEILLNOPTTY	potentially
AEILLNOSSSY	sessionally
AEILLNRSTUV	surveillant
AEILLNRSUVY	universally
AEILLNSSSTY	stainlessly
AEILLNSUUXY	unisexually
AEILLOOPRST	allotropies
AEILLORTTUV	ultraviolet
AEILLPPSUVY	appulsively
AEILLPRRSSU	pluralisers
AEILLPRRSUZ	pluralizers
AEILLPSSSTT	pastellists
AEILLPSTUVY	pulsatively
AEILLRSSTTU	illustrates
AEILMMMSSTY	symmetalism
AEILMMNNOSU	noumenalism
AEILMMNORTY	momentarily
AEILMNNNSSU	unmanliness
AEILMNNOOTU	unemotional
AEILMNNOSSW	womanliness
AEILMNNOSTU	noumenalist
AEILMNNOTUY	noumenality

AEILMNNRTTU	nutrimental
AEILMNNSSTT	instalments
AEILMNOOSTT	molestation
AEILMNOPRRT	trampoliner
AEILMNOPRSS	personalism
AEILMNOPRST	trampolines
AEILMNORSTY	salinometry
AEILMNORTVY	normatively
AEILMOORRST	meliorators
AEILMOPRRSU	leprosarium
AEILMOPRRTY	polarimetry
	temporarily
AEILMOPRTTY	temporality
AEILMOPRTXY	proximately
AEILMOQSTTU	milquetoast
AEILMORSSTV	removalists
AEILMPPSSST	palimpsests
AEILMPRSSST	slipstreams
AEILMRSSTTU	stimulaters
AEILNNOPRSU	unipersonal
AEILNNOPSTT	antileptons
	Saint Pölten
AEILNNORRTY	nonliterary
AEILNNRSTTY	transiently
AEILNNRSTUY	saturninely
AEILNOOPRTX	exploration
AEILNOPPTTY	platinotype
AEILNOPRRST	tripersonal
AEILNOPRSST	interposals
	personalist
AEILNOPRSTY	personality
AEILNOPSSSS	passionless
AEILNORRSTU	serrulation
AEILNORSTTV	ventilators
AEILNORSTUV	voluntaries
AEILNORTTVY	ventilatory
AEILNOSTTUX	exultations
AEILNRSSTTU	neutralists
AEILNSSSSTU	sensualists
AEILOOPRRRT	reportorial
AEILOPPRRSU	populariser
AEILOPPRRUZ	popularizer
AEILOPPRSSU	popularises
AEILOPPRSUZ	popularizes
AEILOPRSSSU	plesiosaurs
AEILORRSTTU	elutriators
AEILOSSSTTY	steatolysis
AEILOSTUVXY	vexatiously
AEILRRSSSTU	surrealists
AEILRSSSTUV	Lévi-Strauss
AEILSSTTTUX	textualists
AEIMMNPRSTT	impartments
AEIMMNRSSSU	summariness
AEIMMNRSTTU	manumitters
AEIMMNSSTZZ	mizzenmasts
AEIMMORSTTU	tautomerism
AEIMMPRSSTU	suprematism
AEIMMRRSSSU	summarisers
AEIMMRRSSUZ	summarizers
AEIMMSSSTTY	systematism
AEIMNNNOSTT	anointments
AEIMNNOPPTT	appointment
AEIMNNORSTU	mensuration
	numerations
AEIMNNSSTTU	sustainment
AEIMNOORSSU	anisomerous
AEIMNOPRTTU	importunate
	permutation
AEIMNOPSTTT	temptations
AEIMNORRSST	ironmasters
AEIMNORRSTT	terminators
AEIMNORRTTY	terminatory
AEIMNORSSTT	monetarists
AEIMNOSSSTY	seismonasty
AEIMNPPRSST	pentaprisms
AEIMNRRSSTT	retransmits
AEIMNRRSTTT	transmitter
AEIMOORSTTU	autoerotism
AEIMOOSSTTU	autotomises
AEIMOOSTTUZ	autotomizes
AEIMOPRRSSU	aspersorium
AEIMOPRRSTT	impetrators
AEIMOPRSTUU	eupatoriums
AEIMPRRTTUY	prematurity
AEIMPRSSTTU	suprematist
AEIMQRSSTUZ	quizmasters
AEIMSSSTTTY	systematist
AEINNNORTTU	antineutron
AEINNOOPRST	personation
AEINNOORSST	resonations
AEINNOORSTV	renovations
AEINNOOSTTT	ostentation
AEINNOPSTTY	spontaneity
AEINNOQRSTU	quaternions
AEINNORSSUZ	Russian Zone
AEINNORSTUV	intravenous
AEINNOSSSUX	anxiousness
AEINNOSSTTV	nonstatives
AEINNPQSSTU	piquantness
AEINNRRSSTY	tyrannisers
AEINNRRSTYZ	tyrannizers
AEINNRSSTTU	unresistant
AEINOOPPRRT	apportioner
	reapportion
AEINOOPPRST	apoproteins
	propionates
AEINOOPRRST	perorations
AEINOOPRSSU	aponeurosis
AEINOOPRTTX	exportation
AEINOORRSTT	restoration
AEINOORSUVX	overanxious
AEINOPPPRST	preappoints
AEINOPRRSST	patronisers
	periastrons
AEINOPRRSTZ	patronizers
AEINOPRSSSU	persuasions
AEINOPRSSSV	vasopressin
AEINOPRSTTU	reputations
AEINOPSTTTU	outpatients
AEINORRSSTT	reinstators
AEINORRSSTU	souterrains
AEINORRSSTV	overstrains
AEINORSSSUV	savouriness
	variousness
AEIOOOPPPRS	prosopopeia
AEIOOPRRSTU	iteroparous
AEIOPPRRRTY	proprietary
AEIOPRRRSST	respirators
AEIOPRRRSTY	respiratory
AEIOPRRRTTU	portraiture
AEIOPRRSTTX	extirpators
AEIOPRRTTUV	vituperator
AEIPPRSTUUV	suppurative
AEIPRSSSTUW	West Prussia
AEKLNNOPSTT	Sankt Pölten
AEKMNOOPSSW	spokeswoman
AEKMORRSSTW	masterworks
AEKOOPRRSTY	prokaryotes
AELLLLRSTUY	stellularly
AELLMOPSSSY	plasmolyses
AELLMOPSSYZ	plasmolyzes
AELLMORSUVY	marvelously
AELLNOOPSTY	Stanley Pool
AELLNOPPRST	propellants
AELLOPRSSTW	wallposters
AELMMNOOPRS	monospermal
AELMMOOPSSS	plasmosomes
AELMMRSSTUU	summersault
AELMNNOOPRT	nontemporal
AELMNNOPSTW	plantswomen
AELMNOPRRSU	supernormal
AELMOOPRSTU	tropaeolums
AELMOPRSTTY	plastometry
AELMOPSSTUY	sympetalous
AELMORSSSTU	somersaults
AELNNOPRSYY	pennyroyals
AELNNSSSUUU	unusualness
AELNOOPPRTT	protoplanet
AELNOORSTTW	Alton Towers
AELNOORSWXY	Lower Saxony
AELNOPRSSSU	parlousness
AELNOPSSSUY	synsepalous
AELNPPRSSTU	supplanters
AELNPRRSUUY	superlunary
AELOOPRRTXY	exploratory
AELOOPSSTTY	osteoplasty
AELOPPRRRSU	pourparlers
AELOPRTTUYY	Port Lyautey
AEMMNORRSTU	mare nostrum
AEMNNNOPSTY	nonpayments
AEMNNOOSSST	stonemasons
AEMNNORRSTT	remonstrant
AEMNNORSTTT	attornments
AEMNNORSTTU	tournaments
AEMNOOPRSTY	trypanosome
AEMNOORRSST	astronomers
AEMNOORSSSU	amorousness
AEMNOORSTUU	neuromatous
AEMNORSSSTT	assortments
AEMNRRSSTTU	transmuters
AEMOOPSSTTY	somatotypes
AEMOPRSSSTT	postmasters
AENNOOPSSTU	spontaneous
AENNOPPRSST	Prestonpans
AENNORRSSTT	nonstarters
AENOOPRRSST	personators

AENOOPRSTXY paroxytones
AENOPRRRSTT transporter
AENOPRRSSST transposers
AENOPRSSTTT protestants
AENORRSTTTU sternutator
AENPPRSSSTU suppressant
AENPRRSSTTU transputers
AEOOPPRRRST propraetors
AEOOPRRSSSV vasopressor
AEOPPRRRSTU rapporteurs
AEOPRRSSSTW sportswears
AEOPRSSTTUW waterspouts
AFFGGHIINRT affrighting
AFFGHLOPSTU ploughstaff
AFFGIIRSSTT graffitists
AFFGIRSSSTU suffragists
AFFILNORSTU insufflator
AFFILNOSSTU sufflations
AFFLLLORUVY flavorfully
AFFLLMOPSUW mallowpuffs
AFGGIINSTTU fustigating
AFGGILNRTUU fulgurating
AFGHHIILNTU highfalutin
AFGHHILLSST flashlights
AFGHIIILNST fishtailing
AFGHILMOPRY filmography
AFGHJNNOOTU John of Gaunt
AFGIIINNRTU infuriating
AFGIILLMNNY inflamingly
AFGIILLNNUY unfailingly
AFGIILMNNTU fulminating
AFGIILMNORS formalising
AFGIILMNORZ formalizing
AFGIILNNOTU antifouling
AFGIIMMNNOY ammonifying
AFGIIMNOSTU fumigations
AFGIIMORSTT sagittiform
AFGIINNOPSY saponifying
AFGIINNQTUY quantifying
AFGIINNRSTX transfixing
AFGIINORSTU figurations
AFGIINOSTTU fustigation
AFGIINRSTTY stratifying
AFGIKLNNOTU outflanking
AFGILLNNTUY flauntingly
AFGILMNORTU formulating
AFGILNORSUV flavourings
AFGILNORTUU fulguration
AFGILNORUVY favouringly
AFGINNRSSTU transfusing
AFGINRRSTTU frustrating
AFGIORSSTTU fustigators
AFGIORSTTUY fustigatory
AFHILORSTWY Solway Firth
AFIIIILNNTV infinitival
AFIIILMNNST infantilism
AFIIILNNTTY infantility
AFIIILNOOSX Alfonso XIII
AFIIINNORTU infuriation
AFIIINNOSTX infixations
AFIILLMORTW Fort William
AFIILMNNOTU fulmination
AFIILMNORTY informality
AFIILNORRTT infiltrator
AFIILNORSTT filtrations flirtations
AFIILORSTTU flirtatious
AFIIMNNOORT information
AFIIMNOORSU omnifarious
AFIIMORSTUV favouritism
AFIINNORSSU infusorians
AFIINNORSTX transfixion
AFIIOPRSSSU fissiparous
AFILLLNOUXY fluxionally
AFILMNOORTU formulation
AFILMNORSTU fulminators
AFILMNORTUY fulminatory
AFIMMORSTUU fumatoriums
AFIMNOORRTY informatory
AFINNORSSTU transfusion
AFINOOPPRST Port of Spain
AFINORRSTTU frustration
AFLMOORRSTU formulators
AGGGINNUWZZ zugzwanging
AGGHHIIILNT hightailing
AGGHHLOPPRY glyphograph
AGGHHOPRRSY hygrographs
AGGHIIJMNTU thingumajig
AGGHIILNNSU languishing
AGGHIILOOST hagiologist
AGGHILNOTUU outlaughing
AGGHMMOPRSY sphygmogram
AGGIIILMNNS misaligning
AGGIIILNNSS signalising
AGGIIILNNSZ signalizing
AGGIIIMMNRT immigrating
AGGIIINNORT originating
AGGIIINNSTT instigating
AGGIIJNNORS jargonising
AGGIIJNNORZ jargonizing
AGGIILMNORS glamorising
AGGIILMNORZ glamorizing
AGGIILNNOSY agonisingly
AGGIILNNOYZ agonizingly
AGGIILNNSTU agglutinins
AGGIILNOOPS apologising
AGGIILNOOPZ apologizing
AGGIILNRSUV vulgarising
AGGIILNRUVZ vulgarizing
AGGIINNORRS garrisoning
AGGIINORTTU gurgitation
AGGILLOOSST algologists
AGGILMNOORY graminology
AGGIMMNOPRR programming
AGGINORRSTU surrogating
AGGLLNOORYY laryngology
AGGLOOORSTY agrostology
AGHHIIJKNNS Jinghis Khan
AGHHIIMNRST nightmarish
AGHHILOPRST lithographs
AGHHILOPRTY lithography
AGHHIMNPRRU harrumphing
AGHHLOOPSUY hylophagous
AGHHNOOPPRS phonographs
AGHHNOOPPRY phonography
AGHHNOORTTY orthognathy
AGHHOOPPRST photographs
AGHHOOPPRTY photography
AGHHOOPRRTY orthography
AGHHOPPRSYY hypsography
AGHHOPPRTYY phytography
AGHHORSTUWY throughways
AGHIIILMNTU humiliating
AGHIIILNNTZ Nizhni Tagil
AGHIIJNNRST Ranjit Singh
AGHIILMNOOS hooliganism
AGHIILNNSVY vanishingly
AGHIILNRSVY ravishingly
AGHIIMNNORS harmonising
AGHIIMNNORZ harmonizing
AGHIIMOPRSU amphigouris
AGHIIMOSTTX thigmotaxis
AGHIINNOSST astonishing
AGHIINNQSUV vanquishing
AGHIINORSTU authorising
AGHIINORTUZ authorizing
AGHIINPRRSS hairsprings
AGHIINPRSTY pharyngitis
AGHIINRSTWW wainwrights
AGHILLNNOUW unhallowing
AGHILNOOSTT anthologist
AGHILOOPSTT pathologist
AGHILOPPSSY gypsophilas
AGHILORSSTT gastroliths
AGHILPRSTWY playwrights
AGHIMNOPRST prognathism
AGHINNOQUUX Hong Xiu Quan
AGHINOOSSTY soothsaying
AGHIOPPRRSS spirographs
AGHJNOOORST John o'Groats
AGHLLOOPSSY hypoglossal
AGHLOOPPSUY polyphagous
AGHLOOPSUXY xylophagous
AGHLOPRSSTY stylographs
AGHLOPRSTYY stylography
AGHMNOOOPSU monophagous
AGHMOOOPRRT graphomotor
AGHNOOPPRRY pornography
AGHNOOPRSTU prognathous
AGIIIILLNNT initialling
AGIIIILNTVX lixiviating
AGIIIJJKMOU Kigoma-Ujiji
AGIIIKLNNOZ kaolinizing
AGIIILLNTTT titillating
AGIIILMNNSU aluminising
AGIIILMNNUZ aluminizing
AGIIILMNSTV vigilantism
AGIIILNNOPV pavilioning
AGIIILNNORS original sin
AGIIILNNPST platinising
AGIIILNNPTZ platinizing

AGIIILNORTV invigilator
AGIIILNORTY originality
AGIIILNOSTT litigations
AGIIILNPSST salpingitis
AGIIILNRSTU ritualising
AGIIILNRSTV virginalist
AGIIILNRTUZ ritualizing
AGIIILNSSUV visualising
AGIIILNSUVZ visualizing
AGIIIMMNORT immigration
AGIIINNNSTU insinuating
AGIIINNOORT origination
AGIIINNOSTT instigation
AGIIINORRST irrigations
AGIIINPRSTV privatising
AGIIINPRTVZ privatizing
AGIIINTTTTV tittivating
AGIIKLMNNOS kalsomining
AGIILLNNOPT pollinating
AGIILLNPQSU pasquilling
AGIILLNPRSU pluralising
AGIILLNPRUZ pluralizing
AGIILMNNORS normalising
AGIILMNNORZ normalizing
AGIILMNNOTY longanimity
AGIILMNPPSY misapplying
AGIILMNSTTU stimulating
AGIILMNSTUU mutualising
AGIILMNTUUZ mutualizing
AGIILNORTUV outrivaling
AGIILNPRSST springtails
AGIILNPSTTU stipulating
AGIILNRSTUY singularity
AGIILNRTUUX luxuriating
AGIILOOSSTX axiologists
AGIIMMNNOPT pantomiming
AGIIMMNNTTU manumitting
AGIIMMNRSSU summarising
AGIIMMNRSUZ summarizing
AGIIMMORRST immigrators
AGIIMMORRTY immigratory
AGIIMMOSSST misogamists
AGIIMNNOPTU impugnation
AGIIMNNPRSS mainsprings
AGIIMNRRSTY martyrising
AGIIMNRRTYZ martyrizing
AGIIMSSSTTT stigmatists
AGIINNNRSTY tyrannising
AGIINNNRTYZ tyrannizing
AGIINNOPRST patronising
AGIINNOPRTZ patronizing
AGIINNPRRST transpiring
AGIINNRSTTU intriguants
AGIINOORRST originators
AGIINOORRTV invigorator
AGIINORSSTT instigators
AGIINRRTTTU triturating
AGIJLNOSTUU jugulations
AGIJNOPSTUX juxtaposing
AGIKLOORSTY karyologist
AGIKMNOPRST postmarking
AGIKNOPRTYY karyotyping
AGILLLNPTUU pullulating
AGILLMNNOOU monolingual
AGILLNPRTTY prattlingly
AGILLNRSTTY startlingly
AGILMNNOOSU longanimous
AGILMNPPRSS Palm Springs
AGILMOOPRTY primatology
AGILMOPSSTY polygamists
AGILMRSTTUU gutturalism
AGILNNPPSTU supplanting
AGILNNPRSUY unsparingly
AGILNOOOPRS sporogonial
AGILNOPPRVY approvingly
AGILNOPRSTU sporulating
AGILNOPSTTU postulating
AGILNPSTTUU pustulating
AGILOOPRSTT patrologist
AGILOORSSTT astrologist
AGILOOSTTTU tautologist
AGILORSSSST glossarists
AGILRTTTUUY gutturality
AGIMMNOOSST monogamists
AGIMNNRSTTU transmuting
AGIMNOOPRST protagonism
AGIMNOORSST agronomists
AGIMNORSTTU outsmarting
AGINNNOPSTU outspanning
AGINNOPRSST transposing
AGINNPPRSTU unstrapping
AGINOOOPRRT prorogation
AGINOOPRSTT protagonist
AGINOORRSTU surrogation
AGINOORRSUV granivorous
AGINOPRRSTT prostrating
AGINPPRSTUU suppurating
AGINRRSSTUU susurrating
AGLLLNOOPYY polygonally
AGLLMOORSUY glamorously
AGLLORRSUUY garrulously
AGLMNOORSUU unglamorous
AGLMNOORTYY laryngotomy
AGLMOOOSTTY stomatology
AGLMOOPRRTU promulgator
AGLMOORRTYY martyrology
AGLNNOPPTUY oppugnantly
AGLOOOSTTUU tautologous
AGMOOORSSTT Matto Grosso
AGMOORSSTTY gastrostomy
AHHIIIPRSST phthiriasis
AHHILMOPSTY halophytism
AHHILNOORTU holothurian
AHHILOPPSYY hypophysial
AHHIMNOPSSW showmanship
AHHIMOPSTYY hypothymias
AHHIOPRSSTU authorships
AHHLLNOPTXY xanthophyll
AHHLNOPSTXY xanthophyls
AHIIIJKNRSS jinrikishas
AHIIILMNOTU humiliation
AHIIILNPPPS Philippians
AHIIIMNNOSY Nishinomiya
AHIILLORSUY hilariously
AHIILMORSTU humiliators
AHIILMORTUY humiliatory
AHIILNPSSTY Hypsilantis
AHIILOPSTTY hospitality
AHIILRSSTTY hairstylist
AHIIMNNOSTU inhumations
AHIIMNNRRTU antirrhinum
AHIIMNOOOSU homoiousian
AHIIMOOPPPT hippopotami
AHIIOPRRSTT traitorship
AHIIRSSSTTW shirtwaists
AHIKKOORRSW kwashiorkor
AHIKMNOPRSW workmanship
AHILLMOOPST Matopo Hills
AHILLMOPRTU prothallium
AHILLNOPSYY anisophylly
AHILLOPSTXY phyllotaxis
AHILMNOPPSW plowmanship
AHILNOORSTZ horizontals
AHILNOPRSTY rhinoplasty
AHILOORRTTY hortatorily
AHILOPPRSXY prophylaxis
AHILOPRRUXY pyrrhuloxia
AHIMNOOOSSU homoousians
AHIMNOORRSU honorariums
AHIMNOPRSTY misanthropy
AHIMOOOPSST opisthosoma
AHIMOORSTUZ rhizomatous
AHINOOPPRST patroonship
AHINOOPSSTX saxophonist
AHINOPRSSUX xiphosurans
AHIOPPRSSST pastorships
AHLMNOTUXYZ zanthoxylum
AHLMOOPPRST trophoplasm
AHLMOOPRSTU photomurals
AHLMOOPRSUY amorphously
AHMMORSSTTU smartmouths
AHMNNOOPRTT Northampton
AHMNOOPRSTU protohumans
AHMNOOPSTTU Southampton
AHNNOSSTTWY shantytowns
AHNORSSTUUY thysanurous
AHOOPPRRSST saprotrophs
AIIIIJNNSTU Justinian II
AIIIILNOTVX lixiviation
AIIIINNOSTT initiations
AIIILLLNPTU lilliputian
AIIILLNOPTX pixillation
AIIILLNOTTT titillation
AIIILLNOTUV illuviation
AIIILMMNSST minimalists
AIIILMNOPST postliminia
AIIILMNOSTT limitations
militations
AIIILMNPRTT tripalmitin
AIIILMRSSTT militarists
AIIILNNOOST lionisation
AIIILNNOOTZ lionization
AIIILNNOTTU intuitional
AIIILNOSTTU utilisation
AIIILNOTTUZ utilization
AIIIMNNOSTT intimations

AIIIMNRSTTU	miniaturist
AIIIMPPRRTY	primiparity
AIIIMPSSTVY	impassivity
AIIINNNOSTU	insinuation
AIIINNOOSST	ionisations
AIIINNOOSTZ	ionizations
AIIINNOPRST	inspiration
AIIINNOSTTU	unitisation
AIIINNOSTTV	invitations
AIIINNOTTUZ	unitization
AIIINORRSTT	irritations
AIIINOSSTTV	visitations
AIIINOSTTTV	titivations
AIIINOTTTTV	tittivation
AIILLMMNOTU	multinomial
AIILLMNNSTU	illuminants
AIILLMNORTU	illuminator
AIILLMNORTY	trinomially
AIILLNNOOPT	pollination
AIILLNORSUY	illusionary
AIILLNRSSTY	sinistrally
AIILLPPRTUY	pupillarity
AIILLPRSTUY	spiritually
AIILLPSTTUY	pulsatility
AIILMMNOOST	immolations
AIILMMORSST	immoralists
AIILMMORTTY	immortality
AIILMNNNOTT	nonmilitant
AIILMNNOSST	nominalists
AIILMNOOPRT	imploration
AIILMNOOPST	malposition
AIILMNOOSST	solmisation
AIILMNOOSTZ	solmization
AIILMNOSSTU	simulations
AIILMNOSTTU	mutilations
	stimulation
AIILMNOSTUY	aluminosity
AIILMOPRRTY	promilitary
AIILMPRTTUY	multiparity
AIILMRSSUVV	survivalism
AIILNNOOSST	insolations
AIILNNORSTU	intrusional
AIILNNORTTU	nutritional
AIILNNOSSTU	insulations
AIILNOOPPST	oppilations
AIILNOOPRSV	provisional
AIILNOORTVY	volitionary
AIILNOPRTUY	unipolarity
AIILNOPSTTU	stipulation
AIILNORTUUX	luxuriation
AIILNOSSTTY	stylisation
AIILNOSTTYZ	stylization
AIILNPRSTUU	unspiritual
AIILNQRTTUY	tranquility
AIILPRSTTUY	spiritualty
AIILRSSTUVV	survivalist
AIIMMNNOSSU	manumission
AIIMMNOPSTT	pantomimist
AIIMMNSSTTU	numismatist
AIIMMPRRSTU	imprimaturs
AIIMNNNOOST	nominations
AIIMNNORSTU	ruminations
AIIMNNRSSTT	ministrants
AIIMNOOPRTT	importation
AIIMNOOPRTX	proximation
AIIMNOOSTTV	motivations
AIIMNOPRSTV	provitamins
AIIMNOPSTTU	imputations
AIIMNORSTTZ	Saint Moritz
AIIMOPPRRSU	primiparous
AIINNNOOSTT	intonations
AIINNNOOSTV	innovations
AIINNNORRTT	nonirritant
AIINNOOOSTZ	ozonisation
AIINNOOOTZZ	ozonization
AIINNORSSTT	transitions
AIINNORSSTU	insinuators
AIINNORSTUY	insinuatory
AIINNRSTTUY	saturninity
AIINOOPPSST	appositions
AIINOPRRSST	inspirators
AIINOPRRSTY	inspiratory
AIINOPRRTTU	parturition
AIINOPRSSST	inspissator
AIINOPRSSTU	suspiration
AIINORRTTTU	trituration
AIINQRSSSTU	sinarquists
AIIOOPPRRTT	propitiator
AIIOPRRSTTT	portraitist
AIIOPRSSTTT	prostatitis
AIIORSTTTTV	tittivators
AIIPRSSSTTU	Pisistratus
AIIPRSSTTVY	varitypists
AIJLNORSSTU	journalists
AIKLLOSSTUW	Lutosławski
AIKMNOSSWYZ	Szymanowski
AIKNOORSTTW	workstation
AILLLNOOPRU	allopurinol
AILLLNOPTUU	pullulation
AILLMNOOPSY	polynomials
AILLMOOPRST	allotropism
AILLMOPSSSY	plasmolysis
AILLNOOPRST	pollinators
AILLNOORSTY	torsionally
AILLNOPRSUU	nulliparous
AILLNORTUVY	voluntarily
AILLNPPSTUY	suppliantly
AILLNRTUUXY	luxuriantly
AILLORRSTTU	illustrator
AILMMNOOSSY	ammonolysis
AILMNNOSUUY	unanimously
AILMNOOOPRT	promotional
AILMNOOPSST	lampoonists
AILMNOORSTT	monolatrist
AILMNOPPSSS	Simplon Pass
AILMNOPRTTY	importantly
AILMNORSTUV	voluntarism
AILMOOPRRTY	imploratory
AILMOOPRUYZ	polyzoarium
AILMOPRSTUU	multiparous
AILMORSSTTU	stimulators
AILNNORTUVY	involuntary
AILNOOPPSTU	populations
AILNOOPRSTU	sporulation
AILNOOPSTTU	postulation
AILNOPPSTTU	postnuptial
AILNOPSTTUU	pustulation
AILNORSSTTU	lustrations
AILNORSTTUV	voluntarist
AILNORSUUVY	unsavourily
AILNOSSTTUU	ustulations
AILNRSSTUUU	laurustinus
AILOOPRSUVY	oviparously
AILOPRSSTTU	stipulators
AILOPRSTTUY	stipulatory
AILORSTTTUY	statutorily
AIMMNORSSTU	stramoniums
AIMMOORRSTU	moratoriums
AIMMOOSSTXY	myxomatosis
AIMNNOOSTUU	mountainous
AIMNNOPRTTU	unimportant
AIMNOOSSTTU	autonomists
AIMNOOSSTTX	taxonomists
AIMNOPSSSTU	assumptions
AIMNRSSTTUU	nasturtiums
AIMOPSSSSTY	symposiasts
AINNNOOORTT	Torontonian
AINNOOPRSTT	antiprotons
AINOOPRRSTT	prostration
AINOOSSTTTU	outstations
AINOPPRSTUU	suppuration
AINOPRSSTUU	usurpations
AINORRSSSTT	transistors
AINORRSSTUU	susurration
AINPRSSTUUV	pursuivants
AIORRRSTTTU	triturators
AKLNNOOOPTZ	zooplankton
ALLLNOOPTYY	polytonally
ALLNOOOPPRR	propranolol
ALLNOPPRUUY	unpopularly
ALLOOOPRSTU	allotropous
ALLOORSTWWW	swallowwort
ALMNNOOSUYY	anonymously
ALMNOOORSTU	monolatrous
ALMNOPRSSTY	sportsmanly
ALNNORSTUYY	tyrannously
ALOOPPRSSTT	protoplasts
ALOOPRSSTTU	postulators
ALOPRRSTUUY	rapturously
AMMNOOORRST	Marston Moor
AMNOOPRSSTW	sportswoman
AMNOOSTTUUY	tautonymous
AMOOPRRRTTY	protomartyr
ANNOOPRSSST	transposons
ANOOOPRRTTY	protonotary
BBBEEIINRSW	winebibbers
BBBEGIIINNW	winebibbing
BBBEOORSSXY	bobbysoxers
BBCCEEHKLOR	breechblock
BBCCEHIOPRY	cyberphobic
BBCDEEEEIKR	Beiderbecke
BBCDEHIRRTU	butcherbird
BBCEEGIILLR	gibberellic
BBCEEKNRRSU	rubbernecks
BBCEELNOOST	cobblestone
BBCEELNOOSU	bubonoceles

BBCEILMOSTU	combustible
BBCEINRSSSU	scrubbiness
BBCEINRSSUU	unsubscribe
BBCEIRRSSSU	subscribers
BBCEJKOORST	stockjobber
BBCEKLORSTU	blockbuster
BBCGIINRSSU	subscribing
BBCGIMOORRY	borborygmic
BBCILMOSTUY	combustibly
BBDDEGILNOS	bobsledding
BBDEEGHILOS	bobsleighed
BBDEEGIILNO	Gideon Bible
BBDEEHHLOOY	hobbledehoy
BBDEELLORWY	Lloyd Webber
BBDEGIIMNOV	divebombing
BBDEGINORUV	overdubbing
BBDEHHOORSY	hobbyhorsed
BBDEIKNOORS	bookbinders
BBDEIKNOORY	bookbindery
BBDEILLMOOO	bloodmobile
BBDELNRSSUU	blunderbuss
BBDGIIKNNOO	bookbinding
BBDGINOSUYY	busybodying
BBDHIIOPRSS	bishopbirds
BBDINOOORSW	ribbonwoods
BBEEEFGRRSU	beefburgers
BBEEEILRRSU	blueberries
BBEEGIILLNR	gibberellin
BBEEGILMRSU	submergible
BBEEHIRRSSU	shrubberies
BBEEILMRSSU	submersible
BBEELLOSTTU	bluebottles
BBEELNNOSTU	bluebonnets
BBEENORRSYY	boysenberry
BBEFILORSUU	bulbiferous
BBEGIIIOSST	gibbosities
BBEGIINRRSU	rubberising
BBEGIINRRUZ	rubberizing
BBEGIKLNOOR	Bolingbroke
BBEGILMNNUY	benumbingly
BBEGINOSSSU	gibbousness
BBEHHILOSST	shibboleths
BBEHHOORSSY	hobbyhorses
BBEHIIILLOP	bibliophile
BBEHINRSSSU	shrubbiness
BBEHLORSTTU	bottlebrush
BBEIILLOOPS	bibliopoles
BBEIILMSSSU	submissible
BBEIKLMOOOS	bookmobiles
BBEKNORSSTU	bonkbusters
BBELLNOTTUY	bellybutton
BBGHILNORTY	throbbingly
BBGHINNRSUU	burning bush
BBGIILLNQUY	quibblingly
BBGMOORRSUY	borborygmus
BBHIIILLOPS	bibliophils
BCCDDEEHKOY	bodychecked
BCCDEILNOTU	conductible
BCCEEEEFINN	beneficence
BCCEEEENRSU	erubescence
BCCEEHHLORT	breechcloth
BCCEEHLORTU	breechclout

BCCEEIILNOR	incoercible
BCCEEIILORT	bioelectric
BCCEEIINOSS	biosciences
BCCEEIIRSST	bisectrices
BCCEEILLLOT	collectible
BCCEEILNNOT	connectible
BCCEEILNOSS	concessible
BCCEEILORRT	correctible
BCCEEIMRRSY	cybercrimes
BCCEEINRSTY	cybernetics
BCCEFIIPSSU	subspecific
BCCEHINOOPR	necrophobic
BCCEIILNNOV	convincible
BCCEIILNORU	ribonucleic
BCCEIILNOTV	convictible
BCCEIINOOOT	biocoenotic
BCCEIINOORT	necrobiotic
BCCEIMOORSX	coxcombries
BCCEIORSSTU	subcortices
BCCHINOOPTY	nyctophobic
BCDDEEEILNS	descendible
BCDDEEEIRRS	redescribed
BCDDEEILSTU	deductibles
BCDDEIIKRSY	dickeybirds
BCDEEEIINNT	Benedictine
BCDEEEIINST	benedicites
BCDEEEIORRS	cerebroside
BCDEEEIRRSS	redescribes
BCDEEFIIJOT	objectified
BCDEEHILNPT	pitchblende
BCDEEHIMORS	chemisorbed
BCDEEHMNOOY	honeycombed
BCDEEHMNOTU	debouchment
BCDEEHMOORS	chemosorbed
BCDEEHORSUU	debouchures
BCDEEIIILRT	liberticide
BCDEEIIIMNO	biomedicine
BCDEEIILNRS	discernible
BCDEEIILRRU	irreducible
BCDEEIILSST	dissectible
BCDEEIINNOT	benediction
BCDEEIINOTU	butenedioic
BCDEEILNNOS	condensible
BCDEEIMNRSU	disencumber
BCDEEINORTY	benedictory
BCDEEINSSSU	subsidences
BCDEELMNTUY	decumbently
BCDEEORRSSS	crossbreeds
BCDEGHNRRSU	bergschrund
BCDEHIILORS	bichlorides
BCDEHILNNOR	hornblendic
BCDEHILORSU	subchloride
BCDEHKOOTTU	bucktoothed
BCDEIIILRTY	credibility
BCDEIILNRSY	discernibly
BCDEIILRRUY	irreducibly
BCDEIILSSSU	discussible
BCDEINORTTU	contributed
BCDEIOOPRSS	proboscides
BCDEIORRSTU	subdirector
BCDEKLOORSU	bloodsucker
BCDELRSTUUU	subcultured

BCDEMMNRSUU	cummerbunds
BCDGIIKMNOR	mockingbird
BCDHHIOOPRY	hydrophobic
BCDHIMOORRY	hydrobromic
BCDIINRTUUY	rubicundity
BCDIIOPRRST	tropicbirds
BCDIIRSSTTU	subdistrict
BCDINOSSTUU	subductions
BCDLORSSTUU	cloudbursts
BCEEEELNNOV	benevolence
BCEEEFILPRT	perfectible
BCEEEGHINRR	Reichenberg
BCEEEGMNRSU	submergence
BCEEEHHINPR	hebephrenic
BCEEEIILRST	celebrities
BCEEEILPPRT	perceptible
BCEEEILPRTX	excerptible
BCEEELLMRSU	cerebellums
BCEEENQSSUU	subsequence
BCEEFIIJOST	objectifies
BCEEFILORRW	Wilberforce
BCEEFIMNORT	fibrocement
BCEEFIOPRSS	fiberscopes
	fibrescopes
BCEEGIIOTVZ	Izetbegović
BCEEGILNOST	congestible
BCEEGIMNNRU	encumbering
BCEEGIMNORY	embryogenic
BCEEGKLMNRU	Mecklenburg
BCEEHHNOOPT	technophobe
BCEEHINORRS	Breconshire
BCEEHIOORRS	seborrhoeic
BCEEHKLNOSU	hucklebones
BCEEHKLRRUY	huckleberry
BCEEHKNORSW	workbenches
BCEEHKOOQSU	chequebooks
BCEEHLMOPTY	phlebectomy
BCEEHMORSUU	embouchures
BCEEHNOOPRS	necrophobes
BCEEIILPSST	plebiscites
BCEEIILRSSS	rescissible
BCEEIINOSST	obscenities
BCEEIJLOTVY	objectively
BCEEIJSSTUV	subjectives
BCEEILLLOSY	bellicosely
BCEEILMNNOT	contemnible
BCEEILMOOST	lobectomies
BCEEILMOSST	comestibles
BCEEILNORST	bristlecone
BCEEILNORTV	convertible
BCEEILORRSU	Le Corbusier
BCEEILPPRTY	perceptibly
BCEEILPRSTU	putrescible
BCEEILPSSTU	susceptible
BCEEINSSSTU	subsistence
BCEEIORRRSW	crowberries
BCEEIPRRRSS	prescribers
BCEEIPRRSSU	superscribe
BCEEIRRSSTT	bittercress
BCEEJLSSSTU	subjectless
BCEEKKLNNOU	knucklebone
BCEEKLNOSTT	bottlenecks

BCEEKORSTUX tuckerboxes
BCEELMMOOTY embolectomy
BCEELMNRTUY recumbently
BCEELNOOSST obsolescent
BCEELNOSTTU cuttlebones
BCEELORSSTU beltcourses
BCEEMMORTYY embryectomy
BCEEMNOSTTU obmutescent
BCEENORSSSU obscureness
BCEEOOORRRS corroborees
BCEFFIORSSU subofficers
BCEFHILLNSU bullfinches
BCEFIIMORRS microfibers
BCEGHHIMOWY High Wycombe
BCEGHIIMNRS besmirching
BCEGIIMMNOS misbecoming
BCEGIIMNNOR recombining
BCEGIIMNNRU incumbering
BCEGIINPRRS prescribing
BCEGILMOORY embryologic
BCEGILNOOOY biocenology
BCEGILNOOSS obsolescing
BCEHHILNOOT holobenthic
BCEHIIIOSTT bioethicist
BCEHIIMOSST biochemists
BCEHILMOOPT phlebotomic
BCEHILNOORS bronchioles
BCEHILNOSST blotchiness
BCEHKKOOSST sketchbooks
BCEHKLOOSSU blockhouses
BCEHLOORSTW blowtorches
BCEHLORRSYY chrysoberyl
BCEHMOORTTY thrombocyte
BCEHMRSSTUW thumbscrews
BCEIIJMOSTV objectivism
BCEIIJOSTTV objectivist
BCEIIJOTTVY objectivity
BCEIIKLLLSS sicklebills
BCEIIKLLRST billsticker
BCEIILLOSTY bellicosity
BCEIIMMRSTY bisymmetric
BCEIINOOOSS biocoenosis
BCEIINOORSS necrobiosis
BCEIIORSSTU obscurities
BCEIJNOSSTU subjections
BCEIJNSTUUV subjunctive
BCEIKLOORST bootlickers
BCEILLORSSU brucellosis
BCEILMNNOTY contemnibly
BCEILMNNTUY incumbently
BCEILMNRSSU crumbliness
BCEILMOOPSS compossible
BCEILMORTUU microtubule
BCEILNNOSUU Cunobelinus
BCEILNORTVY convertibly
BCEILOPRRTU corruptible
BCEILPSSTUY susceptibly
BCEIMOSSTUV combustives
BCEINORSTTU contributes
BCEINOSSSTU subsections
BCEIOOPRSSS proboscises
BCEIOPRRRSS proscribers
BCEIORSTTUV obstructive
BCEJKMPRSUU buckjumpers
BCEKKOOOPST pocketbooks
BCEKKOORRST stockbroker
BCEKLNRSTUU turnbuckles
BCELMOORSYY corymbosely
BCELORSTUUU tuberculous
BCELRSSTUUU subcultures
BCELSTTTTUU scuttlebutt
BCEMNOORSSW crossbowmen
BCEOOOPRSST stroboscope
BCFIIILORTY forcibility
BCGIIILNPSU publicising
BCGIIILNPUZ publicizing
BCGIIKLNOOT bootlicking
BCGIINOOOTT gnotobiotic
BCGIINOPRRS proscribing
BCGIJKMNPUU buckjumping
BCGIKLLNOOS bollockings
bollocksing
BCGIKNPRSSU springbucks
BCGILOOORYY cryobiology
BCGINORSTTU obstructing
BCHHIIMORTY biorhythmic
BCHHIOOOPPT photophobic
BCHIILNOPSY phycobilins
BCHILLOPSYY psychobilly
BCHIMOORSTW witchbrooms
BCIIIILMSTY miscibility
BCIIIILNTVY vincibility
BCIILMMNOUU cumulonimbi
BCIILMOSSTY symbolistic
BCIJNNOSTUU subjunction
BCIKMOORSST broomsticks
BCILLORSUUY lubricously
BCILMNNOOSY nonsymbolic
BCILOPRRTUY corruptibly
BCIMNOOSSTU combustions
BCIMORRSSTU microbursts
BCINOOPRTTY cryptobiont
BCINOORRTTU contributor
BCINOORSTTU obstruction
BCOORRSSTTU obstructors
BDDDEEEINRT interbedded
BDDDEEIIMOS disembodied
BDDDEEINRRU underbidder
BDDDEEINRSU disburdened
BDDDEFILLNO blindfolded
BDDDEFMNOUU dumbfounded
BDDEEEIILSV disbelieved
BDDEEEIMMRS dismembered
BDDEEEIMNRT debridement
BDDEEEIMORR embroidered
BDDEEGIMOSU disembogued
BDDEEIILMOS demobilised
BDDEEIILMOZ demobilized
BDDEEIIMOSS disembodies
BDDEEIINOST disobedient
BDDEEILORSW bowdlerised
BDDEEILORWZ bowdlerized
BDDEEIMNOST disentombed
BDDEEINORSU underbodies
BDDEENSSSUU subduedness
BDDEFINNORU unforbidden
BDDEGGLNOOO boondoggled
BDDEGIINORV overbidding
BDDEHINRRTU thunderbird
BDDEHLNOORS bondholders
BDDEIIRSSUV subdividers
BDDEIIRSTTU distributed
BDDEILLNRUY unbridledly
BDDEILMORSW middlebrows
BDDEINRSTUU undisturbed
BDDELNNOUUY unboundedly
BDDELNOTUUY undoubtedly
BDDGGINOOSY dogsbodying
BDDGIIINSUV subdividing
BDDHIIIMRSY dihybridism
BDDHLNOOOSU bloodhounds
BDEEEHIKRSW bewhiskered
BDEEEHILLMS embellished
BDEEEHILMTW thimbleweed
BDEEEHINRSW New Hebrides
BDEEEHLLNRS hellbenders
BDEEEIILRSV disbeliever
BDEEEIILSSV disbelieves
BDEEEILMNTV bedevilment
BDEEEILMPRT redemptible
BDEEEILPRSS depressible
BDEEEILRRSS redressible
BDEEEILSSTW wildebeests
BDEEEIMMRRS dismemberer
disremember
BDEEEIMNNOU Boumédienne
BDEEEIMNNTZ bedizenment
BDEEEIMORRR embroiderer
BDEEEINRRST interbreeds
BDEEEIRSTTW bitterweeds
BDEEELMSTUW tumbleweeds
BDEEELNSSSS blessedness
BDEEELORSTU doubletrees
BDEEFGIINNR befriending
BDEEFHIRRSU refurbished
BDEEFILRTTU Butterfield
BDEEFLLNORU bellfounder
BDEEGGHIIRW weighbridge
BDEEGHILNTY benightedly
BDEEGHINORU neighboured
BDEEGHOORRT God-botherer
BDEEGIILLNV bedevilling
BDEEGIILNRW bewildering
BDEEGIINNRS inbreedings
BDEEGILMNNO emboldening
BDEEGIMOSSU disembogues
BDEEGINORTU outbreeding
BDEEGLNORSU bludgeoners
BDEEHIINNPU Dien Bien Phu
BDEEHILMNSU unblemished
BDEEHILPRSU republished
BDEEHNNRTUU unburthened
BDEEIILMOSS demobilises
BDEEIILMOSZ demobilizes
BDEEIILNSST distensible

BDEEIIRSTTU	distributee
BDEEIKLNPRS	besprinkled
BDEEILLNPRS	spellbinder
BDEEILMNOTY	molybdenite
BDEEILMOSSW	disembowels
BDEEILMRSSS	dissemblers
BDEEILNORRS	borderlines
BDEEILNPRTU	blueprinted
BDEEILNPSSU	suspendible
BDEEILORRSW	bowdleriser
BDEEILORRWZ	bowdlerizer
BDEEILORSSW	bowdlerises
BDEEILORSWZ	bowdlerizes
BDEEIMMNOST	embodiments
BDEEIMNORST	disrobement
BDEEIMRSTTU	resubmitted
BDEEINORSTX	tinderboxes
BDEEIOORSXY	deoxyribose
BDEELNRRSSU	blurredness
BDEEMNORTUU	outnumbered
BDEENNNOSTU	sunbonneted
BDEENORRSUV	overburdens
BDEENPRRTUU	unperturbed
BDEFGINOORS	forebodings
BDEFGIOORST	footbridges
BDEFGSSSTUU	fussbudgets
BDEFHIILNSS	blindfishes
BDEFILNOOSS	dobsonflies
BDEFILNORSW	brownfields
BDEFLLNORUY	bellfoundry
BDEFORRSSUY	bodysurfers
BDEGGILNNOU	bludgeoning
BDEGGLNOOOR	boondoggler
BDEGGLNOOOS	boondoggles
BDEGHHIINRS	highbinders
BDEGHNORTUU	underbought
BDEGIILMNSS	dissembling
BDEGIKORRSW	bridgeworks
BDEGILNNNUY	unbendingly
BDEGILNNRSU	blunderings
BDEGIMOORRS	bridegrooms
BDEGIMORRSY	dogberryism
BDEGINNNRUU	unburdening
BDEGINNRUUY	underbuying
BDEGIORRSTU	Stourbridge
BDEHHOOORRT	brotherhood
BDEHIIINNTU	uninhibited
BDEHIIKLLTY	Billy the Kid
BDEHIILPRSU	shipbuilder
BDEHIILPSSU	bisulphides
BDEHIIRRSSY	hybridisers
BDEHIIRRSYZ	hybridizers
BDEHIKLNOTU	doublethink
BDEHILLPPUW	bullwhipped
BDEHILLSTTU	bullshitted
BDEHILNPSUU	unpublished
BDEHILOOPRY	hyperboloid
BDEHIMOORSU	rhomboideus
BDEHLNOOTTU	buttonholed
BDEHLNORTTU	thunderbolt
BDEHMOOORST	smoothbored
BDEHNRRSSUU	undershrubs
BDEIIIILNSV	indivisible
BDEIIIILNTY	inedibility
BDEIIILMMOS	immobilised
BDEIIILMMOZ	immobilized
BDEIIILMSSS	dismissible
BDEIIILNTVY	vendibility
BDEIIIMNSTU	bituminised
BDEIIIMNTUZ	bituminized
BDEIIIMORST	morbidities
BDEIIIOSSTU	dubiosities
BDEIILLOSSU	solubilised
BDEIILLOSUZ	solubilized
BDEIILMORSS	disembroils
BDEIILMRSUU	subdelirium
BDEIIRRSTTU	distributer
BDEIIRSSSSU	subsidisers
BDEIIRSSSUZ	subsidizers
BDEIIRSSTTU	distributes
BDEIJNORSSU	subjoinders
BDEIKNORSTU	strikebound
BDEILLORSWY	yellowbirds
BDEILMOOOST	lobotomised
BDEILMOOOTZ	lobotomized
BDEILMOOSSS	disselbooms
BDEILMORSSW	bowdlerisms
BDEILNORSTY	blindstorey
BDEINOSSSUU	dubiousness
BDEIOORSTTW	bitterwoods
BDEISSTTTUU	substituted
BDEKMMNRSUU	kummerbunds
BDELLLOOSSY	bloodlessly
BDELLNOSSUY	boundlessly
BDELLOSSTUY	doubtlessly
BDELMNOOSUY	molybdenous
BDELNOOOSST	bloodstones
BDFGINORSUY	bodysurfing
BDGGHIINNOS	Gobind Singh
BDGGIIILNOS	disobliging
BDGGILRSUUW	Ludwigsburg
BDGHIIINRSY	hybridising
BDGHIIINRYZ	hybridizing
BDGHIILNSST	blindsights
BDGHIIMMNRU	hummingbird
BDGIIINSSSU	subsidising
BDGIIINSSUZ	subsidizing
BDGIILNOTUU	outbuilding
BDGIIMNOSTU	misdoubting
BDGIKMNOSSU	subkingdoms
BDGILLOOTUY	bloodguilty
BDGILNNNSUU	unbundlings
BDHIILRRSWY	whirlybirds
BDHIMNOORSY	monohybrids
BDIIIILNSVY	indivisibly
BDIIINOSSUV	subdivision
BDIILNOOPST	diplobionts
BDIIMNORTUY	moribundity
BDIIORRSTTU	distributor
BDKNNOOORSY	donnybrooks
BDLMNOOTTUU	buttonmould
BDNOOOSTTUW	buttonwoods
BEEEEMMRRRS	rememberers
BEEEFMRRSUZ	bumfreezers
BEEEFOORRST	freebooters
BEEEGGRRSUV	vegeburgers
BEEEGIINNOR	bioengineer
BEEEGIJLLNW	bejewelling
BEEEGILLNRT	belligerent
BEEEGILLNSS	legibleness
BEEEGILMNTU	beguilement
BEEEGILNRUV	Vigée-Lebrun
BEEEGIMMNRR	remembering
BEEEGINRRRS	greenbriers
BEEEGLNORTT	greenbottle
BEEEHILLMRS	embellisher
BEEEHILLMSS	embellishes
BEEEHILLNOR	helleborine
BEEEHLLRSTT	shelterbelt
BEEEHLLRSTW	bellwethers
BEEEHLPSSTU	steeplebush
BEEEIINRRSW	wineberries
BEEEIKLLRRS	bierkellers
BEEEIKMORSU	boeremusiek
BEEEIKNSSTT	Beit Knesset
BEEEIKOPRRS	pokeberries
BEEEILNNORV	nonbeliever
BEEEILNPRTV	preventible
BEEEILNRSUV	unbelievers
BEEEILPRRSS	repressible
BEEEILPRRTV	pervertible
BEEEILPRSSX	expressible
BEEEILRRSSV	reversibles
BEEEIMMMRRS	misremember
BEEEIMRRSTT	embitterers
BEEEINNRRTU	breunnerite
BEEEIOPRRRS	Robespierre
BEEEIRRSSTW	sweetbriers
BEEEIRSTTTW	bittersweet
BEEEKKOOPRS	bookkeepers
BEEELLRSSST	bestsellers
BEEELMNNNOT	ennoblement
BEEEMNRSTTT	betterments
BEEENOPPRTY	teenybopper
BEEENORSSSV	verboseness
BEEENORSSTT	bonesetters
BEEFFIORRSU	febriferous
BEEFGHILOSS	globefishes
BEEFGIINNTT	benefitting
BEEFGINOORT	freebooting
BEEFGINRSUZ	subfreezing
BEEFGLLOORW	globeflower
BEEFGRSSTUU	subterfuges
BEEFHIRRSSU	refurbishes
BEEFIIILRST	febrilities
BEEFILLMRSU	umbellifers
BEEFILNSSSU	fusibleness
BEEFILRSTTU	butterflies
BEEFLLLORSW	bellflowers
BEEFLMNOSTU	befoulments
BEEGGGLOOSX	goggleboxes
BEEGGHNRRTU	Terbrugghen
BEEGGILSSTU	suggestible
BEEGGLOORST	bootleggers
BEEGHINNORR	herringbone

BEEGHINRRST brighteners
BEEGHNOOPRS negrophobes
BEEGIIILLNS ineligibles
BEEGIIINNST benignities
BEEGIILMMNS emblemising
BEEGIILMMNZ emblemizing
BEEGIILNNUV unbelieving
BEEGIIMNRTT embittering
BEEGIIOORSU bourgeoisie
BEEGIKKNOOP bookkeeping
BEEGILLMNOW embowelling
BEEGILLNORW rebellowing
BEEGILLNSST bestselling
BEEGILMNOST obligements
BEEGILNNOSS ignobleness
BEEGIMNNRRU renumbering
BEEGIMNOPRT obtempering
BEEGIMNOSTT misbegotten
BEEGINPRSST Spitsbergen
BEEGIOORSSU bourgeoises
BEEGKLNTTUU Telukbetung
BEEGLMMPTUY mumbletypeg
BEEGLNOSTUU bluetongues
BEEGMNRRSTU Münsterberg
BEEGMNSSSTU subsegments
BEEGMRRTTUW Württemberg
BEEGPRRRSSU Pressburger
BEEHIKORTUW Bourke-White
BEEHILNSSSU blueishness
BEEHILOPRSY hyperbolise
BEEHILOPRYZ hyperbolize
BEEHILPRSSU republishes
BEEHIMMPRSS memberships
BEEHIMNOORT theobromine
BEEHKNOORSU housebroken
BEEHLLNOOPR Bellerophon
BEEHMNOOSST mesobenthos
BEEHMNORSTU burthensome
BEEHOPRRSTT stepbrother
BEEIIJORSTU bijouteries
BEEIILMPRSS impressible
permissible
BEEIILNSSSV visibleness
BEEIILSSSTX bissextiles
BEEIINRRSTW twinberries
BEEIIRRTTUV retributive
BEEIKKNORRS knobkerries
BEEIKLNPRSS besprinkles
BEEIKNORRRT interbroker
BEEILLLNTUV ebulliently
BEEILLMNOPT Bontempelli
BEEILLMRSST belletrisms
BEEILLORRSU irresoluble
BEEILLRRRTU bullterrier
BEEILLRSSTT belletrists
BEEILMMNORT embroilment
BEEILNOPRSS responsible
BEEILNOQSSU obliqueness
BEEILNPRTVY preventibly
BEEILNPSSSU suspensible
BEEILNRSSTT brittleness
BEEILNSSSTU subtileness
BEEILOSSSVY obsessively
BEEIMNNSSSU businessmen
BEEIMRRRSSU reimbursers
BEEINNOORTU boutonniere
BEEINORRSSW snowberries
BEEINORSTTY tenebrosity
BEEINRSSTTU butteriness
BEEINRSSTUV subservient
BEEIRSSSUVV subversives
BEEJLNOSSSS joblessness
BEELLMRSSSU slumberless
BEELLNOSSSU solubleness
BEELLNOSSUV volubleness
BEELMOORSTU troublesome
BEELNNSSSTU bluntnesses
BEELNOOSSTT bottlenoses
BEELOORSSUV overblouses
BEELQRRSSUU burlesquers
BEEMMNNOSTT entombments
BEEMMNOSSST embossments
BEENQRSSSUU brusqueness
BEERRRSTTUU surrebutter
BEFGHILLRTU bullfighter
BEFGIILMORZ gemfibrozil
BEFGIILNTTY befittingly
BEFGIINNTTU unbefitting
BEFGILNORUW furbelowing
BEFHILLMSTU thimblefuls
BEFIIILLTXY flexibility
BEFIILNORRU neurofibril
BEFIILRSSTU filibusters
BEFINORSSSU fibrousness
BEFINORSTTT frostbitten
BEFKKLLOOOS Book of Kells
BEFLLMRSTUU tumblerfuls
BEFLLOOPRTU bulletproof
BEGGGILNOOT bootlegging
BEGGHIINNOR neighboring
BEGGHIINNRT brightening
BEGGHILNORS Helsingborg
BEGGIILLNUY beguilingly
BEGGILSSTUY suggestibly
BEGGINNOORU bourgeoning
BEGGINOORRS Bognor Regis
BEGHIILMRST thimblerigs
BEGHIINRRST rebirthings
BEGHILNORUY neighbourly
BEGIIIILLTY eligibility
BEGIIIMNRST ignimbrites
BEGIIKLRSTZ blitzkriegs
BEGIILLNNTU bulletining
BEGIILMNNRU unlimbering
BEGIILNRSTT bitterlings
BEGIIMNRRSU reimbursing
BEGIINQRTTU briquetting
BEGIKNOOORV overbooking
BEGILLMNRTY tremblingly
BEGILLMNRUY lumberingly
BEGILNOORVW overblowing
BEGILNQRSUU burlesquing
BEGILNRSSTU blusterings
BEGILPSSTTU spittlebugs
BEGINNNNOTU unbonneting
BEGINNORTTU rebuttoning
BEGINRSSTTU buttressing
BEGMNOOORSU ombrogenous
BEGNOORSSTX strongboxes
BEGOOPPRSST gobstoppers
BEGOORRSTTT bogtrotters
BEHIIILLLLS hillbillies
BEHIIINOSTX exhibitions
BEHIIIOPRTV prohibitive
BEHIILMNOST bimonthlies
BEHIILMSTTW thimblewits
BEHIILPSSTU bisulphites
BEHIINPRSTU tribuneship
BEHIIOPRRST prohibiters
BEHIKLNOSSS blokishness
BEHIKNOOSSS bookishness
BEHIKOOSTTX textbookish
BEHIKOPRRSS shipbrokers
BEHILLNSSSU bullishness
BEHILLORSWW willowherbs
BEHILLRSTTU bullshitter
BEHILMNPSTU publishment
BEHILMOPRSY hyperbolism
BEHILOSSSTV bolshevists
BEHIMMORSTU embothriums
BEHINOORSSS boorishness
BEHINORSSTT birthstones
BEHINRSSSTU brutishness
BEHIOORRSUV herbivorous
BEHIORSSTTU soubrettish
BEHLNOOSTTU buttonholes
BEHMNOORTUU Bournemouth
BEHMOOORSST smoothbores
BEHNNOOORRT North Borneo
BEHORRTTTUW Butterworth
BEIIILMMORS immobiliser
BEIIILMMORZ immobilizer
BEIIILMMOSS immobilises
BEIIILMMOSZ immobilizes
BEIIILMNRST libertinism
BEIIILMQRUU equilibrium
BEIIILNSSTY sensibility
BEIIILNSTTY tensibility
BEIIILOQSTU obliquities
BEIIILQRSTU equilibrist
BEIIILSSTTU subtilities
BEIIIMNSSTU bituminises
BEIIIMNSTUZ bituminizes
BEIIIMOPRST improbities
BEIILLNOSSW billowiness
BEIILLNOSTU ebullitions
BEIILLOSSSU solubilises
BEIILLOSSUZ solubilizes
BEIILMPRSSY permissibly
BEIILNOSSSU biliousness
BEIILRSSSTU subtilisers
BEIILRSSTTT librettists
BEIILRSSTUZ subtilizers
BEIINORRTTU retribution
BEILLMPSTUU submultiple

BEILLOPRSST	billposters
BEILLORRSUY	irresolubly
BEILLORSSTT	stilbestrol
BEILMNOOSSW	snowmobiles
BEILNOPRSSY	responsibly
BEILNOSSTUU	botulinuses
BEILORSSSTU	strobiluses
BEILORSTUVY	obtrusively
BEIMNORSSSU	submersions
BEIMPSSTUUV	subsumptive
BEINNOSSTUV	subventions
BEINOOSSSUV	obviousness
BEINOPRSSSU	probusiness
BEINOPRSSTU	subreptions
BEINORSSSUV	subversions
BEINORSSTUU	subroutines
BEINORSTUUV	unobtrusive
BEINSSTTTUU	substituent
BEIOQRSSTUU	soubriquets
BEIORRRTTUY	retributory
BEISSSTTTUU	substitutes
BEKMNORSSSU	mossbunkers
BEKNNNOSTUW	unbeknownst
BELLMOOSSSS	blossomless
BELLNRTTUUY	turbulently
BELNOORSSWW	snowblowers
BELNOOSTUUY	bounteously
BEMOOPRRSTY	Port Moresby
BENNOORSSTW	brownstones
BEORRSTTTUW	butterworts
BERRSSTTTUU	trustbuster
BFFGILNOTUU	outbluffing
BFGIIILNTUY	fungibility
BFHKOOOORSU	book of hours
BFILLNOTUUY	bountifully
BGGIINNPRSU	upbringings
BGGILLMNRUY	grumblingly
BGGINNOORUU	bourguignon
BGHHIIRRSTT	birthrights
BGHIIINOPRT	prohibiting
BGHIIINRRTV	virgin birth Virgin Birth
BGHIMNOORST	thrombosing
BGIIILLLTUY	gullibility
BGIIILNSSTU	subtilising
BGIIILNSTUZ	subtilizing
BGIILLNOPST	billposting
BGIILLNSTTU	Sitting Bull
BGIILMNOSSY	symbolising
BGIILMNOSYZ	symbolizing
BGILLMNSTUY	stumblingly
BGILMNNOOOT	Bloomington
BGILMOOSSTY	symbologist
BGILOORSSTY	bryologists
BGINNNOORSW	brownnosing
BGINNNOTTUU	unbuttoning
BHIIIINNOST	inhibitions
BHIIINOOPRT	prohibition
BHIIIOPRSTU	triphibious
BHIILLRSSTT	stillbirths
BHIIOOPRRST	prohibitors
BHIIOOPRRTY	prohibitory
BHILMOOSTYY	tomboyishly
BHIMNOOPRRT	prothrombin
BHIMNPRSTTU	thumbprints
BHINOORSTUY	Ryobu Shinto
BHKNOOOSTTU	buttonhooks
BIIIILNRSTY	rinsibility
BIIILOPSSTY	possibility
BIIILORSTTY	torsibility
BIIKNOORSSV	Novosibirsk
BIILLNOORTU	tourbillion
BIILLOOSUVY	obliviously
BIILMOOPPTY	popmobility
BIILMORRTUU	lubritorium
BIILOOQSTUU	obliquitous
BIIMNOOSTUX	moxibustion
BIIMNOSSSSU	submissions
BIKLLORSSST	storksbills
BILMOPSTUUY	bumptiously
BILNOOOSTUV	obvolutions
BILNOOOSUXY	obnoxiously
BIMNOORSSTT	trombonists
BIMNOPSSTUU	subsumption
BIMORSSTUUU	rumbustious
BIOOOPPRRSU	opprobrious
BKMOOOPPRST	promptbooks
BLLOORSTUUY	troublously
BLLOOSTTUWY	woollybutts
BMMMMNOSUUU	summum bonum
CCCCDIILOOP	diplococcic
CCCCIMOORSU	micrococcus
CCCDEEEENRS	decrescence
CCCDEEIINNO	coincidence
CCCDEHINOSY	synecdochic
CCCDEIIMRSU	circumcised
CCCDEIIOOSS	coccidioses
CCCDGINOOOO	gonococcoid
CCCDIIIOOSS	coccidiosis
CCCDILOOPSU	diplococcus
CCCEEEENRSX	excrescence
CCCEEENRSXY	excrescency
CCCEEFIIOPS	ecospecific
CCCEEFLLNOU	flocculence
CCCEEIILMST	eclecticism
CCCEEINNOSS	consciences
CCCEENNORRU	concurrence
CCCEENNORST	concrescent
CCCEENORRSU	occurrences
CCCEFIINOPS	conspecific
CCCEFIOORSU	cocciferous
CCCEFLLNOUY	flocculency
CCCEGILLOPY	cycloplegic
CCCEHKORSSS	crosschecks
CCCEIIMRRSU	circumciser
CCCEIIMRSSU	circumcises
CCCEILORSST	Celtic cross
CCCEIMNOOPU	pneumococci
CCCEIMPRSTU	circumspect
CCCEINNOTTU	Connecticut
CCCEIRSSTUY	cysticercus
CCCEKLNOORS	corncockles
CCCENNORRUY	concurrency
CCCGIKNOORW	cockcrowing
CCCHHILOOOS	chocoholics
CCCHIKOPSST	spitchcocks
CCCHILMOTYY	cyclothymic
CCCIIMMOORS	microcosmic
CCCIIMOOPRS	microscopic
CCCILLOPSYY	polycyclics
CCCINNOOOST	concoctions
CCCIOOPSSTY	cystoscopic
CCDDEEENORS	crescendoed decrescendo
CCDDEEERRSU	recrudesced
CCDDEENNOSS	condescends
CCDEEEEINNR	Nicene Creed
CCDEEEIINNS	indecencies
CCDEEEIINRS	iridescence
CCDEEELLORT	recollected
CCDEEEMMNOR	recommenced
CCDEEENNORT	reconnected
CCDEEENORSS	crescendoes
CCDEEERRSSU	recrudesces
CCDEEFIKNOY	cockneyfied
CCDEEFINNOS	confidences
CCDEEHILPSY	psychedelic
CCDEEHIORTT	ricochetted
CCDEEHNOSSY	synecdoches
CCDEEIIINST	insecticide
CCDEEIILRST	dielectrics
CCDEEIKLRSV	cleverdicks
CCDEEILMORU	leucodermic
CCDEEILNOTU	endocuticle
CCDEEILNOTY	conceitedly
CCDEEINNORT	endocentric
CCDEEINORST	concertised concretised
CCDEEINORTV	reconvicted
CCDEEINORTZ	concertized concretized
CCDEEIOPPRU	preoccupied
CCDEEJNORTU	conjectured
CCDEEKORRSW	corkscrewed
CCDEELLLOTY	collectedly
CCDEELLNOTU	uncollected
CCDEELNNOOS	condolences
CCDEELNNORY	concernedly
CCDEELNNOTY	connectedly
CCDEELNORTY	concertedly
CCDEENNNORU	unconcerned
CCDEENNNOTU	unconnected
CCDEENNORTU	unconcerted
CCDEENORRTU	uncorrected
CCDEFIMRSUU	circumfused
CCDEGHILNTU	declutching
CCDEHIINNOS	cinchonised
CCDEHIINNOZ	cinchonized
CCDEHILOPSY	psychodelic
CCDEHIOOPRS	dichroscope
CCDEIILOORT	crocidolite
CCDEIILOPSY	epicycloids
CCDEILNOXYY	doxycycline
CCDEILOPSTY	cyclopedist
CCDEIMNOORS	microsecond

CCDEIMOOOST octodecimos
CCDEINNNOUV unconvinced
CCDEINNOSST disconnects
CCDEINOOPSS picoseconds
CCDEINOPRST conscripted
CCDEINORSST disconcerts
CCDEINORSTT constricted
CCDELLOSTYY cyclostyled
CCDELMOORTY motorcycled
CCDENORSSTU conductress
CCDENORSTTU constructed
deconstruct
CCDGILNNOUY conducingly
CCDHILOOPYY hypocycloid
CCDHIOOPRSY hydroscopic
CCDHIOPRRTY cryptorchid
CCDIMNOSSTU misconducts
CCDINNOOSTU conductions
CCEEEEHIKPS cheekpieces
CCEEEEILNST telescience
CCEEEEINPRT centrepiece
CCEEEELLNSX excellences
CCEEEFHIKNR neckerchief
CCEEEFLNORS florescence
CCEEEFNNORS conferences
CCEEEFNRSTU frutescence
CCEEEGINNOT cenogenetic
CCEEEGINNRS nigrescence
CCEEEGINOSS geosciences
CCEEEGINOTT ectogenetic
CCEEEGINRVY vicegerency
CCEEEGNNORV convergence
CCEEEGNRSTU turgescence
CCEEEHHLOST cheesecloth
CCEEEHINNOR incoherence
CCEEEHINSTT cenesthetic
CCEEEHIPSSS chesspieces
CCEEEIINPPR percipience
CCEEEILNORT coelenteric
CCEEEILNQSU liquescence
CCEEEIMORRT coercimeter
CCEEEINNNOV convenience
CCEEEINNPSS spinescence
CCEEEINOPRV preconceive
CCEEEINOPSS cenospecies
CCEEEINOSTX coexistence
CCEEEINRRST Cirencester
CCEEEINRSSV virescences
CCEEEINRSTV vitrescence
CCEEEIRSTUX executrices
CCEEEKOOPRR Cooper Creek
CCEEELORTTU electrocute
CCEEELORTTY electrocyte
CCEEEMMNORS recommences
CCEEEMNPSSU spumescence
CCEEENNOQSU consequence
CCEEENPRSTU putrescence
CCEEENRRRSU recurrences
CCEEFFIINOT coefficient
CCEEFIIMNNO omnificence
CCEEFIIMNNU munificence
CCEEFIKNOSY cockneyfies
CCEEFLNNOSU confluences
CCEEGHHKRRU Greek Church
CCEEGHIKNPR prechecking
CCEEGINNNOT contingence
CCEEGINOOTT geotectonic
CCEEGINORST egocentrics
CCEEGINOTTY cytogenetic
CCEEGNNOOST cognoscente
CCEEGNNORSU congruences
CCEEGNNORVY convergency
CCEEGNOORRT concertgoer
CCEEGNRSTUY turgescency
CCEEHHKORRY chokecherry
CCEEHINNORY incoherency
CCEEHINORTT theocentric
CCEEHIRRSTU cutcherries
CCEEHKLLLOS cockleshell
CCEEHMOOPRT chemoceptor
CCEEHMOPTYY phycomycete
CCEEHNOSSTU escutcheons
CCEEIILMRSS semicircles
CCEEIILORST isoelectric
CCEEIILPSTU epicuticles
CCEEIILRTTY electricity
CCEEIIMMNSU ecumenicism
CCEEIIMNNOS omniscience
CCEEIIMNOSV misconceive
CCEEIINOPTV nociceptive
CCEEILLNOOS colonelcies
CCEEILLOSTV collectives
CCEEILMOOST colectomies
CCEEILMORTY myoelectric
CCEEILNNOTV conventicle
CCEEILNORRS reconcilers
CCEEILNORST electronics
CCEEILNORTT telocentric
CCEEILNQSUY liquescency
CCEEILOSTUX exocuticles
CCEEIMNOORT econometric
CCEEIMNORRT centromeric
CCEEINNOQTU cinquecento
CCEEINNOSSS conciseness
CCEEINNOSST consistence
CCEEINNOSTV connectives
CCEEINNRRSU incurrences
CCEEINOPRSW crownpieces
CCEEINORSST concertises
concretises
CCEEINORSTZ concertizes
concretizes
CCEEINOSTUV consecutive
CCEEIOPPRSU preoccupies
CCEEIOPRSSS crosspieces
CCEEIORRSTV correctives
CCEEIORTUXX coexecutrix
CCEEJNORRTU conjecturer
CCEEJNORSTU conjectures
CCEELMORSTY cyclometers
CCEELSSSSSU successless
CCEEMNNNORT concernment
CCEENNOORRV overconcern
CCEENOPRRST preconcerts
CCEENORRSST correctness
CCEEOORRRTV overcorrect
CCEEOORSTUX coexecutors
CCEFFIINSUY sufficiency
CCEFHIIISTT fetichistic
CCEFHIIMORS microfiches
CCEFIIIPSTY specificity
CCEFIILNOTV conflictive
CCEFIINNOPS nonspecific
CCEFIINOPRY proficiency
CCEFIMRSSUU circumfuses
CCEFINNOOST confections
CCEFIORRSUU cruciferous
CCEGGILNOOY gynecologic
CCEGHHORRSU churchgoers
CCEGHIIIOPS pichiciegos
CCEGHIILNOR cholinergic
CCEGHIINORT ricocheting
CCEGHIKNORW checkrowing
CCEGHIMNOOR chromogenic
CCEGHINOPSY psychogenic
CCEGIILNNOR reconciling
CCEGIINOOTX toxicogenic
CCEGILMNOPT complecting
CCEGILNOORY eccrinology
CCEGILNOOSY synecologic
CCEGINNNORT concentring
CCEGINNNOTY contingency
CCEGINNOOST cognoscenti
CCEGINOPRTY cryptogenic
CCEGINOPRUY reoccupying
CCEGINORRRU reoccurring
CCEHHHORSUU house church
CCEHHIOSSTT schottische
CCEHHMNORUW churchwomen
CCEHIILNOPR necrophilic
CCEHIINNOSS cinchonises
CCEHIINNOSZ cinchonizes
CCEHIIPRRTY hypercritic
CCEHIKNOPST checkpoints
CCEHILNOPTY polytechnic
CCEHILNORRS chroniclers
CCEHILOOTTY hectocotyli
CCEHIMMNOOR chromonemic
CCEHIMMOOST chemosmotic
CCEHIMNOORT homocentric
CCEHIMOOPRT chemotropic
ectomorphic
CCEHINNRSSU crunchiness
CCEHINOOSTZ zootechnics
CCEHINOPRTY pyrotechnic
CCEHIOOPRTT ectotrophic
CCEHKLOSTTU shuttlecock
CCEHKNOOSST chockstones
CCEHKOOPPRR rock chopper
CCEHMOORSTY cytochromes
CCEHNNORSSU scruncheons
CCEHNOOOPRS chronoscope
CCEHNOPRSUW cowpunchers
CCEIIINSSTT scientistic
CCEIIIRRSST criticisers
CCEIIIRRSTU circuitries

CCEIIIRRSTZ	criticizers
CCEIILMNORT	clinometric
CCEIILMNORU	micronuclei
CCEIILMORST	cliometrics
CCEIIMMORRT	micrometric
CCEIIMNOOST	economistic
CCEIIMOOPRS	microcopies
CCEIIMOORST	sociometric
CCEIIMORSTV	viscometric
CCEIINOORST	coercionist
CCEIIOPRRTY	reciprocity
CCEIJNNOTUV	conjunctive
CCEIKKOPPST	pickpockets
CCEIKLNOPRU	cupronickel
CCEIKMNOSSY	cockneyisms
CCEILLNOOST	collections
CCEILMOORTU	coulometric
CCEILNNOTTU	noctilucent
CCEILNORRTY	incorrectly
CCEILOOQSTU	coquelicots
CCEIMNNNOOO	noneconomic
CCEIMNOORST	centrosomic
CCEIMNOPRTY	pycnometric
CCEIMNRSTUV	circumvents
CCEIMOOPRSS	microscopes
CCEINNNOOST	connections
CCEINNOOPST	conceptions
CCEINNOORST	concretions
CCEINNOOSSS	concessions
CCEINNOOSTU	consecution
CCEINNOSSTY	consistency
CCEINOOOPSS	iconoscopes
CCEINOOPRST	nociceptors
CCEINOORRST	corrections
CCEINOSSSSU	successions
CCEIOOPRSSY	cryoscopies
CCEJNNORTUU	conjuncture
CCEKMOORSTY	comstockery
CCELLNSTUUY	succulently
CCELLOSSTYY	cyclostyles
CCELMOORSTY	motorcycles
CCELMOOSSTY	cyclostomes
CCELNOOOOPS	colonoscope
CCELOOOPPSS	colposcopes
CCELOPRSSUU	corpuscules
CCELORSSSUU	succourless
CCENNORRSTU	concurrents
CCENORRSTTU	constructer reconstruct
CCEOOOPPRST	proctoscope
CCEOOOPRRSS	coprocessor
CCEOOPSSSTY	cystoscopes
CCFGIIKNNOY	cocknifying
CCFGIILNNOT	conflicting
CCFIIINORUX	crucifixion
CCFIILNNOOT	confliction
CCFILMORRUY	cruciformly
CCFILNOORTY	conflictory
CCGGHHIINOU	hiccoughing
CCGGHHINORU	churchgoing
CCGHHINNRUU	unchurching
CCGHIILNNOR	chronicling
CCGHIINORTY	trichogynic
CCGHIKLLNUY	chucklingly
CCGHILNOOOR	chronologic
CCGHILOPTYY	glycophytic
CCGHIOOPRSY	hygroscopic
CCGIIIINRST	criticising
CCGIIIINRTZ	criticizing
CCGIIKKNOTT	ticktocking
CCGIILOOOTX	toxicologic
CCGIOOPRSSY	gyroscopics
CCHIIILMORT	microlithic
CCHIIIOSTTY	histiocytic
CCHIILNOPRR	chlorpicrin
CCHIILOOPPR	coprophilic
CCHIILORSTY	chrysolitic
CCHIIMNOOPR	microphonic
CCHIIMNOORT	monotrichic
CCHIIMNOOST	monostichic
CCHIIMOORTT	trichotomic
CCHIIMOPRTY	microphytic
CCHIIMORSTW	microswitch
CCHIINOOPRS	rhinoscopic
CCHILMNOORY	chylomicron
CCHILMOOPRY	polychromic
CCHILMOPTYY	lymphocytic
CCHIMMNOOOR	monochromic
CCHIMNOOORS	monochroics
CCHIMOOPRTY	cormophytic mycotrophic
CCHINNORSSU	scrunchions
CCHIOOOPRST	orthoscopic
CCHIORRSSST	christcross
CCHIORSSTTY	trichocysts
CCIILLNOPSY	polyclinics
CCIILMORRUU	cirrocumuli
CCIILNOOPRS	ciclosporin
CCIILNSSTUY	unicyclists
CCIILOORSTU	colouristic
CCIILRSSTTY	tricyclists
CCIIMMNOSTU	communistic
CCIIMOOPRRS	microsporic
CCIINNOOSTV	convictions
CCIINOPRTTY	nyctitropic
CCIJNNNOOTU	conjunction
CCIKNOOPSTU	cuckoopints
CCILLNOORSU	councillors
CCILMRRSUUU	curriculums
CCILNNOOSSU	conclusions
CCILNOOPRSY	cyclosporin
CCILNOOSSUY	consciously
CCILOOORSTU	corticolous
CCIMMOOORSS	microcosmos
CCIMNNOOPTU	compunction
CCINNOOSSSU	concussions
CCINNOOSSUU	unconscious
CCINOOPSSUU	conspicuous
CCINOORRSTT	constrictor
CCINOSSSSUU	succussions
CCLLOOORSTU	collocutors
CCLNOOOOPSY	colonoscopy
CCNOORRSTTU	constructor
CCOOOPPRSTY	proctoscopy
CDDDEEEENRS	redescended
CDDDEEEINSS	decidedness
CDDDEEENNSU	undescended
CDDDEEIIRST	discredited
CDDDEEILNUY	undecidedly
CDDDEIMMOOS	discommoded
CDDEEEENPRT	precedented
CDDEEEFFINR	differenced
CDDEEEHLRSU	rescheduled
CDDEEEIIOPT	Pico de Teide
CDDEEEILQSU	deliquesced
CDDEEEIPRTU	decrepitude
CDDEEELNORS	needlecords
CDDEEELRTTU	decluttered
CDDEEEMMNOR	recommended
CDDEEENNOPS	despondence
CDDEEENNOPT	codependent
CDDEEENNORS	recondensed
CDDEEENRSSU	descendeurs
CDDEEEOPRRR	prerecorded
CDDEEFIINST	disinfected
CDDEEFIKLNS	fiddlenecks
CDDEEGILNNU	indulgenced
CDDEEHILNSU	Lüdenscheid
CDDEEHLNSUU	unscheduled
CDDEEIIMRST	misdirected
CDDEEIINORT	rodenticide
CDDEEIINRTT	interdicted
CDDEEILNOOS	decolonised
CDDEEILNOOZ	decolonized
CDDEEILOORS	decolorised
CDDEEILOORZ	decolorized
CDDEEILTUVY	deductively
CDDEEINPRRU	underpriced
CDDEEINPRTU	unpredicted
CDDEEKNOORU	undercooked
CDDEELNOORU	undercooled
CDDEELOORUV	overclouded
CDDEENNOPSY	despondency
CDDEENORRSU	underscored
CDDEENORSSW	crowdedness
CDDEEOORRVW	overcrowded
CDDEFHIINOR	chondrified
CDDEFIIKLST	fiddlestick
CDDEFIIMOST	discomfited
CDDEGHILNOR	godchildren
CDDEGILMNOO	Middle Congo
CDDEGILNOOR	dendrologic
CDDEHIILMNR	childminder
CDDEHIILORS	dichlorides
CDDEIIILNNS	disinclined
CDDEIIILNPS	disciplined
CDDEIILNPTU	duplicident
CDDEIINNOOT	conditioned
CDDEIINOSUU	indeciduous
CDDEILNOOTY	dicotyledon
CDDEILNOSSU	undisclosed
CDDEILOORSU	discoloured
CDDEILOSUUY	deciduously
CDDEIMMNOOS	discommoned
CDDEIMMNOSS	discommends

CDDEIMMOOSS discommodes
CDDEIMOOPSS discomposed
CDDEINNOOST endodontics
CDDEKORRSTU rudderstock
CDDELLLMOOY mollycoddle
CDDEMNOOPSU decompounds
CDDENOORSTU Côtes-du-Nord
CDDEOOPRTUU outproduced
CDDGHILMOST Goldschmidt
CDDIILNORSY cylindroids
CDDINNOOSTY dicynodonts
CDEEEEFFRSV effervesced
CDEEEEFLNSS defenceless
CDEEEEGNRST detergences
CDEEEEINPRX experienced
CDEEEEINPSX expediences
CDEEEELPRST preselected
CDEEEENRRST deterrences
CDEEEFFINRS differences
CDEEEFFLORS effloresced
CDEEEFGLNTU genuflected
CDEEEFHIIPS speechified
CDEEEFIILPS fieldpieces
CDEEEFIILRT electrified
CDEEEFILTVY defectively
CDEEEFLNRTU unreflected
CDEEEFMNORT deforcement
CDEEEGILNST deselecting
CDEEEGILNXY exceedingly
CDEEEGINORS derecognise
CDEEEGINORZ derecognize
CDEEEGINRSV divergences
CDEEEGKNOOS goosenecked
CDEEEHIKLMZ Melchizedek
CDEEEHIPRRS decipherers
CDEEEHLPRSU sepulchered
CDEEEHLRSSU reschedules
CDEEEHRRSTT stretchered
CDEEEIINRSS residencies
CDEEEIJNRTT interjected
CDEEEIKLNST needlestick
CDEEEIKNQRU requickened
CDEEEILNOST deselection
CDEEEILNSTT delitescent
CDEEEILOPSV velocipedes
CDEEEILPTVY deceptively
CDEEEILQSSU deliquesces
CDEEEIMNNOS comediennes
CDEEEINPRST reinspected
CDEEEINPRTT intercepted
CDEEEINPRUV unperceived
CDEEEINRRST interceders
CDEEEINRSTT intersected
CDEEEINRSUV undeceivers
CDEEEINRSUX unexercised
CDEEEINSSTX excitedness
CDEEEIORTVX overexcited
CDEEEJORRTT retrojected
CDEEELNNOOP Ponce de León
CDEEEMMNORR recommender
CDEEEMNNOST encodements
CDEEEMNOPRS recompensed
CDEEENNOPRS respondence
CDEEENNORSS recondenses
CDEEENNORTU encountered
CDEEENOPRRS precensored
CDEEENOQRRU reconquered
CDEEENORRTT retrocedent
CDEEENORRTV reconverted
CDEEEOPRRSS predecessor
reprocessed
CDEEERRRSTU resurrected
CDEEFFHIINR frenchified
CDEEFFHINOR Eichendorff
CDEEFGINRTU centrifuged
CDEEFIIIKRR Frederick II
CDEEFIIKRRV Frederick IV
CDEEFIIKRRX Frederick IX
CDEEFIILNTY deficiently
CDEEFIINPSU unspecified
CDEEFIINRST dentifrices
CDEEFIINRTU uncertified
unrectified
CDEEFILLTUY deceitfully
CDEEFILNNTU uninflected
CDEEFILNORY ecofriendly
CDEEFILNOST deflections
CDEEFILOSST closefisted
CDEEFIMNORR reconfirmed
CDEEFINORRT Fredericton
CDEEFLNORST centerfolds
centrefolds
CDEEFLNOSSY confessedly
CDEEFNNORST frondescent
CDEEFNNSSTU defunctness
CDEEGHIINPR deciphering
CDEEGIILNVY deceivingly
CDEEGIINNRT interceding
CDEEGIINNUV undeceiving
CDEEGIINRRT redirecting
CDEEGILNNSU indulgences
CDEEGILNORS girdlescone
CDEEGILNSUV divulgences
CDEEGINNOTX coextending
CDEEGINOPRS proceedings
CDEEGINORRT retroceding
CDEEHHIMSTT hemstitched
CDEEHIILOPS ophicleides
CDEEHIINNOS Indochinese
CDEEHIINNST indehiscent
CDEEHIKPRSW shipwrecked
CDEEHILOPRR perchloride
CDEEHIMNORS echinoderms
CDEEHIMNORT endothermic
CDEEHIMNOTU endothecium
CDEEHIOPRTV overpitched
CDEEHIOQSTU discotheque
CDEEHMNOPRS comprehends
CDEEHNNORTU truncheoned
CDEEHPRSTTU upstretched
CDEEIIILSTV declivities
CDEEIIKLNSS slickenside
CDEEIILNORT dereliction
CDEEIIMNPSU impudencies
CDEEIIMNRST densimetric
CDEEIIMORRS misericorde
CDEEIIMORTU eudiometric
CDEEIIMOSTZ domesticize
CDEEIIMPRSS spermicides
CDEEIINORRT redirection
CDEEIINRSTV viridescent
CDEEIINRTTU incertitude
CDEEIIOORTV Côte d'Ivoire
CDEEIIORRST directories
CDEEIIORSSV discoveries
CDEEIIPRSTV descriptive
CDEEIIRRSTX directrixes
CDEEIIRSSSV disservices
CDEEIJNORTT introjected
CDEEIKLMORU leukodermic
CDEEIKLNNOO nickelodeon
CDEEIKLNORT interlocked
CDEEILNNOSS declensions
CDEEILNNQUY delinquency
CDEEILNOORS recolonised
CDEEILNOORZ recolonized
CDEEILNOOSS decolonises
CDEEILNOOSZ decolonizes
CDEEILNORTY reconditely
CDEEILNOSSU nucleosides
CDEEILNOSTU nucleotides
CDEEILNSSTU ductileness
CDEEILOORSS decolorises
CDEEILOORSZ decolorizes
CDEEILORSST sclerotised
CDEEILORSTZ sclerotized
CDEEILSTUVY seductively
CDEEIMMORTT recommitted
CDEEIMNNRST discernment
rescindment
CDEEIMNNSTU inducements
CDEEIMNOPRS endospermic
CDEEIMNORTV divorcement
CDEEIMOOSTX sextodecimo
CDEEINNOSTU tendencious
CDEEINNRSSW windscreens
CDEEINOOPSS endoscopies
CDEEINOORTT condottiere
CDEEINORRRT tricornered
CDEEINORRSS considerers
reconsiders
CDEEINORRTU reintroduce
CDEEINPRRSU underprices
CDEEINPRSUU superinduce
CDEEINRSSTY syncretised
CDEEINRSTYZ syncretized
CDEEIORRSSV discoverers
rediscovers
CDEEIORRSVY rediscovery
CDEEIORSTTT detectorist
CDEEIPRSSST disrespects
CDEEIRRRSVW screwdriver

CDEEIRRSSTT	derestricts
CDEEIRSTTUV	destructive
CDEEJKOOTUY	outjockeyed
CDEEKKORSTY	skyrocketed
CDEEKNOORSS	crookedness
CDEEKOOPRSW	woodpeckers
CDEEKOORSTV	overstocked
CDEELMNNOOT	condolement
CDEELMNOPTU	uncompleted
CDEELNNOTTY	contentedly
CDEELNRRTUY	decurrently
CDEELNRTTUU	uncluttered
CDEELOOPRSU	supercooled
CDEEMNNOPRS	precondemns
CDEEMOOPRSS	decomposers
CDEENNOPRSY	respondency
CDEENNOQRUU	unconquered
CDEENNORTUV	unconverted
CDEENNOSTTU	uncontested
CDEENOOSSTT	cottonseeds
CDEENOOSTTW	cottonweeds
CDEENOPRSSU	unprocessed
CDEENOPRTTU	unprotected
CDEENORRSSU	underscores
CDEENOSSTUU	consuetudes
CDEENPSSTUU	unsuspected
CDEEOOPPRRV	overcropped
CDEEOOPRRUV	overproduce
CDEEOPRRRSU	reproducers
CDEFFORRSSU	crossruffed
CDEFGHILNOS	goldfinches
CDEFGIINORY	recodifying
CDEFHIINORS	chondrifies
CDEFHIKOPRT	pitchforked
CDEFIIILMSU	semifluidic
CDEFIILMMOR	microfilmed
CDEFIIMORST	discomfiter
CDEFIINNTUY	infecundity
CDEFIINORST	disinfector
CDEFIINORTU	countrified
CDEFILMNORY	confirmedly
CDEFILNNOTY	confidently
CDEFIMNNORU	unconfirmed
CDEFINOORSV	confervoids
CDEFINORTUY	countryfied
CDEFNNOORSU	confounders
CDEFNORRSTU	undercrofts
CDEGHILNOOS	deschooling
CDEGHINORRS	Schrödinger
CDEGHIOPRTY	copyrighted
CDEGIIJNPRU	prejudicing
CDEGIILNNRY	cylindering
CDEGIINNORS	considering
CDEGIINNPRS	prescinding
CDEGIINOPTY	copyediting
CDEGIINORSV	discovering
CDEGIINPRTU	depicturing
CDEGILNOORU	decolouring
CDEGILNOPSU	decouplings
CDEGIMNNOTU	documenting
CDEGIMNOOPS	decomposing
CDEGIMNORRU	corrigendum
CDEGINNORST	constringed
CDEGINOPRRU	reproducing
CDEGINRSTTU	destructing
CDEGKLOOORS	sockdologer
CDEGMNORSUU	curmudgeons
CDEHHHOORSS	Rosh Chodesh
CDEHHNOOOPR	chordophone
CDEHIIINNOR	enchiridion
CDEHIIINRST	trichinised
CDEHIIINRTZ	trichinized
CDEHIILLNOT	decillionth
CDEHIILOOTT	theodolitic
CDEHIILOPSS	discophiles
CDEHIILORRT	trichloride
CDEHIIMNNOO	Domenichino
CDEHIIMOOST	dichotomies
	dichotomise
CDEHIIMOOTZ	dichotomize
CDEHIIMOSTT	methodistic
CDEHIINOOPV	videophonic
CDEHIKMNPRU	Humperdinck
CDEHILPRTUU	pulchritude
CDEHIMNOOPR	endomorphic
CDEHIMNORST	Christendom
CDEHIMOPRSY	hypodermics
CDEHIMORRTY	hydrometric
CDEHINOOPRT	endotrophic
CDEHINOPRRY	Pondicherry
CDEHINOPSST	docentships
CDEHIOOOPPT	photocopied
CDEHIOOPRST	orthopedics
CDEHKLOORST	stockholder
CDEHLOOPPRS	clodhoppers
CDEHLOOPRSY	copyholders
CDEHOOPRSSY	hydroscopes
CDEIIILLSST	stillicides
CDEIIILNNSS	disinclines
CDEIIILNPRS	discipliner
CDEIIILNPSS	disciplines
CDEIIILNSUV	uncivilised
CDEIIILNUVZ	uncivilized
CDEIIILOPST	politicised
CDEIIILOPTZ	politicized
CDEIIILPSTU	duplicities
CDEIIIMMSTU	mediumistic
CDEIIIMORTX	oxidimetric
CDEIIINNORT	indirection
CDEIIINSTTV	distinctive
CDEIIIOPRTT	peridotitic
CDEIIIOPRTY	periodicity
CDEIIIRSSTV	recidivists
CDEIIISSTUV	vicissitude
CDEIIJNOSTU	jocundities
CDEIIJNSTUV	disjunctive
CDEIILLMNOS	millisecond
CDEIILLOSUY	deliciously
CDEIILLPTUY	pellucidity
CDEIILNNOTY	inconditely
CDEIILNOSTU	unsolicited
CDEIILNRTUY	incredulity
CDEIILNTUVY	inductively
CDEIILOORST	sclerotioid
CDEIILOOSUY	dioeciously
CDEIILOPSSU	pediculosis
CDEIILOSTUV	declivitous
CDEIIMMOOST	commodities
CDEIIMNNSTT	indictments
CDEIIMNORST	modernistic
CDEIIMNOSST	midsections
CDEIIMORRSS	misericords
CDEIIMOSTTY	domesticity
CDEIIMPPRUY	cypripedium
CDEIINNOORT	conditioner
	recondition
CDEIINNOSTU	discontinue
CDEIINOOPRT	periodontic
CDEIINOORTT	condottieri
CDEIINOPRST	description
	predictions
CDEIINORRTT	interdictor
CDEIINORSST	discretions
CDEIINOSSST	dissections
CDEIINRSSTU	scrutinised
CDEIINRSTUZ	scrutinized
CDEIIOOPRTX	dexiotropic
CDEIIOORRSS	sororicides
CDEIJNRSTUU	disjuncture
CDEIKNRRSTU	undertricks
CDEIKNRSSUW	windsuckers
CDEILNORSUU	incredulous
CDEILOORRTU	tricoloured
CDEILORSSSU	disclosures
CDEIMMNOPSU	compendiums
CDEIMMNOTTU	uncommitted
CDEIMMOOPRS	compromised
CDEIMNOOPSU	compendious
CDEIMNOSSTY	syndesmotic
CDEIMOOPSSS	discomposes
CDEINNOORSU	endocrinous
CDEINNOOSTU	contusioned
CDEINNOPRST	nondescript
CDEINNORTUV	uncontrived
CDEINNOSSTT	discontents
CDEINOOPSST	endoscopist
CDEINOOSSTY	endocytosis
CDEINORRSTU	introducers
CDEINORSSTU	discounters
	rediscounts
CDEINORSTTU	destruction
CDEINORSTUY	countryside
CDEINOSTTTU	constituted
CDEIORRSSSU	discoursers
CDEIORSSTUY	discourtesy
CDELLLOSSUY	cloudlessly
CDELLNORSUY	scoundrelly
CDELLORSUUY	credulously
CDELNOORTTY	contortedly
CDEMMOOORSS	cosmodromes
CDEMNOOPRSU	compounders
CDENOOPRRSS	corresponds
CDENOORRTUW	counterword
CDENOPRRTUU	uncorrupted
CDEOOPRSTUU	outproduces
CDEOORSTTUW	woodcutters

CDEORRSSTTU	destructors
CDFFIILLTUY	difficultly
CDFGIIKNORS	disfrocking
CDFGIILNNOY	confidingly
CDFGINNNOOU	confounding
CDFIIMNORSS	disconfirms
CDFIMOORSST	discomforts
CDFINNOSTUY	dysfunction
CDGGIIKLNOR	gridlocking
CDGHIKNOSUV	duckshoving
CDGHILNOOPP	clodhopping
CDGIIINRSTT	districting
CDGIILLOPSY	glycolipids
CDGIILNOORS	discoloring
CDGIILOOSST	discologist
CDGIILOSSTY	dyslogistic
CDGIIMMNNOO	incommoding
CDGIINNORTU	introducing
CDGIINNOSTU	discounting
CDGIINORSSU	discoursing
CDGILLNNOOY	condolingly
CDGILOORTTY	troglodytic
CDGIMNNOOPU	compounding
CDGINOOTTUW	woodcutting
CDHHIILOPRY	hydrophilic
CDHHIOPRTYY	hydrophytic
CDHIIIMOOPR	idiomorphic
CDHIIMNOORS	chironomids
CDHIIMOOSTT	dichotomist
CDHIIOOPRST	chiropodist
CDHILOOOPSU	chilopodous
CDHIMOOOSTU	dichotomous
CDHINOOORTT	orthodontic
CDHINOOPRSY	hydroponics
CDHIOOPRRTY	hydrotropic
CDIIIJNOSUU	injudicious
CDIIILNTTUY	inductility
CDIIINNOSTT	distinction
CDIIINOSSSS	discissions
CDIIIRSSTTX	District Six
CDIIJLOSUUY	judiciously
CDIIJNNOSTU	disjunction
CDIILLOOPPY	polyploidic
CDIILMORSTU	clostridium
CDIILOOPSTU	duopolistic
CDIILOPSTUU	duplicitous
CDIIMMNNOOU	condominium
CDIIMMNOOTY	incommodity
CDIINORSSTT	doctrinists
CDIINOSSSSU	discussions
CDIIOOOOSTV	voodooistic
CDIKLLORSST	drillstocks
CDIKLNOPSSU	spondulicks
CDIKORSSSTW	swordsticks
CDILLORSUUY	ludicrously
CDILMOOORSX	loxodromics
CDILMOOPSUY	lycopodiums
CDILOOORUUU	douroucouli
CDINNOOPRTY	cyprinodont
CDINOOPRSTU	productions
CDNOOOOSTTW	cottonwoods
CEEEEEGMNRR	reemergence
CEEEEFFRSSV	effervesces
CEEEEFNPRRS	preferences
CEEEEFNRRRS	referencers
CEEEEGIMNRS	emergencies
CEEEEHILNST	entelechies
CEEEEILNORT	electioneer
CEEEEIMNNPR	preeminence
CEEEEINPRSX	experiences
CEEEEINRRRV	irreverence
CEEEEJNRSUV	rejuvenesce
CEEEENPPRST	Peter's pence
CEEEENRRRSV	reverencers
CEEEFFHOOSU	coffeehouse
CEEEFFIINTV	ineffective
CEEEFFILTVY	effectively
CEEEFFLNOSS	offenceless
CEEEFFLORSS	effloresces
CEEEFGINNRR	referencing
	refringence
CEEEFHIIPRS	speechifier
CEEEFHIIPSS	speechifies
CEEEFIILRRT	electrifier
CEEEFIILRST	electrifies
CEEEFILTUVX	flexecutive
CEEEFINNQRU	infrequence
CEEEFINQRSU	frequencies
CEEEFIORRST	refectories
CEEEFKLLORR	Rockefeller
CEEEFMNNORT	enforcement
CEEEFNPRSST	perfectness
CEEEFPRRSTU	prefectures
CEEEGGHINNS	gegenschein
CEEEGGILNNS	negligences
CEEEGGNORRR	greengrocer
CEEEGHINORT	heterogenic
CEEEGIINOPR	epeirogenic
CEEEGIKNNOT	kenogenetic
CEEEGIKNORT	greenockite
CEEEGILMNNO	meningocele
CEEEGILNPRT	preelecting
CEEEGILNRST	reselecting
CEEEGINNOSS	cenogenesis
CEEEGINNOTX	xenogenetic
CEEEGINNRRV	reverencing
CEEEGINORSS	recognisees
CEEEGINORSZ	recognizees
CEEEGINORTV	eigenvector
CEEEGINOSST	ectogenesis
CEEEGINRSTV	vicegerents
	viceregents
CEEEGLNORST	electrogens
CEEEGNNOOSS	oncogeneses
CEEEGNRRSSU	resurgences
CEEEHHIRSTT	heresthetic
CEEEHHKLNOP	heckelphone
CEEEHHMOPRS	chemosphere
CEEEHIKNTTT	kitchenette
CEEEHIKPPRS	pikeperches
CEEEHILNSST	Cleisthenes
CEEEHILORTT	heteroclite
CEEEHILSTTT	telesthetic
CEEEHIMNRTU	hermeneutic
CEEEHIMORST	heteroecism
CEEEHIMSSTT	chemisettes
CEEEHINPRRS	encipherers
CEEEHINSSST	cenesthesis
CEEEHIORSSS	coheiresses
CEEEHLLRSSY	cheerlessly
CEEEHLOPRST	Cleethorpes
CEEEHMMNSSY	mesenchymes
CEEEHMNNRRT	trenchermen
CEEEHMORSTT	hectometers
	hectometres
CEEEHNNRRST	entrenchers
CEEEHNORSSS	chersoneses
CEEEHOQRSUU	eurocheques
CEEEIIKLNTT	telekinetic
CEEEIIMNNPT	impenitence
CEEEIINNNRT	internecine
CEEEIINNNST	insentience
CEEEIINNSTX	inexistence
CEEEIINSSST	necessities
CEEEIKNNRSS	snickersnee
CEEEILLSTVY	selectively
CEEEILMNNST	clementines
CEEEILMORST	ceilometers
CEEEILNNOQU	ineloquence
CEEEILNNOTV	nonelective
CEEEILNOPRT	preelection
CEEEILNORST	reelections
	reselection
CEEEILNPRST	percentiles
CEEEILNPSST	pestilences
CEEEILNSTUV	unselective
CEEEILPRTVY	receptively
CEEEILRSSVY	recessively
CEEEILRSTVY	secretively
CEEEILSSVXY	excessively
CEEEILTUVXY	executively
CEEEIMNNNST	incensement
CEEEIMNNSTT	enticements
CEEEIMNRSTT	centimeters
	centimetres
CEEEIMNSTTX	excitements
CEEEINNOPRV	provenience
CEEEINNOSTV	venesection
CEEEINNRSSS	sincereness
CEEEINORTUX	executioner
CEEEINOSTVX	coextensive
CEEEINPRRST	pericenters
	pericentres
CEEEINPRRTT	intercepter
CEEEINPRSSS	preciseness
CEEEINPRSST	persistence
CEEEINPRTUV	unreceptive
CEEEIOPRRSV	overprecise
CEEEIORRSST	corsetieres
CEEEIORSTVX	overexcites
CEEEIPPRSTV	perspective
CEEEIPRSTUV	persecutive
CEEEIRSTUXX	executrixes
CEEEJNNSTUV	juvenescent
CEEEKMNORSS	smokescreen

CEEELLLNTXY	excellently
CEEELLORSTY	electrolyse
CEEELLORTTY	electrolyte
CEEELLORTYZ	electrolyze
CEEELMNOSSW	welcomeness
CEEELMORRST	electromers
	sclerometer
CEEELNNOORT	coelenteron
CEEELNOORSU	neurocoeles
CEEELOPRTTY	electrotype
CEEEMNNNOTU	enouncement
CEEEMNOPRRS	recompenser
CEEEMNOPRSS	recompenses
CEEEMNORRST	centromeres
CEEEMNORTTY	enterectomy
CEEEMNOSTYZ	ectoenzymes
CEEEMNRTTTU	curettement
CEEENNORRTU	encounterer
CEEEOOPRSST	stereoscope
CEEEOPRRSSS	reprocesses
CEEEORRSSSS	sorceresses
CEEEPPRRSST	preceptress
CEEEPRRSSTU	supersecret
CEEFFHIINRS	frenchifies
CEEFFIIINNT	inefficient
CEEFFIILNTY	efficiently
CEEFFIINORT	interoffice
CEEFGIINNNR	inferencing
CEEFGIINNRT	reinfecting
CEEFGINNORR	reenforcing
CEEFGINNRRY	refringency
CEEFGINRSTU	centrifuges
CEEFGLNORTU	genuflector
CEEFGLNPRSU	Spencer Gulf
CEEFHHNORTT	thenceforth
CEEFHIKRSSW	wreckfishes
CEEFHILORSU	cheliferous
CEEFHMOORRR	ferrochrome
CEEFHORSTTU	fourchettes
CEEFHPRRSSU	surfperches
CEEFIILMRTT	flittermice
CEEFIILNORS	Leif Ericson
CEEFIILNTVY	infectively
CEEFIINNORT	reinfection
CEEFIINORST	fictioneers
CEEFIIPRSSU	superficies
CEEFIKKNOPT	pocketknife
CEEFIKLNORR	ferronickel
CEEFIKLOPRS	forcepslike
CEEFILMPRTY	imperfectly
CEEFILNNOSS	confineless
CEEFILNNRSU	influencers
CEEFILNORST	reflections
CEEFILNORSU	fluorescein
CEEFIMNNNOT	confinement
CEEFINNQRUY	infrequency
CEEFINORTTU	counterfeit
CEEFIOOPSST	fetoscopies
CEEFKLORSTT	fetterlocks
CEEFLMOORRT	electroform
CEEFLNOORSW	coneflowers
CEEFLNORSTU	fluorescent
CEEFLOORRSU	foreclosure
CEEFLORRSUU	resourceful
CEEFLPPRSTU	pluperfects
CEEFMNNORST	conferments
CEEFOORRSSU	forecourses
CEEGHIINNPR	enciphering
CEEGHILLNOP	phellogenic
CEEGHILNRSS	Schlesinger
CEEGHIMNORT	thermogenic
CEEGHIMOSST	geochemists
CEEGHINNNRT	entrenching
CEEGHINNRRT	retrenching
CEEGHINRSST	sightscreen
CEEGIILMOOS	semeiologic
CEEGIILNNRS	relicensing
CEEGIIMNRRS	mercerising
CEEGIIMNRRZ	mercerizing
CEEGIINORTV	recognitive
CEEGIINPRST	stringpiece
CEEGIINSSTT	geneticists
CEEGIINSSTU	eugenicists
CEEGILNNOSY	geosyncline
CEEGILNOORS	necrologies
CEEGILNOPST	telescoping
CEEGILNOPTY	polygenetic
CEEGILNOSTT	telegnostic
CEEGIMNNOOT	monogenetic
CEEGIMNORST	egocentrism
CEEGINNNORV	reconvening
CEEGINNOOSS	oncogenesis
CEEGINNOOTT	ontogenetic
CEEGINNORVY	reconveying
CEEGINNRSSU	insurgences
CEEGINOORST	oestrogenic
CEEGINORRSS	recognisers
CEEGINORRSZ	recognizers
CEEGINORSSU	surgeoncies
CEEGINOSSTY	cytogenesis
CEEGINPRSTU	persecuting
CEEGIOPRRTU	picturegoer
CEEGMNNORSS	congressmen
CEEGMOSTYYZ	zygomycetes
CEEGNNOORSU	congenerous
CEEHHIIMPRS	hemispheric
CEEHHILMOOR	heliochrome
CEEHHILNOPT	technophile
CEEHHIMRSTT	hemstitcher
CEEHHIMSSTT	hemstitches
CEEHHIORSVW	whichsoever
CEEHHIPSSTY	hypesthesic
CEEHHMMOORS	hemochromes
CEEHHMORSTT	homestretch
CEEHIIINORS	chinoiserie
CEEHIIKNPST	thinkpieces
CEEHIIKNSTT	kinesthetic
CEEHIILMORT	heliometric
CEEHIIMOOPT	hemopoietic
CEEHIIMPRTU	perithecium
CEEHIIMPSTU	euphemistic
CEEHIIMRSST	chemistries
CEEHIIMSSTT	estheticism
CEEHIINPPRR	perinephric
CEEHIISTTTW	witchetties
CEEHIKNSSST	sketchiness
CEEHIKPPRSS	schipperkes
CEEHILLNOST	clothesline
CEEHILMNORT	thermocline
CEEHILNOPRS	necrophiles
CEEHILNORST	cholesterin
CEEHILOPRST	electorship
	helicopters
CEEHILOPSTT	Philoctetes
CEEHILORSTT	hectoliters
	hectolitres
CEEHILORTTY	heterolytic
CEEHILPRSTU	lectureship
CEEHIMNNRST	enrichments
CEEHIMNOPRS	mesonephric
CEEHIMOPRSS	mesospheric
CEEHIMOPRTT	pitchometer
CEEHIMOPSTU	mouthpieces
CEEHIMOSSTT	somesthetic
CEEHIMPRRTY	hypermetric
CEEHIMRRTUY	eurythermic
CEEHINNRRST	intrenchers
CEEHINOOPPS	phenocopies
CEEHINRRSST	christeners
	rechristens
CEEHINRSSTW	winchesters
CEEHINSSTTY	synesthetic
CEEHIOOPRTT	heterotopic
CEEHIOPRRST	Terpsichore
CEEHIOPRSST	spirochetes
CEEHIOPRSTV	overpitches
CEEHIOPRTTY	heterotypic
CEEHIORSSUV	echoviruses
CEEHIRSSTTT	stretchiest
CEEHKLNOSUY	honeysuckle
CEEHKNORSUY	honeysucker
CEEHLLOORST	cholesterol
CEEHLLORSUY	lecherously
CEEHLMRSTWZ	weltschmerz
CEEHLNOOPRR	chloroprene
CEEHMMOORRS	chromomeres
CEEHMNOORRT	chronometer
CEEHMNOPRTY	nephrectomy
CEEHMNORSST	tschernosem
CEEHMOOPRST	thermoscope
CEEHNOOPPRS	nephroscope
CEEHNOOPPSS	nephoscopes
CEEHNOOPRST	ctenophores
CEEHNOORRTT	orthocenter
	orthocentre
CEEHNOPRSTY	hypocentres
CEEHOOPSSTT	stethoscope
CEEHORRSTTV	overstretch
CEEHORRTTYY	erythrocyte
CEEIIIKNSWZ	Sienkiewicz
CEEIIINNSTV	incentivise
CEEIIINNTVZ	incentivize
CEEIIINRSTZ	citizenries
CEEIIKNNSTZ	zinckenites
CEEIIKNRSST	ricketiness
CEEIILMPRSY	imprecisely

CEEIILMRTUV vermiculite
CEEIILNNORV overincline
CEEIILNNRSY insincerely
CEEIILNNTVY incentively
CEEIILNPRST princeliest
CEEIILNPTVY inceptively
CEEIILNRSTT centiliters
centilitres
CEEIILNTVVY invectively
CEEIILSTTVY selectivity
CEEIIMMPRST metempirics
CEEIIMNNPTY impenitency
CEEIIMNNRST reminiscent
CEEIIMNNSTT incitements
CEEIIMOPRTZ piezometric
CEEIIMOPTTV competitive
CEEIIMORSST esotericism
CEEIIMORSTT meteoritics
CEEIIMORSTX exotericism
CEEIINNNSTY insentiency
CEEIINNORSS incensories
CEEIINNSTXY inexistency
CEEIINOPSST centipoises
CEEIINORSTV insectivore
CEEIINOSTVX convexities
CEEIINPPRST percipients
CEEIINPRSST resipiscent
CEEIINRSSTT interstices
CEEIINRSTVV reviviscent
CEEIIORRSST escritoires
CEEIIPRTTVY receptivity
CEEIIRRSTTV restrictive
CEEIJLOPRST projectiles
CEEIJNORRTT interjector
CEEIKLLNRSS clerkliness
CEEIKLLNRST skillcentre
CEEIKLNNPSU luckpennies
CEEIKLNORRT interlocker
CEEIKNPRSTY persnickety
CEEILLMNNTY inclemently
CEEILLMRSSY mercilessly
CEEILLNRSST stencillers
CEEILLOOPST coleoptiles
CEEILLOQTUV Tocqueville
CEEILLOSSVY voicelessly
CEEILLPRSSY pricelessly
CEEILLSSUVY seclusively
CEEILLSUVXY exclusively
CEEILMNNSTU luminescent
CEEILMNOOPW policewomen
CEEILMNORST clinometers
CEEILMNOSTU contumelies
CEEILMOORRT colorimeter
CEEILMOORSS Îles Comores
CEEILMOOSTU leucotomies
CEEILMOPRSS microsleeps
CEEILNNNOOT nonelection
CEEILNNNOOV nonviolence
CEEILNOOPRS necropoleis
CEEILNOORRT intercooler
CEEILNOORSS recolonises
CEEILNOORSZ recolonizes
CEEILNOPRTU neuroleptic
CEEILNORTTT electrotint
CEEILNPRSTY presciently
CEEILNQSTUY quiescently
CEEILOPSSTY cespitosely
CEEILORSSST sclerotises
CEEILORSSTZ sclerotizes
CEEILORSUVX exclusive or
CEEILRRSTUU sericulture
CEEILRSUVXY excursively
CEEIMMORRST micrometers
micrometres
CEEIMNNOOPT omnipotence
CEEIMNNOPRS prominences
CEEIMNNOPTT incompetent
CEEIMNNORTU countermine
CEEIMNNSTTU intumescent
CEEIMNOORSS economisers
CEEIMNOORST necrotomies
CEEIMNOORSU ceremonious
CEEIMNOORSZ economizers
CEEIMNORSTU emunctories
CEEIMNRRTTU recruitment
CEEIMOOPSSS seismoscope
CEEIMOPRSSV compressive
CEEIMOPRSTU computerise
CEEIMOPRTUZ computerize
CEEIMORSSTV viscometers
CEEIMOSSSTV vicomtesses
CEEINNNOSTT consentient
CEEINNOORRT reconnoiter
reconnoitre
CEEINNOOSTX coextension
CEEINOOPRST retinoscope
CEEINOPPRSS sniperscope
CEEINOPPRST perceptions
CEEINOPRRTT interceptor
CEEINOPRSSS precessions
CEEINOPRSTU persecution
CEEINOPRSTX excerptions
CEEINORRSST intercessor
CEEINORRSTU intercourse
CEEINORSTTV convertites
CEEINOSSSTU necessitous
CEEINOSSSTV costiveness
CEEINPRSSTY persistency
CEEINRRSSTU scrutineers
CEEINRRSSTW wintercress
CEEINRSSSTY syncretises
CEEINRSSTTT trecentists
CEEINRSSTYZ syncretizes
CEEIOPPRSTV prospective
CEEIOPRSTTV protectives
CEEIOPRSTTY stereotypic
CEEIORRSTUU couturieres
CEEIPQRSTUU picturesque
CEEKLNRSTTU turtlenecks
CEEKOORRRTT retrorocket
CEELLMNOUWY unwelcomely
CEELLPRSSSU scrupleless
CEELLRSSTUU cultureless
CEELMMNOPST complements
CEELMNOOPSX complexones
CEELMNOOSSU nucleosomes
CEELMNOPSSX complexness
CEELMNOPSTY splenectomy
CEELMNOPTTY competently
CEELMOOPRVX overcomplex
CEELMOORSTU coulometers
CEELNOOOPRT coleopteron
CEELNRRRTUY recurrently
CEELPSSSSTU suspectless
CEEMMNNOOSS commonsense
CEEMMNOPTUY pneumectomy
CEEMMOSTXYY myxomycetes
CEEMNNNOTTT contentment
CEEMNOORSST centrosomes
CEEMNOORSUV overconsume
CEEMNOORTUV countermove
CEEMNOOSSTU coenosteums
CEEMNOPRRTU procurement
CEEMNOPRSTT contretemps
CEEMNOPRSTU recoupments
CEEMNOPRSTY pycnometers
CEEMOPRRSSU compressure
CEEMOPRRTTY cryptometer
CEENNOORRST cornerstone
CEENNORRSTU rencounters
CEENNRRSSTU currentness
CEENOORRSTV seroconvert
CEENOPPPRRS peppercorns
CEENOPRTTUY countertype
CEENOQRSSTU reconquests
CEENORSTTTU stonecutter
CEENORSTTUX contextures
CEEOOPRRTTV overprotect
CEEOOPRSSTY stereoscopy
CEEOORRSTUU outercourse
CEEOPRRSSSU procuresses
CEEOPRRSSTT protectress
retrospects
CEEOPRRSSTU persecutors
CEEOPRRSTUY persecutory
CEEPRSSSSUU cupressuses
CEERRRSTTUU restructure
CEFFHIINNOR chiffonnier
CEFFHIINORS chiffoniers
CEFFHIKMNOT Metchnikoff
CEFFHILNORT Northcliffe
CEFFHIRSSTT festschrift
CEFFIIRRSTU fructifiers
CEFGHIILNSS clingfishes
CEFGIILNNNU influencing
CEFGIINNORR reinforcing
CEFGIKLNOOR forelocking
CEFGIKLNPSY flyspecking
CEFGILNOORS foreclosing
CEFGILNORSU fluorescing
CEFGINORSSU refocussing
CEFHIIISSTT fetishistic
CEFHIKOSSST stockfishes
CEFHINRSTUW Schweinfurt
CEFIIINTTVY infectivity
CEFIILNNOST inflections

CEFIILNOQSU cinquefoils
CEFIINOPRST proficients
CEFIINORSUZ zinciferous
CEFILMORSUU culmiferous
CEFILNOORTU counterfoil
CEFILOORSUY ferociously
CEFILPRRSUU persulfuric
CEFINNOOSSS confessions
CEFIOPRRSUU cupriferous
CEFLMOORSST comfortless
CEFLNOORRSW cornflowers
CEFLOOOPRSU fluoroscope
CEFNNOORRST confronters
CEFNOORRTTU counterfort
CEFNOPRRTUY perfunctory
CEGGIINNORS recognising
CEGGIINNORZ recognizing
CEGHHKLOSSV Shcheglovsk
CEGHIIKNNST thickenings
CEGHIILLNPR prechilling
CEGHIILNRST Christingle
CEGHIINNNRT intrenching
CEGHIINNRST christening
CEGHIKNNPUY keypunching
CEGHIKNRSTU huckstering
CEGHILLNOOY lichenology
CEGHILNPRSU sepulchring
CEGHIMMNOOS homecomings
CEGHIMNOOPR morphogenic
CEGHIMORRTY hygrometric
CEGHINOOORR gonorrhoeic
CEGHINORRSU chirurgeons
CEGHINORSSU grouchiness
CEGHINORSTY trichogynes
CEGHINSUWZZ zwischenzug
CEGHIOOPRST geostrophic
CEGHIOPRRTY copyrighter
CEGHLOOPRSU glucophores
CEGHLOPSTYY glycophytes
CEGHOOPRSSY hygroscopes
CEGIIIMNNRS reminiscing
CEGIIINOPST poeticising
CEGIIINOPTZ poeticizing
CEGIIINORST eroticising
CEGIIINORTZ eroticizing
CEGIIINSTVV vivisecting
CEGIIKLNNSY sickeningly
CEGIIKLNSST singlestick
CEGIIKPRSST pigstickers
CEGIILLNNST stencilling
CEGIILMNNSU luminescing
CEGIILMOOSS seismologic
CEGIILNNPRS princelings
CEGIILNOOST neologistic
CEGIILNORST cloistering
CEGIILOOPST geopolitics
CEGIIMMNNOU immunogenic
CEGIIMNNOOS economising
CEGIIMNNOOZ economizing
CEGIIMNNSTU intumescing
CEGIIMNOORT goniometric
CEGIINNOORT recognition
CEGIINNOPRS preconising
CEGIINNOPRZ preconizing
CEGIINNRRRU reincurring
CEGIINOPRRV overpricing
CEGIINORSTU congruities
CEGIINRRSTT restricting
CEGIINRSSTY synergistic
CEGIKNOOORV overcooking
CEGIKNORSST stockingers
CEGILLNNOSU counselling
CEGILMNOOOT entomologic
CEGILNNOOSS coolingness
CEGILNNOSST clingstones
CEGILNOOORV overcooling
CEGILNOORST necrologist
CEGILNOOSTY Scientology
CEGILNRRRUY recurringly
CEGILOOOSST oecologists
CEGILOOSSTT cetologists
CEGIMNNNOST consignment
CEGIMNOOOSS cosmogonies
CEGIMNOOPRS recomposing
CEGIMNOPRSS compressing
CEGIMOOORRV microgroove
CEGINNNNSSU cunningness
CEGINNNORTU incongruent
CEGINNNOSTT contingents
CEGINNOOPST copingstone
CEGINNORSST constringes
CEGINNORSTU countersign
CEGINOOOPSS gonioscopes
CEGINOORRSS recognisors
CEGINOORRSV overscoring
CEGINOORRSZ recognizors
CEGINOORRTY recognitory
CEGINOPPRST prospecting
CEGINOPRSTU prosecuting
CEGLMMOORYY myrmecology
CEGLMOOSSTY glossectomy
CEGLNNORTUY congruently
CEGLNOORTUW counterglow
CEGLOPRSUUU groupuscule
CEGNNOPPRSU scuppernong
CEGNOOSSTUY cystogenous
CEGORRRSUYY cryosurgery
CEHHHIIKRST hitchhikers
CEHHIIILLOT heliolithic
CEHHIILMNST helminthics
CEHHIILOTTY ichthyolite
CEHHIIMMOPR hemimorphic
CEHHILMRSUY helichrysum
CEHHIMOOPRR rheomorphic
CEHHIMOOPRT theomorphic
CEHHIMRSTUY eurhythmics
CEHHINOPSTY hyposthenic
CEHHIOPRRST Christopher
CEHHIOPSTYZ schizophyte
CEHHLOOOSSU schoolhouse
CEHHLOOPRST choropleths
CEHHMNORSSY synchromesh
CEHHMOOOPRR chromophore
CEHHMOOPRSY hypsochrome
CEHHMOOPRTY phytochrome
CEHHMOOPSTY chomophytes
CEHHOOOPRRT trochophore
CEHIIINPSTZ citizenship
CEHIIINRSST trichinises
CEHIIINRSTZ trichinizes
CEHIIIRSTTT tritheistic
CEHIIJPSSTU justiceship
CEHIIKLLRSY lickerishly
CEHIILMNTTU multiethnic
CEHIILOOPRT heliotropic
CEHIILOPPRS scripophile
CEHIILPRSTU spherulitic
CEHIIMNOPST phonemicist
CEHIIMNORST thermionics
CEHIIMOPPRR perimorphic
CEHIIMOSSUV mischievous
CEHIIMRSSTY mythicisers
CEHIIMRSTYZ mythicizers
CEHIINOOPRS ionospheric
CEHIINOORSS isochronise
CEHIINOORSZ isochronize
CEHIIOPPTTY epiphytotic
CEHIIOPRRST prehistoric
CEHIIOPRSSY hypocrisies
CEHIIOPRSVY viceroyship
CEHIIOSSSVY vichyssoise
CEHIKMRSSTU hucksterism
CEHILLMOPSY mesophyllic
CEHILLNNOPU punchinello
CEHILLNOOPS colonelship
CEHILMOOPPR pleomorphic
CEHILMOOPRS pleochroism
CEHILMORTTY thermolytic
CEHILNOOQRU chloroquine
CEHILNOORST interschool
CEHILNOPSST clothespins
CEHILNOSSST coltishness
CEHILNOSSSU slouchiness
CEHILOPRSST lectorships
CEHILORSSTY chrysolites
CEHIMMOOPRS mesomorphic
CEHIMMOOSSS chemosmosis
CEHIMNNNOOP nonphonemic
CEHIMNOOPRS microphones
CEHIMNOOPRT phonometric
CEHIMNOOPRX xenomorphic
CEHIMNOPSTY chimneypots
CEHIMOOOPTY homoeotypic
CEHIMOOPRRX xeromorphic
CEHIMOOPRTT photometric
CEHIMOOSSST schistosome
CEHIMOPPRST coppersmith
CEHIMOPRSTY hypsometric
microphytes
CEHIMORSTTY stichometry
CEHINNORSSY synchronise
CEHINNORSYZ synchronize
CEHINOOPRRS coronership
CEHINOORRST orchestrion
CEHINOPRSSS censorships
CEHINOPRSSY hypersonics

CEHINRRSSSU currishness
CEHIOOOPPRT photocopier
CEHIOOOPPST photocopies
CEHIOOOPRSS horoscopies
CEHIOOPSTTY osteophytic
CEHIOORRRST retrochoirs
CEHIOORSSTW switcheroos
CEHIOPRRSST rectorships
CEHIOPRSSTT prosthetics
CEHKOOPPRRS rockhoppers
CEHKOORSSST stockhorses
CEHLLLOPRSY sclerophyll
CEHLMOOPRSY polychromes
CEHLMOPSTYY lymphocytes
CEHMMNOOORS monochromes
CEHMMOOORSS chromosomes
CEHMNOORRTY chronometry
CEHMOOPRSTY cormophytes
CEHMOOSSTUU customhouse
CEHMOPRSTYY psychometry
CEHNNOSSTUU uncouthness
CEHNOOOPPSS phonoscopes
CEHNOOPPRSY nephroscopy
CEHNOOPRRST necrotrophs
CEHNOOPRSTT topnotchers
CEHNOOSSTTU touchstones
CEHNOPRSSTY phenocrysts
CEHOOOPRSST orthoscopes
CEHOOPSSTTY stethoscopy
CEHOORSSTUU courthouses
CEHOPPRTTYY cryptophyte
CEIIIINNNOT Innocent III
CEIIILLMNPU penicillium
CEIIILLNSST illicitness
CEIIILLPTTY ellipticity
CEIIILMORST melioristic
CEIIILNNPTY incipiently
CEIIILOPSST politicises
CEIIILOPSTZ politicizes
CEIIILOSSTW Two Sicilies
CEIIIMNOPRS imprecision
CEIIIMNOSST misoneistic
CEIIIMOSSSS isoseismics
CEIIIMPRSST empiricists
CEIIIMPSSST pessimistic
CEIIIMRSSTV victimisers
CEIIIMRSTVZ victimizers
CEIIINNRSTV vincristine
CEIIINNRSTY insincerity
CEIIINNSTTV instinctive
CEIIINOPRTT peritonitic
CEIIINORSTU cineritious
CEIIINOSTVV vivisection
CEIIINPRSTV inscriptive
CEIIIOPRSTT periostitic
CEIIIORSSTU curiosities
CEIIIOSSSTV viscosities
CEIIIOSSTTV sovietistic
CEIIJLOORTU Joliot-Curie
CEIIKLLPSTT lickspittle
CEIIKLNPRSS prickliness
CEIIKLOOPTY poikilocyte
CEIIKLQRSUV quicksilver
CEIIKNOSSTY cytokinesis
CEIIKNRSSST tricksiness
CEIIKPRSSTT spitsticker
CEIILLLSSSY Scilly Isles
CEIILLNNOST centillions
CEIILLNSUVY inclusively
CEIILMOPSST polemicists
CEIILNNSSUV uncivilness
CEIILNORSUV inclusive or
CEIILNRTUUV viniculture
CEIILORSSTT sclerotitis
CEIILRTTUUV viticulture
CEIILRTTUVY reluctivity
CEIILSTUVXY exclusivity
CEIIMMNOSTU communities
CEIIMMOORST microtomies
CEIIMMORSSS microseisms
CEIIMNOOPTT competition
CEIIMNOPSUU impecunious
CEIIMNORRTT nitrometric
CEIIMNORSTU neuroticism
CEIIMNPRSSS scrimpiness
CEIIMOPRRST spirometric
CEIIMOPRSST semitropics
CEIIMORRRTW microwriter
CEIINNNNOTT incontinent
CEIINNNORTU internuncio
CEIINNOPSST inspections
CEIINNOSTTX extinctions
CEIINOPRSTV voiceprints
CEIINORRSTT restriction
CEIINORSSSS rescissions
CEIINORSSTT trisections
CEIINOSSSUV viciousness
CEIINOSSTUV viscounties
CEIINOSSTUX Six Counties
CEIINRRSSTU scrutiniser
CEIINRRSTUZ scrutinizer
CEIINRSSSTU scrutinises
sinecurists
CEIINRSSTUZ scrutinizes
CEIINRSTTUV instructive
CEIIOPPRSTU precipitous
CEIIORRRSTT terroristic
CEIIORSSTVV vivisectors
CEIIORSTUVY voyeuristic
CEIIPPRSTUY perspicuity
CEIJNOOPRST projections
CEIJNORSSTU surjections
CEIKKORRSST kicksorters
CEIKLNNSSUU unluckiness
CEIKLNOORRT crinkleroot
CEIKLOORSSU cokulorises
CEIKLOPRSST stockpilers
CEIKLOPRTTU leptokurtic
CEIKNNORSTU countersink
CEILLLNOOOV violoncello
CEILMMNOPST compliments
CEILMMOPRUY promycelium
CEILMNOOPST completions
CEILMNOOPSX complexions
CEILMNOOSUY moneciously
CEILMNOTYYZ enzymolytic
CEILMOOOPST colpotomies
cosmopolite
CEILMOOOSST colostomies
CEILMOOOSTV locomotives
CEILMOOPSTY compositely
CEILMOORRTY colorimetry
CEILMOPRTUU pomiculture
CEILMOPSSTT completists
CEILMOPSSUV compulsives
CEILNNNOTTY continently
CEILNNNOTVY connivently
CEILNNOOTVY connotively
CEILNNOSSTU unctionless
CEILNOOOTUV coevolution
CEILNOOPRTU perlocution
CEILNOPRRTW triple crown
CEILNORSSTU courtliness
CEILNRSTUUV ventriculus
CEILOOPRSTT protostelic
CEILOOPRTTU luteotropic
CEILOOPRTTY proteolytic
CEILOORRSTU terricolous
CEILOORRSUV versicolour
CEILOORRSVY corrosively
CEIMMMNOSTT commitments
CEIMMNOQSUU communiques
CEIMMNORSSU consumerism
CEIMMNORSTY metronymics
CEIMMOOPRRS compromiser
CEIMMOOPRSS compromises
CEIMMOORSTV overcommits
CEIMMORSSSU commissures
CEIMMORSTUX commixtures
CEIMNNORSSS crimsonness
CEIMNOOPRSS compression
CEIMNOOPRTU mucoprotein
CEIMNOORSTU coterminous
CEIMNOPRSSU prosceniums
CEIMNOPSTUV consumptive
CEIMNORSSTU consumerist
misconstrue
CEIMNRSSSTY syncretisms
CEIMOOOSSTT costotomies
CEIMOOPRRSS microspores
CEIMOOPRSTT competitors
CEIMOOSSTTY cystotomies
CEINNNOOSTT contentions
CEINNNOOSTV conventions
CEINNOORSSU connoisseur
CEINNOORSSV conversions
CEINNOOSTTU contentious
CEINNOPRSTY encryptions
CEINNOPSTUX expunctions
CEINNORTTUY intercounty
CEINNOSTTTU constituent
CEINOOPRSSS processions
CEINOOPRSTT stenotropic
CEINOOPRSTU prosecution
CEINOOPRSTY retinoscopy
CEINOOPSSSU copiousness

CEINOOPTTTY	totipotency
CEINOPRSSSU	percussions
	supersonics
CEINOPRSSTT	introspects
CEINOPRSSTU	supertonics
CEINORRSSSU	cursoriness
CEINORSSSUU	curiousness
CEINORSSTTT	cornettists
CEINORSTTTU	constituter
CEINOSSSSUV	viscousness
CEINOSSSTUV	viscountess
CEINOSSTTTU	constitutes
CEINRSSSTTY	syncretists
CEIOOPRTTYZ	cryptozoite
CEIOORSSSTT	scooterists
CEIOORSSTTU	ecotourists
CEIOPPRSSUU	perspicuous
CEIOPRRSTWY	copywriters
CEIORRSTUVY	verrucosity
CEIPPRRSSTU	superscript
CEIPPRSSTTY	typescripts
CEKLMPRSSUU	lumpsuckers
CEKNNORSTUU	countersunk
CEKNOORRTUW	counterwork
CEKOORSSTTU	stockroutes
CELLMOOPRRT	comptroller
CELLNOORRST	controllers
CELLNOORSSU	counsellors
CELLNOOTUVY	convolutely
CELLNOPRTUY	corpulently
CELLNRTTUUY	truculently
CELLOOOSSST	closestools
CELMNOORTUU	monoculture
CELMOOPRSTT	complotters
CELMOOPRTYY	pylorectomy
CELNOOPRTTU	counterplot
CELOOPRRSTU	colporteurs
CELOORSTUUY	courteously
CEMMNOOPRTT	comportment
CEMNOORSTUV	covermounts
CEMOOPRRSSS	compressors
CENNOOPRRSU	pronouncers
CENNOOSSSUU	nocuousness
CENOORRSTTV	controverts
CENOORRSTVY	controversy
CENOORSTUUU	uncourteous
CENOPRRSSTU	corruptness
CENORSTTUWY	West Country
CEOOPPRRSST	prospectors
CEOOPRRSSTU	prosecutors
CEPRRSSTTUU	superstruct
CFFGIINRTUY	fructifying
CFFIIINOOSU	inofficious
CFFIILOOSUY	officiously
CFFIINOOSUU	unofficious
CFGHIILLNNY	flinchingly
CFGHIILNNNU	unflinching
CFGHIMNOORT	forthcoming
CFGIIIILNSY	silicifying
CFGIINNNOTU	functioning
CFGILNNOSUY	confusingly
CFGINNNOORT	confronting
CFHIILNOOSS	ichnofossil
CFIIILNNOST	inflictions
CFIIINOSSTT	fictionists
CFIILMOORSS	microfossil
CFIILMORSTU	formulistic
CFIMNOORSST	conformists
CFLLLOORUUY	colourfully
CFLNOORTUWY	Flow Country
CFLNORSUUUU	furunculous
CFLOOOPRSUY	fluoroscopy
CFLORSTUUUY	fructuously
CGGHIIINOST	gothicising
CGGHIIINOTZ	gothicizing
CGGHIILOOPR	logogriphic
CGGIIIKNPST	pigsticking
CGGIILMMNNO	commingling
CGGIILNNRSU	surcingling
CGGIINOORST	gongoristic
CGHHHIIIKNT	hitchhiking
CGHHILOOTYY	ichthyology
CGHHIOPRTYY	hygrophytic
CGHIIIMNSTY	mythicising
CGHIIIMNTYZ	mythicizing
CGHIILMORST	microlights
CGHIILRSSTW	switchgirls
CGHIINPPRRU	chirrupping
CGHILLNOSUY	slouchingly
CGHILLOORSS	schoolgirls
CGHILMOOOPR	morphologic
CGHILOOORST	chorologist
CGHILOOPSTY	phycologist
CGHILOORSTY	Christology
CGHIMNOORST	shortcoming
CGHIMOOOTYZ	homozygotic
CGHIMOOPRYZ	zygomorphic
CGIIIIMNSTV	victimising
CGIIIIMNTVZ	victimizing
CGIIIKLNOPT	politicking
CGIIIKNNPPR	pinpricking
CGIIILNSSTU	linguistics
CGIIILRSTTU	liturgistic
CGIIIMNOSTV	cognitivism
CGIIKLLNORS	rollickings
CGIIKLLNRTY	tricklingly
CGIIKLNOPST	stockpiling
CGIIKLNOPSU	liposucking
CGIILLNOOSU	lignicolous
CGIILLNPPRY	cripplingly
CGIILLOSSTY	syllogistic
CGIILMMNOOU	immunologic
CGIILMNOORY	criminology
CGIILMOOTVY	victimology
CGIILNNNOVY	connivingly
CGIILNNNSUU	cunnilingus
CGIILNOOOST	iconologist
CGIILNOORSU	colourising
CGIILNOORUZ	colourizing
CGIILOOOSST	sociologist
CGIIMMNNOSU	communising
CGIIMMNNOTU	comminuting
CGIIMMNNOUZ	communizing
CGIIMNNOSTU	miscounting
CGIIMNOOPST	compositing
CGIIMNOSSTU	customising
CGIIMNOSTUZ	customizing
CGIINNORTUY	incongruity
CGIINNRSTTU	instructing
CGIINOPRTWY	copywriting
CGIKLMMNOOS	slommocking
CGIKNNORTUY	King Country
CGILLNNOORT	controlling
CGILLNNOOSY	consolingly
CGILMNNOSUY	consumingly
CGILMNOOPTT	complotting
CGILMOOOSST	cosmologist
CGILMOOSSTY	mycologists
CGILNNOOTUV	convoluting
CGILNOOOSST	oncologists
CGILNPRSTUU	sculpturing
CGILOOSSTTY	cytologists
CGIMNOOOSST	cosmogonist
CGINNNOOPRU	pronouncing
CGINNOORSUU	incongruous
CGINOOPPRTU	outcropping
CGINOOPRSST	prognostics
CGINOORSSTU	outcrossing
CGINOORSTUU	outsourcing
CGINRRSTTUU	structuring
CGLNOORSUUY	congruously
CHHIILOOPPS	philosophic
CHHIILOPTTY	lithophytic
CHHIIMORSTY	isorhythmic
CHHIIMRTTYY	rhythmicity
CHHIINORSTY	ichthyornis
CHHILLMOOPY	homophyllic
CHHILMOOOPR	holomorphic
CHHIMMOOOPR	homomorphic
CHHIMOSTTYY	stichomythy
CHHIOORSTTY	orthostichy
CHHLLLOOPRY	chlorophyll
CHIIIMORSST	historicism
CHIIINORSST	histrionics
	trichinosis
CHIIIORSSTT	historicist
CHIIIORSTTY	historicity
CHIILLNOOTT	octillionth
CHIILOOPPRT	protophilic
CHIILOOPRTT	protolithic
CHIILOOSTYZ	hylozoistic
CHIILOPPRSY	scripophily
CHIIMNOORSS	isochronism
CHIIMNOSTWZ	Nimzowitsch
CHIINNOPSSU	pincushions
CHIINOPPRSU	porcupinish
CHIINORRTTY	tyrothricin
CHIIOOPRTTX	thixotropic
CHIIOPPRRTY	porphyritic
CHIIORRSSTY	scirrhosity
CHIIORSSTTU	tristichous
CHIIOSSSTTY	schistosity
CHIKNOQRSTU	quickthorns
CHILLMOPRSY	microphylls
CHILMOOPPRY	polymorphic
CHILNOPSSSU	consulships

CHILOOPPRTY	polytrophic
CHILOORSTUU	ulotrichous
CHIMMNOOOPR	monomorphic
CHIMNNORSSY	synchronism
CHIMNOOPPPY	hypnopompic
CHIMNOOPRRS	prochronism
CHIMOOPRSSY	hypocorisms
CHINOOORSSU	isochronous
CHIOOOPPRTT	phototropic
CHIOOOPRRTT	orthotropic
CHIOOPPRSTY	sporophytic
CHIOOPPRTTY	tropophytic
CHIORSSTTTW	stitchworts
CHMNOOOTTTU	cottonmouth
CHMNOOPSTTU	muttonchops
CHMOOOPRSTY	psychomotor
CHNNOORRSTY	synchrotron
CHNNOORSSUY	synchronous
CIIIIKKKLLN	killikinick
CIIIIKKNNNS	kinnikinics
CIIIIPRSSTT	spiritistic
CIIILLMMNOR	millimicron
CIIILLMOPTY	impoliticly
CIIILLNOSTT	tonsillitic
CIIILNSTUVY	inclusivity
CIIILOPSSST	solipsistic
CIIILRSTTUU	utriculitis
CIIIMNORTTU	micturition
CIIINNOPRST	inscription
CIIINOOSTTY	isotonicity
CIIINORSTUY	incuriosity
CIIJNNNOSTU	injunctions
CIIKKNNOPST	knickpoints
CIILLMORSUV	microvillus
CIILLNNOSST	scintillons
CIILLNOOSTU	illocutions
CIILLOORSTT	torticollis
CIILMMNNOOS	monoclinism
CIILNOOPSTU	liposuction
CIILNOPSTUU	punctilious
CIILNORSUUY	incuriously
CIIMMNNOOTU	comminution
CIIMMNOOSSS	commissions
CIIMMOORSTT	microtomist
CIIMMOPRRSS	microprisms
CIIMNOOOPST	composition
CIIMNOPRRST	microprints
CIIMNRSSTTU	misinstruct
CIIMOPRRSTU	scriptorium
CIIMOPRSTUY	promiscuity
CIINNNOOPST	conniptions
CIINNORSTTU	instruction
CIIOOPRSSUV	piscivorous
CILLMOOQSUU	colloquiums
CILLOOQSSTU	colloquists
CILMNNOOOSU	monoclinous
CILMNOOOSUY	monoicously
CILMNOOPSSU	compulsions
CILNNOOOTUV	convolution
CILNNOOSSUV	convulsions
CILNNOOSUUY	innocuously
CILNOOOPRTU	colourpoint
CILNOPRRTUY	incorruptly
CIMNNOOOPPS	nincompoops
CIMNNOOPSTU	consumption
CIMOOOPRSST	compositors
CIMOOPRSSUU	promiscuous
CIMOPRSSTUU	scrumptious
CINNOOORSTT	contortions
CINOOPRRSTU	corruptions
CINOORSTTTU	constitutor
CINORRSSTTU	instructors
CIOOPRSSSTU	uroscopists
CIOOPRSSTTT	protoctists
CIOPPRSSSTT	postscripts
CKKNORSSTUW	knockwursts
CLLNOOSUUVV	convolvulus
CLOOOPRRSTU	prolocutors
CNNOOOORRRY	Rory O'Connor
DDDDEEEEFIL	fiddledeedee
DDDEEFIOSST	eisteddfods
DDDEEFNNRUU	underfunded
DDDEEGIMOSS	demigoddess
DDDEEGINRRU	undergirded
DDDEEIINSSV	dividedness
DDDEELMNSSU	muddledness
DDDEGHOOOSS	goddesshood
DDDEGIIOORS	didgeridoos
DDDEHLOOORT	toddlerhood
DDDENNOORTW	downtrodden
DDEEEEFIRRZ	freeze-dried
DDEEEEHNPRR	reprehended
DDEEEEILRRV	redelivered
DDEEEEIMSST	disesteemed
DDEEEELOPRV	redeveloped
DDEEEGHHOPP	hedgehopped
DDEEEGINPRS	predesigned
DDEEEGIPRST	predigested
DDEEEHILLSV	dishevelled
DDEEEHNORTY	heterodyned
DDEEEILMNRT	intermeddle
DDEEEILNRSS	slenderised
DDEEEILNRSZ	slenderized
DDEEEIMNOST	demonetised
DDEEEIMNOTZ	demonetized
DDEEEIMPRST	distempered
DDEEEINNNPT	independent
DDEEEINNPRT	interdepend
DDEEEINPRST	predestined
DDEEEIOPRST	redeposited
DDEEEIPPSST	sidestepped
DDEEEIRSSSS	sidedresses
DDEEELLORRW	well-ordered
DDEEELNNPTY	dependently
DDEEELNOPUV	undeveloped
DDEEENOSSTV	devotedness
DDEEENRRRSU	surrendered
DDEEEORRSSV	overdressed
DDEEFIIIMNN	indemnified
DDEEFIIINRT	denitrified
DDEEFIIIRSV	diversified
DDEEFIIIRTV	devitrified
DDEEFIILMSU	demulsified
DDEEFIIMNNU	definiendum
DDEEFIIMSTY	demystified
DDEEFIINSST	disinfested
DDEEFILNORT	interfolded
DDEEFIMORSS	semifreddos
DDEEFIORSST	disforested
DDEEGGHOOPS	hodgepodges
DDEEGHILLTY	delightedly
DDEEGINNRSU	undersigned
DDEEGNOPRSU	groundspeed
DDEEHIILRSS	disrelished
DDEEHINRSSS	reddishness
DDEEIILNSTT	disentitled
DDEEIILPPSS	sideslipped
DDEEIIMNNOS	dimensioned
DDEEIINNSTW	disentwined
DDEEIINORST	disoriented
DDEEIINRRST	disinterred
DDEEIINRSSW	sidewinders
DDEEIINSSTV	disinvested
DDEEIIORSSX	deoxidisers
DDEEIIORSXZ	deoxidizers
DDEEIIQSTUU	disquietude
DDEEIKNNRSS	kindredness
DDEEILORSSV	redissolved
DDEEILPRSSY	dispersedly
DDEEINNNPRU	underpinned
DDEEINORSSW	disendowers
DDEEINSSSTU	studiedness
DDEEIOORRSS	deodorisers
DDEEIOORRSZ	deodorizers
DDEEIOPPRSS	predisposed
DDEENNORSSU	roundedness
DDEENNPRSSU	underspends
DDEENOQRTUU	underquoted
DDEENORSTUY	undestroyed
DDEEOOPPRST	doorstepped
DDEFFIILNTY	diffidently
DDEFGIIILNY	dignifiedly
DDEFGIIINNU	undignified
DDEFHLNORSU	fundholders
DDEFINOPRSU	de profundis
DDEFLNNOUUY	unfoundedly
DDEGHNOTTUU	doughnutted
DDEGIIINOSX	deoxidising
DDEGIIINOXZ	deoxidizing
DDEGIILMSUY	misguidedly
DDEGIILSSUY	disguisedly
DDEGIINNOSW	disendowing
DDEGIINOORS	deodorising
DDEGIINOORZ	deodorizing
DDEGIINORRS	disordering
DDEGIINSSUU	undisguised
DDEGILMNOST	dislodgment
DDEGILNRSTU	disgruntled
DDEGILSSTUY	disgustedly
DDEGNNORRUU	underground
DDEHHIIOPRT	diphtheroid
DDEHIIIPPPS	Phidippides
DDEHIIKNPRS	kindredship
DDEHIIKNSSS	kiddishness
DDEHIILNSSW	windshields

DDEHIILPSSU	disulphides
DDEHIINRSSW	widdershins
DDEHINOORSU	dishonoured
DDEHIOOOPST	photodiodes
DDEHLMOOTUU	loudmouthed
DDEIILNSSTY	dissidently
DDEIIMNNOSU	diminuendos
DDEIIOPRSSS	dispersoids
DDEIKNNRSUW	wunderkinds
DDEILNOSSUV	undissolved
DDEILORSTTY	distortedly
DDEINNOOSTT	endodontist
DDELNNOORRY	Londonderry
DDELNORRSUW	underworlds
DDEOPRRSSTU	rudderposts
DDFGHILNNOU	fundholding
DDFGIMNNOUU	dumfounding
DDIIKLNSTWY	tiddlywinks
DDINOOOPRTT	diprotodont
DEEEEEFHLRW	freewheeled
DEEEEEFPRSZ	deepfreezes
DEEEEELMRTT	telemetered
DEEEEELNTVV	velveteened
DEEEEFLNSSS	defenseless
DEEEEGNNRRS	engenderers
DEEEEHILRSW	sidewheeler
DEEEEHIMPRS	ephemerides
DEEEEHIMRSU	euhemerised
DEEEEHIMRUZ	euhemerized
DEEEEHNPRRR	reprehender
DEEEEIMNRRT	redetermine
DEEEEINORRT	orienteered
DEEEELMNNOW	needlewomen
DEEEELOPRRV	redeveloper
DEEEEMOPRST	speedometer
DEEEENNSTUW	unsweetened
DEEEENPRRST	represented
DEEEEORRSTV	oversteered
DEEEEORRTVX	overexerted
DEEEEQRSSTU	sequestered
DEEEFGINORV	overfeeding
DEEEFHLNSSU	heedfulness
DEEEFHLORRS	freeholders
DEEEFHNRRSU	unrefreshed
DEEEFIILMPX	exemplified
DEEEFIILMRS	demireliefs
DEEEFILMNST	defilements
DEEEFILNSVY	defensively
DEEEFIMRSSW	swimfeeders
DEEEFINORRV	overrefined
DEEEFINRSTW	winterfeeds
DEEEFIOPRRT	profiteered
DEEEFKNOORT	foretokened
DEEEFLNNSSU	needfulness
DEEEFLORRSW	deflowerers
DEEEFLORRTX	retroflexed
DEEEFMNNRTU	unfermented
DEEEFMNRRSU	referendums
DEEEFORRSST	deforesters
DEEEGGINNNR	engendering
DEEEGHHOPPR	hedgehopper
DEEEGHILNNT	enlightened
DEEEGHIORVW	overweighed
DEEEGIIMRSV	demivierges
DEEEGIMORST	geometrised
DEEEGIMORTZ	geometrized
DEEEGINOSXY	deoxygenise
DEEEGINOXYZ	deoxygenize
DEEEGIRRSST	deregisters
DEEEGMNNORS	mondegreens
DEEEGMNNSTU	unsegmented
DEEEHHPRSSS	shepherdess
DEEEHIINNPT	phenetidine
DEEEHILNPRS	replenished
DEEEHILPSST	slipsheeted
DEEEHIMNRST	intermeshed
DEEEHLMORVW	overwhelmed
DEEEHLNNORT	heldentenor
DEEEHLNRSTU	unsheltered
DEEEHMNOSST	Demosthenes
DEEEHNORSTY	heterodynes
DEEEIIMRRST	semiretired
DEEEIINNPTX	inexpedient
DEEEIINRTVW	interviewed
DEEEIINSSST	desensitise
DEEEIINSSTZ	desensitize
DEEEIIRSTTX	dexterities
DEEEIKLLRSW	weedkillers
DEEEILLMOSS	demoiselles
DEEEILLNNST	sentinelled
DEEEILLNPPZ	Led Zeppelin
DEEEILLNRSS	elderliness
DEEEILMMNPT	implemented
DEEEILMMNUV	mendelevium
DEEEILNNOPT	needlepoint
DEEEILNPTXY	expediently
DEEEILNRSSS	slenderises
DEEEILNRSSZ	slenderizes
DEEEILORSTU	deleterious
DEEEILRSSVW	silverweeds
DEEEIMNORST	remonetised
DEEEIMNORTZ	remonetized
DEEEIMNOSST	demonetises
DEEEIMNOSTZ	demonetizes
DEEEIMNRRST	determiners
DEEEIMNRSST	densimeters
DEEEIMORSTU	eudiometers
DEEEINNPSTV	pendentives
DEEEINPRRTT	interpreted
DEEEINPRSST	predestines
DEEEINPRTUX	expenditure
DEEEINRRSST	tenderisers
DEEEINRRSSV	vinedresser
DEEEINRRSTZ	tenderizers
DEEEINRSSSV	diverseness
DEEEINRSSTU	eruditeness
DEEEINRSSTW	westernised
DEEEINRSTWZ	westernized
DEEEIPPRSST	sidestepper
DEEEKLLNNNU	unkennelled
DEEEKLNORSW	needleworks
DEEEKOOPRRS	doorkeepers
DEEELLNRRSU	underseller
DEEELMNNORY	moneylender
DEEELMNOPTV	development
DEEELMNOTVV	devolvement
DEEELNNPRST	resplendent
DEEELNNRSSS	slenderness
DEEELNNSSSS	endlessness
DEEELNORSSS	nesselrodes
DEEELNORTUV	volunteered
DEEELNPPRUX	unperplexed
DEEELNRRTTU	underletter
DEEELOOPPRV	overpeopled
DEEELOOPRVV	overdevelop
DEEELPRRTVY	pervertedly
DEEEMNNORST	endorsement
DEEEMNNOSTT	denotements
DEEEMNNOSTU	denouements
DEEEMNNOSYZ	endoenzymes
DEEEMNORSSV	removedness
DEEEMPRTTUW	trumpetweed
DEEEMRRSSSU	murderesses
DEEENOOSSWZ	sneezewoods
DEEENOPRSUX	underexpose
DEEENOPSSSX	exposedness
DEEENORSTVX	overextends
DEEENPRSSUX	unexpressed
DEEENRRRRSU	surrenderer
DEEENRRSSTU	understeers
DEEENRRSTTT	trendsetter
DEEEOOPRRVW	overpowered
DEEEOOPRSVX	overexposed
DEEEOPPRSTV	overstepped
DEEEOPRSSSS	repossessed
DEEEOPRSTTY	stereotyped
DEEEORRRRST	reredorters
DEEEORRRTTV	retroverted
DEEEORRSSSV	overdresses
DEEEORRTTVX	extroverted
DEEEPRRSSST	prestressed
DEEEPRRSSSU	superseders
DEEEPRRSSUU	supersedure
DEEFFGINNOR	forefending
DEEFFIINNRT	indifferent
DEEFFIIORRT	refortified
DEEFFILNRTY	differently
DEEFFINSSSU	diffuseness
DEEFFIOOPRR	fireproofed
DEEFFORSTUV	overstuffed
DEEFGGILLNS	fledgelings
DEEFGGIOPTT	pettifogged
DEEFGHHORTU	feedthrough
DEEFGHIORST	foresighted
DEEFGILNORW	deflowering
DEEFGINORST	deforesting
DEEFHIILSSV	devilfishes
DEEFHILTTTW	Twelfthtide
DEEFHINRRSU	refurnished
DEEFIIIMNNR	indemnifier
DEEFIIIMNNS	indemnifies
DEEFIIINNST	intensified
DEEFIIINRST	denitrifies
	identifiers
DEEFIIINSTV	definitives
DEEFIIIRRSV	diversifier

DEEFIIIRSSV	diversifies
DEEFIIIRSTV	devitrifies
DEEFIILMNNS	infieldsmen
DEEFIILMNOS	solemnified
DEEFIILMRSU	demulsifier
DEEFIILMSSU	demulsifies
DEEFIILNRST	friendliest
DEEFIIMORST	deformities
DEEFIIMSSTY	demystifies
DEEFIINOPRS	personified
DEEFIINRSVW	viewfinders
DEEFIKLORRW	fieldworker
DEEFILMNNRU	Dunfermline
DEEFILNORTW	interflowed
DEEFILNOSST	fieldstones
DEEFILORSTU	outfielders
DEEFILPRRVY	perfervidly
DEEFINORRSX	ferredoxins
DEEFIORRTTT	retrofitted
DEEFLLNOSSU	dolefulness
DEEFLMNNOST	enfoldments
DEEFLOPRSSY	professedly
DEEFMNOPRRU	unperformed
DEEFNOORSTT	tenderfoots
DEEFNOPRSSU	unprofessed
DEEFNOPRTUY	typefounder
DEEGGIINNRS	redesigning
DEEGGIINRST	redigesting
DEEGGLLOORY	Lloyd George
DEEGGLNOOOS	golden goose
DEEGHHINPRS	shepherding
DEEGHIILNSV	disheveling
DEEGHILLNWY	wheedlingly
DEEGHILNOOP	pigeonholed
DEEGHILOOST	theologised
DEEGHILOOTZ	theologized
DEEGHIMNOOS	homogenised
DEEGHIMNOOZ	homogenized
DEEGHINORSY	hydrogenise
DEEGHINORTV	overnighted
DEEGHINORYZ	hydrogenize
DEEGHINRTUW	underweight
DEEGHNORSTU	groundsheet
DEEGIIILMST	legitimised
DEEGIIILMTZ	legitimized
DEEGIIINSTV	indigestive
DEEGIILSTVY	digestively
DEEGIIMNNOR	domineering
DEEGIIMNNRT	determining
DEEGIINNRST	ingredients
	tenderising
DEEGIINNRTZ	tenderizing
DEEGIINORST	redigestion
DEEGIINRSSV	dissevering
DEEGILLMNOR	remodelling
DEEGILLNPSS	spindlelegs
DEEGILMNOPR	empoldering
DEEGILMNORS	mongrelised
DEEGILMNORZ	mongrelized
DEEGILMNTUV	divulgement
DEEGILNOPRY	redeploying
DEEGILNORUV	overindulge
DEEGILNRSVY	deservingly
DEEGILNRTVY	divergently
DEEGILNRUVY	gerundively
DEEGIMNORSV	misgoverned
DEEGIMORSUU	demiurgeous
DEEGINNORST	rontgenised
DEEGINNORTZ	rontgenized
DEEGINNRSUV	undeserving
DEEGINORSSS	degressions
DEEGINORSTV	stevedoring
DEEGINPRSSU	superseding
DEEGJMNPRTU	prejudgment
DEEGLNORSSY	engrossedly
DEEGLNOSSSS	godlessness
DEEHHILNNNO	Hohenlinden
DEEHHLOORSU	householder
DEEHHOPRRSY	hydrosphere
DEEHIILRSSS	disrelishes
DEEHIIMPRSU	hesperidium
DEEHIIRSSTT	hereditists
DEEHILLORTT	titleholder
DEEHILMNOTU	endothelium
DEEHILMORSS	demolishers
DEEHILOOPRT	heteroploid
DEEHILOOSTT	theodolites
DEEHILOSTTU	silhouetted
DEEHIMNOPRS	premonished
DEEHIMORSST	methodisers
DEEHIMORSTZ	methodizers
DEEHINOOPSV	videophones
DEEHINOPSTY	dehypnotise
DEEHINOPTYZ	dehypnotize
DEEHINOSSSU	hideousness
DEEHINRRSSU	hurriedness
DEEHINSSSTY	synthesised
DEEHINSSTTY	synthetised
DEEHINSSTYZ	synthesized
DEEHINSTTYZ	synthetized
DEEHLLMOPRS	phelloderms
DEEHLMNNOSS	Mendelssohn
DEEHLMNRSUW	underwhelms
DEEHLMOORTY	model theory
DEEHLNORRTW	netherworld
DEEHLOPRSTU	upholstered
DEEHLPRSTUU	sulphureted
DEEHMNNOOOY	honeymooned
DEEHMNOOPTU	openmouthed
DEEHMNOPRRY	hypermodern
DEEHMOORRTY	hydrometeor
DEEHMORRSTY	hydrometers
DEEHNOOORSW	Wooden Horse
DEEIIIMNNST	indemnities
DEEIIIRSSTV	diversities
DEEIIKLLMSS	semiskilled
DEEIIKLNNRT	interlinked
DEEIILLOPST	lepidolites
DEEIILMNSST	limitedness
DEEIILMNSSU	disseminule
DEEIILNOPRS	lepidosiren
DEEIILNPRSV	vilipenders
DEEIILNSSTT	disentitles
DEEIILOPRSY	erysipeloid
DEEIILORSST	siderolites
DEEIILPSTUX	duplexities
DEEIILRSSSV	silversides
DEEIIMMNPST	impediments
DEEIIMMNRST	determinism
DEEIIMNNSTT	inditements
DEEIIMNOPTT	piedmontite
DEEIIMNORST	modernities
DEEIIMNPSST	dissepiment
DEEIIMNRRST	irredentism
DEEIIMNRSSS	minidresses
DEEIIMNRSTT	determinist
DEEIIMNRTTT	intermitted
DEEIINNORTV	inventoried
DEEIINNRTTW	intertwined
DEEIINNSSTT	dissentient
DEEIINNSSTW	disentwines
DEEIINOPSTX	expeditions
DEEIINPRSTY	serendipity
DEEIINRRSTT	irredentist
DEEIINRSSTT	disinterest
DEEIIOPSTUX	expeditious
DEEIIOQSSUX	sesquioxide
DEEIIPRSSSW	sideswipers
DEEIIRSTTUV	divestiture
DEEIJNNOSST	jointedness
DEEIKLLORSV	volkslieder
DEEIKMNPPSU	pumpkinseed
DEEIKNORRTW	interworked
DEEIKORSSST	sidestrokes
DEEILLMPTUX	multiplexed
DEEILLOPRSV	overspilled
DEEILLQRRSU	squirrelled
DEEILMMOPSY	misemployed
DEEILMNOPST	despoilment
DEEILMNRSTW	wilderments
DEEILMOPRSY	polymerised
DEEILMOPRYZ	polymerized
DEEILNNNRSU	underlinens
DEEILNNORST	tenderloins
DEEILNNORVY	nondelivery
DEEILNNQSTU	delinquents
DEEILNOPTUX	unexploited
DEEILNORRSS	orderliness
DEEILNORTVV	intervolved
DEEILNSSSTT	stiltedness
DEEILOPPPTY	polypeptide
DEEILORSSSV	redissolves
DEEIMMNORTU	endometrium
DEEIMMRSSTY	symmetrised
DEEIMMRSTYZ	symmetrized
DEEIMNNNOTU	unmentioned
DEEIMNNNSTT	intendments
DEEIMNNORST	indorsement
DEEIMNNORUU	endoneurium
DEEIMNNRRSU	underminers
DEEIMNOPRST	redemptions
DEEIMNORRSS	modernisers
DEEIMNORRSZ	modernizers
DEEIMNOSSTU	eudemonists
	sedimentous
DEEIMNOTTZZ	mezzotinted

DEEIMNPRSSS	misspenders
DEEIMNPRSSU	unimpressed
DEEIMNRSSTW	stemwinders
DEEIMNSSTTV	divestments
DEEIMOOPRTT	dioptometer
DEEIMOPRRST	misreported
DEEIMOPRSSW	disempowers
DEEINNNOPSU	unpensioned
DEEINNNORST	nonresident
DEEINNOPSST	pointedness
DEEINNOSTTU	tendentious
DEEINNPRSTU	superintend
DEEINNSSTUW	unwitnessed
DEEINOPRRTV	overprinted
DEEINOPRSSS	depressions
DEEINORRSUV	overinsured
DEEINORRTTV	introverted
DEEINOSSSTU	tediousness
DEEINOSSSUV	deviousness
DEEINPRRTTU	interrupted
DEEINRRRTUW	underwriter
DEEINRRSTUW	underwrites
DEEINSSTTTV	vendettists
DEEIOOPRSTU	eurodeposit
DEEIOORRTTV	detritovore
DEEIOPPRSSS	predisposes
DEEIOPPRSST	predeposits
DEEIOPRSSUX	superoxides
DEEIORRSSTV	overstrides
DEEIPRRSSSU	pressurised
DEEIPRRSSUZ	pressurized
DEEIPRRSTUY	eurypterids
DEEKLMRSTTU	kettledrums
DEEKNNNRSSU	drunkenness
DEEKOORTTUY	deuterotoky
DEELMNOPSTY	deployments
DEELMNORTTY	tormentedly
DEELNNOOSST	selenodonts
DEELORRSTXY	dextrorsely
DEELORSTTUV	turtledoves
DEELORSTUXY	dexterously
DEEMNNORSTW	wonderments
DEEMNOORTUY	Deuteronomy
DEEMNOSSSSY	syndesmoses
DEEMOORRSST	drosometers
DEEMOPRRTUV	overtrumped
DEENNOPRSST	respondents
DEENNSSSTTU	stuntedness
DEENOQRSTUU	underquotes
DEENORRSTUY	understorey
DEENOSSSTUU	duteousness
DEEOOPRRSSU	uredospores
DEEOPPPRSSU	presupposed
DEEOPRRRSSU	superorders
DEFFGINNNOU	unoffending
DEFFHIMORSS	sheriffdoms
DEFFIILSUVY	diffusively
DEFFIINORTU	unfortified
DEFFILLLNUU	unfulfilled
DEFGGIILNTY	fidgetingly
DEFGGIJNORU	forejudging
DEFGGLOOOST	footslogged
DEFGHIISTTT	tightfisted
DEFGHMOOORT	Mother of God
DEFGIIIMNNS	misdefining
DEFGIIINNTY	identifying
DEFGIILNNOS	goldfinnies
DEFGIILNPRS	Springfield
DEFGIILNRRS	girlfriends
DEFGIIMNORY	remodifying
DEFGIINNRTY	trendifying
DEFGIINOTXY	detoxifying
DEFGIIRRSSU	disfigurers
DEFGILNNORU	floundering
DEFGIMNOOOR	foredooming
DEFGINNORUV	overfunding
DEFGJMNORTU	forjudgment
DEFHHINOSSU	houndfishes
DEFHIIIMRSU	humidifiers
DEFHIINPRSS	friendships
DEFHINNRSUU	unfurnished
DEFHINPRSTT	spendthrift
DEFHIOORRSX	Oxfordshire
DEFHIORSSSW	swordfishes
DEFHLLMOTUU	fullmouthed
DEFHLMOOTUU	foulmouthed
DEFHMOOOPRT	mothproofed
DEFHORRRSTU	rutherfords
DEFIIILORSS	solidifiers
DEFIIIMNSTY	misidentify
DEFIIINNOST	definitions
DEFIIINNSTU	infinitudes
DEFIIJNSTUU	unjustified
DEFIIMMNORS	misinformed
DEFIIMORRSV	diversiform
DEFIINORRRU	fourdrinier
DEFILLORSWW	wildfowlers
DEFILMNNOST	infoldments
DEFILMNNSSU	mindfulness
DEFILNORSWW	windflowers
DEFILNSSTUU	dutifulness
DEFILPRSSUU	superfluids
DEFILRSSSTU	distressful
DEFINRRSSUW	windsurfers
DEFIOOORRSU	odoriferous
DEFIOORRSSU	dorsiferous
DEFLLNORUWY	wonderfully
DEFOOPSSTUY	pussyfooted
DEGGGIINRSU	ruggedising
DEGGGIINRUZ	ruggedizing
DEGGHHHIILT	highlighted
DEGGHILNOST	longsighted
DEGGHINOSSS	doggishness
DEGGIILNNSY	designingly
DEGGIINNNSU	undesigning
DEGGKLRSUUY	skulduggery
DEGHHOORSUU	roughhoused
DEGHIILMNOS	demolishing
DEGHIIMNOST	methodising
DEGHIIMNOTZ	methodizing
DEGHIINRRST	nightriders
DEGHILMNOOT	moonlighted
DEGHILMOOOS	homologised
DEGHILMOOOZ	homologized
DEGHILNORSU	shouldering
DEGHILNSTUY	unsightedly
DEGHILOPSTT	spotlighted
DEGHINNORSU	enshrouding
DEGHINNRSTU	underthings
DEGHINOSSTU	doughtiness
DEGHIORRRSU	roughriders
DEGHLMOOOTY	methodology
DEGHNOORSUY	hydrogenous
DEGHNOORXYY	oxyhydrogen
DEGHNORRTUW	undergrowth
DEGHOOOPRSW	gopherwoods
DEGIIIINNST	indignities
DEGIIILNNPV	vilipending
DEGIIINNOST	indigestion
DEGIIINPSSW	sideswiping
DEGIIINQSTU	disquieting
DEGIILLNOTU	guillotined
DEGIILMNOPR	impoldering
DEGIILNNNRU	underlining
DEGIILNNOSS	goldsinnies
DEGIILNOTTU	deglutition
DEGIILNRTVY	divertingly
DEGIILOOSST	ideologists
DEGIIMNNNRU	undermining
DEGIIMNNORS	modernising
DEGIIMNNORZ	modernizing
DEGIIMNNPSS	misspending
DEGIIMNOSTU	digoneutism
DEGIINNNRTU	indenturing
DEGIINNORVW	overwinding
DEGIINORRVV	overdriving
DEGIINORSSS	digressions
DEGIINRSSST	distressing
DEGIJMMNSTU	misjudgment
DEGIKLMNOSS	kingdomless
DEGILLNNTUY	indulgently
DEGILLNOPRY	deploringly
DEGILMNORSU	smouldering
DEGILMNOSUW	guildswomen
DEGILMNRSSU	mudslingers
DEGILNNOSSU	ungodliness
DEGILNORUVY	devouringly
DEGILNRSSTU	disgruntles
DEGILOOPRTY	pteridology
DEGILOOPSST	pedologists
DEGINNORSST	grindstones
DEGINOPRSST	topdressing
DEGKOPRRRSU	Krugersdorp
DEGLLNORSUW	groundswell
DEGLOORSTTY	troglodytes
DEGNNOORSTU	stoneground
DEGOOORSSUW	woodgrouses
DEHHIILMNOT	helminthoid
DEHHILMOORS	holohedrism
DEHHILNOOSW	Hinshelwood
DEHHILOPRSS	holderships
DEHHILOPRSY	hydrophiles
DEHHILORSTW	withholders
DEHHIMOORRS	hemorrhoids
DEHHLNOSTUU	sleuthhound

DEHHNOOPRSY hydrophones
DEHHOPRSTYY hydrophytes
DEHIIINOSTT dithionites
DEHIIINRSST disinherits
DEHIILLOOSV livelihoods
DEHIILLOPSY lyophilised
DEHIILLOPYZ lyophilized
DEHIILMNPSU delphiniums
DEHIILPRSTU trisulphide
DEHIIMNOPRS prehominids
DEHIINSTTUW Whitsuntide
DEHIIOOSSTU Theodosius I
DEHIIOPRSST editorships
DEHIKNOORSW hoodwinkers
DEHILLNOSSS dollishness
DEHILNNOOPS indophenols
DEHILNOSSST doltishness
DEHILNOSSTY dishonestly
DEHILNOSTTW thistledown
DEHILNRRUUY unhurriedly
DEHILOPPRYY hyperploidy
DEHILOPSUXY oxysulphide
DEHILPRSSUU sulphurised
DEHILPRSUUZ sulphurized
DEHIMMPSSSY dysphemisms
DEHIMOOPPRS hippodromes
DEHINNNOSSS donnishness
DEHINOORRSS dishonorers
DEHINOORRSU dishonourer
DEHINORRSUV Hudson River
DEHINORSSTT threnodists
DEHINPRSSSU prudishness
DEHINPSSTTU studentship
DEHINRRSSTU undershirts
DEHIOOOPPRT photoperiod
DEHIOOOPRRS odoriphores
DEHIOOORSTX orthodoxies
DEHIOOPRSTT orthopedist
DEHIOORSSST sisterhoods
DEHIOPRRSTY pyrethroids
DEHLNOOPRSY polyhedrons
DEHLORRSSYY hydrolysers
DEHLORRSYYZ hydrolyzers
DEHMMNRSSUU humdrumness
DEHMOOPPRSU pseudomorph
DEHNNORSSUU nursehounds
DEHNOOOOPRT odontophore
DEHNOOOORTX neoorthodox
DEHNOORSSTU undershoots
DEHNOORSSUU roundhouses
DEHNORRSSTU undershorts
DEHNRRSTTUU underthrust
DEIIIKMNRST miniskirted
DEIIILLSSUV disillusive
DEIIILMSSTU similitudes
DEIIILORSTV vitriolised
DEIIILORTVZ vitriolized
DEIIILQRSSU liquidisers
DEIIILQRSUZ liquidizers
DEIIIMNSTUV diminutives
DEIIIMOORST iridotomies
DEIIINNPSSS insipidness
DEIIINORSSV redivisions
DEIIINPRTTY intrepidity
DEIIIOPRRST prioritised
DEIIIOPRRTZ prioritized
DEIIIPSSTTU stupidities
DEIIJKNOORZ Orjonikidze
DEIILLLNUWY unwieldlily
DEIILLMNTUY unlimitedly
DEIILLORSUY deliriously
DEIILMNOOST demolitions
DEIILNOPRRY pyrrolidine
DEIILOSSTUV dissolutive
DEIILOSSTUY seditiously
DEIIMNOOSST endomitosis
DEIIMNOPRTV improvident
DEIIMNORTTT intromitted
DEIIMOORRST dormitories
DEIIMORSSTT dosimetrist
DEIIMORSSTU moisturised
DEIIMORSTUZ moisturized
DEIINNOSSSS dissensions
DEIINNOSSST distensions
DEIINNOSSTT distentions
DEIINOOPRSV provisioned
DEIINOOPSST depositions
DEIINOPRSSS dispersions
DEIINOSSSTU dissentious
DEIINOSTTTU destitution
DEIKMPPRSSU mudskippers
DEIKNNNORRS nondrinkers
DEIKNRRSSTU underskirts
DEILLMOOSUY melodiously
DEILLNORSSW worldliness
DEILLNOTUVY involutedly
DEILLORSTUY desultorily
DEILLOSSTUY dissolutely
DEILMNOOOPS monopolised
DEILMNOOOPZ monopolized
DEILMNOOSUU unmelodious
DEILMNPRTUY imprudently
DEILMOORRTY dolorimetry
DEILNOOSTUV devolutions
DEILNOPRTVY providently
DEILNOSSSTV dissolvents
DEILPRRSSUY surprisedly
DEIMMNNOPTU impoundment
DEIMMNNSTUU indumentums
DEIMMRSSTYY dissymmetry
DEIMNNOOOST monotonised
DEIMNNOOOTZ monotonized
DEIMNNOSSYY synonymised
DEIMNNOSYYZ synonymized
DEIMNOORRRS minor orders
DEIMNOSSSSY syndesmosis
DEIMOOPRTTY dioptometry
DEIMOPPRTTU promptitude
DEINOOPRSTY ponderosity
DEINOOSSTTX exodontists
DEINOPRSTTU outsprinted
DEINOPSSSSU suspensoids
DEINPRRSSUU unsurprised
DEIOPPRSTTU outstripped
DEIOPRSTTTU prostituted
DEIRRSSSTTU distrusters
DEKNOORRSWW wonderworks
DEKOOORRSWW woodworkers
DELLNOPSUUY pendulously
DELLNOSSSUY soundlessly
DELLOOOSWWY yellowwoods
DELMORRSUUY murderously
DELNOOPRSSU splendorous
DELNOOPRSTU pleurodonts
DELNOOPRSUY ponderously
DELNPPRSUUY undersupply
DELOPPRRSSU Lord's Supper
DELOPPRRTUY purportedly
DEMNNOOPSSU modus ponens
DEMNPRRSTUU undertrumps
DENNNOSSSUU unsoundness
DENNOORSTWW downtowners
DENOOOPRSSU endosporous
DENOOORSSSU odorousness
DENOOPPRRSU propounders
DENOPPRSTUU unsupported
DFFIIISTUVY diffusivity
DFGGIIIINRY rigidifying
DFGGIIINRSU disfiguring
DFGHIIIMNUY humidifying
DFGHILLOOST floodlights
DFGIIILNOSY solidifying
DFGIILLNOWW wildfowling
DFGIILNNOTW downlifting
DFGIINNRSUW windsurfing
DFGOOOPRRUX Oxford Group
DFHLOOOOPST photofloods
DFHLOOORSST Lord of Hosts
DFIILMOSTUU multifidous
DFILLMNNUUY unmindfully
DFILRSSTTUU distrustful
DFNOOOPRSSU soundproofs
DGGHIIINNRT nightriding
DGGHIINNOSV Govind Singh
DGGHINORRUY roughdrying
DGGIILLNNUY indulgingly
DGGIILMNNSU mudslinging
DGGILNNORSU groundlings
DGGINNOORSW wrongdoings
DGHHIILNOTW withholding
DGHHIKNOOST knighthoods
DGHIIIIMNNS diminishing
DGHIIINSSTU distinguish
DGHIIKNNOOW hoodwinking
DGHIINNOORS dishonoring
DGHIINNORRT North Riding
DGHILNORSYY hydrolysing
DGHILNORTWY downrightly
DGHILNORYYZ hydrolyzing
DGHILOORSTY hydrologist
DGHLNOORSST strongholds
DGHNOORSSUW showgrounds
DGIIIILNQSU liquidising
DGIIIILNQUZ liquidizing

DGIIIIMNSSU Sigismund II
DGIIIINPRST dispiriting
DGIIIJNNOST disjointing
DGIIILLMNNW windmilling
DGIIILOORST iridologist
DGIIINNOPSS indisposing
DGIIKNNORTU outdrinking
DGIILNNRTUY intrudingly
DGIILNOOPSS podsolising
DGIILNOOPSZ podsolizing
podzolising
DGIILNOOPZZ podzolizing
DGIIMNNOSTU dismounting
DGIINRSSTTU distrusting
DGIKNOOORWW woodworking
DGILLNORSSU groundsills
DGINNOOPPRU propounding
DGINNORRSUU surrounding
DGKNOORRSUW groundworks
DGLNOOPSTTY glyptodonts
DHHIOOPRTYY hypothyroid
DHIIIORSTTY thyroiditis
DHIIMMOPRSS dimorphisms
DHIIMOOSTTW shittim wood
shittimwood
DHIINOORSTW withindoors
DHILLNOOPPY podophyllin
DHILNOOQRUY hydroquinol
DHIMNOORUXY hydroxonium
DHINOOOPRST ornithopods
DHINOPRSSTY dystrophins
DHIOOOPRSUZ rhizopodous
DHIOOPPRRSY porphyroids
DHLOOPRXYYY polyhydroxy
DHMNOOORXYY monohydroxy
DHNNOOOORTX nonorthodox
DIIIIMNOSSV divisionism
DIIIINOSSTV divisionist
DIIILLNOSSU disillusion
DIIILNOSSUY insidiously
DIIILNOSUVY invidiously
DIIIMNNOSTU diminutions
DIIINOOPSST disposition
DIILLNOSSWW windowsills
DIILMNOTUWW multiwindow
DIILNOOSSTU dissolution
DIILNOPSSTY spondylitis
DIINOORSSTT distortions
DIINOPRSSTU disruptions
DIINORSSTUU industrious
DILMOOPSTUY stylopodium
EEEEEGKNPRR greenkeeper
EEEEFIISTWW sweetiewife
EEEEFILQRTU teleferique
EEEEFLRSTTT Fleet Street
EEEEGGINQSU squeegeeing
EEEEGLNNSST genteelness
EEEEGLNRSSV revengeless
EEEEHIMNPRT hemiterpene
EEEEHIMRSSU euhemerises
EEEEHIMRSUZ euhemerizes
EEEEHKLNOUW Leeuwenhoek
EEEEHKOPRSU housekeeper
EEEEHNNSTTV seventeenth
EEEEHORRSVW wheresoever
EEEEIINRTVW interviewee
EEEEIKMPRST timekeepers
EEEEIMNPRSW minesweeper
EEEEIMNRSST mesenteries
EEEEIPRSTTU repetiteuse
EEEEKOPRRST storekeeper
EEEELNPRSST repleteness
EEEELORSSVV oversleeves
EEEELRRSTTT trestletree
EEEEMNRSSTX extremeness
EEEENQRSSSU queernesses
EEEEPPPRRST peppertrees
EEEFFFMNNOT enfeoffment
EEEFFHILRTW whiffletree
EEEFFILORTW Eiffel Tower
EEEFFLNOSSS offenseless
EEEFGINPRRZ prefreezing
EEEFGLLNSSU gleefulness
EEEFHIJLSSW jewelfishes
EEEFHIKNRRT freethinker
EEEFHMNRRST refreshment
EEEFHOORRTT theretofore
EEEFIILMPRX exemplifier
EEEFIILMPSX exemplifies
EEEFIILRRVX irreflexive
EEEFILLRVXY reflexively
EEEFILNRSST fertileness
EEEFIMNNRST refinements
EEEFIMPRRSU perfumeries
EEEFINORRSV overrefines
EEEFINPRRSU superrefine
EEEFINRRRST interferers
EEEFINSSSTV festiveness
EEEFLLORRST foretellers
EEEFMNPRRST preferments
EEEFMOORRRV forevermore
EEEFNNRSSTV ferventness
EEEFNQRRSTU frequenters
EEEGGIINNNR engineering
EEEGGIINNRV Vereeniging
EEEGGMNNORT engorgement
EEEGHHINRST heighteners
EEEGHHINSTT eighteenths
EEEGHILNNRT enlightener
EEEGHIMNOST eighteenmos
EEEGHLNNRST lengtheners
EEEGHNORSSU greenhouses
EEEGHRRSTWY greywethers
EEEGIIKMNPT timekeeping
EEEGIILRSSU religieuses
EEEGIINPSST epigenesist
EEEGIINRSSU seigneuries
EEEGIKNNOSS kenogenesis
EEEGILLOOST teleologies
EEEGILMNSST genteelisms
EEEGILNRSST singletrees
EEEGILNRSTW swingletree
EEEGILOSTTX geotextiles
EEEGIMNNSSS seemingness
EEEGIMORSST geometrises
EEEGIMORSTZ geometrizes
EEEGINNNSSU genuineness
EEEGINNORST roentgenise
EEEGINNORTZ roentgenize
EEEGINNORVW overweening
EEEGINNOSSX xenogenesis
EEEGINNRRTW wintergreen
EEEGINNSSTW sweetenings
EEEGINPRRSV persevering
EEEGIPRRRST preregister
EEEGIRRRSST registerers
EEEGLMNNOTW gentlewomen
EEEGLNOORVY venereology
EEEGMOPRRTY pyrgeometer
EEEGNNORSST greenstones
EEEGNORSSSV governesses
EEEGORSSSTT Grosseteste
EEEHHILLLNP philhellene
EEEHHILOPRS heliosphere
EEEHHIMPRSS hemispheres
EEEHHLOSSUW wheelhouses
EEEHHNPRSTY hypersthene
EEEHIILNNPT nephelinite
EEEHIINNPPR epinephrine
EEEHIIPPRRS peripheries
EEEHILLNPRT telpherline
EEEHILMORST heliometers
EEEHILNPRRS replenisher
EEEHILNPRSS replenishes
EEEHILPPRTW whippletree
EEEHILPSSSS lesseeships
EEEHILRSSTV shirtsleeve
EEEHIMMRSSU euhemerisms
EEEHIMNOPPR Oppenheimer
EEEHIMNRSST intermeshes
smithereens
EEEHIMORRST rheometries
EEEHIMPRSSU euphemisers
EEEHIMPRSUZ euphemizers
EEEHIMRSSTU euhemerists
EEEHINNNSTT nineteenths
EEEHINPSSSV peevishness
EEEHINSSTTV seventieths
EEEHIRRRSTV Three Rivers
EEEHIRRSSST heritresses
EEEHKOPPRSS shopkeepers
EEEHLLRSSST shelterless
EEEHLNNOSST nonetheless
EEEHLNOPRST telephoners
EEEHLNOPSTY polyethenes
EEEHMMNNSST enmeshments
EEEHMMORRTT thermometer
EEEHMOPRRST spherometer
EEEHMPRRSTY hypermeters
EEEHNOQSSUU Queen's House
EEEHNRSSSTT sternsheets
EEEHOPPRRST treehoppers
EEEHOPRRSSU superheroes
EEEIIJQRSTU jequerities
EEEIIKLNSST telekinesis

EEEIIKLRSTW	triweeklies
EEEIIMRSTTX	extremities
EEEIINNPSVX	inexpensive
EEEIINRRTTV	irretentive
EEEIINRRTVW	interviewer
EEEIIORRSTX	exteriorise
EEEIIORRTXZ	exteriorize
EEEIIPRRTTV	preteritive
EEEIKLNORTU	leukotriene
EEEIKLNOSST	skeletonise
EEEIKLNOSTZ	skeletonize
EEEILLPTVXY	expletively
EEEILMMNPRT	implementer
EEEILMMORST	mileometers
EEEILMNNNTV	enlivenment
EEEILMNNTTT	entitlement
EEEILNNPSSS	pensileness
EEEILNNQSSU	queenliness
EEEILNNSSST	tensileness
EEEILNPRRST	terrepleins
EEEILNPRRTT	teleprinter
EEEILNPSVXY	expensively
EEEILNRSSSV	servileness
EEEILNRTTVY	retentively
EEEILNSSSUV	elusiveness
EEEILNSTVXY	extensively
EEEILPRSSST	respiteless
EEEILRRSTTW	telewriters
EEEIMMNNSSS	immenseness
EEEIMMORSST	seismometer
EEEIMMRRSSS	mesmerisers
EEEIMMRRSSZ	mesmerizers
EEEIMNNNTTW	entwinement
EEEIMNNRRTT	reinterment
EEEIMNORSST	remonetises
EEEIMNORSTT	tensiometer
EEEIMNORSTZ	remonetizes
EEEIMNOSSTV	emotiveness
EEEIMNPRSTX	experiments
EEEIMNQQRUU	quinquereme
EEEIMNQRRTU	requirement
EEEIMNQRTTU	requitement
EEEIMNRRSTT	retirements
EEEIMNRSSTT	tensimeters
EEEIMOPRSTX	extemporise
EEEIMOPRSTZ	piezometers
EEEIMOPRTXZ	extemporize
EEEIMRRSSTV	timeservers
EEEINNNSSST	intenseness
EEEINNOPRSS	pensioneers
EEEINNORSTV	overintense
EEEINNPRSST	serpentines
EEEINNPRSTT	presentient
EEEINNPSSSV	pensiveness
EEEINNRRSTV	interveners
EEEINORRRSV	reversioner
EEEINPPPRSS	pepperiness
EEEINPRRRST	enterpriser
EEEINPRRRTT	interpreter
	reinterpret
EEEINPRRSST	enterprises
	intersperse
EEEINPRSSSW	winepresses
EEEINPRSTVV	preventives
EEEINRSSSTV	restiveness
EEEINRSSSTW	westernises
EEEINRSSTWZ	westernizes
EEEIOPRRRST	repertoires
	repertories
EEEIPRRSTTU	repetiteurs
EEEIPRSSSST	priestesses
EEEKLNOOSTX	exoskeleton
EEEKLORRSTW	steelworker
	teleworkers
EEELLLNPRTY	repellently
EEELLLPSSSY	sleeplessly
EEELLNRSSVY	nervelessly
EEELLNSSSSY	senselessly
EEELMNNOPTV	envelopment
EEELMNSSTTT	settlements
EEELMORRSSS	remorseless
EEELNNOOPPS	Peloponnese
EEELNRSSTTW	newsletters
EEELNSSSSSU	uselessness
EEELNSSSSSX	sexlessness
EEELPRRSSTT	letterpress
EEELRSSTTUX	textureless
EEEMMNOPRTW	empowerment
EEEMNNOOPRT	monoterpene
EEEMNNPRSTT	presentment
EEEMNNRSSTT	resentments
EEEMNORSTUV	venturesome
EEEMNPRSSSU	supremeness
EEEMORRSTTY	stereometry
EEEMPRSSSTT	temptresses
EEENOOPRSSS	operoseness
EEENOPRTTUX	open texture
EEENORSSTWZ	sneezeworts
EEEOOPRSSVX	overexposes
EEEOPRRSTTY	stereotyper
EEEOPRSSSSS	repossesses
EEEOPRSSTTY	stereotypes
EEEPRRSSSST	prestresses
EEEPRSSTTTY	typesetters
EEFFGHIIRRT	firefighter
EEFFGIINRSV	fivefingers
EEFFGINORRS	forefingers
EEFFGLLNTUY	effulgently
EEFFIINNOSV	inoffensive
EEFFIIORRST	refortifies
EEFFILNOSVY	offensively
EEFFINNOSUV	unoffensive
EEFFIOORRST	offertories
EEFFIORRRSU	ferriferous
EEFFIORRSTU	forfeitures
EEFFLNRSSTU	fretfulness
EEFGGIIILNR	filigreeing
EEFGGIOPRTT	pettifogger
EEFGHIINRTY	etherifying
EEFGHILMORR	Leigh Fermor
EEFGHILRSST	freightless
EEFGHINRRST	frighteners
EEFGHIOOSSS	goosefishes
EEFGIILNRRT	refiltering
EEFGIINNRRT	interfering
EEFGIINRRST	gentrifiers
EEFGIINRRVY	reverifying
EEFGIINRSTY	esterifying
EEFGILLNNUY	unfeelingly
EEFGILLNORT	foretelling
EEFGILNNOUX	genuflexion
EEFGILNORRW	reflowering
EEFGILNRSTY	freestyling
EEFGIMMORSU	gemmiferous
EEFGIMORTTU	fugitometer
EEFGINNNORZ	nonfreezing
EEFGINNORSS	foreignness
EEFGINNQRTU	frequenting
EEFGINNRTTU	unfettering
EEFGINORRST	reforesting
EEFGINORSSV	forgiveness
EEFGKLLNOST	gentlefolks
EEFGLLMNORS	fellmongers
EEFGLLMNORY	fellmongery
EEFGLLNRTUY	refulgently
EEFGLLOORXY	reflexology
EEFGLLRRTUY	regretfully
EEFGLMNNSTU	engulfments
EEFHHIISSTW	whitefishes
EEFHHILLSSS	shellfishes
EEFHIINPSSS	snipefishes
EEFHIINRRSS	refinishers
EEFHIJLLSSY	jellyfishes
EEFHILLNSSS	fleshliness
EEFHILLSSSW	swellfishes
EEFHILNSSSS	selfishness
EEFHILOSUWY	housewifely
EEFHINOSSST	stonefishes
EEFHINRRSSU	refurnishes
EEFHIORSUWY	housewifery
EEFHLLNPSSU	helpfulness
EEFHLNOPSSU	hopefulness
EEFHMORRRTU	furthermore
EEFHNOORRST	foreshorten
EEFIIINNRST	intensifier
EEFIIINNSST	intensifies
EEFIIISSTTV	festivities
EEFIILLNRTY	infertilely
EEFIILMNOSS	solemnifies
EEFIILMRSSU	emulsifiers
EEFIILNOPSS	Isle of Pines
EEFIILRRSST	fertilisers
EEFIILRRSTZ	fertilizers
EEFIILRTVXY	reflexivity
EEFIINOPRRS	personifier
EEFIINOPRSS	personifies
EEFIIPPRSTT	pipefitters
EEFIIPRRSTT	prettifiers
EEFIKLLNOWY	Yellowknife
EEFILLLMNTU	mellifluent
EEFILLLMRSU	millefleurs
EEFILLMORSU	melliferous
EEFILLNOSSX	flexionless
EEFILLNOSTU	feuilletons
EEFILLRSSTY	lifestylers

EEFILMORRTU fluorimeter
EEFILMRSSTT filmsetters
EEFILNNORST florentines
EEFILNNRTTU interfluent
EEFILNORSSW floweriness
EEFILNRSTUV interfluves
EEFILOOPRRT profiterole
EEFILOORSST loosestrife
EEFILRSSTUX fixtureless
EEFINNORRST interferons
EEFINRSSTUV furtiveness
EEFIOPRSSTU pestiferous
EEFKLLOOSWY yokefellows
EEFLLLNPSUY spleenfully
EEFLLNRSTUY resentfully
EEFLLOPRSUY reposefully
EEFLMNOORTT Montefeltro
EEFLMNOSSSU fulsomeness
EEFLMOORRTU fluorometer
EEFLNNRSTUU unresentful
EEFLNNSSTUU tunefulness
EEFLNORSSTU fortuneless
EEFLNPSSSUU suspenseful
EEFLNRSSSTU restfulness
EEFLNSSSTUZ zestfulness
EEFNNORRRSU forerunners
EEFNOPRSSSU profuseness
EEGGHHIINNT heightening
EEGGHIINSST sightseeing
EEGGHILNNNT lengthening
EEGGHILNRST greenlights
EEGGIILNQSU squilgeeing
EEGGIIMNNRT regimenting
EEGGIINNPRW Winnipegger
EEGGIINRRST registering
EEGGILLNNTY negligently
EEGGILNNRVY revengingly
EEGGILORSUY egregiously
EEGGILRRSST triggerless
EEGGNOOPRST progestogen
EEGHHILRTWW wheelwright
EEGHIILLMRT limelighter
EEGHIILLNNS hellenising
EEGHIILLNNZ hellenizing
EEGHIILOORS hierologies
EEGHIIMNPSU euphemising
EEGHIIMNPUZ euphemizing
EEGHIINSSTW weightiness
EEGHIKNOPPS shopkeeping
EEGHILNNOPT telephoning
EEGHILNNSST lengthiness
EEGHILNOOPS pigeonholes
EEGHILNOPRS negrophiles
EEGHILNOPSY phylogenies
EEGHILOORST theologiser
EEGHILOORTZ theologizer
EEGHILOOSST theologises
EEGHILOOSTZ theologizes
EEGHILRSTTT streetlight
EEGHIMNOORS homogeniser
EEGHIMNOORZ homogenizer
EEGHIMNOOSS homogenises
EEGHIMNOOSZ homogenizes
EEGHIMNOOTY homogeneity
EEGHIMOORST isogeotherm
EEGHINNOSTT ethnogenist
EEGHINNPTWY pennyweight
EEGHINPRSST regentships
EEGHIORSTVW overweights
EEGHLOOPRTY herpetology
EEGHMNOOOSU homogeneous
EEGHMNOORRW whoremonger
EEGHMORRSTY hygrometers
EEGHNNRSSTT strengthens
EEGHNOPSTTY gnetophytes
EEGHNORSTYY hysterogeny
EEGHOSSSTUU guesthouses
EEGIIILMSST legitimises
EEGIIILMSTZ legitimizes
EEGIIILNSTT gentilities
EEGIIIMNPST impetigines
EEGIIINNSTU ingenuities
EEGIIINORSS seigniories
EEGIIINRSTT integrities
EEGIIKLLMMN lemminglike
EEGIIKLPRSS kriegspiels
EEGIILLNNTT intelligent
EEGIILLORSY religiosely
EEGIILMNNRT intermingle
EEGIILNNNST sentineling
EEGIILNNOST lentiginose
EEGIILNNPRV replevining
EEGIILNOPSS lipogenesis
EEGIILNRSSW wirelessing
EEGIIMMNNPT impingement
EEGIIMMNRSS mesmerising
EEGIIMMNRSZ mesmerizing
EEGIIMNNNRS minnesinger
EEGIIMNRSTV timeserving
EEGIINNNRTV intervening
reinventing
EEGIINNORRT reorienting
EEGIINNORST nitrogenise
EEGIINNORTZ nitrogenize
EEGIINNQRUV Virgin Queen
EEGIINNRRRT reinterring
EEGIINNRRST reinserting
EEGIINNRSTT interesting
EEGIINOPRTV progenitive
EEGIINPPQRU reequipping
EEGIINPRSTX expertising
preexisting
EEGIINPRTXZ expertizing
EEGIINRSSSV ingressives
EEGIKLNNNNU unkenneling
EEGIKLNORTW teleworking
EEGILLLSSUY guilelessly
EEGILLMOOST teleologism
EEGILLNORSV overselling
EEGILLOOSTT teleologist
EEGILMNNSST meltingness
EEGILMNOPRY reemploying
EEGILMNORRS mongreliser
EEGILMNORRZ mongrelizer
EEGILMNORSS mongrelises
EEGILMNORSZ mongrelizes
EEGILMOORST metrologies
EEGILMOOSTY etymologies
etymologise
EEGILMOOTYZ etymologize
EEGILNNNRTU unrelenting
EEGILNOORSU neurologies
EEGILNOPRTT teleporting
EEGILNOPSSY polygenesis
EEGILNORSVY sovereignly
EEGILNPRSTY pesteringly
EEGILOOPRST petrologies
EEGILOPRSTT poltergeist
EEGIMNNNORT Montenegrin
EEGIMNNOOSS monogenesis
EEGIMNNORSU monseigneur
EEGIMNNOSTT mignonettes
EEGIMNNRRTU interregnum
EEGIMNNSTTU integuments
EEGIMNOORST goniometers
EEGIMNORSTW swingometer
EEGIMNOSSYZ zymogenesis
EEGINNOOSST ontogenesis
EEGINNORSST rontgenises
EEGINNORSTZ rontgenizes
EEGINNPRSST Springsteen
EEGINNPRSUV supervening
EEGINOPRRTX reexporting
EEGINORRSSS regressions
EEGINORRSTU terrigenous
EEGINORSSXY oxygenisers
EEGINORSTTV oversetting
EEGINORSTVY sovereignty
EEGINORSXYZ oxygenizers
EEGINPRSTTU guttersnipe
EEGINPSTTTY typesetting
EEGINRRSUVY resurveying
EEGIOPRRSSV progressive
EEGKLLMNSUU muskellunge
EEGLMOOORTY meteorology
EEGLNOOSUXY exogenously
EEGLOQRSTUY grotesquely
EEGMNNORSST engrossment
EEGMNNORSSW newsmongers
EEGMNNORSTV governments
EEGOQRRSTUY grotesquery
EEHHILLNSSS hellishness
EEHHILMOPRT thermophile
EEHHILOPRST lithosphere
EEHHILOPSTY heliophytes
EEHHINOSSTT henotheists
EEHHINRSTTT thirteenths
EEHHIOOPSST theosophies
EEHHIOPRRSZ rhizosphere
EEHHIOPSSTY hypothesise
EEHHIOPSTYZ hypothesize
EEHHMNOOPRY hymenophore
EEHHMOORSTU housemother
EEHHMPRRTYY hyperthermy
EEHHNOOPRTY heterophony
EEHHOOPPRST photosphere

EEHHOOPRRTT	heterotroph
EEHHOORSSUW	whorehouses
EEHHOPRSTTY	therophytes
EEHIIIKLNSU	kleinhuisie
EEHIIKNSSST	kinesthesis
EEHIILMPSTU	epitheliums
EEHIILNOOPS	eosinophile
EEHIIMOOPSS	hemopoiesis
EEHIIMPPRRS	premiership
EEHIINRRSST	inheritress
EEHILMMOSTU	mesothelium
EEHILMNNPST	plenishment
EEHILMNORTY	hemielytron
EEHILMOORTT	lithometeor
EEHILMOPPRS	spermophile
EEHILMOPRST	thermopiles
EEHILNOPPRS	nephrolepis
EEHILNOPRRT	leptorrhine
EEHILNOPRTU	neutrophile
EEHILNOPSTT	telephonist
EEHILNORRST	northerlies
EEHILNOSTTV	novelettish
EEHILNPRSTW	printwheels
EEHILOOPRST	heliotropes
EEHILORSSTU	southerlies
EEHILORSSTY	heterolysis
EEHILOSSTTU	silhouettes
EEHIMNNRSTU	minehunters
EEHIMNOPRSS	premonishes
EEHIMNOPRST	hemipterons
EEHIMNPSSSU	humpinesses
EEHIMOPPRRS	emperorship
EEHIMOPRSTU	hemipterous
EEHIMOSSSST	somesthesis
EEHINNOOPTT	thiopentone
EEHINNOPRST	interphones
EEHINNORSST	rhinestones
EEHINNOSSSU	heinousness
EEHINOPSTVY	hypotensive
EEHINPSSSTT	pettishness
EEHINRSSSTU	hirsuteness
EEHINRSSSTY	synthesiser
EEHINRSSTYZ	synthesizer
EEHINSSSSTY	synthesises
EEHINSSSTTY	synthetises
EEHINSSSTYZ	synthesizes
EEHINSSTTYZ	synthetizes
EEHIOPPRRSS	prophesiers
EEHIOPRSSTX	exstrophies
EEHIPRRSSUV	herpesvirus
EEHIPRSSTTU	trusteeship
EEHJNOPRRST	Prester John
EEHKMOORRSW	homeworkers
EEHKMOOSSSU	smokehouses
EEHKNOORSTT	tenterhooks
EEHKNOSTUVY	Yevtushenko
EEHKOORRSUW	houseworker
EEHLLMNOOPS	mellophones
EEHLLMOOSWY	wholesomely
EEHLMNOOSUW	unwholesome
EEHLMNOOSYZ	holoenzymes
EEHLMNOTTVW	twelvemonth
EEHLNOOSSSV	shovelnoses
EEHLOPRRSTU	reupholster
	upholsterer
EEHLORSTTYY	heterostyly
EEHMMORRTTY	thermometry
EEHMMORSSUU	summerhouse
EEHMNNNOOPS	phenomenons
EEHMNNOOORY	honeymooner
EEHMNOOPRSS	mesonephros
EEHMNOOPRST	phonometers
EEHMOOPRSTT	photometers
EEHMOPPRSTY	spermophyte
EEHMOPRSSTT	stepmothers
EEHMOPRSSTY	hypsometers
EEHMOQRSSUU	humoresques
EEHNNORRRST	northerners
EEHNOOOPRSZ	ozonosphere
EEHNOOPRSTY	stereophony
EEHNOPSSSTY	pythonesses
EEHNOPSSTUY	hypotenuses
EEHNORRSSTU	southerners
EEHNORRSTTW	northwester
EEHOOPPRRST	troposphere
EEHOOPRRSTU	porterhouse
EEHOOPRRSTY	heterospory
EEHOOPRSSUW	powerhouses
EEHOOPRSTTT	photosetter
EEHOOPSSTTY	osteophytes
EEHOORSSSTU	storehouses
EEHOPPRRSWY	hyperpowers
EEHORSSTTUW	southwester
EEIIIJQRSTU	jequirities
EEIIIMMNSST	immensities
EEIIIMNNSTU	einsteinium
EEIIINNSSTT	intensities
EEIIINNSSTV	insensitive
EEIIINORRST	interiorise
EEIIINORRTZ	interiorize
EEIIINORSST	seniorities
EEIIINSTTVV	investitive
EEIIJNRSSTT	jitteriness
EEIIKLLNNNS	Enniskillen
EEIIKLLNSTU	unlikeliest
EEIIKLNNRTU	interleukin
EEIIKLNPRSW	periwinkles
EEIILLMMRST	millimeters
	millimetres
EEIILLNRSTY	resiliently
EEIILLNRTUV	Tirunelveli
EEIILLOPRST	pellitories
EEIILLPPRST	pipistrelle
EEIILLPRSTU	spirituelle
EEIILMMNPRT	imperilment
EEIILMNOSST	solemnities
EEIILMNRSSS	miserliness
EEIILMOOSST	ileostomies
EEIILMRSSVY	remissively
EEIILNNRRST	interliners
EEIILNNSTVY	intensively
EEIILNNTVVY	inventively
EEIILNOSSTV	televisions
EEIILNRSSSV	silveriness
EEIILNSSTVY	sensitively
EEIILPRSSTT	priestliest
EEIILQRSTUY	requisitely
EEIILQSTUXY	exquisitely
EEIILRRSSST	sterilisers
EEIILRRSSTZ	sterilizers
EEIILRSSTVY	Sylvester II
EEIIMNNNTTW	intwinement
EEIIMNNPRTT	impertinent
EEIIMNOSSTT	testimonies
EEIIMNPRRUU	perineurium
EEIIMNPRSUU	epineuriums
EEIIMNRSTTW	wintertimes
EEIIMOPRSST	epitomisers
EEIIMOPRSTZ	epitomizers
EEIINNNOSTT	nonentities
EEIINNNTUVV	uninventive
EEIINNOOPRT	Pointe-Noire
EEIINNORRST	reinsertion
EEIINNORSTV	inventories
EEIINNPRRWZ	prizewinner
EEIINNRSSTW	winteriness
EEIINNRSTTW	intertwines
EEIINOPRRTT	preterition
EEIINOPRSTT	petitioners
	repetitions
EEIINRSSSST	sensitisers
EEIINRSSSTZ	sensitizers
EEIINRSTTUV	investiture
EEIINRTTTVY	retentivity
EEIIOPPRRST	proprieties
EEIIOPPRSTV	prepositive
EEIIOPRSTTU	repetitious
EEIIORRRSTT	territories
EEIIORRSSST	rotisseries
EEIIPQRSSTU	perquisites
EEIIRSTTTUV	restitutive
EEIJMNNNOST	enjoinments
EEIJNORSSST	jointresses
EEIKKORSSST	koeksisters
EEIKLLNRSSW	wrinkleless
EEIKLMPRTTU	trumpetlike
EEIKLORRSVW	servile work
EEIKMNORSSS	irksomeness
EEIKMORRSTW	timeworkers
EEILLMMORST	immortelles
EEILLMNOPRT	Montpellier
EEILLMPRTUX	multiplexer
EEILLMPSTUX	multiplexes
EEILLMRSSUW	Weissmuller
EEILLNNPSSY	pennilessly
EEILLNOPQTU	equipollent
EEILLNOSSSY	noiselessly
EEILLNPSSSY	spinelessly
EEILLNPSTTY	pestilently
EEILLOPSVXY	explosively
EEILLORRVWY	Yellow River
EEILLPRRSUW	wirepullers
EEILLPRSUVY	prelusively
	repulsively
EEILLRSUVVY	revulsively
EEILMMNOPRT	implementor

EEILMMRSTTU	multimeters
EEILMNNOSTT	entoilments
EEILMNNOTVV	involvement
EEILMNNSSTT	enlistments
EEILMNOOSST	emotionless
EEILMNORSSS	solemnisers
EEILMNORSSZ	solemnizers
EEILMNOSSSS	lissomeness
EEILMNRTTTY	remittently
EEILMOPRSSY	polymerises
EEILMOPRSYZ	polymerizes
EEILMOPRTUV	pluviometer
EEILMOSSSSU	semisoluses
EEILMPRSSTU	pulsimeters
EEILNNOPPTT	plenipotent
EEILNNOPSSS	pensionless
EEILNNOSSST	tensionless
EEILNNPRTTY	pertinently
EEILNNSSSSS	sinlessness
EEILNOORTVV	overviolent
EEILNOPRRST	interlopers
EEILNORSTVV	intervolves
EEILNOSSTVY	ostensively
EEILNSSSSTW	witlessness
EEILOOPRSST	teliospores
EEILOPPRSTU	superpolite
EEILOPRSSTY	proselytise
EEILOPRSTYZ	proselytize
EEILORRSTTW	rottweilers
EEILPPSSTUV	suppletives
EEILPRRSSUV	pulverisers
EEILPRRSUVZ	pulverizers
EEILPRSSTTU	supertitles
EEIMMNOPRTV	improvement
EEIMMNPRSST	impressment
EEIMMNRSSSU	summeriness
EEIMMPRSUVV	sempervivum
EEIMMRSSSTY	symmetrises
EEIMMRSSTYZ	symmetrizes
EEIMNNNORTV	environment
EEIMNNNRSTT	internments
EEIMNNOOSSS	noisomeness
EEIMNNOPRST	omnipresent
EEIMNNOSSSW	winsomeness
EEIMNNPSSTU	septenniums
EEIMNNSSTTV	investments
EEIMNOORRST	remontoires
EEIMNOORSST	eriostemons
EEIMNOORSTU	neurotomies
EEIMNOPPRST	preemptions
EEIMNOPRSTU	peritoneums
EEIMNOQSTUU	Montesquieu
EEIMNORRSSS	sermonisers
EEIMNORRSSZ	sermonizers
EEIMNORRSTT	nitrometers
EEIMNORRSTU	urinometers
EEIMNORSSST	monitresses
EEIMNORSTTT	tintometers
EEIMNORSTZZ	intermezzos
EEIMNORTTZZ	mezzotinter
EEIMNPPPRST	peppermints
EEIMNRSSSTW	westernisms
EEIMNRSSTTW	Westminster
EEIMOOOSSTT	osteotomies
EEIMOOPRSSX	peroxisomes
EEIMOPPRSSU	superimpose
EEIMOPRRRST	misreporter
	reimporters
EEIMOPRRSST	spirometers
	temporisers
EEIMOPRRSSV	overimpress
EEIMOPRRSTZ	temporizers
EEIMPPRSTUV	presumptive
EEIMPRRSSSU	impressures
EEIMRSSSSTY	systemisers
EEIMRSSSTYZ	systemizers
EEINNNORRTU	interneuron
EEINNNOSTTX	nonexistent
EEINNOPRSST	pretensions
EEINNOPRSTT	septentrion
EEINNOPRSTV	preventions
EEINNORRSTV	intervenors
EEINNOSSSUV	enviousness
EEINNOSSTTU	sententious
EEINNQSSTUU	unquietness
EEINOORRTTX	extortioner
EEINOORSSST	ostensories
EEINOPPRSST	peptonisers
EEINOPPRSTZ	peptonizers
EEINOPRRSSS	repressions
EEINOPRRSST	interposers
EEINOPRRSSV	perversions
EEINOPRSSSX	expressions
EEINOPRSTTU	pretentious
EEINOPSSSTU	piteousness
EEINOQRSSTU	questioners
EEINORRSSUV	overinsures
EEINORRSTUV	enterovirus
EEINORRSTVW	overwinters
EEINORRTTVW	overwritten
EEINORSSSSU	seriousness
EEINPRRRTTU	interrupter
EEINPRTTTWY	typewritten
EEINRRSTUWW	wienerwurst
EEIOPRRSSSU	superioress
EEIOPRSSTTT	operettists
EEIOPSSSSSV	possessives
EEIORRRRSST	terrorisers
EEIORRRRSTZ	terrorizers
EEIPPRSSSUV	suppressive
EEIPRRRSSSU	pressuriser
EEIPRRRSSUZ	pressurizer
EEIPRRSSSSU	pressurises
EEIPRRSSSUZ	pressurizes
EEIPRRSTTWY	typewriters
EEIPRSSSSTT	stepsisters
EEJLNOSSSSY	joylessness
EEKKOORRRTV	voortrekker
EEKLOOORRSV	overlookers
EEKLORRSTTW	trestlework
EEKMNNPSSTU	unkemptness
EEKMNOOPSSW	spokeswomen
EEKNNOSSVYZ	Voznesensky
EEKNOORRSTW	stoneworker
EELLMNNORST	enrollments
EELLNNOSSSW	swollenness
EELLNOOSTWY	Yellowstone
EELLNOPPRST	propellents
EELLNOPSTUY	plenteously
EELLNPRTUUV	pulverulent
EELLOPRSSWY	powerlessly
EELLORRSTTY	storyteller
EELMMNOPSTY	employments
EELMNOOPSTU	Neoptolemus
EELMNOSSSUU	emulousness
EELMNPPSSTU	supplements
EELMOPRSSTU	pulsometers
EELNNSSSSSU	sunlessness
EELNOOPPPRY	polypropene
EELNOOPPSTW	townspeople
EELNOORRSUY	erroneously
EELNOPPRTTY	prepotently
EELNOPRSSSU	leprousness
EELNOPRSTYY	polystyrene
EELNOPSSSST	toplessness
EELOOPRSSTT	protosteles
EELOPPRSSSU	purposeless
EELORRSSSTU	trouserless
EELPRRSSTTU	splutterers
EEMNNOPSSTT	pentstemons
EEMNNRSTTTU	entrustment
EEMNOORSTTY	enterostomy
EEMNORSSTTW	westernmost
EEMOORRSTTU	torturesome
EEMOORSSTTU	metoestrous
EEMOPSSTTUU	tempestuous
EENNOOPRRTU	neuropteron
EENNOORSSSU	onerousness
EENNOORSTTT	rottenstone
EENNOPRSTWW	Newport News
EENNOQRSSTU	quernstones
EENNORSSSUV	nervousness
EENNOSSSTUU	tenuousness
EENOPRSSSTU	Ostpreussen
EENPRRSSSUU	supernurses
EEOOPRRSSSS	repossessor
EEOORRRSSTV	rootservers
EEOPPPRRSTW	pepperworts
EEOPPPRSSSU	presupposes
EEOPPRRSSUW	superpowers
EEOPRRSSSTU	superstores
EEPPRRSSSSU	suppressers
EFFFGIKLNRU	kerfuffling
EFFGHIINRSS	fishfingers
EFFGHILNRSU	reshuffling
EFFGILNRSUY	sufferingly
EFFGLLORTUY	forgetfully
EFFHHINSSSU	huffishness
EFFILLLMNTU	fulfillment
EFFILOORRSU	floriferous
EFGGHIINNRT	frightening
EFGGHIIRRST	triggerfish
EFGGHINRSTU	gunfighters
EFGGIILNNRS	fingerlings
EFGGIINPRRU	prefiguring
EFGGLOOORST	footslogger

EFGHHOORTTU forethought
EFGHIIINNRS refinishing
EFGHIIKNRSS kingfishers
EFGHIILNSST flightiness
EFGHIILOSTW Isle of Wight
EFGHIINORSV overfishing
EFGHIIPRSTZ prizefights
EFGHILORSTV overflights
EFGHIMNORSS fishmongers
EFGHINOORSW foreshowing
EFGHINORSSU surgeonfish
EFGHIOORRTT right-footer
EFGHLLNORSU flugelhorns
EFGHOOPPRRS froghoppers
EFGIIILLNNR fringilline
EFGIIILNNRT interfiling
EFGIIILNRST fertilising
EFGIIILNRTZ fertilizing
EFGIIINPPTT pipefitting
EFGIIINRVVY revivifying
EFGIIKNRSTU kitesurfing
EFGIILLLORW gilliflower
EFGIILLMORU florilegium
EFGIILLNORV overfilling
EFGIILLNSTY stellifying
EFGIILMNSTT filmsetting
EFGIILMNSUY emulsifying
EFGIIMNNORR reinforming
EFGIIMNORSS foreignisms
EFGIINNORTY renotifying
EFGIINNPRRT fingerprint
EFGIINNRSTU interfusing
EFGIINNSSTT fittingness
EFGIINPRRUY repurifying
EFGIINPRTTY prettifying
EFGIKNNOORW foreknowing
EFGILLLORWY gillyflower
EFGILMNNSTU ingulfments
EFGILMNOORT montgolfier
EFGILNOORVW overflowing
EFGILNORSST fosterlings
EFGILNORSTY fosteringly
EFGINNNORRU forerunning
EFGINORRSST fortressing
EFGINORRSUU ferruginous
EFGINPRSSUU superfusing
EFGIOPRSSUY gypsiferous
EFGLNNOSSSU songfulness
EFGNNOORTTU unforgotten
EFHIIIKLLSS killifishes
EFHIILRRSTT shirtlifter
EFHIINRSSTT thriftiness
EFHIKLNOSSS folkishness
EFHIKNRSSTU trunkfishes
EFHILLNSSUY unselfishly
EFHILLSSSTY shiftlessly
EFHILNOOSSS foolishness
EFHILNSSSUW wishfulness
EFHILOOSTUY Isle of Youth
EFHILOPRSST shoplifters
EFHILORRSSU flourishers
EFHINOPPSSS foppishness
EFHLNRSSTUU hurtfulness
ruthfulness
EFHLOOOPRRU fluorophore
EFHMORRSTTU furthermost
EFHOOOPRRSW showerproof
EFHOOOPRRTY proof theory
EFIIIIMNRST infirmities
EFIIIINNSTV infinitives
EFIIILMPRSS simplifiers
EFIIILNRTTY infertility
EFIIILORSTV frivolities
EFIIINORRTY inferiority
EFIIKNNOPST knifepoints
EFIILNPSSTU pitifulness
EFIILNRSSZZ frizzliness
EFIILORSSUV filoviruses
EFIILRSSTTU stultifiers
EFIIMMNORRS misinformer
EFIIMNOPRST profeminist
EFIINNORSTU interfusion
EFIINOPRSSU spiniferous
EFIINORRSUU uriniferous
EFIIOPRRSSU spiriferous
EFIKLLNSSSU skilfulness
EFILLLMOSUU mellifluous
EFILLLNPTUY plentifully
EFILLLNSSUW willfulness
EFILLNOOSUY feloniously
EFILLRSSTUY fruitlessly
EFILMORRTUY fluorimetry
EFILNSSSTUW wistfulness
EFILOOPRRSU proliferous
EFILPRSTUUY superfluity
EFIMNNORSSU uniformness
EFIMNOORSSU somniferous
EFIMNORSSTU misfortunes
EFINOOORSUZ ozoniferous
EFINOOPRSSS professions
EFINOPRSSUU superfusion
EFINORSSSTW frowstiness
EFINORSSSUU furiousness
EFIORRSTTUY yttriferous
EFLLNOSSSUU soulfulness
EFLLNSSSTUU lustfulness
EFLLRSSSTUY stressfully
EFLMNOOORSW moonflowers
EFLMOORRTUY fluorometry
EFLNNOORRSS forlornness
EFLOPRSSUUU superfluous
EFMOOPRRSTU outperforms
EFNNNORRRTU frontrunner
EGGGIILNOOS geologising
EGGGIILNOOZ geologizing
EGGHHHIILRT highlighter
EGGHHIILTTW lightweight
EGGHHINORUW roughhewing
EGGHHINOSSS hoggishness
EGGHIINOSTT ghettoising
EGGHIINOTTZ ghettoizing
EGGHIINOTUW outweighing
EGGHIINPSSS piggishness
EGGHILNNRUY hungeringly
EGGHLNOORSW hornswoggle
EGGIIILNPRV privileging
EGGIIIORRXY Gregory XIII
EGGIILLNNRY lingeringly
EGGIILNNOOS neologising
EGGIILNNOOZ neologizing
EGGIILNRSTY greylisting
EGGIINNOPSW pigeonwings
EGGIINNOSXY oxygenising
EGGIINNOXYZ oxygenizing
EGGIINNRRST restringing
EGGILLNORWY gloweringly
EGGILMMOOST gemmologist
EGGILMOOSST gemologists
EGGILNNRSSU gunslingers
EGGINOORRVW overgrowing
EGGINOPRRSS progressing
EGGINOSSSTU suggestions
EGGINOSSTUU outguessing
EGGLNOOORTY gerontology
EGHHILOPRSY hieroglyphs
hygrophiles
EGHHILOSSTU houselights
lighthouses
EGHHLOSSTTU thoughtless
EGHHOORSSUU roughhouses
EGHHOPRSTYY hygrophytes
EGHIILLNRSV shrivelling
EGHIILLOOST lithologies
EGHIILNOPRS repolishing
EGHIILNPRSY perishingly
EGHIILNRSSS girlishness
EGHIILNRTWY witheringly
EGHIILNSSST sightliness
EGHIILOORST hierologist
EGHIILPRRST sprightlier
EGHIIMMNSTU thingummies
EGHIIMNPRSW whimperings
EGHIINNOPSS sphingosine
EGHIINNOPSU euphonising
EGHIINNOPUZ euphonizing
EGHIINNPSSS ensignships
EGHIIOPPRSU Hippo Regius
EGHIKNOSTTU Königshütte
EGHILLMOSTY lightsomely
EGHILLOOPRS philologers
EGHILLSSSTY sightlessly
EGHILMNOORT moonlighter
EGHILMOOORS homologiser
EGHILMOOORZ homologizer
EGHILMOOOSS homologises
EGHILMOOOSZ homologizes
EGHILMOOSTY mythologies
mythologise
EGHILMOOTYZ mythologize
EGHILNOOOPS phonologies
EGHILNOOPST nephologist
phenologist
EGHILNOOSTT ethnologist
EGHILNOOSTU lithogenous

EGHILNOSSST	ghostliness
EGHILOORSST	rheologists
EGHILOOSSTT	ethologists
	theologists
EGHILORSTUY	righteously
EGHIMNNOOST	smoothening
EGHINNNOSST	nothingness
EGHINNOOSSW	snowshoeing
EGHINNORRST	Sherrington
EGHINNPSSSU	pushingness
EGHINOORSUZ	rhizogenous
EGHINOOSSTT	theogonists
EGHINOPPRSY	prophesying
EGHINOPRSST	hotpressing
EGHINOPRSSU	springhouse
EGHINORSSST	shoestrings
EGHINORSSSU	roguishness
EGHINORSTUU	unrighteous
EGHINPRSSTU	uprightness
EGHINRSSTTU	shutterings
EGHIORRSTTW	ghostwriter
EGHIORSSTTW	ghostwrites
EGHLMOORSTY	mythologers
EGHLOPPRSTY	petroglyphs
EGHMOOOSTYZ	homozygotes
EGHNPRRSTUZ	Hertzsprung
EGHOORRTUVW	overwrought
EGIIILLMNPR	imperilling
EGIIILMNORS	religionism
EGIIILMSSTT	legitimists
EGIIILNNNRT	interlining
EGIIILNNTUZ	luteinizing
EGIIILNORST	religionist
EGIIILNRSST	sterilising
EGIIILNRSTZ	sterilizing
EGIIILNRTUZ	reutilizing
EGIIILORRSU	irreligious
EGIIILORSTY	religiosity
EGIIIMNNRST	ministering
EGIIIMNNRTX	intermixing
EGIIIMNOPST	epitomising
EGIIIMNOPTZ	epitomizing
EGIIIMNORSS	isomerising
EGIIIMNORSZ	isomerizing
EGIIIMRSSST	mistigrises
EGIIINNNOSV	envisioning
EGIIINNOPRT	preignition
EGIIINNOPTT	petitioning
EGIIINNRSTW	winterising
EGIIINNRTWZ	winterizing
EGIIINNSSST	sensitising
EGIIINNSSTZ	sensitizing
EGIIINOPQSU	equipoising
EGIIINOSSTV	sovietising
EGIIINOSTVZ	sovietizing
EGIIJNNOSTT	jettisoning
EGIIKLLNRSS	reskillings
EGIIKLNOOSY	kinesiology
EGIIKNPRSTT	spirketting
EGIILLMNPSS	misspelling
EGIILLNNSSW	willingness
EGIILLNORTU	guillotiner
EGIILLNOSTU	guillotines
EGIILLNPRUW	wirepulling
EGIILLNRSTU	tellurising
EGIILLNRTUZ	tellurizing
EGIILLOOOPS	oligopolies
EGIILLORSUY	religiously
EGIILMNNOSS	solemnising
EGIILMNNOSZ	solemnizing
EGIILMNNSSS	smilingness
EGIILMNPRSY	simperingly
EGIILMOOSST	semiologist
EGIILNNORVV	reinvolving
EGIILNNOSTU	lentiginous
EGIILNNOSTV	Livingstone
EGIILNNOSUY	ingeniously
EGIILNNPRST	splintering
EGIILNORSUU	unreligious
EGIILNPRSUV	pulverising
EGIILNPRUVZ	pulverizing
EGIILNQRRSU	squirreling
EGIILNQRSSU	squirelings
EGIILNQRUVY	quiveringly
EGIILNRSSST	gristliness
EGIILNRTTTY	titteringly
EGIILOOSSTT	etiologists
EGIIMNNOOPS	empoisoning
EGIIMNNORSS	sermonising
EGIIMNNORSZ	sermonizing
EGIIMNNRTTU	unremitting
EGIIMNOPRRT	reimporting
EGIIMNOPRST	temporising
EGIIMNOPRTZ	temporizing
EGIIMNSSSTY	systemising
EGIIMNSSTYZ	systemizing
EGIIMNSTTTU	Mistinguett
EGIINNNNSSW	winningness
EGIINNOPPST	peptonising
EGIINNOPPTZ	peptonizing
EGIINNOPRST	interposing
EGIINNOQSTU	questioning
EGIINNORSSS	ingressions
EGIINNORSUV	souveniring
EGIINNOTTUZ	teutonizing
EGIINNPRSSS	springiness
EGIINNRSSST	stringiness
EGIINNRSSTU	unresisting
EGIINOPRSSU	serpiginous
	spinigerous
EGIINOPRTTU	pirouetting
EGIINORRRST	terrorising
EGIINORRRTZ	terrorizing
EGIINORRTVW	overwriting
EGIINORSSUV	overissuing
EGIINORSTUV	vertiginous
EGIINPRSSUV	supervising
EGIINPRTTWY	typewriting
EGIINSSTTTV	vignettists
EGIIOPRSSTU	prestigious
EGIKLLNNORS	snorkelling
EGIKLNOOORV	overlooking
EGIKNNNOSSW	knowingness
EGIKNNORSTW	networkings
EGIKNOORRVW	overworking
EGILLLNOTXY	extollingly
EGILLLOOVXY	vexillology
EGILLLSSTUY	guiltlessly
EGILLNNOSTW	wellingtons
EGILLNORTVY	revoltingly
EGILLNORVVY	revolvingly
EGILLNPRSSW	wellsprings
EGILLORSSSY	syllogisers
EGILLORSSYZ	syllogizers
EGILMNNOOOS	Mesolóngion
EGILMNOORTY	terminology
EGILMNPRSUY	presumingly
EGILMNRTTUY	mutteringly
EGILMOOORSU	oligomerous
EGILMOORSTT	metrologist
EGILMOOSSTU	museologist
EGILMOOSTTY	etymologist
EGILNNNOOSU	unloosening
EGILNNOPSSS	slopingness
EGILNNOSUUY	ingenuously
EGILNNRSTTY	stringently
EGILNOOOSST	oenologists
EGILNOOPSST	penologists
EGILNOORSTU	neurologist
EGILNOPRRVY	reprovingly
EGILNOPRSTY	proselyting
EGILNORTTTY	totteringly
EGILNPPRSUY	resupplying
EGILNPRSTTU	spluttering
EGILNPSTTUY	upsettingly
EGILNRSSTTU	lutestrings
EGILNSSSTUU	singultuses
EGILOOOPRST	tropologies
EGILOOORSTT	erotologist
EGILOOORSTY	soteriology
EGILOOSSTT	osteologist
EGILOOPRSTT	petrologist
EGILOORSSST	serologists
EGILOOSSSTX	sexologists
EGIMMNNORSU	resummoning
EGIMMNNPSTU	impugnments
EGIMNNOORRS	ironmongers
EGIMNNOORRY	ironmongery
EGIMNOORRSV	misgovernor
EGIMNOORRTT	trimetrogon
EGIMNOORSST	ergonomists
EGIMOOPRSST	geotropisms
EGINNNORRUV	overrunning
EGINNOORSTU	nitrogenous
EGINNOPRSTY	trypsinogen
EGINNORRTUV	overturning
EGINOOPPRTV	overtopping
EGINOOPRRSS	progression
EGINOOPRRST	progenitors
EGINOPPRSSU	superposing
EGINOPPSTTU	outstepping
EGINOPSSTTU	poussetting
EGINORRSSTW	songwriters
EGINORSSTUW	outswingers
EGINPPRSSSU	suppressing
EGINPRRSSTU	superstring

EGIOORRSSSU	gressorious
EGIOPRRSSST	progressist
EGLMNNOOPRT	prolongment
EGLOOORRSWW	woolgrowers
EGMMNOPRSSY	gymnosperms
EGNOOOPRSSU	sporogenous
EGOPPRRSSUU	supergroups
EHHIIMSSTTW	whitesmiths
EHHIINRSSTW	withershins
EHHILMOPRST	thermophils
EHHILOOPPRS	philosopher
EHHILOPSTTY	lithophytes
EHHIMOOPRRT	theriomorph
EHHIMOOPSST	theosophism
EHHINORSSSW	whorishness
EHHINORSTTW	whitethorns
EHHIOOPPRST	phosphorite
EHHIOOPSSTT	theosophist
EHHIOPSSTTY	hypothesist
EHHLOOOPPRS	lophophores
EHHOOOPPRST	photophores
EHHOPPRRTYY	hypertrophy
EHIIILNPPPS	philippines
EHIIILNPSST	philistines
EHIIILOSSTT	hostilities
EHIIIMOSTTU	Thutmose III
EHIIIPRSSVZ	vizierships
EHIIKLNSTTY	kittenishly
EHIIKMNOOSS	Shimonoseki
EHIIKMRRSSS	skirmishers
EHIILLOPSSY	lyophilises
EHIILLOPSYZ	lyophilizes
EHIILMOOSTT	lithotomies
EHIILMRSSTV	silversmith
EHIILNOOPRT	heliotropin
EHIILNOOPSS	eosinophils
EHIILOOPTTX	toxophilite
EHIILORSTTT	lithotrites
EHIIMMOPRST	hemitropism
EHIIMNOSSTT	smithsonite
EHIIMOORSTZ	rhizotomies
EHIINNPRSST	internships
EHIINNSSSSW	swinishness
EHIINOPRTTY	hyponitrite
EHIINPRSSST	spinsterish
EHIINRSSSTT	thirstiness
EHIIOPRSSST	sophistries
EHIKMNNOSSS	monkishness
EHILLMRSSTY	mirthlessly
EHILLOPPSUY	epiphyllous
EHILLORSTTU	little hours
EHILMMNOSTY	semimonthly
EHILMNOOPTY	entomophily
EHILMNPSSSU	lumpishness
EHILMOOPRSU	Hermoupolis
EHILMORSSTY	thermolysis
EHILNOOPPSY	polyphonies
EHILNOORSSZ	horizonless
EHILNOOSTUW	Wilton House
EHILNOPRSTU	neutrophils
EHILNORRSSV	silverhorns
EHILNOSSSTU	loutishness

EHILNSSSSTY	stylishness
EHILOOPRSUX	xerophilous
EHILOPSSTTY	polytheists
EHILPRSSSUU	sulphurises
EHILPRSSUUZ	sulphurizes
EHIMMOOORST	homoerotism
EHIMMOOPSTY	mythopoeism
EHIMMOORSTU	mesothorium
EHIMMOPSSTU	imposthumes
EHIMNNOORSS	moonshiners
EHIMNNORSTU	nourishment
EHIMNNPSSTU	punishments
EHIMNOOPSTY	monophysite
EHIMNOORSTV	von Stroheim
EHIMNOORTTU	nototherium
EHIMNOOSSTT	monotheists
EHIMNORRTUY	erythronium
EHIMOOPRRST	rheotropism
EHIMOOPSSTY	mythopoesis
EHIMOOPSTTY	mythopoeist
EHIMOPRSTXY	xerophytism
EHIMORRSSTT	thermistors
EHINNOOPSTY	hypotension
EHINOOPRRTT	ornithopter
EHINOPRSSTY	hypnotisers
EHINOPRSTYZ	hypnotizers
EHINRSSSTTU	ruttishness
EHINSSSSTTY	synthesists
EHINSSSTTTY	synthetists
EHIOOOPRTTZ	trophozoite
EHIOOPRSTTX	thixotropes
EHIOPPRRSSW	worshippers
EHIOPQRSSTU	questorship
EHJMOPRSSUW	showjumpers
EHLLORSSTWY	worthlessly
EHLMNOPPSTY	nympholepts
EHLMNOPPSYY	nympholepsy
EHLMNOPTUWY	New Plymouth
EHLMOOOSTTY	toothsomely
EHLNOOPSSTY	stylophones
EHLOPRSSUUU	sulphureous
EHMMOOORRTT	thermomotor
EHMNOOOPRST	monostrophe
EHMOOOPRSTU	homopterous
EHMOOPSSTTY	photosystem
EHMOORRSTTW	motherworts
EHMOORSTTYY	hysterotomy
EHNNOPRSTWY	pennyworths
EHNOOOPRRTT	orthopteron
EHNOOPPRSTY	phonotypers
EHOOOPPRRSS	sporophores
EHOOPPRSSTW	showstopper
EHOOPPRSSTY	sporophytes
EHOOPPRSTTY	tropophytes
EHORRSSTTUV	overthrusts
EIIIILNSTTU	inutilities
EIIIINQSTUV	inquisitive
EIIILLLMRST	milliliters
	millilitres
EIIILLOSSTV	villosities
EIIILMNNOPS	epilimnions
EIIILMPRTVY	primitively

EIIILNNPSTY	insipiently
EIIILNTTUVY	intuitively
EIIILORSSST	listeriosis
EIIILORSSTV	vitriolises
EIIILORSTVZ	vitriolizes
EIIIMMNRSTU	ministerium
EIIIMNORSSV	revisionism
EIIIMOPRSTX	proximities
EIIINOPRSTT	peritonitis
EIIINOQRSTU	requisition
EIIINORSSTV	revisionist
EIIINOSSSTU	sinuosities
EIIINPRRSST	inspiriters
EIIINSSTTVY	sensitivity
EIIINSTTTUV	institutive
EIIIOPRRSST	prioritises
EIIIOPRRSTZ	prioritizes
EIIIOPRSSTT	periostitis
EIIIRSSTTVY	resistivity
EIIKKNORSSS	kirk session
EIIKLLNRSTW	winterkills
EIIKMNORSST	ministrokes
EIILLLMSSTY	limitlessly
EIILLMMNNSU	millenniums
EIILLMNNSTT	instillment
EIILLMNORSV	vermillions
EIILLMOPSVY	implosively
EIILLMPRSTU	multipliers
EIILLMPSUVY	impulsively
EIILLNOPSST	septillions
EIILLNOSSTX	sextillions
EIILLOOQSSU	soliloquies
	soliloquise
EIILLOOQSUZ	soliloquize
EIILMOPRSUY	imperiously
EIILNNSSTTY	insistently
EIILNOOPPRT	lipoprotein
EIILNOPRSTV	silverpoint
EIILNRSTUVY	intrusively
EIILNRTTUVY	nutritively
EIILOSSTVVZ	slivovitzes
EIILPRRTUVY	irruptively
EIIMNNOOPRT	premonition
EIIMNNOPRTU	premunition
EIIMNNOPSTU	pneumonitis
EIIMNNORSTU	munitioners
EIIMNOPRRSS	imprisoners
EIIMNOPRSSS	impressions
	permissions
EIIMNOPSSSU	impiousness
EIIMNORRTTT	intermittor
	intromitter
EIIMOOPPSST	pomposities
EIIMOORRSTU	meritorious
EIIMOPPRRTY	impropriety
EIIMOPRRSSV	improvisers
EIIMOPRSSST	prestissimo
EIIMOPSTTUY	impetuosity
EIIMORRSSTU	moisturiser
EIIMORRSTUZ	moisturizer
EIIMORSSSTU	moisturises
EIIMORSSTUZ	moisturizes

EIINNOOSTUV	Soviet Union
EIINNORSSTU	reunionists
EIINOOOPRST	ionotropies
EIINOOPPRST	preposition
EIINOOPRRSV	provisioner
	reprovision
EIINOOPRSST	repositions
EIINOOPSSTX	expositions
EIINOPRSSUV	supervision
EIINORRSSST	sinistrorse
EIINORSTTTU	restitution
EIINORSTTWZ	zwitterions
EIINRSSTTTU	instituters
EIINRSSTTTW	intertwists
EIIOPPRRRTX	proprietrix
EIIOPPSSTUV	suppositive
EIIOPRRSTUY	superiority
EIJKMMRSSUU	Rijksmuseum
EIKLLORRSTW	trelliswork
EIKNNOSSSTT	stinkstones
EIKNOORRRSW	ironworkers
EILLMOORSUV	mellivorous
EILLNOORRST	ritornellos
EILLNOPSSTY	pointlessly
EILLOPRRSUY	prelusorily
EILMMNOPRTY	promimently
EILMNNOPRTY	prominently
EILMNOOOPRS	monopoliser
EILMNOOOPRZ	monopolizer
EILMNOOOPSS	monopolises
EILMNOOOPSZ	monopolizes
EILMNOPRTUY	importunely
EILMNORSUVY	verminously
EILMNOSSYYZ	enzymolysis
EILMOORRSWY	worrisomely
EILMOPRSSTY	proselytism
EILMOPRSTTU	Triptolemus
EILMOPRTUVY	pluviometry
EILMOPSTUUY	impetuously
EILMORSTTUY	multistorey
EILNOOPRSST	portionless
EILNOOPRTTU	luteotropin
EILNOORSSTU	resolutions
EILNOORSTUV	revolutions
EILNOOSSTTU	solution set
EILNOPRSUUY	penuriously
EILNOQRTUVY	ventriloquy
EILNPQSTTUU	quintuplets
EILOOPRRSTY	posteriorly
EILOOPRSSTY	proteolysis
EILOPPRRSTW	slipperwort
EILOPPRSUVY	purposively
EILRRSSTUVW	liverwursts
EIMMNNORSSW	nonswimmers
EIMNNOOOPSS	monopsonies
EIMNNOOOSST	monotonises
EIMNNOOOSTZ	monotonizes
EIMNNOOPSTT	omnipotents
EIMNNOOSSSU	ominousness
EIMNNOSSSYY	synonymises
EIMNNOSSYYZ	synonymizes
EIMNNRSSTTU	instruments
EIMNNRSTTTU	intrustment
EIMNOOPRRTY	premonitory
EIMNOOPRSSS	spoonerisms
EIMNOORSTTU	neurotomist
EIMNOOSSTTT	tenotomists
EIMNOPPRSTU	presumption
EIMNOPRRSTU	importuners
EIMNOPRSSTU	resumptions
EIMOOPRSTTT	optometrist
EIMOORRSUVV	vermivorous
EIMORSSUVXY	myxoviruses
EIMRRSSSTTU	mistrusters
EINNOOPPRTU	inopportune
EINNOORSTUX	neurotoxins
EINNOOSSSUX	noxiousness
EINNOPSSSSU	suspensions
EINNOQRSTUU	non sequitur
EINNORSSSUU	ruinousness
EINNOSSSSUU	sinuousness
EINOOPPRSSS	oppressions
EINOOPRRSST	resorptions
EINOOPSSSSS	possessions
EINOORSSSTU	riotousness
EINOPPRSSST	stroppiness
EINOPPRSSSU	suppression
EINOPRRRSST	ripsnorters
EINOPRRRTTU	interruptor
EINOPSSTTTY	stenotypist
EINOQRSTTUU	tourniquets
EINORSSTTUY	strenuosity
EIOOPPRRRST	proprietors
EIOOPPRRSST	prepositors
EIOORSSTTUZ	zootsuiters
EIOPRRSSSUV	supervisors
EIOPRRSSUVY	supervisory
EIOPRSSTTTU	prostitutes
EIOQRRSTTUU	triquetrous
EIORRSTTTUY	restitutory
EJJMNOOSTUY	jejunostomy
EJKNOORRUWY	journeywork
EKKOOPPRSVY	Prokopyevsk
EKLOOPRRSSW	slopworkers
EKNNNNOSSUW	unknownness
ELLMNNOOSTY	somnolently
ELLMORSTUUY	tremulously
ELLOQRSUUUY	querulously
ELLRSSSTTUY	trustlessly
ELMMNOOSTUY	momentously
ELMMOPSSSTY	symptomless
ELMNOOPSUYY	eponymously
ELNOOPPRTUY	opportunely
ELNORSSTUUY	strenuously
ELOPPRSSSTU	supportless
EMMOOPRSSTT	postmortems
EMNNNOOOSUV	nonvenomous
EMNNOOORSTU	motoneurons
EMNOOPPSSSU	pompousness
EMNOOPRSSTW	sportswomen
EMNOPRRSSTU	prosternums
EMNORRSSTUU	surmounters
EMOOOPRRSST	mosstrooper
EMOOORRSSTV	servomotors
EOPPRRSSSSU	suppressors
FFFGIKLNRUU	kurfuffling
FFGHIIOPPRS	hippogriffs
FFGHILLRTUY	frightfully
FFGIINNOPRT	offprinting
FFIIRRSSTTU	firstfruits
FGGGHIINNTU	gunfighting
FGGHIINOTTU	outfighting
FGGHILNORUU	furloughing
FGGIIKLNNOS	folksinging
FGGIILNORVY	forgivingly
FGGIINNORUV	unforgiving
FGHIILNOPST	shoplifting
FGHIILNORSU	flourishing
FGHIINNRSSU	furnishings
FGHILNORTTY	fortnightly
FGIIILMNPSY	simplifying
FGIIILNOSSS	fossilising
FGIIILNOSSZ	fossilizing
FGIILMNNORY	informingly
FGIILNSTTUY	stultifying
FGIINNOOPSY	opsonifying
FGINOORTTTX	foxtrotting
FGIOORRSUUV	frugivorous
FIIIMNNOSSU	infusionism
FIIIMOPRSTT	stipitiform
FIIINNOSSTU	infusionist
FIILLNOOSUX	solifluxion
FIIMMNOSSTZ	Fitzsimmons
FIIORSSTTTU	fortuitists
FIKLLLNSUUY	unskilfully
FIKLLOORSST	folklorists
FILLOORSUVY	frivolously
FILMRSSTTUU	mistrustful
FILNOORSSTY	frontolysis
FLLOORRSUWY	sorrowfully
GGGIILNNNSU	gunslinging
GGHIIINRSTZ	rightsizing
GGHIILLNSTY	slightingly
GGHIIMNNSTU	gunsmithing
GGHINNNOSTU	shotgunning
GGIILLNOSSY	syllogising
GGIILLNOSYZ	syllogizing
GGIILNOPSSY	gossipingly
GGIINNNRSTU	unstringing
GGIINNOPSST	signposting
GGIINNPPRSU	upspringing
GGILLLNOORS	logrollings
GGILNOOORWW	woolgrowing
GHHIINRSSTT	nightshirts
GHHIIPRSSTW	shipwrights
GHHILOPRTTT	trothplight
GHHINOOPRTU	thoroughpin
GHHINOPRSTT	triphthongs
GHHIOPPPRSY	hippogryphs
GHHMNNOOOPT	monophthong
GHIIIKMNRSS	skirmishing
GHIIKLNNRSY	shrinkingly
GHIIKNNOTTU	outthinking
GHIILLLNRTY	thrillingly
GHIILLMRSTW	millwrights
GHIILLOOPST	philologist

GHIILLOOSTT	lithologist
GHIILMNOOSS	Missolonghi
GHIILNNPSUY	punishingly
GHIILNOORST	rhinologist
GHIILNOPSTY	philogynist
GHIILOOOPST	ophiologist
GHIILOOSSTT	histologist
GHIINNOPSTY	hypnotising
GHIINNOPTYZ	hypnotizing
GHIINNOTTTW	Whittington
GHIINOPPRSW	worshipping
GHIJMNOPSUW	showjumping
GHILLOOOPST	hoplologist
GHILLOOPSYY	syphilology
GHILMNOOSTY	hymnologist
GHILMOOSTTY	mythologist
GHILNNOOSTY	holystoning
GHILNOOOPST	phonologist
GHILNOOORTY	ornithology
GHILNOOPSTY	hypnologist
GHILNOOPSUY	philogynous
GHILOOOPRTY	oligotrophy
GHILOOORSST	horologists
GHILOOPSTTY	phytologist
GHIMMNOORSU	mushrooming
GHIMNOOPSYY	physiognomy
GHIMOOOSSYZ	homozygosis
GHINOOOSTTU	outshooting
GHINOOPPTTY	phototyping
GHLNOOPSSUW	snowploughs
GHNOOOOPRSU	gonophorous
GIIIINNPRST	inspiriting
GIIILLNORTV	vitriolling
GIIILLOSTUY	litigiously
GIIILNNPRSY	inspiringly
GIIILNNQRUY	inquiringly
GIIILNNSSTY	insistingly
GIIIMNNNOTU	munitioning
GIIIMNNOOSU	ignominious
GIIIMNNOPRS	imprisoning
GIIIMNNPRST	imprintings
	misprinting
GIIIMNOPRSV	improvising
GIIINNNOPPT	pinpointing
GIIINNNPRSU	uninspiring
GIIINNOOPST	positioning
GIIINNSTTTU	instituting
GIIINOOPSTV	ovipositing
GIIKLMNOPPS	milksopping
GIIKLNNPRSS	sprinklings
GIILLLNNUWY	unwillingly
GIILLMNOOST	limnologist
GIILLMNOPRY	imploringly
GIILLMNPTUY	multiplying
GIILMNOPRSY	promisingly
GIILMNOPRVY	improvingly
GIILMNQRSUY	squirmingly
GIILMOOSSST	misologists
GIILNNPQTUU	quintupling
GIILNNTTUWY	unwittingly
GIILNOORSUV	lignivorous
GIILNOOSSST	sinologists
GIILNOPSSTY	stylopising
GIILNOPSTYZ	stylopizing
GIILNOSTTUY	glutinosity
GIILOORSSTV	virologists
GIIMNNOPRSU	unpromising
GIIMNNOPRTU	importuning
GIIMNOSSSTY	misogynists
GIIMNRSSTTU	mistrusting
GIINNOOPTTU	outpointing
GIINNOPRRST	ripsnorting
GIINNOPSSSY	synopsising
GIINNOPSSYZ	synopsizing
GIINNPRRSTU	surprinting
GIINOORSTUV	vortiginous
GIINOPRRSUU	pruriginous
GIINOPRSSTU	posturising
GIINOPRSTUZ	posturizing
GIKLNNNOUWY	unknowingly
GIKLNOOPRVY	provokingly
GILLLMNOSUU	slumgullion
GILLMOOPSTY	polyglotism
GILLNOSTUUY	glutinously
GILMMNRRUUY	murmuringly
GILMNOOOSST	monologists
	nomologists
GILMOOOPSST	pomologists
GILMOOSSTYZ	zymologists
GILNNNOPSSU	nonplussing
GILNOOOSSST	nosologists
GILNOPSSTYY	polygynists
GILNORRTTUY	torturingly
GILNRSTTTUY	struttingly
GILOOOPSSTT	topologists
GILOOPSSTTY	typologists
GIMMNNRRUUU	unmurmuring
GIMNNOOSSTY	monogynists
GIMNNORSTUU	surmounting
GIMNOOOPRSU	sporogonium
GINNNOOPRSS	nonprossing
GINNNOOPRST	nonsporting
GINNOOPRSTT	strongpoint
GINOOPRSTUU	outpourings
GKMOORSSSUY	Moussorgsky
GMNOOORRSST	strongrooms
GNOOOPRSTUY	protogynous
HHIMOOPPRSS	phosphorism
HHIMOOPRRSZ	rhizomorphs
HHMNOOOOPSU	homophonous
HHOOOPPRSSU	phosphorous
HHOOOPPRSTT	phototrophs
HIILLNNNOOT	nonillionth
HIILLNORSTT	trillionths
HIILLOQRSUY	liquorishly
HIILMNNOOPY	hypolimnion
HIILMOOPSUY	myiophilous
HIILMOOSTTT	lithotomist
HIILNNPSSST	shinsplints
HIILOPRSTTY	lithotripsy
HIIMMOOPRSS	isomorphism
HIIMMOPRRST	trimorphism
HIIMNOOPRST	monitorship
HILLOOPSUXY	xylophilous
HILLOOSTUWW	Willow South
HILNOOPSTXY	xylophonist
HIMMOOOPRSZ	zoomorphism
HIMNOOPSSUY	symphonious
HIMNOPSSSTY	symphonists
HIMOOOPRSSU	isomorphous
HIMOOPRRSTU	trimorphous
HINOOPPRSSS	sponsorship
HINOOPPSTTY	phonotypist
HINOOPRRTTY	thyrotropin
HINOOPRSTUY	hyponitrous
HINOOPSTTXY	phytotoxins
HIOOPRSSTTT	orthoptists
HLLOOPPRSSY	sporophylls
HLNOOOPPSUY	polyphonous
HMOOOOPRSSU	homosporous
HMOOPSTTTUY	pottymouths
HORRSTTTUWY	trustworthy
IIIILMNNQSU	inquilinism
IIIILNNQTUY	inquilinity
IIIIMMPRSTV	primitivism
IIIIMPPSSSS	Mississippi
IIIIMPRSTTV	primitivist
IIIINNOQSTU	inquisition
IIILLMNOPST	pointillism
IIILLMNOSSU	illusionism
IIILLMNSSTU	illuminists
IIILLNNOQTU	quintillion
IIILLNOPSTT	pointillist
IIILLNOSSTT	tonsillitis
IIILLNOSSTU	illusionist
IIILNNOQSUU	inquilinous
IIIMNOOPSST	impositions
IIINNNORTTU	innutrition
IIINNOSTTTU	institution
IIINOOOPSTV	oviposition
IIINOQRSSTU	inquisitors
IIIOPSSSTTV	positivists
IIJLNORSUUY	injuriously
IIKKLOOSSTV	Tsiolkovski
IILLLOPPSSW	pillowslips
IILLNOOPSST	postillions
IILLOOQSSTU	soliloquist
IILLORSSTUU	illustrious
IILMRSSTTUU	tristimulus
IILNNOOSTUV	involutions
IILNNOOSUXY	innoxiously
IILOOPRRSVY	provisorily
IILOSSSTTXY	stylostixis
IIMNNNNOOSU	nonunionism
IIMNOOPRSTU	positronium
IIMNOPRTTUY	importunity
IINNNNOOSTU	nonunionist
IINOOOPPRST	proposition
IINOOOPPSST	oppositions
IINOOPPSSTU	supposition
IINOPPQRTUY	propinquity
IINORSSTTTU	institutors
IIOOOPRSSTV	ovipositors
ILLORSUUUXY	luxuriously
ILMNNNOOSUU	nonluminous
ILMNOOOPSST	monopolists

ILMOOSSTTXY xylotomists
ILNOOOPRSTY lyosorption
ILNOOOPSSUY poisonously
ILNOOORSTUY notoriously
ILNOOPPRSSU propulsions
ILOOPPRSSST spoilsports
IMNOOPPRSTU opportunism
IMNOORSSTTY monstrosity
IMOOOPPRRTU motu proprio
IMOOOPRSSTU impostorous
IMOOPPRSTTU pittosporum
IMOOPRSSTUU imposturous
IMOPSSTTUUY sumptuosity
INOOOPPRRST proportions
INOOPPRSTTU opportunist
INOOPPRTTUY opportunity
INOOPRRSSTU protrusions
IOOPPRSSTUY suppository
IOOPRRSTTTU prostitutor
LMNOOOPSUYY polyonymous
LMNOOOSSTUY monostylous
LMNOORSSTUY monstrously
LMOPSSTUUUY sumptuously
LOORRSTTUUY torturously
MMNOOOOSSTU monostomous

Twelve Letters

AAAAAALMRSTT	taramasalata
AAAABCCHILNN	bacchanalian
AAAABCLMORST	Malabar Coast
AAAABDEGLMNY	Magdalena Bay
AAAABDEIKNNR	Bandaranaike
AAAABDGGHITV	Bhagavad-Gita
AAAABDHHMRTY	Madhya Bharat
AAAABHILNRSS	Hasan al-Basri
AAAACCCCIRTU	acciaccatura
AAAACDIILPRS	paradisaical
	paradisiacal
AAAACEGGIMNR	Magna Graecia
AAAACEINRRSV	caravanserai
AAAACGILPSSS	passacaglias
AAAACGIMMNRT	anagrammatic
AAAACIMNRSST	antimacassar
AAAADHNPRRUU	Anuradhapura
AAAADLNPRSSU	Sardanapalus
AAAAEGGLNPRU	paralanguage
AAAAEGKKLNNO	Okanagan Lake
AAAAEGNRTVXZ	extravaganza
AAAAEHILMSST	thalassaemia
AAAAEHLLNPST	Pallas Athena
AAAAEIKMNORW	Waikaremoana
AAAAEIMMNRRT	armamentaria
AAAAFGILLNRS	Niagara Falls
AAAAFINRRSST	rastafarians
AAAAGGILMMNT	amalgamating
AAAAGILMMNOT	amalgamation
AAAAIILLMNRT	antimalarial
AAAAILLPRRSS	sarsaparilla
AAAAILNNRSTV	Transvaalian
AAAAILNRSSTU	Australasian
AAAAINNNORTV	Antananarivo
AAAALLLOOPSZ	lalapaloozas
AAABBCEEINRS	Caribbean Sea
AAABBCILLRRY	barbarically
AAABBCORRSTY	Barbary Coast
AAABBEIILLOV	bioavailable
AAABBHMMNORT	Rabbath Ammon
AAABBIIMNRRS	barbarianism
AAABCCDDIRRY	bradycardiac
AAABCCEILLMT	acclimatable
AAABCDEEINRS	abecedarians
AAABCDEHLNNU	Bechuanaland
AAABCDEHNOTY	Daytona Beach
AAABCDEIORSS	scarabaeoids
AAABCEERSSSU	scarabaeuses
AAABCEHILLPT	alphabetical
AAABCEHILNPT	analphabetic
AAABCEHIMRSU	Beaumarchais
AAABCEHLOPPR	approachable
AAABCELNRRTU	tabernacular
AAABCGIINNRT	Cantabrigian
AAABDEELLMNT	Matabeleland
AAABDEILMRST	dramatisable
AAABDEILMRTZ	dramatizable
AAABDEMRSSSS	ambassadress
AAABDIILPTTY	adaptability
AAABDIJMNNRS	Bandjarmasin
AAABDILLOOPR	paraboloidal
AAABDILNNSST	Batan Islands
AAABEEGILMRR	marriageable
AAABEEGLMNNU	unmanageable
AAABEEHIMNPS	amphisbaenae
AAABEEHIRSST	baraesthesia
AAABEELLNPPU	unappealable
AAABEELNPPSU	unappeasable
AAABEHIMNPSS	amphisbaenas
AAABEHINRRST	breatharians
AAABEHLMOSTT	haematoblast
AAABEIILMNNT	maintainable
AAABEILLMNOT	balletomania
AAABEILLNSSU	unassailable
AAABEILNNTTU	unattainable
AAABEINNSSST	San Sebastián
AAABEKLNSSTT	Balkan States
AAABELLNPPUY	unappealably
AAABELLNRSTT	translatable
AAABELNOOPTY	palaeobotany
AAABELQSTTUU	absquatulate
AAABEPRRSSUZ	superbazaars
AAABGGLNNPRU	Luang Prabang
AAABGHPPRRSU	subparagraph
AAABGIILNRRT	Gibraltarian
AAABHHIIMPRS	Ibrahim Pasha
AAABHIILNOTT	habitational
AAABHILNPRSU	Ashurbanipal
AAABHINORSTU	South Arabian
AAABIIILLTVY	availability
AAABIILLPTTY	palatability
AAABIKKLNOTU	Kota Kinabalu
AAABILLNQRRU	Barranquilla
AAABILLNSSUY	unassailably

AAABILNPRSSU Assurbanipal
sublapsarian
AAABIMMNRSTU Ambartsumian
AAACCCCEIRTU acciaccature
AAACCCDHIRTY tachycardiac
AAACCCEILSTT acatalectics
AAACCCISSTTU catacaustics
AAACCDEEGNRS Cascade Range
AAACCDEFHNNR French Canada
AAACCDEIIMNS academicians
AAACCDEILLMY academically
AAACCDEILMNO decalcomania
AAACCDHILORS saccharoidal
AAACCDIINRRT intracardiac
AAACCDILLLOP Dallapiccola
AAACCEGILMTT metagalactic
AAACCEGIORSU agaricaceous
AAACCEHINPSU ipecacuanhas
AAACCEHNOSTU acanthaceous
AAACCEIINPTT incapacitate
AAACCEILLNTU canaliculate
AAACCEILLORS calceolarias
AAACCEINNQTU acquaintance
AAACCELNRSSU crassulacean
AAACCGIINPTT capacitating
AAACCHILLNRY anarchically
AAACCHILNNOR anachronical
AAACCHILNPTY anaphylactic
AAACCIILMRST marcasitical
AAACCIINNPTT incapacitant
AAACCIINOPTT capacitation
AAACCILMNOST acclamations
AAACCILNPTTY anaptyctical
AAACCILORSTU accusatorial
AAACDEGILMOR megalocardia
AAACDEHINRST acidantheras
AAACDEILLMNY maenadically
AAACDEILMPRS paramedicals
AAACDEILNRST cardinalates
AAACDEIMMRSS macadamisers
AAACDEIMMRSZ macadamizers
AAACDEINRSTT tradescantia
AAACDELLLNNW Welland Canal
AAACDENNOPSU pandanaceous
AAACDGHNPRTU Chandragupta
AAACDGIIMMNS macadamising
AAACDGIIMMNZ macadamizing
AAACDGIIMMRT diagrammatic
AAACDGIIMPRT paradigmatic
AAACDIINNNSV Scandinavian
AAACDILLMRTY dramatically
AAACEEENPPRR reappearance
AAACEEGHNNRR carragheenan
AAACEEGNRTVX extravagance
AAACEEHINSST East China Sea
AAACEEJKNPSS jackanapeses
AAACEGGGLOTU galactagogue
AAACEGHILLPS cephalalgias
AAACEGHNRSTW Wasatch Range
AAACEGILLNNS gallinaceans
AAACEGILMMNO megalomaniac
AAACEGIMMNSU Macías Nguema
AAACEGIMNPRT paramagnetic
AAACEGIRRSWY carriageways
AAACEGLPRSSW Pascal's wager
AAACEHHNRTTU Harthacanute
AAACEHILMMTT mathematical
AAACEHIMOPPR pharmacopeia
AAACEHIMRRTT matriarchate
AAACEHINRSSZ Arias Sánchez
AAACEHIPRRTT patriarchate
AAACEHKNSSTW Saskatchewan
AAACEHLMORTY haematocryal
AAACEIILMNRT Latin America
AAACEIJLMNTY Calamity Jane
AAACEILMOOST osteomalacia
AAACEILMPRRT parametrical
AAACEILNORTU aeronautical
AAACEILORSTT aerostatical
AAACELMMORST sarcolemmata
AAACELMNRSST sacramentals
AAACELMOPRST paracetamols
AAACELNOSSTU santalaceous
AAACFIINRRTT antiaircraft
AAACFIMNRRST aircraftsman
AAACGGILLNOY anagogically
AAACGHHILNWY Alcan Highway
AAACGHIINNRT Carthaginian
AAACGHILLNPY anaglyphical
AAACGHIMNOPS phagomaniacs
AAACGIIMNSTT anastigmatic
AAACGILLLNOY analogically
AAACGILLLNVY galvanically
AAACGILLMMMO mammalogical
AAACGILLNPTY anaglyptical
AAACGILMNNOS anglomaniacs
AAACHHIKNRTU Khachaturian
AAACHIKPPRST apparatchiks
AAACHILLLMTY thalamically
AAACHILMNRST charlatanism
AAACHILNOSTU anacoluthias
AAACHIMNORTU tauromachian
AAACHIPPRRST paraphrastic
AAACIIILNNRT catilinarian
AAACIILNNOST canalisation
AAACIILNNOTZ canalization
AAACIILNNRRT intracranial
AAACILLLNTYY analytically
AAACILLMNOTY anatomically
AAACILLMORTY aromatically
AAACILMMNNOO monomaniacal
AAACILMNOPRY pyromaniacal
AAACILNSTTTY anticatalyst
AAACIMNNOTTU catamountain
AAACINPPRSTY parasynaptic
AAACMMOORSWY Coomaraswamy
AAADDEGINSTV disadvantage
AAADDEGLNOPT Ponta Delgada
AAADDGILLMOY amygdaloidal
AAADDIJLRSUU Siraj-ud-daula
AAADDILLNNSS Åland Islands
AAADEEGKPRSS Drake Passage
AAADEEGRTTVX extravagated
AAADEEINRRSV Sierra Nevada

AAADEELNRTTX	Alexandretta
AAADEERSTTVX	extravasated
AAADEFFNNORS	fanfaronades
AAADEGILNRTV	landgraviate
AAADEGILNSSV	Savage Island
AAADEGIMQRSU	Quadragesima
AAADEGLNRSTV	landgravates
AAADEGNOSTUV	advantageous
AAADEILLOPRT	Río de la Plata
AAADEILMNNRS	salamandrine
AAADEIMNNRST	mandarinates
AAADEINOPRTT	readaptation
AAADEINSSSST	assassinated
AAADFIINORST	faradisation
AAADFIINORTZ	faradization
AAADGGINORST	aggradations
AAADGHHIMNSW	Aswan High Dam
AAADGIILLORT	gladiatorial
AAADGINOPRRS	Gran Paradiso
AAADGLNQRRUU	quadrangular
AAADHHMNRSTU	Rhadamanthus
AAADHIILMNOT	amianthoidal
AAADHIINOPRS	anaphrodisia
AAADHILLNRSW	Hadrian's Wall
AAADIILLNOTT	dilatational
AAADIILNORRS	radiolarians
AAADILLLQRTU	Lailat-ul-Qadr
AAADILLNSSTY	All Saints' Day
AAAEEGGLMNTU	metalanguage
AAAEEGILMNRT	Marie Galante
AAAEEGILMSTX	metagalaxies
AAAEEGINNRSX	sexagenarian
AAAEEGMNNPRT	permanganate
AAAEEGRSTTVX	extravagates
AAAEEHIMNSTT	anathematise
AAAEEHIMNTTZ	anathematize
AAAEEHIMRRST	Maria Theresa
AAAEEHIPRSST	paraesthesia
AAAEELLLMNRT	Tell el Amarna
AAAEERSSTTVX	extravasates
AAAEFHIMRRSZ	Mazar-e-Sharif
AAAEFILNRSTT	Santa Fe Trail
AAAEFKLMMSTU	Mustafa Kemal
AAAEGGNNRSTU	Nusa Tenggara
AAAEGHIMMNOS	haemangiomas
AAAEGHIMMNOT	hemangiomata
AAAEGHLOPPRY	palaeography
AAAEGHNPSSTU	agapanthuses
AAAEGIILNRST	egalitarians
AAAEGILLMNRY	managerially
AAAEGILMNNST	galantamines
AAAEGIMNORTV	Moravian Gate
AAAEGIMNPRST	Seringapatam
AAAEGIMRRSTV	margraviates
AAAEGINNNNOR	nonagenarian
AAAEHILNPRST	Rhaetian Alps
AAAEHKORSTUV	katharevousa
AAAEHMOPRRTY	aromatherapy
AAAEHNPRSTTY	parasyntheta
AAAEIILNQRTU	equalitarian
AAAEIINNRSTZ	Saint-Nazaire
AAAEIKLLNNST	antalkalines
AAAEIKNPSSTT	East Pakistan
AAAEILLLNPRT	antiparallel
AAAEILLNPSST	palatialness
AAAEILMNOPPR	paralipomena
AAAEILMRRTTX	extramarital
AAAEILNNNOTX	annexational
AAAEILNPPRRS	prelapsarian
AAAEILNRSTUW	New Australia
AAAEILPPRRSS	reappraisals
AAAEIMNNRSST	transaminase
AAAEIMOOTTUX	autotoxaemia
AAAEINSSSSST	assassinates
AAAEKKLMRTTU	Kemal Atatürk
AAAELLMMMPSS	plasmalemmas
AAAELMNOVYYZ	Novaya Zemlya
AAAELQQRSUUV	quaquaversal
AAAENPPRSSSY	parasynapses
AAAFIILMNNWY	Flaminian Way
AAAFINRRSTTU	trustafarian
AAAGGHINPPRR	paragraphing
AAAGGINORSTV	aggravations
AAAGGIOPPRTU	appoggiatura
AAAGGLNOSSUV	Volsunga Saga
AAAGGMORRSYZ	Magyarország
AAAGHIKNOSTT	kotahitangas
AAAGHINPPRRS	paraphrasing
AAAGHIRSTTWY	straightaway
AAAGHNOPRSTU	paragnathous
AAAGIILLNPST	palatalising
AAAGIILLNPTZ	palatalizing
AAAGIILNNOTV	navigational
AAAGIINNOPST	paganisation
AAAGIINNOPTZ	paganization
AAAGIINRSSTT	sagittarians
AAAGILLLORRT	grallatorial
AAAGLLMOOTUY	autoallogamy
AAAHHHHNORSS	Rosh Hashanah
AAAHHHJNPRSU	Shahjahanpur
AAAHHNOPSTUX	hapaxanthous
AAAHIILNNOTT	antihalation
AAAHIIMNNRTU	humanitarian
AAAHILMNRRTU	Muralitharan
AAAHLLMNPSTY	phantasmally
AAAHLNNOSTXY	Saxony-Anhalt
AAAIILMNPRSU	marsupialian
AAAIILMPRRTY	paramilitary
AAAIILNNORTT	antirational
AAAIILNNOSST	nasalisation
AAAIILNNOSTZ	nasalization
AAAIILNORTTT	totalitarian
AAAIILNPSSTU	saintpaulias
AAAIINNQRSTU	antiquarians
AAAIINRSTTTW	Taiwan Strait
AAAIKLNNOPRT	National Park
AAAILMNOPSSS	anaplasmosis
AAAILMNORTTU	maturational
AAAILNNOSSTY	analysations
AAAILNNOSTYZ	analyzations
AAAILNNRSTVY	Transylvania
AAAILNOPRSTY	paralysation
AAAILNOPRTYZ	paralyzation
AAAIMNNOOSST	antonomasias

AAAIMNOOPRSS	paronomasias
AAAINNNRRSTU	transuranian
AAAINOOPPSST	appassionato
AAAINPPRSSSY	parasynapsis
AAALLLLOOOPZ	lollapalooza
AABBCCEMOOSU	bombacaceous
AABBCDEHLRRS	hardscrabble
AABBCEEKKRRS	backbreakers
AABBCEGIKKNR	backbreaking
AABBCEGMORSW	cabbageworms
AABBCEGNOSTW	cabbagetowns
AABBCEILNOSZ	Blasco Ibáñez
AABBCEINORST	bicarbonates
AABBCGIKLLLN	blackballing
AABBCIIILMNO	bibliomaniac
AABBCIILLNRY	rabbinically
AABBDEEKRSST	breadbaskets
AABBDEELRSST	beadblasters
AABBDEEORRSV	beaverboards
AABBDEGILNST	beadblasting
AABBDILMNOSU	subabdominal
AABBDNNOORRT	Noordbrabant
AABBEEKLLRRS	ballbreakers
AABBEEKLNNOR	nonbreakable
AABBEELLRSST	barbastelles
AABBEFGLRSST	flabbergasts
AABBEGIINRTV	abbreviating
AABBEIIKLLOS	Bielsko-Biała
AABBEIINORTV	abbreviation
AABBEILNNOTU	unobtainable
AABBEILRTTTU	attributable
AABBEIORRSTV	abbreviators
AABBEIRRSTTU	barbiturates
AABBGHIMNOST	thingamabobs
AABBHIIILTTY	habitability
AABBHIKOSSUZ	bashibazouks
AABBHNNORRTT	North Brabant
AABCCDEIILRT	bactericidal
AABCCDEIKNRR	crackbrained
AABCCDEILLSY	decasyllabic
AABCCEELNPTU	unacceptable
AABCCEILLLNU	incalculable
AABCCEILLMOV	clavicembalo
AABCCEILMNOR	microbalance
AABCCEIMORTY	mycobacteria
AABCCEIRRTUU	bureaucratic
AABCCENOORSU	carbonaceous
AABCCGIIKKNP	pickabacking
AABCCGIJKKLN	blackjacking
AABCCGIKKNRT	backtracking
AABCCHHIIMPR	amphibrachic
AABCCIILLLOT	lactobacilli
AABCCIILOTTY	biocatalytic
AABCCILLLNUY	incalculably
AABCCILMOORT	mobocratical
AABCCILOSSTT	cactoblastis
AABCCINRSTTU	subantarctic
AABCCKLNRRTU	blackcurrant
AABCDDDEEKLS	saddlebacked
AABCDDEEKLLP	backpedalled
AABCDDEENORT	decarbonated
AABCDDEENRSU	Secunderabad
AABCDDEGKLRU	blackguarded
AABCDDEHKLNY	backhandedly
AABCDDEJLORS	Jacob's ladder
AABCDDEKLRRW	bladderwrack
AABCDDIKMNOS	diamondbacks
AABCDEEIILNR	ineradicable
AABCDEEILLPS	displaceable
AABCDEEKNRRS	breakdancers
AABCDEELLLSY	decasyllable
AABCDEELNORV	overbalanced
AABCDEENORST	decarbonates
AABCDEENOSTU	subdeaconate
AABCDEFLNOTU	confabulated
AABCDEGIKLNP	backpedaling
AABCDEGIKNNR	breakdancing
AABCDEHHMNRS	chamberhands
AABCDEHIINRT	dibranchiate
AABCDEHIMMRS	chambermaids
AABCDEHMNORR	rhabdomancer
AABCDEHORRTY	carbohydrate
AABCDEIILNNS	cannibalised
AABCDEIILNNZ	cannibalized
AABCDEIILNRY	ineradicably
AABCDEILLSTY	syllabicated
AABCDEINOSTU	subdiaconate
AABCDEKNRSSW	backwardness
AABCDELLNNNO	cannonballed
AABCDELLOORT	collaborated
AABCDELMNRSU	candelabrums
AABCDELOPPRR	clapperboard
AABCDELRSTTY	abstractedly
AABCDENOORRT	decarbonator
AABCDEOPRRRS	scraperboard
AABCDEORRSST	broadcasters
	rebroadcasts
AABCDGGIOORS	braggadocios
AABCDGILNOPR	clapboarding
AABCDGINNOOR	carbonadoing
AABCDGINORST	broadcasting
AABCDGKLLRUY	blackguardly
AABCDIILLLOY	diabolically
AABCDIILMNOY	biodynamical
AABCDIIOPRSS	basidiocarps
AABCDIIQRSTU	biquadratics
AABCDKMNOOSW	backwoodsman
AABCEEEFFILN	ineffaceable
AABCEEEGHLNX	exchangeable
AABCEEEGHLRR	rechargeable
AABCEEEHLRRS	researchable
AABCEEENORTT	betacarotene
AABCEEFFILNY	ineffaceably
AABCEEFIPRRT	prefabricate
AABCEEGGPRRT	carpetbagger
AABCEEGHLNNU	unchangeable
AABCEEGHLNXY	exchangeably
AABCEEGINRTX	exacerbating
AABCEEHKLRST	leatherbacks
AABCEEHLMNRT	merchantable
AABCEEHLOPRR	reproachable
AABCEEHMNRST	antechambers
AABCEEIKMNRT	cabinetmaker
AABCEEILLMMT	emblematical

AABCEEILMNSS amicableness
AABCEEINORTX exacerbation
AABCEEKPPRRS paperbackers
AABCEELLNOOT oblanceolate
AABCEELLNPSS placableness
AABCEELLNSSS scalableness
AABCEELLORRT correlatable
AABCEELNORSV overbalances
AABCEFIILLSS classifiable
AABCEFIILLTY beatifically
AABCEFIILNST sanctifiable
AABCEFLNOSTU confabulates
AABCEGHILPTY bathypelagic
AABCEGHLNNUY unchangeably
AABCEGIKNPPR paperbacking
AABCEHHPSSTY bathyscaphes
AABCEHIIMNPS amphisbaenic
AABCEHILMNRS chamberlains
AABCEHILNRTU uncharitable
AABCEHLMNORS elasmobranch
AABCEHLOPRRY reproachably
AABCEHNOORTY archeobotany
AABCEIIILPST capabilities
AABCEIILLNPP inapplicable
AABCEIILLOSS socialisable
AABCEIILLOSZ socializable
AABCEIILLRTY lacerability
AABCEIILLTVY cleavability
AABCEIILMMRS bicameralism
AABCEIILMNOT alembication
AABCEIILMRST bicameralist
AABCEIILNNSS cannibalises
AABCEIILNNSZ cannibalizes
AABCEIILRTTY traceability
AABCEIILRTUU biauriculate
AABCEIKLLMRS blackmailers
AABCEILLLORT bicollateral
AABCEILLNPPU unapplicable
AABCEILLNSSU suballiances
AABCEILLNSUV vulcanisable
AABCEILLNUVZ vulcanizable
AABCEILLPRRY bicarpellary
AABCEILLSSTY syllabicates
AABCEILLTTUV cultivatable
AABCEILMNNOT contaminable
AABCEILMNOPR incomparable
AABCEILMNRSY carbylamines
AABCEILMORRT barometrical
AABCEILNNOST sanctionable
AABCEILORSST ostracisable
AABCEILORSTZ ostracizable
AABCEILORSUV vocabularies
AABCEILSSTTT Baltic States
AABCEIMRSSTT semiabstract
AABCEINRRSTT scatterbrain
AABCEIORSTTT bacteriostat
AABCEKLLRRST trackerballs
AABCEKQRRSTU quarterbacks
AABCELLOORST collaborates
AABCELNORSTT contrastable
AABCELORSSXY carboxylases
AABCELORSTXY carboxylates
AABCENORSSST contrabasses
AABCEOORSTTZ azotobacters
AABCFIINORST fabrications
AABCFLNOORTU confabulator
AABCGHIILOPR biographical
AABCGHIOOPRS agoraphobics
AABCGIIKLLMN blackmailing
AABCGIINNNNS Canning Basin
AABCGIKLNPPS backslapping
AABCGILLLSUY subglacially
AABCGILNNOTU outbalancing
AABCGLMNNOUZ Guzmán Blanco
AABCHIILMPST amphiblastic
AABCHIIMORTT microhabitat
AABCHIINOOTT cohabitation
AABCHIINORST brachiations
AABCIIILNPTY incapability
AABCIILLNPPY inapplicably
AABCIILLPRSY parisyllabic
AABCIILMRSST strabismical
AABCIILNNOTU incubational
AABCIILRTTTY tractability
AABCILLLLSYY syllabically
AABCILMNOPRY incomparably
AABCILNORSST San Cristóbal
AABCILOSSTTY biocatalysts
AABCILRRSUUU subauricular
AABCINNOORST carbonations
AABCINORRSTU carburations
AABCINORSSTT abstractions
AABCLLOOORRT collaborator
AABCLNORSTTY contrastably
AABCLNORSTUY constabulary
AABCLPRSSSUU subscapulars
AABCMNNNOOTT noncombatant
AABDDDENRRST standardbred
AABDDEEKORST skateboarded
AABDDEELRRTW Albert Edward
AABDDEGGORRS daggerboards
AABDDEHHNRST handsbreadth
AABDDEHLLMOY hebdomadally
AABDDGHORRTU draughtboard
AABDDHIIILMU Abdul-Hamid II
AABDEEEGILRS disagreeable
AABDEEELNRSS readableness
AABDEEGILRSY disagreeably
AABDEEGLNRSS gradableness
AABDEEHHRRSS haberdashers
AABDEEHHRRSY haberdashery
AABDEEHILPST alphabetised
AABDEEHILPTZ alphabetized
AABDEEHLRSTY breathalysed
AABDEEHLRTYZ breathalyzed
AABDEEHORRTW weatherboard
AABDEEILRTTX extraditable
AABDEEJLRSTU readjustable
AABDEEKORRST skateboarder
AABDEELLNSSU laudableness
AABDEELMNNSS damnableness
AABDEELMPRTU perambulated
AABDEFLLNNOR flannelboard
AABDEGIIMSTU disambiguate

AABDEGIKNORW	wakeboarding
AABDEGINORTU	outbargained
AABDEGLLMNOR	balladmonger
AABDEHHIRRST	hairsbreadth
AABDEHILRTWW	withdrawable
AABDEIIKNRSY	bradykinesia
AABDEIILNRST	distrainable
AABDEIKNORST	debarkations
AABDEILLLOSW	disallowable
AABDEILLNOST	labiodentals
AABDEILMNSTU	Ústí nad Labem
AABDEILORRST	bardolatries
	labradorites
AABDEIMNORRS	dermabrasion
AABDEIMNRRSU	barramundies
AABDEIMRRSSS	disembarrass
AABDELNNOPRU	unpardonable
AABDELNRSSST	sandblasters
AABDELOPRRST	plasterboard
AABDFFIILNNS	Baffin Island
AABDGIILNORS	boardsailing
	sailboarding
AABDGIINNOST	bastinadoing
AABDGIINRSST	bastardising
AABDGIINRSTZ	bastardizing
AABDGILNNSST	sandblasting
AABDGINORRST	starboarding
AABDHIOORSUZ	biohazardous
AABDHLOPRSSS	splashboards
AABDHMMOORSY	rhabdomyomas
AABDIIILLTTY	dilatability
AABDIIILSTVY	advisability
AABDIILMQRSU	liquidambars
AABDILOORRSS	boardsailors
AABDIMNORSTU	adumbrations
AABDINOOTTUY	autoantibody
AABDMOORRRST	mortarboards
AABEEEGKMRRS	gamebreakers
AABEEEHKRRRT	heartbreaker
AABEEEILLPRR	irrepealable
AABEEEKRSTVW	basketweaver
AABEEELLNSSS	saleableness
AABEEELMNNSS	amenableness
AABEEELMNRUV	maneuverable
AABEEELMNSST	tameableness
AABEEELNPRTU	unrepeatable
AABEEELNRSST	rateableness
AABEEELNSSSV	saveableness
AABEEFGILLLT	biflagellate
AABEEFGILRRR	irrefragable
AABEEFHINRRT	featherbrain
AABEEFILMNST	manifestable
AABEEFKRRSST	breakfasters
AABEEFLNRRST	transferable
AABEEGGLMORT	mortgageable
AABEEGILMNST	magnetisable
AABEEGILMNTZ	magnetizable
AABEEGLNNTUW	Blaenau Gwent
AABEEGMMORRU	Oberammergau
AABEEHIILRTT	rehabilitate
AABEEHILPRST	alphabetiser
AABEEHILPRTZ	alphabetizer
AABEEHILPSST	alphabetises
AABEEHILPSTZ	alphabetizes
AABEEHLRRSTY	breathalyser
AABEEHLRRTYZ	breathalyzer
AABEEHLRSSTY	breathalyses
AABEEHLRSTYZ	breathalyzes
AABEEIILRSSV	braaivleises
AABEEILLLNPP	inappellable
AABEEILLPRRY	irrepealably
AABEEILMMRSU	immeasurable
AABEEILNRRST	restrainable
AABEEILNRSSV	variableness
AABEEINRRRST	trainbearers
AABEEINRRSST	brainteasers
AABEEINRSSSV	abrasiveness
AABEEKLMNRRU	unremarkable
AABEEKLMNRTU	unmarketable
AABEEKSSSTTW	wastebaskets
AABEELLMNOST	balletomanes
AABEELLNPPSS	palpableness
AABEELLNSSSV	salvableness
AABEELLNSSUV	valuableness
AABEELMNORUV	manoeuvrable
AABEELMNRSUU	unmeasurable
AABEELMPRSTU	perambulates
AABEELNNORSU	unreasonable
AABEELNNOSSU	unseasonable
AABEELNNRSUW	unanswerable
AABEELNPSSSS	passableness
AABEELNRSTTU	entablatures
	subalternate
AABEELPRSSTT	breastplates
AABEENNRRSTU	subterranean
AABEENNRTUUV	Buenaventura
AABEFGIKNRST	breakfasting
AABEFGILRRRY	irrefragably
AABEFHINRRST	Bairnsfather
AABEFHLMNOTU	unfathomable
AABEFIILNOPS	saponifiable
AABEFIILNQTU	quantifiable
AABEFILLMMNS	inflammables
AABEFLLMMNNO	nonflammable
AABEFLNORUUV	unfavourable
AABEFLNRSSTU	transfusable
AABEGGILLNTU	agglutinable
AABEGHIKNRTT	breathtaking
AABEGHILLOSU	Heliogabalus
AABEGHIMNTTW	bantamweight
AABEGIILMNNU	unimaginable
AABEGIINRRTT	Great Britain
AABEGIINSSUU	Guinea-Bissau
AABEGIKLNRSW	lawbreakings
AABEGILNPPRT	palpebrating
	table-rapping
AABEGIMNRRSS	embarrassing
AABEGIRRRSTU	arbitrageurs
AABEGLLMOSST	megaloblasts
AABEGLMMOPRR	programmable
AABEHIINORTZ	hebraization
AABEHILMNORS	harmonisable
AABEHILMNORZ	harmonizable
AABEHILNQSUV	vanquishable

AABEHILNSSTU habitualness
AABEHINRRSSW brainwashers
AABEHIOOPRTT teratophobia
AABEHLMOSSTT hematoblasts
AABEIIILLNTY alienability
AABEIILLLMTY malleability
AABEIILLORST isobilateral
AABEIILLRTTY alterability
AABEIILNRRST libertarians
AABEIILPRRTY reparability
AABEIILPRSTY separability
AABEIILQTTUY equatability
AABEIINOORSS anaerobiosis
AABEIKLMNSTU unmistakable
AABEIKMNORST embarkations
AABEILLNRRTU turbellarian
AABEILLRRSTZ trailblazers
AABEILMMRSSU summarisable
AABEILMMRSUY immeasurably
AABEILMMRSUZ summarizable
AABEILMORSTU ambulatories
AABEILNOORST elaborations
AABEILNPRRST transpirable
AABEILNRRSTT rattlebrains
AABEILOORRST laboratories
AABEILOPPPRR appropriable
AABEIMNRRSTT arbitraments
AABEINNQRSTU barquantines
AABEINSSTTTU substantiate
AABEJNPSSTTU Punjab States
AABELMMNOSTU somnambulate
AABELMNRSTTU transmutable
AABELMNRSUUY unmeasurably
AABELMOPRRTU perambulator
AABELNNORSUY unreasonably
AABELNNOSSUY unseasonably
AABELNNRSUWY unanswerably
AABELNOPRSST transposable
AABFGIILMORY fibromyalgia
AABFHLMNOTUY unfathomably
AABFIILLMMTY flammability
AABFIILLOTTY floatability
AABFLLMNOTYY flamboyantly
AABFLNORUUVY unfavourably
AABGGGILLNRY ballyragging
AABGHIIILNTT habilitating
AABGHIINNRSW brainwashing
AABGIIILNSST assibilating
AABGIIILNTVY navigability
AABGIIINRRTT abirritating
AABGIILLNOOT obligational
AABGIILLNORY aboriginally
AABGIILLNRTZ trailblazing
AABGIILMNNUY unimaginably
AABGIILNOPRS parabolising
AABGIILNOPRZ parabolizing
AABGIILNRSTU tabularising
AABGIILNRTUZ tabularizing
AABGIMNRSTTU masturbating
AABGLLMORSSY syllabograms
AABHIIILNOTT habilitation
AABHIIILRSSZ bilharziasis
AABHIIINNOTT inhabitation
AABHIILNNRTY labyrinthian
AABHIILORSTT habilitators
AABHIINOSTTU habituations
AABHLLLLOOSU hullaballoos
AABIIILNOSST assibilation
AABIIILNSTTY stainability
AABIIINQRTUU ubiquitarian
AABIILNNNTTU tintinnabula
AABIILNOORTY abolitionary
AABIILOPRTVY vaporability
AABIILRSTTUY saturability
AABIIMNNOOST abominations
AABIINNOORTT antiabortion
AABIINNORSTU urbanisation
AABIINNORTUZ urbanization
AABIINOORRST arborisation
AABIINOORRTZ arborization
AABIINORRSTT arbitrations
AABIKLMNSTUY unmistakably
AABILLMRSUXY submaxillary
AABILLNOSTTU blastulation
AABILNSSSTTU substantials
AABILNSSTTUV substantival
AABILOPRRSTU supraorbital
AABIMNOPRSTY parasymbiont
AABIMNORSTTU masturbation
AABINOOPRRTY probationary
AABLMMNNOSTU somnambulant
AABLMNRSTTUY transmutably
AABLORRRSTUY barratrously
AABMORRSSTTU masturbators
AABMORRSTTUY masturbatory
AACCCDHRRSST scratchcards
AACCCEEHILTT catechetical
AACCCEFIINOP Pacific Ocean
AACCCEGNORYY gynaecocracy
AACCCEHIRSTT catachrestic
AACCCEIINRSU inaccuracies
AACCCEJKKRRS crackerjacks
AACCDDEHIIRS disaccharide
AACCDDEMMOOT accommodated
AACCDDHIIRSS disaccharids
AACCDDIILLTY didactically
AACCDDIILOPR diplocardiac
AACCDDIIOTTU autodidactic
AACCDEEHINOX hexadecanoic
AACCDEEINRRT incarcerated
AACCDEEINRTV revaccinated
AACCDEEKMNRR cackermander
AACCDEELLRTU recalculated
AACCDEELNORS accelerandos
AACCDEENNOTT concatenated
AACCDEFHIIRS saccharified
AACCDEHILMOT machicolated
AACCDEHINORS archdiocesan
AACCDEHNORRY archdeaconry
AACCDEIIILNT dialectician
AACCDEIILMST acclimatised
AACCDEIILMTZ acclimatized
AACCDEILLNTY accidentally
AACCDEILOPSY cyclopaedias

AACCDEINNTUV unvaccinated
AACCDELNRTUU carunculated
AACCDELRTTUU acculturated
AACCDEMMOOST accommodates
AACCDENNORST contradances
AACCDIIILRST radicalistic
AACCDIILNOTU claudication
AACCDIIOPRTT catadioptric
AACCDILLLTYY dactylically
AACCDILLNORY draconically
AACCEEEILRTV accelerative
AACCEEFILNST calefacients
AACCEEFKRRSS safecrackers
AACCEEGHILMP megacephalic
AACCEEGHOSST stagecoaches
AACCEEGILNRT accelerating
AACCEEHILNNP anencephalic
AACCEEHIMNOR aeromechanic
AACCEEHIRRST characteries
characterise
AACCEEHIRRTZ characterize
AACCEEHLMNTU catechumenal
AACCEEIILLPR capercaillie
AACCEEIILPRZ capercailzie
AACCEEILNORT acceleration
AACCEEINRRST incarcerates
AACCEEINRSTV revaccinates
AACCEELLRSTU recalculates
AACCEELORRST accelerators
AACCEELORRTY acceleratory
AACCEENNOSTT concatenates
AACCEENRSSTU accurateness
AACCEFHIIRSS saccharifies
AACCEFHLRRTU characterful
AACCEFILNRSS farcicalness
AACCEGHIILPR archipelagic
AACCEGHIIORS hagiocracies
AACCEGHILMOR agrochemical
AACCEGHNRSTT gnatcatchers
AACCEGHOPRRS cacographers
AACCEGINNTTU accentuating
AACCEHHIILRR hierarchical
AACCEHHILNTT chalcanthite
AACCEHHMOSST stomachaches
AACCEHIILNPS chaplaincies
AACCEHIIMNNS mechanicians
AACCEHILLMNO melancholiac
AACCEHILLMNY mechanically
AACCEHILMNNU unmechanical
AACCEHILMOST machicolates
AACCEHILNPRT pentarchical
AACCEHILNRSY saccharinely
AACCEHILOPTU autocephalic
AACCEHILORTT theocratical
AACCEHILPRTY archetypical
AACCEHILRRTT tetrarchical
AACCEHIMORTT metathoracic
AACCEHIMPRTU pharmaceutic
AACCEHINOOSX hexacosanoic
AACCEHIOPRTT cataphoretic
AACCEHLMOPRY macrocephaly
AACCEHLPRSTT scratchplate
AACCEIIINPST incapacities
AACCEIILLNRT anticlerical
AACCEIILMRST acclimatiser
AACCEIILMRTZ acclimatizer
AACCEIILMSST acclimatises
AACCEIILMSTZ acclimatizes
AACCEIILPTVY capacitively
AACCEILLMSTU miscalculate
AACCEILLNNOT cancellation
AACCEILLNOSS neoclassical
AACCEILLOPSU capillaceous
AACCEILLPRSS preclassical
AACCEILLSTTY ecstatically
AACCEILMMORT macroclimate
AACCEILMNOPS complaisance
AACCEILMNOPT cleptomaniac
AACCEILMOOST osteomalacic
AACCEILMOSSU smilacaceous
AACCEILMPRST malpractices
AACCEILMTUUV accumulative
AACCEILNORVY clairvoyance
AACCEILNRRTT recalcitrant
AACCEILNRTUY inaccurately
AACCEILORSSV slavocracies
AACCEILSTUVY accusatively
AACCEIMNNORS necromaniacs
AACCEIMNOPRS accompaniers
AACCEINNORST anacreontics
transoceanic
AACCEINNOTTU accentuation
AACCEINOORTV coacervation
AACCEINORRRT incarcerator
AACCEINORRTY accretionary
AACCEINQSTTU acquittances
AACCEIOPRTVY overcapacity
AACCEKLLNOSY cycloalkanes
AACCELLPPRSW clapperclaws
AACCELNNRSTY transcalency
AACCELPRSSTU spectaculars
AACCELRSTTUU acculturates
AACCENOOPSUY apocynaceous
AACCENOORSSY acrocyanoses
AACCEORSSTUY styracaceous
AACCFIIINOPT pacification
AACCFIILSTTU factualistic
AACCFIINPRST transpacific
AACCFIIOPRTY pacificatory
AACCFIIORRST scarificator
AACCFINNORSS San Francisco
AACCFINOORSS São Francisco
AACCGHHIKNOW Changchiakow
AACCGHHIPRTY tachygraphic
AACCGHHLOPRY chalcography
AACCGHIILLOR oligarchical
AACCGHIILLPR calligraphic
AACCGHIINNNT cachinnating
AACCGHIINRSS saccharising
AACCGHIINRSZ saccharizing
AACCGHIMOPRR macrographic
AACCGHIOPRRT cartographic
AACCGIILMORT tragicomical
AACCGIINRRTU caricaturing

AACCGILLOOPR carpological
AACCGILLOOST scatological
AACCGILMNTUU accumulating
AACCGIMNNOPY accompanying
AACCHHIMOPSY psychomachia
AACCHIIINRTT antirachitic
AACCHIILMSST schismatical
AACCHIILNOTT anti-Catholic
AACCHIILTTUX Ixtaccihuatl
AACCHIILTTUZ Iztaccihuatl
AACCHIINNNOT cachinnation
AACCHIINRSTY saccharinity
AACCHILLLOTY catholically
AACCHILLORTY trochaically
AACCHIMNOPRT panchromatic
AACCHIMOOPRT apochromatic
AACCHINNORTY cachinnatory
AACCHIOPRSTT catastrophic
AACCHLLNORYY acronychally
AACCIIILPSTT capitalistic
AACCIILLLMTY climatically
AACCIILLMSSS classicalism
AACCIILLSSST classicalist
AACCIILLSSTY classicality
AACCIILMORTT timocratical
AACCIILNNOST calcinations
AACCIILNRTUY inarticulacy
AACCIILNTTTY Atlantic City
AACCIILPRTTY practicality
AACCIINNOSTV vaccinations
AACCIINOSSTU acousticians
AACCIIORRSTT aristocratic
AACCIIRRSTTU caricaturist
AACCILLLNOVY volcanically
AACCILLNNOSS nonclassical
AACCILLNOOSY occasionally
AACCILLNORTY narcotically
AACCILLNOSTU calculations
AACCILLORSTY acrostically
AACCILLOSTUY acoustically
AACCILMNOTUU accumulation
AACCILMOPRSS sarcoplasmic
AACCILNNOPRT nonpractical
AACCILNOOPTU occupational
AACCIMNOPSST accompanists
AACCIMNOPSTY accompanyist
AACCINOORSSY acrocyanosis
AACCINOORSTT coarctations
AACCINOPRSTY pantisocracy
AACCIORRSTTT stratocratic
AACCLLNOTTUY contactually
AACCLMORSTUU accumulators
AACCLNPRTUUU acupunctural
AACCOQRSTTUY squattocracy
AACDDDEEHLOR dodecahedral
AACDDEEEHHNR hendecahedra
AACDDEEEHLTY acetaldehyde
AACDDEELPSTU decapsulated
AACDDEIIJTUV adjudicative
AACDDEIILNOT dedicational
AACDDEIINNNR incarnadined
AACDDEIINNRT incardinated
AACDDEIJRUUZ Ciudad Juárez
AACDDEINRSTU candidatures
AACDDEIORRTX dextrocardia
AACDDGIIJNTU adjudicating
AACDDIIJNOTU adjudication
AACDDIJORSTU adjudicators
AACDEEEFFINT decaffeinate
AACDEEFHLMSY shamefacedly
AACDEEFINOST defaecations
AACDEEGHHINR headreaching
AACDEEGHLNNO hendecagonal
AACDEEIINQSU inadequacies
AACDEEILMMNT medicamental
AACDEEILNNOW New Caledonia
AACDEEILNNRS encarnalised
AACDEEILNNRZ encarnalized
AACDEEILNRTT intercalated
AACDEEIMNRTT readmittance
AACDEEINNRRT reincarnated
AACDEEINQRTU reacquainted
AACDEEIPRRTV prevaricated
AACDEELNPSTU encapsulated
AACDEELNRSTU adularescent
AACDEELPSSTU decapsulates
AACDEEMNNSTV advancements
AACDEFFHINRS affranchised
AACDEFILNOST defalcations
AACDEFILNSTY fascinatedly
AACDEFINORTT fractionated
AACDEFMNRTUU manufactured
AACDEGIILOPR cardioplegia
AACDEGIINNRT deracinating
AACDEGIINPTT decapitating
AACDEGIINTTV deactivating
AACDEGILLOOP paedological
AACDEGILMORY cardiomegaly
AACDEGINNPRS parascending
AACDEHIILOPP paedophiliac
AACDEHILLLRY heraldically
AACDEHILLNTU hallucinated
AACDEHIMNRTY diathermancy
AACDEHIMORST achromatised
AACDEHIMORTZ achromatized
AACDEHINORSY hyracoideans
AACDEHINOSTT anticathodes
AACDEHINPPRS handicappers
AACDEHLMOSUY achlamydeous
AACDEHLNOOPP cephalopodan
AACDEHLOPRRT procathedral
AACDEHLORRTT tetrachordal
AACDEHLORSTW Castle Howard
AACDEHMOORRS choreodramas
AACDEHNOPRTY hydnocarpate
AACDEHPRRRSS cardsharpers
AACDEIIINPRT pediatrician
AACDEIIIPRST parasiticide
AACDEIILNRTU clairaudient
AACDEIILRTVY divaricately
AACDEIINNNRS incarnadines
AACDEIINNORT deracination
AACDEIINNRST incardinates
AACDEIINOPTT decapitation

AACDEIINORST	eradications
AACDEIINORTT	ratiocinated
AACDEIINOTTV	deactivation
AACDEIIOSSST	disassociate
AACDEIIPPRTT	participated
AACDEIIPRSSU	parasuicides
AACDEILLMNOY	demoniacally
AACDEILLNOSW	disallowance
AACDEILLNPTY	pedantically
AACDEILMMORT	melodramatic
AACDEILMNOST	declamations
AACDEILMRTTU	matriculated
AACDEILNORST	declarations
AACDEILNOSTT	anecdotalist
AACDEILNPPRU	appendicular
AACDEILNPSTU	incapsulated
AACDEILNRSSS	scandalisers
AACDEILNRSSZ	scandalizers
AACDEIMNNOTT	contaminated
AACDEIMNORST	demarcations
AACDEIMNORSY	aerodynamics
AACDEIMOOSTU	diatomaceous
AACDEIMORRTV	overdramatic
AACDEINNOSSY	Ascension Day
AACDEINNQTUU	unacquainted
AACDEINOPSSU	sapindaceous
AACDEIOPRSTT	decapitators
AACDEIORSTTV	deactivators
AACDELLORSTY	sacerdotally
AACDELNORSTT	translocated
AACDELOPRSSU	pseudoscalar
AACDELORSUVY	cadaverously
AACDELRSTTTY	tetradactyls
AACDENORRSTW	narrowcasted
AACDFGHINNRT	handcrafting
AACDFIIILNNT	infanticidal
AACDFORRRRWY	carryforward
AACDGHIINNPP	handicapping
AACDGHIIOPRR	radiographic
AACDGHILNNRS	crashlanding
AACDGHINPRRS	cardsharping
AACDGHIOPRRS	cardiographs
AACDGHIOPRRY	cardiography
AACDGIIINRTV	divaricating
AACDGIILLOOR	radiological
AACDGIILLOOU	audiological
AACDGIILNNSS	scandalising
AACDGIILNNSZ	scandalizing
AACDGIILRSTU	gradualistic
AACDGILLMOTY	dogmatically
AACDGLMORSTY	dactylograms
AACDHHIKLLRW	Hardwick Hall
AACDHHILORRY	achlorhydria
AACDHIILLLNS	Achill Island
AACDHIILNPRS	cardinalship
AACDHIIOPRSS	aphrodisiacs
AACDHINOPQRU	quadraphonic
AACDHMOPRSSY	psychodramas
AACDIIINORTV	divarication
AACDIIJLORTU	judicatorial
AACDIILLLTYY	dialytically
AACDIILLNOTY	diatonically
AACDIILLSSTY	sadistically
AACDIILMNOST	disclamation
AACDIILNORTV	Victoria Land
AACDIIMNOPSS	dipsomaniacs
AACDIIMNRSTU	traducianism
AACDIINNORRT	doctrinarian
AACDIINNOSTY	cyanidations
AACDIINRSTTU	traducianist
AACDIIORRSTV	divaricators
AACDILLNORSY	sardonically
AACDILLNSTYY	dynastically
AACDILLOPRSY	sporadically
AACDILNOSSTY	anisodactyls
AACDILNPSSST	landscapists
AACDILORSTTY	artiodactyls
AACDIMMNOORT	monodramatic
AACDINNOOSTU	coadunations
AACDLLNOSSUY	scandalously
AACEEEFHLOPS	chapel of ease
AACEEEHLMNPT	metencephala
AACEEEHLMOST	haematoceles
AACEEFFINOTT	affectionate
AACEEFIMNSSS	misfeasances
AACEEFLMRSST	malefactress
AACEEGGILLNO	genealogical
AACEEGGIMNOT	agamogenetic
AACEEGHILLNR	Carnegie Hall
AACEEGHIMNOT	haematogenic
AACEEGHINORT	archegoniate
AACEEGHRRSST	gatecrashers
AACEEGILLNSV	evangelicals
AACEEGILNRRV	vicar general
AACEEGINORSU	geraniaceous
AACEEGLMORTT	galactometer
AACEEGMMORST	macrogametes
AACEEHHMPSTY	chamaephytes
AACEEHIILPRT	perichaetial
AACEEHIINSTT	aesthetician
AACEEHILMRTX	hexametrical
AACEEHILMTTT	metathetical
AACEEHIMNTTX	exanthematic
AACEEHINSSTT	anaesthetics
AACEEHINTTTU	authenticate
AACEEHIOPRST	apothecaries
AACEEHIPRSTT	paraesthetic
AACEEHLMNOPS	encephalomas
AACEEHLMPRST	spermathecal
AACEEHLMRTTY	methacrylate
AACEEHLNPTTU	pentateuchal
AACEEHMNRTTT	reattachment
AACEEHMORSTT	metathoraces
AACEEHNNPPST	happenstance
AACEEHRRSTTT	tetrarchates
AACEEIILPRST	recapitalise
AACEEIILPRTZ	recapitalize
AACEEIIMNPTV	emancipative
AACEEIINRSST	sectarianise
AACEEIINRSTZ	sectarianize
AACEEIIPPRTV	appreciative
AACEEILLMNSS	mesalliances
AACEEILMMMNY	mecamylamine
AACEEILMPPRS	preeclampsia

AACEEILMSTUV	emasculative
AACEEILNNRSS	encarnalises
AACEEILNNRSZ	encarnalizes
AACEEILNORRT	recreational
AACEEILNRSTT	intercalates
AACEEILPRTTU	recapitulate
AACEEIMMNORS	mesoamerican
AACEEINNNRST	centenarians
AACEEINNRRST	reincarnates
AACEEINNRSSS	necessarians
	renaissances
AACEEINPRSST	paracentesis
AACEEIOPRSTT	ectoparasite
AACEEIPRRSST	separatrices
AACEEIPRRSTV	prevaricates
AACEEIRRRRTW	Water Carrier
AACEEIRRSSTT	secretariats
AACEEKLMPRST	marketplaces
AACEELNPSSTU	encapsulates
AACEELNRRTUX	extranuclear
AACEELNRTTVY	tetravalency
AACEELRRSTUW	caterwaulers
AACEEMNORSTU	ramentaceous
AACEENNPPRTU	appurtenance
AACEENNPRRST	transparence
AACEENPRRSSU	preassurance
AACEENRRSSSU	reassurances
AACEFFHHNSSU	Schaffhausen
AACEFFHINRSS	affranchises
AACEFFIIRSTV	affricatives
AACEFFINOSTT	affectations
AACEFFMORTTT	matter of fact
AACEFGHINNRU	French Guiana
AACEFIIILTTV	facilitative
AACEFIIINORT	aerification
AACEFIINORRT	rarefication
AACEFIMNRRST	aircraftsmen
AACEFINORRST	rarefactions
AACEFINORSTT	fractionates
AACEFLNNORRT	confraternal
AACEFMNRRTUU	manufacturer
AACEFMNRSTUU	manufactures
AACEGGHILOPR	geographical
AACEGGHINRST	gatecrashing
AACEGGIKNPPR	prepackaging
AACEGHHIMORR	haemorrhagic
AACEGHHNOSTT	chaetognaths
AACEGHHPRRTY	tachygrapher
AACEGHIILPPR	epigraphical
AACEGHILLMPT	phlegmatical
AACEGHILLPRR	calligrapher
AACEGHILMOOT	haematologic
AACEGHILOPRS	archipelagos
AACEGHIMNOPR	anemographic
	phanerogamic
AACEGHIMOPTT	apothegmatic
AACEGHJKNNNU	Kanchenjunga
AACEGHLSSSTW	watchglasses
AACEGHNOOPRY	oceanography
AACEGHNORSTU	autochangers
AACEGHOPRRRT	cartographer
AACEGIIINRRT	geriatrician
AACEGIILLNNT	geanticlinal
AACEGIILLNRT	interglacial
AACEGIILLOOT	aetiological
AACEGIILMNNS	malignancies
AACEGIILMNRS	caramelising
AACEGIILMNRZ	caramelizing
AACEGIILNSTT	elasticating
AACEGIIMMPRT	epigrammatic
AACEGIIMNNPT	emancipating
AACEGIIMNNTT	antimagnetic
AACEGIIMRRSS	miscarriages
AACEGIIMRSST	magistracies
AACEGIINNRST	ascertaining
AACEGIINPPRT	appreciating
AACEGIINRTTV	reactivating
AACEGIKLNPSW	spacewalking
AACEGILLMNTY	magnetically
AACEGILLMSST	Glamis Castle
AACEGILLNORT	reallocating
AACEGILLNOSU	gallinaceous
AACEGILLOPSS	plagioclases
AACEGILLORSU	argillaceous
AACEGILLPRSU	superglacial
AACEGILMNSTU	emasculating
AACEGILMORST	gasometrical
AACEGILNNOTT	cotangential
AACEGILNOOSU	loganiaceous
AACEGILNRTUW	caterwauling
AACEGIMNORSU	graminaceous
AACEGIMNOSTY	gynecomastia
AACEGINNOORT	octogenarian
AACEGLMNOOPR	campanologer
AACEGLMORTTY	galactometry
AACEGLNOOPSV	galvanoscope
AACEGLNORTTU	congratulate
AACEHHIILMOP	haemophiliac
AACEHIILLPRS	Schiaparelli
AACEHIILLRTY	hieratically
AACEHIILMPRX	alexipharmic
AACEHIILMRTT	arithmetical
AACEHIILNPRS	chaplainries
AACEHIILNTTT	antithetical
AACEHIIMRRST	matriarchies
AACEHIINPTTT	antipathetic
AACEHIIPRRST	patriarchies
AACEHIIPRSST	parastichies
AACEHILLLTTY	athletically
AACEHILLMPTY	empathically
	emphatically
AACEHILLMTTY	thematically
AACEHILLNSTU	hallucinates
AACEHILLPRSY	seraphically
AACEHILLPTTY	pathetically
AACEHILLRTTY	theatrically
AACEHILMNPRU	alphanumeric
AACEHILMOPRS	semaphorical
AACEHILMOPRT	metaphorical
AACEHILMOTXY	haematoxylic
AACEHILMPSTY	metaphysical
AACEHILOPRRS	archesporial
AACEHILQRRSU	squirearchal
AACEHILRRSTU	chartularies

AACEHILRSTTT tetrastichal
AACEHIMNORRT North America
AACEHIMORSST achromatises
AACEHIMORSTT haematocrits
AACEHIMORSTU South America
AACEHIMORSTZ achromatizes
AACEHIMOSSTT haemostatics
AACEHIMPRSTT metaphrastic
AACEHINOSTTY thiocyanates
AACEHIOPRSST cataphoresis
AACEHLLPRTYY archetypally
AACEHMMNOORT chromonemata
AACEHMNNRSTU transhumance
AACEHOPRSSTT catastrophes
AACEHPRRRTTY charterparty
AACEIIINNRSV invariancies
AACEIIINPTTV anticipative
AACEIIKLLMRT alkalimetric
AACEIILLMNSS misalliances
AACEIILLMRTT altimetrical
AACEIILLNRST lacertilians
AACEIILLNRSV incarvilleas
AACEIILMNSTX anticlimaxes
AACEIILNOPPS episcopalian
AACEIILNOSTT elastication
AACEIILNPRTT antiparticle
AACEIILNRTTU inarticulate
AACEIILPRSTU capitularies
AACEIIMNNOPT emancipation
AACEIIMNORST racemisation
AACEIIMNORTZ racemization
AACEIIMNRSST sectarianism
AACEIIMNRSTU aneurismatic
AACEIIMNRSTV carminatives
AACEIINNNTUV annunciative
AACEIINOPPRT appreciation
AACEIINORSTT ratiocinates
AACEIINORTTV reactivation
AACEIINPRSTT pancreatitis
AACEIIOPRSTX exoparasitic
AACEIIPPRSTT participates
AACEIIPRSSTT separatistic
AACEIJKRSTTT straitjacket
AACEIJLLMSTY majestically
AACEIJLNOSTU ejaculations
AACEIJLRSSUU Julius Caesar
AACEIKLLSTTY Salt Lake City
AACEIKLMNOPT kleptomaniac
AACEIKNOPRRT Tarpeian Rock
AACEILLLLMTY metallically
AACEILLLLOPV valpolicella
AACEILLMMTUY immaculately
AACEILLMNRUY unicamerally
AACEILLMNSTY semantically
AACEILLNOORT reallocation
AACEILLNOSTT castellation
AACEILLNPTUY paniculately
AACEILLOPRTY operatically
AACEILLPRRST caterpillars
AACEILLRTTUY articulately
AACEILLRTUUY auriculately
AACEILLSTTUY eustatically
AACEILMMNORT commentarial
manometrical
AACEILMMRSTY asymmetrical
AACEILMNORST reclamations
AACEILMNOSTU emasculation
AACEILMNOSTX exclamations
AACEILMRSTTU matriculates
AACEILMSSTTY systematical
AACEILNNOPTT placentation
AACEILNNRRTU intranuclear
AACEILNOPRTU precautional
AACEILNORSTT altercations
AACEILNOSSTV vacationless
AACEILNPSSTU incapsulates
AACEILNSTTTW West Atlantic
AACEILPRSTTU particulates
AACEILRSTTTU straticulate
AACEILRTTTVY attractively
AACEILSTTUUV auscultative
AACEIMMNORTT commentariat
AACEIMNNOOPT companionate
AACEIMNNOSTT contaminates
AACEIMNOORST erotomaniacs
AACEIMNOPRST emancipators
AACEIMNOPRTY emancipatory
AACEIMNRSTUY aneurysmatic
AACEIMOPRSTV comparatives
AACEINNNORST nonsectarian
AACEINNORSTT recantations
AACEINORRTTT retractation
AACEINPQRSTU preacquaints
AACEINRTTTUV unattractive
AACEIOPPRRST appreciators
AACEIOPPRRTY appreciatory
AACEIOPRRRTV prevaricator
AACEJNNPRRTU Japan Current
AACEKLNOORRT Central Karoo
AACEKLQRSSUV quacksalvers
AACEKNNORSTU cantankerous
AACELLLLORTY collaterally
AACELLMOPSUU ampullaceous
AACELLNNOTVY covenantally
AACELLNRRUVY vernacularly
AACELLOQTTUZ Quetzalcoatl
AACELMNORSTW scarlet woman
AACELMORSSTU emasculators
AACELMORSTUY emasculatory
AACELNORSSTT translocates
AACELOOPPRSS laparoscopes
AACENNPRRSTY transparency
AACENORRSTVY contrayervas
AACFFHIMNNOR Rachmaninoff
AACFFHINOORR Horn of Africa
AACFFIORRSTT trafficators
AACFGGILMNOU camouflaging
AACFGIIILNTT facilitating
AACFGIIINNST fanaticising
AACFGIIINNTZ fanaticizing
AACFGIIINOST gasification
AACFGIILLMNY magnifically
AACFHINNORRT North African
AACFHINORSTU South African

AACFIIIILNRT inartificial
AACFIIILLRTY artificially
AACFIIILMORR microfilaria
AACFIIILNOST salification
AACFIIILNOTT facilitation
AACFIIIMNORT ramification
AACFIIINNOTZ nazification
AACFIIINORTT ratification
AACFIILMNOST factionalism
AACFIILNOOST focalisation
AACFIILNOOTZ focalization
AACFIILNOSTT factionalist
AACFIILORSTT facilitators
AACFIINOSSTT satisfaction
AACFIINSSSTT antifascists
AACFILLLOSUY fallaciously
AACFILLNORTY fractionally
AACFILMORSTT stalactiform
AACFINOORRTT fractionator
AACFIORRSTTT fractostrati
AACFIORSSTTY satisfactory
AACGGHHIIOPR hagiographic
AACGGHIILLOO hagiological
AACGGHIMNOTY gigantomachy
AACGGIILLNTY gigantically
AACGGILMOSTY mystagogical
AACGGINORSTU sugarcoating
AACGHHHIRSTT Chhattisgarh
AACGHHIKLMNS hamshackling
AACGHHOPRRTY chartography
AACGHIILNPST chaptalising
AACGHIILNPTZ chaptalizing
AACGHIKMMNRT matchmarking
AACGHILLNOOT anthological
AACGHILLOOPT pathological
AACGHILNOPPR planographic
AACGHILOOPRZ zoographical
AACGHIMNOPRT camphorating
AACGHIMRTTUU thaumaturgic
AACGHINOPPRT pantographic
AACGHINOPRRU uranographic
AACGHLMOOPRY pharmacology
AACGHLMOORSU chaulmoogras
AACGHMMOORRT chromatogram
AACGHMMOOSSU chasmogamous
AACGHMOOPRSU macrophagous
AACGHNOOPRRS coronagraphs
AACGHOOPPRSU carpophagous
AACGIIILNPST capitalising
AACGIIILNPTZ capitalizing
AACGIIILPRST plagiaristic
AACGIIINNPTT anticipating
AACGIIINNTTV inactivating
vaticinating
AACGIILLMOPX plagioclimax
AACGIILLNNTT cantillating
AACGIILMNNTU calumniating
AACGIILNPTTU capitulating
AACGIILNRTTU articulating
AACGIILOPRST paralogistic
AACGIIMPRSTT pragmatistic
AACGIINNNNTU annunciating
AACGIINNOPRS caparisoning
AACGIINNOSTT antagonistic
AACGIINNRSST incrassating
AACGIINOSSTT castigations
AACGILLMOOST malacologist
AACGILLOOPRT patrological
AACGILLOORST astrological
AACGILLOOTTU tautological
AACGILLPRSYY spagyrically
AACGILLRRTUU agricultural
AACGILNOOSTU coagulations
AACGILNSTTUU auscultating
AACGILOSSTTU cataloguists
AACGIMMOPRRT programmatic
AACGLMOOSTUU glaucomatous
AACGLNOOPSVY galvanoscopy
AACHHIILNPPS chaplainship
AACHHIIMNPRS chairmanship
AACHHILMOPTY hypothalamic
AACHHLNOOTTU autochthonal
AACHIILMOPRS parochialism
AACHIILOPRTY parochiality
AACHIILPRSTY physiatrical
AACHIIMNNOST machinations
AACHIINPPSST captainships
AACHIINRSSSU saurischians
AACHIKLMOOTY Oklahoma City
AACHIKORSTUW autorickshaw
AACHILLMNORY harmonically
AACHILLMOPSY hyaloplasmic
AACHILLNORTU hallucinator
AACHILMNOOPT taphonomical
AACHILOPSTTY hypostatical
AACHIMMNNOPY nymphomaniac
AACHIMMNOSTY mythomaniacs
AACHIMNNORSS anachronisms
AACHIMNOPRRS parachronism
AACHINOPRTTU naturopathic
AACHIOPRSSTU parastichous
AACHIPRSSTTU parachutists
AACHKMOORRSZ Ockham's razor
AACHLLNNNOTY nonchalantly
AACHLLOPPRYY apocryphally
AACHLMORRSTY lachrymators
AACHLMORRTYY lachrymatory
AACHMOORSTTU trachomatous
AACIIILNNORT anticlinoria
AACIIILNNOST laciniations
AACIIILNOSST laicisations
AACIIILNOSTZ laicizations
AACIIINNOPTT anticipation
AACIIINNOTTV inactivation
vaticination
AACIIINNRSSU uncinariasis
AACIIINSSTTT statistician
AACIIJNOSTTT jactitations
AACIILLMNOSY simoniacally
AACIILLMOTTY amitotically
AACIILLNNOTT cantillation
AACIILLNOOST localisation
AACIILLNOOTZ localization
AACIILLNOSTV vacillations

AACIILLNOSTY antisocially
AACIILLORSTY aoristically
AACIILLRSTTY artistically
AACIILMMORSS commissarial
AACIILMNNOTU calumniation
AACIILMNORST lacrimations
AACIILNNNOST lancinations
AACIILNNOOTV invocational
AACIILNOOSTV vocalisation
AACIILNOOTVZ vocalization
AACIILNOPPST applications
AACIILNOPTTU capitulation
AACIILNORTTU articulation
AACIILNRSTTU naturalistic
AACIILORSUVY avariciously
AACIIMMORSST commissariat
AACIIMNNORST animatronics
AACIIMNNOSTU acuminations
AACIIMNOSSTT mastications
AACIIMOTTTUY automaticity
AACIINNNNOTU annunciation
AACIINNNOOST canonisation
AACIINNNOOTZ canonization
AACIINNNORST incarnations
AACIINNNOSTT incantations
AACIINNOPRST nonparasitic
AACIINNORSST incrassation
AACIINOORRTT ratiocinator
AACIINOOSSST associations
AACIINOPRSTT anticipators
AACIINOPRTTY anticipatory
AACIINOPSTTV captivations
AACIINORRSTU curarisation
AACIINORRTUZ curarization
AACIINORSTTV vaticinators
AACIINORTTVY vaticinatory
AACIINOSSTTV vacationists
AACIINPPRSTT participants
AACIIOORSSTX toxocariasis
AACIIOPPRRTT participator
AACIKLMOPRSY karyoplasmic
AACIKLOPRTYY karyotypical
AACILLLMORTY matrilocally
AACILLLNOPTY platonically
AACILLLOPRTY patrilocally
AACILLMNORTY romantically
AACILLMNOSTY monastically
AACILLMOSTUY calamitously
AACILLNNRTYY tyrannically
AACILLNOOTVY vocationally
AACILLNOPPTY panoptically
AACILLNOPRSS rapscallions
AACILLNPSTYY synaptically
AACILLOORRTY oratorically
AACILLPRRTUY particularly
AACILLQRTUUU aquicultural
AACILMNNOPST complainants
AACILMNOOPRT proclamation
AACILMNOORST astronomical
AACILMNORSTU calumniators
AACILMNORSTY microanalyst
AACILMNORTUY calumniatory
AACILMNRSTTU matriculants
AACILMOPSTTY asymptotical
AACILMORRTTU matriculator
AACILNNNOSTU cannulations
AACILNOOSTUV vacuolations
AACILNOPSSTU capsulations
AACILNORSTVY clairvoyants
AACILNOSTTUU auscultation
AACILOPRSTTU capitulators
AACILOPRTTUY capitulatory
AACILORRSTTU articulators
AACILORRTTUY articulatory
AACIMMOPSTTY asymptomatic
AACIMNNNOSTT contaminants
AACIMNNOOPWY companionway
AACIMNNOORTT contaminator
AACIMNNOOSTT antonomastic
AACIMNNOOTTU nonautomatic
AACIMNOOPRST paronomastic
AACIMOORSSST sarcomatosis
AACINNNORSTU annunciators
AACINNNORTUY annunciatory
AACINNOOSTTT constatation
AACINNORSSTT transactions
AACINORSSTTU astronautics
AACLLNNORTUY connaturally
AACLMOOPRRTY proclamatory
AACLNNOPRTTU contrapuntal
AACLNPRSTTYY cryptanalyst
AACLORSSTTUU auscultators
AACLORSTTUUY auscultatory
AACMOOPRSSST astrocompass
AADDDDEGINRS granddaddies
AADDDEEHHLRY hardheadedly
AADDDEGNNRST grandstanded
AADDDEILRRST tarradiddles
AADDDEINRSST standardised
AADDDEINRSTZ standardized
AADDEEEHHMMR hammerheaded
AADDEEHHRTXY hexahydrated
AADDEEHNRSVZ Shevardnadze
AADDEEHNSSWY Ash Wednesday
AADDEEILOPRT Port Adelaide
AADDEEIMNRTV animadverted
AADDEFINORTU defraudation
AADDEGHNRSTU dreadnaughts
AADDEGINORST degradations
AADDEGNNRRST grandstander
AADDEINRRSST standardiser
AADDEINRRSTZ standardizer
AADDEINRSSST standardises
AADDEINRSSTZ standardizes
AADDELNOORTV Volta Redonda
AADDENNSTUVY Advent Sunday
AADDGGINNNOR dragonnading
AADDGHINNRST hardstanding
AADDGIIILNPT dilapidating
AADDGIMNRRTU Martin du Gard
AADDHIILORRT diarthrodial
AADDIIILNOPT dilapidation
AADDIILLNOTY additionally
AADDIILOPRST dilapidators

AADDILNNSSSU Sunda Islands
AADDINNRRUUU Ruanda-Urundi
AADEEEFHHRST featherheads
AADEEEGHLRRT largehearted
AADEEEGHRRTT greathearted
AADEEEGLNNRS Greenland Sea
AADEEEGMMNNT endamagement
AADEEEHHLRST leatherheads
AADEEEHHRTVY heavyhearted
AADEEELNNRWZ New Zealander
AADEEFHINRTT fainthearted
AADEEFLNRSST East Flanders
AADEEGGGIRST disaggregate
AADEEGGLMORT agglomerated
AADEEGHHMORR haemorrhaged
AADEEGHILNTT Tintagel Head
AADEEGHINPRS spearheading
AADEEGILRSTV Elisavetgrad
AADEEGINRSTU aguardientes
AADEEGJMNORU Judaeo-German
AADEEGLPPRSS glasspapered
AADEEHILNQRU harlequinade
AADEEHIMNOTZ diazomethane
AADEEHIMNPTT amphidentate
AADEEHLMRSTY headmasterly
AADEEHLNNRST neanderthals
AADEEHOPRRTZ trapezohedra
AADEEHQRRSTU headquarters
AADEEIIILNRX Alexander III
AADEEIILMMSV mediaevalism
AADEEIILMRST materialised
AADEEIILMRTZ materialized
AADEEIILMSTV mediaevalist
AADEEIILRRST arterialised
AADEEIILRRTZ arterialized
AADEEIIMNNRT antemeridian
AADEEIKNORRT Ekaterinodar
AADEEILLNTUV unalleviated
AADEEILMMORT material mode
AADEEILMMPST semipalmated
AADEEILNNRSX alexandrines
AADEEILNQTUY inadequately
AADEEILNRSST Easter Island
AADEEILNRSTU denaturalise
AADEEILNRTUZ denaturalize
AADEEIMMNNRR remainderman
AADEEIMMNNST misdemeanant
AADEEIMSSSTT metastasised
AADEEIMSSTTZ metastasized
AADEEINOPRST endoparasite
AADEEINOPRTU deuteranopia
AADEEINORSST asteroideans
AADEEIRSSTVV adversatives
AADEELLLNPRU unparalleled
AADEELLNSTTU landaulettes
AADEELMNPRTT departmental
AADEELNRRSTT retranslated
AADEELOPRTTX extrapolated
AADEEMMNRSTW New Amsterdam
AADEEMNNRTUX extramundane
AADEEMNPRRST dermapterans
AADEEMQRRSSU masqueraders
AADEEQRRSTUW quartersawed
AADEFFIIILST disaffiliate
AADEFFIILNTU unaffiliated
AADEFGGILNRT deflagrating
AADEFGGINRSU safeguarding
AADEFGHNRRST grandfathers
AADEFGILNORT deflagration
AADEFHINNOTU fountainhead
AADEFIIILMRS familiarised
AADEFIIILMRZ familiarized
AADEFIILNSUZ sulfadiazine
AADEFILMORTY defamatorily
AADEFILNORTY deflationary
AADEFILNTTUY infatuatedly
AADEGGILNNRR Darling Range
AADEGGILNTTU agglutinated
AADEGGINRRSS aggrandisers
AADEGGINRRSZ aggrandizers
AADEGHILNORU Dún Laoghaire
AADEGHIMMORX hexagrammoid
AADEGHINNRVY Vindhya Range
AADEGHIOPRRR radiographer
AADEGHNOPRRY parahydrogen
AADEGIILMNNT delaminating
AADEGIILMNRS marginalised
AADEGIILMNRZ marginalized
AADEGIILNNST desalinating
AADEGIILPQRU quadriplegia
AADEGIIMMNST diamagnetism
AADEGIINPPRS disappearing
AADEGIKMNRRT trademarking
AADEGILMNSSU salmagundies
AADEGILNNRSV landgravines
AADEGILNPRST plantigrades
AADEGILNRTTU adulterating
triangulated
AADEGIMNNRRT darraignment
AADEGIMNQRSU masquerading
AADEGIMNQSTU desquamating
AADEGINNPPRS sandpapering
AADEGINOPPRS propagandise
AADEGINOPPRZ propagandize
AADEGLNRSTTU strangulated
AADEGMMNORSS Grandma Moses
AADEGMNRRSST grandmasters
AADEGNNPRRST grandparents
AADEGOPRSTTU postgraduate
AADEHHIILLPP Philadelphia
AADEHIKLMORY holidaymaker
AADEHILMNPRS aldermanship
AADEHILNORRT enarthrodial
AADEHINOPRST Herod Antipas
AADEHIOPRRTY radiotherapy
AADEHMNNRSTT Hermannstadt
AADEHPRRSTTU Uttar Pradesh
AADEIIILNOST idealisation
AADEIIILNOTZ idealization
AADEIILLNUVV vaudevillian
AADEIILMNNOT delamination
AADEIILNNOST desalination
nationalised
AADEIILNNOTZ nationalized

AADEIILNNTUV antediluvian
AADEIILNORST rationalised
AADEIILNORTV derivational
AADEIILNORTZ rationalized
AADEIILNRSTT interstadial
AADEIILRRTTY triradiately
AADEIIMNNOST deaminations
AADEIIMNRSTT administrate
AADEIINNSTTT instantiated
AADEIJKLRRSS rijksdaalers
AADEIKMNORST demarkations
AADEILNNNORR noradrenalin
AADEILNNORST Saint Leonard
AADEILNNQRSU quadrennials
AADEILNNSSTT Staten Island
AADEILNORTTU adulteration
AADEILNOSTUV devaluations
AADEILNQRTUV quadrivalent
AADEILNRTUVY valetudinary
AADEILORRSTV advertorials
AADEIMMNRSST disarmaments
AADEIMNOQSTU desquamation
AADEIMNRSSTV maidservants
AADEIMOPPRTX approximated
AADEIMPRRSTY tryparsamide
AADEINNORTTU denaturation
AADEINNRSSTW Saint Andrews
AADEINOPRSTV depravations
AADEINORRSTT retardations
AADEINORSSTT Soenda Strait
AADEINORSTTU desaturation
AADEINOSSTTV devastations
AADEINPQRSSU pasquinaders
AADEIOPPPRRT appropriated
AADELMNNRTUU ultramundane
AADELNNPRSTT transplanted
AADELNNRSTTU untranslated
AADELNOPRSSU San Pedro Sula
AADELORRSTTU adulterators
AADEMNNNRSTU transmundane
AADEMNNOOTTU nonautomated
AADENPRSSTTT standpatters
AADFGHINNSST handfastings
AADFILNNOOTU foundational
AADGGGIINNRS aggrandising
AADGGGIINNRZ aggrandizing
AADGGIINNRRS disarranging
AADGGILMMNOR Mid Glamorgan
AADGGJNNNPUU Ujung Pandang
AADGHHOPRSSW shadowgraphs
AADGHIINPRSU guardianship
AADGIIILNNTV invalidating
AADGIIIMNPRS imparadising
AADGIIIMPRRV primigravida
AADGIILMRSST madrigalists
AADGIILMRTUV multigravida
AADGIILQRUUV Guadalquivir
AADGIINNNPST sandpainting
AADGIINNPQSU pasquinading
AADGILLNPPUY applaudingly
AADGIMNOPPRS propagandism
AADGIMRRSTTU dramaturgist
AADGINOORSTY Rogation Days
AADGINOPPRST propagandist
AADHIIKNSTTZ Tadzhikistan
AADHIILMPRSS admiralships
AADHIILOPPSY diapophysial
AADHIIMOPRSS adiaphorisms
AADHIIOPRSST adiaphorists
AADHILNOOPRT anthropoidal
AADHILNOPSUY diaphanously
AADHIOPRRSTY parathyroids
AADHJKLMMORS Hammarskjöld
AADHKNNOORTT North Dakotan
AADHKNOOSTTU South Dakotan
AADHLORSTUYY Holy Saturday
AADHNNOORSUZ nonhazardous
AADIIILNNOPS Indianapolis
AADIIILNNOTV invalidation
AADIIINORRST irradiations
AADIIKLMNNSU Unimak Island
AADIIKNNRSST Kristiansand
AADIIKNRSSTT Kristianstad
AADIILMNOQRU quadrinomial
AADIILMOPRST prismatoidal
AADIILNOOSTV vasodilation
AADIILNORSTV invalidators
AADIINNOSTTX antioxidants
AADIINOOTTUX autoxidation
AADILLMNOOST amontillados
AADILNOPPRST postprandial
AADILOORSSTV vasodilators
AADINNORSTTU transudation
AADLMNNORUWY laundrywoman
AADLOOOPPPSU Papadopoulos
AADMNOQRSUUU quadrumanous
AADNORRSTTUY transudatory
AAEEEGGIRTVX exaggerative
AAEEEGMNRSSS manageresses
AAEEEHILRTTY aethereality
AAEEEHILSSTT telaesthesia
AAEEEHIMMSST haematemesis
AAEEEHINSSTT anaesthetise
AAEEEHINSTTZ anaesthetize
AAEEEILPRSTT tapsalteerie
AAEEEMNPPSST appeasements
AAEEENPRSSST separateness
AAEEEPRRSSTX exasperaters
AAEEFHMRRRSS sharefarmers
AAEEFNRRSSST transferases
AAEEGGGINRTX exaggerating
AAEEGGIMNOSS agamogenesis
AAEEGGINNRTU guaranteeing
AAEEGGINORTX exaggeration
AAEEGGLMORST agglomerates
AAEEGGORRSTX exaggerators
AAEEGGORRTXY exaggeratory
AAEEGHHMORRS haemorrhages
AAEEGHLMOPTY hepatomegaly
AAEEGHLRSSTW weatherglass
AAEEGHNNORTU Haute-Garonne
AAEEGHNPPRRS paperhangers
AAEEGHNRSSTT Eastern Ghats
AAEEGILLLNSS selaginellas

AAEEGILLNNST gentianellas
AAEEGILMNRTY emarginately
AAEEGILMSSSX sexagesimals
AAEEGILNNORT generational
AAEEGILNOTTV vegetational
AAEEGILNRTUV reevaluating
AAEEGIMNTTUV augmentative
AAEEGIMPSSTU Septuagesima
AAEEGINNORSW Norwegian Sea
AAEEGINNSTUX exsanguinate
AAEEGINPRSTX exasperating
AAEEGINRSSTV asseverating
AAEEGLMNOPST planogametes
AAEEGLMNORTV galvanometer
AAEEGMNNRRST arrangements
AAEEGMNOPRST pomegranates
AAEEGMNSSSTU assuagements
AAEEHHIMPRTT amphitheater
amphitheatre
AAEEHHIPSSTY hypaesthesia
AAEEHHMNRSTW whatshername
AAEEHIIKNSST kinaesthesia
AAEEHIILRTVX exhilarative
AAEEHIIMPRST hemiparasite
AAEEHILPRSTU laureateship
AAEEHIMMNPST amphetamines
AAEEHIMNNPRS arsphenamine
AAEEHIMNRSTT metatherians
AAEEHIMOSSST somaesthesia
AAEEHINNRSTU neurasthenia
AAEEHINSSSTY synaesthesia
AAEEHINSSTTT anaesthetist
AAEEHIPRSSST paresthesias
AAEEHIRRSSTY East Ayrshire
AAEEHKMORRTT katharometer
AAEEHLMOSSTY haematolyses
AAEEHMNORSUW warehouseman
AAEEHMORSTTX metathoraxes
AAEEHOORRSTT steatorrhoea
AAEEIILLRSTT lateralities
AAEEIILLRTTV alliterative
AAEEIILMNRSV naive realism
AAEEIILMNTTV alimentative
AAEEIILMORTV ameliorative
AAEEIILMRRST materialiser
AAEEIILMRRTZ materializer
AAEEIILMRSST materialises
AAEEIILMRSTZ materializes
AAEEIILRRSST arterialises
AAEEIILRRSTZ arterializes
AAEEIIMPRSST semiparasite
AAEEIINNRRTV veterinarian
AAEEIINRSSSV sansevierias
AAEEIIRRSTXX Artaxerxes II
AAEEIKLLMRST alkalimeters
AAEEIKNRRTTU Neturei Karta
AAEEILLMNPST planetesimal
AAEEILLNORTV revelational
AAEEILLPPSTV appellatives
AAEEILLPRSTT septilateral
AAEEILLQRSTU equilaterals
AAEEILMNRSST materialness
AAEEILMORRST alstroemeria
AAEEILNNORTV venerational
AAEEILNORTUV reevaluation
AAEEILNPRSST pleasantries
AAEEILNRSTTV alternatives
AAEEILPRSTVY separatively
AAEEILQRSSTU sesquialtera
AAEEIMNORRRS Sierra Morena
AAEEIMNPPRST appraisement
AAEEIMSSSSTT metastasises
AAEEIMSSSTTZ metastasizes
AAEEINOPRSTX exasperation
AAEEINORSSTV asseveration
AAEEINQRRSTU quaternaries
AAEEIOPRSSTX exoparasites
AAEEIPPRRSTV preparatives
AAEEJKMMNRTZ katzenjammer
AAEEKLNRSSTT rattlesnakes
AAEELLMNSTTT mantellettas
AAEELLNOSTVY Seaton Valley
AAEELLNPRRTY parenterally
AAEELMMNRTTT maltreatment
AAEELMNPRSST malapertness
AAEELNNOSSSS seasonalness
AAEELNNPSSST pleasantness
AAEELNRRSSTT retranslates
AAEELOPRSTTX extrapolates
AAEEMNNPPRSW newspaperman
AAEEMNORSSTW Western Samoa
AAEEMNORSTUX auxanometers
AAEEMNRSTTTY testamentary
AAEEMQRSSSTU marquessates
AAEENNPPRSST apparentness
AAEENNPRSTUU superannuate
AAEEPRRSSTTY state prayers
AAEERRRSTTUU restaurateur
AAEFFIIMRSTV affirmatives
AAEFFILLNSTU affluentials
AAEFFQRRSTTU quarterstaff
AAEFGGILLLNT flagellating
AAEFGHILNRST farthingales
AAEFGHLLNNPR flannelgraph
AAEFGIKLNNRR farnarkeling
AAEFGILLLNOT flagellation
AAEFGINNORTT engraftation
AAEFGLLLORST flagellators
AAEFGLLMNRTY fragmentally
AAEFGLNNRSST flagrantness
AAEFHILLLSTV Festival Hall
AAEFIIILMRRS familiariser
AAEFIIILMRRZ familiarizer
AAEFIIILMRSS familiarises
AAEFIIILMRSZ familiarizes
AAEFIILMNRSS familiarness
AAEFIILMORRV overfamiliar
AAEFIILMPSST fissipalmate
AAEFIILOPRTV parvifoliate
AAEFILMNRRST fraternalism
AAEFILNQRRTU quarterfinal
AAEFILOPRTTU fluorapatite
AAEFILORSSTY forestaysail
AAEFLLLNSSTY Stanley Falls

AAEGGGINORST	aggregations
AAEGGHHIOPRR	hagiographer
AAEGGHILNNOT	halogenating
AAEGGHINNPPR	paperhanging
AAEGGHMNOPRT	magnetograph
AAEGGILNSTTU	agglutinates
AAEGGIMNNORV	overmanaging
AAEGGINNPRRR	prearranging
AAEGGIOPPRTU	appoggiature
AAEGGLLLOSSS	galloglasses
AAEGHHIKNRST	earthshaking
AAEGHHOPPRRS	phraseograph
AAEGHIILNRTX	exhilarating
AAEGHILNNOOT	halogenation
AAEGHIMMNPSS	gamesmanship
AAEGHIMMNSTT	metagnathism
AAEGHIMNPRST	metaphrasing
AAEGHIMNRRTW	heartwarming
AAEGHIMORRRT	metrorrhagia
AAEGHIOPRSTU	autographies
AAEGHLMNRSTU	manslaughter
	slaughterman
AAEGHMNOSTTU	metagnathous
AAEGHMOPRRSS	phraseograms
AAEGHMRSTTUU	thaumaturges
AAEGHNOPPRRT	pantographer
AAEGHNOPRRRU	uranographer
AAEGHNPRRSST	straphangers
AAEGIILLNOST	legalisation
AAEGIILLNOTZ	legalization
AAEGIILLNRTT	alliterating
AAEGIILMNORT	ameliorating
AAEGIILMNRSS	marginalises
AAEGIILMNRSZ	marginalizes
AAEGIILNRSTU	angularities
AAEGIILPRRSS	plagiarisers
AAEGIILPRRSZ	plagiarizers
AAEGIIMMRRSS	mismarriages
AAEGIIMNNORT	emargination
AAEGIINNOSTV	evaginations
AAEGIINNPPRT	appertaining
AAEGIINORSTV	variegations
AAEGIINPPRRS	reappraising
AAEGIINPRRTT	repatriating
AAEGIINPRTTX	expatriating
AAEGIKMNRRTW	watermarking
AAEGILLNNTTY	tangentially
AAEGILLNPPRW	wallpapering
AAEGILMNOORR	oleomargarin
AAEGILNPRSSV	palsgravines
AAEGILNRSTTU	triangulates
AAEGIMNNOTTU	augmentation
AAEGIMNNRRST	arraignments
AAEGIMNNSTTU	antimutagens
AAEGIMNRRSTT	transmigrate
AAEGIMRRSTTU	magistrature
AAEGLLNORTTY	tetragonally
AAEGLLNRSUXY	sexangularly
AAEGLLOPRSTY	pyrogallates
AAEGLMNORTVY	galvanometry
AAEGLMOOPSSU	gamosepalous
AAEGLMOOPSTU	gamopetalous
AAEGLMOPRSST	ergastoplasm
AAEGLMOPRSUY	rampageously
AAEGLNRSSTTU	strangulates
AAEGORRRSSSW	arrowgrasses
AAEHHILMOPTX	exophthalmia
AAEHHIMNSSTW	whatshisname
AAEHHLORSSTT	throatlashes
AAEHHOPPSSST	phosphatases
AAEHIIILNNTV	annihilative
AAEHIILMMPTU	epithalamium
AAEHIILMNOPT	epithalamion
AAEHIILNORTX	exhilaration
AAEHIINOPRTZ	azathioprine
AAEHIKNOSTTV	stakhanovite
AAEHILLMORSV	Villahermosa
AAEHILMNOTXY	haematoxylin
AAEHILMNPSSS	salesmanship
AAEHILMOSSTY	haematolysis
AAEHILMRSTUY	amateurishly
AAEHILNNOSST	Thessalonian
AAEHILORRSTX	exhilarators
AAEHILORRTXY	exhilaratory
AAEHILPPPSST	slaphappiest
AAEHILPPRSTY	hyperspatial
AAEHIMNOPPRR	paramorphine
AAEHIMNPRSTW	watermanship
AAEHIMNSSTTW	whatsitsname
AAEHIMPRSTTW	Matthew Paris
AAEHINOPRSST	Aristophanes
AAEHINRSSTUV	hantaviruses
AAEHLLMOPRSX	morphallaxes
AAEHLMNOOTXY	haematoxylon
AAEHMNOOPRRT	parathormone
AAEHMNOOPRSS	anamorphoses
AAEHMOORSTTU	atheromatous
AAEHMOPRSSTY	massotherapy
AAEHMOPRSTTU	thaumatropes
AAEIIILMSSTV	assimilative
AAEIIILNNNTV	Valentinian I
AAEIIILPRSTT	partialities
AAEIILLLPTVY	palliatively
AAEIILLMMRTY	immaterially
AAEIILLMNNRS	millenarians
AAEIILLNORTT	alliteration
AAEIILLNOSTV	alleviations
AAEIILLNPSTY	sapientially
AAEIILMMNNTT	milatainment
AAEIILMMPRST	Maritime Alps
AAEIILMNNOTT	alimentation
AAEIILMNNRRT	interlaminar
AAEIILMNOORT	amelioration
AAEIILMNOTTZ	metalization
AAEIILMNPTUV	manipulative
AAEIILMOPRRT	imperatorial
AAEIILMRSSTT	materialists
AAEIILMRTTUV	multivariate
AAEIILNNOPST	penalisation
AAEIILNNOPTZ	penalization
AAEIILNNOSST	nationalises
AAEIILNNOSTZ	nationalizes
AAEIILNOQSTU	equalisation
AAEIILNOQTUZ	equalization

AAEIILNORRST	rationaliser
AAEIILNORRTZ	rationalizer
AAEIILNORSST	rationalises
	realisations
AAEIILNORSTT	Aristotelian
	retaliations
AAEIILNORSTV	velarisation
AAEIILNORSTZ	rationalizes
	realizations
AAEIILNORTVZ	velarization
AAEIILNPRSTT	interspatial
AAEIILPPRSVY	appraisively
AAEIIMNNORST	reanimations
AAEIIMNNOSTX	examinations
	exanimations
AAEIIMNOSSTV	avitaminoses
AAEIINNOSTTT	tetanisation
AAEIINNOTTTZ	tetanization
AAEIINNRSSST	sanitariness
AAEIINNSSTTT	instantiates
AAEIINOPRRTT	repatriation
AAEIINOPRTTX	expatriation
AAEIINOPSTTX	expatiations
AAEIINQTTTUV	quantitative
AAEIKNPSSTTW	West Pakistan
AAEILLLMNOST	lamellations
AAEILLLMRTTU	multilateral
AAEILLLNRTUY	unilaterally
AAEILLLOOPSS	soapolallies
AAEILLLPRSST	parallelists
AAEILLLRRTTY	trilaterally
AAEILLMNNSUY	semiannually
AAEILLMNRRTY	artilleryman
AAEILLMNRSUY	aneurismally
AAEILLMPRRXY	premaxillary
AAEILLNNNOTW	Antonine Wall
AAEILLNOOSTV	alveolations
AAEILLNOPPST	appellations
AAEILLNOQTUY	equationally
AAEILLNORSTY	senatorially
AAEILLNSSTTU	Saint Austell
AAEILLNSWWYZ	Wislany Zalew
AAEILLOQRTUY	equatorially
AAEILLQRSSTU	aquarellists
AAEILMNNOSTT	lamentations
AAEILMNORSTV	malversation
AAEILMNPRSTU	planetariums
AAEILMNRRSTU	ultramarines
AAEILMNRSSTT	mistranslate
AAEILMOOPRST	laparotomies
AAEILMOORRST	amelioraters
AAEILNNNPSVY	Pennsylvania
AAEILNNOPRTT	replantation
AAEILNNOPSTX	explanations
AAEILNNOPTTX	explantation
AAEILNNORSST	rationalness
AAEILNNORSTT	alternations
AAEILNNPRSST	transalpines
AAEILNNRSTTU	Saint Laurent
	Saint-Laurent
AAEILNOPRRST	proletarians
AAEILNOPSSTY	passionately
AAEILNORSTUV	revaluations
AAEILNPRSSTT	paternalists
AAEILNQRRTTU	Latin Quarter
AAEILNRRSSTU	sertularians
AAEILNRSSSTU	salutariness
AAEILOPRRSTT	proletariats
AAEILORRSTUW	Lower Austria
AAEIMMMOSSTT	metasomatism
AAEIMMNOOPST	Mesopotamian
AAEIMNOOOOPT	onomatopoeia
AAEIMNOPTUUW	Te Waipounamu
AAEIMOPPRSTX	approximates
AAEINNOPRSTT	trepanations
AAEINNOPRSXY	expansionary
AAEINNORSSTU	Austronesian
AAEINNOSTTTU	attenuations
AAEINOOPRSTV	evaporations
AAEINOPPRRST	preparations
AAEINORRSSTT	arrestations
AAEINOSSTTTT	attestations
AAEINPRSSSTU	East Prussian
AAEIOPPPRRST	appropriates
AAEIPPRRSTUU	Upper Austria
AAEKLMNNORTU	nomenklatura
AAEKLOPRSTTY	keratoplasty
AAELLMNNORTY	ornamentally
AAELLMNRSUYY	aneurysmally
AAELLMRRTUXY	extramurally
AAELLNNPSTUY	unpleasantly
AAELLORRSSTT	stellarators
AAELLORSSSUU	allosauruses
AAELMNNNORTU	unornamental
AAELMNNORTTU	ultramontane
AAELMNOOPRTT	protonematal
AAELMOOPRSTZ	spermatozoal
AAELNNPRRSTT	transplanter
AAELNOOPPRSS	aplanospores
AAELNPRRSTUU	supernatural
AAELNRRSSSTV	transversals
AAELNRRSSTUV	transvaluers
AAELNRSSSTTW	stalwartness
AAELNRSSSTUX	transsexuals
AAELOOPRRTTX	extrapolator
AAEMNNNORSTT	transmontane
AAEMNNOORTUY	neuroanatomy
AAEMNNOPRSST	Montparnasse
AAEMNOOPRSTZ	spermatozoan
AAEMNOPRSTTU	portmanteaus
AAEMNOPRTTUX	portmanteaux
AAEMORSSSTTT	toastmasters
AAENNPPRSTTU	appurtenants
AAEOOPPRRRST	paratroopers
AAFFIIILNOST	affiliations
AAFFIIMNORST	affirmations
AAFGIINNORTT	ingraftation
AAFGIKLMNNOR	frankalmoign
AAFHHLMNNOST	Hofmannsthal
AAFIIILNNOST	finalisation
AAFIIILNNOTZ	finalization
AAFIIILNRTTU	futilitarian
AAFIILLMNRUY	unfamiliarly
AAFIILMMNNOT	inflammation

AAFIILNNORTY	inflationary
AAFIINNOSTTU	infatuations
AAFILMMNOORT	malformation
AAFILMMNORTY	inflammatory
AAFILNNORTTU	Fantin-Latour
AAGGGGILLLNY	lallygagging
AAGGHINNPRST	straphanging
AAGGHINOPRTU	autographing
AAGGHNOOPRRY	organography
AAGGIIILNPRS	plagiarising
AAGGIIILNPRZ	plagiarizing
AAGGIIINNNTV	invaginating
AAGGIIINNRTT	ingratiating
AAGGIIKLLNSS	galligaskins
AAGGIILLNNTV	gallivanting
AAGGIIMNNRRS	misarranging
AAGGIINNNOST	antagonising
AAGGIINNNOTZ	antagonizing
AAGGIINNRTUU	inaugurating
AAGGIKLLNSSY	gallygaskins
AAGGILLMORRS	gorillagrams
AAGGILLNOSST	algolagnists
AAGGLMMOORTY	grammatology
AAGHHIIJNSUZ	Shijiazhuang
AAGHHOPRRRTY	arthrography
AAGHIIILNNNT	annihilating
AAGHIINPSTXY	asphyxiating
AAGHILMOORTY	hamartiology
AAGHILOORSTU	hagiolatrous
AAGHIPRRSTTY	stratigraphy
AAGHLMOOTTUY	thaumatology
AAGHLOOPPRRS	polarographs
AAGHLOOPPRRY	polarography
AAGHOOPPRSSU	saprophagous
AAGIIIILNNST	italianising
AAGIIIILNNTZ	italianizing
AAGIIILMNSST	assimilating
AAGIIILNNSTV	insalivating
AAGIIILNORRT	irrigational
AAGIIIMNNOPR	Parmigianino
AAGIIIMNNOST	imaginations
AAGIIINNNOTV	invagination
AAGIIINNORTT	ingratiation
AAGIIINPRSST	parasitising
AAGIIINPRSTZ	parasitizing
AAGIILLNNUVY	unavailingly
AAGIILMNNPTU	manipulating
AAGIILMRSTTY	magistrality
AAGIILNNRSTU	naturalising
AAGIILNNRSUY	sanguinarily
AAGIILNNRTUZ	naturalizing
AAGIILNPPRSY	appraisingly
AAGIIMNOSTTU	automatising
AAGIIMNOTTUZ	automatizing
AAGIIMNRSTTU	traumatising
AAGIIMNRTTUZ	traumatizing
AAGIINNNQRTU	quarantining
AAGIINNOORST	organisation
AAGIINNOORTZ	organization
AAGIINNORTUU	inauguration
AAGIINNOSSST	assignations
AAGIINOPSSTT	apostatising
AAGIINOPSTTZ	apostatizing
AAGIINORRTTY	ingratiatory
AAGIINORSTTV	gravitations
AAGILLLORSSY	glossarially
AAGILLMNORSY	organismally
AAGILLMNRTUU	multiangular
AAGILLMNTUWY	mulligatawny
AAGILLNOUVVV	vulvovaginal
AAGILLNRRTUY	triangularly
AAGILMMMOSST	mammalogists
AAGILMNNNNOT	nonmalignant
AAGILNNORSTU	granulations
AAGILNNRSTUV	transvaluing
AAGILNORSTTU	gastrulation
	gratulations
AAGILOOPRSTY	parasitology
AAGIMNNOOSST	anastomosing
AAGIMNNRRSTT	transmigrant
AAGINOOOPRSZ	zoosporangia
AAGINOOPPRST	propagations
AAGINORRSTUU	inaugurators
AAGINORRTUUY	inauguratory
AAGLLOPRSTTU	supraglottal
AAGOPRRRSSSW	sparrowgrass
AAHHIOPPRSTU	phosphaturia
AAHHIPRSSTTW	athwartships
AAHHLMOPSTUY	hypothalamus
AAHIIILLOPRU	ailurophilia
AAHIIILNNNOT	annihilation
AAHIILNNORST	annihilators
AAHIIMMNNSTU	antihumanism
AAHIIMNNOSTU	humanisation
AAHIIMNNOTUZ	humanization
AAHIIMOPPRSS	paraphimosis
AAHIINOPSTXY	asphyxiation
AAHIINPPRSST	partisanship
AAHIINPPRSTZ	partizanship
AAHIKKLNOSSV	kalashnikovs
AAHIKLLNNOPT	haliplankton
AAHIKMMNPRSS	marksmanship
AAHIKMNOSSTV	stakhanovism
AAHILLMOOTXY	homotaxially
AAHILLMOPRSX	morphallaxis
AAHILLNNOPTY	antiphonally
AAHILLOPRSTX	trophallaxis
AAHILLOPSSTT	allopathists
AAHILMMOPRTU	prothalamium
AAHILMNOOPRT	prothalamion
AAHILMPRSSTY	amphistylars
AAHIMMNOPRSS	anamorphisms
AAHIMMOPPRRS	paramorphism
AAHIMNOOPRSS	anamorphosis
AAHIOPRSSTXY	asphyxiators
AAHKOPRRSSWW	sparrowhawks
AAHLLMMORSSW	marshmallows
AAHLLMMORSWY	marshmallowy
AAHLNORRSTUY	anarthrously
AAHLOPRRSTTY	arthroplasty
AAHMOOPPRRSU	paramorphous
AAIIIKLLLNOU	Liliuokalani
AAIIILMNOSST	assimilation
AAIIILMPRTTY	impartiality

AAIIILNNOSTV insalivation
AAIIILNNOTTZ latinization
AAIIILNOPRTT Tripolitania
AAIIILNOSTTV visitational
vitalisation
AAIIILNOTTVZ vitalization
AAIIILNRSTTU utilitarians
AAIIILORSTTV visitatorial
AAIIIMMNOSTX maximisation
AAIIIMMNOTXZ maximization
AAIIIMNNRSTU unitarianism
AAIIIMNOSSTV avitaminosis
AAIIINNNOSTT insanitation
AAIIINNOSSTT sanitisation
AAIIINNOSTTZ sanitization
AAIIINNRRTTU Triunitarian
AAIIINORSSTT satirisation
AAIIINORSTTZ satirization
AAIILLMNORTY minatorially
AAIILLMNPRSU supraliminal
AAIILLNNOSTT installation
AAIILLNORRTY irrationally
AAIILMNNOPRS paralimnions
AAIILMNNOPTT implantation
AAIILMNNOPTU manipulation
AAIILMNOORST moralisation
AAIILMNOORTZ moralization
AAIILMNOOTTV motivational
AAIILMNOPSST maintopsails
AAIILMNOSSTV salvationism
AAIILMORSSST assimilators
AAIILMORSSTY assimilatory
AAIILNNNOOTT intonational
AAIILNNNOOTV innovational
AAIILNNORSTT transitional
AAIILNNOSSTT nationalists
AAIILNOOPPST appositional
AAIILNOOPRST polarisation
AAIILNOOPRTZ polarization
AAIILNOORSST solarisation
AAIILNOORSTV valorisation
AAIILNOORSTZ solarization
AAIILNOORTVZ valorization
AAIILNOOSTTT totalisation
AAIILNOOTTTZ totalization
AAIILNOPPSTT palpitations
AAIILNORRSTU ruralisation
AAIILNORRTUZ ruralization
AAIILNORSSTT rationalists
AAIILNORSTTY stationarily
AAIILNOSSTTV salvationist
AAIIMMNNOOST ammoniations
AAIIMNNOORTZ romanization
AAIIMNOORSTT amortisation
AAIIMNOORTTZ amortization
AAIIMNOPRSTT impartations
AAIINNOQSTTU quantisation
AAIINNOQTTUZ quantization
AAIINNORSTTU instauration
AAIINOOPRSTV vaporisation
AAIINOOPRTVZ vaporization
AAIKLNSSSTVY Stanislavsky
AAILLLOSSTWW swallowtails
AAILLMNOTTUY mutationally
AAILLMNRRTUY intramurally
AAILLORSTTUY salutatorily
AAILMMOPPRSS malapropisms
AAILMNOPRSTU manipulators
AAILMNOPRTUY manipulatory
AAILNNORSSTT translations
AAILOORSSTTT totalisators
AAILOORSTTTZ totalizators
AAILOPRSSSTT pastoralists
AAIMMNOPSSTT maintopmasts
AAIMMNOSSSUY immunoassays
AAIMNNRRSTUU transuranium
AAIMNOOSSTTT somatostatin
AAINNORSTTUU unsaturation
AAINOOORTTTU autorotation
AAINORRSSTTU instaurators
AAIOOPPPRRRT appropriator
AAKLNNNNOOPT nanoplankton
AALLMOPRSXYY paroxysmally
AALMNOOPRSTY trypanosomal
AANNORRSSTUY tyrannosaurs
ABBBCEHLOPSY psychobabble
ABBBCIILLTUY clubbability
ABBBDEEIILSS Sidi-bel-Abbès
ABBBEHLMORTU blabbermouth
ABBCCEEHKNRS backbenchers
ABBCCEEHMORS beachcombers
ABBCCEGHIMNO beachcombing
ABBCCEHLMOOR Colomb-Béchar
ABBCCEKKLORS backblockers
ABBCDDEEMRRU breadcrumbed
ABBCDEEIKLRR blackberried
ABBCDGIIKLNR blackbirding
ABBCEEHIILOT bibliothecae
ABBCEEIKLRRS blackberries
ABBCEHIILOST bibliothecas
ABBCFIILORST fibroblastic
ABBDDEEGGORS Bad Godesberg
ABBDDEEILNSS biddableness
ABBDDEGIORRS bridgeboards
ABBDDGINOORY bodyboarding
ABBDEHIILRSY hybridisable
ABBDEHIILRYZ hybridizable
ABBDEIILSSSU subsidisable
ABBDEIILSSUZ subsidizable
ABBDEILNNORS Robben Island
ABBDEINRSSUU suburbanised
ABBDEINRSUUZ suburbanized
ABBDEMMNORST bombardments
ABBEEEILLNUV unbelievable
ABBEEELMORSY Melrose Abbey
ABBEEILLNUVY unbelievably
ABBEEILMRRSU reimbursable
ABBEEILOPQRU equiprobable
ABBEEMNSSSTU subbasements
ABBEENNOTWWY Newtownabbey
ABBEFHIIRSST rabbitfishes
ABBEFHIORRSY Frobisher Bay
ABBEINRSSSUU suburbanises
ABBEINRSSTUU suburbanites

ABBEINRSSUUZ	suburbanizes
ABBGHIILOPRY	bibliography
ABBGHIMNOSTU	thingumabobs
ABBGIILNNOTU	obnubilating
ABBIILOPRSST	probabilists
ABBIIMNNOOST	bombinations
ABCCCIILMSTU	subclimactic
ABCCDEEELPST	bespectacled
ABCCDEEHKORR	checkerboard
ABCCDEEIIRST	bactericides
ABCCDEHIKSTT	backstitched
ABCCDEHILORU	coachbuilder
ABCCDIILORXY	dicarboxylic
ABCCEEELNORT	concelebrate
ABCCEEENORRS	arborescence
ABCCEEGINNRU	buccaneering
ABCCEEIILNSS	inaccessible
ABCCEEILLNOR	reconcilable
ABCCEELLLOST	collectables
ABCCEEMNNRRU	encumbrancer
ABCCEEMNNRSU	encumbrances
ABCCEHIIMNOS	biomechanics
ABCCEHIKSSTT	backstitches
ABCCEHILLRUY	cherubically
ABCCEHINRSTT	tectibranchs
ABCCEHORRSUY	brachycerous
ABCCEIIILRST	criticisable
ABCCEIIILRTZ	criticizable
ABCCEIILNOOT	coenobitical
ABCCEIILNSSY	inaccessibly
ABCCEIKKLSST	sticklebacks
ABCCEIKLLOSU	cockabullies
ABCCEILLNORY	reconcilably
ABCCEILMMNOU	communicable
ABCCEILNNOOS	conscionable
ABCCEILNORTT	contractible
ABCCEILORSTU	scrobiculate
ABCCEIMNNRSU	incumbrances
ABCCGIKNORSS	backcrossing
ABCCHHIMOORT	bathochromic
ABCCHILLMORU	chlorambucil
ABCCIILLSTUY	cubistically
ABCCIIMOORST	macrobiotics
ABCCILLOOSTY	octosyllabic
ABCCILMMNOUY	communicably
ABCCILNNOOSY	conscionably
ABCCILNORTTY	contractibly
ABCCINOOSSTT	tobacconists
ABCCKLNORTUY	Black Country
ABCCNORSSTTU	subcontracts
ABCDDEEEERRT	decerebrated
ABCDDEEINORS	decarbonised
ABCDDEEINORZ	decarbonized
ABCDDEEIRRSU	decarburised
ABCDDEEIRRUZ	decarburized
ABCDEEEERRST	decerebrates
ABCDEEEHHKSS	backsheeshed
ABCDEEEHILPR	decipherable
ABCDEEEHIRSU	debaucheries
ABCDEEEHLORR	breechloader
ABCDEEEHORSS	cheeseboards
ABCDEEEILNUV	undeceivable
ABCDEEELNRTU	uncelebrated
ABCDEEFILNOS	Beaconsfield
ABCDEEHOQRRU	chequerboard
ABCDEEIILLNN	indeclinable
ABCDEEIKKSTY	stickybeaked
ABCDEEILMNSS	dissemblance
ABCDEEILMOST	domesticable
ABCDEEILNORS	considerable
ABCDEEILORSV	discoverable
ABCDEEINORRS	decarboniser
ABCDEEINORRZ	decarbonizer
ABCDEEINORSS	decarbonises
ABCDEEINORSZ	decarbonizes
ABCDEEIRRSSU	decarburises
ABCDEEIRRSUZ	decarburizes
ABCDEELMOOPS	decomposable
ABCDEELMRRSS	descramblers
ABCDEENORRST	centreboards
ABCDEFLNNOOU	confoundable
ABCDEGHIILNR	childbearing
ABCDEGILMNRS	descrambling
ABCDEHHLOOOR	bachelorhood
ABCDEHILSSTW	switchblades
ABCDEHIRRSTW	birdwatchers
ABCDEIIILLRT	liberticidal
ABCDEIILLNNY	indeclinably
ABCDEIILRSTT	distractible
ABCDEIIPSSTU	bicuspidates
ABCDEILMORST	blastodermic
ABCDEILNORSY	considerably
ABCDEILNOSTU	discountable
ABCDEINOOPRS	proboscidean
ABCDEINRSSTU	disturbances
ABCDEIORSVYY	Discovery Bay
ABCDEKMNOOSW	backwoodsmen
ABCDELMNOOPU	compoundable
ABCDEOOORRRT	corroborated
ABCDGHIINNRS	disbranching
ABCDGIINNOOT	bandicooting
ABCDHINOOPRS	branchiopods
ABCDHIORSSTW	switchboards
ABCDHNOORRSY	hydrocarbons
ABCDIILLOPST	diploblastic
ABCDIINOOPRS	proboscidian
ABCEEEFNRSST	benefactress
ABCEEEGKNRRS	greenbackers
ABCEEEHHKSSS	backsheeshes
ABCEEEHLNRRT	retrenchable
ABCEEEHLORTT	bachelorette
ABCEEEILPSTT	battlepieces
ABCEEELMNRSS	resemblances
ABCEEEMMNRRR	remembrancer
ABCEEEMMNRRS	remembrances
ABCEEENORSUV	verbenaceous
ABCEEFFIINRT	febrifacient
ABCEEFIILLNY	beneficially
ABCEEFINNOST	benefactions
ABCEEFINORST	sorbefacient
ABCEEFINRSTU	rubefacients
ABCEEFLLOORS	foreclosable
ABCEEGHNRRSU	Rauschenberg
ABCEEGIILNOT	biogenetical

ABCEEGIINNNS benignancies
ABCEEGIKMNRS greenbackism
ABCEEGILNORS recognisable
ABCEEGILNORZ recognizable
ABCEEHIINRRS chinaberries
ABCEEHKMOSTT Thomas Becket
ABCEEHLORSUY herbaceously
ABCEEHMMNNRT embranchment
ABCEEHORRRST torchbearers
ABCEEHORSTTX chatterboxes
ABCEEIILLNPX inexplicable
ABCEEIILNNNT bicentennial
ABCEEIILNRTX inextricable
ABCEEIILPPRT precipitable
ABCEEILLSSTU subcelestial
ABCEEILMMORS commiserable
ABCEEILNNOTU unnoticeable
ABCEEILNORST celebrations
ABCEEILNORSU ribonuclease
ABCEEILNOSSS sociableness
ABCEEILRSSTU resuscitable
ABCEEINNORSV inobservance
ABCEEINNSSTU subtenancies
ABCEEINOORRT cerebrotonia
ABCEEINORRST cerebrations
ABCEEJKLMRTU lumberjacket
ABCEEKLNNORU unreckonable
ABCEELLLNOSU counsellable
ABCEELLNPSSU culpableness
ABCEELLOOSST blastocoeles
ABCEELOPRSTU prosecutable
ABCEENOPRRTU protuberance
ABCEEOOPRRRT baroreceptor
ABCEEORRSSUU burseraceous
ABCEERRRSTTU carburetters
ABCEFHNOOPRS francophobes
ABCEFIIIINOV Boniface VIII
ABCEGGGIKLLN blacklegging
ABCEGGILNNOO Belgian Congo
ABCEGHILORSY brachylogies
ABCEGHINRSUW Braunschweig
ABCEGHORRRTU turbocharger
ABCEGILNORSY recognisably
ABCEGILNORYZ recognizably
ABCEGILOORTY bacteriology
ABCEGINRRTTU carburetting
ABCEHHINOOPT technophobia
ABCEHHIOOPST theophobiacs
ABCEHHKRSSUW bushwhackers
ABCEHHMOORST bathochromes
ABCEHIKNRSSS brackishness
ABCEHILLOPRY hyperbolical
ABCEHILMNRUU hibernaculum
ABCEHKLRSSUW swashbuckler
ABCEHLNOSTUU untouchables
ABCEIIILLRST liberalistic
ABCEIIILTTXY excitability
ABCEIILLNPXY inexplicably
ABCEIILMNOPT incompatible
ABCEIILNRTXY inextricably
ABCEIILOORST borosilicate
ABCEIILORSTT cristobalite
ABCEIILORTVY revocability
ABCEIILPRSTY plebiscitary
ABCEIIMNNOOZ aminobenzoic
ABCEIINORSTT obstetrician
ABCEIKNPRSTU bankruptcies
ABCEILLMOSTY myeloblastic
ABCEILLNNOOS inconsolable
ABCEILMMNOTU incommutable
ABCEILMMOOST metabolomics
ABCEILMNNOSU inconsumable
ABCEILMNOPTU incomputable
ABCEILNNOTUY unnoticeably
ABCEILNOOPRR incorporable
ABCEILOOSSTT osteoblastic
ABCEILOPRRTT protractible
ABCEILPRTUUV Tuva Republic
ABCEIMNOORST embrocations
ABCEINOORSST obsecrations
ABCEINRRRSST transcribers
ABCELLLMNOOS collembolans
ABCELLLNOORT controllable
ABCELLLOOSTY octosyllable
ABCELLRRTUUY tubercularly
ABCELMNRRSSU unscramblers
ABCELNOPRRUU unprocurable
ABCELNORSTTU counterblast
ABCENOPRRTUY protuberancy
ABCENORSSSSU scabrousness
ABCENOSSTUUU subcutaneous
ABCEOOORRRST corroborates
ABCEORRRSTTU carburettors
ABCFIILLMORY morbifically
ABCFIINORSTU bifurcations
ABCFINOOSSTU obfuscations
ABCFLNOOORRU fluorocarbon
ABCGGGIIKNPY piggybacking
ABCGGILNNOOT conglobating
ABCGHHIKNSUW bushwhacking
ABCGHLOORSUY brachylogous
ABCGIIKLLNST blacklisting
ABCGIILLLOOY biologically
ABCGIINNRRST transcribing
ABCGIKNOPPST backstopping
ABCGILLMOOSY symbological
ABCGILMNNRSU unscrambling
ABCGILNNOOOT conglobation
ABCHIIKLOSTY shockability
ABCHIILNOOPT haplobiontic
ABCHIILRSTUY crushability
ABCHIMNORSSU subharmonics
ABCIIIILRSTY irascibility
ABCIIILMNOTU umbilication
ABCIIILNRTUY incurability
ABCIIIMNORST imbrications
ABCIILLMNOOY bionomically
ABCIILMNOPTY incompatibly
ABCIILNNOTUY connubiality
ABCIILNOPSTU publications
ABCIILNORSTU lubrications
ABCIILNPPRSU subprincipal
ABCIILORRTUY orbicularity
ABCIILRSTTUY scrutability

ABCIIMNNOOST	combinations
ABCIINORRSTU	rubrications
ABCILLLMOSYY	symbolically
ABCILLLOPSYY	polysyllabic
ABCILLMNOOSY	monosyllabic
ABCILLNNOOSY	inconsolably
ABCILMMNOSTU	noctambulism
ABCILMMNOTUY	incommutably
ABCILMNNOSUY	inconsumably
ABCILMNOPTUY	incomputably
ABCILMNOSTTU	noctambulist
ABCILNORSTUU	lucubrations
ABCILOOPSSTU	subapostolic
ABCIMNORSSTU	obscurantism
ABCIMNORSTUU	rambunctious
ABCINNOORSTU	conurbations
ABCINOORSSTU	obscurations
ABCINORSSTTU	obscurantist
	subtractions
ABCLLLNOORTY	controllably
ABCOOOORRRRT	corroborator
ABDDDEEGILRR	griddlebread
ABDDEEEHLNYZ	benzaldehyde
ABDDEEEHLORU	doubleheader
ABDDEEEKORRY	rekeyboarded
ABDDEEELNNPU	undependable
ABDDEEHLLLUY	bullheadedly
ABDDEEIILRST	detribalised
ABDDEEIILRTZ	detribalized
ABDDEEIILSST	destabilised
ABDDEEIILSTZ	destabilized
ABDDEEILMSSS	disassembled
ABDDEEIMNNST	absentminded
ABDDEELMNRRU	drumbledrane
ABDDEELNORSS	bladdernoses
ABDDEENOORUV	overabounded
ABDDEGINORTU	groundbaited
ABDDEILNOOST	bloodstained
ABDDEINORSTU	subordinated
ABDDELORRSTW	bladderworts
ABDEEEEILMRR	irredeemable
ABDEEEERRRTV	reverberated
ABDEEEFIILNS	indefeasible
ABDEEEIILMRR	irremediable
ABDEEEIILRTV	deliberative
ABDEEEILLRTY	deliberately
ABDEEEILMMST	emblematised
ABDEEEILMMTZ	emblematized
ABDEEEILMNRT	determinable
ABDEEEILMRRY	irredeemably
ABDEEEINPRRS	prebendaries
ABDEEELMNTTT	battlemented
ABDEEELMNTZZ	bedazzlement
ABDEEELMPRSS	preassembled
ABDEEELPRSSU	supersedable
ABDEEFIIILNT	identifiable
ABDEEFIILNSY	indefeasibly
ABDEEFILLSTT	battlefields
ABDEEFINSTUU	subinfeudate
ABDEEGIILNRT	deliberating
ABDEEGIMNRST	abridgements
ABDEEGKLLNOW	knowledgable
ABDEEHNPRRSS	sharpbenders
ABDEEIIILTTV	debilitative
ABDEEIIKLRST	East Kilbride
ABDEEIILMRRY	irremediably
ABDEEIILNORT	deliberation
ABDEEIILQRTU	equilibrated
ABDEEIILRSST	detribalises
ABDEEIILRSTZ	detribalizes
ABDEEIILSSST	destabilises
ABDEEIILSSTZ	destabilizes
ABDEEIINORTY	obedientiary
ABDEEIKNRRSW	windbreakers
ABDEEILLNORR	banderillero
ABDEEILMNOPR	imponderable
ABDEEILMNRTY	determinably
ABDEEILMNSST	disablements
ABDEEILMRSSS	disassembler
ABDEEILMSSSS	disassembles
ABDEEILNOSSV	voidableness
ABDEEILNRSSU	undesirables
ABDEEILNRSTY	Libyan Desert
ABDEEILORRST	deliberators
ABDEEILORRUV	boulevardier
ABDEEILPRSTU	disreputable
ABDEEINNORSS	debonairness
ABDEEINNRRSW	breadwinners
ABDEEINNRSTU	Nubian Desert
ABDEEINNSSSU	unbiasedness
ABDEEKMNNOTU	mountebanked
ABDEELLLORRS	rollerblades
ABDEELMNORST	demonstrable
ABDEELNORSSU	labouredness
ABDEENORSSTU	obdurateness
ABDEEOPRRTTU	protuberated
ABDEEORRRSSW	swordbearers
ABDEFFHLORSU	shuffleboard
ABDEFGINORRS	fingerboards
ABDEFIIILLOS	solidifiable
ABDEFIIILNTY	definability
	identifiably
ABDEFLORRTTU	flutterboard
ABDEGHIIOPRS	biographised
ABDEGHIIOPRZ	biographized
ABDEGIIILNTT	debilitating
ABDEGIIKMNRS	disembarking
ABDEGIILLMRU	Millau Bridge
ABDEGIINNNRW	breadwinning
ABDEGIIRRSTU	subirrigated
ABDEGKLLNOWY	knowledgably
ABDEGLNORTTU	battleground
ABDEHHLMOORR	rhombohedral
ABDEHHNOSSUU	househusband
ABDEHIIILMNS	diminishable
ABDEHIILSSST	disestablish
ABDEHILNOORS	dishonorable
ABDEHLLORSYY	hydrolysable
ABDEHLLORYYZ	hydrolyzable
ABDEHMOORRST	motherboards
ABDEIIIILSST	disabilities
ABDEIIILMNSS	inadmissible
ABDEIIILNOTT	debilitation
ABDEIIILRSTY	desirability

ABDEIIILRTVY driveability
ABDEIIIRSSSU subsidiaries
ABDEIILNPSTU indisputable
ABDEIILNRTUY endurability
ABDEIIMNOSST demibastions
ABDEIIOOPRSS basidiospore
ABDEIKORSSTY keyboardists
ABDEILLLSSSY dissyllables
ABDEILMNOPRY imponderably
ABDEILMNOSTU dismountable
ABDEILPRSTUY disreputably
ABDEIMORSTUX ambidextrous
ABDEINORSSTU subordinates
ABDEINRTTTUU unattributed
ABDELMNORSTY demonstrably
ABDELMOORSST bloodstreams
ABDENNORSSTV bondservants
ABDENOPRSSUU superabounds
ABDEOOPPRSTT bootstrapped
ABDFIILNNRUU infundibular
ABDFIILNOOOV bioflavonoid
ABDGHINOOSWX shadowboxing
ABDGHNNOSUUY Younghusband
ABDGIILNPRUY upbraidingly
ABDGIILOOORY radiobiology
ABDGINNOORSW snowboarding
ABDGINOPRRSS springboards
ABDGINORRSST stringboards
ABDHIIIINRST British India
ABDHILNOORSY dishonorably
ABDIIIILNTUY inaudibility
ABDIIILMNSSY inadmissibly
ABDIIILRSSUY subsidiarily
ABDIIIMORSST trombidiasis
ABDIIIRSSTUY subsidiarity
ABDIILLMOTUY modulability
mouldability
ABDIILNNNOSS Bonin Islands
ABDIILNPSTUY indisputably
ABDIINOSSTUU subauditions
ABDIIRRSTTUY distributary
ABDIMNNOSSTU subdominants
ABDLNOOOSSTT odontoblasts
ABEEEEMNRSTV bereavements
ABEEEERRRSTV reverberates
ABEEEFILNNSS fineableness
ABEEEFILNSSS feasibleness
ABEEEFLNQRTU frequentable
ABEEEGGILNRU beleaguering
ABEEEGILNORT renegotiable
ABEEEGILRSSS Gebrselassie
ABEEEHHIRRST heathberries
ABEEEHKORRSU housebreaker
ABEEEIILLRRV irrelievable
ABEEEIKLLNSS likeableness
ABEEEILLNRSS reliableness
ABEEEILLNSSV liveableness
ABEEEILLPRSV replevisable
ABEEEILMMSST emblematises
ABEEEILMMSTZ emblematizes
ABEEEILMNPRT impenetrable
ABEEEILMNRTX exterminable
ABEEEILMRSSS reassemblies
ABEEEILNNSSV enviableness
ABEEEILNRRST East Berliner
ABEEEILNSSSZ sizeableness
ABEEEINRRTTV invertebrate
ABEEEJMMNNST enjambements
ABEEELLNOSSV loveableness
ABEEELMNNSTT entablements
ABEEELNNNORW nonrenewable
ABEEELNSSSSS baselessness
ABEEELQRSSTU sequestrable
ABEEEMPRSTTU subtemperate
ABEEEORRRRTV reverberator
ABEEEPRRSTTY presbyterate
ABEEFFGNRSTU Stauffenberg
ABEEFFILNRSU insufferable
ABEEFGHILNRT frightenable
ABEEFIILLMSU emulsifiable
ABEEFIILLRST fertilisable
ABEEFIILLRTZ fertilizable
ABEEFIILNRST antifebriles
ABEEFIILNRUV unverifiable
ABEEFILLLNSS fallibleness
ABEEFKLNOORW foreknowable
ABEEFLLMNSSU blamefulness
ABEEFNRRRSTU afterburners
ABEEGGIILNOR globigerinae
ABEEGGILNRSS beggarliness
ABEEGHHIKNSS baksheeshing
ABEEGHLRSSSU Burgess Shale
ABEEGIILNSTV investigable
ABEEGIKNRRTU Ekaterinburg
ABEEGILMNRSS reassembling
ABEEGILNNOTU unnegotiable
ABEEGILNNPUX inexpugnable
ABEEGILNNSST tangibleness
ABEEGILNORRS loganberries
ABEEGILNRSUZ gaberlunzies
ABEEGINPRSTT bespattering
ABEEGLNNORUV ungovernable
ABEEGLNNORYY Longyearbyen
ABEEHHPRSSTY bathyspheres
ABEEHIILMPRS imperishable
ABEEHIKLRSTT blatherskite
ABEEHILLMORT thermolabile
ABEEHILLNOSX Bexhill-on-Sea
ABEEHILOPPRS prophesiable
ABEEHILPRSST preestablish
ABEEHILRSSST establishers
ABEEHIQRRSUU harquebusier
ABEEHLLRSSTY breathlessly
ABEEHLMORSTT thermostable
ABEEHLNNOORR blennorrhoea
ABEEHLNNORRS blennorrheas
ABEEHLOPRSST blastosphere
ABEEHLORRSSU barrelhouses
ABEEHLORRSWW wheelbarrows
ABEEHNOPRRSY hyperboreans
ABEEIIILLRST liberalities
ABEEIIILSSTT bestialities
ABEEIIKKMORS bokmakieries
ABEEIILLRRSS liberalisers

ABEEIILLRRSZ	liberalizers
ABEEIILLRSST	sterilisable
ABEEIILLRSTZ	sterilizable
ABEEIILMNNRT	interminable
ABEEIILMNSST	imitableness
ABEEIILMPRTY	permeability
ABEEIILNNSSV	inviableness
ABEEIILNPRTX	inextirpable
ABEEIILNPSST	pitiableness
ABEEIILNRTVY	venerability
ABEEIILNRTWY	renewability
ABEEIILORTTV	obliterative
ABEEIILPRRRS	irrespirable
ABEEIILQRSTU	equilibrates
ABEEIINORSST	enterobiasis
ABEEIIPRSSTT	baptisteries
ABEEIIRSSTUV	subvarieties
ABEEIKLMORRS	boilermakers
ABEEILLNNRUV	invulnerable
	Villeurbanne
ABEEILLNNSTU	unlistenable
ABEEILLNOSSV	violableness
ABEEILLOPRST	boilerplates
ABEEILLORRSV	irresolvable
ABEEILLPRSUV	pulverisable
ABEEILLPRUVZ	pulverizable
ABEEILMMNRSU	immensurable
ABEEILMMOORS	aeroembolism
ABEEILMNORSZ	emblazonries
ABEEILMNPRTY	impenetrably
ABEEILNOPRST	interposable
ABEEILNOQSTU	questionable
ABEEILNSSSTU	suitableness
ABEEILOPPRRX	expropriable
ABEEILPRRSTY	presbyterial
ABEEINNQRSTU	barquentines
ABEEINORRTTV	vertebration
ABEEINPRRSTY	presbyterian
ABEEIQRRSSUU	arquebusiers
ABEEIRRRSSTW	strawberries
ABEEKLMORRTU	troublemaker
ABEEKLNORSSW	workableness
ABEEKLOPRRSW	Parker Bowles
ABEEKORRSSTT	breaststroke
ABEELLMNOPUY	unemployable
ABEELLMNOTTT	ballottement
ABEELLNOSSSV	solvableness
ABEELMMNNOTZ	emblazonment
ABEELMNPRSTU	numberplates
ABEELNNORSTY	Blarney Stone
ABEELNNSSSTU	unstableness
ABEELOPPRSSU	superposable
ABEENRSSSSTU	abstruseness
ABEEOPRRSTTU	protuberates
ABEERRRSSTUU	subtreasurer
ABEFFHIKRSST	Bashkirtseff
ABEFFIIILNTY	ineffability
ABEFFILLLMOR	flabelliform
ABEFFILNRSUY	insufferably
ABEFGILNORRY	forbearingly
ABEFGILNORUV	unforgivable
ABEFGINNRRTU	afterburning
ABEFIILLOSSS	fossilisable
ABEFIILLOSSZ	fossilizable
ABEFIILRTTUY	refutability
ABEFILNOPRTU	unprofitable
ABEFILNRSSTU	transfusible
ABEFLMOORSTT	footlamberts
ABEFLNOSSSTU	boastfulness
ABEFLNOSSSUU	fabulousness
ABEGGHIINNRR	harbingering
ABEGGHIOOPRY	biogeography
ABEGGIILLNST	billingsgate
ABEGGIILNORS	globigerinas
ABEGGIMNNOOR	boomeranging
ABEGHHKORRTU	breakthrough
ABEGHHLOPPRY	phlebography
ABEGHIILNSST	establishing
ABEGHIIOPRSS	biographises
ABEGHIIOPRSZ	biographizes
ABEGHJNNORSU	Johannesburg
ABEGHNOORTTU	Attenborough
ABEGIIILLNRS	liberalising
ABEGIIILLNRZ	liberalizing
ABEGIIILNSST	bestialising
ABEGIIILNSTZ	bestializing
ABEGIILLLMNS	mislabelling
ABEGIILLNOUV	Bougainville
ABEGIILMNNSU	albumenising
ABEGIILMNNUZ	albumenizing
ABEGIILMNOST	metabolising
ABEGIILMNOTZ	metabolizing
ABEGIILNORTT	obliterating
ABEGIILNPRTY	pregnability
ABEGIINRRSTT	Bering Strait
ABEGIINRSSSU	agribusiness
ABEGIIRRSSTU	subirrigates
ABEGILLMORSU	semiglobular
ABEGILLNOOST	balneologist
ABEGILNNPUXY	inexpugnably
ABEGILNNRTTU	table-turning
ABEGINNORRST	interrobangs
ABEGINOOPRTW	powerboating
ABEGLLNORSSU	globularness
ABEGLLORSSSW	glassblowers
ABEGLMORSUUY	umbrageously
ABEGLNNORUVY	ungovernably
ABEGLNORSSSU	glabrousness
ABEGMORRSSTU	burgomasters
ABEHIIILNNSU	Husein ibn-Ali
ABEHIIILRTTY	heritability
ABEHIILMOPST	amphibolites
ABEHIILMPRSY	imperishably
ABEHIILNNRTY	labyrinthine
ABEHIILNOPST	inhospitable
ABEHIIMNOOPS	ambiophonies
ABEHIIMORSSV	behaviorisms
ABEHIIMORSUV	behaviourism
	misbehaviour
ABEHIINNORST	hibernations
ABEHIIORSSTV	behaviorists
ABEHIIORSTUV	behaviourist
ABEHIKLNNRSU	unshrinkable
ABEHILNOPSTY	hypnotisable

ABEHILNOPTYZ	hypnotizable
ABEHILOOPRSU	ailurophobes
ABEHINPRSSTU	paintbrushes
ABEHIOOPRRSS	barophoresis
ABEHLORRSTTY	erythroblast
ABEHMORRRSTX	Marx Brothers
ABEIIILLLMRS	illiberalism
ABEIIILLLRTY	illiberality
ABEIIILLNNRT	brilliantine
ABEIIILLNORS	billionaires
ABEIIILLNSTY	ensilability
ABEIIILMMRSS	miserabilism
ABEIIILMRSST	miserabilist
ABEIIILNOSTT	notabilities
ABEIIILNRRTY	inerrability
ABEIIILOPRST	bipolarities
ABEIIILRTVVY	revivability
ABEIIINNORST	inebriations
ABEIIKLORTVY	revokability
ABEIILLLMPTU	multipliable
ABEIILLMRSTY	bimestrially
ABEIILLMSSTT	bimetallists
ABEIILLORTTY	tolerability
ABEIILLRSSTT	bristletails
ABEIILMMORTY	memorability
ABEIILMNNRTY	interminably
ABEIILMNOOST	embolisation
ABEIILMNOOTZ	embolization
ABEIILMORTVY	removability
ABEIILNNOSTU	nebulisation
ABEIILNNOTUZ	nebulization
ABEIILNNTTUY	untenability
ABEIILNOORTT	obliteration
ABEIILNOPRST	prelibations
ABEIILNQRSTU	equilibrants
ABEIILNRRRTY	interlibrary
ABEIILOQRRTU	equilibrator
ABEIILPRSTUY	superability
ABEIILPRTTUY	reputability
ABEIIMNRSTUU	subminiature
ABEIIMOQRSTU	Barquisimeto
ABEIINORSSTU	suberisation
ABEIINORSTUZ	suberization
ABEIIRSTTTUV	attributives
ABEILLLRSSTY	trisyllables
ABEILLMORSTU	rambouillets
ABEILLNNRUVY	invulnerably
ABEILLNOPPRT	bipropellant
ABEILLNORRTU	interlobular
ABEILLOPRRVY	proverbially
ABEILLORRSVY	irresolvably
ABEILMOSSTUY	abstemiously
ABEILNOQSTUY	questionably
ABEILNORSSUY	Byelorussian
ABEILNORTTXY	exorbitantly
ABEILOORRSTT	obliterators
ABEIMOORSSTT	strabotomies
ABEINOOPRRST	probationers
	reabsorption
ABEINOORSSTV	observations
ABEINOOSSTTT	obtestations
ABEINOPRRTTU	perturbation
ABEINSSSTTUV	substantives
ABELLLLOPSYY	polysyllable
ABELLLMNOOSY	monosyllable
ABELMMNORSUY	membranously
ABELMNNOSTUY	submontanely
ABELMNORSTUU	surmountable
ABELOOPRSSST	blastospores
ABELORRRSTUY	barretrously
ABELRRSSTTUU	surrebuttals
ABEMNORRRSST	barnstormers
ABFGIIILNNTU	infibulating
ABFGIIILNRTY	frangibility
ABFGIILLNSYY	syllabifying
ABFIIILLNORT	fibrillation
ABFIIILNNOTU	infibulation
ABFILMNSSTUU	funambulists
ABFILNOPRTUY	unprofitably
ABGGGILLNRUY	bullyragging
ABGGHINOORSU	Gainsborough
ABGGIILNRRSU	burglarising
ABGGIILNRRUZ	burglarizing
ABGGILLNOSSW	glassblowing
ABGGILOORSST	garbologists
ABGGINOOSSTT	tobogganists
ABGHHOORSSTU	thoroughbass
ABGHIINRSSTT	brattishings
ABGIIIILNTTY	ignitability
ABGIIILLMNSU	bilingualism
ABGIILLMRSUW	Williamsburg
ABGIILLNNOTU	antiglobulin
ABGIILLOORTY	obligatorily
ABGIJNOORSTU	objurgations
ABGIKNRRSSTY	stringybarks
ABGILLNOSTTU	subtotalling
ABGILNOOPSST	spongioblast
ABGILOOORSTY	astrobiology
ABGIMNNORRST	barnstorming
ABGINOORSSTU	subrogations
ABHHILOOPSTU	bathophilous
ABHIIILORSSZ	bilharziosis
ABHIIKMNNPRS	brinkmanship
ABHIILMOPSUY	amphibiously
ABHIILNOPSTY	inhospitably
ABHIINOPRSTV	vibraphonist
ABHIMNNORRTU	Northumbrian
ABHLLMOPSSTY	lymphoblasts
ABHLOOPRSSTT	trophoblasts
ABIIIILRRTTY	irritability
ABIIILLPSTUY	plausibility
ABIIILMMOTVY	immovability
ABIIILMMTTUY	immutability
ABIIILMNOOST	abolitionism
	mobilisation
ABIIILMNOOTZ	mobilization
ABIIILMPTTUY	imputability
ABIIILNOOSTT	abolitionist
ABIIILNPRTTY	printability
ABIIILNRSTUY	insurability
ABIIILSTTTWY	twistability
ABIIINOPRSTT	bipartitions
ABIILLLMNSUY	subliminally
ABIILMOOSTTU	automobilist

ABIILNOORSTT	strobilation
ABIILNORSSUU	insalubrious
ABIILNORSTTU	tribulations
ABIILOPPSTY	opposability
ABIILRSTTTUY	trustability
ABIIMNNOORST	brominations
ABIIMNORSTTU	tambourinist
ABIINOORSSTT	abortionists
ABIINORSTTTU	attributions
ABIIOPRSTTVY	absorptivity
ABILLORSSUUY	salubriously
ABILMMMNOSSU	somnambulism
ABILMMNOSSTU	somnambulist
ABILMNORSTUY	subnormality
ABIMNORSSTTU	nimbostratus
ABINNOORSSTU	subornations
ABNOORRSSTUU	brontosaurus
ACCCDEEEELNS	decalescence
ACCCDEHKOPST	spatchcocked
ACCCDENNOORS	concordances
ACCCEEEELNRS	recalescence
ACCCEEEILNNS	incalescence
ACCCEEEINQSU	acquiescence
ACCCEEELNORS	calorescence
ACCCEEELNOSS	coalescences
ACCCEEHMNOTU	accouchement
ACCCEEHOSSUU	accoucheuses
ACCCEEIILSST	ecclesiastic
ACCCEEILLLTY	eclectically
ACCCEELMNOPS	complacences
ACCCEELNOPST	conceptacles
ACCCEGIINNOR	carcinogenic
ACCCEGINORTY	gynecocratic
ACCCEHILMOTY	cytochemical
ACCCEHILOORS	ochlocracies
ACCCEHILOORT	chloroacetic
ACCCEHINORTT	technocratic
ACCCEIILMOPS	complicacies
ACCCEIILMRST	climacterics
ACCCEIMNNOOT	concomitance
ACCCEIMNRSTU	circumstance
ACCCEINORRST	acrocentrics
ACCCELMNOOPU	pneumococcal
ACCCENOPPRUY	preoccupancy
ACCCHHIILLOT	chalcolithic
ACCCHIIOPRRT	chiropractic
ACCCHIIOPRSZ	schizocarpic
ACCCHILMOTYY	cyclothymiac
ACCCIIILSSST	classicistic
ACCCIILNNOTY	anticyclonic
ACCCIILNOOST	iconoclastic
ACCCILLLNOYY	cyclonically
ACCDDEEEIRRT	reaccredited
ACCDDEEINRTU	unaccredited
ACCDDEEIORTT	decorticated
ACCDDEHINOOP	dodecaphonic
ACCDDEIINORT	endocarditic
ACCDDEIIRSST	disaccredits
ACCDDEINORSS	discordances
ACCDDEINORTT	contradicted
ACCDDGIINORS	disaccording
ACCDEEELLNPR	precancelled
ACCDEEENORST	deconsecrate
ACCDEEFIILRS	decalcifiers
ACCDEEFIIRTT	certificated
ACCDEEFILLMS	Macclesfield
ACCDEEFLLOTU	deflocculate
ACCDEEHHKLSU	chuckleheads
ACCDEEHIILNP	diencephalic
ACCDEEHILNOS	chalcedonies
ACCDEEHIORSS	archdioceses
ACCDEEIIILNS	indelicacies
ACCDEEIILNOT	indoleacetic
ACCDEEILLOPS	peccadilloes
ACCDEEILNOPY	encyclopedia
ACCDEEILRRTU	recirculated
ACCDEEINNNST	incandescent
ACCDEEINNORT	concertinaed
ACCDEEIOPRRT	reciprocated
ACCDEEIORSSS	accessorised
ACCDEEIORSSZ	accessorized
ACCDEEIORSTT	decorticates
ACCDEELNNSTY	candescently
ACCDEEMORSTU	reaccustomed
ACCDEENNNOTU	countenanced
ACCDEENNORTT	concentrated
ACCDEENORTTU	counteracted
ACCDEENOSSUU	succedaneous
ACCDEENRSSSU	accursedness
ACCDEEOOPRRS	Cerro de Pasco
ACCDEFGIILNY	decalcifying
ACCDEFIIMOPT	compactified
ACCDEFLLNOTU	deflocculant
ACCDEGIINNNS	incandescing
ACCDEHHNRRUW	churchwarden
ACCDEHHORSST	crosshatched
ACCDEHIILOST	catholicised
ACCDEHIILOTZ	catholicized
ACCDEHILMOPS	accomplished
ACCDEHILOOPP	cephalopodic
ACCDEHIOORSU	orchidaceous
ACCDEIIILNST	insecticidal
ACCDEIIIPRRT	pericarditic
ACCDEIILLOPY	epicycloidal
ACCDEIILNNOT	coincidental
ACCDEIILRRSU	circularised
ACCDEIILRRUZ	circularized
ACCDEIKLNSST	candlesticks
ACCDEILLNOTY	occidentally
ACCDEILNOPTU	conduplicate
ACCDEILOPSTY	cyclopaedist
ACCDEIMMNOTU	communicated
ACCDEIMNORTU	undemocratic
ACCDEINNORRT	androcentric
ACCDEINORRTT	contradicter
ACCDEIOORRTT	decorticator
ACCDEMNOSTUU	unaccustomed
ACCDFIIINOOT	codification
ACCDHILLNOOY	conchoidally
ACCDIIINNOSS	scincoidians
ACCDIILNOORS	crocodilians
ACCDIINOORST	accordionist
ACCDIINOSTTY	syndiotactic
ACCDILNNOOTU	conductional

ACCDILNOOSSS Cocos Islands
ACCDIMOSSSTU disaccustoms
ACCDINOORRTT contradictor
ACCDLNNOORTY concordantly
ACCEEEGINNOT caenogenetic
ACCEEEHILNPP epencephalic
ACCEEEHILRST chelicerates
ACCEEEHLORRT heterocercal
ACCEEEILSSST Ecclesiastes
ACCEEEINPSTX expectancies
ACCEEENOPRSV vaporescence
ACCEEENORRST reconsecrate
ACCEEFGIIMNN magnificence
ACCEEFHMNORT Franche-Comté
ACCEEFIIRSTT certificates
ACCEEFIKRRRS firecrackers
ACCEEGGIORST secretagogic
ACCEEGHIKMNN namechecking
ACCEEGHIMNOS geomechanics
ACCEEGIINNOT cainogenetic
ACCEEGILNNPR precanceling
ACCEEGINNORS recognisance
ACCEEGINNORZ recognizance
ACCEEHHILORT chalicothere
ACCEEHIILNPT encephalitic
ACCEEHIIORRS hierocracies
ACCEEHILMOPS mesocephalic
ACCEEHILNRST chanticleers
ACCEEHIMORTT tacheometric
ACCEEHINNPST catchpennies
ACCEEHIORTTT heterotactic
ACCEEHIRRTTU architecture
ACCEEHIRSTVZ czarevitches
ACCEEHKORSTW weathercocks
ACCEEHLLORST electroclash
ACCEEHLMNRSY sclerenchyma
ACCEEHMNNORT encroachment
ACCEEIILNRST electricians
ACCEEIINNORT interoceanic
ACCEEIINPPRT precipitance
ACCEEIIOPPSS episcopacies
ACCEEIKRRSSW wisecrackers
ACCEEILLLRTY electrically
ACCEEILLMNUY ecumenically
ACCEEILNPTTU centuplicate
ACCEEILNRTTY tetracycline
ACCEEILRRSTU recirculates
ACCEEIMNOTTY actinomycete
ACCEEINOPPRV Cape Province
ACCEEINORSTV consecrative
ACCEEIOPRRST reciprocates
ACCEEIORSSSS accessorises
ACCEEIORSSSZ accessorizes
ACCEEIORSTTT stereotactic
ACCEELLOORTT collectorate
ACCEELMNNOST concealments
ACCEELMNOPTU accouplement
ACCEELNNOPTY cyclopentane
ACCEELNNOSTV convalescent
ACCEELNNRSTU translucence
ACCEELORSTUY cretaceously
ACCEEMNNORRS necromancers
ACCEEMNOPPSU comeuppances
ACCEEMNORTTU accouterment
accoutrement
ACCEENNNORTU countenancer
ACCEENNNOSTU countenances
ACCEENNORSTT concentrates
ACCEENNORSVY conveyancers
ACCEENOPRRSU precancerous
ACCEFFIIINTY inefficacity
ACCEFGIIINNS significance
ACCEFIILLPSY specifically
ACCEFIIMOPST compactifies
ACCEFMNNOORS conformances
ACCEGGILNOOY gynaecologic
ACCEGHHIOPRR choregraphic
ACCEGHHIOPRT hectographic
ACCEGHHISTTW catchweights
ACCEGHINOPRS scenographic
ACCEGIIKKLNP placekicking
ACCEGIIKNRSW wisecracking
ACCEGIILMOST cleistogamic
ACCEGIINNNOZ incognizance
ACCEGIINRTUX excruciating
ACCEGILLLOOY ecologically
ACCEGILLNOOR necrological
ACCEGILNNOSV convalescing
ACCEGINNNOVY conveyancing
ACCEGINNORST consecrating
ACCEGNOORRTY gerontocracy
ACCEHHILOSSZ eschscholzia
ACCEHHLMNORY chlorenchyma
ACCEHHORSSST crosshatches
ACCEHIILLMRY chimerically
ACCEHIILLNST callisthenic
ACCEHIILNOPR necrophiliac
ACCEHIILNSST calisthenics
ACCEHIILNTTY technicality
ACCEHIILOSST catholicises
ACCEHIILOSTZ catholicizes
ACCEHIIMRSTT chrematistic
ACCEHIIRSTTT tetrastichic
ACCEHILLLORY cholerically
ACCEHILLMNOS melancholics
ACCEHILMOPRS accomplisher
ACCEHILMOPRY microcephaly
pyrochemical
ACCEHILMOPSS accomplishes
ACCEHILNNNOT nontechnical
ACCEHILNOOOT echolocation
ACCEHILOPRTY chalcopyrite
ACCEHIMNORRS chiromancers
ACCEHIMNORST mechatronics
ACCEHIMOORST mesothoracic
ACCEHINNNOPT pantechnicon
ACCEHINNRSSU craunchiness
ACCEHINOPRTY pyrocatechin
ACCEHINOPSSY sycophancies
ACCEHINRSSST scratchiness
ACCEHIOPSTVY psychoactive
ACCEHKLOOSVZ Czechoslovak
ACCEHKLRSSTU saltchuckers
ACCEHLOOPRTY pyrocatechol

ACCEHLOORSSU schorlaceous
ACCEHMNORRTU countermarch
ACCEHMOOORST motorcoaches
ACCEHOOOPRST thoracoscope
ACCEHOPRSSST crosspatches
ACCEIIILNOTV conciliative
ACCEIIILPSST specialistic
ACCEIIINNNPS piccaninnies
ACCEIIINNOST canonicities
ACCEIIISSTTU causticities
ACCEIIKKMNRS camiknickers
ACCEIILLLNTY enclitically
ACCEIILLLPTY ecliptically
ACCEIILLMORT cliometrical
ACCEIILLNNSS clinicalness
ACCEIILLOSST solecistical
ACCEIILLRSST clericalists
ACCEIILMMORT microclimate
ACCEIILMNNOP incompliance
ACCEIILMNOPS compliancies
ACCEIILMOORS seriocomical
ACCEIILMORRT calorimetric
ACCEIILMRRSU semicircular
ACCEIILNOOPS Ascoli Piceno
ACCEIILNORTV intervocalic
ACCEIILNRSST criticalness
ACCEIILNRSTT centralistic
ACCEIILORRTV overcritical
ACCEIILOSSTV viscoelastic
ACCEIILRRRSU circulariser
ACCEIILRRRUZ circularizer
ACCEIILRRSSU circularises
ACCEIILRRSUZ circularizes
ACCEIILRSSTU secularistic
ACCEIIMNORRT craniometric
ACCEIIMNORTT actinometric
ACCEIIMNOSST cosmeticians
ACCEIIMORRTT meritocratic
ACCEIINOPRSS conspiracies
ACCEIINORTUX excruciation
ACCEIINOSSTX exsiccations
ACCEIINPPRTY precipitancy
ACCEIIPPRSTY perspicacity
ACCEIJNNOTUV conjunctivae
ACCEIKLOPRTT kleptocratic
ACCEILLMMORY commercially
ACCEILLMNOOY economically
ACCEILLMOSTY cosmetically
ACCEILLNNORT centroclinal
ACCEILLNOTTY tectonically
ACCEILLOPRRY reciprocally
ACCEILLOPTYY ecotypically
ACCEILMMNORU uncommercial
ACCEILMNNOOU uneconomical
ACCEILMNORTU counterclaim
ACCEILNNNOOT connectional
ACCEILNNOOPT conceptional
ACCEILNNOOTV convectional
ACCEILNNOSTY anticyclones
ACCEILNOORRT correctional
ACCEILNOPRST narcoleptics
ACCEILNOSSSU successional
ACCEILNRRSSU circularness
ACCEILOOSSTT osteoclastic
ACCEILOPRSST ceroplastics
ACCEILOPRSTU plutocracies
ACCEIMMNOSTU communicates
ACCEIMNOSTTY nematocystic
ACCEIMNRTTUU circumnutate
ACCEINNNNOOS inconsonance
ACCEINNNOOSS consonancies
ACCEINNOORST consecration
ACCEINNORSSU coinsurances
ACCEINNORSTV contrivances
ACCEINOOPRRS pornocracies
ACCEINOOPRTU reoccupation
ACCEIOOPRRRT reciprocator
ACCELLMNOPTY complacently
ACCELLNOPTUY conceptually
ACCELLOOORSU corollaceous
ACCELMMNOOPS commonplaces
ACCELMNORSUU macronucleus
ACCELMOOSTTY cyclostomate
ACCELNNRSTUY translucency
ACCELNOOPPRY cyclopropane
ACCELORSUUVY curvaceously
ACCEMOOSSTUY ascomycetous
ACCENNOORRTT concentrator
ACCENOOPRSTU pococurantes
ACCENOORRSST consecrators
ACCENOORRSTY consecratory
ACCENOPRRSTT precontracts
ACCENOPRRSTU counterscarp
ACCENORRSTTU contractures
ACCFGIINNOST confiscating
ACCFGILLNOTU flocculating
ACCFIIIINOTT citification
ACCFIIINOTTY cityfication
ACCFIIMNNOSU Confucianism
ACCFIINNOOST confiscation
ACCFILLNOOTU flocculation
ACCFILMORTUU fractocumuli
ACCFINOORSST confiscators
ACCFINOORSTY confiscatory
ACCGHHIINOPR ichnographic
ACCGHHIINTTT chitchatting
ACCGHHIIOPRR chirographic
ACCGHHIOOPRR chorographic
ACCGHIILLNOO ichnological
ACCGHIILNNOP Chilpancingo
ACCGHIIMOPRR micrographic
ACCGHIIMOTTT thigmotactic
ACCGHIINOOPR iconographic
ACCGHIINOPRZ zincographic
ACCGHIIOPPRT pictographic
ACCGHILLOOPY phycological
ACCGHIMOOPRS cosmographic
ACCGHINORRSS Charing Cross
ACCGIIILNNOT conciliating
ACCGIIILNSSS classicising
ACCGIIILNSSZ classicizing
ACCGIIINORST organicistic
ACCGIILLMOOT climatologic
ACCGIILLNOOO iconological

ACCGIILLOOOS sociological
ACCGIILMNOPT complicating
ACCGIINNOOST consociating
ACCGIKKMMNUU muckamucking
ACCGILLMOOOS cosmological
ACCGILMNOOOS cosmogonical
ACCGILNORTUY granulocytic
ACCGIOOPRSST gastroscopic
ACCHHINOOTTU autochthonic
ACCHHIOPPSTY psychopathic
ACCHIIINSTUV chauvinistic
ACCHIILLOOTY alcoholicity
ACCHIILOPRTY hypocritical
ACCHIIMMORST chromaticism
ACCHIIMNOPTY amphictyonic
ACCHIIMNORST monarchistic
ACCHIIMOORST isochromatic
ACCHIIMORRTT trichromatic
ACCHIIMORTTY chromaticity
ACCHIINOOPTT photoactinic
ACCHIIOPRSTY physiocratic
ACCHILLNNOOO nonalcoholic
ACCHILLOPTTY phyllotactic
ACCHILNOPRTY lycanthropic
ACCHILOOPSSY psychosocial
ACCHILOPPRTY prophylactic
ACCHIMOPRSSY macrophysics
ACCHINOOPSTT phonotactics
ACCHIOOPRRRT chiropractor
ACCHIOOPRRST arthroscopic
ACCHIOORRSSU chiaroscuros
ACCHJKNNNOUY Johnny Canuck
ACCIIILNNOOT conciliation
ACCIIINRSSST narcissistic
ACCIILLRSTTY crystallitic
ACCIILMMOORT microtomical
ACCIILMNNOPY incompliancy
ACCIILMNOOPT complication
ACCIILNNOOTV convictional
ACCIILNNOSTU inculcations
ACCIILNOORST conciliators
ACCIILNOORTY conciliatory
ACCIILNORSTU circulations
ACCIILOPRSUY capriciously
ACCIIMNNOSTY actinomycins
ACCIIMOOPRTT compatriotic
ACCIINNOOOST consociation
ACCIJLNNOTUV conjunctival
ACCIJNNOSTUV conjunctivas
ACCILLMNOOSU malocclusion
ACCILLNOOOST collocations
ACCILNOOSTTU occultations
ACCIMMNNOSTU communicants
ACCIMMNOORTU communicator
ACCIMNNOOSTT concomitants
ACCIMNOOSTUU contumacious
ACCIMOORSSTY macrocytosis
ACCINNOOOSTV convocations
ACCINNOORSTT contractions
ACCINOORSSTU coruscations
ACCIOOPRSSTU stauroscopic
ACCJLNNORTUU conjunctural
ACDDDEEHNOOR dodecahedron
ACDDEEEFNORT confederated
ACDDEEEHIMST semidetached
ACDDEEEILNRT credentialed
ACDDEEEINNPS dependancies
ACDDEEEIPRTT decrepitated
ACDDEEEMMNOR commandeered
ACDDEEEORTUV overeducated
ACDDEEFIILSS declassified
ACDDEEGHNRRU undercharged
ACDDEEGIINRT rededicating
ACDDEEGIKLRS griddlecakes
ACDDEEGKLNOW acknowledged
ACDDEEHIMNRS merchandised
ACDDEEHINNST disenchanted
ACDDEEHLLNOR candleholder
ACDDEEIINORT rededication
ACDDEEILPRTU reduplicated
ACDDEEIMORST democratised
ACDDEEIMORTZ democratized
ACDDEEIMOSTT domesticated
ACDDEEINNRSU redundancies
ACDDEEIQRSTU quadrisected
ACDDEELNPTUU pedunculated
ACDDEENNOSTV Second Advent
ACDDEGHINRSU undischarged
ACDDEHLLOSST saddlecloths
ACDDEIIILMOT domiciliated
ACDDEIILNORU radionuclide
ACDDEIILNPTU induplicated
ACDDEIINNOTV nonaddictive
ACDDEIINORST endocarditis
ACDDEILLMOUY duodecimally
ACDDEILNOOST consolidated
ACDDEILRSTTY distractedly
ACDDEINOSTTU outdistanced
ACDDHIMNORYY hydrodynamic
ACDDILNORSTY discordantly
ACDEEEEGINRS degeneracies
ACDEEEEHLRRS cheerleaders
ACDEEEFFNSST affectedness
ACDEEEFLNRST needlecrafts
ACDEEEFMNNRS Mendès-France
ACDEEEFNORST confederates
ACDEEEGHLLNR rechallenged
ACDEEEGILNRT decelerating
ACDEEEGINOPT paedogenetic
ACDEEEGINPRS predeceasing
ACDEEEHINRUV underachieve
ACDEEEHIORVV overachieved
ACDEEEHIRSTT catheterised
ACDEEEHIRTTZ catheterized
ACDEEEIIPRTV depreciative
ACDEEEILNORT deceleration
ACDEEEILNPRT precedential
ACDEEEILNRST decentralise
ACDEEEILNRSU denuclearise
ACDEEEILNRTV cantilevered
ACDEEEILNRTZ decentralize
ACDEEEILNRUZ denuclearize
ACDEEEILNSST delicateness
delicatessen

ACDEEEIMNOST	adenectomies
ACDEEEIMRSTV	decemvirates
ACDEEEINNRTV	inadvertence
ACDEEEINORTU	auctioneered
ACDEEEINRSSV	disseverance
ACDEEEINRSTV	advertencies
ACDEEEINSSTT	necessitated
ACDEEEIPRSTT	decrepitates
ACDEEELNNOSU	endonuclease
ACDEEELORRST	decelerators
ACDEEEOORRTV	overdecorate
ACDEEEOPRTTX	expectorated
ACDEEEORSTUV	overeducates
ACDEEFFLNTUY	unaffectedly
ACDEEFFNORRT	Fort-de-France
ACDEEFHHIKNR	handkerchief
ACDEEFHILNSS	candlefishes
ACDEEFHINNRS	enfranchised
ACDEEFHINOTT	fianchettoed
ACDEEFHNORRW	henceforward
ACDEEFIILRSS	reclassified
ACDEEFIILRST	federalistic
ACDEEFIILSSS	declassifies
ACDEEFIINRRY	ferricyanide
ACDEEFILMTTU	multifaceted
ACDEEFINORRY	ferrocyanide
ACDEEFNRRSUU	undersurface
ACDEEGHINNRT	interchanged
ACDEEGHLLNNU	unchallenged
ACDEEGHNRRSU	undercharges
ACDEEGHPRRSU	supercharged
ACDEEGIINPRT	depreciating
ACDEEGILLOTY	geodetically
ACDEEGILNRSY	decreasingly
ACDEEGILSTTU	gesticulated
ACDEEGINORRT	redecorating
ACDEEGKLNORW	acknowledger
ACDEEGKLNOSW	acknowledges
ACDEEGNNORTV	Covent Garden
ACDEEGNNOSTT	decongestant
ACDEEHHIMORT	hemichordate
ACDEEHHOPTTY	hypothecated
ACDEEHILMNOR	echinodermal
ACDEEHILMRSS	childermases
ACDEEHILNNOP	diencephalon
ACDEEHIMNRRS	merchandiser
ACDEEHIMNRSS	merchandises
ACDEEHINNRST	disenchanter
ACDEEHINRSTW	windcheaters
ACDEEHINSTTW	Wattenscheid
ACDEEHIORSTT	octahedrites
ACDEEHKKLNSU	knuckleheads
ACDEEHLORTTY	heterodactyl
ACDEEHMORRTU	routemarched
ACDEEHNNOPRU	unchaperoned
ACDEEHOPPRRS	sharecropped
ACDEEHORRSTT	orchestrated
ACDEEIIINNRS	incendiaries
ACDEEIILLMPY	epidemically
ACDEEIILLNTY	indelicately
ACDEEIILLTTY	dietetically
ACDEEIIMNRRT	recriminated
ACDEEIIMNRTY	intermediacy
ACDEEIINNNST	intendancies
ACDEEIINNOST	neonaticides
ACDEEIINOPRT	depreciation
ACDEEIINQSTU	equidistance
ACDEEIINTTUX	inexactitude
ACDEEIIOPPSS	epidiascopes
ACDEEIIPPRTT	precipitated
ACDEEIKLOOPS	kaleidoscope
ACDEEILLMPRY	premedically
ACDEEILLNNOS	declensional
ACDEEILLNNTY	tendencially
ACDEEILLNRTY	interlacedly
ACDEEILLRTUV	revictualled
ACDEEILMNPST	displacement
ACDEEILMORRS	sclerodermia
ACDEEILMRTUV	vermiculated
ACDEEILNORTU	reinoculated
ACDEEILNPQTU	quindecaplet
ACDEEILNRSTT	decentralist
ACDEEILORRST	clearstoried
ACDEEILORTVY	decoratively
ACDEEILPRSTU	reduplicates
ACDEEILRSSTT	decretalists
ACDEEILRTTVY	detractively
ACDEEIMMORST	commiserated
ACDEEIMNNOPR	predominance
ACDEEIMNPRST	predicaments
ACDEEIMOPRST	spermatocide
ACDEEIMORRRS	microreaders
ACDEEIMORRTX	xerodermatic
ACDEEIMORSST	democratises
ACDEEIMORSTZ	democratizes
ACDEEIMOSSTT	domesticates
ACDEEINNRTVY	inadvertency
ACDEEINOORRT	redecoration
ACDEEINOORST	aerodonetics
ACDEEINOPRST	deprecations
ACDEEINOPRTU	deuteranopic
ACDEEINORSTU	reeducations
ACDEEINOSSSU	edaciousness
ACDEEINPRRST	transpierced
ACDEEIOOPRSS	aecidospores
ACDEEIOPPRTU	propaedeutic
ACDEEIOPRRST	depreciators
ACDEEIOPRRTY	depreciatory
ACDEEIORRSTT	directorates
ACDEEIPQRSSU	quadricepses
ACDEEIRSSSTT	dictatresses
ACDEEIRSSTTU	resuscitated
ACDEEKQRRSTU	quarterdecks
ACDEELLNOSTT	constellated
ACDEELMNOPTT	contemplated
ACDEELNRSSSU	underclasses
ACDEEMMMOORT	commemorated
ACDEEMNOPPTY	appendectomy
ACDEEMNRSTTU	traducements
ACDEENNNOPRU	preannounced
ACDEENNNOTUV	uncovenanted
ACDEENNNRSTT	transcendent
ACDEENNORSST	contredanses
ACDEENNORSTT	consternated

ACDEENORRTTU	countertrade
ACDEFFGIINST	disaffecting
ACDEFFIILPST	spifflicated
ACDEFFIINOST	disaffection
ACDEFHIINRSS	disfranchise
ACDEFIIIMOTV	modificative
ACDEFIIINNST	infanticides
ACDEFIIINOST	deifications
ACDEFIILNNOT	confidential
ACDEFIILNSSU	unclassified
ACDEFIINNSTT	disinfectant
ACDEFIINNSTU	unsanctified
ACDEFIINOPTT	pontificated
ACDEFIINORST	fractionised
ACDEFIINORTZ	fractionized
ACDEFIKNORSU	Caudine Forks
ACDEFILLLOTU	folliculated
ACDEFILRTTUX	fluidextract
ACDEGHHNORST	shortchanged
ACDEGHIMOPRS	demographics
ACDEGHIOPRRS	discographer
ACDEGHNNORSU	changerounds
ACDEGIIILMNS	decimalising
ACDEGIIILMNZ	decimalizing
ACDEGIIKNRST	sidetracking
ACDEGIILLNOS	delocalising
ACDEGIILLNOZ	delocalizing
ACDEGIILNOSV	devocalising
ACDEGIILNOVZ	devocalizing
ACDEGIILPQRU	quadriplegic
ACDEGIIMNSTU	miseducating
ACDEGIINNNTU	denunciating
ACDEGIINOTTX	detoxicating
ACDEGIIOOPRT	diageotropic
ACDEGILLOOTY	dialectology
ACDEGILNORTU	edulcorating
ACDEGILNRTTY	detractingly
ACDEGINNNRST	transcending
ACDEGINNOQSU	quindecagons
ACDEGINNORTU	undercoating
ACDEGINNRTTU	detruncating
ACDEGIORRSSU	discouragers
ACDEGKLOORSS	sockdolagers
ACDEHHLOPRYY	hydrocephaly
ACDEHHOOOPTT	photocathode
ACDEHIIINPSS	hispanicised
ACDEHIIINPSZ	hispanicized
ACDEHIILLNOS	Chiloé Island
ACDEHIILMMOT	immethodical
ACDEHIILOPPS	pedophiliacs
ACDEHIIMNNOT	indomethacin
ACDEHIIMORST	radiochemist
ACDEHIINOPRR	perichondria
ACDEHIIOPRST	diaphoretics
ACDEHIIPRTYY	hyperacidity
ACDEHIKLNRST	stickhandler
ACDEHIKLNSST	stickhandles
ACDEHIKMNRSS	scrimshanked
ACDEHILLMOTY	methodically
ACDEHILLPRUY	hyperdulical
ACDEHILMNOTU	unmethodical
ACDEHILORSTY	hydroelastic
ACDEHINOORSS	icosahedrons
ACDEHIOOPRST	orthopaedics
ACDEHKLNNSST	landsknechts
ACDEHLLLOPSY	phylloclades
ACDEHLNPRSTU	thunderclaps
ACDEHLOORSUW	colourwashed
ACDEHMNNOORS	enchondromas
ACDEHMNORRSY	hydromancers
ACDEHMOORSTW	doomwatchers
ACDEHOORRSTU	urochordates
ACDEHORRSTYY	cryohydrates
ACDEIIIILNSV	civilianised
ACDEIIIILNVZ	civilianized
ACDEIIILMNRS	criminalised
ACDEIIILMNRZ	criminalized
ACDEIIILMOST	domiciliates
ACDEIIILNTVY	indicatively
ACDEIIILORST	cordialities
ACDEIIILRTVY	veridicality
ACDEIIIMMORT	radiomimetic
ACDEIIIMNNOT	nicotinamide
ACDEIIIMNNRS	incendiarism
ACDEIIIMNNRT	incriminated
ACDEIIIMNRST	discriminate
ACDEIIIMORST	isodiametric
ACDEIIINOPRT	antiperiodic
ACDEIIINORST	dictionaries
ACDEIIINPPST	appendicitis
ACDEIIINPSST	aspendicitis
ACDEIIINRTTU	antidiuretic
ACDEIIIOPRTY	aperiodicity
ACDEIIIOSSTV	dissociative
ACDEIIIPRRST	pericarditis
ACDEIIJORSTU	judicatories
ACDEIIKLRSTT	Lake District
ACDEIIKPRSTT	Peak District
ACDEIILLNNTY	incidentally
ACDEIILLNSTT	scintillated
ACDEIILLOPRY	periodically
ACDEIILLOPSY	episodically
ACDEIILLPSTY	septicidally
ACDEIILLRTUY	diuretically
ACDEIILMNOST	maledictions
ACDEIILMNSSU	masculinised
ACDEIILMNSUZ	masculinized
ACDEIILMOORT	iodometrical
ACDEIILMORTT	dilatometric
ACDEIILNNNOT	nonidentical
ACDEIILNNOST	declinations
ACDEIILNORST	discretional
ACDEIILNOSTU	elucidations
ACDEIILNOSTV	valedictions
ACDEIILNPSSS	Spice Islands
ACDEIILOPRST	tropicalised
ACDEIILOPRTZ	tropicalized
ACDEIILRRTUV	diverticular
ACDEIIMNORST	dominatrices
	romanticised
ACDEIIMNORTZ	romanticized
ACDEIIMNOSTU	miseducation
ACDEIIMOPRRT	madreporitic
ACDEIINNNOTU	denunciation

ACDEIINNOORT	incoordinate
ACDEIINNORTT	indoctrinate
ACDEIINNRSTY	tyrannicides
ACDEIINOOPPR	propanedioic
ACDEIINOORTV	coordinative
ACDEIINOOTTX	detoxication
ACDEIINOPRST	predications
ACDEIINORRST	doctrinaires
ACDEIINOSTTU	educationist
ACDEIIORSSTT	siderostatic
ACDEIJORSTUX	coadjutrixes
ACDEILLMOSTY	domestically
ACDEILLNOOST	decollations
ACDEILLNSTYY	syndetically
ACDEILLOPSTU	leucoplastid
ACDEILLOPSTY	despotically
ACDEILLRSSTY	crystallised
ACDEILLRSTYZ	crystallized
ACDEILMMNOSU	communalised
ACDEILMMNOUZ	communalized
ACDEILMNOPRU	unproclaimed
ACDEILMNOSUY	mendaciously
ACDEILMOPSTU	deutoplasmic
ACDEILNOOORT	decoloration
ACDEILNOORTU	edulcoration
ACDEILNOORTY	coordinately
ACDEILNOOSST	consolidates
	disconsolate
ACDEILNORSSW	cowardliness
ACDEILNPRSTY	discrepantly
ACDEILNTTUUV	uncultivated
ACDEILOORRUV	varicoloured
ACDEILOPSTTU	deutoplastic
ACDEILRRTTUU	turriculated
ACDEIMMNNOOT	commendation
ACDEIMMNORTY	dynamometric
ACDEIMNNNOOT	condemnation
ACDEIMNNOPRY	predominancy
ACDEIMOORSTT	domesticator
ACDEINNNOOST	condensation
ACDEINNNOSTU	unsanctioned
ACDEINNORSTU	denunciators
ACDEINNORTTU	detruncation
ACDEINNORTUY	denunciatory
ACDEINOOPRRT	incorporated
ACDEINOOPRSS	scorpaenoids
ACDEINOPRTTV	privatdocent
ACDEINOPRTTY	dictyopteran
ACDEINOSSSTU	decussations
ACDEINOSSTTU	outdistances
ACDEINPSSSSU	scindapsuses
ACDEIOOPRRST	corporatised
ACDEIOOPRRTZ	corporatized
ACDELLOPRRUY	procedurally
ACDELNOORTYY	cotyledonary
ACDELOPRRTTY	protractedly
ACDELOPRSTTY	pterodactyls
ACDEMMMNNOST	commandments
ACDEMMNOORTY	commendatory
ACDEMNNOORTY	condemnatory
ACDEMNNORSTU	countermands
ACDEMOORRSST	ostracoderms
ACDEORSTTTUU	autodestruct
ACDFFGILNOSS	scaffoldings
ACDFFIINORST	diffractions
ACDFGIIIINNT	nidificating
ACDFGIILLNUY	fungicidally
ACDFIIIINNOT	nidification
ACDFIIIMNOOT	modification
ACDFIILNNOTU	difunctional
ACDFIIMOORTY	modificatory
ACDGGIINORSU	discouraging
ACDGHHIOPRRY	hydrographic
ACDGHIIOPRTT	dittographic
ACDGHILLOORY	hydrological
ACDGIIINOSST	dissociating
ACDGIILOORST	cardiologist
ACDGIINNOORT	coordinating
ACDGILMMNNOY	commandingly
ACDGINOOOPRT	gonadotropic
ACDGINOORSVW	woodcarvings
ACDHHINOOPRY	hypochondria
ACDHHINOORTX	xanthochroid
ACDHHIOPRRSS	harpsichords
ACDHIILOOPSU	acidophilous
ACDHIIMMORST	dichromatism
ACDHIIMNOORT	mitochondria
ACDHIIMNORSS	diachronisms
ACDHIIOPRSST	rhapsodistic
ACDHIIOPRSTT	dictatorship
ACDHILLOORTY	trochoidally
ACDHIMNOOPTY	photodynamic
ACDHIMNOORST	trichomonads
ACDHINNORSYY	cyanohydrins
ACDHINOOPQRU	quadrophonic
ACDHIORSSTTY	hydrostatics
ACDHLNOOSSUY	Sunday school
ACDIIILNNPST	disciplinant
ACDIIILNPRSY	disciplinary
ACDIIIMNNRST	discriminant
ACDIIINNOSTV	vindications
ACDIIINOOSST	dissociation
ACDIIIOSSTTU	adscititious
ACDIILLLOOTY	colloidality
ACDIILLMNPTU	multiplicand
ACDIILLOOPSU	lapidicolous
ACDIILLOPRTY	dioptrically
ACDIILMNNORU	androclinium
ACDIILMNOPTU	undiplomatic
ACDIILNNOOST	conditionals
ACDIILNOOQTU	coloquintida
ACDIILNOOSST	dislocations
ACDIILNOPSTU	duplications
ACDIILNORTTY	doctrinality
ACDIILNOSSSU	discussional
ACDIIMNORRST	doctrinarism
ACDIINNOOORT	coordination
ACDIINNOSSTY	syndications
ACDIINOPRSST	adscriptions
ACDIINOPSSTU	cuspidations
ACDIINORSSTT	distractions
ACDIINORSSYY	idiosyncrasy
ACDILLLMOOSU	molluscoidal
ACDILLMOOORX	loxodromical

ACDILLORSSTY crystalloids
ACDILMNOOPSU Pamlico Sound
ACDILMNSSTYY syndactylism
ACDILMOORSUY mordaciously
ACDILNOOORST consolidator
ACDILNOOPRTU productional
ACDILORSTTUY tridactylous
ACDINNORSTTU transduction
ACDINOOORRST coordinators
ACDINOOQRSTU conquistador
ACDLOOOPRSTT postdoctoral
ACDNOORSSTTU Sandrocottus
ACEEEEEKPPRS peacekeepers
ACEEEEFNRRSS carefreeness
ACEEEEGIKNPP peacekeeping
ACEEEEGILPTX epexegetical
ACEEEEHLPSST steeplechase
ACEEEELNORTT coelenterate
ACEEEELNPRRS real presence
ACEEEENPRRSV perseverance
ACEEEFFFRSTT aftereffects
ACEEEFLNNOSV Anne of Cleves
ACEEEFLNPSSU peacefulness
ACEEEFLNSSSS facelessness
ACEEEFNNRRST transference
ACEEEGGORSTU secretagogue
ACEEEGHINPRS cheeseparing
ACEEEGHLLNRS rechallenges
ACEEEGIILNNS inelegancies
ACEEEGIKNRRT racketeering
ACEEEGILLTXY exegetically
ACEEEGINNOSS caenogenesis
ACEEEGINNSSW newsagencies
ACEEEGINRRST generatrices
ACEEEGLOSTTT telecottages
ACEEEGNNRRUY unregeneracy
ACEEEHHIRRST heterarchies
ACEEEHILSTTT telaesthetic
ACEEEHIMNQTU cinematheque
ACEEEHIMNSTV achievements
ACEEEHINOSST coenesthesia
ACEEEHIORRVV overachiever
ACEEEHIORSVV overachieves
ACEEEHIRSSTT catheterises
ACEEEHIRSTTZ catheterizes
ACEEEHKLNRST leathernecks
ACEEEHLLNRST chanterelles
ACEEEHLMOPRT cephalometer
ACEEEHLNNOPP epencephalon
ACEEEHMNNNST enhancements
ACEEEHMORSTT tacheometers
ACEEEHPRRSTU superteacher
ACEEEILLLNTT lenticellate
ACEEEILLMRTT telemetrical
ACEEEILMNPST mantelpieces
ACEEEILNNNSV Valenciennes
ACEEEILNORRV overreliance
ACEEEILNRRSV irrelevances
ACEEEILRRTVY recreatively
ACEEEILRTVXY execratively
ACEEEIMMNNPR impermanence
ACEEEIMNNPRS permanencies
ACEEEIMNNPRT intemperance
ACEEEIMPRSST masterpieces
ACEEEINRSSTV creativeness
reactiveness
ACEEEINSSSTT necessitates
ACEEEIPPPRTV apperceptive
ACEEEIPRRTUV recuperative
ACEEEJKLPSST steeplejacks
ACEEELLMNOST metallocenes
ACEEELLOPRTT electroplate
ACEEELLORSVV cloverleaves
ACEEELMMNPST emplacements
ACEEELMNPRST replacements
ACEEELNNSTVY evanescently
ACEEELNOSSUX exonucleases
ACEEELNOTXYY oxyacetylene
ACEEELNRSSSS carelessness
ACEEEMNNNRTT entrancement
ACEEEMNNRSTT reenactments
ACEEENNORSTW Western Ocean
ACEEENNRRTTY tercentenary
ACEEENNRSTXY sexcentenary
ACEEENRRSSSV screensavers
ACEEENRSSSST ancestresses
ACEEEOPPRRTT preceptorate
ACEEEOPRSTTX expectorates
ACEEERRSSSTW watercresses
ACEEFFGINTTU effectuating
ACEEFFILTTUY effectuality
ACEEFFINOTTU effectuation
ACEEFGHIMNST gemeinschaft
ACEEFGHINNRU French Guinea
ACEEFGHINORR forereaching
ACEEFGHLLSST gesellschaft
ACEEFGHNRTUW Feuchtwanger
ACEEFGIINRSS fricasseeing
ACEEFGLNRSSU gracefulness
ACEEFHHIRRSS archerfishes
ACEEFHINNRRS enfranchiser
ACEEFHINNRSS enfranchises
ACEEFHINOSTT fianchettoes
ACEEFHIORSTU chaetiferous
ACEEFHNRRSTU furtherances
ACEEFIIIRTVV verificative
ACEEFIILNQTU liquefacient
ACEEFIILQTUV liquefactive
ACEEFIILRSSS reclassifies
ACEEFIKNNNRS frankincense
ACEEFILLNORT reflectional
ACEEFILLNRTY frenetically
ACEEFILNNORT conferential
ACEEFILOPRRT prefectorial
ACEEFILRRTVY refractively
ACEEFINPRTTU putrefacient
ACEEFINPSTTU stupefacient
ACEEFIORRRST refractories
ACEEFIPRTTUV putrefactive
ACEEFMNOPRRS performances
ACEEGGHNPRSS sprechgesang
ACEEGGINORTV congregative
ACEEGHHIOPRS echographies
ACEEGHHOPRRR choregrapher

ACEEGHILLMNO Michelangelo
ACEEGHILOOST oligochaetes
ACEEGHINNRST interchanges
ACEEGHINOPTT pathogenetic
ACEEGHINORRV overreaching
ACEEGHINRRRT rechartering
ACEEGHLLNSSY changelessly
ACEEGHLOPRRT electrograph
ACEEGHMMORST hectogrammes
ACEEGHMNNORY moneychanger
ACEEGHNOPRRS scenographer
ACEEGHPRRRSU supercharger
ACEEGHPRRSSU supercharges
ACEEGIIKNNOT kainogenetic
ACEEGIILNNPT palingenetic
ACEEGIILNNST geanticlines
ACEEGIILNSTV evangelistic
ACEEGIIMNORT geometrician
ACEEGIINNOSS cainogenesis
ACEEGIINPPRV apperceiving
ACEEGIINRSTV eviscerating
ACEEGIIOTTVX excogitative
ACEEGILLLOOT teleological
ACEEGILLMOOR mereological
ACEEGILLNNRT crenellating
ACEEGILLNTUY geniculately
ACEEGILSSTTU gesticulates
ACEEGIMMNRST centigrammes
ACEEGIMMORST microgametes
ACEEGINNOSSY cyanogenesis
ACEEGINNPRRT carpentering
ACEEGINNRSTV ingravescent
ACEEGINNSSTX exactingness
ACEEGINOORST octogenaries
ACEEGINORRTV overreacting
ACEEGINPRRTU recuperating
ACEEGLMNNOST congealments
ACEEGLMNOORT conglomerate
ACEEGMNORRSS scaremongers
ACEEGOPRRSSU supercargoes
ACEEHHILPRTT terephthalic
ACEEHHIMNOPR archiphoneme
ACEEHHIOPTTT theopathetic
ACEEHHIPSSTY hypaesthesic
ACEEHHMMOORS haemochromes
ACEEHHMOPRTY chemotherapy
ACEEHHNOPRSU Schopenhauer
ACEEHHOPRSTU chapterhouse
ACEEHHOPRTTY tracheophyte
ACEEHHOPSTTY hypothecates
ACEEHHORRSTU Charterhouse
ACEEHIIKNSTT kinaesthetic
ACEEHIILMNOS isocheimenal
ACEEHIILNPST encephalitis
ACEEHIILNSST lecithinases
ACEEHIIMOOPT haemopoietic
ACEEHIIMSSTT aestheticism
ACEEHIINNRST inheritances
ACEEHIINORTT theoretician
ACEEHIINSSTT estheticians
ACEEHIIRRRST trierarchies
ACEEHIKLMNRT merchantlike
ACEEHILLMNOS melancholies
ACEEHILLMORS hemerocallis
ACEEHILLMRTY hermetically
ACEEHILLOPPT leptocephali
ACEEHILLSTTY esthetically
ACEEHILNORSS heroicalness
ACEEHILOORST heterosocial
ACEEHILPRSTY phylacteries
ACEEHIMMNPST impeachments
ACEEHIMMNTTY enthymematic
ACEEHIMNNNST enchainments
ACEEHIMNSSTT chastisement
ACEEHIMOPRTV overemphatic
ACEEHIMOSSTT somaesthetic
ACEEHINNOSST inchoateness
ACEEHINNRSTU neurasthenic
ACEEHINPSSTT pentastiches
ACEEHINSSTTY synaesthetic
ACEEHIOPRSST spirochaetes
ACEEHIPRSTTU therapeutics
ACEEHIRSSTTV tsarevitches
ACEEHLLOORRU leucorrhoeal
ACEEHLMOPRTY cephalometry
ACEEHLOPRRST perchlorates
ACEEHMNNNSTT enchantments
ACEEHMOORSST mesothoraces
ACEEHMORRSTU routemarches
ACEEHNNOPRRT Northern Cape
ACEEHNNORRST archenterons
ACEEHOPPRRRS sharecropper
ACEEHORRSSTT orchestrates
ACEEIIILLSTX lexicalities
ACEEIIILPSST specialities
ACEEIIINNRST itinerancies
ACEEIIINRSTV inveracities
ACEEIILLMNSS miscellanies
ACEEIILLRTTV verticillate
ACEEIILMMPRT metempirical
ACEEIILMPRRT perimetrical
ACEEIILMRRSU mercurialise
ACEEIILMRRUZ mercurialize
ACEEIILNNRST transilience
ACEEIILNORST lectionaries
ACEEIILNOSST sectionalise
ACEEIILNOSTZ sectionalize
ACEEIILNRSTT centralities
ACEEIILRSSTU secularities
ACEEIIMMRSTT meristematic
ACEEIIMNPRSU epicureanism
ACEEIIMNRRST recriminates
ACEEIINNORST containerise
ACEEIINNORTZ containerize
ACEEIINNRTUV renunciative
ACEEIINNSSTV inactiveness
ACEEIINORSSS cessionaries
ACEEIINORSTV evisceration
ACEEIINORTTX exercitation
ACEEIIORSSTV vesicatories
ACEEIIPPRSTT peripatetics
precipitates
ACEEIJORRSTT trajectories
ACEEILLLNTTU intellectual

ACEEILLLPTTT Citlaltépetl
ACEEILLMMRSY mesmerically
ACEEILLMNORY ceremonially
ACEEILLMNSTY centesimally
ACEEILLMORTY meteorically
ACEEILLNNNTY centennially
ACEEILLNNORT crenellation
ACEEILLNORTY neoterically
ACEEILLNRSUV surveillance
ACEEILLORSTY esoterically
ACEEILLORTXY exoterically
ACEEILLRTTUY reticulately
ACEEILMMNPST misplacement
ACEEILMORRST calorimeters
ACEEILMRSTUV vermiculates
ACEEILNNORST crenelations
ACEEILNNOSTU enucleations
ACEEILNNRRTU internuclear
ACEEILNOPPRT perceptional
ACEEILNOPRRT precentorial
ACEEILNOPRSS narcolepsies
precessional
ACEEILNORRST necrolatries
ACEEILNORSSS recessionals
ACEEILNORSTU reinoculates
ACEEILNRRSST centralisers
ACEEILNRRSTZ centralizers
ACEEILOOPSST Apostolic See
ACEEILOPPRRT preceptorial
ACEEILOPSSTY caespitosely
ACEEILORRSST clearstories
ACEEILORRSTV correlatives
ACEEILPPSTTU septuplicate
ACEEILPRSSTU superelastic
ACEEILPSTTUX sextuplicate
ACEEILRRSSSU secularisers
ACEEILRRSSUZ secularizers
ACEEIMMMNOTT committeeman
ACEEIMMNNPRY impermanency
ACEEIMMNORST commentaries
ACEEIMMORSST commiserates
ACEEIMMOSSTT mastectomies
ACEEIMNNOORR oneiromancer
ACEEIMNNOSTT cementations
ACEEIMNOPRST armipotences
ACEEIMNOPSTV compensative
ACEEIMNORRST craniometers
ACEEIMNORSTT actinometers
ACEEIMNORSVW servicewoman
ACEEIMNQRSTU acquirements
ACEEINNRRTTY tricentenary
ACEEINOORRTV overreaction
ACEEINOPPPRT apperception
ACEEINOPRRTU recuperation
ACEEINOPRSTT inspectorate
ACEEINOPSTTX expectations
ACEEINORRSSY recessionary
ACEEINORRSTY secretionary
ACEEINORSTVV conservative
ACEEINPRRSST transpierces
ACEEINRRSSTV transceivers
ACEEINRSSTUV curativeness
ACEEIOOPRSTV cooperatives
ACEEIORRSSTV eviscerators
ACEEIRSSSTTU resuscitates
ACEELLMMNOPT complemental
ACEELLNOPTUY polynucleate
ACEELLNORSSV Roncesvalles
ACEELLNOSSTT constellates
ACEELLPPRTUY perceptually
ACEELMNNORTU nomenclature
ACEELMNOOSTU lomentaceous
ACEELMNOPSTT contemplates
ACEELMNOPTTU outplacement
ACEELMNRSTTY Clytemnestra
ACEELMPRRTUU permaculture
ACEELNOOPRST coleopterans
ACEELNOORRSS Eleanor Cross
ACEELNOOSTUY coetaneously
ACEELNPRSSST spectralness
ACEELNSSSSTT tactlessness
ACEELOOPPPTT Popocatépetl
ACEELOPPPRST copperplates
ACEELPRSSSSU superclasses
ACEELPSSTUUY eucalyptuses
ACEEMMMOORST commemorates
ACEEMMNORSTU commensurate
ACEEMMOPRTTU metacomputer
ACEEMNNNNOTU announcement
ACEEMNNORRST remonstrance
ACEEMOPRSTTY spermatocyte
ACEENNNOPRSU preannounces
ACEENNOPRSTU counterpanes
ACEENNORRSTV contraveners
ACEENNORSSTT consternates
ACEENOORSSTT cotoneasters
ACEENOPRSTTX expectorants
ACEENOPRSTUU percutaneous
ACEEOOPRRTTT protectorate
ACEEOOPRRTTX expectorator
ACEEOPRRRSTU recuperators
ACEEORRSSTUW watercourses
ACEFFFHHIRSS Frisches Haff
ACEFFGHILNRS cliffhangers
ACEFFGHINRUU chauffeuring
ACEFFIIILMOS semiofficial
ACEFFIILPSST spifflicates
ACEFFILNNSSU fancifulness
ACEFFORRSUUU furfuraceous
ACEFGHIINPRY preachifying
ACEFGHILOPRX flexographic
ACEFGHINRSSS grassfinches
ACEFGIIILMNS facsimileing
ACEFGIIILNTT felicitating
ACEFGIINNRST interfacings
ACEFGIINORTV vociferating
ACEFGILNRSTU centrifugals
ACEFGINNRSTT transfecting
ACEFHILNOPRS francophiles
ACEFHLNSSTUW watchfulness
ACEFHNORSTTU countershaft
ACEFIIIILNST finicalities
ACEFIIILNOST fictionalise
ACEFIIILNOTT felicitation

ACEFIIILNOTZ	fictionalize
ACEFIIINORST	reifications
ACEFIIINORTV	verification
ACEFIILLNNOT	inflectional
ACEFIILLRRTY	terrifically
ACEFIILMNORS	infomercials
ACEFIILNOQTU	liquefaction
ACEFIILORSTT	felicitators
ACEFIILORSTU	laticiferous
ACEFIIMNORTV	confirmative
ACEFIINOORTV	vociferation
ACEFIINOPRTT	petrifaction
ACEFIINOPSTT	pontificates
ACEFIINORSST	fractionises
ACEFIINORSTZ	fractionizes
ACEFIIORRTVY	verificatory
ACEFIIRRTTVY	refractivity
ACEFILLNORSY	forensically
ACEFILLORSUW	cauliflowers
ACEFILNNOOSS	confessional
ACEFILORRRTY	refractorily
ACEFIMNOSTTU	tumefactions
ACEFINNORSTT	transfection
ACEFINOORRTT	torrefaction
ACEFINOPRTTU	putrefaction
ACEFINOPSTTU	stupefaction
ACEFINOSSSTU	factiousness
ACEFIOORRSTV	vociferators
ACEFLMOORTTY	olfactometry
ACEGGGINNORT	congregating
ACEGGHINORRV	overcharging
ACEGGIINNSST	giganticness
ACEGGIINORST	categorising
ACEGGIINORTZ	categorizing
ACEGGIINOTTX	excogitating
ACEGGILLLOOY	geologically
ACEGGILLMMOO	gemmological
ACEGGIMNORTY	gyromagnetic
ACEGGINNOORT	congregation
ACEGGNOORRST	congregators
ACEGHHIILOPR	heliographic
ACEGHHILOPRS	helicographs
ACEGHHILRSST	searchlights
ACEGHHINOPRT	ethnographic
ACEGHHIOPRRR	chirographer
ACEGHHIOPRTY	hyetographic
ACEGHHNOPRTY	technography
ACEGHHNORRST	shortchanger
ACEGHHNORSST	shortchanges
ACEGHHOOPRRR	chorographer
ACEGHHOOPRRS	choreographs
ACEGHHOOPRRY	choreography
ACEGHIILLNYY	hygienically
ACEGHIILLOOR	hierological
ACEGHIILNNNS	channelising
ACEGHIILNNNZ	channelizing
ACEGHIIMNSST	schematising
ACEGHIIMNSTZ	schematizing
ACEGHIKLLNSS	shellackings
ACEGHILLNNOU	hallucinogen
ACEGHILLNOOP	nephological
	phenological
ACEGHILLNOOT	ethnological
ACEGHILLRTUY	theurgically
ACEGHILMOPYY	hypoglycemia
ACEGHILNNNTY	enchantingly
ACEGHILNNSTY	chasteningly
ACEGHILOORST	archeologist
ACEGHILOPPRY	pyelographic
ACEGHILOPRXY	lexicography
ACEGHIMNORTV	overmatching
ACEGHIMOOPRT	gametophoric
ACEGHIMOPRRR	micrographer
ACEGHIMOPTTY	gametophytic
ACEGHINOOPRR	iconographer
ACEGHINOPRRZ	zincographer
ACEGHINOPRST	stenographic
ACEGHINORTVW	overwatching
ACEGHINPRRSU	repurchasing
ACEGHIOPPRRR	reprographic
ACEGHIOPPRRT	petrographic
ACEGHIOPRRST	cerographist
ACEGHLNOPSTT	plectognaths
ACEGHMOOPRRS	cosmographer
ACEGHNOOPRSU	necrophagous
ACEGHOPPRRST	spectrograph
ACEGHORRSSTU	roughcasters
ACEGIIILLMTY	illegitimacy
ACEGIIILLNSX	lexicalising
ACEGIIILLNXZ	lexicalizing
ACEGIIILNPSS	specialising
ACEGIIILNPSZ	specializing
ACEGIIILNSST	elasticising
ACEGIIILNSTZ	elasticizing
ACEGIIINNNRT	incinerating
ACEGIIINSTTV	negativistic
ACEGIILLLOTY	collegiality
ACEGIILLMOOS	semiological
ACEGIILLNRRV	Invercargill
ACEGIILLOOPT	geopolitical
ACEGIILLOSTU	eulogistical
ACEGIILLOSTY	egoistically
ACEGIILNNOTU	geniculation
ACEGIILNNOTY	congeniality
ACEGIILNNRST	centralising
ACEGIILNNRSY	increasingly
ACEGIILNNRTZ	centralizing
ACEGIILNPRSS	Alice Springs
ACEGIILNRSSU	secularising
ACEGIILNRSUZ	secularizing
ACEGIILNRTTU	reticulating
ACEGIILNSTUV	vesiculating
ACEGIILORSSU	sacrilegious
ACEGIILOTTVY	cogitatively
ACEGIILRSSST	sacrilegists
ACEGIIMNOSST	isomagnetics
ACEGIIMNTTUY	mutagenicity
ACEGIINNPPRT	apprenticing
ACEGIINNPRST	interspacing
ACEGIINOOTTX	excogitation
ACEGIINOQTUV	equivocating
ACEGIKLLNSSS	gallsickness
ACEGILLLNOOY	neologically
ACEGILLMOORT	metrological

ACEGILLMOOSU museological
ACEGILLMOOTY etymological
ACEGILLNNOSY geosynclinal
ACEGILLNNOTY congenitally
ACEGILLNOORU neurological
ACEGILLNOORY orogenically
ACEGILLNRTTY clatteringly
ACEGILLOOORT erotological
ACEGILLOOOST osteological
ACEGILLOOPRT petrological
ACEGILNNOOST congelations
ACEGILNNOTTU conglutinate
ACEGILNOOPRT organoleptic
ACEGILNOOPTU unapologetic
ACEGILNSTUUU unguiculates
ACEGILOOPSST escapologist
ACEGILORSTTU gesticulator
ACEGIMMNNOTT commentating
ACEGIMMNORSU commeasuring
ACEGIMNNOPRS panicmongers
ACEGIMNNOPSS encompassing
ACEGIMNNOPST compensating
ACEGIMNNORST centimorgans
ACEGIMNOPRTY pyromagnetic
ACEGINNNORTV contravening
ACEGINNORSTT nonstrategic
ACEGINOPRRSU superorganic
ACEGINORSSSU graciousness
ACEGIOOOPPRT apogeotropic
ACEGIOORSTTX excogitators
ACEGLNOOPRSY laryngoscope
ACEGLNOORSUY acrogenously
ACEGLNOPRSTY calyptrogens
ACEGLNORSTUY granulocytes
ACEGLOORSUUY courageously
ACEGMOPRRSST spectrograms
ACEGNOORRSTT gerontocrats
ACEGOOPRSSST gastroscopes
ACEHHIIINRST Chiantishire
ACEHHIILMOPS hemophiliacs
ACEHHIIMMPTU amphithecium
ACEHHIINOPRT hierophantic
ACEHHILMOPTX exophthalmic
ACEHHILMRTUY eurhythmical
ACEHHILOOPST theosophical
ACEHHILOPTTY hypothetical
ACEHHIMOOOPT homoeopathic
ACEHHINOPRTT theanthropic
ACEHHINOSSTX hexastichons
ACEHHINOSTTY osteichthyan
ACEHHLNNNORT North Channel
ACEHHLOOPRTY orthocephaly
ACEHHMOOPRTU chemoautroph
ACEHHMORSTTY chrestomathy
ACEHHNOOSTTU autochthones
ACEHHOOPRTTY hypothecator
ACEHIIINPSSS hispanicises
ACEHIIINPSSZ hispanicizes
ACEHIIINRSST christianise
ACEHIIINRSTZ christianize
ACEHIIKRRSWW Warwickshire
ACEHIILLMPTY mephitically
ACEHIILLMRTY hermitically
ACEHIILLSTTY theistically
ACEHIILMNNTT anthelmintic
ACEHIILNPPRS planispheric
ACEHIILPSTUU euphuistical
ACEHIILSSTWW welwitschias
ACEHIIMOORST rachiotomies
ACEHIINNOPST phoneticians
ACEHIINORRST rhetoricians
ACEHIINSSTTU enthusiastic
ACEHIINTTTUY authenticity
ACEHIIOPSSTT sophisticate
ACEHIIPPRRST periphrastic
ACEHIIQRRSSU squirarchies
ACEHIKMNOSST mackintoshes
ACEHIKRRSSSW kirschwasser
ACEHILLLMNOY melancholily
ACEHILLLPTYY phyletically
ACEHILLMNNTU multichannel
ACEHILLMNOPY phonemically
ACEHILLNOPST plainclothes
ACEHILLNOPTY phonetically
ACEHILLNOPUY euphonically
ACEHILLORRTY rhetorically
ACEHILLRSTYY hysterically
ACEHILMNOOTT nomothetical
ACEHILMOOPSU amphicoelous
ACEHILMOOPTY homeotypical
ACEHILMOPTYY polycythemia
ACEHILNNNSSS clannishness
ACEHILNNOTTT Tenochtitlán
ACEHILNOPPTY phenotypical
ACEHILNPSSSY physicalness
ACEHILPPRSTY hyperplastic
ACEHIMNORSTU euchromatins
ACEHIMOOOSTT homoeostatic
ACEHIMOPRRSU archesporium
ACEHIMOPRSST atmospherics
ACEHIMOPSSTY scyphistomae
ACEHIMORRSST choirmasters
ACEHIMORSTTT thermostatic
ACEHINNOOPRT neoanthropic
ACEHINOOPRTT epanorthotic
ACEHINOPRRSS chairpersons
ACEHINOPRRST chiropterans
ACEHINOPRRTT trichopteran
ACEHINOPRSTY hyperactions
ACEHINORRSST orchestrinas
ACEHIRSSTTWW wristwatches
ACEHKKRRSSSU sharksuckers
ACEHKMRRSSTT stretchmarks
ACEHLLLMOSST smallclothes
ACEHLLLPRSUY sepulchrally
ACEHLLMORSYY lachrymosely
ACEHLLORRSTY orchestrally
ACEHLMMNOOTW commonwealth
ACEHLMOORSST schoolmaster
ACEHLNOOPRTU photonuclear
ACEHLNOPRSTY lycanthropes
ACEHLOOPSTUY polychaetous
ACEHLOOPSUXY oxycephalous
ACEHLOORSSUW colourwashes

ACEHLOPSSUXY	psychosexual
ACEHMMNOOORT	monochromate
ACEHMNOOORSU	anemochorous
ACEHMOORSTTY	tracheostomy
ACEHMOPRRTYY	crymotherapy
ACEHMORRSSTU	chorusmaster
ACEHMOSSSUYY	hyoscyamuses
ACEHNNOOPRST	ctenophorans
ACEHOOPRRSST	arthroscopes
	crapshooters
ACEHOORRRSTT	orchestrator
ACEHOPRRSSSY	chrysoprases
ACEIIIILNSSV	civilianises
ACEIIIILNSVZ	civilianizes
ACEIIIINRSTT	initiatrices
ACEIIIJRSSTU	justiciaries
ACEIIIKNNNPS	pickaninnies
ACEIIILLRSTT	literalistic
ACEIIILMNNSS	inimicalness
ACEIIILMNPSU	municipalise
ACEIIILMNPUZ	municipalize
ACEIIILMNRSS	criminalises
ACEIIILMNRSZ	criminalizes
ACEIIILNNOTT	licentiation
ACEIIILNORTV	Victoria Nile
ACEIIILNOSTT	elicitations
ACEIIILNSTTY	inelasticity
ACEIIILRSTTV	relativistic
ACEIIILRSTVV	revivalistic
ACEIIIMNNRST	incriminates
ACEIIIMNOSST	semioticians
ACEIIIMNPRSS	precisianism
ACEIIINNNORT	incineration
ACEIIINOTTVX	intoxicative
ACEIIIORSSTV	varicosities
ACEIIJLLSTUY	jesuitically
ACEIIJLORSTU	jocularities
ACEIIKKNORTY	karyokinetic
ACEIIKLLMORT	kilometrical
ACEIIKLLOORS	kilocalories
ACEIILLLLPTY	ellipticallly
ACEIILLMNNSU	illuminances
ACEIILLMNSST	miscellanist
ACEIILLMPTTU	multiplicate
ACEIILLNORTY	collinearity
ACEIILLNOSTV	vellications
ACEIILLNSSTT	scintillates
ACEIILMMNRST	mercantilism
ACEIILMMRRSU	mercurialism
ACEIILMMSSTY	semimystical
ACEIILMNORST	salinometric
ACEIILMNOSST	sectionalism
ACEIILMNRSTT	mercantilist
ACEIILMNSSSU	masculinises
ACEIILMNSSUZ	masculinizes
ACEIILMOPPSS	episcopalism
ACEIILMOPRRT	polarimetric
ACEIILMOPRST	semitropical
ACEIILMOPSTT	metapolitics
ACEIILMPRSTU	implicatures
ACEIILMRRTUY	mercuriality
ACEIILNNNRTU	internuncial
ACEIILNNOPST	inspectional
ACEIILNNORSS	ironicalness
ACEIILNNORST	nonrealistic
	reclinations
ACEIILNOORST	coalitioners
ACEIILNOPRST	inspectorial
	replications
ACEIILNOPSTX	explications
ACEIILNOQSTU	equinoctials
ACEIILNORTTU	reticulation
ACEIILNOSSTT	sectionalist
ACEIILNOSTUV	vesiculation
ACEIILNRSSTT	clarinetists
ACEIILNRSTTT	clarinettist
ACEIILOPRSST	tropicalises
ACEIILOPRSTZ	tropicalizes
ACEIILOQSSUU	siliquaceous
ACEIILOQTUVY	equivocality
ACEIILORRRSV	corrivalries
ACEIILPRRSUY	superciliary
ACEIILPRSSST	plasticisers
ACEIILPRSSTZ	plasticizers
ACEIILRRSSTU	surrealistic
ACEIILRRTTTY	retractility
ACEIILRSTTVY	astrictively
ACEIIMMNORST	cremationism
ACEIIMMORSSS	commissaires
	commissaries
ACEIIMNOORST	craniotomies
ACEIIMNOPRST	imprecations
ACEIIMNORRRT	recriminator
ACEIIMNORSST	miscreations
	romanticises
ACEIIMNORSTT	cremationist
ACEIIMNORSTZ	romanticizes
ACEIIMNRSSTU	insectariums
ACEIIMNSSSTT	semanticists
ACEIIMOORSTV	varicotomies
ACEIINNNORTU	renunciation
ACEIINNNOSST	incensations
ACEIINNNOSTT	Constantine I
ACEIINNNOSTU	enunciations
ACEIINNNSTTV	Saint Vincent
ACEIINNOPSTT	pectinations
ACEIINNORRST	incinerators
ACEIINNORRTY	incretionary
ACEIINNORSTT	interactions
ACEIINNOSSST	ascensionist
ACEIINNOTTUV	continuative
ACEIINNSSTTY	nyctinasties
ACEIINOOQTUV	equivocation
ACEIINOORSTV	viscerotonia
ACEIINOORSTX	excoriations
ACEIINOPRRTT	practitioner
ACEIINOPRSTT	crepitations
ACEIINOPRSTU	pertinacious
ACEIINOPSSTT	pectisations
ACEIINOPSTTZ	pectizations
ACEIINORRSTW	contrariwise
ACEIINORSSTT	creationists
	reactionists
ACEIINPPRSTT	precipitants

ACEIINPRSTTY antipyretics
ACEIIOPPRRTT precipitator
ACEIJKLLNOSV Jacksonville
ACEIJLNOOPRT projectional
ACEILLLMNORS lamellicorns
ACEILLMMNNOY mnemonically
ACEILLMMNOOT monometallic
ACEILLMNOOPT compellation
ACEILLMNOOPX complexional
ACEILLMNOSST callistemons
ACEILLMNRTUU multinuclear
ACEILLMNTUVY multivalency
ACEILLMORRTU trimolecular
ACEILLMORTUY molecularity
ACEILLMRRUVY vermicularly
ACEILLMSSTYY systemically
ACEILLMTUUVY cumulatively
ACEILLNNORRU carillonneur
ACEILLNOOTYZ enzootically
ACEILLNORTUY neurotically
ACEILLNOSTTU scutellation
ACEILLOPTUVY copulatively
ACEILLRRSSTY crystalliser
ACEILLRRSTUU sericultural
ACEILLRRSTYZ crystallizer
ACEILLRSSSTY crystallises
ACEILLRSSTTY crystallites
ACEILLRSSTYZ crystallizes
ACEILMMMNOSS commensalism
ACEILMMNOORT monometrical
ACEILMMNOOST commonalties
ACEILMMNORSU communaliser
ACEILMMNORUZ communalizer
ACEILMMNOSSU communalises
ACEILMMNOSTY commensality
ACEILMMNOSUZ communalizes
ACEILMMORSTT recommittals
ACEILMNNOOPT componential
ACEILMNSSSTY mysticalness
ACEILMOOPSTT leptosomatic
ACEILMOPRRTY pyrometrical
ACEILMOPRSTT plastometric
ACEILMOPRSUU primulaceous
ACEILNNNOOTV conventional
ACEILNNNOSTT continentals
ACEILNNNOSTU antinucleons
ACEILNNOORSV conversional
ACEILNNORSTU crenulations
ACEILNNOSSST sanctionless
ACEILNOOPRSS processional
ACEILNOOPRST percolations
ACEILNOOPRTT lactoprotein
ACEILNOORRST correlations
ACEILNOORTUY elocutionary
ACEILNOPSSTU speculations
ACEILNOPSTUX exculpations
ACEILNORSTUV countervails
ACEILNORSUXY exclusionary
ACEILNOSTTUV consultative
ACEILOOPPRSS polariscopes
ACEILOOPRRTY corporeality
ACEILOOPSSTT osteoplastic
ACEILOPRRSUY precariously
ACEILOQSSUUY sequaciously
ACEILPPRSSTU superplastic
ACEILRRSSSTY crystalisers
ACEILRRSSTYZ crystalizers
ACEIMMNOPRTY micropayment
ACEIMMNOSTUV consummative
ACEIMMOORRST commiserator
ACEIMMORRSTU crematoriums
ACEIMNNOOPST compensation
ACEIMNNOOSST Monte Cassino
ACEIMNNOPRTY intercompany
ACEIMNNOPRYZ pancreozymin
ACEIMNOOOOPT onomatopoeic
ACEIMNORSSTV conservatism
ACEIMNPSTTUU mispunctuate
ACEIMNSSTTUY unsystematic
ACEIMOOPRSTZ spermatozoic
zoospermatic
ACEIMOPRRSTY cryptomerias
ACEIMPRSSSTU supremacists
ACEINNOORSTV conservation
conversation
ACEINNOOSTTT contestation
ACEINNORRSST constrainers
contrariness
ACEINNORRTUY renunciatory
ACEINNORSSTT transections
ACEINNORSTTU counterstain
encrustation
ACEINOOOPRST cooperations
ACEINOOPRRST incorporates
ACEINOORRSTT retroactions
ACEINOPPRRTU Port-au-Prince
ACEINOPSSSSU spaciousness
ACEINOPSSSTU captiousness
ACEINOSSSTUU cautiousness
ACEINRRSTUUV incurvatures
ACEIOOPRRSST corporatises
ACEIOOPRRSTZ corporatizes
ACEIOOQRSTUV equivocators
ACEIOOQRTUVY equivocatory
ACEIOORSTUUV overcautious
ACEIORRSSTTU resuscitator
ACEKLNPRSTTU planet-struck
ACEKMMNORTUY mockumentary
ACELLNNOSSUY consensually
ACELLNNOTUVY conventually
ACELLNOTTUXY contextually
ACELMMNOSTUY consummately
ACELMNNOORST nomenclators
ACELMNOOPRTT contemplator
ACELMRSSTUUU musculatures
ACELNNORSTVY conversantly
ACELNNRSSUUU ranunculuses
ACELNOOPRSTU proconsulate
ACELNOSSSTTU sansculottes
ACELOORRSTUW watercolours
ACEMMMOOORRT commemorator
ACEMMNOOPRRY common prayer
ACEMMNOORSTT commentators
ACEMMNOPRSTT compartments

ACEMNOOPRRTY	contemporary
ACEMNOOPRSST	compensators
ACEMNOOPRSTY	compensatory
ACEMOOPRRSTU	macropterous
ACEMORSSSTTU	scoutmasters
ACENNNORSTUV	unconversant
ACENNOORSSSU	canorousness
ACENNRRRSTTU	transcurrent
ACENOOQRTTTU	quattrocento
ACENOORRSSTV	conservators
ACENOORRSTVY	conservatory
ACENOPRRSTTU	counterparts
ACENOPRRTTUY	counterparty
ACEOOPRSSSTU	stauroscopes
ACEOPRRSSSTT	sportscaster
ACFFGGHIILNN	cliffhanging
ACFFIIINOOST	officiations
ACFFIILLNOUY	unofficially
ACFGGHIMNORR	frogmarching
ACFGIIILNOTU	uglification
ACFGIIILNPST	spiflicating
ACFGIILNRSYY	scarifyingly
ACFGIKNRSSTU	starfuckings
ACFHHLNORSSY	synchroflash
ACFHIIIMNOTU	humification
ACFHIILLORRY	horrifically
ACFIIIILNOTV	vilification
ACFIIIIMNNOT	minification
ACFIIIINOTVV	vivification
ACFIIINNOOTT	notification
ACFIIINNORTT	antifriction
ACFIIINNOSTU	unifications
ACFIIINOOSST	ossification
ACFIIINOPRTU	purification
ACFIIINOPTTY	typification
ACFIIINORSTV	vinificators
ACFIILLLOPRY	prolifically
ACFIILLNOPTY	pontifically
ACFIILNNNOOT	nonfictional
ACFIILOSTTUY	factitiously
ACFIIMNNOORT	confirmation
ACFIINNOORST	fornications
ACFIINORRTTU	trifurcation
ACFIIOPRRSTU	purificators
ACFIIOPRRTUY	purificatory
ACFILLNNOTUY	functionally
ACFILLOORSUU	cauliflorous
ACFILMNNOSTU	malfunctions
ACFILNOSTTUU	fluctuations
ACFIMNNOOORT	conformation
ACFIMNOORRTY	confirmatory
ACFINNOOSTTU	confutations
ACFRRSTUUUUY	usufructuary
ACGGHINORSTU	roughcasting
ACGGIILLOOST	glaciologist
ACGGIILNOTTY	cogitatingly
ACGGILLNOORY	laryngologic
ACGHHHIOPTYY	ichthyophagy
ACGHHIILOPRT	lithographic
ACGHHINOOPPR	phonographic
ACGHHIOOPPRT	photographic
ACGHHIOOPRRT	orthographic
ACGHHIOPPRSY	hypsographic
ACGHHIOPPRTY	phytographic
ACGHHNOOPRRS	chronographs
ACGHIIJKNNNU	Kinchinjunga
ACGHIILLLOOP	philological
ACGHIILLLOOT	lithological
ACGHIILLNOOR	rhinological
ACGHIILLNOOS	alcoholising
ACGHIILLNOOZ	alcoholizing
ACGHIILLOOOP	ophiological
ACGHIILLOOST	histological
ACGHIILMNPTY	lymphangitic
ACGHIILNNORT	chlorinating
ACGHIILNORTY	trichogynial
ACGHIIMNRSSW	scrimshawing
ACGHIINNNOST	stanchioning
ACGHIINPRSTY	scintigraphy
ACGHIIOPPRRS	spirographic
ACGHIIPRSSST	sphragistics
ACGHILLMNOOY	hymnological
ACGHILLMOOTY	mythological
ACGHILLNOOOP	phonological
ACGHILLNOOPY	hypnological
ACGHILLOOPRS	oscillograph
ACGHILLOOPTY	phytological
ACGHILLORTTU	logical truth
ACGHILMOORST	cologarithms
ACGHILMOOSST	logomachists
ACGHILNRSSTT	latchstrings
ACGHILOPRSTY	stylographic
ACGHIMMNOOPR	phonogrammic
ACGHIMOOPRSU	microphagous
ACGHINOOPPRR	pornographic
ACGHIOOPSSTY	phagocytosis
ACGHLMOOORTY	chromatology
ACGHNOOOPRRS	coronographs
ACGHOOOPPRSU	coprophagous
ACGHOPPRRSTY	cryptographs
ACGHOPPRRTYY	cryptography
ACGIIILLLOTY	illogicality
ACGIIILMNQTU	quitclaiming
ACGIIILNOSST	logisticians
ACGIIILNOSTY	caliginosity
ACGIIILNPRTT	triplicating
ACGIIILNPSST	plasticising
ACGIIILNPSTZ	plasticizing
ACGIIINNOTTX	intoxicating
ACGIIKKLNSTW	walkingstick
ACGIILLLMNOO	limnological
ACGIILLLOSTY	logistically
ACGIILLLRTUY	liturgically
ACGIILLNNNOR	carillonning
ACGIILLNOOST	colligations
ACGIILMNOSUU	mucilaginous
ACGIILMNSSTU	simulcasting
ACGIILNNOSTU	inosculating
ACGIILNOORST	craniologist
ACGIILNPPSTU	supplicating
ACGIILNRSSTY	crystalising
ACGIILNRSTYZ	crystalizing
ACGIILOOPPRT	plagiotropic
ACGIIMMNOOST	monogamistic

ACGIIMNNNOOP	companioning
ACGIIMORRTVY	microgravity
ACGIINNNOOST	consignation
ACGIINNNORST	constraining
ACGIINNOPSTT	constipating
ACGIINNOSTTW	wainscotting
ACGIJNNOOSTU	conjugations
ACGILLLOOORY	orologically
ACGILLMNNOOY	cognominally
	gnomonically
ACGILLMOORSS	oscillograms
ACGILLOOOPRT	tropological
ACGILMOORRTY	martyrologic
ACGILNNNOTTU	conglutinant
ACGILNOOSTUY	contagiously
ACGILNOPSUUY	pugnaciously
ACGILOOPRSST	carpologists
ACGILOOSSSTT	scatologists
ACGIMMNNOSTU	consummating
ACGIMMOOPRRR	microprogram
ACGIMNOOPRTU	compurgation
ACGINOORRSTU	corrugations
ACGLLNOORSUY	clangorously
ACGLNOOPRSYY	laryngoscopy
ACGMOOPRRSTU	compurgators
ACGMOOPRRTUY	compurgatory
ACGMOOPRSTUY	cryptogamous
ACHHIILLPSTY	ithyphallics
ACHHIILMNOPR	philharmonic
ACHHIIMNOPPS	championship
ACHHIIMOSTTY	stichomythia
ACHHIIMOSTYZ	schizothymia
ACHHIIORSTUY	ichthyosauri
ACHHIKOOSSTV	Shostakovich
ACHHILLMRTYY	rhythmically
ACHHILLOOOST	thioalcohols
ACHHILLOPTTY	thallophytic
ACHHILMNRTUY	unrhythmical
ACHHILOOPRST	holophrastic
ACHHILOPRSSS	scholarships
ACHHIOPPRSTU	phosphaturic
ACHHIORSSTUY	ichthyosaurs
ACHHNNOOOPRY	onychophoran
ACHIIIINOSTU	Antiochus III
ACHIIIINRSST	trichiniasis
ACHIIILMSTWY	whimsicality
ACHIIILNORST	histrionical
ACHIIIMNPSSS	hispanicisms
ACHIIIMNPSSU	musicianship
ACHIIINRSTTY	Christianity
ACHIIIRRSSTU	trichuriasis
ACHIIJKNRSSW	jinrickshaws
ACHIIKLMOPTT	machtpolitik
ACHIILLLOSTY	holistically
ACHIILLMOOTT	lithotomical
ACHIILLNOSSU	hallucinosis
ACHIILLORSTY	historically
ACHIILNNOORT	chlorination
ACHIILNOPRST	rhinoplastic
ACHIILNPSUYY	picayunishly
ACHIILOPRSTT	cartophilist
ACHIILPSSSTY	physicalists
ACHIIMNOOPRS	anisomorphic
ACHIIMNOPRST	misanthropic
ACHIIMNORSST	chrismations
ACHIINNNORST	non-Christian
ACHIINOPRSTT	antistrophic
ACHIIPRSSTTY	psychiatrist
ACHIKLOOPSST	Chilkoot Pass
ACHIKMORTUUV	kurchatovium
ACHILLNOORSY	isochronally
ACHILLNOPTYY	hypnotically
ACHILLORSUVY	chivalrously
ACHILMORSTYY	lachrymosity
ACHILNOOPPTY	phonotypical
ACHILNOORRST	chlorinators
ACHILNORSUUV	unchivalrous
ACHILOOOPTTV	photovoltaic
ACHILOOPPRRS	corporalship
ACHIMNNOORTY	ornithomancy
ACHIMNNORSSY	asynchronism
ACHIMNOOPRTY	actinomorphy
ACHIMOOOPSST	photomosaics
ACHIMOPRSSSY	symposiarchs
ACHIMOPSSSTY	scyphistomas
ACHINNOOPSTY	apocynthions
ACHINOOPTTUY	autohypnotic
ACHIOOPPRRST	saprotrophic
ACHIOOPRRRST	arthrosporic
ACHIOOPRRSUZ	rhizocarpous
ACHIOPRRSSTU	curatorships
ACHIOPRSSSTY	astrophysics
ACHLLOOPRSST	chloroplasts
ACHLMOOPRSST	chromoplasts
ACHMMNOOORST	monochromats
ACHNNOORSSUY	asynchronous
ACHOOPRRRTTU	Port Harcourt
ACIIIILMRSTT	militaristic
ACIIIILNOSTV	civilisation
ACIIIILNOTVZ	civilization
ACIIILMMNPSU	municipalism
ACIIILMNNOST	nominalistic
ACIIILMNOPST	implications
ACIIILMNPSTU	municipalist
ACIIILMNPTUY	municipality
ACIIILMOPSTT	optimistical
ACIIILNNNOST	inclinations
ACIIILNOOSTT	coalitionist
	solicitation
ACIIILNOPRTT	triplication
ACIIILNOSTVV	convivialist
ACIIILNOTVVY	conviviality
ACIIILNPPRTY	principality
ACIIILQTUYZZ	quizzicality
ACIIIMNNORRT	incriminator
ACIIIMNNORST	criminations
ACIIINNOOTTX	intoxication
ACIIINNOSTTT	nictitations
ACIIINNOSTTU	cutinisation
ACIIINNOTTUZ	cutinization
ACIIINOPSSUU	inauspicious
ACIIINOQSSTU	acquisitions
ACIIJLLRSTUY	juristically
ACIIJLNORSTU	journalistic

ACIILLMNOOST	collimations
ACIILLMNOSTY	monistically
ACIILLNNOOPT	nonpolitical
ACIILLNOOSST	colonialists
	oscillations
ACIILLNOPRVY	provincially
ACIILLNORSTT	scintillator
ACIILLNORTTY	tinctorially
ACIILLNRTUUV	vinicultural
ACIILLOOPSTY	isotopically
ACIILLOQTUXY	quixotically
ACIILLOSSUVY	lasciviously
ACIILLPRSTUY	puristically
ACIILLRTTUUV	viticultural
ACIILMMNOOSS	commissional
ACIILMNNOOTU	columniation
ACIILMNNOSTU	culminations
ACIILMNOOPST	compilations
ACIILMNORSTU	matriclinous
ACIILMNSSSTU	masculinists
ACIILNNOOOST	colonisation
ACIILNNOOOTZ	colonization
ACIILNNOOSTU	inoculations
	inosculation
ACIILNNOPSTU	inculpations
ACIILNNOSTUY	insouciantly
ACIILNNOTTUY	continuality
ACIILNOOORTZ	colorization
ACIILNOORSST	consistorial
ACIILNOPPSTU	supplication
ACIILNOPRSTU	patriclinous
ACIILNOSTTUV	cultivations
ACIILNOSTUUY	incautiously
ACIILOPSSUUY	auspiciously
ACIILPRSTTUU	apiculturist
ACIILRSTTUUV	aviculturist
ACIIMMNNOOST	comminations
ACIIMNOPRTTU	protactinium
ACIIMNORSSTT	romanticists
ACIINNNOOTTU	continuation
ACIINNOOPSTT	constipation
ACIINNOORSST	consistorian
ACIINNORSTTU	incrustation
ACIINNORSTUV	incurvations
ACIINOORSTTX	intoxicators
ACIINOPRRSUV	picornavirus
ACIINOPSSUUU	unauspicious
ACIINORSSTTU	rustications
ACIJNNOORSTU	conjurations
ACILLLLOOQUY	colloquially
ACILLLMNNOOY	monoclinally
ACILLMNOORTY	microtonally
ACILLMOOOTYZ	zootomically
ACILLMORSUUY	miraculously
ACILLNNOSTYY	syntonically
ACILLNOOOPST	postcolonial
ACILLNOPSTYY	synoptically
ACILLOOPRRTY	proctorially
ACILLOOQSUUY	loquaciously
ACILLPRRSTUY	scripturally
ACILMMNNOOTT	noncommittal
ACILMMNOSSTU	communalists
ACILMNOOOPST	cosmopolitan
ACILMNOORSTU	matroclinous
ACILMOOPPRST	protoplasmic
ACILMORSTTUU	cumulostrati
	stratocumuli
ACILNNNOSTTY	inconstantly
ACILNNOOORTT	contortional
ACILNNOOOSST	consolations
ACILNNOOSTTU	consultation
ACILNNORTTUY	nocturnality
ACILNOOORSTU	colourations
	iconolatrous
ACILNOOPRSTU	patroclinous
ACILOOPPRSTT	protoplastic
ACILOOPPRTTY	prototypical
ACILOPPRSTUY	supplicatory
ACIMMNNOOSTU	consummation
ACIMMNOOSTTU	commutations
ACIMNNOORSTU	mucronations
ACIMNOOPRSTY	trypanosomic
ACIMNOOPSTTU	computations
ACIMOOOPRSTT	somatotropic
ACINNNOOOSTT	connotations
ACINNNORSTTU	unconstraint
ACINNOOPRSTT	contraptions
ACINNOOPSSTY	syncopations
ACINNOORSTTU	continuators
ACINNOPSTTUU	punctuations
ACINOOOPRRRT	incorporator
ACINOOOPRRST	corporations
ACINOOOPRSTV	provocations
ACINOOPRRSST	conspirators
ACINOOPRRSTT	protractions
ACINOOPRRSTU	procurations
ACINOOPRRSTY	conspiratory
ACINOPRSSTUU	transpicuous
ACIOOPRRSSTT	corporatists
ACIORRRSSTTU	cirrostratus
ACKLNNOOPRTY	cryoplankton
ACLLLPRSTUUY	sculpturally
ACLLOPRSSTYY	polycrystals
ACLLRRSTTUUY	structurally
ACLNOORSTTUY	consultatory
ACMMNOORSSTU	consummators
ACMMNOORSTUY	consummatory
ACMNNOORTUWY	countrywoman
ACMNOOOTTXYY	cytotaxonomy
ACNOOOPPRSTT	contrapposto
ADDDDEEEHLMU	muddleheaded
ADDDDEEEHNRU	dunderheaded
ADDDEEEHNOOW	woodenheaded
ADDDEEFIOSTU	eisteddfodau
ADDDEEIMRSSS	misaddressed
ADDDEEINNRRU	underdrained
ADDDEIIINTUV	individuated
ADDDEIILLLLY	dillydallied
ADDDEMNOOORT	rodomontaded
ADDEEEEFGHRT	featheredged
ADDEEEEGGRST	desegregated
ADDEEEEHLPSY	sleepyheaded
ADDEEEFGNNOR	Garden of Eden
ADDEEEFHLNRY	freehandedly

ADDEEEGGHLOR loggerheaded
ADDEEEGIMNST demagnetised
ADDEEEGIMNTZ demagnetized
ADDEEEGNOTXY deoxygenated
ADDEEEHINRST disheartened
ADDEEEHLNNVY evenhandedly
ADDEEEHLORSY soreheadedly
ADDEEEIIRSTV desiderative
ADDEEEILNPRT interpleaded
ADDEEEILSSUX desexualised
ADDEEEILSUXZ desexualized
ADDEEEIMPRTT premeditated
ADDEEEIORRTT deteriorated
ADDEEEIORTVV overdeviated
ADDEEENNRVWY van der Weyden
ADDEEENOPRVX overexpanded
ADDEEENPRSSV depravedness
ADDEEEOPPRSV eavesdropped
ADDEEFFNRSTU understaffed
ADDEEFHILPSS paddlefishes
ADDEEFHLMORY formaldehyde
ADDEEFHLNORY forehandedly
ADDEEFHOORSW foreshadowed
ADDEEFINOORR foreordained
ADDEEFLNRSSU dreadfulness
ADDEEFMNRSTU defraudments
ADDEEGHNORTY hydrogenated
ADDEEGIINRST desiderating
ADDEEGILNNST disentangled
ADDEEGILNTTU deglutinated
ADDEEGINRRSS readdressing
ADDEEGIRRRSS disregarders
ADDEEGMMOPRR deprogrammed
ADDEEHHIMRTY hemihydrated
ADDEEHHNRSTU thunderheads
ADDEEHLNNOPY openhandedly
ADDEEHMNOTTU muttonheaded
ADDEEHMORSUY hydromedusae
ADDEEHOORSVW overshadowed
ADDEEIIMMNNO demimondaine
ADDEEIIMNRST administered
ADDEEIIMNSST disseminated
ADDEEIINNRST Indian Desert
ADDEEIINORST desideration
ADDEEILMSSTT Middle States
ADDEEILMSTUU demutualised
ADDEEILMTUUZ demutualized
ADDEEILNORSV Slieve Donard
ADDEEILPRSSU displeasured
ADDEEILRRTVY daredeviltry
ADDEEIMMNRST masterminded
ADDEEIMNOPRT predominated
ADDEEIMRSSSS misaddresses
ADDEEINOPRST depredations
ADDEEINPRRSU underpraised
ADDEEINRSTUV unadvertised
ADDEELNOSSTT staddlestone
ADDEEMNORSTT demonstrated
ADDEENPSSWYY Spy Wednesday
ADDEENRRRSUW underdrawers
ADDEFGILRRSU disregardful
ADDEFHILOPST feldspathoid
ADDEFIIIINNR Ferdinand III
ADDEFIIILQSU disqualified
ADDEFIIINNRV Ferdinand VII
ADDEFIIISSST dissatisfied
ADDEFLNNNOUW Newfoundland
ADDEGGHORSTU goddaughters
ADDEGGIIIRST digitigrades
ADDEGGIINRRS disregarding
ADDEGHHOORTU daughterhood
ADDEGHNORSTU dreadnoughts
ADDEGIIMNOSS misdiagnosed
ADDEGIINORSS disorganised
ADDEGIINORSZ disorganized
ADDEGILMNOTU demodulating
ADDEGIOORUZZ Guido d'Arezzo
ADDEHLORSSTT stadtholders
ADDEHMNOORTY monohydrated
ADDEHMNORSUY hydromedusan
ADDEHMORSSUY hydromedusas
ADDEIIILMSST dissimilated
ADDEIIINSTUV individuates
ADDEIILLLLSY dillydallies
ADDEIILLNSSV Devil's Island
ADDEIILMSSTU dissimulated
ADDEIILPSSTY dissipatedly
ADDEIINOPPST disappointed
ADDEILMNOOTU demodulation
ADDEILMNOPRS Promised Land
ADDEILMNSSTW West Midlands
ADDELMOORSTU demodulators
ADDEMNOOORST rodomontades
ADDENNORSSWW downwardness
ADDFIILLNSUY disdainfully
ADDGHILLNNOS landholdings
ADDGHNORSTUW downdraughts
ADDGIILNSSTU studdingsail
ADDGILNNORSW Darling Downs
ADDGINNOOSSW Goodwin Sands
ADDHIIILMOPP amphidiploid
ADDHLLNNOOOR Noordholland
ADDIIILLNUVY individually
ADDIIINORTUV individuator
ADEEEEFGHRST featheredges
ADEEEEGGRSST desegregates
ADEEEEGINRTV degenerative
ADEEEEGLNRTY degenerately
ADEEEEHILRST etherealised
ADEEEEHILRTZ etherealized
ADEEEEIKLNRR Reindeer Lake
ADEEEFFIINRT differentiae
ADEEEFFORRST reafforested
ADEEEFGHORRT foregathered
ADEEEFGIRRRT refrigerated
ADEEEGGILNRT lateenrigged
ADEEEGGINNRT degenerating
ADEEEGGNRSTU unsegregated
ADEEEGHLMMRS sledgehammer
ADEEEGIMNRRS gendarmeries
ADEEEGIMNRST demagnetiser
disagreement
ADEEEGIMNRTZ demagnetizer
ADEEEGIMNSST demagnetises

ADEEEGIMNSTZ	demagnetizes
ADEEEGINNORT	degeneration
ADEEEGINNRST	tragediennes
ADEEEGINOPSS	paedogenesis
ADEEEGINORTT	renegotiated
ADEEEGINPRRT	peregrinated
ADEEEGINPRST	predesignate
ADEEEGINRRTT	redintegrate
	reintegrated
ADEEEGLLNOSS	de los Angeles
ADEEEGLNNNRW	New Englander
ADEEEGLNORTU	outgeneraled
ADEEEGMNNNRT	endangerment
ADEEEGMNNRST	derangements
ADEEEGNOSTXY	deoxygenates
ADEEEHHLORTW	wholehearted
ADEEEHILPSTT	telepathised
ADEEEHILPTTZ	telepathized
ADEEEHIMNRTT	hereditament
ADEEEHIMPRSZ	reemphasized
ADEEEHIMSSTT	metathesised
ADEEEHIMSTTZ	metathesized
ADEEEHINSSSV	adhesiveness
ADEEEHINSSTU	Hauts-de-Seine
ADEEEHINSTTZ	anesthetized
ADEEEHIRRTTT	tetrahedrite
ADEEEHLLORSS	leaseholders
ADEEEHLNNRRT	Netherlander
ADEEEHMNPRSS	hamperedness
ADEEEHMORSST	homesteaders
ADEEEHMORSTV	Mohave Desert
ADEEEHNNNORS	enneahedrons
ADEEEHPRSSST	spreadsheets
ADEEEIILMNRS	demineralise
ADEEEIILMNRZ	demineralize
ADEEEIILNPTX	expediential
ADEEEIILORVZ	overidealize
ADEEEIIMMRST	semidiameter
ADEEEIIMNRTT	intermediate
ADEEEILLMMOS	mademoiselle
ADEEEILMNORT	radioelement
ADEEEILNPRRT	interpleader
ADEEEILNRRTT	interrelated
ADEEEILNRSTX	externalised
ADEEEILNRTXZ	externalized
ADEEEILSSSUX	desexualises
ADEEEILSSUXZ	desexualizes
ADEEEIMMNNRR	remaindermen
ADEEEIMNORST	demonetarise
ADEEEIMNORTZ	demonetarize
ADEEEIMNRTTX	exterminated
ADEEEIMPRSTT	premeditates
ADEEEINOPRSU	europeanised
ADEEEINOPRUZ	europeanized
ADEEEINPRSTT	predestinate
ADEEEIOPPSTX	exopeptidase
ADEEEIORRSTT	deteriorates
ADEEEIORSTVV	overdeviates
ADEEEJMORSTV	Mojave Desert
ADEEEKLLMRSS	Skelmersdale
ADEEEKLLNOST	endoskeletal
ADEEEKLRRSST	deerstalkers
ADEEELLMMNRT	entrammelled
ADEEELLNSSWY	wensleydales
ADEEELNNQRSU	Queenslander
ADEEELNOSSST	desolateness
ADEEELNRSTTU	launderettes
ADEEELOPPRST	tradespeople
ADEEELOPRSSS	leopardesses
ADEEELRSSSTU	adulteresses
ADEEEMNORSST	moderateness
ADEEEMNRSSSU	measuredness
ADEEEMORRSTV	overmastered
ADEEEMOSSTWW	meadowsweets
ADEEENNNORSX	Andersen Nexø
ADEEENOPPRRT	preponderate
ADEEENORRSUV	endeavourers
ADEEENPPRRSS	preparedness
ADEEENPRRTUV	peradventure
ADEEENRRTTWW	Derwentwater
ADEEEOPPRRSV	eavesdropper
ADEEEOPRRSUV	overpersuade
ADEEEORRSSTV	overasserted
ADEEEQRSSTTU	sequestrated
ADEEERSSSSTW	stewardesses
ADEEFFIILNRT	differential
ADEEFGHIIRRT	airfreighted
ADEEFGIILNRS	federalising
ADEEFGIILNRZ	federalizing
ADEEFGILNORS	freeloadings
ADEEFGINNRRS	rangefinders
ADEEFGINNRST	freestanding
ADEEFGKLNPRS	frankpledges
ADEEFHILMSSS	damselfishes
ADEEFHLOPSST	feldspathose
ADEEFHOORRSW	foreshadower
ADEEFILNNSST	inflatedness
ADEEFILNORTV	overinflated
ADEEFILOPRRT	proliferated
ADEEFLMORRTU	reformulated
ADEEFLNRSSTW	West Flanders
ADEEFLNRTUUV	adventureful
ADEEFNOPRRTU	unperforated
ADEEFNSSSSTT	stedfastness
ADEEFOOPRRRS	proofreaders
ADEEFOOPRRTW	waterproofed
ADEEGGHIRSTT	straightedge
ADEEGGILNRTU	deregulating
ADEEGGIRRTTU	regurgitated
ADEEGGLNOPPR	doppelganger
	doppelgänger
ADEEGHHILRTT	lighthearted
ADEEGHIMMOPR	mimeographed
ADEEGHIMNOST	homesteading
ADEEGHIMOPRS	demographies
ADEEGHINNPPR	apprehending
ADEEGHINNRRT	heartrending
ADEEGHINPRSS	grandeeships
ADEEGHINRSTT	straightened
ADEEGHIOPRRV	videographer
ADEEGHLORSUV	overslaughed
ADEEGHLRSSTU	daughterless
ADEEGHMOPRRS	demographers
ADEEGHNNPRSW	grandnephews

ADEEGHNOPRST stenographed
ADEEGHNORSTY hydrogenates
ADEEGHPRSTTU stepdaughter
ADEEGIIMMNNS misdemeaning
ADEEGIIMNNRR remaindering
ADEEGIINRSTT disintegrate
ADEEGIINSTTV investigated
ADEEGIJNNRWW Wandering Jew
ADEEGIKLNRST deerstalking
ADEEGIKNNRRT kindergarten
ADEEGIKNPSST speedskating
ADEEGILLNOPT Point de Galle
ADEEGILMNNRY meanderingly
ADEEGILNNRSU undersealing
ADEEGILNNSST disentangles
ADEEGILNORTU deregulation
ADEEGILNSTTU deglutinates
ADEEGILORTVY derogatively
ADEEGIMNNRST deraignments
ADEEGIMORRST gradiometers
ADEEGIMSSTTU guesstimated
ADEEGINNORUV endeavouring
ADEEGINORRTT interrogated
ADEEGLLRRSSY regardlessly
ADEEGLMNOSSS gladsomeness
ADEEGLNNORSY General Synod
ADEEGLORRRTY retrogradely
ADEEGLORRSTU deregulators
ADEEGLORRTUY deregulatory
ADEEGMMOPRRS deprogrammes
ADEEGMNNRRTU undergarment
ADEEGMNRRRSY gerrymanders
ADEEGNPRTUUX unexpurgated
ADEEGNRRSSST transgressed
ADEEGORRTTXY dextrogyrate
ADEEHHIKNRRS headshrinker
ADEEHHIMRSTY hemihydrates
ADEEHHLORRSS shareholders
ADEEHHNNPTUY unhyphenated
ADEEHHNOPRST heptahedrons
ADEEHIILRRTY hereditarily
ADEEHIIOPRSS isodiapheres
ADEEHILMNOOT endothelioma
ADEEHILMOSSY hemodialyses
ADEEHILNPRRS philanderers
ADEEHIMNPPRS misapprehend
ADEEHIMRSSST headmistress
ADEEHINPSSSU dauphinesses
ADEEHIOOPSST apotheosised
ADEEHIOOPSTZ apotheosized
ADEEHIRRRSSS hairdressers
ADEEHKLORSST stakeholders
ADEEHLLLMOPR phellodermal
ADEEHLLNOSSW hallowedness
ADEEHLLORSSV slaveholders
ADEEHLMMOTUY mealymouthed
ADEEHLOORSTW leatherwoods
ADEEHMNNOSSS handsomeness
ADEEHMNORRSY dysmenorrhea
ADEEHMOPRTTY dermatophyte
ADEEHNNOPRST pentahedrons
ADEEHNORRSTT tetrahedrons
ADEEHNORSTTY stonyhearted
ADEEHORSTTTU stouthearted
ADEEIIILMRST demilitarise
ADEEIIILMRTZ demilitarize
ADEEIIILMTTV delimitative
ADEEIIILORST editorialise
ADEEIIILORTZ editorialize
ADEEIIIMNNPR Indian Empire
ADEEIIJNOORR Rio de Janeiro
ADEEIILLNTVY evidentially
ADEEIILMMNPT impedimental
ADEEIILMMORS memorialised
ADEEIILMMORZ memorialized
ADEEIILMMSSV medievalisms
ADEEIILMNNSS maidenliness
ADEEIILMSSTV medievalists
ADEEIILMTTVY meditatively
ADEEIILNNOST delineations
ADEEIILNNRST internalised
ADEEIILNNRTZ internalized
ADEEIILNORST orientalised
ADEEIILNORTZ orientalized
ADEEIILNPRST presidential
ADEEIILOPRST depilatories
ADEEIILRTVVY derivatively
ADEEIIMMSSTT misestimated
ADEEIIMNNOTV denominative
ADEEIIMNRRRT intermarried
ADEEIIMNRRTY intermediary
ADEEIIMNSSST disseminates
ADEEIINORSTT disorientate
ADEEIINPRSSS dispensaries
ADEEIINRRSTY residentiary
ADEEIINRRTVW water diviner
ADEEIIOPRSST depositaries
ADEEIKLLNSSY ladylikeness
ADEEIKMNRSSS semidarkness
ADEEILLNNTTY tendentially
ADEEILLNPSSW Pelew Islands
ADEEILMMORTY immoderately
ADEEILMNOPRT redemptional
ADEEILMORRSS demoralisers
ADEEILMORRSZ demoralizers
ADEEILMORSTT dilatometers
ADEEILMPRSST slipstreamed
ADEEILMSSTUU demutualises
ADEEILMSTUUZ demutualizes
ADEEILNNPSTU peninsulated
ADEEILNNTTUV unventilated
ADEEILNOPPRT lepidopteran
ADEEILNOPRSS personalised
ADEEILNOPRSZ personalized
ADEEILNOPRTT interpolated
ADEEILNOTTVY denotatively
ADEEILNRRSTY restrainedly
ADEEILOPRRSS depolarisers
ADEEILOPRRSZ depolarizers
ADEEILORSSST idolatresses
ADEEILPRSSSU displeasures
ADEEIMMNORSS misdemeanors
ADEEIMMNORSU misdemeanour
ADEEIMNNRSTT determinants

	detrainments
ADEEIMNNSTTU	edutainments
ADEEIMNOPRST	impersonated
	predominates
ADEEIMNOSSTU	eudaemonists
ADEEIMNRSTUV	misadventure
ADEEIMOPRRTT	premeditator
ADEEIMORSSTT	stadiometers
ADEEIMSSSTTY	systematised
ADEEIMSSTTYZ	systematized
ADEEINNORSTV	denervations
ADEEINNRRSTU	unrestrained
ADEEINNSSSTU	unsteadiness
ADEEINOPPPRT	preappointed
ADEEINORRSTV	overstrained
ADEEINORSSUV	adenoviruses
ADEEINPRRSSU	underpraises
ADEEIOPPRRTX	expropriated
ADEEJMNRSTTU	readjustment
ADEEKLOPRSSU	loudspeakers
ADEELLLRSSSW	Sadler's Wells
ADEELLMMNRTU	untrammelled
ADEELLNNSSSS	landlessness
ADEELMNOORST	demonolaters
ADEELMNOSTTT	Old Testament
ADEELMNRSUUY	unmeasuredly
ADEELMOPRSTU	deuteroplasm
ADEELMORSSTU	somersaulted
ADEELNPPRRUY	unpreparedly
ADEELNRRSUUV	undervaluers
ADEELOPSTTUX	expostulated
ADEEMMNORSTY	dynamometers
ADEEMMOSTUXY	myxedematous
ADEEMNNNORTU	unornamented
ADEEMNNPRSUU	supermundane
ADEEMNNPRTUY	underpayment
ADEEMNORRSTT	remonstrated
ADEEMNORSSTT	demonstrates
ADEENNOORRST	androsterone
ADEENNOPPRRT	preponderant
ADEFFGIMSTUU	suffumigated
ADEFFILNRSTU	faultfinders
ADEFFIORSSST	disafforests
ADEFGHILNSUW	Ludwigshafen
ADEFGHILRSTY	farsightedly
ADEFGIINRSTU	disfeaturing
ADEFGINOOPRR	proofreading
ADEFGINRRSTU	transfigured
ADEFHILLORSS	dollarfishes
ADEFHILLTTWY	halfwittedly
ADEFHILMNORV	Milford Haven
ADEFHILOORST	foolhardiest
ADEFHINRSSSW	dwarfishness
ADEFIIILNNOT	definitional
ADEFIIILQRSU	disqualifier
ADEFIIILQSSU	disqualifies
ADEFIIISSSST	dissatisfies
ADEFIILNOOST	defoliations
ADEFIILNOSTT	deflationist
ADEFIINNOSTU	infeudations
ADEFIINRSTTU	unstratified
ADEFILMNNOSS	manifoldness
ADEFILMORRSU	formularised
ADEFILMORRUZ	formularized
ADEFILNNOOSS	San Ildefonso
ADEFILNOORST	deflorations
ADEFIMNOORST	deformations
ADEFLLNRTUUY	fraudulently
ADEFLMNORTUU	unformulated
ADEGGIINNOPX	Deng Xiaoping
ADEGGIINNRRT	intergrading
ADEGGIINRTTU	ingurgitated
ADEGGIJNNPRU	Junggar Pendi
ADEGGILOORUV	Olduvai Gorge
ADEGGINORRRT	retrograding
ADEGGLNRSSSU	sluggardness
ADEGHHILOPRT	lithographed
ADEGHHOOPPRT	photographed
ADEGHHOPRRRY	hydrographer
ADEGHIILNNPR	philandering
ADEGHIIMNNSU	dehumanising
ADEGHIIMNNUZ	dehumanizing
ADEGHIINRRSS	hairdressing
	sherardising
ADEGHIINRRSZ	sherardizing
ADEGHILLNOSV	slaveholding
ADEGHILNOOST	anthologised
ADEGHILNOOTZ	anthologized
ADEGHILOOPTZ	pathologized
ADEGHIMOPRST	demographist
ADEGHINNORTY	antihydrogen
ADEGHINRSSTU	draughtiness
ADEGHLLNORST	stranglehold
ADEGHLNORSTY	headstrongly
ADEGHMNORRST	grandmothers
ADEGHNOORRTY	hydrogenator
ADEGHOOPRRSX	doxographers
ADEGHORRSTUV	overdraughts
ADEGIIILMNTT	delimitating
ADEGIIILNNSS	desalinising
ADEGIIILNNST	disentailing
ADEGIIILNNSZ	desalinizing
ADEGIIILNRTT	interdigital
ADEGIIILNSTV	devitalising
ADEGIIILNTVZ	devitalizing
ADEGIIJNOPRS	jeopardising
ADEGIIJNOPRZ	jeopardizing
ADEGIILLMNSY	misleadingly
ADEGIILLNNTU	dentilingual
ADEGIILMNORS	demoralising
ADEGIILMNORZ	demoralizing
ADEGIILMNPSS	mispleadings
ADEGIILNNRRT	interlarding
ADEGIILNOPRS	depolarising
ADEGIILNOPRZ	depolarizing
ADEGIILNORSS	digressional
ADEGIILNPRSY	despairingly
ADEGIILNRRRV	Darling River
ADEGIILNRSSU	singularised
ADEGIILNRSUZ	singularized
ADEGIIMNNNOT	denominating
ADEGIIMNNPRR	reprimanding
ADEGIIMNOSSS	misdiagnoses
ADEGIINNOPRR	preordaining

ADEGIINNORST	denigrations
ADEGIINNOSST	designations
ADEGIINNRSTU	denaturising
ADEGIINNRTUZ	denaturizing
ADEGIINOORRT	granodiorite
ADEGIINORRSS	disorganiser
ADEGIINORRSZ	disorganizer
ADEGIINORSSS	disorganises
ADEGIINORSSZ	disorganizes
ADEGIINRSSTT	dissertating
ADEGIKNNRSTU	undertakings
ADEGILNNPRUY	underplaying
ADEGILNNRUUV	undervaluing
ADEGILNOPPTU	depopulating
ADEGILOOPSST	paedologists
ADEGILOORRTY	derogatorily
ADEGILOOSTTU	tautologised
ADEGILOOTTUZ	tautologized
ADEGILRSTTUU	gutturalised
ADEGILRTTUUZ	gutturalized
ADEGIMNORRSS	gormandisers
ADEGIMNORRSZ	gormandizers
ADEGIMNORSSU	gourmandises
ADEGINNOSTUW	Godwin-Austen
ADEGINNRSTTU	understating
ADEGINOPRSTU	outspreading
ADEGINORRSSW	Grosswardein
ADEGINOSSTTU	degustations
ADEGJLMNSTTU	Last Judgment
ADEGMNORSSSU	groundmasses
ADEHHILLPPSU	philadelphus
ADEHHILMOORR	hemorrhoidal
ADEHHIMOORRS	haemorrhoids
ADEHHIOPPSST	phosphatides
	phosphatised
ADEHHIOPPSTZ	phosphatized
ADEHHLMORRTY	hydrothermal
ADEHHOOPPRST	phosphorated
ADEHHOPRRTYY	hydrotherapy
ADEHIILMOSSY	hemodialysis
ADEHIILNSTTT	dilettantish
ADEHIILOPSST	hospitalised
ADEHIILOPSTZ	hospitalized
ADEHIIMNORSS	disharmonies
ADEHIINNRSTY	hydrastinine
ADEHIJLOPSUU	Philo Judaeus
ADEHILLNRSST	disenthralls
ADEHILLOPRSY	spheroidally
ADEHILMNOPSU	sulphonamide
ADEHILMNORSU	malnourished
ADEHINNQSUUV	unvanquished
ADEHINOORSTZ	antherozoids
ADEHINORSTUU	unauthorised
ADEHINORTUUZ	unauthorized
ADEHINPPRSST	transshipped
ADEHINQRRSTU	hindquarters
ADEHINRSSTTW	withstanders
ADEHIOOPRSTT	orthopaedist
ADEHIOPSSSTY	hypostasised
ADEHIOPSSTTY	hypostatised
ADEHIOPSSTYZ	hypostasized
ADEHIOPSTTYZ	hypostatized
ADEHLLLMORSS	smallholders
ADEHLLLORSST	stallholders
ADEHLMNOOPSU	monadelphous
ADEHLORSSTYY	hydrolysates
ADEHMNOORSTY	monohydrates
ADEHOOPSTTTT	photostatted
ADEIIILMNOTT	delimitation
ADEIIILMSSST	dissimilates
ADEIIILORSST	solidarities
ADEIIILORSTT	editorialist
ADEIIIMNORST	dimerisation
ADEIIIMNORTZ	dimerization
ADEIIIMNOSTV	deviationism
ADEIIIMNRSTU	miniaturised
ADEIIIMNRTUZ	miniaturized
ADEIIINNNPPS	pinnipedians
ADEIIINNOOST	deionisation
ADEIIINNOOTZ	deionization
ADEIIINOSTTV	deviationist
ADEIIINSTTTU	attitudinise
ADEIIINTTTUZ	attitudinize
ADEIIIOPSSTV	diapositives
ADEIILLMNORY	meridionally
ADEIILLOSSTY	disloyalties
ADEIILLSTUVV	vaudevillist
ADEIILMMNPRT	malimprinted
ADEIILMMORST	immortalised
ADEIILMMORTZ	immortalized
ADEIILMNSTTT	dilettantism
ADEIILMSSSTU	dissimulates
ADEIILNNORTY	inordinately
ADEIILNOOPST	despoliation
ADEIILNOPRTV	providential
ADEIILNORSST	dilatoriness
ADEIILNQRTUZ	tranquilized
ADEIILORRSTZ	idolatrizers
ADEIILSSSUVY	dissuasively
ADEIIMMNOORT	immoderation
ADEIIMNNNOOT	denomination
ADEIIMNNRSTT	distrainment
ADEIIMNOPRST	postmeridian
ADEIIMNOPRXY	pyridoxamine
ADEIIMNORSSS	readmissions
ADEIIMNORSST	disseminator
ADEIIMOPPRRT	impropriated
ADEIIMORSTTU	audiometrist
ADEIIMRSSTTX	taxidermists
ADEIINNNOSTT	indentations
ADEIINNOPSST	dispensation
ADEIINNORSTT	denitrations
ADEIINNOSSTT	destinations
ADEIINOOPRST	disoperation
ADEIINOOPRTX	peroxidation
ADEIINOPRSTU	repudiations
ADEIINOPRSTV	deprivations
ADEIINORRSVY	diversionary
ADEIINORSSTT	dissertation
ADEIINORSTTX	extraditions
ADEIINOSTTUV	adventitious
ADEIINPRSSSU	prussianised
ADEIINPRSSUZ	prussianized
ADEIINRSSTVY	vineyardists

ADEIIOOOPRST	radioisotope
ADEILLLNOOSY	solenoidally
ADEILLMNRTUY	rudimentally
ADEILLMRRSST	drillmasters
ADEILLNOOTVY	devotionally
ADEILLNOPPRT	dipropellant
ADEILLNPRTUY	prudentially
ADEILMNNNSTU	disannulment
ADEILMNOPSTU	deplumations
ADEILNOOPPTU	depopulation
ADEILNORRSTV	dorsiventral
ADEILNORSSTW	towardliness
ADEILNRSSTWW	windlestraws
ADEILOPPRSSS	predisposals
ADEIMMOPRSUY	praseodymium
ADEIMNNOORST	denominators
ADEIMNNQRSUU	quadrenniums
ADEIMNOOPRRT	predominator
ADEIMNRRSSUY	nurserymaids
ADEIMOOPRSTZ	spermatozoid
ADEINOOPRSTT	deportations
ADEINOPRSSTY	dispensatory
ADEINRSSTTUV	adventurists
ADEIORRSSSTT	dissertators
ADEJMNNORSTU	adjournments
ADEKOOPRSTVZ	Petrozavodsk
ADELLNORSSUY	slanderously
ADELLOOPRRST	petrodollars
ADELLORSTUUY	adulterously
ADELMNNORUWY	laundrywomen
ADELNOORRSTV	dorsoventral
ADELNORSSTVW	strandwolves
ADELOPRRSSWY	swordplayers
ADEMNOORRSTT	demonstrator
ADEMOPRRSSTU	superstardom
ADENNOPRRSST	transponders
ADENNORSSTUW	untowardness
ADEOORRRTTXY	dextrorotary
ADFFGIIIMNRS	disaffirming
ADFFGIILNNTU	faultfinding
ADFGIILNORTU	fluoridating
ADFGIINORSUV	disfavouring
ADFIIILLNNSU	nullifidians
ADFIIILNNOST	disinflation
ADFIIILNNPTY	pinnatifidly
ADFIIILNOSTU	fluidisation
ADFIIILNOTUZ	fluidization
ADFIILNOORTU	fluoridation
ADFIILOSSTUY	fastidiously
ADGGIIIILNST	digitalising
ADGGIIIILNTZ	digitalizing
ADGGIIMNNORS	gormandising
ADGGIIMNNORZ	gormandizing
ADGHHHIILOSY	High Holidays
ADGHIINNSTTW	withstanding
ADGHIINOPRSS	rhapsodising
ADGHIINOPRSZ	rhapsodizing
ADGHILLLMNOS	smallholding
ADGHILNNOPRY	hydroplaning
ADGHIMRRRSYY	hydrargyrism
ADGIIIIMNNTT	intimidating
ADGIIIINOSTT	digitisation
ADGIIIINOTTZ	digitization
ADGIIILNORST	idolatrising
ADGIIILNORTZ	idolatrizing
ADGIIILOOSSS	idioglossias
ADGIIIMNOSSS	misdiagnosis
ADGIILLNNNSU	disannulling
ADGIILLNNOTU	longitudinal
ADGIILMNNOTY	dominatingly
ADGIILNRSTTU	stridulating
ADGIILOORSST	radiologists
ADGIILOOSSTU	audiologists
ADGIINOPPRSV	disapproving
ADGILNNOSTUY	astoundingly
ADGILNOORSST	andrologists
ADGIMMNORSSU	gourmandisms
ADGIMNNOOOST	Santo Domingo
ADGINNOOOPRT	gonadotropin
ADGLLLNOSUUY	glandulously
ADGOOOPRSSTU	gastropodous
ADHHIOPRSTTY	hydropathist
ADHHLLNNOORT	North Holland
ADHHLLNOOSTU	South Holland
ADHHLORSTUYY	Holy Thursday
ADHHNOOPRSUY	hydrophanous
ADHIIIMMRSTT	mithridatism
ADHIILMNOPRU	dolphinarium
ADHIIMOPRSST	diastrophism
ADHILLNOSTUY	outlandishly
ADHILMMOOPTY	lymphomatoid
ADHLNOOOOPRT	odontophoral
ADHOOOPRRSTU	arthropodous
ADIIIIMNNOTT	intimidation
ADIIIINNOSTV	divinisation
ADIIIINNOTVZ	divinization
ADIIILLMRSSY	dissimilarly
ADIIILLNOSTT	distillation
ADIIILLNOSVY	divisionally
ADIIILNOQSTU	liquidations
ADIIIMNORSTT	intimidators
ADIIINOPSSST	dissipations
ADIIINORSTTT	traditionist
ADIIKLLNRSSU	Kuril Islands
ADIILLMOPRRY	primordially
ADIILLNOQRSU	quadrillions
ADIILLNOSSUY	sinusoidally
ADIILLNRSTUY	industrially
ADIILLOPPSST	lipidoplasts
ADIILLOPSTUV	postdiluvial
ADIILLORSTTY	distillatory
ADIILMNNOSST	mandolinists
ADIILMOPSSTT	diplomatists
ADIILMORSSTU	dissimulator
ADIILNOORSTT	distortional
ADIILNOPSTUV	postdiluvian
ADIILNORSTTU	stridulation
ADIINOPSSTTU	disputations
ADIIOPSSTTUU	disputatious
ADIIOPSSTTUY	audiotypists
ADILLMNOOOPY	monopodially
ADILLNRSTTUY	stridulantly
ADILLOORSTUY	idolatrously
ADILORRSSTTU	stridulators

ADILORRSTTUY	stridulatory
ADIOOPRRSSUU	sudoriparous
ADLLMOOORSUY	malodorously
ADLLOOOSSWWW	woodswallows
ADMNNOOSSTTU	Santos-Dumont
ADNNOOPRRSST	transpondors
AEEEEGHMORTT	heterogamete
AEEEEGINRRTV	regenerative
AEEEEGNNRRTU	unregenerate
AEEEEHHPRRSS	sheepshearer
AEEEEHILRSST	etherealises
AEEEEHILRSTZ	etherealizes
AEEEEHLNRSST	etherealness
AEEEEHLRSTTT	leatherettes
AEEEEIMNNRST	Seine-et-Marne
AEEEEKLMRRTT	telemarketer
AEEEFFILMNTY	effeminately
AEEEFFKOSSTW	Feast of Weeks
AEEEFGIRRRST	refrigerates
AEEEFHINRRTT	thereinafter
AEEEFILNPRRT	preferential
AEEEFIMNRTTV	fermentative
AEEEFLLNSSSS	leaflessness
AEEEFLMPRSSU	superfemales
AEEEFLNRSSSS	fearlessness
AEEEFLORSTTW	telesoftware
AEEEFMNORSSS	fearsomeness
AEEEGGHLNSTT	snaggleteeth
AEEEGGINNOSS	angiogeneses
AEEEGGINNRRT	regenerating
AEEEGGINRTTV	revegetating
AEEEGGMMNOSU	emmenagogues
AEEEGHIILMRW	whigmaleerie
AEEEGIILNRST	generalities
AEEEGILMMRRS	lammergeiers
AEEEGILMNOSS	amelogenesis
AEEEGILNNPSS	palingeneses
AEEEGILNRRSS	generalisers
AEEEGILNRRSZ	generalizers
AEEEGILNRSSV	evangelisers
AEEEGILNRSVZ	evangelizers
AEEEGILTTVVY	vegetatively
AEEEGIMNNSTV	envisagement
AEEEGINNORRT	regeneration
AEEEGINNRTTX	exenterating
AEEEGINNSSTV	negativeness
AEEEGINORSTT	renegotiates
AEEEGINORSTV	seronegative
AEEEGINORTTV	revegetation
AEEEGINPRRST	peregrinates
AEEEGINRRSTT	reintegrates
AEEEGIRRSTTV	tergiversate
AEEEGLMMRRSY	lammergeyers
AEEEGLMNNNTT	entanglement
AEEEGLMNNRST	enlargements
AEEEGLNSSSSW	wagelessness
AEEEGMMNORTT	magnetometer
AEEEGMMNOSSS	gamesomeness
AEEEGMNNRSTT	estrangement
AEEEGNORRRST	regenerators
AEEEGOPRRSTU	supererogate
AEEEHHLPSTTT	heptathletes
AEEEHHMNORSX	hexahemerons
AEEEHHNNNPRT	phenanthrene
AEEEHHNOTTXY	ethoxyethane
AEEEHIILNPST	Penthesileia
AEEEHILMPRTY	ephemerality
AEEEHILNNSSV	heavenliness
AEEEHILNRSST	leatheriness
AEEEHILPSSTT	telepathises
AEEEHILPSTTZ	telepathizes
AEEEHIMNNOPP	epiphenomena
AEEEHIMNORSS	Shemona Esrei
AEEEHIMORSTT	metatheories
AEEEHIMPRSSZ	reemphasizes
AEEEHIMSSSTT	metathesises
AEEEHIMSSTTZ	metathesizes
AEEEHINPPRSV	apprehensive
AEEEHINPRSST	parenthesise
AEEEHINPRSTZ	parenthesize
AEEEHINRRTTW	interwreathe
AEEEHINSSTTZ	anesthetizes
AEEEHLMPPRST	pamphleteers
AEEEHLNPSTTT	pentathletes
AEEEHLORSTUX	heterosexual
AEEEHLRRSTTY	Harley Street
AEEEHMNNSTTW	enswathement
AEEEHMNORSUW	warehousemen
AEEEHMOPRSSV	overemphases
AEEEHMORTTTX	methotrexate
AEEEHNOPRRTT	heteropteran
AEEEHNORSSTT	Eratosthenes
AEEEHPRRSSTU	superheaters
AEEEIILMNORT	Maine-et-Loire
AEEEIILMRSTT	semiliterate
AEEEIILNNRTT	interlineate
AEEEIILNPRTX	experiential
AEEEIINNNSTT	Saint-Étienne
AEEEIKNNORST	enterokinase
AEEEILLMMNST	elementalism
AEEEILLMNRTY	elementarily
AEEEILLNPRTT	interpellate
AEEEILMNPRTX	experimental
AEEEILMNRTTY	intemerately
AEEEILNOORST	Saône-et-Loire
AEEEILNRRSTT	interrelates
AEEEILNRSSTV	relativeness
AEEEILNRSSTX	externalises
AEEEILNRSTXZ	externalizes
AEEEILNRTTVY	inveterately
AEEEILRRSTYZ	Eretz Yisrael
AEEEIMNRRTUV	remunerative
AEEEIMNRSTTX	exterminates
AEEEIMOPRRTV	evaporimeter
AEEEIMORSSTT	East Timorese
AEEEIMORSTTV	overestimate
AEEEIMQRRSTU	marqueteries
AEEEINNORTTX	exenteration
AEEEINNRRSTT	entertainers
AEEEINNSSSTV	nativenesses
AEEEINOPRSSU	europeanises
AEEEINOPRSUZ	europeanizes
AEEEINPRSTTV	presentative
AEEEINPRTTVV	preventative

AEEEINRRSTVW	interweavers
AEEEINRRTTUX	extrauterine
AEEEIPRRSTVV	preservative
AEEEIRRSTVVX	extraversive
AEEEJLMNRSUW	New Jerusalem
AEEEKLLPRSSW	sleepwalkers
AEEEKLRRSTTW	streetwalker
AEEELLORSTTT	teetotallers
AEEELLPRSSSU	pleasureless
AEEELMMNNPST	empanelments
AEEELMNNSSSS	namelessness
AEEELMNNSSTV	enslavements
AEEELMNORSYY	eleemosynary
AEEELRRSSSTU	treasureless
AEEEMMNPRSTT	temperaments
AEEEMMNPRTTT	attemperment
AEEEMMNRSSTU	measurements
AEEEMNNNRSST	ensnarements
AEEEMNNPPRSW	newspapermen
AEEEMNNRSTTT	entreatments
AEEEMNNSTTTW	New Testament
AEEEMNRSSSST	reassessment
AEEEMNRSSTTT	restatements
AEEEMOOPRRTV	evaporometer
AEEEMORRSSUV	overmeasures
AEEEMPRRSTTU	temperatures
AEEEMRSSSSST	seamstresses
AEEENOORRSSU	aeroneuroses
AEEENOPRSSTT	stearoptenes
AEEEQRSSSTTU	sequestrates
AEEFFGRSSTTU	suffragettes
AEEFFHLORRTY	forefatherly
AEEFGGIILLNR	fillagreeing
AEEFGHORRSTT	heterografts
AEEFGIKNOPRS	forespeaking
AEEFGILNORRT	foretriangle
AEEFGINRRRST	refrigerants
AEEFGIORRRRT	refrigerator
AEEFGLLPRSUY	presagefully
AEEFGLNRSSTU	gratefulness
AEEFGMNNRSTT	engraftments
AEEFHHNNOSTU	Hohenstaufen
AEEFHHORSSTU	housefathers
AEEFHIKNRSSS	freakishness
AEEFHILNRSST	fatherliness
AEEFHLMNSSSU	shamefulness
AEEFHLMORRTW	flamethrower
AEEFHOOPRRTW	weatherproof
AEEFHPRRRRSY	Harper's Ferry
AEEFIILMPPRR	preamplifier
AEEFIINRRSTT	fraternities
AEEFILNORSTV	overinflates
AEEFILNRSSUW	wearifulness
AEEFILOPRRST	proliferates
AEEFILOPRSTU	petaliferous
AEEFIMNNORTT	fermentation
AEEFIMNNSSST	manifestness
AEEFIMNORSTU	amentiferous
AEEFIMOPRRTV	performative
AEEFINNORSTT	fenestration
AEEFINRRRSST	fraternisers
AEEFINRRRSTZ	fraternizers
AEEFKNNORSSS	forsakenness
AEEFLLNSSSSW	flawlessness
AEEFLLORRSST	forestallers
AEEFLMNORSTT	forestalment
AEEFLMORRSTU	reformulates
AEEFLNSSSTTU	tastefulness
AEEFLNSSSTUW	wastefulness
AEEFLOPQRSUW	pasqueflower
AEEFNRRRRSST	transferrers
AEEFOOPRRSST	professorate
AEEFOQRRRSTU	forequarters
AEEGGGINNNSS	engagingness
AEEGGHIINNRS	garnisheeing
AEEGGHILNPRT	telegraphing
AEEGGHMMMOPR	Memphremagog
AEEGGIILNNRS	generalising
AEEGGIILNNRZ	generalizing
AEEGGIILNNSV	evangelising
AEEGGIILNNVZ	evangelizing
AEEGGIINNNRT	ingenerating
AEEGGIINNOSS	angiogenesis
AEEGGIINORSS	seigniorages
AEEGGILNNORS	sloganeering
AEEGGILNOSST	genealogists
AEEGGILOORST	geratologies
AEEGGILRSSVY	aggressively
AEEGGIMMNOST	geomagnetism
AEEGGINORSST	Saint George's
AEEGGINRSSUV	unaggressive
AEEGGIRRSTTU	regurgitates
AEEGGMNOOSTU	gametogenous
AEEGHHIINNST	heathenising
AEEGHHIINNTZ	heathenizing
AEEGHHILOPRR	heliographer
AEEGHHISTVWY	heavyweights
AEEGHHNOPRRT	ethnographer
AEEGHHOPRRTY	heterography
AEEGHILLMMRT	hellgrammite
AEEGHILORRUV	heliogravure
AEEGHILPRSTT	telegraphist
AEEGHINOPSST	pathogenesis
AEEGHINPRSST	sergeantship
AEEGHINPRSTU	superheating
AEEGHINRRSTT	straightener
AEEGHIPPRSTW	paperweights
AEEGHLMNRSTU	slaughtermen
AEEGHLNOPRSS	selenographs
AEEGHLNOPRSY	selenography
AEEGHLOORRTW	woolgatherer
AEEGHLRRSSTU	slaughterers
AEEGHMNOOSTU	hematogenous
AEEGHMOOPRRT	meteorograph
AEEGHMOOPRST	gametophores
AEEGHMOORSTU	heterogamous
AEEGHMOPSTTY	gametophytes
AEEGHNOOPRTV	photoengrave
AEEGHNOOPSTU	hepatogenous
AEEGHNOPRRST	stenographer
AEEGHNPRSSTV	stevengraphs
AEEGHNRSSTTW	Western Ghats
AEEGHOPPRRRT	petrographer
AEEGHOPRRRSX	xerographers

AEEGHOPRRSST stereographs
AEEGHOPRRSTY stereography
AEEGIIILLLST illegalities
AEEGIIILLMTT illegitimate
AEEGIIILMSTT legitimatise
AEEGIIILMTTZ legitimatize
AEEGIIINSTTV negativities
AEEGIIKNNOSS kainogenesis
AEEGIILLMTTY legitimately
AEEGIILLSSTV legislatives
AEEGIILLSTTU aiguillettes
AEEGIILNNORS legionnaires
AEEGIILNNPSS palingenesis
AEEGIILNNRST eternalising
AEEGIILNNRTV interleaving
AEEGIILNNRTZ eternalizing
AEEGIILNRSST gelatinisers
AEEGIILNRSTZ gelatinizers
AEEGIILRRSTU regularities
AEEGIINNNORT ingeneration
AEEGIINNNRTT entertaining
intenerating
AEEGIINNRTVW interweaving
AEEGIINORRTV reinvigorate
AEEGIINPRRTV privateering
AEEGIINSSTTV investigates
AEEGIJNNRTUV rejuvenating
AEEGIKLLNPSW sleepwalking
AEEGIKNNNSSS sneakingness
AEEGILLMNRTY regimentally
AEEGILLNSSTT tessellating
AEEGILLRSSST legislatress
AEEGILLRSSTU legislatures
AEEGILLRTUVY regulatively
AEEGILMNNRST realignments
AEEGILMNNTTU integumental
AEEGILNNNOPT longipennate
AEEGILNNPSSS pleasingness
AEEGILNNRTTY entreatingly
AEEGILOORSTT teratologies
AEEGIMNNOSTT segmentation
AEEGIMNNRRTU remunerating
AEEGIMNNRSST reassignment
AEEGIMNNRSUV maneuverings
AEEGIMNOSTTW witenagemots
AEEGIMNPRTTT reattempting
AEEGIMNRRSST mastersinger
AEEGIMSSSTTU guesstimates
AEEGINNNSSSU sanguineness
AEEGINOPRRRT peregrinator
AEEGINORRRSZ reorganizers
AEEGINORRSTT interrogates
AEEGINORRTVW overwatering
AEEGINPPRRTT perpetrating
AEEGINPPRTTU perpetuating
AEEGINRRSTTV tergiversant
AEEGIOPRRSTV prerogatives
AEEGKNOORSTU keratogenous
AEEGLLMNOOPR prolegomenal
AEEGLLMNOPSY splenomegaly
AEEGLLMNRUWZ mangelwurzel
AEEGLMNNORTV governmental
AEEGLNNOORTT Lot-et-Garonne
AEEGLOORSTVV overvoltages
AEEGMMNORTTY magnetometry
AEEGMNORRSTV overgarments
AEEGNRRSSSST transgresses
AEEGPRRSSSSU supergrasses
AEEHHHILNSTY heathenishly
AEEHHILMMNTU helianthemum
AEEHHILNSSTU helianthuses
AEEHHILNSTTU unhealthiest
AEEHHILOPRTY heliotherapy
AEEHHIMNPRSW New Hampshire
AEEHHIMPRRTY hyperthermia
AEEHHIRSSTWW whitewashers
AEEHHLLLMOPS Pelham Holles
AEEHHLMPRRTY hyperthermal
AEEHHNOPPRTY phanerophyte
AEEHHNORSSTT hearthstones
AEEHHOPPRTTY phreatophyte
AEEHIIIMNOPT Amenhotep III
AEEHIIKNPRSY hyperkinesia
AEEHIIKNSSST kinaesthesis
AEEHIILMOPST epitheliomas
AEEHIILRSSTV shrievalties
AEEHIIMOOPSS haemopoiesis
AEEHIINORSTT etherisation
AEEHIINORTTZ etherization
AEEHIKLMRRSS sharemilkers
AEEHILLPPRRY peripherally
AEEHILMMOOST mesothelioma
AEEHILMPRRSY hyperrealism
AEEHILNPPRSS planispheres
AEEHILNSSSTT stealthiness
AEEHILPRRSTY hyperrealist
AEEHILPRRTYY hyperreality
AEEHILPSSTTT telepathists
AEEHILSTUVXY exhaustively
AEEHIMNNORTT nitromethane
AEEHIMNOPRTZ promethazine
AEEHIMOPRSSV overemphasis
AEEHIMOSSSST somaesthesis
AEEHINNNOOST hootenannies
AEEHINNOPPRS apprehension
AEEHINOORSTU heteroousian
AEEHINOPRRTY erythropenia
AEEHINOPRSTU neuropathies
AEEHINOPSSTV topheaviness
AEEHINORSTTT titanotheres
AEEHINSSSTTT anesthetists
AEEHIOOPSSST apotheosises
AEEHIOOPSSTZ apotheosizes
AEEHIPPRRXYY hyperpyrexia
AEEHKMPRRSTY hypermarkets
AEEHKNOORRTY heterokaryon
AEEHLLMMORWY yellowhammer
AEEHLLMNNOPY phenomenally
AEEHLLMNNRTT enthrallment
AEEHLLMNOOPT metallophone
AEEHLLMORTXY exothermally
AEEHLMNNRSTT enthralments
AEEHLMNORSTT stenothermal
AEEHLMNRSSSS harmlessness

AEEHLMORSTTW	Tower Hamlets
AEEHLMPRRSUU	superhumeral
AEEHLNOPRTUY	polyurethane
AEEHLOPRSTTY	heteroplasty
AEEHMMNORSST	hammerstones
AEEHMMNRSTUX	xeranthemums
AEEHMMOOPRST	metamorphose
AEEHMNNOPRTY	hymenopteran
AEEHMOORSSTX	mesothoraxes
AEEHMORRSSTW	whoremasters
AEEHMORRSTWY	whoremastery
AEEHMORSSSTU	housemasters
AEEHMORSTTUY	erythematous
AEEHNNOPRSSW	answerphones
AEEHNNORRSTT	northeastern
AEEHNORRSSTT	northeasters
AEEHNORSSTTU	southeastern
AEEHOPRRSSTT	stratosphere
AEEHORSSSTTU	southeasters
AEEIIILLRSTT	literalities
AEEIIILMRRTZ	remilitarize
AEEIIILNQSTU	inequalities
AEEIIKLMNPRS	marlinespike
AEEIILLLRTTY	illiterately
AEEIILLMRSTU	mitrailleuse
AEEIILLNOSTV	televisional
AEEIILLNPSTT	pestilential
AEEIILLNSSSV	villainesses
AEEIILLRRTVY	irrelatively
AEEIILMMORRS	memorialiser
AEEIILMMORRZ	memorializer
AEEIILMMORSS	memorialises
AEEIILMMORSZ	memorializes
AEEIILMNOOST	emotionalise
AEEIILMNOOTZ	emotionalize
AEEIILMNPRSS	imperialness
AEEIILMNRRSS	mineralisers
AEEIILMNRRSZ	mineralizers
AEEIILMNSSST	essentialism
AEEIILMPRTVY	imperatively
AEEIILMRRSST	semitrailers
AEEIILMRSTTU	multiseriate
AEEIILNNPSTT	penitentials
AEEIILNNRSST	internalises
AEEIILNNRSTZ	internalizes
AEEIILNNSSST	inessentials
AEEIILNORSST	orientalises
AEEIILNORSTZ	orientalizes
AEEIILNRRSST	literariness
AEEIILNRSSUV	universalise
AEEIILNRSTTU	neutralities
AEEIILNRSUVZ	universalize
AEEIILNSSSTT	essentialist
AEEIILNSSSTU	sensualities
AEEIILNSSTTY	essentiality
AEEIILOPTTVX	exploitative
AEEIILPPRSSU	Upper Silesia
AEEIIMMSSSTT	misestimates
AEEIIMNNSSTT	intimateness
AEEIIMNRRRST	intermarries
AEEIINNNORTT	inteneration
AEEIINNOPRSS	pensionaries
AEEIINNORSTT	eternisation
AEEIINNORTTZ	eternization
AEEIINNPRTTY	penitentiary
AEEIINNRRTTU	intrauterine
AEEIINOPPRTT	Pointe-à-Pitre
AEEIINORRSTT	reiterations
AEEIINQRSTTU	quaternities
AEEIINRSSTUZ	suzerainties
AEEIINSSTUVV	vesuvianites
AEEIIPRTTUVV	vituperative
AEEIJLOPRTVY	pejoratively
AEEIJMMOPRRS	major premise
AEEIJNNORTUV	rejuvenation
AEEIKMNNSSST	mistakenness
AEEIKMOORSTT	keratotomies
AEEILLLNSTVY	Stanleyville
AEEILLLSTUVY	televisually
AEEILLMNRRTY	artillerymen
AEEILLNNPRTT	interpellant
AEEILLNNPSTY	septennially
AEEILLNNSTTY	sententially
AEEILLNOSSTT	tessellation
AEEILLNOSSTV	volatileness
AEEILLNQSTUY	sequentially
AEEILLNQTUVY	equivalently
AEEILLNRRSTT	interstellar
AEEILLNRRTVY	irrelevantly
AEEILLNSSSST	taillessness
AEEILLNSSSUV	allusiveness
AEEILLOPSTVY	Yelisavetpol
AEEILMMNNPST	impanelments
AEEILMNNNRSS	mannerliness
AEEILMNORSST	salinometers
AEEILMNPSTTU	penultimates
AEEILMNRSSST	masterliness
AEEILMNSSTTU	ultimateness
AEEILMOPRRST	polarimeters
AEEILMORRSST	solarimeters
AEEILMPRRSSU	superrealism
AEEILNNNOSST	nonessential
AEEILNNNRSST	internalness
AEEILNNOPSTX	exponentials
AEEILNNPSSSS	painlessness
AEEILNNPSSTU	peninsulates
AEEILNNSSSTU	unessentials
AEEILNOPRRTT	interpolater
AEEILNOPRSSS	personalises
AEEILNOPRSST	personalties
AEEILNOPRSSX	expressional
AEEILNOPRSSZ	personalizes
AEEILNOPRSTT	interpolates
AEEILNPRRSST	interspersal
AEEILNRRSSTU	neutralisers
AEEILNRRSTUZ	neutralizers
AEEILNRSSTTX	externalists
AEEILPRRSSTU	superrealist
AEEILPRSSTUV	superlatives
AEEILPRSSUVY	persuasively
AEEILRRRSSTT	terrestrials
AEEILRRSTTTU	litterateurs
AEEIMMNORSTT	amortisement
AEEIMMNORTTZ	amortizement

AEEIMMNRSSTU	immatureness
AEEIMMNRSTTT	mistreatment
AEEIMMNSSTTT	misstatement
AEEIMNNNORTT	intermontane
AEEIMNNNRSST	insnarements
AEEIMNNNRSTT	entrainments
AEEIMNNORRTU	remuneration
AEEIMNNORSTT	senarmontite
AEEIMNNORSTU	enumerations
	mountaineers
AEEIMNNOSSTT	maisonnettes
AEEIMNNRSTTT	intreatments
AEEIMNNSSTTT	instatements
AEEIMNOPRSST	impersonates
AEEIMNORRTTX	exterminator
AEEIMOPRRSTV	vaporimeters
AEEIMRSSSTTY	systematiser
AEEIMRSSTTYZ	systematizer
AEEIMSSSSTTY	systematises
AEEIMSSSTTYZ	systematizes
AEEINNOOPRTV	nonoperative
AEEINNOORSTX	exonerations
AEEINNOPRSTT	penetrations
	presentation
AEEINNOSTTUV	eventuations
AEEINNOSTTUX	extenuations
AEEINNPRRRTU	intrapreneur
AEEINOORRSSU	aeroneurosis
AEEINOORTTTX	extortionate
AEEINOPPRRTT	perpetration
AEEINOPPRTTU	perpetuation
AEEINOPPSSST	appositeness
AEEINOPRRSTV	preservation
AEEINOPRRSTY	arsenopyrite
AEEINORRRSVY	reversionary
AEEINORRSSST	reassertions
AEEINORRSSTV	reservations
AEEINORRSTVX	extraversion
AEEINPRSSUUV	unpersuasive
AEEINPRSTUXY	Saint-Exupéry
AEEINRSSTTTV	transvestite
AEEINRSTTTUV	sternutative
AEEIOPPRRSTX	expropriates
AEEIORRSSTTV	restoratives
AEEIPRRSSSTT	stripteasers
AEEIPRRSSSTU	pasteurisers
AEEIPRRSSTUZ	pasteurizers
AEEJNORRSTUV	rejuvenators
AEEKLMNRSSUW	lukewarmness
AEEKLMORRSTW	metalworkers
AEEKMORRSSTT	masterstroke
AEEKMPRRSSTU	supermarkets
AEEKNPRRSSTU	supertankers
AEELLLMNOTVY	malevolently
AEELLMNORSTT	reallotments
AEELLMNPPSTU	supplemental
AEELLMORRSST	steamrollers
AEELLNORSSTW	stonewallers
AEELMMORSTTV	voltammeters
AEELMNOPRSST	temporalness
AEELMNOPRTUY	Merleau-Ponty
AEELMNPRRSTU	premenstrual
AEELMOOPRSTU	somatopleure
AEELMOPRSSTT	plastometers
AEELNORSTUXY	extraneously
AEELNRRSSTVY	transversely
AEELOOPPRTUV	overpopulate
AEELOPSSTTUX	expostulates
AEELQSSTTUUY	statuesquely
AEEMNNNNOPRT	nonpermanent
AEEMNOORTUUV	outmanoeuvre
AEEMNOPRRSTY	pyranometers
AEEMNOQRSTTU	quantometers
AEEMNOQSSSSU	squamoseness
AEEMNORRRSTU	remunerators
AEEMNORRSSTT	remonstrates
AEEMNORSTUUV	outmaneuvers
AEEMPQRRTTUY	Empty Quarter
AEENNOPRRSTU	neuropterans
AEENNORSSSUV	ravenousness
AEENNOSSSSUU	nauseousness
AEENOPRRSSTT	paternosters
AEENORRSSTXY	extrasensory
AEENQRSSSTTU	sequestrants
AEENRRRSSTTV	transverters
AEEOOPRSTUUX	autoexposure
AEEOPPRRRSTT	perpetrators
AEEOPRRSTTTU	tetrapterous
AEEOQRRSSTTU	sequestrator
AEFFGILLLMOR	flagelliform
AEFFGIMSSTUU	suffumigates
AEFFGINORSTV	overstaffing
AEFFHILNSSTU	faithfulness
AEFFIIMNORRS	foraminifers
AEFFILLMMMRS	flimflammers
AEFFILORSSSY	fairyflosses
AEFFKNRRRSTU	frankfurters
AEFGGGILNOPR	leapfrogging
AEFGGHINORRT	forgathering
AEFGGILLNNUY	Lingayen Gulf
AEFGHHINORTY	Fotheringhay
AEFGHHOORRTU	thoroughfare
AEFGHHOORTTU	aforethought
AEFGHHORTTTU	afterthought
AEFGHIINNORS	refashioning
AEFGHIIRSSTU	guitarfishes
AEFGIILRTUVY	figuratively
AEFGIINNRRST	fraternising
AEFGIINNRRTZ	fraternizing
AEFGILLMNNUY	meaningfully
AEFGILLNORST	forestalling
AEFGILLNRSST	fingerstalls
AEFGILLNRTTY	flatteringly
AEFGILLNSSUW	wineglassful
AEFGILLOPRTY	profligately
AEFGILNNOORS	gonfaloniers
AEFGILNNRTTU	unflattering
AEFGIMNNRSTT	ingraftments
AEFGINNNNOTT	nonfattening
AEFGINNRRRST	transferring
AEFGINRRSSTU	transfigures
AEFGLLNRTUUY	ungratefully
AEFGOORRRSTY	agroforestry
AEFHHLOOPSST	photoflashes

AEFHIINNSSST	faintishness
AEFHIOPRRSST	parrotfishes
AEFHKLNNSSTU	thankfulness
AEFHLLMOSSTY	fathomlessly
AEFHLNRSSTUW	wrathfulness
AEFHOOPRRSTT	shatterproof
AEFIIILLRRST	fritillaries
AEFIIILMNSST	semifinalist
AEFIIILNRTTV	infiltrative
AEFIIIMNNOST	feminisation
AEFIIIMNNOTZ	feminization
AEFIILLMOTTU	multifoliate
AEFIILLNOOTU	unifoliolate
AEFIILLNRTUV	interfluvial
AEFIILMNORUV	fluviomarine
AEFIILNOOPRT	perfoliation
AEFIILNOOSTX	exfoliations
AEFIILNORSTT	frontalities
AEFIILRSSUVV	flaviviruses
AEFIIMNNNOTT	infotainment
AEFIINNOSSTT	infestations
	sinfoniettas
AEFIINORSTTU	titaniferous
AEFILLRRSTTU	ultrafilters
AEFILMMNNOOT	monofilament
AEFILMNOSUVX	fluvoxamines
AEFILMORRRSU	formulariser
AEFILMORRRUZ	formularizer
AEFILMORRSSU	formularises
AEFILMORRSUZ	formularizes
AEFILNNOSSTU	fountainless
AEFILNOOPRSS	professional
AEFILNOOPRTV	flavoprotein
AEFILNORSSTW	satinflowers
AEFILOOPRRSS	professorial
AEFILOPPRSUU	papuliferous
AEFIMNNOOSTT	fomentations
AEFIMNNORRST	frontiersman
AEFIMNNOSSSU	infamousness
AEFIMNOOPRRT	preformation
AEFIMNOORRST	reformations
AEFINNORSSTU	stanniferous
AEFINNRRRSST	transferrins
AEFINOOPRRST	perforations
AEFKLLOORRSW	floorwalkers
AEFLLNNSSUUW	unlawfulness
AEFLMMORSSTY	formal system
AEFLNOOPSSTU	teaspoonfuls
AEFLOQRRSUUY	foursquarely
AEFLORRSSTWW	strawflowers
AEFMNORRRSST	transformers
AEFMOOPRSSTT	foretopmasts
AEFNNORSTTUU	unfortunates
AEGGGIINNRRS	grangerising
AEGGGIINNRRZ	grangerizing
AEGGGILNNOTU	agglutinogen
AEGGGILNRSTY	staggeringly
AEGGGILNRSWY	swaggeringly
AEGGGIMNORRT	remortgaging
AEGGHHILNOST	Golan Heights
AEGGHHIMNORR	hemorrhaging
AEGGHIIJLNNO	Heilongjiang
	Heilong Jiang
AEGGHIILNNST	nightingales
AEGGHILNRSTU	slaughtering
AEGGHIOORSTU	South Georgia
AEGGHLNOOSTT	snaggletooth
AEGGHLOOPRRS	logographers
AEGGHOOOPRYZ	zoogeography
AEGGIIILLLNS	illegalising
AEGGIIILLLNZ	illegalizing
AEGGIIILMNTT	legitimating
AEGGIIILNNST	gelatinising
AEGGIIILNNTZ	gelatinizing
AEGGIIIMNNNT	ingeminating
AEGGIIIMNNST	enigmatising
AEGGIIIMNNTZ	enigmatizing
AEGGIILLNORS	allegorising
AEGGIILLNORZ	allegorizing
AEGGIILNRRSU	regularising
AEGGIILNRRUZ	regularizing
AEGGIIMNNPRT	impregnating
AEGGIIMNSTTU	guestimating
AEGGIINNNNSU	ensanguining
AEGGIINNORRS	reorganising
AEGGIINNORRZ	reorganizing
AEGGIINNPRSS	preassigning
AEGGIINNPRSY	panegyrising
AEGGIINNPRYZ	panegyrizing
AEGGIINRSTTU	ingurgitates
AEGGILOORSTT	geratologist
AEGGILORRSUY	gregariously
AEGGIMNNORRW	warmongering
AEGGINNPRSSS	graspingness
AEGGINRRSTTU	regurgitants
AEGGLOOORSTY	astrogeology
AEGGMNNOORRT	rontgenogram
AEGHHIINSTWW	whitewashing
AEGHHILOPRRT	lithographer
AEGHHIPRSUWY	superhighway
AEGHHLOPRSSU	ploughshares
AEGHHMNOPRRY	hymnographer
AEGHHMOPRRST	thermographs
AEGHHMOPRRTY	thermography
AEGHHNOOPPRR	phonographer
AEGHHOOPPRRT	photographer
	rephotograph
AEGHHOOPRRRT	orthographer
AEGHIILMNRST	thermalising
AEGHIILMNRTZ	thermalizing
AEGHIILMNSST	almightiness
AEGHIILNSTTY	hesitatingly
AEGHIILOPPRS	lipographies
AEGHIIMNNRUZ	rehumanizing
AEGHIINNSTTU	unhesitating
AEGHIIPPRSST	epigraphists
AEGHILLMOPSU	melliphagous
AEGHILLMPRST	lamplighters
AEGHILMNNSTU	languishment
AEGHILMOOSTT	hematologist
AEGHILNOOSST	anthologises
AEGHILNOOSTZ	anthologizes
AEGHILNRSTTY	shatteringly
AEGHILOOPSTZ	pathologizes

AEGHILQRRTTU quarterlight
AEGHIMMNOSST mesognathism
AEGHIMNNRSST garnishments
AEGHIMNOOPRS nomographies
AEGHIMNORSUW housewarming
AEGHIMOOPRST mastigophore
AEGHIMOPRSSS seismographs
AEGHIMOPRSSY seismography
AEGHINNNRSSU unharnessing
AEGHINOOPRSS nosographies
AEGHINORSSUW warehousings
AEGHINRRSSTT heartstrings
AEGHINRSSSTT straightness
AEGHIOOPPRST topographies
AEGHIOPPRRSY pyrographies
AEGHIRSSTTWW strawweights
AEGHLMNNOORS longshoreman
AEGHLMOORTUY rheumatology
AEGHLOPRRSXY xylographers
AEGHLORSSTUU slaughterous
AEGHMNOOOPTT photomontage
AEGHMNOOPRRS monographers
nomographers
AEGHMNOOSSTT gnathostomes
AEGHMNOOSSTU mesognathous
AEGHMNOPPRSU pneumographs
AEGHNNOOPRTY anthropogeny
AEGHNOOPPRRR pornographer
AEGHNOOPRRSS nosographers
AEGHNOOPSSTU stenophagous
AEGHOOPPRRST topographers
AEGHOOPRRTUV photogravure
AEGHOPPRRRSY pyrographers
AEGHOPPRRSSS grasshoppers
AEGHOPPRRSTY typographers
AEGHOPPSSYYZ zygapophyses
AEGIIIKNNRST keratinising
AEGIIIKNNRTZ keratinizing
AEGIIILMNNRS mineralising
AEGIIILMNNRZ mineralizing
AEGIIILMNOTT legitimation
AEGIIILNRSTV relativising
revitalising
AEGIIILNRTVZ relativizing
revitalizing
AEGIIIMNNNOT ingemination
AEGIIIMNNNST inseminating
AEGIIINORTVV invigorative
AEGIIINRSTVW West Virginia
AEGIIKLMNPRS marlingspike
AEGIILLMMMRS milligrammes
AEGIILLMRRSU guerrillaism
AEGIILLNNOTW wellingtonia
AEGIILLNNRST reinstalling
AEGIILLNPRVY prevailingly
AEGIILMMNNST misalignment
AEGIILMNNRST streamlining
AEGIILMNORSS regionalisms
AEGIILMNORST mineralogist
AEGIILMOOPRS oligospermia
AEGIILNNNSSU ungainliness
AEGIILNNORTU urinogenital
AEGIILNNPPRT interlapping
AEGIILNNPRUV unprevailing
AEGIILNNRSTU neutralising
AEGIILNNRTTY intreatingly
AEGIILNNRTUZ neutralizing
AEGIILNNSSTV vigilantness
AEGIILNORRSV revalorising
AEGIILNORRVZ revalorizing
AEGIILNORSST regionalists
AEGIILNPPRTV livetrapping
AEGIILNPRSTT earsplitting
AEGIILNRSSSU singularises
AEGIILNRSSUZ singularizes
AEGIILOOSSTT aetiologists
AEGIILRRRTUY irregularity
AEGIIMMNRSSU mismeasuring
AEGIIMNNNORT renominating
AEGIIMNNOPRT impregnation
AEGIIMNNOPTT pigmentation
AEGIIMNSSSUV vaginismuses
AEGIIMRSSSTT stigmatisers
AEGIIMRSSTTZ stigmatizers
AEGIINNNOSST angiotensins
AEGIINNNRSTT intransigent
AEGIINNOOSTT negotiations
AEGIINNOPPRT reappointing
AEGIINNOPTTT potentiating
AEGIINNORRTV overtraining
AEGIINNORSST resignations
AEGIINNORSTT integrations
AEGIINNPPSTU unappetising
AEGIINNPPTUZ unappetizing
AEGIINNRSTTU intriguantes
AEGIINNSTUXY exsanguinity
AEGIINOPRRSV overpraising
AEGIINORRSTT registration
AEGIINORSTTV investigator
AEGIINPRSSTU pasteurising
AEGIINPRSTUZ pasteurizing
AEGIINPRTTUV vituperating
AEGIKLMNORTW metalworking
AEGILLLNPRUY prelingually
AEGILLMPRSSU aspergillums
AEGILLMRSTTU metallurgist
AEGILLNNOSTW stonewalling
AEGILLNOPRTT preallotting
AEGILLNOSTUY gelatinously
AEGILMMNRSTY stammeringly
AEGILMNNNNOT nonalignment
AEGILMNNOQTU magniloquent
AEGILMNOORST glomerations
AEGILMNOPRSU pelargoniums
AEGILMNRSTTY smatteringly
AEGILMOOOSST somatologies
AEGILMORSSTT stigmasterol
AEGILNNNOSTU sanguinolent
AEGILNNOSSTU langoustines
AEGILNNRSSSU singularness
AEGILNNRSTTY astringently
AEGILNOOPRVY parleyvooing
AEGILNOPPRTU repopulating
AEGILNRRSSUY reassuringly

AEGILOORSTTT teratologist
AEGILOOSSTTU tautologises
AEGILOOSTTUZ tautologizes
AEGILORRSSTU grossularite
AEGILRSSTTUU gutturalises
AEGILRSTTUUZ gutturalizes
AEGIMMORSSTU mesogastrium
AEGIMNNORSUV manoeuvrings
AEGIMNNRSTTU menstruating
AEGIMNOPRRST impregnators
AEGIMOORSSTT gastrotomies
AEGINNOORRSV vinegarroons
AEGINNOOSTXY oxygenations
AEGINNOSSUUX exsanguinous
AEGINOORRRTT interrogator
AEGINOORRSTV overroasting
AEGINOPRSTUX expurgations
AEGIPRRSTUVY supergravity
AEGKLORRSSSW glassworkers
AEGLMNOOPTUY pneumatology
AEGLNOOSTUUY autogenously
AEGLNRSSTTUU gutturalness
AEGLOORSTUUY outrageously
AEGMNOORRSST gastronomers
AEGNORRRSSST transgressor
AEGOOPSSTTUY steatopygous
AEHHILNOPPRT philanthrope
AEHHILOPSTTU thiosulphate
AEHHIMNOPRSS horsemanship
AEHHIMOOPSTT homeopathist
AEHHINNOPSTY hyphenations
AEHHINNOPTXY hypoxanthine
AEHHIOPPSSST phosphatises
AEHHIOPPSSTZ phosphatizes
AEHHIORSTTTW whitethroats
AEHHLLOPSTTY thallophytes
AEHHLMOOPRTT photothermal
AEHHLMOOPSTX exophthalmos
AEHHLMOPSTUX exophthalmus
AEHHLOOOPPRT lophophorate
AEHHLOOPRSTU Althorp House
AEHHNOPPRTYY hypnotherapy
AEHHOOPPRSST phosphorates
AEHHOOPPRTTY phototherapy
AEHHOOPRRSST sharpshooter
AEHHOPRSSTTU Theophrastus
AEHIIILNOOPS eosinophilia
AEHIIIMNNOST thiosinamine
AEHIIIMNNSTU inhumanities
AEHIIKLNOSST Thessaloníki
AEHIILLOPRSU ailurophiles
AEHIILLPSSTT philatelists
AEHIILNOPRST relationship
AEHIILOPSSST hospitalises
AEHIILOPSSTZ hospitalizes
AEHIILPRRSTT hairsplitter
AEHIINNOPRTT trephination
AEHIINOORSTT theorisation
AEHIINOORTTZ theorization
AEHIINOPRRSS parishioners
AEHIINOPRRST prehistorian
AEHIINRSSTUW White Russian
AEHIIRRSSTTW shirtwaister
AEHIKMNNNORS Krishna Menon
AEHILLMORSTY isothermally
AEHILLOORSTU heliolatrous
AEHILLOPRSST hospitallers
AEHILLOPSTXY phyllotaxies
AEHILMNNOOPS aminophenols
AEHILMNOOPSU anemophilous
AEHILMNOSTXY hematoxylins
AEHILMNQSSSU qualmishness
AEHILMOOPRST photorealism
AEHILMOOPSST homoplasties
AEHILNOPSTXY phytoalexins
AEHILNPRRSTY platyrrhines
AEHILNPRSSST shinplasters
AEHILOOPRSTT photorealist
AEHIMMMOPRST metamorphism
AEHIMMNNNOOT man in the moon
AEHIMNNOOPRT enantiomorph
AEHIMNNOOSSU Mansion House
AEHIMNNORTTV North Vietnam
AEHIMNNOSSSW womanishness
AEHIMNNOSSTT astonishment
AEHIMNNPRSTT transhipment
AEHIMNNQSTUV vanquishment
AEHIMNOPRSST misanthropes
AEHIMNOSTTUV South Vietnam
AEHIMOOOSSST homoeostasis
AEHIMPRSSSTY sympathisers
AEHIMPRSSTYZ sympathizers
AEHINNPSSSTY synthespians
AEHINOOPRRTT prototherian
AEHINOOPRSST epanorthosis
AEHINOOPSSTT photonasties
AEHINOORSTTX exhortations
AEHINOPRSSTT antistrophes
AEHINOPRSTTY attorneyship
AEHINPPRRSST partnerships
AEHIOOPPRSST apostrophise
AEHIOOPPRSTZ apostrophize
AEHIOOPSSTTT osteopathist
AEHIOOSSSTTU South Ossetia
AEHIOPQRSSTU quaestorship
AEHIOPRRSTWY praiseworthy
AEHIOPSSSSTY hypostasises
AEHIOPSSSTTY hypostatises
AEHIOPSSSTYZ hypostasizes
AEHIOPSSTTYZ hypostatizes
AEHLLLMOOPRS allelomorphs
AEHLLLNOPPSY phylloplanes
AEHLMNPRSUUY superhumanly
AEHLMOPPRRSY lamprophyres
AEHLNOPRSSTU Southern Alps
AEHLNOPRSTUY polyurethans
AEHLNOPSSTUY polyanthuses
AEHLOPPRSTUY pyrosulphate
AEHMMOOOPRST ommatophores
AEHMMOOPRSTU metamorphous
AEHMNOOPRTUX pneumothorax
AEHNOOPRRSSU sarrusophone
AEHNOOPRRSTT orthopterans
AEHNORRSSSTY synarthroses

AEHOOPRRRSST arthrospores
AEHOOPRRSSTT trapshooters
AEIIIILMRSST similarities
AEIIIILNTTVY initiatively
AEIIIILRSTTV trivialities
AEIIIINRSTTX initiatrixes
AEIIILLMNNOR millionnaire
AEIIILLMNORS millionaires
AEIIILLMNTUV illuminative
AEIIILLNORRT trillionaire
AEIIILMMORST immoralities
AEIIILMMPRSS imperialisms
AEIIILMNNOST eliminations
AEIIILMNSSST antimissiles
AEIIILMPRSST imperialists
AEIIILNPRSST pleinairists
AEIIILNRSTTT interstitial
AEIIILPRSSTU spiritualise
AEIIILPRSTUZ spiritualize
AEIIILRSTTUV virtualities
AEIIIMNNNOST insemination
AEIIIMNORSSS missionaries
AEIIIMNOSSTT itemisations
AEIIIMNOSTTZ itemizations
AEIIIMNRSSTU miniaturises
AEIIIMNRSTTV ministrative
AEIIIMNRSTUZ miniaturizes
AEIIINNOOPTV opinionative
AEIIINNORSTT itinerations
AEIIINNRSTTV intransitive
AEIIINORSTTV invitatories
AEIIIOPPRTTV propitiative
AEIIKKNORSSY karyokinesis
AEIIKLLOPRST realpolitiks
AEIIKLMNPRSS marlinspikes
AEIILLLLMNNY millennially
AEIILLLNTUUX luxullianite
AEIILLLPRRTU pluriliteral
AEIILLMMMORY immemorially
AEIILLMSSTTU satellitiums
AEIILLMSTUVY simulatively
AEIILLNNSTTY intestinally
AEIILLNQRSTU tranquillise
AEIILLNQRTUZ tranquillize
AEIILLRSSTTU Little Russia
AEIILLRSTTUV illustrative
AEIILMMNOOST emotionalism
AEIILMMORRST immortaliser
AEIILMMORRTZ immortalizer
AEIILMMORSST immortalises
memorialists
AEIILMMORSTZ immortalizes
AEIILMNNOTVY nominatively
AEIILMNNSSTT militantness
AEIILMNOORST meliorations
AEIILMNOOSTT emotionalist
AEIILMNOOTTY emotionality
AEIILMNOPRSS impressional
AEIILMNORSST misrelations
orientalisms
AEIILMNOSSTT testimonials
AEIILMNRSSUV universalism
AEIILMNRTUVY ruminatively
AEIILMNSTTUY simultaneity
AEIILMPRTTTU multipartite
AEIILMSSTTUV stimulatives
AEIILNNNQQUU quinquennial
AEIILNNOOSTV novelisation
AEIILNNOOTVZ novelization
AEIILNNOSTTV ventilations
AEIILNNPRTTY tripinnately
AEIILNOOPSTX expositional
AEIILNOOPTTX exploitation
AEIILNOOSTVW vowelisation
AEIILNOOTVWZ vowelization
AEIILNOPPSTY inappositely
AEIILNOPTTTY potentiality
AEIILNORSSST solitariness
AEIILNORSSTT orientalists
AEIILNQRRTUZ tranquilizer
AEIILNQRSTUZ tranquilizes
AEIILNQTTUVY quantitively
AEIILNRSSTUV universalist
AEIILNRSTTVY transitively
AEIILNRSTUVY universality
AEIILNSTUUXY unisexuality
AEIILOPPSTVY appositively
AEIILORRRSTT territorials
AEIILPRRTTTY tripartitely
AEIIMMNNSSTT immanentists
AEIIMMNOORST memorisation
AEIIMMNOORTZ memorization
AEIIMNNNOORT renomination
AEIIMNNOOSTT monetisation
AEIIMNNOOTTZ monetization
AEIIMNNOPSSX expansionism
AEIIMNNORSST inseminators
Nestorianism
nitrosamines
AEIIMNNORSTT terminations
AEIIMNNORSTV verminations
AEIIMNNOSSST sensationism
AEIIMNOOPRST operationism
AEIIMNOPRSTT impetrations
AEIIMNRSSSTV transmissive
AEIIMOOORSTV ovariotomies
AEIIMOPPRRST impropriates
AEIIMRRSTTUV triumvirates
AEIINNNORSTV innervations
AEIINNNORTTU antineutrino
AEIINNNQSTTU Saint-Quentin
AEIINNOOPSTT anteposition
AEIINNOORSTT orientations
AEIINNOPRSTU resupination
AEIINNOPSSTX expansionist
AEIINNORSTTT strontianite
AEIINOPPRRST perspiration
AEIINOPPSSTT peptisations
AEIINOPPSTTZ peptizations
AEIINOPRRSTT partitioners
repartitions
AEIINOPRSTTX extirpations
AEIINOPRTTUV vituperation
AEIINPRSSSSU prussianises

AEIINPRSSSUZ	prussianizes
AEIINRRSTTVY	intervarsity
AEIINSSSTTUV	antitussives
AEIIOOPRSSTV	vaporosities
AEIIORSSSTUV	Soviet Russia
AEIJLNORRSSU	journalisers
AEIJLNORRSUZ	journalizers
AEIKLNOPSSTT	kinetoplasts
AEIKMNNRSTTU	Turkmenistan
AEIKMRSSSSTT	taskmistress
AEILLLLPRRRT	pralltriller
AEILLMMMSSTY	symmetallism
AEILLMNNSSTT	installments
AEILLMNOPRSY	impersonally
AEILLMNPRSUU	superluminal
AEILLNNORTTY	intolerantly
AEILLNOOSTTW	wollastonite
AEILLNOQRTUV	ventriloqual
AEILLNORRTTY	torrentially
AEILLNRSSTUV	surveillants
AEILMNNNOOOT	nonemotional
AEILMNNOOPST	Neo-Platonism
AEILMNNORSST	matronliness
AEILMNNOSSTU	noumenalists
AEILMNNOSSTW	Winston-Salem
AEILMNNRSTTU	instrumental
AEILMNOOPRTT	metropolitan
AEILMNOOSSTT	molestations
AEILMNOPRRST	trampoliners
AEILMNOQSUUY	equanimously
AEILMNOSSTUU	simultaneous
AEILMOORSTTT	stromatolite
AEILMOQSSTTU	milquetoasts
AEILMPSSTUVY	assumptively
AEILNNQRSSTU	tranquilness
AEILNOOPRRTT	interpolator
AEILNOOPRSTX	explorations
AEILNOORTUVY	evolutionary
AEILNOPRSSST	personalists
AEILNORRSSTU	serrulations
AEILNORRSUVY	revulsionary
AEILOOOPPPRS	prosopopeial
AEILOOPRSTTY	epistolatory
AEILOPPRRSSU	popularisers
AEILOPPRRSUZ	popularizers
AEILOPRSTUUV	voluptuaries
AEILRRSSTUUV	ultraviruses
AEIMMSSSSTTY	systematisms
AEIMNNOORSTU	Ore Mountains
AEIMNNOPPSTT	appointments
AEIMNNORSTTU	menstruation
AEIMNOOPRRST	impersonator
AEIMNOPRSSTU	reassumption
AEIMNOPRSTTU	permutations
AEIMNRRSSTTT	transmitters
AEIMNRSSSTTV	transvestism
AEIMOPPRRSSU	appressorium
AEIMOPRRSSSU	aspersoriums
AEIMPRSSSTTU	suprematists
AEIMSSSSTTTY	systematists
AEINNNOPRSTT	transpontine
AEINNNORSSTT	nonresistant
AEINNNORSTTU	antineutrons
AEINNOOPRSST	personations
AEINNOOSSTTT	ostentations
AEINNORSSSUV	unsavoriness
AEINNORSTTTU	sternutation
AEINNOSSTTTU	sustentation
AEINOOPPRRST	apportioners
	reapportions
AEINOOPRSTTT	protestation
AEINOOPRSTTX	exportations
AEINOORRSSTT	restorations
AEINOOSSTTTU	ostentatious
AEINOPRRSTTV	transportive
AEINOPRSSSSV	vasopressins
AEIOOOOPPPRS	prosopopoeia
AEIOOOPPPRSS	prosopopeias
AEIOOPPRRRTX	expropriator
AEIOPPRRRSTY	perspiratory
AEIOPRRRSTTU	portraitures
AEIOPRRSSUVV	parvoviruses
AEIOPRRSTTUV	vituperators
AEIORRRSSTTT	Torres Strait
AEIPPRSSTUUV	suppuratives
AEKLMNNOOPRT	meroplankton
AEKLNPPRSTTU	splatterpunk
AELLLMORSUVY	marvellously
AELLMMNNOTUY	monumentally
AELLMNOOOSSS	Solomon's seal
AELLOOPPSSUY	polysepalous
AELLOOPPSTUY	polypetalous
AELMMRSSSTUU	summersaults
AELMNOOOPSSU	monosepalous
AELMNOOOPSTU	monopetalous
AELNOPSSSTUU	patulousness
AELOOPRSTTUX	expostulator
AEMNNOORSSTY	stonemasonry
AEMNNORRSSTT	remonstrants
AEMNOOOPRSTZ	spermatozoon
AEMNOOPRSSTY	trypanosomes
AEMNOORRRSTT	remonstrator
AEMNOQSSSSUU	squamousness
AEMPRRSSTTUU	superstratum
AENOOPRSSSUV	vaporousness
AENOPRRRSSTT	transporters
AENORRSSTTTU	sternutators
AENORRSTTTUY	sternutatory
AENPPRSSSSTU	suppressants
AEOOPRRSSSSV	vasopressors
AEOOPRRSSTTU	tetrasporous
AFFGHLOPSSTU	ploughstaffs
AFFGIILLMMMN	flimflamming
AFFGIILNNSTU	insufflating
AFFHILLNTUUY	unfaithfully
AFFIILNNOSTU	insufflation
AFFILNORSSTU	insufflators
AFFLLLORUUVY	flavourfully
AFGGHHIILNTU	highfaluting
AFGGIILNRTYY	gratifyingly
AFGGIINPPRTW	giftwrapping
AFGHIIKNNRST	rankshifting
AFGHLOOPRRUY	fluorography
AFGIIILNNRTT	infiltrating

AFGIILLMNORU	anguilliform
AFGIILLOSTUY	flagitiously
AFGIILNNORTU	fluorinating
AFGIILNNOSTU	antifoulings
AFGIILNSSTYY	satisfyingly
AFGIINNOOPRR	rainproofing
AFGIINNSSTUY	unsatisfying
AFGIMNNORRST	transforming
AFGIMNORRSTY	transmogrify
AFIIILMNNOST	inflationism
AFIIILMNNSST	infantilisms
AFIIILNNORTT	infiltration
AFIIILNNOSTT	inflationist
AFIILMNNOSTU	fulminations
AFIILMORSTUU	multifarious
AFIILNNOORTU	fluorination
AFIILNORRSTT	infiltrators
AFIILORRSSST	fissirostral
AFIIMMNNORST	misinformant
AFIIMNNOORST	informations
AFILLMNOPSTU	slumpflation
AFILMNOORSTU	formulations
AFIMMNORRSST	transformism
AFIMNORRSSTT	transformist
AFINNORSSSTU	transfusions
AFINORRSSTTU	frustrations
AGGGGILLLNOY	lollygagging
AGGGIIILMNPR	pilgrimaging
AGGGIIJJNNOU	Jiang Jing Guo
AGGGILLNRSTY	stragglingly
AGGHHLOPPRSY	glyphographs
AGGHHLOPPRYY	glyphography
AGGHHMOPPRSY	sphygmograph
AGGHIIINPRST	graphitising
AGGHIIINPRTZ	graphitizing
AGGHIIKNNSTV	thanksgiving
AGGHIILOOSST	hagiologists
AGGHIIMNNRST	hamstringing
AGGHILMNOOOT	homologating
AGGHILNOPRXY	xylographing
AGGHILOOPRST	graphologist
AGGHIMNNOOPR	monographing
AGGHLNOOPRYY	pharyngology
AGGHLOOPRSSY	glossography
AGGHLOPPRTYY	glyptography
AGGHMMOPRSSY	sphygmograms
AGGIIIILNNTV	invigilating
AGGIIIMNSSTT	stigmatising
AGGIIIMNSTTZ	stigmatizing
AGGIIINNORTV	invigorating
AGGIILMNORUZ	glamourizing
AGGIKMNOORST	Magnitogorsk
AGGILMNOPRTU	promulgating
AGGILNOOORST	organologist
AGGILOORSSTT	gastrologist
AGGIMMMNNOOR	monogramming
AGGIMNNORRST	strongarming
AGHHILNOPRTT	triphthongal
AGHHIMNOPSTY	hypognathism
AGHHIOPPRSYY	physiography
AGHHNOOPSTUY	hypognathous
AGHHOOPPSTUY	phytophagous
AGHIILMNPSTY	lymphangitis
AGHIIMNPSSTY	sympathising
AGHIIMNPSTYZ	sympathizing
AGHIINNPPRST	transhipping
AGHILMNOOOOT	homologation
AGHILNNOPSTU	sulphonating
AGHILNOOSSTT	anthologists
AGHILNPRSTUU	sulphurating
AGHILOOPSSTT	pathologists
AGHIMNOOPPPT	photomapping
AGHIMNOOPRST	monographist
AGHIMOPRSTUY	hypogastrium
AGHINOOPRSTT	trapshooting
AGHINOOPSTTT	photostating
AGHINOOSSSTY	soothsayings
AGHIOPPSSYYZ	zygapophysis
AGHLLMOOPSUY	gamophyllous
AGHLLNOOORTY	orthogonally
AGHLLOOPSSSY	hypoglossals
AGHLMOOOPRSU	lagomorphous
AGHLNOOOPRTY	anthropology
AGHMNOOPRTYY	pharyngotomy
AGIIIIILNNST	initialising
AGIIIIILNNTZ	initializing
AGIIIILMNRST	militarising
AGIIIILMNRTZ	militarizing
AGIIIILNNOTV	invigilation
AGIIIILNRSTV	trivialising
AGIIIILNRTVZ	trivializing
AGIIILLMNNTU	illuminating
AGIIILLNOSTV	volatilising
AGIIILLNOTVZ	volatilizing
AGIIILNORSTV	invigilators
AGIIILNRSSTV	virginalists
AGIIIMMNORST	immigrations
AGIIIMNNOPSS	impassioning
AGIIINNOORST	originations
AGIIINNOORTV	invigoration
AGIIINNOPRTT	partitioning
AGIIINNOSSTT	instigations
AGIIINNPSSST	inspissating
AGIIINOPPRTT	propitiating
AGIIJLNNORSU	journalising
AGIIJLNNORUZ	journalizing
AGIIKLMNSTTU	multitasking
AGIILLLMNTUU	multilingual
AGIILLLNRTUY	trilingually
AGIILLNORTUV	outrivalling
AGIILLNRSTTU	illustrating
AGIILLOPSSSS	salpiglossis
AGIILMNNOPRT	trampolining
AGIILMNOOORU	Giulio Romano
AGIILNNSSTUY	sustainingly
AGIILNOORSUV	vainglorious
AGIILNOPPRSU	popularising
AGIILNOPPRUZ	popularizing
AGIIMNNOPSTU	impugnations
AGIIMNNRSTTT	transmitting
AGIIMNOOSTTU	autotomising
AGIIMNOOTTUZ	autotomizing
AGIINNOOPPRT	apportioning
AGIINOORRSTV	invigorators

AGIJKNNOPRTU	Tanjungpriok
AGIKLOORSSTY	karyologists
AGILLMNNOOSU	monolinguals
AGILLMNOPSSY	plasmolysing
AGILLMNOPSYZ	plasmolyzing
AGILLNOOPSTY	palynologist
AGILLNOORRST	longirostral
AGILMNNSSUUY	unassumingly
AGILMNOOOOSY	onomasiology
AGILMNOOPRTU	promulgation
AGILMOOOSSTT	somatologist
AGILMRSSTTUU	gutturalisms
AGILNNOOOPRT	prolongation
AGILNPRSSSUY	surpassingly
AGILOOPPRSTY	papyrologist
AGILOOPRSSTT	patrologists
AGILOORSSSTT	astrologists
AGILOOSSTTTU	tautologists
AGILORSTTUUY	gratuitously
AGIMNNOORRTY	nonmigratory
AGIMNOORSSTT	gastronomist
AGINNOPRRSTT	transporting
AGINOOOPRRST	prorogations
AGINOOPRSSTT	protagonists
AGINOORRSSTU	surrogations
AGLLMOOPSUYY	polygamously
AGLLMOORSUUY	glamourously
AGLLNOORSUUY	languorously
AGLMMNOOOSUY	monogamously
AGLMOOPRRSTU	promulgators
AHHIILMOPSTT	ophthalmitis
AHHILLLLSSYY	shillyshally
AHHILLMMOOST	homothallism
AHHILNOOPSTU	anthophilous
AHHILNOORSTU	holothurians
AHHILNOPPRTY	philanthropy
AHHIMNOPSSSW	showmanships
AHHINNOPRSTT	strophanthin
AHHLLNOPSTXY	xanthophylls
AHHNOPRSSTTU	strophanthus
AHIIILMNOSTU	humiliations
AHIIKMNORSUY	Aum Shinrikyo
AHIILMMPRSTU	triumphalism
AHIILMPRSTTU	triumphalist
AHIILRSSSTTY	hairstylists
AHIIMNNOORSU	inharmonious
AHIIMNOOOSSU	homoiousians
AHILLMMOOPRS	allomorphism
AHILLNOORTYZ	horizontally
AHILMNOORSUY	harmoniously
AHILMNPRTTUY	triumphantly
AHILMOOOPRTY	homopolarity
AHILNOPRSTUU	sulphuration
AHILOPRRSUXY	pyrrhuloxias
AHIMMOOPSSTU	amphistomous
AHIMNNOORSUU	unharmonious
AHIMOOPPPSTU	hippopotamus
AHIMOOPPRSTT	haptotropism
AHIMOOPPRSTU	amphitropous
AHINNOPRSSTU	sinanthropus
AHINOOPSSSTU	sousaphonist
AHINOOPSSSTX	saxophonists
AHINOOPSSTUY	autohypnosis
AHINORRSSSTY	synarthrosis
AHKLLNNOOOPT	holoplankton
AHLMMOOPSTUY	lymphomatous
AHLMNOSTUXYZ	zanthoxylums
AHNOOOPRRTTY	prothonotary
AIIIILNORSTV	virilisation
AIIIILNORTVZ	virilization
AIIIIMMNNOST	minimisation
AIIIIMMNNOTZ	minimization
AIIILLLNPSTU	lilliputians
AIIILLMNNOTU	illumination
AIIILLNNOSTT	instillation
AIIILLNOSTTT	titillations
AIIILMNOOSST	isolationism
AIIILMPRSSTU	spiritualism
AIIILNNOOSST	lionisations
AIIILNNOOSTZ	lionizations
AIIILNOOSSTT	isolationist
AIIILNOSSTTU	utilisations
AIIILNOSTTUZ	utilizations
AIIILPRSSTTU	spiritualist
AIIILPRSTTUY	spirituality
AIIIMMNNOSTU	immunisation
AIIIMMNNOTUZ	immunization
AIIIMNNORSTT	ministration
AIIIMNOOPSTT	optimisation
AIIIMNOOPTTZ	optimization
AIIIMNRSSTTU	miniaturists
AIIINNNOOSTU	unionisation
AIIINNNOOTUZ	unionization
AIIINNNOSSTU	insinuations
AIIINNOPRSST	inspirations
AIIINNOPSSST	inspissation
AIIINNOSSTTU	unitisations
AIIINNOSTTUZ	unitizations
AIIINOOPPRTT	propitiation
AIIINOPRRTTT	tripartition
AIIINOPRSTTT	partitionist
AIIINOSTTTTV	tittivations
AIIINRSTTTVY	transitivity
AIIKMNNOPRSS	parkinsonism
AIILLLNOOTVY	volitionally
AIILLLNOSUVY	villainously
AIILLMMNOSTU	multinomials
AIILLMNOORTY	monitorially
AIILLMNORSTU	illuminators
AIILLNNOOTUV	involutional
AIILLNORSTTU	illustration
AIILLNQRTTUY	tranquillity
AIILMNNORTTU	malnutrition
AIILMNOOPRST	implorations
AIILMNOPRSTT	trampolinist
AIILMNOSSTTU	stimulations
AIILNNOTTUUV	invultuation
AIILNOOOPPST	oppositional
AIILNOOPRSSV	provisionals
AIILNOPSSTTU	stipulations
AIILNORRSSST	sinistrorsal
AIILNORRSTTY	transitorily
AIILNOSSSTTY	stylisations
AIILNOSSTTYZ	stylizations

AIILOPRSUVVY viviparously
AIILRSSSTUVV survivalists
AIIMMNNOSSSU manumissions
AIIMMNOPSSTT pantomimists
AIIMMNOTTUUY autoimmunity
AIIMMNSSSTTU numismatists
AIIMNNORSSST transmission
AIIMNOOORSTT motorisation
AIIMNOOORTTZ motorization
AIIMNOOPRSSU parsimonious
AIIMNOOPRSTT importations
AIIMNOOPRSTX proximations
AIIMNOOQSTTU misquotation
AIIMOOPPRRRT impropriator
AIINNNORRSTT nonirritants
AIINNOOOPSST opsonisation
AIINNOOOPSTZ opsonization
AIINNOOOSSTZ ozonisations
AIINNOOOSTZZ ozonizations
AIINNORRTTUY nutritionary
AIINOOPRRSVY provisionary
AIINOPRSSSST inspissators
AIINOPRSSSTU suspirations
AIINORRSTTTU triturations
AIIOOPPRRSTT propitiators
AIIOOPPRRTTY propitiatory
AIIOPRRSSTTT portraitists
AIJMNRRSTTUY Justin Martyr
AIKNOPRRSTUU Sukarnoputri
AILLLNOOPRSU allopurinols
AILLLNOPSTUU pullulations
AILLMNNOOPRY pronominally
AILLMNOOPSTY polytonalism
AILLMOOPRSST allotropisms
AILLNOOPSTTY polytonalist
AILLNOOPTTYY polytonality
AILLORRSSTTU illustrators
AILMNOORSSTT monolatrists
AILMNORSTUVY voluntaryism
AILNOOOPPRRT proportional
AILNOOPSSTTU postulations
AILNOPPRTUUY unpopularity
AILNORSSTTUV voluntarists
AILNORSTTUVY voluntaryist
AILOOPRRSUUY uproariously
AILOORRSTTUY traitorously
AIMNOOOPRSTT somatotropin
AINOOPRRSSTT prostrations
AIOORRSSTTTU astrotourist
AKLNNOOOPSTZ zooplanktons
AKMOOORSSUUY Yamoussoukro
ALLOORSSTWWW swallowworts
ALMNOOOSTUUY autonomously
ALMNOOPRSUYY paronymously
AMOOPRRRSTTY protomartyrs
BBBCEILMORSU microbubbles
BBBEGIIINNSW winebibbings
BBCCEEHKLORS breechblocks
BBCDEEEKNRRU rubbernecked
BBCDEHIRRSTU butcherbirds
BBCEELNOOSST cobblestones
BBCEGHILNRTU nightclubber
BBCEILMOSSTU combustibles
BBCEINRSSSUU unsubscribes
BBCEJKOORSST stockjobbers
BBCEJKOORSTY stockjobbery
BBCEKLORSSTU blockbusters
BBCELLLOOSWY collywobbles
BBCENOORRSTU broncobuster
BBCGIJKNOOST stockjobbing
BBCGIKLNOSTU blockbusting
BBDDGIILNOUY bodybuilding
BBDEEGGKLOOO gobbledegook
BBDEEHHLOOSY hobbledehoys
BBDEGGKLOOOY gobbledygook
BBDEILLMOOOS bloodmobiles
BBEEGIILLNRS gibberellins
BBEEGILLORRT Robbe-Grillet
BBEEGILMRSSU submergibles
BBEEILLNRSSU lubberliness
BBEEILMRSSSU submersibles
BBEFHIINORSS ribbonfishes
BBEGGHIILNOS bobsleighing
BBEHIIILLOPS bibliophiles
BBEHINNOSSSS snobbishness
BBEILNOSSSUU bibulousness
BBELLNOSTTUY bellybuttons
BBENNORSSSTU stubbornness
BBGHHINOORSY hobbyhorsing
BBHMOOOOPRSU ombrophobous
BBIIILLOOPST bibliopolist
BCCCEIIMRRSU circumscribe
BCCDEEEIMNSU decumbencies
BCCDEGHIKNOY bodychecking
BCCEEEEFINNS beneficences
BCCEEEHKRRRY checkerberry
BCCEEELNOOSS obsolescence
BCCEEEMNOSTU obmutescence
BCCEEHHLORST breechcloths
BCCEEHKLMOOR checkerbloom
BCCEEHLORSTU breechclouts
BCCEEHNORRSS crossbencher
BCCEEHNORSSS crossbenches
BCCEEIIMNNSU incumbencies
BCCEEILLLOST collectibles
BCCEHNOOOPRS bronchoscope
BCCEHORSTTTU butterscotch
BCCEILMOORTY motorbicycle
BCCHIMOORTTY thrombocytic
BCCHNOOOPRSY bronchoscopy
BCCINOOSSSUU subconscious
BCCIOOOPRSST stroboscopic
BCDDEEEIINOS disobedience
BCDDEIIILTUY deducibility
BCDEEEFIILNT indefectible
BCDEEEILNRSS credibleness
BCDEEEIORRSS cerebrosides
BCDEEEKLNOTT bottlenecked
BCDEEEKORRST stockbreeder
BCDEEEMNNRUU unencumbered
BCDEEFIIJSTU subjectified
BCDEEFIILNTY indefectibly
BCDEEGIINRRS redescribing
BCDEEHMNOSTU debouchments

BCDEEIINNOST	benedictions
BCDEEILOPRRU	reproducible
BCDEEILORRSU	cloudberries
BCDEEILRSTTU	destructible
BCDEEIMNNRUU	unincumbered
BCDEEIMNRSSU	disencumbers
BCDEEINPRRSU	unprescribed
BCDEEIPRRSSU	superscribed
BCDEGHNRRSSU	bergschrunds
BCDEHILORSSU	subchlorides
BCDEIIILRTUY	reducibility
BCDEIILNORTU	introducible
BCDEIKMNRSTU	dumbstricken
BCDEILOPRRUY	reproducibly
BCDEIORRSSTU	subdirectors
BCDEKLOORSSU	bloodsuckers
BCDENORSTTUU	unobstructed
BCDFHIOORSTY	Body of Christ
BCDGIIKMNORS	mockingbirds
BCDIIILNOOPT	diplobiontic
BCDIIRSSSTTU	subdistricts
BCEEEEGHRRSU	cheeseburger
BCEEEEGILLNR	belligerence
BCEEEEHORSTW	Beecher Stowe
BCEEEELNNOSV	benevolences
BCEEEFILNNTY	beneficently
BCEEEGHILNSY	beseechingly
BCEEEGIINORT	bioenergetic
BCEEEGILLNRY	belligerency
BCEEEGMNRSSU	submergences
BCEEEHIKORRS	chokeberries
BCEEEIILLNSU	ebulliencies
BCEEEIIPRRSS	spiceberries
BCEEEINRSSUV	subservience
BCEEEIRRRSVY	serviceberry
BCEEENPPRSTU	prepubescent
BCEEENQSSSUU	subsequences
BCEEFIIJSSTU	subjectifies
BCEEFILNORSS	forcibleness
BCEEGHIILNNR	Berlichingen
BCEEGIILOOOS	bioecologies
BCEEGIMNNOSS	becomingness
BCEEHHNOOPST	technophobes
BCEEHIIKRRSW	Berwickshire
BCEEHILLNRSU	Brunelleschi
BCEEIIIILMST	imbecilities
BCEEIILLRSTT	belletristic
BCEEIILNNSSV	vincibleness
BCEEIJLSTUVY	subjectively
BCEEIJNNOOTV	nonobjective
BCEEILMNOPTT	contemptible
BCEEILMOPRSS	compressible
BCEEILNORSTV	convertibles
BCEEILPRSSTU	putrescibles
BCEEIMMOSTTU	subcommittee
BCEEIMORRRWY	microbrewery
BCEEINRSSUVY	subserviency
BCEEIPRRSSSU	superscribes
BCEEKKLNNOSU	knucklebones
BCEELMMOORTU	coulombmeter
BCEELMMORSUY	cumbersomely
BCEFGIIINNOR	fibrinogenic
BCEFGIIJNOTY	objectifying
BCEGHIILNTWY	bewitchingly
BCEGHIIMNORS	chemisorbing
BCEGHIMNNOOY	honeycombing
BCEGHIMNOORS	chemosorbing
BCEGIIILNORR	incorrigible
BCEGIILOOOST	bioecologist
BCEGIKLNOSTU	bluestocking
BCEGILMNNOUY	unbecomingly
BCEGILNOOOOY	biocoenology
BCEHIIIOSSTT	bioethicists
BCEHIIMORSTY	biochemistry
BCEHIINOSTTY	biosynthetic
BCEHIKLNOSSS	blockishness
BCEHIMORSTWW	West Bromwich
BCEHLORRSSYY	chrysoberyls
BCEHMOORSTTY	thrombocytes
BCEIIIIMMORS	biomimicries
BCEIIINOSSTT	bioscientist
BCEIIJMSSTUV	subjectivism
BCEIIJOSSTTV	objectivists
BCEIIJSSTTUV	subjectivist
BCEIIJSTTUVY	subjectivity
BCEIIKLLRSST	billstickers
BCEIIKLMOPRU	Komi Republic
BCEIILNRSTTU	instructible
BCEIINORTTUV	contributive
BCEIIPRSSTUV	subscriptive
BCEIJNSSTUUV	subjunctives
BCEIKNNRSUWW	New Brunswick
BCEILLOOPSUY	ebullioscopy
BCEILMNOPTTY	contemptibly
BCEILMOPRSSY	compressibly
BCEILMORSTUU	microtubules
BCEILORSSTUU	tuberculosis
BCEINNNOSTTU	subcontinent
BCEIORSSTTUV	obstructives
BCEKKOORRSST	stockbrokers
BCELSSTTTTUU	scuttlebutts
BCEMNORSSSUU	cumbrousness
BCEOOOPRSSST	stroboscopes
BCERRSSTTUUU	substructure
BCFIIILNORTY	fibrinolytic
BCGIIIKLLNST	billsticking
BCGIIILNORRY	incorrigibly
BCGIILMOOORY	microbiology
BCGIILOOOOSY	sociobiology
BCGIINNORTTU	contributing
BCGIINOOOSTT	gnotobiotics
BCGIKKNOORST	stockbroking
BCGILLNOORUY	cryoglobulin
BCGILNRSTUUU	subculturing
BCHHIIMORSTY	biorhythmics
BCHHIMOOORRT	orthorhombic
BCHIIIOPSSTY	biophysicist
BCHILMOORTTY	thrombolytic
BCIILLORSUUY	lubriciously
BCIILOOOSTUY	bootylicious
BCIINNOORTTU	contribution
BCIINOPRSSTU	subscription
BCIIOOPRSSTY	cryptobiosis
BCIJNNOSSTUU	subjunctions

BCILMMNOSUUU cumulonimbus
BCINOOPRSTTY cryptobionts
BCINOORRSTTU contributors
BCINOORRTTUY contributory
BCINOORSSTTU obstructions
BDDDEEILMORW middlebrowed
BDDDEEINRRSU underbidders
BDDDEGIINNRU underbidding
BDDEEEEFILMN feebleminded
BDDEEEFINNRU unbefriended
BDDEEEFLMNTU befuddlement
BDDEEEILMOSW disemboweled
BDDEEEIMNRST debridements
BDDEEEINNSST indebtedness
BDDEEENORRUV overburdened
BDDEEFHIORRS Bedfordshire
BDDEEIILMORS disembroiled
BDDEEILMRSTU middlebuster
BDDEGIIMNOSY disembodying
BDDEGIINNRSU disburdening
BDDEHINRRSTU thunderbirds
BDDFGIILLNNO blindfolding
BDDFGIILNORY forbiddingly
BDDFGIMNNOUU dumbfounding
BDEEEEILRRRS elderberries
BDEEEEMMNRRU unremembered
BDEEEFIILNNS indefensible
BDEEEGIILNNR linebreeding
BDEEEHMORRTU mouthbreeder
BDEEEIILRSSV disbelievers
BDEEEIIMORRS embroideries
BDEEEILLNRSU underbellies
BDEEEILMNRTW bewilderment
BDEEEILMNSTV bedevilments
BDEEEILNNSSV vendibleness
BDEEEIMMRRSS dismemberers
disremembers
BDEEEIMNNSTZ bedizenments
BDEEEIMORRRS embroiderers
BDEEFIILNNSY indefensibly
BDEEFIILRSTU filibustered
BDEEFLLNORSU bellfounders
BDEEGGHIIRSW weighbridges
BDEEGGIJRTTU jitterbugged
BDEEGHHIINRS Denbighshire
BDEEGHINNORR herringboned
BDEEGIIILNST indigestible
BDEEGIIILNSV disbelieving
BDEEGIIMMNRS dismembering
BDEEGIIMNORR embroidering
BDEEGIMMRRUU Murrumbidgee
BDEEGINORSST Gibson Desert
BDEEGINORSTU outbreedings
BDEEGLNNORUY Glyndebourne
BDEEHILOPRSY hyperbolised
BDEEHILOPRYZ hyperbolized
BDEEHINOSTUU hebetudinous
BDEEHNORSTUX thunderboxes
BDEEIIILNRTV indivertible
BDEEIILMNTTW nimblewitted
BDEEIIMRRTTU turbidimeter
BDEEIIRRSTTU redistribute
BDEEIIRSSTTU distributees
BDEEILLNPRSS spellbinders
BDEEILORRSSW bowdlerisers
BDEEILORRSWZ bowdlerizers
BDEEIMNORSST disrobements
BDEEIMNRSSTU disbursement
BDEEIOORSSXY desoxyribose
BDEFGILNOORY forebodingly
BDEFLNOSSTUU doubtfulness
BDEGGGILNRUY begrudgingly
BDEGGIIMNOSU disemboguing
BDEGGLNOOORS boondogglers
BDEGHHINOOOR neighborhood
BDEGHHOORRTU thoroughbred
BDEGIIILMNOS demobilising
BDEGIIILMNOZ demobilizing
BDEGIIILNSTY indigestibly
BDEGIILLNNPS spellbinding
BDEGIILNORSW bowdlerising
BDEGIILNORUV overbuilding
BDEGIILNORWZ bowdlerizing
BDEGIIMNNOST disentombing
BDEGILLNNRUY blunderingly
BDEGILLNOOTT bloodletting
BDEHHMNOOORR rhombohedron
BDEHHOOORRST brotherhoods
BDEHIILPRSSU shipbuilders
BDEHIINOPRTU unprohibited
BDEHILOOPRSY hyperboloids
BDEHLNORSTTU thunderbolts
BDEHMOOORRTU mouthbrooder
BDEIIIILLNTY indelibility
BDEIIILNRTVY indivertibly
BDEIIIORSTVY biodiversity
BDEIIIRSTTUV distributive
BDEIILLNOSSU indissoluble
BDEIILMRSSUU subdeliriums
BDEIILNORSST blindstories
BDEIIRRSSTTU distributers
BDEILNORSSTY blindstoreys
BDFIILMNNUUU infundibulum
BDGGGILNNOOO boondoggling
BDGHIIILNPSU shipbuilding
BDGHIIMMNRSU hummingbirds
BDGIIIIILRTY dirigibility
BDGIIINRSTTU distributing
BDGIILNOSTUU outbuildings
BDGIILNRSTUY disturbingly
BDHILOORSTTY bloodthirsty
BDIIIIILSTVY divisibility
BDIIILLNOSUY libidinously
BDIIINORSTTU distribution
BDIIINOSSSUV subdivisions
BDIILLNOSSUY indissolubly
BDIIORRSSTTU distributors
BDLMNOOSTTUU buttonmoulds
BEEEEEFLMNNT enfeeblement
BEEEEFHINORR hereinbefore
BEEEEHILPRSS Peeblesshire
BEEEEIMNSTTW betweentimes
BEEEELMMNTZZ embezzlement
BEEEFILLNSSX flexibleness

BEEEGGGIRRUV veggieburger
BEEEGIINNORS bioengineers
BEEEGILLNRST belligerents
BEEEGILMNSTU beguilements
BEEEGIMNPRSU Supreme Being
BEEEGIOORRSS gooseberries
BEEEGLNORSTT greenbottles
BEEEHIINNRTT terebinthine
BEEEHILLMRSS embellishers
BEEEHILLNORS helleborines
BEEEHNNNOOPZ benzophenone
BEEEHNNOPRRT Open Brethren
BEEEIILNNSTX inextensible
BEEEIILRRRSV irreversible
BEEEILLMNTTT belittlement
BEEEILLMORTU ebulliometer
BEEEILMORTTY biotelemetry
BEEEILNNORSV nonbelievers
BEEEILNNSSSS sensibleness
BEEEILNNSSST tensibleness
BEEEILNRRSST terribleness
BEEEILNRRSTW West Berliner
BEEEIMMMRRSS misremembers
BEEEIMMNRTTT embitterment
BEEEINNNORTZ nitrobenzene
BEEEIPRRSSTY presbyteries
BEEEIRSSTTTW bittersweets
BEEELLNNOTVY benevolently
BEEELNOOSSST obsoleteness
BEEENOPPRSTY teenyboppers
BEEFGIINNRRT birefringent
BEEFGLLOORSW globeflowers
BEEFHIRSSTTU butterfishes
BEEFIILRRSTU filibusterer
BEEFILMNNOOT Bloemfontein
BEEGHIILLMNS embellishing
BEEGHILNORSS neighborless
BEEGHINNORRS herringbones
BEEGHLLNOORU Ellenborough
BEEGHOOPRRTU Peterborough
BEEGIIILLLNT intelligible
BEEGIILNNPUX inexpungible
BEEGIIOORSSU bourgeoisies
BEEGILNORTTX letterboxing
BEEGINORRSUY youngberries
BEEGLOORRTTT globetrotter
BEEGNNORRSTV von Sternberg
BEEHIIILTVXY exhibitively
BEEHIIINORTX exhibitioner
BEEHIKLNOSSS blokeishness
BEEHILLLRSVY Beverly Hills
BEEHILLMOSTY blithesomely
BEEHILMOOPST phlebotomies
phlebotomise
BEEHILMOOPTZ phlebotomize
BEEHILNORRSS horribleness
BEEHILOPRSSY hyperbolises
BEEHILOPRSYZ hyperbolizes
BEEHLORRRTWY whortleberry
BEEHNOOORSSU Osborne House
BEEHOPRRSSTT stepbrothers
BEEIIILMRRSS irremissible
BEEIIILRRSST irresistible
BEEIIINORSST insobrieties
BEEIIKLNSSSU businesslike
BEEIILNOSSTU nebulosities
BEEIILRRRSVY irreversibly
BEEIIORSSTTU tuberosities
BEEILLLORSUY rebelliously
BEEILLMORTUY ebulliometry
BEEILMMNORST embroilments
BEEILPPRSSSU suppressible
BEEILRSSUVVY subversively
BEEINNNOOQUZ benzoquinone
BEEINNOORSTU boutonnieres
BEEINNORRTUW winterbourne
BEEKNNNORSSU unbrokenness
BEELLMNRSSUY numberlessly
BEELLORSSTUY trolleybuses
BEELNNOSSSUU nebulousness
BEELNQSSTUUY subsequently
BEELORSTTUVY oversubtlety
BEEOOPRRSSTU obstreperous
BEERRRSSTTUU surrebutters
BEERRSSSSTTU stressbuster
BEFGHIINRRSU refurbishing
BEFGHILLRSTU bullfighters
BEFGIILMORSZ gemfibrozils
BEFGILMNNSSU fumblingness
BEFIILNORRSU neurofibrils
BEFIILRSTTUY subfertility
BEFILLNSSSSU blissfulness
BEFILMOPRSUU plumbiferous
BEFLLOOPRSTU bulletproofs
BEGGHIINNORU neighbouring
BEGGHILNOORU Ingleborough
BEGGIILNNOSS obligingness
BEGHIILNPRSU republishing
BEGHILNOOOTY ethnobiology
BEGHINNNRTUU unburthening
BEGIIIILLLTY illegibility
BEGIIILLLNTY intelligibly
BEGIIKLNNPRS besprinkling
BEGIILLLNTTY belittlingly
BEGIILLNRSTY blisteringly
BEGIILNNPRTU blueprinting
BEGIILOOOSTX exobiologist
BEGIIMNRSTTU resubmitting
BEGILLNRSTUY blusteringly
BEGILMOORSTY embryologist
BEGILNOOORUY neurobiology
BEGILNPRRTUY perturbingly
BEGIMNNORTUU outnumbering
BEHHOORSSTTU toothbrushes
BEHIIILRSSST British Isles
BEHIIIMNSTTU bismuthinite
BEHIINOSSSTY biosynthesis
BEHILLRSSTTU bullshitters
BEHILMNPSSTU publishments
BEHILMOOPSTT phlebotomist
BEHILMOPRSSY hyperbolisms
BEIIIIILRSST risibilities
BEIIIIILSSTV visibilities
BEIIILLOSSTU solubilities

BEIIILMMORSS immobilisers
BEIIILMMORSZ immobilizers
BEIIILMQRSUU equilibriums
BEIIILMRRSSY irremissibly
BEIIILQRSSTU equilibrists
BEIIILRRSSTY irresistibly
BEIILLORSTUY resolubility
BEIILMSSSUVY submissively
BEIIMNSSSUUV unsubmissive
BEIINORRSTTU retributions
BEIISSTTTUUV substitutive
BEILLMPSSTUU submultiples
BEILLOORSSTT stilboestrol
BEILMOOOPRSY polyribosome
BEILOOQSSUUY obsequiously
BEILOORSSTUY boisterously
BEINSSSTTTUU substituents
BELLMORSSUUY slumberously
BELLNORTTUWY Bulwer-Lytton
BELLORSSTUUY blusterously
BELMNOOPRYYY polyembryony
BERRSSSTTTUU trustbusters
BFFIIILLMORR fibrilliform
BFGGHIILLNTU bullfighting
BFIIIILNSTUY infusibility
BFIIILNORSSY fibrinolysis
BFKMMNOOOOOR Book of Mormon
BGGHHLOOORUU Loughborough
BGHIILLNPPUW bullwhipping
BGHIILLNSTTU bullshitting
BGHILLNNSUUY unblushingly
BGHILNNOOTTU buttonholing
BGHILOOOOPTY photobiology
BGIIIIILNTTY ignitibility
BGIIIILMMNOS immobilising
BGIIIILMMNOZ immobilizing
BGIIIIMNNSTU bituminising
BGIIIIMNNTUZ bituminizing
BGIIILLNOSSU solubilising
BGIIILLNOSUZ solubilizing
BGIIKLLNNNUY unblinkingly
BGIINSSTTTUU substituting
BGILLORSUUUY lugubriously
BGILMOOSSSTY symbologists
BGINRSSTTTUU trustbusting
BHIIINOOPRST prohibitions
BHILMOOOPRSU ombrophilous
BIIIIILNSTVY invisibility
BIIILLNOSTUY insolubility
BIILLNOORSTU tourbillions
BIILOQSTUUUY ubiquitously
BIINOSSTTTUU substitution
BILOORSSTUUY robustiously
BIMNOPSSSTUU subsumptions
CCCCEEENNORS concrescence
CCCCEHINOOSU echinococcus
CCCCHHIOPRTU Coptic Church
CCCDEEEENRSS decrescences
CCCDEEHKORSS crosschecked
CCCDEEIINNOS coincidences
CCCDEEILNOPY encyclopedic
CCCDEIIORSTY cysticercoid
CCCDHIIOOPRS dichroscopic
CCCEEEENRSSX excrescences
CCCEEENORRRU reoccurrence
CCCEEHILORTY heterocyclic
CCCEEHKNORTU countercheck
CCCEEIILMSST eclecticisms
CCCEEIINRTTY eccentricity
CCCEEILNNOTU noctilucence
CCCEGIIMNNOO meningococci
CCCEIIMRRSSU circumcisers
CCCEILOOTTUY leucocytotic
CCCEINNOPSTU concupiscent
CCCEINNSSSTU succinctness
CCCEIOOPRSTT streptococci
CCCEKNORSTTU concertstuck
CCCEMNOOPSUU pneumococcus
CCCGIIIMNRSU circumcising
CCCGIKNOORSW cockcrowings
CCCHHHIRRSTU Christchurch
CCCHIIORSTTY trichocystic
CCCHILMOSTYY cyclothymics
CCCHINOOOPRS chronoscopic
CCCIIIMNORSU circumcision
CCCIIIMORRTU microcircuit
CCCIOOOPPRST proctoscopic
CCDDDEEENNOS condescended
CCDDEEENNOPY codependency
CCDDEEENORSS decrescendos
CCDDEEINNOST disconnected
CCDDEEINORST disconcerted
CCDDEIMNOSTU misconducted
CCDEEEEILNST delitescence
CCDEEEEMNSTU detumescence
CCDEEEENORRT retrocedence
CCDEEEFIIINS deficiencies
CCDEEEFNNORS frondescence
CCDEEEHIINNS indehiscence
CCDEEEHNOSTU escutcheoned
CCDEEEIINRSS iridescences
CCDEEEIINRSV viridescence
CCDEEEINOPRV preconceived
CCDEEELORTTU electrocuted
CCDEEENOPRRT preconcerted
CCDEEENRRSTU recrudescent
CCDEEGILNSUY succeedingly
CCDEEGINNORS crescendoing
CCDEEGINRRSU recrudescing
CCDEEIIINSST insecticides
CCDEEIIMNOSV misconceived
CCDEEILNNORU unreconciled
CCDEEILNOSTU endocuticles
CCDEEIMNRTUV circumvented
CCDEEINNORST disconnecter
CCDEEIORRTTU correctitude
CCDEGIMNNOOS Second Coming
CCDEHIIIINNNO cinchonidine
CCDEHIIOOPRS dichroiscope
CCDEHIMOORTY orchidectomy
CCDEHIOOOPRS dichrooscope
CCDEHIOOPRSS dichroscopes
CCDEIIIIRSTV recidivistic
CCDEIIIRRRTU circuit rider

CCDEILNOTUVY	conductively
CCDEILOPSSTY	cyclopedists
CCDEIMNOORSS	microseconds
CCDEIORRSSSS	crisscrossed
CCDENORSSTTU	deconstructs
CCDHHILOORRY	hydrochloric
CCDHILOOPSYY	hypocycloids
CCDHIOPRRSTY	cryptorchids
CCDIINOTTUVY	conductivity
CCDNNNOOORTU	nonconductor
CCEEEEHRSTTU	cheesecutter
CCEEEEIIKKLO	cockieleekie
CCEEEEILLNSX	excellencies
CCEEEEINPRST	centrepieces
CCEEEEJNNSUV	juvenescence
CCEEEFFIIINS	efficiencies
CCEEEFHIKNRS	neckerchiefs
CCEEEFLNORSU	fluorescence
CCEEEGIIMNST	miscegenetic
CCEEEGILNORT	electrogenic
CCEEEGINNRSS	nigrescences
CCEEEGNNORSV	convergences
CCEEEHHMORST	homescreetch
CCEEEHIIMNPY	chimneypiece
CCEEEHINNORS	incoherences
CCEEEHINOSTT	coenesthetic
CCEEEHKLLPRS	spellchecker
CCEEEIIMNNRS	reminiscence
CCEEEIINPRSS	resipiscence
CCEEEIINRSVV	reviviscence
CCEEEIKLPPRR	Cripple Creek
CCEEEILLORTV	recollective
CCEEEILMNNRT	encirclement
CCEEEILMNNSU	luminescence
CCEEEIMNNOPT	incompetence
CCEEEIMNNSTU	intumescence
CCEEEIMNOPST	competencies
CCEEEIMORRST	coercimeters
CCEEEINNNOST	consentience
CCEEEINNNOSV	conveniences
CCEEEINNORSU	neuroscience
CCEEEINOPRSV	preconceives
CCEEEINORSSV	coerciveness
CCEEEINOSSTX	coexistences
CCEEEINRSSTV	vitrescences
CCEEELNRSTXY	excrescently
CCEEELOOPRST	electroscope
CCEEELORSTTU	electrocutes
CCEEELORSTTY	electrocytes
CCEEEMMMNNOT	commencement
CCEEENNOQSSU	consequences
CCEEENNORSST	concreteness
CCEEFFIIINNY	inefficiency
CCEEFFIINOST	coefficients
CCEEFGINNNOR	conferencing
CCEEFILMRSUX	circumflexes
CCEEFINNOORT	confectioner
CCEEGGILNOTY	glycogenetic
CCEEGILLNORT	recollecting
CCEEGILLOOSY	ecclesiology
CCEEGIMMNNOR	recommencing
CCEEGINNNORT	reconnecting
CCEEGINNNORU	incongruence
CCEEGINNNOST	contingences
CCEEGINNORSU	congruencies
CCEEGINOSTTY	cytogenetics
CCEEGNOORRST	concertgoers
CCEEHHIMOPRS	chemospheric
CCEEHIILNORT	heliocentric
CCEEHIILORTT	heteroclitic
CCEEHIMOSTYZ	schizomycete
CCEEHINNORTT	ethnocentric
CCEEHINNOSTU	inescutcheon
CCEEHIOPTTUY	hypoeutectic
CCEEHKLLLOSS	cockleshells
CCEEHKLOORST	electroshock
CCEEHMOOPRST	chemoceptors
CCEEHMOPSTYY	phycomycetes
CCEEHOPRRRTY	hypercorrect
CCEEIIIORSTV	coercivities
CCEEIILLOSTV	collectivise
CCEEIILLOTVZ	collectivize
CCEEIILOOPTU	leucopoietic
CCEEIIMNORSV	misconceiver
CCEEIIMNOSSV	misconceives
CCEEIIMOPRSS	microspecies
CCEEIINNNNOT	incontinence
CCEEILLLOTVY	collectively
CCEEILLNOORT	recollection
CCEEILLORTTY	electrolytic
CCEEILMORRST	sclerometric
CCEEILNNORTV	conventicler
CCEEILNNOSTV	conventicles
CCEEILNNOTVY	connectively
CCEEILNOORTT	electrotonic
CCEEILNORTVY	concretively
CCEEILOPRRTY	pyroelectric
CCEEILORRTVY	correctively
CCEEILORTTUY	reticulocyte
CCEEILSSSUVY	successively
CCEEIMNNNOTV	convincement
CCEEIMNNOPTY	incompetency
CCEEIMNNSTUY	intumescency
CCEEIMNOORST	econometrics
CCEEIMNRRTUV	circumventer
CCEEIMOSSTTY	cystectomies
CCEEINNNOORT	reconnection
CCEEINNNORTT	interconnect
CCEEINNOORSS	concessioner
CCEEINNOSSST	consistences
CCEEINOOPRRT	nocireceptor
CCEEINOOPRSS	necroscopies
CCEEIOOPRSST	stereoscopic
CCEEJNORRSTU	conjecturers
CCEEKNORSSSU	cocksureness
CCEEMNNNORST	concernments
CCEENOPSSSTU	conspectuses
CCEENORRRUUY	eurocurrency
CCEEOOPPRSST	spectroscope
CCEEOORRRSTV	overcorrects
CCEFGIKNNOYY	cockneyfying
CCEFHHMOORRU	Church of Rome
CCEFHINOORSU	conchiferous
CCEFIIINNSTU	unscientific

CCEFILMNRTUU circumfluent
CCEFKLOOORUW cuckooflower
CCEFLLLNOTUY flocculently
CCEFLLSSSUUY successfully
CCEFLNSSSUUU unsuccessful
CCEGHIINORTT ricochetting
CCEGHILMOPYY hypoglycemic
CCEGIINNORST concertising
concretising
CCEGIINNORTV reconvicting
CCEGIINNORTZ concertizing
concretizing
CCEGIJNNORTU conjecturing
CCEGIKNORRSW corkscrewing
CCEGINOPPRUY preoccupying
CCEHHHOOPSTT hotchpotches
CCEHHIILMOOR heliochromic
CCEHHILNRSSU churchliness
CCEHHIOSSSTT schottisches
CCEHIILLNOPU nucleophilic
CCEHIIMORSTT stichometric
CCEHIINOORRT rhinocerotic
CCEHIIPRRSTY hypercritics
CCEHILLOQRUU Quiller-Couch
CCEHILNOORTU technicolour
CCEHILNOPSTY polytechnics
CCEHIMNOORRT chronometric
CCEHIMOOPRST thermoscopic
CCEHIMOPRSTY psychometric
CCEHINOOPRRT necrotrophic
CCEHINOPRSTY pyrotechnics
CCEHIOOPSSTT stethoscopic
CCEHIORRTTYY erythrocytic
CCEHKLOSSTTU shuttlecocks
CCEHLOOSTTUY hectocotylus
CCEHMMOORRYY myrmecochory
CCEHNNOPRTUU counterpunch
CCEHNOOOPRSS chronoscopes
CCEHNOOPRSSY synchroscope
CCEIIILMOPST complicities
CCEIIIMMORSS microseismic
CCEIIINNNOST concinnities
CCEIIINOORRT oneirocritic
CCEIILLMOSTV collectivism
CCEIILLOSTTV collectivist
CCEIILLOTTVY collectivity
CCEIILMOORRT colorimetric
CCEIILNNOSUV inconclusive
CCEIILNOTVVY convictively
CCEIILPRSTUU pisciculture
CCEIILRRTTUU citriculture
CCEIIMOOPSSS seismoscopic
CCEIINNNNOTY incontinency
CCEIINNOORTV reconviction
CCEIINNORSTT concertinist
CCEIINNOTTVY connectivity
CCEIINOOPRST retinoscopic
CCEIINOORSST coercionists
CCEIINORSTTV constrictive
CCEIINOSSTUV viscountcies
CCEIINRSSTTY syncretistic
CCEIJNNOSTUV conjunctives
CCEIKLOOTTUY leukocytotic
CCEILLNOSUVY conclusively
CCEILLOOOPSS oscilloscope
CCEILMNORSUU micronucleus
CCEILOOPRSUY precociously
CCEILOOSSTUY leucocytosis
CCEIMNORRTUV circumventor
CCEINNOOSSTU consecutions
CCEINNOSTTUY constituency
CCEINOOPRSSU preconscious
CCEINORSTTUV constructive
CCEIOOPSSSTY cystoscopies
CCEIORRSSSSS crisscrosses
CCEJNNORSTUU conjunctures
CCELNNORRTUY concurrently
CCELNOOOOPSS colonoscopes
CCENOPRRSTTU preconstruct
CCENORRRSSTU crosscurrent
CCENORRSSTTU constructers
reconstructs
CCEOOOPPRSST proctoscopes
CCEOOOPRRSSS coprocessors
CCEOOPPRSSTY spectroscopy
CCFGGHIIKNOT cockfighting
CCFGIIMNRSUU circumfusing
CCFIIINORSUX crucifixions
CCFIILNNOOST conflictions
CCFIIMNORSUU circumfusion
CCFILMORSUUU circumfluous
CCFILOOOPRSU fluoroscopic
CCGGHHINORSU churchgoings
CCGHHIILOOTY ichthyologic
CCGHIIINNNOS cinchonising
CCGHIIINNNOZ cinchonizing
CCGHILNOOOST conchologist
CCGIIILMNOOR criminologic
CCGIILNNNOVY convincingly
CCGIINNNNOUV unconvincing
CCGIINNOPRST conscripting
CCGIINNORSTT constricting
CCGILLNOSTYY cyclostyling
CCGILMNOORTY motorcycling
CCGILNNORRUY concurringly
CCGINNORSTTU constructing
CCGINORSSTTU crosscutting
CCHHIIILOTTY ichthyolitic
CCHHIIMOSTTY stichomythic
CCHHIIMOSTYZ schizothymic
CCHHIIOPSTYZ schizophytic
CCHHIMOOOPRR chromophoric
CCHHIMOOOPRT photochromic
CCHHIMOOPRSY hypsochromic
CCHIIINOPRTU Pinturicchio
CCHIILNOOPRR chloropicrin
CCHIIMOPRSSY microphysics
CCHIIOOPRSTY hypocoristic
CCHILMNOORSY chylomicrons
CCHIOOPPRSTY psychotropic
CCHIOPPRTTYY cryptophytic
CCIILNNNSTUU cunnilinctus
CCIILNOOPRSS ciclosporins
CCIILORSTUUY circuitously

CCIIMOOPRSST microscopist
CCIINNOOPRST conscription
CCIINNOORSTT constriction
CCIIOOTTTXYY cytotoxicity
CCIJNNNOOSTU conjunctions
CCILMOORSTTY motorcyclist
CCILMORRSUUU cirrocumulus
CCIMNOOPSTUU compunctious
CCINNOORSTTU construction
CCINOORRSSTT constrictors
CCNOORRSSTTU constructors
CDDDEEFIIOST eisteddfodic
CDDDEEIMMNOS discommended
CDDDEEMNOOPU decompounded
CDDDELLLMOOY mollycoddled
CDDEEEEINNNP independence
CDDEEEEINNPS dependencies
CDDEEEEJNSST dejectedness
CDDEEEGINNRS redescending
CDDEEEGINORS derecognised
CDDEEEGINORZ derecognized
CDDEEEHMNOPR comprehended
CDDEEEINNNPY independency
CDDEEEINORRS reconsidered
CDDEEEIORRSV rediscovered
CDDEEEIPRSST disrespected
CDDEEEIRRSTT derestricted
CDDEEELNSSSU secludedness
CDDEEEMNNOPR precondemned
CDDEEEMOPRSS decompressed
CDDEEHLNNOSU nonscheduled
CDDEEHLNORTU underclothed
CDDEEIIMOSTZ domesticized
CDDEEIINORST rodenticides
CDDEEIJNPRUU unprejudiced
CDDEEILNNSSU includedness
CDDEEINNORSU unconsidered
CDDEEINNOSTT discontented
CDDEEINORRTU reintroduced
CDDEEINORSTU rediscounted
CDDEEINORSUV undiscovered
CDDEEINPRSUU superinduced
CDDEELLNOORT decontrolled
CDDEEMNNOTUU undocumented
CDDEENOOPRRS corresponded
CDDEEOOPRRUV overproduced
CDDEFIIKLSST fiddlesticks
CDDEFIIMNORS disconfirmed
CDDEFIMOORST discomforted
CDDEFLNNOOUY confoundedly
CDDEGIIINRST discrediting
CDDEHIIMOOST dichotomised
CDDEHIIMOOTZ dichotomized
CDDEHILNOSSS cloddishness
CDDEHLNORTUU thundercloud
CDDEIILMNNOO nondomiciled
CDDEIINNOSTU discontinued
CDDEILNOOOTY cotyledonoid
CDDEILNOOPRS scolopendrid
CDDEILNOOSTY dicotyledons
CDDEILOOPSSU diplodocuses
CDDEKORRSSTU rudderstocks
CDDELLLMOORY mollycoddler
CDDELLLMOOSY mollycoddles
CDDEMNNOOPUU uncompounded
CDDGIIMMNOOS discommoding
CDDIIMMOOSTY discommodity
CDDMMNOORSUU McMurdo Sound
CDEEEEFGLLNO Golden Fleece
CDEEEEGINRST detergencies
CDEEEEIILMNT telemedicine
CDEEEEIINNPX inexpedience
CDEEEEIINPSX expediencies
CDEEEEIKLPRW pickerelweed
CDEEEEJNRSUV rejuvenesced
CDEEEELNNPRS resplendence
CDEEEENPRSSU supersedence
CDEEEFFIINNR indifference
CDEEEFHILRST chesterfield
CDEEEFMNORST deforcements
CDEEEGIINRSV divergencies
CDEEEGINORSS derecognises
CDEEEGINORSZ derecognizes
CDEEEHILOPRT helicoptered
CDEEEHIMNPRT decipherment
CDEEEHINRRST rechristened
CDEEEHNRSSTW wretchedness
CDEEEIINNPXY inexpediency
CDEEEIINNSST dissentience
CDEEEIINPRSS presidencies
CDEEEIINSSSV decisiveness
CDEEEIKNSSSW wickednesses
CDEEEILMNORT declinometer
CDEEEILNOSST deselections
CDEEEILNQSTU deliquescent
CDEEEILORRST clerestoried
CDEEEINNNORS nonresidence
CDEEEINRSSST discreetness
discreteness
CDEEEIRRSSST directresses
CDEEELLORSTY electrolysed
CDEEELLORTYZ electrolyzed
CDEEELMMNOPT complemented
CDEEELNNPRSY resplendency
CDEEELNPTUXY unexpectedly
CDEEELOPRTTY electrotyped
CDEEEMMNORRS recommenders
CDEEEMNNNOTU denouncement
CDEEEMOPRSSS decompresses
CDEEENNORRTU rencountered
CDEEEOPRRSSS predecessors
CDEEEOPRRSTT retrospected
CDEEEOPSSSUY pseudocyeses
CDEEERSSSSTU seductresses
CDEEFFGIINNR differencing
CDEEFFIIINOV divine office
CDEEFIIIIKRR Frederick III
CDEEFILNNNUU uninfluenced
CDEEFINNNOSS confinedness
CDEEFNNOSSSU confusedness
CDEEGHILNRSU rescheduling
CDEEGIILNQSU deliquescing
CDEEGIILRRTY triglyceride
CDEEGILNORSS girdlescones

CDEEGILNRTTU declutterring
CDEEGILOPPTY glycopeptide
CDEEGIMMNNOR recommending
CDEEGINNNORS recondensing
CDEEGINNORSU unrecognised
CDEEGINNORUZ unrecognized
CDEEGINOPRRR prerecording
CDEEHHKLLOSS shellshocked
CDEEHILNPRST stepchildren
CDEEHILOPRRS perchlorides
CDEEHINNRSTU unchristened
CDEEHIOPRRRS recordership
CDEEHIOQSSTU discotheques
CDEEHKLLNORS schnorkelled
CDEEHKLNOSUY honeysuckled
CDEEHLMOOSTU closemouthed
CDEEHLNORSTU underclothes
CDEEHORSTTTU outstretched
CDEEIIILNSVY indecisively
CDEEIIILOPST depoliticise
CDEEIIILOPTZ depoliticize
CDEEIIIMORST iridectomies
mediocrities
CDEEIIINNSTV disincentive
CDEEIIINRTTV interdictive
CDEEIIKLNSSS slickensides
CDEEIILNNORV overinclined
CDEEIILNOPRT predilection
CDEEIILNORST derelictions
CDEEIILNRSTY indiscreetly
indiscretely
iridescently
CDEEIILOPSTV velocipedist
CDEEIILPRTVY predictively
CDEEIIMNOOSS diseconomies
CDEEIIMNOPRV improvidence
CDEEIIMNOSTU eudemonistic
CDEEIIMORRSS misericordes
CDEEIIMOSSTZ domesticizes
CDEEIINNORTV nondirective
CDEEIINNRSST indirectness
CDEEIINNSSTY dissentiency
CDEEIINOPRVW provincewide
CDEEIINORRST redirections
CDEEIINOSSSU dieciousness
CDEEIINRSTTU incertitudes
CDEEIKLNNOOS nickelodeons
CDEEIKPPQSTU quickstepped
CDEEILLLOTUV Viollet-le-Duc
CDEEILLNPSSU pellucidness
CDEEILMMNOPT complimented
CDEEILMNOOPX complexioned
CDEEILRRSTTY restrictedly
CDEEIMNNORTU countermined
CDEEIMNNRSST discernments
rescindments
CDEEIMNORSTV divorcements
CDEEIMOOSSTX sextodecimos
CDEEIMOPRSTU computerised
CDEEIMOPRTUZ computerized
CDEEINNNORSY nonresidency
CDEEINNOORRT reconnoitred
CDEEINOOPRSS processioned
CDEEINOPPRRT intercropped
CDEEINOPRSTT introspected
CDEEINORRSST intercrossed
CDEEINORRSTU reintroduces
CDEEINPRSSUU superinduces
CDEEINRRSTTU unrestricted
CDEEIOPRRTUV reproductive
CDEEIOPSSSUY pseudocyesis
CDEEIORRSTUV discoverture
CDEEIORSSTTT detectorists
CDEEIRRRSSVW screwdrivers
CDEELMNNOOST condolements
CDEEMNOOPSSS composedness
CDEEMNOORSUV overconsumed
CDEEMNOORTUV countermoved
covermounted
CDEENNOOPRST corespondent
CDEENNRRRTUU undercurrent
CDEENOOORTXY deoxycortone
CDEENOORRTTV controverted
CDEENOORSSSU decorousness
CDEEOOPRRSUV overproduces
CDEEOOPRSTUV pseudovector
CDEERRRSTTUU restructured
CDEFFIIILSTU difficulties
CDEFGIIINNST disinfecting
CDEFIIINNOST disinfection
CDEFIIMORSST discomfiters
CDEFIIMORSTU discomfiture
CDEFIINORSST disinfectors
CDEGGIILNNNU indulgencing
CDEGIIIMNRST misdirecting
CDEGIIINNRTT interdicting
CDEGIILNNOOS decolonising
CDEGIILNNOOZ decolonizing
CDEGIILNNRSY discerningly
CDEGIILNOORS decolorising
CDEGIILNOORZ decolorizing
CDEGIINNNRSU undiscerning
CDEGIINNPRRU underpricing
CDEGIKNNOORU undercooking
CDEGILMNNNOY condemningly
CDEGILNNNOTY contendingly
CDEGILNNOORU undercooling
CDEGILNOORUV overclouding
CDEGINNORRSU underscoring
CDEGINNRTTUU undercutting
CDEGINOORRVW overcrowding
CDEGKLOOORSS sockdologers
CDEGLMNORUUY curmudgeonly
CDEHHIIIPRTT diphtheritic
CDEHHIILNSSS childishness
CDEHHIIPSTTW whipstitched
CDEHHIOPRRSY hydrospheric
CDEHHNOOOPRS chordophones
CDEHIIILPPSS discipleship
CDEHIIINNORS enchiridions
CDEHIIKNORTY hydrokinetic
CDEHIILORRST trichlorides
CDEHIIMOOSST dichotomises
CDEHIIMOOSTZ dichotomizes

CDEHIIMPSSTY	dysphemistic
CDEHIINOOOPR	conidiophore
CDEHIINOORSS	isochronised
CDEHIINOORSZ	isochronized
CDEHIIOPRRST	directorship
CDEHILLOOPRY	policyholder
CDEHILMNOOOR	monochloride
CDEHIMNOOORS	chondriosome
CDEHINNORSSY	synchronised
CDEHINNORSYZ	synchronized
CDEHIORRTTWY	creditworthy
CDEHKLOORSST	stockholders
CDEIIIILNNPS	indiscipline
CDEIIIJRSTUV	jurisdictive
CDEIIILNPRSS	discipliners
CDEIIILNTVVY	vindictively
CDEIIIMNORST	misdirection
CDEIIINNORST	indiscretion
CDEIIINNORTT	interdiction
CDEIIISSSTUV	vicissitudes
CDEIIJNSSTUV	disjunctives
CDEIILLMNOSS	milliseconds
CDEIILMRTUUV	diverticulum
CDEIILNNPPRU	unprincipled
CDEIILRSSUVY	discursively
CDEIIMMNOOSS	commissioned
	decommission
CDEIIMMRSSTY	dissymmetric
CDEIIMNORSTU	reductionism
CDEIIMPPRSUY	cypripediums
CDEIINNNOOSX	disconnexion
CDEIINNOOPRT	precondition
CDEIINNOORST	conditioners
	reconditions
CDEIINNORSTU	discontinuer
CDEIINNOSSTU	discontinues
CDEIINNSSSTT	distinctness
CDEIINOOPRST	periodontics
CDEIINOOSSSU	dioicousness
CDEIINOPRSST	descriptions
CDEIINORRSTT	interdictors
CDEIINORRTTY	interdictory
CDEIINORSTTU	reductionist
CDEILMNOORST	discolorment
CDEILNOORSUY	indecorously
CDEILOPRTUVY	productively
CDEIMNORSSTU	misconstrued
CDEIMOOPRSSU	discomposure
CDEINNOOORTT	contortioned
CDEINNOPRSST	nondescripts
CDEINNRSTTUU	uninstructed
CDEINOOPRRTU	reproduction
CDEINOOPSSST	endoscopists
CDEINOPRTUUV	unproductive
CDEIOORSSTUU	discourteous
CDELLNNOORTU	uncontrolled
CDELLNOOTUVY	convolutedly
CDELNNOOPRUY	pronouncedly
CDELNOOOSTUY	cotyledonous
CDENNNOOPRUU	unpronounced
CDENOORRSTUW	counterwords
CDENRRSTTUUU	unstructured
CDFGHIINNORY	chondrifying
CDFGIIIMNOST	discomfiting
CDFHILOORRUY	hydrofluoric
CDFINNOSSTUY	dysfunctions
CDGHIKLNOOST	stockholding
CDGIIIILNNNS	disinclining
CDGIIIILNNPS	disciplining
CDGIIINNNOOT	conditioning
CDGIILNOORSU	discolouring
CDGIILOOSSST	discologists
CDGIIMMNNOOS	discommoning
CDGIIMNOOPSS	discomposing
CDGINNNOOORR	noncorroding
CDGINOOPRTUU	outproducing
CDHHILNOORRY	chlorohydrin
CDHIIIMOOPRS	isodimorphic
CDHIILOSSTUY	distichously
CDHIIMOOSSTT	dichotomists
CDHIIOOPRSST	chiropodists
CDHINOOORSTT	orthodontics
CDIIIJNORSTU	jurisdiction
CDIIILNNSTTY	indistinctly
CDIIIMNNSTTU	Nunc Dimittis
CDIIINNOSSTT	distinctions
CDIIJNNOSSTU	disjunctions
CDIILLORSUUY	ridiculously
CDIILMORSSTU	clostridiums
CDIIMMNNOOSU	condominiums
CDIIMMNOOOSU	incommodious
CDIINNOORTTU	introduction
CDIIOPRTTUVY	productivity
CDILMMOOOSUY	commodiously
CDILOOORSUUU	douroucoulis
CDIMNOOORSTU	microdontous
CDINNOOPRSTY	cyprinodonts
CDINOORRTTUY	introductory
CEEEEEGMNRRS	reemergences
CEEEEEINPRRX	reexperience
CEEEEELNPRST	telepresence
CEEEEFFNRSTV	effervescent
CEEEEFINNRRT	interference
CEEEEGHMNORS	cheesemonger
CEEEEHHLORSS	horseleeches
CEEEEHNOPRRY	honeycreeper
CEEEEHNORSVW	whencesoever
CEEEEIINNPRX	inexperience
CEEEEIKKPRTW	wicketkeeper
CEEEEILNORST	electioneers
CEEEEILNSSTV	electiveness
CEEEEINPRSTX	preexistence
CEEEEINRRRSV	irreverences
CEEEEIORRSVX	overexercise
CEEEEJNRSSUV	rejuvenesces
CEEEELMORRTT	electrometer
CEEEENNNOPST	open sentence
CEEEFFGINRSV	effervescing
CEEEFFINNOTV	noneffective
CEEEFFLNORST	efflorescent
CEEEFGHINNRS	greenfinches
CEEEFHIIPRSS	speechifiers
CEEEFHLNRSSU	cheerfulness
CEEEFIILRRST	electrifiers

CEEEFIIMPRTV imperfective
CEEEFILLLMNU mellifluence
CEEEFILLRTVY reflectively
CEEEFILNORSU fluoresceine
CEEEFILNRTUV unreflective
CEEEFILSTUVX flexecutives
CEEEFINNRSST freneticness
CEEEFKLNSSSS fecklessness
CEEEGGILNOOS genecologies
CEEEGGNORRRS greengrocers
CEEEGGNORRRY greengrocery
CEEEGIILLNNT intelligence
CEEEGIINNPRX experiencing
CEEEGIINOPRT epirogenetic
CEEEGILNPRST preselecting
CEEEGINNPRRT Prince Regent
CEEEHHKLNOPS heckelphones
CEEEHHMOPRSS chemospheres
CEEEHIIMRSTU euhemeristic
CEEEHIIPRRSV receivership
CEEEHIKNSTTT kitchenettes
CEEEHILLNPRU Euler-Chelpin
CEEEHILLOPRT electrophile
CEEEHILORSTT heteroclites
CEEEHIMNNPRT encipherment
CEEEHIMNRSTU hermeneutics
CEEEHINOSSST coenesthesis
CEEEHINOSSSV cohesiveness
CEEEHIOORSTU heteroecious
CEEEHLLPSSSY speechlessly
CEEEHLNNOTTU luncheonette
CEEEHLNOOPRT electrophone
CEEEHLOQQSUU quelquechose
CEEEHMNNNRTT entrenchment
CEEEHMNNRRTT retrenchment
CEEEHMOORRST stereochrome
CEEEHNOPRRST centrosphere
CEEEHOOPRRRT rheoreceptor
CEEEIILLNTTV intellective
CEEEIIMNNPRT impertinence
CEEEIIMPPRTV imperceptive
CEEEIINPRTTV interceptive
CEEEIINSSSTZ citizenesses
CEEEIIPRRSTV irrespective
CEEEIKNNRSSS snickersnees
CEEEILLNOPQU equipollence
CEEEILNNOSTV nonselective
CEEEILNORSST reselections
CEEEILORRSST clerestories
CEEEILPPRTVY perceptively
preceptively
CEEEILPRSTVY respectively
CEEEIMMMNOTT committeemen
CEEEIMNNNSST incensements
CEEEIMNNOPRS omnipresence
CEEEIMNNORST mesenteronic
CEEEIMNORSTU neurectomies
CEEEIMNORSVW servicewomen
CEEEIMORRSTT stereometric
CEEEINNNOSTX nonexistence
CEEEINNOSSTV venesections
CEEEINNOTUVX nonexecutive
CEEEINNQSSTU quintessence
CEEEINNRSSSU insecureness
CEEEINORSTUX executioners
CEEEINPPRTUV unperceptive
CEEEINPRRSTT intercepters
CEEEINRRRSTW screenwriter
CEEEIOPPRRST preceptories
CEEEIPPRSSTV perspectives
CEEEIPRRSSUV repercussive
CEEEKLNRSSSS recklessness
CEEELLNPRUUV pulverulence
CEEELLORRSTY electrolyser
CEEELLORRTYZ electrolyzer
CEEELLORSSTY electrolyses
CEEELLORSTTY electrolytes
CEEELLORSTYZ electrolyzes
CEEELMMORTTU telecommuter
CEEELMNOPSST completeness
CEEELMORRSST sclerometers
CEEELMORRTTY electrometry
CEEELOPRRTTY electrotyper
CEEELOPRSTTY electrotypes
CEEELORRSSSU resourceless
CEEEMNNNORTU renouncement
CEEEMNNNOSTU enouncements
CEEEMNOPRRSS recompensers
CEEEMOPRRSTT spectrometer
CEEENNORRSTU encounterers
CEEENNPRTUUV venepuncture
CEEEOOPRRTTX exteroceptor
CEEEOOPRSSST stereoscopes
CEEFFGILNORS efflorescing
CEEFFIILLOTT little office
CEEFFLNORSSU forcefulness
CEEFFNOORRTU counteroffer
CEEFGGILNNTU genuflecting
CEEFGHIINPSY speechifying
CEEFGIILNRTY electrifying
CEEFGILNNOTU genuflection
CEEFGILNNRTU unreflecting
CEEFGLLLNTUY neglectfully
CEEFGLNORSTU genuflectors
CEEFHIKRSSSU suckerfishes
CEEFHILORSSS Ross Ice Shelf
CEEFHILSSTTU cuttlefishes
CEEFHKMORRTU motherfucker
CEEFIIIILNST infelicities
CEEFIILRTTVY reflectivity
CEEFIIMNOPRT imperfection
CEEFIINNORST reinfections
CEEFIINOPRST frontispiece
CEEFILLNOSST flectionless
CEEFILMNRSSU mercifulness
CEEFILNNORST inflorescent
CEEFILNOSSUV voicefulness
CEEFIMNNNOST confinements
CEEFINORSTTU counterfeits
CEEFLLOORRTU electrofluor
CEEFLLPRSTUY respectfully
CEEFLMOORRST electroforms
CEEFLOORRSSU foreclosures
CEEGGILNOSSY glycogenesis

CEEGHIINORTZ	rhizogenetic
CEEGHIINOSTT	histogenetic
CEEGHILNOOST	technologies
CEEGHILNOPTY	phylogenetic
CEEGHILNPRSU	sepulchering
CEEGHILOOPRT	herpetologic
CEEGHIMORSTY	geochemistry
CEEGHINNOPTY	hypnogenetic
CEEGHINOORTT	orthogenetic
CEEGHINOPTTY	phytogenetic
CEEGHINORSTY	hysterogenic
CEEGHINORTUW	counterweigh
CEEGHINRRSTT	stretchering
CEEGHINRSSST	sightscreens
CEEGIIJNNRTT	interjecting
CEEGIIKNNQRU	requickening
CEEGIILLNOTV	vitellogenic
CEEGIINNNSST	enticingness
CEEGIINNPRST	reinspecting
CEEGIINNPRTT	intercepting
CEEGIINNRSSU	insurgencies
CEEGIINNRSTT	intersecting
CEEGIINOPRTV	precognitive
CEEGIINORTVX	overexciting
CEEGIINPRSST	stringpieces
CEEGIJNORRTT	retrojecting
CEEGIKLLNOPS	glockenspiel
CEEGILMOOORT	meteorologic
CEEGILNNOSSY	geosynclines
CEEGIMNNOPRS	recompensing
CEEGINNNORTU	encountering
CEEGINNOPRRS	precensoring
CEEGINNOQRRU	reconquering
CEEGINNORRTV	reconverting
CEEGINOPRRSS	reprocessing
CEEGINRRRSTU	resurrecting
CEEGIOPRRSTU	picturegoers
CEEGMNOORRST	costermonger
CEEHHIILLLNP	philhellenic
CEEHHIINOSTT	henotheistic
CEEHHILMOORS	heliochromes
CEEHHIMRSSTT	hemstitchers
CEEHHINPRSTY	hypersthenic
CEEHHKLRSTTU	kletterschuh
CEEHHLMOOORS	homeschooler
CEEHHLOORSST	clotheshorse
CEEHHMOOPRRS	chromosphere
CEEHHOOPPRSS	phosphoresce
CEEHHOOPRRST	trochosphere
CEEHIIINRRST	inheritrices
CEEHIIKMNOSS	chemokinesis
CEEHIIKNPRTY	hyperkinetic
CEEHIILNNSTT	Lichtenstein
CEEHIINNNPPS	pinchpennies
CEEHIKMNOSSS	homesickness
CEEHILLNOPSU	nucleophiles
CEEHILLNOSST	clotheslines
CEEHILMMOPRY	myrmecophile
CEEHILMNORST	thermoclines
CEEHILMOSSTT	Themistocles
CEEHILNNORTY	incoherently
CEEHILNOOSSS	cohesionless
CEEHILOOPRRT	electrophori
CEEHILOPRSST	electorships
CEEHILPRSSTU	lectureships
CEEHIMMORRTT	thermometric
CEEHIMMOSTTY	thymectomies
CEEHIMMPRSST	sprechstimme
CEEHIMNNNRTT	intrenchment
CEEHIMNOOSTU	Home Counties
CEEHIMNOOSTY	homocysteine
CEEHIMNORSTT	theocentrism
CEEHIMOPRSTT	pitchometers
CEEHINNOPRSV	convenership
CEEHINOOPRST	stereophonic
CEEHINOORRSS	rhinoceroses
CEEHINRSSSTT	stretchiness
CEEHIOPRSTUX	executorship
CEEHIPPRRTYY	hyperpyretic
CEEHKLLNORRS	schnorkeller
CEEHKLNOSSUY	honeysuckles
CEEHKNORSSUY	honeysuckers
CEEHLMOOPRTU	thermocouple
CEEHLOPRSSST	clothespress
CEEHMNOORRST	chronometers
CEEHMNORSTUX	Herstmonceux
CEEHMOOPRSST	thermoscopes
CEEHMOORRSTY	stereochromy
CEEHMOPRRSTY	psychrometer
CEEHMORSTTYY	hysterectomy
CEEHNOOPPRSS	nephroscopes
CEEHNOORRSTT	orthocenters
	orthocentres
CEEHOOPRRSTU	urethroscope
CEEHOOPSSSTT	stethoscopes
CEEHORRSTTYY	erythrocytes
CEEHORSSTTTU	outstretches
CEEIIIMNPPRT	impercipient
CEEIIINNSSSV	incisiveness
CEEIIINPRRTU	perineuritic
CEEIIINRSSTU	insecurities
CEEIIIOPRSST	preciosities
CEEIIIOPSSST	speciosities
CEEIIJNNORTT	interjection
CEEIIJNORTTV	introjective
CEEIIKLNNOTU	kinetonuclei
CEEIIKLOOPTU	leukopoietic
CEEIILLNNOTT	intellection
CEEIILMNNORT	inclinometer
CEEIILMOPSTX	complexities
CEEIILMRSTUV	vermiculites
CEEIILNNORSV	overinclines
CEEIILNNOSSV	insolvencies
CEEIILNNPRSS	princeliness
CEEIILNPPRTY	percipiently
CEEIILNPSSTX	explicitness
CEEIILOOPSSU	leucopoiesis
CEEIILOPRTVX	overexplicit
CEEIIMNNPRTY	impertinency
CEEIIMNOPPRT	imperception
CEEIIMNOSSSS	secessionism
CEEIIMOPRSSU	semiprecious
CEEIIMORRSTU	meretricious
CEEIIMORSSST	esotericisms

CEEIIMORSSTV viscosimeter
CEEIINNNNOTV inconvenient
CEEIINNOPRST reinspection
CEEIINNOPRTT interception
CEEIINNORSST intercession
CEEIINNORSTT intersection
CEEIINOOPSST isoteniscope
CEEIINOPRSTT receptionist
CEEIINORSSTV insectivores
CEEIINOSSSST secessionist
CEEIIPPRRSTV prescriptive
CEEIIPPRTTVY perceptivity
CEEIJLOPRTVY projectively
CEEIJNOORRTT retrojection
CEEIJNORRSTT interjectors
CEEIJNORRTTY interjectory
CEEIKKNOPSTV pocketknives
CEEIKLMNPPRU pumpernickel
CEEIKLNORRST interlockers
CEEIKLNOSSSV lovesickness
CEEILLMNOPTY incompletely
CEEILLNOPQUY equipollency
CEEILLORSSTY electrolysis
CEEILLPRSUVY preclusively
CEEILMMOPSTU lumpectomies
CEEILMOOPRSY copolymerise
CEEILMOOPRYZ copolymerize
CEEILMOORRST colorimeters
CEEILMOORSST sclerotomies
CEEILNNNOTVY conveniently
CEEILNNOSUVX nonexclusive
CEEILNOOPRSS necropolises
CEEILNOOPSTT postelection
CEEILNOORRST intercoolers
CEEILNOPRSTU neuroleptics
CEEILNORSTTT electrotints
CEEILOPRTTVY protectively
CEEILPRSSUVY percussively
CEEIMMMNORTT recommitment
CEEIMMMOOSTY myomectomies
CEEIMNNOPSTT incompetents
CEEIMNNORSTU countermines
CEEIMNOOPRST contemporise
CEEIMNOOPRTZ contemporize
CEEIMNOORSTT econometrist
CEEIMNRRSTTU recruitments
CEEIMOOPSSSS seismoscopes
CEEIMOPRSSTU computerises
CEEIMOPRSTUZ computerizes
CEEINNNOQSTU inconsequent
CEEINNOORRRT reconnoitrer
CEEINNOORRST reconnoiters
reconnoitres
CEEINNOORRSV reconversion
CEEINNOOSSTX coextensions
CEEINNORSSTT contriteness
CEEINNPRTUUV venipuncture
CEEINNRRRTTU intercurrent
CEEINOOPRRTT interoceptor
CEEINOOPRSTT stereopticon
CEEINOOPRSTU counterpoise
CEEINOORRSST retrocession
CEEINOPPRSSS sniperscopes
CEEINOPRRSSU repercussion
CEEINOPRRSTT interceptors
CEEINOPRSSSU preciousness
CEEINOPRSSTU counterspies
persecutions
CEEINOPSSSSU speciousness
CEEINORRRSTU resurrection
CEEINORRSSST intercessors
intercrosses
CEEINORRSSTU intercourses
CEEINORRSSTY intercessory
CEEINORSTTTU reconstitute
CEEINPPRRRTU Prince Rupert
CEEIOOPRRSTT protectories
stereotropic
CEEIOORRRSTT ecoterrorist
CEEKLLNSSSSU lucklessness
CEEKLNOOSTTY cytoskeleton
CEEKOORRRSTT retrorockets
CEELLNOORTTV electronvolt
CEELNNOQSTUY consequently
CEELNOOOPRST coleopterons
CEELNOORSTTU electrotonus
CEELNORSSSUU ulcerousness
CEELOOOPRSTU coleopterous
CEELOPPRSSST prospectless
CEELPRSSSSTU sculptresses
CEEMNOORSSUV overconsumes
CEEMNOORSTUV countermoves
CEEMNOPRRSTU procurements
CEEMOPRRSSSU compressures
CEEMOPRRSTTY cryptometers
spectrometry
CEENNOORRSST cornerstones
CEENNOORRTTU countertenor
CEENNOQSTUUY Queen's County
CEENOOOPPRSS snooperscope
CEENOORRRTTV controverter
CEENOORRSSTV seroconverts
CEENOOSSSTUV covetousness
CEENOPRSTTUY countertypes
CEENORSSTTTU stonecutters
CEEOOPRRSTTV overprotects
CEEOPPRSSSTU prospectuses
CEERRRSSTTUU restructures
CEFFGHIINNRY frenchifying
CEFFHIINNORS chiffonniers
CEFFHIRSSSTT festschrifts
CEFFIIINNSTU insufficient
CEFFIILNSTUY sufficiently
CEFFIORRSTUU fructiferous
CEFFIORSSTUU suffruticose
CEFGGIINNRTU centrifuging
CEFGIIKLLNRY flickeringly
CEFGIIMNNORR reconfirming
CEFHLLLOOOSW schoolfellow
CEFHLMOOORRU fluorochrome
CEFIIILNOSTU infelicitous
CEFIIILORSSU siliciferous
CEFIILLOSTUY felicitously
CEFIILMNNTUY munificently

CEFIILMORRTU fluorimetric
CEFIILNOORRS ferrosilicon
CEFIILNOPRSS prolificness
CEFIILNOPRTY proficiently
CEFIILNORSST frictionless
CEFIILNOSTUY infectiously
CEFIIMNOORST conformities
CEFIIMNOOTUZ Zeno of Citium
CEFILLMNRUUY unmercifully
CEFILLMOORSY frolicsomely
CEFILLORRTUU floriculture
CEFILMOORRTU fluorometric
CEFILNNOSSTU functionless
CEFILNOORSTU counterfoils
CEFILOORSUVY vociferously
CEFLNNORSSSU scornfulness
CEFLOOOPRSSU fluoroscopes
CEFMNNNOORTT confrontment
CEFNOOOPRRTU counterproof
CEFNOORRSTTU counterforts
CEGGIILNNNSS clingingness
CEGGILNOOSTY gynecologist
CEGHHIILNRSY cherishingly
CEGHHIILOPRY hieroglyphic
CEGHHIIMNSTT hemstitching
CEGHHILNOSTT nightclothes
CEGHIIKNPRSW shipwrecking
CEGHIILNRSTT chitterlings
CEGHIINNRSST christenings
CEGHIINOPRTV overpitching
CEGHIIOPSSTY geophysicist
CEGHIKNNOSSS shockingness
CEGHILNOOORS chronologies
CEGHILNOOSTT technologist
CEGHILOOOSTY stoechiology
CEGHILOOPSSY psychologies
psychologise
CEGHILOOPSYZ psychologize
CEGHINNNORTU truncheoning
CEGHINNOSSTU touchingness
CEGHINORRTWY cringeworthy
CEGHINSSUWZZ zwischenzugs
CEGHIOPRRSTY copyrighters
CEGIIIILMSTT legitimistic
CEGIIJNNORTT introjecting
CEGIIKLNNORT interlocking
CEGIIKLNSSST singlesticks
CEGIILLOOSTX lexicologist
CEGIILNNOORS recolonising
CEGIILNNOORZ recolonizing
CEGIILNNPSTY inspectingly
CEGIILNORSST sclerotising
CEGIILNORSTZ sclerotizing
CEGIILOOORST soteriologic
CEGIIMMNORTT recommitting
CEGIINNOOPRT precognition
CEGIINNOORST recognitions
CEGIINNRSSTY syncretising
CEGIINNRSTYZ syncretizing
CEGIINNRTTTU intercutting
CEGIINOPTTYY genotypicity
CEGIJKNOOTUY outjockeying
CEGIKKNORSTY skyrocketing
CEGIKNOORSTV overstocking
CEGILLNRSTUY clusteringly
CEGILNNNOTTY contingently
CEGILNNOSTTY contestingly
CEGILNOOPRSU supercooling
CEGILNOOPRTU glucoprotein
CEGILNOOPRTY glycoprotein
CEGILNOORSST necrologists
CEGIMNNNOSST consignments
CEGIMOOORRSV microgrooves
CEGIMORRRSUY microsurgery
CEGINNNNOSTU unconsenting
CEGINNNORSTT constringent
CEGINNORSSTU countersigns
CEGINNOSTTTU stonecutting
CEGINNPSSTUU unsuspecting
CEGINOOPPRRV overcropping
CEGINORRSSTU stringcourse
CEGINPPRTTUU uppercutting
CEGLNOORSTUW counterglows
CEGLOPRSSUUU groupuscules
CEGMOOSTUYYZ zygomycetous
CEGNNOPPRSSU scuppernongs
CEHHHNOOPRRY rhynchophore
CEHHIILLOSTV Cheviot Hills
CEHHIILMOPRT thermophilic
CEHHIILOSTTY ichthyolites
CEHHIIPSSTTW whipstitches
CEHHILMNORTT trochelminth
CEHHILMRSSUY helichrysums
CEHHILNRSSSU churlishness
CEHHILOOPRTY hypochlorite
CEHHIMMOOOPR homeomorphic
CEHHIMOOPRTT photothermic
CEHHIMOOPSTT photochemist
CEHHIMOPSTTY phytochemist
CEHHIOOPPRST photospheric
CEHHIOPPRRTY hypertrophic
CEHHIOPSSTYZ schizophytes
CEHHLOOOSSSU schoolhouses
CEHHMMOORRTY thermochromy
CEHHMOOOPRRS chromophores
CEHHMOOPRSSY hypsochromes
CEHHOOOPRRST trochophores
CEHIIILNOOPS eosinophilic
CEHIIINPSSTZ citizenships
CEHIIKLNSSST ticklishness
CEHIIKNOOPTT photokinetic
CEHIILLNNORS Lincolnshire
CEHIILMNOPRS necrophilism
CEHIILNQSSSU cliquishness
CEHIILOPPRSS scripophiles
CEHIILOPSTTY polytheistic
CEHIIMMOOSSS chemiosmosis
CEHIIMNOOSTT monotheistic
CEHIIMNOPRUY perionychium
CEHIIMNOPSST phonemicists
CEHIIMOORSTT trichotomies
CEHIINNOPRTY pericynthion
CEHIINOOPRSS rhinoscopies
CEHIINOORSSS isochronises

CEHIINOORSSZ isochronizes
CEHIIOPRRSTU peritrichous
CEHIIOPRSSVY viceroyships
CEHIKLMORSTY locksmithery
CEHIKNOSSSST stockishness
CEHILLNNOPSU punchinellos
CEHILLNOOPSS colonelships
CEHILLOPPTYY polyphyletic
CEHILMMOPRYY myrmecophily
CEHILMNOOPTY monophyletic
CEHILMNOPPTY nympholeptic
CEHILNNOSSSW clownishness
CEHILOOPRTTU luteotrophic
CEHILOQSTTUY coquettishly
CEHILORRTTUU horticulture
CEHILPPRRSUU persulphuric
CEHIMMOOPRRT morphometric
CEHIMMOOPRST chemotropism
CEHIMNORRTYY erythromycin
CEHIMOOPRRTT thermotropic
CEHIMOORSTYZ zoochemistry
CEHIMOOSSSST schistosomes
CEHIMOPPRSST coppersmiths
CEHINNOOPRSV convenorship
CEHINNORRSSY synchroniser
CEHINNORRSYZ synchronizer
CEHINNORSSSY synchronises
CEHINNORSSYZ synchronizes
CEHINOOPRRSS coronerships
CEHINOORRSST orchestrions
CEHIOOOPPRST photocopiers
CEHIOOPPRRST tropospheric
CEHIOOPRSTTY hyperostotic
CEHLLLOPRSSY sclerophylls
CEHMNORSTUUX Hurstmonceux
CEHMOOOOPPST photocompose
CEHMOOOOPRTY oophorectomy
CEHMOOSSSTUU customshouse
CEHNOOOPRRSU necrophorous
CEHNOOPRRTTU photocurrent
CEHOOPRRSTUY urethroscopy
CEHOPPRSTTYY cryptophytes
CEIIIIILNSTV incivilities
CEIIIILMPSST simplicities
CEIIIILPRSTT triplicities
CEIIILLMNPSU penicilliums
CEIIILLNPTXY inexplicitly
CEIIILMNPSST implicitness
CEIIILOPRSTV proclivities
CEIIIMNOPRSS precisionism
CEIIINNORSTU reunionistic
CEIIINNOSSTW Wisconsinite
CEIIINNOSTTU continuities
CEIIINOPRSST precisionist
CEIIINORTTWZ zwitterionic
CEIIINOSSTVV vivisections
CEIIJLNNTUVY injunctively
CEIIJNNOORTT introjection
CEIIKLLPSSTT lickspittles
CEIIKLOOPSTY poikilocytes
CEIIKPRSSSTT spitstickers
CEIILLNOSTUY licentiously
CEIILLRSTUUV silviculture
CEIILMNNOOPT incompletion
CEIILMNNOSTY omnisciently
CEIILMNOSSUX exclusionism
CEIILMOPRTUV pluviometric
CEIILNOOSTTU elocutionist
CEIILNOPRSUY perniciously
CEIILNOSSTUX exclusionist
CEIILOPRSSUU supercilious
CEIILRRTTUUV viticulturer
CEIILRSTTUUV viticultures
CEIIMMNOORSS commissioner
CEIIMMNOPRTU minicomputer
CEIIMNOOPSTT competitions
CEIIMNORSSTU neuroticisms
CEIIMOORSSTT sociometrist
CEIIMORRRSTW microwriters
CEIINNNORSTU internuncios
CEIINNNOSSTT inconsistent
CEIINNORRSTU insurrection
CEIINOOPRRTY incorporeity
CEIINOORSSST consistories
CEIINOPPRRST prescription
CEIINORRSSTT restrictions
CEIINORSSTUX excursionist
CEIINORSTTVY ventricosity
CEIINOSTTTUV constitutive
CEIINRRSSSTU scrutinisers
CEIINRRSSTUZ scrutinizers
CEIIOPPRRSTV proscriptive
CEIIPRRRSTTW scriptwriter
CEIIPSSTTUVY susceptivity
CEIKLNOORRST crinkleroots
CEIKLOOSSTUY leukocytosis
CEIKMNNOORST moonstricken
CEIKNNORSSTU countersinks
CEILLLMNOUUV involucellum
CEILLLNOOOSV violoncellos
CEILLMOOOTVY locomotively
CEILLMOPSUVY compulsively
CEILLMOSTUUY meticulously
CEILLNOSUVVY convulsively
CEILLOPRSSTU portcullises
CEILLRSTUUVY sylviculture
CEILMNOOOSUY monoeciously
CEILMNOOSTUU contumelious
CEILMNOPRSTY polycentrism
CEILMOOOPSSS cosmopolises
CEILMOOOPSST cosmopolites
CEILNNOSSTTY consistently
CEILNOORRTTU interlocutor
CEILNOORSSUY censoriously
CEILNOORSTUW Low Countries
CEILNOSSSSUU lusciousness
CEILNOSSTUUY incestuously
CEILOPRRTUVY corruptively
CEIMMNNORSTY nonsymmetric
CEIMMOOPRRSS compromisers
CEIMNNOOPRSU mispronounce
CEIMNNOORSTU conterminous
CEIMNOOPRSSS compressions
CEIMNOOPRSTU mucoproteins

CEIMNOPRSTTY	streptomycin
CEIMNOPSSTUV	consumptives
CEIMNOPSSTUY	pneumocystis
CEIMNORSSSTU	consumerists
	misconstrues
CEIMOOORRSTV	visceromotor
CEIMOOPRRSTU	micropterous
CEINNOOPRTTU	counterpoint
CEINNOOPRTVW	Provincetown
CEINNOORSSSU	connoisseurs
CEINNOSSTTTU	constituents
CEINOOPRSSTU	prosecutions
CEINORSSTTTU	constituters
CEINPSSSTTUU	intussuscept
CEINRRSSSTTU	instructress
CEIOOOOPRSTT	osteoporotic
CEIOOPRSTTYZ	cryptozoites
CEIPPRRSSSTU	superscripts
CELLLOORSSUY	colourlessly
CELLMOOPRRST	comptrollers
CELMNOPRTUUU	mucopurulent
CELNOOPRSTTU	counterplots
CEMMNNNOOSSU	uncommonness
CEMMOOSTUXYY	myxomycetous
CEMNNOORTUWY	countrywomen
CEMNOOPSTTUU	contemptuous
CENNOSSSTUUU	unctuousness
CEPRRSSSTTUU	superstructs
CFFGINOORSSU	offscourings
CFFGINORRSSU	crossruffing
CFGHIIKNOPRT	pitchforking
CFGIIILMMNOR	microfilming
CFGILMNNOORY	conformingly
CFGILMNOORTY	comfortingly
CFHIILNOOSSS	ichnofossils
CFIIILOSTTUY	fictitiously
CFIIKLLOORST	folkloristic
CFIILLNOOSTU	solifluction
CFIILMOORSSS	microfossils
CFIIMNNOORTY	inconformity
CFILNORSSUUU	furunculosis
CFIMNNOORTUY	unconformity
CFLLOORSSUUY	scrofulously
CGGHIINOPRTY	copyrighting
CGGIINNNORST	constringing
CGHHIINORTUW	witching hour
CGHIIIINNRST	trichinising
CGHIIIINNRTZ	trichinizing
CGHIIKLMNOST	locksmithing
CGHIILOOOPRT	oligotrophic
CGHIILOOOSTY	stoichiology
CGHIILOORSTT	trichologist
CGHIIMNOOPSY	physiognomic
CGHIIMOOPRTT	thigmotropic
CGHILMOOPSSY	psychologism
CGHILNOOORST	chronologist
CGHILOOORSST	chorologists
CGHILOOPSSTY	phycologists
	psychologist
CGHIMNOORSST	shortcomings
CGHINOOOPPTY	photocopying
CGHINOOPSSSY	psychognosis
CGHINORSTTTU	shortcutting
CGIIIILNOPST	politicising
CGIIIILNOPTZ	politicizing
CGIIIMNOSSTY	misogynistic
CGIIINNRSSTU	scrutinising
CGIIINNRSTUZ	scrutinizing
CGIILMOOSSTU	musicologist
CGIILNNNOTUY	continuingly
CGIILNNOPRSY	conspiringly
CGIILNOOOSST	iconologists
CGIILOOOSSST	sociologists
CGIILOOOSTTX	toxicologist
CGIIMMNOOPRS	compromising
CGIINNOSTTTU	constituting
CGILMOOOSSST	cosmologists
CGILNOOSTUUY	contiguously
CGILOOOPRSTT	proctologist
CGILOOPRSTTY	cryptologist
CGIMNOOOSSST	cosmogonists
CGINOOPRSSTY	pyrognostics
CGLMOOOOTXYY	mycotoxology
CHHIIOOPPRST	phosphoritic
CHHILMOPRTYY	polyrhythmic
CHHIMOOOPRRT	orthomorphic
CHHIOOOPPRTT	phototrophic
CHHLMOOPRTUY	chlorophytum
CHHLOOOPRSUY	hypochlorous
CHHMMOOOORSU	homochromous
CHIIIORSSSTT	historicists
CHIILNOOPRTY	Trichinopoly
CHIIMNNRSSTY	strychninism
CHIIMNOOPSTY	monophysitic
CHIINNOORTTY	nonrhoticity
CHIINOOPTTYY	hypotonicity
CHILOOOPPRSU	coprophilous
CHILOOPSSTUY	polystichous
CHIMMNOOORST	monochromist
CHIMNNORSSSY	synchronisms
CHIMNOOOPRST	monostrophic
CHIMNOOORSTU	monotrichous
CHIMNOOOSSTU	monostichous
CHIMNOOPRRSS	prochronisms
CHIMNOPRSTYY	chymotrypsin
CHIMOOOPPRRT	protomorphic
CHIMOOORSTTU	trichotomous
CHINOOOPRSTY	ornithoscopy
CHINOOPPSTTY	posthypnotic
CHIOOOPPRRTT	prototrophic
CHIOOOPRRSTV	Rostropovich
CHKLMOOPRTUY	Plymouth Rock
CHKMNOOORRTT	Throckmorton
CHLMOOOPRSUY	polychromous
CHLOOOPSTUYY	hypocotylous
CHMNOOOSTTTU	cottonmouths
CHNNOORRSSTY	synchrotrons
CHNNOORRTTUY	North Country
CIIIIKKKNNNN	kinnikinnick
CIIIIOPSSTTV	positivistic
CIIILLMMNORS	millimicrons
CIIILLMPTTUY	multiplicity
CIIINNOPRSST	inscriptions
CIILLOOSSTUY	solicitously

CIILMNNORSUY synclinorium
CIILMNOOOPST monopolistic
CIILNNNNOOSU noninclusion
CIILNOOPSSTU liposuctions
CIILOORSTUVY victoriously
CIILOPSSSUUY suspiciously
CIIMMNNOOSTU comminutions
CIIMMOORSSTT microtomists
CIIMNOOOPSST compositions
CIIMNOPRSTTY nyctitropism
CIIMNRSSSTTU misinstructs
CIIMOPRRSSTU scriptoriums
CIINNOOPRRTU incorruption
CIINNOOSTTTU constitution
CIINNORSSTTU instructions
CIINOOPPRRST proscription
CIJLNORSSTUU jurisconsult
CILLMOOPRSUY compulsorily
CILLORRSSUUY scurrilously
CILNNOOOSTUV convolutions
CILNNOOSTUUY continuously
CILNOOOPRSTU colourpoints
CIMMNNNOOSTU noncommunist
CIMMOOORSSTU microstomous
CIMOOOPRRSSU microsporous
CINOORSSTTTU constitutors
CLLOPRSSUUUY scrupulously
CLNOPRSSUUUU unscrupulous
DDDDEEEEEFIL fiddledeedee
DDDEEEILMNRT intermeddled
DDDEEENRRSSU underdressed
DDDEEFHIIIMU dehumidified
DDDEEFHILRSU Huddersfield
DDDEEIIIMPSY epididymides
DDDEEINRSTUU understudied
DDDEHNNOOORR rhododendron
DDEEEEGIRRST deregistered
DDEEEEIMNRRT redetermined
DDEEEEMNNSST dementedness
DDEEEENNSSTX extendedness
DDEEEENORTVX overextended
DDEEEENRRSTU understeered
DDEEEENRSSSV deservedness
DDEEEFGINNRU underfeeding
DDEEEFMNORSS deformedness
DDEEEGINOSXY deoxygenised
DDEEEGINOXYZ deoxygenized
DDEEEHLMNRUW underwhelmed
DDEEEIINSSST desensitised
DDEEEIINSSTZ desensitized
DDEEEILMNRST intermeddles
DDEEEILMNRTY determinedly
DDEEEIMNNRTU undetermined
DDEEEIMOPRSW disempowered
DDEEEINNNPST independents
DDEEEINNPRST interdepends
DDEEEIOPPRST predeposited
DDEEELLMMOSY meddlesomely
DDEEELNOPPRU underpeopled
DDEEELNOPRRT Old Pretender
DDEEELNOPRUV underdevelop
DDEEENOPRRUW underpowered
DDEEENOPRSUX underexposed
DDEEENORSUVZ rendezvoused
DDEEFHIIIMRU dehumidifier
DDEEFHIIIMSU dehumidifies
DDEEFIIINNTU unidentified
DDEEGHHOOPRS Good Shepherd
DDEEGHIILMTW middleweight
DDEEGHINORSY hydrogenised
DDEEGHINORYZ hydrogenized
DDEEGILMNOST dislodgement
DDEEGILNORUV overindulged
DDEEGNOPRSSU groundspeeds
DDEEHIIINRST disinherited
DDEEHIIIPPPS Pheidippides
DDEEHIILNOOT endothelioid
DDEEHINOPSTY dehypnotised
DDEEHINOPTYZ dehypnotized
DDEEIILMMNPS simpleminded
DDEEIILQSTUY disquietedly
DDEEIKNNRRUW wunderkinder
DDEEILNNPSSS splendidness
DDEEILNOPSSS lopsidedness
DDEEIMNNOSTW disendowment
DDEEINNRRSUU underinsured
DDEEINORRSTV overstridden
DDEEINRSSTUU understudies
DDEEIOPSSSSS dispossessed
DDEELNNOPSTY despondently
DDEEMNOOSSTU outmodedness
DDEEMNPRRTUU undertrumped
DDEENOPPPRRU underpropped
DDEFNOOOPRSU soundproofed
DDEGGIINNRRU undergirding
DDEGHILNRSUY shudderingly
DDEGILMNOSST dislodgments
DDEGILNNOPSS ploddingness
DDEGILNNOPSY despondingly
DDEGILNOORST dendrologist
DDEGLNOOORSU dendrologous
DDEGNNORRSUU undergrounds
DDEHIIIMNNSU undiminished
DDEHILNNOOPR philodendron
DDEIIILPRSTY dispiritedly
DDEIIJLNOSTY disjointedly
DDEIILNNOORR liriodendron
DDEIINRSTUWY industrywide
DDEILNOPRUVY unprovidedly
DDEIMOOPPSUU pseudopodium
DDEINNOOSSTT endodontists
DDEJKLNNOORS Nordenskjöld
DDENNORSTTUV von Rundstedt
DDINOOOPRSTT diprotodonts
DEEEEFHILNSS needlefishes
DEEEEGMNNNRT engenderment
DEEEEHILRSSW sidewheelers
DEEEEHLNSSSS heedlessness
DEEEEHNPRRRS reprehenders
DEEEEIILRRSV redeliveries
DEEEEIMNPRRT predetermine
DEEEEIMNPRTX experimented
DEEEEIMNRRST redetermines
DEEEELNNSSSS needlessness

DEEEELOPRRSV redevelopers
DEEEEMOPRSST speedometers
DEEEENRRRVVY Very Reverend
DEEEENRRSSSV reservedness
DEEEFIINNSST definiteness
DEEEFINPRRSU superrefined
DEEEFNNQRTUU unfrequented
DEEEGGHILNRT greenlighted
DEEEGHHOPPRS hedgehoppers
DEEEGHINNPRR reprehending
DEEEGHIORTVW overweighted
DEEEGHNNRSTT strengthened
DEEEGIIILMST delegitimise
DEEEGIIILMTZ delegitimize
DEEEGIILNRRV redelivering
DEEEGIIMNSST disesteeming
DEEEGILNOPRV redeveloping
DEEEGIMNNRTU unregimented
DEEEGINNORST roentgenised
DEEEGINNORTZ roentgenized
DEEEGINNRSSS resignedness
DEEEGINOSSXY deoxygenises
DEEEGINOSXYZ deoxygenizes
DEEEGINRRSTU unregistered
DEEEGJMNPRTU prejudgement
DEEEGORRRSST retrogressed
DEEEHILMNSTV dishevelment
DEEEHIMOPRSV empoverished
DEEEHIMPRSST deemstership
DEEEHMNNORTT dethronement
DEEEIILNORRT Indre-et-Loire
DEEEIIMNPRSY Midi-Pyrénées
DEEEIINRSSST desensitiser
DEEEIINRSSSV derisiveness
DEEEIINRSSTZ desensitizer
DEEEIINSSSST desensitises
DEEEIINSSSTZ desensitizes
DEEEIIORRSTX exteriorised
DEEEIIORRTXZ exteriorized
DEEEIKLNOSST skeletonised
DEEEIKLNOSTZ skeletonized
DEEEILMOPRSY depolymerise
DEEEILMOPRYZ depolymerize
DEEEILMPRTVY redemptively
DEEEILNNOPST needlepoints
DEEEILNRSSSW wildernesses
DEEEILNRSTTY interestedly
DEEEILNSSSUV delusiveness
DEEEILPRSSVY depressively
DEEEIMNOPRRT redemptioner
DEEEIMNORSTT densitometer
DEEEIMNRRSTW Midwesterner
DEEEIMNRSSTV disseverment
DEEEIMOPRSTX extemporised
DEEEIMOPRTXZ extemporized
DEEEIMPRRTTT pretermitted
DEEEINNRSTTU uninterested
DEEEINOPPRTU neuropeptide
DEEEINORRTVW overwintered
DEEEINPRRSST interspersed
DEEEINPRSTUX expenditures
DEEEINRRSSSV vinedressers
DEEEIPPRSSST sidesteppers
DEEEIPRRSSSU depressurise
DEEEIPRRSSUZ depressurize
DEEEKLNNOOST endoskeleton
DEEELLNRRSSU undersellers
DEEELMNNORSY moneylenders
DEEELMNOPRTY redeployment
DEEELMNOPSTV developments
DEEELMNOSTVV devolvements
DEEELMNPPSTU supplemented
DEEELNORSSSV resolvedness
DEEELNRRSTTU underletters
DEEELNRRSUVY unreservedly
DEEELOOPRSVV overdevelops
DEEEMNNORSST endorsements
DEEEMNORRSTV Most Reverend
DEEEMPRSTTUW trumpetweeds
DEEENOPRSSUX underexposes
DEEENRRRRSSU surrenderers
DEEENRRSSTTT trendsetters
DEEEOPPRRSUW superpowered
DEEEOPPRSSSS prepossessed
DEEFFFGINSTU feedingstuff
DEEFFHINRRSU undersheriff
DEEFGHHORSTU feedthroughs
DEEFGIIINPRS presignified
DEEFGJMNORTU forejudgment
DEEFHIIIMNSS semifinished
DEEFHIINNSSS fiendishness
DEEFHJLNNOOY John of Leyden
DEEFIIIILNST infidelities
DEEFIIILNNTY indefinitely
DEEFIIILNTVY definitively
DEEFIIIMNNRS indemnifiers
DEEFIIIRRSSV diversifiers
DEEFIILMRSSU demulsifiers
DEEFIILNNRRU unfriendlier
DEEFIILNNRSS friendliness
DEEFIILNRSTU unfertilised
DEEFIILNRTUZ unfertilized
DEEFILLPSTUY despitefully
DEEFILOPRSTT potter's field
DEEFLOORSTUY surefootedly
DEEFMOOPRRTU outperformed
DEEGGHHINOPP hedgehopping
DEEGGIINNPRS predesigning
DEEGGIINPRST predigesting
DEEGGIMNORST disgorgement
DEEGHIILLNSV dishevelling
DEEGHIINNSTW winding sheet
DEEGHIINSTUX extinguished
DEEGHINNORTY heterodyning
DEEGHINORSSY hydrogenises
DEEGHINORSYZ hydrogenizes
DEEGHINRSSST nightdresses
DEEGHNORSSTU groundsheets
DEEGIIIINNST indigenities
DEEGIILMNNRT intermingled
DEEGIILMOOPY epidemiology
DEEGIILNNRSS slenderising
DEEGIILNNRSZ slenderizing
DEEGIILNNSSY yieldingness

DEEGIILOOPPT oligopeptide
DEEGIILOPSTT epiglottides
DEEGIILRSSVY digressively
DEEGIIMNNOST demonetising
DEEGIIMNNOTZ demonetizing
DEEGIIMNPRST distempering
DEEGIINNORST nitrogenised
DEEGIINNORTZ nitrogenized
DEEGIINNPRST predestining
DEEGIINOPRST predigestion
redepositing
DEEGIINORSST redigestions
DEEGIINPPSST sidestepping
DEEGIJMMNSTU misjudgement
DEEGILLNNRSU underselling
DEEGILLNRSSW well dressing
DEEGILMNNNOY moneylending
DEEGILMNOOOS demonologies
DEEGILMNSTUV divulgements
DEEGILMOOSTY etymologised
DEEGILMOOTYZ etymologized
DEEGILNNRTTU underletting
DEEGILNORSUV overindulges
DEEGILNPRSSY depressingly
DEEGINNNPRTU unpretending
DEEGINNNRSSU enduringness
DEEGINNOPRSV overspending
DEEGINNRRRSU surrendering
DEEGINNRSTTT trendsetting
DEEGINNRSTTU undersetting
DEEGINORRSSV overdressing
DEEGLLOOSTYY dysteleology
DEEGLNNOOSUY endogenously
DEEHHIIMOPRS hemispheroid
DEEHHIOPPRSW horsewhipped
DEEHHIOPSSTY hypothesised
DEEHHIOPSTYZ hypothesized
DEEHHLOORSSU householders
DEEHIILNQRSU relinquished
DEEHIILNSSSV devilishness
DEEHIIMOPRSV impoverished
DEEHIINOSSST dishonesties
DEEHIINPRSST residentship
DEEHILLORSTT titleholders
DEEHILMMNOST demolishment
DEEHILOOPRST heteroploids
DEEHILPRSSUU desulphurise
DEEHILPRSUUZ desulphurize
DEEHIMMNORST endothermism
DEEHINOPSSTY dehypnotises
DEEHINOPSTYZ dehypnotizes
DEEHIOPPRTTY pteridophyte
DEEHKNOOOSUW Kenwood House
DEEHLPRSTTUU sulphuretted
DEEHMOORRSTY hydrometeors
DEEHNNORSTTU thunderstone
DEEIIILLRSST distilleries
DEEIIIMNRTTV divertimenti
DEEIIINORRST interiorised
DEEIIINORRTZ interiorized
DEEIIINSSSVV divisiveness
DEEIIKLLNRTW winterkilled
DEEIIKNNRTTT interknitted
DEEIILMNSSSU disseminules
DEEIILNNSSUW unwieldiness
DEEIILNOPRSS lepidosirens
DEEIILNRSSTU unsterilised
DEEIILNRSTUZ unsterilized
DEEIILOPRSSY erysipeloids
DEEIILPRSSVY dispersively
DEEIIMNNRSTT disinterment
DEEIIMNORSTT endometritis
DEEIIMNORTTV divertimento
DEEIIMNPSSST dissepiments
DEEIIMNRRSST irredentisms
DEEIIMNRSSTT determinists
DEEIIMORRTTU dumortierite
DEEIINNPRSST intrepidness
DEEIINNSSSTT dissentients
DEEIINOOPRST repositioned
DEEIINPRSSST spiritedness
DEEIINQSSSTU disquietness
DEEIINRRSSTT irredentists
DEEIINRSSSTT disinterests
DEEIINRSTTTW intertwisted
DEEIIOOPRSST depositories
DEEIIOQSSSUX sesquioxides
DEEIIRRSSSTW weird sisters
DEEIIRSSTTUV divestitures
DEEIJNORRRSU surrejoinder
DEEIKMNPPSSU pumpkinseeds
DEEILLLLOOPV Léopoldville
DEEILLNNQTUY delinquently
DEEILMNNSSSS mindlessness
DEEILNNOOPRS prednisolone
DEEILNNSSSSW windlessness
DEEILNOOPPRT lepidopteron
DEEILOPPPSTY polypeptides
DEEILOPPRSUV oversupplied
DEEILOPRSSTY proselytised
DEEILOPRSTYZ proselytized
DEEIMNNORSST indorsements
DEEIMNNPSSTU impudentness
DEEIMNNRSTTU instrumented
DEEIMNOOPRSS monodisperse
DEEIMNORSTTY densitometry
DEEIMOOPRSTT dioptometers
DEEIMOPPRRST pteridosperm
DEEIMOPPRSSU superimposed
DEEIMOPRRSTT Redemptorist
DEEINNNORSST nonresidents
DEEINNOQSTUU unquestioned
DEEINNPRSSTU superintends
DEEINNRRTTUW underwritten
DEEINORSSSSU desirousness
DEEINPRSSUUV unsupervised
DEEINRRRSTUW underwriters
DEEIOOPRSSTU eurodeposits
DEEIOORRSTTV detritovores
DEEIOPSSSSSS dispossesses
DEELMNORSTUY tremendously
DEELMOORSTVY overmodestly
DEELNORSSSSW wordlessness
DEELNOSSSSUU sedulousness

DEENNNOSSTUW	unwontedness
DEENOOPRSSST	dessertspoon
DEENOOPRSSTU	uprootedness
DEENOPPPRRRU	underpropper
DEENORRSSTUY	understoreys
DEENORSSSTUX	dextrousness
DEENPPRSSSUU	unsuppressed
DEFGHILLLTUY	delightfully
DEFGIIIMNNNY	indemnifying
DEFGIIINNRTY	denitrifying
DEFGIIINNSST	disinfesting
DEFGIIINRSVY	diversifying
DEFGIIINRTVY	devitrifying
DEFGIILMNSUY	demulsifying
DEFGIILNNORT	interfolding
DEFGIIMNSTYY	demystifying
DEFGIINORSST	disforesting
DEFGINNOPTUY	typefounding
DEFGJMNORSTU	forjudgments
DEFHINPRSSTT	spendthrifts
DEFIIILMSTUY	semifluidity
DEFIILNOORSX	dorsiflexion
DEFIILOPRSUY	perfidiously
DEFIINOPRSTU	profundities
DEFIOORRSSUU	sudoriferous
DEFNNOOPRSSU	profoundness
DEGGHLNOORSW	hornswoggled
DEGGHLOOORYY	hydrogeology
DEGGKLLRSUUY	skullduggery
DEGHHIINOPST	diphthongise
DEGHHIINOPTZ	diphthongize
DEGHHIORSSTT	shortsighted
DEGHIIILNRSS	disrelishing
DEGHIILLNOTT	titleholding
DEGHILMOOSTY	mythologised
DEGHILMOOTYZ	mythologized
DEGHILNNRTUY	thunderingly
DEGHNORRSTUW	undergrowths
DEGIIILNNSTT	disentitling
DEGIIILNPPSS	sideslipping
DEGIIIMNNNOS	dimensioning
DEGIIINNNRTW	interwinding
DEGIIINNNSTW	disentwining
DEGIIINNORST	disorienting
DEGIIINNRRST	disinterring
DEGIIINNSSTV	disinvesting
DEGIIKNNORRV	overdrinking
DEGIILLOOSTT	deltiologist
DEGIILNNOSUY	indigenously
DEGIILNNSSTY	dissentingly
DEGIILNORSSV	redissolving
DEGIINNNNPRU	underpinning
DEGIINNOSSUU	disingenuous
DEGIINNRRTUW	underwriting
DEGIINOPPRSS	predisposing
DEGIINORRSTV	overstriding
DEGIJMMNSSTU	misjudgments
DEGIKMNOPRSU	superkingdom
DEGILMNOOOST	demonologist
DEGILNNORSUY	resoundingly
DEGILNOOOSTT	deontologist
DEGILOOPRSTT	proglottides
DEGINNOQRTUU	underquoting
DEGINOOPPRST	doorstepping
DEGLLNORSSUW	groundswells
DEGLLNORSSUY	groundlessly
DEHHIIILMOOP	hemophilioid
DEHHILOSSSTU	South Shields
DEHHIOPRRTYY	hyperthyroid
DEHHLNOSSTUU	sleuthhounds
DEHIIILNOPRS	siderophilin
DEHIIIMMNNST	diminishment
DEHIIKLLNOOU	unlikelihood
DEHIILPRSSTU	trisulphides
DEHILLOPPSUY	polysulphide
DEHILNOPSSSS	slipshodness
DEHILOOPRRSV	overlordship
DEHIMMNOOPRS	endomorphism
DEHINNOOQRUY	hydroquinone
DEHINNORRSUU	undernourish
DEHINOOPRSST	spinsterhood
DEHINOORRSSU	dishonourers
DEHIOOOPPRST	photoperiods
DEHIOOPRSSTT	orthopedists
DEHLLOORRTWY	otherworldly
DEHLNOORRSUY	horrendously
DEHLNOORSTTW	Old Northwest
DEHLNORSTUUY	thunderously
DEHMNORRSTTU	thunderstorm
DEHMOOPPRSSU	pseudomorphs
DEHNOOOOPRST	odontophores
DEHNOOOORTXY	neoorthodoxy
	neo-orthodoxy
DEHNOOORSTUW	southernwood
DEHNRRSSTTUU	underthrusts
DEIIIILSSTTU	disutilities
DEIIILMNTUVY	diminutively
DEIILLOOQSSU	soliloquised
DEIILLOOQSUZ	soliloquized
DEIILPRSTUVY	disruptively
DEIIMORSSSTT	dosimetrists
DEIJNPRRSTUU	jurisprudent
DEILMNOOOPTU	leontopodium
DEIMNOPSTUYY	pseudonymity
DEINOOOPPRRT	proportioned
DEINOSSSSTUU	studiousness
DEIOOPRSSSSS	dispossessor
DELLMNOOSSTU	modus tollens
DELNNOOPSTYY	polysyndeton
DELNOOORSSSU	dolorousness
DELNOPSSTUUY	stupendously
DEMNOOPSSUUY	pseudonymous
DENNOORSSSUW	wondrousness
DFGHIINNOSTW	downshifting
DFGHIMNOORRY	hydroforming
DGGGILNNRUUY	ungrudgingly
DGGHINNOTTUU	doughnutting
DGGIILNNRSTU	disgruntling
DGGIILNSSTUY	disgustingly
DGHIINNOORSU	dishonouring
DGHILOORSSTY	hydrologists
DGIIILOORSST	iridologists
DGIILOOPRSUY	prodigiously
DGILNOOOOSTT	odontologist

DGINNORRSSUU surroundings
DHHIILOOPPPS phospholipid
DHHILOOPRSUY hydrophilous
DHHIOOPRSTYY hypothyroids
DHIIIMMOOPRS idiomorphism
DHILNOOQRSUY hydroquinols
DHIMOOPRRSTY hydrotropism
DHINOOORSTTT orthodontist
DHIOOORSTTUW withoutdoors
DHLNOOOPPTYY polyphyodont
DHLNOOORTUXY unorthodoxly
DIIIINOQSSTU disquisition
DIIIINOSSSTV divisionists
DIIILLNOSSSU disillusions
DIIINOOPSSST dispositions
DIILMNOSTUWW multiwindows
DIILNOOSSSTU dissolutions
DIILNOOSSTUU solitudinous
DILLORSSTUUY stridulously
EEEEEFGINRRS Friese-Greene
EEEEFGHILNRW freewheeling
EEEEFILQRSTU teleferiques
EEEEGIILNPSS spiegeleisen
EEEEGILLNPSU Eulenspiegel
EEEEGILMNRTT telemetering
EEEEHILPQRTU telepherique
EEEEHIMNPRST hemiterpenes
EEEEHINPRRSV reprehensive
EEEEHKOPRSSU housekeepers
EEEEHLMNOPRT nephelometer
EEEEHLNRSSTV nevertheless
EEEEHNNSSTTV seventeenths
EEEEIINRSTVW interviewees
EEEEIISSTVWW sweetiewives
EEEEIMNPRRTX experimenter
EEEEIMNPRSST presenteeism
EEEEIMNPRSSW minesweepers
EEEEIMNRSTTX extensimeter
EEEEINNQRSTU equestrienne
EEEEINSSSTWY eyewitnesses
EEEEIPRSSTTU repetiteuses
EEEEKOPRRSST storekeepers
EEEELMNRSTTT resettlement
EEEELNRSSSST treelessness
EEEELRRSSTTT trestletrees
EEEEMNOPRRTT penetrometer
EEEEMNORSTTX extensometer
EEEENNPRRRTU entrepreneur
EEEENNRRSSTV reverentness
EEEENPRRSSSV perverseness
EEEFFFMNNOST enfeoffments
EEEFFHILRSTW whiffletrees
EEEFFIMORSTU effusiometer
EEEFFINORRST effronteries
EEEFFINSSSUV effusiveness
EEEFFLLNNORW fennelflower
EEEFGILNNSST fleetingness
EEEFGLLNRUVY revengefully
EEEFGLNNSSUV vengefulness
EEEFGNNOORSS foregoneness
EEEFHIKNRRST freethinkers
EEEFHINRRRSW Renfrewshire
EEEFHINRSSSV feverishness
EEEFHMNRRSST refreshments
EEEFIIKLLNSS lifelikeness
EEEFIILLLLMU millefeuille
EEEFIILMPRSX exemplifiers
EEEFIILNRRTT interfertile
EEEFIIMNNNSS feminineness
EEEFILLNSSSS lifelessness
EEEFILNNORVX nonreflexive
EEEFILNSSTTX self-existent
EEEFINOORSST festooneries
EEEFINPRRSSU superrefines
EEEFLLNSSSSS selflessness
EEEFLNNSSTUV eventfulness
EEEFNNQRSSTU frequentness
EEEGHIIMNRSU euhemerising
EEEGHIIMNRUZ euhemerizing
EEEGHIKNOPSU housekeeping
EEEGHILNNRST enlighteners
EEEGHILRTTWW welterweight
EEEGHIMNOSTU meeting house
meetinghouse
EEEGHLNOPSSY phylogeneses
EEEGHNNRRSTT strengthener
EEEGHNOORSTU heterogenous
EEEGHNORSSTT togetherness
EEEGHOORTTYZ heterozygote
EEEGIILMNNTV inveiglement
EEEGIIMNNPSW minesweeping
EEEGIINNORRT orienteering
EEEGIINORSST generosities
EEEGIINPSSST epigenesists
EEEGIKNOPRST storekeeping
EEEGILLNOOSS selenologies
EEEGILNOPRSV oversleeping
EEEGILNRSSTW swingletrees
EEEGILRRSSVY regressively
EEEGIMNRSSSU messeigneurs
EEEGINNORSST roentgenises
EEEGINNORSTZ roentgenizes
EEEGINNPRRST representing
EEEGINNPSSSW sweepingness
EEEGINOOSSST osteogenesis
EEEGINORRSTV oversteering
EEEGINORRTVX overexerting
EEEGINQRSSTU sequestering
EEEGIOQRRSTU grotesquerie
EEEGIPRRRSST preregisters
EEEGLNOORSTT etonogestrel
EEEGMNORSSSU gruesomeness
EEEGMOPRRSTY pyrgeometers
EEEGNNORSSSU generousness
EEEGNOOPRRST progesterone
EEEGNOORRSUV overgenerous
EEEGNOORSSST stereognoses
EEEGORRRSSST retrogresses
EEEHHILLLNPS philhellenes
EEEHHINPSSSS sheepishness
EEEHHMOPRRST thermosphere
EEEHILNPRRSS replenishers
EEEHILPPRSTW whippletrees
EEEHILRSSSTV shirtsleeves

EEEHIMNNNRST enshrinement
EEEHIMNRSTTU hermeneutist
EEEHIMOPRRSV empoverisher
EEEHIMOPRSSV empoverishes
EEEHIMORSSTX heterosexism
EEEHINNOPRRS reprehension
EEEHINOPRRSU superheroine
EEEHINPRSTVY hypertensive
EEEHIORSSTTX heterosexist
EEEHLLNOPTYY polyethylene
EEEHLLNPSSSS helplessness
EEEHLMNOPRTY nephelometry
EEEHLMNOSSSS homelessness
EEEHLNOPSSSS hopelessness
EEEHMMORRSTT thermometers
EEEHMNNNORTT enthronement
EEEHMOORRSTU heteromerous
EEEHMOPRRSST spherometers
EEEHNOPRRRSY reprehensory
EEEHOPPRSSST prophetesses
EEEIIKLNORSY Kyrie eleison
EEEIILPPRSTX perplexities
EEEIILPRTTVY repetitively
EEEIIMNRSSTT mesenteritis
EEEIINPRRTTV interpretive
EEEIINPRSSVX inexpressive
EEEIINRRSTVW interviewers
EEEIIORRSSTX exteriorises
EEEIIORRSTXZ exteriorizes
EEEIIPPRSTTU perpetuities
EEEIIPQRRSTU prerequisite
EEEIIPRRSSTV perversities
EEEIJLNNSSUV juvenileness
EEEIKLNORSTU leukotrienes
EEEIKLNOSSST skeletonises
EEEIKLNOSSTZ skeletonizes
EEEILLLOPPTT little people
EEEILMMNPRST implementers
EEEILMNNPRTY preeminently
EEEILMNNSSSU unseemliness
EEEILMNNSTTT entitlements
EEEILMNSSSST timelessness
EEEILMPPRTVY preemptively
EEEILNNPRTVY preveniently
EEEILNPRRSTT teleprinters
EEEILNPRTVVY preventively
EEEILNRRRTVY irreverently
EEEILNRSSSST tirelessness
EEEILNRSSSTW westerliness
Western Isles
EEEILPRRSSVY repressively
EEEILPRSSVXY expressively
EEEIMNNNSTTW entwinements
EEEIMNNPRSTT presentiment
EEEIMNNPRSTU supereminent
EEEIMNNRRSTT reinterments
EEEIMNOORSTT enterotomies
EEEIMNORSSST tiresomeness
EEEIMNORSSTT sensitometer
tensiometers
EEEIMNPRRSST misrepresent
EEEIMNQQRSUU quinqueremes
EEEIMNQRRSTU requirements
EEEIMNQRSTTU requitements
EEEIMOORRSST stereoisomer
EEEIMOORSSTT stereotomies
EEEIMOPRRSTX extemporiser
EEEIMOPRRTXZ extemporizer
EEEIMOPRSSTX extemporises
EEEIMOPRSTXZ extemporizes
EEEIMPRRRTTT pretermitter
EEEINNPRSSTX inexpertness
EEEINNPRSTUV supervenient
EEEINNRSSSTV inventresses
EEEINORRRSSV reversioners
EEEINPRRRSST enterprisers
EEEINPRRRSTT interpreters
reinterprets
EEEINPRRSSST intersperses
EEEINPRSSTUV eruptiveness
EEEINPRSSUVX unexpressive
EEEINRRTTTUX intertexture
EEEIORRSTVVX extroversive
EEEKLNOOSSTX exoskeletons
EEEKLOOPPPSS spokespeople
EEEKLORRSSTW steelworkers
EEELLLNRSSTY relentlessly
EEELLMORRTTU tellurometer
EEELLNOSSSSV lovelessness
EEELMMNOPRTY reemployment
EEELMNNOOSSS lonesomeness
EEELMNNOPSTV envelopments
EEELMNNSTTTU unsettlement
EEELMNPPRSTU supplementer
EEELMOPPRRTT teleprompter
EEELNNOSSSST tonelessness
EEELNNSSSSTU tunelessness
EEELNOPRSSSS responseless
EEELNORSSSTU resoluteness
EEELNRSSSSST restlessness
EEELOOPRSTTU teleutospore
EEELPRRSSSSU pressureless
EEEMNNPRSSTT presentments
EEEMPRSSSSST sempstresses
EEENOORSSTTT testosterone
EEEOOPRRSUVX overexposure
EEEOPPRSSSSS prepossesses
EEEOPRRRSSUV overpressure
EEFFGHIIRRST firefighters
EEFFLLORSSTY effortlessly
EEFGGIOPRSTT pettifoggers
EEFGGIOPRTTY pettifoggery
EEFGHIIKNNRT freethinking
EEFGHIILNRRT freightliner
EEFGHIILNRTT Ferlinghetti
EEFGHIILRTTW weightlifter
EEFGHIIPRRTZ prizefighter
EEFGHILNRRSY refreshingly
EEFGIIINPRSS presignifies
EEFGIILMNPXY exemplifying
EEFGIIMNNNRT infringement
EEFGIINNORRV overrefining
EEFGIINOPRRT profiteering
EEFGIINSSTUV fugitiveness

EEFGIKNNOORT foretokening
EEFGILLNSSUU guilefulness
EEFGILNNOSUX genuflexions
EEFGIMORSTTU fugitometers
EEFGINOPPRST Epping Forest
EEFHIILRSSSV silverfishes
EEFHNOORRSST foreshortens
EEFIIINNNSST infiniteness
EEFIIINNRSST intensifiers
EEFIILMOPPRT epileptiform
EEFIIMNOPRST mifepristone
EEFIIMNORSSU seminiferous
EEFIINOPRRSS personifiers
EEFIINORRSSU resiniferous
EEFILLORSSTU stelliferous
EEFILMOOORST tomfooleries
EEFILMORRSTU fluorimeters
EEFILMORSTTU flittermouse
EEFILNNQRTUY infrequently
EEFILNOORRTX retroflexion
EEFILNPSSSTU spitefulness
EEFILOOPRRST profiteroles
EEFIMNNORRST frontiersmen
EEFLLMORRSUY remorsefully
EEFLLNNTUUVY uneventfully
EEFLMNORRSUU unremorseful
EEFLMNORSSSS formlessness
EEFLMOORRSTU fluorometers
EEFLNOPRSSUW powerfulness
EEFNOOORSSST footsoreness
EEGGHIILNNNT enlightening
EEGGHIINORVW overweighing
EEGGIILNNRSS gingerliness
EEGGIIMNORST geometrising
EEGGIIMNORTZ geometrizing
EEGGILSSTUVY suggestively
EEGGLLOOOPSX googolplexes
EEGGNOOPRSST progestogens
EEGGNOORSSSU gorgeousness
EEGHHILRSTWW wheelwrights
EEGHHINOORSS horseshoeing
EEGHIILLMRST limelighters
EEGHIILNNPRS replenishing
EEGHIILNPSST slipsheeting
EEGHIIMNNRST intermeshing
EEGHIINOSSST histogenesis
EEGHIINRSSST tigerishness
EEGHIINRSTUX extinguisher
EEGHIINRTTWW winterweight
EEGHIINSSTUX extinguishes
EEGHILMNORVW overwhelming
EEGHILNOPPST teleshopping
EEGHILNOPSSY phylogenesis
EEGHILOORSST theologisers
EEGHILOORSTZ theologizers
EEGHILRSSTTT streetlights
EEGHIMMRSTUW summerweight
EEGHIMNOORSS homogenisers
EEGHIMNOORSZ homogenizers
EEGHIMOORSST isogeotherms
EEGHINNOPSSY hypnogenesis
EEGHINNOSSTT ethnogenists
EEGHINNPSTWY pennyweights
EEGHINOORSST orthogenesis
EEGHINOPSSTY phytogenesis
EEGHLMNNOORS longshoremen
EEGHLOOORSTU heterologous
EEGHMNOORRSW whoremongers
EEGHMNOORRWY whoremongery
EEGHMNOORSTU thermogenous
EEGHNOOORSTU heterogonous
EEGHNOORSTUY heterogynous
EEGHOORSTUYZ heterozygous
EEGIIINNRTVW interviewing
EEGIILLNNNST sentinelling
EEGIILMMNNPT implementing
EEGIILMNNRST intermingles
EEGIILMOOSST semeiologist
EEGIILNOSTTT stilettoeing
EEGIILOPSSTT epiglottises
EEGIIMMNNPST impingements
EEGIIMNNNRSS minnesingers
EEGIIMNNORST remonetising
EEGIIMNNORTZ remonetizing
EEGIINNORSST nitrogenises
EEGIINNORSTZ nitrogenizes
EEGIINNPRRST enterprising
EEGIINNPRRTT interpreting
EEGIINNRSSTW westernising
EEGIINNRSTWZ westernizing
EEGIINNSTTTW Wittgenstein
EEGIKLLNNNNU unkennelling
EEGIKLNORSTW steelworking
EEGILLNOOSST selenologist
EEGILLNRSTWY swelteringly
EEGILLOOPSST speleologist
EEGILLOOSSTT teleologists
EEGILMNOOOST entomologise
EEGILMNOOOTZ entomologize
EEGILMNOORSU numerologies
EEGILMNORRSS mongrelisers
EEGILMOOPSTY epistemology
EEGILMOOSSTY etymologises
EEGILMOOSTYZ etymologizes
EEGILNNORTUV volunteering
EEGILNNSSSSW winglessness
EEGILNOORRSW lower regions
EEGILOPRSSTT poltergeists
EEGIMNNPSSTT temptingness
EEGIMNNRRSTU interregnums
EEGIMNORSSTW swingometers
EEGINNNRRSSU unerringness
EEGINNPRSSSS pressingness
EEGINOOPRRVW overpowering
EEGINOOPRSSS sporogenesis
EEGINOOPRSVX overexposing
EEGINOORSSST stereognosis
EEGINOPPRSTV overstepping
EEGINOPRSSSS repossessing
EEGINOPRSTTY stereotyping
EEGINORSSSUV grievousness
EEGINOSSSUUX exiguousness
EEGINPRRSSST prestressing
EEGINPRSSTTU guttersnipes

EEGIOPRRSSSV progressives
EEGKLLMNSSUU muskellunges
EEGKPPRSTYYZ Kyrgyz Steppe
EEGLMNNOOOPR prolegomenon
EEGMNNORSSST engrossments
EEGNNOORRSUU neurosurgeon
EEGNORRRSUUY neurosurgery
EEGNORSSSSST songstresses
EEHHIIMMOPRT hemimorphite
EEHHIINSSSTV thievishness
EEHHILLNOPTY theophylline
EEHHILMOPRST thermophiles
EEHHILNNORTY Henry the Lion
EEHHINRSSSSW shrewishness
EEHHIOPPRRSW horsewhipper
EEHHIOPRSSTY hypothesiser
EEHHIOPRSTYZ hypothesizer
EEHHIOPSSSTY hypothesises
EEHHIOPSSTYZ hypothesizes
EEHHLLNNOORZ Hohenzollern
EEHHLLOPPRSY phyllosphere
EEHHLLOPRTYY heterophylly
EEHHMNOOPRSY hymenophores
EEHHMOOPRRTY heteromorphy
EEHHMOORSSTU housemothers
EEHHOOPRRSTT heterotrophs
EEHIIIKLNSSU kleinhuisies
EEHIIINRRSTX inheritrixes
EEHIIKKLRRSS Selkirkshire
EEHIIKNPRSSY hyperkinesis
EEHIILNOOPSS eosinophiles
EEHIILNPRSTY prehensility
EEHIILNQRRSU relinquisher
EEHIILNQRSSU relinquishes
EEHIILNRSSSV liverishness
EEHIIMNPPRRU perinephrium
EEHIIMOPRRSV impoverisher
EEHIIMOPRSSV impoverishes
EEHIIMPPRRSS premierships
EEHIINNSSSVX vixenishness
EEHIIOPRRSST prehistories
EEHIKMNNOSSY monkeyshines
EEHILMMOSSTU mesotheliums
EEHILMNNPSST plenishments
EEHILMNORSST motherliness
EEHILMOORSTT lithometeors
EEHILMOPPRSS spermophiles
EEHILNNPSTWY pennywhistle
EEHILNOOPSST siphonostele
EEHILNOPRSTU neutrophiles
EEHILNOPSSTT telephonists
EEHILOPRSSTU upholsteries
EEHIMNOOPRST nephrotomies
EEHIMOPPRRSS emperorships
EEHINNOPRSTY hypertension
EEHINRSSSSTY synthesisers
EEHINRSSSTYZ synthesizers
EEHIPRSSSTTU trusteeships
EEHKOORRSSUW houseworkers
EEHLMNOSTTVW twelvemonths
EEHLNRSSSSTU ruthlessness
EEHLOPRRSSTU reupholsters
upholsterers
EEHMMORSSSUU summerhouses
EEHMNNOOORRU neurohormone
EEHMNNOOORSY honeymooners
EEHMNNOOPRTY hymenopteron
EEHMNOOORSTU heteronomous
EEHMNOORSTUY heteronymous
EEHMOPPRRTYY hypermetropy
EEHMOPPRSSTY spermophytes
EEHMORRSTUUY eurythermous
EEHNNORRSTTW northwestern
EEHNORRSSTTW northwesters
EEHNORSSTTUW southwestern
EEHOOOPRSTTU heterotopous
EEHOOPPSTTTY phototypeset
EEHOOPRRSSTU porterhouses
EEHOOPRSSSTY hyperostoses
EEHOOPRSSTTT photosetters
EEHORSSSTTUW southwesters
EEIIIJLNSTUV juvenilities
EEIIIMNRSSTV intermissive
EEIIIMOOPSST episiotomies
EEIIINORRSST interiorises
EEIIINORRSTZ interiorizes
EEIIINPRRSTU perineuritis
EEIIINRSSTUV universities
EEIIKLLNNSSU unlikeliness
EEIIKLOOPSSU leukopoiesis
EEIIKNQRSSSU quirkinesses
EEIILLNSSSUV illusiveness
EEIILLPPRSST pipistrelles
EEIILMNNPTTY impenitently
EEIILMNNSSTU untimeliness
EEIILMNOPSST impoliteness
EEIILMNRSSST minstrelsies
EEIILMPRSSVY impressively
permissively
EEIILNNRSSTW winterliness
EEIILNPPRSSS slipperiness
EEIILNPRSSST priestliness
EEIILNPSSSST pitilessness
EEIILNRSSSST sisterliness
EEIILNRSSTUV lentiviruses
EEIILOPSTVXY expositively
EEIIMMNNNSST imminentness
EEIIMMNOPRRS minor premise
EEIIMNNNSTTW intwinements
EEIIMNNRTTTT intermittent
EEIIMNOPRRSS reimpression
EEIIMNOSSSSV omissiveness
EEIIMNPRRSTT misinterpret
EEIIMNPRSSUV unimpressive
EEIIMNPRSTTY sempiternity
EEIIMNRRTTUX intermixture
EEIIMORSSTUV semivitreous
EEIINNNORTTV intervention
EEIINNNOSSTV nonsensitive
EEIINNORRSST reinsertions
EEIINNORSTTT retentionist
EEIINNPPSSST snippetiness
EEIINNPRRSWZ prizewinners
EEIINNPSSTUV punitiveness

EEIINNRSSSST sinisterness
EEIINOORSSTV stereovision
EEIINOPPRSST propensities
EEIINOPRRSSV irresponsive
EEIINOPSSSTV positiveness
EEIINORRSTVV introversive
EEIINORRTTVV introvertive
EEIINPRRTTUV interruptive
EEIINRSSTTUV investitures
EEIIOOPRRSST repositories
EEIIOOPRSSTV seropositive
EEIIOPPRSSTV prepositives
EEIIPRSSTVXY expressivity
EEIKLMNNOSTY Milton Keynes
EEIKLNNNORSV Vernoleninsk
EEIKOPRRRSTW worker-priest
EEILLMOSSTVY motivelessly
EEILLMPRSTUX multiplexers
EEILLNNOQTUY ineloquently
EEILLNNOSSSV slovenliness
EEILLNNOSSUV unloveliness
EEILLNSSSSST listlessness
EEILLORRSTUY irresolutely
EEILLRSSSSTY resistlessly
EEILMMNOPRST implementors
EEILMNNOSTVV involvements
EEILMNOOSSST toilsomeness
EEILMNOOSSTZ Simon Zelotes
EEILMNORSTUV volunteerism
EEILMOOPRSST metropolises
EEILMOOPRSTU pleurotomies
EEILMOPPRRTY peremptorily
EEILMOPRSTUV pluviometers
EEILMORSSSTU moistureless
EEILMPRSTUVY resumptively
EEILNNOOPSVX nonexplosive
EEILNOOORSSU oleoresinous
EEILNOOPPRSY polyisoprene
EEILNOORRSTU resolutioner
EEILNOPRSSSU perilousness
EEILNOPRSSVY responsively
EEILNOQSSSTU questionless
EEILNPRSSTTY persistently
EEILNPSSSUVY suspensively
EEILOPPRSSUV oversupplies
EEILOPPRSSVY oppressively
EEILOPRRSSTY proselytiser
EEILOPRRSTYZ proselytizer
EEILOPRSSSTY proselytises
EEILOPRSSTYZ proselytizes
EEILOPSSSSVY possessively
EEIMMNNOOPST empoisonment
EEIMMNOPRSTV improvements
EEIMMNPRSSST impressments
EEIMMPRSSUVV sempervivums
EEIMNNNORSTV environments
EEIMNNOOPPRS perispomenon
EEIMNNOORSTV normotensive
EEIMNNOPSSTT impotentness
EEIMNOPPRRSS improperness
EEIMNOQRSUUU equinumerous
EEIMNORSSTTY sensitometry
EEIMNORSTTZZ mezzotinters
EEIMOPPRSSSU superimposes
EEIMOPRRRSST misreporters
EEINNNORRSTU interneurons
EEINNOPRSSUV unresponsive
EEINNOPRSTUV supervention
EEINNORSSSSU resinousness
EEINOOPPSSST oppositeness
EEINOOPRRSSS responsories
EEINOOPRSSSS repossession
EEINOORRRSTV retroversion
EEINOORRSTTX extortioners
EEINOORRSTVX extroversion
EEINOORSSSTU interosseous
EEINOPPRSSUV unoppressive
EEINOPRSSSSU supersession
suspensories
EEINOPRSSSTV sportiveness
EEINOPRSSSUV perviousness
previousness
EEINORSSSTUV vitreousness
EEINPRRRSTTU interrupters
EEINRRSSTUWW wienerwursts
EEIOPPRRRSST proprietress
EEIOPRSSTTTY stereotypist
EEIORRRSSTUV retroviruses
EEIORRSSSTWW Swiss Re Tower
EEIPRRRSSSSU pressurisers
EEIPRRRSSSUZ pressurizers
EEKKOORRRSTV voortrekkers
EEKLNORSSSSW worklessness
EEKNNOORSTTT Stoke-on-Trent
EEKNOOPPRSSS spokesperson
EEKNOORRSSTW stoneworkers
EELLNNOORSSV lovelornness
EELLNOSSSSSU soullessness
EELLORRSSTTY storytellers
EELMMNNOPTUY unemployment
EELMOPPRRSUY superpolymer
EELNOOPPPRSY polypropenes
EELNOPRRSTUU seropurulent
EELNOPSSSSST spotlessness
EEMNNOOPPSTT postponement
EEMNNOORSSSU enormousness
EEMNNOOSSSUV venomousness
EEMNNORSSSUU numerousness
EEMNNRSSTTTU entrustments
EENNOOPRRSTU neuropterons
EENNOSSSSSUU sensuousness
EENOOPRRSTUU neuropterous
EENOPRRSSSUY supersensory
EEOOPPRRSSTU preposterous
EEOOPRRSSSSS repossessors
EFFGGHIIINRT firefighting
EFFGIINOOPRR fireproofing
EFFGIINORRTY refortifying
EFFGINORSTUV overstuffing
EFFILNRSSTUU fruitfulness
EFGGGIINOPTT pettifogging
EFGGLOOORSST footsloggers
EFGHHILNTTTW Twelfth Night
EFGHHOORSTTU forethoughts

EFGHIINNRRSU refurnishing
EFGHILNRSSTU rightfulness
EFGIIINNNSTY intensifying
EFGIILLLORSW gilliflowers
EFGIILMNNOSY solemnifying
EFGIILNNORTW interflowing
EFGIILNNRSST triflingness
EFGIILNORSUV griseofulvin
EFGIILNRRTYY terrifyingly
EFGIINNOPRSY personifying
EFGIINNPRRST fingerprints
EFGIINORRTTT retrofitting
EFGILLLORSWY gillyflowers
EFGILLNRTTUY flutteringly
EFGILMNOORST montgolfiers
EFGILNPSTUYY stupefyingly
EFGLNNORSSUW wrongfulness
EFHHILLOOOSY holy of holies
EFHIILQRRSSU squirrelfish
EFHIILRRSSTT shirtlifters
EFHILLRSSTTY thriftlessly
EFHILMNRSSTU mirthfulness
EFHIMNPRSSSU frumpishness
EFHLLNOSSSTU slothfulness
EFHLNOSSTUUY youthfulness
EFHLNRSSTTUU truthfulness
EFHLOOOPRRSU fluorophores
EFIIIILNNTVY infinitively
EFIIIMNORSTU uniformities
EFIILMOPRSVY oversimplify
EFIIMMNORRSS misinformers
EFIIMNOPSSTT postfeminist
EFIINNORSSTU interfusions
EFIINOPRSSTU perfusionist
EFIKLLLNSSSU skillfulness
EFILNOOPSSTT toploftiness
EFILNRSSSTTU tristfulness
EFIOOOPRRSSU soporiferous
EFLLOPPRSUUY purposefully
EFLMNNORSSUU mournfulness
EFLNOPRSSSTU sportfulness
EFLNRSSSTTUU trustfulness
EFNNNORRRSTU frontrunners
EFNNOORRSSSW forswornness
EGGHHHIILRST highlighters
EGGHHIILSTTW lightweights
EGGHIILNNOOP pigeonholing
EGGHIILNOOST theologising
EGGHIILNOOTZ theologizing
EGGHIIMNNOOS homogenising
EGGHIIMNNOOZ homogenizing
EGGHIINNORTV overnighting
EGGHIINPRSSS priggishness
EGGHILNSSSSU sluggishness
EGGHLNOORSSW hornswoggles
EGGHLOOOOPTY photogeology
EGGIIIILMNST legitimising
EGGIIIILMNTZ legitimizing
EGGIILLMMNRY glimmeringly
EGGIILLNNSTY glisteningly
EGGIILLNRSTY glisteringly
EGGIILLNRTTY glitteringly
EGGIILMNNORS mongrelising
EGGIILMNNORZ mongrelizing
EGGIIMNNORSV misgoverning
EGGIINNNORST rontgenising
EGGIINNNORTZ rontgenizing
EGGIINNNSSST stingingness
EGGILLLNORVY grovellingly
EGGILMMOOSST gemmologists
EGGIMNOOPRSS gossipmonger
EGGINORSTYYZ Szent-Györgyi
EGGLNNOOORTY rontgenology
EGHHHOORRTTU throughother
EGHHILNOSSSU ghoulishness
EGHHMORRTTUY merrythought
EGHHNOORSSTU thoroughness
EGHIIKLNNSST knightliness
EGHIIKNNPRRS preshrinking
EGHIILMMNRSY shimmeringly
EGHIILMNOPRS negrophilism
EGHIILMNPRWY whimperingly
EGHIILNOSTTU silhouetting
EGHIILOORSST hierologists
EGHIILPRSSTT sprightliest
EGHIIMNNOPRS premonishing
EGHIINNSSSTY synthesising
EGHIINNSSTTY synthetising
EGHIINNSSTYZ synthesizing
EGHIINNSTTYZ synthetizing
EGHIINORSTWW Wigtownshire
EGHILMNOORST moonlighters
EGHILMOOOPRS morphologies
EGHILMOOORSS homologisers
EGHILMOOORSZ homologizers
EGHILMOORSTY mythologiser
EGHILMOORTYZ mythologizer
EGHILMOOSSTY mythologises
EGHILMOOSTYZ mythologizes
EGHILNOOPRST nephrologist
phrenologist
EGHILNOOPSST nephologists
phenologists
EGHILNOOSSTT ethnologists
EGHILNOPRSTU upholstering
EGHILNPRSTUU sulphureting
EGHILOOPPSST psephologist
EGHIMNNNOOOY honeymooning
EGHIMNPRSSSU grumpishness
EGHINNOOSSST soothingness
EGHINOOORSTV overshooting
EGHINOOPRRSV governorship
EGHINOOPSTTT photosetting
EGHINOORRTVW overthrowing
EGHINOPRSSSU springhouses
EGHINORRTTUW interwrought
EGHINORSTTTW ghostwritten
EGHIORRSSTTW ghostwriters
EGHMNOOPRSTY Grey-Thompson
EGIIIKLNNNRT interlinking
EGIIILNNNRST interlinings
EGIIILNORSST religionists
EGIIIMNNRTTT intermitting
EGIIIMNOPSTU impetiginous

EGIIINNNPRWZ prizewinning
EGIIINNNRTTW intertwining
EGIIINNNSSTV invitingness
EGIIINNOPSSW Winnipegosis
EGIIKKLNRRSS Kriss Kringle
EGIIKLNPPRRS klipspringer
EGIIKNNNSSST stinkingness
EGIIKNNORRTW interworking
EGIIKNNRSSST strikingness
EGIIKNPRSSTT spirkettings
EGIILLMNPSSS misspellings
EGIILLMNPTUX multiplexing
EGIILLNOPRSV overspilling
EGIILLNORSTU guillotiners
EGIILLNPRSUW wirepullings
EGIILLNQRRSU squirrelling
EGIILMMNOPSY misemploying
EGIILMNOPRSY polymerising
EGIILMNOPRYZ polymerizing
EGIILMOOSSST seismologist
semiologists
EGIILNNOORSU nonreligious
EGIILNNORTVV intervolving
EGIILNOOOPSS oligopsonies
EGIILNPPRRSY perspiringly
EGIIMMNRSSTY symmetrising
EGIIMMNRSTYZ symmetrizing
EGIIMNNOPSSS imposingness
EGIIMNNOTTZZ mezzotinting
EGIIMNOOPRRT primogenitor
EGIIMNOORRST risorgimento
EGIIMNOPRRST misreporting
EGIIMRSSSTTU Trismegistus
EGIINNNORTVY inventorying
EGIINNOPRRTV overprinting
EGIINNORRSUV overinsuring
EGIINNORRTTV introverting
EGIINNPRRTTU interrupting
EGIINPRRSSSU pressurising
EGIINPRRSSUZ pressurizing
EGIKLLMNOORY kremlinology
EGILLNORSTTY storytelling
EGILMNNORTTY tormentingly
EGILMNOOOSTT entomologist
EGILMNOORSTU numerologist
EGILMNOOSTYZ enzymologist
EGILMOORSSTT metrologists
EGILMOOSSSTU museologists
EGILMOOSSTTY etymologists
EGILNOOPRSUY pyroligneous
EGILNOORSSSU gloriousness
EGILNOORSSTU neurologists
EGILNOPPRSSY oppressingly
EGILNOPRSTTY protestingly
EGILNRSTTTUY stutteringly
EGILOOORSSTT erotologists
EGILOOOSSSTT osteologists
EGILOOPRSSTT petrologists
EGIMMNOOPRSU spermogonium
EGIMNOORRSSV misgovernors
EGIMNOORRTTY trigonometry
EGIMNOPRRTUV overtrumping
EGINNOPRSTTU unprotesting
EGINNRSSSTTU trustingness
EGINOOPRRSSS progressions
EGINOORRSSSU rigorousness
EGINOORSSSUV vigorousness
EGINOPPPRSSU presupposing
EGIOPRRSSSST progressists
EGLMNNOOPRST prolongments
EHHIILOOPPSS philosophies
philosophise
EHHIILOOPPSZ philosophize
EHHIIMMMOPRS hemimorphism
EHHILOOPPRSS philosophers
EHHILOPPSTUY hyposulphite
EHHIMMOOORTY homoiothermy
EHHIMMOOPRRS rheomorphism
EHHIMMOOPRST theomorphism
EHHIMNOOPRST thermosiphon
EHHIMOOPRRST theriomorphs
EHHINOOOPPRS siphonophore
EHHIOOPPRSST phosphorites
EHHIOOPSSSTT theosophists
EHHIOPSSSTTY hypothesists
EHHMNOOOPRTY phytohormone
EHHOOPPRSSSU phosphoruses
EHIIILORSTTT lithotrities
EHIIIMNPRSST ministership
EHIIKNOOPSST photokinesis
EHIIKNORRSSS Kinross-shire
EHIIKNSSSSTT skittishness
EHIILLMNPSTU phillumenist
EHIILLNOPSTT septillionth
EHIILLNOSTTX sextillionth
EHIILMOOPRST heliotropism
EHIILMRSSSTV silversmiths
EHIILOOPSTTX toxophilites
EHIILOPRRTTT lithotripter
EHIIMMOPPRRS perimorphism
EHIIMNPRSTUX xiphisternum
EHIIMOOPPRSS epimorphosis
EHIINOPRSTTY hyponitrites
EHILLOPPRTYY pyrophyllite
EHILMMOOPPRS pleomorphism
EHILNNOSSTYZ Solzhenitsyn
EHILNOOPRTTU luteotrophin
EHILNOOPSUUY euphoniously
EHILNOORTTWY noteworthily
EHILNPPRSSSU purplishness
EHILNSSSSTTU sluttishness
EHIMMMOOPRSS mesomorphism
EHIMMOORSSTU mesothoriums
EHIMNOOPSSTY monophysites
EHIMNOORSTTU nototheriums
EHIMNORRSTUY erythroniums
EHIMOOPPRRSU perimorphous
EHIMOOPPRRTY pyromorphite
EHIMOOPRSTTT photometrist
EHIMOOPSSTTY mythopoeists
EHIMOPRSSTTY hypsometrist
EHINNORSSTUW unworthiness
EHINOOPRRSTT ornithopters
EHIOOOPRSTTZ trophozoites

EHIOOPRSSSTY hyperostosis
EHIOPQRSSSTU questorships
EHIOPRRSSUVY surveyorship
EHLLMOOPSSUY mesophyllous
EHLMOOOPPRTY photopolymer
EHMMOOOPRSSU mesomorphous
EHMMOOORRSTT thermomotors
EHMNNOORRSTT northernmost
EHMNOOOPRSST monostrophes
EHMNOORSSSUU humorousness
EHMNOORSSTTU southernmost
EHMOOPSSSTTY photosystems
EHNNOOOPRTTU photoneutron
EHOOOPRRSTTU orthopterous
EIIILMNOPSST postliminies
EIIILMNOSSTU luminosities
EIIIMMMNORSS immersionism
EIIIMMNORSST immersionist
EIIIMNNORSST intermission
EIIIMNNPRSTT inspiritment
EIIIMNOOPRST reimposition
EIIIMNORSSTV intromissive
EIIIMPRTTTVY permittivity
EIIINNNOTTUV nonintuitive
EIIINNOORSTT isotretinoin
EIIINOQRSSTU requisitions
EIIINORSSSTV revisionists
EIILLNORSSSU illusoriness
EIILLOOQRSSU soliloquiser
EIILLOOQRSUZ soliloquizer
EIILLOOQSSSU soliloquises
EIILLOOQSSUZ soliloquizes
EIILLPRSSSTY spiritlessly
EIILMNOOSTUV evolutionism
EIILMOOPPRST pleiotropism
EIILMOPRSUVY imperviously
EIILMRSTTUVY multiversity
EIILNOOPPRST lipoproteins
EIILNOORRSTU irresolution
EIILNOOSTTUV evolutionist
EIILNOPRSSTV silverpoints
EIILNOPRSTUY polyneuritis
EIILOOPRSTXY expositorily
EIIMMNNOPRST imprisonment
EIIMMOOPRSTV overoptimism
EIIMNNNQQUUU quinquennium
EIIMNNOOPRST premonitions
EIIMNNORTTTT intromittent
EIIMNORRSTTT intermittors
intromitters
EIIMOOPRSTTV overoptimist
EIIMOPRSSSST prestissimos
EIIMORRSSSTU moisturisers
EIIMORRSSTUZ moisturizers
EIINNOORRSTV introversion
EIINNOPRRTTU interruption
EIINNOPRSSTU interspinous
EIINOOPPRSST prepositions
EIINOOPRRSSV provisioners
reprovisions
EIINOORSTTTX extortionist
EIINOPRSSTTU superstition
EIINORSSTTTU restitutions
EIIOOPPSSTTV postpositive
EIIOORSSTTTU tortuosities
EIIOPPSSSTUV suppositives
EIJLOPRRSUUY perjuriously
EILLMNOOSSTY motionlessly
EILLOPPRSTUY suppletorily
EILMNNOOPTTY omnipotently
EILMNNOSSSUU luminousness
EILMNOOOPRSS monopolisers
EILMNOOOPRSZ monopolizers
EILMOPPRSTUU multipurpose
EILMORSSTTUY multistoreys
EILMORSSTUYY mysteriously
EILNOOPRRSTU retropulsion
EILOORRSSTUY roisterously
EILOPPRSTUVY supportively
EILOPRRSTUVY protrusively
EIMNNOSSSTUU mutinousness
EIMNNRSSTTTU intrustments
EIMNOOOPRRST promontories
EIMNOOORRSST sensorimotor
EIMNOOOSSSTU isostemonous
EIMNOORSSSTU timorousness
EIMNOORSSTTU neurotomists
EIMNOPPRSSTU presumptions
EIMOOPRSSTTT optometrists
EIMOPRSSSSTT postmistress
EINOORSSSUUX uxoriousness
EINOPPRSSSSU suppressions
EINOPRRRSTTU interruptors
EINOPRSSSSUU spuriousness
EINOPSSSTTTY stenotypists
EINORSSSTUUV virtuousness
EIOOOOPRSSST osteoporosis
EKKNNOOSTUVZ Novokuznetsk
ELNOOPPSSSUU populousness
ELNOOPRSTTUY portentously
ELOOPPRRSSUY prosperously
ELOORRSSTTUY stertorously
EMMMNOORSTYY monosymmetry
EMMNOOOPRSSU monospermous
EMOOOPRRSSST mosstroopers
EMOPPRSSTUUU presumptuous
ENNOOORSSSSU sonorousness
ENOOPPRRSSST sportsperson
ENOORSSSTTUU tortuousness
FFGIILNORTYY fortifyingly
FFILLNRTUUUY unfruitfully
FGGGILNOOOST footslogging
FGHHILORRTTY forthrightly
FGHHLLOTTUUY thoughtfully
FGHHLNOTTUUU unthoughtful
FGHIILNORRYY horrifyingly
FGHIMNOOOPRT mothproofing
FGIIIMMNNORS misinforming
FGIILLNOSUUY fuliginously
FGIILMNORTYY mortifyingly
FGIILMNSTYYY mystifyingly
FGILOORSTTUU futurologist
FGINNNNORRTU frontrunning
FGINOOPSSTUY pussyfooting

FHILLOPRSUWY worshipfully
FHLLNRTTUUUY untruthfully
FIIINNOSSSTU infusionists
FIILMMORTTUY multiformity
FIKLLLLNSUUY unskillfully
FILOORSTTUUY fortuitously
GGGHHHIIILNT highlighting
GGGILLNRSTUY strugglingly
GGHHINOORSUU roughhousing
GGHIILMNNOOT moonlighting
GGHIILMNOOOS homologising
GGHIILMNOOOZ homologizing
GGHIILNOPSTT spotlighting
GGHIINORSTTW ghostwriting
GGIIILLNNOTU guillotining
GGIIILNNRTUY intriguingly
GGIILLOORTUY liturgiology
GGILLOOOSSST glossologist
GHHILOOPRSUY hygrophilous
GHHILOPRSTTT trothplights
GHHINOOPRSTU thoroughpins
GHHMNNOOOPST monophthongs
GHHOOORRTTUW thoroughwort
GHIIIILLLNRS Nilgiri Hills
GHIIILLNOPSY lyophilising
GHIIILLNOPYZ lyophilizing
GHIIKLNNNTUY unthinkingly
GHIILLOOPSST philologists
GHIILLOOSSTT lithologists
GHIILNNORSUY nourishingly
GHIILNOORSST rhinologists
GHIILNOPSSTY philogynists
GHIILNPRSSUU sulphurising
GHIILNPRSUUZ sulphurizing
GHIILOOOPSST ophiologists
GHIILOOPSSTY physiologist
GHIILOOSSSTT histologists
GHIIMNOPSSTY physostigmin
GHILLOOOPSST hoplologists
GHILMNOOSSTY hymnologists
GHILMOOOPRST morphologist
GHILMOOSSTTY mythologists
GHILNOOOPSST phonologists
GHILNOOPSSTY hypnologists
GHILOOPSSTTY phytologists
GHIMMOOPRSYZ zygomorphism
GHIMNOOPSSTY gymnosophist
GHLMNOOOOSUY homogonously
GHLMOOOSUYYZ homozygously
GHMOOOPRSUYZ zygomorphous
GIIIIKLLNNNS Inniskilling
GIIIILNORSTV vitriolising
GIIIILNORTVZ vitriolizing
GIIIINOPRRST prioritising
GIIIINOPRRTZ prioritizing
GIIIMNNORTTT intromitting
GIIIMNORSSTU moisturising
GIIIMNORSTUZ moisturizing
GIIINNOOPRSV provisioning
GIILLMNOOSST limnologists
GIILLNOORSUY ingloriously
GIILMMNOOSTU immunologist
GIILMNNOOOPS monopolising
GIILMNNOOOPZ monopolizing
GIILNPRRSSUY surprisingly
GIIMNNNOOOST monotonising
GIIMNNNOOOTZ monotonizing
GIIMNNNOSSYY synonymising
GIIMNNNOSYYZ synonymizing
GIINNOPRSTTU outsprinting
GIINOPPRSTTU outstripping
GIINOPRSTTTU prostituting
GILLLMNOSSUU slumgullions
GILLMOOPSTTY polyglottism
GILLNNNOOPTU nonpolluting
GINNOOPRSSTT strongpoints
GLLNOOSTTUUY gluttonously
GLMMOOOPSTYY symptomology
GLOOOOOPRTYZ protozoology
HHIILNOOPRTY ornithophily
HHILMMOOPRSY hylomorphism
HHILOOOPPSTU photophilous
HHIMMMOOOPRS homomorphism
HHINOOPRRTTY thyrotrophin
HHMMOOOOPRSU homomorphous
HIIIILMNPSST philistinism
HIILLMNOOPSU limnophilous
HIILLNNNOOST nonillionths
HIILLOOPPRWW whippoorwill
HIILMNNOOPSY hypolimnions
HIILMOOSSTTT lithotomists
HIILNOOPRSTU nitrophilous
HIIOPRRSSUVV survivorship
HIKLOOORSSVV Voroshilovsk
HILMMOOPPRSY polymorphism
HILNOOPSSTXY xylophonists
HILOOOPPRSTU tropophilous
HIMMMNOOOPRS monomorphism
HIMOOOPPRSTT phototropism
HIMOOOPRRSTT orthotropism
HINOOPPPRRSY porphyropsin
HINOOPPRSSSS sponsorships
HINOOPPSSTTY phonotypists
HIOOOPRRSTTY protohistory
HJKNNNOOOSTX Knox-Johnston
HLLMNOOOPSUY monophyllous
HLLOPRSSUUUY sulphurously
HLMOOOPPRSUY polymorphous
HLMOOPSSTUUY posthumously
HMMNOOOOPRSU monomorphous
HMOOOPSSSTUY physostomous
HOOOOPRRSTTU orthotropous
IIIIMNNOSTTU intuitionism
IIIIMPRSSTTV primitivists
IIIINNOQSSTU inquisitions
IIIINNOSTTTU intuitionist
IIILLNNOQSTU quintillions
IIILLNOPSSTT pointillists
IIILLNOSSSTU illusionists
IIILMMNOPSTU postliminium
IIILNOQSTUUY iniquitously
IIIMNNOORSST intromission
IIIMNOORTTUV vomiturition
IIINNORSTTTU nutritionist

IIINNORSTTUU	innutritious
IIINNOSSTTTU	institutions
IIINOOOPSSTV	ovipositions
IIIOPRSSTTUY	spirituosity
IILLOOQSSSTU	soliloquists
IILMNOOQSSTU	somniloquist
IILMNOOSTUVY	voluminosity
IILNORSSSTUY	sinistrously
IILNORSTTUUY	nutritiously
IILOOPPRSTUY	propitiously
IIMNOOPRSSTU	positroniums
IINNNNOOSSTU	nonunionists
IINOOOPPRSST	propositions
IINOOOPPSSTT	postposition
IINOOPPRSTUU	unpropitious
IINOOPPSSSTU	suppositions
IINOOPRSTTTU	prostitution
IIOOPPSSSTUU	suppositious
ILLMNOOOSTTY	tonsillotomy
ILLMNOOSUUVY	voluminously
ILMNOOOQSSUU	somniloquous
ILMNOOORSUVY	omnivorously
ILOOPSTTUUVY	voluptuosity
INNNOOOOPSSU	nonpoisonous
INOOPPRSSTTU	opportunists
IOOPRRSSTTTU	prostitutors
LLMOSTTUUUUY	tumultuously
LLOOPSTUUUVY	voluptuously
LMNNOOOOSTUY	monotonously
LMNNOOSSUYYY	synonymously

Thirteen Letters

AAAAACILNNSTT	Santa Catalina
AAAAACINNRSTT	Santa Catarina
AAAABCCEELRTU	baccalaureate
AAAABCCHILMRR	Hamilcar Barca
AAAABDILMORSS	ambassadorial
AAAABEFGKLLLS	Kabalega Falls
AAAACCCCIRSTU	acciaccaturas
AAAACCDIIKLLS	lackadaisical
AAAACCINRSSTU	Transcaucasia
AAAACCLMNORST	malacostracan
AAAACDDGINUUY	Ciudad Guayana
AAAACDEEMRSTT	Atacama Desert
AAAACEGRSSTUU	Caesaraugusta
AAAACEIMMNORS	American Samoa
AAAACEINRRSSV	caravansaries
	caravanserais
AAAACGHILPPRR	paragraphical
AAAACILLLNPTY	aplanatically
AAAACIMNRSSST	antimacassars
AAAADEGHLMNOP	alpha and omega
AAAADGINNOSVY	Sivananda yoga
AAAAEEGNRTUWW	turangawaewae
AAAAEGHIMMNOT	haemangiomata
AAAAEGIMMNRST	anagrammatise
AAAAEGIMMNRTZ	anagrammatize
AAAAEGNRSTVXZ	extravaganzas
AAAAEHILNPPRR	paraphernalia
AAAAGHHIKLSWY	Alaska Highway
AAAAGILMMNOST	amalgamations
AAAAGIMMMNRST	anagrammatism
AAAAGIMMNRSTT	anagrammatist
AAAAHHINPRSSS	Spanish Sahara
AAAAHHKLLMNNU	Amanullah Khan
AAAAHIKMNPSTV	Visakhapatnam
AAAAIILLMNRST	antimalarials
AAAAILLPRRSSS	sarsaparillas
AAAALLPPSSSTU	Uspallata Pass
AAABBIINORRST	barbarisation
AAABBIINORRTZ	barbarization
AAABCCEINORTY	cyanobacteria
AAABCCENNRSSU	bancassurance
AAABCCILLLOTY	catabolically
AAABCCILLORTY	acrobatically
AAABCDEHINRTU	chateaubriand
AAABCDIKNORTW	backwardation
AAABCEEEHKPSY	Chesapeake Bay
AAABCEEILNRST	ascertainable
AAABCEEIMNPRZ	carbamazepine
AAABCEFILNOTT	labefactation
AAABCEGILLLRY	algebraically
AAABCEHILNPST	analphabetics
AAABCEHNOORTY	archaeobotany
AAABCEIILNRTT	antibacterial
AAABCEILLNORY	anaerobically
AAABCEILNOOPT	palaeobotanic
AAABCEILNRSTY	ascertainably
AAABCHHINOOPR	arachnophobia
AAABCIKLLLOTY	katabolically
AAABCILLLOPRY	parabolically
AAABDEEINRRST	Arabian Desert
AAABDEELNPSST	adaptableness
AAABDEGIILMTY	damageability
AAABDELQSTTUU	absquatulated
AAABDFILNNORS	Baranof Island
AAABDHMMOORTY	rhabdomyomata
AAABEEEGKLRRT	Great Bear Lake
AAABEEGLNSSTU	Augean stables
AAABEEILLNSSV	availableness
AAABEELLNPSST	palatableness
AAABEGIILMNTY	manageability
AAABEGILNNOST	antagonisable
AAABEGILNNOTZ	antagonizable
AAABEHLMOSSTT	haematoblasts
AAABEILLMNPTU	manipulatable
AAABELNNRRTUW	unwarrantable
AAABELQSSTTUU	absquatulates
AAABGHPPRRSSU	subparagraphs
AAABHILLMPSTU	amphiblastula
AAABIIILLNOST	labialisation
AAABIIILLNOTZ	labialization
AAABIIILNTTTY	attainability
AAABIIKLNNOST	balkanisation
AAABIIKLNNOTZ	balkanization
AAABILNPRSSSU	sublapsarians
AAABLNNRRTUWY	unwarrantably
AAACCCGHILOPR	cacographical
AAACCDEIINPTT	incapacitated
AAACCDEILLNTU	canaliculated
AAACCDHIILNOR	archidiaconal
AAACCEGILRTTX	extragalactic
AAACCEHILMOPR	macrocephalia
AAACCEIINPSTT	incapacitates
AAACCEILNNOTT	Atlantic Ocean
AAACCEINNQSTU	acquaintances

AAACCELLPRSTY	Crystal Palace
AAACCFINNNRSS	San Franciscan
AAACCGILLLMOO	malacological
AAACCHIILMRRT	matriarchical
AAACCHILLRTTY	cathartically
AAACCHLORSSTY	thalassocracy
AAACCHLORTTTY	thalattocracy
AAACCIILLNSST	anticlassical
AAACCIILLSTTT	stalactitical
AAACCIINNPSTT	incapacitants
AAACCIINOPSTT	capacitations
AAACCILLLTTYY	catalytically
AAACCILLMNORY	macaronically
AAACCILLRSSTY	sarcastically
AAACDDEGHHILT	Gaidhealtachd
AAACDEEILMNNO	Lacedaemonian
AAACDEEINPPRS	disappearance
AAACDEGIMNNPR	Campina Grande
AAACDEHHIKRSV	Chevra Kadisha
AAACDEHHKNRRS	Chandrasekhar
AAACDEHIMNRTY	adiathermancy
AAACDEIIINPRT	paediatrician
AAACDEIINNRRV	Canadian River
AAACDEIIORTTV	radioactivate
AAACDEILLOPSV	Palacio Valdés
AAACDEINRSSTT	tradescantias
AAACDELLNOOST	Llano Estacado
AAACDGHIIMPRT	diaphragmatic
AAACDGILMRRTU	dramaturgical
AAACDHHHINRRS	Harishchandra
AAACDHHILMNST	Chatham Island
AAACDHIINOPRS	anaphrodisiac
AAACDHILNOPTY	anaphylactoid
AAACDIIILPRST	parasiticidal
AAACDIILMNOPS	dipsomaniacal
AAACDILLOPRXY	paradoxically
AAACDILMNNSSY	Cayman Islands
AAACDILNNRSSY	Canary Islands
AAACDMMNNOSTU	Muscat and Oman
AAACEEENPPRRS	reappearances
AAACEEGHILLNP	encephalalgia
AAACEEGHNNRRS	carragheenans
AAACEEGNRSTVX	extravagances
AAACEEHILLLPX	Aix-la-Chapelle
AAACEEHLMNOPT	encephalomata
AAACEENNNOPPR	nonappearance
AAACEEOPPRSUV	papaveraceous
AAACEFILNORRT	rarefactional
AAACEGGGLOSTU	galactagogues
AAACEGHIILNPR	archipelagian
AAACEGHILOPPR	palaeographic
AAACEGILMMNOS	megalomaniacs
AAACEGILMTTUY	Guatemala City
AAACEGIMNOSTY	gynaecomastia
AAACEGIMQRRUZ	García Márquez
AAACEHIIMMNTT	mathematician
AAACEHILLPTTY	apathetically
AAACEHIMOOPPR	pharmacopoeia
AAACEHIMOPPRS	pharmacopeias
AAACEHIMRRSTT	matriarchates
AAACEHIPRRSTT	patriarchates
AAACEIILMNNRT	Latin American
AAACEILLMNOTX	exclamational
AAACEILLMOOST	osteomalacial
AAACEILNNSSST	satanicalness
AAACEILNSSTTT	Caltanissetta
AAACELLMNRSTY	sacramentally
AAACELLNORRTT	contralateral
AAACELNNORSSY	narcoanalyses
AAACELOSSTTUY	autocatalyses
AAACELRRSTUVX	extravascular
AAACFIILLLMOX	maxillofacial
AAACFILLMNSTY	fantasmically
AAACFILLNSTTY	fantastically
AAACFIMNORRTW	aircraftwoman
AAACGGHIIMNOT	gigantomachia
AAACGGILLOPRY	paragogically
AAACGHILOPRTU	autographical
AAACGIILLMSTT	stalagmitical
AAACGILLMMRTY	grammatically
AAACGILLMPRTY	pragmatically
AAACGILMMNRTU	ungrammatical
AAACGILNNOTTU	anticoagulant
AAACHIILLPRSY	pharisaically
AAACHILLMSTTY	asthmatically
AAACHILLNOPRY	anaphorically
AAACHILLPRRTY	patriarchally
AAACHILNRSSSU	Halicarnassus
AAACIILLMOTXY	axiomatically
AAACIILLPRSTY	parasitically
AAACIILLSTTVY	atavistically
AAACIILNNNOTT	incantational
AAACIILNOSSTU	casualisation
AAACIILNOSTTU	actualisation
AAACIILNOSTUZ	casualization
AAACIILNOTTUZ	actualization
AAACIIMNRRSTT	Tractarianism
AAACILLLNOTTY	lactationally
AAACILLLPRTYY	paralytically
AAACILLMNOPRY	panoramically
AAACILLMOTTUY	automatically
AAACILLMRTTUY	traumatically
AAACILNNORSSY	narcoanalysis
AAACILNNORSTT	transactional
AAACILNNRSTTT	transatlantic
AAACILNORSTTU	astronautical
AAACILNPRRSTU	intracapsular
AAACILNSSTTTY	anticatalysts
AAACILOSSTTUY	autocatalysis
AAACIMNNOSTTU	catamountains
AAACLMNPRSTUY	sanctuary lamp
AAADDDEGINSTV	disadvantaged
AAADDEGINSSTV	disadvantages
AAADDEHHMPRSY	Madhya Pradesh
AAADDEHHNPRRS	Andhra Pradesh
AAADEEGILNNSS	Aegean Islands
AAADEEGLMMNRY	Mary Magdalene
AAADEEHIMNSTT	anathematised
AAADEEHIMNTTZ	anathematized
AAADEGILMQRSU	quadragesimal
AAADEGILNRSTV	landgraviates
AAADEHHIMNNRT	rhadamanthine
AAADEHHNPRSSZ	haphazardness
AAADEHIINPRTT	antiapartheid

AAADEILLMPTVY maladaptively
AAADEILLQRRTU quadrilateral
AAADEINOPPRTT preadaptation
AAADEINOPRSTT readaptations
AAADELMMOPSST plasmodesmata
AAADFGKKNOORS Sargon of Akkad
AAADGILLNORTY gradationally
AAADGIMNOORST Good Samaritan
AAADHHILNRRSU Harun al-Rashid
AAADIIMNORSTT dramatisation
AAADIIMNORTTZ dramatization
AAADKLMRRSTTX Karl-Marx-Stadt
AAAEEGGLMNSTU metalanguages
AAAEEGHLOPPRR palaeographer
AAAEEGINNRSSX sexagenarians
AAAEEGKLLRSTT Great Salt Lake
AAAEEGNRSTTVX Extravagantes
AAAEEHIMNSSTT anathematises
AAAEEHIMNSTTZ anathematizes
AAAEEHIPRSSST paraesthesias
AAAEEHNRRSSTW Western Sahara
AAAEEILRSTTVV salva veritate
AAAEFIILMMRST materfamilias
AAAEFIILMPRST paterfamilias
AAAEFILNNPRUZ parainfluenza
AAAEFINNORSTU Anne of Austria
AAAEGGIMNOPRS megasporangia
AAAEGGINRTTVX extravagating
AAAEGIILMMNOR Emilia-Romagna
AAAEGIILMMNRS managerialism
AAAEGIILMNRST managerialist
AAAEGILMNORSU megalosaurian
AAAEGIMMNPRST paramagnetism
AAAEGINNNNORS nonagenarians
AAAEGINORTTVX extravagation
AAAEGINRSTTVX extravasating
AAAEGLLLMOPRR parallelogram
AAAEGLNRTTVXY extravagantly
AAAEHIMNOPRTY hyponatraemia
AAAEHIOSSSTTU Southeast Asia
AAAEIIKNPSSTT East Pakistani
AAAEIILMNNOTX examinational
AAAEIILNQRSTU equalitarians
AAAEILMNPRRTY parliamentary
AAAEIMMMNRRTU armamentarium
AAAEIMNNRSSST transaminases
AAAEINORSTTVX extravasation
AAAGGIOPPRSTU appoggiaturas
AAAGHIRSSTTWY straightaways
AAAGHMNOPRSTY phantasmagory
AAAGIIILMNNOT imaginational
AAAGIIKMOORST Saigo Takamori
AAAGIILNNOSTV galvanisation
AAAGIILNNOTVZ galvanization
AAAGIILNORTTV gravitational
AAAGIINNOPSST paganisations
AAAGIINNOPSTZ paganizations
AAAGIINNSSSST assassinating
AAAGILNOOPPRT propagational
AAAHIIMNNRSTU humanitarians
AAAHIINORRTTU authoritarian
AAAHIIOPPRRUW pipiwharauroa
AAAHIKNRSSTUY Ratushinskaya
AAAHILMMOPSTT amphistomatal
AAAHINRRSTTUZ Zarathustrian
AAAIIILMNNOST animalisation
AAAIIILMNNOTZ animalization
AAAIILLNORTVY variationally
AAAIILNNNORTT intranational
AAAIILNNOSTTT tantalisation
AAAIILNNOTTTZ tantalization
AAAIIMNNOOSTT anatomisation
AAAIIMNNOOTTZ anatomization
AAAIIMNOORSTT aromatisation
AAAIIMNOORTTZ aromatization
AAAIINNORSTTV intravasation
AAAIINNOSSSST assassination
AAAIINORRSTTT tartarisation
AAAIINORRTTTZ tartarization
AAAILLLNOTUVY valuationally
AAAILLNNORSTT translational
AAAILLNNORTTU ultranational
AAAILLNORRSTT translatorial
AAAILMNORSTVY Salvation Army
AAAILNNNORSTT transnational
AAAILNNOPRSTU supranational
AAAILNOPRSSTY paralysations
AAAILNOPRSTYZ paralyzations
AAALLLLOOOPSZ lollapaloozas
AABBBIILORSTY absorbability
AABBCEILNRRST transcribable
AABBCIIILMNOS bibliomaniacs
AABBCIINRRSUU suburbicarian
AABBCILLMOSTY bombastically
AABBDDEEGILOR biodegradable
AABBDEEFGLRST flabbergasted
AABBDEEINRTUV unabbreviated
AABBDIILORSTY adsorbability
AABBDIINOOQSS Qaboos bin Said
AABBEEHILNSST habitableness
AABBEEILLMOST metabolisable
AABBEEILLMOTZ metabolizable
AABBEEILRUVXY Rievaulx Abbey
AABBEHIILNNTU uninhabitable
AABBEHILNOPRT phenobarbital
AABBEIILLOSSU bouillabaisse
AABBEIINORSTV abbreviations
AABBENORRSSSU barbarousness
AABBIIILNOTTY obtainability
AABCCCEHKRRST backscratcher
AABCCDHLRTYYY brachydactyly
AABCCEEFIILRS sacrificeable
AABCCEEIRRSUU bureaucracies
AABCCEHHLPRYY brachycephaly
AABCCEHINOOPR cancerophobia
AABCCEIILMPRT impracticable
AABCCEIILPTTY acceptability
AABCCEILLMOSV clavicembalos
AABCCEILMNORS microbalances
AABCCEILMOTUU bioaccumulate
AABCCEILNPRTU unpracticable
AABCCEIORSSSU brassicaceous
AABCCELMOPRTY campylobacter
AABCCELNNOTUU unaccountable

AABCCGIKKNRST	backtrackings
AABCCIIILNNST	cannibalistic
AABCCIILLLTUY	calculability
AABCCIILMPRTY	impracticably
AABCCILLLOSTU	lactobacillus
AABCCKLNRRSTU	blackcurrants
AABCCLNNOTUUY	unaccountably
AABCDDEKLRRSW	bladderwracks
AABCDDIILORUV	Ciudad Bolívar
AABCDEEEFNRSS	barefacedness
AABCDEEFFHIIN	dieffenbachia
AABCDEEFIPRRT	prefabricated
AABCDEEGHILRS	dischargeable
AABCDEEHLNNOT	nondetachable
AABCDEELLLSSY	decasyllables
AABCDEELORSXY	decarboxylase
AABCDEENNORUV	overabundance
AABCDEENOSSTU	subdeaconates
AABCDEGIKLLNP	backpedalling
AABCDEGINNORT	decarbonating
AABCDEHIILTTY	detachability
AABCDEHIIMORT	thiocarbamide
AABCDEHIINRST	dibranchiates
AABCDEHMNORRS	rhabdomancers
AABCDEHORRSTY	carbohydrates
AABCDEIILTTUY	educatability
AABCDEILOPRRT	particleboard
AABCDEINNOORT	decarbonation
AABCDEINORRTU	decarburation
AABCDELOPPRRS	clapperboards
AABCDENOORRST	decarbonators
AABCDEOPRRRSS	scraperboards
AABCDGGIKLNRU	blackguarding
AABCDGGIOORSU	braggadocious
AABCDGIKLMRSU	blackguardism
AABCDINNORSTT	contrabandist
AABCDKMNORSSW	backswordsman
AABCEEEELNPSS	peaceableness
AABCEEEGHLLLN	challengeable
AABCEEEILLPRR	irreplaceable
AABCEEELLNPRU	unreplaceable
AABCEEELNRSST	traceableness
AABCEEFIPRRST	prefabricates
AABCEEGGPRRST	carpetbaggers
AABCEEGHIOPRT	bacteriophage
AABCEEHILMNPU	unimpeachable
AABCEEHLLRRST	Charles Albert
AABCEEIILLMRR	irreclaimable
AABCEEIILNPPR	inappreciable
AABCEEIKMNRST	cabinetmakers
AABCEEILLPRRY	irreplaceably
AABCEEILMNRSV	vraisemblance
AABCEEILNNPSS	incapableness
AABCEEIRRSTUU	bureaucratise
AABCEEIRRTUUZ	bureaucratize
AABCEELMMORSU	commeasurable
AABCEELNRSSTT	tractableness
AABCEEMMNORSU	membranaceous
AABCEFFGHNRSU	Aschaffenburg
AABCEFIIINOTT	beatification
AABCEFIINORTT	abortifacient
AABCEFIOPRRRT	prefabricator
AABCEGHIIINRV	Virginia Beach
AABCEGHIILNTY	changeability
AABCEGHIILRTY	chargeability
AABCEGIIKMNNT	cabinetmaking
AABCEGILLLNOO	balneological
AABCEGILLMOST	megaloblastic
AABCEGILNNORV	overbalancing
AABCEGILOPSSY	abyssopelagic
AABCEGINOORSU	boraginaceous
AABCEHHHORSTV	Sheva Brachoth
AABCEHIKLPRSU	Sakha Republic
AABCEHILLLMNR	lamellibranch
AABCEHILMNPUY	unimpeachably
AABCEHILMOSTT	hematoblastic
AABCEIILLMRRY	irreclaimably
AABCEIILLPRTU	Altai Republic
AABCEIILMRSST	bicameralists
AABCEIILNPPRY	inappreciably
AABCEIINORRTT	nitrobacteria
AABCEIIRSTTTY	tetrabasicity
AABCEILLLMOTY	metabolically
AABCEILLMOPRT	problematical
AABCEILLOORTV	collaborative
AABCEILLRSSTY	crystalisable
AABCEILLRSTTY	tetrasyllabic
AABCEILLRSTYZ	crystalizable
AABCEILMNNOOP	companionable
AABCEILPRRTTU	Tatar Republic
AABCEILRSTTVY	abstractively
AABCEIMORSSUU	simarubaceous
AABCEIMRRSTUU	bureaucratism
AABCEINRRSSTT	scatterbrains
AABCEIORSSTTT	bacteriostats
AABCELMMNNOSU	somnambulance
AABCELNOOPRTY	polycarbonate
AABCFGILNNOTU	confabulating
AABCFIILORTTY	factorability
AABCFILNNOOTU	confabulation
AABCFILORRSUV	fibrovascular
AABCFLNOORSTU	confabulators
AABCFLNOORTUY	confabulatory
AABCGIIILNNNS	cannibalising
AABCGIIILNNNZ	cannibalizing
AABCGIILLNSTY	syllabicating
AABCGIILLOTUY	coagulability
AABCGILLNNNNO	cannonballing
AABCGILLNOORT	collaborating
AABCHIIILMNTY	machinability
AABCHIIMORSTT	microhabitats
AABCHIINOOSTT	cohabitations
AABCHIMNOPRRS	marsipobranch
AABCHIORRSSUU	brachiosaurus
AABCIIILLMPTY	implacability
AABCIIILLNSTT	antiballistic
AABCIIILLPPTY	applicability
AABCIIILMNORT	antimicrobial
AABCIILLLLSTY	ballistically
AABCIILLNORTU	lubricational
AABCIILLNOSTY	syllabication
AABCIILLOSTTY	biostatically
AABCIILLRSTYY	sybaritically
AABCIILMNNOOT	combinational

AABCIILMNOORT combinatorial
AABCIILMOPRTY comparability
AABCIIMOPRSTY parasymbiotic
AABCIINNOORST carbonisation
AABCIINNOORTZ carbonization
AABCIINORRSTU carburisation
AABCIINORRTUZ carburization
AABCIKLMNNOTU Black Mountain
AABCILLNOOORT collaboration
AABCILMNNOOPY companionably
AABCINORSSSTT contrabassist
AABCLLOOORRST collaborators
AABCMNNNOOSTT noncombatants
AABCNNOOORSST contrabassoon
AABDDDENRRSST standardbreds
AABDDEGIILRTY degradability
AABDDEGIIMSTU disambiguated
AABDDEGINNPRS bandspreading
AABDDEILMNRRY Marie Byrd Land
AABDDGHORRSTU draughtboards
AABDEEFGIILNT indefatigable
AABDEEHIILRTT rehabilitated
AABDEEHORRSTW weatherboards
AABDEEILLNSST dilatableness
AABDEEILNSSSV advisableness
AABDEEKORRSST skateboarders
AABDEELMRRSSY embarrassedly
AABDEEMNRRSSU unembarrassed
AABDEFGIILNTY indefatigably
AABDEFLLNNORS flannelboards
AABDEGIIMSSTU disambiguates
AABDEGIKNORST skateboarding
AABDEGLLMNORS balladmongers
AABDEGLLNRTUY Argyll and Bute
AABDEIIILMNST damnabilities
AABDEIILNRTUY unreadability
AABDEIILPRSTY spreadability
AABDEILMRTUVY adumbratively
AABDEINNNORRS San Bernardino
AABDEINSSTTTU substantiated
AABDELMMNOSTU somnambulated
AABDENNPRSTUU superabundant
AABDFFIILORTY affordability
AABDGLNOORUWY Albury-Wodonga
AABDHIMNORSTT rhabdomantist
AABDIIILLSTYY dialysability
AABDIIILLTYYZ dialyzability
AABDIILNSSTUU Tubuai Islands
AABDKMNOORSTU Dumbarton Oaks
AABEEEEGLNRSS agreeableness
AABEEEHKRRRST heartbreakers
AABEEEKRSSTVW basketweavers
AABEEELLLMNSS malleableness
AABEEELNORSST elaborateness
AABEEELNPRSSS separableness
AABEEELOORRTV overelaborate
AABEEFHIMNNOO Anne of Bohemia
AABEEFHINRRST featherbrains
AABEEFILNNOTU Fontainebleau
AABEEFLNORSSV favorableness
AABEEFLNRRRST transferrable
AABEEGHIKNRRT heartbreaking
AABEEGHLLNSSU laughableness
AABEEGILMNPRT impregnatable
AABEEGILNNSSV navigableness
AABEEHIILRSTT rehabilitates
AABEEHILPRSST alphabetisers
AABEEHILPRSTZ alphabetizers
AABEEHINSSTTW Bassenthwaite
AABEEHLNOPRTY balneotherapy
AABEEHLRRSSTY breathalysers
AABEEHLRRSTYZ breathalyzers
AABEEIILLNNPX inexplainable
AABEEIILLRTVY revealability
AABEEIILNNSSV Évian-les-Bains
AABEEIILPRTTY repeatability
AABEEIKLMNSTU unmistakeable
AABEEILLNNPUX unexplainable
AABEELLLRSTTY tetrasyllable
AABEELMNNORSU nonmeasurable
AABEEMMNRRSST embarrassment
AABEFHILNNOSU unfashionable
AABEFIILLNQUU unqualifiable
AABEFILLMMNNU uninflammable
AABEFILMORSSU balsamiferous
AABEFLMNORRST transformable
AABEGHIILNPST alphabetising
AABEGHIILNPTZ alphabetizing
AABEGHILNRSTY breathalysing
AABEGHILNRTYZ breathalyzing
AABEGHIMNSTTW bantamweights
AABEGIILLNOUV bougainvillea
AABEGIJKLNRWY jawbreakingly
AABEGILMNPRTU perambulating
AABEGILNORRTU gubernatorial
AABEHIINORSTZ hebraizations
AABEHLMOPPRSS blepharospasm
AABEIIKLMRRTY remarkability
AABEIIKLMRTTY marketability
AABEIILLLOSTV volatilisable
AABEIILLLOTVZ volatilizable
AABEIILLNNPXY inexplainably
AABEIILMNORST abnormalities
AABEIILMRSTUY measurability
AABEIILMSTTTY metastability
AABEIILNORSTV verbalisation
AABEIILNORTVZ verbalization
AABEIILNPTTTY patentability
AABEIILNRSTWY answerability
AABEIILOPRTVY evaporability
AABEIIMNNRSTU antisubmarine
AABEIINRRRSST arbitrariness
AABEIKLMNSTUY unmistakeably
AABEILLLRSTTU illustratable
AABEILLNRRSTU turbellarians
AABEILMNNOTTU Table Mountain
AABEILMNOPRTU perambulation
AABEILMNRSTTT transmittable
AABEILNOOPPRT apportionable
AABEILNOORSTV observational
AABEILOQRSTUU subequatorial
AABEIMOPRSSSY parasymbioses
AABEINSSSTTTU substantiates
AABELMMNOSSTU somnambulates

AABELMOPRRSTU	perambulators
AABELMOPRRTUY	perambulatory
AABELNOPRRSTT	transportable
AABELNPRSSSUU	unsurpassable
AABELNRRSTTUU	subternatural
AABFIIMMSSUUX	Fabius Maximus
AABGGIINNORTU	outbargaining
AABGHIIINRSTU	British Guiana
AABGHIINNRSSW	brainwashings
AABGHIOOPRTUY	autobiography
AABGHLLOPRSYY	syllabography
AABGIIILNORTY	aboriginality
AABGIIILNSSTY	assignability
AABGIILLNOOST	globalisation
AABGIILLNOOTZ	globalization
AABGIILOPPRTY	propagability
AABGILLMNRSUY	submarginally
AABHIIILNOSTT	habilitations
AABHIIILNPRRS	librarianship
AABIIIILNRTVY	invariability
AABIIIILNSTTY	insatiability
AABIIILLMPPTY	impalpability
AABIIILMPSSTY	impassability
AABIIILNOSSST	assibilations
AABIIILNOSSTT	stabilisation
AABIIILNOSTTZ	stabilization
AABIIINQRSTUU	ubiquitarians
AABIILNNNRTTU	tintinnabular
AABIILNNSSTTU	insubstantial
AABIILNORSTTU	brutalisation
AABIILNORTTUZ	brutalization
AABIILOPRTUVY	vapourability
AABIILOSTTTUY	autostability
AABIIMOPRSSSY	parasymbiosis
AABIINNNOORTW	rainbow nation
AABIINNORSSTU	urbanisations
AABIINNORSTUZ	urbanizations
AABIINOORRSST	arborisations
AABIINOORRSTZ	arborizations
AABILLNOOPRTY	probationally
AABILLNOSSTTU	blastulations
AABILLNSSTTUY	substantially
AABILMNOOPRST	malabsorption
AABILNNSSTTUU	unsubstantial
AABIMNOPRSSTY	parasymbionts
AABINORSSTTTU	substantiator
AABINORSSTTUU	subsaturation
AABLMMNNOSSTU	somnambulants
AABLMMNOORSTU	somnambulator
AACCCEEILNRRT	recalcitrance
AACCCEENNNOPT	nonacceptance
AACCCEGINORTY	gynaecocratic
AACCCEHIILSTT	catechistical
AACCCEHILMOPR	macrocephalic
AACCCEIILLMRT	climacterical
AACCCFIIILNOT	calcification
AACCCGHHILOPR	chalcographic
AACCCIIILMNTT	anticlimactic
AACCCIILLLMTY	climactically
AACCCIILMMORT	macroclimatic
AACCDDEHIIRSS	disaccharides
AACCDEEELNRSU	adularescence
AACCDEEHINOPT	heptadecanoic
AACCDEEHIRRST	characterised
AACCDEEHIRRTZ	characterized
AACCDEEIILNRU	clairaudience
AACCDEEILNOPY	encyclopaedia
AACCDEEKMNRRS	cackermanders
AACCDEELLPPRW	clapperclawed
AACCDEENNTTUU	unaccentuated
AACCDEHIILMOR	radiochemical
AACCDEHIIRRST	trisaccharide
AACCDEIIILMRT	acidimetrical
AACCDEIIILNST	dialecticians
AACCDEIILLLTY	dialectically
AACCDEIINORTT	accreditation
AACCDEILLMSTU	miscalculated
AACCDEILNNNOT	nonaccidental
AACCDEILNOOTU	coeducational
AACCDEIMMOOTV	accommodative
AACCDEIMNNOPU	unaccompanied
AACCDFIIIINOT	acidification
AACCDGHIIOPRR	cardiographic
AACCDGIILLOOR	cardiological
AACCDGIMMNOOT	accommodating
AACCDIIILLRTY	diacritically
AACCDIILLOPTY	apodictically
AACCDIILNOSSS	Caicos Islands
AACCDIIMNOORT	carcinomatoid
AACCDIMMNOOOT	accommodation
AACCEEEHMNTTU	catechumenate
AACCEEFHINNOR	French Oceania
AACCEEFILORST	calefactories
AACCEEGIORRST	ergatocracies
AACCEEHILMNOT	catecholamine
AACCEEHIMNORS	aeromechanics
AACCEEHIMRRST	saccharimeter
AACCEEHIRRRST	characteriser
AACCEEHIRRRTZ	characterizer
AACCEEHIRRSST	characterises
AACCEEHIRRSTZ	characterizes
AACCEEHLMNPRY	macrencephaly
AACCEEHLRRSST	characterless
AACCEEHMORRST	saccharometer
AACCEEIILLPRS	capercaillies
AACCEEIILPRSZ	capercailzies
AACCEEILNORST	accelerations
AACCEEINRSSSS	accessariness
AACCEELLNSTUZ	Culzean Castle
AACCEELLPPRRW	clapperclawer
AACCEFIIINOTT	acetification
AACCEFILLSTUY	fasciculately
AACCEFILORRSU	calcariferous
AACCEGHHLOPRR	chalcographer
AACCEGHILLOOR	archeological
AACCEGHILMORS	agrochemicals
AACCEGHILOPRR	cerographical
AACCEGHINOOPR	oceanographic
AACCEGIIILNST	Cilician Gates
AACCEGIILNRTT	intergalactic
AACCEGIINNRRT	incarcerating
AACCEGIINNRTV	revaccinating
AACCEGILLNRTU	recalculating
AACCEGILLOOTU	autecological

AACCEGILLORTY	categorically
AACCEGILLOTTY	geotactically
AACCEGINNNOTT	concatenating
AACCEGINOQRSU	quangocracies
AACCEHHLOPPSY	scaphocephaly
AACCEHIILMMNS	mechanicalism
AACCEHIILORRT	hierocratical
AACCEHIILRSTU	eucharistical
AACCEHIINOSTT	catechisation
AACCEHIINOTTZ	catechization
AACCEHILLMNOS	melancholiacs
AACCEHILLMRSV	clishmaclaver
AACCEHILLMSTY	schematically
AACCEHILMNNNO	nonmechanical
AACCEHILMORTT	tachometrical
AACCEHILMRTTY	tachymetrical
AACCEHILOSSTT	scholasticate
AACCEHILRRTTU	architectural
AACCEHIMMORTT	metachromatic
AACCEHIMOOPPR	pharmacopoeic
AACCEHIMPRSTU	pharmaceutics
AACCEHIMRRSTY	saccharimetry
AACCEHLNNOPSU	Nonsuch Palace
AACCEHLPRSSTT	scratchplates
AACCEIILLMNTY	cinematically
AACCEIILLMSSS	semiclassical
AACCEIILLNRST	anticlericals
AACCEIILMNOST	encomiastical
AACCEIILMRSST	acclimatisers
AACCEIILMRSTZ	acclimatizers
AACCEIINNORRT	incarceration
AACCEIINNORTV	revaccination
AACCEIIOPRSTT	ectoparasitic
AACCEIIORRSST	aristocracies
AACCEILLMRTUV	circumvallate
AACCEILLMSSTU	miscalculates
AACCEILLNNOST	cancellations
AACCEILLNSSSS	classicalness
AACCEILLNSTUY	encaustically
AACCEILMMORST	macroclimates
AACCEILMNOPSS	complaisances
AACCEILMNOPST	cleptomaniacs
AACCEILNOPRST	plantocracies
AACCEILNPRSST	practicalness
AACCEILNRRSTT	recalcitrants
AACCEILNRTTUU	nutraceutical
AACCEIMMNNOPT	accompaniment
AACCEINNNOOTT	concatenation
AACCEINOORSTV	coacervations
AACCEINOPSSSU	capaciousness
AACCEINORRRST	incarcerators
AACCEIOORSSTU	aeroacoustics
AACCEIORRSSTT	stratocracies
AACCEKNORTTTU	counterattack
AACCELLPRSTUY	spectacularly
AACCELNPRSTUU	unspectacular
AACCELORSSSUU	crassulaceous
AACCFFILNOPRY	cycloparaffin
AACCFGHIINRSY	saccharifying
AACCFIIILLRSY	sacrificially
AACCFIIILNORT	clarification
AACCFIIINNORT	carnification
AACCFIIINOPRT	caprification
AACCFIIINOPST	pacifications
AACCFIIINORST	scarification
AACCFIILLLORY	calorifically
AACCFIILLSSTY	fascistically
AACCFIILNOSTU	fasciculation
AACCFIIORRSST	scarificators
AACCGGIILLLOO	glaciological
AACCGHHIOPRRT	chartographic
AACCGHIILMNOT	machicolating
AACCGHIKOPRRT	Croagh Patrick
AACCGHILLNOOT	Anglo-Catholic
AACCGIIILMNST	acclimatising
AACCGIIILMNTZ	acclimatizing
AACCGIILLNOOR	craniological
AACCGIILLOPST	plagioclastic
AACCGILLLNTUY	calculatingly
AACCGILNOOPSV	galvanoscopic
AACCGILNRTTUU	acculturating
AACCHHHLNRSUU	Shulchan Aruch
AACCHIIINRSTT	antirachitics
AACCHIILMNOOT	machicolation
AACCHIILMSSST	schismaticals
AACCHIILPRSTY	psychiatrical
AACCHIILQRRSU	squirarchical
AACCHIIMORTTY	achromaticity
AACCHIINNNOST	cachinnations
AACCHIINNORST	anachronistic
AACCHILLMNORY	monarchically
AACCHILLMORTY	chromatically
AACCHILLOPRTT	trophallactic
AACCHILMNOORT	Roman Catholic
AACCHILNNOORU	canonical hour
AACCIIINNOOST	cocainisation
AACCIIINNOOTZ	cocainization
AACCIIINORSTT	cicatrisation
AACCIIINORTTZ	cicatrization
AACCIILLMPRTY	impractically
AACCIILLMSSSS	classicalisms
AACCIILLSSSST	classicalists
AACCIILLSSTUY	casuistically
AACCIILMNOOSS	occasionalism
AACCIILMNORTY	microanalytic
AACCIILNNOPTY	platinocyanic
AACCIIRRSSTTU	caricaturists
AACCILLMORSTU	miscalculator
AACCILLNPRTUY	unpractically
AACCILLNSTTYY	syntactically
AACCILLOPRTTU	plutocratical
AACCILLOPSSST	postclassical
AACCILMNOSTUU	accumulations
AACCILNNOOOTV	convocational
AACCILNORTTUU	acculturation
AACCILNPRTTYY	cryptanalytic
AACCIMNOORSTU	carcinomatous
AACCIMNOPSSTY	accompanyists
AACCINORSSTTY	sacrosanctity
AACCLLNORTTUY	contractually
AACDDEEEFFINT	decaffeinated
AACDDEEEHLLRY	clearheadedly
AACDDEEIIIMMR	Maria de' Medici
AACDDEEIILMMR	Middle America

AACDDEEIQSUUX Duque de Caxias
AACDDEIIOSSST disassociated
AACDDFIIINNOT dandification
AACDDIIJNOSTU adjudications
AACDEEEFFINST decaffeinates
AACDEEEFIMNRR Marie de France
AACDEEEHLNPSS Passchendaele
AACDEEGHNNORR Chandernagore
AACDEEGIMNNOY cyanogenamide
AACDEEGINRRRU undercarriage
AACDEEHINTTTU authenticated
AACDEEHKLORRV Hradec Králové
AACDEEIILPRST recapitalised
AACDEEIILPRTZ recapitalized
AACDEEIINRSST sectarianised
AACDEEIINRSTZ sectarianized
AACDEEILLRTVY declaratively
AACDEEILNQRUV quadrivalence
AACDEEILPRTTU recapitulated
AACDEEIMMNRTY medicamentary
AACDEEIMNNOTT decontaminate
AACDEEIMNRSTT readmittances
AACDEEINPPRTU unappreciated
AACDEEINPQRTU preacquainted
AACDEENNNNOTT nonattendance
AACDEFFIIMNRS disaffirmance
AACDEFINNOSTY Ancient of Days
AACDEGGILLMOY demagogically
AACDEGGILLOPY pedagogically
AACDEGHHIMNOS hochmagandies
AACDEGHIINRRS Cardiganshire
AACDEGHILMOPR demographical
AACDEGHILRSTT straightlaced
AACDEGHIOPRRR cardiographer
AACDEGIILOPRS cardioplegias
AACDEGILNPSTU decapsulating
AACDEGJLNOSUU juglandaceous
AACDEGLMNNORS scandalmonger
AACDEGLNORTTU congratulated
AACDEHIILOPPS paedophiliacs
AACDEHIIMNRRT archimandrite
AACDEHIORRSTT trisoctahedra
AACDEHLNOOPPS cephalopodans
AACDEHLOPRRST procathedrals
AACDEHMNNOORT enchondromata
AACDEHNOPRSTY hydnocarpates
AACDEIIILNRST cardinalities
AACDEIIINPRST pediatricians
AACDEIIIPRSST parasiticides
AACDEIIJLRTUX extrajudicial
AACDEIILLMRTY diametrically
AACDEIILLNNOT declinational
AACDEIILLOPRY aperiodically
AACDEIILNORTV valedictorian
AACDEIILORTVY radioactively
AACDEIILRSTTU disarticulate
AACDEIINNORST deracinations
AACDEIINNPTTU unanticipated
AACDEIINNRSTT transactinide
AACDEIINOPRST endoparasitic
AACDEIINOPSTT decapitations
AACDEIINOSTTV deactivations
AACDEIIOSSSST disassociates
AACDEILLMORTY declamatorily
AACDEILLNORRU Claude Lorrain
AACDEILLNOSSW disallowances
AACDEILLNOTUY educationally
AACDEILLNSTYY asyndetically
AACDEILLORRTY declaratorily
AACDEILMMORST melodramatics
AACDEILMOPRST spermatocidal
AACDEILMORSST sacerdotalism
AACDEILNOPSTU decapsulation
AACDEILNOSSTT anecdotalists
AACDEILNQRUVY quadrivalency
AACDEILNRSTTU ultradistance
AACDEILNRTTUU unarticulated
AACDEILORSSTT sacerdotalist
AACDEILPQRTUU quadruplicate
AACDEIMNNNOTT decontaminant
AACDEINNORSUU arundinaceous
AACDEINOSSSUU audaciousness
AACDELMNNRSSU underclassman
AACDELOPRSSSU pseudoscalars
AACDFIIIMNNOT damnification
AACDFMNOORSTW woodcraftsman
AACDFORRRRSWY carryforwards
AACDGHLOPRTYY dactylography
AACDGIIILLOST dialogistical
AACDGIIINNNNR incarnadining
AACDGIIINNNRT incardinating
AACDGIIINNOST diagnostician
AACDHHILOPRTY hydropathical
AACDHIIIOPRST adiaphoristic
AACDHIILNPRSS cardinalships
AACDHIINNRSST Christiansand
AACDHIKMNOOSU Cahokia Mounds
AACDHILLLRUYY hydraulically
AACDHILLOPRSY rhapsodically
AACDHILMNOORT trichomonadal
AACDHILORSTTY hydrostatical
AACDHIMMOOSSS sadomasochism
AACDHINOPQRSU quadraphonics
AACDIIILLMOTY idiomatically
AACDIIILMOPST idioplasmatic
AACDIIILPQRTU quadricipital
AACDIIINNNORT incardination
AACDIIINORSTV divarications
AACDIIIORTTVY radioactivity
AACDIILLLSTUY dualistically
AACDIILLMPRYY pyramidically
AACDIILLORTTY dictatorially
AACDIILMNOSST disclamations
AACDIILNNOPTU pandiculation
AACDIILNOOORT radiolocation
AACDIIMNOPSST antispasmodic
AACDIINNORRST doctrinarians
AACDIINRSSTTU traducianists
AACDILLLORSTY crystalloidal
AACDILLMOPSSY spasmodically
AACDIMNORSSTY astrodynamics
AACEEEHJKLRTT leatherjacket
AACEEEHLLMNPY myelencephala
AACEEFILOPRRT praefectorial

AACEEFMNRRTUU	remanufacture
AACEEGGILMNOT	gamogenetical
AACEEGHILOPRS	archipelagoes
AACEEGHLLMOPY	megalocephaly
AACEEGHLMNOPR	encephalogram
AACEEGHLMOPSU	megacephalous
AACEEGHNOOPRR	oceanographer
AACEEGILLLNVY	evangelically
AACEEGILMMRTT	telegrammatic
AACEEGINNOSTU	gentianaceous
AACEEGLLOOOPY	palaeoecology
AACEEGLMORSTT	galactometers
AACEEHHILNNPR	rhinencephala
AACEEHIILNPST	elephantiasic
AACEEHIINSSTT	aestheticians
AACEEHILLSTTY	aesthetically
AACEEHILMPRTT	heptametrical
AACEEHILNPRTT	parenthetical
AACEEHIMNNOPT	acetaminophen
AACEEHINSTTTU	authenticates
AACEEHLLMRRST	Charles Martel
AACEEHLMRSTTY	methacrylates
AACEEHLNOPPRS	prosencephala
AACEEHMNOPSUY	nymphaeaceous
AACEEHMNRSTTT	reattachments
AACEEHNNPPSST	happenstances
AACEEHOPRRTXY	archaeopteryx
AACEEIILLMRTT	Little America
AACEEIILNRTTV	intercalative
AACEEIILPRSST	recapitalises
AACEEIILPRSTZ	recapitalizes
AACEEIINNRSST	necessitarian
AACEEIINORRST	reactionaries
AACEEIINRSSST	sectarianises
AACEEIINRSSTZ	sectarianizes
AACEEILLMMRTY	metamerically
AACEEILMMNORT	anemometrical
AACEEILNNPPSU	Cape Peninsula
AACEEILNNRSTW	Saint Lawrence
AACEEILNQRSUV	carnivalesque
AACEEILPRSTTU	recapitulates
AACEEIMNNRSTT	ascertainment
AACEEINSSSTUV	causativeness
AACEEIOPRSSTT	ectoparasites
AACEELLLRRTUX	extracellular
AACEELMRSSSST	masterclasses
AACEELNNOPRTV	convertaplane
AACEELNOPRRTU	palaeocurrent
AACEEMNORSSTU	sarmentaceous
AACEENNPPRSTU	appurtenances
AACEENNPRRSST	transparences
AACEENPRRSSSU	preassurances
AACEFGILNORTV	conflagrative
AACEFIIIILRST	artificialise
AACEFIIIILRTZ	artificialize
AACEFIIILMORR	microfilariae
AACEFIIINORST	aerifications
AACEFIILLNRTY	interfacially
AACEFIILORSSS	Clare of Assisi
AACEFIINORRST	rarefications
AACEFIINRRSVX	Francis Xavier
AACEFILLTTUVY	facultatively
AACEFILMNRSST	Massif Central
AACEFIMNORRTW	aircraftwomen
AACEFIMNORSTU	manufactories
AACEFMNRRSTUU	manufacturers
AACEGGHJKNNNU	Kangchenjunga
AACEGGILLOORT	geratological
AACEGHHIIKKNS	Chiang Kai-shek
AACEGHHOPRRRT	chartographer
AACEGHHPRRSTY	tachygraphers
AACEGHILLLRTY	lethargically
AACEGHILLMOOT	hematological
AACEGHILLMPRY	graphemically
AACEGHILLPRRS	calligraphers
AACEGHILMOPYY	hypoglycaemia
AACEGHILNPRSS	graphicalness
AACEGHILOORST	archaeologist
AACEGHIMNOPRT	cinematograph
AACEGHOPRRRST	cartographers
AACEGHOPRSSSU	sarcophaguses
AACEGIIINRRST	geriatricians
AACEGIILLMNOR	mineralogical
AACEGIILLMNTY	enigmatically
AACEGIILLNNTY	antigenically
AACEGIILLNRST	interglacials
AACEGIILMRRTV	gravimetrical
AACEGIILNNNRS	encarnalising
AACEGIILNNNRZ	encarnalizing
AACEGIILNNRTT	intercalating
AACEGIINNNRRT	reincarnating
AACEGIINNQRTU	reacquainting
AACEGIINPRRTV	prevaricating
AACEGILLLLORY	allegorically
AACEGILLLMRTU	metallurgical
AACEGILLMTUYZ	zeugmatically
AACEGILLNPRYY	panegyrically
AACEGILLOORTT	teratological
AACEGILLRSTTY	strategically
AACEGILMNOOSU	magnoliaceous
AACEGILMNORTV	galvanometric
AACEGILNNPSTU	encapsulating
AACEGINNOORST	octogenarians
AACEGINOSSSSU	sagaciousness
AACEGLLNRRTUY	rectangularly
AACEGLLOOPSUY	polygalaceous
AACEGLMNOOPRS	campanologers
AACEGLNOOPSSV	galvanoscopes
AACEGLNORSTTU	congratulates
AACEHHIILMOPS	haemophiliacs
AACEHHIIMPRTT	amphitheatric
AACEHHILNOPRZ	rhizocephalan
AACEHHINOSSTU	South China Sea
AACEHHLOOPRTX	cephalothorax
AACEHHLORSTTT	throatlatches
AACEHIIIMNRTT	arithmetician
AACEHIIIMPRST	hemiparasitic
AACEHIILLNTUV	hallucinative
AACEHIILLSTTY	atheistically
AACEHIILMPRSX	alexipharmics
AACEHIILNOPST	cephalisation
AACEHIILNOPTZ	cephalization
AACEHIILNPSTT	pantheistical
AACEHIILRTTTY	theatricality

AACEHIIMNNOST mechanisation
AACEHIIMNNOTZ mechanization
AACEHIIMNPSTY metaphysician
AACEHIIOPSSST associateship
AACEHILLMRTUY rheumatically
AACEHILLNTTUY authentically
AACEHILMOPRST atmospherical
AACEHILMOPTYY polycythaemia
AACEHILNNORTT nontheatrical
AACEHIMNNORRT North American
AACEHIMNORSTU South American
AACEHIMPRSTTU pharmaceutist
AACEHINOPRTTY actinotherapy
AACEHINORTTTU authenticator
AACEHINPRSTTY parasynthetic
AACEHLNOPSSYY psychoanalyse
AACEHLNOPSYYZ psychoanalyze
AACEHLOOPSTUU autocephalous
AACEHMSSSSTTU Massachusetts
AACEHNOPPRRTY parthenocarpy
AACEIIILMRSTT materialistic
AACEIIIMPRSST semiparasitic
AACEIIINORTTV ratiocinative
AACEIIKLLMNTY kinematically
AACEIILLLNSTY inelastically
AACEIILLLRSTY realistically
AACEIILLMNPRT planimetrical
AACEIILLMNSSY messianically
AACEIILLMOPTT metapolitical
AACEIILLNRRTY intercalarily
AACEIILLPPTVY applicatively
AACEIILMMNRSU unicameralism
AACEIILMNNRST manneristical
AACEIILMNRSTT maternalistic
AACEIILMNRSTU unicameralist
AACEIILNNORTT interactional
intercalation
AACEIILNOPPRT reapplication
AACEIILNOPPSS episcopalians
AACEIILNORSTT cartelisation
AACEIILNORTTZ cartelization
AACEIILNPRSTT antiparticles
paternalistic
AACEIILNRSSST satiricalness
AACEIILPRRSTU particularise
AACEIILPRRTUZ particularize
AACEIIMMOSTTU semiautomatic
AACEIIMNNOPST emancipations
AACEIIMNNOTTV contaminative
AACEIIMOPRRST microparasite
AACEIIMORSSTT masticatories
AACEIINNNORRT reincarnation
AACEIINOPPRST appreciations
AACEIINOPRRTV prevarication
AACEIINORSTTU cauterisation
AACEIINORSTTV reactivations
AACEIINORTTUZ cauterization
AACEIJKRSSTTT straitjackets
AACEIKLMNOPST kleptomaniacs
AACEIKLOPRSTT keratoplastic
AACEILLLNRRTU intracellular
AACEILLMMPRST metrical psalm
AACEILLMNPTUY pneumatically
AACEILLMORTXY exclamatorily
AACEILLMPRSTY spermatically
AACEILLNOORRT correlational
AACEILLNOORST reallocations
AACEILLNOSSTT castellations
AACEILMNORSSY microanalyses
AACEILMNOSSTU emasculations
AACEILMNRRSUV vernacularism
AACEILMOPRTVY comparatively
AACEILMORRSTT astrometrical
AACEILNNOPSTU encapsulation
AACEILNOSSSSU salaciousness
AACEILNSSSUUV Cassivelaunus
AACEILOOPPRSS laparoscopies
AACEILRSSTTTU Trucial States
AACEIMMNORSTT commentariats
AACEIMMNORTUU communautaire
AACEIMNNOPRRT nonparametric
AACEIMNNRSTTT transmittance
AACEIMNOOPSST compassionate
AACEINOPRRSTT procrastinate
AACEINOPRRTUY precautionary
AACEINOPRSSSU rapaciousness
AACEINORRSTTT retractations
AACEINPRRSSTT transcriptase
AACEIOPRRRSTV prevaricators
AACELLMNORSSW lowerclassman
AACELMMNOPRTT compartmental
AACELNORRSUUV neurovascular
AACELNRSSTTUU sustentacular
AACELOPRRSTUX Castrop-Rauxel
AACEMNNOORSTT entomostracan
AACFFGHIINNRS affranchising
AACFFIIILNOST falsification
AACFGIIIMNNOT magnification
AACFGIIINORTT gratification
AACFGIILNNSTY fascinatingly
AACFGIINNORTT fractionating
AACFGILNNOORT conflagration
AACFGILRSTUVX Carl XVI Gustaf
AACFGIMNNRTUU manufacturing
AACFHIMNPRSST craftsmanship
AACFIIIILRTTY artificiality
AACFIIILMNOPT amplification
AACFIIILNOQTU qualification
AACFIIIMNORST ramifications
AACFIIINORSTT ratifications
AACFIILLORSTV Victoria Falls
AACFIILNOSSTT factionalists
AACFIILOQRTUY qualificatory
AACFIINNOORTT fractionation
AACFIINOORSTT factorisation
AACFIINOORTTZ factorization
AACFIINOSSSTT satisfactions
AACFINOORRSTT fractionators
AACFINORSTTUY anfractuosity
AACFORRSSTTTU fractostratus
AACGGHILLOOPR graphological
logographical
AACGGHINOOPRR organographic
AACGGILLLLOOY algologically

AACGGILLNOOOR	organological
AACGGILLOORST	gastrological
AACGGILMMOORT	logogrammatic
AACGGILNRSTYZ	crystal gazing
AACGHHILMOOPR	homalographic
AACGHHIPRSTTY	tachygraphist
AACGHIILLMORT	logarithmical
AACGHIILLNNTU	hallucinating
AACGHIILLPRST	calligraphist
AACGHIIMNORST	achromatising
AACGHIIMNORTZ	achromatizing
AACGHIIPRRSTT	stratigraphic
AACGHILLNNOTY	gnathonically
AACGHILLOPRXY	xylographical
AACGHILMNOOPR	nomographical
AACGHILNOORST	arachnologist
AACGHILOOPPRR	polarographic
AACGHILOOPPRT	topographical
AACGHILOPPRTY	typographical
AACGHMMOORRST	chromatograms
AACGHMNOOPRSY	pharmacognosy
AACGIIILLMSTY	imagistically
AACGIIILLNOTZ	gallicization
AACGIIILNNOST	anglicisation
AACGIIILNNOTZ	anglicization
AACGIIINNORTT	ratiocinating
AACGIIINPPRTT	participating
AACGIILLLNTVY	vacillatingly
AACGIILLLOOXY	axiologically
AACGIILLNNORY	inorganically
AACGIILMNRTTU	matriculating
AACGIILNNPSTU	incapsulating
AACGIILNORSTU	cartilaginous
AACGIILNPTTVY	captivatingly
AACGIIMNNNOTT	contaminating
AACGIJLNNOOTU	conjugational
AACGILLLNOOPY	palynological
AACGILLLNOSTY	nostalgically
AACGILLMNSTYY	gymnastically
AACGILLMOOOST	somatological
AACGILLMOOSST	malacologists
AACGILLOOPPRY	papyrological
AACGILMNOOPST	campanologist
AACGILMNOORST	gastronomical
AACGILNNORSTT	translocating
AACGILNOOPRTV	galvanotropic
AACGIMMMNOORT	monogrammatic
AACGINNORRSTW	narrowcasting
AACGLNOORRTTU	congratulator
AACHHHIMORSTT	Simchath Torah
AACHHIILNPPSS	chaplainships
AACHHIIMNPRSS	chairmanships
AACHHILPSTXYY	tachyphylaxis
AACHHIMNPSSTY	yachtsmanship
AACHIIINNRSTT	antichristian
AACHIILLNNOTU	hallucination
AACHIIMMOPSTT	amphistomatic
AACHIKORSSTUW	autorickshaws
AACHILLLMPTYY	lymphatically
AACHILLMOOPSU	malacophilous
AACHILLNOPPSY	pansophically
AACHILLNORRTU	Carrantuohill
AACHILLNORSTU	hallucinators
AACHILLNORSTY	thrasonically
AACHILLNORTUY	hallucinatory
AACHILNNOORRT	North Carolina
AACHILNNOPTYY	hypnoanalytic
AACHILNOORSTU	South Carolina
AACHILOPRSSTY	astrophysical
AACHIMMNNOPSY	nymphomaniacs
AACHIMMNOPRST	panchromatism
AACHIMMOOPRST	apochromatism
AACHIMNOPRRSS	parachronisms
AACHIMOPRSSTT	catastrophism
AACHINNOPRRTT	Pontchartrain
AACHIOPRSSTTT	catastrophist
AACHLMMOOPRSY	lymphosarcoma
AACHLNOPSSTYY	psychoanalyst
AACHLOOPRSTTY	thoracoplasty
AACIIIILNOSTT	italicisation
AACIIIILNOTTZ	italicization
AACIIILLMNOPT	implicational
AACIIILLNNNOT	inclinational
AACIIILLNOPTT	antipolitical
AACIIILLPPRTY	participially
AACIIILNNOSTT	nationalistic
AACIIILNOOSST	socialisation
AACIIILNOOSTZ	socialization
AACIIILNORSTT	rationalistic
AACIIINNOORTT	ratiocination
AACIIINNOPSTT	anticipations
AACIIINNOSTTV	vaticinations
AACIIINOPPRTT	participation
AACIIINSSSTTT	statisticians
AACIILLMNNOTY	antinomically
AACIILLMORTTY	matrilocality
	triatomically
AACIILLMOSTTY	atomistically
AACIILLMPRSTY	prismatically
AACIILLNNOSTT	cantillations
AACIILLNOOSST	localisations
AACIILLNOOSTZ	localizations
AACIILLNPRTUY	puritanically
AACIILLNPTTYY	antitypically
AACIILLOPRSTY	piscatorially
AACIILLOPRTTY	patriotically
AACIILLPRSTTY	patristically
AACIILLSSTTTY	statistically
AACIILMNORSSY	microanalysis
AACIILMNORTTU	matriculation
AACIILMPRRSTU	particularism
AACIILNNOOSTV	volcanisation
AACIILNNOOTVZ	volcanization
AACIILNNOPSTU	incapsulation
AACIILNNOSTUV	vulcanisation
AACIILNNOTUVZ	vulcanization
AACIILNOOSSTV	vocalisations
AACIILNOOSTVZ	vocalizations
AACIILNOPSTTU	capitulations
AACIILNORSTTU	articulations
AACIILOPPRSTT	procapitalist
AACIILPRRSTTU	particularist
AACIILPRRTTUY	particularity
AACIIMMNNORTU	communitarian

AACIIMMORSSST commissariats
AACIIMNNNOOTT contamination
AACIIMNNORTUU actinouranium
AACIINNNNOSTU annunciations
AACIINNNOOSST canonisations
AACIINNNOOSTZ canonizations
AACIINNOORSTT narcotisation
AACIINNOORTTZ narcotization
AACIINNORSSST incrassations
AACIINOORRSTT ratiocinators
AACIINORRSSTU curarisations
AACIINORRSTUZ curarizations
AACIIOPPRRSTT participators
AACIIOPPRRTTY participatory
AACILLLOOPSTY apostolically
AACILLMNOOTUY autonomically
AACILLMNOOTXY taxonomically
AACILLMNOPSTY complaisantly
AACILLMPRSTYY sympatrically
AACILLNORTVYY clairvoyantly
AACILMNOOPRST proclamations
AACILMNOOPTTU computational
AACILMNORSSTY microanalysts
AACILMNRRSTUU intramuscular
AACILMOOPSSTT somatoplastic
AACILMORRSTTU matriculators
AACILNNOORSTT translocation
AACILNOSSTTUU auscultations
AACILNPRSSTYY cryptanalysis
AACILOOPRRRTU procuratorial
AACIMNNOOPSWY companionways
AACIMNNOORSTT contaminators
AACIMNNRSTTTY transmittancy
AACIMOPRSTTTU posttraumatic
AACINNOOSSTTT constatations
AACLLNNNOOSTY consonantally
AACLNPRSSTTYY cryptanalysts
AADDEEEEFHHRT featherheaded
AADDEEEHQRRTU headquartered
AADDEEGGILLRT draggletailed
AADDEEGINNRRU underdrainage
AADDEEGNRRTUU undergraduate
AADDEEHHLRRTY hardheartedly
AADDEEHHMMMMO Mohammed Ahmed
AADDEEHLORSTT stadholderate
AADDEEILNRSTU denaturalised
AADDEEILNRTUZ denaturalized
AADDEELMNNQUU Queen Maud Land
AADDEELNRTTUU unadulterated
AADDEFFIIILST disaffiliated
AADDEGGHNRRTU granddaughter
AADDEGINOPPRS propagandised
AADDEGINOPPRZ propagandized
AADDEGNNRRSST grandstanders
AADDEHIMNSSSU Saddam Hussein
AADDEIIMNRSTT administrated
AADDEILNNOSSS Soenda Islands
AADDEILNRSSST dastardliness
AADDEINRRSSST standardisers
AADDEINRRSSTZ standardizers
AADDFIMNNOOSU Usman dan Fodio
AADDGGINNNRST grandstanding
AADDGIINNRSST standardising
AADDGIINNRSTZ standardizing
AADDHILLNNOSW Howland Island
AADDIIILNOTTY additionality
AADDIILMNSSWY Midway Islands
AADEEEGGLRTXY exaggeratedly
AADEEEGGNRTUX unexaggerated
AADEEEGMMNNST endamagements
AADEEEHINSSTT anaesthetised
AADEEEHINSTTZ anaesthetized
AADEEEIILMRST dematerialise
AADEEEIILMRTZ dematerialize
AADEEEIMNNRRT mediterranean
AADEEELPRSTXY exasperatedly
AADEEEMMNRSTU admeasurement
AADEEFHHLLRTY halfheartedly
AADEEFHKLLOTY Lady of the Lake
AADEEFKMNNNOR Anne of Denmark
AADEEFNSSSSTT steadfastness
AADEEGGHILNRT Edgar Atheling
AADEEGILMORRT radiotelegram
AADEEGILMQRSU madrigalesque
AADEEGILRSTVY Yelisavetgrad
AADEEGIMNPRST disparagement
AADEEGINNSTUX exsanguinated
AADEEHILMOSSY haemodialyses
AADEEHILNQRSU harlequinades
AADEEHIMMMNOZ Mohammedanize
AADEEHLLRRTTY tetrahedrally
AADEEHLOPRRTZ trapezohedral
AADEEHLORRTTT tetartohedral
AADEEHMNNSSSU unashamedness
AADEEHPRSSSTT spatterdashes
AADEEIILMMSSV mediaevalisms
AADEEIILMSSTV mediaevalists
AADEEIILNNOST denationalise
AADEEIILNNOTZ denationalize
AADEEIIMNNRSU neuraminidase
AADEEIKNORRTY Yekaterinodar
AADEEILLNPPRS Apple Islander
AADEEILLOPRSY Pays de la Loire
AADEEILMMORST melodramatise
AADEEILMMORTZ melodramatize
AADEEILNNNORR noradrenaline
AADEEILNRSSTU denaturalises
AADEEILNRSTUZ denaturalizes
AADEEIMMNNSST misdemeanants
AADEEIMNNOSUV Madison Avenue
AADEEIMNOPRRT panradiometer
AADEEIMORRSTV overdramatise
AADEEIMORRTVZ overdramatize
AADEEINOPRSST endoparasites
AADEEINPRSSST disparateness
AADEENNPRSTUU superannuated
AADEEORRSTTUV oversaturated
AADEFFIIILSST disaffiliates
AADEFGHLNRRTY grandfatherly
AADEFGILNORST deflagrations
AADEFHINNOSTU fountainheads
AADEFIILNOSTU feudalisation
AADEFIILNOTUZ feudalization
AADEFILMNOORS Maid of Orléans

AADEFILNSSSTY	Safety Islands
AADEFLLMNNTUY	fundamentally
AADEGGHHIMNOU	houghmagandie
AADEGHIIOPPRR	Herod Agrippa I
AADEGHIMMORSX	hexagrammoids
AADEGHIOPRRRS	radiographers
AADEGIIIMPRRV	primigravidae
AADEGIIMNNRTV	animadverting
AADEGILLNNRSW	Wrangel Island
AADEGILNSTTVY	devastatingly
AADEGIMNNRRST	darraignments
AADEGIMNRRSTT	transmigrated
AADEGINOPPRSS	propagandises
AADEGINOPPRSZ	propagandizes
AADEGLMNORSSW	De Morgan's laws
AADEGOPRSSTTU	postgraduates
AADEHHILMOORR	haemorrhoidal
AADEHIILMOSSY	haemodialysis
AADEHIILNPSUZ	sulphadiazine
AADEHIKLMORSY	holidaymakers
AADEHILLLLOTW	Allhallowtide
AADEHILNORSUY	hyaluronidase
AADEHIMMMNOS	Mohammedanism
AADEHIMNORSTU	diathermanous
AADEHNORRSTTW	northeastward
AADEHNORSSSUZ	hazardousness
AADEHORRSSSUU	hadrosauruses
AADEHORSSTTUW	southeastward
AADEIIILNOSST	idealisations
AADEIIILNOSTZ	idealizations
AADEIIIMNNOST	deaminisation
AADEIIIMNNOTZ	deaminization
AADEIIIMNOSTT	mediatisation
AADEIIIMNOTTZ	mediatization
AADEIILLMORTY	mediatorially
AADEIILLMPRXY	maxillipedary
AADEIILLNRRTY	interradially
AADEIILLNSUVV	vaudevillians
AADEIILMMNRST	maladminister
AADEIILMNNOST	delaminations
AADEIILMNSSTU	unassimilated
AADEIILNNSTUV	antediluvians
AADEIIMNNORSV	animadversion
AADEIIMNRSSTT	administrates
AADEIINOPSSST	dispassionate
AADEIIPQRRTTU	quadripartite
AADEIKLNNOORS	Roanoke Island
AADEIKMNRRSTT	Denmark Strait
AADEILLMNRRTY	intradermally
AADEILLNNQRUY	quadrennially
AADEILMMORSTT	melodramatist
AADEILMNNPTUU	unmanipulated
AADEILMNORSST	maladroitness
AADEILMNRSSTT	mistranslated
AADEILNORSTTU	adulterations
AADEILNRSSTTW	Stewart Island
AADEIMPRRSSTY	tryparsamides
AADEINNORSTTU	denaturations
AADEINORRRTXY	extraordinary
AADEINRRSTTWW	Witwatersrand
AADEJLMMNSTTU	maladjustment
AADEKKLNORSSV	Aleksandrovsk
AADEKLLNOOPRS	Aleksandropol
AADELMOOORRST	mater dolorosa
AADELMOPRSTTY	dermatoplasty
AADEMNORSTTUY	tetradynamous
AADFGHIIMPRST	paradigm shift
AADFHIMNPRSST	draftsmanship
AADFINNOORTUY	foundationary
AADGGIILNPRSY	disparagingly
AADGHIINPRSSU	guardianships
AADGHINORSTTT	Saint Gotthard
AADGHMNORSTUW	draughtswoman
AADGIIIMPRRSV	primigravidas
AADGIILLNNSTW	Watling Island
AADGIILMRSTUV	multigravidas
AADGIIMNOOSTT	dogmatisation
AADGIIMNOOTTZ	dogmatization
AADGILLNNOOSS	Lagoon Islands
AADGILNNOPRST	prostaglandin
AADGIMRRSSTTU	dramaturgists
AADGINOPPRSST	propagandists
AADHILNORRSTY	synarthrodial
AADIIILLLRSUV	Livia Drusilla
AADIIILLNPRSS	Lipari Islands
AADIIILNNNOSS	Ionian Islands
AADIIILNNOSTV	invalidations
AADIIINOOSTTZ	diazotisation
AADIIINOOTTZZ	diazotization
AADIILLLNTTUY	latitudinally
AADIILLNOORST	dollarisation
AADIILLNOORTZ	dollarization
AADIILLNORTTY	traditionally
AADIILLOSUUVY	audiovisually
AADIILMNOQRSU	quadrinomials
AADIIMNNOORST	randomisation
AADIIMNNOORTZ	randomization
AADIIMNORRSTT	administrator
AADILMNSSTUUU	Aldus Manutius
AADINNOPSSSUY	Passion Sunday
AADINNORSSTTU	transudations
AAEEEEKKMRRWW	amakwerekwere
AAEEEGILLRSTT	Tate Galleries
AAEEEGMNNRRRT	rearrangement
AAEEEHIILLSSS	Haile Selassie
AAEEEHINSSSTT	anaesthetises
AAEEEHINSSTTZ	anaesthetizes
AAEEEILNNORRS	Sierra Leonean
AAEEEKMNNPPRT	Petermann Peak
AAEEELMMNPRTT	temperamental
AAEEFIIMNSTTV	manifestative
AAEEFIKLLRSTU	Kaieteur Falls
AAEEGGGJNRRUW	Wagner-Jauregg
AAEEGGILMORTV	agglomerative
AAEEGGILNORST	segregational
AAEEGGINORSTX	exaggerations
AAEEGGORSSTTY	Ortega y Gasset
AAEEGHILLMNNT	mental healing
AAEEGHMNOOSTU	haematogenous
AAEEGIIILNUVZ	Venezia Giulia
AAEEGIIMMPRST	epigrammatise
AAEEGIIMMPRTZ	epigrammatize
AAEEGIIMNRRRT	intermarriage
AAEEGIIMNRSTV	vegetarianism

AAEEGILMNOORR	oleomargarine
AAEEGIMMMNNST	mismanagement
AAEEGIMNRTTUV	argumentative
AAEEGIMNSTTUV	augmentatives
AAEEGINNSSTUX	exsanguinates
AAEEGINOPRSTU	eusporangiate
AAEEGLMNORSTV	galvanometers
AAEEGNNNORRTT	Tarn-et-Garonne
AAEEHHIMPRSTT	amphitheaters
	amphitheatres
AAEEHHLMMORTT	hematothermal
AAEEHHMOPPSTT	metaphosphate
AAEEHIILMOPTT	epitheliomata
AAEEHIILNPSST	elephantiasis
AAEEHIIMPRSST	hemiparasites
AAEEHILLNNNPY	phenylalanine
AAEEHILNPRSST	phalansteries
AAEEHILPRSSTU	laureateships
AAEEHINNRRSTY	Tyrrhenian Sea
AAEEHINSSSTTT	anaesthetists
AAEEHIPPRRSTY	hyperparasite
AAEEHKMORRSTT	katharometers
AAEEHMNOSTTUX	exanthematous
AAEEHMOPRRRST	spermatorrhea
AAEEHNOPPRSTU	Parthenopaeus
AAEEIIILMMRST	immaterialise
AAEEIIILMMRTZ	immaterialize
AAEEIILMNNRTT	interlaminate
AAEEIILMRRSST	materialisers
AAEEIILMRRSTZ	materializers
AAEEIILNPRRTT	interparietal
AAEEIILNSSSUV	Aeneas Silvius
AAEEIIMNNNSST	inanimateness
AAEEIIMNNORTX	reexamination
AAEEIIMPRSSST	semiparasites
AAEEIINNRRSSV	anniversaries
AAEEIINNRRSTV	veterinarians
AAEEIINNSSSTT	insatiateness
AAEEIKLMNSSTT	statesmanlike
AAEEIKLNORSTV	Ekaterinoslav
AAEEIKLNSSTTV	talkativeness
AAEEILLLPPTVY	appellatively
AAEEILLLQRTUY	equilaterally
AAEEILLMNPSST	planetesimals
AAEEILLNRTTVY	alternatively
AAEEILMORRSST	alstroemerias
AAEEILNNNOPPT	peneplanation
AAEEILNORSTUV	reevaluations
AAEEILNRRSTTT	transliterate
AAEEILOPRTTVX	extrapolative
AAEEILPPRRTVY	preparatively
AAEEILQRSSSTU	sesquialteras
AAEEIMNPPRSST	appraisements
AAEEIMNPRRSTV	privateersman
AAEEINORSSSTV	asseverations
AAEEJKMMNRSTZ	katzenjammers
AAEELNPRRRTTU	preternatural
AAEEMQRRRSTTU	quartermaster
AAEENNPRSSTUU	superannuates
AAEEQRRSSTTUV	quarterstaves
AAEERRRSSTTUU	restaurateurs
AAEFFIILMNORR	foraminiferal
AAEFFIILMRTVY	affirmatively
AAEFFIIMNORRT	reaffirmation
AAEFFINOORSTT	afforestation
AAEFGHLLNNPRS	flannelgraphs
AAEFGIILLMRSU	gallimaufries
AAEFGIKLNNRRS	farnarkelings
AAEFGILLLMNST	flagellantism
AAEFGILLLNOST	flagellations
AAEFGILMNRRTY	fragmentarily
AAEFGIMNNORTT	fragmentation
AAEFGINNORSTT	engraftations
AAEFHILLOSTUZ	sulfathiazole
AAEFHLMORSTTW	Waltham Forest
AAEFIIIILMRST	familiarities
AAEFIIILMRRSS	familiarisers
AAEFIIILMRRSZ	familiarizers
AAEFIILNNORRU	Alain-Fournier
AAEFIIMNNOSTT	manifestation
AAEFILLOPRRTY	prefatorially
AAEFILMNOORRT	reformational
AAEFILMNPRTUZ	flunitrazepam
AAEFILNQRRSTU	quarterfinals
AAEFILORSSSTY	forestaysails
AAEGGGILMNORT	agglomerating
AAEGGHHIIOPRS	hagiographies
AAEGGHHIMNORR	haemorrhaging
AAEGGHHIOPRRS	hagiographers
AAEGGHMNOPRST	magnetographs
AAEGGIILNTTUV	agglutinative
AAEGGIIMNNORT	aggiornamenti
AAEGGILMNOORT	agglomeration
AAEGGILNPPRSS	glasspapering
AAEGGIMNNOORT	aggiornamento
AAEGGLLLOSSSW	gallowglasses
AAEGGLMNORSTW	West Glamorgan
AAEGGLNOOPRTU	protolanguage
AAEGHHILOPPRS	haplographies
AAEGHHMOOPSTU	hematophagous
AAEGHHOPPRRSS	phraseographs
AAEGHHOPPRRSY	phraseography
AAEGHIINNPSSU	Spanish Guinea
AAEGHIKMNOPRT	kinematograph
AAEGHILMOOSTT	haematologist
AAEGHILNNOOST	halogenations
AAEGHILNOPPRS	planographies
AAEGHIOPRRRTY	arteriography
AAEGHIPRRRSTT	stratigrapher
AAEGHLLMOPRTY	metallography
AAEGHLOPPSYYZ	zygapophyseal
AAEGHLOPRTTUY	telautography
AAEGHLPRTTUUV	truth-value gap
AAEGHMNOOPRSU	phanerogamous
AAEGHMORRTTUY	Great Yarmouth
AAEGHNNOPRSSY	nasopharynges
AAEGHNOOPRRTY	organotherapy
AAEGHNOPPRRST	pantographers
AAEGHNOPRRRSU	uranographers
AAEGIIILMNRST	materialising
AAEGIIILMNRTZ	materializing
AAEGIIILMNTVY	imaginatively
AAEGIIILNRRST	arterialising
AAEGIIILNRRTZ	arterializing

AAEGIIIMMNNST magnanimities
AAEGIIIMNNRSS imaginariness
AAEGIIIMNNTUV unimaginative
AAEGIILLLORST legislatorial
AAEGIILLMRSTY magisterially
AAEGIILLNOSST legalisations
AAEGIILLNOSTZ legalizations
AAEGIILNNTTTY tangentiality
AAEGIIMMMPRST epigrammatism
AAEGIIMMPRSTT epigrammatist
AAEGIIMNNORTZ germanization
AAEGIIMNNOSTT magnetisation
AAEGIIMNNOTTZ magnetization
AAEGIIMNQQSUU Quinquagesima
AAEGIIMNSSSTT metastasising
AAEGIIMNSSTTZ metastasizing
AAEGILLMNOOPT megalopolitan
AAEGILLNRTTUY triangulately
AAEGILMNNOPST Leamington Spa
AAEGILMNOORRS oleomargarins
AAEGILNNRRSTT retranslating
AAEGILNOPRTTX extrapolating
AAEGILOPRRTUX expurgatorial
AAEGIMNNORTTU argumentation
AAEGIMNNOSTTU augmentations
AAEGIMNOOPRST spermatogonia
AAEGIMNRRSSTT transmigrates
AAEGIMRRSSTTU magistratures
AAEGINNOORSTV Stanovoi Range
AAEGINOORSTTY geostationary
AAEGINQRRSTUW quartersawing
AAEGLLNOOOPTY palaeontology
AAEGLLOOOOPYZ palaeozoology
AAEGLNNOOSSSU analogousness
AAEHHILMOPRTX xerophthalmia
AAEHIIILMNSSS leishmaniasis
AAEHIIIMNNSTT antihistamine
AAEHIILNORSTX exhilarations
AAEHIIMNOSTTT thematisation
AAEHIIMNOTTTZ thematization
AAEHIINNOPRST antiphonaries
AAEHIIORTTTUV authoritative
AAEHIKMMOPSST Thomas à Kempis
AAEHIKNOSSTTV stakhanovites
AAEHILMNOSTXY haematoxylins
AAEHILNNOSSST Thessalonians
AAEHIMNPSSSTT statesmanship
AAEHINNNOQRTU anthraquinone
AAEHINOPRSTTU naturopathies
AAEHINPRSSSTY parasynthesis
AAEHLMNOOSTXY haematoxylons
AAEHNNOPRSSXY nasopharynxes
AAEHNNOPRSTTY parasyntheton
AAEIIIILNNNTV Valentinian II
AAEIIILMMMRST immaterialism
AAEIIILMMRSTT immaterialist
AAEIIILMMRTTY immateriality
AAEIIILNNOSTT nationalities
AAEIIILNORSST serialisation
AAEIIILNORSTT rationalities
AAEIIILNORSTZ serialization
AAEIIIMNNPPRT imparipinnate
AAEIIKLMNPSST Semipalatinsk
AAEIILLLMNRTY matrilineally
AAEIILLLNPRTY patrilineally
AAEIILLMNOSTT metallisation
AAEIILLMNOTTZ metallization
AAEIILLMNRSTU unilateralism
AAEIILLNOPSTT palletisation
AAEIILLNOPTTZ palletization
AAEIILLNORSTT alliterations
AAEIILLNPRRTY patrilinearly
AAEIILLNRTTUY unilaterality
AAEIILLQTTUVY qualitatively
AAEIILMMNNSTT milatainments
AAEIILMMNOSTT lemmatisation
AAEIILMMNOTTZ lemmatization
AAEIILMNNORTT terminational
AAEIILMNOORST ameliorations
AAEIILMNOSTTZ metalizations
AAEIILMNPRSST impartialness
AAEIILNNNORTT international
AAEIILNNOORTT orientational
AAEIILNNOPSST penalisations
AAEIILNNOPSTZ penalizations
AAEIILNNORSTV vernalisation
AAEIILNNORTVZ vernalization
AAEIILNOPRRST respirational
AAEIILNOQSSTU equalisations
AAEIILNOQSTUZ equalizations
AAEIILNORRSST rationalisers
AAEIILNORRSTZ rationalizers
AAEIILNORRTTT trilateration
AAEIILNOSSTUX sexualisation
AAEIILNOSTUXZ sexualization
AAEIIMNNNOSTX annexationism
AAEIIMNOOPRST anisometropia
AAEIIMOPPRTVX approximative
AAEIINNNOSTTX annexationist
AAEIINNNSTTTY instantaneity
AAEIINNOSSTTT tetanisations
AAEIINOPPPRRT inappropriate
AAEIINOPRRSTT repatriations
AAEIINOPRSSTT separationist
AAEIIOPPPRRTV appropriative
AAEIKLLNNOPSU Kola Peninsula
AAEILLMNNOPRY praenominally
AAEILLNNOSSTY sensationally
AAEILLNOOPRTY operationally
AAEILLNOPRTXY explanatorily
AAEILMNNORSTU mensurational
AAEILMNOPRTTU permutational
AAEILMNRSSSTT mistranslates
AAEILMNRSSTUX transexualism
AAEILMOPPRTXY approximately
AAEILNNNNPSVY Pennsylvanian
AAEILNNOPRSTT replantations
AAEILNNOPRSTU supernational
AAEILNNOPSTTX explantations
AAEILNNORRSTT retranslation
AAEILNOOORTTV laevorotation
AAEILNOOPRTTX extrapolation
AAEILOPPPRRTY appropriately
AAEILOPPRRRTY preparatorily

AAEILORSSTTVY	assortatively
AAEIMMOOSSSTT	metasomatosis
AAEIMNNNOORTT	ornamentation
AAEIMNORSSTTT	stationmaster
AAEIMNRSTTTUV	transmutative
AAEINNNOSSTTU	instantaneous
AAEINNOPRSTTU	supernatation
AAEKLOPRRSTUX	Kastrop-Rauxel
AAELLMOOPRSTU	somatopleural
AAELLNRRSSTVY	transversally
AAELMNNOOSSSU	anomalousness
AAELMNNORSTTU	ultramontanes
AAELNNNRSSTUU	unnaturalness
AAELNNPRRSSTT	transplanters
AAELNNPRRSTTY	transparently
AAELOOORRTTVY	laevorotatory
AAELOOPRRSTTX	extrapolators
AAELOOPRRTTXY	extrapolatory
AAEMNNNORSSTT	transmontanes
AAFFGHINPRSSU	suffraganship
AAFFIINNOPRRT	nitroparaffin
AAFGIIIILMNRS	familiarising
AAFGIIIILMNRZ	familiarizing
AAFGIINNORSTT	ingraftations
AAFHIJNOORSTU	John of Austria
AAFIIILMNRTUY	unfamiliarity
AAFIIILNNOSST	finalisations
AAFIIILNRSTTU	futilitarians
AAFIIIMNRRSTU	fruitarianism
AAFIILMMNNOST	inflammations
AAFIILMNNOORT	informational
AAFIILMNNOOST	Nation of Islam
AAFIILMNOORST	formalisation
AAFIILMNOORTZ	formalization
AAFILMMNOORST	malformations
AAFILNOOSSSUU	Louis of Nassau
AAFIMOORRSSTT	Formosa Strait
AAGGGIILNNTTU	agglutinating
AAGGHHIIOPRST	hagiographist
AAGGIIILMNNRS	marginalising
AAGGIIILMNNRZ	marginalizing
AAGGIILNNOTTU	agglutination
AAGGIILNNRTTU	triangulating
AAGGILNNRSTTU	strangulating
AAGHHINOOPPRT	anthropophagi
AAGHHNOOPPRTY	anthropophagy
AAGHIILMNORTT	antilogarithm
AAGHIINNNOSTW	Washingtonian
AAGHIMNOOPRST	mastigophoran
AAGHINOPRRSTU	uranographist
AAGIIILMMNORT	immigrational
AAGIIILNNNOST	nationalising
AAGIIILNNNOTZ	nationalizing
AAGIIILNNORST	rationalising
AAGIIILNNORTZ	rationalizing
AAGIIINNNOSTV	invaginations
AAGIIINNNSTTT	instantiating
AAGIIINNORSTT	granitisation
	ingratiations
AAGIIINNORTTZ	granitization
AAGIIJNNOORST	jargonisation
AAGIIJNNOORTZ	jargonization
AAGIIKLNNPSTY	painstakingly
AAGIILLMOORST	malariologist
AAGIILLNNOPST	Gallinas Point
AAGIILLNNSTTY	tantalisingly
AAGIILLNNTTYZ	tantalizingly
AAGIILMNOORST	glamorisation
AAGIILMNOORTZ	glamorization
AAGIILNNORTTU	triangulation
AAGIILNORSTUV	vulgarisation
AAGIILNORTUVZ	vulgarization
AAGIILNRRTTUY	triangularity
AAGIIMNOPPRTX	approximating
AAGIINNOORSST	organisations
AAGIINNOORSTZ	organizations
AAGIINNORSTUU	inaugurations
AAGIINOPPPRRT	appropriating
AAGIKLNNOPQRU	Algonquin Park
AAGIKNNSSUUUY	Aung San Suu Kyi
AAGILLOPRRTUY	purgatorially
AAGILMMNNOSUY	magnanimously
AAGILNNNPRSTT	transplanting
AAGILNNORSTTU	strangulation
AAGILNOOOPRSZ	zoosporangial
AAGILNORSSTTU	gastrulations
AAGIMNNRRSSTT	transmigrants
AAGIMNORRRSTT	transmigrator
AAGINOOOPPRSS	prosopagnosia
AAGIRRSSTTTUU	Tsugaru Strait
AAGLMNOORSTUU	granulomatous
AAHHNOOPPRTTY	anthropopathy
AAHIIILNNNOST	annihilations
AAHIILNNPRRTY	platyrrhinian
AAHIIMNNOORST	harmonisation
AAHIIMNNOORTZ	harmonization
AAHIIMNNOSSTU	humanisations
AAHIIMNNOSTUZ	humanizations
AAHIINOORSTTU	authorisation
AAHIINOORTTUZ	authorization
AAHIINOPSSTXY	asphyxiations
AAHIKLLNNOPST	haliplanktons
AAHILNNOPSSYY	hypnoanalysis
AAIIILMNORRST	irrationalism
AAIIILMNOSSST	assimilations
AAIIILNNOPRST	inspirational
AAIIILNNOPRTT	Tripolitanian
AAIIILNNOPSTT	platinisation
AAIIILNNOPTTZ	platinization
AAIIILNNOSTTZ	latinizations
AAIIILNOORSTV	variolisation
AAIIILNOORTVZ	variolization
AAIIILNORRTTY	irrationality
AAIIILNOSSTUV	visualisation
AAIIILNOSTUVZ	visualization
AAIIILNPRSTTU	antispiritual
AAIIIMMNNNOST	antinomianism
AAIIIMMNOSSTX	maximisations
AAIIIMMNOSTXZ	maximizations
AAIIINNNOSTTT	instantiation
AAIIINOPRSTTV	privatisation
AAIIINOPRTTVZ	privatization
AAIIINORSSSTT	satirisations
AAIILLMMNORTY	matrimonially

AAIILLMNNOTTU multinational
AAIILLMNOPRTY patrimonially
AAIILLNNOSSTT installations
AAIILLNOPRSTU pluralisation
AAIILLNOPRTUZ pluralization
AAIILMNNOORST normalisation
AAIILMNNOORTZ normalization
AAIILMNNOPSTT implantations
AAIILMNNOPSTU manipulations
AAIILMNOOPTTT totipalmation
AAIILMNOORSST moralisations
AAIILMNOORSTZ moralizations
AAIILMNOSTTUU mutualisation
AAIILMNOTTUUZ mutualization
AAIILNOOPRSST polarisations
AAIILNOOPRSTZ polarizations
AAIILNOORSSTV valorisations
AAIILNOORSTVZ valorizations
AAIILNOOSSTTT totalisations
AAIILNOOSTTTZ totalizations
AAIILNORRSSTU ruralisations
AAIILNORRSTUZ ruralizations
AAIILNOSSSTTV salvationists
AAIIMMNORSSTU summarisation
AAIIMMNORSTUZ summarization
AAIIMNNOORSTZ romanizations
AAIIMNOOPPRTX approximation
AAIIMNOORSSTT amortisations
AAIIMNOORSTTZ amortizations
AAIIMNORRSTTY martyrisation
AAIIMNORRTTYZ martyrization
AAIINNOPRRSTT transpiration
AAIINNOQSSTTU quantisations
AAIINNOQSTTUZ quantizations
AAIINNORRSTTY transitionary
AAIINNORSSTTU instaurations
AAIINOOPPPRRT appropriation
AAILLMOOPPSTU papillomatous
AAILMNNNORSTU non-naturalism
AAILMNNORSTUU Ural Mountains
AAILNNOPPSTTU supplantation
AAILNOOOPRRTT protonotarial
AAIMNNORSTTTU transmutation
AAINNORSSTTUU unsaturations
AAINOOORSTTTU autorotations
AAINOPRRRSTTY transpiratory
AAIOOPPPRRRST appropriators
AAKLNNNNNOOPT nannoplankton
AALMOOPSSTTTY stomatoplasty
AANNORRSSTUUY tyrannosaurus
ABBBEHLMORSTU blabbermouths
ABBCDEEIILNRS indescribable
ABBCDEGIMNRRU breadcrumbing
ABBCDEIILNRSY indescribably
ABBCEEIJKORSW jabberwockies
ABBCEEIJLNOOT objectionable
ABBCEGIKLNRRY blackberrying
ABBCEIJLNOOTY objectionably
ABBCEILNORTTU contributable
ABBCGHIIILOPR bibliographic
ABBCIIILMNOTY combinability
ABBCIIILOPRST probabilistic
ABBDEGIINORRW Rainbow Bridge
ABBDEIILRSTTU distributable
ABBDILOOOOSSU Bobo-Dioulasso
ABBEEIIILLTVY believability
ABBEEILLMNRTY Blantyre-Limbe
ABBEEILMPRRTU imperturbable
ABBEEILMSSSSU subassemblies
ABBEELMMNOOTZ bamboozlement
ABBEFHILLNOTY Fonthill Abbey
ABBEGHIILOPRR bibliographer
ABBEIIILOPRST probabilities
ABBEIILORSTVY observability
ABBEILMPRRTUY imperturbably
ABBEILSSTTTUU substitutable
ABBGIINNRSSUU suburbanising
ABBGIINNRSUUZ suburbanizing
ABBIIILMOPRTY improbability
ABCCDDEHIIIKS chickabiddies
ABCCDEEEELNRT credence table
ABCCDEEELNORT concelebrated
ABCCDEEHKORRS checkerboards
ABCCDEHILORSU coachbuilders
ABCCDEILORSTU scrobiculated
ABCCDENORSTTU subcontracted
ABCCEEELNORST concelebrates
ABCCEEIILNNOV inconceivable
ABCCEEJLNORTU conjecturable
ABCCEELNORRTU uncorrectable
ABCCEEMNNRRSU encumbrancers
ABCCEGIILLOOO bioecological
ABCCEHIILLMOY biochemically
ABCCEIIILLLMY imbecilically
ABCCEIIILMPTY impeccability
ABCCEIIILSSTY accessibility
ABCCEIIINOSTV biconcavities
ABCCEIILNNOVY inconceivably
ABCCEIILORTTY bacteriolytic
ABCCEIIMMNRTU circumambient
ABCCEIMMORTUY mycobacterium
ABCCEJLNORTUY conjecturably
ABCCGHIIKNSTT backstitching
ABCCHHIIOPRRS archbishopric
ABCCIILLLNSUY subclinically
ABCCIILORRTXY tricarboxylic
ABCCIIMNOORST combinatorics
ABCCIINORSTTU antiscorbutic
ABCCILLORSTUY scorbutically
ABCCNOORRSTTU subcontractor
ABCDDEEEHNSSU debauchedness
ABCDDEEHKLLOY blockheadedly
ABCDDEEIILRST discreditable
ABCDDEIILRSTY discreditably
ABCDEEEGHNRST Berchtesgaden
ABCDEEEGINRRT decerebrating
ABCDEEEHLORRS breechloaders
ABCDEEEILNRRS candleberries
ABCDEEEINORRT decerebration
ABCDEEELMMNOR recommendable
ABCDEEHOQRRSU chequerboards
ABCDEEIIILTVY deceivability
ABCDEEIILLTTY delectability
ABCDEEIIMOSTY basidiomycete

ABCDEEILNNNOS	incondensable
ABCDEEILNPRTU	unpredictable
ABCDEEINORRSS	decarbonisers
ABCDEEINORRSZ	decarbonizers
ABCDEELMMNNOU	uncommendable
ABCDEFIILSSSU	subclassified
ABCDEGIINNORS	decarbonising
ABCDEGIINNORZ	decarbonizing
ABCDEGIINRRSU	decarburising
ABCDEGIINRRUZ	decarburizing
ABCDEHIILNNRR	brainchildren
ABCDEIIILLNPS	disciplinable
ABCDEIIILNORT	bidirectional
ABCDEIIILNTUY	ineducability
ABCDEIIILPRTY	predicability
ABCDEIIILPSTY	despicability
ABCDEIIILRTTY	creditability
ABCDEIILLOQTU	quodlibetical
ABCDEILNPRTUY	unpredictably
ABCDEINOOPRSS	proboscideans
ABCDEKMNORSSW	backswordsmen
ABCDIIIILNTVY	vindicability
ABCDIIILLPTUY	duplicability
ABCDIIILNNOOT	biconditional
ABCDIINOOPRSS	proboscidians
ABCDILNOOOSTT	odontoblastic
ABCEEEELNRSSX	execrableness
ABCEEEFIIINRS	beneficiaries
ABCEEEFIILLRT	electrifiable
ABCEEEFILLNNU	influenceable
ABCEEEIINNRST	bicentenaries
ABCEEEILNOPTX	exceptionable
ABCEEEILNRSUV	unserviceable
ABCEEEILNSSTX	excitableness
ABCEEEILORRRV	irrecoverable
ABCEEEILORTVX	overexcitable
ABCEEELMNOPRS	recompensable
ABCEEELNSSSUX	excusableness
ABCEEEMMNRRRS	remembrancers
ABCEEFFIINRST	febrifacients
ABCEEFINORSST	sorbefacients
ABCEEGHHIKNSS	backsheeshing
ABCEEGHLMRRSU	schlumbergera
ABCEEGILNOSTT	blastogenetic
ABCEEGIORSSTU	subcategories
ABCEEHILORSTT	heteroblastic
ABCEEHIMNRSTY	chimneybreast
ABCEEHKLLPRTY	Bletchley Park
ABCEEHLNOSSTU	touchableness
ABCEEHMMNNRST	embranchments
ABCEEIILNNNST	bicentennials
ABCEEIILNPRSU	republicanise
ABCEEIILNPRUZ	republicanize
ABCEEIILNRSSS	irascibleness
ABCEEILLORSTV	Belvoir Castle
ABCEEILLSSSTU	subcelestials
ABCEEILMOORSU	bromeliaceous
ABCEEILNNOSTT	incontestable
ABCEEILNNRSSU	incurableness
ABCEEILNOPRRS	cerebrospinal
ABCEEILNOPTXY	exceptionably
ABCEEILNORSSU	ribonucleases
ABCEEILORRRVY	irrecoverably
ABCEEIMNOSSTV	combativeness
ABCEEJKLMRSTU	lumberjackets
ABCEELLRTTUUY	tuberculately
ABCEELMMNORSU	commensurable
ABCEELNNOOPRU	pronounceable
ABCEELNSSSSTU	substanceless
ABCEENNNOORSV	nonobservance
ABCEENOPRRSTU	protuberances
ABCEEOOPRRRST	baroreceptors
ABCEFGHKNOOOS	Book of Changes
ABCEFHIILLMRU	liebfraumilch
ABCEFIIINORTV	verbification
ABCEFIILSSSSU	subclassifies
ABCEFINOORRSU	carboniferous
ABCEFLMNNOORU	unconformable
ABCEFLMNOORTU	uncomfortable
ABCEGHHOORRTU	thoroughbrace
ABCEGHILOPRTY	copyrightable
ABCEGHORRRSTU	turbochargers
ABCEGIIKKNSTY	stickybeaking
ABCEGIINNOOSU	bignoniaceous
ABCEGILLMOORY	embryological
ABCEHIIIORSTV	behavioristic
ABCEHIILMNTTY	bathylimnetic
ABCEHILLMOOPT	phlebotomical
ABCEHILNOPSST	constableship
ABCEHIMPRRSTY	brachypterism
ABCEHKLRSSSUW	swashbucklers
ABCEHLOOPRSTU	claustrophobe
ABCEHOPRRSTUY	brachypterous
ABCEIIIILNOTTY	noticeability
ABCEIIKNNRSSS	brainsickness
ABCEIILLLMPTU	multiplicable
ABCEIILLMNOPU	pneumobacilli
ABCEIILLMORTY	biometrically
ABCEIILMMRSTY	bisymmetrical
ABCEIILMNOPST	incompatibles
ABCEIILMNPRSU	republicanism
ABCEIILNOPRTU	republication
ABCEIILNRSTUY	censurability
ABCEIILOORSST	borosilicates
ABCEIILORSSTY	bacteriolysis
ABCEIIMNNOORT	recombination
ABCEIIMNNOOSZ	aminobenzoics
ABCEIINOORTTX	bacteriotoxin
ABCEIINORSSTT	obstetricians
ABCEIKLPRTUUY	Yakut Republic
ABCEILLMNORYY	embryonically
ABCEILLORSTTY	obstetrically
ABCEILNNOSTTY	incontestably
ABCEILNORTTUU	tuberculation
ABCEILOORSSTU	strobilaceous
ABCEILORRRTUU	arboriculture
ABCEINORRSSTU	subcontraries
ABCEIOOORRRTV	corroborative
ABCELLLOOSSTY	octosyllables
ABCELMMNORSUY	commensurably
ABCELNORSSTTU	counterblasts
ABCFIILNOSTUY	confusability
ABCFLMNNOORUY	unconformably
ABCFLMNOORTUY	uncomfortably

ABCFLNOOORRSU fluorocarbons
ABCGHHNOOPRRY bronchography
ABCGHIKLNSSUW swashbuckling
ABCGIIKLLNSST blacklistings
ABCGIILLNNOOO nonbiological
ABCGILLLNOOTU lactoglobulin
ABCGILLMNOORU macroglobulin
ABCGILNNOOOST conglobations
ABCGINOOORRRT corroborating
ABCHHINOOPRST opisthobranch
ABCHIILLOPSYY biophysically
ABCHILLMOPSTY lymphoblastic
ABCHILOOPRSTT trophoblastic
ABCIIILLNOTUY inoculability
ABCIIILLNPTUY inculpability
ABCIIILLTTUVY cultivability
ABCIIILMNOSTU umbilications
ABCIIILMOPTTY compatibility
ABCIIILNOSTUY unsociability
ABCIILLOORTUY colourability
ABCIILLOPRSTT triploblastic
ABCIILMMOTTUY commutability
ABCIILMOPTTUY computability
ABCIILNPPRSSU subprincipals
ABCILMMNOSSTU noctambulisms
ABCILMNOSSTTU noctambulists
ABCILNOORSTTU obstructional
ABCINOOOORRRT corroboration
ABCINORSSSTTU obscurantists
ABCLRRSSTTUUU substructural
ABCOOOORRRRST corroborators
ABCOOOORRRRTY corroboratory
ABDDDEEEEFHRT featherbedded
ABDDDEEGILRRS griddlebreads
ABDDDEILMNORY broadmindedly
ABDDEEEGHINSS bigheadedness
ABDDEEEHLORSU doubleheaders
ABDDEEEIKLMRR middlebreaker
ABDDEEFINSTUU subinfeudated
ABDDEEHLRTUYY butyraldehyde
ABDDEEIILNPTY dependability
ABDDEEILLNOSS Bedloe's Island
ABDDEELMNRRSU drumbledranes
ABDDEENOPRSUU superabounded
ABDEEEEHINRRS Aberdeenshire
ABDEEEEHLNPRR reprehendable
ABDEEEGKLLNOW knowledgeable
ABDEEEHILRSST reestablished
ABDEEEHKNORRT brokenhearted
ABDEEEHLORRWW wheelbarrowed
ABDEEEIILMRTY redeemability
ABDEEEILMNNST disenablement
ABDEEEILNPRST predestinable
ABDEEEILNRSSS desirableness
ABDEEELMNSTZZ bedazzlements
ABDEEELNNRSSU endurableness
ABDEEELNRSSSS beardlessness
ABDEEELRSSSTT battledresses
ABDEEFGHINRRT fingerbreadth
ABDEEFIIILRSV diversifiable
ABDEEFIIILSTY defeasibility
ABDEEFINSSTUU subinfeudates
ABDEEGIILNRST disintegrable
ABDEEGIKNORRY rekeyboarding
ABDEEGKLLNOWY knowledgeably
ABDEEHILNSSTU unestablished
ABDEEIILMSSSS disassemblies
ABDEEIILNNPSS indispensable
ABDEEIILNNSSU inaudibleness
ABDEEIILNORST deliberations
ABDEEIILNPTXY expendability
ABDEEIILNTTXY extendability
ABDEEIILSTTTY detestability
ABDEEIIMRTTXY ambidexterity
ABDEEIKMMNRST disembarkment
ABDEEILLNORRS banderilleros
ABDEEILMNOPRS imponderables
ABDEEILMRSSSS disassemblers
ABDEEILORRSUV boulevardiers
ABDEEINNSSSSU unbiassedness
ABDEEMNPRSTTU subdepartment
ABDEFFHLORSSU shuffleboards
ABDEFIILLORRT defibrillator
ABDEFIILMORTY deformability
ABDEFIILNNTUU infundibulate
ABDEFLORRSTTU flutterboards
ABDEGHINOORSU boardinghouse
ABDEGIIILNRST detribalising
ABDEGIIILNRTZ detribalizing
ABDEGIIILNSST destabilising
ABDEGIIILNSTZ destabilizing
ABDEGIILMNSSS disassembling
ABDEGINNOORUV overabounding
ABDEGLNORSTTU battlegrounds
ABDEHHNOSSSUU househusbands
ABDEHILMNNSST blandishments
ABDEHILNOORSU dishonourable
ABDEIIILNOSTT debilitations
ABDEIILLNRSTY Liberty Island
ABDEIILLOPRTY deplorability
ABDEIILNNPSSY indispensably
ABDEIILNOPRTY ponderability
ABDEIILPRRTUY perdurability
ABDEIINNORSTU insubordinate
ABDEIINORRSSU subordinaries
ABDEIINORSTUV subordinative
ABDEIIOOPRSSS basidiospores
ABDEILMNNORRU ordinal number
ABDEILNORSTUY subordinately
ABDELNNOPTUUW unputdownable
ABDFIIIILMOTY modifiability
ABDFIIILMORTY formidability
ABDFIILNOOOSV bioflavonoids
ABDGGIINNORTU groundbaiting
ABDGIINNORSTU subordinating
ABDGILMNNORSU bildungsroman
ABDHIIINORSTY hybridisation
ABDHIIINORTYZ hybridization
ABDHILNOORSUY dishonourably
ABDIIIILMSSTY admissibility
ABDIIILNOSSUV subdivisional
ABDIIILOPSSTY disposability
ABDIIILPSTTUY disputability
ABDIIINOSSSTU subsidisation

ABDIIINOSSTUZ	subsidization
ABDIINNOORSTU	subordination
ABEEEEFLNORSU	unforeseeable
ABEEEEILMMPRS	semipermeable
ABEEEEIRRRTVV	reverberative
ABEEEELMNPRSS	permeableness
ABEEEELNNRSSV	venerableness
ABEEEELNPRRST	representable
ABEEEFFILNNSS	ineffableness
ABEEEFIILLMPX	exemplifiable
ABEEEGINRRRTV	reverberating
ABEEEGLMMNNRT	embranglement
ABEEEHILNPPRS	apprehensible
ABEEEHILRSSST	reestablishes
ABEEEHKORRSSU	housebreakers
ABEEEIIKLMNRS	Berkeleianism
ABEEEIILLPRRV	irrepleviable
ABEEEIILRRRTV	irretrievable
ABEEEIKKRRRST	strikebreaker
ABEEEILMNRSSS	miserableness
ABEEEILMNSSST	estimableness
ABEEEILNNRRSS	inerrableness
ABEEEILNPRRTT	interpretable
ABEEEILNQSSTU	equitableness
ABEEEILNRSSTV	veritableness
ABEEEILNSSSST	beastlinesses
ABEEEINORRRTV	reverberation
ABEEEINRRSTTV	invertebrates
ABEEEJLNNOSSY	enjoyableness
ABEEELLMNSSSS	blamelessness
ABEEELLNORSST	tolerableness
ABEEELMMNORSS	memorableness
ABEEELMNORSSV	removableness
ABEEELNNNSSTU	untenableness
ABEEELNNPRSTU	unpresentable
ABEEELNPRSSSU	superableness
ABEEELNRRRTVY	reverberantly
ABEEELNRSSTTU	utterableness
ABEEEMMNPRRSU	supermembrane
ABEEENOSSSTUU	beauteousness
ABEEEORRRRSTV	reverberators
ABEEEORRRRTVY	reverberatory
ABEEEPRRSSTTY	presbyterates
ABEEFGIILNRRR	irrefrangible
ABEEFGILNNRSS	frangibleness
ABEEFGLNORTTU	unforgettable
ABEEFIILNOPRS	personifiable
ABEEFIILPRRTY	preferability
ABEEFILNSSTUU	beautifulness
ABEEGHIKNORSU	housebreaking
ABEEGHILNRSST	rightableness
ABEEGIILMMNST	emblematising
ABEEGIILMMNTZ	emblematizing
ABEEGIILMNNRS	Negri Sembilan
ABEEGIKNRRTUY	Yekaterinburg
ABEEGILNNNOOT	nonnegotiable
ABEEGILNORRVY	overbearingly
ABEEGILNOSSST	blastogenesis
ABEEHIILNSTUX	inexhaustible
ABEEHIKLRSSTT	blatherskites
ABEEHILMNSSTT	establishment
ABEEHILNPPRSY	apprehensibly
ABEEHILOPRTTZ	Port Elizabeth
ABEEHIQRRSSUU	harquebusiers
ABEEHKLNORRTY	heartbrokenly
ABEEHLNNOORRS	blennorrhoeas
ABEEHLNNOORSS	honorableness
ABEEHLOPRSSST	blastospheres
ABEEIIILLMNRS	bimillenaries
ABEEIIILRSSTU	reusabilities
ABEEIILLLNRSS	illiberalness
ABEEIILLMNORS	neoliberalism
ABEEIILLMNSST	limitableness
ABEEIILLRRSUV	Aubervilliers
ABEEIILMPRTTY	temperability
ABEEIILNNORTV	inventoriable
ABEEIILNPRTTY	penetrability
ABEEIILNRRSST	irritableness
ABEEIILRRRTVY	irretrievably
ABEEIIOOPRRRT	Ribeirão Prêto
ABEEILLNPSSSU	plausibleness
ABEEILMMNOSSV	immovableness
ABEEILMMNSSTU	immutableness
ABEEILMNNNOTU	unmentionable
ABEEILMNORRSS	salmonberries
ABEEILMNPSSTU	imputableness
ABEEILNNPRSST	printableness
ABEEILNNRSSSS	brainlessness
ABEEILNNSTTUU	sublieutenant
ABEEILNPRRTTY	interpretably
ABEEILOPRRTVY	reprobatively
ABEEINORRSTTV	vertebrations
ABEEINPRRSSTY	presbyterians
ABEEIOORRSSTV	observatories
ABEEIRRSSSTUU	subtreasuries
ABEEKLMORRSTU	troublemakers
ABEEKMNNORTUY	mountebankery
ABEEKORRSSSTT	breaststrokes
ABEELLMNOSTTT	ballottements
ABEELMMNNOSTZ	emblazonments
ABEELNNNORRTU	nonreturnable
ABEENORRSSTUU	subterraneous
ABEERRRSSSTUU	subtreasurers
ABEFFIIMOPRST	baptism of fire
ABEFGIILNRRRY	irrefrangibly
ABEFGLNORTTUY	unforgettably
ABEFIIIILNSTY	infeasibility
ABEFIIILLRTTY	filterability
ABEFIIJLNSTUU	unjustifiable
ABEFIILNORRRU	neurofibrilar
ABEFLLNOOPSTU	tablespoonful
ABEGHHKORRSTU	breakthroughs
ABEGHIILMOOPS	amphibologies
ABEGIIILNOTTY	negotiability
ABEGIIILNQRTU	equilibrating
ABEGIIILNRTTY	integrability
ABEGIILNORTVY	governability
ABEGIILOOORST	aerobiologist
ABEGIKLMNORTU	troublemaking
ABEGIKMNNNOTU	mountebanking
ABEGILLNOOSST	balneologists
ABEGIMNOSSSUU	ambiguousness
ABEGINOPRRTTU	protuberating
ABEHIIILPRSTY	perishability

ABEHIILNSTUXY	inexhaustibly
ABEHIIMORSSUV	behaviourisms
ABEHIIORSSTUV	behaviourists
ABEHIKLNNNORS	nonshrinkable
ABEHIKMNOORST	thrombokinase
ABEHIKMNQRRTU	Khirbet Qumran
ABEHINNOOSTTT	ethnobotanist
ABEHLLMOPSSUY	blasphemously
ABEHLORRSSTTY	erythroblasts
ABEIIIILLMNTY	eliminability
ABEIIIILNRSST	rinsabilities
ABEIIIILNSSTT	instabilities
ABEIIIILNTTVY	inevitability
ABEIIILLNSTTY	listenability
ABEIIILMMOTVY	immoveability
ABEIIILMNRTTY	terminability
ABEIIILMRSSST	miserabilists
ABEIIILNOPRTY	inoperability
ABEIIILNOQRTU	equilibration
ABEIIILNORSTT	liberationist
ABEIIILNORTXY	inexorability
ABEIIILNPSTXY	expansibility
ABEIIILPRRSTY	respirability
ABEIILLMOPTYY	employability
ABEIILLNRTUVY	vulnerability
ABEIILLORSTVY	resolvability
ABEIILMNOOSST	embolisations
ABEIILMNRSSST	transmissible
ABEIILMNRSTTT	transmittible
ABEIILMNRSTUY	mensurability
ABEIILMPRTTUY	permutability
ABEIILNNOSSTU	nebulisations
ABEIILNNOSTUZ	nebulizations
ABEIILNOORSTT	obliterations
ABEIILNORSSTV	vibrationless
ABEIILNRRTTUY	returnability
ABEIILOPRTTXY	exportability
ABEIILOQRRSTU	equilibrators
ABEIILRTTTUVY	attributively
ABEIIMNOSSSTU	ambitiousness
ABEIIMOORSTUV	overambitious
ABEIINSSSTTUV	substantivise
ABEIINSSTTUVZ	substantivize
ABEIKKNNSSTUZ	Kuznetsk Basin
ABEILLNOOSSSY	obsessionally
ABEILLNOPPRST	bipropellants
ABEILLOOPRSST	ballistospore
ABEILMNNNOTUY	unmentionably
ABEILMNNOSTUU	Blue Mountains
ABEILNNORSTVY	inobservantly
ABEILNOORSSSU	laboriousness
ABEILNOPPRSTU	insupportable
ABEILNSSTTUVY	substantively
ABEIMNNOSSSUW	businesswoman
ABEINNORSTUVY	subventionary
ABEINOOPRRSST	reabsorptions
ABELLLLOPSSYY	polysyllables
ABELLLMNOOSSY	monosyllables
ABELMMNOORTWY	Melton Mowbray
ABELNOPPRSTUU	unsupportable
ABELNOPRRTTUY	protuberantly
ABFIIIILLLMNS	infallibilism
ABFIIIILLLNST	infallibilist
ABFIIIILLLNTY	infallibility
ABFIIILLNORST	fibrillations
ABFIIILNNOSTU	infibulations
ABFIIILOPRTTY	profitability
ABFIIJLNSTUUY	unjustifiably
ABGGHIIINOPRS	biographising
ABGGHIIINOPRZ	biographizing
ABGGIIINRRSTU	subirrigating
ABGGIILOOORST	agrobiologist
ABGIIIILNNTTY	intangibility
ABGIIINORRSTU	subirrigation
ABGIILLNNOSTU	antiglobulins
ABGIIMNNORRST	brainstorming
ABGILNOOPSSST	spongioblasts
ABGINOOPPRSTT	bootstrapping
ABHIIILNPSTUY	punishability
ABHIIILNRSTTY	labyrinthitis
ABHIIINOORSTV	vasoinhibitor
ABHIINOPRSSTV	vibraphonists
ABHLLMOOTUWYZ	Lützow-Holm Bay
ABIIIIILMNTTY	inimitability
ABIIIILLNOTVY	inviolability
ABIIIILMPRTTY	impartibility
ABIIIILMPSSTY	impassibility
ABIIILLNOSTVY	insolvability
ABIIILMNOOSST	mobilisations
ABIIILMNOOSTZ	mobilizations
ABIIILMOPRTTY	importability
ABIIILMOPRTVY	improvability
ABIIILNOOSSTT	abolitionists
ABIIILNOSSTTU	subtilisation
ABIIILNOSTTUZ	subtilization
ABIIILRSTUVVY	survivability
ABIIKLNNOTUWY	unknowability
ABIILMNNNTTUU	tintinnabulum
ABIILMNOOSSTY	symbolisation
ABIILMNOOSTYZ	symbolization
ABIILMOOSSTTU	automobilists
ABIILMORRTTUV	multivibrator
ABIIMNORSSTTU	tambourinists
ABILLMMNOOSSY	monosyllabism
ABILMMNOSSSTU	somnambulists
ABILNOOPPSTUU	subpopulation
ABILNOPPRSTUY	insupportably
ACCCDEEEELNSS	decalescences
ACCCDEEEINNNS	incandescence
ACCCDEEILNOPY	encyclopaedic
ACCCDEEINNNSY	incandescency
ACCCDEHILNOSY	synecdochical
ACCCDEIMNRSTU	circumstanced
ACCCDGIILLOOO	codicological
ACCCEEEILNNSS	incalescences
ACCCEEELNNOSV	convalescence
ACCCEEGINORSY	gynecocracies
ACCCEEHINORST	technocracies
ACCCEEHMNOSTU	accouchements
ACCCEEIILSSST	ecclesiastics
ACCCEEILLNRTY	eccentrically
ACCCEEILMNOPS	complacencies
ACCCEEMOPRRSU	eccremocarpus
ACCCEGILMNNOO	meningococcal

ACCCEHIILMMOR microchemical
ACCCEHIILMOPR microcephalic
ACCCEHIINORTT architectonic
ACCCEHIOOPRST ptochocracies
ACCCEIMMNOOOR macroeconomic
ACCCEIMNNOOST concomitances
ACCCEIMNRSSTU circumstances
ACCCELOOPRSTT streptococcal
ACCCGHIKNOPST spatchcocking
ACCCGHILLNOOO conchological
ACCCHILMOSTYY cyclothymiacs
ACCCHILOOPSTY staphylococci
ACCCIIILMMORT microclimatic
ACCCIILMMOORS microcosmical
ACCCIILMOOPRS microscopical
ACCCIIMNOOTTY actinomycotic
ACCCILOPRSTTY cryptoclastic
ACCDDDEEIIRST disaccredited
ACCDDEEEHHKLU chuckleheaded
ACCDDEEENORST deconsecrated
ACCDDEEFLLOTU deflocculated
ACCDDEIINORSS discordancies
ACCDDEIMOSSTU disaccustomed
ACCDEEEFINORS confederacies
ACCDEEEGLLORS Sacred College
ACCDEEEHKORTW weathercocked
ACCDEEENNNRST transcendence
ACCDEEENORRRT catercornered
ACCDEEENORRST reconsecrated
ACCDEEENORSST deconsecrates
ACCDEEFLLOSTU deflocculates
ACCDEEGIINRRT reaccrediting
ACCDEEHHRSSSU archduchesses
ACCDEEHILLOPR Delphic oracle
ACCDEEIILNOST occidentalise
ACCDEEIILNOTZ occidentalize
ACCDEEIINPRSS discrepancies
ACCDEEILNOPSY encyclopedias
ACCDEEILNPTTU centuplicated
ACCDEENNNRSTY transcendency
ACCDEENNORSTU unconsecrated
ACCDEENOPRRTT precontracted
ACCDEFHIRRRTU Crutched Friar
ACCDEFLLNOSTU deflocculants
ACCDEGIINORTT decorticating
ACCDEGILNOORT Angelic Doctor
ACCDEGILNOOTY accidentology
ACCDEHHILOPRY hydrocephalic
ACCDEHHNRRSUW churchwardens
ACCDEHIMOOSST homoscedastic
ACCDEIIKLOOPS kaleidoscopic
ACCDEIILNNOOT codeclination
ACCDEIINOORTT decortication
ACCDEIINORTTV contradictive
ACCDEILLMOPTY complicatedly
ACCDEILMNOPTU uncomplicated
ACCDEILOPSSSU pseudoclassic
ACCDEILOPSSTY cyclopaedists
ACCDEIMNNOORT nondemocratic
ACCDEIMNRTTUU circumnutated
ACCDEINORRSTT contradicters
ACCDEIOORRSTT decorticators
ACCDFIIILNOTU dulcification
ACCDFIIINOOST codifications
ACCDGIINNORTT contradicting
ACCDHHINOOPRY hypochondriac
ACCDHHIOORRTY hydrothoracic
ACCDHIILORSTV clavichordist
ACCDHILLOOPYY hypocycloidal
ACCDHILOOPRSY hydroscopical
ACCDHIMNOPSYY psychodynamic
ACCDIIILNSSTY syndicalistic
ACCDIIINORSTY idiosyncratic
ACCDIILLLNRYY cylindrically
ACCDIIMMNNOOU incommunicado
ACCDIINNOORTT contradiction
ACCDIINOORSST accordionists
ACCDINOORRSTT contradictors
ACCDINOORRTTY contradictory
ACCEEEELMORRT accelerometer
ACCEEEFINOPPR Prince of Peace
ACCEEEGINNRSV ingravescence
ACCEEEHILLNPT telencephalic
ACCEEEHILLNRS chancelleries
ACCEEEHILMNPS mesencephalic
ACCEEEHILMNPT metencephalic
ACCEEEILLORST ecclesiolater
ACCEEEILNRSTX excrescential
ACCEEENNORRTT reconcentrate
ACCEEENORRSST reconsecrates
ACCEEFIIIPSTV specificative
ACCEEGHIKLORT Greek Catholic
ACCEEGHNNORTU counterchange
ACCEEGHNORRTU countercharge
ACCEEGILLNNPR precancelling
ACCEEGILLNOTY ectogenically
ACCEEGINNORSS recognisances
ACCEEGINNORSZ recognizances
ACCEEHHILORST chalicotheres
ACCEEHHLOORST schoolteacher
ACCEEHHNRRSTU Eastern Church
ACCEEHIILMMOS semiochemical
ACCEEHILLNORS chancellories
ACCEEHILLNOTY acetylcholine
ACCEEHILLOPPT leptocephalic
ACCEEHILMOPRT cephalometric
petrochemical
ACCEEHILMOPSS mesocephalics
ACCEEHILNNSST technicalness
ACCEEHIMMNSTU catechumenism
ACCEEHIRRSTTU architectures
ACCEEHLNNOOXY cyclohexanone
ACCEEHMNNORST encroachments
ACCEEHORRSTTY oystercatcher
ACCEEIILLNRTV interclavicle
ACCEEIILMMNSU ecumenicalism
ACCEEIILMMORS commercialise
ACCEEIILMMORZ commercialize
ACCEEIIMORRST meritocracies
ACCEEIIOPRRTV reciprocative
ACCEEILLMNOUY oecumenically
ACCEEILLORSTY ecclesiolatry
ACCEEILMNOORT econometrical
ACCEEILNOPSTU conceptualise

ACCEEILNOPTUZ	conceptualize
ACCEEILNPSTTU	centuplicates
ACCEEILNQSTUY	acquiescently
ACCEEILORSTTT	electrostatic
ACCEEIMMNOTUX	excommunicate
ACCEEIMNOSTTY	actinomycetes
ACCEEINNORSSV	conservancies
ACCEEINNORTTV	concentrative
ACCEEINOPRTTV	contraceptive
ACCEEINORSSSS	accessoriness
ACCEEINORTTUV	counteractive
ACCEEKLMRRSSU	musselcracker
ACCEELLMMOORU	macromolecule
ACCEELLOORSTT	collectorates
ACCEELMNOPSTU	accouplements
ACCEELNNOSSTV	convalescents
ACCEEMNORRSTT	concertmaster
ACCEEMNORSTTU	accouterments
	accoutrements
ACCEENNNORSTU	countenancers
ACCEENNOORTTY	octocentenary
ACCEEOORRSSTU	stercoraceous
ACCEFFIIINOSU	inefficacious
ACCEFFIIINPRS	infraspecific
ACCEFFIILOSUY	efficaciously
ACCEFGIIINNSS	significances
ACCEFGIIINRTT	certificating
ACCEFGIKRRRSU	Carrickfergus
ACCEFIIINOPST	specification
ACCEFIIINORTT	certification
	rectification
ACCEFIIINPRST	intraspecific
ACCEFIIORRTTY	certificatory
ACCEFINNOORTY	confectionary
ACCEGGILLNOOY	gynecological
ACCEGHHIOOPRR	choreographic
ACCEGHIILOPRX	lexicographic
ACCEGHILLNOOT	technological
ACCEGHILMOPYY	hypoglycaemic
ACCEGHILNNORY	encroachingly
ACCEGHIOPRRVY	cervicography
ACCEGIILLLOOX	lexicological
ACCEGIILNRRTU	recirculating
ACCEGIINNNORT	concertinaing
ACCEGIINOPRRT	reciprocating
ACCEGIINORSSS	accessorising
ACCEGIINORSSZ	accessorizing
ACCEGILLLOOOY	oecologically
ACCEGILLNOOSY	synecological
ACCEGIMNORSTU	reaccustoming
ACCEGINNNNOTU	countenancing
ACCEGINNNORTT	concentrating
ACCEGINNORTTU	counteracting
ACCEGINOORRTT	gerontocratic
ACCEHHIILMOST	histochemical
ACCEHHIINSSTT	chainstitches
ACCEHHILMOOPT	photochemical
ACCEHHILOOPRT	orthocephalic
ACCEHHILOSSSZ	eschscholzias
ACCEHHILOSSTZ	eschscholtzia
ACCEHHIMORSTT	chrestomathic
ACCEHIILLNSST	callisthenics
ACCEHIILNOPRS	necrophiliacs
ACCEHIILPRRTY	hypercritical
ACCEHIIMRSSTT	chrematistics
ACCEHIIOPRSSY	physiocracies
ACCEHILLNOPRT	phallocentric
ACCEHILMOPRSS	accomplishers
ACCEHILNOOOST	echolocations
ACCEHILNOPRTY	pyrotechnical
ACCEHIMMNOORT	chromonematic
ACCEHIMNORSST	chromaticness
ACCEHINNNOPST	pantechnicons
ACCEHIOOPSSTT	tachistoscope
ACCEHOOOPRSST	thoracoscopes
ACCEIIILMNORT	cliometrician
ACCEIIINORSTT	creationistic
ACCEIIKLNOSTW	anticlockwise
ACCEIILLMNORT	clinometrical
ACCEIILMMMORS	commercialism
ACCEIILMMORRT	micrometrical
ACCEIILMMORST	commercialist
	microclimates
ACCEIILMMORTY	commerciality
ACCEIILMNOSSS	neoclassicism
ACCEIILMORSTV	viscometrical
ACCEIILNOSSST	neoclassicist
ACCEIILOPRRTY	reciprocality
ACCEIILPRRSTU	supercritical
ACCEIILRRRSSU	circularisers
ACCEIILRRRSUZ	circularizers
ACCEIIMMNOTUV	communicative
ACCEIINNNOSST	inconstancies
ACCEIINOOPRRT	reciprocation
ACCEIINORSTUX	excruciations
ACCEIIOPPRSSU	perspicacious
ACCEILLLNNOUY	nucleonically
ACCEILLMNOPSU	nucleoplasmic
ACCEILMMNNOOR	noncommercial
ACCEILMNNNOOP	noncompliance
ACCEILMNOPSTU	conceptualism
ACCEILMNORSTU	counterclaims
ACCEILNNOSSTU	consultancies
ACCEILNOPSTTU	conceptualist
ACCEILNORTTVY	contractively
ACCEIMNRSTTUU	circumnutates
ACCEINNNNOOSS	inconsonances
ACCEINNNOORTT	concentration
ACCEINNOOPRTT	contraception
ACCEINNOORRTY	concretionary
ACCEINNOORSST	consecrations
ACCEINNOORSSY	concessionary
ACCEINNOORTTU	counteraction
ACCEINOOPPRTU	preoccupation
ACCEINOOPRSTU	reoccupations
ACCEIOOPRRRST	reciprocators
ACCEIOOPRRRTY	reciprocatory
ACCEJLLNORTUY	conjecturally
ACCEKMMORRTUW	Crummock Water
ACCENNOORRSTT	concentrators
ACCENOPRRSSTU	counterscarps
ACCFGIIMNOPTY	compactifying
ACCFHIIORRSTV	Vicar of Christ
ACCFIIIINOSTT	citifications

ACCFIIINOORST	scorification
ACCFIIINOSTTY	cityfications
ACCFIILNOOPRX	ciprofloxacin
ACCFIINNOOSST	confiscations
ACCFLMORSTUUU	fractocumulus
ACCGHHINOOPRR	chronographic
ACCGHHINORSST	crosshatching
ACCGHIIILNOST	catholicising
ACCGHIIILNOTZ	catholicizing
ACCGHIILLOORT	trichological
ACCGHIILMNOPS	accomplishing
ACCGHILLNOOOR	chronological
ACCGHILLOOPSY	psychological
ACCGHIOPPRRTY	cryptographic
ACCGIIILNRRSU	circularising
ACCGIIILNRRUZ	circularizing
ACCGIILLMOOSU	musicological
ACCGIILLOOOTX	toxicological
ACCGIILMORRSU	microsurgical
ACCGIIMMNNOTU	communicating
ACCGILLLOOTYY	cytologically
ACCGILLOOOPRT	proctological
ACCGILNOOPRSY	laryngoscopic
ACCHHHIMNPRSU	churchmanship
ACCHHIMMOOORT	homochromatic
ACCHIIILPSSTY	physicalistic
ACCHIILMOPRSY	microphysical
ACCHIILMOSSST	scholasticism
ACCHIIMNOOPRT	actinomorphic
ACCHIIMORRSSU	chiaroscurism
ACCHIINOPSTTY	antipsychotic
ACCHIIORRSSTU	chiaroscurist
ACCHILLOOPRST	chloroplastic
ACCHILLOPSTYY	psychotically
ACCHILMMNOOOR	monochromical
ACCHILMOOPRTY	polychromatic
ACCHILOPPRSTY	prophylactics
ACCHIMMNOOORT	monochromatic
ACCHIMOOPSSTY	psychosomatic
ACCHIOOPRRRST	chiropractors
ACCHIOOPRSSUZ	schizocarpous
ACCHLNOOOPSUY	cacophonously
ACCIIILNNOOST	conciliations
ACCIIIMMNOOST	iconomaticism
ACCIILLNNQUUY	quincuncially
ACCIILLPRSTUU	piscicultural
ACCIILMMNOSTU	communalistic
ACCIILMNOOPST	complications
ACCIILNORTTTY	contractility
ACCIIMMNNOOTU	communication
ACCIIMNOOSSTY	actinomycosis
ACCIINNOOOSST	consociations
ACCIINOORRSTY	Socratic irony
ACCIJLNNNOOTU	conjunctional
ACCILMNNOOTTY	concomitantly
ACCIMMNOORSTU	communicators
ACCIMMNOORTUY	communicatory
ACCIMNOOOTTXY	cytotaxonomic
ACCIMNOOPRSTU	pococurantism
ACCINPRSTTUUU	acupuncturist
ACDDDEEENRTUU	undereducated
ACDDDEEHNOORS	dodecahedrons
ACDDEEEFHNRSU	schadenfreude
ACDDEEEHHNNOR	hendecahedron
ACDDEEEHINRUV	underachieved
ACDDEEEHKKLNU	knuckleheaded
ACDDEEEILNRST	decentralised
ACDDEEEILNRSU	denuclearised
ACDDEEEILNRTZ	decentralized
ACDDEEEILNRUZ	denuclearized
ACDDEEEOORRTV	overdecorated
ACDDEEFFILSTY	disaffectedly
ACDDEEHLLNORS	candleholders
ACDDEEHLLORTY	coldheartedly
ACDDEEIINORST	rededications
ACDDEEIMNOOTY	adenoidectomy
ACDDEEMNNORTU	countermanded
ACDDEENORRTTU	countertraded
ACDDEFHIINRSS	disfranchised
ACDDEGHILNNRR	grandchildren
ACDDEGILLNOOR	dendrological
ACDDEGINORSUU	undiscouraged
ACDDEHILMOSUY	dichlamydeous
ACDDEHIMNOOPS	dodecaphonism
ACDDEHINOOPST	dodecaphonist
ACDDEIIIMNRST	discriminated
ACDDEIILLNRTY	dendritically
ACDDEIILNORSU	radionuclides
ACDDEIINNORTT	indoctrinated
ACDDEIINOSSTU	undissociated
ACDDEINNOORTU	uncoordinated
ACDDHIMNORSYY	hydrodynamics
ACDEEEEHLPSST	steeplechased
ACDEEEFINORTV	confederative
ACDEEEHINNRSS	Niedersachsen
ACDEEEHINRRUV	underachiever
ACDEEEHINRSUV	underachieves
ACDEEEILNORST	decelerations
ACDEEEILNRSST	decentralises
ACDEEEILNRSSU	denuclearises
ACDEEEILNRSTZ	decentralizes
ACDEEEILNRSUZ	denuclearizes
ACDEEEILNSSST	delicatessens
ACDEEEILPRTVY	deprecatively
ACDEEEINNRSTV	inadvertences
ACDEEEIOSSTTV	videocassette
ACDEEELLOPRTT	electroplated
ACDEEELNOPRST	preadolescent
ACDEEELNPRRSU	supercalender
ACDEEELOPRSST	Apostles' Creed
ACDEEENNOPPRR	preponderance
ACDEEEOORRSTV	overdecorates
ACDEEFGINNORT	confederating
ACDEEFHHIKNRS	handkerchiefs
ACDEEFHNORRSW	henceforwards
ACDEEFHNORRTW	thenceforward
ACDEEFIINRRSY	ferricyanides
ACDEEFINNOORT	confederation
ACDEEFINORRSY	ferrocyanides
ACDEEFNRRSSUU	undersurfaces
ACDEEGHHOOPRR	choreographed
ACDEEGHIMNNNU	machinegunned
ACDEEGIIMORST	tragicomedies
ACDEEGIINPRTT	decrepitating

ACDEEGILNPRTY	deprecatingly
ACDEEGIMMNNOR	commandeering
ACDEEGINORTUV	overeducating
ACDEEGKLNORSW	acknowledgers
ACDEEGLMNOORT	conglomerated
ACDEEGNNOSSTT	decongestants
ACDEEHHIMORST	hemichordates
ACDEEHILNNOPS	diencephalons
ACDEEHILORRTT	tetrachloride
ACDEEHIMNRRSS	merchandisers
ACDEEHIMOPRRT	Arc de Triomphe
ACDEEHINNRSST	disenchanters
ACDEEHLORSTTY	heterodactyls
ACDEEIIILMNRS	decriminalise
ACDEEIIILMNRZ	decriminalize
ACDEEIIILMSTV	medievalistic
ACDEEIIIMPRTV	impredicative
ACDEEIILLLNSS	Ellice Islands
ACDEEIILMORTU	eudiometrical
ACDEEIILMRRSU	mercurialised
ACDEEIILMRRUZ	mercurialized
ACDEEIILNNNQU	quindecennial
ACDEEIILNNSST	identicalness
ACDEEIILNOSST	sectionalised
ACDEEIILNOSTZ	sectionalized
ACDEEIILNPSSU	unspecialised
ACDEEIILNPSUZ	unspecialized
ACDEEIILORSTV	valedictories
ACDEEIILPRTUV	reduplicative
ACDEEIILPRTVY	predicatively
ACDEEIIMNNRTY	indeterminacy
ACDEEIIMNOPRT	premedication
ACDEEIIMNOSTU	eudaemonistic
ACDEEIIMOSTTV	domesticative
ACDEEIINNORST	containerised
	inconsiderate
ACDEEIINNORTZ	containerized
ACDEEIINNOSST	Ascensiontide
ACDEEIINOPRTT	decrepitation
ACDEEIKLOOPSS	kaleidoscopes
ACDEEILLNNSTY	clandestinely
ACDEEILLNTTUY	denticulately
ACDEEILMNPSST	displacements
ACDEEILNNPTUV	Vincent de Paul
ACDEEILNOORST	reconsolidate
ACDEEILNORSTY	considerately
ACDEEILNORTUV	countervailed
ACDEEILNPPRRU	perpendicular
ACDEEILNPQSTU	quindecaplets
ACDEEILNRSSTT	decentralists
ACDEEILOPRRTY	deprecatorily
ACDEEILPSTTUX	sextuplicated
ACDEEIMNORSTU	documentaries
ACDEEIMOPRSST	spermatocides
ACDEEINNORSSS	secondariness
ACDEEINOORRST	redecorations
ACDEEIOPPRSTU	propaedeutics
ACDEEJORSSSTU	coadjutresses
ACDEELMNNRSSU	underclassmen
ACDEELNPRSSTU	Pure Land sects
ACDEEMNNOPSTU	uncompensated
ACDEENNNRSSTT	transcendents
ACDEENNOPPRRY	preponderancy
ACDEENORRSTTU	countertrades
ACDEFFIILRTVY	diffractively
ACDEFGIILNSSY	declassifying
ACDEFGILLRSUY	disgracefully
ACDEFHIINRSSS	disfranchises
ACDEFIIILMSSS	misclassified
ACDEFIIILNOST	fictionalised
ACDEFIIILNOTZ	fictionalized
ACDEFIIIMMOSS	fideicommissa
ACDEFIILNNOSS	nonclassified
ACDEFIINNSSTT	disinfectants
ACDEFILMNNOTU	malfunctioned
ACDEFILRSTTUX	fluidextracts
ACDEFMNOORSTW	woodcraftsmen
ACDEGGHINNRRU	undercharging
ACDEGGIKLNNOW	acknowledging
ACDEGHHOOPRTU	thoroughpaced
ACDEGHIIMNNRS	merchandising
ACDEGHIINNNST	disenchanting
ACDEGHIIOPRSS	discographies
ACDEGHIMNORTY	hydromagnetic
ACDEGHIOPRRSS	discographers
ACDEGIILLLOOY	ideologically
ACDEGIILLMRUY	demiurgically
ACDEGIILNPRTU	reduplicating
ACDEGIILPQRSU	quadriplegics
ACDEGIIMNORST	democratising
ACDEGIIMNORTZ	democratizing
ACDEGIIMNOSTT	domesticating
ACDEGIIMNOSTY	geodynamicist
ACDEGIINQRSTU	quadrisecting
ACDEGILLMNOOO	demonological
ACDEGILLNOOOT	deontological
ACDEGILLOOSTY	dactylologies
ACDEGILNNOTTU	conglutinated
ACDEHHIOPRRTY	hydrotherapic
ACDEHHLOPRSUY	hydrocephalus
ACDEHHOOOPSTT	photocathodes
ACDEHIIINRSST	christianised
ACDEHIIINRSTZ	christianized
ACDEHIILNOPRR	perichondrial
ACDEHIIMORSST	radiochemists
ACDEHIIOPSSTT	sophisticated
ACDEHIKLNRSST	stickhandlers
ACDEHILMNOPTY	endolymphatic
ACDEHILMORRTY	hydrometrical
ACDEHIMMNOPRS	commandership
ACDEHIMMNORTY	thermodynamic
ACDEHIMOPRTTY	dermatophytic
ACDEHLMOOPRSY	chlamydospore
ACDEHLOOOPPSU	cephalopodous
ACDEHOOOPRRTT	protochordate
ACDEIIILMNPSU	municipalised
ACDEIIILMNPUZ	municipalized
ACDEIIILNOSST	idioticalness
ACDEIIIMNNOST	nicotinamides
ACDEIIIMNORST	dosimetrician
ACDEIIIMNRSST	discriminates
ACDEIIINOPRST	antiperiodics
ACDEIIINRSTTU	antidiuretics
ACDEIIJLLPRUY	prejudicially

ACDEIILLORRTY directorially
ACDEIILNNOTTU denticulation
ACDEIILNOOSTV consolidative
ACDEIILNOPRTU reduplication
ACDEIILRSTTVY distractively
ACDEIIMNNOSTW ancient wisdom
ACDEIIMNOOSTT domestication
ACDEIINNNOSTU denunciations
ACDEIINNOORST consideration
ACDEIINNORSTT indoctrinates
ACDEIINOQRSTU quadrisection
ACDEIINORRSTY discretionary
ACDEIINOSSTTU educationists
ACDEIKNNNORTT Dark Continent
ACDEILLOPSSTU leucoplastids
ACDEILLPPSTYY dyspeptically
ACDEILMNORTUY documentarily
ACDEILNNOPTUU pedunculation
ACDEILNNORSTY constrainedly
ACDEILNNOTTUV noncultivated
ACDEILNOOORST decolorations
ACDEILOPRSSTY perissodactyl
ACDEIMMNNOOST commendations
ACDEIMMOOSTTY mastoidectomy
ACDEIMNNNOOST condemnations
ACDEIMNNOOTTU documentation
ACDEIMNNORRST androcentrism
ACDEIMNPSTTUU mispunctuated
ACDEIMOORSSTT domesticators
ACDEINNNOOSST condensations
ACDEINNNORSTU unconstrained
ACDEINNORSTTU detruncations
ACDEINOPRSTTV privatdocents
ACDEINOPRSTTY dictyopterans
ACDELNOOOSTUY acotyledonous
ACDEMMNNOSTUU unconsummated
ACDEOOPPRSSUU pseudocarpous
ACDEORSSTTTUU autodestructs
ACDFIIIINNOST nidifications
ACDFIIIMNOOST modifications
ACDFIILNNOSTU difunctionals
ACDFILNNOSTUY dysfunctional
ACDGHINOOOPRT gonadotrophic
ACDGIIIILMNOT domiciliating
ACDGIILNNOOST consolidating
ACDGIILNRSTTY distractingly
ACDGIILOORSST cardiologists
ACDGIINNOSTTU outdistancing
ACDGILLLOOOXY doxologically
ACDGILLNOOOOT odontological
ACDGILLOORTTY troglodytical
ACDGILMOSTYYZ zygodactylism
ACDGLOOSTUYYZ zygodactylous
ACDHIILMNOORT mitochondrial
ACDHIINOPSSTU custodianship
ACDHIIOPRSSTT dictatorships
ACDHILMNOOORS chondriosomal
ACDHILOORSSUU dolichosaurus
ACDHIMNOOPSTY photodynamics
ACDHINOOPQRSU quadrophonics
ACDHMNOOORSTU chondromatous
ACDIIILNNOPTU induplication
ACDIIILNNPSST disciplinants
ACDIIIMNNRSST discriminants
ACDIIIMNORRST discriminator
doctrinairism
ACDIIINOOSSST dissociations
ACDIIIOOOPRST radioisotopic
ACDIILLMNPSTU multiplicands
ACDIILLNNOOTY conditionally
ACDIILMNNOOPT nondiplomatic
ACDIILNNNOOTU unconditional
ACDIILNNOOOST consolidation
ACDIILNOOORST discoloration
ACDIILNOOQSTU coloquintidas
ACDIILPQRTUUY quadruplicity
ACDIINNOORRTT indoctrinator
ACDILNOOORSST consolidators
ACDINOOQRSSTU conquistadors
ACDLLOOPSTUYY polydactylous
ACDLMNOOOSTUY condylomatous
monodactylous
ACEEEEHLPRSST steeplechaser
ACEEEEHLPSSST steeplechases
ACEEEELNORSTT coelenterates
ACEEEFFGINOPR peace offering
ACEEEFFINSSTV affectiveness
ACEEEFFLNSSTU effectualness
ACEEEFILNORRT coreferential
ACEEEFMORRRTT refractometer
ACEEEFNNRRSST transferences
ACEEEGGORSSTU secretagogues
ACEEEGHIMNOTT hematogenetic
ACEEEGHIMORTT heterogametic
ACEEEGHINPRSS cheeseparings
ACEEEGILLLNTY telegenically
ACEEEGILLNRTY energetically
ACEEEGILLOPRT precollegiate
ACEEEGLMNORTT electromagnet
ACEEEGLNRSSSS gracelessness
ACEEEGMNNORTU encouragement
ACEEEHIKLLMNO chameleonlike
ACEEEHILMNRTU hermeneutical
ACEEEHIMNQSTU cinematheques
ACEEEHIORRSVV overachievers
ACEEEHLLNNOPT telencephalon
ACEEEHLMNNOPS mesencephalon
ACEEEHLMNNOPT metencephalon
ACEEEHLMOPRST cephalometers
ACEEEHLMPSSSY Champs-Elysées
ACEEEHMMORTTY hemacytometer
ACEEEHNNRSSST enchantresses
ACEEEHPRRSSTU superteachers
ACEEEIILNNSTU lieutenancies
ACEEEIILNRRSV irrelevancies
ACEEEIINSSTTV necessitative
ACEEEILLMPRST capellmeister
ACEEEILMNNRTT interlacement
ACEEEILNNNRTT tercentennial
ACEEEIMNNOSST amniocenteses
ACEEEIMNNRRSS mercenariness
ACEEEINNOPRVX Aix-en-Provence
ACEEEINOSSTVV evocativeness
ACEEEIRSSSTTV state services

ACEEELLNORTTV	electrovalent
ACEEELLOPRRTT	electroplater
ACEEELLOPRSTT	electroplates
ACEEEMNNNRSTT	entrancements
ACEEEOPPRRSTT	preceptorates
ACEEFFHINNPRS	affenpinscher
ACEEFFILLNTUY	ineffectually
ACEEFGHLNNSSU	changefulness
ACEEFGIIMNRRT	ferrimagnetic
ACEEFGIMNORRT	ferromagnetic
ACEEFHHIRSTTT	featherstitch
ACEEFHIMNNRST	franchisement
ACEEFHINNRRSS	enfranchisers
ACEEFHMNOSTUV	vouchsafement
ACEEFIILNQSTU	liquefacients
ACEEFILNOPRSW	Prince of Wales
ACEEFINOSSSTU	facetiousness
ACEEFINPSSTTU	stupefacients
ACEEFLLLNRSTY	crestfallenly
ACEEFMNORSTUU	frumentaceous
ACEEFMORRRTTY	refractometry
ACEEGGHILLNNR	rechallenging
ACEEGGINNOORT	organogenetic
ACEEGHHIOPRRS	choregraphies
ACEEGHHIOPRRT	heterographic
ACEEGHHLLNORS	Öhlenschläger
ACEEGHHOOPRRR	choreographer
ACEEGHHOPRRRS	choregraphers
ACEEGHIINORVV	overachieving
ACEEGHIINRSTT	catheterising
ACEEGHIINRTTZ	catheterizing
ACEEGHILMPRYY	hyperglycemia
ACEEGHILNOPRS	selenographic
ACEEGHILNORSU	clearinghouse
ACEEGHILNSTTW	angletwitches
ACEEGHILOPRRX	lexicographer
ACEEGHINNRSSS	searchingness
ACEEGHIOPRRST	stereographic
ACEEGHLOPRRST	electrographs
ACEEGHLOPRRTY	electrography
ACEEGHMNNORSY	moneychangers
ACEEGHNOPRRSS	scenographers
ACEEGHOOOPPSS	esophagoscope
ACEEGHPRRRSSU	superchargers
ACEEGIILLMOOS	semeiological
ACEEGIILNNRTV	cantilevering
ACEEGIILSTTUV	gesticulative
ACEEGIIMNNOST	miscegenation
ACEEGIIMNOPTZ	piezomagnetic
ACEEGIIMNORST	geometricians
ACEEGIIMNOSTV	vaginectomies
ACEEGIINNNRST	intransigence
ACEEGIINNORTU	auctioneering
ACEEGIINNSSTT	necessitating
ACEEGILLLNOOS	selenological
ACEEGILLLOOPS	speleological
ACEEGILLMORTY	geometrically
ACEEGILLNNOOT	noncollegiate
ACEEGILMNNOQU	magniloquence
ACEEGILNNNOSS	congenialness
ACEEGILNNORRT	Central Region
ACEEGIMMNORTT	magnetometric
ACEEGIMORSSTT	gastrectomies
ACEEGINNNSSSU	unceasingness
ACEEGINOPRTTX	expectorating
ACEEGINORRSTT	gastroenteric
ACEEGJNNOSSTU	conjugateness
ACEEGLMNOORST	conglomerates
ACEEHHIILMPRS	hemispherical
ACEEHHILLORTT	heterothallic
ACEEHHIMNOPRS	archiphonemes
ACEEHHOPRSSTU	chapterhouses
ACEEHHOPRSTTY	tracheophytes
ACEEHIILLMORT	heliometrical
ACEEHIILNPSST	Sistine Chapel
ACEEHIIMOOPTT	hematopoietic
ACEEHIIMPSSTY	metaphysicise
ACEEHIIMPSTYZ	metaphysicize
ACEEHIINORSTT	theoreticians
ACEEHIIQRRSSU	squirearchies
ACEEHIJKPPRRT	Jack the Ripper
ACEEHIKNRSSST	heartsickness
ACEEHILLNPRTY	phrenetically
ACEEHILLORTTY	theoretically
ACEEHILMPRRTY	hypermetrical
ACEEHILNPRSSS	sphericalness
ACEEHILOPRRST	terpsichoreal
ACEEHILOPRSTT	heteroplastic
ACEEHILOPRTTY	heterotypical
ACEEHIMNORSSS	marchionesses
ACEEHIMNSSSTT	chastisements
ACEEHIMOORSTT	tracheotomies
ACEEHIMORRSTT	arthrectomies
ACEEHINOPRRST	terpsichorean
ACEEHINORSSTT	thoracentesis
ACEEHIPRRSSTY	secretaryship
ACEEHIPRSSTTY	cryptesthesia
ACEEHLLMOOORT	alcoholometer
ACEEHLLOPPSTU	leptocephalus
ACEEHLMNORRTU	thermonuclear
ACEEHLMNSSSST	matchlessness
ACEEHLORRSTUY	treacherously
ACEEHMNOPPRRT	rapprochement
ACEEHNNOORSTU	Southern Ocean
ACEEHOORSTTTU	heterotactous
ACEEHOPPRRRSS	sharecroppers
ACEEIIIKKLLNR	Killiecrankie
ACEEIIILPRSTU	peculiarities
ACEEIIILRSTTV	verticalities
ACEEIIIMNRRTV	recriminative
ACEEIIIPPRTTV	precipitative
ACEEIILLLNPTY	penicillately
ACEEIILLLNRTY	rectilineally
ACEEIILLLPPTY	epileptically
ACEEIILLMNRTT	intermetallic
ACEEIILLMPSTY	epistemically
ACEEIILLNRRTY	rectilinearly
ACEEIILMMNORS	ceremonialism
ACEEIILMMNOST	laminectomies
ACEEIILMNOPRS	semiporcelain
ACEEIILMNORST	ceremonialist
ACEEIILMNPRSS	empiricalness
ACEEIILMRRSSU	mercurialises
ACEEIILMRRSUZ	mercurializes

ACEEIILNNNRTT	tricentennial
ACEEIILNNTUVY	enunciatively
ACEEIILNORSTT	intersocietal
ACEEIILNOSSST	sectionalises
ACEEIILNOSSTZ	sectionalizes
ACEEIILORSTVY	viceroyalties
ACEEIILPPRTTY	precipitately
ACEEIIMMORSTV	commiserative
ACEEIIMNNOSST	amniocentesis
ACEEIIMNORRST	mercerisation
ACEEIIMNORRTZ	mercerization
ACEEIIMNPRSSU	epicureanisms
ACEEIIMOORSTV	ovariectomies
ACEEIINNORSST	containerises
ACEEIINNORSTZ	containerizes
ACEEIINNOSSTT	necessitation
ACEEIINNRSSTT	intricateness
ACEEIINNRSTTU	uncertainties
ACEEIINORRSTT	contrarieties
ACEEIINORSSTV	eviscerations
ACEEIINORSTTX	exercitations
ACEEIIRSSTTUV	resuscitative
ACEEIJLNRRTTU	interjectural
ACEEIKLLSSTVW	Sackville-West
ACEEIKLNPSSST	skepticalness
ACEEILLLNOTUV	involucellate
ACEEILLLNPSTY	splenetically
ACEEILLLNRRTU	intercellular
ACEEILLLNSTTU	intellectuals
ACEEILLMNOSSU	miscellaneous
ACEEILLMNTTUU	multinucleate
ACEEILLMOQRUU	equimolecular
ACEEILLNNNSSU	uncleanliness
ACEEILLNNORST	crenellations
ACEEILLNOPTXY	exceptionally
ACEEILLNOSSTY	coessentially
ACEEILLNPRTTY	centripetally
ACEEILLORRTVY	correlatively
ACEEILLPSTUVY	speculatively
ACEEILLRRSSTY	recrystallise
ACEEILLRRSTYZ	recrystallize
ACEEILMNNSSSU	masculineness
ACEEILMNOPTTV	contemplative
ACEEILMNRRSSU	mercurialness
ACEEILNNOPRTV	convertiplane
ACEEILNNOPTUX	unexceptional
ACEEILNNOQSTU	consequential
ACEEILNNRSSUY	unnecessarily
ACEEILNOQSSUV	equivocalness
ACEEILNORSTTU	interosculate
ACEEILNOSTTUX	contextualise
ACEEILNOTTUXZ	contextualize
ACEEILNRSSTUV	lucrativeness
ACEEILNRTTUUV	enculturative
ACEEILOOPRTVY	cooperatively
ACEEILOPRSTTY	stereotypical
ACEEILORRTTVY	retroactively
ACEEILPPSSTTU	septuplicates
ACEEILPSSTTUX	sextuplicates
ACEEIMMMOORTV	commemorative
ACEEIMMNORRTY	Amrit Ceremony
ACEEIMNNOORRS	oneiromancers
ACEEINNNORSST	nonresistance
ACEEINNNOSTTY	consentaneity
ACEEINNNQRTUY	quincentenary
ACEEINNNRSSTU	uncertainness
ACEEINNNSSSST	incessantness
ACEEINNOORSVZ	conversazione
ACEEINNOSSSTU	tenaciousness
ACEEINOOPRRRT	reincorporate
ACEEINOOPRSTU	proteinaceous
ACEEINOOPRTTX	expectoration
ACEEINOOPRTUV	uncooperative
ACEEINOORRSTV	conservatoire
	overreactions
ACEEINOPPPRST	apperceptions
ACEEINOPRRSTU	recuperations
ACEEINOPRSSTT	inspectorates
ACEEINORSSSUV	veraciousness
ACEEINORSSTVV	conservatives
ACEEKLNRSSSST	tracklessness
ACEELLMNORSSW	lowerclassmen
ACEELLNOOPRSU	porcellaneous
ACEELLNSSSSSS	classlessness
ACEELLOORRRST	rollercoaster
ACEELMMNOPRTY	complementary
ACEELNNOOPRTV	convertoplane
ACEELNOOPRRSS	corporealness
ACEEMMNNOPSST	encompassment
ACEEMNNNNOSTU	announcements
ACEEMNNORRSST	remonstrances
ACEEMOPRSSTTY	spermatocytes
ACEENNNOOSSTU	consentaneous
ACEEOOPRRSTTT	protectorates
ACEEOOPRRSTTX	expectorators
ACEEORRRSTTUU	aerostructure
ACEFFHLSSTTUZ	schutzstaffel
ACEFGHIINNNRS	enfranchising
ACEFGHIINNOTT	fianchettoing
ACEFGIIIINSTV	significative
ACEFGIILMNNTY	magnificently
ACEFGIILNRSSY	reclassifying
ACEFGIINORTUV	configurative
ACEFGILLNRTUY	centrifugally
ACEFGINOSSSUU	fugaciousness
ACEFHHIIINPST	chieftainship
ACEFHLLOPRRUY	reproachfully
ACEFHNORSSTTU	countershafts
ACEFIIIJLLNOT	jellification
ACEFIIIJSTTUV	justificative
ACEFIIILMSSSS	misclassifies
ACEFIIILNOSST	fictionalises
ACEFIIILNOSTT	felicitations
ACEFIIILNOSTZ	fictionalizes
ACEFIIINNORTU	reunification
ACEFIIINOPRTT	petrification
ACEFIIINORSTV	verifications
	versification
ACEFIIINOSTTT	testification
ACEFIILLPRSUY	superficially
ACEFIILMMNORT	microfilament
ACEFIILNOQSTU	liquefactions
ACEFIILNORSTY	forensicality
ACEFIINNOOTTU	autoinfection

ACEFIINNORSTU functionaries
ACEFIINOORSTV vociferations
ACEFILNNOOSSS confessionals
ACEFINNOORSSY confessionary
ACEFINNORRTTY confraternity
ACEFINORSSSTU fractiousness
ACEGGHIINNNRT interchanging
ACEGGHINPRRSU supercharging
ACEGGHIOOOPRZ zoogeographic
ACEGGIILNSTTU gesticulating
ACEGGILNNORUY encouragingly
ACEGGILNOOSTY gynaecologist
ACEGGINNOORST congregations
ACEGGLLRSSSTU class struggle
ACEGHHIINOPRS ichnographies
ACEGHHIMOPRRT thermographic
ACEGHHINOPTTY hypothecating
ACEGHHIOOPRRS chorographies
ACEGHHIOPRRRS chirographers
ACEGHHNOOPRRR chronographer
ACEGHHNORRSST shortchangers
ACEGHHOOPRRRS chorographers
ACEGHIIMOPRSS seismographic
ACEGHIINOOPRS iconographies
ACEGHILLLOOTY ethologically
theologically
ACEGHILLNNOSU hallucinogens
ACEGHILLNOOPR phrenological
ACEGHILLOOPPS psephological
ACEGHILOORSST archeologists
ACEGHILOOSSTT eschatologist
ACEGHIMNORRTU routemarching
ACEGHIMOPRRRS micrographers
ACEGHINNOOPRT anthropogenic
ACEGHINOOPRRS iconographers
ACEGHINOPPRRS sharecropping
ACEGHINOPRRSZ zincographers
ACEGHINORRSTT orchestrating
ACEGHIOPRRSST cerographists
ACEGHIORRSSTT gastrotriches
ACEGHLOOOORYZ archeozoology
ACEGHMOOPRRSS cosmographers
ACEGHMOOPSTUY mycetophagous
ACEGHNOOPPRSY pharyngoscope
ACEGHOPPRRRTY cryptographer
ACEGHOPPRRSST spectrographs
ACEGHOPPRRSTY spectrography
ACEGIIILNOOPT geopolitician
ACEGIIIMNNRRT recriminating
ACEGIIINORTTY iatrogenicity
ACEGIIINPPRTT precipitating
ACEGIILLLNOSS illogicalness
ACEGIILLLOOTY etiologically
ACEGIILLMOOSS seismological
ACEGIILLNOOST neologistical
ACEGIILLNRTUV revictualling
ACEGIILLOSTTY egotistically
ACEGIILMNOORT goniometrical
ACEGIILMNRTUV vermiculating
ACEGIILNNORTU reinoculating
ACEGIILNNOSTU geniculations
ACEGIILNOSTTU gesticulation
ACEGIIMMNORST commiserating
ACEGIIMNNOOTT metacognition
ACEGIINNNRSTY intransigency
ACEGIINNPRRST transpiercing
ACEGIINOORSST cosignatories
ACEGIINOOSTTX excogitations
ACEGIINOPRSTY saprogenicity
ACEGIINRSSTTU resuscitating
ACEGILLLNOOPY penologically
ACEGILLMNOOOT entomological
ACEGILLMNOORU numerological
ACEGILLMNOOYZ enzymological
ACEGILLNNOOTY ontogenically
ACEGILLNNOSTT constellating
ACEGILLNOPTYY genotypically
ACEGILLOOPRTY geotropically
ACEGILLSTYYYZ syzygetically
ACEGILMNNOPTT contemplating
ACEGILMNOPSTY salpingectomy
ACEGILMOOSSTU cleistogamous
ACEGILNNNOSUY sanguinolency
ACEGILNNOORSS congressional
ACEGILNNOSTTU conglutinates
ACEGILNORRSUU neurosurgical
ACEGILOOPSSST escapologists
ACEGILORSSTTU gesticulators
ACEGILORSTTUY gesticulatory
ACEGIMMMNOORT commemorating
ACEGIMNOPRSTU pneumogastric
ACEGINNNNOPRU preannouncing
ACEGINNNORSTT consternating
ACEGINOOPRSTT prognosticate
ACEGIOOPRSSST gastroscopies
ACEGLNOOOPSUY polygonaceous
ACEGLNOOPRSSY laryngoscopes
ACEGMNNOORSSW congresswoman
ACEGMOOPRSSSY gyrocompasses
ACEHHIILMNNTT anthelminthic
ACEHHIINOPRSX hieracosphinx
ACEHHIINOPRSZ schizophrenia
ACEHHILMOPRTX xerophthalmic
ACEHHILPPRSYY hyperphysical
ACEHHINOOPTTY hypothecation
ACEHHINOSSTTY osteichthyans
ACEHHINSSSTUZ schizanthuses
ACEHHIOPPSSTY psychopathies
ACEHHMMNRSTUY chrysanthemum
ACEHHMOOOPRRT chromatophore
ACEHHMOOPRSTU chemoautrophs
ACEHHMOOPRTTU chemautotroph
ACEHHOOPRSTTY hypothecators
ACEHHOPPRSTYY psychotherapy
ACEHIIILRSTTT tritheistical
ACEHIIINRRSST christianiser
ACEHIIINRRSTZ christianizer
ACEHIIINRSSST christianises
ACEHIIINRSSTZ christianizes
ACEHIILLLMOTY homiletically
ACEHIILLPPTYY epiphytically
ACEHIILLRSTUY heuristically
ACEHIILMNSSSW whimsicalness
ACEHIILOOPPRT apheliotropic

ACEHIILOPRRST	prehistorical
ACEHIIMNOPSTY	amphictyonies
ACEHIIMORRSST	chrismatories
ACEHIIMPSSTTY	metaphysicist
ACEHIIOPSSSTT	sophisticates
ACEHIIPRTTVYY	hyperactivity
ACEHILLLOPRTY	plethorically
ACEHILLMMOPRY	morphemically
ACEHILLNORSSS	scholarliness
ACEHILLNSTTYY	synthetically
ACEHILLOOPRTY	orthoepically
ACEHILLOPPRTY	prophetically
ACEHILLOPRTTY	prothetically
ACEHILMNOOPRT	phonometrical
ACEHILMOOOPTY	homoeotypical
ACEHILMOPRSTT	thermoplastic
ACEHILMOPRSTY	hypsometrical
ACEHILNOOPPRS	cephalosporin
ACEHILPPRSSUY	superphysical
ACEHIMNOPRRTY	hyperromantic
ACEHIMNPSTTUY	unsympathetic
ACEHIMOOORSTT	thoracotomies
ACEHIMORSSTTT	thermostatics
ACEHINOORRSTT	orchestration
ACEHINOPPRRST	copartnership
ACEHINOPRRSTT	trichopterans
ACEHIOOPRRSST	arthroscopies
ACEHIOPRRSSTT	stratospheric
ACEHIORSSTTTU	tetrastichous
ACEHLMOORSSST	schoolmasters
ACEHLNOORTTTW	Charlottetown
ACEHMMNOOORST	monochromates
ACEHMMOPSTTYY	sympathectomy
ACEHMORRSSSTU	chorusmasters
ACEHOORRRSSTT	orchestrators
ACEIIIILMNRST	criminalities
ACEIIIILMPRST	imperialistic
ACEIIILLMOPST	semipolitical
ACEIIILLMPTVY	implicatively
ACEIIILLNNOPT	penicillation
ACEIIILMNPSSU	municipalises
ACEIIILMNPSUZ	municipalizes
ACEIIILMPSSST	pessimistical
ACEIIILNOSTVV	vivisectional
ACEIIILQSTUVY	acquisitively
ACEIIIMNNORRT	recrimination
ACEIIINNNOSTT	Constantine II
ACEIIINOORSTT	eroticisation
ACEIIINOORTTZ	eroticization
ACEIIINOPPRTT	precipitation
ACEIIINOQRSTU	reacquisition
ACEIIINRTTTVY	interactivity
ACEIILLLNOSVY	Silicon Valley
ACEIILLMNSSST	miscellanists
ACEIILLMORSTY	isometrically
ACEIILLNNOORT	intercolonial
ACEIILLNORRTY	acrylonitrile
ACEIILLNRRTTU	intratelluric
ACEIILLNRRUVY	curvilinearly
ACEIILLNRSTXY	extrinsically
ACEIILLOOPTYZ	epizootically
ACEIILMMNOOST	commonalities
ACEIILMNOPSST	neoplasticism
ACEIILMNORTUV	vermiculation
ACEIILMNOSSSU	maliciousness
ACEIILMNPRRSU	supercriminal
ACEIILMNRSSTT	mercantilists
ACEIILNNOORTU	reinoculation
ACEIILNNOPSST	nonspecialist
ACEIILNOPRRTT	intertropical
ACEIILNOPRSST	personalistic
ACEIILNORSTTU	reticulations
ACEIILNOSSSTT	sectionalists
ACEIILNOSSTUV	vesiculations
ACEIILNPPRTTY	precipitantly
ACEIILNPQTTUU	quintuplicate
ACEIILNRSSTTT	clarinettists
ACEIILORRTTVY	correlativity
ACEIIMMNOORST	commiseration
ACEIIMMNRSTTY	antisymmetric
ACEIIMNNOOOST	economisation
ACEIIMNNOOOTZ	economization
ACEIIMNORRRST	recriminators
ACEIIMNORRRTY	recriminatory
ACEIIMNORRSTT	craniometrist
ACEIIMNORSSTT	cremationists
ACEIIMOORSTTU	autoeroticism
ACEIINNNORSTU	renunciations
ACEIINNNOSTTX	Constantine XI
ACEIINNOOPRST	preconisation
ACEIINNOOPRTZ	preconization
ACEIINNOORSVZ	conversazioni
ACEIINNOSSSST	ascensionists
ACEIINNOSTTUV	continuatives
ACEIINOOPRRTV	incorporative
ACEIINOOQSTUV	equivocations
ACEIINOORRSTV	anticorrosive
ACEIINOORSSTV	viscerotonias
ACEIINOPRRSTT	practitioners
ACEIINORSSSUV	vicariousness
ACEIINORSSTTU	resuscitation
ACEIINOSSSUVV	vivaciousness
ACEIINPRRSTTV	transcriptive
ACEIIOOPRTTVY	cooperativity
ACEIIOPPRRSTT	precipitators
ACEIIORRRSTTV	cirrostrative
ACEIIORRTTTVY	retroactivity
ACEILLLLPSTYY	sylleptically
ACEILLMMNOTYY	metonymically
ACEILLMMRSTYY	symmetrically
ACEILLMNNORTY	conterminally
ACEILLMNOOPST	compellations
ACEILLNNNOSSY	nonsensically
ACEILLNNNOTTY	continentally
ACEILLNNOOSTT	constellation
ACEILLNNORRSU	carillonneurs
ACEILLNOOPRRY	incorporeally
ACEILLNOQUUVY	unequivocally
ACEILLRRSSSTY	crystallisers
ACEILLRRSSTYZ	crystallizers
ACEILMMNOPRTY	complimentary
ACEILMMNORSSU	communalisers
ACEILMMNORSUZ	communalizers
ACEILMMNRSTUY	unsymmetrical

ACEILMMOTTUVY commutatively
ACEILMNNOOPSS companionless
ACEILMNNOOPTT contemplation
ACEILMNNOPSST compliantness
ACEILMNNORRTU intercolumnar
ACEILMNNSSSUU unmusicalness
ACEILMOOPRSTU somatopleuric
ACEILNNNOOSTV conventionals
ACEILNNNOSSTU continualness
ACEILNNOOTTVY connotatively
ACEILNNORTTUU enculturation
ACEILNOOPRSSS processionals
ACEILNOOPRSTT lactoproteins
ACEILNOORRSTV controversial
ACEILNOPRRSTU pronuclearist
ACEILNORSTTVY contrastively
ACEILOOPRTVVY provocatively
ACEILOORRSTTW watercolorist
ACEILPPRSSSTU superplastics
ACEIMMMNOOORT commemoration
ACEIMMOORRSST commiserators
ACEIMNNOOPSST compensations
ACEIMNNORRTTU macronutrient
ACEIMNNOSSTTY nonsystematic
ACEIMNOOOOPTT onomatopoetic
ACEIMNORSSSTU customariness
ACEIMNPSSTTUU mispunctuates
ACEINNNOORSTT consternation
ACEINNNOORTTV contravention
ACEINNOORRSVY conversionary
ACEINNOORSSTV conversations
ACEINNOORSTTW Coniston Water
ACEINNORSSTTU counterstains
encrustations
ACEINOOPRRSSY processionary
ACEINOORRSTUV nectarivorous
ACEINOORSSSTU atrociousness
ACEINOORSSSUV voraciousness
ACEIORRSSSTTU resuscitators
ACELLMMNOOORU monomolecular
ACELLNNRSTTUY translucently
ACELLNOORSTTY constellatory
ACELLOOPRSSSU supercolossal
ACELMNOOPRSTT contemplators
ACELMNOORSSSU clamorousness
ACELMNOPRRSUU supercolumnar
ACELMNORRSUUU neuromuscular
ACELNOOPRSSTU proconsulates
ACELNOPRSSSUU crapulousness
ACELOOPPRRSUU pleurocarpous
ACEMMMOOORRST commemorators
ACEMMMOOORRTY commemoratory
ACEMOOPRSTTTY prostatectomy
ACENNOOOOPRRT noncooperator
ACENNOORRSSSU rancorousness
ACEOPPRRSSTTU streptocarpus
ACEOPRRSSSSTT sportscasters
ACFFGIIILNPST spifflicating
ACFFGILNOSTUY suffocatingly
ACFFIIINOORTT fortification
ACFGIIIILNNOT lignification
ACFGIIIINNNST insignificant
ACFGIIIINNOST signification
ACFGIIILNNSTY significantly
ACFGIIILNOORT glorification
ACFGIIINNOPTT pontificating
ACFGIIINNORST fractionising
ACFGIIINNORTZ fractionizing
ACFGIINNOORTU configuration
ACFHIIIILNOTT lithification
ACFHIIIMNOSTU humifications
ACFHIIINOORRT horrification
ACFHIILLNOORY honorifically
ACFIIIILNOSTV vilifications
ACFIIIINNORTT nitrification
ACFIIIINORTTV vitrification
ACFIIIINOSTVV vivifications
ACFIIIJLLNOOT jollification
ACFIIIJNOSTTU justification
ACFIIILLMNOOT mollification
ACFIIILLNNOTU nullification
ACFIIIMMMNOTU mummification
ACFIIIMNOORTT mortification
ACFIIIMNOSTTY mystification
ACFIIINNOOSTT notifications
ACFIIINOPPTUY yuppification
ACFIIINOPRSTU purifications
ACFIIINOPSTTY typifications
ACFIIJORSTTUY justificatory
ACFIILLLORSTY floristically
ACFIILLOOPRSY soporifically
ACFIILMNNOSTU functionalism
ACFIILNNOSTTU functionalist
ACFIILNNOTTUY functionality
ACFIIMNNOORST confirmations
ACFILLLORRTUU floricultural
ACFILNNNNOOTU nonfunctional
ACFIMNNOOORST conformations
ACFINNNOOORTT confrontation
ACGGHHILOPPRY glyphographic
ACGGHHINNORST shortchanging
ACGGHIKLNOSTU laughingstock
ACGGHILOPPRTY glyptographic
ACGGIILLOOSST glaciologists
ACGGILLLOOOSS glossological
ACGHHHINNSUUU Hung Hsiu-ch'uan
ACGHHIIOPPRSY physiographic
ACGHHILMOOOPR homolographic
ACGHIIIINNPSS hispanicising
ACGHIIIINNPSZ hispanicizing
ACGHIIKMNNRSS scrimshanking
ACGHIILLOOPSY physiological
ACGHILLLMOOOY homologically
ACGHILLMOOOPR morphological
ACGHILLOOPRSS oscillographs
ACGHILLOOPRSY oscillography
ACGHILNOORSUW colourwashing
ACGHIMNNOOOPT pathognomonic
ACGHIMOOPRSST cosmographist
ACGHNOOPPRSYY pharyngoscopy
ACGIIIIILNNSV civilianising
ACGIIIIILNNVZ civilianizing
ACGIIIILMNNRS criminalising
ACGIIIILMNNRZ criminalizing

ACGIIIIMNNNRT incriminating
ACGIIILLNNSTT scintillating
ACGIIILMNNSSU masculinising
ACGIIILMNNSUZ masculinizing
ACGIIILNOPRST tropicalising
ACGIIILNOPRTZ tropicalizing
ACGIIIMNNORST romanticising
ACGIIIMNNORTZ romanticizing
ACGIIILLLOSSTY syllogistical
ACGIIILLMMNOOU immunological
ACGIIILLMNNOPY complainingly
ACGIIILLMOOSTT climatologist
ACGIIILLNRSSTY crystallising
ACGIIILLNRSTYZ crystallizing
ACGIILMMNNOSU communalising
ACGIILMMNNOUZ communalizing
ACGIILMNNNOPU uncomplaining
ACGIILMNOORSU graminicolous
ACGIILNOORSST craniologists
ACGIILRRSTTUU agriculturist
ACGIIMMNOORRS microorganism
ACGIINNNOOSST consignations
ACGIINNNOPRST nonpractising
ACGIINNNOSTUY consanguinity
ACGIINNOOPRRT incorporating
ACGIINOOPRRST corporatising
ACGIINOOPRRTZ corporatizing
ACGILLLMNOOOY nomologically
ACGILLLMOOOPY pomologically
ACGILLLNOOOSY nosologically
ACGILLLNOOOTY ontologically
ACGILLLOOOPTY topologically
ACGILLLOOPTYY typologically
ACGILLNOOOSTV volcanologist
ACGILLNOOSTUV vulcanologist
ACGILLNOOSTYY glycosylation
ACGIMMOOPRRRS microprograms
ACGIMNOOPRSTU compurgations
ACGINNNOOOSTU noncontagious
ACGIOOPRSSSTT gastroscopist
ACHHIIINNORST ornithischian
ACHHIILLOOPPS philosophical
ACHHIILMNOPRS philharmonics
ACHHIILNOPPRT philanthropic
ACHHIIMNOPPSS championships
ACHHIIMOPRSTU amphitrichous
ACHHILMMOORSS schoolmarmish
ACHHIMNOORSTX xanthochroism
ACHHIMNOOSTTU autochthonism
ACHHIORSSTUUY ichthyosaurus
ACHHLLNOOOSTU allochthonous
ACHHNNOOOPRSY onychophorans
ACHHNOOOSTTUU autochthonous
ACHIIIJPRSSTU justiciarship
ACHIIILNPPPRS principalship
ACHIIIMNOSTTY mythicisation
ACHIIIMNOTTYZ mythicization
ACHIILLOPSSTY sophistically
ACHIILMOOOSTY homosociality
ACHIILNNOORST chlorinations
nonhistorical
ACHIILNNRSTUY unchristianly
ACHIILOPRSSTT cartophilists
ACHIIMMORRSTT trichromatism
ACHIIMNNOOPPS companionship
ACHIIOOPRSSTT sophisticator
ACHIIPRSSSTTY psychiatrists
ACHILLMNOPSYY symphonically
ACHILLORRTTUU horticultural
ACHILMOORSSTY chromatolysis
ACHILMOPSTTYY sympatholytic
ACHILOOPPRRSS corporalships
ACHIMNNORSSSY asynchronisms
ACHIMNOOPRRST promonarchist
ACHIMOOOPRSTT somatotrophic
ACHLLMMOOORSY chromosomally
ACHMMNOOOORRT monochromator
ACIIIILNOSSTV civilisations
ACIIIILNOSTVZ civilizations
ACIIIIMNNNORT incrimination
ACIIIIMNOSTTV victimisation
ACIIIIMNOTTVZ victimization
ACIIIILLNNOSTT scintillation
ACIIIILLNNRSTY intrinsically
ACIIIILMNNORTU anticlinorium
ACIIIILMNOPRSV provincialism
ACIIIILMNPSSTU municipalists
ACIIIILNNOPRST inscriptional
ACIIIILNOOSSTT coalitionists
solicitations
ACIIIILNOPRSTT triplications
ACIIIILNOPRTVY provinciality
ACIIIILNOSSTVV convivialists
ACIIIMNNORRST incriminators
ACIIIMNNORRTY incriminatory
ACIIINNOOSTTX intoxications
ACIIINNOSSTTU cutinisations
ACIIINNOSTTUZ cutinizations
ACIILLLMOOQSU colloquialism
ACIILLLNNSTTY scintillantly
ACIILLLRSTUUV silvicultural
ACIILLLSSTTYY stylistically
ACIILLMNNOPTY incompliantly
ACIILLNNSTTUY instinctually
ACIILLNOORTUY illocutionary
ACIILLNORSSTT scintillators
ACIILLNRSTTYY crystallinity
ACIILLOOPRSTY isotropically
ACIILMNNOOSTU columniations
ACIILMNOOOPST compositional
ACIILMNOORSUY acrimoniously
ACIILMNOORTTY microtonality
ACIILMOOOPRST compositorial
ACIILMOORSTTT stromatolitic
ACIILNNOOOSST colonisations
ACIILNNOOOSTZ colonizations
ACIILNNOOSSTU inosculations
ACIILNNORSTTU instructional
ACIILNOOORSTU colourisation
ACIILNOOORSTZ colorizations
ACIILNOOORTUZ colourization
ACIILNOPPSSTU supplications
ACIILNORSTTUV voluntaristic
ACIILPRSSTTUU apiculturists

ACIILQRSTTUUU aquiculturist
ACIILRSSTTUUV aviculturists
ACIIMMNNOOSTU communisation
ACIIMMNNOOTUZ communization
ACIIMMNOORSSY commissionary
ACIIMMOOPRSTT compatriotism
ACIIMNNOOSSTU sanctimonious
ACIIMNOOPRTTU protoactinium
ACIINNNOOPRTU pronunciation
ACIINNNOOSTTU continuations
ACIINNOOOPRRT incorporation
ACIINNOPRRSTT transcription
ACIINNORSSTTU incrustations
ACILLLMRTTUUU multicultural
ACILLMMNNOOUY communionally
ACILLNNOOOTUV convolutional
ACILMMOOPSSSY mycoplasmosis
ACILMNOOOPSST cosmopolitans
ACILMNOSSSTTU sansculottism
ACILMRRSSTTUU structuralism
ACILNNNNOOSTY inconsonantly
ACILNNOORSUVY convulsionary
ACILNNOOSSTTU consultations
ACILNOORRSTUY contrariously
ACILNOORRSUVY carnivorously
ACILNOSSSTTTU sansculottist
ACILRRSSTTTUU structuralist
ACIMMNNOOSSTU consummations
ACINNOPRSTTTU contrapuntist
ACINOOOPRRRST incorporators
ACLMORSSTTUUU cumulostratus
stratocumulus
ACLNNORRSTTUU nonstructural
ACNOOOPPRSSTT contrappostos
ADDDEEHLNNRUY underhandedly
ADDDEFHIILOSV Shield of David
ADDEEEEHNRRTT tenderhearted
ADDEEEGHINPSS pigheadedness
ADDEEEGHNORSY dehydrogenase
ADDEEEGHNORTY dehydrogenate
ADDEEEGINPRST predesignated
ADDEEEGINRRTT redintegrated
ADDEEEGMNRRRY gerrymandered
ADDEEEGNNRRST transgendered
ADDEEEHHNOSST hotheadedness
ADDEEEHINNPSS pinheadedness
ADDEEEIILMNRS demineralised
ADDEEEIILMNRZ demineralized
ADDEEEIILORVZ overidealized
ADDEEEIIMNRTT intermediated
ADDEEEIIRSSTV desideratives
ADDEEEILMNRST Middle Eastern
ADDEEEIMNORST demonetarised
ADDEEEIMNORTZ demonetarized
ADDEEEINOPPST endopeptidase
ADDEEEINPRSTT Painted Desert
predestinated
ADDEEENOPPRRT preponderated
ADDEEEOPRRSUV overpersuaded
ADDEEFFHNNOSS offhandedness
ADDEEFFIORSST disafforested
ADDEEGGHIRSTT straightedged
ADDEEGGINNRSS degradingness
ADDEEGHLNORWY wrongheadedly
ADDEEGIINRSTT disintegrated
ADDEEGIMNNNSS maddeningness
ADDEEGNNRSSUU unguardedness
ADDEEHIKLNRTY kindheartedly
ADDEEHILLNRST disenthralled
ADDEEHLNORTWY downheartedly
ADDEEIIILMRST demilitarised
ADDEEIIILMRTZ demilitarized
ADDEEIIILORST editorialised
ADDEEIIILORTZ editorialized
ADDEEIIMMNNOS demimondaines
ADDEEIINORSST desiderations
ADDEEIINORSTT disorientated
ADDEEIMNRSTUV misadventured
ADDEEINNSSSUV unadvisedness
ADDEELNOSSSTT staddlestones
ADDEEMNOOPSSU pseudomonades
ADDEENNNSSTUU undauntedness
ADDEFGJMNOTUY Day of Judgment
ADDEFIIILMNSU sulfadimidine
ADDEGIIMNRSSS misaddressing
ADDEGIINNNRRU underdraining
ADDEGINNNRSTU understanding
ADDEHHIKNOOSS Dhodhekánisos
ADDEIIIILNSUV individualise
ADDEIIIILNUVZ individualize
ADDEIIINOOSTX deoxidisation
ADDEIIINOOTXZ deoxidization
ADDEIIINSTTTU attitudinised
ADDEIIINTTTUZ attitudinized
ADDEIINOOORST deodorisation
ADDEIINOOORTZ deodorization
ADDEIINOPRSTU superaddition
ADDEILMNOOSTU demodulations
ADDEIMNNRSSTU misunderstand
ADDGIIIINNTUV individuating
ADDGIILLLLNYY dillydallying
ADDGIILNSSSTU studdingsails
ADDGIMNNOOORT rodomontading
ADDHIIILMOPPS amphidiploids
ADDIIIILMNSUV individualism
ADDIIIILNSTUV individualist
ADDIIIILNTUVY individuality
ADDIIIINNOTUV individuation
ADDIIINORSTUV individuators
ADEEEEFHLRRTY freeheartedly
ADEEEEGNNRRTU unregenerated
ADEEEEHLMPPRT pamphleteered
ADEEEENPRSSST desperateness
ADEEEFFIINRTT differentiate
ADEEEFILLNRTY deferentially
ADEEEFNRRRRST retransferred
ADEEEGGGINRST desegregating
ADEEEGGIMNNST disengagement
ADEEEGGINORST desegregation
ADEEEGGNNORST nonsegregated
ADEEEGHLMMRSS sledgehammers
ADEEEGILMNRSY semilegendary
ADEEEGIMNRSST demagnetisers
disagreements

ADEEEGIMNRSTZ demagnetizers
ADEEEGIMORSTU deuterogamies
ADEEEGINNNRSS engrainedness
ADEEEGINNORST degenerations
ADEEEGINPRSST predesignates
ADEEEGINRRSTT redintegrates
ADEEEGIRRSTTV tergiversated
ADEEEGLLNORTU outgeneralled
ADEEEGMNNNRST endangerments
ADEEEGOPRRSTU supererogated
ADEEEGOPRRTUY daguerreotype
ADEEEHINPRSST parenthesised
ADEEEHINPRSTZ parenthesized
ADEEEHINRRTTW interwreathed
ADEEEHLNNNRTW New Netherland
ADEEEHLNOPRTY openheartedly
ADEEEHLNSSSST deathlessness
ADEEEIILMNRSS demineralises
ADEEEIILMNRSZ demineralizes
ADEEEIILNNRTT interlineated
ADEEEIILORSVZ overidealizes
ADEEEIIMMNSST immediateness
ADEEEIIMMRSST semidiameters
ADEEEIIMNNRTT indeterminate
ADEEEIIMNRSTT intermediates
ADEEEIIMNRTTV determinative
ADEEEIIMPRTTV premeditative
ADEEEIINPRSST pedestrianise
ADEEEIINPRSTZ pedestrianize
ADEEEIIORRTTV deteriorative
ADEEEILLNPRTT interpellated
ADEEEILMNORST radioelements
ADEEEILMNRTTY determinately
ADEEEILNOPRSS depersonalise
ADEEEILNOPRSZ depersonalize
ADEEEILNPRRST interpleaders
ADEEEILOPRTTY radioteletype
ADEEEIMNNORTU mountaineered
ADEEEIMNORSST demonetarises
ADEEEIMNORSTZ demonetarizes
ADEEEIMNRSTTU underestimate
ADEEEIMNRSTTV advertisement
ADEEEIMNRTTVZ advertizement
ADEEEIMORSTTV overestimated
ADEEEINNRSSST sedentariness
ADEEEINNRSSUW unweariedness
ADEEEINOPQRTU equiponderate
ADEEEINPRSSTT predestinates
ADEEEIOPPSSTX exopeptidases
ADEEELLMNOPTV developmental
ADEEELLMORRST steamrollered
ADEEELMNRSSSS dreamlessness
ADEEEMNORSTUV adventuresome
ADEEEMNORTUUV outmaneuvered
ADEEENOPPRRST preponderates
ADEEENRSSSTUV adventuresses
ADEEEOPPRRSSV eavesdroppers
ADEEEOPRRSSUV overpersuades
ADEEFFIILNRST differentials
ADEEFGGILNRRS self-regarding
ADEEFGILMNNUV Van Diemen Gulf
ADEEFGILNNRRS Flinders Range
ADEEFGLNRRSSU regardfulness
ADEEFHLORSTTY softheartedly
ADEEFHOORRSSW foreshadowers
ADEEFIILOQRUV overqualified
ADEEFINOORSTT deforestation
ADEEGGGINSSZZ zigzaggedness
ADEEGGHIRSSTT straightedges
ADEEGGIIMNNST demagnetising
ADEEGGIIMNNTZ demagnetizing
ADEEGGINNOTXY deoxygenating
ADEEGGLNOPPRS doppelgangers
ADEEGHIINNRST disheartening
ADEEGHILNRSTY nearsightedly
ADEEGHNOOPRTV photoengraved
ADEEGHPRSSTTU stepdaughters
ADEEGIIILMSTT legitimatised
ADEEGIIILMTTZ legitimatized
ADEEGIIINRTTT interdigitate
ADEEGIILNNPRT interpleading
ADEEGIILNSSUX desexualising
ADEEGIILNSUXZ desexualizing
ADEEGIIMNPRTT premeditating
ADEEGIINNNRSS ingrainedness
ADEEGIINNRRTT intergradient
ADEEGIINORRTT deteriorating
ADEEGIINORRTV reinvigorated
ADEEGIINORSTY Tayside Region
ADEEGIINORTVV overdeviating
ADEEGIINRSSTT disintegrates
ADEEGIKNNRRST kindergartens
ADEEGILNORSTU deregulations
ADEEGIMORSTTU deuterogamist
ADEEGINNOOTXY deoxygenation
ADEEGINNOPRVX overexpanding
ADEEGINOPPRSV eavesdropping
ADEEGINOPRRSV overspreading
ADEEGINORSTTU deuteragonist
ADEEGLNNOORRT Greater London
ADEEGMNNRRSTU undergarments
ADEEGNNORSSSU dangerousness
ADEEGOPRRTUYY daguerreotypy
ADEEHHIKNRRSS headshrinkers
ADEEHHIMOPRRT hermaphrodite
ADEEHHOOORSUW Harewood House
ADEEHIILMNNPY diphenylamine
ADEEHIILNSTTT dilettanteish
ADEEHIIMNORTT trimethadione
ADEEHIMNPPRSS misapprehends
ADEEHIMRSSSTY headmistressy
ADEEHINNORRTY nonhereditary
ADEEHKLLLNOST Kedleston Hall
ADEEHLMNORRSY dysmenorrheal
ADEEHMMOOPRST metamorphosed
ADEEHMNOORRSY dysmenorrhoea
ADEEHMOPRSTTY dermatophytes
ADEEHNNOOSSTU Southend-on-Sea
ADEEHNOOPRRTZ trapezohedron
ADEEHORSSTUVY Shrove Tuesday
ADEEIIILMRRTZ remilitarized
ADEEIIILMRSST demilitarises
ADEEIIILMRSTZ demilitarizes
ADEEIIILORRST editorialiser

ADEEIIILORRTZ editorializer
ADEEIIILORSST editorialises
ADEEIIILORSTZ editorializes
ADEEIIIMNSSTV disseminative
ADEEIIINPRSST stipendiaries
ADEEIILLNRSTY residentially
ADEEIILMNNSTT disentailment
ADEEIILMNOOST emotionalised
ADEEIILMNOOTZ emotionalized
ADEEIILMNPSST dissepimental
ADEEIILMNRSTY sedimentarily
ADEEIILMNSTTT dilettanteism
ADEEIILNRSSUV universalised
ADEEIILNRSUVZ universalized
ADEEIIMMNPRTY impedimentary
ADEEIIMNNORTT determination
ADEEIIMNNOSTT sedimentation
ADEEIIMNOPRTT premeditation
ADEEIIMNORRTT intermediator
ADEEIIMOPRRRV Primo de Rivera
ADEEIINNORSTT tenderisation
ADEEIINNORTTZ tenderization
ADEEIINOORRTT deterioration
ADEEIINOPRRTT repartitioned
ADEEIINOPRTXY expeditionary
ADEEIINORSSTT disorientates
ADEEIINORSSTV disseveration
ADEEILLMNRTTY detrimentally
ADEEILLNNRTTY interdentally
ADEEILMMNNSTT dismantlement
ADEEILMNOORST demonolatries
ADEEILMNOORTZ metronidazole
ADEEILMNOPRTY predominately
ADEEILNNRTTVY inadvertently
ADEEILNOPPRST lepidopterans
ADEEIMMNORSSU misdemeanours
ADEEIMNORSTTV demonstrative
ADEEIMNRRSTTT retransmitted
ADEEIMNRSSTUV misadventures
ADEEIMOPRRSTT premeditators
ADEEINNOPQRTU equiponderant
ADEEINOOPPRRT reapportioned
ADEEINOPRRSST predatoriness
ADEEINOPRRSTU superordinate
ADEEINPRSSTUU unpasteurised
ADEEINPRSTUUZ unpasteurized
ADEEJMNRSSTTU readjustments
ADEELMMRSSTUU summersaulted
ADEELMOPRSSTU deuteroplasms
ADEELNNSSSSTU dauntlessness
ADEELOOPPRTUV overpopulated
ADEEMMOOSTUXY myxoedematous
ADEEMNNPRSTUY underpayments
ADEEMNOORTUUV outmanoeuvred
ADEEMOORRSTUX xerodermatous
ADEENPPRRRSTU understrapper
ADEEORRRSTTUW Wardour Street
ADEFFHIORRSST Staffordshire
ADEFGHINOORSW foreshadowing
ADEFGIINNOORR foreordaining
ADEFHILNNPRTT Pentland Firth
ADEFHILNOORSS foolhardiness
ADEFIIILQRSSU disqualifiers
ADEFIILLNQUUY unqualifiedly
ADEFIILNOSSTT deflationists
ADEFIJMMORRSU Reform Judaism
ADEFILLSSTTUY distastefully
ADEFLLOOPSTYY splayfootedly
ADEFMNNORRSTU untransformed
ADEGGHINNORTY hydrogenating
ADEGGIILNNNST disentangling
ADEGGIILNNRSS niggardliness
ADEGGIILNNTTU deglutinating
ADEGGIMMNOPRR deprogramming
ADEGHHOPRRRSY hydrographers
ADEGHIIOPRSTT dittographies
ADEGHIMOPRSST demographists
ADEGHINNOORTY hydrogenation
ADEGHINNOPPRS pendragonship
ADEGHINNOPRSS androsphinges
ADEGHINOORSVW overshadowing
ADEGHLLNORSST strangleholds
ADEGHLMNORRTY grandmotherly
ADEGHMNORSTUW draughtswomen
ADEGHNOORRSTY hydrogenators
ADEGIIIMNNRST administering
ADEGIIIMNNSST disseminating
ADEGIILLNNSTU dentilinguals
ADEGIILLNPSSY displeasingly
ADEGIILMNSTUU demutualising
ADEGIILMNTTUY unmitigatedly
ADEGIILMNTUUZ demutualizing
ADEGIILNNOTTU deglutination
ADEGIILNPRSSU displeasuring
ADEGIIMMNNRST masterminding
ADEGIIMNNOPRT predominating
ADEGIIMOOPRST diageotropism
ADEGIINNNPRTU underpainting
ADEGIINNPRRSU underpraising
ADEGIINORRSSS disorganisers
ADEGIINORRSSZ disorganizers
ADEGIINORRSTT disintegrator
ADEGILMOORSTT dermatologist
ADEGILNNOQRTU grandiloquent
ADEGILNOOPRTT proglottidean
ADEGIMNNORSTT demonstrating
ADEGJLMNNNOTU nonjudgmental
ADEGLLMNORUWZ mangoldwurzel
ADEHHIIILMOOP haemophilioid
ADEHHLOPRSTUY hydrosulphate
ADEHIIIMRSTTV Mithridates VI
ADEHIILMNPSTY lymphadenitis
ADEHIIMNOOSTT methodisation
ADEHIIMNOOTTZ methodization
ADEHIINNRSSTY hydrastinines
ADEHIKLNNPSSS spindleshanks
ADEHILMNOPSSU sulphonamides
ADEHILMNORXYY hydroxylamine
ADEHILNNOPRSW landownership
ADEHIMOOPRRST moderatorship
ADEHINNNORRTV Northern Dvina
ADEHINNOPRSSX androsphinxes
ADEHINNRSSTWW withdrawnness
ADEHIOOPPRSST apostrophised

ADEHIOOPPRSTZ apostrophized
ADEHIOOPRSSTT orthopaedists
ADEHLLOOPPSUY polyadelphous
ADEHNORRSTTWW northwestward
ADEHORSSTTUWW southwestward
ADEIIIILMSSTV dissimilative
ADEIIILMNOSTT delimitations
ADEIIILMSSTUV dissimulative
ADEIIILNPSTTU platitudinise
ADEIIILNPTTUZ platitudinize
ADEIIILNRSSTU industrialise
ADEIIILNRSTUZ industrialize
ADEIIILORSSTT editorialists
ADEIIILPRSSTU spiritualised
ADEIIILPRSTUZ spiritualized
ADEIIIMNNOSST dissemination
ADEIIINNOOSST deionisations
ADEIIINOOPRST periodisation
ADEIIINOOPRTZ periodization
ADEIIINOSSTTV deviationists
ADEIIINRSTTTU attitudiniser
ADEIIINRTTTUZ attitudinizer
ADEIIINSSTTTU attitudinises
ADEIIINSTTTUZ attitudinizes
ADEIILLMNNOSY dimensionally
ADEIILLMNNTUU unilluminated
ADEIILLNQRSTU tranquillised
ADEIILLNQRTUZ tranquillized
ADEIILLSSTUVV vaudevillists
ADEIILMNOORST Tirso de Molina
ADEIILMNOPSSY impassionedly
ADEIILMNRRTUY rudimentarily
ADEIILNNOOPTY opinionatedly
ADEIILNOOTTVY devotionality
ADEIILNORSSTT traditionless
ADEIILNPRRSTU preindustrial
ADEIILNQSTTUY equidistantly
ADEIILPSTTUVY disputatively
ADEIIMNNNOOST denominations
ADEIIMNNOOPRT predomination
ADEIIMNNOORST modernisation
ADEIIMNNOORTZ modernization
ADEIIMNNOPSSU unimpassioned
ADEIIMNNORSTT antimodernist
ADEIIMNNRSSTT distrainments
ADEIIMNORSSST disseminators
ADEIIMORSSTTU audiometrists
ADEIINNOOPRRT preordination
ADEIINNOPSSST dispensations
ADEIINOOPRSST disoperations
ADEIINORSSSTT dissertations
ADEIIOOOPRSST radioisotopes
ADEILLMNRTTYY tyndallimetry
ADEILLNOPPRST dipropellants
ADEILLNRSTTUU unillustrated
ADEILMNNNSSTU disannulments
ADEILMNNOPRTY predominantly
ADEILNOOPPSTU depopulations
ADEILNOORTUVY devolutionary
ADEIMNNOORSTT demonstration
ADEIMNNOPRSTU superdominant
ADEIMNOOPRRST predominators
ADEIMOOPRSSTZ spermatozoids
ADEINOSSSSSUU assiduousness
ADELNORSTUUVY adventurously
ADEMNOORRSSTT demonstrators
ADENNORSTUUUV unadventurous
ADFFHILNOSSTY standoffishly
ADFGIIILNQSUY disqualifying
ADFGIIINORSTU disfiguration
ADFGIIINSSSTY dissatisfying
ADFHHKLLNOOOO Hook of Holland
ADFIIIILMNOSS solifidianism
ADFIILNOORSTU fluoridations
ADFIKLLNNOORS Norfolk Island
ADGGIIIMNNOSS misdiagnosing
ADGGIIINNORSS disorganising
ADGGIIINNORSZ disorganizing
ADGHILLLMNOSS smallholdings
ADGHINNOOOPRT gonadotrophin
ADGHMNNOOPRRY gynandromorph
ADGIIIILMNSST dissimilating
ADGIIILMNSSTU dissimulating
ADGIIILNNRSSV Virgin Islands
ADGIIILNPRSSY dispraisingly
ADGIIINNOPPST disappointing
ADGIIMNNOSTUU magnitudinous
ADGIJKNNOPRTU Tandjungpriok
ADGIJLNOPPRWY jawdroppingly
ADGILNNOSTTUY outstandingly
ADGINNOOOPRST gonadotropins
ADHHIOPRSSTTY hydropathists
ADHIILLNOQRTU quadrillionth
ADHIILMNOPRSU dolphinariums
ADHIIMNOORSSU disharmonious
ADHILNOORSTYY hydrolysation
ADHILNOORTYYZ hydrolyzation
ADHIMNOPRSSSW swordsmanship
ADIIIILMNOSST dissimilation
ADIIIILMNPRTU platiniridium
ADIIIILMRSSTY dissimilarity
ADIIIIMNNOSTT intimidations
ADIIILLNOSSTT distillations
ADIIILMNOSSTU dissimulation
ADIIILMNRSSTU industrialism
ADIIILMOPRRTY primordiality
ADIIILMORSSTY dissimilatory
ADIIILNOOPSST dispositional
ADIIILNRSSTTU industrialist
ADIIINORSSTTT traditionists
ADIILMORSSSTU dissimulators
ADIILNNNORSTU nonindustrial
ADIILNOOOPSST podsolisation
ADIILNOOOPSTZ podsolization
podzolisation
ADIILNOOOPTZZ podzolization
ADIILNOPSSTUV postdiluvians
ADIILNOPSTTUU platitudinous
ADIINNRSTTUYY Trinity Sunday
ADIKLNRSSUUYY Ryukyu Islands
ADILLLLOOOPPY allopolyploid
ADILLOOOPPTUY autopolyploid
AEEEEGHMORSTT heterogametes
AEEEEGNNRRSTU unregenerates

AEEEEHHNNSTVV seventh heaven
AEEEEHHPRRSSS sheepshearers
AEEEEHLMNPRSS ephemeralness
AEEEEILNRRSST rensselaerite
AEEEEIMNPRSST passementerie
AEEEEKLMRRSTT telemarketers
AEEEEMMNRRSTU remeasurement
AEEEEMNPRSSTT temperateness
AEEEFGHHIRTTW featherweight
AEEEFGIIRRRTV refrigerative
AEEEFINQRTTUV frequentative
AEEEGGIMNOSST gametogenesis
AEEEGHHINPRSS sheepshearing
AEEEGHIILMRSW whigmaleeries
AEEEGHIILNRST etherealising
AEEEGHIILNRTZ etherealizing
AEEEGHIMNOSST hematogenesis
AEEEGHINORSST atherogenesis
AEEEGHLNOPRRS selenographer
AEEEGHMNOPRST magnetosphere
AEEEGIINRSTTV reinvestigate
AEEEGIKLMNRTT telemarketing
AEEEGIKMNQRTU Quaker meeting
AEEEGILLNSTTV televangelist
AEEEGILNNRSSV revealingness
AEEEGIMNNSSTV envisagements
AEEEGIMNPRRTY prayer meeting
AEEEGINNORRST regenerations
AEEEGINORRRTT reinterrogate
AEEEGINORSTTV revegetations
AEEEGIRRSSTTV tergiversates
AEEEGLMNNNSTT entanglements
AEEEGMMNORSTT magnetometers
AEEEGMNNRSSTT estrangements
AEEEGOPRRSSTU supererogates
AEEEGPPPRRSSS peppergrasses
AEEEHHIMRSSTT thermesthesia
AEEEHHIPRSSTY hyperesthesia
AEEEHHNOPRSST asthenosphere
AEEEHILMNNOPP epiphenomenal
AEEEHILNRSSTW weatherliness
AEEEHIMOPRSSV overemphasise
AEEEHIMOPRSVZ overemphasize
AEEEHINPRSSST parenthesises
AEEEHINPRSSTZ parenthesizes
AEEEHINRRSTTW interwreathes
AEEEHLMNSSSSS shamelessness
AEEEHLNPSSSSS shapelessness
AEEEHLNRSSSST heartlessness
AEEEHLOPPRSTY speleotherapy
AEEEHLORSSTUX heterosexuals
AEEEHMNNSSTTW enswathements
AEEEHMNORSSST heartsomeness
AEEEIIILLLNTV Ille-et-Vilaine
AEEEIIIMMNRST Seine-Maritime
AEEEIILNNRSTT interlineates
AEEEIILNRRRTV irreverential
AEEEIILNRSTTX externalities
AEEEIILNSTTUV eventualities
AEEEIILRRTTVY reiteratively
AEEEIIMNRTTVX exterminative
AEEEIINRSSTTV iterativeness
AEEEIKLLMPRST kapellmeister
AEEEILLNPRSTT interpellates
AEEEILLNRRTVY reverentially
AEEEILMNPRSSX exemplariness
AEEEILMNPRTTY intemperately
AEEEILNNPRSUY Eyre Peninsula
AEEEILNNSSSST essentialness
AEEEIMMNNPRST semipermanent
AEEEIMNNNRTTT entertainment
AEEEIMNNRSTTT reinstatement
AEEEIMNORSSSW wearisomeness
AEEEIMNPRRSTV privateersmen
AEEEIMOPRRSTV evaporimeters
AEEEIMORSSTTV overestimates
AEEEINNNSSSST insensateness
AEEEINNPSSSVX expansiveness
AEEEINNSSTTTV attentiveness
tentativeness
AEEEINOPRRSTV perseveration
AEEEINOPRSSTV operativeness
AEEEINORTTTVV overattentive
AEEEINPRSSSVV pervasiveness
AEEEINRSSSSTV assertiveness
AEEEIORRSSTVV overassertive
AEEEIPRRSSTVV preservatives
AEEEKLRRSSTTW streetwalkers
AEEELLMRSSSUY measurelessly
AEEELLNSSSSUV valuelessness
AEEELNNPRSSTV prevalentness
AEEELNSSSSSTT statelessness
tastelessness
AEEEMMNOPRTTU pneumatometer
AEEEMNORSTTTV overstatement
AEEEMNPRRSSTU prematureness
AEEEMNRSSSSST reassessments
AEEEMOOPRRSTV evaporometers
AEEFFGHIMNRTT affreightment
AEEFFGINORRST reafforesting
AEEFGGHINORRT foregathering
AEEFGGIINRRRT refrigerating
AEEFGIINORRRT refrigeration
AEEFGIIPRRTUV prefigurative
AEEFGILNORRST foretriangles
AEEFGINORRSTU argentiferous
AEEFGIORRRRST refrigerators
AEEFGIORRRRTY refrigeratory
AEEFHHLLNSSTU healthfulness
AEEFHILNSSSST faithlessness
AEEFHLMORRSTW flamethrowers
AEEFHOOPRRSTW weatherproofs
AEEFIILLNNRTY inferentially
AEEFIILMPPRRS preamplifiers
AEEFIILMPRSSU superfamilies
AEEFIILOPRRTV proliferative
AEEFIINNORSTT reinfestation
AEEFILLMORSTU metalliferous
AEEFILLMOSSTY Yosemite Falls
AEEFIMNNORSTT fermentations
AEEFIMNORSSTV formativeness
AEEFIMOORRRST reformatories
AEEFINNOQRTTU frequentation
AEEFINNORSSSU nefariousness

AEEFINNORSSTT	fenestrations
AEEFINOORRSTT	reforestation
AEEFINOPRSTTU	superfetation
AEEFIOOPRRSST	professoriate
AEEFLLMNORSTT	forestallment
AEEFLLNSSSSTU	faultlessness
AEEFLMNRSSSTU	masterfulness
AEEFLNPRRSSUY	prayerfulness
AEEFLOPQRSSUW	pasqueflowers
AEEFNNORSSTTU	fortunateness
AEEFOOPRRSSST	professorates
AEEGGHOOOPRRZ	zoogeographer
AEEGGIINNORTT	renegotiating
AEEGGIINNPRRT	peregrinating
AEEGGIINNRRTT	reintegrating
AEEGGILNNORTU	outgeneraling
AEEGGINNOORSS	organogenesis
AEEGGMNNOORRT	roentgenogram
AEEGHHILOPRRS	heliographers
AEEGHHMOPRRRT	thermographer
AEEGHHNOPRRST	ethnographers
AEEGHIILNPSTT	telepathising
AEEGHIILNPTTZ	telepathizing
AEEGHIIMNPRSZ	reemphasizing
AEEGHIIMNSSTT	metathesising
AEEGHIIMNSTTZ	metathesizing
AEEGHIINNSTTZ	anesthetizing
AEEGHILMOORST	isogeothermal
AEEGHILNNRTTY	threateningly
AEEGHILOOPRSS	phraseologies
AEEGHILORRSUV	heliogravures
AEEGHILPRSSTT	telegraphists
AEEGHIMOPRRSS	seismographer
AEEGHINOOPTTV	photonegative
AEEGHINOPRSST	taphrogenesis
AEEGHINRRSSTT	straighteners
AEEGHLLNOOSTU	Longleat House
AEEGHLOORRSTW	woolgatherers
AEEGHMOOPRRST	meteorographs
AEEGHNOOPRRTV	photoengraver
AEEGHNOOPRSTV	photoengraves
AEEGHNOPRRSST	stenographers
AEEGHOPPRRRST	petrographers
AEEGIIILLMSTT	illegitimates
AEEGIIILMSSTT	legitimatises
AEEGIIILMSTTZ	legitimatizes
AEEGIIINSTTVV	investigative
AEEGIILLLSTVY	legislatively
AEEGIILMNORSS	generalissimo
AEEGIILNNORRT	interregional
AEEGIILNNRRTT	interrelating
AEEGIILNNRSTX	externalising
AEEGIILNNRTXZ	externalizing
AEEGIIMNNORTT	regimentation
AEEGIIMNNRSTT	mainstreeting
AEEGIIMNNRTTX	exterminating
AEEGIINNNORST	ingenerations
AEEGIINNOORTT	renegotiation
AEEGIINNOPRRT	peregrination
AEEGIINNOPRSU	europeanising
AEEGIINNOPRUZ	europeanizing
AEEGIINNORRTT	reintegration
AEEGIINORRSTV	reinvigorates
AEEGIINORRTTV	interrogative
AEEGIKLNRSTTW	streetwalking
AEEGILLMMNNRT	entrammelling
AEEGILLMNNSSY	meaninglessly
AEEGILLNRSTVY	everlastingly
AEEGILLOOPSST	spelaeologist
AEEGILLOPRSSS	aspergilloses
AEEGILNNPRTTY	penetratingly
AEEGIMMNOOTTV	magnetomotive
AEEGIMNNNNSSU	unmeaningness
AEEGIMNNOSSTT	segmentations
AEEGIMNNRSSST	reassignments
AEEGIMNNRTTUY	integumentary
AEEGIMNORRSTV	overmastering
AEEGIMNRRSSST	mastersingers
AEEGINNPPRSTT	stepparenting
AEEGINOORSSST	astereognosis
AEEGINOPRRRST	peregrinators
AEEGINORRSSTV	overasserting
AEEGINQRSSTTU	sequestrating
AEEGINRRSSSTV	transgressive
AEEGINRRSSTTV	tergiversants
AEEGIORRRSTTV	tergiversator
AEEGLLMNNNTUY	ungentlemanly
AEEGLLMNNOTWY	gentlewomanly
AEEGLLMNRSUWZ	mangelwurzels
AEEGNNOOPQRTU	rontgenopaque
AEEGOOPRRRSTU	supererogator
AEEGORSSSSTUU	stegosauruses
AEEHHIINNOPTZ	phenothiazine
AEEHHILLMNSVW	Wilhelmshaven
AEEHHILMMNNTT	nemathelminth
AEEHHILMMNSTU	helianthemums
AEEHHILNNSSTU	unhealthiness
AEEHHINOPRRST	tenorrhaphies
AEEHHKMPPRSUY	Humphreys Peak
AEEHHMOPRRTTY	thermotherapy
AEEHHNOPPRSTY	phanerophytes
AEEHHOPPRSTTY	phreatophytes
AEEHIIILNPPPS	Philippine Sea
AEEHIIIMMNRST	Hammerstein II
AEEHIILLNNOTZ	hellenization
AEEHIIMOOPSST	hematopoiesis
AEEHIINORSSTT	etherisations
AEEHIINORSTTZ	etherizations
AEEHILMMNNOPS	phenomenalism
AEEHILMMOOSST	mesotheliomas
AEEHILMNNOPST	phenomenalist
AEEHILNNRSSTU	unearthliness
AEEHILPPRRXYY	hyperpyrexial
AEEHIMNNPSSSS	misshapenness
AEEHIMNORSSTT	thermonasties
AEEHIMNQSSSSU	squeamishness
AEEHIMOPPRRTY	hypermetropia
AEEHINNOPPRSS	apprehensions
AEEHINOORSSTU	heteroousians
AEEHINORSSSTV	overhastiness
AEEHINORSSSTW	seaworthiness
AEEHIOPPRRSXY	hyperprosexia
AEEHIPRRRSSTU	treasurership
AEEHKLNNSSSST	thanklessness

AEEHKNOORRSTY	heterokaryons
AEEHLLMMORSWY	yellowhammers
AEEHLLMNNRSTT	enthrallments
AEEHLLMNOOPST	metallophones
AEEHLMNOOSSST	loathsomeness
AEEHLMPRRSSUU	superhumerals
AEEHLNOPRSTUY	polyurethanes
AEEHLNORRSTTY	northeasterly
AEEHLNOSSTUWW	New South Wales
AEEHLORSSTTUY	southeasterly
AEEHMMOOPRSST	metamorphoses
AEEHMMOPSSTUY	emphysematous
AEEHMNNOPRSTY	hymenopterans
AEEHMNOOPPRTU	pneumatophore
AEEHMOOPPRRST	spermatophore
AEEHMOPPRSTTY	spermatophyte
AEEHNOOPPRRST	parthenospore
AEEIIILMNPRRS	preliminaries
AEEIIILMRRSTZ	remilitarizes
AEEIIILRSSTTV	versatilities
AEEIIIMNSSTTV	imitativeness
AEEIIINRSSSTT	initiatresses
AEEIIKLMNPRSS	marlinespikes
AEEIILLLMNNPR	premillennial
AEEIILLLMOSST	lamellosities
AEEIILLLNNRTY	interlineally
AEEIILLNNPTTY	penitentially
AEEIILLNNRRTY	interlinearly
AEEIILLNSTTXY	existentially
AEEIILMMORRSS	memorialisers
AEEIILMMORRSZ	memorializers
AEEIILMNOOSST	emotionalises
AEEIILMNOOSTZ	emotionalizes
AEEIILMNOPRSS	impersonalise
AEEIILMNOPRSZ	impersonalize
AEEIILMOPRSTT	temporalities
AEEIILNNORRTT	interrelation
AEEIILNNOSSTV	inviolateness
AEEIILNNPSSTV	plaintiveness
AEEIILNNTTTVY	inattentively
AEEIILNOPQTTU	equipotential
AEEIILNOPRSST	personalities
AEEIILNOPRTTV	interpolative
AEEIILNORSTTV	revelationist
AEEIILNORSTVY	televisionary
AEEIILNQRRTTU	interquartile
AEEIILNQSTTUY	sequentiality
AEEIILNRSSSUV	universalises
AEEIILNRSSUVZ	universalizes
AEEIILNSSSSTT	essentialists
AEEIILORRRTTX	exterritorial
AEEIIMMNORSST	mesmerisation
AEEIIMMNORSTZ	mesmerization
AEEIIMNNORTTX	extermination
AEEIIMNPSSSSV	impassiveness
AEEIIMNQRSSTU	equestrianism
AEEIINNNORSTT	intenerations
AEEIINNOORRTT	reorientation
AEEIINNOPSSTT	spontaneities
AEEIINNOQRSTU	questionnaire
AEEIIOPPRRRST	proprietaries
AEEIJNNORSTUV	rejuvenations
AEEIKNOPRSSTT	streptokinase
AEEILLMNNSTTY	sentimentally
AEEILLMNPRSTY	sempiternally
AEEILLNNOPPST	Lepontine Alps
AEEILLNNOPTXY	exponentially
AEEILLNNORSSU	Lons-le-Saunier
AEEILLNNOSTXY	extensionally
AEEILLNNPRSTT	interpellants
AEEILLNNSSTUY	unessentially
AEEILLNOPRRTT	interpellator
AEEILLNORRSVY	reversionally
AEEILLNOSSSTT	tessellations
AEEILLNRSTUXY	intersexually
AEEILLPRSTUVY	superlatively
AEEILLRRRSTTY	terrestrially
AEEILMMNNPRTY	impermanently
AEEILMNNNORTV	environmental
AEEILMNNNSTTU	unsentimental
AEEILMNOOORTV	overemotional
AEEILMOPRRTXY	extemporarily
AEEILMORSTTUV	overstimulate
AEEILNNNOOPPS	Peloponnesian
AEEILNNNOPRST	antipersonnel
AEEILNNNOQTUV	nonequivalent
AEEILNNNOSSST	nonessentials
AEEILNNOPRRST	interpersonal
AEEILNNOPRSTT	septentrional
AEEILNNOSSSST	sensationless
AEEILNNQQTUUV	quinquevalent
AEEILNNRSSSUV	universalness
AEEILNOORRSTV	lateroversion
AEEILNOPRRSTT	interpolaters
AEEILNPRRSSST	interspersals
AEEILOOPSSSTT	osteoplasties
AEEILOPRSSTUY	erysipelatous
AEEILOPSTTUVX	expostulative
AEEILPRRSSSTU	superrealists
AEEIMMNNORSST	momentariness
AEEIMMNORSSTT	amortisements
AEEIMMNORSTTZ	amortizements
AEEIMMNSSSTTT	misstatements
AEEIMNNOPPRTT	reappointment
AEEIMNNORRSTU	remunerations
AEEIMNNORSSTV	normativeness
AEEIMNOPRRSST	temporariness
AEEIMNOPRSSTX	proximateness
AEEIMNORRSTTV	remonstrative
AEEIMNORRSTTX	exterminators
AEEIMNORRTTXY	exterminatory
AEEIMRSSSSTTY	systematisers
AEEIMRSSSTTYZ	systematizers
AEEINNOOPRSVX	overexpansion
AEEINNOPRSSTT	presentations
AEEINNPRRRSTU	intrapreneurs
AEEINOOPRRTTX	reexportation
AEEINOORRSSTV	overassertion
AEEINOORRSTUV	arteriovenous
AEEINOPPRRSTT	perpetrations
AEEINOPRRSSTV	preservations
AEEINOQRSSTTU	sequestration
AEEINOSSSTUVX	vexatiousness
AEEINRSSSTTTV	transvestites

AEEINRSSTTTUV	sternutatives
AEEIOOPPRSTTV	postoperative
AEEKMORRSSSTT	masterstrokes
AEELLMNPPSSTU	supplementals
AEELLMOQRRSUY	quarrelsomely
AEELMNORSSSUV	marvelousness
AEELMNPPRSTUY	supplementary
AEELNOOPSSTTU	stenopetalous
AEELOOPPRSTUV	overpopulates
AEEMMNOPRTTUY	pneumatometry
AEEMNOOPRSTTU	treponematous
AEEMNOORSTUUV	outmanoeuvres
AEEMNPRRRSUUY	supernumerary
AEEOQRRSSSTTU	sequestrators
AEFFGHILOSSTT	Feast of Lights
AEFFGIMRSSTTU	suffragettism
AEFGGHIIINRRT	airfreighting
AEFGHHOORRSTU	thoroughfares
AEFGHHORSTTTU	afterthoughts
AEFGHIILMOPRS	filmographies
AEFGHINNRRSTU	nursing father
AEFGIILLORRSU	argilliferous
AEFGIILNNNSSU	unfailingness
AEFGIILNNORTV	overinflating
AEFGIILNOPRRT	proliferating
AEFGIINOPRRTU	prefiguration
AEFGILLNSSSUW	wineglassfuls
AEFGILMNORRTU	reformulating
AEFGILNNORRWY	forewarningly
AEFGINOOPRRTW	waterproofing
AEFIIIILMNNST	infinitesimal
AEFIIIILNNSTT	infantilities
AEFIIILMNORST	informalities
AEFIIILMNSSST	semifinalists
AEFIIILNORSTT	fertilisation
AEFIIILNORTTZ	fertilization
AEFIILLLNNOXY	inflexionally
AEFIILLLNNTUY	influentially
AEFIILLNNNTUU	uninfluential
AEFIILMNORSUU	aluminiferous
AEFIILMNORTVY	informatively
AEFIILNOOPRRT	proliferation
AEFIILNOPRSTU	platiniferous
AEFIIMNNORTUV	uninformative
AEFIIMNOOPRRT	imperforation
AEFIIMNORSSTU	staminiferous
AEFIINRRSTTTY	interstratify
AEFILMMNNOOST	monofilaments
AEFILMNOORRTU	reformulation
AEFILMORRRSSU	formularisers
AEFILMORRRSUZ	formularizers
AEFILNOOPRSSS	professionals
AEFILNOOPRSSW	passionflower
AEFILNOOPRSTV	flavoproteins
AEFIMNOOPRRST	preformations
AEFIOQRRSTUUZ	quartziferous
AEFLNNORTTUUY	unfortunately
AEGGGIINRRTTU	regurgitating
AEGGGILNNOSTU	agglutinogens
AEGGHHLOPPRRY	glyphographer
AEGGHIILMNNTU	hemagglutinin
AEGGHIIMMNOPR	mimeographing
AEGGHIINNOPST	Teng Hsiao-ping
AEGGHIINNRSTT	straightening
AEGGHILNOORTW	woolgathering
AEGGHILNORSUV	overslaughing
AEGGHINNOPRST	stenographing
AEGGHINOORSTU	South Georgian
AEGGHLOOPRRSS	glossographer
AEGGHLOPPRRTY	glyptographer
AEGGHNNOOPRRT	rontgenograph
AEGGIIINNSTTV	investigating
AEGGIIMNSSTTU	guesstimating
AEGGIINNORRTT	interrogating
AEGGIINORRTTU	regurgitation
AEGGILOORSSTT	geratologists
AEGGINNNOORSS	nonaggression
AEGGINNNORTYZ	Tenzing Norgay
AEGGINNRRSSST	transgressing
AEGGMNNOORRST	rontgenograms
AEGHHILOPRRST	lithographers
AEGHHIOOPRRST	orthographies
AEGHHIOPPRRSY	physiographer
AEGHHIPRSSUWY	superhighways
AEGHHMNOPRRSY	hymnographers
AEGHHNOOPPRRS	phonographers
AEGHHOOPPRRST	photographers
	rephotographs
AEGHHOOPRRRST	orthographers
AEGHIILNNOORT	Lothian Region
AEGHIILNPRTVY	hypervigilant
AEGHIINNSTTUX	extinguishant
AEGHIINOOPSST	apotheosising
AEGHIINOOPSTZ	apotheosizing
AEGHIINOOSTTT	ghettoisation
AEGHIINOOTTTZ	ghettoization
AEGHIIPRRRSST	registrarship
AEGHILMOOSSTT	hematologists
AEGHILOOPRSST	phraseologist
AEGHILQRRSTTU	quarterlights
AEGHIMNORSSUW	housewarmings
AEGHIMNORTTUW	mouthwatering
AEGHIMOOPRSST	mastigophores
AEGHIOPRRSSTU	surrogateship
AEGHLLMOOORTY	moral theology
AEGHLMMOORTTY	thremmatology
AEGHMNOOOPSTT	photomontages
AEGHMNOOOPSTU	entomophagous
AEGHNOOPPRRRS	pornographers
AEGHOOPRRSTUV	photogravures
AEGIIIILNORST	originalities
AEGIIILMMNORS	memorialising
AEGIIILMMNORZ	memorializing
AEGIIILNNNRST	internalising
AEGIIILNNNRTZ	internalizing
AEGIIILNNORST	orientalising
AEGIIILNNORTZ	orientalizing
AEGIIILNORSTU	antireligious
AEGIIILNRSSTU	singularities
AEGIIIMMNSSTT	misestimating
AEGIIIMNNNOST	ingeminations
AEGIIINNOSTTV	investigation
AEGIIINNPPRRS	Pierian Spring
AEGIIINNRSTVW	West Virginian

AEGIIKLMNPRSS	marlingspikes
AEGIILLNNOSTW	wellingtonias
AEGIILLOPRSSS	aspergillosis
AEGIILMMNNSST	misalignments
AEGIILMNNNOOR	Inner Mongolia
AEGIILMNORSST	mineralogists
AEGIILMNORSYY	syringomyelia
AEGIILMNPRSST	slipstreaming
AEGIILMOOSSST	semasiologist
AEGIILNNNPSTU	peninsulating
AEGIILNNOPRSS	personalising
AEGIILNNOPRSZ	personalizing
AEGIILNNOPRTT	interpolating
AEGIIMNNOPRST	impersonating
AEGIIMNNRRRTY	intermarrying
AEGIIMNOPRRTY	primogenitary
AEGIIMNSSSTTY	systematising
AEGIIMNSSTTYZ	systematizing
AEGIINNNRSSTT	intransigents
AEGIINNOORRTT	interrogation
AEGIINNOPPPRT	preappointing
AEGIINNORRSTV	overstraining
AEGIINNORRTUY	genitourinary
AEGIINOPPRRTX	expropriating
AEGIINORRSSTT	registrations
AEGIINORSSTTV	investigators
AEGIINORSTTVY	investigatory
AEGILLMRSSTTU	metallurgists
AEGILMMOPRSUY	gemmiparously
AEGILMNNNNOST	nonalignments
AEGILMNOOORTU	Outer Mongolia
AEGILMNOORSTY	laryngotomies
AEGILMNORSSTU	somersaulting
AEGILMOORRSTY	martyrologies
AEGILNNNORSUY	unreasoningly
AEGILNNOOOSTT	neonatologist
AEGILNOOPRRSS	progressional
AEGILNOPSTTUX	expostulating
AEGILOORSSTTT	teratologists
AEGIMNNOORSTU	Regiomontanus
AEGIMNNORRSTT	remonstrating
AEGIMNOOPRSSU	angiospermous
AEGIMOOOPPRST	apogeotropism
AEGIMOORRRRST	agroterrorism
AEGIMOORSSSTT	gastrostomies
AEGINNNPRSSSU	unsparingness
AEGINNORRSSST	transgression
AEGINOORRRSTT	interrogators
AEGINOORRRTTY	interrogatory
AEGKNPPRSTUUU	Upper Tunguska
AEGLMNOORSSSU	glamorousness
AEGLMOOSSTTYY	systematology
AEGLNORRSSSUU	garrulousness
AEGNORRRSSSST	transgressors
AEHHHINOPRRRY	herniorrhaphy
AEHHHOOPPPSTY	hypophosphate
AEHHIIILMNSST	helminthiasis
AEHHILLMNPTTY	platyhelminth
AEHHILNOPPRST	philanthropes
AEHHILOPSSTTU	thiosulphates
AEHHIMNOPRSTT	theanthropism
AEHHIMOOOPSTT	homoeopathist
AEHHIMOOPSSTT	homeopathists
AEHHINOPRSTTT	theanthropist
AEHHINORRRSTY	North Ayrshire
AEHHIOPPRSTYY	physiotherapy
AEHHIORRSSTUY	South Ayrshire
AEHHLOOPPRSSY	phosphorylase
AEHHNOOPPRTTY	anthropophyte
AEHHNOOPSTTTY	photosynthate
AEHHOOPPPRSTY	pyrophosphate
AEHHOOPRRSSST	sharpshooters
AEHIIILMNOSSS	leishmaniosis
AEHIIILOPSSTT	hospitalities
AEHIILLMNNOPY	aminophylline
AEHIILNOPRSST	relationships
	rhinoplasties
AEHIILNORSSSU	hilariousness
AEHIILPRRSSTT	hairsplitters
AEHIIMOPPRRST	imperatorship
AEHIINNOPRSTT	trephinations
AEHIINOORSSTT	theorisations
AEHIINOORSTTZ	theorizations
AEHIINOPRRSST	prehistorians
AEHIINORRSSTW	airworthiness
AEHIIRRSSSTTW	shirtwaisters
AEHILMMNORTUY	aluminothermy
AEHILMOOSTUXY	homosexuality
AEHILMOPPRSTY	amphiprostyle
AEHILOOPRSSTT	photorealists
AEHIMMMOPRSST	metamorphisms
AEHIMMNOPRTUY	immunotherapy
AEHIMMOOPRSST	metamorphosis
AEHIMNNOOPRST	enantiomorphs
AEHIMNNOSSSTT	astonishments
AEHIMNNPRSSTT	transhipments
	transshipment
AEHIMNPRSTUUY	superhumanity
AEHINOOPRRSTT	prototherians
AEHINOPRSSTTY	attorneyships
AEHIOOPPRSSST	apostrophises
AEHIOOPPRSSTZ	apostrophizes
AEHIOOPSSSTTT	osteopathists
AEHLLNNOORRTT	Northallerton
AEHLMNOOPRTVW	Wolverhampton
AEHLOPPRSSTUY	pyrosulphates
AEHMNOOPRRTTY	anthropometry
AEHMNOOPRSSSU	amorphousness
AEHNOOPRRSSSU	sarrusophones
AEIIILLLMNNST	millennialist
AEIIILLMNNORS	millionnaires
AEIIILLMNORSS	millionairess
AEIIILLMNPRRY	preliminarily
AEIIILLMNRSTY	ministerially
AEIIILLMRRSVY	verisimilarly
AEIIILMNPRTTY	amitriptyline
AEIIILNORSSTT	sterilisation
AEIIILNORSTTZ	sterilization
AEIIILNORTTUZ	reutilization
AEIIILNRSSTTT	interstitials
AEIIILPRRSSTU	spiritualiser
AEIIILPRRSTUZ	spiritualizer
AEIIILPRSSSTU	spiritualises
AEIIILPRSSTTU	spiritualties

AEIIILPRSSTUZ	spiritualizes
AEIIIMMNOSSTT	misestimation
AEIIIMNNNOSST	inseminations
AEIIIMNOOPSTT	epitomisation
AEIIIMNOOPTTZ	epitomization
AEIIIMNOORSST	isomerisation
AEIIIMNOORSTZ	isomerization
AEIIINNORSSSV	visionariness
AEIIINNORSTTW	winterisation
AEIIINNORTTWZ	winterization
AEIIINNOSSSTT	sensitisation
AEIIINNOSSTTZ	sensitization
AEIIINOOSSTTV	sovietisation
AEIIINOOSTTVZ	sovietization
AEIIINOPQRTTU	equipartition
AEIILLNNNOSTY	intensionally
AEIILLNNNOTTY	intentionally
AEIILLNNORTVY	inventorially
AEIILLNOQRTUV	ventriloquial
AEIILLNQRRSTU	tranquilliser
AEIILLNQRRTUZ	tranquillizer
AEIILLNQRSSTU	tranquillises
AEIILLNQRSTUZ	tranquillizes
AEIILLORRRTTY	territorially
AEIILMMORRSST	immortalisers
AEIILMMORRSTZ	immortalizers
AEIILMNNOOPRS	pronominalise
AEIILMNNOOPRZ	pronominalize
AEIILMNNOOSST	solemnisation
AEIILMNNOOSTZ	solemnization
AEIILMNOORSTT	tolerationism
AEIILMNOOSSTT	emotionalists
AEIILMNOPRSTY	impersonality
AEIILMNRSSSUV	universalisms
AEIILNNNNOTTU	unintentional
AEIILNNNORTTU	interlunation
AEIILNNNQQSUU	quinquennials
AEIILNNOOPRTT	interpolation
AEIILNNOOSSTV	novelisations
AEIILNNOOSTVZ	novelizations
AEIILNNOOTTUV	antievolution
AEIILNOOPPRST	prepositional
AEIILNOOPSTTX	exploitations
	sexploitation
AEIILNOORSTTT	tolerationist
AEIILNOPPSTTU	Pontius Pilate
AEIILNOPRSTUV	pulverisation
AEIILNOPRTUVZ	pulverization
AEIILNPRSSSTU	spiritualness
AEIILNQRRSTUZ	tranquilizers
AEIILNRSSSTUV	universalists
AEIILOOPPRRRT	proprietorial
AEIILOPPRRRTY	proprietarily
AEIIMNNNOORST	renominations
AEIIMNNOOPRST	impersonation
AEIIMNOOPRRTT	reimportation
AEIIMNOOPRSTT	temporisation
AEIIMNOOPRTTZ	temporization
AEIIMNOSSSTTY	systemisation
AEIIMNOSSTTYZ	systemization
AEIINNNORSTTU	antineutrinos
AEIINNNORSTTV	nontransitive
AEIINNOOPPSTT	peptonisation
AEIINNOOPPTTZ	peptonization
AEIINNOOPSSTT	antepositions
AEIINNOPSSSTX	expansionists
AEIINOOPPRRTX	expropriation
AEIINOOPRSSTT	Espírito Santo
AEIINOOPRSTTX	extraposition
AEIINOORRRSTT	terrorisation
AEIINOORRRTTZ	terrorization
AEIINOPRSSTTU	Espíritu Santo
AEIINOPRSSTTV	transpositive
AEIINOPRSTTUV	vituperations
AEIINORRRSTTT	antiterrorist
AEIINORRSSSTT	transistorise
AEIINORRSSTTZ	transistorize
AEIKKLMNNORUW	unworkmanlike
AEIKLMNOPRSST	sportsmanlike
AEILLLLPRRRST	pralltrillers
AEILLLMNOOSSS	salmonellosis
AEILLMMMNOOST	monometallism
AEILLMMNOOSTT	monometallist
AEILLNNOOOPSU	Louis Napoleon
AEILLNOPSSSSY	passionlessly
AEILLNORSSUUV	Universal Soul
AEILLOOPRRRTY	reportorially
AEILMMNNORSTU	neutral monism
AEILMMNNOTTUY	monumentality
AEILMNNOOQUYZ	Quezon y Molina
AEILMNNRSSTTU	instrumentals
AEILMNOOPRSTT	metropolitans
AEILMNOPRTTUY	importunately
AEILMNOPSSTUY	pneumatolysis
AEILMOORSSTTT	stromatolites
AEILNNORSSTUV	voluntariness
AEILNNORSTUVY	intravenously
AEILNOOPRRSTT	interpolators
AEILNOOPSTTUX	expostulation
AEILNOORRTUVY	revolutionary
AEILNRSSSTUUU	laurustinuses
AEILOOOOPPPRS	prosopopoeial
AEIMNNNOSSSUU	unanimousness
AEIMNNOOPPRTT	apportionment
AEIMNNOORRSTT	remonstration
AEIMNNORSSTTU	menstruations
AEIMNOOPRRSST	impersonators
AEIMNOPRSSSTU	reassumptions
AEIMNOPRSSTTT	Protestantism
AEIMORSSSSTTT	toastmistress
AEINNORSSSUUV	unsavouriness
AEINNORSSTTTU	sternutations
AEINOOOPPRRTT	proportionate
AEINOOOPRRSTT	protonotaries
AEINOOPRSSTTT	protestations
AEIOOOOPPPRSS	prosopopoeias
AEIOOPPRRRSTX	expropriators
AEKLNPPRSSTTU	splatterpunks
AEKLOOPPRSTVV	Petropavlovsk
AELLMNOPRRSUY	supernormally
AELMNOPRSSTTU	postmenstrual
AELNNOOPSSTUY	spontaneously
AELOOPRSSTTUX	expostulators
AELOOPRSTTUXY	expostulatory

AEMMNOOORSTTU	monotrematous
AEMNNNNOOSSSUY	anonymousness
AEMNOORRRSSTT	remonstrators
AEMPRRSSSTTUU	superstratums
AENNNORSSSTUY	tyrannousness
AENOOOPPRRTXY	proparoxytone
AENOPRRSSSTUU	rapturousness
AFFGGIIMNSTUU	suffumigating
AFFGIIMNOSTUU	suffumigation
AFFIILNNOSSTU	insufflations
AFGGIINNRRSTU	transfiguring
AFGIIILNNRTUY	infuriatingly
AFGIILMNORRSU	formularising
AFGIILMNORRUZ	formularizing
AFIIIILLNNTVY	infinitivally
AFIIILNNORSTT	infiltrations
AFIIILNNOSSTT	inflationists
AFIIILNOOSSST	fossilisation
AFIIILNOOSSTZ	fossilization
AFIILLNOOOPRS	Florianópolis
AFIILLORSTTUY	flirtatiously
AFIILMNOORSUY	omnifariously
AFIILNNOORSTU	fluorinations
AFIILNORSSTUU	sulfurisation
AFIILOPRSSSUY	fissiparously
AFIIMMNNORSST	misinformants
AFILNOPPRRUUV	flavopurpurin
AFIMNORRSSSTT	transformists
AGGGIIINNRTTU	ingurgitating
AGGHHIILNOPRT	lithographing
AGGHHINOOPPRT	photographing
AGGHHMOPPRSSY	sphygmographs
AGGHHMOPPRSYY	sphygmography
AGGHIIKNNSSTV	thanksgivings
AGGHIILLNNSUY	languishingly
AGGHIILNNOOST	anthologising
AGGHIILNNOOTZ	anthologizing
AGGHIILNOOPTZ	pathologizing
AGGHILOOPRSST	graphologists
AGGIIILNNOSTU	isoagglutinin
AGGIIILNNRSSU	singularising
AGGIIILNNRSUZ	singularizing
AGGIIILNNSTTY	instigatingly
AGGIIINNORTTU	ingurgitation
AGGIIJNNRUUXY	Xinjiang Uygur
AGGIILNOOSTTU	tautologising
AGGIILNOOTTUZ	tautologizing
AGGIILNRSTTUU	gutturalising
AGGIILNRTTUUZ	gutturalizing
AGGILLNOORSTY	laryngologist
AGGILNOOORSST	organologists
AGGILOORSSSTT	gastrologists
AGHHIILMNRSTY	nightmarishly
AGHHIINOPPSST	phosphatising
AGHHIINOPPSTZ	phosphatizing
AGHHILMNOPPSU	ploughmanship
AGHHIMNOORSTT	orthognathism
AGHHINOOPPRST	phonographist
	phosphorating
AGHHINOOPRSST	sharpshooting
AGHHIOOPRRSTT	orthographist
AGHHLLMOOOPTY	ophthalmology
AGHHLMNNOOOPT	monophthongal
AGHHNOOORSTTU	orthognathous
AGHIIILLMNTUY	humiliatingly
AGHIIILNOPSST	hospitalising
AGHIIILNOPSTZ	hospitalizing
AGHIIILNPRSTT	hairsplitting
AGHIILNNOSSTY	astonishingly
AGHIINNPPRSST	transshipping
AGHIINOPSSSTY	hypostasising
AGHIINOPSSTTY	hypostatising
AGHIINOPSSTYZ	hypostasizing
AGHIINOPSTTYZ	hypostatizing
AGHILMNOOOOST	homologations
AGHIMNOOPRSST	monographists
AGHIMSSSTTUUU	tsutsugamushi
AGHINOOPSTTTT	photostatting
AGHNNOOOPSUUV	Souphanouvong
AGHOOOPPPRRSY	prosopography
AGIIIILNNOSTV	invigilations
AGIIIIMNNRSTU	miniaturising
AGIIIIMNNRTUZ	miniaturizing
AGIIIILLLNTTTY	titillatingly
AGIIILLMNRSTU	trilingualism
AGIIILMMNNPRT	malimprinting
AGIIILMMNORST	immortalising
AGIIILMMNORTZ	immortalizing
AGIIILNNQRTUZ	tranquilizing
AGIIIMNOPPRRT	impropriating
AGIIINNPRSSSU	prussianising
AGIIINNPRSSUZ	prussianizing
AGIILLMNSTTUY	stimulatingly
AGIILLNOOSSTY	syllogisation
AGIILLNOOSTYZ	syllogization
AGIILMOOPPRST	plagiotropism
AGIILMOOPRSTT	primatologist
AGIILNNOPRSTY	patronisingly
AGIILNNOPRTYZ	patronizingly
AGIIMNOORRSUV	graminivorous
AGILLNOOPSSTY	palynologists
AGILMMNOOSTUY	numismatology
AGILMNOOPRSTU	promulgations
AGILMOOOSSSTT	somatologists
AGILMOORRSTTY	martyrologist
AGILNNOOOPRST	prolongations
AGILOOPPRSSTY	papyrologists
AGIMNOOOPRSUZ	zoosporangium
AGIMNOORSSSTT	gastronomists
AGLLOOOSTTUUY	tautologously
AHHMNOOOPPRRT	anthropomorph
AHHNOOOPPRSTY	anthroposophy
AHIIIILNOOPRRT	horripilation
AHIIILNOPSTTY	inhospitality
AHIILMPRSSTTU	triumphalists
AHIILNOORTTYZ	horizontality
AHIIMNOPRSSTT	misanthropist
AHIINNOOPSTTY	hypnotisation
AHIINNOOPTTYZ	hypnotization
AHIIOPPRTTUYY	hypopituitary
AHIJNNOPRSTUZ	zinjanthropus
AHILLMMOOPRSS	allomorphisms
AHILLNOOPSSUY	anisophyllous
AHILNOPPSSTTU	postulantship

AHIMNOOOPRSTT	somatotrophin
AHIMNOPPRSSST	sportsmanship
AHINOOPSSSSTU	sousaphonists
AHKLNNOOPPTTY	phytoplankton
AHMMOOOOPRSTU	ommatophorous
AHOOOPRRRSSTU	arthrosporous
AIIIILNNOQSTU	inquisitional
AIIIILNOQRSTU	inquisitorial
AIIIIMNPPSSSS	Mississippian
AIIILLMNNOSTU	illuminations
AIIILLMNPSTUY	pusillanimity
AIIILLNNOTTUY	intuitionally
AIIILNNOSTTTU	institutional
AIIILNOOSSSTT	isolationists
AIIILPRSSSTTU	spiritualists
AIIIMMNNOSSTU	immunisations
AIIIMMNNOSTUZ	immunizations
AIIIMNNORSSTT	ministrations
AIIIMNOOPPRRT	impropriation
AIIIMNOOPRSTV	improvisation
AIIIMNOOPSSTT	optimisations
AIIIMNOOPSTTZ	optimizations
AIIINNNOOSSTU	unionisations
AIIINNNOOSTTV	innovationist
AIIINNNOOSTUZ	unionizations
AIIINOOPPRSTT	propitiations
AIIINOPRSSTTT	partitionists
AIIIOOPPRSTTU	propitiatious
AIIIOOPRTVVVY	ovoviviparity
AIIJNOOPSTTUX	juxtaposition
AIILLMNOPSSUU	pusillanimous
AIILLNNOOPTTU	antipollution
AIILLNNORTTUY	nutritionally
AIILLNNORTUVY	involuntarily
AIILLNOOPRSVY	provisionally
AIILLNORSSTTU	illustrations
AIILMMNOPPSUU	Numa Pompilius
AIILMNOPRSSTT	trampolinists
AIILNNOSTTUUV	invultuations
AIILNOOOPPRST	propositional
AIILNOOPPSSTU	suppositional
AIILNOOPSSSTU	San Luis Potosí
AIIMNNORSSSST	transmissions
AIIMNOOQSSTTU	misquotations
AIIMOOPPRRRST	impropriators
AIIMOOPRRSTVY	improvisatory
AIINNNOPSSTUU	Antoninus Pius
AIINNOOOPSSST	opsonisations
AIINNOOOPSSTZ	opsonizations
AIINNOOPRSSTT	transposition
AIIOOOPRSUVVV	ovoviviparous
AILLNOOPSSTTY	polytonalists
AILMNNOOSTUUY	mountainously
AILMOOOPSSSTX	toxoplasmosis
AILNOOOPPRRST	proportionals
AILNORSSTTUVY	voluntaryists
AIMNNNOOSTUWY	Snowy Mountain
AIOORRSSSTTTU	astrotourists
BBCEEGIKNNRRU	rubbernecking
BBCEEIORRSSUV	oversubscribe
BBCEGHILNRSTU	nightclubbers
BBCEIILMNOSTU	incombustible
BBCENOORRSSTU	broncobusters
BBCGIINNRSSUU	unsubscribing
BBCIILMNOSTUY	incombustibly
BBDEEIIKNOORS	bookbinderies
BBDEELNRSSSUU	blunderbusses
BBEEEINORRSSY	boysenberries
BBEEHLORSSTTU	bottlebrushes
BBEGGIMNNORUY	moneygrubbing
BBHIIIILLMOPS	bibliophilism
BBIIILLOOPSST	bibliopolists
BCCCDEIIMRRSU	circumscribed
BCCCEEHILPRUZ	Czech Republic
BCCCEIIMRRRSU	circumscriber
BCCCEIIMRRSSU	circumscribes
BCCCHINOOOPRS	bronchoscopic
BCCEEGNOORTUW	Concertgebouw
BCCEEHKLMOORS	checkerblooms
BCCEEHNORRSSS	crossbenchers
BCCEEIILORRTT	triboelectric
BCCEEIINRSTTY	cyberneticist
BCCEEIKKKNORR	knickerbocker
BCCEEILORRTTU	turboelectric
BCCEFIIIINOST	bioscientific
BCCEHNOOOPRSS	bronchoscopes
BCCEIIIJOSTTV	objectivistic
BCCEIIILNNNOV	inconvincible
BCCEIILLOOPSU	ebullioscopic
BCCEILMOORSTY	motorbicycles
BCCEILNORSTTU	constructible
BCCGIIILMOOOR	microbiologic
BCCGIILLMOOSY	symbolic logic
BCCIIILNNNOVY	inconvincibly
BCDDEEEIINOSS	disobediences
BCDDEEEILNSSU	deducibleness
BCDDEEEIMNRSU	disencumbered
BCDDEEILNNOTU	nondeductible
BCDDEFIINORTY	Forbidden City
BCDDEIIILTTUY	deductibility
BCDDGILLNOORU	bloodcurdling
BCDEEEKORRSST	stockbreeders
BCDEEGIKNORST	stockbreeding
BCDEEGINORRSS	crossbreeding
BCDEEIIILNNRS	indiscernible
BCDEEIILNNNOS	incondensible
BCDEIIIILNRTY	incredibility
BCDEIIILNNRSY	indiscernibly
BCDEIILNORTUY	indolebutyric
BCDEIIMNOOSTY	endosymbiotic
BCDIIILOORRTY	corrodibility
BCDIIILOPRTUY	producibility
BCEEEEFFILRSV	effervescible
BCEEEEGHRRSSU	cheeseburgers
BCEEEFGIINNRR	birefringence
BCEEEGIINORST	bioenergetics
BCEEEGILLNORT	cobelligerent
BCEEEHIKLRRSU	huckleberries
BCEEEHILMOPST	phlebectomies
BCEEEHLNNOORZ	chlorobenzene
BCEEEIILMORTT	biotelemetric
BCEEEIILMPPRT	imperceptible
BCEEEIJNOSSTV	objectiveness
BCEEEILMMOOST	embolectomies

BCEEEIMMORSTY	embryectomies
BCEEEIRRSSSTT	bittercresses
BCEEENPPRSSTU	prepubescents
BCEEGHHNOORST	Hertogenbosch
BCEEGIKLNNOTT	bottlenecking
BCEEGILMNNRUY	encumberingly
BCEEHIKLMPRRU	Khmer Republic
BCEEIILMPPRTY	imperceptibly
BCEEIILNNORTV	inconvertible
BCEEIILNPSSTU	insusceptible
BCEEIILPPRRST	prescriptible
BCEEILNPSSTUU	unsusceptible
BCEEIMMOSSTTU	subcommittees
BCEELLNOOSSTY	obsolescently
BCEELMMOORSTU	coulombmeters
BCEFGIIJNSTUY	subjectifying
BCEGHILNOOOTY	biotechnology
BCEGIIILNORRS	incorrigibles
BCEGIILMNNRUY	incumberingly
BCEGIILOOOSST	bioecologists
BCEGIINPRRSSU	superscribing
BCEGIKLNOSSTU	bluestockings
BCEHIIILPRRSU	Irish Republic
BCEIIIILQRSTU	equilibristic
BCEIIINOSSSTT	bioscientists
BCEIIJSSSTTUV	subjectivists
BCEIILNNORTVY	inconvertibly
BCEIILNOPRRTU	incorruptible
BCEIILNPSSTUY	insusceptibly
BCEIINNOOORSV	bioconversion
BCEIJLNSTUUVY	subjunctively
BCEILMNOOPRYY	polyembryonic
BCEILORSTTUVY	obstructively
BCEINNNOSSTTU	subcontinents
BCELLORSTUUUY	tuberculously
BCERRSSSTTUUU	substructures
BCGHILNOOOORY	chronobiology
BCGHILOOOPSYY	psychobiology
BCGIIIILORRTY	corrigibility
BCGIILOOORSTY	cryobiologist
BCHIIILNOORST	bronchiolitis
BCHIIIOPSSSTY	biophysicists
BCIIIIILMMSTY	immiscibility
BCIIIIILNNTVY	invincibility
BCIILNOPRRTUY	incorruptibly
BCIIMMNOOSSSU	subcommission
BCIINNOORSTTU	contributions
BCIINOPRSSSTU	subscriptions
BDDEEEEIMMRRS	disremembered
BDDEEEGINNRRU	underbreeding
BDDEEEILLMOSW	disembowelled
BDDEEIILNOSTY	disobediently
BDDEEIIMMNOST	disembodiment
BDDEEIIRRSTTU	redistributed
BDDEEILMRSSTU	middlebusters
BDDEEILNNRSSU	unbridledness
BDDEEIMNNRSTU	disburdenment
BDDEENNNOSSUU	unboundedness
BDDEGHILMORSU	Middlesbrough
BDDEIILMMORSW	middlebrowism
BDDEIINRSTTUU	undistributed
BDEEEEIMMMRRS	misremembered
BDEEEFGIKRRRS	Frederiksberg
BDEEEGHINNSST	benightedness
BDEEEGIINNRRT	interbreeding
BDEEEHIINNRRS	Inner Hebrides
BDEEEHILLMNSU	unembellished
BDEEEHIORRSTU	Outer Hebrides
BDEEEHMORRSTU	mouthbreeders
BDEEEIILLNNSS	indelibleness
BDEEEIMMMNRST	dismemberment
BDEEELNNSSSSU	unblessedness
BDEEFIIILNSTY	defensibility
BDEEFILLNORSU	bellfoundries
BDEEFLLOOPRTU	bulletproofed
BDEEGGHIILMRT	thimblerigged
BDEEGIILLNRWY	bewilderingly
BDEEGIILMNOSW	disemboweling
BDEEGIILNRSSV	Blessed Virgin
BDEEGINNNNSSU	unbendingness
BDEEGINNORRUV	overburdening
BDEEGINOORRRS	Borders Region
BDEEHIILMTTTW	thimblewitted
BDEEHILMOOPST	phlebotomised
BDEEHILMOOPTZ	phlebotomized
BDEEIIILNSSSV	divisibleness
BDEEIIILNTTXY	extendibility
BDEEIIMRRSTTU	turbidimeters
BDEEIIRRSSTTU	redistributes
BDEEIMNRSSSTU	disbursements
BDEELLNOOSSSS	bloodlessness
BDEELNNOSSSSU	boundlessness
BDEELNOSSSSTU	doubtlessness
BDEFGGHIIORSS	Bridge of Sighs
BDEFHILOORSTW	Bosworth Field
BDEGHHINOOORS	neighborhoods
BDEGHHINOOORU	neighbourhood
BDEGHHOORRSTU	thoroughbreds
BDEGIIIILSTTY	digestibility
BDEGIIILMNORS	disembroiling
BDEGIILLMNSSY	dissemblingly
BDEGILLNOOSTT	bloodlettings
BDEHHIILLOPPT	Philip the Bold
BDEHHMNOOORRS	rhombohedrons
BDEHMOOORRSTU	mouthbrooders
BDEHNOOOPRSTU	boustrophedon
BDEIIIILLNTUY	ineludibility
BDEIIIRSSTTUV	distributives
BDEIIMNOOSSSY	endosymbiosis
BDEILLOOPRSSW	possible world
BDFFIIIILSTUY	diffusibility
BDGGIIILLNOSY	disobligingly
BDHIIIIINNOST	disinhibition
BDIIILLOSSTUY	dissolubility
BDIIINORSSTTU	distributions
BEEEEEFLMNNST	enfeeblements
BEEEEHILNPRRS	reprehensible
BEEEEHILNSTWW	betweenwhiles
BEEEELMMNSTZZ	embezzlements
BEEEGGGIRRSUV	veggieburgers
BEEEGIILLLNSS	illegibleness
BEEEGIMNORSSY	embryogenesis
BEEEHIKMOPRRS	Pembrokeshire
BEEEHIKRRSSTW	West Berkshire

BEEEHILLMMNST embellishment
BEEEHILLMORSV overembellish
BEEEHILNPRRSY reprehensibly
BEEEIILNPRSSX inexpressible
BEEEIILPRRRSS irrepressible
BEEEILLMNSTTT belittlements
BEEEILLMORSTU ebulliometers
BEEEILNPRSSSU supersensible
BEEEILNRSSSTT brittlenesses
BEEEIMMNRRSTU reimbursement
BEEEINNNORSTZ nitrobenzenes
BEEEINOSSSSSV obsessiveness
BEEEINRSSSTTU butterinesses
BEEELLNORSSSU resolubleness
BEEENNORSSSTU tenebrousness
BEEFGINRRSTTU butterfingers
BEEFHIMNRRSTU refurbishment
BEEFIIILLRTXY reflexibility
BEEFIILNNSSSU infusibleness
BEEFIILRRSSTU filibusterers
BEEFILLMORSUU umbelliferous
BEEGGHIILMRRT thimblerigger
BEEGHHLORSUUY Burghley House
BEEGHILNORSSU neighbourless
BEEGIILLNNUVY unbelievingly
BEEGILMNNRSSU lumberingness
BEEGLOORRSTTT globetrotters
BEEHIIINORSTX exhibitioners
BEEHILMOOPSST phlebotomises
BEEHILMOOPSTZ phlebotomizes
BEEHILNOOORTZ Belo Horizonte
BEEHILNORRSST brotherliness
BEEHIMMNNOPRS nonmembership
BEEHINNOPPRRU buprenorphine
BEEIIIILNSSST sensibilities
BEEIIILMMPRSS impermissible
BEEIIILNNSSSV invisibleness
BEEIIILNSTTXY extensibility
BEEIIILRRSTVY reversibility
BEEIILNOPRRSS irresponsible
BEEIILNPRRTTU interruptible
BEEIILNPRSSXY inexpressibly
BEEIILPRRRSSY irrepressibly
BEEIILRRTTUVY retributively
BEEILLNNOSSSU insolubleness
BEEILNPRSSSUY supersensibly
BEEILNRSSTUVY subserviently
BEEIMNNOSSSUW businesswomen
BEEINNORRSTUW winterbournes
BEEINORSSSTUV obtrusiveness
BEELLMOORSTUY troublesomely
BEENNOOSSSTUU bounteousness
BEERRSSSSSTTU stressbusters
BEFFGINNORRTU burnt offering
BEFGHIINRRSSU refurbishings
BEFGIIILNRSTU filibustering
BEFGIINNOORSU fibrinogenous
BEFGILLOORSUU globuliferous
BEFIIIILLNTXY inflexibility
BEFIIILMRSSTU filibusterism
BEFIIOOORSSST osteofibrosis
BEFILNNOSSTUU bountifulness
BEGGGIIJNRTTU jitterbugging
BEGGHIINNNORR herringboning
BEGGIIIILLNTY negligibility
BEGGILNOORTTT globetrotting
BEGGINNNOORUU bourguignonne
BEGHHIORRRSUX Roxburghshire
BEGHIILLNORTT Little Bighorn
BEGHIILNOPRSY hyperbolising
BEGHIILNOPRYZ hyperbolizing
BEGHILMNOOOXY oxyhemoglobin
BEGHILNNORUUY unneighbourly
BEGIIIIILLNTY ineligibility
BEGIILOOOSSTX exobiologists
BEGILMOORSSTY embryologists
BEGINRSSSSTTU stressbusting
BEHIIIIMNOSTX exhibitionism
BEHIIIINOSTTX exhibitionist
BEHIIILOPRTVY prohibitively
BEHIIMMRSSTUU British Museum
BEHILMOOPSSTT phlebotomists
BEHILOORRSUVY herbivorously
BEHIMNOOSSSTY tomboyishness
BEIIIIIILNRSST rinsibilities
BEIIIILMRSSTY remissibility
BEIIIILNNSSTY insensibility
BEIIIILNRTTVY invertibility
BEIIIILOPSSST possibilities
BEIIIILORSSTT torsibilities
BEIIIILRSSTTY resistibility
BEIIILMMPRSSY impermissibly
BEIIILMNORSST intromissible
BEIIILNOSSTTY ostensibility
BEIILNOOSSSUV obliviousness
BEIILNOPRRSSY irresponsibly
BEIIOPRSSTTUU subreptitious
BEILMOOOPRSSY polyribosomes
BEILNORSTUUVY unobtrusively
BEIMNOPSSSTUU bumptiousness
BEINNOOOSSSUX obnoxiousness
BELNOORSSSTUU troublousness
BFILLOORSTUUU tubuliflorous
BIIIILMOPSSTY impossibility
BIINOSSSTTTUU substitutions
BILMORSSTUUUY rumbustiously
BILOOOPPRRSUY opprobriously
CCCCEEINNOPSU concupiscence
CCCCEIOOPRSTT streptococcic
CCCDEEEENRRSU recrudescence
CCCDEEHIIOPRT cercopithecid
CCCDEIIMNRSUU uncircumcised
CCCDEIIORSSTY cysticercoids
CCCDHIIIOOPRS dichroiscopic
CCCDHIIOOOPRS dichrooscopic
CCCEEEEINRSSX excrescencies
CCCEEEFIMNRRU circumference
CCCEEEIORSTUX coexecutrices
CCCEEENORRRSU reoccurrences
CCCEEFILMNRUU circumfluence
CCCEEHKNORSTU counterchecks
CCCEEILNNOSTU noctilucences
CCCEEILOOPRST electroscopic
CCCEENNNOORRU nonoccurrence

CCCEFHMNOOORR	French Morocco
CCCEGHIKNORSS	crosschecking
CCCEGIMNNOOSU	meningococcus
CCCEHIIMOSTYZ	schizomycetic
CCCEIIILORSUV	vicious circle
CCCEIIMMNOOOR	microeconomic
CCCEIIMNOOOOS	socioeconomic
CCCEIINNORTTY	concentricity
CCCEILMPRSTUY	circumspectly
CCCEIOOPPRSST	spectroscopic
CCCEKNORSSTTU	concertstucks
CCCEOOPRSSTTU	streptococcus
CCCIIIMNORSSU	circumcisions
CCCIIIMORRSTU	microcircuits
CCCIIOOOPRRTT	corticotropic
CCDDEEGINNNOS	condescending
CCDDEENORSTTU	deconstructed
CCDEEEEEFNRSV	defervescence
CCDEEEEILNQSU	deliquescence
CCDEEEEILNSST	delitescences
CCDEEEEMNSSTU	detumescences
CCDEEEINNOSST	conceitedness
CCDEEEINOPSSU	pseudoscience
CCDEEELLNOSST	collectedness
CCDEEENNNORSS	concernedness
CCDEEEOORRRTV	overcorrected
CCDEEHIILNNPY	phencyclidine
CCDEEHILORRTY	hydroelectric
CCDEEHKLOSTTU	shuttlecocked
CCDEEIILLOSTV	collectivised
CCDEEIILLOTVZ	collectivized
CCDEEIINNOSTV	disconnective
CCDEEILMNOPSY	encyclopedism
CCDEEILNOPSTY	encyclopedist
CCDEEIMOORRTT	microdetector
CCDEEINNNOOSS	condescension
CCDEEINNORSST	disconnecters
CCDEEINNOSSUV	conduciveness
CCDEELNNNORUY	unconcernedly
CCDEELNNNOTUY	unconnectedly
CCDEENORRSTTU	reconstructed
CCDEENORSSSTU	conductresses
CCDEGIINNNOST	disconnecting
CCDEGIINNORST	disconcerting
CCDEHIIOOPRSS	dichroiscopes
CCDEHIOOOPRSS	dichrooscopes
CCDEIINNNOOST	disconnection
CCDEIINNOORST	disconcertion
CCDEIMNOORSTU	semiconductor
CCDEINNNOOTUV	nonconductive
CCDEINNORSTTU	unconstricted
CCDGIIMNNOSTU	misconducting
CCDHINOOPRSTU	conductorship
CCDNNNOOORSTU	nonconductors
CCEEEEEFFNRSV	effervescence
CCEEEEFFLNORS	efflorescence
CCEEEEGIINRSV	vicegerencies
CCEEEEJNNSSUV	juvenescences
CCEEEFILNNORS	inflorescence
CCEEEFILORRRT	ferroelectric
CCEEEFNOORRRT	ferroconcrete
CCEEEHHIKORRS	chokecherries
CCEEEHIIMNPSY	chimneypieces
CCEEEHIINNORS	incoherencies
CCEEEHIPRTTUY	hypereutectic
CCEEEHKLLPRSS	spellcheckers
CCEEEHMOOPRRT	chemoreceptor
CCEEEIIIMNPPR	impercipience
CCEEEIILOPRTZ	piezoelectric
CCEEEIIMNNRSS	reminiscences
CCEEEIINNNNOV	inconvenience
CCEEEILLRRSSU	Euler's circles
CCEEEILMNNORT	reconcilement
CCEEEILMNNRST	encirclements
CCEEEILMORRTT	electrometric
CCEEEIMMNSSUU	Science Museum
CCEEEIMNNSSTU	intumescences
CCEEEINNNOQSU	inconsequence
CCEEEINNRRRTU	intercurrence
CCEEELOOPRSST	electroscopes
CCEEEMMMNNOST	commencements
CCEEFFIIINNSU	insufficience
CCEEFFIIINSSU	sufficiencies
CCEEFIIINOPRS	proficiencies
CCEEFIIINPRST	interspecific
	prescientific
CCEEFINNOORST	confectioners
CCEEFINNOORTY	confectionery
CCEEGHIINOSTZ	schizogenetic
CCEEGHILMPRYY	hyperglycemic
CCEEGHINOPSTY	psychogenetic
CCEEGIINNNOST	contingencies
CCEEGIINNOPRV	preconceiving
CCEEGIINORTTY	egocentricity
CCEEGILNORTTU	electrocuting
CCEEGINNNORST	constringence
CCEEGINNOPRRT	preconcerting
CCEEHHNRRSTUW	Western Church
CCEEHIILLOPRT	electrophilic
CCEEHILNOOPRT	electrophonic
CCEEHILOOPRTT	photoelectric
CCEEHIMOSSTYZ	schizomycetes
CCEEHINNOSSTU	inescutcheons
CCEEHINORSSTT	crotchetiness
CCEEHLNOSSSTU	scutcheonless
CCEEIIIOPRRST	reciprocities
CCEEIILLOSSTV	collectivises
CCEEIILLOSTVZ	collectivizes
CCEEIILNOORST	isoelectronic
CCEEIIMNORSSV	misconceivers
CCEEIIMNRTUVV	circumventive
CCEEIINNOSSST	consistencies
CCEEIINNOSTUV	inconsecutive
CCEEIINNQSTTU	cinquecentist
CCEEIJMNORSTU	misconjecture
CCEEILLNNNORT	Lincoln Center
CCEEILLNOORST	recollections
CCEEILLORSTTY	electrolytics
CCEEILNNORSTV	conventiclers
CCEEILNOORTTU	electrocution
CCEEILNOSSSUV	occlusiveness
CCEEILNOSTUVY	consecutively
CCEEILOPRRSTY	pyroelectrics
CCEEILORSTTUY	reticulocytes

CCEEIMNRRSTUV	circumventers
CCEEIMOPRRSTT	spectrometric
CCEEINNNOORST	reconnections
CCEEINNNORSTT	interconnects
CCEEINNOOPPRT	preconception
CCEEINNOORSSS	concessioners
CCEEINNORRSST	incorrectness
CCEEINOOPRRST	nocireceptors
CCEEOOPPRSSST	spectroscopes
CCEFFIIINNSUY	insufficiency
CCEFIIINNNOST	nonscientific
CCEFIILMNORUX	circumflexion
CCEFKLOOORSUW	cuckooflowers
CCEGIIIMNNOSV	misconceiving
CCEGIIMNNRTUV	circumventing
CCEGILMOOOSTY	cosmeticology
CCEGINNNORSTY	constringency
CCEHHIINOPRSZ	schizophrenic
CCEHHIMMOORRT	thermochromic
CCEHHIMOOPRRS	chromospheric
CCEHIIKNOPSTY	psychokinetic
CCEHIILOSSTTY	cholecystitis
CCEHIIMORSSTW	microswitches
CCEHILLOOPRST	collectorship
CCEHIMOPRSSTY	psychometrics
CCEHIMORSTTYY	cytochemistry
CCEHINOPRSSTU	succentorship
CCEHIOOPRRSTU	urethroscopic
CCEHIORRSSSST	christcrosses
CCEHMOOPSTUYY	phycomycetous
CCEHNOOPRSSSY	synchroscopes
CCEIIINOORRST	oneirocritics
CCEIILLOSSTTV	collectivists
CCEIIMNNNOOST	connectionism
CCEIIMNNOOPST	misconception
CCEIIMNNORTUV	circumvention
CCEIIMNOOSSSU	semiconscious
CCEIINNNOSSTY	inconsistency
CCEIINNOOPRTV	preconviction
CCEIINNOORSTV	reconvictions
CCEIINNOOSSTU	conscientious
CCEIINNORSSTT	concertinists
CCEIJLNNOTUVY	conjunctively
CCEILLOOOPSSS	oscilloscopes
CCEILNOOOOPSS	colonoscopies
CCEIMMOOPRRTU	microcomputer
CCEIMNORRSTUV	circumventors
CCEINNOOSSSSU	consciousness
CCEIOOOPPRSST	proctoscopies
CCENNNNOORRTU	nonconcurrent
CCENOORRRSTTU	reconstructor
CCENOPRRSSTTU	preconstructs
CCENORRRSSSTU	crosscurrents
CCFGIILLNNOTY	conflictingly
CCFIIIMMORRST	form criticism
CCFIIMNORSSUU	circumfusions
CCGHILNOOOSST	conchologists
CCGHINOOPSSTY	psychognostic
CCGIIIILNRSTY	criticisingly
CCGIIIILNRTYZ	criticizingly
CCGIINORRSSSS	crisscrossing
CCHHHIIIMNOTY	Ho Chi Minh City
CCHHIILOPPRSY	psychrophilic
CCHHIOPPSSSYY	psychophysics
CCHIILNOOPRSU	councilorship
CCHIINNORSSTY	synchronistic
CCHIINNORSTYY	synchronicity
CCHIIOPRRSSTU	Corpus Christi
CCHILMOOPTTYY	lymphocytotic
CCIIMOOPRSSST	microscopists
CCIINNOOPRSST	conscriptions
CCIINNOOPSSUU	inconspicuous
CCIINNOORSSTT	constrictions
CCILMOORSSTTY	motorcyclists
CCILNNOOSSUUY	unconsciously
CCILNOOPSSUUY	conspicuously
CCINNOORSSTTU	constructions
CDDDEEEINNSSU	undecidedness
CDDEEEELLOPTU	leucodepleted
CDDEEEENNPRTU	unprecedented
CDDEEEIINNRRT	inner-directed
CDDEEELNOORRS	enclosed order
CDDEEEMMNNORU	unrecommended
CDDEEIIILOPST	depoliticised
CDDEEIIILOPTZ	depoliticized
CDDEEIINNOORT	reconditioned
CDDEEILNOOTUY	eudicotyledon
CDDEEINOSSSUU	deciduousness
CDDEGIIMMNNOS	discommending
CDDEGIMNNOOPU	decompounding
CDDEHHILOORRY	hydrochloride
CDDEHLNORSTUU	thunderclouds
CDDEIIILNNPSU	undisciplined
CDDEIINNNOOTU	unconditioned
CDDEILMOOPSSY	discomposedly
CDDEILNOOPRSS	scolopendrids
CDDELLLMOORSY	mollycoddlers
CDDGILLLMNOOY	mollycoddling
CDDIIMMOOOSSU	discommodious
CDEEEEEILNORT	electioneered
CDEEEEEINPRRX	reexperienced
CDEEEEELMORRT	decelerometer
CDEEEEFINSSTV	defectiveness
CDEEEEFLLNSSY	defencelessly
CDEEEEHIILMNW	medicine wheel
CDEEEEIINNPRX	inexperienced
CDEEEEIKLPRSW	pickerelweeds
CDEEEEINNPRUX	unexperienced
CDEEEEINPSSTV	deceptiveness
CDEEEEIORRSVX	overexercised
CDEEEFHILRSST	chesterfields
CDEEEFILNNSST	inflectedness
CDEEEFILNSSTU	deceitfulness
CDEEEFINORTTU	counterfeited
CDEEEFLMOORRT	electroformed
CDEEEGILNORRT	telerecording
CDEEEGLOORRRT	Torre del Greco
CDEEEHMOORRST	stereochromed
CDEEEHORRSTTV	overstretched
CDEEEIIINRSVV	divine service
CDEEEIILNNQSU	delinquencies
CDEEEIIORRSSV	rediscoveries
CDEEEILMNORST	declinometers
CDEEEIMOPRSSV	decompressive

CDEEEINNOORRT	reconnoitered
CDEEEINNOPRVW	New Providence
CDEEEINNORSST	reconditeness
CDEEEINSSSTUV	seductiveness
CDEEEMNNNOSTU	denouncements
CDEEEMNNOPRSU	unrecompensed
CDEEENNNOSSTT	contentedness
CDEEENOORRSTV	seroconverted
CDEEEOOPRRTTV	overprotected
CDEEFHKMOOORT	Dome of the Rock
CDEEFILPRSSTU	disrespectful
CDEEFIMNNORSS	confirmedness
CDEEFINNOORTV	overconfident
CDEEGGIINNORS	derecognising
CDEEGGIINNORZ	derecognizing
CDEEGHIMNNOPR	comprehending
CDEEGIILRRSTY	triglycerides
CDEEGIINNOORT	derecognition
CDEEGIINNORRS	reconsidering
CDEEGIINORRSV	rediscovering
CDEEGIINPRSST	disrespecting
CDEEGIINRRSTT	derestricting
CDEEGILOPPSTY	glycopeptides
CDEEGIMNNNOPR	precondemning
CDEEGIMNOPRSS	decompressing
CDEEGINNORSTU	countersigned
CDEEGLOORSTUX	dextroglucose
CDEEHHIILNORX	chlorhexidine
CDEEHHOOPPRSS	phosphoresced
CDEEHIINOPRTY	dryopithecine
CDEEHILLNSSSS	childlessness
CDEEHIOOPTTUY	hypoeutectoid
CDEEHNNOOOPPS	phonendoscope
CDEEIIIILMSVZ	semicivilized
CDEEIIILOPSST	depoliticises
CDEEIIILOPSTZ	depoliticizes
CDEEIIIMNRSTT	deterministic
CDEEIIIMOSSTT	domesticities
CDEEIIINNSSTV	disincentives
CDEEIILNOPRST	predilections
CDEEIILNOSSSU	deliciousness
CDEEIILOPSSTV	velocipedists
CDEEIILPRSTVY	descriptively
CDEEIIMNORSTT	densitometric
CDEEIINNSSTUV	inductiveness
CDEEIINOOSSSU	dioeciousness
CDEEIINORRSTT	derestriction
CDEEIIORSSSTU	discourtesies
CDEEIJNPRRSUU	jurisprudence
CDEEILMOOPRSY	copolymerised
CDEEILMOOPRYZ	copolymerized
CDEEILNNOOPRS	scolopendrine
CDEEILNNOSTUY	tendenciously
CDEEILRSTTUVY	destructively
CDEEIMMOORTTV	overcommitted
CDEEIMNOOPRSS	decompression
CDEEIMNOOPRST	contemporised
CDEEIMNOOPRTZ	contemporized
CDEEINNORRSTT	nonrestricted
CDEEINOOPRSTU	counterpoised
CDEEINORSTTTU	reconstituted
CDEEKKLNRSTUU	knuckleduster
CDEELLNOSSSSU	cloudlessness
CDEELNORSSSUU	credulousness
CDEELNPSSTUUY	unsuspectedly
CDEENNOOPRRST	correspondent
CDEENNOOPRSST	corespondents
CDEENNOORSSTT	contortedness
CDEENNRRRSTUU	undercurrents
CDEENOOORSTXY	deoxycortones
CDEEOOPRSSTUV	pseudovectors
CDEEPRRSSTTUU	superstructed
CDEFGIINNNOSS	confidingness
CDEFIIINNOSST	disinfections
CDEFIINOOPRRT	indirect proof
CDEGHILNNORTU	underclothing
CDEGHILOOPSSY	psychologised
CDEGHILOOPSYZ	psychologized
CDEGIIIMNOSTZ	domesticizing
CDEGIIMOOOPSS	sigmoidoscope
CDEGIINNNOSTT	discontenting
CDEGIINNORRTU	reintroducing
CDEGIINNORSTU	rediscounting
CDEGIINNPRSUU	superinducing
CDEGIINOOOSUY	gynodioecious
CDEGILLNNOORT	decontrolling
CDEGILNNOOORY	endocrinology
CDEGINNOOPRRS	corresponding
CDEGINOOPRRUV	overproducing
CDEHHIOOORRST	rhodochrosite
CDEHIIILPPSSS	discipleships
CDEHIIIOPRSTY	spheroidicity
CDEHIIKNORSTY	hydrokinetics
CDEHIIMNOPRRU	perichondrium
CDEHIINOOOPRS	conidiophores
CDEHIIOOOPPRT	photoperiodic
CDEHIIOPPRTTY	pteridophytic
CDEHIIOPRRSST	directorships
CDEHILLOOPRSY	policyholders
CDEHILMNOOORS	monochlorides
CDEHIMNOOORSS	chondriosomes
CDEHIMOOPPRSU	pseudomorphic
CDEHIMOORTTYY	thyroidectomy
CDEHKNRRSTTUU	thunderstruck
CDEHMOOOOPPST	photocomposed
CDEIIIINNSTTV	indistinctive
CDEIIILLNSUVY	uncivilisedly
CDEIIILLNUVYZ	uncivilizedly
CDEIIILNSTTVY	distinctively
CDEIIIMMNOOST	incommodities
CDEIIIMNORSST	misdirections
CDEIIIMOOOPRS	Piero di Cosimo
CDEIIIMPRSSTV	descriptivism
CDEIIINNORSST	indiscretions
CDEIIINNORSTT	interdictions
CDEIIIPRSSTTV	descriptivist
CDEIIJLNSTUVY	disjunctively
CDEIIJNOSSSUU	judiciousness
CDEIIMMNOOSSS	decommissions
CDEIIMNOOOPST	decomposition
CDEIIMNORSSTU	reductionisms
CDEIIMNRSSTTU	misinstructed
CDEIINNNOOSSX	disconnexions
CDEIINNOOPRST	preconditions

CDEIINNORSSTU	discontinuers
CDEIINORSSTTU	reductionists
CDEIIRSTTTUVY	destructivity
CDEILLMOORTUU	multicoloured
CDEILLNORSUUY	incredulously
CDEILMNOOPRSU	scolopendrium
CDEILMNOOPSUY	compendiously
CDEILMNOORSST	discolorments
CDEILMNOORSTU	discolourment
CDEILNORSSSUU	ludicrousness
CDEIMNNOOPRSU	mispronounced
CDEIMOOPRSSSU	discomposures
CDEINNOOPRTUV	nonproductive
CDEINOOPPRRTU	preproduction
CDEINOOPRRSTU	reproductions
CDELLNOOOPTYY	polycotyledon
CDELMNNOOOOTY	monocotyledon
CDFGIIIMNNORS	disconfirming
CDFGIIMNOORST	discomforting
CDFIIMNOORSTY	disconformity
CDGHIIIMNOOST	dichotomising
CDGHIIIMNOOTZ	dichotomizing
CDGHIKLNOOSST	stockholdings
CDGIIINNNOSTU	discontinuing
CDGIIMOOOPSSY	sigmoidoscopy
CDHHILNOORRSY	chlorohydrins
CDHHIMNOOPRUY	hypochondrium
CDHIIMNNOOORT	mitochondrion
CDHILMOOOSTUY	dichotomously
CDHIMOOORSSTY	Dio Chrysostom
CDIIIJLNOSUUY	injudiciously
CDIIIJNORSSTU	jurisdictions
CDIIINNOSTTUY	discontinuity
CDIINNOORSTTU	introductions
CDIINNOOSSTUU	discontinuous
CEEEEEINPRRSX	reexperiences
CEEEEFFINSSTV	effectiveness
CEEEEFINNRRST	interferences
CEEEEFLMORRTT	reflectometer
CEEEEGHINORTT	heterogenetic
CEEEEGHMNORSS	cheesemongers
CEEEEGIINOPRT	epeirogenetic
CEEEEHLNRSSSS	cheerlessness
CEEEEIKKPRSTW	wicketkeepers
CEEEEILNSSSTV	selectiveness
CEEEEIMNNPRSU	supereminence
CEEEEIMNORSTT	enterectomies
CEEEEINNPRSUV	supervenience
CEEEEINPRSSTV	receptiveness
CEEEEINPRSSTX	preexistences
CEEEEINRSSSSV	recessiveness
CEEEEINRSSSTV	secretiveness
CEEEEINSSSSVX	excessiveness
CEEEEIOPRTTVX	exteroceptive
CEEEEIORRSSVX	overexercises
CEEEEJNNRSTUV	rejuvenescent
CEEEELMORRSTT	electrometers
CEEEEPPRRSSST	preceptresses
CEEEFFIILNTVY	ineffectively
CEEEFFINNOSTV	noneffectives
CEEEFIIMPRSTV	imperfectives
CEEEFIINNSSTV	infectiveness
CEEEFIMNNORRT	reinforcement
CEEEFIMNPRSST	imperfectness
CEEEFINORRTTU	counterfeiter
CEEEGHIKLNNRS	Gelsenkirchen
CEEEGHILLNOPT	phellogenetic
CEEEGHIMNORTT	thermogenetic
CEEEGIILLNNRT	intelligencer
CEEEGIILLNNST	intelligences
CEEEGIILNOPPT	epileptogenic
CEEEGIJNNRSUV	rejuvenescing
CEEEGIKNNRSSS	greensickness
CEEEHHIPRSTTY	hyperesthetic
CEEEHHKLRSTTU	kletterschuhe
CEEEHIILNNSTT	Liechtenstein
CEEEHILLLMOSU	hemicellulose
CEEEHILLOPRST	electrophiles
CEEEHILMNOPRT	nephelometric
CEEEHIMNOPRST	nephrectomies
CEEEHIMNOPRSV	comprehensive
CEEEHINNPRSST	phreneticness
CEEEHLNNOSTTU	luncheonettes
CEEEHLNOOPRST	electrophones
CEEEHLOQQSSUU	quelquechoses
CEEEHMMOORTTY	hemocytometer
CEEEHMNNNRSTT	entrenchments
CEEEHMNNRRSTT	retrenchments
CEEEHMOORRSST	stereochromes
CEEEHNOPRRSST	centrospheres
CEEEHOOPRRRST	rheoreceptors
CEEEHORRSSTTV	overstretches
CEEEIIMNNPRST	impertinences
CEEEIIMNNRTTT	intermittence
CEEEIIMNPRSSS	impreciseness
CEEEIINNSSTVV	invectiveness
CEEEIINOPRTTV	interoceptive
CEEEILMMORRST	electromerism
CEEEILMNNNSST	inclementness
CEEEILMNOPSST	splenectomies
CEEEILMNRSSSS	mercilessness
CEEEILMOORTTV	electromotive
CEEEILNOSSSSV	voicelessness
CEEEILNOSTVXY	coextensively
CEEEILNPPRRSU	pluripresence
CEEEILNPRSSSS	pricelessness
CEEEILNSSSSUV	seclusiveness
CEEEILNSSSUVX	exclusiveness
CEEEILPPRSTVY	perspectively
CEEEIMMNOPSTU	pneumectomies
CEEEINNOORRRT	reconnoiterer
CEEEINRRRSSTW	screenwriters
CEEEINRRSSSTW	wintercresses
CEEEINRSSSUVX	excursiveness
CEEEIOPRRSTTV	retrospective
CEEELLORRSSTY	electrolysers
CEEELLORRSTYZ	electrolyzers
CEEELMMORSTTU	telecommuters
CEEELMNNOSSUW	unwelcomeness
CEEELOPRRSTTY	electrotypers
CEEEMNNNORSTU	renouncements
CEEEMNNOPSSTT	competentness
CEEEMOPRRSSTT	spectrometers
CEEENNPRSTUUV	venepunctures

CEEEOOPRRSTTX	exteroceptors
CEEEOPRRSSSTT	protectresses
CEEFFHINRSSTT	festschriften
CEEFFIIILNNTY	inefficiently
CEEFFIJNORSTY	Jefferson City
CEEFFNOORRSTU	counteroffers
CEEFGIINNNOTU	eigenfunction
CEEFGILNNOSTU	genuflections
CEEFGINNOORTT	frontogenetic
CEEFHKMORRSTU	motherfuckers
CEEFIIKLNORSU	nickeliferous
CEEFIIMNOPRST	imperfections
	perfectionism
CEEFIINOPRSST	frontispieces
CEEFIINOPRSTT	perfectionist
CEEFILNOORRTT	retroflection
CEEFINOORSSSU	ferociousness
CEEFLLOORRSTU	electrofluors
CEEFLLORRSUUY	resourcefully
CEEGHIILNOPRT	helicoptering
CEEGHIIMOORST	isogeothermic
CEEGHIINNRRST	rechristening
CEEGHIINOSSSZ	schizogenesis
CEEGHIIRRSTUW	cruiserweight
CEEGHIMNOOPRT	morphogenetic
CEEGHINOPSSSY	psychogenesis
CEEGHINORSTUW	counterweighs
CEEGHINORTTUW	counterweight
CEEGIIMMNNOTU	immunogenetic
CEEGIINORRTVX	Vercingetorix
CEEGIKLLNOPSS	glockenspiels
CEEGILLNORSTY	electrolysing
CEEGILLNORTYZ	electrolyzing
CEEGILMMNNOPT	complementing
CEEGILMMNOTTU	telecommuting
CEEGILMOOSSST	glossectomies
CEEGILNOPRTTY	electrotyping
CEEGINNNORRTU	rencountering
CEEGINOPRRSTT	retrospecting
CEEGMNNOORSSW	congresswomen
CEEGMNOORRSST	costermongers
CEEGNNOOOPRST	rontgenoscope
CEEHHIMMORSTT	thermochemist
CEEHHIMOOPRRT	heteromorphic
CEEHHIOOPRRTT	heterotrophic
CEEHHLLOPRSUY	Holy Sepulchre
CEEHHLOORSSST	clotheshorses
CEEHHMNORSSSY	synchromeshes
CEEHHMOOPRRSS	chromospheres
CEEHHOOPPRSSS	phosphoresces
CEEHHOOPRRSST	trochospheres
CEEHIIKLNRSSS	lickerishness
CEEHILMMOPRSY	myrmecophiles
CEEHIMMRSSSTT	Messerschmitt
CEEHIMNNNRSTT	intrenchments
CEEHIMNNOOPRS	comprehension
CEEHIMNNORSTT	ethnocentrism
CEEHIMOORSTTY	stoechiometry
CEEHIMOPPRRTY	hypermetropic
CEEHINNOPRSSV	convenerships
CEEHINOOPPRSS	nephroscopies
CEEHINOPPRRST	precentorship
CEEHIOPPPRRST	preceptorship
CEEHIOPRSSTUX	executorships
CEEHKLLNORRSS	schnorkellers
CEEHLMOOPRSTU	thermocouples
CEEHLNOOOPRTT	photoelectron
CEEHLOOPRRSTU	electrophorus
CEEHMOPRRSSTY	psychrometers
CEEHOOOPPRRTT	photoreceptor
CEEHOOPRRSSTU	urethroscopes
CEEIIIINNRSST	insincerities
CEEIIILRSTTUV	reluctivities
CEEIIIMMPRSTT	metempiricist
CEEIIIMORSTTT	meteoriticist
CEEIIJNNORSTT	interjections
CEEIILLNNOSTT	intellections
CEEIILMNNORST	inclinometers
CEEIILMNNRSTY	reminiscently
CEEIILMOPTTVY	competitively
CEEIILNNSSSUV	inclusiveness
CEEIILNOORSTT	enterocolitis
CEEIILRRSTTVY	restrictively
CEEIIMNNRTTTY	intermittency
CEEIIMNOPPRST	misperception
CEEIIMNOPTTUV	uncompetitive
CEEIIMORSSSTV	viscosimeters
CEEIINNOPRSST	reinspections
CEEIINNOPRSTT	interceptions
CEEIINNORSSST	intercessions
CEEIINNORSSTT	intersections
CEEIINOOPRSST	retinoscopies
CEEIINOOPSSST	isoteniscopes
CEEIINOPRSSTT	receptionists
CEEIINOPRSTTV	introspective
CEEIINOSSSSST	secessionists
CEEIIOPPRRRST	proprietrices
CEEIJNOORRSTT	retrojections
CEEIKLNNOSTUU	kinetonucleus
CEEILMNNOPTTY	incompetently
CEEILMNOORSUY	ceremoniously
CEEILMOOPRSSY	copolymerises
CEEILMOOPRSTY	pylorectomies
CEEILMOOPRSYZ	copolymerizes
CEEILMOPRSSVY	compressively
CEEILNNOOPRTU	nucleoprotein
CEEILNNOOPRXY	clinopyroxene
CEEILNOOPRRST	scleroprotein
CEEILNOORSSSV	venosclerosis
CEEILNOSSSTUY	necessitously
CEEILOOPRSTTU	teleutosporic
CEEILOPPRSTVY	prospectively
CEEILPQRSTUUY	picturesquely
CEEIMMMNORSTT	recommitments
CEEIMMNNOOPTT	omnicompetent
CEEIMNNOORSUU	unceremonious
CEEIMNOOPRSST	contemporises
CEEIMNOOPRSTZ	contemporizes
CEEIMNOOPSSST	compositeness
CEEIMNOORSSTT	econometrists
CEEINNOORRRST	reconnoitrers
CEEINNOORRSSV	reconversions
CEEINNORSTTTU	reconstituent
CEEINNPRSTUUV	venipunctures

CEEINOOPRRSTT	interoceptors
	retrospection
CEEINOOPRSSTT	stereopticons
CEEINOOPRSSTU	counterpoises
CEEINOORRSSST	retrocessions
CEEINOORRSSSV	corrosiveness
CEEINOORRSSTV	controversies
CEEINOPRRSSSU	repercussions
CEEINORRRSSTU	resurrections
CEEINORSSTTTU	reconstitutes
CEEINOSSSSTUV	viscountesses
CEEIOOPRSSSTT	stereoscopist
CEEIOORRRSSTT	ecoterrorists
CEEKLNOOSSTTY	cytoskeletons
CEEKNOORRRTUW	counterworker
CEELLNOORSTTV	electronvolts
CEELPQRSSTUUU	sculpturesque
CEEMMNNOOPTUY	pneumonectomy
CEEMNNNOOPRTU	pronouncement
CEEMNOOPRRTUU	neurocomputer
CEEMOPPRRSTUU	supercomputer
CEENNOORRSTTU	countertenors
CEENOOOPPRSSS	snooperscopes
CEENOORRRSTTV	controverters
CEENOORSSSTUU	courteousness
CEFFIINOOSSSU	officiousness
CEFHIMMOORRRU	ferrochromium
CEFHLLLOOOSSW	schoolfellows
CEFHLMOOORRSU	fluorochromes
CEFIINNNOOSTU	noninfectious
CEFILNOPRRTUY	perfunctorily
CEFLLMOORSSTY	comfortlessly
CEFLLNOORSSUU	colourfulness
CEFMNNNOORSTT	confrontments
CEFNOOOPRRSTU	counterproofs
CEFNORSSSTUUU	fructuousness
CEGGHLNOOOORY	geochronology
CEGGILNOOSSTY	gynecologists
CEGGIMOOORSTU	cogito, ergo sum
CEGHHIILOPRSY	hieroglyphics
CEGHIILOOOSTY	stoicheiology
CEGHIIOPSSSTY	geophysicists
CEGHIKLLNNORS	schnorkelling
CEGHILNOOSSTT	technologists
CEGHILOOOPSYY	ecophysiology
CEGHILOOPSSSY	psychologises
CEGHILOOPSSYZ	psychologizes
CEGHINNOOSTUU	countinghouse
CEGHINORSTTTU	outstretching
CEGHOPRRSSUYY	psychosurgery
CEGIIILNNNORV	overinclining
CEGIIILNOORST	coreligionist
CEGIIINNORSTU	incongruities
CEGIIKNPPQSTU	quickstepping
CEGIILLOOSSTX	lexicologists
CEGIILMMNNOPT	complimenting
CEGIILMNORSYY	syringomyelic
CEGIILNNORRTY	nitroglycerin
CEGIIMNNNORTU	countermining
CEGIIMNOORRTT	trigonometric
CEGIIMNOPRSTU	computerising
CEGIIMNOPRTUZ	computerizing
CEGIINNNOORRT	reconnoitring
CEGIINNOOPRSS	processioning
CEGIINNOPPRRT	intercropping
CEGIINNOPRSTT	introspecting
CEGIINNORRSST	intercrossing
CEGILMMOORSTY	myrmecologist
CEGILNNNORTUY	incongruently
CEGILNOOPRSTU	glucoproteins
CEGILNOOPRSTY	glycoproteins
CEGIMNNOORSUV	overconsuming
CEGIMNNOORTUV	countermoving
	covermounting
CEGINNOORRTTV	controverting
CEGINRRRSTTUU	restructuring
CEGNNOOOPRSTY	rontgenoscopy
CEGNNOORSSSUU	congruousness
CEHHHNOOPRRSY	rhynchophores
CEHHIILLLNRST	Chiltern Hills
CEHHIIMMOOORT	homoiothermic
CEHHIIMOOPRRT	theriomorphic
CEHHIINORSSTY	ichthyornises
CEHHIIOORSSTT	orthostichies
CEHHILMNORSTT	trochelminths
CEHHILOOPRSTY	hypochlorites
CEHHIMMOOOOPR	homoeomorphic
CEHHIMOOPSSTT	photochemists
CEHHIMOPSSTTY	phytochemists
CEHIIKNOPSSSY	psychokinesis
CEHIILMOOPPTY	lymphopoietic
CEHIILMOSSUVY	mischievously
CEHIILNOOPSST	siphonostelic
CEHIIMMOOORST	homoeroticism
CEHIIMNOOPRST	chemisorption
CEHIIMOORSTTY	stoichiometry
CEHIINNOPRSTY	pericynthions
CEHIINOPPRSST	inspectorship
CEHIINOPRTTYY	hypertonicity
CEHIIOOPRSSST	spirochetosis
CEHILNOOPRSSU	counselorship
CEHILNOPSTTYY	polysynthetic
CEHILOPRRSTUY	Holy Scripture
CEHIMMOOPRRST	morphometrics
CEHIMNOOOPRRT	chromoprotein
CEHIMOOPRSTTY	topochemistry
CEHIMOPRSSTTY	psychometrist
CEHINNOOPRSSV	convenorships
CEHINNORRSSSY	synchronisers
CEHINNORRSSYZ	synchronizers
CEHIOOPRRSTTU	trichopterous
CEHMOOOOPPRST	photocomposer
CEHMOOOOPPSST	photocomposes
CEHNOOPRRSTTU	photocurrents
CEIIILMNOPSST	impoliticness
CEIIILNNSTTVY	instinctively
CEIIILNPRSTVY	inscriptively
CEIIIMNOPSTUY	impecuniosity
CEIIIMOPRSSTU	promiscuities
CEIIINOPRSSST	precisionists
CEIIJNNOORSTT	introjections
CEIIJNOOPRSTT	projectionist
CEIILLLNOOSTV	violoncellist
CEIILMNOPSUUY	impecuniously

CEIILNNNNOTTY	incontinently
CEIILNNOORTTU	interlocution
CEIILNOOSSTTU	elocutionists
CEIILNOPRRTUV	proventriculi
CEIILNOPSSSSU	suspicionless
CEIILNORRTTUX	interlocutrix
CEIILNOSSSTUX	exclusionists
CEIILNRSTTUVY	instructively
CEIILOPPRSTUY	precipitously
CEIILRRSSTTUU	sericulturist
CEIILRRSTTUUV	viticulturers
CEIIMMNOORSSS	commissioners
CEIIMMNOPRSTU	minicomputers
CEIIMNNORRTTU	micronutrient
CEIIMNOOOPRST	recomposition
CEIIMNOOPRSTT	protectionism
CEIIMOORSSSTT	sociometrists
CEIINNOOPRSTT	introspection
CEIINNORRSSTU	insurrections
CEIINNORSSSUU	incuriousness
CEIINNRSTTUUV	uninstructive
CEIINOOPRSSTT	retinoscopist
CEIINOOPRSTTT	protectionist
CEIINOORSSTUV	insectivorous
CEIINOPPRRSST	prescriptions
CEIINOPRSSSTU	percussionist
CEIINORSSSTUX	excursionists
CEIIPRRRSSTTW	scriptwriters
CEILLMNOOSTTY	tonsillectomy
CEILMNNOOOSSU	mononucleosis
CEILMNOORSTUY	coterminously
CEILMNOPSTUVY	consumptively
CEILNNOOSTTUY	contentiously
CEILNNOSTTTUY	constituently
CEILNOORRSTTU	interlocutors
CEILNOORRTTUY	interlocutory
CEILOPPRSSUUY	perspicuously
CEIMMMNOORSTY	monosymmetric
CEIMNNOOPRSSU	mispronounces
CEINNNOOSSSUU	innocuousness
CEINNOOPRSTTU	counterpoints
CEINNOPRRSSTU	incorruptness
CEINPSSSSTTUU	intussuscepts
CEIOOOPPPRRRT	proprioceptor
CELLNOOSSUUVV	convolvuluses
CFFIIILNOOSUY	inofficiously
CFGHIILLNNNUY	unflinchingly
CFGHIMNNOORTU	unforthcoming
CFHINNORTTTUU	truth-function
CFIILMNNOTTUU	multifunction
CFIMMNNNOOORS	nonconformism
CFIMNNNOOORST	nonconformist
CFIMNNNOOORTY	nonconformity
CGHHIIINPSTTW	whipstitching
CGHHIILOOSTTY	ichthyologist
CGHIIINNOORSS	isochronising
CGHIIINNOORSZ	isochronizing
CGHIILOORSSTT	trichologists
CGHIINNNORSSY	synchronising
CGHIINNNORSYZ	synchronizing
CGHILNOOORSST	chronologists
CGHILOOPSSSTY	psychologists
CGIIILLOOOPST	oligopolistic
CGIIILMNOORST	criminologist
CGIIILMOOSTTV	victimologist
CGIIILNOOSSTU	sociolinguist
CGIIIMMNNNOOSS	commissioning
CGIIINPRRSTTW	scriptwriting
CGIILMOOSSSTU	musicologists
CGIILOOOSSTTX	toxicologists
CGIIMNNORSSTU	misconstruing
CGILNNOORSUUY	incongruously
CGILOOOPRSSTT	proctologists
CGLOOOOPRTYYZ	cryptozoology
CHHIILOPRSTUU	thiosulphuric
CHHIMOOPRRSTY	hystricomorph
CHHIOOORSSTTU	orthostichous
CHHIOOPRSSTYY	psychohistory
CHHLMOOPRSTUY	chlorophytums
CHHMOOOOPRRSU	chromophorous
CHIIILOOPRSST	solicitorship
CHIIOOOPRRSTT	protohistoric
CHILMMNNOOOUY	Holy Communion
CHILMOOPSSTYY	lymphocytosis
CHILNNOOOPRST	Port Nicholson
CHILNOOORSSUY	isochronously
CHILNOOPPRSSU	proconsulship
CHILOOPSSSTUY	physoclistous
CHILOPPRRSUUY	pyrosulphuric
CHIMMNOOORSST	monochromists
CHLNNOORSSUYY	synchronously
CHMNNOOOPRRUY	Murphy-O'Connor
CIIIIIMPRSTTV	primitivistic
CIIIILLNOSSTU	illusionistic
CIIILNRSTTUUV	viniculturist
CIIILRSTTTUUV	viticulturist
CIILLNOPSTUUY	punctiliously
CIILMMOOOPSST	cosmopolitism
CIIMNNOOOPSST	monopsonistic
CIINNOOORSTTT	contortionist
CIINNOOSSTTTU	constitutions
CIINOOPPRRSST	proscriptions
CIINOOPPRSTTU	opportunistic
CIINOOPRRSTTU	corruptionist
CIJLNORSSSTUU	jurisconsults
CILMOOPRSSUUY	promiscuously
CILMOPRSSTUUY	scrumptiously
CIMMNNNOOSSTU	noncommunists
DDDEEEEINNPRT	interdepended
DDDEEEGIMOSSS	demigoddesses
DDDEHNNOOORRS	rhododendrons
DDEEEEIMNPRRT	predetermined
DDEEEELOOPRVV	overdeveloped
DDEEEENNOPRTV	overdependent
DDEEEGHILNSST	delightedness
DDEEEGHINORSY	dehydrogenise
DDEEEGHINORYZ	dehydrogenize
DDEEEIILLMOTT	Little Diomede
DDEEEIINRSSTT	disinterested
DDEEEILMNRSTW	Middle Western
DDEEEILMOPRSY	depolymerised
DDEEEILMOPRYZ	depolymerized
DDEEEILNNNPTY	independently
DDEEEINNPRSTU	superintended

DDEEEIPRRSSSU depressurised
DDEEEIPRRSSUZ depressurized
DDEEELMNOPRUY underemployed
DDEEELNOPRSUV underdevelops
DDEEFGIIINNSS dignifiedness
DDEEFHIIIMRSU dehumidifiers
DDEEFIIIIMNST misidentified
DDEEFIIINRSUV undiversified
DDEEFNNNOSSUU unfoundedness
DDEEGHHINRTUW hundredweight
DDEEGHIILMSTW middleweights
DDEEGIILMNNRT intermeddling
DDEEGILMNOSST dislodgements
DDEEGINNNPRSU underspending
DDEEGINSSSSTU disgustedness
DDEEHILPRSSUU desulphurised
DDEEHILPRSUUZ desulphurized
DDEEIIKMNRRST Kidderminster
DDEEILNPPRSUU undersupplied
DDEEIMNNOSSTW disendowments
DDEEINORSSSTT distortedness
DDEFGHIIIMNUY dehumidifying
DDEGHHIINOPST diphthongised
DDEGHHIINOPTZ diphthongized
DDEGHHLOOOSSU household gods
DDEGHIIINSSTU distinguished
DDEGIIKMNNOTU United Kingdom
DDEGILNOORSST dendrologists
DDEGINNRSTUUY understudying
DDEHHILOPRSUY hydrosulphide
DDEHIIKNOORZZ Ordzhonikidze
DDEHILNNOOPRS philodendrons
DDEIIIILMSSTU dissimilitude
DDEIIILLNOSSU disillusioned
DDEIILNNOORRS liriodendrons
DDEIMNOORSSTU misunderstood
DEEEEFINNSSSV defensiveness
DEEEEFLLNSSSY defenselessly
DEEEEGIPRRRST preregistered
DEEEEHHPRSSSS shepherdesses
DEEEEIMNPRRRT predeterminer
DEEEEIMNPRRST predetermines
DEEEEINPRRRTT reinterpreted
DEEEELMNOPRTV redevelopment
DEEEENNPRRSTU unrepresented
DEEEENPRRSSTV pervertedness
DEEEFFINNRSST differentness
DEEEFGIINNRTW winterfeeding
DEEEFGJMNORTU forejudgement
DEEEFGKLNOORW foreknowledge
DEEEFHHIORRRS Herefordshire
DEEEFHNOORRST foreshortened
DEEEFIILOPRRT Porţile de Fier
DEEEFINPRRSSV perfervidness
DEEEGGIINRRST deregistering
DEEEGHILNNNTU unenlightened
DEEEGHINRRRTV Right Reverend
DEEEGIIMNNRRT redetermining
DEEEGILLORSTU Rouget de Lisle
DEEEGINNORTVX overextending
DEEEGINNRRSTU understeering
DEEEGINNRSSSV deservingness
DEEEHIMPRSSST deemsterships
DEEEHLOPRRSTU reupholstered
DEEEIILNNORSV nondeliveries
DEEEIILNNPTXY inexpediently
DEEEIINRSSSST desensitisers
DEEEIINRSSSTZ desensitizers
DEEEIKOORSTTU deuterotokies
DEEEILLORSTUY deleteriously
DEEEILMOPRSSY depolymerises
DEEEILMOPRSYZ depolymerizes
DEEEIMNOPRRST redemptioners
DEEEIMNORSSTT densitometers
DEEEIMOPRRSSV overimpressed
DEEEINOPPRSTU neuropeptides
DEEEINSSSTTTU destituteness
DEEEIPRRSSSSU depressurises
DEEEIPRRSSSUZ depressurizes
DEEEKLMMRRTTU kettledrummer
DEEEKLNNOOSST endoskeletons
DEEELLNNPRSTY resplendently
DEEELMNOPRSTY redeployments
DEEELNNSSSTTU unsettledness
DEEENOPRRSUUX underexposure
DEEENORSSSTUX dexterousness
DEEFFHINRRSSU undersheriffs
DEEFFIILNNRTY indifferently
DEEFFIINSSSUV diffusiveness
DEEFFLNNRSSUU unruffledness
DEEFGHILORSTY foresightedly
DEEFGIIMNRSTU disfigurement
DEEFGIINNPRRT fingerprinted
DEEFGJMNORSTU forejudgments
DEEFHHIORRRST Hertfordshire
DEEFHIIMRRSSU Dumfriesshire
DEEFHIMNORSTT Thetford Mines
DEEFIIIIMNSST misidentifies
DEEFIILNNRSTU unfriendliest
DEEFILNOPRSSU splendiferous
DEEFLNNORSSUW wonderfulness
DEEGGHHINOPPS hedgehoppings
DEEGGIINNOSXY deoxygenising
DEEGGIINNOXYZ deoxygenizing
DEEGGIMNORSST disgorgements
DEEGHILMNNRUW underwhelming
DEEGHILMOOOST methodologies
DEEGHILMOOSTY demythologise
DEEGHILMOOTYZ demythologize
DEEGIIINNSSST desensitising
DEEGIIINNSSTZ desensitizing
DEEGIILMNNORY domineeringly
DEEGIILOOPPST oligopeptides
DEEGIIMNOPRSW disempowering
DEEGIINOPPRST predepositing
DEEGIJMMNSSTU misjudgements
DEEGILMNOOOST entomologised
DEEGILMNOOOTZ entomologized
DEEGILMNOOSTY sedimentology
DEEGILNNORTUV overindulgent
DEEGINNOPRSUX underexposing
DEEGINNORSTTW Downing Street
DEEGINNORSUVZ rendezvousing
DEEHHIIMOPRSS hemispheroids

DEEHHIINNOSSS hoidenishness
DEEHHINNOSSSY hoydenishness
DEEHHIOPPRRTY hypertrophied
DEEHHNORRSTUW thundershower
DEEHIINNPRSTU indentureship
DEEHIINPPRSST presidentship
DEEHIINPRSSST residentships
DEEHIKKNNRSUV Verkhne-Udinsk
DEEHILMMNOSST demolishments
DEEHILPRRSSUU desulphuriser
DEEHILPRRSUUZ desulphurizer
DEEHILPRSSSUU desulphurises
DEEHILPRSSUUZ desulphurizes
DEEHINNORSTTY North Tyneside
DEEHINOSSTTUY South Tyneside
DEEHIOPPRSTTY pteridophytes
DEEHNNORSSTTU thunderstones
DEEIIIMMNNRST indeterminism
DEEIIIMNNRSTT indeterminist
DEEIIINOQRSTU derequisition
requisitioned
DEEIILLNNSSUW unwieldliness
DEEIILLNORSSS soldierliness
DEEIILMNNOSSS dimensionless
DEEIILMNNSSTU unlimitedness
DEEIILNNSSTTY dissentiently
DEEIILNORSSSU deliriousness
DEEIILOPPRSST spoiled priest
DEEIILOPPRSTT lepidopterist
DEEIILOPSTUXY expeditiously
DEEIIMMRSSSTY dissymmetries
DEEIIMNNRSSTT disinterments
DEEIIMNNSSTTV disinvestment
DEEIIMNOORSST endometriosis
DEEIIMOORRSTU demeritorious
DEEIINOOPRRSV reprovisioned
DEEIINOPRSSTU serendipitous
DEEIINOSSSSTU seditiousness
DEEIIORRSTVVY overdiversity
DEEIJNORRRSSU surrejoinders
DEEILMNOOSSSU melodiousness
DEEILNNOSTTUY tendentiously
DEEILNOOPPRST lepidopterons
DEEILNORSSSTU desultoriness
DEEILNOSSSSTU dissoluteness
DEEILNPPRSSUU undersupplies
DEEILNPRRTTUY interruptedly
DEEILOOPPRSTU lepidopterous
DEEIMNOORSTTU Deuteronomist
DEEIMNOPRSSST Simpson Desert
DEEIMOPPRRSST pteridosperms
DEEINNPRRTTUU uninterrupted
DEELNNOPSSSUU pendulousness
DEELNNOSSSSSU soundlessness
DEEMNORRSSSUU murderousness
DEEMOOOPRRSST depressomotor
DEENNOOPRSSSU ponderousness
DEENNOPSSSTTU unspottedness
DEENOOPRSSSST dessertspoons
DEENOPPPRRRSU underproppers
DEFHIILLOPSSW disfellowship
DEFHILMRRTTYY Merthyr Tydfil
DEFHIMORRRTUU rutherfordium
DEFIILNOORSSX dorsiflexions
DEFIILPRSTUUY superfluidity
DEFILLRSSSTUY distressfully
DEFILMNNNSSUU unmindfulness
DEFILOOORRSUY odoriferously
DEFLNNOOOORTW Tower of London
DEGGHIINNORSY hydrogenising
DEGGHIINNORYZ hydrogenizing
DEGGIILNNORUV overindulging
DEGHHIILOOPPT Philip the Good
DEGHHIINOPSST diphthongises
DEGHHIINOPSTZ diphthongizes
DEGHHILOPRTTT trothplighted
DEGHHNOOORRTY orthohydrogen
DEGHIIIINNRST disinheriting
DEGHIIINRSSTU distinguisher
DEGHIIINSSSTU distinguishes
DEGHIINNOPSTY dehypnotising
DEGHIINNOPTYZ dehypnotizing
DEGHILMOOOSTT methodologist
DEGHINNOORSTU undershooting
DEGHINNORSSTW downrightness
DEGIIILNPSSTT sidesplitting
DEGIIILNQSTUY disquietingly
DEGIILLOOSSTT deltiologists
DEGIILNRSSSTY distressingly
DEGIILOOPRSTT pteridologist
DEGIINNNNPRSU underpinnings
DEGIINOPSSSSS dispossessing
DEGIKMNOPRSSU superkingdoms
DEGILMNOOOSST demonologists
DEGILNOOOSSTT deontologists
DEGIMNNPRRTUU undertrumping
DEGINNOPPPRRU underpropping
DEHHIILOOPPSS philosophised
DEHHIILOOPPSZ philosophized
DEHHIIOPRRSSY hyperhidrosis
DEHHILOPRSTUY hydrosulphite
DEHHIOPRRSTYY hyperthyroids
DEHHLOOOORSUY Holyroodhouse
DEHIIILNOPRSS siderophilins
DEHIINOOPPSST deipnosophist
DEHILLOPPSSUY polysulphides
DEHMNORRSSTTU thunderstorms
DEIIILMNOOSTT demolitionist
DEIIINNOSSSSU insidiousness
DEIIINNOSSSUV invidiousness
DEIILMNOPRTVY improvidently
DEIILNOOSTTUV devolutionist
DEIINOOOPPRST propositioned
DEIINOOPSSSSS dispossession
DEIJNPRRSSTUU jurisprudents
DEILLNNORSSUW unworldliness
DEILMNOOOPSTU leontopodiums
DEIMMNOOPRSST postmodernism
DEIMNOOPRSSTT postmodernist
DEIOOPRSSSSSS dispossessors
DEIOOPRSSSSSY dispossessory
DFGGHIILLNOOT floodlighting
DFGHIINNOSSTW downshiftings
DFGHIMNOORRSY hydroformings

DFGINNOOOPRSU	soundproofing
DFIINOORSTTUU	fortitudinous
DFILLRSSTTUUY	distrustfully
DGHIIIILMNNSY	diminishingly
DGIIIILNPRSTY	dispiritingly
DGIINNOPPRRTU	roundtripping
DGILNOOOOSSTT	odontologists
DGLMNOOOOSSTU	odontoglossum
DHHIILOOPPPSS	phospholipids
DHIIIMMOOPRSS	isodimorphism
DHIIMOOOPRSSU	isodimorphous
DHILOOPPRSTYY	lipodystrophy
DHINOOORSSTTT	orthodontists
DHNOOOOOPRSTU	odontophorous
DIIIINNOOPSST	indisposition
DIIIINOQSSSTU	disquisitions
DIILMNOSTTUUU	multitudinous
DIILNORSSTUUY	industriously
DIINOOOPPRRST	disproportion
DILNOOOPSSSUY	isospondylous
DLNOOOOPPRTTY	polyprotodont
EEEEELNPRSSSV	Seven Sleepers
EEEEFILNRSSVX	reflexiveness
EEEEGGIINNNRR	reengineering
EEEEGHINORSST	heterogenesis
EEEEGHINORTTY	heterogeneity
EEEEGHNOORSTU	heterogeneous
EEEEGIINOPRSS	epeirogenesis
EEEEHILPQRSTU	telepheriques
EEEEHLMNOPRST	nephelometers
EEEEIMNPRRRTT	preretirement
EEEEIMNPRRSTX	experimenters
EEEEIMNRSSTTX	extensimeters
EEEEINNPSSSVX	expensiveness
EEEEINNQRSSTU	equestriennes
EEEEINNRSSTTV	retentiveness
EEEEINNSSSTVX	extensiveness
EEEEINPQRSSTU	sesquiterpene
EEEELLMOPRRST	Ellesmere Port
EEEELLNPSSSSS	sleeplessness
EEEELMNRSSTTT	resettlements
EEEELNNRSSSSV	nervelessness
EEEELNNSSSSSS	senselessness
EEEEMNOPRRSTT	penetrometers
EEEEMNORSSTTX	extensometers
EEEENNPRRRSTU	entrepreneurs
EEEFFIMORSSTU	effusiometers
EEEFFINNOSSSV	offensiveness
EEEFGILNNNSSU	unfeelingness
EEEFGIMNPRRTU	prefigurement
EEEFGLNRRSSTU	regretfulness
EEEFHILOPPSSY	Isle of Sheppey
EEEFIILLLLMSU	millefeuilles
EEEFINNPRSSSU	superfineness
EEEFLLNORRTTU	fortune-teller
EEEFLNNRSSSTU	resentfulness
EEEFLNOPRSSSU	reposefulness
EEEGGINORSSSU	egregiousness
EEEGHILMNNNTT	enlightenment
EEEGHILRSTTWW	welterweights
EEEGHIMNORSST	thermogenesis
EEEGHNNRRSSTT	strengtheners
EEEGHOORSTTYZ	heterozygotes
EEEGIILMNNSTV	inveiglements
EEEGIILOPRSSU	Siege Perilous
EEEGIIMNNPRTX	experimenting
EEEGIINORSSTV	sovereignties
EEEGILLNSSSSU	guilelessness
EEEGILNNORVWY	overweeningly
EEEGILNOORSTV	venereologist
EEEGILNPRRSVY	perseveringly
EEEGIOQRRSSTU	grotesqueries
EEEGIORRRSSTV	retrogressive
EEEGNOQRSSSTU	grotesqueness
EEEHHIORRSTVW	whithersoever
EEEHIINRRSSST	inheritresses
EEEHILMNNPRST	replenishment
EEEHILMNORSTT	thermotensile
EEEHILMOPRRTY	pyrheliometer
EEEHIMNNNOOPP	epiphenomenon
EEEHIMNRSSTTU	hermeneutists
EEEHIMOPRRSSV	empoverishers
EEEHINNOPRRSS	reprehensions
EEEHIORSSSTTX	heterosexists
EEEHLLNOPSTYY	polyethylenes
EEEHLMNOOSSSW	wholesomeness
EEEHMNOOPRSSS	mesonephroses
EEEHMOORSSSTU	Somerset House
EEEHOOPRRSTTU	heteropterous
EEEIILLNRSSSU	leisureliness
EEEIILNNPSVXY	inexpensively
EEEIINNNSSSTV	intensiveness
EEEIINNNSSTVV	inventiveness
EEEIINNSSSSTV	sensitiveness
EEEIINORSSTVV	oversensitive
EEEIINQRSSSTU	requisiteness
EEEIINQSSSTUX	exquisiteness
EEEIIPQRRSSTU	prerequisites
EEEILNNNPSSSS	pennilessness
EEEILNNOSSSSS	noiselessness
EEEILNNPSSSSS	spinelessness
EEEILNOPSSSVX	explosiveness
EEEILNPRSSSUV	repulsiveness
EEEIMNNPRSSTT	presentiments
EEEIMNOOPRTTT	potentiometer
EEEIMNOORSSTT	enterostomies
EEEIMNORSSSTT	sensitometers
EEEIMNPRRSSST	misrepresents
EEEIMOORRSSST	stereoisomers
EEEIMOPRRSSSV	overimpresses
EEEIMOPRRSSTX	extemporisers
EEEIMOPRRSTXZ	extemporizers
EEEIMPRRRSTTT	pretermitters
EEEINORRSSTUV	enteroviruses
EEEINPRRRSSTT	interpretress
EEEINRRSTTTUX	intertextures
EEEIOPRRSSSSU	superioresses
EEELLMORRSSSY	remorselessly
EEELLMORRSTTU	tellurometers
EEELMNPPRSSTU	supplementers
EEELMOPPRRSTT	teleprompters
EEELNNOPSSSTU	plenteousness
EEELNNOSSSSST	stonelessness
EEELNOPRSSSSW	powerlessness

EEELOOPRSSTTU	teleutospores
EEENNOORRSSSU	erroneousness
EEEOOPRRSSUVX	overexposures
EEEOPRRRSSSUV	overpressures
EEFFGLNORSSTU	forgetfulness
EEFFIILNNOSVY	inoffensively
EEFGGHIIRRSST	triggerfishes
EEFGGILLMNNOR	fellmongering
EEFGHIILNRRST	freightliners
EEFGHIILRSTTW	weightlifters
EEFGHIIPRRSTZ	prizefighters
EEFGHINORSSSU	surgeonfishes
EEFGIILNNRRTY	interferingly
EEFGIIMNNNRST	infringements
EEFGIINNPRRSU	superrefining
EEFGILLOORSTX	reflexologist
EEFGINNOORSST	frontogenesis
EEFHILNNSSSSU	unselfishness
EEFHILNSSSSST	shiftlessness
EEFIIIINORRST	inferiorities
EEFIILLMNOSTU	feuilletonism
EEFIILLNNOSSX	inflexionless
EEFIILLNOSTTU	feuilletonist
EEFIILPRSSTUU	superfluities
EEFILLLLMNTUY	mellifluently
EEFILLNNPSSTU	plentifulness
EEFILLNOOPRSU	polleniferous
EEFILNNOOSSSU	feloniousness
EEFILNOORRSTX	retroflexions
EEFILNRSSSSTU	fruitlessness
EEFILOPRSSTUY	pestiferously
EEFLNRSSSSSTU	stressfulness
EEFMNOORRSSTT	sternforemost
EEGGGHIILNNRT	greenlighting
EEGGHIINORTVW	overweighting
EEGGHINNNRSTT	strengthening
EEGGHMNOOOPRY	geomorphogeny
EEGGIINNNORST	roentgenising
EEGGIINNNORTZ	roentgenizing
EEGGINORRRSST	retrogressing
EEGGLNNOOORTY	roentgenology
EEGHIIKPPRSTZ	Kirghiz Steppe
EEGHIIMNNOOTY	inhomogeneity
EEGHIIMNOPRSV	empoverishing
EEGHIINRSSTUX	extinguishers
EEGHILMNOSSST	lightsomeness
EEGHILNSSSSST	sightlessness
EEGHILOOPRSTT	herpetologist
EEGHIMNNOOOSU	inhomogeneous
EEGHIMNOOPRSS	morphogenesis
EEGHIMNORSTTT	thermosetting
EEGHINORSSSTU	righteousness
EEGHIOORSSTYZ	heterozygosis
EEGHLMNNOOOPY	phenomenology
EEGHLMNOOOSUY	homogeneously
EEGIIINORRSTX	exteriorising
EEGIIINORRTXZ	exteriorizing
EEGIIKLNNOSST	skeletonising
EEGIIKLNNOSTZ	skeletonizing
EEGIILLLNNTTY	intelligently
EEGIILLNNNTTU	unintelligent
EEGIILLNOSTUV	vitelligenous
EEGIILMNOORST	terminologies
EEGIILMOOSSST	semeiologists
EEGIILNNRSTTY	interestingly
EEGIILNORSSSU	religiousness
EEGIIMNOPRRTU	primogeniture
EEGIIMNOPRSTX	extemporising
EEGIIMNOPRTXZ	extemporizing
EEGIIMNPRRTTT	pretermitting
EEGIINNNOSSSU	ingeniousness
EEGIINNNRSTTU	uninteresting
EEGIINNORRTVW	overwintering
EEGIINNPRRSST	interspersing
EEGIINORSSTTV	sovereigntist
EEGILLNNNRTUY	unrelentingly
EEGILLNOOSSST	selenologists
EEGILLNSSSSTU	guiltlessness
EEGILLOOPSSST	speleologists
EEGILMNNPPSTU	supplementing
EEGILMNOOOSST	entomologises
EEGILMNOOOSTZ	entomologizes
EEGILMOOORSTT	meteorologist
EEGILOPRRSSVY	progressively
EEGIMMNNORSTV	misgovernment
EEGINNNOSSSUU	ingenuousness
EEGINOORRRSST	retrogression
EEGINOPPRSSSS	prepossessing
EEGINOPRRSSUV	unprogressive
EEGNNOORRSSUU	neurosurgeons
EEHHIILLLMNPS	philhellenism
EEHHIILLLNPST	philhellenist
EEHHIMNOOPRSW	homeownership
EEHHINOPPRSTT	Pepin the Short
EEHHIOPPRRSSW	horsewhippers
EEHHIOPPRRSTY	hypertrophies
EEHHIOPRSSSTY	hypothesisers
EEHHIOPRSSTYZ	hypothesizers
EEHHLLOPPRSSY	phyllospheres
EEHHMMNOOOPPR	morphophoneme
EEHHOOPRSTTUW	Petworth House
EEHIIILLLPPPV	Philippeville
EEHIIKNNSSSTT	kittenishness
EEHIILNQRRSSU	relinquishers
EEHIIMOOPSSTV	photoemissive
EEHIIMOPRRSSV	impoverishers
EEHIINOPSSSTY	hyposensitise
EEHIINOPSSTYZ	hyposensitize
EEHIKORRSSTWY	West Yorkshire
EEHILLOORSSTT	tortoiseshell
EEHILMNOPPSSY	nympholepsies
EEHILMNRSSSST	mirthlessness
EEHILMOOPPSSY	lymphopoieses
EEHILNNORRSST	northerliness
	Northern Isles
EEHILNOOPSSST	siphonosteles
EEHILNORSSSTU	southerliness
EEHIMOORSSTTY	hysterotomies
EEHIMORSSSSTU	housemistress
EEHLLMNOOSUWY	unwholesomely
EEHLMNORSSSSU	humorlessness
EEHLNORRSTTWY	northwesterly
EEHLNORSSSSTW	worthlessness
EEHLOORSSTTUY	heterostylous

EEHLORSSTTUWY southwesterly
EEHMNNOOORRSU neurohormones
EEHMNNOOPRSTY hymenopterons
EEHMNOOOSSSTT toothsomeness
EEHMNOOPRSTUY hymenopterous
EEHMNOORRSSTT North Somerset
EEHNOOOPRRTXY orthopyroxene
EEHOOOPRRSSTU heterosporous
EEHOOPPSSTTTY phototypesets
EEIIIINSSSTTV sensitivities
EEIIILNNSSTVY insensitively
EEIIIMNPRSSTV primitiveness
EEIIIMOPPRRST improprieties
EEIIINNSSTTUV intuitiveness
EEIIIORRRSSTV Trois-Rivières
EEIILLMNSSSST limitlessness
EEIILMNNPRTTY impertinently
EEIILMNPSSSUV impulsiveness
EEIILMOOSSTTY osteomyelitis
EEIILNNNOSSTV inventionless
EEIILNOORSTUV revolutionise
EEIILNOORTUVZ revolutionize
EEIILNOQRSTUV ventriloquise
EEIILNOQRTUVZ ventriloquize
EEIILOPPRSTVY prepositively
EEIILOPRSTTUY repetitiously
EEIIMNOPRRSSS reimpressions
EEIIMNOPRRSST pretermission
EEIIMNOPRSSSU imperiousness
EEIIMNOPRSSSX expressionism
EEIIMNPRRSSTT misinterprets
EEIIMNRRSTTUX intermixtures
EEIINNNORSTTV interventions
EEIINNOPRRSST interspersion
EEIINNORSSTTT retentionists
EEIINNRSSSTUV intrusiveness
EEIINOPRSSSTX expressionist
EEIJJMNOOSSTU jejunostomies
EEILLLNOPQTUY equipollently
EEILMPPRSTUVY presumptively
EEILNNOPSSSST pointlessness
EEILNNOSSTTUY sententiously
EEILNOOPPRSSY polyisoprenes
EEILNOORRSSTU resolutioners
EEILNOPRSTTUY pretentiously
EEILNPRRSTUUV supervirulent
EEILOOPPRSSST leptospiroses
EEILOPRRSSSTY proselytisers
EEILOPRRSSTYZ proselytizers
EEIMNNNOPRSST prominentness
EEIMNNOOPPRSS perispomenons
EEIMNNORSSSUV verminousness
EEIMNOOPRSSTV promotiveness
EEIMNOOPRTTTY potentiometry
EEIMNOPSSSTUU impetuousness
EEIMOOPRRSSTT stereotropism
EEINNNOPRSSTT nonpersistent
EEINNOPRSSSUU penuriousness
EEINNOPRSTTUU unpretentious
EEINOOPPRSSSS prepossession
EEINOOPRSSSSS repossessions
EEINOORRRSSTV retroversions
EEINOPPRSSSUV purposiveness
EEIOPRSSSTTTY stereotypists
EEKNNOOPSSSTU outspokenness
EEKNOOPPRSSSS spokespersons
EELLNOOPPPRYY polypropylene
EELLOPPRSSSUY purposelessly
EELMNORSSSTUU tremulousness
EELMOPPRRSSUY superpolymers
EELMOPSSTTUUY tempestuously
EELNOQRSSSUUU querulousness
EELNRSSSSSTTU trustlessness
EEMMNNOOSSSTU momentousness
EEMMPRRSSTUYY supersymmetry
EEMNNOOPPSSTT postponements
EENNOOPPRSSTU opportuneness
EENNORSSSSTUU strenuousness
EFFGGILNNORSU longsuffering
EFFGGINOOSTTU gift of tongues
EFFGHILNRSSTU frightfulness
EFFIILOORSSSU fossiliferous
EFGGHIIILNTTW weightlifting
EFGGHIIINPRTZ prizefighting
EFGGHIILNNRTY frighteningly
EFGGIIINNPRSY presignifying
EFGGIINNORSSV forgivingness
EFGHIIILNNSTT thing-in-itself
EFGHIILNORSTT fortnightlies
EFGIKLNNOORWY foreknowingly
EFGIMNOOPRRTU outperforming
EFHIOOPPRRSSS professorship
EFIILLNOOPRSU polliniferous
EFIIMNOPSSSTT postfeminists
EFIINOPRSSSTU perfusionists
EFIKLLNNSSSUU unskilfulness
EFILLLLMOSUUY mellifluously
EFILMNOORSSUY somniferously
EFILNOOORSSTU stoloniferous
EFILNOORSSSUV frivolousness
EFLLOPRSSUUUY superfluously
EFLNOORRSSSUW sorrowfulness
EGGHIIINNSTUX extinguishing
EGGHLMOOOOPRY geomorphology
EGGIIILMNNNRT intermingling
EGGIIINNNORST nitrogenising
EGGIIINNNORTZ nitrogenizing
EGGIILMNOOSTY etymologising
EGGIILMNOOTYZ etymologizing
EGGILNOOORSTT gerontologist
EGGIMNOOPRSSS gossipmongers
EGHHIILOPRSTY hieroglyphist
EGHHIINOPPRSW horsewhipping
EGHHIINOPSSTY hypothesising
EGHHIINOPSTYZ hypothesizing
EGHHILLMNOOTY helminthology
EGHHLLOSSTTUY thoughtlessly
EGHHMORRSTTUY merrythoughts
EGHIIILNNQRSU relinquishing
EGHIIILNRRSST Stirlingshire
EGHIIIMNOPRSV impoverishing
EGHIILMNNOPSY sphingomyelin
EGHIILNNSSSTU unsightliness
EGHIILNPRSSST sprightliness

EGHIILOOOPRST oligotrophies
EGHIIMNOOPSSY physiognomies
EGHIIMNOPSSTY physostigmine
EGHIINPRSSTTU guttersnipish
EGHILMOORSSTY mythologisers
EGHILMOORSTYZ mythologizers
EGHILNOOPRSST nephrologists
phrenologists
EGHILNORSTUUY unrighteously
EGHILNPRSTTUU sulphuretting
EGHILOOPPSSST psephologists
EGHIMNNORRSTU nursing mother
EGHINOOPRRSSV governorships
EGIIIILNORRST irreligionist
EGIIIINNORRST interiorising
EGIIIINNORRTZ interiorizing
EGIIIKLLNNRTW winterkilling
EGIIIKNNNRTTT interknitting
EGIIILLORRSUY irreligiously
EGIIILNOSSSTU litigiousness
EGIIINNOOPRST repositioning
EGIIINNRSTTTW intertwisting
EGIIKLNPPRRSS klipspringers
EGIILLLOOSTVX vexillologist
EGIILLNNNSSUW unwillingness
EGIILLNORSUUY unreligiously
EGIILMNNRTTUY unremittingly
EGIILMNOORSTT terminologist
EGIILMOOSSSST seismologists
EGIILNNOQSTUY questioningly
EGIILNOPRSSTY proselytising
EGIILNOPRSTYZ proselytizing
EGIILNORSTUVY vertiginously
EGIILOOOSSTTV sovietologist
EGIILOPRSSTUY prestigiously
EGIIMNNNNOPSY moneyspinning
EGIIMNNNRSTTU instrumenting
EGIIMNOOPRRST primogenitors
EGIIMNOPPRSSU superimposing
EGIIMOPRRSSSV progressivism
EGIINNNOQSTUU unquestioning
EGIINNNSSTTUW unwittingness
EGIINNOORRSST introgression
EGIIOPRRSSSTV progressivist
EGILLNNOORSST Rolling Stones
EGILMNOOOSSTT entomologists
EGILMNOORSSTU numerologists
EGILMNOOSSTYZ enzymologists
EGILNNOSSSTUU glutinousness
EGILNOPPRSUVY oversupplying
EGMMNOOPRSSUY gymnospermous
EHHHIOOPPPSTY hypophosphite
EHHIILOOPPRSS philosophiser
EHHIILOOPPRSZ philosophizer
EHHIILOOPPSSS philosophises
EHHIILOOPPSSZ philosophizes
EHHILMOOPRSTU thermophilous
EHHIMMMOOOPRS homeomorphism
EHHIMMNOORSTU Monmouthshire
EHHIMNOOPRSST thermosiphons
EHHINOOOPPRSS siphonophores
EHHMMOOOOPRSU homeomorphous
EHHMNOOOPRSTY phytohormones
EHIIILLOPPPSU Louis Philippe
EHIIIMNPRSSST ministerships
EHIIKLMOOPRTY poikilothermy
EHIILLMNPSSTU phillumenists
EHIILLNOPSSTT septillionths
EHIILLNOSSTTX sextillionths
EHIILMOOPPSSY lymphopoiesis
EHIILNOOOPSSU eosinophilous
EHIILNOQRSSSU liquorishness
EHIILOPRRSTTT lithotripters
EHIIMNOOOPSST photoemission
EHIINOOOPRSST iontophoresis
EHIIOOOPPSTTV photopositive
EHILLNNOOPQUY phylloquinone
EHILMNOOOPSTU entomophilous
EHILNOPSSSTYY polysynthesis
EHIMMOOPRRSTT thermotropism
EHIMOOPRSSTTT photometrists
EHIMOPRSSSTTY hypsometrists
EHLLLOOPPSTUY leptophyllous
EHLLNOOPSSTUY stenophyllous
EHLLOPRSSUUUY sulphureously
EHLMOOOPPRSTY photopolymers
EHNNOOOPRSTTU photoneutrons
EIIIILNQSTUVY inquisitively
EIIIINNQSTUUV uninquisitive
EIIIINNSSTTVY insensitivity
EIIILLMOOPSTY poliomyelitis
EIIILNSTTTUVY institutively
EIIIMMNOPRSSS impressionism
EIIIMMNORSSST immersionists
EIIIMNNORSSST intermissions
EIIIMNNPRSSTT inspiritments
EIIIMNOOPRSST reimpositions
EIIIMNOPRSSST impressionist
EIIINNOOPRSTT interposition
EIIJNNORSSSUU injuriousness
EIILLOOQRSSSU soliloquisers
EIILLOOQRSSUZ soliloquizers
EIILMNOQRSTUV ventriloquism
EIILMOORRSTUY meritoriously
EIILNOORRSSTU irresolutions
EIILNOORSSTTU resolutionist
EIILNOORSTTUV revolutionist
EIILNOOSSTTUV evolutionists
EIILNOQRSTTUV ventriloquist
EIILNORRSSSTY sinistrorsely
EIILOOPPRSSST leptospirosis
EIILOPPSSTUVY suppositively
EIIMMNNOPRSST imprisonments
EIIMNOORSSSTT monstrosities
EIIMOOPRSSTTV overoptimists
EIINNNOOSSSUX innoxiousness
EIINNOORRSSTV introversions
EIINNOOSSTTVY tenosynovitis
EIINNOPRRSTTU interruptions
EIINOOPPRSSTU superposition
EIINOOPPRSTTU opportunities
EIINOORSSTTTX extortionists
EIINOPRSSSTTU superstitions
EIIOOPPRSSSTU suppositories

EIIOOPPSSSTTV	postpositives
EIIOPRRSSTTUU	surreptitious
EIIOPRSSSTTUU	superstitious
EILNNOOPPRTUY	inopportunely
EILNORSSSUUUX	luxuriousness
EINNNOOOPSSSS	nonpossession
EINNOOOPSSSSU	poisonousness
EINNOOORSSSTU	notoriousness
EINNOPSSTUUUX	Pontus Euxinus
EMNNOORSSSSTU	monstrousness
EMNOPSSSSTUUU	sumptuousness
ENOOPPRRSSSST	sportspersons
FGILOORSSTTUU	futurologists
FGLMNNOOOOOSS	Song of Solomon
FILLMRSSTTUUY	mistrustfully
GGGHHINOOORTU	thoroughgoing
GGGHILNNOORSW	hornswoggling
GGHIILMNOOSTY	mythologising
GGHIILMNOOTYZ	mythologizing
GGILLOOOSSSST	glossologists
GHIILLOOPSSTY	syphilologist
GHIILNOOORSTT	ornithologist
GHIILOOPSSSTY	physiologists
GHIIMMOOPRSTT	thigmotropism
GHIIMNOOPSSTY	physiognomist
GHILMOOOPRSST	morphologists
GHIMNOOPSSSTY	gymnosophists
GIIIILNNPRSTY	inspiritingly
GIIIKLLLMNSTU	multiskilling
GIIILLNOOQSSU	soliloquising
GIIILLNOOQSUZ	soliloquizing
GIIILMNNOOSUY	ignominiously
GIILMMNOOSSTU	immunologists
GIINNOOOPPRRT	proportioning
GILLLMOOPSSYY	polysyllogism
HHIMOOOPRRSUZ	rhizomorphous
HIIILLNNOQTTU	quintillionth
HIIILLOOPPPPS	Philippopolis
HIILLOOPPRSWW	whippoorwills
HIIMMNOOPSSTY	monophysitism
HILMNOOPSSUYY	symphoniously
HILORRSTTTUWY	trustworthily
HLLNOOOPPSUYY	polyphonously
HNORRSTTTUUWY	untrustworthy
IIIINNOSSTTTU	intuitionists
IIIMNNOORSSST	intromissions
IIIMNOORSTTUV	vomiturítions
IIINNORSSTTTU	nutritionists
IIINOOOPPSSTT	oppositionist
IILLLORSSTUUY	illustriously
IILMNOOQSSSTU	somniloquists
IILNOOOPSSTTU	lotus position
IIMNOOOPPRRST	misproportion
IINNOOPPRTTUY	inopportunity
IINOOOPPSSSTT	postpositions

Fourteen Letters

AAAAAACCEEMRSZ	Caesarea Mazaca
AAAAAADHMNNRST	Sanatana Dharma
AAAAACGILMMNRT	anagrammatical
AAAAACHHKNRRSY	Shankaracharya
AAAAAGGINNRRTT	rangatiratanga
AAAABBCEILRSTY	sabbatical year
AAAABCCEEHIRRT	archaebacteria
AAAABCCEELRSTU	baccalaureates
AAAABCFIIJLNOR	Baja California
AAAABEHKLLLMRU	Mahalla el Kubra
AAAACCDEINORSU	anacardiaceous
AAAACCILLPRTTY	paratactically
AAAACCINNRSSTU	transcaucasian
AAAACCLMNORSST	malacostracans
AAAACDIILLNNST	Catalina Island
AAAACDIILLPRSY	paradisaically
	paradisiacally
AAAACDIIMMNOST	macadamisation
AAAACDIIMMNOTZ	macadamization
AAAACEGILLMMNO	megalomaniacal
AAAACEHMNORSTU	amaranthaceous
AAAACEIMNNRRST	sacramentarian
AAAACHIILNNRSS	Halicarnassian
AAAADDDGIMNNOU	Goa, Daman, and Diu
AAAADDILMNNNSS	Andaman Islands
AAAADEGIMMNRST	anagrammatised
AAAADEGIMMNRTZ	anagrammatized
AAAADEGINNQRRU	quadragenarian
AAAADELLLNORRV	Andorra la Vella
AAAADIILMNNRSS	Mariana Islands
AAAADIKLLNNSSU	Unalaska Island
AAAAEGIMMNRSST	anagrammatises
AAAAEGIMMNRSTZ	anagrammatizes
AAAAFIILNNPRRS	infralapsarian
AAAAGGNOORSTUW	Ogasawara Gunto
AAAAGHIMNOPRST	phantasmagoria
AAAAGIMMNRSSTT	anagrammatists
AAAAHHIKMNPSTV	Vishakhapatnam
AAAAHIIMNNNSST	Mina Hassan Tani
AAAAIILLNOPSTT	palatalisation
AAAAIILLNOPTTZ	palatalization
AAAAILLNPRSSTU	Australian Alps
AAAAILNPPRRSSU	supralapsarian
AAABBEEGLLNOOR	Boolean algebra
AAABBHIIJNNRYY	Jabir ibn Hayyan
AAABBLLNNOORTW	Walloon Brabant
AAABCCDLLLMSUU	lambda calculus
AAABCCEIILLMST	acclimatisable
AAABCCEIILLMTZ	acclimatizable
AAABCCILMNNOOY	cyanocobalamin
AAABCDEGINOSTU	Santiago de Cuba
AAABCDILNNOORY	Calydonian boar
AAABCEFLMNRTUU	manufacturable
AAABCEHILLLPTY	alphabetically
AAABCEHILMOSTT	haematoblastic
AAABCEHILNOPPR	inapproachable
AAABCEHLNOPPRU	unapproachable
AAABCEILMNOSSU	balsaminaceous
AAABCHILNOPPRY	inapproachably
AAABCHLNOPPRUY	unapproachably
AAABDEEMRSSSSS	ambassadresses
AAABDHIMOPRSSS	ambassadorship
AAABDIINORSSTT	bastardisation
AAABDIINORSTTZ	bastardization
AAABEEEGLMNNSS	manageableness
AAABEEGILMNRRU	unmarriageable
AAABEEILNNSSTT	attainableness
AAABEGIILLNOUV	bougainvillaea
AAABEIIIILLSTV	availabilities
AAABEILNOOPSTT	palaeobotanist
AAABELLNNPRSTT	transplantable
AAABELLNNRSTTU	untranslatable
AAABGILNQSTTUU	absquatulating
AAABHHNOPSTTUW	Bophuthatswana
AAABIIKLNNOSST	balkanisations
AAABIIKLNNOSTZ	balkanizations
AAABIILLNRRSTV	Brillat-Savarin
AAABIILNOOPRST	parabolisation
AAABIILNOOPRTZ	parabolization
AAABIILNRRTTWY	warrantability
AAACCCEHILRSTT	catachrestical
AAACCCEINNORTT	Antarctic Ocean
AAACCDEHIINORT	archidiaconate
AAACCDEIMNNOOR	adenocarcinoma
AAACCDEIOPPRSU	capparidaceous
AAACCDILORRSUV	cardiovascular
AAACCEEHILMNOR	aeromechanical
AAACCEEHILMNPR	macrencephalia
AAACCEEILMNRRT	Central America
AAACCEEINNQRTU	reacquaintance
AAACCEGHILLOOR	archaeological
AAACCEHILMPRTU	pharmaceutical
AAACCEHLNNNTUY	Yucatán Channel
AAACCEILNNORTX	extracanonical

AAACCELMNOPSUU	campanulaceous
AAACCGHILOPRRT	cartographical
AAACCGIIINNPTT	incapacitating
AAACCGILLMNOOP	campanological
AAACCHIILNRSTT	charlatanistic
AAACCHIINORSST	saccharisation
AAACCHIINORSTZ	saccharization
AAACCHILLMORTY	achromatically
AAACCHILLNNORY	anachronically
AAACCIIINNOPTT	incapacitation
AAACCILLORTTUY	autocratically
AAACCLMOORSSTU	malacostracous
AAACDDEIIORTTV	radioactivated
AAACDEEINPPRSS	disappearances
AAACDEELOPRRTX	Electra paradox
AAACDEIIINPRST	paediatricians
AAACDEIIORSTTV	radioactivates
AAACDEILLNPRSS	Paracel Islands
AAACDFHIMNNRST	handicraftsman
AAACDGMNORSSTU	coastguardsman
AAACDHHILMNSST	Chatham Islands
AAACDHIINOPRSS	anaphrodisiacs
AAACDHILNOOPRS	achondroplasia
AAACDHINNRSTTU	Tristan da Cunha
AAACDIILNNOSST	scandalisation
AAACDIILNNOSTZ	scandalization
AAACDNOOPRRSTX	Cantor's paradox
AAACEEGIILNSTT	telangiectasia
AAACEEGILMNOPT	palaeomagnetic
AAACEEGILNSSTU	Aguascalientes
AAACEEILLNORRS	Alsace-Lorraine
AAACEEILNORSUV	valerianaceous
AAACEENNNOPPRS	nonappearances
AAACEFGIORSSUX	saxifragaceous
AAACEFIILNORRT	rareficational
AAACEGHILLMOOT	haematological
AAACEGINSSTUWY	Giant's Causeway
AAACEHIILNPTTT	antipathetical
AAACEHIIMMNSTT	mathematicians
AAACEHIIMNPRSS	Spanish America
AAACEHILLLMPRY	alphamerically
AAACEHILLMMTTY	mathematically
AAACEHILMOOPPR	pharmacopoeial
AAACEHILMPRSTT	metaphrastical
AAACEHILNOPPRT	palaeanthropic
AAACEHIMOOPPRS	pharmacopoeias
AAACEILLMNNSTY	anamnestically
AAACEILLMSTTTY	metastatically
AAACEILLNORTUY	aeronautically
AAACEILMMNRSST	sacramentalism
AAACEILMNRSSTT	sacramentalist
AAACEILMNRSTTY	sacramentality
AAACFIILLLSTTY	fatalistically
AAACFIILNSTTTY	fantasticality
AAACFIMNORRSTW	aircraftswoman
AAACGGHHIILOPR	hagiographical
AAACGGHIIMNOST	gigantomachias
AAACGHILLLNPYY	anaglyphically
AAACGHILNOPRRU	uranographical
AAACGHIMNOPRST	phantasmagoric
AAACGIILLMSTTY	astigmatically
AAACGIILLNPSTY	paganistically
AAACGIILMPRTTY	pragmaticality
AAACGILLMNORTY	morganatically
AAACGILNNOSTTU	anticoagulants
AAACGIMNOOPRRS	macrosporangia
AAACGLORRSSTUV	gastrovascular
AAACHIILMMRRST	matriarchalism
AAACHIILNOPSTT	chaptalisation
AAACHIILNOPTTZ	chaptalization
AAACHILLLLOPTY	allopathically
AAACHILLMNPSTY	phantasmically
AAACHILMMNNOPY	nymphomaniacal
AAACHILMOPRTTU	thaumatropical
AAACIIILNOPSTT	capitalisation
AAACIIILNOPTTZ	capitalization
AAACIIILNPSTTT	anticapitalist
AAACIILNOSSSTU	casualisations
AAACIILNOSSTUZ	casualizations
AAACILLLLOPRTY	allopatrically
AAADDEELNORRST	Andrea del Sarto
AAADDEHLLNRRUY	Laurel and Hardy
AAADDGGIINNSTV	disadvantaging
AAADEEGIIKKNRR	Kierkegaardian
AAADEGILMNRRTY	Admiralty Range
AAADEGILNQRSTU	Griqualand East
AAADEGLNOSTUVY	advantageously
AAADEHIMNORSTU	adiathermanous
AAADEIILLNNOSS	Aeolian Islands
AAADEIILNNRTUV	valetudinarian
AAADEILLNNPSST	Pleasant Island
AAADEILLQRRSTU	quadrilaterals
AAADEILNRSTTTY	Latter-day Saint
AAADFHNNOOPTUY	Anthony of Padua
AAADGHIOOPRRTU	autoradiograph radioautograph
AAADGIKLNNOORS	Kangaroo Island
AAADIIILNNRTTU	latitudinarian
AAADIILNNSSSVY	Visayan Islands
AAADIIMNORSSTT	dramatisations
AAADIIMNORSTTZ	dramatizations
AAADIJLNNNSSSU	San Juan Islands
AAADIJNNNORRST	Trans-Jordanian
AAADILLNRSSSTU	Austral Islands
AAAEEEGKLLRSTV	Great Slave Lake
AAAEEGHLOPPRRS	palaeographers
AAAEEGINNPPUUW	Papua New Guinea
AAAEEGINNPRSTU	septuagenarian
AAAEEGLLNPRSTU	Langres Plateau
AAAEEHHLMMORTT	haematothermal
AAAEEHIIMNRRTT	Henrietta Maria
AAAEEIKLMNNRSZ	Mariánské Lázně
AAAEEJMNNRSTVY	Vestmannaeyjar
AAAEFGGLLMNORU	formal language
AAAEFIILMMRSST	matresfamilias
AAAEFIILMPRSST	patresfamilias
AAAEGHHMOOPSTU	haematophagous
AAAEGHIIMNNSTT	anathematising
AAAEGHIIMNNTTZ	anathematizing
AAAEGHLNNOPRSY	nasopharyngeal
AAAEGIIILMNRST	egalitarianism
AAAEGIILMNRSST	managerialists
AAAEGILMNORSSU	megalosaurians
AAAEGINORSTTVX	extravagations

AAAEGLLLMOPRRS	parallelograms
AAAEGMMNORRTTT	tetragrammaton
AAAEHIMOPRRSTT	aromatherapist
AAAEHINOSSSTTU	Southeast Asian
AAAEIIILMPRRST	paramilitaries
AAAEILLMNNPSUY	Malay Peninsula
AAAEIMMMNRRSTU	armamentariums
AAAEIMORRSSTTT	tarsometatarsi
AAAEINORSSTTVX	extravasations
AAAGHINRRSTUUY	Austria-Hungary
AAAGIILNNOORST	organisational
AAAGIILNNOORTZ	organizational
AAAGIINNNOOSTT	antagonisation
AAAGIINNNOOTTZ	antagonization
AAAGINOORRSTTV	astronavigator
AAAHIINORRSTTU	authoritarians
AAAHIIOPPRRSUW	pipiwharauroas
AAAHILORSSTTUU	South Australia
AAAIIIMNNQRSTU	antiquarianism
AAAIILMNNOSTTU	Altai Mountains
AAAIILNNORSTTU	naturalisation
AAAIILNNORTTUZ	naturalization
AAAIILNNOSSTTT	tantalisations
AAAIILNNOSTTTZ	tantalizations
AAAIIMNNOOSSTT	anatomisations
AAAIIMNNOOSTTZ	anatomizations
AAAIIMNOORSSTT	aromatisations
AAAIIMNOOSTTTU	automatisation
AAAIIMNOOTTTUZ	automatization
AAAIIMNORSTTTU	traumatisation
AAAIIMNORTTTUZ	traumatization
AAAIINNORSSTTV	intravasations
AAAIINNOSSSSST	assassinations
AAAILLMPRRSUXY	supramaxillary
AAAILLNNOOPRSY	Annapolis Royal
AAAILMNNOSSTTU	Atlas Mountains
AAAILNNORSTTUV	transvaluation
AAAIMNNNOSSTUY	Sayan Mountains
AAAIMNNORSTTTU	Tatra Mountains
AABBCEEFINORST	absorbefacient
AABBCEHHISSTTW	witches' Sabbath
AABBDGGIINNNOR	brobdingnagian
AABBEEELNNRSSU	unbearableness
AABBEFGGILNRST	flabbergasting
AABBEFHILMNRST	Flemish Brabant
AABBEFINNOSTUY	Fountains Abbey
AABBEIILLOSSSU	bouillabaisses
AABBEILNRTTTUU	unattributable
AABBHIIIILNTTY	inhabitability
AABCCCDHILRTYY	brachydactylic
AABCCCEHHILPRY	brachycephalic
AABCCCEHKRRSST	backscratchers
AABCCCGHIKNRST	backscratching
AABCCDEILMOTUU	bioaccumulated
AABCCDEILNORTT	contradictable
AABCCEEELNPSST	acceptableness
AABCCEELNNORTU	counterbalance
AABCCEGHIIOPRT	bacteriophagic
AABCCEHILLMOPS	accomplishable
AABCCEHNOOORSU	orobanchaceous
AABCCEIIORSTTT	bacteriostatic
AABCCEILMMRTUU	circumambulate
AABCCEILMOSTUU	bioaccumulates
AABCCEIMNORTUY	cyanobacterium
AABCCIIILPRTTY	practicability
AABCCIILNOTTUY	accountability
AABCDDEEHKNNSS	backhandedness
AABCDDEELLLOSY	dodecasyllable
AABCDEEEHLNRRW	Hebrew calendar
AABCDEEFIILLSS	declassifiable
AABCDEEHNNRUZZ	nebuchadnezzar
AABCDEEINRRSTT	scatterbrained
AABCDEEIRRSTUU	bureaucratised
AABCDEEIRRTUUZ	bureaucratized
AABCDEELNORRST	labradorescent
AABCDEENNPRSUU	superabundance
AABCDEENRSSSTT	abstractedness
AABCDEGINORRST	rebroadcasting
AABCDEHHLOSUYZ	Ashby-de-la-Zouch
AABCDEIIILLNOSS	diabolicalness
AABCDEILMNNRRU	cardinal number
AABCDEINORRSTU	decarburations
AABCDELLLORTYY	Barclay de Tolly
AABCDHIKLNOPSU	Bishop Auckland
AABCDIILNNORSS	Nicobar Islands
AABCDINNORSSTT	contrabandists
AABCEEEGHLNNSS	changeableness
AABCEEEGHLNRSS	chargeableness
AABCEEEHILLMNP	Blenheim Palace
AABCEEGHIOPRST	bacteriophages
AABCEEHILNRSST	charitableness
AABCEEHILOPRRR	irreproachable
AABCEEHLMNNRTU	unmerchantable
AABCEEIILLPRTY	replaceability
AABCEEILLLMMTY	emblematically
AABCEEILLMNPSS	implacableness
AABCEEILLNPPSS	applicableness
AABCEEILMNRSSV	vraisemblances
AABCEEIORSSSTT	bacteriostases
AABCEEIRRSSTUU	bureaucratises
AABCEEIRRSTUUZ	bureaucratizes
AABCEELMNOPRSS	comparableness
AABCEFGIINPRRT	prefabricating
AABCEFIIINOSTT	beatifications
AABCEFIIINOTTU	beautification
AABCEFIINOPRRT	prefabrication
AABCEFIINORSTT	abortifacients
AABCEFIOPRRRST	prefabricators
AABCEGHILNORST	branchiostegal
AABCEGIILLOOOR	aerobiological
AABCEHIIILMPTY	impeachability
AABCEHIIMMOSTT	biomathematics
AABCEHILOPRRRY	irreproachably
AABCEHINOORSTT	archeobotanist
AABCEIIILLORSST	aeroballistics
AABCEIILNNPRTU	antirepublican
AABCEIILRRTTTY	retractability
AABCEIILRTTTXY	extractability
AABCEIINOORSTU	bioaeronautics
AABCEIIORSSSTT	bacteriostasis
AABCEILLLRSSTY	crystallisable
AABCEILLLRSTYZ	crystallizable
AABCEILLMORRTY	barometrically
AABCEILNORSSTU	constabularies

AABCEIMOORSSUU	simaroubaceous
AABCELNOOPRSTY	polycarbonates
AABCFILNNOOSTU	confabulations
AABCGGIILLOOOR	agrobiological
AABCGHIILLMOOP	amphibological
AABCGHIILLOPRY	biographically
AABCGHIMOOPRRR	microbarograph
AABCHIILPRSTUY	purchasability
AABCHILOOPRSTU	claustrophobia
AABCIIILLMPRSY	imparisyllabic
AABCIIILNRTTTY	intractability
AABCIILLLOPSTY	collapsability
AABCIILLNOSSTY	syllabications
AABCIIMNORSSTT	abstractionism
AABCIINNOORSST	carbonisations
AABCIINNOORSTZ	carbonizations
AABCIINOOSSSTU	subassociation
AABCIINORRSSTU	carburisations
AABCIINORRSTUZ	carburizations
AABCIINORSSTTT	abstractionist
AABCIKLMNNOSTU	Black Mountains
AABCILLLLOPSYY	polysyllabical
AABCILLNOOORST	collaborations
AABCILLORRRTUU	arboricultural
AABCILMNNOOTTU	noctambulation
AABCILNNOSSTTU	consubstantial
AABCINORSSSSTT	contrabassists
AABCNNOOORSSST	contrabassoons
AABDDEEIMRRSSS	disembarrassed
AABDDEELNNRSTU	understandable
AABDDEGIINOORT	biodegradation
AABDDEIILRSSTY	addressability
AABDDELNNRSTUY	understandably
AABDEEEFHINRRT	featherbrained
AABDEEEHHIRRSS	haberdasheries
AABDEEEHNRRSST	threadbareness
AABDEEELNNRSSU	unreadableness
AABDEEELOORRTV	overelaborated
AABDEEFIIORRRS	barrier of ideas
AABDEEGIKRRSUZ	Gaudier-Brzeska
AABDEEIMNNORSS	Basse-Normandie
AABDEEIMRRSSSS	disembarrasses
AABDEELLMNORSU	Albemarle Sound
AABDEFIIILLQSU	disqualifiable
AABDEGIILMNRSS	Gambier Islands
AABDEIIILMNOPR	imponderabilia
AABDEIIKMNORST	disembarkation
AABDEIILPRSTUY	persuadability
AABDEIINOOSTTU	autoantibodies
AABDGGIIIMNSTU	disambiguating
AABDGIIIMNOSTU	disambiguation
AABDHIMNORSSTT	rhabdomantists
AABDIIIILNSTVY	inadvisability
AABDIIILNOTUVY	unavoidability
AABDIINOOPPRST	disapprobation
AABEEEKLMNRRSS	remarkableness
AABEEEKLMNRSST	marketableness
AABEEELLMNNSST	lamentableness
AABEEELMNRSSSU	measurableness
AABEEELNNORSSS	reasonableness
AABEEELNNOSSSS	seasonableness
AABEEELNNRSSSW	answerableness
AABEEELOORRSTV	overelaborates
AABEEFLNNRRSTU	untransferable
AABEEFLNORSSUV	favourableness
AABEEGLMMOPRRR	reprogrammable
AABEEGLNOPPRSS	propagableness
AABEEHIIILRTTV	rehabilitative
AABEEHIILRTTWY	weatherability
AABEEHKLNNSSSU	unshakableness
AABEEIILMNOTTT	antimetabolite
AABEEIILNNRSSV	invariableness
AABEEIILNNSSST	insatiableness
AABEEILLNNSSUV	invaluableness
AABEEILMNPSSSS	impassableness
AABEELLLRSSTTY	tetrasyllables
AABEELNNRRSTUY	subterraneanly
AABEEMMNRRSSST	embarrassments
AABEFIILNNQTUU	unquantifiable
AABEFILLMMNNNO	noninflammable
AABEGHIIILNRTT	rehabilitating
AABEGHIKLNRTTY	breathtakingly
AABEGHIOOPRRTU	autobiographer
AABEGIILLNOSUV	bougainvilleas
AABEGILMNRRSSY	embarrassingly
AABEGLMNRSSTUU	Albertus Magnus
AABEHIIILNORTT	rehabilitation
AABEHLLOPPRSTY	blepharoplasty
AABEHLMNOOPRST	nephroblastoma
AABEHLMOPPRSSS	blepharospasms
AABEIIIILLNNTY	inalienability
AABEIIILLNORST	liberalisation
AABEIIILLNORTZ	liberalization
AABEIIILLNRTTY	inalterability
AABEIIILMNRRST	libertarianism
AABEIIILNPRSTY	inseparability
AABEIIILPRRRTY	irreparability
AABEIILNORSSTV	verbalisations
AABEIILNORSTVZ	verbalizations
AABEIILNSSSTTU	substantialise
AABEIILNSSTTUZ	substantialize
AABEIINSSTTTUV	substantiative
AABEILMNOPRSTU	perambulations
AABEILNNORSTTU	subalternation
AABEINOOPRRRTY	reprobationary
AABFHIIILNOSTY	fashionability
AABFIIILLMMNTY	inflammability
AABFIILLNPPTUY	unflappability
AABGIINNSSTTTU	substantiating
AABGILMMNNOSTU	somnambulating
AABHIIILNPRRSS	librarianships
AABHIIINPPRSST	bipartisanship
AABIIILLMNPTUY	manipulability
AABIIILNOSSSTT	stabilisations
AABIIILNOSSTTZ	stabilizations
AABIILLNOOPTTX	blaxploitation
AABIILLNPRSSUY	Salisbury Plain
AABIILMNSSSTTU	substantialism
AABIILNNNRTTUY	tintinnabulary
AABIILNORSSTTU	brutalisations
AABIILNORSTTUZ	brutalizations
AABIILNSSSTTTU	substantialist
AABIILNSSTTTUY	substantiality
AABIINNOSSTTTU	substantiation

AABILLLNNOPRRU	Nullarbor Plain
AABILLNSSTTUVY	substantivally
AABILMMNNOOSTU	somnambulation
AABINORSSSTTTU	substantiators
AABINORSSSTTUU	subsaturations
AABLMMNOORSSTU	somnambulators
AACCCEEGINORSY	gynaecocracies
AACCCEEHILLTTY	catechetically
AACCCEEHILMNTU	catechumenical
AACCCEEIILLSST	ecclesiastical
AACCCEHHILOPPS	scaphocephalic
AACCCEHIIRRSTT	characteristic
AACCCFIIILNOST	calcifications
AACCCGHHILNNRU	Anglican Church
AACCCHILLNOOPY	cacophonically
AACCCHLLOOPSTY	staphylococcal
AACCCILNOORSTT	social contract
AACCDDEEILMOPR	El Cid Campeador
AACCDDEMMNOOTU	unaccommodated
AACCDDIIIORTUV	Ciudad Victoria
AACCDEEHINORRS	archdeaconries
AACCDEEILNOPSY	encyclopaedias
AACCDEHIIRRSST	trisaccharides
AACCDEHILOPRSY	polysaccharide
AACCDEHIMNOORS	monosaccharide
AACCDEIILLOPTY	apodeictically
AACCDEIILMNTUZ	unacclimatized
AACCDEIIMNORTT	antidemocratic
AACCDEIINNORTT	contraindicate
AACCDEILLMORTY	democratically
AACCDEILLMRTUV	circumvallated
AACCDFIIILNPSS	Pacific Islands
AACCDGHILOPRTY	dactylographic
AACCDHIMOPRSTY	psychodramatic
AACCDIIINRSTTU	traducianistic
AACCDIINNNORTT	contraindicant
AACCDIMMNOOOST	accommodations
AACCEEEHMNSTTU	catechumenates
AACCEEENORTTUV	overaccentuate
AACCEEGHILLMOP	megalocephalic
AACCEEGIILNTTT	telangiectatic
AACCEEHILMNNSS	mechanicalness
AACCEEHILMNOST	catecholamines
AACCEEHILMORTT	tacheometrical
AACCEEHIMRRSST	saccharimeters
AACCEEHIRRRSST	characterisers
AACCEEHIRRRSTZ	characterizers
AACCEEHMORRSST	saccharometers
AACCEEINNNORSS	reconnaissance
AACCEEINNRSSTU	inaccurateness
AACCEELLPPRRSW	clapperclawers
AACCEFLNORTTUU	counterfactual
AACCEGGILLNOOY	gynaecological
AACCEGHHLOPRRS	chalcographers
AACCEGHIINRRST	characterising
AACCEGHIINRRTZ	characterizing
AACCEGHILLOOST	eschatological
AACCEGHILNOPRS	scenographical
AACCEGIILOOPTT	galactopoietic
AACCEGIIMNRTUV	circumnavigate
AACCEGILLNPPRW	clapperclawing
AACCEGINNOSTUY	nyctaginaceous
AACCEHHIILLRRY	hierarchically
AACCEHHIMNNRRU	Armenian Church
AACCEHIILOPPRS	archiepiscopal
AACCEHIILQRRSU	squirearchical
AACCEHIINOSSTT	catechisations
AACCEHIKLOOSVZ	Czechoslovakia
AACCEHILLORTTY	theocratically
AACCEHILLPRTYY	archetypically
AACCEHINOPPRRT	parthenocarpic
AACCEHLMOOPRSU	macrocephalous
AACCEHLOOPRSSY	polysaccharose
AACCEIIILPRSTT	practicalities
AACCEIILLMORRT	calorimetrical
AACCEIILMNORRT	craniometrical
AACCEIILMNORTT	actinometrical
AACCEIINNORRST	incarcerations
AACCEIINNORSTV	revaccinations
AACCEIINOPRSST	pantisocracies
AACCEILLLOPPTY	apoplectically
AACCEILLLOPRVY	prevocalically
AACCEILLMRSTUV	circumvallates
AACCEILLMTUUVY	accumulatively
AACCEIMMNNOPST	accompaniments
AACCEINNNOOSTT	concatenations
AACCEIOQRSSTTU	squattocracies
AACCEKNORSTTTU	counterattacks
AACCELLMMOORRU	macromolecular
AACCELNNORSUUU	ranunculaceous
AACCELOOPRSTUU	portulacaceous
AACCENNORSSSST	sacrosanctness
AACCFFILNOPRSY	cycloparaffins
AACCFHILNOOSSU	Nicholas of Cusa
AACCFIIILNORST	clarifications
AACCFIIILNOSST	classification
AACCFIIINNORST	carnifications
AACCFIIINNOSTT	sanctification
AACCFIIINOPRST	caprifications
AACCFIILORSSTY	classificatory
AACCGHHIILNOPR	ichnographical
AACCGHHIILOPRR	chirographical
AACCGHHILOOPRR	chorographical
AACCGHHILOPRST	chalcographist
AACCGHIILLLORY	oligarchically
AACCGHIILNOOPR	iconographical
AACCGHIILNOPRZ	zincographical
AACCGHILMOOPRS	cosmographical
AACCGHILNOPSVY	psychogalvanic
AACCGIILLLMOOT	climatological
AACCGIILLMNSTU	miscalculating
AACCGIILLMORTY	tragicomically
AACCGILLLNOOOV	volcanological
AACCGILLLNOOUV	vulcanological
AACCHHIIMMOPRT	amphichromatic
AACCHHIMNORRUV	Moravian Church
AACCHIILLMSSTY	schismatically
AACCHIILMNOOST	machicolations
AACCHILLLOSSTY	scholastically
AACCHILLOSSTTY	stochastically
AACCHILNOPSTYY	psychoanalytic
AACCIIILMPRTTY	impracticality
AACCIIIMOPRRST	microparasitic
AACCIIINNOOSST	cocainisations

AACCIIINNOOSTZ	cocainizations
AACCIIINORSSTT	cicatrisations
AACCIIINORSTTZ	cicatrizations
AACCIILLMNOSTU	miscalculation
AACCIILMNRSTTU	circumstantial
AACCIILNPRTTUY	unpracticality
AACCIILOOPRSTV	vicar apostolic
AACCIIMNOORSST	carcinomatosis
AACCILLMORSSTU	miscalculators
AACCILLNOOPTUY	occupationally
AACDDEEIILMMNR	Middle American
AACDDEEILOSTVV	devil's advocate
AACDDEEIMNNOTT	decontaminated
AACDDEELLORSSS	Dead Sea Scrolls
AACDDEIILRSTTU	disarticulated
AACDDEILPQRTUU	quadruplicated
AACDDHILMNORYY	hydrodynamical
AACDEEEFHMNSSS	shamefacedness
AACDEEFFGIINNT	decaffeinating
AACDEEFMNRRTUU	remanufactured
AACDEEGIILMORS	cardiomegalies
AACDEEGINRRRSU	undercarriages
AACDEEHIIMNRST	diathermancies
AACDEEHIJLNRSW	Jewish calendar
AACDEEIIILMSTV	mediaevalistic
AACDEEIJKRSTTT	straitjacketed
AACDEEILOPPRTU	propaedeutical
AACDEEIMNNOSTT	decontaminates
AACDEEJLOQRSUZ	Jaques-Dalcroze
AACDEELLNNSUVY	Lucas van Leyden
AACDEELNNNRSTT	transcendental
AACDEENNNNOSTT	nonattendances
AACDEENORSSSUV	cadaverousness
AACDEFFIIMNRSS	disaffirmances
AACDEFHIMNNRST	handicraftsmen
AACDEFIIIILRST	artificialised
AACDEFIIIILRTZ	artificialized
AACDEFIIINNOTZ	denazification
AACDEFMNNRTUUU	unmanufactured
AACDEGHIOPRRRS	cardiographers
AACDEGHLOPRRTY	dactylographer
AACDEGILLMOORT	dermatological
AACDEGLMNNORSS	scandalmongers
AACDEGMNORSSTU	coastguardsmen
AACDEHIIMNRRST	archimandrites
AACDEHILLNNNSS	Channel Islands
AACDEHILORRSTT	trisoctahedral
AACDEHLNOPSSYY	psychoanalysed
AACDEHLNOPSYYZ	psychoanalyzed
AACDEHMOPRSTUY	pachydermatous
AACDEIIILLLSTY	idealistically
AACDEIIILMNOST	decimalisation
AACDEIIILMNOTZ	decimalization
AACDEIILLNOOST	delocalisation
AACDEIILLNOOTZ	delocalization
AACDEIILNNOPTY	platinocyanide
AACDEIILNOSTTU	educationalist
AACDEIILPRRSTU	particularised
AACDEIILPRRTUZ	particularized
AACDEIILRSSTTU	disarticulates
AACDEIIMNORSTY	aerodynamicist
AACDEIINNOORTV	nonradioactive

AACDEIINNRSSTT	transactinides
AACDEILLMMORTY	dermatomically
AACDEILMMNORTY	dynamometrical
AACDEILMOPRSTT	dermatoplastic
AACDEILNNNOOST	condensational
AACDEILNOPRSSS	sporadicalness
AACDEILORSSSTT	sacerdotalists
AACDEILPQRSTUU	quadruplicates
AACDEIMNNNOSTT	decontaminants
AACDEIMNNNOTTU	uncontaminated
AACDEIMNNOORTT	decontaminator
AACDEINOPRRSTT	procrastinated
AACDELNNOSSSSU	scandalousness
AACDELORSTTTUY	tetradactylous
AACDFHJMNOOSSU	John of Damascus
AACDFIIIILNOPT	lapidification
AACDFIIIMNNOST	damnifications
AACDGHHILOPRRY	hydrographical
AACDGHIMOOPRRY	myocardiograph
AACDGIIILNRTVY	divaricatingly
AACDGIIINNOSST	diagnosticians
AACDGIIINOSSST	disassociating
AACDGIILLLOORY	radiologically
AACDGIILLLOOUY	audiologically
AACDGIILLNOSTY	diagnostically
AACDHIMOOPRTYY	cardiomyopathy
AACDIIIILNNPRS	disciplinarian
AACDIIILNNPRST	Pitcairn Island
AACDIIILNOPPST	disapplication
AACDIIILNORSTV	Victoria Island
AACDIIINNNORST	incardinations
AACDIIINOOSSST	disassociation
AACDIILLLMOPTY	diplomatically
AACDIILORRSTTU	disarticulator
AACDIIMNOPSSST	antispasmodics
AACDILLNNOOSSV	Volcano Islands
AACDILNOOSSTUY	anisodactylous
AACDILOORSTTUY	artiodactylous
AACEEEFLMRSSST	malefactresses
AACEEEGHIMNOTT	haematogenetic
AACEEEGILNSSTT	telangiectases
AACEEEHJKLRSTT	leatherjackets
AACEEEHLMOSTUY	thymelaeaceous
AACEEEHMMORTTY	haemacytometer
AACEEFFILNOTTY	affectionately
AACEEFMNRRSTUU	remanufactures
AACEEGGILLLNOY	genealogically
AACEEGHHLNOPPR	encephalograph
AACEEGHILMPRYY	hyperglycaemia
AACEEGHLMNOPRS	encephalograms
AACEEGHNOOPRRS	oceanographers
AACEEGIILLMNSV	evangelicalism
AACEEGIILNSSTT	telangiectasis
AACEEGILLLOOPS	spelaeological
AACEEGILLNNPTY	pangenetically
AACEEGILMORSTT	galactometries
AACEEHHIRRTTUY	Château-Thierry
AACEEHHLNOPPTY	encephalopathy
AACEEHHMNOPRTY	mechanotherapy
AACEEHIIMOOPTT	haematopoietic
AACEEHILLLPTTY	telepathically
AACEEHILLMPTTY	empathetically

AACEEHILLMRTXY hexametrically
AACEEHILMMNTTY enthymematical
AACEEHILNRSSTT theatricalness
AACEEHILRRTUVX extravehicular
AACEEHIPRSSTTY cryptaesthesia
AACEEIIINPPRTV inappreciative
AACEEIILOPRSTV overcapitalise
AACEEIILOPRTVZ overcapitalize
AACEEIILPPRTVY appreciatively
AACEEIILPRTTUV recapitulative
AACEEIIMNNRSSS necessarianism
AACEEIINNRSSST necessitarians
AACEEIINPPRTUV unappreciative
AACEEILMMNSSTU immaculateness
AACEEILNRSSTTU articulateness
AACEEINNPRRSST transparencies
AACEEINRSSTTTV attractiveness
AACEEKLOSSSTTY Stokesay Castle
AACEELNNOPRSTV convertaplanes
AACEELNOPRRSTU palaeocurrents
AACEELOOPRRRTX extracorporeal
AACEFFHIILORTT article of faith
AACEFFILNORSSS Francis of Sales
AACEFIIIILRSST artificialises
AACEFIIIILRSTZ artificializes
AACEFIINPRRTTU parturifacient
AACEFILLNOSSSU fallaciousness
AACEFIMNORRSTW aircraftswomen
AACEGGHIIMNOST gigantomachies
AACEGGHILLOPRY geographically
AACEGGILNNOORT congregational
AACEGHHIILLOPR heliographical
AACEGHHILNOPRT ethnographical
AACEGHHILOPRTY hyetographical
AACEGHHIMOPPTT apophthegmatic
AACEGHHIOPPRRS phraseographic
AACEGHHOPRRRST chartographers
AACEGHIILLPPRY epigraphically
AACEGHIILMOPSU malpighiaceous
AACEGHIINNTTTU authenticating
AACEGHIJKRSTTT straightjacket
AACEGHILLLMPTY phlegmatically
AACEGHILLMNOPY megaphonically
AACEGHILLMOPRT metallographic
AACEGHILLOOPRS phraseological
AACEGHILLOOPRW Low Archipelago
AACEGHILNOPRST stenographical
AACEGHILOORSST archaeologists
AACEGHILOPPRRT petrographical
AACEGHILOPRTTU telautographic
AACEGHIMNOPRST cinematographs
AACEGHIMNOPRTY cinematography
AACEGHLNNSTUUW weltanschauung
AACEGHLOOOORYZ archaeozoology
AACEGIIILNPRST recapitalising
AACEGIIILNPRTZ recapitalizing
AACEGIIINNRSST sectarianising
AACEGIIINNRSTZ sectarianizing
AACEGIILLLLSTY legalistically
AACEGIILLLOOTY aetiologically
AACEGIILLMOOSS semasiological
AACEGIILLMOPSX plagioclimaxes
AACEGIILNPRTTU recapitulating
AACEGIILOOPSST galactopoiesis
AACEGIINNPQRTU preacquainting
AACEGIINOORSTT categorisation
AACEGIINOORTTZ categorization
AACEGILLLMORTY algometrically
AACEGILLLOOPTY apologetically
AACEGILLMNOORT organometallic
AACEGILNOOPSSV galvanoscopies
AACEGILNORTTUV congratulative
AACEGILNRRTTUY rectangularity
AACEGIMNOSSTTT magnetostatics
AACEHHILNNOPTY phthalocyanine
AACEHHILNOPRSZ rhizocephalans
AACEHIIIMNRSTT arithmeticians
AACEHIILLLLPTY philatelically
AACEHIILLMRTTY arithmetically
AACEHIILNOPSST cephalisations
AACEHIILNOPSTZ cephalizations
AACEHIIMNOSSTT schematisation
AACEHIIMNOSTTZ schematization
AACEHIIMNPSSTY metaphysicians
AACEHIINNOTTTU authentication
AACEHIIOPSSSST associateships
AACEHILLMNNORY enharmonically
AACEHILLMOPRSY semaphorically
AACEHILLMOPRTY metaphorically
AACEHILLMPSTYY metaphysically
AACEHILMORRSTY lachrymatories
AACEHIMMMORSTT metachromatism
AACEHIMOOPPRST pharmacopoeist
AACEHIMPRSSTTU pharmaceutists
AACEHINORSTTTU authenticators
AACEHLNNOORSSU Chalon-sur-Saône
AACEHLNOPRSSYY psychoanalyser
AACEHLNOPRSYYZ psychoanalyzer
AACEHLNOPSSSYY psychoanalyses
AACEHLNOPSSYYZ psychoanalyzes
AACEHLOOPSSTTY photocatalyses
AACEHLQRRSTTUU Urquhart Castle
AACEHMNOOOPPRS anamorphoscope
AACEHMNOPRSTUY parenchymatous
AACEIIILLNOSTX lexicalisation
AACEIIILLNOTXZ lexicalization
AACEIIILNOPSST specialisation
AACEIIILNOPSTZ specialization
AACEIIILNPTTVY anticipatively
AACEIIINNOPPRT inappreciation
AACEIILLLMRTTY altimetrically
AACEIILLNPSTTY antiseptically
AACEIILLNRTTUY inarticulately
AACEIILMNRSSTU unicameralists
AACEIILNNORSTT centralisation
intercalations
AACEIILNNORTTZ centralization
AACEIILNNRSTTU antinuclearist
AACEIILNOOPPSU papilionaceous
AACEIILNOPPRST reapplications
AACEIILNOPRTTU recapitulation
AACEIILNORSSTT cartelisations
AACEIILNORSSTU secularisation
AACEIILNORSTTZ cartelizations

AACEIILNORSTUZ	secularization
AACEIILOPPRRTY	appreciatorily
AACEIILPRRRSTU	particulariser
AACEIILPRRRTUZ	particularizer
AACEIILPRRSSTU	particularises
AACEIILPRRSTUZ	particularizes
AACEIIMMOSSTTU	semiautomatics
AACEIIMOPRRSST	microparasites
AACEIINNNORRST	reincarnations
AACEIINOPRRSTV	prevarications
AACEIINORSSSUV	avariciousness
AACEIINORSSTTU	cauterisations
AACEIINORSTTUZ	cauterizations
AACEILLLNOPSTY	pleonastically
AACEILLMMNORTY	manometrically
AACEILLMMRSTYY	asymmetrically
AACEILLMNORRTU	intramolecular
AACEILLMSSTTYY	systematically
AACEILMNNOOPST	compensational
AACEILMNOSSSTU	calamitousness
AACEILMNRRSSUV	vernacularisms
AACEILNNNRSSTY	tyrannicalness
AACEILNNOORSTV	conservational
	conversational
AACEILNNOPSSTU	encapsulations
AACEILNORSTTUX	exclaustration
AACEILOPRRRTUV	overparticular
AACEILOPRRTTUY	recapitulatory
AACEINNORSTTUU	intracutaneous
AACEINOPRRSSTT	procrastinates
AACEKLNNORSTUY	cantankerously
AACELLLOPPRRYY	polycarpellary
AACELLMNOOPRRY	monocarpellary
AACELLMOPRRSUU	supramolecular
AACEMOOPRSSSST	astrocompasses
AACFFIIILNOSST	falsifications
AACFGIIIMNNOST	magnifications
AACFGIIINORSTT	gratifications
AACFGILNNOORST	conflagrations
AACFIIIILLNRTY	inartificially
AACFIIILMNOPST	amplifications
AACFIIILNOQSTU	qualifications
AACFIIIMMNNOOT	ammonification
AACFIIINNOOPST	saponification
AACFIIINNOQTTU	quantification
AACFIIINORSTTT	stratification
AACFIILLMORTTU	multifactorial
AACFIILMNOPSST	Pontifical Mass
AACFIILORSSTTY	satisfactorily
AACFIINNOORSTT	fractionations
AACFIINOORSSTT	factorisations
AACFIINOORSTTZ	factorizations
AACFILMNNOOORT	conformational
AACFINORSSTTUY	unsatisfactory
AACGGILLLNOORY	laryngological
AACGGILLMOSTYY	mystagogically
AACGGILNNORTTU	congratulating
AACGHHIILLOPRT	lithographical
AACGHHILOOPRRT	orthographical
AACGHHILOPPRSY	hypsographical
AACGHHINOOPPRT	anthropophagic
AACGHHIPRSSTTY	tachygraphists

AACGHHMOOPRRTY	chromatography
AACGHIILLPRSST	calligraphists
AACGHILLLOOPTY	pathologically
AACGHILLMOPRYY	myographically
AACGHILLOOPRRY	orographically
AACGHILLOPRSTY	stylographical
AACGHILMOOPRST	pharmacologist
AACGHILNOORSST	arachnologists
AACGHLOOPPRSYY	parapsychology
AACGIIILNNOSST	anglicisations
AACGIIILNNOSTZ	anglicizations
AACGIIILNPRSTU	paralinguistic
AACGIILLMMOOST	logical atomism
AACGIIMNOOPRRS	microsporangia
AACGILLLOORSTY	astrologically
AACGILLLOOTTUY	tautologically
AACGILLLRRTUUY	agriculturally
AACGILLMOOOSTT	stomatological
AACGILLMOORRTY	martyrological
AACGILLORSTTYY	gyrostatically
AACGILMNOOPSST	campanologists
AACGILMOOPRRTU	compurgatorial
AACGILNNOORTTU	congratulation
AACGINNORRSSTW	narrowcastings
AACGLNOORRSTTU	congratulators
AACGLNOORRTTUY	congratulatory
AACHHINOOPPRTT	anthropopathic
AACHIIILLPRRTU	Tiruchirapalli
AACHIILLNNOSTU	hallucinations
AACHIILLNOOOST	alcoholisation
AACHIILLNOOOTZ	alcoholization
AACHIILMNOPRST	misanthropical
AACHIIMNNORSTT	antimonarchist
AACHIINPRSTTYY	antipsychiatry
AACHILLNOPSTYY	hyponastically
AACHILLOPSTTYY	hypostatically
AACHILLOPTTUYY	autophytically
AACHILNOPSSSYY	psychoanalysis
AACHILOOPSSTTY	photocatalysis
AACHIOPRSSSTTT	catastrophists
AACHLLLMOOPSUY	malacophyllous
AACHLNOPSSSTYY	psychoanalysts
AACIIIILNOSSTT	italicisations
AACIIIILNOSTTZ	italicizations
AACIIILLMMRSTU	multiracialism
AACIIILLNRSTTY	inartistically
AACIIILMNOPPST	misapplication
AACIIILNOPRTTY	anticipatorily
AACIIILNOPSSTT	plasticisation
AACIIILNOPSTTZ	plasticization
AACIIIMNOOSSST	associationism
AACIIINNOORSTT	ratiocinations
AACIILLLMORSTY	moralistically
AACIILLLRSTTUY	altruistically
AACIILLMMNSTUY	numismatically
AACIILMNORSTTU	matriculations
AACIILNNOPSSTU	incapsulations
AACIILNNOSSTTT	nonstatistical
AACIILNOOPRRST	conspiratorial
AACIILNORSSTTY	crystalisation
AACIILNORSTTTU	straticulation
AACIILNORSTTYZ	crystalization

AACIILOPPRSSTT procapitalists
AACIILPRRSSTTU particularists
AACIIMMNNORSTU communitarians
AACIIMNNNOOSTT contaminations
AACILLLLOOPRTY allotropically
AACILLLNORSTUY ultrasonically
AACILLMNOORSTY astronomically
AACILLMOPSTTYY asymptotically
AACILNNNOSTTUV anticonvulsant
AACILNNOORSSTT translocations
AACIMNNOOSSTTU Coast Mountains
AACINOOPRRRSTT procrastinator
AACLLNNOPRTTUY contrapuntally
AADDDEEEHHNRSS hardheadedness
AADDDEMNNOORSW Waddesdon Manor
AADDDFGILMPWYY Dafydd ap Gwilym
AADDEEEIILMRST dematerialised
AADDEEEIILMRTZ dematerialized
AADDEEFLLORRTU Fort Lauderdale
AADDEEGHLLRTUY glutaraldehyde
AADDEEGNRRSTUU undergraduates
AADDEEHLORSSTT stadholderates
AADDEEHLORSTTT stadtholderate
AADDEEIILNNOST denationalised
AADDEEIILNNOTZ denationalized
AADDEEILLNRSSW Leeward Islands
AADDEEILMMORST melodramatised
AADDEEILMMORTZ melodramatized
AADDEEILMNNNSV Van Diemen's Land
AADDEEIMORRSTV overdramatised
AADDEEIMORRTVZ overdramatized
AADDEENRRSTTUU undersaturated
AADDEFFINNNRRZ Franz Ferdinand
AADDEGGHNRRSTU granddaughters
AADDEHHINPRSVY Vindhya Pradesh
AADDEILLNNORSS Ladrone Islands
AADDEILLNNORTV Torvill and Dean
AADDHILNNOSSTU Thousand Island
AADDHILNRSSTUY Thursday Island
AADDHMNRSTUUYY Maundy Thursday
AADEEEELNNRRTW Ennerdale Water
AADEEEFGHLRRTT Alfred the Great
AADEEEGMNNQRUU Queen Maud Range
AADEEEIILMRSST dematerialises
AADEEEIILMRSTZ dematerializes
AADEEEILLLPPPR parallelepiped
AADEEEILNRRSST Easter Islander
AADEEEMMNRSSTU admeasurements
AADEEFGILLLNOT dinoflagellate
AADEEFIILNORST federalisation
AADEEFIILNORTZ federalization
AADEEFMNNOOTTY Day of Atonement
AADEEGGIMNNRST aggrandisement
AADEEGGIMNNRTZ aggrandizement
AADEEGHILOPRRT radiotelegraph
AADEEGHINQRRTU headquartering
AADEEGHIPPPRSU pseudepigrapha
AADEEGIIMMPRST epigrammatised
AADEEGIIMMPRTZ epigrammatized
AADEEGILMORRST radiotelegrams
AADEEGIMNNRRST disarrangement
AADEEHHIMPRSST headmastership
AADEEHILMNOOTT endotheliomata
AADEEHIMNNORTU Haute-Normandie
AADEEHNNNOSTTY Thadentsonyane
AADEEIIILMMRST immaterialised
AADEEIIILMMRTZ immaterialized
AADEEIILMNNRTT interlaminated
AADEEIILNNOSST denationalises
AADEEIILNNOSTZ denationalizes
AADEEIILNPQSSU sesquipedalian
AADEEIILNRSTUV valetudinaries
AADEEIINNPRRST predestinarian
AADEEILLLOPPPR parallelopiped
AADEEILMMORSST melodramatises
AADEEILMMORSTZ melodramatizes
AADEEILMNORTTT tatterdemalion
AADEEILNRRSTTT transliterated
AADEEIMNOPRRST panradiometers
AADEEIMORRSSTV overdramatises
AADEEIMORRSTVZ overdramatizes
AADEEINNPRSSTT antidepressant
AADEEINNQSSTTU antiquatedness
AADEELLMNPRTTY departmentally
AADEEPRRSSTTUU supersaturated
AADEFFJLNNORSZ Franz Josef Land
AADEFHILLNNPRZ Rheinland-Pfalz
AADEFILLNRSSSU Fur Seal Islands
AADEFILMMNNSTU fundamentalism
AADEFILMNNSTTU fundamentalist
AADEFILMNNTTUY fundamentality
AADEFILNOOOPRS Leonardo of Pisa
AADEGGGIINORST disaggregation
AADEGGHHIMNOSU houghmagandies
AADEGHIIIOPPRR Herod Agrippa II
AADEGIILNNRSTU denaturalising
AADEGIILNNRTUZ denaturalizing
AADEGIIMRRUUWY Yerwa-Maiduguri
AADEGIINNORRTT intergradation
AADEGILNQRSTUW Griqualand West
AADEGINOORRRTT retrogradation
AADEHHKLLNNOOV Hoek van Holland
AADEHIILLMNPSU sulphanilamide
AADEHIIMNNOSTU dehumanisation
AADEHIIMNNOTUZ dehumanization
AADEHIINORRSST sherardisation
AADEHIINORRSTZ sherardization
AADEHIIOPRRSTT radiotherapist
AADEHILLMORTUY rheumatoidally
AADEHILMORSTUY Admiralty House
AADEHINNOPSSSU diaphanousness
AADEHNORRSSTTW northeastwards
AADEHORSSSTTUW southeastwards
AADEIIILNNOSST desalinisation
AADEIIILNNOSTZ desalinization
AADEIIILNOSTTV devitalisation
AADEIIILNOTTVZ devitalization
AADEIIIMNNOSST deaminisations
AADEIIIMNNOSTZ deaminizations
AADEIIIMNRSTTV administrative
AADEIILMMNRSST maladministers
AADEIILMNNNOOT denominational
AADEIILMNOORST demoralisation
AADEIILMNOORTZ demoralization

AADEIILNNOPSST dispensational
AADEIILNOOPRST depolarisation
AADEIILNOOPRTZ depolarization
AADEIILNORSSTT dissertational
AADEIIMNNORSSV animadversions
AADEIINNRRSSTT Transdniestria
AADEIINORRSSTT radioresistant
AADEILMMORSSTT melodramatists
AADEILNNORTUUV undervaluation
AADEILOPRTTTVY total depravity
AADEINOPPPRRTU unappropriated
AADEJLMMNSSTTU maladjustments
AADFFGIIIILNST disaffiliating
AADFFIIIILNOST disaffiliation
AADFFIIIMNORST disaffirmation
AADFHLLNOOPRST Parts of Holland
AADFIIILNNRSSS Frisian Islands
AADFILLNNOOTUY foundationally
AADGGIINNOPPRS propagandising
AADGGIINNOPPRZ propagandizing
AADGIIIILNOSTT digitalisation
AADGIIIILNOTTZ digitalization
AADGIIIMNNRSTT administrating
AADGIIMNOOSSTT dogmatisations
AADGILNNOPRSST prostaglandins
AADIIILMNORSTT traditionalism
AADIIILNORSTTT traditionalist
AADIIILNORTTTY traditionality
AADIIIMNNORSTT administration
AADIIIMNRRSTTX administratrix
AADIIINOOSSTTZ diazotisations
AADIILNNNOORTT nontraditional
AADIIMNNOORSST randomisations
AADIIMNNOORSTZ randomizations
AADIIMNORRSSTT administrators
AADILLNPRSSSTY Spratly Islands
AAEEEFGHLLLMOT hemoflagellate
AAEEEFGMNNORRS ferromanganese
AAEEEGHIMNOSST haematogenesis
AAEEEGHLMNRRSY Hamersley Range
AAEEEGHLRSSSTW weatherglasses
AAEEEGMNNPRRRT prearrangement
AAEEEGMNNRRRST rearrangements
AAEEEHHIMRSSTT thermaesthesia
AAEEEHHIPRSSTY hyperaesthesia
AAEEEINPRSSSTV separativeness
AAEEFGIMNNORRS ferromagnesian
AAEEFHILMNSTUZ sulfamethazine
AAEEFILNNRRSTT transferential
AAEEFINNORSSTT aftersensation
AAEEGGGILNRTXY exaggeratingly
AAEEGGHILMNTTU hemagglutinate
AAEEGHIINNSSTT anaesthetising
AAEEGHIINNSTTZ anaesthetizing
AAEEGHIMMNOPSY hypomagnesemia
AAEEGHLLMOPRRT metallographer
AAEEGHLLNOOPTY palaeethnology
AAEEGIILNNORST generalisation
AAEEGIILNNORTZ generalization
AAEEGIILNNOSTV evangelisation
AAEEGIILNNOTVZ evangelization
AAEEGIIMMPRSST epigrammatises
AAEEGIIMMPRSTZ epigrammatizes
AAEEGIIMNRRRST intermarriages
AAEEGILMNOORRS oleomargarines
AAEEGILMNTTUVY augmentatively
AAEEGILNNPPSSU Gaspé Peninsula
AAEEGILNPRSTXY exasperatingly
AAEEGIMMNNRRST misarrangement
AAEEGLMNPRSSTU suprasegmental
AAEEGLNNORSSTT tetragonalness
AAEEGMNOPRSSSU rampageousness
AAEEHHILMNORTT trihalomethane
AAEEHHMOPPSSTT metaphosphates
AAEEHIIMOOPSST haematopoiesis
AAEEHIKKLNOPTT Alte Pinakothek
AAEEHILMMOOSTT mesotheliomata
AAEEHILMPPRSSS plasmapheresis
AAEEHIMNNNOOPZ aminophenazone
AAEEHIMNRSSSTU amateurishness
AAEEHIPPRRSSTY hyperparasites
AAEEHMOOPRRRST spermatorrhoea
AAEEIIILMMRSST immaterialises
AAEEIIILMMRSTZ immaterializes
AAEEIILLMNNPRR premillenarian
AAEEIILMMNRSST immaterialness
AAEEIILMMPRSST Alpes-Maritimes
AAEEIILMNNRSTT interlaminates
AAEEIILNNORSTT eternalisation
AAEEIILNNORTTZ eternalization
AAEEIILNNOSSST sensationalise
AAEEIILNNOSSTZ sensationalize
AAEEIIMNNORSTX reexaminations
AAEEIKLNORSTVY Yekaterinoslav
AAEEIKLNRRSSTU Kaiserslautern
AAEEIKLOPRSSTT keratoplasties
AAEEILNNNOPPST peneplanations
AAEEILNNOPRSTT presentational
AAEEILNNPRRTTY interplanetary
AAEEILNRRSSTTT transliterates
AAEEINNOPSSSST passionateness
AAEELNNNPSSSTU unpleasantness
AAEEMNNOPPRSWW newspaperwoman
AAEEMQRRRSSTTU quartermasters
AAEFFIIMNORRST reaffirmations
AAEFFINOORSSTT afforestations
AAEFGIMNNORSTT fragmentations
AAEFHINNORRRST Finsteraarhorn
AAEFIIMNNOSSTT manifestations
AAEFIINNORRSTT fraternisation
AAEFIINNORRTTZ fraternization
AAEFIMNORRSTTV transformative
AAEGGGNOOORRTY Góngora y Argote
AAEGGHIILMNNTU haemagglutinin
AAEGGIIMNNOPRR Grampian Region
AAEGGIINNNSTUX exsanguinating
AAEGGIINNORRST grangerisation
AAEGGIINNORRTZ grangerization
AAEGGILMMOORST grammatologies
AAEGGILMNOORST agglomerations
AAEGGIMMNOPRSU megasporangium
AAEGGLNOOPRSTU protolanguages
AAEGHHIOPRRRST arthrographies
AAEGHIILLNRTXY exhilaratingly

AAEGHIIMPRSSTT	magistrateship
AAEGHIIPRRSSTT	stratigraphies
AAEGHIKMNOPRST	kinematographs
AAEGHIKMNOPRTY	kinematography
AAEGHILMOOSSTT	haematologists
AAEGHIPRRRSSTT	stratigraphers
AAEGIIILLLNOST	illegalisation
AAEGIIILLLNOTZ	illegalization
AAEGIIILMRSSTT	magistralities
AAEGIIILNNOSTT	gelatinisation
AAEGIIILNNOTTZ	gelatinization
AAEGIILLNOORST	allegorisation
AAEGIILLNOORTZ	allegorization
AAEGIILNORRSTT	registrational
AAEGIILNORRSTU	regularisation
AAEGIILNORRTUZ	regularization
AAEGIIMMMPRSST	epigrammatisms
AAEGIIMMPRSSTT	epigrammatists
AAEGIIMNNOSSTT	magnetisations
AAEGIIMNNOSTTZ	magnetizations
AAEGIIMNRRSTTV	transmigrative
AAEGIINNNOSTUX	exsanguination
AAEGIINNNRSSSU	sanguinariness
AAEGIINNOORRST	reorganisation
AAEGIINNOORRTZ	reorganization
AAEGIINNSSTTUU	Saint Augustine
AAEGILLMNOOPST	megalopolitans
AAEGILMNOOPRST	spermatogonial
AAEGILNOOPRSTT	progestational
AAEGIMNNORSTTU	argumentations
AAEGINNNPRSTUU	superannuating
AAEGMMNOORRSTU	Gesta Romanorum
AAEHHILLOPSTUZ	sulphathiazole
AAEHHIMOPRRSST	amphiarthroses
AAEHIIIMNNSSTT	antihistamines
AAEHIILMNORSTT	thermalisation
AAEHIILMNORTTZ	thermalization
AAEHIIMNOSSTTT	thematisations
AAEHIIMNOSTTTZ	thematizations
AAEHILOPRRSSTT	arthroplasties
AAEHIMOPRSSSTT	massotherapist
AAEHLMOOPPRRST	spermatophoral
AAEHNNORRSSSTU	anarthrousness
AAEIIIIILNNNTV	Valentinian III
AAEIIIKNNORSTT	keratinisation
AAEIIIKNNORTTZ	keratinization
AAEIIILLMMNNRS	millenarianism
AAEIIILLMSSTVY	assimilatively
AAEIIILMMRSSTT	immaterialists
AAEIIILMNNORST	mineralisation
AAEIIILMNNORTZ	mineralization
AAEIIILNORSSST	serialisations
AAEIIILNORSSTZ	serializations
AAEIIILNORSTTV	relativisation
	revitalisation
AAEIIILNORTTVZ	relativization
	revitalization
AAEIIIMMPRSSST	semiparasitism
AAEIIINNNRSSST	insanitariness
AAEIIINNPPRTTT	pinnatipartite
AAEIILLMNOSSTT	metallisations
AAEIILLMNOSTTZ	metallizations

AAEIILLMNPTUVY	manipulatively
AAEIILLMOPRRTY	imperatorially
AAEIILLNNORSTT	reinstallation
AAEIILLNPRSTTY	interspatially
AAEIILMMNOSSTT	lemmatisations
AAEIILMMNOSTTZ	lemmatizations
AAEIILMNNOSSST	sensationalism
AAEIILMNOOPRST	operationalism
AAEIILMNOPRRST	proletarianism
AAEIILNNNORSTT	internationals
AAEIILNNORRSST	irrationalness
AAEIILNNORSTTU	neutralisation
AAEIILNNORTTUZ	neutralization
AAEIILNNOSSSTT	sensationalist
AAEIILNOORRSTV	revalorisation
AAEIILNOORRTVZ	revalorization
AAEIILNORRSTTT	trilaterations
AAEIILNOSSSTUX	sexualisations
AAEIILNOSSTUXZ	sexualizations
AAEIILNQTTTUVY	quantitatively
AAEIIMOPPPRRST	misappropriate
AAEIINNNOSSTTX	annexationists
AAEIINNORSSSTT	stationariness
AAEIINNPPRRSTT	antiperspirant
AAEIINOPRSSSTT	separationists
AAEIINOPRSSTTU	pasteurisation
AAEIINOPRSTTUZ	pasteurization
AAEIKKKLMNRSSU	Kamensk-Uralski
AAEIKKMMMNOPUZ	Kommunizma Peak
AAEILLLLMORRST	lamellirostral
AAEILLLLMRTTUY	multilaterally
AAEILMNRSSSTUX	transsexualism
AAEILMOOPPRSTT	spatiotemporal
AAEILNNNOOOPRT	nonoperational
AAEILNNORRSSTT	retranslations
AAEILNOOORSTTV	laevorotations
AAEILNOOPRSTTX	extrapolations
AAEILNORRRSTTT	transliterator
AAEILNRRSTTUUV	natural virtues
AAEIMNNNOORSTT	ornamentations
AAEIMNNOORSTTU	neuroanatomist
AAEIMNORSSSTTT	stationmasters
AAEINNNOPRSTUU	superannuation
AAEINNOPRSSTTU	supernatations
AAELLNPRRSTUUY	supernaturally
AAELMNOOPPSSTU	postmenopausal
AAELNNNOPRSTTX	xenotransplant
AAFFIINNOPRRST	nitroparaffins
AAFIIIMNNORRTU	uniformitarian
AAFIILLMMNORTY	inflammatorily
AAFIILMNOORSST	formalisations
AAFIILMNOORSTZ	formalizations
AAFILLNNOOPSUU	Paulinus of Nola
AAFIMNNOORRSTT	transformation
AAGGHHIIOPRSST	hagiographists
AAGGHINOOPRRST	organographist
AAGGHLMNOORSTU	South Glamorgan
AAGGIIILNNRTTY	ingratiatingly
AAGGIILNNOSTTU	agglutinations
AAGGIIMNNRRSTT	transmigrating
AAGGILMMOORSTT	grammatologist
AAGHHNOOPPRSTU	anthropophagus

AAGHIIINOPRSTT	graphitisation
AAGHIIINOPRTTZ	graphitization
AAGHIILMNORSTT	antilogarithms
AAGHIIPRRSSTTT	stratigraphist
AAGHIMNOOPRSST	mastigophorans
AAGHINOPRRSSTU	uranographists
AAGIIIMNOSSTTT	stigmatisation
AAGIIIMNOSTTTZ	stigmatization
AAGIIINNORSSTT	granitisations
AAGIIINNORSTTZ	granitizations
AAGIIJNNOORSST	jargonisations
AAGIIJNNOORSTZ	jargonizations
AAGIILLMOORSST	malariologists
AAGIILLNOOSTUY	Ignatius Loyola
AAGIILMNNRSSTT	mistranslating
AAGIILNNORSTTU	triangulations
AAGIILOOPRSSTT	parasitologist
AAGIIMNNORRSTT	transmigration
AAGILMNOOPRSTV	galvanotropism
AAGIMNORRRSSTT	transmigrators
AAGIMNORRRSTTY	transmigratory
AAHHIIMOPRRSST	amphiarthrosis
AAHIILNNPRRSTY	platyrrhinians
AAHIIMNNOORSST	harmonisations
AAHIIMNNOORSTZ	harmonizations
AAHIINOORSSTTU	authorisations
AAHIINOORSTTUZ	authorizations
AAHILMOPPRRSTY	amphiprostylar
AAHILNOOOPRRTT	prothonotarial
AAHLLOPPSSTTYY	staphyloplasty
AAIIIIILNNOSTT	initialisation
AAIIIIILNNOTTZ	initialization
AAIIIILMMNRSTT	antimilitarism
AAIIIILMNORSTT	militarisation
AAIIIILMNORTTZ	militarization
AAIIIILMNRSTTT	antimilitarist
AAIIIILMNRSTTU	utilitarianism
AAIIIILNORSTTV	trivialisation
AAIIIILNORTTVZ	trivialization
AAIIILLLMNNOTU	illuminational
AAIIILLNOOSTTV	volatilisation
AAIIILLNOOTTVZ	volatilization
AAIIILMNORRSST	irrationalisms
AAIIILNNOPSSTT	platinisations
AAIIILNNOPSTTZ	platinizations
AAIIILNOSSSTUV	visualisations
AAIIILNOSSTUVZ	visualizations
AAIIINNNOSSTTT	instantiations
AAIIINNOOOSTTU	autoionisation
AAIIINNOOOTTUZ	autoionization
AAIIINOPRSSTTV	privatisations
AAIIINOPRSTTVZ	privatizations
AAIIJLNNOORSTU	journalisation
AAIIJLNNOORTUZ	journalization
AAIILLLMNPRSUY	supraliminally
AAIILLLNORSTTU	illustrational
AAIILLMNNOSTTU	multinationals
AAIILLMOOPPSST	papillomatosis
AAIILLNNORSTTY	transitionally
AAIILLNOPRSSTU	pluralisations
AAIILLNOPRSTUZ	pluralizations
AAIILNOOPPRSTU	popularisation
AAIILNOOPPRTUZ	popularization
AAIIMMNOSSSTUY	immunoassayist
AAIIMNNNOSTTUU	Uinta Mountains
AAIIMNOOPPRSTX	approximations
AAIIMNOORRSSTZ	Zoroastrianism
AAIIMNORRSSTTY	martyrisations
AAIIMNORRSTTYZ	martyrizations
AAIINNOPRRSSTT	transpirations
AAIINOOPPPRRST	appropriations
AAIINOOQQSTTUU	quasi-quotation
AAIKMNNOORSTUZ	Ozark Mountains
AAILLLMOORRRYZ	Zorrilla y Moral
AAILMMNNORSTTU	ultramontanism
AAILMNNORSTTTU	ultramontanist
AAILNNOPPSSTTU	supplantations
AAIMNNORSSTTTU	transmutations
AAINNOOPRRSTTT	transportation
ABBCDEEEIORRSU	berberidaceous
ABBCDEILMOOSTU	discombobulate
ABBCEIIJLSTTUY	subjectability
ABBCEILPRRTUUY	Buryat Republic
ABBDDEEEILNSSS	biddablenesses
ABBDEEGNNNRRUU	Neubrandenburg
ABBDIIIILNTTUY	indubitability
ABBEEELNORSSSV	observableness
ABBEEHINNOOPRT	phenobarbitone
ABBEEILMNOPRSS	improbableness
ABBEEINNOOPRTT	pentobarbitone
ABBEGHIIILOPRS	bibliographies
ABBEGHIILOPRRS	bibliographers
ABCCCEEIIMMNRU	circumambience
ABCCCEIIMMNRUY	circumambiency
ABCCCEIORSTUUU	cucurbitaceous
ABCCEEGILNNORT	concelebrating
ABCCEEIILLNORR	irreconcilable
ABCCEEILMMNOUX	excommunicable
ABCCEEILNNOORT	concelebration
ABCCEHIINORSST	bronchiectasis
ABCCEIIILNOTVY	conceivability
ABCCEIILLNORRY	irreconcilably
ABCCEIILMMNNOU	incommunicable
ABCCEIILRRSTUV	cruciverbalist
ABCCEILNNNOOSU	unconscionable
ABCCGINNORSTTU	subcontracting
ABCCHHIIOPRRSS	archbishoprics
ABCCHILOOPRSTU	claustrophobic
ABCCIILMMNNOUY	incommunicably
ABCCIINORSSTTU	antiscorbutics
ABCCILLOOPRXYY	polycarboxylic
ABCCILNNNOOSUY	unconscionably
ABCCILOOOPRSST	stroboscopical
ABCCNOORRSSTTU	subcontractors
ABCDDEEILMMNOS	discommendable
ABCDEEEEILNSSV	deceivableness
ABCDEEEELLNSST	delectableness
ABCDEEEHIILNPR	indecipherable
ABCDEEEHILNPRU	undecipherable
ABCDEEEIILRSSV	disserviceable
ABCDEEEILNPRSS	predicableness
ABCDEEEILNPSSS	despicableness
ABCDEEEILNRSST	creditableness
ABCDEEEILPRSST	disrespectable

ABCDEEEINORRST	decerebrations
ABCDEEGHIIMRRS	Cambridgeshire
ABCDEEGIILPRUY	Adygei Republic
ABCDEEHIILNPRY	indecipherably
ABCDEEIILNNORS	inconsiderable
ABCDEEIILNPRSU	republicanised
ABCDEEIILNPRUZ	republicanized
ABCDEEIIMOSSTY	basidiomycetes
ABCDEFILMOORST	discomfortable
ABCDEGHHOORRTU	thoroughbraced
ABCDEIIILPRTTY	predictability
ABCDEIILNNORSY	inconsiderably
ABCDEIILNNOSTY	condensability
ABCDENOOORRRTU	uncorroborated
ABCDHILNOOORRT	bronchodilator
ABCDIIIILOSSTY	dissociability
ABCDIIILNNOOST	biconditionals
ABCEEEEEILNPRX	experienceable
ABCEEEEFNRSSST	benefactresses
ABCEEEEKLLRSTY	Berkeley Castle
ABCEEELNNRSSSU	censurableness
ABCEEFIILNORTY	enforceability
ABCEEGHLMRRSSU	schlumbergeras
ABCEEGIILLNOTY	biogenetically
ABCEEGIINORSUZ	zingiberaceous
ABCEEGILNNORSU	unrecognisable
ABCEEGILNNORUZ	unrecognizable
ABCEEGKKOORRST	stockbrokerage
ABCEEHIOOPRSUU	euphorbiaceous
ABCEEIIILPRTVY	perceivability
ABCEEIIILRSTVY	serviceability
ABCEEIILLMPRRU	Mari El Republic
ABCEEIILNPRSSU	republicanises
ABCEEIILNPRSUZ	republicanizes
ABCEEIILORRTVY	recoverability
ABCEEIILPRSTTY	respectability
ABCEEILLMNOPSS	compliableness
ABCEEILLNNPSSU	inculpableness
ABCEEILMNOPSST	compatibleness
ABCEEILNNOSSSU	unsociableness
ABCEEILNNSTUUY	sublieutenancy
ABCEEINOPRRSTU	protuberancies
ABCEEINORRRSST	Cartier-Bresson
ABCEELLNOORSSU	colourableness
ABCEELMMNOSSTU	commutableness
ABCEFIIINORSTV	verbifications
ABCEGHLNORRTTU	Charlottenburg
ABCEGIILOORSTT	bacteriologist
ABCEGINQRSTTUY	cybersquatting
ABCEHIIIORSTUV	behaviouristic
ABCEHIILRSTTTY	stretchability
ABCEHILLLOPRYY	hyperbolically
ABCEHILLNNORST	Bristol Channel
ABCEHILORRSTTY	erythroblastic
ABCEHLOOPRSSTU	claustrophobes
ABCEIIILLNTTUY	ineluctability
ABCEIIILNSTUXY	inexcusability
ABCEIIILORRTVY	irrevocability
ABCEIIILRRTTTY	retractibility
ABCEIILNOPPRTU	prepublication
ABCEIILNOPRSTU	republications
ABCEIILNOSTTTY	contestability
ABCEIIMNORRTTU	nitrobacterium
ABCEIIMOSSSTTY	biosystematics
ABCEIINOORSTTX	bacteriotoxins
ABCEILLLMOORTY	bolometrically
ABCEILLLNNOORT	incontrollable
ABCEILLMNOPSUU	pneumobacillus
ABCEILLMNOSSSY	symbolicalness
ABCEILNNNOSTTU	subcontinental
ABCELLLNNOORTU	uncontrollable
ABCELNOSSTUUUY	subcutaneously
ABCEMMMNOORSUU	mucomembranous
ABCFGIILNSSSUY	subclassifying
ABCFIIIMNOORST	bioinformatics
ABCFIILMNOORTY	conformability
ABCGIIIILNOTTY	incogitability
ABCGIILLMOOOTY	bioclimatology
ABCGIILNOOPSST	spongioblastic
ABCGILLLNOOSTU	lactoglobulins
ABCGILLMNOORSU	macroglobulins
ABCHHINOOPRSST	opisthobranchs
ABCHIILNOTTUUY	untouchability
ABCHILMOOPRSTT	thromboplastic
ABCIIIIJLSTTUY	justiciability
ABCIIILLLOPSTY	collapsibility
ABCIIILNRSTTUY	inscrutability
ABCIILLMNOSTYY	symbiontically
ABCIILMMNOSSTU	somnambulistic
ABCIILNORSTTUY	construability
ABCILLLNNOORTY	incontrollably
ABCILMNORSTUUY	rambunctiously
ABCINOOOORRRST	corroborations
ABCLLLNNOORTUY	uncontrollably
ABDDEEEELNNPSS	dependableness
ABDDEEEFGHINRT	featherbedding
ABDDEEEHLLNSSU	bullheadedness
ABDDEEEIKLMRRS	middlebreakers
ABDDEEHIILSSST	disestablished
ABDDEEILMNNSTY	absentmindedly
ABDDEFGIMORRST	Stamford Bridge
ABDEEEEFILNSSS	defeasibleness
ABDEEEEILNRSST	deliberateness
ABDEEEELNSSSTT	detestableness
ABDEEEFFIILNRT	differentiable
ABDEEEGHINRSST	bigheartedness
ABDEEEHILPRSST	preestablished
ABDEEEIIINORST	obedientiaries
ABDEEEIILLRTVY	deliberatively
ABDEEEIILMNNRT	indeterminable
ABDEEEIINNOPZZ	benzodiazepine
ABDEEEILMNNSST	disenablements
ABDEEEILNNNSSU	undeniableness
ABDEEELLNOPRSS	deplorableness
ABDEEFGHINRRST	fingerbreadths
ABDEEFIIIILNST	definabilities
ABDEEFIIILNNTU	unidentifiable
ABDEEFIILMNOSS	modifiableness
ABDEEFILMNORSS	formidableness
ABDEEGILNNOOTU	double negation
ABDEEGIPRRRRTY	partridgeberry
ABDEEHIIILRTTY	hereditability
ABDEEHIILSSSST	disestablishes
ABDEEIIILLRTVY	deliverability

ABDEEIIIMNOORT bioremediation
ABDEEIILMNNRTY indeterminably
ABDEEIILMNSSSS admissibleness
ABDEEIILNNPSSS indispensables
ABDEEIILRRSSTY redressability
ABDEEIKMMNRSST disembarkments
ABDEEILMNNORST indemonstrable
ABDEEILNOPSSSS disposableness
ABDEEILNPSSSTU disputableness
ABDEELMNNORSTU undemonstrable
ABDEEMNPRSSTTU subdepartments
ABDEFGIINNSTUU subinfeudating
ABDEFIIILLNORT defibrillation
ABDEFIILLORRST defibrillators
ABDEFIINNOSTUU subinfeudation
ABDEFINORSTUUY subinfeudatory
ABDEGGIKNNORRU groundbreaking
ABDEGIILLNRSST Gilbert Islands
ABDEGINNOPRSUU superabounding
ABDEHINNORRSTU Dunbartonshire
ABDEHLMNNORRTU Northumberland
ABDEIIILMNOOST demobilisation
ABDEIIILMNOOTZ demobilization
ABDEIIILNPSSTY dispensability
ABDEIIILNRSTUY undesirability
ABDEIIINRSSSSU subsidiariness
ABDEIIIRRSSTTU distributaries
ABDEIILNOORSTW bowdlerisation
ABDEIILNOORTWZ bowdlerization
ABDEIINNORSSTU insubordinates
ABDEIINSSSTTUV substantivised
ABDEIINSSTTUVZ substantivized
ABDEILMNNORSTY indemonstrably
ABDEILMORSTUXY ambidextrously
ABDGIIILOOORST radiobiologist
ABDGILMNNORSSU bildungsromans
ABDHIIINORSSTY hybridisations
ABDHIIINORSTYZ hybridizations
ABDHILNNOORTTY labyrinthodont
ABDIIIILMNOTTY indomitability
ABDIIILLOSSTVY dissolvability
ABDIIILNORSTTU distributional
ABDIIINOSSSSTU subsidisations
ABDIIINOSSSTUZ subsidizations
ABDIIOOOPRSSSU basidiosporous
ABEEEEFLNPRRSS preferableness
ABEEEENPRSSSSY Basses-Pyrénées
ABEEEFIILNNSSS infeasibleness
ABEEEFIILNRSSV verifiableness
ABEEEFILLNRSST filterableness
ABEEEGLMMNNRST embranglements
ABEEEGLNNORSSV governableness
ABEEEHIILLLSTV Élisabethville
ABEEEHILNPRSSS perishableness
ABEEEHILPRSSST preestablishes
ABEEEHLNRSSSST breathlessness
ABEEEIILLPRRSV irreplevisable
ABEEEIILNNPSSX inexpiableness
ABEEEIILNNSSTV inevitableness
ABEEEIKKRRRSST strikebreakers
ABEEEILMMNOSSV immoveableness
ABEEEILMNNRSST terminableness
ABEEEILNNOPRSS inoperableness
ABEEEILNNORSSX inexorableness
ABEEEILNRRRTTV intervertebral
ABEEEINORRRSTV reverberations
ABEEELLNNRSSUV vulnerableness
ABEEELLNORSSSV resolvableness
ABEEELMNPRSSTU permutableness
ABEEELNNOPRSSS personableness
ABEEELNORRSSST restorableness
ABEEEMMNPRRSSU supermembranes
ABEEFHIMNOORST Bohemian Forest
ABEEFIILLLNNSS infallibleness
ABEEFIILMNRTTY fermentability
ABEEFILNOPRSST profitableness
ABEEGHIILNRSST reestablishing
ABEEGHIILNSTUX extinguishable
ABEEGHILMMNOOT methaemoglobin
ABEEGHILNORRWW wheelbarrowing
ABEEGIIKKNRRST strikebreaking
ABEEGIILNNNSST intangibleness
ABEEGMNORSSSUU umbrageousness
ABEEGNOORRRTTU turbogenerator
ABEEHILMNSSSTT establishments
ABEEHILNOPSSST hospitableness
ABEEHLNNOORSSU honourableness
ABEEHLNNOPTUYZ phenylbutazone
ABEEIIIILLNSST ensilabilities
ABEEIIILMMPRTY impermeability
ABEEIIILMNNSST inimitableness
ABEEIIILRRTTVY retrievability
ABEEIILLNNOSSV inviolableness
ABEEIILMNOPRSS impressionable
ABEEIILMNPSSSS impassibleness
ABEEIILMNRRTUY remunerability
ABEEIILNPRSTTY presentability
ABEEIILNPRTTVY preventability
ABEEIILPRRSTVY preservability
ABEEILLPRRSTYY presbyterially
ABEEILMNNNOSTU unmentionables
ABEEILMNOPRSSV improvableness
ABEEILNNOQSTUU unquestionable
ABEEILNNSSTTUU sublieutenants
ABEEILRRRSSTTU subterrestrial
ABEEIMNOSSSSTU abstemiousness
ABEEKLNNNOSSUW unknowableness
ABEFGIIILNRRTY refrangibility
ABEFIIILRRTTUY irrefutability
ABEFIILLNORRRU neurofibrillar
ABEFLLNOOPSSTU tablespoonfuls
ABEGHIILMNOORU hemoglobinuria
ABEGHILMNOOOXY oxyhaemoglobin
ABEGHLMNRRSSTU bremsstrahlung
ABEGIIILMNPRTY impregnability
ABEGIILOOORSST aerobiologists
ABEGIILORRSSTY gyrostabiliser
ABEGIILORRSTYZ gyrostabilizer
ABEHHIJNOPSTTT John the Baptist
ABEHHINOOPPSST bisphosphonate
ABEHIIIILNRTTY inheritability
ABEHIIILSTTUXY exhaustibility
ABEHIIMNOPSSSU amphibiousness
ABEHINNOOSSTTT ethnobotanists

ABEIIIILMNSTTY inestimability
ABEIIILLNORTTY intolerability
ABEIIILMNNRTUY innumerability
ABEIIILMORRTVY irremovability
ABEIIILNORSSTT liberationists
ABEIIILNPRSTUY insuperability
ABEIIILPRSSTUY persuasibility
ABEIIIMNRSSTUU subminiaturise
ABEIIIMNRSTUUZ subminiaturize
ABEIIMNOPRRTTU imperturbation
ABEIIMOPRSSTUU superambitious
ABEIINSSSSTTUV substantivises
ABEIINSSSTTUVZ substantivizes
ABEILLOOPRSSST ballistospores
ABEILMNNORSTUU insurmountable
ABEILNNOQSTUUY unquestionably
ABEILNOOOPPRRT proportionable
ABEILNORSSSSUU salubriousness
ABELMNNORSTUUU unsurmountable
ABENNOOPSSSTUU subspontaneous
ABENOORRSSSTUU brontosauruses
ABFGIIIILNNRTY infrangibility
ABFIIIIILRTTVY vitrifiability
ABFIIIIJLSTTUY justifiability
ABFIIIILLLNSST infallibilists
ABFIIIILNOSSTY fissionability
ABGGIILOOORSST agrobiologists
ABGIIIIILMMTTY immitigability
ABGIIMNNORRSST brainstormings
ABHIIIKLNNTTUY unthinkability
ABHIIINOOPRRTY prohibitionary
ABHIIINOORSSTV vasoinhibitors
ABHIIINOORSTVY vasoinhibitory
ABHIILLOPPPRTY Port Phillip Bay
ABHILMNOOPRSTT thromboplastin
ABIIIIILLLMTTY illimitability
ABIIIILLMPSTUY implausibility
ABIIIILMMNOOST immobilisation
ABIIIILMMNOOTZ immobilization
ABIIIIMNNOSTTU bituminisation
ABIIIIMNNOTTUZ bituminization
ABIILLNORSSUUY insalubriously
ABIILMNOOSSSTY symbolisations
ABIILMNOOSSTYZ symbolizations
ABIILMORRSTTUV multivibrators
ABIILNNNOSTTUU tintinnabulous
ABIILOPPRSTTUY supportability
ABILMNNORSTUUY insurmountably
ABILNOOOPPRRTY proportionably
ABILNOOPPSSTUU subpopulations
ACCCCHHHILORTU Catholic Church
ACCCCHILOOPSTY staphylococcic
ACCCDEEEINNNSS incandescences
ACCCEEHINOORSS onchocerciases
ACCCEEIILSSSTU Ecclesiasticus
ACCCEEINOPPRSU preoccupancies
ACCCEHHILMOPSY psychochemical
ACCCEHIINOORSS onchocerciasis
ACCCEHIINORSTT architectonics
ACCCEILLNNORTY concentrically
ACCCEIMMNOOORS macroeconomics
ACCCFIIIKNNOOT cocknification
ACCCGIIMNNRSTU circumstancing
ACCCHIIOOPSSTT tachistoscopic
ACCCHLOOPSSTUY staphylococcus
ACCDDEEIILNOST occidentalised
ACCDDEEIILNOTZ occidentalized
ACCDDEGIIINRST disaccrediting
ACCDDEINNORTTU uncontradicted
ACCDEEEELNOPRS preadolescence
ACCDEEEHHIKNRT chickenhearted
ACCDEEEINORSST cardiocenteses
ACCDEEENNORRTT reconcentrated
ACCDEEGHNNORTU counterchanged
ACCDEEGHNORRTU countercharged
ACCDEEGINNORST deconsecrating
ACCDEEHMNORRTU countermarched
ACCDEEIILLLRTY dielectrically
ACCDEEIILMMORS commercialised
ACCDEEIILMMORZ commercialized
ACCDEEIILNOSST occidentalises
ACCDEEIILNOSTZ occidentalizes
ACCDEEIINORSST cardiocentesis
ACCDEEILMNOPSY encyclopaedism
ACCDEEILMNORTU counterclaimed
ACCDEEILMNORTY dynamoelectric
electrodynamic
ACCDEEILNNNSTY incandescently
ACCDEEILNOPSTU conceptualised
ACCDEEILNOPSTY encyclopaedist
ACCDEEILNOPTUZ conceptualized
ACCDEEIMMNOTUX excommunicated
ACCDEEIMNOPPTY appendicectomy
ACCDEEINNNOSTU discountenance
ACCDEEINNOORST deconsecration
ACCDEEINOPRRTU unreciprocated
ACCDEFGILLNOTU deflocculating
ACCDEFIIINOORT recodification
ACCDEFILLNOOTU deflocculation
ACCDEHHILLOOPY dolichocephaly
ACCDEHHIMNORSY hydromechanics
ACCDEHILMNOPSU unaccomplished
ACCDEHIMOORSTT Socratic method
ACCDEIILLNNOTY coincidentally
ACCDEIILNNOOST codeclinations
ACCDEIINNNOSTU discontinuance
ACCDEIINOORSTT decortications
ACCDGIIMNOSSTU disaccustoming
ACCDHHHINNORTY chondrichthyan
ACCDHHINOOPRSY hypochondriacs
ACCDHIIIMMORST dichromaticism
ACCDHIILORSSTV clavichordists
ACCDHIMNOPSSYY psychodynamics
ACCDHIOORSSTUY hydroacoustics
ACCDIIILLNRTYY cylindricality
ACCDIILNNOOPTU conduplication
ACCDIINNOORSTT contradictions
ACCDIINOORSTTU contradictious
ACCEEEELLNORTV electrovalence
ACCEEEELMORRST accelerometers
ACCEEEFFIINSTU efficient cause
ACCEEEHHILMRRS Schleiermacher
ACCEEEHILLMNPY myelencephalic
ACCEEEILLORSST ecclesiolaters

ACCEEELLNORTVY electrovalency
ACCEEELORRTTUY electrocautery
ACCEEENNORRSTT reconcentrates
ACCEEFIMORRRTT refractometric
ACCEEGHIKNORTW weathercocking
ACCEEGHILMPRYY hyperglycaemic
ACCEEGHILOPRRT electrographic
ACCEEGHNNORSTU counterchanges
ACCEEGHNORRSTU countercharges
ACCEEGIINNORSS carcinogenesis
ACCEEGILLNORTY geocentrically
ACCEEGINNORRST reconsecrating
ACCEEGINOORRST gerontocracies
ACCEEHHIILNNPR rhinencephalic
ACCEEHHILMMORT thermochemical
ACCEEHHLOORSST schoolteachers
ACCEEHIIILNSTT technicalities
ACCEEHIILMMOSS semiochemicals
ACCEEHIILMNRSS chimericalness
ACCEEHILLNORTT centrolecithal
ACCEEHILMOPRST petrochemicals
ACCEEHILNOPPRS prosencephalic
ACCEEHMNORRSTU countermarches
ACCEEHORRSSTTY oystercatchers
ACCEEIILLNRSTV interclavicles
ACCEEIILMMORSS commercialises
ACCEEIILMMORSZ commercializes
ACCEEIIMNNOORT econometrician
ACCEEIINNOORSS concessionaire
ACCEEILLLNORTY electronically
ACCEEILLLOPSTY telescopically
ACCEEILMOOPRTV overcomplicate
ACCEEILMOPRSTU proceleusmatic
ACCEEILNOPSSTU conceptualises
ACCEEILNOPSTUZ conceptualizes
ACCEEILORSSTTT electrostatics
ACCEEILORSSTUU sterculiaceous
ACCEEIMMNOSTUX excommunicates
ACCEEINNNOORSS reconnoissance
ACCEEINNOORRST reconsecration
ACCEEINOPRSTTV contraceptives
ACCEEKLMRRSSSU musselcrackers
ACCEELLMMOORSU macromolecules
ACCEELLNNOSTVY convalescently
ACCEEMNORRSSTT concertmasters
ACCEFGIIIINNNS insignificance
ACCEFIIIINNSTT antiscientific
ACCEFIIILLNSTY scientifically
ACCEFIIINOPSST specifications
ACCEFIIINORSTT certifications
rectifications
ACCEGHHILNOOST schoolteaching
ACCEGHIILLNNOU hallucinogenic
ACCEGHIOPPRRST spectrographic
ACCEGIILNNPTTU centuplicating
ACCEGIILNRTUXY excruciatingly
ACCEGILLMMOORY myrmecological
ACCEGINNOPRRTT precontracting
ACCEHHILLNOPRS chancellorship
ACCEHHILOSSSTZ eschscholtzias
ACCEHIIIMORSTT chromaticities
ACCEHIILMORSTT stichometrical
ACCEHILLMOPRYY pyrochemically
ACCEHILLNNOORR Iron Chancellor
ACCEHILMMNOPST accomplishment
ACCEHILMNOORRT chronometrical
ACCEHILMOOPRST thermoscopical
ACCEHILMOOPRSU microcephalous
ACCEHILMOPRSTY psychometrical
ACCEHILOORSSTU Horatius Cocles
ACCEHIMOORRTYZ ectomycorrhiza
ACCEHIOOPSSSTT tachistoscopes
ACCEHLNNNORTUY Channel Country
ACCEIIILMMORSS microseismical
ACCEIIILMNNOPS incompliancies
ACCEIIILMNORST cliometricians
ACCEIIILNNOORT reconciliation
ACCEIIILNOORRT oneirocritical
ACCEIILLLOSSTY solecistically
ACCEIILLMOORRT colorimetrical
ACCEIILLMOORSY seriocomically
ACCEIILLMRRSUY semicircularly
ACCEIILLOPPRSY periscopically
ACCEIILMMORSST commercialists
ACCEIILNNOPTTU centuplication
ACCEIILNOORRTY reconciliatory
ACCEIILNOSSSST neoclassicists
ACCEIINNOORSTT concretisation
ACCEIINNOORTTZ concretization
ACCEIINOOPRRST reciprocations
ACCEIINOPRSSSU capriciousness
ACCEILLNOSSSUY successionally
ACCEILMMNNOOSS commonsensical
ACCEILNOPSSTTU conceptualists
ACCEIMMNOORTUX excommunicator
ACCEIMNOOPRSTU pococuranteism
ACCEINNNOORSTT concentrations
ACCEINNOORSTTU counteractions
ACCEINOOPPRSTU preoccupations
ACCFFIIINORTTU fructification
ACCFGIIIINNNSY insignificancy
ACCFHHILLLLRSU Churchill Falls
ACCFIIIIILNOST silicification
ACCGGHHIIKNNOU Chiang Ching-kuo
ACCGHHIILLOOTY ichthyological
ACCGHHIOPPRSSY psychographics
ACCGHIILLOOPRS oscillographic
ACCGHILOPRSSUY psychosurgical
ACCGHINOOPPRSY pharyngoscopic
ACCGIIILLMNOOR criminological
ACCGIILLLOOOSY sociologically
ACCGIIMNNRTTUU circumnutating
ACCGILLLMOOOSY cosmologically
ACCGILLOOPRSYY gyroscopically
ACCGILMOOOORSY macrosociology
ACCHHILOPPSSYY psychophysical
ACCHHIMOOOPRRT chromatophoric
ACCHHIMOOORRTT orthochromatic
ACCHIIILNORSTT antichloristic
ACCHIIINNNOOST cinchonisation
ACCHIIINNNOOTZ cinchonization
ACCHIILLOPRTYY hypocritically
ACCHIIMMNNOSTU Communist China
ACCHIIORRSSSTU chiaroscurists

ACCHILLNNORSYY	synchronically
ACCHIMMNOOORST	monochromatics
ACCHIMNOOOPRSS	Spanish Morocco
ACCIIILLNOORTY	conciliatorily
ACCIIILLOOOPST	sociopolitical
ACCIIIMMNOOSST	iconomaticisms
ACCIIMMNNOOSTU	communications
ACCIIMNNORTTUU	circumnutation
ACCILLOPPRRTYY	procryptically
ACCILMNOOSTUUY	contumaciously
ACCILNNOORSTTU	constructional
ACCINPRSSTTUUU	acupuncturists
ACCLMOOOSSTTUY	cyclostomatous
ACDDEEEHHNNORS	hendecahedrons
ACDDEEGKLNNOUW	unacknowledged
ACDDEEIIILMNRS	decriminalised
ACDDEEIIILMNRZ	decriminalized
ACDDEEILNOORST	reconsolidated
ACDDEEIMNOSTTU	undomesticated
ACDDEEINRSSSTT	distractedness
ACDDEELOOORRST	Colorado Desert
ACDDEEORSTTTUU	autodestructed
ACDDEFILOOPPRS	apple of discord
ACDDEHHILOOPRY	hydrocephaloid
ACDDEHINOOPSST	dodecaphonists
ACDDEIINOOORSU	androdioecious
ACDDIIJLLORTUU	Ciudad Trujillo
ACDEEEELLPRRUZ	Pérez de Cuéllar
ACDEEEFFNNSSTU	unaffectedness
ACDEEEHINRRSUV	underachievers
ACDEEEIILNNSST	indelicateness
ACDEEEIINNRSTV	inadvertencies
ACDEEEILLNPRTY	precedentially
ACDEEEIMNOPPST	appendectomies
ACDEEEINNOPQRU	equiponderance
ACDEEEINORSSTV	decorativeness
ACDEEELNOPRSST	preadolescents
ACDEEELNPRRSSU	supercalenders
ACDEEENOPRSSSU	predaceousness
ACDEEENRRRSTUY	undersecretary
ACDEEFFIMORRTT	diffractometer
ACDEEFGHOOOOPP	Cape of Good Hope
ACDEEFHIIKRSSU	Fischer-Dieskau
ACDEEFHIINNRSS	disenfranchise
ACDEEFHNORRSTW	thenceforwards
ACDEEFINNOORST	confederations
ACDEEGGILNNORR	Recording Angel
ACDEEGHIINNRUV	underachieving
ACDEEGHINNTUUW	Dutch New Guinea
ACDEEGIILNNRST	decentralising
ACDEEGIILNNRSU	denuclearising
ACDEEGIILNNRTZ	decentralizing
ACDEEGIILNNRUZ	denuclearizing
ACDEEGIILNPRTY	depreciatingly
ACDEEGILNNOQRU	grandiloquence
ACDEEGIMNORSTU	discouragement
ACDEEGINOORRTV	overdecorating
ACDEEGKLMNNOTW	acknowledgment
ACDEEHIIINNRST	disinheritance
ACDEEHIIMPSSTY	metaphysicised
ACDEEHIIMPSTYZ	metaphysicized
ACDEEHILMNOSST	methodicalness
ACDEEHILORRSTT	tetrachlorides
ACDEEHIMNNNSTT	disenchantment
ACDEEHLMOORSST	schoolmastered
ACDEEIIIILRSTV	veridicalities
ACDEEIIILMNRSS	decriminalises
ACDEEIIILMNRSZ	decriminalizes
ACDEEIILMNOSTU	eudemonistical
ACDEEIILNNNQSU	quindecennials
ACDEEIILNNNSST	incidentalness
ACDEEIILNRSSTU	diureticalness
ACDEEIIMNOPRST	premedications
ACDEEIINOPRSTT	decrepitations
ACDEEIIORRSTTV	Victoria Desert
ACDEEILLLNNOSY	declensionally
ACDEEILLLNOTUV	involucellated
ACDEEILLRRSSTY	recrystallised
ACDEEILLRRSTYZ	recrystallized
ACDEEILNOORSST	reconsolidates
ACDEEILNORSTTU	interosculated
ACDEEILNOSTTUX	contextualised
ACDEEILNOTTUXZ	contextualized
ACDEEILNPPRRSU	perpendiculars
ACDEEILOPRSSTY	perissodactyle
ACDEEIMMNNOORT	recommendation
ACDEEIMNNOOPST	decompensation
ACDEEIMNNOSSSU	mendaciousness
ACDEEINNNOORST	recondensation
ACDEEINNOORSST	coordinateness
ACDEEINNOPQRUY	equiponderancy
ACDEEINNORSTTU	counterstained
ACDEEINOOPRRRT	reincorporated
ACDEEINOPRSSSU	predaciousness
ACDEELNNNRSTTY	transcendently
ACDEEMMNOORRTY	recommendatory
ACDEENOPRRSSTT	protractedness
ACDEFGHLNNOORT	French Togoland
ACDEFIIIINNOTT	identification
ACDEFIIINOOTTX	detoxification
ACDEFIILLNNOTY	confidentially
ACDEGHILLMOOOT	methodological
ACDEGHIMNORSTY	hydromagnetics
ACDEGHINNORSTU	countershading
ACDEGIILLOOPRT	pteridological
ACDEGIILLOOSTT	dialectologist
ACDEGIIMNOSSTY	geodynamicists
ACDEGILNNNRSTY	transcendingly
ACDEGIMNNNORTU	countermanding
ACDEGINNORRTTU	countertrading
ACDEGINOOPRSTT	prognosticated
ACDEHHIILOORTZ	chlorothiazide
ACDEHHIIMOPRRT	hermaphroditic
ACDEHHILLNOORT	chlorthalidone
ACDEHHIOOPRRST	archpriesthood
ACDEHHLOOPRSUY	hydrocephalous
ACDEHIIKLNORTY	hydrokinetical
ACDEHIILLMMOTY	immethodically
ACDEHIILLOPRSY	spheroidically
ACDEHIIMORRSTY	radiochemistry
ACDEHILLMOPRYY	hypodermically
ACDEHILLNOORRY	hydrocoralline
ACDEHILLNOPTYY	endophytically
ACDEHILMOOPPRR	chlorpropamide

ACDEHIMMNOPRSS	commanderships
ACDEHIMMNORSTY	thermodynamics
ACDEHINNOOPRTY	endocrinopathy
ACDEHINOORRSTT	trisoctahedron
ACDEHLMOOPRSSY	chlamydospores
ACDEHOOOPRRSTT	protochordates
ACDEIIIIMNNRST	indiscriminate
ACDEIIIIMNRSTV	discriminative
ACDEIIILMNRSTY	discriminately
ACDEIIILNNORTU	unidirectional
ACDEIIILNORSTT	doctrinalities
ACDEIIILNORTTY	directionality
ACDEIIIMNORSST	dosimetricians
ACDEIIINORSSSY	idiosyncrasies
ACDEIILLMOORTY	iodometrically
ACDEIILLNORSTY	discretionally
ACDEIILMMRSSTY	dissymmetrical
ACDEIILNNNOORT	nondirectional
ACDEIILNNOOOST	decolonisation
ACDEIILNNOOOTZ	decolonization
ACDEIILNNOSTTU	denticulations
ACDEIILNOOORST	decolorisation
ACDEIILNOOORTZ	decolorization
ACDEIILNOPRSTU	reduplications
ACDEIILNOSSSTY	Society Islands
ACDEIILNPQTTUU	quintuplicated
ACDEIIMNOOSSTT	domestications
ACDEIINNOORSST	considerations
ACDEIINOQRSSTU	quadrisections
ACDEILLMNOOSTY	endosmotically
ACDEILLNOOSSTY	disconsolately
ACDEILNNOPSTUU	pedunculations
ACDEILOPRSSSTY	perissodactyls
ACDEIMMNNOPSUY	pneumodynamics
ACDEIMNNOOSTTU	documentations
ACDEIMNOORSSSU	mordaciousness
ACDEINNOOPRRTU	unincorporated
ACDEINNORSTUUY	consuetudinary
ACDEINOOQRSSTU	conquistadores
ACDELLOOPSTTUY	leptodactylous
ACDFGHIIINNRSS	disfranchising
ACDFGHILMNNTUY	Flying Dutchman
ACDFHIIIIMNOTU	humidification
ACDFIIIILNOOST	solidification
ACDGGIILNORSUY	discouragingly
ACDGHILLLOORYY	hydrologically
ACDGIIIIMNNRST	discriminating
ACDGIIINNNORTT	indoctrinating
ACDHHIIOPRRSST	harpsichordist
ACDHIIIMNOOPPR	panidiomorphic
ACDHIIOOOPPRTT	diaphototropic
ACDHILLNOOPRYY	hydroponically
ACDIIIILNNNOST	disinclination
ACDIIIIMNNORST	discrimination
ACDIIIJLNORSTU	jurisdictional
ACDIIILNNOOTTY	conditionality
ACDIIILNNOPSTU	induplications
ACDIIILOSSTTUY	adscititiously
ACDIIIMNORRSST	discriminators
ACDIIIMNORRSTY	discriminatory
ACDIIINNNOOORT	incoordination
ACDIIINNNOORTT	indoctrination
ACDIILNNOOOSST	disconsolation
ACDIILNOOORSTU	discolouration
ACDIINNOORRSTT	indoctrinators
ACDILLLMOOORXY	loxodromically
ACEEEEGILLPTXY	epexegetically
ACEEEEHLPRSSST	steeplechasers
ACEEEEINNRRSTT	tercentenaries
ACEEEFGHIMNNST	gemeinschaften
ACEEEFGHINNRSU	French Guianese
ACEEEFGHLLNSST	gesellschaften
ACEEEFGNOORSTT	Congo Free State
ACEEEFINRRSSTV	refractiveness
ACEEEFMORRRSTT	refractometers
ACEEEGHHLLNORS	Oehlenschläger
ACEEEGHILNPSST	steeplechasing
ACEEEGHLNNSSSS	changelessness
ACEEEGIILLNPTY	epigenetically
ACEEEGLMNORSTT	electromagnets
ACEEEGMNNORSTU	encouragements
ACEEEHHIINRSTT	heresthetician
ACEEEHHILLMMOS	Sholem Aleichem
ACEEEHHILLORTT	heterolecithal
ACEEEHHIPRSTTY	hyperaesthetic
ACEEEHILLMORSS	hemerocallises
ACEEEHILNORSST	cholinesterase
ACEEEHLLMNNOPY	myelencephalon
ACEEEHLLMORRTT	electrothermal
ACEEEHLLNNOPST	telencephalons
ACEEEHLMNNOPSS	mesencephalons
ACEEEHLMNNOPST	metencephalons
ACEEEHLOPRRTTY	electrotherapy
ACEEEHMMOORTTY	haemocytometer
ACEEEHMMORSTTY	hemacytometers
ACEEEIILMNNNST	semicentennial
ACEEEIILOPRSSV	overspecialise
ACEEEIILOPRSVZ	overspecialize
ACEEEIINNRRSTT	tricentenaries
ACEEEILLLMRTTY	telemetrically
ACEEEILLMPRSST	capellmeisters
ACEEEILLOPPPRU	peculiar people
ACEEEILMNNRSTT	interlacements
ACEEEILMORRSTT	stereometrical
ACEEEILNNNOQUV	nonequivalence
ACEEEILNNNRSTT	tercentennials
ACEEEILNNQQUUV	quinquevalence
ACEEEILNRRSSTU	creatureliness
ACEEELLOPRRSTT	electroplaters
ACEEELMNOPRTUX	counterexample
ACEEEMNOOPRSTV	overcompensate
ACEEEMNORRSTUU	countermeasure
ACEEENNOOSSSTU	coetaneousness
ACEEFFHINNPRSS	affenpinschers
ACEEFFIILNTTUY	ineffectuality
ACEEFHIIINORTT	etherification
ACEEFHIMNNRSST	franchisements
ACEEFHMNOSSTUV	vouchsafements
ACEEFIIINORSTT	esterification
ACEEFINORRRSST	refractoriness
ACEEGGIMNNORRS	scaremongering
ACEEGHHILLNNNS	English Channel
ACEEGHHIOOPRRS	choreographies
ACEEGHHOOPRRRS	choreographers

ACEEGHIKLNNRSU	Recklinghausen
ACEEGHILLNOPRY	hypoallergenic
ACEEGHILLOOPRT	herpetological
ACEEGHILMNPSST	phlegmaticness
ACEEGHILOPRRSX	lexicographers
ACEEGHIMMNORTT	thermomagnetic
ACEEGHIMNOPRST	magnetospheric
ACEEGHIMOOPRRT	meteorographic
ACEEGHINOPRTTU	Pinochet Ugarte
ACEEGHMMMNNOOR	Greenham Common
ACEEGHOOOOPPSS	oesophagoscope
ACEEGIINORTTTY	teratogenicity
ACEEGIINOSSTTV	cogitativeness
ACEEGILLLLOOTY	teleologically
ACEEGILLMOOORT	meteorological
ACEEGILLNOORTY	orogenetically
ACEEGILLNOPRTT	electroplating
ACEEGILLNORSTY	estrogenically
ACEEGILLNRSTYY	synergetically
ACEEGILNNNOSST	congenitalness
ACEEGNOORSSSUU	courageousness
ACEEHHILNNNOPR	rhinencephalon
ACEEHHIMOPRSTT	chemotherapist
ACEEHHIMORSSTT	chrestomathies
ACEEHIIILNPSTT	licentiateship
ACEEHIILMOOPRR	microaerophile
ACEEHIILPRRSTY	hyperrealistic
ACEEHIIMPSSSTY	metaphysicises
ACEEHIIMPSSTYZ	metaphysicizes
ACEEHIINPPPRST	apprenticeship
ACEEHIKOPRRTTY	hyperkeratotic
ACEEHILLLNOPTY	telephonically
ACEEHILLMNNOSS	melancholiness
ACEEHILLMORTXY	exothermically
ACEEHILLRSTTYY	hysteretically
ACEEHILMMORRTT	thermometrical
ACEEHIMMNORSSV	servomechanism
ACEEHIMOORSSTT	tracheostomies
ACEEHLLMOOORST	alcoholometers
ACEEHLLOOPPSTU	leptocephalous
ACEEHLNNOOPPRS	prosencephalon
ACEEHLNPPRSSTU	Penshurst Place
ACEEHMMNOSSTUY	mesenchymatous
ACEEHMNOPPRRST	rapprochements
ACEEIIILLLMPST	semielliptical
ACEEIIJLNNORTT	interjectional
ACEEIILLLNPSST	ellipticalness
ACEEIILLLRTTVY	verticillately
ACEEIILLMMPRTY	metempirically
ACEEIILLMORSTT	microsatellite
ACEEIILLMPRRTY	perimetrically
ACEEIILLRRSTTV	verticillaster
ACEEIILMNOPSTX	exceptionalism
ACEEIILMNORSST	ceremonialists
ACEEIILNNNNQTU	quincentennial
ACEEIILNNNOPTT	epicontinental
ACEEIILNNNRSTT	tricentennials
ACEEIILNNORSST	intercessional
ACEEIILNNORSTT	intersectional
ACEEIILNORRSST	intercessorial
ACEEIILNOSSTTY	coessentiality
ACEEIINNOSSSTT	necessitations
ACEEIKMMNORSTU	mockumentaries
ACEEILLLLNTTUY	intellectually
ACEEILLLNNTTUU	unintellectual
ACEEILLMNORRTU	intermolecular
ACEEILLNOPRSSY	precessionally
ACEEILLRRSSSTY	recrystallises
ACEEILLRRSSTYZ	recrystallizes
ACEEILMNOOOPSU	polemoniaceous
ACEEILMNOPSTTV	contemplatives
ACEEILMNSSTUUV	cumulativeness
ACEEILNNOPRSTV	convertiplanes
ACEEILNNOPSTUV	nonspeculative
ACEEILNNQQUUVY	quinquevalency
ACEEILNORRRSTU	resurrectional
ACEEILNORSSTTU	interosculates
ACEEILNORSTVVY	conservatively
ACEEILNOSSTTUX	contextualises
ACEEILNOSTTUXZ	contextualizes
ACEEIMMMNOOTTW	committeewoman
ACEEIMMNNORSTU	incommensurate
ACEEIMNOOPRRST	contemporaries
ACEEIMNOPPRRTU	mercaptopurine
ACEEINNNORSSST	nonresistances
ACEEINNOOOPRTV	noncooperative
ACEEINNOORSSVZ	conversaziones
ACEEINOOPRRRST	reincorporates
ACEEINOOPRSTTX	expectorations
ACEEINOORRSSTV	conservatoires
	conservatories
ACEEINOPRRSSSU	precariousness
ACEEINOPRRSTTU	counterparties
ACEELLLMMNOPTY	complementally
ACEELMMNORSTUY	commensurately
ACEELNNOOPRSTV	convertoplanes
ACEEORRRSSTTUU	aerostructures
ACEFFHIIJMOOOR	Joachim of Fiore
ACEFFLORRSUUUY	furfuraceously
ACEFGIIINNORTT	gentrification
ACEFGIINNORTTU	centrifugation
ACEFHHIIINPSST	chieftainships
ACEFHHLNORSSSY	synchroflashes
ACEFIIIILMPSTV	simplificative
ACEFIIIINORTVV	revivification
ACEFIIIJLLNOST	jellifications
ACEFIIILMNOSTU	emulsification
ACEFIIILPRSTUY	superficiality
ACEFIIINNORSTU	reunifications
ACEFIIINOPRTTT	prettification
ACEFIIINORSSTV	versifications
ACEFIIINOSSTTT	testifications
ACEFIILLLNNOTY	inflectionally
ACEFIILMMNORST	microfilaments
ACEFIIMNNOORRT	reconfirmation
ACEFIINOSSSTTU	factitiousness
ACEFINRRRSTTUU	infrastructure
ACEFIRRSSTUUUU	usufructuaries
ACEFLLNOORSTTW	Wollstonecraft
ACEFLNOORSSSTU	colourfastness
ACEGGHHINOOPRR	choreographing
ACEGGHIIMNNNNU	machinegunning
ACEGGILLNOOORT	gerontological
ACEGGILMNNOORT	conglomerating

ACEGGILNOOSSTY	gynaecologists
ACEGHHIILLOPRY	hieroglyphical
ACEGHHNOOPRRRS	chronographers
ACEGHIILLNOSTY	histogenically
ACEGHILLLNOOTY	ethnologically
ACEGHILLNOOPTY	photogenically
ACEGHILLNOORTY	orthogenically
ACEGHILOORRRTY	chloroargyrite
ACEGHILOOSSSTT	eschatologists
ACEGHLMOOPSTYY	metapsychology
ACEGHLNNNOOOTY	nanotechnology
ACEGHMMOOPRSUY	myrmecophagous
ACEGHNOOPPRSSY	pharyngoscopes
ACEGHOOOOPPSSY	oesophagoscopy
ACEGHOPPRRRSTY	cryptographers
ACEGIIIILLLOST	illogicalities
ACEGIIILMNRRSU	mercurialising
ACEGIIILMNRRUZ	mercurializing
ACEGIIILNNOSST	sectionalising
ACEGIIILNNOSTZ	sectionalizing
ACEGIIILNOOPST	geopoliticians
ACEGIIINNNORST	containerising
ACEGIIINNNORTZ	containerizing
ACEGIIKMMNORRT	micromarketing
ACEGIILLLOSTUY	eulogistically
ACEGIILLMNOORT	terminological
ACEGIILLOOORST	soteriological
ACEGIILLORSSUY	sacrilegiously
ACEGIILNNORTUV	countervailing
ACEGIILNNOTTUV	conglutinative
ACEGIILNOQTUVY	equivocatingly
ACEGIILNOSSTTU	gesticulations
ACEGIILNPSTTUX	sextuplicating
ACEGILLLMOORTY	metrologically
ACEGILLLMOOTYY	etymologically
ACEGILLLOOOSTY	osteologically
ACEGILLLOOPRTY	petrologically
ACEGILMNNOOORT	conglomeration
ACEGILNOOPRSSY	laryngoscopies
ACEGINNNOOSSUU	consanguineous
ACEGINNOOSSSTU	contagiousness
ACEGINNOPSSSUU	pugnaciousness
ACEGINOOPRSSTT	prognosticates
ACEHHIIILMNNTT	antihelminthic
ACEHHIINOPPRTT	pithecanthropi
ACEHHIINOPRRTT	therianthropic
ACEHHIINOPRSSZ	schizophrenias
ACEHHIIPPRRSST	archpriestship
ACEHHILLOOPSTY	theosophically
ACEHHILLOPTTYY	hypothetically
ACEHHILOOPRSUZ	rhizocephalous
ACEHHIMOOPPRST	metaphosphoric
ACEHHINOOPPRST	phosphocreatin
ACEHHINOOPSTTY	hypothecations
ACEHHLMOOOPPST	ophthalmoscope
ACEHHLOOOPRSTU	orthocephalous
ACEHHMMNRSSTUY	chrysanthemums
ACEHHMOOOPRRST	chromatophores
ACEHHMOOPRSTTU	chemautotrophs
ACEHIIIILMSSTW	whimsicalities
ACEHIIINRRSSST	christianisers
ACEHIIINRRSSTZ	christianizers
ACEHIILLLOPSTY	phyllosilicate
ACEHIILLPSTUUY	euphuistically
ACEHIILNORSSST	historicalness
ACEHIIMNNOOPRT	enantiomorphic
ACEHIIMPSSSTTY	metaphysicists
ACEHIINNOPRSST	anticensorship
ACEHIINNPSSSUY	picayunishness
ACEHIINNSSTTUU	unenthusiastic
ACEHIINOOPRTTU	eutrophication
ACEHIINOPPRSST	spinthariscope
ACEHIIOOPRSSST	spirochaetosis
ACEHIIOORRSTTT	osteoarthritic
ACEHILLMNOPRST	phallocentrism
ACEHILLNOPPTYY	phenotypically
ACEHILLNOPRSTT	phallocentrist
ACEHILLOPRSTTY	prosthetically
ACEHILLOPRTXYY	xerophytically
ACEHILMNOOPRRZ	chlorpromazine
ACEHILMOPRSSTT	thermoplastics
ACEHILNOOPPRSS	cephalosporins
ACEHILNORSSSUV	chivalrousness
ACEHIMNOOPRRTT	anthropometric
ACEHIMOPPRSTTY	spermatophytic
ACEHIMORRSSTTY	astrochemistry
ACEHINOORRSSTT	orchestrations
ACEHINOPPRRSST	copartnerships
ACEHLLMOORSSTY	schoolmasterly
ACEHLLOPSSUXYY	psychosexually
ACEIIIILMNPSTU	municipalities
ACEIIIILNPPRST	principalities
ACEIIIILQSTUZZ	quizzicalities
ACEIIILLMPTTUV	multiplicative
ACEIIILLNNOPST	penicillations
ACEIIILLNORTTV	verticillation
ACEIIILLOPSSTY	isopiestically
ACEIIILMNOOSTT	emotionalistic
ACEIIILNRRTUVY	curvilinearity
ACEIIILNRSSTUV	universalistic
ACEIIIMMNOORSS	commissionaire
ACEIIIMNNORRST	recriminations
ACEIIIMNNORSTT	interactionism
ACEIIINNNOSTTV	Constantine VII
ACEIIINNOPSSTX	expansionistic
ACEIIINOORSSTT	eroticisations
ACEIIINOORSTTZ	eroticizations
ACEIIINOPPRSTT	precipitations
ACEIIINOPQRSTU	preacquisition
ACEIIINOQRSSTU	reacquisitions
ACEIIINORSSTTU	securitisation
ACEIIINORSTTUZ	securitization
ACEIILLLNRTUUY	unicellularity
ACEIILLMNNOOOS	neocolonialism
ACEIILLNNOOOST	neocolonialist
ACEIILMNNNOSTT	continentalism
ACEIILMNORSTUV	vermiculations
ACEIILMNPRRSSU	supercriminals
ACEIILNNNOSSTY	nonsensicality
ACEIILNNNOSTTT	continentalist
ACEIILNNOOORST	recolonisation
ACEIILNNOOORTZ	recolonization
ACEIILNNOORSTU	reinoculations
ACEIILNNORRSTU	insurrectional

ACEIILNNORSTTU nocturnalities
ACEIILNNOTTUVY continuatively
ACEIILNOOPRRTY incorporeality
ACEIILNOORSSTT sclerotisation
ACEIILNOORSTTZ sclerotization
ACEIILNOPRSTUY pertinaciously
ACEIILNOSSSSUV lasciviousness
ACEIILNPQSTTUU quintuplicates
ACEIIMMNNOORTU immunoreaction
ACEIIMMNOORSST commiserations
ACEIIMNORRSSTT craniometrists
ACEIINNORSSTTY syncretisation
ACEIINNORSTTYZ syncretization
ACEIINNOSSSTUU incautiousness
ACEIINOOOPRSTT cooperationist
ACEIINOOPRSTTV contrapositive
ACEIINOPSSSSUU auspiciousness
ACEIINORSSSTTU resuscitations
ACEILLLMORTUVY volumetrically
ACEILLLNOOQSSU colloquialness
ACEILLMMOORSTY osmometrically
ACEILLMOPRRTYY pyrometrically
ACEILLNNNOOTVY conventionally
ACEILLNNOOSSTT constellations
ACEILLNOOPRSSY processionally
ACEILLNOPRSSUY supersonically
ACEILLNOSTTUVY consultatively
ACEILMNOOORTUV macroevolution
ACEILMNOOPRRTY contemporarily
ACEILMNORSSSUU miraculousness
ACEILNNNNOOTUV unconventional
ACEILNNNOOPSTT Constantinople
ACEILNNOOOPRST spironolactone
ACEILNOOPRRTUY perlocutionary
ACEILNOOQSSSUU loquaciousness
ACEILNOPRRRTUV proventricular
ACEILNOPRRSSTU pronuclearists
ACEILOORRSSTTW watercolorists
ACEILOORRSTTUW watercolourist
ACEIMMMNOOORST commemorations
ACEIMMNNOORSTU commensuration
ACEIMNNNOOPRTU pronunciamento
ACEIMNNORRSTTU macronutrients
ACEIMNOORRSTUV conservatorium
ACEINNNOOOOPRT noncooperation
ACEINNNOORSTTV contraventions
ACEKLMMNOORSTT Kelmscott Manor
ACELRRRSTTTUUU ultrastructure
ACEMNOOORSSTTU entomostracous
ACENNOOOOPRRST noncooperators
ACFFIIINOORSTT fortifications
ACFGIIIIILNNOST fictionalising
ACFGIIIILNNOTZ fictionalizing
ACFGIIIINNOSST significations
ACFGIIILMNSSSY misclassifying
ACFGIIILNOORST glorifications
ACFGIIINNNNOST nonsignificant
ACFGIILMNNNOTU malfunctioning
ACFGIINNOORSTU configurations
ACFHIIINOORRST horrifications
ACFIIIILMNOPST simplification
ACFIIIINNORSTT nitrifications
ACFIIIINORSTTV vitrifications
ACFIIIJLLNOOST jollifications
ACFIIIJNOSSTTU justifications
ACFIIILNOSTTTU stultification
ACFIIIMNOORSTT mortifications
ACFIIIMNOSSTTY mystifications
ACFIIINNOOOPST opsonification
ACFIILLNNNOOTY nonfictionally
ACFIILLRSTTUUY futuristically
ACFIILNNOSSTTU functionalists
ACFINNNOOORSTT confrontations
ACGGHHIMOPPRSY sphygmographic
ACGGIILNNNOTTU conglutinating
ACGHHHIOOPSTUY ichthyophagous
ACGHIIIINNRSST christianising
ACGHIIIINNRSTZ christianizing
ACGHIIILNOPSTT antiphlogistic
ACGHIIINOPSSTT sophisticating
ACGHIILLLLOOPY philologically
ACGHIILLLLOOTY lithologically
ACGHIILLLOOSTY histologically
ACGHIILLNOOORT ornithological
ACGHIILMNOOPSY physiognomical
ACGHILLLMOOTYY mythologically
ACGHILLLNOOOPY phonologically
ACGHILLLOOPTYY phytologically
ACGHILMOOORSTT chromatologist
ACGHIMOOPRSSST cosmographists
ACGHIOPPRRSTTY cryptographist
ACGIIIILMNNPSU municipalising
ACGIIIILMNNPUZ municipalizing
ACGIIIJLLNOSTY jingoistically
ACGIIILLLNSTUY linguistically
ACGIIILLLPSTUY pugilistically
ACGIIILNNOTTXY intoxicatingly
ACGIILLLLMNOOY limnologically
ACGIILLMNOSUUY mucilaginously
ACGIILLMOOSSTT climatologists
ACGIILNNNOOTTU conglutination
ACGIILRRSSTTUU agriculturists
ACGIIMMNOORRSS microorganisms
ACGIIMNNPSTTUU mispunctuating
ACGILLNOOOSSTV volcanologists
ACGILLNOOSSTUV vulcanologists
ACGILNOOPRSSTY laryngoscopist
ACGINOOOPRRSTT prognosticator
ACGIOOPRSSSSTT gastroscopists
ACHHIIINNORSST ornithischians
ACHHILLMNOOOPY homophonically
ACHHIMMMOOORST homochromatism
ACHHINOOOPPRST anthroposophic
ACHHLMOOOPPSTY ophthalmoscopy
ACHIIIINNORSTT trichinisation
ACHIIIINNORTTZ trichinization
ACHIIIJPRSSSTU justiciarships
ACHIIILLLPSTYY syphilitically
ACHIIILLNORSTY histrionically
ACHIIILNPPPRSS principalships
ACHIIIMNOORSST trichomoniasis
ACHIIINOOPSSTT sophistication
ACHIILLLMNOOTY monolithically
ACHIILLLOSTTYY histolytically

ACHIIMMOPRSSSY	commissaryship
ACHIIOOPRSSSTT	sophisticators
ACHIIOPRSSSTTY	astrophysicist
ACHILLLNOOPPYY	polyphonically
ACHILLOOPPTTYY	phototypically
ACHILMMOOPRSTY	polychromatism
ACHILMOPSSTTYY	sympatholytics
ACHIMMMNOOORST	monochromatism
ACHIMNOOOPRSTU	actinomorphous
ACHIOOPPRRRSTU	procuratorship
ACHLNNOORSSUYY	asynchronously
ACHMMNOOOORRST	monochromators
ACIIIILNOOPSTT	politicisation
ACIIIILNOOPTTZ	politicization
ACIIIILPRSSTTU	spiritualistic
ACIIIIMNOSSTTV	victimisations
ACIIIIMNOSTTVZ	victimizations
ACIIILLLMPSSTY	simplistically
ACIIILLMNOPTTU	multiplication
ACIIILLMOPSTTY	optimistically
ACIIILLNNOSSTT	scintillations
ACIIILNOPSSUUY	inauspiciously
ACIILLLMOOQSSU	colloquialisms
ACIILNNOOSTTTU	constitutional
ACIILNOOORSSTU	colourisations
ACIILNOOORSTUZ	colourizations
ACIILQRSSTTUUU	aquiculturists
ACIIMMNNOOSSTU	communisations
ACIIMMNNOOSTUZ	communizations
ACIIMMNOOPSTTU	miscomputation
ACIIMNNOPSTTUU	mispunctuation
ACIINNNOOPRSTU	pronunciations
ACIINNOOOPRRST	incorporations
ACIINNOOOPRSTT	contraposition
ACIINNOPRRSSTT	transcriptions
ACIKMNNOORSTUY	Rocky Mountains
ACILLOOPPRTTYY	prototypically
ACILNNOOORTUVY	convolutionary
ACILNOPRSSTUUY	transpicuously
ACILNOSSSSTTTU	sansculottists
ACILRRSSSTTTUU	structuralists
ACIMMOOORSSTTU	microstomatous
ACIMNOOOSTTTXY	cytotaxonomist
ACINNOPRSSTTTU	contrapuntists
ADDDEEEEHLRRTW	Edward the Elder
ADDDEEEGHNORTY	dehydrogenated
ADDDEEIILMNOSS	Diomede Islands
ADDDEIIIILNSUV	individualised
ADDDEIIIILNUVZ	individualized
ADDEEEEFHNNRSS	freehandedness
ADDEEEEGHLMMRS	sledgehammered
ADDEEEEHNNNSSV	evenhandedness
ADDEEEEHNORSSS	soreheadedness
ADDEEEFFIINRTT	differentiated
ADDEEEFHNNORSS	forehandedness
ADDEEEFHNOSSST	softheadedness
ADDEEEGHLNNOSS	longheadedness
ADDEEEGHNORSSY	dehydrogenases
ADDEEEGHNORSTY	dehydrogenates
ADDEEEHIMNPPRS	misapprehended
ADDEEEHNNNOPSS	openhandedness
ADDEEEIINPRSST	pedestrianised
ADDEEEIINPRSTZ	pedestrianized
ADDEEEILMPRTTY	premeditatedly
ADDEEEILNOPRSS	depersonalised
ADDEEEILNOPRSZ	depersonalized
ADDEEEIMNPRTTU	unpremeditated
ADDEEEIMNRSTTU	underestimated
ADDEEEINOPQRTU	equiponderated
ADDEEFFHLRRUUY	furfuraldehyde
ADDEEFLNNNORUW	Newfoundlander
ADDEEGIIINRTTT	interdigitated
ADDEEHIIMNNRTY	dimenhydrinate
ADDEEIINPSSSST	dissipatedness
ADDEEINOPRRSTU	superordinated
ADDEELNOPPRTUU	underpopulated
ADDEFGILLRRSUY	disregardfully
ADDEFIIILSSSTY	dissatisfiedly
ADDEFIILLNNRSS	Flinders Island
ADDEFIILNNSSSU	disdainfulness
ADDEGILNOORRSU	Rio Grande do Sul
ADDEGINNNRSSTU	understandings
ADDEHHILOPRSST	stadholdership
ADDEHILLNOORSW	Lord Howe Island
ADDEIIIILNRSUV	individualiser
ADDEIIIILNRUVZ	individualizer
ADDEIIIILNSSUV	individualises
ADDEIIIILNSUVZ	individualizes
ADDEIIILNPSTTU	platitudinised
ADDEIIILNPTTUZ	platitudinized
ADDEIIILNRSSTU	industrialised
ADDEIIILNRSTUZ	industrialized
ADDEIIINOOSSTX	deoxidisations
ADDEIIINOOSTXZ	deoxidizations
ADDEIILNOPPSTY	disappointedly
ADDEIMNNRSSSTU	misunderstands
ADDIIIILMNSSUV	individualisms
ADDIIIILNSSTUV	individualists
ADDIIIINNOSTUV	individuations
ADEEEEEGNNRSST	degenerateness
ADEEEEHHLMMPST	Hemel Hempstead
ADEEEEIMNPRRTT	predeterminate
ADEEEFFIINRSTT	differentiates
ADEEEFGILORRTU	Tierra del Fuego
ADEEEFGLNNNSSW	newfangledness
ADEEEFHOOPRRTW	weatherproofed
ADEEEFIMNNOORT	aforementioned
ADEEEFIMNRSTTU	disfeaturement
ADEEEFINNORSTT	defenestration
ADEEEGGIMNNSST	disengagements
ADEEEGIILMNRST	legerdemainist
ADEEEGIINRRTTV	redintegrative
ADEEEGIINRSTTV	reinvestigated
ADEEEGIKNNRRRT	kindergartener
ADEEEGINORRRTT	reinterrogated
ADEEEGLNRRSSSS	regardlessness
ADEEEGOPRRRTUY	daguerreotyper
ADEEEGOPRRSTUY	daguerreotypes
ADEEEHHLLORTWY	wholeheartedly
ADEEEHIINRRSST	hereditariness
ADEEEHILNOOPRT	radiotelephone
ADEEEHIMNNRSTT	disheartenment
ADEEEHIMNORRSV	Mies van der Rohe
ADEEEHIMOPRSSV	overemphasised

ADEEEHIMOPRSVZ overemphasized
ADEEEHIMRSSSST headmistresses
ADEEEIIIMNRRST intermediaries
ADEEEIIINRRSST residentiaries
ADEEEIILLNPTXY expedientially
ADEEEIILMNRTTY intermediately
ADEEEIIMMQRSUV demisemiquaver
ADEEEIIMNRSTTV determinatives
ADEEEIIMNSSTTV meditativeness
ADEEEIINPRSSST pedestrianises
ADEEEIINPRSSTZ pedestrianizes
ADEEEILMORRTTY radiotelemetry
ADEEEILNOPRSSS depersonalises
ADEEEILNOPRSSZ depersonalizes
ADEEEILOPRSTTY radioteletypes
ADEEEIMMNORSST immoderateness
ADEEEIMNRSSTTU underestimates
ADEEEIMNRSSTTV advertisements
ADEEEIMNRSTTVZ advertizements
ADEEEINNRSTTUW Wiener Neustadt
ADEEEINOPQRSTU equiponderates
ADEEELNOPPRRTY preponderately
ADEEEMNNRSTTTU understatement
ADEEENNNOSSSSU unseasonedness
ADEEENNPPRRSSU unpreparedness
ADEEFFIILLNRTY differentially
ADEEFFIINORRTT differentiator
ADEEFGHINRSSST farsightedness
ADEEFHILNSSTTW halfwittedness
ADEEFHKLOOOSTW Lake of the Woods
ADEEFIMNNOORRT foreordainment
ADEEGGHLNOOSTT snaggletoothed
ADEEGGIINNPRST predesignating
ADEEGGIINNRRTT redintegrating
ADEEGGILLNNORT golden triangle
ADEEGGIMNNRRRY gerrymandering
ADEEGHHILLRTTY lightheartedly
ADEEGHHOOPPRRT rephotographed
ADEEGHILNNRRTY heartrendingly
ADEEGHILNRSSTU daughterliness
ADEEGHNNORSSST headstrongness
ADEEGIIILMNNRS demineralising
ADEEGIIILMNNRZ demineralizing
ADEEGIIILNORVZ overidealizing
ADEEGIIIMNNRTT intermediating
ADEEGIIINRSTTT interdigitates
ADEEGIIINRSTTV disintegrative
ADEEGIIKLLNNSS Keeling Islands
ADEEGIIMNNORST demonetarising
ADEEGIIMNNORTZ demonetarizing
ADEEGIINNORRTT redintegration
ADEEGIINNPRSTT predestinating
ADEEGIINNRRRVW Wind River Range
ADEEGIINORRSTT deregistration
ADEEGIMORSSTTU deuterogamists
ADEEGINNOPPRRT preponderating
ADEEGINOORRSST derogatoriness
ADEEGINOPRRSUV overpersuading
ADEEGINORSSTTU deuteragonists
ADEEGJLMNNNOTU nonjudgemental
ADEEHHIILMOPRS hemispheroidal
ADEEHHILLPPSSU philadelphuses
ADEEHHIMOPRRST hermaphrodites
ADEEHIIILMPPRY hyperlipidemia
ADEEHIIMNOORTT triiodomethane
ADEEHIKLORRSSY Yorkshire Dales
ADEEHILMNNRSTT disenthralment
ADEEHILNOOPRTY radiotelephony
ADEEHIMORRSTTT tetartohedrism
ADEEHLMNOORRSY dysmenorrhoeal
ADEEHLORSTTTUY stoutheartedly
ADEEHNOOPRRSTZ trapezohedrons
ADEEHOPRRSSSTU pseudarthroses
ADEEIIILORRSST editorialisers
ADEEIIILORRSTZ editorializers
ADEEIIIMNNORTT intermediation
ADEEIIINORSSTV radiosensitive
ADEEIILLLLMNSV Melville Island
ADEEIILLNPRSTY presidentially
ADEEIILMNNOTVY denominatively
ADEEIILMNNSSTT disentailments
ADEEIILMNOPRSS impersonalised
ADEEIILMNOPRSZ impersonalized
ADEEIILNNNORST nonresidential
ADEEIIMNNOOSTT demonetisation
ADEEIIMNNOOTTZ demonetization
ADEEIIMNORRSTT intermediators
ADEEIINNNORSST inordinateness
ADEEIINNOPRSTT predestination
ADEEIINOPRSSST dispensatories
ADEEIINSSSSSUV dissuasiveness
ADEEILMMNNSSTT dismantlements
ADEEILMORSTTUV overstimulated
ADEEILNNOOSSTV devotionalness
ADEEILNNRRSTUY unrestrainedly
ADEEIMNNORRSST arrondissement
ADEEIMNORSSTTV demonstratives
ADEEINNOOPPRRT preponderation
ADEEINOPRRSSTU superordinates
ADEELNNOPPRRTY preponderantly
ADEELNNORSSSSU slanderousness
ADEEMNNNORRUWY Newry and Mourne
ADEENPPRRRSSTU understrappers
ADEFFGIINORSST disafforesting
ADEFGIIMNORRST transmogrified
ADEFIIINNOSSTT disinfestation
ADEFIINNOOORRT foreordination
ADEFIINOORSSTT disforestation
ADEFIINOSSSSTU fastidiousness
ADEFIIOORSSTUV overfastidious
ADEFILNOPRSSTY Parts of Lindsey
ADEGGIIINNRSTT disintegrating
ADEGGILLNRSSSU sluggardliness
ADEGHHHIILNRSS Shire Highlands
ADEGHIILLNNRST disenthralling
ADEGHIILMNPSTY lymphangitides
ADEGHINNOORSTY hydrogenations
ADEGHNNOOOPRRY androgynophore
ADEGIIIILMNRST demilitarising
ADEGIIIILMNRTZ demilitarizing
ADEGIIIILNORST editorialising
ADEGIIIILNORTZ editorializing
ADEGIIINNORSTT disintegration
disorientating

ADEGIINNNPRSTU underpaintings
ADEGIINORRSSTT disintegrators
ADEGILMOORSSTT dermatologists
ADEGINNNPSSSTU upstandingness
ADEGLLMNORSUWZ mangoldwurzels
ADEHHIILLLLSSY shillyshallied
ADEHHIMOPRRSTU Hermaphroditus
ADEHHIOPRRSTTY hydrotherapist
ADEHHLLMORRTYY hydrothermally
ADEHHLOPRSSTUY hydrosulphates
ADEHIILNNOPSSX Phoenix Islands
ADEHILNNOPRSSW landownerships
ADEHILNNOSSSTU outlandishness
ADEHIMOOOPPRSS paedomorphosis
ADEHIMOOPRRSST moderatorships
ADEHINOORRSSTW roadworthiness
ADEHIOPRRSSSTU pseudarthrosis
ADEHNORRSSTTWW northwestwards
ADEHORSSSTTUWW southwestwards
ADEIIILMNNORST tridimensional
ADEIIILMNNOSTY dimensionality
ADEIIILNPRSTTU platitudiniser
ADEIIILNPRTTUZ platitudinizer
ADEIIILNPSSTTU platitudinises
ADEIIILNPSTTUZ platitudinizes
ADEIIILNRSSSTU industrialises
ADEIIILNRSSTUZ industrializes
ADEIIIMNNOSSST disseminations
ADEIIINNOORSTT disorientation
ADEIIINOOPRSST periodisations
ADEIIINOOPRSTZ periodizations
ADEIIINRSSTTTU attitudinisers
ADEIIINRSTTTUZ attitudinizers
ADEIILLNOPRTVY providentially
ADEIILMNNOOPRS pronominalised
ADEIILMNNOOPRZ pronominalized
ADEIILNOSTTUVY adventitiously
ADEIIMNNOORSST modernisations
ADEIIMNNOORSTZ modernizations
ADEIIMNNOPPSTT disappointment
ADEIIMNNORSSTT antimodernists
ADEIINNOOPRRST preordinations
ADEIINORRSSSTT transistorised
ADEIINORRSSTTZ transistorized
ADEILLNORRSTVY dorsiventrally
ADEILMMNORRSTU ultramodernism
ADEILMNORRSTTU ultramodernist
ADEILNOORSSSTU idolatrousness
ADEIMNNOORSSTT demonstrations
ADEIMNNOPRSSTU superdominants
ADEINOOOPPRRTT proportionated
ADEINOOORRTTTX dextrorotation
ADELLNOORRSTVY dorsoventrally
ADELMNOOORSSSU malodorousness
ADEOOORRRTTTXY dextrorotatory
ADFGIIINORSSTU disfigurations
ADFIIIMNNOORST disinformation
ADGHILOOORRSVV Voroshilovgrad
ADGHINNOOOPRST gonadotrophins
ADGHMNNOOPRRSY gynandromorphs
ADGHMNNOOPRRYY gynandromorphy
ADGIIIINNSTTTU attitudinising
ADGIIIINNTTTUZ attitudinizing
ADGIILLLNNOTUY longitudinally
ADGIILNOPPRSVY disapprovingly
ADHIIMMMMNRTUU Urim and Thummim
ADHILNOORSSTYY hydrolysations
ADHILNOORSTYYZ hydrolyzations
ADIIIILMNOSSST dissimilations
ADIIIILMNPRSTU platiniridiums
ADIIIILNOQSSTU disquisitional
ADIIILMNOSSSTU dissimulations
ADIIILNRSSSTTU industrialists
ADIILLOPRRSSTU Lords Spiritual
ADIILNOPRSSTTU postindustrial
ADIILOPSSTTUUY disputatiously
ADILLLLOOOPPSY allopolyploids
ADILLLLOOOPPYY allopolyploidy
ADILLMNNOOOSSS Solomon Islands
ADILLOOOPPSTUY autopolyploids
ADILLOOOPPTUYY autopolyploidy
AEEEEFFIMNNSST effeminateness
AEEEEGILNORRVZ overgeneralize
AEEEEGILNRRTVY regeneratively
AEEEEGINSSTTVV vegetativeness
AEEEEGLNNRRTUY unregenerately
AEEEEHMNOPPRRT ephemeropteran
AEEEEHNPRSSTUY Hautes-Pyrénées
AEEEEILMNNRSST elementariness
AEEEEIMNNRSSTT intemerateness
AEEEEIMNNRTTVW interweavement
AEEEEINNPRRTTT interpenetrate
AEEEEINNRSSTTV inveterateness
AEEEEINNRSSTVV venerativeness
AEEEEINPRRSTTV representative
AEEEEMMNRRSSTU remeasurements
AEEEFGHHIRSTTW featherweights
AEEEFHIIRRSSTT Irish Free State
AEEEFIILNNRRTT interferential
AEEEFILLNPRRTY preferentially
AEEEFILMNRTTVY fermentatively
AEEEFINQRSTTUV frequentatives
AEEEGGINRSSSSV aggressiveness
AEEEGGIORRSSVV overaggressive
AEEEGHHINPRSSS sheepshearings
AEEEGHHIOPRRST heterographies
AEEEGHILMNPPRT pamphleteering
AEEEGIILMNSSTT legitimateness
AEEEGIINRSSTTV reinvestigates
AEEEGILLNSSTTV televangelists
AEEEGILLRSSSST legislatresses
AEEEGINORRRSTT reinterrogates
AEEEGNNOOPQRTU roentgenopaque
AEEEGNNOORRSTT enterogastrone
AEEEHHHINNSSST heathenishness
AEEEHHLMNNOSTY Henley-on-Thames
AEEEHIIMNRSSST Shemini Atseres
AEEEHIINNPPRSV inapprehensive
AEEEHILNPPRSVY apprehensively
AEEEHILNPRTTVY hyperventilate
AEEEHILOPRSSTT heteroplasties
AEEEHIMOPRSSSV overemphasises
AEEEHIMOPRSSVZ overemphasizes
AEEEHINNPPRSUV unapprehensive

AEEEHINSSSTUVX	exhaustiveness
AEEEIIINNPRSTT	penitentiaries
AEEEIILLNPRTXY	experientially
AEEEIILLNRSSTT	illiterateness
AEEEIILMNNSSTT	sentimentalise
AEEEIILMNNSTTZ	sentimentalize
AEEEIILNRRSSTV	irrelativeness
AEEEIIMNPRSSTV	imperativeness
AEEEIINPRRTTTV	interpretative
AEEEILLLNRSSST	Lesser Antilles
AEEEILLMNPRTXY	experimentally
AEEEILMNORRTTV	intervalometer
AEEEILMNRRTUVY	remuneratively
AEEEILNOPRSTUV	superelevation
AEEEIMNNNRSTTT	entertainments
AEEEIMNNRRTUUV	unremunerative
AEEEIMNNRSSTTT	reinstatements
AEEEINNNPRRTTT	interpenetrant
AEEEINNOPRRSTT	representation
AEEEINOPRRSSTV	perseverations
AEEEINPRSSSSUV	persuasiveness
AEEELMNNNRSSSS	mannerlessness
AEEEMMNOPRSTTU	pneumatometers
AEEEMNNOPPRSWW	newspaperwomen
AEEEMNOOPRSTUX	extemporaneous
AEEEMNORSSSSTV	overassessment
AEEEMNORSSTTTV	overstatements
AEEENNORSSSTUX	extraneousness
AEEENNRRSSSSTV	transverseness
AEEENQSSSSTTUU	statuesqueness
AEEFFGHIMNRSTT	affreightments
AEEFGIIMMNRRST	ferrimagnetism
AEEFGIINRSSTUV	figurativeness
AEEFGILMNNNSSU	meaningfulness
AEEFGIMMNORRST	ferromagnetism
AEEFGINNRRRRST	retransferring
AEEFGLNNRSSTUU	ungratefulness
AEEFHLMNOSSSST	fathomlessness
AEEFIILNNOPRRU	infopreneurial
AEEFIILNOQQTUU	quinquefoliate
AEEFIINNORSSTT	reinfestations
AEEFILMOPRRTVY	performatively
AEEFIOOPRRSSST	professoriates
AEEFNOQRRSSSUU	foursquareness
AEEGGHNNOOPRRT	roentgenograph
AEEGGHOOOPRRSZ	zoogeographers
AEEGGIINORSSTT	segregationist
AEEGGIINRRSTTV	tergiversating
AEEGGILLNNORTU	outgeneralling
AEEGGINOPRRSTU	supererogating
AEEGGINORRSSSU	gregariousness
AEEGGIOSSTTUUV	autosuggestive
AEEGGMNNOORRST	roentgenograms
AEEGHHLORSSTUU	slaughterhouse
AEEGHIINNPRSST	parenthesising
AEEGHIINNPRSTZ	parenthesizing
AEEGHIINNRRTTW	interwreathing
AEEGHIIPRRRSST	parish register
AEEGHILNOOSSTY	anesthesiology
AEEGHILNOPRSST	selenographist
AEEGHIMNSSSTTT	steamtightness
AEEGHIMOPRRSSS	seismographers
AEEGHINRSSTTTW	watertightness
AEEGHNOOPRRSTV	photoengravers
AEEGIIILLLMTTY	illegitimately
AEEGIIILLLNNTT	intelligential
AEEGIIILLNNSTT	intelligentsia
AEEGIIILNNNRTT	interlineating
AEEGIIILRRRSTU	irregularities
AEEGIILLNNPRTT	interpellating
AEEGIILMNORSSS	generalissimos
AEEGIILNNNRTTY	entertainingly
AEEGIIMMNOPSTZ	piezomagnetism
AEEGIIMNNNORTU	mountaineering
AEEGIIMNORSTTV	overestimating
AEEGIINNNNRTTU	unentertaining
AEEGIINNOORSTT	renegotiations
AEEGIINNOPRRST	peregrinations
AEEGIINNORRSTT	reintegrations
AEEGIINORRSTTV	interrogatives
	tergiversation
AEEGILLMNORRST	steamrollering
AEEGILLOOPSSST	spelaeologists
AEEGILNNOSSSTU	gelatinousness
AEEGIMNNNORSTU	Green Mountains
AEEGIMNNORTUUV	outmaneuvering
AEEGIMNRRRTUWZ	gewurztraminer
AEEGINOOPRRSTU	supererogation
AEEGIORRRSSTTV	tergiversators
AEEGIORRRSTTVY	tergiversatory
AEEGLLMNNORTVY	governmentally
AEEGNOORSSSTUU	outrageousness
AEEGOOPRRRSSTU	supererogators
AEEGOOPRRRSTUY	supererogatory
AEEHHIINNOPSTZ	phenothiazines
AEEHHILLMORSTT	heterothallism
AEEHHILMMNNSTT	nemathelminths
AEEHHLMNNOPSTU	sulphonmethane
AEEHHOPPPRSSTU	superphosphate
AEEHIILLNNOSTZ	hellenizations
AEEHIJNNOPRSST	Saint-John Perse
AEEHIKOPRRSSTY	hyperkeratosis
AEEHILLMRSSSTW	Wilhelmstrasse
AEEHILMNNOPSST	phenomenalists
AEEHILMNOOPRTY	hyperemotional
AEEHILOOPRRTTY	heteropolarity
AEEHIMNNOPRSST	Pontine Marshes
AEEHIMNORSSTUV	overenthusiasm
AEEHINPPPPRRSW	whippersnapper
AEEHLMNOORRTTT	thermotolerant
AEEHMNNPRSSSUU	superhumanness
AEEHMNOOPPRSTU	pneumatophores
AEEHMOOPPRRSST	spermatophores
AEEHMOPPRSSTTY	spermatophytes
AEEHNOOPPRRSST	parthenospores
AEEIIILMNSSTTX	existentialism
AEEIIILNNNORTT	interlineation
AEEIIILNNSSTTY	inessentiality
AEEIIILNOPSTTT	potentialities
AEEIIILNSSTTTX	existentialist
AEEIIILORRRSTT	territorialise
AEEIIILORRRTTZ	territorialize
AEEIILLLNOSTVY	televisionally
AEEIILLLNPSTTY	pestilentially

AEEIILLNNOPRTT	interpellation
AEEIILMMNNOPTT	implementation
AEEIILMMNNSSTT	sentimentalism
AEEIILMNNOSSTX	extensionalism
AEEIILMNNSSTTT	sentimentalist
AEEIILMNNSTTTY	sentimentality
AEEIILMNOORSTT	telomerisation
AEEIILMNOORTTZ	telomerization
AEEIILMNOPRSSS	impersonalises
AEEIILMNOPRSSZ	impersonalizes
AEEIILMNRSSTUX	intersexualism
AEEIILNNNORTTV	interventional
AEEIILNNORRSTT	interrelations
AEEIILNNOSTTXY	extensionality
AEEIILNNQSSTTU	quintessential
AEEIILNORSSTTV	revelationists
AEEIILNRSTTUXY	intersexuality
AEEIILPRTTUVVY	vituperatively
AEEIIMNNOORSTT	remonetisation
AEEIIMNNOORTTZ	remonetization
AEEIIMNNORSTTX	exterminations
AEEIIMNOORSTTV	overestimation
AEEIINNOORRSTT	reorientations
AEEIINNOPPSSST	inappositeness
AEEIINNOPRRTTT	interpretation
AEEIINNOQRSSTU	questionnaires
AEEIINNORSSTTW	westernisation
AEEIINNORSTTWZ	westernization
AEEIINNRSSSTTV	transitiveness
AEEIINPQQRTTUU	quinquepartite
AEEIKLNNOPRSUY	Yorke Peninsula
AEEIKMRSSSSSTT	taskmistresses
AEEILLLNNNPSUY	Lleyn Peninsula
AEEILLNNRSSSTT	slatternliness
AEEILLNOPRRSTT	interpellators
AEEILMNNNNRSSU	unmannerliness
AEEILMNOSSSTUU	simultaneouses
AEEILMORSSTTUV	overstimulates
AEEILNNPPPRSUU	Upper Peninsula
AEEILNOORRSSTV	lateroversions
AEEILNOORTTTXY	extortionately
AEEILNOPRSSTTU	reputationless
AEEIMNNOPPRSTT	reappointments
AEEINNOOPRSSVX	overexpansions
AEEINOOPRRSTTX	reexportations
AEEINOORRSSSTV	overassertions
AEEINOQRSSSTTU	sequestrations
AEEINORRSSTTTU	sternutatories
AEELLLMNPPSTUY	supplementally
AEELLMNORSSSUV	marvellousness
AEFFHILNNSSTUU	unfaithfulness
AEFFIIMNOORRSU	foraminiferous
AEFGGNOORRSSYY	Gregory of Nyssa
AEFGIILNOSSSTU	flagitiousness
AEFGIIMNORRSST	transmogrifies
AEFGIINOPRRSTU	prefigurations
AEFHHLNNOPRTWY	halfpennyworth
AEFHIILNNOPRTY	hyperinflation
AEFIIIILMNNSST	infinitesimals
AEFIIILNORSSTT	fertilisations
AEFIIILNORSTTZ	fertilizations
AEFIILNOOPRRST	proliferations
AEFILLNOOPRSSY	professionally
AEFILLOOPRRSSY	professorially
AEFILMNOORRSTU	formation rules
	reformulations
AEFILNNOOPRSSU	unprofessional
AEFILNOOPRSSSW	passionflowers
AEFIMNNOORRSTW	frontierswoman
AEGGHHLOPPRRSY	glyphographers
AEGGHHOOPPRTYY	phytogeography
AEGGHILOOPRSSS	glossographies
AEGGHILOPPRSTY	glyptographies
AEGGHINNOOPRTV	photoengraving
AEGGHLOOPRRSSS	glossographers
AEGGHLOPPRRSTY	glyptographers
AEGGHNNOOPRRST	rontgenographs
AEGGIIIIILMNSTT	legitimatising
AEGGIIIIILMNTTZ	legitimatizing
AEGGIIINNORRTV	reinvigorating
AEGGIINORRSTTU	regurgitations
AEGGINOOSSTTUU	autosuggestion
AEGHHIOPPRRSSY	physiographers
AEGHHLMOPPRSTY	plethysmograph
AEGHIILLOPRSST	legislatorship
AEGHIILNNSTTUY	unhesitatingly
AEGHIILNOOOSTT	theologisation
AEGHIILNOOOTTZ	theologization
AEGHIIMNNOOOST	homogenisation
AEGHIIMNNOOOTZ	homogenization
AEGHIINNSSTTUX	extinguishants
AEGHIINOOSSTTT	ghettoisations
AEGHIINOOSTTTZ	ghettoizations
AEGHIIPRRRSSST	registrarships
AEGHILMOORSTTU	rheumatologist
AEGHILOOPRSSST	phraseologists
AEGHIMMNOOPRST	metamorphosing
AEGHIMNOOPRSTY	pharyngotomies
AEGHLLMOOPPRSY	megasporophyll
AEGHLNOOOPRTUY	neuropathology
AEGHMMOOPRRTTY	photogrammetry
AEGHOOOPPPRRRS	prosopographer
AEGIIIILMNOSTT	legitimisation
AEGIIIILMNOTTZ	legitimization
AEGIIIILMNRRTZ	remilitarizing
AEGIIILMNNOOST	emotionalising
AEGIIILMNNOOTZ	emotionalizing
AEGIIILNNRSSUV	universalising
AEGIIILNNRSUVZ	universalizing
AEGIIILNORTVVY	invigoratively
AEGIIIMNNORRTT	intermigration
AEGIIINNOORRTV	reinvigoration
AEGIIINNOPRRTT	repartitioning
AEGIIINNORSTTT	integrationist
AEGIIINNOSSTTV	investigations
AEGIILMNNOORST	mongrelisation
AEGIILMNNOORTZ	mongrelization
AEGIILMOOSSSST	semasiologists
AEGIILNNNRSTTY	intransigently
AEGIIMNNRRSTTT	retransmitting
AEGIINNNOORSTT	rontgenisation
AEGIINNNOORTTZ	rontgenization
AEGIINNOOPPRRT	reapportioning
AEGIINNOORRSTT	interrogations

AEGILLMNNOQTUY magniloquently
AEGILMMNRSSTUU summersaulting
AEGILMNOOORSTU osmoregulation
AEGILMNOOPSTTU pneumatologist
AEGILNNNOSSSUU lanuginousness
AEGILNNOOOSSTT neonatologists
AEGILNOOPPRTUV overpopulating
AEGIMMNOOPRSTU spermatogonium
AEGIMNNNSSSSUU unassumingness
AEGIMNNOORTUUV outmanoeuvring
AEGINNORRSSSST transgressions
AEGINORSSSTTUU gratuitousness
AEGKKMNOORSSTU Ust-Kamenogorsk
AEGLLMOPRRTUYY pyrometallurgy
AEGLMNOORSSSUU glamourousness
AEGLNNOORSSSUU languorousness
AEGMMNNOOOSSSU monogamousness
AEHHHOOOPPRSTT orthophosphate
AEHHHOOPPPSSTY hypophosphates
AEHHIILLLLRSSY shillyshallier
AEHHIILLLLSSSY shillyshallies
AEHHIILNOPPRST philanthropies
AEHHILLMNPSTTY platyhelminths
AEHHIMOOOPSSTT homoeopathists
AEHHINOPPRSTTY hypnotherapist
AEHHINOPRSSTTT theanthropists
AEHHLLMOOPRTTY photothermally
AEHHLOOPPRSSSY phosphorylases
AEHHNOOPPRSTTY anthropophytes
AEHHNOOPSSTTTY photosynthates
AEHHOOPPPRSSTY pyrophosphates
AEHIIKLLMOOPRT poikilothermal
AEHIILLMNNOPSY aminophyllines
AEHIILMOOPPRST apheliotropism
AEHIILOPRRSTWY praiseworthily
AEHIIMNNOSTTUW White Mountains
AEHIIMOPPRRSST imperatorships
AEHIINNOSSTTTY synthetisation
AEHIINNOSSTTYZ synthesization
AEHIINNOSTTTYZ synthetization
AEHIIOORRSSTTT osteoarthritis
AEHIIPPRRTTUYY hyperpituitary
AEHILMOPPRSSTY amphiprostyles
AEHILNNOORSSTZ horizontalness
AEHIMNNPRSSSTT transshipments
AEHIMOOPPPSSTU hippopotamuses
AEHINNOPRSSSTU sinanthropuses
AEHINOOOPRRSTT prothonotaries
AEHLMNOOOPSSTU haplostemonous
AEIIIILMNRSSTT ministerialist
AEIIIILPRSSTTU spiritualities
AEIIILLLMNNSST millennialists
AEIIILLMNNORSS millionnairess
AEIIILLNRSTTTY interstitially
AEIIILMNPRSTTY amitriptylines
AEIIILMORRRSTT territorialism
AEIIILNNNOTTTY intentionality
AEIIILNNOOPTVY opinionatively
AEIIILNNRSTTVY intransitively
AEIIILNORSSSTT sterilisations
AEIIILNORSSTTZ sterilizations
AEIIILNORSTTUZ reutilizations
AEIIILORRRSTTT territorialist
AEIIILORRRTTTY territoriality
AEIIILPRRSSSTU spiritualisers
AEIIILPRRSSTUZ spiritualizers
AEIIIMMNOSSSTT misestimations
AEIIIMNOOPSSTT epitomisations
AEIIIMNOOPSTTZ epitomizations
AEIIIMNOORSSST isomerisations
AEIIIMNOORSSTZ isomerizations
AEIIINNORSSTTW winterisations
AEIIINNORSTTWZ winterizations
AEIIINNOSSSSTT sensitisations
AEIIINNOSSSTTZ sensitizations
AEIIINOOPRRSSV provisionaries
AEIIINOPQRSTTU equipartitions
AEIIINOQRRSTUY requisitionary
AEIIIOOPPRRSTT propitiatories
AEIILLLMNNOPST postmillennial
AEIILLLRSTTUVY illustratively
AEIILLMNOPRSSY impressionally
AEIILLNNNQQUUY quinquennially
AEIILLNNOSSSUV villainousness
AEIILLNQRRSSTU tranquillisers
AEIILLNQRRSTUZ tranquillizers
AEIILMNNOOPRSS pronominalises
AEIILMNNOOPRSZ pronominalizes
AEIILMNOOPRSTY polymerisation
AEIILMNOOPRTYZ polymerization
AEIILMNRSSSTVY transmissively
AEIILNNNORSTTU interlunations
AEIILNNOOPRSTT interpolations
AEIILNNOPRSTUY unipersonality
AEIILNOORSSTTT tolerationists
AEIILNOPRRSTTY tripersonality
AEIIMMNORSSTTY symmetrisation
AEIIMMNORSTTYZ symmetrization
AEIIMNNOOPRSST impersonations
AEIIMNNORRSSST retransmission
AEIIMNOOPRRSTT reimportations
AEIIMNOORRSSTT restorationism
AEIIMNOSSSSTTY systemisations
AEIIMNOSSSTTYZ systemizations
AEIIMNRSSSTTTV transvestitism
AEIINNOOPPSSTT peptonisations
AEIINNOOPPSTTZ peptonizations
AEIINNORRSSSTT transitoriness
AEIINOOPPRRSTX expropriations
AEIINOOPRSSTTX extrapositions
AEIINOORRSSTTT restorationist
AEIINOPRRSSSTU pressurisation
AEIINOPRRSSTUZ pressurization
AEIINOPRSSSUVV viviparousness
AEIINORRSSSSTT transistorises
AEIINORRSSSTTZ transistorizes
AEIIORRRSTTWYZ Swazi Territory
AEILLMMMNOOSST monometallisms
AEILLMMNOOSSTT monometallists
AEILLMNNRSTTUY instrumentally
AEILLMNOSSTUUY simultaneously
AEILMNOPRRSTUY supernormality
AEILNOOOPPRTUV overpopulation
AEILNOOPSSTTUX expostulations

AEILNOOSSTTTUY	ostentatiously
AEIMMNOOOSSTUU	semiautonomous
AEIMNNOOPPRSTT	apportionments
AEIMNNOORRSSTT	remonstrations
AEIMNOPPRRSTTU	superimportant
AEINNOOSSTTTUU	unostentatious
AEINOOOPPRRSTT	proportionates
AEINOOPRRSSSUU	uproariousness
AELLMNNOOOPPRT	monopropellant
AENOOOPPRRSTXY	proparoxytones
AFFGIIMNOSSTUU	suffumigations
AFIIILNOOSSSST	fossilisations
AFIIILNOOSSSTZ	fossilizations
AFIIIMMNNOORST	misinformation
AFIILLMORSTUUY	multifariously
AGGHIILNPRSTUW	Walpurgis Night
AGGHILNOOPRSTY	pharyngologist
AGGIIILNNORTVY	invigoratingly
AGGILLNOORSSTY	laryngologists
AGGLLNOOOORTYY	otolaryngology
AGHHIIOOPRRSTY	historiography
AGHHILOOOPSTTY	histopathology
AGHHINOOPPRSST	phonographists
AGHHIOOPRRSSTT	orthographists
AGHHLOOOPPTTYY	phytopathology
AGHIINOOPPRSST	apostrophising
AGHIINOOPPRSTZ	apostrophizing
AGHILNOOOPRSTT	anthropologist
AGHIMOOOPRSSTU	mastigophorous
AGIIIILNPRSSTU	spiritualising
AGIIIILNPRSTUZ	spiritualizing
AGIIILLLMNNTUY	illuminatingly
AGIIILLMNNNTUU	unilluminating
AGIIILLNNQRSTU	tranquillising
AGIIILLNNQRTUZ	tranquillizing
AGIIILNOSTUVVV	vulvovaginitis
AGIILMOOPRSSTT	primatologists
AGILMOORRSSTTY	martyrologists
AGLMMOOOPSTTYY	symptomatology
AHHIILNOPPRSTT	philanthropist
AHHLLNOOPSTUXY	xanthophyllous
AHHMNOOOPPRRST	anthropomorphs
AHIILMNNOORSUY	inharmoniously
AHIILMOOPSSSST	histoplasmosis
AHIILNNOOOPSTT	Polish notation
AHIILNOPRSSTUU	sulphurisation
AHIILNOPRSTUUZ	sulphurization
AHIIMNOPRSSSTT	misanthropists
AHIINNOOPSSTTY	hypnotisations
AHIINNOOPSTTYZ	hypnotizations
AIIIILMNNOSTTU	intuitionalism
AIIIILNNOSTTTU	intuitionalist
AIIIILNOORSTTV	vitriolisation
AIIIILNOORTTVZ	vitriolization
AIIIINNRSTTTVY	intransitivity
AIIIINOOPRRSTT	prioritisation
AIIIINOOPRRTTZ	prioritization
AIIIKLLNSSVVYZ	Vislinsky Zaliv
AIIILLMPPSSUUU	Suppiluliumas I
AIIILOOPPRRTTY	propitiatorily
AIIIMNOOPPRRST	impropriations
AIIIMNOOPRSSTV	improvisations
AIIIMNRSSSTTVY	transmissivity
AIIIMNRSTTTTVY	transmittivity
AIIINNNOOSSTTV	innovationists
AIIINNORSTTTUY	institutionary
AIIJNOOPSSTTUX	juxtapositions
AIILLNNOOPSTTU	antipollutions
AIILMNNOOOOPST	monopolisation
AIILMNNOOOOPTZ	monopolization
AIILMNOOPRSSUY	parsimoniously
AIILNOOOPPSSTT	postpositional
AIINNOOPRSSSTT	transpositions
AIKKKMOORRSSVY	Rimsky-Korsakov
AIKMMNNOOSSTUY	Smoky Mountains
AILLNOOOPPRRTY	proportionally
AIMNNNOOSSTUWY	Snowy Mountains
BBCCDEIIMNRSUU	circumbendibus
BBCDEEIORRSSUV	oversubscribed
BBCEEIORRSSSUV	oversubscribes
BBCEIILMNOSSTU	incombustibles
BBCEILMNNOOSTU	noncombustible
BBCIIILMOSTTUY	combustibility
BBDEEGILNOOOSU	Bois de Boulogne
BBEGIIILMRSTUY	submergibility
BBEIIILMRSSTUY	submersibility
BBEIIKLLNOOSSY	Sibylline Books
BCCCEIIMRRRSSU	circumscribers
BCCCGIIIMNRRSU	circumscribing
BCCCIIMOOPRSSU	submicroscopic
BCCDIIILNOTTUY	conductibility
BCCEEEEHIKRRRS	checkerberries
BCCEEHORSSTTTU	butterscotches
BCCEEIIILORTTY	bioelectricity
BCCEEIILMORRTY	microcelebrity
BCCEEIINRSSTTY	cyberneticists
BCCEEIKKKNORRS	knickerbockers
BCCEEJNORSTTUU	countersubject
BCCEIIIJSSTTUV	subjectivistic
BCCHINOOOPRSST	bronchoscopist
BCCILNOOSSSUUY	subconsciously
BCDEEEIILNNRSS	incredibleness
BCDEEGIIMNNRSU	disencumbering
BCDEEHHNOORSUU	Bouches-du-Rhône
BCDEEIILNRSTTU	indestructible
BCDEIIIIILRRTUY	irreducibility
BCDEIIIILNNOSTY	condensibility
BCDEIILNRSTTUY	indestructibly
BCDEILMPRRTUUU	Udmurt Republic
BCEEEEIIRRRSSV	serviceberries
BCEEEGILLNORST	cobelligerents
BCEEEHILMNOPRS	comprehensible
BCEEEHIOORRRST	Oberösterreich
BCEEEIJNSSSTUV	subjectiveness
BCEEEMMNORSSSU	cumbersomeness
BCEEFIIILPRTTY	perfectibility
BCEEGIMNNNOSSU	unbecomingness
BCEEHILMNOPRSY	comprehensibly
BCEEIIILNNNSSV	invincibleness
BCEEIIILPPRTTY	perceptibility
BCEEIILLOOPSSU	ebullioscopies
BCEEIILMNNOSTU	bioluminescent
BCEEIILMNOPRSS	incompressible
BCEEIKNNRRSUWW	New Brunswicker

BCEEILNNNOORTV nonconvertible
BCEEILNOORRTTV controvertible
BCEEIMNNPRSTUU superincumbent
BCEEIMORRRRSTY cyberterrorism
BCEGHIILNPRSUU Ingush Republic
BCEGIINOOPPRST bioprospecting
BCEIIILNORTTVY convertibility
BCEIIILPRSTTUY putrescibility
BCEIIILPSSTTUY susceptibility
BCEIILMNOPRSSY incompressibly
BCEIILNORTTUVY contributively
BCEIINNOOORSSV bioconversions
BCEIINOORRSTTU contributories
BCEILMMNOSSUUU cumulonimbuses
BCEILNOORRTTVY controvertibly
BCEMNNOOPRTTTU Compton-Burnett
BCGIIILMOOORST microbiologist
BCGIIILOOOOSST sociobiologist
BCGIILOOORSSTY cryobiologists
BCIIILOPRRTTUY corruptibility
BCIIMMNOOSSSSU subcommissions
BCIIMNOORSSTTU obstructionism
BCIINOORSSTTTU obstructionist
BDDEEEEFILLMNY feeblemindedly
BDDEFGIINNORSS forbiddingness
BDEEEEFILNNSSS defensibleness
BDEEEFGINRRTTU butterfingered
BDEEEGIILNSSST digestibleness
BDEEEGIIMMNRRS disremembering
BDEEEGIMMNOSTU disemboguement
BDEEEIINNNORTZ dinitrobenzene
BDEEEILMMNOSTW disembowelment
BDEEEIMMMNRSST dismemberments
BDEEEMNOORRSUV overburdensome
BDEEFFIILNSSSU diffusibleness
BDEEFGINNOORSS forebodingness
BDEEGIIILLNSVY disbelievingly
BDEEGIILLMNOSW disembowelling
BDEEGILLNRSTUW Tunbridge Wells
BDEEIIIIORSSTV biodiversities
BDEEIIIRRSTTUV redistributive
BDEEILLNOSSSSU dissolubleness
BDEGHHINOOORSU neighbourhoods
BDEGHIILNNNSST nightblindness
BDEGIIINRRSTTU redistributing
BDEHIILOORRSTT bloodthirstier
BDEIIIIIILSSTV divisibilities
BDEIIIILMQRSUU disequilibrium
BDEIIIILNSSTTY distensibility
BDEIIILNNOSSSU libidinousness
BDEIIILNPSSTUY suspendibility
BDEIIILRSTTUVY distributively
BDEIIINORRSTTU redistribution
BDHIIIIINNOSST disinhibitions
BDHIILLOORSTTY bloodthirstily
BDIIIIIILNSTVY indivisibility
BEEEEIILMORSTT biotelemetries
BEEEEILNNSSSTX extensibleness
BEEEFIILLNNSSX inflexibleness
BEEEGGIIINNNOR bioengineering
BEEEGGIILLNNSS negligibleness
BEEEGIIILLNNSS ineligibleness
BEEEGIIMMMNRRS misremembering
BEEEGILLNNNORT nonbelligerent
BEEEHILLMMNSST embellishments
BEEEHILMNOSSST blithesomeness
BEEEHILORRRSTW whortleberries
BEEEHLORRRSTVY Everly Brothers
BEEEIILMNRSSSS remissibleness
BEEEIILNNNSSSS insensibleness
BEEEILLNORSSSU rebelliousness
BEEEILORSSTTUV oversubtleties
BEEEIMMNRRSSTU reimbursements
BEEEINNORSSSTU tenebriousness
BEEEINRSSSSUVV subversiveness
BEEELMNNRSSSSU numberlessness
BEEENNQSSSSTUU subsequentness
BEEFHIMNRRSSTU refurbishments
BEEGGHIILMRRST thimbleriggers
BEEGHIILNNORSS neighborliness
BEEGIIILLLNNTU unintelligible
BEEGILMOOOORTY biometeorology
BEEHHKNOORSTUW Knebworth House
BEEHLOOORRSTTU troubleshooter
BEEIIIILNPRTTVY preventibility
BEEIILMNOPSSSS impossibleness
BEEIILNPPRSSSU insuppressible
BEEIIMNSSSSSUV submissiveness
BEEINNOPRSSSSU businessperson
BEEINOOQSSSSUU obsequiousness
BEEINOORSSSSTU boisterousness
BEELMNORSSSSUU slumberousness
BEELOOPRRSSTUY obstreperously
BEFGILLNOOPRTU bulletproofing
BEGGGHIIILMNRT thimblerigging
BEGGHILLNOORUW Wellingborough
BEGGIIILSSTTUY suggestibility
BEGGILNOORSTTT globetrottings
BEGHIILMNOOPST phlebotomising
BEGHIILMNOOPTZ phlebotomizing
BEGHILNNNSSSUU unblushingness
BEGIILNOOORSTU neurobiologist
BEGILNORSSSUUU lugubriousness
BEHIIIINOSSTTX exhibitionists
BEIIIILMPRSSTY permissibility
BEIIILLORRSTUY irresolubility
BEIIILNOPRSSTY responsibility
BEIILNPPRSSSUY insuppressibly
BEIILSSTTTUUVY substitutively
BEIINOQSSSTUUU ubiquitousness
BEINOORSSSSTUU robustiousness
BGHIILOOOOPSTT photobiologist
BGIILLMMNNOOUU immunoglobulin
BHIIIIMNOOPRST prohibitionism
BHIIIINOOPRSTT prohibitionist
BIIISSTTTTUUVY substitutivity
CCCDDEEEENNNOS condescendence
CCCDEEEENRRSSU recrudescences
CCCDEEEHKNORTU counterchecked
CCCDEEHIIOOPRT cercopithecoid
CCCDEEHIIOPRST cercopithecids
CCCDGIILOOORTU glucocorticoid
CCCEEEFIMNRRSU circumferences
CCCEEEHHHIINNR chincherinchee

CCCEEEIIINRSTT eccentricities
CCCEEEILNNOSSS conscienceless
CCCEEIIMPRSTUV circumspective
CCCEENNNOORRSU nonoccurrences
CCCEIIILLOSTTV collectivistic
CCCEIIILMRSSSU circumscissile
CCCEIIMMNOOORS microeconomics
CCCEIIMNOPRSTU circumspection
CCCHIIOOOPRRTT corticotrophic
CCCIIIMNNORSUU uncircumcision
CCCIIIMORRRTUY microcircuitry
CCCIILMNOORTUU circumlocution
CCCILMOORRTUUY circumlocutory
CCDDEEILNNOSTY disconnectedly
CCDDEEILNORSTY disconcertedly
CCDEEEEEFNRSSV defervescences
CCDEEEEILNQSSU deliquescences
CCDEEEELNNOSST closed sentence
CCDEEEFINNOORV overconfidence
CCDEEEIINNNNOV inconvenienced
CCDEEEINNNORTT interconnected
CCDEEEINOPSSSU pseudosciences
CCDEEENNOOPRRS correspondence
CCDEEHIIMOORST orchidectomies
CCDEEHILNOORTU technicoloured
CCDEEHNNOPRTUU counterpunched
CCDEEIILOORRRV Crocodile River
CCDEEIJMNORSTU misconjectured
CCDEEILNOPSSTY encyclopedists
CCDEEIMNNORSTT disconcertment
CCDEEIMOORRSTT microdetectors
CCDEEINNNOOSSS condescensions
CCDEENOPRRSTTU preconstructed
CCDEGIILNNOOOR endocrinologic
CCDEGINNORSTTU deconstructing
CCDEIIINORSTTU reductionistic
CCDEIIINOSTTUV conductivities
CCDEIILMOORTTY clitoridectomy
CCDEIIMNNOOSTU semiconduction
CCDEIINNNOOSST disconnections
CCDEIINNOORSST disconcertions
CCDEIIOOORRSTT corticosteroid
CCDEIMNOORSSTU semiconductors
CCDEINNOORSTTU deconstruction
CCDENOOPRRSTUU superconductor
CCDGIIIMOOOPSS sigmoidoscopic
CCDHHHOOORRTUX Orthodox Church
CCDHIIMOPRRSTY cryptorchidism
CCDHINOOPRSSTU conductorships
CCDHNOOOOPRTTU photoconductor
CCEEEEEFLNNORT teleconference
CCEEEEEJNNRSUV rejuvenescence
CCEEEEFFLNORSS efflorescences
CCEEEEHHMORSST homescreetches
CCEEEEMMMNNORT recommencement
CCEEEFFIIIINNS inefficiencies
CCEEEFIIOPRSST stereospecific
CCEEEFILNNORSS inflorescences
CCEEEHILMORRTT electrothermic
thermoelectric
CCEEEHILMORSTT electrochemist
CCEEEHMOOPRRST chemoreceptors
CCEEEIIKLNORTT electrokinetic
CCEEEIIMNNSSTU intumescencies
CCEEEIINNNNOSV inconveniences
CCEEEILLLORTVY recollectively
CCEEEILLNOSSTV collectiveness
CCEEEILMNNORST reconcilements
CCEEEILNNNOOTT teleconnection
CCEEEIMMNNOOPT omnicompetence
CCEEEINNRRRSTU intercurrences
CCEEEINORRRSUU eurocurrencies
CCEEEINSSSSSUV successiveness
CCEEFLNSSSSSUU successfulness
CCEEGHIORRRSUU churrigueresco
CCEEGIILLOOSST ecclesiologist
CCEEGIINOSTTTY cytogeneticist
CCEEGINOORRRTV overcorrecting
CCEEHHIMNOSTTY chemosynthetic
CCEEHIIMNORSTT theocentricism
CCEEHIIMOORSTT stoechiometric
CCEEHIINORTTTY theocentricity
CCEEHNNOPRSTUU counterpunches
CCEEIIILLOSTTV collectivities
CCEEIILNORRTTU interlocutrice
CCEEIINNOSSTTU constituencies
CCEEIINNQSSTTU cinquecentists
CCEEIJMNORSSTU misconjectures
CCEEILMMOOPRTX complexometric
CCEEILMNORSSUU micronucleuses
CCEEILNNOSSSUV conclusiveness
CCEEILNOOOPRTT optoelectronic
CCEEILNOORSTTU electrocutions
CCEEINNNOOSTUV nonconsecutive
CCEEINNOOPPRST preconceptions
CCEEINOOORRRTV overcorrection
CCEEINOOORRSTT corticosterone
CCEEINOOPRSSSU precociousness
CCEEINORRSTTUV reconstructive
CCEELNORRTTUUU counterculture
CCEFIILMNORSUX circumflexions
CCEFILNNOORTTU Council of Trent
CCEFLLNSSSUUUY unsuccessfully
CCEGHIKLNOSTTU shuttlecocking
CCEGIIILLNOSTV collectivising
CCEGIIILLNOTVZ collectivizing
CCEGIINNNNOSSV convincingness
CCEGINNOOOPRST rontgenoscopic
CCEGINNORRSTTU reconstructing
CCEHHIINOPRSSZ schizophrenics
CCEHHIOOPSSUYZ schizophyceous
CCEHIIIMOORSTT stoichiometric
CCEHIIIMPRRSTY hypercriticism
CCEHIIMMORRSTY microchemistry
CCEHILLOOPRSST collectorships
CCEHIMOOSSTUYZ schizomycetous
CCEHINOOPRSSUY hyperconscious
CCEHINOOPRSTUY psychoneurotic
CCEHINOPRSSSTU succentorships
CCEHNNOOOPRSSY synchronoscope
CCEIIILMORRSTW lower criticism
CCEIILLNNOSUVY inconclusively
CCEIILNORSTTVY constrictively
CCEIIMNNOOPSST misconceptions

CCEIIMNNORSTUV circumventions
CCEIINNOOPRSTV preconvictions
CCEIINORSSSTUU circuitousness
CCEILNOOPRSSUY preconsciously
CCEILNORSTTUVY constructively
CCEILOOORRSSTU stercoricolous
CCEIMMOOPRRSTU microcomputers
CCEIMOOOPRRRSS microprocessor
CCEIMORRRSTTUU microstructure
CCEINNOORRSTTU reconstruction
CCEIOOPPRSSSTT spectroscopist
CCENOORRRSSTTU reconstructors
CCFGIILNNNNOOT nonconflicting
CCGHIILOOPSSTY psychologistic
CCGHIIOOPRSTYY hygroscopicity
CCHIILLNOOPRSU councillorship
CCHIILNOOPRSSU councilorships
CCHIINOOOPRRTT corticotrophin
CCIIIJNNOSTTUV conjunctivitis
CCIIILPRSSTTUU pisciculturist
CCIIILRRSTTTUU citriculturist
CCIILMNOORTUUV circumvolution
CCIIMNORSSTTUV constructivism
CCIINORSSTTTUV constructivist
CCILMNOOPSTUUY compunctiously
CCILMOORRTUUVY circumvolutory
CDDDDEEEILLMUX excluded middle
CDDEEEEENNOPRV overdependence
CDDEEEEIINNNPS independencies
CDDEEENNOPRSSY Ross Dependency
CDDEEFNNNOOSSU confoundedness
CDDEEIIMMNOOSS decommissioned
CDDEEIINNOOPRT preconditioned
CDDEEIJLNPRUUY unprejudicedly
CDDEEILNNOSTTY discontentedly
CDDEEILNOOSTUY eudicotyledons
CDDEEKNOORSSTY Eddystone Rocks
CDDEHHILOORRSY hydrochlorides
CDDEIIIMMOOSST discommodities
CDDEILNOOOSTUY dicotyledonous
CDEEEEELMORRST decelerometers
CDEEEEILLLNOST Leconte de Lisle
CDEEEENNPSSTUX unexpectedness
CDEEEFHIKNRRRY Frederick Henry
CDEEEGHINORTUW counterweighed
CDEEEGILNNORUV overindulgence
CDEEEHIOPRTTUY hypereutectoid
CDEEEIIINNSSSV indecisiveness
CDEEEIINNRSSST indiscreetness
indiscreteness
CDEEEILOOPRSTT electrodeposit
CDEEEINNNOORRU neuroendocrine
CDEEEINRRSSSTT restrictedness
CDEEFINNOPRSTU superconfident
CDEEHIIILPRVYZ hypercivilized
CDEEHIIMOOPRRT thermoperiodic
CDEEHKOOORSUYZ Chudskoye Ozero
CDEEHLLLOORSUY hydrocellulose
CDEEHNNOOOPPSS phonendoscopes
CDEEIIIILNRTTVY interdictively
CDEEIIIINNSSTVV vindictiveness
CDEEIINORRSSTT derestrictions
CDEEIINRSSSSUV discursiveness
CDEEIJNPRRSSUU jurisprudences
CDEEILLNOOPTUY polynucleotide
CDEEILOPRRTUVY reproductively
CDEEIMNNNOSTTT discontentment
CDEEIMNOOPRSSS decompressions
CDEEINNOOPRTTU counterpointed
CDEEINNOORSSSU indecorousness
CDEEINNORSTTUV nondestructive
CDEEINOPRSSTUV productiveness
CDEEINPSSSTTUU intussuscepted
CDEEKKLNRSSTUU knuckledusters
CDEELNNOOSSTUV convolutedness
CDEELNOOPRTTTU counterplotted
CDEENNOOPRRSST correspondents
CDEFIIIMMMOSSU fideicommissum
CDEGIIIILNOPST depoliticising
CDEGIIIILNOPTZ depoliticizing
CDEGIIINNNOORT reconditioning
CDEGIIMOOOPSSS sigmoidoscopes
CDEHINOOORRSTY hydrocortisone
CDEIIIILRSTTUV diverticulitis
CDEIIILORSSTUV diverticulosis
CDEIIINNNOSTTV nondistinctive
CDEIIINNNSSSTT indistinctness
CDEIILNORSSSUU ridiculousness
CDEIINNOORRTTU reintroduction
CDEIINNOPRSTUU superinduction
CDEIINORSSTTTU destructionist
CDEILMNOOPRSSU scolopendriums
CDEILMNOORSSTU discolourments
CDEILNOPRTUUVY unproductively
CDEILOORSSTUUY discourteously
CDEIMMNOOOSSSU commodiousness
CDEINOOOPRRTUV overproduction
CDELLNOOOPSTYY polycotyledons
CDELMNNOOOOSTY monocotyledons
CDGIILMNOOPSSY discomposingly
CDHHILLLOOOPRY chlorophylloid
CDHIILOOOPRRRS Polish Corridor
CDHIINNOORTTTU truth-condition
CDHIINOOOOPRSU conidiophorous
CDHINOOOPRSSTT prosthodontics
CDIIJNNNNOOSTU nondisjunction
CDIILMMNOOOSUY incommodiously
CDIILNOORRTTUY introductorily
CDINOOOPPRSTTU postproduction
CEEEEFFIPRSTUV supereffective
CEEEEFFLNRSTVY effervescently
CEEEEFGINNQRUY eigenfrequency
CEEEEFILNRSSTV reflectiveness
CEEEEFLMORRSTT reflectometers
CEEEEGGINORRRS greengroceries
CEEEEGHINPRRTY hyperenergetic
CEEEEGIILNNORT electioneering
CEEEEGIINNPRRX reexperiencing
CEEEEHIILRRSST Leicestershire
CEEEEHLNPSSSSS speechlessness
CEEEEINPPRSSTV perceptiveness
CEEEEINPRSSSTV respectiveness
CEEEFFGILNRSVY effervescingly
CEEEFFIINPRSTU superefficient

CEEEFGLLNNSSTU	neglectfulness
CEEEFIILMPRTVY	imperfectively
CEEEFILLNRTUVY	unreflectively
CEEEFIMNNORRST	reinforcements
CEEEFINORRSTTU	counterfeiters
CEEEFLNPRSSSTU	respectfulness
CEEEGHIIMORSST	geochemistries
CEEEGIILLNNNTU	unintelligence
CEEEGIILLNNRST	intelligencers
CEEEGIIMNOPRST	spermiogenetic
CEEEGIINORRSVX	overexercising
CEEEGILNOPRSST	teleprocessing
CEEEGLORRRSTUY	electrosurgery
CEEEGNNOOOPRST	roentgenoscope
CEEEHIIILRRRUV	Richelieu River
CEEEHIMNOPRSSV	comprehensives
CEEEHIMORSSTTY	hysterectomies
	hysterectomise
CEEEHIMORSTTYZ	hysterectomize
CEEEHINNNORSST	incoherentness
CEEEHIORRRSSTW	Worcestershire
CEEEHLMNOORRTT	thermoelectron
CEEEHLOPRSSSST	clothespresses
CEEEHMMOORSTTY	hemocytometers
CEEEHMMOPSSSTY	metempsychoses
CEEEIIIMNNPRST	impertinencies
CEEEIIKNNPRSST	pernicketiness
CEEEIILLLNTTVY	intellectively
CEEEIILMPPRTVY	imperceptively
CEEEIILPRRSTVY	irrespectively
CEEEIIMMOORRTT	micrometeorite
CEEEILMMNOPRTZ	complementizer
CEEEILMNNOPSST	incompleteness
CEEEILNOPRSSTU	pleurocentesis
CEEEIMMMNOOTTW	committeewomen
CEEEIMNNORTTUX	extreme unction
CEEEINNOORRRST	reconnoiterers
CEEEINOPRSSTTV	protectiveness
CEEEINPRSSSSUV	percussiveness
CEEEINPSSSSTUV	susceptiveness
CEEEIOOPRRTTVV	overprotective
CEEEIOPRRSSTTV	retrospectives
CEEFGIINNNOSTU	eigenfunctions
CEEFGIINNORTTU	counterfeiting
CEEFGILMNOORRT	electroforming
CEEFIILLNNOSST	inflectionless
CEEFIILNOSSSTU	felicitousness
CEEFIIMNNNSSTU	munificentness
CEEFIINNOSSSTU	infectiousness
CEEFIINOPRSSTT	perfectionists
CEEFIJOOSSSTUY	Society of Jesus
CEEFILMNNRSSUU	unmercifulness
CEEFILMNOORSSS	frolicsomeness
CEEFILNOORRSTT	retroflections
CEEFINOORSSSUV	vociferousness
CEEGHIIRRSSTUW	cruiserweights
CEEGHIMNOORRST	stereochroming
CEEGHINORRSTTV	overstretching
CEEGHINORSTTUW	counterweights
CEEGHLNOOORTTY	terotechnology
CEEGIIINOPSTTY	genotypicities
CEEGIILNNORRTY	nitroglycerine
CEEGIIMMNNOSTU	immunogenetics
CEEGIINNNOORRT	reconnoitering
CEEGILLLLNOOSU	lignocellulose
CEEGINNOORRSTV	seroconverting
CEEGINOOPRRTTV	overprotecting
CEEGNNOOOPRSST	rontgenoscopes
CEEGNNOOOPRSTY	roentgenoscopy
CEEHHIMMORSSTT	thermochemists
CEEHHIMNOSSSTY	chemosynthesis
CEEHHMOOORRSTU	heterochromous
CEEHHNOOPPRSST	phosphorescent
CEEHIILMOPRRTY	pyrheliometric
CEEHIIMOORSTTY	stoicheiometry
CEEHIIMOPRSTYZ	piezochemistry
CEEHIIOOPRRTTY	erythropoietic
CEEHIMMOPSSSTY	metempsychosis
CEEHIMNNOOPRSS	comprehensions
CEEHIMOOOPRST	oophorectomies
CEEHIMOPRRSTTY	petrochemistry
CEEHINOQSSSTTU	coquettishness
CEEHLNOOOPRSTT	photoelectrons
CEEHNOOPRSSSUY	psychoneuroses
CEEHOOOPPRRSTT	photoreceptors
CEEIIILNNPSSTX	inexplicitness
CEEIIIMMPRSSTT	metempiricists
CEEIIIMORSSTTT	meteoriticists
CEEIIIMPPRTTVY	imperceptivity
CEEIILLMNORSTT	scintillometer
CEEIILMORRSTUY	meretriciously
CEEIILNNNNOTVY	inconveniently
CEEIILNNOSSSTU	licentiousness
CEEIILPPRRSTVY	prescriptively
CEEIIMNNOOPTTV	noncompetitive
CEEIIMNOOPRTTT	potentiometric
CEEIINNOPRSSSU	perniciousness
CEEIINNORRSTTV	nonrestrictive
CEEIIOOPPPRRTV	proprioceptive
CEEILLLNOORSTU	nitrocellulose
CEEILMNOOOSSTV	locomotiveness
CEEILMNOPSSSUV	compulsiveness
CEEILMNOSSSTUU	meticulousness
CEEILMOOORSSST	electroosmosis
CEEILNNNOQSTUY	inconsequently
CEEILNNOOPRSTU	nucleoproteins
CEEILNNOOPRSXY	clinopyroxenes
CEEILNNOSSSUVV	convulsiveness
CEEILNNRRRTTUY	intercurrently
CEEILNOOPRRSST	scleroproteins
CEEILNORRSSTTU	interlocutress
CEEIMMOOPRRRTY	micropyrometer
CEEINNNOPRSTTU	supercontinent
CEEINNOOORRSSV	seroconversion
CEEINNOORSSSSU	censoriousness
CEEINNORSSTTTU	reconstituents
CEEINNOSSSSTUU	incestuousness
CEEINOOPRRSSTT	retrospections
CEEINRRSSSSTTU	instructresses
CEEIOOPRSSSSTT	stereoscopists
CEEKKLNOOOSSSV	Československo
CEEKNNOOOSSTTT	Stockton-on-Tees
CEEKNOORRRSTUW	counterworkers
CEELLNOORSSSSU	colourlessness

CEEMNNNOOPRSTU	pronouncements
CEEMNOOPRRSTUU	neurocomputers
CEEMOPPRRSSTUU	supercomputers
CEEPRRRSSTTUUU	superstructure
CEFFIIILNNSTUY	insufficiently
CEFFILORRSTUUY	fructiferously
CEFGHINOORSSST	sign of the cross
CEFHHJNOOORSST	John of the Cross
CEFIIILLNOSTUY	infelicitously
CEFIIILNPPRRST	first principle
CEFIIINOSSSTTU	fictitiousness
CEFIIMNNOORSTU	unconformities
CEFLNOORSSSSUU	scrofulousness
CEGGHILMOOOOPR	geomorphologic
CEGGIINNNORSTU	countersigning
CEGHHINOOPPRSS	phosphorescing
CEGHNNOOORSSUY	geosynchronous
CEGIIILNOORSST	coreligionists
CEGIIKNNNORSTU	countersinking
CEGIILMNOOPRSY	copolymerising
CEGIILMNOOPRYZ	copolymerizing
CEGIIMMNOORTTV	overcommitting
CEGIIMNNOOPRST	contemporising
CEGIIMNNOOPRTZ	contemporizing
CEGIINNNNOOORT	nonrecognition
CEGIINNOOPRSTU	counterpoising
CEGIINNORSTTTU	reconstituting
CEGILMMOORSSTY	myrmecologists
CEGILNNPSSTUUY	unsuspectingly
CEGIMNNOOOOSUY	gynomonoecious
CEGINNOOSSSTUU	contiguousness
CEGINPRRSSTTUU	superstructing
CEHHIIMORSSTTY	histochemistry
CEHHIMMMOORRST	thermochromism
CEHHIMMNOOOPPR	morphophonemic
CEHHIMNOOPRSTY	phonochemistry
CEHHIMOOPRSTTY	photochemistry
CEHHIMOPRSTTYY	phytochemistry
CEHHINOOPSTTTY	photosynthetic
CEHHOOOOPPPRSS	phosphoroscope
CEHIIIKLMOOPRT	poikilothermic
CEHIIMNOOPRSST	chemisorptions
CEHIINOPPRSSST	inspectorships
CEHIINOPRRSTTT	streptothricin
CEHIJMNNOORTTU	thermojunction
CEHILLNOOPRRST	controllership
CEHILLNOOPRSSU	counsellorship
CEHILMMOOPRSUY	myrmecophilous
CEHILMOORSSSST	schoolmistress
CEHILNOOPRSSSU	counselorships
CEHIMNOOOPRRST	chromoproteins
CEHIMOPRSSSTTY	psychometrists
CEHINOOPRSSSUY	psychoneurosis
CEHLLLOOPRSSUY	sclerophyllous
CEHMOOOOPPRSST	photocomposers
CEIIIILLMPSTTU	multiplicities
CEIIIINOSSTTVV	vivisectionist
CEIIILNOOSTTUV	evolutionistic
CEIIIMOOPRSTTV	overoptimistic
CEIIIMPPRRSSTV	prescriptivism
CEIIINORRSSTTT	restrictionist
CEIIJNOOPRSSTT	projectionists
CEIILLLNOOSSTV	violoncellists
CEIILLOPRSSUUY	superciliously
CEIILNNNOSSTTY	inconsistently
CEIILNOORRRSTT	trinitrocresol
CEIILNOOSSSSTU	solicitousness
CEIILNOSTTTUVY	constitutively
CEIILOOORSSTUV	oversolicitous
CEIILOPPRRSTVY	proscriptively
CEIILRRSSSTTUU	sericulturists
CEIIMMNNNOORTU	intercommunion
CEIIMMNNORTTUY	intercommunity
CEIIMNNOOOPSSU	pneumoconiosis
CEIIMNNORRSTTU	micronutrients
CEIIMNOOOPRSST	recompositions
CEIINNOOPRSSTT	introspections
CEIINNOORSTTTU	reconstitution
CEIINOOPRSSSTT	retinoscopists
CEIINOOPRSSTTT	protectionists
CEIINOORSSSTUV	victoriousness
CEIINOPPRRSSTU	superscription
CEIINOPRSSSSTU	percussionists
CEIINOPSSSSSUU	suspiciousness
CEIIOOPRSSSUUV	oversuspicious
CEILLMNOOSTUUY	contumeliously
CEILMNNOORSTUY	conterminously
CEILMNOOPRSSSU	compulsoriness
CEILMOOPRRSSTU	multiprocessor
CEILNOPRRSTUUV	proventriculus
CEILNORRSSSSUU	scurrilousness
CEINNNOOSSSTUU	continuousness
CEIOOOPPPRRRST	proprioceptors
CELMNOOPSTTUUY	contemptuously
CELNOPRSSSSUUU	scrupulousness
CELOOPRRSSUUUV	overscrupulous
CFIILLORRSTTUU	floriculturist
CFIMNNNOOORSST	nonconformists
CGGHIILNOOPSSY	psychologising
CGGHIILNOOPSYZ	psychologizing
CGHHIILOOSSTTY	ichthyologists
CGHIILNOPSSTUY	psycholinguist
CGHILOOOOPSTYY	phytosociology
CGHIMNOOOOPPST	photocomposing
CGIIILMNOORSST	criminologists
CGIIILMOOSSTTV	victimologists
CGIIILNOOOPSST	oligopsonistic
CGIIILNOOSSSTU	sociolinguists
CGIIIMNNNOOSTV	noncognitivism
CGIIIMNNRSSTTU	misinstructing
CGIILMMNOOPRSY	compromisingly
CGIIMMNNOOPRSU	uncompromising
CGIIMNNNOOPRSU	mispronouncing
CGILLNNNNOOORT	noncontrolling
CHHHIOOOPPPRSY	hypophosphoric
CHHILOOOPPPRSY	polyphosphoric
CHHIMOOPRRSSTY	hystricomorphs
CHHIOOOPPPRRSY	pyrophosphoric
CHHJMNOOORSSTY	John Chrysostom
CHHLLLOOOPRSUY	chlorophyllous
CHIILORRSTTTUU	horticulturist
CHIINOPRRSSTTU	instructorship
CHIIOOORSSTTXY	thyrotoxicosis
CHILMOOORSTTUY	trichotomously

CHILNOOPPRSSSU	proconsulships
CHILOOOPPRRSTU	prolocutorship
CIIILLRSSTTUUV	silviculturist
CIIILNRSSTTUUV	viniculturists
CIIILRSSTTTUUV	viticulturists
CIIIMNNORSSTTU	misinstruction
CIINNOOORSSTTT	contortionists
CIINOOPRRSSTTU	corruptionists
CILNOPRSSTUUUY	unscrupulosity
CLLNOPRSSUUUUY	unscrupulously
DDDEEEELNOPRUV	underdeveloped
DDDEEEGHINORSY	dehydrogenised
DDDEEEGHINORYZ	dehydrogenized
DDEEEEIMNNRSST	determinedness
DDEEEEINNNPRTT	interdependent
DDEEEELMMNOSSS	meddlesomeness
DDEEEGHINORSSY	dehydrogenises
DDEEEGHINORSYZ	dehydrogenizes
DDEEEGIINNNPRT	interdepending
DDEEEIINQSSSTU	disquietedness
DDEEEILNNNNRTU	Unter den Linden
DDEEEIMNNNORTU	undermentioned
DDEEGHHINRSTUW	hundredweights
DDEEGHILMOOSTY	demythologised
DDEEGHILMOOTYZ	demythologized
DDEEHILNOORRTY	dehydroretinol
DDEEHINNORRSUU	undernourished
DDEEIIINPRSSST	dispiritedness
DDEEIIJNNOSSST	disjointedness
DDEEIILLMMNPSY	simplemindedly
DDEEIILNORRSSS	disorderliness
DDEHHILOPRSSUY	hydrosulphides
DDEHIILNOPSSSS	slipshoddiness
DDEIIIILMSSSTU	dissimilitudes
DEEEEHMNORRRTV	Reverend Mother
DEEEEIILNNORSS	Oder-Neisse Line
DEEEEILLMMOSSS	mesdemoiselles
DEEEEIMNPRRRST	predeterminers
DEEEEIMNPRRSST	misrepresented
DEEEEINNRSSSTT	interestedness
DEEEEINPRSSSSV	depressiveness
DEEEELMNOPRSTV	redevelopments
DEEEENNRRSSSUV	unreservedness
DEEEFGJMNORSTU	forejudgements
DEEEFIIINNNSST	indefiniteness
DEEEFIIINNSSTV	definitiveness
DEEEFILNNRSSSS	friendlessness
DEEEFILNPSSSTU	despitefulness
DEEEFNOORSSSTU	surefootedness
DEEEGIIMNNPRRT	predetermining
DEEEGIINRSSSSV	digressiveness
DEEEGILNOOPRVV	overdeveloping
DEEEGNNOPRRTUY	Young Pretender
DEEEHIIKLNOOTT	kinetheodolite
DEEEIIMNPRRSTT	misinterpreted
DEEEIIMNRSSTTV	divertissement
DEEEIINORRSSVV	Revised Version
DEEEIINPRSSSSV	dispersiveness
DEEEILNNRSTTUY	uninterestedly
DEEEILNPRRSSTY	interspersedly
DEEEILOPRSSTVX	Prévost d'Exiles
DEEEIMMNOPRSTW	disempowerment
DEEEINNNPRSTTU	superintendent
DEEEKLMMRRSTTU	kettledrummers
DEEEMNNORSSSTU	tremendousness
DEEENOPRRSSUUX	underexposures
DEEFFHILLOORST	Lord of the Flies
DEEFFIIIMNNRST	indifferentism
DEEFFIIINNRSTT	indifferentist
DEEFGHILLNSSTU	delightfulness
DEEFGIIMNRSSTU	disfigurements
DEEFHOOORRSSTW	Sherwood Forest
DEEFIIILMOPRSV	oversimplified
DEEFIILNNNRSSU	unfriendliness
DEEFIINOPRSSSU	perfidiousness
DEEFMMNOOORTVX	Oxford Movement
DEEGHIINNSTUUX	unextinguished
DEEGHILMOOSSTY	demythologises
DEEGHILMOOSTYZ	demythologizes
DEEGHLNOORSSYY	hydrogenolyses
DEEGIIILMOOPST	epidemiologist
DEEGIIINNRSSTT	disinteresting
DEEGIILMNOPRSY	depolymerising
DEEGIILMNOPRYZ	depolymerizing
DEEGIINNNOSSSU	indigenousness
DEEGIINNNPRSTU	superintending
DEEGIINPRRSSSU	depressurising
DEEGIINPRRSSUZ	depressurizing
DEEGILLOOSSTTY	dysteleologist
DEEGILMNNRSTTU	disgruntlement
DEEGLNNORSSSSU	groundlessness
DEEHHNORRSSTUW	thundershowers
DEEHIINNPRSSTU	indentureships
DEEHIINOPSSSTY	hyposensitised
DEEHIINOPSSTYZ	hyposensitized
DEEHIINORTTTYY	identity theory
DEEHIINPPRSSST	presidentships
DEEHILPRRSSSUU	desulphurisers
DEEHILPRRSSUUZ	desulphurizers
DEEHINNORRSSUU	undernourishes
DEEIIIILMRSTUV	verisimilitude
DEEIIILNOPRSTV	vespertilionid
DEEIIIMNNRSSTT	indeterminists
DEEIIIMNNSSTUV	diminutiveness
DEEIIINOQRSSTU	derequisitions
DEEIILLNNOPVYY	polyvinylidene
DEEIILNOORSTUV	revolutionised
DEEIILNOORTUVZ	revolutionized
DEEIILNOQRSTUV	ventriloquised
DEEIILNOQRTUVZ	ventriloquized
DEEIILOPPRSSTT	lepidopterists
DEEIJNOPQRSSSU	Josquin des Prés
DEEKNOOPPRRSTV	Dnepropetrovsk
DEEMOOOPRRSSST	depressomotors
DEENNOPSSSSTUU	stupendousness
DEFGIIIIMNNSTY	misidentifying
DEGGHILOOORSTY	hydrogeologist
DEGHHILORSSTTY	shortsightedly
DEGHIIINRSSSTU	distinguishers
DEGHIILNPRSSUU	desulphurising
DEGHIILNPRSUUZ	desulphurizing
DEGHILMOOOSSTT	methodologists
DEGHILNOORSSYY	hydrogenolysis
DEGIILNNOSSUUY	disingenuously

DEGIILOOPRSSTT	pteridologists
DEGIINOOPRSSSU	prodigiousness
DEGILNNPPRSUUY	undersupplying
DEGILNOOOOPRTY	periodontology
DEHIIMOOOPPRST	photoperiodism
DEHIINOOPPSSST	deipnosophists
DEHILNOOPRRXYY	hydroxyproline
DEHIMMOOPPRSSU	pseudomorphism
DEHIOOPPRSTTUY	pteridophytous
DEHLLMMOPRSUUY	Sully-Prudhomme
DEHMOOOPPRSSUU	pseudomorphous
DEIIILMNOOSSTT	demolitionists
DEIIINOOPPRSST	predisposition
DEIILNOOSSTTUV	devolutionists
DEILMNOOOPSSTU	diplostemonous
DEILNORSSSSTUU	stridulousness
DEIMNOOPRSSSTT	postmodernists
DELMNOOPSSUUYY	pseudonymously
DFGHIIKMNORSST	Kingsford-Smith
DGGHHIIINNOPST	diphthongising
DGGHHIIINNOPTZ	diphthongizing
DGGHIIIINNSSTU	distinguishing
DGHIINNNOOORVZ	Nizhni Novgorod
DGIIIILLNNOSSU	disillusioning
DGLMNOOOOSSSTU	odontoglossums
DHHIIMOOPRSTYY	hypothyroidism
DHINOOOPRSSTTT	prosthodontist
DIIIINNOOPSSST	indispositions
DIINOOOPPRRSST	disproportions
DLNOOOOPPRSTTY	polyprotodonts
EEEEFGLNNRSSUV	revengefulness
EEEEFIMNNORRTV	overrefinement
EEEEFIMNORRRTT	interferometer
EEEEGINRRSSSSV	regressiveness
EEEEHHIMPRRTTT	Peter the Hermit
EEEEHILMNOPRST	nephelometries
EEEEHILNPRRSVY	reprehensively
EEEEIIMMNRRSTT	semiretirement
EEEEIINPRSSTTV	repetitiveness
EEEEILPRRTTTWY	teletypewriter
EEEEIMNPRRRSST	misrepresenter
EEEEINNPRSSTVV	preventiveness
EEEEINPRRSSSSV	repressiveness
EEEEINPRSSSSVX	expressiveness
EEEELLNNRSSSST	relentlessness
EEEFFHKORRSSST	Sheffer's stroke
EEEFFHLNOORTUW	wheel of fortune
EEEFFLNORSSSST	effortlessness
EEEFGIMNPRRSTU	prefigurements
EEEFIMNORRRTTY	interferometry
EEEFLMNORRSSSU	remorsefulness
EEEFLNNNSSTUUV	uneventfulness
EEEGGIINPRRRST	preregistering
EEEGGINSSSSTUV	suggestiveness
EEEGHILNSSSSTW	weightlessness
EEEGIILLNOSSTV	vitellogenesis
EEEGIIMNOPRSSS	spermiogenesis
EEEGIINNPRRRTT	reinterpreting
EEEGIINNRSSSSV	ingressiveness
EEEGILNOORSSTV	venereologists
EEEHHIIMNORRST	Merionethshire
EEEHHILMOPPSST	Mephistopheles
EEEHIINNNOPPRR	norepinephrine
EEEHIINNRRSSSV	Inverness-shire
EEEHIINPRSSSTY	hypersensitise
EEEHIINPRSSTVY	hypersensitive
EEEHIINPRSSTYZ	hypersensitize
EEEHILMNNPRSST	replenishments
EEEHILMOPRRSTY	pyrheliometers
EEEHIMMNOPRSTV	empoverishment
EEEHINNOPRSTXY	hyperextension
EEEIILMNOPSSST	impolitenesses
EEEIILNPRRTTVY	interpretively
EEEIILNPRSSVXY	inexpressively
EEEIIMNNNPSSTT	impenitentness
EEEIIMNNNRTTTW	intertwinement
EEEIIMNPRRRSTT	misinterpreter
EEEIIMNPRSSSSV	impressiveness
	permissiveness
EEEIINPRSSSTUV	supersensitive
EEEILLNOSSSTUV	Îles sous le Vent
EEEILMNNPRSTUY	supereminently
EEEILMNOSSSSTV	motivelessness
EEEILNOPRSSSSX	expressionless
EEEILNORRSSSTU	irresoluteness
EEEILORRSTVVXY	extroversively
EEEIMNOOPRSTTT	potentiometers
EEEIMNOPPRRSST	peremptoriness
EEEINNOPRSSSSV	responsiveness
EEEINNPSSSSSUV	suspensiveness
EEEINOPPRSSSSV	oppressiveness
EEEINOPSSSSSSV	possessiveness
EEEIOPPRRRSSST	proprietresses
EEFGHINNOORRST	foreshortening
EEFGILLOORSSTX	reflexologists
EEFHIILQRRSSSU	squirrelfishes
EEFHILNRSSSSTT	thriftlessness
EEFIIILMOPRSSV	oversimplifies
EEFIIILNRRTTTY	interfertility
EEFIILLNOSSTTU	feuilletonists
EEFIMNNOORRSTW	frontierswomen
EEFLNOPPRSSSUU	purposefulness
EEGHIIMNNSTTUX	extinguishment
EEGHILLMNORVWY	overwhelmingly
EEGHILNOPRRSTU	reupholstering
EEGHILOOPRSSTT	herpetologists
EEGHINOOPPRRTY	porphyrogenite
EEGHLNOOORSTUY	heterogonously
EEGIIILNORRSTU	interreligious
EEGIILMNORTTUU	ultimogeniture
EEGIILMOOPSSTT	epistemologist
EEGIILNNPRRSTY	enterprisingly
EEGIIMNOPRRSSV	overimpressing
EEGIINNNPRRSTU	unenterprising
EEGIINORSSSTTV	sovereigntists
EEGILMOOORSSTT	meteorologists
EEGILNOOPRRVWY	overpoweringly
EEGINNOOPRRSSV	nonprogressive
EEGINOORRRSSST	retrogressions
EEHHIILLLNPSST	philhellenists
EEHHIILMNNOTTY	methylthionine
EEHHIMMOOPRRST	heteromorphism
EEHHLLOOPRSTUY	heterophyllous
EEHHMMNOOOPPRS	morphophonemes

EEHHMOOOPRRSTU	heteromorphous
EEHIILMNNQRSTU	relinquishment
EEHIILNOPPRSTY	pyelonephritis
EEHIIMMNOPRSTV	impoverishment
EEHIINOOPRRTTY	erythropoietin
EEHIINOOPSSSTT	photosensitise
EEHIINOOPSSTTV	photosensitive
EEHIINOOPSSTTZ	photosensitize
EEHIINOPSSSSTY	hyposensitises
EEHIINOPSSSTYZ	hyposensitizes
EEHIIOOPRRSSTY	erythropoiesis
EEHIMOOPRRRSTU	mother superior
EEHINNOOPSSSUU	euphoniousness
EEHINNOORSSTTW	noteworthiness
EEHINNORSSSTWW	newsworthiness
EEHLMNOOORSTUY	heteronomously
EEHLMNOORSTUYY	heteronymously
EEHLMNORSSSSUU	humourlessness
EEHMOOOPPRRTTY	pyrophotometer
EEHNOOOPRRSTXY	orthopyroxenes
EEIIIIMPRSTTTV	permittivities
EEIILMNNRTTTTY	intermittently
EEIILMNOSSSTTY	Simeon Stylites
EEIILNOORRSTUV	revolutioniser
EEIILNOORRTUVZ	revolutionizer
EEIILNOORSSTUV	revolutionises
EEIILNOORSTUVZ	revolutionizes
EEIILNOPRRSSVY	irresponsively
EEIILNOQRSSTUV	ventriloquises
EEIILNOQRSTUVZ	ventriloquizes
EEIILNPRRTTUVY	interruptively
EEIILNPRSSSSST	spiritlessness
EEIIMNOPRSSSUV	imperviousness
EEIINNOPRRSSST	interspersions
EEIINOPRSSSSTX	expressionists
EEILLNOQSSSTUY	questionlessly
EEILMNNNNOOTVV	noninvolvement
EEILMNNOOSSSST	motionlessness
EEIMNORSSSSTUY	mysteriousness
EEIMOPRSSSSSTT	postmistresses
EEINOOPPRSSSSS	prepossessions
EEINOPPRSSSTUV	supportiveness
EEINOPRRSSSTUV	protrusiveness
EELLNOOPPPRSYY	polypropylenes
EELOOPPRRSSTUY	preposterously
EENNOOPRSSSTTU	portentousness
EENOOPPRRSSSSU	prosperousness
EENOORRSSSSTTU	stertorousness
EFFGHHLOORTTUU	forethoughtful
EFFGHIIJNORRTY	Griffith-Joyner
EFFILNNRSSTUUU	unfruitfulness
EFGGIIINNNPRRT	fingerprinting
EFGGOOORRRSTUY	Gregory of Tours
EFGHHINORRSSTT	forthrightness
EFGHHLNOSSTTUU	thoughtfulness
EFGHINOOOPRRSW	showerproofing
EFGIILNNOSSSUU	fuliginousness
EFHILMNOOOSSST	tomfoolishness
EFHILNOPRSSSUW	worshipfulness
EFHIOOPPRRSSSS	professorships
EFHLNNRSSTTUUU	untruthfulness
EFIKLLLNNSSSUU	unskillfulness
EFINOORSSSTTUU	fortuitousness
EGGIILMNNOOOST	entomologising
EGGIILMNNOOOTZ	entomologizing
EGGILNNOOORSTT	rontgenologist
EGGILNOOORSSTT	gerontologists
EGHHIILOPRSSTY	hieroglyphists
EGHHINOPPRRTYY	hypertrophying
EGHIIILMNRSSTV	silversmithing
EGHIIKNNNNSSTU	unthinkingness
EGIIIILNORRSST	irreligionists
EGIIIINNOQRSTU	requisitioning
EGIIILMNNRTTTY	intermittingly
EGIIILNNNRTTWY	intertwiningly
EGIIINNOOPRRSV	reprovisioning
EGIIKLLMNOORST	kremlinologist
EGIILLLOOSSTVX	vexillologists
EGIILMNOORSSTT	terminologists
EGIILNNOORSSSU	ingloriousness
EGIILOOOSSSTTV	sovietologists
EGIIMNOOPRRSSS	progressionism
EGIINNOORRSSST	introgressions
EGIINNPRRSSSSU	surprisingness
EGIINOOPRRSSST	progressionist
EGIIOPRRSSSSTV	progressivists
EGILMMOOOPSSTY	symptomologies
EHHHIOOPPPSSTY	hypophosphites
EHHIILOOPPRSSS	philosophisers
EHHIILOOPPRSSZ	philosophizers
EHHIKNOORRRSTY	North Yorkshire
EHHIKOORRSSTUY	South Yorkshire
EHHIMMMOOOOPRS	homoeomorphism
EHHIMMMOOOPRSS	homeomorphisms
EHHIMOOOPRRSTU	theriomorphous
EHHINOOOPPPRST	phosphoprotein
EHHINOOPSSSTTY	photosynthesis
EHHLLMOOPRSTUY	thermophyllous
EHHMMOOOOOPRSU	homoeomorphous
EHIILNNOOPRRTT	trinitrophenol
EHIIMNOOOPSSST	photoemissions
EHIIOOPPPRRRST	proprietorship
EHIIOPPRRSSSUV	supervisorship
EHILMNOPSSSTYY	polysynthesism
EHLNOPRSSSSUUU	sulphurousness
EHMOOOPPRRTTYY	pyrophotometry
EIIIMNOPRSSSST	impressionists
EIIINNOOPRSSTT	interpositions
EIIINNOQSSSTUU	iniquitousness
EIILLMNOOOSSTT	tonsillotomies
EIILNOOOPPSSST	oppositionless
EIILNOORSSSTTU	resolutionists
EIILNOORSSTTUV	revolutionists
EIILNOQRSSTTUV	ventriloquists
EIILOOPPSSTTVY	postpositively
EIINNOORRRTTUY	union territory
EIINNORSSSTTUU	nutritiousness
EIINOOPPPRSSTU	presupposition
EIINOOPPRSSSTU	propitiousness
EIINOPRSSSSTUU	spirituousness
EILMNNOOSSSUUV	voluminousness
EILOPRRSSUUUUX	superluxurious
EIMNNOOOPPRRTT	proportionment
EIMNNOOORSSSUV	omnivorousness

EINOOOOPPRRRTV overproportion
ELMNOSSSTTUUUU tumultuousness
ELMOPPRSSTUUUY presumptuously
ELNOOPSSSTUUUV voluptuousness
EMNNNOOOOSSSTU monotonousness
EMNNNOOSSSSUYY synonymousness
EMNOPPRSSTUUUU unpresumptuous
GGHHIILNOPRTTT trothplighting
GHHIIILNOOPPSS philosophising
GHHIIILNOOPPSZ philosophizing
GHIILLOOPSSSTY syphilologists
GHIILNOOORSSTT ornithologists
GHIIMNOOPSSSTY physiognomists
GIIINNOOOPPRST propositioning
GILLLMOOPSSSYY polysyllogisms
GILOOOOOPRSTTZ protozoologist
HHIILNOOOPRSTU ornithophilous
HHINOOOOPPRSSU siphonophorous
HHLOOPPRSSUUUY hyposulphurous
HINOOOPPPRRRTY protoporphyrin
IIIIINNOQSSTTU inquisitionist
IIINOOOPPSSSTT oppositionists
IIIOOPPSSSTTUU supposititious
IILLNOOORRTTTU trinitrotoluol
IILOOPPSSSTUUY suppositiously
IIMNOOOPPRRSST misproportions

Fifteen Letters

AAAAACELMNNNOPZ Panama Canal Zone
AAAAACGLMOOPRRY Macapagal Arroyo
AAAAAGIKMORTTUW Kitagawa Utamaro
AAAABBCCIIILLMR Biblical Aramaic
AAAABCCDEJMSSUU Judas Maccabaeus
AAAABCEHHIILLTT Baile Átha Cliath
AAAABCEILLNOOPT palaeobotanical
AAAABEGNNRRSTTY Narragansett Bay
AAAABFHILMNOPRS Plains of Abraham
AAAABIJNNSSTTUU San Juan Bautista
AAAACCDEILLNNNO Caledonian Canal
AAAACCDIIKLLLSY lackadaisically
AAAACCEHHLNNOPT acanthocephalan
AAAACCILLLLPRTY parallactically
AAAACDEEHINNRST Athanasian Creed
AAAACDIIMMNOSST macadamisations
AAAACDIIMMNOSTZ macadamizations
AAAACEEHHLLMNPT thalamencephala
AAAACEGHILLOPPR palaeographical
AAAACEHIKNNSSTW Saskatchewanian
AAAACEIIJLLLSTV Castilla la Vieja
AAAACGHILLPPRRY paragraphically
AAAADEGINNQRRSU quadragenarians
AAAAEIILMNNPRRT parliamentarian
AAAAEIKLLNNPSSU Alaska Peninsula
AAAAELMORRSSTTT tarsometatarsal
AAAAFIILNNPRRSS infralapsarians
AAAAGGIIMMNNRST anagrammatising
AAAAGGIIMMNNRTZ anagrammatizing
AAAAGHIMNOPRSST phantasmagorias
AAAAIILLNOPSSTT palatalisations
AAAAIILLNOPSTTZ palatalizations
AAAAILNPPRRSSSU supralapsarians
AAABBIIIILLOTVY bioavailability
AAABCCEEHILRRST characterisable
AAABCCEEHILRRTZ characterizable
AAABCCFINNORSSY San Francisco Bay
AAABCDEIILLNRSS Balearic Islands
AAABCEEHINRRTTT tetrabranchiate
AAABCEEIIMNNRTT metacinnabarite
AAABCEEILMNSTTU semantic tableau
AAABCEEILNNRSTU unascertainable
AAABCEHINOORSTT archaeobotanist
AAABCEILLLRSTTY tetrasyllabical
AAABCHIILOPPRTY approachability
AAABCIIILNNNOST cannibalisation
AAABCIIILNNNOTZ cannibalization
AAABDEEGIIILMST damageabilities
AAABDHIMOPRSSSS ambassadorships
AAABDIINORSSSTT bastardisations
AAABDIINORSSTTZ bastardizations
AAABEGIIILMRRTY marriageability
AAABEGIILLNOSUV bougainvillaeas
AAABEHIILNOPSTT alphabetisation
AAABEHIILNOPTTZ alphabetization
AAABEHIMNNORRTY Erymanthian boar
AAABEIKLLNNNPSU Balkan Peninsula
AAABEILNOOPSSTT palaeobotanists
AAABIILLNRSTTTY translatability
AAABIILMNPRSSSU sublapsarianism
AAABIILNOOPRSST parabolisations
AAABIILNOOPRSTZ parabolizations
AAABIKLMNNNOSTU Balkan Mountains
AAABILNNRSSTTTU transubstantial
AAACCCGHHILLOPR chalcographical
AAACCCILLLMSTYY cataclysmically
AAACCDEEILOPSSU asclepiadaceous
AAACCDEHIINORST archidiaconates
AAACCDEIMNNOORS adenocarcinomas
AAACCDGHIILOPRR cardiographical
AAACCDHIMMNOPRY pharmacodynamic
AAACCEEILMNNRRT Central American
AAACCEEINNQRSTU reacquaintances
AAACCEEINORRSSU sarraceniaceous
AAACCEGHILNOOPR oceanographical
AAACCEHILORSSST thalassocracies
AAACCEHILORSTTT thalattocracies
AAACCEHMNORTTTT chemoattractant
AAACCEILNOPRRST practical reason
AAACCEMOPPRRSTU carpometacarpus
AAACCFIILNRRSTU intrafascicular
AAACCGHHILOPRRT chartographical
AAACCGHILLMOOPR pharmacological
AAACCHIILMNNORT antimonarchical
AAACCIIILMNOSTT acclimatisation
AAACCIIILMNOTTZ acclimatization
AAACCIIINNOPSTT incapacitations
AAACCIILLMNORTY microanalytical
AAACCILLLOPPTYY apocalyptically
AAACDDEILNOPRSS Nord-Pas-de-Calais
AAACDDIKLLNNSSU Auckland Islands
AAACDEEHIIMNRST adiathermancies
AAACDEEHILMMOSU hamamelidaceous
AAACDEGIILLMNTY diamagnetically

AAACDEHHHILMPRS	Himachal Pradesh
AAACDEILLLMNNTT	Mittelland Canal
AAACDEILLMNORYY	aerodynamically
AAACDEILLMORSUY	amaryllidaceous
AAACDGIIINORTTV	radioactivating
AAACDGILLMRRTUY	dramaturgically
AAACDGILNNNNORU	Grand Union Canal
AAACDIIINOORTTV	radioactivation
AAACDIILLNOOORT	radiolocational
AAACEEGILLNPRTY	paragenetically
AAACEEGILNORTTV	lactovegetarian
AAACEEHILLMORTT	Charlotte Amalie
AAACEEHIMMMSTTT	metamathematics
AAACEEHIOPRRSST	acroparesthesia
AAACEELMNNRSSST	sacramentalness
AAACEFILNNSSSTT	fantasticalness
AAACEGILLMNORTV	galvanometrical
AAACEGILMMNRSST	grammaticalness
AAACEGILMNOPRTY	malacopterygian
AAACEHHIILMPRTT	amphitheatrical
AAACEHIIMNNPRSS	Spanish-American
AAACEHIINNRSSTT	Saint Catharines
AAACEHIKNOPRRTU	Carpatho-Ukraine
AAACEHILMMNNOTT	nonmathematical
AAACEHIMPPRSTTY	parasympathetic
AAACEILMNRSSSTT	sacramentalists
AAACGGHILNOOPRR	organographical
AAACGHIILPRRSTT	stratigraphical
AAACGHILLOPRTUY	autographically
AAACGIILLMRSTTY	magistratically
AAACGIILLOOPRST	parasitological
AAACGIMMORSSTUX	Saxo Grammaticus
AAACHIILLLNNOTU	hallucinational
AAACHIILMNOPRST	sharia-compliant
AAACHIILNOPSSTT	chaptalisations
AAACHIILNOPSTTZ	chaptalizations
AAACHIIMNOORSTT	achromatisation
AAACHIIMNOORTTZ	achromatization
AAACIIILNOPSSTT	capitalisations
AAACIIILNOPSTTZ	capitalizations
AAACIIILNPSSTTT	anticapitalists
AAACIILLLMNOSTY	anomalistically
AAACIILNORSSTUV	vascularisation
AAACIILNORSTUVZ	vascularization
AAACILLNNOORTTV	contravallation
AAACILLNNORSTTY	transactionally
AAACILLNORSTTUY	astronautically
AAADDEGINOSSTUV	disadvantageous
AAADDEGINPRSSWW	Windward Passage
AAADDFIKLLLNNSS	Falkland Islands
AAADDHIMNNOPSTY	Damon and Pythias
AAADDIINNORSSTT	standardisation
AAADDIINNORSTTZ	standardization
AAADEEELNNPRSST	lares and penates
AAADEGIILLNNPSS	Pelagian Islands
AAADEIILLNNSSTU	Aleutian Islands
AAADEIILNNRSTUV	valetudinarians
AAADFHILNQRRSSU	Farquhar Islands
AAADGHIOOPRRSTU	autoradiographs
	radioautographs
AAADGHIOOPRRTUY	autoradiography
AAADHIJKMMMNRSU	Jammu and Kashmir
AAADHILLLMNRSSS	Marshall Islands
AAADHIMNNORRSTU	Hardouin Mansart
AAADIIILNNRSTTU	latitudinarians
AAAEEEFGHLLLMOT	haemoflagellate
AAAEEELMNRSVYYZ	Severnaya Zemlya
AAAEEGGHILMNTTU	haemagglutinate
AAAEEGGHLOOPPRY	palaeogeography
AAAEEGGILNPRTUV	private language
AAAEEGHIMMNOPSY	hypomagnesaemia
AAAEEGILMMNOPST	palaeomagnetism
AAAEEGINNPRSSTU	septuagenarians
AAAEEHILNNORTTT	National Theatre
AAAEEINNORRSSTT	Saorstat Eireann
AAAEELMMMNORRRT	Moral Rearmament
AAAEFGGLLMNOORV	Vale of Glamorgan
AAAEFGJMNOORRTU	Margaret of Anjou
AAAEFIILMNNOSTT	manifestational
AAAEGGMMMNORRTU	Montague grammar
AAAEGHIMNOPRSST	phantasmagories
AAAEGHLLOOOPPTY	palaeopathology
AAAEGHLNOOPPRTY	palaeontography
AAAEGIIILMNRSST	egalitarianisms
AAAEGIINNNQQRUU	quinquagenarian
AAAEGIKOSTUUWYY	Tokugawa Iyeyasu
AAAEGILLLNNORTY	National Gallery
AAAEGILLNNPRSTU	Transalpine Gaul
AAAEHHLOPRSSTTY	thalassotherapy
AAAEHIMOPRRSSTT	aromatherapists
AAAEIIILMNORSTT	materialisation
AAAEIIILMNORTTZ	materialization
AAAEIIILMNQRSTU	equalitarianism
AAAEIIILNORRSTT	arterialisation
AAAEIIILNORRTTZ	arterialization
AAAEIILMMNPRRST	parliamentarism
AAAEILLNNNOPSUV	Avalon Peninsula
AAAEILMNNPRRTUY	unparliamentary
AAAEMORRSSSTTTU	tarsometatarsus
AAAFFIKMMNNRRTU	Frankfurt am Main
AAAFIIIILMNORST	familiarisation
AAAFIIIILMNORTZ	familiarization
AAAGHIILLMNSUVW	Vaughan Williams
AAAGHINNORRSTUU	Austro-Hungarian
AAAGIIILMNNORST	marginalisation
AAAGIIILMNNORTZ	marginalization
AAAGIILLNORTTVY	gravitationally
AAAGIINNNOOSSTT	antagonisations
AAAGIINNNOOSTTZ	antagonizations
AAAGIINNOORSTTV	astronavigation
AAAGINOORRSSTTV	astronavigators
AAAHIIIMMNNRSTU	humanitarianism
AAAHIIIMNNRSTTU	humanitarianist
AAAHILNORSSTTUU	South Australian
AAAIIIINNNRRTTT	antitrinitarian
AAAIIILLMMNOSST	malassimilation
AAAIIILMNNORSTT	antirationalism
AAAIIILMNORSTTT	totalitarianism
AAAIIILNNNOOSTT	nationalisation
AAAIIILNNNOOTTZ	nationalization
AAAIIILNNNOSTTT	antinationalist
AAAIIILNNOORSTT	rationalisation
AAAIIILNNOORTTZ	rationalization
AAAIIMNOOSSTTTU	automatisations

AAAIINNNPRRSTTT antitranspirant
AAAILLNNOPRSTUY supranationally
AAAILMNNORSTTTU transmutational
AAAILNNNOPRSTTT transplantation
AAAILNNORSSTTUV transvaluations
AABBCEEFINORSST absorbefacients
AABBCGHIIILLOPR bibliographical
AABCCCEHHIILOPR brachiocephalic
AABCCCEHHILPRSY brachycephalics
AABCCDEEHILLNSY hendecasyllabic
AABCCDEELNNORTU counterbalanced
AABCCDEGHHLMNNO Mönchengladbach
AABCCDEGHHLMNNU München-Gladbach
AABCCDEILMMRTUU circumambulated
AABCCDHILMRSTYY brachydactylism
AABCCDHLORSTUYY brachydactylous
AABCCEEILNPRSST practicableness
AABCCEELNNORSTU counterbalances
AABCCEELORRRSUV cerebrovascular
AABCCEGIILLOORT bacteriological
AABCCEGIILMNRUV circumnavigable
AABCCEHHILMPRSY brachycephalism
AABCCEHHLOPRSUY brachycephalous
AABCCEILMMRSTUU circumambulates
AABCCGIILMNOTUU bioaccumulating
AABCCIIIILLLNTUY incalculability
AABCCILMMORRTUU circumambulator
AABCDDEELLLOSSY dodecasyllables
AABCDEEEGKLLNOW acknowledgeable
AABCDEEEHLLLNSY hendecasyllable
AABCDEEHIIILSTT detachabilities
AABCDEIINNOORST decarbonisation
AABCDEIINNOORTZ decarbonization
AABCDEIINORRSTU decarburisation
AABCDEIINORRTUZ decarburization
AABCDEILNOORTXY decarboxylation
AABCDGIIILLOOOR radiobiological
AABCDHIILLMRTYY dithyrambically
AABCEEEGHILNNRT interchangeable
AABCEEEGHLLLNNU unchallengeable
AABCEEFFIIILNTY ineffaceability
AABCEEGHIILNTXY exchangeability
AABCEEGHILNNRTY interchangeably
AABCEEILNNRSSTT intractableness
AABCEEINOQRSSTU sesquicarbonate
AABCEFIINOPRRST prefabrications
AABCEGGHIILOOPR biogeographical
AABCEGGHOORSTUX Saxe-Coburg-Gotha
AABCEGHIOOPRSTU bacteriophagous
AABCEGIINRRSTUU bureaucratising
AABCEGIINRRTUUZ bureaucratizing
AABCEGILMNOPSUU plumbaginaceous
AABCEHHIILMNPRS chamberlainship
AABCEHHILNOOPRT lophobranchiate
AABCEHIKKLPRSSU Khakass Republic
AABCEHILLMORTTY bathometrically
AABCEHILLMRTTYY bathymetrically
AABCEHINOORSSTT archeobotanists
AABCEHIORRSSSUU brachiosauruses
AABCEIILNNPRSTU antirepublicans
AABCEILLLMOPRTY problematically
AABCEILLLMORSTY meroblastically
AABCEILMNNNOOPU uncompanionable
AABCEINNOSSTTTU consubstantiate
AABCELLOOPRTXYY polycarboxylate
AABCFIIILLNOSTY syllabification
AABCGHIMOOPRRRS microbarographs
AABCHIILLLNRTYY labyrinthically
AABCHILLLLOOSTY holoblastically
AABCIIIILLNPPTY inapplicability
AABCIIILMNOPRTY incomparability
AABCIILLLLRSTYY trisyllabically
AABCIINOORSSTTU bioastronautics
AABCIINOOSSSSTU subassociations
AABCIINORSSSTTT abstractionists
AABCILMNNOOSTTU noctambulations
AABDDEEGHLOOPRT photodegradable
AABDDEEGIIILRST degradabilities
AABDDEGIINOORST biodegradations
AABDEEGHINORRTW weatherboarding
AABDEEGIIILRSTY disagreeability
AABDEEGILMNRRTU Bermuda Triangle
AABDEEIILNNSSSV inadvisableness
AABDEEILNNOSSUV unavoidableness
AABDEFGHHLMOORU Flamborough Head
AABDEGIIMNRRSSS disembarrassing
AABDEIIILNORSTT detribalisation
AABDEIIILNORTTZ detribalization
AABDEIIILNOSSTT destabilisation
AABDEIIILNOSTTZ destabilization
AABDEIIKMNORSST disembarkations
AABDEIILNSSSTTU substantialised
AABDEIILNSSTTUZ substantialized
AABDEINNSSTTTUU unsubstantiated
AABDELLLMMOOSTU medulloblastoma
AABDIINOOPPRSST disapprobations
AABEEEGLLMNRSSY General Assembly
AABEEEHKLNNSSSU unshakeableness
AABEEEIILLNNNSS inalienableness
AABEEEILLNNRSST inalterableness
AABEEEILNNPRSSS inseparableness
AABEEEILNPRRRSS irreparableness
AABEEEKLNNPSSSU unspeakableness
AABEEELLNPRSSSU pleasurableness
AABEEELNNORSSST treasonableness
AABEEFHILNNOSSS fashionableness
AABEEFILLMMNNSS inflammableness
AABEEFLLNNPPSSU unflappableness
AABEEFLNNNORRST nontransferable
AABEEFLNNORSSUV unfavorableness
AABEEGHIKLNRRTY heartbreakingly
AABEEGIKLLNRRRV Granville-Barker
AABEEGILNOORRTV overelaborating
AABEEIIILLPRRTY irrepealability
AABEEIILMNOSTTT antimetabolites
AABEEIILMNRTUVY maneuverability
AABEEILNOOORRTV overelaboration
AABEFGIIILRRRTY irrefragability
AABEFIILNRRSTTY transferability
AABEGHHMOOPRRRT thermobarograph
AABEGHIILMNOORU haemoglobinuria
AABEGHIIOOPRSTU autobiographies
AABEGHIOOPRRSTU autobiographers
AABEHIIILNORSTT rehabilitations

AABEHLNOOPRTTTT	Neath Port Talbot
AABEIIILLNORSST	liberalisations
AABEIIILLNORSTZ	liberalizations
AABEIIILMMRSTUY	immeasurability
AABEIILMNORTUVY	manoeuvrability
AABEIILNORSSSTU	atrabiliousness
AABEIILNSSSSTTU	substantialises
AABEIILNSSSTTUZ	substantializes
AABEILLNOORSTVY	observationally
AABEILNNSSSSTTU	substantialness
AABGGIIILLNTTUY	agglutinability
AABGIILMMOPRRTY	programmability
AABHIIIKKMRSSUU	Murasaki Shikibu
AABIIIIMNQRSTUU	ubiquitarianism
AABIIINNOORSTTT	antiabortionist
AABIILLNNSSTTUY	insubstantially
AABIILMNRSTTTUY	transmutability
AABIILNOPRSSTTY	transposability
AABIILNSSSSTTTU	substantialists
AABIINNOSSSTTTU	substantiations
AABILLNNSSTTUUY	unsubstantially
AACCCDEFIIILNOT	decalcification
AACCCEEHILPRTTY	hypercatalectic
AACCCEHHILOOPRT	cephalothoracic
AACCCEHIILLSTTY	catechistically
AACCCEHIIOPPRSY	archiepiscopacy
AACCCEHIIRRSSTT	characteristics
AACCCEHILLMOTTY	chemotactically
AACCCEIILLLMRTY	climacterically
AACCCEIILLLSTYY	acetylsalicylic
AACCCILLMMOORSY	macrocosmically
AACCCILLMOOPRSY	macroscopically
AACCDDEIINNORTT	contraindicated
AACCDEEENORTTUV	overaccentuated
AACCDEEHHLOOPRT	cephalochordate
AACCDEEKNORTTTU	counterattacked
AACCDEFHLLOORUU	La Rochefoucauld
AACCDEGHIILOORS	oligosaccharide
AACCDEGIILLLOOT	dialectological
AACCDEGIIMNRTUV	circumnavigated
AACCDEHHILMNORY	hydromechanical
AACCDEHILOPRSSY	polysaccharides
AACCDEHIMNOORSS	monosaccharides
AACCDEIIILLMRTY	acidimetrically
AACCDEIINNORSTT	contraindicates
AACCDEILLNOOTUY	coeducationally
AACCDELMNOOORST	Coromandel Coast
AACCDFGHHIILNOS	Chichagof Island
AACCDGILMMNOOTY	accommodatingly
AACCDGIMMNNOOTU	unaccommodating
AACCDHHILNOOPRY	hypochondriacal
AACCDHIIMOOSSST	sadomasochistic
AACCDHILNOOPRST	achondroplastic
AACCDIILLOOPRSY	radioscopically
AACCDIINNNORSTT	contraindicants
AACCEEENORSTTUV	overaccentuates
AACCEEGHILMMNOT	magnetochemical
AACCEEGILNORSST	categoricalness
AACCEEHHLOOPRST	cephalothoraces
AACCEEHIIMRRSST	saccharimetries
AACCEEHIIMRRSTZ	mischaracterize
AACCEEHIIOPPRST	archiepiscopate
AACCEEHILMNORSV	servomechanical
AACCEEILLNNOPRT	precancellation
AACCEEILLNORTTY	electroanalytic
AACCEEINNNORSSS	reconnaissances
AACCEFIILNRRSTU	interfascicular
AACCEFIILOOPRSU	caprifoliaceous
AACCEFLNORSTTUU	counterfactuals
AACCEGHIILLOPRX	lexicographical
AACCEGHIIMNOPRT	cinematographic
AACCEGHILLLOORY	archeologically
AACCEGIILOOPSTT	galactopoietics
AACCEGIIMNRSTUV	circumnavigates
AACCEHHILMNOOPT	photomechanical
AACCEHIIKMNOPRT	pharmacokinetic
AACCEHIILLMNSTY	mechanistically
AACCEHIKLNOOSVZ	Czechoslovakian
AACCEHILLLLMNOY	melancholically
AACCEHILLMORTTY	tachometrically
AACCEHILLRRTTUY	architecturally
AACCEHLOOPRSSSY	polysaccharoses
AACCEIIIILLMNRST	anticlericalism
AACCEIILLMNOSTY	encomiastically
AACCEIILLNRRTUV	interclavicular
AACCEIILMNPRSST	impracticalness
AACCEIIMNRSTTTU	circumstantiate
AACCEILLMNOPSTU	nucleoplasmatic
AACCEILMNNORTTU	counterclaimant
AACCEILNNPRSSTU	unpracticalness
AACCEILRRRRTUUX	extracurricular
AACCFIIILNOSSST	classifications
AACCGHHILOPRSST	chalcographists
AACCGHHIMOOPRRT	chromatographic
AACCGHILOPPRRTY	cryptographical
AACCGHIMMNOORRT	chronogrammatic
AACCGHIMNOOPRST	pharmacognostic
AACCGIIILLLNOORY	craniologically
AACCGIILLMNRTUV	circumvallating
AACCGIIMNORRTUV	circumnavigator
AACCGILLNNOOSTT	logical constant
AACCHIIILNOOSTT	catholicisation
AACCHIIILNOOTTZ	catholicization
AACCHIIINNORSTT	Christian Action
AACCHIILLMOSSTY	masochistically
AACCHIILLPRSTYY	psychiatrically
AACCHILLNOPSTYY	sycophantically
AACCHIMNNOOPRSS	Spanish Moroccan
AACCIIILLLOSSTY	socialistically
AACCIIILNORRSTU	circularisation
AACCIIILNORRTUZ	circularization
AACCIIILPRRSTTU	particularistic
AACCIILLMNORTUV	circumvallation
AACCIILLMNOSSTU	miscalculations
AACCILLLOPRTTUY	plutocratically
AACDDEEEEHLNRSS	clearheadedness
AACDDEEGHNPRSSU	Gadsden Purchase
AACDDEGGIINRSST	Giscard d'Estaing
AACDDEHHILNNOPS	Daphnis and Chloe
AACDDEIILNNOORV	Leonardo da Vinci
AACDDHIILNNSSSW	Sandwich Islands
AACDEEGHIMNOPRT	cinematographed
AACDEEHIIORRSTT	icositetrahedra
AACDEEHINNTTTUU	unauthenticated

AACDEEIILMNOSTU	eudaemonistical
AACDEEIILNPRSTU	undercapitalise
AACDEEIILNPRTUZ	undercapitalize
AACDEEIILOPRSTV	overcapitalised
AACDEEIILOPRTVZ	overcapitalized
AACDEEIIMNNOTTV	decontaminative
AACDEGHILLMOPRY	demographically
AACDEGHLOPRRSTY	dactylographers
AACDEGIIMNNNOTT	decontaminating
AACDEGILLMNOUVY	many-valued logic
AACDEGILNOOPRSS	diagonal process
AACDEHHIILNPRST	Christadelphian
AACDEHILMMNORTY	thermodynamical
AACDEIIILMNOSST	idiomaticalness
AACDEIIJLLRTUXY	extrajudicially
AACDEIILLMNRRTY	intradermically
AACDEIILLMORTUY	audiometrically
AACDEIILLNNORSS	Caroline Islands
AACDEIILNNOPSTY	platinocyanides
AACDEIILNORSSTT	dictatorialness
AACDEIILNOSSTTU	educationalists
AACDEIILNRRSTUV	cardinal virtues
AACDEIIMNNNOOTT	decontamination
AACDEIIMNOORSTT	democratisation
AACDEIIMNOORTTZ	democratization
AACDEIIMNORSSTY	aerodynamicists
AACDEILLMORRTTU	courtmartialled
AACDEIMNNOORSTT	decontaminators
AACDEINOOOPRRTT	Pietro da Cortona
AACDFIIIILNOPST	lapidifications
AACDFIIINOSSSTT	dissatisfaction
AACDFIIORSSSTTY	dissatisfactory
AACDGHIMOOPRRSY	myocardiographs
AACDGIIILNRSTTU	disarticulating
AACDGIILNPQRTUU	quadruplicating
AACDHIILLNOOPRY	radiophonically
AACDHIILMNRSSST	Christmas Island
AACDHILLORSTTYY	hydrostatically
AACDIIIILNNPRSS	disciplinarians
AACDIIILLMNOTUY	unidiomatically
AACDIIILNOPPSST	disapplications
AACDIIILNORSTTU	disarticulation
AACDIIINOOSSSST	disassociations
AACDIILNOPQRTUU	quadruplication
AACDIILORRSSTTU	disarticulators
AACDILMNOOPRRUY	cardiopulmonary
AACDLLNOOPRSTUX	Castor and Pollux
AACDMNOORRRSSTY	Ross and Cromarty
AACEEEGHHLRRSTT	Charles the Great
AACEEEGILLMNTTY	metagenetically
AACEEEHHHLNORTX	hexachlorethane
AACEEEHILMORTTT	metatheoretical
AACEEEHMMORSTTY	haemacytometers
AACEEELLNORSSTY	electroanalyses
AACEEENNQRRTTUY	quatercentenary
AACEEFFHIMNNRST	affranchisement
AACEEGGILLMNOTY	gamogenetically
AACEEGHHILOPRRT	heterographical
AACEEGHHLNOPPRS	encephalographs
AACEEGHHLNOPPRY	encephalography
AACEEGHILLLPRTY	telegraphically
AACEEGHILLNOPRS	selenographical
AACEEGHILOPRRST	stereographical
AACEEGHIMMNORST	archeomagnetism
AACEEGHIMNOPRRT	cinematographer
AACEEGHLLMOOPSU	megalocephalous
AACEEGIKMORSTTY	category mistake
AACEEGILLOOOPST	palaeoecologist
AACEEHHIMNRRRST	Carmarthenshire
AACEEHHLOOPRSTX	cephalothoraxes
AACEEHIINORSTTT	catheterisation
AACEEHIINORTTTZ	catheterization
AACEEHILLMORTTY	theorematically
AACEEHILLNPRTTY	parenthetically
AACEEHILLPRTTUY	therapeutically
AACEEHINNORRRSV	Caernarvonshire
AACEEIILLPPRTTY	peripatetically
AACEEIILOPRSSTV	overcapitalises
AACEEIILOPRSTVZ	overcapitalizes
AACEEILLNORSSTY	electroanalysis
AACEEIMNOPRSSTV	comparativeness
AACEELLLLRRTUXY	extracellularly
AACEENNOOPSSSSU	saponaceousness
AACEFGIMNNRRTUU	remanufacturing
AACEFHHIMRRSSTT	Father Christmas
AACEFHIORSSTTUW	South West Africa
AACEFIILLNOORRW	Lower California
AACEFIINORSSTTU	anfractuosities
AACEFILOOPRSSSU	passifloraceous
AACEGGHILOOOPRZ	zoogeographical
AACEGHHMOOPRRRT	chromatographer
AACEGHIIKMNOPRT	kinematographic
AACEGHIJKRSSTTT	straightjackets
AACEGHILLMOORTU	rheumatological
AACEGHILLOPRRXY	xerographically
AACEGHILLOPRSUU	Sulu Archipelago
AACEGIIJKNRSTTT	straitjacketing
AACEGIILLLMNORY	mineralogically
AACEGIILLMRRTVY	gravimetrically
AACEGIINOORSSTT	categorisations
AACEGIINOORSTTZ	categorizations
AACEGILLLLMRTUY	metallurgically
AACEGILLMNOOPTU	pneumatological
AACEGLNOORSSTUY	agranulocytoses
AACEHHILLMOOPTY	homeopathically
AACEHHILNNOPSTY	phthalocyanines
AACEHIILLNPSTTY	pantheistically
AACEHIINNOSTTTU	authentications
AACEHILLMOPRSTY	atmospherically
AACEHILLMPSTTYY	sympathetically
AACEHILLNOPRTUY	neuropathically
AACEHILLOOPSTTY	osteopathically
AACEHILOOPRSSTT	thoracoplasties
AACEHILOPRRSSTT	stratospherical
AACEHIMOOPPRSST	pharmacopoeists
AACEHLNOPRSSSYY	psychoanalysers
AACEHLNOPRSSYYZ	psychoanalyzers
AACEHMNOOOPPRSS	anamorphoscopes
AACEHMNOOORRSTY	archeoastronomy
AACEHNOOPPRRSTU	parthenocarpous
AACEIIILLMNOSTU	aluminosilicate
AACEIIILLNOSSTX	lexicalisations
AACEIIILLNOSTXZ	lexicalizations
AACEIIILMNOPPSS	episcopalianism

AACEIIILNOPSSST specialisations
AACEIIILNOPSSTZ specializations
AACEIIILNPRSTTT antiperistaltic
AACEIIILPRRSTTU particularities
AACEIIIMMNOSTTT metamictisation
AACEIIIMMNOTTTZ metamictization
AACEIIIMNNOPSTT emancipationist
AACEIILLLMNSTTY mentalistically
AACEIILLLPRSTTY peristaltically
AACEIILLMNNRSTY manneristically
AACEIILMNOPRRTT malpractitioner
AACEIILNNORSSTT centralisations
AACEIILNNORSTTZ centralizations
AACEIILNNPRSSTU puritanicalness
AACEIILNNRSSTTU antinuclearists
AACEIILNOPRSTTU recapitulations
AACEIILPRRRSSTU particularisers
AACEIILPRRRSTUZ particularizers
AACEILLLLNRRTUY intracellularly
AACEILLLMNOPRTY planometrically
AACEILLLNNOOSTT constellational
AACEILMMMNOOORT commemorational
AACEILMNOOPSSTY compassionately
AACEILMNOOSSSTY ancylostomiases
AACEILNOOORRTTU autocorrelation
AACEILNORSSTTUX exclaustrations
AACELLMMNOPRTTY compartmentally
AACFFIIINORSSSS Francis of Assisi
AACFGIIIIILNRST artificialising
AACFGIIIIILNRTZ artificializing
AACFGIILNNOORTU configurational
AACFIIIMMNNOOST ammonifications
AACFIIINNOORSTT fractionisation
AACFIIINNOORTTZ fractionization
AACFIIINNOQSTTU quantifications
AACFIIINORSSTTT stratifications
AACFIILLLMORSTY formalistically
AACFILNNNOOORTT confrontational
AACGGHHILLOPPRY glyphographical
AACGGHHILNOOPRY cholangiography
AACGGHILLLOOPRY logographically
AACGGHILLNOOPRY pharyngological
AACGGHILLOPPRTY glyptographical
AACGHHIILOPPRSY physiographical
AACGHHILLLOOPRY holographically
AACGHIIILMNORTT antilogarithmic
AACGHIILLLMORTY algorithmically
logarithmically
AACGHILLLOPPRYY polygraphically
AACGHILLMNOOPRY monographically
nomographically
AACGHILLNOOOPRT anthropological
AACGHILLOOPPRTY topographically
AACGHILLOPPRTYY typographically
AACGHILMOOPRSST pharmacologists
AACGHILNNOPSSYY psychoanalysing
AACGHILNNOPSYYZ psychoanalyzing
AACGHIMNOOPRSST pharmacognosist
AACGHLLOPRRSTYY crystallography
AACGIIILNPRRSTU particularising
AACGIIILNPRRTUZ particularizing
AACGIIILNPRSSTU paralinguistics
AACGIILLRRSTTUU agriculturalist
AACGIINNOPRRSTT procrastinating
AACGIJLLNNOOTUY conjugationally
AACGILLLMOOOSTY somatologically
AACGILLMNOORSTY gastronomically
AACGILLNNORRTUU nonagricultural
AACGILNNOORSTTU congratulations
AACGILNOORSSTUY agranulocytosis
AACGIMMNOOPRRSU macrosporangium
AACHHIILLNOPPRT philanthropical
AACHIILLMNORSTY harmonistically
AACHIILNNNOORRT North Carolinian
AACHIILNNOORSTU South Carolinian
AACHIIMNNORSSTT antimonarchists
AACHILLLMOOPSTY homoplastically
AACHILLOPPRSTYY saprophytically
AACHILLOPPSSTTY staphyloplastic
AACIIIILMNNORST criminalisation
AACIIIILMNNORTZ criminalization
AACIIILLLRSTTUY ritualistically
AACIIILMNNOSSTU masculinisation
AACIIILMNNOSTUZ masculinization
AACIIILMNOPPSST misapplications
AACIIILNOOPRSTT tropicalisation
AACIIILNOOPRTTZ tropicalization
AACIIIMNNOORSTT romanticisation
AACIIIMNNOORTTZ romanticization
AACIILLNOOPRSTY anisotropically
AACIILLNORSSTTY crystallisation
AACIILLNORSTTYZ crystallization
AACIILMMNNOOSTU communalisation
AACIILMMNNOOTUZ communalization
AACIILMNOOSSSTY ancylostomiasis
AACIILNNOOOTTUU autoinoculation
AACIILNNOPRRSTT transcriptional
AACIILNORSSSTTY crystalisations
AACIILNORSSTTTU straticulations
AACIILNORSSTTYZ crystalizations
AACIINNOOPRRSTT procrastination
AACILLLLMOPSTYY plasmolytically
AACILLMMOPSTTYY symptomatically
AACILLMNRRSTUUY intramuscularly
AACILNNNOSSTTUV anticonvulsants
AACILNNOPRSTTTU contrapuntalist
AACINOOPRRRSSTT procrastinators
AACLLRRRSTTTUUU ultrastructural
AACLNNNOOOPSSTT postconsonantal
AADDDIILNNRSSWW Windward Islands
AADDEEEHHNRRSST hardheartedness
AADDEEELMMNNPUY Eupen and Malmédy
AADDEEHMRRRTTWY Edward the Martyr
AADDEEIILMMNRST maladministered
AADDEIILNOPRSTU superadditional
AADDHILNNOSSSTU Thousand Islands
AADEEEFHHLNRSST halfheartedness
AADEEEGGLNNNNRW New England Range
AADEEEHMNRRSSTW warmheartedness
AADEEEIKLNNRSVX Alexander Nevski
AADEEEILLLPPPRS parallelepipeds
AADEEEILMNPRSTT departmentalise
AADEEEILMNPRTTZ departmentalize
AADEEFLMNNNSSTU fundamentalness

AADEEGGHILMNTTU	hemagglutinated
AADEEGHILOPRRST	radiotelegraphs
AADEEGHILOPRRTY	radiotelegraphy
AADEEGIIILMNRST	dematerialising
AADEEGIIILMNRTZ	dematerializing
AADEEGIIMNNOSTT	demagnetisation
AADEEGIIMNNOTTZ	demagnetization
AADEEGIMNNRRSST	disarrangements
AADEEHIIILMPPRY	hyperlipidaemia
AADEEHIIIMNRRST	hereditarianism
AADEEHLLORRTTTY	tetartohedrally
AADEEIIILNNOSSST	sensationalised
AADEEIIILNNOSSTZ	sensationalized
AADEEIIILNOSSTUX	desexualisation
AADEEIIILNOSTUXZ	desexualization
AADEEIINNPRRSST	predestinarians
AADEEILLLOPPPRS	parallelopipeds
AADEEILMMNPRSTT	departmentalism
AADEEILMNORSTTT	tatterdemalions
AADEEILMOPRSSTT	dermatoplasties
AADEEILNNPRSSUW	Seward Peninsula
AADEEINNPRSSSTT	antidepressants
AADEELMNNNOPRTT	nondepartmental
AADEFHLLLNRSSTU	Sutherland Falls
AADEFILMNNSSTTU	fundamentalists
AADEGHIMNOOORRS	Angra do Heroísmo
AADEGIIILNNNOST	denationalising
AADEGIIILNNNOTZ	denationalizing
AADEGIILMMNORST	melodramatising
AADEGIILMMNORTZ	melodramatizing
AADEGIIMNORRSTV	overdramatising
AADEGIIMNORRTVZ	overdramatizing
AADEGIINNORRSTT	intergradations
AADEGINOORRRSTT	retrogradations
AADEHHLMNOPPTYY	lymphadenopathy
AADEHIIOPRRSSTT	radiotherapists
AADEHILNOSSSSTU	South Sea Islands
AADEHLNORRSTTWY	northeastwardly
AADEIILMNOSTTUU	demutualisation
AADEIILMNOTTUUZ	demutualization
AADEIILNOPSSSTY	dispassionately
AADEIILNORRRTXY	extraordinarily
AADEIIMOPPPRRST	misappropriated
AADEILLNOOPRSUX	Alexandroúpolis
AADEILMNNOORSTT	demonstrational
AADEILNNORSTUUV	undervaluations
AADELLOPRRSSSUX	Russell's paradox
AADELNOPRSTTUUY	polyunsaturated
AADEMNNOORSTTUU	monounsaturated
AADFFIIIMNORSST	disaffirmations
AADFGHILNNNOOSY	laying on of hands
AADFGHIORRRSTTW	straightforward
AADFNNOOORRSTTV	Stratford-on-Avon
AADGHHIMNPRSSTU	draughtsmanship
AADGIIINNOORSST	disorganisation
AADGIIINNOORSTZ	disorganization
AADHILLNORRSTYY	synarthrodially
AADIIILNORSSTTT	traditionalists
AADIIIMNNORSSTT	administrations
AAEEEEFGNORRSTT	Orange Free State
AAEEEFGHLLLMOST	hemoflagellates
AAEEEGILLNRRSTT	Greater Antilles
AAEEEGILRRRSTVV	Great Slave River
AAEEEGMNNPRRRST	prearrangements
AAEEEHHIMMMNPTT	methamphetamine
AAEEEHIILNORSTT	etherealisation
AAEEEHIILNORTTZ	etherealization
AAEEEHIMNNNOPRS	neoarsphenamine
AAEEEIIMNNORTTT	Marie Antoinette
AAEEEILMNNPTTTU	antepenultimate
AAEEEILNNRSSTTV	alternativeness
AAEEELLMMNPRTTY	temperamentally
AAEEFFINOORRSTT	reafforestation
AAEEFFLNNORSSTT	Feast of Lanterns
AAEEFGILLRRTTVY	Great Rift Valley
AAEEFGIMNNRRSST	fragmentariness
AAEEFHILPPRSTTY	past life therapy
AAEEFINNORSSSTT	aftersensations
AAEEGGHILMNSTTU	hemagglutinates
AAEEGHIKMNOPRRT	kinematographer
AAEEGHILLMORRTY	erythromelalgia
AAEEGHILNOOSSTY	anaesthesiology
AAEEGHLLMOPRRST	metallographers
AAEEGIIIMNNSSTV	imaginativeness
AAEEGIIIMNORTVV	overimaginative
AAEEGIILMNRSSST	magisterialness
AAEEGIILNNORSST	generalisations
AAEEGIILNNORSTZ	generalizations
AAEEGILMNRTTUVY	argumentatively
AAEEGIMMNNRRSST	misarrangements
AAEEGLMNOQRUZZZ	González Márquez
AAEEHHILMNORSTT	trihalomethanes
AAEEHIINNOSTTTZ	anesthetization
AAEEHIMNNNOOPSZ	aminophenazones
AAEEHLMMMNOSSUU	Ashmolean Museum
AAEEIILLMNNPRRS	premillenarians
AAEEIILLNOQRTTU	Loire-Atlantique
AAEEIILNNORSTTX	externalisation
AAEEIILNNORTTXZ	externalization
AAEEIILNNOSSSST	sensationalises
AAEEIILNNOSSSTZ	sensationalizes
AAEEIKLMNNSSTTU	unstatesmanlike
AAEEILLLMORRSTT	lamellirostrate
AAEEILLMNNPPRSU	Palmer Peninsula
AAEEILNNOPRRSST	proletarianness
AAEEIMNNPRRSSTT	semitransparent
AAEEINOPPPRRSST	appropriateness
AAEELLNPRRRTTUY	preternaturally
AAEENNNPRRSSSTT	transparentness
AAEFIIILMORRTVY	overfamiliarity
AAEFMNOORRRSTTU	autotransformer
AAEGGIIIMMNPRST	epigrammatising
AAEGGIIIMMNPRTZ	epigrammatizing
AAEGHHINOOPPRTT	anthropophagite
AAEGHHNOOOPPRST	organophosphate
AAEGHILLMOPRSTT	metallographist
AAEGHLLNOORTTUY	natural theology
AAEGIIIILMMNRST	immaterialising
AAEGIIIILMMNRTZ	immaterializing
AAEGIIILMNNNRTT	interlaminating
AAEGIIILMNNTUVY	unimaginatively
AAEGIIILNNOSTTV	investigational
AAEGIIKNNNPSSST	painstakingness
AAEGIILLNOORSST	allegorisations

AAEGIILLNOORSTZ allegorizations
AAEGIILNNOORRTT interrogational
AAEGIILNNRRSTTT transliterating
AAEGIILNORRSSTU regularisations
AAEGIILNORRSTUZ regularizations
AAEGIINNOORRSST reorganisations
AAEGIINNOORRSTZ reorganizations
AAEGILLNOOOPSTT palaeontologist
AAEGILLOOOOPSTZ palaeozoologist
AAEGIMMNNNOSSSU magnanimousness
AAEGIMNOPRRSTTU tetrasporangium
AAEHIIKLMNRSSTU Karelian Isthmus
AAEHIILORTTTUVY authoritatively
AAEHIMOPRSSSSTT massotherapists
AAEIIIILNORRSTT irrationalities
AAEIIILMMNOORST memorialisation
AAEIIILMMNOORTZ memorialization
AAEIIILMNNNORTT interlamination
AAEIIILNNNORSTT internalisation
AAEIIILNNNORTTZ internalization
AAEIIILNPRSSSTT antiperistalsis
AAEIILLMNNRSTTU transilluminate
AAEIILLNNNORTTY internationally
AAEIILLNNORSSTT reinstallations
AAEIILMNNPRSTUY Taimyr Peninsula
AAEIILNNOOPRSST personalisation
AAEIILNNOOPRSTZ personalization
AAEIILNNORRSTTT transliteration
AAEIILNNOSSSSTT sensationalists
AAEIILNOORRSSTV revalorisations
AAEIILNOORRSTVZ revalorizations
AAEIILNOPPPRRTY inappropriately
AAEIIMNOSSSTTTY systematisation
AAEIIMNOSSTTTYZ systematization
AAEIIMOPPPRRSST misappropriates
AAEIINNPPRRSSTT antiperspirants
AAEIKLMNOOSSSTY ankylostomiases
AAEILLNNOPRSTUY supernationally
AAEILMNNPRSTUYY Taymyr Peninsula
AAEILMNPRRSSTUU supernaturalism
AAEILNNNOSSTTUY instantaneously
AAEILNORRRSSTTT transliterators
AAEILNPRRSSTTUU supernaturalist
AAEIMNNNORRSTTT Antiremonstrant
AAEIMNNOORSSTTU neuroanatomists
AAEINNNOPRSSTUU superannuations
AAEINOPRRSSTTUU supersaturation
AAELNNNOPRSSTTX xenotransplants
AAENNORRSSSTUUY tyrannosauruses
AAFGIINNORRSTTU transfiguration
AAFIIIILMNRSTTU futilitarianism
AAFIIIMNNORRSTU uniformitarians
AAFIILLNORRTTTU ultrafiltration
AAFIILMNOORRSTU formularisation
AAFIILMNOORRTUZ formularization
AAFIMNNOORRSSTT transformations
AAGGHINOOPRRSST organographists
AAGGILMMOORSSTT grammatologists
AAGHHNOOOPPRSTU anthropophagous
AAGHIIPRRSSSTTT stratigraphists
AAGHLNOOPRRSTUY ultrasonography
AAGHMNOOOSSTTTU gnathostomatous
AAGIIILNNORSSTU singularisation
AAGIIILNNORSTUZ singularization
AAGIIIMNOSSSTTT stigmatisations
AAGIIIMNOSSTTTZ stigmatizations
AAGIILNORSTTTUU gutturalisation
AAGIILNORTTTUUZ gutturalization
AAGIILOOPRSSSTT parasitologists
AAGIIMNNORRSSTT transmigrations
AAGILMNOOPRSSTV galvanotropisms
AAGIMNNOORSSTUZ Zagros Mountains
AAHHHLOPPRRSTYY staphylorrhaphy
AAHHIINOOPPSSTT phosphatisation
AAHHIINOOPPSTTZ phosphatization
AAHHIMNOOPPRSTT anthropopathism
AAHIIILNOOPSSTT hospitalisation
AAHIIILNOOPSTTZ hospitalization
AAHIINNNOPPRSST nonpartisanship
AAHIINNNOPPRSTZ nonpartizanship
AAHIINOOPSSSTTY hypostasisation
AAHIINOOPSSTTTY hypostatisation
AAHIINOOPSSTTYZ hypostasization
AAHIINOOPSTTTYZ hypostatization
AAIIIIILNNOSSTT initialisations
AAIIIIILNNOSTTZ initializations
AAIIIILMNORSSTT militarisations
AAIIIILMNORSTTZ militarizations
AAIIIILMNRSSTTT antimilitarists
AAIIIIMNNORSTTU miniaturisation
AAIIIIMNNORTTUZ miniaturization
AAIIILLNNOPRSTY inspirationally
AAIIILMMNOORSTT immortalisation
AAIIILMMNOORTTZ immortalization
AAIIILMNOOPRSTV improvisational
AAIIILNNOQRTTUZ tranquilization
AAIIINNOOOSSTTU autoionisations
AAIIINNOOOSTTUZ autoionizations
AAIIJLNNOORSSTU journalisations
AAIIJLNNOORSTUZ journalizations
AAIIJLNOOPSTTUX juxtapositional
AAIIKLMNOOSSSTY ankylostomiasis
AAIILNNOOPRSSTT transpositional
AAIILNOOPPRSSTU popularisations
AAIILNOOPPRSTUZ popularizations
AAIIMMNOSSSSTUY immunoassayists
AAIIMNOOPRSSSTY trypanosomiasis
AAILMMMNNOOOSSU anomalous monism
AAILMNNORSSTTTU ultramontanists
AAIMNNORSSTTUUU Taurus Mountains
AAINNOOPRRSSTTT transportations
ABBCCCEIILMRRSU circumscribable
ABBCDDEILMOOSTU discombobulated
ABBCDEEGIMNRSUZ Brześć nad Bugiem
ABBCDEILMOOSSTU discombobulates
ABBCEEELNNNORYZ benzenecarbonyl
ABBCEEIILNNRSSS inscribableness
ABBCEEIJLNNOOTU unobjectionable
ABBCEHIIKLPRRSU Bashkir Republic
ABBCHIIILMORSTU British Columbia
ABBCIKLLMOOOSSY symbolical books
ABBDEEELNORSSTU redoubtableness
ABBDEEIILNNSSTU indubitableness
ABBEEIIIILLNTUVY unbelievability

ABBEIIIILMOPRST	improbabilities
ABBEIIILOPQRTUY	equiprobability
ABCCEEEILNNOSSV	conceivableness
ABCCEEIILLNORRS	irreconcilables
ABCCEEILNNOORST	concelebrations
ABCCEFIIIJNOOTT	objectification
ABCCEFIILLPSSUY	subspecifically
ABCCEGIILLLOOOY	bioecologically
ABCCEHHILPRSUUV	Chuvash Republic
ABCCEHHINNRTUYZ	Byzantine Church
ABCCEHHINOORRST	brachistochrone
ABCCEIIIILNSSTY	inaccessibility
ABCCEIIILLNORTY	reconcilability
ABCCEIKKLLMPRUU	Kalmuck Republic
ABCCGIIILLMOOOR	microbiological
ABCCIIILMMNOTUY	communicability
ABCDDEEEHKLNOSS	blockheadedness
ABCDEEEIILMMNSS	immedicableness
ABCDEEEILNPRSST	predictableness
ABCDEEELMMNNOSS	commendableness
ABCDEEHIIILPRTY	decipherability
ABCDEEHMNORRRTU	Camborne-Redruth
ABCDEEIILNOSSSS	dissociableness
ABCDEIILLLOQTUY	quodlibetically
ABCDEIILMOOPSTY	decomposability
ABCDEIIMOOSSTUY	basidiomycetous
ABCDHILNOOORRST	bronchodilators
ABCDIIIILRSTTTY	distractibility
ABCEEEEILNRSSSV	serviceableness
ABCEEEELNPRSSST	respectableness
ABCEEEILNNOPTUX	unexceptionable
ABCEEEILNNSSSUX	inexcusableness
ABCEEEILNORRSSV	irrevocableness
ABCEEEIMNORRTTU	enterobacterium
ABCEEELNNOQRSSU	conquerableness
ABCEEELNNORSSSV	conversableness
ABCEEELNNOSSSTT	contestableness
ABCEEFKLLNORRST	Bracknell Forest
ABCEEFLMNNOORSS	conformableness
ABCEEFLMNOORSST	comfortableness
ABCEEGHHKLNOSSV	Blagoveshchensk
ABCEEHHLMNNOOPR	rhombencephalon
ABCEEILMMNNORSU	incommensurable
ABCEEILNNOPTUXY	unexceptionably
ABCEEILNNRSSSTU	inscrutableness
ABCEEINOPQRSSUV	Basque Provinces
ABCEELNNNOOPRUU	unpronounceable
ABCEGHHIIKMNRSU	Buckinghamshire
ABCEGHILMPPRSUU	Schaumburg-Lippe
ABCEGIIILNNPRSU	republicanising
ABCEGIIILNNPRUZ	republicanizing
ABCEGIIILNORSTY	recognisability
ABCEGIIILNORTYZ	recognizability
ABCEGIILOORSSTT	bacteriologists
ABCEGILLLMOORYY	embryologically
ABCEHIILMOOPSTT	histocompatible
ABCEIIIILLNPTXY	inexplicability
ABCEIIIILNRTTXY	inextricability
ABCEIIIILPPRTTY	precipitability
ABCEIILLMMRSTYY	bisymmetrically
ABCEILMMNNORSUY	incommensurably
ABCEILOOORRRTVY	corroboratively
ABCELLLNNNOOORT	noncontrollable
ABCGHHIOOPPRSYY	psychobiography
ABCGHIILLOOOOPT	photobiological
ABCGIILLNOOOTTY	gnotobiotically
ABCHHIILLMORTYY	biorhythmically
ABCIIIILMNOPTTY	incompatibility
ABCIIILLNNOOSTY	inconsolability
ABCIIILMMNOTTUY	incommutability
ABCIIILMNOPTTUY	incomputability
ABCIILLLMOSSTYY	symbolistically
ABCIILLLNOORTTY	controllability
ABCIILORRRSTTUU	arboriculturist
ABCILLNOORSTTUY	obstructionally
ABDDDEEIMNNORSS	broadmindedness
ABDDEEELLNNORTV	Oldenbarneveldt
ABDEEEEILMNPRRT	predeterminable
ABDEEEFIILNNNSS	indefinableness
ABDEEEGKLLNNOUW	unknowledgeable
ABDEEEHKLNORRTY	brokenheartedly
ABDEEEIIILMRRTY	irredeemability
ABDEEEIINNOPSZZ	benzodiazepines
ABDEEEILNNPSSSS	dispensableness
ABDEEEILNNRSSSU	undesirableness
ABDEEFIIIILNSTY	indefeasibility
ABDEEGLORRTTUUW	Teutoburger Wald
ABDEEIILMNNOSST	indomitableness
ABDEEILLNOSSSSV	dissolvableness
ABDEEINNORSSSTU	subordinateness
ABDEFIIILLNORST	defibrillations
ABDEGHHINNOORTV	Brighton and Hove
ABDEGHIIILNSSST	disestablishing
ABDEGHIIILNSSTU	distinguishable
ABDEIIILMNOOSST	demobilisations
ABDEIIILMNOOSTZ	demobilizations
ABDEIIILMNOPRTY	imponderability
ABDEIIILPRSTTUY	disreputability
ABDEIIIMNRSSTUU	subminiaturised
ABDEIIIMNRSTUUZ	subminiaturized
ABDEIILMNORSTTY	demonstrability
ABDEIILNNORSTUY	insubordinately
ABDEIILNOORSSTW	bowdlerisations
ABDEIILNOORSTWZ	bowdlerizations
ABDFIIILLNOPRSS	Pribilof Islands
ABDGHIIILNSSTUY	distinguishably
ABDGIIILOOORSST	radiobiologists
ABDHHIINORRSSTU	British Honduras
ABDHHIMOOOPPRSY	dysmorphophobia
ABDHILNNOORSTTY	labyrinthodonts
ABDIIIIILMNSSTY	inadmissibility
ABDIIIILNPSTTUY	indisputability
ABDIIILMNORSTTU	maldistribution
ABDIIINNNOORSTU	insubordination
ABEEEEILMMNPRSS	impermeableness
ABEEEEILNNPRRTT	interpenetrable
ABEEEEIORRRRSTV	reverberatories
ABEEEELNNPRSSST	presentableness
ABEEEFGILNNRRSS	refrangibleness
ABEEEFHHLMORSTT	Star of Bethlehem
ABEEEFILNRRSSTU	irrefutableness
ABEEEGILMNNPRSS	impregnableness
ABEEEHIILNNRSST	inheritableness
ABEEEHILMNRSSTT	reestablishment

ABEEEHKNNORRSST heartbrokenness
ABEEEHMMOORRRTT thermobarometer
ABEEEIILMNNSSST inestimableness
ABEEEIILNNQSSTU inequitableness
ABEEEILLNNORSST intolerableness
ABEEEILMNNNRSSU innumerableness
ABEEEILMNORRSSV irremovableness
ABEEEILNNPRSSSU insuperableness
ABEEELNNRSSTTUU unutterableness
ABEEFGIILNNNRSS infrangibleness
ABEEFIIJLNSSSTU justifiableness
ABEEFILORSTTTUY Statue of Liberty
ABEEGHHLLMNNOTW Bethmann Hollweg
ABEEGHIILNPRSST preestablishing
ABEEGIIIILNOSTT negotiabilities
ABEEGINPRRSSTTU Saint Petersburg
ABEEGNOORRRSTTU turbogenerators
ABEEHIKLNNNSSTU unthinkableness
ABEEHILMNORSSTW blameworthiness
ABEEIIILLLMNSST illimitableness
ABEEIIILLNRSTUV vulnerabilities
ABEEIIILMNPRTTY impenetrability
ABEEIILLMNPSSSU implausibleness
ABEEIIMNPRRSSTY presbyterianism
ABEEIINRSSTTTUV attributiveness
ABEEILNNNPRSSTU unprintableness
ABEEINNSSSSTTUV substantiveness
ABEELNOPPRSSSTU supportableness
ABEELNORRSSTUUY subterraneously
ABEFIILLNORRRUY neurofibrillary
ABEFINNORRRSSUW Barrow-in-Furness
ABEGIIILNNPTUXY inexpugnability
ABEGIILORRSSSTY gyrostabilisers
ABEGIILORRSSTYZ gyrostabilizers
ABEHHHOOORRRTUY boo-hurrah theory
ABEHHINOOPPSSST bisphosphonates
ABEHIIIILMPRSTY imperishability
ABEHIILMORSTTTY thermostability
ABEHILMNOOORRTT tribromoethanol
ABEHMNNORSSTUUY Sunbury-on-Thames
ABEIIIILMNNRTTY interminability
ABEIIILLNNRTUVY invulnerability
ABEIIILLORRSTVY irresolvability
ABEIIILNOQSTTUY questionability
ABEIIIMNRSSSTUU subminiaturises
ABEIIIMNRSSTUUZ subminiaturizes
ABEIILLMNOPTUYY unemployability
ABEILMNNORSTUUZ Elburz Mountains
ABFHIJLNOORSSUY John of Salisbury
ABFIIILNOPRTTUY unprofitability
ABGIIINNSSSTTUV substantivising
ABGIIINNSSTTUVZ substantivizing
ABHIIILNOPSTTYY hypnotisability
ABHIIILNOPTTYYZ hypnotizability
ACCCDEEEIINNNSS incandescencies
ACCCDEEIIINNNOT anticoincidence
ACCCDEHHIILLOOP dolichocephalic
ACCCDEHILLNOSYY synecdochically
ACCCEEEHILLMORT electrochemical
ACCCEEEMOPRRSSU eccremocarpuses
ACCCEEFHILLLOOR cholecalciferol
ACCCEEGIILLLOOS ecclesiological
ACCCEEIIILMSSST ecclesiasticism
ACCCEEILOORSTTU electroacoustic
ACCCEFIIKNNOOTY cockneyfication
ACCCEGIIINNORTY carcinogenicity
ACCCEHHIILMOPSY physicochemical
ACCCEHHILMOPSSY psychochemicals
ACCCEHHILOPPRSU Episcopal Church
ACCCEHIILOORRTT trichloroacetic
ACCCEIIIILMMORST commercialistic
ACCCEIILNOPSTTU conceptualistic
ACCCEIKLNOORSTW contraclockwise
ACCCEILOOPPRSST spectroscopical
ACCCFIIIKNNOOST cocknifications
ACCCHIOOPSSSTUY psychoacoustics
ACCCIILLMOOPRSY microscopically
ACCDDEEINNNOSTU discountenanced
ACCDEEEHIORSSTT heteroscedastic
ACCDEEEILNNOPTY cyclopentadiene
ACCDEEFIIINORTT decertification
ACCDEEHILLLPSYY psychedelically
ACCDEEHINOOOPSU chenopodiaceous
ACCDEEILMNOPSST complicatedness
ACCDEEILMNORSTY electrodynamics
ACCDEEILMOOPRTV overcomplicated
ACCDEEILNOPSSTY encyclopaedists
ACCDEEINNNOSSTU discountenances
ACCDEEINNOORSST deconsecrations
ACCDEFGHHLNNORU Church of England
ACCDEFHHIINNNOR French Indochina
ACCDEFIIINOORST recodifications
ACCDEFILLNOOSTU deflocculations
ACCDEHIINNOOPRT endocrinopathic
ACCDEHILLLOPSYY psychodelically
ACCDEIIILLNNRSSY cylindricalness
ACCDEIILNORTTVY contradictively
ACCDEIINNNOSSTU discontinuances
ACCDEIINOORRSTT contradictories
ACCDFHIIINNOORT chondrification
ACCDFIIIMMNOOOT commodification
ACCDHHHINNORSTY chondrichthyans
ACCDIILNNOOPSTU conduplications
ACCDIILNOORRTTY contradictorily
ACCEEEELLNORSTV electrovalences
ACCEEEGILLNNOTY cenogenetically
ACCEEEGILMNORTT electromagnetic
magnetoelectric
ACCEEEHMNOOPRRT mechanoreceptor
ACCEEEILLMORRTT electrometrical
ACCEEEINNOORSTT octocentenaries
ACCEEFFIINOSSSU efficaciousness
ACCEEFHIIINOPST speechification
ACCEEFHMNNOORRS French Cameroons
ACCEEFIIILNORTT electrification
ACCEEFIILMNRRTU circumferential
ACCEEFIINNOORST confectionaries
ACCEEGIIMOPRSUV Amerigo Vespucci
ACCEEGILLNOTTYY cytogenetically
ACCEEGILLORRSTU electrosurgical
ACCEEGINNNORRTT reconcentrating
ACCEEHHIMOORRTT heterochromatic
ACCEEHILLMOPRTY petrochemically
ACCEEHILLOOPRTT photoelectrical

ACCEEHILOORRSTT	atherosclerotic
ACCEEHINOORSSTT	thoracocentesis
ACCEEIIILMMORST	commercialities
ACCEEIIMMNOTUVX	excommunicative
ACCEEIIMNNOORST	econometricians
ACCEEIINNOORSSS	concessionaires
	concessionaries
ACCEEIIOPPRRTTY	cryoprecipitate
ACCEEILMOOPRSTV	overcomplicates
ACCEEILMOPRSSTU	proceleusmatics
ACCEEILNNORTTVY	concentratively
ACCEEILNORTTUVY	counteractively
ACCEEILNORTTXYY	oxytetracycline
ACCEEINNNOORRTT	reconcentration
ACCEEINNNOORSSS	reconnoissances
ACCEEINNOORRSST	reconsecrations
ACCEEINNORSSTTV	contractiveness
ACCEELMMNNOOPSS	commonplaceness
ACCEFFIIILNOSUY	inefficaciously
ACCEGGHINNNORTU	counterchanging
ACCEGGHINNORRTU	countercharging
ACCEGHIIILNNORT	anticholinergic
ACCEGHIILLOOOST	stoechiological
ACCEGHIIOPRRSTY	psychogeriatric
ACCEGHILLLNOOTY	technologically
ACCEGHILLNOPSYY	psychogenically
ACCEGHIMNNORRTU	countermarching
ACCEGIIILMMNORS	commercialising
ACCEGIIILMMNORZ	commercializing
ACCEGIILLLLOOXY	lexicologically
ACCEGIILMNNORTU	counterclaiming
ACCEGIILNNOPSTU	conceptualising
ACCEGIILNNOPTUZ	conceptualizing
ACCEGIIMMNNOTUX	excommunicating
ACCEGILLLNOOSYY	synecologically
ACCEHHILLMNOOPR	chloramphenicol
ACCEHHILLMOOPTY	photochemically
ACCEHHILLNOPRSS	chancellorships
ACCEHHIMOOPRTTU	chemautotrophic
ACCEHIIILMOOPRR	microaerophilic
ACCEHIILLPRRTYY	hypercritically
ACCEHIILNORSSTT	interscholastic
ACCEHIIMNOPRSTY	psychometrician
ACCEHIIMNORSTTY	actinochemistry
ACCEHILLMNOORTY	homocentrically
ACCEHILLMOOPRTY	chemotropically
ACCEHILMMNOPSST	accomplishments
ACCEHINNOOPRRTT	anthropocentric
ACCEHLLMNOOSTUY	collenchymatous
ACCEIIILNNOORST	reconciliations
ACCEIIILOSSTTVY	viscoelasticity
ACCEIIIMMNNOTUV	incommunicative
ACCEIILMMNOTUVY	communicatively
ACCEIILNNOPSTTU	centuplications
ACCEIILOPPRSSUY	perspicaciously
ACCEIIMMNNOOTUX	excommunication
ACCEIIMMNNOTUUV	uncommunicative
ACCEIINNOORSSTT	concretisations
ACCEIINNOORSTTZ	concretizations
ACCEILMOOPRRSTU	ultramicroscope
ACCEIMMNOORSTUX	excommunicators
ACCEIMMNOORTUXY	excommunicatory
ACCELLNOOOSUUVV	convolvulaceous
ACCFIINNOOORTTT	act of contrition
ACCGHIIILLOOOST	stoichiological
ACCGHILLLNOOORY	chronologically
ACCGHILLLOOPSYY	psychologically
ACCGHILLOOPRSYY	hygroscopically
ACCGIILLLMOOSUY	musicologically
ACCGIILLLOOOTXY	toxicologically
ACCHHILMOOOPPST	ophthalmoscopic
ACCHIIINNNOOSST	cinchonisations
ACCHIIINNNOOSTZ	cinchonizations
ACCHIILNNOORTTY	thyrocalcitonin
ACCIILLLPRSTUUY	pisciculturally
ACCIILLMMNOSTUY	communistically
ACCIIMNNORSTTUU	circumnutations
ACCIJLLNNNOOTUY	conjunctionally
ACCILMOOPRRSTUY	ultramicroscopy
ACCINOOORRSSTTV	vasoconstrictor
ACDDEEEELNPRRSU	supercalendered
ACDDEEEFFINSSST	disaffectedness
ACDDEEEHHIKNSST	thickheadedness
ACDDEEEHLNORSST	coldheartedness
ACDDEEEIIMNOOST	adenoidectomies
ACDDEEFHIINNRSS	disenfranchised
ACDDEEHIINSSTTU	Dutch East Indies
ACDDEFLMOOORSSW	Sword of Damocles
ACDDEIIMMNNOOST	discommendation
ACDDIIIIILNSTUV	individualistic
ACDEEEFHHIRSTTT	featherstitched
ACDEEEGKLMNNOTW	acknowledgement
ACDEEEHIINNOPTT	acetophenetidin
ACDEEEIILOPRSSV	overspecialised
ACDEEEIILOPRSVZ	overspecialized
ACDEEEILLORSSTY	electrodialyses
ACDEEEILNNNSSST	clandestineness
ACDEEEINNORSSST	considerateness
ACDEEEMNOOPRSTV	overcompensated
ACDEEFFIINRSSTV	diffractiveness
ACDEEFFIMORRSTT	diffractometers
ACDEEFGILNRSSSU	disgracefulness
ACDEEFHIINNRSSS	disenfranchises
ACDEEFIIINORSTT	desertification
ACDEEFLMNNORRRT	Clermont-Ferrand
ACDEEGGHIMOOPRS	geodemographics
ACDEEGIIILLMOOP	epidemiological
ACDEEGILLLOOSTY	dysteleological
ACDEEGILLOORRTY	Coleridge-Taylor
ACDEEGIMNORSSTU	discouragements
ACDEEGKLMNNOSTW	acknowledgments
ACDEEGNNOPPRSUY	pseudopregnancy
ACDEEHHILMNOORT	dichloromethane
ACDEEHIIIKNNRRS	Kincardineshire
ACDEEHIIINNRSST	disinheritances
ACDEEHIILNOOPRT	radiotelephonic
ACDEEHILLMNORTY	endothermically
ACDEEHIMNNNSSTT	disenchantments
ACDEEHIMNOORSTU	echinodermatous
ACDEEIIILMNPSTT	simplicidentate
ACDEEIILLMNORTT	dominical letter
ACDEEIILLMORTUY	eudiometrically
ACDEEIILLORSSTY	electrodialysis
ACDEEIILNNORSTY	inconsiderately

ACDEEIIMMOORRRT	radiomicrometer
ACDEEIIMMOOSSTT	mastoidectomies
ACDEEIIMNNOORTT	codetermination
ACDEEIINNOORRST	reconsideration
ACDEEILLNPPRRUY	perpendicularly
ACDEEILOPRSSSTY	perissodactyles
ACDEEIMMNNOORST	recommendations
ACDEEIMMNORSTUY	semidocumentary
ACDEEIMNNOOPSST	decompensations
ACDEEINNNOORSST	recondensations
ACDEEIORSTTTUUV	autodestructive
ACDEELMOORRSSTU	sclerodermatous
ACDEEMMMNNNOSTT	Ten Commandments
ACDEFGHIINOOSTZ	sign of the zodiac
ACDEFIIIIMNNNOT	indemnification
ACDEFIIIINNORTT	denitrification
ACDEFIIIINNOSTT	identifications
ACDEFIIIINORSTV	diversification
ACDEFIIIINORTTV	devitrification
ACDEFIIILMNOSTU	demulsification
ACDEFIIILNNOTTY	confidentiality
ACDEFIIIMMORSSY	fideicommissary
ACDEFIIIMNOSTTY	demystification
ACDEFIILNNNNOOT	nonconfidential
ACDEGGHILLOOORY	hydrogeological
ACDEGHIILNNNSTY	disenchantingly
ACDEGHILMOPRSTY	dermatoglyphics
ACDEGIIIILMNNRS	decriminalising
ACDEGIIIILMNNRZ	decriminalizing
ACDEGIILLOOSSTT	dialectologists
ACDEGIILNNOORST	reconsolidating
ACDEGINORSTTTUU	autodestructing
ACDEHHIOOPRRSST	archpriesthoods
ACDEHHLMMOOOSUY	homochlamydeous
ACDEHIILOPSSTTY	sophisticatedly
ACDEHIINOPSSTTU	unsophisticated
ACDEHILLMORRTYY	hydrometrically
ACDEHILLNOOPRTY	polychlorinated
ACDEHILLNOORRSY	hydrocorallines
ACDEHILNNOSSSTU	Schouten Islands
ACDEHILOORSSSUU	dolichosauruses
ACDEHINOORRSSTT	trisoctahedrons
ACDEHLLOOPRSSUY	pseudoscholarly
ACDEHLMMNOOOSUY	monochlamydeous
ACDEHMNNOOORSTU	enchondromatous
ACDEIIILMNNOORT	omnidirectional
ACDEIIILNORRSTY	discretionarily
ACDEIIINNNOORST	inconsideration
ACDEIIINNORRSTY	indiscretionary
ACDEIILLMNORSTY	modernistically
ACDEIILLNOOPRTY	periodontically
ACDEIILNNOOORST	reconsolidation
ACDEIILNNOOOSST	decolonisations
ACDEIILNNOOOSTZ	decolonizations
ACDEIILNOOORSST	decolorisations
ACDEIILNOOORSTZ	decolorizations
ACDEIMNNOOOORSU	andromonoecious
ACDFHIIIIMNOSTU	humidifications
ACDFIIIMNNOORST	disconfirmation
ACDGHIMNNOOPRRY	gynandromorphic
ACDGIILLLOSSTYY	dyslogistically
ACDGILNOOOPRRSS	Colorado Springs
ACDHHIINOOPRSSY	hypochondriasis
ACDHHIIOPRRSSST	harpsichordists
ACDHIIILLMOOPRY	idiomorphically
ACDHIIIMNOOOSTT	dichotomisation
ACDHIIIMNOOOTTZ	dichotomization
ACDHILLOOPRRTYY	hydrotropically
ACDIIIILNNNOSST	disinclinations
ACDIIIIMNNORSST	discriminations
ACDIIIINRSSTUVY	vicissitudinary
ACDIIINNNOORSTT	indoctrinations
ACDIIINNNOOSTTU	discontinuation
ACDIILLNNNOOTUY	unconditionally
ACDIILNNOOOSSST	disconsolations
ACEEEEGILNORTTV	electronegative
ACEEEFFILNNSSTU	ineffectualness
ACEEEFHHIRSSTTT	featherstitches
ACEEEFHIMNNNRST	enfranchisement
ACEEEFIIILMPTVX	exemplificative
ACEEEGHINNOPRTT	parthenogenetic
ACEEEGIILLNORTT	intercollegiate
ACEEEGIKLLNNOTY	kenogenetically
ACEEEGIMNOPRSTT	spermatogenetic
ACEEEHHHLNOOPRX	hexachlorophene
ACEEEHHIINRSSTT	herestheticians
ACEEEHILLMNRTUY	hermeneutically
ACEEEHILLMOORST	cholesterolemia
ACEEEHLLMNNOPSY	myelencephalons
ACEEEHMMOORSTTY	haemocytometers
ACEEEHNORRSSSTU	treacherousness
ACEEEIILLLNSTTU	intellectualise
ACEEEIILLLNTTUZ	intellectualize
ACEEEIILMNNNSST	semicentennials
ACEEEIILOPRSSSV	overspecialises
ACEEEIILOPRSSVZ	overspecializes
ACEEEIINNNQRSTU	quincentenaries
ACEEEIINPPRSSTT	precipitateness
ACEEEILNNOSSSST	coessentialness
ACEEEILNORRSSTV	correlativeness
ACEEEILNPSSSTUV	speculativeness
ACEEEIMMNOPRSSU	menispermaceous
ACEEEINNNRSSSSU	unnecessariness
ACEEEINOOPRSSTV	cooperativeness
ACEEEINORRSSTTV	retroactiveness
ACEEELLLNORTTVY	electrovalently
ACEEELMNOPRSTUX	counterexamples
ACEEEMNOOPRSSTV	overcompensates
ACEEEMNORRSSTUU	countermeasures
ACEEFFHNOORRSST	father confessor
ACEEFGIIMNNNSST	magnificentness
ACEEFGILNRRTTUU	ultracentrifuge
ACEEFHIIINORSTT	etherifications
ACEEFHILNNOPRSY	French Polynesia
ACEEFHLNOPRRSSU	reproachfulness
ACEEFIIILMNOPTX	exemplification
ACEEFIIINORSSTT	esterifications
ACEEFIILNPRSSSU	superficialness
ACEEFIINNORRSTT	confraternities
ACEEFILNORSSSTU	lactiferousness
ACEEGHHIINOPRSS	hieracosphinges
ACEEGHINNOOPRTT	anthropogenetic
ACEEGHOOOOPPSSS	oesophagoscopes
ACEEGIILLMOOPST	epistemological

ACEEGIILMMNNOTU	immunogenetical
ACEEGIILMNOPSST	salpingectomies
ACEEGIINOPPRRTV	graviperception
ACEEGIINORRSTTT	gastroenteritic
ACEEGILLLNOPTYY	polygenetically
ACEEGILLNNOOTTY	ontogenetically
ACEEGILLNOORSTY	oestrogenically
ACEEHHIINOPRSSX	hieracosphinxes
ACEEHHILNNNOPRS	rhinencephalons
ACEEHHILNOORRTT	trichloroethane
ACEEHHIMNOORRTT	heterochromatin
ACEEHHIMOPRSSTT	chemotherapists
ACEEHHINOOPPRST	phosphocreatine
ACEEHIIILNPSSTT	licentiateships
ACEEHIILLLMORTY	heliometrically
ACEEHIILLMNRSTY	hemicrystalline
ACEEHIILLMPSTUY	euphemistically
ACEEHIILMOOPRRS	microaerophiles
ACEEHIILOORSTTY	heterosociality
ACEEHIINPPPRSST	apprenticeships
ACEEHILMOPPRRTY	hypermetropical
ACEEHILOORRSSST	atherosclerosis
ACEEHIMMNORSSSV	servomechanisms
ACEEHIMMOPSSTTY	sympathectomies
ACEEHINOOPRSTTU	Poitou-Charentes
ACEEIIINQSSSTUV	acquisitiveness
ACEEIILLLMNSTTU	intellectualism
ACEEIILLLNSTTTU	intellectualist
ACEEIILLLNTTTUY	intellectuality
ACEEIILLMOPRTYZ	piezometrically
ACEEIILLRRSSTTV	verticillasters
ACEEIILMMORSTVY	commiseratively
ACEEIILNNNNQSTU	quincentennials
ACEEIILNNNOOSTV	conventionalise
ACEEIILNNNOOTVZ	conventionalize
ACEEIILNNNOQSTU	inconsequential
ACEEIINOSSSSUVV	vivaciousnesses
ACEEILLLMNOSSUY	miscellaneously
ACEEILLLNNNOTTU	nonintellectual
ACEEILLMMNOPRTY	complementarily
ACEEILLMNOPTTVY	contemplatively
ACEEILLMNORSSTV	Costermansville
ACEEILLNNOPTUXY	unexceptionally
ACEEILLNNOQSTUY	consequentially
ACEEILLNOORSTTY	electrolysation
ACEEILLNOORTTYZ	electrolyzation
ACEEILMMMOORTVY	commemoratively
ACEEILMMNNOOPTT	complementation
ACEEILMMNOPRTTY	complementarity
ACEEILMMNRSSSTY	symmetricalness
ACEEILMMORRRTTU	ultramicrometer
ACEEILMNNRSSTTU	semitranslucent
ACEEILNNNNOSSSS	nonsensicalness
ACEEILNNOQSSUUV	unequivocalness
ACEEIMNNOOPRTTY	contemporaneity
ACEEIMOOPRSSTTT	prostatectomies
ACEEINOOPRSSTVV	provocativeness
ACEEINORRRRSTUY	resurrectionary
ACEELLOORSTTUUU	Toulouse-Lautrec
ACEELMNOOQRRSUU	Lourenço Marques
ACEELNNNOOSSTUY	consentaneously
ACEEMNNOOOPRSTU	contemporaneous
ACEEOPPRRSSSTTU	streptocarpuses
ACEFGIIIILNSTVY	significatively
ACEFGIINNORSTTU	centrifugations
ACEFHILNNOPRTUY	hyperfunctional
ACEFIIIINNNOSTT	intensification
ACEFIIIINORSTVV	revivifications
ACEFIIILMNNOOST	solemnification
ACEFIIINNOOPRST	personification
ACEFIIMNNOORRST	reconfirmations
ACEFINRRRSSTTUU	infrastructures
ACEGGHHIOOPPRTY	phytogeographic
ACEGGILLNNOOORT	rontgenological
ACEGHIIIMNNPSTY	pachymeningitis
ACEGHIIIMNPSSTY	metaphysicising
ACEGHIIIMNPSTYZ	metaphysicizing
ACEGHILLLOOPPSY	psephologically
ACEGHILLMORRTYY	hygrometrically
ACEGHILMNOORSST	schoolmastering
ACEGHILOOOORSTZ	archeozoologist
ACEGHIMMOOPRRTT	photogrammetric
ACEGHLLOOPSUYYZ	zygophyllaceous
ACEGIILLLMOOSSY	seismologically
ACEGIILLLNOOSTY	neologistically
ACEGIILLMMNNOUY	immunogenically
ACEGIILLMNOORTY	goniometrically
ACEGIILLNRRSSTY	recrystallising
ACEGIILLNRRSTYZ	recrystallizing
ACEGIILLNRSSTYY	synergistically
ACEGIILMNOORRTT	trigonometrical
ACEGIILNNORSTTU	interosculating
ACEGIILNNOSTTUX	contextualising
ACEGIILNNOTTUXZ	contextualizing
ACEGIIMNOPRRSSU	superorganicism
ACEGIINNNORSTTU	counterstaining
ACEGIINNOOPRRRT	reincorporating
ACEGIINOOPRSTTV	prognosticative
ACEGIINOPRRSSTU	superorganicist
ACEGILLLMNOOOTY	entomologically
ACEGILLNNOORSSY	congressionally
ACEGILLNORRSUUY	neurosurgically
ACEGILMNNOOORST	conglomerations
ACEGILMOORSTUVY	cytomegalovirus
ACEGINOOPRRSSTY	crossopterygian
ACEHHHOORSSTTUW	Chatsworth House
ACEHHIILLMNPTTY	platyhelminthic
ACEHHIIPPRRSSST	archpriestships
ACEHHILLPPRSYYY	hyperphysically
ACEHHILMOORSSST	schoolmasterish
ACEHHINOPPRSTTU	pithecanthropus
ACEHHINORRSSSTW	crashworthiness
ACEHHIOPPRSSTTY	psychotherapist
ACEHHIORSSSTUUY	ichthyosauruses
ACEHHLMOOOPPSST	ophthalmoscopes
ACEHIILLLOOPRTY	heliotropically
ACEHIILLLOPSSTY	phyllosilicates
ACEHIILLOPRRSTY	prehistorically
ACEHIILMMNNOSTT	Mont-Saint-Michel
ACEHIILOOPSTTTY	photoelasticity
ACEHIIMMMOPSTTY	sympathomimetic
ACEHIINOPPRSSST	spinthariscopes
ACEHIIOORRSSTTT	osteoarthritics
ACEHILLLNOORSTY	holocrystalline

ACEHILLMNOOPRXY xenomorphically
ACEHILLMOOPRTTY photometrically
ACEHILLMOPRSTYY hypsometrically
ACEHILLNOPRSSTT phallocentrists
ACEHILLNOPRSTYY hypocrystalline
ACEHILMNOOPPTYY lymphocytopenia
ACEHILOPSSTUXYY psychosexuality
ACEHINOPRRSTUYY neuropsychiatry
ACEHMNOOPRSSTUY prosenchymatous
ACEIIIINNOSTTVV antivivisection
ACEIIILLMPSSSTY pessimistically
ACEIIILLNORSTTV verticillations
ACEIIILLNOSTVVY vivisectionally
ACEIIILNNOPRRTV interprovincial
ACEIIILNPRSSTTU spiritual incest
ACEIIIMMNOORSSS commissionaires
ACEIIINOPQRSSTU preacquisitions
ACEIIINORRRSTVX Saint Croix River
ACEIILLMMNOPRTY complimentarily
ACEIILLNNOOOSST neocolonialists
ACEIILLORSTUVYY voyeuristically
ACEIILMNNNOOSTV conventionalism
ACEIILNNNOOSTTV conventionalist
ACEIILNNNOOTTVY conventionality
ACEIILNNOOORSST recolonisations
ACEIILNNOOORSTZ recolonizations
ACEIILNNOOPRSTT introspectional
ACEIILNNOORSTTU interosculation
ACEIILNPRRSTTVY transcriptively
ACEIILPPRSSTTUY superplasticity
ACEIIMMNNOORSTU immunoreactions
ACEIIMNNOORSSSU acrimoniousness
ACEIIMNOOPRSTTU computerisation
ACEIIMNOOPRTTUZ computerization
ACEIINNOOOPRRRT reincorporation
ACEIINNOORSSTTV conservationist
conversationist
ACEIINNORRRSTUY insurrectionary
ACEIINNORRRTTTU counterirritant
ACEIINOOOPRSSTT cooperationists
ACEIINOOPRSSTTV contrapositives
ACEILLNOORRSTVY controversially
ACEILMMMNOORSTY monosymmetrical
ACEILMMNNOPRTUY uncomplimentary
ACEILMNOOORSTUV macroevolutions
ACEILNNNNNOOOTV nonconventional
ACEILNNOORRSTUV uncontroversial
ACEILOORRSSTTUW watercolourists
ACEIMNNNOOPRSTU pronunciamentos
ACEIMNOORRSSTUV conservatoriums
ACEINNOORRSSSTU contrariousness
ACEINNOORRSSSUV carnivorousness
ACELNOOOPPRRSTU counterproposal
ACELPRRRSSTTUUU superstructural
ACELRRRSSTTTUUU ultrastructures
ACEMNNNOOOPRRTY noncontemporary
ACFFHKLNOORRSTU Frankfurt School
ACFGIIIILNNNSTY insignificantly
ACFHIIJLNNOORUW Julian of Norwich
ACFIIIILMNOPSST simplifications
ACFIIINNOOOPSST opsonifications
ACFIILLMNNOTTUU multifunctional
ACGGIINNNOOPRSTT prognosticating
ACGHHIIIOOPRRST historiographic
ACGHHIMOOOPPRRT microphotograph
photomicrograph
ACGHHINOOOPPRTZ photozincograph
ACGHHLOOOPPSTYY psychopathology
ACGHIIILNOPSSTT antiphlogistics
ACGHIILLLOOPSYY physiologically
ACGHILLLMOOOPRY morphologically
ACGHILMOOORSSTT chromatologists
ACGHIOPPRRSSTTY cryptographists
ACGIIILLLNNSTTY scintillatingly
ACGIIILNNPQTTUU quintuplicating
ACGIIINNNNOOTTX nonintoxicating
ACGIILLLLOSSTYY syllogistically
ACGIILLLMMNOOUY immunologically
ACGIILNNNOOSTTU conglutinations
ACGIILNNOSSSSUU Cassius Longinus
ACGIIMMNOOPRRSU microsporangium
ACGIINNOOOPRSTT prognostication
ACGILLOOOOOPRTZ protozoological
ACGILNOOPRSSSTY laryngoscopists
ACGINOOOPRRSSTT prognosticators
ACHHIILLLOOPPSY philosophically
ACHHIILLNOOPPSU unphilosophical
ACHHIMMOOORRSTT orthochromatism
ACHHIMNOOOPPRRT anthropomorphic
ACHHIOOPRRSTTYY orthopsychiatry
ACHHLNOOOSTTUUY autochthonously
ACHHMOOOOPRRSTU chromatophorous
ACHIIIMOOSSSSST schistosomiasis
ACHIIINOOPSSSTT sophistications
ACHIILLLOOSTYYZ hylozoistically
ACHIIMMOPRSSSSY commissaryships
ACHIINNNOORSSTY synchronisation
ACHIINNNOORSTYZ synchronization
ACHIIOPRSSSSTTY astrophysicists
ACHIKLNNOOPPTTY phytoplanktonic
ACHILLLORRTTUUY horticulturally
ACHIOOPPRRRSSTU procuratorships
ACHMNNNOORRTTUY northcountryman
ACIIILLMNOPSTTU multiplications
ACIIILNNOPQTTUU quintuplication
ACIILMMNOOOPSST cosmopolitanism
ACIILMNNOOSSTUY sanctimoniously
ACIIMMNOOPSSTTU miscomputations
ACIIMNNOPSSTTUU mispunctuations
ACIINNOOOPRSSTT contrapositions
ACIMNOOOSSTTTXY cytotaxonomists
ADDDEEEHNNNRSSU underhandedness
ADDDEIIIINNOTUV deindividuation
ADDEEEEEHLLNSSV levelheadedness
ADDEEEEHLNRRTTY tenderheartedly
ADDEEEGHNNORSSW wrongheadedness
ADDEEEHIKNNRSST kindheartedness
ADDEEEHNNORSSTW downheartedness
ADDEEEIIJLMMNNT middelmannetjie
ADDEEEILNNSSSVY seven deadly sins
ADDEEFIILORRSTT Distrito Federal
ADDEEGGHINNORTY dehydrogenating
ADDEEGHINNOORTY dehydrogenation
ADDEEIIILNRSSTU deindustrialise

ADDEEIIILNRSTUZ deindustrialize
ADDEEJKLNNOORSS Nordenskjöld Sea
ADDEFGIKLLLOORS Kolar Gold Fields
ADDEFIILLNNRSSY Friendly Islands
ADDEGGIIINORRST rigid designator
ADDEGILNNNRSTUY understandingly
ADDEHHILOPRSSST stadholderships
ADDEHHILOPRSSTT stadtholdership
ADDEIIIIILNSTUV individualities
ADDEIIIILNRSSUV individualisers
ADDEIIIILNRSUVZ individualizers
ADDGIIIIILNNSUV individualising
ADDGIIIIILNNUVZ individualizing
ADDHIJMOOORSTUX Orthodox Judaism
ADEEEEGILNORRVZ overgeneralized
ADEEEEHNNOPRSST openheartedness
ADEEEEILLLMNRSS Ellesmere Island
ADEEEEIMNNRSSTT determinateness
ADEEEEINNPRRTTT interpenetrated
ADEEEFHNORSSSTT softheartedness
ADEEEFIMNRSSTTU disfeaturements
ADEEEFINNORSSTT defenestrations
ADEEEGGHILMMNRS sledgehammering
ADEEEGHINNRSSST nearsightedness
ADEEEGIILMNRSST legerdemainists
ADEEEGIKNNPRRRT prekindergarten
ADEEEGIKNNRRRST kindergarteners
ADEEEGILMNNNSTT disentanglement
ADEEEGOPRRRSTUY daguerreotypers
ADEEEHILNNORSST lionheartedness
ADEEEHILNOOPRST radiotelephones
ADEEEIIINNNSSST Seine-Saint-Denis
ADEEEIILMNNRTTY indeterminately
ADEEEIILMNNSSTT sentimentalised
ADEEEIILMNNSTTZ sentimentalized
ADEEEIILMNRTTVY determinatively
ADEEEIIMMQRSSUV demisemiquavers
ADEEEIIMOORRSST diastereoisomer
ADEEELLLMNOPTVY developmentally
ADEEEMNNRSSTTTU understatements
ADEEFFGIIINNRTT differentiating
ADEEFFIIINNORTT differentiation
ADEEFFIINORRSTT differentiators
ADEEFFIMNORSSTT disafforestment
ADEEFIIINRRSTTT interstratified
ADEEFIILNNQSSUU unqualifiedness
ADEEFILNSSSSTTU distastefulness
ADEEFIMNNOORRST foreordainments
ADEEGGMMNORRTTU Götterdämmerung
ADEEGHIILNNRSTY dishearteningly
ADEEGHIIMNNPPRS misapprehending
ADEEGIIINNPRSST pedestrianising
ADEEGIIINNPRSTZ pedestrianizing
ADEEGIILNNOPRSS depersonalising
ADEEGIILNNOPRSZ depersonalizing
ADEEGIIMNNRSTTU underestimating
ADEEGIIMNOOORRT radiogoniometer
ADEEGIINNOPQRTU equiponderating
ADEEGIINNORRSTT redintegrations
ADEEGIINOPRSTUU Portuguese India
ADEEGIINORRSSTT deregistrations
ADEEGIOPRRSTTUY daguerreotypist
ADEEHHNOOPPSSYY adenohypophyses
ADEEHILLMNNRSTT disenthrallment
ADEEHILMNNRSSTT disenthralments
ADEEHILNNNORRRT Northern Ireland
ADEEHILNNORRSTU Southern Ireland
ADEEHLNNNORSTUY Ashton-under-Lyne
ADEEIIILORRRSTT territorialised
ADEEIIILORRRTTZ territorialized
ADEEIIIMNNNORTT indetermination
ADEEIIINNOSSSTT desensitisation
ADEEIIINNOSSTTZ desensitization
ADEEIIMNNOPRTTU unpremeditation
ADEEIIMNNOPSSSS impassionedness
ADEEIIMNNORSTTU underestimation
ADEEIINNNOOPSST opinionatedness
ADEEIINPSSSTTUV disputativeness
ADEEILMNORSTTVY demonstratively
ADEEIMNNORRSSST arrondissements
ADEEIMNNORSTTUV undemonstrative
ADEFFHINNOSSSST standoffishness
ADEFIIINNOSSSTT disinfestations
ADEFIINNOOORRST foreordinations
ADEGGIIIINNRTTT interdigitating
ADEGHIINNOORSTY hydrogenisation
ADEGHIINNOORTYZ hydrogenization
ADEGHIMNNORSTUY Mothering Sunday
ADEGHLLMORRTUYY hydrometallurgy
ADEGHNNOOOPRRSY androgynophores
ADEGIIIMNORRSSY Missionary Ridge
ADEGIIINNORSSTT disintegrations
ADEGIIIOPRRSTTT prestidigitator
ADEGIINNOPRRSTU superordinating
ADEGILLNNOQRTUY grandiloquently
ADEHHIIMMOPRRST hermaphroditism
ADEHHINOOPPSSYY adenohypophysis
ADEHHIOPRRSSTTY hydrotherapists
ADEHIINNOOPSTTY dehypnotisation
ADEHIINNOOPTTYZ dehypnotization
ADEHIKNNOPRRSST Perth and Kinross
ADEHIMOOPRSSTTY dermatophytosis
ADEHLNNOPRSSTUU Southern Uplands
ADEHLNORRSTTWWY northwestwardly
ADEHLORSSTTUWWY southwestwardly
ADEIIIIILMRSSST dissimilarities
ADEIIILNPRSSTTU platitudinisers
ADEIIILNPRSTTUZ platitudinizers
ADEIIINORSSSTTT dissertationist
ADEIIJLNPRRSTUU jurisprudential
ADEIILMNNOORTTU intermodulation
ADEIILNORRSSTTX sinistrodextral
ADEIILNORRSTTVY dorsiventrality
ADEIIMNNOPPSSTT disappointments
ADEILMNOPRSSSUY Duplessis-Mornay
ADEILMNORRSSTTU ultramodernists
ADEILMOPSTTUUUY pseudomutuality
ADEILNOORRSTTVY dorsoventrality
ADEINOOORRSTTTX dextrorotations
ADGHIINNNOSTTTW notwithstanding
ADGIIIILNNPSTTU platitudinising
ADGIIIILNNPTTUZ platitudinizing
ADGIIIILNNRSSTU industrialising
ADGIIIILNNRSTUZ industrializing

ADGIIILNNOPPSTY	disappointingly
ADGLMOOOORSSSTU	Mato Grosso do Sul
ADHIILMNOORSSUY	disharmoniously
ADHIIMOOOPPRSTT	diaphototropism
ADHIKMNNOOOORSU	Norodom Sihanouk
AEEEEFKKMNOOPSW	Okefenokee Swamp
AEEEEFLNRSSSSTU	featurelessness
AEEEEGILNORRSVZ	overgeneralizes
AEEEEHMNOPPRRST	ephemeropterans
AEEEEIILMNPRSTX	experimentalise
AEEEEIILMNPRTXZ	experimentalize
AEEEEILNNPRRRTU	entrepreneurial
AEEEEIMNNPRSSTT	intemperateness
AEEEEIMNNRSTTVW	interweavements
AEEEEINNPRRSTTT	interpenetrates
AEEEEINPRRSSTTV	representatives
AEEEELMNRSSSSSU	measurelessness
AEEEFGIIORRRRST	refrigeratories
AEEEFIILNPRRTTY	preferentiality
AEEEFILMMOPRSTT	Temple of Artemis
AEEEFKNOPRSSTTV	Parts of Kesteven
AEEEGHINNOPRSST	parthenogenesis
AEEEGILLMNNNSST	gentlemanliness
AEEEGILMNNNSSSS	meaninglessness
AEEEGILNNRSSSTV	everlastingness
AEEEGIMNOPRSSST	spermatogenesis
AEEEHHIMOPRRSTT	thermotherapies
AEEEHIIMNPPRSSV	misapprehensive
AEEEHILLMNNOPPY	epiphenomenally
AEEEHILNORRSSTT	northeasterlies
AEEEHILORSSSTTU	southeasterlies
AEEEHILORSTTUXY	heterosexuality
AEEEHIMNOSSTTUV	South Vietnamese
AEEEIILMMNPRSTX	experimentalism
AEEEIILMNNSSSTT	sentimentalises
AEEEIILMNNSSTTZ	sentimentalizes
AEEEIILMNPRSTTX	experimentalist
AEEEIIMNNOPRTTX	experimentation
AEEEIINNNSSTTTV	inattentiveness
AEEEIINNOPRSSTV	inoperativeness
AEEEILMNORRSTTV	intervalometers
AEEEILMNPPRSSTU	supplementaries
AEEEILNOPRSSTUV	superelevations
AEEEILNPRSSSTUV	superlativeness
AEEEILNRRRSSSTT	terrestrialness
AEEEIMNNORSSSTV	normativenesses
AEEEIMNOPRRSSTX	extemporariness
AEEEIMNPRRRSSUU	supernumeraries
AEEEINNOPRRSSTT	representations
AEEELMNOQRRSSSU	quarrelsomeness
AEEEMNOPRRSSTUW	Weston-super-Mare
AEEEMNORSSSSSTV	overassessments
AEEFGHHLNNOORTT	Angel of the North
AEEFGHINOOPRRTW	weatherproofing
AEEFGIILPRRTUVY	prefiguratively
AEEFGIMNNRRSTTU	transfigurement
AEEFIIINRRSSTTT	interstratifies
AEEFIILNOOPRSSS	professionalise
AEEFIILNOOPRSSZ	professionalize
AEEFIIMNNORSSTV	informativeness
AEEFNNNORSSTTUU	unfortunateness
AEEGGHHOOPPRRTY	phytogeographer
AEEGGHNNOOPRRST	roentgenographs
AEEGGIIINNRSTTV	reinvestigating
AEEGGIINNORRRTT	reinterrogating
AEEGGIINORSSSTT	segregationists
AEEGHHLOOPPRTTY	telephotography
AEEGHHLORSSSTUU	slaughterhouses
AEEGHIIILLPRSTT	Tiglath-pileser I
AEEGHIIMNOPRSSV	overemphasising
AEEGHIIMNOPRSVZ	overemphasizing
AEEGHIKLMNNNORS	Kamerlingh-Onnes
AEEGHILNOPRSSST	selenographists
AEEGHINNOOPRSST	anthropogenesis
AEEGHNNOOPRRTTY	rontgenotherapy
AEEGIIILLNNSSTT	intelligentsias
AEEGIIINNNSTTTW	Wittgensteinian
AEEGIIINNORSTTV	reinvestigation
AEEGIIILNORRTTVY	interrogatively
AEEGIINNNOORSTT	roentgenisation
AEEGIINNNOORTTZ	roentgenization
AEEGIINNOORRRTT	reinterrogation
AEEGIINOORRRSTT	interrogatories
AEEGIINOPRRRSTT	preregistration
AEEGIINORRSSTTT	gastroenteritis
AEEGIINORRSSTTV	tergiversations
AEEGILNRRSSSTVY	transgressively
AEEGILRRTTTUUXZ	Tuxtla Gutiérrez
AEEGINNNOSSSSUU	sanguineousness
AEEGLMNNNNOORTV	nongovernmental
AEEHHHIINOPRRRS	herniorrhaphies
AEEHHHILLNNOPPT	phenolphthalein
AEEHHIJNOSSSTVW	Jehovah's Witness
AEEHIILMOOPSTTU	epitheliomatous
AEEHIIMNNOPPRSS	misapprehension
AEEHIKLNNOPRTUY	phenylketonuria
AEEHINPPPPRRSSW	whippersnappers
AEEIIILLMNORSSS	millionairesses
AEEIIILNSSSTTTX	existentialists
AEEIIILORRRSSTT	territorialises
AEEIIILORRRSTTZ	territorializes
AEEIIINOORRSTTX	exteriorisation
AEEIIINOORRTTXZ	exteriorization
AEEIILLNNOPRSTT	interpellations
AEEIILLORRRTTXY	exterritorially
AEEIILMNNSSSTTT	sentimentalists
AEEIILNNOPPRTTY	plenipotentiary
AEEIILNOORRSTUV	revolutionaries
AEEIIMNNOPRSSTT	presentationism
AEEIIMNOOPRSTTX	extemporisation
AEEIIMNOOPRTTXZ	extemporization
AEEIIMNOORSSTTV	overestimations
AEEIINNOPRRSTTT	interpretations
AEEIINNOPRSSTTT	presentationist
AEEILLMNNNORTVY	environmentally
AEEILLMNPPRSTUY	supplementarily
AEEILMNNOOPPRUU	pleuropneumonia
AEEILMNNOPPSTTU	supplementation
AEEILNNOPSSSSSS	passionlessness
AEEILOOPPRSTTVY	postoperatively
AEEIMNNOOPPRRTT	reapportionment
AEEIMNNOPRSSTTU	importunateness
AEEIMORSSSSSTTT	toastmistresses
AEENNNOOPSSSSTU	spontaneousness

AEFHHLNNOPRSTWY halfpennyworths
AEFIIIILLMNNSTY infinitesimally
AEFIILMNOOPRSSS professionalism
AEFIILNOOPRSSST professionalist
AEFIILNORSSSTTU flirtatiousness
AEFIIMNNOORSSSU omnifariousness
AEFIINOPRSSSSSU fissiparousness
AEFILNNNOOOPRSS nonprofessional
AEGGHHINOOPPRRT rephotographing
AEGGHINNOOPRSTV photoengravings
AEGGIILNNORRTTY interrogatingly
AEGHHIIMNNORSTT Nottinghamshire
AEGHHIIMNNRSSST nightmarishness
AEGHHIIOOPRRRST historiographer
AEGHHLMOPPRSSTY plethysmographs
AEGHIILLOPRSSST legislatorships
AEGHIIMNNOOOSST homogenisations
AEGHIIMNNOOOSTZ homogenizations
AEGHILMOORSSTTU rheumatologists
AEGHIOOOPPPRRSS prosopographies
AEGHLLMOOPPRSSY megasporophylls
AEGHOOOPPPRRRSS prosopographers
AEGIIILMNNOPRSS impersonalising
AEGIIILMNNOPRSZ impersonalizing
AEGIIIMNNORRSTT intermigrations
AEGIIINNNOORSTT nitrogenisation
AEGIIINNNOORTTZ nitrogenization
AEGIIINNNRSSTTT intransigentist
AEGIIINNOORRSTV reinvigorations
AEGIIINNORSSTTT integrationists
AEGIILMNORSTTUV overstimulating
AEGIILNOORRRTTY interrogatorily
AEGILLNOOPRRSSY progressionally
AEGILLNOPSTTUXY expostulatingly
AEGILMNOOPSSTTU pneumatologists
AEHHHOOOPPRSSTT orthophosphates
AEHHIIILRRSSTWW Lewis with Harris
AEHHIILLLLRSSSY shillyshalliers
AEHHIIMNOPRRSTT therianthropism
AEHHIIOPPRSSTTY physiotherapist
AEHHINOPPRSSTTY hypnotherapists
AEHIIMMNNOOPRST enantiomorphism
AEHIINNOSSSTTYZ synthesizations
AEHIINOPRRSSTTT trainspotterish
AEHIMNOOPRRSTTT anthropometrist
AEHLMNNOOPRRSTT Palmerston North
AEIIIILMNRSSSTT ministerialists
AEIIIKNNSSSTTTV Saint Kitts-Nevis
AEIIILORRRSSTTT territorialists
AEIILLLNOQRTUVY ventriloquially
AEIILLNNNNOTTUY unintentionally
AEIILLNOOPPRSTY prepositionally
AEIILLNOORRTUVY revolutionarily
AEIILMMNNRSSTTU instrumentalism
AEIILMMNOOPRSTT metropolitanism
AEIILMNNRSSTTTU instrumentalist
AEIILMNNRSTTTUY instrumentality
AEIILMNOOPRSSTY polymerisations
AEIILMNOOPRSTYZ polymerizations
AEIILNNNORSSTUV involuntariness
AEIILNOOPRSSTTY proselytisation
AEIILNOOPRSTTYZ proselytization
AEIIMMNORSSSTTY symmetrisations
AEIIMMNORSSTTYZ symmetrizations
AEIIMNNNORSTTTU instrumentation
AEIIMNNORRSSSST retransmissions
AEIINOORRSSSTTT restorationists
AEIINOPRRSSSSTU pressurisations
AEIINOPRRSSSTUZ pressurizations
AEIKLMMNNOOPRST Palmer-Tomkinson
AEIKLMNNOPRSSTU unsportsmanlike
AEILNOOOPPRRTTY proportionately
AEIMMNNNOORSTUU Mourne Mountains
AEIMNNNOOSSSTUU mountainousness
AELLMNNOOOPPRST monopropellants
AFGGIIMNNORRSTY transmogrifying
AFGHLMOOOOPRRTU photofluorogram
AGGHILNOOPRSSTY pharyngologists
AGHHHILOOOPPRTT photolithograph
AGHHIILLLLNSSYY shillyshallying
AGHHIIMNOOPSSTT opisthognathism
AGHHILLMOOOPSTT ophthalmologist
AGHHINOOOPSSTTU opisthognathous
AGHHOOOOPPPRTTY phototopography
AGHHOOOPPPRTTYY phototypography
AGHIILMNOOOSTTY mythologisation
AGHIILMNOOOTTYZ mythologization
AGHILNOOOPRSSTT anthropologists
AGIIILMNNNOOPRS pronominalising
AGIIILMNNNOOPRZ pronominalizing
AGIIINNORRSSSTT transistorising
AGIIINNORRSSTTZ transistorizing
AGIILMMNOOSSTTU numismatologist
AGIINNOOOPPRRTT proportionating
AHHIILNOPPRSSTT philanthropists
AHHILLMOOOPPRSY moral philosophy
AHHILNOOOPPRSTY phosphorylation
AHHINOOOPPRSSTT anthroposophist
AHIIIMOPPRSTTUY hypopituitarism
AHIJLMNOOOPRSTU photojournalism
AHIJLNOOOPRSTTU photojournalist
AHINOOOPRRSSTTT phototransistor
AIIIILLNOQRSTUY inquisitorially
AIIIILNNOSSTTTU intuitionalists
AIIIILNOORSSTTV vitriolisations
AIIIILNOORSTTVZ vitriolizations
AIIIINOOPRRSSTT prioritisations
AIIILLNNOSTTTUY institutionally
AIILLLMNOPSSUUY pusillanimously
AIILLNOOOPPRSTY propositionally
AIILLNOOPPSSTUY suppositionally
AIILMNNOOOOPSST monopolisations
AIILMNNOOOOPSTZ monopolizations
AIILNOOOPPRRTTY proportionality
BBBBEEFGIIILRTT flibbertigibbet
BBCEEILMNOSSSTU combustibleness
BBCEGIINORRSSUV oversubscribing
BBCHIIIIILLOPST bibliophilistic
BBDDEILMMNOOPRY mind-body problem
BBEEEGHIILLNNSW New English Bible
BBEEEIILMMRSSSU semisubmersible
BBEHILMMMOOORST thromboembolism
BCCCEEEHHILNPRU Chechen Republic
BCCDEEEEIJKOSUV České Budějovice

BCCEEEIILMNNOSU	bioluminescence
BCCEEEIMNNPRSUU	superincumbence
BCCEEILNORRSTTU	reconstructible
BCCEEIMNNPRSUUY	superincumbency
BCCEEJNORSSTTUU	countersubjects
BCCHINOOOPRSSST	bronchoscopists
BCDDEEIIIILSTTU	deductibilities
BCDDGILLLNOORUY	bloodcurdlingly
BCDEEEIILNRRSSU	irreducibleness
BCDEEEIMMNNRSTU	disencumberment
BCDEEFIIIILNTTY	indefectibility
BCDEHIOORRSSSTT	Scottish Borders
BCDEIIILOPRRTUY	reproducibility
BCDEIIILRSTTTUY	destructibility
BCEEEHLLOOPRSSS	phleboscleroses
BCEEEILNNORSSTV	convertibleness
BCEEEILNPSSSSTU	susceptibleness
BCEEGHIILNOOOST	biotechnologies
BCEEHILLOOPRSSS	phlebosclerosis
BCEEIIILMPPRRST	imperscriptible
	imprescriptible
BCEEILNOPRRSSTU	corruptibleness
BCEEINORSSSTTUV	obstructiveness
BCEGHIILNOOOSTT	biotechnologist
BCEHIIIIINOSTTX	exhibitionistic
BCEIIILMNOPTTTY	contemptibility
BCEIIILMOPRSSTY	compressibility
BCEIIILMPPRRSTY	imprescriptibly
BCEIIMMNOORSSSU	subcommissioner
BCGHIILNOOOORST	chronobiologist
BCGHIILOOOPSSTY	psychobiologist
BCGIIIIILNORRTY	incorrigibility
BCGIIILMOOORSST	microbiologists
BCGIIILOOOOSSST	sociobiologists
BCIINOORSSSTTTU	obstructionists
BCINNNOOORRTTUY	noncontributory
BDDEEIIMRRSTTTU	distributed term
BDEEEEHILLMORSV	overembellished
BDEEEGIMMNOSSTU	disemboguements
BDEEEIINNNORSTZ	dinitrobenzenes
BDEEEILMMNOSSTW	disembowelments
BDEEFIIIILNNSTY	indefensibility
BDEEFLMMNOORRUY	ferromolybdenum
BDEEIIIILNNSSSV	indivisibleness
BDEFGILLNOOOORW	Robin Goodfellow
BDEGGIIILNNOSSS	disobligingness
BDEGIIIIILNSTTY	indigestibility
BDEGIILLNOOSSTU	bloodguiltiness
BDEHIILOORSSTTT	bloodthirstiest
BDEIIINORRSSTTU	redistributions
BDFFIIILMNNORUU	infundibuliform
BDIIIILLNOSSTUY	indissolubility
BEEEEHILLMORSSV	overembellishes
BEEEGGILNSSSSTU	suggestibleness
BEEEGIILNNNSSUV	unbelievingness
BEEEIINNNORRTTZ	trinitrobenzene
BEEEILNNOPRSSSS	responsibleness
BEEELMNOORSSSTU	troublesomeness
BEEGHIILNNORSSU	neighbourliness
BEEHIIINOPRSSTV	prohibitiveness
BEEHINOORRSSSUV	herbivorousness
BEEHLOOORRSSTTU	troubleshooters
BEEIIIILNNSTTXY	inextensibility
BEEIIIILRRRSTVY	irreversibility
BEEINNORSSSTUUV	unobtrusiveness
BEGHHINOOOPTUUY	Houphouet-Boigny
BEGHILNOOORSTTU	troubleshooting
BEGIIIIILLLNTTY	intelligibility
BEGIILNOOORSSTU	neurobiologists
BEGILNNOOORSSTT	Toronto Blessing
BEHIIIIKLLORRSU	Kirribilli House
BEIIIIILMOPSSST	impossibilities
BEIIIIILMRRSSTY	irremissibility
BEIIIIILRRSSTTY	irresistibility
BEIMNORSSSSTUUU	rumbustiousness
BEINOOOPPRRSSSU	opprobriousness
BENNNOOPRRTTTUU	Burton-upon-Trent
BGHIIILOOOOPSSTT	photobiologists
BGIILLMMNNOOSUU	immunoglobulins
BHIIIINOOPRSSTT	prohibitionists
CCCDDEEEENNNOSS	condescendences
CCCDEEHIIOOPRST	cercopithecoids
CCCDEIIMNOORTTU	conductiometric
CCCDGIILOOORSTU	glucocorticoids
CCCEEEHHHIINNRS	chincherinchees
CCCEEEHILNORSTT	electrotechnics
CCCEEGHIKNNORTU	counterchecking
CCCEEHLMOOSTTYY	cholecystectomy
CCCEEIILMNOORRT	microelectronic
CCCEIIIMPRRSTUV	circumscriptive
CCCIIIMNOPRRSTU	circumscription
CCCIILMNOORSTUU	circumlocutions
CCDDEEGILNNNOSY	condescendingly
CCDEEENNNNORSSU	unconcernedness
CCDEEENNNNOSSTU	unconnectedness
CCDEEENNOOPRRSS	correspondences
CCDEEIMNNORSSTT	disconcertments
CCDEEINOPRSTUUV	superconductive
CCDEENNORRSTTUU	unreconstructed
CCDEGIILNNORSTY	disconcertingly
CCDEGINNOPRSTUU	superconducting
CCDEHINOOOPTTUV	photoconductive
CCDEIIOOORRSSTT	corticosteroids
CCDEINNOOPRSTUU	superconduction
CCDEINNOORSSTTU	deconstructions
CCDENOOPRRSSTUU	superconductors
CCDHINNOOOOPTTU	photoconduction
CCDHNOOOOPRSTTU	photoconductors
CCEEEEEFLNNORST	teleconferences
CCEEEEFILNRRSTT	Fertile Crescent
CCEEEELOOPRRRTT	electroreceptor
CCEEEEMMMNNORST	recommencements
CCEEEFIINNOORST	confectioneries
CCEEEHHNOOPPRSS	phosphorescence
CCEEEHILMORSSTT	electrochemists
CCEEEHILOOPRRTT	electrophoretic
CCEEEIIKLNORSTT	electrokinetics
CCEEEILNNNOOSTT	teleconnections
CCEEEINNORRSSST	incorrectnesses
CCEEEINNOSSSTUV	consecutiveness
CCEEFFIIIINNSSU	insufficiencies
CCEEGIIINNNNNOV	inconveniencing
CCEEGIILLOOSSST	ecclesiologists
CCEEGIINNNNORTT	interconnecting

CCEEGIINOSSTTTY	cytogeneticists
CCEEGINNOOOPRST	roentgenoscopic
CCEEHIIILMNORST	heliocentricism
CCEEHIIILNORTTY	heliocentricity
CCEEHIIIMOORSTT	stoicheiometric
CCEEHIIMNORSSTT	theocentricisms
CCEEHIINNORTTTY	ethnocentricity
CCEEHINOOPRRRTY	hypercorrection
CCEEHNORRSTTTUU	technostructure
CCEEIIINNNOSSST	inconsistencies
CCEEIILNNOSTUVY	inconsecutively
CCEEIILNORRSTTU	interlocutrices
CCEEIILOPRRTTYY	pyroelectricity
CCEEIINNNNOORTT	interconnection
CCEEILNOOOPRSTT	optoelectronics
CCEEINOOORRRSTV	overcorrections
CCEELNORRSTTUUU	countercultures
CCEFILNNOOSSSUU	unselfconscious
CCEGHHIIIIMRRST	higher criticism
CCEGHILMNOOORTY	microtechnology
CCEGHINNNOPRTUU	counterpunching
CCEGIIJMNNORSTU	misconjecturing
CCEGINNOPRRSTTU	preconstructing
CCEHIIIMPRRSSTY	hypercriticisms
CCEHIIKLNNOOSTY	cholecystokinin
CCEHIIMMOOPSTTY	psychotomimetic
CCEHNNOOOPRSSSY	synchronoscopes
CCEIILMNOOSSSUY	semiconsciously
CCEIILNNOOSSTUY	conscientiously
CCEIINNNOOSSTUU	unconscientious
CCEIMOOOPRRRSSS	microprocessors
CCEIMORRRSSTTUU	microstructures
CCEINNNOORSTTUV	nonconstructive
CCEINNNOOSSSSUU	unconsciousness
CCEINNOOPSSSSUU	conspicuousness
CCEINNOORRSSTTU	reconstructions
CCEIOOPPRSSSSTT	spectroscopists
CCGIIIILNOOSSTU	sociolinguistic
CCHHIIMOOPRRSTY	hystricomorphic
CCHIILLNOOPRSSU	councillorships
CCIIILPRSSSTTUU	pisciculturists
CCIIILRRSSTTTUU	citriculturists
CCIIINNOOORSTTT	contortionistic
CCIILMNOORSTUUV	circumvolutions
CCIILNNOOPSSUUY	inconspicuously
CCIIMNNOORSSTTU	misconstruction
CCIINNOORSSTTTU	constructionist
CCIINORSSSTTTUV	constructivists
CDDEEEEEINNNPRT	interdependence
CDDEEEEINNNPRTY	interdependency
CDDEEEELNNPRTUY	unprecedentedly
CDDEEHIINSSTTUW	Dutch West Indies
CDDEFILLNOOSTTU	Sutton Coldfield
CDDEFINOOSSUUUX	Eudoxus of Cnidus
CDDEINNOOPRRTUU	underproduction
CDDIILMMOOOSSUY	discommodiously
CDDIILOORSSSUUU	Diodorus Siculus
CDEEEEEFLNNSSSS	defencelessness
CDEEEEINNNPRSTU	superintendence
CDEEEGHINORTTUW	counterweighted
CDEEEGILNNORSUV	overindulgences
CDEEEHHILPRSTUW	whited sepulchre
CDEEEHIMORSSTTY	hysterectomised
CDEEEHIMORSTTYZ	hysterectomized
CDEEEIINPRSSSTV	descriptiveness
CDEEEILOOPRSSTT	electrodeposits
CDEEEIMNNPRSTUU	superinducement
CDEEEINNNOSSSTU	tendenciousness
CDEEEINNNPRSTUY	superintendency
CDEEEINRSSSTTUV	destructiveness
CDEEENNPSSSSTUU	unsuspectedness
CDEEFILLPRSSTUY	disrespectfully
CDEEGHIMNNNOPRU	uncomprehending
CDEEGIILLNOOOTU	oligonucleotide
CDEEHIIMOORSTTY	thyroidectomies
CDEEHIKNNRRSTTU	thunderstricken
CDEEHKLNNOOORST	chondroskeleton
CDEEIIIIMNNRSTT	indeterministic
CDEEIIILNNSSSUV	uncivilisedness
CDEEIIILNNSSUVZ	uncivilizedness
CDEEIIINNSSSTTV	distinctiveness
CDEEIINNOPRSTUV	United Provinces
CDEEILLNOOPSTUY	polynucleotides
CDEEILNNORSSSUU	incredulousness
CDEEIMNNOOPSSSU	compendiousness
CDEFIIIMNOORSST	disconformities
CDEGIIIMMNNOOSS	decommissioning
CDEGIIINNNOOPRT	preconditioning
CDEGIILNNOOORST	endocrinologist
CDEGILNNOOPRRSY	correspondingly
CDEIIIIILNNSTTVY	indistinctively
CDEIIIINNOSSTTU	discontinuities
CDEIIIJNNOSSSUU	injudiciousness
CDEIIMMNNNOOOSS	noncommissioned
CDEIINNOORRSTTU	reintroductions
CDEIINORSSSTTTU	destructionists
CDHHNNOOOORSTUY	odontorhynchous
CDHIILNOPRSTUUU	pulchritudinous
CDIIIINOSSSTUUV	vicissitudinous
CDIILNNOOSSTUUY	discontinuously
CDIIMOOPPRRSTUY	cryptosporidium
CDIINNOOPRTTUVY	nonproductivity
CEEEEELOOPRSSTT	telestereoscope
CEEEEFFIINNSSTV	ineffectiveness
CEEEEHHLNOOPRRT	perchloroethene
CEEEEHIILNNRSTT	Liechtensteiner
CEEEEHIMNPRTTXY	hyperexcitement
CEEEFIIMNORRRTT	interferometric
CEEEFLNORRSSSUU	resourcefulness
CEEEGGILNNOOSSU	gluconeogenesis
CEEEGGILNNOOSSY	glyconeogenesis
CEEEGHILORRSSTU	Gloucestershire
CEEEGHIQRRRSUUU	churrigueresque
CEEEGHLLOOORRTY	electrorheology
CEEEGNNOOOPRSST	roentgenoscopes
CEEEHIIMNNOPRSV	incomprehensive
CEEEHILMNOPRSVY	comprehensively
CEEEHILOOPRRSST	electrophoresis
CEEEHIMORRSSTTY	stereochemistry
CEEEHIMORSSSTTY	hysterectomises
CEEEHIMORSSTTYZ	hysterectomizes
CEEEHLMNOORRSTT	thermoelectrons
CEEEHLOOPRRSSTU	electrophoruses
CEEEIIKNNPRSSST	persnicketiness

CEEEIILOOPRSTTV	electropositive
CEEEIIMMOORRSTT	micrometeorites
CEEEIIMNOPSSTTV	competitiveness
CEEEIIMNORSTTUX	excrementitious
CEEEIIMOORRSSTT	stereoisometric
CEEEIINRRSSSTTV	restrictiveness
CEEEIKLNNOSSTUU	kinetonucleuses
CEEEILMMNOPRSTZ	complementizers
CEEEILOPRRSTTVY	retrospectively
CEEEIMMNNOOPSTU	pneumonectomies
CEEEIMNNOORSSSU	ceremoniousness
CEEEINNOPRRSTVW	Western Province
CEEEINPQRSSSTUU	picturesqueness
CEEEMMNNOORTTUV	countermovement
CEEFIIILLNOSTTU	feuilletonistic
CEEFINNOPRRSSTU	perfunctoriness
CEEFLMNOORSSSST	comfortlessness
CEEGGHIINNORTUW	counterweighing
CEEGGHILNOOOORS	geochronologies
CEEGIINNNNORSTT	nonintersecting
CEEHHIMMORRSTTY	thermochemistry
CEEHHIMOPPRTTYY	hemicryptophyte
CEEHIIMNNNOOPRS	incomprehension
CEEHIIMNOSSSSUV	mischievousness
CEEHILLNOORRSXY	hexylresorcinol
CEEHILNNOSSSTUY	nucleosynthesis
CEEHIMMOPSSSTTY	metempsychosist
CEEIIINOPRSSSTX	expressionistic
CEEIILLMNOOSSTT	tonsillectomies
CEEIILLMNORSSTT	scintillometers
CEEIILNOPRSTTVY	introspectively
CEEIILNORRSTTUX	interlocutrixes
CEEIIMNNOPSSSUU	impecuniousness
CEEIIMNORRRSSTU	resurrectionism
CEEIINNNOORRSTV	interconversion
CEEIINNRSSSTTUV	instructiveness
CEEIINOPPRSSSTU	precipitousness
CEEIINORRRSSTTU	resurrectionist
CEEIINPSSSTTUUV	intussusceptive
CEEILMNNOORSUUY	unceremoniously
CEEIMMOOPRRRSTY	micropyrometers
CEEIMNNOPSSSTUV	consumptiveness
CEEINNNOOSSSTTU	contentiousness
CEEINNNOPRSSTTU	supercontinents
CEEINOPPRSSSSUU	perspicuousness
CEELLPQRSSTUUUY	sculpturesquely
CEEPRRRSSSTTUUU	superstructures
CEFFIIINNOOSSSU	inofficiousness
CEFGHIMNNOORSST	forthcomingness
CEFIIMNNNOOORST	nonconformities
CEGHILMNOOOSTUY	ethnomusicology
CEGHLNOOOPRSUYY	neuropsychology
CEGIINNNOOPRTTU	counterpointing
CEGIINNPSSSTTUU	intussuscepting
CEGILNNOOPRTTTU	counterplotting
CEGILOOOOPRSTYZ	cryptozoologies
CEGINNNOORSSSUU	incongruousness
CEHHHILMOOOPRTT	chemolithotroph
CEHHIIOOPRSSSTY	psychohistories
CEHHIMMNOOOPPRS	morphophonemics
CEHHINOPSSSSTYY	psychosynthesis
CEHHOOOOPPPRSSS	phosphoroscopes
CEHIIMMMNORSTUY	immunochemistry
CEHIINNOOPRSSSU	connoisseurship
CEHIJMNNOORSTTU	thermojunctions
CEHILLMOOPPRRST	comptrollership
CEHILLNOOPRRSST	controllerships
CEHILLNOOPRSSSU	counsellorships
CEHILMOORSSSSTY	schoolmistressy
CEHILOPPRRSUUXY	peroxysulphuric
CEHMNNNOORRTTUY	northcountrymen
CEHNNNOORSSSSUY	synchronousness
CEIIIIMNOPRSSST	impressionistic
CEIIIINOSSSTTVV	vivisectionists
CEIIILNOQRSTTUV	ventriloquistic
CEIIIMNNORRSSTU	insurrectionism
CEIIINNORRSSTTU	insurrectionist
CEIIINORRSSSTTT	restrictionists
CEIILLNOORRTTUY	interlocutorily
CEIILNNOPSSSTUU	punctiliousness
CEIINNOPSSSTTUU	intussusception
CEIINOPPRRSSSTU	superscriptions
CEILMOOPRRSSSTU	multiprocessors
CEIMNNOOOPRSTUV	overconsumption
CEIMNOOPRSSSSUU	promiscuousness
CEIMNOPRSSSSTUU	scrumptiousness
CFHILMNOOOORRRT	nitrochloroform
CFIILLORRSSTTUU	floriculturists
CGHIILNOPSSSTUY	psycholinguists
CHHHINNOORRSTUY	ornithorhynchus
CHHHIOOOOPPRRST	orthophosphoric
CHIILORRSSTTTUU	horticulturists
CHIINOPRRSSSTTU	instructorships
CHILLMOOOPPRRSY	microsporophyll
CHILOOOPPRRSSTU	prolocutorships
CIIILLRSSSTTUUV	silviculturists
CIIIMNNORSSSTTU	misinstructions
DDEEEEHINOPPRSU	pseudoephedrine
DDEEEEILMNRRSTW	Middle Westerner
DDEEEGIILNPRRUV	underprivileged
DDEEEGILNNOPRUV	underdeveloping
DDEEEIIINOQRSTU	derequisitioned
DDEEEIILNRSSTTY	disinterestedly
DDEEGGHIINNORSY	dehydrogenising
DDEEGGHIINNORYZ	dehydrogenizing
DDEEHILNOORRSTY	dehydroretinols
DDEGHIIINNSSTUU	undistinguished
DDEIINOOOPPRRST	disproportioned
DDEIINOOPSSSUUY	Pseudo-Dionysius
DEEEEEFLNNSSSSS	defenselessness
DEEEEHNOPRRSTUY	superheterodyne
DEEEEILNORSSSTU	deleteriousness
DEEEELMNOOPRTVV	overdevelopment
DEEEFFIIOPRRSTT	Petrified Forest
DEEEFGHINORSSST	foresightedness
DEEEGIIMNNNORSS	domineeringness
DEEEHIIKLNOOSTT	kinetheodolites
DEEEHIINPRSSSTY	hypersensitised
DEEEHIINPRSSTYZ	hypersensitized
DEEEIIMNRSSSTTV	divertissements
DEEEIINOPSSSTUX	expeditiousness
DEEEIMMNOPRSSTW	disempowerments

DEEEINNNOSSSTTU	tendentiousness
DEEEINNNPRSSTTU	superintendents
DEEELMMNNOPRTUY	underemployment
DEEFFIIINNRSSTT	indifferentists
DEEFILLNOPRSSUY	splendiferously
DEEFILNRSSSSSTU	distressfulness
DEEFINOOORRSSSU	odoriferousness
DEEGGHILNNOSSST	longsightedness
DEEGIIILMOOPSST	epidemiologists
DEEGIILMNOOSSTT	sedimentologist
DEEGILLOOSSSTTY	dysteleologists
DEEHHHILOOPRSSU	householdership
DEEHIIMMOOPRRST	thermoperiodism
DEEHIINOOPSSSTT	photosensitised
DEEHIINOOPSSTTZ	photosensitized
DEEIIIILMRSSTUV	verisimilitudes
DEEIIILNOPRSSTV	vespertilionids
DEEIILMOORRSTUY	demeritoriously
DEFILNRSSSSTTUU	distrustfulness
DEGGHIILMNOOSTY	demythologising
DEGGHIILMNOOTYZ	demythologizing
DEGGHILOOORSSTY	hydrogeologists
DEGHHIINNNORSTU	Huntingdonshire
DEGHIINNNORRSUU	undernourishing
DEHHIIMOPRRSTYY	hyperthyroidism
DEIIILLMNNOSSTU	disillusionment
DEIIINOOPPRSSST	predispositions
DEIINNORSSSSTUU	industriousness
DFILMMNOOOOOSSW	Wisdom of Solomon
DGIILNOOORSSSTY	strongyloidosis
DHHIIMOOPRSSTYY	hypothyroidisms
DHHLOOPRRSSUUUY	hydrosulphurous
DHINOOOPRSSSTTT	prosthodontists
DIILLMNOSTTUUUY	multitudinously
EEEEFIMNNORRSTV	overrefinements
EEEEFIMNORRRSTT	interferometers
EEEEGHLNOORSTUY	heterogeneously
EEEEGILNPSTTTTY	teletypesetting
EEEEGINNNORSSVW	overweeningness
EEEEIIMMNRRSSTT	semiretirements
EEEEIINNNPSSSVX	inexpensiveness
EEEEIINNRRSSTTV	irretentiveness
EEEEILPRRSTTTWY	teletypewriters
EEEEIMNPRRRSSST	misrepresenters
EEEEINPRRRSSSTT	interpretresses
EEEELMNORRSSSSS	remorselessness
EEEFFIINNNOSSSV	inoffensiveness
EEEFHHHILMOORST	Home of the Hirsel
EEEFHIILNOSSSUW	housewifeliness
EEEFINOPRSSSSTU	pestiferousness
EEEGHMNNOOOSSSU	homogeneousness
EEEGIIMNNPRRSST	misrepresenting
EEEGIINNNRSSSTT	interestingness
EEEGIINNOPRSSTV	progenitiveness
EEEGILNNNNRSSTU	unrelentingness
EEEGILORRRSSTVY	retrogressively
EEEGINOPRRSSSSV	progressiveness
EEEHIINPPRRRSTT	interpretership
EEEHIINPRSSSSTY	hypersensitises
EEEHIINPRSSSTYZ	hypersensitizes
EEEHILNORRSSTTW	northwesterlies
EEEHILORSSSTTUW	southwesterlies
EEEHIMORSSSSSTU	housemistresses
EEEHINNOPRSSTXY	hyperextensions
EEEHLMNNOOSSSUW	unwholesomeness
EEEIIILNNOPRSTV	vespertilionine
EEEIIINNNSSSSTV	insensitiveness
EEEIILLNNRSSUUY	Neuilly-sur-Seine
EEEIIMMOORRSSST	stereoisomerism
EEEIIMNNNRSTTTW	intertwinements
EEEIIMNPRRRSSTT	misinterpreters
EEEIINOPRSSSTTU	repetitiousness
EEEIMNPPRSSSTUV	presumptiveness
EEEINNNOSSSSTTU	sententiousness
EEEINNOPRSSSTTU	pretentiousness
EEELNOPPRSSSSSU	purposelessness
EEEMNOPSSSSTTUU	tempestuousness
EEFILLLMNOSSSUU	mellifluousness
EEFLNOPRSSSSUUU	superfluousness
EEGGILNNOOORSTT	roentgenologist
EEGHHLNOSSSSTTU	thoughtlessness
EEGHILMNNOOOPST	phenomenologist
EEGHIMMNOORRSTY	Montgomeryshire
EEGHINNORSSSTUU	unrighteousness
EEGHINOOPPRRSTY	porphyrogenites
EEGIIILNORRSSSU	irreligiousness
EEGIIIMNNPRRSTT	misinterpreting
EEGIILLLNNNTTUY	unintelligently
EEGIILMOOPSSSTT	epistemologists
EEGIIMNNNRSSTTU	unremittingness
EEGIINNORSSSTUV	vertiginousness
EEGIINOPRSSSSTU	prestigiousness
EEGILNOPPRSSSSY	prepossessingly
EEGIMOOPRRSTTUU	Portuguese Timor
EEGINNOPPRSSSSU	unprepossessing
EEHHINOOPSSSTTY	photosynthesise
EEHHINOOPSSTTYZ	photosynthesize
EEHHNOOPPRSSUYY	neurohypophyses
EEHIINOOPSSSSTT	photosensitises
EEHIINOOPSSSTTZ	photosensitizes
EEHLNOPRSSSSUUU	sulphureousness
EEHMOOOPPRRSTTY	pyrophotometers
EEIIIINNQSSSTUV	inquisitiveness
EEIIIMNNNORSTTV	interventionism
EEIIINNNORSTTTV	interventionist
EEIIINNRRSTTUVY	interuniversity
EEIILNNOORRTTTU	trinitrotoluene
EEIILNOORRSSTUV	revolutionisers
EEIILNOORRSTUVZ	revolutionizers
EEIIMNOORRSSSTU	meritoriousness
EEIINNNNNOORTTV	nonintervention
EEINNNOOPPRSSTU	inopportuneness
EFGIIILMNOPRSVY	oversimplifying
EFILMNRSSSSTTUU	mistrustfulness
EGGILNNOOORSSTT	rontgenologists
EGHHIILLMNOOSTT	helminthologist
EGHIIINNOPSSSTY	hyposensitising
EGHIIINNOPSSTYZ	hyposensitizing
EGHILNOOOPRSUYY	neurophysiology
EGIIILNNOORSTUV	revolutionising
EGIIILNNOORTUVZ	revolutionizing
EGIIILNNOQRSTUV	ventriloquising
EGIIILNNOQRTUVZ	ventriloquizing
EGIIIMNNNOOSSSU	ignominiousness

EGIINOOPRRSSSST	progressionists
EHHIMMMOOOOPRSS	homoeomorphisms
EHHINOOOPPPRSST	phosphoproteins
EHHINOOPPRSSUYY	neurohypophysis
EHIIIKLMMOOPRST	poikilothermism
EHIIILMNNPRSSUY	hyperinsulinism
EHIILLMOOPPRTTU	photomultiplier
EHIIOOPPPRRRSST	proprietorships
EHINORRSSSTTTUW	trustworthiness
EIIIMNOOPPRSSTU	superimposition
EIIKLLMNPRSSTTU	Rumpelstiltskin
EIILLMMNNOOORTT	montmorillonite
EIILLNORSSSSTUU	illustriousness
EIILNOOPPSSSSTU	suppositionless
EIILOPRRSSTTUUY	surreptitiously
EIILOPRSSSTTUUY	superstitiously
EIINOOPPPRSSSTU	presuppositions
EINOOOOPPRRRSTV	overproportions
GGGHHILNOOORTUY	thoroughgoingly
GILOOOOOPRSSTTZ	protozoologists
HHHOOOOPPPRSSUY	hypophosphorous
IIIIINNOQSSSTTU	inquisitionists
IIILLOOPRSTUUVV	Vitruvius Pollio
ILNNOORRRSSSTUU	Snorri Sturluson

Supplement

Word Play

Contents

Internet Resources for Word Games 3

Introduction to Cryptic Crosswords 8

Anagrams and Other Grams 14

Short Words 23

J, Q, X, and Z 28

2

Internet Resources for Word Games

RESOURCES FOR SOLVING CROSSWORDS

Collins English Dictionary is available online at:
http://www.collins.co.uk/wordexchange/

GENERAL CROSSWORD SITES

The Crossword Centre
www.crossword.org.uk
Crossword resource centre with puzzles, history, competitions, features and book reviews.

About.com Crosswords
www.crosswords.about.com
American daily crossword and puzzle site including tutorials.

Crossword Tournament
www.crosswordtournament.com
From the New York Times Puzzle Editor, a site which includes puzzles and crosswords, links and histories.

Lexcentrics
www.lexcentrics.com/Crosswords/
Cryptic crosswords, wordgames and tutorials.

Thinks.com
www.thinks.com
Includes a daily crossword and other puzzles such as jigsaws and wordsearches.

The Tantalus Crossword
http://tantalus-crossword.co.uk/

RESOURCES FOR COMPILING CROSSWORDS

Crossword Compiler
http://crossword-compiler.com/Scrabble
Software for compiling 'everyday' crosswords.

Crossword Maestro
http://crosswordmaestro.com/
Software for solving cryptic crosswords.

CROSSWORD CLUBS

The Times Crossword Club
www.timesonline.co.uk/section/0,,252,00.html
An annual fee allows you to access the Listener crossword and many others.

The Crossword Club
www.thecrosswordclub.co.uk/
Cryptic crossword site with monthly magazine for subscribers.

The Australian Crossword Club
http://crosswordclub.org/

ONLINE CROSSWORDS

The Guardian
www.guardian.co.uk/
The Guardian Annual registration allows you to access Araucaria, Bunthorne & co.

The Independent
http://enjoyment.independent.co.uk/crosswords/cryptic/
The Independent Annual subscription. Good cryptic puzzles by an increasingly well-respected team of compilers.

The Atlantic Monthly
www.theatlantic.com/doc/200506
The Atlantic Monthly US cryptic puzzles by Emily Cox and Henry Rathvon

The Telegraph
www.telegraph.co.uk/arts/main.jhtml
Access the puzzles online.

Private Eye
www.privateeye.co.uk/content/showitem.cfm/issue.1131/section.xword
Fun puzzles with typically scurrilous clues.

Auctor
http://mysite.wanadoo-members.co.uk/Classical_Studies
Puzzles to test your Latin

The Scotsman
http://thescotsman.scotsman.com/games.cfm?id=501162005

Free Crosswords
http://quicksitebuilder.cnet.com/neilshepherd/
Alberich's crossword site

Pub Crosswords
www.pubcrosswords.com/
Fun puzzles and cash prizes

Globe and Mail (Canada)
Crosswords are available online to subscribers at:
www.theglobeandmail.com/

The Toronto Star
www.thestar.com/cgibin/star_static.cgi?section=AandE&page=/Third_Party/xword/index.html

A1 Puzzles
www.a1puzzles.com
Subscription site with interactive crosswords, jigsaw puzzles and trivia. Twenty-five new crosswords and puzzles added every month.

LINKS FOR SCRABBLE®

MATTEL's official Scrabble site
www.mattelscrabble.com/en/adults/index.html

SCRABBLE CLUBS AND ASSOCIATIONS

Association of British Scrabble Players
www.absp.org.uk/index.html

Scottish Scrabble Association
www.scottishscrabble.org/

Singapore Scrabble Association
www.toucanet.com/

South African Scrabble Players' Association
www.geocities.com/sanspa/home.html

Australian Scrabble Players' Association
www.scrabble.org.au/

New Zealand Association of Scrabble Players
www.scrabble.co.nz/

Scrabble in Nigeria
www.nigerianscrabble.com/

Bahrain Scrabble League
http://mywebpage.netscape.com/bahrainscrabble/main.html

Netherlands English Scrabble Club
www.nesc.nl/

Maltese Scrabble Club
www.maltascrab.net.tf/

National Scrabble Association (North America)
www.scrabble-assoc.com/

Scrabble in Canada
www.scrabble-assoc.com/canada/

OTHER WORDGAMES

Countdown
www.channel4.com/entertainment/tv/showcards/C/countdown.html
www.thecountdownpage.com/

Introduction to Cryptic Crosswords

Many people who enjoy quick crosswords find the cryptic variety daunting. This is a shame, as cryptic crosswords require very much the same attributes as quick ones; a good vocabulary and an ability to think laterally. If you have been put off by cryptic crosswords before, it's well worth giving them another try – once you have learned how to speak their language. While the compilers of cryptic puzzles have infinite depths of devilish cunning, they tend to rely on a fairly limited set of clue structures with which to torment crossword addicts.

Cryptic clues generally come in two parts: the first element is a literal definition of the answer, while the second is a play on words that is used to work the answer out. Of course, it can be difficult to work out which is which, but that is part of the fun! The following are some of the more common clue structures.

ANAGRAM INDICATORS

Compilers often use 'trigger' words, or anagram indicators, to suggest that the solution can be found in the form of an anagram. The list of these words is virtually endless; any word that suggests change, upset or disorder can be used. Here is a list of some examples:

about
adjust
annoy
another
anyhow
anyway
arrange
awkward
badly
bend
blend
broken
chaotic
cocktail
crazy
deform
derange
devastated
different
disfigure
distress
doctor
garble
jumble
mixed
order
strange
transform
wild

Whenever you encounter an anagram indicator, look at the length of the solution. This will help you narrow down the elements of the clue that may be an anagram of the answer. For example, consider the following:

Meat merchant who blends cut herb (7)

Here, *blends* indicates that an anagram of the solution may be contained in the clue. As the solution has seven letters, the next step is to look for one or more consecutive words that contain exactly seven letters. Here, the obvious candidates are *cut* and *herb*. We can then look for a hint in the first part of the clue, which leads us easily from *Meat merchant* to an anagram of *cut herb – butcher*.

REVERSALS

A common compiler's ruse is to indicate (cryptically of course!) that a word in the clue should be reversed to provide the solution. Often, the reversal indicator depends on whether the required word is Down or Across in the crossword grid. The following is a Down clue:

Rising evil may breathe (4)

If evil is written so that it 'rises', rather than descends, the grid, we are left with a synonym for breathe – live. Other reversal indicators include:

returning
retreating
turning
going back
climbing
northwards
westwards

CHARADES

Some clues work like a game of charades, with one part of the clue describing the solution and others indicating words that can be put together to form it. For example:

Goblin Lima comes out in force (5)

Another word for *goblin* is *imp*, while Lima stands for L in the Nato Phonetic Alphabet. *Imp* plus *L* "comes out in" a synonym for *force* – *impel*. It's always worth examining a clue to see if there is a word or phrase – like 'comes out in' in this instance – that suggests that certain elements work together to form another.

READ-THROUGHS

A common clue type is that which includes the solution within other words in the clue, either 'hidden' in the middle of a longer word, or spelt out by adjacent letters in two or more consecutive words. These clues are often indicated by words such as:

buried
embedded
hidden
in
inside
swallowed

When you find any word that hints at one thing inside another, it's a good idea to scan the other parts of the clue to see if you can spot a complete word nestling inside others. Here's an example of a relatively simple 'read-through':

Item of clothing found in dog-lover's wardrobe (5)

'Found in' is a signal that a read-through may be involved, and the clue structure tells us that we should be looking for an item of clothing in *dog-lover's wardrobe*. As *wardrobe* seems to continue the clothing imagery of the first part of the clue, we can deduce that we should look at *dog-lover's*. And here we find the answer – *glove*.

DOUBLE DEFINITIONS

Crossword clues sometimes divide into two sections, each of which defines the solution in a different way. Awareness of this makes clues like the following appear much less baffling:

Assault the pancake mix (6)

A synonym for the verb *assault* is, of course, *batter* – which also happens to be a synonym for *pancake mix*. It's therefore a good idea to see if you can break a given clue into two constituent parts; if no common word springs to mind, try checking one of the parts in this dictionary – you may find that the book points out a sense of the word that previously eluded you.

DELETIONS

One kind of crossword clue is solved by simply removing a letter from one of its constituent words. The compiler will usually hint at this obliquely by using words such as the following:

tailless
headless
beheaded
eviscerated
gutless
heartless
topless
endless

Each of these words indicates that another word in, or suggested by, the clue will yield the solution if a letter is removed from within the word, or from its beginning or end, as in the following:

Great Scots endless noisy fight (4)

Once you have worked out that a noisy fight is a *brawl*, the word *endless* should encourage you to remove the L, leaving you with the Scots word for 'great', *braw*.

&LIT

An important type of clue is the '&lit', short for 'and literally so'. This is perhaps the most satisfying clue to solve, as it represents a perfect composition on the part of the compiler. Often indicated by an exclamation mark, the &lit consists of a phrase that can be read literally to provide the solution – but is also one of the other types of cryptic clue. Probably the most famous example of this sort of clue is:

Terribly angered! (7)

Here, terribly is an anagram indicator; if the letters of angered are terribly messed up, we get enraged – for which the whole clue is also a literal definition. Most '&lit' clues are far trickier than this, however, but the principle remains the same.

Anagrams and other -grams

ANAGRAMS

Here are some more anagrams which transform
the names of contemporary figures and events.
Some of the transformations are most appropriate!

Elvis Aaron Presley	>	Seen alive? Sorry, pal!
Madonna Louise Ciccone	>	one cool dance musician
Albert Einstein	>	ten elite brains
William Butler Yeats	>	a really sublime twit
Diego Maradona	>	an adored amigo
Elle MacPherson	>	her men collapse
Arnold Schwarzenegger	>	he's grown large'n'crazed
Clint Eastwood	>	Old West Action
President Boris Yeltsin	>	tipsiness done terribly
Florence Nightingale	>	angel of the reclining
The Houses of Parliament	>	loonies far up the Thames

There are some anagrams which are quite uncanny in their coincidental meanings, such as the one below:

> 'To be or not to be? That is the question.
> Whether 'tis nobler in the mind to suffer the
> slings and arrows of outrageous fortune.'

Which becomes:

> 'In one of the Bard's best-thought-of tragedies,
> our insistent hero, Hamlet, queries on two fronts
> about how life turns rotten.'

The following poem is a very clever anagram. See if you can guess what it refers to and remember, the clue is in the title!

> Viva United States of America
> Monk? Hmm . . . jivin', man!
> Honk, known champ – damn!
> Calmly twirl, mystic vox,
> And dancing skyward, waltz.

ANAGRAM GAMES

ANAGRAM (1)

You should have between two and six players. Prepare 100 cards with a letter of the alphabet written on each. There should be four of the majority of letters such as C and M, seven or eight of very common letters such as A and E, and only one each of rare letters such as X and Z. The cards should be placed down, and turned over one at a time by each player in turn. When a word is spotted from the letters showing, the first player to shout it out claims the points. So it pays to be quick-thinking! The minimum length of word is four letters. So, for example, if the letters L, E, A, and P are turned over one by one, the fastest player to shout out 'Leap!', 'Pale!', or 'Peal!' will win the points. A player may also add a letter to the list of words already declared, to form a new word, or they may rearrange an existing word.

ANAGRAM (2)

This game asks you to solve anagrams set by other players. Going round a group one by one, each player says an anagram to the next person, who then attempts to solve it. For example:

Barbara: (*to Ray*) Ok, I'll start with *team.*

Ray: *Meat.* (*to Milo*): *Trap.*

Milo: *Part.* (*to Lizzie*): *Face.*

Lizzie: *Café!* Ok, now for some more difficult ones! (*to Jessie*) *Nectar.*

Jessie: Ummm, *train?*

Lizzie: Wrong, you're out! It's *trance.* (*to Maggie*) How about *auction?*

Maggie: *Caution.*

ANAGRAM PAIRS

Try to compose phrases comprising two words that are anagrams of each other, then give your fellow players a clue to the phrase and see if they can guess what you're thinking of. Here are some examples to get you started:

Clue: current snake
Answer: present serpent

Clue: aircraft to Asian kingdom
Answer: Nepal plane

Clue: leftover autumn fruit
Answer: spare pears

Clue: impeccable school monitor
Answer: perfect prefect

Clue: hidden gift
Answer: latent talent

Clue: Teutonic horse trough
Answer: German manger

Clue: Oriental seriousness
Answer: Eastern earnest

Clue: conceited herb
Answer: arrogant tarragon

A *pangram* is a short phrase formed using all 26 letters of the alphabet. The very best pangrams use each letter only once. Here is an example of one formed from the minimum 26 letters:

Mr Jock, TV quiz PhD, bags few lynx.

As most 26-letter pangrams have to resort to using obscure or dubiously valid words, the result can be a little difficult to decipher, as in the example below:

Pyx vang quiz: komb crwth fjelds.

This, roughly explained, means 'A quiz about coin chest nautical rope tackle: German combination ancient Celtic string instrument, high Scandinavian rocky plateau.' Much clearer now!

Using just a few extra letters, normally vowels, can make your pangram a lot more comprehensible, as these examples show:

How quickly daft jumping zebras vex. (30 letters)

The five boxing wizards jump quickly. (31 letters)

Probably the best-known of these more 'coherent' pangrams is:

The quick brown fox jumps over a lazy dog.

This sentence is often used in to practice typing, as it uses every letter key on the keyboard, and is easy to remember.

Try making up your own pangrams. The 'perfect' pangram, which has not yet been devised, would contain 26 letters only, make complete grammatical sense and avoid resorting to proper names or abbreviations. As the twenty-six letters of the alphabet can be put together in over 403,000,000,000,000,000,000,000,000 different ways, this may keep you occupied for some time!

As well as devising your own pangrams, try making up a themed sentence containing 26 words, each word beginning with a different letter of the alphabet. You may use a certain degree of artistic licence, as you will be unable to use words like *a* and *the* more than once, and allowances are made for words starting with the letter X, as there are not many possibilities to choose from!

How about:

Dog breeding
All British Crufts dog enthusiasts favour gestation; however, I jest; keen Labrador minders never order poor quadrupeds, rightly sceptical, to undertake vexing whelping. X-cellent yearling zealots!

or

Finding Nirvana
Adults bicker concerning discovering enlightenment, for good honest Indians joke kindly: love must nourish. Oriental philosophy quite right. Serene tai-chi uncovers Vishnu; with x-citing yoga – Zen.

(For more of these, see: http://puzzles.about.com/library/weekly)

OTHER TYPES OF GRAM

ANTIGRAMS

An antigram is an anagram which means the opposite to the starting phrase. They are difficult to deliberately devise, and most are simply discovered by chance. They are often witty and apt, as you will see from the examples below:

filled	>	ill-fed
Santa	>	Satan
misfortune	>	it's more fun
funeral	>	real fun!
infection	>	fine tonic
militarism	>	I limit arms
saintliness	>	entails sins
antagonist	>	not against
a picture of health	>	oft pale, I ache, hurt
evangelists	>	evil's agents
within earshot	>	I won't hear this
sweltering heat	>	the winter gales
the man who laughs	>	he's glum, won't ha-ha
the Oscar Nominations	>	It's not a cinema honor

LIPOGRAMS

A lipogram is a piece of writing from which all examples of a certain letter have been omitted. It is simple to devise one of these when the letter is, for example, Q or Z, but more difficult when you are trying to avoid using a common letter. Work out which letter is missing from the passage below, then have a go yourself:

> Alas, for lack of application, lipogrammatists can slip up and with what upshot? Inclusion of that symbol you had sought to avoid. Oh my, my, such a pity. A shambolic lipogram! Sham! So that you do not miss my point: all of this stuff and rubbish was a Q-lipogram. But, no, it isn't! What is still missing is that symbol twixt I and K! But is it just that symbol? Oh, no! A slip up! This is as difficult as writing a dictionary! My typing digits, in pain, must follow my brain's commands, and no slip-ups must occur if I want to do this right!
> (from http://en.wikipedia.org/wiki/Lipogram)

ANUGRAMS

An *anugram* is an anagram, both parts of which are mutually true. The best-known of these is:

Eleven plus two > *twelve plus one*

These are very rare – well done if you can come up with one of your own!

Short Words

TWO-LETTER WORDS

In certain word games, such as Scrabble®, Hangman and crosswords, it is useful to be aware of the many two-letter words that you can play, as these will help you gain an advantage over your opponent, or complete a tricky puzzle. Most of these terms are uncommon in everyday speech and writing, so their meanings are given here for interest and to help you memorize the words.

aa	rough volcanic rock
ad	advertisement
ae	*Scot* one
ai	three-toed sloth
aw	*Scot* all
ax	*US* axe
ba	*myth* a bird with a human head, representing the soul in Egyptian mythology.
di	diameter, didymium
ee	*Scot* eye
el	*US* elevated railroad
em	a print measurement
en	print measurement, half the length of an em
es	einsteinium
ex	a former partner
fa	*music* the fourth note in a scale
gi	judo or karate suit
id	*psychoanal* unconscious instincts
io	ionium
ja	*S Afr* yes
jo	*Scot* sweetheart
ka	*myth* a guardian spirit in Egyptian mythology
la	*music* the sixth note in a scale
li	Chinese unit of length: The li is approximately equal to 590 yards.

mi	*music* the third note in a scale
mo	molybdenum
mu	the twelfth letter of the Greek alphabet
ne	neon
nu	the thirteenth letter of the Greek alphabet
od	a force supposedly responsible for many natural phenomena
om	a sacred symbol of Hinduism, repeated as a mantra
os	*anat* bone
ou	*S Afr* man or chap
ox	type of male cattle
pa	a Maori village
pi	the sixteenth letter of the Greek alphabet
po	chamber pot
qi	vital bodily energy flow
re	with reference to
si	silicon
te	*music* the seventh note in a scale
ti	plant with reddish flowers
ut	a note in medieval music
wo	old spelling of woe
xi	the fourteenth letter of the Greek alphabet
yo	informal greeting
zo	a Tibetan breed of cattle

There are many hundreds of well-known three-letter words available to choose from when playing word games, but here we list some of the more unusual ones that you may not be familiar with. Knowledge of unusual three-letter words can be very useful for solving crossword puzzles or in word games such as Hangman. Challenge your opponent with the word *cwm*, for example, and watch as the noose is drawn tighter and tighter ...

aba	a type of cloth from Syria
adz	a heavy tool with a steel blade
ala	*zoology* a winglike structure
alb	a long white robe worn by priests
alt	*music* high in pitch
ani	a black tropical American bird
awn	a bristle on certain types of grass
bel	a unit of power
ben	*Scot* the inner room in a cottage
bey	a title used in the Ottoman Empire
bon	a Japanese Buddhist religion
caz	*slang* short for casual
col	a mountain pass connecting two peaks
cos	a type of lettuce
cru	in France, a wine-producing region
cwm	*Welsh* a valley
dag	*Aust & NZ* an eccentric person
dak	in India, a system of mail delivery
dal	an Indian lentil dish
dan	a black-belt grade in karate
daw	*archaic* jackdaw
dop	*S Afr* a small drink, usually alcoholic
dor	a type of dung beetle
dun	a brownish-grey colour
duo	a pair of performers
dzo	a Tibetan breed of cattle

edh	a character in the Runic alphabet
eft	*archaic* newt
ell	an obsolete unit of length
erg	a unit of work or energy
ern	the European sea eagle
eta	the seventh letter in the Greek alphabet
gam	a school of whales
hap	*archaic* luck, chance
hoy	*naut* a freight barge
hui	*NZ* a Maori social gathering
ide	a small silver European fish
iff	*logic* if and only if
ism	an unspecified doctrine
jol	*S Afr* slang a party
jot	to write a brief note of
jus	*cookery* a type of sauce
kai	NZ food
kat	a white-flowered evergreen shrub
kea	*NZ* a large native parrot
ked	a sheep parasite
kex	a large hollow-stemmed plant
kif	another name for marijuana
kir	a drink made from white wine and cassis
lox	a type of smoked salmon
max	*informal* the greatest or most significant
nix	*mythol* a friendly water sprite
nth	*maths* of an unspecified number
pax	a Christian greeting
pyx	a chest used at the British Mint to check coin weights

qat	a white-flowered evergreen shrub
qua	*prep* by virtue of being
rad	formerly, a unit of radiation
rai	a type of Algerian popular music
raj	in India, government; rule
rav	*Judaism* a religious mentor
reo	*NZ* a language
ret	to moisten or soak fabric
rex	part of a king's official title
roy	*Austral slang* a trendy male
sax	a tool resembling a small axe
sik	*Austral slang* excellent
ska	type of West Indian pop music
suq	in Muslim countries, an open-air marketplace
tay	*Irish dialect* tea
ted	to shake and loosen hay in order to dry it
tef	a type of grass with edible grain
teg	a two-year-old sheep
tor	a high rocky hill
tux	*US* dinner jacket
vex	to anger or annoy
vie	to contend for superiority with
wat	a Thai Buddhist monastery
wha	*Scot* who
wok	a large Chinese cooking pot
xis	plural of *xi*
zax	a variant of *sax*
zen	a Japanese school of Buddhism
zho	a Tibetan breed of cattle

J, Q, X , and Z

Did you know that J, Q, X, and Z are the least-used letters in the English alphabet? This fact was discovered in a highly scientific manner by a certain Alfred Butts, the inventor of Scrabble®, when he was devising one of the forerunners of the game. He scoured the front page of the New York Times, counted the occurrence of each letter, and concluded a frequency for each, on which the value of the letter tiles in his 'Lexiko' game were based. Here is a list of some of the more unusual words that use J, Q, X and Z, which are helpful in many different word games. Try some of these out the next time you play Hangman!

J

dojo	a room or hall for the practice of martial arts
haji	a Muslim who has made a pilgrimage to Mecca
hajj	the pilgrimage to Mecca that every Muslim should make at least once
jake	*Aust & NZ* slang all right; satisfactory
jamb	the vertical side of a door or window frame
jape	a joke
jarl	a Scandinavian chieftain or noble
jato	*aeronautics* jet-assisted takeoff
jazz	a type of popular music of African-American origin
jess	a short leather strap used in falconry
jebel	a hill or mountain in an Arab country
ajiva	in the Jain philosophy, an object without a soul
ajuga	a type of plant with medicinal uses
bijou	something small but often elegant
djinn	supernatural beings or spirits (in Muslim belief)
hadji	a Muslim who has made a pilgrimage to Mecca
jabot	a frill or ruffle on the neck of a garment
abjure	to solemnly renounce or retract

Q

qadi	a variant spelling of cadi, a judge in a Muslim community
qoph	the nineteenth letter in the Hebrew alphabet
quag	another word for quagmire, a soft wet area of land
quay	a wharf, typically built parallel to the shoreline
quod	*Brit slang* jail
faqir	a variant spelling of *fakir*, a member of any religious order of Islam
maquis	shrubby aromatic vegetation found in Mediterranean areas
pique	a feeling of resentment or irritation
qanat	an underground irrigation system, mostly found in Iran
qorma	a variant spelling of korma, a type of Indian dish made with cream
quaff	to drink heartily or in one draught
quale	*philosophy* an essential property or quality
quist	*West Midland and southwestern English dialect* a wood pigeon
barque	a sailing ship with three or more masts
bisque	a thick soup made from shellfish
claque	a group of people hired to applaud
loquat	an ornamental evergreen tree with small yellow plumlike fruits
aliquot	*maths* relating to an exact divisor of a number
bezique	a card game similar to whist

x

axel	a type of jump used in skating
axon	the part of a nerve cell that conducts impulses
calx	a powdery metal oxide formed when an ore or mineral is roasted
coxa	the technical name for the hipjoint
doxy	opinion or doctrine, especially concerning religious matters
ixia	a plant with ornamental funnel-shaped flowers
oryx	a large African antelope with long straight horns
addax	a large light-coloured antelope with spiralling horns
auxin	a type of plant hormone which promotes growth
ataxia	lack of muscular coordination
calyx	the part of a flower that protects the developing bud
coccyx	a small triangular bone at the base of the spine
extant	still in existance; surviving
magnox	an alloy consisting mostly of magnesium
oxalis	a plant with cloverlike leaves and white, pink, red or yellow flowers
axolotl	a North American aquatic salamander
bandbox	a lightweight box used for small items such as hats
bauxite	a claylike substance containing aluminium oxides
coaxial	*maths* mounted on a common axis

z

adze	a heavy hand tool with a steel blade
azan	*Islam* the call to prayer
lutz	a type of jump used in skating
meze	a starter eaten in Greece and other Mediterranean countries
zarf	an ornamental holder for a hot coffee cup
zebu	a domesticated ox used in India and East Asia
zein	a protein found in maize used to make plastics, adhesives etc
zila	an administrative district in India
azote	*obsolete* nitrogen
gloze	*archaic* to explain away; minimize the importance of
kudzu	a fast-growing climbing plant with purple fragrant flowers
matzo	a thin biscuit of unleavened bread, traditionally eaten at Passover
winze	*mining* a steeply inclined shaft for ventilation
zenith	the highest point; peak
zephyr	a light breeze
zinnia	a brightly-coloured flower native to America
zorbing	*informal* the activity of travelling downhill inside a large ball
zydeco	a type of Black Cajun music
zymase	a mixture of enzymes that ferments sugars